TH.

ENCYCLOPÆDIA bRITANNICA

A

DICTIONARY

OF

ARTS, SCIENCES, LITERATURE AND GENERAL INFORMATION

ELEVENTH EDITION

VOLUME XVI

L to LORD ADVOCATE

NEW YORK
THE ENCYCLOPÆDIA BRITANNICA COMPANY
1911

INITIALS USED IN VOLUME XVI. TO IDENTIFY INDIVIDUAL CONTRIBUTORS,[1] WITH THE HEADINGS OF THE ARTICLES IN THIS VOLUME SO SIGNED.

A. B. Ch.	A. B. Chatwood, B.Sc., A.M.Inst.C.E., M.Inst.Elec.E.	Lock.
A. B. R.	Alfred Barton Rendle, M.A., D.Sc., F.R.S., F.L.S. Keeper, Department of Botany, British Museum. Author of *Text Book on Classification of Flowering Plants, &c.*	Leaf.
A. C. F.	Alexander Campbell Fraser, LL.D. See the biographical article: Fraser, A. C.	Locke, John.
A. C. S.	Algernon Charles Swinburne. See the biographical article: Swinburne, A. C.	Landor.
A. D.	Henry Austin Dobson, LL.D. See the biographical article: Dobson, Henry Austin.	Locker-Lampson.
A. Fi.	Pierre Marie Auguste Filon. See the biographical article: Filon, P. M. A.	Labiche.
A. F. P.	Albert Frederick Pollard, M.A., F.R.Hist.Soc. Professor of English History in the University of London. Fellow of All Souls' College, Oxford. Assistant editor of the Dictionary of National Biography, 1893–1901. Lothian Prizeman, Oxford, 1892; Arnold Prizeman, 1898. Author of *England under the Protector Somerset*, *Henry VIII*; *Life of Thomas Cranmer*; &c.	Lambert, Francis; Lambert, Nicholson.
A. Gl.	Arnold Glover, M.A., LL.B. (d. 1905). Trinity College, Cambridge; Joint-editor of *Beaumont and Fletcher* for the Cambridge University Press.	Layard.
A. Go.*	Rev. Alexander Gordon, M.A. Lecturer in Church History in the University of Manchester.	Laurentius, Paul; Libertines.
A. G. D.	Arthur George Doughty, C.M.G., M.A., Litt.D., F.R.Hist.S., F.R.S.(Canada). Dominion Archivist of Canada. Member of the Geographical Board of Canada. Author of *The Cradle of New France*; &c. Joint editor of *Documents relating to the Constitutional History of Canada*.	Lafontaine.
A. H. S.	Rev. Archibald Henry Sayce, Litt.D., LL.D. See the biographical article: Sayce, A. H.	Laodicea.
A. J. G.	Rev. Alexander James Grieve, M.A., B.D. Professor of New Testament and Church History, Yorkshire United Independent College, Bradford. Sometime Registrar of Madras University, and Member of Mysore Educational Service.	Logos (*in part*).
A. J. L.	Andrew Jackson Lamoureux. Librarian, College of Agriculture, Cornell University. Editor of the *Rio News* (Rio de Janeiro), 1879–1901.	Lima (*Peru*).
A. L.	Andrew Lang. See the biographical article: Lang, Andrew.	La Cloche.
A. M. An.	Adelaide Mary Anderson, M.A. H.M. Principal Lady Inspector of Factories, Home Office. Clerk to the Royal Commission on Labour, 1892–1894. Gamble Gold Medallist, Girton College, Cambridge, 1893. Author of various articles on Industrial Life and Legislation, &c.	Labour Legislation.
A. M. C.	Agnes Mary Clerke. See the biographical article: Clerke, A. M.	Lagrange; Laplace; Leverrier.
A. N.	Alfred Newton, F.R.S. See the biographical article: Newton, Alfred.	Lämmergeyer; Lapwing; Lark; Linnet; Loom.
A. P. C.	Arthur Philemon Coleman, M.A., Ph.D., F.R.S. Professor of Geology in the University of Toronto. Geologist, Bureau of Mines, Toronto, 1893–1910. Author of *Reports of the Bureau of Mines of Ontario*.	Labrador (*in part*).

[1] A complete list, showing all individual contributors, appears in the final volume.

A. P. Lo.	Albert Peter Low. Deputy Minister of Department of Mines, Canada. Member of Geological Survey of Canada. Author of *Report on the Exploration in the Labrador Peninsula*; &c.	Labrador (*in part*).
A. Se.*	Adam Sedgwick, M.A., F.R.S. Professor of Zoology at the Imperial College of Science and Technology, London. Fellow, and formerly Tutor, of Trinity College, Cambridge. Professor of Zoology in the University of Cambridge, 1907–1909.	Larval Forms.
A. Sh.	Arthur Shadwell, M.A., M.D., LL.D., F.R.C.P. Member of Council of Epidemiological Society. Author of *The London Water-Supply*; *Industrial Efficiency*; *Drink, Temperance and Legislation*.	Liquor Laws.
A. So.	Albrecht Socin, Ph.D. (1844–1899). Formerly Professor of Semitic Philology in the Universities of Leipzig and Tübingen. Author of *Arabische Grammatik*; &c.	Lebanon (*in part*).
A. S. C.	Alan Summerly Cole, C.B. Assistant Secretary for Art, Board of Education, 1900–1908. Author of *Ancient Needle Point and Pillow Lace*; *Embroidery and Lace*; *Ornament in European Silks*; &c.	Lace.
A. St H. G.	Alfred St Hill Gibbons. Major, East Yorkshire Regiment. Explorer in South Central Africa. Author of *Africa from South to North through Marotseland*.	Lewanika.
A. S. M.	Alexander Stuart Murray, LL.D. See the biographical article: Murray, Alexander Stuart.	Lamp.
A. S. W.	Augustus Samuel Wilkins, M.A., LL.D., Litt.D. (1843–1905). Professor of Latin, Owens College, Manchester, 1869–1905. Author of *Roman Literature*; &c.	Latin Language (*in part*).
A. T. T.	A. T. Thorson. Official in Life Saving Service, U.S.A.	Life-boat: *United States*.
A. W. H.*	Arthur William Holland. Formerly Scholar of St John's College, Oxford. Bacon Scholar of Gray's Inn, 1900.	Leopold I. (*Roman Emperor*); Levellers.
A. W. Hu.	Rev. Arthur Wollaston Hutton, M.A. Rector of Bow Church, Cheapside. Librarian National Liberal Club, 1889–1899. Author of *Life of Cardinal Newman*; *Life of Cardinal Manning*; &c.	Leo XIII.
A. W. R.	Alexander Wood Renton, M.A., LL.B. Puisne Judge of the Supreme Court of Ceylon. Editor of *Encyclopaedia of the Laws of England*.	Landlord and Tenant; Letters Patent; Lodger and Lodgings.
A. W. W.	Adolphus William Ward, Litt.D., LL.D. See the biographical article: Ward, Adolphus William.	Lodge, Thomas.
B. D. J.	Benjamin Daydon Jackson, Ph.D. General Secretary of the Linnean Society. Secretary to Departmental Committee of H.M. Treasury on Botanical Work, 1900–1901. Author of *Glossary of Botanic Terms*; &c.	Linnaeus.
C.	The Rt. Hon. the Earl of Crewe. See the biographical article: Crewe, 1st Earl of.	Laprade.
C. C. W.	Charles Crawford Whinery, A.M. Cornell University. Assistant editor 11th Edition of the *Encyclopaedia Britannica*.	La Salle; Lincoln, Abraham (*in part*).
C. Di.	Charles Dibdin, F.R.G.S. Secretary of the Royal National Life-boat Institution. Hon. Secretary of the Civil Service Life-boat Fund, 1870–1906.	Life-boat: *British*.
C. D. W.	Hon. Carroll Davidson Wright. See the biographical article: Wright, Hon. Carroll Davidson.	Labour Legislation: *United States*.
C. E.*	Charles Everitt, M.A., F.C.S., F.G.S., F.R.A.S. Formerly Scholar of Magdalen College, Oxford.	Light: *Introduction* and *History*.
C. F. A.	Charles Francis Atkinson. Formerly Scholar of Queen's College, Oxford. Captain, 1st City of London (Royal Fusiliers). Author of *The Wilderness and Cold Harbour*.	Long Island (*Battle*).
C. F.-Br.	Charles Fortescue-Brickdale. Barrister-at-Law, Lincoln's Inn. Registrar of the Office of the Land Registry, Lincoln's Inn Fields. Author of *Registration of Title to Land*; *The Practice of the Land Registry*; *Land Transfer in Various Countries*; &c.	Land Registration.
C. H.*	Sir Charles Holroyd. See the biographical article: Holroyd, Sir Charles.	Legros.
C. H. Ha.	Carlton Huntley Hayes, A.M., Ph.D. Assistant Professor of History in Columbia University, New York City. Member of the American Historical Association.	Leo I.-X. (*Popes*)
C. J. B.*	Rev. Charles James Ball, M.A. University Lecturer in Assyriology, Oxford. Author of *Light from the East*.	Lamentations.
C. L. K.	Charles Lethbridge Kingsford, M.A., F.R.Hist.S., F.S.A. Assistant Secretary, Board of Education. Author of *Life of Henry V*. Editor of *Chronicles of London* and Stow's *Survey of London*.	Lancaster, John of Gaunt, duke of.
C. M.	[illegible] Mirbt, D.Th. [illegible] Church History in the University of Marburg. Author of *Publizistik* [illegible] *Gregor VII.*; *Quellen zur Geschichte des Papsttums*; &c.	Lateran Councils.

C. Mo.	WILLIAM COSMO MONKHOUSE. See the biographical article: MONKHOUSE, W. C.	Leighton, Lord.
C. R. B.	CHARLES RAYMOND BEAZLEY, M.A., D.LITT., F.R.G.S., F.R.HIST.S. Professor of Modern History in the University of Birmingham. Formerly Fellow of Merton College, Oxford, and University Lecturer in the History of Geography. Lothian Prizeman, Oxford, 1889. Lowell Lecturer, Boston, 1908. Author of *Henry the Navigator*; *The Dawn of Modern Geography*; &c.	Leif Ericsson; Leo, Johannes.
De B.	HENRI G. S. A. DE BLOWITZ. See the biographical article: BLOWITZ, H. DE.	Lesseps, Ferdinand de.
D. F. T.	DONALD FRANCIS TOVEY. Author of *Essays in Musical Analysis*: comprising *The Classical Concerto*, *The Goldberg Variations*, and analysis of many other classical works.	Lasso, Orlando.
D. G. H.	DAVID GEORGE HOGARTH, M.A. Keeper of the Ashmolean Museum, Oxford. Fellow of Magdalen College, Oxford. Fellow of the British Academy. Excavated at Paphos, 1888; Naucratis, 1899 and 1903; Ephesus, 1904–1905; Assiut, 1906–1907; Director, British School at Athens, 1897–1900; Director, Cretan Exploration Fund, 1899.	Latakia; Lebanon (*in part*)
D. H.	DAVID HANNAY. Formerly British Vice-Consul at Barcelona. Author of *Short History of the Royal Navy*; *Life of Emilio Castelar*, &c.	La Hogue, Battle of; Lauria, Roger de; Lepanto, Battle of; Lima.
D. Ll. T.	DANIEL LLEUFER THOMAS. Barrister-at-Law, Lincoln's Inn. Stipendiary Magistrate at Pontypridd and Rhondda.	Llantwit Major.
D. Mn.	REV. DUGALD MACFADYEN, M.A. Minister of South Grove Congregational Church, Highgate. Author of *Constructive Congregational Ideals*, &c.	Leighton, Robert (*in part*).
D. M. W.	SIR DONALD MACKENZIE WALLACE, K.C.I.E., K.C.V.O. Extra Groom of the Bedchamber to H.M. King George V. Director of the Foreign Department of *The Times*, 1891–1899. Member of the Institut de Droit International and Officier de l'Instruction Publique (France). Joint-editor of New Volumes (10th ed.) of the *Encyclopaedia Britannica*. Author of *Russia*; *Egypt and the Egyptian Question*; *The Web of Empire*; &c.	Lobánov-Rostovski.
E. B.*	ERNEST CHARLES FRANÇOIS BABELON. Professor at the Collège de France. Keeper of the department of Medals and Antiquities at the Bibliothèque Nationale. Member of the Académie des Inscriptions et de Belles Lettres, Paris. Chevalier of the Legion of Honour. Author of *Descriptions Historiques des Monnaies de la République Romaine*; *Traités des Monnaies Grecques et Romaines*, *Catalogue des Camées de la Bibliothèque Nationale*.	Lepta.
E. C. B.	EDWARD CUTHBERT BUTLER, O.S.B., M.A., D.LITT. (Dublin) Abbot of Downside Abbey, Bath. Author of "The Lausiac History of Palladius," in *Cambridge Texts and Studies*, vol. vi.	Leo, Brother.
E. Da.	EDWARD GEORGE DANNREUTHER (1844–1905). Member of Board of Professors, Royal College of Music, 1895–1905. Conducted the first Wagner Concerts in London, 1873–1874. Author of *The Music of the Future*, &c. Editor of a critical edition of Liszt's *Études*.	Liszt.
E. D. J. W.	EDWARD D. J. WILSON. Formerly Leader-writer on *The Times*.	Londonderry, 2nd Marquess of.
E. G.	EDMUND GOSSE, LL.D., D.C.L. See the biographical article GOSSE, EDMUND.	Lampoon; Lie, Jonas L. E.
E. Ga.	EMILE GARCKE, M.INST.E.E. Managing Director of British Electric Traction Co., Ltd. Author of *Manual of Electrical Undertakings*, &c.	Lighting: *Electric* (*Commercial Aspects*).
E. He.	EDWARD HEAWOOD, M.A. Gonville and Caius College, Cambridge. Librarian of the Royal Geographical Society, London.	Livingstone Mountains.
E. J. D.	EDWARD JOSEPH DENT, M.A., MUS.BAC. Formerly Fellow of King's College, Cambridge. Author of *A. Scarlatti: his Life and Works*.	Leo, Leonardo.
E. O.*	EDMUND OWEN, M.B., F.R.C.S., LL.D., D.SC. Consulting Surgeon to St Mary's Hospital, London, and to the Children's Hospital, Great Ormond Street, London. Chevalier of the Legion of Honour. Late Examiner in Surgery at the Universities of Cambridge, London and Durham. Author of *A Manual of Anatomy for Senior Students*.	Liver: *Surgery of Liver and Gall Bladder*.
E. Pr.	EDGAR PRESTAGE. Special Lecturer in Portuguese Literature in the University of Manchester. Examiner in Portuguese in the Universities of London, Manchester, &c. Commendador, Portuguese Order of S. Thiago. Corresponding Member of Lisbon Royal Academy of Sciences, Lisbon Geographical Society, &c. Author of *Letters of a Portuguese Nun*, *Azurara's Chronicle of Guinea*; &c.	Lobo, F. R.; Lopes, Fernão.
E. R. L.	SIR EDWIN RAY LANKESTER, K.C.B., F.R.S., D.SC. Hon. Fellow of Exeter College, Oxford. Director of the Natural History Departments of the British Museum, 1898–1907. President of the British Association, 1906. Professor of Zoology and Comparative Anatomy in University College, London, 1874–1890. Linacre Professor of Comparative Anatomy at Oxford, 1891–1898. Vice-President of the Royal Society, 1896. Romanes Lecturer at Oxford, 1905. Author of *Degeneration*, *The Advancement of Science*; *The Kingdom of Man*; &c.	Lamellibranchia (*in part*).

E. V. L.	EDWARD VERRALL LUCAS. Editor of *Works of Charles Lamb*. Author of *Life of Charles Lamb*.	**Lamb, Charles.**
F. E. B.	FRANK EVERS BEDDARD, M.A., F.R.S. Prosector of Zoological Society, London. Formerly Lecturer in Biology at Guy's Hospital, London. Naturalist to "Challenger" Expedition Commission, 1882–1884. Author of *Monograph of the Oligochaeta, Animal Colouration*; &c.	**Leech.**
F. E. W.	REV. FREDERICK EDWARD WARREN, M.A., B.D., F.S.A Rector of Bardwell, Bury St Edmunds. Fellow of St John's College, Oxford, 1865–1882. Author of *The Old Catholic Ritual done into English and compared with the Corresponding Offices in the Roman and Old German Manuals*; *The Liturgy and Ritual of the Celtic Church*; &c.	**Lection, Lectionary; Lector; Litany; Liturgy.**
F. G. M. B.	FREDERICK GEORGE MEESON BECK, M.A Fellow and Lecturer in Classics, Clare College, Cambridge.	**Lombards** (*in part*).
F. G. P.	FREDERICK GYMER PARSONS, F.R.C.S., F.Z.S., F.R.ANTHROP.INST Vice-President, Anatomical Society of Great Britain and Ireland. Lecturer on Anatomy at St Thomas's Hospital and the London School of Medicine for Women. Formerly Hunterian Professor at the Royal College of Surgeons.	**Liver:** *Anatomy*.
F. J. H.	FRANCIS JOHN HAVERFIELD, M.A., LL.D., F.S.A. Camden Professor of Ancient History in the University of Oxford. Fellow of Brasenose College. Ford's Lecturer, 1906–1907. Fellow of the British Academy. Author of Monographs on Roman History, especially Roman Britain; &c.	**Legion** (*in part*); **Limes Germanicus.**
F. L.*	SIR FRANKLIN LUSHINGTON, M.A. Formerly Chief Police Magistrate for London. Author of *Wagers of Battle*.	**Lear, Edward.**
F. V. B.	F. VINCENT BROOKS.	**Lithography.**
F. v. H.	BARON FRIEDRICH VON HÜGEL. Member of Cambridge Philological Society; Member of Hellenic Society. Author of *The Mystical Element of Religion*.	**Loisy.**
F. Wa.	FRANCIS WATT, M.A. Barrister-at-Law, Middle Temple. Author of *Law's Lumber Room*; *Scotland of to-day*; &c	**Law, John.**
F. W. R.*	FREDERICK WILLIAM RUDLER, I.S.O., F.G.S. Curator and Librarian of the Museum of Practical Geology, London, 1879–1902. President of the Geologists' Association, 1887–1889.	**Labradorite; Lapis Lazuli.**
F. W. Ra.	FRANCIS WILLIAM RAIKES, K.C., LL.D. (1842–1906). Judge of County Courts, Hull, 1898–1906. Joint-author of *The New Practice*; &c.	**Lien.**
G. A. Gr.	GEORGE ABRAHAM GRIERSON, C.I.E., PH.D., D.LITT. (Dubl.) Member of the Indian Civil Service, 1873–1903. In charge of Linguistic Survey of India, 1898–1902. Gold Medallist, Royal Asiatic Society, 1909. Vice-President of the Royal Asiatic Society. Formerly Fellow of Calcutta University. Author of *The Languages of India*; &c.	**Lahnda.**
G. E.	REV GEORGE EDMUNDSON, M.A., F.R HIST.S. Formerly Fellow and Tutor of Brasenose College, Oxford. Ford's Lecturer, 1909–1910. Employed by British Government in preparation of the British Case in the British Guiana-Venezuelan and British Guiana-Brazilian boundary arbitrations.	**Limburg.**
G. F. B.	GEORGE FREDERICK BARWICK Assistant-Keeper of Printed Books and Superintendent of Reading-room, British Museum.	**Lavigerie.**
G. F. K.	GEORGE FREDERICK KUNZ, A.M., PH.D., D.Sc. Gem Expert to Messrs Tiffany & Co., New York. Hon. Curator of Precious Stones, American Museum of Natural History, New York. Fellow of Geological Society of America. Author of *Precious Stones of North America*, &c. Senior Editor of *Book of the Pearl*.	**Lapidary and Gem-cutting.**
G. H. C.	GEORGE HERBERT CARPENTER, B.Sc. Professor of Zoology in the Royal College of Science, Dublin. Author of *Insects: Their Structure and Life*.	**Lepidoptera.**
[illegible]	GEORGE SAINTSBURY, D.C.L., LL.D. See the biographical article: SAINTSBURY, GEORGE E. B.	**La Bruyère; La Fontaine; Lamartine; La Rochefoucauld; Le Sage.**
[illegible]	GEORGE SOMES LAYARD. Trinity College, Cambridge. Barrister-at-Law, Inner Temple. Author of *Charles Keene*; *Shirley Brooks*; &c.	**Linton, William James.**
[illegible]	REV. GRIFFITHES WHEELER THATCHER, M.A., B.D. Warden of Camden College, Sydney, N.S.W. Formerly Tutor in Hebrew and Old Testament History at Mansfield College, Oxford.	**Labid.**
[illegible]	HENDRIK ANTOON LORENTZ. Professor of Physics in the University of Leiden. Author of *La théorie électromagnétique de Maxwell et son application aux corps mouvants*.	**Light:** *Nature of*.
[illegible]	HENRY BENJAMIN WHEATLEY, F.S.A. Assistant Secretary, Royal Society of Arts, 1879–1909. President of the Samuel [illegible] Vice-President of the Bibliographical Society, 1908–1910. [illegible] *London*; *London Past and Present*; &c.	**London:** *History*.
[illegible]	[illegible]WARD, F.R.S., F.G.S. [illegible] of the Geological Survey of England and Wales. [illegible] Association, 1893–1894. Wollaston Medallist, 1908.	**Logan, Sir William E.; Lonsdale, William.**

H. Ch.	Hugh Chisholm, M.A. Formerly Scholar of Corpus Christi College, Oxford. Editor of the 11th edition of the *Encyclopaedia Britannica*; Co-editor of the 10th edition.	Lloyd George, D.
H. De.	Rev. Hippolyte Delehaye, S.J. Bollandist. Joint-author of the *Acta Sanctorum*.	Lawrence, St; Linus.
H. F. G.	Hans Friedrich Gadow, M.A., F.R.S., Ph.D. Strickland Curator and Lecturer on Zoology in the University of Cambridge. Author of *Amphibia and Reptiles* (Cambridge Natural History).	Lizard.
H. F. P.	Henry Francis Pelham, LL.D. See the biographical article: Pelham, H. F.	Livy (*in part*).
H. H. J.	Sir Henry Hamilton Johnston, K.C.B., G.C.M.G. See the biographical article: Johnston, Sir Henry Hamilton.	Liberia.
H. M. S.	Henry Morse Stephens, M.A., Litt.D. Professor of History and Director of University Extension, University of California. Author of *History of the French Revolution*; *Revolutionary Europe*; &c.	Littré.
H. R. T.	Henry Richard Tedder, F.S.A. Secretary and Librarian of the Athenaeum Club, London.	Libraries (*in part*).
H. St.	Henry Sturt, M.A. Author of *Idola Theatri*; *The Idea of a Free Church*; and *Personal Idealism*.	Lange, Friedrich Albert.
H. T. A.	Rev. Herbert Thomas Andrews. Professor of New Testament Exegesis, New College, London. Author of the "Commentary on Acts," in the *Westminster New Testament*; *Handbook on the Apocryphal Books* in the "Century Bible."	Logia.
H. W. B.*	Herbert William Blunt, M.A. Student, Tutor, and Librarian, Christ Church, Oxford. Formerly Fellow of All Souls' College.	Logic: *History*.
H. W. C. D.	Henry William Carless Davis, M.A. Fellow and Tutor of Balliol College, Oxford. Fellow of All Souls' College, Oxford, 1895–1902. Author of *Charlemagne*; *England under the Normans and Angevins*; &c.	Lanfranc; Langton, Stephen.
H. Y.	Sir Henry Yule, K.C.S.I. See the biographical article: Yule, Sir Henry.	Lhasa (*in part*).
I. A.	Israel Abrahams. Reader in Talmudic and Rabbinic Literature in the University of Cambridge. Formerly President, Jewish Historical Society of England. Author of *A Short History of Jewish Literature*; *Jewish Life in the Middle Ages*; *Judaism*; &c.	Lazarus, Emma; Leon, Moses; Leon of Modena.
J. An.	Joseph Anderson, LL.D. Keeper of the National Museum of Antiquities, Edinburgh. Assistant Secretary to the Society of Antiquaries of Scotland, and Rhind Lecturer, 1879–1882 and 1892. Editor of Drummond's *Ancient Scottish Weapons*; &c.	Lake Dwellings.
J. A. F.	John Ambrose Fleming, M.A., D.Sc., F.R.S. Pender Professor of Electrical Engineering in the University of London. Fellow of University College, London. Formerly Fellow of St John's College, Cambridge. Vice-President of the Institution of Electrical Engineers. Author of *The Principles of Electric Wave Telegraphy*; *Magnets and Electric Currents*; &c.	Leyden Jar; Lighting: *Electric*.
J. A. F. M.	John Alexander Fuller Maitland, M.A., F.S.A. Musical critic of *The Times*. Author of *Life of Schumann*; *The Musician's Pilgrimage*; *Masters of German Music*; *English Music in the Nineteenth Century*; *The Age of Bach and Handel*. Editor of Grove's *Dictionary of Music and Musicians*; &c.	Lind, Jenny.
J. A. H.	John Allen Howe, B.Sc. Curator and Librarian of the Museum of Practical Geology, London. Author of *The Geology of Building Stones*; &c.	Lias; Llandovery Group.
J. Dr.	Sir James Dewar, F.R.S., LL.D. See the biographical article: Dewar, Sir J.	Liquid Gases.
J. D. B.	James David Bourchier, M.A., F.R.G.S. King's College, Cambridge. Correspondent of *The Times* in South-Eastern Europe. Commander of the Orders of Prince Danilo of Montenegro and of the Saviour of Greece, and Officer of the Order of St Alexander of Bulgaria.	Larissa.
J. D. Br.	James Duff Brown. Borough Librarian, Islington Public Libraries. Vice-President of the Library Association. Author of *Guide to Librarianship*; &c.	Libraries (*in part*).
J. F.-K.	James Fitzmaurice-Kelly, Litt.D., F.R.Hist.S. Gilmour Professor of Spanish Language and Literature, Liverpool University. Norman McColl Lecturer, Cambridge University. Fellow of the British Academy. Member of the Royal Spanish Academy. Knight Commander of the Order of Alphonso XII. Author of *A History of Spanish Literature*; &c.	La Cueva; Larra; Literature.
J. F. St.	John Frederick Stenning, M.A. Dean and Fellow of Wadham College, Oxford. University Lecturer in Aramaic. Lecturer in Divinity and Hebrew at Wadham College.	Leviticus.
J. Ga.	James Gairdner, C.B., LL.D. See the biographical article: Gairdner, James.	Lancaster, House of; Leicester, Robert Dudley, earl of.
J. G. F.	Sir Joshua Girling Fitch, LL.D. See the biographical article: Fitch, Sir J. G.	Lancaster, Joseph.

INITIALS AND HEADINGS OF ARTICLES

J. G. N.	**John George Nicolay** (1832–1901) Marshal of the U.S. Supreme Court, 1872–1887. Joint-author of *Abraham Lincoln:* &c.	Lincoln, Abraham (*in part*).
J. G. P.*	**James Gordon Parker, D.Sc., F.C.S.** Principal of Leathersellers Technical College, London. Gold Medallist, Society of Arts. Author of *Leather for Libraries*; *Principles of Tanning*; &c.	Leather.
J. G. R.	**John George Robertson, M.A., Ph.D.** Professor of German Language and Literature, University of London. Editor of the *Modern Language Journal*. Author of *History of German Literature*; *Schiller after a Century*; &c.	Lessing (*in part*).
J. Ha.	**Justus Hashagen, Ph.D.** Privat-dozent in Medieval and Modern History, University of Bonn. Author of *Das Rheinland unter der französische Herrschaft*.	Lang, Karl Heinrich; Ledochowski; Leo, Heinrich.
J. H. F.	**John Henry Freese, M.A.** Formerly Fellow of St John's College, Cambridge.	Leo VI. (*Emperor of the East*).
J. Hl. R.	**John Holland Rose, M.A., Litt.D.** Lecturer on Modern History to the Cambridge University Local Lectures Syndicate. Author of *Life of Napoleon I.*; *Napoleonic Studies*; *The Development of the European Nations*; *The Life of Pitt*; &c.	Las Cases.
J. J. L.*	**Rev. John James Lias, M.A.** Chancellor of Llandaff Cathedral. Formerly Hulsean Lecturer in Divinity and Lady Margaret Preacher, University of Cambridge.	Langen.
J. K. I.	**John Kells Ingram, LL.D.** See the biographical article: Ingram, J. K.	Leslie, Thomas E. C.
J. Le.	**Rev. James Legge, M.A.** See the biographical article: Legge, James.	Lao-Tsze.
J. L. M.	**John Linton Myres, M.A., F.S.A., F.R.G.S.** Wykeham Professor of Ancient History in the University of Oxford. Formerly Gladstone Professor of Greek and Lecturer in Ancient Geography, University of Liverpool. Lecturer in Classical Archaeology in University of Oxford.	Lelegas; Locri (*Greece*).
J. L. W.	**Jessie Laidlay Weston.** Author of *Arthurian Romances unrepresented in Malory*.	Lancelot.
J. Mu.	**Sir John Murray, K.C.B., F.R.S.** See the biographical article: Murray, Sir John.	Lake.
J. M. C.	**Rev. James M. Crombie.** Author of *Braemar: its Topography and Natural History*; *Lichenes Britannici*.	Lichens (*in part*).
J. M. G.	**John Miller Gray** (1850–1894) Art Critic and Curator of the Scottish National Portrait Gallery, 1884–1894. Author of *David Scott, R.S.A.*; *James and William Tassie*.	Leech, John.
J. P. E.	**Jean Paul Hippolyte Emmanuel Adhémar Esmein** Professor of Law in the University of Paris. Officer of the Legion of Honour Member of the Institute of France. Author of *Cours élémentaire d'histoire du droit français*; &c.	Lettres de Cachet.
J. P. P.	**John Percival Postgate, M.A., Litt.D** Professor of Latin in the University of Liverpool. Fellow of Trinity College, Cambridge. Fellow of the British Academy. Editor of the *Classical Quarterly*. Editor-in-chief of the *Corpus Poetarum Latinorum*; &c.	Latin Literature (*in part*).
J. P. Pe.	**Rev. John Punnett Peters, Ph.D., D.D** Canon Residentiary, P. E. Cathedral of New York. Formerly Professor of Hebrew in the University of Pennsylvania. Director of the University Expedition to Babylonia, 1888–1895. Author of *Nippur, or Explorations and Adventures on the Euphrates*; *Scriptures, Hebrew and Christian*.	Lagash; Larsa.
J. S.	**James Sully, LL.D.** See the biographical article: Sully, James.	Lewes, George Henry (*in part*).
J. Si.	**James Sime, M.A.** (1843–1895). Author of *A History of Germany*; &c.	Lessing (*in part*).
J. S. F.	**John Smith Flett, D.Sc., F.G.S.** Petrographer to the Geological Survey. Formerly Lecturer on Petrology in Edinburgh University. Neill Medallist of the Royal Society of Edinburgh. Bigsby Medallist of the Geological Society of London.	Laccolite; Lamprophyres; Laterite; Leucite: *Leucite Rocks*; Limestone.
J. S. K.	**John Scott Keltie, LL.D., F.S.S., F.S.A. (Scot.).** Secretary, Royal Geographical Society. Hon. Member, Geographical Societies of Paris, Berlin, Rome, &c. Editor of the *Statesman's Year Book*. Editor of the *Geographical Journal*.	Livingstone.
J. S. W.	**John Stephen Willison, LL.D., F.R.S. (Canada).** Editor of *The News* (Toronto). Canadian Correspondent of *The Times*. Author of *Sir Wilfrid Laurier and the Liberal Party*; &c.	Laurier.
J. T. Be.	**John Thomas Bealby.** Joint-author of Stanford's *Europe*. Formerly Editor of the *Scottish Geographical Magazine*. Translator of Sven Hedin's *Through Asia*, *Central Asia and Tibet*; &c.	Ladoga (*in part*); Livonia (*in part*); Lop-nor.
[illegible]	**[illegible]lor Brown.**	Leighton, Robert (*in part*).

J. T. C.	**Joseph Thomas Cunningham, M.A., F.Z.S.** Lecturer on Zoology at the South-Western Polytechnic, London. Formerly Fellow of University College, Oxford. Assistant Professor of Natural History in the University of Edinburgh. Naturalist to the Marine Biological Association.	**Lamellibranchia** (*in part*).
J. T. S.*	**James Thomson Shotwell, Ph.D.** Professor of History in Columbia University, New York City.	**Languedoc.**
J. V.*	**Jules Viard.** Archivist at the National Archives, Paris. Officer of Public Instruction. Author of *La France sous Philippe VI. de Valois*; &c.	**Le Maçon.**
J. W. D.	**Captain J. Whitly Dixon, R.N.** Nautical Assessor to the Court of Appeal.	**Log.**
J. W. He.	**James Wycliffe Headlam, M.A.** Staff Inspector of Secondary Schools under the Board of Education. Formerly Fellow of King's College, Cambridge. Professor of Greek and Ancient History at Queen's College, London. Author of *Bismarck and the Foundation of the German Empire*; &c.	**Lasker.**
J. W. L. G.	**James Whitbread Lee Glaisher, M.A., D.Sc., F.R.S.** Fellow of Trinity College, Cambridge. Formerly President of the Cambridge Philosophical Society, and the Royal Astronomical Society. Editor of *Messenger of Mathematics* and the *Quarterly Journal of Pure and Applied Mathematics.*	**Legendre, A. M.;** **Logarithm.**
K. H.	**Killingworth Hedges, M.Inst.C.E., M.Inst.Elect.E.** Hon. Secretary of the Lightning Research Committee. Author of *Modern Lightning Conductors*; &c.	**Lightning Conductor.**
K. S.	**Kathleen Schlesinger.** Editor of *The Portfolio of Musical Archaeology.* Author of *The Instruments of the Orchestra.*	**Lituus.**
L. A. W.	**Laurence Austine Waddell, C.B., C.I.E., LL.D., M.B.** Lieut.-Colonel I.M.S. (retired). Author of *Lhasa and its Mysteries*, &c.	**Lhasa** (*in part*).
L. B.	**Laurence Binyon.** See the biographical article: Binyon, L.	**Lawson, Cecil Gordon.**
L. D.*	**Louis Marie Olivier Duchesne.** See the biographical article: Duchesne, L. M. O.	**Liberius.**
L. J. S.	**Leonard James Spencer, M.A.** Assistant in the Department of Mineralogy, British Museum. Formerly Scholar of Sidney Sussex College, Cambridge, and Harkness Scholar. Editor of the *Mineralogical Magazine.*	**Leadhillite;** **Lepidolite;** **Leucite** (*in part*); **Liroconite.**
L. T. D.	**Sir Lewis Tonna Dibdin, M.A., D.C.L., F.S.A.** Dean of the Arches; Master of the Faculties; and First Church Estates Commissioner. Bencher of Lincoln's Inn. Author of *Monasticism in England*, &c.	**Lincoln Judgment, The.**
L. V.*	**Luigi Villari.** Italian Foreign Office (Emigration Dept.). Formerly Newspaper Correspondent in east of Europe. Italian Vice-Consul in New Orleans, 1906, Philadelphia, 1907, and Boston, U.S.A., 1907–1910. Author of *Italian Life in Town and Country*, &c.	**Leopold II.** (*Grand Duke of Tuscany*).
M. Br.	**Margaret Bryant.**	**Landor:** *Bibliography*; **La Salle.**
M. Ca.	**Moritz Cantor, Ph.D.** Honorary Professor of Mathematics in the University of Heidelberg. Author of *Vorlesungen über die Geschichte der Mathematik*, &c.	**Leonardo of Pisa.**
M. H. S.	**Marion H. Spielmann, F.S.A.** Formerly Editor of the *Magazine of Art.* Member of Fine Art Committee of International Exhibitions of Brussels, Paris, Buenos Aires, Rome, and the Franco-British Exhibition, London. Author of *History of "Punch"*; *British Portrait Painting to the Opening of the Nineteenth Century*; *Works of G. F. Watts, R.A.*; *British Sculpture and Sculptors of To-day*; *Henriette Ronner*; &c.	**Line Engraving** (*in part*).
M. N. T.	**Marcus Niebuhr Tod, M.A.** Fellow and Tutor of Oriel College, Oxford. University Lecturer in Epigraphy. Joint-author of *Catalogue of the Sparta Museum.*	**Laconia;** **Leonidas; Leotychides.**
M. O. B. C.	**Maximilian Otto Bismarck Caspari, M.A.** Reader in Ancient History at London University. Lecturer in Greek at Birmingham University, 1905–1908.	**Leo I.–V.** (*Emperors of the East*); **Lesbos; Leuctra.**
M. P.*	**Leon Jacques Maxime Prinet.** Formerly Archivist to the French National Archives. Auxiliary of the Institute of France (Academy of Moral and Political Sciences).	**L'Aubespine.**
N. G. G.	**Nicholas G. Gedye.** Chief Engineer to the Tyne Improvement Commission.	**Lighthouse** (*in part*).
O. Hr.	**Otto Henker, Ph.D.** On the Staff of the Carl Zeiss Factory, Jena, Germany.	**Lens.**
P. A. K.	**Prince Peter Alexeivitch Kropotkin.** See the biographical article: Kropotkin, Prince P. A.	**Ladoga** (*in part*), **Lithuanians and Letts:** *History*; **Livonia** (*in part*).

P. C. M.	**Peter Chalmers Mitchell, M.A., F.R.S., D.Sc., LL.D.** Secretary to the Zoological Society of London. University Demonstrator in Comparative Anatomy and Assistant to Linacre Professor at Oxford, 1888–1891. Lecturer on Biology at Charing Cross Hospital, 1892–1894; at London Hospital, 1894. Examiner in Biology to the Royal College of Physicians, 1892–1896, 1901–1903. Examiner in Zoology to the University of London, 1903.	**Life; Longevity.**
P. C. Y.	**Philip Chesney Yorke, M.A.** Magdalen College, Oxford.	**Laud, Archbishop; Lauderdale, Duke of; Leeds, 1st Duke of.**
P. G.	**Percy Gardner, Litt.D., LL.D., F.S.A.** See the biographical article. Gardner, Percy.	**Leochares.**
P. Gi.	**Peter Giles, M.A., LL.D., Litt.D.** Fellow and Classical Lecturer of Emmanuel College, Cambridge, and University Reader in Comparative Philology. Late Secretary of the Cambridge Philological Society. Author of *Manual of Comparative Philology*, &c.	**L.**
P. G. H.	**Philip Gilbert Hamerton.** See the biographical article: Hamerton, Philip Gilbert.	**Line Engraving** (*in part*).
R. A. S. M.	**Robert Alexander Stewart Macalister, M.A., F.S.A.** St John's College, Cambridge. Director of Excavations for the Palestine Exploration Fund.	**Lachish.**
R. G.	**Richard Garnett, LL.D.** See the biographical article: Garnett, Richard.	**Leopardi.**
R. I. P.	**Reginald Innes Pocock, F.Z.S.** Superintendent of the Zoological Gardens, London.	**Leaf-insect; Locust** (*in part*).
R. J. M.	**Ronald John McNeill, M.A.** Christ Church, Oxford. Barrister-at-Law. Formerly Editor of the *St James's Gazette*, London.	**Lawn Tennis; Leicester, R. Sidney, earl of; Lockhart, George.**
R. K. D.	**Sir Robert Kennaway Douglas.** Formerly Professor of Chinese, King's College, London. Keeper of Oriental Printed Books and MSS. at British Museum, 1892–1907. Member of the Chinese Consular Service, 1858–1865. Author of *The Language and Literature of China: Europe and the Far East*; &c.	**Li Hung Chang.**
R. L.*	**Richard Lydekker, F.R.S., F.G.S., F.Z.S.** Member of the Staff of the Geological Survey of India, 1874–1882. Author of *Catalogue of Fossil Mammals, Reptiles and Birds in the British Museum*; *The Deer of all Lands*, *The Game Animals of Africa*; &c.	**Langur; Lemming** (*in part*); **Lemur; Leopard** (*in part*); **Lion** (*in part*); **Litopterna.**
R. McL.	**Robert M'Lachlan.** Editor of the *Entomologists' Monthly Magazine*.	**Locust** (*in part*).
R. M. B.	**Robert Michael Ballantyne.** See the biographical article: Ballantyne, R. M.	**Life-boat:** *British* (*in part*).
R. N. B.	**Robert Nisbet Bain** (d. 1909). Assistant Librarian, British Museum, 1883–1909. Author of *Scandinavia*, *the Political History of Denmark, Norway and Sweden, 1513–1900*; *The First Romanovs, 1613–1725*; *Slavonic Europe: the Political History of Poland and Russia from 1469 to 1796*; &c.	**Ladislaus I. and IV. of Hungary; Laski.**
R. S. C.	**Robert Seymour Conway, M.A., D.Litt** (Cantab.) Professor of Latin and Indo-European Philology in the University of Manchester. Formerly Professor of Latin in University College, Cardiff, and Fellow of Gonville and Caius College, Cambridge. Author of *The Italic Dialects*.	**Latin Language** (*in part*). **Liguria:** *Archaeology and Philology*.
R. W.	**Richard Webster, A.M.** Formerly Fellow in Classics, Princeton University. Editor of *The Elegies of Maximianus*; &c.	**Long Island.**
R. W. C.	**The Very Rev. R. W. Church, D.D.** See the biographical article: Church, R. W.	**Lombards:** *The Kingdom in Italy*.
S. A. C.	**Stanley Arthur Cook, M.A.** Lecturer in Hebrew and Syriac, and formerly Fellow, Gonville and Caius College, Cambridge. Editor for Palestine Exploration Fund. Examiner in Hebrew and Aramaic, London University, 1904–1908. Author of *Glossary of Aramaic Inscriptions*; *The Laws of Moses and the Code of Hammurabi*; *Critical Notes on Old Testament History*; *Religion of Ancient Palestine*; &c.	**Levites.**
S. C.	**Sidney Colvin, LL.D.** See the biographical article. Colvin, Sidney.	**Leonardo da Vinci.**
St C.	**Viscount St Cyres.** See the biographical article. Iddesleigh, 1st Earl of.	**Liguori.**
S. D. F. S.	**Rev. Stewart Dingwall Fordyce Salmond, M.A., D.D** (1838–1905). Professor of Systematic Theology and Exegesis of the Epistles, U.F.C. College, Aberdeen, 1876–1905. Author of *The Parables of our Lord*; &c. Editor of *The International Library of Theology*; &c.	**Logos** (*in part*).
S. N.	**Simon Newcomb, LL.D., D.Sc.** See the biographical article: Newcomb, Simon.	**Latitude; Light:** *Velocity*.

T. As. — Thomas Ashby, M.A., D.Litt., F.S.A.
Director of the British School of Archaeology at Rome. Corresponding Member of the Imperial German Archaeological Institute. Formerly Scholar of Christ Church, Oxford. Craven Fellow, Oxford, 1897. Author of *The Classical Topography of the Roman Campagna*; &c.
— **Labicana, Via; Labici; Lampedusa; Lanciano; Lanuvium; Larino; Latina, Via; Latium; Laurentina, Via; Lavinium; Lecce; Leghorn; Leontini; Licodia Eubea; Ligures Baebiani; Liguria:** *History*; **Locri:** *Italy.*

T. A. I. — Thomas Allan Ingram, M.A., LL.D.
Trinity College, Dublin.
— **Livery Companies; London:** *Finance.*

T. Ca. — Thomas Case, M.A.
President of Corpus Christi College, Oxford. Formerly Waynflete Professor of Moral and Metaphysical Philosophy at Oxford and Fellow of Magdalen College. Author of *Physical Realism*; &c.
— **Logic.**

T. C. A. — Sir Thomas Clifford Allbutt, K.C.B., M.A., M.D., D.Sc., LL.D., F.R.S.
Regius Professor of Physic in the University of Cambridge. Physician to Addenbrooke's Hospital, Cambridge. Fellow of Gonville and Caius College, Cambridge. Editor of *Systems of Medicine*.
— **Lister, 1st Baron.**

T. Da. — Thomas Davidson, LL.D.
— **Longfellow.**

T. F. C. — Theodore Freylinghuysen Collier, Ph.D.
Assistant Professor of History, Williams College, Williamstown, Mass., U.S.A.
— **Laodicea, Synod of.**

T. F. H. — Thomas F. Henderson.
Author of *Mary Queen of Scots and the Casket Letters*; &c.
— **Latimer.**

T. H. H.* — Sir Thomas Hungerford Holdich, K.C.M.G., K.C.I.E., D.Sc., F.R.G.S.
Colonel in the Royal Engineers. Superintendent, Frontier Surveys, India, 1892–1898. Gold Medallist, R.G.S. (London), 1887. H.M. Commissioner for the Perso-Beluch Boundary, 1896. Author of *The Indian Borderland*; *The Gates of India*; &c.
— **Ladakh and Baltistan.**

T. K. — Thomas Kirkup, M.A., LL.D.
Author of *An Inquiry into Socialism*; *Primer of Socialism*; &c.
— **Lassalle.**

T. Mo. — Thomas Moore, F.L.S. (1821–1887).
Curator of the Garden of the Apothecaries Company at Chelsea, 1848–1887. Editor of the *Gardeners' Magazine of Botany*; Author of *Handbook of British Ferns*; *Index Filicum*; *Illustrations of Orchidaceous Plants*.
— **Labyrinth.**

T. M. L. — Rev. Thomas Martin Lindsay, LL.D., D.D.
Principal of the United Free Church College, Glasgow. Formerly Assistant to the Professor of Logic and Metaphysics in the University of Edinburgh. Author of *History of the Reformation*; *Life of Luther*; &c.
— **Lollards.**

T. Se. — Thomas Seccombe, M.A.
Lecturer in History, East London and Birkbeck Colleges, University of London. Stanhope Prizeman, Oxford, 1887. Assistant Editor of *Dictionary of National Biography*, 1891–1900. Author of *The Age of Johnson*; &c.
— **Lever, Charles.**

T. W. R. D. — Thomas William Rhys Davids, LL.D., Ph.D.
Professor of Comparative Religion, Manchester University. Professor of Pali and Buddhist Literature, University College, London, 1882–1904. President of the Pali Text Society. Fellow of the British Academy. Secretary and Librarian of Royal Asiatic Society, 1885–1902. Author of *Buddhism*, *Sacred Books of the Buddhists*; *Early Buddhism*; *Buddhist India*; *Dialogues of the Buddha*; &c.
— **Lāmāism.**

T. Wo. — Thomas Woodhouse.
Head of the Weaving and Textile Designing Department, Technical College, Dundee.
— **Linen and Linen Manufactures.**

V. B. L. — Vivian Byam Lewes, F.I.C., F.C.S.
Professor of Chemistry, Royal Naval College. Chief Superintendent Gas Examiner to the Corporation of the City of London.
— **Lighting:** *Oil and Gas.*

V. H. B. — Vernon Herbert Blackman, M.A., D.Sc.
Professor of Botany in the University of Leeds. Formerly Fellow of St John's College, Cambridge.
— **Lichens** (*in part*).

W. A. B. C. — Rev. William Augustus Brevoort Coolidge, M.A., F.R.G.S.
Fellow of Magdalen College, Oxford. Professor of English History, St David's College, Lampeter, 1880–1881. Author of *Guide to Switzerland*; *The Alps in Nature and in History*; &c. Editor of *The Alpine Journal*, 1880–1889.
— **Lausanne; Leuk; Liechtenstein; Linth; Locarno; Locle, Le.**

W. A. P. — Walter Alison Phillips, M.A.
Formerly Exhibitioner of Merton College and Senior Scholar of St John's College, Oxford. Author of *Modern Europe*; &c.
— **Laibach, Congress of; Lights, Ceremonial use of.**

W. E. Co. — The Rt. Rev. William Edward Collins, M.A., D.D.
Bishop of Gibraltar. Formerly Professor of Ecclesiastical History, King's College, London. Lecturer of Selwyn and St John's Colleges, Cambridge. Author of *The Study of Ecclesiastical History*; *Beginnings of English Christianity*; &c.
— **Libellatici.**

W. F. I. — William Fergusson Irvine, Hon. M.A. (Liverpool).
Hon. Secretary and General Editor of Historical Society of Lancashire and Cheshire. Hon. Local Secretary for Cheshire of the Society of Antiquaries. Author of *Liverpool in the reign of Charles II.*; *Old Halls of Wirral*; &c.
— **Liverpool.**

W. H. Be.	**William Henry Bennett, M.A., D.D., D.Litt.** (Cantab.). Professor of Old Testament Exegesis in New and Hackney Colleges, London. Formerly Fellow of St John's College, Cambridge. Lecturer in Hebrew at Firth College, Sheffield. Author of *Religion of the Post-Exilic Prophets*; &c.	**Lamech.**
W. H. F.	**Sir William Henry Flower, F.R.S.** See the biographical article: Flower, Sir W. H.	**Lemming** (*in part*); **Leopard** (*in part*); **Lion** (*in part*).
W. M. R.	**William Michael Rossetti.** See the biographical article: Rossetti, Dante Gabriel.	**Lely, Sir Peter; Lippi.**
W. P. T.	**William Peterfield Trent, LL.D., D.C.L.** Professor of English Literature, Columbia University. Author of *English Culture in Virginia*; *A Brief History of American Literature*; &c.	**Lanier.**
W. R. So.	**William Ritchie Sorley, M.A., Litt.D., LL.D.** Professor of Moral Philosophy in the University of Cambridge. Fellow of King's College, Cambridge. Fellow of the British Academy. Formerly Fellow of Trinity College. Author of *The Ethics of Naturalism*; *The Interpretation of Evolution*; &c.	**Leibnitz.**
W. R. S.-R.	**William Ralston Shedden-Ralston, M.A.** Formerly Assistant in the Department of Printed Books, British Museum. Author of *Russian Folk Tales*; &c.	**Lermontov.**
W. T. Ca.	**William Thomas Calman, D.Sc., F.Z.S.** Assistant in charge of Crustacea, Natural History Museum, South Kensington. Author of "Crustacea" in *A Treatise on Zoology*, edited by Sir E. Ray Lankester.	**Lobster.**
W. T. D.	**William Tregarthen Douglass, M.Inst.C.E., M.I.M.E.** Consulting Engineer to Governments of Western Australia, New South Wales, Victoria, Cape of Good Hope, &c. Erected the Eddystone and Bishop Rock Lighthouses. Author of *The New Eddystone Lighthouse*; &c.	**Lighthouse** (*in part*).
W. W. R.*	**William Walker Rockwell, Lic.Theol.** Assistant Professor of Church History, Union Theological Seminary, New York.	**Leo XI. and XII.** (*popes*).
W. W. S.	**Walter William Skeat, Litt.D., LL.D., D.C.L.** See the biographical article: Skeat, W. W.	**Layamon.**
W. Y. S.	**William Young Sellar, LL.D.** See the biographical article: Sellar, William Young.	**Latin Literature** (*in part*).

PRINCIPAL UNSIGNED ARTICLES

[illegible]
[illegible]
Lagos.
Lahore.
Lake District.
Lambeth Conferences.
Lanarkshire.
Lancashire.
Lantern.
Lapland.
Larceny.
Larch.
Lead Poisoning.
Leeds.
Legitimacy.
Leguminosae.
Leicestershire.
Leipzig.
Leith.
Lemnos.
Lemon.
Lent.
Leprosy.
Libel.
Liberal Party.
Liliaceae.
Lille.
Lily.
Limitation, Statutes of
Lincoln.
Lincolnshire.
Lippe.
Lisbon.

S.
St
S. 1
S. H.

ENCYCLOPÆDIA BRITANNICA

ELEVENTH EDITION

VOLUME XVI

L a letter which was the twelfth letter of the Phoenician alphabet. It has in its history passed through many changes of form, ending curiously enough in its usual manuscript form with a shape almost identical with that which it had about 900 B.C. (𐤋 ∠). As was the case with B and some other letters the Greeks did not everywhere keep the symbol in the position in which they had borrowed it ⅃. This, which was its oldest form in Attica and in the Chalcidian colonies of Italy, was the form adopted by the Romans, who in time converted it into the rectangle L, which passed from them to the nations of western Europe. In the Ionic alphabet, however, from which the ordinary Greek alphabet is derived it appeared as Λ. A still more common form in other parts of Greece was Ʌ, with the legs of unequal length. The editors of Herodotus have not always recognized that the name of Labda, the mother of Cypselus, in the story (v. 92) of the founding of the great family of Corinthian despots, was derived from the fact that she was lame and so suggested the form of the Corinthian Ʌ. Another form ⊢ or ⊢ was practically confined to the west of Argolis. The name of the Greek letter is ordinarily given as *Lambda*, but in Herodotus (above) and in Athenaeus x. p. 453 *e*, where the names of the letters are given, the best authenticated form is *Labda*. The Hebrew name, which was probably identical with the Phoenician, is *Lamed*, which, with a final vowel added as usual, would easily become *Lambda*, *b* being inserted between *m* and another consonant. The pronunciation of *l* varies a great deal according to the point at which the tongue makes contact with the roof of the mouth. The contact, generally speaking, is at the same point as for *d*, and this accounts for an interchange between these sounds which occurs in various languages, *e.g.* in Latin *lacrima* from the same root as the Greek *δάκρυ* and the English *tear*. The change in Latin occurs in a very limited number of cases and one explanation of their occurrence is that they are borrowed (Sabine) words. In pronunciation the breath may be allowed to escape at one or both sides of the tongue. In most languages *l* is a fairly stable sound. Orientals, however, have much difficulty in distinguishing between *l* and *r*. In Old Persian *l* is found in only two foreign words, and in Sanskrit different dialects employ *r* and *l* differently in the same words. Otherwise, however, the interchanges between *r* and *l* were somewhat exaggerated by the older philologists. Before other consonants *l* becomes silent in not a few languages, notably in French, where it is replaced by *u*, and in English where it has occasionally been restored in recent times, *e.g.* in *fault* which earlier was spelt without *l* (as in French whence it was borrowed), and which Goldsmith could still rhyme with *aught*. In the 15th century the Scottish dialect of English dropped *l* largely both before consonants and finally after *a* and *u*, *a'* = all, *fa'* = fall, *pu'* = pull, *'oo'* = wool, *bulk* pronounced like *book*, &c., while after *o* it appears as *w*, *row* (pronounced *rau*) = roll, *know* = knoll, &c. It is to be observed that L = 50 does not come from this symbol, but was an adaptation of ↓, the western Greek form of χ, which had no corresponding sound in Latin and was therefore not included in the ordinary alphabet. This symbol was first rounded into ⊥ and then changed first to ⊥ and ultimately to L. (P. Gi.)

LAACHER SEE, a lake of Germany, in the Prussian Rhine Province, 5 m. W. of Brohl on the Rhine, and N. of the village of Niedermendig. It occupies what is supposed to be a crater of the Eifel volcanic formation, and the pumice stone and basalt found in great quantities around it lend credence to this theory. It lies 850 ft. above the sea, is 5 m. in circumference and 160 ft. deep, and is surrounded by an amphitheatre of high hills. The water is sky blue in colour, very cold and bitter to the taste. The lake has no natural outlet and consequently is subjected to a considerable rise and fall. On the western side lies the Benedictine abbey of St Maria Laach (*Abbatia Lacensis*) founded in 1093 by Henry II., count palatine of the Rhine. The abbey church, dating from the 12th century, was restored in 1838. The history of the monastery down to modern times appears to have been uneventful. In 1802 it was abolished and at the close of the Napoleonic wars it became a Prussian state demesne. In 1863 it passed into the hands of the Jesuits, who, down to their expulsion in 1873, published here a periodical, which still appears, entitled *Stimmen aus Maria Laach*. In 1892 the monastery was again occupied by the Benedictines.

LAAGER, a South African Dutch word (Dutch *leger*, Ger. *lager*, connected with Eng. "lair") for a temporary defensive encampment, formed by a circle of wagons. The English word is "leaguer," an armed camp, especially that of a besieging or "beleaguering" army. The Ger. *lager*, in the sense of "store," is familiar as the name of a light beer (see BREWING).

LAAS, ERNST (1837–1885), German philosopher, was born on the 16th of June 1837 at Fürstenwalde. He studied theology and philosophy under Trendelenburg at Berlin, and eventually became professor of philosophy in the new university of Strassburg. In *Kant's Analogien der Erfahrung* (1876) he keenly criticized Kant's transcendentalism, and in his chief work *Idealismus und Positivismus* (3 vols., 1879–1884), he drew a clear contrast between Platonism, from which he derived transcendentalism, and positivism, of which he considered Protagoras the founder. Laas in reality was a disciple of Hume. Throughout his philosophy he endeavours to connect metaphysics with ethics and the theory of education.

His chief educational works were *Der deutsche Aufsatz in den obern Gymnasialklassen* (1868; 3rd ed., part i., 1898, part ii., 1894), and *Der deutsche Unterricht auf höhern Lehranstalten* (1872; 2nd ed. 1886). He contributed largely to the *Vierteljahrsschr. f. wiss. Philos.* (1880–1882); the *Litterarischer Nachlass*, a posthumous collection, was published at Vienna (1887). See Hanisch, *Der Positivismus von Ernst Laas* (1902); Gjurits, *Die Erkenntnisstheorie des Ernst Laas* (1903); Falckenberg, *Hist. of Mod. Philos.* (Eng. trans., 1895).

LA BADIE, JEAN DE (1610–1674), French divine, founder of the school known as the Labadists, was born at Bourg, not far from Bordeaux, on the 13th of February 1610, being the son of [illegible] Charles de la Badie, governor of Guienne. He was sent [illegible] the Jesuit school at Bordeaux, and when fifteen entered the [illegible] college there. In 1626 he began to study philosophy [illegible] theology. He was led to hold somewhat extreme views [illegible] the efficacy of prayer and the direct influence of the Holy [illegible] upon believers, and adopted Augustinian views about [illegible] free will and predestination, which brought him into [illegible] with his order. He therefore separated from the [illegible] and then became a preacher to the people, carrying on [illegible] at Bordeaux, Paris and Amiens. At Amiens in 1640 [illegible] appointed a canon and teacher of theology. The hostility [illegible] Mazarin, however, forced him to retire to the Car[illegible] hermitage at Graville. A study of Calvin's *Institutes* [illegible] that he had more in common with the Reformed [illegible] the Roman Catholic Church, and after various [illegible] joined the Reformed Church of France and [illegible] of theology at Montauban in 1650. His reasons [illegible] published in the same year in his *Déclaration* [illegible] Rome. His accession to the ranks of the Pro[illegible] a great triumph; no such man since Calvin [illegible] had left the Roman Catholic Church. [illegible] the pastorate of the church at Orange on the [illegible] at once became noted for his severity of [illegible] his face zealously against dancing, card[illegible] entertainments. The unsettled state of [illegible] annexed to France, compelled him to leave [illegible] he became a pastor in Geneva. He then [illegible] the French church in London, but after [illegible] settled at Middelburg, where he was pastor [illegible] congregation at a Walloon church. [illegible] by this time (1666) well known, and [illegible] found themselves in conflict with the [illegible] The result was that la Badie and his [illegible] church in a neighbouring town. [illegible] He had enthusiastic disciples, [illegible] at Montauban, Pierre Dulignon [illegible] (d. 1670), Theodor Untereyk (d. [illegible]), and, more important than [illegible]–1678), whose book *Eucleria* [illegible] of the tenets of her master. At [illegible] congregation, la Badie developed his [illegible] Reformed Churches: the church [illegible] who have been born again from [illegible] of this regeneration, and is [illegible] believers; the Holy Spirit guides [illegible] the church possesses throughout [illegible] which it had in the ancient days; [illegible] the continual type of every [illegible] should be a community [illegible] together, eat together, dance [illegible] between two believers, [illegible] are born without original [illegible] is not binding. [illegible] so they said—their [illegible] and separatism of the [illegible] collision with their [illegible] and in 1670 they accepted the invitation of the princess Elizabeth, abbess of Herford in Westphalia, to take up their abode within her territories, and settled in Herford to the number of about fifty. Not finding the rest they expected they migrated to Bremen in 1672, and afterwards to Altona, where they were dispersed on the death of the leaders. Small communities also existed in the Rhineland, and a missionary settlement was established in New York. Jean de la Badie died in February 1674.

La Badie's works include *La Prophétie* (1668), *Manuel de piété* (1669), *Protestation de bonne foi et saine doctrine* (1670), *Brève déclaration de nos sentiments touchant l'Église* (1670). See H. van Berkum, *De Labadie en de Labadisten* (Sneek, 1851); Max Göbel (1811–1857), *Gesch. d. christl. Lebens in der rheinisch-westphälischen Kirche* (Coblenz, 3 vols., 1849–1860); Heinrich Heppe (1820–1879), *Geschichte des Pietismus* (Leiden, 1879); Albrecht Ritschl, *Geschichte des Pietismus*, vol. i. (Bonn, 1880); and especially Peter Yvon, *Abrégé précis de la vie et de la conduite et des vrais sentiments de feu Mr de Labadie*, and Anna Maria v. Schürman, *Eucleria* (Altona, 1673, 1678). Cf. the article in Herzog-Hauck, *Realencyklopädie*.

LABARUM, the sacred military standard of the early Christian Roman emperors, first adopted by Constantine the Great after his miraculous vision in 312, although, according to Gibbon, he did not exhibit it to the army till 323. The name seems to have been known before, and the banner was simply a Christianized form of the Roman cavalry standard. Eusebius (*Life of Const.* i. 31) describes the first labarum as consisting of a long gilded spear, crossed at the top by a bar from which hung a square purple cloth, richly jewelled. At the upper extremity of the spear was a golden wreath encircling the sacred monogram, formed of the first two letters of the name of Christ. In later banners the monogram was sometimes embroidered on the cloth. A special guard of fifty soldiers was appointed to protect the sacred standard. The derivation of the word labarum is disputed; it appears to be connected with the Basque *labarva*, signifying standard. See FLAG.

LABÉ, LOUISE CHARLIN PERRIN (c. 1525–1566), French poet, called *La Belle Cordière*, was born at Lyons about 1525, the daughter of a rich ropemaker, named Charley or Charlin. At the siege of Perpignan she is said to have fought on horseback in the ranks of the Dauphin, afterwards Henry II. Some time before 1551 she married Ennemond Perrin, a ropemaker. She formed a library and gathered round her a society which included many of the learned ladies of Lyons,—Pernette du Guillet, Claudine and Sibylle Scève and Clémence de Bourges, and the poets Maurice Scève, Charles Fontaine, Pontus de Tyard; and among the occasional visitors were Clément Marot and his friend Melin de Saint-Gelais, with probably Bonaventure des Périers and Rabelais. About 1550 the poet Olivier de Magny passed through Lyons on his way to Italy in the suite of Jean d'Avanson, the French envoy to the Holy See. As the friend of Ronsard, "Prince of Poets," he met with an enthusiastic reception from Louise, who straightway fell in love with him. There seems little doubt that her passion for Magny inspired her eager, sincere verse, and the elegies probably express her grief at his first absence. A second short visit to Lyons was followed by a second longer absence. Magny's influence is shown more decisively in her *Sonnets*, which, printed in 1555, quickly attained great popularity. During his second visit to Italy Magny had apparently consoled himself, and Louise, despairing of his return, encouraged another admirer, Claude Rubys, when her lover returned unexpectedly. Louise dismissed Rubys, but Magny's jealousy found vent in an ode addressed to the Sire Aymon (Ennemond), which ruined her reputation; while Rubys, angry at his dismissal, avenged himself later in his *Histoire véritable de Lyons* (1573). This scandal struck a fatal blow at Louise's position. Shortly afterwards her husband died, and she returned to her country house at Parcieu, where she died on the 25th of April 1566, leaving the greater part of the fortune she was left to the poor. Her works include, besides the *Elegies* and *Sonnets* mentioned, a prose *Débat de folie et d'amour* (translated into English by Robert Greene in 1608).

See editions of her *Œuvres* by P. Blanchemain (1875), and by C. Boy (2 vols., 1887). A sketch of Louise Labé and of the Lyonnese

Society is in Miss Edith Sichel's *Women and Men of the French Renaissance* (1901). See also J. Favre, *Olivier de Magny* (1885).

LABEL (a French word, now represented by *lambeau*, possibly a variant; it is of obscure origin and may be connected with a Teutonic word appearing in the English "lap," a flap or fold), a slip, ticket, or card of paper, metal or other material, attached to an object, such as a parcel, bottle, &c., and containing a name, address, description or other information, for the purpose of identification. Originally the word meant a band or ribbon of linen or other material, and was thus applied to the fillets (*infulae*) attached to a bishop's mitre. In heraldry the "label" is a mark of "cadency."

In architecture the term "label" is applied to the outer projecting moulding over doors, windows, arches, &c., sometimes called "Dripstone" or "Weather Moulding," or "Hood Mould." The former terms seem scarcely applicable, as this moulding is often inside a building where no rain could come, and consequently there is no drip. In Norman times the label frequently did not project, and when it did it was very little, and formed part of the series of arch mouldings. In the Early English styles they were not very large, sometimes slightly undercut, sometimes deeply, sometimes a quarter round with chamfer, and very frequently a "roll" or "scroll-moulding," so called because it resembles the part of a scroll where the edge laps over the body of the roll. Labels generally resemble the string-courses of the period, and, in fact, often return horizontally and form strings. They are less common in Continental architecture than in English.

LABEO, MARCUS ANTISTIUS (*c.* 50 B.C.–A.D. 18), Roman jurist, was the son of Pacuvius Antistius Labeo, a jurist who caused himself to be slain after the defeat of his party at Philippi. A member of the plebeian nobility, and in easy circumstances, the younger Labeo early entered public life, and soon rose to the praetorship; but his undisguised antipathy to the new régime, and the somewhat brusque manner in which in the senate he occasionally gave expression to his republican sympathies—what Tacitus (*Ann.* iii. 75) calls his *incorrupta libertas*—proved an obstacle to his advancement, and his rival, Ateius Capito, who had unreservedly given in his adhesion to the ruling powers, was promoted by Augustus to the consulate, when the appointment should have fallen to Labeo, smarting under the wrong done him, Labeo declined the office when it was offered to him in a subsequent year (Tac. *Ann* iii. 75; Pompon, in fr. 47, *Dig.* i. 2). From this time he seems to have devoted his whole time to jurisprudence. His training in the science had been derived principally from Trebatius Testa. To his knowledge of the law he added a wide general culture, devoting his attention specially to dialectics, philology (*grammatica*), and antiquities, as valuable aids in the exposition, expansion, and application of legal doctrine (Gell. xiii. 10). Down to the time of Hadrian his was probably the name of greatest authority; and several of his works were abridged and annotated by later hands. While Capito is hardly ever referred to, the dicta of Labeo are of constant recurrence in the writings of the classical jurists, such as Gaius, Ulpian and Paul; and no inconsiderable number of them were thought worthy of preservation in Justinian's *Digest*. Labeo gets the credit of being the founder of the Proculian sect or school, while Capito is spoken of as the founder of the rival Sabinian one (Pomponius in fr 47, *Dig* i. 2), but it is probable that the real founders of the two *scholae* were Proculus and Sabinus, followers respectively of the methods of Labeo and Capito

Labeo's most important literary work was the *Libri Posteriorum*, so called because published only after his death. It contained a systematic exposition of the common law His *Libri ad Edictum* embraced a commentary, not only on the edicts of the urban and peregrine praetors, but also on that of the curule aediles His *Probabilium (πιθανῶν) lib VIII*, a collection of definitions and axiomatic legal propositions, seems to have been one of his most characteristic productions.

See van Eck, "De vita, moribus, et studiis M Ant Labeonis" (Franeker, 1692), in Oelrichs's *Thes nov*, vol. i, Mascovius, *De sectis Sabinianor et Proculianor* (1728), Pernice, *M Antistius Labeo. Das röm Privatrecht im ersten Jahrhunderte der Kaiserzeit* (Halle, 1873–1892).

LABERIUS, DECIMUS (*c.* 105–43 B.C.), Roman knight and writer of mimes. He seems to have been a man of caustic wit, who wrote for his own pleasure. In 45 Julius Caesar ordered him to appear in one of his own mimes in a public contest with the actor Publilius Syrus. Laberius pronounced a dignified prologue on the degradation thus thrust on his sixty years, and directed several sharp allusions against the dictator. Caesar awarded the victory to Publilius, but restored Laberius to his equestrian rank, which he had forfeited by appearing as a mimus (Macrobius, *Sat.* ii. 7). Laberius was the chief of those who introduced the mimus into Latin literature towards the close of the republican period. He seems to have been a man of learning and culture, but his pieces did not escape the coarseness inherent to the class of literature to which they belonged; and Aulus Gellius (xvi. 7, 1) accuses him of extravagance in the coining of new words. Horace (*Sat.* i. 10) speaks of him in terms of qualified praise.

In addition to the prologue (in Macrobius), the titles of forty-four of his mimi have been preserved; the fragments have been collected by O Ribbeck in his *Comicorum Latinorum reliquiae* (1873).

LABIATAE (*i.e* "lipped," Lat *labium*, lip), in botany, a natural order of seed-plants belonging to the series Tubiflorae of the dicotyledons, and containing about 150 genera with 2800 species. The majority are annual or perennial herbs

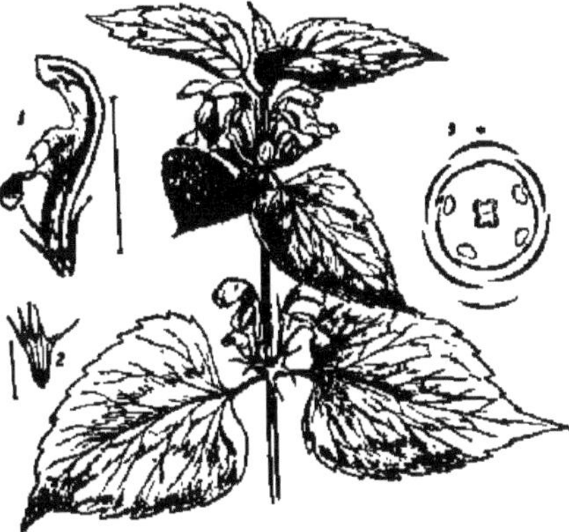

FIG. 1.—Flowering Shoot of Dead-nettle (*Lamium album*). *1*, Flower cut lengthwise, enlarged; *2* calyx, enlarged, *3*, floral diagram.

inhabiting the temperate zone, becoming shrubby in warmer climates. The stem is generally square in section and the simple exstipulate leaves are arranged in decussating pairs (*i.e.* each pair is in a plane at right angles to that of the pairs immediately above and below it); the blade is entire, or toothed, lobed or more or less deeply cut. The plant is often hairy, and the hairs are frequently glandular, the secretion containing a scent characteristic of the genus or species. The flowers are borne in the axils of the leaves or bracts; they are rarely solitary as in *Scutellaria* (skull-cap), and generally form an apparent whorl (*verticillaster*) at the node, consisting of a pair of cymose inflorescences each of which is a simple three-flowered dichasium as in *Brunella*, *Salvia*, &c., or more generally a dichasium passing over into a pair of monochasial cymes as in *Lamium* (fig 1), *Ballota*, *Nepeta*, &c A number of whorls may be crowded at the apex of the stem and the subtending leaves reduced to small bracts, the whole forming a raceme- or spike-like inflorescence as in *Mentha* (fig 2, 5) *Brunella*, &c, the bracts are sometimes large and coloured as in *Monarda*, species of *Salvia*, &c, in the latter the apex of the stem is sometimes occupied with a cluster of sterile coloured bracts. The plan of the flower is remarkably uniform (fig. 1, 3); it is bisexual, and zygomorphic in the [illegible] posterior pair is [illegible] the pistil consisting [illegible] anatropous ovule attached [illegible] style springs from the [illegible] segments (gynobasic), and [illegible] comprises four one-seeded [illegible] the seed has a thin [illegible] Although [illegible] the flower is very [illegible] Thus the calyx [illegible] or straight [illegible] teeth or lobes varies [illegible] (fig. 2, [illegible] as in thyme [illegible] the number [illegible] of genera, [illegible] which simple or [illegible] developed. The shape

[illegible] 2. Corolla of same [illegible] flower of spearmint (*Mentha* [illegible] showing stamens; 6, flower-[illegible] diagram of *Salvia*.

[illegible] the differences being doubtless [illegible] pollination of the flowers by insect-[illegible] or variously bent and often [illegible] occasionally the limb is equally [illegible] (fig. 2, 3, 4) an almost [illegible] of the two posterior teeth. [illegible] lip being formed by the two [illegible] anterior petals (see fig 1, [illegible] the lower lip is generally [illegible] for the bee or other [illegible] for honey, the upper lip shows [illegible] (fig. 1), *Stachys*, &c., [illegible] from rain for the stamens, [illegible] the tribe *Ocimoideae* the four [illegible] and the single anterior one [illegible] the upper lip is absent, all five [illegible] the lower. The posterior [illegible] staminode, but generally [illegible] reduced to staminodes [illegible] in *Salvia* (fig. 2, 2, 6), [illegible] pair reduced. In [illegible] In *Nepeta* and allied [illegible] but this is rare, the [illegible] of the anterior [illegible] two-celled, each cell [illegible] be more or less [illegible] is seen in *Salvia* [illegible] where the connective is filiform and jointed to the [illegible] while the anterior anther-cell is reduced to a sterile appendage. Honey is secreted by a hypogynous disk. In the more general type of flower the anthers and stigmas are protected by the arching upper lip as in dead-nettle (fig. 1) and many other British genera; the lower lip affords a resting-place for the insect which in probing the flower for the honey, secreted on the lower side of the disk, collects pollen on its back. Numerous variations in detail are found in the different genera; in *Salvia* (fig. 2), for instance, there is a lever mechanism, the barren half of each anther forming a knob at the end of a short arm which when touched by the head of an insect causes the anther at the end of the longer arm to descend on the insect's back. In the less common type, where the anterior part of the flower is more developed, as in the *Ocimoideae*, the stamens and style lie on the under lip and honey is secreted on the upper side of the hypogynous disk; the insect in probing the flower gets smeared with pollen on its belly and legs. Both types include brightly-coloured flowers with longer tubes adapted to the visits of butterflies and moths, as species of *Salvia*, *Stachys*, *Monarda*, &c.; some South American species of *Salvia* are pollinated by humming-birds. In *Mentha* (fig. 2, 3), thyme, marjoram (*Origanum*), and allied genera, the flowers are nearly regular and the stamens spread beyond the corolla.

The persistent calyx encloses the ripe nutlets, and aids in their distribution in various ways, by means of winged spiny or hairy lobes or teeth, sometimes it forms a swollen bladder. A scanty endosperm is sometimes present in the seed; the embryo is generally parallel to the fruit axis with a short inferior radicle and generally flat cotyledons.

The order occurs in all warm and temperate regions; its chief centre is the Mediterranean region, where some genera such as *Lavandula*, *Thymus*, *Rosmarinus* and others form an important feature in the vegetation. The tribe *Ocimoideae* is exclusively tropical and subtropical and occurs in both hemispheres. The order is well represented in Britain by seventeen native genera; *Mentha* (mint) including also *M. piperita* (peppermint) and *M. Pulegium* (pennyroyal); *Origanum vulgare* (marjoram); *Thymus Serpyllum* (thyme); *Calamintha* (calamint), including also *C. Clinopodium* (wild basil) and *C. Acinos* (basil thyme); *Salvia* (sage), including *S. Verbenaca* (clary); *Nepeta Cataria* (catmint), *N. Glechoma* (ground-ivy), *Brunella* (self-heal); *Scutellaria* (skull-cap); *Stachys* (woundwort); *S. Betonica* is wood betony; *Galeopsis* (hemp-nettle); *Lamium* (dead-nettle); *Ballota* (black horehound); *Teucrium* (germander); and *Ajuga* (bugle).

Labiatae are readily distinguished from all other orders of the series excepting Verbenaceae, in which, however, the style is terminal; but several genera, e.g. *Ajuga*, *Teucrium* and *Rosmarinus*, approach Verbenaceae in this respect, and in some genera of that order the style is more or less sunk between the ovary lobes. The fruit-character indicates an affinity with Boraginaceae from which, however, they differ in habit and by characters of ovule and embryo.

The presence of volatile oil renders many genera of economic use, such are thyme, marjoram (*Origanum*), sage (*Salvia*), lavender (*Lavandula*), rosemary (*Rosmarinus*), patchouli (*Pogostemon*). The tubers of *Stachys Sieboldi* are eaten in France.

LABICANA, VIA, an ancient highroad of Italy, leading E.S.E. from Rome It seems possible that the road at first led to Tusculum, that it was then prolonged to Labici, and later still became a road for through traffic, it may even have superseded the Via Latina as a route to the S E, for, while the distance from Rome to their main junction at Ad Bivium (or to another junction at Compitum Anagninum) is practically identical, the summit level of the former is 725 ft. lower than that of the latter, a little to the west of the pass of Algidus. After their junction it is probable that the road bore the name Via Latina rather than Via Labicana. The course of the road after the first six miles from Rome is not identical with that of any modern road, but can be clearly traced by remains of pavement and buildings along its course.

See T. Ashby in *Papers of the British School at Rome*, i. 215 sqq. (T. As.)

LABICHE, EUGÈNE MARIN (1815–1888), French dramatist, was born on the 5th of May 1815, of *bourgeois* parentage. He read for the bar, but literature had more powerful attractions, and he was hardly twenty when he gave to the *Chérubin*—an impertinent little magazine, long vanished and forgotten—a short story, entitled, in the cavalier style of the period, *Les plus belles sont les plus fausses*. A few others followed much in the same strain, but failed to catch the attention of the public. He tried his hand at dramatic criticism in the *Revue des théâtres*, and in 1838 made a double venture on the stage. The small Théâtre du Panthéon produced, amid some signs of popular favour, a drama of his, *L'Avocat Loubet*, while a vaudeville, *Monsieur de Coislin ou l'homme infiniment poli*, written in collaboration with Marc Michel, and given at the Palais Royal, introduced for the first time to the Parisians a provincial actor who was to become and to remain a great favourite with them, Grassot, the famous low comedian. In the same year Labiche, still doubtful about his true vocation, published a romance called *La Clé des champs*. M. Léon Halévy, his successor at the Academy and his panegyrist, informs us that the publisher became a bankrupt soon after the novel was out. "A lucky misadventure, for," the biographer concludes, "this timely warning of Destiny sent him back to the stage, where a career of success was awaiting him." There was yet another obstacle in the way. When he married, he solemnly promised his wife's parents that he would renounce a profession then considered incompatible with moral regularity and domestic happiness. But a year afterwards his wife spontaneously released him from his vow, and Labiche recalled the incident when he dedicated the first edition of his complete works: "To my wife." Labiche, in conjunction with Varin,[1] Marc Michel,[2] Clairville,[3] Dumanoir,[4] and others contributed comic plays interspersed with couplets to various Paris theatres. The series culminated in the memorable farce in five acts, *Un Chapeau de paille d'Italie* (August 1851). It remains an accomplished specimen of the French *imbroglio*, in which some one is in search of something, but does not find it till five minutes before the curtain falls. Prior to that date Labiche had been only a successful *vaudevilliste* among a crowd of others; but a twelvemonth later he made a new departure in *Le Misanthrope et l'Auvergnat*. All the plays given for the next twenty-five years, although constructed on the old plan, contained a more or less appreciable dose of that comic observation and good sense which gradually raised the French farce almost to the level of the comedy of character and manners. "Of all the subjects," he said, "which offered themselves to me, I have selected the *bourgeois*. Essentially mediocre in his vices and in his virtues, he stands half-way between the hero and the scoundrel, between the saint and the profligate." During the second period of his career Labiche had the collaboration of Delacour,[5] Choler,[6] and others. When it is asked what share in the authorship and success of the plays may be claimed for those men, we shall answer in Émile Augier's words: "The distinctive qualities which secured a lasting vogue for the plays of Labiche are to be found in all the comedies written by him with different collaborators, and are conspicuously absent from those which they wrote without him." A more useful and more important collaborator he found in Jean Marie Michel Geoffroy (1813–1883) whom he had known as a *débutant* in his younger days, and who remained his faithful interpreter to the last. Geoffroy impersonated the *bourgeois* not only to the public, but to the author himself; and it may be assumed that Labiche, when writing, could see and hear Geoffroy acting the character and uttering, in his pompous, fussy way, the words that he had just committed to paper. *Célimare le bien-aimé* (1863), *Le Voyage de M. Perrichon* (1860), *La Grammaire*, *Un Pied dans le crime*, *La Cagnotte* (1864), may be quoted as the happiest productions of Labiche.

In 1877 he brought his connexion with the stage to a close, and retired to his rural property in Sologne. There he could be seen, dressed as a farmer, with low-brimmed hat, thick gaiters and an enormous stick, superintending the agricultural work and busily engaged in reclaiming land and marshes. His life-long friend, Augier, visited him in his principality, and, being left alone in the library, took to reading his host's dramatic productions, scattered here and there in the shape of theatrical *brochures*. He strongly advised Labiche to publish a collected and revised edition of his works. The suggestion, first declined as a joke and long resisted, was finally accepted and carried into effect. Labiche's comic plays, in ten volumes, were issued during 1878 and 1879. The success was even greater than had been expected by the author's most sanguine friends. It had been commonly believed that these plays owed their popularity in great measure to the favourite actors who had appeared in them; but it was now discovered that all, with the exception of Geoffroy, had introduced into them a grotesque and caricatural element, thus hiding from the spectator, in many cases, the true comic vein and delightful delineation of human character. The amazement turned into admiration, and the *engouement* became so general that very few dared grumble or appear scandalized when, in 1880, Labiche was elected to the French Academy. It was fortunate that, in former years, he had never dreamt of attaining this high distinction; for, as M. Pailleron justly observed, while trying to get rid of the little faults which were in him, he would have been in danger of losing some of his sterling qualities. But when the honour was bestowed upon him, he enjoyed it with his usual good sense and quiet modesty. He died in Paris on the 23rd of January 1888.

Some foolish admirers have placed him on a level with Molière, but it will be enough to say that he was something better than a public *amuseur*. Many of his plays have been transferred to the English stage. They are, on the whole, as sound as they are entertaining. Love is practically absent from his theatre. In none of his plays did he ever venture into the depths of feminine psychology, and womankind is only represented in them by pretentious old maids and silly, insipid, almost dumb, young ladies. He ridiculed marriage according to the invariable custom of French playwrights, but in a friendly and good-natured manner which always left a door open to repentance and timely amendment. He is never coarse, never suggestive. After he died the French farce, which he had raised to something akin to literature, relapsed into its former grossness and unmeaning complexity. (A. Fi.)

His *Théâtre complet* (10 vols., 1878–1879) contains a preface by Émile Augier.

LABICI, an ancient city of Latium, the modern Monte Compatri, about 17 m. S.E. from Rome, on the northern slopes of the Alban Hills, 1739 ft. above sea-level. It occurs among the thirty cities of the Latin League, and it is said to have joined the Aequi in 419 B.C. and to have been captured by the Romans in 418. After this it does not appear in history, and in the time of Cicero and Strabo was almost entirely deserted if not destroyed. Traces of its ancient walls have been noticed. Its place was taken by the *respublica Lavicanorum Quintanensium*, the post-station established in the lower ground on the Via Labicana (see LABICANA, VIA), a little S.W. of the modern village of Colonna, the site of which is attested by various inscriptions and by the course of the road itself.

See T. Ashby in *Papers of the British School at Rome*, i. 256 sqq. (T. As.)

LABID (Abū 'Aqīl Labīd ibn Rabī'a) (*c.* 560–*c.* 661), Arabian poet, belonged to the Banī 'Āmir, a division of the tribe of the Hawāzin. In his younger years he was an active warrior and his verse is largely concerned with inter-tribal disputes. Later, he was sent by a sick uncle to get a remedy from Mahomet at Medina and on this occasion was much influenced by a part of the Koran. He accepted Islam soon after, but seems then to have ceased writing. In Omar's caliphate he is said to have settled in Kufa. Tradition ascribes to him a long life, but dates given are uncertain and contradictory. One of his poems is contained in the *Mo'allakat* (*q.v.*).

Twenty of his poems were edited by Chālidī (Vienna, 1880); another thirty-five, with fragments and a German translation of the

[1] Victor Varin, pseudonym of Charles Voirin (1798–1869).

[2] Marc Antoine Amédée Michel (1812–1868), vaudevillist.

[3] Louis François Nicolaïe, called Clairville (1811–1879), part-author of the famous *Fille de Mme Angot* (1872).

[4] Philippe François Pinel, called Dumanoir (1806–1865).

[5] Alfred Charlemagne Lartigue, called Delacour (1815–1885). For a list of this author's pieces see O. Lorenz, *Catalogue Général* (vol. ii., 1868).

[6] Adolphe Joseph Choler (1822–1889).

whole, were edited (partly from the remains of A. Huber) by C. Brockelmann (Leiden, 1892); cf. A. von Kremer, *Über die Gedichte des Lebyd* (Vienna, 1881). Stories of Labid are contained in the *Kitâbul-Aghâni*, xiv. 93 ff. and xv. 137 ff. (G. W. T.)

LABIENUS, the name of a Roman family, said (without authority) to belong to the gens Atia. The most important member was TITUS LABIENUS. In 63 B.C., at Caesar's instigation, he prosecuted Gaius Rabirius (*q.v.*) for treason; in the same year, as tribune of the plebs, he carried a plebiscite which indirectly secured for Caesar the dignity of pontifex maximus (Dio Cassius xxxvii. 37). He served as a legatus throughout Caesar's Gallic campaigns and took Caesar's place whenever he went to Rome. His chief exploits in Gaul were the defeat of the Treviri under Indutiomarus in 54, his expedition against Lutetia (Paris) in 52, and his victory over Camulogenus and the Aedui in the same year. On the outbreak of the civil war, however, he was one of the first to desert Caesar, probably owing to an overweening sense of his own importance, not adequately recognized by Caesar. He was rapturously welcomed on the Pompeian side; but he brought no great strength with him, and his ill fortune under Pompey was as marked as his success had been under Caesar. From the defeat at Pharsalus, to which he had contributed by affecting to despise his late comrades, he fled to Corcyra, and thence to Africa. There he was able by mere force of numbers to inflict a slight check upon Caesar at Ruspina in 46. After the defeat at Thapsus he joined the younger Pompey in Spain, and was killed at Munda (March 17th, 45).

LABLACHE, LUIGI (1794–1858), Franco-Italian singer, was born at Naples on the 6th of December 1794, the son of a merchant of Marseilles who had married an Irish lady. In 1806 he entered the Conservatorio della Pieta de Turchini, where he studied music under Gentili and singing under Valesi, besides learning to play the violin and violoncello. As a boy he had a beautiful alto voice, and by the age of twenty he had developed a magnificent bass with a compass of two octaves from E♭ below to E♭ above the bass stave. After making his first appearance at Naples he went to Milan in 1817, and subsequently travelled to Turin, Venice and Vienna. His first appearances in London and Paris in 1830 led to annual engagements in both the English and French capitals. His reception at St Petersburg a few years later was no less enthusiastic. In England he took part in many provincial musical festivals, and was engaged by Queen Victoria to teach her singing. On the operatic stage he was equally successful in comic or tragic parts, and with his wonderfully powerful voice he could express either humour or pathos. Among his friends were Rossini, Bellini, Donizetti and Mercadante. He was one of the thirty-two torch-bearers chosen to surround the coffin at Beethoven's funeral in 1827. He died at Naples on the 23rd of January 1858 and was buried at Maison Lafitte, [illegible] Lablache's Leporello in *Don Giovanni* was perhaps his [illegible] impersonation; among his principal other rôles [illegible] in *Cenerentola* (Rossini), Assur in *Semiramide* [illegible] in *La Gazza Ladra* (Rossini), Henry VIII. [illegible] (Donizetti), the Doge in *Marino Faliero* [illegible] in *Don Pasquale* (Donizetti), Geronimo [illegible] *Segreto* (Cimarosa), Gritzenko in *L'Étoile du* [illegible] Caliban in *The Tempest* (Halévy).

[illegible] United States, a legal holiday in nearly [illegible] Territories, where the first Monday in [illegible] by parades and meetings of labour [illegible] the Knights of Labor paraded in New [illegible] 1884 another parade was held, and it [illegible] should be set apart for this purpose. [illegible] first Monday in September a legal [illegible] Labor Day was observed as a holiday [illegible] except in Arizona and North [illegible] holiday only in New Orleans [illegible] Wyoming and New Mexico [illegible] statute, but in each may [illegible] the governor.

[illegible] of central France, in [illegible] Dore by road. Pop. (1906) 1401. La Bourboule is situated on the right bank of the Dordogne at a height of 2790 ft. Its waters, of which arsenic is the characteristic constituent, are used in cases of diseases of the skin and respiratory organs, rheumatism, neuralgia, &c. Though known to the Romans they were not in much repute till towards the end of the 19th century. The town has three thermal establishments and a casino.

LABOUR CHURCH, THE, an organization intended to give expression to the religion of the labour movement. This religion is not theological—it leaves theological questions to private individual conviction—but "seeks the realization of universal well-being by the establishment of Socialism—a commonwealth founded upon justice and love." It asserts that "improvement of social conditions and the development of personal character are both essential to emancipation from social and moral bondage, and to that end insists upon the duty of studying the economic and moral forces of society." The first Labour Church was founded at Manchester (England) in October 1891 by a Unitarian minister, John Trevor. This has disappeared, but vigorous successors have been established not only in the neighbourhood, but in Bradford, Birmingham, Nottingham, London, Wolverhampton and other centres of industry, about 30 in all, with a membership of 3000. Many branches of the Independent Labour Party and the Social Democratic Federation also hold Sunday gatherings for adults and children, using the Labour Church hymn-book and a similar form of service, the reading being chosen from Dr Stanton Coit's *Message of Man*. There are special forms for child-naming, marriages and burials. The separate churches are federated in a Labour Church Union, which holds an annual conference and business meeting in March. At the conference of 1909, held in Ashton-under-Lyne, the name "Labour Church" was changed to "Socialist Church."

LA BOURDONNAIS, BERTRAND FRANÇOIS, COUNT MAHÉ DE (1699–1753), French naval commander, was born at Saint Malo on the 11th of February 1699. He went to sea when a boy, and in 1718 entered the service of the French India Company as a lieutenant. In 1724 he was promoted captain, and displayed such bravery in the capture of Mahé of the Malabar coast that the name of the town was added to his own. For two years he was in the service of the Portuguese viceroy of Goa, but in 1735 he returned to French service as governor of the Île de France and the Île de Bourbon. His five years' administration of the islands was vigorous and successful. A visit to France in 1740 was interrupted by the outbreak of hostilities with Great Britain, and La Bourdonnais was put at the head of a fleet in Indian waters. He saved Mahé, relieved General Dupleix at Pondicherry, defeated Lord Peyton, and in 1746 participated in the siege of Madras. He quarrelled with Dupleix over the conduct of affairs in India, and his anger was increased on his return to the Île de France at finding a successor to himself installed there by his rival. He set sail on a Dutch vessel to present his case at court, and was captured by the British, but allowed to return to France on parole. Instead of securing a settlement of his quarrel with Dupleix, he was arrested (1748) on a charge of gubernatorial peculation and maladministration, and secretly imprisoned for over two years in the Bastille. He was tried in 1751 and acquitted, but his health was broken by the imprisonment and by chagrin at the loss of his property. To the last he made unjust accusations against Dupleix. He died at Paris on the 10th of November 1753. The French government gave his widow a pension of 2400 livres.

La Bourdonnais wrote *Traité de la mâture des vaisseaux* (Paris 1723), and left valuable memoirs which were published by his grandson, a celebrated chess player, Count L. C. Mahé de la Bourdonnais (1795–1840) (latest edition, Paris, 1890). His quarrel with Dupleix has given rise to much debate; for a long while the fault was generally laid to the arrogance and jealousy of Dupleix, but W. Cartwright and Colonel Malleson have pointed out that La Bourdonnais was proud, suspicious and over-ambitious.

See P. de Gennes, *Mémoire pour le sieur de la Bourdonnais, avec les pièces justificatives* (Paris, 1750); *The Case of Mde la Bourdonnais, in a Letter to a Friend* (London, 1748); Fantin des Odoards, *Révolutions de l'Inde* (Paris, 1796); Collin de Bar, *Histoire de l'Inde ancienne et moderne* (Paris, 1814); Barchou de Penhoën, *Histoire de la conquête et de la fondation de l'empire anglais dans l'Inde* (Paris, 1840); Margry, "Les Isles de France et de Bourbon sous le gouvernement de La Bourdonnais," in *La Revue maritime et coloniale* (1862); W. Cartwright, "Dupleix et l'Inde française," in *La Revue britannique* (1882); G. B. Malleson, *Dupleix* (Oxford, 1895); Anandaranga Pillai, *Les Français dans l'Inde, Dupleix et Labourdonnais, extraits du journal d'Anandaran-gappoullé 1736–1748*, trans. in French by Vinson in *École spéciale des langues orientales vivantes*, series 3, vol. xv. (Paris, 1894).

LABOUR EXCHANGE, a term very frequently applied to registries having for their principal object the better distribution of labour (see UNEMPLOYMENT). Historically the term is applied to the system of equitable labour exchanges established in England between 1832 and 1834 by Robert Owen and his followers. The idea is said to have originated with Josiah Warren, who communicated it to Owen. Warren tried an experiment in 1828 at Cincinnati, opening an exchange under the title of a "time store." He joined in starting another at Tuscarawas, Ohio, and a third at Mount Vernon, Indiana, but none were quite on the same line as the English exchanges. The fundamental idea of the English exchanges was to establish a currency based upon labour; Owen in *The Crisis* for June 1832 laid down that all wealth proceeded from labour and knowledge; that labour and knowledge were generally remunerated according to the time employed, and that in the new exchanges it was proposed to make *time* the standard or measure of wealth. This new currency was represented by "labour notes," the notes being measured in hours, and the hour reckoned as being worth sixpence, this figure being taken as the mean between the wage of the best and the worst paid labour. Goods were then to be exchanged for the new currency. The exchange was opened in extensive premises in the Gray's Inn Road, near King's Cross, London, on the 3rd of September 1832. For some months the establishment met with considerable success, and a considerable number of tradesmen agreed to take labour notes in payment for their goods. At first, an enormous number of deposits was made, amounting in seventeen weeks to 445,501 hours. But difficulties soon arose from the lack of sound practical valuators, and from the inability of the promoters to distinguish between the labour of the highly skilled and that of the unskilled. Tradesmen, too, were quick to see that the exchange might be worked to their advantage; they brought unsaleable stock from their shops, exchanged it for labour notes, and then picked out the best of the saleable articles. Consequently the labour notes began to depreciate; trouble also arose with the proprietors of the premises, and the experiment came to an untimely end early in 1834.

See F. Podmore's *Robert Owen*, ii. c. xvii. (1906); B. Jones, *Co-operative Production*, c. viii. (1894); G. J. Holyoake, *History of Co-operation*, c. viii. (1906).

LABOUR LEGISLATION. Regulation of labour,[1] in some form or another, whether by custom, royal authority, ecclesiastical rules or by formal legislation in the interests of a community, is no doubt as old as the most ancient forms of civilization. And older than all civilization is the necessity for the greater part of mankind to labour for maintenance, whether freely or in bonds, whether for themselves and their families or for the requirements or superfluities of others. Even while it is clear, however, that manual labour, or the application of the bodily forces—with or without mechanical aid—to personal maintenance and the production of goods, remains the common lot of the majority of citizens of the most developed modern communities, still there is much risk of confusion if modern technical terms such as "labour," "employer," "labour legislation" are freely applied to conditions in bygone civilizations with wholly different industrial organization and social relationships.

[1] The term "labour" (Lat. *labor*) means strictly any energetic work, though in general it implies hard work, but in modern parlance it is specially confined to industrial work of the kind done by the "working-classes."

In recent times in England there has been a notable disappearance from current use of correlative terms implying a social relationship which is greatly changed, for example, in the rapid passage from the Master and Servant Act 1867 to the Employer and Workman Act 1875. In the 18th century the term "manufacturer" passed from its application to a working craftsman to its modern connotation of at least some command of capital, the employer being no longer a small working master. An even more significant later change is seen in the steady development of a labour legislation, which arose in a clamant social need for the care of specially helpless "protected" persons in factories and mines, into a wider legislation for the promotion of general industrial health, safety and freedom for the worker from fraud in making or carrying out wage contracts.

If, then, we can discern these signs of important changes within so short a period, great caution is needed in rapidly reviewing long periods of time prior to that industrial revolution which is traced mainly to the application of mechanical power to machinery in aid of manual labour, practically begun and completed within the second half of the 18th century. "In 1740 save for the fly-shuttle the loom was as it had been since weaving had begun . . . and the law of the land was" (under the Act of Apprentices of 1563) "that wages in each district should be assessed by Justices of the Peace."[2] Turning back to still earlier times, legislation—whatever its source or authority—must clearly be devoted to aims very different from modern aims in regulating labour, when it arose before the labourer, as a man dependent on an "employer" for the means of doing work, had appeared, and when migratory labour was almost unknown through the serfdom of part of the population and the special status secured in towns to the artisan.

In the great civilizations of antiquity there were great aggregations of labour which was not solely, though frequently it was predominantly, slave labour; and some of the features of manufacture and mining on a great scale arose, producing the same sort of evils and industrial maladies known and regulated in our own times. Some of the maladies were described by Pliny and classed as "diseases of slaves." And he gave descriptions of processes, for example in the metal trades, as belonging entirely to his own day, which modern archaeological discoveries trace back through the earliest known Aryan civilizations to a prehistoric origin in the East, and which have never died out in western Europe, but can be traced in a concentrated manufacture with almost unchanged methods, now in France, now in Germany, now in England.

Little would be gained in such a sketch as this by an endeavour to piece together the scattered and scanty materials for a comparative history of the varying conditions and methods of labour regulation over so enormous a range. While our knowledge continually increases of the remains of ancient craft, skill and massed labour, much has yet to be discovered that may throw light on methods of organization of the labourers. While much, and in some civilizations most, of the labour was compulsory or forced, it is clear that too much has been sometimes assumed, and it is by no means certain that even the pyramids of Egypt, much less the beautiful earliest Egyptian products in metal work, weaving and other skilled craft work, were typical products of slave labour. Even in Rome it was only at times that the proportion of slaves valued as property was greater than that of hired workers, or, apart from capture in war or self-surrender in discharge of a debt, that purchase of slaves by the trader, manufacturer or agriculturist was generally considered the cheapest means of securing labour. As in early England the various stages of village industrial life, medieval town manufacture, and organization in craft gilds, and the beginnings of the mercantile system, were parallel with a greater or less prevalence of serfdom and even with the presence in part of slavery, so in other ages and civilizations the various methods of organization of labour are found to some extent together. The Germans in their primitive settlements were accustomed to the notion of slavery, and in the decline of the

[2] H. D. Traill, *Social England*, v. 602 (1896).

completely altered the face of industrial England. From time to time, in respect of particular trades, provisions against truck and for payment of wages in current coin, similar to the act of Edward IV. in the woollen industry, were found necessary, and this branch of labour legislation developed through the reigns of Anne and the four Georges until consolidation and amendment were effected, after the completion of the industrial revolution, in the Truck Act of 1831. From the close of the 17th century and during the 18th century the legislature is no longer mainly engaged in devising means for compelling labourers and artisans to enter into involuntary service, but rather in regulating the summary powers of justices of the peace in the matter of dispute between masters and servants in relation to contracts and agreements, express or implied, presumed to have been entered into voluntarily on both sides. While the movement to refer labour questions to the jurisdiction of the justices thus gradually developed, the main subject matter for their exercise of jurisdiction in regard to labour also changed, even when theoretically for a time the two sets of powers—such as (*a*) moderation of craft gild ordinances and punishment of workers refusing hire, or (*b*) fixing scales of wages and enforcement of labour contracts—might be concurrently exercised. Even in an act of George II. (1746) for settlement of disputes and differences as to wages or other conditions under a contract of labour, power was retained for the justices, on complaint of the masters of misdemeanour or ill-behaviour on the part of the servant, to discharge the latter from service or to send him to a house of correction "there to be corrected," that is, to be held to hard labour for a term not exceeding a month or to be corrected by whipping. In an act with similar aims of George IV. (1823), with a rather wider scope, the power to order corporal punishment, and in 1867 to hard labour, for breach of labour contracts had disappeared, and soon after the middle of the 19th century the right to enforce contracts of labour also disappeared. Then breach of such labour contracts became simply a question of recovery of damages, unless both parties agreed that security for performance of the contract shall be given instead of damages.

While the endeavour to enforce labour apart from a contract died out in the latter end of the 18th century, sentiment for some time had strongly grown in favour of developing early industrial training of children. It appears to have been a special object of charitable and philanthropic endeavour in the 17th century, as well as the 18th, to found *houses of industry*, in which little children, even under five years of age, might be trained for apprenticeship with employers. Connected as this development was with poor relief, one of its chief aims was to prevent future unemployment and vagrancy by training in habits and knowledge of industry, but not unavowed was another motive: "from children thus trained up to constant labour we may venture to hope the lowering of its price."[1] The evils and excesses which lay enfolded within such a movement gave the first impulse to the new ventures in labour legislation which are specially the work of the 19th century. Evident as it is "that before the Industrial Revolution very young children were largely employed both in their own homes and as apprentices under the Poor Law," and that "long before Peel's time there were misgivings about the apprenticeship system," still it needed the concentration and prominence of suffering and injury to child life in the factory system to lead to parliamentary intervention.

3. *From 1800 to the Codes of 1872 and 1878.*—A serious outbreak of fever in 1784 in cotton mills near Manchester appears to have first drawn widespread and influential public opinion to the overwork of children, under terribly dangerous and insanitary conditions, on which the factory system was then largely being carried on. A local inquiry, chiefly by a group of medical men presided over by Dr Percival, was instituted by the justices of the peace for Lancashire, and in the forefront of the resulting report stood a recommendation for limitation and control of the working hours of the children. A resolution by the county justices followed, in which they declared their intention in future to refuse "indentures of parish Apprentices whereby they shall be bound to Owners of Cotton Mills and other works in which children are obliged to work in the night or more than ten hours in the day." In 1795 the Manchester Board of Health was formed, which, with fuller information, more definitely advised legislation for the regulation of the hours and conditions of labour in factories. In 1802 the Health and Morals of Apprentices Act was passed, which in effect formed the first step towards prevention of injury to and protection of labour in factories. It was directly aimed only at evils of the apprentice system, under which large numbers of pauper children were worked in cotton and woollen mills without education, for excessive hours, under wretched conditions. It did not apply to places employing fewer than twenty persons or three apprentices, and it applied the principle of limitation of hours (to twelve a day) and abolition of night work, as well as educational requirements, only to apprentices. Religious teaching and suitable sleeping accommodation and clothing were provided for in the act, also as regards apprentices. Lime-washing and ventilation provisions applied to all cotton and woollen factories employing more than twenty persons. "Visitors" were to be appointed by county justices for repression of contraventions, and were empowered to "direct the adoption of such sanitary regulations as they might on advice think proper." The mills were to be registered by the clerk of the peace, and justices had power to inflict fines of from £2 to £5 for contraventions. Although enforcement of the very limited provisions of the act was in many cases poor or non-existent, in some districts excellent work was done by justices, and in 1803 the West Riding of Yorkshire justices passed a resolution substituting the ten hours' limit for the twelve hours' limit of the act, as a condition of permission for indenturing of apprentices in mills.

Rapid development of the application of steam power to manufacture led to growth of employment of children in populous centres, otherwise than on the apprenticeship system, and before long the evils attendant on this change brought the general question of regulation and protection of child labour in textile factories to the front. The act of 1819, limited as it was, was a noteworthy step forward, in that it dealt with this wider scope of employment of children in cotton factories, and it is satisfactory to record that it was the outcome of the efforts and practical experiments of a great manufacturer, Robert Owen. Its provisions fell on every point lower than the aims he put forward on his own experience as practicable, and notably in its application only to cotton mills instead of all textile factories. Prohibition of child labour under nine years of age and limitation of the working day to twelve in the twenty-four (without specifying the precise hour of beginning and closing) were the main provisions of this act. No provision was made for enforcement of the law beyond such as was attempted in the act of 1802. Slight amendments were attempted in the acts of 1825 and 1831, but the first really important factory act was in 1833 applying to textile factories generally, limiting employment of young persons under eighteen years of age, as well as children, prohibiting night work between 8.30 P.M. and 5.30 A.M., and first providing for "inspectors" to enforce the law. This is the act which was based on the devoted efforts of Michael Sadler, with whose name in this connexion that of Lord Ashley, afterwards earl of Shaftesbury, was from 1832 associated. The importance of this act lay in its provision for skilled inspection and thus for enforcement of the law by an independent body of men unconnected with the locality in which the manufactures lay, whose specialization in their work enabled them to acquire information needed for further development of legislation for protection of labour. Their powers were to a certain extent judicial, being assimilated to those possessed by justices; they could administer oaths and make such "rules regulations and orders" as were necessary for execution of the act, and could hear complaints and impose penalties under the act. In 1844 a textile factory act modified these extensive

[1] From an "Essay on Trade" (1770), quoted in *History of Factory Legislation*, by B. L. Hutchins and A. Harrison (1903), pp. 5, 6.

inspectoral powers, organizing the service on lines resembling those of our own time, and added provision for certifying surgeons to examine workers under sixteen years of age as to physical fitness for employment and to grant certificates of age and ordinary strength. Hours of labour, by the act of 1833, were limited for children under eleven to 9 a day or 48 in the week, and for young persons under eighteen to 12 a day or 69 in the week. Between 1833 and 1844 the movement in favour of a ten hours' day, which had long been in progress, reached its height in a time of great commercial and industrial distress, but could not be carried into effect until 1847. By the act of 1844 the hours of adult women were first regulated, and were limited (as were already those of "young persons") to 12 a day; children were permitted either to work the same hours on alternate days or "half-time," with compulsory school attendance as a condition of their employment. The aim in thus adjusting the hours of the three classes of workers was to provide for a practical standard working-day. For the first time detailed provisions for health and safety began to make their appearance in the law. Penal compensation for preventible injuries due to unfenced machinery was also provided, and appears to have been the outcome of a discussion by witnesses before the Royal Commission on Labour of Young Persons in Mines and Manufactures in 1841.

From this date, 1841, begin the first attempts at protective legislation for labour in mining. The first Mines Act of 1842 following the terrible revelations of the Royal Commission referred to excluded women and girls from underground working, and limited the employment of boys, excluding from underground working those under ten years, but it was not until 1850 that systematic reporting of fatal accidents and until 1855 that other safeguards for health, life and limb in mines were seriously provided by law. With the exception of regulations against truck there was no protection for the miner before 1842; before 1814 it was not customary to hold inquests on miners killed by accidents in mines. From 1842 onwards considerable interaction in the development of the two sets of acts (mines and factories), as regards special protection against industrial injury to health and limb, took place, both in parliament and in the department (Home Office) administering them. Another strong influence tending towards ultimate development of scientific protection of health and life in industry began in the work and reports of the series of sanitary commissions and Board of Health reports from 1843 onwards. In 1844 the mines inspector made his first report, but two years later women were still employed to some extent underground. Organized inspection began in 1850, and in 1854 the Select Committee on Accidents adopted a suggestion of the inspectors for legislative extension of the practice of several colliery owners in framing special safety rules for working in mines. The act of 1855 provided seven general rules, relating to ventilation, fencing of disused shafts, proper means for signalling, proper gauges and valve for steam-boiler, indicator and brake for machine lowering and raising; also it provided that detailed special rules submitted by mine-owners to the secretary of state, might, on his approval, have the force of law and be enforceable by penalty. The Mines Act of 1860, besides extending the law to ironstone mines, following as it did on a series of disastrous accidents and explosions, strengthened some of the provisions for safety. At several inquests strong evidence was given of incompetent management and neglect of rules, and a demand was made for enforcing employment only of certificated managers of coal mines. This was not met until the act of 1872, but in 1860 certain sections relating to wages and education were introduced. Steady development of the coal industry, increasing association among miners, and increased scientific knowledge of means of ventilation and of other methods for securing safety, all paved the way to the Coal Mines Act of 1872, and in the same year health and safety in metalliferous mines received their first legislative treatment in a code of similar scope and character to that of the Coal Mines Act. This act was amended in 1886, and repealed and recodified in 1887; its principal provisions are still in force, with certain revised special rules and modifications as regards reporting of accidents (1906) and employment of children (1903). It was based on the recommendations of a Royal Commission, which had reported in 1864, and which had shown the grave excess of mortality and sickness among metalliferous miners, attributed to the inhalation of gritty particles, imperfect ventilation, great changes of temperature, excessive physical exertion, exposure to wet, and other causes. The prohibition of employment of women and of boys under ten years underground in this class of mines, as well as in coal mines, had been effected by the act of 1842, and inspection had been provided for in the act of 1860; these were in amended form included in the code of 1872, the age of employment of boys underground being raised to twelve. In the Coal Mines Act of 1872 we see the first important effort to provide a complete code of regulation for the special dangers to health, life and limb in coal mines apart from other mines; it applied to "mines of coal, mines of stratified ironstone, mines of shale and mines of fire-clay." Unlike the companion act—applying to all other mines—it maintained the age limit of entering underground employment for boys at ten years, but for those between ten and twelve it provided for a system of working analogous to the half-time system in factories, including compulsory school attendance. The limits of employment for boys from twelve to sixteen were 10 hours in any one day and 54 in any one week. The chief characteristics of the act lay in extension of the "general" safety rules, improvement of the method of formulating "special" safety rules, provision for certificated and competent management, and increased inspection. Several important matters were transferred from the special to the general rules, such as compulsory use of safety lamps where needed, regulation of use of explosives, and securing of roofs and sides. Special rules, before being submitted to the secretary of state for approval, must be posted in the mine for two weeks, with a notice that objections might be sent by any person employed to the district inspector. Wilful neglect of safety provisions became punishable in the case of employers as well as miners by imprisonment with hard labour. But the most important new step lay in the sections relating to daily control and supervision of every mine by a manager holding a certificate of competency from the secretary of state, after examination by a board of examiners appointed by the secretary of state, power being retained for him to cause later inquiry into competency of the holder of the certificate, and to cancel or suspend the certificate in case of proved unfitness.

Returning to the development of factory and workshop law from the year 1844, the main line of effort—after the act of 1847 had restricted hours of women and young persons to 10 a day and fixed the daily limits between 6 A.M. and 6 P.M. (Saturday 6 A.M. to 2 P.M.)—lay in bringing trade after trade in some degree under the scope of this branch of law, which had hitherto only regulated conditions in textile factories. Bleaching and dyeing works were included by the acts of 1860 and 1862; lace factories by that of 1861; calendering and finishing by acts of 1863 and 1864; bakehouses became partially regulated by an act of 1863, with special reference to local authorities for administration of its clauses. The report of the third Children's Employment Commission brought together in accessible form the miserable facts relating to child labour in a number of unregulated industries in the year 1862, and the act of 1864 brought some of (these earthenware-making, lucifer match-making, percussion cap and cartridge making, paper-staining, and fustian cutting) partly under the scope of the various textile factory acts in force. A larger addition of trades was made three years later, but the act of 1864 is particularly interesting in that it first embodied some of the results of inquiries of expert medical and sanitary commissioners, by requiring ventilation to be applied to the removal of injurious gases, dust, and other impurities generated in manufacture, and made a first attempt to engraft part of the special rules system from the mines acts. The provisions for framing such rules disappeared in the Consolidating Act of 1878, to be revived in a better form later.

[illegible] Act of 1866, administered by local authorities, [illegible] sanitation in any factories and workshops [illegible] factory acts, and the Workshops Regulation [illegible] similarly to be administered by local authorities, [illegible] practically completed the application of the [illegible] factory acts to all places in which manual [illegible] for gain in the making or finishing of [illegible] of articles for sale. A few specially dangerous [illegible] brought under regulation in 1864 and 1867 [illegible] and lucifer match making, glass-making) [illegible] "factories," although not using mechanical power, [illegible] of less than fifty persons relegated [illegible] to the category of "workshops," but broadly [illegible] of such motor power in aid of process [illegible] the distinction between factories [illegible]. The Factory Act of 1874, the last of the series [illegible] Act of 1878, raised the minimum [illegible] for children to ten years in textile factories. [illegible] inquiries into conditions of child labour [illegible] to light, in regard to textile and non-[illegible] that parents as much as any employers [illegible] for too early employment and excessive [illegible] of children, and from early times until [illegible] it has been recognised that they [illegible] be held responsible for due observation of [illegible] example, in 1831 it was found necessary [illegible] against parental responsibility for false [illegible] 1833 parents of a child or "any Person [illegible] the wages of such child" were made [illegible] employment of children without school [illegible] hours.

[illegible] on the bill which became law in 1874, [illegible] that revision and consolidation of the [illegible] regulating manufacturing industry [illegible]; modifications and exceptions [illegible] in separate industries needed re-[illegible] on clear principles, and the [illegible] the law could with great advantage be [illegible] to all the industries. In particular, [illegible] of employment, pauses for meals, [illegible] factories and [illegible] working-day, and [illegible] establishments to [illegible]

to compute the total amount of wages payable to them; (*e*) extension of the act to laundries; (*f*) a tentative effort to limit the too early employment of mothers after childbirth.

II. Law of United Kingdom, 1910

Factories and Workshops.—The act of 1878 remained until 1901, although much had been meanwhile superimposed, a monument to the efforts of the great factory reformers of the first half of the 19th century, and the general groundwork of safety for workers in factories and workshops in the main divisions of sanitation, security against accidents, physical fitness of workers, general limitation of hours and times of employment for young workers and women. The act of 1901, which came into force 1st January 1902 (and became the principal act), was an amending as well as a consolidating act. Comparison of the two acts shows, however, that, in spite of the advantages of further consolidation and helpful changes in arrangement of sections and important additions which tend towards a specialized hygiene for factory life, the fundamental features of the law as fought out in the 19th century remain undisturbed. So far as the law has altered in character, it has done so chiefly by gradual development of certain sanitary features, originally subordinate, and by strengthening provision for security against accidents and not by retreat from its earlier aims. At the same time a basis for possible new developments can be seen in the protection of "outworkers" as well as factory workers against fraudulent or defective particulars of piece-work rates of wages.

Later acts directly and indirectly affecting the law are certain acts of 1903, 1906, 1907, to be touched on presently.

The act of 1878, in a series of acts from 1883 to 1895, received striking additions, based (1) on the experience gained in other branches of protective legislation, *e.g.* development of the method of regulation of dangerous trades by "special rules" and administrative inquiry into accidents under Coal Mines Acts; (2) on the findings of royal commissions and parliamentary inquiries, *e.g.* increased control of "outwork" and domestic workshops, and limitation of "overtime"; (3) on the development of administrative machinery for enforcing the more modern law relating to public health, *e.g.* transference of administration of sanitary provisions in workshops to the local sanitary authorities; (4) on the trade-union demand for means for securing trustworthy records of wage-contracts between employer and workman, *e.g.* the section requiring particulars of work and wages for piece-workers. The first additions to the act of 1878 were, however, almost purely attempts to deal more adequately than had been attempted in the code of 1878 with certain striking instances of trades injurious to health. Thus the Factory and Workshop Act of 1883 provided that white-lead factories should not be carried on without a certificate of conformity with certain conditions, and also made provision for special rules, on lines later superseded by those laid down in the act of 1891, applicable to any employment in a factory or workshop certified as dangerous or injurious by the secretary of state. The act of 1883 also dealt with sanitary conditions in bakehouses. Certain definitions and explanations of previous enactments touching overtime and employment of a child in any factory or workshop were also included in the act. A class of factories in which excessive heat and humidity seriously affected the health of operatives was next dealt with in the Cotton Cloth Factories Act 1889. This provided for special notice to the chief inspector from all occupiers of cotton cloth factories (*i.e.* any room, shed, or workshop or part thereof in which weaving of cotton cloth is carried on) who intend to produce humidity by artificial means; regulated both temperature of workrooms and amount of moisture in the atmosphere, and provided for tests and records of the same; and fixed a standard minimum volume of fresh air (600 cub. ft.) to be admitted in every hour for every person employed in the factory. Power was retained for the secretary of state to modify by order the standard for the maximum limit of humidity of the atmosphere at any given temperature. A short act in 1870 extended this power to other measures for the protection of health.

Additions to act of 1878.

The special measures from 1878 to 1889 gave valuable precedents for further developments of special hygiene in factory life, but the next advance in the Factory and Workshop Act 1891, following the House of Lords Committee on the sweating system and the Berlin International Labour Conference, extended over much wider ground. Its principal objects were: (*a*) to render administration of the law relating to workshops more efficient, particularly as regards sanitation; with this end in view it made the primary controlling authority for sanitary matters in workshops the local sanitary authority (now the district council), acting by their officers, and giving them the powers of the less numerous body of factory inspectors, while at the same time the provisions of the Public Health Acts replaced in workshops the very similar sanitary provisions of the Factory Acts; (*b*) to provide for greater security against accidents and more efficient fencing of machinery in factories; (*c*) to extend the method of regulation of unhealthy or dangerous occupations by application of special rules and requirements to any incident of employment (other than in a domestic workshop) certified by the secretary of state to be dangerous or injurious to health or dangerous to life or limb, (*d*) to raise the age of employment of children and restrict the employment of women immediately after childbirth; (*e*) to require particulars of rate of wages to be given with work to piece-workers in certain branches of the textile industries; (*f*) to amend the act of 1878 in various subsidiary ways, with the view of improving the administration of its principles, *e.g.* by increasing the means of checking the amount of overtime worked, empowering inspectors to enter work-places used as dwellings without a justice's warrant, and the imposition of minimum penalties in certain cases. On this act followed four years of greatly accelerated administrative activity. No fewer than sixteen trades were scheduled by the secretary of state as dangerous to health. The manner of preparing and establishing suitable rules was greatly modified by the act of 1901 and will be dealt with in that connexion.

The Factory and Workshop Act 1895 followed thus on a period of exercise of new powers of administrative regulation (the period being also that during which the Royal Commission on Labour made its wide survey of industrial conditions), and after two successive annual reports of the chief inspector of factories had embodied reports and recommendations from the women inspectors, who in 1893 were first added to the inspectorate. Again, the chief features of an even wider legislative effort than that of 1891 were the increased stringency and definiteness of the measures for securing hygienic and safe conditions of work. Some of these measures, however, involved new principles, as in the provision for the prohibition of the use of a dangerous machine or structure by the order of a magistrate's court, and the power to include in the special rules drawn up in pursuance of section 8 of the act of 1891, the prohibition of the employment of any class of persons, or the limitation of the period of employment of any class of persons in any process scheduled by order of the secretary of state. These last two powers have both been exercised, and with the exercise of the latter passed away, without opposition, the absolute freedom of the employer of the adult male labourer to carry on his manufacture without legislative limitation of the hours of labour. Second only in significance to these new developments was the addition, for the first time since 1867, of new classes of workplaces not covered by the general definitions in section 93 of the Consolidating Act of 1878, viz.: (*a*) laundries (with special conditions as to hours, &c.); (*b*) docks, wharves, quays, warehouses and premises on which machinery worked by power is temporarily used for the purpose of the construction of a building or any structural work in connexion with the building (for the purpose only of obtaining security against accidents). Other entirely new provisions in the act of 1895, later strengthened by the act of 1901, were the requirement of a reasonable temperature in workrooms, the requirement of lavatories for the use of persons employed in any department where poisonous substances are used, the obligation on occupiers and medical practitioners to report cases of industrial poisoning; and the penalties imposed on an employer wilfully allowing wearing apparel to be made, cleaned or repaired in a dwelling-house where an inmate is suffering from infectious disease. Another provision empowered the secretary of state to specify classes of outwork and areas with a view to the regulation of the sanitary condition of premises in which outworkers are employed. Owing to the conditions attached to its exercise, no case was found in which this power could come into operation, and the act of 1901 deals with the matter on new lines. The requirement of annual returns from occupiers of persons employed, and the competency of the person charged with infringing the act to give evidence in his defence, were important new provisions, as was also the adoption of the powers to direct a formal investigation of any accident on the lines laid down in section 45 of the Coal Mines Regulation Act 1887. Other sections, relating to sanitation and safety, were developments of previous regulations, *e.g.* the fixing of a standard of overcrowding, provision of sanitary accommodation separate for each sex where the standard of the Public Health Act Amendment Act of 1890 had not been adopted by the competent local sanitary authority, power to order a fan or other mechanical means to carry off injurious gas, vapour or other impurity (the previous power covering only dust). The fencing of machinery and definition of accidents were made more precise, young persons were prohibited from cleaning dangerous machinery, and additional safeguards against risk of injury by fire or panic were introduced. On the question of employment the foremost amendments lay in the almost complete prohibition of overtime for young persons, and the restriction of the power of an employer to employ protected persons outside his factory or workshop on the same day that he had employed them in the factory or workshop. Under the head of particulars of work and wages to piece-workers an important new power, highly valued by the workers, was given to apply the principle with the necessary modifications by order of the secretary of state to industries other than textile and to outworkers as well as to those employed inside factories and workshops.

The act of 1901.

In 1899 an indirect modification of the limitation to employment of children was effected by the Elementary Education Amendment Act, which, by raising from eleven to twelve the minimum age at which a child may, by the by-laws of a local authority, obtain total or partial exemption from the obligation to attend school, made it unlawful for an occupier to take into employment any child under twelve in such a manner as to prevent full-time attendance at school. The age of employment became generally thereby the same as it has been for employment at a mine above ground since 1887. The act of 1901 made the prohibition of employment of a child under twelve in a factory or workshop direct and absolute. Under the divisions of sanitation, safety, fitness for employment, special regulation of dangerous trades, special control of bakehouses, exceptional treatment of creameries, new methods of dealing with home work and outworkers, important additions were made to the general law by the act of 1901, as also in regulations for strengthened administrative control. New general sanitary provisions were those prescribing: (*a*) ventilation *per se* for every workroom, and empowering the secretary of state to fix a standard of sufficient ventilation; (*b*) drainage of wet floors; (*c*) the power of the secretary of state to define in certain cases what shall constitute sufficient and suitable sanitary accommodation. New safety provisions were those relating to—(*a*) Examination and report on steam boilers; (*b*) prohibition of employment of a child in cleaning below machinery in motion; (*c*) power of the district council to make by-laws for escape in case of fire. The most important administrative alterations were: (*a*) a justice engaged in the same trade as, or being officer of an association of persons engaged in the same trade as, a person charged with an offence may not act at the hearing and determination of the charge; (*b*) ordinary supervision of sanitary conditions under which outwork is carried on was transferred to the district council, power being reserved to the Home Office to intervene in case of neglect or default by any district council.

[illegible]

[illegible] any offence against the act com-[illegible] who is employed in connexion with the [illegible] and is in the employment or pay of the [illegible] deemed to be the occupier of the factory; [illegible] of reporting accidents, the actual employer [illegible] in any factory or workshop is bound under [illegible] to report the same to the occupier; (*d*) so far [illegible] sanitary conditions, fencing of machinery, affixing of [illegible] factories, the *owner* (as defined by the Public [illegible] 1875), generally speaking, takes the place of the occupier. [illegible] in a factory or workshop includes work whether for [illegible] not, (*a*) in a manufacturing process or handicraft, (*b*) in [illegible] any place used for the same, (*c*) in cleaning or oiling any part [illegible] machinery, (*d*) any work whatsoever incidental to the process [illegible] handicraft, or connected with the article made. Persons found in [illegible] part of the factory or workshop, where machinery is used or manufacture carried on, except at meal-times, or when machinery [illegible] stopped, are deemed to be employed until the contrary is proved. The act, however, does not apply to employment for the sole purpose of repairing the premises or machinery, nor to the process of preserving and curing fish immediately upon its arrival in the fishing boats in order to prevent the fish from being destroyed or spoiled, nor to the process of cleaning and preparing fruit so far as is necessary to prevent it from spoiling during the months of June, July, August and September. Certain light handicrafts carried on by a family only in a private house or room at irregular intervals are also outside the scope of the act.

The foremost provisions are those relating to the sanitary condition of the workplaces and the general security of every class of worker. Every factory must be kept in a cleanly condition, free from noxious effluvia, ventilated in such a manner as to render harmless, so far as practicable, gases, vapours, dust or other impurities generated in the manufacture; must be provided with sufficient and suitable sanitary conveniences separate for the sexes; must not be overcrowded (not less than 250 cubic ft. during the day, 400 during overtime, for each worker). In these matters the law of public health takes in workshops the place of the Factory Act, the requirements being substantially the same. Although, however, primarily the officers of the district council enforce the sanitary provisions in workshops, the government factory inspectors may give notice of any defect in them to the district council in whose district they are situate; and if proceedings are not taken within one month by the latter, the factory inspector may act in default and recover expenses from the district council. This power does not extend to domestic workshops which are under the law relating to public health so far as general sanitation is concerned. General powers are reserved to the secretary of state, where he is satisfied that the Factory Act or law relating to public health as regards workplaces has not been carried out by any district council, to authorize a factory inspector during a period named in his order to act instead of the district council. Other general sanitary provisions administered by the government inspectors are the requirement in factories and workshops of washing conveniences where poisonous substances are used; adequate measures for securing and maintaining a reasonable temperature of such a kind as will not interfere with the purity of the air in each room in which any person is employed; maintenance of sufficient means of ventilation in every room in a factory or workshop (in conformity with such standard as may be prescribed by order of the secretary of state); provision of a fan to carry off injurious dust, gas or other impurity, and prevent their inhalation in any factory or workshop; drainage of floors where wet processes are carried on. For laundries and bakehouses there are further sanitary regulations; *e.g.* in laundries all stoves for heating irons shall be sufficiently separated from any ironing-room or ironing-table, and the floors shall be "drained in such a manner as will allow the water to flow off freely"; and in bakehouses a cistern supplying water to a bakehouse must be quite separate from that supplying water to a water-closet, and the latter may not communicate directly with the bakehouse. Use of underground bakehouses (*i.e.* a baking room with floor more than 3 ft. below the ground adjoining) is prohibited, except where already used at the passing of the act; further, in these cases, after 1st January 1904, a certificate as to suitability in light, ventilation, &c., must be obtained from the district council. In other trades certified by the secretary of state further sanitary regulations may be made to increase security for health by special rules to be presently touched on. The secretary of state may also make sanitary requirements a condition of granting such exceptions to the general law as he is empowered to grant. In factories, as distinct from workshops, a periodical lime washing (or washing with hot water and soap where paint and varnish have been used) of all inside walls and ceilings once at least in every fourteen months is generally required; in bakehouses once in six months. As regards sufficiency and suitability of sanitary accommodation, the standards determined by order of the secretary of state shall be observed in the districts to which it is made applicable. An order was made called the Sanitary Accommodation Order, on the 4th of February 1903, the definitions and standards in which have also been widely adopted by local sanitary authorities in districts where the Order has no legal force, the local authority having parallel power under the Public Health Act of 1890.

Sanitation.

Security and accidents.

Security in the use of machinery is provided for by precautions as regards the cleaning of machinery in motion and working between the fixed and traversing parts of self-acting machines driven by power, by fencing of machinery, and by empowering inspectors to obtain an order from a court of summary jurisdiction to prohibit the use, temporarily or absolutely, of machinery, ways, works or plant, including use of a steam boiler, which cannot be used without danger to life and limb. Every hoist and fly-wheel directly connected with mechanical power, and every part of a water-wheel or engine worked by mechanical power, and every wheel race, must be fenced, whatever its position, and every part of mill-gearing or dangerous machinery must either be fenced or be in such position that it is as safe as if fenced. No protected persons may clean any part of mill-gearing in motion, and children may further not clean any part of or below manufacturing machinery in motion by aid of mechanical power; young persons further may not clean any machinery if the inspector notifies it to the occupier as dangerous. Security as regards the use of dangerous premises is provided for by empowering courts of summary jurisdiction, on the application of an inspector, to prohibit their use until the danger has been removed. The district council, or, in London, the county council, or in case of their default the factory inspector, can require certain provisions for escape in case of fire in factories and workshops in which more than forty persons are employed; special powers to make by-laws for means of escape from fire in any factory or workshop are, in addition to any powers for prevention of fire that they possess, given to every district council, in London to the county council. The means of escape must be kept free from obstruction. Provisions are made for doors to open outwards in each room in which more than ten persons are employed, and to prevent the locking, bolting or fastening of doors so that they cannot easily be opened from inside when any person is employed or at meals inside the workplace. Further, provisions for security may be provided in special regulations. Every boiler for generating steam in a factory or workshop or place where the act applies must have a proper safety valve, a steam gauge, and a water gauge, and every such boiler, valve and gauge must be maintained in proper condition. Examination by a competent person must take place at least once in every fourteen months. The occupier of any factory or workshop may be liable for penal compensation not exceeding £100 in case of injury or death due to neglect of any provision or special rule, the whole or any part of which may be applied for the benefit of the injured person or his family, as the secretary of state determines. When a death has occurred by accident in a factory or workshop, the coroner must advise the factory inspector for the district of the place and time of the inquest. The secretary of state may order a formal investigation of the circumstances of any accident as in the case of mines. Careful and detailed provisions are made for the reporting by occupiers to inspectors, and entry in the registers at factories and workshops of accidents which occur in a factory or workshop and (*a*) cause loss of life to a person employed there, or (*b*) are due to machinery moved by mechanical power, molten metal, hot liquid, explosion, escape of gas or steam, electricity, so disabling any person employed in the factory or workshop as to cause him to be absent throughout at least one whole day from his ordinary work, (*c*) are due to any other special cause which the secretary of state may determine, (*d*) not falling under the previous heads and yet cause disablement for more than seven days' ordinary work to any person working in the factory or workshop. In the case of (*a*) or (*b*) notice has also to be sent to the certifying surgeon by the occupier. Cases of lead, phosphorus, arsenical and mercurial poisoning, or anthrax, contracted in any factory or workshop must similarly be reported and registered by the occupier, and the duty of reporting these cases is also laid on medical practitioners under whose observation they come. The list of classes of poisoning can be extended by the secretary of state's order.

Physical fitness of workers.

Certificates of physical fitness for employment must be obtained by the occupier from the certifying surgeon for the district for all persons under sixteen years of age employed in a factory, and in any class of workshops to which the requirement has been extended by order of the secretary of state, and an inspector may suspend any such persons for re-examination in a factory, or for examination in a workshop, when "disease or bodily infirmity" unfits the person, in his opinion, for the work of the place. The certifying surgeon may examine the process as well as the person submitted, and may qualify the certificate he grants by conditions as to the work on which the person is fit to be employed. An occupier of a factory or workshop or laundry shall not knowingly allow a woman to be employed therein within four weeks after childbirth.

Hours of protected persons.

The employment of children, young persons and women is regulated as regards ordinary and exceptional hours of work, ordinary and exceptional meal-times, length of spells and holidays. The outside limits of ordinary periods of employment and holidays are, broadly, the same for textile factories as for non-textile factories and workshops; the main difference lies in the requirement of not less than a total two hours' interval for meals out of the twelve, and a limit of four and a half hours for any spell of work, a longer weekly half holiday, and a prohibition of overtime, in textile factories, as compared with a total one and a half hours' interval for meals and a limit of five hours for spells and (conditional) permission of overtime in non-textile factories. The hours of work must be specified, and from Monday to Friday may be between 6 A.M. and 6 P.M., or 7 A.M. to 7 P.M.; in non-textile factories and workshops the hours also may be taken between 8 A.M. and 8 P.M. or by order of the secretary of state for special industries 9 A.M. to 9 P.M. Between these outside limits, with the proviso that meal-times must be fixed and limits as to spells observed, women and young persons may be employed the full time, children on the contrary only half time, on alternate days, or in alternate sets attending school half time regularly. On Saturdays, in textile factories in which the period commences at 6 A.M. all manufacturing work must cease at 12 if not less than one hour is given for meals, or 11.30 if less than one hour is given for meals (half an hour extra allowed for cleaning), and in non-textile factories and workshops at 2 P.M., 3 P.M. or 4 P.M., according as the hour of beginning is 6 A.M., 7 A.M. or 8 A.M. In "domestic workshops" the total number of hours for young persons and children must not exceed those allowed in ordinary workshops, but the outside limits for beginning and ending are wider; and the case is similar as regards hours of women in "women's workshops." Employment outside a factory or workshop in the business of the same is limited in a manner similar to that laid down in the Shop Hours Act, to be touched on presently. Overtime in certain classes of factories, workshops and warehouses attached to them is permitted, under conditions specified in the acts, for women, to meet seasonal or unforeseen pressure of business, or where goods of a perishable nature are dealt with, for young persons only in a very limited degree in factories liable to stoppage for drought or flood, or for an unfinished process. These and other cases of exceptional working are under minute and careful administrative regulations. Broadly these same regulations as to exceptional overtime may apply in *laundries* but the act of 1907 granted to laundries not merely ancillary to the manufacture carried on in a factory or workshop (*e.g.* shirt and collar factories), additional power to fix different periods of employment for different days of the week, and to make use of one or other of two exceptional methods of arranging the daily periods so as to permit of periods of different length on different days; these exceptional periods cannot be worked in addition to overtime permissible under the general law. Laundries carried on in connexion with charitable or reformatory institutions were brought in 1907 within the scope of the law, but special schemes for regulation as to hours, meals, holidays, &c., may be submitted by the managers to the secretary of state, who is empowered to approve them if he is satisfied that they are not less favourable than the corresponding provisions of the principal act; such schemes shall be laid as soon as possible before both Houses of Parliament.

Night work is allowed in certain specified industries, under conditions, for male young persons, but for no other workers under eighteen, and overtime for women may never be later than 10 P.M. or before 6 A.M. Sunday work is prohibited except, under conditions, for Jews; and in factories, workshops and laundries six holidays (generally the Bank holidays) must be allowed in the year. In creameries in which women and young persons are employed the secretary of state may by special order vary the beginning and end of the daily period of employment, and allow employment for not more than three hours on Sundays and holidays.

Dangerous and unhealthy industries.

The general provisions of the act may be supplemented where specially dangerous or unhealthy trades are carried on, by special regulations. This was provided for in the law in force until 31st December 1901, as in the existing principal act, and the power to establish rules had been exercised between 1892 and 1901 in twenty-two trades or processes where injury arose either from handling of dangerous substances, such as lead and lead compounds, phosphorus, arsenic or various chemicals, or where there is inhalation of irritant dust or noxious fumes, or where there is danger of explosion or infection of anthrax. Before the rule could be drawn up under the acts of 1891 to 1895, the secretary of state had to certify that in the particular case or class of cases in question (*e.g.* process or machinery), there was, in his opinion, danger to life or limb or risk of injury to health; thereupon the chief inspector might propose to the occupier of the factory or workshop such special rules or measures as he thought necessary to meet the circumstances. The occupier might object or propose modifications, but if he did not the rules became binding in twenty-one days; if he objected, and the secretary of state did not assent to any proposed modification, the matters in difference had to be referred to arbitration, the award in which finally settled the rules or requirement to be observed. In November 1901, in the case of the earthenware and china industry, the last arbitration of the kind was opened and was finally concluded in 1903. The parties to the arbitration were the chief inspector, on behalf of the secretary of state, and the occupier or occupiers, but the workmen interested might be and were represented on the arbitration. In the establishing of the twenty-two sets of existing special rules only thrice has arbitration been resorted to, and only on two of these occasions were workmen represented. The provisions as to the arbitration were laid down in the first schedule to the Act of 1891, and were similar to those under the Coal Mines Regulation Acts. Many of these codes have still the force of law and will continue until in due [illegible] under the amended procedure of the act of 1901. [illegible] regulate conditions of employment, but also [illegible] employment of any class of workers; where [illegible] regulations affected adult workers the rules had to [illegible] laid before both Houses of Parliament before [illegible] operation. The obligation to observe the rules in [illegible] workers as well as on occupiers, and the section in [illegible] providing a penalty for non-observance was drafted, [illegible] the rules, so as to provide for a simultaneous fine [illegible] exceeding two pounds for the worker, not exceeding ten [illegible] the occupier.)

[illegible] special regulations of the act of 1901 touch [illegible] of procedure for making the regulations, but [illegible] the first time domestic workshops and added a [illegible] regulations that may be made; further, [illegible] sanction for observance of any rules that may [illegible] the occupier in the same general position [illegible] non-observance as in other matters under the [illegible] of the secretary of state that any manu[illegible] process or manual labour used in factories [illegible] or injurious to life, health or limb, such [illegible] the secretary of state to meet the necessity [illegible] by him after he has duly published notice: [illegible] the place where copies of the draft regu[illegible] and (3) of the time during which objections [illegible] persons affected. The secretary of state [illegible] to meet the objections made. If not, [illegible] withdrawn or appears to him frivolous, he [illegible] regulations, appoint a competent person to [illegible] with regard to the draft regulations and to [illegible] The inquiry is to be made under such rules [illegible] may lay down, and when the regulations are [illegible] as soon as possible before parliament. Either [illegible] regulations or any of them, without prejudice [illegible] secretary of state to make new regulations. [illegible] to all factories or workshops in which the [illegible] process, &c., is used, or to a specified class. [illegible] things, (a) prohibit or limit employment [illegible] persons; (b) prohibit, limit, or control use [illegible]; (c) modify or extend special regulations [illegible] Regulations have been established among [illegible] trades and processes: felt hat-making where [illegible] is used; file-cutting by hand; manu[illegible] electric accumulators; docks, processes of loading, un[illegible] tar distilling; factories in which self-acting mules are [illegible] locomotives; spinning and weaving of flax, hemp and [illegible] manufacture of paints and colours; beading of yarn dyed by [illegible] lead compounds.

[illegible] the Factory and Workshop Acts have not directly [illegible] wages, they have made certain provision for securing to [illegible] worker that the amount agreed upon shall be received: [illegible] by extending every act in force relating to the inspec[illegible] of weights, measures and weighing machines for use [illegible] the sale of goods to those used in a factory or workshop [illegible] checking or ascertaining the wages of persons em[illegible] (2) by ensuring that piece-workers in the textile [illegible] other trades specified by the secretary of state) shall [illegible] any piece of work, clear particulars of [illegible] applicable to the work to be done and of the work to which [illegible] be applied. Unless the particulars of work are ascer[illegible] an automatic indicator, they must be given to textile [illegible] and in the case of weavers in the cotton, worsted [illegible] trades the particulars of wages must be supplied [illegible] to each worker, and also shown on a placard in a con[illegible] position. In other textile processes, it is sufficient to [illegible] particulars separately to each worker. The secretary of [illegible] his powers to extend this protection to non-textile [illegible] with suitable modifications, in various hardware industries, [illegible] making, locks, chains, in wholesale tailoring and [illegible] wearing apparel, in fustian cutting, umbrella-making, [illegible] and a number of other piece-work trades. He [illegible] most of these and other trades used his power to extend [illegible] to outworkers.

With a view to efficient administration of the act (a) certain [illegible] have to be conspicuously exhibited at the factory or work[illegible] (b) registers and lists kept, and (c) notices sent [illegible] to the inspector by the occupier. Among the first the [illegible] important are the prescribed abstract of the act, the names and addresses of the inspector and certifying surgeon, [illegible] of employment, and specified meal-times (which may not [illegible] without fresh notice to the inspector), the air space and [illegible] of persons who may legally be employed in each room, and [illegible] particulars of exceptional employment; among the [illegible] are the general registers of children and young persons em[illegible] of accidents, of limewashing, of overtime, and lists of out[illegible] among the third are the notice of beginning to occupy a [illegible] or workshop, which the occupier must send within one [illegible] of overtime employment, notice of accident, poisoning [illegible] and returns of persons employed, with such other par[illegible] as may be prescribed. These must [illegible] chief inspector at intervals of not less than one and not more than three years, as may be directed by the secretary of state.

The secretary of state for the Home Department controls the administration of the acts, appoints the inspectors referred to in the acts, assigns to them their duties, and regulates the manner and cases in which they are to exercise the powers of inspectors. The act, however, expressly assigns certain duties and powers to a chief inspector and certain to district inspectors. Many provisions of the acts depend as to their operation on the making of orders by the secretary of state. These orders may impose special obligations on occupiers and increase the stringency of regulations, may apply exceptions as to employment, and may modify or relax regulations to meet special classes of circumstances. In certain cases, already indicated, his orders guide or determine the action of district councils, and, generally, in case of default by a council he may empower his inspectors to act as regards workplaces, instead of the council, both under the Factory Acts and Public Health Acts.

The powers of an inspector are to enter, inspect and examine, by day or by night, at any reasonable time, any factory or workshop (or laundry, dock, &c.), or part of one, when he has reason to believe that any person is employed there; to take with him a constable if he has reasonable cause to expect obstruction; to require production of registers, certificates, &c., under the acts; to examine, alone or in the presence of any other person, as he sees fit, every person in the factory or workshop, or in a school where the children employed are being educated; to prosecute, conduct or defend before a court of summary jurisdiction any proceeding under the acts; and to exercise such other powers as are necessary for carrying the act into effect. The inspector has also the duty of enforcing the Truck Acts in places, and in respect of persons, under the Factory Acts. Certifying surgeons are appointed by the chief inspector subject to the regulations of the secretary of state, and their chief duties are (a) to examine workers under sixteen, and persons under special rules, as to physical fitness for the daily work during legal periods, with power to grant qualified certificates as to the work for which the young worker is fit, and (b) to investigate and report on accidents and cases of lead, phosphorus or other poisoning and anthrax.

In 1907 there were registered as under inspection 110,276 factories, including laundries with power, 146,917 workshops (other than men's workshops), including laundries without power; of works under special rules or regulations (included in the figures just given) there were 10,586 and 19,687 non-textile works under orders for supply of particulars to piece-workers. Of notices of accidents received there were 124,325, of which 1179 were fatal; of reported cases of poisoning there were 653, of which 40 were fatal. Prosecutions were taken by inspectors in 4474 cases and convictions obtained in 4211 cases. Of persons employed there were, according to returns of occupiers, 1904, 4,165,791 in factories and 688,756 in workshops.

Coal Mines.—The mode of progress to be recorded in the regulation of coal mines since 1872 can be contrasted in one aspect with the progress just recorded of factory legislation since 1878. Consolidation was again earlier adopted when large amendments were found necessary, with the result that by far the greater part of the law is to be found in the act of 1887, which repealed and re-enacted, with amendments, the Coal Mines Acts of 1872 and 1886, and the Stratified Ironstone Mines (Gunpowder) Act, 1881. The act of 1881 was simply concerned with rules relating to the use of explosives underground. The act of 1886 dealt with three questions: (a) The election and payment of checkweighers (*i.e.* the persons appointed and paid by miners in pursuance of section 13 of the act of 1887 for the purpose of taking a correct account on their behalf of the weight of the mineral gotten by them, and for the correct determination of certain deductions for which they may be liable); (b) provision for new powers of the secretary of state to direct a formal investigation of any explosion or accident, and its causes and circumstances, a provision which was later adopted in the law relating to factories; (c) provision enabling any relatives of persons whose death may have been caused by explosions or accidents in or about mines to attend in person, or by agent, coroners' inquests thereon, and to examine witnesses. The act of 1887, which amended, strengthened and consolidated these acts and the earlier Consolidating Act of 1872, may also be contrasted in another aspect with the general acts of factory legislation. In scope it formed, as its principal forerunner had done, a general code; and in some measure it went farther in the way of consolidation than the Factory Acts had done, inasmuch as certain questions, which in factories are dealt with by statutes distinct from the Factory Acts, have been included in the Mines Regulation Acts, *e.g.* the prohibition of the payment of wages in public-houses, and the machinery relating to weights and measures whereby miners control their payment; further, partly from the less changing nature of the industry, but probably mainly from the power of expression gained for miners by their organization, the code, so far as it went, at each stage answered apparently on the whole more nearly to the views and needs of the persons protected than the parallel law relating to factories. This was strikingly seen in the evidence before the Royal Commission on Labour in 1892–1894, where the repeated expression of satisfaction on the part of the miners with the provisions as distinct from the administration of the code (" with a few trifling exceptions ") is in marked contrast with the long and varied series of claims and contentions put forward for amendment of the Factory Acts.

Since the act of 1887 there have followed five minor acts, based on the recommendation of the officials acting under the acts, while two of them give effect to claims made by the miners before the Royal Commission on Labour. Thus, in 1894, the Coal Mines (Checkweigher) Act rendered it illegal for an employer (" owner, agent, or manager of any mine, or any person employed by or acting under the instructions of any such owner, agent, or manager ") to make the removal of a particular checkweigher a condition of employment, or to exercise improper influence in the appointment of a checkweigher. The need for this provision was demonstrated by a decision of the Court of Session in Edinburgh, which upheld an employer in his claim to the right of dismissing all the workmen and re-engaging them on condition that they would dismiss a particular checkweigher. In 1896 a short act extended the powers to propose, amend and modify special rules, provided for representation of workmen on arbitration under the principal act on any matter in difference, modified the provision for plans of mines in working and abandoned mines, amended three of the general rules (inspection before commencing work, use of safety lamp and non-inflammable substances for stemming), and empowered the secretary of state by order to prohibit or regulate the use of any explosive likely to become dangerous. In 1900 another brief act raised the age of employment of boys underground from twelve to thirteen. In 1903 another amending act allowed as an alternative qualification for a manager's certificate a diploma in scientific and mining training after at least two years' study at a university mining school or other educational institution approved by the secretary of state, coupled with practical experience of at least three years in a mine. In the same year the Employment of Children Act affected children in mines to the extent already indicated in connexion with factories. In 1905 a Coal Mines (Weighing of Minerals) Act improved some provisions relating to appointment and pay of checkweighers and facilities for them and their duly appointed deputies in carrying out their duties. In 1906 the Notice of Accidents Act provided for improved annual returns of accidents and for immediate reporting to the district inspector of accidents under newly-defined conditions as they arise in coal and metalliferous mines.

Act of 1887.

While the classes of mines regulated by the act of 1887 are the same as those regulated by the act of 1872 (*i.e.* mines of coal, of stratified ironstone, of shale and of fire-clay, including works above ground where the minerals are prepared for use by screening, washing, &c.) the interpretation of the term " mine," is wider and simpler, including " every shaft in the course of being sunk, and every level and inclined plane in the course of being driven, and all the shafts, levels, planes, works, tramways and sidings, both below ground and above ground, in and adjacent to and belonging to the mine." Of the persons responsible under penalty for the observance of the acts the term " owner " is defined precisely as in the act of 1872, but the term " agent " is modified to mean " any person appointed as the representative of the owner in respect of any mine or any part thereof, and, as such, superior to a manager appointed in pursuance of this act." Of the persons protected, the term " young person " disappeared from the act, and " boy," *i.e.* " a male under the age of sixteen years," and " girl," *i.e.* " a female under the age of sixteen years," take their place, and the term " woman " means, as before, " a female of the age of sixteen years and upwards." The prohibition of employment underground of women and girls remains untouched, and the prohibition of employment underground of boys has been successively extended from boys of the age of ten in 1872 to boys of twelve in 1887 and to boys of thirteen in 1900. The age of employment of boys and girls above ground in connexion with any mine is raised from ten years in 1872 to twelve years since 1887. The hours of employment of a boy below ground may not exceed fifty-four in any one week, nor ten in any one day from the time of leaving the surface to the time of returning to the surface. Above ground any boy or girl under thirteen (and over twelve) may not be employed on more than six days in any one week; if employed on more than three days in one week, the daily total must not exceed six hours, or in any other case ten hours. Protected persons above thirteen are limited to the same daily and weekly total of hours as boys below ground, but there are further provisions with regard to intervals for meals and prohibiting employment for more than five hours without an interval of at least half an hour for a meal. Registers must be kept of all protected persons, whether employed above or below ground. Section 38 of the Public Health Act 1875, which requires separate and sufficient sanitary conveniences for persons of each sex, was first extended by the act of 1887 to the portions of mines above ground in which girls and women are employed; underground this matter is in metalliferous mines in Cornwall now provided for by special rules. Ventilation, the only other requirement in the acts that can be classed as sanitary, is provided for in every mine in the " general rules " which are aimed at securing safety of mines, and which, so far as ventilation is concerned, seek to dilute and render harmless noxious or inflammable gases. The provision which prohibits employment of any persons in mines not provided with at least two shafts is made much more stringent by the act of 1887 than in the previous code, by increasing the distance between the two shafts from 10 to 15 yds., and increasing the height of communications between them. Other provisions amended or strengthened are those relating to the following points: (*a*) Daily personal supervision of the mine by the certificated manager; (*b*) classes of certificates and constitution of board for granting certificates of competency; (*c*) plan of workings of any mine to be kept up to a date not more than three months previously at the office of the mine; (*d*) notice to be given to the inspector of the district by the owner, agent or manager, of accidents in or about any mine which cause loss of life or serious personal injury, or are caused by explosion of coal or coal dust or any explosive or electricity or any other special cause that the secretary of state specifies by order, and which causes any personal injury to any person employed in or about the mine; it is provided that the place where an explosion or accident occurs causing loss of life or serious personal injury shall be left for inspection for at least three days, unless this would tend to increase or continue a danger or impede working of the mine: this was new in the act of 1887; (*e*) notice to be given of opening and abandonment of any mine: this was extended to the opening or abandonment of any seam; (*f*) plan of an abandoned mine or seam to be sent within three months; (*g*) formal investigation of any explosion or accident by direction of the secretary of state: this provision, first introduced by the act of 1886, was modified in 1887 to admit the appointment by the secretary of state of " any competent person " to hold the investigation, whereas under the earlier section only an inspector could be appointed.

General rules.

The " general rules " for safety in mines have been strengthened in many ways since the act of 1872. Particular mention may be made of rule 4 of the act of 1887, relating to the inspection of conditions as to gas ventilation beyond appointed stations at the entrance to the mine or different parts of the mine; this rule generally removed the earlier distinction between mines in which inflammable gas has been found within the preceding twelve months, and mines in which it has not been so found; of rules 8, 9, 10 and 11, relating to the construction, use, &c., of safety lamps, which are more detailed and stringent than rule 7 of the act of 1872, which they replaced; of rule 12, relating to the use of explosives below ground; of rule 24, which requires the appointment of a competent male person not less than twenty-two years of age for working the machinery for lowering and raising persons at the mine; of rule 34, which first required provision of ambulances or stretchers with splints and bandages at the mine ready for immediate use; of rule 38, which strengthened the provision for periodical inspection of the mine by practical miners on behalf of the workmen at their own cost. With reference to the last-cited rule, during 1898 a Prussian mining commission visited Great Britain, France and Belgium, to study and compare the various methods of inspection by working miners established in these three countries. They found that, so far as the method had been applied, it was most satisfactory in Great Britain, where the whole cost is borne by the workers' own organizations, and they attributed part of the decrease in number of accidents per thousand employed since 1872 to the inauguration of this system.

Special rules.

The provisions as to the proposal, amendment and modification of " special rules," last extended by the act of 1896, may be contrasted with those of the Factory Act. In the latter it is not until an industry or process has been scheduled as dangerous or injurious by the secretary of state's order that occasion arises for the formation of special rules, and then the initiative rests with the Factory Department whereas in mines it is incumbent in every case on the owner, agent or manager [illegible] within three months of the commencement of any working, for the approval of the secretary of state, special rules best calculated to prevent dangerous accidents, and to provide for the safety, convenience and proper discipline of the persons employed in or about the mine. These rules may, if they relate to lights and lamps used in the mine, description of explosives, watering and damping of the mine, or prevention of accidents from inflammable gas or coal dust, supersede any general rule in the principal act. Apart from the initiation of the rules, the methods of establishing them, whether by agreement or by resort to arbitration of the parties (i.e. the mine owners and the secretary of state), are practically the same as under the Factory Act, but there is special provision in the Mines Acts for enabling the persons working in the mine to [illegible] objections to the proposed rules, in addition to their subsequent right to be represented on the arbitration, if any.

Of the sections touching on wages questions, the prohibition of the payment of wages in public-houses remains unaltered, being re-enacted in 1887; the sections relating to payment by weight for amount of mineral gotten by persons employed, and for check-weighing the amount by a "checkweigher" stationed by the majority of workers at each place appointed for the weighing of the material, were secured, particularly as to the determination of deductions by the act of 1887, with a view to meeting some problems raised by decisions on cases under the act of 1872. The attempt seems not to have been wholly successful, the highest legal authorities having expressed conflicting opinions on the precise meaning of the terms "mineral contracted to be gotten." The whole history of the development of this means of securing the fulfilment of wage contract to the workers may be compared with the history of the sections affording protection to piece-workers by particulars of work and wages in the textile trades since the Factory Act of 1891.

As regards legal proceedings, the chief amendments of the act of 1872 are, the extension of the provision that the "owner, agent, or manager" charged in respect of any contravention by another person might be sworn and examined as an ordinary witness, to any person charged with any offence under the act. The result of the proceedings against workmen by the owner, agent or manager in respect of an offence under the act is to be reported within twenty-one days to the inspector of the district. The powers of inspectors were extended to cover an inquiry as to the care and treatment of horses and other animals in the mine, and as to the control, management or direction of the mine by the manager.

An important act was passed in 1908 (Coal Mines Regulation Act [illegible]) limiting the hours of work for workmen below ground. It enacted that, subject to various provisions, a workman was not to be below ground in a mine for the purpose of his work, [illegible] going to and from his work, for more than eight hours [illegible] consecutive twenty-four hours. Exception was made [illegible] the case of those below ground for the purpose of rendering assistance in the event of an accident, or for meeting any danger, [illegible] dealing with any emergency or work incompleted, through [illegible] circumstances, which requires to be dealt with to [illegible] interference in the work of the mine. The [illegible] of every mine must fix the times for the lowering [illegible] raising of the men to begin and be completed, and such [illegible] must be conspicuously posted at the pit head. These [illegible] must be approved by an inspector. The term "workman" [illegible] means any person employed in a mine below ground [illegible] an official of the mine (other than a fireman, examiner [illegible]), or a mechanic or a horse keeper or a person engaged [illegible] surveying or measuring. In the case of a fireman, [illegible] deputy, onsetter, pump minder, fanman or furnace [illegible] the maximum period for which he may be below ground [illegible] hours and a half. A register must be kept by the [illegible] of the mine of the times of descent and ascent, [illegible] the workmen may, at their own cost, station persons [illegible] holding the office of checkweigher or not) at the pit [illegible] observe the times. The authorities of the mine may [illegible] the hours of working by one hour a day on not more than [illegible] days in one calendar year (s. 3). The act may be suspended [illegible] in council in the event of war or of imminent national [illegible] great emergency, or in the event of any grave economic [illegible] due to the demand for coal exceeding the supply [illegible] at any time. The act came into force on the 1st of [illegible] except for the counties of Northumberland and Durham [illegible] its operation was postponed until the 1st of January 1910. [illegible] the number of coal-mines reported on was 3126, and the [illegible] persons employed below ground was 691,112 of whom [illegible] under 16 years of age. Above ground 167,261 were [illegible] women and girls. The number of separate fatal accidents was 1006, causing the loss of 1205 lives. (prosecutions by far the greater number were against workme numbering in coal and metalliferous mines 951; owners ar managers were prosecuted in 72 cases, and convictions obtained i 43 cases.

Quarries.—From 1878 until 1894 open quarries (as distin from underground quarries regulated by the Metalliferou Mines Regulation Act) were regulated only by the Factor Acts so far as they then applied. It was laid down in sectio 93 of the act of 1878 (41 Vict. c. 16), that "any premises or plac shall not be excluded from the definition of a factory or worksho by reason only that such premises, &c., are or is in the ope air," thereby overruling the decision in *Kent* v. *Astley* tha quarries in which the work, as a whole, was carried on in the ope air were not factories; in a schedule to the same act quarrie were defined as "any place not being a mine in which person work in getting slate, stone, coprolites or other minerals.' The Factory Act of 1891 made it possible to bring these place in part under "special rules" adapted to meet the special risk and dangers of the operations carried on in them, and by orde of the secretary of state they were certified, December 1891 as dangerous, and thereby subject to special rules. Until then as reported by one of the inspectors of factories, quarries ha been placed under the Factory Acts without insertion of appro priate rules for their safe working, and many of them wer "developed in a most dangerous manner without any regar for safety, but merely for economy," and managers of many ha "scarcely seen a quarry until they became managers." In hi report for 1892 it was recommended by the chief inspector o factories that quarries should be subject to the jurisdiction o the government inspectors of mines. At the same time currenc was given, by the published reports of the evidence before th Royal Commission on Labour, to the wish of large number of quarrymen that open as well as underground quarries shoul come under more specialized government inspection. In 189 a committee of experts, including inspectors of mines and o factories, was appointed by the Home Office to investigate th conditions of labour in open quarries, and in 1894 the Quarrie Act brought every quarry, as defined in the Factory Act 187 any part of which is more than 20 ft. deep, under certain of th provisions of the Metalliferous Mines Acts, and under th inspection of the inspectors appointed under those acts; furthe it transferred the duty of enforcing the Factory and Worksho Acts, so far as they apply in quarries over 20 ft. deep, from th Factory to the Metalliferous Mines inspectors.

The provisions of the Metalliferous Mines Acts 1872 and 187 applied to quarries, are those relating to payment of wages i public-houses, notice of accidents to the inspector, appointmen and powers of inspectors, arbitration, coroners' inquests, speci rules, penalties, certain of the definitions, and the powers o the secretary of state finally to decide disputed questions whethe places come within the application of the acts. For othe matters, and in particular fencing of machinery and employmen of women and young persons, the Factory Acts apply, with proviso that nothing shall prevent the employment of youn persons (boys) in three shifts for not more than eight hou each. In 1899 it was reported by the inspectors of mines tha special rules for safety had been established in over 2000 quarrie In the reports for 1905 it was reported that the accounts of blas ing accidents indicated that there was "still much laxity i observance of the Special rules, and that many irregular an dangerous practices are in vogue." The absence or deficienc of external fencing to a quarry dangerous to the public has bee since 1887 (50 & 51 Vict. c. 19) deemed a nuisance liable to b dealt with summarily in the manner provided by the Publi Health Act 1875.

In 1905, 94,819 persons were employed, of whom 59,978 worke inside the actual pits or excavations, and 34,841 outside. Compare with 1900, there was a total increase of 924 in the number of perso employed. Fatal accidents resulted in 1900 in 127 deaths; compare with 1899 there was an increase of 10 in the number of deaths, and, Professor Le Neve Foster pointed out, this exceeded the averag death-rate of underground workers at mines under the Coal Min Acts during the previous ten years, in spite of the quarrier "havin nothing to fear from explosions of gas, underground fires or inundations." He attributed the difference to a lax observance of precautions which might in time be remedied by stringent administration of the law. In 1905 there were 97 fatal accidents resulting in 99 deaths. In 1900 there were 92 prosecutions against owners or agents, with 67 convictions, and 13 prosecutions of workers, with 12 convictions, and in 1905 there were 45 prosecutions of owners or agents with 43 convictions and 9 prosecutions of workmen with 5 convictions.

Payment of wages in public-houses.

In 1883 a short act extended to all "workmen" who are manual labourers other than miners, with the exception of domestic or menial servants, the prohibition of payment of wages in public-houses, beer-shops and other places for the sale of spirituous or fermented liquor, laid down in the Coal Mines Regulations and Metalliferous Mines Regulation Acts. The places covered by the prohibition include any office, garden or place belonging to or occupied with the places named, but the act does not apply to such wages as are paid by the resident, owner or occupier of the public-house, beer-shop and other places included in the prohibition to any workman *bona fide* employed by him. The penalty for an offence against this act is one not exceeding £10 (compare the limit of £20 for the corresponding offence under the Coal Mines Act), and all offences may be prosecuted and penalties recovered in England and Scotland under the Summary Jurisdiction Acts. The act does not apply to Ireland, and no special inspectorate is charged with the duty of enforcing its provisions.

Shop Hours.—In four brief acts, 1892 to 1899, still in force, the first very limited steps were taken towards the positive regulation of the employment of shop assistants. In the act of 1904 certain additional optional powers were given to any local authority making a "closing order" fixing the hour (not earlier than 7 P.M. or on one day in the week 1 P.M.) at which shops shall cease to serve customers throughout the area of the authority or any specified part thereof as regards all shops or as regards any specified class of shops. Before such an order can be made (1) a prima facie case for it must appear to the local authority; (2) the local authority must inquire and agree; (3) the order must be drafted and sent for confirmation or otherwise to the central authority, that is, the secretary of state for the Home Department; (4) the order must be laid before both Houses of Parliament. The Home Office has given every encouragement to the making of such orders, but their number in England is very small, and the act is practically inoperative in London and many large towns where the need is greatest. As the secretary of state pointed out in the House of Commons on the 1st of May 1907, the local authorities have not taken enough initiative, but at the same time there is a great difficulty for them in obtaining the required two-thirds majority, among occupiers of the shops to be affected, in favour of the order, and at the same time shop assistants have no power to set the law in motion. In England 364 local authorities have taken no steps, but in Scotland rather better results have been obtained. The House resolved, on the date named, that more drastic legislation is required. As regards shops, therefore, in place of such general codes as apply to factories, laundries, mines—only three kinds of protective requirement are binding on employers of shop assistants: (1) Limitation of the weekly total of hours of work of persons under eighteen years of age to seventy-four inclusive of meal-times; (2) prohibition of the employment of such persons in a shop on the same day that they have, to the knowledge of the employer, been employed in any factory or workshop for a longer period than would, in both classes of employment together, amount to the number of hours permitted to such persons in a factory or workshop; (3) provision for the supply of seats by the employer, in all rooms of a shop or other premises where goods are retailed to the public, for the use of female assistants employed in retailing the goods—the seats to be in the proportion of not fewer than one to every three female assistants. The first two requirements are contained in the act of 1892, which also prescribed that a notice, referring to the provisions of the act, and stating the number of hours in the week during which a young person may be lawfully employed in the shop, shall be kept exhibited by the employer; the third requirement was first provided by the act of 1899. The intervening acts of 1893 and 1895 are merely supplementary to the act of 1892; the former providing for the salaries and expenses of the inspectors which the council of any county or borough (and in the City of London the Common Council) were empowered by the act of 1892 to appoint; the latter providing a penalty of 40s. for failure of an employer to keep exhibited the notice of the provisions of the acts, which in the absence of a penalty it had been impossible to enforce. The penalty for employment contrary to the acts is a fine not exceeding £1 for each person so employed, and for failure to comply with the requirements as to seats, a fine not exceeding £3 for a first offence, and for any subsequent offence a fine of not less than £1 and not exceeding £5.

Meaning of "shop."

A wide interpretation is given by the act of 1892 to the class of workplace to which the limitation of hours applies. "Shop" means retail and wholesale shops, markets, stalls and warehouses in which assistants are employed for hire, and includes licensed public-houses and refreshment houses of any kind. The person responsible for the observance of the acts is the "employer" of the "young persons" (*i.e.* persons under the age of eighteen years), whose hours are limited, and of the "female assistants" for whom seats must be provided. Neither the term "employer" nor "shop assistant" (used in the title of the act of 1899) is defined; but other terms have the meaning assigned to them in the Factory and Workshop Act 1878. The "employer" has, in case of any contravention alleged, the same power as the "occupier" in the Factory Acts to exempt himself from fine on proof of due diligence and of the fact that some other person is the actual offender. The provisions of the act of 1892 do not apply to members of the same family living in a house of which the shop forms part, or to members of the employer's family, or to any one wholly employed as a domestic servant.

In London, where the County Council has appointed men and women inspectors to apply the acts of 1892 to 1899, there were, in 1900, 73,929 premises, and in 1905, 84,269, under inspection. In the latter year there were 22,035 employing persons under 18 years of age. In 1900 the number of young persons under the acts were: indoors, 10,239 boys and 4428 girls; outdoors, 35,019 boys, 206 girls. In 1905 the ratio between boys and girls had decidedly altered: indoors, 6602 boys, 4668 girls; outdoors, 22,654 boys, 308 girls. The number of irregularities reported in 1900 were 9204 and the prosecutions were 117; in 1905 the irregularities were 6966 and the prosecutions numbered 34. As regards the act of 1899, in only 1088 of the 14,844 shops affected in London was there found in 1900 to be failure to provide seats for the women employed in retailing goods. The chief officer of the Public Control Department reported that with very few exceptions the law was complied with at the end of the first year of its application.

As regards cleanliness, ventilation, drainage, water-supply and sanitary condition generally, shops have been since 1878 (by 41 Vict. c. 16, s. 101) subject to the provisions of the Public Health Act 1875, which apply to all buildings, except factories under the Factory Acts, in which any persons, whatever their number be, are employed. Thus, broadly, the same sanitary provisions apply in shops as in workshops, but in the former these are enforced solely by the officers of the local authority, without reservation of any power, as in workshops for the Home Office inspectorate, to act in default of the local authority.

Shop assistants, so far as they are engaged in manual, not merely clerical labour, come under the provisions of the Truck Acts 1831 to 1887, and in all circumstances they fall within the sections directed against unfair and unreasonable fines in the Truck Act of 1896; but, unlike employés in factories, workshops, laundries and mines, they are left to apply these provisions so far as they can themselves, since neither Home Office inspectors nor officers of the local authority have any specially assigned powers to administer the Truck Acts in shops.

Truck.—Setting aside the special Hosiery Manufacture (Wages) Act 1874, aimed at a particular abuse appearing chiefly in the hosiery industry—the practice of making excessive charges on wages for machinery and frame rents—only two acts, those of 1887 and 1896, have been added to the general law against truck since the act of 1831, which repealed all prior Truck Acts and which remains the principal act. Further amendments of the law have been widely and strenuously demanded, and are hoped for as the result of the long inquiry by a departmental committee appointed early in 1906. The Truck Act Amendment Act 1887, amended and extended the act without adding any distinctly new principle; the Truck Act of 1896 was directed towards providing remedies for matters shown by decisions under the earlier Truck Acts to be outside the scope of the principles and provisions of those acts. Under the earlier acts the main objects were: (1) to make the wages of workmen, *i.e.* the reward of labour, payable only in current coin of the realm, and to prohibit whole or part payment of wages in food or drink or clothes or any other articles; (2) to forbid agreements, express or implied, between employer and workmen as to the manner or place in which, or articles on which, a workman shall expend his wages, or for the deduction from wages of the price of articles (other than materials to be used in the labour of the workmen) supplied by the employer. The act of 1887 added a further prohibition by making it illegal for an employer to charge interest on any advance of wages, "whenever by agreement, custom, or otherwise a workman is entitled to receive in anticipation of the regular period of the payment of his wages an advance as part or on account thereof." Further, it strengthened the section [illegible] which provided that no employer shall have [illegible] workman for goods supplied at any shop [illegible] the employer, or in which the employer is interested, [illegible] workman suing an employer for wages against [illegible] in respect of goods supplied to the workman [illegible] any order or direction of the employer, [illegible] expressly prohibiting an employer from dismissing any workman on account of any particular time, place or manner of expending his wages. Certain exemptions to the prohibition of payment otherwise than in coin were provided for in the act [illegible], if an agreement were made in writing and signed by the workman, [illegible] rent, victuals dressed and consumed under the employer's roof, medicine, fuel, provender for beasts of burden used in the trade, materials and tools for use by miners, advances for friendly societies or savings banks; in the case of fuel, provender and tools there was also a proviso that the charge should not exceed the real and true value. The act of 1887 amended these provisions by requiring a correct annual audit in the case of deductions for medicine or tools, by permitting part payment of servants in husbandry in food, drink (not intoxicants) or other allowances, and by prohibiting any deductions for sharpening or repairing workmen's tools except by agreement not forming part of the condition of hiring. Two important administrative amendments were made by the act of 1887: (1) a section similar to that in the Factory and Mines Acts was added, empowering the employer to exempt himself from penalty for contravention of the acts on proof that any other person was the actual offender and of his own due diligence in enforcing the execution of the acts; (2) the duty of enforcing the acts in factories, workshops, and mines was imposed upon the inspectors of the Factory and Mines Departments, respectively, of the Home Office, and to their task they were empowered to bring all the authorities and powers which they possessed in virtue of the acts under which they are appointed; these inspectors thus prosecute defaulting employers and recover penalties under the Summary Jurisdiction Acts, but they do not undertake civil proceedings for improper deductions or payments, proceedings for which would lie with workmen under the Employers and Workmen Act 1875. The persons to whom the benefits of the act applied were added to by the act of 1887, which repealed the complicated list of trades contained in the principal act and substituted the simpler definition of the Employers and Workmen Act, 1875. Thus the acts 1831 to 1887, and also the act of 1896, apply to all workers (men, women and children) engaged in manual labour, except domestic servants; they apply not only in mines, factories and workshops, but, to quote the published Home Office Memorandum on the acts, "in all places where workpeople are engaged in manual labour under a contract with an employer, whether or no the employer be an owner or agent or a servant, or be himself a workman; and therefore a workman who employs and pays others under him must also observe the Truck Acts." The law thus in certain circumstances covers outworkers for a contractor or sub-contractor. A decision of the High Court at Dublin in 1900 (*Squire* v. *Sweeney*) strengthened the inspectors in investigation of offences committed amongst outworkers by supporting the contention that inquiry and exercise of all the powers of an inspector could legally take place in parts of an employer's premises other than those in which the work is given out. It defined for Ireland, in a narrower sense than h[illegible] understood and acted upon by the Factory Department, the classes of outworkers protected by deciding that only such as were under a contract personally to execute the work were covered. In 1905 the law in England was similarly declared in the decided case of *Squire* v. *The Midland Lace Co.* The judges (Lord Alverstone, C.J.; and Kennedy and Ridley, J.J.) stated that they came to the conclusion with "reluctance," and said: "We venture to express the hope that some amendment of the law may be made so as to extend the protection of the Truck Act to a class of workpeople indistinguishable from those already within its provisions." The workers in question were lace-clippers taking out work to do in their homes, and in the words of the High Court decision "though they do sometimes employ assistants are evidently, as a class, wage-earning manual labourers and not contractors in the ordinary and popular sense." The principle relied on in the decision was that in the case of *Ingram* v. *Barnes*.

The Truck Act 1887.

Persons benefited by Truck Acts.

At the time of the passing of the act of 1887 it seems to have been generally believed that the obligation under the principal act to pay the "entire amount of wages earned" in coin rendered illegal any deductions from wages in respect of fines. Important decisions in 1888 and 1889 showed this belief to have been ill-founded. The essential point lies in the definition of the word "wages" as the "recompense, reward or remuneration of labour," which implies not necessarily any gross sum in question between employer and workmen where there is a contract to perform a certain piece of work, but that part of it, the real *net* wage, which the workman was to get as his *recompense* for the labour performed. As soon as it became clear that excessive deductions from wages as well as payments by workers for materials used in the work were not illegal, and that deductions or payments by way of compensation to employers or by way of discipline might legally (with the single exception of fines for lateness for women and children, regulated by the Employers and Workmen Act 1875) even exceed the degree of loss, hindrance or damage to the employer, it also came clearly into view that further legislation was desirable to extend the principles at the root of the Truck Acts. It was desirable, that is to say, to hinder more fully the unfair dealing that may be encouraged by half-defined customs in work-places, on the part of the employer in making a contract, while at the same time leaving the principle of freedom of contract as far as possible untouched. The Truck Act of 1896 regulates the conditions under which deductions can be made by or payments made to the employer, out of the "sum contracted to be paid to the worker," *i.e.* out of any gross sum whatever agreed upon between employer and workman. It makes such deductions or payments illegal unless they are in pursuance of a contract; and it provides that deductions (or payments) for (*a*) fines, (*b*) bad work and damaged goods, (*c*) materials, machines, and any other thing provided by the employer in relation to the work shall be reasonable, and that particulars of the same in writing shall be given to the workman. In none of the cases mentioned is the employer to make any profit; neither by fines, for they may only be imposed in respect of acts or omissions which cause, or are likely to cause, loss or damage; nor by sale of materials, for the price may not exceed the cost to the employer; nor by deductions or payments for damage, for these may not exceed the actual or estimated loss to the employer. Fines and charges for damage must be "fair and reasonable having regard to all the circumstances of the case," and no contract could make legal a fine which a court held to be unfair to the workman in the sense of the act. The contract between the employer and workman must either be in writing signed by the workman, or its terms must be clearly stated in a notice constantly affixed in a place easily accessible to the workman to whom, if a party to the contract, a copy shall be given at the time of making the contract, and who shall be entitled, on request, to obtain from the employer a copy of the notice free of charge. On each occasion when a deduction or payment is made, full particulars in writing must be supplied to the workman. The employer is bound to keep a register of deductions or payments, and to enter therein particulars of any fine made under the contract, specifying the amount and nature of the act or omission in respect of which the fine was imposed. This register must be at all times open to inspectors of mines or factories, who are entitled to make a copy of the contract or any part of it. This act as a whole applies to all workmen included under the earlier Truck Acts; the sections relating to fines apply also to shop assistants. The latter, however, apparently are left to enforce the provisions of the law themselves, as no inspectorate is empowered to intervene on their behalf. In these and other cases a prosecution under the Truck Acts may be instituted by any person. Any workman or shop assistant may recover any sum deducted by or paid to his employer contrary to the act of 1896, provided that proceedings are commenced within six months, and that where he has acquiesced in the deduction or payment he shall only recover the excess over the amount which the court may find to have been fair and reasonable in all the circumstances of the case. It is expressly declared in the act that nothing in it shall affect the provisions

Meaning of "wages."

The Truck Act 1896.

of the Coal Mines Acts with reference to payment by weight, or legalize any deductions, from payments made, in pursuance of those provisions. The powers and duties of inspectors are extended to cover the case of a laundry, and of any place where work is given out by the occupier of a factory or workshop or by a contractor or sub-contractor. Power is reserved for the secretary of state to exempt by order specified trades or branches of them in specified areas from the provisions of the act of 1896, if he is satisfied that they are unnecessary for the protection of the workmen. This power has been exercised only in respect of one highly organised industry, the Lancashire cotton industry. The effect of the exemption is not to prevent fines and deductions from being made, but the desire for it demonstrated that there are cases where leaders among workers have felt competent to make their own terms on their own lines without the specific conditions laid down in this act. The reports of the inspectors of factories have demonstrated that in other industries much work has had to be done under this act, and knowledge of a highly technical character to be gradually acquired, before opinions could be formed as to the reasonableness and fairness, or the contrary, of many forms of deduction. Owing partly to difficulties of legal interpretation involving the necessity of taking test cases into court, partly to the margin for differences of opinion as to what constitutes "reasonableness" in a deduction, the average number of convictions obtained on prosecutions is not so high as under the Factory Acts, though the average penalty imposed is higher. In 1904, 61 cases were taken into court resulting in 34 convictions with an average penalty of £1, 10s. In 1905, 38 cases resulting in 34 convictions were taken with an average penalty of £1, 3s. In 1906, 37 cases resulting in 25 convictions were taken with an average penalty of £1, 10s.

Reference should here be made to the Shop Clubs Act of 1902 as closely allied with some of the provisions of the Truck Acts by its provision that employers shall not make it a condition of employment that any workman shall become a member of a shop club unless it is registered under the Friendly Societies Act of 1896. As in the case of payment of wages in Public Houses Act, no special insoectorate has the duty of enforcing this act.

III. Continental Europe

In comparing legislation affecting factories, mines, shops and truck in the chief industrial countries of the continent with that of Great Britain, it is essential to a just view that inquiry should be extended beyond the codes themselves to the general social order and system of law and administration in each country. Further, special comparison of the definitions and the sanctions of each industrial code must be recognized as necessary, for these vary in all. In so brief a summary as is appended here no more is possible than an outline indication of the main general requirements and prohibitions of the laws as regards: (1) hours and times of employment, (2) ordinary sanitation and special requirements for unhealthy and dangerous industries, (3) security against accidents, and (4) prevention of fraud and oppression in fulfilment of wage contracts. As regards the first of these subdivisions, in general in Europe the ordinary legal limit is rather wider than in Great Britain, being in several countries not less than 11 hours a day, and while in some, as in France, the normal limit is 10 hours daily, yet the administrative discretion in granting exceptions is rather more elastic. The weekly half-holiday is a peculiarly British institution. On the other hand, in several European countries, notably France, Austria, Switzerland and Russia, the legal maximum day applies to adult as well as youthful labour, and not only to specially protected classes of persons. As regards specialized sanitation for unhealthy factory industries, German regulations appear to be most nearly comparable with British. Mines' labour regulation in several countries, having an entirely different origin linked with ownership of mines, is only in few and most recent developments comparable with British Mines Regulation Acts. In regulation of shops, Germany, treating this matter as an integral part of her imperial industrial code, has advanced farther than has Great Britain. In truck legislation most European countries (with the exception of France) appear to have been influenced by the far earlier laws of Great Britain, although in some respects Belgium, with her rapid and recent industrial development, has made interesting original experiments. The rule of Sunday rest (see Sunday) has been extended in several countries, most recently in Belgium and Spain. In France this partially attempted rule has been so modified as to be practically a seventh day rest; not necessarily Sunday.

France.—Hours of labour were, in France, first limited in factories (*usines et manufactures*) for adults by the law of the 9th of September 1848 to 12 in the 24. Much uncertainty existed as to the class of workplaces covered. Finally, in 1885, an authoritative decision defined them as including: (1) Industrial establishments with motor power or continual furnaces, (2) workshops employing over 20 workers. In 1851, under condition of notification to the local authorities, exceptions, still in force, were made to the general limitation, in favour of certain industries or processes, among others for letterpress and lithographic printing, engineering works, work at furnaces and in heating workshops, manufacture of projectiles of war, and any work for the government in the interests of national defence or security. The limit of 12 hours was reduced, as regards works in which women or young workers are employed, in 1900 to 11, and was to be successively reduced to 10½ hours and to 10 hours at intervals of two years from April 1900. This labour law for adults was preceded in 1841 by one for children, which prevented their employment in factories before 8 years of age and prohibited night labour for any child under 13. This was strengthened in 1874, particularly as regards employment of girls under 21, but it was not until 1892 that the labour of women was specially regulated by a law, still in force, with certain amendments in 1900. Under this law factory and workshop labour is prohibited for children under 13 years, though they may begin at 12 if qualified by the prescribed educational certificate and medical certificate of fitness. The limit of daily hours of employment is the same as for adult labour, and, similarly, from the 1st of April 1902 was 10½, and two years later became 10 hours in the 24. Notice of the hours must be affixed, and meal-times or pauses with absolute cessation of work of at least one hour must be specified. By the act of 1892 one day in the week, not necessarily Sunday, had to be given for entire absence from work, in addition to eight recognized annual holidays, but this was modified by a law of 1906 which generally requires Sunday rest, but allows substitution of another day in certain industries and certain circumstances. Night labour—work between 9 P.M. and 5 A.M.—is prohibited for workers under 18, and only exceptionally permitted, under conditions, for girls and women over 18 in specified trades. In mines and underground quarries employment of women and girls is prohibited except at surface works, and at the latter is subject to the same limits as in factories. Boys of 13 may be employed in certain work underground, but under 16 may not be employed more than 8 hours in the 24 from bank to bank. A law of 1905 provided for miners a 9 hours' day and in 1907 an 8 hours' day from the foot of the entrance gallery back to the same point.

As in Great Britain, distinct services of inspection enforce the law in factories and mines respectively. In factories and workshops an inspector may order re-examination as to physical fitness for the work imposed of any worker under 16; certain occupations and processes are prohibited—*e.g.* girls under 16 at machines worked by treadles, and the weights that may be lifted, pushed or carried by girls or boys under 18 are carefully specified. The law applies generally to philanthropic and religious institutions where industrial work is carried on, as in ordinary trading establishments; and this holds good even if the work is by way of technical instruction. Domestic workshops are not controlled unless the industry is classed as dangerous or unhealthy; introduction of motor power brings them under inspection. General sanitation in industrial establishments is provided for in a law of 1893, amended in 1903, and is supplemented by administrative regulations for special risks due to poisons, dust, explosive substances, gases, fumes, &c. Ventilation, both general and special, lighting, provision of lavatories, cloakrooms, good drinking water, drainage and cleanliness are required in all workplaces, shops, warehouses, restaurant kitchens, and where workers are lodged by their employers hygienic conditions are prescribed for dormitories. In many industries women, children and young workers are either absolutely excluded from specified unhealthy processes, or are admitted only under conditions. As regards shops and offices, the labour laws are: one which protects apprentices against overwork (law of 22nd February 1851), one (law of 29th December 1900) which requires that seats shall be provided for women and girls employed in retail sale of articles, and a decree of the 28th of July 1904 defining in detail conditions of hygiene in dormitories for workmen and shop assistants. The law relating to seats is enforced by the inspectors of factories. In France there is no special penal legislation against abuses of the truck system, or excessive fines and deductions from wages, although bills with that end in view have frequently been before parliament. Indirect protection to workers is no doubt in many cases afforded in organized industries by the action of the *Conseils de Prud'hommes.*

Belgium.—In 1848 in Belgium the Commission on Labour proposed legislation to limit, as in France, the hours of labour for adults, but this proposal was never passed. Belgian regulation of labour in industry remains essentially, in harmony with its earliest beginnings in 1863 and onwards, a series of specialized provisions to meet particular risks of individual trades, and did not, until 1889, give any adherence to a common principle of limitation of hours and times of labour for "protected" persons. This was in the law of the 13th of December 1889, which applies to mines, quarries, factories, workshops classed as unhealthy, wharves and docks, transports. As in France, industrial establishments having a charitable or philanthropic [illegible] character are included. The persons protected are [illegible] under 21 years, and boys under 16; and women [illegible] a place in the law through the prohibition of their [illegible] within four weeks after childbirth. As the hours of [illegible] women remain ordinarily unlimited by law, so are [illegible] boys from 16 to 21. The law of Sunday rest dated the [illegible] 1905, however, applies to labour generally in all in[illegible] commercial undertakings except transport and fisheries, [illegible] regulated exceptions for (a) cases of breakdown or [illegible] *force majeure*, (b) certain repairs and cleaning, (c) [illegible] materials, (d) retail food supply. Young workers are [illegible] the exceptions. The absolute prohibitions of em[illegible] for children under 12 years in any industry, manu[illegible] or transport, and for women and girls under 21 [illegible] surface in working of mines. Boys under 16 years and girls under 21 years may in general not be em[illegible] 5 A.M. or after 9 P.M., and one day in the seven is to be [illegible] from employment; to these rules exception may [illegible] by royal decree for classes or groups of processes, or [illegible] authorities in exceptional cases. The exceptions may be [illegible] only to workers over 14 years, but in mines, by [illegible] boys over 12 years may be employed from 4 A.M. The [illegible] fixes only a maximum of 12 hours of effective work, to be [illegible] by pauses for rest of not less than 1½ hours, empowering [illegible] by decree to formulate more precise limits suited to the [illegible] circumstances of individual industries. Royal decrees have laid down the conditions for many groups, including [illegible] manufacture of paper, pottery, glass, clothing, mines, [illegible] engineering and printing works. In some the daily limit [illegible] in more 10½ or 11 hours. In a few exceptionally un[illegible] trades, such as the manufacture of lucifer matches, vulcaniza[illegible] india-rubber by means of carbon bi-sulphide, the age of ex[illegible] employment has been raised, and in the last-named [illegible] hours have been reduced to 5, broken into two spells of 2½ [illegible]. As a rule the conditions of health and safeguarding of [illegible] in exceptionally injurious trades have been sought by [illegible] decrees under the law of 1863 relating to public health in [illegible]. Special regulations for safety of workers have been [illegible] in manufactures of white-lead, oxides of lead, chromate [illegible] lucifer match works, rag and shoddy works; and for dangers [illegible] to many industries, provisions against dust, poisons, [illegible] and other risks to health or limb have been codified in a [illegible] of 1895. A royal decree of the 31st of March 1903 prohibits [illegible] of persons under 16 years in fur-pulling and in carotting [illegible] skins, and another of the 13th of May 1905 regulates use of [illegible] house-painting. In 1898 a law was passed to enable the [illegible] to deal with risks in quarries under the same procedure. [illegible] mines (which are not private property, but state conces[illegible] to be worked under strict state control) has been provided for [illegible] in matters of hygiene, until 1899 the powers of the [illegible] authorities to intervene were insufficient, and a law [illegible] authorizing the government to make regulations for every [illegible] undertaking, whether classed under the law of [illegible] or not. By a special law of 1888 children and young [illegible] under 18 years are excluded from employment as pedlars, [illegible] circuses, except by their parents, and then only if they [illegible] 14 years. Abuses of the truck system have, since 1887, [illegible] with care. The chief objects of the law of 1887 were [illegible] in full to all workers, other than those in agri[illegible] service, of wages in legal tender, to prohibit [illegible] public-houses, and to secure prompt payment of [illegible] deductions were permitted under careful control for [illegible] objects: lodging, use of land, uniforms, food, [illegible] of the 10th of October 1903 required use of [illegible] for estimating wages in certain cases in textile [illegible] the 13th of June 1896 regulates the affixing in [illegible] at least five workers are employed, of a notice [illegible] nature and rate of fines, if any, and the mode [illegible] central services the mines inspectorate [illegible] workshop inspectorate, divide the duties above [illegible] a system of local administration of the [illegible] industries classed as unhealthy, but the [illegible] supreme control in these matters to the [illegible] expert staff.

[illegible] regulation of labour in manufacture [illegible] only to employment of children. [illegible] was established in the law of the [illegible] to all industrial undertakings, ex[illegible] fishing, stock-rearing. Employ[illegible] is prohibited, and hours are limited [illegible] for women of any age. These pro[illegible] by royal decree from unhealthy [illegible] are specified in a decree of 1897 [illegible] regulations. Hours of employment [illegible] for rest must be [illegible] be spent in a [illegible] day work, and [illegible] but there are [illegible] is allowed [illegible] women, for example, in butter and cheese making, and night work for boys over 14 in certain industries. Employment of women within four weeks of childbirth is prohibited. Notices of working hours must be affixed in workplaces. Underground work in mines is prohibited for women and young persons under 16, but in Holland mining is a very small industry. In 1895 the first legislative provision was made for protection of workers against risk of accident or special injury to health. Sufficient cubic space, lighting, ventilation, sanitary accommodation, reasonable temperature, removal of noxious gases or dust, fencing of machinery, precautions against risk from fire and other matters are provided for. The manufacture of lucifer matches by means of white phosphorus was forbidden and the export, importation and sale was regulated by a law of the 28th of May 1901. By a regulation of the 16th of March 1904 provisions for safety and health of women and young workers were strengthened in processes where lead compounds or other poisons are used, and their employment at certain dangerous machines and in cleaning machinery or near driving belts was prohibited. No penal provision against truck exists in Holland, but possibly abuses of the system are prevented by the existence of industrial councils representing both employers and workers, with powers to mediate or arbitrate in case of disputes.

Switzerland.—In Switzerland separate cantonal legislation prepared the way for the general Federal labour law of 1877 on which subsequent legislation rests. Such legislation is also cantonal as well as Federal, but in the latter there is only amplification or interpretation of the principles contained in the law of 1877, whereas cantonal legislation covers industries not included under the Federal law, *e.g.* single workers employed in a trade (*métier*) and employment in shops, offices and hotels. The Federal law is applied to factories, workshops employing young persons under 18 or more than 10 workers, and workshops in which unhealthy or dangerous processes are carried on. Mines are not included, but are regulated in some respects as regards health and safety by cantonal laws. Further, the Law of Employers' Liability 1881–1887, which requires in all industries precautions against accidents and reports of all serious accidents to the cantonal governments, applies to mines. This led, in 1896, to the creation of a special mining department, and mines, of which there are few, have to be inspected once a year by a mining engineer. The majority of the provisions of the Federal labour law apply to adult workers of both sexes, and the general limit of the 11-hours' day, exclusive of at least one hour for meals, applies to men as well as women. The latter have, however, a legal claim, when they have a household to manage, to leave work at the dinner-hour half an hour earlier than the men. Men and unmarried women may be employed in such subsidiary work as cleaning before or after the general legal limits. On Saturdays and eves of the eight public holidays the 11-hours' day is reduced to 10. Sunday work and night work are forbidden, but exceptions are permitted conditionally. Night work is defined as 8 P.M. to 5 A.M. in summer, 8 P.M. to 6 A.M. in winter. Children are excluded from employment in workplaces under the law until 14 years of age, and until 16 must attend continuation schools. Zürich canton has fixed the working day for women at 10 hours generally, and 9 hours on Saturdays and eves of holidays. Bâle-Ville canton has the same limits and provides that the very limited Sunday employment permitted shall be compensated by double time off on another day. In the German-speaking cantons girls under 18 are not permitted to work overtime; in all cantons except Glarus the conditional overtime of 2 hours must be paid for at an enhanced wage.

Sanitary regulations and fencing of machinery are provided for with considerable minuteness in a Federal decree of 1897. The plans of every new factory must be submitted to the cantonal government. In the case of lucifer match factories, not only the building but methods of manufacture must be submitted. Since 1901 the manufacture, sale and import of matches containing white phosphorus have been forbidden. Women must be absent from employment during eight weeks before and after childbirth. In certain dangerous occupations, *e.g.* where lead or lead compounds are in use, women may not legally be employed during pregnancy. A resolution of the federal council in 1901 classed thirty-four different substances in use in industry as dangerous and laid down that in case of clearly defined illness of workers directly caused by use of any of these substances the liability provided by article 3 of the law of the 25th of June 1881, and article 1 of the law of the 26th of April 1887, should apply to the manufacture. Legislative provision against abuses of the truck system appears to be of earlier origin in Switzerland (17th century) than any other European country outside England (15th century). The Federal Labour Law 1877 generally prohibits payment of wages otherwise than in current coin, and provides that no deduction shall be made without an express contract. Some of the cantonal laws go much farther than the British act of 1896 in forbidding certain deductions; *e.g.* Zürich prohibits any charge for cleaning, warming or lighting workrooms or for hire of machinery. By the Federal law fines may not exceed half a day's wage. Administration of the Labour laws is divided between inspectors appointed by the Federal Government and local authorities, under supervision of the cantonal governments. The Federal Government forms a court of appeal against decisions of the cantonal governments.

Germany.—Regulation of the conditions of labour in industry throughout the German empire is provided for in the Imperial Industrial Code and the orders of the Federal Council based thereon. By far the most important recent amendment socially is the law regulating child-labour, dated the 30th of March 1903, which relates to establishments having industrial character in the sense of the Industrial Code. This Code is based on earlier industrial codes of the separate states, but more especially on the Code of 1869 of the North German Confederation. It applies in whole or in part to all trades and industrial occupations, except transport, fisheries and agriculture. Mines are only included so far as truck, Sunday and holiday rest, prohibition of employment underground of female labour, limitation of the hours of women and young workers are concerned; otherwise the regulations for protection of life and limb of miners vary, as do the mining laws of the different states. To estimate the force of the Industrial Code in working, it is necessary to bear in mind the complicated political history of the empire, the separate administration by the federated states, and the generally considerable powers vested in administration of initiating regulations. The Industrial Code expressly retains power for the states to initiate certain additions or exceptions to the Code which in any given state may form part of the law regulating factories there. The Code (unlike the Austrian Industrial Code) lays down no general limit for a normal working day for adult male workers, but since 1891 full powers were given to the Imperial government to limit hours for any classes of workers in industries where excessive length of the working day endangers the health of the worker (R.G.O. § 120e). Previously application had been made of powers to reduce the working day in such unhealthy industries as silvering of mirrors by mercury and the manufacture of white-lead. Separate states had, under mining laws, also limited hours of miners. Sunday rest was, in 1891, secured for every class of workers, commercial, industrial and mining. Annual holidays were also secured on church festivals. These provisions, however, are subject to exceptions under conditions. An important distinction has to be shown when we turn to the regulations for hours and times of labour for protected persons (women, young persons and children). Setting aside for the moment hours of shop assistants (which are under special sections since 1900), it is to "factory workers" and not to industrial workers in general that these limits apply, although they may be, and in some instances have been, further extended—for instance, in ready-made clothing trades—by imperial decree to workshops, and by the Child Labour Law of 1903 regulation of the scope and duration of employment of children is much strengthened in workshops, commerce, transport and domestic industries. The term "factory" (*Fabrik*) is not defined in the Code, but it is clear from various decisions of the supreme court that it only in part coincides with the English term, and that some workplaces, where processes are carried on by aid of mechanical power, rank rather as English workshops. The distinction is rather between wholesale manufacturing industry, with subdivision of labour, and small industry, where the employer works himself. Certain classes of undertaking, viz. forges, timber-yards, dock-yards, brickfields and open quarries, are specifically ranked as factories. Employment of protected persons at the surface of mines and underground quarries, and in salt works and ore-dressing works, and of boys underground comes under the factory regulations. These exclude children from employment under 13 years, and even later if an educational certificate has not been obtained; until 14 years hours of employment may not exceed 6 in the 24. In processes and occupations under the scope of the Child Labour Law children may not be employed by their parents or guardians before 10 years of age or by other employers before 12 years of age; nor between the hours of 8 P.M. and 8 A.M., nor otherwise than in full compliance with requirements of educational authorities for school attendance and with due regard to prescribed pauses. In school term time the daily limit of employment for children is three hours, in holiday time three hours. As regards factories Germany, unlike Great Britain, France and Switzerland, requires a shorter day for young persons than for women—10 hours for the former, 11 hours for the latter. Women over 16 years may be employed 11 hours. Night work is forbidden, i.e. work between 8.30 P.M. and 5.30 A.M. Overtime may be granted to meet unforeseen pressure or for work on perishable articles, under conditions, by local authorities and the higher administrative authorities. Prescribed meal-times are—an unbroken half-hour for children in their 6 hours; for young persons a mid-day pause of one hour, and half an hour respectively in the morning and afternoon spells; for women, an hour at mid-day, but women with the care of a household have the claim, on demand, to an extra half-hour, as in Switzerland. No woman may be employed within four weeks after childbirth, and unless a medical certificate can then be produced, the absence must extend to six weeks. Notice of working periods and meal-times must be affixed, and copies sent to the local authorities. Employment of protected persons in factory industries where there are special risks to health or morality may be forbidden or made dependent on special conditions. By the Child Labour Law employment of children is forbidden in brickworks, stone breaking, chimney sweeping, street cleaning and other processes and occupations. By an order of the Federal Council in 1902 female workers were excluded from main processes in forges and rolling mills. All industrial employers alike are bound to organize labour in such a manner as to secure workers against injury to health and to ensure good conduct and propriety. Sufficient light, suitable cloakrooms and sanitary accommodation, and ventilation to carry off dust, vapours and other impurities are especially required. Dining-rooms may be ordered by local authorities. Fencing and provision for safety in case of fire are required in detail. The work of the trade accident insurance associations in preventing accidents is especially recognized in provisions for special rules in dangerous or unhealthy industries. Officials of the state factory departments are bound to give opportunity to trustees of the trade associations to express an opinion on special rules. In a large number of industries the Federal Council has laid down special rules comparable with those for unhealthy occupations in Great Britain. Among the regulations most recently revised and strengthened are those for manufacture of lead colours and lead compounds, and for horse-hair and brush-making factories. The relations between the state inspectors of factories and the ordinary police authorities are regulated in each state by its constitution. Prohibitions of truck in its original sense—that is, payment of wages otherwise than in current coin—apply to any persons under a contract of service with an employer for a specified time for industrial purposes; members of a family working for a parent or husband are not included; outworkers are covered. Control of fines and deductions from wages applies only in factory industries and shops employing at least 20 workers. Shop hours are regulated by requiring shops to be closed generally between 9 P.M. and 5 A.M., by requiring a fixed mid-day rest of 1½ hours and at least 10 hours' rest in the 24 for assistants. These limits can be modified by administrative authority. Notice of hours and working rules must be affixed. During the hours of compulsory closing sale of goods on the streets or from house to house is forbidden. Under the Commercial Code, as under the Civil Code, every employer is bound to adopt every possible measure for maintaining the safety, health and good conduct of his employés. By an order of the Imperial Chancellor under the Commercial Code seats must be provided for commercial assistants and apprentices.

Austria.—The Industrial Code of Austria, which in its present outline (modified by later enactments) dates from 1883, must be carefully distinguished from the Industrial Code of the kingdom of Hungary. The latter is, owing to the predominantly agricultural character of the population, of later origin, and hardly had practical force before the law of 1893 provided for inspection and prevention of accidents in factories. No separate mining code exists in Hungary, and conditions of labour are regulated by the Austrian law of 1854. The truck system is repressed on lines similar to those in Austria and Germany. As regards limitation of hours of adult labour, Hungary may be contrasted with both those empires in that no restriction of hours applies either to men's or women's hours, whereas in Austrian factories both are limited to an 11-hours' day with exceptional overtime for which payment must always be made to the worker. The Austrian Code has its origin, however, like the British Factory Acts, in protection of child labour. Its present scope is determined by the Imperial "Patent" of 1859, and all industrial labour is included except mining, transport, fisheries, forestry, agriculture and domestic industries. Factories are defined as including industries in which a "manufacturing process is carried on in an enclosed place by the aid of not less than twenty workers working with machines, with subdivision of labour, and under an employer who does not himself manually assist in the work." In smaller handicraft industries the compulsory gild system of organization still applies. In every industrial establishment, large or small, the sanitary and safety provisions, general requirement of Sunday rest, and annual holidays (with conditional exceptions), prohibition of truck and limitation of the ages of child labour apply Night work for women, 8 P.M. to 5 A.M., is prohibited only in factory industries; for young workers it is prohibited in any industry. Pauses in work are required in all industries; one hour at least must be given at mid-day, and if the morning and afternoon spells exceed 5 hours each, another half-hour's rest at least must be given. Children may not be employed in industrial work before 12 years, and then only 8 hours a day at work that is not injurious and if educational requirements are observed. The age of employment is raised to 14 for "factories," and the work must be such as will not hinder physical development. Women may not be employed in regular industrial occupation within one month after childbirth. In certain scheduled unhealthy industries, where certificates of authorization from local authorities must be obtained by intending occupiers, conditions of health and safety for workers can be laid down in the certificate. The Minister of the Interior is empowered to draw up regulations prohibiting or making conditions for the employment of young workers or women in dangerous or unhealthy industries. The provisions against truck cover not only all industrial workers engaged in manual labour under a contract with an employer, but also shop-assistants; the special regulations against fines and deductions apply to factory workers and shops where at least 20 workers are employed. In mines under the law of 1884, which supplements the general mining law, employment of women and girls underground is prohibited; boys from 12 to 16 and girls from 12 to 18 may only be employed at light work above ground; 14 is the earliest age of admission for boys underground. The shifts from bank to bank [illegible] not exceed 12 hours, of which not more than 10 may be work. Sunday rest must begin not later than 6 A.M., and must be of 24 hours' duration. These last two provisions do not hold in case of pressing danger for safety, health or property. Sick and accident funds and mining associations are legislated for in minutest detail. The general law provides for safety in working, but special rules drawn up by the district authorities lay down in detail the conditions of health and safety. As regards manufacturing industry, the Industrial Code lays no obligation on employers to report accidents, and until the Accident Insurance Law of 1889 came into force no statistics were available. In Austria, unlike Germany, the factory inspectorate is organized throughout under a central chief inspector.

Scandinavian Countries.—In Sweden the Factory Law was amended in January 1901; in Denmark in July 1901. Until that year, however, Norway was in some respects in advance of the other two countries by its law of 1892, which applied to industrial works, including metal works of all kinds and mining. Women were thereby prohibited from employment: (*a*) underground; (*b*) in cleaning or oiling machinery in motion; (*c*) during six weeks after childbirth, unless provided with a medical certificate stating that they might return at the end of four weeks without injury to health; (*d*) in dangerous, unhealthy or exhausting trades during pregnancy. Further, work on Sundays and public holidays is prohibited to all workers, adult and youthful, with conditional exceptions under the authority of the inspectors. Children over 12 are admitted to industrial work on obtaining certificates of birth, of physical fitness and of elementary education. The hours of children are limited to 6, with pauses, and of young persons (of 14 to 18 years) to 10, with pauses. Night work between 8 P.M. and 6 A.M. is prohibited. All workers are entitled to a copy of a code of factory rules containing the terms of the [illegible] of work drawn up by representatives of employés with the [illegible] and sanctioned by the inspector. Health and safety in [illegible] are provided for in detail in the same law of 1892. Special rules [illegible] be made for dangerous trades, and in 1899 such rules were [illegible] for match factories, similar to some of the British rules, [illegible] notably providing for a dental examination four times yearly by a doctor. In Denmark, regulation began with unhealthy industries, and it was not until the law of 1901 came into force, on the 1st of January 1902, that children under 12 years have been excluded from factory labour. Control of child labour can be strengthened by municipal regulations, and this has been done in Copenhagen by an order of the 23rd of May [illegible]. In Sweden the 12 years' limit had for some time held in the larger factories; the scope has been extended so that it corresponds with the Norwegian law. The hours of children are in Denmark, as for those under 14 years; in Sweden 6 for those under 13 years. Young persons may not in either country work more than 10 hours daily, and night work, which is forbidden for persons under 18 years, is now defined as in Norway. Women may not be employed in industry within four weeks of childbirth, except on authority of a medical certificate. All factories in Sweden where young persons are employed are subject to [illegible] inspection once a year. Fencing of machinery and hygienic [illegible] (ventilation, [illegible], light) are regulated [illegible] white phosphorus in manufacture [illegible] In Denmark the [illegible] special regulations [illegible] administrative orders which strengthen [illegible] dangerous industries, e.g. dry-cleaning [illegible] and engineering [illegible] regulates labour [illegible] works.

[illegible] the industrial [illegible]

The law of 1886 prohibits employment of children under 9 years in industry and under 10 years in underground mining. Night work for women was in Italy first prohibited by the law of the 19th of June 1902, and at the same time also for boys under 15, but this regulation was not to take full effect for 5 years as regards persons already employed; by the same law persons under 15 and women of any age were accorded the claim to one day's complete rest of 24 hours in the week; the age of employment of children in factories, workshops, laboratories, quarries, mines, was raised to 12 years generally and 14 years for underground work; the labour of female workers of any age was prohibited in underground work, and power was reserved to further restrict and regulate their employment as well as that of male workers under 15. Spain and Italy, the former by the law of the 13th of March 1900, the latter by the law of the 19th of June 1902, prohibit the employment of women within a fixed period of childbirth; in Spain the limit is three weeks, in Italy one month, which may be reduced to three weeks on a medical certificate of fitness. Sunday rest is secured in industrial works, with regulated exceptions in Spain by the law of the 3rd of March 1904. It is in the direction of fencing and other safeguards against accidents and as regards sanitary provisions, both in industrial workplaces and in mines, that Italy has made most advance since her law of 1890 for prevention of accidents. Special measures for prevention of malaria are required in cultivation of rice by a ministerial circular of the 23rd of April 1903; work may not begin until an hour after sunrise and must cease an hour before sunset; children under 13 may not be employed in this industry.

(A. M. An.)

IV. United States.

History.

Under the general head of Labour Legislation all American statute laws regulating labour, its conditions, and the relation of employer and employé must be classed. It includes what is properly known as factory legislation. Labour legislation belongs to the latter half of the 19th century, so far as the United States is concerned. Like England in the far past, the Americans in colonial days undertook to regulate wages and prices, and later the employment of apprentices. Legislation relating to wages and prices was long ago abandoned, but the laws affecting the employment of apprentices still exist in some form, although conditions of employment have changed so materially that apprenticeships are not entered as of old; but the laws regulating the employment of apprentices were the basis on which English legislation found a foothold when parliament wished to regulate the labour of factory operatives. The code of labour laws of the present time is almost entirely the result of the industrial revolution during the latter part of the 18th century, under which the domestic or hand-labour system was displaced through the introduction of power machinery. As this revolution took place in the United States at a somewhat later date than in England, the labour legislation necessitated by it belongs to a later date. The factory, so far as textiles are concerned, was firmly established in America during the period from 1820 to 1840, and it was natural that the English legislation found friends and advocates in the United States, although the more objectionable conditions accompanying the English factory were not to be found there.

Early attempts to regulate hours.

The first attempt to secure legislation regulating factory employment related to the hours of labour, which were very long—from twelve to thirteen hours a day. As machinery was introduced it was felt that the tension resulting from speeded machines and the close attention required in the factory ought to be accompanied by a shorter work-day. This view took firm hold of the operatives, and was the chief cause of the agitation which has resulted in a great body of laws applying in very many directions. As early as 1806 the caulkers and shipbuilders of New York City agitated for a reduction of hours to ten per day, but no legislation followed. There were several other attempts to secure some regulation relative to hours, but there was no general agitation prior to 1831. As Massachusetts was the state which first recognized the necessity of regulating employment (following in a measure, and so far as conditions demanded, the English labour or factory legislation), the history of such legislation in that state is indicative of that in the United States, and as it would be impossible in this article to give a detailed history of the origin of laws in the different states, the dates of their enactment, and their provisions, it is best to follow primarily the course of the Eastern states, and especially that of Massachusetts, where the first general agitation took place and the first laws were enacted. That state in 1836 regulated by law the question of the education of young persons employed in manufacturing establishments. The regulation of hours of labour was warmly discussed in 1832, and several legislative committees and commissions reported upon it, but no specific action on the general question of hours of labour secured the indorsement of the Massachusetts legislature until 1874, although the day's labour of children under twelve years of age was limited to ten hours in 1842. Ten hours constituted a day's labour, on a voluntary basis, in many trades in Massachusetts and other parts of the country as early as 1853, while in the shipbuilding trades this was the work-day in 1844. In April 1840 President Van Buren issued an order "that all public establishments will hereafter be regulated, as to working hours, by the ten-hours system." The real aggressive movement began in 1845, through numerous petitions to the Massachusetts legislature urging a reduction of the day's labour to eleven hours, but nothing came of these petitions at that time. Again, in 1850, a similar effort was made, and also in 1851 and 1852, but the bills failed. Then there was a period of quiet until 1865, when an unpaid commission made a report relative to the hours of labour, and recommended the establishment of a bureau of statistics for the purpose of collecting data bearing upon the labour question. This was the first step in this direction in any country. The first bureau of the kind was established in Massachusetts in 1869, but meanwhile, in accordance with reports of commissions and the address of Governor Bullock in 1866, and the general sentiment which then prevailed, the legislature passed an act regulating in a measure the conditions of the employment of children in manufacturing establishments; and this is one of the first laws of the kind in the United States, although the first legislation in the United States relating to the hours of labour which the writer has been able to find, and for which he can fix a date, was enacted by the state of Pennsylvania in 1849, the law providing that ten hours should be a day's work in cotton, woollen, paper, bagging, silk and flax factories.

Employment of children.

The Massachusetts law of 1866 provided, firstly, that no child under ten should be employed in any manufacturing establishment, and that no child between ten and fourteen should be so employed unless he had attended some public or private school at least six months during the year preceding such employment, and, further, that such employment should not continue unless the child attended school at least six months in each and every year; secondly, a penalty not exceeding $50 for every owner or agent or other person knowingly employing a child in violation of the act; thirdly, that no child under the age of fourteen should be employed in any manufacturing establishment more than eight hours in any one day; fourthly, that any parent or guardian allowing or consenting to employment in violation of the act should forfeit a sum not to exceed $50 for each offence; fifthly, that the Governor instruct the state constable and his deputies to enforce the provisions of all laws for regulating the employment of children in manufacturing establishments. The same legislature also created a commission of three persons, whose duty it was to investigate the subject of hours of labour in relation to the social, educational and sanitary condition of the working classes. In 1867 a fundamental law relating to schooling and hours of labour of children employed in manufacturing and mechanical establishments was passed by the Massachusetts legislature. It differed from the act of the year previous in some respects, going deeper into the general question. It provided that no child under ten should be employed in any manufacturing or mechanical establishment of the commonwealth, and that no child between ten and fifteen should be so employed unless he had attended school, public or private, at least three months during the year next preceding his employment. There were provisions relating to residence, &c., and a further provision that no time less than 120 half-days of actual schooling should be deemed an equivalent of three months, and that no child under fifteen should be employed in any manufacturing or mechanical establishment more than sixty hours any one week. The law also provided penalties for violation. It repealed the act of 1866.

In 1869 began the establishment of that chain of offices in the United States, the principle of which has been adopted by other countries, known as bureaus of statistics of labour, their especial purpose being the collection and dissemination of information relating to all features of industrial employment. As a result of the success of the first bureau, bureaus are in existence in thirty-three states, in addition to the United States Bureau of Labour.

A special piece of legislation which belongs to the commonwealth of Massachusetts, so far as experience shows, was that in 1872, providing for cheap morning and evening trains for the accommodation of working men living in the vicinity of Boston. Great Britain had long had such trains, which were called parliamentary trains. Under the Massachusetts law some of the railways running out of Boston furnished the accommodation required, and the system has since been in operation.

Factory legislation, 1877.

In different parts of the country the agitation to secure legislation regulating the hours of labour became aggressive again in 1870 and the years immediately following, there being a constant repetition of attempts to secure the enactment of a ten-hours law, but in Massachusetts all the petitions failed till 1874, when the legislature of that commonwealth established the hours of labour at sixty per week not only for children under eighteen, but for women, the law providing that no minor under eighteen and no woman over that age should be employed by any person, firm or corporation in any manufacturing establishment more than ten hours in any one day. In 1876 Massachusetts reconstructed its laws relating to the employment of children, although it did not abrogate the principles involved in earlier legislation, while in 1877 the commonwealth passed Factory Acts covering the general provisions of the British laws. It provided for the general inspection of factories and public buildings, the provisions of the law relating to dangerous machinery, such as belting, shafting, gearing, drums, &c., which the legislature insisted must be securely guarded, and that no machinery other than steam engines should be cleaned while running. The question of ventilation and cleanliness was also attended to. Dangers connected with hoistways, elevators and well-holes were minimized by their protection by sufficient trap-doors, while fire-escapes were made obligatory on all establishments of three or more storeys in height. All main doors, both inside and outside, of manufacturing establishments, as well as those of churches, school-rooms, town halls, theatres and every building used for public assemblies, should open outwardly whenever the factory inspectors of the commonwealth deemed it necessary. These provisions remain in the laws of Massachusetts, and other states have found it wise to follow them.

The labour legislation in force in 1910 in the various states of the Union might be classified in two general branches: (A) protective labour legislation, or laws for the aid of workers who, on account of their economic dependence, are not in a position fully to protect themselves; (B) legislation having for its purpose the fixing of the legal status of the worker as an employé, such as laws relating to the making and breaking of the labour contract, the right to form organizations and to assemble peaceably, the settlement of labour disputes, the licensing of occupations, &c.

Factory and workshop acts.

(A) The first class includes factory and workshop acts, laws relating to hours of labour, work on Sundays and holidays, the payment of wages, the liability of employers for injuries to their employés, &c. Factory acts have been passed by nearly all the states of the Union. These may be considered in two groups—first, laws which relate to conditions of employment and affect only children, young persons and women; and second, laws which relate to the sanitary condition of factories and workshops and to the safety of employés generally. The states adopting such laws have usually made provision for factory inspectors, whose duties are to enforce these laws and who have power to enter and inspect factories and workshops. The most common provisions of the factory acts in the various states are those which fix an age limit below which employment is unlawful. All but five states have enacted such provisions, and these five states have practically no manufacturing industries. In some states the laws fixing an age limit are restricted in their application to factories, while in others they extend also to workshops, bakeries, mercantile establishments and other work places where children are employed. The prescribed age limit varies from ten to fourteen years. Provisions concerning the education of children in factories and workshops may be considered in two groups, those relating to apprenticeship and those requiring a certain educational qualification as a pre-requisite to employment. Apprenticeship laws are numerous, but they do not now have great force, because of the practical abrogation of the apprenticeship system through the operation of modern methods of production. Most states have provisions prohibiting illiterates under a specified age, usually sixteen, from being employed in factories and workshops. The provisions of the factory acts relating to hours of labour and night work generally affect only the employment of women and young persons. Most of the states have enacted such provisions, those limiting the hours of children occurring more frequently than those limiting the hours of women. The hour limit for work in such cases ranges from six per day to sixty-six per week. Where the working time of children is restricted, the minimum age prescribed for such children ranges from twelve to twenty-one years. In some cases the restriction of the hours of labour of women and children is general, while in others it applies only to employment in one or more classes of industries. Other provisions of law for the protection of women and children, but not usually confined in their operation to factories and workshops, are such as require seats for females and separate toilet facilities for the sexes, and prohibit employment in certain occupations as in mines, places where intoxicants are manufactured or sold, in cleaning or operating dangerous machinery, &c. Provisions of factory acts relating to the sanitary condition of factories and workshops and the safety of employés have been enacted in nearly all the manufacturing states of the Union. They prohibit overcrowding, and require proper ventilation, sufficient light and heat, the lime-washing or painting of walls and ceilings, the provision of exhaust fans and blowers in places where dust or dangerous fumes are generated, guards on machinery, mechanical belts and gearing shifters, guards on elevators and hoistways, hand-rails on stairs, fire-escapes, &c.

Hours of labour.

The statutes relating to hours of labour may be considered under five groups, namely: (1) general laws which merely fix what shall be regarded as a day's labour in the absence of a contract; (2) laws defining what shall constitute a day's work on public roads; (3) laws limiting the hours of labour per day on public works; (4) laws limiting the hours of labour in certain occupations; and (5) laws which specify the hours per day or per week during which women and children may be employed. The statutes included in the first two groups place no restrictions upon the number of hours which may be agreed upon between employers and employés, while those in the other three groups usually limit the freedom of contract and provide penalties for their violation. A considerable number of states have enacted laws which fix a day's labour in the absence of any contract, some at eight and others at ten hours, so that when an employer and an employé make a contract and they do not specify what shall constitute a day's labour, eight or ten hours respectively would be ruled as the day's labour in an action which might come before the courts. In a number of the states it is optional with the citizens to liquidate certain taxes either by cash payments or by rendering personal service. In the latter case the length of the working day is defined by law, eight hours being usually specified. The Federal government and nearly one-half of the states have laws providing that eight hours shall constitute a day's work for employés on public works. Under the Federal Act it is unlawful for any officer of the government or of any contractor or subcontractor for public works to permit labourers and mechanics to work longer than eight hours per day. The state laws concerning hours of labour have similar provisions. Exceptions are provided for cases of extraordinary emergencies, such as danger to human life or property. In many states the hours of labour have been limited by law in occupations in which, on account of their dangerous or insanitary character, the health of the employés would be jeopardized by long hours of labour, or in which the fatigue occasioned by long hours would endanger the lives of the employés or of the public. The occupations for which such special legislation has been enacted are those of employés on steam and street railways, in mines and other underground workings, smelting and refining works, bakeries and cotton and woollen mills. Laws limiting the hours of labour of women and children have been considered under factory and workshop acts.

Sunday labour.

Nearly all states and Territories of the Union have laws prohibiting the employment of labour on Sunday. These laws usually make it a misdemeanour for persons either to labour themselves or to compel or permit their apprentices, servants or other employés, to labour on the first day of the week. Exceptions are made in the case of household duties or works of necessity or charity, and in the case of members of religious societies who observe some other than the first day of the week.

Payment of wages.

Statutes concerning the payment of wages of employés may be considered in two groups: (1) those which relate to the employment contract, such as laws fixing the maximum period of wage payments, prohibiting the payment of wages in scrip or other evidences of indebtedness in lieu of lawful money, prohibiting wage deductions on account of fines, breakage of machinery, discounts for prepayments, medical attendance, relief funds or other purposes, requiring the giving of notice of reduction of wages, &c.; (2) legislation granting certain privileges or affording special protection to working people with respect to their wages, such as laws exempting wages from attachment, preferring wage claims in assignments, and granting workmen liens upon buildings and other constructions on which they have been employed.

Employers' liability.

Employers' liability laws have been passed to enable an employé to recover damages from his employer under certain conditions when he has been injured through accident occurring in the works of the employer. The common-law maxim that the principal is responsible for the acts of his agent does not apply where two or more persons are working together under the same employer and one of the employés is injured through the carelessness of his fellow-employé, although the one causing the accident is the agent of the principal, who under the common law would be responsible. The old Roman law and the English and American practice under it held that the co-employé was a party to the accident. The injustice of this rule is seen by a single illustration. A weaver in a cotton factory, where there are hundreds of operatives, is injured by the neglect or carelessness of the engineer in charge of the motive power. Under the common law the weaver could not recover damages from the employer, because he was the co-employé of the engineer. So, one of thousands of employés of a railway system, sustaining injuries through the carelessness of a switchman whom he never saw, could recover no damages from the railway company, both being co-employés of the same employer. The injustice of this application of the common-law rule has been recognized, but the only way to avoid the difficulty was through specific legislation providing that under such conditions as those related, and similar ones, the doctrine of co-employment should not apply, and that the workman should have the same right to recover damages as a passenger upon a railway train. This legislation has upset some of the most notable distinctions of law.

The first agitation for legislation of this character occurred in England in 1880. A number of states in the Union have now enacted statutes fixing the liability of employers under certain conditions and relieving the employé from the application of the common-law rule. Where the employé himself is contributory to the injuries resulting from an accident he cannot recover, nor can he recover in some cases where he knows of the danger from the defects of tools or implements employed by him. The legislation upon the subject involves many features of legislation which need not be described here, such as those concerning the power of employés to make a contract, and those defining the conditions, often elaborate, which lead to the liability of the employer and the duties of the employé, and the relations in which damages for injuries sustained in employment may be recovered from the employer.

(B) The statutes thus far considered may be regarded as protective labour legislation. There is, besides, a large body of statutory laws enacted in the various states for the purpose of fixing the legal status of employers and employés and defining their rights and privileges as such.

Labour contract.

A great variety of statutes have been enacted in the various states relating to the labour contract. Among these are laws defining the labour contract, requiring notice of termination of contract, making it a misdemeanour to break a contract of service and thereby endanger human life or expose valuable property to serious injury, or to make a contract of service and accept transportation or pecuniary advancements with intent to defraud, prohibiting contracts of employment whereby employés waive the right to damages in case of injury, &c. A Federal statute makes it a misdemeanour for any one to prepay the transportation or in any way assist or encourage the importation of aliens under contract to perform labour or service of any kind in the United States, exceptions being made in the case of skilled labour that cannot otherwise be obtained, domestic servants and persons belonging to any of the recognized professions.

Licensed occupations.

The Federal government and nearly all the states and territories have statutory provisions requiring the examination and licensing of persons practising certain trades other than those in the class of recognized professions. The Federal statute relates only to engineers on steam vessels, masters, mates, pilots, &c. The occupations for which examinations and licences are required by the various state laws are those of barbers, horseshoers, elevator operators, plumbers, stationary firemen, steam engineers, telegraph operators on railroads and certain classes of mine workers and steam and street railway employés.

Labour organizations.

The right of combination and peaceable assembly on the part of employés is recognized at common law throughout the United States. Organizations of working-men formed for their mutual benefit, protection and improvement, such as for endeavouring to secure higher wages, shorter hours of labour or better working conditions, are nowhere regarded as unlawful. A number of states and the Federal government have enacted statutes providing for the incorporation of trade unions, but owing to the freedom from regulation or inspection enjoyed by unincorporated trade unions, very few have availed themselves of this privilege. A number of states have enacted laws tending to give special protection to and encourage trade unions. Thus, nearly one-half of the states have passed acts declaring it unlawful for employers to discharge workmen for joining labour organizations, or to make it a condition of employment that they shall not belong to such bodies. Laws of this kind have generally been held to be unconstitutional. Nearly all the states have laws protecting trade unions in the use of the union label, insignia of membership, credentials, &c., and making it a misdemeanour to counterfeit or fraudulently use them. A number of the states exempt labour organizations from the operations of the anti-trust and insurance acts.

Labour disputes.

Until recent years all legal action concerning labour disturbances was based upon the principles of the common law. Some of the states have now fairly complete statutory enactments concerning labour disturbances, while others have little or no legislation of this class. The right of employés to strike for any cause or for no cause is sustained by the common law everywhere in the United States. Likewise an employer has a right to discharge any or all of his employés when they have no contract with him, and he may refuse to employ any person or class of persons for any reason or for no reason. Agreements among strikers to take peaceable means to induce others to remain away from the works of an employer until he yields to the demands of the strikers are not held to be conspiracies under the common law, and the carrying out of such a purpose by peaceable persuasion and without violence, intimidation or threats, is not unlawful. However, any interference with the constitutional rights of another to employ whom he chooses or to labour when, where or on what terms he pleases, is illegal. The boycott has been held to be an illegal conspiracy in restraint of trade. The statutory enactments of the various states concerning labour disturbances are in part re-enactments of the rules of common law and in part more or less departures from or additions to the established principles. The list of such statutory enactments is a large one, and includes laws relating to blacklisting, boycotting, conspiracy against working-men, interference with employment, intimidation, picketing and strikes of railway employés; laws requiring statements of causes of discharge of employés and notice of strikes in advertisements for labour; laws prohibiting deception in the employment of labour and the hiring of armed guards by employers; and laws declaring that certain labour agreements do not constitute conspiracy. Some of these laws have been held to be unconstitutional, and some have not yet been tested in the courts.

Arbitration and conciliation.

The laws just treated relate almost entirely to acts either of employers or of employés, but there is another form of law, namely, that providing for action to be taken by others in the effort to prevent working people from losing employment, either by their own acts or by those of their employers, or to settle any differences which arise out of controversies relating to wages, hours of labour, terms and conditions of employment, rules, &c. These laws provide for the mediation and the arbitration of labour disputes (see Arbitration and Conciliation). Twenty-three states and the Federal government have laws or constitutional provisions of this nature. In some cases they provide for the appointment of state boards, and in others of local boards only. A number of states provide for local or special boards in addition to the regular state boards. In some states it is required that a member of a labour organization must be a member of the board, and, in general, both employers and employés must be represented. Nearly all state boards are required to attempt to mediate between the parties to a dispute when information is received of an actual or threatened labour trouble. Arbitration may be undertaken in some states on application from either party, in others on the application of both parties. An agreement to maintain the *status quo* pending arbitration is usually required. The modes of enforcement of obedience to the awards of the boards are various. Some states depend on publicity alone, some give the decisions the effect of judgments of courts of law which may be enforced by execution, while in other states disobedience to such decisions is punishable as for contempt of court. The Federal statute applies only to common carriers engaged in interstate commerce, and provides for an attempt to be made at mediation by two designated government officials in controversies between common carriers and their employés, and, in case of the failure of such an attempt, for the formation of a board of arbitration consisting of the same officials together with certain other parties to be selected. Such arbitration boards are to be formed only at the request or upon the consent of both parties to the controversy.

The judicial enforcement of labour laws.

The enforcement of laws by executive or judicial action is an important matter relating to labour legislation, for without action such laws would remain dead letters. Under the constitutions of the states, the governor is the commander-in-chief of the military forces, and he has the power to order the militia or any part of it into active service in case of insurrection, invasion, tumult, riots or breaches of the peace or imminent danger thereof. Frequent action has been taken in the case of strikes with the view of preventing or suppressing violence threatened or happening to persons or property, the effect being, however, that the militia protects those working or desiring to work, or the employers. The president of the United States may use the land and naval forces whenever by reason of insurrection, domestic violence, unlawful obstructions, conspiracy, combinations or assemblages of persons it becomes impracticable to enforce the laws of the land by the ordinary course of judicial proceedings, or when the execution of the laws is so hindered by reason of such events that any portion or class of the people are deprived thereby of their rights and privileges under the constitution and laws of the country. Under this general power the United States forces have been used for the protection of both employers and employés indirectly, the purpose being to protect mails and, as in the states, to see that the laws are carried out.

The power of the courts to interfere in labour disputes is through the injunction and punishment thereunder for contempt of court. It is a principle of law that when there are interferences, actual or threatened, with property or with rights of a pecuniary nature, and the common or statute law offers no adequate and immediate remedy for the prevention of injury, a court of equity may interpose and issue its order or injunction as to what must or must not be done, a violation of which writ gives the court which issued it the power to punish for contempt. The doctrine is that something is necessary to be done to stop at once the destruction of property and the obstruction of business, and the injunction is immediate in its action. This writ has been resorted to frequently for the indirect protection of employés and of employers. (C. D. W.)

Authorities.—English: (*a*) **Factory Legislation**: Abraham and Davies, *Law relating to Factories and Workshops* (London, 1897 and 1902); Redgrave, *Factory Acts* (London, 1897); Royal Commission on Labour, *Minutes of Evidence and Digests*, Group "C" (3 vols., 1892–1893), *Assistant Commissioner's Report on Employment of Women* (1893), *Fifth and Final Report of the Commission* (1894); International Labour Conference at Berlin, *Correspondence, Commercial Series* (C. 6042) (1890); House of Lords Committee on the Sweating System, *Report* (1891); *Home Office Reports*: Annual Reports of H.M. Chief Inspector of Factories (1879 to 1901), Committee on White Lead and Various Lead Industries (1894), Working of the Cotton Cloth Factories Acts (1897), Dangerous Trades (Anthrax) Committee, Do., Miscellaneous Trades (1896–97–98–99), Conditions of Work in Fish-Curing Trade (1898), Lead Compounds in Pottery (1899), Phosphorus in Manufacture of Lucifer Matches (1899), &c., &c.; Whately Cooke-Taylor, *Modern Factory System* (London, 1891); Oliver, *Dangerous Trades* (London, 1902); Cunningham, *Growth of English Commerce and Industry* (1907); Hutchins and Harrison, *History of Factory Legislation* (1903); Traill, *Social England*, &c., &c. (*b*) **Mines and Quarries**: *Statutes*: Coal Mines Regulation Acts 1886, 1894, 1896, 1899; Metalliferous Mines Regulation Acts 1872, 1875; Quarries Act 1894; Royal Commission on Labour, *Minutes of Evidence and Digests*, Group "A" (1892–1893, 3 vols.); Royal Commission on Mining Royalties, *Appendices* (1894); *Home Office Reports*: Annual General Report upon the Mining Industry (1894–1897), Mines and Quarries, General Reports and Statistics (1898 to 1899), Annual Reports of H.M. Chief Inspector of Factories (1893–1895) (Quarries); Macswinney and Bristowe, *Coal Mines Regulation Act 1887* (London, 1888). (*c*) **Shops**: *Statutes*: Shop Hours Acts 1892, 1893, 1896, Seats for Shop Assistants Act 1899; *Report of Select Committee of House of Commons on the Shop Hours Regulation Bill 1886* (Eyre and Spottiswoode). (*d*) **Truck**: *Home Office Reports*: Annual Reports of H.M. Chief Inspector of Factories, especially 1895–1900, Memorandum on the Law relating to Truck and Checkweighing Clauses of the Coal Mines Acts 1896, Memorandum relating to the Truck Acts, by Sir Kenelm Digby, with text of Acts (1897).

CONTINENTAL EUROPE: *Annuaire de la législation du travail* (Bruxelles, 1898–1905); *Hygiène et sécurité des travailleurs dans les ateliers industriels* (Paris, 1895); *Bulletin de l'inspection du travail* (Paris, 1895–1902); *Bulletin de l'office international du travail* (Paris, 1902–1906); *Congrès international de législation du travail* (1898); *Die Gewerbeordnung für das deutsche Reich*, (1) Landmann (1897); (2) Neukamp (1901); *Gesetz betr. Kinderarbeit in gewerblichen Betrieben, 30. März 1903*; [illegible] *Manz'sche Gesetzausgabe*, [illegible] Band und siebenter Band (Wien, 1897–1898); *Legge sugli infortunii del lavoro* (Milan, 1900).

UNITED STATES: See the *Twenty-Second Annual Report of the Commissioner of Labor* (1907) giving all labour laws in force in the United States in 1907, with annotations of decisions of courts; bi-monthly *Bulletins* of the U.S. Bureau of Labor, containing laws [illegible] since those contained in the foregoing, and decisions of courts relating to employees and employers; also special articles in these [illegible] "Employer and Employé under the Common Law" [illegible] "Protection of Workmen in their Employment" (No. 26), [illegible] Arbitration" (No. 60), "Laws relating [illegible] Women and Children, and to Factory In[illegible] and Safety of Employés" (No. 74), [illegible] Labor in Manufacturing Industries, 1890 to [illegible] of Labor Legislation of 1908 and 1909" (No. [illegible] Industrial Commission on Labor Legisla[illegible] Report); C. D. Wright, *Industrial* [illegible] (1882); Stimson, *Handbook to the Labor* [illegible] and *Labor in its Relation to Law*; Adams [illegible] Labatt, *Commentaries on the Law of* [illegible]

LABOUR PARTY, in Great Britain, the name given to the [illegible] in parliament composed of working-class representatives. [illegible] the Reform Act of 1884, extending the franchise [illegible] working-class electorate, the votes of "labour" [illegible] more and more a matter of importance for politicians; [illegible] the Liberal party, seeking for the support of organized [illegible] the trade unions, found room for a few working-class [illegible]sentatives, who, however, acted and voted as Liberals. [illegible] till 1893 that the Independent Labour party, splitting [illegible] Mr J. Keir Hardie (b. 1856) from the socialist organiza[illegible] known as the Social Democratic Federation (founded 1881), [illegible] formed at Bradford, with the object of getting independent [illegible] returned to parliament on a socialist programme. [illegible] Mr Keir Hardie, who as secretary of the Lanarkshire [illegible] Union had stood unsuccessfully as a labour candidate [illegible] Lanark in 1888, and sat as M.P. for West Ham in [illegible] was elected to parliament for Merthyr-Tydvil by its [illegible] and in 1906 it obtained the return of 30 members, Mr [illegible] Hardie being chairman of the group. Meanwhile in 1899 [illegible] Trade Union Congress instructed its parliamentary com[illegible] call a conference on the question of labour representa[illegible] and in February 1900 this was attended by trade union [illegible] and also by representatives of the Independent Labour [illegible] Social Democratic Federation and the Fabian Society. [illegible] was carried "to establish a distinct labour group [illegible] who shall have their own whips, and agree upon [illegible], which must embrace a readiness to co-operate [illegible] which for the time being may be engaged in [illegible] legislation in the direct interest of labour," and the [illegible] Labour Representation Committee) was elected [illegible]. Under their auspices 29 out of 51 candidates [illegible] at the election of 1906. These groups were distinct [illegible] members ("Lib.-Labs") who obeyed the Liberal [illegible] with the Liberals. In 1908 the attempts to [illegible] parliamentary representatives of the Independent [illegible] with the Trades Union members were successful. [illegible] that year the Miners' Federation, returning 15 [illegible] joined the Independent Labour party, now known [illegible] purposes as the "Labour Party"; other [illegible] such as the Amalgamated Society of Railway [illegible] took the same step. This arrangement came into [illegible] general election of 1910, when the bulk of the [illegible] representatives signed the constitution of the Labour [illegible] after the election numbered 40 members of parlia-

LABRADOR,[1] a great peninsula in British North Americ[illegible] bounded E. by the North Atlantic, N. by Hudson Strait, [illegible] by Hudson and James Bays, and S. by an arbitrary line extendi[illegible] eastwards from the south-east corner of Hudson Bay, near [illegible] N., to the mouth of the Moisie river, on the Gulf of St Lawren[illegible] in 50° N., and thence eastwards by the Gulf of St Lawrence. [illegible] extends from 50° to 63° N., and from 55° to 80° W., and embra[illegible] an approximate area of 511,000 sq. m. Recent exploratio[illegible] and surveys have added greatly to the knowledge of this va[illegible] region, and have shown that much of the peninsula is not [illegible] land of "awful desolation," but a well-wooded country, contai[illegible] ing latent resources of value in its forests, fisheries and miner[illegible]

Physical Geography.—Labrador forms the eastern limb of the [illegible] in the Archaean protaxis of North America (see CANADA), and in[illegible]cludes most of the highest parts of that area. Along some portio[illegible] of the coasts of Hudson and also of Ungava Bay there is a fringe [illegible] lowland, but most of the interior is a plateau rising toward the sou[illegible] and east. The highest portion extends east and west between [illegible] and 54° N., where an immense granite area lies between the head[illegible]waters of the larger rivers of the four principal drainage basins; th[illegible] lowest area is between Hudson Bay and Ungava Bay in the north[illegible] west, where the general level is not more than 500 ft. above the se[illegible] The only mountains are the range along the Atlantic coast, extendin[illegible] from the Strait of Belle Isle to Cape Chidley; in their southern hal[illegible] they rarely exceed 1500 ft., but increase in the northern half to [illegible] general elevation of upwards of 2000 ft., with numerous sharp peak[illegible] between 3000 and 5000 ft., some say 7000 or 8000 ft. The coasts ar[illegible] deeply indented by irregular bays and fringed with rocky islands[illegible] especially along the high Atlantic coast, where long narrow fiord[illegible] penetrate inland. Hamilton Inlet, 250 m. north of the Strait of Bell[illegible] Isle, is the longest of these bays, with a length of 150 m. and [illegible] breadth varying from 2 to 30 m. The surface of the outer portions of the plateau is deeply seamed by valleys, cut into the crystallin[illegible] rocks by the natural erosion of rivers, depending for their length and depth upon the volume of water flowing through them. The valley of the Hamilton river is the greatest, forms a continuation of the valley of the Inlet and extends 300 m. farther inland, while its bottom lies from 500 to 1500 ft. below the surface of the plateau into which it is cut. The depressions between the low ridges of the interior are occupied by innumerable lakes, many of great size, including Mistassini, Mishikamau, Clearwater, Kaniapiskau and Seal, all from 50 to 100 m. long. The streams discharging these lakes, before entering their valleys, flow on a level with the country and occupy all depressions, so that they frequently spread out into lake-expansions and are often divided into numerous channels by large islands. The descent into the valleys is usually abrupt, being made by heavy rapids and falls; the Hamilton, from the level interior, in a course of 12 m. falls 760 ft. into the head of its valley, this descent including a sheer drop of 315 ft. at the Grand Falls, which, taken with the large volume of the river, makes it the greatest fall in North America. The rivers of the northern and western watersheds drain about two-thirds of the peninsula; the most important of the former are the Koksoak, the largest river of Labrador (over 500 m. long), the George, Whale and Payne rivers, all flowing into Ungava Bay. The large rivers flowing westwards into Hudson Bay are the Povungnituk, Kogaluk, Great Whale, Big, East Main and Rupert, varying in length from 300 to 500 m. The rivers flowing south are exceedingly rapid, the Moisie, Romaine, Natashkwan and St Augustine being the most important; all are about 300 m. long. The Atlantic coast range throws most of the drainage northwards into the Ungava basin, and only small streams fall into the ocean, except the Hamilton, North-west and Kenamou, which empty into the head of Hamilton Inlet.

Geology.—The peninsula is formed largely of crystalline schists and gneisses associated with granites and other igneous rocks, all of archaean age; there are also large areas of non-fossiliferous, stratified limestones, cherts, shales and iron ores, the unaltered equivalents of part of the schists and gneisses. Narrow strips of Animikie (Upper Huronian or perhaps Cambrian) rocks occur along the low-lying southern and western shores, but there are nowhere else indications of the peninsula having been below sea-level since an exceedingly remote time. During the glacial period the country was covered by a thick mantle of ice, which flowed out radially from a central collecting-ground. Owing to the extremely long exposure to denudation, to the subsequent removal of the greater part of the decomposed rock by glaciers, and to the unequal weathering of the component rocks, it is now a plateau, which ascends somewha[illegible] abruptly within a few miles of the coast-line to heights of betwee[illegible]

[1] From the Portuguese *llavrador* (a yeoman farmer). The nam[illegible] was originally given to Greenland (1st half of 16th century) and wa[illegible] transferred to the peninsula in the belief that it formed part of the same country as Greenland. The name was bestowed "because h[illegible] who first gave notice of seeing it [Greenland] was a farmer (*llavrador*) from the Azores." See the historical sketch of Labrador by W. S. Wallace in Grenfell's *Labrador, &c.*, 1909.

500 and 2000 ft. The interior is undulating, and traversed by ridges of low, rounded hills, seldom rising more than 500 ft. above the surrounding general level.

Minerals.—The mineral wealth is undeveloped. Thick beds of excellent iron ore cover large areas in the interior and along the shores of Hudson and Ungava Bays. Large areas of mineralized Huronian rocks have also been discovered, similar to areas in other parts of Canada, where they contain valuable deposits of gold, copper, nickel and lead; good prospects of these metals have been found.

Climate.—The climate ranges from cold temperate on the southern coasts to arctic on Hudson Strait, and is generally so rigorous that it is doubtful if the country is fit for agriculture north of 51°, except on the low grounds near the coast. On James Bay good crops of potatoes and other roots are grown at Fort George, 54° N., while about the head of Hamilton Inlet, on the east coast, and in nearly the same latitude, similar crops are easily cultivated. On the outer coasts the climate is more rigorous, being affected by the floating ice borne southwards on the Arctic current. In the interior at Mistassini, 50° 30′ N., a crop of potatoes is raised annually, but they rarely mature. No attempts at agriculture have been made elsewhere inland. Owing to the absence of grass plains, there is little likelihood that it will ever be a grazing district. There are only two seasons in the interior: winter begins early in October, with the freezing of the small lakes, and lasts until the middle of June, when the ice on rivers and lakes melts and summer suddenly bursts forth. From unconnected observations the lowest temperatures of the interior range from −50° F. to −60° F., and are slightly higher along the coast. The mean summer temperature of the interior is about 55° F., with frosts during every month in the northern portion. On the Atlantic coast and in Hudson Bay the larger bays freeze solid between the 1st and 15th of December, and these coasts remain ice-bound until late in June. Hudson Strait is usually sufficiently open for navigation about the 10th of July.

Vegetation.—The southern half is included in the sub-Arctic forest belt, and nine species of trees constitute the whole arborescent flora of this region; these species are the white birch, poplar, aspen, cedar, Banksian pine, white and black spruce, balsam fir and larch. The forest is continuous over the southern portion to 53° N., the only exceptions being the summits of rocky hills and the outer islands of the Atlantic and Hudson Bay, while the low margins and river valleys contain much valuable timber. To the northward the size and number of barren areas rapidly increase, so that in 55° N. more than half the country is treeless, and two degrees farther north the limit of trees is reached, leaving, to the northward, only barrens covered with low Arctic flowering plants, sedges and lichens.

Fisheries.—The fisheries along the shores of the Gulf of St Lawrence and of the Atlantic form practically the only industry of the white population scattered along the coasts, as well as of a large proportion of the inhabitants of Newfoundland. The census (1891) of Newfoundland gave 10,478 men, 2081 women and 828 children employed in the Labrador fishery in 861 vessels, of which the tonnage amounted to 33,689; the total catch being 488,788 quintals of cod, 1275 tierces of salmon and 3828 barrels of herring, which, compared with the customs returns for 1880, showed an increase of cod and decreases of salmon and herring. The salmon fishery along the Atlantic coast is now very small, the decrease being probably due to excessive use of cod-traps. The cod fishery is now carried on along the entire Atlantic coast and into the eastern part of Ungava Bay, where excellent catches have been made since 1893. The annual value of the fisheries on the Canadian portion of the coast is about $350,000. The fisheries of Hudson Bay and of the interior are wholly undeveloped, though both the bay and the large lakes of the interior are well stocked with several species of excellent fish, including Arctic trout, brook trout, lake trout, white fish, sturgeon and cod.

Population.—The population is approximately 14,500 or about one person to every 35 sq. m.; it is made up of 3500 Indians, 2000 Eskimo and 9000 whites. The last are confined to the coasts and to the Hudson Bay Company's trading posts of the interior. On the Atlantic coast they are largely immigrants from Newfoundland, together with descendants of English fishermen and Hudson Bay Company's servants. To the north of Hamilton Inlet they are of more or less mixed blood from marriage with Eskimo women. The Newfoundland census of 1901 gave 3634 as the number of permanent white residents along the Atlantic coast, and the Canadian census (1891) gave a white population of 5728, mostly French Canadians, scattered along the north shore of the Gulf of St Lawrence, while the whites living at the inland posts did not exceed fifty persons. It is difficult to give more than a rough approximation of the number of the native population, owing to their habits of roving from one trading post to another, and the consequent liability of counting the same family several times if the returns are computed from the books of the various posts, the only available data for an enumeration. The following estimate is arrived at in this manner: Indians—west coast, 1200; Ungava Bay, 200; east coast, 200; south coast, 1900. Eskimo—Atlantic coast, 1000; south shore of Hudson Strait, 800; east coast of Hudson Bay, 500. The Indians roam over the southern interior in small bands, their northern limit being determined by that of the trees on which they depend for fuel. They live wholly by the chase, and their numbers are dependent upon the deer and other animals; as a consequence there is a constant struggle between the Indian and the lower animals for existence, with great slaughter of the latter, followed by periodic famines among the natives, which greatly reduce their numbers and maintain an equilibrium. The native population has thus remained about stationary for the last two centuries. The Indians belong to the Algonquin family, and speak dialects of the Cree language. By contact with missionaries and fur-traders they are more or less civilized, and the great majority of them are Christians. Those living north of the St Lawrence are Roman Catholic, while the Indians of the western watershed have been converted by the missionaries of the Church Mission Society; the eastern and northern bands have not yet been reached by the missionaries, and are still pagans. The Eskimo of the Atlantic coast have long been under the guidance of the Moravian missionaries, and are well advanced in civilization; those of Hudson Bay have been taught by the Church Mission Society, and promise well; while the Eskimo of Hudson Strait alone remain without teachers, and are pagans. The Eskimo live along the coasts, only going inland for short periods to hunt the barren-ground caribou for their winter clothing; the rest of the year they remain on the shore or the ice, hunting seals and porpoises, which afford them food, clothing and fuel. The christianized Indians and Eskimo read and write in their own language; those under the teaching of the Church Mission Society use a syllabic character, the others make use of the ordinary alphabet.

Political Review.—The peninsula is divided politically between the governments of Canada, Newfoundland and the province of Quebec. The government of Newfoundland, under Letters Patent of the 28th of March 1876, exercises jurisdiction along the Atlantic coast; the boundary between its territory and that of Canada is a line running due north and south from Anse Sablon, on the north shore of the Strait of Belle Isle, to 52° N., the remainder of the boundary being as yet undetermined. The northern boundary of the province of Quebec follows the East Main river to its source in Patamisk lake, thence by a line due east to the Ashuanipi branch of the Hamilton river; it then follows that river and Hamilton Inlet to the coast area under the jurisdiction of Newfoundland. The remainder of the peninsula, north of the province of Quebec, by order in council dated the 18th of December 1897, was constituted Ungava District, an unorganized territory under the jurisdiction of the government of the Dominion of Canada.

AUTHORITIES.—W. T. Grenfell and others, *Labrador: the Country and the People* (New York, 1909); R. F. Holmes, "A Journey in the Interior of Labrador," *Proc. R.G.S.* x. 189-205 (1887); A. S. Packard, *The Labrador Coast* (New York, 1891); Austen Cary, "Exploration on Grand River, Labrador," *Bul. Am. Geo. Soc.* vol. xxiv., 1892; R. Bell, "The Labrador Peninsula," *Scottish Geo. Mag.* July 1895. Also the following reports by the Geological Survey of Canada:—R. Bell, "Report on an Exploration of the East Coast of Hudson Bay," 1877–1878; "Observations on the Coast of Labrador and on Hudson Strait and Bay," 1882–1884; A. P. Low, "Report on the Mistassini Expedition," 1885; "Report on James Bay and the Country East of Hudson Bay," 1887–1888; "Report on Explorations in the Labrador Peninsula, 1892–1895," 1896; "Report on a Traverse of the Northern Part of the Labrador Peninsula," 1898; "Report on the South Shore of Hudson Strait," 1899. For History: W. G. Gosling, *Labrador* (1910). (A. P. Lo.; A. P. C.)

LABRADORITE, or LABRADOR SPAR, a lime-soda felspar of the plagioclase (*q.v.*) group, often cut and polished as an ornamental stone. It takes its name from the coast of Labrador, where it was discovered, as boulders, by the Moravian Mission about 1770, and specimens were soon afterwards sent to the secretary in London, the Rev. B. Latrobe. The felspar itself is generally of a dull grey colour, with a rather greasy lustre, but many specimens exhibit in certain directions a magnificent play of colours—blue, green, orange, purple or red; the colour in some specimens changing when the stone is viewed in different directions. This optical effect, known sometimes as "labradorescence," seems due in some cases to the presence of minute laminae of certain minerals, like göthite or haematite, arranged parallel to the surface which reflects the colour; but in other cases it may be caused not so much by inclusions as by a delicate lamellar structure in the felspar. An aventurine effect is produced by the presence of microscopic enclosures. The original labradorite was found in the neighbourhood of Nain, notably in a lagoon about 50 m. inland, and in St Paul's Island. Here it occurs with hypersthene, of a rich bronzy sheen, forming a coarse-grained norite. When wet, the stones are remarkably brilliant, and have been called by the natives "fire rocks." Russia has also yielded chatoyant labradorite, especially near Kiev and in Finland; a fine blue labradorite has been brought from Queensland; and the mineral is also known in several localities in the United States, as at Keeseville, in Essex county, New York. The ornamental stone from south Norway, now largely used as a decorative material in architecture, owes its beauty to a felspar with a blue opalescence, often called labradorite, but really a kind of orthoclase which Professor W. C. Brögger has termed cryptoperthite, whilst the rock in which it occurs is an augite-syenite called by him laurvigite, from its chief locality, Laurvik in Norway. Common labradorite, without play of colour, is an important constituent of such rocks as gabbro, diorite, andesite, dolerite and basalt. (See PLAGIOCLASE.) Ejected crystals of labradorite are found on Monti Rossi, a double parasitic cone on Etna.

The term labradorite is unfortunately used also as a rock-name, having been applied by Fouqué and Lévy to a group of basic rocks rich in augite and poor in olivine. (F. W. R.*)

LABRADOR TEA, the popular name for a species of *Ledum*, a small evergreen shrub growing in bogs and swamps in Greenland and the more northern parts of North America. The leaves are tough, densely covered with brown wool on the under face, fragrant when crushed and have been used as a substitute for tea. The plant is a member of the heath family (Ericaceae).

LABRUM (Lat. for "lip"), the large vessel of the warm bath in the Roman thermae. These were cut out of great blocks of marble and granite, and have generally an overhanging lip. There is one in the Vatican of porphyry over 12 ft. in diameter. The term *labrum* is used in zoology, of a lip or lip-like part; in entomology it is applied specifically to the upper lip of an insect, the lower lip being termed *labium*.

LA BRUYÈRE, JEAN DE (1645–1696), French essayist and moralist, was born in Paris on the 16th of August 1645, and not, as was once the common statement, at Dourdan (Seine-et-Oise) in 1639. His family was of the middle class, and his reference to a certain Geoffroy de la Bruyère, a crusader, is only a satirical illustration of a method of self-ennoblement common in France as in some other countries. Indeed he himself always signed the name Delabruyère in one word, thus avowing his *roture*. His progenitors, however, were of respectable position, and he could trace them back at least as far as his great-grandfather, who had been a strong Leaguer. La Bruyère's own father was controller-general of finance to the Hôtel de Ville. The son was educated by the Oratorians and at the university of Orleans; he was called to the bar, and in 1673 bought a post in the revenue department at Caen, which gave the status of noblesse and a certain income. In 1687 he sold this office. His predecessor in it was a relation of Bossuet, and it is thought that the transaction was the cause of La Bruyère's introduction to the great orator. Bossuet, who from the date of his own preceptorship of the dauphin, was a kind of agent-general for tutorships in the royal family, introduced him in 1684 to the household of the great Condé, to whose grandson Henri Jules de Bourbon as well as to that prince's girl-bride Mlle de Nantes, one of Louis XIV.'s natural children, La Bruyère became tutor. The rest of his life was passed in the household of the prince or else at court, and he seems to have profited by the inclination which all the Condé family had for the society [illegible] Very little is known of the events of this part—or, indeed, of any part—of his life. The impression derived from the few notices of him is of a silent observant, but somewhat awkward man, resembling in manner Joseph Addison, whose master in literature La Bruyère undoubtedly was. Yet despite the numerous enemies which his book raised up for him, most of these notices are favourable—notably that of Saint-Simon, an acute judge and one bitterly prejudiced against *roturiers* generally. There is, however, a curious passage in a letter from Boileau to Racine in which he regrets that "nature has not made La Bruyère as agreeable as he would like to be." His *Caractères* appeared in 1688, and at once, as Nicolas de Malezieu had predicted, brought him "bien des lecteurs et bien des ennemis." At the head of these were Thomas Corneille, Fontenelle and Benserade, who were pretty clearly aimed at in the book, as well as innumerable other persons, men and women of letters as well as of society, on whom the cap of La Bruyère's fancy-portraits was fitted by manuscript "keys" compiled by the scribblers of the day. The friendship of Bossuet and still more the protection of the Condés sufficiently defended the author, and he continued to insert fresh portraits of his contemporaries in each new edition of his book, especially in the 4th (1689). Those, however, whom he had attacked were powerful in the Academy, and numerous defeats awaited La Bruyère before he could make his way into that guarded hold. He was defeated thrice in 1691, and on one memorable occasion he had but seven votes, five of which were those of Bossuet, Boileau, Racine, Pellisson and Bussy-Rabutin. It was not till 1693 that he was elected, and even then an epigram, which, considering his admitted insignificance in conversation, was not of the worst, *haesit lateri*:—

"Quand la Bruyère se présente
Pourquoi faut il crier haro?
Pour faire un nombre de quarante
Ne falloit il pas un zéro?"

His unpopularity was, however, chiefly confined to the subjects of his sarcastic portraiture, and to the hack writers of the time, of whom he was wont to speak with a disdain only surpassed by that of Pope. His description of the *Mercure galant* as "*immédiatement au dessous de rien*" is the best-remembered specimen of these unwise attacks; and would of itself account for the enmity of the editors, Fontenelle and the younger Corneille. La Bruyère's discourse of admission at the Academy, one of the best of its kind, was, like his admission itself, severely criticized, especially by the partisans of the "Moderns" in the "Ancient and Modern" quarrel. With the *Caractères*, the translation of Theophrastus, and a few letters, most of them addressed to the prince de Condé, it completes the list of his literary work, with the exception of a curious and much-disputed posthumous treatise. La Bruyère died very suddenly, and not long after his admission to the Academy. He is said to have been struck with dumbness in an assembly of his friends, and, being carried home to the Hôtel de Condé, to have expired of apoplexy a day or two afterwards, on the 10th of May 1696. It is not surprising that, considering the recent panic about poisoning, the bitter personal enmities which he had excited and the peculiar circumstances of his death, suspicions of foul play should have been entertained, but there was apparently no foundation for them. Two years after his death appeared certain *Dialogues sur le Quiétisme*, alleged to have been found among his papers incomplete, and to have been completed by the editor. As these dialogues are far inferior in literary merit to La Bruyère's other works, their genuineness has been denied. But the straightforward and circumstantial account of their appearance given by this editor, the Abbé du Pin, a man of acknowledged probity, the intimacy of La Bruyère with Bossuet, whose views in his contest with Fénelon these dialogues are designed to further, and the entire absence, at so short a time after the alleged author's death, of the least protest on the part of his friends and representatives, seem to be decisive in their favour.

Although it is permissible to doubt whether the value of the *Caractères* has not been somewhat exaggerated by traditional French criticism, they deserve beyond all question a high place.

The plan of the book is thoroughly original, if that term may be accorded to a novel and skilful combination of existing elements. The treatise of Theophrastus may have furnished the first idea, but it gave little more. With the ethical generalizations and social Dutch painting of his original La Bruyère combined the peculiarities of the Montaigne essay, of the *Pensées* and *Maximes* of which Pascal and La Rochefoucauld are the masters respectively, and lastly of that peculiar 17th-century product, the "portrait" or elaborate literary picture of the personal and mental characteristics of an individual. The result was quite unlike anything that had been before seen, and it has not been exactly reproduced since, though the essay of Addison and Steele resembles it very closely, especially in the introduction of fancy portraits. In the titles of his work, and in its extreme desultoriness, La Bruyère reminds the reader of Montaigne, but he aimed too much at sententiousness to attempt even the apparent continuity of the great essayist. The short paragraphs of which his chapters consist are made up of maxims proper, of criticisms literary and ethical, and above all of the celebrated sketches of individuals baptised with names taken from the plays and romances of the time. These last are the great feature of the work, and that which gave it its immediate if not its enduring popularity. They are wonderfully piquant, extraordinarily life-like in a certain sense, and must have given great pleasure or more frequently exquisite pain to the originals, who were in many cases unmistakable and in most recognizable.

But there is something wanting in them. The criticism of Charpentier, who received La Bruyère at the Academy, and who was of the opposite faction, is in fact fully justified as far as it goes. La Bruyère literally "est [trop] descendu dans le particulier." He has neither, like Molière, embodied abstract peculiarities in a single life-like type, nor has he, like Shakespeare, made the individual pass *sub speciem aeternitatis*, and serve as a type while retaining his individuality. He is a photographer rather than an artist in his portraiture. So, too, his maxims, admirably as they are expressed, and exact as their truth often is, are on a lower level than those of La Rochefoucauld. Beside the sculpturesque precision, the Roman brevity, the profoundness of ethical intuition "piercing to the accepted hells beneath," of the great Frondeur, La Bruyère has the air of a literary *petit-maître* dressing up superficial observation in the finery of *esprit*. It is indeed only by comparison that he loses, but then it is by comparison that he is usually praised. His abundant wit and his personal "malice" have done much to give him his rank in French literature, but much must also be allowed to his purely literary merits. With Racine and Massillon he is probably the very best writer of what is somewhat arbitrarily styled classical French. He is hardly ever incorrect—the highest merit in the eyes of a French academic critic. He is always well-bred, never obscure, rarely though sometimes "precious" in the turns and niceties of language in which he delights to indulge, in his avowed design of attracting readers by form, now that, in point of matter, "tout est dit." It ought to be added to his credit that he was sensible of the folly of impoverishing French by ejecting old words. His chapter on "Les ouvrages de l'esprit" contains much good criticism, though it shows that, like most of his contemporaries except Fénelon, he was lamentably ignorant of the literature of his own tongue.

The editions of La Bruyère, both partial and complete, have been extremely numerous. *Les Caractères de Théophraste traduits du Grec, avec les caractères et les mœurs de ce siècle*, appeared for the first time in 1688, being published by Michallet, to whose little daughter, according to tradition, La Bruyère gave the profits of the book as a dowry. Two other editions, little altered, were published in the same year. In the following year, and in each year until 1694, with the exception of 1693, a fresh edition appeared, and, in all these five, additions, omissions and alterations were largely made. A sixth edition, not much altered, was put forth in the year of the author's death. The Academy speech appeared in the eighth edition. The Quietist dialogues were published in 1699; most of the letters, including those addressed to Condé, not till 1867. In recent times numerous editions of the complete works have appeared, notably those of Walckenaer (1845), Servois (1867, in the series of *Grands écrivains de la France*), Asselineau (a scholarly reprint of the last original edition, 1872) and finally Chassang (1876); the last is one of the most generally useful, as the editor has collected almost everything of value in his predecessors. The literature of "keys" to La Bruyère is extensive and apocryphal. Almost everything that can be done in this direction and in that of general illustration was done by Edouard Fournier in his learned and amusing *Comédie de La Bruyère* (1866); M. Paul Morillot contributed a monograph on La Bruyère to the series of *Grands écrivains français* in 1904.
(G. SA.)

LABUAN (a corruption of the Malay word *labuh-an*, signifying an "anchorage"), an island of the Malay Archipelago, off the north-west coast of Borneo in 5° 16′ N., 115° 15′ E. Its area is 30·23 sq. m.; it is distant about 6 m. from the mainland of Borneo at the nearest point, and lies opposite to the northern end of the great Brunei Bay. The island is covered with low hills rising from flats near the shore to an irregular plateau near the centre. About 1500 acres are under rice cultivation, and there are scattered patches of coco-nut and sago palms and a few vegetable gardens, the latter owned for the most part by Chinese. For the rest Labuan is covered over most of its extent by vigorous secondary growth, amidst which the charred trunks of trees rise at frequent intervals, the greater part of the forest of the island having been destroyed by great accidental conflagrations. Labuan was ceded to Great Britain in 1846, chiefly through the instrumentality of Sir James Brooke, the first raja of Sarawak, and was occupied two years later.

At the time of its cession the island was uninhabited, but in 1881 the population numbered 5731, though it had declined to 5361 in 1891. The census returns for 1901 give the population at 8411. The native population consists of Malay fishermen, Chinese, Tamils and small shifting communities of Kadayans, Tutongs and other natives of the neighbouring Bornean coast. There are about fifty European residents. At the time of its occupation by Great Britain a brilliant future was predicted for Labuan, which it was thought would become a second Singapore. These hopes have not been realized. The coal deposits, which are of somewhat indifferent quality, have been worked with varying degrees of failure by a succession of companies, one of which, the Labuan & Borneo Ltd., liquidated in 1902 after the collapse of a shaft upon which large sums had been expended. It was succeeded by the Labuan Coalfields Ltd. The harbour is a fine one, and the above-named company possesses three wharves capable of berthing the largest Eastern-going ocean steamers. To-day Labuan chiefly exists as a trading depôt for the natives of the neighbouring coast of Borneo, who sell their produce—beeswax, edible birds-nests, camphor, gutta, trepang, &c.,—to Chinese shopkeepers, who resell it in Singapore. There is also a considerable trade in sago, much of which is produced on the mainland, and there are three small sago-factories on the island where the raw product is converted into flour. The Eastern Extension Telegraph Company has a central station at Labuan with cables to Singapore, Hong-Kong and British North Borneo. Monthly steam communication is maintained by a German firm between Labuan, Singapore and the Philippines. The colony joined the Imperial Penny Postage Union in 1889. There are a few miles of road on the island and a metre-gauge railway from the harbour to the coal mines, the property of the company. There is a Roman Catholic church with a resident priest, an Anglican church, visited periodically by a clergyman from the mainland, two native and Chinese schools, and a sailors' club, built by the Roman Catholic mission. The bishop of Singapore and Sarawak is also bishop of Labuan. The European graveyard has repeatedly been the scene of outrages perpetrated, it is believed, by natives from the mainland of Borneo, the graves being rifled and the hair of the head and other parts of the corpses being carried off to furnish ornaments to weapons and ingredients in the magic philtres of the natives. Pulau Dat, a small island in the near neighbourhood of Labuan, is the site of a fine coco-nut plantation whence nuts and copra are exported in bulk. The climate is hot and very humid.

Until 1869 the expenditure of the colony was partly defrayed by imperial grants-in-aid, but after that date it was left to its own resources. A garrison of imperial troops was maintained until 1871, when the troops were withdrawn after many deaths from fever and dysentery had occurred among them. Since then law and or [illegible] without difficulty by a small mixed police [illegible]. From the 1st of January 1890 to the [illegible] was transferred for administrative [illegible] North Borneo Company, the governor for the [illegible] territories holding also the royal com[illegible]. This arrangement did not work [illegible] with frequent petitions and protests from [illegible] was then placed under the government of [illegible] and is administered by a deputy governor [illegible] Straits Civil Service.

[illegible] botanically as *Laburnum vulgare* (or [illegible]) a familiar tree of the pea family (Legu[illegible] known as "golden chain" and "golden rain." [illegible] mountains of France, Switzerland, southern [illegible] &c., has long been cultivated as an [illegible] throughout Europe, and was introduced into [illegible] the European colonists. Gerard records [illegible] in 1597 under the names of anagyris, [illegible] (*Herball*, p. 1239), but the date of [illegible] England appears to be unknown. In [illegible] a corruption from laburnum [illegible] as also *arbois, i.e. arc-bois*, "the [illegible] by the ancient Gauls for bows. It [illegible] some parts of the Mâconnois, where the [illegible] their strength and elasticity for half [illegible] *Arboretum*, ii. 590).

[illegible] the tree are cultivated, differing in the [illegible] the form of the foliage, &c., such as the [illegible]), *pendulum, crispum*, &c.; var. [illegible] leaves. One of the most remarkable [illegible] (C. *purpurascens*), which bears three [illegible] racemes of pure yellow flowers, others [illegible] others of an intermediate brick-red tint. [illegible] blossoms, and are sterile, with malformed [illegible] appears to be good. The yellow [illegible]" are fertile. It originated in Paris [illegible] who inserted a "shield" of the bark of [illegible] a stock of Laburnum. A vigorous shoot [illegible] subsequently propagated. Hence it would [illegible] distinct species became united by their [illegible] the trees propagated therefrom subsequently [illegible] respective parentages in bearing both yellow [illegible] but produce as well blossoms of an inter[illegible] character. Such a result may be called a [illegible] For full details see Darwin's *Animals and* [illegible]

[illegible] has highly poisonous properties. The roots [illegible] which is a member of the same family as [illegible] has proved fatal to cattle, though hares and [illegible] bark of it with avidity (*Gardener's Chronicle*, [illegible]). The seeds also are highly poisonous, [illegible] as well as acrid narcotic principles, especially [illegible] Gerard (*loc. cit.*) alludes to the powerful effect [illegible] by taking the bruised leaves medicinally. [illegible] bees will not visit the flowers (*N.H.* xvi. 31), [illegible] bees and butterflies play an important [illegible] as bees, of the flowers, which they visit for the [illegible]

[illegible] of the laburnum is of a dark reddish-brown [illegible] and durable, and takes a good polish. Hence it [illegible] and used with other coloured woods [illegible]. The laburnum has been called false [illegible] of its wood.

[illegible] (Gr. λαβύρινθος, Lat. *labyrinthus*), the name [illegible] by the Greeks and Romans to buildings, entirely or partly [illegible] containing a number of chambers and intricate [illegible] egress puzzling and difficult. The word [illegible] to be of Egyptian origin, while others [illegible] with the Gr. λαύρα, the passage of a mine. Another [illegible] from λάβρυς, a Lydian or Carian word [illegible] *Hellenic Studies*, [illegible] a labyrinth or [illegible], the symbol [illegible]

Pliny (*Nat. Hist.* xxxvi. 19, 91) mentions the following as the four famous labyrinths of antiquity.

1. The Egyptian: of which a description is given by Herodotus (ii. 148) and Strabo (xvii. 811). It was situated to the east of Lake Moeris, opposite the ancient site of Arsinoë or Crocodilopolis. According to Egyptologists, the word means "the temple at the entrance of the lake." According to Herodotus, the entire building, surrounded by a single wall, contained twelve courts and 3000 chambers, 1500 above and 1500 below ground. The roofs were wholly of stone, and the walls covered with sculpture. On one side stood a pyramid 40 orgyiae, or about 243 ft. high. Herodotus himself went through the upper chambers, but was not permitted to visit those underground, which he was told contained the tombs of the kings who had built the labyrinth, and of the sacred crocodiles. Other ancient authorities considered that it was built as a place of meeting for the Egyptian nomes or political divisions; but it is more likely that it was intended for sepulchral purposes. It was the work of Amenemhê III., of the 12th dynasty, who lived about 2300 B.C. It was first located by the Egyptologist Lepsius to the north of Hawara in the Fayum, and (in 1888) Flinders Petrie discovered its foundation, the extent of which is about 1000 ft. long by 800 ft. wide. Immediately to the north of it is the pyramid of Hawara, in which the mummies of the king and his daughter have been found (see W. M. Flinders Petrie, *Hawara, Biahmu, and Arsinoë*, 1889).

2. The Cretan: said to have been built by Daedalus on the plan of the Egyptian, and famous for its connexion with the legend of the Minotaur. It is doubtful whether it ever had any real existence and Diodorus Siculus says that in his time it had already disappeared. By the older writers it was placed near Cnossus, and is represented on coins of that city, but nothing corresponding to it has been found during the course of the recent excavations, unless the royal palace was meant. The rocks of Crete are full of winding caves, which gave the first idea of the legendary labyrinth. Later writers (for instance, Claudian, *De sexto Cons. Honorii*, 634) place it near Gortyna, and a set of winding passages and chambers close to that place is still pointed out as the labyrinth; these are, however, in reality ancient quarries.

3. The Lemnian: similar in construction to the Egyptian. Remains of it existed in the time of Pliny. Its chief feature was its 150 columns.

4. The Italian: a series of chambers in the lower part of the tomb of Porsena at Clusium. This tomb was 300 ft. square and 50 ft. high, and underneath it was a labyrinth, from which

Fig. 1.—Labyrinth of London and Wise.

it was exceedingly difficult to find an exit without the assistance of a clew of thread. It has been maintained that this tomb is to be recognized in the mound named Poggio Gajella near Chiusi.

Lastly, Pliny (xxxvi. 19) applies the word to a rude drawing on the ground or pavement, to some extent anticipating the modern or garden maze.

On the Egyptian labyrinth see A. Wiedemann, *Ägyptische Geschichte* (1884), p. 258, and his edition of the second book of Herodotus (1890); on the Cretan, C. Höck, *Kreta* (1823–1829), and

A. J. Evans in *Journal of Hellenic Studies*; on the subject generally, articles in Roscher's *Lexikon der Mythologie* and Daremberg and Saglio's *Dictionnaire des antiquités*.

In gardening, a labyrinth or *maze* means an intricate network of pathways enclosed by hedges or plantations, so that those

Fig. 2.—Labyrinth of Batty Langley.

who enter become bewildered in their efforts to find the centre or make their exit. It is a remnant of the old geometrical style of gardening. There are two methods of forming it. That which is perhaps the more common consists of walks, or alleys as they

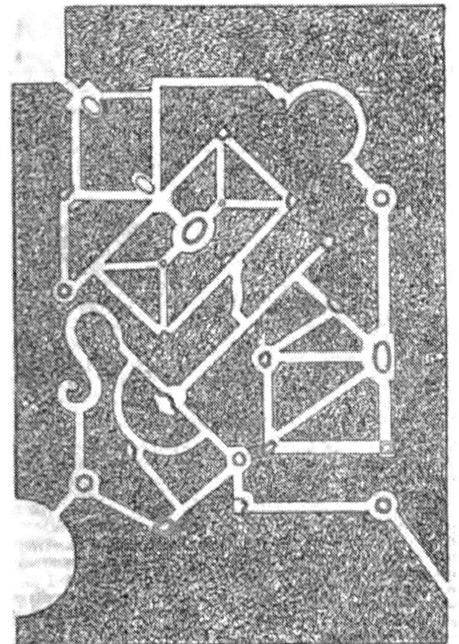

Fig. 3.—Labyrinth at Versailles.

were formerly called, laid out and kept to an equal width or nearly so by parallel hedges, which should be so close and thick that the eye cannot readily penetrate them. The task is to get to the centre, which is often raised, and generally contains a covered seat, a fountain, a statue or even a small group of trees. After reaching this point the next thing is to return to the entrance, when it is found that egress is as difficult as ingress. To every design of this sort there should be a key, but even those who know the key are apt to be perplexed. Sometimes the design consists of alleys only, as in fig. 1, published in 1706 by London and Wise. In such a case, when the farther end is reached, there only remains to travel back again. Of a more pretentious character was a design published by Switzer in 1742.

Fig. 4.—Maze at Hampton Court.

This is of octagonal form, with very numerous parallel hedges and paths, and "six different entrances, whereof there is but one that leads to the centre, and that is attended with some difficulties and a great many stops." Some of the older designs for labyrinths, however, avoid this close parallelism of the alleys, which, though equally involved and intricate in their windings, are carried through blocks of thick planting, as shown in fig. 2, from a design published in 1728 by Batty Langley. These blocks of shrubbery have been called wildernesses. To this latter class belongs the celebrated labyrinth at Versailles (fig. 3), of which Switzer observes, that it "is allowed by all to be the noblest of its kind in the world."

Whatever style be adopted, it is essential that there should be a thick healthy growth of the hedges or shrubberies that confine the wanderer. The trees used should be impenetrable to the eye, and so tall that no one can look over them; and the paths should be of gravel and well kept. The trees chiefly used for the hedges, and the best for the purpose, are the hornbeam among deciduous trees, or the yew among evergreens. The beech might be used instead of the hornbeam on suitable soil. The green holly might be planted

Fig. 5.—Maze at Somerleyton Hall.

as an evergreen with very good results, and so might the American arbor vitae if the natural soil presented no obstacle. The ground must be well prepared, so as to give the trees a good start, and a mulching of manure during the early years of their growth would be of much advantage. They must be kept trimmed in or clipped, especially in their earlier stages; trimming with the knife is much to be preferred to clipping with shears. Any plants getting much in advance of the rest should be topped, and the whole kept to some 4 ft. or 5 ft. in height until the lower parts are well thickened, when it may be allowed to acquire the allotted height by moderate annual increments. In cutting, the hedge (as indeed all hedges) should be kept broadest at the base and narrowed upwards, which prevents it from getting thin and bare below by the stronger growth being drawn to the tops.

The maze in the gardens at Hampton Court Palace (fig. 4) is considered one of the finest examples in England. It was planted in the early part of the reign of William III., though it has been supposed that a maze had existed there since the time of Henry VIII. It is constructed on the hedge and alley system, and was, it is believed, originally planted with hornbeam, but many of the plants have been replaced by hollies, yews, &c., so that the vegetation is mixed. The walks are about half a mile in length, and the ground occupied is a little over a quarter of an acre. The centre contains two large trees, with a seat beneath each. The key to reach this resting place is to keep the right hand continuously in contact with the hedge from first to last, going round all the stops.

The maze in the gardens at Somerleyton Hall, near Lowestoft (fig. 5), was designed by Mr John Thomas. The hedges are of English

Fig. 6.—Labyrinth in Horticultural Society's Garden.

yew, are about 6½ ft. high, and have been planted about sixty years. In the centre is a grass mound, raised to the height of the hedges, and on this mound is a pagoda, approached by a curved grass path. At the two corners on the western side are banks of laurels 15 or 16 ft. high. On each side of the hedges throughout the labyrinth is a small strip of grass.

There was also a labyrinth at Theobald's Park, near Cheshunt, when this place passed from the earl of Salisbury into the possession of James I. Another is said to have existed at Wimbledon House, the seat of Earl Spencer, which was probably laid out by Brown in the 18th century. There is an interesting labyrinth, somewhat after the plan of fig 2, at Mistley Place, Manningtree.

When the gardens of the Royal Horticultural Society at South Kensington were being planned, Albert, Prince Consort, the president of the society, especially desired that there should be a maze formed in the ante-garden, which was made in the form shown in fig. 6. This labyrinth, designed by Lieut. W. A. Nesfield, was for many years the chief point of attraction to the younger visitors to the gardens; but it was allowed to go to ruin, and had to be destroyed. The gardens themselves are now built over. (T. Mo.)

LABYRINTHULIDEA, the name given by Sir Ray Lankester (1885) to Sarcodina (*q.v.*) forming a reticulate plasmodium, the denser masses united by fine pseudopodical threads, hardly distinct from some Proteomyxa, such as *Archerina*.

This is a small and heterogeneous group. *Labyrinthula*, discovered by L. Cienkowsky, forms a network of relatively stiff threads on which are scattered large spindle-shaped enlargements, each representing an amoeba, with a single nucleus. The threads are pseu… slowly emitted and withdrawn. The amoebae m… active state. The nearest approach to a "reproductive" state is the approximation of the amoebae, and their separate encystment in an irregular heap,

Labyrinthulidea.

1. A colony or "cell-heap" of *Labyrinthula vitellina*, Cienk., crawling upon an Alga.
2. A colony or "cell-heap" of *Chlamydomyxa labyrinthuloides*, Archer, with fully expanded network of threads on which the oat-shaped corpuscles (cells) are moving. *o*, Is an ingested food particle; at *c* a portion of the general protoplasm has detached itself and become encysted.
3. A portion of the network of *Labyrinthula vitellina*, Cienk., more highly magnified. *p*, Protoplasmic mass apparently produced by fusion of several filaments. *p'*, Fusion of several cells which have lost their definite spindle-shaped contour. *s*, Corpuscles which have become spherical and are no longer moving (perhaps about to be encysted).
4. A single spindle cell and threads of *Labyrinthula macrocystis*, Cienk. *n*, Nucleus.
5. A group of encysted cells of *L. Macrocystis*, embedded in a tough secretion.

6, 7. Encysted cells of *L. macrocystis*, with enclosed protoplasm divided into four spores.

8, 9. Transverse division of a non-encysted spindle-cell of *L. macrocystis*.

recalling the Acrasieae. From each cyst ultimately emerges a single amoebae, or more rarely four (figs. 6, 7). The saprophyte *Diplophrys (?) stercorea* (Cienk.) appears closely allied to this.

Chlamydomyxa (W. Archer) resembles *Labyrinthula* in its freely branched plasmodium, but contains yellowish chromatophores, and minute oval vesicles ("physodes") filled with a substance allied to tannin—possibly phloroglucin—which glide along the plasmodial tracks. The cell-body contains numerous nuclei; but in its active state is not resolvable into distinct oval amoeboids. It is amphitrophic, ingesting and digesting other Protista, as well as "assimilating" by its chromatophores, the product being oil, not starch. The whole body may form a laminated cellulose resting cyst, from which it may only temporarily emerge (fig. 2), or it may undergo resolution into nucleate cells which then encyst, and become multinucleate before rupturing the cyst afresh.

Leydenia (F. Schaudinn) is a parasite in malignant diseases of the pleura. The pseudopodia of adjoining cells unite to form a network; but its affinities seem to such social naked Foraminifera as *Mikrogromia*.

See Cienkowsky, *Archiv f. Microscopische Anatomie*, iii. 274 (1867), xii. 44 (1876); W. Archer, *Quart. Jour. Microscopic Science*, xv. 107 (1875); E. R. Lankester, *Ibid.*, xxxix., 233 (1896); Hieronymus and Jenkinson, *Ibid.*, xlii. 89 (1899); W. Zopf, *Beiträge zur Physiologie und Morphologie niederer Organismen*, ii. 36 (1892), iv. 60 (1894); Pénard, *Archiv für Protistenkunde*, iv. 296 (1904); F. Schaudinn and Leyden, *Sitzungsberichte der Königlich preussischen Akademie der Wissenschaft*, vi. (1896).

LAC, a resinous incrustation formed on the twigs and young branches of various trees by an insect, *Coccus lacca*, which infests them. The term lac (*laksha*, Sanskrit; *lakh*, Hindi) is the same as the numeral lakh—a hundred thousand—and is indicative of the countless hosts of insects which make their appearance with every successive generation. Lac is a product of the East Indies, coming especially from Bengal, Pegu, Siam and Assam, and is produced by a number of trees of the species *Ficus*, particularly *F. religiosa*. The insect which yields it is closely allied to the cochineal insect, *Coccus cacti*; kermes, *C. ilicis* and Polish grains, *C. polonicus*, all of which, like the lac insect, yield a red colouring matter. The minute larval insects fasten in myriads on the young shoots, and, inserting their long proboscides into the bark, draw their nutriment from the sap of the plant. The insects begin at once to exude the resinous secretion over their entire bodies; this forms in effect a cocoon, and, the separate exudations coalescing, a continuous hard resinous layer regularly honeycombed with small cavities is deposited over and around the twig. From this living tomb the female insects, which form the great bulk of the whole, never escape. After their impregnation, which takes place on the liberation of the males, about three months from their first appearance, the females develop into a singular amorphous organism consisting in its main features of a large smooth shining crimson-coloured sac—the ovary—with a beak stuck into the bark, and a few papillary processes projected above the resinous surface. The red fluid in the ovary is the substance which forms the lac dye of commerce. To obtain the largest amount of both resin and dye-stuff it is necessary to gather the twigs with their living inhabitants in or near June and November. Lac encrusting the twigs as gathered is known in commerce as "stick lac", the resin crushed to small fragments and washed in hot water to free it from colouring matter constitutes "seed lac"; and this, when melted, strained through thick canvas, and spread out into thin layers, is known as "shellac," and is the form in which the resin is usually brought to European markets. Shellac varies in colour from a dark amber to an almost pure black; the palest, known as "orange-lac," is the most valuable; the darker varieties —"liver-coloured," "ruby," "garnet," &c.—diminish in value as the colour deepens. Shellac may be bleached by dissolving it in a boiling lye of caustic potash and passing chlorine through the solution till all the resin is precipitated, the product being known as white shellac. Bleached lac takes light delicate shades of colour, and dyed a golden yellow it is much used in the East Indies for working into chain ornaments for the head and for other personal adornments. Lac is a principal ingredient in sealing-wax, and forms the basis of some of the most valuable varnishes, besides being useful in various cements, &c. Average stick lac contains about 68 % of resin, 10 of lac dye and 6 of a waxy substance. Lac dye is obtained by evaporating the water in which stick lac is washed, and comes into commerce in the form of small square cakes. It is in many respects similar to, although not identical with, cochineal.

LACAILLE, NICOLAS LOUIS DE (1713–1762), French astronomer, was born at Rumigny, in the Ardennes, on the 15th of March 1713. Left destitute by the death of his father, who held a post in the household of the duchess of Vendôme, his theological studies at the Collège de Lisieux in Paris were prosecuted at the expense of the duke of Bourbon. After he had taken deacon's orders, however, he devoted himself exclusively to science, and, through the patronage of J. Cassini, obtained employment, first in surveying the coast from Nantes to Bayonne, then, in 1739, in remeasuring the French arc of the meridian. The success of this difficult operation, which occupied two years, and achieved the correction of the anomalous result published by J. Cassini in 1718, was mainly due to Lacaille's industry and skill. He was rewarded by admission to the Academy and the appointment of mathematical professor in Mazarin college, where he worked in a small observatory fitted for his use. His desire to observe the southern heavens led him to propose, in 1750, an astronomical expedition to the Cape of Good Hope, which was officially sanctioned, and fortunately executed. Among its results were determinations of the lunar and of the solar parallax (Mars serving as an intermediary), the first measurement of a South African arc of the meridian, and the observation of 10,000 southern stars. On his return to Paris in 1754 Lacaille was distressed to find himself an object of public attention; he withdrew to Mazarin college, and there died, on the 21st of March 1762, of an attack of gout aggravated by unremitting toil. Lalande said of him that, during a comparatively short life, he had made more observations and calculations than all the astronomers of his time put together. The quality of his work rivalled its quantity, while the disinterestedness and rectitude of his moral character earned him universal respect.

His principal works are: *Astronomiae Fundamenta* (1757), containing a standard catalogue of 398 stars, re-edited by F. Baily (*Memoirs Roy. Astr. Society*, v. 93); *Tabulae Solares* (1758); *Coelum australe stelliferum* (1763) (edited by J. D. Maraldi), giving zone-observations of 10,000 stars, and describing fourteen new constellations; "Observations sur 515 étoiles du Zodiaque" (published in t. vi. of his *Éphémérides*, 1763); *Leçons élémentaires de Mathématiques* (1741), frequently reprinted; ditto *de Mécanique* (1743), &c.; ditto *d'Astronomie* (1746), 4th edition augmented by Lalande (1779); ditto *d'Optique* (1750), &c. Calculations by him of eclipses for eighteen hundred years were inserted in *L'Art de vérifier les dates* (1750); he communicated to the Academy in 1755 a classed catalogue of forty-two southern nebulae, and gave in t. ii. of his *Éphémérides* (1755) practical rules for the employment of the lunar method of longitudes, proposing in his additions to Pierre Bouguer's *Traité de Navigation* (1760) the model of a nautical almanac.

See G. de Fouchy, "Éloge de Lacaille," *Hist. de l'Acad. des Sciences*, p. 197 (1762); G. Brotier, Preface to Lacaille's *Coelum australe*; Claude Carlier, *Discours historique*, prefixed to Lacaille's *Journal historique du voyage fait au Cap* (1763); J. J. Lalande, *Connaissance des temps*, p. 185 (1767); *Bibl. astr.* pp. 422, 456, 461, 482; J. Delambre, *Hist. de l'astr. au XVIIIe siècle*, pp. 457–542; J. S. Bailly, *Hist. de l'astr. moderne*, tomes ii., iii., *passim*; J. C. Poggendorff, *Biog. Lit. Handwörterbuch*; R. Grant, *Hist. of Physical Astronomy*, pp. 486, &c.; R. Wolf, *Geschichte der Astronomie*. A catalogue of 9766 stars, reduced from Lacaille's observations by T. Henderson, under the supervision of F. Baily, was published in London in 1847.

LACAITA, SIR JAMES [GIACOMO] (1813–1895), Anglo-Italian politician and writer. Born at Manduria in southern Italy, he practised law in Naples, and having come in contact with a number of prominent Englishmen and Americans in that city, he acquired a desire to study the English language. Although a moderate Liberal in politics, he never joined any secret society, but in 1851 after the restoration of Bourbon autocracy he was arrested for having supplied Gladstone with information on Bourbon misrule. Through the intervention of the British and Russian ministers he was liberated, but on the publication [illegible] letters to Lord Aberdeen he was obliged [illegible] Naples. He first settled in Edinburgh, where he married [illegible] and then in London where he made numerous [illegible] and political circles, and was professor of [illegible] at Queen's College from 1853 to 1856. In the latter year [illegible] Lord Minto to Italy, on which occasion he [illegible] From 1857 to 1863 he was private secretary [illegible] to Lord Lansdowne, and in 1858 he accompanied [illegible] to the Ionian Islands as secretary, for which services [illegible] K.C.M.G. the following year. In 1860 Francis II. [illegible] had implored Napoleon III. to send a squadron to [illegible] Garibaldi from crossing over from Sicily to Calabria; [illegible] expressed himself willing to do so provided Great [illegible] cooperated, and Lord John Russell was at first inclined [illegible] At this juncture Cavour, having heard of the scheme, [illegible] Lacaita, at the suggestion of Sir James Hudson, the [illegible] at Turin, with the task of inducing Russell to [illegible] Lacaita, who was an intimate friend both [illegible] and his wife, succeeded, with the help of the latter, [illegible] over the British statesman just as he was about to [illegible] the Franco-Neapolitan proposal, which was in consequence abandoned. He returned to Naples late in 1860 and the [illegible] year was elected member of parliament for Bitonto, [illegible] he had been naturalized a British subject in 1855, [illegible] took part in parliamentary politics, but in 1876 was [illegible] senator. He was actively interested in a number of [illegible] operating in Italy, and was made one of the [illegible] of the Italian Southern Railway Co. He had a wide [illegible] in many European countries and in America, [illegible] a number of the most famous men in politics and [illegible] He died in 1895 at Posilipo near Naples.

[illegible] he gave many lectures on Italian literature [illegible] in England; and among his writings may be [illegible] number of articles on Italian subjects in the [illegible] (1860), and an edition of Benvenuto [illegible] on Dante delivered in 1375; he co-[illegible] in the latter's great edition of Dante's [illegible] and he compiled a catalogue in four [illegible] of Devonshire's library at Chatsworth (London, [illegible]).

LA CALLE, a seaport of Algeria, in the arrondissement of [illegible] of Constantine, 56 m. by rail E. of Bona and 10 [illegible] Tunisian frontier. It is the centre of the Algerian [illegible] coral fisheries and has an extensive industry in [illegible] sardines, but the harbour is small and exposed [illegible] and W. winds. The old fortified town, now almost [illegible] is built on a rocky peninsula about 400 yds. long, [illegible] united to the mainland by a bank of sand. Since the [illegible] of La Calle by the French in 1836 a new town has [illegible] the coast. Pop. (1906) of the town, 2774; of the [illegible]

La Calle [illegible] the site of its earliest records in the 10th century [illegible] has been the residence of coral merchants. In the 16th century [illegible] privileges of fishing for coral were granted by the [illegible] of Algiers to the French, who first established themselves [illegible] a bay to the westward of La Calle, naming their settlement [illegible] de France, [illegible] still exist of this town. In 1677 [illegible] they moved their headquarters to La Calle. The company—[illegible] Compagnie d'Afrique—[illegible] owned the concession for the fishery [illegible] was suppressed in 1798 on the outbreak of war between France [illegible] and Algiers. In 1806 the British consul-general at Algiers [illegible] obtained the right to occupy Bona and La Calle for an annual [illegible] sum of £11,000; but though the money was paid for several [illegible] years no practical effect was given to the agreement. The [illegible] French regained possession in 1817, were expelled during the [illegible] war of 1827, when La Calle was burnt, but returned and rebuilt [illegible] the place in 1836. The boats engaged in the fishery were mainly [illegible] Italian, but [illegible] during the last quarter of the 19th [illegible] century of heavy taxes on alien French boats drove the foreign [illegible] [illegible] was abandoned, [illegible]

[illegible] Sir Alex. Pellat [illegible] 1789); E. [illegible] (1839) and Sir [illegible] R. L. Playfair [illegible] 1877).

LA CALPRENÈDE, GAUTHIER DE COSTES, Seigneur de (c. 1610–1663), French novelist and dramatist, was b[illegible] Château of Tolgou, near Sarlat (Dordogne), in 16[illegible] After studying at Toulouse, he came to Paris and e[illegible] regiment of the guards, becoming in 1650 gentleman-i[illegible] of the royal household. He died in 1663 in conseq[illegible] kick from his horse. He was the author of several lo[illegible] romances ridiculed by Boileau. They are: *Cassandre* (1642–1650); *Cléopâtre* (1648); *Faramond* (1661); *Nouvelles, ou les Divertissements de la princesse Alcidiane*, published under his wife's name, but generally attri[illegible] him. His plays lack the spirit and force that occasionall[illegible] the novels. The best is *Le Comte d'Essex*, represented [illegible] which supplied some ideas to Thomas Corneille for his [illegible] of the same name.

LA CARLOTA, a town of the province of Negros Oc[illegible] Philippine Islands, on the W. coast of the island and [illegible] bank of San Enrique river, about 18 m. S. of Baco[illegible] capital of the province. Pop. (1903), after the annex[illegible] San Enrique, 19,492. There are fifty-four villages or [illegible] in the town; the largest had a population in 1903 of [illegible] two others had each more than 1000 inhabitants. The P[illegible] dialect of the Visayan language is spoken by most of the [illegible] tants. At La Carlota the Spanish government establ[illegible] station for the study of the culture of sugar-cane; [illegible] American government this has been converted into a [illegible] agricultural experiment station, known as "Government [illegible]

LACCADIVE ISLANDS, a group of coral reefs and isl[illegible] the Indian Ocean, lying between 10° and 12° 20′ N. a[illegible] 40′ and 74° E. The name Laccadives (*laksha dwipa*, the "h[illegible] thousand isles") is that given by the people of the M[illegible] coast, and was probably meant to include the Maldives [illegible] are called by the natives simply *Divi*, "islands," or *Am*[illegible] from the chief island. There are seventeen separate [illegible] "round each of which the 100-fathom line is contin[illegible] (J. S. Gardiner). There are, however, only thirteen island[illegible] of these only eight are inhabited. They fall into two g[illegible] —the northern, belonging to the collectorate of South K[illegible] and including the inhabited islands of Amini, Kardamat, [illegible] and Chetlat; and the southern, belonging to the administ[illegible] district of Malabar, and including the inhabited islands of A[illegible] Kavaratti, Androth and Kalpeni. Between the Lacca[illegible] and the Maldives to the south lies the isolated Minikoi, [illegible] physically belongs to neither group, though somewhat [illegible] to the Maldives (*q.v.*). The principal submerged banks lie [illegible] of the northern group of islands; they are Munyal, Cor[illegible] and Sesostris, and are of greater extent than those on w[illegible] the islands lie. The general depth over these is from 23 [illegible] fathoms, but Sesostris has shallower soundings "indic[illegible] patches growing up, and some traces of a rim" (J. S. Gardi[illegible]). The islands have in nearly all cases emerged from the eas[illegible] and protected side of the reef, the western being compl[illegible] exposed to the S.W. monsoon. The islands are small, [illegible] exceeding a mile in breadth, while the total area is only a[illegible] 80 sq. m. They lie so low that they would be hardly discern[illegible] but for the coco-nut groves with which they are thickly cove[illegible] The soil is light coral sand, beneath which, a few feet do[illegible] lies a stratum of coral stretching over the whole of the islan[illegible] This coral, generally a foot to a foot and a half in thickne[illegible] has been in the principal islands wholly excavated, whereb[illegible] the underlying damp sand is rendered available for cereals. These excavations—a work of vast labour—were made at a [illegible] remote period, and according to the native tradition by giants. In these spaces (*tolam*, "garden") coarse grain, pulse, bananas and vegetables are cultivated; coco-nuts grow abundantly everywhere. For rice the natives depend upon the mainland.

Population and Trade.—The population in 1901 was 10,274. The people are Moplas, *i.e.* of mixed Hindu and Arab descent, and are Mahommedans. Their manners and customs are similar to those of the coast Moplas; but they maintain their [illegible] ancient caste distinctions. The language spoken is M[illegible] but it is written in the Arabic character. [illegible] are common accomplishments among the men. The chief industry is the manufacture of coir. The various processes are entrusted to the women. The men employ themselves with boatbuilding and in conveying the island produce to the coast. The exports from the Laccadives are of the annual value of about £17,000.

History.—No data exist for determining at what period the Laccadives were first colonized. The earliest mention of them as distinguished from the Maldives seems to be by Albirūni (*c.* 1030), who divides the whole archipelago (Dībajāt) into the *Dīvah Kūzah* or Cowrie Islands (the Maldives), and the *Dīvah Kanbar* or Coir Islands (the Laccadives). (See *Journ. Asiat. Soc.*, September 1844, p. 265). The islanders were converted to Islam by an Arab apostle named Mumba Mulyaka, whose grave at Androth still imparts a peculiar sanctity to that island. The kazee of Androth was in 1847 still a member of his family, and was said to be the twenty-second who had held the office in direct line from the saint. This gives colour to the tradition that the conversion took place about 1250. It is also further corroborated by the story given by the Ibn Batuta of the conversion of the Maldives, which occurred, as he heard, four generations (say one hundred and twenty years) before his visit to these islands in 1342. The Portuguese discovered the Laccadives in May 1498, and built forts upon them, but about 1545 the natives rose upon their oppressors. The islands subsequently became a suzerainty of the raja of Cannanore, and after the peace of Seringapatam, 1792 the southern group was permitted to remain under the management of the native chief at a yearly tribute. This was often in arrear, and on this account these islands were sequestrated by the British government in 1877.

See *The Fauna and Geography of the Maldive and Laccadive Archipelagoes*, ed. J. Stanley Gardiner (Cambridge 1901–1905); *Malabar District Gazetteer* (Madras, 1908); G. Pereira, "As Ilhas de Dyve" (*Boletim da Soc. Geog.*, Lisbon, 1898–1899) gives details relating to the Laccadives from the 16th-century MS. volume *De insulis et peregrinatione lusitanorum* in the National Library, Lisbon.

LACCOLITE (Gr. λάκκος, cistern, λίθος, stone), in geology, the name given by Grove K. Gilbert to intrusive masses of igneous rock possessing a cake-like form, which he first described from the Henry Mountains of southern Utah. Their characteristic is that they have spread out along the bedding planes of the strata, but are not so broad and thin as the sheets or intrusive sills which, consisting usually of basic rocks, have spread over immense distances without attaining any great thickness. Laccolites cover a comparatively small area and have greater thickness. Typically they have a domed upper surface while their base is flat. In the Henry Mountains they are from 1 to 5 m. in diameter and range in thickness up to about 5000 ft. The cause of their peculiar shape appears to be the viscosity of the rock injected, which is usually of intermediate character and comparatively rich in alkalis, belonging to the trachytes and similar lithological types. These are much less fluid than the basalts, and the latter in consequence spread out much more readily along the bedding planes, forming thin flat-topped sills. At each side the laccolites thin out rapidly so that their upper surface slopes steeply to the margins. The strata above them which have been uplifted and bent are often cracked by extension, and as the igneous materials well into the fissures a large number of dikes is produced. At the base of the laccolite, on the other hand, the strata are flat and dikes are rare, though there may be a conduit up which the magma has flowed into the laccolite. The rocks around are often much affected by contact alteration, and great masses of them have sometimes sunk into the laccolite, where they may be partly melted and absorbed.

Gilbert obtained evidence that these laccolites were filled at depths of 7000 to 10,000 ft. and did not reach the surface, giving rise to volcanoes. From the effects on the drainage of the country it seemed probable that above the laccolites the strata swelled up in flattish eminences. Often they occur side by side in groups belonging to a single period, though all the members of each group are not strictly of the same age. One laccolite may be formed on the side of an earlier one, and compound laccolites also occur. When exposed by erosion they give rise to hills, and their appearance varies somewhat with the stage of development.

In the western part of South America laccolites agreeing in all essential points with those described by Gilbert occur in considerable numbers and present some diversity of types. Occasionally they are asymmetrical, or have one steep or vertical side while the other is gently inclined. In other cases they split into a number of sheets spreading outwards through the rocks around. But the term laccolite has also been adopted by geologists in Britain and elsewhere to describe a variety of intrusive masses not strictly identical in character with those of the Henry Mountains. Some of these rest on a curved floor, like the gabbro masses of the Cuillin Hills in Skye; others are injected along a flattish plane of unconformability where one system of rocks rests on the upturned and eroded edges of an older series. An example of the latter class is furnished by the felsite mass of the Black Hill in the Pentlands, near Edinburgh, which has followed the line between the Silurian and the Old Red Sandstone, forcing the rocks upwards without spreading out laterally to any great extent.

The term laccolite has also been applied to many granite intrusions, such as those of Cornwall. We know from the evidence of mining shafts which have been sunk in the country near the edge of these granites that they slope downwards underground with an angle of twenty to thirty degrees. They have been proved also to have been injected along certain well-marked horizons; so that although the rocks of the country have been folded in a very complicated manner the granite can often be shown to adhere closely to certain members of the stratigraphical sequence for a considerable distance. Hence it is clear that their upper surfaces are convex and gently arched, and it is conjectured that the strata must extend below them, though at a great depth, forming a floor. The definite proof of this has not been attained for no borings have penetrated the granites and reached sedimentary rocks beneath them. But often in mountainous countries where there are deep valleys the bases of great granite laccolites are exposed to view in the hill sides. These granite sills have a considerable thickness in proportion to their length, raise the rocks above them and fill them with dikes, and behave generally like typical laccolites. In contradistinction to intrusions of this type with a well-defined floor we may place the batholiths, bysmaliths, plutonic plugs and stocks, which have vertical margins and apparently descend to unknown depths. It has been conjectured that masses of this type eat their way upwards by dissolving the rock above them and absorbing it, or excavate a passage by breaking up the roof of the space they occupy while the fragments detached sink downwards and are lost in the ascending magma. (J. S. F.)

LACE (corresponding to Ital. *merletto, trina*; Genoese *pizzo*; Ger. *spitzen*; Fr. *dentelle*; Dutch *kanten*; Span. *encaje*; the English word owes something to the Fr. *lassis* or *lacis*, but both are connected with the earlier Lat. *laqueus*; early French laces were also called *passements* or insertions and *dents* or edgings), the name applied to ornamental open work formed of threads of flax, cotton, silk, gold or silver, and occasionally of mohair or aloe fibre, looped or plaited or twisted together by hand, (1) with a needle, when the work is distinctively known as "needlepoint lace"; (2) with bobbins, pins and a pillow or cushion, when the work is known as "pillow lace"; and (3) by steam-driven machinery, when imitations of both needlepoint and pillow laces are produced. Lace-making implies the production of ornament and fabric concurrently. Without a pattern or design the fabric of lace cannot be made.

The publication of patterns for needlepoint and pillow laces dates from about the middle of the 16th century. Before that period lace described such articles as cords and narrow braids of plaited and twisted threads, used not only to fasten shoes, sleeves and corsets together, but also in a decorative manner to braid the hair, to wind round hats, and to be sewn as trimmings upon costumes. In a Harleian MS. of the time of Henry VI. and Edward IV., about 1471, directions are given for the making of "lace Bascon, lace indented, lace bordered, lace covert, a brode lace, a round lace, a thynne lace, an open lace, lace for hattys," &c. The MS. opens with an illuminated capital letter, in which is the figure of a woman making these articles. The MS. supplies a clear description how threads in combinations of twos, threes, fours, fives, to tens and fifteens, were to be twisted and plaited together. Instead of the pillow, bobbins and pins with which pillow lace soon afterwards was made, the hands were used, each finger of a hand serving as a peg upon which was placed a "bowys" or "bow," or little ball of thread. Each ball might be of different colour from the other. The writer of the MS. says that the first finger next the thumb shall be called A, the next B, and so on. According to the sort of cord or braid to be made, so each of the four fingers, A, B, C, D might be called into service. A "thynne lace" might be made with three threads, and then only fingers A, B, C would be required. A [illegible] piece, stouter than the "thynne" lace, might require [illegible] four or more fingers. By occasionally dropping [illegible] threads from certain fingers a sort of indented lace or [illegible] be made. But when laces of more importance [illegible] such as a broad lace for "hattys," the fingers on [illegible] assistants were required. The smaller cords or [illegible] laces," when fastened in simple or fantastic loops along [illegible] collars and cuffs, were called "purls" (see the small edges [illegible] collar worn by Catherine de' Medici, Pl. II. fig. 4). [illegible] to the direction from which some suggestion may be derived [illegible] another evolution of lace-making, notice should be taken of the fact that at an early period the darning of varied ornamental devices, stiff and geometric in treatment into hand-made network of small square meshes (see squares of "lacis," Pl. I. fig. 1) became specialised in many European countries. This is held by some writers to be "opus filatorium," or "opus araneum" (spider work). Examples of this "opus filatorium," said to date from the [illegible]th century exist in public collections. The productions of this darning in the early part of the 16th century came to be known as "punto a maglia quadra" in Italy and as "lacis" in France, and through a growing demand for household and wearing linen, very much of the "lacis" was made in white threads not only in Italy and France but also in Spain. In appearance it is a filmy fabric. With white threads also were the "purlings" above mentioned made, by means of leaden bobbins or "fuxli," and were called "merletti a piombini" (see lower border, Pl. II. fig. 3). Cut and drawn thread linen work (the latter known as "tela tirata" in Italy and as "deshilado" in Spain) were other forms of embroidery as much in vogue as the darning on net and the "purling." The ornament of much of this cut and drawn linen work (see collar of Catherine de' Medici, Pl. II. fig. 4), more restricted in scope than that of the darning on net, was governed by the recurrence of open squares formed by the withdrawal of the threads. Within these squares and rectangles radiating devices usually were worked by means of whipped and buttonhole stitches (Pl. fig. 5). The general effect in the linen was a succession of insertions or borders of plain or enriched reticulations, whence the name "punto a reticella" given to this class of embroidery in Italy. Work of similar style and especially that with whipped stitches was done rather earlier in the Grecian islands, which derived it from Asia Minor and Persia. The close connexion of the Venetian republic with Greece and the eastern islands, as well as its commercial relations with the East, sufficiently explains an early transplanting of this kind of embroidery into Venice, as well as in southern Spain. At Venice besides being called "reticella," cut work was also called "punto tagliato." Once fairly established as home industries such arts were quickly exploited with a beauty and variety of pattern, complexity of stitch and delicacy of execution, until insertions and edgings made independently of any linen as a starting base (see first two borders, Pl. II. fig. 3) came into being under the name of "Punto in aria" (Pl. II. fig. 7). This was the first variety of Venetian and Italian needlepoint lace in the middle of the 16th century,[1] and its appearance then almost coincides in date with that of the "merletti a piombini," which was the earliest Italian cushion or pillow lace (see lower edging, Pl. II. fig. 3).

The many varieties of needlepoint and pillow laces will be touched on under the heading allotted to each of these methods of making lace. Here, however, the general circumstances of their genesis may be briefly alluded to. The activity in cord and braid-making and in the particular sorts of ornamental needlework already mentioned clearly postulated such special labour as was capable of being converted into lace-making. And from the 16th century onwards the stimulus to the industry in Europe was afforded by regular trade demand, coupled with the exertions of those who encouraged their dependents or protégés to give their spare time to remunerative home occupations. Thus the origin and perpetuation of the industry have come to be associated with the women folk of peasants and fishermen in circumstances which present little dissimilarity whether in regard to needle lace workers now making lace in whitewashed cottages and cabins at Youghal and Kenmare in the south of Ireland, or those who produced their "punti in aria" during the 16th century about the lagoons of Venice, or Frenchwomen who made the sumptuous "Points de France" at Alençon and elsewhere in the 17th and 18th centuries; or pillow lace workers to be seen at the present day at little seaside villages tucked away in Devonshire dells, or those who were engaged more than four hundred years ago in "merletti a piombini" in Italian villages or on "Dentelles au fuseau" in Flemish lowlands. The ornamental character, however, of these several laces would be found to differ much; but methods, materials, appliances and opportunities of work would in the main be alike. As fashion in wearing laces extended, so workers came to be drawn together into groups by employers who acted as channels for general trade.[2] Nuns in the past as in the present have also devoted attention to the industry, often providing in the convent precincts workrooms not only for peasant women to carry out commissions in the service of the church or for the trade, but also for the purpose of training children in the art. Elsewhere lace schools have been founded by benefactors or organized by some leading local lace-maker[3] as much for trading as for education. In all this variety of circumstance, development of finer work has depended upon the abilities of the workers being exercised under sound direction, whether derived through their own intuitions, or supplied by intelligent and tasteful employers. Where any such direction has been absent the industry viewed commercially has suffered, its productions being devoid of artistic effect or adaptability to the changing tastes of demand.

It is noteworthy that the two widely distant regions of Europe where pictorial art first flourished and attained high perfection, north Italy and Flanders, were precisely the localities where lace-making first became an industry of importance both from an artistic and from a commercial point of view. Notwithstanding more convincing evidence as to the earlier development of pillow lace making in Italy the invention of pillow lace is often credited to the Flemings; but there is no distinct trace of the time or the locality. In a picture said to exist in the church of St Gomar at Lierre, and sometimes attributed to Quentin Matsys (1495), is introduced a girl apparently working at some sort of lace with pillow, bobbins, &c., which are somewhat similar to the implements in use in more recent times.[4] From the very infancy of Flemish art an active intercourse was maintained between the Low Countries and the great centres of Italian art; and it is therefore only what might be expected that the wonderful examples of the art and handiwork of Venice in lace-making should soon have come to be known to and rivalled among the equally industrious, thriving and artistic Flemings. At the end of the 16th century pattern-books were issued in Flanders having the same general character as those published for the guidance of the Venetian and other Italian lace-makers.

[1] The prevalence of fashion in the above-mentioned sorts of embroidery during the 16th century is marked by the number of pattern-books then published. In Venice a work of this class was issued by Alessandro Paganino in 1527; another of a similar nature, printed by Pierre Quinty, appeared in the same year at Cologne; and *La Fleur de la science de pourtraicture et patrons de broderie, façon arabicque et ytalique*, was published at Paris in 1530. From these early dates until the beginning of the 17th century pattern-books for embroidery in Italy, France, Germany and England were published in great abundance. The designs contained in many of those dating from the 16th century were to be worked for costumes and hangings, and consisted of scrolls, arabesques, birds, animals, flowers, foliage, herbs [illegible]. So far, however, as their reproduction as laces might be concerned, the execution of complicated work was involved which [illegible] practised lace-workers, such as those who arose a century [illegible] would be expected

[2] A very complete account of how these conditions began and developed at Alençon, for instance, is given in Madame Despierre's *Histoire du Point d'Alençon* (1886) to which is appended an interesting and annotated list of merchants, designers and makers of Point d'Alençon.

[3] *E.g.* The family of Camusat at Alençon from 1602 until 1795.

[4] The picture, however, as Seguin has pointed out, was probably painted some thirty years later, and by Jean Matsys.

France and England were not far behind Venice and Flanders in making needle and pillow lace. Henry III. of France (1574–1589) appointed a Venetian, Frederic Vinciolo, pattern maker for varieties of linen needle works and laces to his court. Through the influence of this fertile designer the seeds of a taste for lace in France were principally sown. But the event which *par excellence* would seem to have fostered the higher development of the French art of lace-making was the aid officially given it in the following century by Louis XIV., acting on the advice of his minister Colbert. Intrigue and diplomacy were put into action to secure the services of Venetian lace-workers; and by an edict dated 1665 the lace-making centres at Alençon, Quesnoy, Arras, Reims, Sedan, Château Thierry, Loudun and elsewhere were selected for the operations of a company in aid of which the state made a contribution of 36,000 francs; at the same time the importation of Venetian, Flemish and other laces was strictly forbidden.[1] The edict contained instructions that the lace-makers should produce all sorts of thread work, such as those done on a pillow or cushion and with the needle, in the style of the laces made at Venice, Genoa, Ragusa and other places; these French imitations were to be called "points de France." By 1671 the Italian ambassador at Paris writes, "Gallantly is the minister Colbert on his way to bring the 'lavori d'aria' to perfection." Six years later an Italian, Domenigo Contarini, alludes to the "punto in aria," "which the French can now do to admiration." The styles of design which emanated from the chief of the French lace centre, Alençon, were more fanciful and less severe than the Venetian, and it is evident that the Flemish lace-makers later on adopted many of these French patterns for their own use. The provision of French designs (fig. 24) which owes so much to the state patronage, contrasts with the absence of corresponding provision in England and was noticed early in the 18th century by Bishop Berkeley. "How," he asks, "could France and Flanders have drawn so much money from other countries for figured silk, lace and tapestry, if they had not had their academies of design?"

Fig. 24.—Portion of a Flounce of Needlepoint Lace, French, early 18th century, "Point de France." The honeycomb ground is considered to be a peculiarity of "Point d'Argentan": some of the fillings are made in the manner of the "Point d'Alençon" *réseau*.

It is fairly evident too that the French laces themselves, known as "bisette," "gueuse," "campane" and "mignonette," were small and comparatively insignificant works, without pretence to design.

[1] See the poetical skit *Révolte des passements et broderies*, written by Mademoiselle de la Tousse, cousin of Madame de Sévigné, in the middle of the 17th century, which marks the favour which foreign laces at that time commanded amongst the leaders of French fashion.

The humble endeavours of peasantry in England (which could boast of no schools of design), Germany, Sweden, Russia and Spain could not result in work of so high artistic pretension as that of France and Flanders. In the 18th century good lace was made in Devonshire, but it is only in recent years that to some extent the hand lace-makers of England and Ireland have become impressed with the necessity of well-considered designs for their work. Pillow lace making under the name of "bone lace making" was pursued in the 17th century in Buckinghamshire, Hertfordshire and Bedfordshire, and in 1724 Defoe refers to the manufacture of bone lace in which villagers were "wonderfully exercised and improved within these few years past." "Bone" lace dates from the 17th century in England and was practically the counterpart of Flemish "dentelles au fuseau," and related also to the Italian "merletti a piombini" (see Pl. fig. 10). In Germany, Barbara Uttmann, a native of Nuremberg, instructed peasants of the Harz mountains to twist and plait threads in 1561. She was assisted by certain refugees from Flanders. A sort of "purling" or imitation of the Italian "merletti a piombini" was the style of work produced then.

Lace of comparatively simple design has been made for centuries in villages of Andalusia as well as in Spanish conventual establishments. The "point d'Espagne," however, appears to have been a commercial name given by French manufacturers of a class of lace made in France with gold or silver threads on the pillow and greatly esteemed by Spaniards in the 17th century. No lace pattern-books have been found to have been published in Spain. The needle-made laces which came out of Spanish monasteries in 1830, when these institutions were dissolved, were mostly Venetian needle-made laces. The lace vestments preserved at the cathedral at Granada hitherto presumed to be of Spanish work are verified as being Flemish of the 17th century (similar in style to Pl. fig. 14). The industry is not alluded to in Spanish ordinances of the 15th, 16th or 17th centuries, but traditions which throw its origin back to the Moors or Saracens are still current in Seville and its neighbourhood, where a twisted and knotted arrangement of fine cords is often worked[1] under the name of "Morisco" fringe, elsewhere called macramé lace. Black and white silk pillow laces, or "blondes," date from the 18th century. They were made in considerable quantity in the neighbourhood of Chantilly, and imported for mantillas by Spain, where corresponding silk lace making was started. Although after the 18th century the making of silk laces more or less ceased at Chantilly and the neighbourhood, the craft is now carried on in Normandy—at Bayeux and Caen—as well as in Auvergne, which is also noted for its simple "torchon" laces. Silk pillow lace making is carried on in Spain, especially at Barcelona. The patterns are almost entirely imitations from 18th-century French ones of a large and free floral character. Lace-making is said to have been promoted in Russia through the patronage of the court, after the visit of Peter the Great to Paris in the early days of the 18th century. Peasants in the districts of Vologda, Balakhua (Nijni-Novgorod), Bieleff (Tula) and Mzensk (Orel) make pillow laces of simple patterns. Malta is noted for producing a silk pillow lace of black or white, or red threads, chiefly of patterns in which repetitions of circles, wheels and radiations of shapes resembling grains of wheat are the main features. This characteristic of design, appearing in white linen thread laces of similar make which have been identified as Genoese pillow laces of the early 17th century, reappears in Spanish and Paraguayan work. Pillow lace in imitation of Maltese, Buckinghamshire and Devonshire laces is made to a small extent in Ceylon, in different parts of India and in Japan. A successful effort has also been made to re-establish the industry in the island of Burano near Venice, and pillow and needlepoint lace of good design is made there.

At present the chief sources of hand-made lace are France, Belgium, Ireland and England.

France is faithful to her traditions in maintaining a lively and graceful taste in lace-making. Fashion of late years has called for ampler and more boldly effective laces, readily produced with both braids and cords and far less intricate needle or pillow work than was required for the dainty and smaller laces of earlier date.

In Belgium the social and economic conditions are, as they have been in the past, more conducive and more favourable than elsewhere to lace-making at a sufficiently remunerative

Fig. 25.—Collar and Berthe of Irish Crochet Lace.

rate of wages. The production of hand-made laces in Belgium was in 1900 greater than that of France. The principal modern needle-made lace of Belgium is the "Point de Gaze"; "Duchesse" and Bruges laces are the chief pillow-made laces; whilst "Point Appliqué" and "Plat Appliqué" are frequently the results not only of combining needle-made and pillow work, but also of using them in conjunction with machine-made net. Ireland is the best producer of that substantial looped-thread

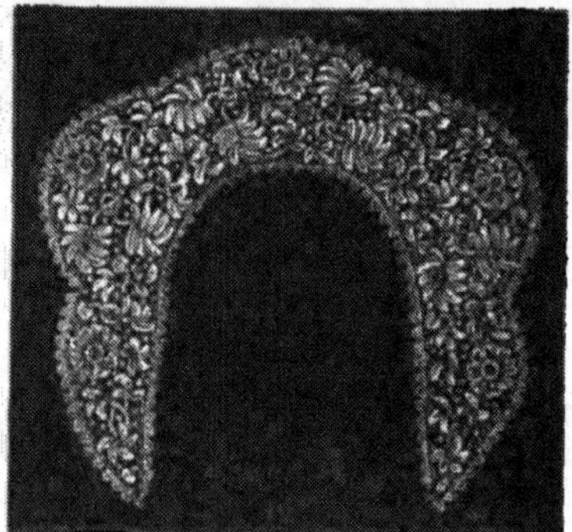

Fig. 26.—Collar of Irish Crochet Lace.

work known as crochet (see figs. 25, 26, 27), which must be regarded as a hand-made lace fabric although not classifiable as a needlepoint or pillow lace. It is also quite distinct in character from pseudo-laces, which are really embroideries with a lace-like appearance, *e.g.* embroideries on net, cut and embroidered cambrics and fine linen. For such as these Ireland maintains a reputation in its admirable Limerick and Carrickmacross laces, made not only in Limerick and Carrickmacross, but also

[1] Useful information has been communicated to the writer of the present article on lace by Mrs B. Wishaw of Seville.

in Kinsale, Newry, Crossmaglen and elsewhere. The demand from France for Irish crochet is now far beyond the supply, a condition which leads not only to the rapid repetition by Irish workers of old patterns, but tends also to a gradual debasement of both texture and ornament. Attempts have been made to counteract this tendency, with some success, as the specimens of Irish crochet in figs. 25, 26 and 27 indicate.

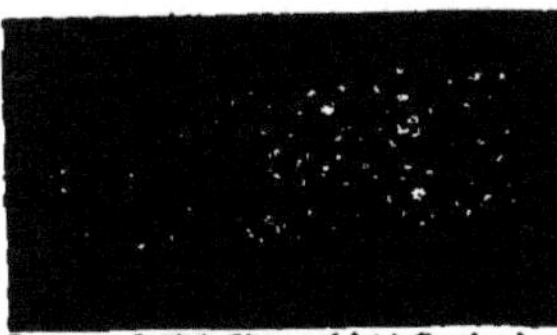
Fig. 27.—Lady's Sleeve of Irish Crochet Lace.

An appreciable amount of pillow-made lace is annually supplied from Devonshire, Buckinghamshire, Bedfordshire and Northampton, but it is bought almost wholly for home use. The English laces are made almost entirely in accordance with the precedents of the 19th century—that is to say, in definite lengths and widths, as for borders, insertions and flounces, although large shaped articles, such as panels for dresses, long sleeves complete skirts, jackets, blouses, and fancifully shaped collars of considerable dimensions have of late been freely made elsewhere. To make such things entirely of lace necessitates many modifications in the ordinary methods; the English lace-workers are slow to adapt their work in the manner requisite, and hence are far behind in the race to respond to the fashionable demand. No countries succeed so well in promptly answering the variable call of fashion as France and Belgium.

As regards trade in lace, America probably buys more from Belgium than from France; France and England come next as purchasers of nearly equal quantities, after which come Russia and Italy.

The greatest amount of lace now made is that which issues from machines in England, France and Germany. The total number of persons employed in the lace industry in England in 1871 was 49,370, and in 1901 about 34,929, of whom not more than 5000 made lace by hand.

The early history[1] of the lace-making machine coincides with that of the stocking frame, that machine having been adapted about the year 1768 for producing open-looped fabrics which had a net-like appearance. About 1786 frames for making point nets by machinery first appear at Mansfield and later at Ashbourne and Nottingham and soon afterwards modifications were introduced into such frames in order to make varieties of meshes in the point nets which were classed as figured nets. In 1808 and 1809 John Heathcoat of Nottingham obtained patents for machines for making bobbin net with a simpler and more readily produced mesh than that of the point net just mentioned. For at least thirty years thousands of women had been employed in and about Nottingham in the embroidery of simple ornament on net. In 1813 John Leavers began to improve the figured net weaving machines above mentioned, and from these the lace-making machines in use at the present time were developed. But it was the application of the celebrated Jacquard apparatus to such machines that enabled manufacturers to produce all sorts of patterns in thread-work in imitation of the patterns for hand-made lace. A French machine called the "dentellière" was devised (see *La Nature* for the 3rd of March 1881), and the patterns produced by it were of plaited threads. The expense, however, attending the production of plaited lace by the "dentellière" is as great as that of pillow lace made by the hand, and so the machine has not succeeded for ordinary trade purposes. More successful results have been secured by the new patent circular lace machine of Messrs. Birkin & Co. of Nottingham, the productions of which, all of simple design, cannot be distinguished from hand-made pillow lace of the same style (see figs. 57, 58, 59).

Before dealing with technical details in processes of making lace whether by hand or by the machine, the component parts of different makes of lace may be considered. These are governed by the ornaments or patterns, which may be so designed, as they were in the earlier laces, that the different component parts may touch one another without any intervening ground-work. But as a wish arose to vary the effect of the details in a pattern ground-works were gradually developed and at first consisted of links or ties between the substantial parts of the pattern. The bars or ties were succeeded by grounds of meshes, like nets. Sometimes the substantial parts of a pattern were outlined with a single thread or by a strongly marked raised edge of buttonhole-stitched or of plaited work. Minute fanciful devices were then introduced to enrich various portions of the pattern. Some of the heavier needle-made laces resemble low relief carving in ivory, and the edges of the relief portions are often decorated with clusters of small loops. For the most part all this elaboration was brought to a high pitch of variety and finish by French designers and workers; and French terms are more usual in speaking of details in laces. Thus the solid part of the pattern is called the *toilé* or clothing, the links or ties are called *brides*, the meshed grounds are called *réseaux*, the outline to the edges of a pattern is called *cordonnet* or *brodé*, the insertions of fanciful devices *modes*, the little loops *picots*. These terms are applicable to the various portions of laces made with the needle, on the pillow or by the machine.

[1] See Felkin's *Machine-wrought Hosiery and Lace Manufactures*.

The sequence of patterns in lace (which may be verified upon referring to figs 1 to 23) is roughly as follows. From about 1540 to 1590 they were composed of geometric forms set within squares, or of crossed and radiating line devices, resulting in a very open fabric, stiff and almost wiry in effect, without *brides* or *réseaux*. From 1590 may be dated the introduction into patterns of very conventional floral and even human and animal forms and slender scrolls, rendered in a tape-like texture, held together by *brides*. To the period from 1620 to 1670 belongs the development of long continuous scroll patterns with *réseaux* and *brides*, accompanied in the case of needle-made laces with an elaboration of details, *e.g. cordonnet* with massings of *picots*. Much of these laces enriched with fillings or *modes* was made at this time. From 1650 to 1700 the scroll patterns gave way to arrangements of detached ornamental details (as in Pl. VI. fig. 22): and about 1700 to 1760 more important schemes or designs were made (as in Pl. fig. 19, and in fig. 24 in text), into which were introduced naturalistic renderings of garlands, flowers, birds, trophies, architectural ornament and human figures. Grounds composed entirely of varieties of *modes* as in the case of the *réseau rosacé* (Pl. V. fig. 21) were sometimes made then. From 1760 to 1800 small details consisting of bouquets, sprays of flowers, single flowers, leaves, buds, spots and such like were adopted, and sprinkled over meshed grounds, and the character of the texture was gauzy and filmy (as in figs. 40 and 42). Since that time variants of the foregoing styles of pattern and textures have been used according to the bent of fashion in favour of simple or complex ornamentation, or of stiff, compact or filmy textures.

Needlepoint Lace.—The way in which the early Venetian "punto in aria" was made corresponds with that in which needlepoint lace is now worked. The pattern is first drawn upon a piece of parchment. The parchment is then stitched to two pieces of linen. Upon the leading lines drawn on the parchment a thread is laid, and fastened through to the parchment and linen by means of stitches, thus constructing a skeleton thread pattern (see left-hand part of fig. 30). Those portions which are to be represented as the "clothing" or *toilé* are usually worked as indicated in the enlarged diagram (fig. 29), and then edged as a rule with buttonhole stitching (fig. 28).

Fig. 28. Fig. 29.

Between these *toilé* portions of the pattern are worked ties (*brides*) or meshes (*réseaux*), and thus the various parts united into one fabric are wrought on to the face of the parchment pattern and reproducing it (see right-hand part of fig. 30). A knife is passed between the two pieces of linen at the back of the parchment, cutting the stitches which have passed through the parchment and linen, and so releasing the lace itself from its pattern parchment. In the earlier stages, the lace was made in lengths to serve as insertions (*passements*) and also in vandykes (*dentelles*)

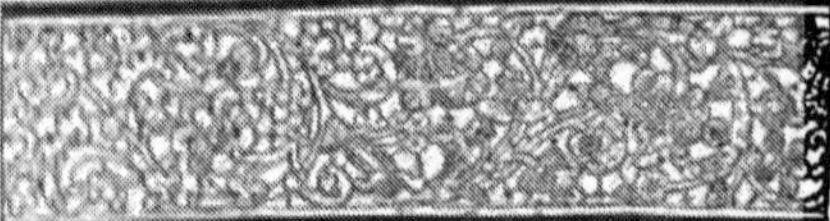

FIG. 30.—Parchment Pattern showing work in progress: the more complete lace is on the right half of the pattern.

to serve as edgings. Later on insertions and vandykes were made in one piece. All of such were at first of a geometric style of pattern (Pl. figs. 3-5 and 6).

Following closely upon them came the freer style of design already mentioned, without and then with links or ties—*brides*—interspersed between the various details of the patterns (Pl. II. fig. 7), which were of flat tapelike texture. In elaborate specimens of this flat point lace some lace workers occasionally used gold thread with the white thread. These flat laces ("Punto in Aria") are also called "flat Venetian point." About 1640 "rose (raised) point" laces began to be made (Pl. III. fig. 12). They were done in relief and those of bold design with stronger reliefs are called "gros point de Venise." Lace of this latter class was used for altar cloths, flounces, *jabots* or neckcloths which hung beneath the chin over the breast (Pl. III. fig. 11), as well as for trimming the turned-over tops of jack boots. *Tabliers* and ladies' aprons were also made of such lace. In these no regular ground was introduced. All sorts of minute embellishments, like little knots, stars and loops or *picots*, were worked on to the irregularly arranged *brides* or ties holding the main patterns together, and the more dainty of these raised laces (Pl. fig. 17) exemplify the most subtle uses to which the buttonhole stitch appears capable of being put in making ornaments. But about 1660 came laces with *brides* or ties arranged in a honeycomb reticulation or regular ground. To them succeeded lace in which the compact relief gave place to daintier and lighter material combined with a ground of meshes or *réseau*. The needle-made meshes were sometimes of single and sometimes of double threads. A diagram is given of an ordinary method of making such meshes (fig. 31). At the end of the 17th century the lightest of the Venetian needlepoint laces were made; and this class which was of the filmiest texture is usually known as "point de Venise à réseau" (Pl. V. fig. 20*a*). It was contemporary with the needle-made French laces of Alençon and Argentan[1] that became famous towards the latter part of the 17th century (Pl. V. fig. 20*b*). "Point d'Argentan" has been thought to be especially distinguished on account of its delicate honeycomb ground of hexagonally arranged *brides* (fig. 32), a peculiarity already referred to in certain antecedent Venetian point laces. Often intermixed with this hexagonal *brides* ground is the fine-meshed ground or *réseau* (fig. 20*b*), which has been held to be distinctive of "point d'Alençon." But the styles of patterns and the methods of working them, with rich variety of insertions or *modes*, with the *brodé* or *cordonnet* of raised buttonhole stitched edging, are alike in Argentan and Alençon needle-made laces (Pl. V. fig. 20*b* and fig. 32). Besides the hexagonal *brides*

FIG. 31.

[1] After 1650 the lace-workers at Alençon and its neighbourhood produced work of a daintier kind than that which was being made by the Venetians. As a rule the hexagonal *bride* grounds of Alençon laces are smaller than similar details in Venetian laces. The average size of a diagonal taken from angle to angle in an Alençon (or so-called Argentan) hexagon was about one-sixth of an inch, and each side of the hexagon was about one-tenth of an inch. An idea of the minuteness of the work can be formed from the fact that a side of a hexagon would be overcast with some nine or ten buttonhole stitches.

ground and the ground of meshes another variety of grounding (*réseau rosacé*) was used in certain Alençon designs. This ground consisted of buttonhole-stitched skeleton hexagons within each of which was worked a small hexagon of *toilé* connected with the outer surrounding hexagon by means of six little ties or *brides* (Pl. V. fig. 21). Lace with this particular ground has been called "Argentella," and some writers have thought that it was a specialty of Genoese or Venetian work. But the character of the work and the style of the floral patterns are those of Alençon laces. The industry at Argentan was virtually an offshoot of that nurtured at Alençon, where "lacis," "cut work" and "vélin" (work on parchment) had been made for years before the well-developed needle-made "point d'Alençon" came into vogue under the favouring patronage of the state-aided lace company mentioned as having been formed in 1665.

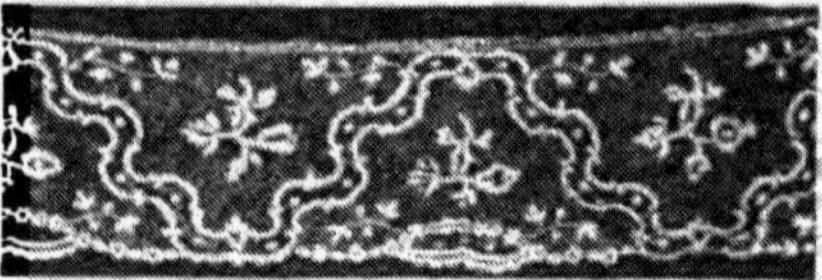

FIG. 32.—Border of Needlepoint Lace made in France about 1740–1750, the clear hexagonal mesh ground, which is compactly stitched, being usually regarded as characteristic of the point de France made at Argentan.

Madame Despierre in her *Histoire du point d'Alençon* gives an interesting and trustworthy account of the industry.

In Belgium, Brussels has acquired some celebrity for needle-made laces. These, however, are chiefly in imitation of those made at Alençon, but the *toilé* is of less compact texture and sharpness in definition of pattern. Brussels needlepoint lace is often worked with meshed grounds made on a pillow, and a plain

FIG. 33.—Shirt decorated with Insertions of Flat Needlepoint Lace. (English, 17th century. Victoria and Albert Museum.)

thread is used as a *cordonnet* for their patterns instead of a thread overcast with buttonhole stitches as in the French needlepoint laces. Note the bright sharp outline to the various ornamental details in Pl. V. fig. 20*b*.

Needlepoint lace has also been occasionally produced in

England. Whilst the character of its design in the early 17th century was rather more primitive, as a rule, than that of the contemporary Italian, the method of its workmanship is virtually the same and an interesting specimen of English needle-made lace inset into an early 17th-century shirt is illustrated in fig. 33. Specimens of needle-made work done by English school children may be met with in samplers of the 17th and 18th centuries. Needlepoint lace is successfully made at Youghal, Kenmare and New Ross in Ireland, where of late years attention has been given to the study of designs for it. The lace-making school at Burano near Venice produces hand-made laces which are, to a great extent, careful reproductions of the more celebrated classes of point laces, such as "punto in aria," "rose point de Venise," "point de Venise à réseau," "point d'Alençon," "point d'Argentan" and others. Some good needlepoint lace is made in Bohemia and elsewhere in the Austrian empire.

Pillow-made Lace.—Pillow-made lace is built upon no substructure corresponding with a skeleton thread pattern such as is used for needlepoint lace, but is the representation of a pattern obtained by twisting and plaiting threads.

These patterns were never so strictly geometric in style as those adopted for the earliest point lace making from the antecedent cut linen and drawn thread embroideries. Curved forms, almost at the outset of pillow lace, seem to have been found easy of execution (see lower border, Pl. II. fig. 3); its texture was more lissom and less crisp and wiry in appearance than that of contemporary needle-made lace. The early twisted and plaited thread laces, which had the appearance of small cords merging into one another, were soon succeeded by laces of similar make but with flattened and broader lines more like fine braids or tapes (Pl. I. fig. 2, and Pl. fig. 10). But pillow laces of this tapey character must not be confused with laces in which actual tape or braid is used. That peculiar class of lace-work does not arise until after the beginning of the 17th century when the weaving of tape is said to have commenced in Flanders. In England this sort of tape-lace dates no farther back than 1747, when two Dutchmen named Lanfort were invited by an English firm to set up tape looms in Manchester.

The process by which lace is made on the pillow is roughly and briefly as follows. A pattern is first drawn upon a piece of paper or parchment. It is then pricked with holes by a skilled "pattern pricker," who determines where the principal pins shall be stuck for guiding the threads. This pricked pattern is then fastened to the pillow. The pillow or cushion varies in shape in different countries. Some lace-makers use a circular pad, backed with a flat board, in order that it may be placed upon a table and easily moved. Other lace-workers use a well-stuffed round pillow or short bolster, flattened at the two ends, so that they may hold it conveniently on their laps. From the upper part of pillow with the pattern fastened on it hang the threads from the bobbins. The bobbin threads thus hang across the pattern. Fig. 34 shows the commencement, for instance, of a double set of three-thread plaitings. The compact portion in a pillow lace has a woven appearance (fig. 35).

Fig. 34.—Diagram showing six Bobbins in use.

Fig. 35.

About the middle of the 17th century pillow lace of formal scroll patterns somewhat in imitation of those for point lace was made, chiefly in Flanders. The earlier of these had grounds of ties or *brides* and was often called "point de Flandres" (Pl. fig. 14) in contradistinction to scroll patterns with a mesh ground, which were called "point d'Angleterre" (Pl. fig. 16). Into Spain and France much lace from Venice and Flanders was imported as well as into England, where from the 16th century the manufacture of the simple pattern "bone lace" by peasants in the midland and southern counties was still being carried on. In Charles II.'s time its manufacture was threatened with extinction by the preference given to the more artistic and finer Flemish laces. The importation of the latter was accordingly prohibited. Dealers in Flemish lace sought to evade the prohibitions by calling certain of their laces "point d'Angleterre,"

Fig. 36.—Border of English Pillow-made (Devonshire) Lace in the style of a Brussels design of the middle of the 18th century.

and smuggling them into England. But smuggling was made so difficult that English dealers were glad to obtain the services of Flemish lace-makers and to induce them to settle in England. It is from some such cause that the better 17th- and 18th-century

Fig. 37.—Border of English (Bucks. or Beds.) Pillow-made Lace in the style of a Mechlin design of the latter part of the 18th century.

English pillow laces bear resemblance to pillow laces of Brussels, of Mechlin and of Valenciennes.

As skill in the European lace-making developed soon after the middle of the 17th century, patterns and particular plaitings

Fig. 38.—Border of Pillow-made Lace, Mechlin, from a design similar to such as was used for point d'Alençon of the Louis XV. period.

came to be identified with certain localities. Mechlin, for instance, enjoyed a high reputation for her productions. The chief technical features of this pillow lace lie in the plaiting of the meshes, and the outlining of the clothing or *toilé* with a thread *cordonnet*. The ordinary Mechlin mesh is hexagonal in shape. Four of the sides are of double twisted threads, two are of four threads plaited three times (fig. 39).

Fig. 39.—Mechlin Mesh.

In Brussels pillow lace, which has greater variety of design, the mesh is also hexagonal; but in contrast with the Mechlin mesh whilst four of its sides are of double-twisted threads the other two are of four threads plaited four times (fig. 41). The finer specimens of Brussels lace are remarkable for the fidelity and grace with which the botanical forms in many of its patterns are rendered (Pl. VI. fig. 23). These are mainly reproductions or adaptations of designs for point d'Alençon, and the soft quality imparted to them in the texture of pillow-made lace contrasts with the harder and more crisp appearance in needlepoint lace. An example of dainty Brussels pillow lace is given in fig. 42. In the Brussels pillow lace a delicate modelling effect

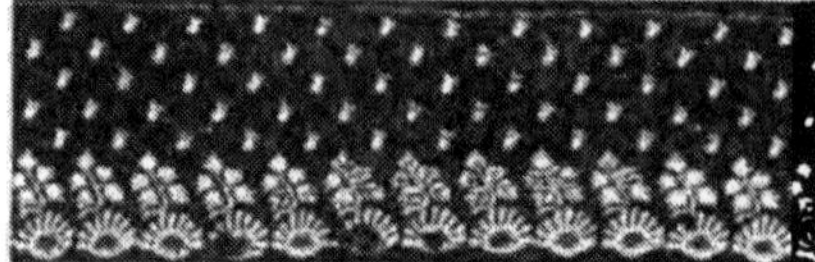

Fig. 40.—Border of Pillow-made Lace, Mechlin, end of the 18th century.

is often imparted to the close textures of the flowers by means of pressing them with a bone instrument which gives concave shapes to petals and leaves, the edges of which consist in part of slightly raised *cordonnet* of compact plaited work.

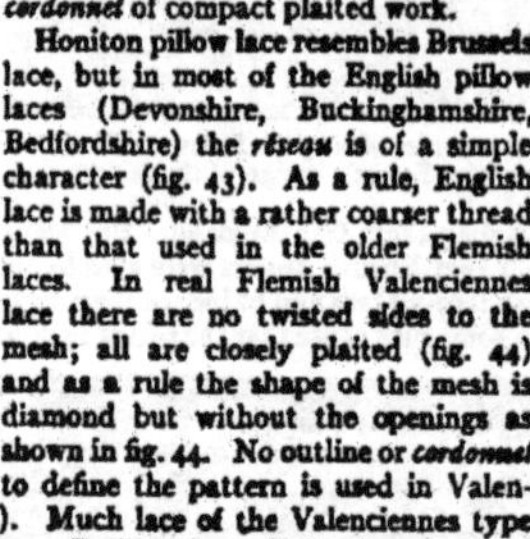

Fig. 41.—Enlargement of Brussels Mesh.

Honiton pillow lace resembles Brussels lace, but in most of the English pillow laces (Devonshire, Buckinghamshire, Bedfordshire) the *réseau* is of a simple character (fig. 43). As a rule, English lace is made with a rather coarser thread than that used in the older Flemish laces. In real Flemish Valenciennes lace there are no twisted sides to the mesh; all are closely plaited (fig. 44) and as a rule the shape of the mesh is diamond but without the openings as shown in fig. 44. No outline or *cordonnet* to define the pattern is used in Valenciennes lace (see fig. 45). Much lace of the Valenciennes type (fig. 54) is made at Ypres. Besides these distinctive classes of pillow-like laces, there are others in which equal care in plaiting and twisting threads is displayed, though the character of the design is comparatively simple, as for instance in ordinary pillow laces from Italy, from the Auvergne, from Buckinghamshire, or rude and primitive as in laces from Crete, southern Spain and Russia. Pillow lace-making in Crete is now said to be extinct. The laces were made chiefly of silk. The patterns in many specimens are outlined with one, two or three bright-coloured silken threads. Uniformity in simple character of design may also be observed in many Italian, Spanish, Bohemian, Swedish and Russian pillow laces (see the lower edge of fig. 46).

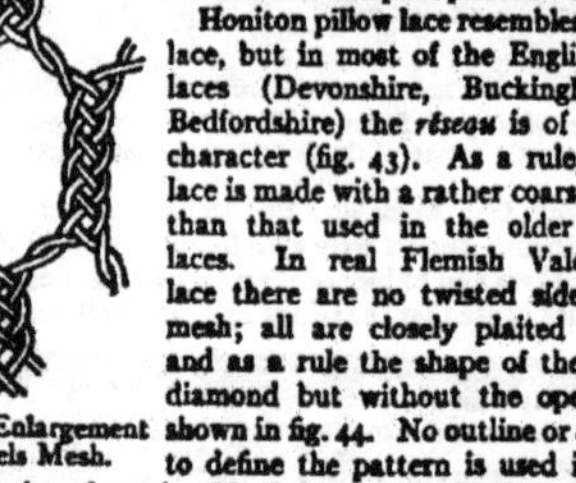

Fig. 42.—Portion of a Wedding Veil, 7 ft. 6 in.×6 ft. 6 in., of Pillow-made Lace, Brussels, late 18th century. The design consists of light leafy garlands of orange blossoms and other flowers daintily festooned. Little feathery spirals and stars are powdered over the ground, which is of Brussels *vrai réseau*. In the centre upon a more open ground of pillow-made hexagonal *brides* is a group of two birds, one flying towards the other which appears ready to take wing from its nest; an oval frame containing two hearts pierced by an arrow, and a hymeneal torch. Throughout this veil is a profusion of pillow renderings of various *modes*, the *réseau rosacé*, star devices, &c. The ornamental devices ' ... 'd and partly worked into the ground (Victoria

Fig. 43. Fig. 44.

Guipure.—This name is often applied to needlepoint and pillow laces in which the ground consists of ties or *brides*, but it more properly designates a kind of lace or "passementerie," made with gimp of fine wires whipped round with silk, and with cotton thread. An earlier kind of gimp was formed with "Cartisane," a little strip of thin parchment or vellum covered with silk, gold or silver thread. These stiff gimp threads, formed into a pattern, were held together by stitches worked with the needle. Gold and silver thread laces have been usually made on the pillow, though gold thread has been used with fine effect in 17th-century Italian needlepoint laces.

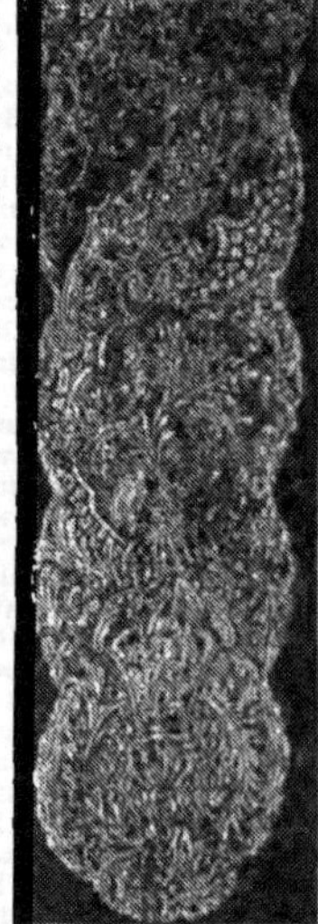

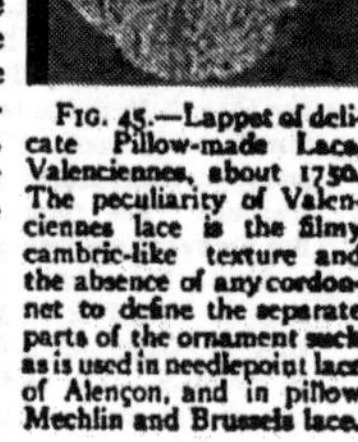

Fig. 45.—Lappet of delicate Pillow-made Lace, Valenciennes, about 1750. The peculiarity of Valenciennes lace is the filmy cambric-like texture and the absence of any cordonnet to define the separate parts of the ornament such as is used in needlepoint lace of Alençon, and in pillow Mechlin and Brussels lace.

Machine-made Lace.—We have already seen that a technical peculiarity in making needlepoint lace is that a single thread and needle are alone used to form the pattern, and that the buttonhole stitch and other loopings which can be worked by means of a needle and thread mark a distinction between lace made in this manner and lace made on the pillow. For the process of pillow lace making a series of threads are in constant employment, plaited and twisted the one with another. A buttonhole stitch is not producible by it. The Leavers lace machine does not make either a buttonhole stitch or a plait. An essential principle of this machine-made work is that the threads are twisted together as in stocking net. The Leavers lace machine is that generally in use at Nottingham and Calais. French ingenuity has developed improvements in this machine whereby laces of delicate thread are made; but as fast as France makes an improvement England follows with another, and both countries virtually maintain an equal position in this branch of industry. The number of threads brought into operation in a Leavers machine is regulated by the pattern to be produced, the threads being of two sorts, beam or warp threads and bobbin or weft threads. Upwards of 8880 are sometimes used, sixty pieces of lace being made simultaneously, each piece requiring 148 threads—100 beam threads and 48 bobbin threads. The ends of both sets of threads are fixed to a cylinder upon which as the manufacture proceeds the lace becomes wound.

Fig. 46.—Border to a Cloth. The wide part bearing the double-headed eagle of Russia is of drawn thread embroidery; the scalloped edging is of Russian pillow-made lace, though the style of its pattern is often seen in pillow laces made by peasants in Danubian provinces as well as in the south of Spain.

The supply of the beam or warp threads is held upon reels, and that of the bobbins or weft threads is held in bobbins. The beam or warp thread reels are arranged in frames or trays beneath the stage, above which and between it and the cylinder the twisting of the bobbin or weft with beam or warp threads takes place. The bobbins containing the bobbin or weft threads are flattened in shape so as to pass conveniently between the stretched beam or warp threads. Each bobbin can contain about 120 yds. of thread. By most ingenious mechanism varying degrees of tension can be imparted to warp and weft threads as required. As the bobbins or weft threads pass like pendulums between the warp threads the latter are made to oscillate, thus causing them to become twisted with the bobbin threads. As the twistings take place, combs passing through both warp and weft threads compress the twistings. Thus the texture of the clothing or *toilé* in machine-made lace may generally be detected by its ribbed appearance, due to the compressed twisted threads. Figs. 47 and 48 are intended to show effects obtained by varying the tensions of weft and warp threads. For instance, if the weft, as threads *b, b, b, b* in fig. 47, be tight and the warp thread slack, the warp thread *a* will be twisted upon the weft threads. But if the warp thread *a* be tight and the weft threads *b, b, b, b*, be slack, as in fig. 48, then the weft threads will be twisted on the warp thread. At the same time the twisting in both these cases arises from the conjunction of movements given to the two sets of threads, namely, an oscillation or movement from side to side of the beam or warp threads, and the swinging or pendulum-like movement of the bobbin or weft threads between the warp threads.

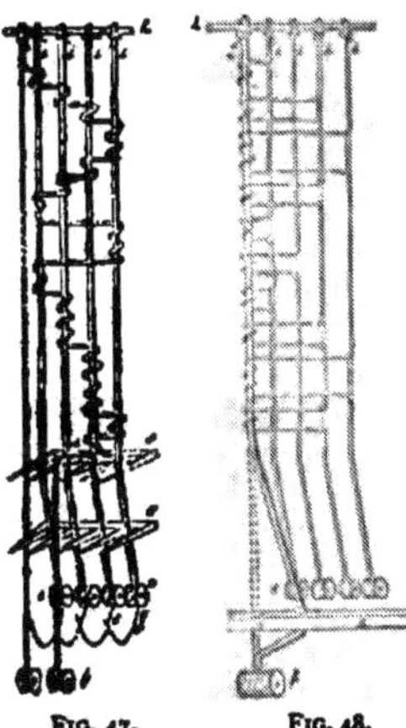

Fig. 47. Fig. 48.

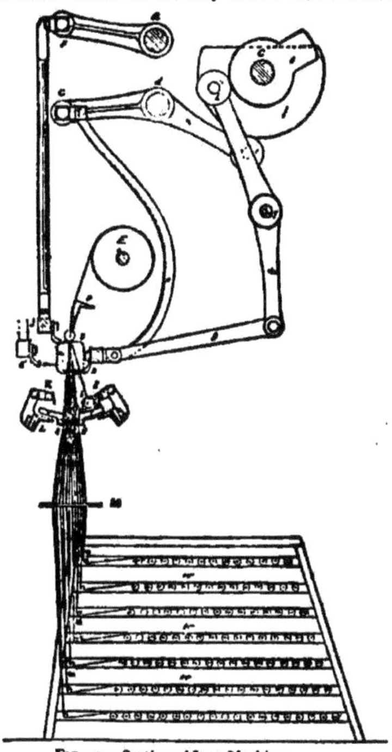

Fig. 49.—Section of Lace Machine.

Fig. 49 is a diagram of a sectional elevation of a lace machine representing its more essential parts. E is the cylinder or beam upon which the lace is rolled as made, and upon which the ends of both warp and weft threads are fastened at starting. Beneath are *w, w, w*, a series of trays or beams, one above the other, containing the reels of the supplies of warp threads; *c, c* represent the slide bars for the passage of the bobbin *b* with its thread from *k* to *k*, the landing bars, one on each side of the rank of warp threads; *s, s* are the combs which take it in turns to press together the twistings as they are made. The combs come away clear from the threads as soon as they have pressed them together and fall into positions ready

Fig. 50.—Machine-made Lace in imitation of 16th-century Needle-point "Reticella" Lace.

to perform their pressing operations again. The contrivances for giving each thread a particular tension and movement at a certain time are connected with an adaptation of the Jacquard system of pierced cards. The machine lace pattern drafter has to calculate how many holes shall be punched in a card, and to determine the position of such holes. Each hole regulates the mechanism for giving movement to a thread. Fig. 54 displays a piece of hand-made Valenciennes (Ypres) lace and fig. 55 a corresponding piece woven by the machine. The latter shows the advantage that can be gained by using very fine gauge machines, thus enabling a very close imitation of the real lace to be made by securing a very open and clear *réseau* or net, such as would be made on a coarse machine, and at the same time to keep the pattern fine and solid and standing out well from the net, as is the case with the real lace, which cannot be done by using a coarse gauge machine. In this example the machine used is a 16 point (that is 32 carriages to the inch), and the ground is made half gauge, that is 8 point,

Fig. 51.—Border of Machine-made Lace in the style of 17th-century Pillow Guipure Lace.

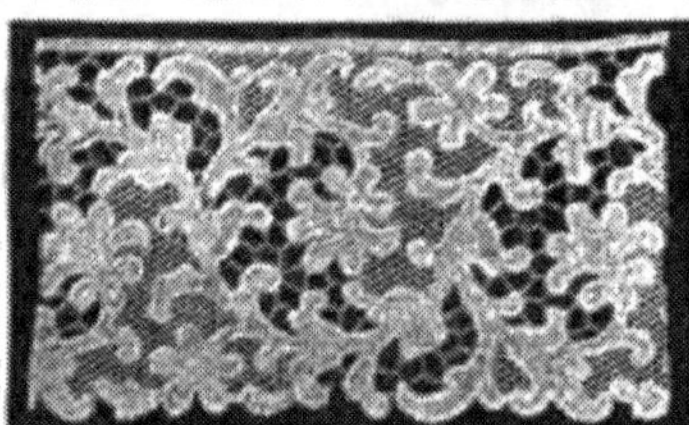

Fig. 52.—Border of Machine-made Lace in imitation of 17th-century Pillow Lace.

and the weaving is made the full gauge of the machine, that is 16 point. Fig. 56 gives other examples of hand- and machine-made Valenciennes lace. The machine-made lace (*b*) imitating the real (*a*) is made on a 14-point machine (that is 28 carriages to the inch), the ground being 7 point and the pattern being full gauge or 14 point. Although the principle in these examples of machine work is exactly the same, in so far that they use half gauge net and full gauge clothing to produce the contrast as mentioned above, the fabrication of these two examples is quite different, that in fig. 55 being an example of tight bobbins or weft, and slack warp threads as shown in fig. 47. Whereas the example in fig. 56 is made with slack bobbins or weft threads and tight warp threads as in fig. 48. In fig. 57 is a piece of hand-made lace of stout thread, very similar to much Cluny lace made in the Auvergne and to the Buckinghamshire "Maltese" lace. Close to it are specimens of lace (figs. 58 and 59) made by the new patent circular lace machine of Messrs Birkin of Nottingham. This machine although very slow in production actually reproduces the real lace, at a cost slightly below that of the hand-made lace. In another branch of lace-making by machinery, mechanical ingenuity, combined with chemical treatment, has led to surprising results (figs. 53 and 50). Swiss, German and other manufacturers use machines in which a principle of the sewing-machine is involved. A fine silken tissue is thereby enriched with an elaborately raised cotton or thread embroidery. The whole fabric is then treated with chemical mordants which, whilst dissolving the silky web, do not attack the cotton or thread embroidery. A relief embroidery possessing the appearance of hand-made raised needlepoint lace is thus produced.

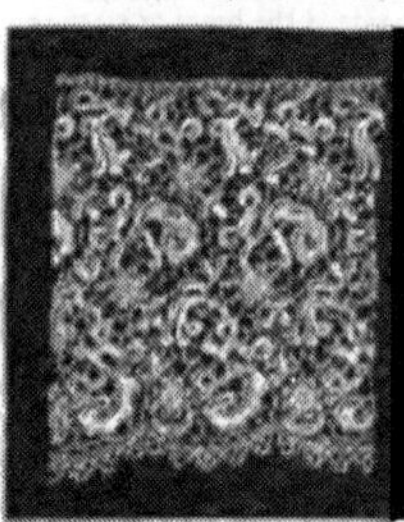

Fig. 53.—Machine-made Trimming Border in imitation of Irish Crochet Lace.

Fig. 54.—A Piece of Hand-made Pillow Lace, Belgian (Ypres), 20th century. (The machine imitation is given in fig. 55.)

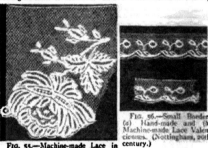

Fig. 55.—Machine-made Lace in imitation of the Hand-made Specimen of fig. 54. (Nottingham, 20th century.)

Fig. 56.—Small Borders (*a*) Hand-made and (*b*) Machine-made Lace Valenciennes. (Nottingham, 20th century.)

Fig. 57.—Specimen of Hand-made Pillow Lace.

Fig. 58.—Specimen of Machine-made Lace in which the twisting and plaiting of the threads are identical with those of the hand-made specimen of fig. 57. (Nottingham, 20th century.)

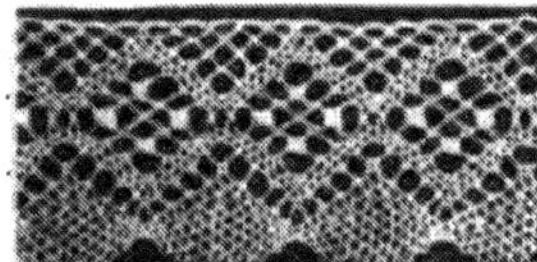

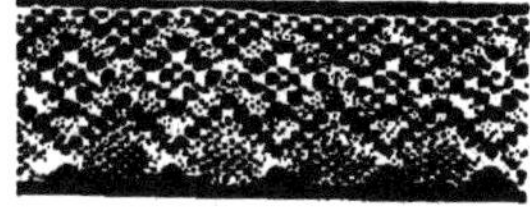

FIG. 59.—Specimens of Machine-made Torchon Lace, in the same manner as such lace is made on the pillow by hand. (Nottingham, 20th century.)

Figs. 60 and 61 give some idea of the high quality to which this admirable counterfeit has been brought.

Collections of hand-made lace chiefly exist in museums and technical institutions, as for instance the Victoria and Albert

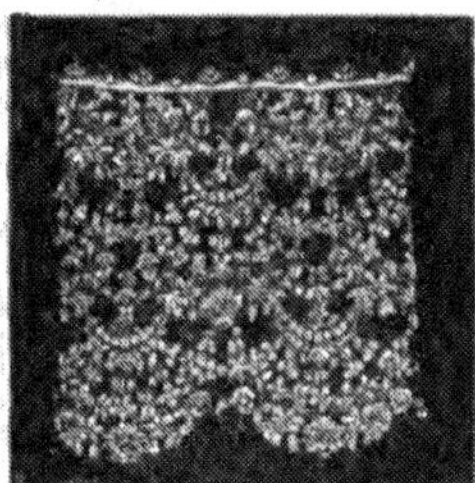

FIG. 60.—Machine-made Lace of Modern Design.

Museum in London, the Musée des Arts Décoratifs in Paris, and museums at Lyons, Nuremberg, Berlin, Turin and elsewhere.

FIG. 61.—Machine-made Lace in imitation of 17th-century Needlepoint Lace, "Gros point de Venise."

In such places the opportunity is presented of tracing in chronological sequence the stages of pattern and texture development.

Literature.—The literature of the art of lace-making is considerable. The series of 16th- and 17th-century lace pattern-books, of which the more important are perhaps those by F. Vinciolo (Paris, 1587), Cesare Vecellio (Venice, 1592), and Isabetta Catanea Parasole (Venice, 1600), not to mention several kindred works of earlier and later date published in Germany and the Netherlands, supplies a large field for exploration. Signor Ongania of Venice published a limited number of facsimiles of the majority of such works. M. Alvin of Brussels issued a brochure in 1863 upon these patterns, and in the same year the marquis Girolamo d'Adda contributed two bibliographical essays upon the same subject to the *Gazette des Beaux-Arts* (vol. xv. p. 342 seq., and vol. xvii. p. 421 seq.). In 1864 Cavaliere A. Merli wrote a pamphlet (with illustrations) entitled *Origine ed uso delle trine a filo di rete*; Mons F. de Fertiault compiled a brief and rather fanciful *Histoire de la dentelle* in 1843, in which he reproduced statements to be found in Diderot's *Encyclopédie*, subsequently quoted by Roland de la Platière. The first *Report of the Department of Practical Art* (1853) contains a "Report on Cotton Print Works and Lace-Making" by Octavius Hudson, and in the first *Report of the Department of Science and Art* are some "Observations on Lace." Reports upon the International Exhibitions of 1851 (London) and 1867 (Paris), by M. Aubry, Mrs Palliser and others contain information concerning lace-making. The most important work first issued upon the history of lace-making is that by Mrs Bury Palliser (*History of Lace*, 1869). In this work the history is treated rather from an antiquarian than a technical point of view; and wardrobe accounts, inventories, state papers, fashionable journals, diaries, plays, poems, have been laid under contribution with surprising diligence. A new edition published in 1902 presents the work as entirely revised, re-written and enlarged under the editorship of M. Jourdain and Alice Dryden. In 1875 the Arundel Society brought out *Ancient Needle-point and Pillow Lace*, a folio volume of permanently printed photographs taken from some of the finest specimens of ancient lace collected for the International Exhibition of 1874. These were accompanied by a brief history of lace, written from the technical aspect of the art, by Alan S. Cole. At the same time appeared a bulky imperial 4to volume by Seguin, entitled *La Dentelle*, illustrated with wood-cuts and fifty photo-typographical plates. Seguin divides his work into four sections. The first is devoted to a sketch of the origin of laces; the second deals with pillow laces, bibliography of lace and a review of sumptuary edicts; the third relates to needle-made lace; and the fourth contains an account of places where lace has been and is made, remarks upon commerce in lace, and upon the industry of lace makers. Without sufficient conclusive evidence Seguin accords to France the palm for having excelled in producing practically all the richer sorts of laces, notwithstanding that both before and since the publication of his otherwise valuable work, many types of them have been identified as being Italian in origin. Descriptive catalogues are issued of the lace collections at South Kensington Museum, at the Science and Art Museum, Dublin, and at the Industrial Museum, Nuremberg. In 1881 a series of four Cantor Lectures on the art of lace-making were delivered before the Society of Arts by Alan S. Cole.

A Technical History of the Manufacture of Venetian Laces, by G. M. Urbani de Gheltof, with plates, was translated by Lady Layard, and published at Venice by Signor Ongania. The *History of Machine-wrought Hosiery and Lace Manufacture* (London, 1867), by Felkin, has already been referred to. There is also a technological essay upon lace made by machinery, with diagrams of lace stitches and patterns (*Technologische Studien im sächsischen Erzgebirge*, Leipzig, 1878), by Hugo Fischer. In 1886 the Libraire Renouard, Paris, published a *History of Point d'Alençon*, written by Madame G. Despierres, which gives a close and interesting account of the industry, together with a list, compiled from local records, of makers and dealers from 1602 onwards.—*Embroidery and Lace: their manufacture and history from the remotest antiquity to the present day*, by Ernest Lefebure, lace-maker and administrator of the École des Arts Décoratifs, translated and enlarged with notes by Alan S. Cole, was published in London in 1888. It is a well-illustrated handbook for amateurs, collectors and general readers.—Irish laces made from modern designs are illustrated in a *Renascence of the Irish Art of Lace-making*, published in 1888 (London).—*Anciennes Dentelles belges formant la collection de feue madame Augusta Baronne Liedts et données au Musée de Gruuthuis à Bruges*, published at Antwerp in 1889, consists of a folio volume containing upwards of 181 phototypes—many full size—of fine specimens of lace. The ascriptions of country and date of origin are occasionally inaccurate, on account of a too obvious desire to credit Bruges with being the birthplace of all sorts of lace-work, much of which shown in this work is distinctly Italian in style.—The *Encyclopaedia of Needlework*, by Thérèse de Dillmont-Dornach (Alsace, 1891), is a detailed guide to several kinds of embroidery, knitting, crochet, tatting, netting and most of the essential stitches for needlepoint lace. It is well illustrated with wood-cuts and process blocks.—An exhaustive history of Russian lace-making is given in *La Dentelle russe*, by Madame Sophie Davidoff, published at Leipzig, 1895. Russian lace is principally pillow-work with rather heavy thread, and upwards of eighty specimens are reproduced by photo-lithography in this book.

A short account of the best-known varieties of *Point and Pillow Lace*, by A. M. S. (London, 1899), is illustrated with typical specimens of Italian, Flemish, French and English laces, as well as with magnified details of lace, enabling any one to identify the plaits, the twists and loops of threads in the actual making of the fabric.—*L'Industrie* [illegible] *dans le Pas de Calais, 1815–1900*, [illegible] is an important volume of over 600 [illegible] with abundant process blocks of [illegible] machine nets and laces made at Calais since 1815. [illegible] of the Arras hand-made laces, the pro- [illegible] now almost extinct. The book was sold for the [illegible] towards the erection of a statue in [illegible] of the apparatus by means of which [illegible] manufactured. It is of some interest to [illegible] at Calais owe their origin to [illegible] R. Webster arrivé à St Pierre- [illegible] venant d'Angleterre, est l'un des [illegible] la communauté une fabrique de tulles," [illegible] *Past and Present*, by C. C. [illegible] 1900) upon the lace-making [illegible] Bedfordshire and Northamptonshire [illegible] laces made in these counties from the [illegible] *Musée rétrospectif. Dentelles à* [illegible] *de 1900 à Paris. Rapport de* [illegible] good illustrations, especially of [illegible] France of the 17th and 18th [illegible] *dentelliers au XVIIe et au* [illegible] de Laprade (Paris, 1905), brings [illegible] information throwing light upon [illegible] France where the industry has been [illegible] periods. The book is well and usefully [illegible] plates), with a short historical [illegible] (Stuttgart, 1902); *Pillow Lace*, a [illegible] and Margaret S. Marriage [illegible] *Lace*, a practical text-book of [illegible] (London, 1907); *Antiche trine* [illegible] well illustrated; *Seven* [illegible] Pollen (London and New York, 1908). [illegible]

(A. S. C.)

LACE-BARK TREE, a native of Jamaica, known botanically as *Lagetta lintearia*, from its native name lagetto. The inner bark consists of numerous concentric layers of interlacing fibres resembling in appearance lace. Collars and other articles of apparel have been made of the fibre, which is also used in the manufacture of whips, &c. The tree belongs to the natural order Thymelaeaceae, and is grown in hothouses in Britain.

LACEDAEMON, in historical times an alternative name of Laconia (*q.v.*). Homer uses only the former, and in some passages seems to denote by it the Achaean citadel, the Therapnae of later times, in contrast to the lower town Sparta (G. Gilbert, *Studien zur altspartanischen Geschichte*, Göttingen, 1872, p. 34 [illegible]). It is described by the epithets [illegible] (hollow) and [illegible] [illegible] or hollow), and is probably connected etymologically [illegible] any hollow place. Lacedaemon is now the name of a separate department, which had in 1907 a population of [illegible].

LACÉPÈDE, BERNARD GERMAIN ÉTIENNE DE LA VILLE, [illegible] (1756–1825), French naturalist, was born at Agen in [illegible] on the 26th of December 1756. His education was [illegible] conducted by his father, and the early perusal of [illegible] *Natural History* awakened his interest in that branch [illegible] absorbed his chief attention. His leisure he [illegible] in which, besides becoming a good performer [illegible] and organ, he acquired considerable mastery of [illegible] two of his operas (which were never published) [illegible] the high approval of Gluck; in 1781–1785 he also [illegible] volumes his *Poétique de la musique*. Mean- [illegible] treatises, *Essai sur l'électricité* (1781) and [illegible] *générale et particulière* (1782–1784), which gained him [illegible] of Buffon, who in 1785 appointed him sub- [illegible] Jardin du Roi, and proposed to him to become [illegible] of his *Histoire naturelle*. This continuation [illegible] the titles *Histoire des quadrupèdes ovipares* [illegible] 1788–1789) and *Histoire naturelle des* [illegible] the Revolution Lacépède became a [illegible] assembly, but during the Reign of [illegible] having become endangered by his [illegible] the Jardin du Roi was [illegible] Lacépède was appointed, [illegible]

appeared his *Histoire des cétacés*. From this period till his death the part he took in politics prevented him making any further contribution of importance to science. In 1799 he became a senator, in 1801 president of the senate, in 1803 grand chancellor of the legion of honour, in 1804 minister of state, and at the Restoration in 1819 he was created a peer of France. He died at Épinay on the 6th of October 1825. During the latter part of his life he wrote *Histoire générale physique et civile de l'Europe*, published posthumously in 18 vols., 1826.

A collected edition of his works on natural history was published in 1826.

LACEWING-FLY, the name given to neuropterous insects of the families *Hemerobiidae* and *Chrysopidae*, related to the ant-lions, scorpion-flies, &c., with long filiform antennae, longish bodies and two pairs of large similar richly veined wings. The larvae are short grubs beset with hair-tufts and tubercles. They feed upon *Aphidae* or "green fly" and cover themselves with the emptied skins of their prey. Lacewing-flies of the genus *Chrysopa* are commonly called golden-eye flies.

LA CHAISE, FRANÇOIS DE (1624–1709), father confessor of Louis XIV., was born at the château of Aix in Forey on the 25th of August 1624, being the son of Georges d'Aix, seigneur de la Chaise, and of Renée de Rochefort. On his mother's side he was a grandnephew of Père Coton, the confessor of Henry IV. He became a novice of the Society of Jesus before completing his studies at the university of Lyons, where, after taking the final vows, he lectured on philosophy to students attracted by his fame from all parts of France. Through the influence of Camille de Villeroy, archbishop of Lyons, Père de la Chaise was nominated in 1674 confessor of Louis XIV., who intrusted him during the lifetime of Harlay de Champvallon, archbishop of Paris, with the administration of the ecclesiastical patronage of the crown. The confessor united his influence with that of Madame de Maintenon to induce the king to abandon his liaison with Madame de Montespan. More than once at Easter he is said to have had a convenient illness which dispensed him from granting absolution to Louis XIV. With the fall of Madame de Montespan and the ascendancy of Madame de Maintenon his influence vastly increased. The marriage between Louis XIV. and Madame de Maintenon was celebrated in his presence at Versailles, but there is no reason for supposing that the subsequent coolness between him and Madame de Maintenon arose from his insistence on secrecy in this matter. During the long strife over the temporalities of the Gallican Church between Louis XIV. and Innocent XI. Père de la Chaise supported the royal prerogative, though he used his influence at Rome to conciliate the papal authorities. He must be held largely responsible for the revocation of the Edict of Nantes, but not for the brutal measures applied against the Protestants. He exercised a moderating influence on Louis XIV.'s zeal against the Jansenists, and Saint-Simon, who was opposed to him in most matters, does full justice to his humane and honourable character. Père de la Chaise had a lasting and unalterable affection for Fénelon, which remained unchanged by the papal condemnation of the *Maximes*. In spite of failing faculties he continued his duties as confessor to Louis XIV. to the end of his long life. He died on the 20th of January 1709. The cemetery of Père-la-Chaise in Paris stands on property acquired by the Jesuits in 1826, and not, as is often stated, on property personally granted to him.

See R. Chantelauze, *Le Père de la Chaise. Études d'histoire religieuse* (Paris and Lyons, 1859).

LA CHAISE-DIEU, a town of central France, in the department of Haute Loire, 29 m. N.N.W. of Le Puy by rail. Pop. (1906) 1203. The town, which is situated among fir and pine woods, 3500 ft. above the sea, preserves remains of its ramparts and some houses of the 14th and 15th centuries, but owes its celebrity to a church, which, after the cathedral of Clermont-Ferrand, is the most remarkable Gothic building in Auvergne. The west façade, approached by a flight of steps, is flanked by two massive towers. The nave and aisles are of equal height and are separated from the choir by a stone rood screen. The

Fig. 1.—Portion of a Coverlet composed of squares of "lacis" or darned netting, divided by linen cut-work bands.

The squares are worked with groups representing the twelve months, and with scenes from the old Spanish dramatic story "Celestina." Spanish or Portuguese. 16th century. (Victoria and Albert Museum.)

Fig. 2.—Corner of a Bed-cover of pillow-made lace of a tape-like texture with characteristics in the twisted and plaited threads relating the work to Italian "merletti a piombini" or early English "bone lace."

Possibly made in Flanders or Italy during the early part of the 17th or at the end of the 16th century. The design includes the Imperial double-headed eagle of Austria with the ancient crown of the German Empire. (Victoria and Albert Museum.)

Fig. 3.—Three Vandyke or Dentated Borders of Italian Lace of the late 16th century.

Style usually called "Reticella" on account of the patterns being based on repeated squares or reticulations. The two first borders are of needlepoint work; the lower border is of such pillow lace as was known in Italy as "merletti a piombini."

Fig. 4.—Catherine de Medici, wearing a linen upturned collar of cut work and needlepoint lace. Louvre. About 1540.

Fig. 7.—Border of flat Needlepoint Lace of fuller texture than that of fig. 3, and from a freer style of design in which conventionalized floral forms held together by small bars or tyes are used.

Style called "punto in aria," chiefly on account of its independence of squares or reticulations. Italian. Early 17th century.

Fig. 6.—Amelie Elisabeth, Comtesse de Hainault, wearing a ruff of needlepoint Reticella lace. By MORCELSE. The Hague. About 1600.

(Figs. 4 and 6 by permission of Messrs. Braun, Clement & Co., Dornach (Alsace), and Paris.)

Fig. 8.—Mary, Countess of Pembroke, Wearing a Coif and Cuffs of Reticella Lace. National Portrait Gallery. Dated 1614.

Fig. 9.—Henri II., Duc de Montmorency, Wearing a Falling Lace Collar. By LE NAIN. Louvre. About 1628.

(By permission of Messrs Braun, Clement & Co., Dornach (Alsace), and Paris.)

Fig. 11.—James II. Wearing a Jabot and Cuffs of Raised Needlepoint Lace. By RILEY. National Portrait Gallery. About 1685.

(Figs. 8 and 11, photo by Emery Walker.)

Fig. 12.—Jabot of Needlepoint Lace Worked Partly in Relief, and Usually known as "Gros Point de Venise."

Middle of 17th century. Conventional scrolling stems with off-shooting pseudo-blossoms and leafs are specially characteristic in design for this class of lace. Its texture is typical of a development in needle-made lace later than the flat "punto in aria" of Pl. II. fig. 7.

Fig. 13.—Mme Verbiest, Wearing Pillow-made Lace *à réseau*.
From the family group by GONZALEZ COQUES. Buckingham Palace. About 1664.
(By permission of Messrs Braun, Clement & Co., Dornach (Alsace), and Paris.)

Fig. 15.—Princess Maria Teresa Stuart, Wearing a Flounce or Tablier of Lace Similar to that in fig. 17. Dated 1695.
From a group by LARGILLIÈRE. National Portrait Gallery.
(Photo by Emery Walker.)

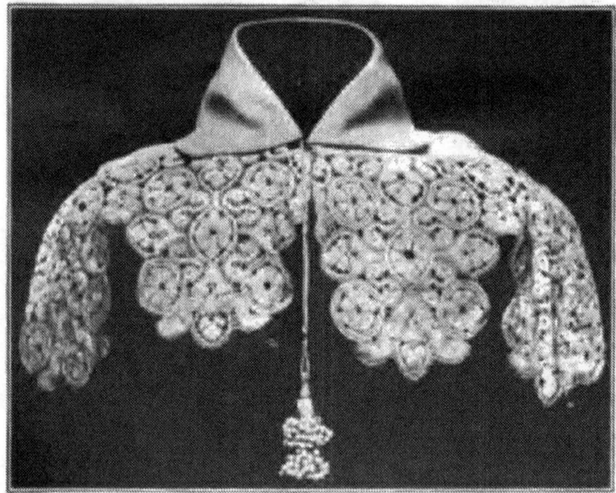

Fig. 10.—Scallopped Collar of Tape-like Pillow-made Lace.
Possibly of Engl[illegible] century work. Its texture is typical of a development in pillow-[illegible] han that of the lower edge of "merletti a piombini" in Pl. I[illegible]

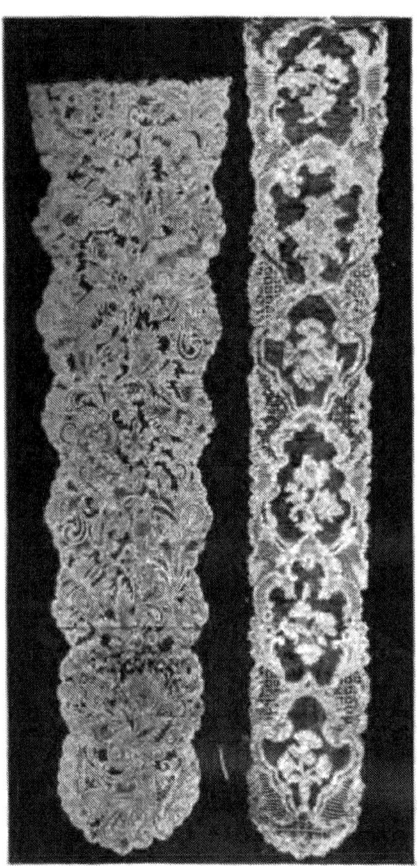

A Fig. 20. B

A.—A Lappet of "Point de Venise à Réseau."

The conventional character of the pseudo-leaf and floral forms contrasts with that of the realistic designs of contemporary French laces. Italian. Early 18th century.

B.—A Lappet of Fine "Point d'Alençon."

Louis XV. period. The variety of the fillings of geometric design is particularly remarkable in this specimen, as is the button-hole stitched cordonnat or outline to the various ornamental forms.

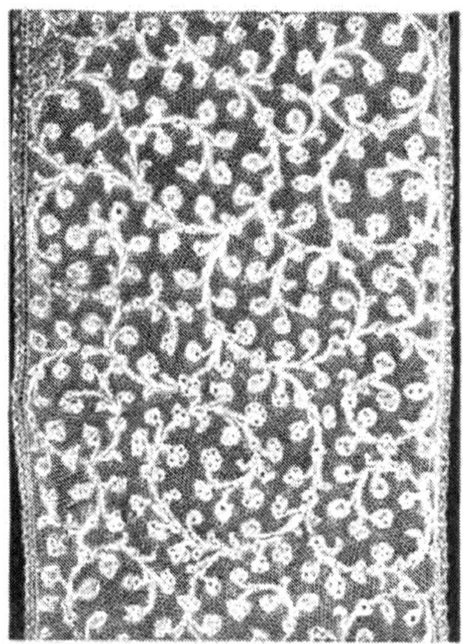

Fig. 16.—Flounce of Pillow-made Lace *à Réseau.*

Flemish, of the middle of the 17th century. This lace is usually thought to be the earliest type of "Point d'Angleterre" in contradistinction to the "Point de Flandres" (fig. 14).

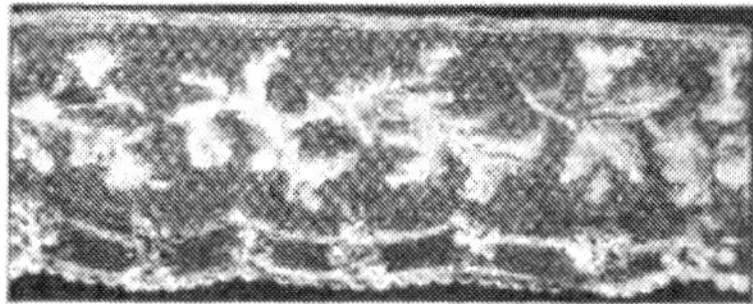

Fig. 21.—Border of French Needlepoint Lace, with Ground of "Réseau Rosacé." 18th century.

Fig. 14.—Piece of Pillow-made Lace Usually Known as "Point de Flandres à brides."

Of the middle of the 17th century, the designs for which were often adaptations from those made for such needlepoint lace as that of the Jabot in fig. 12.

[illegible] napkin or handkerchief bordered with [illegible] lace in [illegible] ch acorns [illegible] lations.

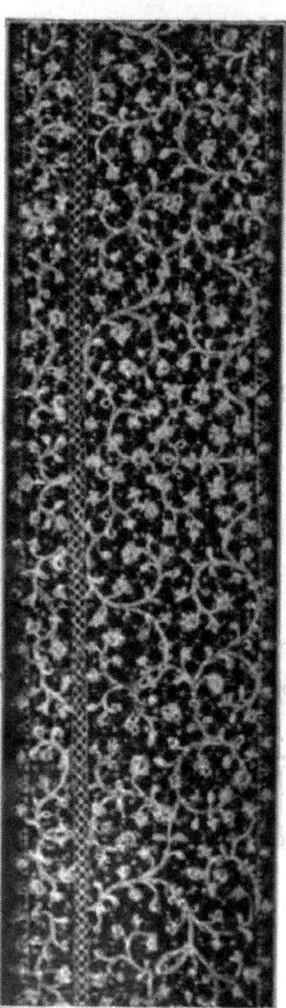

Fig. 17.—Very delicate needle-point lace with clusters of small relief work.

Venetian, middle of the 17th century, and often called "rose-point lace," and sometimes "Point de Neige."

Fig. 19.—Portion of flounce, needlepoint lace copied at the Burano Lace School from the original of the so-called "Point de Venise à Brides Picotées."

17th century. Formerly belonging to Pope Clement XIII., but now the property of the queen of Italy. The design and work, however, are indistinguishable from those of important flounces of "Point de France." The pattern consists of repetitions of two vertically-arranged groups of fantastic pine-apples and vases with flowers, intermixed with bold rococo bands and large leaf devices. The hexagonal meshes of the ground, although similar to the Venetian "brides picotées," are much akin to the button-hole stitched ground of "Point d'Argentan." (Victoria and Albert Museum.)

Fig. 18.—Charles Gaspard Guillaume de Vintimille, wearing lace similar in style of design shown in fig. 19. About 1730.

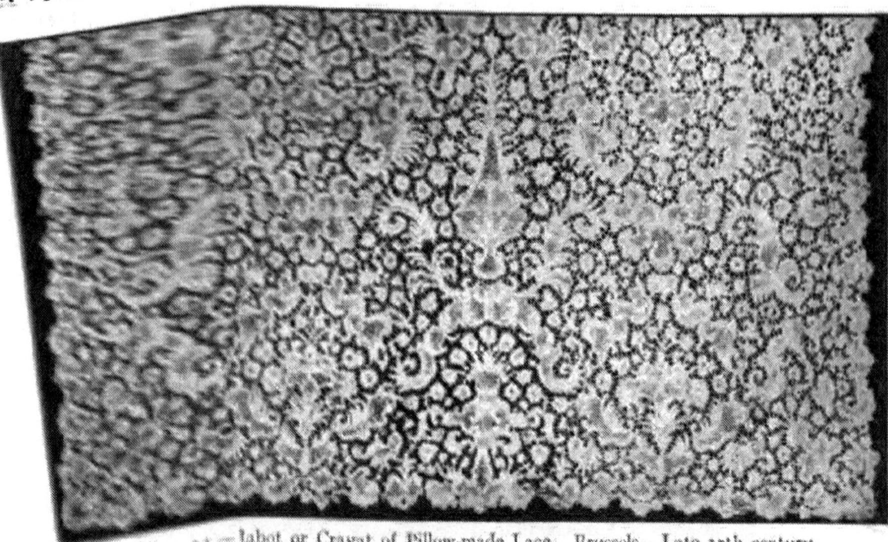

Fig. ...—Jabot or Cravat of Pillow-made Lace. Brussels. Late 17th century.
(Victoria and Albert Museum.)

...tastic Floral Design, the Ground of Which is
...d Within Small Openwork Vertical Strips.
...ria and Albert Museum.)

choir, terminating in an apse with radiating chapel, contains the fine tomb and statue of Clement VI., carved stalls and some admirable Flemish tapestries of the early 16th century. There is a ruined cloister on the south side. The church, which dates from the 14th century, was built at the expense of Pope Clement VI., and belonged to a powerful Benedictine abbey founded in 1043. There are spacious monastic buildings of the 18th century. The abbey was formerly defended by fortifications, the chief survival of which is a lofty rectangular keep to the south of the choir. Trade in timber and the making of lace chiefly occupy the inhabitants of the town.

LA CHALOTAIS, LOUIS RENÉ DE CARADEUC DE (1701–1785), French jurist, was born at Rennes, on the 6th of March 1701. He was for 60 years procureur général at the parliament of Brittany. He was an ardent opponent of the Jesuits; drew up in 1761 for the parliament a memoir on the constitutions of the Order, which did much to secure its suppression in France; and in 1763 published a remarkable "Essay on National Education," in which he proposed a programme of scientific studies as a substitute for those taught by the Jesuits. The same year began the conflict between the Estates of Brittany and the governor of the province, the duc d'Aiguillon (*q.v.*). The Estates refused to vote the extraordinary imposts demanded by the governor in the name of the king. La Chalotais was the personal enemy of d'Aiguillon, who had served him an ill turn with the king, and when the parliament of Brittany sided with the Estates, he took the lead in its opposition. The parliament forbade by decrees the levy of imposts to which the Estates had not consented. The king annulling these decrees, all the members of the parliament but twelve resigned (October 1764 to May 1765). The government considered La Chalotais one of the authors of this affair. At this time the secretary of state who administered the affairs of the province, Louis Phélypeaux, duc de la Vrillière, comte de Saint-Florentin (1705–1777), received two anonymous and abusive letters. La Chalotais was suspected of having written them, and three experts in handwriting declared that they were by him. The government therefore arrested him, his son and four other members of the parliament. The arrest made a great sensation. There was much talk of "despotism." Voltaire stated that the procureur général, in his prison of Saint Malo, was reduced, for lack of ink, to write his defence with a toothpick dipped in vinegar—which was apparently pure legend; but public opinion all over France was strongly aroused against the government. On the 16th of November 1765 a commission of judges was named to take charge of the trial. La Chalotais maintained that the trial was illegal; being procureur général he claimed the right to be judged by the parliament of Rennes, or failing this by the parliament of Bordeaux, according to the custom of the province. The judges did not dare to pronounce a condemnation on the evidence of experts in handwriting, and at the end of a year, things remained where they were at the first. Louis XV. then decided on a sovereign act, and brought the affair before his council, which without further formality decided to send the accused into exile. That expedient but increased the popular agitation; *philosophes*, members of the parliament, patriot Bretons and Jansenists all declared that La Chalotais was the victim of the personal hatred of the duc d'Aiguillon and of the Jesuits. The government at last gave way, and consented to recall the members of the parliament of Brittany who had resigned. This parliament, when it met again, after the formal accusation of the duc d'Aiguillon, demanded the recall of La Chalotais. This was accorded in 1775, and La Chalotais was allowed to transmit his office to his son. In this affair public opinion showed itself stronger than the absolutism of the king. The opposition to the royal power gained largely through it, and it may be regarded as one of the preludes to the revolution of 1789. La Chalotais, who was personally a violent, haughty and unsympathetic character, died at Rennes on the 12th of July 1785.

See, besides the *Comptes-Rendus des Constitutions des Jésuites* and the *Essai d'éducation nationale*, the *Mémoires de la Chalotais* (3 vols., 1766–1767). Two works containing detailed bibliographies are Marion; *La Bretagne et le duc d'Aiguillon* (Paris, 1893), and B. Pocquet, *Le Duc d'Aiguillon et La Chalotais* (Paris, 1901). See also a controversy between these two authors in the *Bulletin critique* for 1902.

LA CHARITÉ, a town of central France in the department of Nièvre, on the right bank of the Loire, 17 m. N.N.W. of Nevers on the Paris-Lyon-Méditerranée railway. Pop. (1906) 3990. La Charité possesses the remains of a fine Romanesque basilica, the church of Sainte-Croix, dating from the 11th and early 12th centuries. The plan consists of a nave, rebuilt at the end of the 17th century, transept and choir with ambulatory and side chapels. Surmounting the transept is an octagonal tower of one story, and a square Romanesque tower of much beauty flanks the main portal. There are ruins of the ramparts, which date from the 14th century. The manufacture of hosiery, boots and shoes, files and iron goods, lime and cement and woollen and other fabrics are among the industries; trade is chiefly in wood and iron.

La Charité owes its celebrity to its priory, which was founded in the 8th century and reorganized as a dependency of the abbey of Cluny in 1052. It became the parent of many priories and monasteries, some of them in England and Italy. The possession of the town was hotly contested during the wars of religion of the 16th century, at the end of which its fortifications were dismantled.

LA CHAUSSÉE, PIERRE CLAUDE NIVELLE DE (1692–1754), French dramatist, was born in Paris in 1692. In 1731 he published an *Épître à Clio*, a didactic poem in defence of Lériget de la Faye in his dispute with Antoine Houdart de la Motte, who had maintained that verse was useless in tragedy. La Chaussée was forty years old before he produced his first play, *La Fausse Antipathie* (1734). His second play, *Le Préjugé à la mode* (1735) turns on the fear of incurring ridicule felt by a man in love with his own wife, a prejudice dispelled in France, according to La Harpe, by La Chaussée's comedy. *L'École des amis* (1737) followed, and, after an unsuccessful attempt at tragedy in *Maximinien*, he returned to comedy in *Mélanide* (1741). In *Mélanide* the type known as *comédie larmoyante* is fully developed. Comedy was no longer to provoke laughter, but tears. The innovation consisted in destroying the sharp distinction then existing between tragedy and comedy in French literature. Indications of this change had been already offered in the work of Marivaux, and La Chaussée's plays led naturally to the domestic drama of Diderot and of Sedaine. The new method found bitter enemies. Alexis Piron nicknames the author "*le Révérend Père Chaussée*," and ridiculed him in one of his most famous epigrams. Voltaire maintained that the *comédie larmoyante* was a proof of the inability of the author to produce either of the recognized kinds of drama, though he himself produced a play of similar character in *L'Enfant prodigue*. The hostility of the critics did not prevent the public from shedding tears nightly over the sorrows of La Chaussée's heroine. *L'École des mères* (1744) and *La Gouvernante* (1747) form, with those already mentioned, the best of his work. The strict moral aims pursued by La Chaussée in his plays seem hardly consistent with his private preferences. He frequented the same gay society as did the comte de Caylus and contributed to the *Recueils de ces messieurs*. La Chaussée died on the 14th of May 1754. Villemain said of his style that he wrote prosaic verses with purity, while Voltaire, usually an adverse critic of his work, said he was "*un des premiers après ceux qui ont du génie*."

For the *comédie larmoyante* see G. Lanson, *Nivelle de la Chaussée et la comédie larmoyante* (1887).

LACHES (from Anglo-French *lachesse*, negligence, from *lasche*, modern *lâche*, unloosed, slack), a term for slackness or negligence, used particularly in law to signify negligence on the part of a person in doing that which he is by law bound to do, or unreasonable lapse of time in asserting a right, seeking relief, or claiming a privilege. Laches is frequently a bar to a remedy which might have been had if prosecuted in proper time. Statutes of limitation specify the time within which various classes of actions may be brought. Apart from statutes of limitation courts of equity will often refuse relief to those [illegible] unreasonable time to elapse in seeking it, [illegible] *vigilantibus ac non dormientibus jura sub-* [illegible]

LACHINE, [illegible] incorporated town in Jacques Cartier county, [illegible] m. W. of Montreal, on Lake St Louis, an [illegible] St Lawrence river, and at the upper end of [illegible] Pop. (1901) 5361. It is a station on the [illegible] and a port of call for steamers plying [illegible] the Great Lakes. It is a favourite summer [illegible] at Montreal. It was named in 1669 in [illegible] Robert Cavelier de la Salle (1643– [illegible] a westward passage to China. In 1689 [illegible] a terrible massacre of the French by the [illegible]

LACHISH, [illegible] of great importance in S. Palestine, often [illegible] Tell el-Amarna tablets. It was destroyed [illegible] the league against the Gibeonites (Joshua [illegible] the tribe of Judah (xv. 39) Rehoboam [illegible] King Amaziah having fled hither, [illegible] conspirators (2 Kings xiv. 19). [illegible] conducted a campaign (2 Kings xviii. 13) [illegible] endeavoured to make terms with him: [illegible] commemorated by bas-reliefs found in Nineveh, [illegible] see G. Smith's *History of Sennacherib*, [illegible] the last cities that resisted Nebuchadnezzar [illegible] meaning of Micah's denunciation (i. 13) [illegible] The *Onomasticon* places it 7 m. from [illegible] road, which agrees with the generally [illegible] Tell el-Hesi, an important mound [illegible] Exploration Fund by Petrie and [illegible] The name is preserved in a small Roman [illegible] Umm Lakis, which probably repre- [illegible] the descendants of the ancient [illegible]

[illegible] *Tell el-Hesy*, and F. J. Bliss, *A Mound* [illegible] by the Palestine Exploration Fund.
(R. A. S. M.)

LACHMANN, KARL KONRAD FRIEDRICH WILHELM [illegible] philologist and critic, was born at Bruns- [illegible] 1793. He studied at Leipzig and [illegible] mainly to philological studies. [illegible] army as a volunteer *chasseur* and [illegible] to Paris, but did not encounter the [illegible] an assistant master in the Friedrich [illegible] and a *privat-docent* at the university. [illegible] one of the principal masters in [illegible] at Königsberg, where he assisted [illegible] Friedrich Karl Köpke (1785–1865) [illegible] von Ems' *Barlaam und Josaphat* [illegible] in a contemplated edition [illegible] von der Vogelweide. In January 1818 [illegible] extraordinarius of classical philology in [illegible] and at the same time began to [illegible] grammar and the Middle High German [illegible] during the following seven years [illegible] study of those subjects, and in [illegible] in order that he might search [illegible] Germany for further materials. [illegible] nominated extraordinary professor [illegible] philology in the university of Berlin [illegible] 1830 he was admitted a member [illegible] The remainder of his laborious [illegible] and a teacher was uneventful. [illegible] 1851.

[illegible] of the first volume of P. E. [illegible] *Altertums* (1816), is a [illegible] the history of German philology [illegible] *germanischen Philologie*, 1870). [illegible] *die ursprüngliche Gestalt des* [illegible] and still more in his review of [illegible] contributed in 1817 to [illegible] already laid down the rules of [illegible] and metrical principles [illegible] which [illegible] advance in that branch of investigation. The rigidly scientific character of his method becomes increasingly apparent in the *Auswahl aus den hochdeutschen Dichtern des dreizehnten Jahrhunderts* (1820), in the edition of Hartmann's *Iwein* (1827), in those of Walther von der Vogelweide (1827) and Wolfram von Eschenbach (1833), in the papers "Über das Hildebrandslied," "Über althochdeutsche Betonung und Verskunst," "Über den Eingang des Parzivals," and "Über drei Bruchstücke niederrheinischer Gedichte" published in the *Abhandlungen* of the Berlin Academy, and in *Der Nibelunge Not und die Klage* (1826, 11th ed., 1892), which was followed by a critical commentary in 1836. Lachmann's *Betrachtungen über Homer's Ilias*, first published in the *Abhandlungen* of the Berlin Academy in 1837 and 1841, in which he sought to show that the *Iliad* consists of sixteen independent "lays" variously enlarged and interpolated, have had considerable influence on modern Homeric criticism (see HOMER), although his views are no longer accepted. His smaller edition of the New Testament appeared in 1831, 3rd ed. 1846; the larger, in two volumes, in 1842–1850. The plan of Lachmann's edition, explained by himself in the *Stud. u. Krit.* of 1830, is a modification of the unaccomplished project of Bentley. It seeks to restore the most ancient reading current in Eastern MSS., using the consent of the Latin authorities (Old Latin and Greek Western Uncials) as the main proof of antiquity of a reading where the oldest Eastern authorities differ. Besides *Propertius* (1816), Lachmann edited *Catullus* (1829); *Tibullus* (1829); *Genesius* (1834); *Terentianus Maurus* (1836); *Babrius* (1845); *Avianus* (1845); *Gaius* (1841–1842); the *Agrimensores Romani* (1848–1852); *Lucilius* (edited after his death by Vahlen, 1876); and *Lucretius* (1850). The last, which was the main occupation of the closing years of his life, from 1845, was perhaps his greatest achievement, and has been characterized by Munro as "a work which will be a landmark for scholars as long as the Latin language continues to be studied." Lachmann also translated Shakespeare's sonnets (1820) and *Macbeth* (1829).

See M. Hertz, *Karl Lachmann, eine Biographie* (1851), where a full list of Lachmann's works is given; F. Leo, *Rede zur Säcularfeier K. Lachmanns* (1893); J. Grimm, biography in *Kleine Schriften*; W. Scherer in *Allgemeine deutsche Biographie*, xvii., and J. E. Sandys, *Hist. of Classical Scholarship*, iii. (1908), pp. 127–131.

LACINIUM, PROMUNTURIUM (mod. Capo delle Colonne), 7 m S.E. of Crotona (mod. Cotrone); the easternmost point of Bruttii (mod. Calabria). On the cape still stands a single column of the temple erected to Hera Lacinia, which is said to have been fairly complete in the 16th century, but to have been destroyed to build the episcopal palace at Cotrone. It is a Doric column with capital, about 27 ft. in height. Remains of marble roof-tiles have been seen on the spot (Livy xlii. 3) and architectural fragments were excavated in 1886–1887 by the Archaeological Institute of America. The sculptures found were mostly buried again, but a few fragments, some decorative terra-cottas and a dedicatory inscription to Hera of the 6th century B.C., in private possession at Cotrone, are described by F. von Duhn in *Notizie degli scavi*, 1897, 343 seq. The date of the erection of the temple may be given as 480–440 B.C.; it is not recorded by any ancient writer.

See R. Koldewey and O. Puchstein, *Die griechischen Tempel in Unteritalien und Sicilien* (Berlin 1899, 41).

LA CIOTAT, a coast town of south-eastern France in the department of Bouches-du-Rhône, on the west shore of the Bay of La Ciotat, 26 m. S.E. of Marseilles by rail. Pop. (1906) 10,562. The port is easily accessible and well sheltered. The large shipbuilding yards and repairing docks of the Messageries Maritimes Company give employment to between 2000 and 3000 workmen. Fishing and an active coasting trade are carried on; the town is frequented for sea-bathing. La Ciotat was in ancient times the port of the neighbouring town of *Citharista* (now the village of Ceyreste).

LA CLOCHE, JAMES DE ["Prince James Stuart"] (1644 ?–1669), a character who was brought into the history of England by Lord Acton in 1862 (*Home and Foreign Review*, i. 146–174: "The Secret History of Charles II."). From information discovered by Father Boero in the archives of the Jesuits in Rome, Lord Acton averred that Charles II., when a lad at Jersey, had a natural son, James. The evidence follows. On the 2nd of April 1668, as the register of the Jesuit House of Novices at Rome attests, "there entered Jacobus de la Cloche." His baggage was exiguous, his attire was clerical. He is described as "from the island of Jersey, under the king of England, aged 24." He possessed two documents in French, purporting to have been written by Charles II. at Whitehall, on the 25th of

September 1665, and on the 7th of February 1667. In both Charles acknowledges James to be his natural son, he styles him "James de la Cloche de Bourg du Jersey," and avers that to recognize him publicly "would imperil the peace of the kingdoms"—why is not apparent. A third certificate of birth, in Latin, undated, was from Christina of Sweden, who declares that James, previously a Protestant, has been received into the church of Rome at Hamburg (where in 1667–1668 she was residing) on the 29th of July 1667. The next paper purports to be a letter from Charles II. of August 3/13 to Oliva, general of the Jesuits. The king writes, in French, that he has long wished to be secretly received into the church. He therefore desires that James, his son by a young lady "of the highest quality," and born to him when he was about sixteen, should be ordained a priest, come to England and receive him. Charles alludes to previous attempts of his own to be secretly admitted (1662). James must be sent secretly to London at once, and Oliva must say nothing to Christina of Sweden (then meditating a journey to Rome), and must never write to Charles except when James carries the letter. Charles next writes on August 29/September 9. He is most anxious that Christina should not meet James; if she knows Charles's design of changing his creed she will not keep it secret, and Charles will infallibly lose his life. With this letter there is another, written when the first had been sealed. Charles insists that James must not be accompanied, as novices were, when travelling, by a Jesuit *socius* or guardian. Charles's wife and mother have just heard that this is the rule, but the rule must be broken. James, who is to travel as "Henri de Rohan," must not come by way of France. Oliva will supply him with funds. On the back of this letter Oliva has written the draft of his brief reply to Charles (from Leghorn, October 14, 1668). He merely says that the bearer, a French gentleman (James spoke only French), will inform the king that his orders have been executed. Besides these two letters is one from Charles to James, of date August 4/14. It is addressed to "Le Prince Stuart," though none of Charles's bastards was allowed to bear the Stuart name. James is told that he may desert the clerical profession if he pleases. In that case "you may claim higher titles from us than the duke of Monmouth." (There was no higher title save prince of Wales!) If Charles and his brother, the duke of York, die childless, "the kingdoms belong to you, and parliament cannot legally oppose you, unless as, at present, they can only elect Protestant kings." This letter ought to have opened the eyes of Lord Acton and other historians who accept the myth of James de la Cloche. Charles knew that the crown of England was not elective, that there was no Exclusion Act, and that there were legal heirs if he and his brother died without issue. The last letter of Charles is dated November 18/28, and purports to have been brought from England to Oliva by James de la Cloche on his return to Rome. It reveals the fact that Oliva, despite Charles's orders, did send James by way of France, with a *socius* or guardian whom he was to pick up in France on his return to England. Charles says that James is to communicate certain matters to Oliva, and come back at once. Oliva is to give James all the money he needs, and Charles will later make an ample donation to the Jesuits. He acknowledges a debt to Oliva of £800, to be paid in six months. The reader will remark that the king has never paid a penny to James or to Oliva, and that Oliva has never communicated directly with Charles. The truth is that all of Charles's letters are forgeries. This is certain because in all he writes frequently as if his mother, Henrietta Maria, were in London, and constantly in company with him. Now she had left England for France in 1665, and to England she never returned. As the letters—including that to "Prince Stuart"—are all forged, it is clear that de la Cloche was an impostor. His aim had been to get money from Oliva, and to pretend to travel to England, meaning to enjoy himself. He did not quite succeed, for Oliva sent a *socius* with him into France. His precautions to avoid a meeting with Christina of Sweden were necessary. She knew no more of him than did Charles, and would have exposed him.

The name of James de la Cloche appears no more in documents. He reached Rome in December 1668, and in January a person calling himself "Prince James Stuart" appears in Naples, accompanied by a *socius* styling himself a French knight of Malta. Both are on their way to England, but Prince James falls ill and stays in Naples, while his companion departs. The knight of Malta may be a Jesuit. In Naples, Prince James marries a girl of no position, and is arrested on suspicion of being a coiner. To his confessors (he had two in succession) he says that he is a son of Charles II. Our sources are the despatches of Kent, the English agent at Naples, and the *Lettere*, vol. iii., of Vincenzo Armanni (1674), who had his information from one of the confessors of the "Prince." The viceroy of Naples communicated with Charles II., who disowned the impostor; Prince James, however, was released, and died at Naples in August 1669, leaving a wild will, in which he claims for his son, still unborn, the "apanage" of Monmouth or Wales, "which it is usual to bestow on natural sons of the king." The son lived till about 1750, a penniless pretender, and writer of begging letters.

It is needless to pursue Lord Acton's conjectures about later mysterious appearances of James de la Cloche at the court of Charles, or to discuss the legend that his mother was a lady of Jersey—or a sister of Charles! The Jersey myths may be found in *The Man of the Mask* (1908), by Monsignor Barnes, who argued that James was the man in the iron mask (see IRON MASK). Later Monsignor Barnes, who had observed that the letter of Charles to Prince James Stuart is a forgery, noticed the impossibility that Charles, in 1668, should constantly write of his mother as resident in London, which she left for ever in 1665.

Who de la Cloche really was it is impossible to discover, but he was a bold and successful swindler, who took in, not only the general of the Jesuits, but Lord Acton and a generation of guileless historians. (A. L.)

LA CONDAMINE, CHARLES MARIE DE (1701–1774), French geographer and mathematician, was born at Paris on the 28th of January 1701. He was trained for the military profession, but turned his attention to science and geographical exploration. After taking part in a scientific expedition in the Levant (1731), he became a member with Louis Godin and Pierre Bouguer of the expedition sent to Peru in 1735 to determine the length of a degree of the meridian in the neighbourhood of the equator. His associations with his principals were unhappy; the expedition was beset by many difficulties, and finally La Condamine separated from the rest and made his way from Quito down the Amazon, ultimately reaching Cayenne. His was the first scientific exploration of the Amazon. He returned to Paris in 1744 and published the results of his measurements and travels with a map of the Amazon in *Mém. de l'académie des sciences*, 1745 (English translation 1745–1747). On a visit to Rome La Condamine made careful measurements of the ancient buildings with a view to a precise determination of the length of the Roman foot. The journal of his voyage to South America was published in Paris in 1751. He also wrote in favour of inoculation, and on various other subjects, mainly connected with his work in South America. He died at Paris on the 4th of February 1774.

LACONIA (Gr. Λακωνική), the ancient name of the south-eastern district of the Peloponnese, of which Sparta was the capital. It has an area of some 1,048,000 acres, slightly greater than that of Somersetshire, and consists of three well-marked zones running N. and S. The valley of the Eurotas, which occupies the centre, is bounded W. by the chain of Taygetus (mod. Pentedaktylon, 7900 ft.), which starts from the Arcadian mountains on the N., and at its southern extremity forms the promontory of Taenarum (Cape Matapan). The eastern portion of Laconia consists of a far more broken range of hill country, rising in Mt. Parnon to a height of 6365 ft. and terminating in the headland of Malea. The range of Taygetus is well watered and was in ancient times covered with forests which afforded excellent hunting to the Spartans, while it had also large iron mines and quarries of an inferior bluish marble, as well as of the famous *rosso antico* of Taenarum. Far poorer are the slopes of

LACONIA—LACONICUM

[illegible] consisting for the most part of barren limestone uplands [illegible] watered. The Eurotas valley, however, is fertile, and produces at the present day maize, olives, oranges and mulberries in great abundance. Laconia has no rivers of importance except the Eurotas and its largest tributary the Oenus (mod. Kelefina). The coast, especially on the east, is rugged and dangerous. Laconia has few good harbours, nor are there any islands lying off its shores with the exception of Cythera (Cerigo), S. of Cape Malea. The most important towns, besides Sparta and Gythium, were Bryseae, Amyclae and Pharis in the Eurotas plain, Pellana and Belbina on the upper Eurotas, Sellasia on the Oenus, Caryae on the Arcadian frontier, Prasiae, Zarax and Epidaurus Limera on the east coast, Geronthrae on the slopes of Parnon, Boeae, Asopus, Helos, Las and Teuthrone on the Laconian Gulf, and Hippola, Messa and Oetylus on the Messenian Gulf.

The earliest inhabitants of Laconia, according to tradition, were the autochthonous Leleges [illegible]. Minyan immigrants then [illegible] places on the coast and even appear to have [illegible] into the interior and to have founded Amyclae. [illegible], too, visited the shores of the Laconian Gulf, [illegible] of trade at a very early period between [illegible] e.g. a number of blocks of green Laconian [illegible] the quarries at Croceae have been found in the [illegible]. In the Homeric poems Laconia [illegible] of an Achaean prince, Menelaus, whose [illegible] Therapne on the left bank of the Eurotas, [illegible] Achaean conquerors, however, probably [illegible] a suzerainty over Laconia and part [illegible] too few to occupy the whole land. [illegible] the incoming Dorians, and [illegible] the history of Laconia is that [illegible] B.C. the Laconian coast towns [illegible] the Roman general T. Quinctius [illegible] the Achaean League. When [illegible] remained independent under [illegible] the Lacedaemonians" or [illegible] Λακεδαιμονίων or Ἐλευθερο- [illegible] which was a στρατηγός (general) [illegible]. Augustus seems to have [illegible], for Pausanias (iii. 21, 6) [illegible] the twenty-four cities which [illegible] only eighteen remained as [illegible] (see ACHAEAN LEAGUE). In [illegible] devastated Laconia, and [illegible] large bands of Slavic immigrants. [illegible] the scene of vigorous struggles [illegible], Turks and Venetians, the [illegible] ruined strongholds of Mistra [illegible]) and Monemvasia, "the [illegible] east coast, and Passava near [illegible] the War of Independence was [illegible], the inhabitants of the [illegible] part of Taygetus. They [illegible] independence of the Turks [illegible] their medieval customs, living [illegible] the vendetta or blood-feud. [illegible] two departments (nomes), [illegible] capitals at Sparta and [illegible]

[illegible] Laconia [illegible] under- [illegible] important [illegible] out by [illegible] in 1904 by [illegible] Taygetus, [illegible] avated in [illegible] interest, while [illegible] unearthed [illegible] found at [illegible] Edictum [illegible] British Archaeological [illegible] of the ancient and medieval remains in Laconia. The results, of which the most important are summarized in the article SPARTA, are published in the British School *Annual*, x. ff. The acropolis of Geronthrae, a hero-shrine at Angelona in the south-eastern highlands, and the sanctuary of Ino-Pasiphae at Thalamae have also been investigated.

BIBLIOGRAPHY.—Besides the Greek histories and many of the works cited under SPARTA, see W. M. Leake, *Travels in the Morea* (London, 1830), cc. iv.-viii., xxii., xxiii.; E. Curtius, *Peloponnesos* (Gotha, 1852), ii. 203 ff.; C. Bursian, *Geographie von Griechenland* (Leipzig, 1868), ii. 102 ff.; Strabo viii. 5; Pausanias iii. and the commentary in J. G. Frazer, *Pausanias's Description of Greece* (London, 1898), vol. iii.; W. G. Clark, *Peloponnesus* (London, 1858), 155 ff.; E. P. Boblaye, *Recherches géographiques sur les ruines de la Morée* (Paris, 1835), 65 ff.; L. Ross, *Reisen im Peloponnes* (Berlin, 1841), 158 ff.; W. Vischer, *Erinnerungen u. Eindrücke aus Griechenland* (Basel, 1857), 360 ff.; J. B. G. M. Bory de Saint-Vincent, *Relation du voyage de l'expédition scientifique de Morée* (Paris, 1836), cc. 9, 10; G. A. Blouet, *Expédition scientifique de Morée* (Paris, 1831–1838), ii. 58 ff.; A. Philippson, *Der Peloponnes* (Berlin, 1892), 155 ff.; *Annual* of British School at Athens, 1907–8. *Inscriptions*: Le Bas-Foucart, *Voyage archéologique: Inscriptions*, Nos. 160-290; *Inscriptiones Graecae*, v.; *Corpus Inscriptionum Graecarum* (Berlin, 1828), Nos. 1237-1510; Collitz-Bechtel, *Sammlung der griech. Dialektinschriften*, iii. 2 (Göttingen, 1898), Nos. 4400-4613. *Coins*: *Catalogue of Greek Coins in the British Museum: Peloponnesus* (London, 1887), xlvi. ff., 121 ff.; B. V. Head, *Historia Numorum* (Oxford, 1887), 363 ff. *Cults*: S. Wide, *Lakonische Kulte* (Leipzig, 1893). *Ancient roads*: W. Loring, "Some Ancient Routes in the Peloponnese" in *Journal of Hellenic Studies*, xv. 25 ff.

(M. N. T.)

LACONIA, a city and the county-seat of Belknap county, New Hampshire, U.S.A., on both sides of the Winnepesaukee river, 28 m. N.N.E. of Concord. Pop. (1900) 8042 (1770 foreign-born); (1910) 10,183. Laconia is served by two divisions of the Boston & Maine railway, which has a very handsome granite passenger station (1892) and repair shops here. It is pleasantly situated in the lake district of central New Hampshire, and in the summer season Lake Winnisquam on the S. and W. and Lake Winnepesaukee on the N.E. attract many visitors. The city covers an area of 24·65 sq. m. (5·47 sq. m. annexed since 1890). Within the city limits, and about 6 m. from its centre, are the grounds of the Winnepesaukee Camp-Meeting Association, and the camping place for the annual reunions of the New Hampshire Veterans of the Civil War, both at The Weirs, the northernmost point in the territory claimed by colonial Massachusetts; about 2 m. from the centre of Laconia is Lakeport (pop. 1900, 2137), which, like The Weirs, is a summer resort and a ward in the city of Laconia. Among the public institutions are the State School for Feeble-minded Children, a cottage hospital and the Laconia Public Library, lodged in the Gale Memorial Library building (1903). Another fine building is the Congregational Church (1906). The New Hampshire State Fish Hatchery is in Laconia. Water-power is furnished by the river. In 1905 Laconia ranked first among the cities of the state in the manufacture of hosiery and knit goods, and the value of these products for the year was 48·4% of the total value of the city's factory product; among its other manufactures are yarn, knitting machines, needles, sashes and blinds, axles, paper boxes, boats, gas and gasolene engines, and freight, passenger and electric cars. The total value of the factory products increased from $2,152,379 in 1900 to $3,096,878 in 1905, or 43·9%. The portion of the city N. of the river, formerly known as Meredith Bridge, was set apart from the township of Meredith and incorporated as a township under the name of Laconia in 1855; a section S. of the river was taken from the township of Gilford in 1874; and Lakeport was added in 1893, when Laconia was chartered as a city. The name Laconia was first applied in New England to the region granted in 1629 to Mason and Gorges (see MASON, JOHN).

LACONICUM (*i.e.* Spartan, *sc. balneum*, bath), the dry sweating room of the Roman thermae, contiguous to the caldarium or hot room. The name was given to it as being the only form of warm bath that the Spartans admitted. The laconicum was usually a circular room with niches in the axes of the diagonals and was covered by a conical roof with a circular opening at the top.

according to Vitruvius (v. 10), "from which a brazen shield is suspended by chains, capable of being so lowered and raised as to regulate the temperature." The walls of the laconicum were plastered with marble stucco and polished, and the conical roof covered with plaster and painted blue with gold stars. Sometimes, as in the old baths at Pompeii, the laconicum was provided in an apse at one end of the caldarium, but as a rule it was a separate room raised to a higher temperature and had no bath in it. In addition to the hypocaust under the floor the wall was lined with flue tiles. The largest laconicum, about 75 ft. in diameter, was that built by Agrippa in his thermae on the south side of the Pantheon, and is referred to by Cassius (liii. 23), who states that, in addition to other works, "he constructed the hot bath chamber which he called the Laconicum Gymnasium." All traces of this building are lost; but in the additions made to the thermae of Agrippa by Septimius Severus another laconicum was built farther south, portions of which still exist in the so-called Arco di Giambella.

LACORDAIRE, JEAN BAPTISTE HENRI (1802–1861), French ecclesiastic and orator, was born at Recey-sur-Ource, Côte d'Or, on the 12th of March 1802. He was the second of a family of four, the eldest of whom, Jean Théodore (1801–1870), travelled a great deal in his youth, and was afterwards professor of comparative anatomy at Liége. For several years Lacordaire studied at Dijon, showing a marked talent for rhetoric; this led him to the pursuit of law, and in the local debates of the advocates he attained a high celebrity. At Paris he thought of going on the stage, but was induced to finish his legal training and began to practise as an advocate (1817–1824). Meanwhile Lamennais had published his *Essai sur l'Indifférence*,—a passionate plea for Christianity and in particular for Roman Catholicism as necessary for the social progress of mankind. Lacordaire read, and his ardent and believing nature, weary of the theological negations of the Encyclopaedists, was convinced. In 1823 he became a theological student at the seminary of Saint Sulpice; four years later he was ordained and became almoner of the college Henri IV. He was called from it to co-operate with Lamennais in the editorship of *L'Avenir*, a journal established to advocate the union of the democratic principle with ultramontanism. Lacordaire strove to show that Catholicism was not bound up with the idea of dynasty, and definitely allied it with a well-defined liberty, equality and fraternity. But the new propagandism was denounced from Rome in an encyclical. In the meantime Lacordaire and Montalembert, believing that, under the charter of 1830, they were entitled to liberty of instruction, opened an independent free school. It was closed in two days, and the teachers fined before the court of peers. These reverses Lacordaire accepted with quiet dignity; but they brought his relationship with Lamennais to a close. He now began the course of Christian *conférences* at the Collège Stanislas, which attracted the art and intellect of Paris; thence he went to Nôtre Dame, and for two years his sermons were the delight of the capital. His presence was dignified, his voice capable of indefinite modulation, and his gestures animated and attractive. He still preached the gospel of the people's sovereignty in civil life and the pope's supremacy in religion, but brought to his propagandism the full resources of a mind familiar with philosophy, history and literature, and indeed led the reaction against Voltairean scepticism. He was asked to edit the *Univers*, and to take a chair in the university of Louvain, but he declined both appointments, and in 1838 set out for Rome, revolving a great scheme for christianizing France by restoring the old order of St Dominic. At Rome he donned the habit of the preaching friar and joined the monastery of Minerva. His *Mémoire pour le rétablissement en France de l'ordre des frères prêcheurs* was then prepared and dedicated to his country; at the same time he collected the materials for the life of St Dominic. When he returned to France in 1841 he resumed his preaching at Nôtre Dame, but he had small success in re-establishing the order of which he ever afterwards called himself monk. His funeral orations are the most notable in their kind of any delivered during his time, those devoted to Marshal Drouet and Daniel O'Connell being especially marked by point and clearness. He next thought that his presence in the National Assembly would be of use to his cause; but being rebuked by his ecclesiastical superiors for declaring himself a republican, he resigned his seat ten days after his election. In 1850 he went back to Rome and was made provincial of the order, and for four years laboured to make the Dominicans a religious power. In 1854 he retired to Sorrèze to become director of a private lyceum, and remained there until he died on the 22nd of November 1861. He had been elected to the Academy in the preceding year.

The best edition of Lacordaire's works is the *Œuvres complètes* (6 vols., Paris, 1872–1873), published by C. Poussielgue, which contains, besides the *Conférences*, the exquisitely written, but uncritical, *Vie de Saint Dominique* and the beautiful *Lettres à un jeune homme sur la vie chrétienne*. For a complete list of his published correspondence see L. Petit de Julleville's *Histoire de la langue et de la littérature française*, vii. 598.

The authoritative biography is by Ch. Foisset (2 vols., Paris, 1870). The religious aspect of his character is best shown in Père B. Chocarne's *Vie du Père Lacordaire* (2 vols., Paris, 1866—English translation by A. Th. Drane, London, 1868); see also Count C. F. R. de Montalembert's *Un Moine au XIXème siècle* (Paris, 1862—English translation by F. Aylward, London, 1867). There are lives by Mrs H. L. Lear (London, 1882); by A. Ricard (1 vol. of *L'École menaisienne*, Paris, 1883); by Comte O. d'Haussonville (1 vol., *Les Grands écrivains français* series, Paris, 1897); by Gabriel Ledos (Paris, 1901); by Dora Greenwell (1867); and by the duc de Broglie (Paris, 1889). The *Correspondance inédite du Père Lacordaire*, edited by H. Villard (Paris, 1870), may also be consulted. See also Saint-Beuve in *Causeries du Lundi*. Several of Lacordaire's *Conférences* have been translated into English, among these being, *Jesus Christ* (1869); *God* (1870); *God and Man* (1872); *Life* (1875). For a theological study of the *Conférences de Nôtre Dame*, see an article by Bishop J. C. Hedley in *Dublin Review* (October 1870).

LACQUER, or **LACKER**, a general term for coloured and frequently opaque varnishes applied to certain metallic objects and to wood. The term is derived from the resin lac, which substance is the basis of lacquers properly so called. Technically, among Western nations, lacquering is restricted to the coating of polished metals or metallic surfaces, such as brass, pewter and tin, with prepared varnishes which will give them a golden, bronze-like or other lustre as desired. Throughout the East Indies the lacquering of wooden surfaces is universally practised; large articles of household furniture, as well as small boxes, trays, toys and papier-mâché objects, being decorated with bright-coloured and variegated lacquer. The lacquer used in the East is, in general, variously coloured sealing-wax, applied, smoothed and polished in a heated condition; and by various devices intricate marbled, streaked and mottled designs are produced. Quite distinct from these, and from all other forms of lacquer, is the lacquer work of Japan, for which see JAPAN, § *Art*.

LACRETELLE, PIERRE LOUIS DE (1751–1824), French politician and writer, was born at Metz on the 9th of October 1751. He practised as a barrister in Paris; and under the Revolution was elected as a *député suppléant* in the Constituent Assembly, and later as deputy in the Legislative Assembly. He belonged to the moderate party known as the "Feuillants," but after the 10th of August 1792 he ceased to take part in public life. In 1803 he became a member of the Institute, taking the place of La Harpe. Under the Restoration he was one of the chief editors of the *Minerve française*; he wrote also an essay, *Sur le 18 Brumaire* (1799), some *Fragments politiques et littéraires* (1817), and a treatise *Des partis politiques et des factions de la prétendue aristocratie d'aujourd'hui* (1819).

His younger brother, JEAN CHARLES DOMINIQUE DE LACRETELLE, called Lacretelle *le jeune* (1766–1855), historian and journalist, was also born at Metz on the 3rd of September 1766. He was called to Paris by his brother in 1787, and during the Revolution belonged, like him, to the party of the *Feuillants*. He was for some time secretary to the duc de la Rochefoucauld-Liancourt, the celebrated philanthropist, and afterwards joined the staff of the *Journal de Paris*, then managed by Suard, and where he had as colleagues André Chénier and Antoine Roucher. He made no attempt to hide his monarchist sympathies, and this, together with the way in which he reported the trial and death of Louis XVI., brought him in peril of his life; to avoid this [illegible] in the army, but after Thermidor he returned [illegible] his newspaper work. He was involved in the [illegible] of the 13th Vendémiaire, and condemned to [illegible] after the 18th Fructidor; but, thanks to powerful [illegible] "forgotten" in prison till after the 18th Bru[illegible] he was set at liberty by Fouché. Under the Empire [illegible] professor of history in the *Faculté des lettres* [illegible] and elected as a member of the Académie fran[illegible] in 1827 he was prime mover in the protest made by [illegible] Academy against the minister Peyronnet's law on the [illegible] to the failure of that measure, but this step cost [illegible], his post as *censeur royal*. Under Louis [illegible] himself entirely to his teaching and literary [illegible] he retired to Mâcon; but there, as in Paris, he [illegible] of a brilliant circle, for he was a wonderful *causeur*, [illegible] equally good listener, and had many interesting ex[illegible] to recall. He died on the 26th of March 1855. [illegible] Pierre Henri (1815–1899) was a humorous writer and [illegible] of purely contemporary interest.

[illegible] Lacretelle's chief work is a series of histories of the 18th [illegible] Revolution and its sequel: *Précis historique de la [illegible] française* appended to the history of Rabaud St Étienne, [illegible] written in the prison of La Force (5 vols., 1801–1806); [illegible] *France pendant le XVIIIe siècle* (6 vols., 1808); *Histoire* [illegible] (2 vols., 1821); *L'Assemblée Législative* [illegible] *Convention Nationale* (3 vols., 1824–1825); *Histoire de* [illegible] (1829–1835); *Histoire du consulat et* [illegible] vols. 1846. The author was a moderate and fair-[illegible] possessed neither great powers of style, nor striking [illegible] the special historian's power of writing minute [illegible] breadth of view. Carlyle's sarcastic remark [illegible] of the Revolution, that it "exists, but does [illegible]" a pretty true of all his books. He had been an eye-[illegible] actor in the events which he describes, but his [illegible] be accepted with caution.

LACROIX, ANTOINE FRANÇOIS ALFRED (1863–), [illegible] and geologist, was born at Mâcon, Saône et [illegible] of February 1863. He took the degree of [illegible] In 1893 he was appointed professor of [illegible] *Jardin des Plantes*, Paris, and in 1896 director [illegible] laboratory in the *École des Hautes Études*. [illegible] to minerals connected with volcanic [illegible] rocks, to the effects of metamorphism, [illegible] various parts of the world, notably in [illegible] numerous contributions to scientific [illegible] the mineralogy and petrology of Mada-[illegible] elaborate and exhaustive volume [illegible] *La Montagne Pelée et ses érup-*[illegible] an important work entitled *Minéra-*[illegible] (1893–1898), and other works [illegible] Michel Levy. He was elected member [illegible] 1904.

LACROIX, PAUL (1806–1884), French author and journalist, [illegible] of April 1806, the son of a novelist. [illegible] pseudonym of P. L. Jacob, *bibliophile*, [illegible] suggested by the constant interest he [illegible] books generally. Lacroix was an [illegible] writer. Over twenty historical [illegible] and he also wrote a variety [illegible] a history of Napoleon III., [illegible] Nicholas I. of Russia. He [illegible] of a five-volume work, [illegible] a standard work on the [illegible] the chief merit of [illegible] illustrations it contains. He [illegible] of the history of culture [illegible] published an exhaustive [illegible] which has always been [illegible] bibliography were also [illegible] appointed librarian of the [illegible] the 16th of October [illegible]

LACROMA, [illegible]

and lying less than half a mile south of Ragusa. Though barely 1¼ m. in length, Lacroma is remarkable for the beauty of its subtropical vegetation. It was a favourite resort of the archduke Maximilian, afterwards emperor of Mexico (1832–1867), who restored the château and park; and of the Austrian crown prince Rudolph (1857–1889). It contains an 11th-century Benedictine monastery; and the remains of a church, said by a very doubtful local tradition to have been founded by Richard I. of England (1157–1199), form part of the imperial château.

See *Lacroma*, an illustrated descriptive work by the crown princess Stéphanie (afterwards Countess Lónyay)(Vienna, 1892).

LA CROSSE, a city and the county-seat of La Crosse county, Wisconsin, U.S.A., about 180 m. W.N.W. of Milwaukee, and about 120 m. S.E. of St Paul, Minnesota, on the E. bank of the Mississippi river, at the mouth of the Black and of the La Crosse rivers. Pop. (1900) 28,895; (1910 census) 30,417. Of the total population in 1900, 7222 were foreign-born, 3130 being German and 2023 Norwegian, and 17,555 were of foreign-parentage (both parents foreign-born), including 7853 of German parentage, 4422 of Norwegian parentage, and 1062 of Bohemian parentage. La Crosse is served by the Chicago & North Western, the Chicago, Milwaukee & St Paul, the Chicago, Burlington & Quincy, the La Crosse & South Eastern, and the Green Bay & Western railways, and by river steamboat lines on the Mississippi. The river is crossed here by a railway bridge (C.M. & St P.) and wagon bridge. The city is situated on a prairie, extending back from the river about 2½ m. to bluffs, from which fine views may be obtained. Among the city's buildings and institutions are the Federal Building (1886–1887), the County Court House (1902–1903), the Public Library (with more than 20,000 volumes), the City Hall (1891), the High School Building (1905–1906), the St Francis, La Crosse and Lutheran hospitals, a Young Men's Christian Association Building, a Young Women's Christian Association Building, a U.S. Weather Station (1907), and a U.S. Fish Station (1905). La Crosse is the seat of a state Normal School (1909). Among the city's parks are Pettibone (an island in the Mississippi), Riverside, Burns, Fair Ground and Myrick. The city is the see of a Roman Catholic bishop. La Crosse is an important lumber and grain market, and is the principal wholesale distributing centre for a large territory in S.W. Wisconsin, N. Iowa and Minnesota. Proximity to both pine and hardwood forests early made it one of the most important lumber manufacturing places in the North-west; but this industry has now been displaced by other manufactures. The city has grain elevators, flour mills (the value of flour and grist mill products in 1905 was $2,166,116), and breweries (product value in 1905, $1,440,659). Other important manufactures are agricultural implements ($542,425 in 1905), lumber and planing mill products, leather, woollen knit and rubber goods, tobacco, cigars and cigarettes, carriages, foundry and machine-shop products, copper and iron products, cooperage, pearl buttons, brooms and brushes. The total value of the factory product in 1905 was $8,139,432, as against $7,676,581 in 1900. The city owns and operates its water-works system, the wagon bridge (1890–1891) across the Mississippi, and a toll road (2½ m. long) to the village of La Crescent, Minn.

Father Hennepin and du Lhut visited or passed the site of La Crosse as early as 1680, but it is possible that adventurous *coureurs-des-bois* preceded them. The first permanent settlement was made in 1841, and La Crosse was made the county-seat in 1855 and was chartered as a city in 1856.

LACROSSE, the national ball game of Canada. It derives its name from the resemblance of its chief implement used, the curved netted stick, to a bishop's crozier. It was borrowed from the Indian tribes of North America. In the old days, according to Catlin, the warriors of two tribes in their war-paint would form the sides, often 800 or 1000 strong. The goals were placed from 500 yds. to ½ m. apart with practically no side boundaries. A solemn dance preceded the game, after which the ball was tossed into the air and the two sides rushed to catch it on "crosses," similar to those now in use. The medicine-men acted as umpires, and the squaws urged on the men by beating them with switches. The game attracted much attention from the early French settlers in Canada. In 1763, after Canada had become British, the game was used by the aborigines to carry out an ingenious piece of treachery. On the 4th of June, when the garrison of Fort Michilimackinac (now Mackinac) was celebrating the king's birthday, it was invited by the Ottawas, under their chief Pontiac, to witness a game of "baggataway" (lacrosse). The players gradually worked their way close to the gates, when, throwing aside their crosses and seizing their tomahawks which the squaws suddenly produced from under their blankets, they rushed into the fort and massacred all the inmates except a few Frenchmen.

The game found favour among the British settlers, but it was not until 1867, the year in which Canada became a Dominion, that G. W. Beers, a prominent player, suggested that Lacrosse should be recognized as the national game, and the National Lacrosse Association of Canada was formed. From that time the game has flourished vigorously in Canada and to a less extent in the United States. In 1868 an English Lacrosse Association was formed, but, although a team of Indians visited the United Kingdom in 1867, it was not until sometime later that the game became at all popular in Great Britain. Its progress was much encouraged by visits of teams representing the Toronto Lacrosse Club in 1888 and 1902, the methods of the Canadians and their wonderful "short-passing" exciting much admiration. In 1907 the Capitals of Ottawa visited England, playing six matches, all of which were won by the Canadians. The match North *v.* South has been played annually in England since 1882. A county championship was inaugurated in 1905. A North of England League, embracing ten clubs, began playing league matches in 1897; and a match between the universities of Oxford and Cambridge has been played annually since 1903. A match between England and Ireland was played annually from 1881 to 1904.

Implements of the Game.—The ball is made of indiarubber sponge, weighs between $4\frac{1}{2}$ and $4\frac{3}{4}$ oz., and measures 8 to $8\frac{1}{4}$ in. in circumference. The "crosse" is formed of a light staff of hickory wood, the top being bent to form a kind of hook, from the tip of which a thong is drawn and made fast to the shaft about 2 ft. from the other end. The oval triangle thus formed is covered with a network of gut or rawhide, loose enough to hold the ball but not to form a bag. At no

The Crosse.

part must the crosse measure more than 12 in. in breadth, and no metal must be used in its manufacture. It may be of any length to suit the player. The goals are set up not less than 100 nor more than 150 yds. apart, the goal-posts being 6 ft. high and the same distance apart. They are set up in the middle of the "goal-crease," a space of 12 ft. square marked with chalk. A net extends from the top rail and sides of the posts back to a point 6 ft. behind the middle of the line between the posts. Boundaries are agreed upon by the captains. Shoes may have indiarubber soles, but must be without spikes.

The Game.—The object of the game is to send the ball, by means of the crosse, through the enemy's goal-posts as many times as possible during the two periods of play, precisely as in football and hockey. There are twelve players on each side. In every position save that of goal there are two men, one of each side, whose duties are to "mark" and neutralize each other's efforts. The game is opened by the act of "facing," in which the two centres, each with his left shoulder towards his opponents' goal, hold their crosses, wood downwards, on the ground, the ball being placed between them. When the signal is given the centres draw their crosses sharply inwards in order to gain possession of the ball. The ball may be kicked or struck with the crosse, as at hockey, but the goal-keeper alone may handle it, and then only to block and not to throw it. Although the ball may be thrown with the crosse for a long distance—220 yds. is about the limit—long throws are seldom tried, it being generally more advantageous for a player to run with the ball resting on the crosse, until he can pass it to a member of his side who proceeds with the attack, either by running, passing to another, or trying to throw the ball through the opponents' goal. The crosse, usually held in both hands, is made to retain the ball by an ingenious rocking motion only acquired by practice. As there is no "off-side" in Lacrosse, a player may pass the ball to the front, side or rear. No charging is allowed, but one player may interfere with another by standing directly in front of him ("body-check"), though without holding, tripping or striking with the crosse. No one may interfere with a player who is not in possession of the ball. Fouls are penalized either by the suspension of the offender until a goal has been scored or until the end of the game; or by allowing the side offended against a "free position." When a "free position" is awarded each player must stand in the position where he is, excepting the goal-keeper who may get back to his goal, and any opponent who may be nearer the player getting the ball than 5 yds.; this player must retire to that distance from the one who has been given the "free position," who then proceeds with the game as he likes when the referee says "play." This penalty may not be carried out nearer than 10 yds. from the goal. If the ball crosses a boundary the referee calls "stand," and all players stop where they are, the ball being then "faced" not less than 4 yds. within the boundary line by the two nearest players.

See the official publications of the English Lacrosse Union; and *Lacrosse* by W. C. Schmeisser, in Spalding's "Athletic Library." Also *Manners, Customs and Condition of the North American Indians*, by George Catlin.

LA CRUZ, RAMÓN DE (1731–1794), Spanish dramatist, was born at Madrid on the 28th of March 1731. He was a clerk in the ministry of finance, and is the author of three hundred *sainetes*, little farcical sketches of city life, written to be played between the acts of a longer play. He published a selection in ten volumes (Madrid, 1786–1791), and died on the 5th of March 1794. The best of his pieces, such as *Las Tertulias de Madrid*, are delightful specimens of satiric observation.

See E. Cotarelo y Mori, *Don Ramón de la Cruz y sus obras* (Madrid, 1899); C. Cambronero, *Sainetes inéditos existentes en la Biblioteca Municipal de Madrid* (Madrid, 1900).

LACRYMATORY (from Lat. *lacrima*, a tear), a class of small vessels of terra-cotta, or, more frequently, of glass, found in Roman and late Greek tombs, and supposed to have been bottles into which mourners dropped their tears. They contained unguents, and to the use of unguents at funeral ceremonies the finding of so many of these vessels in tombs is due. They are shaped like a spindle, or a flask with a long small neck and a body in the form of a bulb.

LACTANTIUS FIRMIANUS (*c.* 260–*c.* 340), also called Lucius Caelius (or Caecilius) Lactantius Firmianus, was a Christian writer who from the beauty of his style has been called the "Christian Cicero." His history is very obscure. He was born of heathen parents in Africa about 260, and became a pupil of Arnobius, whom he far excelled in style though his knowledge of the Scriptures was equally slight. About 290 he went to Nicomedia in Bithynia while Diocletian was emperor, to teach rhetoric, but found little work to do in that Greek-speaking city. In middle age he became a convert to Christianity, and about 306 he went to Gaul (Trèves) on the invitation of Constantine the Great, and became tutor to his eldest son, Crispus. He probably died about 340.

Lactantius' chief work, *Divinarum Institutionum Libri Septem*, is an "apology" for and an introduction to Christianity, written in exquisite Latin, but displaying such ignorance as to have incurred the charge of favouring the Arian and Manichaean heresies. It seems to have been begun in Nicomedia about 304 and finished in Gaul before 311. Two long eulogistic addresses and most of the brief apostrophes to the emperor are from a later hand, which has added some dualistic touches. The seven books of the institutions have separate titles given to them either by the author or by a later editor. The first, *De Falsa Religione*, and the second, *De Origine Erroris*, attack the polytheism of heathendom, show the unity of the God of creation and providence, and try to explain how men have been corrupted by demons. The third book, *De Falsa Sapientia*, describes and criticizes the various systems of prevalent philosophy. The fourth book, *De Vera Sapientia et Religione*, insists upon the inseparable union of true wisdom and true religion, and maintains that this union is made real in the person of Christ. The fifth book, *De Justitia*, maintains that true righteousness is not to be found apart from Christianity, and that it springs from piety which consists in the knowledge of God. The sixth book, *De Vero Cultu*, describes the true worship of God, which is righteousness.

[illegible] chiefly in the exercise of Christian love towards [illegible]. The seventh book, *De Vita Beata*, discusses, [illegible] variety of subjects, the chief good, immortality, the [illegible] and the resurrection. Jerome states that [illegible] wrote an epitome of these *Institutions*, and such a [illegible] may well be authentic, was discovered in MS. in the [illegible] in 1711 by C. M. Pfaff.

[illegible] Lactantius wrote several treatises: [illegible] addressed to one Donatus and directed against [illegible] philosophy. (2) *De Opificio Dei sive de Formatione* [illegible] work, and one which reveals very little [illegible]. He exhorts a former pupil, Demetrianus, [illegible] by wealth from virtue; and he demonstrates [illegible] from the adaptability and beauty of the [illegible]. A [illegible] incendiary treatise, *De Mortibus* [illegible] describes God's judgments on the persecutors [illegible] Nero to Diocletian, and has served as a model [illegible]. *De Mort. Persecut.* is not in the earlier [illegible] it was discovered and printed by Baluze [illegible] ascribe it to an unknown Lucius Caecilius; [illegible] differences of grammar, style and [illegible] the writings already mentioned. It was [illegible] at Nicomedia, c. 315. Jerome speaks of [illegible] and several poems have been attributed [illegible] which Harnack thinks makes use of [illegible] and *De Resurrectione (Domini)* [illegible]. The first of these may [illegible] days, the second is a product of [illegible] the third was written by Venantius [illegible].

[illegible] Gersdorf's *Bibl. patr. eccl.* x., xi. [illegible]; S. Brandt and G. [illegible] *Lat.* xix., xxvii. 1 and [illegible] Fletcher in *Ante-Nicene Fathers*, [illegible] early Christian literature, [illegible] A. Ebert, A. Ehrhard, G. Krüger's [illegible] *Realencyk.* vol. xi., give [illegible] on the subject.

[illegible] Two lactic [illegible] from each other in the position [illegible] group in the molecule; they are [illegible] acid (fermentation or [illegible] hydroxypropionic [illegible]. Although [illegible] two hydroxypropionic [illegible] are known. The third [illegible] (J. v. Liebig), [illegible] on [illegible] It is identical with [illegible], except with [illegible] formed [illegible] resembles [illegible] on polarized [illegible]

[illegible]

It forms a colourless syrup, of specific gravity 1·2485 (15°/4°), and decomposes on distillation under ordinary atmospheric pressure; but at very low pressures (about 1 mm.) it distils at about 85° C., and then sets to a crystalline solid, which melts at about 18° C. It possesses the properties both of an acid and of an alcohol. When heated with dilute sulphuric acid to 130° C., under pressure, it is resolved into formic acid and acetaldehyde. Chromic acid oxidises it to acetic acid and carbon dioxide; potassium permanganate oxidizes it to pyruvic acid; nitric acid to oxalic acid, and a mixture of manganese dioxide and sulphuric acid to acetaldehyde and carbon dioxide. Hydrobromic acid converts it into α-brompropionic acid, and hydriodic acid into propionic acid.

Lactide, $O<\begin{matrix}CH(CH_3)\cdot CO\\ CO\cdot CH(CH_3)\end{matrix}>O$, a crystalline solid, of melting-point 124° C., is one of the products obtained by the distillation of lactic acid.

LACTONES, the cyclic esters of hydroxy acids, resulting from the internal elimination of water between the hydroxyl and carboxyl groups, this reaction taking place when the hydroxy acid is liberated from its salts by a mineral acid. The α and β-hydroxy acids do not form lactones, the tendency for lactone formation appearing first with the γ-hydroxy acids, thus γ-hydroxybutyric acid, $CH_2OH\cdot CH_2\cdot CH_2\cdot CO_2H$, yields γ-butyrolactone, $CH_2\cdot CH_2\cdot CH_2\cdot CO\cdot O$. These compounds may also be prepared by the distillation of the γ-halogen fatty acids, or by the action of alkaline carbonates on these acids, or from βγ- or γδ-unsaturated acids by digestion with hydrobromic acid or dilute sulphuric acid. The lactones are mostly liquids which are readily soluble in alcohol, ether and water. On boiling with water, they are partially reconverted into the hydroxy acids. They are easily saponified by the caustic alkalis.

On the behaviour of lactones with ammonia, see H. Meyer, *Monatshefte*, 1899, 20, p. 717; and with phenylhydrazine and hydrazine hydrate, see R. Meyer, *Ber.*, 1893, 26, p. 1273; L. Gattermann, *Ber.*, 1899, 32, p. 1133, E. Fischer, *Ber.*, 1889, 22, p. 1889.

γ-Butyrolactone is a liquid which boils at 206° C. It is miscible with water in all proportions and is volatile in steam. *γ-valerolactone*, $CH_3\cdot CH\cdot CH_2\cdot CH_2\cdot CO\cdot O$, is a liquid which boils at 207–208° C. *δ-lactones* are also known, and may be prepared by distilling the δ-chlor acids.

LA CUEVA, JUAN DE (1550?–1609?), Spanish dramatist and poet, was born at Seville, and towards 1579 began writing for the stage. His plays, fourteen in number, were published in 1588, and are the earliest manifestations of the dramatic methods developed by Lope de Vega. Abandoning the Senecan model hitherto universal in Spain, Cueva took for his themes matters of national legend, historic tradition, recent victories and the actualities of contemporary life: this amalgam of epical and realistic elements, and the introduction of a great variety of metres, prepared the way for the Spanish romantic drama of the 17th century. A peculiar interest attaches to *El Infamador*, a play in which the character of Leucino anticipates the classic type of Don Juan. As an initiative force, Cueva is a figure of great historical importance; his epic poem, *La Conquista de Bética* (1603), shows his weakness as an artist. The last work to which his name is attached is the *Ejemplar poético* (1609), and he is believed to have died shortly after its publication.

See the editions of *Saco de Roma* and *El Infamador*, by E. de Ochoa, in the *Tesoro del teatro español* (Paris, 1838), vol. i. pp. 251-285; and of *Ejemplar poético*, by J. J. López de Sedano, in the *Parnaso español*, vol. viii. pp. 1-68; also E. Walberg, "Juan de la Cueva et son Exemplar poétice" in the *Acta Universitatis Lundensis* (Lund, 1904), vol. xxix.; "Poèmes inédits de Juan de la Cueva (Viaje de Sannio)" edited by F. A. Wulff, in the *Acta Universitatis Lundensis* (Lund, 1886-1887), vol. xxiii.; F. A. Wulff, "De la rimas de Juan de la Cueva, Primera Parte" in the *Homenaje a Menéndez y Pelayo* (Madrid, 1899), vol. ii. pp. 143-148. (J. F.-K.)

LACUNAR, the Latin name in architecture for a panelled or coffered ceiling or soffit. The word is derived from *lacuna*, a cavity or hollow, a blank, hiatus or gap. The panels or coffers of a ceiling are by Vitruvius called *lacunaria*.

LACUZON (Fr. *la cuzon*, disturbance), the name given to the Franc Comtois leader CLAUDE PROST (1607–1681), who was born at Longchaumois (department of Jura) on the 17th June 1607. He gained his first military experience when [illegible] invaded Burgundy in 1636, harrying the French troops from the castles of Montaigu and St Laurent-la-Roche, and devastating the frontier districts of Bresse and Bugey with fire and sword (1640–1642). In the first invasion of Franche-Comté by Louis XIV. in 1668 Lacuzon was unable to make any effective resistance, but he played an important part in Louis's second invasion. In 1673 he defended Salins for some time; after the capitulation of the town he took refuge in Italy. He died at Milan on the 21st of December 1681.

LACY, FRANZ MORITZ, Count (1725–1801), Austrian field marshal, was born at St Petersburg on the 21st of October 1725. His father, Peter, Count Lacy, was a distinguished Russian soldier, who belonged to an Irish family, and had followed the fortunes of the exiled James II. Franz Moritz was educated in Germany for a military career, and entered the Austrian service. He served in Italy, Bohemia, Silesia and the Netherlands during the War of the Austrian Succession, was twice wounded, and by the end of the war was a lieut.-colonel. At the age of twenty-five he became full colonel and chief of an infantry regiment. In 1756 with the opening of the Seven Years' War he was again on active service, and in the first battle (Lobositz) he distinguished himself so much that he was at once promoted major-general. He received his third wound on this occasion and his fourth at the battle of Prague in 1757. Later in 1757 Lacy bore a conspicuous part in the great victory of Breslau, and at Leuthen, where he received his fifth wound, he covered the retreat of the defeated army. Soon after this began his association with Field-Marshal Daun, the new generalissimo of the empress's forces, and these two commanders, powerfully assisted later by the genius of Loudon, made head against Frederick the Great for the remainder of the war. A general staff was created, and Lacy, a lieutenant field-marshal at thirty-two, was made chief of staff (quartermaster-general) to Daun. That their cautiousness often degenerated into timidity may be admitted—Leuthen and many other bitter defeats had taught the Austrians to respect their great opponent—but they showed at any rate that, having resolved to wear out the enemy by Fabian methods, they were strong enough to persist in their resolve to the end. Thus for some years the life of Lacy, as of Daun and Loudon, is the story of the war against Prussia (see Seven Years' War). After Hochkirch (October 15, 1758) Lacy received the grand cross of the Maria Theresa order. In 1759 both Daun and Lacy fell into disfavour for failing to win victories, and Lacy owed his promotion to Feldzeugmeister only to the fact that Loudon had just received this rank for the brilliant conduct of his detachment at Kunersdorf. His responsibilities told heavily on Lacy in the ensuing campaigns, and his capacity for supreme command was doubted even by Daun, who refused to give him the command when he himself was wounded at the battle of Torgau.

After the peace of Hubertusburg a new sphere of activity was opened, in which Lacy's special gifts had the greatest scope. Maria Theresa having placed her son, the emperor Joseph II., at the head of Austrian military affairs, Lacy was made a field-marshal, and given the task of reforming and administering the army (1766). He framed new regulations for each arm, a new code of military law, a good supply system. As the result of his work the Austrian army was more numerous, far better equipped, and cheaper than it had ever been before. Joseph soon became very intimate with his military adviser, but this did not prevent his mother, after she became estranged from the young emperor, from giving Lacy her full confidence. His activities were not confined to the army. He was in sympathy with Joseph's innovations, and was regarded by Maria Theresa as a prime mover in the scheme for the partition of Poland. But his self-imposed work broke down Lacy's health, and in 1773, in spite of the remonstrances of Maria Theresa and of the emperor, he laid down all his offices and went to southern France. On returning he was still unable to resume office, though as an unofficial adviser in political and military matters he was far from idle. In the brief and uneventful War of the Bavarian Succession, Lacy and Loudon were the chief Austrian commanders against the king of Prussia, and when Joseph II. at Maria Theresa's death, became the sovereign of the Austrian dominions as well as emperor, Lacy remained his most trusted friend. More serious than the War of the Bavarian Succession was the Turkish war which presently broke out. Lacy was now old and worn out, and his tenure of command therein was not marked by any greater measure of success than in the case of the other Austrian generals. His active career was at an end, although he continued his effective interest in the affairs of the state and the army throughout the reign of Joseph's successor, Leopold I. His last years were spent in retirement at his castle of Neuwaldegg near Vienna. He died at Vienna on the 24th of November 1801.

See memoir by A. v. Arneth in *Allgemeine deutsche Biographie* (Leipzig, 1883).

LACY, HARRIETTE DEBORAH (1807–1874), English actress, was born in London, the daughter of a tradesman named Taylor. Her first appearance on the stage was at Bath in 1827 as Julia in *The Rivals*, and she was immediately given leading parts there in both comedy and tragedy. Her first London appearance was in 1830 as Nina, in Dimond's *Carnival of Naples*. Her Rosalind, Aspatia (to Macready's Melantius) in *The Bridal*, and Lady Teazle to the Charles Surface of Walter Lacy (1809–1898)—to whom she was married in 1839—confirmed her position and popularity. She was the original Helen in *The Hunchback* (1832), and also created Nell Gwynne in Jerrold's play of that name, and the heroine in his *Housekeeper*. She was considered the first Ophelia of her day. She retired in 1848.

LACY, MICHAEL ROPHINO (1795–1867), Irish musician, son of a merchant, was born at Bilbao and appeared there in public as a violinist in 1801. He was sent to study in Paris under Kreutzer, and soon began a successful career, being known as "*Le Petit Espagnol*." He played in London for some years after 1805, and then became an actor, but in 1818 resumed the musical profession, and in 1820 became leader of the ballet at the King's theatre, London. He composed or adapted from other composers a number of operas and an oratorio, *The Israelites in Egypt*. He died in London on the 20th of September 1867.

LACYDES OF CYRENE, Greek philosopher, was head of the Academy at Athens in succession to Arcesilaus about 241 B.C. Though some regard him as the founder of the New Academy, the testimony of antiquity is that he adhered in general to the theory of Arcesilaus, and, therefore, that he belonged to the Middle Academy. He lectured in a garden called the Lacydeum, which was presented to him by Attalus I. of Pergamum, and for twenty-six years maintained the traditions of the Academy. He is said to have written treatises, but nothing survives. Before his death he voluntarily resigned his position to his pupils, Euander and Telecles. Apart from a number of anecdotes distinguished rather for sarcastic humour than for probability, Lacydes exists for us as a man of refined character, a hard worker and an accomplished orator. According to Athenaeus (x. 438) and Diogenes Laërtius (iv. 60) he died from excessive drinking, but the story is discredited by the eulogy of Eusebius (*Praep. Ev.* xiv. 7), that he was in all things moderate.

See Cicero, *Acad.* ii. 6; and Aelian, *V.H.* ii. 41; also articles Academy, Arcesilaus, Carneades.

LADAKH AND BALTISTAN, a province of Kashmir, India. The name Ladak, commonly but less correctly spelt Ladakh, and sometimes Ladag, belongs primarily to the broad valley of the upper Indus in West Tibet, but includes several surrounding districts in political connexion with it; the present limits are between 75° 40′ and 80° 30′ E., and between 32° 25′ and 36° N. It is bounded N. by the Kuenlun range and the slopes of the Karakoram, N.W. and W. by the dependency of Baltistan or Little Tibet, S.W. by Kashmir proper, S. by British Himalayan territory, and E. by the Tibetan provinces of Ngari and Rudok. The whole region lies very high, the valleys of Rupshu in the south-east being 15,000 ft., and the Indus near Leh 11,000 ft., while the average height of the surrounding ranges is 19,000 ft. The proportion of arable and even possible pasture land to barren rock and gravel is very small. Pop., including Baltistan (1901)

165,991, of whom 30,216 in Ladakh proper are Buddhists, whereas the Baltis have adopted the Shiah form of Islam.

The natural features of the country may be best explained by reference to two native terms, under one or other of which every part is included; viz. *changtang*, *i.e.* "northern, or high plain," where the amount of level ground is considerable, and *rong*, *i.e.* "deep valley," where the contrary condition prevails. The former predominates in the east, diminishing gradually westwards. There, although the vast alluvial deposits which once filled the valley to a remarkably uniform height of about 5,000 ft. have left their traces on the mountain sides, they have undergone immense denudation, and their débris now forms secondary deposits, flat bottoms or shelving slopes, the only spots available for cultivation or pasture. These masses of alluvium are often either metamorphosed to a subcrystalline rock still showing the composition of the strata, or simply consolidated by lime.

Grand scenery is exceptional, for the valleys are confined, and from the higher points the view is generally of a confused mass of brown or yellow hills, absolutely barren, and of no great apparent height. The parallelism characteristic of the Himalayan ranges continues here, the direction being north-west and south-east. A central range divides the Indus valley, here 4 to 8 m. wide, from that of its north branch the Shyok, which with its fertile tributary valley of Nubra is again bounded on the north by the Karakoram. This central ridge is mostly syenitic gneiss, [illegible] north-east from it are found, successively, Silurian slates, [illegible] shales and Triassic limestones, the gneiss recurring [illegible] the Turkestan frontier. The Indus lies along the line which [illegible] the crystalline rocks from the Eocene sandstones and [illegible] of the lower range of hills on the left bank, the lofty [illegible] behind them consisting of parallel bands of rocks [illegible] Silurian to Cretaceous.

[illegible] lakes in the east districts at about 14,000 ft. have been [illegible] greater extent, and connected with the river systems of [illegible], but they are now mostly without outlet, saline, [illegible] process of desiccation.

[illegible] the capital of Ladakh, and the road to Leh from Srinagar [illegible] the lovely Sind valley to the sources of the river at the [illegible] Pass (11,300 ft.) in the Zaskar range. This is the range [illegible] the southern edge of the upland plains of Deosai [illegible] divides them from the valley of Kashmir, and then [illegible] Nanga Parbat (26,620 ft.) and beyond that mountain [illegible] the north of Swat and Bajour. To the south-east it [illegible] chain till it merges into the line of snowy peaks [illegible] and the plains of India—the range which reaches [illegible] the famous peaks of Gangotri, Nandadevi and [illegible] the most central and conspicuous range in the [illegible] Zoji La, which curves from the head of the Sind [illegible] uplands of Dras (where lies the road to the [illegible] and Leh), is, in spite of its altitude, a pass [illegible] but for local accumulations, it would [illegible] It affords a typical instance of that [illegible] by which a river-head may erode a channel [illegible] the plateau behind, there being no steep [illegible] on the northern side of the range. From [illegible] by easy gradients, following the [illegible] to the Indus, when it turns up the [illegible] Leh there are many routes into Tibet, [illegible] from the Indus valley to the Tibetan [illegible] La to Lake Pangkong and Rudok (14,000 [illegible] position on the western Tibetan [illegible] of Leh in Kashmir. The chief trade [illegible] however, follows the line offered by [illegible] of the Brahmaputra (or Tsanpo), [illegible] rivers north of Lake Mana- [illegible]

[illegible] the most elevated observatory [illegible] Indus valley is remarkably [illegible] of the sun is very great. [illegible] than [illegible] feet [illegible] the read- [illegible] tempera-ture in the shade, and this difference has occasionally exceeded 90° . . . . The mean annual temperature at Leh is 40°, that of the coldest months (January and February) only 18° and 19°, but it rises rapidly from February to July, in which month it reaches 62° with a mean diurnal maximum of 80° both in that month and August, and an average difference of 29° or 30° between the early morning and afternoon. The mean highest temperature of the year is 90°, varying between 84° and 93° in the twelve years previous to 1893. On the other hand, in the winter the minimum thermometer falls occasionally below 0°, and in 1878 reached as low as 17° below zero. The extreme range of recorded temperature is therefore not less than 110°. The air is as dry as Quetta, and rather more uniformly so. . . . The amount of rain and snow is insignificant. The average rain (and snow) fall is only 2·7 in. in the year."[1] The winds are generally light, and depend on the local direction of the valleys. At Leh, which stands at the entrance of the valley leading to the Kardang Pass, the most common directions are between south and west in the daytime and summer, and from north-east in the night, especially in the later months of the year. In January and February the air is generally calm, and April and May are the most windy months of the year.

Vegetation is confined to valleys and sheltered spots, where a stunted growth of tamarisk and *Myricaria*, *Hippophae* and *Elaeagnus*, furze, and the roots of *burtsi*, a salsolaceous plant, supply the traveller with much-needed firewood. The trees are the pencil cedar (*Juniperus excelsa*), the poplar and willow (both extensively planted, the latter sometimes wild), apple, mulberry, apricot and walnut. Irrigation is skilfully managed, the principal products being wheat, a beardless variety of barley called *grim*, millet, buckwheat, pease, beans and turnips. Lucerne and prangos (an umbelliferous plant) are used as fodder.

Among domestic animals are the famous shawl goat, two kinds of sheep, of which the larger (*huniya*) is used for carrying burdens, and is a principal source of wealth, the yak and the dso, a valuable hybrid between the yak and common cow. Among wild animals are the kiang or wild ass, ibex, several kinds of wild sheep, antelope (*Pantholops*), marmot, hare and other Tibetan fauna.

The present value of the trade between British India and Tibet passing through Ladakh is inconsiderable. Ladakh, however, is improving in its trade prospects apart from Tibet. It is curious that both Ladakh and Tibet import a considerable amount of treasure, for on the borders of western Tibet and within a radius of 100 or 200 m. of Leh there centres a gold-mining industry which apparently only requires scientific development to render it enormously productive. Here the surface soil has been for many centuries washed for gold by bands of Tibetan miners, who never work deeper than 20 to 50 ft., and whose methods of washing are of the crudest description. They work in winter, chiefly because of the binding power of frost on the friable soil, suffering great hardships and obtaining but a poor return for their labour. But the remoteness of Ladakh and its extreme altitude still continue to bar the way to substantial progress, though its central position naturally entitles it to be a great trade mart.

The adjoining territory of Baltistan forms the west extremity of Tibet, whose natural limits here are the Indus from its abrupt southward bend in 74° 45′ E., and the mountains to the north and west, separating a comparatively peaceful Tibetan population from the fiercer Aryan tribes beyond. Mahommedan writers about the 16th century speak of Baltistan as "Little Tibet," and of Ladakh as "Great Tibet," thus ignoring the really Great Tibet altogether. The Balti call Gilgit "a Tibet," and Dr Leitner says that the Chilasi call themselves Bot or Tibetans; but, although these districts may have been overrun by the Tibetans, or have received rulers of that race, the ethnological frontier coincides with the geographical one given. Baltistan is a mass of lofty mountains, the prevailing formation being gneiss. In the north is the Baltoro glacier, the largest out of the arctic regions, 35 m. long, contained between two ridges whose highest peaks to the south are 25,000 and to the north 28,265 ft. The Indus, as in Lower Ladakh, runs in a narrow gorge, widening for nearly 20 m. after receiving the Shyok. The capital, Skardu, a scattered collection of houses, stands here, perched on a rock 7250 ft. above the sea. The house roofs are flat, occupied only in part by a second story, the remaining space being devoted to drying apricots, the chief staple of the main valley, which supports little cultivation. But the rapid slope westwards is seen generally in the vegetation. Birch, plane, spruce and *Pinus excelsa* appear; the fruits are finer, including pomegranate, pear, peach, vine and melon, and where irrigation is available, as in the North Shigar, and at the deltas of the tributary valleys, the crops are more luxuriant and varied.

History.—The earliest notice of Ladakh is by the Chinese pilgrim Fa-hien, A.D. 400, who, travelling in search of a purer

[1] H. F. Blandford, *Climate and Weather of India* (London, 1889).

faith, found Buddhism flourishing there, the only novelty to him being the prayer-cylinder, the efficacy of which he declares is incredible. Ladakh formed part of the Tibetan empire until its disruption in the 10th century, and since then has continued ecclesiastically subject, and sometimes tributary, to Lhasa. Its inaccessibility saved it from any Mussulman invasion until 1531, when Sultan Said of Kashgar marched an army across the Karakoram, one division fighting its way into Kashmir and wintering there. Next year they invaded eastern Tibet, where nearly all perished from the effects of the climate.

Early in the 17th century Ladakh was invaded by its Mahommedan neighbours of Baltistan, who plundered and destroyed the temples and monasteries; and again, in 1685–1688, by the Sokpa, who were expelled only by the aid of the lieutenant of Aurangzeb in Kashmir, Ladakh thereafter becoming tributary. The gyalpo or king then made a nominal profession of Islam, and allowed a mosque to be founded at Leh, and the Kashmiris have ever since addressed his successors by a Mahommedan title. When the Sikhs took Kashmir, Ladakh, dreading their approach, offered allegiance to Great Britain. It was, however, conquered and annexed in 1834–1841 by Gulab Singh of Jammu—the unwarlike Ladakhis, even with nature fighting on their side, and against indifferent generalship, being no match for the Dogra troops. These next turned their arms successfully against the Baltis (who in the 18th century were subject to the Mogul), and were then tempted to revive the claims of Ladakh to the Chinese provinces of Rudok and Ngari. This, however, brought down an army from Lhasa, and after a three days' fight the Indian force was almost annihilated—chiefly indeed by frostbite and other sufferings, for the battle was fought in mid-winter, 15,000 ft. above the sea. The Chinese then marched on Leh, but were soon driven out again, and peace was finally made on the basis of the old frontier. The widespread prestige of China is illustrated by the fact that tribute, though disguised as a present, is paid to her, for Ladakh, by the maharaja of Kashmir.

The principal works to be consulted are F. Drew, *The Jummoo and Kashmir Territories*; Cunningham, *Ladak*; Major J. Biddulph, *The Tribes of the Hindoo Koosh*; Ramsay, *Western Tibet*; Godwin-Austen, "The Mountain Systems of the Himalaya," vol. vi., *Proc. R.G.S.* (1884); W. Lawrence, *The Valley of Kashmir* (1895); H. F. Blandford, *The Climate and Weather of India* (1889). (T. H. H.*)

LADD, GEORGE TRUMBULL (1842–), American philosopher, was born in Painesville, Lake county, Ohio, on the 19th of January 1842. He graduated at Western Reserve College in 1864 and at Andover Theological Seminary in 1869; preached in Edinburg, Ohio, in 1869–1871, and in the Spring Street Congregational Church of Milwaukee in 1871–1879; and was professor of philosophy at Bowdoin College in 1879–1881, and Clark professor of metaphysics and moral philosophy at Yale from 1881 till 1901, when he took charge of the graduate department of philosophy and psychology; he became professor emeritus in 1905. In 1879–1882 he lectured on theology at Andover Theological Seminary, and in 1883 at Harvard, where in 1895–1896 he conducted a graduate seminary in ethics. He lectured in Japan in 1892, 1899 (when he also visited the universities of India) and 1906–1907. He was much influenced by Lotze, whose *Outlines of Philosophy* he translated (6 vols., 1877), and was one of the first to introduce (1879) the study of experimental psychology into America, the Yale psychological laboratory being founded by him.

Publications.—*The Principles of Church Polity* (1882); *The Doctrine of Sacred Scripture* (1884); *What is the Bible?* (1888); *Essays on the Higher Education* (1899), defending the "old" (Yale) system against the Harvard or "new" education, as praised by George H. Palmer; *Elements of Physiological Psychology* (1889, rewritten as *Outlines of Physiological Psychology*, in 1890); *Primer of Psychology* (1894); *Psychology, Descriptive and Explanatory* (1894); and *Outlines of Descriptive Psychology* (1898); in a "system of philosophy," *Philosophy of the Mind* (1891); *Philosophy of Knowledge* (1897); *A Theory of Reality* (1899); *Philosophy of Conduct* (1902); and *Philosophy of Religion* (2 vols., 1905); *In Korea with Marquis Ito* (1908); and *Knowledge, Life and Reality* (1909).

LADDER, (O. Eng. *hlaeder*; of Teutonic origin, cf. Dutch *leer*, Ger. *Leiter*; the ultimate origin is in the root seen in "lean," Gr. κλῖμαξ), a set of steps or "rungs" between two supports to enable one to get up and down; usually made of wood and sometimes of metal or rope. Ladders are generally movable, and differ from a staircase also in having only treads and no "risers." The term "Jacob's ladder," taken from the dream of Jacob in the Bible, is applied to a rope ladder with wooden steps used at sea to go aloft, and to a common garden plant of the genus *Polemonium* on account of the ladder-like formation of the leaves. The flower known in England as Solomon's seal is in some countries called the "ladder of heaven."

LADING (from "to lade," O. Eng. *hladan*, to put cargo on board; cf. "load"), **BILL OF**, the document given as receipt by the master of a merchant vessel to the consignor of goods, as a guarantee for their safe delivery to the consignee. (See Affreightment.)

LADISLAUS [I.], Saint (1040–1095), king of Hungary, the son of Béla I., king of Hungary, and the Polish princess Richeza, was born in Poland, whither his father had sought refuge, but was recalled by his elder brother Andrew I. to Hungary (1047) and brought up there. He succeeded to the throne on the death of his uncle Geza in 1077, as the eldest member of the royal family, and speedily won for himself a reputation scarcely inferior to that of Stephen I., by nationalizing Christianity and laying the foundations of Hungary's political greatness. Instinctively recognizing that Germany was the natural enemy of the Magyars, Ladislaus formed a close alliance with the pope and all the other enemies of the emperor Henry IV., including the anti-emperor Rudolph of Swabia and his chief supporter Welf, duke of Bavaria, whose daughter Adelaide he married. She bore him one son and three daughters, one of whom, Piriska, married the Byzantine emperor John Comnenus. The collapse of the German emperor in his struggle with the pope left Ladislaus free to extend his dominions towards the south, and colonize and Christianize the wildernesses of Transylvania and the lower Danube. Hungary was still semi-savage, and her native barbarians were being perpetually recruited from the hordes of Pechenegs, Kumanians and other races which swept over her during the 11th century. Ladislaus himself had fought valiantly in his youth against the Pechenegs, and to defend the land against the Kumanians, who now occupied Moldavia and Wallachia as far as the Alt, he built the fortresses of Turnu-Severin and Gyula Fehérvár. He also planted in Transylvania the Szeklers, the supposed remnant of the ancient Magyars from beyond the Dnieper, and founded the bishoprics of Nagy-Várad, or Gross-Wardein, and of Agram, as fresh foci of Catholicism in south Hungary and the hitherto uncultivated districts between the Drave and the Save. He subsequently conquered Croatia, though here his authority was questioned by the pope, the Venetian republic and the Greek emperor. Ladislaus died suddenly in 1095 when about to take part in the first Crusade. No other Hungarian king was so generally beloved. The whole nation mourned for him for three years, and regarded him as a saint long before his canonization. A whole cycle of legends is associated with his name.

See J. Babik, *Life of St Ladislaus* (Hung.) (Eger, 1892); György Pray, *Dissertatio de St Ladislao* (Pressburg, 1774); Antal Gánóczy, *Diss. hist. crit. de St Ladislao* (Vienna, 1775). (R. N. B.)

LADISLAUS IV., The Kumanian (1262–1290), king of Hungary, was the son of Stephen V., whom he succeeded in 1272. From his tenth year, when he was kidnapped from his father's court by the rebellious vassals, till his assassination eighteen years later, his whole life, with one bright interval of military glory, was unrelieved tragedy. His minority, 1272–1277, was an alternation of palace revolutions and civil wars, in the course of which his brave Kumanian mother Elizabeth barely contrived to keep the upper hand. In this terrible school Ladislaus matured precociously. At fifteen he was a man, resolute, spirited, enterprising, with the germs of many talents and virtues, but rough, reckless and very imperfectly educated. He was married betimes to Elizabeth of Anjou, who had been brought up at the Hungarian court. The marriage was a purely political one, arranged by his father and a section of the Hungarian magnates to counterpoise hostile German and Czech influences. During [illegible] of his reign, Ladislaus obsequiously followed the [illegible] and the Neapolitan court in foreign affairs. In Hungary [illegible] party was in favour of the Germans, but the civil [illegible] raged between the two factions from 1276 to 1278 [illegible] Ladislaus, at the head of 20,000 Magyars and [illegible] co-operating with Rudolph of Habsburg in the [illegible] (August 26th, 1278), which destroyed [illegible] the empire of the Premyslidae. A month later [illegible] arrived in Hungary to inquire into the conduct of [illegible] was accused by his neighbours, and many of his own [illegible] of adopting the ways of his Kumanian kinsfolk and [illegible] abandoning Christianity. Ladislaus was not really a pagan, [illegible] he would not have devoted his share of the spoil of Durnkrut to the building of the Franciscan church at Pressburg, nor would he have venerated as he did his aunt St Margaret. Political necessity was largely responsible for the movement against him, yet the result of a very careful investigation (1279–1281) by Philip, bishop of Fermo, more than justified many of the accusations brought against Ladislaus. He clearly preferred the society of the semi-heathen Kumanians to that of the Christians; wore, and made his court wear, Kumanian dress; surrounded himself with Kumanian concubines, and neglected and ill-used his ill-favoured Neapolitan consort. He was finally compelled to take up arms against his Kumanian friends, whom he routed at Hodmézö (May 1282) with fearful loss; but, previously to this, he had arrested the legate, whom he subsequently attempted to starve into submission, and his conduct generally was regarded as so unsatisfactory that, after repeated warnings, the Holy See resolved to supersede him by his Angevin kinsfolk, whom he had also alienated, and on the 8th of August 1288 Pope Nicholas IV. proclaimed a crusade against him. For the next two years all Hungary was convulsed by a horrible civil war, during which the unhappy young king, who fought for his heritage to the last with desperate valour, was driven from one end of his kingdom to the other like a hunted beast. On the 25th of December 1289 he issued a manifesto to the lesser gentry, a large portion of whom sided with him, urging them to continue the struggle against the magnates and their foreign supporters; but on the 10th of July 1290 he was murdered in his camp at Korosszeg by the Kumanians, who never forgave him for deserting them.

See Karoly Szabó, *Ladislaus the Cumanian* (Hung.), (Budapest, 1886); and Acsády, *History of the Hungarian Realm*, i. 2 (Budapest, 1903). The latter is, however, too favourable to Ladislaus.

(R. N. B.)

LADISLAUS V. (1440–1457), king of Hungary and Bohemia, the only son of Albert, king of Hungary, and Elizabeth, daughter of the emperor Sigismund, was born at Komárom on the 22nd of February 1440, four months after his father's death, and was [illegible] called Ladislaus Posthumus. The estates of Hungary [illegible] elected Wladislaus III. of Poland their king, but [illegible] caused the holy crown to be stolen from its [illegible] and compelled the primate to crown the [illegible] on the 15th of May 1440; where[illegible] she placed the child beneath the guardian[ship] [illegible] emperor Frederick III. On the death of [illegible] Ladislaus V. was elected [illegible] though not without considerable [illegible] was sent to Vienna to induce the [illegible] and the holy crown; but it was [illegible] was compelled to relinquish both. [illegible] the pernicious guardianship [illegible] who corrupted him [illegible] a jealous hatred of the [illegible] he was crowned king [illegible] of his time at Prague [illegible] to the Turkish [illegible] to hinder the [illegible] and fled from the [illegible] On the death [illegible]

for his murderous attempt on Lászlo Hunyadi at Belgrade, Ladislaus procured the decapitation of young Hunyadi (16th of March 1457), after a mock trial which raised such a storm in Hungary that the king fled to Prague, where he died suddenly (Nov. 23rd, 1457), while making preparations for his marriage with Magdalena, daughter of Charles VII. of France. He is supposed to have been poisoned by his political opponents in Bohemia.

See F. Palacky, *Zeugenverhör über den Tod König Ladislaus von Ungarn u. Böhmen* (Prague, 1856); Ignacz Acsády, *History of the Hungarian State* (Hung.), vol. i. (Budapest, 1903).

LA DIXMERIE, NICOLAS BRICAIRE DE (c. 1730–1791), French man of letters, was born at Lamothe (Haute-Marne). While still young he removed to Paris, where the rest of his life was spent in literary activity. He died on the 26th of November 1791. His numerous works include *Contes philosophiques et moraux* (1765), *Les Deux Âges du goût et du génie sous Louis XIV. et sous Louis XV.* (1769), a parallel and contrast, in which the decision is given in favour of the latter; *L'Espagne littéraire* (1774); *Éloge de Voltaire* (1779) and *Éloge de Montaigne* (1781).

LADO ENCLAVE, a region of the upper Nile formerly administered by the Congo Free State, but since 1910 a province of the Anglo-Egyptian Sudan. It has an area of about 15,000 sq. m., and a population estimated at 250,000 and consisting of Bari, Madi, Kuku and other Nilotic Negroes. The enclave is bounded S.E. by the north-west shores of Albert Nyanza—as far south as the port of Mahagi—E. by the western bank of the Nile (Bahr-el-Jebel) to the point where the river is intersected by 5° 30′ N., which parallel forms its northern frontier from the Nile westward to 30° E. This meridian forms the west frontier to 4° N., the frontier thence being the Nile-Congo watershed to the point nearest to Mahagi and from that point direct to Albert Nyanza.

The country is a moderately elevated plateau sloping northward from the higher ground marking the Congo-Nile watershed. The plains are mostly covered with bush, with stretches of forest in the northern districts. Traversing the plateau are two parallel mountainous chains having a general north to south direction. One chain, the Kuku Mountains (average height 2000 ft.), approaches close to the Nile and presents, as seen from the river, several apparently isolated peaks. At other places these mountains form precipices which stretch in a continuous line like a huge wall. From Dufile in 3° 34′ N. to below the Bedden Rapids in 4° 40′ N. the bed of the Nile is much obstructed and the river throughout this reach is unnavigable (see NILE). Below the Bedden Rapids rises the conical hill of Rejaf, and north of that point the Nile valley becomes flat. Ranges of hill, however, are visible farther westwards, and a little north of 5° N. is Jebel Lado, a conspicuous mountain 2500 ft. high and some 12 m. distant from the Nile. It has given its name to the district, being the first hill seen from the Nile in the ascent of some 1000 m. from Khartum. On the river at Rejaf, at Lado, and at Kiro, 28 m. N. of Lado, are government stations and trading establishments. The western chain of hills has loftier peaks than those of Kuku, Jebel Loka being about 3000 ft. high. This western chain forms a secondary watershed separating the basin of the Yei, a large river, some 400 m. in length, which runs almost due north to join the Nile, from the other streams of the enclave, which have an easterly or north-easterly direction and join the Nile, after comparatively short courses.

The northern part of the district was first visited by Europeans in 1841–1842, when the Nile was ascended by an expedition despatched by Mehemet Ali to the foot of the rapids at Bedden. The neighbouring posts of Gondokoro, on the east bank of the Nile, and Lado, soon became stations of the Khartum ivory and slave traders. After the discovery of Albert Nyanza by Sir Samuel Baker in 1864, the whole country was overrun by Arabs, Levantines, Turks and others, whose chief occupation was slave raiding. The region was claimed as part of the Egyptian [S]udan, but it was not until the arrival of Sir Samuel Baker at [Gon]dokoro in 1870 as governor of the equatorial provinces, that any effective control of the slave traders was attempted. Baker was succeeded by General C. G. Gordon, who established a separate administration for the Bahr-el-Ghazal. In 1878 Emin Pasha became governor of the Equatorial Province, a term henceforth confined to the region adjoining the main Nile above the Sobat confluence, and the region south of the Bahr-el-Ghazal province. (The whole of the Lado Enclave thus formed part of Emin's old province.) Emin made his headquarters at Lado, whence he was driven in 1885 by the Mahdists. He then removed to Wadelai, a station farther south, but in 1889 the pasha, to whose aid H. M. Stanley had conducted an expedition from the Congo, evacuated the country and with Stanley made his way to the east coast. While the Mahdists remained in possession at Rejaf, Great Britain in virtue of her position in Uganda claimed the upper Nile region as within the British sphere; a claim admitted by Germany in 1890. In February 1894 the union jack was hoisted at Wadelai, while in May of the same year Great Britain granted to Leopold II., as sovereign of the Congo State, a lease of large areas lying west of the upper Nile inclusive of the Bahr-el-Ghazal and Fashoda. Pressed however by France, Leopold II. agreed to occupy only that part of the leased area east of 30° E. and south of 5° 30′ N., and in this manner the actual limits of the Lado Enclave, as it was thereafter called, were fixed. Congo State forces had penetrated to the Nile valley as early as 1891, but it was not until 1897, when on the 17th of February Commandant Chaltin inflicted a decisive defeat on the Mahdists at Rejaf, that their occupation of the Lado Enclave was assured. After the withdrawal of the French from Fashoda, Leopold II. revived (1899) his claim to the whole of the area, leased to him in 1894. In this claim he was unsuccessful, and the lease, by a new agreement made with Great Britain in 1906, was annulled (see AFRICA, § 5). The king however retained the enclave, with the stipulation that six months after the termination of his reign it should be handed over to the Anglo-Sudanese government (see *Treaty Series*. No. 4, 1906).

See *Le Mouvement géographique* (Brussels) *passim*, and especially articles in the 1910 issues.

LADOGA (formerly NEVO), a lake of northern Russia, between 59° 56′ and 61° 46′ N., and 29° 53′ and 32° 50′ E., surrounded by the governments of St Petersburg and Olonets, and of Viborg in Finland. It has the form of a quadrilateral, elongated from N.W. to S.E. Its eastern and southern shores are flat and marshy, the north-western craggy and fringed by numerous small rocky islands, the largest of which are Valamo and Konnevitz, together having an area of 14 sq. m. Ladoga is 7000 sq. m. in area, that is, thirty-one times as large as the Lake of Geneva; but, its depth being less, it contains only nineteen times as much water as the Swiss lake. The greatest depth, 730 ft., is in a trough in the north-western part, the average depth not exceeding 250 to 350 ft. The level of Lake Ladoga is 55 ft. above the Gulf of Finland, but it rises and falls about 7 ft., according to atmospheric conditions, a phenomenon very similar to the *seiches* of the Lake of Geneva being observed in connexion with this.

The western and eastern shores consist of boulder clay, as well as a narrow strip on the southern shore, south of which runs a ridge of crags of Silurian sandstones. The hills of the north-western shore afford a variety of granites and crystalline slates of the Laurentian system, whilst Valamo island is made up of a rock which Russian geologists describe as orthoclastic hypersthenite. The granite and marble of Serdobol, and the sandstone of Putilovo, are much used for buildings at St Petersburg; copper and tin from the Pitkäranta mine are exported.

No fewer than seventy rivers enter Ladoga, pouring into it the waters of numberless smaller lakes which lie at higher levels round it. The Volkhov, which conveys the waters of Lake Ilmen, is the largest; Lake Onega discharges its waters by the Svir; and the Saima system of lakes of eastern Finland contributes the Vuoxen and Taipale rivers; the Syas brings the waters from the smaller lakes and marshes of the Valdai plateau. Ladoga discharges its surplus water by means of the Neva, which flows from its south-western corner into the Gulf of Finland, rolling down its broad channel 104,000 cubic ft. of water per second.

The water of Ladoga is very pure and cold; in May the surface temperature does not exceed 36° Fahr., and even in August it reaches only 50° and 53°, the average yearly temperature of the air at Valamo being 36·8°. The lake begins to freeze in October, but it is only about the end of December that it is frozen in its deeper parts; and it remains ice-bound until the end of March, though broad ice-fields continue to float in the middle of the lake until broken up by gales. Only a small part of the Ladoga ice is discharged by the Neva; but it is enough to produce in the middle of June a return of cold in the northern capital. The thickness of the ice does not exceed 3 or 4 ft.; but during the alternations of cold and warm weather, with strong gales, in winter, stacks of ice, 70 and 80 ft. high, are raised on the shores and on the icefields. The water is in continuous rotatory motion, being carried along the western shore from north to south, and along the eastern from south to north. The vegetation on the shores is poor; immense forests, which formerly covered them, are now mostly destroyed. But the fauna of the lake is somewhat rich; a species of seal which inhabits its waters, as well as several species of arctic crustaceans, recall its former connexion with the Arctic Ocean. The sweet water *Diatomaceae* which are found in great variety in the ooze of the deepest parts of the lake also have an arctic character.

Fishing is very extensively carried on. Navigation, which is practicable for only one hundred and eighty days in the year, is rather difficult owing to fogs and gales, which are often accompanied, even in April and September, with snow-storms. The prevailing winds blow from N.W. and S.W.; N.E. winds cause the water to rise in the south-western part, sometimes 3 to 5 ft. Steamers ply regularly in two directions from St Petersburg—to the monasteries of Konnevitz and Valamo, and to the mouth of the Svir, whence they go up that river to Lake Onega and Petrozavodsk; and small vessels transport timber, firewood, planks, iron, kaolin, granite, marble, fish, hay and various small wares from the northern shore to Schlüsselburg, and thence to St Petersburg. Navigation on the lake being too dangerous for small craft, canals with an aggregate length of 104 m. were dug in 1718–1731, and others in 1861–1886 having an aggregate length of 101 m. along its southern shore, uniting with the Neva at Schlüsselburg the mouths of the rivers Volkhov, Syas and Svir, all links in the elaborate system of canals which connect the upper Volga with the Gulf of Finland.

The population (35,000) on the shores of the lake is sparse, and the towns—Schlüsselburg (5285 inhabitants in 1897), New Ladoga (4144), Kexholm (1325) and Serdobol—are small. The monasteries of Valamo, founded in 992, on the island of the same name, and Konnevskiy, on Konnevitz island, founded in 1393, are visited every year by many thousands of pilgrims. (P. A. K.; J. T. BE.)

LADY (O. Eng. *hlaefdige*, Mid. Eng. *lăfdi*, *lăvedi*; the first part of the word is *hlāf*, loaf, bread, as in the corresponding *hlāford*, lord; the second part is usually taken to be from the root *dig*-, to knead, seen also in "dough"; the sense development from bread-kneader, bread-maker, to the ordinary meaning, though not clearly to be traced historically, may be illustrated by that of "lord"), a term of which the main applications are two, (1) as the correlative of "lord" (*q.v.*) in certain of the usages of that word, (2) as the correlative of "gentleman" (*q.v.*). The primary meaning of mistress of a household is, if not obsolete, in present usage only a vulgarism. The special use of the word as a title of the Virgin Mary, usually "Our Lady," represents the Lat. *Domina Nostra*. In Lady Day and Lady Chapel the word is properly a genitive, representing the O. Eng. *hlaefdigan*. As a title of nobility the uses of "lady" are mainly paralleled by those of "lord." It is thus a less formal alternative to the full title giving the specific rank, of marchioness, countess, viscountess or baroness, whether as the title of the husband's rank by right or courtesy, or as the lady's title in her own right. In the case of the younger sons of a duke or marquess, who by courtesy have lord prefixed to their Christian and family name, the wife is known by the husband's Christian and family name with Lady prefixed, *e.g.* Lady John B.; the daughters of dukes, marquesses and earls are by courtesy Ladies; here that title is prefixed to the Christian and family name of the lady, *e.g.* Lady Mary B., and this is preserved if the lady marry a commoner, *e.g.* Mr and Lady Mary C. "Lady" is also the customary title of the wife of a baronet or knight; the proper title, now only used in legal documents or on sepulchral monuments, is "dame" (*q.v.*); in the latter case the usage is to prefix Dame to the Christian name of the wife followed by the surname of the husband, thus Dame Eleanor B., but in the former, Lady with the surname of the husband only, Sir A. and Lady B. During the 15th and 16th centuries "princesses" or daughters of the blood royal were usually known by their Christian names with "the Lady" prefixed, *e.g.* the Lady Elizabeth.

[illegible] its original application as a title [illegible], an example which has been [illegible] "lady" has been extended [illegible] correlative of "gentleman" [illegible], and in this is paralleled by [illegible] French, *donna* in Spanish, &c. [illegible] woman of a certain social position

[illegible] burgh of Fifeshire, Scotland, 5½ m. [illegible] British railway, ½ m. from the left [illegible] Besides having a station [illegible] also connected with Perth and [illegible] junction of some importance and [illegible] It is an industrial centre, linen [illegible] being the principal industries. [illegible] has prehistoric barrows and a fort. [illegible] a standing stone, a mound and [illegible] while urns and coins have been [illegible] of Collessie and Monimail the [illegible] of a crescent known as the Bow [illegible] the Mount, the residence of Sir [illegible]-1555). Its lofty site is now [illegible] Here, too, is the Doric pillar, [illegible] memory of John Hope, 4th earl of [illegible] the seat of the earls of Leven, lies

[illegible] the Orange Free State, 80 m. E. of [illegible] railway connects it with Natal [illegible] of whom 2334 were whites. [illegible] situated at the foot of a flat-topped hill [illegible] of the Caledon river, which [illegible] Basutoland. Ladybrand is the [illegible] has a large wheat market and is [illegible] owing to the proximity of the [illegible] even during the summer [illegible] Coal and petroleum are found in [illegible] after the wife of Sir. J. H. Brand, [illegible] State.

[illegible] dedicated to the Blessed Virgin [illegible] Generally the chapel was [illegible] and formed a projection from the [illegible] Salisbury, Exeter, Wells, St [illegible] and Norwich cathedrals,—in [illegible] The earliest Lady-chapel [illegible] of Canterbury; this was [illegible] Archbishop Lanfranc to the [illegible] shifted in 1450 to the chapel on [illegible] The Lady-chapel at Ely [illegible] attached to the north transept; [illegible] west of the south transept. [illegible] was that built by Henry III. [illegible] which was 30 ft. wide, much in [illegible] and extended to the end of the [illegible] chapel. Among other [illegible] Lady-chapels are those at Ottery- [illegible] Edmund's, Wimborne, Christ- [illegible] Church, Surrey, and Compton [illegible] Kent, it was built over the [illegible] there were two Lady-chapels. [illegible] French cathedrals and churches, [illegible] in Belgium they were not [illegible] in some cases they are [illegible] of the chevet, but in others, [illegible] they became much more [illegible] Spain during the Renais- [illegible] examples.

[illegible] the days in the church [illegible] Mary's life, but now [illegible] held on the 25th of [illegible] medieval and later times [illegible] In 1752 this was [illegible] March remains one of the Quarter Days; though in some parts old Lady Day, on the 6th of April, is still the date for rent paying. See Annunciation.

LADYSMITH, a town of Natal, 189 m. N.W. of Durban by rail, on the left bank of the Klip tributary of the Tugela. Pop. (1904) 5568, of whom 2269 were whites. It lies 3284 ft. above the sea and is encircled by hills, while the Drakensberg are some 30 m. distant to the N.W. Ladysmith is the trading centre of northern Natal, and is the chief railway junction in the province, the main line from the south dividing here. One line crosses Van Reenen's pass into the Orange Free State, the other runs northwards to the Transvaal. There are extensive railway workshops. Among the public buildings are the Anglican church and the town hall. The church contains tablets with the names of 3200 men who perished in the defence and relief of the town in the South African War (see below), while the clock tower of the town hall, partially destroyed by a Boer shell, is kept in its damaged condition.

Ladysmith, founded in 1851, is named after Juana, Lady Smith, wife of Sir Harry Smith, then governor of Cape Colony. It stands near the site of the camp of the Dutch farmers who in 1848 assembled for the purpose of trekking across the Drakensberg. Here they were visited by Sir Harry Smith, who induced the majority of the farmers to remain in Natal. The growth of the town, at first slow, increased with the opening of the railway from Durban in 1886 and the subsequent extension of the line to Johannesburg.

In the first and most critical stage of the South African War of 1899–1902 (see Transvaal) Ladysmith was the centre of the struggle. During the British concentration on the town there were fought the actions of Talana (or Dundee) on the 20th, Elandslaagte on the 21st and Rietfontein on the 24th of October 1899. On the 30th of October the British sustained a serious defeat in the general action of Lombard's Kop or Farquhar's Farm, and Sir George White decided to hold the town, which had been fortified, against investment and siege until he was relieved directly or indirectly by Sir Redvers Buller's advance. The greater portion of Buller's available troops were despatched to Natal in November, with a view to the direct relief of Ladysmith, which meantime the Boers had closely invested. His first attempt was repelled on the 15th of December in the battle of Colenso, his second on the 24th of January 1900 by the successful Boer counterstroke against Spion Kop, and his third was abandoned without serious fighting (Vaalkranz, Feb. 5). But two or three days after Vaalkranz, almost simultaneously with Lord Roberts's advance on Bloemfontein Sir Redvers Buller resumed the offensive in the hills to the east of Colenso, which he gradually cleared of the enemy, and although he was checked after reaching the Tugela below Colenso (Feb. 24) he was finally successful in carrying the Boer positions (Pieter's Hill) on the 27th and relieving Ladysmith, which during these long and anxious months (Nov. 2–Feb. 28) had suffered very severely from want of food, and on one occasion (Caesar's Camp, Jan. 6, 1900) had only with heavy losses and great difficulty repelled a powerful Boer assault. The garrison displayed its unbroken resolution on the last day of the investment by setting on foot a mobile column, composed of all men who were not too enfeebled to march out, in order to harass the Boer retreat. This expedition was however countermanded by Buller.

LAELIUS, the name of a Roman plebeian family, probably settled at Tibur (Tivoli). The chief members were:—

Gaius Laelius, general and statesman, was a friend of the elder Scipio, whom he accompanied on his Spanish campaign (210–206 B.C.). In Scipio's consulship (205), Laelius went with him to Sicily, whence he conducted an expedition to Africa. In 203 he defeated the Massaesylian prince Syphax, who, breaking his alliance with Scipio, had joined the Carthaginians, and at Zama (202) rendered considerable service in command of the cavalry. In 197 he was plebeian aedile and in 196 praetor of Sicily. As consul in 190 he was employed in organizing the recently conquered territory in Cisalpine Gaul. Placentia and Cremona were repeopled, and a new colony founded at Bononia.

He is last heard of in 170 as ambassador to Transalpine Gaul. Though little is known of his personal qualities, his intimacy with Scipio is proof that he must have been a man of some importance. Silius Italicus (*Punica*, xv. 450) describes him as a man of great endowments, an eloquent orator and a brave soldier.

See Index to Livy; Polybius x. 3. 9, 39, xi. 32, xiv. 4. 8, xv. 9. 12, 14; Appian, *Hisp.* 25-29; Cicero, *Philippica*, xi. 7.

His son, Gaius Laelius, is known chiefly as the friend of the younger Scipio, and as one of the speakers in Cicero's *De senectute*, *De amicitia* (or *Laelius*) and *De Republica*. He was surnamed *Sapiens* ("the wise"), either from his scholarly tastes or because, when tribune, he "prudently" withdrew his proposal (151 B.C.) for the relief of the farmers by distributions of land, when he saw that it was likely to bring about disturbances. In the third Punic War (147) he accompanied Scipio to Africa, and distinguished himself at the capture of the Cothon, the military harbour of Carthage. In 145 he carried on operations with moderate success against Viriathus in Spain; in 140 he was elected consul. During the Gracchan period, as a staunch supporter of Scipio and the aristocracy, Laelius became obnoxious to the democrats. He was associated with P. Popilius Laenas in the prosecution of those who had supported Tiberius Gracchus, and in 131 opposed the bill brought forward by C. Papirius Carbo to render legal the election of a tribune to a second year of office. The attempts of his enemies, however, failed to shake his reputation. He was a highly accomplished man and belonged to the so-called "Scipionic circle." He studied philosophy under the Stoics Diogenes Babylonius and Panaetius of Rhodes; he was a poet, and the plays of Terence, by reason of their elegance of diction, were sometimes attributed to him. With Scipio he was mainly instrumental in introducing the study of the Greek language and literature into Rome. He was a gifted orator, though his refined eloquence was perhaps less suited to the forum than to the senate. He delivered speeches *De Collegiis* (145) against the proposal of the tribune C. Licinius Crassus to deprive the priestly colleges of their right of co-optation and to transfer the power of election to the people; *Pro Publicanis* (139), on behalf of the farmers of the revenue; against the proposal of Carbo noticed above; *Pro Se*, a speech in his own defence, delivered in answer to Carbo and Gracchus; funeral orations, amongst them two on his friend Scipio. Much information is given concerning him in Cicero, who compares him to Socrates.

See Index to Cicero; Plutarch, *Tib. Gracchus*, 8; Appian, *Punica*, 126; Horace, *Sat.* ii. 1. 72; Quintilian, *Instit.* xii. 10. 10; Suetonius, *Vita Terentii*; Terence, *Adelphi*, Prol. 15, with the commentators.

LAENAS, the name of a plebeian family in ancient Rome, notorious for cruelty and arrogance. The two most famous of the name[1] are:—

Gaius Popilius Laenas, consul in 172 B.C. He was sent to Greece in 174 to allay the general disaffection, but met with little success. He took part in the war against Perseus, king of Macedonia (Livy xliii. 17, 22). When Antiochus Epiphanes, king of Syria, invaded Egypt, Laenas was sent to arrest his progress. Meeting him near Alexandria, he handed him the decree of the senate, demanding the evacuation of Egypt. Antiochus having asked time for consideration, Laenas drew a circle round him with his staff, and told him he must give an answer before he stepped out of it. Antiochus thereupon submitted (Livy xlv. 12; Polybius xxix. 11; Cicero, *Philippica*, viii. 8; Vell. Pat. i. 10).

Publius Popilius Laenas, son of the preceding. When consul in 132 B.C. he incurred the hatred of the democrats by his harsh measures as head of a special commission appointed to take measures against the accomplices of Tiberius Gracchus. In 123 Gaius Gracchus brought in a bill prohibiting all such commissions, and declared that, in accordance with the old laws of appeal, a magistrate who pronounced sentence of death against a citizen, without the people's assent, should be guilty of high treason. It is not known whether the bill contained a retrospective clause against Laenas, but he left Rome and sentence of banishment from Italy was pronounced against him. After the restoration of the aristocracy the enactments against him were cancelled, and he was recalled (121).

See Cicero, *Brutus*, 25. 34, and *De domo sua*, 31; Vell. Pat. ii. 7; Plutarch, *C. Gracchus*, 4.

[1] The name is said by Cicero to be derived from *laena*, the sacerdotal cloak carried by Marcus Popilius (consul 359) when he went to the forum to quell a popular rising.

LAER (or Laar), **PIETER VAN** (1613–c. 1675), Dutch painter, was born at Laaren in Holland. The influence of a long stay in Rome begun at an early age is seen in his landscape and backgrounds, but in his subjects he remained true to the Dutch tradition, choosing generally lively scenes from peasant life, as markets, feasts, bowling scenes, farriers' shops, robbers, hunting scenes and peasants with cattle. From this taste, or from his personal deformity, he was nicknamed Bamboccio by the Italians. On his return to Holland about 1639, he lived chiefly at Amsterdam and Haarlem, in which latter city he died in 1674 or 1675. His pictures are marked by skilful composition and good drawing; he was especially careful in perspective. His colouring, according to Crowe, is "generally of a warm, brownish tone, sometimes very clear, but oftener heavy, and his execution broad and spirited." Certain etched plates are also attributed to him.

LAESTRYGONES, a mythical race of giants and cannibals. According to the *Odyssey* (x. 80) they dwelt in the farthest north, where the nights were so short that the shepherd who was driving out his flock met another driving it in. This feature of the tale contains some hint of the long nightless summer in the Arctic regions, which perhaps reached the Greeks through the merchants who fetched amber from the Baltic coasts. Odysseus in his wanderings arrived at the coast inhabited by the Laestrygones, and escaped with only one ship, the rest being sunk by the giants with masses of rock. Their chief city was Telepylus, founded by a former king Lamus, their ruler at that time being Antiphates. This is a purely fanciful name, but Lamus takes us into a religious world where we can trace the origin of the legend, and observe the god of an older religion becoming the subject of fairy tales (see Lamia) in a later period.

The later Greeks placed the country of the Laestrygones in Sicily, to the south of Aetna, near Leontini; but Horace (*Odes*, iii. 16. 34) and other Latin authors speak of them as living in southern Latium, near Formiae, which was supposed to have been founded by Lamus.

LAETUS, JULIUS POMPONIUS [Giulio Pomponio Leto], (1425–1498), Italian humanist, was born at Salerno. He studied at Rome under Laurentius Valla, whom he succeeded (1457) as professor of eloquence in the Gymnasium Romanum. About this time he founded an academy, the members of which adopted Greek and Latin names, met on the Quirinal to discuss classical questions and celebrated the birthday of Romulus. Its constitution resembled that of an ancient priestly college, and Laetus was styled pontifex maximus. The pope (Paul II.) viewed these proceedings with suspicion, as savouring of paganism, heresy and republicanism. In 1468 twenty of the academicians were arrested during the carnival; Laetus, who had taken refuge in Venice, was sent back to Rome, imprisoned and put to the torture, but refused to plead guilty to the charges of infidelity and immorality. For want of evidence, he was acquitted and allowed to resume his professorial duties; but it was forbidden to utter the name of the academy even in jest. Sixtus IV. permitted the resumption of its meetings, which continued to be held till the sack of Rome (1527) by Constable Bourbon during the papacy of Clement VII. Laetus continued to teach in Rome until his death on the 9th of June 1498. As a teacher, Laetus, who has been called the first head of a philological school, was extraordinarily successful; in his own words, like Socrates and Christ, he expected to live on in the person of his pupils, amongst whom were many of the most famous scholars of the period. His works, written in pure and simple Latin, were published in a collected form (*Opera Pomponii Laeti varia*, 1521). They contain treatises on the Roman magistrates, priests and lawyers, and a compendium of Roman history from the death of the younger Gordian to the time of Justin III. Laetus also wrote commentaries on classical authors, and promoted the publication of the editio princeps of Virgil at Rome in 1469.

See *The Life of Leto* by Sabellicus (Strassburg, 1510); G. Voigt, *Die Wiederbelebung des klassischen Alterthums*, ii.; F. Gregorovius, *Geschichte der Stadt Rom im Mittelalter*, vii. (1894), p. 576, for an account of the academy; Sandys, *History of Classical Scholarship* (1908), ii. 92.

LAEVIUS (? *c.* 80 B.C.), a Latin poet of whom practically nothing is known. The earliest reference to him is perhaps in Suetonius (*De grammaticis*, 3), though it is not certain that the Laevius Milissus there referred to is the same person. Definite references do not occur before the 2nd century (Fronto, *Ep. ad M. Caes.* i. 3; Aulus Gellius, *Noct. Att.* ii. 24, xii. 10, xix. 9; Apuleius, *De magia*, 30; Porphyrion, *Ad Horat. carm.* iii. 1, 2). Some sixty miscellaneous lines are preserved (see Bährens, *Fragm. poët. rom.* pp. 287-293), from which it is difficult to see how ancient critics could have regarded him as the master of Ovid or Catullus. Gellius and Ausonius state that he composed an *Erotopaegnia*, and in other sources he is credited with *Adonis, Alcestis, Centauri, Helena, Ino, Protesilaudamia, Sirenocirca, Phoenix*, which may, however, be only the parts of the *Erotopaegnia*. They were not serious poems, but light and often licentious skits on the heroic myths.

See O. Ribbeck, *Geschichte der römischen Dichtung*, i.; H. de la Ville de Mirmont, *Étude biographique et littéraire sur le poète Laevius* (Paris, 1900), with critical ed. of the fragments, and remarks on vocabulary and syntax; A. Weichert, *Poëtarum latinorum reliquiae* (Leipzig, 1830); M. Schanz, *Geschichte der römischen Litteratur* (2nd ed.), pt. i. p. 163; W. Teuffel, *Hist. of Roman Literature* (Eng. tr.), § 150, 4; a convenient summary in F. Plessis, *La Poésie latine* (1909), pp. 139-142.

LAEVULINIC ACID (β-acetopropionic acid), $C_5H_8O_3$ or $CH_3CO{\cdot}CH_2{\cdot}CH_2{\cdot}CO_2H$, a ketonic acid prepared from laevulose, inulin, starch, &c., by boiling them with dilute hydrochloric or sulphuric acids. It may be synthesized by condensing sodium acetoacetate with monochloracetic ester, the acetosuccinic ester produced being then hydrolysed with dilute hydrochloric acid (M. Conrad, *Ann.*, 1877, 188, p. 222).

$$\underset{\displaystyle CO_2R}{CH_3{\cdot}CO{\cdot}CH{\cdot}Na} \rightarrow \underset{\displaystyle CO_2R}{CH_3{\cdot}CO{\cdot}CH{\cdot}CH_2{\cdot}CO_2R} \rightarrow CH_3COCH_2{\cdot}CH_2{\cdot}CO_2OH.$$

It may also be prepared by heating the anhydride of γ-methyloxy-[illegible] acid with concentrated sulphuric acid, and by oxidation [illegible] methyl heptenone and of geraniol. It crystallizes in plates, which melt at 32·5-33° C. and boil at 148-149° (15 mm.) (A. [illegible] *Journ. prak. Chem.*, 1891 [2], 44, p. 114). It is readily [illegible] alcohol, ether and water. The acid, when distilled [illegible] decomposed and yields α and β-angelica lactones. [illegible] heated with hydriodic acid and phosphorus, it yields [illegible] acid; and with iodine and caustic soda solution it [illegible] even in the cold. With hydroxylamine it yields [illegible] which by the action of concentrated sulphuric acid [illegible] to N-methylsuccinimide $(CH_2{\cdot}CO)_2N{\cdot}CH_3$.

[illegible] (1835–1910), American artist, was born [illegible] the 31st of March 1835, of French parentage. [illegible] instruction in drawing from his grandfather, [illegible] a painter of miniatures; studied law and [illegible] entered the atelier of Thomas Couture in Paris, [illegible] a short time, giving especial attention to the [illegible] masters at the Louvre; and began [illegible] to the poets (1859). An intimacy with [illegible] had a strong influence on him, [illegible] Newport, Rhode Island. La Farge [illegible] and figure alike in the early sixties. [illegible] time incapacitated for work, [illegible] he did some decorative work [illegible] and turned his attention [illegible] of the Society of Mural [illegible] commissions include windows [illegible] Peter's church, the Paulist [illegible] New York [illegible]

Buffalo, and the "Battle Window" in Memorial Hall at Harvard; ceilings and windows for the house of Cornelius Vanderbilt, windows for the houses of W. H. Vanderbilt and D. O. Mills, and panels for the house of Whitelaw Reid, New York; panels for the Congressional Library, Washington; Bowdoin College, the Capitol at St Paul, Minn., besides designs for many stained glass windows. He was also a prolific painter in oil and water colour, the latter seen notably in some water-colour sketches, the result of a voyage in the South Seas, shown in 1895. His influence on American art was powerfully exhibited in such men as Augustus St Gaudens, Wilton Lockwood, Francis Lathrop and John Humphreys Johnston. He became president of the Society of American Artists, a member of the National Academy of Design in 1869; an officer of the Legion of Honour of France; and received many medals and decorations. He published *Considerations on Painting* (New York, 1895), *Hokusai: A Talk about Hokusai* (New York, 1897), and *An Artist's Letters from Japan* (New York, 1897).

See Cecilia Waern, *John La Farge, Artist and Writer* (London, 1896, No. 26 of *The Portfolio*).

LA FARINA, GIUSEPPE (1815–1863), Italian author and politician, was born at Messina. On account of the part he took in the insurrection of 1837 he had to leave Sicily, but returning in 1839 he conducted various newspapers of liberal tendencies, until his efforts were completely interdicted, when he removed to Florence. In 1840 he had published *Messina ed i suoi monumenti*, and after his removal to Florence he brought out *La Germania coi suoi monumenti* (1842), *L' Italia coi suoi monumenti* (1842), *La Svizzera storica ed artistica* (1842–1843), *La China*, 4 vols. (1843–1847), and *Storia d' Italia*, 7 vols. (1846–1854). In 1847 he established at Florence a democratic journal, *L'Alba*, in the interests of Italian freedom and unity, but on the outbreak of the revolution in Sicily in 1848 he returned thither and was elected deputy and member of the committee of war. In August of that year he was appointed minister of public instruction and later of war and marine. After vigorously conducting a campaign against the Bourbon troops, he was forced into exile, and repaired to France in 1849. In 1850 he published his *Storia documentata della Rivoluzione Siciliana del 1848–1849*, and in 1851–1852 his *Storia d' Italia dal 1815 al 1848*, in 6 vols. He returned to Italy in 1854 and settled at Turin, and in 1856 he founded the *Piccolo Corriere d' Italia*, an organ which had great influence in propagating the political sentiments of the Società Nazionale Italiana, of which he ultimately was chosen president. With Daniele Manin (*q.v.*), one of the founders of that society, he advocated the unity of Italy under Victor Emmanuel even before Cavour, with whom at one time he had daily interviews, and organized the emigration of volunteers from all parts of Italy into the Piedmontese army. He also negotiated an interview between Cavour and Garibaldi, with the result that the latter was appointed commander of the Cacciatori delle Alpi in the war of 1859. Later he supported Garibaldi's expedition to Sicily, where he himself went soon after the occupation of Palermo, but he failed to bring about the immediate annexation of the island to Piedmont as Cavour wished. In 1860 he was chosen a member of the first Italian parliament and was subsequently made councillor of state. He died on the 5th of September 1863.

See A. Franchi, *Epistolario di Giuseppe La Farina* (2 vols., 1869) and L. Carpi, *Il Risorgimento Italiano*, vol. i. (Milan, 1884).

LA FAYETTE, GILBERT MOTIER DE (1380–1462), marshal of France, was brought up at the court of Louis II., 3rd duke of Bourbon. He served under Marshal Boucicaut in Italy, and on his return to France after the evacuation of Genoa in 1409 became seneschal of the Bourbonnais. In the English wars he was with John I., 4th duke of Bourbon, at the capture of Soubise in 1413, and of Compiègne in 1415. The duke then made him lieutenant-general in Languedoc and Guienne. He failed to defend Caen and Falaise in the interest of the dauphin (afterwards Charles VII.) against Henry V. in 1417 and 1418, but in the latter year he held Lyons for some time against Jean sans [illegible]ur, duke of Burgundy. A series of successes over the English and Burgundians on the Loire was rewarded in 1420 with the government of Dauphiny and the office of marshal of France. La Fayette commanded the Franco-Scottish troops at the battle of Baugé (1421), though he did not, as has been sometimes stated, slay Thomas, duke of Clarence, with his own hand. In 1424 he was taken prisoner by the English at Verneuil, but was released shortly afterwards, and fought with Joan of Arc at Orleans and Patay in 1429. The marshal had become a member of the grand council of Charles VII., and with the exception of a short disgrace about 1430, due to the ill-will of Georges de la Trémouille, he retained the royal favour all his life. He took an active part in the army reform initiated by Charles VII., and the establishment of military posts for the suppression of brigandage. His last campaign was against the English in Normandy in 1449. He died on the 23rd of February 1462. His line was continued by Gilbert IV. de La Fayette, son of his second marriage with Jeanne de Joyeuse.

LA FAYETTE, LOUISE DE (*c.* 1616–1665), was one of the fourteen children of John, comte de La Fayette, and Marguerite de Bourbon-Busset. Louise became maid of honour to Anne of Austria, and Richelieu sought to attract the attention of Louis XIII. to her in the hope that she might counterbalance the influence exercised over him by Marie de Hautefort. The affair did not turn out as the minister wished. The king did indeed make her the confidante of his affairs and of his resentment against the cardinal, but she, far from repeating his confidences to the minister, set herself to encourage the king in his resistance to Richelieu's dominion. She refused, nevertheless, to become Louis's mistress, and after taking leave of the king in Anne of Austria's presence retired to the convent of the Filles de Sainte-Marie in 1637. Here she was repeatedly visited by Louis, with whom she maintained a correspondence. Richelieu intercepted the letters, and by omissions and falsifications succeeded in destroying their mutual confidence. The cessation of their intercourse was regretted by the queen, who had been reconciled with her husband through the influence of Louise. At the time of her death in January 1665 Mlle de La Fayette was superior of a convent of her order which she had founded at Chaillot.

See *Mémoires de Madame de Motteville*; Victor Cousin, *Madame de Hautefort* (Paris, 1868); L'Abbé Sorin, *Louise-Angèle de La Fayette* (Paris, 1893).

LA FAYETTE, MARIE JOSEPH PAUL YVES ROCH GILBERT DU MOTIER, Marquis de (1757–1834), was born at the château of Chavaniac in Auvergne, France, on the 6th of September 1757. His father[1] was killed at Minden in 1759, and his mother and his grandfather died in 1770, and thus at the age of thirteen he was left an orphan with a princely fortune. He married at sixteen Marie Adrienne Françoise de Noailles (d. 1807), daughter of the duc d'Ayen and granddaughter of the duc de Noailles, then one of the most influential families in the kingdom. La Fayette chose to follow the career of his father, and entered the Guards.

La Fayette was nineteen and a captain of dragoons when the English colonies in America proclaimed their independence. "At the first news of this quarrel," he afterwards wrote in his memoirs, "my heart was enrolled in it." The count de Broglie, whom he consulted, discouraged his zeal for the cause of liberty. Finding his purpose unchangeable, however, he presented the young enthusiast to Johann Kalb, who was also seeking service in America, and through Silas Deane, American agent in Paris, an arrangement was concluded, on the 7th of December 1776, by which La Fayette was to enter the American service as major-general. At this moment the news arrived of grave disasters to the American arms. La Fayette's friends again advised him to abandon his purpose. Even the American envoys, Franklin and Arthur Lee, who had superseded Deane, withheld further encouragement and the king himself forbade his leaving. At the instance of the British ambassador at Versailles orders were issued to seize the ship La Fayette was fitting out at Bordeaux, and La Fayette himself was arrested. But the ship was sent from Bordeaux to a neighbouring port in Spain, La Fayette escaped from custody in disguise, and before a second *lettre de cachet* could reach him he was afloat with eleven chosen companions. Though two British cruisers had been sent in pursuit of him, he landed safely near Georgetown, S.C., after a tedious voyage of nearly two months, and hastened to Philadelphia, then the seat of government of the colonies.

When this lad of nineteen, with the command of only what little English he had been able to pick up on his voyage, presented himself to Congress with Deane's authority to demand a commission of the highest rank after the commander-in-chief, his reception was a little chilly. Deane's contracts were so numerous, and for officers of such high rank, that it was impossible for Congress to ratify them without injustice to Americans who had become entitled by their service to promotion. La Fayette appreciated the situation as soon as it was explained to him, and immediately expressed his desire to serve in the American army upon two conditions—that he should receive no pay, and that he should act as a volunteer. These terms were so different from those made by other foreigners, they had been attended with such substantial sacrifices, and they promised such important indirect advantages, that Congress passed a resolution, on the 31st of July 1777, "that his services be accepted, and that, in consideration of his zeal, illustrious family and connexions, he have the rank and commission of major-general of the United States." Next day La Fayette met Washington, whose lifelong friend he became. Congress intended his appointment as purely honorary, and the question of giving him a command was left entirely to Washington's discretion. His first battle was Brandywine (*q.v.*) on the 11th of September 1777, where he showed courage and activity and received a wound. Shortly afterwards he secured what he most desired, the command of a division—the immediate result of a communication from Washington to Congress of November 1, 1777, in which he said:—

"The marquis de La Fayette is extremely solicitous of having a command equal to his rank. I do not know in what light Congress will view the matter, but it appears to me, from a consideration of his illustrious and important connexions, the attachment which he has manifested for our cause, and the consequences which his return in disgust might produce, that it will be advisable to gratify his wishes, and the more so as several gentlemen from France who came over under some assurances have gone back disappointed in their expectations. His conduct with respect to them stands in a favourable point of view—having interested himself to remove their uneasiness and urged the impropriety of their making any unfavourable representations upon their arrival at home. Besides, he is sensible, discreet in his manners, has made great proficiency in our language, and from the disposition he discovered at the battle of Brandywine possesses a large share of bravery and military ardour."

Of La Fayette's military career in the United States there is not much to be said. Though the commander of a division, he never had many troops in his charge, and whatever military talents he possessed were not of the kind which appeared to conspicuous advantage on the theatre to which his wealth and family influence rather than his soldierly gifts had called him. In the first months of 1778 he commanded troops detailed for the projected expedition against Canada. His retreat from Barren Hill (May 28, 1778) was commended as masterly; and he fought at the battle of Monmouth (June 28,) and received from Congress a formal recognition of his services in the Rhode Island expedition (August 1778).

The treaties of commerce and defensive alliance, signed by the insurgents and France on the 6th of February 1778, were promptly followed by a declaration of war by England against the latter, and La Fayette asked leave to revisit France and to consult his king as to the further direction of his services. This leave was readily granted; it was not difficult for Washington to replace the major-general, but it was impossible to find another equally competent, influential and devoted champion of the American cause near the court of Louis XVI. In fact, he went on a mission rather than a visit. He embarked on the 11th of January 1779, was received with enthusiasm, and was made a colonel in the French cavalry. On the 4th of March following Franklin wrote to the president of Congress: "The marquis de La Fayette... is infinitely esteemed and beloved here, and I am persuaded will

[1] The family of La Fayette, to the cadet branch of which he belonged, received its name from an estate in Aix, Auvergne, which belonged in the 13th century to the Motier family.

the death of the y[illegible]
Laetus also wrote [illegible]
moted the publica[illegible]
in 1460.

See *The Life of* [illegible] *Die Wiederbelebung* [illegible] *Geschichte der Sta*[illegible] account of the ac[illegible] (1908), ii. 93.

LAEVIUS (? [illegible] nothing is know[illegible] Suetonius (*De* [illegible] Laevius Milis[illegible] references do [illegible] *M. Caes.* i. 3 [illegible] Apuleius, *De* [illegible] Some sixty [illegible] *Fragm. poet* [illegible] how ancien[illegible] Ovid or Ca[illegible] an *Erotop*[illegible] *Alcestis*, [illegible] *Phoenix*, [illegible] *Sirenocirca*[illegible] *Protesilaodamia*, [illegible] licentiou[illegible]

See O[illegible] Ville de [illegible] (Paris, [illegible] vocabula[illegible] (Leipzig, [illegible] (and ed[illegible] iv), § 1[illegible] (1909), pp[illegible]

LAEVU[illegible] CH_3CO[illegible] inulin, st[illegible] sulphuric [illegible] acetoacet[illegible] produced [illegible] (M. Conra[illegible] $CH_3CO \cdot C$[illegible]

It may also [illegible] glutaric ac[illegible] of methyl [illegible] which melt[illegible] Michael, *J*[illegible] soluble in al[illegible] slowly, in [illegible] When heate[illegible] *n*-valeric ac[illegible] gives isovaler[illegible] an oxime, wh[illegible] re-arranges its[illegible]

LA FARGE [illegible] in New York, [illegible] He received [illegible] Mount St. [illegible] architecture, [illegible] where he rema[illegible] study and rep[illegible] by making illu[illegible] the artist Will[illegible] the two working[illegible] to mural landsca[illegible] But from 1860 [illegible] and when he re[illegible] for Trinity chur[illegible] to stained glass[illegible] Puvis a. Savio[illegible] for St Thomas's [illegible] church, the Brick [illegible] (1885), and the [illegible]

[illegible] his friends from proposing him for the mayoralty of Paris in opposition to Pétion.

When, in December 1791, three armies were formed on the eastern frontier to attack Austria, La Fayette was placed in command of one of them. But events moved faster than La Fayette's moderate and humane republicanism, and seeing that the lives of the king and queen were each day more and more in danger, he definitely opposed himself to the further advance of the Jacobin party, intending eventually to use his army for the restoration of a limited monarchy. On the 19th of August the Assembly declared him a traitor. He was compelled [to take] refuge in the neutral territory of Liége, whence as one [of the] prime movers in the Revolution he was taken and held as a prisoner of state for five years, first in Prussian and [afterw]ards in Austrian prisons, in spite of the intercession of [America] and the pleadings of his wife. Napoleon, however, [thou]gh he had a low opinion of his capacities, stipulated in the [treaty] of Campo Formio (1797) for La Fayette's release. He [was] not allowed to return to France by the Directory. He [return]ed in 1799; in 1802 voted against the life consulate of [Napol]eon; and in 1804 he voted against the imperial title. [He liv]ed in retirement during the First Empire, but returned [to pu]blic affairs under the First Restoration and took some [part] in the political events of the Hundred Days. From 1818 [to 1]824 he was deputy for the Sarthe, speaking and voting [alw]ays on the Liberal side, and even becoming a *carbonaro*. He then revisited America (July 1824–September 1825) where he was overwhelmed with popular applause and voted the sum of $200,000 and a township of land. From 1825 to his death he sat in the Chamber of Deputies for Meaux. During the revolution of 1830 he again took command of the National Guard and pursued the same line of conduct, with equal want of success, as in the first revolution. In 1834 he made his last speech—on behalf of Polish political refugees. He died at Paris on the 20th of May 1834. In 1876 in the city of New York a monument was erected to him, and in 1883 another was erected at Puy.

Few men have owed more of their success and usefulness to their family rank than La Fayette, and still fewer have abused it less. He never achieved distinction in the field, and his political career proved him to be incapable of ruling a great national movement; but he had strong convictions which always impelled him to study the interests of humanity, and a pertinacity in maintaining them, which, in all the strange vicissitudes of his eventful life, secured him a very unusual measure of public respect. No citizen of a foreign country has ever had so many and such warm admirers in America, nor does any statesman in France appear to have ever possessed uninterruptedly for so many years so large a measure of popular influence and respect. He had what Jefferson called a "canine appetite" for popularity and fame, but in him the appetite only seemed to make him more anxious to merit the fame which he enjoyed. He was brave to rashness, and he never shrank from danger or responsibility if he saw the way open to spare life or suffering, to protect the defenceless, to sustain the law and preserve order.

His son, GEORGES WASHINGTON MOTIER DE LA FAYETTE ([illegible]), entered the army and was aide-de-camp to General Grouchy through the Austrian, Prussian and Polish (1805–07) campaigns. Napoleon's distrust of his father rendering promotion improbable, Georges de La Fayette retired into private life in [illegible] until the Restoration, when he entered the Chamber of Representatives and voted consistently on the Liberal side. He was away from Paris during the revolution of July 1830, but he took an active part in the "campaign of the banquets," which led up to that of 1848. He died in December of the next year. His son, OSCAR THOMAS GILBERT MOTIER DE LA FAYETTE ([illegible]), was educated at the École Polytechnique, and served as an artillery officer in Algeria. He entered the Chamber of Deputies in [illegible] and voted, like his father, with the extreme left. After the revolution of 1848 he received a post in the provisional government, and as a member of the Constituent Assembly he became secretary of the war committee. [illegible] in the Legislative Assembly in 1851, he [illegible] protest against the establishment of the third republic, becoming a life senator in 1875. His brother EDMOND MOTIER DE LA FAYETTE (1818–1890) shared his political opinions. He was one of the secretaries of the Constituent Assembly, and a member of the senate from 1876 to 1888.

See *Mémoires historiques et pièces authentiques sur M. de La Fayette pour servir à l'histoire des révolutions* (Paris, An II., 1793–1794); B. Sarrans, *La Fayette et la Révolution de 1830, histoire des choses et des hommes de Juillet* (Paris, 1834); *Mémoires, correspondances et manuscrits de La Fayette*, published by his family (6 vols., Paris, 1837–1838); Regnault Warin, *Mémoires pour servir à la vie du général La Fayette* (Paris, 1824); A. Bardoux, *La Jeunesse de La Fayette* (Paris, 1892); *Les Dernières années de La Fayette* (Paris, 1893); E. Charavaray, *Le Général La Fayette* (Paris, 1895); A. Levasseur, *La Fayette en Amérique 1824* (Paris, 1829); J. Cloquet, *Souvenirs de la vie privée du général La Fayette* (Paris, 1836); Max Büdinger, *La Fayette in Oesterreich* (Vienna, 1898); and M. M. Crawford, *The Wife of Lafayette* (1908); Bayard Tuckerman, *Life of Lafayette* (New York, 1889); Charlemagne Tower, *The Marquis de La Fayette in the American Revolution* (Philadelphia, 1895).

LA FAYETTE, MARIE-MADELEINE PIOCHE DE LA VERGNE, COMTESSE DE (1634–1692), French novelist, was baptized in Paris, on the 18th of March 1634. Her father, Marc Pioche de la Vergne, commandant of Havre, died when she was sixteen; and her mother seems to have been more occupied with her own than her daughter's interests. Mme de la Vergne married in 1651 the chevalier de Sévigné, and Marie thus became connected with Mme de Sévigné, who was destined to be a lifelong friend. She studied Greek, Latin and Italian, and inspired in one of her tutors, Gilles de Ménage, an enthusiastic admiration which he expressed in verse in three or four languages. Marie married in 1655 François Motier, comte de La Fayette. They lived on the count's estates in Auvergne, according to her own account (in a letter to Ménage) quite happily; but after the birth of her two sons her husband disappeared so effectually that it was long supposed that he died about 1660, though he really lived until 1683. Mme de La Fayette had returned to Paris, and about 1665 contracted an intimacy with the duc de la Rochefoucauld, then engaged on his *Maximes*. The constancy and affection that marked this liaison on both sides justified it in the eyes of society, and when in 1680 La Rochefoucauld died Mme de La Fayette received the sincerest sympathy. Her first novel, *La Princesse de Montpensier*, was published anonymously in 1662; *Zayde* appeared in 1670 under the name of J. R. de Segrais; and in 1678 her masterpiece, *La Princesse de Clèves*, also under the name of Segrais. The history of the modern novel of sentiment begins with the *Princesse de Clèves*. The interminable pages of Mlle de Scudéry with the *Précieuses* and their admirers masquerading as Persians or ancient Romans had already been discredited by the burlesques of Paul Scarron and Antoine Furetière. It remained for Mme de La Fayette to achieve the more difficult task of substituting something more satisfactory than the disconnected episodes of the *roman comique*. This she accomplished in a story offering in its shortness and simplicity a complete contrast to the extravagant and lengthy romances of the time. The interest of the story depends not on incident but on the characters of the personages. They act in a perfectly reasonable way and their motives are analysed with the finest discrimination. No doubt the semi-autobiographical character of the material partially explains Mme de La Fayette's refusal to acknowledge the book. Contemporary critics, even Mme de Sévigné amongst them, found fault with the avowal made by Mme de Clèves to her husband. In answer to these criticisms, which her anonymity prevented her from answering directly, Mme de La Fayette wrote her last novel, the *Comtesse de Tende*.

The character of her work and her history have combined to give an impression of melancholy and sweetness that only represents one side of her character, for a correspondence brought to light comparatively recently showed her as the acute diplomatic agent of Jeanne de Nemours, duchess of Savoy, at the court of Louis XIV. She had from her early days also been intimate with Henrietta of England, duchess of Orleans, under whose immediate direction she wrote her *Histoire de Madame Henriette d'Angleterre*, which only appeared in 1720. She wrote memoirs of the reign of Louis XIV., which, with the exception of two chapters, for the years 1688 and 1689 (published at Amsterdam, 1731), were lost through her son's carelessness. Madame de La Fayette died on the 25th of May 1692.

See Sainte-Beuve, *Portraits de femmes*; the comte d'Haussonville, *Madame de La Fayette* (1891), in the series of *Grands écrivains français*; M. de Lescure's notice prefixed to an edition of the *Princesse de Clèves* (1881); and a critical edition of the historical memoirs by Eugène Asse (1890). See also L. Rea, *Marie Madeleine, comtesse de La Fayette* (1908).

LAFAYETTE, a city and the county-seat of Tippecanoe county, Indiana, U.S.A., situated at the former head of navigation on the Wabash river, about 64 m. N.W. of Indianapolis. Pop. (1900) 18,116, of whom 2266 were foreign-born; (1910 census) 20,081. It is served by the Chicago, Indianapolis & Louisville, the Cleveland, Cincinnati, Chicago & St Louis, the Lake Erie & Western, and the Wabash railways, and by the Terre Haute, Indianapolis & Eastern (electric), and the Fort Wayne & Wabash Valley (electric) railways. The river is not now navigable at this point. Lafayette is in the valley of the Wabash river, which is sunk below the normal level of the plain, the surrounding heights being the walls of the Wabash basin. The city has an excellent system of public schools, a good public library, two hospitals, the Wabash Valley Sanitarium (Seventh Day Adventist), St Anthony's Home for old people and two orphan asylums. It is the seat of Purdue University, a co-educational, technical and agricultural institution, opened in 1874 and named in honour of John Purdue (1802–1876), who gave it $150,000. This university is under state control, and received the proceeds of the Federal agricultural college grant of 1862 and of the second Morrill Act of 1890; in connexion with it there is an agricultural experiment station. It had in 1908–1909 180 instructors, 1900 students, and a library of 25,000 volumes and pamphlets. Just outside the city is the State Soldiers' Home, where provision is also made for the wives and widows of soldiers; in 1908 it contained 553 men and 700 women. The city lies in the heart of a rich agricultural region, and is an important market for grain, produce and horses. Among its manufactures are beer, foundry and machine shop products (the Chicago, Indianapolis & Louisville railway has shops here), straw board, telephone apparatus, paper, wagons, packed meats, canned goods, flour and carpets; the value of the factory product increased from $3,514,276 in 1900 to $4,631,415 in 1905, or 31·8%. The municipality owns its water works.

Lafayette is about 5 m. N.E. of the site of the ancient Wea (Miami) Indian village known as Ouiatanon, where the French established a post about 1720. The French garrison gave way to the English about 1760; the stockade fort was destroyed during the conspiracy of Pontiac, and was never rebuilt. The head-quarters of Tecumseh and his brother, the "Prophet," were established 7 m. N. of Lafayette near the mouth of the Tippecanoe river, and the settlement there was known as the "Prophet's Town." Near this place, and near the site of the present village of Battle Ground (where the Indiana Methodists now have a summer encampment and a camp meeting in August), was fought on the 7th of November 1811 the battle of Tippecanoe, in which the Indians were decisively defeated by Governor William Henry Harrison, the whites losing 188 in killed and wounded and the Indians about an equal number. The battle ground is owned by the state; in 1907 the state legislature and the United States Congress each appropriated $12,500 for a monument, which took the form of a granite shaft 90 ft. high. The first American settlers on the site of Lafayette appeared about 1820, and the town was laid out in 1825, but for many years its growth was slow. The completion of the Wabash and Erie canal marked a new era in its development, and in 1853 Lafayette was incorporated.

LA FERTÉ, the name of a number of localities in France, differentiated by agnomens. La Ferté Imbault (department of Loir-et-Cher) was in the possession of Jacques d'Étampes (1590–1668), marshal of France and ambassador in England, who was known as the marquis of La Ferté Imbault. La Ferté Nabert (the modern La Ferté Saint Aubin, department of Loiret) was acquired in the 16th century by the house of Saint Nectaire (corrupted to Sennéterre), and erected into a duchy in the peerage of France (*duché-pairie*) in 1665 for Henri de Saint Nectaire, marshal of France. It was called La Ferté Lowendal after it had been acquired by Marshal Lowendal in 1748.

LA FERTÉ-BERNARD, a town of western France, in the department of Sarthe, on the Huisne, 27 m. N.E. of Le Mans, on the railway from Paris to that town. Pop. (1906) 4358. La Ferté carries on cloth manufacture and flour-milling and has trade in horses and cattle. Its church of Notre Dame has a choir (16th century) with graceful apse-chapels of Renaissance architecture and remarkable windows of the same period; the remainder of the church is in the Flamboyant Gothic style. The town hall occupies the superstructure and flanking towers of a fortified gateway of the 15th century.

La Ferté-Bernard owes its origin and name to a stronghold ([illegible]) built about the 11th century and afterwards held by the family of Bernard. In 1424 it did not succumb to the English [illegible] till after a four months' siege. It belonged in the 16th century to the family of Guise and supported the League, but was captured by the royal forces in 1590.

LA FERTÉ-MILON, a town of northern France in the department of Aisne on the Ourcq, 47 m. W. by S. of Reims by rail. [illegible] 1663. The town has imposing remains comprising [illegible] flanked by four towers of an unfinished castle built [illegible] the beginning of the 15th century by Louis of Orleans, [illegible] Charles VI. The churches of St Nicholas and Notre-Dame, of the 16th century, both contain fine old stained [illegible] Jean Racine, the poet, was born in the town, and a [illegible] David d'Augers has been erected to him.

LAFFITTE, JACQUES (1767–1844), French banker and [illegible], was born at Bayonne on the 24th of October 1767, [illegible] ten children of a carpenter. He became clerk in [illegible] house of Perregaux in Paris, was made a partner [illegible] in 1800, and in 1804 succeeded Perregaux as [illegible]. The house of Perregaux, Laffitte et Cie. [illegible] of the greatest in Europe, and Laffitte became [illegible] governor (1814) of the Bank of France and [illegible] the Chamber of Commerce (1814). He raised large [illegible] for the provisional government in 1814 and for [illegible] during the Hundred Days, and it was with him [illegible] five million francs in gold before [illegible] the last time. Rather than permit the govern[illegible] the money from the Bank he supplied [illegible] his own pocket for the arrears of the imperial [illegible]. He was returned by the department [illegible] Chamber of Deputies in 1816, and took his seat [illegible] He spoke chiefly on financial questions; his known [illegible] did not prevent Louis XVIII. from insisting on [illegible] on the commission on the public finances. In [illegible] from a financial crisis by buying a large [illegible] but next year, in consequence of his heated [illegible] the press and the electoral law of 1867, [illegible] the Bank was taken from him. One of the [illegible] of the partisans of a constitutional [illegible] the duke of Orleans, he was deputy for Bayonne [illegible] his house in Paris became the headquarters [illegible]. When Charles X., after retracting [illegible] the comte d'Argout[1] to Laffitte to [illegible] the banker replied, "It is too late. [illegible] Charles X." and it was he who secured [illegible] Louis Philippe as lieutenant-general of the [illegible] August he became president of the [illegible] on the 9th he received in this capacity [illegible] to the new constitution. The clamour [illegible] the death of the imprisoned ministers of [illegible] culminated in riots, induced the more moderate members of the government—including Guizot, the duc de Broglie and Casimir-Périer—to hand over the administration to a ministry which, possessing the confidence of the revolutionary Parisians, should be in a better position to save the ministers from their fury. On the 5th of November, accordingly, Laffitte became minister-president of a government pledged to progress (*mouvement*), holding at the same time the portfolio of finance. The government was torn between the necessity for preserving order and the no less pressing necessity (for the moment) of conciliating the Parisian populace; with the result that it succeeded in doing neither one nor the other. The impeached ministers were, indeed, saved by the courage of the Chamber of Peers and the attitude of the National Guard; but their safety was bought at the price of Laffitte's popularity. His policy of a French intervention in favour of the Italian revolutionists, by which he might have regained his popularity, was thwarted by the diplomatic policy of Louis Philippe. The resignation of Lafayette and Dupont de l'Eure still further undermined the government, which, incapable even of keeping order in the streets of Paris, ended by being discredited with all parties. At length Louis Philippe, anxious to free himself from the hampering control of the agents of his fortune, thought it safe to parade his want of confidence in the man who had made him king. Thereupon, in March 1831, Laffitte resigned, begging pardon of God and man for the part he had played in raising Louis Philippe to the throne. He left office politically and financially a ruined man. His affairs were wound up in 1836, and next year he created a credit bank, which prospered as long as he lived, but failed in 1848. He died in Paris on the 26th of May 1844.

See P. Thureau-Dangin, *La Monarchie de Juillet* (vol. i. 1884).

[1] [illegible] comte d'Argout (1782–1858), after[illegible] and a member of the Laffitte, [illegible]

LAFFITTE, PIERRE (1823–1903), French Positivist, was born on the 21st of February 1823 at Béguey (Gironde). Residing at Paris as a teacher of mathematics, he became a disciple of Comte, who appointed him his literary executor. On the schism of the Positivist body which followed Comte's death, he was recognized as head of the section which accepted the full Comtian doctrine; the other section adhering to Littré, who rejected the religion of humanity as inconsistent with the materialism of Comte's earlier period. From 1853 Laffitte delivered Positivist lectures in the room formerly occupied by Comte in the rue Monsieur le Prince. He published *Les Grands Types de l'humanité* (1875) and *Cours de philosophie première* (1889). In 1893 he was appointed to the new chair founded at the Collège de France for the exposition of the general history of science, and it was largely due to his inspiration that a statue to Comte was erected in the Place de la Sorbonne in 1902. He died on the 4th of January 1903.

LA FLÈCHE, a town of western France, capital of an arrondissement in the department of Sarthe on the Loire, 31 m. S.S.W. of Le Mans by rail. Pop. (1906) town 7800; commune 10,663. The chief interest of the town lies in the Prytanée, a famous school for the sons of officers, originally a college founded for the Jesuits in 1607 by Henry IV. The buildings, including a fine chapel, were erected from 1620 to 1633 and are surrounded by a park. A bronze statue of Henry IV. stands in the market-place. La Flèche is the seat of a sub-prefect and of a tribunal of first instance, and carries on tanning, flour-milling, and the manufacture of paper, starch, wooden shoes and gloves. It is an agricultural market.

The lords of La Flèche became counts of Maine about 1100, but the lordship became separate from the county and passed in the 16th century to the family of Bourbon and thus to Henry IV.

LAFONT, PIERRE CHÉRI (1797–1873), French actor, was born at Bordeaux on the 15th of May 1797. Abandoning his profession as assistant ship's doctor in the navy, he went to Paris to study singing and acting. He had some experience at a small theatre, and was preparing to appear at the Opéra Comique when the director of the Vaudeville offered him an engagement. Here he made his *début* in 1821 in *La Somnambule*, and his good looks and excellent voice soon brought him into public favour. After several years at the Nouveautés and the Vaudeville, on the burning of the latter in 1838 he went to England, and married, at Gretna Green, Jenny Colon, from whom he was soon divorced. On his return to Paris he joined the Variétés, where he acted for fifteen years in such plays as *Le Chevalier de Saint Georges*, *Le Lion empaillé*, *Une dernière conquête*, &c. Another engagement at the Vaudeville followed, and one at the Gaîté, and he ended his brilliant career at the Gymnase in the part of the noble father in such plays as *Les Vieux Garçons* and *Nos bons villageois*. He died in Paris on the 19th of April 1873.

LA FONTAINE, JEAN DE (1621–1695), French poet, was born at Château Thierry in Champagne, probably on the 8th of July 1621. His father was Charles de La Fontaine, "maître des eaux et forêts"—a kind of deputy-ranger—of the duchy of Château Thierry; his mother was Françoise Pidoux. On both sides his family was of the highest provincial middle class, but was not noble; his father was also fairly wealthy. Jean, the eldest child, was educated at the *collège* (grammar-school) of Reims, and at the end of his school days he entered the Oratory in May 1641, and the seminary of Saint-Magloire in October of the same year; but a very short sojourn proved to him that he had mistaken his vocation. He then apparently studied law, and is said to have been admitted as *avocat*, though there does not seem to be actual proof of this. He was, however, settled in life, or at least might have been so, somewhat early. In 1647 his father resigned his rangership in his favour, and arranged a marriage for him with Marie Héricart, a girl of sixteen, who brought him twenty thousand livres, and expectations. She seems to have been both handsome and intelligent, but the two did not get on well together. There appears to be absolutely no ground for the vague scandal as to her conduct, which was, for the most part long afterwards, raised by gossips or personal enemies of La Fontaine. All that is positively said against her is that she was a negligent housewife and an inveterate novel reader; La Fontaine himself was constantly away from home, was certainly not strict in point of conjugal fidelity, and was so bad a man of business that his affairs became involved in hopeless difficulty, and a *séparation de biens* had to take place in 1658. This was a perfectly amicable transaction for the benefit of the family; by degrees, however, the pair, still without any actual quarrel, ceased to live together, and for the greater part of the last forty years of La Fontaine's life he lived in Paris while his wife dwelt at Château Thierry, which, however, he frequently visited. One son was born to them in 1653, and was educated and taken care of wholly by his mother.

Even in the earlier years of his marriage La Fontaine seems to have been much at Paris, but it was not till about 1656 that he became a regular visitor to the capital. The duties of his office, which were only occasional, were compatible with this non-residence. It was not till he was past thirty that his literary career began. The reading of Malherbe, it is said, first awoke poetical fancies in him, but for some time he attempted nothing but trifles in the fashion of the time—epigrams, ballades, rondeaux, &c. His first serious work was a translation or adaptation of the *Eunuchus* of Terence (1654). At this time the Maecenas of French letters was the Superintendant Fouquet, to whom La Fontaine was introduced by Jacques Jannart, a connexion of his wife's. Few people who paid their court to Fouquet went away empty-handed, and La Fontaine soon received a pension of 1000 livres (1659), on the easy terms of a copy of verses for each quarter's receipt. He began too a medley of prose and poetry, entitled *Le Songe de Vaux*, on Fouquet's famous country house. It was about this time that his wife's property had to be separately secured to her, and he seems by degrees to have had to sell everything of his own; but, as he never lacked powerful and generous patrons, this was of small importance to him. In the same year he wrote a ballad, *Les Rieurs du Beau-Richard*, and this was followed by many small pieces of occasional poetry addressed to various personages from the king downwards. Fouquet soon incurred the royal displeasure, but La Fontaine, like most of his literary protégés, was not unfaithful to him, the well-known elegy *Pleurez, nymphes de Vaux*, being by no means the only proof of his devotion. Indeed it is thought not improbable that a journey to Limoges in 1663 in company with Jannart, and of which we have an account written to his wife, was not wholly spontaneous, as it certainly was not on Jannart's part. Just at this time his affairs did not look promising. His father and himself had assumed the title of esquire, to which they were not strictly entitled, and, some old edicts on the subject having been put in force, an informer procured a sentence against the poet fining him 2000 livres. He found, however, a new protector in the duke and still more in the duchess of Bouillon, his feudal superiors at Château Thierry, and nothing more is heard of the fine. Some of La Fontaine's liveliest verses are addressed to the duchess, Anne Mancini, the youngest of Mazarin's nieces, and it is even probable that the taste of the duke and duchess for Ariosto had something to do with the writing of his first work of real importance, the first book of the *Contes*, which appeared in 1664. He was then forty-three years old, and his previous printed productions had been comparatively trivial, though much of his work was handed about in manuscript long before it was regularly published. It was about this time that the quartette of the Rue du Vieux Colombier, so famous in French literary history, was formed. It consisted of La Fontaine, Racine, Boileau and Molière, the last of whom was almost of the same age as La Fontaine, the other two considerably younger. Chapelle was also a kind of outsider in the coterie. There are many anecdotes, some pretty obviously apocryphal, about these meetings. The most characteristic is perhaps that which asserts that a copy of Chapelain's unlucky *Pucelle* always lay on the table, a certain number of lines of which was the appointed punishment for offences against the company. The coterie furnished under feigned names the personages of La Fontaine's version of the Cupid and Psyche story, which, however, with *Adonis*, was not printed till 1669. Meanwhile the poet continued to find friends. In 1664 he was regularly commissioned and sworn in as gentleman to the duchess dowager of Orleans, and was installed in the Luxembourg. He still retained his rangership, and in 1666 we have something like a reprimand from Colbert suggesting that he should look into some malpractices at Château Thierry. In the same year appeared the second book of the *Contes*, and in 1668 the first six books of the *Fables*, with more of both kinds in 1671. In this latter year a curious instance of the docility with which the poet lent himself to any influence was afforded by his officiating, at the instance of the Port-Royalists, as editor of a volume of sacred poetry dedicated to the prince de Conti. A year afterwards his situation, which had for some time been decidedly flourishing, showed signs of changing very much for the worse. The duchess of Orleans died, and he apparently had to give up his rangership, probably selling it to pay debts. But there was always a providence for La Fontaine. Madame de la Sablière, a woman of great beauty, of considerable intellectual power and of high character, invited him to make his home in her house, where he lived for some twenty years. He seems to have had no trouble whatever about his affairs thenceforward; and could devote himself to his two different lines of poetry, as well as to that of theatrical composition.

In 1682 he was, at more than sixty years of age, recognised as one of the first men of letters of France. Madame de Sévigné, one of the soundest literary critics of the time, and by no means given to praise mere novelties, had spoken of his second collection of *Fables* published in the winter of 1678 as divine; and it is pretty certain that this was the general opinion. It was not unreasonable, therefore, that he should present himself to the Academy, and, though the subjects of his *Contes* were scarcely calculated to propitiate that decorous assembly, while his attachment to Fouquet and to more than one representative of the old Frondeur party made him suspect to Colbert and the king, most of the members were his personal friends. He was first proposed in 1682, but was rejected for Dangeau. The next year Colbert died and La Fontaine was again nominated. Boileau was also a candidate, but the first ballot gave the fabulist

[illegible] worth, and who received them from his father, La [F]ontaine's attached friend for more than thirty years. Perhaps the best worth recording of all these stories is one of the Vieux [C]olombier quartette, which tells how Molière, while Racine and Boileau were exercising their wits upon "le bonhomme" or "le bon" (by both which titles La Fontaine was familiarly known), remarked to a bystander, "Nos beaux esprits ont beau faire, ils n'effaceront pas le bonhomme." They have not.

The works of La Fontaine, the total bulk of which is considerable, fall no less naturally than traditionally into three divisions, the *Fables*, the *Contes* and the miscellaneous works. Of these the first may be said to be known universally, the second to be known to all lovers of French literature, the third to be with a few exceptions practically forgotten. This distribution of the judgment of posterity is as usual just in the main, but not wholly. There are excellent things in the *Œuvres Diverses*, but their excellence is only occasional, and it is not at the best equal to that of the *Fables* or the *Contes*. It was thought by contemporary judges who were both competent and friendly that La Fontaine attempted too many styles, and there is something in the criticism. His dramatic efforts are especially weak. The best pieces usually published under his name—*Ragotin*, *Le Florentin*, *La Coupe enchantée*, were originally fathered not by him but by Champmeslé, the husband of the famous actress who captivated Racine and Charles de Sévigné. His avowed work was chiefly in the form of opera, a form of no great value at its best. *Psyche* has all the advantages of its charming story and of La Fontaine's style, but it is perhaps principally interesting nowadays because of the framework of personal conversation already alluded to. The mingled prose and verse of the *Songe de Vaux* is not uninteresting, but its best things, such as the description of night—

> "Laissant tomber les fleurs et ne les semant pas,"

which has enchanted French critics, are little more than conceits, though as in this case sometimes very beautiful conceits. The elegies, the epistles, the epigrams, the ballades, contain many things which would be very creditable to a minor poet or a writer of vers de société, but even if they be taken according to the wise rule of modern criticism, each in its kind, and judged simply according to their rank in that kind, they fall far below the merits of the two great collections of verse narratives which have assured La Fontaine's immortality.

Between the actual literary merits of the two there is not much to choose, but the change of manners and the altered standard of literary decency have thrown the *Contes* into the shade. These tales are identical in general character with those which amused Europe from the days of the early *fabliau* writers. Light love, the misfortunes of husbands, the cunning of wives, the breach of their vows by ecclesiastics, constitute the staple of their subject. In some respects La Fontaine is the best of such tale-tellers, while he is certainly the latest who deserves such excuse as may be claimed by a writer who does not choose indecent subjects from a deliberate knowledge that they are considered indecent, and with a deliberate desire to pander to a vicious taste. No one who followed him in the style can claim this excuse; he can, and the way in which contemporaries of stainless virtue such as Madame de Sévigné speak of his work shows that, though the new public opinion was growing up, it was not finally accepted. In the *Contes* La Fontaine for the most part attempts little originality of theme. He takes his stories (varying them, it is true, in detail not a little) from Boccaccio, from Marguerite, from the *Cent Nouvelles Nouvelles*, &c. He applies to them his marvellous power of easy sparkling narration, and his hardly less marvellous faculty of saying more or less outrageous things in the most polite and gentlemanly manner. These *Contes* have indeed certain drawbacks. They are not penetrated by the half pagan ardour for physical beauty and the delights of sense which animates and excuses the early Italian Renaissance. They have not the subtle mixture of passion and sensuality, of poetry and appetite, which distinguishes the work of Marguerite and of the Pléiade. They are emphatically *contes pour rire*, a genuine expression of the *esprit gaulois* of the fabliau writers and of Rabelais, destitute of the grossness of envelope which had formerly covered that spirit. A comparison of "La Fiancée du roi de Garbe" with its original in Boccaccio (especially if the reader takes M. Émile Montégut's admirable essay as a commentary) will illustrate better than anything else what they have and what they have not. Some writers have pleaded hard for the admission of actual passion of the poetical sort in such pieces as "La Courtisane amoureuse," but as a whole it must be admitted to be absent.

The *Fables*, with hardly less animation and narrative art than the *Contes*, are free from disadvantages (according to modern notions) of subject, and exhibit the versatility and fecundity of the author's talent perhaps even more fully. La Fontaine had many predecessors in the fable and especially in the beast fable. In his first issue, comprising what are now called the first six books, he adhered to the path of these predecessors with some closeness; but in the later collections he allowed himself far more liberty, and it is in these parts that his genius is most fully manifested. The boldness of the politics is as much to be considered as the ingenuity of the moralizing, as the intimate knowledge of human nature displayed in the substance of the narratives, or as the artistic mastery shown in their form. It has sometimes been objected that the view of human character which La Fontaine expresses is unduly dark, and resembles too much that of La Rochefoucauld, for whom the poet certainly had a profound admiration. The discussion of this point would lead us too far here. It may only be said that satire (and La Fontaine is eminently a satirist) necessarily concerns itself with the darker rather than with the lighter shades. Indeed the objection has become pretty nearly obsolete with the obsolescence of what may be called the sentimental-ethical school of criticism. Its last overt expression was made by Lamartine, excellently answered by Sainte-Beuve. Exception has also been taken to the *Fables* on more purely literary, but hardly less purely arbitrary grounds by Lessing. Perhaps the best criticism ever passed upon La Fontaine's *Fables* is that of Silvestre de Sacy, to the effect that they supply three several delights to three several ages: the child rejoices in the freshness and vividness of the story, the eager student of literature in the consummate art with which it is told, the experienced man of the world in the subtle reflections on character and life which it conveys. Nor has any one, with the exception of a few paradoxers like Rousseau and a few sentimentalists like Lamartine, denied that the moral tone of the whole is as fresh and healthy as its literary interest is vivid. The book has therefore naturally become the standard reading book of French both at home and abroad, a position which it shares in verse with the *Télémaque* of Fénelon in prose. It is no small testimony to its merit that not even this use or misuse has interfered with its popularity.

The general literary character of La Fontaine is, with allowance made for the difference of subject, visible equally in the *Fables* and in the *Contes*. Perhaps one of the hardest sayings in French literature for an English student is the dictum of Joubert to the effect that "*Il y a dans La Fontaine une plénitude de poésie qu'on ne trouve nulle part dans les autres auteurs français.*" The difficulty arises from the ambiguity of the terms. For inventiveness of fancy and for diligent observation of the rules of art La Fontaine deserves, if not the first, almost the first place among French poets. In his hands the oldest story becomes novel, the most hackneyed moral piquant, the most commonplace details fresh and appropriate. As to the second point there has not been such unanimous agreement. It used to be considered that La Fontaine's ceaseless diversity of metre, his archaisms, his licences in rhyme and orthography, were merely ingenious devices for the sake of easy writing, intended to evade the trammels of the stately couplet and *rimes difficiles* enjoined by Boileau. Lamartine in the attack already mentioned affects contempt of the "vers boiteux, disloqués, inégaux, sans symmétrie ni dans l'oreille ni sur la page." This opinion may be said to have been finally exploded by the most accurate metrical critic and one of the most skilful metrical practitioners that France has ever had, Théodore de Banville; and it is only surprising that it should ever have been entertained by any professional maker of verse. La Fontaine's irregularities are strictly regulated, his cadences carefully arranged, and the whole effect may be said to be (though, of course, in a light and tripping measure instead of a stately one) similar to that of the stanzas of the English pindaric ode in the hands of Dryden or Collins. There is therefore nothing against La Fontaine on the score of invention and nothing on the score of art. But something more, at least according to English standards, is wanted to make up a "plenitude of poesy," and this something more La Fontaine seldom or never exhibits. In words used by Joubert himself elsewhere, he never "transports." The faculty of transporting is possessed and used in very different manners by different poets. In some it takes the form of passion, in some of half mystical enthusiasm for nature, in some of commanding eloquence, in some of moral fervour. La Fontaine has none of these things: he is always amusing, always sensible, always clever, sometimes even affecting, but at the same time always more or less prosaic, were it not for his admirable versification. He is not a great poet, perhaps not even a great humorist; but he is the most admirable teller of light tales in verse that has ever existed in any time or country; and he has established in his verse-tale a model which is never likely to be surpassed.

La Fontaine did not during his life issue any complete edition of his works, nor even of the two greatest and most important divisions of them. The most remarkable of his separate publications have already been noticed. Others were the *Poème de la captivité de St Malc* (1673), one of the pieces inspired by the Port-Royalists, the *Poème du Quinquina* (1692), a piece of task work also, though of a very different kind, and a number of pieces published either in small pamphlets or with the works of other men. Among the latter may be singled out the pieces published by the poet with the works of his friend Maucroix (1685). The year after his death some posthumous works appeared, and some years after his son's death the scattered poems, letters, &c., with the addition of some unpublished work bought from the family in manuscript, were carefully edited and published as *Œuvres diverses* (1729). During the 18th century two of the most magnificent illustrated editions ever published of any poet reproduced the two chief works of La Fontaine. The *Fables* were illustrated by Oudry (1755–1759), the *Contes* by Eisen (1762). This latter under the title of "Édition des Fermiers-Généraux" fetches a high price. During the first thirty years of the 19th century Walckenaer, a great student of French 17th-century classics, published for the house of Didot three successive editions of La Fontaine, the last (1826–1827) being perhaps entitled to the rank of the standard edition, as his *Histoire de la vie et des ouvrages de La Fontaine* is the standard biography and bibliography. The later editions of M. Marty-Laveaux in the *Bibliothèque elzévirienne*, A. Pauly in the *Collection des classiques françaises* of M. Lemerre and L. Moland in that of M. Garnier supply in different forms all that can be wished. The second is the handsomest, the third, which is complete, perhaps the most generally useful. Editions, selections, translations, &c., of the *Fables*, especially for school use, are innumerable; but an illustrated edition published by the *Librairie des Bibliophiles* (1874) deserves to be mentioned as not unworthy of its 18th-century predecessors. The works of M. Grouchy, *Documents inédits sur La Fontaine* (1893); of G. Lafenestre, *Jean de La Fontaine* (1895); and of Émile Faguet, *Jean de La Fontaine* (1900), should be mentioned. (G. Sa.)

LAFONTAINE, SIR LOUIS HIPPOLYTE, Bart. (1807–1864), Canadian statesman and judge, third son of Antoine Ménard LaFontaine (1772–1813) and Marie-J-Fontaine Bienvenue, was born at Boucherville in the province of Quebec on the 4th of October 1807. LaFontaine was educated at the Collège de Montréal under the direction of the Sulpicians, and was called to the bar of the province of Lower Canada on the 18th of August 1829. He married firstly Adèle, daughter of A. Berthelot of Quebec; and, secondly, Jane, daughter of Charles Morrison, of Berthier, by whom he had two sons. In 1830 he was elected a member of the House of Assembly for the county of Terrebonne, and became an ardent supporter of Louis Joseph Papineau in opposing the administration of the governor-in-chief, which led to the rebellion of 1837. LaFontaine, however, did not approve the violent methods of his leader, and after the hostilities at Saint Denis he presented a petition to Lord Gosford requesting him to summon the assembly and to adopt measures to stem the revolutionary course of events in Lower Canada. The rebellion broke out afresh in the autumn of 1838; the constitution of 1791 was suspended; LaFontaine was imprisoned for a brief period; and Papineau, who favoured annexation by the United States, was in exile. At this crisis in Lower Canada the French Canadians turned to LaFontaine as their leader, and under his direction maintained their opposition to the special council, composed of nominees of the crown. In 1839 Lord Sydenham, the governor-general, offered the solicitor generalship to LaFontaine, which he refused; and after the Union of 1841 LaFontaine was defeated in the county of Terrebonne through the governor's influence. During the next year he obtained a seat in the assembly of the province of Canada, and on the death of Sydenham he was called by Sir Charles Bagot to form an administration with Robert Baldwin. The ministry resigned in November 1843, as a protest against the actions of Lord Metcalfe, who had succeeded Bagot. In 1848 LaFontaine formed a new administration with Baldwin, and remained in office until 1851, when he retired from public life. It was during the ministry of LaFontaine-Baldwin that the Amnesty Bill was passed, which occasioned grave riots in Montreal, personal violence to Lord Elgin and the destruction of the parliament buildings. After the death of Sir James Stuart in 1853 LaFontaine was appointed chief justice of Lower Canada and president of the seigneurial court, which settled the vexed question of land tenure in Canada; and in 1854 he was created a baronet. He died at Montreal on the 26th of February 1864.

LaFontaine was well versed in constitutional history and French law; he reasoned closely and presented his conclusions with directness. He was upright in his conduct, sincerely attached to the traditions of his race, and laboured conscientiously to establish responsible government in Canada. His principal works are: *L'Analyse de l'ordonnance du conseil spécial sur les bureaux d'hypothèques* (Montreal, 1842); *Observations sur les questions seigneuriales* (Montreal, 1854); see *LaFontaine*, by A. DeCelles (Toronto, 1906). (A. G. D.)

LAFOSSE, CHARLES DE (1640–1716), French painter, was born in Paris. He was one of the most noted and least servile pupils of Le Brun, under whose direction he shared in the chief of the great decorative works undertaken in the reign of Louis XIV. Leaving France in 1662, he spent two years in Rome and three in Venice, and the influence of his prolonged studies of Veronese is evident in his "Finding of Moses" (Louvre), and in his "Rape of Proserpine" (Louvre), which he presented to the Royal Academy as his diploma picture in 167-

sixteen votes against
assent was necessary
ballot in case of the fa
and the election wa
however, some mon
The king hastened
“ Vous pouvez ince
d'être sage.” His
only serious literar
between the Acade
on the subject of
decided to be a b
Furetière, a man of
he considered to b
whose unlucky C
second collection
police condemnati
Bourgeois, howeve
wards La Fontai
the celebrated A
and Perrault were
he had been spe
comparison with
About the same
of the last of h
Madame d'Herv
Ulrich, a lady of
acquaintance wa
Vendôme, Chauli
Temple; but, th
herself up almost
La Fontaine cont
in 1693. What f
the many stories
bearing of the de
He met him in the
his home at his h
He had already
a severe illness t
M. Poucet, had b
acknowledge the i
the destruction of
submitted to as a
of the young duke
only eleven years
present of his own
for the time, he w
hosts had to nur
did very carefully
pleting his *Fables*
Madame de la Sab
13th of April 1695
in the cemetery of
nearly fifteen yea

The curious pe
some other men of
by literary traditi
indifference to bus
His later contemp
century finally acce
his son, being tol
thought I had seen
a duel with a supp
him to visit at his h
with his stockings
those of his awkwa
in company. It ou
unfavourable descr
special friend and s
enemy. But after
when it is rememb
anecdotes in Louis

[illegible] This temple had been rased and
[illegible], in the Greek or Seleucid period,
[illegible] bearing the inscription in Aramaic
[illegible] Hadad-nadin-akhe, king of a small
[illegible] It was beneath this fortress that the
[illegible] Gudea were found, which constitute the
[illegible] collections at the Louvre. These had
[illegible] otherwise mutilated, and thrown into the
[illegible] new fortress. From this stratum came also
[illegible] of bas reliefs of high artistic excellence. The
[illegible] other larger mound resulted in the discovery
[illegible] buildings containing objects of all sorts in
[illegible], dating from the earliest Sumerian period
[illegible] enabling us to trace the art history of Babylonia
[illegible] hundreds of years before the time of Gudea.
[illegible] mound had been occupied largely by store
[illegible] which were stored not only grain, figs, &c., but also
[illegible], sculptures and every possible object connected
[illegible] and administration of palace and temple. In a
[illegible] mound de Sarzec discovered the archives of
[illegible], about 30,000 inscribed clay tablets, containing
[illegible] records, and revealing with extraordinary minute-
[illegible] administration of an ancient Babylonian temple, the
[illegible] of its property, the method of farming its lands, herding
[illegible], and its commercial and industrial dealings and enter-
[illegible] for an ancient Babylonian temple was a great industrial,
[illegible]ercial, agricultural and stock-raising establishment. Un-
[illegible]ately, before these archives could be removed, the galleries
[illegible]ing them were rifled by the Arabs, and large numbers
[illegible] tablets were sold to antiquity dealers, by whom they have
[illegible] scattered all over Europe and America. From the inscrip-
[illegible] found at Tello, it appears that Lagash was a city of great
[illegible]portance in the Sumerian period, some time probably in the
[illegible] millennium B.C. It was at that time ruled by independent
[illegible]ngs, Ur-Nina and his successors, who were engaged in contests
[illegible]ith the Elamites on the east and the kings of Kengi and Kish
[illegible] the north. With the Semitic conquest it lost its independence,
[illegible] rulers becoming *patesis*, dependent rulers, under Sargon and
[illegible]is successors; but it still remained Sumerian and continued to
[illegible]e a city of much importance, and, above all, a centre of artistic
[illegible]evelopment. Indeed, it was in this period and under the
[illegible]mmediately succeeding supremacy of the kings of Ur, Ur-Gur
[illegible]nd Dungi, that it reached its highest artistic development. At
[illegible]his period, also, under its *patesis*, Ur-bau and Gudea, Lagash had
[illegible]xtensive commercial communications with distant realms.
According to his own records, Gudea brought cedars from the Amanus and Lebanon mountains in Syria, diorite or dolorite from eastern Arabia, copper and gold from central and southern Arabia and from Sinai, while his armies, presumably under his over-lord, Ur-Gur, were engaged in battles in Elam on the east. His was especially the era of artistic development. Some of the earlier works of Ur-Nina, En-anna-tum, Entemena and others, before the Semitic conquest, are also extremely interesting, especially the famous stele of the vultures and a great silver vase ornamented with what may be called the coat of arms of Lagash, a lion-headed eagle with wings outspread, grasping a lion in each talon. After the time of Gudea, Lagash seems to have lost its importance; at least we know nothing more about it until the construction of the Seleucid fortress mentioned, when it seems to have become part of the Greek kingdom of Characene. The objects found at Tello are the most valuable art treasures up to this time discovered in Babylonia.

See E. de Sarzec, *Découvertes en Chaldée* (1887 foll.).

(J. P. Pe.)

LAGHMAN, a district of Afghanistan, in the province of Jalalabad, between Jalalabad and Kabul, on the northern side of the Peshawar road, one of the richest and most fertile tracts in Afghanistan. It is the valley of the Kabul river between the Tagao and the Kunar and merges on the north into Kafiristan. The inhabitants, Ghilzais and Tajiks, are supposed to be the cleverest business people in the country. Sugar, cotton and [illegible] are exported to Kabul. The Laghman route between Kabul and India crossing the Kunar river into the Mohmand country is the route followed by Alexander the Great and Baber; but it has now been supplanted by the Khyber.

LAGOON (Fr. *lagune*, Lat. *lacuna*, a pool), a term applied to (1) a sheet of salt or brackish water near the sea, (2) a sheet of fresh water of no great depth or extent, (3) the expanse of smooth water enclosed by an atoll. Sea lagoons are formed only where the shores are low and protected from wave action. Under these conditions a bar may be raised above sea-level or a spit may grow until its end touches the land. The enclosed shallow water is then isolated in a wide stretch, the seaward banks broaden, and the lagoon becomes a permanent area of still shallow water with peculiar faunal features. In the old lake plains of Australia there are occasional wide and shallow depressions where water collects permanently. Large numbers of aquatic birds, black swans, wild duck, teal, migrant spoon-bills or pelicans, resort to these fresh-water lagoons.

LAGOS, the western province of Southern Nigeria, a British colony and protectorate in West Africa. The province consists of three divisions: (1) the coast region, including Lagos Island, being the former colony of Lagos; (2) small native states adjacent to the colony; and (3) the Yoruba country, farther inland. The total area is some 27,000 sq. m., or about the size of Scotland. The province is bounded S. by the Gulf of Guinea, (from 2° 46′ 55″ to 4° 30′ E.); W. by the French colony of Dahomey; N. and E. by other provinces of Nigeria.

Physical Features.—The coast is low, marshy and malarious, and all along the shore the great Atlantic billows cause a dangerous surf. Behind the coast-line stretches a series of lagoons, in which are small islands, that of Lagos having an area of 3¾ sq. m. Beyond the lagoons and mangrove swamps is a broad zone of dense primeval forest—"the bush"—which completely separates the arable lands from the coast lagoons. The water-parting of the streams flowing north to the Niger, and south to the Gulf of Guinea, is the main physical feature. The general level of Yorubaland is under 2000 ft. But towards the east, about the upper course of the river Oshun, the elevation is higher. Southward from the divide the land, which is intersected by the nearly parallel courses of the rivers Ogun, Omi, Oshun, Oni and Oluwa, falls in continuous undulations to the coast, the open cultivated ground gradually giving place to forest tracts, where the most characteristic tree is the oil-palm. Flowering trees, certain kinds of rubber vines, and shrubs are plentiful. In the northern regions the shea-butter tree is found. The fauna resembles that of the other regions of the Guinea coast, but large game is becoming scarce. Leopards, antelopes and monkeys are common, and alligators infest the rivers.

The lagoons, lying between the outer surf-beaten beach and the inner shore line, form a navigable highway of still waters, many miles in extent. They are almost entirely free from rock, though they are often shallow, with numerous mud banks. The most extensive are Lekki in the east, and Ikoradu (Lagos) in the west. At its N.W. extremity the Lagos lagoon receives the Ogun, the largest river in Yorubaland, whose current is strong enough to keep the seaward channel open throughout the year. Hence the importance of the port of Lagos, which lies in smooth water at the northern end of this channel. The outer entrance is obstructed by a dangerous sand bar.

Climate and Health.—The climate is unhealthy, especially for Europeans. The rainfall has not been ascertained in the interior. In the northern districts it is probably considerably less than at Lagos, where it is about 70 in. a year. The variation is, however, very great. In 1901 the rainfall was 112 in., in 1902 but 47, these figures being respectively the highest and lowest recorded in a period of seventeen years. The mean temperature at Lagos is 82·5° F., the range being from 68° to 91°. At certain seasons sudden heavy squalls of wind and rain that last for a few hours are common. The hurricane and typhoon are unknown. The principal diseases are malarial fever, smallpox, rheumatism, peripheral neuritis, dysentery, chest diseases and guinea-worm. Fever not unfrequently assumes the dangerous form known as "black-water fever." The frequency of smallpox is being much diminished outside the larger towns in the interior, in which vaccination is neglected. The absence of plague, yellow fever, cholera, typhoid fever and scarlatina is noteworthy. A mild form of yaws is endemic.

Inhabitants.—The population is estimated at 1,750,000. The Yoruba people, a Negro race divided into many tribes, form the majority of the inhabitants. Notwithstanding their political feuds and their proved capacity as fighting men, the Yoruba are distinguished above all the surrounding races for their generally peaceful disposition, industry, friendliness, courtesy and hospitality towards strangers. They are also intensely patriotic. Physically they resemble closely their Ewe and Dahomey neighbours, but are of somewhat lighter complexion, taller and of less pronounced Negro features. They exhibit high administrative ability, possess a marked capacity for trade, and have made remarkable progress in the industrial arts. The different tribes are distinguished by tattoo markings, usually some simple pattern of two or more parallel lines, disposed horizontally or vertically on the cheeks or other parts of the face. The feeling for religion is deeply implanted among the Yoruba. The majority are pagans, or dominated by pagan beliefs, but Islam has made great progress since the cessation of the Fula wars, while Protestant and Roman Catholic missions have been at work since 1848 at Abeokuta, Oyo, Ibadan and other large towns. Samuel Crowther, the first Negro bishop in the Anglican church, who was distinguished as an explorer, geographer and linguist, was a native of Yorubaland, rescued (1822) by the English from slavery and educated at Sierra Leone (see YORUBAS).

Towns.—Besides Lagos (*q.v.*), pop. about 50,000, the chief towns in the colony proper are Epe, pop. 16,000, on the northern side of the lagoons, and Badagry (a notorious place during the slave-trade period) and Lekki, both on the coast. Inland the chief towns are Abeokuta (*q.v.*), pop. about 60,000, and Ibadan (*q.v.*), pop. estimated at 150,000.

Agriculture and Trade.—The chief wealth of the country consists in forest produce, the staple industries being the collection of palm-kernels and palm oil. Besides the oil-palm forests large areas are covered with timber trees, the wood chiefly cut for commercial purposes being a kind of mahogany. The destruction of immature trees and the fluctuations in price render this a very uncertain trade. The rubber industry was started in 1894, and in 1896 the rubber exported was valued at £347,000. In 1899, owing to reckless methods of tapping the vines, 75% of the rubber plants died. Precautions were then taken to preserve the remainder and allow young plants to grow. The collection of rubber recommenced in 1904 and the industry again became one of importance. A considerable area is devoted to cocoa plantations, all owned by native cultivators. Coffee and tobacco of good quality are cultivated and shea-butter is largely used as an illuminant. The Yoruba country is the greatest agricultural centre in West Africa. For home consumption the Yoruba grow yams, maize and millet, the chief articles of food, cassava, sweet potatoes, sesame and beans. Model farms have been established for experimental culture and for the tuition of the natives. A palatable wine is obtained from the *Raphia vinifera* and native beers are also brewed. Imported spirits are largely consumed. There are no manufactures on a large scale save the making of "country cloths" (from cotton grown, spun and woven in the country) and mats. Pottery and agricultural implements are made, and tanning, dyeing and forging practised in the towns, and along the rivers and lagoons boats and canoes are built. Fishing is extensively engaged in, the fish being dried and sent up country. Except iron there are no valuable minerals in the country.

The cotton plant from which the "country cloths" are made is native to the country, the soil of which is capable of producing the very finest grades of cotton. The Egba branch of the Yoruba have always grown the plant. In 1869 the cotton exported was valued at £76,957, but owing to low prices the natives ceased to grow cotton for export, so that in 1879 the value of exported cotton was only £526. In 1902 planting for export was recommenced by the Egba on scientific lines, and was started in the Abeokuta district with encouraging results.

The Yoruba profess to be unable to alienate land in perpetuity, but native custom does not preclude leasing, and land concessions have been taken up by Europeans on long leases. Some concessions are only for cutting and removing timber; others permit of cultivation. The northern parts of the protectorate are specially suitable for stock raising and poultry culture.

The chief exports are palm-kernels, palm-oil, timber, rubber and cocoa. Palm-kernels alone constitute more than a half in value of the total exports, and with palm-oil over three-fourths.

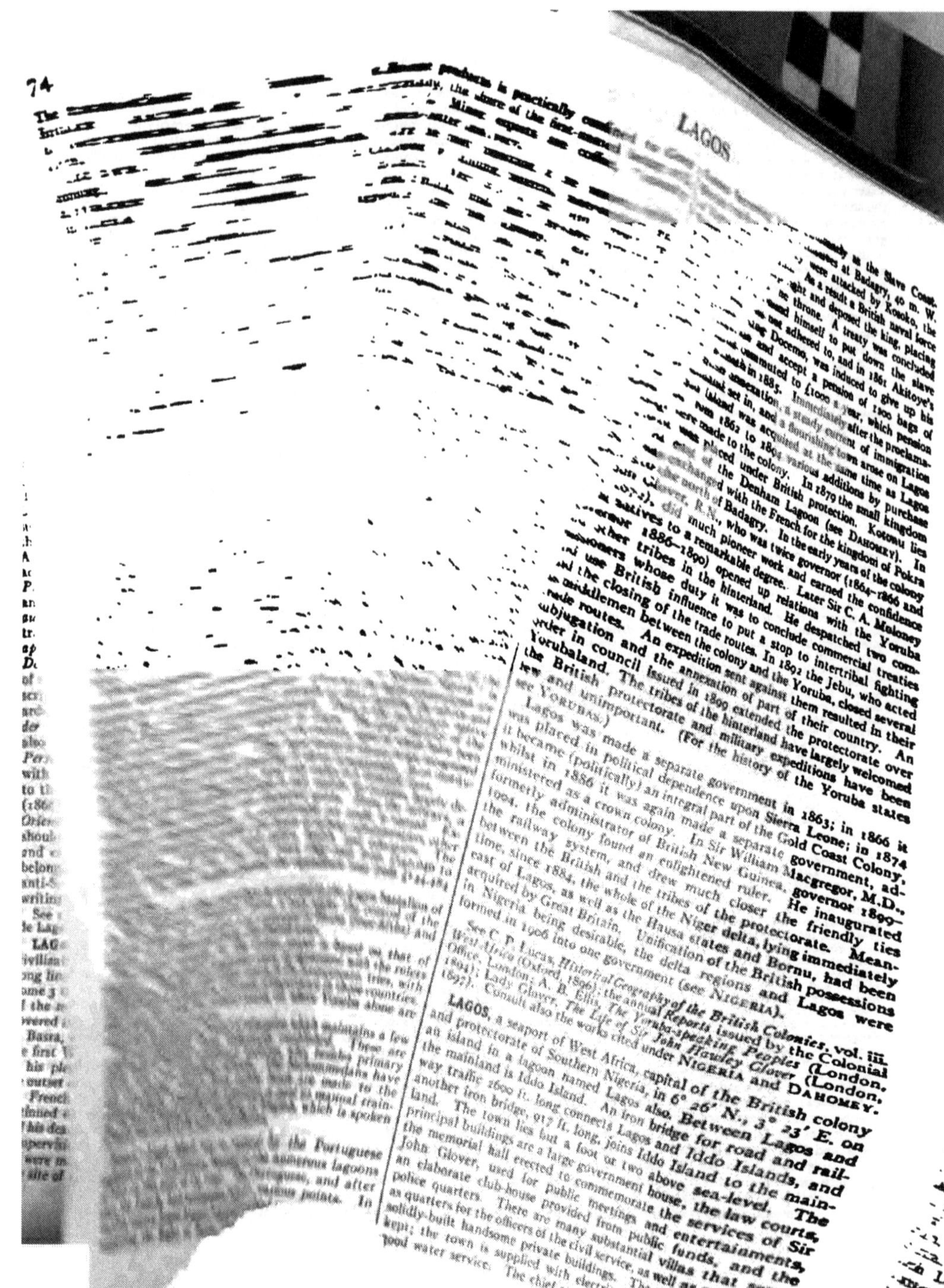

...products is practically confined ... the share of the first-named ... Minor exports are coffee ...

...Slave Coast. ...at Badagry, 40 m. W. ...were attacked by Kosoko, the ... As a result a British naval force ...ght and deposed the king, placing ...he throne. A treaty was concluded ...bound himself to put down the slave ...not adhered to, and in 1861 Akitoye's ...Docemo, was induced to give up his ...and accept a pension of 1200 bags of ...commuted to £1000 a year, which pension ...in 1885. Immediately after the proclama... annexation, a steady current of immigration ...set in, and a flourishing town arose on Lagos ...island was acquired at the same time as Lagos ...from 1862 to 1864 various additions by purchase ...were made to the colony. In 1879 the small kingdom ...was placed under British protection. Kotonu lies ...of the Denham Lagoon (see DAHOMEY). In ...exchanged with the French for the kingdom of Pokra ...the north of Badagry. In the early years of the colony ...John Glover, R.N., who was twice governor (1864–1866 and ...1872), did much pioneer work and earned the confidence ...natives to a remarkable degree. Later Sir C. A. Moloney ...governor 1886–1890) opened up relations with the Yoruba ...other tribes in the hinterland. He despatched two commissioners whose duty it was to conclude commercial treaties ...and use British influence to put a stop to intertribal fighting ...and the closing of the trade routes. In 1892 the Jebu, who acted ...as middlemen between the colony and the Yoruba, closed several ...trade routes. An expedition sent against them resulted in their subjugation and the annexation of part of their country. An order in council issued in 1899 extended the protectorate over Yorubaland. The tribes of the hinterland have largely welcomed the British protectorate and military expeditions have been few and unimportant. (For the history of the Yoruba states see YORUBAS.)

Lagos was made a separate government in 1863; in 1866 it was placed in political dependence upon Sierra Leone; in 1874 it became (politically) an integral part of the Gold Coast Colony, whilst in 1886 it was again made a separate government, administered as a crown colony. In Sir William Macgregor, M.D., formerly administrator of British New Guinea, governor 1899–1904, the colony found an enlightened ruler. He inaugurated the railway system, and drew much closer the friendly ties between the British and the tribes of the protectorate. Meantime, since 1884, the whole of the Niger delta, lying immediately east of Lagos, as well as the Hausa states and Bornu, had been acquired by Great Britain. Unification of the British possessions in Nigeria being desirable, the delta regions and Lagos were formed in 1906 into one government (see NIGERIA).

See C. P. Lucas, *Historical Geography of the British Colonies*, vol. iii. *West Africa* (Oxford, 1896); the annual *Reports* issued by the Colonial Office, London; A. B. Ellis, *The Yoruba-speaking Peoples* (London, 1894); Lady Glover, *The Life of Sir John Hawley Glover* (London, 1897). Consult also the works cited under NIGERIA and DAHOMEY.

LAGOS, a seaport of West Africa, capital of the British colony and protectorate of Southern Nigeria, in 6° 26′ N., 3° 23′ E. on an island in a lagoon named Lagos also. Between Lagos and the mainland is Iddo Island. An iron bridge for road and railway traffic 2600 ft. long connects Lagos and Iddo Islands, and another iron bridge, 917 ft. long, joins Iddo Island to the mainland. The town lies but a foot or two above sea-level. The principal buildings are a large government house, the law courts, the memorial hall erected to commemorate the services of Sir John Glover, used for public meetings and entertainments, an elaborate club-house provided from public funds, and the police quarters. There are many substantial villas that serve as quarters for the officers of the civil service, as well as numerous solidly-built handsome private buildings. The ... kept; the town is supplied with electric ... good water service. The chief stre...

all on the banks of the lagoon. The swamps of which originally Lagos Island entirely consisted have been reclaimed. In connexion with this work a canal, 25 ft. wide, has been cut right through the island and a sea-wall built round its western half. There is a commodious public hospital, of the cottage type, on a good site. There is a racecourse, which also serves as a general public recreation ground. Shifting banks of sand form a bar at the sea entrance of the lagoon. Extensive works were undertaken in 1908 with a view to making Lagos an open port. A mole has been built at the eastern entrance to the harbour and dredgers are at work on the bar, which can be crossed by vessels drawing 13 ft. Large ocean-going steamers anchor not less than 2 m. from land, and goods and passengers are there transhipped into smaller steamers for Lagos. Heavy cargo is carried by the large steamers to Forcados, 200 m. farther down the coast, transhipped there into branch boats, and taken via the lagoons to Lagos. The port is 4279 m. from Liverpool, 1203 from Freetown, Sierra Leone (the nearest safe port westward), and 315 from Cape Coast.

The inhabitants, about 50,000, include, besides the native tribes, Sierra Leonis, Fanti, Krumen and the descendants of some 6000 Brazilian *emancipados* who were settled here in the early days of British rule. The Europeans number about 400. Rather more than half the populace are Moslems.

LAGOS, a seaport of southern Portugal, in the district of Faro (formerly the province of Algarve); on the Atlantic Ocean, and on the estuary of the small river Lagos, here spanned by a fine stone bridge. Pop. (1900) 8291. The city is defended by fortifications erected in the 17th century. It is supplied with water by an aqueduct 800 yds. long. The harbour is deep, capacious, and completely sheltered on the north and west; it is frequently visited by the British Channel fleet. Vines and figs are extensively cultivated in the neighbourhood, and Lagos is the centre of important sardine and tunny fisheries. Its trade is chiefly carried on by small coasting vessels, as there is no railway. Lagos is on or near the site of the Roman *Lacobriga*. Since the 15th century it has held the formal rank and title of city. Cape St Vincent, the ancient *Promontorium Sacrum*, and the south-western extremity of the kingdom, is 22 m. W. It is famous for its connexion with Prince Henry (*q.v.*), the Navigator, who here founded the town of Sagres in 1421; and for several British naval victories, the most celebrated of which was won in 1797 by Admiral Jervis (afterwards Earl St Vincent) over a larger Spanish squadron. In 1759 Admiral Boscawen defeated a French fleet off Lagos. The great earthquake of 1755 destroyed a large part of the city.

LA GRÂCE, or LES GRÂCES, a game invented in France during the first quarter of the 19th century and called there *le jeu des Grâces*. It is played with two light sticks about 16 in. long and a wicker ring, which is projected into the air by placing it over the sticks crossed and then separating them rapidly. The ring is caught upon the stick of another player and thrown back, the object being to prevent it from falling to the ground.

LA GRAND' COMBE, a town of southern France, in the department of Gard on the Gardon, 30 m. N.N.W. of Nîmes by rail. Pop. (1906) town, 6406; commune, 11,292. There are extensive coal mines in the vicinity.

LAGRANGE, JOSEPH LOUIS (1736–1813), French mathematician, was born at Turin, on the 25th of January 1736. He was of French extraction, his great grandfather, a cavalry captain, having passed from the service of France to that of Sardinia, and settled in Turin under Emmanuel II. His father, Joseph Louis Lagrange, married Maria Theresa Gros, only daughter of a rich physician at Cambiano, and had by her eleven children, of whom only the eldest (the subject of this notice) and the youngest survived infancy. His emoluments as treasurer at war, together with his wife's fortune, provided him with ample means, which he lost by rash speculations, a circumstance regarded by his son as the prelude to his own good fortune; for had he been rich, he used to say, he might never have known mathematics.

The genius of Lagrange did not at once take its true bent. His earliest tastes were literary rather than scientific, and he learned the rudiments of geometry during his first year at the college of Turin, without difficulty, but without distinction. The perusal of a tract by Halley (*Phil. Trans.* xviii. 960) roused his enthusiasm for the analytical method, of which he was destined to develop the utmost capabilities. He now entered, unaided save by his own unerring tact and vivid apprehension, upon a course of study which, in two years, placed him on a level with the greatest of his contemporaries. At the age of nineteen he communicated to Leonhard Euler his idea of a general method of dealing with "isoperimetrical" problems, known later as the Calculus of Variations. It was eagerly welcomed by the Berlin mathematician, who had the generosity to withhold from publication his own further researches on the subject, until his youthful correspondent should have had time to complete and opportunity to claim the invention. This prosperous opening gave the key-note to Lagrange's career. Appointed, in 1754, professor of geometry in the royal school of artillery, he formed with some of his pupils—for the most part his seniors—friendships based on community of scientific ardour. With the aid of the marquis de Saluces and the anatomist G. F. Cigna, he founded in 1758 a society which became the Turin Academy of Sciences. The first volume of its memoirs, published in the following year, contained a paper by Lagrange entitled *Recherches sur la nature et la propagation du son*, in which the power of his analysis and his address in its application were equally conspicuous. He made his first appearance in public as the critic of Newton, and the arbiter between d'Alembert and Euler. By considering only the particles of air found in a right line, he reduced the problem of the propagation of sound to the solution of the same partial differential equations that include the motions of vibrating strings, and demonstrated the insufficiency of the methods employed by both his great contemporaries in dealing with the latter subject. He further treated in a masterly manner of echoes and the mixture of sounds, and explained the phenomenon of grave harmonics as due to the occurrence of beats so rapid as to generate a musical note. This was followed, in the second volume of the *Miscellanea Taurinensia* (1762) by his "Essai d'une nouvelle méthode pour déterminer les maxima et les minima des formules intégrales indéfinies," together with the application of this important development of analysis to the solution of several dynamical problems, as well as to the demonstration of the mechanical principle of "least action." The essential point in his advance on Euler's mode of investigating curves of maximum or minimum consisted in his purely analytical conception of the subject. He not only freed it from all trammels of geometrical construction, but by the introduction of the symbol δ gave it the efficacy of a new calculus. He is thus justly regarded as the inventor of the "method of variations"—a name supplied by Euler in 1766.

By these performances Lagrange found himself, at the age of twenty-six, on the summit of European fame. Such a height had not been reached without cost. Intense application during early youth had weakened a constitution never robust, and led to accesses of feverish exaltation culminating, in the spring of 1761, in an attack of bilious hypochondria, which permanently lowered the tone of his nervous system. Rest and exercise, however, temporarily restored his health, and he gave proof of the undiminished vigour of his powers by carrying off, in 1764, the prize offered by the Paris Academy of Sciences for the best essay on the libration of the moon. His treatise was remarkable, not only as offering a satisfactory explanation of the coincidence between the lunar periods of rotation and revolution, but as containing the first employment of his radical formula of mechanics, obtained by combining with the principle of d'Alembert that of virtual velocities. His success encouraged the Academy to propose, in 1766, as a theme for competition, the hitherto unattempted theory of the Jovian system. The prize was again awarded to Lagrange; and he earned the same distinction with essays on the problem of three bodies in 1772, on the secular equation of the moon in 1774, and in 1778 on the theory of cometary perturbations.

[illegible] a long felt desire by a visit [illegible] delight of conversing [illegible] A. C. Clairault, d'Alembert, [illegible] prevented him from [illegible] of the mathematical [illegible] of which he had been a [illegible] by the removal of Euler [illegible] d'Alembert united to recommend [illegible] was enhanced by [illegible] by his dread of a royal [illegible] was that an invita- [illegible] king in Europe" to [illegible] at his court, was sent to [illegible] Lagrange was installed [illegible] francs, ample leisure [illegible] sufficient to secure him [illegible] The national jealousy of [illegible] to him; but such [illegible] the inoffensiveness of his [illegible] example of his [illegible] society, impelled [illegible] of the Conti family, [illegible] Soon after marriage [illegible] to which she suc- [illegible] and a considerable store

[illegible] complete treatises [illegible] communicated by [illegible] the years 1767 and [illegible] His *Mécanique* [illegible] itself, was [illegible] great work was the [illegible] the author almost [illegible] published essay.[1] [illegible] of the theory [illegible] from the simple [illegible] the equations necessary [illegible] From the funda- [illegible] then acquired a new [illegible] aid of the calculus [illegible] truths, by pro- [illegible] constitute, in Sir [illegible] poem." This [illegible] By his mode of [illegible] characterized by the [illegible] between [illegible] aggregation finally [illegible] was for [illegible] hydrodynamics.[2] [illegible] was derived, by [illegible] principle; [illegible] complete form

[illegible] the book [illegible] Legendre. [illegible] After [illegible] completed [illegible] [illegible]

with miscellaneous studies, especially with that of chemistry, which, in the new form given to it by Lavoisier, he found "aisée comme l'algèbre." The Revolution roused him once more to activity and cheerfulness. Curiosity impelled him to remain and watch the progress of such a novel phenomenon; but curiosity was changed into dismay as the terrific character of the phenomenon unfolded itself. He now bitterly regretted his temerity in braving the danger. "Tu l'as voulu" he would repeat self-reproachfully. Even from revolutionary tribunals, however, the name of Lagrange uniformly commanded respect. His pension was continued by the National Assembly, and he was partially indemnified for the depreciation of the currency by remunerative appointments. Nominated president of the Academical commission for the reform of weights and measures, his services were retained when its "purification" by the Jacobins removed his most distinguished colleagues. He again sat on the commission of 1799 for the construction of the metric system, and by his zealous advocacy of the decimal principle largely contributed to its adoption.

Meanwhile, on the 31st of May 1792 he married Mademoiselle Lemonnier, daughter of the astronomer of that name, a young and beautiful girl, whose devotion ignored disparity of years, and formed the one tie with life which Lagrange found it hard to break. He had no children by either marriage. Although specially exempted from the operation of the decree of October 1793, imposing banishment on foreign residents, he took alarm at the fate of J. S. Bailly and A. L. Lavoisier, and prepared to resume his former situation in Berlin. His design was frustrated by the establishment of and his official connexion with the École Normale, and the École Polytechnique. The former institution had an ephemeral existence; but amongst the benefits derived from the foundation of the École Polytechnique one of the greatest, it has been observed,[4] was the restoration of Lagrange to mathematics. The remembrance of his teachings was long treasured by such of his auditors—amongst whom were J. B. J. Delambre and S. F. Lacroix—as were capable of appreciating them. In expounding the principles of the differential calculus, he started, as it were, from the level of his pupils, and ascended with them by almost insensible gradations from elementary to abstruse conceptions. He seemed, not a professor amongst students, but a learner amongst learners; pauses for thought alternated with luminous exposition; invention accompanied demonstration; and thus originated his *Théorie des fonctions analytiques* (Paris, 1797). The leading idea of this work was contained in a paper published in the *Berlin Memoirs* for 1772.[5] Its object was the elimination of the, to some minds, unsatisfactory conception of the infinite from the metaphysics of the higher mathematics, and the substitution for the differential and integral calculus of an analogous method depending wholly on the serial development of algebraical functions. By means of this "calculus of derived functions" Lagrange hoped to give to the solution of all analytical problems the utmost "rigour of the demonstrations of the ancients";[6] but it cannot be said that the attempt was successful. The validity of his fundamental position was impaired by the absence of a well-constituted theory of series; the notation employed was inconvenient, and was abandoned by its inventor in the second edition of his *Mécanique*; while his scruples as to the admission into analytical investigations of the idea of limits or vanishing ratios have long since been laid aside as idle. Nowhere, however, were the keenness and clearness of his intellect more conspicuous than in this brilliant effort, which, if it failed in its immediate object, was highly effective in secondary results. His purely abstract mode of regarding functions, apart from any mechanical or geometrical considerations, led the way to a new and sharply characterized development of the higher analysis in the hands of A. Cauchy, C. G. Jacobi, and others.[7] The *Théorie des fonctions* is divided into three parts, of which the first explains the general doctrine of functions, the second deals with its

[4] By J. Delambre, *Œuvres de Lagrange*, i. p. xlii.
[5] iii. 441. [6] *Théorie des fonctions*, p. 6.
[7] Geschichte der math. Wiss. ii. 322-323.

application to geometry, and the third with its bearings on mechanics.

On the establishment of the Institute, Lagrange was placed at the head of the section of geometry; he was one of the first members of the Bureau des Longitudes; and his name appeared in 1791 on the list of foreign members of the Royal Society. On the annexation of Piedmont to France in 1796, a touching compliment was paid to him in the person of his aged father. By direction of Talleyrand, then minister for foreign affairs, the French commissary repaired in state to the old man's residence in Turin, to congratulate him on the merits of his son, whom they declared "to have done honour to mankind by his genius, and whom Piedmont was proud to have produced, and France to possess." Bonaparte, who styled him "la haute pyramide des sciences mathématiques," loaded him with personal favours and official distinctions. He became a senator, a count of the empire, a grand officer of the legion of honour, and just before his death received the grand cross of the order of réunion.

The preparation of a new edition of his *Mécanique* exhausted his already failing powers. Frequent fainting fits gave presage of a speedy end, and on the 8th of April 1813 he had a final interview with his friends B. Lacépède, G. Monge and J. A. Chaptal. He spoke with the utmost calm of his approaching death; "c'est une dernière fonction," he said, "qui n'est ni pénible ni désagréable." He nevertheless looked forward to a future meeting, when he promised to complete the autobiographical details which weakness obliged him to interrupt. They remained untold, for he died two days later on the 10th of April, and was buried in the Pantheon, the funeral oration being pronounced by Laplace and Lacépède.

Amongst the brilliant group of mathematicians whose magnanimous rivalry contributed to accomplish the task of generalization and deduction reserved for the 18th century, Lagrange occupies an eminent place. It is indeed by no means easy to distinguish and apportion the respective merits of the competitors. This is especially the case between Lagrange and Euler on the one side, and between Lagrange and Laplace on the other. The calculus of variations lay undeveloped in Euler's mode of treating isoperimetrical problems. The fruitful method, again, of the variation of elements was introduced by Euler, but adopted and perfected by Lagrange, who first recognised its supreme importance to the analytical investigation of the planetary movements. Finally, of the grand series of researches by which the stability of the solar system was ascertained, the glory must be almost equally divided between Lagrange and Laplace. In analytical invention, and mastery over the calculus, the Turin mathematician was admittedly unrivalled. Laplace owned that he had despaired of effecting the integration of the differential equations relative to secular inequalities until Lagrange showed him the way. But Laplace unquestionably surpassed his rival in practical sagacity and the intuition of physical truth. Lagrange saw in the problems of nature so many occasions for analytical triumphs; Laplace regarded analytical triumphs as the means of solving the problems of nature. One mind seemed the complement of the other; and both, united in honourable rivalry, formed an instrument of unexampled perfection for the investigation of the celestial machinery. What may be called Lagrange's first period of research into planetary perturbations extended from 1774 to 1784 (see ASTRONOMY: *History*). The notable group of treatises communicated, 1781–1784, to the Berlin Academy was designed, but did not prove to be his final contribution to the theory of the planets. After an interval of twenty-four years the subject, re-opened by S. D. Poisson in a paper read on the 20th of June 1808, was once more attacked by Lagrange with all his pristine vigour and fertility of invention. Resuming the inquiry into the invariability of mean motions, Poisson carried the approximation, with Lagrange's formulae, as far as the squares of the disturbing forces, hitherto neglected, with the same result as to the stability of the system. He had not attempted to include in his calculations the orbital variations of the disturbing bodies; but Lagrange, by the happy artifice of transferring the origin of coordinates from the centre of the sun to the centre of gravity of the sun and planets, obtained a simplification of the formulae, by which the same analysis was rendered equally applicable to each of the planets severally. It deserves to be recorded as one of the numerous coincidences of discovery that Laplace, on being made acquainted by Lagrange with his new method, produced analogous expressions, to which his independent researches had led him. The final achievement of Lagrange in this direction was the extension of the method of the variation of arbitrary constants, successfully used by him in the investigation of periodical as well as of secular inequalities, to any system whatever of mutually interacting bodies.[1] "Not without astonishment," even to himself, regard being had to the great generality of the differential equations, he reached a result so wide as to include, as a particular case, the solution of the planetary problem recently obtained by him. He proposed to apply the same principles to the calculation of the disturbances produced in the rotation of the planets by external action on their equatorial protuberances, but was anticipated by Poisson, who gave formulae for the variation of the elements of rotation strictly corresponding with those found by Lagrange for the variation of the elements of revolution. The revision of the *Mécanique analytique* was undertaken mainly for the purpose of embodying in it these new methods and final results, but was interrupted, when two-thirds completed, by the death of its author.

In the advancement of almost every branch of pure mathematics Lagrange took a conspicuous part. The calculus of variations is indissolubly associated with his name. In the theory of numbers he furnished solutions of many of P. Fermat's theorems, and added some of his own. In algebra he discovered the method of approximating to the real roots of an equation by means of continued fractions, and imagined a general process of solving algebraical equations of every degree. The method indeed fails for equations of an order above the fourth, because it then involves the solution of an equation of higher dimensions than they proposed. Yet it possesses the great and characteristic merit of generalizing the solutions of his predecessors, exhibiting them all as modifications of one principle. To Lagrange, perhaps more than to any other, the theory of differential equations is indebted for its position as a science, rather than a collection of ingenious artifices for the solution of particular problems. To the calculus of finite differences he contributed the beautiful formula of interpolation which bears his name; although substantially the same result seems to have been previously obtained by Euler. But it was in the application to mechanical questions of the instrument which he thus helped to form that his singular merit lay. It was his just boast to have transformed mechanics (defined by him as a "geometry of four dimensions") into a branch of analysis, and to have exhibited the so-called mechanical "principles" as simple results of the calculus. The method of "generalized coordinates," as it is now called, by which he attained this result, is the most brilliant achievement of the analytical method. Instead of following the motion of each individual part of a material system, he showed that, if we determine its configuration by a sufficient number of variables, whose number is that of the degrees of freedom to move (there being as many equations as the system has degrees of freedom), the kinetic and potential energies of the system can be expressed in terms of those, and the differential equations of motion thence deduced by simple differentiation. Besides this most important contribution to the general fabric of dynamical science, we owe to Lagrange several minor theorems of great elegance,—among which may be mentioned his theorem that the kinetic energy imparted by given impulses to a material system under given constraints is a maximum. To this entire branch of knowledge, in short, he successfully imparted that character of generality and completeness towards which his labours invariably tended.

His share in the gigantic task of verifying the Newtonian theory would alone suffice to immortalize his name. His co-operation was indeed more indispensable than at first sight appears. Much as was done *by* him, what was done *through* him was still more important. Some of his brilliant rival's most conspicuous discoveries were implicitly contained in his writings, and wanted but one step for completion. But that one step, from the abstract to the concrete, was precisely that which the character of Lagrange's mind indisposed him to make. As notable instances may be mentioned Laplace's discoveries relating to the velocity of sound and the secular acceleration of the moon, both of which were led close up to by Lagrange's analytical demonstrations. In the *Berlin Memoirs* for 1778 and 1783 Lagrange gave the first direct and theoretically perfect method of determining cometary orbits. It has not indeed proved practically available; but his system of calculating cometary perturbations by means of "mechanical quadratures" has formed the starting-point of all subsequent researches on the subject. His determination[2] of maximum and minimum values for the slowly varying planetary eccentricities was the earliest attempt to deal with the problem. Without a more accurate knowledge of the masses of the planets than was then possessed a satisfactory solution was impossible; but the upper limits assigned by him agreed closely with those obtained later by U. J. J. Leverrier.[3] As a mathematical writer Lagrange has perhaps never been surpassed. His treatises are not only storehouses of ingenious methods, but models of symmetrical form. The clearness, elegance and originality of his mode of presentation give lucidity to what is obscure, novelty to what is familiar, and simplicity to what is abstruse. His genius was one of generalization and abstraction; and the aspirations of the time towards unity and perfection received, by his serene labours, an embodiment denied to them in the troubled world of politics.

BIBLIOGRAPHY.—Lagrange's numerous scattered memoirs have been collected and published in seven 4to volumes, under the title

[1] *Œuvres*, vi. 771.

[2] *Œuvres*, v. 211 seq.

[3] Grant, *History of Physical Astronomy*, p. 117.

[illegible] 1477 the chapel was presented by Ferdinand and Isabella to the monks of the Parral, a neighbouring Hieronymite monastery. The original *granja* (i.e. grange or farm), established by the monks, was purchased in 1719 by Philip V., after the destruction of his summer palace at Valsain, the ancient *Vallis Sapinorum*, 2 m. S. Philip determined to convert the estate into a second Versailles. The palace was built between 1721 and 1723. Its façade is fronted by a colonnade in which the pillars reach to the roof. The state apartments contain some valuable 18th-century furniture, but the famous collection of sculptures was removed to Madrid in 1836, and is preserved there in the Museo del Prado. At La Granja it is represented by facsimiles in plaster. The collegiate church adjoining the palace dates from 1724, and contains the tombs of Philip V. and his consort Isabella Farnese. An artificial lake called El Mar, 4095 ft. above sea-level, irrigates the gardens, which are imitated from those of Versailles, and supplies water for the fountains. These, despite the antiquated and sometimes tasteless style of their ornamentation, are probably the finest in the world; it is noteworthy that, owing to the high level of the lake, no pumps or other mechanism are needed to supply pressure. There are twenty-six fountains besides lakes and waterfalls. Among the most remarkable are the group of "Perseus, Andromeda and the Sea-Monster," which sends up a jet of water 110 ft. high, the "Fame," which reaches 125 ft., and the very elaborate "Baths of Diana." It is of the last that Philip V. is said to have remarked, "It has cost me three millions and amused me three minutes." Most of the fountains were made by order of Queen Isabella in 1727, during the king's absence. The glass factory of San Ildefonso was founded by Charles III.

It was in La Granja that Philip V. resigned the crown to his son in January 1724, to resume it after his son's death seven months later; that the treaties of 1777, 1778, 1796 and 1800 were signed (see SPAIN: *History*); that Ferdinand VII. summoned Don Carlos to the throne in 1832, but was induced to alter the succession in favour of his own infant daughter Isabella, thus involving Spain in civil war; and that in 1836 a military revolt compelled the Queen-regent Christina to restore the constitution of 1812.

LAGRENÉE, LOUIS JEAN FRANÇOIS (1724–1805), French painter, was a pupil of Carle Vanloo. Born at Paris on the 30th of December 1724, in 1755 he became a member of the Royal Academy, presenting as his diploma picture the "Rape of Deianira" (Louvre). He visited St Petersburg at the call of the empress Elizabeth, and on his return was named in 1781 director of the French Academy at Rome; he there painted the "Indian Widow," one of his best-known works. In 1804 Napoleon conferred on him the cross of the legion of honour, and on the 19th of June 1805 he died in the Louvre, of which he was honorary keeper.

LA GUAIRA, or LA GUAYRA (sometimes LAGUAIRA, &c.), a town and port of Venezuela, in the Federal district, 23 m. by rail and 6½ m. in a direct line N. of Caracas. Pop. (1904, estimate) 14,000. It is situated between a precipitous mountain side and a broad, semicircular indentation of the coast line which forms the roadstead of the port. The anchorage was long considered one of the most dangerous on the Caribbean coast, and landing was attended with much danger. The harbour has been improved by the construction of a concrete breakwater running out from the eastern shore line 2044 ft., built up from an extreme depth of 46 ft. or from an average depth of 29½ ft., and rising 10½ ft. above sea-level. This encloses an area of 76½ acres, having an average depth of nearly 28 ft. The harbour is further improved by 1870 ft. of concrete quays and 1397 ft. of retaining sea-wall, with several piers (three covered) projecting into deep water. These works were executed by a British company, known as the La Guaira Harbour Corporation, Ltd., and were completed in 1891 at a cost of about one million sterling. The concession is for 99 years and the additional charges which the company is authorized to impose are necessarily heavy. These improvements and the restrictions placed upon the direct trade between West Indian ports and the Orinoco have greatly increased the foreign trade of La Guaira, which in 1903 was 52% of [illegible] of the [illegible] *puertos habilitados* of the republic [illegible] entries of that year numbered 277, of which 263 entered with general cargo and 14 with coal exclusively. The exports included 152,625 bags coffee, 124,047 bags cacao and 152,891 hides. For 1905–1906 the imports at La Guaira were valued officially at £767,365 and the exports at £665,708. The city stands on sloping ground stretching along the circular coast line with a varying width of 130 to 330 ft. and having the appearance of an amphitheatre. The port improvements added 18 acres of reclaimed land to La Guaira's area, and the removal of old shore batteries likewise increased its available breadth. In this narrow space is built the town, composed in great part of small, roughly-made cabins, and narrow, badly-paved streets, but with good business houses on its principal street. From the mountain side, reddish-brown in colour and bare of vegetation, the solar heat is reflected with tremendous force, the mean annual temperature being 84° F. The seaside towns of Maiquetia, 2 m. W. and Macuto, 3 m. E., which have better climatic and sanitary conditions and are connected by a narrow-gauge railway, are the residences of many of the wealthier merchants of La Guaira.

La Guaira was founded in 1588, was sacked by filibusters under Amias Preston in 1595, and by the French under Grammont in 1680, was destroyed by the great earthquake of the 26th of March 1812, and suffered severely in the war for independence. In 1903, pending the settlement of claims of Great Britain, Germany and Italy against Venezuela, La Guaira was blockaded by a British-German-Italian fleet.

LA GUÉRONNIÈRE, LOUIS ÉTIENNE ARTHUR DUBREUIL HÉLION, VICOMTE DE (1816–1875), French politician, was the scion of a noble Poitevin family. Although by birth and education attached to Legitimist principles, he became closely associated with Lamartine, to whose organ, *Le Bien Public*, he was a principal contributor. After the stoppage of this paper he wrote for *La Presse*, and in 1850 edited *Le Pays*. A character sketch of Louis Napoleon in this journal caused differences with Lamartine, and La Guéronnière became more and more closely identified with the policy of the prince president. Under the Empire he was a member of the council of state (1853), senator (1861), ambassador at Brussels (1868), and at Constantinople (1870), and grand officer of the legion of honour (1866). He died in Paris on the 23rd of December 1875. Besides his *Études et portraits politiques contemporains* (1856) his most important works are those on the foreign policy of the Empire: *La France, Rome et Italie* (1851), *L'Abandon de Rome* (1862), *De la politique intérieure et extérieure de la France* (1862).

His elder brother, ALFRED DUBREUIL HÉLION, Comte de La Guéronnière (1810–1884), who remained faithful to the Legitimist party, was also a well-known writer and journalist. He was consistent in his opposition to the July Monarchy and the Empire, but in a series of books on the crisis of 1870–1871 showed a more favourable attitude to the Republic.

LAGUERRE, JEAN HENRI GEORGES (1858–), French lawyer and politician, was born in Paris on the 24th of June 1858. Called to the bar in 1879, he distinguished himself by brilliant pleadings in favour of socialist and anarchist leaders, defending Prince Kropotkine at Lyons in 1883, Louise Michel in the same year; and in 1886, with A. Millerand as colleague he defended Ernest Roche and Duc Quercy, the instigators of the Decazeville strike. His strictures on the *procureur de la République* on this occasion being declared libellous he was suspended for six months and in 1890 he again incurred suspension for an attack on the attorney-general, Quesnay de Beaurepaire. He also pleaded in the greatest criminal cases of his time, though from 1893 onwards exclusively in the provinces, his exclusion from the Parisian bar having been secured on the pretext of his connexion with *La Presse*. He entered the Chamber of Deputies for Apt in 1883 as a representative of the extreme revisionist programme, and was one of the leaders of the Boulangist agitation. He had formerly written for Georges Clemenceau's organ *La Justice*, but when Clemenceau refused to impose any shibboleth on the radical party he became director of *La Presse*. He rallied to the republican party in May 1891, some months before General Boulanger's suicide. He was not re-elected to the Chamber in 1893. Laguerre was an excellent lecturer on the revolutionary period of French history, concerning which he had collected many valuable and rare documents. He interested himself in the fate of the "Little Dauphin" (Louis XVII.), whose supposed remains, buried at Ste Marguerite, he proved to be those of a boy of fourteen.

LAGUNA, or LA LAGUNA, an episcopal city and formerly the capital of the island of Teneriffe, in the Spanish archipelago of the Canary Islands. Pop. (1900) 13,074. Laguna is 4 m. N. by W. of Santa Cruz, in a plain 1800 ft. above sea-level, surrounded by mountains. Snow is unknown here, and the mean annual temperature exceeds 63° F.; but the rainfall is very heavy, and in winter the plain is sometimes flooded. The humidity of the atmosphere, combined with the warm climate and rich volcanic soil, renders the district exceptionally fertile; wheat, wine and tobacco, oranges and other fruits, are produced in abundance. Laguna is the favourite summer residence of the wealthier inhabitants of Santa Cruz. Besides the cathedral, the city contains several picturesque convents, now secularized, a fine modern town hall, hospitals, a large public library and some ancient palaces of the Spanish nobility. Even the modern buildings have often an appearance of antiquity, owing to the decay caused by damp, and the luxuriant growth of climbing plants.

LA HARPE, JEAN FRANÇOIS DE (1739–1803), French critic, was born in Paris of poor parents on the 20th of November 1739. His father, who signed himself Delharpe, was a descendant of a noble family originally of Vaud. Left an orphan at the age of nine, La Harpe was taken care of for six months by the sisters of charity, and his education was provided for by a scholarship at the Collège d'Harcourt. When nineteen he was imprisoned for some months on the charge of having written a satire against his protectors at the college. La Harpe always denied his guilt, but this culminating misfortune of an early life spent entirely in the position of a dependent had possibly something to do with the bitterness he evinced in later life. In 1763 his tragedy of *Warwick* was played before the court. This, his first play, was perhaps the best he ever wrote. The many authors whom he afterwards offended were always able to observe that the critic's own plays did not reach the standard of excellence he set up. *Timoléon* (1764), *Pharamond* (1765) and *Gustave Wasa* (1766) were failures. *Mélanie* was a better play, but was never represented. The success of *Warwick* led to a correspondence with Voltaire, who conceived a high opinion of La Harpe, even allowing him to correct his verses. In 1764 La Harpe married the daughter of a coffee house keeper. This marriage, which proved very unhappy and was dissolved, did not improve his position. They were very poor, and for some time were guests of Voltaire at Ferney. When, after Voltaire's death, La Harpe in his praise of the philosopher ventured on some reasonable, but rather ill-timed, criticism of individual works, he was accused of treachery to one who had been his constant friend. In 1768 he returned from Ferney to Paris, where he began to write for the *Mercure*. He was a born fighter and had small mercy on the authors whose work he handled. But he was himself violently attacked, and suffered under many epigrams, especially those of Lebrun-Pindare. No more striking proof of the general hostility can be given than his reception (1776) at the Academy, which Sainte-Beuve calls his "execution." Marmontel, who received him, used the occasion to eulogize La Harpe's predecessor, Charles Pierre Colardeau, especially for his pacific, modest and indulgent disposition. The speech was punctuated by the applause of the audience, who chose to regard it as a series of sarcasms on the new member. Eventually La Harpe was compelled to resign from the *Mercure*, which he had edited from 1770. On the stage he produced *Les Barmécides* (1778), *Philoctète*, *Jeanne de Naples* (1781), *Les Brames* (1783), *Coriolan* (1784), *Virginie* (1786). In 1786 he began a course of literature at the newly-established Lycée. In these lectures, published as the *Cours de littérature ancienne et moderne*, La Harpe is at his best, for he found a standpoint more or less independent of contemporary polemics. He is said to be inexact in dealing with the ancients, [illegible] of the middle ages, but he [illegible] writers. Sainte-Beuve [illegible] French school of tragedy, which [illegible]. La Harpe was a disciple of the [illegible] party through the [illegible]. In [illegible] he edited the *Mercure de France* [illegible] to the revolutionary leaders. But in April [illegible] seized as a "suspect." In prison he [illegible] which he described in convincing [illegible] an ardent Catholic and a [illegible]. When he resumed his chair at the Lycée, he [illegible] politics and literature. He was [illegible] the publication (1801–1807) of his *Correspondance* [illegible] with the grand-duke, afterwards the [illegible]. In these letters he surpassed the [illegible]. He contracted a second marriage, which was dissolved after a few weeks by his wife. He died on the [illegible] of February 1803 in Paris, leaving in his will an [illegible] to his fellow countrymen to maintain peace and [illegible]. Among his posthumous works was a *Prophétie de Cazotte* which Sainte-Beuve pronounces his best work. It is a [illegible] of a dinner-party of notables long before the Revolution, when Jacques Cazotte is made to prophesy the [illegible] awaiting the various individuals of the company.

Among his works [illegible]—*Commentaire sur Racine* (1795–1796), [illegible] *sur le théâtre de Voltaire* [illegible] in 1814), and an epic poem *La Religion* (1814). His [illegible] has been often reprinted. To the edition of [illegible] is prefixed a notice by [illegible]. See also Sainte-Beuve, *Causeries du lundi*, vol. v.; [illegible], *Recherches historiques, bibliographiques et littéraires* . . . *sur La Harpe* ([illegible]).

LAHIRE, LAURENT DE ([illegible]), French painter, was born at Paris on the [illegible] of February [illegible]. He became a pupil of Lallemand, studied the works of Primaticcio at Fontainebleau, but never visited Italy, and belongs wholly to that transition period which preceded the school of Simon Vouet. His picture of Nicolas V opening the crypt in which he discovers the corpse of St Francis of Assisi standing (Louvre) was executed in 1630 for the Capuchins of the Marais; it shows a gravity and sobriety of character which marked Lahire's best work, and seems not to have been without influence on Le Sueur. The Louvre contains eight other works, and paintings by Lahire are in the museums of Strasburg, Rouen and Le Mans. His drawings, of which the British Museum possesses a fine example, "Presentation of the Virgin in the Temple," are treated as seriously as his paintings, and [illegible] simplicity and dignity [illegible]. The example of the Capuchins, for whom he executed [illegible], was followed [illegible] other works in Paris, Rouen and Fécamp, was followed [illegible] goldsmiths' company, for whom he produced in 1635 "St [illegible] healing the Sick" (Louvre) and the "Conversion of St Paul" [illegible]. In 1648, with eleven other artists, he founded [illegible] Royal Academy of Painting and Sculpture. Richelieu [illegible] Palais Royal, Chancellor Séguier, Tallemant [illegible] with important [illegible] a series of [illegible] a great number of [illegible] the town-hall of [illegible] municipality.

[illegible] of the [illegible] Rothaar [illegible] elevation [illegible] eastward to [illegible] course [illegible] and [illegible] sides [illegible] and [illegible]

Burgstein and Nassau, and the well-known health resort of Ems. The Lahn is about 135 m. long; it is navigable from its mouth to Giessen, and is partly canalized. A railway follows the valley practically throughout. In 1796 there were here several encounters between the French under General Jourdan and the troops of the archduke Johan, which resulted in the retreat of the French across the Rhine.

LAHNDA (properly *Lahndā* or *Lahindā*, western, or *Lahndē-dī bōlī*, the language of the West), an Indo-Aryan language spoken in the western Punjab. In 1901 the number of speakers was 3,337,917. Its eastern boundary is very indefinite as the language gradually merges into the Panjabi immediately to the east, but it is conventionally taken as the river Chenab from the Kashmir frontier to the town of Ramnagar, and thence as a straight line to the south-west corner of the district of Montgomery. Lahnda is also spoken in the north of the state of Bahawalpur and of the province of Sind, in which latter locality it is known as Siraiki. Its western boundary is, roughly speaking, the river Indus, across which the language of the Afghan population is Pashto (Pushtu), while the Hindu settlers still speak Lahnda. In the Derajat, however, Lahnda is the principal language of all classes in the plains west of the river.

Lahnda is also known as Western Panjabi and as Jatki, or the language of the Jats, who form the bulk of the population whose mother-tongue it is. In the Derajat it is called Hindko or the language of Hindus. In 1819 the Serampur missionaries published a Lahnda version of the New Testament. They called the language Uchchi, from the important town of Uch near the confluence of the Jhelam and the Chenab. This name is commonly met with in old writings. It has numerous dialects, which fall into two main groups, a northern and a southern, the speakers of which are separated by the Salt Range. The principal varieties of the northern group are Hindki (the same in meaning as Hindko) and Pōthwārī. In the southern group the most important are Khētrānī, Multānī, and the dialect of Shahpur. The language possesses no literature.

Lahnda belongs to the north-western group of the outer band of Indo-Aryan languages (*q.v.*), the other members being Kashmiri (*q.v.*) and Sindhi, with both of which it is closely connected. See Sindhi; also Hindostani. (G. A. Gr.)

LA HOGUE, BATTLE OF, the name now given to a series of encounters which took place from the 19th to the 23rd (O.S.) of May 1692, between an allied British and Dutch fleet and a French force, on the northern and eastern sides of the Cotentin in Normandy. A body of French troops, and a number of Jacobite exiles, had been collected in the Cotentin. The government of Louis XIV. prepared a naval armament to cover their passage across the Channel. This force was to have been composed of the French ships at Brest commanded by the count of Tourville, and of a squadron which was to have joined him from Toulon. But the Toulon ships were scattered by a gale, and the combination was not effected. The count of Tourville, who had put to sea to meet them, had with him only 45 or 47 ships of the line. Yet when the reinforcement failed to join him, he steered up Channel to meet the allies, who were known to be in strength. On the 15th of May the British fleet of 63 sail of the line, under command of Edward Russell, afterwards earl of Orford, was joined at St Helens by the Dutch squadron of 36 sail under Admiral van Allemonde. The apparent rashness of the French admiral in seeking an encounter with very superior numbers is explained by the existence of a general belief that many British captains were discontented, and would pass over from the service of the government established by the Revolution of 1688 to their exiled king, James II. It is said that Tourville had orders from Louis XIV. to attack in any case, but the story is of doubtful authority. The British government, aware of the Jacobite intrigues in its fleet, and of the prevalence of discontent, took the bold course of appealing to the loyalty [illegible]tism of its officers. At a meeting of the flag-officers on [illegible] Britannia," Russell's flag-ship, on the 15th of May, [illegible]d their loyalty, and the whole allied fleet put to sea [illegible]. On the 19th of May, when Cape Barfleur, the north-eastern point of the Cotentin, was 21 m. S.W. of them, they sighted Tourville, who was then 20 m. to the north of Cape La Hague, the north-western extremity of the peninsula, which must not be confounded with La Houque, or La Hogue, the place at which the fighting ended. The allies were formed in a line from S.S.W. to N.N.E. heading towards the English coast, the Dutch forming the White or van division, while the Red or centre division under Russell, and the Blue or rear under Sir John Ashby, were wholly composed of British ships. The wind was from the S.W. and the weather hazy. Tourville bore down and attacked about mid-day, directing his main assault on the centre of the allies, but telling off some ships to watch the van and rear of his enemy. As this first encounter took place off Cape Barfleur, the battle was formerly often called by the name. On the centre, where Tourville was directly opposed to Russell, the fighting was severe. The British flag-ship the "Britannia" (100), and the French, the "Soleil Royal" (100), were both completely crippled. After several hours of conflict, the French admiral, seeing himself outnumbered, and that the allies could outflank him and pass through the necessarily wide intervals in his extended line, drew off without the loss of a ship. The wind now fell and the haze became a fog. Till the 23rd, the two fleets remained off the north coast of the Cotentin, drifting west with the ebb tide or east with the flood, save when they anchored. During the night of the 19th/20th some British ships became entangled, in the fog, with the French, and drifted through them on the tide, with loss. On the 23rd both fleets were near La Hague. About half the French, under D'Amfreville, rounded the cape, and fled to St Malo through the dangerous passage known as the Race of Alderney (le Ras Blanchard). The others were unable to get round the cape before the flood tide set in, and were carried to the eastward. Tourville now transferred his own flag, and left his captains free to save themselves as they best could. He left the "Soleil Royal," and sent her with two others to Cherbourg, where they were destroyed by Sir Ralph Delaval. The others now ran round Cape Barfleur, and sought refuge on the east side of the Cotentin at the anchorage of La Houque, called by the English La Hogue, where the troops destined for the invasion were encamped. Here 13 of them were burnt by Sir George Rooke, in the presence of the French generals and of the exiled king James II. From the name of the place where the last blow was struck, the battle has come to be known by the name of La Hogue.

Sufficient accounts of the battle may be found in Lediard's *Naval History* (London, 1735), and for the French side in Tronde's *Batailles navales de la France* (Paris, 1867). The escape of D'Amfreville's squadron is the subject of Browning's poem "Hervé Riel."

(D. H.)

LAHORE, an ancient city of British India, the capital of the Punjab, which gives its name to a district and division. It lies in 31° 35′ N. and 74° 20′ E. near the left bank of the River Ravi, 1706 ft. above the sea, and 1252 m. by rail from Calcutta. It is thus in about the same latitude as Cairo, but owing to its inland position is considerably hotter than that city, being one of the hottest places in India in the summer time. In the cold season the climate is pleasantly cool and bright. The native city is walled, about 1¼ m. in length W. to E. and about ¾ m. in breadth N. to S. Its site has been occupied from early times, and much of it stands high above the level of the surrounding country, raised on the remains of a succession of former habitations. Some old buildings, which have been preserved, stand now below the present surface of the ground. This is well seen in the mosque now called Masjid Niwin (or sunken) built in 1560, the mosque of Mullah Rahmat, 7 ft. below, and the Shivali, a very old Hindu temple, about 12 ft. below the surrounding ground. Hindu tradition traces the origin of Lahore to Loh or Lava, son of Rama, the hero of the *Ramayana*. The absence of mention of Lahore by Alexander's historians, and the fact that coins of the Graeco-Bactrian kings are not found among the ruins, lead to the belief that it was not a place of any importance during the earliest period of Indian history. On the other hand, Hsüan Tsang, the Chinese Buddhist, notices the city in his *Itinerary* (A.D. 630); and it seems probable, therefore, that Lahore first rose into prominence between the 1st and 7th centuries A.D. Governed originally by a family of Chauhan Rajputs, a branch of the house of Ajmere, Lahore fell successively under the dominion of the Ghazni and Ghori sultans, who made it the capital of their Indian conquests, and adorned it with numerous buildings, almost all now in ruins. But it was under the Mogul empire that Lahore reached its greatest size and magnificence. The reigns of Humayun, Akbar, Jahangir, Shah Jahan and Aurangzeb form the golden period in the annals and architecture of the city. Akbar enlarged and repaired the fort, and surrounded the town with a wall, portions of which remain, built into the modern work of Ranjit Singh. Lahore formed the capital of the Sikh empire of that monarch. At the end of the second Sikh War, with the rest of the Punjab, it came under the British dominion.

The architecture of Lahore cannot compare with that of Delhi. Jahangir in 1622–1627 erected the Khwabgah or "sleeping-place," a fine palace much defaced by the Sikhs but to some extent restored in modern times; the Moti Masjid or "pearl mosque" in the fort, used by Ranjit Singh and afterwards by the British as a treasure-house; and also the tomb of Anarkali, used formerly as the station church and now as a library. Shah Jahan erected a palace and other buildings near the Khwabgah, including the beautiful pavilion called the Naulakha from its cost of nine lakhs, which was inlaid with precious stones. The mosque of Wazir Khan (1634) provides the finest example of *kashi* or encaustic tile work. Aurangzeb's Jama Masjid, or "great mosque," is a huge bare building, stiff in design, and lacking the detailed ornament typical of buildings at Delhi. The buildings of Ranjit Singh, especially his mausoleum, are common and meretricious in style. He was, moreover, responsible for much of the despoiling of the earlier buildings. The streets of the native city are narrow and tortuous, and are best seen from the back of an elephant. Two of the chief features of Lahore lie outside its walls at Shahdara and Shalamar Gardens respectively. Shahdara, which contains the tomb of the emperor Jahangir, lies across the Ravi some 6 m. N. of the city. It consists of a splendid marble cenotaph surrounded by a grove of trees and gardens. The Shalamar Gardens, which were laid out in A.D. 1637 by Shah Jahan, lie 6 m. E. of the city. They are somewhat neglected except on festive occasions, when the fountains are playing and the trees are lit up by lamps at night.

The modern city of Lahore, which contained a population of 202,964 in 1901, may be divided into four parts: the native city, already described; the civil station or European quarter, known as Donald Town; the Anarkali bazaar, a suburb S. of the city wall; and the cantonment, formerly called Mian Mir. The main street of the civil station is a portion of the grand trunk road from Calcutta to Peshawar, locally known as the Mall. The chief modern buildings along this road, west to east, are the Lahore museum, containing a fine collection of Graeco-Buddhist sculptures, found by General Cunningham in the Yusufzai country, and arranged by Mr Lockwood Kipling, a former curator of the museum; the cathedral, begun by Bishop French, in Early English style, and consecrated in 1887; the Lawrence Gardens and Montgomery Halls, surrounded by a garden that forms the chief meeting-place of Europeans in the afternoon; and opposite this government house, the official residence of the lieutenant-governor of the Punjab; next to this is the Punjab club for military men and civilians. Three miles beyond is the Lahore cantonment, where the garrison is stationed, except a company of British infantry, which occupies the fort. It is the headquarters of the 3rd division of the northern army. Lahore is an important junction on the North-Western railway system, but has little local trade or manufacture. The chief industries are silk goods, gold and silver lace, metal work and carpets which are made in the Lahore gaol. There are also cotton mills, flour mills, an ice-factory, and several factories for mineral waters, oils, soap, leather goods, &c. Lahore is an important educational centre. Here are the Punjab University with five colleges, medical and law colleges, a central training

manufactures of pottery, bricks, oil, linen and woollen cloth, hose and paper.

Laibach is supposed to occupy the site of the ancient Emona or Aemona, founded by the emperor Augustus in 34 B.C. It was besieged by Alaric in 400, and in 451 it was desolated by the Huns. In 900 Laibach suffered much from the Magyars, who were, however, defeated there in 914. In the 12th century the town passed into the hands of the dukes of Carinthia; in 1270 it was taken by Ottocar of Bohemia; and in 1277 it came under the Habsburgs. In the early part of the 15th century the town was several times besieged by the Turks. The bishopric was founded in 1461. On the 17th of March 1797 and again on the 3rd of June 1809 Laibach was taken by the French, and from 1809 to 1813 it became the seat of their general government of the Illyrian provinces. From 1816 to 1849 Laibach was the capital of the kingdom of Illyria. The town is also historically known from the congress of Laibach, which assembled here in 1821 (see below). Laibach suffered severely on the 14th of April 1895 from an earthquake.

Congress or Conference of Laibach.—Before the break-up of the conference of Troppau (*q.v.*), it had been decided to adjourn it till the following January, and to invite the attendance of the king of Naples, Laibach being chosen as the place of meeting. Castlereagh, in the name of Great Britain, had cordially approved this invitation, as "implying negotiation" and therefore as a retreat from the position taken up in the Troppau Protocol. Before leaving Troppau, however, the three autocratic powers, Russia, Austria and Prussia, had issued, on the 8th of December 1820, a circular letter, in which they reiterated the principles of the Protocol, *i.e.* the right and duty of the powers responsible for the peace of Europe to intervene to suppress any revolutionary movement by which they might conceive that peace to be endangered (Hertslet, No. 105). Against this view Castlereagh once more protested in a circular despatch of the 19th of January 1821, in which he clearly differentiated between the objectionable general principles advanced by the three powers, and the particular case of the unrest in Italy, the immediate concern not of Europe at large, but of Austria and of any other Italian powers which might consider themselves endangered (Hertslet, No. 107).

The conference opened on the 26th of January 1821, and its constitution emphasized the divergences revealed in the above circulars. The emperors of Russia and Austria were present in person, and with them were Counts Nesselrode and Capo d'Istria, Metternich and Baron Vincent; Prussia and France were represented by plenipotentiaries. But Great Britain, on the ground that she had no immediate interest in the Italian question, was represented only by Lord Stewart, the ambassador at Vienna, who was not armed with full powers, his mission being to watch the proceedings and to see that nothing was done beyond or in violation of the treaties. Of the Italian princes, Ferdinand of Naples and the duke of Modena came in person; the rest were represented by plenipotentiaries.

It was soon clear that a more or less open breach between Great Britain and the other powers was inevitable. Metternich was anxious to secure an apparent unanimity of the powers to back the Austrian intervention in Naples, and every device was used to entrap the English representative into subscribing a formula which would have seemed to commit Great Britain to the principles of the other allies. When these devices failed, attempts were made unsuccessfully to exclude Lord Stewart from the conferences on the ground of defective powers. Finally he was forced to an open protest, which he caused to be inscribed on the journals, but the action of Capo d'Istria in reading to the assembled Italian ministers, who were by no means reconciled to the large claims implied in the Austrian intervention, a declaration in which as the result of the "intimate union established by solemn acts between all the European powers" the Russian emperor offered to the allies "the aid of his arms, should new revolutions threaten new dangers," an attempt to revive that idea of a "universal union" based on the Holy Alliance (*q.v.*) against which Great Britain had consistently protested.

The objections of Great Britain were, however, not so much to an Austrian intervention in Naples as to the far-reaching principles by which it was sought to justify it. King Ferdinand had been invited to Laibach, according to the circular of the

8th of December, in order that he might be free to act as "mediator between his erring peoples and the states whose tranquillity they threatened." The cynical use he made of his "freedom" to repudiate obligations solemnly contracted is described elsewhere (see NAPLES, *History*). The result of this action was the Neapolitan declaration of war and the occupation of Naples by Austria, with the sanction of the congress. This was preceded, on the 10th of March, by the revolt of the garrison of Alessandria and the military revolution in Piedmont, which in its turn was suppressed, as a result of negotiations at Laibach, by Austrian troops. It was at Laibach, too, that, on the 19th of March, the emperor Alexander received the news of Ypsilanti's invasion of the Danubian principalities, which heralded the outbreak of the War of Greek Independence, and from Laibach Capo d'Istria addressed to the Greek leader the tsar's repudiation of his action.

The conference closed on the 12th of May, on which date Russia, Austria and Prussia issued a declaration (Hertslet, No. 108) "to proclaim to the world the principles which guided them" in coming "to the assistance of subdued peoples," a declaration which once more affirmed the principles of the Troppau Protocol. In this lay the European significance of the Laibach conference, of which the activities had been mainly confined to Italy. The issue of the declaration without the signatures of the representatives of Great Britain and France proclaimed the disunion of the alliance, within which—to use Lord Stewart's words—there existed "a triple understanding which bound the parties to carry forward their own views in spite of any difference of opinion between them and the two great constitutional governments."

No separate history of the congress exists, but innumerable references are to be found in general histories and in memoirs, correspondence, &c., of the time. See Sir E. Hertslet, *Map of Europe* (London, 1875); Castlereagh, *Correspondence*; Metternich, *Memoirs*; N. Bianchi, *Storia documentata della diplomazia Europea in Italia* (8 vols., Turin, 1865–1872); Gentz's correspondence (see GENTZ, F. VON). Valuable unpublished correspondence is preserved at the Record Office in the volumes marked F. O., Austria, Lord Stewart, January to February 1821, and March to September 1821. (W. A. P.)

LAIDLAW, WILLIAM (1780–1845), friend and amanuensis of Sir Walter Scott, was born at Blackhouse, Selkirkshire, on the 19th of November 1780, the son of a sheep farmer. After an elementary education in Peebles he returned to work upon his father's farm. James Hogg, the shepherd poet, who was employed at Blackhouse for some years, became Laidlaw's friend and appreciative critic. Together they assisted Scott by supplying material for his *Border Minstrelsy*, and Laidlaw, after two failures as a farmer in Midlothian and Peeblesshire, became Scott's steward at Abbotsford. He also acted as Scott's amanuensis at different times, taking down a large part of *The Bride of Lammermoor*, *The Legend of Montrose* and *Ivanhoe* from the author's dictation. He died at Contin near Dingwall, Ross-shire, on the 18th of May 1845. Of his poetry, little is known except *Lucy's Flittin'* in Hogg's *Forest Minstrel*.

LAING, ALEXANDER GORDON (1793–1826), Scottish explorer, the first European to reach Timbuktu, was born at Edinburgh on the 27th of December 1793. He was educated by his father, William Laing, a private teacher of classics, and at Edinburgh University. In 1811 he went to Barbados as clerk to his maternal uncle Colonel (afterwards General) Gabriel Gordon. Through General Sir George Beckwith, governor of Barbados, he obtained an ensigncy in the York Light Infantry. He was employed in the West Indies, and in 1822 was promoted to a company in the Royal African Corps. In that year, while with his regiment at Sierra Leone, he was sent by the governor, Sir Charles MacCarthy, to the Mandingo country, with the double object of opening up commerce and endeavouring to abolish the slave trade in that region. Later in the same year Laing visited Falaba, the capital of the Sulima country, and ascertained the source of the Rokell. He endeavoured to reach the source of the Niger, but was stopped by the natives. He was, however, enabled to fix it with approximate accuracy. He took an active part in the Ashanti War of 1823–24, and was sent home with the despatches containing the news of the death in action of Sir Charles MacCarthy. Henry, 3rd Earl Bathurst, then secretary for the colonies, instructed Captain Laing to undertake a journey, via Tripoli and Timbuktu, to further elucidate the hydrography of the Niger basin. Laing left England in February 1825, and at Tripoli on the 14th of July following he married Emma Warrington, daughter of the British consul. Two days later, leaving his bride behind, he started to cross the Sahara, being accompanied by a sheikh who was subsequently accused of planning his murder. Ghadames was reached, by an indirect route, in October 1825, and in December Laing was in the Tuat territory, where he was well received by the Tuareg. On the 10th of January 1826 he left Tuat, and made for Timbuktu across the desert of Tanezroft. Letters from him written in May and July following told of sufferings from fever and the plundering of his caravan by Tuareg, Laing being wounded in twenty-four places in the fighting. Another letter dated from Timbuktu on the 21st of September announced his arrival in that city on the preceding 18th of August, and the insecurity of his position owing to the hostility of the Fula chieftain Bello, then ruling the city. He added that he intended leaving Timbuktu in three days' time. No further news was received from the traveller. From native information it was ascertained that he left Timbuktu on the day he had planned and was murdered on the night of the 26th of September 1826. His papers were never recovered, though it is believed that they were secretly brought to Tripoli in 1828. In 1903 the French government placed a tablet bearing the name of the explorer and the date of his visit on the house occupied by him during his thirty-eight days' stay in Timbuktu.

While in England in 1824 Laing prepared a narrative of his earlier journeys, which was published in 1825 and entitled *Travels in the Timannee, Kooranko and Soolima Countries, in Western Africa*.

LAING, DAVID (1793–1878), Scottish antiquary, the son of William Laing, a bookseller in Edinburgh, was born in that city on the 20th of April 1793. Educated at the Canongate Grammar School, when fourteen he was apprenticed to his father. Shortly after the death of the latter in 1837, Laing was elected to the librarianship of the Signet Library, which post he retained till his death. Apart from an extraordinary general bibliographical knowledge, Laing was best known as a lifelong student of the literary and artistic history of Scotland. He published no original volumes, but contented himself with editing the works of others. Of these, the chief are—*Dunbar's Works* (2 vols., 1834), with a supplement added in 1865; *Robert Baillie's Letters and Journals* (3 vols., 1841–1842); *John Knox's Works* (6 vols., 1846–1864); *Poems and Fables of Robert Henryson* (1865); *Andrew of Wyntoun's Orygynale Cronykil of Scotland* (3 vols., 1872–1879); *Sir David Lyndsay's Poetical Works* (3 vols., 1879). Laing was for more than fifty years a member of the Society of Antiquaries of Scotland, and he contributed upwards of a hundred separate papers to their *Proceedings*. He was also for more than forty years secretary to the Bannatyne Club, many of the publications of which were edited by him. He was struck with paralysis in 1878 while in the Signet Library, and it is related that, on recovering consciousness, he looked about and asked if a proof of Wyntoun had been sent from the printers. He died a few days afterwards, on the 18th of October, in his eighty-sixth year. His library was sold by auction, and realized £16,137. To the university of Edinburgh he bequeathed his collection of MSS.

See the Biographical Memoir prefixed to *Select Remains of Ancient, Popular and Romance Poetry of Scotland*, edited by John Small (Edinburgh, 1885); also T. G. Stevenson, *Notices of David Laing with List of his Publications, &c.* (privately printed 1878).

LAING, MALCOLM (1762–1818), Scottish historian, son of Robert Laing, and elder brother of Samuel Laing the elder, was born on his paternal estate on the Mainland of Orkney. Having studied at the grammar school of Kirkwall and at Edinburgh University, he was called to the Scotch bar in 1785, but devoted his time mainly to historical studies. In 1793 he completed the sixth and last volume of Robert Henry's *History of Great Britain*, the portion which he wrote being in its strongly liberal tone at variance with the preceding part of the work; and in 1802 he published his *History of Scotland from the Union of the Crowns to the Union of the Kingdoms*, a work showing considerable research. Attached to the *History* was a dissertation on the Gowrie conspiracy, and another on the supposed authenticity of Ossian's poems. In another dissertation, prefixed to a second and corrected edition of the *History* published in 1804, Laing endeavoured to prove that Mary, queen of Scots, wrote the Casket Letters, and was partly responsible for the murder of Lord Darnley. In the same year he edited the *Life and Historie of King James VI.*, and in 1805 brought out in two volumes an edition of Ossian's poems. Laing, who was a friend of Charles James Fox, was member of parliament for Orkney and Shetland from 1807 to 1812. He died on the 6th of November 1818.

LAING, SAMUEL (1810–1897), British author and railway [illegible], was born at Edinburgh on the 12th of December [illegible]. He was the nephew of Malcolm Laing, the historian of [illegible]; and his father, Samuel Laing (1780–1868), was also a well-known author, whose books on Norway and Sweden [illegible] much attention. Samuel Laing the younger entered [illegible]'s College, Cambridge, in 1827, and after graduating as [illegible] wrangler and Smith's prizeman, was elected a fellow, [illegible] at Cambridge temporarily as a coach. He was [illegible] to the bar in 1837, and became private secretary to Mr [illegible] (afterwards Lord Taunton), the president of the Board of Trade. In 1842 he was made secretary to the railway [illegible], and retained this post till 1847. He had by then [illegible] an authority on railway working, and had been a member [illegible] Railway Commission; it was at his suggestion [illegible] "parliamentary" rate of a penny a mile was instituted. [illegible] was appointed chairman and managing director of [illegible] Brighton & South Coast Railway, and his business [illegible] itself in the largely increased prosperity of the [illegible] became chairman (1852) of the Crystal Palace [illegible] retired from both posts in 1855. In 1852 he [illegible] parliament as a Liberal for Wick, and after losing his [illegible] was re-elected in 1859, in which year he was ap[illegible] secretary to the Treasury; in 1860 he was [illegible] minister in India. On returning from India, he [illegible] parliament for Wick in 1865. He was defeated [illegible] he was returned for Orkney and Shetland, [illegible] seat till 1885. Meanwhile he had been re[illegible] of the Brighton line in 1867, and continued [illegible] being generally recognized as an admirable [illegible] also chairman of the Railway Debenture [illegible] Railway Share Trust. In later life he became [illegible] author, his *Modern Science and Modern* [illegible] *of the Future* (1889) and *Human* [illegible] read, not only by reason of the [illegible] experience of affairs and clear [illegible] popular and at the same time [illegible] the scientific problems of the day. [illegible] 6th of August 1897.

[illegible] a pass through the Drakensberg, [illegible] of Majuba (*q.v.*), at an elevation [illegible] part of a ridge which slopes [illegible], and before the opening of [illegible] the nek was the main artery [illegible] and Pretoria. The railway [illegible] ft. long. When the Boers [illegible] they occupied Laing's Nek [illegible] ments into the Transvaal. [illegible] British force endeavoured [illegible] was forced to retire.

[illegible]), Scottish merchant, [illegible] was born at Greenock in [illegible] founder of the Birken[illegible]. In 1831 Laird and [illegible] company for the commercial [illegible] of the Niger [illegible] der. [illegible] er, one, the "Alburkah," a paddle-wheel steamer of 55 tons designed by Laird, being the first iron vessel to make an ocean voyage. Macgregor Laird went with the expedition, which was led by Richard Lander and numbered forty-eight Europeans, of whom all but nine died from fever or, in the case of Lander, from wounds. Laird went up the Niger to the confluence of the Benue (then called the Shary or Tchadda), which he was the first white man to ascend. He did not go far up the river but formed an accurate idea as to its source and course. The expedition returned to Liverpool in 1834, Laird and Surgeon R. A. K. Oldfield being the only surviving officers besides Captain (then Lieut.) William Allen, R.N., who accompanied the expedition by order of the Admiralty to survey the river. Laird and Oldfield published in 1837 in two volumes the *Narrative of an Expedition into the Interior of Africa by the River Niger . . . in 1832, 1833, 1834*. Commercially the expedition had been unsuccessful, but Laird had gained experience invaluable to his successors. He never returned to Africa but thenceforth devoted himself largely to the development of trade with West Africa and especially to the opening up of the countries now forming the British protectorates of Nigeria. One of his principal reasons for so doing was his belief that this method was the best means of stopping the slave trade and raising the social condition of the Africans. In 1854 he sent out at his own charges, but with the support of the British government, a small steamer, the "Pleiad," which under W. B. Baikie made so successful a voyage that Laird induced the government to sign contracts for annual trading trips by steamers specially built for navigation of the Niger and Benue. Various stations were founded on the Niger, and though government support was withdrawn after the death of Laird and Baikie, British traders continued to frequent the river, which Laird had opened up with little or no personal advantage. Laird's interests were not, however, wholly African. In 1837 he was one of the promoters of a company formed to run steamships between England and New York, and in 1838 the "Sirius," sent out by this company, was the first ship to cross the Atlantic from Europe entirely under steam. Laird died in London on the 9th of January 1861.

His elder brother, John Laird (1805–1874), was one of the first to use iron in the construction of ships; in 1829 he made an iron lighter of 60 tons which was used on canals and lakes in Ireland; in 1834 he built the paddle steamer "John Randolph" for Savannah, U.S.A., stated to be the first iron ship seen in America. For the East India Company he built in 1839 the first iron vessel carrying guns and he was also the designer of the famous "Birkenhead." A Conservative in politics, he represented Birkenhead in the House of Commons from 1861 to his death.

LAÏS, the name of two Greek courtesans, generally distinguished as follows. (1) The elder, a native of Corinth, born *c.* 480 B.C., was famous for her greed and hardheartedness, which gained her the nickname of *Axinē* (the axe). Among her lovers were the philosophers Aristippus and Diogenes, and Eubatas (or Aristoteles) of Cyrene, a famous runner. In her old age she became a drunkard. Her grave was shown in the Craneion near Corinth, surmounted by a lioness tearing a ram. (2) The younger, daughter of Timandra the mistress of Alcibiades, born at Hyccara in Sicily *c.* 420 B.C., taken to Corinth during the Sicilian expedition. The painter Apelles, who saw her drawing water from the fountain of Peirene, was struck by her beauty, and took her as a model. Having followed a handsome Thessalian to his native land, she was slain in the temple of Aphrodite by women who were jealous of her beauty. Many anecdotes are told of a Laïs by Athenaeus, Aelian, Pausanias, and she forms the subject of many epigrams in the Greek Anthology; but, owing to the similarity of names, there is considerable uncertainty to whom they refer. The name itself, like Phryne, was used as a general term for a courtesan.

See F. Jacobs, *Vermischte Schriften*, iv. (1830).

LAISANT, CHARLES ANNE (1841–), French politician, was born at Nantes on the 1st of November 1841, and was educated at the École Polytechnique as a military engineer.

He defended the fort of Issy at the siege of Paris, and served in Corsica and in Algeria in 1873. In 1876 he resigned his commission to enter the Chamber as deputy for Nantes in the republican interest, and in 1879 he became director of the *Petit Parisien*. For alleged libel on General Courtot de Cissey in this paper he was heavily fined. In the Chamber he spoke chiefly on army questions; and was chairman of a commission appointed to consider army legislation, resigning in 1887 on the refusal of the Chamber to sanction the abolition of exemptions of any kind. He then became an adherent of the revisionist policy of General Boulanger and a member of the League of Patriots. He was elected Boulangist deputy for the 18th Parisian arrondissement in 1889. He did not seek re-election in 1893, but devoted himself thenceforward to mathematics, helping to make known in France the theories of Giusto Bellavitis. He was attached to the staff of the École Polytechnique, and in 1903–1904 was president of the French Association for the Advancement of Science.

In addition to his political pamphlets *Pourquoi et comment je suis Boulangiste* (1887) and *L'Anarchie bourgeoise* (1887), he published mathematical works, among them *Introduction à l'étude des quaternions* (1881) and *Théorie et applications des équipollences* (1887).

LAI-YANG, a city in the Chinese province of Shan-tung, in 37° N., 120° 55′ E., about the middle of the eastern peninsula, on the highway running south from Chi-fu to Kin-Kia or Ting-tsu harbour. It is surrounded by well-kept walls of great antiquity, and its main streets are spanned by large *pailous* or monumental arches, some dating from the time of the emperor Tai-ting-ti of the Yuan dynasty (1324). There are extensive suburbs both to the north and south, and the total population is estimated at 50,000. The so-called Ailanthus silk produced by *Saturnia cynthia* is woven at Lai-yang into a strong fabric; and the manufacture of the peculiar kind of wax obtained from the la-shu or wax-tree insect is largely carried on in the vicinity.

LAKANAL, JOSEPH (1762–1845), French politician, was born at Serres (Ariège) on the 14th of July 1762. His name, originally Lacanal, was altered to distinguish him from his Royalist brothers. He joined one of the teaching congregations, and for fourteen years taught in their schools. When elected by his native department to the Convention in 1792 he was acting as vicar to his uncle Bernard Font (1723–1800), the constitutional bishop of Pamiers. In the Convention he held apart from the various party sections, although he voted for the death of Louis XVI. He rendered great service to the Revolution by his practical knowledge of education. He became a member of the Committee of Public Instruction early in 1793, and after carrying many useful decrees on the preservation of national monuments, on the military schools, on the reorganization of the Museum of Natural History and other matters, he brought forward on the 26th of June his *Projet d'éducation nationale* (printed at the Imprimerie Nationale), which proposed to lay the burden or primary education on the public funds, but to leave secondary education to private enterprise. Provision was also made for public festivals, and a central commission was to be entrusted with educational questions. The scheme, in the main the work of Sieyès, was refused by the Convention, who submitted the whole question to a special commission of six, which under the influence of Robespierre adopted a report by Michel le Peletier de Saint Fargeau shortly before his tragic death. Lakanal, who was a member of the commission, now began to work for the organization of higher education, and abandoning the principle of his *Projet* advocated the establishment of state-aided schools for primary, secondary and university education. In October 1793 he was sent by the Convention to the south-western departments and did not return to Paris until after the revolution of Thermidor. He now became president of the Education Committee and promptly abolished the system which had had Robespierre's support. He drew up schemes for departmental normal schools, for primary schools (reviving in substance the *Projet*) and central schools. He presently acquiesced in the supersession of his own system, but continued his educational reports after his election to the Council of the Five Hundred. In 1799 he was sent by the Directory to organize the defence of the four departments on the left bank of the Rhine threatened by invasion. Under the Consulate he resumed his professional work, and after Waterloo retired to America, where he became president of the university of Louisiana. He returned to France in 1834, and shortly afterwards, in spite of his advanced age, married a second time. He died in Paris on the 14th of February 1845; his widow survived till 1881. Lakanal was an original member of the Institute of France. He published in 1838 an *Exposé sommaire des travaux de Joseph Lakanal*.

His *éloge* at the Academy of Moral and Political Science, of which he was a member, was pronounced by the comte de Rémusat (February 16, 1845), and a *Notice historique* by F. A. M. Mignet was read on the 2nd of May 1857. See also notices by Émile Darnaud (Paris, 1874), "Marcus" (Paris, 1879), P. Legendre in *Hommes de la révolution* (Paris, 1882), E. Guillon, *Lakanal et l'instruction publique* (Paris, 1881). For details of the reports submitted by him to the government see M. Tourneux, "Histoire de l'instruction publique, actes et délibérations de la convention, &c." in *Bibliog. de l'hist. de Paris* (vol. iii., 1900); also A. Robert and G. Cougny, *Dictionnaire des parlementaires* (vol. ii., 1890).

LAKE, GERARD LAKE, 1st Viscount (1744–1808), British general, was born on the 27th of July 1744. He entered the foot guards in 1758, becoming lieutenant (captain in the army) 1762, captain (lieut.-colonel) in 1776, major 1784, and lieut.-colonel in 1792, by which time he was a general officer in the army. He served with his regiment in Germany in 1760–1762 and with a composite battalion in the Yorktown campaign of 1781. After this he was equerry to the prince of Wales, afterwards George IV. In 1790 he became a major-general, and in 1793 was appointed to command the Guards Brigade in the duke of York's army in Flanders. He was in command at the brilliant affair of Lincelles, on the 18th of August 1793, and served on the continent (except for a short time when seriously ill) until April 1794. He had now sold his lieut.-colonelcy in the guards, and had become colonel of the 53rd foot and governor of Limerick. In 1797 he was promoted lieut.-general. In the following year the Irish rebellion broke out. Lake, who was then serving in Ireland, succeeded Sir Ralph Abercromby in command of the troops in April 1798, issued a proclamation ordering the surrender of all arms by the civil population of Ulster, and on the 21st of June routed the rebels at Vinegar Hill (near Enniscorthy, Co. Wexford). He exercised great, but perhaps not unjustified, severity towards all rebels found in arms. Lord Cornwallis now assumed the chief command in Ireland, and in August sent Lake to oppose the French expedition which landed at Killala Bay. On the 29th of the same month Lake arrived at Castlebar, but only in time to witness the disgraceful rout of the troops under General Hely-Hutchinson (afterwards 2nd earl of Donoughmore); but he retrieved this disaster by compelling the surrender of the French at Ballinamuck, near Cloone, on the 8th of September. In 1799 Lake returned to England, and soon afterwards obtained the command in chief in India. He took over his duties at Calcutta in July 1801, and applied himself to the improvement of the Indian army, especially in the direction of making all arms, infantry, cavalry and artillery, more mobile and more manageable. In 1802 he was made a full general.

On the outbreak of war with the Mahratta confederacy in 1803 General Lake took the field against Sindhia, and within two months defeated the Mahrattas at Coel, stormed Aligahr, took Delhi and Agra, and won the great victory of Laswari (November 1st, 1803), where the power of Sindhia was completely broken, with the loss of thirty-one disciplined battalions, trained and officered by Frenchmen, and 426 pieces of ordnance. This defeat, followed a few days later by Major-General Arthur Wellesley's victory at Argaum, compelled Sindhia to come to terms, and a treaty with him was signed in December 1803. Operations were, however, continued against his confederate, Holkar, who, on the 17th of November 1804, was defeated by Lake at Farrukhabad. But the fortress of Bhurtpore held out against four assaults early in 1805, and Cornwallis, who succeeded Wellesley as governor-general in July of that year—superseding Lake at the same time as commander-in-chief—determined

liber[illegible]
and i[illegible]
the Cr[illegible]
able r[illegible]
the Go[illegible]
of Ossia[illegible]
and corr[illegible]
endeavo[illegible]
Casket L[illegible]
Lord Dar[illegible]
of King J[illegible]
edition of
James Fox
from 1807 t[illegible]
LAING, S[illegible]
administrat[illegible]
1810. He w[illegible]
Scotland; an[illegible]
a well-know[illegible]
attracted mu[illegible]
St John's Col[illegible]
second wrang[illegible]
and remained
called to the [illegible]
Labouchere (a
Board of Trad[illegible]
department, a[illegible]
become an auth[illegible]
of the Dalhous[illegible]
that the "parl[illegible]
In 1848 he wa[illegible]
the London, B[illegible]
faculty showe[illegible]
line. He also
Company, but
entered parlia[illegible]
seat in 1857, [illegible]
pointed financ[illegible]
made finance [illegible]
was re-elected [illegible]
in 1868, but in
and retained hi[illegible]
appointed chair[illegible]
in that post till
administrator.
Trust and the [illegible]
well known as
Thought (1885),
Origins (1892) b[illegible]
writer's influent[illegible]
style, but also [illegible]
well-informed tre[illegible]
Laing died at Syd[illegible]
LAING'S [or LA[illegible]
South Africa, imm[illegible]
of 5400 to 6000 ft
from Majuba to [illegible]
the railway in 18[illegible]
of communication
pierces the nek b[illegible]
rose in revolt in [illegible]
to oppose the entry
On the 28th of Jan[illegible]
to drive the Boers f[illegible]
LAIRD, MACGR[illegible]
pioneer of British tr[illegible]
1808, the younger s[illegible]
head firm of shipbu[illegible]
certain Liverpool men
development of the [illegible]
having been made [illegible]
In 1832 the compa[illegible]

[illegible] *Roofs*.—When the roofs of great limestone caves or underground [illegible] at the surface what are called *limestone* [illegible]. Lakes similar to these are also found in regions abounding in rock-salt deposits; the Jura range offers many such lakes.

[illegible] *Erosion*.—A. C. Ramsay has shown that innumerable [illegible] hemisphere do not lie in fissures produced by [illegible] disturbances, nor in areas of subsidence, nor in syn[illegible] strata, but are the results of glacial erosion. Many [illegible] above gorges in Switzerland, as well as in the [illegible], were, without doubt, what Sir Archibald [illegible], or true rock-basins, which have been filled [illegible] brought into them by their tributary streams.

[illegible] *Basins*.—These may be due to the following causes:—
[illegible] occurs in mountainous regions, where strata [illegible] the valley, rest on soft layers; the hard rocks slip [illegible] heavy rains, damming back the drainage, which [illegible] basin. Many small lakes high up in the Alps [illegible] formed by a river being dammed back in this way.

[illegible] *Glacier*.—In Alaska, in Scandinavia and in the Alps a [illegible] the mouth of a tributary valley, the stream flowing [illegible] back, and a lake is thus formed. The best-known [illegible] is the Märjelen Lake in the Alps, near the great [illegible]. Lake Castain in Alaska is barred by the Malaspina [illegible] 3 m. long and 1 m. in width when at its highest [illegible] through a tunnel 9 m. in length beneath the ice-[illegible] parallel roads of Glen Roy in Scotland are suc[illegible] formed along the shores of a glacial lake during the [illegible]. Lake Agassiz, which during the glacial period [illegible] valley of the Red River, and of which the present Lake [illegible] remnant, was formed by an ice-dam along the margin [illegible] sheets. It is estimated to have been 700 m. in length, [illegible] an area of 110,000 sq. m., thus exceeding the [illegible] five great North American lakes: Superior (31,200), [illegible] Huron with Georgian Bay (23,800), Erie (9960) [illegible].

[illegible] *Moraine of an Actual Glacier*.—These lakes some[illegible] the Alps of Central Europe and in the Pyrenees [illegible].

[illegible] *Moraine of an Ancient Glacier*.—The barrier in [illegible] the last moraine left by the retreating glacier. [illegible] abundant in the northern hemisphere, especially in [illegible] the Alps.

[illegible] *Deposition of Glacial Drift*.—After the retreat of [illegible] glaciers great masses of glacial drift are left on the land-[illegible] on account of the manner in which these masses were [illegible] in depressions that become filled with water. [illegible] are without visible outlets, the water frequently [illegible] through the glacial drift. These lakes are so numerous [illegible] part of North America that one can trace the [illegible] of the great ice-sheet by following the southern [illegible] region, where lakes may be counted by tens [illegible] from the size of a tarn to that of the great [illegible] above mentioned.

[illegible] *into Dunes*.—It is a well-known fact that sand [illegible] a country for several miles in the direction of the [illegible]. When these sand-dunes obstruct a valley a lake [illegible]. A good example of such a lake is found in Moses [illegible] Washington; but the sand-dunes may also fill up [illegible] and lakes, for instance, in the Sahara, [illegible] are like vast lakes in the early morning, and in [illegible] much evaporation has taken place, like vast [illegible].

[illegible] *Matter deposited by Lateral Streams*.—If the current [illegible] be not powerful enough to sweep away detrital matter [illegible] a lateral stream, a dam is formed causing a lake. [illegible] frequently met with in the narrow valleys of the [illegible] Scotland.

[illegible].—Lakes of this kind are met with in volcanic [illegible].

[illegible] *Basins*.—In the vast tundras that skirt the Arctic [illegible] the old and the new world a great number of frozen [illegible] are met with, surrounded by banks of vegetation. [illegible] are generally accumulated every season at the same [illegible] the growth of the tundra vegetation is [illegible] snow-drifts that last longest are surrounded [illegible] vegetation. When such accumulations of snow [illegible] vegetation on the place they occupied is much less [illegible]. Year after year such places become more [illegible] compared to the general surface, where [illegible] abundant and thus give origin to lakes. [illegible] regions small bays are cut off [illegible] by the growth of corals, and thus ultimately fresh-[illegible].

[illegible].—From the time of its formation a lake [illegible]. The historical period has not been [illegible] to have watched the birth, life and [illegible] a considerable size, still by studying the various stages of development a fairly good idea of the course they run can be obtained.

In humid regions two processes tend to the extinction of a lake, viz. the deposition of detrital matter in the lake, and the lowering of the lake by the cutting action of the outlet stream on the barrier. These outgoing streams, however, being very pure and clear, all detrital matter having been deposited in the lake, have less eroding power than inflowing streams. One of the best examples of the action of the filling-up process is presented by Lochs Doine, Voil and Lubnaig in the Callander district of Scotland. In post-glacial times these three lochs formed, without doubt, one continuous sheet of water, which subsequently became divided into three different basins by the deposition of sediment. Loch Doine has been separated from Loch Voil by alluvial cones laid down by two opposite streams. At the head of Loch Doine there is an alluvial flat that stretches for 1½ m., formed by the Lochlarig river and its tributaries. The long stretch of alluvium that separates Loch Voil from Loch Lubnaig has been laid down by Calair Burn in Glen Buckie, by the Kirkton Burn at Balquhidder, and by various streams on both sides of Strathyre. Loch Lubnaig once extended to a point ¾ m. beyond its present outlet, the level of the loch being lowered about 20 ft. by the denuding action of the river Leny on its rocky barrier.

In arid regions, where the rainfall is often less than 10 ins. in the year, the action of winds in the transport of sand and dust is more in evidence than that of rivers, and the effects of evaporation greater than of precipitation. Salt and bitter lakes prevail in these regions. Many salt lakes, such as the Dead Sea and the Great Salt Lake, are descended from fresh-water ancestors, while others, like the Caspian and Aral Seas, are isolated portions of the ocean. Lakes of the first group have usually become salt through a decrease in the rainfall of the region in which they occur. The water begins to get salt when the evaporation from the lake exceeds the inflow. The inflowing waters bring in a small amount of saline and alkaline matter, which becomes more and more concentrated as the evaporation increases. In lakes of the second group the waters were salt at the outset. If inflow exceeds evaporation they become fresher, and may ultimately become quite fresh. If the evaporation exceeds the inflow they diminish in size, and their waters become more and more salt and bitter. The first lake which occupied the basin of the Great Salt Lake of Utah appears to have been fresh, then with a change of climate to have become a salt lake. Another change of climate taking place, the level of the lake rose until it overflowed, the outlet being by the Snake river; the lake then became fresh. This expanded lake has been called Lake Bonneville, which covered an area of about 17,000 sq. m. Another change of climate in the direction of aridity reduced the level of the lake below the level of the outlet, the waters became gradually salt, and the former great fresh-water lake has been reduced gradually to the relatively small Great Salt Lake of the present day. The sites of extinct salt lakes yield salt in commercial quantities.

The Water of Lakes.—(*a*) *Composition.*—It is interesting to compare the quantity of solid matter in, and the chemical composition of, the water of fresh and salt lakes:—

	Total Solids by Evaporation expressed in Grams per Litre.
Great Salt Lake (Russell)	238·12
Lake of Geneva (Delebecque)	0·1775

The following analysis of a sample of the water of the Great Salt Lake (Utah, U.S.A.) is given by I. C. Russell:—

	Grams per Litre.	Probable Combination.	
Na	75·825	NaCl	192·860
K	3·925	K_2SO_4	8·756
Li	0·021	Li_2SO_4	0·166
Mg	4·844	$MgCl_2$	15·044
Ca	2·424	$MgSO_4$	5·216
Cl	128·278	$CaSO_4$	8·240
SO_3	12·522	$Fe_2O_3+Al_2O_3$	0·004
O in sulphates	2·494	SiO_2	0·018
$Fe_2O_3+Al_2O_3$	0·004	Surplus SO_3	0·051
SiO_2	0·018		
Bo_2O_3	trace		
Br_2	faint trace		

The following analyses of the waters of other salt lakes are given by Mr J. Y. Buchanan (Art. "Lake," *Ency. Brit.*, 9th Ed.), an analysis of sea-water from the Suez Canal being added for comparison:—

	Koko-nor.	Aral Sea.	Caspian Sea. Open.	Caspian Sea. Karabugas.	Urmia Sea.	Dead Sea.	Lake Van.	Suez Canal, Ismailia.
Specific Gravity	1·00907	..	1·01106	1·26217	1·17500	..	1·01800	1·03898
Percentage of Salt	1·11	1·09	1·30	28·5	22·28	22·13	1·73	5·1
Name of Salt.	Grams of Salt per 1000 Grams of Water.							
Bicarbonate of Lime	0·6804	0·2185	0·1123	..	..	..	..	0·0072
" Iron	0·0053	..	0·0014	..	..	..	..	0·0069
" Magnesia	0·6598	..	..	..	..	..	0·4031	..
Carbonate of Soda	..	..	..	..	..	..	5·3976	..
Phosphate of Lime	0·0028	..	0·0021	..	..	..	..	0·0029
Sulphate of Lime	..	1·3499	0·9004	..	0·7570	0·8600	..	1·8593
" Magnesia	0·9324	2·9799	3·0855	61·9350	13·5460	..	0·2595	3·2231
" Soda	1·7241	..	..	..	..	..	2·5673	..
" Potash	..	..	..	..	..	..	0·5363	..
Chloride of Sodium	6·9008	6·2356	8·1163	83·2840	192·4100	76·5000	8·0500	40·4336
" Potassium	0·2209	0·1145	0·1339	9·9560	..	23·3000	..	0·6231
" Rubidium	0·0055	..	0·0034	0·2510	..	..	..	0·0265
" Magnesium	..	0·0003	0·6115	129·3770	15·4610	95·6000	..	4·7632
" Calcium	..	..	..	..	0·5990	22·4500	..	..
Bromide of Magnesium	0·0045	..	0·0081	0·1930	..	2·3100	..	0·0779
Silica	0·0098	..	0·0024	..	..	0·2400	0·0761	0·0027
Total Solid Matter	11·1463	10·8987	12·9773	284·9960	222·7730	221·2600	17·2899	51·0264

This table embraces examples of several types of salt lakes. In the Koko-nor, Aral and open Caspian Seas we have examples of the moderately salt, non-saturated waters. In the Karabugas, a branch gulf of the Caspian, Urmia and the Dead Seas we have examples of saturated waters containing principally chlorides. Lake Van is an example of the alkaline seas which also occur in Egypt, Hungary and other countries. Their peculiarity consists in the quantity of carbonate of soda dissolved in their waters, which is collected by the inhabitants for domestic and commercial purposes.

The following analyses by Dr Bourcart give an idea of the chemical composition of the water of fresh-water lakes in grams per litre:—

	Tanay.	Bleu.	Märjelen.	St Gothard.
SiO_2	0·003	0·0042	0·0014	0·0008
$Fe_2O_3+Al_2O_3$	0·0012	0·0006	0·0008	trace
NaCl	0·0017	..	..	..
Na_2SO_4	0·0011	0·0038	0·0031	0·00085
Na_2CO_3	..	..	..	0·00128
K_2SO_4	0·0021	0·0028	0·0044	..
K_2CO_3	..	..	0·0003	0·00130
$MgSO_4$	0·006	0·0305	..	..
$MgCO_3$	0·0046	0·0158	0·0008	0·00015
$CaSO_4$	..	..	..	..
$CaCO_3$	0·107	0·1189	0·0061	0·00178
MnO	0·001	..	..	..

end. When the wind ceases, a temperature-seiche is started, just as an ordinary seiche is started in a basin of water which has been tilted. This temperature-seiche has been studied experimentally and rendered visible by superimposing a layer of paraffin on a layer of water.

Wedderburn estimates the quantity of heat that enters Loch Ness and is given out again during the year to be approximately sufficient to raise about 30,000 million gallons of water from freezing-point to boiling-point. Lakes thus modify the climate of the region in which they occur, both by increasing its humidity and by decreasing its range of temperature. They cool and moisten the atmosphere by evaporation during summer, and when they freeze in winter a vast amount of latent heat is liberated, and moderates the fall of temperature.

Lakes act as reservoirs for water, and so tend to restrain floods, and to promote regularity of flow. They become sources of mechanical power, and as their waters are purified by allowing the sediment which enters them to settle, they become valuable sources of water-supply for towns and cities. In temperate regions small and shallow lakes are likely to freeze all over in winter, but deep lakes in similar regions do not generally freeze, owing to the fact that the low temperature of the air does not continue long enough to cool down the entire body of water to the maximum density point. Deep lakes are thus the best sources of water-supply for cities, for in summer they supply relatively cool water and in winter relatively warm water. Besides, the number of organisms in deep lakes is less than in small shallow lakes, in which there is a much higher temperature in summer, and consequently much greater organic growth. The deposits, which are formed along the shores and on the floors of lakes, depend on the geological structure and nature of the adjacent shores.

Biology.—Compared with the waters of the ocean those of lakes may safely be said to contain relatively few animals and plants. Whole groups of organisms—the Echinoderms, for instance—are unrepresented. In the oceans there is a much greater uniformity in the physical and chemical conditions than obtains in lakes. In lakes the temperature varies widely. To underground lakes light does not penetrate, and in these some of the organisms may be blind, for example, the blind crayfish (*Cambarus pellucidus*) and the blind fish (*Amblyopsis spelaeus*) of the Kentucky caves. The majority of lakes are fresh, while some are so salt that no organisms have been found in them. The peaty matter in other lakes is so abundant that light does not penetrate to any great depth, and the humic acids in solution prevent the development of some species. Indeed, every lake has an individuality of its own, depending upon climate, size, nature of the bottom, chemical composition and connexion with other lakes. While the ocean contains many families and genera not represented in lakes, almost every genus in lakes is represented in the ocean.

The vertebrates, insects and flowering plants inhabiting lakes vary much according to latitude, and are comparatively well known to zoologists and botanists. The micro-fauna and flora have only recently been studied in detail, and we cannot yet be said to know much about tropical lakes in this respect. Mr James Murray, who has studied the Scottish lakes, records in over 400 Scottish lochs 724 species (the fauna including 447 species, all invertebrates, and the flora comprising 277 species) belonging to the following groups; the list must not be regarded as in any way complete:—

Fauna.		*Flora.*	
Mollusca	7 species	Phanerogamia	65 species
Hydrachnida	17 "	Equisetaceae	1 "
Tardigrada	30 "	Selaginellaceae	1 "
Insecta	7 "	Characeae	6 "
Crustacea	78 "	Musci	18 "
Bryozoa	7 "	Hepaticae	2 "
Worms	25 "	Florideae	2 "
Rotifera	181 "	Chlorophyceae	142 "
Gastrotricha	2 "	Bacillariaceae	26 "
Coelenterata	1 "	Myxophyceae	10 "
Porifera	1 "	Peridiniaceae	4 "
Protozoa	91 "		
	447 "		277 "

These organisms are found along the shores, in the deep waters, and in the surface waters of the lakes.

The *littoral region* is the most populous part of lakes; the existence of a rooted vegetation is only possible there, and this in turn supports a rich littoral fauna. The greater heat of the water along the margins also favours growth. The great majority of the species in Scottish lochs are met with in this region. Insect larvae of many kinds are found under stones or among weeds. Most of the Cladocera, and the

Copepoda of the genus *Cyclops*, and the Harpacticidae are only found in this region. Water-mites, nearly all the Rotifers, Gastrotricha, Tardigrada and Molluscs are found here, and Rhizopods are abundant. A large number of the littoral species in Loch Ness extends down to a depth of about 300 ft.

The abyssal region, in Scottish lochs, lies, as a rule, deeper than 300 ft., and in this deep region a well-marked association of animals appears in the muds on the bottom, but none of them are peculiar to it: they all extend into the littoral zone, from which they were originally derived. In Loch Ness the following sparse population was recorded:—

1 Mollusc:	*Pisidium pusillum* (Gmel).
3 Crustacea:	*Cyclops viridis*, Jurine.
	Candona candida (Müll).
	Cypria ophthalmica, Jurine.
3 Worms:	*Stylodrilus gabretae*, Vejd.
	Oligochaete, not determined.
	Automolos morgiensis (Du Plessis).
1 Insect:	*Chironomus* (larva).
Infusoria:	Several, ectoparasites on *Pisidium* and *Cyclops*, not determined.

In addition, the following were found casually at great depths in Loch Ness: *Hydra*, *Limnaea peregra*, *Proales daphnicola* and *Lynceus affinis*.

The pelagic region of the Scottish lakes is occupied by numerous microscopic organisms, belonging to the Zooplankton and Phytoplankton. Of the former group 30 species belonging to the Crustacea, Rotifera and Protozoa were recorded in Loch Ness. Belonging to the second group 150 species were recorded, of which 120 were Desmids. Some of these species of plankton organisms are almost universal in the Scottish lochs, while others are quite local. Some of the species occur all the year through, while others have only been recorded in summer or in winter. The great development of Algae in the surface waters, called "flowering of the water" (*Wasserblüthe*), was observed in August in Loch Lomond; a distinct "flowering," due to Chlorophyceae, has been observed in shallow lochs as early as July. It is most common in August and September, but has also been observed in winter.

The plankton animals which are dominant or common, both over Scotland and the rest of Europe, are:—

Diaptomus gracilis.
Daphnia hyalina.
Diaphanosoma brachyurum.
Leptodora hindtii.
Conochilus unicornis.
Asplanchna priodonta.
Polyarthra platyptera.
Anuraea cochlearis.
Notholca longispina.
Ceratium hirundinella.
Asterionella.

All of these, according to Dr Lund, belong to the general plankton association of the European plain, or are even cosmopolitan.

The Scottish plankton on the whole differs from the plankton of the central European plateau, and from the cosmopolitan fresh-water plankton, in the extraordinary richness of the Phytoplankton in species of Desmids, in the conspicuous arctic element among the Crustacea, in the absence or comparative rarity of the species commonest in the general European plankton. Another peculiarity is the local distribution of some of the Crustacea and many of the Desmids.

The derivation of the whole lacustrine population of the Scottish lochs does not seem to present any difficulty. The abyssal forms have been traced to the littoral zone without any perceptible modifications. The plankton organisms are a mingling of European and arctic species. The cosmopolitan species may enter the lochs by ordinary migration. It is probable that if the whole plankton could be annihilated, it would be replaced by ordinary migration within a few years. The eggs and spores of many species can be dried up without injury, and may be carried through the air as dust from one lake to another; others, which would not bear desiccation, might be carried in mud adhering to the feet of aquatic birds and in various other ways. The arctic species may be survivors from a period when arctic conditions prevailed over a great part of Europe. What are known as "relicts" of a marine fauna have not been found in the Scottish fresh-water lochs.

It is somewhat remarkable that none of the organisms living in fresh-water lochs has been observed to exhibit the phenomenon of phosphorescence, although similar organisms in the salt-water lochs a few miles distant exhibit brilliant phosphorescence. At similar depths in the sea-lochs there is usually a great abundance of life when compared with that found in fresh-water lochs.

Length, Depth, Area and Volume of Lakes.—In the following table will be found the length, depth, area and volume of some of the principal lakes of the world.[1] Sir John Murray estimates the volume of water in the 560 Scottish lochs recently surveyed at 7 cub. m., and the approximate volume of water in all the lakes of the world at about 2000 cub. m., so that this last number is but a small fraction of the volume of the ocean, which he previously estimated at 324 million cub. m. It may be recalled that the total rainfall on the land of the globe is estimated at 29,350 cub. m., and the total discharge from the rivers of the globe at 6524 cub. r

British Lakes

	Length in Miles.	Depth in Feet.		Area in sq. m.	Volume in million cub. ft.
I. *England*—		Max.	Mean.		
Windermere	10·50	219	78·5	5·69	12,250
Ullswater	7·35	205	83	3·44	7,870
Wastwater	3·00	258	134·5	1·12	4,128
Coniston Water	5·41	184	79	1·89	4,000
Crummock Water	2·50	144	87·5	0·97	2,343
Ennerdale Water	2·40	148	62	1·12	1,978
Bassenthwaite Water	3·83	70	18	2·06	1,023
Derwentwater	2·87	72	18	2·06	1,010
Haweswater	2·33	103	39·5	0·54	589
Buttermere	1·26	94	54·5	0·36	537
II. *Wales*—					
Llyn Cawlyd	1·62	222	109·1	0·18	941
Llyn Cwellyn	1·20	122	74·1	0·35	713
Llyn Padarn	2·00	94	52·4	0·43	632
Llyn Llydaw	1·11	190	77·4	0·19	409
Llyn Peris	1·10	114	63·9	0·19	344
Llyn Dulyn	0·31	189	104·2	0·05	156
III. *Scotland*—					
Ness	24·23	754	433·02	21·78	263,162
Lomond	22·64	623	121·29	27·45	92,805
Morar	11·68	1017	284·00	10·30	81,482
Tay	14·55	508	199·08	10·19	56,550
Awe	25·47	307	104·95	14·85	43,451
Maree	13·46	367	125·30	11·03	38,539
Lochy	9·78	531	228·95	5·91	37,726
Rannoch	9·70	440	167·46	7·37	34,387
Shiel	17·40	420	132·73	7·56	27,986
Arkaig	12·00	359	152·71	6·24	26,573
Earn	6·46	287	137·83	3·91	14,421
Treig	5·10	436	207·37	2·41	13,907
Shin	17·22	162	51·04	8·70	12,380
Fannich	6·92	282	108·76	3·60	10,920
Assynt	6·36	282	101·10	3·10	8,731
Quoich	6·95	281	104·60	2·86	8,345
Glass	4·03	365	159·07	1·86	8,265
Fionn (Carnmore)	5·76	144	57·79	3·52	5,667
Laggan	7·04	174	67·68	2·97	5,601
Loyal	4·46	217	65·21	2·55	4,628
IV. *Ireland*—					
Neagh	17	102	40	153	161,000
Erne (Lower)	24	226	43	43	62,000
Erne (Upper)	13	89	10	15	5,000
Corrib	27	152	30	68	59,000
Mask	10	191	52	35	55,000
Derg	24	119	30	49	47,000

European Continental Lakes

	Length in Miles.	Depth in Feet.		Area in sq. m.	Volume in million cub. ft.
		Max.	Mean.		
Ladoga	125	732	300	7000	43,200,000
Onega	145	740	200	3800	21,000,000
Vener	93	292	108	2149	6,357,000
Geneva	45	1015	506	225	3,175,000
Vetter	68	413	128	733	2,543,000
Mjösen	57	1483	..	139	2,882,000
Garda	38	1124	446	143	1,766,000
Constance	42	827	295	208	1,711,000
Ochrida	19	942	479	105	1,391,000
Maggiore	42	1220	574	82	1,310,000
Como	30	1345	513	56	794,000
Hornafvan	7	1391	253	93	777,000

[1] Divergence between certain of these figures and those quoted elsewhere in this work may be accounted for by the slightly different results arrived at by various authorities.

African Lakes

	Length in Miles.	Depth in Feet.		Area in sq. m.	Volume in million cub. ft.
		Max.	Mean.		
Victoria Nyanza	200	240	..	26,200	5,800,000
Nyasa . . .	350	2580	..	14,200	396,000,000
Tanganyika . .	420	2100	..	12,700	283,000,000

Asiatic Lakes

	Length in Miles.	Depth in Feet.		Area in sq. m.	Volume in million cub. ft.
		Max.	Mean.		
Aral	265	222	52	24,400	43,600,000
Baikal . . .	330	5413	..	11,580	274,000,000
Balkash . . .	323	33	..	7,000	4,880,000
Urmia . . .	80	50	15	1,750	732,000

American Lakes

	Length in Miles.	Depth in Feet.		Area in sq. m.	Volume in million cub. ft.
		Max.	Mean.		
Superior . . .	412	1008	475	31,200	413,000,000
Huron . . .	263	730	250	23,800	166,000,000
Michigan . .	335	870	325	22,450	203,000,000
Erie	240	210	70	9,960	19,500,000
Ontario . . .	190	738	300	7,240	61,000,000
Titicaca . . .	120	924	347	3,200	30,900,000

New Zealand Lakes

	Length in Miles	Depth in Feet.		Area in sq. m.	Volume in million cub. ft.
		Max.	Mean.		
Taupo . . .	25	534	367	238·0	2,435,000
Wakatipu . .	49	1242	707	112·3	2,205,000
Manapouri . .	19	1458	328	56·0	512,000
Rotorua . . .	7·5	120	39	31·6	34,000
Waikarimoana .	7·25	846	397	14·7	166,000
Wairaumoana .	5·25	375	175	6·1	30,000
Rotoiti . . .	10·7	230	69	14·2	27,000

Authorities.—F. A. Forel, "Handbuch der Seenkunde, allgemeine Limnologie," *Bibliothek geogr. Handbücher* (Stuttgart, 1901), *Le Léman, monographie limnologique* (3 vols., Lausanne, 1892–1901); A. Delebecque, *Les Lacs français*, text and plates (Paris, 1898); H. R. Mill, "Bathymetrical Survey of the English Lakes," *Geogr. Journ.* vol. vi pp. 46 and 135 (1895); Jehu, "Bathymetrical and Geological Study of the Lakes of Snowdonia," *Trans. Roy. Soc. Edin.* vol. xl p. 419 (1902); Sir John Murray and Laurence Pullar, "Bathymetrical Survey of the Fresh-water Lochs of Scotland," *Geogr. Journ.* (1900 to 1908, re-issued in six volumes, Edinburgh, 1910); W. Halbfass, "Die Morphometrie der europäischen Seen," *Zeitschr. Gesell. Erdkunde Berlin* (Jahrg. 1903, p. 592; 1904, p. 204). I. C. Russell, *Lakes of North America* (Boston and London, 1895); O. Zacharias, "Forschungsberichte aus der biologischen Station zu Plön" (Stuttgart); F. E. Bourcart, *Les Lacs alpins suisses, étude chimique et physique* (Geneva, 1906); G. P. Magrini, *Limnologia* (Milan, 1907). (J. Mu.)

LAKE CHARLES, a city of Louisiana, U.S.A., capital of Calcasieu Parish, 30 m. from the Gulf of Mexico and about 218 m. (by rail) W. of New Orleans. Pop. (1889) 838, (1890) 3442, (1900) 6680 (2407 negroes); (1910) 11,449. It is served by the Louisiana & Texas (Southern Pacific System), the St Louis, Watkins & Gulf, the Louisiana & Pacific and the Kansas City Southern railways. The city is charmingly situated on the shore of Lake Charles, and on the Calcasieu river, which with some dredging can be made navigable for large vessels for 132 m. from the Gulf. It is a winter resort. Among the principal buildings are a Carnegie library, the city hall, the Government building, the court house, St Patrick's sanatorium, the masonic temple and the Elks' club. Lake Charles is in the prairie region of southern Louisiana, to the N. of which, covering a large part of the state, are magnificent forests of long-leaf pine, and lesser lowland growths of oak, ash, magnolia, cypress and other valuable timber. The Watkins railway extending to the N.E. and the Kansas City Southern extending to the N.W. have opened up the very best of the forest. The country to the S. and W. is largely given over to rice culture. Lake Charles is the chief centre of lumber manufacture in the state, and has rice mills, car shops and an important trade in wool. Ten miles W. are sulphur mines (product in 1907 about 362,000 tons), which with those of Sicily produce a large part of the total product of the world. Jennings, about 34 m. to the E., is the centre of oil fields, once very productive but now of diminishing importance. Welsh, 23 m. E., is the centre of a newer field; and others lie to the N. Lake Charles was settled about 1852, largely by people from Iowa and neighbouring states, was incorporated as a town in 1857 under the name of Charleston and again in 1867 under its present name, and was chartered as a city in 1886. The city suffered severely by fire in April 1910.

LAKE CITY, a town and the county-seat of Columbia county, Florida, U.S.A., 59 m. by rail W. by S. of Jacksonville. Pop. (1900) 4013, of whom 2159 were negroes: (1905) 6509; (1910) 5032. Lake City is served by the Atlantic Coast Line, the Seaboard Air Line and the Georgia Southern & Florida railways. There are ten small lakes in the neighbourhood, and the town is a winter and health resort. It is the seat of Columbia College (Baptist, 1907); the Florida Agricultural College was opened here in 1883, became the university of Florida in 1903, and in 1905 was abolished by the Buckman Law. Vegetables and fruits grown for the northern markets, sea-island cotton and tobacco are important products of the surrounding country, and Lake City has some trade in cotton, lumber, phosphates and turpentine. The town was first settled about 1826 as Alligator; it was incorporated in 1854; adopted the present name in 1859; and in 1901, with an enlarged area, was re-incorporated.

LAKE DISTRICT, in England, a district containing all the principal English lakes, and variously termed the Lake Country, Lakeland and "the Lakes." It falls within the north-western counties of Cumberland, Westmorland and Lancashire (Furness district), about one-half being within the first of these. Although celebrated far outside the confines of Great Britain as a district of remarkable and strongly individual physical beauty, its area is only some 700 sq. m., a circle with radius of 15 m. from the central point covering practically the whole. Within this circle, besides the largest lake, Windermere, is the highest point in England, Scafell Pike; yet Windermere is but 10½ m. in length, and covers an area of 5·69 sq. m., while Scafell Pike is only 3210 ft. in height. But the lakes show a wonderful variety of character, from open expanse and steep rock-bound shores to picturesque island-groups and soft wooded banks; while the mountains have always a remarkable dignity, less from the profile of their summits than from the bold sweeping lines of their flanks, unbroken by vegetation, and often culminating in sheer cliffs or crags. At their feet, the flat green valley floors of the higher elevations give place in the lower parts to lovely woods. The streams are swift and clear, and numerous small waterfalls are characteristic of the district. To the north, west and south, a flat coastal belt, bordering the Irish Sea, with its inlets Morecambe Bay and Solway Firth, and broadest in the north, marks off the Lake District, while to the east the valleys of the Eden and the Lune divide it from the Pennine mountain system. Geologically, too, it is individual. Its centre is of volcanic rocks, complex in character, while the Coal-measures and New Red Sandstone appear round the edges. The district as a whole is grooved by a main depression, running from north to south along the valleys of St John, Thirlmere, Grasmere and Windermere, surmounting a pass (Dunmail Raise) of only 783 ft.; while a secondary depression, in the same direction, runs along Derwentwater, Borrowdale, Wasdale and Wastwater, but here Sty Head Pass, between Borrowdale and Wasdale, rises to 1600 ft. The centre of the 15-m. radius lies on the lesser heights between Langstrath and Dunmail Raise, which may, however, be the crown of an ancient dome of rocks, "the dissected skeleton of which, worn by the warfare of air and rain and ice, now alone remains" (Dr H. R. Mill, "Bathymetrical Survey of the English Lakes," *Geographical Journal*, vi. 48). The principal features of the district may be indicated by following this circle round from north, by west, south and east.

The river Derwent (*q.v.*), rising in the tarns and "gills" or "ghylls" (small streams running in deeply-grooved clefts) north of Sty Head Pass and the Scafell mass flows north through the wooded Borrowdale and forms Derwentwater and Bassenthwaite. These two lakes are in a class apart from all the rest, being broader for their length, and quite shallow (about 18 ft. average and 70 ft. maximum), as distinct from the long, narrow and deep troughs occupied by the other chief lakes, which average from 40 to 135 ft. deep. Derwentwater (*q.v.*), studded with many islands, is perhaps the most beautiful of all. Borrowdale is joined on the east by the bare wild dale of Langstrath, and the Greta joins the Derwent immediately below Derwentwater; the town of Keswick lying near the junction. Derwentwater and Bassenthwaite occupy a single depression, a flat alluvial plain separating them. From Seatoller in Borrowdale a road traverses Honister Pass (1100 ft.), whence it descends westward, beneath the majestic Honister Crags, where green slate is quarried, into the valley containing Buttermere (94 ft. max. depth) and Crummock Water (144 ft.), drained by the Cocker. Between this and the Derwent valley the principal height is Grasmoor (2791 ft.); southward a steep narrow ridge (High Style, 2643) divides it from Ennerdale, containing Ennerdale Water (148 ft. max. depth), which is fed by the Liza and drained by the Ehen. A splendid range separates this dale from Wasdale and its tributary Mosedale, including Great Gable (2949 ft.), Pillar (2927), with the precipitous Pillar Rock on the Ennerdale flank and Steeple (2746). Wasdale Head, between Gable and the Scafell range, is peculiarly grand, with dark grey screes and black crags frowning above its narrow bottom. On this side of Gable is the fine detached rock, Napes Needle. Wastwater, 3 m. in length, is the deepest lake of all (258 ft.), its floor, like those of Windermere and Ullswater, sinking below sea-level. Its east shore consists of a great range of screes. East of Wasdale lies the range of Scafell (*q.v.*), its chief points being Scafell (3162 ft.), Scafell Pike (3210), Lingmell (2649) and Great End (2984), while the line is continued over Esk Hause Pass (2490) along a fine line of heights (Bow Fell, 2960; Crinkle Crags, 2816), to embrace the head of Eskdale. The line then descends to Wrynose Pass (1270 ft.), from which the Duddon runs south through a vale of peculiar richness in its lower parts; while the range continues south to culminate in the Old Man of Coniston (2633) with the splendid Dow Crags above Goats Water. The pleasant vale of Yewdale drains south to Coniston Lake (5½ m. long, 184 ft. max. depth), east of which a lower, well-wooded tract, containing two beautiful lesser lakes, Tarn Hows and Esthwaite Water, extends to Windermere (*q.v.*). This lake collects waters by the Brathay from Langdale, the head of which, between Bow Fell and Langdale Pikes (2401 ft.), is very fine; and by the Rothay from Dunmail Raise and the small lakes of Grasmere and Rydal Water, embowered in woods. East of the Rothay valley and Thirlmere lies the mountain mass including Helvellyn (3118 ft.), Fairfield (2863) and other points, with magnificent crags at several places on the eastern side towards Grisedale and Patterdale. These dales drain to Ullswater (205 ft. max., second to Windermere in area), and so north-east to the Eden. To the east and south-east lies the ridge named High Street (2663 ft.), from the Roman road still traceable from south to north along its summit, and sloping east again to the sequestered Hawes Water (103 ft. max.), a curiously shaped lake nearly divided by the delta of the Measand Beck. There remains the Thirlmere valley. Thirlmere itself was raised in level, and adapted by means of a dam at the north end, as a reservoir for the water-supply of Manchester in 1890–1894. It drains north by St John's Vale into the Greta, north of which again rises a mountain-group of which the chief summits are Saddleback or Blencathra (2847 ft.) and the graceful peak of Skiddaw (3054). The most noteworthy waterfalls are—Scale Force (Dano-Norwegian *fors, foss*), besides Crummock, Lodore near Derwentwater, Dungeon Gill Force, beside Langdale, Dalegarth Force in Eskdale, Aira near Ullswater, sung by Wordsworth, Stock Gill Force and Rydal Falls near Ambleside.

The principal centres in the Lake District are Keswick (Derwentwater), Ambleside, Bowness, Windermere and Lakeside (Windermere), Coniston and Boot (Eskdale), all of which, except Ambleside and Bowness (which nearly joins Windermere) are accessible by rail. The considerable village of Grasmere lies beautifully at the head of the lake of that name; and above Esthwaite is the small town of Hawkshead, with an ancient church, and picturesque houses curiously built on the hill-slope and sometimes spanning the streets. There are regular steamer services on Windermere and Ullswater. Coaches and cars traverse the main roads during the summer, but many of the finest dales and passes are accessible only on foot or by ponies. All the mountains offer easy routes to pedestrians, but some of them, as Scafell, Pillar, Gable (Napes Needle), Pavey Ark above Langdale and Dow Crags near Coniston, also afford ascents for experienced climbers.

This mountainous district, having the sea to the west, records an unusually heavy rainfall. Near Seathwaite, below Styhead Pass, the largest annual rainfall in the British Isles is recorded, the average (1870–1899) being 133·53 in., while 173·7 was measured in 1903 and 243·98 in. in 1872. At Keswick the annual mean is 60·02, at Grasmere about 80 ins. The months of maximum rainfall at Seathwaite are November, December and January and September.

Fish taken in the lakes include perch, pike, char and trout in Windermere, Ennerdale, Bassenthwaite, Derwentwater, &c., and the gwyniad or fresh-water herring in Ullswater. The industries of the Lake District include slate quarrying and some lead and zinc mining, and weaving, bobbin-making and pencil-making.

Setting aside London and Edinburgh, no locality in the British Isles is so intimately associated with the history of English literature as the Lake District. In point of time the poet whose name is first connected with the region is Gray, who wrote a journal of his tour in 1769. But it was Wordsworth, a native of Cumberland, born on the outskirts of the Lake District itself, who really made it a Mecca for lovers of English poetry. Out of his long life of eighty years, sixty were spent amid its lakes and mountains, first as a schoolboy at Hawkshead, and afterwards as a resident at Grasmere (1799–1813) and Rydal Mount (1813–1850). In the churchyard of Grasmere the poet and his wife lie buried; and very near to them are the remains of Hartley Coleridge (son of the poet), who himself lived many years at Keswick, Ambleside and Grasmere. Southey, the friend of Wordsworth, was a resident of Keswick for forty years (1803–1843), and was buried in Crosthwaite churchyard. Samuel Taylor Coleridge lived some time at Keswick, and also with the Wordsworths at Grasmere. From 1807 to 1815 Christopher North (John Wilson) was settled at Windermere. De Quincey spent the greater part of the years 1809 to 1828 at Grasmere, in the first cottage which Wordsworth had inhabited. Ambleside, or its environs, was also the place of residence of Dr Arnold (of Rugby), who spent there the vacations of the last ten years of his life; and of Harriet Martineau, who built herself a house there in 1845. At Keswick Mrs Lynn Linton was born in 1822. Brantwood, a house beside Coniston Lake, was the home of Ruskin during the last years of his life. In addition to these residents or natives of the locality, Shelley, Scott, Nathaniel Hawthorne, Clough, Crabb Robinson, Carlyle, Keats, Tennyson, Matthew Arnold, Mrs Hemans, Gerald Massey and others of less reputation made longer or shorter visits, or were bound by ties of friendship with the poets already mentioned. The Vale of St John, near Keswick, recalls Scott's *Bridal of Triermain*. But there is a deeper connexion than this between the Lake District and English letters. German literature tells of several literary schools, or groups of writers animated by the same ideas, and working in the spirit of the same principles and by the same poetic methods. The most notable instance—indeed it is almost the only instance—of the kind in English literature is the Lake School of Poets. Of this school the acknowledged head and founder was Wordsworth, and the tenets it professed are those laid down by the poet himself in the famous preface to the edition of *The Lyrical Ballads* which he published in 1800. Wordsworth's theories of poetry—the objects best suited for poetic treatment, the characteristics of such treatment and the choice of diction suitable for the purpose—may be said to have grown out of the soil and substance of the lakes and mountains, and out of the homely lives of the people, of Cumberland and Westmoreland.

See CUMBERLAND, LANCASHIRE, WESTMORLAND. The following is a selection from the literature of the subject: Harriet Martineau, *The English Lakes* (Windermere, 1858); Mrs Lynn Linton, *The Lake Country* (London, 1864); E. Waugh, *Rambles in the Lake Country* (1861) and *In the Lake Country* (1880); W. Knight, *Through the Wordsworth Country* (London, 1890); H. D. Rawnsley, *Literary Associations of the English Lakes* (2 vols., Glasgow, 1894) and *Life and Nature of the English Lakes* (Glasgow, 1899); Stopford Brooke, *Dove Cottage, Wordsworth's Home from 1800 to 1808*; A. G. Bradley, *The Lake District, its Highways and Byeways* (London, 1901); Sir John Harwood, *History of the Thirlmere Water Scheme* (1895); for mountain-climbing, Col. J. Brown, *Mountain Ascents in Westmorland and Cumberland* (London, 1888); Haskett-Smith, *Climbing in the British Isles*, part. i.; Owen G. Jones, *Rock-climbing in the English Lake District*, 2nd ed. by W. M. Crook (Keswick, 1900).

LAKE DWELLINGS, the term employed in archaeology for habitations constructed, not on the dry land, but within the margins of lakes or creeks at some distance from the shore.

The villages of the Guajiros in the Gulf of Maracaibo are described by Goering as composed of houses with low sloping roofs perched on lofty piles and connected with each other by bridges of planks. Each house consisted of two apartments; the floor was formed of split stems of trees set close together and covered with mats; they were reached from the shore by dug-out canoes poled over the shallow waters, and a notched tree trunk served as a ladder. The custom is also common in the estuaries of the Orinoco and Amazon. A similar system prevails in New Guinea. Dumont d'Urville describes four such villages in the Bay of Dorei, containing from eight to fifteen blocks or clusters of houses, each block separately built or and consisting of a row of distinct dwellings. C. D. Cameron describes three villages thus built on piles in Lake Mohrya, or Moria, in Central Africa, the motive here being to prevent surprise by bands of slave-catchers. Similar constructions have been described by travellers, among the Dyaks of Borneo, in Celebes, in the Caroline Islands, on the Gold Coast of Africa, and in other places.

Hippocrates, writing in the 5th century B.C., says of the people of the Phasis that their country is hot and marshy and subject to frequent inundations, and that they live in houses of timber and reeds constructed in the midst of the waters, and use boats of a single tree trunk. Herodotus, writing also in the 5th century B.C., describes the people of Lake Prasias as living in houses constructed on platforms supported on piles in the middle of the lake, which are approached from the land by a single narrow bridge. Abulfeda the geographer, writing in the 13th century, notices the fact that part of the Apamaean Lake was inhabited by Christian fishermen who lived on the lake in wooden huts built on piles, and Sir John Lubbock (Lord Avebury) mentions that the Rumelian fishermen on Lake Prasias "still inhabit wooden cottages built over the water, as in the time of Herodotus."

The records of the wars in Ireland in the 16th century show that the petty chieftains of that time had their defensive strongholds constructed in the "freshwater lochs" of the country, and there is record evidence of a similar system in the western parts of Scotland. The archaeological researches of the past fifty years have shown that such artificial constructions in lakes were used as defensive dwellings by the Celtic people from an early period to medieval times (see CRANNOG). Similar researches have also established the fact that in prehistoric times nearly all the lakes of Switzerland, and many in the adjoining countries—in Savoy and the north of Italy, in Austria and Hungary and in Mecklenburg and Pomerania—were peopled, so to speak, by lake-dwelling communities, living in villages constructed on platforms supported by piles at varying distances from the shores. The principal groups are those in the Lakes of Bourget, Geneva, Neuchâtel, Bienne, Zürich and Constance lying to the north of the Alps, and in the Lakes Maggiore, Varese, Isco and Garda lying to the south of that mountain range. Many smaller lakes, however, contain them, and they are also found in peat moors on the sites of ancient lakes now drained or silted up, as at Laibach in Carniola. In some of the larger lakes the number of settlements has been very great. Fifty are enumerated in the Lake of Neuchâtel, thirty-two in the Lake of Constance, twenty-four in the Lake of Geneva, and twenty in the Lake of Bienne. The site of the lake dwelling of Wangen, in the Untersee, Lake of Constance, forms a parallelogram more than 700 paces in length by about 120 paces in breadth. The settlement at Morges, one of the largest in the Lake of Geneva, is 1200 ft. long by 150 ft. in breadth. The settlement of Sutz, one of the largest in the Lake of Bienne, extends over six acres, and was connected with the shore by a gangway nearly 100 yds. long and about 40 ft. wide.

The substructure which supported the platforms on which the dwellings were placed was most frequently of piles driven into the bottom of the lake. Less frequently it consisted of a mass of brushwood or fascines built up from the bottom and strengthened by stakes penetrating the mass so as to keep it from spreading. When piles were used they were the rough stems of trees of a length proportioned to the depth of the water, sharpened sometimes by fire and at other times chopped to a point by hatchets. On their level tops the beams supporting the platforms were laid and fastened by wooden pins, or inserted in mortises cut in the heads of the piles. In some cases the substructure was further steadied and strengthened by cross beams notched into the piles below the supports of the platform. The platform itself was usually composed of rough undressed stems, but occasionally it was formed of [illegible] from larger stems. When the mud was too soft to [illegible] the piles [illegible]d into a framework [illegible] placed h[illegible]tom of the lake. On the other hand, when the bottom was rocky so that the piles could not be driven, they were steadied at their bases by being enveloped in a mound of loose stones, in the manner in which the foundations of piers and breakwaters are now constructed. In cases where piles have not been used, as at Niederwil and Wauwyl, the substructure is a mass of fascines or faggots laid parallel and crosswise upon one another with intervening layers of brushwood or of clay and gravel, a few piles here and there being fixed throughout the mass to serve as guides or stays. At Niederwil the platform was formed of split boards, many of which were 2 ft. broad and 2 or 3 in. in thickness.

On these substructures were the huts composing the settlement; for the peculiarity of these lake dwellings is that they were pile villages, or clusters of huts occupying a common platform. The huts themselves were quadrilateral in form. The size of each dwelling is in some cases marked by boards resting edgeways on the platform, like the skirting boards over the flooring of the rooms in a modern house. The walls, which were supported by posts, or by piles of greater length, were formed of wattle-work, coated with clay. The floors were of clay, and in each floor there was a hearth constructed of flat slabs of stone. The roofs were thatched with bark, straw, reeds or rushes. As the superstructures are mostly gone, there is no evidence as to the position and form of the doorways, or the size, number and position of the windows, if there were any. In one case, at Schussenried, the house, which was of an oblong quadrangular form, about 33 by 23 ft., was divided into two rooms by a partition. The outer room, which was the smaller of the two, was entered by a doorway 3 ft. in width facing the south. The access to the inner room was by a similar door through the partition. The walls were formed of split tree-trunks set upright and plastered with clay; and the flooring of similar timbers bedded in clay. In other cases the remains of the gangways or bridges connecting the settlements with the shore have been discovered, but often the village appears to have been accessible only by canoes. Several of these single-tree canoes have been found, one of which is 43 ft. in length and 4 ft. 4 in. in its greatest width. It is impossible to estimate with any degree of certainty the number of separate dwellings of which any of these villages may have consisted, but at Niederwil they stood almost contiguously on the platform, the space between them not exceeding 3 ft. in width. The size of the huts also varied considerably. At Niederwil they were 20 ft. long and 12 ft. wide, while at Robenhausen they were about 27 ft. long by about 22 ft. wide.

The character of the relics shows that in some cases the settlements have been the dwellings of a people using no materials but stone, bone and wood for their implements, ornaments and weapons; in others, of a people using bronze as well as stone and bone; and in others again the occasional use of iron is disclosed. But, though the character of the relics is thus changed, there is no corresponding change in the construction and arrangements of the dwellings. The settlement in the Lake of Moosseedorf, near Bern, affords the most perfect example of a lake dwelling of the Stone age. It was a parallelogram 70 ft. long by 50 ft. wide, supported on piles, and having a gangway built on faggots connecting it with the land. The superstructure had been destroyed by fire. The implements found in the relic bed under it were axe-heads of stone, with their haftings of stag's horn and wood; a flint saw, set in a handle of fir wood and fastened with asphalt; flint flakes and arrow-heads; harpoons of stag's horn with barbs; awls, needles, chisels, fish-hooks and other implements of bone; a comb of yew wood 5 in. long; and a skate made out of the leg bone of a horse. The pottery consisted chiefly of roughly-made vessels, some of which were of large size, others had holes under the rims for suspension, and many were covered with soot, the result of their use as culinary vessels. Burnt wheat, barley and linseed, with many varieties of seeds and fruits, were plentifully mingled with the bones of the stag, the ox, the swine, the sheep and the goat, representing the ordinary food of the inhabitants, while remains of the beaver, the fox, the hare, the dog, the bear, the horse, the elk and the bison were also found.

The settlement of Robenhausen, in the moor which was formerly the bed of the ancient Lake of Pfäffikon, seems to have continued in occupation after the introduction of bronze. The site covers nearly 3 acres, and is estimated to have contained 100,000 piles. In some parts three distinct successions of inhabited platforms have been traced. The first had been destroyed by fire. It is represented at the bottom of the lake by a layer of charcoal mixed with implements of stone and bone and other relics highly carbonized. The second is represented above the bottom by a series of piles with burnt heads, and in the bottom by a layer of charcoal mixed with corn, apples, cloth, bones, pottery and implements of stone and bone, separated from the first layer of charcoal by 3 ft. of peaty sediment intermixed with relics of the occupation of the platform. The piles of the third settlement do not reach down to the shell marl, but are fixed in the layers representing the first and second settlements. They are formed of split oak trunks, while those of the two first settlements are round stems chiefly of soft wood. The huts of this last settlement appear to have had cattle stalls between them, the droppings and litter forming heaps at the lake bottom. The bones of the animals consumed as food at this station were found in such numbers that 5 tons were collected in the construction of a watercourse which crossed the site. Among the wooden objects recovered from the relic beds were tubs, plates, ladles and spoons, a flail for threshing corn, a last for stretching shoes of hide, celt handles, clubs, long-bows of yew, floats and implements of fishing and a dug-out canoe 12 ft. long. No spindle-whorls were found, but there were many varieties of cloth, platted and woven, bundles of yarn and balls of string. Among the tools of bone and stag's horn were awls, needles, harpoons, scraping tools and haftings for stone axe-heads. The implements of stone were chiefly axe-heads and arrow-heads. Of clay and earthenware there were many varieties of domestic dishes, cups and pipkins, and crucibles or melting pots made of clay and horse dung and still retaining the drossy coating of the melted bronze.

The settlement of Auvernier in the Lake of Neuchatel is one of the richest and most considerable stations of the Bronze age. It has yielded four bronze swords, ten socketed spear-heads, forty celts or axe-heads and sickles, fifty knives, twenty socketed chisels, four hammers and an anvil, sixty rings for the arms and legs, several highly ornate torques or twisted neck rings, and upwards of two hundred hair pins of various sizes up to 16 in. in length, some having spherical heads in which plates of gold were set. Moulds for sickles, lance-heads and bracelets were found cut in stone or made in baked clay. From four to five hundred vessels of pottery finely made and elegantly shaped are indicated by the fragments recovered from the relic bed. The Lac de Bourget, in Savoy, has eight settlements, all of the Bronze age. These have yielded upwards of 4000 implements, weapons and ornaments of bronze, among which were a large proportion of moulds and founders' materials. A few stone implements suggest the transition from stone to bronze; and the occasional occurrence of iron weapons and pottery of Gallo-Roman origin indicates the survival of some of the settlements to Roman times.

The relative antiquity of the earlier settlements of the Stone and Bronze ages is not capable of being deduced from existing evidence. "We may venture to place them," says Dr F. Keller, "in an age when iron and bronze had been long known, but had not come into our districts in such plenty as to be used for the common purposes of household life, at a time when amber had already taken its place as an ornament and had become an object of traffic." It is now considered that the people who erected the lake dwellings of Central Europe were also the people who were spread over the mainland. The forms and the ornamentation of the implements and weapons of stone and bronze found in the lake dwellings are the same as those of the implements and weapons in these materials found in the soil of the adjacent regions, and both groups must therefore be ascribed to the industry of one and the same people. Whether dwelling on the land or dwelling in the lake, they have exhibited so many indications of capacity, intelligence, industry and social organization that they cannot be considered as presenting, even in their Stone age, a very low condition of culture or civilization. Their axes were made of tough stones, sawn from the block and ground to the fitting shape. They were fixed by the butt in a socket of stag's horn, mortised into a handle of wood. Their knives and saws of flint were mounted in wooden handles and fixed with asphalt. They made and used an endless variety of bone tools. Their pottery, though roughly finished, is well made, the vessels often of large size and capable of standing the fire as cooking utensils. For domestic dishes they also made wooden tubs, plates, spoons, ladles and the like. The industries of spinning and weaving were largely practised. They made nets and fishing lines, and used canoes. They practised agriculture, cultivating several varieties of wheat and barley, besides millet and flax. They kept horses, cattle, sheep, goats and swine. Their clothing was partly of linen and partly of woollen fabrics and the skins of their beasts. Their food was nutritious and varied, their dwellings neither unhealthy nor incommodious. They lived in the security and comfort obtained by social organization, and were apparently intelligent, industrious and progressive communities.

There is no indication of an abrupt change from the use of stone to the use of metal such as might have occurred had the knowledge of copper and bronze, and the methods of working them, been introduced through the conquest of the original inhabitants by an alien race of superior culture and civilization. The improved cultural conditions become apparent in the multiplication of the varieties of tools, weapons and ornaments made possible by the more adaptable qualities of the new material; and that the development of the Bronze age culture in the lake dwellings followed the same course as in the surrounding regions where the people dwelt on the dry land is evident from the correspondence of the types of implements, weapons, ornaments and utensils common to both these conditions of life.

Other classes of prehistoric pile-structures akin to the lake dwellings are the Terremare of Italy and the Terpen of Holland. Both of these are settlements of wooden huts erected on piles, not over the water, but on flat land subject to inundations. The terremare (so named from the marly soil of which they are composed) appear as mounds, sometimes of very considerable extent, which when dug into disclose the remains and relic beds of the ancient settlements. They are most abundant in the plains of northern Italy traversed by the Po and its tributaries, though similar constructions have been found in Hungary in the valley of the Theiss. These pile-villages were often surrounded by an earthen rampart within which the huts were erected in more or less regular order. Many of them present evidence of having been more than once destroyed by fire and reconstructed, while others show one or more reconstructions at higher levels on the same site. The contents of the relic beds indicate that they belong for the most part to the age of bronze, although in some cases they may be referred to the latter part of the Stone age. Their inhabitants practised agriculture and kept the common domestic animals, while their tools, weapons and ornaments were mainly of similar character to those of the contemporary lake dwellers of the adjoining regions. Some of the Italian terremare show quadrangular constructions made like the modern log houses, of undressed tree trunks superposed longitudinally and overlapping at the ends, as at Castione in the province of Parma. A similar mode of construction is found in the pile-village on the banks of the Save, near Donja Dolina in Bosnia, described in 1904 by Dr Truhelka. Here the larger houses had platforms in front of them forming terraces at different levels descending towards the river. There was a cemetery adjacent to the village in which both unburnt and cremated interments occurred, the former predominating. From the general character of the relics this settlement appeared to belong to the early Iron age. The Terpen of Holland appear as mounds somewhat similar to those of the terremare, and were also pile structures, on low or marshy lands subject to inundations from the sea. Unlike the terremare and the lake dwellings they do not seem to belong to the prehistoric ages, but yield indications of occupation in post-Roman and medieval times.

AUTHORITIES.—The materials for the investigation of this singular phase of prehistoric life were first collected and systematized by Dr Ferdinand Keller (1800–1881), of Zürich, and printed in *Mittheilungen der Antiquarischen Gesellschaft in Zürich*, vols. ix.-xxii., 4to (1855–1886). The substance of these reports has been issued as a separate work in England, *The Lake Dwellings of Switzerland and other parts of Europe*, by Dr Ferdinand Keller, translated and arranged by John Edward Lee, 2nd ed. (2 vols. 8vo, London, 1878). Other works on the same subject are Frédéric Troyon, *Habitations lacustres des temps anciens et modernes* (Lausanne, 1860); E. Desor, *Les Palafittes ou constructions lacustres du lac de Neuchâtel* (Paris, 1865); E. Desor and L. Favre, *Le Bel Âge du bronze lacustre en Suisse* (Paris, 1874); A. Perrin, *Étude préhistorique sur la Savoie spécialement à l'époque lacustre* (*Les Palafittes du lac de Bourget*, Paris, 1870); Ernest Chantre, *Les Palafittes ou constructions lacustres du lac de Paladru* (Chambéry, 1871); Bartolomeo Gastaldi, *Lake Habitations and Prehistoric Remains in the Turbaries and Marl-beds of Northern and Central Italy*, translated by C. H. Chambers (London, 1865); Sir John Lubbock (Lord Avebury), *Prehistoric Times* (4th ed., London, 1878); Robert Munro, *The Lake-Dwellings of Europe* (London, 1890), with a bibliography of the subject. (J. An.)

LAKE GENEVA, a city of Walworth county, Wisconsin, U.S.A., 65 m. N.W. of Chicago. Pop. (1900) 2585, of whom 493 were foreign-born; (1905) 3449; (1910) 3079. It is served by the Chicago & Northwestern railway. The city is picturesquely situated on the shores of Lake Geneva (9 m. long and [illegible] m. wide), a beautiful body of remarkably clear water, fed by springs, and encircled by rolling hills covered with thick groves of hardwood trees. The region is famous as a summer resort, particularly for Chicago people. The city is the seat of Oakwood Sanitarium, and at Williams Bay, 6 m. distant, is the Yerkes Observatory of the University of Chicago. Dairying is the most important industrial interest. The first settlement at Lake Geneva was made about 1833. The city was chartered in 1886.

LAKE OF THE WOODS, a lake in the south-west of the province of Ontario, Canada, bordering west on the province of Manitoba, and south on the state of Minnesota. It is of an exceedingly irregular shape, and contains many islands. Its length is [illegible] m., breadth 10 to 50 m., area 1500 sq. m. It lies in the centre of the Laurentian region between Lakes Winnipeg and Superior, and an area of 36,000 sq. m. drains into it. It collects the waters of many rivers, the chief being Rainy river from the east, draining Rainy Lake. By the Winnipeg river on the north-east it discharges into Lake Winnipeg. The source of Winnipeg river is 1057 ft. above the sea, and drops [illegible] ft. in the course of 165 m. The scenery both on and around the lake is exceedingly beautiful, and the islands are largely occupied by the summer residences of city merchants. Kenora, a flourishing town at the source of the Winnipeg river, is the centre of the numerous lumbering and mining enterprises of the vicinity.

LAKE PLACID, a village in Essex county, New York, U.S.A., on the W. shore of Mirror Lake, near the S. end of Lake Placid, about 42 m. N.W. of Ticonderoga. Pop. (1905) 1514; (1910) [illegible]. The village is served by the Delaware & Hudson railway. The region is one of the most attractive in the Adirondacks, and is a much frequented summer resort. There are four good golf courses here, and the village has a well-built club house, called the "Neighborhood House." The village lies on the narrow strip of land (about ½ m.) between Mirror Lake (about 1 m. long, N. and S., and ½ m. wide), and Lake Placid, about 5 m. long (N.N.E. by S.S.W.), and about 1½ m. (maximum) [illegible] broad; its altitude is 1864 ft. The lake is roughly divided, from N. to S. by three islands—Moose, the largest, and Hawk, both privately owned, and Buck—and is a beautiful sheet of water in a picturesque setting of forests and heavily wooded hills and mountains. Among the principal peaks in the vicinity [illegible] Whiteface Mountain (4871 ft.), about 3 m. N.W. of the N. end of the lake; McKenzie Mountain (3872 ft.), about 1 m. [illegible] and Pulpit Mountain (2658 ft.), on the E. shore. [illegible] of Whiteface Mountain commands a fine view, [illegible] ft.), Saddleback (4530 ft.), Basin (4825 ft.), [illegible] and McIntyre (5110 [illegible] about 10 m. to the S. and Lake Champlain to the E., and to the N.E. may be seen, on clear days, the spires of Montreal. In the valleys E. and S. are the headwaters of the famous Ausable river. About 2 m. E. of the village, at North Elba, is the grave of the abolitionist, John Brown, with its huge boulder monument, and near it is another monument which bears the names of the 20 persons who bought the John Brown farm and gave it to the state. The railway to the village was completed in 1893. The village was incorporated in 1900.

LAKEWOOD, a village of Ocean county, New Jersey, U.S.A., in the township of Lakewood, 59 m. S. by W. of New York city, and 8 m. from the coast, on the Central Railroad of New Jersey. Pop. (1900) of the township, including the village, 3094; (1905) 4265, (1910) 5149. Lakewood is a fashionable health and winter resort, and is situated in the midst of a pine forest, with two small lakes, and many charming walks and drives. In the village there are a number of fine residences, large hotels, a library and a hospital. The winter temperature is 10-12° F. warmer than in New York. The township of Lakewood was incorporated in 1892.

LAKH (from the Sans. *laksha*, one hundred thousand), a term used in British India, in a colloquial sense to signify a lakh of rupees (written 1,00,000), which at the face value of the rupee would be worth £10,000, but now is worth only £6666. The term is also largely used in trade returns. A hundred lakhs make a crore.

LAKHIMPUR, a district of British India in the extreme east of the province of Eastern Bengal and Assam. Area, 4529 sq. m. It lies along both banks of the Brahmaputra for about 400 m.; it is bounded N. by the Daphla, Miri, Abor and Mishmi hills, E. by the Mishmi and Kachin hills, S. by the watershed of the Patkai range and the Lohit branch of the Brahmaputra, and W. by the districts of Darrang and Sibsagar. The Brahmaputra is navigable for steamers in all seasons as far as Dibrugarh, in the rainy season as far as Sadiya; its navigable tributaries within the district are the Subansiri, Dibru and Dihing. The deputy-commissioner in charge exercises political control over numerous tribes beyond the inner surveyed border. The most important of these tribes are the Miris, Abors, Mishmis, Khamtis, Kachins and Nagas. In 1901 the population was 371,396, an increase of 46% in the decade. The district has enjoyed remarkable and continuous prosperity. At each successive census the percentage of increase has been over 40, the present population being more than three times as great as that of 1872. This increase is chiefly due to the numerous tea gardens and to the coal mines and other enterprises of the Assam Railways and Trading Company. Lakhimpur was the first district into which tea cultivation was introduced by the government, and the Assam Company began operations here in 1840. The railway, known as the Dibru-Sadiya line, runs from Dibrugarh to Makum, with two branches to Talap and Margherita, and has been connected across the hills with the Assam-Bengal railway. The coal is of excellent quality, and is exported by river as far as Calcutta. The chief oil-wells are at Digboi. The oil is refined at Margherita, producing a good quality of kerosene oil and first-class paraffin, with wax and other by-products. The company also manufactures bricks and pipes of various kinds. Another industry is cutting timber, for the manufacture of tea-chests, &c.

Lakhimpur figures largely in the annals of Assam as the region where successive invaders from the east first reached the Brahmaputra. The Bara Bhuiyas, originally from the western provinces of India, were driven out by the Chutias (a Shan race), and these in their turn gave place to their more powerful brethren, the Ahoms, in the 13th century. The Burmese, who had ruined the native kingdoms, at the end of the 18th century, were in 1825 expelled by the British, who placed the southern part of the country, together with Sibsagar under the rule of Raja Purandhar Singh; but it was not till 1838 that the whole was taken under direct British administration. The headquarters are at Dibrugarh.

See *Lakhimpur District Gazetteer* (Calcutta, 1905).

LAKSHMI (Sans. for "mark," "sign," generally used in composition with *punya*, "prosperous"; hence "good sign," "good fortune"), in Hindu mythology, the wife of Vishnu.

worshipped as the goddess of love, beauty and prosperity. She has many other names, the chief being *Loka mata* ("mother of the world"), *Padma* ("the lotus"), *Padma laya* ("she who dwells on a lotus") and *Jaladhija* ("the ocean-born"). She is represented as of a bright golden colour and seated on a lotus. She is said to have been born from the sea of milk when it was churned from ambrosia. Many quaint myths surround her birth. In the Rig Veda her name does not occur as a goddess.

LALAING, JACQUES DE (*c.* 1420–1453), Flemish knight, was originally in the service of the duke of Cleves and afterwards in that of the duke of Burgundy, Philip III., the Good, gaining great renown by his prowess in the tiltyard. The duke of Burgundy entrusted him with embassies to the pope and the king of France (1451), and subsequently sent him to put down the revolt of the inhabitants of Ghent, in which expedition he was killed. His biography, *Le Livre des faits de messire Jacques de Lalaing*, which has been published several times, is mainly the work of the Burgundian herald and chronicler Jean le Fèvre, better known as *Toison d'or*; the Flemish historiographer Georges Chastellain and the herald Charolais also took part in its compilation.

LALANDE, JOSEPH JÉRÔME LEFRANÇAIS DE (1732–1807), French astronomer, was born at Bourg (department of Ain), on the 11th of July 1732. His parents sent him to Paris to study law; but the accident of lodging in the Hôtel Cluny, where J. N. Delisle had his observatory, drew him to astronomy, and he became the zealous and favoured pupil of both Delisle and Pierre Lemonnier. He, however, completed his legal studies, and was about to return to Bourg to practise there as an advocate, when Lemonnier obtained permission to send him to Berlin, to make observations on the lunar parallax in concert with those of N. L. Lacaille at the Cape of Good Hope. The successful execution of his task procured for him, before he was twenty-one, admission to the Academy of Berlin, and the post of adjunct astronomer to that of Paris. He now devoted himself to the improvement of the planetary theory, publishing in 1759 a corrected edition of Halley's tables, with a history of the celebrated comet whose return in that year he had aided Clairault to calculate. In 1762 J. N. Delisle resigned in his favour the chair of astronomy in the Collège de France, the duties of which were discharged by Lalande for forty-six years. His house became an astronomical seminary, and amongst his pupils were J. B. J. Delambre, G. Piazzi, P. Mechain, and his own nephew Michel Lalande. By his publications in connexion with the transit of 1769 he won great and, in a measure, deserved fame. But his love of notoriety and impetuous temper compromised the respect due to his scientific zeal, though these faults were partially balanced by his generosity and benevolence. He died on the 4th of April 1807.

Although his investigations were conducted with diligence rather than genius, the career of Lalande must be regarded as of eminent service to astronomy. As a lecturer and writer he gave to the science unexampled popularity; his planetary tables, into which he introduced corrections for mutual perturbations, were the best available up to the end of the 18th century; and the Lalande prize, instituted by him in 1802 for the chief astronomical performance of each year, still testifies to his enthusiasm for his favourite pursuit. Amongst his voluminous works are *Traité d'astronomie* (2 vols., 1764; enlarged edition, 4 vols., 1771–1781, 3rd ed., 3 vols., 1792); *Histoire céleste française* (1801), giving the places of 50,000 stars; *Bibliographie astronomique* (1803), with a history of astronomy from 1781 to 1802; *Astronomie des dames* (1785); *Abrégé de navigation* (1793); *Voyage d'un françois en Italie* (1769), a valuable record of his travels in 1765–1766. He communicated above one hundred and fifty papers to the Paris Academy of Sciences, edited the *Connoissance des temps* (1759–1774), and again (1794–1807), and wrote the concluding 2 vols. of the 2nd edition of Montucla's *Histoire des mathématiques* (1802).

See *Mémoires de l'Institut*, t. viii. (1807) (J. B. J. Delambre); Delambre, *Hist. de l'astr. au XVIIIe siècle*, p. 547; *Magasin encyclopédique*, ii. 288 (1810) (Mme de Salm); J. S. Bailly, *Hist. de l'astr. moderne*, t. iii. (ed. 1785); J. Mädler, *Geschichte der Himmelskunde*, ii. 141; R. Wolf, *Gesch. der Astronomie*; J. J. Lalande, *Bibl. astr.* p. 428; J. C. Poggendorff, *Biog. Lit. Handwörterbuch*; M. Marie, *Hist. des sciences*, ix. 35.

LALÍN, a town of north-western Spain, in the province of Pontevedra. Pop. (1900) 16,238. Lalín is the centre of the trade in agricultural products of the fertile highlands between the Deza and Arnego rivers. The local industries are tanning and the manufacture of paper. Near Lalín are the ruins of the Gothic abbey of Carboeiro.

LA LINEA, or LA LINEA DE LA CONCEPCION, a town of Spain, in the province of Cadiz, between Gibraltar and San Roque. Pop. (1900) 31,802. La Linea, which derives its name from the *line* or boundary dividing Spanish territory from the district of Gibraltar, is a town of comparatively modern date and was formerly looked upon as a suburb of San Roque. It is now a distinct frontier post and headquarters of the Spanish commandant of the lines of Gibraltar. The fortifications erected here in the 16th century were dismantled by the British in 1810, to prevent the landing of French invaders, and all the existing buildings are modern. They include barracks, casinos, a theatre and a bull-ring, much frequented by the inhabitants and garrison of Gibraltar. La Linea has some trade in cereals, fruit and vegetables; it is the residence of large numbers of labourers employed in Gibraltar.

LALITPUR, a town of British India, in Jhansi district, United Provinces. Pop. (1901) 11,560. It has a station on the Great Indian Peninsula railway, and a large trade in oil-seeds, hides and *ghi*. It contains several beautiful Hindu and Jain temples. It was formerly the headquarters of a district of the same name, which was incorporated with that of Jhansi in 1891. The Bundela chiefs of Lalitpur were among those who most eagerly joined the Mutiny, and it was only after a severe struggle that the district was pacified.

LALLY, THOMAS ARTHUR, COMTE DE, Baron de Tollendal (1702–1766), French general, was born at Romans, Dauphiné, in January 1702, being the son of Sir Gerard O'Lally, an Irish Jacobite who married a French lady of noble family, from whom the son inherited his titles. Entering the French army in 1721 he served in the war of 1734 against Austria; he was present at Dettingen (1743), and commanded the regiment de Lally in the famous Irish brigade at Fontenoy (May 1745). He was made a brigadier on the field by Louis XV. He had previously been mixed up in several Jacobite plots, and in 1745 accompanied Charles Edward to Scotland, serving as aide-de-camp at the battle of Falkirk (January 1746). Escaping to France, he served with Marshal Saxe in the Low Countries, and at the capture of Maestricht (1748) was made a *maréchal de camp*. When war broke out with England in 1756 Lally was given the command of a French expedition to India. He reached Pondicherry in April 1758, and at the outset met with some trifling military success. He was a man of courage and a capable general; but his pride and ferocity made him disliked by his officers and hated by his soldiers, while he regarded the natives as slaves, despised their assistance, and trampled on their traditions of caste. In consequence everything went wrong with him. He was unsuccessful in an attack on Tanjore, and had to retire from the siege of Madras (1758) owing to the timely arrival of the British fleet. He was defeated by Sir Eyre Coote at Wandiwash (1760), and besieged in Pondicherry and forced to capitulate (1761). He was sent as a prisoner of war to England. While in London, he heard that he was accused in France of treachery, and insisted, against advice, on returning on parole to stand his trial. He was kept prisoner for nearly two years before the trial began; then, after many painful delays, he was sentenced to death (May 6, 1766), and three days later beheaded. Louis XV. tried to throw the responsibility for what was undoubtedly a judicial murder on his ministers and the public, but his policy needed a scapegoat, and he was probably well content not to exercise his authority to save an almost friendless foreigner.

See G. B. Malleson, *The Career of Count Lally* (1865); "Z's" (the marquis de Lally-Tollendal) article in the *Biographie Michaud*; and Voltaire's *Œuvres complètes*. The legal documents are preserved in the Bibliothèque Nationale.

LALLY-TOLLENDAL, TROPHIME GÉRARD, MARQUIS DE (1751–1830), was born at Paris on the 5th of March 1751. He was the legitimized son of the comte de Lally and only discove-

[illegible] the [illegible] the case [illegible] Lally's [illegible] innocence [illegible] In 1779 Lally-[illegible] Strasbourg, and in [illegible] of Paris. [illegible] Revolution, but [illegible] all even of its [illegible] to the [illegible] of re-[illegible] August 1789 [illegible] Later in the [illegible] Louis XVI. [illegible] to defend the [illegible] France. He did not [illegible] Louis XVIII. created [illegible] became a member of the [illegible] his death, on the 11th [illegible] philanthropic work, French Academy [illegible] of March 1830, he [illegible] Lally-[illegible] 1793); Lally-[illegible] Mémoires, attributed [illegible] he further [illegible] Biographie Michaud; see also [illegible] M. le marquis de Lally-[illegible] Necrologie de [illegible] (Paris, undated); Voltaire, Œuvres [illegible] see the analytical table of contents, vol. ii.

LALO, ÉDOUARD (1823–1892), French composer, was born at Lille, on the 27th of January 1823. He began his musical studies at the conservatoire at Lille, and in Paris attended the violin classes of Habeneck. For several years Lalo led a modest and retired existence, playing the viola in the quartet party organized by Armingaud and Jacquard, and in composing chamber music. His early works include two trios, a quartet, and several pieces for violin and pianoforte. In 1867 he took part in an operatic competition, an opera from his pen, entitled *Fiesque*, obtaining the third place out of forty-three. This work was accepted for production at the Paris Opéra, but delays occurred, and nothing was done. *Fiesque* was next offered to the Théâtre de la Monnaie, Brussels, and was about to be produced there when the manager became bankrupt. Thus, when nearly fifty years of age, Lalo found himself in difficulties. *Firsque* [illegible] but the composer published the pianoforte [illegible] of the music in other works. [illegible] French composers found their [illegible] Lalo was one of these, and [illegible] several interesting works from [illegible] a sonata for violoncello, a [illegible] violin concerto and the [illegible] orchestra, one of his best-[illegible] he had written a second [illegible] would be produced at the [illegible] him the "scenario" of a [illegible] be content with this, and [illegible] he fell ill, the last scenes [illegible] *Namouna*, the [illegible] the Opéra in 1882. Six [illegible] *Le Roi d'Ys* was brought [illegible] at last enabled to taste [illegible] came to him too [illegible] the music to *Néron*, a [illegible] in 1891, were his [illegible] opera, but had only [illegible] he died. [illegible]

employment of curious rhythmic devices. His music is ever ingenious and brilliantly effective.

LA MADDALENA, an island 2½ m. from the N.E. coast of Sardinia. Pop. (1901) 8361. Napoleon bombarded it in 1793 without success, and Nelson made it his headquarters for some time. It is now an important naval station of the Italian fleet, the anchorage being good, and is strongly fortified. A bridge and an embankment connect it with Caprera. It appears to have been inhabited in Roman times.

LĀMĀISM, a system of doctrine partly religious, partly political. Religiously it is the corrupt form of Buddhism prevalent in Tibet and Mongolia. It stands in a relationship to primitive Buddhism similar to that in which Roman Catholicism, so long as the temporal power of the pope was still in existence, stood to primitive Christianity. The ethical and metaphysical ideas most conspicuous in the doctrines of Lāmāism are not confined to the highlands of central Asia, they are accepted in great measure also in Japan and China. It is the union of these ideas with a hierarchical system, and with the temporal sovereignty of the head of that system in Tibet, which constitutes what is distinctively understood by the term Lāmāism. Lāmāism has acquired a special interest to the student of comparative history through the instructive parallel which its history presents to that of the Church of Rome.

The "Great Vehicle."

The central point of primitive Buddhism was the doctrine of "Arahatship"—a system of ethical and mental self-culture, in which deliverance was found from all the mysteries and sorrows of life in a change of heart to be reached here on earth. This doctrine seems to have been held very nearly in its original purity from the time when it was propounded by Gotama in the 6th century B.C. to the period in which northern India was conquered by the Huns about the commencement of the Christian era. Soon after that time there arose a school of Buddhist teachers who called their doctrine the "Great Vehicle." It was not in any contradiction to the older doctrine, which they contemptuously called the "Little Vehicle," but included it all, and was based upon it. The distinguishing characteristic of the newer school was the importance which it attached to "Bodhisatship." The older school had taught that Gotama, who had propounded the doctrine of Arahatship, was a Buddha, that only a Buddha is capable of discovering that doctrine, and that a Buddha is a man who by self-denying efforts, continued through many hundreds of different births, has acquired the so-called *Ten Pāramitās* or cardinal virtues in such perfection that he is able, when sin and ignorance have gained the upper hand throughout the world, to save the human race from impending ruin. But until the process of perfection has been completed, until the moment when at last the sage, sitting under the Wisdom tree acquires that particular insight or wisdom which is called Enlightenment or Buddhahood, he is still only a Bodhisat. The link of connexion between the various Bodhisats in the future Buddha's successive births is not a soul which is transferred from body to body, but the *karma*, or character, which each successive Bodhisat inherits from his predecessors in the long chain of existences. Now the older school also held, in the first place, that, when a man had, in this life, attained to Arahatship, his karma would not pass on to any other individual in another life—or in other words, that after Arahatship there would be no rebirth; and, secondly, that four thousand years after the Buddha had proclaimed the *Dhamma* or doctrine of Arahatship, his teaching would have died away, and another Buddha would be required to bring mankind once more to a knowledge of the truth. The leaders of the Great Vehicle urged their followers to seek to attain, not so much to Arahatship, which would involve only their own salvation, but to Bodhisatship, by the attainment of which they would be conferring the blessings of the Dhamma upon countless multitudes in the long ages of the future. By thus laying stress upon Bodhisatship, rather than upon Arahatship, the new school, though they doubtless merely thought themselves to be carrying the older orthodox doctrines to their logical conclusion, were really changing the central point of

Buddhism, and were altering the direction of their mental vision. It was of no avail that they adhered in other respects in the main to the older teaching, that they professed to hold to the same ethical system, that they adhered, except in a few unimportant details, to the old regulations of the order of the Buddhist mendicant recluses. The ancient books, preserved in the *Pāli Piṭakas*, being mainly occupied with the details of Arahatship, lost their exclusive value in the eyes of those whose attention was being directed to the details of Bodhisatship. And the opinion that every leader in their religious circles, every teacher distinguished among them for his sanctity of life, or for his extensive learning, was a Bodhisat, who might have and who probably had inherited the karma of some great teacher of old, opened the door to a flood of superstitious fancies.

It is worthy of note that the new school found its earliest professors and its greatest expounders in a part of India outside the districts to which the personal influence of Gotama and of his immediate followers had been confined. The home of early Buddhism was round about Kosala and Magadha; in the district, that is to say, north and south of the Ganges between where Allahabad now lies on the west and Rajgir on the east. The home of the Great Vehicle was, at first, in the countries farther to the north and west. Buddhism arose in countries where Sanskrit was never more than a learned tongue, and where the exclusive claims of the Brahmins had never been universally admitted. The Great Vehicle arose in the very stronghold of Brahminism, and among a people to whom Sanskrit, like Latin in the middle ages in Europe, was the literary *lingua franca*. The new literature therefore, which the new movement called forth, was written, and has been preserved, in Sanskrit—its principal books of *Dharma*, or doctrine, being the following nine: (1) *Prajñā-pāramitā*, (2) *Gaṇḍa-vyūha*; (3) *Daśa-bhūmīś-vara*; (4) *Samādhi-rāja*; (5) *Lankāvatāra*; (6) *Saddharma-puṇḍarīka*; (7) *Tathāgata-guhyaka*; (8) *Lalita-vistara*; (9) *Suvarṇa-prabhāsa*. The date of none of these works is known with any certainty, but it is highly improbable that any one of them is older than the 6th century after the death of Gotama. Copies of all of them were brought to Europe by Mr B. H. Hodgson, and other copies have been received since then; but only one of them has as yet been published in Europe (the *Lalita Vistara*, edited by Lefmann), and only two have been translated into any European language. These are the *Lalita Vistara*, translated into French, through the Tibetan, by M. Foucaux, and the *Saddharma Puṇḍarīka*, translated into English by Professor Kern. The former is legendary work, partly in verse, on the life of Gotama, the historical Buddha; and the latter, also partly in verse, is devoted to proving the essential identity of the Great and the Little Vehicles, and the equal authenticity of both as doctrines enunciated by the master himself.

Of the authors of these nine works, as of all the older Buddhist works with one or two exceptions, nothing has been ascertained. The founder of the system of the Great Vehicle is, however, often referred to under the name of Nāgārjuna, whose probable date is about A.D. 200.

Together with Nāgārjuna, other early teachers of the Great Vehicle whose names are known are Vasumitra, Vasubandhu, Āryadeva, Dharmapāla and Gunamati—all of whom were looked upon as Bodhisats. As the newer school did not venture so far as to claim as Bodhisats the disciples stated in the older books to have been the contemporaries of Gotama (they being precisely the persons known as Arahats), they attempted to give the appearance of age to the Bodhisat theory by representing the Buddha as being surrounded, not only by his human companions the Arahats, but also by fabulous beings, whom they represented as the Bodhisats existing at that time. In the opening words of each Mahāyāna treatise a list is given of such Bodhisats, who were beginning, together with the historical Bodhisats, to occupy a position in the Buddhist church of those times similar to that occupied by the saints in the corresponding period of the history of Christianity in the Church of Rome. And these lists of fabulous Bodhisats have now a distinct historical importance. For they grow in length in the later works; and it is often possible by comparing them one with another to fix, not the date, but the comparative age of the books in which they occur. Thus it is a fair inference to draw from the shortness of the list in the opening words of the *Lalita Vistara*, as compared with that in the first sections of the *Saddharma Puṇḍarīka*, that the latter work is much the younger of the two, a conclusion supported also by other considerations.

Among the Bodhisats mentioned in the *Saddharma Puṇḍarīka*, and not mentioned in the *Lalita Vistara*, as attendant on the Buddha are Manju-śrī and Avalokiteśvara. That these saints were already acknowledged by the followers of the Great Vehicle at the beginning of the 5th century is clear from the fact that Fa Hien, who visited India about that time, says that "men of the Great Vehicle" were then worshipping them at Mathura, not far from Delhi (F. H., chap. xvi.). These were supposed to be celestial beings who, inspired by love of the human race, had taken the so-called Great Resolve to become future Buddhas, and who therefore descended from heaven when the actual Buddha was on earth, to pay reverence to him, and to learn of him. The belief in them probably arose out of the doctrine of the older school, which did not deny the existence of the various creations of previous mythology and speculation, but allowed of their actual existence as spiritual beings, and only deprived them of all power over the lives of men, and declared them to be temporary beings liable, like men, to sin and ignorance, and requiring, like men, the salvation of Arahatship. Among them the later Buddhists seem to have placed their numerous Bodhisats; and to have paid especial reverence to Manju-śrī as the personification of wisdom, and to Avalokiteśwara as the personification of overruling love. The former was afterwards identified with the mythical first Buddhist missionary, who is supposed to have introduced civilization into Tibet about two hundred and fifty years after the death of the Buddha.

The five mystic trinities.

The way was now open to a rapid fall from the simplicity of early Buddhism, in which men's attention was directed to the various parts of the system of self-culture, to a belief in a whole pantheon of saints or angels, which appealed more strongly to the half-civilized races among whom the Great Vehicle was now professed. A theory sprang up which was supposed to explain the marvellous powers of the Buddhas by representing them as only the outward appearance, the reflection, as it were, or emanation, of ethereal Buddhas dwelling in the skies. These were called *Dhyāni Buddhas*, and their number was supposed to be, like that of the Buddhas, innumerable. Only five of them, however, occupied any space in the speculative world in which the ideas of the later Buddhists had now begun to move. But, being Buddhas, they were supposed to have their Bodhisats; and thus out of the five last Buddhas of the earlier teaching there grew up five mystic trinities, each group consisting of one of these five Buddhas, his prototype in heaven the Dhyāni Buddha, and his celestial Bodhisat. Among these hypothetical beings, the creations of a sickly scholasticism, hollow abstractions without life or reality, the particular trinity in which the historical Gotama was assigned a subordinate place naturally occupied the most exalted rank. Amitābha, the Dhyāni-Buddha of this trinity, soon began to fill the largest place in the minds of the new school; and Avalokiteśwara, his Bodhisat, was looked upon with a reverence somewhat less than his former glory. It is needless to add that, under the overpowering influence of these vain imaginations, the earnest moral teachings of Gotama became more and more hidden from view. The imaginary saints grew and flourished. Each new creation, each new step in the theory, demanded another, until the whole sky was filled with forgeries of the brain, and the nobler and simpler lessons of the founder of the religion were hidden beneath the glittering stream of metaphysical subtleties.

Still worse results followed on the change of the earlier point of view. The acute minds of the Buddhist pandits, no longer occupied with the practical lessons of Arahatship, turned their

Amitâbha, who occupies the higher place in the mythology of the Great Vehicle, would be superior to the latter, as the spiritual representative of Avalokitesvara. But practically the Dalai Lâma, owing to his position in the capital,[1] has the political supremacy, and is actually called the *Gyalpo Rinpotshe*, "the glorious king"—his companion being content with the title *Pantshen Rinpotshe*, "the glorious teacher." When either of them dies it is necessary for the other to ascertain in whose body the celestial being whose outward form has been dissolved has been pleased again to incarnate himself. For that purpose the names of all male children born just after the death of the deceased Great Lâma are laid before his survivor. He chooses three out of the whole number; their names are thrown into a golden casket provided for that purpose by a former emperor of China. The Chutuktus, or abbots of the great monasteries, then assemble, and after a week of prayer, the lots are drawn in their presence and in presence of the surviving Great Lâma and of the Chinese political resident. The child whose name is first drawn is the future Great Lâma; the other two receive each of them 500 pieces of silver. The Chutuktus just mentioned correspond in many respects to the Roman cardinals. Like the Great Lâmas, they bear the title of Rinpotshe or Glorious, and are looked upon as incarnations of one or other of the celestial Bodhisats of the Great Vehicle mythology. Their number varies from ten to a hundred; and it is uncertain whether the honour is inherent in the abbacy of certain of the greatest cloisters, or whether the Dalai Lâma exercises the right of choosing them. Under these high officials of the Tibetan hierarchy there come the Chubil Khâns, who fill the post of abbot to the lesser monasteries, and are also incarnations. Their number is very large; there are few monasteries in Tibet or in Mongolia which do not claim to possess one of these living Buddhas. Besides these mystical persons there are in the Tibetan church other ranks and degrees, corresponding to the deacon, full priest, dean and doctor of divinity in the West. At the great yearly festival at Lhasa they make in the cathedral an imposing array, not much less magnificent than that of the clergy in Rome; for the ancient simplicity of dress has disappeared in the growing differences of rank, and each division of the spiritual army is distinguished in Tibet, as in the West, by a special uniform. The political authority of the Dalai Lâma is confined to Tibet itself, but he is the acknowledged head also of the Buddhist church throughout Mongolia and China. He has no supremacy over his co-religionists in Japan, and even in China there are many Buddhists who are not practically under his control or influence.

The best work on Lâmaism is still Köppen's *Die Lamaische Hierarchie und Kirche* [illegible]. See also Bushell, "The Early History of Tibet," in the [illegible] *Royal Asiatic Society*, 1879–1880, vol. [illegible]; Ssanang Ssetsen, [illegible] *of the East Mongols* (in Mongolian, translated into German by I. J. Schmidt, *Geschichte der Ost-Mongolen*); [illegible] by M. Léon Feer, in *Annales du Musée* [illegible] *des Buddhismus in Hoch-Asien*; [illegible]; Huc and Gabet, [illegible] *Tibet, et la Chine* [illegible] *Nachrichten über die* [illegible] Sarat Chunder Das's "Contributions [illegible] Religion and History of Tibet," in the *Journal of the* [illegible] 1881, L. A. Waddell, *The Buddhism of* [illegible]; A. H. Francke, *History of Western Tibet* [illegible] Grünwedel, *Mythologie des Buddhismus in Tibet* [illegible] Berlin, 1900). (T. W. R. D.)

LAMALOU-LES-BAINS, a watering-place of southern France [illegible] department of Hérault, 53½ m. W. of Montpellier by rail, [illegible] in a valley of the southern Cévennes. Pop. (1906) 720. The [illegible] waters, which are both hot and cold, are used in cases of rheumatism, sciatica, locomotor ataxy and nervous maladies.

LAMA-MIAO, or Dolon-nor, a city of the province of Chih-li, China, 150 m. N. of Peking, in a barren sandy plain watered by the Urtingol, a tributary of the Shang-tu-ho. The town proper, almost exclusively occupied by Chinese, is about a mile in length by half a mile in breadth, has narrow and dirty streets, and contains a population of about 26,000. Unlike the ordinary Chinese town of the same rank, it is not walled. A busy trade is carried on between the Chinese and the Mongolians, who bring in their cattle, sheep, camels, hides and wool to barter for tea, tobacco, cotton and silk. At some distance from the Chinese town lies the Mongolian quarter, with two groups of lama temples and villages occupied by about 2300 priests. Dr Williamson (*Journeys in North China*, 1870) described the chief temple as a huge oblong building with an interior not unlike a Gothic church. Lama-miao is the seat of a manufactory of bronze idols and other articles of ritual, which find their way to all parts of Mongolia and Tibet. The craftsmen work in their own houses.

LAMAR, LUCIUS QUINTUS CINCINNATUS (1825–1893), American statesman and judge, was born at the old "Lamar Homestead," in Putnam county, Georgia, on the 17th of September 1825. His father, Lucius Q. C. Lamar (1797–1834), was an able lawyer, a judge of the superior court of Georgia, and the compiler of the *Laws of Georgia from 1810 to 1819* (1821). In 1845 young Lamar graduated from Emory College (Oxford, Ga.), and in 1847 was admitted to the bar. In 1849 he removed to Oxford, Mississippi, and in 1850–1852 was adjunct professor of mathematics in the state university. In 1852 he removed to Covington, Ga., to practise law, and in 1853 was elected a member of the Georgia House of Representatives. In 1855 he returned to Mississippi, and two years later became a member of the National House of Representatives, where he served until December 1860, when he withdrew to become a candidate for election to the "secession" convention of Mississippi. He was elected to the convention, and drafted for it the Mississippi ordinance of secession. In the summer of 1860 he had accepted an appointment to the chair of ethics and metaphysics in the university of Mississippi, but, having been appointed a lieutenant-colonel in the Confederate Army in the spring of 1861, he resigned his professorship. The colonel of his regiment (Nineteenth Mississippi) was killed early in the battle of Williamsburg, on the 5th of May 1862, and the command then fell to Lamar, but in October he resigned from the army. In November 1862 he was appointed by President Jefferson Davis special commissioner of the Confederacy to Russia; but he did not proceed farther than Paris, and his mission was soon terminated by the refusal of the Confederate Senate to confirm his appointment. In 1866 he was again appointed to the chair of ethics and metaphysics in the university of Mississippi, and in the next year was transferred to the chair of law, but in 1870, Republicans having become trustees of the university upon the readmission of the state into the Union, he resigned. From 1873 to 1877 he was again a Democratic representative in Congress; from 1877 to 1885 he was a United States senator; from 1885 to January 1888 he was secretary of the interior; and from 1888 until his death at Macon, Ga., on the 23rd of January 1893, he was an associate justice of the Supreme Court of the United States. In Congress Lamar fought the silver and greenback craze and argued forcibly against the protective tariff; in the department of the interior he introduced various reforms; and on the Supreme Court bench his dissenting opinion in the *Neagle Case* (based upon a denial that certain powers belonging to Congress, but not exercised, were by implication vested in the department of justice) is famous. But he is perhaps best known for the part he took after the Civil War in helping to effect a reconciliation between the North and the South. During the early secession movement he strove to arouse the white people of the South from their indifference, declaring that secession alone could save them from a doom similar to that of the former whites of San Domingo. He probably never changed his convictions as to the righteousness of the "lost cause"; but he accepted the result of the war as a final settlement of the differences leading to it, and strove to restore the South in the Union, and to effect the reunion of the nation in feeling as well as in government. This is in part [illegible]en from such speeches as his eulogy on Charles Sumner (27th April 1874), his leadership in reorganizing the Democratic

[1] This statement, representing the substantial and historical position, is retained, in spite of the crises of March [illegible] Dalai Lâma took refuge from the Chinese in [illegible] the British expedition occupied Lhasa and [illegible] China (see Tibet).

party of his own state, and his counsels of peace in the disputed presidential election of 1876.

See Edward Mayes, *Lucius Q. C. Lamar: His Life, Times and Speeches* (Nashville, Tenn., 1896).

LAMARCK, JEAN BAPTISTE PIERRE ANTOINE DE MONET, CHEVALIER DE (1744–1829), French naturalist, was born on the 1st of August 1744, at Bazantin, a village of Picardy. He was an eleventh child; and his father, lord of the manor and of old family, but of limited means, having placed three sons in the army, destined this one for the church, and sent him to the Jesuits at Amiens, where he continued till his father's death. After this he would remain with the Jesuits no longer, and, not yet seventeen years of age, started for the seat of war at Bergen-op-Zoom, before which place one of his brothers had already been killed. Mounted on an old horse, with a boy from the village as attendant, and furnished by a lady with a letter of introduction to a colonel, he reached his destination on the evening before a battle. Next morning the colonel found that the new and very diminutive volunteer had posted himself in the front rank of a body of grenadiers, and could not be induced to quit the position. In the battle, the company which he had joined became exposed to the fire of the enemy's artillery, and in the confusion of retreat was forgotten. All the officers and subalterns were killed, and not more than fourteen men were left, when the oldest grenadiers seeing there were no more French in sight proposed to the young volunteer so soon become commandant to withdraw his men. This he refused to do without orders. These at last arrived; and for his bravery he was made an officer on the spot, and soon after was named to a lieutenancy.

After the peace, the regiment was sent to Monaco. There one of his comrades playfully lifted him by the head, and to this it was imputed that he was seized with disease of the glands of the neck, so severe as to put a stop to his military career. He went to Paris and began the study of medicine, supporting himself by working in a banker's office He early became interested in meteorology and in physical and chemical speculations of a chimerical kind, but happily threw his main strength into botany, and in 1778 published his *Flore française*, a work in which by a dichotomous system of contrasting characters he enabled the student with facility to determine species. This work, which went through several editions and long kept the field, gained for its author immediate popularity as well as admission to the Academy of Sciences.

In 1781 and 1782, under the title of botanist to the king, an appointment obtained for him by Buffon, whose son accompanied him, he travelled through various countries of Europe, extending his knowledge of natural history; and on his return he began those elaborate contributions to botany on which his reputation in that science principally rests, namely, the *Dictionnaire de Botanique* and the *Illustrations de Genres*, voluminous works contributed to the *Encyclopédie Méthodique* (1785). In 1793, in consequence of changes in the organization of the natural history department at the Jardin du Roi, where he had held a botanical appointment since 1788, Lamarck was presented to a zoological chair, and called on to lecture on the *Insecta* and *Vermes* of Linnaeus, the animals for which he introduced the term *Invertebrata*. Thus driven, comparatively late in life, to devote his principal attention to zoology instead of botany, he had the misfortune soon after to suffer from impaired vision; and the malady resulted subsequently in total blindness. Yet his greatest zoological work, the *Histoire naturelle des animaux sans vertèbres*, was published from 1815 to 1822, with the assistance, in the last two volumes, of his eldest daughter and of P. A. Latreille (1762–1833). A volume of plates of the fossil shells of the neighbourhood of Paris was collected in 1823 from his memoirs in the *Annales des Muséums*. He died on the 18th of December 1829.

The character of Lamarck as a naturalist is remarkable alike for its excellences and its defects. His excellences were width of scope, fertility of ideas and a pre-eminent faculty of precise description, arising not only from a singularly terse style, but from a clear insight into both the distinctive features and the resemblances of forms. That part of his zoological work which constitutes his solid claim to the highest honour as a zoologist is to be found in his extensive and detailed labours in the departments of living and fossil *Invertebrata*. His endeavours at classification of the great groups were necessarily defective on account of the imperfect knowledge possessed in his time in regard to many of them, *e.g.* echinoderms, ascidians and intestinal worms; yet they are not without interest, particularly on account of the comprehensive attempt to unite in one great division as *Articulata* all those groups that appeared to present a segmented construction. Moreover, Lamarck was the first to distinguish vertebrate from invertebrate animals by the presence of a vertebral column, and among the Invertebrata to found the groups *Crustacea*, *Arachnida* and *Annelida*. In 1785 (*Hist. de l'Acad.*) he evinced his appreciation of the necessity of natural orders in botany by an attempt at the classification of plants, interesting, though crude and falling immeasurably short of the system which grew in the hands of his intimate friend A. L. de Jussieu. The problem of taxonomy has never been put more philosophically than he subsequently put it in his *Animaux sans vertèbres*: "What arrangement must be given to the general distribution of animals to make it conformable to the order of nature in the production of these beings?"

The most prominent defect in Lamarck must be admitted to have been want of control in speculation. Doubtless the speculative tendency furnished a powerful incentive to work, but it outran the legitimate deductions from observation, and led him into the production of volumes of worthless chemistry without experimental basis, as well as into spending much time on fruitless meteorological predictions. His *Annuaires Météorologiques* were published yearly from 1800 to 1810, and were not discontinued until after an unnecessarily public and brutal tirade from Napoleon, administered on the occasion of being presented with one of his works on natural history.

To the general reader the name of Lamarck is chiefly interesting on account of his theory of the origin of life and of the diversities of animal forms. The idea, which appears to have been favoured by Buffon before him, that species were not through all time unalterable, and that the more complex might have been developed from pre-existent simpler forms, became with Lamarck a belief or, as he imagined, a demonstration. Spontaneous generation, he considered, might be easily conceived as resulting from such agencies as heat and electricity causing in small gelatinous bodies an utricular structure, and inducing a "singular tension," a kind of "éréthisme" or "orgasme"; and, having thus accounted for the first appearance of life, he explained the whole organization of animals and formation of different organs by four laws (introduction to his *Histoire naturelle des animaux sans vertèbres*, 1815):—

1. "Life by its proper forces tends continually to increase the volume of every body possessing it, and to enlarge its parts, up to a limit which it brings about.

2. "The production of a new organ in an animal body results from the supervention of a new want (*besoin*) continuing to make itself felt, and a new movement which this want gives birth to and encourages.

3. "The development of organs and their force of action are constantly in ratio to the employment of these organs.

4. "All which has been acquired, laid down, or changed in the organization of individuals in the course of their life is conserved by generation and transmitted to the new individuals which proceed from those which have undergone those changes.

The second law is often referred to as Lamarck's hypothesis of the evolution of organs in animals by appetence or longing, although he does not teach that the animal's desires affect its conformation directly, but that altered wants lead to altered habits, which result in the formation of new organs as well as in modification, growth or dwindling of those previously existing. Thus, he suggests that, ruminants being pursued by carnivora, their legs have grown slender; and, their legs being only fit for support, while their jaws are weak, they have made attack with the crown of the head, and the determination of fluids thither has led to the growth of horns. So also the stretching of the giraffe's neck to reach the foliage he supposes to have led to its elongation; and the kangaroo, sitting upright to support the young in its pouch, he imagines to have had its fore-limbs dwarfed by disuse, and its hind legs and tail exaggerated by using them in leaping. The fourth law expresses the inheritance of acquired characters, which is denied by August Weismann and his followers. For a more detailed account of Lamarck's place in the history of the doctrine of evolution, see Evolution.

LA MARGHERITA, CLEMENTE SOLARO, Count del (1792–1869), Piedmontese statesman, was born at Mondovi. He studied law at Siena and Turin, but Piedmont was at that time under French domination, and being devoted to the house of Savoy he refused to take his degree, as this proceeding would have obliged him to recognize the authority of the usurper; after the restoration of the Sardinian kingdom, however, he graduated. In 1816 he entered the diplomatic service. Later he returned to Turin, and succeeded in gaining the confidence and esteem of King Charles Albert, who in 1835 appointed him minister of foreign affairs. A fervent Roman Catholic, devoted to the pope and to the Jesuits, friendly to Austria and firmly attached to the principles of autocracy, he strongly opposed every attempt at political innovation, and was in consequence bitterly hated by the liberals. When the popular agitation in favour of constitutional reform first broke out the king felt obliged to dispense with La Margherita's services, although he had conducted public affairs with considerable ability and absolute loyalty, even upholding the dignity of the kingdom in the face of the arrogant attitude of the cabinet of Vienna. He expounded his political creed and his policy as minister to Charles Albert (from February 1835 to October 1847) in his *Memorandum storico-politico*, published in 1851, a document of great interest for the study of the conditions of Piedmont and Italy at that time. In 1853 he was elected deputy for San Quirico, but he persisted in regarding his mandate as derived from the royal authority rather than as an emanation of the popular will. As leader of the Clerical Right in the parliament he strongly opposed Cavour's policy, which was eventually to lead to Italian unity, and on the establishment of the kingdom of Italy he retired from public life.

LA MARMORA, ALFONSO FERRERO (1804–1878), Italian general and statesman, was born at Turin on the 18th of November 1804. He entered the Sardinian army in 1823, and was a captain in March 1848, when he gained distinction and the rank of major at the siege of Peschiera. On the 5th of August 1848 he liberated Charles Albert, king of Sardinia, from the Milan revolutionaries, and in October was promoted general and appointed minister of war. After suppressing the revolt of Genoa in 1849, he again assumed in November 1849 the portfolio of war, which, save during the period of his command of the Crimean expedition, he retained until 1859. Having reconstructed the Piedmontese army, he took part in the war of 1859 against Austria; and in July of that year succeeded Cavour in the premiership. In 1860 he was sent to Berlin and St Petersburg to arrange for the recognition of the kingdom of Italy, and subsequently he held the offices of governor of Milan and royal lieutenant at Naples, until, in September 1864, he succeeded Minghetti as premier. In this capacity he modified the scope of the September Convention by a note in which he claimed for Italy full freedom of action in respect of national aspirations to the possession of Rome, a document of which Visconti Venosta afterwards took advantage when justifying the Italian occupation of Rome in 1870. In April 1866 La Marmora concluded an alliance with Prussia against Austria, and, on the outbreak of war in June, took command of an army corps, but was defeated at Custozza on the 23rd of June. Accused of treason by his fellow-countrymen, and of duplicity by the Prussians, he eventually published in defence of his tactics (1873) a series of documents entitled *Un po' più di luce sugli eventi dell' anno 1866* (More light on the events of 1866) a step which caused irritation in Germany, and exposed him to the charge of having violated state secrets. Meanwhile he had been sent to Paris in 1867 to oppose the French expedition to Rome, and in 1870, after the occupation of Rome by the Italians, had been appointed lieutenant-general at the new capital. He died at Florence on the 5th of January 1878. La Marmora's writings include *Un episodio del risorgimento italiano* (Florence, 1875); and *I segreti di stato nel governo constituzionale* (Florence, 1877).

See G. Massani, *Il generale Alfonso La Marmora* (Milan, 1880).

LAMARTINE, ALPHONSE MARIE LOUIS DE PRAT DE (1790–1869), French poet, historian and statesman, was born at Mâcon on the 21st of October 1790. The order of his surnames is a controversial matter, and they are sometimes reversed. The family of Lamartine was good, and the title of Prat was taken from an estate in Franche Comté. His father was imprisoned during the Terror, and only released owing to the events of the 9th Thermidor. Lamartine's early education was received from his mother. He was sent to school at Lyons in 1805, but not being happy there was transferred to the care of the Pères de la Foi at Belley, where he remained until 1809. For some time afterwards he lived at home, reading romantic and poetical literature, but in 1811 he set out for Italy, where he seems to have sojourned nearly two years. His family having been steady royalists, he entered the Gardes du corps at the return of the Bourbons, and during the Hundred Days he sought refuge first in Switzerland and then at Aix-en-Savoie, where he fell in love, with abundant results of the poetical kind. After Waterloo he returned to Paris. In 1818–1819 he revisited Switzerland, Savoy and Italy, the death of his beloved affording him new subjects for verse. After some difficulties he had his first book, the *Méditations, poétiques et religieuses*, published (1820). It was exceedingly popular, and helped him to make a position. He had left the army for some time; he now entered the diplomatic service and was appointed secretary to the embassy at Naples. On his way to his post he married, in 1823, at Geneva a young English lady, Marianne Birch, who had both money and beauty, and in the same year his *Nouvelles méditations poétiques* appeared.

In 1824 he was transferred to Florence, where he remained five years. His *Last Canto of Childe Harold* appeared in 1825, and he had to fight a duel (in which he was wounded) with an Italian officer, Colonel Pepe, in consequence of a phrase in it. Charles X., on whose coronation he wrote a poem, gave him the order of the Legion of Honour. The *Harmonies poétiques et religieuses* appeared in 1829, when he had left Florence. Having refused an appointment in Paris under the Polignac ministry, he went on a special mission to Prince Leopold of Saxe-Coburg. In the same year he was elected to the Academy. Lamartine was in Switzerland, not in Paris, at the time of the Revolution of July, and, though he put forth a pamphlet on "Rational Policy," he did not at that crisis take any active part in politics, refusing, however, to continue his diplomatic services under the new government. In 1832 he set out with his wife and daughter for Palestine, having been unsuccessful in his candidature for a seat in the chamber. His daughter Julia died at Beirut, and before long he received the news of his election by a constituency (Bergues) in the department of the Nord. He returned through Turkey and Germany, and made his first speech shortly after the beginning of 1834. Thereafter he spoke constantly, and acquired considerable reputation as an orator,—bringing out, moreover, many books in prose and verse. His Eastern travels (*Voyage en Orient*) appeared in 1835, his *Chute d'un ange* and *Jocelyn* in 1837, and his *Recueillements*, the last remarkable volume of his poetry, in 1839. As the reign of Louis Philippe went on, Lamartine, who had previously been a liberal royalist, something after the fashion of Chateaubriand, became more and more democratic in his opinions. He set about his greatest prose work, the *Histoire des Girondins*, which at first appeared periodically, and was published as a whole in 1847. Like many other French histories, it was a pamphlet as well as a chronicle, and the subjects of Lamartine's pen became his models in politics.

At the revolution of February Lamartine was one of the first to declare for a provisional government, and became a member of it, with the post of minister for foreign affairs. He was elected for the new constituent assembly in ten different departments, and was chosen one of the five members of the Executive Committee. For a few months indeed Lamartine, from being a distinguished man of letters, an official of inferior rank in diplomacy, and an eloquent but unpractical speaker in parliament, became one of the foremost men in Europe. His inexperience in the routine work of government, the utterly unpractical nature of his colleagues, and the turbulence of the Parisian mob, proved fatal to his chances. He gave some proofs of statesmanlike ability, and his eloquence was repeatedly called into requisition to pacify the Parisians. But no one can permanently carry on the government of a great country by speeches from the balcony of a house in the capital, and Lamartine found himself in a dilemma. So long as he held aloof from Ledru-Rollin and the more radical of his colleagues, the disunion resulting weakened the government; as soon as he effected an approximation to them the middle classes fell off from him. The quelling of the insurrection of the 15th of May was his last successful act. A month later the renewal of active disturbances brought on the fighting of June, and Lamartine's influence was extinguished in favour of Cavaignac. Moreover, his chance of renewed political pre-eminence was gone. He had been tried and found wanting, having neither the virtues nor the vices of his situation. In January 1849, though he was nominated for the presidency, only a few thousand votes were given to him, and three months later he was not even elected to the Legislative Assembly.

The remaining story of Lamartine's life is somewhat melancholy. He had never been a rich man, nor had he been a saving one, and during his period of popularity and office he had incurred great expenses. He now set to work to repair his fortune by unremitting literary labour. He brought out in the *Presse* (1849) a series of *Confidences*, and somewhat later a kind of autobiography, entitled *Raphael*. He wrote several historical works of more or less importance, the *History of the Revolution of 1848*, *The History of the Restoration*, *The History of Turkey*, *The History of Russia*, besides a large number of small biographical and miscellaneous works. In 1858 a subscription was opened for his benefit. Two years afterwards, following the example of Chateaubriand, he supervised an elaborate edition of his own works in forty-one volumes. This occupied five years, and while he was engaged on it his wife died (1863). He was now over seventy; his powers had deserted him, and even if they had not the public taste had entirely changed. His efforts had not succeeded in placing him in a position of independence; and at last, in 1867, the government of the Empire (from which he had perforce stood aloof, though he never considered it necessary to adopt the active protesting attitude of Edgar Quinet and Victor Hugo) came to his assistance, a vote of £20,000 being proposed in April of that year for his benefit by Émile Ollivier. This was creditable to both parties, for Lamartine, both as a distinguished man of letters and as a past servant of the state, had every claim to the bounty of his country. But he was reproached for accepting it by the extreme republicans and irreconcilables. He did not enjoy it long, dying on the 28th of February 1869.

As a statesman Lamartine was placed during his brief tenure of office in a position from which it would have been almost impossible for any man, who was not prepared and able to play the dictator, to emerge with credit. At no time in history were unpractical crotchets so rife in the heads of men as in 1848. But Lamartine could hardly have guided the ship of state safely even in much calmer weather. He was amiable and even estimable, the chief fault of his character being vanity and an incurable tendency towards theatrical effect, which makes his travels, memoirs and other personal records as well as his historical works radically untrustworthy. Nor does it appear that he had any settled political ideas. He did good by moderating the revolutionary and destructive ardour of the Parisian populace in 1848; but he had been perhaps more responsible than any other single person for bringing about the events of that year by the vague and frothy republican declamation of his *Histoire des Girondins*.

More must be said of his literary position. Lamartine had the advantage of coming at a time when the literary field, at least in the departments of belles lettres, was almost empty. The feeble school of descriptive writers, epic poets of the extreme decadence, fabulists and miscellaneous verse-makers, which the Empire had nourished could satisfy no one. Madame de Staël was dead; Chateaubriand, though alive, was something of a classic, and had not effected a full revolution. Lamartine did not himself go the complete length of the Romantic revival, but he went far in that direction. He availed himself of the reviving interest in legitimism and Catholicism which was represented by Bonald and Joseph de Maistre, of the nature worship of Rousseau and Bernardin de Saint Pierre, of the sentimentalism of Madame de Staël, of the medievalism and the romance of Chateaubriand and Scott, of the *maladie du siècle* of Chateaubriand and Byron. Perhaps if his matter be very closely analysed it will be found that he added hardly anything of his own. But if the parts of the mixture were like other things the mixture itself was not. It seemed indeed to the immediate generation so original that tradition has it that the *Méditations* were refused by a publisher because they were in none of the accepted styles. They appeared when Lamartine was nearly thirty years old. The best of them, and the best thing that Lamartine ever did, is the famous *Lac*, describing his return to the little mountain tarn of Le Bourget after the death of his mistress, with whom he had visited it in other days. The verse is exquisitely harmonious, the sentiments conventional but refined and delicate, the imagery well chosen and gracefully expressed. There is an unquestionable want of vigour, but to readers of that day the want of vigour was entirely compensated by the presence of freshness and grace. Lamartine's chief misfortune in poetry was not only that his note was a somewhat weak one, but that he could strike but one. The four volumes of the *Méditations*, the *Harmonies* and the *Recueillements*, which contained the prime of his verse, are perhaps the most monotonous reading to be found anywhere in work of equal bulk by a poet of equal talent. They contain nothing but meditative lyrical pieces, almost any one of which is typical of the whole, though there is considerable variation of merit. The two narrative poems which succeeded the early lyrics, *Jocelyn* and the *Chute d'un ange*, were, according to Lamartine's original plan, parts of a vast "Epic of the Ages," some further fragments of which survive. *Jocelyn* had at one time more popularity in England than most French verse. *La Chute d'un ange*, in which the Byronic influence is more obvious than in any other of Lamartine's works, and in which some have also seen that of Alfred de Vigny, is more ambitious in theme, and less regulated by scrupulous conditions of delicacy in handling, than most of its author's poetry. It does, however, little more than prove that such audacities were not for him.

As a prose writer Lamartine was very fertile. His characteristics in his prose fiction and descriptive work are not very different from those of his poetry. He is always and everywhere sentimental, though very frequently, as in his shorter prose tales (*The Stone Mason of Saint Point*, *Graziella*, &c.), he is graceful as well as sentimental. In his histories the effect is worse. It has been hinted that Lamartine's personal narratives are doubtfully trustworthy; with regard to his Eastern travels some of the episodes were stigmatized as mere inventions. In his histories proper the special motive for embellishment disappears, but the habit of inaccuracy remains. As an historian he belongs exclusively to the rhetorical school as distinguished from the philosophical on the one hand and the documentary on the other.

It is not surprising when these characteristics of Lamartine's work are appreciated to find that his fame declined with singular rapidity in France. As a poet he had lost his reputation many years before he died. He was entirely eclipsed by the brilliant and vigorous school who succeeded him with Victor Hugo at their head. His power of initiative in poetry was very small, and the range of poetic ground which he could cover strictly limited. He could only carry the picturesque sentimentalism of Rousseau, Bernardin de Saint Pierre and Chateaubriand a little farther, and clothe it in language and verse a little less antiquated than that of Chênedollé and Millevoye. He has been said to be a French Cowper, and the parallel holds good in respect of versification and of his relative position to the more daringly innovating school that followed, though not in respect of individual peculiarities. Lamartine in short occupied a kind of half-way house between the 18th century and the Romantic movement, and he never got any farther. When Matthew Arnold questioned his importance in conversation with Sainte-Beuve, the answer was, "He is important to *us*," and it was a true answer; but the limitation is obvious. In more recent years, however, efforts have been made by Brunetière and others to remove it. The usual revolution of critical as of other taste, the oblivion of personal and political unpopularity, and above all the reaction against Hugo and the extreme Romantics, have been the main agents in this. Lamartine has been extolled as a pattern of combined passion and restraint, as a model of nobility of sentiment, and as a harmoniser of pure French classicism in taste and expression with much, if not all, the better part of Romanticism itself. These oscillations of opinion are frequent, if not universal, and it is only after more than one or two swings that the pendulum remains at the perpendicular. The above remarks are an attempt to correct extravagance in either direction. But it is difficult to believe that Lamartine can ever permanently take rank among the first order of poets.

The edition mentioned is the most complete one of Lamartine, but there are many issues of his separate works. After his death some poems and *Mémoires inédits* of his youth were published, and also two volumes of correspondence, while in 1893 Mlle V. de Lamartine added a volume of *Lettres* to him. The change of views above referred to may be studied in the detached articles of MM. Brunetière, [illegible] *Lamartine, &c.*, and in the more substantive work of Ch. de [illegible] *Lamartine* (1889); E. Deschanel, *Lamartine* (1893); [illegible] *Lamartine* (1896); and perhaps best of all in the [illegible] Emile Legouis' Clarendon Press edition of *Jocelyn* (1906), [illegible] effort is made to combat the idea of Lamartine's [illegible] as a poet. (G. Sa.)

[illegible] (1775–1834), English essayist and critic, [illegible] Office Row, Inner Temple, London, on the [illegible] 1775. His father, John Lamb, a Lincolnshire [illegible] the situation of clerk and servant-companion [illegible] Salt, a member of parliament and one of the benchers [illegible] Temple, was successful in obtaining for Charles, [illegible] of three surviving children, a presentation to [illegible] Hospital where the boy remained from his eighth to [illegible] (1782–1789). Here he had for a schoolfellow [illegible] Taylor Coleridge, his senior by rather more than two [illegible] and a close and tender friendship began which lasted for [illegible] the lives of both. When the time came for leaving [illegible] he had learned some Greek and acquired consider- [illegible] Latin composition, Lamb, after a brief stay at [illegible] spent, as his school holidays had often been, [illegible] in Salt's library) was condemned to the [illegible] "an inconquerable impediment" in his [illegible] him for the clerical profession, which, as [illegible] were usually only given to those preparing [illegible] deprived him of the only means by which [illegible] a university education. For a short [illegible] of Joseph Paice, a London merchant, [illegible] weeks, until the 8th of February 1792, [illegible] the Examiner's Office of the South Sea [illegible] John was established, a period which, [illegible] sixteen, was to provide him nearly [illegible] materials for the first of the *Essays of* [illegible] 1792, he entered the Accountant's [illegible] House, where during the next three and [illegible] official folios of what he used to call [illegible]

[illegible] little. At the end of 1794 [illegible] joined him in writing sonnets in [illegible] to eminent persons: early in [illegible] much in the company of James [illegible] helped in the composition of the [illegible] *Salstaff*; and at the end of the year [illegible] mentally as to necessitate [illegible] The cause, it is probable, was an [illegible] Simmons, the Hertfordshire [illegible] are addressed, whom he would [illegible] as a youth to Blakesware House, [illegible] of the Plumer family, of which [illegible] Field, was for many years, until [illegible]

[illegible] 1796 that a dreadful calamity [illegible] seemed to blight all Lamb's [illegible] On the 22nd of September [illegible] a state of extreme nervous [illegible] by day and to her mother [illegible] acute mania, in which she [illegible] The calm self-mastery and [illegible] Charles Lamb, by constitution [illegible] displayed at this crisis [illegible] of those nearest him, will ever [illegible] to the reverence and affection of [illegible] the heroisms of common [illegible] he succeeded in obtaining his [illegible] restraint to which she would [illegible] the express condition that he [illegible] responsibility for her safe keeping. [illegible] though no one was capable of [illegible] affectionate companionship than [illegible] health, there was ever present [illegible] of her malady; and when [illegible] become [illegible] which took place in quietness and tears. How deeply the whole course of Lamb's domestic life must have been affected by his singular loyalty as a brother needs not to be pointed out.

Lamb's first appearance as an author was made in the year of the great tragedy of his life (1796), when there were published in the volume of *Poems on Various Subjects* by Coleridge four sonnets by "Mr Charles Lamb of the India House." In the following year he contributed, with Charles Lloyd, a pupil of Coleridge, some pieces in blank verse to the second edition of Coleridge's *Poems*. In 1797 his short summer holiday was spent with Coleridge at Nether Stowey, where he met the Wordsworths, William and Dorothy, and established a friendship with both which only his own death terminated. In 1798, under the influence of Henry Mackenzie's novel *Julie de Roubigné*, he published a short and pathetic prose tale entitled *Rosamund Gray*, in which it is possible to trace beneath disguised conditions references to the misfortunes of the author's own family, and many personal touches; and in the same year he joined Lloyd in a volume of *Blank Verse*, to which Lamb contributed poems occasioned by the death of his mother and his aunt Sarah Lamb, among them being his best-known lyric, "The Old Familiar Faces." In this year, 1798, he achieved the unexpected publicity of an attack by the *Anti-Jacobin* upon him as an associate of Coleridge and Southey (to whose *Annual Anthology* he had contributed) in their Jacobin machinations. In 1799, on the death of her father, Mary Lamb came to live again with her brother, their home then being in Pentonville; but it was not until 1800 that they really settled together, their first independent joint home being at Mitre Court Buildings in the Temple, where they lived until 1809. At the end of 1801, or beginning of 1802, appeared Lamb's first play *John Woodvil*, on which he set great store, a slight dramatic piece written in the style of the earlier Elizabethan period and containing some genuine poetry and happy delineation of the gentler emotions, but as a whole deficient in plot, vigour and character; it was held up to ridicule by the *Edinburgh Review* as a specimen of the rudest condition of the drama, a work by "a man of the age of Thespis." The dramatic spirit, however, was not thus easily quenched in Lamb, and his next effort was a farce, *Mr H——*, the point of which lay in the hero's anxiety to conceal his name "Hogsflesh"; but it did not survive the first night of its appearance at Drury Lane, in December 1806. Its author bore the failure with rare equanimity and good humour—even to joining in the hissing—and soon struck into new and more successful fields of literary exertion. Before, however, passing to these it should be mentioned that he made various efforts to earn money by journalism, partly by humorous articles, partly as dramatic critic, but chiefly as a contributor of sarcastic or funny paragraphs, "sparing neither man nor woman," in the *Morning Post*, principally in 1803.

In 1807 appeared *Tales founded on the Plays of Shakespeare*, written by Charles and Mary Lamb, in which Charles was responsible for the tragedies and Mary for the comedies; and in 1808, *Specimens of English Dramatic Poets who lived about the time of Shakespeare*, with short but felicitous critical notes. It was this work which laid the foundation of Lamb's reputation as a critic, for it was filled with imaginative understanding of the old playwrights, and a warm, discerning and novel appreciation of their great merits. In the same year, 1808, Mary Lamb, assisted by her brother, published *Poetry for Children*, and a collection of short school-girl tales under the title *Mrs Leicester's School*; and to the same date belongs *The Adventures of Ulysses*, designed by Lamb as a companion to *The Adventures of Telemachus*. In 1810 began to appear Leigh Hunt's quarterly periodical, *The Reflector*, in which Lamb published much (including the fine essays on the tragedies of Shakespeare and on Hogarth) that subsequently appeared in the first collective edition of his *Works*, which he put forth in 1818.

Between 1811, when *The Reflector* ceased, and 1820, he wrote almost nothing. In these years we may imagine him at his most social period, playing much whist and entertaining his friends on Wednesday or Thursday nights; meanwhile gathering that reputation as a conversationalist or inspirer of conversation in others, which Hazlitt, who was at one time one of Lamb's closest friends, has done so much to celebrate. When in 1818 appeared the *Works* in two volumes, it may be that Lamb considered his literary career over. Before coming to 1820, and an event which was in reality to be the beginning of that career as it is generally known—the establishment of the *London Magazine*—it should be recorded that in the summer of 1819 Lamb, with his sister's full consent, proposed marriage to Fanny Kelly, the actress, who was then in her thirtieth year. Miss Kelly could not accept, giving as one reason her devotion to her mother. Lamb bore the rebuff with characteristic humour and fortitude.

The establishment of the *London Magazine* in 1820 stimulated Lamb to the production of a series of new essays (the *Essays of Elia*) which may be said to form the chief corner-stone in the small but classic temple of his fame. The first of these, as it fell out, was a description of the old South Sea House, with which Lamb happened to have associated the name of a "gay light-hearted foreigner" called Elia, who was a clerk in the days of his service there. The pseudonym adopted on this occasion was retained for the subsequent contributions, which appeared collectively in a volume of essays called *Elia*, in 1823. After a career of five years the *London Magazine* came to an end; and about the same period Lamb's long connexion with the India House terminated, a pension of £450 (£441 net) having been assigned to him. The increased leisure, however, for which he had long sighed, did not prove favourable to literary production, which henceforth was limited to a few trifling contributions to the *New Monthly* and other serials, and the excavation of gems from the mass of dramatic literature bequeathed to the British Museum by David Garrick, which Lamb laboriously read through in 1827, an occupation which supplied him for a time with the regular hours of work he missed so much. The malady of his sister, which continued to increase with ever shortening intervals of relief, broke in painfully on his lettered ease and comfort; and it is unfortunately impossible to ignore the deteriorating effects of an over-free indulgence in the use of alcohol, and, in early life, tobacco, on a temperament such as his. His removal on account of his sister to the quiet of the country at Enfield, by tending to withdraw him from the stimulating society of the large circle of literary friends who had helped to make his weekly or monthly "at homes" so remarkable, doubtless also tended to intensify his listlessness and helplessness. One of the brightest elements in the closing years of his life was the friendship and companionship of Emma Isola, whom he and his sister had adopted, and whose marriage in 1833 to Edward Moxon, the publisher, though a source of unselfish joy to Lamb, left him more than ever alone. While living at Edmonton, whither he had moved in 1833 so that his sister might have the continual care of Mr and Mrs Walden, who were accustomed to patients of weak intellect, Lamb was overtaken by an attack of erysipelas brought on by an accidental fall as he was walking on the London road. After a few days' illness he died on the 27th of December, 1834. The sudden death of one so widely known, admired and beloved, fell on the public as well as on his own attached circle with all the poignancy of a personal calamity and a private grief. His memory wanted no tribute that affection could bestow, and Wordsworth commemorated in simple and solemn verse the genius, virtues and fraternal devotion of his early friend.

Charles Lamb is entitled to a place as an essayist beside Montaigne, Sir Thomas Browne, Steele and Addison. He unites many of the characteristics of each of these writers—refined and exquisite humour, a genuine and cordial vein of pleasantry and heart-touching pathos. His fancy is distinguished by great delicacy and tenderness; and even his conceits are imbued with human feeling and passion. He had an extreme and almost exclusive partiality for earlier prose writers, particularly for Fuller, Browne and Burton, as well as for the dramatists of Shakespeare's time; and the care with which he studied them is apparent in all he ever wrote. It shines out conspicuously in his style, which has an antique air and is redolent of the peculiarities of the 17th century. Its quaintness has subjected the author to the charge of affectation, but there is nothing really affected in his writings. His style is not so much an imitation as a reflexion of the older writers; for in spirit he made himself their contemporary. A confirmed habit of studying them in preference to modern literature had made something of their style natural to him; and long experience had rendered it not only easy and familiar but habitual. It was not a masquerade dress he wore, but the costume which showed the man to most advantage. With thought and meaning often profound, though clothed in simple language, every sentence of his essays is pregnant.

He played a considerable part in reviving the dramatic writers of the Shakesperian age; for he preceded Gifford and others in wiping the dust of ages from their works. In his brief comments on each specimen he displays exquisite powers of discrimination: his discernment of the true meaning of his author is almost infallible. His work was a departure in criticism. Former editors had supplied textual criticism and alternative readings: Lamb's object was to show how our ancestors felt when they placed themselves by the power of imagination in trying situations, in the conflicts of duty or passion or the strife of contending duties; what sorts of loves and enmities theirs were.

As a poet Lamb is not entitled to so high a place as that which can be claimed for him as essayist and critic. His dependence on Elizabethan models is here also manifest, but in such a way as to bring into all the greater prominence his native deficiency in "the accomplishment of verse." Yet it is impossible, once having read, ever to forget the tenderness and grace of such poems as "Hester," "The Old Familiar Faces," and the lines "On an infant dying as soon as born" or the quaint humour of "A Farewell to Tobacco." As a letter writer Lamb ranks very high, and when in a nonsensical mood there is none to touch him.

Editions and memoirs of Lamb are numerous. The *Letters*, with a sketch of his life by Sir Thomas Noon Talfourd, appeared in 1837; the *Final Memorials of Charles Lamb* by the same hand, after Mary Lamb's death, in 1848; Barry Cornwall's *Charles Lamb: A Memoir*, in 1866. Mr P. Fitzgerald's *Charles Lamb: his Friends, his Haunts and his Books* (1866); W. Carew Hazlitt's *Mary and Charles Lamb* (1874). Mr Fitzgerald and Mr Hazlitt have also both edited the *Letters*, and Mr Fitzgerald brought Talfourd to date with an edition of Lamb's works in 1870–1876. Later and fuller editions are those of Canon Ainger in 12 volumes, Mr Macdonald in 12 volumes and Mr E. V. Lucas in 7 volumes, to which in 1905 was added *The Life of Charles Lamb*, in 2 volumes. (E. V. L.)

LAMB (a word common to Teutonic languages; cf. Ger. *Lamm*), the young of sheep. The Paschal Lamb or Agnus Dei is used as a symbol of Jesus Christ, the Lamb of God (John i. 29), and "lamb," like "flock," is often used figuratively of the members of a Christian church or community, with an allusion to Jesus' charge to Peter (John xxi. 15). The "lamb and flag" is an heraldic emblem, the dexter fore-leg of the lamb supporting a staff bearing a banner charged with the St George's cross. This was one of the crests of the Knights Templars, used on seals as early as 1241; it was adopted as a badge or crest by the Middle Temple, the Inner Temple using another crest of the Templars, the winged horse or Pegasus. The old Tangier regiment, now the Queen's Royal West Surrey Regiment, bore a Paschal Lamb as its badge. From their colonel, Percy Kirke (*q.v.*), they were known as Kirke's Lambs. The exaggerated reputation of the regiment for brutality, both in Tangier and in England after Sedgmoor, lent irony to the nickname.

LAMBALLE, MARIE THÉRÈSE LOUISE OF SAVOY-CARIGNANO, PRINCESSE DE (1749–1792), fourth daughter of Louis Victor of Carignano (d. 1774) (great-grandfather of King Charles Albert of Sardinia), and of Christine Henriette of Hesse-Rheinfels-Rothenburg, was born at Turin on the 8th of September 1749. In 1767 she was married to Louis Alexandre Stanislaus de Bourbon, prince of Lamballe, son of the duke of Penthièvre, a grandson of Louis XIV.'s natural son the count of Toulouse. Her husband dying the following year, she retired with her father-in-law to Rambouillet, where she lived until the marriage of the [illegible] she returned to court. Marie Antoinette, [illegible] gentle and naïve manners, singled her out for [illegible] confidante. The impetuous character of the [illegible] in Madame de Lamballe that submissive [illegible] which yields to force of environment, and the two [illegible] friends. After her accession Marie Antoinette, in [illegible] king's opposition, had her appointed superintendent [illegible] household. Between 1776 and 1785 the comtesse de [illegible] succeeded in supplanting her, but when the queen [illegible] avarice of the Polignacs, she turned again to Madame [illegible]. From 1785 to the Revolution she was Marie Antoinette's closest friend and the pliant instrument of her [illegible]. She came with the queen to the Tuileries and as her [illegible] served as a meeting-place for the queen and the members [illegible] Assembly whom she wished to gain over, the people believed [illegible] the soul of all the intrigues. After a visit to England in [illegible] to appeal for help for the royal family she made her will [illegible] returned to the Tuileries, where she continued her services [illegible] until the 10th of August, when she shared her [illegible] the queen in the Temple. On the 19th of August she was [illegible] La Force, and having refused to take the oath [illegible] the monarchy, she was on the 3rd of September delivered [illegible] the fury of the populace, after which her head was [illegible] a pike and carried before the windows of the queen.

[illegible] Madame de Lamballe (Paris, 1888); Austin [illegible] (1890); B. C. Hardy, *Princesse de* [illegible] Comte de Lescure, *La Princesse de Lamballe* . . . [illegible] (1864); some letters of the princess [illegible] Schmidt in *La Révolution française* (vol. xxxix., [illegible] *Essai sur la mort de madame la princesse de* [illegible] Montefiore, *The Princesse de Lamballe* (1896). [illegible] *of the Royal Family of France . . . now first* [illegible] *Journal, Letters and Conversations of the Princesse* [illegible] 2 vols., 1826) have since appeared in various [illegible] and in French. They are attributed to Catherine [illegible] Broglio-Solari, and are apocryphal.

LAMBALLE, a town of north-western France, in the department of Côtes-du-Nord, on the Gouessant 13 m. E.S.E. of St [illegible]. Pop. (1906) 4347. Crowning the eminence on [illegible] is built is a beautiful Gothic church (13th and [illegible] the chapel of the castle of the counts of [illegible]. La Noue, the famous Huguenot leader, was mortally [illegible] in the siege of the castle, which was dismantled [illegible] Richelieu. Of the other buildings, the church of St [illegible] and 16th centuries) is the chief. Lamballe [illegible] (depot for stallions) and carries on trade [illegible] leather-dressing; earthenware is manufactured [illegible]. Lamballe was the capital of the territory [illegible] who in 1569 were made dukes.

LAMBAYEQUE, a coast department of northern Peru, [illegible] E. and S. by Cajamarca and Libertad. [illegible] 1,070. It belongs to the [illegible] is settled along the river valleys [illegible] one of the chief sugar-producing [illegible] valleys, especially near [illegible] of Eten, and in some valleys [illegible] largely produced. Four railways connect its [illegible] with the small ports of Eten and [illegible] Eten to Cayalti, 25 m., [illegible] and Chiclayo to Pátapo, 15 m. [illegible] the departmental capital, [illegible] of 12,500, Ferreñafe 6000, [illegible].

LAMBEAUX, JEF (JOSEPH MARIE THOMAS), (1852–1908), [illegible] He studied at the [illegible] Antwerp [illegible] and was a pupil of Jean Geefs. [illegible] and was followed [illegible] "Children [illegible] "The Lucky Number" and [illegible] he went to Paris, where he [illegible] "The Beggar" and "The Blind [illegible] (1881), generally regarded [illegible] Italy, where he was [illegible]

are his fountain at Antwerp (1886), "Robbing the Eagle's Eyrie" (1890), "Drunkenness" (1893), "The Triumph of Woman," "The Bitten Faun" (which created a great stir at the Exposition Universelle at Liége in 1905), and "The Human Passions," a colossal marble bas-relief, elaborated from a sketch exhibited in 1889. Of his numerous busts may be mentioned those of Hendrik Conscience, and of Charles Bals, the burgomaster of Brussels. He died on the 6th of June 1908.

LAMBERMONT, AUGUSTE, BARON (1819–1905), Belgian statesman, was born at Dion-le-Val in Brabant on the 25th of March 1819. He came of a family of small farmer proprietors, who had held land during three centuries. He was intended for the priesthood and entered the seminary of Floreffe, but his energies claimed a more active sphere. He left the monastery for Louvain University. Here he studied law, and also prepared himself for the military examinations. At that juncture the first Carlist war broke out, and Lambermont hastened to the scene of action. His services were accepted (April 1838) and he was entrusted with the command of two small cannon. He also acted as A.D.C. to Colonel Durando. He greatly distinguished himself, and for his intrepidity on one occasion he was decorated with the Cross of the highest military Order of St Ferdinand. Returning to Belgium he entered the Ministry for Foreign Affairs in 1842. He served in this department sixty-three years. He was closely associated with several of the most important questions in Belgian history during the last half of the 19th century—notably the freeing of the Scheldt. He was one of the very first Belgians to see the importance of developing the trade of their country, and at his own request he was attached to the commercial branch of the foreign office. The tolls imposed by the Dutch on navigation on the Scheldt strangled Belgian trade, for Antwerp was the only port of the country. The Dutch had the right to make this levy under treaties going back to the treaty of Munster in 1648, and they clung to it still more tenaciously after Belgium separated herself in 1830–1831 from the united kingdom of the Netherlands—the London conference in 1839 fixing the toll payable to Holland at 1·50 florins (3s.) per ton. From 1856 to 1863 Lambermont devoted most of his energies to the removal of this impediment. In 1856 he drew up a plan of action, and he prosecuted it with untiring perseverance until he saw it embodied in an international convention seven years later. Twenty-one powers and states attended a conference held on the question at Brussels in 1863, and on the 15th of July the treaty freeing the Scheldt was signed. For this achievement Lambermont was made a baron. Among other important conferences in which Lambermont took a leading part were those of Brussels (1874) on the usages of war, Berlin (1884–1885) on Africa and the Congo region, and Brussels (1890) on Central African Affairs and the Slave Trade. He was joint reporter with Baron de Courcel of the Berlin conference in 1884–1885, and on several occasions he was chosen as arbitrator by one or other of the great European powers. But his great achievement was the freeing of the Scheldt, and in token of its gratitude the city of Antwerp erected a fine monument to his memory. He died on the 7th of March 1905.

LAMBERT, DANIEL (1770–1809), an Englishman famous for his great size, was born near Leicester on the 13th of March 1770, the son of the keeper of the jail, to which post he succeeded in 1791. About this time his size and weight increased enormously, and though he had led an active and athletic life he weighed in 1793 thirty-two stone (448 lb). In 1806 he resolved to profit by his notoriety, and resigning his office went up to London and exhibited himself. He died on the 21st of July 1809, and at the time measured 5 ft. 11 in. in height and weighed 52½ stone (739 lb). His waistcoat, now in the Kings Lynn Museum, measures 102 in. round the waist. His coffin contained 112 ft. of elm and was built on wheels. His name has been used as a synonym for immensity. George Meredith describes London as the "Daniel Lambert of cities," and Herbert Spencer uses the phrase "a Daniel Lambert of learning." His enormous [illegible] were depicted on a number of tavern signs, but the portrait of him, a large mezzotint, is preserved at the [illegible]

LAMBERT, FRANCIS (*c* 1486–1530), Protestant reformer, was the son of a papal official at Avignon, where he was born between 1485 and 1487. At the age of 15 he entered the Franciscan monastery at Avignon, and after 1517 he was an itinerant preacher, travelling through France, Italy and Switzerland. His study of the Scriptures shook his faith in Roman Catholic theology, and by 1522 he had abandoned his order, and became known to the leaders of the Reformation in Switzerland and Germany. He did not, however, identify himself either with Zwinglianism or Lutheranism; he disputed with Zwingli at Zurich in 1522, and then made his way to Eisenach and Wittenberg, where he married in 1523. He returned to Strassburg in 1524, being anxious to spread the doctrines of the Reformation among the French-speaking population of the neighbourhood. By the Germans he was distrusted, and in 1526 his activities were prohibited by the city of Strassburg. He was, however, befriended by Jacob Sturm, who recommended him to the Landgraf Philip of Hesse, the most liberal of the German reforming princes. With Philip's encouragement he drafted that scheme of ecclesiastical reform for which he is famous. Its basis was essentially democratic and congregational, though it provided for the government of the whole church by means of a synod. Pastors were to be elected by the congregation, and the whole system of canon-law was repudiated. This scheme was submitted by Philip to a synod at Homburg; but Luther intervened and persuaded the Landgraf to abandon it. It was far too democratic to commend itself to the Lutherans, who had by this time bound the Lutheran cause to the support of princes rather than to that of the people. Philip continued to favour Lambert, who was appointed professor and head of the theological faculty in the Landgraf's new university of Marburg. Patrick Hamilton (*q.v.*), the Scottish martyr, was one of his pupils; and it was at Lambert's instigation that Hamilton composed his *Loci communes*, or *Patrick's Pleas* as they were popularly called in Scotland. Lambert was also one of the divines who took part in the great conference of Marburg in 1529; he had long wavered between the Lutheran and the Zwinglian view of the Lord's Supper, but at this conference he definitely adopted the Zwinglian view. He died of the plague on the 18th of April 1530, and was buried at Marburg.

A catalogue of Lambert's writings is given in Haag's *La France protestante*. See also lives of Lambert by Baum (Strassburg, 1840); F. W. Hessencamp (Elberfeld, 1860), Stieve (Breslau, 1867) and Louis Ruffet (Paris, 1873); Lorimer, *Life of Patrick Hamilton* (1857); A. L. Richter, *Die evangelischen Kirchenordnungen des 16. Jahrh.* (Weimar, 1846); Hessencamp, *Hessische Kirchenordnungen im Zeitalter der Reformation*; Philip of Hesse's *Correspondence with Bucer*, ed. M. Lenz; Lindsay, *Hist. Reformation*; *Allgemeine deutsche Biographie*. (A. F. P.)

LAMBERT, JOHANN HEINRICH (1728–1777), German physicist, mathematician and astronomer, was born at Mulhausen, Alsace, on the 26th of August 1728. He was the son of a tailor; and the slight elementary instruction he obtained at the free school of his native town was supplemented by his own private reading. He became book-keeper at Montbéliard ironworks, and subsequently (1745) secretary to Professor Iselin, the editor of a newspaper at Basel, who three years later recommended him as private tutor to the family of Count A. von Salis of Coire. Coming thus into virtual possession of a good library, Lambert had peculiar opportunities for improving himself in his literary and scientific studies. In 1759, after completing with his pupils a tour of two years' duration through Göttingen, Utrecht, Paris, Marseilles and Turin, he resigned his tutorship and settled at Augsburg. Munich, Erlangen, Coire and Leipzig became for brief successive intervals his home. In 1764 he removed to Berlin, where he received many favours at the hand of Frederick the Great and was elected a member of the Royal Academy of Sciences of Berlin, and in 1774 edited the Berlin *Ephemeris*. He died of consumption on the 25th of September 1777. His publications show him to have been a man of original and active mind with a singular facility in applying mathematics to practical questions.

His mathematical discoveries were extended and overshadowed by his contemporaries. His development of the equation $x^m + px = q$ in an infinite series was extended by Leonhard Euler, and particularly by Joseph Louis Lagrange. In 1761 he proved the irrationality of π; a simpler proof was given somewhat later by Legendre. The introduction of hyperbolic functions into trigonometry was also due to him. His geometrical discoveries are of great value, his *Die freie Perspective* (1759–1774) being a work of great merit. Astronomy was also enriched by his investigations, and he was led to several remarkable theorems on conics which bear his name. The most important are: (1) To express the time of describing an elliptic arc under the Newtonian law of gravitation in terms of the focal distances of the initial and final points, and the length of the chord joining them. (2) A theorem relating to the apparent curvature of the geocentric path of a comet.

Lambert's most important work, *Pyrometrie* (Berlin, 1779), is a systematic treatise on heat, containing the records and full discussion of many of his own experiments. Worthy of special notice also are *Photometria* (Augsburg, 1760), *Insigniores orbitae cometarum proprietates* (Augsburg, 1761), and *Beiträge zum Gebrauche der Mathematik und deren Anwendung* (4 vols., Berlin, 1765–1772). The *Memoires* of the Berlin Academy from 1761 to 1784 contain many of his papers, which treat of such subjects as resistance of fluids, magnetism, comets, probabilities, the problem of three bodies, meteorology, &c. In the *Acta Helvetica* (1752–1760) and in the *Nova acta erudita* (1763–1769) several of his contributions appear. In Bode's *Jahrbuch* (1776–1780) he discusses nutation, aberration of light, Saturn's rings and comets; in the *Nova acta Helvetica* (1787) he has a long paper "Sur le son des corps élastiques," in Bernoulli and Hindenburg's *Magazin* (1787–1788) he treats of the roots of equation and of parallel lines; and in Hindenburg's *Archiv* (1798–1799) he writes on optics and perspective. Many of these pieces were published posthumously. Recognized as among the first mathematicians of his day, he was also widely known for the universality and depth of his philological and philosophical knowledge. The most valuable of his logical and philosophical memoirs were published collectively in 2 vols. (1782).

See Huber's *Lambert nach seinem Leben und Wirken*; M. Chasles, *Geschichte der Geometrie*; and Baensch, *Lamberts Philosophie und seine Stellung zu Kant* (1902).

LAMBERT [*alias* NICHOLSON], **JOHN** (d. 1538), English Protestant martyr, was born at Norwich and educated at Cambridge, where he graduated B.A. and was admitted in 1521 a fellow of Queen's College on the nomination of Catherine of Aragon. After acting for some years as a "mass-priest," his views were unsettled by the arguments of Bilney and Arthur; and episcopal persecution compelled him, according to his own account, to assume the name Lambert instead of Nicholson. He likewise removed to Antwerp, where he became chaplain to the English factory, and formed a friendship with Frith and Tyndale. Returning to England in 1531, he came under the notice of Archbishop Warham, who questioned him closely on his religious beliefs. Warham's death in August 1532 relieved Lambert from immediate danger, and he earned a living for some years by teaching Latin and Greek near the Stocks Market in London. The duke of Norfolk and other reactionaries accused him of heresy in 1536, but reforming tendencies were still in the ascendant, and Lambert escaped. In 1538, however, the reaction had begun, and Lambert was its first victim. He singled himself out for persecution by denying the Real Presence: and Henry VIII., who had just rejected the Lutheran proposals for a theological union, was in no mood to tolerate worse heresies. Lambert had challenged some views expressed by Dr John Taylor, afterwards bishop of Lincoln; and Cranmer as archbishop condemned Lambert's opinions. He appealed to the king as supreme head of the Church, and on the 16th of November Henry heard the case in person before a large assembly of spiritual and temporal peers. For five hours Lambert disputed with the king and ten bishops; and then, as he boldly denied that the Eucharist was the body of Christ, he was condemned to death by Cromwell as vicegerent. Henry's condescension and patience produced a great impression on his Catholic subjects; but Cromwell is said by Foxe to have asked Lambert's pardon before his execution, and Cranmer eventually adopted the views he condemned in Lambert. Lambert was burnt at Smithfield on the 22nd of November.

dauphin, wher
charmed by h
a companion
dauphiness fo
temperament
became fast f
spite of the ki
of the royal h
Polignac succ
tired of the av
de Lamballe.
Antoinette's c
caprices. She
salon served
of the Assembl
her to be the s
1791 to appea
and returned
to the queen
imprisonment
transferred to
against the mc
over to the f
placed on a pi

See George B
Dobson, *Four*
Lamballe (1908
d'après des docu
published by C
1900); L. Lamb
Lamballe (1902);
The Secret Memo
published from the
de Lamballe (Lon
editions in English
Hyde, Marchione

LAMBALLE, a
ment of Côtes-d
Brieuc by rail.
which the town i
14th centuries),
Penthièvre. La
wounded in 1591
in 1626 by Riche
Martin (11th, 15
has an important
in grain, tanning
factured in the en
tory of the count

LAMBAYEQUE
bounded N. by
Area, 4614 sq. m.
arid region of the
where irrigation is
departments of
Ferreñafe, rice is
principal produci
Pimentel, viz.: Et
Pimentel to Lamb
The principal to
with a population
and Lambayeque

LAMBEAUX, J.
Belgian sculptor,
Antwerp Academy
His first work, " W
by a long series
dancing," " Say ' G
" An Accident " (
executed for the Bel
Pauper," and produ
as his masterpiece.
impressed by the w
predilection for effects

... XIII.; Foxe's *Acts and Monu-*... *Queen History*; Gairdner, ... *Bag.* and authorities. (A. F. P.)

[illegible]

the English army, and had his horse shot under him. Parliament now conferred on him a grant of lands in Scotland worth £1000 per annum.

In October 1651 Lambert was made a commissioner to settle the affairs of Scotland, and on the death of Ireton he was appointed lord deputy of Ireland (January 1652). He accepted the office with pleasure, and made magnificent preparations; parliament, however, soon afterwards reconstituted the Irish administration and Lambert refused to accept office on the new terms. Henceforward he began to oppose the Rump. In the council of officers he headed the party desiring representative government, as opposed to Harrison who favoured a selected oligarchy of " God-fearing " men, but both hated what remained of the Long parliament, and joined in urging Cromwell to dissolve it by force. At the same time Lambert was consulted by the parliamentary leaders as to the possibility of dismissing Cromwell from his command, and on the 15th of March 1653 Cromwell refused to see him, speaking of him contemptuously as " bottomless Lambert." On the 20th of April, however, Lambert accompanied Cromwell when he dismissed the council of state, on the same day as the forcible expulsion of the parliament. Lambert now favoured the formation of a small executive council, to be followed by an elective parliament whose powers should be limited by a written instrument of government. Being at this time the ruling spirit in the council of state, and the idol of the army, there were some who looked on him as a possible rival of Cromwell for the chief executive power, while the royalists for a short time had hopes of his support. He was invited, with Cromwell, Harrison and Desborough, to sit in the nominated parliament of 1653; and when the unpopularity of that assembly increased, Cromwell drew nearer to Lambert. In November 1653 Lambert presided over a meeting of officers, when the question of constitutional settlement was discussed, and a proposal made for the forcible expulsion of the nominated parliament. On the 1st of December he urged Cromwell to assume the title of king, which the latter refused. On the 12th the parliament resigned its powers into Cromwell's hands, and on the 13th Lambert obtained the consent of the officers to the Instrument of Government (*q.v.*), in the framing of which he had taken a leading part. He was one of the seven officers nominated to seats in the council created by the Instrument. In the foreign policy of the protectorate he was the most clamorous of those who called for alliance with Spain and war with France in 1653, and he firmly withstood Cromwell's design for an expedition to the West Indies.

In the debates in parliament on the Instrument of Government in 1654 Lambert proposed that the office of protector should be made hereditary, but was defeated by a majority which included members of Cromwell's family. In the parliament of this year, and again in 1656, Lord Lambert, as he was now styled, sat as member for the West Riding. He was one of the major-generals appointed in August 1655 to command the militia in the ten districts into which it was proposed to divide England, and who were to be responsible for the maintenance of order and the administration of the law in their several districts. Lambert took a prominent part in the committee of council which drew up instructions to the major-generals, and he was probably the originator, and certainly the organizer, of the system of police which these officers were to control. Gardiner conjectures that it was through divergence of opinion between the protector and Lambert in connexion with these " instructions " that the estrangement between the two men began. At all events, although Lambert had himself at an earlier date requested Cromwell to take the royal dignity, when the proposal to declare Oliver king was started in parliament (February 1657) he at once declared strongly against it. A hundred officers headed by Fleetwood and Lambert waited on the protector, and begged him to put a stop to the proceedings. Lambert was not convinced by Cromwell's arguments, and their complete estrange-
personal as well as political, followed. On his refusal
the oath of allegiance to the protector, Lambert was
d of his commissions, receiving, however, a pension of

£2000 a year. He retired to his garden at Wimbledon, and appeared no more in public during Oliver Cromwell's lifetime; but shortly before his death Cromwell sought a reconciliation, and Lambert and his wife visited him at Whitehall.

When Richard Cromwell was proclaimed protector his chief difficulty lay with the army, over which he exercised no effective control. Lambert, though holding no military commission, was the most popular of the old Cromwellian generals with the rank and file of the army, and it was very generally believed that he would instal himself in Oliver's seat of power. Richard's adherents tried to conciliate him, and the royalist leaders made overtures to him, even proposing that Charles II. should marry Lambert's daughter. Lambert at first gave a lukewarm support to Richard Cromwell, and took no part in the intrigues of the officers at Fleetwood's residence, Wallingford House. He was a member of the parliament which met in January 1659, and when it was dissolved in April under compulsion of Fleetwood and Desborough, he was restored to his commands. He headed the deputation to Lenthall in May inviting the return of the Rump, which led to the tame retirement of Richard Cromwell into obscurity; and he was appointed a member of the committee of safety and of the council of state. When the parliament, desirous of controlling the power of the army, withheld from Fleetwood the right of nominating officers, Lambert was named one of a council of seven charged with this duty. The parliament's evident distrust of the soldiers caused much discontent in the army; while the entire absence of real authority encouraged the royalists to make overt attempts to restore Charles II., the most serious of which, under Sir George Booth and the earl of Derby, was crushed by Lambert near Chester on the 19th of August. He promoted a petition from his army that Fleetwood might be made lord-general and himself major-general. The republican party in the House took offence. The Commons (October 12th, 1659) cashiered Lambert and other officers, and retained Fleetwood as chief of a military council under the authority of the speaker. On the next day Lambert caused the doors of the House to be shut and the members kept out. On the 26th a "committee of safety" was appointed, of which he was a member. He was also appointed major-general of all the forces in England and Scotland, Fleetwood being general. Lambert was now sent with a large force to meet Monk, who was in command of the English forces in Scotland, and either negotiate with him or force him to terms. Monk, however, set his army in motion southward. Lambert's army began to melt away, and he was kept in suspense by Monk till his whole army fell from him and he returned to London almost alone. Monk marched to London unopposed. The "excluded" Presbyterian members were recalled. Lambert was sent to the Tower (March 3rd, 1660), from which he escaped a month later. He tried to rekindle the civil war in favour of the Commonwealth, but was speedily recaptured and sent back to the Tower (April 24th). On the Restoration he was exempted from danger of life by an address of both Houses to the king, but the next parliament (1662) charged him with high treason. Thenceforward for the rest of his life Lambert remained in custody in Guernsey. He died in 1694.

Lambert would have left a better name in history if he had been a cavalier. His genial, ardent and excitable nature, easily raised and easily depressed, was more akin to the royalist than to the puritan spirit. Vain and sometimes overbearing, as well as ambitious, he believed that Cromwell could not stand without him; and when Cromwell was dead, he imagined himself entitled and fitted to succeed him. Yet his ambition was less selfish than that of Monk. Lambert is accused of no ill faith, no want of generosity, no cold and calculating policy. As a soldier he was far more than a fighting general and possessed many of the qualities of a great general. He was, moreover, an able writer and speaker, and an accomplished negotiator and took pleasure in quiet and domestic pursuits. He learnt his love of gardening from Lord Fairfax, who was also his master in the art of war. He painted flowers, besides cultivating them, and incurred the blame of Mrs Hutchinson by "dressing his flowers in his garden and working at the needle with his wife and his maids." He made no special profession of religion; but no imputation is cast upon his moral character by his detractors. It has been said that he became a Roman Catholic before his death.

LAMBERT OF HERSFELD (d. *c.* 1088), German chronicler, was probably a Thuringian by birth and became a monk in the Benedictine abbey of Hersfeld in 1058. As he was ordained priest at Aschaffenburg he is sometimes called Lambert of Aschaffenburg, or Schafnaburg. He made a pilgrimage to the Holy Land, and visited various monasteries of his order; but he is famous as the author of some *Annales*. From the creation of the world until about 1040 these *Annales* are a jejune copy of other annals, but from 1040 to their conclusion in 1077 they are interesting for the history of Germany and the papacy. The important events during the earlier part of the reign of the emperor Henry IV., including the visit to Canossa and the battle of Hohenburg, are vividly described. Their tone is hostile to Henry IV. and friendly to the papacy; their Latin style is excellent. The *Annales* were first published in 1525 and are printed in the *Monumenta Germaniae historica*, Bände iii. and v. (Hanover and Berlin, 1826 fol.). Formerly Lambert's reputation for accuracy and impartiality was very high, but both qualities have been somewhat discredited.

Lambert is also regarded as the author of the *Historia Hersfeldensis*, the extant fragments of which are published in Band v. of the *Monumenta* of a *Vita Lulli*, Lullus, archbishop of Mainz, being the founder of the abbey of Hersfeld; and of a *Carmen de bello Saxonico*. His *Opera* have been edited with an introduction by O. Holder-Egger (Hanover, 1894).

See H. Delbrück, *Über die Glaubwürdigkeit Lamberts von Hersfeld* (Bonn, 1873); A. Eigenbrodt, *Lampert von Hersfeld und die neuere Quellenforschung* (Cassel, 1896); L. von Ranke, *Zur Kritik fränkisch-deutscher Reichsannalisten* (Berlin, 1854); W. Wattenbach, *Deutschlands Geschichtsquellen* Band ii. (Berlin, 1906) and A. Potthast, *Bibliotheca Historica* (Berlin, 1896).

LAMBESSA, the ancient Lambaesa, a village of Algeria, in the arrondissement of Batna and department of Constantine, 7 m. S.E. of Batna and 17 W. of Timgad. The modern village, the centre of an agricultural colony founded in 1848, is noteworthy for its great convict establishment (built about 1850). The remains of the Roman town, and more especially of the Roman camp, in spite of wanton vandalism, are among the most interesting ruins in northern Africa. They are now preserved by the *Service des Monuments historiques* and excavations have resulted in many interesting discoveries. The ruins are situated on the lower terraces of the Jebel Aures, and consist of triumphal arches (one to Septimius Severus, another to Commodus), temples, aqueducts, vestiges of an amphitheatre, baths and an immense quantity of masonry belonging to private houses. To the north and east lie extensive cemeteries with the stones standing in their original alignments; to the west is a similar area, from which, however, the stones have been largely removed for building the modern village. Of the temple of Aesculapius only one column is standing, though in the middle of the 19th century its façade was entire. The capitol or temple dedicated to Jupiter, Juno and Minerva, which has been cleared of débris, has a portico with eight columns. On level ground about two-thirds of a mile from the centre of the ancient town stands the camp, its site now partly occupied by the penitentiary and its gardens. It measures 1640 ft. N. to S. by 1476 ft. E. to W., and in the middle rise the ruins of a building commonly called, but incorrectly, the praetorium. This noble building, which dates from A.D. 268, is 92 ft. long by 66 ft. broad and 49 ft. high; its southern façade has a splendid peristyle half the height of the wall, consisting of a front row of massive Ionic columns and an engaged row of Corinthian pilasters. Behind this building (which was roofed), is a large court giving access to other buildings, one being the arsenal. In it have been found many thousands of projectiles. To the S.E. are the remains of the baths. The ruins of both city and camp have yielded many inscriptions (Renier edited 1500, and there are 4185 in the *Corpus Inscr. Lat.* vol. viii.); and, though a very large proportion are epitaphs of the barest kind, the more important pieces supply an outline of the history of the place. Over 2500 inscriptions relating to the camp have been deciphered. In a museum in the village are objects of antiquity discovered in the vicinity. Besides inscriptions, statues, &c., are some fine mosaics found in 1905 near the arch of Septimius Severus. The statues include [illegible] taken from the temple of [illegible]

[illegible] The camp of the third [illegible] its origin, appears to [illegible] and 129, in the time of [illegible] was found inscribed on a [illegible] at the great camp still extant. [illegible] a vicus, 10 curiae of which [illegible] a municipium probably [illegible] of the newly founded [illegible] removed by Gordianus, but [illegible] and its final departure did [illegible] soon afterwards declined. [illegible] and no Christian inscriptions [illegible]

[illegible] of Markuna, the ancient [illegible]

[illegible] *l'Algérie* (Paris, 1901) and [illegible] L. Renier, *Inscriptions* [illegible] Wilmann, "Die röm [illegible] *phil. in honorem Th.* [illegible] *Travels in the Footsteps* [illegible] *Africa* (London, 1902).

[illegible] borough of London, [illegible] Thames, N.E. by Southwark, [illegible] Wandsworth and Battersea, [illegible] of the county of London. [illegible] commonly confined to the [illegible] the river; but the [illegible] and Vauxhall (north [illegible] Norwood (south). Four [illegible] the limits of the borough, [illegible] Lambeth and Vauxhall, of [illegible] dates from 1817, and is [illegible] within the county of London. [illegible] Westminster Bridge Road [illegible] Road and Brixton [illegible] it at Kennington. [illegible] Vauxhall Bridge, and [illegible] Bridge the river [illegible]

[illegible] in various forms. [illegible] to the meaning of a haven, [illegible] word signifying mud is [illegible] mentioned in Domesday; [illegible] of Falkes de Breauté, [illegible] of John and Henry III. [illegible] Lambeth was given to the [illegible] of Edward the Confessor, [illegible] the 11th century. They did [illegible] the close of the 12th [illegible] see of Canterbury. The [illegible] and forms, with the parish [illegible] lying close to the river [illegible], and to some extent [illegible] of the Thames one of [illegible] The oldest part of the palace [illegible] The so-called Lollard's [illegible] its use as a prison, dates [illegible] of brick, and the hall [illegible] by the archbishops [illegible] quadrangle. Among [illegible] are examples by Holbein, [illegible] There is a valuable library. [illegible] 1830, though the ancient [illegible] of antiquity. Here [illegible] including Bancroft (d. [illegible] collectors, and a memorial [illegible] in the Ashmolean [illegible] which he presented the collec- [illegible] Tradescant (d. 1662). In the [illegible] was a circus, well known in [illegible] as Astley's, and near [illegible] Vauxhall Gardens.

[illegible] are Kennington Park (20 [illegible] of Brixton, and near the southern end of Kennington Road is Kennington Oval, the ground of the Surrey County Cricket Club, the scene of its home matches and of other important fixtures. Among institutions the principal is St Thomas' Hospital, the extensive buildings of which front the Albert Embankment. The original foundation dated from 1213, was situated in Southwark, and was connected with the priory of Bermondsey. The existing buildings, subsequently enlarged, were opened in 1871, are divided into a series of blocks, and include a medical school. Other hospitals are the Royal, for children and women, Waterloo Road, the Lying-in Hospital, York Road, and the South-western fever hospital in Stockwell. There are technical institutes in Brixton and Norwood; and on Brixton Hill is Brixton Prison. In the northern part of the borough are numerous factories, including the great Doulton pottery works. The parliamentary borough of Lambeth has four divisions, North, Kennington, Brixton and Norwood, each returning one member. The borough council consists of a mayor, 10 aldermen and 60 councillors. Area, 4080·4 acres.

LAMBETH CONFERENCES, the name given to the periodical assemblies of bishops of the Anglican Communion (Pan-Anglican synods), which since 1867 have met at Lambeth Palace, the London residence of the archbishop of Canterbury. The idea of these meetings was first suggested in a letter to the archbishop of Canterbury by Bishop Hopkins of Vermont in 1851, but the immediate impulse came from the colonial Church in Canada. In 1865 the synod of that province, in an urgent letter to the archbishop of Canterbury (Dr Longley), represented the unsettlement of members of the Canadian Church caused by recent legal decisions of the Privy Council, and their alarm lest the revived action of Convocation "should leave us governed by canons different from those in force in England and Ireland, and thus cause us to drift into the status of an independent branch of the Catholic Church." They therefore requested him to call a "national synod of the bishops of the Anglican Church at home and abroad," to meet under his leadership. After consulting both houses of the Convocation of Canterbury, Archbishop Longley assented, and convened all the bishops of the Anglican Communion (then 144 in number) to meet at Lambeth in 1867. Many Anglican bishops (amongst them the archbishop of York and most of his suffragans) felt so doubtful as to the wisdom of such an assembly that they refused to attend it, and Dean Stanley declined to allow Westminster Abbey to be used for the closing service, giving as his reasons the partial character of the assembly, uncertainty as to the effect of its measures and "the presence of prelates not belonging to our Church." Archbishop Longley said in his opening address, however, that they had no desire to assume "the functions of a general synod of all the churches in full communion with the Church of England," but merely to "discuss matters of practical interest, and pronounce what we deem expedient in resolutions which may serve as safe guides to future action." Experience has shown how valuable and wise this course was. The resolutions of the Lambeth Conferences have never been regarded as synodical decrees, but their weight has increased with each conference. Apprehensions such as those which possessed the mind of Dean Stanley have long passed away.

Seventy-six bishops accepted the primate's invitation to the first conference, which met at Lambeth on the 24th of September 1867, and sat for four days, the sessions being in private. The archbishop opened the conference with an address: deliberation followed; committees were appointed to report on special questions; resolutions were adopted, and an encyclical letter was addressed to the faithful of the Anglican Communion. Each of the subsequent conferences has been first received in Canterbury cathedral and addressed by the archbishop from the chair of St Augustine. It has then met at Lambeth, and after sitting for five days for deliberation upon the fixed subjects and appointment of committees, has adjourned, to meet again at the end of a fortnight and sit for five days more, to receive reports, adopt resolutions and to put forth the encyclical letter.

I. *First Conference* (September 24-28, 1867), convened and presided over by Archbishop Longley. The proposed order of subjects was entirely altered in view of the Colenso case, for which urgency was claimed; and most of the time was spent in discussing it. Of the thirteen resolutions adopted by the conference, two have direct reference to this case; the rest have to do with the creation of new sees and missionary jurisdictions, commendatory letters, and a "voluntary spiritual tribunal" in cases of doctrine and the due subordination of synods. The reports of the committees were not ready, and were carried forward to the conference of 1878.

II. *Second Conference* (July 2-27, 1878), convened and presided over by Archbishop Tait. On this occasion no hesitation appears to have been felt; 100 bishops were present, and the opening sermon was preached by the archbishop of York. The reports of the five special committees (based in part upon those of the committee of 1867) were embodied in the encyclical letter, viz. on the best mode of maintaining union; voluntary boards of arbitration, missionary bishops and missionaries, continental chaplains and the report of a committee on difficulties submitted to the conference.

III. *Third Conference* (July 3-27, 1888), convened and presided over by Archbishop Benson; 145 bishops present; the chief subject of consideration being the position of communities which do not possess the historic episcopate. In addition to the encyclical letter, nineteen resolutions were put forth, and the reports of twelve special committees are appended upon which they are based, the subjects being intemperance, purity, divorce, polygamy, observance of Sunday, socialism, care of emigrants, mutual relations of dioceses of the Anglican Communion, home reunion, Scandinavian Church, Old Catholics, &c., Eastern Churches, standards of doctrine and worship. Perhaps the most important of these is the famous "Lambeth Quadrilateral," which laid down a fourfold basis for home reunion—the Holy Scriptures, the Apostles' and Nicene creeds, the two sacraments ordained by Christ himself and the historic episcopate.

IV. *Fourth Conference* (July 5-31, 1897), convened by Archbishop Benson, presided over by Archbishop Temple; 194 bishops present. One of the chief subjects for consideration was the creation of a "tribunal of reference"; but the resolutions on this subject were withdrawn, owing, it is said, to the opposition of the American bishops, and a more general resolution in favour of a "consultative body" was substituted. The encyclical letter is accompanied by sixty-three resolutions (which include careful provision for provincial organization and the extension of the title "archbishop" to all metropolitans, a "thankful recognition of the revival of brotherhoods and sisterhoods, and of the office of deaconess," and a desire to promote friendly relations with the Eastern Churches and the various Old Catholic bodies), and the reports of the eleven committees are subjoined.

V. *Fifth Conference* (July 6-August 5, 1908), convened by Archbishop Randall Davidson, who presided; 241 bishops were present. The chief subjects of discussion were: the relations of faith and modern thought, the supply and training of the clergy, education, foreign missions, revision and "enrichment" of the Prayer-Book, the relation of the Church to "ministries of healing" (Christian Science, &c.), the questions of marriage and divorce, organization of the Anglican Church, reunion with other Churches. The results of the deliberations were embodied in seventy-eight resolutions, which were appended to the encyclical issued, in the name of the conference, by the Archbishop of Canterbury on the 8th of August.

The fifth Lambeth conference, following as it did close on the great Pan-Anglican congress, is remarkable mainly as a proof of the growth of the influence and many-sided activity of the Anglican Church, and as a conspicuous manifestation of her characteristic principles. Of the seventy-eight resolutions none is in any sense epoch-making, and their spirit is that of the traditional Anglican *via media*. In general they are characterized by a firm adherence to the fundamental articles of Catholic orthodoxy, tempered by a tolerant attitude towards those not of "the household of the faith." The report of the committee on faith and modern thought is "a faithful attempt to show how the claim of our Lord Jesus Christ, which the Church is set to present to each generation, may, under the characteristic conditions of our time, best command allegiance." On the question of education (Res. 11-19) the conference reaffirmed strongly the necessity for definite Christian teaching in schools, "secular systems" being condemned as "educationally as well as morally unsound, since they fail to co-ordinate the training of the whole nature of the child" (Res. 11). The resolutions on questions affecting foreign missions (20-26) deal with *e.g.* the overlapping of episcopal jurisdictions (22) and the establishment of Churches on lines of race or colour, which is condemned (20). The resolutions on questions of marriage and divorce (37-43) reaffirm the traditional attitude of the Church; it is, however, interesting to note that the resolution (40) deprecating the remarriage in church of the innocent party to a divorce was carried only by eighty-seven votes to eighty-four. In resolutions 44 to 53 the conference deals with the duty of the Church towards modern democratic ideals and social problems, affirms the responsibility of investors for the character and conditions of the concerns in which their money is placed (49); "while frankly acknowledging the moral gains sometimes won by war" strongly supports the extension of international arbitration (52), and emphasizes the duty of a stricter observance of Sunday (53). On the question of reunion, the ideal of corporate unity was reaffirmed (58). It was decided to send a deputation of bishops with a letter of greeting to the national council of the Russian Church about to be assembled (60) and certain conditions were laid down for intercommunion with certain of the Churches of the Orthodox Eastern Communion (62) and the "ancient separated Churches of the East" (63-65). Resolution 67 warned Anglicans from contracting marriages, under actual conditions, with Roman Catholics. By resolution 68 the conference stated its desire to "maintain and strengthen the friendly relations" between the Churches of the Anglican Communion and "the ancient Church of Holland" (Jansenist, see UTRECHT) and the old Catholic Churches; and resolutions 70-73 made elaborate provisions for a projected corporate union between the Anglican Church and the *Unitas Fratrum* (Moravian Brethren). As to "home reunion," however, it was made perfectly clear that this would only be possible "on lines suggested by such precedents as those of 1610," *i.e.* by the Presbyterian Churches accepting the episcopal model. So far as the organization of the Anglican Church is concerned, the most important outcome of the conference was the reconstruction of the Central Consultative Body on representative lines (54-56); this body to consist of the archbishop of Canterbury and seventeen bishops appointed by the various Churches of the Anglican Communion throughout the world. A notable feature of the conference was the presence of the Swedish bishop of Kalmar, who presented a letter from the archbishop of Upsala, as a tentative advance towards closer relations between the Anglican Church and the Evangelical Church of Sweden.

See Archbishop R. T. Davidson, *The Lambeth Conferences of 1867, 1878 and 1888* (London, 1896); *Conference of Bishops of the Anglican Communion, Encyclical Letter*, &c. (London, 1897 and 1908).

LAMBINUS, DIONYSIUS, the Latinized name of DENIS LAMBIN (1520-1572), French classical scholar, born at Montreuil-sur-mer in Picardy. Having devoted several years to classical studies during a residence in Italy, he was invited to Paris in 1560 to fill the professorship of Latin in the Collège de France, which he soon afterwards exchanged for that of Greek. His lectures were frequently interrupted by his ill-health and the religious disturbances of the time. His death (September 1572) is said to have been caused by his apprehension that he might share the fate of his friend Peter Ramus (Pierre de la Ramée), who had been killed in the massacre of St Bartholomew. Lambinus was one of the greatest scholars of his age, and his editions of classical authors are still useful. In textual criticism he was a conservative, but by no means a slavish one; indeed, his opponents accused him of rashness in emendation. His chief defect is that he refers vaguely to his MSS. without specifying the source of his readings, so that their relative importance cannot be estimated. But his commentaries, with their wealth of illustration and parallel passages, are a mine of information. In the opinion of the best scholars, he preserved the happy mean in his annotations, although his own countrymen have coined the word *lambiner* to express trifling and diffuseness.

His chief editions are: Horace (1561); Lucretius (1564), on which see H. A. J. Munro's preface to his edition; Cicero (1566); Cornelius Nepos (1569); Demosthenes (1570), completing the unfinished work of Guillaume Morel; Plautus (1576).

See Peter Lazer, *De Dionysio Lambino narratio*, printed in Orelli's *Onomasticon Tullianum* (i. 1836), and *Trium disertissimorum virorum praefationes ac epistolae familiares aliquot: Mureti, Lambini, Regii* (Paris, 1579); also Sandys, *Hist. of Classical Scholarship* (1908, ii. 188), and A. Horawitz in Ersch and Gruber's *Allgemeine Encyclopädie*.

LAMBOURN, a market town in the Newbury parliamentary division of Berkshire, England, 65 m. W. of London, the terminus of the Lambourn Valley light railway from Newbury. Pop. (1901) 2071. It lies high up the narrow valley of the Lambourn, a tributary of the Kennet famous for its trout-fishing, among the Berkshire Downs. The church of St Michael is cruciform and principally late Norman, but has numerous additions of later periods and has been considerably altered by modern restoration. The inmates of an almshouse founded by John Estbury, *c.* 1500, by his desire still hold service daily at his tomb in the church. A Perpendicular market-cross stands without the church. The town has agricultural trade, but its chief importance is derived from large training stables in the neighbourhood. To the north of the town is a large group of *tumuli* known as the Seven Barrows, ascertained by excavation to be a British burial-place.

LAMECH (לֶמֶךְ), the biblical patriarch, appears in each of the antediluvian genealogies, Gen. iv. 16-24 J., and Gen. v. P. In the former he is a descendant of Cain, and through his sons the author of primitive civilization; in the latter he is the father of Noah. But it is now generally held that these two genealogies are variant adaptations of the Babylonian list of primitive

whether Lamech is to be
of these kings; he may
from another tradition.
Lamech's family are the
civilization; he himself
'Adah ("ornament,"
("shadow"). He has
the last-named qualified by
The assonance of these
brothers Hasan and Hosein
Jabal institutes the life of
of music, Tubal-Cain
be forms of a root used in
horn (*i.e.* trumpet),
may be the eponymous
mentioned in Ezekiel in
All three names are
of offspring, so that
"son," and there are
Lamech has
pleasant," "comely";
narrative clearly
arts as they
likely that he thought
age by a universal
suggest that the
of civilization as
the passage was
told of Cain and
variant of Abel. An
genealogy:

my speech.

interpreted as expressing
he expects to derive
worker in bronze will
so that he will be
injury. But the poem
with the genealogy. It
the prowess
some relation to
a hero and not a

the Priestly Code, *c.*
ancient tradition in
noteworthy that
MSS. Lamech dies

original meaning are
deity, or both.
the Babylonian
with *Ubara*
is the ninth
of the hero of
patriarch,
cannot be
connected with the

the Bible in I
and inter-
(W. H. Be.)

district of Vizeu
by road
Pop. (1900)
is possible that

on iv. 19.
stratification
Times.

9471. The nearest railway station is Peso da Regoa, on the opposite side of the Douro and on the Barca d'Alva-Oporto railway. Lamego is an ancient and picturesque city, in the midst of a beautiful mountain region. Its principal buildings are the 14th-century Gothic cathedral, Moorish citadel, Roman baths and a church which occupies the site of a mosque, and, though intrinsically commonplace, is celebrated in Portugal as the seat of the legendary cortes of 1143 or 1144 (see PORTUGAL, *History*). The principal industries are viticulture and the rearing of swine, which furnish the so-called "Lisbon hams." Lamego was a Moorish frontier fortress of some importance in the 9th and 10th centuries. It was captured in 1057 by Ferdinand I. of Castile and Leon.

LAMELLIBRANCHIA (Lat. *lamella*, a small or thin plate, and Gr. βράγχια, gills), the fourth of the five classes of animals constituting the phylum Mollusca (*q.v.*). The Lamellibranchia are mainly characterized by the rudimentary condition of the head, and the retention of the primitive bilateral symmetry, the latter feature being accentuated by the lateral compression of the body and the development of the shell as two bilaterally symmetrical plates or valves covering each one side of the animal. The foot is commonly a simple cylindrical or ploughshare-shaped organ, used for boring in sand and mud, and more rarely presents a crawling disk similar to that of Gastropoda; in some forms it is aborted. The paired ctenidia are very greatly developed right and left of the elongated body, and form the most prominent organ of the group. Their function is chiefly not respiratory but nutritive, since it is by the currents produced by their ciliated surface that food-particles are brought to the feebly-developed mouth and buccal cavity.

The Lamellibranchia present as a whole a somewhat uniform structure. The chief points in which they vary are—(1) in the structure of the ctenidia or branchial plates; (2) in the presence of one or of two chief muscles, the fibres of which run across the animal's body from one valve of the shell to the other (adductors); (3) in the greater or less elaboration of the posterior portion of the mantle-skirt so as to form a pair of tubes, by one of which water is introduced into the sub-pallial chamber, whilst by the other it is expelled; (4) in the perfect or deficient symmetry of the two valves of the shell and the connected soft parts, as compared with one another; (5) in the development of the foot as a disk-like crawling organ (*Arca*, *Nucula*, *Pectunculus*, *Trigonia*, *Lepton*, *Galeomma*), as a simple plough-like or tongue-shaped organ (*Unionidae*, &c.), as a re-curved saltatory organ (*Cardium*, &c.), as a long burrowing cylinder (*Solenidae*, &c.), or its partial (Mytilacea) or even complete abortion (Ostraeacea).

The essential Molluscan organs are, with these exceptions, uniformly well developed. The mantle-skirt is always long, and hides the rest of the animal from view, its dependent margins meeting in the middle line below the ventral surface when the animal is retracted; it is, as it were, slit in the median line before and behind so as to form two flaps, a right and a left; on these the right and the left calcareous valves of the shell are borne respectively, connected by an uncalcified part of the shell called the ligament. In many embryo Lamellibranchs a centro-dorsal primitive shell-gland or follicle has been detected. The mouth lies in the median line anteriorly, the anus in the median line posteriorly.

Both ctenidia, right and left, are invariably present, the axis of each taking origin from the side of the body as in the schematic archi-Mollusc (see fig. 15). A pair of renal tubes opening right and left, rather far forward on the sides of the body, are always present. Each opens by its internal extremity into the pericardium. A pair of genital apertures, connected by genital ducts with the paired gonads, are found right and left near the nephridial pores, except in a few cases where the genital duct joins that of the renal organ (*Spondylus*). The sexes are often, but not always, distinct. No accessory glands or copulatory organs are ever present in Lamellibranchs. The ctenidia often act as brood-pouches.

A dorsal contractile heart, with symmetrical right and left auricles receiving aerated blood from the ctenidia and mantle-skirt, is present, being unequally developed only in those few forms which are inequivalve. The typical pericardium is well developed It, as in other Mollusca, is not a blood-space but develops from the coelom, and it communicates with the exterior by the pair of renal tubes. As in Cephalopoda (and possibly other Mollusca) water can be introduced through the nephridia into this space. The alimentary canal keeps very nearly to the median vertical plane whilst exhibiting a number of flexures and loopings in this plane. A pair of large glandular outgrowths, the so-called "liver" or great digestive gland, exists as in other Molluscs. A pair of pedal otocysts, and a pair of osphradia at the base of the gills, appear to be always present. A typical nervous system is present (fig. 19), consisting of a cerebro-pleural ganglion-pair, united by connectives to a pedal ganglion-pair and a visceral ganglion-pair (parieto-splanchnic).

A pyloric caecum connected with the stomach is commonly found, containing a tough flexible cylinder of transparent cartilaginous appearance, called the "crystalline style" (*Mactra*). In many Lamellibranchs a gland is found on the hinder surface of the foot in the mid line, which secretes a substance which sets into the form of threads—the so-called "byssus"—by means of which the animal can fix itself. Sometimes this gland is found in the young and not in the adult (*Anodonta, Unio, Cyclas*). In some Lamellibranchs (*Pecten, Spondylus, Pholas, Mactra, Tellina, Pectunculus, Galeomma*, &c.), although cephalic eyes are generally absent, special eyes are developed on the free margin of the mantle-skirt, apparently by the modification of tentacles commonly found there. There are no pores in the foot or elsewhere in Lamellibranchia by which water can pass into and out of the vascular system, as formerly asserted.

The Lamellibranchia live chiefly in the sea, some in fresh waters. A very few have the power of swimming by opening and shutting the valves of the shell (*Pecten, Lima*); most can crawl slowly or burrow rapidly; others are, when adult, permanently fixed to stones or rocks either by the shell or the byssus. In development some Lamellibranchia pass through a free-swimming trochosphere stage with preoral ciliated band; other fresh-water forms which carry the young in brood-pouches formed by the ctenidia have suppressed this larval phase.

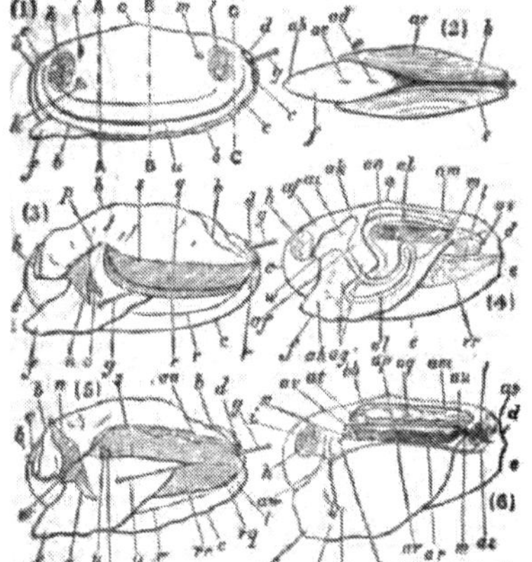

Fig. 1.—Diagrams of the external form and anatomy of *Anodonta cygnea*, the Pond-Mussel; in figures 1, 3, 4, 5, 6 the animal is seen from the left side, the centro-dorsal region uppermost. (1) Animal removed from its shell, a probe *g* passed into the sub-pallial chamber through the excurrent siphonal notch. (2) View from the ventral surface of an Anodon with its foot expanded and issuing from between the gaping shells. (3) The left mantle-flap reflected upwards so as to expose the sides of the body. (4) Diagrammatic section of Anodon to show the course of the alimentary canal. (5) The two gill-plates of the left side reflected upwards so as to expose the fissure between foot and gill where the probe *g* passes. (6) Diagram to show the positions of the nerve-ganglia, heart and nephridia.

Letters in all the figures as follows:

a, Centro-dorsal area.
b, Margin of the left mantle-flap.
c, Margin of the right mantle-flap.
d, Excurrent siphonal notch of the mantle margin.
e, Incurrent siphonal notch of the mantle margin.
f, Foot.
g, Probe passed into the superior division of the sub-pallial chamber through the excurrent siphonal notch, and issuing by the side of the foot into the inferior division of the sub-pallial chamber.
h, Anterior (pallial) adductor muscle of the shells.
i, Anterior retractor muscle of the foot.
k, Protractor muscle of the foot.
l, Posterior (pedal) adductor muscle of the shells.
m, Posterior retractor muscle of the foot.
n, Anterior labial tentacle.
o, Posterior labial tentacle.
p, Base-line of origin of the reflected mantle-flap from the side of the body.
q, Left external gill-plate.
r, Left internal gill-plate.
rr, Inner lamella of the right inner gill-plate.
rg, Right outer gill-plate.
s, Line of concrescence of the outer lamella of the left outer gill-plate with the left mantle-flap.
t, Pallial tentacles.
u, The thickened muscular pallial margin which adheres to the shell and forms the pallial line of the left side.
v, That of the right side.
w, The mouth.
x, Aperture of the left organ of Bojanus (nephridium) exposed by cutting the attachment of the inner lamella of the inner gill-plate.
y, Aperture of the genital duct.
z, Fissure between the free edge of the inner lamella of the inner gill-plate and the side of the foot, through which the probe *g* passes into the upper division of the sub-pallial space.
aa, Line of concrescence of the inner lamella of the right inner gill-plate with the inner lamella of the left inner gill-plate.
ab, ac, ad, Three pit-like depressions in the median line of the foot supposed by some writers to be pores admitting water into the vascular system.
ae, Left shell valve.
af, Space occupied by liver.
ag, Space occupied by gonad.
ah, Muscular substance of the foot.
ai, Duct of the liver on the wall of the stomach.
ak, Stomach.
al, Rectum traversing the ventricle of the heart.
am, Pericardium.
an, Glandular portion of the left nephridium.
ap, Ventricle of the heart.
aq, Aperture by which the left auricle joins the ventricle.
ar, Non-glandular portion of the left nephridium.
as, Anus.
at, Pore leading from the pericardium into the glandular sac of the left nephridium.
au, Pore leading from the glandular into the non-glandular portion of the left nephridium.
av, Internal pore leading from the non-glandular portion of the left nephridium to the external pore *x*.
aw, Left cerebro-pleuro-visceral ganglion.
ax, Left pedal ganglion.
ay, Left otocyst.
az, Left olfactory ganglion (parieto-splanchnic).
bb, Floor of the pericardium separating that space from the non-glandular portion of the nephridia.

As an example of the organization of a Lamellibranch, we shall review the structure of the common pond-mussel or swan mussel (*Anodonta cygnea*), comparing it with other Lamellibranchia.

The swan-mussel has superficially a perfectly developed bilateral symmetry. The left side of the animal is seen as when removed from its shell in fig. 1 (1). The valves of the shell have been removed by severing their adhesions to the muscular areae *h, i, k, l, m, u*. The free edge of the left half of the mantle-skirt *b* is represented as a little contracted in order to show the exactly similar free edge of the right half of the mantle-skirt *c*. These edges are not attached to, although they touch, one another; each flap (right or left) can be freely thrown back in the way carried out in fig. 1 (3) for that of the left side. This is not always the case with Lamellibranchs; there is in the group a tendency for the corresponding edges of the mantle-skirt to fuse together by concrescence, and so to form a more or less completely closed bag, as in the Scaphopoda (*Dentalium*). In this way the notches *d, e* of the hinder part of the mantle-skirt of *Anodonta* are in the siphonate forms converted into two separate holes, the edges of the mantle being elsewhere fused together along this hinder margin. Further than this, the part of the mantle-skirt bounding the two holes is frequently drawn out so as to form a pair of tubes which project from the shell (figs. 8, 29). In such Lamellibranchs as the oysters, scallops and many others which have the edges of the mantle-skirt quite free, there are numerous tentacles upon those edges.

In *Anodonta* these pallial tentacles are confined to a small area surrounding the inferior siphonal notch (fig. 1 [3], *l*). When the edges of the mantle ventral to the inhalant orifice are united, an anterior aperture is left for the protrusion of the foot, and thus there are three pallial apertures altogether, and species in this condition are called "Tripora." This is the usual condition in the Eulamellibranchia and Septibranchia. When the pedal aperture is small and far forward there may be a fourth aperture in the region of the fusion behind the pedal aperture. This occurs in *Solen*, and such forms are called "Quadrifora."

The centro dorsal point *a* of the animal of *Anodonta* (fig. 1 [1]) is called the umbonal area; the great anterior muscular surface *k* is that of the anterior adductor muscle, the posterior similar surface *i* is that of the posterior adductor muscle; the long line of attachment *w* is the simple "pallial muscle,"—a thickened ridge which is seen to run parallel to the margin of the mantle-skirt in this Lamellibranch. In siphonate forms the pallial muscle is not simple, but is indented posteriorly by a sinus formed by the muscles which retract the siphons.

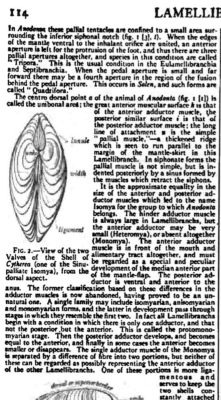

Fig. 2.—View of the two Valves of the Shell of *Cytherea* (one of the Sinupalliate Isomya), from the dorsal aspect.

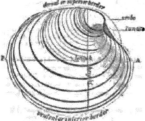

It is the approximate equality in the size of the anterior and posterior adductor muscles which led to the name Isomya for the group to which *Anodonta* belongs. The hinder adductor muscle is always large in Lamellibranchs, but the anterior adductor may be very small (Heteromya), or absent altogether (Monomya). The anterior adductor muscle is in front of the mouth and alimentary tract altogether, and must be regarded as a special and peculiar development of the median anterior part of the mantle-flap. The posterior adductor is ventral and anterior to the anus. The former classification based on these differences in the adductor muscles is now abandoned, having proved to be an unnatural one. A single family may include isomyarian, anisomyarian and monomyarian forms, and the latter in development pass through stages in which they resemble the first two. In fact all Lamellibranchs begin with a condition in which there is only one adductor, and that not the posterior but the anterior. This is called the protomonomyarian stage. Then the posterior adductor develops, and becomes equal to the anterior, and finally in some cases the anterior becomes smaller or disappears. The single adductor muscle of the Monomya is separated by a difference of fibre into two portions, but neither of these can be regarded as possibly representing the anterior adductor of the other Lamellibranchs. One of these portions is more ligamentous and serves to keep the two shells constantly attached to one another, whilst the more fleshy portion serves to close the shell rapidly when it has been gaping.

In removing the valves of the shell from an *Anodonta*, it is necessary not only to cut through the muscular attachments of the body-wall to the shell but to sever also a strong elastic ligament, or spring resembling india-rubber, joining the two shells about the umbonal area. The shell of *Anodonta* does not present these parts in the most strongly marked condition, and accordingly our figures (figs. 2, 3, 4) represent the valves of the sinupalliate genus *Cytherea*. The corresponding parts are recognizable in *Anodonta*. Referring to the figures (2, 3) for an explanation of terms applicable to the parts of the valve and the markings on its inner surface—corresponding to the muscular areas already noted on the surface of the animal's body—we must specially note here the position of that denticulated thickening of the dorsal margin of the valve which is called the hinge (fig. 4). By this hinge one valve is closely fitted to the other. Below this hinge each shell becomes concave, above it each shell rises a little to form the umbo, and it is into this ridge-like upgrowth of each valve that the elastic ligament or spring is fixed (fig. 4). As shown in the diagram (fig. 5) representing a transverse section of the two valves of a Lamellibranch, the two shells form a double lever, of which the toothed-hinge is the fulcrum. The adductor muscles placed in the concavity of the shells act upon the long arms of the lever at a mechanical advantage; their contraction keeps the shells shut, and stretches the ligament or spring *h*. On the other hand, the ligament *h* acts upon the short arm formed by the umbonal ridge of the shells; whenever the adductors relax, the elastic substance of the ligament contracts, and the shells gape. It is on this account that the valves of a dead Lamellibranch always gape; the elastic ligament is no longer counteracted by the effort of the adductors. The state of closure of the valves of the shell is not, therefore, one of rest; when it is at rest—that is, when there is no muscular effort—the valves of a Lamellibranch are slightly gaping, and are closed by the action of the adductors when the animal is disturbed. The ligament is simple in *Anodonta*; in many Lamellibranchs it is separated into two layers, an outer and an inner (thicker and denser). That the condition of gaping of the shell-valves is essential to the life of the Lamellibranch appears from the fact that food to nourish it, water to aerate its blood, and spermatozoa to fertilize its eggs, are all introduced into this gaping chamber by currents of water, set going by the highly-developed ctenidia. The current of water enters into the sub-pallial space at the spot marked *e* in fig. 1 (1), and, after passing as far forward as the mouth *w* in fig. 1 (5), takes an outward course and leaves the sub-pallial space by the upper notch *d*. These notches are known in *Anodonta* as the afferent and efferent siphonal notches respectively, and correspond to the long tube-like afferent inferior and efferent superior "siphons" formed by the mantle in many other Lamellibranchs (fig. 8).

Fig. 3.—Right Valve of the same Shell from the Outer Face.

Fig. 4.—Left Valve of the same Shell from the Inner Face. (Figs. 2, 3, 4 from Owen.)

Whilst the valves of the shell are equal in *Anodonta* we find in many Lamellibranchs (*Ostraea*, *Chama*, *Corbula*, &c.) one valve larger, and the other smaller and sometimes flat, whilst the larger shell may be fixed to rock or to stones (*Ostraea*, &c.). A further variation consists in the development of additional shelly plates upon the dorsal line between the two large valves (*Pholadidae*). In *Pholas dactylus* we find a pair of umbonal plates, a dors-umbonal plate and a dorsal plate. It is to be remembered that the whole of the cuticular hard product produced on the dorsal surface and on the mantle-flaps is to be regarded as the "shell," of which a median band-like area, the ligament, usually remains uncalcified, so as to result in the production of two valves united by the elastic ligament. But the shelly substance does not always in boring forms adhere to this form after its first growth. In *Aspergillum* the whole of the tubular mantle area secretes a continuous shelly tube, although in the young condition two valves were present. These are seen (fig. 7) set in the firm substance of the adult tubular shell, which has even replaced the ligament, so that the tube is complete. In *Teredo* a similar tube is formed as the animal elongates (boring in wood), the original shell-valves not adhering to it but remaining movable and provided with a special muscular apparatus in place of a ligament. In the shell of Lamellibranchs three distinct layers can be distinguished: an external chitinous, non-calcified layer, the periostracum; a middle layer composed of calcareous prisms perpendicular to the surface, the prismatic layer; and an internal layer composed of laminae parallel to the surface, the nacreous layer. The last is secreted by the whole surface of the mantle except the border, and additions to its thickness continue to be made through life. The periostracum is produced by the extreme edge of the mantle border, the prismatic layer by the part of the border within the edge. These two layers, therefore, when once formed cannot increase in thickness; as the mantle grows in extent its border passes beyond the formed parts of the two outer layers, and the latter are covered internally by a deposit of nacreous matter. Special deposits of the nacreous matter around foreign bodies form pearls, the foreign nucleus being usually of parasitic origin (see Pearl).

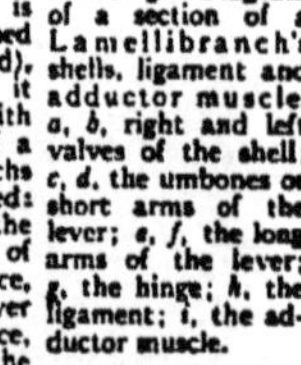

Fig. 5.—Diagram of a section of a Lamellibranch's shells, ligament and adductor muscle. *a*, *b*, right and left valves of the shell; *c*, *d*, the umbones or short arms of the lever; *e*, *f*, the long arms of the lever; *g*, the hinge; *h*, the ligament; *i*, the adductor muscle.

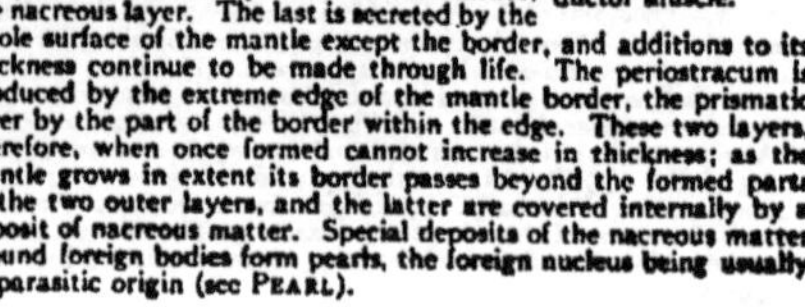

Let us now examine the organs which lie beneath the mantle-skirt of *Anodonta*, and are bathed by the current of water which circulates through it. This can be done by lifting up and throwing back the left half of the mantle-skirt as is represented in fig. 1 (3). We thus expose the plough-like foot (*f*), the two left labial tentacles, and the two left gill-plates or left ctenidium. In fig. 1 (5), one of the labial tentacles *n* is also thrown back to show the mouth *w*, and the two left gill-plates are reflected to show the gill-plates of the right side (*rr*, *ry*) projecting behind the foot, the inner or median plate of each side being united by concrescence to its fellow of the opposite side along a continuous line (*aa*). The left inner gill-plate is also snipped to show the subjacent orifices of the left renal organ *x*, and of the genital gland (testis or ovary) *y*. The foot thus exposed in *Anodonta* is a simple muscular tongue-like organ. It can be protruded between the flaps of the mantle (fig. 1 [1] [2]) so as to issue from the shell, and by its action the *Anodonta* can slowly crawl or burrow in soft mud or sand. Other Lamellibranchs may have a larger foot relatively than has *Anodonta*. In *Arca* it has a sole-like surface. In *Arca* too and many others it carries a byssus-forming gland and a byssus-cementing gland. In the cockles, in *Cardium* and in *Trigonia*, it is capable of a sudden stroke, which causes the animal to jump when out of the water, in the latter genus to a height of four feet. In *Mytilus* the foot is reduced to little more than a tubercle carrying the apertures of these glands. In the oyster it is absent altogether.

FIG. 6.—Shell of *Aspergillum vaginiferum*. (From Owen.)

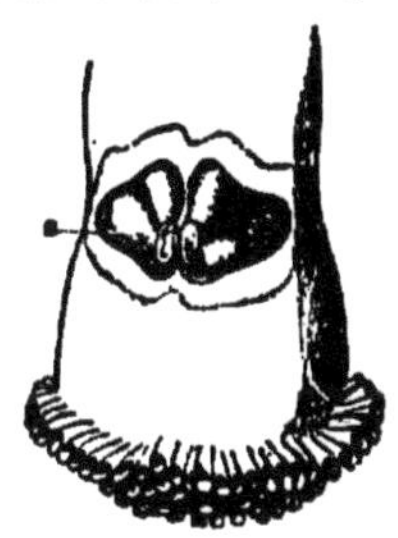

FIG. 7.—Shell of *Aspergillum vaginiferum* to show the original valves *a*, now embedded in a continuous calcification of tubular form. (From Owen.)

The labial tentacles or palps of *Anodonta* (*n*, *o* in fig. 1 [3], [5]) are highly vascular flat processes richly supplied with nerves. The left anterior tentacle (seen in the figure) is joined at its base in front of the mouth (*w*) to the right anterior tentacle, and similarly the left (*o*) and right posterior tentacles are joined behind the mouth. Those of *Arca* (*i*, *k* in fig. 9) show this relation to the mouth (*a*). These organs are characteristic of all Lamellibranchs; they do not vary except in size, being sometimes drawn out to streamer-like dimensions. Their appearance and position suggest that they are in some way related morphologically to the gill-plates, the anterior labial tentacle being a continuation of the outer gill-plate, and the posterior a continuation of the inner gill-plate. There is no embryological evidence to support this suggested connexion, and, as will appear immediately, the history of the gill-plates in various forms of Lamellibranchs does not directly favour it. The palps are really derived from part of the velar area of the larva.

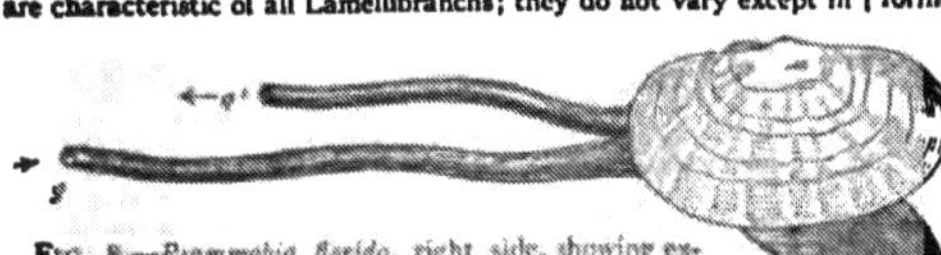

FIG. 8.—*Psammobia florida*, right side, showing expanded foot *e*, and *g* incurrent and *g'* excurrent siphons. (From Owen.)

The gill-plates have a structure very different from that of the labial tentacles, and one which in *Anodonta* is singularly complicated as compared with the condition presented by these organs in some other Lamellibranchs, and with what must have been their original condition in the ancestors of the whole series of living Lamellibranchia. The phenomenon of "concrescence" which we have already had to note as showing itself so importantly in regard to the free edges of the mantle-skirt and the formation of the siphons, is what, above all things, has complicated the structure of the Lamellibranch ctenidium. Our present knowledge of the interesting series of modifications through which the Lamellibranch gill-plates have developed to their most complicated form is due to R. H. Peck, K. Mitsukuri and W. G. Ridewood. The Molluscan ctenidium is typically a plume-like structure, consisting of a vascular axis, on each side of which is set a row of numerous lamelliform or filamentous processes. These processes are hollow, and receive the venous blood from, and return it again aerated into, the hollow axis, in which an afferent and an efferent blood-vessel may be differentiated. In the genus *Nucula* (fig. 10) we have an example of a Lamellibranch retaining this plume-like form of gill. In the Arcacea (*e.g.* *Arca* and *Pectunculus*) the lateral processes which are set on the axis of the ctenidium are not lamellae, but are slightly flattened, very long tubes or hollow filaments. These filaments are so fine and are set so closely together that they appear to form a continuous membrane until examined with a lens. The microscope shows that the neighbouring filaments are held together by patches of cilia, called "ciliated junctions," which interlock with one another just as two brushes may be made to do. In fig. 11, A a portion of four filaments of a ctenidium of the sea-mussel (*Mytilus*) is represented, having precisely the same structure as those of *Arca*. The filaments of the gill (ctenidium) of *Mytilus* and *Arca* thus form two closely set rows which depend from the axis of the gill like two parallel plates. Further, their structure is profoundly modified by the curious condition of the free ends of the depending filaments. These are actually reflected at a sharp angle—doubled on themselves in fact—and thus form an additional row of filaments (see fig. 11 B). Consequently, each primitive filament has a descending and an ascending ramus, and instead of each row forming a simple plate, the plate is double, consisting of a descending and an ascending lamella. As the axis of the ctenidium lies by the side of the body, and is very frequently connate with the body, as so often happens in Gastropods also, we find it convenient to speak of the two plate-like structures formed on each ctenidial axis as the outer and the inner gill-plate; each of these is composed of two lamellae, an outer (the reflected) and an adaxial in the case of the outer gill-plate, and an adaxial and an inner (the reflected) in the case of the inner gill-plate. This is the condition seen in *Arca* and *Mytilus*, the so-called plates dividing upon the slightest touch into their constituent filaments, which are but loosely conjoined by their "ciliated junctions." Complications follow upon this in other forms. Even in *Mytilus* and *Arca* a connexion is here and there formed between the ascending and descending rami of a filament by hollow extensible outgrowths called "interlamellar junctions" (*il. j* in B, fig. 11). Nevertheless the filament is a complete tube formed of chitinous substance and clothed externally by ciliated epithelium, internally by endothelium and lacunar tissue—a form of connective tissue—as shown in fig. 11, C. Now let us suppose as happens in the genus *Dreissensia*—a genus not far removed from *Mytilus*—that the ciliated inter-filamentar junctions (fig. 12) give place to solid permanent inter-filamentar junctions, so that the filaments are converted, as it were, into a trellis-work. Then let us suppose that the inter-lamellar junctions already noted in *Mytilus* become very numerous, large and irregular; by them the two trellis-works of filaments would be united so as to leave only a sponge-like set of spaces between them. Within the trabeculae of the sponge-work blood circulates, and between the trabeculae the water passes, having entered by the apertures left in the trellis-work formed by the united gill-filaments (fig. 14). The larger the

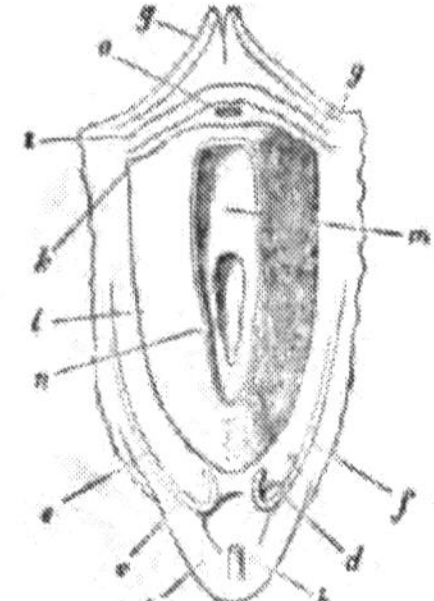

FIG. 9.—View from the ventral (pedal) aspect of the animal of *Arca noae*, the mantle-flap and gill-filaments having been cut away. (Lankester.)
a, Mouth.
b, Anus.
c, Free spirally turned extremity of the gill-axis or ctenidial axis of the right side.
d, Do. of the left side.
e, *f*, Anterior portions of these axes fused by concrescence to the wall of the body.
g, Anterior adductor muscle.
h, Posterior adductor.
i, Anterior labial tentacle.
k, Posterior labial tentacle.
l, Base line of the foot.
m, Sole of the foot.
n, Callosity.

intralamellar spongy growth becomes, the more do the original gill-filaments lose the character of blood-holding tubes, and tend to become dense elastic rods for the simple purpose of supporting the spongy growth. This is seen both in the section of *Dreissensia* gill (fig. 12) and in those of *Anodonta* (fig. 13, A,B,C). In the drawing of *Dreissensia* the individual filaments *f f f* are cut across in one lamella at the

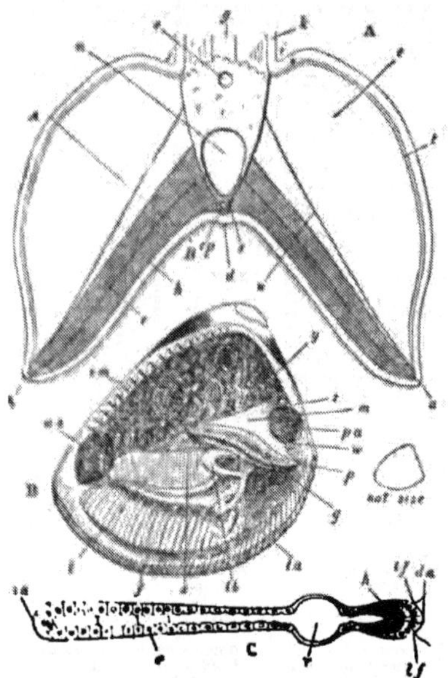

FIG. 10.—Structure of the Ctenidia of *Nucula*. (After Mitsukuri.) See also fig. 2.

A. Section across the axis of a ctenidium with a pair of plates — flattened and shortened filaments—attached.
i,j,h,g Are placed on or near the membrane which attaches the axis of the ctenidium to the side of the body.
a,b, Free extremities of the plates (filaments).
d, Mid-line of the inferior border.
e, Surface of the plate.
i, Its upper border.
h, Chitinous lining of the plate.
r, Dilated blood-space.
u, Fibrous tract.
o, Upper blood-vessel of the axis.
n, Lower blood-vessel of the axis.
s, Chitinous framework of the axis.
sp, Canal in the same.
A, *B*, Line along which the cross-section C of the plate is taken.
B. Animal of a male *Nucula proxima*, Say, as seen when the left valve of the shell and the left half of the mantle-skirt are removed
a.a, Anterior adductor muscle.
p.a, Posterior adductor muscle.
v.m, Visceral mass.
f, Foot.
g, Gill.
l, Labial Tentacle.
l.a, Filamentous appendage of the labial tentacle.
lb, Hood-like appendage of the labial tentacle.
m, Membrane suspending the gill and attached to the body along the line *x*, *y*, *z*, *w*.
p, Posterior end of the gill (ctenidium).
C. Section across one of the gill-plates (*A*, *B*, in A) comparable with fig. 11 C.
t.a, Outer border.
d.a, Axial border.
l.f, Latero-frontal epithelium.
e, Epithelium of general surface.
r, Dilated blood-space.
h, Chitinous lining (compare A).

horizon of an inter-filamentar junction, in the other (lower in the figure) at a point where they are free. The chitinous substance *ch* is observed to be greatly thickened as compared with what it is in fig. 11, C, tending in fact to obliterate altogether the lumen of the filament. And in *Anodonta* (fig. 13, C) this obliteration is effected. In *Anodonta*, besides being thickened, the skeletal substance of the filament develops a specially dense, rod-like body on each side of each filament. Although the structure of the ctenidium is thus highly complicated in *Anodonta*, it is yet more so in some of the siphonate genera of Lamellibranchs. The filaments take on a secondary grouping, the surface of the lamella being thrown into a series of half-cylindrical ridges, each consisting of ten or twenty filaments; a filament of much greater strength and thickness than the others may be placed between each pair of groups. In *Anodonta*, as in many other Lamellibranchs, the ova and hatched embryos are carried for a time in the ctenidia or gill apparatus, and in this particular case the space between the two lamellae of the outer gill-plate is that which serves to receive the ova (fig. 13, A). The young are nourished by a substance formed by the cells which cover the spongy inter-lamellar outgrowths.

Other points in the modification of the typical ctenidium must be noted in order to understand the ctenidium of *Anodonta*. The axis of each ctenidium, right and left, starts from a point well forward

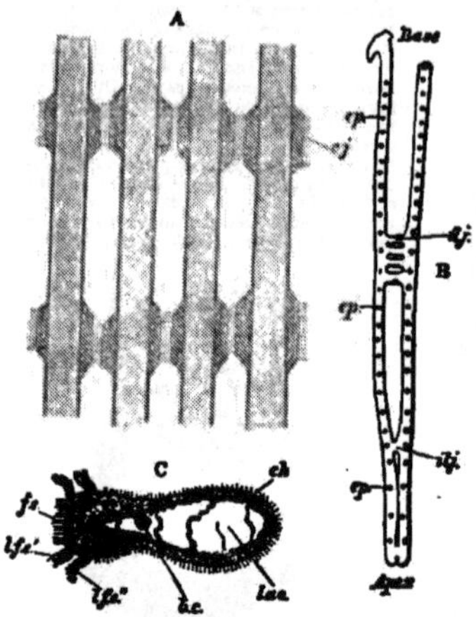

FIG. 11.—Filaments of the Ctenidium of *Mytilus edulis*. (After R. H. Peck.)

A, Part of four filaments seen from the outer face in order to show the ciliated junctions *c.j.*

B, Diagram of the posterior face of a single complete filament with descending ramus and ascending ramus ending in a hook-like process; *cp.*, *cp.*, the ciliated junctions; *il.j.*, inter-lamellar junction.

C, Transverse section of a filament taken so as to cut neither a ciliated junction nor an inter-lamellar junction. *f.e.*, Frontal epithelium; *l.f.e'.*, *l.f.e"*., the two rows of latero-frontal epithelial cells with long cilia; *ch*, chitinous tubular lining of the filament; *lac.*, blood lacuna traversed by a few processes of connective tissue cells; *b.c.*, blood-corpuscle.

near the labial tentacles, but it is at first only a ridge, and does not project as a free cylindrical axis until the back part of the foot is reached. This is difficult to see in *Anodonta*, but if the mantle-skirt be entirely cleared away, and if the dependent lamellae which spring from the ctenidial axis be carefully cropped so as to leave the axis itself intact, we obtain the form shown in fig. 15, where *g* and *h* are respectively the left and the right ctenidial axes projecting freely beyond the body. In *Arca* this can be seen with far less trouble, for the filaments are more easily removed than are the consolidated lamellae formed by the filaments of *Anodonta*, and in *Arca* the free axes of the ctenidia are large and firm in texture (fig. 9, *c*,*d*).

If we were to make a vertical section across the long axis of a Lamellibranch which had the axis of its ctenidium free from its origin onwards, we should find such relations as are shown in the diagram fig. 16, A. The gill axis *d* is seen lying in the sub-pallial chamber between the foot *b* and the mantle *c*. From it depend the gill-filaments or lamellae—formed by united filaments—drawn as black lines *f*. On the left side these lamellae are represented as having only a small reflected growth, on the right side the reflected ramus or lamella is complete (*fr* and *er*). The actual condition in *Anodonta* at the region where the gills begin anteriorly is shown in fig. 16, B. The axis of the ctenidium is seen to be adherent to, or fused by concrescence with, the body-wall, and moreover on each side the outer lamella of the outer gill-plate is fused to the mantle, whilst the inner lamella of the inner gill-plate is fused to the foot. If we take another section nearer the hinder margin of the foot, we get the arrangement

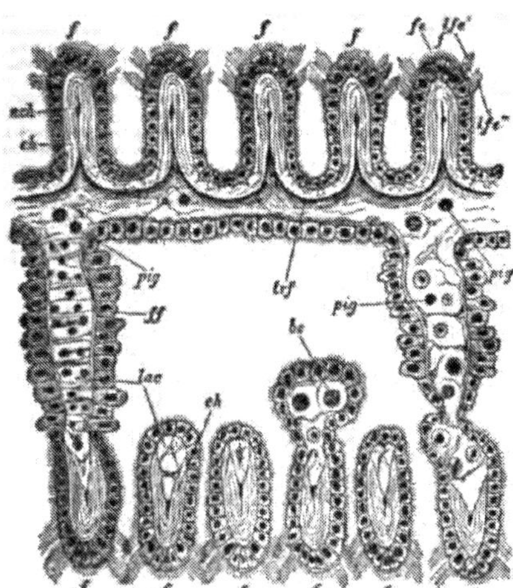

FIG. 12.—Transverse Section of the Outer Gill-plate of *Dreissensia polymorpha*. (After R. H. Peck.)

f, Constituent gill-filaments.
ff, Fibrous sub-epidermic tissue.
ch, Chitonous substance of the filaments.
sch, Cells related to the chitonous substance.
lac, Lacunar tissue.
pig, Pigment-cells.
bc, Blood-corpuscles.
fe, Frontal epithelium.
lfe', *lfe"*, Two rows of latero-frontal epithelial cells with long cilia.
trf, Fibrous, possibly muscular, substance of the inter-filamentar junctions.

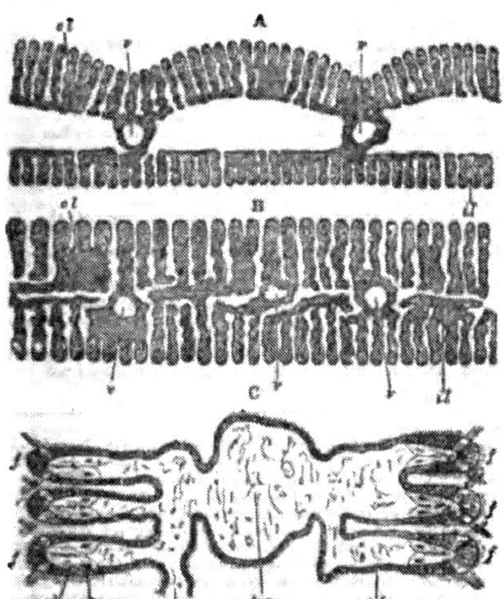

FIG. 13.—Transverse Sections of Gill-plates of *Anodonta*. (After R. H. Peck.)

A, Outer gill-plate.
B, Inner gill-plate.
C, A portion of B more highly [magnified.
ol, Outer lamella.
il, Inner lamella.
v, Blood-vessel.
f, Constituent filaments.
lac, Lacunar tissue.
ch, Chitonous substance of the filament.
chr, Chitonous rod embedded in the softer substance *ch*.'

shown diagrammatically in fig. 16, C, and more correctly in fig. 17. In this region the inner lamellae of the inner gill-plates are no longer

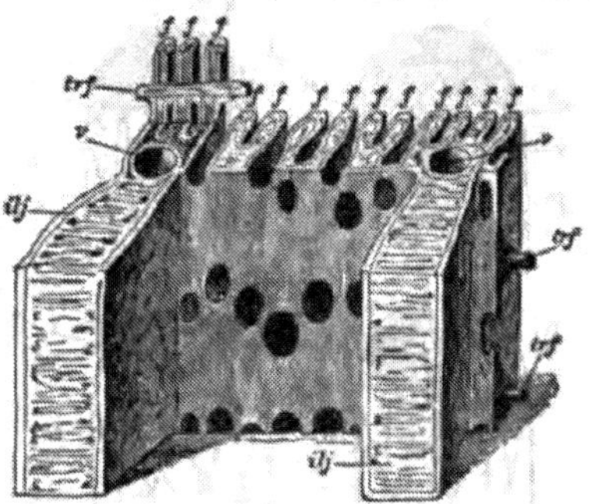

FIG. 14.—Gill-lamellae of *Anodonta*. (After R. H. Peck.)

Diagram of a block cut from the outer lamella of the outer gill-plate and seen from the inter-lamellar surface. *f*, Constituent filaments; *trf*, fibrous tissue of the transverse inter-filamentar junctions; *v*, blood-vessel *ilj*, Inter-lamellar junction. The series of oval holes on the back of the lamella are the water-pores which open between the filaments in irregular rows separated horizontally by the transverse inter-filmentar junctions.

affixed to the foot Passing still farther back behind the foot, we find in *Anodonta* the condition shown in the section D, fig. 16. The axes *i* are now free; the outer lamellae of the outer gill-plates (*er*) still adhere by concrescence to the mantle-skirt, whilst the inner lamellae of the inner gill-plates meet one another and fuse by concrescence at *g*. In the lateral view of the animal with reflected mantle-skirt and gill-plates, the line of concrescence of the inner lamellae of the inner gill-plates is readily seen; it is marked *aa* in fig. 1 (5). In the same figure the free part of the inner lamella of the inner gill-plate resting on the foot is marked *z*, whilst the attached part—the most anterior—has been snipped with scissors so as to show the genital and nephridial apertures *x* and *y*. The concrescence, then, of the free edge of the reflected lamellae of the gill-plates of Anodon is very extensive. It is important, because such a concrescence is by no means universal, and does not occur, for example, in *Mytilus* or in *Arca*; further, because when its occurrence is once appreciated, the reduction of the gill-plates of *Anodonta* to the plume-type of the simplest ctenidium presents no difficulty; and, lastly, it has importance in reference to its physiological significance. The mechanical result of the concrescence of the outer lamellae to the mantle-flap, and of the inner lamellae to one another as shown in section D, fig. 16, is that the sub-pallial space is divided into two spaces by a horizontal septum. The upper space (*i*) communicates with the outer world

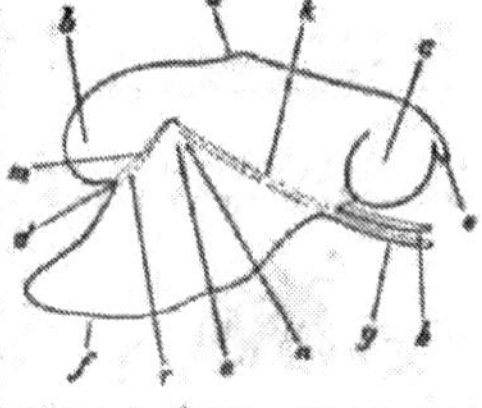

FIG. 15.—Diagram of a view from the left side of the animal of *Anodonta cygnaea*, from which the mantle-skirt, the labial tentacles and the gill-filaments have been entirely removed so as to show the relations of the axis of the gill-plumes or ctenidia *g*, *k*. (Original.)

a, Centro-dorsal area.
b, Anterior adductor muscle.
c, Posterior adductor muscle.
d, Mouth.
e, Anus.
f, Foot.
g, Free portion of the axis of left ctenidium.
h, Axis of right ctenidium.
k, Portion of the axis of the left ctenidium which is fused with the base of the foot, the two dotted lines indicating the origins of the two rows of gill-filaments.
m, Line of origin of the anterior labial tentacle.
n, Nephridial aperture.
o, Genital aperture.
r, Line of origin of the posterior labial tentacle.

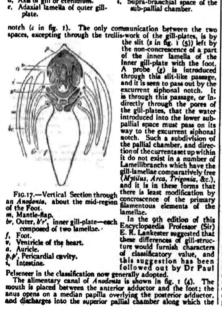

by the excurrent or superior siphonal notch of the mantle (fig. 1, *d*); the lower space communicates by the lower siphonal

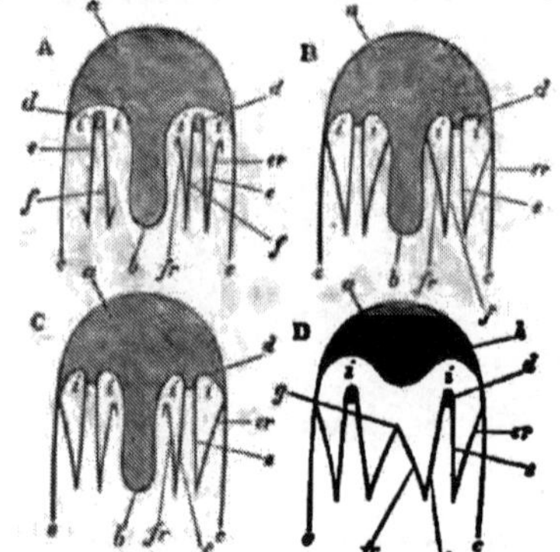

FIG. 16.—Diagrams of Transverse Sections of a Lamellibranch to show the Adhesion, by Concrescence, of the Gill-Lamellae to the Mantle-flaps, to the foot and to one another. (Lankester.)

A, Shows two conditions with free gill-axis.
B, Condition at foremost region in *Anodonta*.
C, Hind region of foot in *Anodonta*.
D, Region altogether posterior to the foot in *Anodonta*.
a, Visceral mass.
b, Foot.
c, Mantle flap.
d, Axis of gill or ctenidium.
e, Adaxial lamella of outer gill-plate.
er, Reflected lamella of outer gill-plate.
f, Adaxial lamella of inner gill-plate.
fr, Reflected lamella of inner gill-plate.
g, Line of concrescence of the reflected lamellae of the two inner gill-plates.
h, Rectum.
i, Supra-branchial space of the sub-pallial chamber.

notch (*c* in fig. 1). The only communication between the two spaces, excepting through the trellis-work of the gill-plates, is by the slit (*s* in fig. 1 (5)) left by the non-concrescence of a part of the inner lamella of the inner gill-plate with the foot. A probe (*g*) is introduced through this slit-like passage, and it is seen to pass out by the excurrent siphonal notch. It is through this passage, or indirectly through the pores of the gill-plates, that the water introduced into the lower sub-pallial space must pass on its way to the excurrent siphonal notch. Such a subdivision of the pallial chamber, and direction of the current set up within it do not exist in a number of Lamellibranchs which have the gill-lamellae comparatively free (*Mytilus*, *Arca*, *Trigonia*, &c.), and it is in these forms that there is least modification by concrescence of the primary filamentous elements of the lamellae.

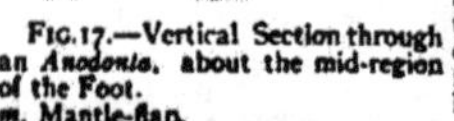

FIG. 17.—Vertical Section through an *Anodonta*, about the mid-region of the Foot.

m, Mantle-flap.
br, Outer, *b'r'*, inner gill-plate—each composed of two lamellae.
f, Foot.
v, Ventricle of the heart.
a, Auricle.
p, *p'*, Pericardial cavity.
i, Intestine.

In the 9th edition of this Encyclopaedia Professor (Sir) E. R. Lankester suggested that these differences of gill-structure would furnish characters of classificatory value, and this suggestion has been followed out by Dr Paul Pelseneer in the classification now generally adopted.

The alimentary canal of *Anodonta* is shown in fig. 1 (4). The mouth is placed between the anterior adductor and the foot; the anus opens on a median papilla overlying the posterior adductor, and discharges into the superior pallial chamber along which the excurrent stream passes. The coil of the intestine in *Anodonta* is similar to that of other Lamellibranchs. The rectum traverses the pericardium, and has the ventricle of the heart wrapped, as it were, around it. This is not an unusual arrangement in Lamellibranchs, and a similar disposition occurs in some Gastropoda (*Haliotis*). A pair of ducts (*as*) lead from the first enlargement of the alimentary tract called stomach into a pair of large digestive glands, the so-called liver, the branches of which are closely packed in this region (*af*). The food of the *Anodonta*, as of other Lamellibranchs, consists of microscopic animal and vegetable organisms, brought to the mouth by the stream which sets into the sub-pallial chamber at the lower siphonal notch (*e* in fig. 1) Probably a straining of water from solid particles is effected by the lattice-work of the ctenidia or gill-plates.

The heart of *Anodonta* consists of a median ventricle embracing the rectum (fig. 18, A), and giving off an anterior and a posterior artery,

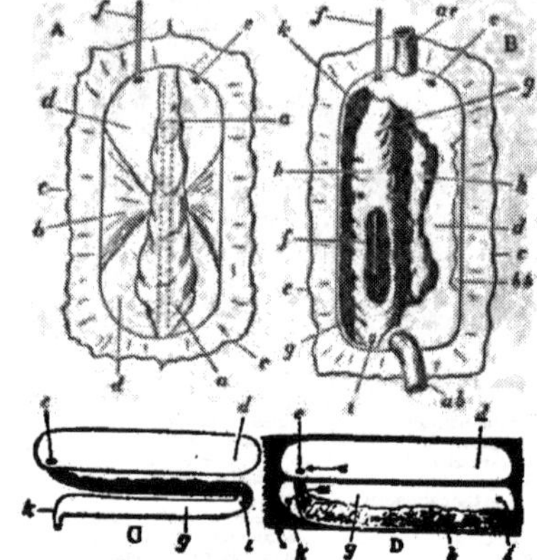

FIG. 18.—Diagrams showing the Relations of Pericardium and Nephridia in a Lamellibranch such as *Anodonta*.

A, Pericardium opened dorsally so as to expose the heart and the floor of the pericardial chamber *d*.
B, Heart removed and floor of the pericardium cut away on the left side so as to open the non-glandular sac of the nephridium, exposing the glandular sac *b*, which is also cut into so as to show the probe *f*.
C, Ideal pericardium and nephridium viewed laterally.
D, Lateral view showing the actual relation of the glandular and non-glandular sacs of the nephridium. The arrows indicate the course of fluid from the pericardium outwards.
a, Ventricle of the heart.
b, Auricle.
bb, Cut remnant of the auricle.
c, Dorsal wall of the pericardium cut and reflected.
e, Reno-pericardial orifice.
f, Probe introduced into the left reno-pericardial orifice.
g, Non-glandular sac of the left nephridium.
h, Glandular sac of the left nephridium.
i, Pore leading from the glandular into the non-glandular sac of the left nephridium.
k, Pore leading from the non-glandular sac to the exterior.
ac, Anterior.
ab, Posterior, cut remnants of the intestine and ventricle.

and of two auricles which open into the ventricle by orifices protected by valves.

The blood is colourless, and has colourless amoeboid corpuscles floating in it. In *Ceratisolen legumen*, various species of *Arca* and a few other species the blood is crimson, owing to the presence of corpuscles impregnated with haemoglobin. In *Anodonta* the blood is driven by the ventricle through the arteries into vessel-like spaces, which soon become irregular lacunae surrounding the viscera, but in parts—*e.g.* the labial tentacles and walls of the gut—very fine vessels with endothelial cell-lining are found. The blood makes its way by large veins to a venous sinus which lies in the middle line below the heart, having the paired renal organs (nephridia) placed between it and that organ. Hence it passes through the vessels of the glandular walls of the nephridia right and left into the gill-lamellae, whence it returns through many openings into the widely-stretched auricles. In the filaments of the gill of Protobranchia and many Filibranchia the tubular cavity is divided by a more or less complete fibrous septum into two channels, for an afferent and efferent blood-current. The ventricle and auricles of *Anodonta* lie in a pericardium which is clothed with a pavement endothelium (*d*, fig. 18).

It does not contain blood or communicate directly with the blood-system; this isolation of the pericardium we have noted already in Gastropods and Cephalopoda. A good case for the examination of the question as to whether blood enters the pericardium of Lamellibranchs, or escapes from the foot, or by the renal organs when the animal suddenly contracts, is furnished by the *Ceratisolen legumen*, which has red blood-corpuscles. According to observations made by Penrose on an uninjured *Ceratisolen legumen*, no red corpuscles are to be seen in the pericardial space, although the heart is filled with them, and no such corpuscles are ever discharged by the animal when it is irritated.

FIG. 19.—Nerve-ganglia and Cords of three Lamellibranchs. (From Gegenbaur.)
A, Of *Teredo*.
B, Of *Anodonta*.
C, Of *Pecten*.
a, Cerebral ganglion-pair (=cerebro-pleuro-visceral).
b, Pedal ganglion-pair
c, Olfactory (osphradial) ganglion-pair.

The pair of renal organs of *Anodonta*, called in Lamellibranchs the organs of Bojanus, lie below the membranous floor of the pericardium, and open into it by two well-marked apertures (*e* and *f* in fig. 18). Each nephridium, after being bent upon itself as shown in fig. 18, C, D, opens to the exterior by a pore placed at the point marked *x* in fig. 1 (5) (6). One half of each nephridium is of a dark-green colour and glandular (*h* in fig. 18). This opens into the reflected portion which overlies it as shown in the diagram fig. 18, D, *i*; the latter has non-glandular walls, and opens by the pore *k* to the exterior. The renal organs may be more ramified in other Lamellibranchs than they are in *Anodonta*. In some they are difficult to discover. That of the common oyster was described by Hoek. Each nephridium in the oyster is a pyriform sac, which communicates by a narrow canal with the urino-genital groove placed to the front of the great adductor muscle; by a second narrow canal it communicates with the pericardium. From all parts of the pyriform sac narrow stalk-like tubes are given off, ending in abundant widely-spread branching glandular caeca, which form the essential renal secreting apparatus. The genital duct opens by a pore into the urino-genital groove of the oyster (the same arrangement being repeated on each side of the body) close to but distinct from the aperture of the nephridial canal. Hence, except for the formation of a urino-genital groove, the apertures are placed as they are in *Anodonta*. Previously to Hoek's discovery a brown-coloured investment of the auricles of the heart of the oyster had been supposed to represent the nephridia in a rudimentary state. This investment, which occurs also in many Filibranchia, forms the pericardial glands, comparable to the pericardial accessory glandular growths of Cephalopoda. In *Unionidae* and several other forms the pericardial glands are extended into diverticula of the pericardium which penetrate the mantle and constitute the organ of Heber. The glands secrete hippuric acid which passes from the pericardium into the renal organs.

FIG. 20.—Otocyst of *Cyclas*. (From Gegenbaur.)
c, Capsule.
e, Ciliated cells lining the same.
o, Otolith.

Nervous System and Sense-Organs.—In *Anodonta* there are three well-developed pairs of nerve ganglia (fig. 19, B, and fig. 1 (6)). An anterior pair, lying one on each side of the mouth (fig. 19, B, *a*) and connected in front of it by a commissure, are the representatives of the cerebral and pleural ganglia of the typical Mollusc, which are not here differentiated as they are in Gastropoda. A pair placed close together in the foot (fig. 19, B, *b*, and fig. 1 (6), *ax*) are the typical pedal ganglia; they are joined to the cerebro-pleural ganglia by connectives.

Posteriorly beneath the posterior adductors, and covered only by a thin layer of elongated epidermal cells, are the visceral ganglia. United with these ganglia on the outer sides are the osphradial ganglia, above which the epithelium is modified to form a pair of sense-organs, corresponding to the osphradia of other Molluscs. In some Lamellibranchs the osphradial ganglia receive nerve-fibres, not from the visceral ganglia, but from the cerebral ganglia along the visceral commissure. Formerly the posterior pair of ganglia were identified as simply the osphradial ganglia, and the anterior pair as the cerebral, pleural and visceral ganglia united into a single pair. But it has since been discovered that in the Protobranchia the cerebral ganglia and the pleural are distinct, each giving origin to its own connective which runs to the pedal ganglion. The cerebro-pedal and pleuro-pedal connectives, however, in these cases are only separate in the initial parts of their course, and unite together for the lower half of their length, or for nearly the whole length. Moreover, in many forms, in which in the adult condition there is only a single pair of anterior ganglia and a single pedal connective, a pleural ganglion distinct from the cerebral has been recognized in the course of development. There is, however, no evidence of the union of a visceral pair with the cerebro-pleural.

The sense-organs of *Anodonta* other than the osphradia consist of a pair of otocysts attached to the pedal ganglia (fig. 1 (6), *ay*). The otocysts of *Cyclas* are peculiarly favourable for study on account of the transparency of the small foot in which they lie, and may be taken as typical of those of Lamellibranchs generally. The structure of

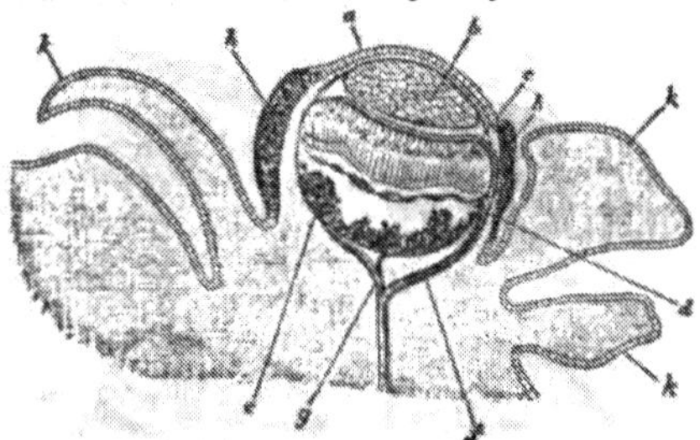

FIG. 21.—Pallial Eye of *Spondylus*. (From Hickson.)
a, Prae-corneal epithelium.
b, Cellular lens.
c, Retinal body.
d, Tapetum.
e, Pigment.
f, Retinal nerve.
g, Complementary nerve.
h, Epithelial cells filled with pigment.
k, Tentacle.

one is exhibited in fig. 20. A single otolith is present as in the veliger embryos of Opisthobranchia. In Filibranchia and many Protobranchia the otocyst (or statocyst) contains numerous particles (otoconia). The organs are developed as invaginations of the epidermis of the foot, and in the majority of the Protobranchia the orifice of invagination remains open throughout life; this is also the case in *Mytilus* including the common mussel.

Anodonta has no eyes of any sort, and the tentacles on the mantle edge are limited to its posterior border. This deficiency is very usual in the class; at the same time, many Lamellibranchs have tentacles on the edge of the mantle supplied by a pair of large well-developed nerves, which are given off from the cerebro-pleural ganglion-pair,

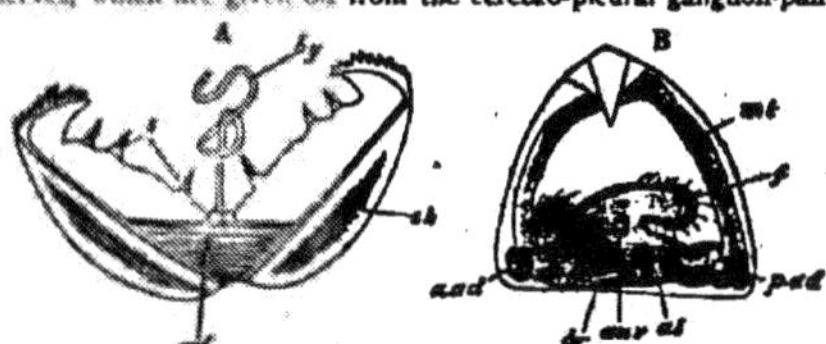

FIG. 22.—Two Stages in the Development of *Anodonta*. (From Balfour.) Both figures represent the glochidium stage.
A. When free swimming, shows the two dentigerous valves widely open.
B. A later stage, after fixture to the fin of a fish.
sh, Shell.
ad, Adductor muscle.
s, Teeth of the shell.
by, Byssus.
a.ad, Anterior adductor.
p.ad, Posterior adductor.
mt, Mantle-flap.
f, Foot.
br, Branchial filaments.
au.v, Otocyst.
al, Alimentary canal.

and very frequently some of these tentacles have undergone a special metamorphosis converting them into highly-organized eyes. Such eyes on the mantle-edge are found in *Pecten*, *Spondylus*, *Lima*, *Pinna*, *Pectunculus*, *Modiola*, *Cardium*, *Tellina*, *Mactra*, *Venus*, *Solen*, *Pholas* and *Galeomma*. They are totally distinct from the cephalic eyes of typical Mollusca, and have a different structure and historical development. They have originated not as pits but as tentacles. They agree with the dorsal eyes of *Oncidium* (Pulmonata) in the curious fact that the optic nerve penetrates the capsule of the eye and passes in front of the retinal body (fig. 21), so that its fibres join the anterior faces of the nerve-end cells as in Vertebrates, instead of their posterior faces as in the cephalic eyes of Mollusca and Arthropoda; moreover, the lens is not a cuticular product but a cellular structure, which, again, is a feature of agreement with the Vertebrate eye. It must, however, be distinctly borne in mind that there is a fundamental difference between the eye of Vertebrates and of all other groups in the fact that in the Vertebrata the retinal body is itself a part of the central nervous system, and not a separate

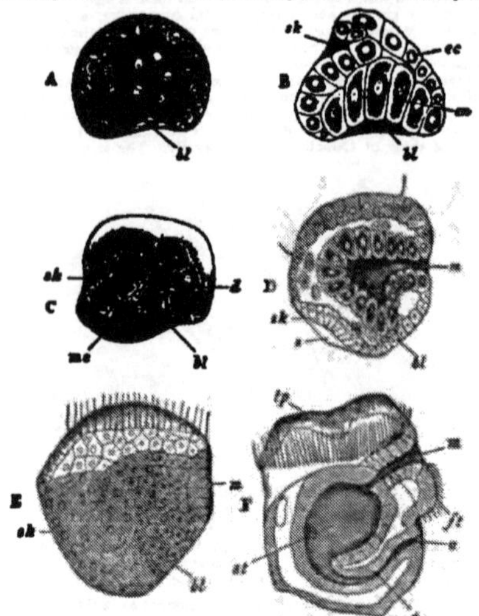

FIG. 23.—Development of the Oyster, *Ostrea edulis*. (Modified from Horst.)

A, Blastula stage (one-cell-layered sac), with commencing invagination of the wall of the sac at *bl*, the blastopore.
B, Optical section of a somewhat later stage, in which a second invagination has begun—namely, that of the shell-gland *sh*.
bl, Blastopore.
en, Invaginated endoderm (wall of the future arch-enteron).
ec, Ectoderm.
C, Similar optical section at a little later stage. The invagination connected with the blastopore is now more contracted, *d*; and cells, *me*, forming the mesoblast from which the cœlom and muscular and skeleto-trophic tissues develop, are separated.
D, Similar section of a later stage. The blastopore, *bl*, has closed; the anus will subsequently perforate the corresponding area. A new aperture, *m*, the mouth, has eaten its way into the invaginated endodermal sac, and the cells pushed in with it constitute the stomodaeum. The shell-gland, *sh*, is flattened out, and a delicate shell, *s*, appears on its surface. The ciliated velar ring is cut in the section, as shown by the two projecting cilia on the upper part of the figure. The embryo is now a Trochosphere.
E, Surface view of an embryo at a period almost identical with that of D.
F, Later embryo seen as a transparent object.
m, Mouth.
ft, Foot.
a, Anus.
e, Intestine.
st, Stomach.
tp, Velar area of the prostomium. The extent of the shell and commencing upgrowth of the mantle-skirt is indicated by a line forming a curve from *a* to F.

N.B.—In this development, as in that of *Pisidium* (fig. 25), no part of the blastopore persists either as mouth or as anus, but the aperture closes—the pedicle of invagination, or narrow neck of the invaginated arch-enteron, becoming the intestine. The mouth and the anus are formed as independent in-pushings, the mouth with stomodaeum first, and the short anal proctodaeum much later. This interpretation of the appearances is contrary to that of Horst, from whom our drawings of the oyster's development are taken. The account given by the American William K. Brooks differs greatly as to matter of fact from that of Horst, and appears to be erroneous in some respects.

modification of the epidermis—myelonic as opposed to epidermic. The structure of the reputed eyes of several of the above-named genera has not been carefully examined. In *Pecten* and *Spondylus*, however, they have been fully studied (see fig. 21, and explanation). Rudimentary cephalic eyes occur in the *Mytilidae* and in *Avicula* at the base of the first filament of the inner gill, each consisting of a pigmented epithelial fossa containing a cuticular lens. In the *Arcidae* the pallial eyes are compound or faceted somewhat like those of Arthropods.

Generative Organs.—The gonads of *Anodonta* are placed in distinct male and female individuals. In some Lamellibranchs—for instance, the European Oyster and the *Pisidium pusillum*—the sexes are united in the same individual; but here, as in most hermaphrodite animals, the two sexual elements are not ripe in the same individual at the same moment. It has been conclusively shown that the *Ostrea edulis* does not fertilize itself. The American Oyster (*O. virginiana*) and the Portuguese Oyster (*O. angulata*) have the sexes separate, and fertilization is effected in the open water after the discharge of the ova and the spermatozoa from the females and males respectively. In the *Ostrea edulis* fertilization of the eggs is effected at the moment of their escape from the uro-genital groove, or even before, by means of spermatozoa drawn into the sub-pallial chamber by the incurrent ciliary stream, and the embryos pass through the early stages of development whilst entangled between the gill-lamellae of the female parent (fig. 23). In *Anodonta* the eggs pass into the space between the two lamellae of the outer gill-plate, and are there fertilized, and advance whilst still in this position to the glochidium phase of development (fig. 22). They may be found here in thousands in the summer and autumn months. The gonads themselves are extremely simple arborescent glands which open to the exterior by two simple ducts, one right and one left, continuous with the tubular branches of the gonads. In the most primitive Lamellibranchs there is no separate generative aperture but the gonads discharge into the renal cavity, as in *Patella* among Gastropods. This is the case in the Protobranchia, *e.g. Solenomya*, in which the gonad opens into the reno-pericardial duct. But the generative products do not pass through the whole length of the renal tube: there is a direct opening from the pericardial end of the tube to the distal end, and the ova or sperms pass through this. In *Arca*, in *Anomiidae* and in *Pectinidae* the gonad opens into the external part of the renal tube. The next stage of modification is seen in *Ostraea*, *Cyclas* and some *Lucinidae*, in which the generative and renal ducts

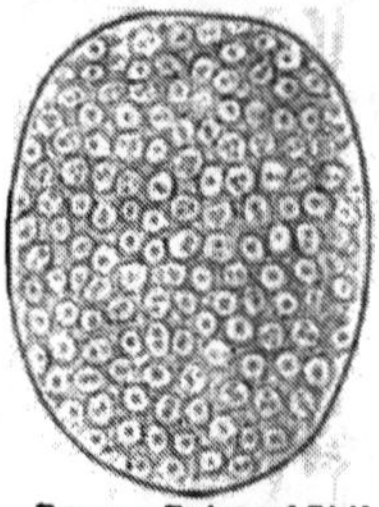

FIG. 24.—Embryo of *Pisidium pusillum* in the diblastula stage, surface view (after Lankester). The embryo has increased in size by accumulation of liquid between the outer and the invaginated cells. The blastopore has closed.

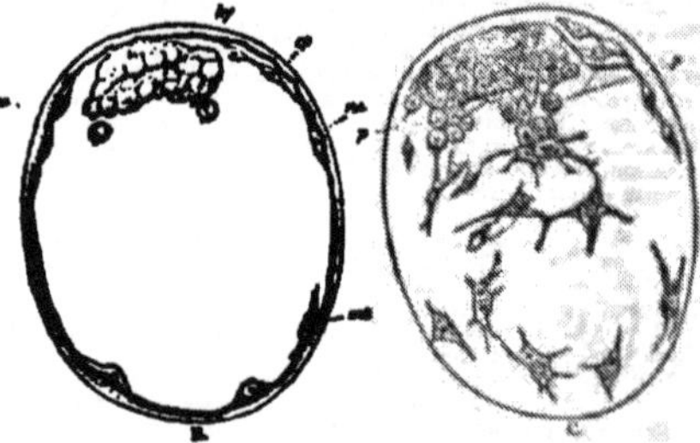

FIG. 25.—B, Same embryo as fig. 24, in optical median section, showing the invaginated cells *hy* which form the arch-enteron, and the mesoblastic cells *me* which are budded off from the surface of the mass *hy*, and apply themselves to the inner surface of the epiblastic cell-layer *ep*. C, The same embryo focused so as to show the mesoblastic cells which immediately underlie the outer cell-layer.

open into a cloacal slit on the surface of the body. In *Mytilus* the two apertures are on a common papilla, in other cases the two apertures are as in *Anodonta*. The Anatinacea and *Poromya* among the Septibranchia are, however, peculiar in having two genital apertures on each side, one male and one female. These forms are hermaphrodite, with an ovary and testis completely separate from each other on each side of the body, each having its own duct and aperture.

The development of *Anodonta* is remarkable for the curious larval form known as *glochidium* (fig. 22). The glochidium quits the gill-pouch of its parent and swims by alternate opening and shutting of the valves of its shell, as do adult *Pecten* and *Lima*, trailing at the same time a long byssus thread. This byssus is not homologous with that of other Lamellibranchs, but originates from a single glandular epithelial cell embedded in the tissues on the dorsal anterior side of the adductor muscle. By this it is brought into contact with the fin of a fish, such as perch, stickleback or others, and effects a hold thereon by means of the toothed edge of its shells. Here it becomes encysted, and is nourished by the exudations of the fish. It remains in this condition for a period of two to six weeks, and during this time the permanent organs are developed from the cells of two symmetrical cavities behind the adductor muscle. The early larva of *Anodonta* is not unlike the trochosphere of other Lamellibranchs, but the mouth is wanting. The glochidium is formed by the precocious development of the anterior adductor and the retardation of all the other organs except the shell. Other Lamellibranchs exhibit either a trochosphere larva which becomes a veliger differing only from the Gastropod's and Pteropod's veliger in having bilateral shell-calcifications instead of a single central one; or, like *Anodonta*, they may develop within the gill-plates of the mother, though without presenting such a specialized larva as the glochidium. An example of the former is seen in the development of the European oyster, to the figure of which and its explanation the reader is specially referred (fig. 23). An example of the latter is seen in a common little freshwater bivalve, the *Pisidium pusillum*, which has been studied by Lankester. The gastrula is formed in this case by invagination. The embryonic cells continue to divide, and form an oval vesicle containing liquid (fig. 24); within this, at one pole, is seen the mass of invaginated cells (fig. 25, *hy*). These invaginated cells are the archenteron; they proliferate and give off branching cells, which apply themselves (fig. 25, C) to the inner face of the vesicle, thus forming the mesoblast. The outer single layer of cells which constitutes the surface of the vesicle is the ectoderm or epiblast. The little mass of hypoblast or enteric cell-mass now enlarges, but remains connected with the cicatrix of the blastopore or orifice of invagination by a stalk, the rectal peduncle. The enteron itself becomes bilobed and is joined by a new invagination, that of the mouth and stomodaeum. The mesoblast multiplies its cells, which become partly muscular and partly skeleto-trophic. Centro-dorsally now appears the embyronic shell-gland. The pharynx or stomodaeum is still small, the foot not yet prominent. A later stage is seen in fig. 26, where the pharynx is widely open and the foot prominent. No ciliated velum or pre-oral (cephalic) lobe ever develops. The shell-gland disappears, the mantle-skirt is raised as a ridge, the paired shell-valves are secreted, the anus opens by a proctodaeal ingrowth into the rectal peduncle, and the rudiments of the gills (*br*) and of the renal organs (B) appear (fig. 26, lateral view), and thus the chief organs and general form of the adult are acquired. Later changes consist in the growth of the shell-valves over the whole area of the mantle-flaps, and in the multiplication of the gill-filaments and their consolidation to form gill-plates. It is important to note that the gill-filaments are formed one by one *posteriorly*. The labial tentacles are formed late. In the allied genus *Cyclas*, a byssus gland is formed in the foot and subsequently disappears, but no such gland occurs in *Pisidium*.

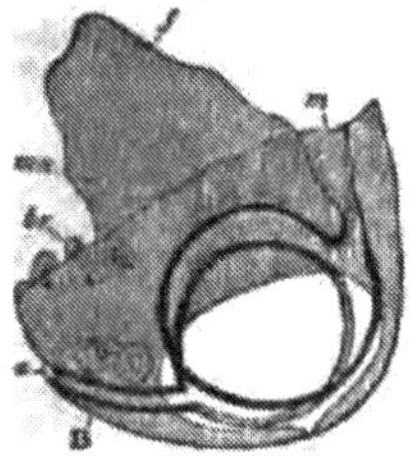

FIG. 26.—Diagram of Embryo of *Pisidium*. The unshaded area gives the position of the shell-valve. (After Lankester.)

m, Mouth.
x, Anus.
f, Foot.
br, Branchial filaments.
ms, Margin of the mantle-skirt.
B, Organ of Bojanus.

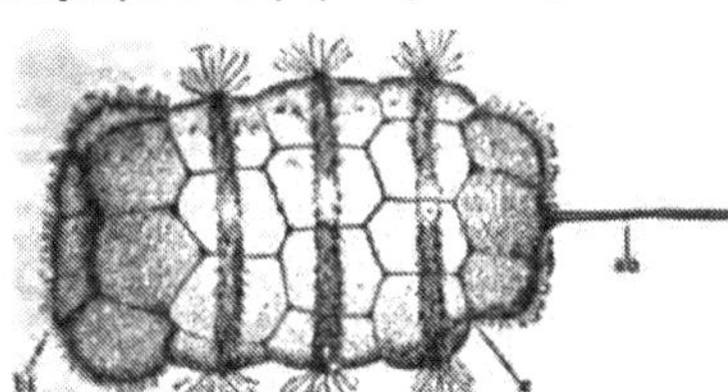

After Drew, in Lankester's *Treatise on Zoology*. (A. & C. Black.)

FIG. 27.—Surface view of a forty-five hour embryo of *Yoldia limatula*. *a.c*, Apical cilia. *bl*, Blastopore. *x*, Depression where the cells that form the cerebral ganglia come to the surface.

An extraordinary modification of the veliger occurs in the development of *Nucula* and *Yoldia* and probably other members of the same families. After the formation of the gastrula by epibole the larva becomes enclosed by an ectodermic test covering the whole of the original surface of the body, including the shell-gland, and leaving only a small opening at the posterior end in which the stomodaeum and proctodaeum are formed. In *Yoldia* and *Nucula proxima* the test consists of five rows of flattened cells, the three median rows bearing circlets of long cilia. At the anterior end of the test is the apical plate from the centre of which projects a long flagellum as in many other Lamellibranch larvae. In *Nucula delphinodonta* the test is uniformly covered with short cilia, and there is no flagellum. When the larval development is completed the test is cast off, its cells breaking apart and falling to pieces leaving the young animal with a well-developed shell exposed and the internal organs in an advanced state. The test is really a ciliated velum developed in the normal position at the apical pole but reflected backwards in such a way as to cover the original ectoderm except at the posterior end. In *Yoldia* and *Nucula proxima* the ova are set free in the water and the test-larvae are free-swimming, but in *Nucula delphinodonta* the female forms a thin-walled egg-case of mucus attached to the posterior end of the shell and in communication with the pallial chamber; in this case the eggs develop and the test-larva is enclosed. A similar modification of the velum occurs in *Dentalium* and in *Myzomenia* among the Amphineura.

Classification of Lamellibranchia

The classification originally based on the structure of the gills by P. Pelseneer included five orders, viz.: the Protobranchia in which the gill-filaments are flattened and not reflected; the Filibranchia in which the filaments are long and reflected, with non-vascular junctions; the Pseudo-lamellibranchia in which the gill-lamellae are vertically folded, the interfilamentar and interlamellar junctions being vascular or non-vascular; the Eulamellibranchia in which the interfilamentar and interlamellar junctions are vascular; and lastly the Septibranchia in which the gills are reduced to a horizontal partition. The Pseudolamellibranchia included the oyster, scallop and their allies which formerly constituted the order Monomyaria, having only a single large adductor muscle or in addition a very small anterior adductor. The researches of W. G. Ridewood have shown that in gill-structure the Pectinacea agree with the Filibranchia and the Ostraeacea with the Eulamellibranchia, and accordingly the order Pseudolamellibranchia is now suppressed and its members divided between the two other orders mentioned. The four orders now retained exhibit successive stages in the modification of the ctenidia by reflection and concrescence of the filament, but other organs, such as the heart, adductors, renal organs, may not show corresponding stages. On the contrary considerable differences in these organs may occur within any single order. The Protobranchia, however, possess several primitive characters besides that of the branchiae. In them the foot has a flat ventral surface used for creeping, as in Gastropods, the byssus gland is but slightly developed, the pleural ganglia are distinct, there is a relic of the pharyngeal cavity, in some forms with a pair of glandular sacs, the gonads retain their primitive connexion with the renal cavities, and the otocysts are open.

Order I. Protobranchia

In addition to the characters given above, it may be noted that the mantle is provided with a hypobranchial gland on the outer side of each gill, the auricles are muscular, the kidneys are glandular through their whole length, the sexes are separate.

Fam. 1. *Solenomyidae*.—One row of branchial filaments is directed dorsally, the other ventrally; the mantle has a long postero-ventral suture and a single posterior aperture; the labial palps of each side are fused together; shell elongate; hinge without teeth; periostracum thick. *Solenomya*.

Fam. 2. *Nuculidae*.—Labial palps free, very broad, and provided with a posterior appendage; branchial filaments transverse; shell has an angular dorsal border; mantle open along its whole border. *Nucula*. *Acila*. *Pronucula*.

Fam. 3. *Ledidae*.—Like the *Nuculidae*, but mantle has two posterior sutures and two united siphons. *Leda*. *Yoldia*. *Malletia*.

[illegible]—Extinct; Silurian.

[illegible] Palaeoconcha is connected with the Proto- [illegible]. It contains the following extinct [illegible]

[illegible]—Shell equivalve with hinge dentition as in [illegible] Silurian and Devonian.

[illegible]—Shell inequivalve. *Antipleura*; Silurian.

[illegible] Shell equivalve and ventricose; hinge [illegible]. Silurian and Devonian.

[illegible]—Shell thin, equivalve, oval or elongate; [illegible] *Grammysia*; Silurian and Devonian. [illegible] *Cardiomorpha*; Silurian to Carbon- [illegible]

[illegible]—Shell very inequivalve; hinge without teeth.

[illegible]—Shell equivalve, greatly elongated, um- [illegible]. *Solenopsis*; Devonian to Trias.

Order II. Filibranchia

[illegible] ventrally directed and reflected, connected by [illegible]. Foot generally provided with a highly [illegible] apparatus.

Sub-order I.—*Anomiacea.*

[illegible] with a single large posterior adductor. The [illegible] the pericardium, lies dorsad of the rectum [illegible] anteriorly. The reflected borders of the [illegible] are fused together in the middle line. [illegible] kidneys and the right gonad extends into [illegible] animal fixed.

[illegible]—Foot small; inferior (right) valve of adult [illegible] passage of the byssus. *Anomia*; byssus [illegible] British. *Placuna*; byssus atrophied in [illegible]. *Ephippium*. *Placunanomia*.

Sub-order II.—*Arcacea.*

[illegible] open throughout its extent; generally with [illegible] and posterior adductors. The heart lies in [illegible] of two aortae. Gills without inter- [illegible] renal and genital apertures separate.

[illegible] of the mantle bear compound pallial [illegible] direct continuations of the lips. [illegible] it has numerous teeth on either [illegible] the teeth are perpendicular to the edge. [illegible] British. *Pectunculus*; foot without [illegible]; freshwater; India. *Argina*. [illegible] *Anadara*. *Adacnarca*.

[illegible]—Shell as in *Arca*, but the posterior [illegible] parallel to the cardinal border. [illegible] from the Jurassic. All the other [illegible]; Devonian to Tertiary. *Cur-* [illegible]

[illegible] orbicular, hinge curved, ligament [illegible] antero-posteriorly; foot elongate, [illegible] posteriorly. *Limopsis*. *Trinacria*; [illegible]

[illegible]—Shell thin, very inequilateral, anterior part [illegible] *Philobrya*.

[illegible]; shell equivalve and inequi- [illegible]; Silurian and Devonian. [illegible]; Silurian.

[illegible] foot elongated, pointed in [illegible] border sharp; byssus absent. *Tri-* [illegible] directed backwards. [illegible] in the Secondary epoch, especially [illegible] six living species, all in Australian [illegible] first discovered in 1827. *Schiz-* [illegible] Trias.

[illegible] shell inequilateral, posterior [illegible] teeth in form of a fan. *Lyrodesma*; [illegible]

Sub-order III.—*Mytilacea.*

[illegible] small or absent. Heart gives [illegible] gills smooth, gill-filaments all [illegible] Gonads generally extend into [illegible] linguiform and byssiferous. [illegible] anterior end short; [illegible] Mantle has a posterior [illegible] British. *Modiola*; [illegible] British. *Crenella*. *Stavelia*.

[illegible] Silurian to Cretaceous; ad- [illegible] *Modiomorpha*. *Myo-* [illegible]

[illegible]; ligament sub- [illegible] adductor absent. [illegible] *Bakevellia*. *Gervilleia*; [illegible]

Sub-order IV.—*Pectinacea.*

Monomyarian, with open mantle. Gills folded and the filaments at summits and bases of the folds are different from the others. Gonads contained in the visceral mass and generally open into renal cavities. Foot usually rudimentary.

Fam. 1. *Vulsellidae.*—Shell high; hinge toothless; foot without byssus. *Vulsella*.

Fam. 2. *Aviculidae.*—Shell very inequilateral; cardinal border straight with two auriculae, the posterior the longer. Foot with a very stout byssus. Gills fused to the mantle. *Avicula*; British. *Meleagrina*. Pearls are obtained from a species of this genus in the Persian Gulf, Indian Ocean, &c. *Malleus*. Several extinct genera.

Fam. 3. *Prasinidae.*—Shell inequilateral, with anterior umbones and prominent antérior auricula; cardinal border arched. *Prasina*.

Fam. 4. *Pterinoidae.*—Extinct; Palaeozoic.

Fam. 5. *Lunulicardiidae.*—Extinct; Silurian and Devonian.

Fam. 6. *Conocardiidae.*—Extinct; Silurian to Carboniferous.

Fam. 7. *Ambonychiidae.*—Extinct; Silurian and Devonian. The last two families are dimyarian, with small anterior adductor.

Fam. 8. *Myalinidae.*—Extinct; Silurian to Cretaceous; adductors sub-equal.

Fam. 9. *Amussiidae.*—Shell orbicular, smooth externally with radiating costae internally. Gills without interlamellar junctions. *Amussium*.

Fam. 10. *Spondylidae.*—Shell very inequivalve, fixed by the right valve which is the larger. No byssus. *Spondylus*; shell with spiny ribs, adherent by the spines. *Plicatula*.

Fam. 11. *Pectinidae.*—Shell with radiating ribs; dorsal border with two auriculae. Foot byssiferous. Mantle borders with well developed eyes. *Pecten*; shell orbicular, with equal auriculae; without a byssal sinus; British. *Chlamys*; anterior auricula the larger and with a byssal sinus; British. *Pedum*. *Hinnites*. *Pseudamussium*. *Camptonectes*. *Hyalopecten*; abyssal.

Sub-order V.—*Dimyacea.*

Dimyarian, with orbicular and almost equilateral shell; adherent; hinge without teeth and ligament internal. Gills with free non-reflected filaments.

Fam. *Dimyidae.*—Characters of the sub-order. *Dimya*; recent in abyssal depths and fossil since the Jurassic.

Order III. Eulamellibranchia

Edges of the mantle generally united by one or two sutures. Two adductors usually present. Branchial filaments united by vascular interfilamentar junctions and vascular interlamellar junctions; the latter contain the afferent vessels. The gonads always have their own proper external apertures.

Sub-order I.—*Ostraeacea.*

Monomyarian or with a very small anterior adductor. Mantle open; foot rather small, branchiae folded; shell inequivalve.

Fam. 1. *Limidae.*—Shell with auriculae. Foot digitiform, with byssus. Borders of mantle with long and numerous tentacles. Gills not united with mantle. *Lima*; members of this genus form a nest by means of the byssus, or swim by clapping the valves of the shell together. *Limaea*.

Fam. 2. *Ostraeidae.*—Foot much reduced and without byssus. Heart usually on the ventral side of the rectum. Gills fused to the mantle. Shell irregular, fixed in the young by the left and larger valve. *Ostraea*; foot absent in the adult; edible and cultivated; some species, as the British *O. edulis*, are hermaphrodite.

Fam. 3. *Eligmidae.*—Extinct; Jurassic.

Fam. 4. *Pinnidae.*—Shell elongated, truncated and gaping posteriorly. Dimyarian, with a very small anterior adductor. Foot with byssus. *Pinna*; British. *Cyrtopinna*. *Aviculopinna*; fossil, Carboniferous and Permian. *Pinnigena*; Jurassic and Cretaceous. *Atrina*; fossil and recent, from Carboniferous to present day.

Sub-order II.—*Submytilacea.*

Mantle only slightly closed; usually there is only a single suture. Siphons absent or very short. Gills smooth. Nearly always dimyarian. Shell equivalve, with an external ligament.

Fam. 1. *Dreissensiidae.*—Shell elongated; hinge without teeth; summits of valves with an internal septum. Siphons short. *Dreissensia*; lives in fresh water, but originated from the Caspian Sea; introduced into England about 1824.

Fam. 2. *Modiolarcidae.*—Foot with a plantar surface; the two branchial plates serve as incubatory pouches. *Modiolarca*.

Fam. 3. *Astartidae.*—Shell concentrically striated; foot elongate, without byssus. *Astarte*; British. *Woodia*. *Opis*; Secondary. *Prosocoelus*; Devonian.

Fam. 4. *Crassatellidae*.—Shell thick, with concentric striae, ligament external; foot short. *Crassatella*. *Cuna*.

Fam. 5. *Carditidae*.—Shell thick, with radiating costae; foot carinated, often byssiferous. *Cardita*. *Thecalia*. *Milneria*. *Venericardia*.

Fam. 6. *Condylocardiidae*.—Like *Carditidae*, but with an external ligament. *Condylocardia*. *Carditella*. *Carditopsis*.

Fam. 7. *Cyprinidae*.—Mantle open in front, with two pallial sutures; external gill-plates smaller than the internal. *Cyprina*; British. *Cypricardia*. *Pleurophorus*; Devonian to Trias. *Anisocardia*; Jurassic to Tertiary. *Veniella*; Cretaceous to Tertiary.

Fam. 8. *Isocardiidae*.—Mantle largely closed, pedal orifice small; gill-plates of equal size; shell globular, with prominent and coiled umbones. *Isocardia*; British.

Fam. 9. *Callocardiidae*.—Siphons present; external gill-plate smaller than the internal; umbones not prominent. *Callocardia*; abyssal.

Fam. 10. *Lucinidae*.—Labial palps very small; gills without an external plate. *Lucina*; British. *Montacuta*; British. *Cryptodon*.

Fam. 11. *Corbidae*.—Shell thick, with denticulated borders; anal aperture with valve but no siphon; foot elongated and pointed. *Corbis*. *Gonodon*; Trias and Jurassic. *Mutiella*; Upper Cretaceous.

Fam. 12. *Ungulinidae*.—Foot greatly elongated, vermiform, ending in a glandular enlargement. *Ungulina*. *Diplodonta*; British. *Axinus*; British.

Fam. 13. *Cyrenellidae*.—Two elongated, united, non-retractile siphons; freshwater. *Cyrenella*. *Joanisiella*.

Fam. 14. *Tancrediidae*.—Shell elongate, sub-triangular. Extinct. *Tancredia*; Trias to Cretaceous. *Meekia*; Cretaceous.

Fam. 15. *Unicardiidae*.—Shell sub-orbicular, nearly equilateral, with concentric striae. Extinct, Carboniferous to Cretaceous. *Unicardium*. *Scaldia*. *Pseudedmondia*.

Fam. 16. *Leptonidae*.—Shell thin; no siphons; foot long and byssiferous; marine; hermaphrodite and incubatory. *Kellya*; British. *Lepton*; commensal with the Crustacean *Gebia*; British. *Erycina*; Tertiary. *Pythina*. *Scacchia*. *Sportella*. *Cyamium*.

Fam. 17. *Galeommidae*.—Mantle reflected over shell; shell thin, gaping; adductors much reduced. *Galeomma*; British. *Scintilla*. *Hindsiella*. *Ephippodonta*; commensal with shrimp *Axius*. The three following genera with an internal shell probably belong to this family:—*Chlamydoconcha*. *Scioberetia*; commensal with a Spatangid. *Entovalva*; parasitic in *Synapta*.

Fam. 18. *Kellyellidae*.—Shell ovoid; anal aperture with very short siphon; foot elongated. *Kellyella*. *Turtonia*; British. *Allopagus*; Eocene. *Lutetia*; Eocene.

Fam. 19. *Cyrenidae*.—Two siphons, more or less united, with papillose orifices; pallial line with a sinus; freshwater. *Cyrena*. *Corbicula*. *Batissa*. *Velorita*. *Galatea*. *Fischeria*.

FIG. 28.—Lateral view of a *Mactra*, the right valve of the shell and right mantle-flap removed, and the siphons retracted. (From Gegenbaur.)

br, *br'*, Outer and inner gill-plates.
l, Labial tentacle.
ts, *tr*, Upper and lower siphons
ms, Siphonal muscle of the mantle-flap.
ma Anterior adductor muscle.
mp, Posterior adductor muscle.
p, Foot.
c, Umbo.

Fam. 20. *Cycladidae*.—One siphon or two free siphons with simple orifices; pallial line simple; hermaphrodite, embryos incubated in external gill-plate; freshwater, *Cyclas*; British. *Pisidium*; British.

Fam. 21. *Rangiidae*.—Two short siphons; shell with prominent umbones and internal ligament. *Rangia*; brackish water, Florida.

Fam. 22. *Cardiniidae*.—Shell elongated, inequilateral. Extinct. *Cardinia*; Trias and Jurassic. *Anthracosia*; Carboniferous and Permian. *Anoplophora*; Trias. *Pachycardia*; Trias.

Fam. 23. *Megalodontidae*.—Shell inequilateral, thick; posterior adductor impression on a myophorous apophysis. Extinct. *Megalodon*; Devonian to Jurassic. *Pachyrisma*; Trias and Jurassic. *Durga*; Jurassic. *Dicerocardium*; Jurassic.

Fam. 24. *Unionidae*.—Shell equilateral; mantle with a single pallial suture and no siphons; freshwater; larva a glochidium. *Unio*; British. *Anodonta*; British. *Pseudodon*. *Quadrula*. *Arconaia*. *Monocondylea*. *Solenaia*. *Mycetopus*.

Fam. 25. *Mutelidae*.—Differs from *Unionidae* in having two pallial sutures; freshwater. *Mutela*. *Pliodon*. *Spatha*. *Iridina*. *Hyria*. *Castalia*. *Aplodon*. *Plagiodon*.

Fam. 26. *Aetheriidae*.—Shell irregular, generally fixed in the adult; foot absent; freshwater. *Aetheria*. *Mulleria*. *Bartlettia*.

Sub-order III.—*Tellinacea*.

Mantle not extensively closed; two pallial sutures and two well-developed siphons. Gills smooth. Foot compressed and elongated. Labial palps very large. Dimyarian; pallial line with a deep sinus.

Fam. 1. *Tellinidae*.—External gill-plate directed upwards; siphons separate and elongated; foot with byssus; palps very large; ligament external. *Tellina*; British. *Gastrana*; British. *Capsa*. *Macoma*.

Fam. 2. *Scrobiculariidae*.—External gill-plates directed upwards; siphons separate and excessively long; foot without byssus. *Scrobicularia*; estuarine; British. *Syndosmya*; British. *Cumingia*.

Fam. 3. *Donacidae*.—External gill-plate directed ventrally; siphons separate, of moderate length, anal siphon the longer. *Donax*; British. *Iphigeneia*.

Fam. 4. *Mesodesmatidae*.—External gill-plate directed ventrally; siphons separate and equal. *Mesodesma*. *Ervilia*; British.

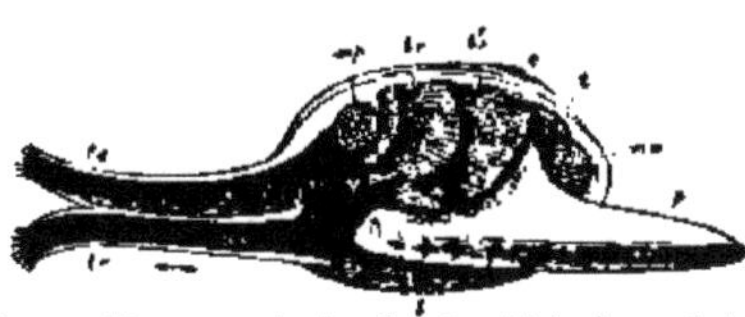

FIG. 29.—The same animal as fig. 28, with its foot and siphons expanded. Letters as in fig. 28. (From Gegenbaur.)

Fam. 5. *Cardiliidae*.—Shell very high and short; dimyarian; posterior adductor impression on a prominent apophysis. *Cardilia*.

Fam. 6. *Mactridae*.—External gill-plate directed ventrally; siphons united, invested by a chitinous sheath; foot long, bent at an angle, without byssus. *Mactra*; British (figs. 28, 29). *Mulinia*. *Harvella*. *Raeta*. *Eastonia*. *Heterocardia*. *Vanganella*.

Sub-order IV.—*Veneracea*.

Two pallial sutures, siphons somewhat elongated and partially or wholly united. Gills slightly folded. A bulb on the posterior aorta. Ligament external.

Fam. 1. *Veneridae*.—Foot well developed; pallial sinus shallow or absent. *Venus*; British. *Dosinia*; British. *Tapes*; British. *Cyclina*. *Lucinopsis*; British. *Meretrix*. *Circe*; British. *Venerupis*.

Fam. 2. *Petricolidae*.—Boring forms with a reduced foot; shell elongated, with deep pallial sinus. *Petricola*. *P. pholadiformis*, originally an inhabitant of the coast of the United States, has been acclimatized for some years in the North Sea.

Fam. 3. *Glaucomyidae*.—Siphons very long and united; foot small; shell thin, with deep pallial sinus; fresh or brackish water. *Glaucomya*. *Tanysiphon*.

Sub-order V.—*Cardiacea*.

Two pallial sutures. Siphons generally short. Foot cylindrical, more or less elongated, byssogenous. Gills much folded. Shell equivalve, with radiating costae and external ligament.

Fam. 1. *Cardiidae*.—Mantle slightly closed; siphons very short, surrounded by papillae which often bear eyes; foot very long, geniculated; pallial line without sinus; two adductors. *Cardium*; British. *Pseudo-kellya*. *Byssocardium*; Eocene. *Lithocardium*; Eocene.

Fam. 2. *Limnocardiidae*.—Siphons very long, united throughout; shell gaping; two adductors; brackish waters. *Limnocardium*; Caspian Sea and fossil from the Tertiary. *Archicardium*; Tertiary.

Fam. 3. *Tridacnidae*.—Mantle closed to a considerable extent; apertures distant from each other; no siphons; a single adductor; shell thick. *Tridacna*. *Hippopus*.

Sub-order VI.—*Chamacea*.

Asymmetrical, inequivalve, fixed, with extensive pallial sutures; no siphons. Two adductors. Foot reduced and without byssus. Shell thick, without pallial sinus.

Fam. 1. *Chamidae*.—Shell with sub-equal valves and prominent umbones more or less spirally coiled; ligament external. *Chama*. *Diceras*; Jurassic. *Requienia*; Cretaceous. *Matheronia*; Cretaceous.

Fam. 2. *Caprinidae*.—Shell inequivalve; fixed valve spiral or conical; free valve coiled or spiral; Cretaceous. *Caprina*. *Caprotina*. *Caprinula*, &c.

Fam. 3. *Monopleuridae*.—Shell very inequivalve; fixed valve conical or spiral; free valve operculiform; Cretaceous. *Monopleuron*. *Baylea*. The two following families, together known as Rudistae, are closely allied to the preceding; they are extinct marine forms from Secondary deposits. They were fixed by the

Fam. 4. *Clen*
The fossil g
branchia throu
families.
Fam. 1. *Pr*
Arca, *Pra*
Fam. 2. *Ar*
Fam. 3. *Ca*
without t
Fam. 4. *Gr*
hinge wi
Prolomya
iferous.
Fam. 5. *Vl*
Vlasta; S
Fam. 6. *Sc*
bones ve

Gill-filame
ciliated jun
developed b

Very asyn
heart is not
and gives of
inner gill-pla
The gonads
the mantle.
Fam. 1.
perforat
large a
adult.

Symmetri
well develop
the pericar
lamellar jun
Fam. 1.
eyes.
Hinge
side of
Arca;
byssus;
Bathyar
Fam. 2.
hinge
Cucullae
genera
bonaria;
Fam. 3.
longer
pointed
Tertiary
Fam. 4. *Pl*
atrophie
Fam. 5. *C*
lateral,
Cypricar
Fam. 6. *T*
front an
gonia;
This gen
in Juras
seas. Li
odus; Pe
Fam. 7. *L*
side shor
Silurian.

Symmetrica
off only an an
similar, with i
mantle and op
Fam. 1. *M*
hinge wit
suture.
British.
Dacrydium
Fam. 2. *Mc*
ductor mu
concha.
Fam. 3. *Pe*
divided;
Perna. *C*
Trias to
to Cretace

[illegible] [illegible] [illegible] prolonged backwards into a calcareous tube [illegible] [illegible] *Clavagella*. *Brechites* (*Aspergillum*). [illegible]—Foot byssiferous; siphons short, in- [illegible] British. *Entodesma*. *Mytilimeria*. [illegible]—Siphons short, gills papillose; foot [illegible] Many species abyssal. *Verticordia*. [illegible] *Halicardia*.

Order IV. Septibranchia

[illegible] their respiratory function, and are transformed [illegible] septum on each side between mantle and foot. [illegible] at considerable depths, and are carnivorous.

[illegible] [illegible]*idae*.—Siphons short and separate; branchial [illegible] a large valve; branchial septum bears two groups [illegible] on either side; hermaphrodite. *Poromya*; British. [illegible] *Liopistha*; Cretaceous.

[illegible] [illegible]*rachidae*.—Branchial septum with three groups of [illegible] each side; siphons short, separate, branchial siphon [illegible] *Cetoconcha* (*Silenia*).

[illegible] 3. *Cuspidariidae*.—Branchial septum with four or five pairs [illegible] narrow symmetrical orifices; siphons long, united, their [illegible] surrounded by tentacles; sexes separate. *Cuspi-* [illegible] British.

[illegible]—T. Barrois, "Le Stylet crystallin des Lamelli- [illegible] *Revue biol. Nord France*, i. (1890); Jameson, "On the [illegible] Pearls," *Proc. Zool. Soc.* (London, 1902); R. H. Peck, [illegible] Minute Structure of the Gills of Lamellibranch Mollusca," [illegible] *Micr. Sci.* xvii. (1877); W. G. Ridewood, "On the [illegible] of the Gills of the Lamellibranchia," *Phil. Trans. B.* cxcv. [illegible] K. Mitsukuri, "On the Structure and Significance of some [illegible] forms of Lamellibranchiate Gills," *Quart. Journ. Micr. Sci.* [illegible]; A. H. Cooke, "Molluscs," *Cambridge Natural History*, [illegible]; Paul Pelseneer, "Mollusca," *Treatise on Zoology*, edited by [illegible] Ray Lankester, pt. v. (E. R. L.; J. T. C.)

LAMENNAIS, HUGUES FÉLICITÉ ROBERT DE (1782–1854), French priest, and philosophical and political writer, was born at Saint Malo, in Brittany, on the 19th of June 1782. He was the son of a shipowner of Saint Malo ennobled by Louis XVI. for public services, and was intended by his father to follow mercantile pursuits. He spent long hours in the library of an uncle, devouring the writings of Rousseau, Pascal and others. He thereby acquired a vast and varied, though superficial, erudition, which determined his subsequent career. Of a sickly and sensitive nature, and impressed by the horrors of the French Revolution, his mind was early seized with a morbid view of life, and this temper characterized him throughout all his changes of opinion and circumstance. He was at first inclined towards rationalistic views, but partly through the influence of his brother Jean Marie (1775–1861), partly as a result of his philosophical and historical studies, he felt belief to be indispensable to action and saw in religion the most powerful leaven of the community. He gave utterance to these convictions in the *Réflexions sur l'état de l'église en France pendant le 18ème siècle et sur sa situation actuelle*, published anonymously in Paris in 1808. Napoleon's police seized the book as dangerously ideological, with its eager recommendation of religious revival and active clerical organization, but it awoke the ultramontane spirit which has since played so great a part in the politics of churches and of states.

As a rest from political strife, Lamennais devoted most of the following year to a translation, in exquisite French, of the *Speculum Monachorum* of Ludovicus Blosius (Louis de Blois) which he entitled *Le Guide spirituel* (1809). In 1811 he received the tonsure and shortly afterwards became professor of mathematics in an ecclesiastical college founded by his brother at Saint Malo. Soon after Napoleon had concluded the Concordat with Pius VII. he published, in conjunction with his brother, *De la tradition de l'église sur l'institution des évêques* (1814), a writing occasioned by the emperor's nomination of Cardinal Maury to the archbishopric of Paris, in which he strongly condemned the Gallican principle which allowed bishops to be created irrespective of the pope's sanction. He was in Paris at the first Bourbon restoration in 1814, which he hailed with satisfaction, less as a monarchist than as a strenuous apostle of religious regeneration. Dreading the *Cent Jours*, he escaped to London, where he obtained a meagre livelihood by giving French lessons in a school founded by the abbé Jules Carron for French émigrés;

he also became tutor at the house of Lady Jerningham, whose first impression of him as an imbecile changed into friendship. On the final overthrow of Napoleon in 1815 he returned to Paris, and in the following year, with many misgivings as to his calling, he yielded to his brother's and Carron's advice, and was ordained priest by the bishop of Rennes.

The first volume of his great work, *Essai sur l'indifférence en matière de religion*, appeared in 1817 (Eng. trans. by Lord Stanley of Alderley, London, 1898), and affected Europe like a spell, investing, in the words of Lacordaire, a humble priest with all the authority once enjoyed by Bossuet. Lamennais denounced toleration, and advocated a Catholic restoration to belief. The right of private judgment, introduced by Descartes and Leibnitz into philosophy and science, by Luther into religion and by Rousseau and the Encyclopaedists into politics and society, had, he contended, terminated in practical atheism and spiritual death. Ecclesiastical authority, founded on the absolute revelation delivered to the Jewish people, but supported by the universal tradition of all nations, he proclaimed to be the sole hope of regenerating the European communities. Three more volumes (Paris, 1818–1824) followed, and met with a mixed reception from the Gallican bishops and monarchists, but with the enthusiastic adhesion of the younger clergy. The work was examined by three Roman theologians, and received the formal approval of Leo XII. Lamennais visited Rome at the pope's request, and was offered a place in the Sacred College, which he refused. On his return to France he took a prominent part in political work, and together with Chateaubriand, the vicomte de Villèle, was a regular contributor to the *Conservateur*, but when Villèle became the chief of the supporters of absolute monarchy, Lamennais withdrew his support and started two rival organs, *Le Drapeau blanc* and *Le Mémorial catholique*. Various other minor works, together with *De la religion considérée dans ses rapports avec l'ordre civil et politique* (2 vols., 1825–1826), kept his name before the public.

He retired to La Chênaie and gathered round him a host of brilliant disciples, including C. de Montalembert, Lacordaire and Maurice de Guérin, his object being to form an organized body of opinion to persuade the French clergy and laity to throw off the yoke of the state connexion. With Rome at his back, as he thought, he adopted a frank and bold attitude in denouncing the liberties of the Gallican church. His health broke down and he went to the Pyrenees to recruit. On his return to La Chênaie in 1827 he had another dangerous illness, which powerfully impressed him with the thought that he had only been dragged back to life to be the instrument of Providence. *Les Progrès de la révolution et de la guerre contre l'église* (1828) marked Lamennais's complete renunciation of royalist principles, and henceforward he dreamt of the advent of a theocratic democracy. To give effect to these views he founded *L'Avenir*, the first number of which appeared on the 16th of October 1830, with the motto "God and Liberty." From the first the paper was aggressively democratic; it demanded rights of local administration, an enlarged suffrage, universal freedom of conscience, freedom of instruction, of meeting, and of the press. Methods of worship were to be criticized, improved or abolished in absolute submission to the spiritual, not to the temporal authority. With the help of Montalembert, he founded the *Agence générale pour la défense de la liberté religieuse*, which became a far-reaching organization, it had agents all over the land who noted any violations of religious freedom and reported them to headquarters. As a result, *L'Avenir's* career was stormy, and the opposition of the Conservative bishops checked its circulation; Lamennais, Montalembert and Lacordaire resolved to suspend it for a while, and they set out to Rome in November 1831 to obtain the approval of Gregory XVI. The "pilgrims of liberty" were, after much opposition, received in audience by the pope, but only on the condition that the object which brought them to Rome should not be mentioned. This was a bitter disappointment to such earnest ultramontanes, who received, a few days after the audience, a letter from Cardinal Pacca, advising their departure from Rome and suggesting that the Holy See, whilst admitting the justice of their intentions, would like the matter left open for the present. Lacordaire and Montalembert obeyed; Lamennais, however, remained in Rome, but his last hope vanished with the issue of Gregory's letter to the Polish bishops, in which the Polish patriots were reproved and the tsar was affirmed to be their lawful sovereign. He then "shook the dust of Rome from off his feet." At Munich, in 1832, he received the encyclical *Mirari vos*, condemning his policy; as a result *L'Avenir* ceased and the *Agence* was dissolved.

Lamennais, with his two lieutenants, submitted, and deeply wounded, retired to La Chênaie. His genius and prophetic insight had turned the entire Catholic church against him, and those for whom he had fought so long were the fiercest of his opponents. The famous *Paroles d'un croyant*, published in 1834 through the intermediary of Sainte-Beuve, marks Lamennais's severance from the church. "A book, small in size, but immense in its perversity," was Gregory's criticism in a new encyclical letter. A tractate of aphorisms, it has the vigour of a Hebrew prophecy and contains the choicest gems of poetic feeling lost in a whirlwind of exaggerations and distorted views of kings and rulers. The work had an extraordinary circulation and was translated into many European languages. It is now forgotten as a whole, but the beautiful appeals to love and human brotherhood are still reprinted in every hand-book of French literature.

Henceforth Lamennais was the apostle of the people alone. *Les Affaires de Rome, des maux de l'église et de la société* (1837) came from old habit of religious discussions rather than from his real mind of 1837, or at most it was but a last word. *Le Livre du peuple* (1837), *De l'esclavage moderne* (1839), *Politique à l'usage du peuple* (1839), three volumes of articles from the journal of the extreme democracy, *Le Monde*, are titles of works which show that he had arrived among the missionaries of liberty, equality and fraternity, and he soon got a share of their martyrdom. *Le Pays et le gouvernement* (1840) caused him a year's imprisonment. He struggled through difficulties of lost friendships, limited means and personal illnesses, faithful to the last to his hardly won dogma of the sovereignty of the people, and, to judge by his contribution to Louis Blanc's *Revue du progrès* was ready for something like communism. He was named president of the "Société de la solidarité républicaine," which counted half a million adherents in fifteen days. The Revolution of 1848 had his sympathies, and he started *Le Peuple constituant*; however, he was compelled to stop it on the 10th of July, complaining that silence was for the poor, but again he was at the head of *La Révolution démocratique et sociale*, which also succumbed. In the constituent assembly he sat on the left till the *coupe d'état* of Napoleon III. in 1851 put an end to all hopes of popular freedom. While deputy he drew up a constitution, but it was rejected as too radical. Thereafter a translation of Dante chiefly occupied him till his death, which took place in Paris on the 27th of February 1854. He refused to be reconciled to the church, and was buried according to his own directions at Père La Chaise without funeral rites, being mourned by a countless concourse of democratic and literary admirers.

During the most difficult time of his republican period he found solace for his intellect in the composition of *Une voix de prison*, written during his imprisonment in a similar strain to *Les paroles d'un croyant*. This is an interesting contribution to the literature of captivity; it was published in Paris in 1846. He also wrote *Esquisse de philosophie* (1840). Of the four volumes of this work the third, which is an exposition of art as a development from the aspirations and necessities of the temple, stands pre-eminent, and remains the best evidence of his thinking power and brilliant style.

There are two so-called *Œuvres complètes de Lamennais*, the first in 10 volumes (Paris, 1836–1837), and the other in 10 volumes (Paris, 1844); both these are very incomplete and only contain the works mentioned above. The most noteworthy of his writings subsequently published are: *Amschaspands et Darvands* (1843), *Le Devil de la Pologne* (1846), *Mélanges philosophiques et politiques* (1856), *Les Évangiles* (1846) and *La Divine Comédie*, these latter being translations of the Gospels and of Dante.

Part of his voluminous correspondence has also appeared. The most interesting volumes are the following: *Correspondance de F. de Lamennais*, edited by E. D. Forgues (2 vols., 1855–1858); *Œuvres inédites de F. Lamennais*, edited by Ange Blaize (2 vols., 1866); *Correspondance inédite entre Lamennais et le baron de Vitrolles*, edited by E. D. Forgues (1819–1853); *Confidences de Lamennais, lettres inédites de 1821 à 1848*, edited by A. du Bois de la Villerabel (1886); *Lamennais d'après des documents inédits*, by Alfred Roussel (Rennes, 2 vols., 1892), *Lamennais intime, d'après une correspondance inédite*, by A. Roussel (Rennes, 1897); *Un Lamennais inconnu*, edited by A. Laveille (1898); *Lettres de Lamennais à Montalembert*, edited by E. D. Forgues (1898), and many other letters published in the *Revue bleue*, *Revue britannique* &c.

A list of lives or studies on Lamennais would fill several columns. The following may be mentioned. A Blaize, *Essai biographique sur M. de Lamennais* (1858), E. D. Forgues *Notes et souvenirs* (1859); F. Brunetière, *Nouveaux essais sur la littérature contemporaine* (1893), E. Faguet, *Politiques et moralistes*, ii. (1898), P. Janet, *La Philosophie de Lamennais* (1890); P. Mercier, S.J., *Lamennais d'après sa correspondance et les travaux les plus récents* (1893), A Mollien et F. Duine, *Lamennais, sa vie et ses idées; Pages choisies* (Lyons, 1898); The Hon. W. Gibson, *The Abbé de Lammenais and the Liberal Catholic Movement in France* (London, 1896); E. Renan *Essais de morale et de critique* (1857); E. Schérer, *Mélanges de critique religieuse* (1859); G. E. Spuller, *Lamennais, étude d'histoire et de politique religieuse* (1892); Mgr. Ricard, *L'école menaisienne* (1882), and Sainte-Beuve, *Portraits contemporains*, tome i. (1832), and *Nouveaux Lundis*, tome i. p. 22; tome xi. p. 347.

LAMENTATIONS (*Lamentations of Jeremiah*), a book of the Old Testament. In Hebrew MSS. and editions this little collection of liturgical poems is entitled איכה *Ah how!*, the first word of ch. i. (and chs. ii., iv.); cf. the books of the Pentateuch, and the Babylonian Epic of Creation (a far older example). In the Septuagint it is called Θρῆνοι, "Funeral-songs" or "Dirges," the usual rendering of Heb. קינה (Am. v. 1; Jer. vii. 29; 2 Sam. i. 17), which is, in fact, the name in the Talmud (*Baba Bathra* 15*a*) and other Jewish writings; and it was known as such to the Fathers (Jerome, *Cinoth*). The Septuagint (B) introduces the book thus: "And it came to pass, after Israel was taken captive and Jerusalem laid waste, Jeremiah sat weeping, and lamented with this lamentation over Jerusalem, and said . . ." a notice which may have related originally to the first poem only. Some Septuagint MSS., and the Syriac and other versions, have the fuller title *Lamentations of Jeremiah*. In the Hebrew Bible Lamentations is placed among the *Cetubim* or Hagiographa, usually as the middle book of the five *Megilloth* or Ferial Rolls (Canticles, Ruth, Lamentations, Ecclesiastes, Esther) according to the order of the days on which they are read in the Synagogue, Lamentations being read on the 9th of Ab (6th of August), when the destruction of the Temple is commemorated (*Mass. Sopherim* 18). But the Septuagint appends the book to Jeremiah (*Baruch* intervening), just as it adds Ruth to Judges; thus making the number of the books in the Hebrew Canon the same as that of the letters of the Hebrew alphabet, viz. twenty-two (so Jos. c. Ap. i. 8), instead of the Synagogal twenty-four (see *Baba Bathra* 14*b*).

Special features and poetical structure.—These poems exhibit a peculiar metre, the so-called "limping verse," of which Am. v. 2 is a good instance:

"She is fállen, to ríse no móre—
Maid Isráël!
Left lórn upón her lánd—
none raising hér!"

A longer line, with three accented syllables, is followed by a shorter with two. Chs. i.-iii. consist of stanzas of three such couplets each, chs. iv. and v. of two like Am. v. 2. This metre [illegible] to be distinctive of elegy. The text of Lamentations, however, so often deviates from it, that we can only [illegible] a tendency of the poet to cast his couplets into this [illegible]. Some anomalies, both of metre and of sense, [illegible] removed by judicious emendation; and many lines [illegible] enough, if we assume a crasis of open vowels [illegible], or a diphthongal pronunciation of others, or [illegible] of certain suffixes as in Syriac. The oldest [illegible] are not couched in this metre; *e.g.* David's [illegible] i. 19-27 Saul and Jonathan). Yet the [illegible] *'ek nafĕlu 'ha gibbōrī*[illegible] heroes [illegible] longer line. [illegible] of this Hebrew metre may be recognised in the Babylonian epic of Gilgamesh, written at least a thousand years earlier:—

Ea-bâni ibri kuḍâni | *Nimru sha çêri*
"Eabani, my friend, my little brother! | Leopard of the Wild!"

and again:—

Kîki lúshut | *Kîki luqûl-ma*
Íbri shá arámmu | *Itémi ṭiṭṭish*
"How shall I be dumb? | How shall I bewail?
The friend whom I love | is turned to clay!"

Like a few of the Psalms, Lamentations i.-iv. are alphabetical acrostics. Each poem contains twenty-two stanzas, corresponding to the twenty-two letters of the Hebrew alphabet; and each stanza begins with its proper letter. (In ch. iii. each of the three couplets in a stanza begins with the same letter, so that the alphabet is repeated thrice: cf. Psalm cxix. for an eight-fold repetition.) The alphabet of Lamentations ii. iii. iv. varies from the usual order of the letters by placing *Pe* before *Ain*. The same was doubtless the case in ch. i. also until some scribe altered it. He went no further, because the sense forbade it in the other instances. The variation may have been one of local use, either in Judea or in Babylonia; or the author may have had some fanciful reason for the transposition, such as, for example, that *Pe* following *Samech* (ספ) might suggest the word ספדו, "Wail ye!" (2 Sam. iii. 31). Although the oldest Hebrew elegies are not alphabetic acrostics, it is a curious fact that the word הנבל, "Was he a coward?" (Sc. [illegible]; Is. vii. 4), is formed by the initial letters of the four lines on Abner (om. ו, line 3); and the initials of the verses of David's great elegy are [illegible], which may be read as a sentence meaning, perhaps, "Lo, I the Avenger" (cf. Deut. xxxii. 41, 43) "will go forth!"; or the first two letters (ה׳א׳) may stand for [illegible], "Alas, my brother!" (Jer. xxii. 18; cf. xxxiv. 5). In cryptic fashion the poet thus registers a vow of vengeance on the Philistines. Both kinds of acrostic occur side by side in the Psalms. Psalm cx., an acrostic of the same kind as David's elegy, is followed by Psalms cxi. cxii., which are alphabetical acrostics, like the Lamentations. Such artifices are not in themselves greater clogs on poetic expression than the excessive alliteration of old Saxon verse or the strict rhymes of modern lyrics. (Alliteration, both initial and internal, is common in Lamentations.)

As the final piece, ch. v. may have suffered more in transmission than those which precede it—even to the extent of losing the acrostic form (like some of the Psalms and Nahum i.), besides half of its stanzas. If we divide the chapter into quatrains, like ch. iv., we notice several vestiges of an acrostic. The *Aleph* stanza (verses 7, 8) still precedes the *Beth* (verses 9, 10), and the *Ain* is still quite clear (verses 17, 18; cf. i. 16). Transposing verses 5, 6, and correcting their text, we see that the *Jod* stanza (verses 3, 4) precedes the *Lamed* (verses 6, 5), *Caph* having disappeared between them. With this clue, we may rearrange the other quatrains in alphabetical sequence, each according to its initial letter. We thus get a broken series of eleven stanzas, beginning with the letters א (verses 7, 8), ב (9, 10), ה (21, 22), ו (19, cf. Psalm cii. 13; and 20), ז (1, 2), ח (13, בחורים; 14), י (3, 4), ל (6, [illegible]; 5, [illegible] . . . על), נ (11; 12), ע (17, 18), and ש (15, 16), successively. An internal connexion will now be apparent in all the stanzas.

General subject and outline of contents.—The theme of Lamentations is the final siege and fall of Jerusalem (586 B.C.), and the attendant and subsequent miseries of the Jewish people.

In ch. i. we have a vivid picture of the distress of Zion, after all is over. The poet does not describe the events of the siege, nor the horrors of the capture, but the painful experience of subjection and tyranny which followed. Neither this nor ch. ii. is strictly a "dirge." Zion is not dead. She is personified as a widowed princess, bereaved and desolate, sitting amid the ruins of her former joys, and brooding over her calamities. From verse 11*c* to the end (except verse 17) she herself is the speaker:—

"O come, ye travellers all!
Behold and see
If grief there be like mine!"

She images her sorrows under a variety of metaphors (cf. ch. iii. 1-18); ascribing all her woes to Yahweh's righteous wrath, provoked by her sins, and crying for vengeance on the malicious rivals who had rejoiced at her overthrow.

The text has suffered much. Verse 5c read: בשבי (v. 18), "into captivity," צרים (v. 7), "adversaries." For verse 7, see Budde, V. 14: נשקד, read נקשר, "was bound." Verse 19c read: כי בקשו אכל להשיב נפש ולא מצאו "For they sought food to restore life, and found it not:" cf. Septuagint; and verses 11, 16. Verse 20: the incongruous כי מרו מריתי, "For I grievously rebelled," should be נכמרו מעי, "My inwards burn"; Hos. xi. 8. Verses 21 f.: "All my foes heard, rejoiced That IT" (cf. Psalm ix. 13). "Thou didst. Bring Thou" (הבא אתה), "the Day Thou hast proclaimed; Let them become like me! Let the time" (עת; see Septuagint) "of their calamity come!"

Chapter ii.—"Ah how in wrath the Lord | Beclouds Bath-Sion!" The poet laments Yahweh's anger as the true cause which destroyed city and kingdom, suspended feast and Sabbath, rejected altar and sanctuary. He mentions the uproar of the victors in the Temple; the dismantling of the walls; the exile of king and princes (verses 1-9). He recalls the mourning in the doomed city; the children dying of hunger in the streets; the prophets deluding the people with vain hopes. Passers-by jeered at the fallen city; and all her enemies triumphed over her (verses 10-17). Sion is urged to cry to the Lord in protest against His pitiless work (verses 18-22).

Here too emendation is necessary. Verse 4a: הציב חצו, "He fixed His arrow," sc. on the string (Septuagint, ἐστερέωσεν); cf. Psalm xi. 2. Add at the end אפו (חמתו) כלה, "He spent His anger:" see iv. 11, Ezek. vii. 8, xx. 8, 21. Verse 6: ויפרץ גדר משכנו, "And He broke down the wall of His dwelling-place" (Septuagint τὸ σκήνωμα αὐτοῦ, cf. Psalm lxxxiv. 7f., where שכו follows, as here). Is. v 5, Psalms lxxx. 13, lxxxix. 41. Perhaps חרס, verses 2, 17. But Septuagint καὶ διεπέτασεν = ויפרש (i. 13, 17) = הרס (iv. 4) or even ויפרץ. Verse 9, perhaps: "He sunk (טבע) her gates in the ground,—He shattered her bars; He made her king and her princes wander (הניע, Jer. xxiii. 1)—Among the nations without Torah" (cf. Ezek. vii. 26 f.). Verse 18: "Cry much" (הרבי; or bitterly, מר, Zeph. i. 14) "unto the Lord, O Virgin Daughter of Zion!" Verse 19 is metrically redundant, and the last clauses do not agree with what follows. "For the life of thy children" was altered from "for what He hath done to thee" (על שעולל לך); and then the rest was added. The uniform gloom of this, the most dirge-like of all the pieces, is unrelieved by a single ray of hope, even the hope of vengeance, cf. chapters i. iii. iv. *ad fin.*

Chapter iii.—Here the nation is personified as a man (cf. Hos. xi. 1), who laments his own calamities. In view of i. 12-22, ii. 20-22, this is hardly a serious deviation from the strict form of elegy (*Klagelied*). Budde makes much of "the close external connexion with ch. ii." The truth is that the break is as great as between any two of these poems. Chapter ii. ends with a mother's lament over her slaughtered children; chapter iii. makes an entirely new beginning, with its abruptly independent "I am the Man!" The suppression of the Divine Name is intentional. Israel durst not breathe it, until compelled by the climax, verse 18: cf. Am. vi. 10. Contrast its frequency afterwards, when ground of hope is found in the Divine pity and purpose (verses 22-40), and when the contrite nation turns to its God in prayer (verses 55-66). The spiritual aspect of things is now the main topic. The poet deals less with incident, and more with the moral significance of the nation's sufferings. It is the religious culmination of the book. His poem is rather lyrical than narrative, which may account for some obscurities in the connexion of thought; but his alphabetic scheme proves that he *designed* twenty-two stanzas, not sixty-six detached couplets. There is something arresting in that bold "I am the Man"; and the lyrical intensity, the religious depth and beauty of the whole, may well blind us to occasional ruggedness of metre and language, abrupt transitions from figure to figure and other alleged blemishes, some of which may not have seemed such to the poet's contemporaries (*e.g.* the repetition of the acrostic word, far more frequent in Psalm cxix.); and some disappear on revision of the text.

Verse 5, perhaps: "He swallowed me up" (Jer. li. 34) "and begirt my head" (Septuagint) "with gloom" (אפלה Is. lviii. 10, cf. verse 6, yet cf. also תלאה, Neh. ix. 32). Verse 14: "all my people," rather *all peoples* (Heb. MSS. and Syr.). Verse 16b, rd. הפלשני, "He made me bore" (*i.e.* grovel) "in the ashes:" cf. Jer. vi. 26; Ezek. xxvii. 30. Verse 17a should be: ותזנח לעולם נפשי "And He cast off my soul for ever:" see verse 31; Psalm lxxxviii. 15. Verse 26: "It is good *to wait*" (לחיל) "*in silence*" (דומם Is. xlvii. 5); or "It is good *that he wait and be silent*" (כי יחיל ודמם; cf. verse 27). Verse 31, add נפשו, "his soul." The verse is a reply to 17a. Verses 34-36 render: "To crush under His feet . . . Adonai *purposed* not" (Gen. xx. 10; Psalm lxvi. 18). Verse 39, חי (Gen. v. 5; or חיה Neh. ix. 29) is the necessary second verb: "Why doth a mortal complain?" (or "What . . . lament?"). "Doth a man live by his sins?": Man "lives by" righteousness (Ezek. xxxiii. 19). For the wording, cf. Psalm lxxxix. 49. Verse 43a: "Thou didst encompass with" (rg. תסכה; Hos. xii. 1) "anger and pursue us." Syntax as verse 66a. Verse 49, rd. תגרה (cf. ii. 18 also). Verse 51: "Mine eye did hurt to herself" (לנפשה), "By weeping over my people." Verse 48 rh. i. 16; Jer. xxxi. 15. Verse 52: "They quelled my life in the pit" (Sheol; Psalms xxx. 4, lxxxviii. 4, 7; verse 55): "They *brought me down to Abaddon*" (ירדוני אבדון; cf. Psalm lxxxviii. 12). Verse 58: "O plead, Lord, the cause of my soul! O redeem my life!", cf. Psalm cxix. 154. If the prayer for vengeance begins here, Budde's "deep division in the middle of an acrostic letter-group" vanishes. Verse 59, rd. עותי, "my perverting," inf. pi. c. suff. obj.; cf. verse 36. Verse 61b repeated by mistake from 60b. Perhaps: "Wherewith they dogged my steps:" עקבו פעמי: Psalm lxxxix. 51 f. Verse 63, rd. קומם, as usual, and נגינתם, as in verse 14 and Job xxx. 9. Verse 65: "Thou wilt give them madness" (cf. Arab. *gunûn*; *magnûn*, mad) "of heart; Thou wilt curse and consume them!" (תאלם תכלם).

Chapter iv. "Ah, how doth gold grow dim,—
The finest ore change hue!"

The poet shows how famine and the sword desolated Zion (verses 1-10). All was Yahweh's work; a wonder to the heathen world, but accounted for by the crimes of prophets and priests (Jer xxiii. 11, 14, xxvi. 8, 20 ff., xxix. 21-23), who, like Cain, became homeless wanderers and outcasts (verses 11-16). Vainly did the besieged watch for succours from Egypt (Jer xxxvii. 5 ff.), and even the last forlorn hope, the flight of "Yahweh's Anointed," King Zedekiah, was doomed to fail (verses 17-20, Jer xxxix. 4 ff). Edom rejoiced in her ruin (Ezek. xxv 12, xxxv. 15, Obad.; Psalm cxxxvii. 7); but Zion's sin is now atoned for (cf Is. xl. 2), and she may look forward to the judgment of her foe (verses 21-22).

Verse 6d, perhaps: "And their ruin tarried not" (ולא חיל פידם), cf. Pro. xxiv. 22. Verse 7d: "Their body" (rd. גרמם) "was a sapphire:" see Ct. v. 14; Dn. x. 6. Verse 9: "Happier were the slain of the sword Than the slain of famine! For they" (Septuagint om.), "they passed away" (הלכו Septuagint; Psalm xxxix. 14) "with a stab" (Ju. ix. 54; Is. xiii. 15; Jer. li. 4), "Suddenly, in the field" (פתאם בש'; Jer xiv. 18). Verse 13, add היא after נביאיה; cf. Ju. xiv. 4; Jer. xxii. 16. Verse 17c: "While we watched" (Septuagint) "continually:" בצפותנו. Verse 18: "Our steps were curbed" (צרו MSS.; see Pro. iv. 12; Job xviii. 7) "from walking In our open places" (before the city gates: Neh. viii. 1, 3); "The completion of our days drew nigh" (קרב יום מלאת ימינו; cf. Lev. viii. 33; Job xx. 22), "For our end was come" (Ezek. vii. 2, 6, &c.). Verse 21, Septuagint om. Uz (dittogr. ?); "Settler in the Land!" (*i.e.* of Judah; cf. Ezek. xxxv. 10, xxxvi. 5. Perhaps יורשת הא' "Seizer of the Land").

Chapter v.—A sorrowful supplication, in which the speakers deplore, not the fall of Jerusalem, but their own state of galling dependence and hopeless poverty. They are still suffering for the sins of their fathers, who perished in the catastrophe (verse 7). They are at the mercy of "servants" (verse 8, cf 2 Kings xxv. 24; Neh. v. 15: "Yea, even their 'boys' lorded it over the people"), under a tyranny of pashas of the worst type (verses 11 f.). The soil is owned by aliens; and the Jews have to buy their water and firewood (verses 2, 4; cf. Neh. ix. 36 f.) While busy harvesting, they are exposed to the raids of the Bedouins (verse 9). Jackals prowl among the ruins of Zion (verse 18; cf. Neh. iv. 3).. And this condition of things has already lasted a very long time (verse 20).

Verses 5 f. transpose and read: "To adversaries" (לצרים) "we submitted, Saying" (לאמר), "'We shall be satisfied with bread'" (cf. Jer. xlii. 14); "The yoke of our neck they made heavy" (Neh. v. 15: הכבידו על העם), "We toil, and no rest is allowed us." Verse 13: "Nobles endured to grind, And princes staggered under logs" (חרים for בחורים, which belongs to verse 14; שרים for נערים. Eccl. x. 7; Is. xxxiv. 12; Neh. iv. 14;

v. 7; vi. 17). Verse 19, "But Thou . . ." Psalm cii. 13 ([illegible] fell out after preceding [illegible], verse 18). Verse 22, omit [illegible]; dittogr. of following [illegible].

Authorship and date.—The tradition of Jeremiah's authorship cannot be traced higher than the Septuagint version. The prefatory note there may come from a Hebrew MS., but perhaps refers to chapter i. only ("Jeremiah sang *this dirge*"). The idea that Lamentations was originally appended to Jeremiah in the Hebrew Canon, as it is in the old versions, and was afterwards separated from it and added to the other Megilloth for the liturgical convenience of the Synagogue, rests on the fact that Josephus (Ap. i. 1, 8) and, following him, Jerome and Origen reckon 22 books, taking Ruth with Judges and Lamentations with Jeremiah; whereas the ordinary Jewish reckoning gives 24 books, as in our Hebrew Bibles. There is no evidence that this artificial reckoning according to the number of letters in the Hebrew alphabet was ever much more than a fanciful suggestion. Even in the Septuagint the existing order may not be original. It appears likely that Lamentations was not translated by the same hand as Jeremiah (Nöldeke) Unlike the latter, the Septuagint Lamentations sticks closely to the Massoretic text. The two books can hardly have been united from the first. On the strength of 2 Chron. xxxv. 25, some ancient writers (*e.g.* Jerome *ad* Zech. xii. 11) held that Jeremiah composed Lamentations. When, however, Josephus (Ant. x. 5, 1) states that Jeremiah wrote an elegy on Josiah still extant in his day, he may be merely quoting a little too much of Chron. *loc. cit.*; and it is obvious that he need not mean our book (see Whiston's note). It is urged, indeed, that the author of Chronicles could not have imagined a prophet to have sympathized with such a king as Zedekiah so warmly as is implied by Lamentations iv. 20; and, therefore, he must have connected the passage with Josiah, the last of the good kings. However that may have been, the Chronicler neither says that Jeremiah wrote *all* the elegies comprised in *The Qinoth*, nor does he imply that the entire collection consisted of only five pieces. Rather, the contrary; for he implies that *The Qinoth* contained not only Jeremiah's single dirge on Josiah, but also the elegies of "all the singing men and singing women," from the time of Josiah's death (608) down to his own day (3rd century). The untimely fate of Josiah became a stock allusion in dirges. It is not meant that for three centuries the dirge-writers had nothing else to sing of; much less, that they sang of the fall of Jerusalem (presupposed by our book) before its occurrence. Upon the whole, it does not seem probable, either that the Chronicler mistook Lamentations iv. for Jeremiah's dirge on Josiah, or that the book he calls *The Qinoth* was identical with our Qinoth. Later writers misunderstood him, because—on the ground of certain obtrusive similarities between Jeremiah and Lamentations (see Driver, L.O.T. p. 433 f.), and the supposed reference in Lamentations iii. 53 ff. to Jeremiah xxxviii. 6 ff., as well as the fact that Jeremiah was the one well-known inspired writer who had lived through the siege of Jerusalem—they naturally enough ascribed this little book to the prophet. It is certainly true that the same emotional temperament, dissolving in tears at the spectacle of the country's woes, and expressing itself to a great extent in the same or similar language, is noticeable in the author(s) of Lamentations i.-iv. and in Jeremiah. And both refer these woes to the same cause, viz. the sins of the nation, and particularly of its prophets and priests.

This, however, is not enough to prove identity of authorship; and the following considerations militate strongly against the tradition. (i.) The language and style of Lamentations are in general very unlike those of Jeremiah (see the details in Nägelsbach and Löhr); whatever allowance may be made for conventional differences in the phraseology of elegiac poetry and prophetic prose, even of a more or less lyrical cast. (ii.) Lamentations i.-iv. show a knowledge of Ezekiel (cf. Lamentations ii. 4*c*; Ez. xx. 8, 21; Lam. ii. 14; Ez. xii. 24; xiii. 10, 14; Lam. ii. 15; Ez. xxvii. 3; xxviii. 12; Lam. iv. 20; Ez. xix. 4, 8) and of Is. xl.-lxvi. (Lam. i. 10, [illegible]; Is. lxiv. 10; Lam. i. 15; Is. lxiii. 2; Lam. ii. 1; Is. lxvi. 1; Lam. ii. 2*c*; Is. xliii. 28; Lam. ii. 13 *the 3 verbs*; Is. xl. 18, 25; Lam. ii. 15*c*; Is. lx. 15*b*; Lam. iii. 26 [illegible]; Is. xlvii. 5; Lam. iii. 30; Is. l. 6; Lam. iv. 14; Is. lix. 3, 10; Lam. iv. 15; Is. lii. 11; Lam. iv. 17*c*; Is. xlv. 20; Lam. iv. 22; Is. xl. 2). Jeremiah does not quote Ezekiel; and he could hardly have quoted writings of the age of Cyrus. (iii.) The coincidences of language between Lamentations and certain late Psalms, such as Psalms lxix., lxxiv., lxxx., lxxxviii., lxxxix., cxix., are numerous and significant, at least as a general indication of date. (iv.) The point of view of Lamentations sometimes differs from that of the prophet. This need not be the case in i. 21 f. where the context shows that the "enemies" are not the Chaldeans, but Judah's ill neighbours, Edom, Ammon, Moab and the rest (cf. iv. 21 f.; iii. 59-66 may refer to the same foes). Ch. ii. 9*c* may refer to popular prophecy ("*her* prophets"; cf. verse 14), which would naturally be silenced by the overwhelming falsification of its comfortable predictions (iv. 14 ff.; cf. Jer. xiv. 13; Ezek. vii. 26 f.; Psalm lxxiv. 9). But though Jeremiah was by no means disloyal (Jer. xxxiv. 4 f.), he would hardly have spoken of Zedekiah in the terms of Lam. iv. 20; and the prophet never looked to Egypt for help, as the poet of iv. 17 appears to have done. It must be admitted that Lamentations exhibits, upon the whole, "a poet (more) in sympathy with the old life of the nation, whose attitude towards the temple and the king is far more popular than Jeremiah's" (W. Robertson Smith); cf. i. 4, 10, 19, ii. 6, 7, 20*c*. (v.) While we find in Lamentations some things that we should not have expected from Jeremiah, we miss other things characteristic of the prophet. There is no trace of his confident faith in the restoration of both Israel and Judah (Jer. iii. 14-18, xxiii. 3-8, xxx.-xxxiii.), nor of his unique doctrine of the New Covenant (Jer. xxxi. 31-34), as a ground of hope and consolation for Zion. The only hope expressed in Lamentations i. is the hope of Divine vengeance on Judah's malicious rivals (i. 21 f.); and even this is wanting from ch. ii. Chapter iii. finds comfort in the thought of Yahweh's unfailing mercy; but ends with a louder cry for vengeance. Chapter iv. suggests neither hope nor consolation, until the end, where we have an assurance that Zion's punishment is complete, and she will not again be exiled (iv. 21 f.). The last word is woe for Edom. In chapter v. we have a prayer for restoration: "Make us return, O Yahweh, and we shall return!" (*i.e.* to our pristine state). Had Jeremiah been the author, we should have expected something more positive and definitely prophetic in tone and spirit. (The author of chapter iii. seems to have felt this. It was apparently written in view of chapter ii. as a kind of religious counterpoise to its burden of despair, which it first takes up, verses 1-20, and then dissipates, verses 21 ff.). (vi.) It seems almost superfluous to add that, in the brief and troubled story of the prophet's life after the fall of the city Jer. xxxix.-xliv.), it is difficult to specify an occasion when he may be supposed to have enjoyed the necessary leisure and quiet for the composition of these elaborate and carefully constructed pieces, in a style so remote from his ordinary freedom and spontaneity of utterance. And if at the very end of his stormy career he really found time and inclination to write anything of this nature, we may wonder why it was not included in the considerable and somewhat miscellaneous volume of his works, or at least mentioned in the chapters which relate to his public activity after the catastrophe.

Budde's date, 550 B.C., might not be too early for chapter v., if it stood alone. But it was evidently written as the close of the book, and perhaps to complete the number of five divisions, after the model of the Pentateuch; which would bring it below the date of Ezra (457 B.C.). And this date is supported by internal indications. The Divine forgetfulness has already lasted a very long time since the catastrophe ("for ever," verse 20); which seems to imply the lapse of much more than thirty-six years (cf. Zech. i. 12). The hill of Zion is still a deserted site haunted by jackals, as it was when Nehemiah arrived, 445 B.C. (Neh. i. 3, ii. 3, 13, 17, iv. 3). And the conditions, political and economic, seem to agree with what is told us by Nehemiah of the state of things which he found, and which prevailed before his coming: cf. esp. Neh. v. 2-5 with Lamentations

v. 2, 10, and Neh. v. 15 with Lamentations v. 5, 8. There is nothing in chapter i. which Nehemiah himself might not have written, had he been a poet (cf. Neh. i. 4). The narrative of Neh. xiii. throws light on verse 10; and there are many coincidences of language, *e.g.* "The Province" (of Judea), Neh. i. 3, cf. verse 1; "adversaries" (צרים), of Judah's hostile neighbours, verse 7, Neh. iv. 11; "made my strength stumble," verse 14, cf. Neh. iv. 4 (Heb.); the prayers, verses 21 f., Neh. iv. 4 f. (Heb. iii. 36 f.), are similar. The memory of what is told in Neh. iv. 5 (11), Ezra iv. 23 f., v. 5, may perhaps have suggested the peculiar term [illegible], *stoppage, arrest*, verse 7. With verse 3 "Judah migrated from oppression; From greatness of servitude; She settled among the nations, Without finding a resting-place," cf. Neh. v. 18 end, Jer. xl. 11 f. The "remnant of the captivity" (Neh. i. 2 f.) became much attenuated (cf. verse 4), because all who could escape from the galling tyranny of the foreigner left the country (cf. verse 6). Verses 11, 19 (dearth of food), 20 (danger in the field, starvation in the house) agree curiously with Neh. v. 6, 9 f.

[illegible]. Chapters ii. and iv. can hardly be dated earlier than the beginning of the Persian period. They might then have been written by one who, as a young man of sixteen or twenty, had witnessed the terrible scenes of fifty years before. If, however, as is generally recognized, these poems are not the spontaneous and unstudied outpourings of passionate grief, but compositions of calculated art and studied effects, written for a purpose, it is obvious that they need not be contemporary. A poet of a later generation might have sung of the great drama in this fashion. The chief incidents and episodes would be deeply graven in the popular memory; and it is the poet's function to make the past live again. There is much metaphor (i. 13-15, ii. 1-4, iii. 1-18, iv. 1 ff.), and little detail beyond the horrors usual in long sieges (see Deut. xxviii. 52 ff.; 2 Kings vi. 28 f.) Acquaintance with the existing literature and the popular reminiscences of the last days of Jerusalem would supply an ample foundation for all that we find in these poems.

Literature.—The older literature is fully given by Nägelsbach in Lange's *Bibelwerk A.T.* xv. (1868, Eng. trans., 1871, p. 17). Among commentaries may be noticed those of Kalkar (in Latin) (1836); O. Thenius in *Kurzgefasstes Exeg. Handbuch* (1855), who ascribes chapters ii. and iv. to Jeremiah (comp. K. Budde in *Z.A.T.W.*, 1882, p. 45); Vaihinger (1857); Neumann (1858); H. Ewald in his *Dichter*, vol. i. pt. ii. (2nd ed., 1866); Engelhardt (1867); Nägelsbach, *op. cit.* (1868); E. Gerlach, *Die Klagelied. Jer.* (1868); A. Kamphausen in Bunsen's *Bibelwerk* iii. (1868); C. F. Keil (1872) (Eng. trans., 1874); Payne Smith in *The Speaker's Commentary*; Reuss, *La Bible: poésie lyrique* (1879); T. K. Cheyne, at end of "Jeremiah," *Pulpit Commentary* (1883-1885); E. H. Plumptre, in Ellicott's *O.T. for English Readers* (1884); S. Oettli in Strack-Zöckler's *Kurzgef. Komm. A.T.* vii. (1889); M. Löhr (1891) and again *Handkommentar zum A.T.* (1893); F. Baethgen *ap.* Kautzsch, *Die Heilige Schrift d. A.T.* (1894); W. F. Adeney, *Expositor's Bible* (1895); S. Minocchi, *Le Lamentazioni di Geremia* (Rome, 1897); and K. Budde, "Fünf Megilloth," in *Kurzer Hd.-Comm. zum A.T.* (1898).

For textual and literary criticism see also Houbigant, *Notae Criticae*, ii. 477-483 (1777); E. H. Rodhe, *Num Jeremias Threnos scripserit quaestiones* (Lundae, 1871); F. Montet, *Étude sur le livre des Lamentations* (Geneva, 1875); G. Bickell, *Carmina V. T. metrice*, 112-120 (1882), and *Wiener Zeitschrift für Kunde des Morgenlandes*, viii. 101 ff. (1894) (cf. also his *Dichtungen der Hebräer*, i. 87-108, 1882); Merkel, *Über das A.T. Buch der Klagelieder* (Halle, 1889); J. Dyserinck, *Theologisch Tijdschrift*, xxvi. 359 ff. (1892); S. A. Fries, "Parallele zwischen Thr. iv., v. und der Makkabäerzeit," *Z.A.T.W.*, xiii. 110 ff. (1893) (chaps. iv. v. Maccabean; i.-iii. Jeremiah's); and on the other side Löhr, *Z.A.T.W.* xiv. 51 ff. (1894); *id. ib.*, p. 31 ff., *Der Sprachgebrauch des Buches der Klagelieder*; and Löhr, "Threni iii. und die jeremianische Autorschaft des Buches der Klagelieder," *Z.A.T.W.*, xxiv. 1 ff. (1904).

On the prosody, see (besides the works of Bickell and Dyserinck) K. Budde, "Das hebräische Klagelied," *Z.A.T.W.*, ii. 1 ff. (1882), iii. 299 ff. (1883), xi. 234 ff. (1891), xii. 31 ff. 261 ff. (1892); *Preussische Jahrbücher*, lxxiii. 461 ff. (1893); and C. J. Ball, "The Metrical Structure of Qinoth," *P.S.B.A.* (March 1887). (The writer was then unacquainted with Budde's previous labours.)

The following may also be consulted, Nöldeke, *Die A.T. Literatur*, pp. 142-148 (1868); Seinecke, *Gesch. des Volkes Israel*, ii. 29 ff. (1884); Stade, *Gesch.* p. 701, n. 1 (1887); Smend in *Z.A.T.W.* (1888), p. 62 f.; Steinthal, "Die Klagelieder Jer." in *Bibel und Rel.-philosophie*, 16-33 (1890); Driver, *L.O.T.* (1891), p. 428, "The Lamentations"; and Cheyne's article "Lamentations (Book)," in *Enc. Bibl.* iii. (C. J. B.*)

LAMETH, ALEXANDRE THÉODORE VICTOR, Comte de (1760–1829), French soldier and politician, was born in Paris on the 20th of October 1760. He served in the American War of Independence under Rochambeau, and in 1789 was sent as deputy to the States General by the nobles of the *bailliage* of Péronne. In the Constituent Assembly he formed with Barnave and Adrien Duport a sort of association called the "Triumvirate," which controlled a group of about forty deputies forming the advanced left of the Assembly. He presented a famous report in the Constituent Assembly on the organization of the army, but is better known by his eloquent speech on the 28th of February 1791, at the Jacobin Club, against Mirabeau, whose relations with the court were beginning to be suspected, and who was a personal enemy of Lameth. However, after the flight of the king to Varennes, Lameth became reconciled with the court. He served in the army as *maréchal-de-camp* under Luckner and Lafayette, but was accused of treason on the 15th of August 1792, fled the country, and was imprisoned by the Austrians. After his release he engaged in commerce at Hamburg with his brother Charles and the duc d'Aiguillon, and did not return to France until the Consulate. Under the Empire he was made prefect successively in several departments, and in 1810 was created a baron. In 1814 he attached himself to the Bourbons, and under the Restoration was appointed prefect of Somme, deputy for Seine-Inférieure and finally deputy for Seine-et-Oise, in which capacity he was a leader of the Liberal opposition. He died in Paris on the 18th of March 1829. He was the author of an important *History of the Constituent Assembly* (Paris, 2 vols., 1828–1829).

Of his two brothers, Théodore Lameth (1756–1854) served in the American war, sat in the Legislative Assembly as deputy from the department of Jura, and became *maréchal-de-camp*; and Charles Malo François Lameth (1757–1832), who also served in America, was deputy to the States General of 1789, but emigrated early in the Revolution, returned to France under the Consulate, and was appointed governor of Würzburg under the Empire. Like Alexandre, Charles joined the Bourbons, succeeding Alexandre as deputy in 1829.

See F. A. Aulard, *Les Orateurs de l'Assemblée Constituante* (Paris, 1905); also M. Tourneux, *Bibliog. de l'histoire de Paris* (vol. iv., 1906, *s.v.* "Lameth").

LAMETTRIE, JULIEN OFFRAY DE (1709–1751), French physician and philosopher, the earliest of the materialistic writers of the Illumination, was born at St Malo on the 25th of December 1709. After studying theology in the Jansenist schools for some years, he suddenly decided to adopt the profession of medicine. In 1733 he went to Leiden to study under Boerhaave, and in 1742 returned to Paris, where he obtained the appointment of surgeon to the guards. During an attack of fever he made observations on himself with reference to the action of quickened circulation upon thought, which led him to the conclusion that psychical phenomena were to be accounted for as the effects of organic changes in the brain and nervous system. This conclusion he worked out in his earliest philosophical work, the *Histoire naturelle de l'âme*, which appeared about 1745. So great was the outcry caused by its publication that Lamettrie was forced to take refuge in Leiden, where he developed his doctrines still more boldly and completely, and with great originality, in *L'Homme machine* (Eng. trans., London, 1750; ed. with introd. and notes, J. Assézat, 1865), and *L'Homme plante*, treatises based upon principles of the most consistently materialistic character. The ethics of these principles were worked out in *Discours sur le bonheur*, *La Volupté*, and *L'Art de jouir*, in which the end of life is found in the pleasures of the senses, and virtue is reduced to self-love. Atheism is the only means of ensuring the happiness of the world, which has been rendered impossible by the wars brought about by theologians. The soul is only the thinking part of the body, and with the body it passes away. When death comes, the farce is over (*la farce est jouée*), therefore let us take our pleasure while we can. Lamettrie has been called "the Aristippus of modern materialism." So strong was the feeling against him that in 1748 he was compelled to quit Holland for Berlin, where Frederick the Great not only allowed him to practise as a physician, but appointed him court reader. He died on the 11th of November 1751. His collected *Œuvres philosophiques* appeared after his death in several editions, published in London, Berlin and Amsterdam respectively.

The chief authority for his life is the *Éloge* written by Frederick the Great (printed in Assézat's ed. of *Homme machine*). In modern times Lamettrie has been judged less severely; see F. A. Lange, *Geschichte des Materialismus* (Eng. trans. by E. C. Thomas, ii. 1880); Nérée Quépat (*i.e.* René Paquet), *La Mettrie, sa vie et ses œuvres* (1873, with complete history of his works); J. E. Poritzky, *J. O. de Lamettrie, Sein Leben und seine Werke* (1900); F. Picavet, "La Mettrie et la critique allemande," in *Compte rendu des séances de l'Acad. des Sciences morales et politiques*, xxxii. (1889), a reply to German rehabilitations of Lamettrie.

LAMIA, in Greek mythology, queen of Libya. She was beloved by Zeus, and when Hera robbed her of her children out of jealousy, she killed every child she could get into her power (Diod. Sic. xx. 41; Schol. Aristophanes, *Pax*, 757). Hence Lamia came to mean a female bogey or demon, whose name was used by Greek mothers to frighten their children; from the Greek she passed into Roman demonology. She was represented with a woman's face and a serpent's tail. She was also known as a sort of fiend, the prototype of the modern vampire, who in the form of a beautiful woman enticed young men to her embraces, in order that she might feed on their life and heart's blood. In this form she appears in Goethe's *Die Braut von Corinth*, and Keats's *Lamia*. The name Lamia is clearly the feminine form of Lamus, king of the Laestrygones (*q.v.*). At some early period, or in some districts, Lamus and Lamia (both, according to some accounts, children of Poseidon) were worshipped as gods; but the names did not attain general currency. Their history is remarkably like that of the malignant class of demons in Germanic and Celtic folk-lore. Both names occur in the geographical nomenclature of Greece and Asia Minor; and it is probable that the deities belong to that religion which spread from Asia Minor over Thrace into Greece.

LAMMAS (O. Eng. *hlammaesse*, *hlafmaesse*, from *hlaf*, loaf, and *maesse*, mass, "loaf-mass"), originally in England the festival of the wheat harvest celebrated on the 1st of August, O.S. It was one of the old quarter-days, being equivalent to midsummer, the others being Martinmas, equivalent to Michaelmas, Candlemas (Christmas) and Whitsuntide (Easter). Some rents are still payable in England at Lammastide, and in Scotland it is generally observed, but on the 12th of August, since the alteration of the calendar in George II.'s reign. Its name was in allusion to the custom that each worshipper should present in the church a loaf made of the new wheat as an offering of the first-fruits.

A relic of the old "open-field" system of agriculture survives in the so-called "Lammas Lands." These were lands enclosed and held in severalty during the growing of corn and grass and thrown open to pasturage during the rest of the year for those who had common rights. These commoners might be the several owners, the inhabitants of a parish, freemen of a borough, tenants of a manor, &c. The opening of the fields by throwing down the fences took place on Lammas Day (12th of August) for corn-lands and on Old Midsummer Day (6th of July) for grass. They remained open until the following Lady Day. Thus, in law, "lammas lands" belong to the several owners in fee-simple subject for half the year to the rights of pasturage of other people (*Baylis* v. *Tyssen-Amherst*, 1877, 6 Ch. D., 50).

See further F. Seebohm, *The English Village Community*; C. I. Elton, *Commons and Waste Lands*; P. Vinogradoff, *Villainage in England*.

LÄMMERGEYER (Ger. *Lämmergeier*, *Lamm*, lamb, and *Geier*, vulture), or bearded vulture, the *Falco barbatus* of Linnaeus and the *Gypaetus barbatus* of modern ornithologists, one of the grandest birds-of-prey of the Palaearctic region—inhabiting lofty mountain chains from Portugal to the borders of China, though within historic times it has been exterminated in several of its ancient haunts. Its northern range in Europe does not seem to have extended farther than the southern frontier of Bavaria, or the neighbourhood of Salzburg;[1] but in Asia it formerly reached a higher latitude, having been found even so lately as 1830 in the Amur region where, according to G. F. Radde (*Beitr. Kenntn. Russ. Reichs*, xxiii. p. 467), it has now left but its name. It is not uncommon on many parts of the Himalayas, where it breeds; and on the mountains of Kumaon and the Punjab, and is the "golden eagle" of most Anglo-Indians. It is found also in Persia, Palestine, Crete and Greece, the Italian Alps, Sicily, Sardinia and Mauritania.

In some external characters the lämmergeyer is intermediate between the families *Vulturidae* and *Falconidae*, and the opinion of systematists has from time to time varied as to its proper position. It is now generally agreed, however, that it is more closely allied with the eagles than with the vultures, and the sub-family *Gypaëtinae* of the *Falconidae* has been formed to contain it.

The whole length of the bird is from 43 to 46 in., of which, however, about 20 are due to the long cuneiform tail, while the pointed wings measure more than 30 in. from the carpal joint to the tip. The top of the head is white, bounded by black, which, beginning in stiff bristly feathers turned forwards over the base of the beak, proceeds on either side of the face in a well-defined band to the eye, where it bifurcates into two narrow stripes, of which the upper one passes above and beyond that feature till just in front of the scalp it suddenly turns upwards across the head and meets the corresponding stripe from the opposite side, enclosing the white forehead already mentioned, while the lower stripe extends beneath the eye about as far backwards and then suddenly stops. A tuft of black, bristly feathers projects beardlike from the base of the mandible, and gives the bird one of its commonest epithets in many languages. The rest of the head, the neck, throat and lower parts generally are clothed with lanceolate feathers of a pale tawny colour—sometimes so pale as to be nearly white beneath; while the scapulars, back and wing-coverts generally, are of a glossy greyish-black, most of the feathers having a white shaft and a median tawny line. The quill-feathers, both of the wings and tail, are of a dark blackish-grey. The irides are of a light orange, and the sclerotic tunics—equivalent to the "white of the eye" in most animals—which in few birds are visible, are in this very conspicuous and of a bright scarlet, giving it an air of great ferocity. In the young of the year the whole head, neck and throat are clothed in dull black, and most of the feathers of the mantle and wing-coverts are broadly tipped and mesially streaked with tawny or lightish-grey.

The lämmergeyer breeds early in the year. The nest is of large size, built of sticks, lined with soft material and placed on a ledge of rock—a spot being chosen, and often occupied for many years, which is nearly always difficult of access. Here in the month of February a single egg is usually laid. This is more than 3 in. in length by nearly 2½ in breadth, of a pale but lively brownish-orange. The young when in the nest are clad in down of a dirty white, varied with grey on the head and neck, and with ochraceous in the iliac region.

There is much discrepancy as to the ordinary food of the lämmergeyer, some observers maintaining that it lives almost entirely on carrion, offal and even ordure; but there is no question of its frequently taking living prey, and it is reasonable to suppose that this bird, like so many others, is not everywhere uniform in its habits. Its name shows it to be the reputed enemy of shepherds, and it is in some measure owing to their hostility that it has been exterminated in so many parts of its European range. But the lämmergeyer has also a great partiality for bones, which when small enough it swallows. When they are too large, it is said to soar with them to a great height and drop them on a rock or stone that they may be broken into pieces of convenient size. Hence its name ossifrage,[2] by which the

[1] See a paper by Dr Girtanner on this bird in Switzerland (*Verhandl. St-Gall. naturw. Gesellschaft*, 1869–1870, pp. 147–244).

[2] Among other crimes attributed to the species is that, according to Pliny (*Hist. Nat.* x. cap. 3), of having caused the death of the poet Aeschylus, by dropping a tortoise on his bald head! In the

Hebrew *Peres* is rightly translated in the Authorized Version of the Bible (Lev. xi. 13; Deut. xiv. 12)—a word corrupted into osprey, and applied to a bird which has no habit of the kind.

The lammergeyer of north-eastern and south Africa is specifically distinct, and is known as *Gypaetus meridionalis* or *G. nudipes*. In habits it resembles the northern bird, from which it differs in little more than wanting the black stripe below the eye and having the lower part of the tarsus bare of feathers. It is the "golden eagle" of Bruce's *Travels*, and has been beautifully figured by Joseph Wolf in E. Rüppell's *Syst. Übers. der Vögel Nord-Ost-Afrika's* (Taf. 1). (A. N.)

LAMOIGNON, a French family, which takes its name from Lamoignon, a place said to have been in its possession since the 13th century. One of its several branches is that of Lamoignon de Malesherbes. Several of the Lamoignons have played important parts in the history of France and the family has been specially distinguished in the legal profession. GUILLAUME DE LAMOIGNON (1617–1677), attained eminence as a lawyer and became president of the parlement of Paris in 1658. First on the popular, and later on the royalist side during the Fronde, he presided at the earlier sittings of the trial of Fouquet, whom he regarded as innocent, and he was associated with Colbert, whom he was able more than once to thwart. Lamoignon tried to simplify the laws of France and sought the society of men of letters like Boileau and Racine. Having received rich rewards for his public services, he died in Paris on the 10th of December 1677. Guillaume's second son, NICOLAS DE LAMOIGNON (1648–1724), took the surname of Basville. Following his hereditary calling he filled many public offices, serving as intendant of Montauban, of Pau, of Poitiers and of Languedoc before his retirement in 1718. His administration of Languedoc was chiefly remarkable for vigorous measures against the Camisards and other Protestants, but in other directions his work in the south of France was more beneficent, as, following the example of Colbert, he encouraged agriculture and industry generally and did something towards improving the means of communication. He wrote a *Mémoire*, which contains much interesting information about his public work. This was published at Amsterdam in 1724. Lamoignon, who is called by Saint Simon, "the king and tyrant of Languedoc," died in Paris on the 17th of May 1724. CHRÉTIEN FRANÇOIS DE LAMOIGNON (1735–1789) entered public life at an early age and was an actor in the troubles which heralded the Revolution. First on the side of the parlement and later on that of the king he was one of the assistants of Loménie de Brienne, whose unpopularity and fall he shared. He committed suicide on the 15th of May 1789.

LAMONT, JOHANN VON (1805–1879), Scottish-German astronomer and magnetician, was born at Braemar, Aberdeenshire, on the 13th of December 1805. He was sent at the age of twelve to be educated at the Scottish monastery in Regensburg, and apparently never afterwards returned to his native country. His strong bent for scientific studies was recognized by the head of the monastery, P. Deasson, on whose recommendation he was admitted in 1827 to the then new observatory of Bogenhausen (near Munich), where he worked under J. Soldner. After the death of his chief in 1835 he was, on H. C. Schumacher's recommendation, appointed to succeed him as director of the observatory. In 1852 he became professor of astronomy at the university of Munich, and held both these posts till his death, which took place on the 6th of August 1879. Lamont was a member of the academies of Brussels, Upsala and Prague, of the Royal Society of Edinburgh, of the Cambridge Philosophical Society and of many other learned corporations. Among his contributions to astronomy may be noted his eleven zone-catalogues of 34,674 stars, his measurements, in 1836–1837, of nebulae and clusters, and his determination of the mass of Uranus from observations of its satellites (*Mem. Astron. Soc.* xi. 51, 1838). A magnetic observatory was equipped at Bogenhausen in 1840 through his initiative; he executed comprehensive magnetic surveys 1849–1858; announced the magnetic decennial period in 1850, and his discovery of earth-currents in 1862. His *Handbuch des Erdmagnetismus* (Berlin, 1849) is a standard work on the subject.

See *Allgemeine Deutsche Biographie* (S. Günther); V. J. Schrift, *Astr. Gesellschaft*, xv. 60; *Monthly Notices Roy. Astr. Society*, xl. 203; *Nature*, xx. 425; *Quart. Journal Meteor. Society*, vi. 72; *Proceedings Roy. Society of Edinburgh*, x. 358; *The Times* (12 Aug., 1879); Sir F. Ronalds's *Cat. of Books relating to Electricity and Magnetism*, pp. 281–283; *Royal Society's Cat. of Scientific Papers*, vols. iii. vii.

LAMORICIÈRE, CHRISTOPHE LÉON LOUIS JUCHAULT DE (1806–1865), French general, was born at Nantes on the 11th of September 1806, and entered the Engineers in 1828. He served in the Algerian campaigns from 1830 onwards, and by 1840 he had risen to the grade of *maréchal-de-camp* (major-general). Three years later he was made a general of division. He was one of the most distinguished and efficient of Bugeaud's generals, rendered special service at Isly (August 14, 1844), acted temporarily as governor-general of Algeria, and finally effected the capture of Abd el-Kader in 1847. Lamoricière took some part in the political events of 1848, both as a member of the Chamber of Deputies and as a military commander. Under the régime of General Cavaignac he was for a time minister of war. From 1848 to 1851 Lamoricière was one of the most conspicuous opponents of the policy of Louis Napoleon, and at the *coup d'état* of the 2nd of December 1851 he was arrested and exiled. He refused to give in his allegiance to the emperor Napoleon III., and in 1860 accepted the command of the papal army, which he led in the Italian campaign of 1860. On the 18th of September of that year he was severely defeated by the Italian army at Castelfidardo. His last years were spent in complete retirement in France (he had been allowed to return in 1857), and he died at Prouzel (Somme) on the 11th of September 1865.

See E. Keller, *Le Général de Lamoricière* (Paris, 1873).

LA MOTHE LE VAYER, FRANÇOIS DE (1588–1672), French writer, was born in Paris of a noble family of Maine. His father was an *avocat* at the parlement of Paris and author of a curious treatise on the functions of ambassadors, entitled *Legatus, seu De legatorum privilegiis, officio et munere libellus* (1579) and illustrated mainly from ancient history. François succeeded his father at the parlement, but gave up his post about 1647 and devoted himself to travel and *belles lettres*. His *Considérations sur l'éloquence française* (1638) procured him admission to the Academy, and his *De l'instruction de Mgr. le Dauphin* (1640) attracted the attention of Richelieu. In 1649 Anne of Austria entrusted him with the education of her second son and subsequently with the completion of Louis XIV.'s education, which had been very much neglected. The outcome of his pedagogic labours was a series of books comprising the *Géographie, Rhétorique, Morale, Économique, Politique, Logique*, and *Physique du prince* (1651–1658). The king rewarded his tutor by appointing him historiographer of France and councillor of state. La Mothe Le Vayer died in Paris. Modest, sceptical, and occasionally obscene in his Latin pieces and in his verses, he made himself a *persona grata* at the French court, where libertinism in ideas and morals was hailed with relish. Besides his educational works, he wrote *Jugement sur les anciens et principaux historiens grecs et latins* (1646); a treatise entitled *Du peu de certitude qu'il y a en histoire* (1668), which in a sense marks the beginning of historical criticism in France; and sceptical *Dialogues*, published posthumously under the pseudonym of Orosius Tubero. An incomplete edition of his works was published at Dresden in 1756–1759.

See Bayle, *Dictionnaire critique*, article "Vayer"; L. Étienne, *Essai sur La Mothe Le Vayer* (Paris, 1849).

LA MOTTE, ANTOINE HOUDAR DE (1672–1731), French author, was born in Paris on the 18th of January 1672. In 1693 his comedy *Les Originaux* proved a complete failure, which so depressed the author that he contemplated joining the Trappists, but four years later he again began writing operas and ballets, *e.g. L'Europe galante* (1697), and tragedies, one of

Atlas range the food of this bird is said to consist chiefly of the *Testudo mauritanica*, which "it carries to some height in the air, and lets fall on a stone to break the shell" (*Ibis*, 1859, p. 177). It was the φήνη and ὀσσίφραγος of Greek classical writers.

which, *Inès de Castro* (1723), was produced with immense success at the Théâtre Français. He was a champion of the moderns in the revived controversy of the ancients and moderns. Madame Dacier had published (1699) a translation of the *Iliad*, and La Motte, who knew no Greek, made a translation (1714) in verse founded on her work. The nature of his work may be judged from his own expression: "I have taken the liberty to change what I thought disagreeable in it." He defended the moderns in the *Discours sur Homère* prefixed to his translation, and in his *Réflexions sur la critique* (1716). Apart from the merits of the controversy, it was conducted on La Motte's side with a wit and politeness which compared very favourably with his opponent's methods. He was elected to the Academy in 1710, and soon after became blind. La Motte carried on a correspondence with the duchesse du Maine, and was the friend of Fontenelle. He had the same freedom from prejudice, the same inquiring mind as the latter, and it is on the excellent prose in which his views are expressed that his reputation rests. He died in Paris on the 26th of December 1731.

His *Œuvres du théâtre* (2 vols.) appeared in 1730, and his *Œuvres* [illegible] vols.) in 1754. See A. H. Rigault, *Histoire de la querelle des anciens et des modernes* (1859).

LAMOUREUX, CHARLES (1834–1899), French conductor and violinist, was born at Bordeaux on the 28th of September [illegible]. He studied at the Pau Conservatoire, was engaged as [illegible] at the Opéra, and in 1864 organized a series of concerts [illegible] to chamber music. Having journeyed to England [illegible] at a Handel festival, he thought he would attempt [illegible] similar in Paris. At his own expense he founded [illegible] Société de l'Harmonie Sacrée," and in 1873 conducted [illegible] performance in Paris of Handel's *Messiah*. He also [illegible] performances of Bach's *St Matthew Passion*, Handel's [illegible], Gounod's *Gallia*, and Massenet's *Eve*. In [illegible] conducted the festival given at Rouen to celebrate the [illegible] of Boïeldieu. The following year he became *chef* [illegible] at the Opéra Comique. In 1881 he founded the [illegible] associated with his name, which contributed [illegible] popularize Wagner's music in Paris. The perform[illegible] pieces taken from the German master's works [illegible] satisfy him, and he matured the project to [illegible], which at that time had not been heard in [illegible] the purpose he took the Eden Theatre, and on the [illegible] he conducted the first performance of Wagner's [illegible] French capital. Owing to the opposition of the [illegible] the performance was not repeated; but it doubtless [illegible] way for the production of the same masterpiece [illegible] Opéra a few years later. Lamoureux was successively [illegible] at the Conservatoire, first *chef d'orchestre* [illegible] Comique, and twice first *chef d'orchestre* at the [illegible] visited London on several occasions, and gave [illegible] at the Queen's Hall. Lamoureux died at [illegible] of December 1899. *Tristan und Isolde* had [illegible] in Paris, owing to his initiative and under [illegible] conducting one of the performances of this [illegible] he was taken ill and succumbed in a few days, [illegible] before his death of witnessing the [illegible] he had so courageously championed.

[illegible], a torch, λάμπειν, to shine), the general [illegible] in which some combustible substance, [illegible] is held. Lamps are usually [illegible] the term is also employed in [illegible]; and as now employed [illegible] they are dealt with in the article [illegible] point of view, in modern times, [illegible] here; but their archaeo[illegible]

[illegible] (c. 700) that the [illegible] Greece, it had [illegible] by the 4th [illegible] been employed [illegible]

sees nothing strange in the "festival of lamps," Lychnokaie, which was held at Sais in Egypt, except in the vast number of them. Each was filled with oil so as to burn the whole night. Again he speaks of evening as the time of lamps (περὶ λύχνων, vii. 215). Still, the scarcity of lamps in a style anything like that of an early period, compared with the immense number of them from the late Greek and Roman age, seems to justify the remark of Athenaeus. The commonest sort of domestic lamps were of terra-cotta and of the shape seen in figs. 1 and 2 with a spout or nozzle (μυκτήρ) in which the wick (θρυαλλίς) burned, a round hole on the top to pour in oil by, and a handle to carry the lamp with. A lamp with two or more spouts was δίμυξος, τρίμυξος, &c., but these terms would not apply strictly to the large class of lamps with numerous holes for wicks but without nozzles. Decoration was confined to the front of the handle, or more commonly to the circular space on the top of the lamp, and it consisted almost always of a design in relief, taken from mythology or legend, from objects of daily life or scenes such as displays of gladiators or chariot races, from animals and the chase. A lamp in the British Museum has a view of the interior of a Roman circus with spectators looking on at a chariot race. In other cases the lamp is made altogether of a fantastic shape, as in the form of an animal, a bull's head, or a human foot. Naturally colour was excluded from the ornamentation except in the form of a red or black glaze, which would resist the heat. The typical form of hand lamp (figs. 1, 2) is a combination of the flatness necessary for carrying steady and remaining steady when set down, with the roundness evolved from the working in clay and characteristic of vessels in that material. In the bronze lamps this same type is retained, though the roundness was less in keeping with metal. Fanciful shapes are equally common in bronze. The standard form of handle consists of a ring for the forefinger and above it a kind

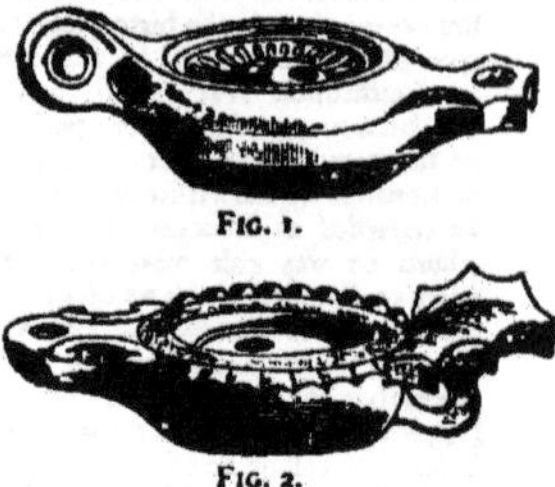

Fig. 1.

Fig. 2.

Fig. 3.

of palmette for the thumb. Instead of the palmette is sometimes a crescent, no doubt in allusion to the moon. It would only be with bronze lamps that the cover protecting the flame from the wind could be used, as was the case out of doors in Athens. Such a lamp was in fact a lantern. Apparently it was to the lantern that the Greek word *lampas*, a torch, was first transferred, probably from a custom of having guards to protect the torches also. Afterwards it came to be employed for the lamp itself (λύχνος, *lucerna*). When Juvenal (*Sat.* iii. 277) speaks of the *aenea lampas*, he may mean a torch with a bronze handle, but more probably either a lamp or a lantern. Lamps used for suspension were mostly of bronze, and in such cases the decoration was on the under part, so as to be seen from below. Of [illegible] the best example is the lamp at Cortona, found there in

1840 (engraved, *Monumenti d. inst. arch.* iii. pls. 41, 42, and in Dennis, *Cities and Cemeteries of Etruria*, 2nd ed. ii. p. 403). It is set round with sixteen nozzles ornamented alternately with a siren and a satyr playing on a double flute. Between each pair of nozzles is a head of a river god, and on the bottom of the lamp is a large mask of Medusa, surrounded by bands of animals. These designs are in relief, and the workmanship,

Fig. 4.—Bronze Lamp in British Museum.

which appears to belong to the beginning of the 5th century B.C., justifies the esteem in which Etruscan lamps were held in antiquity (Athenaeus xv. 700). Of a later but still excellent style is a bronze lamp in the British Museum found in the baths of Julian in Paris (figs. 3, 4, 5). The chain is attached by means of two dolphins very artistically combined. Under the nozzles are heads of Pan (fig. 3); and from the sides project the foreparts of lions (fig. 5). To what extent lamps may have been used in temples is unknown. Probably the Erechtheum on the acropolis of Athens was an exception in having a gold one kept burning day and night, just as this lamp itself must have been an exception in its artistic merits. It was the work of the sculptor Callimachus, and was made apparently for the newly rebuilt temple a little before 400 B.C. When once filled with oil and lit it burned continuously for a whole year. The wick was of a fine flax called Carpasian (now understood to have been a kind of cotton), which proved to be the least combustible of all flax (Pausanias i. 26. 7). Above the lamp a palm tree of bronze rose to the roof for the purpose of carrying off the fumes. But how this was managed it is not easy to determine unless the palm be supposed to have been inverted and to have hung above the lamp spread out like a reflector, for which purpose the polished bronze would have served fairly well. The stem if left hollow would collect the fumes and carry them out through the roof.

Fig. 5.

This lamp was refilled on exactly the same day each year, so that there seems to have been an idea of measuring time by it, such as may also have been the case in regard to the lamp stand (λύχνιον) capable of holding as many lamps as there were days of the year, which Dionysius the Sicilian tyrant placed in the Prytaneum of Tarentum. At Pharae in Achaia there was in the market-place an oracular statue of Hermes with a marble altar before it to which bronze lamps were attached by means of lead. Whoever desired to consult the statue went there in the evening and first filled the lamps and lit them, placing also a bronze coin on the altar. A similar custom prevailed at the oracle of Apis in Egypt (Pausanias vii. 22. 2). At Argos he speaks of a chasm into which it was a custom continued to his time to let down burning lamps, with some reference to the goddess of the lower world, Persephone (ii. 22. 4). At Cnidus a large number of terra-cotta lamps were found crowded in one place a little distance below the surface, and it was conjectured that there must have been there some statue or altar at which it had been a custom to leave lamps burning at night (Newton, *Discoveries at Halicarnassus, &c.*, ii. 394). These lamps are of terra-cotta, but with little ornamentation, and so like each other in workmanship that they must all have come from one pottery, and may have been all brought to the spot where they were found on one occasion, probably the funeral of a person with many friends, or the celebration of a festival in his honour, such as the *parentalia* among the Romans, to maintain which it was a common custom to bequeath property. For example, a marble slab in the British Museum has a Latin inscription describing the property which had been left to provide among other things that a lighted lamp with incense on it should be placed at the tomb of the deceased on the kalends, nones and ides of each month (*Mus. Marbles*, v. pl. 8, fig. 2). For birthday presents terra-cotta lamps appear to have been frequently employed, the device generally being that of two figures of victory holding between them a disk inscribed with a good wish for the new year: ANNV NOV FAVSTV FELIX. This is the inscription on a lamp in the British Museum, which besides the victories has among other symbols a disk with the head of Janus. As the torch gave way to the lamp in fact, so also it gave way in mythology. In the earlier myths, as in that of Demeter, it is a torch with which she goes forth to search for her daughter, but in the late myth of Cupid and Psyche it is an oil lamp which Psyche carries, and from which to her grief a drop of hot oil falls on Cupid and awakes him. Terra-cotta lamps have very frequently the name of the maker stamped on the foot. Clay moulds from which the lamps were made exist in considerable numbers. (A. S. M.)

LAMP-BLACK, a deep black pigment consisting of carbon in a very fine state of division, obtained by the imperfect combustion of highly carbonaceous substances. It is manufactured from scraps of resin and pitch refuse and inferior oils and fats, and other similar combustible bodies rich in carbon, the finest lamp-black being procured by the combustion of oils obtained in coal-tar distillation (see Coal-Tar). Lamp-black is extensively used in the manufacture of printing ink, as a pigment for oil painting and also for "ebonizing" cabinet work, and in the waxing and lacquering of leather. It is the principal constituent of China ink.

LAMPEDUSA, a small island in the Mediterranean, belonging to the province of Girgenti, from which it is about 112 m. S.S.W. Pop. (1901, with Linosa—see below) 2276. Its greatest length is about 7 m., its greatest width about 2 m.; the highest point is 400 ft. above sea-level. Geologically it belongs to Africa, being situated on the edge of the submarine platform which extends along the east coast of Tunisia, from which (at Mahadia) it is 90 m. distant eastwards. The soil is calcareous; it was covered with scrub (chiefly the wild olive) until comparatively recent times, but this has been cut, and the rock is now bare. The valleys are, however, fairly fertile. On the south, near the only village, is the harbour, which has been dredged to a depth of 13 ft. and is a good one for torpedo boats and small craft.

The island was, as remains of hut foundations show, inhabited [illegible] prehistoric times. Punic tombs and Roman buildings also [illegible] the harbour. The island is the Lopadusa of Strabo, [illegible] the Lipadosa of Ariosto's *Orlando Furioso*, the scene of the [illegible] of Roger of Sicily and of his conversion by the hermit. [illegible] slaves were taken from its population in 1553. [illegible] it was given by Alfonso of Aragon to Don Giovanni [illegible], baron of Montechiaro. In 1661, Ferdinand Tommasi, [illegible] received the title of prince from Charles II. of [illegible]. In 1737 the earl of Sandwich found only one inhabitant [illegible] in 1760 some French settlers established themselves [illegible]. Catherine II. of Russia proposed to buy it as a Russian [illegible] station, and the British government thought of doing [illegible] if Napoleon had succeeded in seizing Malta. In 1800 [illegible] it was leased to Salvatore Gatt of Malta, who in 1810 [illegible] of it to Alessandro Fernandez. In 1843 onwards [illegible] II. of Naples established a colony there. There is [illegible] penal colony for *domicilio coatto*, with some 400 [illegible] B. Sanvisente, *L'Isola di Lampedusa eretta a* [illegible] Naples, 1849). Eight miles W. is the islet of Lampione. [illegible] 30 m. to the N.N.E., measures about 2 by 2 m., [illegible] volcanic; its highest point is 610 ft. above sea-[illegible]. Pop. [illegible] about 200. It has landing-places on the S. [illegible] and is more fertile than Lampedusa; but it suffers from [illegible] springs. Sanvisente says the water in Lampedusa [illegible]. A few fragments of undoubtedly Roman pottery and [illegible] coins have been found there, but the cisterns and [illegible] are probably of later date (P. Calcara, [illegible] *di Linosa*, Palermo, 1851, 29). (T. As.)

[illegible], a town in the grand-duchy of Hesse-[illegible] from Mannheim by the railway to Frankfort-[illegible] and at the junction of lines to Worms and [illegible] a Roman Catholic church and a fine [illegible] and has chemical and cigar factories. Pop. [illegible]

[illegible] (*...-pont-Stephan*), a market town, muni-[illegible] town of Cardiganshire, Wales, on [illegible] Teifi, here crossed by an ancient stone [illegible]. Lampeter is a station on the so-[illegible] Milford branch line of the Great Western [illegible] a [illegible] origin, the town is entirely modern [illegible] object being the Gothic [illegible] College, founded in 1822, which cover [illegible] a valuable library of English, Welsh [illegible]. The modernized parish [illegible] some old monuments of [illegible] the town are the park and mansion [illegible] family.

[illegible] goes to prove the early [illegible], a Celtic missionary of the [illegible] was the original builder of the [illegible] outpost in the upper [illegible] a castle, which was [illegible] the 12th century. In 1188 [illegible] Baldwin on his way [illegible] and the Crusade was vigor-[illegible] was first incorporated [illegible] known charter dates from [illegible]

[illegible]

Littré derives it from a term of Parisian argot, *lamper*, to drink greedily, in great mouthfuls. This word appears to have begun to be prevalent in the middle of the 17th century, and Furetière has preserved a fragment from a popular song, which says:—

> Jacques fuyant de Dublin
> Dit à Lauzun, son cousin,
> " Prenez soin de ma couronne,
> J'aurai soin de ma personne,
> Lampons! lampons! "

—that is to say, let us drink heavily, and begone dull care. Scarron speaks of a wild troop, singing *leridas* and *lampons*. There is, also, a rare French verb, *lamponner*, to attack with ridicule, used earlier in the 17th century by Brantôme. In its English form, lampoon, the word is used by Evelyn in 1645, " Here they still paste up their drolling lampoons and scurrilous papers," and soon after it is a verb,—" suppose we lampooned all the pretty women in Town." Both of these forms, the noun and the verb, have been preserved ever since in English, without modification, for violent and reckless literary censure. Tom Brown (1663–1704) was a past master in the art of lampooning, and some of his attacks on the celebrities of his age have a certain vigour. When Dryden became a Roman Catholic, Brown wrote:—

> Traitor to God and rebel to thy pen,
> Priest-ridden Poet, perjured son of Ben,
> If ever thou prove honest, then the nation
> May modestly believe in transubstantiation.

Several of the heroes of the *Dunciad*, and in particular John Oldmixon (1673–1742), were charged without unfairness with being professional lampooners. The coarse diatribes which were published by Richard Savage (1697–1743), mainly against Lady Macclesfield, were nothing more nor less than lampoons, and the word may with almost equal justice be employed to describe the coarser and more personal portions of the satires of Churchill. As a rule, however, the lampoon possessed no poetical graces, and in its very nature was usually anonymous. The notorious *Essay on Woman* (1764) of John Wilkes was a lampoon, and was successfully proceeded against as an obscene libel. The progress of civilization and the discipline of the law made it more and more impossible for private malice to take the form of baseless and scurrilous attack, and the lampoon, in its open shape, died of public decency in the 18th century. Malice, especially in an anonymous form, and passing in manuscript from hand to hand, has continued, however, to make use of this very unlovely form of literature. It has constantly reappeared at times of political disturbance, and the French have seldom failed to exercise their wicked wit upon their unpopular rulers. See also PASQUINADE. (E. G.)

LAMPREY, a fish belonging to the family *Petromyzontidae* (from πέτρος and μύζω, literally, stone-suckers), which with the hag-fishes or *Myxinidae* forms a distinct subclass of fishes, the *Cyclostomata*, distinguished by the low organization of their skeleton, which is cartilaginous, without vertebral segmentation, without ribs or real jaws, and without limbs. The lampreys are readily recognized by their long, eel-like, scaleless body, terminating anteriorly in the circular, suctorial mouth characteristic of the whole sub-class. On each side, behind the head, there is a row of seven branchial openings, through which the water is conveyed to and from the gills. By means of their mouth they fasten to stones, boats, &c., as well as to other fishes, their object being to obtain a resting-place on the former, whilst they attach themselves to the latter to derive nourishment from them. The inner surface of their cup-shaped mouth is armed with pointed teeth, with which they perforate the integuments of the fish attacked, scraping off particles of the flesh and sucking the blood. Mackerel, cod, pollack and flat-fishes are the kinds most frequently attacked by them in the sea; of river-fish the migratory *Salmonidae* and the shad are sometimes found with the marks of the teeth of the lamprey, or with the fish actually attached to them. About fifteen species are known from the coasts and rivers of the temperate regions of the northern and southern hemispheres. In Great Britain and Europe generally three species occur, viz. the large spotted sea-lamprey (*Petromyzon marinus*), the river-lamprey or lampern (*P. fluviatilis*), and the small lampern or "pride" or "sand-piper" (*P. branchialis*). The first two are migratory, entering rivers in the spring to spawn; of the river-lamprey, however, specimens are met with in fresh water all the year round. In North America about ten species of lamprey occur, while in South America and Australasia still others are found. Lampreys, especially the sea-lamprey, are esteemed as food, formerly more so than at present; but their flesh is not easy of digestion. Henry I. of England is said to have fallen a victim to this, his favourite dish. The species of greatest use is the river-lamprey, which as bait is preferred to all others in the cod and turbot fisheries of the North Sea. Yarrell states that formerly the Thames alone supplied from 1,000,000 to 1,200,000 lamperns annually, but their number has so much fallen off that, for instance, in 1876 only 40,000 were sold to the cod-fishers. That year, however, was an unusually bad year; the lamperns, from their scarcity, fetched £8, 10s. a thousand, whilst in ordinary years £5 is considered a fair price. The season for catching lamperns closes in the Thames about the middle of March. The origin of the name lamprey is obscure; it is an adaptation of Fr. *lamproie*, Med. Lat. *lampreda*; this has been taken as a variant of another Med. Lat. form *Lampetra*, which occurs in ichthyological works of the middle ages; the derivation from *lambere petras*, to lick stones, is a specimen of etymological ingenuity. The development of lampreys has received much attention on the part of naturalists, since Aug. Müller discovered that they undergo a metamorphosis, and that the minute worm-like lamperns previously known under the name of *Ammocoetes*, and abundant in the sand and mud of many streams, were nothing but the undeveloped young of the river-lampreys and small lamperns. See Cyclostomata.

LAMPROPHYRES (from Gr. λαμπρός, bright, and the terminal part of the word porphyry, meaning rocks containing bright porphyritic crystals), a group of rocks containing phenocrysts, usually of biotite and hornblende (with bright cleavage surfaces), often also of olivine and augite, but not of felspar. They are thus distinguished from the porphyries and porphyrites in which the felspar has crystallized in two generations. They are essentially "dike rocks," occurring as dikes and thin sills, and are also found as marginal facies of plutonic intrusions. They furnish a good example of the correlation which often exists between petrographical types and their mode of occurrence, showing the importance of physical conditions in determining the mineralogical and structural characters of rocks. They are usually dark in colour, owing to the abundance of ferro-magnesian silicates, of relatively high specific gravity and liable to decomposition. For these reasons they have been defined as a *melanocrate* series (rich in the dark minerals); and they are often accompanied by a complementary *leucocrate* series (rich in the white minerals felspar and quartz) such as aplites, porphyries and felsites. Both have been produced by differentiation of a parent magma, and if the two complementary sets of rocks could be mixed in the right proportions, it is presumed that a mass of similar chemical composition to the parent magma would be produced.

Both in the hand specimens and in microscopic slides of lamprophyric rocks biotite and hornblende are usually conspicuous. Though black by reflected light they are brown by transmitted light and highly pleochroic. In some cases they are yellow-brown, in other cases chestnut-brown and reddish brown; in the same rock the two minerals have strikingly similar colour and pleochroism. Augite, when it occurs, is sometimes green, at other times purple. Felspar is restricted to the ground mass; quartz occurs sometimes but is scarce. Although porphyritic structure is almost universal, it is sometimes not very marked. The large biotites and hornblendes are not sharply distinct from those of intermediate size, which in turn graduate into the small crystals of the same minerals in the ground mass. As a rule all the ingredients have rather perfect crystalline forms (except quartz), hence these rocks have been called "panidiomorphic." In many lamprophyres the pale quartz and felspathic ingredients tend to occur in rounded spots, or *ocelli*, in which there has been progressive crystallization from the margins towards the centre. These spots may consist of radiate or brush-like felspars (with some mica and hornblende) or of quartz and felspar. A central area of quartz or of analcite probably represents an original miarolitic cavity infilled at a later period.

There are two great groups of lamprophyres differing in composition while retaining the general features of the class. One of these accompanies intrusions of granite and diorite and includes the minettes, kersantites, vogesites and spessartites. The other is found in association with nepheline syenites, essexites and teschenites, and is exemplified by camptonites, monchiquites and alnoites. The complementary facies of the first group is the aplites, porphyrites and felsites; that of the second group includes bostonites, tinguaites and other rocks.

The *granito-dioritic-lamprophyres* (the first of these two groups) are found in many districts where granites and diorites occur, *e.g.* the Scottish Highlands and Southern Uplands, the Lake district, Ireland, the Vosges, Black Forest, Harz, &c. As a rule they do not proceed directly from the granite, but form separate dikes which may be later than, and consequently may cut, the granites and diorites. In other districts where granites are abundant no rocks of this class are known. It is rare to find only one member of the group present, but minettes, vogesites, kersantites, &c., all appear and there are usually transitional forms. For this reason these rock species must not be regarded as sharply distinct from one another. The group as a whole is a well-characterized one and shows few transitions to porphyries, porphyrites and other dike types; its subdivisions, however, tend to merge into one another and especially when they are weathered are hard to differentiate. The presence or absence of the four dominant minerals, orthoclase, plagioclase, biotite and hornblende, determines the species. Minettes contain biotite and orthoclase; kersantites, biotite and plagioclase. Vogesites contain hornblende and orthoclase; spessartites, hornblende and plagioclase. Each variety of lamprophyre may and often does contain all four minerals but is named according to the two which preponderate. These rocks contain also iron oxides (usually titaniferous), apatite, sometimes sphene, augite and olivine. The hornblende and biotite are brown or greenish brown, and as a rule their crystals even when small are very perfect and give the micro-sections an easily recognizable character. Green hornblende occurs in some of these rocks. The augite builds eumorphic crystals of pale green colour, often zonal and readily weathering. Olivine in the fresh state is rare; it forms rounded, corroded grains; in many cases it is decomposed to green or colourless hornblende in radiating nests (pilite). The plagioclase occurs as small rectangular crystals; orthoclase may have similar shapes or may be fibrous and grouped in sheaflike aggregates which are narrow in the middle and spread out towards both ends. If quartz is present it is the last product of crystallization and the only mineral devoid of idiomorphism; it fills up the spaces between the other ingredients of the rock. As all lamprophyres are prone to alteration by weathering a great abundance of secondary minerals is usually found in them; the principal are calcite and other carbonates, limonite, chlorite, quartz and kaolin.

Ocellar structure is common; the ocelli consist mainly of orthoclase and quartz, and may be a quarter of an inch in diameter. Another feature of these rocks is the presence of large foreign crystals or xenocrysts of felspar and of quartz. Their forms are rounded, indicating partial resorption by the solvent action of the lamprophyric magma; and the quartz may be surrounded by corrosion borders of minerals such as augite and hornblende produced where the magma is attacking the crystal. These crystals are of doubtful origin; they are often of considerable size and may be conspicuous in hand-specimens of the rocks. It is supposed that they did not crystallize in the lamprophyre dike but in some way were caught up by it. Other enclosures, more certainly of foreign origin, are often seen, such as quartzite, schists, garnetiferous rocks, granite, &c. These may be baked and altered or in other cases partly dissolved. Cordierite may be formed either in the enclosure or in the lamprophyre, where it takes the shape of hexagonal prisms which in polarized light break up into six sectors, triangular in shape, diverging from the centre of the crystal.

The second group of lamprophyric dike rocks (*the camptonite, monchiquite, alnoite series*) is much less common than those above described. As a rule they occur together, and there are transitions between the different sub-groups as in the granito-dioritic lamprophyres. In Sweden, Brazil, Portugal, Norway, the north of Scotland, Bohemia, Arkansas and other places this assemblage of rock types has been met with, always presenting nearly identical features. In most cases, though not in all, they have a close association with nepheline or leucite syenites and similar rocks rich in alkalies. This indicates a genetic affinity like that which exists between the granites and the minettes, &c., and further proof of this connexion is furnished [illegible] the occasional occurrence in these lamprophyres of leucite, haüyne and other felspathoid minerals.

The camptonites (called after Campton, New Hampshire) are dark brown, nearly black rocks often with large hornblende phenocrysts. Their essential minerals in thin section are hornblende of a strong brown colour; augite purple, pleochroic and rich in titanium, olivine and plagioclase felspar. They have the porphyritic and panidiomorphic structures described in the rocks of the previous group, and like them also have an ocellar character, often very conspicuous under the microscope. The accessory minerals are biotite, apatite, iron oxides and analcite. They decompose readily and are then often filled with carbonates. Many of these rocks prove on analysis to be exceedingly rich in titanium; they may contain 4 or 5% of titanium dioxide.

The monchiquites (called after the Serra de Monchique, Portugal) are fine grained and devoid of felspar. Their essential constituents are olivine and purplish augite. Brown hornblende, like that of the camptonites, occurs in many of them. An interstitial substance is present, which may sometimes be a brown glass, but at other times is colourless and is believed by some petrographers to be primary analcite. They would define the monchiquites as rocks consisting of olivine, augite and analcite; others regard the analcite as secondary, and consider the base as essentially glassy. Some monchiquites contain haüyne; while in others small leucites are present. Ocellar structure is occasionally present, though less marked than in the camptonites. A special group of monchiquites rich in large brown biotite has been called fourchites (after the Fourche Mountains, Arkansas).

The alnöites (called after the island of Alnö in Norway) are rare rocks found in Norway, Montreal and other parts of North America and in the north of Scotland. They contain olivine, augite, brown biotite and melilite. They are free from felspar, and contain very low percentages of silica.

The chemical composition of some of these rocks will be indicated by the analyses of certain well-known examples.

	SiO_2	TiO_2	Al_2O_3	Fe_2O_3	FeO	MgO	CaO	Na_2O	K_2O
I.	[illegible]	1·71	15·07	8·41	...	7·23	5·33	3·12	4·81
II.	[illegible]	1·20	13·52	2·56	4·83	6·36	5·78	2·34	5·36
III.	[illegible]	...	15·39	2·76	5·04	6·38	8·83	2·67	2·77
IV.	[illegible]	...	12·68	11·68	2·13	6·11	4·96	3·85	3·65
V.	[illegible]	4·15	15·36	3·27	9·89	5·01	9·47	8·15	0·19
VI.	[illegible]	2·80	14·82	2·40	7·52	6·98	10·81	3·06	2·90
VII.	[illegible]	2·54	8·80	3·92	5·42	17·66	17·86	0·77	2·45

In addition to the oxides given these rocks contain small quantities of water (combined and hygroscopic), CO_2, S, MnO, P_2O_5, Cr_2O_3, &c. (J. S. F.)

LAMPSACUS, an ancient Greek colony in Mysia, Asia Minor, known as Pityusa or Pityussa before its colonization by Ionian Greeks from Phocaea and Miletus, was situated on the Hellespont, opposite Callipolis (Gallipoli) in Thrace. It possessed a good harbour; and the neighbourhood was *famous for its wine*, so that, having fallen into the hands of the Persians during the Ionian revolt, it was assigned by Artaxerxes I. to Themistocles to provide him with wine, as Percote did with meat and Magnesia with bread. After the battle of Mycale (479 B.C.), Lampsacus joined the Athenians, but, having revolted from them in 411, was reduced by force. It was defended in 196 B.C. against Antiochus the Great of Syria, after which its inhabitants were received [illegible] Rome. Lampsacus was the chief seat of the worship [illegible] a gross nature-god closely connected with the culture [illegible]. The ancient name is preserved in that of the modern [illegible] Lapsaki but the Greek town possibly lay at Chardak opposite Gallipoli.

[illegible], *Lettres sur la Morée, l'Hellespont, &c.* (Paris, [illegible]), *Voyage pittoresque dans l'empire ottoman* [illegible]

[illegible], a pillar, tripod or figure extending to the [illegible] holding a lamp. The lampstand (*lampa-* [illegible] French origin; it appears to have been in [illegible] the end of the 17th century.

[illegible] municipal and police burgh, and county [illegible] Scotland, standing on high ground about [illegible] right bank of the Clyde, 31 m. S.E. of [illegible] railway. Pop. (1901) 6440. It is a favourite holiday resort, being the point from which the falls of the Clyde are usually visited. The principal buildings are the town hall, the county buildings, the assembly rooms, occupying the site of an old Franciscan monastery, three hospitals, a convalescent home, the Smyllum orphanage and the Queen Victoria Jubilee fountain. The industries include cotton-spinning, weaving, nail-making and oilworks, and there are frequent markets for cattle and sheep. Lanark is a place of considerable antiquity. Kenneth II. held a parliament here in 978, and it was sometimes the residence of the Scottish kings, one of whom, William the Lion (d. 1214), granted it a charter. Several of the earlier exploits of William Wallace were achieved in the neighbourhood. He burned the town and slew the English sheriff William Hezelrig. About 1 m. N.W. are Cartland Craigs, where Mouse Water runs through a precipitous red sandstone ravine, the sides of which are about 400 ft. high. The stream is crossed by a bridge of single span, supposed to be Roman, and by a three-arched bridge, designed by Thomas Telford and erected in 1823. On the right bank, near this bridge, is the cave in which Wallace concealed himself after killing Hezelrig and which still bears his name. Lanark was the centre of much activity in the days of the Covenanters. William Lithgow (1582–1645), the traveller, William Smellie (1697–1763), the obstetrician and Gavin Hamilton (1730–1797), the painter, were born at Lanark. The town is one of the Falkirk district group of parliamentary burghs, the other constituents being Airdrie, Hamilton, Falkirk and Linlithgow.

[illegible] II. Kersantite (Neubrunn, Thur- [illegible] Mountain, Montana). IV. Spes- [illegible] (Campton Falls). [illegible] VII. Alnöite (Alnö).

New Lanark (pop. 795), 1 m. S., is famous in connexion with the socialist experiments of Robert Owen. The village was founded by David Dale (1739–1806) in 1785, with the support of Sir Richard Arkwright, inventor of the spinning-frame, who thought the spot might be made the Manchester of Scotland. In ten years four cotton mills were running, employing nearly 1400 hands. They were sold in 1799 to a Manchester company, who appointed Owen manager. In the same year he married Dale's daughter. For many years the mills were successfully conducted, but friction ultimately arose and Owen retired in 1828. The mills, however, are still carried on.

There are several interesting places near Lanark. Braxfield, on the Clyde, gave the title of Lord Braxfield to Robert Macqueen (1722–1799), who was born in the mansion and acquired on the bench the character of the Scottish Jeffreys. Robert Baillie, the patriot who was executed for conscience' sake (1684), belonged to Jerviswood, an estate on the Mouse. Lee House, the home of the Lockharts, is 3 m. N.W. The old castle was largely rebuilt in the 19th century. It contains some fine tapestry and portraits, and the Lee Penny—familiar to readers of Sir Walter Scott's *Talisman*—which was brought from Palestine in the 14th century by the Crusading knight, Sir Simon Lockhart. It is described as a cornelian encased in a silver coin. Craignethan Castle on the Nethan, a left-hand tributary joining the Clyde at Crossford, is said to be the original of the "Tillietudlem" of Scott's *Old Mortality*.

LANARKSHIRE, a south-western county of Scotland, bounded N. by the shires of Dumbarton and Stirling, E. by Linlithgowshire, Mid-Lothian and Peeblesshire, S. by Dumfriesshire and W. by the counties of Ayr, Renfrew and Dumbarton. Its area is 879 sq. m. (562,821 acres). It may be described as embracing the valley of the Clyde; and, in addition to the gradual descent from the high land in the south, it is also characterized by a gentle slope towards both banks of the river. The shire is divided into three wards, the Upper, comprising all the southern section, or more than half the whole area (over 330,000 acres); the Middle, with Hamilton for its chief town, covering fully 190,000 acres; and the Lower, occupying the northern area of about 40,000 acres. The surface falls gradually from the uplands in the south to the Firth of Clyde. The highest hills are nearly all on or close to the borders of Peeblesshire and Dumfriesshire, and include Culter Fell (2454 ft.) and Lowther Hill (2377). The loftiest heights exclusively belonging to Lanarkshire are Green Lowther (2403), Tinto (2335), Ballencleuch Law (2267), Rodger Law (2257), Dun Law (2216), Shiel Dod (2190), Dungrain Law (2186) and Comb Law (2107). The principal rivers are the Clyde and its head waters and affluents (on the right, the Medwin, Mouse, South Calder, North

Calder and Kelvin; on the left, the Douglas, Nethan, Avon, Rotten Calder and Cart). There are no lochs of considerable size, the few sheets of water in the north—Woodend Reservoir, Bishop Loch, Hogganfield Loch, Woodend Loch, Lochend Loch—mainly feeding the Monkland and the Forth and Clyde Canals. The most famous natural features are the Falls of Clyde at Bonnington, Corra, Dundaff and Stonebyres.

Geology.—The southern upland portion is built up of Silurian and Ordovician rocks; the northern lower-lying tracts are formed of Carboniferous and Old Red Sandstone rocks. Ordovician strata cross the county from S.W. to N.E. in a belt 5-7 m. in breadth which is brought up by a fault against the Old Red and the Silurian on the northern side. This fault runs by Lamington, Roberton and Crawfordjohn. The Ordovician rocks lie in a synclinal fold with beds of Caradoc age in the centre flanked by graptolitic shales, grits and conglomerates, including among the last-named the local "Haggis-rock"; the well-known lead mines of Leadhills are worked in these formations. Silurian shales and sandstones, &c., extend south of the Ordovician belt to the county boundary; and again, on the northern side of the Ordovician belt two small tracts appear through the Old Red Sandstone on the crests of anticlinal folds. The Old Red Sandstone covers an irregular tract north of the Ordovician belt; a lower division consisting of sandstone, conglomerates and mud-stones is the most extensively developed; above this is found a series of contemporaneous porphyrites and melaphyres, conformable upon the lower division in the west of the county but are not so in the east. An upper series of sandstones and grits is seen for a short distance west of Lamington. Lanark stands on the Old Red Sandstone and the Falls of Clyde occur in the same rocks. Economically the most important geological feature is the coal basin of the Glasgow district. The axis of this basin lies in a N.E.-S.W. direction; in the central part, including Glasgow, Airdrie, Motherwell, Wishaw, Carluke, lie the coal-measures, consisting of sandstones, shales, marls and fireclays with seams of coal and ironstone. There are eleven beds of workable coal, the more important seams being the Ell, Main, Splint, Pyotshaw and Virtuewell. Underlying the coal-measures is the Millstone Grit seen on the northern side between Glenboig and Hogganfield—here the fireclays of Garnkirk, Gartcosh and Glenboig are worked—and on the south and south-east of the coal-measures, but not on the western side, because it is there cut out by a fault. Beneath the last-named formation comes the Carboniferous Limestone series with thin coals and ironstones, and again beneath this is the Calciferous Sandstone series which in the south-east consists of sandstones, shales, &c., but in the west the greater part of the series is composed of interbedded volcanic rocks—porphyrites and melaphyres. It will be observed that in general the younger formations lie nearer the centre of the basin and the older ones crop out around them. Besides the volcanic rocks mentioned there are intrusive basalts in the Carboniferous rocks like that in the neighbourhood of Shotts, and the smaller masses at Hogganfield near Glasgow and elsewhere. Volcanic necks are found in the Carluke and Kilcadzow districts, marking the vents of former volcanoes and several dikes of Tertiary age traverse the older rocks. An intrusion of pink felsite in early Old Red times has been the cause of Tinto Hill. Evidences of the Glacial period are abundant in the form of kames and other deposits of gravel, sand and boulder clay. The ice in flowing northward and southward from the higher ground took an easterly direction when it reached the lower ground. In the lower reaches of the Clyde the remains of old beaches at 25, 50 and 100 ft. above the present sea-level are to be observed.

Climate and Agriculture.—The rainfall averages 42 in. annually, being higher in the hill country and lower towards the north. The temperature for the year averages 48° F., for January 38° and for July 59°. The area under grain has shown a downward tendency since 1880. Oats is the principal crop, but barley and wheat are also grown. Potatoes and turnips are raised on a large scale. In the Lower Ward market-gardening has increased considerably, and the quantity of vegetables, grapes and tomatoes reared under glass has reached great proportions. An ancient industry in the vale of the Clyde for many miles below Lanark is the cultivation of fruit, several of the orchards being said to date from the time of Bede. The apples and pears are of good repute. There has been a remarkable extension in the culture of strawberries, hundreds of acres being laid down in beds. The sheep walks in the upper and middle wards are heavily stocked and the herds of cattle are extensive, the favoured breeds being Ayrshire and a cross between this and "improved Lanark." Dairy-farming flourishes, the cheeses of Carnwath and Lesmahagow being in steady demand. Clydesdale draught-horses are of high class. They are supposed to have been bred from Flanders horses imported early in the 18th century by the 5th duke of Hamilton. Most of the horses are kept for agricultural work, but a considerable number of unbroken horses and mares are maintained for stock. Pigs are numerous, being extensively reared by the miners. The largest farms are situated in the Upper Ward, but the general holding runs from 50 to 100 acres. More than 21,000 acres are under wood.

Other Industries.—The leading industries are those in connexion with the rich and extensive coal and iron field to the east and south-east of Glasgow; the shipbuilding at Govan and Partick and in Glasgow harbour; the textiles at Airdrie, Blantyre, Hamilton, Lanark, New Lanark, Rutherglen and Glasgow; engineering at Cambuslang, Carluke, Coatbridge, Kinning Park, Motherwell and Wishaw, and the varied and flourishing manufactures centred in and around Glasgow.

Communications.—In the north of the county, where population is most dense and the mineral field exceptionally rich, railway facilities are highly developed, there being for 10 or 12 m. around Glasgow quite a network of lines. The Caledonian Railway Company's main line to the south runs through the whole length of the shire, sending off branches at several points, especially at Carstairs Junction. The North British Railway Company serves various towns in the lower and middle wards and its lines to Edinburgh cross the north-western corner and the north of the county. Only in the immediate neighbourhood of Glasgow does the Glasgow and South Western system compete for Lanarkshire traffic, though it combines with the Caledonian to work the Mid-Lanarkshire and Ayrshire railway. The Monkland Canal in the far north and the Forth and Clyde Canal in the north and north-west carry a considerable amount of goods, and before the days of railways afforded one of the principal means of communication between east and west.

Population and Administration.—The population amounted in 1891 to 1,105,899 and in 1901 to 1,339,327, or 1523 persons to the sq. m. Thus though only tenth in point of extent, it is much the most populous county in Scotland, containing within its bounds nearly one-third of the population of the country. In 1901 there were 104 persons speaking Gaelic only, and 26,905 speaking Gaelic and English. The chief towns, with populations in 1901, apart from Glasgow, are Airdrie (22,288), Cambuslang (12,252), Coatbridge (36,991), Govan (82,174), Hamilton (32,775), Kinning Park (13,852), Larkhall (11,879), Motherwell (30,418), Partick (54,298), Rutherglen (17,220), Shettleston (12,154), Wishaw (20,873). Among smaller towns are Bellshill, Carluke, Holytown, Lanark, Stonefield, Tollcross and Uddingston; and Lesmahagow and East Kilbride are populous villages and mining centres. The county is divided into six parliamentary divisions:—North-east, North-west, Mid and South Lanark, Govan and Partick each returning one member. The royal burghs are Glasgow, Lanark and Rutherglen; the municipal and police burghs Airdrie, Biggar, Coatbridge, Glasgow, Govan, Hamilton, Kinning Park, Lanark, Motherwell, Partick, Rutherglen and Wishaw. Glasgow returns seven members to Parliament; Airdrie, Hamilton and Lanark belong to the Falkirk group and Rutherglen to the Kilmarnock group of parliamentary burghs. Lanarkshire is a sheriffdom, whose sheriff-principal is confined to his judicial duties in the county, and he has eight substitutes, five of whom sit constantly in Glasgow, and one each at Airdrie, Hamilton and Lanark. The shire is under school-board jurisdiction, many schools earning grants for higher education. For advanced education, besides the university and many other institutions in Glasgow there are a high school in Hamilton, and technical schools at Coatbridge and Wishaw. The county council expends the "residue" grant in supporting lectures and classes in agriculture and agricultural chemistry, mining, dairying, cookery, laundry work, nursery and poultry-keeping, in paying fees and railway fares and providing bursaries for technical students, and in subsidizing science and art and technical classes in day and evening schools. A director of technical education is maintained by the council. Lanark, Motherwell and Biggar entrust their shares of the grant to the county council, and Coatbridge and Airdrie themselves subsidize science and art and evening classes and continuation schools.

History.—At an early period Lanarkshire was inhabited by a Celtic tribe, the Damnonii, whose territory was divided by the wall of Antoninus between the Forth and Clyde (remains of which are found in the parish of Cadder), but who were never wholly subjugated by the Romans. Traces of their fortifications, mounds and circles exist, while stone axes, bronze celts, querns and urns belonging to their age are occasionally unearthed. Of the Romans there are traces in the camp on Beattock summit near Elvanfoot, in the fine bridge over the Mouse near Lanark, in the road to the south of Strathaven, in the wall already mentioned and in the coins and other relics that have been dug up. After their departure the country which included Lanarkshire formed part of the kingdom of Strathclyde, which, in the 7th century, was subdued by Northumbrian Saxons, when great numbers of the Celts migrated into Wales. The county once embraced a portion of Renfrewshire, but this was disjoined in the time of Robert III. The shire was then divided into two wards, the Over (with Lanark as its chief town) and the Nether (with Rutherglen as its capital). The present division into three wards was not effected till the 18th century. Independently of Glasgow, Lanarkshire has not borne any part continuously in the general history of Scotland, but has been the scene of

follows where necessary. The figures show population in 1901.

Northern Division.—This embraces almost all the county N. of the Ribble, including Furness, and a small area S. of the Ribble estuary. It is considerably the largest of the divisions. *Parliamentary divisions*, from N. to S.—North Lonsdale, Lancaster, Blackpool, Chorley. *Parliamentary, county and municipal boroughs*—Barrow-in-Furness (57,586; one member); Preston (112,989; two members). *Municipal boroughs*—Blackpool (county borough; 47,348), Chorley (26,852), Lancaster (40,329; county town), Morecambe (11,798). *Urban districts*—Adlington (4523; Chorley), Bispham-with-Norbreck (Blackpool), Carnforth (3040; Lancaster), Croston (2102; Chorley), Dalton-in-Furness (13,020), Fleetwood (12,082), Fulwood (5238; Preston), Grange (1993), Heysham (3381; Morecambe), Kirkham (3693, Preston), Leyland (6865; Chorley), Longridge (4304; Preston), Lytham (7185), Poulton-le-Fylde (2223; Blackpool), Preesall-with-Hackinsall (1423; Fleetwood), St Anne's-on-the-Sea (6838, a watering-place between Blackpool and Lytham), Thornton (3108, Fleetwood), Ulverston (10,064, in Furness), Withnell (3349; Chorley).

North-Eastern Division.—This lies E. of Preston, and is the smallest of the four. *Parliamentary divisions*—Accrington, Clitheroe, Darwen, Rossendale. *Parliamentary, county and municipal boroughs*—Blackburn (127,626; two members); Burnley (97,043; one member). *Municipal boroughs*—Accrington (43,122), Bacup (22,505), Clitheroe (11,414), Colne (23,000), Darwen (38,212), Haslingden (18,543, extending into South-Eastern division), Nelson (32,816), Rawtenstall (31,053). *Urban districts*—Barrowford (4959; Colne), Brierfield (7288; Burnley), Church (6463; Accrington), Clayton-le-Moors (8153; Accrington), Great Harwood (12,015; Blackburn), Oswaldtwistle (14,192; Blackburn), Padiham (12,205; Burnley), Rishton (7031, Blackburn), Trawden (2641; Colne), Walton-le-Dale (11,271, Preston).

South-Western Division.—This division represents roughly a quadrant with radius of 20 m. drawn from Liverpool. *Parliamentary divisions*—Bootle, Ince, Leigh, Newton, Ormskirk, Southport, Widnes. *Parliamentary boroughs*—the city and county and municipal borough of Liverpool (684,958, nine members); the county and municipal boroughs of St Helens (84,410; one member); Wigan (60,764; one member), Warrington (64,242; a part only of the parliamentary borough is in this county). *Municipal boroughs*—Bootle (58,566), Leigh (40,001), Southport (county borough; 48,083), Widnes (28,580). *Urban districts*—Abram (6306; Wigan), Allerton (1101; Liverpool), Ashton-in-Makerfield (18,687), Atherton (16,211), Billinge (4232; Wigan), Birkdale (14,197; Southport), Childwall (219; Liverpool), Formby (6060), Golborne (6789; St Helens), Great Crosby (7555; Liverpool), Haydock (8575; St Helens), Hindley (23,504; Wigan), Huyton-with-Roby (4661; St Helens), Ince-in-Makerfield (21,262), Lathom-and-Burscough (7113; Ormskirk), Litherland (10,592; Liverpool), Little Crosby (563; Liverpool), Little Woolton (1001; Liverpool), Much Woolton (4731; Liverpool), Newton-in-Makerfield (16,699), Ormskirk (6857), Orrell ([illegible]; Wigan), Prescot (7855; St Helens), Rainford (3359; St Helens), [illegible] (6699; Ormskirk), Standish-with-Langtree ([illegible]; Wigan), Tyldesley-with-Shakerley (14,843), Upholland ([illegible]; Wigan), Waterloo-with-Seaforth (23,102; Liverpool).

South-Eastern Division.—This is of about the same area as the [illegible] division, and it constitutes the heart of the industrial [illegible]. *Parliamentary divisions*—Eccles, Gorton, Heywood, Middleton, [illegible], Radcliffe-cum-Farnworth, Stretford, Westhoughton. [illegible] *boroughs*—the city and county of a city of Manchester ([illegible] members); with which should be correlated the adjacent [illegible] municipal borough of Salford (220,957; three [illegible]), the county and municipal boroughs of Bolton ([illegible]), Bury (58,029; one member), Rochdale ([illegible]; one member), Oldham (137,246; two members), and the [illegible] of Ashton-under-Lyne (43,890). Part only of [illegible] borough is within the county, and this [illegible] of the parliamentary boroughs of Staly- [illegible] *Municipal boroughs*—Eccles (34,369), Hey- [illegible] (25,178), Mossley (13,452). *Urban districts* [illegible] Audenshaw (7216; Ashton-under-Lyne), [illegible] Chadderton (24,892; Oldham), Crump- [illegible] Denton (14,934; Ashton-under-Lyne), [illegible]), Failsworth (14,152; Manchester), [illegible] Gorton (26,564; Manchester), Heaton [illegible] Horwich (15,084; Bolton), Hurst (7145; [illegible]; Eccles), Kearsley (9218; Bolton), [illegible] (11,485; Manchester), Little- [illegible] Little Hulton (7294; Bolton), Little [illegible] (4341; Rochdale), Norden (3907; [illegible] Manchester), Radcliffe (25,368; [illegible]), Royton (14,881; Oldham), [illegible] Swinton-and-Pendlebury (27,005; [illegible]; Bolton), [illegible]), West- [illegible]; Bury),

Lancashire is one of the counties palatine. It is attached to the duchy of Lancaster, a crown office, and retains the chancery court for the county palatine. The chancery of the duchy of Lancaster was once a court of appeal for the chancery of the county palatine, but now even its jurisdiction in regard to the estates of the duchy is merely nominal. The chancery of the county palatine has concurrent jurisdiction with the High Court of Chancery in all matters of equity within the county palatine, and independent jurisdiction in regard to a variety of other matters. The county palatine comprises six hundreds.

Lancashire is in the northern circuit, and assizes are held at Lancaster for the north, and at Liverpool and Manchester for the south of the county. There is one court of quarter sessions, and the county is divided into 33 petty sessional divisions. The boroughs of Blackburn, Bolton, Burnley, Liverpool, Manchester, Oldham, Salford and Wigan have separate commissions of the peace and courts of quarter sessions; and those of Accrington, Ashton-under-Lyne, Barrow-in-Furness, Blackpool, Bolton, Bury, Clitheroe, Colne, Darwen, Eccles, Heywood, Lancaster, Middleton, Mossley, Nelson, Preston, Rochdale, St Helens, Southport and Warrington have separate commissions of the peace only. There are 430 civil parishes. Lancashire is mainly in the diocese of Manchester, but parts are in those of Liverpool, Carlisle, Ripon, Chester and Wakefield. There are 787 ecclesiastical parishes or districts wholly or in part within the county.

Manchester and Liverpool are each seats of a university and of other important educational institutions. Within the bounds of the county there are many denominational colleges, and near Clitheroe is the famous Roman Catholic college of Stonyhurst. There is a day training college for schoolmasters in connexion with University College, Liverpool, and a day training college for both schoolmasters and schoolmistresses in connexion with Owens College, Manchester. At Edgehill, Liverpool, there is a residential training college for schoolmistresses which takes day pupils, at Liverpool a residential Roman Catholic training college for schoolmasters, and at Warrington a residential training college (Chester, Manchester and Liverpool diocesan) for schoolmistresses.

***History*.—The district afterwards known as Lancashire was after the departure of the Romans for many years apparently little better than a waste. It was not until the victory of Æthelfrith, king of Deira, near Chester in 613 cut off the Britons of Wales from those of Lancashire and Cumberland that even Lancashire south of the Ribble was conquered. The part north of the Ribble was not absorbed in the Northumbrian kingdom till the reign of Ecgfrith (670–685). Of the details of this long struggle we know nothing, but to the stubborn resistance made by the British leaders are due the legends of Arthur; and of the twelve great battles he is supposed to have fought against the English, four are traditionally, though probably erroneously, said to have taken place on the river Douglas near Wigan. In the long struggle for supremacy between Mercia and Northumbria, the country between the Mersey and Ribble was sometimes under one, sometimes under the other kingdom. During the 9th century Lancashire was constantly invaded by the Danes, and after the peace of Wedmore (878) it was included in the Danish kingdom of Northumbria. The *A.S. Chronicle* records the reconquest of the district between the Ribble and Mersey in 923 by the English king, when it appears to have been severed from the kingdom of Northumbria and united to Mercia, but the districts north of the Ribble now comprised in the county belonged to Northumbria until its incorporation with the kingdom of England. The names on the Lancashire coast ending in *by*, such as Crosby, Formby, Roby, Kirkby, Derby, show where the Danish settlements were thickest. William the Conqueror gave the lands between the Ribble and Mersey, and Amounderness to Roger de Poictou, but at the time of Domesday Book these had passed out of his hand and belonged to the king.**

The name Lancashire does not appear in Domesday; the lands between the Ribble and Mersey were included in Cheshire and those north of the Ribble in Yorkshire. Roger de Poictou soon regained his lands, and Rufus added to his possessions the rest of Lonsdale south of the Sands, of which he already held a part; and as he had the Furness fells as well, he owned all that is now known as Lancashire. In 1102 he finally forfeited all his lands, which Henry I. held till, in 1118, he created the honour of Lancaster by incorporating with Roger's forfeited

lands certain escheated manors in the counties of Nottingham, Derby and Lincoln, and certain royal manors, and bestowed it upon his nephew Stephen, afterwards king. During Stephen's reign the history of the honour presents certain difficulties, for David of Scotland held the lands north of the Ribble for a time, and in 1147 the earl of Chester held the district between the Ribble and Mersey. Henry II. gave the whole honour to William, Stephen's son, but in 1164 it came again into the king's hands until 1189, when Richard I. granted it to his brother John. In 1194, owing to John's rebellion, it was confiscated and the honour remained with the crown till 1267. In 1229, however, all the crown demesne between the Ribble and Mersey was granted to Ranulf, earl of Chester, and on his death in 1232 came to William Ferrers, earl of Derby, in right of his wife Agnes, sister and co-heir of Ranulf. The Ferrers held it till 1266, when it was confiscated owing to the earl's rebellion. In 1267 Henry III. granted the honour and county and all the royal demesne therein to his son Edmund, who was created earl of Lancaster. His son, Earl Thomas, married the heiress of Henry de Lacy, earl of Lincoln, and thus obtained the great estates belonging to the de Lacys in Lancashire. On the death of Henry, the first duke of Lancaster, in 1361, the estates, title and honour fell to John of Gaunt in right of his wife Blanche, the duke's elder daughter, and by the accession of Henry IV., John of Gaunt's only son, to the throne, the duchy and honour became merged in the crown.

The county of Lancaster is first mentioned in 1169 as contributing 100 marks to the Royal Exchequer for defaults and fines. The creation of the honour decided the boundaries, throwing into it Furness and Cartmel, which geographically belong to Westmorland; Lonsdale and Amounderness, which in Domesday had been surveyed under Yorkshire; and the land between the Ribble and Mersey. In Domesday this district south of the Ribble was divided into the six hundreds of West Derby, Newton, Warrington, Blackburn, Salford and Leyland, but before Henry II.'s reign the hundreds of Warrington and Newton were absorbed in that of West Derby. Neither Amounderness nor Lonsdale was called a hundred in Domesday, but soon after that time the former was treated as a hundred. Ecclesiastically the whole of the county originally belonged to the diocese of York, but after the reconquest of the district between the Ribble and Mersey in 923 this part was placed under the bishop of Lichfield in the archdeaconry of Chester, which was subdivided into the rural deaneries of Manchester, Warrington and Leyland. Up to 1541 the district north of the Ribble belonged to the archdeaconry of Richmond in the diocese of York, and was subdivided into the rural deaneries of Amounderness, Lonsdale and Coupland. In 1541 the diocese of Chester was created, including all Lancashire, which was divided into two archdeaconries: Chester, comprising the rural deaneries of Manchester, Warrington and Blackburn, and Richmond, comprising the deaneries of Amounderness, Furness, Lonsdale and Kendal. In 1847 the diocese of Manchester was created, which included all Lancashire except parts of West Derby, which still belonged to the diocese of Chester, and Furness and Cartmel, which were added to Carlisle in 1856. In 1878 by the creation of the diocese of Liverpool the south-eastern part of the county was subtracted from the Manchester diocese.

No shire court was ever held for the county, but as a duchy and county palatine it has its own special courts. It may have enjoyed palatine jurisdiction under Earl Morcar before the Conquest, but these privileges, if ever exercised, remained in abeyance till 1351, when Henry, duke of Lancaster, received power to have a chancery in the county of Lancaster and to issue writs therefrom under his own seal, as well touching pleas of the crown as any other relating to the common laws, and to have all *Jura Regalia* belonging to a county palatine. In 1377 the county was erected into a palatinate for John of Gaunt's life, and in 1396 these rights of jurisdiction were extended and settled in perpetuity on the dukes of Lancaster. The county palatine courts consist of a chancery which dates back at least to 1376, a court of common pleas, the jurisdiction of which was transferred in 1873 by the Judicature Act to the high court of justice, and a court of criminal jurisdiction which in no way differs from the king's ordinary court. In 1407 the duchy court of Lancaster was created, in which all questions of revenue and dignities affecting the duchy possessions are settled. The chancery of the duchy has been for years practically obsolete. The duchy and county palatine each has its own seal. The office of chancellor of the duchy and county palatine dates back to 1351.

Lancashire is famed for the number of old and important county families living within its borders. The most intimately connected with the history of the county are the Stanleys, whose chief seat is Knowsley Hall. Sir John Stanley early in the 15th century married the heiress of Lathom and thus obtained possession of Lathom and Knowsley. In 1456 the head of the family was created a peer by the title of Baron Stanley and in 1485 raised to the earldom of Derby. The Molyneuxes of Sephton and Croxteth are probably descended from William de Molines, who came to England with William the Conqueror, and is on the roll of Battle Abbey. Roger de Poictou gave him the manor of Sephton, and Richard de Molyneux who held the estate under Henry II. is undoubtedly an ancestor of the family. In 1628 Sir Richard Molyneux was advanced to the peerage of Ireland by the title of Viscount Maryborough, and in 1771 Charles, Lord Maryborough, became earl of Sefton in the peerage of Ireland. His son was created a peer of the United Kingdom as Baron Sefton of Croxteth. The Bootle Wilbrahams, earls of Lathom, are, it is said, descended from John Botyll of Melling, who was alive in 1421, and from the Wilbrahams of Cheshire, who date back at least to Henry III.'s reign. In 1755 the two families intermarried. In 1828 the title of Baron Skelmersdale was bestowed on the head of the family and in 1880 that of earl of Lathom. The Gerards of Bryn are said to be descended from an old Tuscan family, one of whom came to England in Edward the Confessor's time, and whose son is mentioned in Domesday. Bryn came into this family by marriage early in the 14th century. Sir Thomas Gerard was created a baronet by James I. in 1611, and in 1876 a peerage was conferred on Sir Robert Gerard. The Gerards of Ince were a collateral branch. The Lindsays, earls of Crawford and Balcarres, are representative on the female side of the Bradshaighs of Haigh Hall, who are said to be of Saxon origin. Other great Lancashire families are the Hoghtons of Hoghton Tower, dating back to the 12th century, the Blundells of Ince Blundell, who are said to have held the manor since the 12th century, now represented by the Weld-Blundells, the Tyldesleys of Tyldesley, now extinct, and the Butlers of Dewsey, barons of Warrington, of whom the last male heir died in 1586.

At the close of the 12th and during the 13th century there was a considerable advance in the importance of the towns; in 1199 Lancaster became a borough, in 1207 Liverpool, in 1230 Salford, in 1246 Wigan, and in 1301 Manchester. The Scottish wars were a great drain to the county, not only because the north part was subject to frequent invasions, as in 1322, but because some of the best blood was taken for these wars. In 1297 Lancashire raised 1000 men, and at the battle of Falkirk (1298) 1000 Lancashire soldiers were in the vanguard, led by Henry de Lacy, earl of Lincoln. In 1349 the county was visited by the Black Death and a record exists of its ravages in Amounderness. In ten parishes between September 1349 and January 1350, 13,180 persons perished. At Preston 3000 died, at Lancaster 3000, at Garstang 2000 and at Kirkham 3000. From the effects of this plague Lancashire was apparently slow to recover; its boroughs ceased to return members early in the 14th century and trade had not yet made any great advance. The drain of the Wars of the Roses on the county must also have been heavy, although none of the battles was fought within its borders; Lord Stanley's force of 5000 raised in Lancashire and Cheshire virtually decided the battle of Bosworth Field. The poverty of the county is shown by the fact that out of £40,000 granted in 1504 by parliament to the king, Lancashire's share was only £318. At the battle of Flodden (1513) the Lancashire archers led by Sir Edward Stanley almost totally destroyed the Highlanders on the right Scottish wing and greatly contributed to the victory. Under the Tudors the county prospered; the parliamentary boroughs once more began to return members, the towns increased in size, many halls were built by the gentry and trade increased.

In 1617 James I. visited Lancashire, and in consequence of a petition presented to him at Hoghton, complaining of the restrictions imposed upon Sunday amusements, he issued in 1618 the famous *Book of Sports*. Another of James's works, the *Daemonologie*, is closely connected with the gross superstitions concerning witches which were specially prevalent in Lancashire. The great centre of this witchcraft was Pendle Forest, in the parish of Whalley, and in 1612 twelve persons from Pendle and eight from Samlesbury were tried for witchcraft, nine of whom were hanged. In 1633 another batch of seventeen witches from Pendle were tried and all sentenced to be executed, but the king pardoned them. This was the last important case of witchcraft in Lancashire.

In the assessment of ship money in 1636 the county was put down for £1000, towards which Wigan was to raise £50, Preston £40, Lancaster £30, and Liverpool £25, and these figures compared with the assessments of £140 on Hull and £200 on Leeds show the comparative unimportance of the Lancashire boroughs. On the eve of the Great Rebellion in 1641 parliament resolved to take command of the militia, and Lord Strange, Lord Derby's eldest son, was removed from the lord lieutenancy. On the whole, the county was Royalist, and the moving spirit among the Royalists was Lord Strange, who became Lord Derby in 1642. Manchester was the headquarters of the Parliamentarians, and was besieged by Lord Derby in September 1642 for seven days, but not taken. Lord Derby himself took up his headquarters at Warrington and garrisoned Wigan. At the opening of 1643 Sir Thomas Fairfax made Manchester his headquarters. Early in February the Parliamentarians from Manchester successfully assaulted Preston, which was strongly Royalist; thence the Parliamentarians marched to Hoghton Tower, which they took, and within a few days captured Lancaster. On the Royalist side Lord Derby made an unsuccessful attack on Bolton from Wigan. In March a large Spanish ship, laden with ammunition for the use of parliament, was driven by a storm on Rossall Point and seized by the Royalists; Lord Derby ordered the ship to be burned, but the parliament forces from Preston succeeded in carrying off some of the guns to Lancaster castle. In March Lord Derby captured the town of Lancaster but not the castle, and marching to Preston regained it for the king, but was repulsed in an attack on Bolton. In April Wigan, one of the chief Royalist strongholds in the county, was taken by the parliament forces, who also again captured Lancaster, and the guns from the Spanish ship were moved for use against Warrington, which was obliged to surrender in May after a week's siege. Lord Derby also failed in an attempt on Liverpool, and the tide of war had clearly turned against the Royalists in Lancashire. In June Lord Derby went to the Isle of Man, which was threatened by the king's enemies. Soon after, the Parliamentarians captured Hornby castle, and only two strongholds, Thurland castle and Lathom house, remained in Royalist hands. In the summer, after a seven weeks' siege by Colonel Alexander Rigby, Thurland castle surrendered and was demolished. In February 1644 the Parliamentarians, under Colonel Rigby, Colonel Ashton and Colonel Moore, besieged Lathom house, the one refuge left to the Royalists, which was bravely defended by Lord Derby's heroic wife, Charlotte de la Trémoille. The siege lasted nearly four months and was raised on the approach of Prince Rupert, who marched to Bolton and was joined on his arrival outside the town by Lord Derby. Bolton was captured by storm; Rupert ordered that no quarter should be given, and it is usually said at least 1500 of the garrison were slain. Prince Rupert advanced without delay to Liverpool, which was defended by Colonel Moore, and took it after a siege of three weeks. After the battle of Marston Moor Prince Rupert soon appeared in Lancashire and small engagements took place at Ormskirk, Upholland and Preston; in November Liverpool was handed to the Parliamentarians. Lathom house was again the only strong place in Lancashire left to the Royalists, and in December 1645 after a five months' siege it was compelled to surrender through lack of provisions, and was almost entirely destroyed. For the moment the war in Lancashire was over. In 1648, however, the Royalist forces under the duke of Hamilton and Sir Marmaduke Langdale marched through Lancaster to Wigan, hoping to reach Manchester; but near Preston were routed by Cromwell in person. The remnant retreated through Wigan towards Warrington, and after being again defeated at Winwick surrendered at Warrington. In 1651 Charles II. advanced through Lancaster, Preston and Chorley on his southward march, and Lord Derby after gathering forces was on his way to meet him when he was defeated at Wigan. In 1658, after Cromwell's death, a Royalist rebellion was raised in which Lancashire took a prominent part, but it was quickly suppressed. During the Rebellion of 1715 Manchester was the chief centre of Roman Catholic and High Church Toryism. On the 7th of November the Scottish army entered Lancaster, where the Pretender was proclaimed king, and advanced to Preston, at which place a considerable body of Roman Catholics joined it. The rebels remained at Preston a few days, apparently unaware of the advance of the government troops, until General Wills from Manchester and General Carpenter from Lancaster surrounded the town, and on the 13th of November the town and the rebel garrison surrendered. Several of the rebels were hanged at Preston, Wigan, Lancaster and other places. In 1745 Prince Charles Edward passed through the county and was joined by about 200 adherents, called the Manchester regiment and placed under the command of Colonel Townley, who was afterwards executed.

The first industry established in Lancashire was that of wool, and with the founding of Furness abbey in 1127 wool farming on a large scale began here, but the bulk of the wool grown was exported, not worked up in England. In 1282, however, there was a mill for fulling or bleaching wool in Manchester, and by the middle of the 16th century there was quite a flourishing trade in worsted goods. In an act of 1552 Manchester "rugs and frizes" are specially mentioned, and in 1566 another act regulated the fees of the aulnager who was to have his deputies at Manchester, Rochdale, Bolton, Blackburn and Bury; the duty of the aulnagers was to prevent "cottons frizes and rugs" from being sold unsealed, but it must be noted that by cottons is not meant what we now understand by the word, but woollen goods. The 17th century saw the birth of the class of clothiers, who purchased the wool in large quantities or kept their own sheep, and delivered it to weavers who worked it up into cloth in their houses and returned it to the employers. The earliest mention of the manufacture of real cotton goods is in 1641, when Manchester made fustians, vermilions and dimities, but the industry did not develop to any extent until after the invention of the fly shuttle by John Kay in 1733, of the spinning jenny by James Hargreaves of Blackburn in 1765, of the water frame throstle by Richard Arkwright of Bolton in 1769, and of the mule by Samuel Crompton of Hall-in-the-Wood near Bolton in 1779. So rapid was the development of the cotton manufacture that in 1787 there were over forty cotton mills in Lancashire, all worked by water power. In 1789, however, steam was applied to the industry in Manchester, and in 1790 in Bolton a cotton mill was worked by steam. The increase in the import of raw cotton from 3,870,000 lb in 1769 to 1,083,600,000 in 1860 shows the growth of the industry. The rapid growth was accompanied with intermittent periods of depression, which in 1819 in particular led to the formation of various political societies and to the Blanketeers' Meeting and the Peterloo Massacre. During the American Civil War the five years' cotton famine caused untold misery in the county, but public and private relief mitigated the evils, and one good result was the introduction of machinery capable of dealing with the shorter staple of Indian cotton, thus rendering the trade less dependent for its supplies on America.

During the 18th century the only town where maritime trade increased was Liverpool, where in the last decade about 4500 ships arrived annually of a tonnage about one-fifth that of the London shipping. The prosperity of Liverpool was closely bound up with the slave trade, and about one-fourth of its ships were employed in this business. With the increase of trade the means of communication improved. In 1758 the duke of Bridgewater began the Bridgewater canal from Worsley to Salford and across the Irwell to Manchester, and before the end of the century the county was intersected by canals. In 1830 the first railway in England was opened between Manchester and Liverpool, and other railways rapidly followed.

The first recorded instance of parliamentary representation in Lancashire was in 1295, when two knights were returned for the county and two burgesses each for the boroughs of Lancaster, Preston, Wigan and Liverpool. The sheriff added to this return "There is no city in the county of Lancaster." The boroughs were, however, excused one after another from parliamentary repesentation, which was felt as a burden owing to the compulsory payment of the members' wages. Lancaster ceased to send members in 1331 after making nineteen returns, but renewed its privileges in 1529; from 1529 to 1547 there are no parliamentary returns, but from 1547 to 1867 Lancaster continued to return two members. Preston similarly was excused after 1331, after making eleven returns, but in 1529 and from 1547 onwards returned two members. Liverpool and Wigan sent members in 1295 and 1307, but not again till 1547. To the writ issued in 1362 the sheriff in his return says: "There is not any City or Borough in this County from which citizens or burgesses ought or are accustomed to come as this Writ requires." In 1559 Clitheroe and Newton-le-Willows first sent two members. Thus in all Lancashire returned fourteen members, and, with a brief exception during the Commonwealth, this continued to be the parliamentary representation till 1832. By the Reform Act of 1832 Lancashire was assigned four members, two for the northern and two for the southern division. Lancaster, Preston, Wigan and Liverpool continued to send two members, Clitheroe returned one and Newton was disfranchised. The following new boroughs were created: Manchester, Bolton, Blackburn, Oldham, returning two members each; Ashton-under-Lyne, Bury, Rochdale, Salford and Warrington, one each. In 1861 a third member was given to South Lancashire and in 1867 the county was divided into four constituencies, to each of which four members were assigned; since 1885 the county returns twenty-three members. The boroughs returned from 1867 to 1885 twenty-five members, and since 1885 thirty-four.

Antiquities.—The Cistercian abbey of Furness (*q.v.*) is one of the finest and most extensive ecclesiastical ruins in England. Whalley abbey, first founded at Stanlawe in Cheshire in 1178, and removed in 1296, belonged to the same order. There was a priory of Black Canons at Burscough, founded in the time of Richard I., one at Conishead dating from Henry II.'s reign, and one at Lancaster. A convent of Augustinian friars was founded at Cartmel in 1188, and one at Warrington about 1280. There are some remains of the Benedictine priory of Upholland, changed from a college of secular priests in 1318; and the same order had a priory at Lancaster founded in 1094, a cell at Lytham, of the reign of Richard I., and a priory at Penwortham, founded shortly after the time of the Conqueror. The Premonstratensians had Cockersand abbey, changed in 1190 from a hospital founded in the reign of Henry II., of which the chapter-house remains. At Kersal, near Manchester, there was a cell of Cluniac monks founded in the reign of John, while at Lancaster there were convents of Dominicans and Franciscans, and at Preston a priory of Grey Friars built by Edmund, earl of Lancaster, son of Henry III.

Besides the churches mentioned under the several towns, the more interesting are those of Aldingham, Norman doorway; Aughton; Cartmel priory church (see FURNESS); Hawkshead; Heysham, Norman with traces of earlier date; Hoole; Huyton; Kirkby, rebuilt, with very ancient font; Kirkby Irleth, late Perpendicular, with Norman doorway; Leyland; Melling (in Lonsdale), Perpendicular, with stained-glass windows; Middleton, rebuilt in 1524, but containing part of the Norman church and several monuments; Ormskirk, Perpendicular with traces of Norman, having two towers, one of which is detached and surmounted by a spire; Overton, with Norman doorway; Radcliffe, Norman; Sefton, Perpendicular, with fine brass and recumbent figures of the Molyneux family, also a screen exquisitely carved; Stidd, near Ribchester, Norman arch and old monuments; Tunstall, late Perpendicular; Upholland priory church, Early English, with low massy tower; Urswick, Norman, with embattled tower and several old monuments; Walton-on-the-hill, anciently the parish church of Liverpool; Walton-le-Dale; Warton, with old font; Whalley abbey church, Decorated and Perpendicular, with Runic stone monuments.

The principal old castles are those of Lancaster; Dalton, a small rude tower occupying the site of an older building; two towers of Gleaston castle, built by the lords of Aldingham in the 14th century; the ruins of Greenhalgh castle, built by the first earl of Derby, and demolished after a siege by order of parliament in 1649; the ruins of Fouldrey in Piel Island near the entrance to Barrow harbour, erected in the reign of Edward III., now most dilapidated. There are many old timber houses and mansions of interest, as well as numerous modern seats.

See *Victoria History of Lancashire* (1906–1907); E. Baines, *The History of the County Palatine and Duchy of Lancaster* (1888); H. Fishwick, *A History of Lancashire* (1894); W. D. Pink and A. B. Beavan, *The Parliamentary Representation of Lancashire* (1889).

LANCASTER, HOUSE OF. The name House of Lancaster is commonly used to designate the line of English kings immediately descended from John of Gaunt, the fourth son of Edward III. But the history of the family and of the title goes back to the reign of Henry III., who created his second son, Edmund, earl of Lancaster in 1267. This Edmund received in his own day the surname of Crouchback, not, as was afterwards supposed, from a personal deformity, but from having worn a cross upon his back in token of a crusading vow. He is not a person of much importance in history except in relation to a strange theory raised in a later age about his birth, which we shall notice presently. His son Thomas, who inherited the title, took the lead among the nobles of Edward II.'s time in opposition to Piers Gaveston and the Despensers, and was beheaded for treason at Pontefract. At the commencement of the following reign his attainder was reversed and his brother Henry restored to the earldom; and Henry being appointed guardian to the young king Edward III., assisted him to throw off the yoke of Mortimer. On this Henry's death in 1345 he was succeeded by a son of the same name, sometimes known as Henry Tort-Col or Wryneck, a very valiant commander in the French wars, whom the king advanced to the dignity of a duke. Only one duke had been created in England before, and that was fourteen years previously, when the king's son Edward, the Black Prince, was made duke of Cornwall. This Henry Wryneck died in 1361 without heir male. His second daughter, Blanche, became the wife of John of Gaunt, who thus succeeded to the duke's inheritance in her right; and on the 13th of November 1362, when King Edward attained the age of fifty, John was created duke of Lancaster, his elder brother, Lionel, being at the same time created duke of Clarence. It was from these two dukes that the rival houses of Lancaster and York derived their respective claims to the crown. As Clarence was King Edward's third son, while John of Gaunt was his fourth, in ordinary course on the failure of the elder line the issue of Clarence should have taken precedence of that of Lancaster in the succession. But the rights of Clarence were conveyed in the first instance to an only daughter, and the ambition and policy of the house of Lancaster, profiting by advantageous circumstances, enabled them not only to gain possession of the throne but to maintain themselves in it for three generations before they were dispossessed by the representatives of the elder brother.

As for John of Gaunt himself, it can hardly be said that this sort of politic wisdom is very conspicuous in him. His ambition was generally more manifest than his discretion; but fortune favoured his ambition, even as to himself, somewhat beyond expectation, and still more in his posterity. Before the death of his father he had become the greatest subject in England, his three elder brothers having all died before him. He had even added to his other dignities the title of king of Castile, having married, after his first wife's death, the daughter of Peter the Cruel. The title, however, was an empty one, the throne of Castile being actually in the possession of Henry of Trastamara, whom the English had vainly endeavoured to set aside. His military and naval enterprises were for the most part disastrous failures, and in England he was exceedingly unpopular. Nevertheless, during the later years of his father's reign the weakness of the king and the declining health of the Black Prince threw the government very much into his hands. He even aimed, or was suspected of aiming, at the succession to the crown; but in this hope he was disappointed by the action of the Good Parliament a year before Edward's death, in which it was settled that Richard the son of the Black Prince should be king after his grandfather. Nevertheless the suspicion with which he was regarded was not altogether quieted when Richard came to the throne, a boy in the eleventh year of his age. The duke himself complained in parliament of the way he was spoken of out of doors, and at the outbreak of Wat Tyler's insurrection the peasants stopped pilgrims on the road to Canterbury and made them swear never to accept a king of the name of John. On gaining possession of London they burnt his magnificent palace of the Savoy. Richard found a convenient way to get rid of John of Gaunt by sending him to Castile to make good his barren title, and on this expedition he was away three years. He succeeded so far as to make a treaty with his rival, King John, son of Henry of Trastamara, for the succession, by virtue of which his daughter Catherine became the wife of Henry III. of Castile some years later. After his return the king seems to have regarded him with greater favour, created him duke of Aquitaine, and employed him in repeated embassies to France, which at length resulted in a treaty of peace, and Richard's marriage to the French king's daughter.

Another marked incident of his public life was the support which he gave on one occasion to the Reformer Wycliffe. How far this was due to religious and how far to political considerations may be a question; but not only John of Gaunt but his immediate descendants, the three kings of the house of Lancaster, all took deep interest in the religious movements of the times. A reaction against Lollardy, however, had already begun in the days of Henry IV., and both he and his son felt obliged to discountenance opinions which were believed to be politically and theologically dangerous.

Accusations had been made against John of Gaunt more than once during the earlier part of Richard II.'s reign of entertaining designs to supplant his nephew on the throne. But these Richard never seems to have wholly credited, and during his three years' absence his younger brother, Thomas of Woodstock, duke of Gloucester, showed himself a far more dangerous intriguer. Five confederate lords with Gloucester at their head took up arms against the king's favourite ministers, and the Wonderful Parliament put to death without remorse almost every agent of his former administration who had not fled the country. Gloucester even contemplated the dethronement of the king, but found that in this matter he could not rely on the support of his associates, one of whom was Henry, earl of Derby, the duke of Lancaster's son. Richard soon afterwards, by declaring himself of age, shook off his uncle's control, and within ten years the acts of the Wonderful Parliament were reversed by a parliament no less arbitrary. Gloucester and his allies were then brought to account; but the earl of Derby and Thomas Mowbray, earl of Nottingham, were taken into favour as having opposed the more violent proceedings of their associates. As if to show his entire confidence in both these noblemen, the king created the former duke of Hereford and the latter duke of Norfolk. But within three months from this time the one duke accused the other of treason, and the truth of the charge, after much consideration, was referred to trial by battle according to the laws of chivalry. But when the combat was about to commence it was interrupted by the king, who, to preserve the peace of the kingdom, decreed by his own mere authority that the duke of Hereford should be banished for ten years—a term immediately afterwards reduced to five—and the duke of Norfolk for life.

This arbitrary sentence was obeyed in the first instance by both parties, and Norfolk never returned. But Henry, duke of Hereford, whose milder sentence was doubtless owing to the fact that he was the popular favourite, came back within a year, having been furnished with a very fair pretext for doing so by a new act of injustice on the part of Richard. His father, John of Gaunt, had died in the interval, and the king, troubled with a rebellion in Ireland, and sorely in want of money, had seized the duchy of Lancaster as forfeited property. Henry at once sailed for England, and landing in Yorkshire while King Richard was in Ireland, gave out that he came only to recover his inheritance. He at once received the support of the northern lords, and as he marched southwards the whole kingdom was soon practically at his command. Richard, by the time he had recrossed the channel to Wales, discovered that his cause was lost. He was conveyed from Chester to London, and forced to execute a deed by which he resigned his crown. This was recited in parliament, and he was formally deposed. The duke of Lancaster then claimed the kingdom as due to himself by virtue of his descent from Henry III.

The claim which he put forward involved, to all appearance, a strange falsification of history, for it seemed to rest upon the supposition that Edmund of Lancaster, and not Edward I., was the eldest son of Henry III. A story had gone about, even in the days of John of Gaunt, who, if we may trust the chronicler John Hardyng (*Chronicle*, pp. 290 [illegible]) had got it inserted in chronicles deposited in various monasteries, that this Edmund, surnamed Crouchback, was really hump-backed, and that he was set aside in favour of his younger brother Edward on account of his deformity. No chronicle, however, is known to exist which actually states that Edmund Crouchback was thus set aside; and in point of fact he had no deformity at all, while Edward was six years his senior. Hardyng's testimony is, moreover, suspicious as reflecting the prejudices of the Percys after they had turned against Henry IV., for Hardyng himself expressly says that the earl of Northumberland was the source of his information (see note, p. 353 of his *Chronicle*). But a statement in the continuation of the chronicle called the *Eulogium* (vol. iii. pp. 369, 370) corroborates Hardyng to some extent; for we are told that John of Gaunt had once desired in parliament that his son should be recognized on this flimsy plea as heir to the crown; and when Roger Mortimer, earl of March, denied the story and insisted on his own claim as descended from Lionel, duke of Clarence, Richard imposed silence on both parties. However this may be, it is certain that this story, though not directly asserted to be true, was indirectly pointed at by Henry when he put forward his claim, and no one was then bold enough to challenge it.

This was partly due, no doubt, to the fact that the true lineal heir after Richard was then a child, Edmund, who had just succeeded his father as earl of March. Another circumstance was unfavourable to the house of Mortimer—that it derived its title through a woman. No case precisely similar had as yet arisen, and, notwithstanding the precedent of Henry II., it might be doubted whether succession through a female was favoured by the constitution. If not, Henry could say with truth that he was the direct heir of his grandfather, Edward III. If, on the other hand, succession through females was valid, he could trace his descent through his mother from Henry III. by a very illustrious line of ancestors. And, in the words by which he formally made his claim, he ventured to say no more than that he was descended from the king last mentioned "by right line of the blood." In what particular way that "right line" was to be traced he did not venture to indicate.

A brief epitome of the reigns of the three successive kings belonging to the house of Lancaster (Henry IV., V. and VI.) will be found elsewhere. With the death of Henry VI. the direct male line of John of Gaunt became extinct. But by his daughters he became the ancestor of more than one line of foreign kings, while his descendants by his third wife, Catherine Swynford, conveyed the crown of England to the house of Tudor. It is true that his children by this lady were born before he married her; but they were made legitimate by act of parliament, and, though Henry IV. in confirming the privilege thus granted to them endeavoured to debar them from the succession to the crown, it is now ascertained that there was no such reservation in the original act, and the title claimed by Henry VII. was probably better than he himself supposed.

We show on the following page a pedigree of the royal and illustrious houses that traced their descent from John of Gaunt. (J. GA.)

LANCASTER, HENRY, EARL OF (*c.* 1281–1345), was the second son of Edmund, earl of Lancaster (d. 1296), and consequently a grandson of Henry III. During his early days he took part in campaigns in Flanders, Scotland and Wales, but was quite overshadowed by his elder brother Thomas (see below). In 1324, two years after Thomas had lost his life for opposing the king, Henry was made earl of Leicester by his cousin, Edward II., but he was not able to secure the titles and estates of Lancaster to which he was heir, and he showed openly that his sympathies were with his dead brother. When Queen Isabella took up arms against her husband in 1326 she was joined at once by the earl, who took a leading part in the proceedings against the king and his favourites, the Despensers, being Edward's gaoler at Kenilworth castle. Edward III. being now on the throne, Leicester secured the earldom of Lancaster and his brother's lands, becoming also steward of England; he knighted the young king and was the foremost

TABLE OF THE PRINCIPAL DESCENDANTS OF JOHN OF GAUNT.

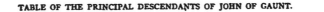

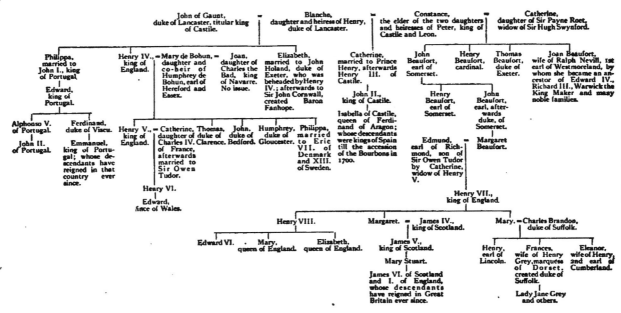

John of Gaunt, duke of Lancaster, titular king of Castile. = Blanche, daughter and heiress of Henry, duke of Lancaster. = Constance, the elder of the two daughters and heiresses of Peter, king of Castile and Leon. = Catherine, daughter of Sir Payne Roet, widow of Sir Hugh Swynford.

Issue of John of Gaunt and Blanche:

- Philippa, married to John I., king of Portugal.
  - Edward, king of Portugal.
    - Alphonso V. of Portugal.
      - John II. of Portugal.
    - Ferdinand, duke of Viseu.
      - Emmanuel, king of Portugal; whose descendants have reigned in that country ever since.
- Henry IV., king of England. = Mary de Bohun, daughter and co-heir of Humphrey de Bohun, earl of Hereford and Essex. = Joan, daughter of Charles the Bad, king of Navarre. No issue.
  - Henry V., king of England. = Catherine, daughter of Charles IV. of France, afterwards married to Sir Owen Tudor.
    - Henry VI.
      - Edward, prince of Wales.
  - Thomas, duke of Clarence.
  - John, duke of Bedford.
  - Humphrey, duke of Gloucester.
  - Philippa, married to Eric VII. of Denmark and XIII. of Sweden.
- Elizabeth, married to John Holand, duke of Exeter, who was beheaded by Henry IV.; afterwards to Sir John Cornwall, created Baron Fanhope.

Issue of John of Gaunt and Constance:

- Catherine, married to Prince Henry, afterwards Henry III. of Castile.
  - John II., king of Castile.
    - Isabella of Castile, queen of Ferdinand of Aragon; whose descendants were kings of Spain till the accession of the Bourbons in 1700.

Issue of John of Gaunt and Catherine:

- John Beaufort, earl of Somerset.
  - Henry Beaufort, earl of Somerset.
  - John Beaufort, earl, afterwards duke, of Somerset.
    - Margaret Beaufort. = Edmund, earl of Richmond, son of Sir Owen Tudor by Catherine, widow of Henry V.
      - Henry VII., king of England.
        - Henry VIII.
          - Edward VI.
          - Mary, queen of England.
          - Elizabeth, queen of England.
        - Margaret. = James IV., king of Scotland.
          - James V., king of Scotland.
            - Mary Stuart.
              - James VI. of Scotland and I. of England, whose descendants have reigned in Great Britain ever since.
        - Mary. = Charles Brandon, duke of Suffolk.
          - Henry, earl of Lincoln.
          - Frances, wife of Henry Grey, marquess of Dorset, created duke of Suffolk.
            - Lady Jane Grey and others.
          - Eleanor, wife of Henry, 2nd earl of Cumberland.
- Henry Beaufort, cardinal.
- Thomas Beaufort, duke of Exeter.
- Joan Beaufort, wife of Ralph Nevill, 1st earl of Westmoreland, by whom she became an ancestor of Edward IV., Richard III., Warwick the King Maker and many noble families.

[illegible]

East Indies . . . , ed. Sir Clements Markham, Hakluyt Soc. (1877), *Calendars of State Papers, East Indies.* The original journals of Lancaster's voyage of 1601–1603 have disappeared, and here we have only Purchas to go on.

LANCASTER, JOHN OF GAUNT, Duke of (1340–1399), fourth son of Edward III. and Queen Philippa, was born in March 1340 at Ghent, whence his name. On the 29th of September 1342 he was made earl of Richmond; as a child he was present at the sea fight with the Spaniards in August 1350, but his first military service was in 1355, when he was knighted. On the 19th of May 1359 he married his cousin Blanche, daughter and ultimately sole heiress of Henry, duke of Lancaster. In her right he became earl of Lancaster in 1361, and next year was created duke. His marriage made him the greatest lord in England, but for some time he took no prominent part in public affairs. In 1366 he joined his eldest brother, Edward the Black Prince, in Aquitaine, and in the year after led a strong contingent to share in the campaign in support of Pedro the Cruel of Castile. With this began the connexion with Spain, which was to have so great an influence on his after-life. John fought in the van at Najera on the 3rd of April 1367, when the English victory restored Pedro to his throne. He returned home at the end of the year. Pedro proved false to his English allies, and was finally overthrown and killed by his rival, Henry of Trastamara, in 1369. The disastrous Spanish enterprise led directly to renewed war between France and England. In August 1369 John had command of an army which invaded northern France without success. In the following year he went again to Aquitaine, and was present with the Black Prince at the sack of Limoges. Edward's health was broken down, and he soon after went home, leaving John as his lieutenant. For a year John maintained the war at his own cost, but whilst in Aquitaine a greater prospect was opened to him. The duchess Blanche had died in the autumn of 1369 and now John married Constance (d. 1394), the elder daughter of Pedro the Cruel, and in her right assumed the title of king of Castile and Leon. For sixteen years the pursuit of his kingdom was the chief object of John's ambition. No doubt he hoped to achieve his end, when he commanded the great army which invaded France in 1373. But the French would not give battle, and though John marched from Calais right through Champagne, Burgundy and Auvergne, it was with disastrous results; only a shattered remnant of the host reached Bordeaux.

The Spanish scheme had to wait, and when John got back to England he was soon absorbed in domestic politics. The king was prematurely old, the Black Prince's health was broken, John, in spite of the unpopularity of his ill-success, was forced into the foremost place. As head of the court party he had to bear the brunt of the attack on the administration made by the Good Parliament in 1376. It was not perhaps altogether just, and John was embittered by reflections on his loyalty. As soon as the parliament was dissolved he had its proceedings reversed, and next year secured a more subservient assembly. There came, however, a new development. The duke's politics were opposed by the chief ecclesiastics, and in resisting them he had made use of Wycliffe. With Wycliffe's religious opinions he had no sympathy. Nevertheless when the bishops arraigned the reformer for heresy John would not abandon him. The conduct over the trial led to a violent quarrel with the Londoners, and a riot in the city during which John was in danger of his life from the angry citizens. The situation was entirely altered by the death of Edward III. on the 21st of June. Though his enemies had accused him of aiming at the throne, John was without any taint of disloyalty. In his nephew's interests he accepted a compromise, disclaimed before parliament the truth of the malicious rumours against him, and was reconciled formally with his opponents. Though he took his proper place in the ceremonies at Richard's coronation, he showed a tactful moderation by withdrawing for a time from any share in the government. However, in the summer of 1378, he commanded in an attack on St Malo, which through no fault of his failed. To add to this misfortune, during his absence some of his supporters violated the sanctuary at Westminster. He vindicated himself somewhat bitterly in a parliament at Gloucester, but still avoiding a prominent part in the government, accepted the command on the Scottish border. He was there engaged when his palace of the Savoy in London was burnt during the peasants' revolt in June 1381. Wild reports that even the government had declared him a traitor made him seek refuge in Scotland. Richard had, however, denounced the calumnies, and at once recalled his uncle.

John's self-restraint had strengthened his position, and he began again to think of his Spanish scheme. He urged its undertaking in parliament in 1382, but nearer troubles were more urgent, and John himself was wanted on the Scottish border. There he sought to arrange peace, but against his will was forced into an unfortunate campaign in 1384. His ill-success renewed his unpopularity, and the court favourites of Richard II. intrigued against him. They were probably responsible for the allegation, made by a Carmelite, called Latemar, that John was conspiring against his nephew. Though Richard at first believed it, the matter was disposed of by the friar's death. However, the court party soon after concocted a fresh plot for the duke's destruction; John boldly denounced his traducers, and the quarrel was appeased by the intervention of the king's mother. The intrigue still continued, and broke out again during the Scottish campaign in 1385. John was not the man to be forced into treason to his family, but the impossibility of the position at home made his foreign ambitions more feasible.

The victory of John of Portugal over the king of Castile at Aljubarrota, won with English help, offered an opportunity. In July 1386 John left England with a strong force to win his Spanish throne. He landed at Corunna, and during the autumn conquered Galicia. Juan, who had succeeded his father Henry as king of Castile, offered a compromise by marriage. John of Gaunt refused, hoping for greater success with the help of the king of Portugal, who now married the duke's eldest daughter Philippa. In the spring the allies invaded Castile. They could achieve no success, and sickness ruined the English army. The conquests of the previous year were lost, and when Juan renewed his offers, John of Gaunt agreed to surrender his claims to his daughter by Constance of Castile, who was to marry Juan's heir. After some delay the peace was concluded at Bayonne in 1388. The next eighteen months were spent by John as lieutenant of Aquitaine, and it was not till November 1389 that he returned to England. By his absence he had avoided implication in the troubles at home. Richard, still insecure of his own position, welcomed his uncle, and early in the following year marked his favour by creating him duke of Aquitaine. John on his part was glad to support the king's government; during four years he exercised his influence in favour of pacification at home, and abroad was chiefly responsible for the conclusion of a truce with France. Then in 1395 he went to take up the government of his duchy; thanks chiefly to his lavish expenditure his administration was not unsuccessful, but the Gascons had from the first objected to government except by the crown, and secured his recall within less than a year. Almost immediately after his return John married as his third wife Catherine Swynford; Constance of Castile had died in 1394. Catherine had been his mistress for many years, and his children by her, who bore the name of Beaufort, were now legitimated. In this and in other matters Richard found it politic to conciliate him. But though John presided at the trial of the earl of Arundel in September 1397, he took no active part in affairs. The exile of his son Henry in 1398 was a blow from which he did not recover. He died on the 3rd of February 1399, and was buried at St Paul's near the high altar.

John was neither a great soldier nor a statesman, but he was a chivalrous knight and loyal to what he believed were the interests of his family. In spite of opportunities and provocations he never lent himself to treason. He deserves credit for his protection of Wycliffe, though he had no sympathy with his religious or political opinions. He was also the patron of Chaucer, whose *Boke of the Duchesse* was a lament for Blanche of Lancaster.

The chief original sources for John's life are Froissart, the maliciously hostile *Chronicon Angliae* (1328–1388), and the eulogistic *Chronicle* of Henry Knighton (both the latter in the Rolls Series). But fuller information is to be found in the excellent biography by S. Armytage-Smith, published in 1904. For his descendants see the table under LANCASTER, HOUSE OF. (C. L. K.)

LANCASTER, JOSEPH (1778–1838), English educationist, was born in Southwark in 1778, the son of a Chelsea pensioner. He had few opportunities of regular instruction, but he very early showed unusual seriousness and desire for learning. At sixteen he looked forward to the dissenting ministry; but soon after his religious views altered, and he attached himself to the Society of Friends, with which he remained associated for many years, until long afterwards he was disowned by that body. At the age of twenty he began to gather a few poor children under his father's roof, and to give them the rudiments of instruction, without a fee, except in cases in which the parent was willing to pay a trifle. Soon a thousand children were assembled in the Borough Road; and, the attention of the duke of Bedford, Mr Whitbread, and others having been directed to his efforts, he was provided with means for building a schoolroom and supplying needful materials. The main features of his plan were the employment of older scholars as monitors, and an elaborate system of mechanical drill, by means of which these young teachers were made to impart the rudiments of reading, writing and arithmetic to large numbers at the same time. The material appliances for teaching were very scanty—a few leaves torn out of spelling-books and pasted on boards, some slates and a desk spread with sand, on which the children wrote with their fingers. The order and cheerfulness of the school and the military precision of the children's movements began to attract much public observation at a time when the education of the poor was almost entirely neglected. Lancaster inspired his young monitors with fondness for their work and with pride in the institution of which they formed a part. As these youths became more trustworthy, he found himself at leisure to accept invitations to expound what he called "his system" by lectures in various towns. In this way many new schools were established, and placed under the care of young men whom he had trained. In a memorable interview with George III., Lancaster was encouraged by the expression of the king's wish that every poor child in his dominions should be taught to read the Bible. Royal patronage brought in its train resources, fame and public responsibility, which proved to be beyond Lancaster's own powers to sustain or control. He was vain, reckless and improvident. In 1808 a few noblemen and gentlemen paid his debts, became his trustees and founded the society at first called the Royal Lancasterian Institution, but afterwards more widely known as the British and Foreign School Society. The trustees soon found that Lancaster was impatient of control, and that his wild impulses and heedless extravagance made it impossible to work with him. He quarrelled with the committee, set up a private school at Tooting, became bankrupt, and in 1818 emigrated to America. There he met at first a warm reception, gave several courses of lectures which were well attended, and wrote to friends at home letters full of enthusiasm. But his fame was short-lived. The miseries of debt and disappointment were aggravated by sickness, and he settled for a time in the warmer climate of Carácas. He afterwards visited St Thomas and Santa Cruz, and at length returned to New York, the corporation of which city made him a public grant of 500 dollars in pity for the misfortunes which had by this time reduced him to lamentable poverty. He afterwards visited Canada, where he gave lectures at Montreal, and was encouraged to open a school which enjoyed an ephemeral success, but was soon abandoned. A small annuity provided by his friends in England was his only means of support. He formed a plan for returning home and giving a new impetus to his "system," by which he declared it would be possible "to teach ten thousand children in different schools, not knowing their letters, all to read fluently in three weeks to three months." But these visions were never realized. He was run over by a carriage in the streets of New York on the 24th of October 1838, and died in a few hours.

As one of the two rival inventors of what was called the "monitorial" or "mutual" method of instruction, Lancaster's name was prominent for many years in educational controversy. Dr Andrew Bell (*q.v.*) had in 1797 published an account of his experiments in teaching; and Lancaster in his first pamphlet, published in 1803, frankly acknowledges his debt to Bell for some useful hints. The two worked independently, but Lancaster was the first to apply the system of monitorial teaching on a large scale. As an economical experiment his school at the Borough Road was a signal success. He had one thousand scholars under discipline, and taught them to read, write and work simple sums at a yearly cost of less than 5s. a head. His tract *Improvements in Education* described the gradation of ranks, the system of signals and orders, the functions of the monitors, the method of counting and of spelling and the curious devices he adopted for punishing offenders. Bell's educational aims were humbler, as he feared to "elevate above their station those who were doomed to the drudgery of daily labour," and therefore did not desire to teach even writing and ciphering to the lower classes. The main difference between them was that the system of the one was adopted by ecclesiastics and Conservatives,—the "National Society for the Education of the Poor in the principles of the Established Church" having been founded in 1811 for its propagation; while Lancaster's method was patronized by the *Edinburgh Review*, by Whig statesmen, by a few liberal Churchmen and by Nonconformists generally. It was the design of Lancaster and his friends to make national education Christian, but not sectarian,—to cause the Scriptures to be read, explained and reverenced in the schools, without seeking by catechisms or otherwise to attract the children to any particular church or sect. This principle was at first vehemently denounced as deistic and mischievous, and as especially hostile to the Established Church. To do them justice, it must be owned that the rival claims and merits of Bell and Lancaster were urged with more passion and unfairness by their friends than by themselves. Yet neither is entitled to hold a very high place among the world's teachers. Bell was cold, shrewd and self-seeking. Lancaster had more enthusiasm, a genuine and abounding love for children, and some ingenuity in devising plans both for teaching and governing. But he was shiftless, wayward and unmethodical, and incapable of sustained and high-principled personal effort. His writings were not numerous. They consist mainly of short pamphlets descriptive of the successes he attained at the Borough Road. His last publication, *An Epitome of the Chief Events and Transactions of my Own Life*, appeared in America in 1833, and is characterized, even more strongly than his former writings, by looseness and incoherency of style, by egotism and by a curious incapacity for judging fairly the motives either of his friends or his foes. We have since come to believe that intelligent teaching requires skill and previous training, and that even the humblest rudiments are not to be well taught by those who have only just acquired them for themselves, or to be attained by mere mechanical drill. But in the early stages of national education the monitorial method served a valuable purpose. It brought large numbers of hitherto neglected children under discipline, and gave them elementary instruction at a very cheap rate. Moreover, the little monitors were often found to make up in brightness, tractability and energy for their lack of experience, and to teach the arts of reading, writing and computing with surprising success. And one cardinal principle of Bell and Lancaster is of prime importance. They regarded a school, not merely as a place to which individual pupils should come for guidance from teachers, but as an organized community whose members have much to learn from each other. They sought to place their scholars from the first in helpful mutual relations, and to make them feel the need of common efforts towards the attainment of common ends. (J. G. F.)

LANCASTER, THOMAS, Earl of (*c.* 1277–1322), was the eldest son of Edmund, earl of Lancaster and titular king of Sicily, and a grandson of the English king, Henry III.; while he was related to the royal house of France both through his mother, Blanche, a granddaughter of Louis VIII., and his step-sister, Jeanne, queen of Navarre, the wife of Philip IV. A minor when Earl Edmund died in 1296, Thomas received his father's earldoms of Lancaster and Leicester in 1298, but did not become prominent in English affairs until after the accession of his cousin, Edward II., in July 1307. Having married Alice (d. 1348), daughter and heiress of Henry Lacy, earl of Lincoln, and added the earldom of Derby to those which he already held, he was marked out both by his wealth and position as the leader of the barons in their resistance to the new king. With his associates he produced the banishment of the royal favourite, Piers Gaveston, in 1308; compelled Edward in 1310 to surrender his power to a committee of "ordainers," among whom he himself was numbered; and took up arms when Gaveston returned to England in January 1312. Lancaster, who had just obtained the earldoms of Lincoln and Salisbury on the death of his father-in-law in 1311, drove the king and his favourite from Newcastle to Scarborough, and was present at the execution of Gaveston in June 1312. After lengthy efforts at mediation, he made his submission and received a full pardon from Edward in October 1313; but he refused to accompany the king on his march into Scotland, which ended at Bannockburn, and took advantage of the English disaster to wrest the control of affairs from the hands of Edward. In 1315 he took command of the forces raised to fight the Scots, and was soon appointed to the "chief place in the council," while his supporters filled the great offices of state, but his rule was as feeble as that of the monarch whom he had superseded. Quarrelling with some of the barons, he neglected both the government and the defence of the kingdom, and in 1317 began a private war with John, Earl Warrenne, who had assisted his countess to escape from her husband. The capture of Berwick by the Scots, however, in April 1318 led to a second reconciliation with Edward. A formal treaty, made in the following August, having been ratified by parliament, the king and earl opened the siege of Berwick; but there was no cohesion between their troops, and the undertaking was quickly abandoned. On several occasions Lancaster was suspected of intriguing with the Scots, and it is significant that his lands were spared when Robert Bruce ravaged the north of England. He refused to attend the councils or to take any part in the government until 1321, when the Despensers were banished, and war broke out again between himself and the king. Having conducted some military operations against Lancaster's friends on the Welsh marches, Edward led his troops against the earl, who gradually fell back from Burton-on-Trent to Pontefract. Continuing this movement, Lancaster reached Boroughbridge, where he was met by another body of royalists under Sir Andrew Harclay. After a skirmish he was deserted by his troops, and was obliged to surrender. Taken to his own castle at Pontefract, where the king was, he was condemned to death as a rebel and a traitor, and was beheaded near the town on the 22nd of March 1322. He left no children.

Although a coarse, selfish and violent man, without any of the attributes of a statesman, Lancaster won a great reputation for patriotism; and his memory was long cherished, especially in the north of England, as that of a defender of popular liberties. Over a hundred years after his death miracles were said to have been worked at his tomb at Pontefract; thousands visited his effigy in St Paul's Cathedral, London, and it was even proposed to make him a saint.

See *Chronicles of the Reigns of Edward I. and Edward II.*, edited with introduction by W. Stubbs (London, 1882–1883); and W. Stubbs, *Constitutional History*, vol. ii. (Oxford, 1896).

LANCASTER, a market town and municipal borough, river port, and the county town of Lancashire, England, in the Lancaster parliamentary division, 230 m. N.W. by N. from London by the London & North-Western railway (Castle Station); served also by a branch of the Midland railway (Green Ayre station). Pop. (1891) 33,256, (1901) 40,329. It lies at the head of the estuary of the river Lune, mainly on its south bank, 7 m. from the sea. The site slopes sharply up to an eminence crowned by the castle and the church of St Mary. Fine views over the rich valley and Morecambe Bay to the west are commanded from the summit. St Mary's church was originally attached by Roger de Poictou to his Benedictine priory founded at the close of the 11th century. It contains some fine Early English work in the nave arcade, but is of Perpendicular workmanship in general appearance, while the tower dates from 1759. There are some beautiful Decorated oak stalls in the chancel, brought probably from Cockersand or Furness Abbey.

The castle occupies the site of a Roman *castrum*. The Saxon foundations of a yet older structure remain, and the tower at the south-west corner is supposed to have been erected during the reign of Hadrian. The Dungeon Tower, also supposed to be of Roman origin, was taken down in 1818. The greater part of the old portion of the present structure was built by Roger de Poictou, who utilized some of the Roman towers and the old walls. In 1322 much damage was done to the castle by Robert

Bruce, whose attack it successfully resisted, but it was restored and strengthened by John of Gaunt, who added the greater part of the Gateway Tower as well as a turret on the keep or Lungess Tower, which on that account has been named "John o' Gaunt's Chair." During the Civil War the castle was captured by Cromwell. Shortly after this it was put to public use, and now, largely modernized, contains the assize courts and gaol. Its appearance, with massive buildings surrounding a quadrangle, is picturesque and dignified. Without the walls is a pleasant terrace walk. Other buildings include several handsome modern churches and chapels (notably the Roman Catholic church); the Storey Institute with art gallery, technical and art schools, museum and library, presented to the borough by Sir Thomas Storey in 1887; Palatine Hall, Ripley hospital (an endowed school for the children of residents in Lancaster and the neighbourhood), the asylum, the Royal Lancaster infirmary and an observatory in the Williamson Park. A new town hall, presented by Lord Ashton in 1909, is a handsome classical building from designs of E. W. Mountford. The Ashton Memorial in Williamson Park, commemorating members of the Ashton family, is a lofty domed structure. The grammar school occupies modern buildings, but its foundation dates from the close of the 15th century, and in its former Jacobean house near the church William Whewell and Sir Richard Owen were educated. A horseshoe inserted in the pavement at Horseshoe Corner in the town, and renewed from time to time, is said to mark the place where a shoe was cast by John of Gaunt's horse.

The chief industries are cotton-spinning, cabinet-making, oil cloth-making, railway wagon-building and engineering. Glasson Dock, 5 m. down the Lune, with a graving dock, is accessible to vessels of 600 tons. The Kendal and Lancaster canal reaches the town by an aqueduct over the Lune, which is also crossed by a handsome bridge dated 1788. The town has further connexion by canal with Preston. The corporation consists of a mayor, 8 aldermen and 24 councillors. Area, 3506 acres.

History.—Lancaster (Lone-caster or Lunecastrum) was an important Roman station, and traces of the Roman fortification wall remain. The Danes left few memorials of their occupation, and the Runic Cross found here, once supposed to be Danish, is now conclusively proved to be Anglo-Saxon. At the Conquest, the place, reduced in size and with its Roman castrum almost in ruins, became a possession of Roger de Poictou, who founded or enlarged the present castle on the old site. The town and castle had a somewhat chequered ownership till in 1266 they were granted by Henry III. to his son Edmund, first earl of Lancaster, and continued to be a part of the duchy of Lancaster till the present time. A town gathered around the castle, and in 1193 John, earl of Mertoun, afterwards king, granted it a charter, and another in 1199 after his accession. Under these charters the burgesses claimed the right of electing a mayor, of holding a yearly fair at Michaelmas and a weekly market on Saturday. Henry III. in 1226 confirmed the charter of 1199; in 1291 the style of the corporation is first mentioned as *Ballivus et communitas burgi*, and Edward III.'s confirmation and extension (1362) is issued to the mayor, bailiffs and commonalty. Edward III.'s charter was confirmed by Richard II. (1389), Henry IV. (1400), Henry V. (1421), Henry VII. (1488) and Elizabeth (1563). James I. (1604) and Charles II. (1665 and 1685) ratified, with certain additions, all previous charters, and again in 1819 a similar confirmation was issued. John of Gaunt in 1362 obtained a charter for the exclusive right of holding the sessions of pleas for the county in Lancaster itself, and up to 1873 the duchy appointed a chief justice and a puisne justice for the court of common pleas at Lancaster. In 1322 the Scots burnt the town, the castle alone escaping; the town was rebuilt but removed from its original position on the hill to the slope and foot. Again in 1389, after the battle of Otterburn, it was destroyed by the same enemy. At the outbreak of the Great Rebellion the burgesses sided with the king, and the town and castle were captured in February 1643 by the Parliamentarians. In March 1643 Lord Derby assaulted and took the town with great slaughter, but the castle remained in the hands of the Parliamentarians. In May and June of the same year the castle was again besieged in vain, and in 1648 the Royalists under Sir Thomas Tyldesley once more fruitlessly besieged it. During the rebellion of 1715 the northern rebels occupied Lancaster for two days and several of them were later executed here. During the 1745 rebellion Prince Charles Edward's army passed through the town in its southward march and again in its retreat, but the inhabitants stood firm for the Hanoverians.

Two chartered markets are held weekly on Wednesday and Saturday and three annual fairs in April, July and October. A merchant gild existed here, which was ratified by Edward III.'s charter (1362), and in 1688 six trade companies were incorporated. The chief manufactures used to be sailcloth, cabinet furniture, candles and cordage. The borough returned two members to parliament from 1295 to 1331 and again from some time in Henry VIII.'s reign before 1529 till 1867, when it was merged in the Lancaster division of north Lancashire. A church existed here, probably on the site of the parish church of St Mary's, in Anglo-Saxon times, but the present church dates from the early 15th century. An act of parliament was passed in 1792 to make the canal from Kendal through Lancaster and Preston, which is carried over the Lune about a mile above Lancaster by a splendid aqueduct.

See Fleury, *Time-Honoured Lancaster* (1891); E. Baines, *History of Lancashire* (1888).

LANCASTER, a city and the county-seat of Fairfield county, Ohio, U.S.A., on the Hocking river (non-navigable), about 32 m. S.E. of Columbus. Pop. (1900) 8991, of whom 442 were foreign-born and 212 were negroes; (1910 census) 13,093. Lancaster is served by the Hocking Valley, the Columbus & Southern and the Cincinnati & Muskingum Valley (Pennsylvania Lines) railways, and by the electric line of the Scioto Valley Traction Company, which connects it with Columbus. Near the centre of the city is Mt. Pleasant, which rises nearly 200 ft. above the surrounding plain and about which cluster many Indian legends; with 70 acres of woodland and fields surrounding it, this has been given to the city for a park. On another hill is the county court house. Lancaster has a public library and a children's home; and 6 m. distant is the State Industrial School for Boys. The manufactures include boots and shoes, glass and agricultural implements. The total value of the city's factory product in 1905 was $4,159,410, being an increase of 118·3% over that of 1900. Lancaster is the trade centre of a fertile agricultural region, has good transportation facilities, and is near the Hocking Valley and Sunday Creek Valley coal-fields; its commercial and industrial importance increased greatly, after 1900, through the development of the neighbouring natural gas fields and, after 1907–1908, through the discovery of petroleum near the city. Good sandstone is quarried in the vicinity. The municipality owns and operates its waterworks and natural gas plant. Lancaster was founded in 1800 by Ebenezer Zane (1747–1811), who received a section of land here as part compensation for opening a road, known as "Zane's Trace," from Wheeling, West Virginia, to Limestone (now Maysville), Kentucky. Some of the early settlers were from Lancaster, Pennsylvania, whence the name. Lancaster was incorporated as a village in 1831 and twenty years later became a city of the third class.

LANCASTER, a city and the county-seat of Lancaster county, Pennsylvania, U.S.A., on the Conestoga river, 68 m. W. of Philadelphia. Pop. (1900) 41,459, of whom 3492 were foreign-born and 777 were negroes; (1910 census) 47,227. It is served by the Pennsylvania, the Philadelphia & Reading and the Lancaster, Oxford & Southern railways, and by tramways of the Conestoga Traction Company, which had in 1909 a mileage of 152 m. Lancaster has a fine county court house, a soldiers' monument about 43 ft. in height, two fine hospitals, the Thaddeus Stevens Industrial School (for orphans), a children's home, the Mechanics' Library, and the Library of the Lancaster Historical Society. It is the seat of Franklin and Marshall College (Reformed Church), of the affiliated Franklin and Marshall Academy, and of the Theological Seminary of the Reformed Church, conducted in connexion with the college. The college was founded in 1852 by the consolidation of Franklin College, founded at Lancaster in 1787, and Marshall College, founded at Mercersburg in 1836, both of which had earned a high standing among the educational institutions of Pennsylvania. Franklin College was named in honour of Benjamin Franklin, an early patron; Marshall College was founded by the Reformed Church and was named in honour of John Marshall. The Theological Seminary was opened in 1825 at Carlisle, Pa., and was removed to York, Pa., in 1829, to Mercersburg, Pa., in 1837 and to Lancaster in 1871; in 1831 it was chartered by the Pennsylvania legislature. Among its teachers have been John W. Nevin and Philip Schaff, whose names, and that of the seminary, are associated with the so-called "Mercersburg Theology." At Millersville, 4 m. S.W. of Lancaster, is the Second Pennsylvania State Normal School. At Lancaster are the graves of General John F. Reynolds, who was born here; Thaddeus Stevens, who lived here after 1842; and President James Buchanan, who lived for many years on an estate, "Wheatland," near the city and is buried in the Woodward Hill Cemetery. The city is in a productive tobacco and grain region, and has a large tobacco trade and important manufactures. The value of the city's factory products increased from $12,750,429 in 1900 to $14,647,681 in 1905, or 14·9%. In 1905 the principal products were umbrellas and canes (valued at $2,782,879), cigars and cigarettes ($1,951,972), and foundry and machine-shop products ($1,036,526). Lancaster county has long been one of the richest agricultural counties in the United States, its annual products being valued at about $10,000,000; in 1906 the value of the tobacco crop was about $3,225,000, and there were 824 manufactories of cigars in the county.

Lancaster was settled about 1717 by English Quakers and Germans, was laid out as a town in 1730, incorporated as a borough in 1742, and chartered as a city in 1818. An important treaty with the Iroquois Indians was negotiated here by the governor of Pennsylvania and by commissioners from Maryland and Virginia in June 1744. Some of General Burgoyne's troops, surrendered at Saratoga, were confined here after the autumn of 1780. The Continental Congress sat here on the 27th of September 1777 after being driven from Philadelphia by the British; and subsequently, after the organization of the Federal government, Lancaster was one of the places seriously considered when a national capital was to be chosen. From 1799 to 1812 Lancaster was the capital of Pennsylvania.

LANCE, a form of spear used by cavalry (see SPEAR). The use of the lance, dying away on the decay of chivalry and the introduction of pistol-armed cavalry, was revived by the Polish and Cossack cavalry who fought against Charles XII. and Frederick the Great. It was not until Napoleon's time, however, that lancer regiments appeared in any great numbers on European battlefields. The effective use of the weapon—long before called by Montecucculi the "queen of weapons"—by Napoleon's lancers at Waterloo led to its introduction into the British service, and except for a short period after the South [illegible] War, in which it was condemned as an anachronism, [illegible] has shared, or rather contested, with the sword the premier [illegible] amongst cavalry arms. In Great Britain and other [illegible] lances are carried by the front rank of cavalry, except [illegible] cavalry, regiments, as well as by lancer regiments. In [illegible] since 1880, the *whole* of the cavalry has been armed [illegible] In Russia, on the other hand, line cavalry [illegible] recently, considered as a sort of mounted infantry [illegible] the lance was restricted to the Cossacks, and in [illegible] enjoys less favour than in Germany. Altogether [illegible] few questions of armament or military detail more [illegible] in the present day as in the past, than this of [illegible]

[illegible] used in the British service are of two kinds, those [illegible] with bamboo staves. The latter are much pre- [illegible] generally used, the "male" bamboo being peculiarly [illegible] The lance is provided with a sling, through [illegible] his right arm when the lance is carried slung, [illegible] shoe fitting into a bucket attached to the right [illegible] loop is also provided, by which the lance [illegible] the saddle when the trooper dismounts. The [illegible] service. The head is of the best steel. [illegible] owing to difficulty in obtaining [illegible] straight enough in the grain [illegible]

able length, for lance staves, have adopted a stave of steel tubing as well as one of pine (figs. 2, 3 and 4).

As to the question of the relative efficiency of the lance and the sword as the principal arm for cavalry, it is alleged that the former is heavy and fatiguing to carry, conspicuous, and much in the way when reconnoitring in close country, working through woods and the like; that, when unslung ready for the charge, it is awkward to handle, and may be positively dangerous if a horse becomes restive and the rider has to use both hands on the reins; that unless the thrust be delivered at full speed, it is easily parried; and, lastly, that in the *mêlée*, when the trooper has not room to use his lance, he will be helpless until he either throws it away or slings it, and can draw his sword. While admitting the last-mentioned objection, those who favour the lance contend that success in the first shock of contact is all-important, and that this success the lancer will certainly obtain, owing to his long reach enabling him to deliver a blow before the swordsman can retaliate, while, when the *mêlée* commences, the rear rank will come to the assistance of the front rank. Further, it is claimed that the power of delivering the first blow gives confidence to the young soldier; that the appearance of a lancer regiment, preceded as it were by a hedge of steel, has an immense moral effect; that in single combat a lancer, with room to turn, can always defeat an opponent armed with a sword; and, lastly, that in pursuit a lancer is terrible to an enemy, whether the latter be mounted or on foot. As in the case of the perennial argument whether a sword should be designed mainly for cutting or thrusting, it is unlikely that the dispute as to the merits of the lance over the sword will ever be definitely settled, since so many other factors — horsemanship, the training of the horse, the skill and courage of the adversary—determine the trooper's success quite as much as the weapon he happens to wield. The following passage from *Cavalry: its History and Tactics* (London, 1853), by Captain Nolan, explains how the lance gained popularity in Austria:—"In the last Hungarian war (1848–49) the Hungarian Hussars were . . . generally successful against the Austrian heavy cavalry—cuirassiers and dragoons; but when they met the Polish Lancers, the finest regiments of light horse in the Austrian service, distinguished for their discipline, good riding, and, above all, for their *esprit de corps* and gallantry in action, against those the Hungarians were not successful, and at once attributed this to the lances of their opponents. The Austrians then extolled the lance above the sword, and armed all their light cavalry regiments with it."

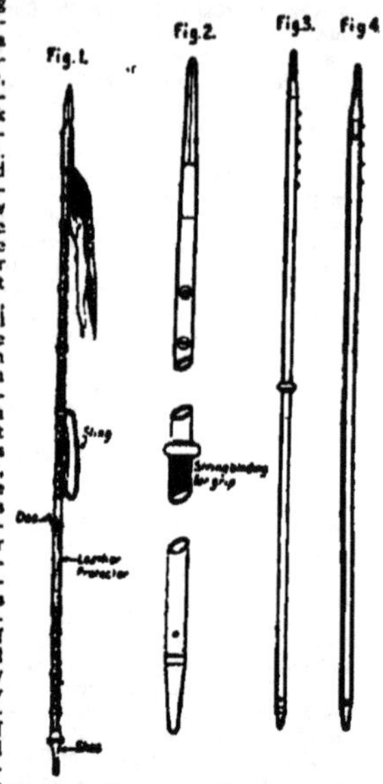

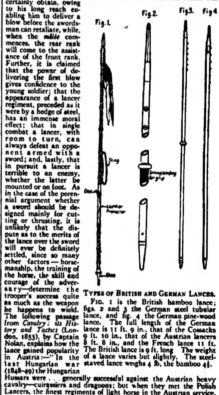

TYPES OF BRITISH AND GERMAN LANCES.

FIG. 1 is the British bamboo lance; figs. 2 and 3 the German steel tubular lance, and fig. 4 the German pine-wood lance. The full length of the German lance is 11 ft. 9 in., that of the Cossacks 9 ft. 10 in., that of the Austrian lancers 8 ft. 8 in., and the French lance 11 ft. The British lance is 9 ft. long. The weight of a lance varies but slightly. The steel-staved lance weighs 4 lb, the bamboo 4½.

The lancer regiments in the British service are the 5th, the 9th, the 12th, the 16th, the 17th and the 21st. All these were converted at different dates from hussars and light dragoons, the last-named in 1896. The typical lancer uniform is a light-fitting short-skirted tunic with a double-breasted front, called the plastron, of a different colour, a girdle, and a flat-topped lancer "cap," adapted from the Polish czapka (see UNIFORMS: *Naval and Military*). The British lancers, with the exception of the 16th, who wear scarlet with blue facings, are clad in blue, the 5th, 9th and 12th having scarlet facings and green, black and red plumes respectively, the 17th (famous as the "death or glory boys" and wearing a skull and crossbones badge) white facings and white plume, and the 21st light-blue facings and plume.

LANCELOT (Lancelot du Lac, or Lancelot of the Lake), a famous figure in the Arthurian cycle of romances. To the great majority of English readers the name of no knight of King Arthur's court is so familiar as is that of Sir Lancelot. The mention of Arthur and the Round Table at once brings him to mind as the most valiant member of that brotherhood and the secret lover of the Queen. Lancelot, however, is not an original member of the cycle, and the development of his story is still a source of considerable perplexity to the critic.

Briefly summarized, the outline of his career, as given in the German *Lanzelet* and the French prose *Lancelot*, is as follows: Lancelot was the only child of King Ban of Benoic and his queen Helaine. While yet an infant, his father was driven from his kingdom, either by a revolt of his subjects, caused by his own harshness (*Lanzelet*), or by the action of his enemy Claudas de la Deserte (*Lancelot*). King and queen fly, carrying the child with them, and while the wife is tending her husband, who dies of a broken heart on his flight, the infant is carried off by a friendly water-fairy, the Lady of the Lake, who brings the boy up in her mysterious kingdom. In the German poem this is a veritable "Isle of Maidens," where no man ever enters, and where it is perpetual spring. In the prose *Lancelot*, on the other hand, the Lake is but a mirage, and the Lady's court does not lack its complement of gallant knights; moreover the boy has the companionship of his cousins, Lionel and Bohort, who, like himself, have been driven from their kingdom by Claudas. When he reaches the customary age (which appears to be fifteen), the young Lancelot, suitably equipped, is sent out into the world. In both versions his name and parentage are concealed, in the *Lanzelet* he is genuinely ignorant of both; here too his lack of all knightly accomplishments (not unnatural when we remember he has here been brought up entirely by women) and his inability to handle a steed are insisted upon. Here he rides forth in search of what adventure may bring. In the prose *Lancelot* his education is complete, he knows his name and parentage, though for some unexplained reason he keeps both secret, and he goes with a fitting escort and equipment to Arthur's court to demand knighthood. The subsequent adventures differ widely: in the *Lanzelet* he ultimately reconquers his kingdom, and, with his wife Iblis, reigns over it in peace, both living to see their children's children, and dying on the same day, in good old fairy-tale fashion. In fact, the whole of the *Lanzelet* has much more the character of a fairy or folk-tale than that of a knightly romance.

In the prose version, Lancelot, from his first appearance at court, conceives a passion for the queen, who is very considerably his senior, his birth taking place some time after her marriage to Arthur. This infatuation colours all his later career. He frees her from imprisonment in the castle of Meleagant, who has carried her off against her will—(a similar adventure is related in *Lanzelet*, where the abductor is Valerin, and Lanzelet is not the rescuer)—and, although he recovers his kingdom from Claudas, he prefers to remain a simple knight of Arthur's court, bestowing the lands on his cousins and half-brother Hector. Tricked into a liaison with the Fisher King's daughter Elaine, he becomes the father of Galahad, the Grail winner, and, as a result of the queen's jealous anger at his relations with the lady, goes mad, and remains an exile from the court for some years. He takes part, fruitlessly, in the Grail quest, only being vouchsafed a fleeting glimpse of the sacred Vessel, which, however, is sufficient to cast him into unconsciousness, in which he remains for as many days as he has spent years in sin. Finally, his relations with Guenevere are revealed to Arthur by the sons of King Lot, Gawain, however, taking no part in the disclosure. Surprised together, Lancelot escapes, and the queen is condemned to be burnt alive. As the sentence is about to be carried into execution Lancelot and his kinsmen come to her rescue, but in the fight that ensues many of Arthur's knights, including three of Gawain's brothers, are slain. Thus converted into an enemy, Gawain urges his uncle to make war on Lancelot, and there follows a desperate struggle between Arthur and the race of Ban. This is interrupted by the tidings of Mordred's treachery, and Lancelot, taking no part in the last fatal conflict, outlives both king and queen, and the downfall of the Round Table. Finally, retiring to a hermitage, he ends his days in the odour of sanctity.

The process whereby the independent hero of the *Lanzelet* (who, though his mother is Arthur's sister, has but the slightest connexion with the British king), the faithful husband of Iblis, became converted into the principal ornament of Arthur's court, and the devoted lover of the queen, is by no means easy to follow, nor do other works of the cycle explain the transformation. In the pseudo-chronicles, the *Historia* of Geoffrey and the translations by Wace and Layamon, Lancelot does not appear at all; the queen's lover, whose guilty passion is fully returned, is Mordred. Chrétien de Troyes' treatment of him is contradictory; in the *Erec*, his earliest extant poem, Lancelot's name appears as third on the list of the knights of Arthur's court. (It is well, however, to bear in mind the possibility of later addition or alteration in such lists.) In *Cligès* he again ranks as third, being overthrown by the hero of the poem. In *Le Chevalier de la Charrette*, however, which followed *Cligès*, we find Lancelot alike as leading knight of the court and lover of the queen, in fact, precisely in the position he occupies in the prose romance, where, indeed, the section dealing with this adventure is, as Gaston Paris clearly proved, an almost literal adaptation of Chrétien's poem. The subject of the poem is the rescue of the queen from her abductor Meleagant; and what makes the matter more perplexing is that Chrétien handles the situation as one with which his hearers are already familiar; it is Lancelot, and not Arthur or another, to whom the office of rescuer naturally belongs. After this it is surprising to find that in his next poem, *Le Chevalier au Lion*, Lancelot is once, and only once, casually referred to, and that in a passing reference to his rescue of the queen. In the *Perceval*, Chrétien's last work, he does not appear at all, and yet much of the action passes at Arthur's court.

In the continuations added at various times to Chrétien's unfinished work the rôle assigned to Lancelot is equally modest. Among the fifteen knights selected by Arthur to accompany him to Chastel Orgueilous he only ranks ninth. In the version of the *Luite Tristran* inserted by Gerbert in his *Perceval*, he is publicly overthrown and shamed by Tristan. Nowhere is he treated with anything approaching the importance assigned to him in the prose versions. Welsh tradition does not know him; early Italian records, which have preserved the names of Arthur and Gawain, have no reference to Lancelot; among the group of Arthurian knights figured on the architrave of the north doorway of Modena cathedral (a work of the 12th century) he finds no place; the real cause for his apparently sudden and triumphant rise to popularity is extremely difficult to determine. What appears the most probable solution is that which regards Lancelot as the hero of an independent and widely diffused folk-tale, which, owing to certain special circumstances, was brought into contact with, and incorporated in, the Arthurian tradition. This much has been proved certain of the adventures recounted in the *Lanzelet*; the theft of an infant by a water-fairy; the appearance of the hero three consecutive days, in three different disguises, at a tournament; the rescue of a queen, or princess, from an Other-World prison, all belong to one well-known and widely-spread folk-tale, variants of which are found in almost every land, and of which numerous examples have been collected alike by M. Cosquin in his *Contes Lorrains*, and by Mr J. F. Campbell in his *Tales of the West Highlands*.

The story of the loves of Lancelot and Guenevere, as related by Chrétien, has about it nothing spontaneous and genuine; in no way can it be compared with the story of Tristan and Iseult. It is the exposition of a relation governed by artificial and arbitrary rules, to which the principal actors in the drama must perforce conform. Chrétien states that he composed the poem (which he left to be completed by Godefroi de Leigni) at the request of the countess Marie of Champagne, who provided him with *matière et san*. Marie was the daughter of Louis VII. of France and of Eleanor of Aquitaine, subsequently wife of [illegible] Anjou and England. It is a matter of history that [illegible] daughters were active agents in fostering that [illegible] relations of the sexes which found its most [illegible] in the "Courts of Love," and which was [illegible] the dictum that love between husband and wife [illegible]. The logical conclusion appears to be that the [illegible] a "Tendenz-Schrift," composed under certain [illegible], in response to a special demand. The story [illegible] Iseult, immensely popular as it was, was too [illegible] we say too crude?)—to satisfy the taste of the [illegible] Chrétien was writing. Moreover, the Arthurian [illegible] popular story of the day, and Tristan did not [illegible] circle, though he was ultimately introduced, [illegible], it must be admitted, within its bounds. [illegible] cycle must have its own love-tale; Guenevere, [illegible] of that cycle, could not be behind the courtly [illegible] and lack a lover; one had to be found for her. [illegible] popular hero of a tale in which an adventure [illegible] the Charrette figured prominently, was pressed [illegible] Modred, Guenevere's earlier lover, being too [illegible] character; moreover, Modred was required for [illegible].

[illegible] the story to be assigned? Here we must [illegible] between the Lancelot proper and the Lancelot- [illegible] so far as the latter are concerned, we cannot [illegible] version of Chrétien,—nowhere, prior to the [illegible] Chevalier de la Charrette is there any evidence [illegible] such a story. Yet Chrétien does not claim to [illegible] the situation. Did it spring from the fertile [illegible] lady, Marie, or another? The authorship [illegible], on the other hand, is invariably ascribed [illegible] Map, the chancellor of Henry II., but so [illegible] of the Arthurian prose Romances. The [illegible] opinion is towards accepting Map as the [illegible] romance, which formed the basis for later [illegible] and there is a growing tendency to identify [illegible] original Lancelot with the source of the German [illegible]. The author, Ulrich von Zatzikhoven, tells us that he [illegible] from a French (welsches) book in the posses- [illegible] de Morville, one of the English hostages, who, in [illegible] Richard Cœur de Lion in the prison of Leopold [illegible]. Further evidence on the point is, unfortunately, [illegible]. To the student of the original texts [illegible] less interesting hero than Gawain, [illegible], each of whom possesses a well-marked [illegible] is the centre of what we may call individual [illegible] and excepting the incident of his being [illegible] by a water-fairy (from a Lai relating [illegible] story probably started), there is [illegible] Lancelot's character or career to distin- [illegible] romantic hero of the period. The [illegible] is good, easy and graceful, but [illegible] and interest, and the situations [illegible] manner. English readers, [illegible] through the medium of Malory's noble [illegible], carry away an impression [illegible] by a study of the original [illegible], in its rise and development, [illegible] stage of Arthurian romance; [illegible] for the folk, and it lacks alike [illegible] of the genuine "popular" [illegible]

[illegible] printed, J. C. Brunet chronicles [illegible] of this last date there [illegible] by Philippe Lenoire, [illegible] from a much fuller manu- [illegible] the only version available [illegible] text published [illegible] Roman de la Table Ronde, [illegible] was published by [illegible] Roman van Lancet [illegible] the Agravain [illegible] from Meleagant [illegible] closely with the Lenoire edition of 1533. The Books devoted by Malory to Lancelot are also drawn from this latter section of the romance; there is no sign that the English translator had any of the earlier part before him. Malory's version of the *Charrette* adventure differs in many respects from any other extant form, and the source of this special section of his work is still a question of debate among scholars. The text at his disposal, especially in the *Queste* section, must have been closely akin to that used by the Dutch translator and the compiler of Lenoire, 1533. Unfortunately, Dr Sommer, in his study on the *Sources of Malory*, omitted to consult these texts, with the result that the sections dealing with *Lancelot* and *Queste* urgently require revision.

[illegible] with [illegible] ferred [illegible] tough [illegible] which [illegible] the po[illegible] stirrup [illegible] can be [illegible] small [illegible] The G[illegible] ash in [illegible]

Bibliography.—*Lanzelet* (ed. Hahn, 1845, out of print and extremely difficult to obtain). Chrétien's poem has been published by Professor Wendelin Foerster, in his edition of the works of that poet, *Der Karrenritter* (1899). A Dutch version of a short episodic poem, *Lancelot et le cerf au pied blanc* will be found in M. Jonckbloet's volume, and a discussion of this and other *Lancelot* poems, by Gaston Paris, is contained in vol. xxx. of *Histoire littéraire de la France*. For critical studies on the subject cf. Gaston Paris's articles in *Romania*, vols. x. and xii.; Wechssler, *Die verschiedenen Redaktionen des Graal-Lancelot Cyklus*; J. L. Weston, *The Legend of Sir Lancelot du Lac* (Grimm Library, vol. xii.); and *The Three Days' Tournament* (Grimm Library, vol. xv.) an appendix to the previous vol. (J. L. W.)

LANCET (from Fr. *lancette*, dim. of *lance*, lance), the name given to a surgical instrument, with a narrow two-edged blade and a lance-shaped point, used for opening abscesses, &c. The term is applied, in architecture, to a form of the pointed arch, and to a window of which the head is a lancet-arch.

LANCEWOOD, a straight-grained, tough, light elastic wood obtained from the West Indies and Guiana. It is brought into commerce in the form of taper poles of about 20 ft. in length and from 6 to 8 in. in diameter at the thickest end. Lancewood is used by carriage-builders for shafts; but since the practice of employing curved shafts has come largely into use it is not in so great demand as formerly. The smaller wood is used for whip-handles, for the tops of fishing-rods, and for various minor purposes where even-grained elastic wood is a desideratum. The wood is obtained from two members of the natural order Anonaceae. The black lancewood or carisiri of Guiana (*Guatteria virgata*) grows to a height of 50 ft., is of remarkably slender form, and seldom yields wood more than 8 in. diameter. The yellow lancewood tree (*Duguetia quitarensis*, yari-yari, of Guiana) is of similar dimensions, found in tolerable abundance throughout Guiana, and used by the Indians for arrow-points, as well as for spars, beams, &c.

LAN-CHOW-FU, the chief town of the Chinese province of Kan-suh, and one of the most important cities of the interior part of the empire, on the right bank of the Hwang-ho. The population is estimated at 175,000. The houses, with very few exceptions, are built of wood, but the streets are paved with blocks of granite and marble. Silks, wood-carvings, silver and jade ornaments, tin and copper wares, fruits and tobacco are the chief articles of the local trade. Tobacco is very extensively cultivated in the vicinity.

LANCIANO (anc. *Anxanum*), a town and episcopal see of the Abruzzi, Italy, in the province of Chieti, situated on three hills, 984 ft. above sea-level, about 8 m. from the Adriatic coast and 12 m. S.E. of Chieti. Pop. (1901) 7642 (town), 18,316 (commune). It has a railway station on the coast railway, 19 m. S.E. of Castellammare Adriatico. It has broad, regular streets, and several fine buildings. The cathedral, an imposing structure with a fine clock-tower of 1619, is built upon bridges of brickwork, dating perhaps from the Roman period (though the inscription attributing the work to Diocletian is a forgery), that span the gorge of the Feltrino, and is dedicated to S. Maria del Ponte, Our Lady of the Bridge. The Gothic church of S. Maria Maggiore dates from 1227 and has a fine façade, with a portal of 1317 by a local sculptor. The processional cross by the silversmith Nicola di Guardiagrele (1422) is very beautiful. In S. Nicola is a fine reliquary of 1445 by Nicola di Francavilla. The church of the Annunziata has a good rose window of 1362. The industries of the town, famous in the middle ages, have declined. Anxanum belonged originally to the tribe of the Frentani and later became a *municipium*. It lay on the ancient highroad, which abandoned the coast at Ortona 10 m. to the N. and returned to it at Histonium (Vasto) Remains of a Roman theatre exist under the bishop's palace.

See V. Bindi, *Monumenti degli Abruzzi* (Naples, 1889, 690 sqq.), and for discoveries in the neighbourhood see A. de Nino in *Notizie degli scavi* (1884), 431. (T. As.)

LANCRET, NICOLAS (1660–1743), French painter, was born in Paris on the 22nd of January 1660, and became a brilliant depicter of light comedy which reflected the tastes and manners of French society under the regent Orleans. His first master was Pierre d'Ulin, but his acquaintance with and admiration for Watteau induced him to leave d'Ulin for Gillot, whose pupil Watteau had been. Two pictures painted by Lancret and exhibited on the Place Dauphine had a great success, which laid the foundation of his fortune, and, it is said, estranged Watteau, who had been complimented as their author. Lancret's work cannot now, however, be taken for that of Watteau, for both in drawing and in painting his touch, although intelligent, is dry, hard and wanting in that quality which distinguished his great model, these characteristics are due possibly in part to the fact that he had been for some time in training under an engraver. The number of his paintings (of which over eighty have been engraved) is immense; he executed a few portraits and attempted historical composition, but his favourite subjects were balls, fairs, village weddings, &c. The British Museum possesses an admirable series of studies by Lancret in red chalk, and the National Gallery, London, shows four paintings—the "Four Ages of Man" (engraved by Desplaces and l'Armessin), cited by d'Argenville amongst the principal works of Lancret. In 1719 he was received as Academician, and became councillor in 1735; in 1741 he married a grandchild of Boursault, author of *Aesop at Court*. He died on the 14th of September 1743.

See d'Argenville, *Vies des peintres*; and Ballot de Sovot, *Éloge de M. Lancret* (1743, new ed. 1874).

LAND, the general term for that part of the earth's surface which is solid and dry as opposed to sea or water. The word is common to Teutonic languages, mainly in the same form and with essentially the same meaning. The Celtic cognate forms are Irish *lann*, Welsh *llan*, an enclosure, also in the sense of "church," and so of constant occurrence in Welsh place-names, Cornish *lan* and Breton *lann*, health, which has given the French *lande*, an expanse or tract of sandy waste ground. The ultimate root is unknown. From its primary meaning have developed naturally the various uses of the word, for a tract of ground or country viewed either as a political, geographical or ethnographical division of the earth, as property owned by the public or state or by a private individual, or as the rural as opposed to the urban or the cultivated as opposed to the built on part of the country; of particular meanings may be mentioned that of a building divided into tenements or flats, the divisions being known as "houses," a Scottish usage, and also that of a division of a ploughed field marked by the irrigating channels, hence transferred to the smooth parts of the bore of a rifle between the grooves of the rifling.

For the physical geography of the land, as the solid portion of the earth's surface, see GEOGRAPHY. For land as the subject of cultivation see AGRICULTURE and SOIL, also RECLAMATION OF LAND. For the history of the holding or tenure of land see VILLAGE COMMUNITIES and FEUDALISM; a particular form of land tenure is dealt with under MÉTAYAGE. The article AGRARIAN LAWS deals with the disposal of the public land (*Ager publicus*) in Ancient Rome, and further information with regard to the part played by the land question in Roman history will be found under ROME: § *History*. The legal side of the private ownership of land is treated under REAL PROPERTY and CONVEYANCING (see also LANDLORD AND TENANT, and LAND REGISTRATION).

LANDAU, a town in the Bavarian Palatinate, on the Queich, lying under the eastern slope of the Hardt Mountains, 32 m by rail S.W. from Mannheim, at the junction of lines to Neustadt an der Hardt, Weissenburg and Saarbrücken. Pop. (1905) 17,165. Among its buildings are the Gothic Evangelical church, dating from 1285; the chapel of St Catherine built in 1344; the church of the former Augustinian monastery, dating from 1405; and the Augustinian monastery itself, founded in 1276 and now converted into a brewery. There are manufactures of cigars, beer, hats, watches, furniture and machines, and a trade in wine, fruit and cereals. Large cattle-markets are held here. Landau was founded in 1224, becoming an imperial city fifty years later. This dignity was soon lost, as in 1317 it passed to the bishopric of Spires and in 1331 to the Palatinate, recovering its former position in 1511. Captured eight times during the Thirty Years' War the town was ceded to France by the treaty of Westphalia in 1648, although with certain ill-defined reservations. In 1679 Louis XIV. definitely took possession of Landau. Its fortifications were greatly strengthened; nevertheless it was twice taken by the Imperialists and twice recovered by the French during the Spanish Succession War. In 1815 it was given to Austria and in the following year to Bavaria. The fortifications were finally dismantled in 1871.

The town is commonly supposed to have given its name to the four-wheeled carriage, with an adjustable divided top for use either open or closed, known as a "landau" (Ger. *Landauer*). But this derivation is doubtful, the origin of the name being also ascribed to that of an English carriage-builder, Landow, who introduced this form of equipage.

See E. Heuser, *Die Belagerungen von Landau in den Jahren 1702 und 1703* (Landau, 1894); Lehmann, *Geschichte der ehemaligen freien Reichsstadt Landau* (1851); and Jost, *Interessante Daten aus der 600 jährigen Geschichte der Stadt Landau* (Landau, 1879).

LANDECK, a town and spa in the Prussian province of Silesia, on the Biele, 73 m. by rail S. of Breslau and close to the Austrian frontier. Pop. (1905) 3,481. It is situated at an altitude of 1400 ft. It has manufactures of gloves. Landeck is visited by nearly 10,000 people annually on account of its warm sulphur baths, which have been known since the 13th century. In the neighbourhood are the ruins of the castle of Karpenstein.

See Langner, *Bad Landeck* (Glatz, 1872); Schütze, *Die Thermen von Landeck* (Berlin, 1895); Wehse, *Bad Landeck* (Breslau, 1886); Joseph, *Die Thermen von Landeck* (Berlin, 1887), and Patschovsky, *Führer durch Bad Landeck und Umgebung* (Schweidnitz, 1902).

LANDEN, JOHN (1719–1790), English mathematician, was born at Peakirk near Peterborough in Northamptonshire on the 23rd of January 1719, and died on the 15th of January 1790 at Milton in the same county. He lived a very retired life, and saw little or nothing of society; when he did mingle in it, his dogmatism and pugnacity caused him to be generally shunned. In 1762 he was appointed agent to the Earl Fitzwilliam, and held that office to within two years of his death. He was first known as a mathematician by his essays in the *Ladies' Diary* for 1744. In 1766 he was elected a fellow of the Royal Society. He was well acquainted with the works of the mathematicians of his own time, and has been called the "English d'Alembert." In his *Discourse* on the "Residual Analysis," he proposes to avoid the metaphysical difficulties of the method of fluxions by a purely algebraical method. The idea may be compared with that of Joseph Louis Lagrange's *Calcul des Fonctions*. His memoir (1775) on the rotatory motion of a body contains (as the author was aware) conclusions at variance with those arrived at by Jean le Rond, d'Alembert and Leonhard Euler in their researches on the same subject. He reproduces and further develops and defends his own views in his *Mathematical Memoirs*, and in his paper in the *Philosophical Transactions* for 1785. But Landen's capital discovery is that of the theorem known by his name (obtained in its complete form in the memoir of 1775, and reproduced in the first volume of the *Mathematical Memoirs*) for the expression of the arc of an hyperbola in terms of two elliptic arcs. His researches on elliptic functions are of considerable elegance, but their great merit lies in the stimulating effect which they had on later mathematicians. He also showed that the roots of a cubic equation can be derived by means of the infinitesimal calculus.

The list of his writings is as follows:—*Ladies' Diary*, various communications (1744–1760); papers in the *Phil. Trans.* (1754, 1760, 1768, 1771, 1775, 1777, 1785); *Mathematical Lucubrations* (1755); *A Discourse concerning the Residual Analysis* (1758); *The Residual Analysis*, book i. (1764); *Animadversions on Dr Stewart's Method of computing the Sun's Distance from the Earth* (1771); *Mathematical Memoirs* (1780, 1789).

[illegible], a town in the province of Liège, Belgium, an important [illegible] from Limburg, Liège and [illegible]. It is the birthplace of the first [illegible] of Landen from his grandson [illegible]. In [illegible] the French under Marshal Luxemburg [illegible] the Anglo-Dutch army under William III. This [illegible] from a village 3 m. W. of Landen. [illegible] under Frederick of Saxe-Coburg [illegible] the French under Dumouriez.

[illegible] ([illegible]–1834) and **JOHN** (1807–[illegible]), [illegible] of the Niger, were natives of Cornwall, [illegible]. At the age of eleven Richard [illegible] West Indies in the service of a merchant. Returning [illegible] of three years he took service with [illegible] with whom he travelled on the continent. [illegible] Major (afterwards General Sir) [illegible] through Cape Colony. In 1825 [illegible] to Hugh Clapperton, then preparing [illegible] to West Africa. He was Clapperton's [illegible] in this expedition, and on [illegible] in April 1827 Richard Lander, [illegible] parts of the Hausa states, returned [illegible] Yoruba bringing with him Clapper-[illegible] its publication (1829) was added [illegible] from *Kano to the Coast*, and in [illegible] another account of the expedi-[illegible] *Clapperton's Last Expedition* [illegible] *Adventures of the Author*. [illegible] autobiographical note. Richard [illegible] scientific attainments, had ex-[illegible] that the British government [illegible] determine the course of the lower [illegible] was accompanied by his brother [illegible] better educated than Richard, who [illegible]. Leaving England in January [illegible] Badagry on the Guinea coast on [illegible] travelled by the route previously [illegible] on the right bank of the Niger, [illegible]. Thence they ascended the river [illegible] the travellers began, [illegible] of the river, not knowing [illegible] in canoes accom-[illegible] instrument a common [illegible] river, ascertaining when [illegible] its stream, that their [illegible] the beginning of the delta [illegible] whom they were ransomed [illegible] they were taken to [illegible] a passage was obtained to [illegible]. The Landers [illegible] correctness the [illegible]

[illegible]

died on the 16th of November 1839 of a disease contracted in Africa.

See, besides the books mentioned, the *Narrative* of the Niger expedition of 1832–1834, published in 1837 by Macgregor Laird and R. A. K. Oldfield.

LANDES, a department in the south-west of France, formed in 1790 of portions of the ancient provinces of Guyenne (Landes, Condomois Chalosse), Gascony and Béarn, and bounded N. by Gironde, E. by Lot-et-Garonne and Gers, S. by Basses Pyrenées, and W (for 68 m.) by the Bay of Biscay. Pop. (1906) 293,397. Its area, 3615 sq. m., is second only to that of the department of Gironde. The department takes its name from the *Landes*, which occupy three-quarters of its surface, or practically the whole region north of the Adour, the chief river of the department. They are separated from the sea by a belt of dunes fringed on the east by a chain of lakes. South of the Adour lies the Chalosse—a hilly region, intersected by the Gabas, Luy and Gave de Pau, left-hand tributaries of the Adour, which descend from the Pyrenees. On the right the Adour is joined by the Midouze, formed by the junction of the Douze and the Midou. The climate of Landes is the Girondine, which prevails from the Loire to the Pyrenees. Snow is almost unknown, the spring is rainy, the summer warm and stormy. The prevailing wind is the south-west, and the mean temperature of the year is 53° F., the thermometer hardly ever rising above 82° or falling below 14°. The annual rainfall in the south of the department in the neighbourhood of the sea reaches 55 in., but diminishes by more than half towards the north-east.

The fertility of La Chalosse is counterbalanced by the comparative poorness of the soil of the Landes, and small though the population is, the department does not produce wheat enough for its own consumption. The chief cereal is maize; next in importance are rye, wheat and millet. Of vegetables, the bean is most cultivated. The vine is grown in the Chalosse, sheep are numerous, and the "Landes" breed of horses is well known. Forests, chiefly composed of pines, occupy more than half the department, and their exploitation forms the chief industry. The resin of the maritime pine furnishes by distillation essence of turpentine, and from the residue are obtained various qualities of resin, which serve to make varnish, tapers, sealing-wax and lubricants. Tar, and an excellent charcoal for smelting purposes, are also obtained from the pine-wood. The department has several mineral springs, the most important being those of Dax, which were frequented in the time of the Romans, and of Eugénie-les-Bains and Préchacq. The cultivation of the cork tree is also important. There are salt-workings and stone quarries. There are several iron-works in the department, those at Le Boucau, at the mouth of the Adour, are the most important. There are also saw-mills, distilleries, flour-mills, brick and tile works and potteries. Exports include resinous products, pine-timber, metal, brandy, leading imports are grain, coal, iron, millinery and furniture. In its long extent of coast the department has no considerable port. Opposite Cape Breton, however, where the Adour formerly entered the sea, there is, close to land, a deep channel where there is safe anchorage. It was from this once important harbour of Capbreton that the discoverers of the Canadian island of that name set out. Landes includes three arrondissements (Mont-de-Marsan, Dax and St Sever), 28 cantons and 334 communes.

Mont-de-Marsan is the capital of the department, which comes within the circumscription of the appeal court of Pau, the académie (educational division) of Bordeaux and the archbishopric of Auch, and forms part of the region of the 18th army corps. It is served by the Southern railway; there is some navigation on the Adour, but that upon the other rivers is of little importance. Mont-de-Marsan, Dax, St Sever and Aire-sur-l'Adour, the most noteworthy towns, receive separate notice. Hagetmau has a church built over a Romanesque crypt, the roof of which is supported on columns with elaborately-carved capitals. Sorde has an interesting abbey-church of the 13th and 14th centuries.

LANDES, an extensive natural region of south-western France, known more strictly as the Landes de Gascogne. It has an area of 5400 sq. m., and occupies three-quarters of the department of Landes, half of that of Gironde, and some 175,000 acres of Lot-et-Garonne. The Landes, formerly a vast tract of moorland and marsh, now consist chiefly of fields and forests of pines. They form a plateau, shaped like a triangle, the base of which is the Atlantic coast while the apex is situated slightly west of Nérac (Lot-et-Garonne). Its limits are, on the S. the river Adour; on the E. the hills of Armagnac, Eauzan, Condomois, Agenais and Bazadais; and on the N.E. the Garonne, the hills of Médoc and the Gironde. The height of the plateau ranges in general from 130 to 260 ft.; the highest altitude (498 ft.) is found in the east near Baudignan (department of Landes), from which point there is a gradual slope towards north, south, east and west. The soil is naturally sterile. It is composed of fine sand resting on a subsoil of tufa (*alios*) impermeable by water; for three-quarters of the year, consequently, the waters, settling on the almost level surface and unable to filter through, used to transform the country into unwholesome swamps, which the Landesats could only traverse on stilts. About the middle of the 18th century an engineer, François Chambrelent, instituted a scheme of draining and planting to remedy these evils. As a result about 1600 m. of ditches have been dug which carry off superficial water either to streams or to the lakes which fringe the landes on the west, and over 1,600,000 acres have been planted with maritime pines and oaks. The coast, for a breadth of about 4 m., and over an area of about 225,000 acres, is bordered by dunes, in ranges parallel to the shore, and from 100 to 300 ft. in height. Driven by the west wind, which is most frequent in these parts, the dunes were slowly advancing year by year towards the east, burying the cultivated lands and even the houses. Nicolas Thomas Brémontier, towards the end of the 18th century, devised the plan of arresting this scourge by planting the dunes with maritime pines. Upwards of 210,000 acres have been thus treated. In the south-west, cork trees take the place of the pines. To prevent the formation of fresh dunes, a "dune littorale" has been formed by means of a palisade. This barrier, from 20 to 30 ft high, presents an obstacle which the sand cannot cross. On the eastern side of the dunes is a series of lakes (Hourtin et Carcans, Lacanau, Cazau or Sanguinet, Biscarrosse, Aureilhan, St Julien, Léon and Soustons) separated from the sea by the heaping up of the sand. The salt water has escaped by defiltration, and they are now quite fresh The Basin of Arcachon, which lies midway between the lakes of Lacanau and Cazau, still communicates with the ocean, the current of the Leyre which flows into it having sufficient force to keep a passage open.

LANDESHUT, a town in the Prussian province of Silesia, at the north foot of the Riesengebirge, and on the river Bober, 65 m. S.W. of Breslau by rail. Pop. (1905) 9000. Its main industries are flax-spinning, linen-weaving and manufactures of cloth, shoes and beer. The town dates from the 13th century, being originally a fortress built for protection against the Bohemians. There the Prussians defeated the Austrians in May 1745, and in June 1760 the Prussians were routed by a greatly superior force of Austrians.

See Perschke, *Beschreibung und Geschichte der Stadt Landeshut* (Breslau, 1829).

LANDGRAVE (Ger. *Landgraf*, from *Land*, "a country" and *Graf*, "count"), a German title of nobility surviving from the times of the Holy Roman Empire. It originally signified a count of more than usual power or dignity, and in some cases implied sovereignty The title is now rare; it is borne by the former sovereign of Hesse-Homburg, now incorporated in Prussia, the heads of the various branches of the house of Hesse, and by a branch of the family of Fürstenberg. In other cases the title of landgrave is borne by German sovereigns as a subsidiary title, e.g. the grand-duke of Saxe-Weimar is landgrave of Thuringia.

LANDLORD AND TENANT. In *Roman Law*, the relationship of landlord and tenant arose from the contract of letting and hiring (*locatio conductio*), and existed also with special incidents, under the forms of tenure known as *emphyteusis*—the long lease of Roman law—and *precarium*, or tenancy at will (see ROMAN LAW).

Law of England.—The law of England—and the laws of Scotland and Ireland agree with it on this point—recognizes no absolute private ownership of land. The absolute and ultimate owner of all land is the crown, and the highest interest that a subject can hold therein—viz. an estate in fee simple—is only a tenancy. But this aspect of the law, under which the landlord, other than the crown, is himself always a tenant, falls beyond the scope of the present article, which is restricted to those holdings that arise from the hiring and leasing of land.

The legal relationship of landlord and tenant is constituted by a lease, or an agreement for a lease, by assignment, by attornment and by estoppel. And first of a lease and an agreement for a lease. All kinds of interests and property, whether corporeal, such as lands or buildings, or incorporeal, such as rights of common or of way, may be let The Benefices Act 1898, however, now prohibits the grant of a lease of an advowson. Titles of honour, offices of trust or relating to the administration of justice, and pensions granted by the crown for military services are also inalienable. Generally speaking, any person may grant or take a lease. But there are a number of common-law and statutory qualifications and exceptions. A lease by or to an infant is voidable at his option. But extensive powers of leasing the property of infants have been created by the Settled Estates Act 1877 and the Settled Land Act 1882 A person of unsound mind can grant or take a lease if he is capable of contracting. Leases may be made on behalf of lunatics subject to the jurisdiction in lunacy under the provisions of the Lunacy Act 1890 and the Settled Land Act 1882. A married woman can lease her "separate property" apart from or under the Married Women's Property Acts, as if she were a single woman (*feme sole*). As regards other property, the concurrence of her husband is generally necessary. An alien was, at common law, incapable of being either a lessor or a lessee. But this disqualification is removed by the Naturalization Act 1870. The right to deal with the property of a convict while he is undergoing sentence (but not while he is out of prison on leave) is, by the Forfeiture Act 1870, vested in his administrator Leases by or to corporations must be by deed under their common seal, and the leasing powers of ecclesiastical corporations in particular are subject to complicated statutory restrictions which cannot here be examined (see Phillimore, *Eccl Law*, 2nd ed., p. 1281). Powers of granting building and other leases have been conferred by modern legislation on municipal corporations and other local authorities.

Leases.

A person having an interest in land can, in general, create a valid interest only to the extent of that interest. Thus a tenant for years, or even from year to year only, may stand in his turn as landlord to another tenant. If he profess, however, to create a tenancy for a period longer than that to which his own interest extends, he does not thereby give to his tenant an interest available against the reversioner or remainder man. The subtenant's interest will expire with the interest of the person who created it. But as between the subtenant and his immediate lessor the subtenancy will be good, and should the interest of the lessor become greater than it was when the subtenancy was created the subtenant will have the benefit of it. On his side, again, the subtenant, by accepting that position, is estopped from denying that his lessor's title (whatever it be) is good. There are also special rules of law with reference to leases by persons having only a limited interest in the property leased, e.g. a tenant for life under the Settled Land Acts, or a mortgagor or mortgagee.

The Letting.—To constitute the relationship of landlord and tenant in the mode under consideration, it is necessary not only that there should be parties capable of entering into the contract, but that there should be a letting, as distinct from a mere agreement to let, and that the right conveyed should be a right to the exclusive possession of the subject of the letting and not a simple licence to use it. Whether a particular instrument is a lease, or an agreement for a lease, or a bare licence, is a question the answer to which depends to a large extent on the circumstances of individual cases; and the only general rule

express contract or by implication, as where premises are occupied with the consent of the owner, but without any express or implied agreement as to the duration of the tenancy, or where a house is lent rent free by one person to another. A tenancy at will is determined by either party alienating his interest as soon as such alienation comes to the knowledge of the other. (vi.) *Tenancy at Sufferance.*—A tenant who comes into possession by a lawful demise, but "holds over" or continues in possession after his estate is ended, is said to be a "tenant at sufferance." Properly speaking, tenancy at sufferance is not a tenancy at all, inasmuch as if the landlord acquiesces in it, it becomes a tenancy at will; and it is to be regarded merely as a legal fiction which prevented the rightful owner from treating the tenant as a trespasser until he had himself made an actual entry on or had brought an action to recover the land. The Distress for Rent Act 1737, however, enables a landlord to recover double rent from a tenant who holds over after having himself given notice to quit; while another statute in the reign of George II.—the Landlord and Tenant Act 1730—makes a tenant who holds over after receiving a notice from his landlord liable to the extent of double the value of the premises. There is no tenancy by sufferance against the crown.

Form of a Lease.—The component parts of a lease are the parties, the recitals (when necessary) setting out such matters as the title of the lessor; the demise or actual letting (the word "demise" is ordinarily used, but any term indicating an express intention to make a present letting is sufficient); the parcels in which the extent of the premises demised is stated, the *habendum* (which defines the commencement and the term of the lease), the *reddendum* or reservation of rent, and the covenants and conditions. The Conveyancing Act 1881 provides that, as regards conveyances subsequent to 1881, unless a contrary intention is expressed, a lease of "land" is to be deemed to include all buildings, fixtures, easements, &c., appertaining to it; and, if there are houses or other buildings on the land demised, all out-houses, erections, &c., are to pass with the lease of the land. Rights which the landlord desires to retain over the lands let are excepted or reserved. Sporting rights will pass to the lessee unless reserved (see GAME LAWS). A grant or reservation of mines in general terms confers, or reserves, a right to work the mines, subject to the obligation of leaving a reasonable support to the surface as it exists at the time of the grant or reservation. It is not necessary that a lease should be dated. In the absence of a date, it will take effect from the day of delivery

Covenants in Leases.—These may be roughly divided into four groups. (i.) *Implied Covenants.*—A covenant is said to be implied when it is raised by implication of law without any express provision being made for it in the lease. Thus a lessee is under an implied obligation to treat the premises demised in a tenant-like or "husband-like" manner, and again, where in a lease by deed the word "demise" is used, the lessor probably covenants impliedly for his own title and for the quiet enjoyment of the premises by the lessee. (ii.) "*Usual*" *Covenants.*—Where an agreement for a lease specifies only such essential conditions as the payment of rent, and either mentions no other terms, or provides that the lease shall contain the "usual" covenants, the parties are entitled to have inserted in the lease made in pursuance of the agreement such other provisions as are "usual" in leases of property of the same character, and in the same district, not being provisions tending to abridge or qualify the legal incidents of the estate intended to be granted to the lessee. The question what covenants are "usual" is a question of fact. A covenant by the lessor, limited to his own acts and those of persons claiming under or through him, for the "quiet enjoyment" by the lessee of the demised premises, and covenants by the lessee to pay rent, to pay taxes, except such as fall upon the landlord, to keep the premises in repair, and to allow the landlord to enter and view the condition of the premises may be taken as typical instances of "usual" covenants. Covenants by the lessee to build and repair, not to assign or underlet without license, or to insure, or not to carry on a particular trade on the premises leased, have been held not to be "usual." Where the agreement provides for the insertion in the lease of "proper" covenants, such covenants only are pointed at as are calculated to secure the full effect of the contract, and a covenant against assignment or under-letting would not ordinarily be included. (iii.) *The Covenants running with the Land.*—A covenant is said to "run with the land" when the rights and duties which it creates are not merely personal to the immediate parties (in which case a covenant is said to be "collateral"), but pass also to their assignees. At common law, it was said that covenants "ran with the land" but not with the reversion, the assignee of the reversion not having the rights of the original lessor. But the assignees of both parties were placed on the same footing by a statute of Henry VIII. (1540). A covenant "runs with the land" if it relates either to a thing in esse, which is part and parcel of the demise, *e.g.* the payment of rent, the repair of houses or fixtures or machinery already built or set up, or to a thing not *in esse* at the time of the demise, but touching the land, provided that the word "assigns" is used in the covenant. All implied covenants run with the land. As instances of "collateral" covenants, we may take a covenant by a lessor to give the lessee a right of pre-emption over a piece of land adjoining the subject of the demise, or in the case of a lease of a beer-shop, not to keep any similar shop within a prescribed distance from the premises demised, or a covenant by a lessee to pay rates on premises not demised. A covenant not to assign without the lessor's assent runs with the land and applies to a re-assignment to the original lessee (iv.) *Restrictive Covenants.*—These may be subdivided into two classes—covenants not to assign or underlet without the lessor's consent (it may be noted that such consent must be applied for even if, under the covenant, it cannot be withheld); and covenants in restraint of trade, *e.g.* not to use the demised premises for certain trading purposes, and in the case of "tied houses" a covenant by the lessees to purchase all beer required from the lessors.

In addition a lease frequently contains covenants for renewal of the lease at the option of the lessee, and for repairs or insurance against damage by fire by the lessee. Leases frequently contain a covenant by the lessee to bear and pay rates, taxes, assessments and other "impositions" or "charges," or "duties" or "outgoings," or "burdens" (except property tax) imposed upon the demised premises during the term. Considerable difficulty has arisen as to the scope of the terms "impositions," "charges," "duties," "outgoings," "burdens." The words, "rates, taxes, assessments" point to payments of a periodical or recurring character. Are the latter words in such covenants limited to payments of this kind, or do they include single and definite payments demanded, for example, by a local authority, acting under statutory powers, for improvements of a permanent kind affecting the premises demised? The decisions on the point are numerous and difficult to reconcile, but the main test is whether, on the true construction of the particular covenant, the lessee has undertaken to indemnify the landlord against payments of all kinds. The stronger current of modern authority is in favour of the landlords and not in favour of restricting the meaning of covenants of this class. It may be added that, if a lessee covenants to pay rates and taxes, no demand by the collector apparently is necessary to constitute a breach of the covenant; where a rate is duly made and published it is the duty of the parties assessed to seek out the collector and pay it.

Mutual Rights and Liabilities of Landlord and Tenant.—These are to a large extent regulated by the covenants of the lease. (i.) The landlord generally covenants—and, in the absence of such a proviso, a covenant will be implied from the fact of letting—that the tenant shall have quiet enjoyment of the premises for the time agreed upon. This obligation makes the landlord responsible for any lawful eviction of the tenant during the term, but not for wrongful eviction unless he is himself the wrongdoer or has expressly made himself responsible for evictions of all kinds. It may be noted here that at common law no lease for years is complete till actual entry has been made by the lessee. Till then, he has only a right of entry or *interesse termini*. (ii.) The tenant, on his part, is presumed to undertake to use the property in a reasonable manner, according to the purposes for which it was let, and to do reasonable repairs.

Repairs. A landlord is not presumed to have undertaken to put the premises in repair, nor to execute repairs. But the respective obligations of parties where repairs are, as they always are in leases for years, the subject of express covenant, may vary indefinitely. The obligation is generally imposed upon the tenant to keep the premises in "good condition" or "tenantable repair." The amount and quality of the repairs necessary to fulfil the covenant are always relative to the age, class and condition of the premises at the time of the lease. A tenant is not responsible, under such a covenant, for deterioration due to diminution in value caused by lapse of time or by the elements. Where there is an unqualified covenant to repair, and the premises during the tenancy are burnt down, or destroyed by some other inevitable calamity, the tenant is bound to rebuild and restore them at his own expense, even although the landlord has taken out a policy on his own account and been paid by the insurance company in respect of it. A covenant to keep in repair requires the tenant to put the premises in repair if they are out of it, and to maintain them in that condition up to and at the end of the tenancy. A breach of the covenant to repair gives the landlord an action for damages which will be measured by the estimated injury to the reversion if the action be brought during the tenancy, and by the sum necessary to execute the repairs, if the action be brought later. (iii.) The improper user of the premises to the injury of the reversioner is *waste* (*q.v.*). (iv.) Covenants by the tenants to insure the premises and keep them insured are also common; and if the premises are left uninsured for the smallest portion of the term, though there is no damage by fire, the covenant is broken. (v.) Covenants to bear and pay rates and taxes have been discussed above. (vi.) As to the tenant's obligation to pay rent, see RENT.

Assignment, Attornment, Estoppel.—The relationship of landlord and tenant may be altered either voluntarily, by the act of the parties, or involuntarily, by the operation of law, and may also be dissolved. The principal mode of voluntary alteration is an assignment either by the tenant of his term or by the landlord of his reversion. An assignment which creates the relationship of landlord and tenant between the lessor or lessee and the assignee, must be by deed, but the acceptance by a landlord of rent from a tenant under an invalid assignment may create an implied tenancy from year to year; and similarly payment of rent by a tenant may amount to an acknowledgment of his landlord's title. This is one form of tenancy by estoppel. The principle of all tenancies of this kind is that something has been done by the party estopped, amounting to an admission which he cannot be allowed to contradict. "Attornment," or the agreement by a tenant to become tenant to a new landlord, is a term now often used to indicate an acknowledgment of the existence of the relationship of landlord and tenant. It may be noted that it is still common to insert in mortgage deeds what is called an "attornment clause," by which the mortgagor "attorns" tenant to the mortgagee, and the latter thereupon acquires a power of distress as an additional security. If the lands assigned are situated in Middlesex or Yorkshire, the assignment should be registered under the Middlesex Registry or Yorkshire Registries Acts, as the case may be; and similar provision is now made for the registration by an assignee of his title under the Land Transfer Acts 1875 and 1897.

Underlease.—Another form of alteration in a contract of tenancy is an under-lease, which differs from assignment in this—that the lessor parts with a portion of his estate instead of, as in assignment, with the whole of it. There is no privity of contract between an underlessee and the superior landlord; but the latter can enforce against the former restrictive covenants of which he had notice, it is the duty of the underlessee to inform himself as to the covenants of the original lease, and, if he enters and takes possession, he will be considered to have had full notice of, and will be bound by, these covenants.

Bankruptcy, Death.—The contract of tenancy may also be altered by operation of law. If a tenant become bankrupt, his interest passes to his trustee in bankruptcy—unless, as is frequently the case, the lease makes the occurrence of that contingency determine the lease. So, on the death of a tenant, his interest passes to his legal representatives.

Dissolution of Tenancy.—Tenancy is dissolved by the expiry of the term for which it was created, or by forfeiture of the tenant's interest on the ground of the breach of some condition by the tenant and re-entry by the landlord. A breach of condition may, however, be waived by the landlord, and the legislature has made provision for the relief of the tenant from the consequences of such breaches in certain cases. Relief from forfeiture and rights of re-entry are now regulated chiefly by the Conveyancing Acts 1881 and 1882. Under these acts a right of re-entry or forfeiture is not to be enforceable unless and until the lessor has served on the lessee a written notice specifying the breach of covenant or condition complained of, and requiring him to remedy it or make compensation, and this demand has not within a reasonable time been complied with; and when a lessor is proceeding to enforce such a right the court may, if it think fit, grant relief to the lessee. A forfeiture is also waived if the landlord elects not to take advantage of it—and shows his election either expressly or impliedly by some act, which acknowledges the continuance of the tenancy, *e.g.* by the acceptance of, or even by an absolute and unqualified demand for,

[illegible]

meaning an agricultural holding which exceeds one acre, and either does not exceed fifty acres, or, if exceeding fifty acres, is at the date of sale or letting of an annual value for the purposes of income tax not exceeding fifty pounds; the expression "allotment" includes a field garden). Section 47 of the act gives the tenant the same rights to compensation as if his holding had been a holding under the Agricultural Holdings Act 1908 (*vide supra*). Compensation was given to market gardeners for unexhausted improvements by the Market Gardeners' Compensation Act 1895 and by the Agricultural Holdings Act 1906 for improvements effected before the commencement of that act on a holding cultivated to the knowledge of the landlord as a market garden, if the landlord had not dissented in writing to the improvements. The important sections of these acts were incorporated in the Agricultural Holdings Act 1908, s. 42.

Scots Law.—The original lease in Scots law took the form of a grant by the proprietor or lessor. But, with advancing civilization and the consequent increase in the number of the conditions to be imposed on both parties, leases became mutual contracts, bilateral in form. The law of Scotland as to landlord and tenant may be considered under two main heads:—I. *Ordinary Leases, Common Law and Statutory*; II. *Building or Long Leases.*

I *Ordinary Leases, Common Law and Statutory.*—A verbal lease for a year is good. Such a lease for more than a year is not effectual even for a year, except where the lessee has taken possession. At common law, while a lease was binding on the grantor and his heirs, it was not good against "singular successors," *i.e.* persons acquiring by purchase or adjudication, and the lessee was liable to be ejected by such persons, unless (a precaution usually taken) sasine of the subjects demised was expressly conferred on him by the lease. To obviate this difficulty, the Scots Act 1449, c. 18, made possession of the subjects of the lease equivalent to sasine. This enactment applies to leases of agricultural subjects, houses, mills, fisheries and whatever is *fundo annexum*; provided that (*a*) the lease, when for more than one year, must be in writing, (*b*) it must be definite as to subject, rent (which may consist of money, grain or services, if the *reddendum* is not illusory) and term of duration, (*c*) possession must follow on the lease. Special powers of granting leases are conferred by statute on trustees. (Trusts [Scotland] Act 1867, s. 2), *curatores bonis* (Judicial Factors [Scotland] Act 1889) and heirs of entail (cf. Entail Act 1882, ss. 5, 6, 8, 9). The requisites of the statutory leases, last mentioned, are similar to those imposed in England upon tenants for life by the Settled Land Acts (*v. sup.* p. 3). The rent stipulated for must not be illusory, and must fairly represent the value of the subjects leased, and the term of the lease must not be excessive (as to rent generally, see RENT). A life-renter can only grant a lease that is effectual during the subsistence of the life-rent. There is practically no limitation, but the will of the parties, as to the persons to whom a lease may be granted. A lease granted to a tenant by name will pass, on his death during the subsistence of the term to his heir-at-law, even if the lease contains no destination to heirs. The rights and obligations of the lessor and the tenant (*e.g.* as to the use of the produce, the payment of rent, the quiet possession of the subjects demised, and as to the payment of rates and taxes) are similar to those existing under English law. An agricultural lease does not, apart from stipulation, confer any right to kill game, other than hares and rabbits (as to which, see the Ground Game Act 1880, and GAME LAWS) or any right of fishing. A tenant is not entitled, without the landlord's consent, to change the character of the subjects demised, and, except under an agricultural lease, he is bound to quit the premises on the expiration of the lease. In the case of urban leases, however, ejectment (*q.v.*)—called in Scots Law "removing"—will not be authorized unless the tenant received 40 days' warning before the term of removal. In the absence of such notice, the parties are held, if there be nothing in their conduct or in the lease inconsistent with this presumption, to renew their agreement in all its terms, and so on from year to year till due notice is given. This is called "tacit relocation." A lease may be transmitted (i.) by "assignation," intimated to the landlord, and followed by possession on the part of the assignee; (ii.) by sub-lease—the effect of which is equivalent to that of under-lease in English law; (iii.) by succession, as of the heir of a tenant; (iv.) in the case of agricultural holdings, by bequest (Agricultural Holdings [Scotland] Act 1883, s. 29). A lease terminates (i.) by the expiration of its term or by advantage being taken by the party in whose favour it is stipulated, of a "break" in the term; (ii.) by the occurrence of an "irritancy" of ground of forfeiture, either conventional, or statutory, e.g. where a tenant's rent is in arrear, or he fails to remove on the expiry of his lease (Act of Sederunt, 14th of Dec. 1756 Agricultural Holdings Act 1883, s. 27); (iii.) by the bankruptcy or insolvency of the tenant, at the landlord's option, if it is so stipulated in the lease; (iv.) by the destruction, e.g by fire, of the subject leased, unless the landlord is bound to restore it. Complete destruction of the subject leased, e.g. where a house is burnt down, or a farm is reduced to "sterility" by flood or hurricane, discharges the tenant from the obligation to pay rent. The effect of partial destruction has given rise to some uncertainty "The distinction seems to be that if the destruction be permanent, though partial, the failure of the subject let will give relief by entitling the tenant to renounce the lease, unless a deduction shall be allowed, but that if it be merely temporary or occasional, it will not entitle the tenant to relief" (Bell's *Prin.* s. 1208) Agricultural leases usually contain special provisions as to the order of cropping, the proper stocking of the farm, and the rights of the incoming and outgoing tenant with regard to the way-going crop. Where the rent is in money, it is generally payable at Whitsunday and Martinmas—the two "legal terms." Sometimes the term of payment is *before* the crop is reaped, sometimes *after*. "The terms thus stipulated are called 'the conventional terms'; the rent payable by anticipation being called 'forehand rent,' that which is payable after the crop is reaped, 'back rent.' Where the rent is in grain, or otherwise payable in produce, it is to be satisfied from the produce of the farm, if there be any. If there be none the tenant is bound and entitled to deliver fair marketable grain of the same kind." (Bell's *Principles*, ss. 1204, 1205). The general rule with regard to "waygoing crops" on arable farms is that the tenant is entitled to reap the crop sown before the term of removal (whether or not that be the natural termination of the lease), the right of exclusive possession being his during seed time. But he is not entitled to the use of the barns in threshing, &c., the corn.

The Agricultural Holdings (Scotland) Acts 1883 and 1900, already referred to incidentally, contain provisions—similar to those of the English acts—as to a tenant's right to compensation for unexhausted improvements, removal for non-payment of rent, notice to quit at the termination of a tenancy, and a tenant's property in fixtures. The Crofters' Holdings (Scotland) Acts 1886, 1887 and 1888, confer on "crofters" special rights. A crofter is defined as "a tenant of a holding"—being arable or pasture land, or partly arable and partly pasture land—"from year to year who resides on his holding, the annual rent of which does not exceed £30 in money, and which is situated in a 'crofting parish.'" Nearly all the parishes in Argyll, Inverness, Ross, Cromarty, Sutherland, Caithness and Orkney and Shetland answer to this description. The crofter enjoys a perpetual tenure subject to the fulfilment of certain conditions as to payment of rent, non-assignment of tenancy, &c., and to defeasance at his own option on giving one year's notice to the landlord. A Crofters' Commission constituted under the acts has power to fix fair rents, and the crofter on renunciation of his tenancy or removal from his holding is entitled to compensation for permanent improvements. The Small Holdings Act 1892 applies to Scotland.

Under the law of Scotland down to 1880, a landlord had as security for rent due on an agricultural lease a "hypothec"—*i.e.* a preferential right over ordinary creditors, and extending, subject to certain limitations, over the whole stock and crop of the tenant. This right was enforceable by sequestration and sale. It was abolished in 1880 as regards all leases entered into after the 11th of November 1881, where the land demised exceeded two acres in extent, and the landlord was left to remedies akin to ejectment (Hypothec Abolition, Scotland, Act 1880).

II. *Building or Long Leases.*—Under these leases, the term of which is usually 99 and sometimes 999 years, the tenant is to a certain extent in the position of a fee simple proprietor, except that his right is terminable, and that he can only exercise such rights of ownership as are conferred on him either by statute or by the terms of his lease. Extensive powers of entering into such leases have been given by statute to trustees subject to the authority of the Court (Trusts [Scotland] Act 1867, s. 3) and to heirs of entail (Entail Acts 1840, 1849, 1882). Where long leases are "probative," *i.e.* holograph or duly tested, do not exceed 31 years, or, except as regards leases of mines and minerals, and of lands held by burgage tenure, relate to an extent of land exceeding 50 acres, and contain provisions for renewal, they may be recorded for publication in the *Register of Sasines*, and such publication has the effect of possession (Registration of Leases [Scotland] Act 1857).

Ireland.—The law of landlord and tenant was originally substantially the same as that described for England is. But the modern Land Acts have readjusted the relation between landlords and tenants, while the Land Purchase Acts have aimed at abolishing those relations by enabling the tenant to become the owner of his holding. The way was paved for these changes by the existence in Ulster of a local custom having virtually the force of law, which had two main features—fixity of tenure, and free right of sale by the tenant of his interest. These principles, with the addition of that of fair rents settled by judicial means, were gradually established by the Land Acts of 1870 and subsequent years, and the whole system was remodelled by the Land Purchase Acts (see IRELAND).

United States.—The law of landlord and tenant in the United States is in its principles similar to those of English law It is only possible to indicate, by way of example, some of the points of similarity. The relationship of landlord and tenant is created, altered and dissolved in the same way, and the rights and duties of parties are substantially identical. A lease must contain, either in itself or by clear reference, all the terms of a complete contract—the names of the parties, description of the property let, the rent (see RENT) and the conditions. The date is not essential. That is a matter of identification as to time only In Pennsylvania, parol evidence of the date is allowed. The general American doctrine is that where the contract is contained in separate writings they must connect themselves by reference, and that parol evidence is not admissible to connect them. The English doctrine that a verbal lease may be specifically enforced if there has been part performance by the person seeking the remedy has been fully adopted in nearly all the American states. The law as to the rights and obligations of assignees and sub-lessees and as to surrender is the same as in England. Forfeiture only renders a lease void as regards the lessee; it may be waived by the lessor, and acceptance by the landlord of rent due after forfeiture, with notice of such forfeiture, amounts to waiver. Where there is a lease for a certain period, no notice to quit is necessary. In uncertain tenancies there must be reasonable notice—*i.e.* at common law six months generally. The notice necessary to determine a monthly or weekly tenancy is generally a month or a week (see further under LODGER; LODGINGS). In the United States, as in England, the covenant for quiet enjoyment only extends, so far as relates to the acts of third parties, to lawful acts of disturbance in the enjoyment of the subject agreed to be let.

Laws of other Countries.—It is impossible here to deal with the systems of land tenure in force in other countries. Only the question of the legal relations between landlord and tenant can be touched upon. In France, the Code Civil recognizes two such relationships, the letting to hire of houses (*bail à loyer*) and the letting to farm of rural properties (*bail à ferme*). To a certain extent, both forms of tenancy are governed by the same rules. The letting may be either written or verbal. But a verbal lease presents this disadvantage that, if it is unperformed and one of the parties denies its existence, it cannot be proved by witnesses. The party who denies the letting can only be put to his oath (Arts. 1714-1715). It may further be noted that in the case of a verbal lease, notice to quit is regulated by the custom of the place (Art. 1736). The tenant or farmer has the right of underletting or assigning his lease, in the absence of prohibiting stipulation (Art. 1717). The lessor is bound by the nature of his contract and without the need of any particular stipulation (i.) to deliver to the lessee the thing hired in a good state of repair; (ii.) to maintain it in a state to serve the purpose for which it has been hired; (iii.) to secure to the lessee peaceable enjoyment during the continuance of the lease (Arts. 1719-1720). He is bound to warrant the lessee against, and to indemnify him for, any loss arising from any faults or defects in the thing hired which prevent its use, even though he was not aware of them at the time of the lease (Art. 1721). If during the continuance of the letting, the thing hired is entirely destroyed by accident, the lease is cancelled. In case of partial destruction, the lessee may, according to circumstances, demand either a diminution of the price, or the cancellation of the lease. In neither case is there ground for damages (Art. 1722). The lessor cannot, during the lease, change the form of the thing hired (Art. 1723). The lessee is bound, on his side (i.) to use the thing hired like a good head of a household (*bon père de famille*), in accordance with the express or presumed purpose of the hiring, (ii.) to pay the price of the hiring at the times agreed (Art. 1728). On breach of the former obligation, the lease may be judicially cancelled (Art. 1729) As to the consequences of breach of the latter, see RENT. If a statement of the condition of the property (*état des lieux*) has been prepared, the lessee must give it up such as he received it according to the statement, except what has perished or decayed by age or by means of *force majeure* (Art. 1730). In the absence of an *état des lieux*, the lessee is presumed to have received the thing hired in a good state of tenantable repair, and must so yield it up, saving proof to the contrary (Art. 1731). He is liable for injuries or losses happening during his enjoyment, unless he prove that they have taken place without his fault (Art. 1732); in particular, for loss by fire unless he show that the fire happened by accident, *force majeure*, or defect of construction, or through communication from a neighbouring house (Art. 1733) The lessee is

nt, which h[illegible]
n action for [illegible]
efore or after
A tenancy [illegible]
greater and a
person, with[illegible]
a tenant for
surrender, c
determine a
to some ac[illegible]
denying an[illegible]
continued t[illegible]
The land[illegible]
law the ab[illegible]
may have t
certain cas[illegible]
contending
fixtures (w[illegible]
to the soil
remove th[illegible]
for the pu[illegible]
In respect
may be [illegible]
happenin[illegible]
(3) A si[illegible]
tenants
of the d[illegible]
would [illegible]
on the [illegible]
right or
stantial
tenant [illegible]
assigna[illegible]
and int[illegible]
the exce[illegible]
over at
added to
or by the
of the ac[illegible]
whatever
they plea[illegible]
The law
Statutor[illegible]
a few mod[illegible]
tenant. [illegible]
Agricultur[illegible]
cultural te[illegible]
improveme[illegible]
writing, an[illegible]
landlord's c[illegible]
may be m[illegible]
down of pe[illegible]
of hops, em[illegible]
land, clay [illegible]
purchased m[illegible]
making prov[illegible]
In the case [illegible]
must be give[illegible]
ments himsel[illegible]
5% per annu[illegible]
for a period [illegible]
repay the outl[illegible]
of the act a[illegible]
when he is com[illegible]
for reasons inc[illegible]
cultural tenant
to compensatio[illegible]
hibited with reg[illegible]
1900 to remove f[illegible]
otherwise entitle[illegible]
landlord, unless
valuation. The
every tenant (wit[illegible]
of disposal of pro[illegible]
or explicit agreem[illegible]
EJECTMENT, FIXTU[illegible]
Act 1908, which rep[illegible]
on terms similar to
with small holdi[illegible]

[illegible] to some extent in Italy (Civil Code, Arts. 1568 et seq.), Spain [illegible] Civil Code, Arts 1542 et seq.), and Portugal (Civil Code, Arts. [illegible] et seq., 1595 et seq.). In all these countries there are varieties of emphyteutic tenure; and in Italy the mezzadria or metayer system (see Civil Code, Arts. 1647 et seq.) exists. The German Civil Code adopts the distinction between *bail à loyer* [illegible] Miehl, Arts. 535 et seq.) and *bail à ferme* (Pacht, Arts. 581 et seq.). Dutch law also (Civil Code, Arts. 1583 et seq.) is similar to the French.

The Indian law of landlord and tenant is described in the article INDIAN LAW. The laws of the various British colonies on the subject are too numerous and too different to be dealt with here. In Mauritius, the provisions of the Code Civil are in force without modification. In Quebec (Civil Code, Arts. [illegible] et seq.) and St Lucia (Civil Code, Arts. 1512 et seq.) they have been reproduced by the local law. In many of the colonies, parts of the English law of landlord and tenant, common law and statutory, have been introduced by local enactments (cf. British Guiana, Ord. 4 of 1846; Jamaica, 1 Vict. c. 26). In [illegible] (e.g. Victoria, Landlord and Tenant Act 1890, No. 1108; Ontario, Rev. Stats. 1897, c. 170) consolidating statutes have been passed.

AUTHORITIES.—English Law: Wolstenholme, Brinton and Cherry, *Conveyancing and Settled Land Acts* (London, 9th ed., 1905); Hood and Challis, *Conveyancing and Settled Land Acts* (London, 7th ed., [illegible]); Foa, on *Landlord and Tenant* (London, 4th ed., 1907); Woodfall, on *Landlord and Tenant* (London, 18th ed., 1907); Fawcett, *Landlord and Tenant* (London, 3rd ed., 1905). Scots Law: Hunter, on *Landlord and Tenant* (Edinburgh, 4th ed., 1876); Rankine, on *Land Ownership* (Edinburgh, 3rd ed., 1891); Rankine, on *Leases* (Edinburgh, 2nd ed., [illegible]); Hunter, *Landlord and Tenant* (4th ed. [illegible], Edinburgh, 1876). Irish Law: Kelly's *Statute Law of Landlord and Tenant in Ireland* (Dublin, 1898); Barton and Cherry's *Land Act 1896* (Dublin, [illegible]); Quill, Hamilton and Longworth, *Irish Land Acts of 1903 and 1904* (Dublin, 1904). American Law: Bouvier, *Law Dictionary* (ed. Rawle) (London, 1897); McAdam, [illegible], *Remedies and Liabilities of Landlord and Tenant* (New York, [illegible]); Wood, *Law of Landlord and Tenant* (New York, 1888). Foreign and Colonial Laws: Field, *Landholding and the relation of Landlord and Tenant in various Countries*; *Ruling Cases* (American Notes), London and Boston, 1894–1901). (A. W. R.)

LANDON, CHARLES PAUL (1760–1826), French painter and art-author, was born at Nonant in 1760. He entered the studio of Regnault, and won the first prize of the Academy in 1792. After his return from Italy, disturbed by the Revolution, he seems to have abandoned painting for letters, but he began to exhibit in [illegible], and continued to do so at various intervals up to [illegible]. His "Leda" obtained an award of merit in 1801, and is now in the Louvre. His "Mother's Lesson," "Paul and Virginia Bathing," and "Daedalus and Icarus" have been engraved; but his works on painting and painters, which reach nearly one hundred volumes, form his chief title to be remembered. In spite of a complete want of critical accuracy, an extreme carelessness in the biographical details, and the feebleness of the line engravings by which they are illustrated, Landon's *Annales du Musée*, in [illegible] vols., form a vast repertory of compositions by masters of every age and school of permanent value. Landon also published *Lives of Celebrated Painters*, in 22 vols.; *An Historical Description of Paris*, 2 vols.; a *Description of London*, with [illegible] plates, and descriptions of the Luxembourg, of the [illegible] collection, and of the gallery of the duchesse de Berry. He died at Paris in 1826.

LANDON, LETITIA ELIZABETH (1802–1838), English poet and novelist, better known by her initials L. E. L. than as Miss Landon or Mrs Maclean, was descended from an old Herefordshire family, and was born at Chelsea on the 14th of August [illegible]. She went to a school in Chelsea where Miss Mitford also received her education. Her father, an army agent, amassed a large property, which he lost by speculation shortly before his death. About 1815 the Landons made the acquaintance of William Jerdan, and Letitia began her contributions to the [illegible] and to various Christmas annuals. She also [illegible] volumes of verse, which soon won for her a wide [illegible]. The gentle melancholy and romantic sentiment [illegible] embodied suited the taste of the period, and would in any case have secured her the sympathy and approval of a wide class of readers. She displays richness of fancy and aptness of language, but her work suffered from hasty production, and has not stood the test of time. The large sums she earned by her literary labours were expended on the support of her family. An engagement to John Forster, it is said, was broken off through the intervention of scandalmongers. In June 1838 she married George Maclean, governor of the Gold Coast, but she only survived her marriage, which proved to be very unhappy, by a few months. She died on the 15th of October 1838 at Cape Coast from an overdose of prussic acid, which, it is supposed, was taken accidentally.

For some time L. E. L. was joint editor of the *Literary Gazette*. Her first volume of poetry appeared in 1820 under the title *The Fate of Adelaide*, and was followed by other collections of verses with similar titles. She also wrote several novels, of which the best is *Ethel Churchill* (1837). Various editions of her *Poetical Works* have been published since her death, one in 1880 with an introductory memoir by W. B. Scott. *The Life and Literary Remains of Letitia Elizabeth Landon*, by Laman Blanchard, appeared in 1841, and a second edition in 1855.

LANDOR, WALTER SAVAGE (1775–1864), English writer, eldest son of Walter Landor and his wife Elizabeth Savage, was born at Warwick on the 30th of January 1775. [He was sent to Rugby school, but was removed at the headmaster's request and studied privately with Mr Langley, vicar of Ashbourne. In 1793 he entered Trinity College, Cambridge. He adopted republican principles and in 1794 fired a gun at the windows of a Tory for whom he had an aversion. He was rusticated for a year, and, although the authorities were willing to condone the offence, he refused to return. The affair led to a quarrel with his father in which Landor expressed his intention of leaving home for ever. He was, however, reconciled with his family through the efforts of his friend Dorothea Lyttelton. He entered no profession, but his father allowed him £150 a year, and he was free to live at home or not as he pleased.]

In 1795 appeared in a small volume, divided into three books, *The Poems of Walter Savage Landor*, and, in pamphlet form of nineteen pages, an anonymous *Moral Epistle, respectfully dedicated to Earl Stanhope*. No poet at the age of twenty ever had more vigour of style and fluency of verse; nor perhaps has any ever shown such masterly command of epigram and satire, made vivid and vital by the purest enthusiasm and most generous indignation. Three years later appeared the first edition of the first great work which was to inscribe his name for ever among the great names in English poetry. The second edition of *Gebir* appeared in 1803, with a text corrected of grave errors and improved by magnificent additions. About the same time the whole poem was also published in a Latin form, which for might and melody of line, for power and perfection of language, must always dispute the palm of precedence with the English version. [His father's death in 1805 put him in possession of an independent fortune. Landor settled in Bath. Here in 1808 he met Southey, and the mutual appreciation of the two poets led to a warm friendship.] In 1808, under an impulse not less heroic than that which was afterwards to lead Byron to a glorious death in redemption of Greece and his own good fame, Landor, then aged thirty-three, left England for Spain as a volunteer to serve in the national army against Napoleon at the head of a regiment raised and supported at his sole expense. After some three months' campaigning came the affair of Cintra and its disasters; "his troop," in the words of his biographer, "dispersed or melted away, and he came back to England in as great a hurry as he had left it," but bringing with him the honourable recollection of a brave design unselfishly attempted, and the material in his memory for the sublimest poem published in our language, between the last masterpiece of Milton and the first masterpiece of Shelley—one equally worthy to stand unchallenged beside either for poetic perfection as well as moral majesty—the lofty tragedy of *Count Julian*, which appeared in 1812, without the name of its author. No comparable work is to be found in English poetry between the date of *Samson Agonistes* and the date of *Prometheus Unbound*; and with both these great works it has some points of greatness in common. The superhuman isolation of agony and endurance which encircles and exalts the hero is in each case expressed with equally appropriate magnificence of effect. The style of *Count Julian*, if somewhat deficient in dramatic ease and the fluency of natural dialogue, has such might and purity and majesty of speech as elsewhere we find only in Milton so long and so steadily sustained.

In May 1811 Landor had suddenly married Miss Julia Thuillier, with whose looks he had fallen in love at first sight in a ball-room at Bath; and in June they settled for a while at Llanthony Abbey in Monmouthshire, from whence he was worried in three years' time by the combined vexation of neighbours and tenants, lawyers and lords-lieutenant; not before much toil and money had been nobly wasted on attempts to improve the sterility of the land, to relieve the wretchedness and raise the condition of the peasantry. He left England for France at first, but after a brief residence at Tours took up his abode for three years at Como; "and three more wandering years he passed," says his biographer, "between Pisa and Pistoja, before he pitched his tent in Florence in 1821."

In 1835 he had an unfortunate difference with his wife which ended in a complete separation. In 1824 appeared the first series of his *Imaginary Conversations*, in 1826 "the second edition, corrected and enlarged"; a supplementary third volume was added in 1828; and in 1829 the second series was given to the world. Not until 1846 was a fresh instalment added, in the second volume of his collected and selected works. During the interval he had published his three other most famous and greatest books in prose: *The Citation and Examination of William Shakespeare* (1834), *Pericles and Aspasia* (1836), *The Pentameron* (1837). To the last of these was originally appended *The Pentalogia*, containing five of the very finest among his shorter studies in dramatic poetry. In 1847 he published his most important Latin work, *Poemata et inscriptiones*, comprising, with large additions, the main contents of two former volumes of idyllic, satiric, elegiac and lyric verse; and in the same golden year of his poetic life appeared the very crown and flower of its manifold labours, the *Hellenics of Walter Savage Landor*, enlarged and completed. Twelve years later this book was re-issued, with additions of more or less value, with alterations generally to be regretted, and with omissions invariably to be deplored. In 1853 he put forth *The Last Fruit off an Old Tree*, containing fresh conversations, critical and controversial essays, miscellaneous epigrams, lyrics and occasional poems of various kind and merit, closing with *Five Scenes* on the martyrdom of Beatrice Cenci, unsurpassed even by their author himself for noble and heroic pathos, for subtle and genial, tragic and profound, ardent and compassionate insight into character, with consummate mastery of dramatic and spiritual truth. In 1856 he published *Antony and Octavius—Scenes for the Study*, twelve consecutive poems in dialogue which alone would suffice to place him high among the few great masters of historic drama.

In 1858 appeared a metrical miscellany bearing the title of *Dry Sticks Fagoted by W. S. Landor*, and containing among other things graver and lighter certain epigrammatic and satirical attacks which reinvolved him in the troubles of an action for libel; and in July of the same year he returned for the last six years of his life to Italy, which he had left for England in 1835. [He was advised to make over his property to his family, on whom he was now dependent. They appear to have refused to make him an allowance unless he returned to England. By the exertions of Robert Browning an allowance was secured. Browning settled him first at Siena and then at Florence.] Embittered and distracted by domestic dissensions, if brightened and relieved by the affection and veneration of friends and strangers, this final period of his troubled and splendid career came at last to a quiet end on the 17th of September 1864. In the preceding year he had published a last volume of *Heroic Idyls, with Additional Poems*, English and Latin,—the better part of them well worthy to be indeed the "last fruit" of a genius which after a life of eighty-eight years had lost nothing

[illegible]

[illegible] could neither heighten nor lessen the fulness of [illegible] and ready generosity. To the poets of his own and [illegible] generation he was not readier to do honour than to [illegible] a later growth, and not seldom of deserts far lower and [illegible] claims than theirs. That he was not unconscious of [illegible], and avowed it with the frank simplicity of nobler [illegible], is not more evident or more certain than that in company with his friends and fellows he was liable rather to undervalue than to overrate himself. He was a classic, and no formalist; the wide range of his just and loyal admiration had room for a genius so far from classical as Blake's. Nor in his own highest mood or method of creative as of critical work was he a classic only, in any narrow or exclusive sense of the term. On either side, immediately or hardly below his mighty masterpiece of *Pericles and Aspasia*, stand the two scarcely less beautiful and vivid studies of medieval Italy and Shakespearean England. The very finest flower of his immortal dialogues is probably to be found in the single volume comprising only "Imaginary Conversations of Greeks and Romans"; his utmost command of passion and pathos may be tested by its transcendent success in the distilled and concentrated tragedy of *Tiberius and Vipsania*, where for once he shows a quality more proper to romantic than classical imagination—the subtle and sublime and terrible power to enter the dark vestibule of distraction, to throw the whole force of his fancy, the whole fire of his spirit, into the "shadowing passion" (as Shakespeare calls it) of gradually imminent insanity. Yet, if this and all other studies from ancient history or legend could be subtracted from the volume of his work, enough would be left whereon to rest the foundation of a fame which time could not sensibly impair.

(A. C. S.)

BIBLIOGRAPHY.—See *The Works and Life of Walter Savage Landor* (8 vols., 1846), the life being the work of John Forster. Another edition of his works (1891–1893), edited by C. G. Crump, comprises *Imaginary Conversations, Poems, Dialogues in Verse and Epigrams* and *The Longer Prose Works*. His *Letters and other Unpublished Writings* were edited by Mr Stephen Wheeler (1897). There are many volumes of selections from his works, notably one (1882) for the "Golden Treasury" series, edited by Sidney Colvin, who also contributed the monograph on *Landor* (1881) in the "English Men of Letters" series. A bibliography of his works, many of which are very rare, is included in Sir Leslie Stephen's article on Landor in the *Dictionary of National Biography* (vol. xxxii., 1892). (M. Br.)

LANDOUR, a hill station and sanatorium in India, in Dehra Dun district of the United Provinces, adjoining Mussoorie. Pop. (1901) 1720, rising to 3700 in the hot season. Since 1827 it has been a convalescent station for European troops, with a school for their children.

LAND REGISTRATION, a legal process connected with the transfer of landed property, comprising two forms—registration of deeds and registration of title, which may be best described as a species of machinery for assisting a purchaser or mortgagee in his inquiries as to his vendor's or mortgagor's title previously to completing his dealing, and for securing his own position afterwards. The expediency of making inquiry into the vendor's title before completing a purchase of land (and the case of a mortgage is precisely similar) is obvious. In the case of goods possession may ordinarily be relied on as proof of full ownership; in the case of land, the person in ostensible possession is very seldom the owner, being usually only a tenant, paying rent to someone else. Even the person to whom the rent is paid is in many cases—probably, in England, in most cases—not the full owner, but only a life owner, or a trustee, whose powers of disposing of the property are of a strictly limited nature. Again, goods are very seldom the subject of a mortgage, whereas land has from time immemorial been the frequent subject of this class of transaction. Evidently, therefore, some sort of inquiry is necessary to enable a purchaser to obtain certainty that the land for which he pays full price is not subject to an unknown mortgage or charge which, if left undiscovered, might afterwards deprive him of a large part or even the whole of its value. Again, the probability of serious consequences to the purchaser ensuing from a mistake as to title is infinitely greater in the case of land [illegible] the case of goods. Before the rightful owner can recover misappropriated goods, he has to find out where they are. This is usually a matter of considerable difficulty. By the time they have reached the hands of a *bonâ fide* purchaser all chance of their recovery by the true owner is practically at an end. But with land the case is far otherwise. A dispossessed rightful owner never has any difficulty in tracing his property, for it is immovable. All he has to do is to bring an action for ejectment against the person in possession. For these reasons, among others, any attempt to deal with land on the simple and unsuspecting principles which obtain in regard to goods would be fraught with grave risks.

Apart from very early and primitive social conditions, there appear to be only two ways in which the required certainty as to title to land can be obtained. Either the purchaser must satisfy himself, by an exhaustive scrutiny and review of all the deeds, wills, marriages, heirships and other documents and events by which the property has been conveyed, mortgaged, leased, devised or transmitted during a considerable period of time, that no loophole exists whereby an adverse claim can enter or be made good—this is called the system of private investigation of title—or the government must keep an authoritative list or register of the properties within its jurisdiction, together with the names of the owners and particulars of the encumbrances in each case, and must protect purchasers and others dealing with land, on the faith of this register, from all adverse claims. This second system is called Registration of Title. To these two alternatives may perhaps be added a third, of very recent growth—Insurance of Title. This is largely used in the United States. But it is in reality only a phase of the system of private investigation. The insurance company investigates the title, and charges the purchaser a premium to cover the expense and the risk of error. Registration of deeds is an adjunct of the system of private investigation, and, except in England, is a practically invariable feature of it. It consists in the establishment of public offices in which all documents affecting land are to be recorded—partly to preserve them in a readily accessible place, partly to prevent the possibility of any material deed or document being dishonestly concealed by a vendor. Where registration is effected by depositing a full copy of the deed, it also renders the subsequent falsification of the original document dangerous. Registration of deeds does not (except perhaps to a certain extent indirectly) cheapen or simplify the process of investigation—the formalities at the registry add something to the trouble and cost incurred—but it prevents the particular classes of fraud mentioned.

The history of land registration follows, as a general rule, a fairly uniform course of development. In very early times, and in small and simple communities, the difficulty afterwards found in establishing title to land does not arise, owing to the primitive habit of attaching ceremony and publicity to all dealings. The parties meet on the land, with witnesses; symbolical acts (such as handing over a piece of earth, or the bough of a tree) are performed; and a set form of words is spoken, expressive of the intention to convey. By this means the ownership of each estate in the community becomes to a certain extent a matter of common knowledge, rendering fraud and mistake difficult. But this method leaves a good deal to be desired in point of security. Witnesses die, and memory is uncertain; and one of the earliest improvements consists in the establishment of a sort of public record kept by the magistrate, lord or other local authority, containing a series of contemporary notes of the effect of the various transactions that take place. This book becomes the general title-deed of the whole community, and as long as transactions remain simple, and not too numerous, the results appear to be satisfactory. Of this character are the Manorial Court Rolls, which were in the middle ages the great authorities on title, both in England and on the continent. The entries in them in early times were made in a very few words. The date, the names of the parties, the name or short verbal description of the land, the nature of the transaction, are all that appear. In the land registry at Vienna there is a continuous series of registers of this kind going back to 1368, in Prague to 1377, in Munich to 1440. No doubt there are extant (though in a less easily accessible form) manorial records in England of equal or greater antiquity. This may be considered the first stage in the history of Land Registration. It can hardly be said to be in active operation at the present day in any civilized country—in the sense in which that term is usually understood. Where dealings become more numerous and complicated, written instruments are required to express the intentions of the parties, and afterwards to supply evidence of the landowner's title. It appears, too, that as a general rule the public books already described continue to be used, notwithstanding this change; only (as would be expected) the entries in them, once plain and simple, either grow into full copies of the long and intricate deeds, or consist of mere notes stating that such and such deeds have been executed, leaving the persons interested to inquire for the originals, in whose custody soever they may be found. This system, which may be regarded as the second stage in the history of land registration, is called Registration of Deeds. It prevails in France, Belgium, parts of Switzerland, in Italy, Spain, India, in almost all the British colonies (except Australasia and Canada), in most of the states of the American Union, in the South American republics, in Scotland and Ireland, and in the English counties of Yorkshire and Middlesex. Where it exists, there is generally a law to the effect that in case of dispute a registered deed shall prevail over an unregistered one. The practical effect is that a purchaser can, by searching the register, find out exactly what deeds he ought to inquire for, and receives an assurance that if, after completion, he registers his own conveyance, no other deeds—even if they exist—will prevail against him.

The expenses and delays, not to mention the occasional actual losses of property through fraud or mistake, attendant on the system of making every purchaser responsible for the due examination of his vendor's title—whether or not assisted by registration of deeds—have induced several governments to establish the more perfect system of Registration of Title, which consists in collecting the transactions affecting each separate estate under a separate head, keeping an accurate account of the parcels of which each such estate is composed, and summarizing authoritatively, as each fresh transaction occurs, the subsisting rights of all parties in relation to the land itself. This system prevails in Germany, Austria, Hungary, parts of Switzerland, the Australasian colonies, nearly the whole of Canada, some of the states of the American Union, to a certain extent in Ireland, and is in course of establishment in England and Wales. The Register consists of three portions:— (1) The description of the land, usually, but not necessarily, accompanied by a reference to a map; (2) the ownership, giving the name and address of the person who can sell and dispose of the land; and (3) the encumbrances, in their order of priority, and the names of the persons for the time being entitled to them. When any fresh transaction takes place the instrument effecting it is produced, and the proper alterations in, or additions to, the register are made: if it be a sale, the name of the vendor is cancelled from the register, and that of the purchaser is entered instead; if it be a mortgage, it is added to the list of encumbrances; if a discharge, the encumbrance discharged is cancelled; if it is a sale of part of the land, the original description is modified or the plan is marked to show the piece conveyed, while a new description or plan is made and a new register is opened for the detached parcel. In the English and Australian registries a "land certificate" is also issued to the landowner containing copies of the register and of the plan. This certificate takes the place more or less of the old documents of title. On a sale, the process is as follows: The vendor first of all produces to the purchaser his land certificate, or gives him the number of his title and an authority to inspect the register. In Austria and in some colonial registries this is not necessary, the register being open to public inspection, which in England is not the case. The purchaser, on inspecting this, can easily see for himself whether the land he wishes to buy is comprised in the registered description or plan, whether the vendor's name appears on the register as the owner

[illegible] the crowded antique school and ask, "Where is my [illegible] dog-boy?" Although his pictures sold easily [illegible] the prices he received at this time were compara[illegible]. In 1818 Landseer sent to the Society of Painters [illegible] Water Colours, which then held its exhibitions in [illegible], his picture of "Fighting Dogs getting Wind." [illegible] of this work to Sir George Beaumont vastly enhanced [illegible] of the painter, who soon became "the fashion." This [illegible] illustrates the prime strength of Landseer's earlier style. [illegible] the productions of his later life, it displays not an iota [illegible] sentiment. Perfectly drawn, solidly and minutely finished, [illegible] carefully composed, its execution attested the skill acquired [illegible] ten years' studies from nature. Between 1818 and 1825 Landseer did a great deal of work, but on the whole gained [illegible] besides facility of technical expression, a greater zest for humour and a larger style. The work of this stage ended with [illegible] production of the painting called "The Cat's Paw," which was sent to the British Institution in 1824, and made an enormous sensation. The price obtained for this picture, £100, enabled Landseer to set up for himself in the house No. 1 St John's Wood Road, where he lived nearly fifty years and in which he died. During this period Landseer's principal pictures were "The Cat Disturbed", "Alpine Mastiffs reanimating a Distressed Traveller," a famous work engraved by his father; "The Ratcatchers"; "Pointers to be"; "The Larder Invaded"; and "Neptune," the head and shoulders of a Newfoundland dog. In 1824 Landseer and C. R. Leslie made a journey to the Highlands—a momentous visit for the former, who thenceforward [illegible] failed annually to repeat it in search of studies and subjects.

In 1826 Landseer was elected an A.R.A. In 1827 appeared "The Monkey who has seen the World," a picture which marked the growth of a taste for humorous subjects in the mind of the painter that had been evoked by the success of the "Cat's Paw" "Taking a Buck" (1825) was the painter's first Scottish picture. Its execution marked a change in his style which, in increase of largeness, was a great improvement. In other respects, however, there was a decrease of solid qualities; indeed, finish, searching modelling, and elaborate draughtsmanship rarely appeared in Landseer's work after 1823. The subject, as such, soon after this time became a very distinct element in his pictures; ultimately it dominated, and in effect the artist enjoyed a greater degree of popularity than technical judgment justified, so that later criticism has put Landseer's position in art much lower than the place he once occupied. Sentiment gave new charm to his works, which had previously depended on the expression of animal passion and character, and the exhibition of noble qualities of draughtsmanship. Sentimentality ruled in not a few pictures of later dates, and *quasi*-human humour, or pathos, superseded that masculine animalism which rioted in its energy, and enabled the artist to rival Snyders, if not Velazquez, as a painter of beasts. After "High Life" and "Low Life," now in the Tate Gallery, London, Landseer's dogs, and even his lions and birds, were sometimes more than half civilized. It was not that these later pictures were less true to nature than their forerunners, but the models were chosen from different grades of animal society. As Landseer prospered he kept finer company, and his new patrons did not care about rat-catching and dog-fighting, however vigorously and learnedly those subjects might be depicted. It cannot be said that the world lost much when, in exchange for the "Cat Disturbed" and "Fighting Dogs getting Wind," came "Jack in Office," "The Old Shepherd's Chief Mourner," and "The Swannery invaded by Eagles," three pictures which are types of as many diverse moods of Landseer's art, and each a noble one.

Landseer was elected a Royal Academician in 1831. "Chevy Chase" (1826), which is at Woburn, "The Highland Whisky Still" (18·9), "High Life" (1829) and "Low Life" (1829), besides other important works, had appeared in the interval. Landseer had by this time attained such amazing mastery that he painted "Spaniel and Rabbit" in two hours and a half, [illegible] "Rabbits," which was at the British Institution, in three-[illegible] of an hour; and the fine dog-picture "Odin" (1836) was the work of one sitting, *i.e.* painted within twelve hours. But perhaps the most wonderful instance of his rapid but sure and dexterous brush-handling was "The Cavalier's Pets" (1845), the picture of two King Charles's spaniels in the National Gallery, which was executed in two days. Another remarkable feat consisted in drawing, simultaneously, a stag's head with one hand and a head of a horse with the other. "Harvest in the Highlands," and that masterpiece of humour, "Jack in Office," were exhibited in 1833. In 1834 a noble work of sentiment was given to the world in "Suspense," which is now at South Kensington, and shows a dog watching at the closed door of his wounded master. Many think this to be Landseer's finest work, others prefer "The Old Shepherd's Chief Mourner" (1837). The over-praised and unfortunate "Bolton Abbey in the Olden Time," a group of portraits in character, was also shown in 1834, and was the first picture for which the painter received £400. A few years later he sold "Peace" and "War" for £1500, and for the copyrights alone obtained £6000. In 1881 "Man proposes, God Disposes" (1864) was resold for 6300 guineas, and a cartoon of "The Chase" (1866) fetched 5000 guineas. "A Distinguished Member of the Humane Society," a dog reclining on a quay wall (1838), was succeeded by "Dignity and Impudence" (1839). The "Lion Dog of Malta," and "Laying down the Law" appeared in 1840. In 1842 was finished the capital "Highland Shepherd's Home" (Sheepshanks Gift), together with the beautiful "Eos," a portrait of Prince Albert's most graceful of greyhounds, to which Thomas Landseer added an ineffable charm and solidity not in the painting. The "Rout of Comus" was painted in the summerhouse of Buckingham Palace garden in 1843. The "Challenge" was accompanied (1844) by "Shoeing the Bay Mare" (Bell Gift), and followed by "Peace" and "War," and the "Stag at Bay" (1846) "Alexander and Diogenes," and a "Random Shot," a dead kid lying in the snow, came forth in 1848. In 1850 Landseer received a national commission to paint in the Houses of Parliament three subjects connected with the chase. Although they would have been worth three times as much money, the House of Commons refused to grant £1500 for these pictures, and the matter fell through, more to the artist's profit than the nation's gain. The famous "Monarch of the Glen" (1851) was one of these subjects. "Night" and "Morning," romantic and pathetic deer subjects, came in due order (1853). For "The Sanctuary" (1842) the Fine Arts jury of experts awarded to the artist the great gold medal of the Exposition Universelle, Paris, 1855.

The "Dialogue at Waterloo" (1850), which he afterwards regarded with strong disapproval, showed how Landseer, like nearly all English artists of original power and considerable fertility, owed nothing to French or Italian training. In the same year he received the honour of knighthood. Next came "Geneva" (1851), "Titania and Bottom" (1851), which comprises a charming queen of the fairies, and the "Deer Pass" (1852), followed by "The Children of the Mist" (1853), "Saved" (1856), "Braemar," a noble stag, "Rough and Ready," and "Uncle Tom and his Wife for Sale" (1857). "The Maid and the Magpie" (1858), the extraordinarily large cartoon called "Deer Browsing" (1857), "The Twa Dogs" (1858), and one or two minor paintings were equal to any previously produced by the artist. Nevertheless, signs of failing health were remarked in "Doubtful Crumbs" and a "Kind Star" (1859). The immense and profoundly dramatic picture called "A Flood in the Highlands" (1860) more than reinstated the painter before the public, but friends still saw ground for uneasiness. Extreme nervous excitability manifested itself in many ways, and in the choice (1864) of the dreadful subject of "Man Proposes, God Disposes," bears clumsily clambering among relics of Sir John Franklin's party, there was occult pathos, which some of the artist's intimates suspected, but did not avow. In 1862 and 1863 Landseer produced nothing; but "A Piper and a Pair of Nutcrackers" (1864) revealed his old power. He declined the presidentship of the Royal Academy in 1865, in succession to Sir Charles Eastlake. In 1867 the four lions which he had modelled for the base of the Nelson Monument in Trafalgar Square, London, were unveiled, and with "The Swannery invaded by Eagles" (1869) he achieved his last triumph. After four years more, full of suffering, mainly of broken art and shattered mental powers, Sir Edwin Landseer died on the 1st of October 1873, and was buried, ten days later, in St Paul's Cathedral. Those who would see the full strength of Landseer's brush should examine his sketches and the like in the Victoria and Albert Museum and similar works. In these he shows himself endowed with the strength of Paul Potter.

See Algernon Graves's *Catalogue of the Works of the late Sir Edwin Landseer, R.A.* (London, n.d.), Frederic G. Stephens's *Sir Edwin Landseer* (1880); W Cosmo Monkhouse's *The Studies of Sir Edwin Landseer, R.A., with a History of his Art-Life* (London, n.d), W P. Frith's *My Autobiography and Reminiscences* (1887), Vernon Heath's *Recollections* (1892); and James A. Manson's "Sir Edwin Landseer, R.A.," *The Makers of British Art* (London, 1902).

LAND'S END, a promontory of Cornwall, forming the westernmost point of England. It is a fine headland of granite, pierced by a natural arch, on a coast renowned for its cliff scenery. Dangerous reefs lie off the point, and one group a mile from the mainland is marked by the Longships Lighthouse, in 50° 4′ N., 5° 43′ W. The Land's End is the westernmost of the granite masses which rise at intervals through Cornwall from Dartmoor. The phenomenon of a raised beach may be seen here, but indications of a submerged forest have also been discovered in the neighbourhood.

LANDSHUT, a town in the kingdom of Bavaria, on the right bank of the Isar, 40 m. N.E. of Munich on the main line of railway to Regensburg. Pop. (1905) 24,217 Landshut is still a quaint, picturesque place; it consists of an old and a new town and of four suburbs, one part of it lying on an island in the Isar. It contains a fine street, the Altstadt, and several interesting medieval buildings. Among its eleven churches the most noteworthy are those of St Martin, with a tower 432 ft. high, of St Jodocus, and of the Holy Ghost, or the Hospital church, all three begun before 1410. The former Dominican convent, founded in 1271, once the seat of the university, is now used as public offices. The post-office, formerly the meeting-house of the Estates, a building adorned with old frescoes; the royal palace, which contains some very fine Renaissance work; and the town-hall, built in 1446 and restored in 1860, are also noteworthy. The town has monuments to the Bavarian king, Maximilian II., and to other famous men; it contains a botanical garden and a public park. On a hill overlooking Landshut is the castle of Trausnitz, called also Burg Landshut, formerly a stronghold of the dukes of Lower Bavaria, whose burial-place was at Seligenthal also near the town. The original building was erected early in the 13th century, but the chapel, the oldest part now existing, dates from the 14th century. The upper part of the castle has been made habitable. The industries of Landshut are not important; they include brewing, tanning and spinning, and the manufacture of tobacco and cloth. Market gardening and an extensive trade in grain are also carried on.

Landshut was founded about 1204, and from 1255 to 1503 it was the principal residence of the dukes of Lower Bavaria and of their successors, the dukes of Bavaria-Landshut. During the Thirty Years' War it was captured several times by the Swedes and in the 18th century by the Austrians. In April 1809 Napoleon defeated the Austrians here and the town was stormed by his troops. From 1800 to 1826 the university, formerly at Ingolstadt and now at Munich, was located at Landshut. Owing to the three helmets which form its arms the town is sometimes called "Dreihelm Stadt."

See Staudenraus, *Chronik der Stadt Landshut*, (Landshut 1832); Wiesend, *Topographische Geschichte von Landshut* (Landshut, 1858); Rosenthal, *Zur Rechtsgeschichte der Städte Landshut und Straubing* (Würzberg, 1883); Kalcher, *Führer durch Landshut* (Landshut, 1887), Haack, *Die gotische Architektur und Plastik der Stadt Landshut* (Munich, 1894); and *Geschichte der Stadt Landshut* (Landshut, 1835).

LANDSKNECHT, a German mercenary foot-soldier of the 16th century. The name (German for "man of the plains") was given to mark the contrast between the force of these

... emperor Maximilian I. about the end ... century, and the Swiss, the "men of the mountains," ... mercenary infantry of Europe. After ... Marignano and Pavia, where the military reputa- ... been broken, the Swabian *landsknechte* ... best fighting troops in Europe. Though ... and always the mainstay of imperial ... bodies as mercenaries elsewhere ... they fought for the League and for the ... In fact *landsknecht*, and more ... corruption *lansquenet*, became in western ... mercenary foot-soldiers. It is owing ... long pike or lance), the typical weapon ... that the corrupted French form, ... *landsknecht*, and an English "lance- ...

... raised by colonels (*Oberst*), to whom ... commissions corresponding to the ... were organized in regiments made up ... and regimental staff, with a varying ... (*Fähnlein*), commanded by ... subaltern officers were lieutenants ... In thus defining the titles and duties ... every detail of regimental customs ... and interior economy, the lands- ... as the founders of the modern ... see further Army).

... of Sweden, on the east side of the ... Pop. (1900) 14,300. The ... depth of 35 ft., with 15 ft. beside ... among the first twelve manufacturing ... the principal industries ... manufacture and refining from beetroot. ... opposite the town, Tycho ... observatory of Uranien- ... 16th century. Landskrona, ... owed its first importance ... a body of Carmelite monks ... the place the privileges ... 16th and 17th centuries it ... its own prosperity. On the ... was fought in the neigh- ... the Danes.

... of the *levée en masse*, ... bearing arms and not ... forces, standing army ... nations. ... "defence of the ... insurrectional militia ... mentioned in [illegible] ... Ages, i. 262, 10th ed. ... by a royal edict of ... up all men capable of ... and forty-five, and ... of the country. ... an integral part of ... composed of one line and ... the mobiliza- ... line, and by the ... relegated to ... a totally different ... alongside ... such recruits as, ... In Switzer- ... all citizens ... "Auszug" or ... Arabic ... Hereford.

church, but this purpose was abandoned, and for some time he studied the art of engraving. Failure of health compelled him to throw aside the burin, and in 1825 he started for Egypt, where he spent three years, twice ascended the Nile, proceeding as far as the second cataract, and composed a complete description of Egypt, with a portfolio of one hundred and one drawings. This work was never published, but the account of the modern Egyptians, which formed a part of it, was accepted for separate publication by the Society for the Diffusion of Useful Knowledge. To perfect this work Lane again visited Egypt in 1833–1835, residing mainly in Cairo, but retiring to Luxor during the plague of 1835. Lane took up his residence in the Mahommedan quarter, and under the name of Mansur Effendi lived the life of an Egyptian scholar. He was fortunate in the time when he took up his work, for Cairo had not then become a modern city, and he was thus able to describe aspects of Arabian life that no longer exist there. Perfected by the additional observations collected during these years, the *Modern Egyptians* appeared in 1836, and at once took the place which it has never lost as the best description of Eastern life and an Eastern country ever written. It was followed from 1838 to 1840 by a translation of the *Arabian Nights*, with notes and illustrations, designed to make the book a sort of encyclopaedia of Eastern manners. The translation itself is an admirable proof of scholarship, but is characterized by a somewhat stilted mannerism, which is not equally appropriate to all parts of the motley-coloured original. The character of some of the tales and the tedious repetitions of the same theme in the Arabic collection induced Lane to leave considerable parts of the work untranslated. The value of his version is increased by the exhaustive notes on Mahommedan life and customs. In 1840 Lane married a Greek lady. A useful volume of *Selections from the Kur-án* was published in 1843, but before it passed through the press Lane was again in Egypt, where he spent seven years (1842–1849) collecting materials for a great Arabic lexicon, which the munificence of Lord Prudhoe (afterwards duke of Northumberland) enabled him to undertake. The most important of the materials amassed during this sojourn (in which he was accompanied by his wife and by his sister, Mrs Poole, authoress of the *Englishwoman in Egypt*, with her two sons, afterwards well known in Eastern letters) was a copy in 24 thick quarto volumes of Sheikh Murtadā's great lexicon, the *Tāj el 'Arūs*, which, though itself a compilation, is so extensive and exact that it formed the main basis of Lane's subsequent work. The author, who lived in Egypt in the 18th century, used more than a hundred sources, interweaving what he learned from them with the *al-Qāmūs* of Fairūzābādī in the form of a commentary. By far the larger part of this commentary was derived from the *Lisān el 'Arab* of Ibn Mokarram, a work of the 13th century, which Lane was also able to use while in Cairo.

Returning to England in 1849, Lane devoted the remaining twenty-seven years of his life to digesting and translating his Arabic material in the form of a great thesaurus of the lexicographical knowledge of the Arabs. In spite of weak health he continued this arduous task with unflagging diligence till a few days before his death at Worthing on the 10th of August 1876. Five parts appeared during his lifetime (1863–1874), and three posthumous parts were afterwards edited from his papers by S. Lane-Poole. Even in its imperfect state the *Lexicon* is an enduring monument, the completeness and finished scholarship with which it is executed making each article an exhaustive monograph. Two essays, the one on Arabic lexicography and the other on Arabic pronunciation, contributed to the magazine of the German Oriental Society, complete the record of Lane's publications. His scholarship was recognized by many learned European societies. He was a member of the German Oriental Society, a correspondent of the French Institute, &c. In 1863 he was awarded a small civil list pension, which was after his death continued to his widow. Lane was not an original mind; ... were those of observation, industry and sound ... His personal character was elevated and pure, his ... of religious and moral duty being of the type that characterized the best circles of English evangelicalism in the early part of the 19th century.

A Memoir, by his grand-nephew, S. Lane-Poole, was prefixed to part vi. of the *Lexicon*. It was published separately in 1877.

LANE, GEORGE MARTIN (1823–1897), American scholar, was born at Charlestown, Massachusetts, on the 24th of December 1823. He graduated in 1846 at Harvard, and in 1847–1851 studied at the universities of Berlin, Bonn, Heidelberg and Göttingen. In 1851 he received his doctor's degree at Göttingen for his dissertation *Smyrnaeorum Res Gestae et Antiquitates*, and on his return to America he was appointed University Professor of Latin in Harvard College. From 1869 until 1894, when he resigned and became professor emeritus, he was Pope Professor of Latin in the same institution. His *Latin Pronunciation*, which led to the rejection of the English method of Latin pronunciation in the United States, was published in 1871. He died on the 30th of June 1897. His *Latin Grammar*, completed and published by Professor M. H. Morgan in the following year, is of high value. Lane's assistance in the preparation of Harper's Latin lexicons was also invaluable. English light verse he wrote with humour and fluency, and his song *Jonah* and the *Ballad of the Lone Fishball* were famous.

LANE, JAMES HENRY (1814–1866), American soldier and politician, was born at Lawrenceburg, Indiana, on the 22nd of June 1814. He was the son of Amos Lane (1778–1849), a political leader in Indiana, a member of the Indiana House of Representatives in 1816–1818 (speaker in 1817–1818), in 1821–1822 and in 1839–1840, and from 1833 to 1837 a Democratic representative in Congress. The son received a common school education, studied law and in 1840 was admitted to the bar. In the Mexican War he served as a colonel under General Taylor, and then commanded the Fifth Indiana regiment (which he had raised) in the Southern Campaign under General Scott. Lane was lieutenant-governor of Indiana from 1849 to 1853, and from 1853 to 1855 was a Democratic representative in Congress. His vote in favour of the Kansas-Nebraska Bill ruined his political future in his own state, and he emigrated in 1855 to the Territory of Kansas, probably as an agent of Stephen A. Douglas to organize the Democratic party there. He soon joined the Free State forces, however, was a member of the first general Free State convention at Big Springs in September 1855, and wrote its "platform," which deprecated abolitionism and urged the exclusion of negroes from the Territory; and he presided over the Topeka Constitutional Convention, composed of Free State men, in the autumn of 1855. Lane was second in command of the forces in Lawrence during the "Wakarusa War"; and in the spring of 1856 was elected a United States senator under the Topeka Constitution, the validity of which, however, and therefore the validity of his election, Congress refused to recognize. In May 1856, with George Washington Deitzler (1826–1884), Dr Charles Robinson, and other Free State leaders, he was indicted for treason; but he escaped from Kansas, made a tour of the northern cities, and by his fiery oratory aroused great enthusiasm in behalf of the Free State movement in Kansas. Returning to the Territory with John Brown in August 1856, he took an active part in the domestic feuds of 1856–1857. After Kansas became a state, Lane was elected in 1861 to the United States Senate as a Republican. Immediately on reaching Washington he organized a company to guard the President; and in August 1861, having gained the ear of the Federal authorities and become intimate with President Lincoln, he went to Kansas with vague military powers, and exercised them in spite of the protests of the governor and the regular departmental commanders. During the autumn, with a brigade of 1500 men, he conducted a devastating campaign on the Missouri border, and in July 1862 he was appointed commissioner of recruiting for Kansas, a position in which he rendered faithful service, though he frequently came into conflict with the state authorities. At this time he planned a chimerical "great Southern expedition" against New Mexico, but this came to nothing. In 1864 he laboured earnestly for the re-election of Lincoln. When President Johnson quarrelled with the Radical Republicans, Lane deserted the latter and defended the Executive. Angered by his defection, certain senators accused him of being implicated in Indian contracts of a fraudulent character; and in a fit of depression following this accusation he took his own life, dying near Fort Leavenworth, Kansas, on the 11th of July 1866, ten days after he had shot himself in the head. Ambitious, unscrupulous, rash and impulsive, and generally regarded by his contemporaries as an unsafe leader, Lane was a man of great energy and personal magnetism, and possessed oratorical powers of a high order.

See the article by L. W. Spring entitled "The Career of a Kansas Politician," in vol. iv. (October 1898) of the *American Historical Review*; and for the commoner view, which makes him not a coward as does Spring, but a "grim chieftain" and a hero, see John Speer, *Life of Gen. James H. Lane, "The Saviour of Kansas,"* (Garden City, Kansas, 1896).

Senator Lane should not be confused with James Henry Lane (1833–1907), who served on the Confederate side during the Civil War, attaining the rank of brigadier-general in 1862, and after the war was professor of natural philosophy and military tactics in the Virginia Agricultural and Mechanical College from 1872 to 1880, and professor of civil engineering and drawing in the Alabama Polytechnic Institute from 1882 until his death.

LANESSAN, JEAN MARIE ANTOINE DE (1843–), French statesman and naturalist, was born at Sainte-André de Cubzac (Gironde) on the 13th of July 1843. He entered the navy in 1862, serving on the East African and Cochin-China stations in the medical department until the Franco-German War, when he resigned and volunteered for the army medical service. He now completed his studies, taking his doctorate in 1872. Elected to the Municipal Council of Paris in 1879, he declared in favour of communal autonomy and joined with Henri Rochefort in demanding the erection of a monument to the Communards; but after his election to the Chamber of Deputies for the 5th arrondissement of Paris in 1881 he gradually veered from the extreme Radical party to the Republican Union, and identified himself with the cause of colonial expansion. A government mission to the French colonies in 1886–1887, in connexion with the approaching Paris exhibition, gave him the opportunity of studying colonial questions, on which, after his return, he published three works: *La Tunisie* (Paris, 1887); *L'Expansion coloniale de la France* (*ib.*, 1888), *L'Indo-Chine française* (*ib.*, 1889). In 1891 he was made civil and military governor of French Indo-China, where his administration, which involved him in open rupture with Admiral Fournier, was severely criticized. Nevertheless he consolidated French influence in Annam and Cambodia, and secured a large accession of territory on the Mekong river from the kingdom of Siam. He was recalled in 1894, and published an apology for his administration (*La Colonisation française en Indo-Chine*) in the following year. In the Waldeck-Rousseau cabinet of 1899 to 1902 he was minister of marine, and in 1901 he secured the passage of a naval programme intended to raise the French navy during the next six years to a level befitting the place of France among the great powers. At the general election of 1906 he was not re-elected. He was political director of the *Siècle*, and president of the French Colonization Society, and wrote, besides the books already mentioned, various works on political and biological questions.

LANFRANC (d. 1089), archbishop of Canterbury, was a Lombard by extraction. He was born in the early years of the 11th century at Pavia, where his father, Hanbald, held the rank of a magistrate. Lanfranc was trained in the legal studies for which northern Italy was then becoming famous, and acquired such proficiency that tradition links him with Irnerius of Bologna as a pioneer in the renaissance of Roman law. Though designed for a public career Lanfranc had the tastes of a student. After his father's death he crossed the Alps to found a school in France; but in a short while he decided that Normandy would afford him a better field. About 1039 he became the master of the cathedral school at Avranches, where he taught for three years with conspicuous success. But in 1142 he embraced the monastic profession in the newly founded house of Bec. Until 1145 he lived at Bec in absolute seclusion. He was then persuaded by Abbot Herluin to open a school in the

ratified the Federal Constitution for New Hampshire; a member of the United States Senate in 1789–1801, and its president *pro tem.* during the first Congress and the second session of the second Congress; a member of the New Hampshire House of Representatives in 1801–1805 and its speaker in 1803–1805; and governor of the state in 1805–1809 and in 1810–1812. He received nine electoral votes for the vice-presidency in 1808, and in 1812 was an elector on the Madison ticket. He died in Portsmouth on the 18th of September 1819. He was an able leader during the Revolutionary period, when his wealth and social position were of great assistance to the patriot party. In the later years of his life in New Hampshire he was the most prominent of the local Republican leaders and built up his party by partisan appointments. He refused the naval portfolio in Jefferson's cabinet.

His elder brother, Woodbury Langdon (1739–1805), was a delegate to the Continental Congress in 1779–1780, a member of the executive council of New Hampshire in 1781–1784, judge of the Supreme Court of the state in 1782 and in 1786–1790 (although he had had no legal training), and a state senator in 1784–1785.

Alfred Langdon Elwyn has edited *Letters by Washington, Adams, Jefferson and Others, Written During and After the Revolution, to John Langdon of New Hampshire* (Philadelphia, 1880), a book of great interest and value. See a biographical sketch of John Langdon by Charles R. Corning in the *New England Magazine*, vol. xxii. (Boston, 1897).

LANGE, ANNE FRANÇOISE ELIZABETH (1772–1816), French actress, was born in Genoa on the 17th of September 1772, the daughter of a musician and an actress at the Comédie Italienne. She made her first appearance on the stage at Tours in 1787 and a successful début at the Comédie Française in 1788 in *L'Écossaise* and *L'Oracle*. She followed Talma and the others in 1791 to the Rue Richelieu, but returned after a few months to the Comédie Française. Here her talent and beauty gave her an enormous success in François de Neuchâteau's *Paméla*, the performance of which brought upon the theatre the vials of wrath of the Committee of Safety. With the author and the other members of the caste, she was arrested and imprisoned. After the 9th Thermidor she rejoined her comrades at the Feydeau, but retired on the 16th of December 1797, reappearing only for a few performances in 1807. She had, meantime, married the son of a rich Belgian named Simons. She died on the 25th of May 1816.

LANGE, ERNST PHILIPP KARL (1813–1899), German novelist, who wrote under the pseudonym *Philipp Galen*, was born at Potsdam on the 21st of December 1813. He studied medicine at Berlin (1835–1840), and on taking his degree, in 1840, entered the Prussian army as surgeon. In this capacity he saw service in the Schleswig-Holstein campaign of 1849. He settled at Bielefeld as medical practitioner and here issued his first novel, *Der Inselkönig* (1852. 3rd ed., 1858), which enjoyed considerable popularity. In Bielefeld he continued to work at his profession and to write, until his retirement, with the rank of *Oberstabsarzt* (surgeon-general) to Potsdam in 1878; there he died on the 20th of February 1899. Lange's novels are distinguished by local colouring and pretty, though not powerful, descriptions of manners and customs. He particularly favoured scenes of English life, though he had never been in that country, and on the whole he succeeded well in his descriptions. Chief among his novels are, *Der Irre von St James* (1853, 5th ed., 18[illegible]), and *Emery Glandon* (3rd ed., Leip., 1865), while of those dealing with the Schleswig-Holstein campaign *Andreas Burns* (1860) and *Die Tochter des Diplomaten* (1865) commanded considerable attention.

His *[illegible] Schriften* appeared in 36 vols. (1857–1866).

LANGE, FRIEDRICH ALBERT (1828–1875), German philosopher and sociologist, was born on the 28th of September 1828, at Wald, near Solingen, the son of the theologian, J. P. Lange [illegible]. He was educated at Duisburg, Zürich and Bonn, distinguished himself by gymnastics as much as by [illegible] 1852 he became schoolmaster at Cologne; in 1855 [illegible] in philosophy at Bonn; in 1858 schoolmaster at Duisburg, resigning when the government forbade schoolmasters to take part in political agitation. Lange then entered on a career of militant journalism in the cause of political and social reform. He was also prominent in the affairs of his town, yet found leisure to write most of his best-known books, *Die Leibesübungen* (1863), *Die Arbeiterfrage* (1865, 5th ed. 1894), *Geschichte des Materialismus und Kritik seiner Bedeutung in der Gegenwart* (1866; 7th ed. with biographical sketch by H. Cohen, 1902; Eng. trans., E. C. Thomas, 1877), and *J. S. Mill's Ansichten über die sociale Frage* (1866). In 1866, discouraged by affairs in Germany, he moved to Winterthur, near Zürich, to become connected with the democratic newspaper, *Winterthurer Landbote*. In 1869 he was *Privatdozent* at Zürich, and next year professor. The strong French sympathies of the Swiss in the Franco-German War led to his speedy resignation. Thenceforward he gave up politics. In 1872 he accepted a professorship at Marburg. Unhappily, his vigorous frame was already stricken with disease, and, after a lingering illness, he died at Marburg, on the 23rd of November 1875, diligent to the end. His *Logische Studien* was published by H. Cohen in 1877 (2nd ed., 1894). His main work, the *Geschichte des Materialismus*, which is brilliantly written, with wide scientific knowledge and more sympathy with English thought than is usual in Germany, is rather a didactic exposition of principles than a history in the proper sense. Adopting the Kantian standpoint that we can know nothing but phenomena, Lange maintains that neither materialism nor any other metaphysical system has a valid claim to ultimate truth. For empirical phenomenal knowledge, however, which is all that man can look for, materialism with its exact scientific methods has done most valuable service. Ideal metaphysics, though they fail of the inner truth of things, have a value as the embodiment of high aspirations, in the same way as poetry and religion. In Lange's *Logische Studien*, which attempts a reconstruction of formal logic, the leading idea is that reasoning has validity in so far as it can be represented in terms of space. His *Arbeiterfrage* advocates an ill-defined form of socialism. It protests against contemporary industrial selfishness, and against the organization of industry on the Darwinian principle of struggle for existence.

See O. A. Ellissen, *F. A. Lange* (Leipzig, 1891), and in *Monatsch. d. Comeniusgesell.* iii., 1894, 210 ff.; H. Cohen in *Preuss. Jahrb.* xxvii., 1876, 353 ff.; Vaihinger, *Hartmann, Dühring und Lange* (Iserlohn, 1876); J. M. Bösch, *F. A. Lange und sein Standpunkt d. Ideals* (Frauenfeld, 1890); H. Braun, *F. A. Lange, als Socialökonom* (Halle, 1881). (H. St.)

LANGE, JOHANN PETER (1802–1884), German Protestant theologian, was of peasant origin and was born at Sonneborn near Elberfeld on the 10th of April 1802. He studied theology at Bonn (from 1822) under K. I. Nitzsch and G. C. F. Lücke, held several pastorates, and eventually (1854) settled at Bonn as professor of theology in succession to Isaac A. Dorner, becoming also in 1860 counsellor to the consistory. He died on the 9th of July 1884. Lange has been called the poetical theologian *par excellence*: "It has been said of him that his thoughts succeed each other in such rapid and agitated waves that all calm reflection and all rational distinction become, in a manner, drowned" (F. Lichtenberger). As a dogmatic writer he belonged to the school of Schleiermacher. His *Christliche Dogmatik* (3 vols., 1849–1852, new edition, 1870) "contains many fruitful and suggestive thoughts, which, however, are hidden under such a mass of bold figures and strange fancies, and suffer so much from want of clearness of presentation, that they did not produce any lasting effect" (Otto Pfleiderer).

His other works include *Das Leben Jesu* (3 vols., 1844–1847), *Das apostolische Zeitalter* (2 vols., 1853–1854), *Grundriss der theologischen Enzyklopädie* (1877), *Grundriss der christlichen Ethik* (1878), and *Grundriss der Bibelkunde* (1881). In 1857 he undertook with other scholars a *Theologisch-homiletisches Bibelwerk*, to which he contributed commentaries on the first four books of the Pentateuch, Haggai, Zechariah, Malachi, Matthew, Mark Revelation. The *Bibelwerk* has been translated, enlarged and revised under the general editorship of Dr Philip Schaff.

LANGEAIS, a town of west-central France in the department of Indre-et-Loire, on the right bank of the Loire, 16 m. W.S.W. of Tours by rail. Pop. (1906) town, 1755; commune, 3550. Langeais has a church of the 11th, 12th and 15th centuries but is chiefly interesting for the possession of a large château built soon after the middle of the 15th century by Jean Bourré, minister of Louis XI. Here the marriage of Charles VIII. and Anne of Brittany took place in 1491. In the park are the ruins of a keep of late 10th-century architecture, built by Fulk Nerra, count of Anjou.

LANGEN, JOSEPH (1837–1901), German theologian, was born at Cologne on the 3rd of June 1837. He studied at Bonn, was ordained priest in 1859, was nominated professor extraordinary at the university of Bonn in 1864, and a professor in ordinary of the exegesis of the New Testament in 1867—an office which he held till his death. He was one of the able band of professors who in 1870 supported Döllinger in his resistance to the Vatican decrees, and was excommunicated with Ignaz v. Döllinger, Johann Huber, Johann Friedrich, Franz Heinrich Reusch, Joseph Hubert Reinkens and others, for refusing to accept them. In 1878, in consequence of the permission given to priests to marry, he ceased to identify himself with the Old Catholic movement, although he was not reconciled with the Roman Catholic Church. Langen was more celebrated as a writer than as a speaker. His first work was an inquiry into the authorship of the Commentary on St Paul's Epistles and the Treatise on Biblical Questions, ascribed to Ambrose and Augustine respectively. In 1868 he published an *Introduction to the New Testament*, a work of which a second edition was called for in 1873. He also published works on the *Last Days of the Life of Jesus*, on *Judaism in the Time of Christ*, on *John of Damascus* (1879) and an *Examination of the Vatican Dogma in the Light of Patristic Exegesis of the New Testament*. But he is chiefly famous for his *History of the Church of Rome to the Pontificate of Innocent III.* (4 vols., 1881–1893), a work of sound scholarship, based directly upon the authorities, the most important sources being woven carefully into the text. He also contributed largely to the *Internationale theologische Zeitschrift*, a review started in 1893 by the Old Catholics to promote the union of National Churches on the basis of the councils of the Undivided Church, and admitting articles in German, French and English. Among other subjects, he wrote on the School of Hierotheus, on Romish falsifications of the Greek Fathers, on Leo XIII., on Liberal Ultramontanism, on the Papal Teaching in regard to Morals, on Vincentius of Lerins and he carried on a controversy with Professor Willibald Beyschlag, of the German Evangelical Church, on the respective merits of Protestantism and Old Catholicism regarded as a basis for teaching the Christian faith. An attack of apoplexy put an end to his activity as a teacher and hastened his death, which occurred in July 1901. (J. J. L.*)

LANGENBECK, BERNHARD RUDOLF KONRAD VON (1810–1887), German surgeon, was born at Horneburg on the 9th of November 1810, and received his medical education at Göttingen, where he took his doctor's degree in 1835 with a thesis on the structure of the retina. After a visit to France and England, he returned to Göttingen as *Privatdozent*, and in 1842 became professor of surgery and director of the Friedrichs Hospital at Kiel. Six years later he succeeded J. F. Dieffenbach (1794–1847) as director of the Clinical Institute for Surgery and Ophthalmology at Berlin, and remained there till 1882, when failing health obliged him to retire. He died at Wiesbaden on the 30th of September 1887. Langenbeck was a bold and skilful operator, but was disinclined to resort to operation while other means afforded a prospect of success. He devoted particular attention to military surgery, and was a great authority in the treatment of gunshot wounds. Besides acting as general field-surgeon of the army in the war with Denmark in 1848, he saw active service in 1864, 1866, and again in the Franco-German campaign of 1870–71. He was in Orleans at the end of 1870, after the city had been taken by the Prussians, and was unwearied in his attentions, whether as operator or consultant, to wounded men with whom every public building was packed. He also utilized the opportunities for instruction that thus arose, and the "Militär-Aerztliche Gesellschaft," which met twice a week for some months, and in the discussions of which

[illegible]work about half a mile east of the town; (*e*) Fort Dampierre, 8 m [illegible] of the town, which commands all the main approaches from [illegible] north, and completes the circle by crossing its fire with that of [illegible] St Menge.

LANGTOFT, PETER (d. *c.* 1307), English chronicler, took [illegible] name from the village of Langtoft in Yorkshire, and was [illegible] canon of the Augustinian priory in Bridlington. His name [illegible] given as Langetoft and Langetost. He wrote in French [illegible] a *Chronicle* dealing with the history of England from the [illegible] times to the death of Edward I. in 1307. It consists of [illegible] parts and contains about 9000 rhyming verses. The [illegible] part of the *Chronicle* is taken from Geoffrey of Monmouth [illegible] other writers; for the period dealing with the reign of [illegible] I. Langtoft is a contemporary and valuable authority, [illegible] for affairs in the north of England and in Scotland. [illegible] *Chronicle* seems to have enjoyed considerable popu[illegible] in the north, and the latter part of it was translated into [illegible] by Robert Mannyng, sometimes called Robert of Brunne, [illegible] It has been edited for the Rolls Series by T. Wright [illegible]

[illegible] preface, and also O. Preussner, *Robert Mannyng of* [illegible] *von Pierre de Langtofts Chronicle und ihr* [illegible] (Breslau, 1891).

LANGTON, JOHN (d. 1337), chancellor of England and bishop [illegible], was a clerk in the royal chancery, and became [illegible] in 1292. He obtained several ecclesiastical appoint[illegible] to the resistance of Pope Boniface VIII. he [illegible] the bishopric of Ely in 1298, although he was [illegible] Edward I. and visited Rome to attain his end. [illegible] as chancellor in 1302, he was chosen bishop [illegible] and again became chancellor shortly after [illegible] Edward II. in 1307. Langton was one of the [illegible] elected in 1310, and it was probably his connexion [illegible] that led to his losing the office of chancellor about [illegible] however, to take part in public affairs; [illegible] between the king and Earl Thomas of Lancaster in [illegible] to do so between Edward and his rebellious [illegible] He died in June or July 1337. Langton built [illegible] at Chichester, and was a benefactor of the [illegible]

LANGTON, STEPHEN (d. 1228), cardinal and archbishop of [illegible] the son of English parents; but the date and [illegible] are unknown. Since he became early in his [illegible] of York, and since his brother Simon [illegible] to that see in 1215, we may suppose the [illegible] of northern extraction. Stephen, however, [illegible] and having graduated in that university [illegible] most celebrated theologians. This was [illegible] when he composed his voluminous com[illegible] which still exist in manuscript) and divided [illegible] At Paris also he contracted the friend[illegible] the future Innocent III., which played [illegible] shaping his career. Upon becoming pope, [illegible] Langton to Rome, and in 1206 designated [illegible] S. Chrysogonus. Immediately after[illegible] into the vortex of English politics. [illegible] Walter had died in 1205, and the [illegible] had raised thorny questions. The [illegible] claimed a share in choosing the new [illegible] had been exclusively reserved to [illegible] a papal privilege; and John [illegible] were prepared to give their [illegible] de Gray, bishop of Norwich. A [illegible] made the double pressure of [illegible] their sub-prior Reginald [illegible] The plot leaked out; [illegible] to elect John de Gray, and [illegible] the case Innocent [illegible] this election, and the [illegible] contest between the [illegible] and the pope on the [illegible] and was appointed [illegible] Pope Gregory IX. [illegible]

declared both elections void; and with John's consent ordered that a new election should be made in his presence by the representatives of the monks. The latter, having confessed that they had given John a secret pledge to elect none but the bishop of Norwich, were released from the promise by Innocent, and at his suggestion elected Stephen Langton, who was consecrated by the pope on the 17th of June 1207. On hearing the news the king banished the monks of Canterbury and lodged a protest with the pope, in which he threatened to prevent any English appeals from being brought to Rome. Innocent replied by laying England under an interdict (March 1208), and excommunicating the king (November 1209). As John still remained obstinate, the pope at length invited the French king Philip Augustus to enter England and depose him. It was this threat which forced John to sue for a reconciliation; and the first condition exacted was that he should acknowledge Langton as archbishop. During these years Langton had been residing at Pontigny, formerly the refuge of Becket. He had addressed to the English people a dignified protest against the king's conduct, and had at last pressed the pope to take extreme measures. But he had consistently adopted towards John as conciliatory an attitude as his duty to the church would allow, and had more than once entered upon negotiations for a peaceful compromise. Immediately after entering England (July 1213) he showed his desire for peace by absolving the king. But, unlike the pope, he gave ear to the popular cry for redress of political grievances; and persisted in associating with the baronial opposition, even after he was ordered by Innocent to excommunicate them as disturbers of the peace. Langton encouraged the barons to formulate their demands, and is said to have suggested that they should take their stand upon the charter of Henry I. It is uncertain what further share he took in drafting Magna Carta. At Runnymede he appeared as a commissioner on the king's side, and his influence must therefore be sought in those clauses of the Charter which differ from the original petitions of the barons. Of these the most striking is that which confirms the "liberties" of the church; and this is chiefly remarkable for its moderation.

Soon after the issue of the charter the archbishop left England to attend the Fourth Lateran Council. At the moment of his departure he was suspended by the representatives of Innocent for not enforcing the papal censures against the barons. Innocent confirmed the sentence, which remained in force for two years. During this time the archbishop resided at Rome. He was allowed to return in 1218, after the deaths of Innocent and John. From that date till his death he was a tower of strength to the royal party. Through his influence Pandulf was recalled to Rome (1221) and Honorius III. promised that no legate should be sent to reside in England during the archbishop's lifetime. In 1222, in a synod held at Oseney, he promulgated a set of Constitutions still recognized as forming a part of the law of the English Church. Beyond this little is recorded of his latter years. He died on the 9th of July 1228, and was buried in Canterbury Cathedral, where his tomb, unless tradition errs, may still be seen.

The authorities are mainly those for the reign of John. No contemporary biography has come down to us. Some letters, by Langton and others, relating to the quarrel over his election are preserved in a Canterbury Chronicle (ed. W. Stubbs in the "Rolls" edition of *Gervase of Canterbury*, vol. ii.). There are many references to him in the correspondence of Innocent III. (Migne's *Patrologia Latina*, vols. ccxiv.-ccxvii.). Of modern works see F. Hurter, *Geschichte Papst Innocenz III.* (Hamburg, 1841–1844); W. F. Hook, *Lives of the Archbishops of Canterbury* (London, 1860–1876), and W. Stubbs's preface to the second volume of *Walter of Coventry* ("Rolls" ed.), which devotes special attention to Langton. The MSS. of Langton's writings are noticed in J. Bale's *Index Britanniae scriptorum* (ed. R. L. Poole, 1902); his Constitutions are printed in D. Wilkin's *Concilia*, vol. ii. (London, 1737). (H. W. C. D.)

Another English prelate who bore the name of Langton was Thomas Langton, bishop of Winchester, chaplain to Edward IV. In 1483 he was chosen bishop of St Davids; in 1485 he was made bishop of Salisbury and provost of Queen's College, Oxford, and he became bishop of Winchester in 1493. In 1501 he was elected archbishop of Canterbury, but he died on the 27th of January 1501, [illegible]fore his election had been confirmed.

LANGTON, WALTER (d. 1321), bishop of Lichfield and treasurer of England, was probably a native of Langton West in Leicestershire. Appointed a clerk in the royal chancery, he became a favourite servant of Edward I., taking part in the suit over the succession to the Scottish throne in 1292, and visiting France more than once on diplomatic business. He obtained several ecclesiastical preferments, became treasurer in 1295, and in 1296 bishop of Lichfield. Having become unpopular, the barons in 1301 vainly asked Edward to dismiss him; about the same time he was accused of murder, adultery and simony. Suspended from his office, he went to Rome to be tried before Pope Boniface VIII., who referred the case to Winchelsea, archbishop of Canterbury; the archbishop, although Langton's lifelong enemy, found him innocent, and this sentence was confirmed by Boniface in 1303. Throughout these difficulties, and also during a quarrel with the prince of Wales, afterwards Edward II., the treasurer was loyally supported by the king. Visiting Pope Clement V. on royal business in 1305, Langton appears to have persuaded Clement to suspend Winchelsea; after his return to England he was the chief adviser of Edward I., who had already appointed him the principal executor of his will. His position, however, was changed by the king's death in July 1307. The accession of Edward II. and the return of Langton's enemy, Piers Gaveston, were quickly followed by the arrest of the bishop and his removal from office. His lands, together with a great hoard of movable wealth, were seized, and he was accused of misappropriation and venality. In spite of the intercession of Clement V. and even of the restored archbishop, Winchelsea, who was anxious to uphold the privileges of his order, Langton, accused again by the barons in 1309, remained in prison after Edward's surrender to the "ordainers" in 1310. He was released in January 1312 and again became treasurer; but he was disliked by the "ordainers," who forbade him to discharge the duties of his office. Excommunicated by Winchelsea, he appealed to the pope, visited him at Avignon, and returned to England after the archbishop's death in May 1313. He was a member of the royal council from this time until his dismissal at the request of parliament in 1315. He died in November 1321, and was buried in Lichfield cathedral, which was improved and enriched at his expense. Langton appears to have been no relation of his contemporary, John Langton, bishop of Chichester.

LANGTRY, LILLIE (1852–), English actress, was the daughter of the Rev. W. C. le Breton, dean of Jersey, and married in 1874 Edward Langtry (d. 1897). For many years she was famous as one of the most beautiful women in England. It was not till 1881 that she definitely went on the stage, appearing from that time under her own management both in London and in America. In 1899 she married Sir Hugo de Bathe, Bart.

LANGUAGE (adapted from the Fr. *langage*, from *langue*, tongue, Lat. *lingua*), the whole body of words and combinations of words as used in common by a nation, people or race, for the purpose of expressing or communicating their thoughts; also, more widely, the power of expressing thought by verbal utterance. See generally under PHILOLOGY, PHONETICS, VOICE, WRITING, GRAMMAR, &c.; and the articles on the various languages, or under headings of countries and races.

LANGUEDOC, one of the old provinces of France, the name of which dates from the end of the 13th century. In 1290 it was used to refer to the country in whose tongue (*langue*) the word for "yes" was *oc*, as opposed to the centre and north of France, the *langue d'oïl* (the *oui* of to-day). Territorially Languedoc varied considerably in extent, but in general from 1360 until the French Revolution it included the territory of the following departments of modern France: part of Tarn et Garonne, Tarn, most of Haute-Garonne, Ariège, Aude, Pyrénées-Orientales, Hérault, Gard, Lozère, part of Ardèche and Haute-Loire. The country had no natural geographical unity. Stretching over the Cevennes into the valleys of the upper Loire on the north and into that of the upper Garonne on the west, it reached the Pyrenees on the south and the rolling hills along the Rhone on the east. Its unity was entirely a political creation, but none the less real, as it was the great state of the Midi, the representative of its culture and, to some degree, the defence of its peculiar civilization. Its climate, especially in Hérault (Montpellier), is especially delightful in spring and early summer, and the scenery still holds enough ruined remains of Roman and feudal times to recall the romance and the tragedy of its history.

Although the name is of comparatively late medieval origin, the history of Languedoc, which had little in common with that of northern France, begins with the Roman occupation. Toulouse was an important place as early as 119 B.C.; the next year Narbonne, the seaport, became a Roman colony. By the time of Julius Caesar the country was sufficiently Romanized to furnish him with men and money, and though at first involved in the civil wars which followed, it prospered under Roman rule as perhaps no other part of the empire did. While it corresponded exactly to no administrative division of the Roman empire, it was approximately the territory included in *Gallia Narbonensis*, one of the seventeen provinces into which the empire was divided at the death of Augustus. It was rich and flourishing, crowded with great and densely populated towns, Nîmes, Narbonne, Béziers, Toulouse; with schools of rhetoric and poetry still vigorous in the 5th century; theatres, amphitheatres and splendid temples. In the 5th century this high culture was an open prize for the barbarians; and after the passing of the Vandals, Suebi and Visigoths into Spain, the Visigoths returned under Wallia, who made his capital at Toulouse in 419. This was the foundation of the Visigothic kingdom which Clovis dismembered in 507, leaving the Visigoths only Septimania—the country of seven cities, Narbonne, Carcassonne, Elne, Béziers, Maguelonne, Lodève and Agde—that is, very nearly the area occupied later by the province of Languedoc. At the council of Narbonne in 589 five races are mentioned as living in the province, Visigoths, Romans, Jews—of whom there were a great many—Syrians and Greeks. The repulse of the Arabs by Charles Martel in 732 opened up the country for the Frankish conquest, which was completed by 768. Under the Carolingians Septimania became part of the kingdom of Aquitaine, but became a separate duchy in 817.

Until the opening of the 13th century there is no unity in the history of Languedoc, the great houses of Toulouse and Carcassonne and the swarm of warlike counts and barons practically ignoring the distant king of France, and maintaining a chronic state of civil war. The feudal régime did not become at all universal in the district, as it tended to become in the north of France. Allodial tenures survived in sufficient numbers to constitute a considerable class of non-vassal subjects of the king, with whose authority they were little troubled. By the end of the 11th century the house of the counts of Toulouse began to play the predominant rôle; but their court had been famous almost a century before for its love of art and literature and its extravagance in dress and fashions, all of which denoted its wealth. Constance, wife of King Robert II. and daughter of the count of Toulouse, gave great offence to the monks by her following of gallant gentlemen. They owed their tastes, not only to their Roman blood, and the survival of their old love for rhetoric and poetry, but also to their intercourse with the Mahommedans, their neighbours and enemies, and their friends when they were not fighting. Under Raymond of Saint Gilles, at the end of the 11th century, the county of Toulouse began its great career, but Raymond's ambition to become an Oriental prince, which led him—and the hundred thousand men who, according to the chroniclers, followed him—away on the first crusade, left a troubled heritage to his sons Bertrand and Alphonse Jourdain. The latter successfully beat off William IX., duke of Aquitaine, and won from the count of Barcelona that part of Provence between the Drôme and the Durance. The reign of Alphonse lasted from 1109 to 1148. By the opening of the 13th century the sovereignty of the counts of Toulouse was recognized through about half of Provence, and they held the rich cities of the most cultured and wealthiest portion of France, cities which had a high degree of local independence. Their local governments, with their consuls at the head, show, at least in name, the influence of Roman ideas. It is still an open question how much of their autonomy had remained untouched by the barbarian invasions from the Roman period. The citizens of these free cities were in continual intercourse with Saracens of Palestine and Moors of Spain; they had never entirely abandoned pagan customs, their poetry—the poetry of the troubadours—taught them the joys of life rather than the fear of death, the licence of their chivalry with its courts of love led to the other extreme of asceticism in such as were of religious temperament; all things combined to make Languedoc the proper soil for heresy. The Church never had the hold upon the country that it had in the north, the people of the Midi were always lukewarm in the faith; there was no noteworthy ecclesiastical literature in Languedoc from the end of the Carolingian period until after the Albigensian crusade, no theological centre like Paris, Bec or Laon. Yet Languedoc furnished the most heroic martyrs for the ascetic Manichaean creed. The era of heresy began with the preaching of Peter de Bruеys and his follower, Henry of Lausanne, who emptied the churches and taught contempt for the clergy. Saint Bernard himself was able to make but temporary headway against this rebellion from a sacramental and institutionalized Christianity. In the first decade of the 13th century came the inevitable conflict. The whole county of Toulouse, with its fiefs of Narbonne, Béziers, Foix, Montpellier and Quercy, was in open and scornful secession from the Catholic Church, and the suppression of this Manichaean or Cathar religion was the end of the brilliant culture of Languedoc. (See ALBIGENSES, CATHARS, INQUISITION.) The crusade against the Albigenses, as the Cathars were locally termed, in 1209, resulted in the union to the crown of France in 1229 of all the country from Carcassonne to the Rhone, thus dividing Languedoc into two. The western part left to Raymond VII., by the treaty of 1229, included the Agenais, Quercy, Rouergue, the Toulousain and southern Albigeois. He had as well the Venaissin across the Rhone. From 1229 to his death in 1249 Raymond VII. worked tirelessly to bring back prosperity to his ruined country, encouraging the foundation of new cities, and attempting to gain reconciliation with the Church. He left only a daughter, Jeanne, who was married to Alphonse of Poitiers. Alphonse, a sincere Catholic, upheld the Inquisition, but although ruling the country from Paris, maintained peace. Jeanne died without heirs four days after her husband, upon their return from the crusade in Africa, in 1271, and although she attempted by will to prevent the reversion of her lands to the crown, they were promptly seized by King Philip III., who [illegible] intervention of Roger Bernard, count of Foix, as an [illegible] appear with a formidable army, which had little to [illegible] entire submission. Thus the county of Toulouse [illegible] though Philip III. turned over the Agenais [illegible] England in 1279. In 1274 he ceded the county [illegible] Gregory X., the papacy having claimed [illegible] since the Albigensian crusade (see [illegible]

[illegible] the reduced county of Toulouse. At the [illegible] 1229 Louis IX. was given all the [illegible] to the Rhone. This royal Languedoc [illegible] treachery on the part of northern [illegible] officials. In 1248 Louis IX. sent [illegible] Charlemagne's *missi dominici*, to [illegible] to inquire concerning peculation [illegible] of their investigations the king [illegible] which organized the admini- [illegible] *sénéchaussées* were created— [illegible] each with its lesser [illegible] During the reign of Philip [illegible] employed securing justice for [illegible] of lands, and in 1270 [illegible] established at Toulouse. In [illegible] Languedoc, but in the [illegible]

government than one for securing money, thus aiding the *enquêteurs*, who during the Hundred Years' War became mere revenue hunters for the king. In 1355 the Black Prince led a savage plundering raid across the country to Narbonne. After the battle of Poitiers, Languedoc supported the count of Armagnac, but there was no enthusiasm for a national cause. Under Charles V., Louis of Anjou, the king's brother, was governor of Languedoc, and while an active opponent of the English, he drained the country of money. But his extortions were surpassed by those of another brother, the duc de Berry, after the death of Charles V. In 1382 and 1383 the infuriated peasantry, abetted by some nobles, rose in a rebellion— known as the Tuchins— which was put down with frightful butchery, while still greater sums were demanded from the impoverished country. In the anarchy which followed brigandage increased. Redress did not come until 1420, when the dauphin, afterwards Charles VII., came to Languedoc and reformed the administration. Then the country he saved furnished him with the means for driving out the English in the north. For the first time, in the climax of its miseries, Languedoc was genuinely united to France. But Charles VII. was not able to drive out the brigands, and it was not until after the English were expelled in 1453 that Languedoc had even comparative peace. Charles VII. united Comminges to the crown; Louis XI. Roussillon and Cerdagne, both of which were ceded to Aragon by Charles VIII. as the price of its neutrality during his expedition into Italy. From the reign of Louis XI. until 1523 the governorship of Languedoc was held by the house of Bourbon. After the treason of the constable Bourbon it was held by the Montmorency family with but slight interruption until 1632.

The Reformation found Languedoc orthodox. Persecution had succeeded. The Inquisition had had no victims since 1340, and the cities which had been centres of heresy were now strongly orthodox. Toulouse was one of the most fanatically orthodox cities in Europe, and remained so in Voltaire's day. But Calvinism gained ground rapidly in the other parts of Languedoc, and by 1560 the majority of the population was Protestant. It was, however, partly a political protest against the misrule of the Guises. The open conflict came in 1561, and from that until the edict of Nantes (1598) there was intermittent civil war, accompanied with iconoclasm on the one hand, massacres on the other and ravages on both.

The main figure in this period is that of Henri de Montmorency, seigneur de Damville, later duc de Montmorency, governor of the province from 1563, who was, at first, hostile to the Protestants, then from 1574 to 1577, as leader of the "*Politiques*," an advocate of compromise. But peace was hardly ever established, although there was a yearly truce for the ploughing. By the edict of Nantes, the Protestants were given ten places of safety in Languedoc; but civil strife did not come to an end, even under Henry IV. In 1620 the Protestants in Languedoc rose under Henri, duc de Rohan (1579–1638), who for two years defied the power of Louis XIII. When Louis took Montpellier in 1622, he attempted to reconcile the Calvinists by bribes of money and office, and left Montauban as a city of refuge. Richelieu's extinction of Huguenotism is less the history of Languedoc than of the Huguenots (*q.v.*). By 1629 Protestantism was crushed in the Midi as a political force. Then followed the tragic episode of the rebellion of Henri II., duc de Montmorency, son of the old governor of Languedoc. As a result, Languedoc lost its old provincial privilege of self-assessment until 1649, and was placed under the governorship of Marshal Schomberg. During Louis XIV.'s reign Languedoc prospered until the revocation of the edict of Nantes. Industries and agriculture were encouraged, roads and bridges were built, and the great canal giving a water route from the Atlantic to the Mediterranean increased the trade of its cities. Colbert especially encouraged its manufactures. The religious persecutions which accompanied the revocation of the edict of Nantes bore hardest on Languedoc, and resulted in a guerilla warfare known as the rebellion of the Camisards (*q.v.*). On the eve of the Revolution some of the brightest scenes of contentment and prosperity which surprised

Arthur Young, the English traveller in France, were those of the grape harvests in Languedoc vineyards.

In 1790 Languedoc disappeared from the map of France, with the other old provinces; and the departments mentioned took its place. But the peculiar characteristics of the men of the Midi remain as clearly distinct from those of the north as the Scottish type is distinct from the English. The "peaceful insurrection" of the Languedoc vine-growers in the summer of 1907 revealed to the astonished Parisians the same spirit of independence as had underlain the resistance to Simon de Montfort and Richelieu.

The one monumental history of Languedoc is that of the Benedictines, Dom Claude Devic and Dom J. J. Vaissete, *Histoire générale de la province de Languedoc* (5 vols., Paris, 1730–1745). This has been re-edited, and continued and increased by the addition of important monographs, to 15 volumes (Toulouse, 1872–1892). It is the great library of sources, critical apparatus and bibliographies concerning Languedoc, and carries the history up to 1790. The fine article "Languedoc" in *La Grande Encyclopédie* is by A. Mollinier, perhaps the greatest modern authority on Languedoc. (J. T. S.*)

LANGUET, HUBERT (1518–1581), French Huguenot writer and diplomat, was born at Vitteaux in Burgundy, of which town his father was governor. He received his early education from a distinguished Hellenist, Jean Perelle, and displayed remarkable ability in Greek and Latin. He studied law, theology and science at the university of Poitiers from 1536 to 1539; then, after some travel, attended the universities of Bologna and Padua, receiving the doctorate from the latter in 1548. At Bologna he read Melanchthon's *Loci communes theologiae* and was so impressed by it that in 1549 he went to Wittenberg to see the author, and shortly afterwards became a Protestant. He made his headquarters at Wittenberg until the death of Melanchthon in 1560, although during that period, as well as throughout the rest of his life, he travelled extensively in France, Italy, Spain, Germany, Sweden, and even Finland and Lapland. In 1557 he declined the invitation of Gustavus I. to enter the service of Sweden, but two years later accepted a similar invitation of Augustus I., elector of Saxony. He showed great ability in diplomacy, particularly in organizing the Protestants. He represented the elector at the French court from 1561 to 1572 except when the religious and political troubles in France occasionally compelled him temporarily to withdraw. He performed many minor diplomatic missions for the elector, and in 1567 accompanied him to the siege of Gotha. He delivered a violent harangue before Charles IX. of France in 1570 on behalf of the Protestant princes, and escaped death on St Bartholomew's Day (1572) only through the intervention of Jean de Morvilliers, the moderate and influential bishop of Orleans. He represented the elector of Saxony at the imperial court from 1573 to 1577. Financial embarrassment and disgust at the Protestant controversies in which he was forced to participate caused him to seek recall from the imperial court. His request being granted, Languet spent the last years of his life mainly in the Low Countries, and though nominally still in the service of the elector, he undertook a mission to England for John Casimir of Bavaria and was a valuable adviser to William the Silent, prince of Orange. Languet died at Antwerp on the 30th of September 1581.

His correspondence is important for the history of the 16th century. Three hundred and twenty-nine letters to Augustus of Saxony dating from the 17th of November 1565 to the 8th of September 1581, and one hundred and eleven letters to the chancellor Mordeisen dating from November 1559 to the summer of 1565, are preserved in MS. in the Saxon archives, and were published by Ludovicus at Halle in 1699 under the title *Arcana seculi decimi sexti*. One hundred and eight letters to Camerarius were published at Groningen in 1646 under the title *Langueti Epistolae ad Joach. Camerarium, patrem et filium*; and ninety-six to his great friend Sir Philip Sidney, dating from the 22nd of April 1573 to the 28th of October 1580, appeared at Frankfort in 1633 and have been translated into English by S. A. Pears (London, 1845). The *Historica Descriptio* of the siege and capture of Gotha appeared in 1568 and has been translated into French and German. The authorship of the work by which Languet is best known has been disputed. It is entitled *Vindiciae contra tyrannos, sive de principis in populum populique in principem legitima potestate, Stephano Junio Bruto Celta auctore*, and is thought to have been published at Basel (1579) although it bears the imprint of Edinburgh. It has been attributed to Beza, Hotman, Casaubon and Duplessis-Mornay, by divers writers on various grounds—to the last-named on the very respectable authority of Grotius. The authorship of Languet was supported by Peter Bayle (for reasons stated in the form of a supplement to the *Dictionnaire*) and confirmed by practically all later writers. The work has been frequently reprinted, the Leipzig edition (1846) containing a life of Languet by Treitschke. A French translation appeared in 1581 and an English translation in 1689. The work upholds the doctrine of resistance, but affirms that resistance must come from properly constituted authorities and objects to anything which savours of anabaptism or other extreme views. The *Apologie ou défence du très illustre Prince Guillaume contre le ban et l'édit du roi d'Espagne* (Leiden, 1581) is sometimes attributed to Languet. There seems little doubt, however, that it was really the work of the prince himself, with the help either of Languet (Groen van Prinsterer, *Archives*) or of Pierre de Villiers (Motley, *Rise of the Dutch Republic*; and Blok, *History of the People of the Netherlands*).

See Ph. de la Mare, *Vie d'Hubert Languet* (Halle, 1700); E. and E. Haag, *La France protestante*; H. Chevreul, *Hubert Languet* (Paris, 1852); J. Blasel, *Hubert Languet* (Breslau, 1872); O. Scholz, *Hubert Languet als kursächsischer Berichterstatter u. Gesandter in Frankreich während 1560–1572* (Halle, 1875); G. Touchard, *De politica Huberti Langueti* (Paris, 1898). There is a good article on Languet by P. Tschackert in Hauck's *Real-Encyklopädie*, 3rd ed., xi. 274–280.

LANGUR, one of the two Hindu names (the other being *hanuman*) of the sacred Indian monkey scientifically known as *Semnopithecus entellus*, and hence sometimes called the entellus monkey. A prodigiously long tail, beetling eyebrows with long black hairs, black ears, face, feet and hands, and a general greyish-brown colour of the fur are the distinctive characteristics of the langur. These monkeys roam at will in the bazaars of Hindu cities, where they help themselves freely from the stores of the grain-dealers, and they are kept in numbers at the great temple in Benares. In a zoological sense the term is extended to embrace all the monkeys of the Asiatic genus *Semnopithecus*, which includes a large number of species, ranging from Ceylon, India and Kashmir to southern China and the Malay countries as far east as Borneo and Sumatra. These monkeys are characterized by their lank bodies, long slender limbs and tail, well-developed thumbs, absence of cheek-pouches, and complex stomachs. They feed on leaves and young shoots. (R. L.*)

LANG VON WELLENBURG, MATTHÄUS (1469–1540), German statesman and ecclesiastic, was the son of a burgher of Augsburg. He afterwards assumed the name of Wellenburg from a castle that came into his possession. After studying at Ingolstadt, Vienna and Tübingen he entered the service of the emperor Frederick III. and quickly made his way to the front. He was also one of the most trusted advisers of Frederick's son and successor Maximilian I., and his services were rewarded in 1500 with the provostship of the cathedral at Augsburg and in the following year with the bishopric of Gurk. In 1511 he was made a cardinal by Pope Julius II., and in 1514 he became coadjutor to the archbishop of Salzburg, whom he succeeded in 1519. He also received the bishopric of Cartagena in Murcia in 1521, and that of Albano in 1535. Lang's adherence to the older faith, together with his pride and arrogance, made him very unpopular in his diocese of Salzburg; in 1523 he was involved in a serious struggle with his subjects, and in 1525, during the Peasants' War, he had again to fight hard to hold his own. He was one of the chief ministers of Charles V., he played an important part in the tangled international negotiations of his time; and he was always loyal to his imperial masters. Not without reason has he been compared with Cardinal Wolsey. He died on the 30th of March 1540.

LANIER, SIDNEY (1842–1881), American poet, was born at Macon, Georgia, on the 3rd of February 1842. He was of Huguenot descent on his father's side, and of Scottish and Virginian on his mother's. From childhood he was passionately fond of music. His subsequent mastery of the flute helped to support him and greatly increased his reputation. At the age of fourteen he entered Oglethorpe College, where, after graduating with distinction, he held a tutorship. He enlisted in the Confederate army in April 1861, serving first in Virginia, and finding opportunities to continue his studies. After the Seven Days' battles around Richmond, he was transferred to the signal service.

[illegible] time the first symptoms of consumption appeared. [illegible] served in a blockade-runner, but his vessel was [illegible] and he was confined for five months in a Federal [illegible] porting the best of companions. Exchanged [illegible] he started home on foot, arriving in a state of [illegible]. In 1867 he visited New [illegible] his novel *Tiger Lilies*—an immature [illegible] his war experiences, and now difficult [illegible] the same year he took charge of a country [illegible] and was married to Miss Mary Day of his [illegible] he returned to Macon in low health, [illegible] with his father. In 1872 [illegible] for his health, but was forced to return, and he [illegible] in the Peabody concerts at [illegible]. He wrote a guide-book to Florida [illegible] from Froissart, Malory, the Mabinogion [illegible]. He now made congenial [illegible] his reputation gradually in- [illegible] he was enabled to study music and literature, [illegible] poetry. In 1876 he wrote his ambitious [illegible] Centennial [illegible], and brought his family [illegible] volume of verse appeared in the next year. In [illegible] English literature at Johns Hopkins [illegible] became the basis of his *Science of* [illegible] his most important prose work, and an [illegible] the relations of music and poetry—and [illegible] (New York, 1883), which, devoted [illegible] suggestive, but one-sided. Work had [illegible] growing feebleness, and in the [illegible] to Lynn, North Carolina, to try [illegible] there on the 7th of September. Since his [illegible] steadily and greatly, an enlarged and [illegible] prepared by his wife, his *Letters*, [illegible] volumes of miscellaneous prose [illegible] keeping his name before the public. A [illegible] *Shakspere and his Forerunners* (London, [illegible] edited by H. W. Lanier. Among his more [illegible] "The Revenge of Hamish," [illegible] "The Marshes of Glynn." [illegible] rather than poetic, and [illegible] he is held to be one of [illegible] modern American poets. [illegible] the New South, the greatest [illegible] of heroic and exquisite [illegible]

[illegible] "Memorial" by William Hayes Ward, prefixed to the [illegible] (1899), edited by [illegible] *Sidney Lanier* (1905). [illegible] writings in *Select Poems* [illegible] edited by Morgan Callaway.

(W. P. T.)

[illegible] DENIS, COMTE (1753–1827), French [illegible] (Ille-et-Vilaine) on the 12th of [illegible] college career, which made him [illegible] barrister at nineteen, he was [illegible] and in 1775 professor of [illegible]. At this period he wrote two [illegible] the distracted state of public [illegible] *juris ecclesiastici* [illegible]. He had begun his career at [illegible] *du colombier*, and [illegible] to the states-general of [illegible] and the substitution of [illegible] and the Navarrese for king of [illegible] the civil constitution [illegible] Convention in September 1792 [illegible] views, becoming one [illegible] Mountain, though he never [illegible] principles. He refused to [illegible] that the nation had no [illegible]. His daily attacks on [illegible] April 1793, in a demand by the commune for his exclusion from the assembly, but, undaunted, when the Parisian populace invaded the Chamber on the 2nd of June, Lanjuinais renewed his defiance of the victorious party. Placed under arrest with the Girondins, he escaped to Rennes where he drew up a pamphlet denouncing the constitution of 1793 under the curious title *Le Dernier Crime de Lanjuinais* (Rennes, 1793). Pursued by J. B. Carrier, who was sent to stamp out resistance in the west, he lay hidden until some time after the revolution of Thermidor (July 1794), but he was readmitted to the Convention on the 8th of March 1795. He maintained his liberal and independent attitude in the Conseil des Anciens, the Senate and the Chamber of Peers, being president of the upper house during the Hundred Days. Together with G. J. B. Target, J. E. M. Portalis and others he founded under the empire an academy of legislation in Paris, himself lecturing on Roman law. Closely associated with oriental scholars, and a keen student of oriental religions, he entered the Academy of Inscriptions in 1808. After the Bourbon restoration Lanjuinais consistently defended the principles of constitutional monarchy, but most of his time was given to religious and political subjects. Besides many contributions to periodical literature he wrote, among other works, *Constitutions de la nation française* (1819); *Appréciation du projet de loi relatif aux trois concordats* (1806, 6th ed. 1827), in defence of Gallicanism; and *Études biographiques et littéraires sur Antoine Arnauld, P. Nicole et Jacques Necker* (1823). He died in Paris on the 13th of January 1827.

His son, VICTOR AMBROISE, VICOMTE DE LANJUINAIS (1802–1869), was also a politician, becoming a deputy in 1838. His interests lay chiefly in financial questions and in 1849 he became minister of commerce and agriculture in the cabinet of Odilon Barrot. He wrote a *Notice historique sur la vie et les ouvrages du comte de Lanjuinais*, which was prefixed to an edition of his father's *Œuvres* (4 vols., 1832).

For the life of the comte de Lanjuinais see also A. Robert and G. Cougny, *Dictionnaire des parlementaires*, vol. ii. (1890); and F. A. Aulard, *Les Orateurs de la Législative et de la Convention* (Paris, 1885–1886). For a bibliography of his works see J. M. Quérard, *La France littéraire*, vol. iii. (1829).

LANMAN, CHARLES ROCKWELL (1850–), American Sanskrit scholar, was born in Norwich, Connecticut, on the 8th of July 1850. He graduated at Yale in 1871, was a graduate student there (1871–1873) under James Hadley and W. D. Whitney, and in Germany (1873–1876) studied Sanskrit under Weber and Roth and philology under Georg Curtius and Leskien. He was professor of Sanskrit at Johns Hopkins University in 1876–1880 and subsequently at Harvard University. In 1889 he travelled in India and bought for Harvard University Sanskrit and Prākrit books and manuscripts, which, with those subsequently bequeathed to the university by Fitzedward Hall, make the most valuable collection of its kind in America, and made possible the *Harvard Oriental Series*, edited by Professor Lanman. In 1879–1884 he was secretary and editor of the *Transactions*, and in 1889–1890 president of the American Philological Association, and in 1884–1894 he was corresponding secretary of the American Oriental Society, in 1897–1907 vice-president, and in 1907–1908 president. In the *Harvard Oriental Series* he translated (vol. iv.) into English Rājaçekhara's Karpūra-Mañjarī (1900), a Prākrit drama, and (vols. vii. and viii.) revised and edited Whitney's translation of, and notes on, the *Atharva-Veda Samhitā* (2 vols., 1905); he published *A Sanskrit Reader, with Vocabulary and Notes* (2 vols., 1884–1888); and he wrote on early Hindu pantheism and contributed the section on Brahmanism to *Messages of the World's Religions*.

LANNES, JEAN, duke of Montebello (1769–1809), marshal of France, was born at Lectoure (Gers) on the 11th of April 1769. He was the son of a livery stables keeper, and was apprenticed to a dyer. He had had little education, but his great strength and proficiency in all manly sports caused him in 1792 to be elected sergeant-major of the battalion of volunteers of Gers, which he had joined on the breaking out of war between Spain and the French republic. He served through the campaigns in the Pyrenees in 1793 and 1794, and rose by distinguished conduct to the rank of *chef de brigade*. However, in 1795, on the reform of the army introduced by the Thermidorians, he was dismissed from his rank. He re-enlisted as a simple volunteer in the army of Italy, and in the famous campaign of 1796 he again fought his way up to high rank, being eventually made a general of brigade by Bonaparte. He was distinguished in every battle, and was wounded at Arcola. He was chosen by Bonaparte to accompany him to Egypt as commander of one of Kléber's brigades, in which capacity he greatly distinguished himself, especially on the retreat from Syria. He went with Bonaparte to France, assisted at the 18th Brumaire, and was appointed general of division, and commandant of the consular guard. He commanded the advanced guard in the crossing of the Alps in 1800, was instrumental in winning the battle of Montebello, from which he afterwards took his title, and bore the brunt of the battle of Marengo. In 1801 Napoleon sent him as ambassador to Portugal. Opinions differ as to his merits in this capacity; Napoleon never made such use of him again. On the establishment of the empire he was created a marshal of France, and commanded once more the advanced guard of a great French army in the campaign of Austerlitz. At Austerlitz he had the left of the Grand Army. In the 1806–07 campaign he was at his best, commanding his corps with the greatest credit in the march through the Thuringian Forest, the action of Saalfeld (which is studied as a model to-day at the French Staff College) and the battle of Jena. His leadership of the advanced guard at Friedland was even more conspicuous. He was now to be tried as a commander-in-chief, for Napoleon took him to Spain in 1808, and gave him a detached wing of the army, with which he won a victory over Castaños at Tudela on November 22. In January 1809 he was sent to attempt the capture of Saragossa, and by February 21, after one of the most stubborn defences in history, was in possession of the place. Napoleon then created him duc de Montebello, and in 1809, for the last time, gave him command of the advanced guard. He took part in the engagements around Eckmühl and the advance on Vienna. With his corps he led the French army across the Danube, and bore the brunt, with Masséna, of the terrible battle of Aspern-Essling (*q.v.*). On the 22nd of May he had to retreat. During the retreat Lannes exposed himself as usual to the hottest fire, and received a mortal wound, to which he succumbed at Vienna on the 31st of May. As he was being carried from the field to Vienna he met the emperor hurrying to the front. It was reported that the dying man reproached Napoleon for his ambition, but this rests on little evidence save the fact that Lannes was the most blunt and outspoken of all Napoleon's marshals. He was one of the few men for whom the emperor felt a real and deep affection, and at this their last meeting Napoleon gave way to a passionate burst of grief, even in the midst of the battle. His eldest son was made a peer of France by Louis XVIII.

Lannes ranks with Davout and Masséna as the ablest of all Napoleon's marshals, and consciously or unconsciously was the best exponent of the emperor's method of making war. Hence his constant employment in tasks requiring the utmost resolution and daring, and more especially when the emperor's combinations depended upon the vigour and self-sacrifice of a detachment or fraction of the army. It was thus with Lannes at Friedland and at Aspern as it was with Davout at Austerlitz and Auerstädt, and Napoleon's estimate of his subordinates' capacities can almost exactly be judged by the frequency with which he used them to prepare the way for his own shattering blow. Routine generals with the usual military virtue, or careful and exact troop leaders like Soult and Macdonald, Napoleon kept under his own hand for the final assault which he himself launched, but the long hours of preparatory fighting against odds of two to one, which alone made the final blow possible, he entrusted only to men of extraordinary courage and high capacity for command. In his own words, he found Lannes a pigmy, and lost him a giant. Lannes's place in his affections was never filled.

See R. Périn, *Vie militaire de Jean Lannes* (Paris, 1809).

LANNION, a town of north-western France, capital of an arrondissement in the department of Côtes-du-Nord, on the right bank of the Léguer, 45 m. W.N.W. of St Brieuc by rail. Pop. (1906) 5336. Lannion is 5 m. in direct line from the mouth of the Léguer; its port does a small trade (exports of agricultural produce, imports of wine, salt, timber, &c.), and there is an active fishing industry. The town contains many houses of the 15th and 16th centuries and other old buildings, the chief of which is the church of St Jean-du-Baly (16th and 17th centuries). On an eminence close to Lannion is the church of Brélevenez of the 12th century, restored in the 15th or 16th century; it has an interesting 16th-century Holy Sepulchre.

Some 6 m. S.E. of the town are the imposing ruins of the château of Tonquédec (*c.* 1400) styled the "Pierrefonds of Brittany," and there are other buildings of antiquarian interest in the vicinity. The coast north of Lannion at Trégastel and Ploumanac presents curious rock formations.

Lannion is the seat of a subprefect and has a tribunal of first instance and a communal college. Its industries include saw-milling, tanning and the manufacture of farm implements. The town was taken in 1346 by the English; it was defended against them by Geoffroy de Pontblanc whose valour is commemorated by a cross close to the spot where he was slain.

LANNOY, GUILLEBERT DE (1386–1462), Flemish diplomatist, was chamberlain to the duke of Burgundy, governor of the fort of Sluys, and a knight of the Golden Fleece. He discharged several diplomatic missions in France, England, Prussia, Poland and Lithuania, and was one of the negotiators of the treaty of Troyes (1420). In 1421 he was sent by Henry V. of England to Palestine to inquire into the possibility of reviving the kingdom of Jerusalem, and wrote an account of his travels, *Les Pèlerinages de Surye et de Egipte*, which was published in 1826 and again in 1842.

LANOLIN (Lat. *lana*, wool, and *oleum*, oil), the commercial name of the preparation styled *adeps lanae hydrosus* in the British Pharmacopoeia, and which consists of 7 oz. of neutral wool-fat (*adeps lanae*) mixed with 3 fluid oz. of water. The wool-fat is obtained by purification of the "brown grease," "recovered grease" or dégras extracted from raw sheep's wool in the process of preparing it for the spinner. It is a translucent unctuous substance which has the property of taking up large quantities of water and forming emulsions which are very slow to separate into their constituents. Owing to the ease with which it penetrates the skin, wool-fat both in the anhydrous form and as lanolin, sometimes mixed with such substances as vaseline or fatty oils, is largely employed as a basis for ointments. It is slightly antiseptic and does not become rancid.

LA NOUE, FRANÇOIS DE (1531–1591), called Bras-de-Fer, one of the Huguenot captains of the 16th century, was born near Nantes in 1531, of an ancient Breton family. He served in Italy under Marshal Brissac, and in the first Huguenot war, but his first great exploit was the capture of Orleans at the head of only fifteen cavaliers in 1567, during the second war. At the battle of Jarnac in March 1569 he commanded the rearguard, and at Moncontour in the following October he was taken prisoner; but he was exchanged in time to resume the governorship of Poitou, and to inflict a signal defeat on the royalist troops before Rochefort. At the siege of Fontenay (1570) his left arm was shattered by a bullet; but a mechanic of Rochelle made him an iron arm (hence his sobriquet) with a hook for holding his reins. When peace was made in France in the same year, La Noue carried his sword against the Spaniards in the Netherlands, but was taken at the recapture of Mons by the Spanish in 1572. Permitted to return to France, he was commissioned by Charles IX., after the massacre of St Bartholomew, to reconcile the inhabitants of La Rochelle, the great stronghold of the Huguenots, to the king. But the Rochellois were too much alarmed to come to terms; and La Noue, perceiving that war was imminent, and knowing that his post was on the Huguenot side, gave up his royal commission, and from 1574 till 1578 acted as general of La Rochelle. When peace was again concluded La Noue once more went to aid the Protestants of the Low Countries. He took several towns and captured Count Egmont in 1580; but a few weeks afterwards he fell into the hands of the Spaniards. Thrust into a loathsome prison at Limburg, La Noue, the admiration of all, of whatever faith, for his gallantry, honour and purity of character, was kept confined for five years by a powerful nation, whose reluctance to set him [illegible] adheres to his reputation. It was in [illegible] that he wrote his celebrated *Discours politiques et militaires*, a work which was published at Basel in 1587 (reprinted at La Rochelle 1590, Frankfort on Main (in German) 1592 and 1612, and London (in English) 1597) and had an immense influence on the soldiers of all nations. The abiding value of La Noue's "Discourses" lies in the fact that he wrote of war as a human drama, before it had been elaborated and codified. At length, in June 1585, La Noue was exchanged for Egmont and other prisoners of consideration, while a heavy ransom and a pledge not to bear arms against his Catholic majesty were also exacted from him. Till 1580 La Noue took no part in public matters, but in that year he joined Henry of Navarre against the Leaguers. He was present at both sieges of Paris, at Ivry and other battles. At the siege of Lamballe in Brittany he received a wound of which he died at Moncontour on the 4th of August 1591.

[illegible] *Déclaration pour prise d'armes et* [illegible] *Observations sur l'histoire de* [illegible] and notes on *Plutarch's Lives*. His [illegible] See *La Vie de François,* [illegible] Amirault Leiden, 1661); Bran- [illegible] C. Vincent's *Les Héros de la* [illegible] and Hauser, *François de La Noue* [illegible]

LANSDOWNE, WILLIAM PETTY FITZMAURICE, 1st marquess of [illegible] British statesman, better known under [illegible] Shelburne, was born at Dublin on the [illegible] He was a descendant of the lords of Kerry [illegible] and his grandfather Thomas Fitzmaurice, [illegible] married the daughter of [illegible] Petty [illegible] On the death without issue of Sir [illegible] the first earl of Shelburne, the estates [illegible] John Fitzmaurice advanced in 1753 to the [illegible] of Shelburne, who [illegible] took the additional name of Petty. [illegible] his childhood "in the remotest [illegible] Ireland," and according to his own account, [illegible] Christ Church, Oxford, in 1755, he had both [illegible] everything to unlearn." From a [illegible] he describes as "narrow-minded" he received [illegible] guidance in his studies, but he attributes his [illegible] knowledge of the world chiefly [illegible] he fell in "with [illegible] conversation." Shortly after leaving the [illegible] regiment during the Seven Years' [illegible] at Minden and Kloster-Kampen [illegible] colonel and appointed aide-de- [illegible] Being thus brought into near com- [illegible] he was in 1761 employed by that [illegible] the support of Henry Fox, Lord [illegible] House of Commons as member [illegible] he succeeded his father as earl of [illegible] and Baron Wycombe in the [illegible] Though he declined [illegible] negotiations to induce [illegible] the Commons to the peace of [illegible] and, although [illegible] through good [illegible] Shelburne [illegible] of the Board [illegible] Pitt in the cabinet, [illegible] on account [illegible] expulsion from [illegible] of the king, he [illegible] return to power [illegible] Pitt's illness [illegible] thwarted [illegible] dismissed [illegible] office under the [illegible] the king would [illegible] Lord Rockingham [illegible] the accession of [illegible] of Fox with

North, which caused his resignation in the following February, his fall being perhaps hastened by his plans for the reform of the public service. He had also in contemplation a bill to promote free commercial intercourse between England and the United States. When Pitt acceded to office in 1784, Shelburne, instead of receiving a place in the cabinet, was created marquess of Lansdowne. Though giving a general support to the policy of Pitt, he from this time ceased to take an active part in public affairs. He died on the 7th of May 1805. During his lifetime he was blamed for insincerity and duplicity, and he incurred the deepest unpopularity, but the accusations came chiefly from those who were dissatisfied with his preference of principles to party, and if he had had a more unscrupulous regard to his personal ambition, his career as a statesman would have had more outward success. He was cynical in his estimates of character, but no statesman of his time possessed more enlightened political views, while his friendship with those of his contemporaries eminent in science and literature must be allowed considerable weight in qualifying our estimate of the moral defects with which he has been credited. He was twice married, first to Lady Sophia (1745–1771), daughter of John Carteret, Earl Granville, through whom he obtained the Lansdowne estates near Bath, and secondly to Lady Louisa (1755–1789), daughter of John Fitzpatrick, 1st earl of Upper Ossory. John Henry Petty Fitzmaurice (1765–1809), his son by the first marriage, succeeded as 2nd marquess, after having sat in the House of Commons for twenty years as member for Chipping Wycombe.

Henry Petty Fitzmaurice, 3rd marquess of Lansdowne (1780–1863), son of the 1st marquess by his second marriage, was born on the 2nd of July 1780 and educated at Edinburgh University and at Trinity College, Cambridge. He entered the House of Commons in 1802 as member for the family borough of Calne and quickly showed his mettle as a politician. In February 1806, as Lord Henry Petty, he became chancellor of the exchequer in the ministry of "All the Talents," being at this time member for the university of Cambridge, but he lost both his seat and his office in 1807. In 1809 he became marquess of Lansdowne; and in the House of Lords and in society he continued to play an active part as one of the Whig leaders. His chief interest was perhaps in the question of Roman Catholic emancipation, a cause which he consistently championed, but he sympathized also with the advocates of the abolition of the slave-trade and with the cause of popular education. Lansdowne, who had succeeded his cousin, Francis Thomas Fitzmaurice, as 4th earl of Kerry in 1818, took office with Canning in May 1827 and was secretary for home affairs from July of that year until January 1828; he was lord president of the council under Earl Grey and then under Lord Melbourne from November 1830 to August 1841, with the exception of the few months in 1835 when Sir Robert Peel was prime minister. He held the same office during the whole of Lord John Russell's ministry (1846–1852), and, having declined to become prime minister, sat in the cabinets of Lord Aberdeen and of Lord Palmerston, but without office. In 1857 he refused the offer of a dukedom, and he died on the 31st of January 1863. Lansdowne's social influence and political moderation made him one of the most powerful Whig statesmen of the time; he was frequently consulted by Queen Victoria on matters of moment, and his long official experience made his counsel invaluable to his party. He married Louisa (1785–1851), daughter of the 2nd earl of Ilchester, and was succeeded by his son Henry, the 4th marquess (1816–1866). The latter, who was member of parliament for Calne for twenty years and chairman of the Great Western railway, married for his second wife Emily (1819–1895), daughter of the comte de Flahaut de la Billarderie, a lady who became Baroness Nairne in her own right in 1867. By her he had two sons, the 5th marquess and Lord Edmond Fitzmaurice (Baron Fitzmaurice of Leigh).

Henry Charles Keith Petty Fitzmaurice, 5th marquess of Lansdowne (b. 1845), was educated at Balliol, Oxford, where he became one of Jowett's favourite pupils. In 1869 he married the daughter of the 1st duke of Abercorn. As a member of the Liberal party he was a lord of the treasury (1869–1872), under-secretary of war (1872–1874), and under-secretary of India (1880); in 1883 he was appointed governor-general of Canada, and from 1888 to 1893 he was viceroy of India. He joined the Liberal Unionist party when Mr Gladstone proposed home rule for Ireland, and on returning to England became one of its most influential leaders. He was secretary of state for war from 1895 to 1900, and foreign secretary from 1900 to 1906, becoming leader of the Unionist party in the House of Lords on Lord Salisbury's death.

His brother Edmond George Fitzmaurice, Baron Fitzmaurice (b. 1846), was educated at Trinity, Cambridge, where he took a first class in classics. Unlike Lord Lansdowne, he remained a Liberal in politics and followed Mr Gladstone in his home rule policy. As Lord Edmond Fitzmaurice he entered the House of Commons in 1868, and was under-secretary for foreign affairs from 1882 to 1885. He then had no seat in parliament till 1898, when he was elected for the Cricklade division of Wilts, and retiring in 1905, he was created Baron Fitzmaurice of Leigh in 1906, and made under-secretary for foreign affairs in Sir Henry Campbell-Bannerman's ministry. In 1908 he became chancellor of the duchy of Lancaster and a member of the Liberal cabinet, but resigned his post in 1909. He devoted much time to literary work, and was the author of excellent biographies of the 1st marquess, of Sir William Petty (1895), and of Lord Granville (1905), under whom he had served at the foreign office.

For the 1st marquess, see Lord Fitzmaurice, *Life of William, Earl of Shelburne* (3 vols., London, 1875–1876).

LANSDOWNE, a hill cantonment in India, in Garhwal district of the United Provinces, about 6000 ft. above the sea, 19 m. by cart road from the station of Kotdwara on the Oudh and Rohilkhand railway. Pop. (1901) 3943. The cantonment, founded in 1887, extends for more than 3 m. through pine and oak forests, and can accommodate three Gurkha battalions.

LANSING, the capital of Michigan, U.S.A., in Ingham county, at the confluence of the Grand and Cedar rivers, about 85 m. W.N.W. of Detroit and about 64 m. E.S.E. of Grand Rapids. Pop. (1900) 16,485, of whom 2397 were foreign-born; (1910 census) 31,229. It is served by the Michigan Central, the Lake Shore & Michigan Southern, the Grand Trunk and the Père Marquette railways, and by interurban electric lines. The Grand river on its way through the city makes a horse-shoe bend round a moderately elevated plateau; this is the commercial centre of the city, and here, in a square covering 10 acres, is the State Capitol, erected in 1873–1878 and containing the State library. On the opposite side of the river, farther N., and also extending across the southern portion of the city, are districts devoted largely to manufacturing. Lansing has a public library and a city hospital. About 3 m. E. of the city, at East Lansing, is the State Agricultural College (coeducational), the oldest agricultural college in the United States, which was provided for by the state constitution of 1850, was organized in 1855 and opened in 1857. Its engineering course was begun in 1885; a course in home economics for women was established in 1896; and a forestry course was opened in 1902. In connexion with the college there is an agricultural experiment station. Lansing is the seat of the Michigan School for the Blind, and of the State Industrial School for Boys, formerly the Reform School. The city has abundant water-power and is an important manufacturing centre. The value of the factory products increased from $2,942,306 in 1900 to $6,887,415 in 1904, or 134·1%. The municipality owns and operates the water-works and the electric-lighting plant. The place was selected as the site for the capital in 1847, when it was still covered with forests, and growth was slow until 1862, when the railways began to reach it. Lansing was chartered as a city in 1859 and rechartered in 1893.

LANSING MAN, the term applied by American ethnologists to certain human remains discovered in 1902 during the digging of a cellar near Lansing, Kansas, and by some authorities believed to represent a prehistoric type of man. They include a skull and several large adult bones and a child's jaw. They were found beneath 20 ft. of undisturbed silt, in a position indicating intentional burial. The skull is preserved in the U. S. National Museum at Washington. It is similar in shape to those of historic Indians of the region. Its ethnological value as indicating the existence of man on the Missouri in the glacial period is very doubtful, it being impossible accurately to determine the age of the deposits.

See *Handbook of American Indians* (Washington, 1907).

LANSQUENET, the French corrupted form of the German *Landsknecht* (*q.v.*), a mercenary foot-soldier of the 16th century. It is also the name of a card game said to have been introduced into France by the *Landsknechte*. The pack of 52 cards is cut by the player at the dealer's right. The dealer lays the two first cards face upwards on the table to his left; the third he places in front of him and the fourth, or *réjouissance* card, in the middle of the table. The players, usually called (except in the case of the dealer) *punters*, stake any sum within the agreed limit upon this réjouissance card; the dealer, who is also the banker, covers the bets and then turns up the next card. If this fails to match any of the cards already exposed, it is laid beside the réjouissance card and then punters may stake upon it. Other cards not matching are treated in the same manner. When a card is turned which matches the réjouissance card, the banker wins everything staked on it, and in like manner he wins what is staked on any card (save his own) that is matched by the card turned. The banker pays all stakes, and the deal is over as soon as a card appears that matches his own; excepting that should the two cards originally placed at his left both be matched before his own, he is then entitled to a second deal. In France matching means winning, not losing, as in Great Britain. There are other variations of play on the continent of Europe.

LANTARA, SIMON MATHURIN (1729–1778), French landscape painter, was born at Oncy on the 24th of March 1729. His father was a weaver, and he himself began life as a herdboy; but, having attracted the notice of Gille de Reumont, a son of his master, he was placed under a painter at Versailles. Endowed with great facility and real talent, his powers found ready recognition; but he found the constraint of a regular life and the society of educated people unbearably tiresome; and as long as the proceeds of the last sale lasted he lived careless of the future in the company of obscure workmen. Rich amateurs more than once attracted him to their houses, only to find that in ease and high living Lantara could produce nothing. He died in Paris on the 22nd of December 1778. His works, now much prized, are not numerous; the Louvre has one landscape, "Morning," signed and dated 1761. Bernard, Joseph Vernet, and others are said to have added figures to his landscapes and sea-pieces. Engravings after Lantara will be found in the works of Lebas, Piquenot, Duret, Mouchy and others. In 1809 a comedy called *Lantara, or the Painter in the Pothouse*, was brought out at the Vaudeville with great success.

See E. Bellier de la Chavignerie, *Recherches sur le peintre Lantara* (Paris, 1852).

LANTERN (an adaptation of the Fr. *lanterne* from Lat. *lanterna* or *laterna*, supposed to be from Gr. λαμπτήρ, a torch or lamp, λάμπειν, to shine, cf. "lamp"; the 16th- and 17th-century form "lanthorn" is due to a mistaken derivation from "horn," as a material frequently used in the making of lanterns), a metal case filled in with some transparent material, and used for holding a light and protecting it from rain or wind. The appliance is of two kinds—the hanging lantern and the hand lantern—both of which are ancient. At Pompeii and Herculaneum have been discovered two cylindrical bronze lanterns, with ornamented pillars, to which chains are attached for carrying or hanging the lantern. Plates of horn surrounded the bronze lamp within, and the cover at the top can be removed for lighting and for the escape of smoke. The hanging lantern for lighting rooms was composed of ornamental metal work, of which iron and brass were perhaps [illegible] Silver, and even gold, were, however, [illegible] metal of the 17th and [illegible] exceedingly artistic work of this [illegible] bronze were often very [illegible] has sides of horn, talc, bladder or [illegible] shape remains in the common [illegible] glass sides, to carry a candle. [illegible] a much more modest appliance [illegible] although in great houses it was some- [illegible]. As glass grew cheaper it [illegible] materials, but the horn lantern which [illegible] century was still being used in [illegible]. By the end of the 18th century [illegible] had been superseded by the candlestick. [illegible] China and Japan, usually known [illegible] or cylindrical in shape, and the [illegible] in use folds flat. For illuminative [illegible] they are coloured with patterns of [illegible] carried by the ordinary foot passenger [illegible]. In China the "Feast of Lanterns" [illegible] New Year and lasts for four days. In [illegible] is sometimes known as the "feast of [illegible] that the spirits of the dead ancestors return [illegible]. The festival takes place in July. The [illegible] has a convex lens which concentrates the [illegible] in the shape of a diverging cone. [illegible] a shutter or slide arrangement by which [illegible] at will. Ships' lanterns are used as [illegible]. On Trajan's column is a repre- [illegible] lantern on a ship. The ships' lanterns [illegible] were highly ornamental, especially [illegible]. At the Armeria Real in Madrid is a [illegible] ships' lanterns. The protected [illegible] lights used in lighthouses are also known [illegible].

[illegible] a lantern is primarily a framework of timber, [illegible] to admit ample light, placed on the top [illegible], it is applied to those portions of [illegible] perforated with windows, and more [illegible] part of the towers of cathedrals and [illegible] of Ely cathedral, or the tower of [illegible]. The term is also applied to the [illegible] of Bath Abbey church, which was [illegible]" from the number of its windows, [illegible], the "lantern of Ireland," on [illegible] side of the choir which was [illegible] the lantern was looked upon [illegible] surmounting the dome, as in St Peter's, [illegible] Paris, and St Paul's, London.

Magic or Optical Lantern.

[illegible] is an instrument for projecting [illegible] magnified representations of [illegible] photographed on glass, or of [illegible] on glass slides or in [illegible]. If the light traverses the object, the projection [illegible] by reflected light, episcopic.

[illegible] magic lantern is usually attributed to [illegible], who described it in the first edition (1646) [illegible], but it is very probably of earlier [illegible]. For a long period the magic lantern was used chiefly [illegible], or in the hands of so-called wizards [illegible] and perform other tricks, astonishing to [illegible] optical principles employed. Within [illegible], the optical lantern has been greatly [illegible] construction, and its use widely extended. By [illegible] photographs on glass can be shown [illegible] to large audiences, thus saving the trouble [illegible] large diagrams. When suitably [illegible] in the form of a microscope to exhibit [illegible] of minute [illegible] organisms, [illegible] ri- [illegible] delicate phys- [illegible] ments which could otherwise be seen only by a few at a time. Another application of the optical lantern is found in the cinematograph (*q.v.*).

The optical lantern, in its simpler forms, consists of the following parts: (1) the lantern body, (2) a source of light, (3) an optical system for projecting the images. The lantern body is a rectangular casing usually made of Russian iron, but sometimes covered with wood (which must be protected by asbestos at parts liable to damage by heat), provided with the openings necessary to the insertion of the source of light, windows for viewing the same, a chimney for conveying away the products of combustion, fittings to carry the slides and the optical system. In the earlier and simpler lanterns, oil lamps were commonly used, and in the toy forms either an oil flame or an ordinary gas jet is still employed. Natural petroleum burnt in a specially constructed lamp by means of two or three parallel wicks set edgeways to the lenses was employed in the sciopticon, an improved lantern invented in America which gave well-defined pictures 6 to 10 ft. in diameter. The Argand gas burner also found application. A great improvement attended the introduction of lime-light, *i.e.* the light emitted by a block of lime made incandescent by an impinging oxyhydrogen or oxygen-coal-gas flame, and the readiness with which hydrogen and oxygen can be prepared and rendered available by compression in steel cylinders and the increased commercial supply of coal-gas greatly popularized these illuminants. Many improvements have been made on the original apparatus. The lime-cylinders are specially prepared to withstand better the disintegrating effects of the flame, and are mounted on a rotating pin in order that fresh surfaces may be brought into play. Cones of zirconia are also used in the same way; or a thorium mantle in conjunction with alcohol vapour may be employed. Two types of burner are in use: (1) the "blow-through jet," in which the oxygen is forced through the jet of the burning gas (this is the safest type), and (2) where the gases are mixed before combustion (this is the more dangerous but also the more powerful type). Ether burners are also in use. In one type the oxygen supply is divided into two streams, one of which passes through a chamber containing cotton wool soaked with ether, and then rejoins the undiverted stream at the jet. The application of the incandescent gas mantle is limited by the intensity of the heat emitted and the large area of the source. Of electrical illuminants the platinum and carbon filament lamps are not much used, the Nernst lamp (in which the preliminary heating is effected by a spirit lamp and not by an auxiliary coil) being preferred. But the arc light is undoubtedly the best illuminant for use in the projecting lantern. The actual size of the source is comparatively small, and hence it is necessary to mount the carbons so that the arc remains at one point on the axis of the optical system. It is also advisable to set back the carbons relatively to one another and to tilt them, so that the brightest part of the "crater" faces the lens.

Optical System.—In the ordinary (or vertically) projecting lantern the rays are transmitted through a lens termed the "condenser," then through the object, and finally through another lens termed the "objective." In the horizontally projecting types the light, after passing through the condenser, is reflected vertically by a plane mirror inclined at 45° to the direction of the light; it then traverses another lens, then the object, then the objective, and is finally projected horizontally by a plane mirror inclined at 45°, or by a right angled glass prism, the hypothenuse face of which is silvered. In episcopic projection, the light, having traversed the condenser, is reflected on to the object, placed horizontally, by an inclined mirror. The rays reflecting the object then traverse the objective, and are then projected horizontally by a mirror or prism. This device inverts the object; a convenient remedy is to place an erecting prism before the lens. The object of the condenser is to collect as much light as possible from the source, and pass it through the object in a uniform beam. For this purpose the condenser should subtend as large an angle as possible at the source of light. To secure this, it should be tolerably large, and its distance from the light, that is, its focal length, small. Since effective single lenses of large diameter are necessarily of long focus, a really good condenser of considerable diameter and yet of short focus must be a combination of two or more lenses. It is essential that the condenser be white and limpid and free from defects or striae.

In the earlier lanterns, as still in the cheaper forms, only a single plano-convex lens or bull's-eye was employed as a condenser. A good compound condenser for ordinary work is that proposed by Herschel, consisting of a biconvex lens and a meniscus mounted together with the concave side of the meniscus next the light. Other types employ two plano-convex lenses, the curved surfaces nearly in contact; or a concavo-convex and a plano-convex lens. Or it may be a triple combination, the object always being to increase the aperture. The focus must not be so short as to bring the lens too near the light, and render it liable to crack from the intense heat. In some lanterns this is guarded against by placing a plate of thin glass between the condenser and the light. If the source of light be broad, an iris diaphragm may be introduced so as to eliminate inequalities in illumination.

The function of the objective is to produce a magnified inverted image of the picture on the screen. In toy lanterns it is a simple double-convex lens of short focus. This, however, can only produce a small picture, and that not very distinct at the edges. The best objective is the portrait combination lens usually of the Petzval type as used in ordinary photographic cameras. These are carefully corrected both for spherical and chromatic aberration, which is absolutely essential in the objective, although not so necessary in the condenser.

Objects.—The commonest objects used for exhibiting with the optical lantern are named " slides " and consist of pictures printed on transparent surfaces. Solid objects mounted on glass after the ordinary manner of mounting microscopic objects are also possible of exhibition, and hollow glass tanks containing organisms or substances undergoing some alteration are also available for use with the lantern. If it be necessary to eliminate the heat rays, which may act deleteriously on the object, a vessel is introduced containing either water or a 5% solution of ferric chloride. In the ordinary slide the pictures are painted with transparent water or oil colours, or photographed on pieces of glass. If parts of the picture are to be movable, two disks of glass are employed, the one movable in front of the other, the fixed part of the picture being painted on the fixed disk and the movable part on the other. By means of a lever the latter disk is moved in its own plane; and in this way a cow, for instance, can be represented drinking, or a donkey cutting amusing capers. In the chromatrope slide two circular disks of glass are placed face to face, each containing a design radiating from the centre, and painted with brilliant transparent colours. By a small pinion gearing in toothed wheels or endless bands the disks are made to move in opposite directions in their own plane. The effect produced is a singularly beautiful change of design and colour. In astronomical slides the motions of the heavenly bodies, eclipses, the phases of the moon or the like are similarly represented by mechanical means.

Dissolving Views.—For this purpose two magic lanterns are necessary, arranged either side by side or the one on the top of the other. The fronts of the lanterns are slightly inclined to each other so as to make the illuminated disks on the screen due to each lantern coincide. By means of a pair of thin metallic shutters terminating in comb-like teeth, and movable by a rack or lever, the light from either lantern can be gradually cut off at the same time that the light from the other is allowed gradually to fall on the screen. In this way one view appears to melt or dissolve into another. This arrangement was first adopted by Childe in 1811.

Phantasmagoria.—In this arrangement the pictures on the screen appear gradually to increase or diminish in size and brightness. To effect this a semi-transparent screen of cotton or other material is used, the lantern being behind and the audience in front. The lantern is mounted on wheels so that it can be rapidly moved up to or withdrawn from the screen; and an automatic arrangement is provided whereby simultaneously with this the objective is made to approach or recede from the slide so as to focus the picture on the screen in any position of the lantern. In this way a very small picture appears gradually to grow to enormous dimensions.

See L. Wright, *Optical Projection* (1891); E. Trutat, *Traité des Projections* (Paris, 1897 and 1901); P. E. Liesegang, *Die Projektions-Kunst* (Leipzig, 1909).

LANTERN-FLY, the name given to insects belonging to the homopterous division of the Hemiptera, and referable to the genus *Fulgora* and allied forms. They are mostly of large size, with a superficial resemblance to lepidoptera due to their brilliant and varied coloration. Characteristic of the group is the presence on the front of the head of a hollow process, simulating a snout, which is sometimes inflated and as large as the rest of the insect, sometimes elongated, narrow and apically upturned. It was believed, mainly on the authority of Marie Sibylle de Mérian, that this process, the so-called " lantern," was luminous at night. Linnaeus adopted the statement without question and made use of a number of specific names, such as *lanternaria*, *phosphorea*, *candelaria*, &c., to illustrate the supposed fact, and thus aided in disseminating a belief which subsequent observations have failed to establish and which is now generally rejected.

LANTERNS OF THE DEAD, the architectural name for the small towers in stone, found chiefly in the centre and west of France, pierced with small openings at the top, where a light was exhibited at night to indicate the position of a cemetery. These towers were usually circular, with a small entrance in the lower part giving access to the interior, so as to raise the lamps by a pulley to the required height. One of the most perfect in France is that at Cellefrouin (Charente), which consists of a series of eight attached semicircular shafts, raised on a pedestal, and is crowned with a conical roof decorated with fir cones; it has only one aperture, towards the main road. Other examples exist at Ciron (Indre) and Antigny (Vienne).

Lantern of the Dead at Cellefrouin (Charente).

LANTHANUM [symbol La, atomic weight 139·0 (O = 16)] one of the metals of the cerium group of rare earths. Its name is derived from the Gr. λανθάνειν, to lie hidden. It was first isolated in 1839 by C. G. Mosander from the " cerium " of J. Berzelius. It is found in the minerals gadolinite, cerite, samarskite and fergusonite, and is usually obtained from cerite. For details of the complex process for the separation of the lanthanum salts from cerite, see R. Bunsen (*Pogg. Ann.*, 1875, 155, p. 377); P. T. Cleve (*Bull. de la soc. chim.*, 1874, 21, p. 196); and A. v. Welsbach (*Monats. f. Chem.*, 1884, 5, p. 508). The metal was obtained by Mosander on heating its chloride with potassium, and by W. F. Hillebrand and T. Norton (*Pogg. Ann.*, 1875, 156, p. 466) on electrolysis of the fused chloride, while C. Winkler (*Ber.*, 1890, 23, p. 78) prepared it by heating the oxide with a mixture of magnesium and magnesia. Muthmann and Weiss (*Ann.*, 1904, 331, p. 1) obtained it by electrolysing the anhydrous chloride. It may be readily hammered, but cannot be drawn. Its specific gravity is 6·1545, and it melts at 810°. It decomposes cold water slowly, but hot water violently. It burns in air, and also in chlorine and bromine, and is readily oxidized by nitric acid.

Lanthanum oxide, La_2O_3, is a white powder obtained by burning the metal in oxygen, or by ignition of the carbonate, nitrate or sulphate. It combines with water with evolution of heat, and on heating with magnesium powder in an atmosphere of hydrogen forms a hydride of probable composition La_2H_3 (C. Winkler, *Ber.* 1891, 24, p. 890). *Lanthanum hydroxide*, $La(OH)_3$, is a white amorphous powder formed by precipitating lanthanum salts by potassium hydroxide. It decomposes ammonium salts. *Lanthanum chloride*, $LaCl_3$, is obtained in the anhydrous condition by heating lanthanum ammonium chloride or, according to C. Matignon (*Compt. rend.*, 1905, 40, p. 1181), by the action of chlorine or hydrochloric acid on the residue obtained by evaporating the oxide with hydrochloric acid. It forms a deliquescent crystalline mass. By evaporation of a solution of lanthanum oxide in hydrochloric acid to the consistency of a syrup, and allowing the solution to stand, large colourless crystals of a hydrated chloride of the composition $2LaCl_3 \cdot 15H_2O$ are obtained. *Lanthanum sulphide*, La_2S_3, is a yellow powder, obtained when the oxide is heated in the vapour of carbon bisulphide. It is decomposed by water, with evolution of sulphuretted hydrogen. *Lanthanum sulphate*, $La_2(SO_4)_3 \cdot 9H_2O$, forms six-sided prisms, isomorphous with those of the corresponding cerium salt. By careful heating it may be made to yield the anhydrous salt. *Lanthanum nitrate*, $La(NO_3)_3 \cdot 6H_2O$, is obtained by dissolving the oxide in nitric acid. It crystallizes in plates, and is soluble in water and alcohol. *Lanthanum carbide*, LaC_2, is prepared by heating the oxide with carbon in the electric furnace (H. Moissan, *Compt. rend.*, 1896, 123, p. 148). It is decomposed by water with the formation of acetylene, methane, ethylene, &c. *Lanthanum carbonate*, $La_2CO_3 \cdot 8H_2O$, occurs as the rare mineral lanthanite, forming greyish-white, pink or yellowish rhombic prisms. The atomic weight of lanthanum has been determined by B. Brauner (*Proc. Chem. Soc.*, 1901, 17, p. 63) by ignition of lanthanum sulphate at 500° C., the value obtained being 139 (O = 16).

LANUVIUM (more frequently *Lanivium* in imperial times, mod. *Civita Lavinia*), an ancient city of Latium, some 19 m. S.E. of Rome, a little S.W. of the Via Appia. It was situated on an isolated hill projecting S. from the main mass of the Alban Hills, and commanding an extensive view over the low country between it and the sea. It was one of the members of the Latin League, and remained independent until conquered by Rome in 338 B.C. At first it did not enjoy the right of Roman citizenship, but acquired it later; and even in imperial times its chief magistrate and municipal council kept the titles of *dictator* and *senatus* respectively. It was especially famous for its rich and much venerated temple of Juno Sospes, from which Octavian borrowed money in 31 B.C., and the possessions of which extended as far as the sea-coast (T. Ashby in *Mélanges de l'école française*, 1905, 203). It possessed many other temples, repaired by Antoninus Pius, who was born close by, as was also Commodus. Remains of the ancient theatre and of the city walls exist in the modern village, and above it is an area surrounded by a portico, in *opus reticulatum*, upon the north side of which is a rectangular building in *opus quadratum*, probably connected with the temple of Juno. Here archaic decorative terra-cottas were discovered in excavations carried on by Lord Savile. The acropolis of the primitive city was probably on the highest point above the temple to the north. The neighbourhood, which is now covered with vineyards, contains remains of many Roman villas, one of which is traditionally attributed to Antoninus Pius.

See *Notizie degli Scavi, passim*. (T. As.)

LANZA, DOMENICO GIOVANNI GIUSEPPE MARIA (1810–1882), Italian politician, was born at Casale, Piedmont, on the 15th of February 1810. He studied medicine at Turin, and practised for some years in his native place. He was one of the promoters of the agrarian association in Turin, and took an active part in the rising of 1848. He was elected to the Piedmontese parliament in that year, and attached himself to the party of Cavour, devoting his attention chiefly to questions of economy and finance. He became minister of public instruction in 1855 in the cabinet of Cavour, and in 1858 minister of finance. He followed Cavour into his temporary retirement in July 1859 after the peace of Villafranca, and for a year (1860–1861) was president of the Chamber. He was minister of the interior (1864–1865) in the La Marmora cabinet, and arranged the transference of the capital to Florence. He maintained a resolute opposition to the financial policy of Menabrea, who resigned when Lanza was a second time elected, in 1869, president of the Chamber. Lanza formed a new cabinet in which he was himself minister of the interior. With Quintino Sella as minister of finance he sought to reorganize Italian finance, and resigned office when Sella's projects were rejected in 1873. His cabinet had seen the accomplishment of Italian unity and the installation of an Italian government in Rome. He died in Rome on the 9th of March 1882.

See Enrico Tavallini, *La Vita ed i tempi di Giovanni Lanza* (2 vols., Turin and Naples, 1887).

LANZAROTE, an island in the Atlantic Ocean, forming part of the Spanish archipelago of the Canary Islands (*q.v.*). Pop. (1900) 17,546; area, 326 sq. m. Lanzarote, the most easterly of the Canaries, has a length of 31 m. and a breadth varying from 5 to 10 m. It is naked and mountainous, bearing everywhere marks of its volcanic origin. Montaña Blanca, the highest point (2000 ft.), is cultivated to the summit. In 1730 the appearance of half the island was altered by a volcanic outburst. A violent earthquake preceded the catastrophe, by which nine villages were destroyed. In 1825 another volcanic eruption took place accompanied by earthquakes, and two hills were thrown up. The port of Naos on the south-east of the island affords safe anchorage. It is protected by two forts. A short distance inland is the town of Arrecife (pop. 3082). The climate is hot and dry. There is only a single spring of fresh water on the island, and that in a position difficult of access. From the total failure of water the inhabitants were once compelled to abandon the island. Dromedaries are used as beasts of burden. Teguise (pop. 3786), on the north-west coast, is the residence of the local authorities. A strait about 6 m. in width separates Lanzarote from Fuerteventura.

Graciosa, a small uninhabited island, is divided from the north-eastern extremity of Lanzarote by a channel 1 m. in width, which affords a capacious and safe harbour for large ships; but basaltic cliffs, 1500 ft. high, prevent intercourse with the inhabited part of Lanzarote. A few persons reside on the little island Allegranza, a mass of lava and cinders ejected at various times from a now extinct volcano, the crater of which has still a well-defined edge.

LANZI, LUIGI (1732–1810), Italian archaeologist, was born in 1732 and educated as a priest. In 1773 he was appointed keeper of the galleries of Florence, and thereafter studied Italian painting and Etruscan antiquities and language. In the one field his labours are represented by his *Storia Pittorica della Italia*, the first portion of which, containing the Florentine, Sienese, Roman and Neapolitan schools, appeared in 1792, the rest in 1796. The work is translated by Roscoe. In archaeology his great achievement was *Saggio di lingua Etrusca* (1789), followed by *Saggio delle lingue Ital. antiche* (1806). In his memoir on the so-called Etruscan vases (*Dei vasi antichi dipinti volgarmente chiamati Etruschi*, 1806) Lanzi rightly perceived their Greek origin and characters. What was true of the antiquities would be true also, he argued, of the Etruscan language, and the object of the *Saggio di lingua Etrusca* was to prove that this language must be related to that of the neighbouring peoples—Romans, Umbrians, Oscans and Greeks. He was allied with E. Q. Visconti in his great but never accomplished plan of illustrating antiquity altogether from existing literature and monuments. His notices of ancient sculpture and its various styles appeared as an appendix to the *Saggio di lingua Etrusca*, and arose out of his minute study of the treasures then added to the Florentine collection from the Villa Medici. The abuse he met with from later writers on the Etruscan language led Corssen (*Sprache der Etrusker*, i. p. vi.) to protest in the name of his real services to philology and archaeology. Among his other productions was an edition of Hesiod's *Works and Days*, with valuable notes, and a translation in *terza rima*. Begun in 1785, it was recast and completed in 1808. The list of his works closes with his *Opere sacre*, a series of treatises on spiritual subjects. Lanzi died on the 30th of March 1810. He was buried in the church of the Santa Croce at Florence by the side of Michelangelo.

LAOAG, a town, port for coasting vessels, and capital of the province of Ilocos Norte, Luzon, Philippine Islands, on the Laoag river, about 5 m. from its mouth, and in the N.W. part of the island. Pop. (1903) 34,454; in 1903, after the census had been taken, the municipality of San Nicolás (pop. 1903, 10,880) was added to Laoag. Laoag is on an extensive coast plain, behind which is a picturesque range of hills; it is well built and is noted for its fine climate, the name "Laoag" signifying "clear." It is especially well equipped for handling rice, which is shipped in large quantities; Indian corn, tobacco and sugar are also shipped. Cotton is grown in the vicinity, and is woven by the women into fabrics, which find a ready sale among the pagan tribes of the mountains. The language is Ilocano.

LAOCOON, in Greek legend a brother of Anchises, who had been a priest of Apollo, but having profaned the temple of the god he and his two sons were attacked by serpents while preparing to sacrifice a bull at the altar of Poseidon, in whose service Laocoon was then acting as priest. An additional motive for his punishment consisted in his having warned the Trojans against the wooden horse left by the Greeks. But, whatever his crime may have been, the punishment stands out even among the tragedies of Greek legend as marked by its horror—particularly so as it comes to us in Virgil (*Aeneid*, ii. 199 sq.), and as it is represented in the marble group, the Laocoon, in the Vatican. In the oldest existing version of the legend—that of Arctinus of Miletus, which has so far been preserved in the excerpts of Proclus—the calamity is lessened by the fact that only one of the two sons is killed; and this, as has been pointed out (*Arch. Zeitung*, 1879, p. 167), agrees with the interpretation which Goethe in his *Propylaea* had put on the marble group without reference to the literary tradition. He says: "The younger son struggles and is powerless, and is alarmed; the father struggles ineffectively, indeed his efforts only increase the opposition; the elder son is least of all injured, he feels neither anguish nor pain, but he is horrified at what he sees happening to his father, and he screams while he pushes the coils of the serpent off from his legs. He is thus an observer, witness, and participant in the incident, and the work is then complete." Again, "the gradation of the incident is this: the father has become powerless among the coils of the serpent; the younger son has still strength for resistance but is wounded; the elder has a prospect of escape." Lessing, on the other hand, maintained the view that the marble group illustrated the version of the legend given by Virgil, with such differences as were necessary from the different limits of representation imposed on the arts of sculpture and of poetry. These limits required a new definition, and this he undertook in his still famous work, *Laokoon* (see the edition of Hugo Blümner, Berlin, 1876, in which the subsequent criticism is collected). The date of the Laocoon being now fixed (see AGESANDER) to 40–20 B.C., there can be no question of copying Virgil. The group represents the extreme of a pathetic tendency in sculpture (see GREEK ART, Plate I. fig. 52).

LAODICEA, the name of at least eight cities, founded or renovated in the later Hellenic period. Most of them were founded by the Seleucid kings of Syria. Seleucus, founder of the dynasty, is said by Appian to have named five cities after his mother Laodice. Thus in the immense realm of the Seleucidae from the Aegean Sea to the borders of India we find cities called Laodicea, as also Seleucia (*q.v.*). So long as Greek civilization held its ground, these were the commercial and social centres. The chief are Laodicea *ad Lycum* (see below); *Combusta* on the borders of Phrygia, Lycaonia and Pisidia; a third in Pontus; a fourth, *ad mare*, on the coast of Syria; a fifth, *ad Libanum*, beside the Lebanon mountains; and three others in the far east—Media, Persia and the lower Tigris valley. In the latter countries Greek civilization was short-lived, and the last three cities disappeared; the other five continued great throughout the Greek and Roman period, and the second, third and fourth retain to the present day the ancient name under the pronunciation Ladik, Ladikiyeh or Latakia (*q.v.*).

LAODICEA AD LYCUM (mod. *Denizli*, *q.v.*) was founded probably by Antiochus II. Theos (261–46 B.C.), and named after his wife Laodice. Its site is close to the station of Gonjeli on the Anatolian railway. Here was one of the oldest homes of Christianity and the seat of one of the seven churches of the Apocalypse. Pliny states (v. 29) that the town was called in older times Diospolis and Rhoas; but at an early period Colossae, a few miles to the east, and Hierapolis, 6 m. to the north, were the great cities of the neighbourhood, and Laodicea was of no importance till the Seleucid foundation (Strabo, p. 578). A favourable site was found on some low hills of alluvial formation, about 2 m. S. of the river Lycus (Churuk Su) and 9 m. E. of the confluence of the Lycus and Maeander. The great trade route from the Euphrates and the interior passed to it through Apamea. There it forked, one branch going down the Maeander valley to Magnesia and thence north to Ephesus, a distance of about 90 m., and the other branch crossing the mountains by an easy pass to Philadelphia and the Hermus valley, Sardis, Thyatira and at last Pergamum. St Paul (Col. iv. 15) alludes to the situation of Laodicea beside Colossae and Hierapolis; and the order in which the last five churches of the Apocalypse are enumerated (Rev. i. 11) is explained by their position on the road just described. Placed in this situation, in the centre of a very fertile district, Laodicea became a rich city. It was famous for its money transactions (Cic. *Ad Fam.* ii. 17, iii. 5), and for the beautiful soft wool grown by the sheep of the country (Strabo 578). Both points are referred to in the message to the church (Rev. iii. 17, 18).

Little is known of the history of the town. It suffered greatly from a siege in the Mithradatic war, but soon recovered its prosperity under the Roman empire. The *Zeus of Laodicea*, with the curious epithet *Azeus* or *Azeis*, is a frequent symbol on the city coins. He is represented standing, holding in the extended right hand an eagle, in the left a spear, the *hasta pura*. Not far from the city was the temple of Men Karou, with a great medical school; while Laodicea itself produced some famous Sceptic philosophers, and gave origin to the royal family of Polemon and Zenon, whose curious history has been illustrated in recent times (W. H. Waddington, *Mélanges de Numism.* ser. ii.; Th. Mommsen, *Ephem. Epigraph* i. and ii.; M. O. Rayet, *Milet et le Golfe Latmique*, chap. v.). The city fell finally into decay in the frontier wars with the Turkish invaders. Its ruins are of wide extent, but not of great beauty or interest; there is no doubt, however, that much has been buried beneath the surface by the frequent earthquakes to which the district is exposed (Strabo 580; Tac. *Ann.* xiv. 27).

See W. M. Ramsay, *Cities and Bishoprics of Phrygia*, i.-ii. (1895); *Letters to the Seven Churches* (1904), and the beautiful drawings of Cockerell in the *Antiquities of Ionia*, vol. iii. pl. 47–51. (A. H. S.)

LAODICEA, SYNOD OF, held at Laodicea ad Lycum in Phrygia, some time between 343 and 381 (so Hefele; but Baronius argues for 314, and others for a date as late as 399), adopted sixty canons, chiefly disciplinary, which were declared ecumenical by the council of Chalcedon, 451. The most significant canons are those directly affecting the clergy, wherein the clergy appear as a privileged class, far above the laity, but with sharply differentiated and carefully graded orders within itself. For example, the priests are not to be chosen by the people; penitents are not to be present at ordinations (lest they should hear the failings of candidates discussed); bishops are to be appointed by the metropolitan and his suffragan; sub-deacons may not distribute the elements of the Eucharist; clerics are forbidden to leave a diocese without the bishop's permission. Other canons treat of intercourse with heretics, admission of penitent heretics, baptism, fasts, Lent, angel-worship (forbidden as idolatrous) and the canonical books, from which the Apocrypha and Revelation are wanting.

See Mansi ii. 563-614; Hardouin i. 777-792; Hefele, 2nd ed., i. 746-777 (Eng. trans. ii. 295-325). (T. F. C.)

LAOMEDON, in Greek legend, son of Ilus, king of Troy and father of Podarces (Priam). The gods Apollo and Poseidon served him for hire, Apollo tending his herds, while Poseidon built the walls of Troy. When Laomedon refused to pay the reward agreed upon, Apollo visited the land with a pestilence, and Poseidon sent up a monster from the sea, which ravaged the land. According to the oracle, the wrath of Poseidon could only be appeased by the sacrifice of one of the king's daughters. The lot fell upon Hesione, who was chained to a rock to await the monster's coming. Heracles, on his way back from the land of the Amazons, offered to slay the monster and release Hesione, on condition that he should receive the wonderful horses presented by Zeus to Tros, the father of Ganymede, to console him for the loss of his son. Again Laomedon broke his word; whereupon Heracles returned with a band of warriors, attacked Troy, and slew Laomedon and all his sons except Priam. According to Diodorus Siculus, Laomedon aggravated his offence by imprisoning Iphiclus and Telamon, who had been sent by Heracles to demand the surrender of the horses. Laomedon was buried near the Scaean gate, and it was said that so long as his grave remained undisturbed, so long would the walls of Troy remain impregnable.

See Homer, *Iliad*, v. 265, 640, vii. 452, xxi. 443; Apollodorus ii. 5. 9 and 6. 4; Diod. Sic. iv. 32, 42, 49; Hyginus, *Fab.* 89; Horace, *Odes* iii. 3, 22; Ovid, *Metam.* xi. 194.

LAON, a town of northern France, capital of the department of Aisne, 87 m. N.E. of Paris on the Northern railway. Pop. (1906), town, 9787, commune (including troops) 15,288. It is situated on an isolated ridge, forming two sides of a triangle, which rises some 330 ft. above the surrounding plain and the little river of Ardon. The suburbs of St Marcel and Vaux extend along the foot of the ridge to the north. From the railway station, situated in the plain to the north, a straight staircase of several hundred steps leads to the gate of the town, and all the roads connecting Laon with the surrounding district are cut in zigzags on the steep slopes, which are crowned by promenades on the site of the old ramparts. The 13th-century gates of Ardon, Chenizelles and Soissons, the latter in a state of ruin, have been preserved. At the eastern extremity of the ridge rises the citadel; at its apex is the parade-ground of St Martin, and at the southern end stands the ancient abbey of St Vincent. The deep depression between the arms of the ridge, known as the Cuve St Vincent, has its slopes covered with trees, vegetable gardens and vineyards. From the promenade along the line of the ramparts there is an extensive view northward beyond St Quentin, westward to the forest of St Gobain, and southward over the wooded hills of the Laonnais and Soissonnais.

The cathedral of Laon (see Architecture, Romanesque and Gothic Architecture in France) is one of the most important creations of the art of the 12th and 13th centuries. It took the place of the old cathedral, burned at the beginning of the communal struggles mentioned below. The building is cruciform, and the choir terminates in a straight wall instead of in an apse. Of the six towers flanking the façades, only four are complete to the height of the base of the spires, two at the west front with hugh figures of oxen beneath the arcades of their upper portion, and one at each end of the transept. A square central tower forms a lantern within the church. The west front, with three porches, the centre one surmounted by a fine rose window, ranks next to that of Notre-Dame at Paris in purity. The cathedral has stained glass of the 13th century and a choir grille of the 18th century. The chapter-house and the cloister contain beautiful specimens of the architecture of the beginning of the 13th century. The old episcopal palace, contiguous to the cathedral, is now used as a court-house. The front, flanked by turrets, is pierced by great pointed windows. There is also a Gothic cloister and an old chapel of two storeys, of a date anterior to the cathedral. The church of St Martin dates from the middle of the 12th century. The old abbey buildings of the same foundation are now used as the hospital. The museum of Laon has collections of sculpture and painting. In its garden there is a chapel of the Templars belonging to the 12th century. The church of the suburb of Vaux near the railway station dates from the 11th and 12th centuries. Numerous cellars of two or three storeys have taken the place of the old quarries in the hill-side. Laon forms with La Fère and Reims a triangle of important fortresses. Its fortifications consist of an inner line of works on the summit of Laon itself, and two groups of detached forts, one some 3½ m. S.E. about the village of Bruyères, the other about 3 m. W.S.W., near Laniscourt. To the S.S.W. forts [illegible] and Condé connect Laon with the Aisne and with Reims.

Laon is the seat of a prefect and a court of assizes, and possesses a tribunal of first instance, a lycée for boys, a college for girls, a school of agriculture and training colleges. Sugar-making and metal-founding are carried on, but neither industry nor trade, which is in grain and wine, are of much importance.

[illegible] of Laon (Laudunum) has always had some [illegible]. In the time of Caesar there was a Gallic [illegible] the Remi (inhabitants of the country round Reims) [illegible] the seat of the confederated Belgae. Whatever may [illegible] locality of that battlefield, Laon was fortified [illegible] successively checked the invasions of the Franks, [illegible] Vandals, Alans and Huns. St Remigius, the arch-[illegible] baptized Clovis, was born in the Laonnais, and [illegible] the end of the 5th century, instituted the bishopric [illegible] and Laon was one of the principal towns of [illegible] Franks, and the possession of it was often dis-[illegible] enriched its church with the gift of very [illegible] the fall of the Carolingians Laon took the [illegible] their heir, and Hugh Capet only succeeded [illegible] the town by the [illegible] bishop, who, in return for this service, was made second ecclesiastical peer of the kingdom. Early in the 12th century the communes of France set about emancipating themselves, and the history of the commune of Laon is one of the richest and most varied. The citizens had profited by a temporary absence of Bishop Gaudry to secure from his representatives a communal charter, but he, on his return, purchased from the king of France the revocation of this document, and recommenced his oppressions. The consequence was a revolt, in which the episcopal palace was burnt and the bishop and several of his partisans were put to death. The fire spread to the cathedral, and reduced it to ashes. Uneasy at the result of their victory, the rioters went into hiding outside the town, which was anew pillaged by the people of the neighbourhood, eager to avenge the death of their bishop. The king alternately interfered in favour of the bishop and of the inhabitants till 1239. After that date the liberties of Laon were no more contested till 1331, when the commune was abolished. During the Hundred Years' War it was attacked and taken by the Burgundians, who gave it up to the English, to be retaken by the French after the consecration of Charles VII. Under the League Laon took the part of the Leaguers, and was taken by Henry IV. During the campaign of 1814 Napoleon tried in vain to dislodge Blücher from it. In 1870 an engineer blew up the powder magazine of the citadel at the moment when the German troops were entering the town. Many lives were lost; and the cathedral and the old episcopal palace were damaged. At the Revolution Laon permanently lost its rank as a bishopric.

LAOS, a territory of French Indo-China, bounded N. by the Chinese province of Yun-nan, W. by the British Shan states and Siam, S. by Cambodia and Annam, E. by Annam and N.E. by Tongking. Northern Laos is traversed by the Mekong (*q.v.*) which from Chieng-Khan to a point below Stung-Treng forms the boundary between Laos (on the left bank) and Siam and Cambodia (on the right). French Laos constitutes a strip of territory between 700 and 800 m. in length with an average breadth of 155 m., an approximate area of 88,780 sq. m., and a population of about 550,000. Its northern region between the Mekong and Tongking is covered by a tangle of mountain chains clothed with dense forests and traversed by the Nam-Hou, the Nam-Ta and other tributaries of the Mekong. The culminating point exceeds 6500 ft. in height. South of this is the extensive wooded plateau of Tran-Ninh with an average altitude of between 3000 and 5000 ft. Towards the 18th degree of latitude this mountain system narrows into a range running parallel to and closely approaching the coast of the China Sea as it descends south. The boundary between Laos and Annam follows the crest-line of this range, several peaks of which exceed 6500 ft. (Pu-Atwat, over 8000 ft.). On the west its ramifications extend to the Mekong enclosing wide plains watered by the affluents of that river.

Laos is inhabited by a mixed population falling into three main groups—the Thais (including the Laotions (see below)); various aboriginal peoples classed as Khas; and the inhabitants of neighbouring countries, *e.g.* China, Annam, Cambodia, Siam, Burma, &c.

Laos has a rainy season lasting from June to October and corresponding to the S.W. monsoon and a dry season coinciding with the N.E. monsoon and lasting from November to May. Both in northern and southern Laos the heat during April and May is excessive, the thermometer reaching 104° F. and averaging 95° F. With the beginning of the rains the heat becomes more tolerable. December, January and February are cool months, the temperature in south Laos (south of 19°) averaging 77°, in north Laos from 50° to 53°. The plateau of Tran-Ninh and, in the south, that of the Bolovens are distinguished by the wholesomeness of their climate.

The forests contain bamboo and many valuable woods amongst which only the teak of north Laos and rattan are exploited to any extent; other forest products are rubber, stick lac, gum, benjamin, cardamoms, &c. Rice and maize, and cotton, indigo, tobacco, sugar-cane and cardamoms are among the cultivated plants. Elephants are numerous and the forests are inhabited by tigers, panthers, bears, deer and buffalo. Hunting and fishing are leading occupations of the inhabitants. Many species of monkeys, as well as peacocks, pheasants and woodcock are found, and the reptiles include crocodiles, turtles, pythons and cobras.

Scarcity of labour and difficulty of communication hinder

the working of the gold, tin, copper, argentiferous lead, precious stones and other minerals of the country and the industries in general are of a primitive kind and satisfy only local needs.

The buffalo, the ox, the horse and the elephant are domesticated, and these together with cardamoms, rice, tobacco and the products of the forests form the bulk of the exports. Swine are reared, their flesh forming an important article of diet. Imports are inconsiderable, comprising chiefly cotton fabrics, garments and articles for domestic use. Trade is chiefly in the hands of the Chinese and is carried on for the most part with Siam. The Mekong is the chief artery of transit; elsewhere communication is afforded by tracks sometimes passable only for pedestrians. Luang-Prabang (*q.v.*) is the principal commercial town. Before the French occupation of Laos, it was split up into small principalities (*muongs*) of which the chief was that of Vien-Tiane. Vien-Tiane was destroyed in 1828 by the Siamese who annexed the territory. In 1893 they made it over to the French, who grouped the *muongs* into provinces. Of these there are twelve each administered by a French commissioner and, under his surveillance, by native officials elected by the people from amongst the members of an hereditary nobility. At the head of the administration there is a resident-superior stationed at Savannaket. Up till 1896 Laos had no special budget, but was administered by Cochin-China, Annam and Tongking. The budget for 1899 showed receipts £78,988 and expenditure £77,417. For 1904 the budget figures were, receipts £82,942, expenditure £76,344. The chief sources of revenue are the direct taxes (£15,606 in 1904), especially the poll-tax, and the contribution from the general budget of Indo-China (£54,090 in 1904). The chief items of expenditure in 1904 were Government house, &c., £22,558, transport, £19,191, native guard, £17,327.

See M. J. F. Garnier, *Voyage d'exploration en Indo-Chine* (Paris, 1873); C. Gosselin, *Le Laos et le protectorat français* (Paris, 1900); L. de Reinach, *Le Laos* (Paris, 1902) and *Notes sur le Laos* (Paris, 1906); and bibliography under Indo-China, French.

LAOS, or Laotions, an important division of the widespread Thai or Shan race found throughout Indo-China from 28° N. and the sources of the Irrawaddy as far as Cambodia and 7° N. in the Malay Peninsula. This Thai family includes the Shans proper, and the Siamese. The name Lao, which appears to mean simply "man," is the collective Siamese term for all the Thai peoples subject to Siam, while Shan, said to be of Chinese origin, is the collective Burmese term for those subject to Burma. Lao is therefore rather a political than an ethnical title, and the people cordially dislike the name, insisting on their right to be called Thai. Owing to the different circumstances which have attended their migrations, the Thai peoples have attained to varying degrees of civilization. The Lao, who descended from the mountain districts of Yunnan, Szechuen and Kweichow to the highland plains of upper Indo-China, and drove the wilder Kha peoples whom they found in possession into the hills, mostly adopted Buddhism, and formed small settled communities or states in which laws were easy, taxes light and a very fair degree of comfort was attained. There are two main divisions, the Lao Pong Dam ("Black Paunch Laos"), so-called from their habit of tattooing the body from the waist to the knees, and the Lao Pong Kao ("White Paunch Laos") who do not tattoo. Lao tattooing is of a most elaborate kind. The Lao Pong Dam now form the western branch of the Lao family, inhabiting the Siamese Lao states of Chieng Mai Lapaun, 'Tern Pre and Nan, and reaching as far south as 17° N. Various influences have contributed to making the Lao the pleasant, easy-going, idle fellow that he is. The result is that practically all the trade of these states is in the hands of Bangkok Chinese firms, of a certain number of European houses and others, while most of the manual labour connected with the teak industry is done by Ka Mus, who migrate in large numbers from the left bank of the Mekong. The Lao Pong Kao, or eastern branch, appear to have migrated southwards by the more easterly route of the Nam-u and the Mekong valley. In contradistinction to the Lao Pong Dam, who have derived their written language from the Burmese character, the eastern race has retained what appears to be the early form of the present Siamese writing, from which it differs little. They formed important settlements at various points on the Mekong, notably Luang Prabang, Wieng Chan (Vien-Tiane) Ubon and Bassac; and, heading inland as far as Korat on the one side and the Annamite watershed in the east, they drove out the less civilized Kha peoples, and even the Cambodians, as the Lao Pong Dam did on the west. Vien-Tiane during the 18th century was the most powerful of the Lao principalities, and was feared and respected throughout Indo-China. It was destroyed by the Siamese in 1828. The inhabitants, in accordance with the Indo-Chinese custom of the day, were transported to Lower Siam. The Lao Pong Kao below 18° N. are a less merry and less vivacious people, and are for the most part shorter and more thick-set than those of Luang Prabang and the north. If possible, they are as a race lazier than the western Lao, as they are certainly more musical. The "khen," or mouth organ, which is universal among them, is the sweetest-toned of eastern instruments.

After 1828 the Laos became entirely subject to Siam, and were governed partly by khiao, or native hereditary princes, partly by mandarins directly nominated by the Bangkok authorities. The khiao were invested by a gold dish, betel-box, spittoon and teapot, which were sent from Bangkok and returned at their death or deposition. Of all the khiao the most powerful was the prince of Ubon (15° N., 105° E.), whose jurisdiction extended nearly from Bassac on the Mekong northwards to the great southern bend of that river. Nearly all the Laos country is now divided between France and Siam, and only a few tribes retain a nominal independence.

The many contradictory accounts of the Laos are due to the fact that the race has become much mixed with the aboriginal inhabitants. The half-castes sprung from alliances with the wild tribes of Caucasic stock present every variety between that type and the Mongolian. But the pure Laos are still distinguished by the high cheek-bones, small flat nose, oblique eyes, wide mouth, black lank hair, sparse beard, and yellow complexion of the Thai and other branches of the Mongol family. In disposition the Laos are an apathetic, peace-loving, pleasant-mannered race. Though the women have to work, they are free and well treated, and polygamy is rare. The Laos are very superstitious, believe in wer-wolves, and that all diseases are caused by evil spirits. Their chief food is rice and fish. Men, women and children all smoke tobacco. The civilized Laos were long addicted to slave-hunting, not only with the sanction but even with the co-operation of their rulers, the Lao mandarins heading regular expeditions against the wilder tribes.

Closely allied with the Lao are a number of tribes found throughout the hill regions of the upper Mekong, between Yunnan and Kwangsi in China and the upper waters of the Menam in Siam. They have all within recent times been partakers in the general movement towards the south-west from the highland districts of southern China, which has produced so many recruits for the peopling of the Indo-Chinese peninsula. Of this group of people, among whom may be named the Yao, Yao Yin, Lanten, Meo, Musur (or Muhso) and Kaw, perhaps the best known and most like the Lao are the Lu—both names meaning originally "man"—who have in many cases adopted a form of Buddhism (flavoured strongly by their natural respect for local spirits as well as tattooing) and other relatively civilized customs, and have forsaken their wandering life among the hills for a more settled village existence. Hardy, simple and industrious, fond of music, kind-hearted, and with a strangely artistic taste in dress, these people possess in a wonderful degree the secret of cheerful contentment.

Authorities.—M. J. F. Garnier, *Voyage d'exploration en Indo-Chine*; A. H. Mouhot, *Travels in the Central Parts of Indo-China, Cambodia and Laos* (1864); Holt S. Hallett, *A Thousand Miles on an Elephant in the Shan States* (1890); A. R. Colquhoun, *Amongst the Shans* (1885); Lord Lamington, *Proc. R.G.S.* vol. xiii. No. 12; Archer, *Report on a Journey in the Mekong Valley*; Prince Henri d'Orléans, *Around Tonkin and Siam* (1894); M'Carthy, *Report on a Survey in Siam* (1895); Bulletins, Paris Geographical Society: H. Warington Smyth, *Notes of a Journey on the Upper Mekong* (1895); *Five Years in Siam* (1898); Harmand, *Le Laos et les populations sauvages de l'Indo-Chine* (1880). See also bibliography to preceding article.

LÂO-TSZE, or Laou-Tsze, the designation of the Chinese author of the celebrated treatise called *Tâo Teh King*, and the reputed founder of the religion called *Tâoism*. The Chinese

Accepting the *Tâo Teh King* as the veritable work of Lâo-tsze, we may now examine its contents. Consisting of not more than between five and six thousand characters, it is but a short treatise—not half the size of the Gospel of St Mark. The nature of the subject, however, the want of any progress of thought or of logical connexion between its different parts, and the condensed style, with the mystic tendencies and poetical temperament of the author, make its meaning extraordinarily obscure. Divided at first into two parts, it has subsequently and conveniently been subdivided into chapters. One of the oldest, and the most common, of these arrangements makes the chapters eighty-two.

Supposed harmony with Biblical teaching.

Some Roman Catholic missionaries, two centuries ago, fancied that they found a wonderful harmony between many passages and the teaching of the Bible. Montucci of Berlin ventured to say in 1808: "Many things about a Triune God are so clearly expressed that no one who has read this book can doubt that the mystery of the Holy Trinity was revealed to the Chinese five centuries before the coming of Jesus Christ." Even Rémusat, the first occupant of a Chinese chair in Europe, published at Paris in 1823 his *Mémoire sur la vie et les opinions de Lâo-tsze*, to vindicate the view that the Hebrew name Yahweh was phonetically represented in the fourteenth chapter by Chinese characters. These fancies were exploded by Stanislas Julien, when he issued in 1842 his translation of the whole treatise as *Le Livre de la voie et de la vertu*.

The most important thing is to determine what we are to understand by the *Tâo*, for *Teh* is merely its outcome, especially in man, and is rightly translated by "virtue." Julien translated *Tâo* by "la voie." Chalmers leaves it untranslated. "No English word," he says (p. xi.), "is its exact equivalent. Three terms suggest themselves—the way, reason and the word; but they are all liable to objection. Were we guided by etymology, 'the way' would come nearest the original, and in one or two passages the idea of a way seems to be in the term; but this is too materialistic to serve the purpose of a translation. 'Reason,' again, seems to be more like a quality or attribute of some conscious being than *Tâo* is. I would translate it by 'the Word,' in the sense of the Logos, but this would be like settling the question which I wish to leave open, viz. what resemblance there is between the Logos of the New Testament and this Chinese Tâo." Later Sinologues in China have employed "nature" as our best analogue of the term. Thus Watters (*Lâo-tsze, A Study in Chinese Philosophy*, p. 45) says:— "In the *Tâo Teh King* the originator of the universe is referred to under the names Non-Existence, Existence, Nature (*Tâo*) and various designations—all which, however, represent one idea in various manifestations. It is in all cases Nature (*Tâo*) which is meant." This view has been skilfully worked out; but it only hides the scope of "the Venerable Philosopher." "Nature" cannot be accepted as a *translation* of *Tâo*. That character was, primarily, the symbol of a way, road or path; and then, figuratively, it was used, as we also use *way*, in the senses of means and method—the *course* that we pursue in passing from one thing or concept to another as its end or result. It is the name of a quality. Sir Robert Douglas has well said (*Confucianism and Tâoism*, p. 189): "If we were compelled to adopt a single word to represent the *Tâo* of Lâo-tsze, we should prefer the sense in which it is used by Confucius, 'the way,' that is, μέθοδος."

The doctrine of "the way."

What, then, was the quality which Lâo-tsze had in view, and which he thought of as the *Tâo*—there in the library of Chow, at the pass of the valley of Han, and where he met the end of his life beyond the limits of the civilized state? It was the simplicity of spontaneity, action (which might be called non-action) without motive, free from all selfish purpose, resting in nothing but its own accomplishment. This is found in the phenomena of the material world. "All things spring up without a word spoken, and grow without a claim for their production. They go through their processes without any display of pride in them; and the results are realized without any assumption of ownership. It is owing to the absence of such assumption that the results and their processes do not disappear" (chap. ii.). It only needs the same quality in the arrangements and measures of government to make society beautiful and happy. "A government conducted by sages would free the hearts of the people from inordinate desires, fill their bellies, keep their ambitions feeble and strengthen their bones. They would constantly keep the people without knowledge and free from desires; and, where there were those who had knowledge, they would have them so that they would not dare to put it in practice" (chap. iii.). A corresponding course observed by individual man in his government of himself becoming again "as a little child" (chaps. x. and xxviii.) will have corresponding results. "His constant virtue will be complete, and he will return to the primitive simplicity" (chap. xxviii.).

Such is the subject matter of the *Tâo Teh King*—the operation of this method or *Tâo*, "without striving or crying," in nature, in society and in the individual. Much that is very beautiful and practical is inculcated in connexion with its working in the individual character. The writer seems to feel that he cannot say enough on the virtue of humility (chap. viii., &c.). There were three things which he prized and held fast—gentle compassion, economy and the not presuming to take precedence in the world (chap. lxvii.). His teaching rises to its highest point in chap. lxiii.:—"It is the way of *Tâo* not to act from any personal motive, to conduct affairs without feeling the trouble of them, to taste without being aware of the flavour, to account the great as small and the small as great, to recompense injury with kindness." This last and noblest characteristic of the *Tâo*, the requiting "good for evil," is not touched on again in the treatise; but we know that it excited general attention at the time, and was the subject of conversation between Confucius and his disciples (*Confucian Analects*, xiv. 36).

What is said in the *Tâo* on government is not, all of it, so satisfactory. The writer shows, indeed, the benevolence of his heart. He seems to condemn the infliction of capital punishment (chaps. lxxiii. and lxxiv.), and he deplores the practice of war (chap. lxix.); but he had no sympathy with the progress of society or with the culture and arts of life. He says (chap. lxv.):—"Those who anciently were skilful in practising the *Tâo* did not use it to enlighten the people; their object rather was to keep them simple. The difficulty in governing the people arises from their having too much knowledge, and therefore he who tries to govern a state by wisdom is a scourge to it, while he who does not try to govern thereby is a blessing." The last chapter but one is the following:—"In a small state with a few inhabitants, I would so order it that the people, though supplied with all kinds of implements, would not (care to) use them; I would give them cause to look on death as a most grievous thing, while yet they would not go away to a distance to escape from it. Though they had boats and carriages, they should have no occasion to ride in them. Though they had buff-coats and sharp weapons, they should not don or use them. I would make them return to the use of knotted cords (instead of written characters). They should think their coarse food sweet, their plain clothing beautiful, their poor houses places of rest and their common simple ways sources of enjoyment. There should be a neighbouring state within sight, and the sound of the fowls and dogs should be heard from it to us without interruption, but I would make the people to old age, even to death, have no intercourse with it."

On reading these sentiments, we must judge of Lâo-tsze that, with all his power of thought, he was only a dreamer. But thus far there is no difficulty arising from his language in regard to the *Tâo*. It is simply a quality, descriptive of the style of character and action, which the individual should seek to attain in himself, and the ruler to impress on his administration. The language about the *Tâo* in nature is by no means so clear. While Sir Robert Douglas says that "the way" would be the best translation of *Tâo*, he immediately adds:—"But *Tâo* is more than the way. It is the way and the way-goer. It is an eternal road; along it all beings and things walk; but no being made it, for it is being itself; it is everything, and nothing and the cause and effect of all. All things originate from *Tâo*, conform to *Tâo* and to *Tâo* at last they return."

Some of these representations require modification; but no thoughtful reader of the treatise can fail to be often puzzled by what is said on the point in hand. Julien, indeed, says with truth (p. xiii.) that "it is impossible to take *Tâo* for the primordial Reason, for the sublime Intelligence, which has created and governs the world"; but many of Lâo-tsze's statements are unthinkable if there be not behind the *Tâo* the unexpressed recognition of a personal creator and ruler. Granted that he does not affirm positively the existence of such a Being, yet certainly he does not deny it, and his language even implies it. It has been said, indeed, that he denies it, and we are referred in proof to the fourth chapter:—"*Tâo* is like the emptiness of a vessel; and the use of it, we may say, must be free from all self-sufficiency. How deep and mysterious it is, as if it were the author of all things! We should make our sharpness blunt, and unravel the complications of things; we should attemper our brightness, and assimilate ourselves to the obscurity caused by dust. How still and clear is *Tâo*, a phantasm with the semblance of permanence! I do not know whose son it is. It might appear to have been before God (*Tî*)." *The Tâo and the Deity.*

The reader will not overlook the cautious and dubious manner in which the predicates of *Tâo* are stated in this remarkable passage. The author does not say that it was before God, but that "it might appear" to have been so. Nowhere else in his treatise does the nature of *Tâo* as a method or style of action come out more clearly. It has no positive existence of itself; it is but like the emptiness of a vessel, and the manifestation of it by men requires that they endeavour to free themselves from all self-sufficiency. Whence came it? It does not shock Lâo-tsze to suppose that it had a father, but he cannot tell whose son it is. And, as the feeling of its mysteriousness grows on him, he ventures to say that "it might appear to have been before God."

There is here no denial but express recognition of the existence of God, so far as it is implied in the name *Tî*, which is the personal name for the concept of heaven as the ruling power, by means of which the fathers of the Chinese people rose in prehistoric time to the idea of God. Again and again Lâo-tsze speaks of heaven just as "we do when we mean thereby the Deity who presides over heaven and earth." These last words are taken from Watters (p. 81); and, though he adds, "We must not forget that this heaven is inferior and subsequent to the mysterious *Tâo*, and was in fact produced by it," it has been shown how rash and unwarranted is the ascription of such a sentiment to "the Venerable Philosopher." He makes the *Tâo* prior to heaven and earth, which is a phrase denoting what we often call "nature," but he does not make it prior to heaven in the higher and immaterial usage of that name. The last sentence of his treatise is:—"It is the *Tâo*—the way—of Heaven to benefit and not injure; it is the *Tâo*—the way—of the sage to do and not strive."

Since Julien laid the *Tâo Teh King* fairly open to Western readers in 1842, there has been a tendency to overestimate rather than to underestimate its value as a scheme of thought and a discipline for the individual and society. There are in it lessons of unsurpassed value, such as the inculcation of simplicity, humility and self-abnegation, and especially the brief enunciation of the divine duty of returning good for ill; but there are also the regretful representations of a primitive society when men were ignorant of the rudiments of culture, and the longings for its return.

When it was thought that the treatise made known the doctrine of the Trinity, and even gave a phonetic representation of the Hebrew name for God, it was natural, even necessary, to believe that its author had had communication with more western parts of Asia, and there was much speculation about visits to India and Judaea, and even to Greece. The necessity for assuming such travels has passed away. If we can receive Sze-mâ Ch'ien's histories as trustworthy, Lâo-tsze might have heard, in the states of Chow and among the wild tribes adjacent to them, views about society and government very like his own. Ch'ien relates how an envoy came in 624 B.C.—twenty years before the date assigned to the birth of Lâo-tsze—to the court of Duke Mû of Ch'in, sent by the king of some rude hordes on the west. The duke told him of the histories, [illegible] laws which they had in the middle [illegible] were of frequent occurrence, [illegible] was secured among the wild people, who [illegible]. The envoy smiled, and replied that [illegible] were occasioned by those very things of which [illegible] that there had been a gradual degenera- [illegible] states, as their professed civilization had [illegible] since the days of the ancient sage, Hwang Ti, whereas [illegible] where there was nothing but the primitive [illegible] showed a pure virtue in their treatment of [illegible] responded to them with loyalty and good faith. [illegible] of a state," said he in conclusion, "is like a man's [illegible] single person. He rules it, and does not know how [illegible] and this was indeed the method of the sages." Lâo-tsze [illegible] to go further afield to find all that he has said about [illegible]

[illegible] confined ourselves to the Tâoism of the *Tâo Teh King* [illegible] on the religion Tâoism now existing in China, but [illegible] which did not take shape until more than five hundred years after the death of Lâo-tsze, though he now occupies the second place in its trinity of "The three Pure or Holy Ones." There is hardly a word in his treatise that savours of superstition or religion. In the works of Lieh-tsze and his earliest followers of note, we find abundance of superstitions; but their beliefs (if indeed we can say that they had beliefs) had not become embodied in any religious institu- [illegible]. When we come to the Ch'in dynasty (221–206 B.C.), we meet with a Tâoism in the shape of a search for the fairy islands of the [illegible], where the herb of immortality might be gathered. In [illegible] A.D. a magician, called Chang Tâo-ling, comes before [illegible] professor and controller of this Tâoism, preparing in [illegible] "the pill" which renewed his youth, supreme over all [illegible] destroying millions of demons by a stroke of his pencil. [illegible] books, talismans and charms, with his sword and seal, [illegible] and one of them, professing to be animated by his [illegible] the Lung-hû mountain in Kiang-si, the acknowledged [illegible] of Tâoism. But even then the system was not yet a [illegible] temples or monasteries, liturgies and forms of public [illegible] borrowed all these from Buddhism, which first obtained [illegible] in China between A.D. 65 and 70, though at least a [illegible] passed before it could be said to have free course [illegible]

[illegible] with the form of a religion, Tâoism is in reality a [illegible] of base and dangerous superstitions. Alchemy, [illegible] have dwelt and dwell under its shadow. [illegible] Holy Ones" has the title of *Thien Tsun*, "the [illegible] Honoured," taken from Buddhism, and also of *Sheng* [illegible] from the old religion of the country. The most [illegible] is not one of them, but has the title of *Yü* [illegible] "God, the Perfect King." But it would take long [illegible] celestial gods," "great gods," "divine rulers" and [illegible] been doubted whether Lâo-tsze acknowledged the [illegible] at all, but modern Tâoism is a system of the [illegible]. The science and religion of the West meet from [illegible] opposition. The "Venerable Philosopher" [illegible] have welcomed them; but he ought not to bear [illegible] the founder of the Tâoist religion. (J. Le.)

[illegible] department of Bolivia, bounded N. by [illegible] of Caupolican and El Beni, E. by El [illegible] S. by Cochabamba and Oruro and W. [illegible] Pop. (1900) 445,616, the majority of whom [illegible] sq. m. The department belongs to [illegible] and its greater part to the cold, [illegible] region. The Cordillera Real crosses it [illegible] in the snow-crowned summits of [illegible]. The west of the department includes [illegible] with about half of the lake. This [illegible] is partially barren and inhospitable, [illegible] permitting the production of little besides [illegible] *quinoa*) and barley, with a [illegible] in favoured localities. Some atten- [illegible] rearing of llamas, and a few cattle, sheep [illegible] south of Lake Titicaca. There is a [illegible] in this region, living chiefly in [illegible] of their own industry. In the [illegible] slopes, where climatic conditions [illegible] tropical, wheat, Indian corn, oats and [illegible] of the temperate zone are cultivated. [illegible] coca, rice, sugar cane, tobacco, [illegible] tropical fruits are grown, and the [illegible] and rubber. The mineral wealth [illegible] silver, tin, copper and bismuth. Tin [illegible] important of these, the principal tin mines being in the vicinity of the capital and known under the names of Huayna-Potosi, Milluni and Chocoltaga. The chief copper mines are the famous Corocoro group, about 75 m. S.S.E. of Lake Titicaca by the Desaguadero river, the principal means of transport. The output of the Corocoro mines, which also includes gold and silver, finds its way to market by boat and rail to Mollendo, and by pack animals to Tacna and rail to Arica. There are no roads in La Paz worthy of the name except the 5 m. between the capital and the "Alto," though stage-coach communication with Oruro and Chililaya has been maintained by the national government. The railway opened in 1905 between Guaqui and La Paz (54 m.) superseded the latter of these stage lines, and a railway is planned from Viacha to Oruro to supersede the other. The capital of the department is the national capital La Paz. Corocoro, near the Desaguadero river, about 75 m. S.S.E. of Lake Titicaca and 13,353 ft. above sea-level, has an estimated population (1906) of 15,000, chiefly Aymará Indians.

LA PAZ (officially La Paz de Ayacucho), the capital of Bolivia since 1898, the see of a bishopric created in 1605 and capital of the department of La Paz, on the Rio de la Paz or Rio Chuquiapo, 42 m. S.E. of Lake Titicaca (port of Chililaya) in 16° 30′ S., 68° W. Pop. (1900) 54,713, (1906, estimate) 67,235. The city is built in a deeply-eroded valley of the Cordillera Real which is believed to have formed an outlet of Lake Titicaca, and at this point descends sharply to the S.E., the river making a great bend southward and then flowing northward to the Beni. The valley is about 10 m. long and 3 m. wide, and is singularly barren and forbidding. Its precipitous sides, deeply gullied by torrential rains and diversely coloured by mineral ores, rise 1500 ft. above the city to the margin of the great plateau surrounding Lake Titicaca, and above these are the snow-capped summits of Illimani and other giants of the Bolivian Cordillera. Below, the valley is fertile and covered with vegetation, first of the temperate and then of the tropical zone. The elevation of La Paz is 12,120 ft. above sea-level, which places it within the *puna* climatic region, in which the summers are short and cold. The mean annual temperature is a little above the *puna* average, which is 54° F., the extremes ranging from 19° to 75°. Pneumonia and bronchial complaints are common, but consumption is said to be rare. The surface of the valley is very uneven, rising sharply from the river on both sides, and the transverse streets of the city are steep and irregular. At its south-eastern extremity is the Alameda, a handsome public promenade with parallel rows of exotic trees, shrubs and flowers, which are maintained with no small effort in so inhospitable a climate. The trees which seem to thrive best are the willow and eucalyptus. The streets are generally narrow and roughly paved, and there are numerous bridges across the river and its many small tributaries. The dwellings of the poorer classes are commonly built with mud walls and covered with tiles, but stone and brick are used for the better structures. The cathedral, which was begun in the 17th century when the mines of Potosi were at the height of their productiveness, was never finished because of the revolutions and the comparative poverty of the city under the republic. It faces the Plaza Mayor and is distinguished for the finely-carved stonework of its façade. Facing the same plaza are the government offices and legislative chambers. Other notable edifices and institutions are the old university of San Andrés, the San Francisco church, a national college, a seminary, a good public library and a museum rich in relics of the Inca and colonial periods. La Paz is an important commercial centre, being connected with the Pacific coast by the Peruvian railway from Mollendo to Puno (via Arequipa), and a Bolivian extension from Guaqui to the Alto de La Paz (Heights of La Paz)—the two lines being connected by a steamship service across Lake Titicaca. An electric railway 5 m. long connects the Alto de La Paz with the city, 1493 ft. below. This route is 496 m. long, and is expensive because of trans-shipments and the cost of handling cargo at Mollendo. The vicinity of La Paz abounds with mineral wealth; most important are the tin deposits of Huayna-Potosi, Milluni and Chocoltaga. The La Paz valley is auriferous, and since the foundation of the city gold has been taken from the soil washed down from the mountain sides.

La Paz was founded in 1548 by Alonzo de Mendoza on the site of an Indian village called Chuquiapu. It was called the Pueblo Nuevo de Nuestra Señora de la Paz in commemoration of the reconciliation between Pizarro and Almagro, and soon became an important colony. At the close of the war of independence (1825) it was rechristened La Paz de Ayacucho, in honour of the last decisive battle of that protracted struggle. It was made one of the four capitals of the republic, but the revolution of 1898 permanently established the seat of government here because of its accessibility, wealth, trade and political influence.

LA PÉROUSE, JEAN-FRANÇOIS DE GALAUP, Comte de (1741–c. 1788), French navigator, was born near Albi, on the 22nd of August 1741. His family name was Galaup, and La Pérouse or La Peyrouse was an addition adopted by himself from a small family estate near Albi. As a lad of eighteen he was wounded and made prisoner on board the "Formidable" when it was captured by Admiral Hawke in 1759; and during the war with England between 1778 and 1783 he served with distinction in various parts of the world, more particularly on the eastern coasts of Canada and in Hudson's Bay, where he captured Forts Prince of Wales and York (August 8th and 21st, 1782). In 1785 (August 1st) he sailed from Brest in command of the French government expedition of two vessels ("La Boussole" under La Pérouse himself, and "L'Astrolabe," under de Langle) for the discovery of the North-West Passage, vainly essayed by Cook on his last voyage, from the Pacific side. He was also charged with the further exploration of the north-west coasts of America, and the north-east coasts of Asia, of the China and Japan seas, the Solomon Islands and Australia; and he was ordered to collect information as to the whale fishery in the southern oceans and as to the fur trade in North America. He reached Mount St Elias, on the coast of Alaska, on the 23rd of June 1786. After six weeks, marked by various small discoveries, he was driven from these regions by bad weather; and after visiting the Hawaiian Islands, and discovering Necker Island (November 5th, 1786), he crossed over to Asia (Macao, January 3rd, 1787). Thence he passed to the Philippines, and so to the coasts of Japan, Korea and "Chinese Tartary," where his best results were gained. Touching at Quelpart, he reached De Castries Bay, near the modern Vladivostok, on the 28th of July 1787; and on the 2nd of August following discovered the strait, still named after him, between Sakhalin and the Northern Island of Japan. On the 7th of September he put in at Petropavlovsk in Kamchatka, where he was well received by special order of the Russian empress, Catherine II.; thence he sent home Lesseps, overland, with the journals, notes, plans and maps recording the work of the expedition. He left Avacha Bay on the 29th of September, and arrived at Mauna in the Samoan group on the 8th of December; here de Langle and ten of the crew of the "Astrolabe" were murdered. He quitted Samoa on the 14th of December, touched at the Friendly Islands and Norfolk Island and arrived in Botany Bay on the 26th of January 1788. From this place, where he interchanged courtesies with some of the English pioneers in Australia, he wrote his last letter to the French Ministry of Marine (February 7th). After this no more was heard of him and his squadron till in 1826 Captain Peter Dillon found the wreckage of what must have been the "Boussole" and the "Astrolabe" on the reefs of Vanikoro, an island to the north of the New Hebrides. In 1828 Dumont d'Urville visited the scene of the disaster and erected a monument (March 14th).

See Milet Mureau, *Voyage de la Pérouse autour du monde* (Paris, 1797) 4 vols.; Gérard, *Vies . . . des . . . marins français* (Paris, 1825), 197-200; Peter Dillon, *Narrative . . . of a Voyage in the South Seas for the Discovery of the Fate of La Pérouse* (London, 1829), 2 vols.; Dumont d'Urville, *Voyage pittoresque autour du monde*; Quoy and Paul Gaimard, *Voyage de . . . l'Astrolabe*; Domeny de Rienzi, *Océanie*; Van Tenac, *Histoire général de la marine*, iv. 258-264; *Moniteur universel*, 13th of February 1847.

LAPIDARY, and GEM CUTTING (Lat. *lapidarius*, *lapis*, a stone). The earliest examples of gem cutting and carving known (see also Gem) are the ancient engraved seals, which are of two principal types, the cylindrical or "rolling" seals of Babylonia and Assyria, suggested by a joint of the bamboo or the central whorl of a conch-like shell, and the peculiar scarabaeoid seals of Egypt. Recent researches make it appear that both these types were in use as far back as 4500 B.C., though with some variations. The jewels of Queen Zer, and other jewels consisting of cut turquoise, lapis lazuli and amethyst, found by the French mission, date from 4777 B.C. to 4515 B.C. Until about 2500 B.C., the cylinder seals bore almost wholly animal designs; then cuneiform inscriptions were added. In the 6th century B.C., the scarabaeoid type was introduced from Egypt, while the rolling seals began to give place to a new form, that of a tall cone. These, in a century or two, were gradually shortened; the hole by which they were suspended was enlarged until it could admit the finger, and in time they passed into the familiar form of seal-rings. This later type, which prevailed for a long period, usually bore Persian or Sassanian inscriptions. The scarabaeoid seals were worn as rings in Egypt apparently from the earliest times.

The most ancient of the cylinder seals were cut at first from shell, then largely from opaque stones such as diorite and serpentine. After 2500 B.C., varieties of chalcedony and milky quartz were employed, translucent and richly coloured; sometimes even rock crystal, and also frequently a beautiful compact haematite. Amazone stone, amethyst and fossil coral were used, but no specimen is believed to be known of ruby, sapphire, emerald, diamond, tourmaline or spinel.

The date of about 500 B.C. marks the beginning of a period of great artistic taste and skill in gem carving, which extended throughout the ancient civilized world, and lasted until the 3rd or 4th century A.D. Prior to this period, all the work appears to have been done by hand with a sapphire point, or else with a bow-drill; thenceforward the wheel came to be largely employed. The Greek cutters, in their best period, the 5th and 6th centuries B.C., knew the use of disks and drills, but preferred the sapphire point for their finest work, and continued to use it for two or three hundred years. Engraving by the bow-drill was introduced in Assyrian and Babylonian work as early as perhaps 3000 B.C., the earlier carving being all done with the sapphire point, which was secured in a handle for convenient application. This handwork demanded the utmost skill and delicacy of touch in the artist. The bow-drill consisted of a similar point fastened in the end of a stick, which could be rotated by means of a horizontal cross-bar attached at each end to a string wound around the stick; as the cross-bar was moved up and down, the stick was made to rotate alternately in opposite directions. This has been a frequent device for such purposes among many peoples, both ancient and modern, civilized and uncivilized. The point used by hand, and the bow-drill, were afterwards variously combined in executing such work. Another modification was the substitution for the point, in either process, of a hollow tube or drill, probably in most cases the joint of a hollow reed, whereby very accurate circles could be made, as also crescent figures and the like. This process, used with fine hard sand, has also been widely employed among many peoples. It may perhaps have been suggested by the boring of other shells by carnivorous molluscs of the *Murex* type, examples of which may be picked up on any sea-beach. It is possible that the cylinder seals were drilled in this way out of larger pieces by means of a hollow reed or bamboo, the cylinder being left as the core.

The Egyptian scarabs were an early and very characteristic type of seal cutting. The Greek gem cutters modified them by adding Greek and Etruscan symbols and talismanic signs; many of them also worked in Egypt and for Egyptians. Phoenician work shows a mixture of Assyrian and Egyptian designs; and Cypriote seals, principally on the agate gems, are known that are referred to the 9th century B.C.

Scarabs are sometimes found that have been sliced in two, and the new flat faces thus produced carved with later inscriptions and set in rings. This secondary work is of many kinds. An Assyrian cylinder in the Metropolitan Museum, New York, referred to 3000 B.C., bears such a cutting of Mediterranean [illegible] remarkable results are sometimes produced [illegible] touches of the drill, which under the glass [illegible] nevertheless yield strong effects. [illegible] seen now in many of the Japanese sketches, where a whole landscape is depicted [illegible] few simple but powerful [illegible] some of these seals may [illegible] and also that they [illegible] who could not afford [illegible] been made by [illegible] went on until in the [illegible] it had reached a very [illegible] show drill-work [illegible] is occasionally seen.

[illegible]

inclining more to a violet cast than the pyrope, and can be obtained in larger pieces. The ancient garnets, from Etruscan and Byzantine remains, some of which are flat plates set in gold, or carved with mythological designs, were probably obtained from India or perhaps from the remarkable locality for large masses of garnet in German East Africa. Many are cut with the portraits of Sassanian kings with their characteristic pearl earrings. The East Indians carve small dishes out of a single garnet.

The carving of elegant objects from transparent quartz, or rock crystal, has been carried on since the 16th century, first in Italy, by the greatest masters of the time, and afterwards in Prague, under Rudolph II., until the Thirty Years' War, when the industry was wiped out. Splendid examples of this work are in the important museums of Europe. Many of these are reproduced now in Vienna, and fine examples are included in some American museums. Among them are rock-crystal dishes several inches across, beautifully engraved in intaglio and mounted in silver with gems. Other varieties of quartz minerals, such as agate, jasper, &c., and other ornamental stones of similar hardness, are likewise wrought into all manner of art objects. Caskets, vases, ewers, coupés and animal and other fanciful forms, are familiar in these opaque and semi-transparent stones, either carved out of single masses or made of separate pieces united with gold, silver or enamel in the most artistic manner. Cellini, and other masters in the 16th and 17th centuries, vied with each other in such work.

The greatest development of agate (*q.v.*), however, has been seen in Germany, at Waldkirch in Breisgau, and especially at Idar and Oberstein on the Nahe, in Oldenburg. The industry began in the 14th century, at the neighbouring town of Freiburg, but was transferred to Waldkirch, where it is still carried on, employing about 120 men and women, the number of workmen having increased nearly threefold since the middle of the 19th century. The Idar and Oberstein industry was founded somewhat later, but is much more extensive. Mills run by water-power line the Nahe river for over 30 m., from above Kreuznach to below Idar, and gave employment in 1908 to some 5000 people—1625 lapidaries, 160 drillers, 100 engravers, 2900 cutters, &c., besides 300 jewellers and 300 dealers. The industry began here in consequence of the abundance of agates in the amygdaloid rocks of the vicinity; and it is probable that many of the Cinque Cento gems, and perhaps even some of the Roman ones, were obtained in this region. By the middle of the 18th century the best material was about exhausted, but the industry had become so firmly established that it has been kept up and increased by importing agates. In 1540 there were only three mills; in 1740, twenty-five; in 1840, fifty; in 1870, one hundred and eighty-four. Agents and prospectors are sent all over the world to procure agates and other ornamental stones, and enormous quantities are brought there and stored. The chief source of agate supply has been in Uruguay, but much has been brought from other distant lands. It was estimated that fifty thousand tons were stored at Salto in Uruguay at one time.

The grinding is done on large, horizontal wheels like grindstones, some 6 ft. in diameter and one-fourth as thick, run by water-wheels. The faces of some of these grindstones are made with grooves of different sizes so that round objects or convex surfaces can be ground very easily and rapidly. An agate ball or marble, for instance, is made from a piece broken to about the right size and held in one of these semicircular grooves until one-half of it is shaped, and then turned over and the other half ground in the same way. The polishing is done on wooden wheels, with tripoli found in the vicinity; any carving or ornamentation is then put on with a wheel-edge or a drill by skilled workmen.

In the United States the Drake Company at Sioux Falls, South Dakota, has done cutting and polishing in hard materials on a grand scale. It is here, and here only, that the agatized wood from Chalcedony Park, Arizona, has been cut and polished, large sections of tree-trunks having been made into table-tops and columns of wonderful beauty, with a polish like that of a mirror.

Much of the finest lapidary work, both on a large and a small scale, is done in Russia. Catherine II. sought to develop the precious stone resources of the Ural region, and sent thither two Italian lapidaries. This led to the founding of an industry which now employs at least a thousand people. The work is done either at the great imperial lapidary establishment at Ekaterinburg, or in the vicinity of the mines by lapidary masters, as they are called, each of whom has his peculiar style. The products are sold to dealers at the great Russian fairs at Nishniy Novgorod, Moscow and Ekaterinburg. The imperial works at the last-named place have command of an immense water-power, and are on such a scale that great masses of hard stones can be worked as marble is in other countries. Much of the machinery is primitive, but the applications are ingenious and the results unsurpassed anywhere. The work done is of several classes, ranging from the largest and most massive to the smallest and most delicate. There is (1) the cutting of facetted gems, as topaz, aquamarine, amethyst, &c., from the mines of the Ural, and of other gem-stones also; this is largely done by means of the cadrans, a small machine held in the hand, by which the angle of the facets can be adjusted readily when once the stone has been set, and which produces work of great beauty and accuracy. Then there is (2) a vast variety of ornamental objects, large and small, some weighing 2000 lb and over, and requiring years to complete; they are made from the opaque minerals of the Ural and Siberia—malachite, rhodonite, lapis-lazuli, aventurine and jasper. A peculiar type of work is (3) the production of beautiful groups of fruit, flowers and leaves, in stones selected to match exactly the colour of each object represented. These are chosen with great care and skill, somewhat as in the Florentine mosaics, not to produce a flat inlaid picture, however, but a perfect reproduction of form, size and colour. These groups are carved and polished from hard stones, whereas the Florentine mosaic work includes many substances that are much softer, as glass, shell, &c.

Enormous masses of material are brought to these works; the supply of rhodonite, jade, jaspers of various colours, &c., sometimes amounting to hundreds of tons. One mass of Kalkansky jasper weighed nearly 9 tons, and a mass of rhodonite above 50 tons; the latter required a week of sledging, with ninety horses, to bring it from the quarry, only 14 m. from the works. About seventy-five men are employed, at twenty-five roubles a month (£2, 11s. 6d.), and ten boys, who earn from two to ten roubles (4s. to £1). A training school is connected with the works, where over fifty boys are pupils; on graduating they may remain as government lapidaries or set up on their own account.

There are two other great Russian imperial establishments of the same kind. One of these, founded by Catherine II., is at Peterhof, a short distance from the capital; it is a large building fitted up with imperial elegance. Here are made all the designs and models for the work done at Ekaterinburg; these are returned and strictly preserved. In the Peterhof works are to be seen the largest and most remarkable achievements of the lapidarian art, vases and pedestals and columns of immense size, made from the hardest and most elegant stones, often requiring the labour of years for their completion. The third great establishment is at Kolyvan, in Siberia, bearing a like relation to the minerals and gem-stones of the Altai region that the works of Ekaterinburg do to the Ural. The three establishments are conducted at large expense, from the private revenue of the tsar. The Russian emperors have always taken special interest in lapidary work, and the products of these establishments have made that country famous throughout the world. The immense monolithic columns of the Hermitage and of St Isaac's Cathedral, of polished granite and other hard and elegant stones, are among the triumphs of modern architectural work; and the Alexander column at St Petersburg is a single polished shaft, 13 ft. in diameter and 82 ft. in height, of the red Finland granite.

The finest lapidary work of modern France is done at Moulin la Vacherie Saint Simon, Seine-et-Marne, where some seventy-five of the most skilful artisans are engaged. The products are all manner of ornamental objects of every variety of beautiful stone, all finished with absolute perfection of detail. Columns and other ornaments of porphyry and the like, of ancient workmanship, are brought hither from Egypt and elsewhere, and recut into smaller objects for modern artistic tastes. Here, too, are made spheres of transparent quartz—"crystal balls"—up to 6 in. in diameter, the material for which is obtained in Madagascar.

A few words may be said, by way of comparison and contrast, about the lapidary art of Japan and China, especially in relation to the crystal balls, now reproduced in France and elsewhere. The tools are the simplest, and there is no machinery; but the lack of it is made up by time and patience, and by hereditary pride, as a Japanese artisan can often trace back his art through many generations continuously. To make a quartz ball, a large crystal or mass is chipped or broken into available shape, and then the piece is trimmed into a spherical form with a small steel hammer. The polishing is effected by grinding with emery and garnet-powder and plenty of water, in semi-cylindrical pieces of cast iron, of sizes varying with that of the ball to be ground, which is kept constantly turning as it is rubbed. Small balls are fixed in the end of a bamboo tube, which the worker continually revolves. The final brilliant polish is given by the hand, with rouge-powder (haematite). This process is evidently very slow, and only the cheapness of labour prevents the cost from being too great.

The spheres are now made quite freely but very differently in France, Germany and the United States. They are ground in semicircular grooves in a large horizontal wheel of hard stone, such as is used for grinding garnets at Oberstein and Idar, or else by gradually revolving them on a lathe and fitting them into hollow cylinders. Plenty of water must be used, to prevent heating and cracking. The polishing is effected on a wooden wheel with tripoli. Work of this kind is now done in the United States, in the production of the spheres and carved ornaments of rock-crystal, that is equal to any in the world. But most of the material for these supposed Japanese balls now comes from Brazil or Madagascar, and the work is done in Germany or France.

The cutting of amber is a special branch of lapidary work developed along the Baltic coast of Germany, where amber is chiefly obtained. The amber traffic dates back to prehistoric times; but the cutting industry in northern Europe cannot be definitely traced further back than the 14th century, when gilds of amber-workers were known at Bruges and Lübeck. Fine carving was also done at Königsberg as early as 1399. The latter city and Danzig have become the chief seats of the amber industry, and the business has increased immensely

[illegible] not only for all the [illegible] and even [illegible] colours

[illegible] its extreme hardness, [illegible] for use in jewelry [illegible] of the lapidary's art. [illegible] cleaved or sawed [illegible] the desired form, and [illegible] have been cut. The stages [illegible] cleavage or division; [illegible] point of fact there are four [illegible] the stone for cutting is a somewhat [illegible] are classed in four groups— [illegible]

[illegible]—Diamonds are always found as [illegible] though often irregular or [illegible] in each case is twofold: [illegible] stone possible, and (2) to remove [illegible] flaws or defects. These ends are generally [illegible] causing it to split along certain [illegible] weakness, which are parallel with [illegible] This process requires the utmost [illegible] skill on the part of the operator, as any [illegible] great loss of valuable material; hence expert [illegible] high wages. The stone is first examined [illegible] the directions of the cleavage planes, [illegible] only by an expert. The cleaver then cuts [illegible] at the place selected, with another diamond [illegible] a rather dull iron or steel edge is then laid [illegible] and a smart blow struck upon it. If all has been [illegible] the diamond divides at once in the direction [illegible] mentions knowing some one who could [illegible] like mica or talc. In this process, each of the [illegible] cement on the end of a stick or handle, [illegible] firmly while one is applied to the other.

[illegible] large and very valuable, the cleaving is a [illegible] Wollaston in 1790 made many favourable [illegible] by buying very poor-looking flawed stones and [illegible] the good parts. In the case of the immense Excelsior [illegible] carats, which was divided at Amsterdam in [illegible] splendid stones, the most elaborate [illegible] over two months was given to the work before- [illegible] models were made of the very irregular stone [illegible] ways to determine those most advan- [illegible] applied to the most remark- [illegible] ever undertaken—the cutting [illegible] diamond of 3025¾ English carats. The [illegible] be treated by the old-fashioned [illegible] precautions of every kind at [illegible] successfully accomplished after [illegible] 1908). The two [illegible] one a pendeloque or [illegible] brilliant, were given 72 [illegible] table and cullet) [illegible]

[illegible] one, still used [illegible] But a different [illegible] of sawing,[1] which is [illegible] The stone is placed in a [illegible] melted aluminium; [illegible] exposed, [illegible] or thin [illegible] phosphor [illegible] made [illegible]

cutters for centuries. Two patents were taken out, however, by different parties, with some distinctions of method. The process is much slower than hand-cleavage, but greatly diminishes the loss of material involved. It is claimed that not only can flaws or defective portions be thus easily taken off, but that any well-formed crystal of the usual octahedral shape (known in the trade as "six-point") can be divided in half very perfectly at the "girdle," making two stones, in each of which the sawed face can be used with advantage to form the "table" of a brilliant. By another method the stone is sawed at a tangent with the octahedron, and then each half into three pieces; for this Wood method a total saving of 5% is claimed. Occasionally the finest material is only a small spot in a large mass of impure material, and this is taken out by most skilful cleaving.

After the cleaving or sawing, however, the diamond is rarely yet in a form for cutting the facets, and requires considerable shaping. This rough "blocking-out" of the final form it is to assume, by removing irregularities and making it symmetrical, is called "brutage." Well-shaped and flawless crystals, indeed may not require to be cleaved, and then the brutage is the first process. Here again, the old hand methods are beginning to give place to mechanism. In either case two diamonds are taken, each fixed in cement on the end of a handle or support, and are rubbed one against the other until the irregularities are ground away and the general shape desired is attained. The old method was to do this by hand—an extremely tedious and laborious process. The machine method, invented about 1885 and first used by Field and Morse of Boston, is now used at Antwerp exclusively. In this, one diamond is fixed at the centre of a rotating apparatus, and the other, on an arm or handle, is placed so as to press steadily against the other stone at the proper angle. The rotating diamond thus becomes rounded and smoothed; the other one is then put in its place at the centre and their mutual action reversed.

At Amsterdam a hand-process is employed, which lies between the cleavage and the brutage. This consists in cutting or trimming away angles and irregularities all over the stone by means of a sharp-edged or pointed diamond, both being mounted in cement on pear-shaped handles for firm holding. This work is largely done by women. In all these processes the dust and fragments are caught and carefully saved.

2. *Cutting and Setting.*—The next process is that of cutting the facets; but an intervening step is the fixing or "setting" of the stone for that purpose. This is done by embedding it in a fusible alloy, melting at 440° Fahr., in a little cup-shaped depression on the end of a handle, the whole being called a "dop." Only the portion to be ground off is left exposed; and two such mounted diamonds are then rubbed against each other until a face is produced. This is the work of the cutter; it is very laborious, and requires great care and skill. The hands must be protected with leather gloves. The powder produced is carefully saved, as in the former processes, for use in the final polishing. When one face has been produced, the alloy is softened by heating, and the stone re-set for grinding another surface; and as this process is necessary for every face cut, it must be repeated many times for each stone. An improved dop has lately been devised in which the diamond is held by a system of claws so that all this heating and resetting can, it is claimed, be obviated, and the cutting completed with only two changes.

3. *Polishing.*—The faces having thus been cut, the last stage is the polishing. This is done upon horizontal iron wheels called "skaifs," made to rotate up to 2500 revolutions per minute. The diamond-powder saved in the former operations, and also made by crushing very inferior diamonds, here comes into use as the only material for polishing. It is applied with oil, and the stones are fixed in a "dop" in much the same way as in the cutting process. Again, the utmost skill and watchfulness are necessary, as the angles of the faces must be mathematically exact, in order to yield the best effects by refraction and reflection of light, and their sizes must be accurately regulated to pr[illegible]try of the stone. In this process, also,

the old hand method is already replaced in part by an improved device whereby the diamond is held by adjustable claws, on a base that can be rotated, so as to apply it in any desired position. By this means the time and trouble of repeated re-setting in the dop are saved, as well as the liability to injury from the heating and cooling; the services of special "setters" are also made needless.

The rapid development of mechanical devices for the several stages of diamond cutting has already greatly influenced the art. A very interesting comparison was brought out in the thirteenth report of the American Commissioner of Labour, as to the aspects and relations of hand-work and machinery in this branch of industry. It appeared from the data gathered that the advantage lay with machinery as to time and with hand-work as to cost, in the ratios respectively of 1 to 3·38 and 1·76 to 1. In other words, about half the gain in time is lost by increased expense in the use of machine methods. A great many devices and applications have been developed within the last few years, owing to the immense increase in the production of diamonds from the South African mines, and their consequent widespread use.

History of Diamond Cutting.—The East Indian diamonds, many of which are doubtless very ancient, were polished in the usual Oriental fashion by merely rounding off the angles. Among church jewels in Europe are a few diamonds of unknown age and source, cut four-sided, with a table above and a pyramid below. Several cut diamonds are recorded among the treasures of Louis of Anjou in the third quarter of the 14th century. But the first definite accounts of diamond polishing are early in the century following, when one Hermann became noted for such work in Paris. The modern method of "brilliant" cutting, however, is generally ascribed to Louis de Berquem, of Bruges, who in 1475 cut several celebrated diamonds sent to him by Charles the Bold, duke of Burgundy. He taught this process to many pupils, who afterwards settled in Antwerp and Amsterdam, which have been the chief centres of diamond cutting ever since. Peruzzi was the artist who worked out the theory of the well-proportioned brilliant of 58 facets. Some very fine work was done early in London also, but most of the workmen were Jews, who, being objectionable in England, finally betook themselves to Amsterdam and Antwerp. Efforts have been lately made to re-establish the art in London, where, as the great diamond mart of the world, it should peculiarly belong.

The same unwise policy was even more marked in Portugal. That nation had its colonial possessions in India, following the voyages and discoveries of Da Gama, and thus became the chief importer of diamonds into Europe. Early in the 18th century, also, the diamond-mines were discovered in Brazil, which was then likewise a Portuguese possession; thus the whole diamond product of the world came to Portugal, and there was naturally developed in Lisbon an active industry of cutting and polishing diamonds. But in time the Jews were forced away, and went to Holland and Belgium, where diamond cutting has been concentrated since the middle of the 18th century.

It is of interest to trace the recent endeavours to establish diamond cutting in the United States. The pioneer in this movement was Henry D. Morse of Boston, associated with James W. Yerrington of New York. He opened a diamond-cutting establishment about 1860 and carried it on for some years, training a number of young men and women, who became the best cutters in the country. But the chief importance of his work lay in its superior quality. So long had it been a monopoly of the Dutch and Belgians that it was declining into a mere mechanical trade. Morse studied the diamond scientifically and taught his pupils how important mathematical exactitude in cutting was to the beauty and value of the gem. He thus attained a perfection rarely seen before, and gave a great stimulus to the art. Shops were opened in London as well, in consequence of Morse's success; and many valuable diamonds were recut in the United States after his work became known. This fact in turn reacted upon the cutter abroad, especially in France and Switzerland; and thus the general standard of the art was greatly advanced.

Diamond cutting in the United States is now a well-established industry. From 1882 to 1885 a number of American jewelers undertook such work, but for various reasons it was not found practicable then. Ten years later, however, there were fifteen firms engaged in diamond cutting, giving employment to nearly 150 men in the various processes involved. In the year 1894 a number of European diamond workers came over; some foreign capital became engaged; and a rapid development of diamond cutting took place. This movement was caused by the low tariff on uncut diamonds as compared with that on cut stones. It went so far as to be felt seriously abroad; but in a year or two it declined, owing partly to strikes and partly to legal questions as to the application of some of the tariff provisions. At the close of 1895, however, there were still some fourteen establishments in and near New York, employing about 500 men. Since then the industry has gradually developed. Many of the European diamond workers who came over to America remained and carried on their art; and the movement then begun has become permanent. New York is now recognized as one of the chief diamond-cutting centres; there are some 500 cutters, and the quality of work done is fully equal, if not superior, to any in the Old World. So well is this fact established that American-cut diamonds are exported and sold in Europe to a considerable and an increasing extent.

In the Brazilian diamond region of Minas Geraes an industry of cutting has grown up since 1875. Small mills are run by water power, and the machinery, as well as the methods, are from Holland. This Brazilian diamond work is done both well and cheaply, and supplies the local market.

The leading position in diamond working still belongs to Amsterdam, where the number of persons engaged in the industry has trebled since about 1875, in consequence of the enormous increase in the world's supply of diamonds. The number now amounts to 15,000, about one-third of whom are actual cleavers, cutters, polishers, &c. The number of cutting establishments in Amsterdam is about seventy, containing some 7000 mills.

Antwerp comes next with about half as many mills and a total of some 4500 persons engaged in all departments, including about seventy women. These are distributed among thirty-five or forty establishments. A majority of the workers are Belgians, but there are many Dutch, Poles and Austro-Hungarians, principally Jews. Among these numerous employees there is much opportunity for dishonesty, and but little surveillance, actual or possible; yet losses from this cause are almost unknown. The wages paid are good, averaging from £2, 9s. 6d. to £2, 17s. 6d. a week. Sorters receive from 28s. to £2; cutters from £2, 9s. 6d to £3, 6s., and cleavers from £3, 14s. upwards.

With the recent introduction of electricity in diamond cutting there has been a revolution in that industry. Whereas formerly wheels were made to revolve by steam, they are now placed in direct connexion with electric motors, although there is not a motor to each machine. The saws for slitting the diamond can thus be made to revolve much more rapidly, and there is a cleanliness and a speed about the work never before attained. (C. F. K.)

LAPILLI (pl. of Ital. *lapillo*, from Lat. *lapillus*, dim. of *lapis*, a stone), a name applied to small fragments of lava ejected from a volcano. They are generally subangular in shape and vesicular in structure, varying in size from a pea to a walnut. In the Neapolitan dialect the word becomes *rapilli*—a form sometimes used by English writers on volcanoes. (See VOLCANOES.)

LAPIS LAZULI, or azure stone,[1] a mineral substance valued for decorative purposes in consequence of the fine blue colour which it usually presents. It appears to have been the sapphire of ancient writers: thus Theophrastus describes the *σάπφειρος* as being spotted with gold-dust, a description quite inappropriate to modern sapphire, but fully applicable to lapis lazuli, for this stone frequently contains disseminated particles of iron-pyrites of gold-like appearance. Pliny, too, refers to the *sapphirus* as a stone sprinkled with specks of gold; and possibly an allusion to the same character may be found in Job xxviii. 6. The Hebrew *sappir*, denoting a stone in the High Priest's breastplate, was probably lapis lazuli, as acknowledged in the Revised Version of the Bible. With the ancient Egyptians lapis lazuli was a favourite stone for amulets and ornaments such as scarabs; it was also used to a limited extent by the Assyrians and Babylonians for cylinder seals. It has been suggested that the Egyptians obtained it from Persia in exchange for their emeralds. When the lapis lazuli contains pyrites, the brilliant spots in the deep blue matrix invite comparison with the stars in the firmament. The stone seems to have been sometimes called by ancient writers *κύανος*. It was a favourite material with the Italians of the *Cinquecento* for vases, small busts and other ornaments. Magnificent examples of the decorative use of lapis lazuli are to be seen in St Petersburg, notably in the columns of St Isaac's cathedral. The beautiful blue colour of lapis lazuli led to its employment, when ground and levigated, as a valuable pigment known as ultramarine (*q.v.*), a substance now practically displaced by a chemical product (artificial ultramarine).

Lapis lazuli occurs usually in compact masses, with a finely granular structure; and occasionally, but only as a great rarity,

[1] The Med. Gr. *λαζούριον*, Med. Lat. *lazurius* or *lazulus*, as the names of this mineral substance, were adaptations of the Arab. *al-lazward*, Pers. *lājward*, blue colour, lapis lazuli. The same word appears in Med. Lat. as *azura*, whence O.F. *azur*, Eng. "azure," blue, particularly used of that colour in heraldry (*q.v.*) and represented conventionally in black and white by horizontal lines.

[illegible] iron. Its specific [illegible] 5, so that being [illegible] to lose its lustre [illegible] azure or rich [illegible] violet and even red [illegible] colour is sometimes [illegible] illumination [illegible] black. The mineral [illegible] edges.

[illegible] variation in composition [illegible] as to its homogeneity. [illegible] microscopic studies of L. H. [illegible] who found that sections [illegible] minerals, but it was reserved [illegible] H. Bäckström, of Christiania, [illegible] and subject them to analysis, [illegible] true constitution of lapis lazuli, and [illegible] rather than a definite mineral species. [illegible] part of most lapis lazuli is a blue mineral allied to [illegible] crystallized in the cubic system, which Brögger [illegible] as lazurite, but this is intimately associated with [illegible] related mineral which has long been known as haüyne, [illegible] The lazurite, sometimes regarded as true lapis [illegible] a sulphur-bearing sodum and aluminium silicate, [illegible] the formula: $Na_4(NaS_3Al)Al_2(SiO_4)_3$. As the lazurite and the haüynite seem to occur in molecular intermixture, [illegible] kinds of lapis lazuli are formed; and it has been proposed to distinguish some of them as lazurite-lapis and haüyne-lapis, according as one or the other mineral prevails. The lazurite of lapis lazuli is to be carefully distinguished from lazulite, an aluminium-magnesium phosphate, related to turquoise. In addition to the blue cubic minerals in lapis lazuli, the following minerals have also been found: a non-ferriferous diopside, an amphibole called, from the Russian mineralogist, koksharovite, orthoclase, plagioclase, a muscovite-like mica, apatite, titanite, zircon, calcite and pyrite. The calcite seems to form in some cases a great part of the lapis; and the pyrite, which may occur in patches, is often altered to limonite.

Lapis lazuli usually occurs in crystalline limestone, and seems to be a product of contact metamorphism. It is recorded from Persia, Tartary, Tibet and China, but many of the localities are vague and some doubtful. The best known and probably the most important locality is in Badakshan. There it occurs in limestone, in the valley of the river Kokcha, a tributary to the Oxus, south of Firgamu. The mines were visited by Marco Polo in 1271, by J. B. Fraser in 1825, and by Captain John Wood in 1837–1838. The rock is split by aid of fire. Three varieties of the lapis lazuli are recognized by the miners: *nili* of indigo-blue colour, *asmani* sky-blue, and *sabzi* of green tint. Another locality for lapis lazuli is in Siberia near the western extremity of Lake Baikal, where it occurs in limestone at its contact with granite. Fine masses of lapis lazuli occur in the Andes, in the vicinity of Ovalle, Chile. In Europe lapis lazuli is found as a rarity in the peperino of Latium, near Rome, and in the ejected blocks of Monte Somma, Vesuvius. (F. W. R.*)

LAPITHAE, a mythical race, whose home was in Thessaly in the valley of the Peneus. The genealogies make them a kindred race with the Centaurs, their king Peirithoüs being the son, and the Centaurs the grandchildren (or sons) of Ixion. The best-known legends with which they are connected are those of Ixion (*q.v.*) and the battle with the Centaurs (*q.v.*). A well-known Lapith was Caeneus, said to have been originally a girl named Caenis, the favourite of Poseidon, who changed her into a man and made her invulnerable (Ovid, *Metam.* xii. 146 ff). In the Centaur battle, having been crushed by rocks and trunks of trees, he was changed into a bird; or he disappeared into the depths of the earth unharmed. According to some, the Lapithae are representatives of the giants of fable, or spirits of the storm; according to others, they are a semi-legendary, semi-historical race, like the Myrmidons and other Thessalian tribes. The Greek sculptors of the school of Pheidias conceived of the battle of the Lapithae and Centaurs as a struggle between mankind and mischievous monsters, and symbolical of the great conflict between the Greeks and Persians. Sidney Colvin (*Journ. Hellen. Stud.* i. 64) explains it as a contest of the physical powers of nature, and the mythical expression of the terrible effects of swollen waters.

LA PLACE (Lat. *Placaeus*), **JOSUÉ DE** (1606?–1665), French Protestant divine, was born in Brittany. He studied and afterwards taught philosophy at Saumur. In 1625 he became pastor of the Reformed Church at Nantes, and in 1632 was appointed professor of theology at Saumur, where he had as his colleagues, appointed at the same time, Moses Amyraut and Louis Cappell. In 1640 he published a work, *Theses theologicae de statu hominis lapsi ante gratiam*, which was looked upon with some suspicion as containing liberal ideas about the doctrine of original sin. The view that the original sin of Adam was not imputed to his descendants was condemned at the synod of Charenton (1645), without special reference being made to La Place, whose position perhaps was not quite clear. As a matter of fact La Place distinguished between a direct and indirect imputation, and after his death his views, as well as those of Amyraut, were rejected in the *Formula consensus* of 1675. He died on the 17th of August 1665.

La Place's defence was published with the title *Disputationes academicae* (3 vols., 1649–1651; and again in 1665); his work *De imputatione primi peccati Adami* in 1655. A collected edition of his works appeared at Franeker in 1699, and at Aubencit in 1702.

LAPLACE, PIERRE SIMON, Marquis de (1749–1827), French mathematician and astronomer, was born at Beaumont-en-Auge in Normandy, on the 28th of March 1749. His father was a small farmer, and he owed his education to the interest excited by his lively parts in some persons of position. His first distinctions are said to have been gained in theological controversy, but at an early age he became mathematical teacher in the military school of Beaumont, the classes of which he had attended as an extern. He was not more than eighteen when, armed with letters of recommendation, he approached J. B. d'Alembert, then at the height of his fame, in the hope of finding a career in Paris. The letters remained unnoticed, but Laplace was not crushed by the rebuff. He wrote to the great geometer a letter on the principles of mechanics, which evoked an immediate and enthusiastic response. "You," said d'Alembert to him, "needed no introduction; you have recommended yourself; my support is your due." He accordingly obtained for him an appointment as professor of mathematics in the École Militaire of Paris, and continued zealously to forward his interests.

Laplace had not yet completed his twenty-fourth year when he entered upon the course of discovery which earned him the title of "the Newton of France." Having in his first published paper [1] shown his mastery of analysis, he proceeded to apply its resources to the great outstanding problems in celestial mechanics. Of these the most conspicuous was offered by the opposite inequalities of Jupiter and Saturn, which the emulous efforts of L. Euler and J. L. Lagrange had failed to bring within the bounds of theory. The discordance of their results incited Laplace to a searching examination of the whole subject of planetary perturbations, and his maiden effort was rewarded with a discovery which constituted, when developed and completely demonstrated by his own further labours and those of his illustrious rival Lagrange, the most important advance made in physical astronomy since the time of Newton. In a paper read before the Academy of Sciences, on the 10th of February 1773 (*Mém. présentés par divers savans*, tom. vii., 1776), Laplace announced his celebrated conclusion of the invariability of planetary mean motions, carrying the proof as far as the cubes of the eccentricities and inclinations. This was the first and most important step in the establishment of the stability of the solar system. It was followed by a series of profound investigations, in which Lagrange and Laplace alternately surpassed and supplemented each other in assigning limits of variation to the several elements of the planetary orbits. The analytical tournament closed with the communication to the Academy by Laplace,

[1] "Recherches sur le calcul intégral," *Mélanges de la Soc. Roy. de Turin* (1766–1769).

in 1787, of an entire group of remarkable discoveries. It would be difficult, in the whole range of scientific literature, to point to a memoir of equal brilliancy with that published (divided into three parts) in the volumes of the Academy for 1784, 1785 and 1786. The long-sought cause of the "great inequality" of Jupiter and Saturn was found in the near approach to commensurability of their mean motions; it was demonstrated in two elegant theorems, independently of any except the most general considerations as to mass, that the mutual action of the planets could never largely affect the eccentricities and inclinations of their orbits; and the singular peculiarities detected by him in the Jovian system were expressed in the so-called "laws of Laplace." He completed the theory of these bodies in a treatise published among the Paris *Memoirs* for 1788 and 1789; and the striking superiority of the tables computed by J. B. J. Delambre from the data there supplied marked the profit derived from the investigation by practical astronomy. The year 1787 was rendered further memorable by Laplace's announcement on the 19th of November (*Memoirs*, 1786), of the dependence of lunar acceleration upon the secular changes in the eccentricity of the earth's orbit. The last apparent anomaly, and the last threat of instability, thus disappeared from the solar system.

With these brilliant performances the first period of Laplace's scientific career may be said to have closed. If he ceased to make striking discoveries in celestial mechanics, it was rather their subject-matter than his powers that failed. The general working of the great machine was now laid bare, and it needed a further advance of knowledge to bring a fresh set of problems within reach of investigation. The time had come when the results obtained in the development and application of the law of gravitation by three generations of illustrious mathematicians might be presented from a single point of view. To this task the second period of Laplace's activity was devoted. As a monument of mathematical genius applied to the celestial revolutions, the *Mécanique céleste* ranks second only to the *Principia* of Newton.

The declared aim of the author [1] was to offer a complete solution of the great mechanical problem presented by the solar system, and to being theory to coincide so closely with observation that empirical equations should no longer find a place in astronomical tables. His success in both respects fell little short of his lofty ideal. The first part of the work (2 vols. 4to, Paris, 1799) contains methods for calculating the movements of translation and rotation of the heavenly bodies, for determining their figures, and resolving tidal problems; the second, especially dedicated to the improvement of tables, exhibits in the third and fourth volumes (1802 and 1805) the application of these formulae; while a fifth volume, published in three instalments, 1823–1825, comprises the results of Laplace's latest researches, together with a valuable history of progress in each separate branch of his subject. In the delicate task of apportioning his own large share of merit, he certainly does not err on the side of modesty; but it would perhaps be as difficult to produce an instance of injustice, as of generosity in his estimate of others. Far more serious blame attaches to his all but total suppression in the body of the work—and the fault pervades the whole of his writings—of the names of his predecessors and contemporaries. Theorems and formulae are appropriated wholesale without acknowledgment, and a production which may be described as the organized result of a century of patient toil presents itself to the world as the offspring of a single brain. The *Mécanique céleste* is, even to those most conversant with analytical methods, by no means easy reading. J. B. Biot, who assisted in the correction of its proof sheets, remarked that it would have extended, had the demonstrations been fully developed, to eight or ten instead of five volumes; and he saw at times the author himself obliged to devote an hour's labour to recovering the dropped links in the chain of reasoning covered by the recurring formula. "Il est aisé à voir." [2]

The *Exposition du système du monde* (Paris, 1796) has been styled by Arago "the *Mécanique céleste* disembarrassed of its analytical paraphernalia." Conclusions are not merely stated in it, but the methods pursued for their attainment are indicated. It has the strength of an analytical treatise, the charm of a popular dissertation. The style is lucid and masterly, and the summary of astronomical history with which it terminates has been reckoned one of the masterpieces of the language. To this linguistic excellence the writer owed the place accorded to him in 1816 in the Academy, of which institution he became president in the following year. The famous "nebular hypothesis" of Laplace made its appearance in the *Système du monde*. Its being relegated to a note (vii.), and propounded "Avec la défiance que doit inspirer tout ce qui n'est point un résultat de l'observation ou du calcul," it is plain, from the complacency with which he recurred to it [3] at a later date, that he regarded the speculation with considerable interest. That it formed the starting-point, and largely prescribed the course of thought on the subject of planetary origin is due to the simplicity of its assumptions, and the clearness of the mechanical principles involved, rather than to any cogent evidence of its truth. It is curious that Laplace, while bestowing more attention than they deserved on the crude conjectures of Buffon, seems to have been unaware that he had been, to some extent, anticipated by Kant, who had put forward in 1755, in his *Allgemeine Naturgeschichte*, a true though defective nebular cosmogony.

The career of Laplace was one of scarcely interrupted prosperity. Admitted to the Academy of Sciences as an associate in 1773, he became a member in 1785, having, about a year previously, succeeded E. Bezout as examiner to the royal artillery. During an access of revolutionary suspicion, he was removed from the commission of weights and measures; but the slight was quickly effaced by new honours. He was one of the first members, and became president of the Bureau of Longitudes, took a prominent place at the Institute (founded in 1796), professed analysis at the École Normale, and aided in the organization of the decimal system. The publication of the *Mécanique céleste* gained him world-wide celebrity, and his name appeared on the lists of the principal scientific associations of Europe, including the Royal Society. But scientific distinctions by no means satisfied his ambition. He aspired to the rôle of a politician, and has left a memorable example of genius degraded to servility for the sake of a riband and a title. The ardour of his republican principles gave place, after the 18th Brumaire, to devotion towards the first consul, a sentiment promptly rewarded with the post of minister of the interior. His incapacity for affairs was, however, so flagrant that it became necessary to supersede him at the end of six weeks, when Lucien Bonaparte became his successor. "He brought into the administration," said Napoleon, "the spirit of the infinitesimals." His failure was consoled by elevation to the senate, of which body he became chancellor in September 1803. He was at the same time named grand officer of the Legion of Honour, and obtained in 1813 the same rank in the new order of Reunion. The title of count he had acquired on the creation of the empire. Nevertheless he cheerfully gave his voice in 1814 for the dethronement of his patron, and his "suppleness" merited a seat in the chamber of peers, and, in 1817, the dignity of a marquisate. The memory of these tergiversations is perpetuated in his writings. The first edition of the *Système du monde* was inscribed to the Council of Five Hundred; to the third volume of the *Mécanique céleste* (1802) was prefixed the declaration that, of all the truths contained in the work, that most precious to the author was the expression of his gratitude and devotion towards the "pacificator of Europe"; upon which noteworthy protestation the suppression in the editions of the *Théorie des probabilités* subsequent to the restoration, of the original dedication to the emperor formed a fitting commentary.

During the later years of his life, Laplace lived much at Arcueil, where he had a country-place adjoining that of his friend C. L. Berthollet. With his co-operation the Société d'Arcueil was formed, and he occasionally contributed to its *Memoirs*. In this peaceful retirement he pursued his studies with unabated ardour, and received with uniform courtesy distinguished visitors from all parts of the world. Here, too, he died, attended by his physician, Dr Majendie, and his mathematical coadjutor, Alexis Bouvard, on the 5th of March 1827. His last words were: "Ce que nous connaissons est peu de chose, ce que nous ignorons est immense."

Expressions occur in Laplace's private letters inconsistent

[1] "Plan de l'Ouvrage," *Œuvres*, tom. i. p. 1.

[2] *Journal des savants* (1850).

[3] *Méc. cél.*, tom. v. p. 346.

with the atheistical opinions he is commonly believed to have held. His character, notwithstanding the egotism by which it was disfigured, had an amiable and engaging side. Young men of science found in him an active benefactor. His relations with these "adopted children of his thought" possessed a singular charm of affectionate simplicity; their intellectual progress and material interests were objects of equal solicitude to him, and he demanded in return only diligence in the pursuit of knowledge. Biot relates that, when he himself was beginning his career, Laplace introduced him at the Institute for the purpose of explaining his supposed discovery of equations of mixed differences, and afterwards showed him, under a strict pledge of secrecy, the papers, then yellow with age, in which he had long before obtained the same results. This instance of [illegible] is the more worthy of record that it formed a marked exception to Laplace's usual course. Between him and A. M. Legendre there was a feeling of "more than coldness," owing to his [illegible], with scant acknowledgment, of the fruits of the other's labours; and Dr Thomas Young counted himself, rightly or wrongly, amongst the number of those similarly aggrieved by him. With Lagrange, on the other hand, he always remained on the best of terms. Laplace left a son, Charles Emile Pierre Joseph Laplace (1789–1874), who succeeded to his title, and rose to the rank of general in the artillery.

It might be said that Laplace was a great mathematician by the original structure of his mind, and became a great discoverer through the [illegible] sentiment which animated it. The regulated [illegible] with which he regarded the system of nature was [illegible] first to last. It can be traced in his earliest essay, [illegible] the ravings of his final illness. By it his extra[illegible] analytical powers became strictly subordinated to [illegible]. To this lofty quality of intellect he [illegible] sagacity in perceiving analogies, and in detecting [illegible] that lay concealed in his formulae, and a tenacity [illegible] by which problems, once seized, were held fast, [illegible] until they yielded up their solutions. In every [illegible] astronomy, accordingly, deep traces of his [illegible]. "He would have completed the science of the [illegible] Fourier remarked," had the science been capable [illegible]

[illegible] that he first examined the conditions of stability [illegible] by Saturn's rings, pointed out the necessity for [illegible] for it a period ($10^h 33^m$) virtually identical [illegible] by the observations of Herschel; that he [illegible] in the solar system of an invariable plane such [illegible] the products of the planetary masses by the pro[illegible] described by their radii vectores in a given [illegible] and made notable advances in the theory of [illegible] tom. iv. p. 258), besides construct[illegible] for the barometrical determination of [illegible] p. 324). His removal of the considerable [illegible] actual and Newtonian velocities of sound,[1] [illegible] the increase of elasticity due to the heat of [illegible] have sufficed to illustrate a lesser name. [illegible] his notice, and he announced in [illegible] the subject in a separate work. With [illegible] series of experiments on specific [illegible] of which the "ice calorimeter" was [illegible] jointly to the *Memoirs* of the [illegible] development of electricity by evapora[illegible] the first to offer a complete analysis [illegible] a definite hypothesis—that of forces [illegible]"; and he made strenuous but [illegible] phenomena of light on an identical [illegible] his that chemical affinity and [illegible] be included under the same [illegible] recalcitrance to this cherished [illegible] theory of light was distasteful to [illegible]

[illegible] equilibrium of a rotating fluid [illegible] of Laplace. His first memoir [illegible] 1773, when he was only twenty-[illegible] twenty-eight. The results of his [illegible] by him as "un des points [illegible]"—are embodied in the [illegible] the most remarkable proofs [illegible] Legendre and d'Alembert [illegible] problem, confining their attention to the possible figures which would satisfy the conditions of equilibrium. Laplace treated the subject from the point of view of the gradual aggregation and cooling of a mass of matter, and demonstrated that the form which such a mass would ultimately assume must be an ellipsoid of revolution whose equator was determined by the primitive plane of maximum areas.

The related subject of the attraction of spheroids was also signally promoted by him. Legendre, in 1783, extended Maclaurin's theorem concerning ellipsoids of revolution to the case of any spheroid of revolution where the attracted point, instead of being limited to the axis or equator, occupied any position in space; and Laplace, in his treatise *Théorie du mouvement et de la figure elliptique des planètes* (published in 1784), effected a still further generalization by proving, what had been suspected by Legendre, that the theorem was equally true for any confocal ellipsoids. Finally, in a celebrated memoir, *Théorie des attractions des sphéroïdes et de la figure des planètes*, published in 1785 among the Paris *Memoirs* for the year 1782, although written after the treatise of 1784, Laplace treated exhaustively the general problem of the attraction of any spheroid upon a particle situated outside or upon its surface.

These researches derive additional importance from having introduced two powerful engines of analysis for the treatment of physical problems, Laplace's coefficients and the potential function. By his discovery that the attracting force in any direction of a mass upon a particle could be obtained by the direct process of differentiating a single function, Laplace laid the foundations of the mathematical sciences of heat, electricity and magnetism. The expressions designated by Dr Whewell, Laplace's coefficients (see SPHERICAL HARMONICS) were definitely introduced in the memoir of 1785 on attractions above referred to. In the figure of the earth, the theory of attractions, and the sciences of electricity and magnetism this powerful calculus occupies a prominent place. C. F. Gauss in particular employed it in the calculation of the magnetic potential of the earth, and it received new light from Clerk Maxwell's interpretation of harmonics with reference to poles on the sphere.

Laplace nowhere displayed the massiveness of his genius more conspicuously than in the theory of probabilities. The science which B. Pascal and P. de Fermat had initiated he brought very nearly to perfection; but the demonstrations are so involved, and the omissions in the chain of reasoning so frequent, that the *Théorie analytique* (1812) is to the best mathematicians a work requiring most arduous study. The theory of probabilities, which Laplace described as common sense expressed in mathematical language, engaged his attention from its importance in physics and astronomy; and he applied his theory, not only to the ordinary problems of chances, but also to the inquiry into the causes of phenomena, vital statistics and future events.

The device known as the method of least squares, for reducing numerous equations of condition to the number of unknown quantities to be determined, had been adopted as a practically convenient rule by Gauss and Legendre; but Laplace first treated it as a problem in probabilities, and proved by an intricate and difficult course of reasoning that it was also the most advantageous, the mean of the probabilities of error in the determination of the elements being thereby reduced to a minimum.

Laplace published in 1779 the method of generating functions, the foundation of his theory of probabilities, and the first part of his *Théorie analytique* is devoted to the exposition of its principles, which in their simplest form consist in treating the successive values of any function as the coefficients in the expansion of another function with reference to a different variable. The latter is therefore called the generating function of the former. A *direct* and an *inverse* calculus is thus created, the object of the former being to determine the coefficients from the generating function, of the latter to discover the generating function from the coefficients. The one is a problem of interpolation, the other a step towards the solution of an equation in finite differences. The method, however, is now obsolete owing to the more extended facilities afforded by the calculus of operations.

The first formal proof of Lagrange's theorem for the development in a series of an implicit function was furnished by Laplace, who gave to it an extended generality. He also showed that every equation of an even degree must have at least one real quadratic factor, reduced the solution of linear differential equations to definite integrals, and furnished an elegant method by which the linear partial differential equation of the second order might be solved. He was also the first to consider the difficult problems involved in equations of mixed differences, and to prove that an equation in finite differences of the first degree and the second order might always be converted into a continued fraction.

In 1842, the works of Laplace being nearly out of print, his widow was about to sell a farm to procure funds for a new impression, when the government of Louis Philippe took the matter in hand. A grant of 40,000 francs having been obtained from the chamber, a national edition was issued in seven 4to vols., bearing the title *Œuvres de Laplace* (1843–1847). The *Mécanique céleste* with its four supplements occupies the first 5 vols., the 6th contains the *Système du monde*, and the 7th the *Th. des probabilités*, to which the more popular *Essai philosophique* forms an introduction. Of the four supplements added by the author (1816–1825) he tells us that the problems in the last were contributed by his son. An enumeration of Laplace's memoirs and papers (about one hundred in number) is rendered superfluous by their embodiment in his principal works. The *Th. des prob.* was first published in 1812, the *Essai* in 1814; and both works as well as the *Système du monde* went through repeated editions. An English version of the *Essai* appeared in New York in 1902. Laplace's first separate work, *Théorie du mouvement et de la figure elliptique des planètes* (1784), was published at the expense of President Bochard de Saron. The *Précis de l'histoire de l'astronomie* (1821), formed the fifth book of the 5th edition of the *Système du monde*. An English translation, with copious elucidatory notes, of the first 4 vols. of the *Mécanique céleste*, by N. Bowditch, was published at Boston, U.S. (1829–1839), in 4 vols. 4to.; a compendium of certain portions of the same work by Mrs Somerville appeared in 1831, and a German version of the first 2 vols. by Burckhardt at Berlin in 1801. English translations of the *Système du monde* by J. Pond and H. H. Harte were published, the first in 1809, the second in 1830. An edition entitled *Les Œuvres complètes de Laplace* (1878), &c., which is to include all his memoirs as well as his separate works, is in course of publication under the auspices of the Academy of Sciences. The thirteenth 4to volume was issued in 1904. Some of Laplace's results in the theory of probabilities are simplified in S. F. Lacroix's *Traité élémentaire du calcul des probabilités* and De Morgan's *Essay*, published in Lardner's *Cabinet Cyclopaedia*. For the history of the subject see *A History of the Mathematical Theory of Probability*, by Isaac Todhunter (1865). Laplace's treatise on specific heat was published in German in 1892 as No. 40 of W. Ostwald's *Klassiker der exacten Wissenschaften*.

Authorities.—Baron Fourier's *Éloge*, *Mémoires de l'institut*, x. lxxxi. (1831); *Revue encyclopédique*, xliii. (1829); S. D. Poisson's Funeral Oration (*Conn. des Temps*, 1830, p. 19); F. X. von Zach, *Allg. geographische Ephemeriden*, iv. 70 (1799); F. Arago, *Annuaire du Bureau des Long.* 1844, p. 271, translated among Arago's Biographies of Distinguished Men (1857); J. S. Bailly, *Hist. de l'astr. moderne*, t. iii.; R. Grant, *Hist. of Phys. Astr.* p. 50, &c.; A. Berry, *Short Hist. of Astr.* p. 306; Max Marie, *Hist. des sciences* t. x. pp. 69–98; R. Wolf, *Geschichte der Astronomie*; J. Mädler, *Gesch. der Himmelskunde*, i. 17; W. Whewell, *Hist. of the Inductive Sciences*, ii. *passim*; J. C. Poggendorff, *Biog.-lit. Handwörterbuch*. (A. M. C.)

LAPLAND, or Lappland, a name used to indicate the region of northern Europe inhabited by the Lapps, though not applied to any administrative district. It covers in Norway the division (*amter*) of Finmarken and the higher inland parts of Tromsö and Nordland; in Russian territory the western part of the government of Archangel as far as the White Sea and the northern part of the Finnish district of Uleåborg; and in Sweden the inland and northern parts of the old province of Norrland, roughly coincident with the districts (*län*) of Norbotten and Vesterbotten, and divided into five divisions—Torne Lappmark, Lule Lappmark, Pite Lappmark, Lycksele Lappmark and Åsele Lappmark. The Norwegian portion is thus insignificant; of the Russian only a little lies south of the Arctic circle, and the whole is less accessible and more sparsely populated than the Swedish, the southern boundary of which may be taken arbitrarily at about 64° N., though scattered families of Lapps occur much farther south, even in the Hardanger Fjeld in Norway.

The Scandinavian portion of Lapland presents the usual characteristics of the mountain plateau of that peninsula—on the west side the bold headlands and fjords, deeply-grooved valleys and glaciers of Norway, on the east the long mountain lakes and great lake-fed rivers of Sweden. Russian Lapland is broadly similar to the lower-lying parts of Swedish Lapland, but the great lakes are more generally distributed, and the valleys are less direct. The country is low and gently undulating, broken by detached hills and ridges not exceeding in elevation 2500 ft. In the uplands of Swedish Lapland, and to some extent in Russian Lapland, the lakes afford the principal means of communication; it is almost impossible to cross the forests from valley to valley without a native guide. In Sweden the few farms of the Swedes who inhabit the region are on the lake shores, and the traveller must be rowed from one to another in the typical boats of the district, pointed at bow and stern, unusually low amidships, and propelled by short sculls or paddles. Sailing is hardly ever practised, and squalls on the lakes are often dangerous to the rowing-boats. On a few of the lakes wood-fired steam-launches are used in connexion with the timber trade, which is considerable, as practically the whole region is forested. Between the lakes all journeying is made on foot. The heads of the Swedish valleys are connected with the Norwegian fjords by passes generally traversed only by tracks; though from the head of the Ume a driving road crosses to Mo on Ranen Fjord. Each principal valley has a considerable village at or near the tail of the lake-chain, up to which a road runs along the valley. The village consists of wooden cottages with an inn (*gästgifvaregård*), a church, and frequently a collection of huts without windows, closed in summer, but inhabited by the Lapps when they come down from the mountains to the winter fairs. Sometimes there is another church and small settlement in the upper valley, to which, once or twice in a summer, the Lapps come from great distances to attend service. To these, too, they sometimes bring their dead for burial, bearing them if necessary on a journey of many days. Though Lapland gives little scope for husbandry, a bad summer being commonly followed by a winter famine, it is richly furnished with much that is serviceable to man. There are copper-mines at the mountain of Sulitelma, and the iron deposits in Norrland are among the most extensive in the world. Their working is facilitated by the railway from Stockholm to Gellivara, Kirunavara and Narvik on the Norwegian coast, which also connects them with the port of Luleå on the Gulf of Bothnia. The supply of timber (pine, fir, spruce and birch) is unlimited. Though fruit-trees will not bear there is an abundance of edible berries; the rivers and lakes abound with trout, perch, pike and other fish, and in the lower waters with salmon; and the cod, herring, halibut and Greenland shark in the northern seas attract numerous Norwegian and Russian fishermen.

The climate is thoroughly Arctic. In the northern parts unbroken daylight in summer and darkness in winter last from two to three months each; and through the greater part of the country the sun does not rise at mid-winter or set at midsummer. In December and January in the far north there is little more daylight than a cold glimmer of dawn; by February, however, there are some hours of daylight; in March the heat of the sun is beginning to modify the cold, and now and in April the birds of passage begin to appear. In April the snow is melting from the branches; spring comes in May; spring flowers are in blossom, and grain is sown. At the end of this month or in June the ice is breaking up on the lakes, woods rush into leaf, and the unbroken daylight of the northern summer soon sets in. July is quite warm; the great rivers come down full from the melting snows in the mountains. August is a rainy month, the time of harvest; night-frosts may begin already about the middle of the month. All preparations for winter are made during September and October, and full winter has set in by November.

The Lapps.—The Lapps (Swed. *Lappar*; Russian *Lopari*; Norw. *Finner*) call their country *Sabme* or *Same*, and themselves *Samelats*—names almost identical with those employed by the Finns for their country and race, and probably connected with a root signifying "dark." Lapp is almost certainly a nickname imposed by foreigners, although some of the Lapps apply it contemptuously to those of their countrymen whom they think to be less civilized than themselves.[1]

In Sweden and Finland the Lapps are usually divided into fisher, mountain and forest Lapps. In Sweden the first class includes many impoverished mountain Lapps. As described by Laestadius (1827–1832), their condition was very miserable; but since his time matters have improved. The principal colony has its summer quarters on the Stora-Lule Lake, possesses good boats and nets, and, besides catching and drying fish, makes money by the shooting of wild fowl and the gathering of eggs. When he has acquired a little means it is not unusual for the fisher to settle down and reclaim a bit of land. The mountain and forest Lapps are the true representatives of the race. In the wandering life of the mountain Lapp his autumn residence, on the borders of the forest district, may be considered as the central point; it is there that he erects his *njalla*, a small wooden storehouse raised high above the ground by one or more piles. About the beginning of November he begins to wander south or east into the forest land, and in the winter he may visit, not only

[1] The most probable etymology is the Finnish *lappu*, and in this case the meaning would be the "land's end folk."

such places as Jokkmokk and Arjepluog, but even Gefle, Upsala or Stockholm. About the beginning of May he is back at his njalla, but as soon as the weather grows warm he pushes up to the mountains, and there throughout the summer pastures his herds and prepares his store of cheese. By autumn or October he is busy at his njalla killing the surplus reindeer bulls and curing meat for the winter. From the mountain Lapp the forest (or, as he used to be called, the spruce-fir) Lapp is mainly distinguished by the narrower limits within which he pursues his nomadic life. He never wanders outside of a certain district, in which he possesses hereditary rights, and maintains a series of camping-grounds which he visits in regular rotation. In May or April he lets his reindeer loose, to wander as they please; but immediately after midsummer, when the mosquitoes become troublesome, he goes to collect them. Catching a single deer and belling it, he drives it through the wood; the other deer, whose instinct leads them to gather into herds for mutual protection against the mosquitoes, are attracted by the sound. Should the summer be very cool and the mosquitoes few, the Lapp finds it next to impossible to bring the creatures together. About the end of August they are again let loose, but they are once more collected in October, the forest Lapp during winter pursuing the same course of life as the mountain Lapp.

In Norway there are three classes—the sea Lapps, the river Lapps and the mountain Lapps, the first two settled, the third nomadic. The mountain Lapps have a rather ruder and harder life than the same class in Sweden. About Christmas those of Kautokeino and Karasjok are usually settled in the neighbourhood of the churches; in summer they visit the coast, and in autumn they return inland. Previous to 1852, when they were forbidden by imperial decree, they were wont in winter to move south across the Russian frontiers. It is seldom possible for them to remain more than three or four days in one spot. Flesh is their favourite, in winter almost their only food, though they also use reindeer milk, cheese and rye or barley cakes. The sea Lapps are in some respects hardly to be distinguished from the other coast dwellers of Finmark. Their food consists mainly of cooked fish. The river Lapps, many of whom, however, are descendants of Finns proper, breed cattle, attempt a little tillage and entrust their reindeer to the care of mountain Lapps.

In Finland there are comparatively few Laplanders, and the great bulk of them belong to the fisher class. Many are settled in the neighbourhood of the Enare Lake. In the spring they go down to the Norwegian coast and take part in the sea fisheries, returning to the lake about midsummer. Formerly they found the capture of wild reindeer a profitable occupation, using for this purpose a palisaded avenue gradually narrowing towards a pitfall.

The Russian Lapps are also for the most part fishers, as is natural in a district with such an extent of coast and such a number of lakes, not to mention the advantage which the fisher has over the reindeer keeper in connexion with the many fasts of the Greek Church. They maintain a half nomadic life, very few having become settlers in the Russian villages. It is usual to distinguish them according to the district of the coast which they frequent, as Murman (Murmanski) and Terian (Terski) Lapps. A separate tribe, the Filmans, *i.e.* Finnmans, wander about the Pazyets, Motov and Pechenga tundras, and retain the peculiar dialect and the Lutheran creed which they owe to a former connexion with Sweden. They were formerly known as the "twice and thrice tributary" Lapps, because they paid to two or even three states—Russia, Denmark and Sweden.

The Lapps within the historical period have considerably recruited themselves from neighbouring races. Shortness of stature[1] is their most obvious characteristic, though in regard to this much exaggeration has prevailed. Düben found an average of 4·9 ft. for males and a little less for females; Mantegazza, who made a number of anthropological observations in Norway in 1879, gives 5 ft. and 4·75 ft., respectively (*Archivio per l'antrop.*, 1880). Individuals much above or much below the average are rare. The body is usually of fair proportions, but the legs are rather short, and in many cases somewhat bandy. Dark, swarthy, yellow, copper-coloured are all adjectives employed to describe their complexion—the truth being that their habits of life do not conduce either to the preservation or display of the natural colour of their skin, and that some of them are really fair, and others, perhaps the majority, really dark. The colour of the hair ranges from blonde and reddish to a bluish or greyish black; the eyes are black, hazel, blue or grey. The shape of the skull is the most striking peculiarity of the Lapp. He is the most brachycephalous type of man in Europe, perhaps in the world.[2] According to Virchow, the women in width of face are more Mongolian in type than the men, but neither in men nor women does the opening of the eye show any true obliquity. In children the eye is large, open and round. The nose is always low and broad, more markedly retroussé among the females than the males. Wrinkled and puckered by exposure to the weather, the faces even of the younger Lapps assume an appearance of old age. The muscular system is usually well developed, but there is deficiency of fatty tissue, which affects the features (particularly by giving relative prominence to the eyes) and the general character of the skin. The thinness of the skin, indeed, can but rarely be paralleled among other Europeans. Among the Lapps, as among other lower races, the index is shorter than the ring finger.

The Lapps are a quiet, inoffensive people. Crimes of violence are almost unknown, and the only common breach of law is the killing of tame reindeer belonging to other owners. In Russia, however, they have a bad reputation for lying and general untrustworthiness, and drunkenness is well-nigh a universal vice. In Scandinavia laws have been directed against the importation of intoxicating liquors into the Lapp country since 1723.

Superficially at least the great bulk of the Lapps have been Christianized—those of the Scandinavian countries being Protestants, those of Russia members of the Greek Church. Although the first attempt to convert the Lapps to Christianity seems to have been made in the 11th century, the worship of heathen idols was carried on openly in Swedish Lappmark as late as 1687, and secretly in Norway down to the first quarter of the 18th century, while the practices of heathen rites survived into the 19th century, if indeed they are extinct even yet. Lapp graves, prepared in the heathen manner, have been discovered in upper Namdal (Norway), belonging to the years 1820 and 1826. In education the Scandinavian Lapps are far ahead of their Russian brethren, to whom reading and writing are arts as unfamiliar as they were to their pagan ancestors. The general manner of life is patriarchal. The father of the family has complete authority over all its affairs; and on his death this authority passes to the eldest son. Parents are free to disinherit their children; and, if a son separates from the family without his father's permission, he receives no share of the property except a gun and his wife's dowry.[3]

The Lapps are of necessity conservative in most of their habits, many of which can hardly have altered since the first taming of the reindeer. But the strong current of mercantile enterprise has carried a few important products of southern civilization into their huts. The lines in which James Thomson describes their simple life—

> The reindeer form their riches: these their tents,
> Their robes, their beds, and all their homely wealth
> Supply; their wholesome fare and cheerful cups—

are still applicable in the main to the mountain Lapps; but even they have learned to use coffee as an ordinary beverage and to wear stout Norwegian cloth (*vadmal*).

Linguistically the Lapps belong to the Finno-Ugrian group (*q.v.*); the similarity of their speech to Finnish is evident though

[1] Hence they have been supposed by many to be the originals of the "little folk" of Scandinavian legend.

[2] Bertillon found in one instance a cephalic index of 94. The average obtained by Pruner Bey was 84·7, by Virchow 82·5.

[3] A valuable paper by Ephimenko, on "The Legal Customs of the Lapps, especially in Russian Lapland," appeared in vol. viii. of the *Mem. of Russ. Geog. Soc.*, Ethnog. Section, 1878.

the phonetics are different and more complicated. It is broken up into very distinct and even mutually unintelligible dialects, the origin of several of which is, however, easily found in the political and social dismemberment of the people. Düben distinguishes four leading dialects; but a much greater number are recognizable. In Russian Lapland alone there are three, due to the influence of Norwegian, Karelian and Russian (Lönnrot, *Acta Soc. Sci. Fennicae*, vol. iv.). "The Lapps," says Castren, "have had the misfortune to come into close contact with foreign races while their language was yet in its tenderest infancy, and consequently it has not only adopted an endless number of foreign words, but in many grammatical aspects fashioned itself after foreign models." That it began at a very early period to enrich itself with Scandinavian words is shown by the use it still makes of forms belonging to a linguistic stage older even than that of Icelandic. Düben has subjected the vocabulary to a very interesting analysis for the purpose of discovering what stage of culture the people had reached before their contact with the Norse. Agricultural terms, the names of the metals and the word for smith are all of Scandinavian origin, and the words for "taming" and "milk" would suggest that the southern strangers taught the Lapps how to turn the reindeer to full account. The important place, however, which this creature must always have held in their estimation is evident from the existence of more than three hundred native words in connexion with reindeer.

Language.

The Lapp tongue was long ago reduced to writing by the missionaries; but very little has been printed in it except school-books and religious works. A number of popular tales and songs, indeed, have been taken down from the lips of the people. The songs are similar to those of the Finns, and a process of mutual borrowing seems to have gone on. In one of the saga-like pieces—Pishan-Peshan's son—there seems to be a mention of the Baikal Lake, and possibly also of the Altai Mountains. The story of Njavvisena, daughter of the Sun, is full of quaint folk-lore about the taming of the reindeer. Giants, as well as a blind or one-eyed monster, are frequently introduced, and the Aesopic fable is not without its representatives. Many of the Lapps are able to speak one or even two of the neighbouring tongues.

The reputation of the Laplanders for skill in magic and divination is of very early date, and in Finland is not yet extinct. When Erik Blood-axe, son of Harold Haarfager, visited Bjarmaland in 922, he found Gunhild, daughter of Asur Tote, living among the Lapps, to whom she had been sent by her father for the purpose of being trained in witchcraft; and Ivan the Terrible of Russia sent for magicians from Lapland to explain the cause of the appearance of a comet. One of the powers with which they were formerly credited was that of raising winds. "They tye three knottes," says old Richard Eden, "on a strynge hangyng at a whyp. When they lose one of these they rayse tollerable wyndes. When they lose an other the wynde is more vehement; but by losing the thyrd they rayse playne tempestes as in old tyme they were accustomed to rayse thunder and lyghtnyng" (*Hist. of Trauayle*, 1577). Though we are familiar in English with allusions to "Lapland witches," it appears that the art, according to native custom, was in the hands of the men. During his divination the wizard fell into a state of trance or ecstasy, his soul being held to run at large to pursue its inquiries. Great use was made of a curious divining-drum, oval in shape and made of wood, 1 to 4 ft. in length. Over the upper surface was stretched a white-dressed reindeer skin, and at the corners (so to speak) hung a variety of charms—tufts of wool, bones, teeth, claws, &c. The area was divided into several spaces, often into three, one for the celestial gods, one for the terrestrial and one for man. A variety of figures and conventional signs were drawn in the several compartments: the sun, for instance, is frequently represented by a square and a stroke from each corner, Thor by two hammers placed crosswise; and in the more modern specimens symbols for Christ, the Virgin, and the Holy Ghost are introduced. An *arpa* or divining-rod was laid on a definite spot, the drum beaten by a hammer, and conclusions drawn from the position taken up by the arpa. Any Lapp who had attained to manhood could in ordinary circumstances consult the drum for himself, but in matters of unusual moment the professional wizard (*naid*, *noide* or *noaide*) had to be called in.

Witchcraft.

History.—The Lapps have a dim tradition that their ancestors lived in a far eastern land, and they tell rude stories of conflicts with Norsemen and Karelians. But no answer can be obtained from them in regard to their early distribution and movements. It has been maintained that they were formerly spread over the whole of the Scandinavian peninsula, and they have even been considered the remnants of that primeval race of cave-dwellers which hunted the reindeer over the snow-fields of central and western Europe. But much of the evidence adduced for these theories is highly questionable. The contents of the so-called Lapps' graves found in various parts of Scandinavia are often sufficient in themselves to show that the appellation must be a misnomer, and the syllable Lap or Lapp found in many names of places can often be proved to have no connnexion with the Lapps.[1] They occupied their present territory when they are first mentioned in history. According to Düben the name first occurs in the 13th century—in the *Fundinn Noregr*, composed about 1200, in Saxo Grammaticus, and in a papal bull of date 1230; but the people are probably to be identified with those Finns of Tacitus whom he describes as wild hunters with skins for clothing and rude huts as only means of shelter, and certainly with the Skrithiphinoi of Procopius (*Goth.* ii. 15), the Scritobini of Paulus Warnefridus, and the Scridifinni of the geographer of Ravenna. Some of the details given by Procopius, in regard for instance to the treatment of infants, show that his informant was acquainted with certain characteristic customs of the Lapps.

In the 9th century the Norsemen from Norway began to treat their feeble northern neighbours as a subject race. The wealth of Ottar, "northmost of the northmen," whose narrative has been preserved by King Alfred, consisted mainly of six hundred of those "deer they call hrenas" and in tribute paid by the natives; and the Eigils saga tells how Brynjulf Bjargulfson had his right to collect contributions from the Finns (*i.e.* the Lapps) recognized by Harold Haarfager. So much value was attached to this source of wealth that as early as 1050 strangers were excluded from the fur-trade of Finmark, and a kind of coast-guard prevented their intrusion. Meantime the Karelians were pressing on the eastern Lapps, and in the course of the 11th century the rulers of Novgorod began to treat them as the Norsemen had treated their western brethren. The ground-swell of the Tatar invasion drove the Karelians westward in the 13th century, and for many years even Finmark was so unsettled that the Norsemen received no tribute from the Lapps. At length in 1326 a treaty was concluded between Norway and Russia by which the supremacy of the Norwegians over the Lapps was recognized as far east as Voljo beyond Kandalax on the White Sea, and the supremacy of the Russians over the Karelians as far as Lyngen and the Målself. The relations of the Lapps to their more powerful neighbours were complicated by the rivalry of the different Scandinavian kingdoms. After the disruption of the Calmar Union (1523) Sweden began to assert its rights with vigour, and in 1595 the treaty of Teusina between Sweden and Russia decreed "that the Lapps who dwell in the woods between eastern Bothnia and Varanger shall pay their dues to the king of Sweden." It was in vain that Christian IV. of Denmark visited Kola and exacted homage in 1599, and every year sent messengers to protest against the collection of his tribute by the Swedes (a custom which continued down to 1806). Charles of Sweden took the title of "king of the Kajans and Lapps," and left no means untried to establish his power over all Scandinavian Lapland. By the peace of Knäröd (1613) Gustavus Adolphus gave up the Swedish claim to Finmark; and in 1751 mutual renunciations brought the relations of Swedish and Norwegian (Danish) Lapland to their present position. Meanwhile Russian influence had been spreading westward; and in 1809, when Alexander I. finally obtained the cession of Finland, he also added to his dominions the whole of Finnish Lapland to the east of the Muonio and the Köngämä. It may be interesting to mention that Lapps, armed with bows and arrows, were attached to certain regiments of Gustavus Adolphus in Germany during the Thirty Years' War.

The Lapps have had the ordinary fate of a subject and defenceless people; they have been utilized with little regard to their own interest or inclinations. The example set by the early Norwegians was followed by the Swedes: a peculiar class of adventurers known as the Birkarlians (from *Bjark* or *Birk*, "trade") began in the 13th century to farm the Lapps, and, receiving very extensive privileges from the kings, grew to great wealth and influence. In 1606 there were twenty-two Birkarlians in Tornio, seventeen in Lule, sixteen in Pite, and sixty-six in Ume Lappmark. They are regularly spoken of as having or owning Lapps, whom they dispose of as any other piece of property. In Russian Lapland matters followed much the same course. The very institutions of the Solovets monastery, intended by St Tryphon for the benefit of the poor neglected pagans, turned out the occasion of much injustice towards them. By a charter of Ivan Vasilivitch (November 1556), the monks are declared masters of the Lapps of the Motoff and Petchenga districts, and they soon sought to extend their control over those not legally assigned to them (Ephimenko). Other monasteries were gifted

[1] The view that the Lapps at one time occupied the whole of the Scandinavian peninsula, and have during the course of centuries been driven back by the Swedes and Norwegians is disproved by the recent investigations of Yngvar Nielsen, K. B. Wiklund and others. The fact is, the Lapps are increasing in numbers, as well as pushing their way farther and farther south. In the beginning of the 16th century their southern border-line in Norway ran on the upper side of 64° N. In 1890 they forced their way to the head of the Hardanger Fjord in 60° N. In Sweden the presence of Lapps as far south as Jämtland (or Jemtland) is first mentioned in 1864. In 1881 they pushed on into the north of Dalecarlia, about 61° 45′ N.

[illegible] rights; and the supplication of the patriarch [illegible], for example, shows clearly the [illegible] Lapps were subjected.

[illegible] these abuses were abolished; and in [illegible] the Lapps of the present day enjoy the [illegible] a large amount of philanthropic legisla- [illegible] rulers. There seems to be no fear of their [illegible] may be by gradual amalgamation with [illegible]. In Norway the total number of [illegible], and in Sweden in 1904 it was officially [illegible]. Add to these some 3000 for Russian [illegible] Lapp population approximates to 30,000. [illegible] are gradually abandoning their nomadic [illegible] in the Swedish population. The [illegible] Lapps lead a semi-nomadic existence; [illegible] nomads can scarcely reach 1500 at [illegible] there are about 3500 nomads.

[illegible] Dubeu, *Om Lappland och Lapparne* [illegible] list of over 200 authorities; C. Rabot, [illegible] les récentes explorations de MM. [illegible] *La Géographie*, Soc. Géog. de Paris VII. [illegible] Bayard Taylor, *Northern Travel* [illegible] *White Sea Peninsula* (London, 1883), [illegible] London, 1875); P. B. du Chaillu, [illegible] S. Tromholt, *Under* [illegible] (London, 1885); Y. Nielsen, *Det* [illegible] H. H. Reusch, *Folk og natur* [illegible] *De Svenska nomadlapparnas* [illegible] (Upsala, 1908); see also [illegible] Scheffer, *Lapponia* [illegible] (1674); Regnard, *Voyage* [illegible] in Danish [illegible] Sir A. de C. Brooke, *A* [illegible] *Journal* (1831).

[illegible] of Lapp in the university [illegible] *Sprogprover: en samling* [illegible] and *Lappisk* [illegible] See also G. [illegible] Friis, [illegible] Grammars of the Lapp [illegible] Leem (1748), Rask [illegible] Among more [illegible] by J. A. Friis; [illegible] by J. Qvigstad, a [illegible] of the Lulea [illegible] by K. B. [illegible] the Kola dialect [illegible] by [illegible] and Finnish by [illegible] and others in the [illegible] *der lappischen* [illegible]

[illegible] a notable addition by [illegible] preserved in the [illegible] to the [illegible] the younger. On [illegible] (1896). [illegible] translated into [illegible] Bible was [illegible] dialect of Lappish [illegible]

[illegible] the province [illegible] with [illegible] (1907), [illegible] two years [illegible]

La[illegible] not [illegible] life [illegible] Ka[illegible] of [illegible] they [illegible] by [illegible] the [illegible] more [illegible] in wi[illegible] milk, [illegible] some [illegible] dwell[illegible] fish. [illegible] of Finn[illegible] their re[illegible]

In Fi[illegible] great bu[illegible] in the [illegible] down to [illegible] returning [illegible] the captur[illegible] this purpo[illegible] a pitfall.

The Russ[illegible] natural in a [illegible] number of la[illegible] has over the [illegible] of the Greek [illegible] few having be[illegible] to distinguish [illegible] they frequent, [illegible] Lapps. A sepa[illegible] about the Pazy[illegible] the peculiar dial[illegible] a former connexi[illegible] as the "twice an[illegible] to two or even thr[illegible]

The Lapps wit[illegible] recruited themselv[illegible] stature[1] is their mo[illegible] to this much exag[illegible] average of 4·9 ft. for [illegible] gazza, who made a [illegible] Norway in 1879, give[illegible]

[1] Hence they [illegible] the "little folk" [illegible]

museum, originally presented by Dr Moreno, has become one of the most important in South America, its palaeontological and anthropological collections being unique. There are also a university, national college, public library, astronomical observatory, several churches, two hospitals and two theatres. A noteworthy public park is formed by a large plantation of eucalyptus trees, which have grown to a great height and present an imposing appearance on the level, treeless plain. Electricity is in general use for public and private lighting, and tramways are laid down in the principal streets and extend eastward to the port. The harbour of the port of La Plata consists of a large artificial basin, 1450 yds. long by 150 yds. wide, with approaches, in addition to the old port of Ensenada, which are capable of receiving the largest vessels that can navigate the La Plata estuary. Up to the opening of the new port works of Buenos Aires a large part of the ocean-going traffic of Buenos Aires passed through the port of La Plata. It has good railway connexions with the interior, and exports cattle and agricultural produce.

LAPORTE, ROLAND (1675–1704), Camisard leader, better known as "Roland," was born at Mas Soubeyran (Gard) in a cottage which has become the property of the Société de l'Histoire du Protestantisme français, and which contains relics of the hero. He was a nephew of Laporte, the Camisard leader who was hunted down and shot in October 1702, and he himself became the leader of a band of a thousand men which he formed into a disciplined army with magazines, arsenals and hospitals. For daring in action and rapidity of movement he was second only to Cavalier. These two leaders in 1702 secured entrance to the town of Sauve under the pretence of being royal officers, burnt the church and carried off provisions and ammunition for their forces. Roland, who called himself "general of the children of God," terrorised the country between Nîmes and Alais, burning churches and houses, and slaying those suspected of hostility against the Huguenots, though without personally taking any part of the spoil. Cavalier was already in negotiation with Marshal Villars when Roland cut to pieces a Catholic regiment at Fontmorte in May 1704. He refused to lay down his arms without definite assurance of the restoration of the privileges accorded by the Edict of Nantes. Villars then sought to negotiate, offering Roland the command of a regiment on foreign service and liberty of conscience, though not the free exercise of their religion, for his co-religionists. This parley had no results, but Roland was betrayed to his enemies, and on the 14th of August 1704 was shot while defending himself against his captors. The five officers who were with him surrendered, and were broken on the wheel at Nîmes. Roland's death put an end to the effective resistance of the Cévenols.

See A. Court, *Histoire des troubles des Cévennes* (Villefranche, 1760); H. M. Baird, *The Huguenots and the revocation of the Edict of Nantes* (2 vols., London, 1895), and other literature dealing with the Camisards.

LA PORTE, a city and the county seat of La Porte county, Indiana, U.S.A., 12 m. S. of Lake Michigan and about 60 m. S.E. of Chicago. Pop. (1890) 7126; (1900) 7113 (1403 foreign-born); (1910) 10,525. It is served by the Lake Erie & Western, the Lake Shore & Michigan Southern, the Père Marquette, the Chicago, South Bend & Northern Indiana (electric), and the Chicago-New York Electric Air Line railways. La Porte lies in the midst of a fertile agricultural region, and the shipment of farm and orchard products is one of its chief industries. There are also numerous manufactures. La Porte's situation in the heart of a region of beautiful lakes (including Clear, Pine and Stone lakes) has given it a considerable reputation as a summer resort. The lakes furnish a large supply of clear ice, which is shipped to the Chicago markets. La Porte was settled in 1830, laid out in 1833, incorporated as a town in 1835, and first chartered as a city in 1852.

LAPPA, an island directly opposite the inner harbour of [illegible] the distance across being from 1 to 1½ m. It is a station [illegible] imperial maritime customs which collects duties [illegible] between China and the Portuguese colony of Macao. The arrangement is altogether abnormal, and was consented to by the Portuguese government in 1887 to assist the Chinese authorities in the suppression of opium smuggling. A similar arrangement prevails at the British colony of Hong-Kong, where the Chinese customs station is Kowloon. In both cases the customs stations levy duties on vessels entering and leaving the foreign port in lieu of levying them, as ought to be done, on entering or leaving a Chinese port.

LAPPARENT, ALBERT AUGUSTE COCHON DE (1839–1908), French geologist, was born at Bourges on the 30th of December 1839. After studying at the École Polytechnique from 1858 to 1860 he became *ingénieur au corps des mines*, and took part in drawing up the geological map of France; and in 1875 he was appointed professor of geology and mineralogy at the Catholic Institute, Paris. In 1879 he prepared an important memoir for the geological survey of France on *Le Pays de Bray*, a subject on which he had already published several memoirs, and in 1880 he served as president of the French Geological Society. In 1881–1883 he published his *Traité de géologie* (5th ed., 1905), the best European text-book of stratigraphical geology. His other works include *Cours de minéralogie* (1884, 3rd ed., 1899), *La Formation des combustibles minéraux* (1886), *Le Niveau de la mer et ses variations* (1886), *Les Tremblements de terre* (1887), *La Géologie en chemin de fer* (1888), *Précis de minéralogie* (1888), *Le Siècle du fer* (1890), *Les Anciens Glaciers* (1893), *Leçons de géographie physique* (1896), *Notions générales sur l'écorce terrestre* (1897), *Le Globe terrestre* (1899), and *Science et apologétique* (1905). With Achille Delesse he was for many years editor of the *Revue de géologie* and contributed to the *Extraits de géologie*, and he joined with A. Potier in the geological surveys undertaken in connexion with the Channel Tunnel proposals. He died in Paris on the 5th of May 1908.

LAPPENBERG, JOHANN MARTIN (1794–1865), German historian, was born on the 30th of July 1794 at Hamburg, where his father, Valentin Anton Lappenberg (1759–1819), held an official position. He studied medicine, and afterwards history, at Edinburgh. He continued to study history in London, and at Berlin and Göttingen, graduating as doctor of laws at Göttingen in 1816. In 1820 he was sent by the Hamburg senate as resident minister to the Prussian court. In 1823 he became keeper of the Hamburg archives; an office in which he had the fullest opportunities for the laborious and critical research work upon which his reputation as an historian rests. He retained this post until 1863, when a serious affection of the eyes compelled him to resign. In 1850 he represented Hamburg in the German parliament at Frankfort, and his death took place at Hamburg on the 28th of November 1865. Lappenberg's most important work is his *Geschichte von England*, which deals with the history of England from the earliest times to 1154, and was published in two volumes at Hamburg in 1834–1837. It has been translated into English by B. Thorpe as *History of England under the Anglo-Saxon Kings* (London 1845, and again 1881), and *History of England under the Norman Kings* (Oxford, 1857), and has been continued in three additional volumes from 1154 to 1509 by R. Pauli. His other works deal mainly with the history of Hamburg, and include *Hamburgische Chroniken in Niedersächsischer Sprache* (Hamburg, 1852–1861); *Geschichtsquellen des Erzstiftes und der Stadt Bremen* (Bremen, 1841); *Hamburgisches Urkundenbuch* (Hamburg, 1842); *Urkundliche Geschichte des Hansischen Stahlhofes zu London* (Hamburg, 1851); *Hamburgische Rechtsalterthümer* (Hamburg, 1845); and *Urkundliche Geschichte des Ursprunges der deutschen Hanse* (Hamburg, 1830), a continuation of the work of G. F. Sartorius. For the *Monumenta Germaniae historica* he edited the *Chronicon* of Thietmar of Merseburg, the *Gesta Hammenburgensis ecclesiae pontificum* of Adam of Bremen and the *Chronica Slavorum* of Helmold, with its continuation by Arnold of Lübeck. Lappenberg, who was a member of numerous learned societies in Europe, wrote many other historical works.

See E. H. Meyer, *Johann Martin Lappenberg* (Hamburg, 1867); and R. Pauli in the *Allgemeine deutsche Biographie*, Band xvii. (Leipzig, 1883).

LAPRADE, PIERRE MARTIN VICTOR RICHARD DE (1812–1883), known as VICTOR DE LAPRADE, French poet and critic, was born on the 13th of January 1812 at Montbrison, in the department of the Loire. He came of a modest provincial family. After completing his studies at Lyons, he produced in 1839 a small volume of religious verse, *Les Parfums de Madeleine*. This was followed in 1840 by *La Colère de Jésus*, in 1841 by the religious fantasy of *Psyché*, and in 1844 by *Odes et poèmes*. In 1845 Laprade visited Italy on a mission of literary research, and in 1847 he was appointed professor of French literature at Lyons. The French Academy, by a single vote, preferred Émile Augier at the election in 1857, but in the following year Laprade was chosen to fill the chair of Alfred de Musset. In 1861 he was removed from his post at Lyons owing to the publication of a political satire in verse (*Les Muses d'État*), and in 1871 took his seat in the National Assembly on the benches of the Right. He died on the 13th of December 1883. A statue has been raised by his fellow-townsmen at Montbrison. Besides those named above, Laprade's poetical works include *Poèmes évangéliques* (1852), *Idylles héroïques* (1858), *Les Voix du silence* (1864), *Pernette* (1868), *Poèmes civiles* (1873), *Le Livre d'un père* (1877), *Varia* and *Livre des adieux* (1878–1879). In prose he published, in 1840, *Des habitudes intellectuelles de l'avocat*. *Questions d'art et de morale* appeared in 1861, succeeded by *Le Sentiment de la nature, avant le Christianisme* in 1866, and *Chez les modernes* in 1868, *Éducation libérale* in 1873. The material for these books had in some cases been printed earlier, after delivery as a lecture. He also contributed articles to the *Revue des deux mondes* and the *Revue de Paris*. No writer represents more perfectly than Laprade the admirable genius of French provincial life, its homely simplicity, its culture, its piety and its sober patriotism. As a poet he belongs to the school of Chateaubriand and Lamartine. Devoted to the best classical models, inspired by a sense of the ideal, and by worship of nature as revealing the divine—gifted, too, with a full faculty of expression—he lacked only fire and passion in the equipment of a romantic poet. But the want of these, and the pressure of a certain chilly facility and of a too conscious philosophizing have prevented him from reaching the first rank, or from even attaining the popularity due to his high place in the second. Only in his patriotic verse did he shake himself clear from these trammels. Speaking generally, he possessed some of the qualities, and many of the defects, of the English Lake School. Laprade's prose criticisms must be ranked high. Apart from his classical and metaphysical studies, he was widely read in the literatures of Europe, and built upon the groundwork of a naturally correct taste. His dislike of irony and scepticism probably led him to underrate the product of the 18th century, and there are signs of a too fastidious dread of Philistinism. But a constant love of the best, a joy in nature and a lofty patriotism are not less evident than in his poetry. Few writers of any nation have fixed their minds so steadily on whatsoever things are pure, and lovely and of good report.

See also Edmond Biré, *Victor de Laprade, sa vie et ses œuvres*. (C.)

LAPSE (Lat. *lapsus*, a slip or departure), in law, a term used in several senses. (1) In ecclesiastical law, when a patron has neglected to present to a void benefice within six months next after the avoidance, the right of presentation is said to lapse. In such case the patronage or right of presentation devolves from the neglectful patron to the bishop as ordinary, to the metropolitan as superior and to the sovereign as patron paramount. (2) The failure of a testamentary disposition in favour of any person, by reason of the decease of its object in the testator's lifetime, is termed a lapse. See LEGACY, WILL.

LAPWING (O.Eng. *hlēapewince* = "one who turns about in running or flight").[1] a bird, the *Tringa vanellus* of Linnaeus and the *Vanellus vulgaris* or *V. cristatus* of modern ornithologists.

[1] Skeat, *Etym. Dict.* (1898), *s.v.* Caxton in 1481 has "lapwynches" (*Reynard the Fox*, cap. 27). The first part of the word is from *hleapan*, to leap; the second part is "wink" (O.H.G. *winchan*, Ger. *wanken*, to waver). Popular etymology has given the word its present form, as if it meant "wing-flapper," from "lap," a fold or flap of a garment.

In the temperate parts of the Old World this species is perhaps the most abundant of the plovers, *Charadriidae*, breeding in almost every suitable place from Ireland to Japan—the majority migrating towards winter to southern countries, as the Punjab, Egypt and Barbary—though in the British Islands some are always found at that season. As a straggler it has occurred within the Arctic Circle (as on the Varanger Fjord in Norway), as well as in Iceland and even Greenland; while it not unfrequently appears in Madeira and the Azores. Conspicuous as the strongly contrasted colours of its plumage and its very peculiar flight make it, it is remarkable that it maintains its ground when so many of its allies have been almost exterminated, for the lapwing is the object perhaps of greater persecution than any other European bird that is not a plunderer. Its eggs are the well-known "plovers' eggs" of commerce,[1] and the bird, wary and wild at other times of the year, in the breeding-season becomes easily approachable, and is shot to be sold in the markets for "golden plover." Its growing scarcity in Great Britain was very perceptible until the various acts for the protection of wild birds were passed. It is now abundant and is of service both for the market and to agriculture. What seems to be the secret of the lapwing holding its position is the adaptability of its nature to various kinds of localities. It will find sustenance equally on the driest of soils as on the fattest pastures; upland and fen, arable and moorland, are alike to it, provided only the ground be open enough. The wailing cry[2] and the frantic gestures of the cock bird in the breeding-season will tell any passer-by that a nest or brood is near; but, unless he knows how to look for it, nothing save mere chance will enable him to find it. The nest is a slight hollow in the ground, wonderfully inconspicuous even when deepened, as is usually the case, by incubation, and the black-spotted olive eggs (four in number) are almost invisible to the careless or untrained eye. The young when first hatched are clothed with mottled down, so as closely to resemble a stone, and to be overlooked as they squat motionless on the approach of danger. At a distance the plumage of the adult appears to be white and black in about equal proportions, the latter predominating above; but on closer examination nearly all the seeming black is found to be a bottle-green gleaming with purple and copper; the tail-coverts, both above and below, are of a bright bay colour, seldom visible in flight. The crest consists of six or eight narrow and elongated feathers, turned slightly upwards at the end, and is usually carried in a horizontal position, extending in the cock beyond the middle of the back; but it is capable of being erected so as to become nearly vertical. Frequenting parts of the open country so very divergent in character, and as remarkable for the peculiarity of its flight as for that of its cry, the lapwing is far more often observed in nearly all parts of the British Islands than any other of the group *Limicolae*. The peculiarity of its flight seems due to the [illegible] and rounded wings it possesses, the steady and ordinarily somewhat slow flapping of which impels the body at each stroke with a manifest though easy jerk. Yet on occasion, as when performing its migrations, or even its almost daily transits from one feeding-ground to another, and still more when being pursued by a falcon, the speed with which it moves through the air is very considerable. On the ground this bird runs nimbly, and is nearly always engaged in searching for its food, which is wholly animal.

Allied to the lapwing are several forms that have been placed by ornithologists in the genera *Hoplopterus*, *Chettusia*, *Lobivanellus*, *Defilippia*. In some of them the hind toe, which has already ceased to have any function in the lapwing, is wholly wanting. In others the wings are armed with a tubercle or even a sharp spur on the carpus. Few have any occipital crest, but several have the face ornamented by the outgrowth of a fleshy lobe or lobes. With the exception of North America, they are found in most parts of the world, but perhaps the greater number in Africa. Europe has three species—*Hoplopterus spinosus*, the spur-winged plover, and *Chettusia gregaria* and *C. leucura*; but the first and last are only stragglers from Africa and Asia. (A. N.)

[1] There is a prevalent belief that many of the eggs sold as [illegible] are those of rooks, but no notion can be more absurd, [illegible] the appearance of the two is wholly unlike. Those of the [illegible] of the golden plover (to a small extent), and enormous [illegible] those of the black-headed gull, and in certain places of [illegible] are, however, sold as lapwings', having a certain [illegible] and a difference of flavour only to be [illegible] value.

[2] [illegible] with some variety of intonation, [illegible] peewit and tewhit, commonly ap- [illegible] to the bird—though the first is that [illegible] gull, *Larus ridibundus* (see GULL), is [illegible] In Swedish *Vipa*, in Germany [illegible] and in France *Dixhuit* are names of [illegible]. Other English names are [illegible] from its long hornlike crest and [illegible] to have been [illegible] among English writers of the middle [illegible] *Upupa* properly hoopoe, by [illegible] with which they were best ac- [illegible] writers of the same or an earlier [illegible] (plural), and rendered that [illegible] tuft of feathers on leading them [illegible] the lapwing for winnowing [illegible] of the bird's wings.

LAPWORTH, CHARLES (1842–), English geologist, was born at Faringdon in Berkshire on the 30th of September 1842. He was educated partly in the village of Buckland in the same county, and afterwards in the training college at Culham, near Oxford (1862–1864). He was then appointed master in a school connected with the Episcopal church at Galashiels, where he remained eleven years. Geology came to absorb all his leisure time, and he commenced to investigate the Silurian rocks of the Southern Uplands, and to study the graptolites and other fossils which mark horizons in the great series of Lower Palaeozoic rocks. His first paper on the Lower Silurian rocks of Galashiels was published in 1870, and from that date onwards he continued to enrich our knowledge of the southern uplands of Scotland until the publication by the Geological Society of his masterly papers on *The Moffat Series* (1878) and *The Girvan Succession* (1882). Meanwhile in 1875 he became an assistant master in the Madras College, St Andrews, and in 1881 professor of geology and mineralogy (afterwards geology and physiography) in the Mason College, now University of Birmingham. In 1882 he started work in the Durness-Eriboll district of the Scottish Highlands, and made out the true succession of the rocks, and interpreted the complicated structure which had baffled most of the previous observers. His results were published in "The Secret of the Highlands" (*Geol. Mag.*, 1883). His subsequent work includes papers on the Cambrian rocks of Nuneaton and the Ordovician rocks of Shropshire. The term Ordovician was introduced by him in 1879 for the strata between the base of the Lower Llandovery formation and that of the Lower Arenig; and it was intended to settle the confusion arising from the use by some writers of Lower Silurian and by others of Upper Cambrian for the same set of rocks. The term Ordovician is now generally adopted. Professor Lapworth was elected F.R.S. in 1888, he received a royal medal in 1891, and was awarded the Wollaston medal by the Geological Society in 1899. He was president of the Geological Society, 1902–1904. His *Intermediate Text-book of Geology* was published in 1899.

See article, with portrait and bibliography, in *Geol. Mag.* (July 1901).

LAR, a city of Persia, capital of Laristan, in 27° 30′ N., 53° 58′ E., 180 m. from Shiraz and 75 from the coast at Bander Lingah. It stands at the foot of a mountain range in an extensive plain covered with palm trees, and was once a flourishing place, but a large portion is in ruins, and the population which early in the 18th century numbered 50,000 is reduced to 8000. There are still some good buildings, of which the most prominent are the old bazaar consisting of four arcades each 180 ft. long, 14 broad and 22 high, radiating from a domed centre 30 ft. high, an old stone mosque and many cisterns. The crest of a steep limestone hill immediately behind the town and rising 150 ft. above the plain is crowned by the ruins of a castle formerly deemed impregnable. Just below the castle is a well sunk 200 ft. in the rock. The tower-flanked mud wall which surrounds the town is for the most part in ruins.

LARA, western state of Venezuela, lying in the angle formed by the parting of the N. and N.E. ranges of the Cordillera de Mérida and extending N.E. with converging frontiers to the Caribbean. Pop. (1905 estimate) 272,252. The greater part of its surface is mountainous, with elevated fertile valleys which have a temperate climate. The Tocuyo river rises in the S.W. angle of the state and flows N.E. to the Caribbean with a total length of 287 m. A narrow-gauge railway, the "South-western," owned by British capitalists, runs from the port of Tucacas 55 m. S.W. to Barquisimeto by way of the Aroa copper-mining district. Lara produces wheat and other cereals, coffee, sugar, tobacco, neat cattle, sheep and various mineral ores, including silver, copper, iron, lead, bismuth and antimony. The capital, Barquisimeto, is one of the largest and most progressive of the inland cities of Venezuela. Carora is also prominent as a commercial centre. Tocuyo (pop. in 1891, 15,383), 40 m. S.W. of Barquisimeto, is an important commercial and mining town, over 2000 ft. above sea-level, in the midst of a rich agricultural and pastoral region. Yaritagua (pop. about 12,000), 20 m. E. of Barquisimeto, and 1026 ft. above the sea, is known for its cigar manufactories.

LARAISH (*El Araish*), a port in northern Morocco on the Atlantic coast in 35° 13′ N., 6° 9′ W., 43 m. by sea S. by W. of Tangier, picturesquely situated on the left bank of the estuary of the Wad Lekkus. Pop. 6000 to 7000. The river, being fairly deep inside the bar, made this a favourite port for the Salli rovers to winter in, but the quantity of alluvial soil brought down threatens to close the port. The town is well situated for defence, its walls are in fair condition, and it has ten forts, all supplied with old-fashioned guns. Traces of the Spanish occupation from 1610–1689 are to be seen in the towers whose names are given by Tissot as those of St Stephen, St James and that of the Jews, with the Castle of Our Lady of Europe, now the kasbah or citadel. The most remarkable feature of Laraish is its fine large market-place inside the town with a low colonnade in front of very small shops. The streets, though narrow and steep, are generally paved. Its chief exports are oranges, millet, dra and other cereals, goat-hair and skins, sheepskins, wool and fullers' earth. The wool goes chiefly to Marseilles. The annual value of the trade is from £400,000 to £500,000.

In 1780 all the Europeans in Laraish were expelled by Mohammed XVI., although in 1786 the monopoly of its trade had been granted to Holland, even its export of wheat. In 1787 the Moors were still building pirate vessels here, the timber for which came from the neighbouring forest of M'amora. Not far from the town are the remains of what is believed to be a Phoenician city, Shammish, mentioned by Idrisi, who makes no allusion to Laraish. It is not, however, improbable from a passage in Scylax that the site of the present town was occupied by a Libyan settlement. Tradition also connects Laraish with the garden of the Hesperides, *'Arâsi* being the Arabic for "pleasure-gardens," and the "golden apples" perhaps the familiar oranges.

LARAMIE, a city and the county-seat of Albany county, Wyoming, U.S.A., on the Laramie river, 57 m. by rail N.W. of Cheyenne. Pop. (1900) 8207, of whom 1280 were foreign-born; (1905) 7601; (1910) 8237. It is served by the Union Pacific and the Laramie, Hahn's Peak & Pacific railways, the latter extending from Laramie to Centennial (30 m.). The city is situated on the Laramie Plains, at an elevation of 7165 ft., and is hemmed in on three sides by picturesque mountains. It has a public library, a United States Government building and hospitals, and is the seat of the university of Wyoming and of a Protestant Episcopal missionary bishopric. There is a state fish hatchery in the vicinity. The university (part of the public school system of the state) was founded in 1886, was opened in 1887, and embraces a College of Liberal Arts and Graduate School, a Normal School, a College of Agriculture and the Mechanic Arts, an Agricultural Experiment Station (established by a Federal appropriation), a College of Engineering, a School of Music, a Preparatory School and a Summer School. Laramie is a supply and distributing centre for a live-stock raising and mining region—particularly coal mining, though gold, silver, copper and iron are also found. The Union Pacific Railroad Company has machine shops, repair shops and rolling mills at Laramie, and, a short distance S. of the city, ice-houses and a tie-preserving plant. The manufactures include glass, leather, flour, plaster and pressed brick, the brick being made from shale obtained in the vicinity. The municipality owns and operates the water-works; the water is obtained from large springs about 2½ m. distant. Laramie was settled in 1868, by people largely from New England, Michigan, Wisconsin and Iowa, and was named in honour of Jacques Laramie, a French fur trader. It was first chartered as a city in 1868 by the legislature of Dakota, and was rechartered by the legislature of Wyoming in 1873.

LARBERT, a parish and town of Stirlingshire, Scotland. Pop. of parish (1901) 6500, of town, 1442. The town is situated on the Carron, 8 m. S. by E. of Stirling by the North British and Caledonian railways, the junction being an important station for traffic from the south by the West Coast route. Coal-mining is the chief industry. The principal buildings are the church, finely placed overlooking the river, the Stirling district asylum and the Scottish National Institution for imbecile children. In the churchyard is a monument to James Bruce, the Abyssinian traveller, who was born and died at Kinnaird House, 2½ m. N.E. Two m. N. by W. are the ruins of Torwood Castle and the remains of Torwood forest, to which Sir William Wallace retired after his defeat at Falkirk (1298). Near "Wallace's oak," in which the patriot concealed himself, Donald Cargill (1619–1681), the Covenanter, excommunicated Charles II. and James, duke of York, in 1680. The fragment of an old round building is said to be the relic of one of the very few "brochs," or round towers, found in the Lowlands.

LARCENY (an adaptation of Fr. *larcin*, O. Fr. *larrecin*, from Lat. *latrocinium*, theft, *latro*, robber), the unlawful taking and carrying away of things personal, with intent to deprive the rightful owner of the same. The term *theft*, sometimes used as a synonym of larceny, is in reality a broader term, applying to all cases of depriving another of his property whether by removing or withholding it, and includes larceny, robbery, cheating, embezzlement, breach of trust, &c.

Larceny is, in modern legal systems, universally treated as a crime, but the conception of it as a crime is not one belonging to the earliest stage of law. To its latest period Roman law regarded larceny or theft (*furtum*) as a delict *prima facie* pursued by a civil remedy—the *actio furti* for a penalty, the *vindicatio* or *condictio* for the stolen property itself or its value. In later times, a criminal remedy to meet the graver crimes gradually grew up by the side of the civil, and in the time of Justinian the criminal remedy, where it existed, took precedence of the civil (*Cod.* iii. 8. 4). But to the last criminal proceedings could only be taken in serious cases, *e.g.* against stealers of cattle (*abigei*) or the clothes of bathers (*balnearii*). The punishment was death, banishment, or labour in the mines or on public works. In the main the Roman law coincides with the English law. The definition as given in the *Institutes* (iv. 1. 1) is "furtum est contrectatio rei fraudulosa, vel ipsius rei, vel etiam ejus usus possessionisve," to which the *Digest* (xlvii. 2. 1, 3) adds "lucri faciendi gratia." The earliest English definition, that of Bracton (150*b*), runs thus: "furtum est secundum leges contrectatio rei alienae fraudulenta cum animo furandi invito illo domino cujus res illa fuerit." Bracton omits the "lucri faciendi gratia" of the Roman definition, because in English law the motive is immaterial,[1] and the "usus ejus possessionisve," because the definition includes an intent to deprive the owner of his property permanently. The "animo furandi" and "invito domino" of Bracton's definition are expansions for the sake of greater clearness. They seem to have been implied in Roman law. *Furtum* is on the whole a more comprehensive term than larceny. This

[1] Thus destruction of a letter by a servant, with a view of suppressing inquiries into his or her character, makes the servant guilty of larceny in English law.

[illegible] arises from the tendency to extend the bounds [illegible] to limit the bounds of a crime. Thus it was [illegible] would not be theft at English common law) to use [illegible] contrary to the wishes of the owner, to retain [illegible], or to steal a human being, such as a slave or *filius* [illegible] a special form of *furtum* called *plagium*). The latter [illegible] English law an abduction under certain circumstances [illegible]. One of two married persons could not commit [illegible] against the other, but larceny may be so committed [illegible] the Married Women's Property Act 1882. [illegible] was merely a delict, the *obligatio ex delicto* could be [illegible] by agreement between the parties; this cannot [illegible] in England. In another direction English law is more [illegible] the rights of third parties than was Roman. [illegible] a good title to stolen goods; in Roman law [illegible], except in the single case of a *hereditas* acquired [illegible]. The development of the law of *furtum* at Rome [illegible] interesting, for even in its latest period is found a [illegible] the most primitive theories of law adopted by [illegible]. They took as their guide the measure of [illegible] to be exacted by an aggrieved person under [illegible] of the case" (Maine, *Ancient Law*, ch. x.). [illegible] reason of the division of *furtum* into *mani-*[illegible]. The manifest thief was one taken [illegible] with the manner," in the language of old [illegible] Twelve Tables denounced the punishment of [illegible] manifest thief, for that would be the penalty [illegible] owner in whose place the judge stood. [illegible] penalty was afterwards mitigated by the [illegible] for it the payment of quadruple the [illegible]. The same penalty was also given by [illegible] from a fire or a wreck, or of prevention [illegible] inflicted the non-manifest thief in [illegible] stolen. The actions for penalties [illegible] for the stolen goods themselves or [illegible] and double penalties still remain [illegible]. The search for stolen goods, as it [illegible] was a survival of a period when the [illegible] of summons (*in jus vocatio*), [illegible] such a search, by the Twelve Tables, [illegible] of the supposed thief by the [illegible] a cincture, and carrying a [illegible] apparently against any possi-[illegible] by depositing some of his own [illegible]. This mode of search [illegible] Justinian. Robbery (*bona vi* [illegible]. By the *actio vi bonorum* [illegible] be recovered if the action [illegible] value if brought after the [illegible] value included the stolen [illegible] in effect only a triple one. [illegible] as in *furtum*.

[illegible] to have been very early [illegible] calling for special attention. [illegible] laws are full of provisions on [illegible] to regard it as a delict [illegible] payment. Considerable [illegible] in regard to the owner [illegible] Æthelberht, if a freeman [illegible] fold, if from a freeman [illegible] stole, he had only to [illegible] laws of Alfred ordinary [illegible] stole in a church was [illegible] laws of Ina named as [illegible] to the wer-gild of [illegible] might be slain if he fled [illegible] punishment increased. [illegible] form was inflicted. [illegible] placed a thief in the [illegible]. Putting out the [illegible] the parish [illegible]

century, and until 1827 theft or larceny of certain kinds remained capital. Both before and after the Conquest local jurisdiction over thieves was a common franchise of lords of manors, attended with some of the advantages of modern summary jurisdiction.

Under the common law larceny was a felony. It was affected by numerous statutes, the main object of legislation being to bring within the law of larceny offences which were not larcenies at common law, either because they were thefts of things of which there could be no larceny at common law, *e.g.* beasts *ferae naturae*, title deeds or choses in action, or because the common law regarded them merely as delicts for which the remedy was by civil action, *e.g.* fraudulent breaches of trust. The earliest act in the statutes of the realm dealing with larceny appears to be the *Carta Forestae* of 1225, by which fine or imprisonment was inflicted for stealing the king's deer. The next act appears to be the statute of Westminster the First (1275), dealing again with stealing deer. It seems as though the beginning of legislation on the subject was for the purpose of protecting the chases and parks of the king and the nobility. A very large number of the old acts are named in the repealing act of 1827. An act of the same date removed the old distinction between grand and petit larceny.[1] The former was theft of goods above the value of twelve pence, in the house of the owner, not from the person, or by night, and was a capital crime. It was petit larceny where the value was twelve pence or under, the punishment being imprisonment or whipping. The gradual depreciation in the value of money afforded good ground for Sir Henry Spelman's sarcasm that, while everything else became dearer, the life of man became continually cheaper. The distinction between grand and petit larceny first appears in statute law in the Statute of Westminster the First, c. 15, but it was not created for the first time by that statute. It is found in some of the pre-Conquest codes, as that of Æthelstan, and it is recognized in the *Leges Henrici Primi*. A distinction between simple and compound larceny is still found in the books. The latter is larceny accompanied by circumstances of aggravation, as that it is in a dwelling-house or from the person. The law of larceny is now contained chiefly in the Larceny Act 1861 (which extends to England and Ireland), a comprehensive enactment including larceny, embezzlement, fraud by bailees, agents, bankers, factors, and trustees, sacrilege, burglary, housebreaking, robbery, obtaining money by threats or by false pretences, and receiving stolen goods, and prescribing procedure, both civil and criminal. There are, however, other acts in force dealing with special cases of larceny, such as an act of Henry VIII. as to stealing the goods of the king, and the Game, Post-Office and Merchant Shipping Acts. There are separate acts providing for larceny by a partner of partnership property, and by a husband or wife of the property of the other (Married Women's Property Act 1882). Proceedings against persons subject to naval or military law depend upon the Naval Discipline Act 1866 and the Army Act 1881. There are several acts, both before and after 1861, directing how the property is to be laid in indictments for stealing the goods of counties, friendly societies, trades unions, &c. The principal conditions which must exist in order to constitute larceny are these: (1) there must be an actual taking into the possession of the thief, though the smallest removal is sufficient; (2) there must be an intent to deprive the owner of his property for an indefinite period, and to assume the entire dominion over it, an intent often described in Bracton's words as *animus furandi*; (3) this intent must exist at the time of taking; (4) the thing taken must be one capable of larceny either at common law or by statute. One or two cases falling under the law of larceny are of special interest. It was held more than once that a servant taking corn to feed his master's horses, but without any intention of applying it for his own benefit, was guilty of larceny. To remedy this hardship, the Misappropriation of Servants Act 1863 was passed to declare such an act not to be felony. The case of appropriation of goods which have been found has led to some difficulty. It now seems to be the law that in order to constitute a larceny of lost goods there must be a felonious intent at the time of finding, that is, an intent to deprive the owner of them, coupled with reasonable means at the same time of knowing the owner. The mere retention of the goods when the owner has become known to the finder does not make the retention criminal. Larceny of money may be committed when the money is paid by mistake, if the prisoner took it *animo furandi*. In two noteworthy cases the question was argued before a very full court for crown cases reserved, and in each case there was a striking difference of opinion. In *R.* v. *Middleton*, 1873, L.R. 2 C.C.R., 38, the prisoner, a depositor in a post-office savings bank, received by the mistake of the clerk a larger sum that he was entitled to. The jury found that he had the *animus furandi* at the time of taking the money, and that he knew it to be the money of the postmaster-general. The majority of the court held it to be larceny. In a case in 1885 (*R.* v. *Ashwell*, L.R. 16 Q.B.D. 190), where the prosecutor gave the prisoner a sovereign believing it to be a shilling, and the prisoner

[1] This provision was most unnecessarily repeated in the Larceny Act of 1861.

took it under that belief, but afterwards discovered its value and retained it, the court was equally divided as to whether the prisoner was guilty of larceny at common law, but held that he was not guilty of larceny as a bailee. Legislation has considerably affected the procedure in prosecutions for larceny. The inconveniences of the common law rules of interpretation of indictments led to certain amendments of the law, now contained in the Larceny Act, for the purpose of avoiding the frequent failures of justice owing to the strictness with which indictments were construed. Three larcenies of property of the same person within six months may now be charged in one indictment. On an indictment for larceny the prisoner may be found guilty of embezzlement, and *vice versa*; and if the prisoner be indicted for obtaining goods by false pretences, and the offence turn out to be larceny, he is not entitled to be acquitted of the misdemeanour. A count for receiving may be joined with the count for stealing. In many cases it is unnecessary to allege or prove ownership of the property the subject of the indictment. The act also contains numerous provisions as to venue and the apprehension of offenders. In another direction the powers of courts of Summary Jurisdiction (*q.v.*) have been extended, in the case of charges of larceny, embezzlement and receiving stolen goods, against children and young persons and against adults pleading guilty or waiving their right to trial by jury. The maximum punishment for larceny is fourteen years' penal servitude, but this can only be inflicted in certain exceptional cases, such as horse or cattle stealing and larceny by a servant or a person in the service of the crown or the police. The extreme punishment for simple larceny after a previous conviction for felony is ten years' penal servitude. Whipping may be part of the sentence on boys under sixteen.

Scotland.—A vast number of acts of the Scottish parliament dealt with larceny. The general policy of the acts was to make larceny what was not larceny at common law, *e.g.* stealing fruit, dogs, hawks or deer, and to extend the remedies, *e.g.* by giving the justiciar authority throughout the kingdom, by making the master in the case of theft by the servant liable to give the latter up to justice, or by allowing the use of firearms against thieves. The general result of legislation in England and Scotland has been to assimilate the law of larceny in both kingdoms. As a rule, what would be larceny in one would be larceny in the other.

United States.—The law depends almost entirely upon state legislation, and is in general accordance with that of England. The only acts of Congress bearing on the subject deal with larceny in the army and navy, and with larceny and receiving on the high seas or in any place under the exclusive jurisdiction of the United States, *e.g.* Alaska.

Alaska.—Stealing any goods, chattels, government note, bank note, or other thing in action, books of account, &c., is larceny: punishment, imprisonment for not less than one nor more than ten years if the property stolen is in value over $35. Larceny in any dwelling-house, warehouse, steamship, church, &c., is punishable by imprisonment for not less than one nor more than seven years. Larceny of a horse, mule, ass, bull, steer, cow or reindeer is punishable by imprisonment for not less than one nor more than fifteen years. Wilfully altering or defacing marks or brands on such animals is larceny (Pen. Code Alaska, § 45, 1899).

Arizona.—Appropriating property found without due inquiry for the owner is larceny (Penal Code, § 442). "Dogs are property and of the value of *one dollar each* within the meaning of the terms 'property' and 'value' as used in this chapter" (*id.* § 448). Property includes a passage ticket though never issued. Persons stealing property in another state or county, or who receive it knowing it to be stolen and bring it into Arizona, may be convicted and punished as if the offence was committed there (*id.* § 454). Stealing gas or water from a main is a misdemeanour.

Iowa.—It is larceny to steal electricity, gas or water from wires, meters or mains (L. 1903, ch. 132).

New York.—Larceny as defined by § 528 of the Penal Code includes also embezzlement, obtaining property by false pretences, and felonious breach of trust (*People* v. *Dumar*, 106 N.Y. 508), but the method of proof required to establish these offences has not been changed. Grand larceny in the *first degree* is (*a*) stealing property of any value in the night time; (*b*) of $25 in value or more at night from a dwelling house, vessel or railway car; (*c*) of the value of more than $500 in any manner; in the *second degree* (*a*) stealing in any manner property of the value of over $25 and under $500, (*b*) taking from the person property of any value; (*c*) stealing any record of a court or other record filed with any public officer. Every other larceny is petit larceny. "Value" of any stock, bond or security having a market value is the amount of money due thereon or what, in any contingency, might be collected thereon, of any passenger ticket the price it is usually sold at. The value of anything else not fixed by statute is its market value. Grand larceny, in the first degree, is punishable by imprisonment not exceeding ten years; in the second degree, not exceeding five years. Petit larceny is a misdemeanour (Penal Code, §§ 530-535). Bringing stolen goods into the state knowing them to be stolen is punishable as larceny within the state (*id.* § 540). A "pay ticket" for removing a load of snow may be the subject of larceny and its value the amount to be paid on it. (*People* v. *Fletcher* [1906] 110 App. D. 231).

Kansas.—The owner of goods who takes them from a railroad company with intent to defeat its lien for transportation charges is guilty of larceny. (*Atchison Co.* v. *Hinsdell* [1907] 90 Pac. Rep. 800).

Massachusetts.—Larceny includes embezzlement and obtaining money by false pretences. (Rev. L. 1902, ch. 218, § 40.) The failing to restore to or to notify the owner of property removed from premises on fire is larceny (*id.* ch. 208, § 22). It is larceny to purchase property (payment for which is to be made on or before delivery) by means of a false pretence as to means or ability to pay, provided such pretence is signed by the person to be charged. Indictment for stealing a will need not contain an allegation of value (*id.* § 29). A person convicted either as accessory or principal of three distinct larcenies shall be adjudged "a common and notorious thief" and may be imprisoned for not more than twenty years (*id.* 31). On second conviction for larceny of a bicycle, the thief may be imprisoned for not more than five years. Larceny of things annexed to realty is punishable as if it were a larceny of personal property (*id.* §§ 33, 35).

Ohio.—Stealing "anything of value" is larceny (Bates Stats. § 6856). Tapping gas pipes is punishable by fine or imprisonment for not more than thirty days. Stealing timber having "timber dealers'" trade mark, or removing it from a stream, is punishable by a fine of not less than $20.

Utah.—It is grand larceny to alter the mark or brand on an animal (L. 1905, ch. 38).

Wyoming.—For branding or altering or defacing the brand on cattle with intent to steal, the penalty is imprisonment for not more than five years. It is larceny for a bailee to convert with intent to steal goods left with or found by him (Rev. Stats. §§ 4986, 4989).

Washington.—A horse not branded, but under Code § 6861 an "outlaw," the owner being unknown, can be the subject of a larceny, having been held to be property of the state. (*State* v. *Eddy* [1907], 90 Pac. Rep. 641). For the third offence of such a larceny the penalty is imprisonment for *life* (L. 1903, ch. 86).

See also EMBEZZLEMENT; CHEATING; FALSE PRETENCES; ROBBERY; STOLEN GOODS.

LARCH (from the Ger. *Lärche*, M.H.G. *Lerche*, Lat. *larix*), a name applied to a small group of coniferous trees, of which the common larch of Europe is taken as the type. The members of the genus *Larix* are distinguished from the firs, with which they were formerly placed, by their deciduous leaves, scattered singly, as in *Abies*, on the young shoots of the season, but on all older branchlets growing in whorl-like tufts, each surrounding the extremity of a rudimentary or abortive branch; they differ from cedars (*Cedrus*), which also have the fascicles of leaves on arrested branchlets, not only in the deciduous leaves, but in the cones, the scales of which are thinner towards the apex, and are persistent, remaining attached long after the seeds are discharged. The trees of the genus are closely allied in botanic features, as well as in general appearance, so that it is sometimes difficult to assign to them determinate specific characters, and the limit between species and variety is not always very accurately defined. Nearly all are natives of Europe, or the northern plains and mountain ranges of Asia and North America, though one (*Larix Griffithii*) occurs only on the Himalayas.

The common larch (*L. europaea*) is, when grown in perfection, a stately tree with tall erect trunk, gradually tapering from root to summit, and horizontal branches springing at irregular intervals from the stem, and in old trees often becoming more or less drooping, but rising again towards the extremities; the branchlets or side shoots, very slender and pendulous, are pretty thickly studded with the spurs each bearing a fascicle of thirty or more narrow linear leaves, of a peculiar bright light green when they first appear in the spring, but becoming of a deeper hue when mature. The yellow stamen-bearing flowers are in sessile, nearly spherical catkins; the fertile ones vary in colour, from red or purple to greenish-white, in different varieties; the erect cones, which remain long on the branches, are above an inch in length and oblong-ovate in shape, with reddish-brown scales somewhat waved on the edges, the lower bracts usually rather longer than the scales. The tree flowers in April or May, and the winged seeds are shed the following autumn. When standing in an open space, the larch grows of a nearly conical shape, with the lower branches almost reaching the ground, while those above gradually diminish in length towards the top of the trunk, presenting a very symmetrical form; but in dense woods the lower parts become bare of foliage, as with the firs under similar circumstances. When springing up among rocks or on ledges, the stem sometimes becomes much curved, and, with its spreading boughs and pendent branchlets, often forms a striking and picturesque object in alpine passes and steep ravines. In the prevalent European varieties the bark is reddish-grey, and rather rough and scarred in old trees, which are often much lichen-covered. The trunk attains a height of from 80 to 140 ft., with a diameter of from 3 to 5 ft. near the ground, but in close woods is comparatively slender in proportion to its altitude. The larch abounds on the Alps of Switzerland, on which it flourishes at an elevation of 5000 ft., and also on those of Tirol and Savoy, on the Carpathians, and in most of the hill regions of central Europe; it is not wild on the Apennine

Branchlet of Larch (*Larix europaea*).

chain, or the Pyrenees, and in the wild state is unknown in the Spanish peninsula. It forms extensive woods in Russia, but does not extend to Scandinavia, where its absence is somewhat remarkable, as the tree grows freely in Norway and Sweden where planted, and even multiplies itself by self-sown seed, according to F. C. Schübeler, in the neighbourhood of Trondhjem In the north-eastern parts of Russia, in the country towards the Petchora river, and on the Ural, a peculiar variety prevails, regarded by some as a distinct species (*L. sibirica*), this form is abundant nearly throughout Siberia, extending to the Pacific coast of Kamchatka and the hills of the Amur region. The Siberian larch has smooth grey bark and smaller cones, approaching in shape somewhat to those of the American hackmatack; it seems even hardier than the Alpine tree, growing up to latitude 68°, but, as the inclement climate of the polar shores is neared, dwindling down to a dwarf and even trailing bush.

The larch, from its lofty straight trunk and the high quality of its wood, is one of the most important of coniferous trees; its growth is extremely rapid, the stem attaining a large size in from sixty to eighty years, while the tree yields good useful timber at forty or fifty; it forms firm heartwood at an early age, and the sapwood is less perishable than that of the firs, rendering it more valuable in the young state.

The wood of large trees is compact in texture, in the best varieties of a deep reddish colour varying to brownish-yellow, but apt to be lighter in tint, and less hard in grain, when grown in rich soils or in low sheltered situations. It is remarkably tough, resisting a rending strain better than any of the fir or pine woods in common use, though not as elastic as some; properly seasoned, it is as little liable to shrink as to split; the boughs being small compared to the trunk, the timber is more free from large knots, and the small knots remain firm and undecayed. The only drawback to these good qualities is a certain liability to warp and bend, unless very carefully seasoned; for this purpose it is recommended to be left floating in water for a year after felling, and then allowed some months to dry slowly and completely before sawing up the logs; barking the trunk in winter while the tree is standing, and leaving it in that state till the next year, has been often advised with the larch as with other timber, but the practical inconveniences of the plan have prevented its adoption on any large scale. When well prepared for use, larch is one of the most durable of coniferous woods. Its strength and toughness render it valuable for naval purposes, to which it is largely applied; its freedom from any tendency to split adapts it for clinker-built boats. It is much employed for house-building; most of the picturesque log-houses in Vaud and the adjacent cantons are built of squared larch trunks, and derive their fine brown tint from the hardened resin that slowly exudes from the wood after long exposure to the summer sun; the wooden shingles, that in Switzerland supply the place of tiles, are also frequently of larch. In Germany it is much used by the cooper as well as the carpenter, while the form of the trunk admirably adapts it for all purposes for which long straight timber is needed. It answers well for fence-posts and river piles; many of the foundations of Venice rest upon larch, the lasting qualities of which were well known and appreciated, not only in medieval times, but in the days of Vitruvius and Pliny. The harder and darker varieties are used in the construction of cheap solid furniture, being fine in grain and taking polish better than many more costly woods. A peculiarity of larch wood is the difficulty with which it is ignited, although so resinous, and, coated with a thin layer of plaster, beams and pillars of larch might probably be found to justify Caesar's epithet "igni impenetrabile lignum"; even the small branches are not easily kept alight, and a larch fire in the open needs considerable care. Yet the forests of larch in Siberia often suffer from conflagration. When these fires occur while the trees are full of sap, a curious mucilaginous matter is exuded from the half-burnt stems; when dry it is of pale reddish colour, like some of the coarser kinds of gum-arabic, and is soluble in water, the solution resembling gum-water, in place of which it is sometimes used; considerable quantities are collected and sold as "Orenburg gum"; in Siberia and Russia it is occasionally employed as a semi-medicinal food, being esteemed an antiscorbutic. For burning in close stoves and furnaces, larch makes tolerably good fuel, its value being estimated by Hartig as only one-fifth less than that of beech; the charcoal is compact. and is in demand for iron-smelting and other metallurgic uses in some parts of Europe.

In the trunk of the larch, especially when growing in climates where the sun is powerful in summer, a fine clear turpentine exists in great abundance; in Savoy and the south of Switzerland, it is collected for sale, though not in such quantity as formerly, when, being taken to Venice for shipment, it was known in commerce as "Venice turpentine" Old trees are selected, from the bark of which it is observed to ooze in the early summer; holes are bored in the trunk, somewhat inclined upward towards the centre of the stem, in which, between the layers of wood, the turpentine is said to collect in small lacunae; wooden gutters placed in these holes convey the viscous fluid into little wooden pails hung on the end of each gutter, the secretion flows slowly all through the summer months, and a tree in proper condition yields from 6 to 8 lb a year, and will continue to give an annual supply for thirty or forty years, being, however, rendered quite useless for timber by subjection to this process. In Tirol, a single hole is made near the root of the tree in the spring; this is stopped with a plug, and the turpentine is removed by a scoop in the autumn; but each tree yields only from a few ounces to ½ lb by this process. Real larch turpentine is a thick tenacious fluid, of a deep yellow colour, and nearly transparent; it does not harden by time, it contains 15% of the essential oil of turpentine, also resin, succinic, pinic and sylvic acids, and a bitter extractive matter. According to Pereira, much sold under the name of Venice turpentine is a mixture of common resin and oil of turpentine. On the French Alps a sweet exudation is found on the small branchlets of young larches in June and July, resembling manna in taste and laxative properties, and known as *Manna de Briançon* or *Manna Brigantina*; it occurs in small whitish irregular granular masses, which are removed in the morning before they are too much dried by the sun; this manna seems to differ little in composition from the sap of the tree, which also contains *mannite*; its cathartic powers are weaker than those of the manna of the manna ash (*Fraximus ornus*), but it is employed in France for the same purposes.

The bark of the larch is largely used in some countries for tanning; it is taken from the trunk only, being stripped from the trees when felled; its value is about equal to that of birch bark; but, according to the experience of British tanners, it is scarcely half as strong as that of the oak. The soft inner bark is occasionally used in Siberia as a ferment, by hunters and others, being boiled and mixed with rye-meal, and buried in the snow for a short time, when it is employed as a substitute for other leaven, and in making the sour liquor called "quass." In Germany a fungus (*Polyporus Laricis*) grows on the roots and stems of decaying larches, which was formerly in esteem as a drastic purgative. The young shoots of the larch are sometimes given in Switzerland as fodder to cattle.

The larch, though mentioned by Parkinson in 1629 as "nursed up" by a few "lovers of variety" as a rare exotic, does not seem to have been much grown in England till early in the 18th century. In Scotland the date of its introduction is a disputed point, but it seems to have been planted at Dunkeld by the 2nd duke of Athole in 1727, and about thirteen or fourteen years later considerable plantations were made at that place, the commencement of one of the largest planting experiments on record; it is estimated that 14 million larches were planted on the Athole estates between that date and 1826. The cultivation of the tree rapidly spread, and the larch has become a conspicuous feature of the scenery in many parts of Scotland. It grows as rapidly and attains as large a size in British habitats suited to it as in its home on the Alps, and often produces equally good timber. The larch of Europe is essentially a mountain tree, and requires not only free air above, but a certain moderate amount of moisture in the soil beneath, with, at the same time, perfect drainage, to bring the timber to perfection. Where there is complete freedom from stagnant water in the ground, and abundant room for the spread of its branches to light and air, the larch will flourish in a great variety of soils, stiff clays, wet or mossy peat, and moist alluvium being the chief exceptions; in its native localities it seems partial to the debris of primitive and metamorphic rocks, but is occasionally found growing luxuriantly on calcareous subsoils; in Switzerland it attains the largest size, and forms the best timber, on the northern declivities of the mountains; but in Scotland a southern aspect appears most favourable.

The best variety for culture in Britain is that with red female flowers; the light-flowered kinds are said to produce inferior wood, and the Siberian larch does not grow in Scotland nearly as fast as the Alpine tree. The larch is raised from seed in immense numbers in British nurseries; that obtained from Germany is preferred, being more perfectly ripened than the cones of home growth usually are. The seeds are sown in April, on rich ground, which should not be too highly manured; the young larches are planted out when two years old, or sometimes transferred to a nursery bed to attain a larger size; but, like all conifers, they succeed best when planted young; on the mountains, the seedlings are usually put into a mere slit made in the ground by a spade with a triangular blade, the place being first cleared of any heath, bracken, or tall herbage that might smother the young tree; the plants should be from 3 to 4 ft. apart, or even more, according to the growth intended before thinning, which should be begun as soon as the boughs begin to overspread much; little or no pruning is needed beyond the careful removal of dead branches. The larch is said not to succeed on arable land, especially where corn has been grown, but experience does not seem to support this view; that against the previous occupation of the ground by Scotch fir or Norway spruce is probably better founded, and, where timber is the object, it should not be planted with other conifers. On the Grampians and neighbouring hills the larch will flourish at a greater elevation than the pine, and will grow up to an altitude of 1700 or even 1800 ft.; but it attains its full size on lower slopes. In very dry and bleak localities, the Scotch fir will probably be more successful up to 900 ft. above the sea, the limit of the luxuriant growth of that hardy conifer in Britain; and in moist valleys or on imperfectly drained acclivities Norway spruce is more suitable. The growth of the larch while young is exceedingly rapid; in the south of England it will often attain a height of 25 ft. in the first ten years, while in favourable localities it will grow upwards of 80 ft. in half a century or less; one at Dunkeld felled sixty years after planting was 110 ft. high; but usually the tree does not increase so rapidly after the first thirty or forty years. Some larches in Scotland rival in size the most gigantic specimens standing in their native woods; a tree at Dalwick, Peeblesshire, attained 5 ft. in diameter; one at Glenarbuck, near the Clyde, grew above 140 ft. high, with a circumference of 13 ft. The annual increase in girth is often considerable even in large trees; the fine larch near the abbey of Dunkeld figured by Strutt in his *Sylva Britannica* increased 2½ ft. between 1796 and 1825, its measurement at the latter date being 13 ft., with a height of 97½ ft.

In the south of England, the larch is much planted for the supply of hop-poles, though in parts of Kent and Sussex poles formed of Spanish chestnut are regarded as still more lasting. In plantations made with this object, the seedlings are placed very close (from 1½ to 2 ft. apart), and either cut down all at once, when the required height is attained or thinned out, leaving the remainder to gain a greater length; the land is always well trenched before planting. The best month for larch planting, whether for poles or timber, is November; larches are sometimes planted in the spring, but the practice cannot be commended, as the sap flows early, and, if a dry period follows, the growth is sure to be checked. The thinnings of the larch woods in the Highlands are in demand for railway sleepers, scaffold poles, and mining timber, and are applied to a variety of agricultural purposes. The tree generally succeeds on the Welsh hills.

The young seedlings are sometimes nibbled by the hare and rabbit; and on parts of the highland hills both bark and shoots are eaten in the winter by the roe-deer; larch woods should always be fenced in to keep out the hill-cattle, which will browse upon the shoots in spring. The "woolly aphis," "American blight," or "larch blight" (*Eriosoma laricis*) often attacks the trees in close valleys, but rarely spreads much unless other unhealthy conditions are present. The larch suffers from several diseases caused by fungi; the most important is the larch-canker caused by the parasitism of *Peziza Willkommii*. The spores germinate on a damp surface and enter the cortex through small cracks or wounds in the protecting layer. The fungus-mycelium will go on growing indefinitely in the cambium layer, thus killing and destroying a larger area year by year. The most effective method of treatment is to cut out the diseased branch or patch as early as possible. Another disease which is sometimes confused with that caused by the *Peziza* is "heart-rot"; it occasionally attacks larches only ten years old or less, but is more common when the trees have acquired a considerable size, sometimes spreading in a short time through a whole plantation. The trees for a considerable period show little sign of unhealthiness, but eventually the stem begins to swell somewhat near the root, and the whole tree gradually goes off as the disease advances; when cut down, the trunk is found to be decayed at the centre, the "rot" usually commencing near the ground. Trees of good size are thus rendered nearly worthless, often showing little sign of unhealthiness till felled. Great difference of opinion exists among foresters as to the cause of this destructive malady; but it is probably the direct result of unsuitable soil, especially soil containing insufficient nourishment.

Considerable quantities of larch timber are imported into Britain for use in the dockyards, in addition to the large home supply. The quality varies much, as well as the colour and density; an Italian sample in the museum at Kew (of a very dark red tint) weighs about 24½ lb to the cub. ft., while a Polish specimen, of equally deep hue, is 44 lb 1 oz. to the same measurement.

For the landscape gardener, the larch is a valuable aid in the formation of park and pleasure ground; but it is never seen to such advantage as when hanging over some tumbling burn or rocky pass among the mountains. A variety with very pendent boughs, known as the "drooping" larch var. *pendula*, is occasionally met with in gardens.

The bark of the larch has been introduced into pharmacy, being given, generally in the form of an alcoholic tincture, in chronic bronchitic affections and internal haemorrhages. It contains, in addition to tannin, a peculiar principle called *larixin*, which may be obtained in a pure state by distillation from a concentrated infusion of the bark; it is a colourless substance in long crystals, with a bitter and astringent taste, and a faint acid reaction; hence some term it *larixinic acid*.

The European larch has long been introduced into the United States, where, in suitable localities, it flourishes as luxuriantly as in Britain. Plantations have been made in America with an economic view, the tree growing much faster, and producing good timber at an earlier age than the native hackmatack (or tamarack), while the wood is less ponderous, and therefore more generally applicable.

The genus is represented in the eastern parts of North America by the hackmatack (*L. americana*), of which there are several varieties, two so well marked that they are by some botanists considered specifically distinct. In one (*L. microcarpa*) the cones are very small, rarely exceeding ½ in. in length, of a roundish-oblong shape; the scales are very few in number, crimson in the young state, reddish-brown when ripe; the tree much resembles the European larch in general appearance but is of more slender growth; its trunk is seldom more than 2 ft. in diameter and rarely above 80 ft. high; this form is the red larch, the *épinette rouge* of the French Canadians. The black larch (*L. pendula*) has rather larger cones, of an oblong shape, about ¾ in. long, purplish or green in the immature state, and dark brown when ripe, the scales somewhat more numerous, the bracts all shorter than the scales. The bark is dark bluish-grey, smoother than in the red larch, on the trunk and lower boughs often glossy; the branches are more or less pendulous and very slender.

The red larch grows usually on higher and drier ground, ranging from the Virginian mountains to the shores of Hudson Bay; the black larch is found often on moist land, and even in swamps. The hackmatack is one of the most valuable timber trees of America; it is in great demand in the ports of the St Lawrence for shipbuilding. It is far more durable than any of the oaks of that region, is heavy and close-grained, and much stronger, as well as more lasting, than that of the pines and firs of Canada. In many parts all the finer trees have been cut down, but large woods of it still exist in the less accessible districts; it abounds especially near Lake St John, Quebec, and in Newfoundland is the prevalent tree in some of the forest tracts; [illegible] common in Maine and Vermont. In the timber and building yards the "red" hackmatack is the kind preferred, the produce, probably, of *L. microcarpa*; the "grey" is less esteemed; but the varieties from which these woods are obtained cannot always be traced with certainty. Several fine specimens of the red larch exist in English parks, but its growth is much slower than that of *L. europaea*; the more pendulous forms of *L. pendula* are elegant trees for the garden. The hackmatacks might perhaps be grown with advantage in places too wet for the common larch.

In western America a larch (*L. occidentalis*) occurs more nearly resembling *L. europaea*. The leaves are short, thicker and more rigid than in any of the other larches; the cones are much larger than those of the hackmatacks, egg-shaped or oval in outline; the scales are of a fine red in the immature state, the bracts green and extending far beyond the scales in a rigid leaf-like point. The bark of the trunk has the same reddish tint as that of the common larch of Europe. It is the largest of all larches and one of the most useful timber trees of North America. Some of the trees are 250 ft. high and 6 to 8 ft. in diameter. The wood is the hardest and strongest of all the American conifers; it is durable and adapted for construction work or household furniture.

LARCHER, PIERRE HENRI (1726–1812), French classical scholar and archaeologist, was born at Dijon on the 12th of October 1726. Originally intended for the law, he abandoned it for the classics. His (anonymous) translation of Chariton's *Chaereas and Callirrhoë* (1763) marked him as an excellent Greek scholar. His attack upon Voltaire's *Philosophie de l'histoire* (published under the name of l'Abbé Bazin) created considerable interest at the time. His archaeological and mythological *Mémoire sur Vénus* (1775), which has been ranked with similar works of Heyne and Winckelmann, gained him admission to the Académie des Inscriptions (1778). After the [illegible] university was founded, he was appointed professor [illegible] literature (1809) with Boissonade as his assistant. [illegible] December 1812. Larcher's best work [illegible] of Herodotus (1786, new ed. by L. Humbert, [illegible] of which he had spent fifteen years. [illegible] though correct, is dull, but the com- [illegible] into English, London, 1829, new ed. [illegible] dealing with historical, geographical [illegible] and enriched by a wealth of illus- [illegible] modern authors, is not without value. [illegible] *et les écrits de P. L.* (1813); [illegible] i. 205; D. A. Wyttenbach, [illegible]

LARTIUS [illegible], **TITUS**, probably sur- [illegible] of an Etruscan family (cf. Lars [illegible] settled in Rome. When consul [illegible] the title and office being [illegible] to command against the [illegible] to reinstate Tarquin in [illegible] appointment three years [illegible] against the Latins [illegible] burden of their debts. [illegible] the Latins, and also inte- [illegible] of the plebeians. [illegible] Cocles in the [illegible] the Etruscans.

[illegible] vi. 37; Cicero, [illegible]

LARD [illegible] related to [illegible] and strained [illegible] from the "leaf" [illegible] the term [illegible] from other [illegible] "lard" at [illegible]

America. "Neutral lard" is prepared at a temperature of 40°–50° C. from freshly killed hogs; the finest quality, used for making oleomargarine, is got from the leaf, while the second, employed by biscuit and pastry bakers, is obtained from the fat of the back. Steam heat is utilized in extracting inferior qualities, such as "choice lard" and "prime steam lard," the source of the latter being any fat portion of the animal. Lard is a pure white fat of a butter-like consistence; its specific gravity is about 0·93, its solidifying point about 27°–30° C., and its melting point 35°–45° C. It contains about 60% of olein and 40% of palmitin and stearin. Adulteration is common, the substances used including "stearin" both of beef and of mutton, and vegetable oils such as cotton seed oil: indeed, mixtures have been sold as lard that contain nothing but such adulterants. In the pharmacopoeia lard figures as *adeps* and is employed as a basis for ointments. Benzoated lard, used for the same purpose, is prepared by heating lard with 3% of powdered benzoin for two hours; it keeps better than ordinary lard, but has slightly irritant properties.

Lard oil is the limpid, clear, colourless oil expressed by hydraulic pressure and gentle heat from lard; it is employed for burning and for lubrication. Of the solid residue, lard "stearine," the best qualities are utilized for making oleomargarine, the inferior ones in the manufacture of candles.

See J. Lewkowitsch, *Oils, Fats and Waxes* (London, 1909).

LARDNER, DIONYSIUS (1793–1859), Irish scientific writer, was born at Dublin on the 3rd of April 1793. His father, a solicitor, wished his son to follow the same calling. After some years of uncongenial desk work, Lardner entered Trinity College, Dublin, and graduated B.A. in 1817. In 1828 he became professor of natural philosophy and astronomy at University College, London, a position he held till 1840, when he eloped with a married lady, and had to leave the country. After a lecturing tour through the principal cities of the United States, which realized £40,000, he returned to Europe in 1845. He settled at Paris, and resided there till within a few months of his death, which took place at Naples on the 29th of April 1859.

Though lacking in originality or brilliancy, Lardner showed himself to be a successful populariser of science. He was the author of numerous mathematical and physical treatises on such subjects as algebraic geometry (1823), the differential and integral calculus (1825), the steam engine (1828), besides hand-books on various departments of natural philosophy (1854–1856); but it is as the editor of *Lardner's Cabinet Cyclopaedia* (1830–1844) that he is best remembered. To this scientific library of 134 volumes many of the ablest savants of the day contributed, Lardner himself being the author of the treatises on arithmetic, geometry, heat, hydrostatics and pneumatics, mechanics (in conjunction with Henry Kater) and electricity (in conjunction with C. V. Walker). The *Cabinet Library* (12 vols., 1830–1832) and the *Museum of Science and Art* (12 vols., 1854–1856) are his other chief undertakings. A few original papers appear in the Royal Irish Academy's *Transactions* (1824), in the Royal Society's *Proceedings* (1831–1836) and in the Astronomical Society's *Monthly Notices* (1852–1853); and two *Reports* to the British Association on railway constants (1838, 1841) are from his pen.

LARDNER, NATHANIEL (1684–1768), English theologian, was born at Hawkhurst, Kent. After studying for the Presbyterian ministry in London, and also at Utrecht and Leiden, he took licence as a preacher in 1709, but was not successful. In 1713 he entered the family of a lady of rank as tutor and domestic chaplain, where he remained until 1721. In 1724 he was appointed to deliver the Tuesday evening lecture in the Presbyterian chapel, Old Jewry, London, and in 1729 he became assistant minister to the Presbyterian congregation in Crutched Friars. He was given the degree of D.D. by Marischal College, Aberdeen, in 1745. He died at Hawkhurst on the 24th of July 1768.

An anonymous volume of *Memoirs* appeared in 1769; and a life by Andrew Kippis is prefixed to the edition of the *Works* of Lardner, published in 11 vols., 8vo in 1788, in 4 vols. 4to in 1817, and 10 vols. 8vo in 1827. The full title of his principal work—a work which, though now out of date, entitles its author to be regarded as the [illegible] modern critical research in the field of early Christian [illegible] *The Credibility of the Gospel History; or the Principal* [illegible] *New Testament confirmed by Passages of Ancient Authors, who were contemporary with our Saviour or his Apostles, or lived near their time*. Part i., in 2 vols. 8vo, appeared in 1727, the publication of part ii., in 12 vols. 8vo, began in 1733 and ended in 1755. In 1730 there was a second edition of part i., and the *Additions and Alterations* were also published separately. A *Supplement*, otherwise entitled *A History of the Apostles and Evangelists, Writers of the New Testament*, was added in 3 vols. (1756–1757), and reprinted in 1760. Other works by Lardner are *A Large Collection of Ancient Jewish and Heathen Testimonies to the Truth of the Christian Revelation, with Notes and Observations* (4 vols., 4to, 1764–1767); *The History of the Heretics of the two first Centuries after Christ*, published posthumously in 1780 and a considerable number of occasional sermons.

LAREDO, a city and the county-seat of Webb county, Texas, U.S.A., and a sub-port of entry, on the Rio Grande opposite Nuevo Laredo, Mexico, and 150 m. S. of San Antonio. Pop. (1900) 13,429, of whom 6882 were foreign-born (mostly Mexicans) and 82 negroes; (1910 census) 14,855. It is served by the International & Great Northern, the National of Mexico, the Texas Mexican and the Rio Grande & Eagle Pass railways, and is connected by bridges with Nuevo Laredo. Among the principal buildings are the U.S. Government Building, the City Hall and the County Court House; and the city's institutions include the Laredo Seminary (1882) for boys and girls, the Mercy Hospital, the National Railroad of Mexico Hospital and an Ursuline Convent. Loma Vista Park (65 acres) is a pleasure resort, and immediately W. of Laredo on the Rio Grande is Fort McIntosh (formerly Camp Crawford), a United States military post. Laredo is a jobbing centre for trade between the United States and Mexico, and is a sub-port of entry in the Corpus Christi Customs District. It is situated in a good farming and cattle-raising region, irrigated by water from the Rio Grande. The principal crop is Bermuda onions; in 1909 it was estimated that 1500 acres in the vicinity were devoted to this crop, the average yield per acre being about 20,000 ℔. There are coal mines about 25 m. above Laredo on the Rio Grande, and natural gas was discovered about 28 m. E. in 1908. The manufacture of bricks is an important industry. Laredo was named from the seaport in Spain, and was founded in 1767 as a Mexican town; it originally included what is now Nuevo Laredo, Mexico, and was long the only Mexican town on the left bank of the river. It was captured in 1846 by a force of Texas Rangers, and in 1847 was occupied by U.S. troops under General Lamar. In 1852 it was chartered as a city of Texas.

LA RÉOLE, a town of south-western France, capital of an arrondissement in the department of Gironde, on the right bank of the Gironde, 38 m. S.E. of Bordeaux by rail. Pop. (1906) 3469. La Réole grew up round a monastery founded in the 7th or 8th century, which was reformed in the 11th century and took the name of *Regula*, whence that of the town. A church of the end of the 12th century and some of the buildings (18th century) are left. There is also a town hall of the 12th and 14th centuries. The town fortifications were dismantled by order of Richelieu, but remains dating from the 12th and 14th centuries are to be seen, as well as a ruined château built by Henry II. of England. La Réole has a sub-prefecture, a tribunal of first instance, a communal college and an agricultural school. The town is the centre of the district in which the well-known breed of Bazadais cattle is reared. It is an agricultural market and carries on trade in the wine of the region together with liqueur distillery and the manufacture of casks, rope, brooms, &c.

LARES (older form *Lases*), Roman tutelary deities. The word is generally supposed to mean "lords," and identified with Etruscan *larth*, *lar*; but this is by no means certain. The attempt to harmonize the Stoic demonology with Roman religion led to the Lares being compared with the Greek "heroes" during the period of Greco-Roman culture, and the word is frequently translated ἥρωες. In the later period of the republic they are confounded with the Penates (and other deities), though the distinction between them was probably more sharply marked in earlier times. They were originally gods of the cultivated fields, worshipped by each household where its allotment joined those of others (see below). The distinction between public and private Lares existed from early times. The latter were worshipped in the house by the family alone, and the household Lar (*familiaris*) was conceived of as the centre-point of the family and of the family cult. The word itself (in the singular) came to be used in the general sense of "home." It is certain that originally each household had only one Lar; the plural was at first only used to include other classes of Lares, and only gradually, after the time of Cicero, ousted the singular. The image of the Lar, made of wood, stone or metal, sometimes even of silver, stood in its special shrine (*lararium*), which in early times was in the atrium, but was afterwards transferred to other parts of the house, when the family hearth was removed from the atrium. In some of the Pompeian houses the *lararium* was represented by a niche only, containing the image of the *lar*. It was usually a youthful figure, dressed in a short, high-girt tunic, holding in one hand a *rhyton* (drinking-horn), in the other a *patera* (cup). Under the Empire we find usually two of these, one on each side of the central figure of the Genius of the head of the household, sometimes of Vesta the hearth-deity. The whole group was called indifferently Lares or Penates. A prayer was said to the Lar every morning, and at each meal offerings of food and drink were set before him; a portion of these was placed on the hearth and afterwards shaken into the fire. Special sacrifices were offered on the kalends, nones, and ides of every month, and on the occasion of important family events. Such events were the birthday of the head of the household; the assumption of the *toga virilis* by a son; the festival of the Caristia in memory of deceased members of the household; recovery from illness; the entry of a young bride into the house for the first time; return home after a long absence. On these occasions the Lares were crowned with garlands, and offerings of cakes and honey, wine and incense, but especially swine, were laid before them. Their worship persisted throughout the pagan period, although its character changed considerably in later times. The emperor Alexander Severus had images of Abraham, Christ and Alexander the Great among his household Lares.

The public Lares belonged to the state religion. Amongst these must be included, at least after the time of Augustus, the *Lares compitales*. Originally two in number, mythologically the sons of Mercurius and Lara (or Larunda), they were the presiding deities of the cross-roads (*compita*), where they had their special chapels. It has been maintained by some that they are the twin brothers so frequent in early religions, the Romulus and Remus of the Roman foundation legends. Their sphere of influence included not only the cross-roads, but the whole neighbouring district of the town and country in which they were situated. They had a special annual festival, called Compitalia, to which public games were added some time during the republican period. When the colleges of freedmen and slaves, who assisted the presidents of the festival, were abolished by Julius Caesar, it fell into disuse. Its importance was revived by Augustus, who added to these Lares his own Genius, the religious personification of the empire.

The state itself had its own Lares, called *praestites*, the protecting patrons and guardians of the city. They had a temple and altar on the Via Sacra, near the Palatine, and were represented on coins as young men wearing the chlamys, carrying lances, seated, with a dog, the emblem of watchfulness, at their feet. Mention may also be made of the *Lares grundules*, whose worship was connected with the white sow of Alba Longa and its thirty young (the epithet has been connected with *grunnire*, to grunt): the *viales*, who protected travellers; the *hostilii*, who kept off the enemies of the state; the *permarini*, connected with the sea, to whom L. Aemilius Regillus, after a naval victory over Antiochus (190 B.C.), vowed a temple in the Campus Martius, which was dedicated by M. Aemilius Lepidus the censor in 179.

The old view that the Lares were the deified ancestors of the family has been rejected lately by Wissowa, who holds that the Lar was originally the protecting spirit of a man's lot of arable land, with a shrine at the *compitum*, *i.e.* the spot where the path bounding his arable met that of another holding; and thence found his way into the house.

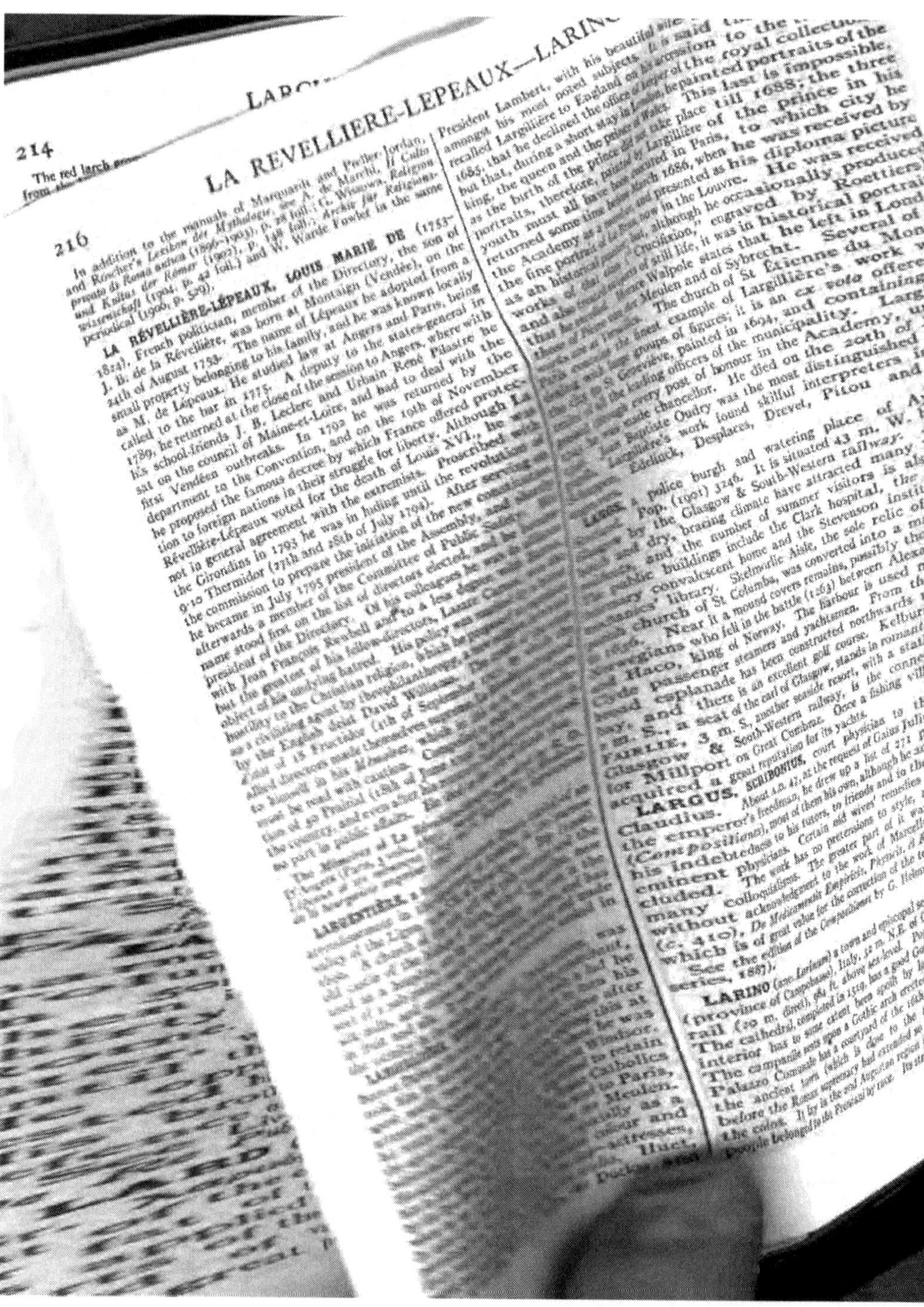

214
216
LA REVELLIERE-LEPEAUX—LARINO
LA RÉVELLIÈRE-LÉPEAUX, LOUIS MARIE DE
LARGUS, SCRIBONIUS
LARINO

it importance in the military history of Italy from the Hannibalic wars onwards. The town was a *municipium*, situated on the main road to the S E., which left the coast at Histonium (Vasto) and ran from Larinum E. to Sipontum From Larinum a branch road ran to Bovianum Vetus. Remains of its city walls, of its amphitheatre and also of baths, &c., exist, and it did not cease to be inhabited until after the earthquake of 1300, when the modern city was established. Cluentius, the client of Cicero, who delivered a speech in his favour, was a native of Larinum, his father having been praetor of the allied forces in the Social War (T As)

LARISSA (Turk. *Yeni Shehr*, "new town"), the most important town of Thessaly, situated in a rich agricultural district on the right bank of the Salambria (Peneios, Peneus, Peneius), about 35 m N W of Volo, with which it is connected by rail Pop. (1889) 13,610, (1907) 18,001 Till 1881 it was the seat of a pasha in the vilayet of Jannina, it is now the capital of the Greek province and the seat of a nomarch. Its long subjection to Turkey has left little trace of antiquity, and the most striking features in the general view are the minarets of the disused mosques (only four are now in use) and the Mahommedan burying-grounds. It was formerly a Turkish military centre and most of the people were of Turkish blood. In the outskirts is a village of Africans from the Sudan—a curious remnant of the forces collected by Ali Pasha. The manufactures include Turkish leather, cotton, silk and tobacco, trade and industry, however, are far from prosperous, though improving owing to the immigration of the Greek commercial element. Fevers and agues are prevalent owing to bad drainage and the overflowing of the river, and the death-rate is higher than the birth-rate. A considerable portion of the Turkish population emigrated in 1881; a further exodus took place in 1898. The department of Larissa had in 1907 a population of 95,066.

Larissa, written Larisa on ancient coins and inscriptions, is near the site of the Homeric Argissa. It appears in early times, when Thessaly was mainly governed by a few aristocratic families, as an important city under the rule of the Aleuadae, whose authority extended over the whole district of Pelasgiotis. This powerful family possessed for many generations before 369 B C the privilege of furnishing the Tagus, or generalissimo, of the combined Thessalian forces. The principal rivals of the Aleuadae were the Scopadae of Crannon, the remains of which (called by the Turks *Old Larissa*) are about 14 m. to the S.W. The inhabitants sided with Athens during the Peloponnesian War, and during the Roman invasion their city was of considerable importance. Since the 5th century it has been the seat of an archbishop, who has now fifteen suffragans. Larissa was the headquarters of Ali Pasha during the Greek War of Independence, and of the crown prince Constantine during the Greco-Turkish War; the flight of the Greek army from this place to Pharsala took place on the 23rd of April 1897. Notices of some ancient inscriptions found at Larissa are given by Miller in *Mélanges philologiques* (Paris, 1880); several sepulchral reliefs were found in the neighbourhood in 1882 A few traces of the ancient acropolis and theatre are still visible

The name Larissa was common to many "Pelasgian" towns, and apparently signified a fortified city or *burg*, such as the citadel of Argos. Another town of the name in Thessaly was Larissa Cremaste, surnamed Pelasgia (Strabo ix. p. 440), situated on the slope of Mt. Othrys. (J. D. B.)

LĀRISTĀN, a sub-province of the province of Fars in Persia, bounded E. and N.E. by Kerman and S. by the Persian Gulf. It lies between 26° 30′ and 28° 25′ N. and between 52° 30′ and 55° 30′ E. and has an extreme breadth and length of 120 and 210 m. respectively, with an area of about 20,000 sq. m. Pop about 90,000. Laristan consists mainly of mountain ranges in the north and east, and of arid plains varied with rocky hills and sandy valleys stretching thence to the coast. In the highlands, where some fertile upland tracts produce corn, dates and other fruits, the climate is genial, but elsewhere it is extremely sultry, and on the low-lying coast lands malarious. Good water is everywhere so scarce that but for the rain preserved in cisterns the country would be mostly uninhabitable. Many cisterns are infested with Guinea worm (*filaria medinensis*, Gm.) The coast is chiefly occupied by Arab tribes who were virtually independent, paying merely a nominal tribute to the shah's government until 1898 They reside in small towns and mud forts scattered along the coast. The people of the interior are mostly of the old Iranian stock, and there are also a few nomads of the Turkish Bahārlū tribe which came to Persia in the 11th century when the province was subdued by a Turkish chief. Laristan remained an independent state under a Turkish ruler until 1602, when Shah Ibrahim Khan was deposed and put to death by Shah 'Abbas the Great. The province is subdivided into eight districts (1) Lar, the capital and environs, with 34 villages, (2) Bikhah Ihsham with 11, (3) Bikhah Fal with 10, (4) Jehangiriyeh with 30, (5) Shibkuh with 36, (6) Fumistan with 13, (7) Kauristan with 4, (8) Mazayijan with 6 villages. Lingah, with its principal place Bander Lingah and 11 villages, formerly a part of Laristan, is now included in the "Persian Gulf Ports," a separate administrative division Laristan is famous for the condiment called *māhidbeh* (fish-jelly), a compound of pounded small sprat-like fish, salt, mustard, nutmeg, cloves and other spices, used as a relish with nearly all foods.

LARIVEY, PIERRE (*c.* 1550–1612), French dramatist, of Italian origin, was the son of one of the Giunta, the famous printers of Florence and Venice. The family was established at Troyes and had taken the name of Larivey or L'Arrivey, by way of translation from *giunto* Pierre Larivey appears to have cast horoscopes, and to have acted as clerk to the chapter of the church of St Étienne, of which he eventually became a canon. He has no claim to be the originator of French comedy. The *Corrivaux* of Jean de la Taille dates from 1562, but Larivey naturalized the Italian comedy of intrigue in France. He adapted, rather than translated, twelve Italian comedies into French prose. The first volume of the *Comédies facétieuses* appeared in 1579, and the second in 1611. Only nine in all were printed.[1] The licence of the manners depicted in these plays is matched by the coarseness of the expression. Larivey's merit lies in the use of popular language in dialogue, which often rises to real excellence, and was not without influence on Molière and Regnard. Molière's *L'Avare* owes something to the scene in Larivey's masterpiece, *Les Esprits*, where Séverin laments the loss of his purse, and the opening scene of the piece seems to have suggested Regnard's *Retour imprévu*. It is uncertain whether Larivey's plays were represented, though they were evidently written for the stage. In any case prose comedy gained very little ground in popular favour before the time of Molière. Larivey was the author of many translations, varying in subject from the *Facétieuses nuits* (1573) of Straparola to the *Humanité de Jésus-Christ* (1604) from Pietro Aretino.

LARK (O. Eng. *lāwerce*, Ger. *Lerche*, Dan. *Laerke*, Dutch *Leeuwerik*), a bird's name used in a rather general sense, the specific meaning being signified by a prefix, as skylark, titlark, woodlark. It seems to be nearly conterminous with the Latin *Alauda* as used by older authors; and, though this was to some extent limited by Linnaeus, several of the species included by him under the genus he so designated have long since been referred elsewhere. By Englishmen the word lark, used without qualification, almost invariably means the skylark, *Alauda arvensis*, which, as the best-known and most widely spread species throughout Europe, has been invariably considered the type of the genus. Of all birds it holds unquestionably the foremost place in English literature. It is one of the most favourite cage birds, as it will live for many years in captivity, and, except in the season of moult, will pour forth its thrilling song many times in an hour for weeks or months together. The skylark is probably the most plentiful of the class in western Europe. Not only does it frequent almost all unwooded districts in that quarter of the globe, but, unlike most birds, its numbers increase with the spread of agricultural improvement. Nesting chiefly in the growing corn, its eggs and young are protected in a great measure from molestation, and, as each pair of birds will rear several broods

[1] *Le Laquais*, from the *Ragazzo* of Ludovico Dolce; *La Veuve*, from the *Vedova* of Nicolo Buonaparte; *Les Esprits*, from the *Aridosio* of Lorenzino de Medicis; *Le Morfondu*, from the *Gelosia* of Antonio Grazzini, *Les Jaloux*, from the *Gelosi* of Vincent Gabbiani; and *Les Escolliers*, from the *Cecca* of Girolamo Razzi, in the first volume; and in the second, *Constance*, from the *Costanza* of Razzi; *Le Fidèle*, from the *Fedele* of Luigi Pasqualigo; and *Les Tromperies*, from the *Inganni* of N. Secchi.

LARK

... may be set down ... eggs in each ... When the ... flocks. ... to others ... succeeds ... previously ... flocks arrive ... Scotland ... as occurring ... in succession. ... numbers simply ... these migrations ... but the rate of ... so favourable ... diminution

... World from the ... occurs in North ... Lower Egypt ... and has been ... appearance there is ... on Long Island, ... New Zealand— ... a denizen as are ... societies have

... Alauda arvensis.

... number of species have ... may be deemed valid, ... the difference ... shown in the annexed ... work by H. E. Dresser, in ... These are found

... more local and, there- ... skylark, from which it ... shorter tail, more ... Though not actually ... imply, it is seldom ... variety and power of ... peculiarly its own. ... activity. It has by ... and perhaps the most ... while its appearance ... rare.

... group of larks char- ... more curved bill, ... features. This ... has for its type ... a bird common ... countries of the ... obtained several ... of this group ... and such as ... whereby they are

assimilated in hue to that of their haunts. The same characteristic may be observed in several other groups—especially those known as belonging to the genera *Calandrella*, *Ammomanes* and *Certhilauda*, some species of which are of a light sandy or cream colour The genus last named is of very peculiar appearance, presenting in some respects an extraordinary resemblance to the hoopoes, so much so that the first specimen described was referred to the genus *Upupa*, and named *U alaudipes*. The resemblance, however, is merely one of analogy

Fig. 2.—A, *Lullula arborea*; B, *Certhilauda.*

Fig. 3.—A, *Melanocorypha calandra*; B, *Rhamphocorys clot-bey.*

There is, however, abundant evidence of the susceptibility of the Alaudine structure to modification from external circumstances—in other words, of its plasticity, and perhaps no homogeneous group of *Passeres* could be found which better displays the working of natural selection. Almost every character that among Passerine birds is accounted most sure is in the larks found subject to modification. The form of the bill varies in an extraordinary degree In the woodlark (fig. 2, A), already noticed, it is almost as slender as a warbler's, in *Ammomanes* it is short, in *Certhilauda* (fig 2, B) it is elongated and curved, in *Pyrrhulauda* and *Melanocorypha* (fig 3, A) it is stout and finchlike, while in *Rhamphocorys* (fig. 3, B) it is exaggerated to an extent that surpasses almost any Fringilline form, exceeding in its development that found in some members of the perplexing genus *Paradoxornis*, and even presenting a resemblance to the same feature in the far-distant *Anastomus*—the tomia of the maxilla not meeting those of the mandibula along their whole length, but leaving an open space between them The hind claw, generally greatly elongated in larks, is in *Calandrella* (fig 4) and some other genera reduced

Fig. 4 —*Calandrella brachydactyla.*

to a very moderate size. The wings exhibit almost every modification, from the almost entire abortion of the first primary in the skylark to its considerable development (fig. 5), and from tertials and scapulars of ordinary length to the extreme elongation found in the *Motacillidae* and almost in certain *Limicolae*. The most constant character indeed of the *Alaudidae* would seem to be that afforded by the *podotheca* or covering of the tarsus, which is scutellate behind as well as in front, but a character easily overlooked.[1]

In the Old World larks are found in most parts of the

[1] By assigning far too great an importance to this superficial character (in comparison with others), C. J. Sundevall (*Tentamen*, pp. 53-63) was induced to array the larks, hoopoes and several other heterogeneous groups in one "series," to which he applied the name of *Scutelliplantares*.

Palaearctic, Ethiopian and Indian regions, but only one genus, *Mirafra*, inhabits Australia, where it is represented by, so far as is ascertained, a single species, *M. horsfieldi*, and there is no true lark indigenous to New Zealand. In the New World there is also only one genus, *Otocorys*, where it is represented by many races, some of which closely approach the Old World shore-lark, *O alpestris*. The shore-lark is in Europe a native of only the extreme north, but is very common near the shores of the Varanger Fjord, and likewise breeds on mountain-tops farther south-west, though still well within the Arctic circle. The mellow tone of its call-note has obtained for it in Lapland a name signifying "bell-bird," and the song of the cock is lively, though not very loud. The bird trustfully resorts to the neighbourhood of houses, and even enters the villages of East Finmark in search of its food. It produces at least two broods in the season, and towards autumn migrates to lower latitudes in large flocks. These have been observed in winter on the east coast of Great Britain, and the species instead of being regarded, as it once was, in the light of an accidental visitor to the United Kingdom, must now be deemed an almost regular visitor, though in very varying numbers. The observations on its habits made by Audubon in Labrador have long been known, and often reprinted. Other congeners of this bird are the *O. penicillata* of south-eastern Europe, Palestine and central Asia—to which are referred by H. E. Dresser (*B Europe*, iv. 401) several other forms originally described as distinct. All these birds, which have been termed horned larks, from the tuft of elongated black feathers growing on each side of the head, form a little group easily recognized by their peculiar coloration, which calls to mind some of the ringed plovers, *Aegialitis*.

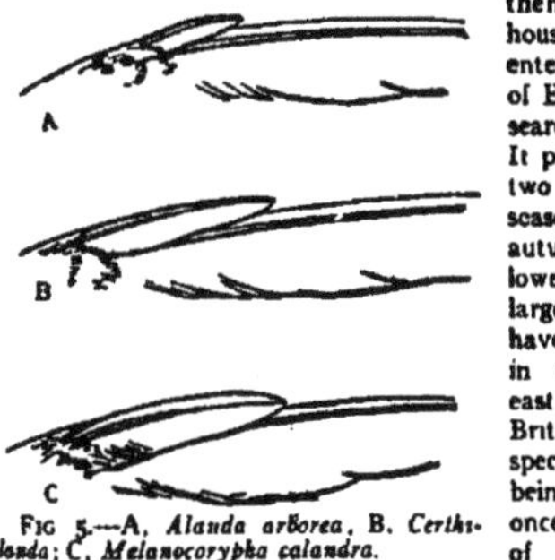

FIG 5.—A, *Alauda arborea*, B. *Certhilauda*; C, *Melanocorypha calandra*.

The name of lark is also frequently applied to many birds which do not belong to the *Alaudidae* as now understood. The mud-lark, rock-lark, tit-lark and tree-lark are pipits (*q.v.*). The grasshopper-lark is one of the aquatic warblers (*q.v.*), while the so-called meadow-lark of America is an Icterus (*q.v.*) Sand-lark and sea-lark are likewise names often given to some of the smaller members of the *Limicolae*. Of the true larks, *Alaudidae*, there may be perhaps about one hundred species, and it is believed to be a physiological character of the family that they moult but once in the year, while the pipits, which in general appearance much resemble them, undergo a double moult, as do others of the *Motacillidae*, to which they are most nearly allied. (A. N.)

LARKHALL, a mining and manufacturing town of Lanarkshire, Scotland, near the left bank of the Clyde, 1 m. S.E. of Glasgow by the Caledonian railway. Pop. (1901) 11,879. The highest bridge in Scotland has been thrown across the river Avon, which flows close by. Brick-making is carried on at several of the adjoining collieries. Other industries include bleaching, silk-weaving, fire-clay and enamelling works, and a sanitary appliances factory. The town has a public hall and baths.

LARKHANA, a town and district of British India, in Sind, Bombay. The town is on a canal not far from the Indus, and has a station on the North-Western railway, 281 m. N. by E. of Karachi. It is pleasantly situated in a fertile locality, and is well laid out with wide streets and spacious gardens. It is a centre of trade, with manufactures of cotton, silk, leather, metal-ware and paper. Pop (1901) 14,543

The DISTRICT OF LARKHANA, lying along the right bank of the Indus, was formed out of portions of Sukkur and Karachi districts in 1901, and has an area of 5091 sq. m.; pop. (1901) 656,083, showing an increase of 10% in the decade. Its western part is mountainous, but the remainder is a plain of alluvium watered by canals and well cultivated, being the most fertile part of Sind. The staple grain-crops are rice, wheat and millets, which are exported, together with wool, cotton and other agricultural produce. Cotton cloth, carpets, salt and leather goods are manufactured, and dyeing is an important industry. The district is served by the North-Western railway.

LARKSPUR, in botany, the popular name for species of *Delphinium*, a genus of hardy herbaceous plants belonging to the natural order Ranunculaceae (*q.v.*). They are of erect branching habit, with the flowers in terminal racemes, often of considerable length. Blue is the predominating colour, but purple, pink, yellow (*D. Zalil* or *sulphureum*), scarlet (*D. cardinale*) and white also occur; the "spur" is produced by the elongation of the upper sepal. The field or rocket larkspur (*D Ajacis*), the branching larkspur (*D. consolida*), *D. cardiopetalum* and their varieties, are charming annuals, height about 18 in. The spotted larkspur (*D requienii*) and a few others are biennials. The perennial larkspurs, however, are the most gorgeous of the family. There are numerous species of this group, natives of the old and new worlds, and a great number of varieties, raised chiefly from *D. exaltatum*, *D. formosum* and *D. grandiflorum*. Members of this group vary from 2 ft. to 6 ft. in height.

The larkspurs are of easy cultivation, either in beds or herbaceous borders, the soil should be deeply dug and manured. The annual varieties are best sown early in April, where they are intended to flower, and suitably thinned out as growth is made. The perennial kinds are increased by the division of existing plants in spring, or by cuttings taken in spring or autumn and rooted in pots in cold frames. The varieties cannot be perpetuated with certainty by seed. Seed is the most popular means, however, of raising larkspurs in the majority of gardens, and is suitable for all ordinary purposes; it should be sown as soon as gathered, preferably in rows in nursery beds, and the young plants transplanted when ready. They should be fit for the borders in the spring of the following year, and if strong, should be planted in groups about 3 ft. apart. Delphiniums require exposure to light and air. Given plenty of space in a rich soil, the plants rarely require to be staked except in windy localities.

LARNACA, LARNICA or LARNECA (anc. *Citium*, Turk. *Tusla*), a town of the island of Cyprus, at the head of a bay on the south coast, 23 m. S.S.E. from Nicosia. Pop. (1901) 7964. It is the principal port of the island, exporting barley, wheat, cotton, raisins, oranges, lemons and gypsum. There is an iron pier 450 ft. long, but vessels anchor in the bay in from 16 to 70 ft. of water. Larnaca occupies the site of the ancient *Citium*, but the citadel of the ancient city was used to fill up the ancient harbour in 1879. The modern and principal residential part of the town is called Scala. Mycenaean tombs and other antiquities have been found (see CYPRUS).

LA ROCHE, a small town in the Belgian Ardennes, noticeable for its antiquity and its picturesque situation. Pop. (1904) 2065. Its name is derived from its position on a rock commanding the river Ourthe, which meanders round the little place, and skirts the rock on which are the interesting ruins of the old castle of the 11th century. This is supposed to have been the site of a hunting box of Pippin, and certainly the counts of La Roche held it in fief from his descendants, the Carolingian rulers. In the 12th century they sold it to the counts of Luxemburg. In the 16th and 17th centuries the French and Imperialists frequently fought in its neighbourhood, and at Tenneville, not far distant, is shown the tomb of an English officer named Barnewall killed in one of these encounters in 1692. La Roche is famous as a tourist centre on account of its fine sylvan scenery. Among the local curiosities is the Diable-Château, a freak of nature, being the apparent replica of a medieval castle. La [illegible] by steam tramway with Melreux, a station [illegible] from Marloie to Liége.

LA ROCHEFOUCAULD, the name of an old French family [illegible] from a castle[1] in the province of Angoumois [illegible] Charente), which was in its possession in the [illegible] François de La Rochefoucauld [illegible] Francis I., was made count in 1515. At the time [illegible] of religion the family fought for the Protestant [illegible] François (1588–1650) was created duke and peer of France [illegible] XIII in 1622. His son François was the author of [illegible] Maximes, and the son of the latter acquired for his house [illegible] of La Roche-Guyon and Liancourt by his marriage [illegible] Charlotte du Plessis-Liancourt. Alexandre [illegible] (d. 1762), left two daughters, who married [illegible] of the family. Of the numerous branches [illegible] most famous are those of Roucy, Roye, Bayers, [illegible] and Estissac, which all furnished distin[illegible] and soldiers.

LA ROCHEFOUCAULD, FRANÇOIS DE [illegible] writer of France, one of her best memoir writers, [illegible] most complete and accomplished [illegible] was born at Paris in the Rue des [illegible] of September 1613. The author [illegible] the lifetime of his father [illegible] stirring years [illegible] neglected in the matter [illegible] kind, but he joined the army [illegible] immediately began [illegible] had been nominally married [illegible] who seems to have been [illegible] scandal touches [illegible] was perhaps more [illegible] years Marcillac continued [illegible] where he displayed [illegible] for much military [illegible] Madame de Chevreuse [illegible] who successively influenced [illegible] he became attached [illegible] of her quarrels [illegible] seems to have [illegible] was to carry [illegible] against Richelieu [illegible]

[illegible]

fighting and intriguing except impaired health, a seriously embarrassed fortune, and some cause for bearing a grudge against almost every party and man of importance in the state. He spent some years in this retirement, and he was fortunate enough (thanks chiefly to the fidelity of Gourville, who had been in his service, and who, passing into the service of Mazarin and of Condé, had acquired both wealth and influence) to be able to repair in some measure the breaches in his fortune. He did not, however, return to court life much before Mazarin's death, when Louis XIV. was on the eve of assuming absolute power, and the turbulent aristocratic anarchy of the Fronde was a thing utterly of the past.

Somewhat earlier, La Rochefoucauld had taken his place in the salon of Madame de Sablé, a member of the old Rambouillet coterie, and the founder of a kind of successor to it. It was known that he, like almost all his more prominent contemporaries, had spent his solitude in writing memoirs, while the special literary employment of the Sablé salon was the fabrication of *Sentences* and *Maxims*. In 1662, however, more trouble than reputation, and not a little of both, was given to him by a surreptitious publication of his memoirs, or what purported to be his memoirs, by the Elzevirs. Many of his old friends were deeply wounded, and he hastened to deny flatly the authenticity of the publication, a denial which (as it seems, without any reason) was not very generally accepted. Three years later (1665) he published, though without his name, the still more famous *Maxims*, which at once established him high among the men of letters of the time. About the same date began the friendship with Madame de la Fayette, which lasted till the end of his life. The glimpses which we have of him henceforward are chiefly derived from the letters of Madame de Sévigné, and, though they show him suffering agonies from gout, are on the whole pleasant. He had a circle of devoted friends; he was recognized as a moralist and man of letters of the first rank; he might have entered the Academy for the asking, and in the altered measure of the times his son, the prince de Marcillac, to whom some time before his death he resigned his titles and honours, enjoyed a considerable position at court. Above all, La Rochefoucauld was generally recognized by his contemporaries from the king downward as a type of the older noblesse as it was before the sun of the great monarch dimmed its brilliant qualities. This position he has retained until the present day. He died at Paris on the 17th of March 1680, of the disease which had so long tormented him.

La Rochefoucauld's character, if considered without the prejudice which a dislike to his ethical views has sometimes occasioned, is thoroughly respectable and even amiable. Like almost all his contemporaries, he saw in politics little more than a chessboard where the people at large were but pawns. The weight of testimony, however, inclines to the conclusion that he was unusually scrupulous in his conduct, and that his comparative ill success in the struggle arose more from this scrupulousness than from anything else. He has been charged with irresolution, and there is some ground for admitting the charge so far as to pronounce him one of those the keenness of whose intellect, together with their apprehension of both sides of a question, interferes with their capacity as men of action. But there is no ground whatever for the view which represents the *Maxims* as the mere outcome of the spite of a disappointed intriguer, disappointed through his own want of skill rather than of fortune.

His importance as a social and historical figure is, however, far inferior to his importance in literature. His work in this respect consists of three parts—letters, *Memoirs* and the *Maxims*. His letters exceed one hundred in number, and are biographically valuable, besides displaying not a few of his literary characteristics, but they need not further detain us. The *Memoirs*, when they are read in their proper form, yield in literary merit, in interest, and in value to no memoirs of the time, not even to those of Retz, between whom and La Rochefoucauld there was [illegible] mixture of enmity and esteem which resulted in a [illegible] most characteristic "portraits." But their history is unique in its strangeness. It has been said that a pirated edition appeared in Holland, and this, despite the author's protest, continued to be reprinted for some thirty years. It has been now proved to be a mere cento of the work of half a dozen different men, scarcely a third of which is La Rochefoucauld's, and which could only have been possible at a time when it was the habit of persons who frequented literary society to copy pell-mell in commonplace books the MS. compositions of their friends and others. Some years after La Rochefoucauld's death a new recension appeared, somewhat less incorrect than the former, but still largely adulterated, and this held its ground for more than a century. Only in 1817 did anything like a genuine edition (even then by no means perfect) appear. The *Maxims*, however, had no such fate. The author re-edited them frequently during his life, with alterations and additions; a few were added after his death, and it is usual now to print the whole of them, at whatever time they appeared, together. Thus taken, they amount to about seven hundred in number, in hardly any case exceeding half a page in length, and more frequently confined to two or three lines. The view of conduct which they illustrate is usually and not quite incorrectly summed up in the words "everything is reducible to the motive of self-interest." But though not absolutely incorrect, the phrase is misleading. The *Maxims* are in no respect mere deductions from or applications of any such general theory. They are on the contrary independent judgments on different relations of life, different affections of the human mind, and so forth, from which, taken together, the general view may be deduced or rather composed. Sentimental moralists have protested loudly against this view, yet it is easier to declaim against it in general than to find a flaw in the several parts of which it is made up. With a few exceptions La Rochefoucauld's maxims represent the matured result of the reflection of a man deeply versed in the business and pleasures of the world, and possessed of an extraordinarily fine and acute intellect, on the conduct and motives which have guided himself and his fellows. There is as little trace in them of personal spite as of *forfanterie de vice*. But the astonishing excellence of the literary medium in which they are conveyed is even more remarkable than the general soundness of their ethical import. In uniting the four qualities of brevity, clearness, fulness of meaning and point, La Rochefoucauld has no rival. His *Maxims* are never mere epigrams; they are never platitudes; they are never dark sayings. He has packed them so full of meaning that it would be impossible to pack them closer, yet there is no undue compression; he has sharpened their point to the utmost, yet there is no loss of substance. The comparison which occurs most frequently, and which is perhaps on the whole the justest, is that of a bronze medallion, and it applies to the matter no less than to the form. Nothing is left unfinished, yet none of the workmanship is finical. The sentiment, far from being merely hard, as the sentimentalists pretend, has a vein of melancholy poetry running through it which calls to mind the traditions of La Rochefoucauld's devotion to the romances of chivalry. The maxims are never shallow; each is the text for a whole sermon of application and corollary which any one of thought and experience can write. Add to all this that the language in which they are written is French, still at almost its greatest strength, and chastened but as yet not emasculated by the reforming influence of the 17th century, and it is not necessary to say more. To the literary critic no less than to the man of the world La Rochefoucauld ranks among the scanty number of pocket-books to be read and re-read with ever new admiration, instruction and delight.

The editions of La Rochefoucauld's *Maxims* (as the full title runs, *Réflexions ou sentences et maximes morales*) published in his lifetime bear the dates 1665 (*editio princeps*), 1666, 1671, 1675, 1678. An important edition which appeared after his death in 1693 may rank almost with these. As long as the *Memoirs* remained in the state above described, no edition of them need be mentioned, and none of the complete works was possible. The previous more or less complete editions are all superseded by that of MM Gilbert and Gourdault (1868–1883), in the series of "Grands Écrivains de la France," 3 vols. There are still some puzzles as to the text; but this edition supplies all available material in regard to them. The handsomest separate edition of the *Maxims* is the so-called *Édition des bibliophiles* (1870); but cheap and handy issues are plentiful. See the English version by G. H. Powell (1903). Nearly all the great French critics of the 19th century have dealt more or less with La Rochefoucauld the chief recent monograph on him is that of J. Bourdeau in the *Grands écrivains français* (1893). (G. Sa.)

LA ROCHEFOUCAULD-LIANCOURT, FRANÇOIS ALEXANDRE FRÉDÉRIC, Duc de (1747–1827), French social reformer, was born at La Roche Guyon on the 11th of January 1747, the son of François Armand de La Rochefoucauld, duc d'Estissac, grand master of the royal wardrobe. The duc de Liancourt became an officer of carbineers, and married at seventeen. A visit to England seems to have suggested the establishment of a model farm at Liancourt, where he reared cattle imported from England and Switzerland. He also set up spinning machines on his estate, and founded a school of arts and crafts for the sons of soldiers, which became in 1788 the École des Enfants de la Patrie under royal protection. Elected to the states-general of 1789 he sought in vain to support the cause of royalty while furthering the social reforms he had at heart. On the 12th of July, two days before the fall of the Bastille, he warned Louis XVI. of the state of affairs in Paris, and met his exclamation that there was a revolt with the answer, "*Non, sire, c'est une révolution.*" On the 18th of July he became president of the Assembly. Established in command of a military division in Normandy, he offered Louis a refuge in Rouen, and, failing in this effort, assisted him with a large sum of money. After the events of the 10th of August 1792 he fled to England, where he was the guest of Arthur Young, and thence passed to America. After the assassination of his cousin, Louis-Alexandre, duc de La Rochefoucauld d'Enville, at Gisors on the 14th of September 1792 he assumed the title of duc de La Rochefoucauld. He returned to Paris in 1799, but received small favour from Napoleon. At the Restoration he entered the House of Peers, but Louis XVIII. refused to reinstate him as master of the wardrobe, although his father had paid 400,000 francs for the honour. Successive governments, revolutionary and otherwise, recognized the value of his institutions at Liancourt, and he was for twenty-three years government inspector of his school of arts and crafts, which had been removed to Châlons. He was one of the first promoters of vaccination in France; he established a dispensary in Paris, and he was an active member of the central boards of administration for hospitals, prisons and agriculture. His opposition to the government in the House of Peers led to his removal in 1823 from the honorary positions he held, while the vaccination committee, of which he was president, was suppressed. The academies of science and of medicine admitted him to their membership by way of protest. Official hostility pursued him even after his death (27th of March 1827), for the old pupils of his school were charged by the military at his funeral. His works, chiefly on economic questions, include books on the English system of taxation, poor-relief and education.

His eldest son, François, duc de La Rochefoucauld (1765–1848), succeeded his father in the House of Peers. The second, Alexandre, comte de La Rochefoucauld (1767–1841), married a San Domingo heiress allied to the Beauharnais family. Mme de La Rochefoucauld became dame d'honneur to the empress Joséphine, and their eldest daughter married a brother-in-law of Pauline Bonaparte, Princess Borghese. La Rochefoucauld became ambassador successively to Vienna (1805) and to the Hague (1808–1810), where he negotiated the union of Holland with France. During the "Hundred Days" he was made a peer of France. He subsequently devoted himself to philanthropic work, and in 1822 became deputy to the Chamber and sat with the constitutional royalists. He was again raised to the peerage in 1831.

The third son, Frédéric Gaëtan, marquis de La Rochefoucauld-Liancourt (1779–1863), was a zealous philanthropist and a partisan of constitutional monarchy. He took no part in politics after 1848. The marquis wrote on social questions, notably on prison administration; he edited the works of La Rochefoucauld, and the memoirs of Condorcet; and he was the author of some vaudevilles, tragedies and poems.

LA ROCHEJACQUELEIN, DE, the name of an ancient French family of La Vendée, celebrated for its devotion to the throne during and after the Revolution. Its original name was Duverger, derived from a fief near Bressuire in Poitou, and its pedigree

Peninsula with his family in 1812. In 1817 Larra returned to Spain, knowing less Spanish than French. His nature was disorderly, his education was imperfect, and, after futile attempts to obtain a degree in medicine or law, he made an imprudent marriage at the age of twenty, broke with his relatives and became a journalist. On the 27th of April 1831 he produced his first play, *No más mostrador*, based on two pieces by Scribe and Dieulafoy. Though wanting in originality, it is brilliantly written, and held the stage for many years. On the 24th of September 1834 he produced *Macías*, a play based on his own historical novel, *El Doncel de Don Enrique el Doliente* (1834). The drama and novel are interesting as experiments, but Larra was essentially a journalist, and the increased liberty of the press after the death of Ferdinand VII. gave his caustic talent an ampler field. He was already famous under the pseudonyms of "Juan Pérez de Munguía" and "Figaro" which he used in *El Pobrecito Hablador* and *La Revista Española* respectively. Madrid laughed at his grim humour; ministers feared his vitriolic pen and courted him assiduously; he was elected as deputy for Ávila, and a great career seemed to lie before him. But the era of military *pronunciamientos* ruined his personal prospects and patriotic plans. His writing took on a more sombre tinge; domestic troubles increased his pessimism, and, in consequence of a disastrous love-affair, he committed suicide on the 13th of February 1837. Larra lived long enough to prove himself the greatest prose-writer that Spain can boast during the 19th century. He wrote at great speed with the constant fear of the censor before his eyes, but no sign of haste is discernible in his work, and the dexterity with which he aims his venomous shafts is amazing. His political instinct, his abundance of ideas and his forcible, mordant style would have given him a foremost position at any time and in any country; in Spain, and in his own period, they placed him beyond all rivalry. (J. F.-K.)

LARSA (Biblical *Ellasar*, Gen. xiv. 1), an important city of ancient Babylonia, the site of the worship of the sun-god, Shamash, represented by the ancient ruin mound of Senkereh (Senkera). It lay 15 m. S.E. of the ruin mounds of Warka (anc. *Erech*), near the east bank of the Shatt-en-Nil canal. Larsa is mentioned in Babylonian inscriptions as early as the time of Ur-Gur, 2700 or 2800 B.C., who built or restored the *ziggurat* (stage-tower) of E-Babbar, the temple of Shamash. Politically it came into special prominence at the time of the Elamite conquest, when it was made the centre of Elamite dominion in Babylonia, perhaps as a special check upon the neighbouring Erech, which had played a prominent part in the resistance to the Elamites. At the time of Khammurabi's successful struggle with the Elamite conquerors it was ruled by an Elamite king named Eriaku, the Arioch of the Bible, called Rim-Sin by his Semitic subjects. It finally lost its independence under Samsu-iluna, son of Khammurabi, *c.* 1900 B.C. and from that time until the close of the Babylonian [illegible] it was a subject city of Babylon. Loftus conducted [illegible] at this site in 1854. He describes the ruins as [illegible] of a low, circular platform, about 4½ m. in circum[illegible] [illegible] gradually from the level of the plain to a central [illegible] ft. high. This represents the ancient *ziggurat* of the [illegible] of Shamash, which was in part explored by Loftus. From the inscriptions found there it appears that, besides the [illegible] mentioned, Khammurabi, Burna-buriash (buryas) [illegible] Nebuchadrezzar restored or rebuilt the temple [illegible]. The excavations at Senkereh were peculiarly [illegible] in the discovery of inscribed remains, consisting [illegible] tablets, early contracts, but including also an im[illegible] tablet and a number of tablets of a [illegible] to Senkereh, exhibiting in bas-[illegible] life. Loftus found also the remains [illegible] cemetery. From the ruins it would [illegible] to be inhabited at or soon after [illegible] [illegible] (1857). (J. P. Pe.)

[illegible] 1871), French [illegible]ist, [illegible] Bar[illegible] of

Gers, France, where his family had lived for more than five hundred years. He was educated for the law at Auch and Toulouse, but having private means elected to devote himself to science. The then recent work of Cuvier on fossil mammalia encouraged Lartet in excavations which led in 1834 to his first discovery of fossil remains in the neighbourhood of Auch. Thenceforward he devoted his whole time to a systematic examination of the French caves, his first publication on the subject being *The Antiquity of Man in Western Europe* (1860), followed in 1861 by *New Researches on the Coexistence of Man and of the Great Fossil Mammifers characteristic of the Last Geological Period*. In this paper he made public the results of his discoveries in the cave of Aurignac, where evidence existed of the contemporaneous existence of man and extinct mammals. In his work in the Périgord district Lartet had the aid of Henry Christy (*q.v.*). The first account of their joint researches appeared in a paper descriptive of the Dordogne caves and contents, published in *Revue archéologique* (1864). The important discoveries in the Madeleine cave and elsewhere were published by Lartet and Christy under the title *Reliquiae Aquitanicae*, the first part appearing in 1865. Christy died before the completion of the work, but Lartet continued it until his breakdown in health in 1870. The most modest and one of the most illustrious of the founders of modern palaeontology, Lartet's work had previously been publicly recognized by his nomination as an officer of the Legion of Honour; and in 1848 he had had the offer of a political post. In 1857 he had been elected a foreign member of the Geological Society of London, and a few weeks before his death he had been made professor of palaeontology at the museum of the Jardin des Plantes. He died at Seissan in January 1871.

LARVAL FORMS, in biology. As is explained in the article on Embryology (*q.v.*), development and life are coextensive, and it is impossible to point to any period in the life of an organism when the developmental changes cease. Nevertheless it is customary to speak of development as though it were confined to the early period of life, during which the important changes occur by which the uninucleated zygote acquires the form characteristic of the species. Using the word in this restricted sense, it is pointed out in the same article that the developmental period frequently presents two phases, the embryonic and the larval. During the embryonic phase the development occurs under protection, either within the egg envelopes, or within the maternal body, or in a brood pouch. At the end of this phase the young organism becomes free and uses, as a rule, its own mouth and digestive organs. If this happens before it has approximately acquired the adult form, it is called a larva (Lat. *larva*, ghost, spectre, mask), and the subsequent development by which the adult form is acquired constitutes the larval phase. In such forms the life-cycle is divided into three phases, the embryonic, the larval and the adult. The transition between the first two of these is always abrupt; whereas the second and third, except in cases in which a metamorphosis occurs (see METAMORPHOSIS), graduate into one another, and it is not possible to say when the larval stage ends and the adult begins. This is only what would be expected when it is remembered that the developmental changes never cease. It might be held that the presence of functional reproductive organs, or the possibility of rapidly acquiring them, marks off the adult phase of life from the larval. But this test sometimes fails. In certain of the Ctenophora there is a double sexual life; the larva becomes sexually mature and lays eggs, which are fertilized and develop; it then loses its generative organs and develops into the adult, which again develops reproductive organs (*dissogony*; see Chun, *Die Ctenophoren des Golfes von Neapel*, 1880). In certain Amphibia the larva may develop sexual organs and breed (axolotl), but in this case (*neoteny*) it is doubtful whether further development may occur in the larva. A very similar phenomenon is found in certain insect larvae (*Cecidomyia*), but in this case ova alone are produced and develop parthenogenetically (paedogenesis). Again in certain Trematoda larval stages known as the sporocyst and redia produce ova which have the power of developing unfertilized; in this case the larva probably has not the power of continuing its development. It is very generally held by philosophers that the end of life is reproduction, and there is much to be said for this view; but, granting its truth, it is difficult to see why the capacity for reproduction should so generally be confined to the later stages of life. We know by more than one instance that it is possible for the larva to reproduce by sexual generation; why should not the phenomenon be more common? It is impossible in the present state of our knowledge to answer this question.

The conclusion, then, that we reach is that the larval phase of life graduates into the later phases, and that it is impossible to characterize it with precision, as we can the embryonic phase. Nevertheless great importance has been attached, in certain cases, to the forms assumed by the young organism when it breaks loose from its embryonic bonds. It has been widely held that the study of larvae is of greater importance in determining genetic affinity than the study of adults. What justification is there for this view? The phase of life, chosen for the ordinary anatomical and physiological studies and labelled as the adult phase, is merely one of the large number of stages of structure through which the organism passes during its free life In animals with a well-marked larval phase, by far the greater number of the stages of structure are included in the larval period, for the developmental changes are more numerous and take place with greater rapidity at the beginning of life than in its later periods. As each of the larval stages is equal in value for the purposes of our study to the adult phase, it clearly follows that, if there is anything in the view that the anatomical study of organisms is of importance in determining their mutual relations, the study of the organism in its various larval stages must have a greater importance than the study of the single and arbitrarily selected stage of life called the adult.

The importance, then, of the study of larval forms is admitted, but before proceeding to it this question may be asked. What is the meaning of the larval phase? Obviously this is part of a larger problem: Why does an organism, as soon as it is established at the fertilization of the ovum, enter upon a cycle of transformations which never cease until death puts an end to them? It is impossible to give any other answer to this question than this, viz. that it is a property of living matter to react in a remarkable way to external forces without undergoing destruction. As is explained in EMBRYOLOGY, development consists of an orderly interaction between the organism and its environment The action of the environment produces certain morphological changes in the organism. These changes enable the organism to move into a new environment, which in its turn produces further structural changes in the organism. These in their turn enable, indeed necessitate, the organism to move again into a new environment, and so the process continues until the end of the life-cycle. The essential condition of success in this process is that the organism should always shift into the environment to which its new structure is suited, any failure in this leading to impairment of the organism. In most cases the shifting of the environment is a very gradual process, and the morphological changes in connexion with each step of it are but slight. In some cases, however, jumps are made, and whenever such jumps occur we get the morphological phenomenon termed metamorphosis. It would be foreign to our purpose to consider this question further here, but before leaving it we may suggest, if we cannot answer, one further question. Has the duration and complexity of the life-cycle expanded or contracted since organisms first appeared on the earth? According to the current view, the life-cycle is continually being shortened at one end by the abbreviation of embryonic development and by the absorption of larval stages into the embryonic period, and lengthened at the other by the evolutionary creation of new adult phases. What was the condition of the earliest organisms? Had they the property of reacting to external forces to the same extent and in the same orderly manner that organisms have to-day?

For the purpose of obtaining light upon the genetic affinities of an organism, a larval stage has as much importance as has the adult stage. According to the current views of naturalists, which are largely a product of Darwinism, it has its counterpart, as has the adult stage, in the ancestral form from which the living organism has been derived by descent with modification. Just as the adult phase of the living form differs owing to evolutionary modification from the adult phase of the ancestor, so each larval phase will differ for the same reason from the corresponding larval phase in the ancestral life-history. Inasmuch as the organism is variable at every stage of its existence, and is exposed to the action of natural selection, there is no reason why it should escape modification at any stage. But, as the characters of the ancestor are unknown, it is impossible to ascertain what the modification has been, and the determination of which of the characters of its descendant (whether larval or adult) are new and which ancient must be conjectural. It has been customary of late years to distinguish in larvae those characters which are supposed to have been recently acquired as *caenogenetic*, the ancient characters being termed *palingenetic*. These terms, if they have any value, are applicable with equal force to adults, but they are cumbrous, and the absence of any satisfactory test which enables us to distinguish between a character which is ancestral and one which has been recently acquired renders their utility very doubtful. Just as the adult may be supposed, on evolution doctrine, to be derived from an ancestral adult, so the various larval stages may be supposed to have been derived from the corresponding larval stage of the hypothetical ancestor. If we admit organic evolution at all, we may perhaps go so far, but we are not in a position to go further, and to assert that each larval stage is representative of and, so to speak, derived from some adult stage in the remote past, when the organism progressed no further in its life-cycle than the stage of structure revealed by such a larval form. We may perhaps have a right to take up this position, but it is of no advantage to us to do so, because it leads us into the realm of pure fancy. Moreover, it assumes that an answer can be given to the question asked above—has the life-cycle of organisms contracted or expanded as the result of evolution? This question has not been satisfactorily answered. Indeed we may go further and say that naturalists have answered it in different ways according to the class of facts they were contemplating at the moment. If we are to consider larvae at all from the evolution point of view, we must treat them as being representative of ancestral larvae from which they have been derived by descent with modification; and we must leave open the question whether and to what extent the first organisms themselves passed through a complicated life-cycle.

From the above considerations it is not surprising to find that the larvae of different members of any group resemble each other to the same kind of degree as do the adults, and that the larvae of allied groups resemble one another more closely than do the larvae of remote groups, and finally that a study of larvae does in some cases reveal affinities which would not have been evident from a study of adults alone. Though it is impossible to give here an account of the larval forms of the animal kingdom, we may illustrate these points, which are facts of fundamental importance in the study of larvae, by a reference to specific cases.

The two great groups, Annelida and Mollusca, which by their adult structure present considerable affinity with one another, agree in possessing a very similar larval form, known as the *trochosphere* or *trochophore*.

A typical trochosphere larva (figs. 1, 2) possesses a small, transparent body divided into a large preoral lobe and a small postoral region. The mouth (4) is on the ventral surface at the junction of the preoral lobe with the hinder part of the body, and there is an anus (7) at the hind end. Connecting the two is a curved alimentary canal which is frequently divided into oesophagus, stomach and intestine. There is a preoral circlet of powerful cilia, called the "velum" (2), which encircles the body just anterior to the mouth and marks off the preoral lobe, and there is very generally a second ring of cilia immediately behind the mouth (3). At the anterior end of the preoral lobe is a nervous thickening of the ectoderm called

Peninsula with his fan
Spain, knowing less
disorderly, his educatio
to obtain a degree in
marriage at the age
became a journalist.
first play, *No más mo*
Dieulafoy. Though
written, and held th
September 1834 he
historical novel, *El*
The drama and nov
was essentially a jou
after the death of
ampler field. He w
"Juan Pérez de M
El Pobrecito Habl
Madrid laughed
vitriolic pen and
deputy for Ávila,
But the era of m
prospects and p
sombre tinge; do
in consequence o
on the 13th of F
himself the grea
the 19th century
of the censor b
in his work, an
shafts is amazi
and his forcibl
position at an
own period, t

LARSA (B
of ancient B.
Shamash, rep
(Senkera). I
(anc. *Erech*),
Larsa is men
time of Ur-G
ziggurat (stag
Politically it
Elamite conq
dominion in
neighbouring
resistance to
successful stru
by an Elamite
called Rim-Sin
dependence un
B.C., and from
period it was
excavations at
consisting of a
ference, rising g
mound 70 ft. hi
temple of Sha
From the inscri
kings already m
and the great N
of Shamash. T
successful in th
of clay tablets,
portant mathem.
description almo
relief scenes of
of an ancient Ba
appear that Senk
the Persian conq
See W. K. Loftus

LARTET, EDO
was born in 180

... form, a small transparent creature, ... a postoral longitudinal ciliated band (fig. ... the band of cilia becomes divided in such a way ... bands, the one preoral, encircling the preoral ... postoral (fig. 5, B). In the other ... single and longitudinal. In all cases the

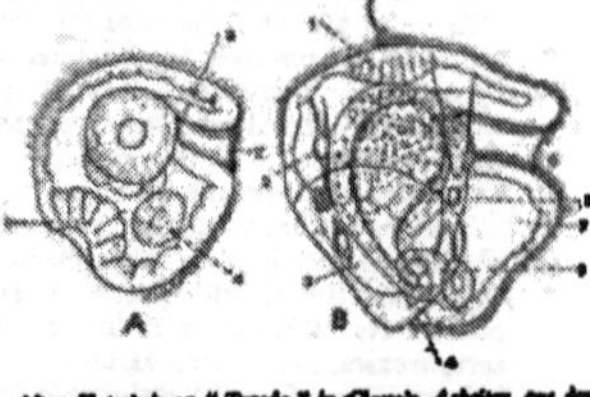

After Hatschek on "Teredo" in Claus's *Arbeiten aus dem zoolog. Institut der Wien.*

FIG. 4.—A, Embryo, and B, Young Trochosphere Larva of the Lamellibranch *Teredo*.

In A the shell-gland (1) and the mouth (2) and the rudiment of the enteron (3) are shown; (4) primitive mesoderm cells.

In B the shell-gland has flattened out and the shell is formed. 1, Apical plate; 2, muscles; 3, shell; 4, anal invagination; 5, mesoblast; 6, mouth; 7, foot.

The cilia of the preoral and postoral bands are not clearly differentiated at this stage.

... these forms ... obviously distinct but as obviously modifications of a common ... and related to one another. They present certain remarkable ... features which differentiate them from other larval ... except the tornaria larvae of the Enteropneusta. They ... an alimentary canal with a mouth and anus as does the ... trochosphere, but they differ altogether from that larva in having a ... diverticulum of the alimentary canal which gives rise to the coelom ... to a considerable part of the meso... Further, they are without an apical plate with its tuft of sensory hairs. In Crinoids the type is different (fig. 10), and might belong to a different phylum. The body is opaque, and encircled by five ciliary bands, and is without either mouth, anus or arms, and there is a tuft of cilia on the preoral lobe. A resemblance to the other Echinoderm larvae is found in the fact that coelomic diverticula of the enteron are present.

The larvae of two other groups present certain resemblances to the typical Echinoderm larvae. The one of these is the tor-

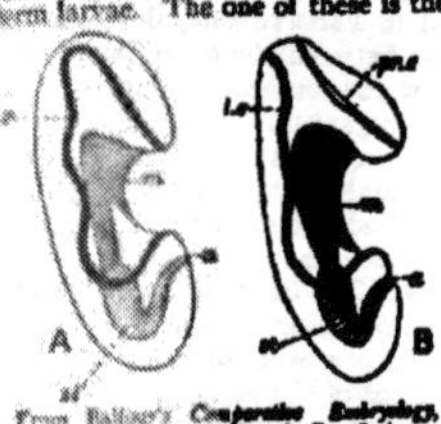

From Balfour's *Comparative Embryology*, by permission of Macmillan & Co., Ltd.

FIG. 5.—Diagrams of side views of two young Echinoderm Larvae, showing the course of the ciliary bands. A, auricularia larva of a Holothurian; B, bipinnaria larva of an Asteroid; *a*, anus; *l.c.*, in A primitive longitudinal ciliary band, in B postoral longitudinal ciliary band; *m*, mouth; *pr.c.*, preoral ciliary band; *st*, stomach.

After J. Müller.

FIG. 6.—*Auricularia stelligera*, ventral view, somewhat diagrammatic. The larva of a Holothurian.

1. Frontal area.
2. Preoral arm.
3. Anterior transverse portion of ciliary band.
4. Posterior transverse portion of same.
5. Postoral arm.
6. Anal area.
7. Posterior lateral arm.
8. Posterior dorsal arm.
9. Oral depression.
10. Middle dorsal arm.
11. Anterior dorsal arm.
12. Anterior lateral arm.
13. Ventral median arm.
14. Dorsal median arm.
15. Unpaired posterior arm.

naria larva of the Enteropneusta (fig. 11), which recalls Echinoderms in the possession of two ciliary bands, the one preoral and the other postoral and partly longitudinal, and in the presence of gut diverticula which give rise to the coelom; but, like the trochosphere, it possesses an apical plate with sensory organs on the preoral lobe. The resemblance of the tornaria to the bipinnaria is so close that, taking into consideration certain additional resemblances in the arrangement of the coelomic vesicles which arise from the original gut diverticulum, it is impossible to resist the conclusion that there is affinity between the Echinoderm and Enteropneust phyla. Here we have a case like that of the Tunicata in which an affinity which is not

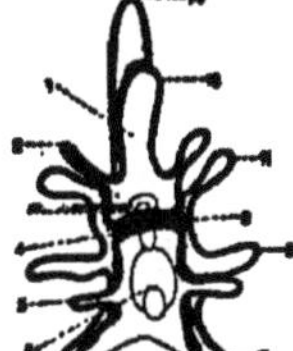

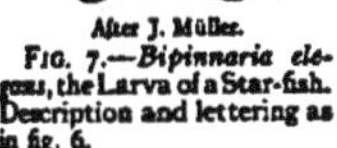

After J. Müller.

FIG. 7.—*Bipinnaria elegans*, the Larva of a Star-fish. Description and lettering as in fig. 6.

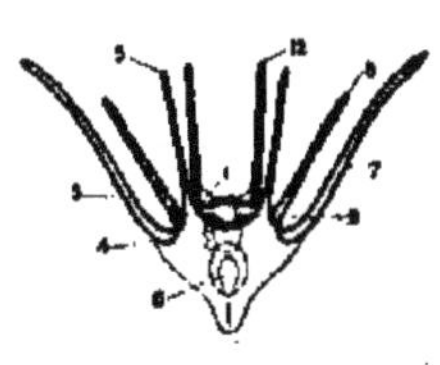

After J. Müller.

FIG. 8.—*Ophiopluteus bimaculatus*, the Larva of an Ophiurid. Description and lettering as in fig. 6.

evident from a study of the adult alone is revealed by a study of the young form. The other larva which recalls the Echinoderm type is the Actinotrocha of *Phoronis* (fig. 12), but the resemblance

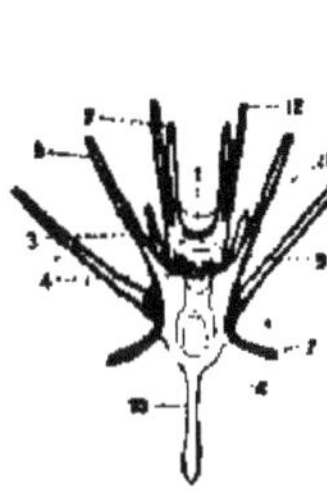

After J. Müller.

FIG. 9.—*Echinopluteus*, the Larva of a Spatangid. Description and lettering as in fig. 6.

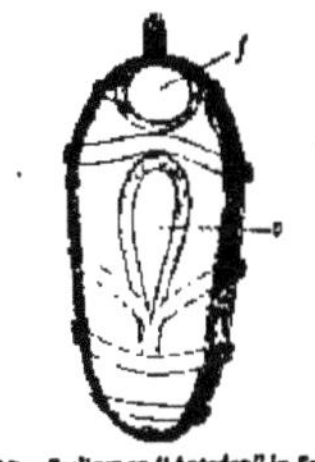

After Seeliger on "Antedon" in Spengel's *Zoologische Jahrbücher*.

FIG. 10.—A free-swimming Larva of Antedon, ventral view. It has an apical tuft of cilia, five ciliated bands, and a depression—the vestibular depression—on its ventral surface. *v*, Vestibular depression; *f*, adhesive pit.

is not nearly so close, being confined to the presence of a postoral longitudinal band of cilia which is prolonged into arm-like processes.

The following groups have larvae which cannot be related to other larvae: the Porifera, Coelenterata, Turbellaria and

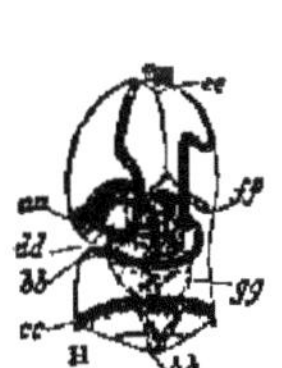

After Metschnikoff.

FIG. 11.—Tornaria Larva of an Enteropneust, side view.
ee, Apical plate.
aa, Preoral ciliary band.
bb, Postoral ciliary band.
dd, Mouth.
ff, Anterior coelomic vesicle and pore.
gg, Alimentary canal.
hh, Anus.

FIG. 12.—Actinotrocha Larva of *Phoronis*, side view. (Modified after Benham.)
1. Apical plate.
2. Mouth.
3. Postoral ciliary band and arms.
4. Perianal ciliary band.

Nemertea, Brachiopoda, Myriapoda, Insecta, Crustacea, Tunicata. We may shortly notice the larvae of the two latter.

In the Crustacea the larvae are highly peculiar and share, in a striking manner, certain of the important features of specialization presented by the adult, viz. the presence of a strong cuticle and of articulated appendages and the absence of cilia. They are remarkable among larvae for the number of stages which they pass through in attaining the adult state. However numerous these may be, they almost always have, when first set free from the egg, one of two forms, that of the *nauplius* (fig. 13, A) or that of the *zoaea* (fig. 13, B). The nauplius is found throughout the group and is the more important of the two; the zoaea is confined to the higher members, in some of which it merely forms a stage through which the larva, hatched as a nauplius, passes in its gradual development. The nauplius larva is of classic interest because its occurrence has enabled zoologists to determine with precision the position in the animal kingdom of a group, the Cirripedia, which was placed by the illustrious Cuvier among the Mollusca.

In the Tunicata the remarkable tadpole larva, the structure and development of which was first elucidated by the great Russian naturalist, A. Kowalevsky, possesses a similar interest to that of the nauplius larva of Cirripeds, and of the tornaria larva of the Enteropneusta, in that it pointed the way to the recognition of the affinities of the Tunicata, affinities which were entirely unsuspected till they were revealed by a study of the larvae.

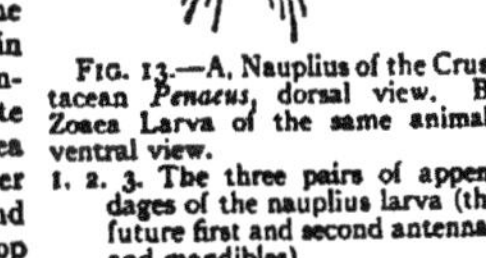

FIG. 13.—A, Nauplius of the Crustacean *Penaeus*, dorsal view. B, Zoaea Larva of the same animal, ventral view.
1, 2, 3. The three pairs of appendages of the nauplius larva (the future first and second antennae and mandibles).
3. Mandible.
4. First maxilla.
5. Second maxilla.
6. First maxilliped.
7. Second maxilliped.
8. Third maxilliped.

With regard to the occurrence of larvae, three general statements may be made. (1) They are always associated with a small egg in which the amount of food yolk is not sufficient to enable the animal to complete its development in the embryonic state. (2) A free-swimming larva is usually found in cases in which the adult is attached to foreign objects. (3) A larval stage is, as a rule, associated with internal parasitism of the adult. The object gained by the occurrence of a larva in the two last cases is to enable the species to distribute itself over as wide an area as possible. It may further be asserted that land and fresh-water animals develop without a larval stage much more frequently than marine forms. This is probably partly due to the fact that the conditions of land and fresh-water life are not so favourable for the spread of a species over a wide area by means of simply-organized larvae as are those of marine life, and partly to the fact that, in the case of fresh-water forms at any rate, a feebly-swimming larva would be in danger of being swept out to sea by currents.

1. The association of larvae with small eggs. This is a true statement as far as it goes, but in some cases small eggs do not give rise to larvae, some special form of nutriment being provided by the parent, e.g. Mammalia, in which there is a uterine nutrition by means of a placenta; some Gastropoda (e.g. *Helix waltoni*, *Bulimus*), in which, though the ovum is not specially large, it floats in a large quantity of albumen at the expense of which the development is completed; some Lamellibranchiata (*Cyclas*, &c.), Echinodermata (many *Ophiurids*, &c.), &c., in which development takes place in a brood

by means of a brush, spray or insufflation. Overheated and ill-ventilated rooms must be avoided, as entrance into them immediately aggravates the trouble and causes a paroxysm of coughing.

Oedematous Laryngitis is a very fatal condition, which may occur, though rarely, as a sequence of acute laryngitis. It is far more commonly seen in syphilitic and tubercular conditions of the larynx, in kidney disease, in certain fevers, and in cases of cellulitis of the neck. The larynx is also one of the sites of *Angeioneurotic oedema.* In this form of laryngitis there are all the symptoms of acute laryngitis, but on a very much exaggerated scale. The dyspnoea, accompanied by marked stridor, may arise and reach a dangerous condition within the space of an hour, and demand the most prompt treatment. On examination the mucous membrane round the epiglottis is seen to be enormously swollen. The treatment is ice round the throat and internally, scarification of the swollen parts, and should that not relieve the asphyxial symptoms, tracheotomy must be performed immediately.

Tubercular Laryngitis is practically always associated with phthisis. The mucous membrane is invaded by the tubercles, which first form small masses. These later break down and ulcerate; the ulceration then spreads up and down, causing an immense amount of destruction. The first indication is hoarseness, or, in certain forms, pain on swallowing. The cough is, as a rule, a late symptom. A sudden oedema may bring about a rapid fatal termination. The general treatment is the same as that advised for phthisis; locally, the affected parts may be removed by one or a series of operations, generally under local anaesthesia, or they may be treated with some destructive agent such as lactic acid. The pain on swallowing can be best alleviated by painting with a weak solution of cocaine. The condition is a very grave one; the prognosis depends largely on the associated pulmonary infection—if that be extensive, a very small amount of laryngeal mischief resists treatment, while, if the case be the contrary, a very extensive mischief may be successfully dealt with.

Syphilitic Laryngitis.—Invasion of the larynx in syphilis is very common. It may occur in both stages of the disease and in the inherited form. In the secondary stage the damage is superficial, and the symptoms those of a slight acute laryngitis. The injury in the tertiary stage is much more serious, the deeper structures are invaded with the formation of deep ulcers, which may when they heal form strong cicatrices, which produce a narrowing of the air-passage which may eventually require surgical interference. Occasionally a fatal oedema may arise. The treatment consists of administering constitutional remedies, local treatment being of comparatively slight importance.

Paroxysmal Laryngitis, or *Laryngismus stridulus*, is a nervous affection of the larynx that occurs in infants. It appears to be associated with adenoids. The disease consists of a reflex spasm of the glottis, which causes a complete blocking of the air-passages. The attacks, which are recurrent, cause acute asphyxiation. They may cease for no obvious reason, or one may prove fatal. The whole attack is of such short duration that the infant has either recovered or succumbed before assistance can be called. After an attack, careful examination should be made, and the adenoids, if present, removed by operation.

LA SABLIÈRE, MARGUERITE DE (*c.* 1640–1693), friend and patron of La Fontaine, was the wife of Antoine Rambouillet, sieur de la Sablière (1624–1679), a Protestant financier entrusted with the administration of the royal estates, her maiden name being Marguerite Hessein. She received an excellent education in Latin, mathematics, physics and anatomy from the best scholars of her time, and her house became a meeting-place for poets, scientists and men of letters, no less than for brilliant members of the court of Louis XIV. About 1673 Mme de la ... received into her house La Fontaine, whom for twenty ... relieved of every kind of material anxiety. Another inmate of the house was the traveller and physician ...ernier, whose abridgment of the works of Gassendi ... for Mme de la Sablière. The abbé Chaulieu and his fellow-poet, Charles Auguste, marquis de La Fare, were among her most intimate associates. La Fare sold his commission in the army to be able to spend his time with her. This liaison, which seems to have been the only serious passion of her life, was broken in 1679. La Fare was seduced from his allegiance, according to Mme de Sévigné by his love of play, but to this must be added a new passion for the actress La Champmeslé. Mme de la Sablière thenceforward gave more and more attention to good works, much of her time being spent in the hospital for incurables. Her husband's death in the same year increased her serious tendencies, and she was presently converted to Roman Catholicism. She died in Paris on the 8th of January 1693.

LA SALE (or La Salle), **ANTOINE DE** (c. 1388–1462?), French writer, was born in Provence, probably at Arles. He was a natural son of Bernard de la Salle,[1] a famous soldier of fortune, who served many masters, among others the Angevin dukes. In 1402 Antoine entered the court of Anjou, probably as a page, and in 1407 he was at Messina with Duke Louis II., who had gone there to enforce his claim to the kingdom of Sicily. The next years he perhaps spent in Brabant, for he was present at two tournaments given at Brussels and Ghent. With other gentlemen from Brabant, whose names he has preserved, he took part in the expedition of 1415 against the Moors, organized by John I. of Portugal. In 1420 he accompanied Louis III. on another expedition to Naples, making in that year an excursion from Norcia to the Monte della Sibilla, and the neighbouring Lake of Pilate. The story of his adventures on this occasion, and an account, with some sceptical comments, of the local legends regarding Pilate, and the Sibyl's grotto,[2] form the most interesting chapter of *La Salade*, which is further adorned with a map of the ascent from Montemonaco. La Sale probably returned with Louis III. of Anjou, who was also comte de Provence, in 1426 to Provence, where he was acting as *viguier* of Arles in 1429. In 1434 René, Louis's successor, made La Sale tutor to his son Jean d'Anjou, duc de Calabre, to whom he dedicated, between the years 1438 and 1447, his *La Salade*, which is a text-book of the studies necessary for a prince. The primary intention of the title is no doubt the play on his own name, but he explains it on the ground of the miscellaneous character of the book—a salad is composed "of many good herbs." In 1439 he was again in Italy in charge of the castle of Capua, with the duc de Calabre and his young wife, Marie de Bourbon, when the place was besieged by the king of Aragon. René abandoned Naples in 1442, and Antoine no doubt returned to France about the same time. His advice was sought at the tournaments which celebrated the marriage of the unfortunate Margaret of Anjou at Nancy in 1445; and in 1446, at a similar display at Saumur, he was one of the umpires. La Sale's pupil was now twenty years of age, and, after forty years' service of the house of Anjou, La Sale left it to become tutor to the sons of Louis de Luxembourg, comte de Saint Pol, who took him to Flanders and presented him at the court of Philippe le Bon, duke of Burgundy. For his new pupils he wrote at Châtelet-sur-Oise, in 1451, a moral work entitled *La Salle*.

He was nearly seventy years of age when he wrote the work that has made him famous, *L'Hystoire et plaisante cronicque du petit Jehan de Saintré et de la jeune dame des Belles-Cousines, Sans autre nom nommer*, dedicated to his former pupil, Jean de Calabre. An *envoi* in MS. 10,057 (nouv. acq. fr.) in the Bibliothèque Nationale, Paris, states that it was completed at Châtelet on the 6th of March 1455 (*i.e.* 1456). La Sale also announces an intention, never fulfilled, apparently, of writing a romance of *Paris et Vienne*. The MSS. of *Petit Jehan de Saintré* usually contain in addition *Floridam et Elvide*, translated by Rasse de Brunhamel from the Latin of Nicolas de Clamange, and dedicated to La Sale; also *Addiction extraite des Cronicques de Flandres*, of which only a few lines are original. Brunhamel says in his dedication that La Sale had delighted to write honourable histories from the time of his "florie jeunesse," which confirms a reasonable inference from the style of *Petit Jehan de Saintré* that its author was no novice in the art of romance-writing. The *Réconfort à Madame de Neufville*, a consolatory epistle including two stories of parental fortitude, was written at Vendeuil-sur-Oise about 1458, and in 1459 La Sale produced his treatise *Des anciens tournois et faicts d'armes* and the *Journée d'Onneur et de Prouesse*. He followed his patron to Genappe in Brabant when the Dauphin (afterwards Louis XI.) took refuge at the Burgundian court.

La Sale is generally accepted as the author of one of the most famous satires in the French language, *Les Quinze Joyes de mariage*, because his name has been disengaged from an acrostic at the end of the Rouen MS. He is also supposed to have been the "acteur" in the collection of licentious stories supposed to be narrated by various persons at the court of Philippe le Bon, and entitled the *Cent Nouvelles Nouvelles*. One only of the stories is given in his name, but he is credited with the compilation of the whole, for which Louis XI. was long held responsible. A completed copy of this was presented to the Duke of Burgundy at Dijon in 1462. If then La Sale was the author, he probably was still living; otherwise the last mention of him is in 1461.

Petit Jehan de Saintré gives, at the point when the traditions of chivalry were fast disappearing, an account of the education of an ideal knight and rules for his conduct under many different circumstances. When Petit Jehan, aged thirteen, is persuaded by the Dame des Belles-Cousines to accept her as his lady, she gives him systematic instruction in religion, courtesy, chivalry and the arts of success. She materially advances his career until Saintré becomes an accomplished knight, the fame of whose prowess spreads throughout Europe. This section of the romance—apparently didactic in intention—fits in with the author's other works of edification. But in the second part this virtuous lady falls a victim to a vulgar intrigue with Damp Abbé. One of La Sale's commentators, M. Joseph Nève, ingeniously maintains that the last section is simply to show how the hero, after passing through the other grades of education, learns at last by experience to arm himself against coquetry. The book may, however, be fairly regarded as satirizing the whole theory of "courteous" love, by the simple method of fastening a repulsive conclusion on an ideal case. The contention that the *fabliau*-like ending of a romance begun in idyllic fashion was due to the corrupt influences of the Dauphin's exiled court, is inadmissible, for the last page was written when the prince arrived in Brabant in 1456. That it is an anti-clerical satire seems unlikely. The profession of the seducer is not necessarily chosen from that point of view. The language of the book is not disfigured by coarseness of any kind, but, if the brutal ending was the expression of the writer's real views, there is little difficulty in accepting him as the author of the *Quinze Joyes de mariage* and the *Cent Nouvelles Nouvelles*.—Both these are masterpieces in their way and exhibit a much greater dramatic power and grasp of dialogue than does *Petit Jehan*. Some light is thrown on the romance by the circumstances of the duc de Calabre, to whom it was dedicated. His wife, Marie de Bourbon, was one of the "Belles-Cousines" who contended for the favour of Jacques or Jacquet de Lalaing in the *Livre des faits de Jacques Lalaing* which forms the chief source of the early exploits of Petit Jehan.

The incongruities of La Sale's aims appear in his method of construction. The hero is not imaginary. Jehan de Saintré flourished in the Hundred Years' War, was taken prisoner after Poitiers, with the elder Boucicaut, and was employed in negotiating the treaty of Brétigny. Froissart mentioned him as "le meilleur et le plus vaillant chevalier de France." His exploits as related in the romance are, however, founded on those of Jacques de Lalaing (*c.* 1422–1453), who was brought up at the Burgundian court, and became such a famous knight that he excited the rivalry of the "Belles-Cousines," Marie de Bourbon and Marie de Clèves, duchesse d'Orléans. Lalaing's exploits are related by more than one chronicler, but M. Gustave Raynaud thinks that the *Livre des faits de Jacques de Lalaing*, published among the works of Georges Chastelain, to which textual parallels may be found in *Petit Jehan*, should also be attributed to La Sale, who in that case undertook two accounts of the same hero, one historical and the other fictitious. To complicate matters, he drew, for the later exploits of Petit Jehan, on the *Livres des faits de Jean Boucicaut*, which gives the history of the younger Boucicaut. The atmosphere of the book is not the rough realities of the English wars in which the real Saintré figured but that of the courts to which La Sale was accustomed.

The title of *Les Quinze Joyes de mariage* is, with a profanity characteristic of the time, borrowed from a popular litany, *Les Quinze Joies de Notre Dame*, and each chapter terminates with a liturgical

[1] For his career, see Paul Durrieu, *Les Gascons en Italie* (Auch, 1885, pp. 107-71).

[2] For the legend of the Sibyl current in Italy at the time, given by La Sale, and its inter-relation with the Tannhäuser story, see W. Soederhjelm, "A. de la Salle et la légende de Tannhäuser" in *Mémoires de la soc. néo-philologique d'Helsingfors* (1897, vol. ii.); and Gaston Paris, "Le Paradis de la Reine Sibylle," and "La Légende du Tannhäuser," in the *Revue de Paris* (Dec. 1897 and March 1898).

[illegible] the miseries of marriage. Evidence in favour of [illegible] brought forward by M. E. Gossart (*Bibliophile* [illegible]), who quotes from his didactic treatise of *La* [illegible] [illegible] from St Jerome's treatise against [illegible] the chief elements of the satire. Gaston [illegible] Dec. 1897) expressed an opinion that to find [illegible] penetration by which La Sale divines [illegible] of married life, and the painful exactness [illegible] necessary to travel as far as Balzac. The [illegible] enough in the middle ages in France, but [illegible] *Joyes* is unusually natural and pregnant. [illegible] is perfect in its kind. There is no re- [illegible] of romance is replaced by the methods [illegible]

[illegible] *Nouvelles* the Italian *novella* is naturalized in [illegible] modelled on the *Decameron* of Boccaccio, and [illegible] *Facetiae* of the contemporary scholar [illegible] are rarely borrowed, and in cases where the [illegible] models they appear to be independent [illegible] the general immorality of the conception is [illegible] the details, but the ninety-eighth story [illegible] a genuine tragedy, and is of an entirely [illegible]. It is another version of the [illegible] already mentioned.

[illegible] these achievements to La Sale, some [illegible] ascribe to him also the farce of *Maître* [illegible]

[illegible] undoubted and reputed works are:— [illegible] Guichard (1843); *Les Cent Nouvelles* [illegible] Bibl. elzévirienne, 1858); *Les Quinze* [illegible] Bibl. elzév., 1857). *La Salade* was [illegible] 16th century. *La Salle* was never [illegible] E. Gossart in the *Bibliophile belge* [illegible] the authorities quoted above, and [illegible] *sa vie et ses ouvrages . . . suivi du* [illegible] *et de fragments et documents* [illegible] of *Les Quinze Joyes* and the [illegible] La Sale's works; Pietro Toldo, [illegible] *del XV e XVI secolo* [illegible] in the *Journal des Savants* [illegible] über Antoine de la Salle," in [illegible] *Sprachen*, vol. xlvi.; and G. [illegible] du Petit Jehan de Saintré," in [illegible]

(M. Br.)

[illegible] LOUIS COLLINET, [illegible] belonged to a noble family [illegible] Abraham Fabert, marshal [illegible] army at the age of eleven, [illegible] when the Revolution [illegible] his commission, but he [illegible] bravery and innate [illegible] him. By 1795 he had [illegible] a staff-officer in the army [illegible] he rivalled Seydlitz's [illegible] of a bridge to avoid [illegible] Davout's life in action. [illegible] combat in that year [illegible] broke seven swords. [illegible] general of brigade, [illegible] cavalry at Austerlitz. [illegible] he had but 600 hussars [illegible] terrified the com- [illegible] surrender, a feat [illegible] Denhingdon House. [illegible] in the Polish [illegible] Murat, grand [illegible], Lasalle was [illegible] at Medina de [illegible] body of troops [illegible] the cavalry [illegible] Austrian war. [illegible] With the [illegible] still unknown, [illegible] Wild [illegible] more than [illegible] that [illegible] true gift [illegible] in [illegible]

LA SALLE, RENÉ ROBERT CAVELIER, Sieur de (1643–1687), French explorer in North America, was born at Rouen on the 22nd of November 1643. He taught for a time in a school (probably Jesuit) in France, and seems to have forfeited his claim to his father's estate by his connexion with the Jesuits. In 1666 he became a settler in Canada, whither his brother, a Sulpician abbé, had preceded him. From the Seminary of St Sulpice in Montreal La Salle received a grant on the St Lawrence about 8 m. above Montreal, where he built a stockade and established a fur-trading post. In 1669 he sold this post (partly to the Sulpicians who had granted it to him) to raise funds for an expedition to China[1] by way of the Ohio,[2] which he supposed, from the reports of the Indians, to flow into the Pacific. He passed up the St Lawrence and through Lake Ontario to a Seneca village on the Genesee river; thence with an Iroquois guide he crossed the mouth of the Niagara (where he heard the noise of the distant falls) to Ganastogue, an Iroquois colony at the head of Lake Ontario, where he met Louis Joliet and received from him a map of parts of the Great Lakes. La Salle's missionary comrades now gave up the quest for China to preach among the Indians. La Salle discovered the Ohio river, descended it at least as far as the site of Louisville, Kentucky, and possibly, though not probably, to its junction with the Mississippi, and in 1669–1670, abandoned by his few followers, made his way back to Lake Erie. Apparently he passed through Lake Erie, Lake Huron and Lake Michigan, and some way down the Illinois river. Little is known of these explorations, for his journals are lost, and the description of his travels rests only on the testimony of the anonymous author of a *Histoire de M. de la Salle*. Before 1673 La Salle had returned to Montreal. Becoming convinced, after the explorations of Marquette and Joliet in 1673, that the Mississippi flowed into the Gulf of Mexico, he conceived a vast project for exploring that river to its mouth and extending the French power to the lower Mississippi Valley. He secured the support of Count Frontenac, then governor of Canada, and in 1674 and 1677 visited France, obtaining from Louis XIV. on his first visit a patent of nobility and a grant of lands about Fort Frontenac, on the site of the present Kingston, Ontario, and on his second visit a patent empowering him to explore the West at his own expense, and giving him the buffalo-hide monopoly. Late in the year 1678, at the head of a small party, he started from Fort Frontenac. He established a post above Niagara Falls, where he spent the winter, and where, his vessel having been wrecked, he built a larger ship, the "Griffon," in which he sailed up the Great Lakes to Green Bay (Lake Michigan), where he arrived in September 1679. Sending back the "Griffon" freighted with furs, by which he hoped to satisfy the claims of his creditors, he proceeded to the Illinois river, and near what is now Peoria, Illinois, built a fort, which he called Fort Crèvecœur. Thence he detached Father Hennepin, with one companion, to explore the Illinois to its mouth, and, leaving his lieutenant, Henri de Tonty (*c.* 1650–*c.* 1702),[3] with about fifteen men, at Fort Crèvecœur, he returned by land, afoot, to Canada to obtain needed supplies, discovering the fate of the "Griffon" (which proved to have been lost), thwarting the intrigues of his enemies and appeasing his creditors. In July 1680 news reached him at Fort Frontenac that nearly all Tonty's men had deserted, after destroying or appropriating most of the supplies; and that twelve of them were on their way to kill him as the surest means of escaping punishment.

[1] The name La Chine was sarcastically applied to La Salle's settlement on the St Lawrence.

[2] The Iroquois seem to have used the name Ohio for the Mississippi, or at least for its lower part; and this circumstance makes the story of La Salle's exploration peculiarly difficult to disentangle.

[3] Tonty (or Tonti), an Italian, born at Gaeta, was La Salle's principal lieutenant, and was the equal of his chief in intrepidity. Before his association with La Salle he had engaged in military service in Europe, during which he had lost a hand. He accompanied La Salle to the mouth of the Mississippi, and was in command of Fort St Louis from the time of its erection until 1702, except during his journeys down the Mississippi in search of his chief. In 1702 he joined d'Iberville in lower Louisiana, and soon after was despatched [illegible] mission to the Chickasaw Indians. This is the last authentic [illegible] im

These he met and captured or killed. He then returned to the Illinois, to find the country devastated by the Iroquois, and his post abandoned. He formed a league of the Western Indians to fight the Iroquois, then went to Michilimackinac, where he found Tonty, proceeded again to Fort Frontenac to obtain supplies and organize his expedition anew, and returned in December 1681 to the Illinois. Passing down the Illinois to the Mississippi, which he reached in February 1682, he floated down that stream to its mouth, which he reached on the 9th of April, and, erecting there a monument and a cross, took formal possession in the name of Louis XIV., in whose honour he gave the name "Louisiana" to the region. He then returned to Michilimackinac, whence, with Tonty, he went again to the Illinois and established a fort, Fort St Louis, probably on Starved Rock (near the present Ottawa, Illinois), around which nearly 20,000 Indians (Illinois, Miamis and others seeking protection from the Iroquois) had been gathered. La Salle then went to Quebec, and La Barre, who had succeeded Frontenac, being unfriendly to him, again visited France (1684), where he succeeded in interesting the king in a scheme to establish a fort at the mouth of the Mississippi and to seize the Spanish posts in the vicinity. On the 24th of July 1684, with four vessels under the command of himself and Captain Beaujeu, a naval officer, he sailed from La Rochelle. Mistaking, it appears, the inlets of Matagorda Bay (which La Salle called St Louis's Bay) in the present state of Texas, for the mouth of an arm of the Mississippi, he landed there, and Beaujeu, soon afterwards returned to France. The expedition had met with various misfortunes; one vessel had been captured by the Spaniards and another had been wrecked; and throughout La Salle and Beaujeu had failed to work in harmony. Soon finding that he was not at the mouth of the Mississippi, La Salle established a settlement and built a fort, Fort St Louis, on the Lavaca (he called it La Vache) river, and leaving there the greater part of his force, from October 1685 to March 1686 he vainly sought for the Mississippi. He also made two attempts to reach the Illinois country and Canada, and during the second, after two months of fruitless wanderings, he was assassinated, on the 19th of March 1687, by several of his followers, near the Trinity river in the present Texas.

His colony on the Lavaca, after suffering terribly from privation and disease and being attacked by the Indians, was finally broken up, and a force of Spaniards sent against it in 1689 found nothing but dead bodies and a dismantled fort; the few survivors having become domesticated in the Indian villages near by. Some writers, notably J. G. Shea, maintain that La Salle never intended to fortify the mouth of the Mississippi, but was instructed to establish an advanced post near the Spanish possessions, where he was to await a powerful expedition under a renegade Spaniard, Peñalosa, with whom he was to co-operate in expelling the Spaniards from this part of the continent.[1]

La Salle was one of the greatest of the explorers in North America. Besides discovering the Ohio and probably the Illinois, he was the first to follow the Mississippi from its upper course to its mouth and thus to establish the connexion between the discoveries of Radisson, Joliet and Marquette in the north with those of De Soto in the south. He was stern, indomitable and full of resource.

The best accounts of La Salle's explorations may be found in Francis Parkman's *La Salle and the Discovery of the Great West* (Boston, 1879; later revised editions), in Justin Winsor's *Cartier to Frontenac* (Boston, 1894), and in J. G. Shea's *Discovery and Exploration of the Mississippi Valley* (New York, 1852); see also P. Chesnel, *Histoire de Cavelier de La Salle, exploration et conquête du bassin du Mississippi* (Paris, 1901). Of the early narratives see Louis Hennepin, *Description de la Louisiane* (1683); Joutel, *Journal historique du dernier voyage que feu M. de la Salle fit dans le Golfe de Mexique, etc.* (Paris, 1713); and Henri de Tonty, *Dernières Découvertes dans l'Amérique septentrionale de M. de La Salle* (Paris, 1697). Original narratives may be found, translated into English, in *The Journeys of René Robert Cavelier, Sieur de La Salle, as related by his Faithful Lieutenant Henri de Tonty, &c.* (2 vols., New York, 1905), edited by I. J. Cox; in Benjamin F. French's *Historical Collections of Louisiana* (6 series, New York, 1846–1853), and in Shea's *Early Voyages Up and Down the Mississippi* (Albany, 1861); and an immense collection of documents relating to La Salle may be found in Pierre Margry's *Découvertes et établissements des Français dans l'ouest et dans le sud de l'Amérique septentrionale, 1614–1754. Mémoires et documents originaux recueillis et publiés* (6 vols., Paris, 1875–1886), especially in vol. ii. (C. C. W.)

[1] Although La Salle and Don Diego de Peñalosa (1624–1687) presented to the French government independent plans for an expedition against the Spaniards and Peñalosa afterwards proposed their co-operation, there is no substantial evidence that this project was adopted. Parkman is of the opinion that La Salle proposed his expedition against the Spaniards in the hope that the conclusion of peace between France and Spain would prevent its execution and that he might then use the aid he had thus received in establishing a fortified commercial colony at the mouth of the Mississippi. See E. T. Miller, "The Connection of Peñalosa with the La Salle Expedition," in the *Quarterly* of the Texas State Historical Association, vol. v. (Austin, Tex., 1902).

LA SALLE, ST JEAN BAPTISTE DE (1651–1719), founder of the order of Christian Brothers, was born at Reims. The son of a rich lawyer, his father's influence early secured him a canonry in the cathedral; there he established a school, where free elementary instruction was given to poor children. The enterprise soon broadened in scope; a band of enthusiastic assistants gathered round him; he resolved to resign his canonry, and devote himself entirely to education. His assistants were organized into a community, which gradually rooted itself all over France; and a training-school for teachers, the Collège de Saint-Yon, was set up at Rouen. In 1725, six years after the founder's death, the society was recognized by the pope, under the official title of "Brothers of the Christian Schools"; its members took the usual monastic vows, but did not aspire to the priesthood. During the first hundred years of its existence its activities were mainly confined to France; during the 19th century it spread to most of the countries of western Europe, and has been markedly successful in the United States. When La Salle was canonized in 1900, the total number of brothers was estimated at 15,000. Although the order has been chiefly concerned with elementary schools, it undertakes most branches of secondary and technical education; and it has served as a model for other societies, in Ireland and elsewhere, slightly differing in character from the original institute.

LA SALLE, a city of La Salle county, Illinois, U.S.A., on the Illinois river, near the head of navigation, 99 m. S.W. of Chicago. Pop. (1900) 10,446, of whom 3471 were foreign-born; (1910 census) 11,537. The city is served by the Chicago, Burlington & Quincy, the Chicago, Rock Island & Pacific, and the Illinois Central railways, and by the Illinois & Michigan Canal, of which La Salle is the western terminus. The city has a public library. The principal industries are the smelting of zinc and the manufacture of cement, rolled zinc, bricks, sulphuric acid and clocks; in 1905 the city's factory products were valued at $3,158,173. In the vicinity large quantities of coal are mined, for which the city is an important shipping point. The municipality owns and operates the waterworks and the electric lighting plant. The first settlement was made here in 1830; and the place which was named in honour of the explorer, René Robert Cavelier, Sieur de La Salle, was chartered as a city in 1852 and rechartered in 1876.

LASAULX, ARNOLD CONSTANTIN PETER FRANZ VON (1839–1886), German mineralogist and petrographer, was born at Castellaun near Coblenz on the 14th of June 1839. He was educated at Berlin, where he took his Ph. D. in 1868. In 1875 he became professor of mineralogy at Breslau, and in 1880 professor of mineralogy and geology at Bonn. He was distinguished for his researches on minerals and on crystallography, and he was one of the earlier workers on microscopic petrography. He described in 1878 the eruptive rocks of the district of Saar and Moselle. In 1880 he edited *Der Aetna* from the MSS. of Dr W. Sartorius von Waltershausen, the results of observations made between the years 1834–1869. He was author of *Elemente der Petrographie* (1875), *Einführung in die Gesteinslehre* (1885), and *Précis de pétrographie* (1887). He died at Bonn on the 25th of January 1886.

...expedition under Columbus to the West Indies, and in 1502 ... with Nicolás de Ovando, the governor, to Hayti, where ... he was admitted to holy orders, being the first priest ordained in the American colonies. In 1511 he passed over to Cuba to take part in the work of "population and pacification," and in 1513 or 1514 he witnessed and vainly endeavoured to check the massacre of Indians at Caonao. Soon afterwards there was assigned to him and his friend Renteria a large village in the neighbourhood of Zagua, with a number of Indians attached to it in what was known as *repartimiento* (allotment); like the rest of his countrymen he made the most of this opportunity for growing rich, but occasionally celebrated mass and preached. Soon, however, having become convinced of the injustice connected with the *repartimiento* system, he began to preach against it, at the same time giving up his own slaves. With the consent of his partner he resolved to go to Spain on behalf of the oppressed natives, and the result of his representations was that in 1516 Cardinal Jimenes caused a commission to be sent out for the reform of abuses, Las Casas himself, with the title of "protector of the Indians," being appointed to advise and report on them. This commission had not been long at San Domingo before Las Casas perceived the indifference of his coadjutors to the cause which he himself had at heart, and July 1517 found him again in Spain, where he developed his scheme for the complete liberation of the Indians—a scheme which not only included facilities for emigration from Spain, but was intended to give to each Spanish resident in the colonies the right of importing twelve negro slaves. The emigration movement proved a failure, and Las Casas lived long enough to express his shame for having been so slow to see that Africans were as much entitled to freedom as were the natives of the New World. Overwhelmed with disappointment, he retired to the Dominican monastery in Haiti; he joined the order in 1522 and devoted eight years to study. About 1530 he appears to have revisited the Spanish court, but on what precise errand is not known; the confusion concerning this period of his life extends to the time when, after visits to Mexico, Nicaragua, Peru and Guatemala, he undertook an expedition in 1537 into Tuzulutlan, the inhabitants of which were, chiefly through his tact, peaceably converted to Christianity, mass being celebrated for the first time amongst them in the newly founded town of Rabinal in 1538. In 1539 Las Casas was sent to Spain to obtain Dominican recruits, and through Loaysa, general of the order, and confessor of Charles V., he was successful in obtaining royal orders and letters favouring his enterprise. During this stay in Europe, which lasted more than four years, he visited Germany to see the emperor; he also (1542) wrote his *Veynte Rasones*, in defence of the liberties of the Indians and the *Brevisima Relacion de la Destruycion des las Indias occidentales*, the latter of which was published some twelve years later. In 1543 he refused the Mexican bishopric of Cuzco, but was prevailed upon to accept that of Chiapa, for which he sailed in 1544. Thwarted at every point by the officials, and outraged by his countrymen in his attempt to carry out the new laws which his humanity had procured, he returned to Spain and resigned his dignity (1547). In 1550 he met Sepúlveda in public debate on the theses drawn from the recently published *Apologia pro libro de justis belli causis*, in which the latter had maintained the lawfulness of waging unprovoked war upon the natives of the New World. The course of the discussion may be traced in the account of the *Disputa* contained in the *Obras* (1552). In 1565 Las Casas successfully remonstrated with Philip II. against the financial project for selling the reversion of the *encomiendas*—a project which would have involved the Indians in hopeless bondage. In July of the following year he died at Madrid, whither he had gone to urge (and with success) the necessity of restoring a court of justice which had been suppressed in Guatemala. His *Historia de las Indias* was not published till 1875–1876.

Sir Arthur Helps' *Life of Las Casas* (London, 1868) has not been superseded; but see also F. A. MacNutt, *Bartholomew de Las Casas* (1909).

LAS CASES, EMMANUEL AUGUSTIN DIEUDONNÉ MARIN JOSEPH, MARQUIS (1766–1842), French official, was born at the castle of Las Cases near Revel in Languedoc. He was educated at the military schools of Vendôme and Paris; he entered the navy and took part in various engagements of the years 1781–1782. The outbreak of the Revolution in 1789 caused him to "emigrate," and he spent some years in Germany and England, sharing in the disastrous Quiberon expedition (1795). He was one of the few survivors and returned to London, where he lived in poverty. He returned to France during the Consulate with other royalists who rallied to the side of Napoleon, and stated afterwards to the emperor that he was "conquered by his glory." Not until 1810 did he receive much notice from Napoleon, who then made him a chamberlain and created him a count of the empire (he was marquis by hereditary right). After the first abdication of the emperor (11th of April 1814), Las Cases retired to England, but returned to serve Napoleon during the Hundred Days. The second abdication opened up for Las Cases the most noteworthy part of his career. He withdrew with the ex-emperor and a few other trusty followers to Rochefort; and it was Las Cases who first proposed and strongly urged the emperor to throw himself on the generosity of the British nation. Las Cases made the first overtures to Captain Maitland of H.M.S. "Bellerophon" and received a guarded reply, the nature of which he afterwards misrepresented. Las Cases accompanied the ex-emperor to St Helena and acted informally but very assiduously as his secretary, taking down numerous notes of his conversations which thereafter took form in the famous *Mémorial de Ste Hélène*. The limits of this article preclude an attempt at assessing the value of this work. It should be read with great caution, as the compiler did not scruple to insert his own thoughts and to colour the expressions of his master. In some cases he misstated facts and even fabricated documents. It is far less trustworthy than the record penned by Gourgaud in his *Journal*. Disliked by Montholon and Gourgaud, Las Cases seems to have sought an opportunity to leave the island when he had accumulated sufficient literary material. However that may be, he infringed the British regulations in such a way as to lead to his expulsion by the governor, Sir Hudson Lowe (November, 1816). He was sent first to the Cape of Good Hope and thence to Europe, but was not at first allowed by the government of Louis XVIII. to enter France. He resided at Brussels; but, gaining permission to come to Paris after the death of Napoleon, he took up his residence there, published the *Mémorial*, and soon gained an enormous sum from it. He died in 1842 at Passy.

See *Mémoires de E. A. D., comte de Las Cases* (Brussels, 1818); *Mémorial de Ste Hélène* (4 vols., London and Paris, 1823; often republished and translated); *Suite au mémorial de Ste Hélène, ou observations critiques, &c.* (2 vols., Paris, 1824), anonymous, but known to be by Grille and Musset-Pathay. See too GOURGAUD, MONTHOLON, and LOWE, SIR HUDSON. (J. HL. R.)

LASHIO, the headquarters of the superintendent, northern Shan States, Burma, situated in 22° 56′ N. and 97° 45′ E. at an altitude of 3100 ft., on a low spur overlooking the valley of the Nam Yao. It is the present terminus of the Mandalay-Kun Lông railway and of the government cart road from Mandalay, from which it is 178 m. distant. It consists of the European station, with court house and quarters for the civil officers; the military police post, the headquarters of the Lashio battalion of military police; the native station, in which the various nationalities, Shans, Burmans, Hindus and Mahommedans, are divided into separate quarters, with reserves for government servants and for the temporary residences of the five sawbwas of the northern Shan States; and a bazaar. Under Burmese rule Lashio was also the centre of authority for the northern Shan States, but the Burmese post in the valley was close to the Nam Yao, in an old Chinese fortified camp. The Lashio valley was formerly very populous; but a rebellion, started by the sawbwa of Hsenwi, about ten years before the British occupation, ruined it, and it is only slowly approaching the prosperity it formerly enjoyed; pop. (1901) 2565. The annual rainfall averages 54 in. The average maximum temperature is 80·5° and the average minimum 55·5°.

LASKER, EDUARD (1829–1884), German publicist, was born on the 14th of October 1829, at Jarotschin, a village in Posen, being the son of a Jewish tradesman. He attended the gymnasium, and afterwards the university of Breslau. In 1848 after the outbreak of the revolution, he went to Vienna and entered the students' legion which took so prominent a part in the disturbances; he fought against the imperial troops during the siege of the city in October. He then continued his legal studies at Breslau and Berlin, and after a visit of three years to England, then the model state for German liberals, entered the Prussian judicial service. In 1870 he left the government service, and in 1873 was appointed to an administrative post in the service of the city of Berlin. He had been brought to the notice of the political world by some articles he wrote from 1861 to 1864, which were afterwards published under the title *Zur Verfassungsgeschichte Preussens* (Leipzig, 1874), and in 1865 he was elected member for one of the divisions of Berlin in the Prussian parliament. He joined the radical or *Fortschritts* party, and in 1867 was also elected to the German parliament, but he helped to form the national liberal party, and in consequence lost his seat in Berlin, which remained faithful to the radicals; after this he represented Magdeburg and Frankfort-on-Main in the Prussian, and Meiningen in the German, parliament. He threw himself with great energy into his parliamentary duties, and quickly became one of its most popular and most influential members. An optimist and idealist, he joined to a fervent belief in liberty an equal enthusiasm for German unity and the idea of the German state. His motion that Baden should be included in the North German Confederation in January 1870 caused much embarrassment to Bismarck, but was not without effect in hastening the crisis of 1870. His great work, however, was the share he took in the judicial reform during the ten years 1867–1877. To him more than to any other single individual is due the great codification of the law. While he again and again was able to compel the government to withdraw or amend proposals which seemed dangerous to liberty, he opposed those liberals who, unable to obtain all the concessions which they called for, refused to vote for the new laws as a whole. A speech made by Lasker on the 7th of February 1873, in which he attacked the management of the Pomeranian railway, caused a great sensation, and his exposure of the financial mismanagement brought about the fall of Hermann Wagener, one of Bismarck's most trusted assistants. By this action he caused, however, some embarrassment to his party. This is generally regarded as the beginning of the reaction against economic liberalism by which he and his party were to be deprived of their influence. He refused to follow Bismarck in his financial and economic policy after 1878; always unsympathetic to the chancellor, he was now selected for his most bitter attacks. Between the radicals and socialists on the one side and the government on the other, like many of his friends, he was unable to maintain himself. In 1879 he lost his seat in the Prussian parliament; he joined the *Secession*, but was ill at ease in his new position. Broken in health and spirits by the incessant labours of the time when he did "half the work of the Reichstag," he went in 1883 for a tour in America, and died suddenly in New York on the 5th of January 1884.

Lasker's death was the occasion of a curious episode, which caused much discussion at the time. The American House of Representatives adopted a motion of regret, and added to it these words: "That his loss is not alone to be mourned by the people of his native land, where his firm and constant exposition of, and devotion to, free and liberal ideas have materially advanced the social, political and economic conditions of these people, but by the lovers of liberty throughout the world." This motion was sent through the American minister at Berlin to the German foreign office, with a request that it might be communicated to the president of the Reichstag. It was to ask Bismarck officially to communicate a resolution in which a foreign parliament expressed an opinion in German affairs exactly opposed to that which the emperor at his advice had always followed. Bismarck therefore refused to communicate the resolution, and returned it through the German minister at Washington.

Among Lasker's writings may be mentioned: *Zur Geschichte der parlamentarischen Entwickelung Preussens* (Leipzig, 1873), *Die Zukunft des Deutschen Reichs* (Leipzig, 1877) and *Wege und Ziele der*

Kulturentwickelung (Leipzig, 1881). After his death his *Fünfzehn Jahre parlamentarischer Geschichte 1866–1880* appeared edited by W. Cahn (Berlin, 1902). See also L. Bamberger, *Eduard Lasker, Gedenkrede* (Leipzig, 1884); A. Wolff, *Zur Erinnerung an Eduard Lasker* (Berlin, 1884); Freund, *Einiges über Eduard Lasker* (Leipzig, 1885); and *Eduard Lasker, seine Biographie und letzte öffentliche Rede*, by various writers (Stuttgart, 1884). (J. W. He.)

LASKI, the name of a noble and powerful Polish family, is taken from the town of Lask, the seat of their lordship.

Jan Laski, the elder (1456–1531), Polish statesman and ecclesiastic, appears to have been largely self-taught and to have owed everything to the remarkable mental alertness which was hereditary in the Laski family. He took orders betimes, and in 1495 was secretary to the Polish chancellor Zawisza Kurozwecki, in which position he acquired both influence and experience. The aged chancellor entrusted the sharp-witted young ecclesiastic with the conduct of several important missions. Twice, in 1495 and again in 1500, he was sent to Rome, and once on a special embassy to Flanders, of which he has left an account. On these occasions he had the opportunity of displaying diplomatic talent of a high order. On the accession to the Polish throne in 1501 of the indolent Alexander, who had little knowledge of Polish affairs and chiefly resided in Lithuania, Laski was appointed by the senate the king's secretary, in which capacity he successfully opposed the growing separatist tendencies of the grand-duchy and maintained the influence of Catholicism, now seriously threatened there by the Muscovite propaganda. So struck was the king by his ability that on the death of the Polish chancellor in 1503 he passed over the vice-chancellor Macics Dzewicki and confided the great seal to Laski. As chancellor Laski supported the *szlachta*, or country-gentlemen, against the lower orders, going so far as to pass an edict excluding henceforth all plebeians from the higher benefices of the church. Nevertheless he approved himself such an excellent public servant that the new king, Sigismund I., made him one of his chief counsellors. In 1511 the chancellor, who ecclesiastically was still only a canon of Cracow, obtained the coveted dignity of archbishop of Gnesen which carried with it the primacy of the Polish church. In the long negotiations with the restive and semi-rebellious Teutonic Order, Laski rendered Sigismund most important political services, proposing as a solution of the question that Sigismund should be elected grand master, while he, Laski, should surrender the primacy to the new candidate of the knights, Albert of Brandenburg, a solution which would have been far more profitable to Poland than the ultimate settlement of 1525. In 1513 Laski was sent to the Lateran council, convened by Pope Julius II., to plead the cause of Poland against the knights, where both as an orator and as a diplomatist he brilliantly distinguished himself. This mission was equally profitable to his country and himself, and he succeeded in obtaining from the pope for the archbishops of Gnesen the title of *legati nati*. In his old age Laski's partiality for his nephew, Hieronymus, led him to support the candidature of John Zapolya, the protégé of the Turks, for the Hungarian crown so vehemently against the Habsburgs that Clement VII. excommunicated him, and the shock of this disgrace was the cause of his sudden death in 1531. Of his numerous works the most noteworthy are his collection of Polish statutes entitled: *Statuta provinciae gnesnensis antiqua, &c.* (Cracow, 1525–1528) and *De Ruthenorum nationibus eorumque erroribus*, printed at Nuremberg.

See Heinrich R. von Zeissberg, *Joh. Laski, Erzbischof in Gnesen* (Vienna, 1874); and Jan Korytkowski, *Jan Laski, Archbishop of Gnesen* (Gnesen, 1880).

Hieronymus Jaroslaw Laski (1496–1542), Polish diplomatist, nephew of Archbishop Laski, was successively palatine of Inowroclaw and of Sieradia. His first important mission was to Paris in 1524, ostensibly to contract an anti-Turkish league with the French king, but really to bring about a matrimonial alliance between the dauphin, afterwards Henry II., and the daughter of King Sigismund I., a project which failed through no fault of Laski's. The collapse of the Hungarian monarchy at Mohacs (1526) first opened up a wider career to Laski's adventurous activity. Contrary to the wishes of his own sovereign, Sigismund I., whose pro-Austrian policy he detested, Laski entered the service of John Zapolya, the Magyar competitor for the Hungarian throne, thereby seriously compromising Poland both with the emperor and the pope. Zapolya despatched him on an embassy to Paris, Copenhagen and Munich for help, but on his return he found his patron a refugee in Transylvania, whither he had retired after his defeat by the German king Ferdinand I. at Tokay in 1527. In his extremity Zapolya placed himself under the protection of the sultan, Laski being sent to Constantinople as his intermediary. On his way thither he was attacked and robbed of everything, including his credentials and the rich presents without which no negotiations were deemed possible at the Porte. But Laski was nothing if not audacious. Proceeding on his way to the Turkish capital empty-handed, he nevertheless succeeded in gaining the confidence of Gritti, the favourite of the grand vizier, and ultimately persuaded the sultan to befriend Zapolya and to proclaim him king of Hungary. He went still further, and without the slightest authority for his action concluded a ten years' truce between his old master King Sigismund of Poland and the Porte. He then returned to Hungary at the head of 10,000 men, with whose aid he enabled Zapolya to re-establish his position and defeat Ferdinand at Saros-Patak. He was rewarded with the countship of Zips and the governor-generalship of Transylvania. But his influence excited the jealousy of the Magyars, and Zapolya was persuaded to imprison him. On being released by the interposition of the Polish grand hetman, Tarnowski, he became the most violent opponent of Zapolya. Shortly after his return to Poland, Laski died suddenly at Cracow, probably poisoned by one of his innumerable enemies.

See Alexander Hirschberg, *Hieronymus Laski* (Pol.) (Lemberg, 1888).

Jan Laski, the younger (1499–1560), also known as *Johannes a Lasco*, Polish reformer, son of Jaroslaw (d. 1523) voivode of Sieradia and nephew of the famous Archbishop Laski. During his academical course abroad he made the acquaintance of Zwingli and Erasmus and returned to Poland in 1526 saturated with the new doctrines. Nevertheless he took orders, and owing to the influence of his uncle obtained the bishopric of Veszprem in Hungary from King John Zapolya, besides holding a canonry of Cracow and the office of royal secretary. In 1531 he resigned all his benefices rather than give up a woman whom he had secretly married, and having incurred general reprobation and the lasting displeasure of his uncle the archbishop, he fled to Germany, where ultimately (1543) he adopted the Augsburg Confession. For the next thirteen years Laski was a wandering apostle of the new doctrines. He was successively superintendent at Emden and in Friesland, passed from thence to London where he became a member of the so-called *ecclesia peregrinorum*, a congregation of foreign Protestants exiled in consequence of the Augsburg Interim of 1548 and, on being expelled by Queen Mary, took refuge first in Denmark and subsequently at Frankfort-on-Main, where he was greatly esteemed. From Frankfort he addressed three letters (printed at Basel) to King Sigismund, Augustus, and the Polish gentry and people, urging the conversion of Poland to Protestantism. In 1556, during the brief triumph of the anti-catholics, he returned to his native land, took part in the synod of Brzesc, and published a number of polemical works, the most noteworthy of which were *Forma ac ratio tota ecclesiastici ministerii in peregrinorum Ecclesiae instituta* (Pinczow, 1560), and in Polish, *History of the Cruel Persecution of the Church of God in 1567*, republished in his *Opera*, edited by A. Kuyper at Amsterdam in 1866. He died at Pinczow in January 1560 and was buried with great pomp by the Polish Protestants, who also struck a medal in his honour. Twice married, he left two sons and two daughters. His nephew (?) Albert Laski, who visited England in 1583, wasted a fortune in aid of Dr Dee's craze for the "philosopher's stone." Laski's writings are important for the organization of the *ecclesia peregrinorum*, and he was concerned in the Polish version of the Bible, not published till 1563.

See H. Dalton, *Johannes a Lasco* (1881), English version of the earlier portion by J. Evans (1886); Bartels, *Johannes a Lasco* (1860); Harboe, *Schicksale des Johannes a Lasco* (1758); R. Wallace,

Antitrinitarian Biography (1850); Bonet-Maury, *Early Sources of Eng. Unit. Christianity* (1884); W. A. J. Archbold in *Dict. Nat. Biog.* (1892) under "Laski," George Pascal, *Jean de Lasco* (Paris, 1894); *Life* in Polish by Antoni Walewski (Warsaw, 1872); and Juljan Bukowski, *History of the Reformation in Poland* (Pol.) (Cracow, 1883). (R. N. B.)

LAS PALMAS, the capital of the Spanish island of Grand Canary, in the Canary archipelago, and of an administrative district which also comprises the islands of Lanzarote and Fuerteventura; on the east coast, in 28° 7′ N. and 5° 24′ W. Pop. (1900) 44,517. Las Palmas is the largest city in the Canary Islands, of which it was the capital until 1833. It is the seat of a court of appeal, of a brigadier, who commands the military forces in the district, of a civil lieutenant-governor, who is independent of the governor-general except in connexion with elections and municipal administration, and of a bishop, who is subordinate to the archbishop of Seville. The palms from which the city derives its name are still characteristic of the fertile valley which it occupies. Las Palmas is built on both banks of a small river, and although parts of it date from the 16th century, it is on the whole a clean and modern city, well drained, and supplied with pure water, conveyed by an aqueduct from the highlands of the interior. Its principal buildings include a handsome cathedral, founded in the 16th century but only completed in the 19th, a theatre, a museum, an academy of art, and several hospitals and good schools. The modern development of Las Palmas is largely due to the foreign merchants, and especially to the British who control the greater portion of the local commerce. La Luz, the port, is connected with Las Palmas by a railway 4 m. long; it is a free port and harbour of refuge, officially considered the third in importance of Spanish ports, but actually the first in the matter of tonnage. It is strongly fortified. The harbour, protected by the promontory of La Isleta, which is connected with the mainland by a narrow bar of sand, can accommodate the largest ships, and affords secure anchorage in all weathers. Ships can discharge at the breakwater (1257 yds. long) or at the Santa Catalina mole, constructed in 1883–1902. The minimum depth of water alongside the quays is 4½ ft. There are floating water-tanks, numerous lighters, titan and other cranes, repairing workshops, and very large supplies of coal afloat and ashore. La Luz is one of the principal Atlantic coaling stations, and the coal-trade is entirely in British hands. Other important industries are shipbuilding, fishing, and the manufacture of glass, leather and hats. The chief exports are fruit, vegetables, sugar, wine and cochineal; coal, iron, cement, timber, petroleum, manure, textiles and provisions are the chief imports. (See also CANARY ISLANDS.)

LASSALLE, FERDINAND (1825–1864), German socialist, was born at Breslau on the 11th of April 1825, of Jewish extraction. His father, a prosperous merchant in Breslau, intended Ferdinand for a business career, and sent him to the commercial school at Leipzig; but the boy got himself transferred to the university, first at Breslau, and afterwards at Berlin. His favourite studies were philology and philosophy; he became an ardent Hegelian. Having completed his university studies in 1845, he began to write a work on Heraclitus from the Hegelian point of view; but it was soon interrupted by more stirring interests, and did not see the light for many years. It was in Berlin, towards the end of 1845, that he met the lady with whom his life was to be associated in so remarkable a way, the Countess Hatzfeldt. She had been separated from her husband for many years, and was at feud with him on questions of property and the custody of their children. Lassalle attached himself to the cause of the countess, whom he believed to have been outrageously wronged, made special study of law, and, after bringing the case before thirty-six tribunals, reduced the powerful count to a compromise on terms most favourable to his client. The process, which lasted ten years, gave rise to not a little scandal, especially that of the *Cassettengeschichte* which pursued Lassalle all the rest of his life. This "affair of the casket" arose out of an attempt by the countess's friends to get possession of a bond for a large life annuity settled by the count on his mistress, a Baroness Meyendorf, to the prejudice of the countess and her children. Two of Lassalle's comrades succeeded in carrying off the casket, which contained the lady's jewels, from the baroness's room at an hotel in Cologne. They were prosecuted for theft, one of them being condemned to six months' imprisonment. Lassalle, accused of moral complicity, was acquitted on appeal. He was not so fortunate in 1849, when he underwent a year's durance for resistance to the authorities of Düsseldorf during the troubles of that stormy period. But going to prison was a familiar experience in Lassalle's life. Till 1859 Lassalle resided mostly in the Rhine country, prosecuting the suit of the countess, finishing the work on Heraclitus, which was not published till 1858, taking little part in political agitation, but ever a helpful friend of the working men. He was not allowed to live in Berlin because of his connexion with the disturbances of '48. In 1859, however, he entered the city disguised as a carter, and, through the influence of Humboldt with the king, got permission to stay there. The same year he published a remarkable pamphlet on the *Italian War and the Mission of Prussia*, in which he warned his countrymen against going to the rescue of Austria in her war with France. He pointed out that if France drove Austria out of Italy she might annex Savoy, but could not prevent the restoration of Italian unity under Victor Emmanuel. France was doing the work of Germany by weakening Austria; Prussia should form an alliance with France to drive out Austria and make herself supreme in Germany. After their realization by Bismarck these ideas have become sufficiently commonplace; but they were nowise obvious when thus published by Lassalle. In 1861 he published a great work in two volumes, *System der erworbenen Rechte* (*System of Acquired Rights*).

Now began the short-lived activity which was to give him an historical significance. It was early in 1862, when the struggle of Bismarck with the Prussian liberals was already begun. Lassalle, a democrat of the most advanced type, saw that an opportunity had come for asserting a third great cause—that of the working men—which would outflank the liberalism of the middle classes, and might even command the sympathy of the government. His political programme was, however, entirely subordinate to the social, that of bettering the condition of the working classes, for which he believed the schemes of Schulze-Delitzsch were utterly inadequate. Lassalle flung himself into the career of agitator with his accustomed vigour. His worst difficulties were with the working men themselves, among whom he met the most discouraging apathy. His mission as organizer and emancipator of the working class lasted only two years and a half. In that period he issued about twenty separate publications, most of them speeches and pamphlets, but one of them, that against Schulze-Delitzsch, a considerable treatise, and all full of keen and vigorous thought. He founded the "Allgemeiner Deutscher Arbeiterverein," was its president and almost single-handed champion, conducted its affairs, and carried on a vast correspondence, not to mention about a dozen state prosecutions in which he was during that period involved. Berlin, Leipzig, Frankfort and the industrial centres on the Rhine were the chief scenes of his activity. His greatest success was on the Rhine, where in the summers of 1863 and 1864 his travels as missionary of the new gospel resembled a triumphal procession. The agitation was growing rapidly, but he had achieved little substantial success when a most unworthy death closed his career.

While posing as the messiah of the poor, Lassalle was a man of decidedly fashionable and luxurious habits. His suppers were well known as among the most exquisite in Berlin. It was the most piquant feature of his life that he, one of the gilded youth, a connoisseur in wines, and a learned man to boot, had become agitator and the champion of the working man. In one of the literary and fashionable circles of Berlin he had met a Fräulein von Dönniges, for whom he at once felt a passion, which was ardently reciprocated. In the summer of 1864 he met her again on the Rigi, when they resolved to marry. She was a young lady of twenty, decidedly unconventional and original in character, but the daughter of a Bavarian [illegible] then resident at Geneva, who would have nothing to [illegible] with Lassalle. The lady was imprisoned in her own room, [illegible], apparently under the influence of very questionable [illegible], renounced Lassalle in favour of another admirer, a [illegible], Count von Racowitza. Lassalle sent a challenge [illegible] the lady's father and her betrothed, which was accepted [illegible] latter. At the Carouge, a suburb of Geneva, the meeting [illegible] on the morning of August 28, 1864, when Lassalle [illegible] wounded, and he died on the 31st of August. [illegible] such a foolish ending, his funeral was that of a martyr, [illegible] of his adherents he has been regarded since with [illegible] of religious devotion.

[illegible] lay claim to any special originality as a socialistic [illegible] he publish any systematic statement of his views. [illegible] ideas are sufficiently clear and simple. Like a true [illegible] three stages in the development of labour: the [illegible] period, which, through the subjection of the [illegible] without freedom; the reign of capital and [illegible] established in 1789, which sought freedom by [illegible] and the new era, beginning in 1848, which [illegible] with freedom by introducing the principle [illegible] the basis and starting-point of his opinions [illegible] of capital and so long as the working man [illegible] wages, no improvement in his condition [illegible] position he founded on the law of wages [illegible] accepted by all the leading economists, [illegible] by the ordinary relations of supply and [illegible] wages leads to an increase in the labouring [illegible] the supply of labour, is followed by a [illegible]. Thus population increases or decreases [illegible] or fall of wages. The condition of the [illegible] rise above the mere standard of [illegible], and the continued supply of his [illegible] the co-operative schemes of Schulze-[illegible] self-help" were utterly inadequate, [illegible] the working classes were destitute of [illegible] working man helping himself with his [illegible] capitalists he compared to a battle with [illegible] modern artillery. In short, Lassalle ac-[illegible] economy to show that the inevitable [illegible] for the working classes, and that no [illegible] abolishing the conditions in which [illegible] other words, by abolishing the [illegible] capital altogether. And this could [illegible] association of the working men with [illegible]. And he held that such association [illegible] the working men, the government [illegible] examine the books of the various [illegible] should be carried out according to [illegible] such transactions. But how [illegible] a loan? Simply by introducing [illegible] working men were an overwhelming [illegible] and should control the government. [illegible] organize the working classes into [illegible] was thus indicated, by peaceful [illegible] insurrection, might attain the [illegible] In this way the fourth estate would [illegible] the capitalist, and a great step [illegible] social question."

[illegible] Lassalle's life was to produce [illegible] a socialistic movement in [illegible] returned to the Reichstag [illegible] votes, and at the election [illegible] polled 3,258,068 votes. [illegible] returned in 1907 was due [illegible] political groups.) This [illegible] been commensurate with [illegible] day of his passion for [illegible] be enthroned as the [illegible] at his side. With [illegible] organizing, he might [illegible] with him as the [illegible] combat the Prussian [illegible] Reichstag, he spoke of him [illegible] and ability [illegible] Ketteler of Mainz [illegible] advocated.

[illegible] von Ephesus [illegible] (Leipzig, 1861) [illegible] power. But of [illegible] and pamphlets con-[illegible] the most important [illegible] Franz von Sickingen, Herr Bastiat-[illegible] drama, Franz [illegible]

The best biography of Lassalle is H. Oncken's *Lassalle* (Stuttgart, 1904); another excellent work on his life and writings is George Brandes's Danish work, *Ferdinand Lassalle* (German translation, 4th ed., Leipzig, 1900). See also A. Aaberg, *Ferdinand Lassalle* (Leipzig, 1883); C. v. Plener, *Lassalle* (Leipzig, 1884); G. Meyer, *Lassalle als Sozialokonom* (Berlin, 1894); Brandt, *F. Lassalles sozialokonomische Anschauungen und praktische Vorschläge* (Jena, 1895); Seillière, *Études sur Ferdinand Lassalle* (Paris, 1897); E. Bernstein, *Ferd. Lassalle und seine Bedeutung für die Arbeiterklasse* (Berlin, 1904). There is a considerable literature on his love affair and death; the most notable books are: *Meine Beziehungen zu F. Lassalle*, by Helene von Racowitza, a very strange book; *Enthullungen uber das tragische Lebensende F. Lassalle's* by B. Becker; *Im Anschluss an die Memoiren der H. von Racowitza*, by A. Kutschbach, and George Meredith's *Tragic Comedians* (1880). (T. K.)

LASSEN, CHRISTIAN (1800–1876), German orientalist, was born on the 22nd of October 1800, at Bergen in Norway. Having received his earliest university education at Christiania, he went to Germany, and continued his studies at Heidelberg and Bonn. In the latter university Lassen acquired a sound knowledge of Sanskrit. He next spent three years in Paris and London, engaged in copying and collating MSS., and collecting materials for future research, especially in reference to the Hindu drama and philosophy. During this period he published, jointly with E. Burnouf, his first work, *Essai sur le Pâli* (Paris, 1826). On his return to Bonn he studied Arabic, and took the degree of Ph.D., his dissertation discussing the Arabic notices of the geography of the Punjab (*Commentatio geographica atque historica de Pentapotamia Indica*, Bonn, 1827). Soon after he was admitted *Privatdozent*, and in 1830 was appointed extraordinary and in 1840 ordinary professor of Old Indian language and literature. In spite of a tempting offer from Copenhagen, in 1841, Lassen remained faithful to the university of his adoption to the end of his life. He died at Bonn on the 8th of May 1876, having been affected with almost total blindness for many years. As early as 1864 he was relieved of the duty of lecturing.

In 1829–1831 he brought out, in conjunction with August W. von Schlegel, a critical annotated edition of the *Hitopadeśa*. The appearance of this edition marks the starting-point of the critical study of Sanskrit literature. At the same time Lassen assisted von Schlegel in editing and translating the first two cantos of the epic *Râmâyana* (1829–1838). In 1832 he brought out the text of the first act of Bhavabhûti's drama, *Mâlatîmâdhava*, and a complete edition, with a Latin translation, of the *Sânkhya-kârikâ*. In 1837 followed his edition and translation of Jayadeva's charming lyrical drama, *Gîtagovinda* and his *Institutiones linguae Pracriticae*. His *Anthologia Sanscritica*, which came out the following year (new ed. by Johann Gildemeister, 1868), contained several hitherto unpublished texts, and did much to stimulate the study of Sanskrit in German universities. In 1846 Lassen brought out an improved edition of Schlegel's text and translation of the "Bhagavad-gîtâ." He did not confine himself to the study of Indian languages but acted likewise as a scientific pioneer in other fields of philological inquiry. In his *Beiträge zur Deutung der Eugubinischen Tafeln* (1833) he prepared the way for the correct interpretation of the Umbrian inscriptions; and the *Zeitschrift fur die Kunde des Morgenlandes* (7 vols., 1837–1850), started and largely conducted by him, contains among other valuable papers from his pen, grammatical sketches of the Beluchi and Brahui languages, and an essay on the Lycian inscriptions.

Soon after the appearance of Burnouf's *Commentaire sur le Yaçna* (1833), Lassen also directed his attention to the Zend, and to Iranian studies generally; and in *Die altpersischen Keilinschriften von Persepolis* (1836) he first made known the true character of the Old Persian cuneiform inscriptions, thereby anticipating, by one month, Burnouf's *Memoire* on the same subject, while Sir Henry Rawlinson's famous memoir on the Behistun inscription, though drawn up in Persia, independently of contemporaneous European research, at about the same time, did not reach the Royal Asiatic Society until three years later. Subsequently Lassen published, in the sixth volume of his journal (1845), a collection of all the Old Persian cuneiform inscriptions known up to that date. He also was the first scholar in Europe who took up, with signal success, the decipherment of the newly-discovered Bactrian coins, which furnished him the materials for *Zur Geschichte der griechischen und indo-skythischen Konige in Baktrien, Kabul, und Indien* (1838). He contemplated bringing out a critical edition of the *Vendidad*; but, after publishing the first five fargards (1852), he felt that his whole energies were required for the successful accomplishment of the great undertaking of his life—his *Indische Altertumskunde*. In this work—completed in four volumes, published respectively in 1847 (2nd ed., 1867), 1849 (2nd ed., 1874), 1858 and 1861—which forms one of the greatest monuments of untiring industry and critical scholarship, everything that could be gathered from native and foreign sources, relative to [illegible] political, social and intellectual development of India, from the earliest times down to the Mahommedan invasion, was worked up by him into a connected historical account.

LASSEN, EDUARD (1830–1904), Belgian musical composer, was born in Copenhagen, but was taken as a child to Brussels and educated at the Brussels Conservatoire. He won the *prix de Rome* in 1851, and went for a long tour in Germany and Italy. He settled at Weimar, where in 1861 he succeeded Liszt as conductor of the opera, and he died there on the 15th of January 1904. Besides many well-known songs, he wrote operas—*Landgraf Ludwig's Brautfahrt* (1857), *Frauenlob* (1861), *Le Captif* (1868)—instrumental music to dramas, notably to Goethe's *Faust* (1876), two symphonies and various choral works.

LASSO (LASSUS), **ORLANDO** (*c.* 1530–1594), Belgian musical composer, whose real name was probably Roland Delattre, was born at Mons, in Hainault, probably not much earlier than 1532, the date given by the epitaph printed at the end of the volumes of the *Magnum opus musicum*; though already in the 16th century the opinions of his biographers were divided between the years 1520 and 1530 Much is reported, but very little known, of his connexions and his early career. The discrepancy as to the date of his birth appears also in connexion with his appointment at the church of St John Lateran in Rome. If he was born in 1530 or 1532 he could not have obtained that appointment in 1541 What is certain is that his first book of madrigals was published in Venice in 1555, and that in the same year he speaks of himself in the preface of Italian and French songs and Latin motets as if he had recently come from Rome. He seems to have visited England in 1554 and to have been introduced to Cardinal Pole, to whom an adulatory motet appears in 1556. (This is not, as might hastily be supposed, a confusion resulting from the fact that the ambassador from Ferdinand, king of the Romans, Don Pedro de Lasso, attended the marriage of Philip and Mary in England in the same year.) His first book of motets appeared at Antwerp in 1556, containing the motet in honour of Cardinal Pole. The style of Orlando had already begun to purify itself from the speculative and chaotic elements that led Burney, who seems to have known only his earlier works, to call him "a dwarf on stilts" as compared with Palestrina. But where he is orthodox he is as yet stiff, and his secular compositions are, so far, better than his more serious efforts.

In 1557, if not before, he was invited by Albrecht IV., duke of Bavaria, to go to Munich. The duke was a most intelligent patron of all the fine arts, a notable athlete, and a man of strict principles. Munich from henceforth never ceased to be Orlando's home; though he sometimes paid long visits to Italy and France, whether in response to royal invitations or with projects of his own. In 1558 he made a very happy marriage by which he had four sons and two daughters. The four sons all became good musicians, and we owe an inestimable debt to the pious industry of the two eldest sons, who (under the patronage of Duke Maximilian I., the second successor of Orlando's master) published the enormous collection of Orlando's Latin motets known as the *Magnum opus musicum*.

Probably no composer has ever had more ideal circumstances for artistic inspiration and expression than had Orlando. His duty was to make music all day and every day, and to make it according to his own taste. Nothing was too good, too severe or too new for the duke. Church music was not more in demand than secular. Instrumental music, which in the 16th century had hardly any independent existence, accompanied the meals of the court; and Orlando would rise from dessert to sing trios and quartets with picked voices. The daily prayers included a full mass with polyphonic music. This amazing state of things becomes more intelligible and less alarming when we consider that 16th-century music was no sooner written than it could be performed. With such material as Orlando had at his disposal, musical performance was as unattended by expense and tedious preliminaries as a game of billiards in a good billiard room. Not even Haydn's position at Esterhaz can have enabled him, as has been said, to "ring the bell" for musicians to come and try a new orchestral effect with such ease as that with which Orlando could produce his work at Munich. His fame soon became world-wide, and every contemporary authority is full of the acclamation with which Orlando was greeted wherever his travels took him.

Very soon, with this rapid means of acquiring experience, Orlando's style became as pure as Palestrina's; while he always retained his originality and versatility. His relations to the literary culture of the time are intimate and fascinating; and during his stay at the court of France in 1571 he became a friend of the poet Ronsard. In 1579 Duke Albrecht died Orlando's salary had already been guaranteed to him for life, so that his outward circumstances did not change, and the new duke was very kind to him. But the loss of his master was a great grief and seems to have checked his activity for some time. In 1589, after the publication of six Masses, ending with a beautiful *Missa pro defunctis*, his strength began to fail; and a sudden serious illness left him alarmingly depressed and inactive until his death on the 14th of June 1594.

If Palestrina represents the supreme height attained by 16th-century music, Orlando represents the whole century. It is impossible to exaggerate the range and variety of his style, so long as we recognise the limits of 16th-century musical language. Even critics to whom this language is unfamiliar cannot fail to notice the glaring differences between Orlando's numerous types of art, though such critics may believe all those types to be equally crude and archaic. The swiftness of Orlando's intellectual and artistic development is astonishing. His first four volumes of madrigals show a very intermittent sense of beauty. Many a number in them is one compact mass of the fashionable harsh play upon the "false relation" between twin major and minor chords, which is usually believed to be the unenviable distinction of the English madrigal style from that of the Italians. It must be confessed that in the Italian madrigal (as distinguished from the *villanella* and other light forms), Orlando never attained complete certainty of touch, though some of his later madrigals are indeed glorious. But in his French chansons, many of which are settings of the poems of his friend Ronsard, his wit and lightness of touch are unfailing. In setting other French poems he is sometimes unfortunately most witty where the words are most gross, for he is as free from modern scruples as any of his Elizabethan contemporaries. In 1562, when the Council of Trent was censuring the abuses of Flemish church music, Orlando had already purified his ecclesiastical style; though he did not go so far as to Italianize it in order to oblige those modern critics who are unwilling to believe that anything appreciably unlike Palestrina can be legitimate. At the same time Orlando's Masses are not among his greatest works. This is possibly partly due to the fact that the proportions of a musical Mass are at the mercy of the local practice of the liturgy; and that perhaps the uses of the court at Munich were not quite so favourable to broadly designed proportion (not length) as the uses of Rome. Differences which might cramp the 16th-century composer need not amount to anything that would draw down the censure of ecclesiastical authorities. Be this as it may, Orlando's other church music is always markedly different from Palestrina's, and often fully as sublime. It is also in many ways far more modern in resource. We frequently come upon things like the *Justorum animae* [Magnum Opus, No. 260 (301)] which in their way are as overpoweringly touching as, for example, the Benedictus of Beethoven's *Mass in D* or the soprano solo in Brahms's *Deutsches Requiem*.

No one has approached Orlando in the ingenuity, quaintness and humour of his tone-painting. He sometimes descends to extremely elaborate musical puns, carrying farther than any other composer since the dark ages the absurd device of setting syllables that happened to coincide with the *sol-fa* system to the corresponding *sol-fa* notes. But in the most absurd of such cases he evidently enjoys twisting these notes into a theme of pregnant musical meaning. The quaintest instance is the motet *Quid estis pusillanimes* [Magnum Opus, No. 92 (69)] where extra *sol-fa* syllables are introduced into the text to make a good theme in combination with the syllables already there by accident! (*An nescitis Justitiae Ut Sol* [*Fa Mi*] *Re Laxatas*

civilian settlement, the former a Gallic customs station, the latter, which may be compared to the *canabae* of the Roman camps, containing the booths and taverns used by soldiers and sailors. He also considers the older station to have been, not as usually supposed, Helvetic, but pre- or proto-Helvetic, the character of which changed with the advance of the Helvetii into Switzerland (*c.* 110–100 B.C.). La Tène has given its name to a period of culture (*c.* 500 B.C.–A.D. 100), the phase of the Iron age succeeding the Hallstatt phase, not as being its starting-point, but because the finds are the best known of their kind. The latter are divided into early (*c.* 500–250 B.C.), middle (250–100 B.C.) and late (100 B.C.–A.D. 100), and chiefly belong to the middle period. They are mostly of iron, and consist of swords, spear-heads, axes, scythes and knives, which exhibit a remarkable agreement with the description of the weapons of the southern Celts given by Diodorus Siculus. There are also brooches, bronze kettles, torques, small bronze ear-rings with little glass pearls of various colours, belt-hooks and pins for fastening articles of clothing. The La Tène culture made its way through France across to England, where it has received the name of "late Celtic"; a remarkable find has been made at Aylesford in Kent.

See F. Keller, *Lake Dwellings of Switzerland*, vi. (Eng. trans., 1878); V. Gross, *La Tène un oppidum helvète* (1886); E. Vouga, *Les Helvètes à La Tène* (1886); P. Reinecke, *Zur Kenntnis der la Tène Denkmäler der Zone nordwärts der Alpen* (Mainzer Festschrift, 1902); R. Forrer, *Reallexikon der prähistorischen . . . Altertümer* (1907), where many illustrations are given.

LATERAN COUNCILS, the ecclesiastical councils or synods held at Rome in the Lateran basilica which was dedicated to Christ under the title of Salvator, and further called the basilica of Constantine or the church of John the Baptist. Ranking as a papal cathedral, this became a much-favoured place of assembly for ecclesiastical councils both in antiquity (313, 487) and more especially during the middle ages. Among these numerous synods the most prominent are those which the tradition of the Roman Catholic church has classed as ecumenical councils.

1. The first Lateran council (the ninth ecumenical) was opened by Pope Calixtus II. on the 18th of March 1123; its primary object being to confirm the concordat of Worms, and so close the conflict on the question of investiture (*q.v.*). In addition to this, canons were enacted against simony and the marriage of priests; while resolutions were passed in favour of the crusaders, of pilgrims to Rome and in the interests of the truce of God. More than three hundred bishops are reported to have been present.

For the resolutions see *Monumenta Germaniae, Leges*, iv., i. 574–576 (1893); Mansi, *Collectio Conciliorum*, xxi. p. 281 sq.; Hefele, *Conciliengeschichte*, v. 378–384 (ed. 2, 1886).

2. The second Lateran, and tenth ecumenical, council was held by Pope Innocent II. in April 1139, and was attended by close on a thousand clerics. Its immediate task was to neutralize the after-effects of the schism, which had only been terminated in the previous year by the death of Anacletus II. (d. 25th January 1138). All consecrations received at his hands were declared invalid, his adherents were deposed, and King Roger of Sicily was excommunicated. Arnold of Brescia, too, was removed from office and banished from Italy.

Resolutions, *ap.* Mansi, *op. cit.* xxi., 525 sq.; Hefele, *Conciliengeschichte*, v. 438–445 (ed. 2).

3. At the third Lateran council (eleventh ecumenical), which met in March 1179 under Pope Alexander III., the clergy present again numbered about one thousand. The council formed a sequel to the peace of Venice (1177), which marked the close of the struggle between the papacy and the emperor Frederick I. Barbarossa; its main object being to repair the direct or indirect injuries which the schism had inflicted on the life of the church and to display to Christendom the power of the see of Rome. Among the enactments of the council, the most important concerned the appointment to the papal throne (Canon 1), the electoral law of 1059 being supplemented by a further provision declaring a two-thirds majority to be requisite for the validity of the cardinals' choice. Of the participation of the Roman clergy and populace, or of the imperial ratification, there was no longer any question. Another resolution, of importance for the history of the treatment of heresy, was the canon which decreed that armed force should be employed against the Cathari in southern France, that their goods were liable to confiscation and their persons to enslavement by the princes, and that all who took up weapons against them should receive a two years' remission of their penance and be placed—like the crusaders—under the direct protection of the church.

Resolutions, *ap.* Mansi, *op. cit.* xxii. 212 sq.; Hefele, *Conciliengeschichte*, v. 710–719 (ed. 2).

4. The fourth Lateran council (twelfth ecumenical), convened by Pope Innocent III. in 1215, was the most brilliant and the most numerously attended of all, and marks the culminating point of a pontificate which itself represents the zenith attained by the medieval papacy. Prelates assembled from every country in Christendom, and with them the deputies of numerous princes. The total included 412 bishops, with 800 priors and abbots, besides the representatives of absent prelates and a number of inferior clerics. The seventy decrees of the council begin with a confession of faith directed against the Cathari and Waldenses, which is significant if only for the mention of a transubstantiation of the elements in the Lord's Supper. A series of resolutions provided in detail for the organized suppression of heresy and for the institution of the episcopal inquisition (Canon 3). On every Christian, of either sex, arrived at years of discretion, the duty was imposed of confessing at least once annually and of receiving the Eucharist at least at Easter (Canon 21). Enactments were also passed touching procedure in the ecclesiastical courts, the creation of new monastic orders, appointments to offices in the church, marriage-law, conventual discipline, the veneration of relics, pilgrimages and intercourse with Jews and Saracens. Finally, a great crusade was resolved upon, to defray the expenses of which it was determined that the clergy should lay aside one-twentieth—the pope and the cardinals one-tenth—of their revenues for the next three years; while the crusaders were to be held free of all burdens during the period of their absence.

Resolutions, *ap.* Mansi, *op. cit.* xxii. 953 sq.; Hefele, *Conciliengeschichte*, v. 872–905 (ed. 2). See also INNOCENT III.

5. The fifth Lateran council (eighteenth ecumenical) was convened by Pope Julius II. and continued by Leo X. It met from the 3rd of May 1512 to the 16th of March 1517, and was the last great council anterior to the Reformation. The change in the government of the church, the rival council of Pisa, the ecclesiastical and political dissensions within and without the council, and the lack of disinterestedness on the part of its members, all combined to frustrate the hopes which its convocation had awakened. Its resolutions comprised the rejection of the pragmatic sanction, the proclamation of the pope's superiority over the council, and the renewal of the bull *Unam sanctam* of Boniface VIII. The theory that it is possible for a thing to be theologically true and philosophically false, and the doctrine of the mortality of the human soul, were both repudiated; while a three years' tithe on all church property was set apart to provide funds for a war against the Turks.

See Hardouin, *Coll. Conc.* ix. 1570 sq.; Hefele-Hergenröther, *Conciliengeschichte*, viii. 454 sq.; (1887). Cf. bibliography under LEO X. (C. M.)

LATERITE (Lat. *later*, a brick), in petrology, a red or brown superficial deposit of clay or earth which gathers on the surface of rocks and has been produced by their decomposition; it is very common in tropical regions. In consistency it is generally soft and friable, but hard masses, nodules and bands often occur in it. These are usually rich in iron. The superficial layers of laterite deposits are often indurated and smooth black or dark-brown crusts occur where the clays have long been exposed to a dry atmosphere; in other cases the soft clays are full of hard nodules, and in general the laterite is perforated by tubules, sometimes with veins of different composition and appearance from the main mass. The depth of the laterite beds varies up to 30 or 40 ft., the deeper layers often being soft when the surface is hard or stony; the transition to fresh, sound rock below may be very sudden. That laterite is merely rotted crystalline rock is proved by its often preserving the structures, veins and even the outlines of the minerals of the parent mass below; the felspars and other components of granite gneiss having evidently been converted *in situ* into a soft argillaceous material.

Laterite occurs in practically every tropical region of the earth, and is very abundant in Ceylon, India, Burma, Central and West Africa, Central America, &c. It is especially well developed where the underlying rock is crystalline and felspathic (as granite gneiss, syenite and diorite), but occurs also on basalts in the Deccan and in other places, and is found even on mica schist, sandstone and quartzite, though in such cases it tends to be more sandy than argillaceous. Many varieties have been recognized. In India a calcareous laterite with large concretionary blocks of carbonate of lime is called kankar (kunkar), and has been much used in building bridges, &c., because it serves as a hydraulic cement. In some districts (*e.g.* W. Indies) similar types of laterite have been called "puzzuolans" and are also used as mortar and cement. Kankar is also known and worked in British East Africa. The clay called cabook in Ceylon is essentially a variety of laterite. Common laterite contains very little lime, and it seems that in districts which have an excessive rainfall that component may be dissolved out by percolating water, while kankar, or calcareous laterite, is formed in districts which have a smaller rainfall. In India also a distinction is made between "high-level" and "low-level" laterites. The former are found at all elevations up to 5000 ft. and more, and are the products of the decomposition of rock *in situ*; they are often fine-grained and sometimes have a very well-marked concretionary structure. These laterites are subject to removal by running water, and are thus carried to lower grounds forming transported or "low-level" laterites. The finer particles tend to be carried away into the rivers, while the sand is left behind and with it much of the heavy iron oxides. In such situations the laterites are sandy and ferruginous, with a smaller proportion of clay, and are not intimately connected with the rocks on which they lie. On steep slopes laterite also may creep or slip when soaked with rain, and if exposed in sections on roadsides or river banks has a bedded appearance, the stratification being parallel to the surface of the ground.

Chemical and microscopical investigations show that laterite is not a clay like those which are so familiar in temperate regions; it does not consist of hydrous silicate of alumina, but is a mechanical mixture of fine grains of quartz with minute scales of hydrates of alumina. The latter are easily soluble in acid while clay is not, and after treating laterite with acids the alumina and iron leave the silica as a residue in the form of quartz. The alumina seems to be combined with variable proportions of water, probably as the minerals hydrargillite, diaspore and gibbsite, while the iron occurs as goethite, turgite, limonite, haematite. As already remarked, there is a tendency for the superficial layers to become hard, probably by a loss of the water contained in these aluminous minerals. These chemical changes may be the cause of the frequent concretionary structure and veining in the laterite. The great abundance of alumina in some varieties of laterite is a consequence of the removal of the fine particles of gibbsite, &c., from the quartz by the action of gentle currents of water. We may also point out the essential chemical similarity between laterite and the seams of bauxite which occur, for example, in the north of Ireland as reddish clays between flows of Tertiary basalt. The bauxite is rich in alumina combined with water, and is used as an ore of aluminium. It is often very ferruginous. Similar deposits occur at Vogelsberg in Germany, and we may infer that the bauxite beds are layers of laterite produced by sub-aerial decomposition in the same manner as the thick laterite deposits which are now in course of formation in the plateau basalts of the Deccan in India.

The conditions under which laterite are formed include, first, a high seasonal temperature, for it occurs only in tropical districts and in plains or mountains up to about 5000 ft. in height; secondly, a heavy rainfall, with well-marked alternation of wet and dry seasons (in arid countries laterite is seldom seen, and where the rainfall is moderate the laterite is often calcareous); third, the presence of rocks containing aluminous minerals such as felspar, augite, hornblende and mica. On pure limestones such as coral rocks and on quartzites laterite deposits do not originate except where the material has been transported.

Many hypotheses have been advanced to account for the essential difference between lateritization and the weathering processes exhibited by rocks in temperate and arctic climates. In the tropics the rank growth of vegetation produces large amounts of humus and carbonic acid which greatly promote rock decomposition, igneous and crystalline rocks of all kinds are deeply covered under rich dark soils, so that in tropical forests the underlying rocks are rarely to be seen. In the warm soil nitrification proceeds rapidly and bacteria of many kinds flourish. It has also been argued that the frequent thunderstorms produce much nitric acid in the atmosphere and that this may be a cause of lateritization, but it is certainly not a necessary factor, as beds of laterite occur in oceanic islands lying in regions of the ocean where lightning is rarely seen. Sir Thomas Holland has brought forward the suggestion that the development of laterite may depend on the presence in the soil of bacteria which are able to decompose silicate of alumina into quartz and hydrates of alumina. The restricted distribution of laterite deposits might then be due to the inhibiting effect of low temperatures on the reproduction of these organisms. This very ingenious hypothesis has not yet received the experimental confirmation which seems necessary before it can be regarded as established. Malcolm Maclaren, rejecting the bacterial theory, directs special attention to the alternate saturation of the soil with rain water in the wet season and desiccation in the subsequent drought. The laterite beds are porous, in fact they are traversed by innumerable tubules which are often lined with deposits of iron oxide and aluminous minerals. We may be certain that, as in all soils during dry weather, there is an ascent of water by capillary action towards the surface, where it is gradually dissipated by evaporation. The soil water brings with it mineral matter in solution, which is deposited in the upper part of the beds. If the alumina be at one time in a soluble condition it will be drawn upwards and concentrated near the surface. This process explains many peculiarities of laterites, such as their porous and slaggy structure, which is often so marked that they have been mistaken for slaggy volcanic rocks. The concretionary structure is undoubtedly due to chemical re-arrangements, among which the escape of water is probably one of the most important; and many writers have recognized that the hard ferruginous crust, like the induration which many soft laterites undergo when dug up and exposed to the air, is the result of desiccation and exposure to the hot sun of tropical countries. The brecciated structure which many laterites show may be produced by great expansion of the mass consequent on absorption of water after heavy rains, followed by contraction during the subsequent dry season.

Laterites are not of much economic use. They usually form a poor soil, full of hard concretionary lumps and very unfertile because the potash and phosphates have been removed in solution, while only alumina, iron and silica are left behind. They are used as clays for puddling, for making tiles, and as a mortar in rough work. Kankar has filled an important part as a cement in many large engineering works in India. Where the iron concretions have been washed out by rains or by artificial treatment (often in the form of small shot-like pellets) they serve as an iron ore in parts of India and Africa. Attempts are being made to utilize laterite as an ore of aluminium, a purpose for which some varieties seem well adapted. There are also deposits of manganese associated with some laterites in India which may ultimately be valuable as mineral ores. (J. S. F.)

LATH (O. Eng. *laett*, Mid. Eng. *lappe*, a form possibly due to the Welsh *llath*; the word appears in many Teutonic languages, cf. Dutch *lat*, Ger. *Latte*, and has passed into Romanic, cf. Ital. *latta*, Fr. *latte*); a thin flat strip of wood or other material used in building to form a base or groundwork for plaster, or for tiles, slates or other covering for roofs. Such strips of wood are employed to form lattice-work, or for the bars of Venetian blinds or shutters. A "lattice" (O. Fr. *lattis*) is an interlaced structure of laths fastened together so as to form a screen with diamond-shaped or square interstices. Such a screen was used, as it still is in the East, as a shutter for a window admitting air rather than light; it was hence used of the window closed by such a screen. In modern usage the term is applied to a window with diamond-shaped panes set in lead-work. A window with a lattice painted red was formerly a common inn-sign (cf. Shakespeare, *2 Hen. IV.* ii. 2. 86); frequently the window was dispensed with, and the sign remained painted on a board.

LATHE. (1) A mechanical appliance in which material is held and rotated against a tool for cutting, scraping, polishing or other purpose (see TOOLS). This word is of obscure origin. It may be a modified form of "lath," for in an early form of lathe the rotation is given by a treadle or spring lath attached to the ceiling. The *New English Dictionary* points out a possible source of the word in Dan. *lad*, meaning apparently a supporting framework, found in the name of the turning-lathe, *drejelad*, and also in *savelad*, saw-bench, *vaeverlad*, loom, &c. (2) One of five, formerly six, districts containing three or more hundreds, into which the county of Kent was divided. Though the division survives, it no longer serves any administrative purpose. It was formerly a judicial division, the court of the lathe being superior to that of the hundred. In this it differs from the rape (*q.v.*) of Sussex, which was a geographical rather than an administrative division. In O. Eng. the word was *læð*, the origin of which is doubtful. The *New English Dictionary* considers it almost certainly identical with O. Norse *lað*, landed possessions, territory, with a possible association in meaning with such words as *leið*, court, *móllaeaða*, attendance at a meeting or moot, or with Mod. Dan. *laegd*, a division of the country for military purposes.

LATHROP, FRANCIS (1849–1909), American artist, was born at sea, near the Hawaiian Islands, on the 22nd of June 1849, being the great-grandson of Samuel Holden Parsons, and the son of George Alfred Lathrop (1819–1877), who for some time was United States consul at Honolulu. He was a pupil of T. C. Farrar (1838–1891) in New York, and studied at the Royal academy of Dresden. In 1870–1873 he was in England, studying under Ford Madox Brown and Burne-Jones, and working in the school of William Morris, where he devoted particular attention to stained glass. Returning to America in 1873, he became known as an illustrator, painted portraits, designed stained glass, and subsequently confined himself to decorative work. He [illegible] the chancel of Trinity church, Boston, and decorated the interior of Bowdoin college chapel, at Brunswick, Maine, and several churches in New York. The Marquand memorial [illegible] Princeton chapel, is an example of his work in stained glass. His latest work was a series of medallions for the building of the [illegible]-American society in New York. He was one of the [illegible] members of the Society of American Artists, and [illegible] an associate of the National Academy of Design, New [illegible] which also William L. Lathrop (b. 1859) an artist [illegible] be distinguished from him, became a member in [illegible]. He died at Woodcliff, New Jersey, on the 18th of [illegible].

[illegible] younger brother, George Parsons Lathrop (1851–1898), [illegible] on the 25th of August 1851, took up litera[illegible]. He was an assistant editor of the *Atlantic* [illegible], and editor of the Boston *Courier* in 1877– [illegible] one of the founders (1883) of the American [illegible] was prominent in the movement for Roman [illegible] schools, and wrote several novels, some [illegible] essays. He was the author of *A Study of* [illegible] (1876), and edited the standard edition [illegible] Hawthorne's works. In 1871 he married [illegible] daughter of Nathaniel Hawthorne— [illegible] Lathrop (b. 1851). After his death Mrs [illegible] entirely to charity. She was instru[illegible] (1896) and subsequently conducted St [illegible] in New York City. In 1900 she [illegible] taking the name of Mother Mary [illegible] of the Dominican community [illegible] established in 1901 and subsequently [illegible] Hill home (for cancerous patients) [illegible]. She published a volume of poems (1888); [illegible] and, with her husband, *A Story* [illegible] *Convent of the Visitation* [illegible]

[illegible]), English bishop, and one [illegible] Reformation in England, was born [illegible]. He was the son of a yeoman, [illegible] four pounds by year at the [illegible] as much as kept half a [illegible] hundred sheep and thirty [illegible] birth is not definitely known. [illegible] 1470, a palpable error, and [illegible] validity possibly a misprint for 1490.[1] Foxe states that at "the age of fourteen years he was sent to the university of Cambridge," and as he was elected fellow of Clare in 1509, his year of entrance was in all likelihood 1505. Latimer himself also, in mentioning his conversion from Romanism about 1523, says that it took place after he was thirty years of age. According to Foxe, Latimer went to school "at the age of four or thereabout." The purpose of his parents was to train him up "in the knowledge of all good literature," but his father "was as diligent to teach him to shoot as any other thing." As the yeomen of England were then in comparatively easy circumstances, the practice of sending their sons to the universities was quite usual, indeed Latimer mentions that in the reign of Edward VI., on account of the increase of rents, the universities had begun wonderfully to decay. He graduated B.A. in 1510 and M.A. in 1514. Before the latter date he had taken holy orders. While a student he was not unaccustomed "to make good cheer and be merry," but at the same time he was a punctilious observer of the minutest rites of his faith and "as obstinate a Papist as any in England." So keen was his opposition to the new learning that his oration on the occasion of taking his degree of bachelor of divinity was devoted to an attack on the opinions of Melanchthon. It was this sermon that determined his friend Thomas Bilney to go to Latimer's study, and ask him "for God's sake to hear his confession," the result being that "from that time forward he began to smell the word of God, and forsook the school doctors and such fooleries." Soon his discourses exercised a potent influence on learned and unlearned alike; and, although he restricted himself, as indeed was principally his custom through life, to the inculcation of practical righteousness, and the censure of clamant abuses, a rumour of his heretical tendencies reached the bishop of Ely, who resolved to become unexpectedly one of his audience. Latimer, on seeing him enter the church, boldly changed his theme to a portrayal of Christ as the pattern priest and bishop. The points of comparison were, of course, deeply distasteful to the prelate, who, though he professed his "obligations for the good admonition he had received," informed the preacher that he "smelt somewhat of the pan." Latimer was prohibited from preaching in the university or in any pulpits of the diocese, and on his occupying the pulpit of the Augustinian monastery, which enjoyed immunity from episcopal control, he was summoned to answer for his opinions before Wolsey, who, however, was so sensible of the value of such discourses that he gave him special licence to preach throughout England.

At this time Protestant opinions were being disseminated in England chiefly by the surreptitious circulation of the works of Wycliffe, and especially of his translations of the New Testament. The new leaven had begun to communicate its subtle influence to the universities, but was working chiefly in secret and even to a great extent unconsciously to those affected by it, for many were in profound ignorance of the ultimate tendency of their own opinions. This was perhaps, as regards England, the most critical conjuncture in the history of the Reformation, both on this account and on account of the position in which Henry VIII. then stood related to it. In no small degree its ultimate fate seemed also to be placed in the hands of Latimer. In 1526 the imprudent zeal of Robert Barnes had resulted in an ignominious recantation, and in 1527 Bilney, Latimer's most trusted coadjutor, incurred the displeasure of Wolsey, and did humiliating penance for his offences. Latimer, however, besides possessing sagacity, quick insight into character, and a ready and formidable wit which thoroughly disconcerted and confused his opponents, had naturally a distaste for mere theological discussion, and the truths he was in the habit of inculcating could scarcely be controverted, although, as he stated them, they were diametrically contradictory of prevailing errors both in

[1] The only reasons for assigning an earlier date are that he was commonly known as "old Hugh Latimer," and that Bernher, his Swiss servant, states incidentally that he was "above threescore and seven years" in the reign of Edward VI. Bad health and anxieties probably made him look older than his years, but under Edward VI. his powers as an orator were in full vigour, and he was at his book winter and summer at two o'clock in the morning.

doctrine and practice. In December 1529 he preached his two "sermons on the cards," which awakened a turbulent controversy in the university, and his opponents, finding that they were unable to cope with the dexterity and keenness of his satire, would undoubtedly have succeeded in getting him silenced by force, had it not been reported to the king that Latimer "favoured his cause," that is, the cause of the divorce. While, therefore, both parties were imperatively commanded to refrain from further dispute, Latimer was invited to preach before Henry in the Lent of 1530. The king was so pleased with the sermon that after it "he did most familiarly talk with him in a gallery." Of the special regard which Henry seemed to have conceived for him Latimer took advantage to pen the famous letter on the free circulation of the Bible, an address remarkable, not only for what Froude justly calls "its almost unexampled grandeur," but for its striking repudiation of the aid of temporal weapons to defend the faith, "for God," he says, "will not have it defended by man or man's power, but by His Word only, by which He hath evermore defended it, and that by a way far above man's power and reason." Though the appeal was without effect on the immediate policy of Henry, he could not have been displeased with its tone, for shortly afterwards he appointed Latimer one of the royal chaplains. In times so "out of joint" Latimer soon became "weary of the court," and it was with a sense of relief that he accepted the living of West Kington, or West Kineton, Wiltshire, conferred on him by the king in 1531. Harassed by severe bodily ailments, encompassed by a raging tumult of religious conflict and persecution, and aware that the faint hopes of better times which seemed to gild the horizon of the future might be utterly darkened by a failure either in the constancy of his courage or in his discernment and discretion, he exerted his eloquence with unabating energy in the furtherance of the cause he had at heart. At last a sermon he was persuaded to preach in London exasperated John Stokesley, bishop of the diocese, and seemed to furnish that fervent persecutor with an opportunity to overthrow the most dangerous champion of the new opinions. Bilney, of whom Latimer wrote, "if such as he shall die evil, what shall become of me?" perished at the stake in the autumn of 1531, and in January following Latimer was summoned to answer before the bishops in the consistory. After a tedious and captious examination, he was in March brought before convocation, and, on refusing to subscribe certain articles, was excommunicated and imprisoned; but through the interference of the king he was finally released after he had voluntarily signified his acceptance of all the articles except two, and confessed that he had erred not only "in discretion but in doctrine." If in this confession he to some extent tampered with his conscience, there is every reason to believe that his culpable timidity was occasioned, not by personal fear, but by anxiety lest by his death he should hinder instead of promoting the cause of truth. After the consecration of Cranmer to the archbishopric of Canterbury in 1533 Latimer's position was completely altered. A commission appointed to inquire into the disturbances caused by his preaching in Bristol severely censured the conduct of his opponents; and, when the bishop prohibited him from preaching in his diocese, he obtained from Cranmer a special licence to preach throughout the province of Canterbury. In 1534 Henry formally repudiated the authority of the pope, and from this time Latimer was the chief co-operator with Cranmer and Cromwell in advising the king regarding the series of legislative measures which rendered that repudiation complete and irrevocable.

It was, however, the preaching of Latimer more than the edicts of Henry that established the principles of the Reformation in the minds and hearts of the people; and from his preaching the movement received its chief colour and complexion. The sermons of Latimer possess a combination of qualities which constitute them unique examples of that species of literature. It is possible to learn from them more regarding the social and political condition of the period than perhaps from any other source, for they abound, not only in exposures of religious abuses, and of the prevailing corruptions of society, but in references to many varieties of social injustice and unwise customs, in racy sketches of character, and in vivid pictures of special features of the time, occasionally illustrated by interesting incidents in his own life. The homely terseness of his style, his abounding humour—rough, cheery and playful, but irresistible in its simplicity, and occasionally displaying sudden and dangerous barbs of satire—his avoidance of dogmatic subtleties, his noble advocacy of practical righteousness, his bold and open denunciation of the oppression practised by the powerful, his scathing diatribes against ecclesiastical hypocrisy, the transparent honesty of his fervent zeal, tempered by sagacious moderation—these are the qualities which not only rendered his influence so paramount in his lifetime, but have transmitted his memory to posterity as perhaps that of the one among his contemporaries most worthy of our interest and admiration.

In September 1535 Latimer was consecrated bishop of Worcester. While holding this office he was selected to officiate as preacher when the friar, John Forest, whom he vainly endeavoured to move to submission, was burned at the stake for denying the royal supremacy. In 1539, being opposed to the "act of the six articles," Latimer resigned his bishopric, learning from Cromwell that this was the wish of the king. It would appear that on this point he was deceived, but as he now declined to accept the articles he was confined within the precincts of the palace of the bishop of Chichester. After the attainder of Cromwell little is known of Latimer until 1546, when, on account of his connexion with the preacher Edward Crome, he was summoned before the council at Greenwich, and committed to the Tower of London. Henry died before his final trial could take place, and the general pardon at the accession of Edward VI. procured him his liberty. He declined to resume his see, notwithstanding the special request of the Commons, but in January 1548 again began to preach, and with more effectiveness than ever, crowds thronging to listen to him both in London and in the country. Shortly after the accession of Mary in 1553 a summons was sent to Latimer to appear before the council at Westminster. Though he might have escaped by flight, and though he knew, as he quaintly remarked, that "Smithfield already groaned for him," he at once joyfully obeyed. The pursuivant, he said, was "a welcome messenger." The hardships of his imprisonment, and the long disputations at Oxford, told severely on his health, but he endured all with unbroken cheerfulness. On the 16th of October 1555 he and Ridley were led to the stake at Oxford. Never was man more free than Latimer from the taint of fanaticism or less dominated by "vainglory," but the motives which now inspired his courage not only placed him beyond the influence of fear, but enabled him to taste in dying an ineffable thrill of victorious achievement. Ridley he greeted with the words, "Be of good comfort, Master Ridley, and play the man; we shall this day light such a candle by God's grace in England as (I trust) shall never be put out." He "received the flame as it were embracing it. After he had stroked his face with his hands, and (as it were) bathed them a little in the fire, he soon died (as it appeared) with very little pain or none."

Two volumes of Latimer's sermons were published in 1549. A complete edition of his works, edited by G. E. Corrie for the Parker Society, appeared in two volumes (1844–1845). His *Sermon on the Ploughers* and *Seven Sermons preached before Edward VI.* were reprinted by E. Arber (1869). The chief contemporary authorities for his life are his own *Sermons*, John Stow's *Chronicle* and Foxe's *Book of Martyrs*. In addition to memoirs prefixed to editions of his sermons, there are lives of Latimer by R. Demaus (1869, new and revised ed. 1881), and by R. M. and A. J. Carlyle (1899). (T. F. H.)

LATINA, VIA, an ancient highroad of Italy, leading S.E. from Rome. It was probably one of the oldest of Roman roads, leading to the pass of Algidus, so important in the early military history of Rome; and it must have preceded the Via Appia as a route to Campania, inasmuch as the Latin colony at Cales was founded in 334 B.C. and must have been accessible from Rome by road, whereas the Via Appia was only made twenty-two years later. It follows, too, a far more natural line of communication, without the engineering difficulties which the Via Appia had to encounter. As a through route it no doubt [illegible] the Via Labicana (see Labicana, Via), though the latter may have been preferred in later times. After their junction, the Via Latina continued to follow the valley of the Trerus (Sacco), following the line taken by the modern railway to Naples, and passing below the Hernican hill-towns, Anagnia, Ferentinum, Frusino, &c. At Fregellae it crossed the Liris, and then passed through Aquinum and Casinum, both of them comparatively low-lying towns. It then entered the interval between the Apennines and the volcanic group of Rocca Monfina, and the original road, instead of traversing it, turned abruptly N.E. over the mountains to Venafrum, thus giving a direct communication with the interior of Samnium by roads to [illegible] and Telesia. In later times, however, there was in all probability a short cut by Rufrae along the line taken by the modern highroad and railway. The two lines rejoined near the modern railway station of Caianello and the road ran to Teanum [illegible], and so to Casilinum, where was the crossing of the [illegible] and the junction with the Via Appia. The distance from Rome to Casilinum was 129 m. by the Via Appia, 135 m. by the Via Latina through Venafrum, 126 m. by the short cut by Rufrae. Considerable remains of the road exist in the neighbourhood of Rome; for the first 40 m., as far as Compitum [illegible], it is not followed by any modern road; while farther [illegible] it is in the main identical with the modern highway.

[illegible] in *Papers of the British School at Rome* iv. 1 sqq.
(T. As.)

LATINI, BRUNETTO (*c.* 1210–*c.* 1294), Italian philosopher [illegible] born in Florence, and belonged to the Guelph [illegible] disaster of Montaperti he took refuge for some [illegible] in France, but in 1269 returned to Tuscany [illegible] years held successive high offices. Giovanni [illegible] he was a great philosopher and a consummate [illegible] not only in knowing how to speak well, but [illegible]. He both began and directed the growth [illegible] in making them ready in speaking well [illegible] to guide and direct our republic according [illegible]. He was the author of various works [illegible]. While in France he wrote in French his [illegible] of the encyclopaedic knowledge of the [illegible] as *Tesoro* by Bono Giamboni in the [illegible] his poem *Tesoretto*, rhymed couplets [illegible] a sort of abridgment put in allegorical [illegible] didactic verse. He is famous as the [illegible] (see *Inferno*, xv. 82-87).

[illegible] edition (1863); for the *Tesoro*, [illegible] the *Tesoretto*, B. Wiese's study in [illegible] vii. See also the biographical [illegible] Latini by Thor Sundby (1884), [illegible]

[illegible] *Records of its Area.*—Latin [illegible] Rome and in the plain of Latium [illegible] the earliest period from which [illegible] of its existence. But it is [illegible] on the one hand, whether [illegible] (see below), which is as- [illegible] at that epoch, represents exactly [illegible] on the other, over how [illegible] peninsula, or even of the lands [illegible] language may at that date [illegible] we find its limits within [illegible] south-west by Etruscan [illegible] south-east, and probably [illegible] dialects (of the Marsi, [illegible]); but on the [illegible] speech, nor of any [illegible] Asculum or earlier [illegible] Picenum). [illegible] from the archaeo- [illegible] 5th century B.C. [illegible] their younger folk, [illegible] peninsula. Of the [illegible] save in the case of Etruscan in Campania, but it may be reasonably inferred from the evidence of place-names and tribal names, combined with that of the Faliscan inscriptions, that before the Sabine invasion some idiom, not remote from Latin, was spoken by the pre-Etruscan tribes down the length of the west coast (see Falisci; Volsci; also Rome: *History*; Liguria; Siculi).

2. *Earliest Roman Inscriptions.*—At Rome, at all events, it is clear from the unwavering voice of tradition that Latin was spoken from the beginning of the city. Of the earliest Latin inscriptions found in Rome which were known in 1909, the oldest, the so-called "Forum inscription," can hardly be referred with confidence to an earlier century than the 5th; the later, the well-known *Duenos* (= later Latin *bonus*) inscription, certainly belongs to the 4th; both of these are briefly described below (§§ 40, 41). At this date we have probably the period of the narrowest extension of Latin; non-Latin idioms were spoken in Etruria, Umbria, Picenum and in the Marsian and Volscian hills. But almost directly the area begins to expand again, and after the war with Pyrrhus the Roman arms had planted the language of Rome in her military colonies throughout the peninsula. When we come to the 3rd century B.C. the Latin inscriptions begin to be more numerous, and in them (*e.g.* the oldest epitaphs of the Scipio family) the language is very little removed from what it was in the time of Plautus.

3. *The Italic Group of Languages.*—For the characteristics and affinities of the dialects that have just been mentioned, see the article Italy: *Ancient Languages and Peoples*, and to the separate articles on the tribes. Here it is well to point out that the only one of these languages which is not akin to Latin is Etruscan; on the other hand, the only one very closely resembling Latin is Faliscan, which with it forms what we may call the Latinian dialect of the Italic group of the Indo-European family of languages. Since, however, we have a far more complete knowledge of Latin than of any other member of the Italic group, this is the most convenient place in which to state briefly the very little than can be said as yet to have been ascertained as to the general relations of Italic to its sister groups. Here, as in many kindred questions, the work of Paul Kretschmer of Vienna (*Einleitung in die Geschichte der griechischen Sprache*, Göttingen, 1896) marked an important epoch in the historical aspects of linguistic study, as the first scientific attempt to interpret critically the different kinds of evidence which the Indo-European languages give us, not in vocabulary merely, but in phonology, morphology, and especially in their mutual borrowings, and to combine it with the non-linguistic data of tradition and archaeology. A certain number of the results so obtained have met with general acceptance and may be briefly treated here. It is, however, extremely dangerous to draw merely from linguistic kinship deductions as to racial identity, or even as to an original contiguity of habitation. Close resemblances in any two languages, especially those in their inner structure (morphology), may be due to identity of race, or to long neighbourhood in the earliest period of their development; but they may also be caused by temporary neighbourhood (for a longer or shorter period), brought about by migrations at a later epoch (or epochs). A particular change in sound or usage may spread over a whole chain of dialects and be in the end exhibited alike by them all, although the time at which it first began was long after their special and distinctive characteristics had become clearly marked. For example, the limitation of the word-accent to the last three syllables of a word in Latin and Oscan (see below)—a phenomenon which has left deep marks on all the Romance languages—demonstrably grew up between the 5th and 2nd centuries B.C.; and it is a permissible conjecture that it started from the influence of the Greek colonies in Italy (especially Cumae and Naples), in whose language the same limitation (although with an accent whose actual character was probably more largely musical) had been established some centuries sooner.

4. *Position of the Italic Group.*—The Italic group, then, when [illegible]red with the other seven main "families" of Indo-

European speech, in respect of their most significant differences, ranges itself thus:

(i.) *Back-palatal and Velar Sounds.*—In point of its treatment of the Indo-European back-palatal and velar sounds, it belongs to the western or *centum* group, the name of which is, of course, taken from Latin; that is to say, like German, Celtic and Greek, it did not sibilate original *k* and *g*, which in Indo-Iranian, Armenian, Slavonic and Albanian have been converted into various types of sibilants (Ind.-Eur.* *kmtom* = Lat. *centum*, Gr. (ἑ)-κατόν, Welsh *cant*, Eng. *hund-*(*red*), but Sans. *śatam*, Zend *satəm*); but, on the other hand, in company with just the same three western groups, and in contrast to the eastern, the Italic languages labialized the original velars (Ind.-Eur. * *qod* = Lat. *quod*, Osc. *pod*, Gr. πο-(δαπός), Welsh *pwy*, Eng. *what*, but Sans. *kás*, " who ?").

(ii.) *Indo-European Aspirates.*—Like Greek and Sanskrit, but in contrast to all the other groups (even to Zend and Armenian), the Italic group largely preserves a distinction between the Indo-European *mediae aspiratae* and *mediae* (*e.g.* between Ind.-Eur. *dh* and *d*, the former when initial becoming initially regularly Lat. *f* as in Lat. *fēc-ī* [cf. Umb. *feia*, "*faciat*"], beside Gr. ἔ-θηκ-α [cf. Sans. *da-dhā-ti*, " he places "], the latter simply *d* as in *domus*, Gr. δόμος). But the *aspiratae*, even where thus distinctly treated in Italic, became fricatives, not pure aspirates, a character which they only retained in Greek and Sanskrit.

(iii.) *Indo-European ŏ.*—With Greek and Celtic, Latin preserved the Indo-European *ŏ*, which in the more northerly groups (Germanic, Balto-Slavonic), and also in Indo-Iranian, and, curiously, in Messapian, was confused with *ă*. The name for olive-oil, which spread with the use of this commodity from Greek (ἔλαιϝον) to Italic speakers and thence to the north, becoming by regular changes (see below) in Latin first **ŏlaivom*, then **ŏleivom*, and then taken into Gothic and becoming *alēv*, leaving its parent form to change further (not later than 100 B.C.) in Latin to *oleum*, is a particularly important example, because (*a*) of the chronological limits which are implied, however roughly, in the process just described, and (*b*) of the close association in time of the change of *o* to *a* with the earlier stages of the " sound-shifting " (of the Indo-European plosives and aspirates) in German; see Kretschmer, *Einleit.* p. 116, and the authorities he cites.

(iv.) *Accentuation.*—One marked innovation common to the western groups as compared with what Greek and Sanskrit show to have been an earlier feature of the Indo-European parent speech was the development of a strong expiratory (sometimes called stress) accent upon the first syllable of all words. This appears early in the history of Italic, Celtic, Lettish (probably, and at a still later period) in Germanic, though at a period later than the beginning of the " sound-shifting." This extinguished the complex system of Indo-European accentuation, which is directly reflected in Sanskrit, and was itself replaced in Latin and Oscan by another system already mentioned, but not in Latin till it had produced marked effects upon the language (*e.g.* the degradation of the vowels in compounds as in *cōnficio* from *cón-facio*, *inclūdo* from *ín-claudo*). This curious wave of accentual change (first pointed out by Dieterich, *Kuhn's Zeitschrift*, i., and later by Thurneysen, *Revue celtique*, vi. 312, *Rheinisches Museum*, xliii. 349) needs and deserves to be more closely investigated from a chronological standpoint. At present it is not clear how far it was a really connected process in all the languages. (See further Kretschmer, *op. cit.* p. 115, K. Brugmann, *Kurze vergleichende Grammatik* (1902–1904), p. 57, and their citations, especially Meyer-Lübke, *Die Betonung im Gallischen* (1901).)

To these larger affinities may be added some important points in which the Italic group shows marked resemblances to other groups.

5. *Italic and Celtic.*—It is now universally admitted that the Celtic languages stand in a much closer relation than any other group to the Italic. It may even be doubted whether there was any real frontier-line at all between the two groups before the Etruscan invasion of Italy (see ETRURIA: *Language*; LIGURIA). The number of morphological innovations on the Indo-European system which the two groups share, and which are almost if not wholly peculiar to them, is particularly striking. Of these the chief are the following.

(i.) Extension of the abstract-noun stems in *-ti-* (like Greek φάτις with Attic φάσις, &c.) by an *-n-* suffix, as in Lat. *mentio* (stem *menti-ōn-*) = Ir. (*ar-*)*mitiu* (stem *miti-n-*), contrasted with the same word without the *n*-suffix in Sans. *mati-*, Lat. *mens*, Ind.-Eur. **mn̥-ti-*. A similar extension (shared also by Gothic) appears in Lat. *iuventūt-i-*, O. Ir. *oitiu* (stem *oitiut-*) beside the simple *-tu-* in nouns like *senātus*.

(ii.) Superlative formation in *-is-ṃmo-* as in Lat. *aegerrimus* for **aegr-isṃmos*, Gallic Οὐξισάμη the name of a town meaning " the highest."

(iii.) Genitive singular of the *o*-stems (second declension) in *-ī* Lat. *agri*, O. Ir. (Ogam inscriptions) *maqi*, " of a son."

(iv.) Passive and deponent formation in *-r*, Lat. *sequitur* = Ir. *sechedar*, " he follows." The originally active meaning of this curious *-r* suffix was first pointed out by Zimmer (*Kuhn's Zeitschrift*, 1888, xxx. 224), who thus explained the use of the accusative pronouns with these " passive " forms in Celtic; Ir. *-m-berar*, " I am carried," literally " folk carry me "; Umb. *pir ferar*, literally *ignem feratur*, though as *pir* is a neuter word (= Gr. πῦρ) this example was not so convincing. But within a twelvemonth of the appearance of Zimmer's article, an Oscan inscription (Conway, *Camb. Philol. Society's Proceedings*, 1890, p. 16, and *Italic Dialects*, p. 113) was discovered containing the phrase *ultiumam* (*iiuklam*) *sakrafir*, " ultimam (imaginem) consecraverint " (or " ultima consecretur ") which demonstrated the nature of the suffix in Italic also. This originally active meaning of the *-r* form (in the third person singular passive) is the cause of the remarkable fondness for the " impersonal " use of the passive in Latin (*e.g.*, *itur in antiquam silvam*, instead of *eunt*), which was naturally extended to all tenses of the passive (*ventum est*, &c.), so soon as its origin was forgotten. Fuller details of the development will be found in Conway, *op. cit.* p. 561, and the authorities there cited (very little is added by K. Brugmann, *Kurze vergl. Gramm.* 1904, p. 596).

(v.) Formation of the perfect passive from the *-to-* past participle, Lat. *monitus* (*est*), &c., Ir. *léic-the*, " he was left," *ro-léiced*, " he has been left." In Latin the participle maintains its distinct adjectival character, in Irish (J. Strachan, *Old Irish Paradigms*, 1905, p. 50) it has sunk into a purely verbal form, just as the perfect participles in *-us* in Umbrian have been absorbed into the future perfect in *-ust* (*entelust*, " intenderit "; *benust*, " venerit ") with its impersonal passive or third plural active *-us(s)o* (probably standing for *-ussor*) as in *benuso*, " ventum erit " (or " venerint ").

To these must be further added some striking peculiarities in phonology.

(vi.) Assimilation of *p* to a *qu* in a following syllable as in Lat. *quinque* = Ir. *cóic*, compared with Sans. *pañca*, Gr. πέντε, Eng. *five*, Ind.-Eur. **penqe*.

(vii.) Finally—and perhaps this parallelism is the most important of all from the historical standpoint—both Italic and Celtic are divided into two sub-families which differ, and differ in the same way, in their treatment of the Ind.-Eur. velar tenuis *q*. In both halves of each group it was labialized to some extent; in one half of each group it was labialized so far as to become *p*. This is the great line of cleavage (i.) between Latinian (Lat. *quod*, *quando*, *quinque*; Falisc. *cuando*) and Osco-Umbrian, better called Safine (Osc. *pod*, Umb. *pane* [for **panda*], Osc.-Umb. *pompe-*, " five," in Osc. *pümperias* " nonae," Umb. *pumperia-*, " fifth day of the month "); and (ii.) between Goidelic (Gaelic) (O. Ir. *cóic*, " five," *maq*, " son "; modern Irish and Scotch *Mac* as in *MacPherson*) and Brythonic (Britannic) (Welsh *pump*, " five," *Ap* for *map*, as in *Powel* for *Ap Howel*).

The same distinction appears elsewhere; Germanic belongs, broadly described, to the *q*-group, and Greek, broadly described, to the *p*-group. The ethnological bearing of the distinction within Italy is considered in the articles SABINI and VOLSCI, but the wider questions which the facts suggest have as yet been only scantily discussed; see the references for the " Sequanian " dialect of Gallic (in the inscription of Coligny, whose language preserves *q*) in the article CELTS: *Language*.

From these primitive affinities we must clearly distinguish the numerous words taken into Latin from the Celts of north Italy within the historic period; for these see especially an interesting study by J. Zwicker, *De vocabulis et rebus Gallicis sive Transpadanis apud Vergilium* (Leipzig dissertation, 1905).

6. *Greek and Italic.*—We have seen above (§ 4, i., ii., iii.) certain broad characteristics which the Greek and the Italic groups of language have in common. The old question of the degree of their affinity may be briefly noticed. There are deep-seated differences in morphology, phonology and vocabulary between the two languages—such as (*a*) the loss of the forms of the ablative in Greek and of the middle voice in Latin; (*b*) the decay of the fricatives (*s*, *v*, *j*) in Greek and the cavalier treatment of the aspirates in Latin; and (*c*) the almost total discrepancy of the vocabularies of law and religion in the two languages—which altogether forbid the assumption that the two groups can ever have been completely identical after their first dialectic separation from the parent language. On the other hand, in the first early periods of that dialectic development in the Indo-European family, the precursors of Greek and Italic cannot have been separated by any very wide boundary. To this primitive neighbourhood may be referred such peculiarities as (*a*) the genitive plural feminine ending in *-āsōm* (Gr. -άων, later in various dialects -έων, -ῶν, -ᾶν; cf. Osc. *egmazum* " rerum "; Lat. *mensarum*, with *-r-* from *-s-*), (*b*) the feminine gender of many nouns of the *-o-* declension, cf. Gr. ἡ ὁδός, Lat. *haec fāgus*; and some important and ancient syntactical features, especially in the uses of the cases (*e.g.* (*c*) the genitive of price) of the (*d*) infinitive and of the (*e*) participles passive (though in

each case the forms differ widely in the two groups), and perhaps (*f*) of the dependent moods (though here again the forms have been vigorously reshaped in Italic). These syntactic parallels, which are hardly noticed by Kretschmer in his otherwise careful discussion (*Einleit.* p. 155 seq.), serve to confirm his general conclusion which has been here adopted; because syntactic peculiarities have a long life and may survive not merely complete revolutions in morphology, but even a complete change in the speaker's language, *e.g.* such Celticisms in Irish-English as "What are you after doing?" for "What have you done?" or in Welsh-English as "whatever" for "anyhow." A few isolated correspondences in vocabulary, as in *remus* from **ret-s-mo-*, with ἐρετμός and in a few plant-names (*e.g.* πράσον and *porrum*), cannot disturb the general conclusion, though no doubt they have some historical significance, if it could be determined.

7. *Indo-Iranian and Italo-Celtic.*—Only a brief reference can here be made to the striking list of resemblances between the Indo-Iranian and Italo-Celtic groups, especially in vocabulary, which Kretschmer has collected (*ibid.* pp. 126-144). The most striking of these are *rēx*, O. Ir. *rīg-*, Sans. *rāj-*, and the political meaning of the same root in the corresponding verb in both languages (contrast *regere* with the merely physical meaning of Gr. ὀρέγνυμι); Lat. *flāmen* (for **flag-men*) exactly = Sans. *brahman-* (neuter), meaning probably "sacrificing," "worshipping," and then "priesthood," "priest," from the Ind.-Eur. root **bhelgh-*, "blaze," "make to blaze"; *rēs*, *rem* exactly = Sans. *rās*, *rām* in declension and especially in meaning; and *Ārio-*, "noble," in Gallic *Ariomanus*, &c., = Sans. *ārya-*, "noble" (whence "Aryan"). So *argentum* exactly = Sans. *rajata-*, Zend *erezata-*; contrast the different (though morphologically kindred) suffix in Gr. ἄργυρος. Some forty-two other Latin or Celtic words (among them *crēdere*, *caesariēs*, *probus*, *castus* (cf. Osc. *kasit*, Lat. *caret*, Sans. *šišta-*), *Volcānus*, *Neptūnus*, *ensis*, *erus*, *pruina*, *rūs*, *novācula*) have precise Sanskrit or Iranian equivalents, and none so near in any other of the eight groups of languages. Finally the use of an *-r* suffix in the third plural is common to both Italo-Celtic (see above) and Indo-Iranian. These things clearly point to a fairly close, and probably in part political, intercourse between the two communities of speakers at some early epoch. A shorter, but interesting, list of correspondences in vocabulary with Balto-Slavonic (*e.g.* the words *mentīri*, *rūs*, *ignis* have close equivalents in Balto-Slavonic) suggests that at the same period the precursor of this dialect too was a not remote neighbour.

8. *Date of the Separation of the Italic Group.*—The date at which the Italic group of languages began to have (so far as it had at all) a separate development of its own is at present only a matter of conjecture. But the combination of archaeological and linguistic research which has already begun can have no more interesting object than the approximate determination of this date (or group of dates); for it will give us a point of cardinal importance in the early history of Europe. The only consideration which can here be offered as a starting-point for the inquiry is the chronological relation of the Etruscan invasion, which is probably referable to the 12th century B.C. (see ETRURIA), to the two strata of Indo-European population—the -CO- folk (*Falisci*, *Marruci*, *Volsci*, *Hernici* and others), to whom the Tuscan invaders owe the names *Etrusci* and *Tusci*, and the -NO- folk, who, on the West coast, in the centre and south of Italy, appear at a distinctly later epoch, in some places (as in the Bruttian peninsula, see BRUTTII) only at the beginning of our historical record. If the view of Latin as mainly the tongue of the -CO- folk prove to be correct (see ROME: *History*; ITALY: *Ancient Languages and Peoples*; SABINI; VOLSCI) we must regard it (*a*) as the southern or earlier half of the Italic group, firmly rooted in Italy in the 12th century B.C., but (*b*) by no means yet isolated from contact with the northern or later half; such is at least the suggestion of the striking peculiarities in morphology which it shares with not merely Oscan and Umbrian, but also, as we have seen, with Celtic. The progress in time of this isolation ought before long to be traced with some approach to certainty.

THE HISTORY OF LATIN

9. We may now proceed to notice the chief changes that arose in Latin after the (more or less) complete separation of the Italic group whenever it came about. The contrasted features of Oscan and Umbrian, to some of which, for special reasons, occasional reference will be here made, are fully described under OSCA LINGUA and IGUVIUM respectively.

It is rarely possible to fix with any precision the date at which a particular change began or was completed, and the most serviceable form for this conspectus of the development will be to present, under the heads of Phonology, Morphology and Syntax, the chief characteristics of Ciceronian Latin which we know to have been developed after Latin became a separate language. Which of these changes, if any, can be assigned to a particular period will be seen as we proceed. But it should be remembered that an enormous increase of exact knowledge has accrued from the scientific methods of research introduced by A. Leskien and K. Brugmann in 1879, and finally established by Brugmann's great *Grundriss* in 1886, and that only a brief enumeration can be here attempted. For adequate study reference must be made to the fuller treatises quoted, and especially to the sections bearing on Latin in K. Brugmann's *Kurze vergleichende Grammatik* (1902).

I. PHONOLOGY

10. *The Latin Accent.*—It will be convenient to begin with some account of the most important discovery made since the application of scientific method to the study of Latin, for, though it is not strictly a part of phonology, it is wrapped up with much of the development both of the sounds and, by consequence, of the inflexions. It has long been observed (as we have seen § 4, iv. above) that the restriction of the word-accent in Latin to the last three syllables of the word, and its attachment to a long syllable in the penult, were certainly not its earliest traceable condition; between this, the classical system, and the comparative freedom with which the word-accent was placed in pro-ethnic Indo-European, there had intervened a period of first-syllable accentuation to which were due many of the characteristic contractions of Oscan and Umbrian, and in Latin the degradation of the vowels in such forms as *accentus* from *ad*+*cantus* or *praecipitem* from *prae*+*caput-* (§ 19 below). R. von Planta (*Osk.-Umbr. Grammatik*, 1893, i. p. 594) pointed out that in Oscan also, by the 3rd century B.C., this first-syllable-accent had probably given way to a system which limited the word-accent in some such way as in classical Latin. But it remained for C. Exon, in a brilliant article (*Hermathena* (1906), xiv. 117, seq.), to deduce from the more precise stages of the change (which had been gradually noted, see *e.g.* F. Skutsch in Kroll's *Altertumswissenschaft im letzten Vierteljahrhundert*, 1905) their actual effect on the language.

11. *Accent in Time of Plautus.*—The rules which have been established for the position of the accent in the time of Plautus are these:

(i.) The quantity of the final syllable had no effect on accent.
(ii.) If the penult was long, it bore the accent (*amābāmus*).
(iii.) If the penult was short, then
  (*a*) if the ante-penult was long, it bore the accent (*amābimus*);
  (*b*) if the ante-penult was short, then
    (i.) if the ante-ante-penult was long, the accent was on the ante-penult (*amīcitia*); but
    (ii.) if the ante-ante-penult was also short, it bore the accent (*columine*, *puĕritia*).

Exon's Laws of Syncope.—With these facts are now linked what may be called Exon's Laws, viz.—

In pre-Plautine Latin in all words or word-groups of four or more syllables whose chief accent is on one long syllable, a short unaccented medial vowel was syncopated: thus **quinquedecem* became **quinqdecem* and thence *quindecim* (for the *-im* see § 19), **sups-emere* became **supsmere* and that *sūmere* (un -*psm-* v. *inf.*) **surregere*, **surregimus*, and the like became *surgere*, *surgimus*, and the rest of the paradigm followed; so probably *validē bonus* became *valdē bonus*, *exterā viam* became *extrā viam*; so **supo-lendo* became *sublendo* (pronounced *sup-lendo*), **āridēre*, **avidēre* (from *āridus*, *avidus*) became *ārdēre*, *audēre*. But the influence of cognate forms often interfered; *posteri-diē* became *postrīdiē*, but in *posterōrum*, *posterārum* the short syllable was restored by the influence of the trisyllabic cases, *posterus*, *posterī*, &c., to which the law did not apply. Conversely, the nom. **āridor* (more correctly at this period **āridōs*), which would not have been contracted, followed the form of *ārdōrem* (from **āridōrem*), *ārdēre*, &c.

The same change produced the monosyllabic forms *nec*, *ac*, *neu*, *seu*, from *neque*, &c., before consonants, since they had no accent of their own, but were always pronounced in one breath with the following word, *neque tantum* becoming *nec tantum*, and the like. So in Plautus (and probably always in spoken Latin) the words *semp(e)*, *ind(e)*, *quipp(e)*, *ill(e)*, are regularly monosyllables

12. *Syncope of Final Syllables.*—It is possible that the frequent but far from universal syncope of final syllables in Latin (especially before *-s*, as in *mēns*, which represents both Gr. μένος and Sans. *matis* = Ind.-Eur. *mn̥tis*, Eng. *mind*) is due also to this law operating on such combinations as *bona mēns* and the like, but this has not yet been clearly shown. In any case the effects of any such phonetic change have been very greatly modified by analogical changes. The Oscan and Umbrian syncope of short vowels before final *s* seems to be an independent change, at all events in its detailed working. The outbreak of the unconscious affection of slurring final syllables may have been contemporaneous.

13. *In post-Plautine Latin* words accented on the ante-antepenult:—

(i.) suffered syncope in the short syllable following the accented syllable (*bálineae* became *bálneae*, *puéritia* became *puértia* (Horace), *cólumine*, *tégimine*, &c., became *cúlmine*, *tégmine*, &c., beside the trisyllabic *columen*, *tegimen*) unless

(ii.) that short vowel was *e* or *i*, followed by another vowel (as in *párietem*, *múlierem*, *Púteoli*), when, instead of contraction, the accent shifted to the penult, which at a later stage of the language became lengthened, *pariétem* giving Ital. *parète*, Fr. *paroi*, *Puteóli* giving Ital. *Pozzuóli*.

The restriction of the accent to the last three syllables was completed by these changes, which did away with all the cases in which it had stood on the fourth syllable.

14. *The Law of the Brevis Brevians.*—Next must be mentioned another great phonetic change, also dependent upon accent, which had come about before the time of Plautus, the law long known to students as the *Brevis Brevians*, which may be stated as follows (Exon, *Hermathena* (1903), xii. 491, following Skutsch in, *e.g.*, Vollmöller's *Jahresbericht für romanische Sprachwissenschaft*, i. 33): a syllable long by nature or position, and preceded by a short syllable, was itself shortened if the word-accent fell immediately before or immediately after it—that is, on the preceding short syllable or on the next following syllable. The sequence of syllables need not be in the same word, but must be as closely connected in utterance as if it were. Thus *mŏdō* became *mŏdă*, *vŏlŭ̄ptātem* became *vŏlŭ(p)tātem*, *quid ĕst?* became *quid ĕst?* either the *s* or the *t* or both being but faintly pronounced.

It is clear that a great number of flexional syllables so shortened would have their quantity immediately restored by the analogy of the same inflexion occurring in words not of this particular shape; thus, for instance, the long vowel of *ămō* and the like is due to that in other verbs (*pulsō*, *agitō*) not of iambic shape. So ablatives like *modō*, *sonō* get back their *-ō*, while in particles like *modo*, "only," *quōmodo*, "how," the shortened form remains. Conversely, the shortening of the final *-a* in the nom. sing. fem. of the *a*-declension (contrast *terră* with Gr. χώρᾱ) was probably partly due to the influence of common forms like *eă*, *bonă*, *mală*, which had come under the law.

15. *Effect on Verb Inflexion.*—These processes had far-reaching effects on Latin inflexion. The chief of these was the creation of the type of conjugation known as the *capio*-class. All these verbs were originally inflected like *audio*, but the accident of their short root-syllable (in such early forms as **fŭgīs*, **fŭgītūrus*, **fŭgītōtis*, &c., becoming later *fŭgĭs*, *fŭgĭtūrus*, *fŭgĭtōtis*) brought great parts of their paradigm under this law, and the rest followed suit; but true forms like *fugīre*, *cupīre*, *morīri*, never altogether died out of the spoken language. St Augustine, for instance, confessed in 387 A.D. (*Epist.* iii. 5, quoted by Exon, *Hermathena* (1901), xi. 383,) that he does not know whether *cupi* or *cupiri* is the pass. inf. of *cupio*. Hence we have Ital. *fuggire*, *morire*, Fr. *fuir*, *mourir*. (See further on this conjugation, C. Exon, *l.c.*, and F. Skutsch, *Archiv für lat. Lexicographie*, xii. 210, two papers which were written independently.)

16. The question has been raised how far the true phonetic shortening appears in Plautus, produced not by word-accent but by metrical ictus—*e.g.* whether the reading is to be trusted in such lines as *Amph.* 761, which gives us *dedisse* as the first foot (tribrach) of a trochaic line "because the metrical ictus fell on the syllable *ded-*"—but this remarkable theory cannot be discussed here. See the articles cited and also F. Skutsch, *Forschungen zu Latein. Grammatik und Metrik*, i. (1892); C. Exon, *Hermathena* (1903) xii. p. 492, W. M. Lindsay, *Captivi* (1900), appendix.

In the history of the vowels and diphthongs in Latin we must distinguish the changes which came about independently of accent and those produced by the preponderance of accent in another syllable.

17. *Vowel-Changes independent of Accent.*—In the former category the following are those of chief importance:—

(i.) ĭ became ĕ (*e*) when final, as in *ant-e* beside Gr. ἀντί, *triste* besides *tristi-s*, contrasted with *e.g.*, the Greek neuter ἴδρι (the final *-e* of the infinitive—*regere*, &c.—is the *-ĭ* of the locative, just as in the so-called ablatives *genere*, &c.); (*b*) before *-r-* which has arisen from *-s-*, as in *cineris* beside *cinis*, *cinisculus*; *serō* beside Gr. ἵ(σ)ημι (Ind.-Eur. **si-sēmi*, a reduplicated non-thematic present).

(ii.) Final ŏ became ĕ; imperative *sequere* = Gr. ἕπε(σ)ο; Lat. *ille* may contain the old pronoun **so*, "he," Gr. ὁ, Sans. *sa* (otherwise Skutsch, *Glotta*, i. Hefte 2-3).

(iii.) *el* became *ol* when followed by any sound save *e*, *i* or *l*, as in *volō*, *volt* beside *velle*; *colō* beside Gr. πέλλομαι, πολεῖν, Att. τέλος; *colōnus* for **quelōnus*, beside *inquilīnus* for **en-quelenus*.

(iv.) *e* became *i* (i.) before a nasal followed by a palatal or velar consonant (*tingo*, Gr. τέγγω; *in-cipio* from **en-capio*); (ii.) under certain conditions not yet precisely defined, one of which was *i* in a following syllable (*nihil*, *nisi*, *similis*). From these forms *in-* spread and banished *en-*, the earlier form.

(v.) The "neutral vowel" ("schwa Indo-Germanicum") which arose in pro-ethnic Indo-European from the reduction of long *ā*, *ē* or *ō* in unaccented syllables (as in the *-tós* participles of such roots as *stā-*, *dhē-*, *dō-*, **statós*, **dhatós*, **datós*) became *a* in Latin (*status*, *con-ditus* [from **con-dhatos*], *datus*), and it is the same sound which is represented by *a* in most of the forms of *dō* (*damus*, *dabō*, &c.).

(vi.) When a long vowel came to stand before another vowel in the same word through loss of *i̯* or *u̯*, it was always shortened; thus the *-eō* of intransitive verbs like *candeō*, *caleō* is for *-ējō* (where the *ē* is identical with the η in Gr. ἐμάνην, ἐφάνην) and was thus confused with the causative *-eiō* (as in *moneō*, "I make to think," &c.), where the short *e* is original. So *audīvī* became **audiī* and thence *audiī* (the form *audīvi* would have disappeared altogether but for being restored from *audīveram*, &c.; conversely *audieram* is formed from *audiī*). In certain cases the vowels contracted, as in *trēs*, *partēs*, &c. with *-ēs* from *ejes*. **amō* from *amā(i̯)ō*.

18. *Of the Diphthongs.*

(vii.) *eu* became *ou* in pro-ethnic Italic, Lat. *novus*: Gr. νέος, Lat. *novem*, Umbr. *nuviper* (*i.e.* *noviper*, "usque ad noviens": Gr. (ἐν-)νέα; in unaccented syllables this *-ov-* sank to *-u(v)-* as in *dēnuō* from *dē novō*, *suus* (which is rarely anything but an enclitic word), Old Lat. *sovos*: Gr. ἑ(Ϝ)ός.

Changes of the diphthongs independent of accent.

(viii.) *ou*, whether original or from *eu*, when in one syllable became *-ū-*, probably about 200 B.C., as in *dūcō*, Old Lat. *doucō*, Goth. *tiuhan*, Eng. *tow*, Ind.-Eur. **deucō*.

(ix.) *ei* became ī (as in *dīcō*, Old Lat. *deico*: Gr. δείκνυμι, *fīdo*: Gr. πείθομαι, Ind.-Eur. **bheidhō*) just before the time of Lucilius, who prescribes the spellings *puerei* (nom. plur.) but *puerī* (gen. sing.), which indicates that the two forms were pronounced alike in his time, but that the traditional distinction in spelling had been more or less preserved. But after his time, since the sound of *ei* was merely that of ī, *ei* is continually used merely to denote a long ī, even where, as in *faxeis* for *faxīs*, there never had been any diphthongal sound at all.

(x.) In rustic Latin (Volscian and Sabine) *au* became ō as in the vulgar terms *explōdere*, *plōstrum*. Hence arose interesting doublets of meaning;—*lautus* (the Roman form), "elegant," but *lōtus*, "washed"; *haustus*, "draught," but *hōstus* (Cato), "the season's yield of fruit."

(xi.) *oi* became *oe* and thence *ū* some time after Plautus, as in *ūnus*, Old Lat. *oenus*: Gr. οἰνή "ace." In Plautus the forms have nearly all been modernized, save in special cases, *e.g.* in *Trin.* i. 1, 2, *immoene facinus*, "a thankless task," has not been changed to *immune* because that meaning had died out of the adjective so that *immune facinus* would have made nonsense; but at the end of the same line *utile* has replaced *oetile*. Similarly in a small group of words the old form was preserved through their frequent use in legal or religious documents where tradition was strictly preserved—*poena*, *foedus* (neut.), *foedus* (adj.), "ill-omened." So the archaic and poetical *moenia*, "ramparts," beside the true classical form *mūnia*, "duties"; the historic *Poeni* beside the living and frequently used *Pūnicum* (*bellum*)—an example which demonstrates conclusively (*pace* Sommer) that the variation between *ū* and *oe* is not due to any difference in the surrounding sounds.

(xii.) *ai* became *ae* and this in rustic and later Latin (2nd or 3rd century A.D.) simple *ē*, though of an open quality—Gr. αἴθος, αἴθω, Lat. *aedēs* (originally "the place for the fire"); the country forms of *haedus*, *praetor* were *edus*, *pretor* (Varro, *Ling. Lat.* v. 97, Lindsay, *Lat. Lang.* p. 44).

19. *Vowels and Diphthongs in unaccented Syllables.*—The changes of the short vowels and of the diphthongs in unaccented syllables are too numerous and complex to be set forth here. Some took place under the first-syllable system of accent, some later (§§ 9, 10). Typical examples are *pepĕrci* from **péparcai* and *ŏnustus* from **ónostos* (before two consonants); *concĭno* from **cóncano* and *hospitis* from **hóstipotes*, *legimus* beside Gr. λέγομεν (before one consonant); *Siculi* from **Sicĕloi* (before a thick *l*, see § 17, 3); *dīligit* from **dísleget* (contrast, however, the preservation of the second *e* in *neglĕgit*); *occupat* from **ópcapat* (contrast *accipit* with *i* in the following syllable); the varying spelling in *monumentum* and *monimentum*, *maxumus* and *maximus*, points to an intermediate sound (ü) between *u* and *i* (cf. Quint. i. 4. 8, reading *optumum* and *optimum* [not *opimum*] with W. M. Lindsay, *Latin Language* §§ 14, 16, *seq.*), which could not be correctly represented in spelling; this difference may, however, be due merely to the effect of differences in the neighbouring sounds, an effect greatly obscured by analogical influences.

Inscriptions of the 4th or 3rd century, B.C. which show original *-es* and *-os* in final syllables (*e.g.* *Venerës*, gen. sing., *nāvebos* abl. pl.) compared with the usual forms in *-is*, *-us* a century later, give us roughly the date of these changes. But final *-os*, *-om*, remained after *-u-* (and *v*) down to 50 B.C. as in *servos*.

20. Special mention should be made of the change of *-rĭ-* and *-ro-* to *-er-* (*incertus* from **encritos*; *ager*, *ācer* from **agros*, **ācris*; the

feminine *ācris* was restored in Latin (though not in North Oscan) by the analogy of other adjectives, like *tristis*, while the masculine *ācer* was protected by the parallel masculine forms of the *-o-* declension, like *tener*, *niger* [from **teneros*, **nigros*]).

21. Long vowels generally remained unchanged, as in *compāgo*, *condōno*.

22. Of the diphthongs, *ai* and *oi* both sank to *ei*, and with original *ei* further to *ī*, in unaccented syllables, as in *Achīvi* from Gr. Ἀχαιϝοί, *olīvom*, earlier **oleivom* (borrowed into Gothic and there becoming *alēv*) from Gr. ἐλαιϝον. This gives us interesting chronological data, since the *ai-* must have changed to *ol-* (§ 16, 3) before the change of *-ai-* to *-ei-*, and that before the change of the accent from the first syllable to the penultimate (§ 9); and the borrowing took place after *-ai-* had become *-ei-*, but before *-eivom* had become *-eum*, as it regularly did before the time of Plautus.

But cases of *oi*, *ae*, which arose later than the change to *ei*, *ī*, were unaffected by it; thus the nom. plur. of the first declension originally ended in *-ās* (as in Oscan), but was changed at some period before Plautus to *-ae* by the influence of the pronominal nom. plur. ending *-ae* in *quae*, *hae*, &c., which was accented in these monosyllables and had therefore been preserved. The history of the *-ae* of the dative, genitive and locative is hardly yet clear (see Exon, *Hermathena* (1905), xiii. 555; K. Brugmann, *Grundriss*, 1st ed. ii. 571, 601).

The diphthongs *au*, *ou* in unaccented syllables sank to *-ū-*, as in *inclūdō* beside *claudō*; the form *clūdō*, taken from the compounds, superseded *claudo* altogether after Cicero's time. So *cūdō*, taken from *incūdō*, *excūdō*, banished the older **caudō*, "I cut, strike," with which is probably connected *cauda*, "the striking member, tail," and from which comes *caussa*, "a cutting, decision, legal case," whose *-ss-* shows that it is derived from a root ending in a dental (see §25 (*b*) below and Conway, *Verner's Law in Italy*, p. 72).

Consonants.—Passing now to the chief changes of the consonants we may notice the following points:—

23. Consonant *i* (wrongly written *j*; there is no *g*-sound in the letter), conveniently written *i̯* by phoneticians,

(i.) was lost between vowels, as in *trēs* for **treies*, &c. (§ 17, 6);

(ii.) in combination: *-mi̯-* became *-ni-*, as in *veniō*, from Ind.-Eur. **gʷm̥i̯ō*, "I come," Sans. *gam-*, Eng. *come*; *-ni̯-* probably (under certain conditions at least) became *-nd-*, as in *tendō* beside Gr. τείνω, *fendō* = Gr. θείνω, and in the gerundive stem *-endus*, *-undus*, probably for *-eni̯os*, *-oni̯os*; cf. the Sanskrit gerundive in *-an-īya-s*; *-gi̯-*, *-di̯-* became *-i̯-* as in *māior* from **mag-ior*, *pēior* from **ped-ior*;

(iii.) otherwise *-i̯-* after a consonant became generally syllabic (*-ii̯-*), as in *capiō* (trisyllabic) beside Goth. *hafya*.

24. Consonant *u* (formerly represented by English *v*), conveniently written *u̯*,

(i.) was lost between similar vowels when the first was accented, as in *audīvī*, which became *audiī* (§ 17 [6]), but not in *amāvī*, nor in *avārus*.

(ii.) in combination: *du̯-* became *b*, as in *bonus*, *bellum*, O. Lat. *duonus*, **duellum* (though the poets finding this written form in old literary sources treated it as trisyllabic); *pu̯-*, *fu̯-*, *bu̯-*, lost the *u̯*, as in *ap-erio*, *op-erio* beside Lith. *-veriu*, "I open," Osc. *veru*, "gate," and in the verbal endings *-bam*, *-bō*, from *-bhu̯-ām*, *-bhu̯ō* (with the root of Lat. *fui*), and *fīo*, *du-bius*, *super-bus*, *vasti-bundus*, &c., from the same; *-su̯-* between vowels (at least when the second was accented) disappeared (see below § 25 (*a*), iv.), as in *pruīna* for *prus-uīna*, cf. Eng. *fros-t*, Sans. *pruṣvā*, "hoar-frost." Contrast *Minérva* from an earlier **menes-u̯ā*; *su̯e-*, *su̯o-*, both became *so-*, as in *sorōr(em)* beside Sans. *svasār-am*, Ger. *schwes-t-er*, Eng. *sister*, *sordēs*, beside O. Ger. *swart-s*, mod. *schwarz*. *-u̯o-* in final syllables became *-u-*, as in *cum* from *quom*, *parum* from *paru̯om*; but in the declensional forms *-u̯u-* was commonly restored by the analogy of the other cases, thus (*a*) *seru̯os seru̯om*, *seru̯ī* became (*b*) **serus*, **serum*, **seru̯ī*, but finally (*c*) *seru̯us*, *seru̯um*, *seru̯ī*.

(iii.) In the 2nd century A.D., Lat. *v* (*i.e.* *u̯*) had become a voiced labio-dental fricative, like Eng. *v*; and the voiced labial plosive *b* had broken down (at least in certain positions) into the same sound; hence they are frequently confused as in spellings like *vene* for *bene*, *Bictorinus* for *Victorinus*.

25. (*a*) Latin *s*

(i.) became *r* between vowels between 450 and 350 B.C. (for the date see R. S. Conway, *Verner's Law in Italy*, pp. 61-64), as in *āra*, beside O. Lat. *āsa*, *generis* from **geneses*, Gr. γένεος; *eram*, *erō* for **esām*, **esō*, and so in the verbal endings *-erām*, *-erō*, *-erim*. But a considerable number of words came into Latin, partly from neighbouring dialects, with *-s-* between vowels, after 350 B.C., when the change ceased, and so show *-s-*, as *rosa* (probably from S. Oscan for **rodia* "rose-bush" cf. Gr. ῥόδον), *cāseus*, "cheese," *miser*, a term of abuse, beside Gr. μυσαρός (probably also borrowed from south Italy), and many more, especially the participles in *-sus* (*fūsus*), where the *-s-* was *-ss-* at the time of the change of *-s-* to *-r-* (so in *causa*, see above). All attempts to explain the retention of the *-s-* otherwise must be said to have failed (*e.g.* the theory of accentual difference in *Verner's Law in Italy*, or that of dissimilation, given by Brugmann, *Kurze vergl. Gram.* p. 242).

(ii.) *-s-* became *-br-* (= Eng. *thr* in [illegible] ethnic Italic, and [illegible] initially *fr-* as in *fr*[illegible] [illegible]ur. **srīgos*), but medially *-br-*, as in *funebris*, [illegible]

(iii.) *-rs-*, *ls-* became *-rr-*, *-ll-*, as in *ferre*, *velle*, for **fer-se*, **vel-se* (cf. *es-se*).

(iv.) Before *m*, *n*, *l*, and *v*, *-s-* vanished, having previously caused the loss of any preceding plosive or *-n-*, and the preceding vowel, if short, was lengthened as in

prīmus from **prismos*, Paelig. *prismu*, "prima," beside *pris-cus*.
iūmentum from O. Lat. *iouxmentum*, older **ieugsmentom*; cf. Gr. ζεῦγμα, ζύγον, Lat. *iugum*, *iungo*.
lūna from **leucsnā-*, Praenest. *losna*, Zend *raoχšna-*; cf. Gr. λεῦκος, "white-ness" neut. *e.g.* λευκός, "white," Lat. *lūceō*.
tēlum from **tens-lom* or **tends-lom*, *trānāre* from **trāns-nāre*.
sēvirī from **sex-virī*, *ēvehō* from **ex-vehō*, and so *ē-mittō*, *ē-lidō*, *ē-numerō*, and from these forms arose the preposition *ē* instead of *ex*.

(v.) Similarly *-sd-* became *-d-*, as in *īdem* from *is-dem*.

(vi.) Before *n-*, *m-*, *l-*, initially *s-* disappeared, as in *nūbo* beside Old Church Slavonic *snubiti*, "to love, pay court to"; *mīror* beside Sans. *smáyatē*, "laughs," Eng. *smi-le*; *lūbricus* beside Goth. *sliupan*, Eng. *slip*.

(*b*) Latin *-ss-* arose from an original *-t* + *t-*, *-d* + *t-*, *-dh* + *t-* (except before *-r*), as in *missus*, earlier **mit-tos*; *tōnsus*, earlier **tond-tos*, but *tonstrix* from **tond-trix*. After long vowels this *-ss-* became a single *-s-* some time before Cicero (who wrote *caussa* [see above], *divissio*, &c., but probably only pronounced them with *-s-*, since the *-ss-* came to be written single directly after his time).

26. Of the Indo-European velars the breathed *q* was usually preserved in Latin with a labial addition of *-u̯-* (as in *sequor*, Gr. ἕπομαι, Goth. *saihwan*, Eng. *see*; *quod*, Gr. ποδ-(απός), Eng. *what*); but the voiced *gʷ* remained (as *-gu-*) only after *-n-* (*unguo* beside Ir. *imb*, "butter") and (as *g*) before *r*, *l*, and *u* (as in *grātis*, Gr. βαρύς; *glans*, Gr. βάλανος; *legūmen*, Gr. λοβός, λοβίον). Elsewhere it became *v*, as in *veniō* (see § 23, ii.), *nūdus* from **nouedos*, Eng. *naked*. Hence *bōs* (Sans. *gāus*, Eng. *cow*) must be regarded as a farmer's word borrowed from one of the country dialects (*e.g.* Sabine); the pure Latin would be **vōs*, and its oblique cases, *e.g.* acc. **vovem*, would be inconveniently close in sound to the word for sheep *ovem*.

27. The treatment of the Indo-European voiced aspirates (*bh*, *dh*, *g̑h*, *gʷh*) in Latin is one of the most marked characteristics of the language, which separates it from all the other Italic dialects, since the fricative sounds, which represented the Indo-European aspirates in pro-ethnic Italic, remained fricatives medially if they remained at all in that position in Oscan and Umbrian, whereas in Latin they were nearly always changed into voiced explosives. Thus—

Ind.-Eur. *bh*: initially Lat. *f-* (*ferō*; Gr. φέρω).
medially Lat. *-b-* (*tibi*; Umb. *tefe*; Sans. *tubhy-(am)*, "to thee"; the same suffix in Gr. βίη-φι, &c.).

Ind.-Eur. *dh*: initially Lat. *f-* (*fa-cere*, *fē-c-ī*; Gr. θετός (instead of *θατός), ἔθηκα).
medially *-d-* (*medius*; Osc. *mefiai*; Gr. μέσσος, μέσος from *μεθιος); except after *u* (*iubeo* beside *iussus* for **iudh-tos*; Sans. *yudhati*, "rouses to battle"); before *l* (*stabulum*, but Umb. *stafla-*, with the suffix of Gr. στέγεθρον, &c.); before or after *r* (*verbum*: Umb. *verfale*: Eng. *word*. Lat. *glaber* [v. inf.]: Ger. *glatt*: Eng. *glad*).

Ind.-Eur. *g̑h*: initially *h-* (*humī*: Gr. χαμαί); except before *-u-* (*fundo*: Gr. χέ(ϝ)ω, χύτρα).
medially *-h-* (*veho*: Gr. ἔχω, ὄχος; cf. Eng. *wagon*); except after *-n-* (*fingere*: Osc. *feiho*, "wall"; Gr. θιγγάνω: Ind.-Eur. *dheig̑h-*, *dhing̑h-*); and before *l* (*fig(u)lus*, from the same root).

Ind.-Eur *gʷh*: initially *f-* (*formus* and *furnus*, "oven", Gr. θερμός, θέρος, cf. Ligurian *Bormiō*, "a place with hot springs," *Bormanus*, "a god of hot springs"; *fendō*: Gr. θείνω, φόνος, πρόσ-φατος).
medially *v*, *-gu-* or *-g-* just as Ind.-Eur. *gʷ* (*ninguere*, *nivem* beside Gr. νίφα, νίφει; *frāgrāre* beside Gr. ὀσφραίνομαι [ὀσ- for *ods-*, cf. Lat. *odor*], a reduplicated verb from a root *gʷhrā-*).

For the "non-labializing velars" (*hostis*, *congius*, *glaber*) reference must be made to the fuller accounts in the handbooks.

28. AUTHORITIES.—This summary account of the chief points in Latin phonology may serve as an introduction to its principles, and give some insight into the phonetic character of the language. For systematic study reference must be made to the standard books, Karl Brugmann, *Grundriss der vergleichenden Grammatik der Indo-Germanischen Sprachen* (vol. i., *Lautlehre*, 2nd ed. Strassburg, 1897; Eng. trans. of ed. 1 by Joseph Wright, Strassburg, 1888) and his *Kurze vergleichende Grammatik* (Strassburg, 1902); these contain still by far the best accounts of Latin; Max Niederman, *Précis de phonétique du Latin* (Paris, 1906), a very convenient handbook, excellently planned; F. Sommer, *Lateinische Laut- und Flexionslehre* (Heidelberg, 1902), containing many new conjectures; W. M. Lindsay, *The Latin Language* (Oxford, 1894), translated into German (with corrections) by Nohl (Leipzig, 1897), a most valuable collection of material, especially from the ancient grammarians, but not always accurate in phonology; F. Stolz, vol. i. of a joint *Historische Grammatik d. lat. Sprache* by Blase, Landgraf, Stolz and others (Leipzig, 1894); Neue-Wagener, *Formenlehre d. lat. Sprache* (3 vols., 3rd ed.

Leipzig, 1888, foll.); H. J. Roby's *Latin Grammar* (from Plautus to Suetonius; London, 7th ed., 1896) contains a masterly collection of material, especially in morphology, which is still of great value. W. G. Hale and C. D. Buck's *Latin Grammar* (Boston, 1903), though on a smaller scale, is of very great importance, as it contains the fruit of much independent research on the part of both authors; in the difficult questions of orthography it was, as late as 1907, the only safe guide.

II. MORPHOLOGY

In morphology the following are the most characteristic Latin innovations:—

29. *In nouns.*

(i.) The complete loss of the dual number, save for a survival in the dialect of Praeneste (*C.I.L.* xiv. 2891, = Conway, *Ital. Dial.* p. 285, where *Q. k. Cestio Q. f.* seems to be nom. dual); so *C.I.L.* xi. 6706, T. C. Vomanio, see W. Schulze, *Lat. Eigennamen*, p. 117.

(ii.) The introduction of new forms in the gen. sing. of the -*o*- stems (*domini*), of the -*ā*- stems (*mensae*) and in the nom. plural of the same two declensions; innovations mostly derived from the pronominal declension.

(iii.) The development of an adverbial formation out of what was either an instrumental or a locative of the -*o*- stems, as in *longē*. And here may be added the other adverbial developments, in -*m* (*palam*, *sensim*) probably accusative, and -*iter*, which is simply the accusative of *iter*, "way," crystallized, as is shown especially by the fact that though in the end it attached itself particularly to adjectives of the third declension (*molliter*), it appears also from adjectives of the second declension whose meaning made their combination with *iter* especially natural, such as *longiter*, *firmiter*, *largiter* (cf. English *straightway*, *longways*). The only objections to this derivation which had any real weight (see F. Skutsch, *De nominibus no- suffixi ope formatis*, 1890, pp. 4-7) have been removed by Exon's Law (§ 11), which supplies a clear reason why the contracted type *constanter* arose in and was felt to be proper to Participial adverbs, while *firmiter* and the like set the type for those formed from adjectives.

(iv.) The development of the so-called fifth declension by a re-adjustment of the declension of the nouns formed with the suffix -*iē*-: -*iā*- (which appears, for instance, in all the Greek feminine participles, and in a more abstract sense in words like *māteriēs*) to match the inflexion of two old root-nouns *rēs* and *diēs*, the stems of which were originally *rēj*- (Sans. *rās*, *rāyas*, cf. Lat. *reor*) and *diēy*-.

(v.) The disuse of the -*ti*- suffix in an abstract sense. The great number of nouns which Latin inherited formed with this suffix were either (1) marked as abstract by the addition of the further suffix -*ōn*- (as in *natio* beside the Gr. γνῆσι-ος, &c.) or else (2) confined to a concrete sense; thus *vectis*, properly "a carrying, lifting," came to mean "pole, lever"; *ratis*, properly a "reckoning, devising," came to mean "an (improvised) raft" (contrast *ratio*); *postis*, a "placing," came to mean "post."

(vi.) The confusion of the consonantal stems with stems ending in -*i*-. This was probably due very largely to the forms assumed through phonetic changes by the gen. sing. and the nom. and acc. plural. Thus at say 300 B.C. the inflexions probably were:

	conson. stem	-*i*- stem
Nom. plur.	**rēg-ēs*	*host-ēs*
Acc. plur.	*rēg-ēs*	*host-īs*

The confusing difference of signification of the long -*ēs* ending led to a levelling of these and other forms in the two paradigms.

(vii.) The disuse of the *u* declension (Gr. ἡδύς, ἐλάχυς) in adjectives; this group in Latin, thanks to its feminine form (Sans. fem. *svādvī*, "sweet"), was transferred to the *i* declension (*suavis*, *gravis*, *levis*, *dulcis*).

30. *In verbs.*

(i.) The disuse of the distinction between the personal endings of primary and secondary tenses, the -*t* and -*nt*, for instance, being used for the third person singular and plural respectively in all tenses and moods of the active. This change was completed after the archaic period, since we find in the oldest inscriptions -*d* regularly used in the third person singular of past tenses, *e.g.* *deded*, *feced* in place of the later *dedit*, *fecit*; and since in Oscan the distinction was preserved to the end, both in singular and plural, *e.g.* *faamat* (perhaps meaning "auctionatur"), but *deded* ("dedit"). It is commonly assumed from the evidence of Greek and Sanskrit (Gr. ἐστι, Sans. *asti* beside Lat. *est*) that the primary endings in Latin have lost a final -*i*, partly or wholly by some phonetic change.

(ii.) The non-thematic conjugation is almost wholly lost, surviving only in a few forms of very common use, *est*, "is"; *ēst*, "eats"; *volt*, "wills," &c.

(iii.) The complete fusion of the aorist and perfect forms, and in the same tense the fusion of active and middle endings; thus *tutudī*, earlier **tutudai*, is a true middle perfect; *dīxī* is an *s* aorist with the same ending attached; *dīxit* is an aorist active; *tutudistī* is a conflation of perfect and aorist with a middle personal ending.

(iv.) The development of perfects in -*uī* and -*vī*, derived partly from true perfects of roots ending in *v* or *u*, *e.g.* *mōvī* *rūī*. For the origin of *monuī* see Exon, *Hermathena* (1901), xi. 396 sq.

(v.) The complete fusion of conjunctive and optative into a single mood, the subjunctive; *regam*, &c., are conjunctive forms, whereas *rexerim*, *rexissem* are certainly and *regerem* most probably optative; the origin of *amem* and the like is still doubtful. Notice, however, that true conjunctive forms were often used as futures, *regēs*, *reget*, &c., and also the simple thematic conjunctive in forms like *ero*, *rexero*, &c.

(vi.) The development of the future in -*bo* and imperfect in -*bam* by compounding some form of the verb, possibly the Present Participle with forms from the root of *fui*, **amans-fuo* becoming *amabo*, **amans-fuam* becoming *amabam* at a very early period of Latin; see F. Skutsch, *Atti d. Congresso Storico Intern.* (1903), vol. ii. p. 191.

(vii.) We have already noticed the rise of the passive in -*r* (§ 5 (d)). Observe, however, that several middle forms have been pressed into the service, partly because the -*r*- in them which had come from -*s*- seemed to give them a passive colour (*legere* = Gr. λέγε(σ)ο, Attic λέγου). The interesting forms in -*minī* are a confusion of two distinct inflexions, namely, an old infinitive in -*menai*, used for the imperative, and the participial -*menoi*, masculine, -*menai*, feminine, used with the verb "to be" in place of the ordinary inflexions. Since these forms had all come to have the same shape, through phonetic change, their meanings were fused; the imperative forms being restricted to the plural, and the participial forms being restricted to the second person.

31. *Past Participle Passive.*—Next should be mentioned the great development in the use of the participle in -*tos* (*factus*, *fusus*, &c.). This participle was taken with *sum* to form the perfect tenses of the passive, in which, thanks partly to the fusion of perfect and aorist active, a past aorist sense was also evolved. This reacted on the participle itself giving it a prevailingly past colour, but its originally timeless use survives in many places, *e.g.* in the participle *ratus*, which has as a rule no past sense, and more definitely still in such passages as Vergil, *Georg.* i. 206 (*vectis*), *Aen.* vi. 22 (*ductis*), both of which passages demand a present sense. It is to be noticed also that in the earliest Latin, as in Greek and Sanskrit, the *passive* meaning, though the commonest, is not universal. Many traces of this survive in classical Latin, of which the chief are

1. The active meaning of deponent participles, in spite of the fact that some of them (*e.g.* *adeptus*, *commeus*, *expertus*) have also a passive sense, and
2. The familiar use of these participles by the Augustan poets with an accusative attached (*galeam indutus*, *traiectus lora*). Here no doubt the use of the Greek middle influenced the Latin poets, but no doubt they thought also that they were reviving an old Latin idiom.

32. *Future Participle.*—Finally may be mentioned together (*a*) the development of the future participle active (in -*ūrus*, never so freely used as the other participles, being rare in the ablative absolute even in Tacitus) from an old infinitive in -*ūrum* ("scio inimicos meos hoc dicturum," C. Gracchus (and others) *apud* Gell. i. 7, and Priscian ix. 864 (p. 475 Keil), which arose from combining the dative or locative of the verbal noun in -*tu* with an old infinitive *esom* "esse" which survives in Oscan, **dictu esom* becoming *dicturum*. This was discovered by J. P. Postgate (*Class. Review*, v. 301, and *Idg. Forschungen* iv. 252). (*b*) From the same infinitival accusative with the post-position -*dō*, meaning "to," "for," "in" (cf. *quandō* for **quam-dō*, and Eng. *to*, Germ. *zu*) was formed the so-called gerund *agen-dō*, "for doing," "in doing," which was taken for a Case, and so gave rise to the accusative and genitive in -*dum* and -*dī*. The form in -*dō* still lives in Italian as an indeclinable present participle. The modal and purposive meanings of -*dō* appear in the uses of the gerund.

The authorities giving a fuller account of Latin morphology are the same as those cited in § 28 above, save that the reader must consult the second volume of Brugmann's *Grundriss*, which in the English translation (by Conway and Rouse, Strassburg, 1890-1896) is divided into volumes ii, iii. and iv.; and that Niedermann does not deal with morphology.

III. SYNTAX

The chief innovations of syntax developed in Latin may now be briefly noted.

33. *In nouns.*

(i.) Latin restricted the various Cases to more sharply defined uses than either Greek or Sanskrit; the free use of the internal accusative in Greek (*e.g.* ὕβριν ὑβρίζειν, τυφλὸς τά ὦτα) is strange to Latin, save in poetical imitations of Greek; and so is the freedom of the Sanskrit instrumental, which often covers meanings expressed in Latin by *cum*, *ab*, *inter*.

(ii.) The syncretism of the so-called ablative case, which combines the uses of (*a*) the true ablative which ended in -*d* (O. Lat. *praidād*); (*b*) the instrumental sociative (plural forms like *dominīs*, the ending being that of Sans. *çivāis*); and (*c*) the locative (*noct-e*, "at night"; *itiner-e*, "on the road," with the ending of Greek ποιμέν-ι). The so-called absolute construction is mainly derived from the second of these, since it is regularly attached fairly closely to the subject of the clause in which it stands, and when accompanied by a passive participle most commonly denotes an action performed by that subject. But the other two sources cannot be altogether excluded (*orto sole*, "starting from sunrise"; *campo patente*, "on, in sight of, the open plain").

34. *In verbs.*

(i.) The rich development and fine discrimination of the uses of the subjunctive mood, especially (*a*) in indirect questions (based on [illegible] questions and not fully developed by the time [illegible], who constantly writes such phrases as *dic quis es* for the [illegible]; (*b*) after the relative of essential definition [illegible] and the circumstantial *cum* (" at such a time [illegible]"). The two uses (*a*) and (*b*) with (*c*) the common Purpose [illegible] clauses spring from the " prospective " or " antici[illegible]" meaning of the mood. (*d*) Observe further its use in sub[illegible] clauses, [illegible] *quod abierim*, " he is angry because [illegible]"). This and all the uses of the mood in [illegible] are derived partly from (*a*) and (*b*) and partly from [illegible] of past time (*Non illi argentum redderem?* [illegible]. " Ought I not to have returned the money to him?" [illegible] ought not to have," or, more literally, " You were not [illegible]

[illegible] chapter of Latin syntax see W.G. Hale's " Cum-[illegible]," *Cornell University Studies in Classical Philology*, [illegible], and *The Anticipatory Subjunctive* (Chicago, 1894).

[illegible] system of oratio obliqua with the sequence of [illegible] growth of the latter see Conway, *Livy II.*, Appendix ii., [illegible]

[illegible] construction of the gerundive (*ad capiendam* [illegible]) a present (and future?) passive participle, but re-[illegible] by being linked with the so-called gerund (see § 32,*b*). [illegible] probably not the restriction, appears in Oscan and [illegible]

[illegible] use of the impersonal passive has already been [illegible]

[illegible] authorities for the study of Latin syntax are: [illegible] *Gramm.*, vol. ii. (see § 28); Landgraf's [illegible] (vol. ii. of the joint *Hist. Gram.*, see § 28); [illegible] Grammar (see § 28); Draeger's *Historische* [illegible] 2nd ed., Leipzig, 1878–1881), useful but not [illegible]; the Latin sections in Delbrück's *Vergleichende* [illegible] volume of Brugmann's *Grundriss* (§ 28).

[illegible] OF GREEK WORDS

[illegible], before proceeding to describe the develop-[illegible] in its various epochs, to notice briefly [illegible] vocabulary to Greek, since it affords an indication [illegible] influence of Greek life and literature [illegible] the younger idiom. Corssen (*Lat. Aus-*[illegible] four different stages in the process, [illegible] by no means sharply divided in time, [illegible] different degrees and kinds of intercourse. [illegible] the period of the early intercourse of Rome [illegible] with the colonies in the south of [illegible] belong many names of nations, [illegible], *Tarentum*, *Graeci*, *Achivi*, *Poenus*; [illegible] articles of industry and [illegible], *talentum*, *purpura*, [illegible]. Words like *amurca*, *scutula*, [illegible] familiarity with Greek [illegible] of naturalization. To these [illegible] heroes, like *Apollo*, *Pollux* and [illegible] naturalized Latin words and [illegible] which took place in the Latin [illegible] (cf. §§ 9-27 *supra*). (*b*) The [illegible] of the closer intercourse re-[illegible] Italy, and the wars in Sicily, [illegible] imitations of Greek litera-[illegible] references to Greek life and [illegible] hybrid forms, whether made [illegible] Greek stems as *ballistarius*, [illegible] or of Greek [illegible]; or by derivation, [illegible] composition as *inexschemi*, [illegible]. The character of many of [illegible] who coined them must have [illegible] of colloquial Greek on [illegible] audience. The most [illegible] the burlesque lines in [illegible] himself as

[illegible]

[illegible] inflected according [illegible] in which the [illegible], *Orestes*, *Ci-*[illegible]. Cicero [illegible] *e.g.* *Pyrasmum* as [illegible] some fluctu-[illegible] to the [illegible] and [illegible]

This is equally true whatever was the precise nature of the sound which at that period the Greek aspirates had reached in their secular process of change from pure aspirates (as in Eng. *ant-hill*, &c.) to fricatives (like Eng. *th* in *thin*). (See Arnold and Conway, *The Restored Pronunciation of Greek and Latin*, 4th ed., Cambridge, 1908, p. 21.)

(*d*) A fourth stage is marked by the practice of the Augustan poets, who, especially when writing in imitation of Greek originals, freely use the Greek inflexions, such as *Arcadis*, *Tethȳ*, *Aegida*, *Echus*, &c. Horace probably always used the Latin form in his *Satires* and *Epistles*, the Greek in his Odes. Later prose writers for the most part followed the example of his *Odes*. It must be added, however, in regard to these literary borrowings that it is not quite clear whether in this fourth class, and even in the unmodified forms in the preceding class, the words had really any living use in spoken Latin.

V. PRONUNCIATION

This appears the proper place for a rapid survey of the pronunciation[1] of the Latin language, as spoken in its best days.

37. CONSONANTS.—(i.) *Back palatal*. Breathed plosive *c*, pronounced always as *k* (except that in some early inscriptions—probably none much later, if at all later, than 300 B.C.—the character is used also for *g*) until about the 7th century after Christ. *K* went out of use at an early period, except in a few old abbreviations for words in which it had stood before *a*, *e.g.*, *kal.* for *kalendae*. *Q*, always followed by the consonantal *u*, except in a few old inscriptions, in which it is used for *c* before the vowel *u*, *e.g.* *pequnia*. *X*, an abbreviation for *cs*; *xs* is, however, sometimes found. Voiced plosive *g*, pronounced as in English *gone*, but never as in English *gem* before about the 6th century after Christ. Aspirate *h*, the rough breathing as in English.

(ii.) *Palatal*.—The consonantal *i*, like the English *y*; it is only in late inscriptions that we find, in spellings like *Zanuario*, *Giove*, any definite indication of a pronunciation like the English *j*. The precise date of the change is difficult to determine (see Lindsay's *Latin Lang.* p. 49), especially as we may, in isolated cases, have before us merely a dialectic variation; see PAELIGNI.

(iii.) *Lingual*.—*r* as in English, but probably produced more with the point of the tongue. *l* similarly more dental than in English. *s* always breathed (as Eng. *ce* in *ice*). *z*, which is only found in the transcription of Greek words in and after the time of Cicero, as *dz* or *zz*.

(iv.) *Dental*.—Breathed, *t* as in English. Voiced, *d* as in English, but by the end of the 4th century *di* before a vowel was pronounced like our *j* (cf. *diurnal* and *journal*). Nasal, *n* as in English; but also (like the English *n*) a guttural nasal (*ng*) before a guttural. Apparently it was very lightly pronounced, and easily fell away before *s*.

(v.) *Labial*.—Breathed, *p* as in English. Voiced, *b* as in English; but occasionally in inscriptions of the later empire *v* is written for *b*, showing that in some cases *b* had already acquired the fricative sound of the contemporary *β* (see § 24, iii.). *b* before a sharp *s* was pronounced *p*, *e.g.* in *urbs*. Nasal, *m* as in English, but very slightly pronounced at the end of a word. Spirant, *v* like the *ou* in French *oui*, but later approximating to the *w* heard in some parts of Germany, Ed. Sievers, *Grundzüge d. Phonetik*, ed. 4, p. 117, *i.e.* a labial *v*, not (like the English *v*) a labio-dental *v*.

(vi.) *Labio-dental*.—Breathed fricative, *f* as in English.

38. VOWELS.—*ā*, *ū*, *ī*, as the English *ah*, *oo*, *ee*; *ō*, a sound coming nearer to Eng. *aw* than to Eng. *ō*; *ē* a close Italian *ē*, nearly as the *a* of Eng. *mate*, *ée* of Fr. *passée*. The short sound of the vowels was not always identical in quality with the long sound. *ă* was pronounced as in the French *chatte*, *ŭ* nearly as in Eng. *pull*, *ĭ* nearly as in *pit*, *ŏ* as in *dot*, *ĕ* nearly as in *pet*. The diphthongs were produced by pronouncing in rapid succession the vowels of which they were composed, according to the above scheme. This gives, *au* somewhat broader than *ou* in *house*; *eu* like *ow* in the " Yankee " pronunciation of *town*; *ae* like the vowel in *hat* lengthened, with perhaps somewhat more approximation to the *i* in *wine*; *oe*, a diphthongal sound approximating to Eng. *oi*; *ui*, as the French *oui*.

To this it should be added that the Classical Association, acting

[1] The grounds for this pronunciation will be found best stated in Postgate, *How to pronounce Latin* (1907), Arnold and Conway, *The Restored Pronunciation of Greek and Latin* (4th ed., Cambridge, 1908); and in the grammars enumerated in § 28 above, especially the preface to vol. i. of Roby's *Grammar*. The chief points about *c* may be briefly given as a specimen of the kind of evidence. (1) In some words the letter following *c* varies in a manner which makes it impossible to believe that the pronunciation of the *c* depended upon this, *e.g.* *decumus* and *decimus*, *dic* from Plaut. *dice*; (2) if *c* was pronounced before *e* and *i* otherwise than before *a*, *o* and *u*, it is hard to see why *k* should not have been retained for the latter use; (3) no ancient writer gives any hint of a varying pronunciation of *c*; (4) a Greek *κ* is always transliterated by *c*, and *c* by *κ*; (5) Latin words containing *c* borrowed by Gothic and early High German are always spelt with *k*. (6) the varying pronunciations of *ca*, *ci* in the Romance languages [illegible] explicable except as derived independently from an original

on the advice of a committee of Latin scholars, has recommended for the diphthongs *ae* and *oe* the pronunciation of English *i* (really *ai*) in *wine* and *oi* in *boil*, sounds which they undoubtedly had in the time of Plautus and probably much later, and which for practical use in teaching have been proved far the best.

VI. The Language as recorded

39. Passing now to a survey of the condition of the language at various epochs and in the different authors, we find the earliest monument of it yet discovered in a donative inscription on a fibula or brooch found in a tomb of the 7th century B.C. at Praeneste. It runs "Manios med fhefhaked Numasioi," *i.e.* "Manios made me for Numasios." The use of *f* (*fh*) to denote the sound of Latin *f* supplied the explanation of the change of the symbol *f* from its Greek value (= Eng. *w*) to its Latin value *f*, and shows the Chalcidian Greek alphabet in process of adaptation to the needs of Latin (see Writing). The reduplicated perfect, its 3rd sing. ending *-ed*, the dative masculine in *-oi* (this is one of the only two recorded examples in Latin), the *-s-* between vowels (§ 25, 1), and the *-a-* in what was then (see §§ 9, 10) certainly an unaccented syllable and the accusative *med*, are all interesting marks of antiquity.[1]

40. The next oldest fragment of continuous Latin is furnished by a vessel dug up in the valley between the Quirinal and the Viminal early in 1880. The vessel is of a dark brown clay, and consists of three small round pots, the sides of which are connected together. All round this vessel runs an inscription, in three clauses, two nearly continuous, the third written below; the writing is from right to left, and is still clearly legible; the characters include one sign not belonging to the later Latin alphabet, namely ꟼ for R, while the M has five strokes and the Q has the form of a Koppa.

The inscription is as follows:—

"iovesat deivos qoi med mitat, nei ted endo cosmis virco sied, asted noisi opetoitesiai pacari vois.
dvenos med feced en manom einom duenoi ne med malo statod."

The general style of the writing and the phonetic peculiarities make it fairly certain that this work must have been produced not later than 300 B.C. Some points in its interpretation are still open to doubt,[2] but the probable interpretation is—

"Deos iurat ille (*or* iurant illi) qui me mittat (*or* mittant) ne in te Virgo (*i.e.* Proserpina) comis sit, nisi quidem optimo (?) Theseae (?) pacari vis. Duenos me fecit contra Manum, Dueno autem ne per me malum stato (= imputetur, imponatur)."

"He (or they) who dispatch me binds the gods (by his offering) that Proserpine shall not be kind to thee unless thou wilt make terms with (or "for") Opetos Thesias (?). Duenos made me against Manus, but let no evil fall to Duenos on my account."

41. Between these two inscriptions lies in point of date the famous stele discovered in the Forum in 1899 (G. Boni, *Notiz. d. scavi*, May 1899). The upper half had been cut off in order to make way for a new pavement or black stone blocks (known to archaeologists as the *niger lapis*) on the site of the comitium, just to the north-east of the Forum in front of the Senate House. The inscription was written lengthwise along the (pyramidal) stele from foot to apex, but with the alternate lines in reverse directions, and one line not on the full face of any one of the four sides, but up a roughly-flattened fifth side made by slightly broadening one of the angles. No single sentence is complete and the mutilated fragments have given rise to a whole literature of conjectural "restorations."

R. S. Conway examined it *in situ* in company with F. Skutsch in 1903 (cf. his article in Vollmöller's *Jahresbericht*, vi. 453), and the only words that can be regarded as reasonably certain are *regei* (*regi*) on face 2, *kalatorem* and *iouxmenta* on face 3, and *iouestod* (*iusto*) on face 4.[3] The date may be said to be fixed by the variation of the sign for *m* between ꟿ and Ꟊ (with ᴑ for *r*) and other alphabetic indications which suggest the 5th century B.C. It has been suggested also that the reason for the destruction of the stele and the repavement may have been either (1) the pollution of the comitium by the Gallic invasion of 390 B.C., all traces of which, on their departure, could be best removed by a repaving; or (2) perhaps more probably, the Augustan restorations (Studniczka, *Jahresheft d. Österr. Institut*, 1903, vi. 129 ff.). (R. S. C.)

42. Of the earlier long inscriptions the most important would be the *Columna Rostrata*, or column of Gaius Duilius (*q.v.*), erected to commemorate his victory over the Carthaginians in 260 B.C., but for the extent to which it has suffered from the hands of restorers. The shape of the letters plainly shows that the inscription, as we have it, was cut in the time of the empire. Hence Ritschl and Mommsen pointed out that the language was modified at the same time, and that, although many archaisms have been retained, some were falsely introduced, and others replaced by more modern forms. The most noteworthy features in it are—C always written for G (Cesset = *gessit*), single for double consonants (*clases-classes*), *d* retained in the ablative (*e.g.*, *in altod marid*), *e* for *u* in inflexions (*praesat, exfociont* = *exfugiunt*), *e* for *i* (*navebos* = *navibus*, *exemet* = *exemit*); of these the first is probably an affected archaism, G having been introduced some time before the assumed date of the inscription. On the other hand, we have *preda* where we should have expected *praida*; no final consonants are dropped; and the forms *-es*, *-eis* and *-is* for the accusative plural are interchanged capriciously. The doubts hence arising preclude the possibility of using it with confidence as evidence for the state of the language in the 3rd century B.C.

43. Of unquestionable genuineness and the greatest value are the *Scipionum Elogia*, inscribed on stone coffins, found in the monument of the Scipios outside the Capene gate (*C.I.L.*[2] i. 32). The earliest of the family whose epitaph has been preserved is L. Cornelius Scipio Barbatus (consul 298 B.C.), the latest C. Cornelius Scipio Hispanus (praetor in 139 B.C.); but there are good reasons for believing with Ritschl that the epitaph of the first was not contemporary, but was somewhat later than that of his son (consul 259 B.C.). This last may therefore be taken as the earliest specimen of any length of Latin and it was written at Rome; it runs as follows:—

honcoino . ploirume . cosentiont . r[omai]
duonoro . optumo . fuise . uiro [virorum]
luciom . scipione . filios . barbati
consol . censor . aidilis . hic . fuet a [pud uos]
hec . cepit . corsica . aleriaque . urbe[m]
de]det . tempestatebus. aide . meretod [uotam].

The archaisms in this inscription are—(1) the retention of *o* for *u* in the inflexion of both nouns and verbs; (2) the diphthongs *oi* (= later *u*) and *ai* (= later *ae*); (3) *-et* for *-it*, *hec* for *hic*, and *-ebus* for *-ibus*; (4) *duon-* for *bon*; and (5) the dropping of a final *m* in every case except in *Luciom*, a variation which is a marked characteristic of the language of this period.

44. The oldest specimen of the Latin language preserved to us in any literary source is to be found in two fragments of the Carmina Saliaria (Varro, *De ling. Lat.* vii. 26, 27), and one in Terentianus Scaurus, but they are unfortunately so corrupt as to give us little real information (see B. Maurenbrecher, *Carminum Saliarium reliquiae*, Leipzig, 1894; G. Hempl, *American Philol. Assoc. Transactions*, xxxi., 1900, 184). Rather better evidence is supplied in the *Carmen Fratrum Arvalium*, which was found in 1778 engraved on one of the numerous tablets recording the transactions of the college of the Arval brothers, dug up on the site of their grove by the Tiber, 5 m. from the city of Rome; but this also has been so corrupted in its oral tradition that even its general meaning is by no means clear (*C.I.L.*[2] i. 28; Jordan, *Krit. Beiträge*, pp. 203-211).

45. The text of the Twelve Tables (451-450 B.C.), if preserved in its integrity, would have been invaluable as a record of antique Latin; but it is known to us only in quotations. R. Schoell, whose edition and commentary (Leipzig, 1866) is the most complete, notes the following traces, among others, of an archaic syntax: (1) both the subject and the object of the verb are often left to be understood from the context, *e.g. ni it antestamino, igitur, em capito*; (2) the imperative is used even for permissions, "si volet, plus dato," "if he choose, he may give him more"; (3) the subjunctive is apparently never used in conditional,

[1] The inscription was first published by Helbig and Dümmler in *Mittheilungen des deutschen archäol. Inst. Rom.* ii. 40; since in *C.I.L.* xiv. 4123 and Conway, *Italic Dial.* 280, where other references will be found.

[2] This inscription was first published by Dressel, *Annali dell' Inst. Archeol. Romano* (1880), p. 158, and since then by a multitude of commentators. The view of the inscription as a curse, translating a Greek cursing-formula, which has been generally adopted, was first put forward by R. S. Conway in the *American Journal of Philology*, x. (1889), 453; see further his commentary *Italic Dialects*, p. 329, and since then G. Hempl, *Trans. Amer. Philol. Assoc.* xxxiii. (1902), 150, whose interpretation of *iovesat* = *iurat* and *Opetoi Tesiai* has been here adopted, and who gives other references.

[3] The most important writings upon it are those of Domenico Comparetti, *Iscriz. arcaica del Foro Romano* (Florence-Rome, 1900); Hülsen, *Berl. philolog. Wochenschrift* (1899), No. 40; and Thurneysen, *Rheinisches Museum* (Neue Folge), iii. 2. Prof. G. Tropea gives a *Cronaca della discussione* in a series of very useful articles in the *Rivista di storia antica* (Messina, 1900 and 1901). Skutsch's article already cited puts the trustworthy results in an exceedingly brief compass.

only in final sentences, but the future perfect is common; (4) the connexion between sentences is of the simplest kind, and conjunctions are rare. There are, of course, numerous isolated archaisms of form and meaning, such as *calvitur*, *pacunt*, *endo*, *escit*. Later and less elaborate editions are contained in *Fontes iuris Romani*, by Bruns-Mommsen-Gradenwitz (1892); and P. Girard, *Textes de droit romain* (1895).

46. Turning now to the language of literature we may group the Latin authors as follows:—

I. *Ante-Classical* (240–80 B.C.).—Naevius (? 269–204), Plautus (254–184), Ennius (239–169), Cato the Elder (234–149), Terentius (? [illegible]), Pacuvius (220–132), Accius (170–94), Lucilius (? [illegible]).

II. *Classical—Golden Age* (80 B.C.–A.D. 14).—Varro (116–28), [illegible]. Lucretius (99–55), Caesar (102–44), Catullus [illegible], Sallust (86–34), Virgil (70–19), Horace (65–8), Propertius [illegible], Tibullus (? 54–? 18), Ovid (43 B.C.–A.D. 18), [illegible] A.D. 18).

III. *Classical—Silver Age* (A.D. 14–180).—Velleius (? 19 B.C.–[illegible]), M. Seneca (d. c. A.D. 30), Persius (34–62), Petronius [illegible], Lucan [illegible] 65), L. Seneca (d. A.D. 65), Plinius major [illegible], Martial (40–102), Quintilian (42–118), Pliny the younger [illegible], Tacitus (? 60–? 118), Juvenal (? 47–? 138), Suetonius [illegible], Fronto (c. 90–170).

47. *Naevius and Plautus.*—In Naevius we find archaisms [illegible] much more numerous than in Plautus, especially [illegible] of the original length of vowels, and early forms [illegible], such as the genitive in -*as* and the ablative in -*d*. The number of archaic words preserved is perhaps due to the fact that a large proportion of his fragments have been preserved only by grammarians, who cited them for the express purpose of [illegible] them.

48. [illegible] of Plautus important features have already been mentioned. [illegible] for its more general characteristics see Plautus.

49. *Ennius.*—The language of Ennius deserves especial study [illegible] influence which he exerted in fixing the [illegible]. He first established the rule that in hexameter [illegible] followed by two consonants (except in the case [illegible] a liquid, or a double consonant), must be treated [illegible]. The number of varying quantities [illegible], and the elision of final -*s* becomes the [illegible]. On the other hand he very [illegible] the original length of verbal terminations [illegible] in *o* and *a*, and elides final [illegible]. In declension he never uses -*ae* [illegible] the older and shorter form of the [illegible] of pronouns are [illegible]; and in verbal [illegible] (§ 17, vi.), [illegible] the way of tmesis [illegible] *altisonum* [illegible] regarded as failures, [illegible] simple and straight- [illegible] style, and con- [illegible] time forward the [illegible] with the popular [illegible] was in a certain [illegible] not identical with [illegible] would lend new [illegible] drawn from [illegible] ever-increasing [illegible] language of the [illegible] genuine current of [illegible] Plautus and Terence, [illegible] products of [illegible]

[illegible] is noteworthy [illegible] use of compounds [illegible] in the classical [illegible]

times to be unsuited to the genius of the Latin language, Quintilian censures severely his line—

Nerei repandirostrum incurvicervicum pecus.

Accius, though probably the greatest of the Roman tragedians, is only preserved in comparatively unimportant fragments. We know that he paid much attention to grammar and orthography; and his language is much more finished than that of Ennius. It shows no marked archaisms of form, unless the infinitive in -*ier* is to be accounted as such.

Lucilius furnishes a specimen of the language of the period, free from the restraints of tragic diction and the imitation of Greek originals. Unfortunately the greater part of his fragments are preserved only by a grammarian whose text is exceptionally corrupt; but they leave no doubt as to the justice of the criticism passed by Horace on his careless and "muddy" diction. The *urbanitas* which is with one accord conceded to him by ancient critics seems to indicate that his style was free from the taint of provincial Latinity, and it may be regarded as reproducing the language of educated circles in ordinary life; the numerous Graecisms and Greek quotations with which it abounds show the familiarity of his readers with the Greek language and literature. Varro ascribes to him the *gracile genus dicendi*, the distinguishing features of which were *venustas* and *subtilitas*. Hence it appears that his numerous archaisms were regarded as in no way inconsistent with grace and precision of diction. But it may be remembered that Varro was himself something of an archaiser, and also that the grammarians' quotations may bring this aspect too much into prominence. Lucilius shares with the comic poets the use of many plebeian expressions, the love for diminutives, abstract terms and words of abuse; but occasionally he borrows from the more elevated style of Ennius forms like *simitu* (= simul), *noenu* (= non), *facul* (= facile), and the genitive in -*ai*, and he ridicules the contemporary tragedians for their *scenatica*, their high-flown diction and *sesquipedalia verba*, which make the characters talk "not like men but like portents, flying winged snakes." In his ninth book he discusses questions of grammar, and gives some interesting facts as to the tendencies of the language. For instance, when he ridicules a *praetor urbanus* for calling himself *pretor*, we see already the intrusion of the rustic degradation of *ae* into *e*, which afterwards became universal. He shows a great command of technical language, and (partly owing to the nature of the fragments) ἅπαξ λεγόμενα are very numerous.

50. *Cato.*—The treatise of Cato the elder, *De re rustica*, would have afforded invaluable material, but it has unfortunately come down to us in a text greatly modernized, which is more of interest from the point of view of literature than of language. We find in it, however, instances of the accusative with *uti*, of the old imperative *praefamino* and of the fut. sub. *servassis*, *prohibessis* and such interesting subjunctive constructions as *dato bubus bibant omnibus*, "give all the oxen (water) to drink."

51. *Growth of Latin Prose.*—It is unfortunately impossible to trace the growth of Latin prose diction through its several stages with the same clearness as in the case of poetry. The fragments of the earlier Latin prose writers are too scanty for us to be able to say with certainty when and how a formed prose style was created. But the impulse to it was undoubtedly given in the habitual practice of oratory. The earliest orators, like Cato, were distinguished for strong common sense, biting wit and vigorous language, rather than for any graces of style; and probably personal *auctoritas* was of far more account than rhetoric both in the law courts and in the assemblies of the people. The first public speaker, according to Cicero, who aimed at a polished style and elaborate periods was M. Aemilius Lepidus Porcina, in the middle of the 2nd century B.C.[2] On his model the Gracchi and Carbo fashioned themselves, and, if we may judge from the fragments of the orations of C. Gracchus which are preserved, there were few traces of archaism remaining. A more perfect example of the *urbanitas* at which good speakers aimed was supplied by a famous speech of C. Fannius against C. Gracchus,

[2] [illegible]cero also refers to certain *scripta dulcissima* of the son of Scipio [illegible]us Maior, which must have possessed some merits of style.

which Cicero considered the best oration of the time. No small part of the *urbanitas* consisted in a correct urban pronunciation; and the standard of this was found in the language of the women of the upper classes, such as Laelia and Cornelia.

In the earliest continuous prose work which remains to us the four books *De Rhetorica ad Herennium*, we find the language already almost indistinguishable from that of Cicero. There has been much discussion as to the authorship of this work, now commonly, without very convincing reasons, ascribed to Q. Cornificius; but, among the numerous arguments which prove that it cannot have been the work of Cicero, none has been adduced of any importance drawn from the character of the language. It is worth while noticing that not only is the style in itself perfectly finished, but the treatment of the subject of style, *elocutio* (iv. 12. 17), shows the pains which had already been given to the question. The writer lays down three chief requisites—(1) *elegantia*, (2) *compositio* and (3) *dignitas*. Under the first come *Latinitas*, a due avoidance of solecisms and barbarisms, and *explanatio*, clearness, the employment of familiar and appropriate expressions. The second demands a proper arrangement, hiatus, alliteration, rhyme, the repetition or displacement of words, and too long sentences are all to be eschewed. Dignity depends upon the selection of language and of sentiments.

52. *Characteristics of Latin Prose.*—Hence we see that by the time of Cicero Latin prose was fully developed. We may, therefore, pause here to notice the characteristic qualities of the language at its most perfect stage. The Latin critics were themselves fully conscious of the broad distinction in character between their own language and the Greek. Seneca dwells upon the stately and dignified movement of the Latin period, and uses for Cicero the happy epithet of *gradarius*. He allows to the Greeks *gratia*, but claims *potentia* for his own countrymen. Quintilian (xii. 10. 27 seq.) concedes to Greek more euphony and variety both of vocalization and of accent; he admits that Latin words are harsher in sound, and often less happily adapted to the expression of varying shades of meaning. But he too claims "power" as the distinguishing mark of his own language. Feeble thought may be carried off by the exquisite harmony and subtleness of Greek diction; his countrymen must aim at fulness and weight of ideas if they are not to be beaten off the field. The Greek authors are like lightly moving skiffs; the Romans spread wider sails and are wafted by stronger breezes; hence the deeper waters suit them. It is not that the Latin language fails to respond to the calls made upon it. Lucretius and Cicero concur, it is true, in complaints of the poverty of their native language; but this was only because they had had no predecessors in the task of adapting it to philosophic utterance, and the long life of Latin technical terms like *qualitas*, *species*, *genus*, *ratio*, shows how well the need was met when it arose. H. A. J. Munro has said admirably of this very period:—

"The living Latin for all the higher forms of composition, both prose and verse, was a far nobler language than the living Greek. During the long period of Grecian pre-eminence and literary glory, from Homer to Demosthenes, all the manifold forms of poetry and prose which were invented one after the other were brought to such exquisite perfection that their beauty of form and grace of language were never afterwards rivalled by Latin or any other people. But hardly had Demosthenes and Aristotle ceased to live when that Attic which had been gradually formed into such a noble instrument of thought in the hands of Aristophanes, Euripides, Plato and the orators, and had superseded for general use all the other dialects, became at the same time the language of the civilized world and was stricken with a mortal decay. . . . Epicurus, who was born in the same year as Menander, writes a harsh jargon that does not deserve to be called a style; and others of whose writings anything is left entire or in fragments, historians and philosophers alike, Polybius, Chrysippus, Philodemus, are little if any better. When Cicero deigns to translate any of their sentences, see what grace and life he instils into their clumsily expressed thoughts, how satisfying to the ear and taste are the periods of Livy when he is putting into Latin the heavy and uncouth clauses of Polybius! This may explain what Cicero means when at one time he gives to Greek the preference over Latin, at another to Latin over Greek; in reading Sophocles or Plato he could acknowledge their unrivalled excellence; in translating Panaetius or Philodemus he would feel his own immeasurable superiority."

The greater number of long syllables, combined with the paucity of diphthongs and the consequent monotony of vocalization, and the uniformity of the accent, lent a weight and dignity of movement to the language which well suited the national *gravitas*. The precision of grammatical rules and the entire absence of dialectic forms from the written literature contributed to maintain the character of unity which marked the Roman republic as compared with the multiplicity of Greek states. It was remarked by Francis Bacon that artistic and imaginative nations indulge freely in verbal compounds, practical nations in simple concrete terms. In this respect, too, Latin contrasts with Greek. The attempts made by some of the earlier poets to indulge in novel compounds was felt to be out of harmony with the genius of the language. Composition, though necessarily employed, was kept within narrow limits, and the words thus produced have a sharply defined meaning, wholly unlike the poetical vagueness of some of the Greek compounds. The vocabulary of the language, though receiving accessions from time to time in accordance with practical needs, was rarely enriched by the products of a spontaneous creativeness. In literature the taste of the educated town circles gave the law; and these, trained in the study of the Greek masters of style, required something which should reproduce for them the harmony of the Greek period. Happily the orators who gave form to Latin prose were able to meet the demand without departing from the spirit of their own language.[1]

53. *Cicero and Caesar.*—To Cicero especially the Romans owed the realization of what was possible to their language in the way of artistic finish of style. He represents a protest at once and the same time against the inroads of the *plebeius sermo*, vulgarized by the constant influx of non-Italian provincials into Rome, and the "jargon of spurious and partial culture" in vogue among the Roman pupils of the Asiatic rhetoricians. His essential service was to have caught the tone and style of the true Roman *urbanitas*, and to have fixed it in extensive and widely read speeches and treatises as the final model of classical prose. The influence of Caesar was wholly in the same direction. His cardinal principle was that every new-fangled and affected expression, from whatever quarter it might come, should be avoided by the writer, as rocks by the mariner. His own style for straightforward simplicity and purity has never been surpassed; and it is not without full reason that Cicero and Caesar are regarded as the models of classical prose. But, while they fixed the type of the best Latin, they did not and could not alter its essential character. In subtlety, in suggestiveness, in many-sided grace and versatility, it remained far inferior to the Greek. But for dignity and force, for cadence and rhythm, for clearness and precision, the best Latin prose remains unrivalled.

It is needless to dwell upon the grammar or vocabulary of Cicero. His language is universally taken as the normal type of Latin; and, as hitherto the history of the language has been traced by marking differences from his usage, so the same method may be followed for what remains.

54. *Varro*, "the most learned of the ancients," a friend and contemporary of Cicero, seems to have rejected the periodic rhythmical style of Cicero, and to have fallen back upon a more archaic structure. Mommsen says of one passage "the clauses of the sentence are arranged on the thread of the relative like dead thrushes on a string." But, in spite (some would say, because) of his old-fashioned tendencies, his language shows great vigour and spirit In his Menippean satires he intentionally made free use of plebeian expressions, while rising at times to a real grace and showing often fresh humour. His treatise *De Re Rustica*, in the form of a dialogue, is the most agreeable of his works, and where the nature of his subject allows it there is

[1] The study of the rhythm of the *Clausulae*, *i.e.* of the last dozen (or half-dozen) syllables of a period in different Latin authors, has been remarkably developed in the last three years, and is of the highest importance for the criticism of Latin prose. It is only possible to refer to Th. Zielinski's *Das Clauselgesetz in Cicero's Reden* (St. Petersburg, 1904), reviewed by A. C. Clark in *Classical Review*, 1905, p. 164, and to F. Skutsch's important comments in Vollmöller's *Jahresberichten uber die Fortschritte der romanischen Philologie* (1905) and *Glotta* (i. 1908, esp. p. 413), also to A. C. Clark's *Fontes Prosae Numerosae* (Oxford, 1909), *The Cursus in Mediaeval and Vulgar Latin* (*ibid.* 1910), and article CICERO.

only in final sentences, the connexion between [illegible] conjunctions are rare. [illegible] archaisms of form and [illegible] *escit*. Later and less [illegible] *Iuris Romani*, by [illegible] P. Girard, *Textes de* [illegible]

46. Turning now [illegible] the Latin authors a[illegible]

I. *Ante-Classical* [illegible] (254–184), Ennius [illegible] (? 195–159), Pac[illegible] (? 168–103).

II. *Classical*—[illegible] Cicero (106–44), [illegible] (87–? 47), Sallu[illegible] pertius (? 50– [illegible] Livy (59 B.C.–A[illegible]

III. *Classic*[illegible] ? A.D. 31), M[illegible] (d. 66), Lucan [illegible] (23–A.D. 79), [illegible] Younger (61–? [illegible] Suetonius (75[illegible]

47. *Naeviu*[illegible] proportionally [illegible] in the retentio[illegible] of inflexion, s[illegible] The number o[illegible] that so large [illegible] only by the gr[illegible] of explaining [illegible]

Of the lang[illegible] been mention[illegible] see PLAUTUS.

48. *Ennius*.– [illegible] because of the [illegible] literary style. [illegible] verse all vowe[illegible] of a mute and [illegible] as lengthened [illegible] is also much d[illegible] rule, though no [illegible] commonly reta[illegible] (*essit*, *facitt*) a[illegible] *s* before an ini[illegible] as the genitive, [illegible] gen. plur. is -*u*[illegible] used, as *mis*, *o*[illegible] inflexion there a[illegible] *potestur* (cf. § 5[illegible] (*saxo cere comm*[illegible] cael, *replet te la*[illegible] and never came [illegible] forward, with th[illegible] junctions are co[illegible] literary languag[illegible] dialect. Even to [illegible] sense a dead lan[illegible] that of ordinary [illegible] vigour to his sty[illegible] homely speech. [illegible] measure, the lang[illegible] schools, adapted [illegible] Italian speech is al[illegible] and reappears clea[illegible] the early Romance [illegible]

49. *Pacuvius*, *A*[illegible] especially for his at[illegible] after the fashion of [illegible]

[illegible]

[illegible] his lyrics, and Persius and Juvenal, [illegible] on the whole there are few [illegible] on the language of later [illegible] *Epodes* the diction is that of the [illegible] hardly at all from that of [illegible] The occasional archaisms, [illegible] *surrexe*, the infinitives [illegible] may be explained as still [illegible] ceasing to be current in [illegible] may account for plebeian [illegible] *soppa*, *caldus*, *soldus*, [illegible] and for such pronouns, [illegible] as were common [illegible] in elevated poetry. [illegible] with the licence which he [illegible] are framed according [illegible] the other hand the language is [illegible] There are practically no archaisms [illegible] or plebeian [illegible] but not with the [illegible] like *Tethyi* [illegible] numerous, *e.g.* the [illegible] and with [illegible] accusative, the [illegible] the transitive [illegible] as *orgadatus*, [illegible] "vocative" use of the [illegible] adjectives, where prose would have [illegible] though not limited to [illegible] with other poets. [illegible] apparently only [illegible] innovations in voca- [illegible] have [illegible] skill in the use [illegible] existing stores, [illegible] much less marked [illegible] either Virgil [illegible]

[illegible] reached its full [illegible] Virgil was to the [illegible] wrought were still [illegible] admits of [illegible] most artistic prose. [illegible] Lucretius and [illegible] fiction, rich [illegible] of inspiration. [illegible] literally with [illegible], or again some [illegible] was equally familiar [illegible] the earlier Latin [illegible] sense of fitness and [illegible] which recalls [illegible] the lofty strains [illegible] of antiquarianism [illegible] never passes into [illegible] are often such as [illegible] graceful flavour of [illegible] unintelligible. Forms [illegible]

[illegible] any peculiarly [illegible] language, like that of [illegible] were accounted [illegible] constructions a [illegible] more definite con- [illegible] *caelo*, [illegible], and many [illegible] substantives as [illegible] *sublitens*; [illegible] involving [illegible] frequent occurrence of [illegible] *tulor*, *pascor*.

[1] For further infor[illegible] and LATIN LITERATU[illegible]

60. *Livy*.—In the singularly varied and beautiful style of Livy we find Latin prose in rich maturity. To a training in the rhetorical schools, and perhaps professional experience as a teacher of rhetoric, he added a thorough familiarity with contemporary poetry and with the Greek language; and these attainments have all deeply coloured his language. It is probable that the variety of style naturally suggested by the wide range of his subject matter was increased by a half-unconscious adoption of the phrases and constructions of the different authorities whom he followed in different parts of his work; and the industry of German critics has gone far to demonstrate a conclusion likely enough in itself. Hence perhaps comes the fairly long list of archaisms, especially in formulae (cf. Kühnast, *Liv. Synt.* pp. 14-18). These are, however, purely isolated phenomena, which do not affect the general tone. It is different with the poetical constructions and Graecisms, which appear on every page. Of the latter we find numerous instances in the use of the cases, *e.g.* in genitives like *via praedae omissae*, *oppidum Antiochiae*, *aequum campi*; in datives like *quibusdam volentibus erat*; in accusatives like *iurare calumniam*, *certare multam*; an especially frequent use of transitive verbs absolutely; and the constant omission of the reflexive pronoun as the subject of an infinitive in reported speech. To the same source must be assigned the very frequent pregnant construction with prepositions, an attraction of relatives, and the great extension of the employment of relative adverbs of place instead of relative pronouns, *e.g. quo = in quem*. Among his poetical characteristics we may place the extensive list of words which are found for the first time in his works and in those of Virgil or Ovid, and perhaps his common use of concrete words for collective, *e.g. eques* for *equitatus*, of abstract terms such as *remigium*, *servitia*, *robora*, and of frequentative verbs, to say nothing of poetical phrases like *haec ubi dicta dedit*, *adversum montium*, &c. Indications of the extended use of the subjunctive, which he shares with contemporary writers, especially poets, are found in the construction of *ante quam*, *post quam* with this mood, even when there is no underlying notion of anticipation, of *donec*, and of *cum* meaning "whenever." On the other hand, *forsitan* and *quamvis*, as in the poets, are used with the indicative in forgetfulness of their original force. Among his individual peculiarities may be noticed the large number of verbal nouns in *-tus* (for which Cicero prefers forms in *-tio*) and in *-tor*, and the extensive use of the past passive participle to replace an abstract substantive, *e.g. ex dictatorio imperio concusso*. In the arrangement of words Livy is much more free than any previous prose writer, aiming, like the poets, at the most effective order. His periods are constructed with less regularity than those of Cicero, but they gain at least as much in variety and energy as they lose in uniformity of rhythm and artistic finish. His style cannot be more fitly described than in the language of Quintilian, who speaks of his *mira iucunditas* and *lactea ubertas*.

61. *Propertius*.—The language of Propertius is too distinctly his own to call for detailed examination here. It cannot be taken as a specimen of the great current of the Latin language; it is rather a tributary springing from a source apart, tinging to some slight extent the stream into which it pours itself, but soon ceasing to affect it in any perceptible fashion. "His obscurity, his indirectness and his incoherence" (to adopt the words of J. P. Postgate) were too much out of harmony with the Latin taste for him to be regarded as in any sense representative; sometimes he seems to be hardly writing Latin at all. Partly from his own strikingly independent genius, partly from his profound and not always judicious study of the Alexandrian writers, his poems abound in phrases and constructions which are without a parallel in Latin poetry. His archaisms and Graecisms, both in diction and in syntax, are very numerous; but frequently there is a freedom in the use of cases and prepositions which can only be due to bold and independent innovations. His style well deserves a careful study for its own sake (cf. J. P. Postgate's *Introduction*, pp. lvii.-cxxv.); but it is of comparatively little significance in the history of the language.

62. *Ovid*.—The brief and few poems of Tibullus supply only what is given much more fully in the works of Ovid. In these we have the language recognized as that best fitted for poetry by the fashionable circles in the later years of Augustus. The style of Ovid bears many traces of the imitation of Virgil, Horace and Propertius, but it is not less deeply affected by the rhetoric of the schools. His never-failing fertility of fancy and command of diction often lead him into a diffuseness which mars the effect of his best works; according to Quintilian it was only in his (lost) tragedy of *Medea* that he showed what real excellence he might have reached if he had chosen to control his natural powers. His influence on later poets was largely for evil; if he taught them smoothness of versification and polish of language, he also co-operated powerfully with the practice of recitation to lead them to aim at rhetorical point and striking turns of expression, instead of a firm grasp of a subject as a whole, and due subordination of the several parts to the general impression. Ovid's own influence on language was not great; he took the diction of poetry as he found it, formed by the labours of his predecessors; the conflict between the archaistic and the Graecizing schools was already settled in favour of the latter; and all that he did was to accept the generally accepted models as supplying the material in moulding which his luxuriant fancy could have free play. He has no deviations from classical syntax but those which were coming into fashion in his time (*e.g forsitan* and *quamvis* with the indic., the dative of the agent with passive verbs, the ablative for the accusative of time, the infinitive after adjectives like *certus*, *aptus*, &c.), and but few peculiarities in his vocabulary. It is only in the letters from the Pontus that laxities of construction are detected, which show that the purity of his Latin was impaired by his residence away from Rome, and perhaps by increasing carelessness of composition.

63. *The Latin of Daily Life*.—While the leading writers of the Ciceronian and Augustan eras enable us to trace the gradual development of the Latin language to its utmost finish as an instrument of literary expression, there are some less important authors who supply valuable evidence of the character of the *sermo plebeius*. Among them may be placed the authors of the *Bellum Africanum* and the *Bellum Hispaniense* appended to Caesar's Commentaries. These are not only far inferior to the exquisite *urbanitas* of Caesar's own writings; they are much rougher in style even than the less polished *Bellum Alexandrinum* and *De Bello Gallico Liber VIII*, which are now with justice ascribed to Hirtius. There is sufficient difference between the two to justify us in assuming two different authors, but both freely employ words and constructions which are at once antiquated and vulgar. The writer of the *Bellum Alexandrinum* uses a larger number of diminutives within his short treatise than Caesar in nearly ten times the space; *postquam* and *ubi* are used with the pluperfect subjunctive; there are numerous forms unknown to the best Latin, like *tristimonia*, *exporrigere*, *cruciabiliter* and *convulnero*; *potior* is followed by the accusative, a simple relative by the subjunctive. There is also a very common use of the pluperfect for the imperfect, which seems a mark of this *plebeius sermo* (Nipperdey, *Quaest. Caes.* pp. 13-30).

Another example of what we may call the Latin of business life is supplied by Vitruvius. Besides the obscurity of many of his technical expressions, there is a roughness and looseness in his language, far removed from a literary style; he shares the incorrect use of the pluperfect, and uses plebeian forms like *calefaciuntur*, *facilitet*, *expertiones* and such careless phrases as *rogavit Archimedem uti in se sumeret sibi de eo cogitationem*. At a somewhat later stage we have, not merely plebeian, but also provincial Latin represented in the *Satyricon* of Petronius. The narrative and the poems which are introduced into it are written in a style distinguished only by the ordinary peculiarities of silver Latinity; but in the numerous conversations the distinctions of language appropriate to the various speakers are accurately preserved, and we have in the talk of the slaves and provincials a perfect storehouse of words and constructions of the greatest linguistic value. Among the unclassical forms and constructions may be noticed masculines like *fatus*, *vinus*, *balneus*, *fericulus* and *lactem* (for *lac*), *striga* for *strix*, *gaudimonium* and *tristimonium*, *sanguen*, *manducare*, *nutricare*, *molestare*, *nesapius* (*sapius* = Fr. *sage*), *rostrum* (= *os*), *ipsimus* (= master), *scordalias*, *baro*, and numerous diminutives like *camella*, *audaculus*, *potiuncula*.

much vivacity and
precepts are necessa
sentences are as a
links; his diction co

55. *Sallust.*—In S
we have the earlie
It is probably due
style is marked b
be ascribed to int
which led him
ineruditissimus fu
phrases used in a
e.g. cum animo h
prosapia, dolus,
collibeo, and the
for frequentativ
partly in inflecti
soleo, comperior
syntax his con
contemporary

56. *Lucretius*
eum, endo for
for *aliud, rabi*
ablatives in *-i*
colos, vapos,
confluxet = co
simple forms
usual compo
forms from
in, tmesis w
supata, ordic
poetical pur
masters of
his style, wl
But the purit
to a recogn
has noted m
he alone am
on familiar
others are dir
view to swee
(forty or mo
the classical
terriloquus, p
in the history
fashionable in
Virgil, and th

57. *Catullus*
circles, lifted
it is used to g
he did not esc
his genius is
lyrical poems
says: "No Lat
the perfect gra
all in Catullus,
of these poems
intimate letters
language, of th
Greek words are
are employed ar
Archaisms are
reasons he has fo
contracted forms;
antiquated *lotuli*
language in the
analytic perfect *p*
that of the indefin

58. *Horace.*—Th
of a new chapter i
influence of Horace
temporary Virgil; fo

[illegible] In his contemporary Lucan we have another example [illegible] a style especially attractive to the young, handled [illegible] brilliant but ill-disciplined powers. The *Pharsalia* [illegible] rhetoric, in striking epigram, in high sounding [illegible] but there are no flights of sustained imagination, [illegible], no self-control in avoiding the exaggerated or [illegible], no mature philosophy of life or human destiny. [illegible] poets he is the least Virgilian. It has been said [illegible] corrupted the style of poetry, not less than Seneca [illegible].

[illegible], *Frontinus.*—In the elder Pliny the same [illegible] seen occasionally breaking out in the midst of the [illegible] form in which he gives out the stores of his [illegible]. Wherever he attempts a loftier tone than [illegible] compiler, he falls into the tricks of Seneca. [illegible] encyclopaedic subject matter naturally makes [illegible] very extensive; but in syntax and general tone [illegible] he does not differ materially from contemporary [illegible] is of interest especially for the sound judg[illegible] to a true appreciation of the writers of [illegible] age. He set himself strenuously to resist the [illegible] fashionable in his own time, and to hold up [illegible] purer and loftier models. His own criticisms [illegible] taste, and often by great happiness of [illegible] pointed without being unduly epigrammatic. [illegible] style did not escape, as indeed it hardly could, the [illegible]; and in many small points his language [illegible] classical purity. There is more approach to the [illegible] the best models in Frontinus, who furnishes a [illegible] that it was rather the corruption of literary taste [illegible] change in the language of ordinary cultivated [illegible] the prevalent style was due. Writing on practical [illegible] art of war and the water-supply of Rome—he goes [illegible] the point without rhetorical flourishes, and the [illegible] style which he occasionally introduces serve to [illegible] to distort his thought.

[illegible] *Age.*—The epic poets of the Flavian age [illegible] a striking contrast to the writers of the Claudian period. [illegible] was the cardinal fault of the one school, [illegible] and slavish following of authority is the mark of [illegible]. The general correctness of this period may perhaps [illegible] (with Merivale) partly to the political conditions, [illegible] the establishment of professional schools. Teachers [illegible] must have done much to repress extravagance [illegible] language, but they could not kindle the spark [illegible] Flaccus, Silius Italicus and Papinius Statius [illegible] and in rhythm, and abound in learning; [illegible] drawn from books and not from nature or [illegible] are elaborated to the injury of the impression [illegible], every line is laboured, and overcharged with [illegible] rhetoric. Statius shows by far the greatest [illegible] freshness; but he attempts to fill a broad [illegible] and colouring suited only to a miniature. [illegible] tendencies of the language of his time, [illegible] powerful mind. A careful study of [illegible] Virgil and Lucan, has kept his [illegible] a high standard of purity. His style is eminently [illegible] of real power. The concise brevity [illegible] seems to have been the result of a deliberate [illegible] diffuseness into the form recognized [illegible]. In his verses we notice a few [illegible] which represent the pronunciation of his [illegible] of the final *-o* in verbs, but as a [illegible] Virgilian standard. In Martial the [illegible] epigram finds its most perfect [illegible] finished versification.

[illegible] *and Tacitus.*—The typical prose-writers [illegible] the younger and Tacitus. Some features [illegible] are peculiar to himself; but on the whole [illegible] represents the tendencies shared in [illegible] all the writers of this period. The [illegible] in the direction of a more varied and occasionally more effective syntax; its most striking defect is a lack of harmony in the periods, of arrangements in words, of variety in particles arising from the loose connexion of sentences The vocabulary is extended, but there are losses as well as gains. Quintilian's remarks are fully borne out by the evidence of extant authorities: on the one hand, *quid quod nihil iam proprium placet, dum parum creditur disertum, quod et alius dixisset* (viii. *prooem.* 24); *a corruptissimo quoque poetarum figuras seu translationes mutuamur; tum demum ingeniosi scilicet, si ad intelligendos nos opus sit ingenio* (*ib.* 25); *sordet omne quod natura dictavit* (*ib.* 26); on the other hand, *nunc utique, cum haec exercitatio procul a veritate seiuncta laboret incredibili verborum fastidio, ac sibi magnam partem sermonis absciderit* (viii. 3, 23), *multa cotidie ab antiquis ficta moriuntur* (*ib.* 6, 32). A writer like Suetonius therefore did good service in introducing into his writings terms and phrases borrowed, not from the rhetoricians, but from the usage of daily life.

69. In the vocabulary of Tacitus there are to be noted:—

1. Words borrowed (consciously or unconsciously) from the classical poets, especially Virgil, occurring for the most part also in contemporary prose. Of these Dräger gives a list of ninety-five (*Syntax und Stil des Tacitus*, p. 96).

2. Words occurring only, or for the first time, in Tacitus. These are for the most part new formations or compounds from stems already in use, especially verbal substantives in *-tor* and *-sor*, *-tus* and *-sus*, *-tura* and *-mentum*, with new frequentatives.

3. Words used with a meaning (*a*) not found in earlier prose, but sometimes borrowed from the poets, *e.g. componere*, "to bury"; *scriptura*, "a writing"; *ferratus* "armed with a sword"; (*b*) peculiar to later writers, *e.g. numerosus*, "numerous"; *famosus*, "famous"; *decollare*, "to behead"; *imputare*, "to take credit for," &c.; (*c*) restricted to Tacitus himself, *e.g. dispergere = divolgare*.

Generally speaking, Tacitus likes to use a simple verb instead of a compound one, after the fashion of the poets, employs a pluperfect for a perfect, and (like Livy and sometimes Caesar) aims at vividness and variety by retaining the present and perfect subjunctive in indirect speech even after historical tenses. Collective words are followed by a plural far more commonly than in Cicero. The ellipse of a verb is more frequent. The use of the cases approximates to that of the poets, and is even more free. The accusative of limitation is common in Tacitus, though never found in Quintilian. Compound verbs are frequently followed by the accusative where the dative might have been expected; and the Virgilian construction of an accusative with middle and passive verbs is not unusual. The dative of purpose and the dative with a substantive in place of a genitive are more common with Tacitus than with any writer. The ablative of separation is used without a preposition, even with names of countries and with common nouns; the ablative of place is employed similarly without a preposition; the ablative of time has sometimes the force of duration; the instrumental ablative is employed even of persons. A large extension is given to the use of the quantitative genitive after neuter adjectives and pronouns, and even adverbs, and to the genitive with active participles; and the genitive of relation after adjectives is (probably by a Graecism) very freely employed. In regard to prepositions, there are special uses of *extra*, *erga*, *iuxta* and *tenus* to be noted, and a frequent tendency to interchange the use of a preposition with that of a simple case in corresponding clauses. In subordinate sentences *quod* is used for "the fact that," and sometimes approaches the later use of "that"; the infinitive follows many verbs and adjectives that do not admit of this construction in classical prose, the accusative and infinitive are used after negative expressions of doubt, and even in modal and hypothetical clauses.

Like Livy, the writers of this time freely employ the subjunctive of repeated action with a relative, and extend its use to relative conjunctions, which he does not. In clauses of comparison and proportion there is frequently an ellipse of a verb (with *nihil aliud quam*, *ut*, *tanquam*); *tanquam*, *quasi* and *velut* are used to imply not comparison but alleged reason; *quin* and *quominus* are interchanged at pleasure. *Quamquam* and *quamvis* are commonly followed by the subjunctive, even when denoting facts. The free use of the genitive and dative of the gerundive to denote purpose is common in Tacitus, the former being almost limited to him. Livy's practice in the use of participles is extended even beyond the limits to which he restricts it. It has been calculated that where Caesar uses five participial clauses, Livy has sixteen, Tacitus twenty-four.

In his compressed brevity Tacitus may be said to be individual; but in the poetical colouring of his diction, in the rhetorical cast of his sentences, and in his love for picturesqueness and variety he is a true representative of his time.

70. *Suetonius.*—The language of Suetonius is of interest as giving a specimen of silver Latinity almost entirely free from personal idiosyncrasies; his expressions are regular and straightforward, clear and business-like; and, while in grammar he does not attain to classical purity, he is comparatively free from rhetorical affectations.

71. *The African Latinity.*—A new era commences with the accession of Hadrian (117). As the preceding half century had been marked by the influence of Spanish Latinity (the Senecas, Lucan, Martial, Quintilian), so in this the African style was paramount. This is the period of affected archaisms and pedantic learning, combined at times with a reckless love of innovation and experiment, resulting in the creation of a large number of new formations and in the adoption of much of the plebeian dialect. Fronto and Apuleius mark a strong reaction against the culture of the preceding century, and for evil far more than for good the chain of literary tradition was broken. The language which had been unduly refined and elaborated now relapsed into a tasteless and confused patch-work, without either harmony or brilliance of colouring. In the case of the former the subject matter is no set-off against the inferiority of the style. He deliberately attempts to go back to the obsolete diction of writers like Cato and Ennius. We find compounds like *altipendulus*, *nudiustertianus*, *tolutiloquentia*, diminutives such as *matercella*, *amulla*, *passercula*, *studiolum*, forms like *congarrire*, *disconcinnus*, *pedetemptius*, *desiderantissimus* (passive), *conticinium*; *gaudeo*, *oboedio* and *perfungor* are used with an accusative, *modestus* with a genitive. On the other hand he actually attempts to revive the form *asa* for *ara*. In Apuleius the archaic element is only one element in the queer mixture which constitutes his style, and it probably was not intended to give the tone to the whole. Poetical and prosaic phrases, Graecisms, solecisms, jingling assonances, quotations and coinages apparently on the spur of the moment, all appear in this wonderful medley. There are found such extraordinary genitives as *sitire beatitudinis*, *cenae pignerarer*, *incoram omnium*, *foras corporis*, sometimes heaped one upon another as *fluxos vestium Arsacidas et frugum pauperes Ityraeos et odorum divites Arabas*. Diminutives are coined with reckless freedom, *e.g. diutule*, *longule*, *mundule amicia et altiuscule sub ipsas papillas succinctula*. He confesses himself that he is writing in a language not familiar to him: *In urbe Latia advena studiorum Quiritium indigenam sermonem aerumnabili labore, nullo magistro praeeunte, aggressus excolui*; and the general impression of his style fully bears out his confession. Melanchthon is hardly too severe when he says that Apuleius brays like his own ass. The language of Aulus Gellius is much superior in purity; but still it abounds in rare and archaic words, *e.g. edulcare*, *recentari*, *aeruscator*, and in meaningless frequentatives like *solitavisse*. He has some admirable remarks on the pedantry of those who delighted in obsolete expressions (xi. 7) such as *apluda*, *flocus* and *bovinator*; but his practice falls far short of his theory.

72. *The Lawyers.*—The style of the eminent lawyers of this period, foremost among whom is Gaius, deserves especial notice as showing well one of the characteristic excellences of the Latin language. It is for the most part dry and unadorned, and in syntax departs occasionally from classical usages, but it is clear, terse and exact. Technical terms may cause difficulty to the ordinary reader, but their meaning is always precisely defined; new compounds are employed whenever the subject requires them, but the capacities of the language rise to the demands made upon it; and the conceptions of jurisprudence have never been more adequately expressed than by the great Romanist jurists. (A. S. W.; R. S. C.)

For the subsequent history of the language see ROMANCE LANGUAGES.

LATIN LITERATURE. The germs of an indigenous literature had existed at an early period in Rome and in the country districts of Italy, and they have an importance as indicating natural wants in the Italian race, which were ultimately satisfied by regular literary forms. The art of writing was first employed in the service of the state and of religion for books of ritual, treaties with other states, the laws of the Twelve Tables and the like. An approach to literature was made in the *Annales Maximi*, records of private families, funeral orations and inscriptions on busts and tombs such as those of the Scipios in

[illegible] of amusement, such as the chariot races. The [illegible] was mainly of educative value. The [illegible] translation of the *Odyssey*, which was [illegible] in the days of Horace, and the religious [illegible] called upon to compose in 207 had no high [illegible]. He was, however, the first to familiarise [illegible] the forms of the Greek drama and the Greek [illegible] determine the main lines which Latin literature [illegible] than a century afterwards.

[illegible] successor, Cn. Naevius (d. *c.* 200 B.C.), was not, [illegible] Greek, but either a Roman citizen or, more probably, [illegible] who enjoyed the limited citizenship of a [illegible] had served in the Roman army in the [illegible] war. His first appearance as a dramatic author was [illegible] he adapted both tragodies and comedies from the [illegible] the bent of his genius, the tastes of his audience, [illegible] of the language developed through the active [illegible] and business of life, gave a greater impulse to comedy [illegible] tragedy. Naevius tried to use the theatre, as it had been [illegible] writers of the Old Comedy of Athens, for the purposes [illegible] warfare, and thus seems to have anticipated by a [illegible] the part played by Lucilius. But his attacks upon the [illegible] aristocracy, especially the Metelli, were resented by their [illegible], and Naevius, after being imprisoned, had to retire in [illegible] age into banishment. He was not only the first in point [illegible], and according to ancient testimony one of the first in [illegible] of merit, among the comic poets of Rome, and in spirit, [illegible] not in form, the earliest of the line of Roman satirists, [illegible] he was also the oldest of the national poets. Besides cele[illegible] the success of M. Claudius Marcellus in 222 over the Gauls [illegible] a play called *Clastidium*, he gave the first specimen of the [illegible] *praetexta* in his *Alimonium Romuli et Remi*, based on the most national of all Roman traditions. Still more important [illegible] was rendered by him in his long Saturnian poem on the [illegible] Punic war, in which he not only told the story of contem[illegible] events but gave shape to the legend of the settlement of [illegible] in Latium,—the theme ultimately adopted for the great national epic of Rome.

Naevius.

His younger contemporary T. Maccius Plautus (*c.* 254–184) was the greatest comic dramatist of Rome. He lived and wrote only to amuse his contemporaries, and thus, although more popular in his lifetime and more fortunate than any of the older authors in the ultimate survival of a large number of his works, he is less than any of the great writers of Rome in sympathy with either the serious or the caustic spirit in Latin literature. Yet he is the one extant witness to the humour and vivacity of the Italian temperament at a stage between its early rudeness and rigidity and its subsequent degeneracy.

Plautus.

Thus far Latin literature, of which the predominant characteristics are dignity, gravity and fervour of feeling, seemed likely to become a mere vehicle of amusement adapted to all classes of the people in their holiday mood. But a new spirit, which henceforth became predominant, appeared in the time of Plautus. Latin literature ceased to be in close sympathy with the popular spirit, either politically or as a form of amusement, but became the expression of the ideas, sentiment and culture of the aristocratic governing class. It was by Q. Ennius (239–169) of Rudiae in Messapia, that a new direction was given to Latin literature. Deriving from his birthplace the culture, literary and philosophical, of Magna Graecia, and having gained the friendship of the greatest of the Romans living in that great age, he was of all the early writers most fitted to be the medium of conciliation between the serious genius of ancient Greece and the serious genius of Rome. Alone among the older writers he was endowed with the gifts of a poetical imagination and animated with enthusiasm for a great ideal.

Ennius.

First among his special services to Latin literature was the fresh impulse which he gave to tragedy. He turned the eyes of his contemporaries from the commonplace social humours of later Greek life to the contemplation of the heroic age. But he did not thereby denationalise the Roman drama. He animated the heroes of early Greece with the martial spirit of Roman soldiers and the ideal magnanimity and sagacity of Roman senators, and imparted weight and dignity to the language and verse in which their sentiments and thoughts were expressed. Although Rome wanted creative force to add a great series of tragic dramas to the literature of the world, yet the spirit of elevation and moral authority breathed into tragedy by Ennius passed into the ethical and didactic writings and the oratory of a later time.

Another work was the *Saturae*, written in various metres, but chiefly in the trochaic tetrameter. He thus became the inventor of a new form of literature; and, if in his hands the *satura* was rude and indeterminate in its scope, it became a vehicle by which to address a reading public on matters of the day, or on the materials of his wide reading, in a style not far removed from the language of common life. His greatest work, which made the Romans regard him as the father of their literature, was his epic poem, in eighteen books, the *Annales*, in which the record of the whole career of Rome was unrolled with idealizing enthusiasm and realistic detail. The idea which inspired Ennius was ultimately realized in both the national epic of Virgil and the national history of Livy. And the metrical vehicle which he conceived as the only one adequate to his great theme was a rude experiment, which was ultimately developed into the stately Virgilian hexameter. Even as a grammarian he performed an important service to the literary language of Rome, by fixing its prosody and arresting the tendency to decay in its final syllables. Although of his writings only fragments remain, these fragments are enough, along with what we know of him from ancient testimony, to justify us in regarding him as the most important among the makers of Latin literature before the age of Cicero.

There is still one other name belonging partly to this, partly to the next generation, to be added to those of the men of original force of mind and character who created Latin literature, that of M. Porcius Cato the Censor (234–149), the younger contemporary of Ennius, whom he brought to Rome. More than Naevius and Plautus he represented the pure native element in that literature, the mind and character of Latium, the plebeian pugnacity, which was one of the great forces in the Roman state. His lack of imagination and his narrow patriotism made him the natural leader of the reaction against the new Hellenic culture. He strove to make literature ancillary to politics and to objects of practical utility, and thus started prose literature on the chief lines that it afterwards followed. Through his industry and vigorous understanding he gave a great impulse to the creation of Roman oratory, history and systematic didactic writing. He was one of the first to publish his speeches and thus to bring them into the domain of literature. Cicero, who speaks of 150 of these speeches as extant in his day, praises them for their acuteness, their wit, their conciseness. He speaks with emphasis of the impressiveness of Cato's eulogy and the satiric bitterness of his invective.

Cato.

Cato was the first historical writer of Rome to use his native tongue. His *Origines*, the work of his old age, was written with that thoroughly Roman conception of history which regarded actions and events solely as they affected the continuous and progressive life of a state. Cato felt that the record of Roman glory could not be isolated from the story of the other Italian communities, which, after fighting against Rome for their own independence, shared with her the task of conquering the world. To the wider national sympathies which stimulated the researches of the old censor into the legendary history of the Italian towns we owe some of the most truly national parts of Virgil's *Aeneid*.

In Naevius, Plautus, Ennius and Cato are represented the contending forces which strove for ascendancy in determining what was to be the character of the new literature. The work, begun by them, was carried on by younger contemporaries and successors; by Statius Caecilius (*c.* 220–168), an Insubrian Gaul, in comedy; in tragedy by M. Pacuvius (*c.* 220–132), the nephew of Ennius, called by Cicero the greatest of Roman tragedians; and, in the following generation, by L. Accius (*c.* 170–86), who was more usually placed in this position. The impulse given to oratory by Cato, Ser. Sulpicius Galba and others, and along with it the development of prose composition, went on with increased momentum till the age of Cicero. But the interval between the death of Ennius (169) and the beginning of Cicero's career, while one of progressive advance in the appreciation of literary form and style, was much less distinguished by original force than the time immediately before and after the end of the second Punic war. The one complete survival of the generation after the death of Ennius, the comedy of P. Terentius Afer or Terence (*c.* 185–159), exemplifies the gain in literary accomplishment and the loss in literary freedom. Terence has nothing Roman or Italian except his pure and idiomatic Latinity. His Athenian elegance affords the strongest contrast to the Italian rudeness of Cato's *De Re Rustica*. By looking at them together we understand how much the comedy of Terence was able to do to refine and humanize the manners of Rome, but at the same time what a solvent it was of the discipline and ideas of the old republic. What makes Terence an important witness of the culture of his time is that he wrote from the centre of the Scipionic circle, in which what was most humane and liberal in Roman statesmanship was combined with the appreciation of what was most vital in the Greek thought and literature of the time. The comedies of Terence may therefore be held to give some indication of the tastes of Scipio, Laelius and their friends in their youth. The influence of Panaetius and Polybius was more adapted to their maturity, when they led the state in war, statesmanship and oratory, and when the humaner teaching of Stoicism began to enlarge the sympathies of Roman jurists. But in the last years during which this circle kept together a new spirit appeared in Roman politics and a new power in Roman literature,—the revolutionary spirit evoked by the Gracchi in opposition to the long-continued ascendancy of the senate, and the new power of Roman satire, which was exercised impartially and unsparingly against both the excesses of the revolutionary spirit and the arrogance and incompetence of the extreme party among the nobles. Roman satire, though in form a legitimate development of the indigenous dramatic *satura* through the written *satura* of Ennius and Pacuvius, is really a birth of this time, and its author was the youngest of those admitted into the intimacy of the Scipionic circle, C. Lucilius of Suessa Aurunca (*c.* 180–103). Among the writers before the age of Cicero he alone deserves to be named with Naevius, Plautus, Ennius and Cato as a great originative force in literature. For about thirty years the most important event in Roman literature was the production of the satires of Lucilius, in which the politics, morals, society and letters of the time were criticized with the utmost freedom and pungency, and his own personality was brought immediately and familiarly before his contemporaries. The years that intervened between his death and the beginning of the Ciceronian age are singularly barren in works of original value. But in one direction there was some novelty. The tragic writers had occasionally taken their subjects from Roman life (*fabulae praetextae*), and in comedy we find the corresponding *togatae* of Lucius Afranius and others, in which comedy, while assuming a Roman dress, did not assume the virtue of a Roman matron.

Terence.

Lucilius.

The general results of the last fifty years of the first period (130 to 80) may be thus summed up. In poetry we have the satires of Lucilius, the tragedies of Accius and of a few successors among the Roman aristocracy, who thus exemplified the affinity of the Roman stage to Roman oratory; various annalistic poems intended to serve as continuations of the great poem of Ennius; minor poems of an epigrammatic and erotic character, unimportant anticipations of the Alexandrian tendency operative in the following period; works of criticism in trochaic tetrameters by Porcius Licinus and others, forming part of the critical and grammatical movement which almost from the first accompanied the creative movement in Latin literature, and which may be

General results from 130 to 80.

[illegible]

may most appropriately be taken as marking the end of one period and the beginning of another.

Second Period: from 80 to 42 B.C.

The last age of the republic coincides with the first half of the Golden age of Roman literature. It is generally known as the Ciceronian age from the name of its greatest literary representative, whose activity as a speaker and writer was unremitting during nearly the whole period. It is the age of purest excellence in prose, and of a new birth of poetry, characterized rather by great original force and artistic promise than by perfect accomplishment. The five chief representatives of this age who still hold their rank among the great classical writers are Cicero, Caesar and Sallust in prose, Lucretius and Catullus in verse. The works of other prose writers, Varro and Cornelius Nepos, have been partially preserved; but these writers have no claim to rank with those already mentioned as creators and masters of literary style. Although literature had not as yet become a trade or profession, an educated reading public already existed, and books and intellectual intercourse filled a large part of the leisure of men actively engaged in affairs. Even oratory was intended quite as much for readers as for the audiences to which it was immediately addressed; and some of the greatest speeches which have come down from that great age of orators were never delivered at all, but were published as manifestoes after the event with the view of influencing educated opinion, and as works of art with the view of giving pleasure to educated taste.

Thus the speeches of M. Tullius Cicero (106–43) belong to the domain of literature quite as much as to that of forensic or political oratory. And, although Demosthenes is a master of style unrivalled even by Cicero, the literary *Cicero.* interest of most of Cicero's speeches is stronger than that of the great mass of Greek oratory. It is urged with justice that the greater part of Cicero's *Defence of Archias* was irrelevant to the issue and would not have been listened to by a Greek court of justice or a modern jury. But it was fortunate for the interests of literature that a court of educated Romans could be influenced by the considerations there submitted to them. In this way a question of the most temporary interest, concerning an individual of no particular eminence or importance, has produced one of the most impressive vindications of literature ever spoken or written. Oratory at Rome assumed a new type from being cultivated as an art which endeavoured to produce persuasion not so much by intellectual conviction as by appeal to general human sympathies. In oratory, as in every other intellectual province, the Greeks had a truer sense of the limits and conditions of their art. But command over form is only one element in the making of an orator or poet. The largeness and dignity of the matter with which he has to deal are at least as important. The Roman oratory of the law courts had to deal not with petty questions of disputed property, of fraud, or violence, but with great imperial questions, with matters affecting the well-being of large provinces and the honour and safety of the republic; and no man ever lived who, in these respects, was better fitted than Cicero to be the representative of the type of oratory demanded by the condition of the later republic. To his great [illegible] accomplishment, perfected by practice and elaborate study, to the power of his patriotic, his moral, and personal sympathies, and his passionate emotional nature, must be added his vivid imagination and the rich and copious stream of his [illegible] had no rival among Roman writers or [illegible] said that Roman poetry has produced [illegible] of character. But the Verres, Catiline, [illegible] living and permanent types. The story [illegible] may be true or false, but the picture of [illegible] it presents is vividly dramatic. Had [illegible] in his speeches we should have ranked [illegible] as one who had realized the highest [illegible] should think of him also as the creator and [illegible] and, moreover, not only as a great orator [illegible] appreciative critic of oratory. But to his [illegible] we have to add his services not indeed to philosophy but to the literature of philosophy. Though not a philosopher he is an admirable interpreter of those branches of philosophy which are fitted for practical application, and he presents us with the results of Greek reflection vivified by his own human sympathies and his large experience of men. In giving a model of the style in which human interest can best be imparted to abstract discussions, he used his great oratorical gift and art to persuade the world to accept the most hopeful opinions on human destiny and the principles of conduct most conducive to elevation and integrity of character.

The *Letters* of Cicero are thoroughly natural—*colloquia absentium amicorum*, to use his own phrase. Cicero's letters to Atticus, and to the friends with whom he was completely at his ease, are the most sincere and immediate expression of the thought and feeling of the moment. They let us into the secret of his most serious thoughts and cares, and they give a natural outlet to his vivacity of observation, his wit and humour, his kindliness of nature. It shows how flexible an instrument Latin prose had become in his hand, when it could do justice at once to the ample and vehement volume of his oratory, to the calmer and more rhythmical movement of his philosophical meditation, and to the natural interchange of thought and feeling in the everyday intercourse of life.

Among the many rival orators of the age the most eminent were Quintus Hortensius Ortalus and C. Julius Caesar. The former was the leading representative of the Asiatic or florid style of oratory, and, like other members of the aristocracy, such as C. Memmius and L. Manlius Torquatus, and like Q. Catulus in the preceding generation, was a kind of dilettante poet and a precursor of the poetry of pleasure, which attained such prominence in the elegiac poets of the Augustan age. Of C. Julius Caesar (102–44) as an orator we can judge only by his reputation and by the testimony of his great rival and adversary Cicero; but we are able to appreciate the special praise of perfect taste in the use of language attributed to him.[1] In his *Commentaries*, by laying aside the ornaments of oratory, he created the most admirable style of prose narrative, the style which presents interesting events in their sequence of time and dependence on the will of the actor, rapidly and vividly, with scarcely any colouring of personal or moral feeling, any oratorical passion, any pictorial illustration. While he shows the persuasive art of an orator by presenting the subjugation of Gaul and his own action in the Civil War in the light most favourable to his claim to rule the Roman world, he is entirely free from the Roman fashion of self-laudation or disparagement of an adversary. The character of the man reveals itself especially in a perfect simplicity of style, the result of the clearest intelligence and the strongest sense of personal dignity. He avoids not only every unusual but every superfluous word; and, although no writing can be more free from rhetorical colouring, yet there may from time to time be detected a glow of sympathy, like the glow of generous passion in Thucydides, the more effective from the reserve with which it betrays itself whenever he is called on to record any act of personal heroism or of devotion to military duty.

Caesar.

In the simplicity of his style, the directness of his narrative, the entire absence of any didactic tendency, Caesar presents a marked contrast to another prose writer of that age—the historian C. Sallustius Crispus or Sallust (c. 87–36). Like Varro, he survived Cicero by some years, but the tone and spirit in which his works are written assign him to the republican era. He was the first of the purely artistic historians, as distinct from the annalists and the writers of personal memoirs. He imitated the Greek historians in taking particular actions—the *Jugurthan War* and the *Catilinarian Conspiracy*—as the subjects of artistic treatment. He wrote also a continuous work, *Historiae*, treating of the events of the twelve years following the death of Sulla, of which only fragments are preserved. His two extant works are more valuable as artistic studies of the rival parties in the state and of personal character than as trustworthy narratives of facts. His style aims at effectiveness by pregnant expression, sententiousness, archaism. He produces the impression of caring more for the manner of saying a thing than for its truth. Yet he has great value as a painter of historical portraits, some of them those of his contemporaries, and as an author who had been a political partisan and had taken some part in making history before undertaking to write it; and he gives us, from the popular side, the views of a contemporary on the politics of the time. Of the other historians, or rather annalists, who belong to this period, such as Q. Claudius Quadrigarius, Q. Valerius Antias, and C. Licinius Macer, the father of Calvus, we have only fragments remaining.

Sallust.

The period was also remarkable for the production of works which we should class as technical or scientific rather than literary. The activity of one of these writers was so great that he is entitled to a separate mention. This was M. Terentius Varro, the most learned not only of the Romans but of the Greeks, as he has been called. The list of Varro's writings includes over seventy treatises and more than six hundred books dealing with topics of every conceivable kind. His *Menippeae Saturae*, miscellanies in prose and verse, of which unfortunately only fragments are left, was a work of singular literary interest.

Varro.

Since the *Annals* of Ennius no great and original poem had appeared. The powerful poetical force which for half a century continued to be the strongest force in literature, and which created masterpieces of art and genius, first revealed itself in the latter part of the Ciceronian age. The conditions which enabled the poetic genius of Italy to come to maturity in the person of T. Lucretius Carus (96–55) were entire seclusion from public life and absorption in the ideal pleasures of contemplation and artistic production. This isolation from the familiar ways of his contemporaries, while it was, according to tradition and the internal evidence of his poem, destructive to his spirit's health, resulted in a work of genius, unique in character, which still stands forth as the greatest philosophical poem in any language. In the form of his poem he followed a Greek original; and the stuff out of which the texture of his philosophical argument is framed was derived from Greek science; but all that is of deep human and poetical meaning in the poem is his own. While we recognize in the *De Rerum Natura* some of the most powerful poetry in any language and feel that few poets have penetrated with such passionate sincerity and courage into the secret of nature and some of the deeper truths of human life, we must acknowledge that, as compared with the great didactic poem of Virgil, it is crude and unformed in artistic design, and often rough and unequal in artistic execution. Yet, apart altogether from its independent value, by his speculative power and enthusiasm, by his revelation of the life and spectacle of nature, by the fresh creativeness of his diction and the elevated movement of his rhythm, Lucretius exercised a more powerful influence than any other on the art of his more perfect successors.

Lucretius.

While the imaginative and emotional side of Roman poetry was so powerfully represented by Lucretius, attention was directed to its artistic side by a younger generation, who moulded themselves in a great degree on Alexandrian models. Such were Valerius Cato also a distinguished literary critic, and C. Licinius Calvus, an eminent orator. Of this small group of poets one only has survived, fortunately the man of most genius among them, the bosom-friend of Calvus, C. Valerius Catullus (84–54). He too was a new force in Roman literature. He was a provincial by birth, although early brought into intimate relations with members of the great Roman families. The subjects of his best art are taken immediately from his own life—his loves, his friendships, his travels, his animosities, personal and political. His most original contribution to the substance of Roman literature was that he first shaped into poetry the experience of his own heart, as it had been shaped by Alcaeus and Sappho in the early days of Greek poetry. No poet has surpassed him in the power of vitally reproducing the pleasure and pain of the passing hour, not recalled by idealizing reflection as in Horace, nor overlaid with mythological ornament as in Propertius, but in all the keenness

Catullus.

[1] *Latine loqui elegantissime.*

[illegible] introduced into Roman [illegible] political or social satire [illegible] Horace and the *Epigrams* [illegible] recalling the stories of Greek [illegible] his greatest contribution to [illegible] which he attained in the [illegible] metres, and in the [illegible] the language of familiar [illegible] the creative imagination, [illegible] at once a lifelike and an [illegible] the interest of being [illegible] life and in his art he [illegible] their genius as the [illegible] rises above them [illegible] his affection for his [illegible] simple pleasures, [illegible] to these feelings.

[illegible]

taste for ethical analysis and reflection introduced by Cicero. One great work had still to be done in prose—a retrospect of the past history of the state from an idealizing and romanticizing point of view. For that work the Augustan age, as the end of one great cycle of events and the beginning of another, was eminently suited, and a writer who, by his gifts of imagination and sympathy, was perhaps better fitted than any other man of antiquity for the task, and who through the whole of this period lived a life of literary leisure, was found to do justice to the subject.

Although the age did not afford free scope and stimulus to individual energy and enterprise, it furnished more material and social advantages for the peaceful cultivation of letters. The new influence of patronage, which in other times has chilled the genial current of literature, became, in the person of Maecenas, the medium through which literature and the imperial policy were brought into union. Poetry thus acquired the tone of the world, kept in close connexion with the chief source of national life, while it was cultivated to the highest pitch of artistic perfection under the most favourable conditions of leisure [illegible] freedom from the distractions and anxieties of life.

The earliest in the order of time of the poets who ado[illegible] [illegible] Virgil (70–19)—is also the [illegible] genius, the most richly cultivated, and the most [illegible] in art. He is the idealizing poet of the hopes [illegible] aspirations and of the purer and happier life of which the age seemed to contain the promise. He elevates the present by associating it with the past and future of the world, and [illegible] it by seeing in it the fulfilment of a divine purpose. [illegible] is the true representative poet of Rome and Italy, of [illegible] and of the beauty of nature, the artist in whom [illegible] of the past were made perfect, and the unapproach[illegible] to future times. While more richly [illegible] sensibility to all native influences, he was more [illegible] than any of his contemporaries with the poetry, [illegible] and the learning of Greece. The earliest efforts [illegible] reproduce the cadences, the diction [illegible] of Theocritus; but even in these imi[illegible] of his youth Virgil shows a perfect mastery of his materials. The Latin hexameter, which in Ennius and Lucretius [illegible] the more dignified and majestic emotions, [illegible] the most perfect measure in which the [illegible] sentiment of nature has been expressed. The sentiment of Italian scenery and the love which [illegible] the familiar sights and sounds of his [illegible] which never can pass away.

[illegible] we are struck by the great advance in the [illegible] and self-dependence of the artist, in the mature [illegible] in the deepening and strengthen[illegible] convictions. His genius still works [illegible] by Greek art, and under the disadvantage [illegible] and utilitarian aim imposed on it. But [illegible] surpassed his originals that he alone [illegible] poem a place among the highest [illegible] while he has so transmuted his material [illegible] truth, he has made the whole poem [illegible] The homeliest details of the farmer's [illegible] through the poet's love of nature; through [illegible] his pious sympathy with the sanctities [illegible] through his patriotic sympathy with the [illegible] and through the rich allusiveness of his [illegible] in poetry and legend which can illustrate and [illegible]

[illegible] Virgil is the idealizing poet of [illegible] life of Italy, as the imagination could [illegible] an altered world. In the *Aeneid* he is the [illegible] glory, as manifested in the person of [illegible] life, vividly conceived but [illegible] was perfected in the years that [illegible] victory at Actium. To do justice to his [illegible] with a greater poet than those [illegible] in his previous works. And,

though he cannot unroll before us the page of heroic ...ure in the
the power and majesty of Homer, yet by the sym... ...f a fresh
which he realizes the idea of Rome, and by the power ...just as
he has used the details of tradition, of local scenes, ... the
usage, to embody it, he has built up in the form ...as,
poem the most enduring and the most artistically
monument of national grandeur.

The second great poet of the time—Q. Horatiu...
Horace (68–8) is both the realist and the idealist of
Horace. we want to know the actual lives, mann...
of thinking of the Romans of the generati...
the overthrow of the republic it is in the *Satires* an...
the *Epistles* of Horace that we shall find them. If
that time provided to stir the fancy and move
imaginative reflection, it is in the lyrical poems o...
we shall find the most varied and trustworthy
literary activity extends over about thirty years
divides itself into three periods, each marked
character. The first—extending from about 40 t...
the *Epodes* and *Satires*. In the former he imitates
Archilochus, but takes his subjects from the m...
incidents of the day. Personality is the essence ...
the *Satires* it is used merely as illustrative of ge...
In the *Satires* we find realistic pictures of soci...
conduct and opinions of the world submitted to the stan...
good feeling and common sense. The style of the *Epodes* is pointed and epigrammatic, that of the *Satires* natural and familiar. The hexameter no longer, as in Lucilius, moves awkwardly as if in fetters, but, like the language of Terence, of Catullus in his lighter pieces, of Cicero in his letters to Atticus, adapts itself to the everyday intercourse of life. The next period is the meridian of his genius, the time of his greatest lyrical inspiration, which he himself associates with the peace and leisure secured to him by his Sabine farm. The life of pleasure which he had lived in his youth comes back to him, not as it was in its actual distractions and disappointments, but in the idealizing light of meditative retrospect. He had not only become reconciled to the new order of things, but was moved by his intimate friendship with Maecenas to aid in raising the world to sympathy with the imperial rule through the medium of his lyrical inspiration, as Virgil had through the glory of his epic art. With the completion of the three books of *Odes* he cast aside for a time the office of the *vates*, and resumed that of the critical spectator of human life, but in the spirit of a moralist rather than a satirist. He feels the increasing languor of the time as well as the languor of advancing years, and seeks to encourage younger men to take up the rôle of lyrical poetry, while he devotes himself to the contemplation of the true art of living. Self-culture rather than the fulfilment of public or social duty, as in the moral teaching of Cicero, is the aim of his teaching; and in this we recognize the influence of the empire in throwing the individual back on himself. As Cicero tones down his oratory in his moral treatises, so Horace tones down the fervour of his lyrical utterances in his *Epistles*, and thus produces a style combining the ease of the best epistolary style with the grace and concentration of poetry—the style, as it has been called, of "idealized common sense," that of the *urbanus* and cultivated man of the world who is also in his hours of inspiration a genuine poet. In the last ten years of his life Horace resumed his lyrical function for a time, under pressure of the imperial command, and produced some of the most exquisite and mature products of his art. But his chief activity is devoted to criticism. He first vindicates the claims of his own age to literary pre-eminence, and then seeks to stimulate the younger writers of the day to what he regarded as the manlier forms of poetry, and especially to the tragic drama, which seemed for a short time to give promise of an artistic revival.

But the poetry of the latter half of the Augustan age destined to survive did not follow the lines either of lyrical or of dramatic art marked out by Horace. The latest form of poetry adopted from Greece and destined to gain and permanently to hold the ear of the world was the *elegy*. From the time of Mimnermus this

amoenum attributed to him by Tacitus, the fruit of which is sometimes seen in the "honeyed phrases" mentioned by Petronius—pure aspirations combined with inconsistency of purpose—the inconsistency of one who tries to make the best of two worlds, the ideal inner life and the successful real life in the atmosphere of a most corrupt court. The *Pharsalia* of Lucan (39–65), with Cato as its hero, is essentially a Stoic manifesto of the opposition. It is written with the force and fervour
...extreme youth and with the literary ambition of a race as
...new to the discipline of intellectual culture, and is charac-
...d by rhetorical rather than poetical imagination. The
...*Satires* of Persius (34–62) are the purest product of
...a Stoicism that had found in a contemporary, Thrasea,
...nal and practical hero than Cato. But no important
...iquity has less literary charm than Persius. In
...erary conceits and fopperies which he satirizes
...the most unnatural contortions of expression.
...ngth are the seven eclogues of T. Calpurnius
...he beginning of the reign of Nero, which
...and facility of diction. Of the works
...om a human point of view is perhaps
...lest literature has the most genuine
...of a prose novel—the *Satyricon*—
...ost sincere in its representation,
...penetrating in its satire, most

Cyn... ...introduced both into life
intelligible ... ...espasian. The time was
idolatry and a... ...d sense and
pertius is a less accomp... ...Vespasian Age of
writer than either Tibullus ... ...ller of the Domitian.
of dealing gravely with a great or ... ...23–79),
them, and his diction and rhythm give ... Valerius Flaccus
concentrated force of conception and a correspon... ...90), the most
of imaginative feeling which remind us of Lucretius. ...f Domitian,

The most facile and brilliant of the elegiac poets ... the time,
least serious in tone and spirit is P. Ovidius Naso or Ovid (43 ... ...ributions
A.D. 18). As an amatory poet he is the poet of pleasure ... among
and intrigue rather than of tender sentiment or ... ...licus,
absorbing passion. Though he treated his subject in relation to ... ...ial.
himself with more levity and irony than real feeling, yet by his sparkling wit and fancy he created a literature of sentiment and adventure adapted to amuse the idle and luxurious society of which the elder Julia was the centre. His power of continuous narrative is best seen in the *Metamorphoses*, written in hexameters to which he has imparted a rapidity and precision of movement more suited to romantic and picturesque narrative than the weighty self-restrained verse of Virgil. In his *Fasti* he treats a subject of national interest; it is not, however, through the strength of Roman sentiment but through the power of vividly conceiving and narrating stories of strong human interest that the poem lives. In his latest works—the *Tristia* and *Ex Ponto*—he imparts the interest of personal confessions to the record of a unique experience. Latin poetry is more rich in the expression of personal feeling than of dramatic realism. In Ovid we have both. We know him in the intense liveliness of his feeling and the human weakness of his nature more intimately than any other writer of antiquity, except perhaps Cicero. As Virgil marks the point of maturest excellence in poetic diction and rhythm, Ovid marks that of the greatest facility.

The Augustan age was one of those great eras in the world like the era succeeding the Persian War in Greece, the Elizabethan age in England, and the beginning of the 19th Livy. century in Europe, in which what seems a new spring of national and individual life calls out an idealizing retrospect of the past. As the present seems full of new life, the past seems rich in glory and the future in hope. The past of Rome had always a peculiar fascination for Roman writers. Virgil in a supreme degree, and Horace, Propertius and Ovid in a less degree, had expressed in their poetry the romance of the past. But it was in the great historical work of T. Livius or Livy (59 B.C.–A.D. 17) that the record of the national life received its most systematic exposition. Its execution was the work of a life prolonged through the languor and dissolution following so soon upon the promise of the new era, during which time the past became glorified by contrast with the disheartening aspect of the present. The value of the work consists not in any power of critical investigation or weighing of historical evidence but in the intense sympathy of the writer with the national ideal, and the vivid imagination with which under the influence of this sympathy he gives life to the events and personages, the wars and political struggles, of times remote from his own. He makes us feel more than any one the majesty of the Roman state, of its great magistracies, and of the august council by which its policy was guided. And, while he makes the words *senatus populusque Romanus* full of significance for all times, no one realizes with more enthusiasm all that is implied in the words *imperium Romanum*, and the great military qualities of head and heart by which that empire was acquired and maintained. The vast scale on which the work was conceived and the thoroughness of artistic execution with which the details are finished are characteristically Roman. The prose style of Rome, as a vehicle for the continuous narration of events coloured by a rich and picturesque imagination and instinct with dignified emotion, attained its perfection in Livy.

Fourth Period: The Silver Age, from A.D. *17 to about 130.*

Characteristics of post-Augustan age.

For more than a century after the death of Augustus Roman literature continues to flow in the old channels. Though drawing from the provinces, Rome remains the centre of the literary movement. The characteristics of the great writers are essentially national, not provincial nor cosmopolitan. In prose the old forms—oratory, history, the epistle, treatises or dialogues on ethical and literary questions—continue to be cultivated. Scientific and practical subjects, such as natural history, architecture, medicine, agriculture, are treated in more elaborate literary style. The old Roman *satura* is developed into something like the modern prose novel. In the various provinces of poetry, while there is little novelty or inspiration, there is abundance of industry and ambitious effort. The national love of works of large compass shows itself in the production of long epic poems, both of the historic and of the imitative Alexandrian type. The imitative and rhetorical tastes of Rome showed themselves in the composition of exotic tragedies, as remote in spirit and character from Greek as from Roman life, of which the only extant specimens are those attributed to the younger Seneca. The composition of didactic, lyrical and elegiac poetry also was the accomplishment and pastime of an educated dilettante class, the only extant specimens of any interest being some of the *Silvae* of Statius. The only voice with which the poet of this age can express himself with force and sincerity is that of satire and satiric epigram. We find now only imitative echoes of the old music created by Virgil and others, as in Statius, or powerful declamation, as in Lucan and Juvenal. There is a deterioration in the diction as well as in the music of poetry. The elaborate literary culture of the Augustan age has done something to impair the native force of the Latin idiom. The language of [illegible], in the most elaborate kind of prose as well as poetry, [illegible] of popular speech. The old oratorical tastes and [illegible] their outlet in public recitations and the practice of [illegible]. Forced and distorted expression, exaggerated [illegible] and antithesis, an affected prettiness, are studied [illegible] the applause of audiences who thronged [illegible] rooms in search of temporary excitement. [illegible] widely diffused, but is less thorough, [illegible], derived less than before from the [illegible]. The precocious immaturity of Lucan's [illegible] contrast to the long preparation of [illegible] office. Although there are some [illegible] and one at [illegible] into the [illegible] its effect on [illegible] doubted that the steady literary decline which characterized the last centuries of paganism was beginning before the death of Ovid and Livy.

The influences which had inspired republican and Augustan literature were the artistic impulse derived from a familiarity with the great works of Greek genius, becoming more intimate with every new generation, the spell of Rome over the imagination of the kindred Italian races, the charm of Italy, and the vivid sensibility of the Italian temperament. These influences were certainly much less operative in the first century of the empire. The imitative impulse, which had much of the character of a creative impulse, and had resulted in the appropriation of the forms of poetry suited to the Roman and Italian character and of the metres suited to the genius of the Latin language, no longer stimulated to artistic effort. The great sources of Greek poetry were no longer regarded, as they were by Lucretius and Virgil, as sacred, untasted springs, to be approached in a spirit of enthusiasm tempered with reverence. We have the testimony of two men of shrewd common sense and masculine understanding—Martial and Juvenal—to the stale and lifeless character of the art of the Silver Age, which sought to reproduce in the form of epics, tragedies and elegies the bright fancies of the Greek mythology.

The idea of Rome, owing to the antagonism between the policy of the government and the sympathies of the class by which literature was favoured and cultivated, could no longer be an inspiring motive, as it had been in the literature of the republic and of the Augustan age. The spirit of Rome appears only as animating the protest of Lucan, the satire of Persius and Juvenal, the sombre picture which Tacitus paints of the annals of the empire. Oratory is no longer an independent voice appealing to sentiments of Roman dignity, but the weapon of the "informers" (*delatores*), wielded for their own advancement and the destruction of that class which, even in their degeneracy, retained most sympathy with the national traditions. Roman history was no longer a record of national glory, stimulating the patriotism and flattering the pride of all Roman citizens, but a personal eulogy or a personal invective, according as servility to a present or hatred of a recent ruler was the motive which animated it.

The charm of Italian scenes still remained the same, but the fresh and inspiring feeling of nature gave place to the mere sensuous gratification derived from the luxurious and artificial beauty of the country villa. The idealizing poetry of passion, which found a genuine voice in Catullus and the elegiac poets, could not prolong itself through the exhausting licence of successive generations. The vigorous vitality which gives interest to the personality of Catullus, Propertius and Ovid no longer characterizes their successors. The pathos of natural affection is occasionally recognized in Statius and more rarely in Martial, but it has not the depth of tenderness found in Lucretius and Virgil. The wealth and luxury of successive generations, the monotonous routine of life, the separation of the educated class from the higher work of the world, have produced their enervating and paralysing effect on the mainsprings of poetic and imaginative feeling.

New literary elements.

New elements, however, appear in the literature of this period. As the result of the severance from the active interests of life, a new interest is awakened in the inner life of the individual. The immorality of Roman society not only affords abundant material to the satirist, but deepens the consciousness of moral evil in purer and more thoughtful minds. To these causes we attribute the pathological observation of Seneca and Tacitus, the new sense of purity in Persius called out by contrast with the impurity around him, the glowing if somewhat sensational exaggeration of Juvenal, the vivid characterization of Martial. The literature of no time presents so powerfully the contrast between moral good and evil. In this respect it is truly representative of the life of the age. Another new element is the influence of a new race. In the two preceding periods the rapid diffusion of literary culture following the Social War and the first Civil War was seen to awaken into new life the elements of original genius in Italy and Cisalpine Gaul. In the first century of the empire a similar result was produced by the diffusion of that culture in the Latinized districts of Spain. The fervid temperament of a fresh and vigorous race, which received the Latin discipline just as Latium had two or three centuries previously received the Greek discipline, revealed itself in the writings of the Senecas, Lucan, Quintilian, Martial and others, who in their own time added literary distinction to the Spanish towns from which they came. The new extraneous element introduced into Roman literature draws into greater prominence the characteristics of the last great representatives of the genuine Roman and Italian spirit—the historian Tacitus and the satirist Juvenal.

On the whole this century shows, in form, language and substance, the signs of literary decay. But it is still capable of producing men of original force; it still maintains the traditions of a happier time; it is still alive to the value of literary culture, and endeavours by minute attention to style to produce new effects. Though it was not one of the great eras in the annals of literature, yet the century which produced Martial, Juvenal and Tacitus cannot be pronounced barren in literary originality, nor that which produced Seneca and Quintilian devoid of culture and literary taste.

This fourth period is itself subdivided into three divisions: (1) from the accession of Tiberius to the death of Nero, 68—the most important part of it being the Neronian age, 54 to 68; (2) the Flavian era, from the death of Nero to the death of Domitian, 96; (3) the reigns of Nerva and Trajan and part of the reign of Hadrian.

Period from Tiberius to Nero.

1. For a generation after the death of Augustus no new original literary force appeared. The later poetry of the Augustan age had ended in trifling dilettantism, for the continuance of which the atmosphere of the court was no longer favourable. The class by which literature was encouraged had become both enervated and terrorized. The most remarkable poetical product of the time is the long-neglected astrological poem of Manilius which was written at the beginning of Tiberius's reign. Its vigour and originality have had scanty justice done to them owing to the difficulty of the subject-matter and the style, and the corruptions which still disfigure its text. Very different has been the fate of the *Fables* of Phaedrus. This slight work of a Macedonian freedman, destitute of national significance and representative in its morality only of the spirit of cosmopolitan individualism, owes its vogue to its easy Latinity and popular subject-matter. Of the prose writers C. Velleius Paterculus, the historian, and Valerius Maximus, the collector of anecdotes, are the most important. A. Cornelius Celsus composed a series of technical handbooks, one of which, upon medicine, has survived. Its purity of style and the fact that it was long a standard work entitle it to a mention here. The traditional culture was still, however, maintained, and the age was rich in grammarians and rhetoricians. The new profession of the *delator* must have given a stimulus to oratory. A high ideal of culture, literary as well as practical, was realized in Germanicus, which seems to have been transmitted to his daughter Agrippina, whose patronage of Seneca had important results in the next generation. The reign of Claudius was a time in which antiquarian learning, grammatical studies, and jurisprudence were cultivated, but no important additions were made to literature. A fresh impulse was given to letters on the accession of Nero, and this was partly due to the theatrical and artistic tastes of the young emperor. Four writers of the Neronian age still possess considerable interest,—L. Annaeus Seneca, M. Annaeus Lucanus, A. Persius Flaccus and Petronius Arbiter. The first three represent the spirit of their age by exhibiting the power of the Stoic philosophy as a moral, political and religious force; the last is the most cynical exponent of the depravity of the time. Seneca (*c.* 5 B.C.–A.D. 65) is less than Persius a pure Stoic, and more of a moralist and pathological observer of man's inner life. He makes the commonplaces of a cosmopolitan philosophy interesting by his abundant illustration drawn from the private and social life of his contemporaries. He has knowledge of the world, the suppleness of a courtier, Spanish vivacity, and the *ingenium amoenum* attributed to him by Tacitus, the fruit of which is sometimes seen in the "honeyed phrases" mentioned by Petronius—pure aspirations combined with inconsistency of purpose—the inconsistency of one who tries to make the best of two worlds, the ideal inner life and the successful real life in the atmosphere of a most corrupt court. The *Pharsalia* of Lucan (39–65), with Cato as its hero, is essentially a Stoic manifesto of the opposition. It is written with the force and fervour of extreme youth and with the literary ambition of a race as yet new to the discipline of intellectual culture, and is characterized by rhetorical rather than poetical imagination. The six short *Satires* of Persius (34–62) are the purest product of Stoicism—a Stoicism that had found in a contemporary, Thrasea, a more rational and practical hero than Cato. But no important writer of antiquity has less literary charm than Persius. In avoiding the literary conceits and fopperies which he satirizes he has recourse to the most unnatural contortions of expression. Of hardly greater length are the seven eclogues of T. Calpurnius Siculus, written at the beginning of the reign of Nero, which are not without grace and facility of diction. Of the works of the time that which from a human point of view is perhaps the most detestable in ancient literature has the most genuine literary quality, the fragment of a prose novel—the *Satyricon*—of Petronius (d. 66). It is most sincere in its representation, least artificial in diction, most penetrating in its satire, most just in its criticism of art and style.

Age of Domitian.

2. A greater sobriety of tone was introduced both into life and literature with the accession of Vespasian. The time was, however, characterized rather by good sense and industry than by original genius. Under Vespasian C. Plinius Secundus, or Pliny the elder (compiler of the *Natural History*, an encyclopaedic treatise, 23–79), is the most important prose writer, and C. Valerius Flaccus Setinus Balbus, author of the *Argonautica* (d. *c.* 90), the most important among the writers of poetry. The reign of Domitian, although it silenced the more independent spirits of the time, Tacitus and Juvenal, witnessed more important contributions to Roman literature than any age since the Augustan,—among them the *Institutes* of Quintilian, the *Punic War* of Silius Italicus, the epics and the *Silvae* of Statius, and the *Epigrams* of Martial. M. Fabius Quintilianus, or Quintilian (*c.* 35–95), is brought forward by Juvenal as a unique instance of a thoroughly successful man of letters, of one not belonging by birth to the rich or official class, who had risen to wealth and honours through literature. He was well adapted to his time by his good sense and sobriety of judgment. His criticism is just and true rather than subtle or ingenious, and has thus stood the test of the judgment of after-times. The poem of Ti. Catius Silius Italicus (25–101) is a proof of the industry and literary ambition of members of the rich official class. Of the epic poets of the Silver Age P. Papinius Statius (*c.* 45–96) shows the greatest technical skill and the richest pictorial fancy in the execution of detail; but his epics have no true inspiring motive, and, although the recitation of the *Thebaid* could attract and charm an audience in the days of Juvenal, it really belongs to the class of poems so unsparingly condemned both by him and Martial. In the *Silvae*, though many of them have little root in the deeper feelings of human nature, we find occasionally more than in any poetry after the Augustan age something of the purer charm and pathos of life. But it is not in the *Silvae*, nor in the epics and tragedies of the time, nor in the cultivated criticism of Quintilian that the age of Domitian lives for us. It is in the *Epigrams* of M. Valerius Martialis or Martial (*c.* 41–104) that we have a true image of the average sensual frivolous life of Rome at the end of the 1st century, seen through a medium of wit and humour, but undistorted by the exaggeration which moral indignation and the love of effect add to the representation of Juvenal. Martial represents his age in his *Epigrams*, as Horace does his in his *Satires* and *Odes*, with more variety and incisive force in his sketches, though with much less poetic charm and serious meaning. We know the daily life, the familiar personages, the outward aspect of Rome in the age of Domitian

[illegible] a little later than Fronto and was [illegible] parts. In his *Metamorphoses*, [illegible] Greek original, he takes the [illegible] adventures of Lucius of Madaura, [illegible] famous legend of Cupid and Psyche. His [illegible] has a strange fascination for the [illegible] Roman or Italian about it. Two [illegible] historians may be mentioned: Justinus [illegible] abridged the history of Pompeius Trogus, [illegible] Annius Florus, who wrote in the [illegible] historical sketch based upon Livy. The [illegible] includes the lives of the emperors [illegible] (117–284), is the work of six [illegible] wrote under Diocletian and two under [illegible] a collection of personal memoirs of little [illegible] and marked by puerility and poverty [illegible] Marcellinus (*c.* 330–400) had a higher [illegible] historian's function. His narrative of the [illegible] now remains) is honest and straightfor[illegible] is awkward and obscure. The last pagan [illegible] mentioned is Q. Aurelius Symmachus [illegible] author of some speeches and a collection of [illegible] ornate and courtly periods cannot [illegible] there was nothing now for paganism to say. [illegible] writers alone that we find the vigour of life. [illegible] Christian apologetics is the *Octavius* of [illegible] contemporary of Fronto. It is [illegible] strongly tinged by classical [illegible] different is the work of "the [illegible] Septimius Florens Tertullianus (*c.* 150–230), [illegible] the most vigorous of the Latin champions [illegible] shows the African revolt of which we [illegible] its medley of archaisms, Graecisms [illegible] the strength of the disintegrating forces [illegible] language. A more commanding figure [illegible] St Augustine (354–430), bishop [illegible] and dialectical power [illegible] or St Jerome (*c.* 331 [illegible] in Dalmatia, does for many-[illegible]

Christian writers.

[illegible] was attended by an increased [illegible] studies. From the time of [illegible] who was the teacher of [illegible] had been taken in [illegible] at Rome. Varro [illegible] Flaccus in the Augustan [illegible] lexicography and etymology. [illegible] Probus (*c.* A.D. 60) was the first [illegible] In the next century we have [illegible], and then a much [illegible] of Aulus Gellius, and [illegible] Terentianus, an African, upon [illegible] and metre. Somewhat later [illegible] Terence and Horace, Helenius Acro [illegible] The tradition was continued in [illegible] and C. Marius Victorinus, [illegible] the grammarian and commen[illegible] Flavius Sosipater Charisius and [illegible] the author of a valuable commentary [illegible] Theodosius (*c.* 400) wrote a [illegible] and seven books of [illegible] Capella (*c.* 430), a [illegible] a compendium of the seven liberal [illegible] prose and verse, with some literary [illegible] grammarian who need be named is the [illegible] celebrated Priscianus, who pub[illegible] probably in the middle [illegible]

Grammarians.

[illegible] which may be regarded as one of the outlying [illegible] genius had had some of its greatest [illegible] of the "codes," was active [illegible] distinguished of the early jurists (whose works are lost) were Q. Mucius Scaevola, who died in 82 B.C., and following him Ser. Sulpicius Rufus, who died in 43 B.C.

Jurists. In the Augustan age M. Antistius Labeo and C. Ateius Capito headed two opposing schools in jurisprudence, Labeo being an advocate of method and reform, and Capito being a conservative and empiricist. The strife, which reflects the controversy between the "analogists" and the "anomalists" in philology, continued long after their death. Salvius Julianus was entrusted by Hadrian with the task of reducing into shape the immense mass of law which had grown up in the edicts of successive praetors—thus taking the first step towards a code. Sex. Pomponius, a contemporary, wrote an important legal manual of which fragments are preserved. The most celebrated handbook, however, is the *Institutiones* of Gaius, who lived under Antonius Pius—a model of what such treatises should be. The most eminent of all the Roman jurists was Aemilius Papinianus, the intimate friend of Septimius Severus; of his works only fragments remain. Other considerable writers were the prolific Domitius Ulpianus (*c.* 215) and Julius Paulus, his contemporary. The last juristical writer of note was Herennius Modestinus (*c.* 240). But though the line of great lawyers had ceased, the effects of their work remained and are clearly visible long after in the "codes"—the code of Theodosius (438) and the still more famous code of Justinian (529 and 533), with which is associated the name of Tribonianus.

BIBLIOGRAPHY.—The most full and satisfactory modern account of Latin literature is M. Schanz's *Geschichte der römischen Litteratur*. The best in English is the translation by C. C. Warr of W. S. Teuffel and L. Schwabe's *History of Roman Literature*. J. W. Mackail's short *History of Latin Literature* is full of excellent literary and aesthetic criticisms on the writers. C. Lamarre's *Histoire de la littérature latine* (1901, with specimens) only deals with the writers of the republic. W. Y. Sellar's *Roman Poets of the Republic and Poets of the Augustan Age*, and R. Y. Tyrrell's *Lectures on Latin Poetry*, will also be found of service. A concise account of the various Latin writers and their works, together with bibliographies, is given in J. E. B. Mayor's *Bibliographical Clue to Latin Literature* (1879), which is based on a German work by E. Hübner. See also the separate bibliographies to the articles on individual writers.

(W. Y. S.; J. P. P.)

LATINUS, in Roman legend, king of the aborigines in Latium, and eponymous hero of the Latin race. In Hesiod (*Theogony*, 1013) he is the son of Odysseus and Circe, and ruler of the Tyrsenians; in Virgil, the son of Faunus and the nymph Marica, a national genealogy being substituted for the Hesiodic, which probably originated from a Greek source. Latinus was a shadowy personality, invented to explain the origin of Rome and its relations with Latium, and only obtained importance in later times through his legendary connexion with Aeneas and the foundation of Rome. According to Virgil (*Aeneid*, vii. xii.), Aeneas, on landing at the mouth of the Tiber, was welcomed by Latinus, the peaceful ruler whose seat of government was Laurentum, and ultimately married his daughter Lavinia.

Other accounts of Latinus, differing considerably in detail, are to be found in the fragments of Cato's *Origines* (in Servius's commentary on Virgil) and in Dionysius of Halicarnassus; see further authorities in the article by J. A. Hild, in Daremberg and Saglio, *Dictionnaire des antiquités*.

LATITUDE (Lat. *latitudo*, *latus*, broad), a word meaning breadth or width, hence, figuratively, freedom from restriction, but more generally used in the geographical and astronomical sense here treated. The latitude of a point on the earth's surface is its angular distance from the equator, measured on the curved surface of the earth. The direct measure of this distance being impracticable, it has to be determined by astronomical observations. As thus determined it is the angle between the direction of the plumb-line at the place and the plane of the equator. This is identical with the angle between the horizontal planes at the place and at the equator, and also with the elevation of the celestial pole above the horizon (see ASTRONOMY). Latitude thus determined by the plumb-line is termed *astronomical*. The *geocentric latitude* of a place is the angle which the line from the earth's centre to the place makes with the plane of the equator. *Geographical latitude*, which is used in mapping, is based on the supposition that the earth is an elliptic spheroid of known compression, and is the angle which the normal to this spheroid makes with the equator. It differs from the astronomical latitude only in being corrected for local deviation of the plumb-line.

The latitude of a celestial object is the angle which the line drawn from some fixed point of reference to the object makes with the plane of the ecliptic.

Variability of Terrestrial Latitudes.—The latitude of a point on the earth's surface, as above defined, is measured from the equator. The latter is defined by the condition that its plane makes a right angle with the earth's axis of rotation. It follows that if the points in which this axis intersects the earth's surface, *i.e.* the poles of the earth, change their positions on the earth's surface, the position of the equator will also change, and therefore the latitudes of places will change also. About the end of the 19th century research showed that there actually was a very minute but measurable periodic change of this kind. The north and south poles, instead of being fixed points on the earth's surface, wander round within a circle about 50 ft. in diameter. The result is a variability of terrestrial latitudes generally.

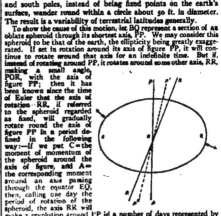

To show the cause of this motion, let BQ represent a section of an oblate spheroid through its shortest axis, PP. We may consider this spheroid to be that of the earth, the ellipticity being greatly exaggerated. If set in rotation around its axis of figure PP, it will continue to rotate around that axis for an indefinite time. But if, instead of rotating around PP, it rotates around some other axis, RR, making a small angle, POR, with the axis of figure PP; then it has been known since the time of Euler that the axis of rotation RR, if referred to the spheroid regarded as fixed, will gradually rotate round the axis of figure PP in a period defined in the following way:—If we put C = the moment of momentum of the spheroid around the axis of figure, and A = the corresponding moment around an axis passing through the equator EQ, then, calling one day the period of rotation of the spheroid, the axis RR will make a revolution around PP in a number of days represented by the fraction $C/(C-A)$. In the case of the earth, this ratio is 1/0·0032813 or 305. It follows that the period in question is 305 days.

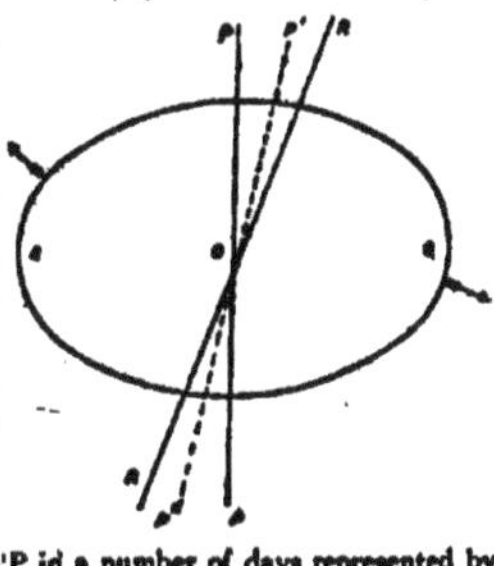

Up to 1890 the most careful observations and researches failed to establish the periodicity of such a rotation, though there was strong evidence of a variation of latitude. Then S. C. Chandler, from an elaborate discussion of a great number of observations, showed that there was really a variation of the latitude of the points of observation; but, instead of the period being 305 days, it was about 428 days. At first sight this period seemed to be inconsistent with dynamical theory. But a defect was soon found in the latter, the correction of which reconciled the divergence. In deriving a period of 305 days the earth is regarded as an absolutely rigid body, and no account is taken either of its elasticity or of the mobility of the ocean. A study of the figure will show that the centrifugal force round the axis RR will act on the equatorial protuberance of the rotating earth so as to make it tend in the direction of the arrows. A slight deformation of the earth will thus result; and the axis of figure of the distorted spheroid will no longer be PP, but a line P′P′ between PP and RR. As the latter moves round, P′P′ will continually follow it through the incessant change of figure produced by the change in the direction of the centrifugal force. Now the rate of motion of RR is determined by the actual figure at the moment. It is therefore less than the motion in an absolutely rigid spheroid in the proportion RP : RP. It is found that, even though the earth were no more elastic than steel, its yielding combined with the mobility of the ocean would make this ratio about 2 : 3, resulting in an increase of the period by one-half, making it about 457 days. Thus this small flexibility is even

the last seven years deviate but slightly from Chandler's formulae though they show a markedly smaller value of the annual term. In consequence, the change in the amplitude of the fluctuation through the seven-year period is not so well marked as before 1900.

Chandler's investigations are found in a series of papers published in the *Astronomical Journal*, vols. xi. to xv. and xviii. Newcomb's explanation of the lengthening of the Eulerian period is found in the *Monthly Notices of the Royal Astronomical Society* for March 1892. Later volumes of the *Astronomical Journal* contain discussions of the causes which may produce the annual fluctuation. An elaborate mathematical discussion of the theory is by Vito Volterra: "Sulla teoria dei movimenti del Polo terrestre" in the *Astronomische Nachrichten*, vol. 138; also, more fully in his memoir "Sur la théorie des variations des latitudes," *Acta Mathematica*, vol. xxii. The results of the international observations are discussed from time to time by Albrecht in the publications of the International Geodetic Association, and in the *Astronomische Nachrichten* (see also EARTH, FIGURE OF). (S. N.)

LATIUM,[1] in ancient geography, the name given to the portion of central Italy which was bounded on the N.W. by Etruria, on the S.W. by the Tyrrhenian Sea, on the S.E. by Campania, on the E. by Samnium and on the N.E. by the mountainous district inhabited by the Sabini, Aequi and Marsi. The name was, however, applied very differently at different times. Latium originally means the land of the Latini, and in this sense, which alone is in use historically, it was a tract of limited extent; but after the overthrow of the Latin confederacy, when the neighbouring tribes of the Rutuli, Hernici, Volsci and Aurunci, as well as the Latini properly so called, were reduced to the condition of subjects and citizens of Rome, the name of Latium was extended to comprise them all. It thus denoted the whole country from the Tiber to the mouth of the Savo, and just included the Mons Massicus, though the boundary was not very precisely fixed (see below). The change thus introduced, though already manifest in the composition of the Latin league (see below) was not formally established till the reign of Augustus, who formed of this larger Latium and Campania taken together the first region of Italy; but it is already recognized by Strabo (v. 3. 2. p. 228), as well as by Pliny, who terms the additional territory thus incorporated *Latium Adjectum*, while he designates the original Latium, extending from the Tiber to Circeii, as *Latium Antiquum*.

1. LATIUM ANTIQUUM consisted principally of an extensive plain, now known as the Campagna di Roma, bounded towards the interior by the Apennines, which rise very abruptly from the plains to a height of between 4000 and 5000 ft. Several of the Latin cities, including Tibur and Praeneste, were situated on the terrace-like underfalls of these mountains,[2] while Cora, Norba and Setia were placed in like manner on the slopes of the Volscian mountains (Monti Lepini), a rugged and lofty limestone range, which runs parallel to the main mass of the Apennines, being separated from them, however, by the valley of the Trerus (Sacco), and forms a continuous barrier from there to Terracina. No volcanic eruptions are known to have taken place in these mountains within the historic period, though Livy sometimes speaks of it "raining stones in the Alban hills" (I. 31, xxv. 9—on the latter occasion it even did so on the Aventine). It is asserted, too, that some of the earliest tombs of the necropolis of Alba Longa (*q.v.*) were found beneath a stratum of peperino. Earthquakes (not of a violent character within recent centuries, though the ruin of the Colosseum is probably to be ascribed to this cause) are not unknown even at the present day in Rome and in the Alban Hills, and a seismograph has been established at Rocca di Papa. The surface is by no means a uniform plain, but is a broad undulating tract, furrowed throughout by numerous depressions, with precipitous banks, serving as water-courses, though rarely traversed by any considerable stream. As the general level of the plain rises gradually, though almost imperceptibly, to the foot of the Apennines, these channels by degrees assume the character of ravines of a formidable description.

[1] *Latium*, from the same root as *lātus*, side; *later*, brick; πλατύς, flat; flat, broad: not connected with *lātus*, wide.

... time of Augustus the boundary of Latium extended as ... Treba (Trevi), 12 m. S.E. of Sublaqueum (Subiaco).

Geology. Four main periods may be distinguished in the geological history of Rome and the surrounding district. The hills on the right bank of the Tiber culminating in Monte Mario (455 ft.) belong to the first of these, being of the Pliocene formation, they consist of a lower bluish-grey clay and an upper group of yellow sands and gravels. This clay since Roman times has supplied the material for brick-making, and the valleys which now separate the different summits (Janiculum, Vatican, Monte Mario) are in considerable measure artificial On the left bank this clay has been reached at a lower level, at the foot of the Pincian Hill, while in the Campagna it has been found to extend below the later volcanic formations. The latter may be divided into two groups, corresponding to the second and third periods. In the second period volcanic activity occurred at the bottom of the Pliocene sea, and the tufa, which extends over the whole Campagna to a thickness of 300 ft. or more, was formed. At the same time, hot springs, containing abundant carbonate of lime in solution, produced deposits of travertine at various points. In the third, after the Campagna, by a great general uplift, had become a land surface, volcanic energy found an outlet in comparatively few large craters, which emitted streams of hard lava as well as fragmentary materials, the latter forming sperone (*lapis Gabinus*) and peperino (*lapis Albanus*), while upon one of the former, which runs from the Alban Hills to within 2 m. of Rome, the Via Appia was carried. The two main areas near Rome are formed by the group of craters on the north (Bracciano, Bolsena, &c.) and the Alban Hills on the south, the latter consisting of one great crater with a base about 12 m. in diameter, in the centre of which a smaller crater was later on built up (the basin is now known as the Campo di Annibale) with several lateral vents (the Lake of Albano, the Lake of Nemi, &c.). The Alban Mount (Monte Cavo) is almost the highest point on the rim of the inner crater, while Mount Algidus and Tusculum are on the outer ring wall of the larger (earlier) crater

The fourth period is that in which the various subaerial agencies of abrasion, and especially the streams which drain the mountain chain of the Apennines, have produced the present features of the Campagna, a plain furrowed by gullies and ravines. The communities which inhabited the detached hills and projecting ridges which later on formed the city of Rome were in a specially favourable position. These hills (especially the Palatine, the site of the original settlement) with their naturally steep sides, partly surrounded at the base by marshes and situated not far from the confluence of the Anio with the Tiber, possessed natural advantages not shared by the other primitive settlements of the district; and their proximity to one another rendered it easy to bring them into a larger whole The volcanic materials available in Rome and its neighbourhood were especially useful in building. The tufa, sperone and peperino were easy to quarry, and could be employed by those who possessed comparatively elementary tools, while travertine, which came into use later, was an excellent building stone, and the lava (*selce*) served for paving stones and as material for concrete The strength of the renowned Roman concrete is largely due to the use of pozzolana (see PUTEOLI), which also is found in plenty in the Campagna.

Between the volcanic tract of the Campagna and the sea there is a broad strip of sandy plain, evidently formed merely by the accumulation of sand from the sea, and constituting a barren tract, still covered almost entirely with wood as it was in ancient times, except for the almost uninterrupted line of villas along the ancient coast-line, which is now marked by a line of sandhills, some ½ m or more inland (see LAVINIUM, TIBER) This long belt of sandy shore extends without a break for a distance of above 30 m from the mouth of the Tiber to the promontory of Antium (Porto d'Anzio), a low rocky headland, projecting out into the sea, and forming the only considerable angle in this line of coast Thence again a low sandy shore of similar character, but with extensive shore lagoons which served in Roman times and serve still for fish-breeding, extends for about 24 m to the foot of the Monte Circeo (*Circeius Mons, q.v.*) The region of the Pomptine Marshes (*q.v.*) occupies almost the whole tract between the sandy belt on the sea-shore and the Volscian mountains, extending from the southern foot of the Alban Hills below Velletri to the sea near Terracina.

Drainage. The district sloping down from Velletri to the dead level of the Pontine (Pomptine) Marshes has not, like the western and northern slopes of the Alban Hills, drainage towards the Tiber The subsoil too is differently formed. the surface consists of very absorbent materials, then comes a stratum of less permeable tufa or peperino (sometimes clay is present), and below that again more permeable materials. In ancient, and probably pre-Roman, times this district was drained by an elaborate system of *cuniculi*, small drainage tunnels, about 5 ft high and 2 ft. wide, which ran, not at the bottom of the valleys, where there were sometimes streams already, and where, in any case, erosion would have broken through their roofs, but along their slopes, through the less permeable tufa, their object being to drain the hills on each side of the valleys. They had probably much to do with the relative healthiness of this district in early times. Some of them have been observed to be earlier in date than the Via Appia (312 B.C.). They were studied in detail by R. de la Blanchère When they fell into desuetude, malaria gained the upper hand, the lack of drainage providing breeding-places for the malarial mosquito. Remains of similar drainage channels exist in many parts of the Campagna Romana and of southern Etruria at points where the natural drainage was not sufficient, and especially in cultivated or inhabited hills (though it was not necessary here, as in the neighbourhood of Velletri, to create a drainage system, as streams and rivers were already present as natural collectors) and streams very frequently pass through them at the present day. The drainage channels which were dug for the various crater lakes in the neighbourhood of Rome are also interesting in this regard. That of the Alban Lake is the most famous; but all the other crater lakes are similarly provided. As the drainage by *cuniculi* removed the moisture in the subsoil, so the drainage of the lakes by *emissaria*, outlet channels at a low level, prevented the permeable strata below the tufa from becoming impregnated with moisture which they would otherwise have derived from the lakes of the Alban Hills. The slopes below Velletri, on the other hand, derive much of their moisture from the space between the inner and outer ring of the Alban volcano, which it was impossible to drain and this in turn receives much moisture from the basin of the extinct inner crater.[1]

Pre-historic remains. Numerous isolated palaeolithic objects of the Mousterian type have been found in the neighbourhood of Rome in the quaternary gravels of the Tiber and Anio, but no certain traces of the neolithic period have come to light, as the many flint implements found sporadically round Rome probably belong to the period which succeeded neolithic (called by Italian archaeologists the eneolithic period) inasmuch as both stone and metal (not, however, bronze, but copper) were in use[2] At Sgurgola, in the valley of the Sacco, a skeleton was found in a rock-cut tomb of this period which still bears traces of painting with cinnabar A similar rock-cut tomb was found at Mandela, in the Anio valley. Both are outside the limits of the Campagna in the narrower sense; but similar tombs were found (though less accurately observed) in travertine quarries between Rome and Tivoli. Objects of the Bronze age too have only been found sporadically The earliest cemeteries and hut foundations of the Alban Hills belong to the Iron age, and cemeteries and objects of a similar character have been found in Rome itself and in southern Etruria, especially the characteristic hut-urns. The objects found in these cemeteries show close affinity with those found in the terremare of Emilia, these last being of earlier date, and hence Pigorini and Helbig consider that the Latini were close descendants of the inhabitants of the terremare. On the other hand, the ossuaries of the Villanova type, while they occur as far south as Veii and Caere, have never so far been found on the left bank of the Tiber, in Latium proper (see L. Pigorini in *Rendiconti dei Lincei*, ser. v vol. xvi., 1907, p. 676, and xviii., 1909). We thus have at the beginning of the Iron age two distinct currents of civilization in central Italy, the Latin and that of Villanova. As to the dates to which these are to be attributed, there is not as yet complete accord, *e.g* some archaeologists assign to the 11th, others (and with far better reasons) to the 8th century B.C., the earliest tombs of the Alban necropolis and the coeval tombs of the necropolis recently discovered in the Forum at Rome. In this last necropolis cremation seems slightly to precede inhumation in date.

For the prehistoric period see *Bullettino di paleontologia Italiana*, *passim*, B. Modestov, *Introduction à l'histoire romaine* (Paris, 1907), and T. E. Peet, *The Stone and Bronze Ages in Italy* (Oxford, 1909).

Latin League. It is uncertain to what extent reliance can be placed upon the traditional accounts of the gradual spread of the supremacy of Rome in Latium, and the question cannot be discussed here[3] The list of the thirty communities belonging to the Latin league, given by Dionysius of Halicarnassus

[1] See R. de la Blanchère in Daremberg and Saglio, *Dictionnaire des antiquités*, s.vv *Cuniculus*, *Emissarium*, and the same author's *Chapitre d'histoire pontine* (Paris, 1889)

[2] See G. A. Colini in *Bullettino di paletnologia Italiana*, xxxi. (1905)

[3] The most important results will be found stated at the outset of the articles ROME *History* (the chief being that the Plebeians of Rome probably consisted of Latins and the Patricians of Sabines), LIGURIA, SICULI and ARICIA. For the Etruscan dominion in the Latin plain see ETRURIA Special mention may here be made of one or two points of importance The legends represent the Latins of the historical period as a fusion of different races, Ligures, Veneti and Siculi among them, the story of the alliance of the Trojan settler Aeneas with the daughter of Latinus, king of the aborigines, and the consequent enmity of the Rutulian prince Turnus, well known to readers of Virgil, is thoroughly typical of the reflection of these distant ethnical phenomena in the surviving traditions. In view of the historical significance of the NO- ethnicon (see SABINI) it is important to observe that the original form of the ethnic adjective no doubt appears in the title of *Juppiter Latiaris* (not *Latinus*); and that Virgil's description of the descent of the noble Drances at Latinus's court (Aen. xi 340)—*genus huic materna superbum Nobilitas dabat, incertum de patre ferebat*—indicates a very different system of family ties from the famous *patria potestas* and agnation of the Patrician and Sabine clans. (R. S C)

(v. 61), is, however, of great importance. It is considered by Th. Mommsen (*Roman History*, i. 445) that it dates from about the year 370 B.C., to which period belong the closing of the confederacy, no fresh communities being afterwards admitted to it, and the consequent fixing of the boundaries of Latium. The list is as follows: Ardeates, Aricini, Bovillani,[1] Bubentani, Cabani, Carventani, Circeienses, Coriolani, Corbintes, Corni (probably Corani), Fortinei (?), Gabini, Laurentini, Lavinates, Labicani, Lanuvini, Nomentani, Norbani, Praenestini, Pedani, Querquetulani, Satricani, Scaptini, Setini, Tellenii, Tiburtini, Tolerienses, Tusculani, Veliterni.

These communities may be briefly described according to their geographical arrangement. Laurentum and Lavinium, names so conspicuous in the legendary history of Aeneas, were situated in the strip near the sea-coast—the former only 8 m. S.E. of Ostia, which was from the first merely the port of Rome, and never figured as an independent city. Farther S.E. again lay Ardea, the ancient capital of the Rutuli, and some distance beyond that Antium, situated on the sea-coast, which does not occur in the list of Dionysius, and is, in the early annals of Rome, called a Volscian town—even a chief city. On the southern underfalls of the Alban mountains, commanding the plain at the foot, stood Lanuvium and Velitrae, Aricia rose on a neighbouring hill, and Corioli was probably situated on the lower slopes. The village of the Cabani (probably identical with the Cabenses) is possibly to be sought on the site of the modern Rocca di Papa, N. of Monte Cavo. The more important city of Tusculum occupied one of the northern summits of the same group, while opposite to it, in a commanding situation on a lofty offshoot of the Apennines, rose Praeneste, now Palestrina. Bola and Pedum were probably in the same neighbourhood, Labici on an outlying summit (Monte Compatri) of the Alban Hills below Tusculum, and Corbio (probably at Rocca Priora) on a rocky summit east of the same city. Tibur (Tivoli) occupied a height commanding the outlet of the river Anio. Corniculum, farther west, stood on the summit of one of three conical hills that rise abruptly out of the plain at the distance of a few miles from Monte Gennaro, the nearest of the Apennines, and which were thence known as the Montes Corniculani. Nomentum was a few miles farther north, between the Apennines and the Tiber, and close to the Sabine frontier. The boundary between the two nations was indeed in this part very fluctuating. Nearly in the centre of the plain of the Campagna stood Gabii; Bovillae was also in the plain, but close to the Appian Way, where it begins to ascend the Alban Hills. Several other cities—Tellenae, Scaptia and Querquetulum—mentioned in the list of Dionysius were probably situated in the Campagna, but the site cannot be determined. Satricum, on the other hand, was certainly south of the Alban Hills, between Velitrae and Antium; while Cora, Norba and Setia (all of which retain their ancient names with little modification) crowned the rocky heights which form advanced posts from the Volscian mountains towards the Pontine Marshes. Carventum possibly occupied the site of Rocca Massima N. of Cori, and Tolerium was very likely at Valmontone in the valley of the Sacco (anc. Trerus or Tolerus). The cities of the Bubentani and Fortinei are quite unknown.

A considerable number of the Latin cities had before 370 B.C. either been utterly destroyed or reduced to subjection by Rome, and had thus lost their independent existence. Such were Antemnae and Caenina, both of them situated within a few miles of Rome to the N., the conquest of which was ascribed to Romulus, Fidenae, about 5 m. N. of the city, and close to the Tiber, and Crustumerium, in the hilly tract farther north towards the Sabine frontier. Suessa Pometia also, on the borders of the Pontine Marshes, to which it was said to have given name, was a city of importance, the destruction of which was ascribed to Tarquinius Superbus. In any case it had disappeared before 370 B.C., as it does not occur in the list of the Latin league attributable to that date. It is probably to be sought between Velletri and Cisterna. But by far the most important of these extinct cities was Alba, on the lake to which it gave its name, which was, according to universally received tradition, the parent of Rome, as well as of numerous other cities within the limits of Latium, including Gabii, Fidenae, Collatia, Nomentum and other well-known towns. Whether or not this tradition deserves to rank as historical, it appears certain that at a still earlier period there existed a confederacy of thirty towns, of which Alba was the supreme head. A list of those who were wont to participate in the sacrifices on the Alban Mount is given us by Pliny (*N.H.* iii. 5. 69) under the name of *populi albenses*, which includes only six or at most eight of those found in the list of Dionysius,[2] and these for the most part among the more obscure and least known of the names given by him. Many of the rest are unknown, while the more powerful cities of Aricia, Lanuvium and Tusculum, though situated immediately on the Alban Hills, are not included, and appear to have maintained a wholly independent position. This earlier league was doubtless broken up by the fall of Alba, it was probably the increasing power of the Volsci and Aequi that led to the formation of the later league, including all the more powerful cities of Latium, as well as to the alliance concluded by them with the Romans in the consulship of Spurius Cassius (493 B.C.). Other cities of the Latin league had already (according to the traditional dates) received Latin colonies—Velitrae (494 B.C.), Norba (492), Ardea (442), Labici (418), Circei (393), Satricum (385), Setia (382).

The cities of the Latin league continued to hold general meetings or assemblies from time to time at the grove of the Aqua Ferentina, a sanctuary at the foot of the Alban Hills, perhaps in a valley below Marino, while they had also a common place of worship on the summit of the Alban Mount (Monte Cavo), where stood the celebrated temple of Jupiter Latiaris. The participation in the annual sacrifices at this sanctuary was regarded as typical of a Latin city (hence the name "prisci Latini" given to the participating peoples), and they continued to be celebrated long after the Latins had lost their independence and been incorporated in the Roman state.[3]

Roman supremacy.

We are on firmer ground in dealing with the spread of the supremacy of Rome in Latium when we take account of the foundation of new colonies and of the formation of new tribes, processes which as a rule go together. The information that we have as to the districts in which the sixteen earliest clans (*tribus rusticae*)[4] were settled shows us that, except along the Tiber, Rome's dominion extended hardly more than 5 m. beyond the city gates (Mommsen, *History of Rome*, i. 58). Thus, towards the N. and E. we find the towns of Antemnae, Fidenae, Caenina and Gabii,[5] on the S.E., towards Alba, the boundary of Roman territory was at the Fossae Cluiliae, 5 m. from Rome, where Coriolanus encamped (Livy ii. 39), and, on the S., towards Laurentum at the 6th mile, where sacrifice to Terminus was made (Ovid, *Fasti*, ii. 682): the Ambarvalia too were celebrated even in Strabo's day (v. 3. 3. p. 230) at a place called Φῆστοι between the 5th and 6th mile. The identification (cf. Hulsen in Pauly-Wissowa, *Realencyclopädie*, vi. 2223) of this locality with the grove of the Arval brothers at the 5th mile of the Via Portuensis, to the W. of Rome, and of the Ambarvalia with the festival celebrated by this brotherhood in May of each year, is now generally accepted. But Roman sway must either from the first, or very soon, have extended to Ostia, the port of Rome at the mouth of the Tiber and it was as the emporium of Latium that Rome acquired her first importance.[6]

[1] The MSS. read Βοιλλανῶν or Βοιλανῶν the Latin translation has Bolanorum. It is difficult to say which is to be preferred. The list gives only twenty-nine names, and Mommsen proposes to insert Signini.

[2] Albani, Aesolani (probably E. of Tibur), Accienses, Abolani, Bubetani, Bolani, Cusuetani (Carventani ?), Coriolani, Fidenates, Foreti (Fortinei ?), Hortenses (near Corbio), Latinienses (near Rome itself), Longani, Manates, Macrales, Munienses (Castrimoenienses ?), Numinienses, Olliculani, Octulani, Pedani, Polletaurini, Querquetulani, Sicani, Sisolenses, Tolerienses, Tutienses (not, one would think, connected with the small stream called Tutia at the 6th mile of the Via Salaria, Liv. xxvi. 11), Vimitellari, Velienses, Venetulani, Vitellenses (not far from Corbio).

[3] To an earlier stage of the Latin league, perhaps to about 430 B.C. (Mommsen, *op. cit.* 445 n. 2) belongs the dedication of the grove of Diana by a *dictator Latinus*, in the name of the people of Tusculum, Aricia, Lanuvium, Laurentum, Cora, Tibur, Suessa Pometia and Ardea.

[4] Of the *gentes* from which these tribes took their names, six entirely disappeared in later days, while the other ten can be traced as patrician—a proof that the patricians were not noble families in origin (Mommsen, *Römische Forschungen*, i. 106). For the tribes see W. Kubitschek, *De Romanarum tribuum origine* (Vienna, 1882).

[5] We have various traces of the early antagonism to Gabii, *e.g.* the opposition between *ager Romanus* and *ager Gabinus* in the augural law.

[6] For the early extension of Roman territory towards the sea, cf. Festus, p. 213, Müll., *s.v.* "Pectuscum:" *Pectuscum Palati dicta est ea regio urbis, quam Romulus obversam posuit, ea parte, in qua plurimum erat agri Romani ad mare versus et qua mollissime adibatur Urbs, cum Etruscorum agrum a Romano Tiberis discluderet, ceterae vicinae civitates colles aliquos haberent oppositos.*

The boundary of the *Ager Romanus antiquus* towards the north-west is similarly fixed by the festival of the Robigalia at the 5th milestone of the Via Clodia. Within this area fall the districts inhabited by the earliest tribes, so far as these are known to us. The *tribus Romilia* was settled on the right bank of the Tiber near the sanctuary of the Arvales, the *Galeria* perhaps a little farther west on the lower course of the stream now known as Galera, and the *Fabia* perhaps on the Cremera towards Veii. We know that the *pagus Lemonius* was on the Via Latina, and that the *tribus Pupinia* dwelt between Tusculum and the city, while the territory of the *Papiria* possibly lay nearer Tusculum, as it was to this tribe that the Roman citizens in Tusculum belonged in later days. It is possible that the *Camilia* was situated in the direction of Tibur, inasmuch as this town was afterwards enrolled in this tribe. The *tribus Claudia*, probably the last of the 16 older *tribus rusticae*, was according to tradition founded in 504 B.C. Its territory lay beyond the Anio, between Fidenae and Ficulea (Liv. ii. 16, Dion. Hal. v. 40). The locality of the *pagi* round which the other tribes were grouped is not known to us.

The primitive tribes.

With the earliest extensions of the Roman territory coincided the first beginnings of the Roman road system. The road to Ostia may have existed from the first but after the Latin communities on the lower Anio had fallen under the dominion of Rome, we may well believe that the first portion of the Via Salaria, leading to Antemnae, Fidenae (the fall of which is placed by tradition in 428 B.C.) and Crustumerium, came into existence. The formation (according to the traditional dating in 495 or 471 B.C.) of the *tribus Clustumina* (the only one of the earlier twenty-one tribes which bears a local name) is both a consequence of an extension of territory and of the establishment of the assembly of the plebs by tribes, for which an inequality of the total number of divisions was desirable (Mommsen, *History of Rome*, i. 360). The correlative of the Via Salaria was the Via Campana, so called because it led past the grove of the Arvales along the right bank of the Tiber to the Campus Salinarum Romanarum,[1] the salt marshes, from which the Via Salaria took its name, inasmuch as it was the route by which Sabine traders came from the interior to fetch the salt. To this period would also belong the Via Ficulensis, leading to Ficulea, and afterwards prolonged to Nomentum, and the Via Collatina, which led to Collatia. Gabii became Roman in fairly early times, though at what period is uncertain, and with its subjugation must have originated the Via Gabina, afterwards prolonged to Praeneste. The Via Latina too must be of very early origin, and tradition places the foundation of the Latin colony at Signia (to which it led) as early as 495 B.C. Not long after the capture of Fidenae, the main outpost of Veii, the chief city itself fell (396 B.C.) and a road (still traceable) was probably made thither. There was also probably a road to Caere in early times, inasmuch as we hear of the flight of the Vestals thither in 389 B.C. The origin of the rest of the roads is no doubt to be connected with the gradual establishment of the Latin league. We find that while the later (long distance) roads bear as a rule the name of their constructor, all the short distance roads on the left bank of the Tiber bear the names of towns which belonged to the league—Nomentum, Tibur, Praeneste, Labici, Ardea, Laurentum—while Ficulea and Collatia do not appear. The Via Pedana, leading to Pedum, is known to us only from an inscription (*Bull. Soc. Antiquaires de France*, 1905, p. 177) discovered in Tunisia in 1905, and may be of much later origin, it was a branch of the Via Praenestina. There must too have been a road, along the line of the later Via Appia, to Bovillae, Aricia, Lanuvium and Velitrae, going thence to Cora, Norba and Setia along the foot of the Volscian Mountains, while nameless roads, which can still be traced, led direct from Rome to Satricum and to Lavinium.

Road system.

We can trace the advance of the Roman supremacy with greater ease after 387 B.C., inasmuch as from this year (adopting the traditional dating for what it is worth) until 299 B.C. every accession of territory is marked by the foundation of a group of new tribes, the limit of 35 in all was reached in the latter year. In 387, after the departure of the Gauls, southern Etruria was conquered, and four new tribes were formed: *Arnensis* (probably derived from Aro, mod. Arrone—though the ancient name does not occur in literature—the stream which forms the outlet to the lake of Bracciano, anc. *Lacus Sabatinus*),[2] *Sabatina* (called after this lake), *Stellatina* (named from the Campus Stellatinus, near Capena, cf. Festus p. 343 Müll.) and *Tromentina* (which, Festus tells us, was so called from the Campus Tromentus, the situation of which we do not know). Four years later were founded the Latin colonies of Sutrium and Nepet. In 358 B.C. Roman preponderance in the Pomptine territory was shown by the formation of the *tribus Pomptina* and *Publilia*, while in 338 and 329 respectively Antium and Tarracina became colonies of Roman citizens, the former having been founded as a Latin colony in 494 B.C.

[1] The ancient name is known from an inscription discovered in 1888.

[2] So Kubitschek in Pauly-Wissowa, *Realencyclopädie*, ii. 1204.

After the dissolution of the Latin league which followed upon the defeat of the united forces of the Samnites and of those Latin and Volscian cities which had revolted against Rome, two new tribes, *Maecia* and *Scaptia*,[3] were created in 332 B.C. in connexion with the distribution of the newly acquired lands (Mommsen, *History*, i. 462). A further advance in the same direction ending in the capture of Privernum in 329 B.C. is marked by the establishment in 318 B.C. of the *tribus Oufentina* (from the river Ufens which runs below Setia, mod. *Sezze*, and Privernum, mod. *Piperno*, and the *tribus Falerna* (in the Ager Falernus), while the foundation of the colonies of Cales (334) and Fregellae (328) secured the newly won south Volscian and Campanian territories and led no doubt to a prolongation of the Via Latina. The moment had now come for the pushing forward of another line of communication, which had no doubt reached Tarracina in 329 B.C. but was now definitely constructed (*munita*) as a permanent military highway as far as Capua in 312 B.C. by Appius Claudius, after whom it was named. To him no doubt is due the direct line of road through the Pontine Marshes from Velitrae to Terracina. Its construction may fairly be taken to mark the period at which the roads of which we have spoken, hitherto probably mere tracks, began to be transformed into real highways. In the same year (312) the colony of Interamna Lirenas was founded, while Luceria, Suessa (Aurunca) and Saticula had been established a year or two previously. Sora followed nine years later. In 299 B.C. further successes led to the establishment of two new tribes—the *Teretina* in the upper valley of the Trerus (Sacco) and the *Aniensis*, in the upper valley of the Anio—while to about the same time we must attribute the construction of two new military roads, both secured by fortresses. The southern road, the Via Valeria led to Carsioli and Alba Fucens (founded as Latin colonies respectively in 298 and 303 B.C.), and the northern (afterwards the Via Flaminia[4]) to Narnia (founded as a Latin colony in 299 B.C.). There is little doubt that the formation of the *tribus Quirina* (deriving its name possibly from the town of Cures) and the *tribus Velina* (from the river Velinus, which forms the well-known waterfalls near Terni) is to be connected with the construction of the latter high road, though its date is not certainly known. The further history of Roman supremacy in Italy will be found in the article ROME: *History*. We notice, however, that the continual warfare in which the Roman state was engaged led to the decadence of the free population of Latium, and that the extension of the empire of Rome was fatal to the prosperity of the territory which immediately surrounded the city.[5]

What had previously, it seems, been a well-peopled region, with peasant proprietors, kept healthy by careful drainage, became in the 4th and 3rd centuries B.C. a district consisting in large measure of huge estates (*latifundia*) owned by the Roman aristocracy, cultivated by gangs of slaves. This led to the disappearance of the agricultural population, to a decline in public safety, and to the spread of malaria in many parts, indeed, it is quite possible that it was not introduced into Latium before the 4th century B.C. The evil increased in the later period of the Republic, and many of the old towns of Latium sank into a very decayed condition, with this the continual competition of the provinces as sources of food-supply no doubt had a good deal to do. Cicero

Causes of depopulation.

[3] Festus tells us (p. 136 Müll.) that the Maecia derived its name "a quodam castro." Scaptia was the only member of the Latin league that gave its name to a tribe.

[4] See FLAMINIA, VIA and VALERIA, VIA.

[5] L. Caetani indeed (*Nineteenth Century and After*, 1908) attributes the economic decadence of the Roman Campagna to the existence of free trade throughout the Roman empire.

speaks of Gabii, Labici and Bovillae as places that had fallen into abject poverty, while Horace refers to Gabii and Fidenae as mere "deserted villages," and Strabo as "once fortified towns, but now villages, belonging to private individuals." Many of the smaller places mentioned in the list of Dionysius, or the early wars of the Romans, had altogether ceased to exist, but the statement of Pliny that fifty-three communities (*populi*) had thus perished within the boundaries of Old Latium is perhaps exaggerated. By the end of the Republic a good many parts of Latium were infected, and Rome itself was highly malarious in the warm months (see W. H. S. Jones in *Annals of Archaeology and Anthropology*, ii. 97, Liverpool, 1909). The emperors Claudius, Nerva and Trajan turned their attention to the district, and under their example and exhortation the Roman aristocracy erected numerous villas within its boundaries, and used them at least for summer residences. During the 2nd century the Campagna seems to have entered on a new era of prosperity The system of roads radiating in all directions from Rome (see ITALY: *History*, § B) belonged to a much earlier period, but they were connected by a network of crossroads (now mostly abandoned, while the main lines are still almost all in use) leading to the very numerous villas with which the Campagna was strewn (even in districts which till recently were devastated by malaria), and which seem in large measure to belong to this period. Some of these are of enormous extent, *e.g* the villa of the Quintilii on the Via Appia, that known as Setta Bassi on the Via Latina, and that of Hadrian near Tibur, the largest of all.

When the land tax was introduced into Italy in 292, the first region of Augustus obtained the name of *provincia Campania*. Later on the name Latium entirely disappeared, and the name Campania extended as far as Veii and the Via Aurelia, whence the medieval and modern name Campagna di Roma. The donation made by Constantine to various churches of Rome of numerous estates belonging to the *patrimonium Caesaris* in the neighbourhood of Rome was of great historical importance, as being the origin of the territorial dominion of the papacy. His example was followed by others, so that the church property in the Campagna soon became considerable; and, owing to the immunities and privileges which it enjoyed, a certain revival of prosperity ensued. The invasions of the barbarian hordes did great harm, but the formation of centres (*domusculiae*) in the 8th and 9th centuries was a fact of great importance. the inhabitants, indeed, formed the medieval militia of the papacy Smaller centres (the *colonia*—often formed in the remains of an ancient villa—the *curtis* or *curia*, the *castrum*, the *casale*) grew up later. We may note that, owing to the growth of the temporal power of the popes, there was never a *dux Romae* dependent on the exarchate of Ravenna, similar to those established by Narses in the other districts of Italy.

The papal influence was also retained by means of the suburban bishoprics, which took their rise as early as the 4th and 5th centuries. The rise of the democratic commune of Rome[1] about 1143 and of the various trade corporations which we already find in the early 11th century led to struggles with the papacy; the commune of Rome made various attempts to exercise supremacy in the Campagna and levied various taxes from the 12th century until the 15th. The commune also tried to restrict the power of the barons, who, in the 13th century especially, though we find them feudatories of the holy see from the 10th century onwards, threatened to become masters of the whole territory, which is still dotted over with the baronial castles and lofty solitary towers of the rival families of Rome—Orsini, Colonna, Savelli, Conti, Caetani—who ruthlessly destroyed the remains of earlier edifices to obtain materials for their own, and whose castles, often placed upon the high roads, thus following a strategic line to a stronghold in the country, did not contribute to the undisturbed security of traffic upon them, but rather led to their abandonment. On a list of the inhabited centres of the Campagna of the 14th century with the amount of salt (which was a monopoly of the commune of Rome) consumed by each, Tomassetti bases an estimate of the population. this was about equal to that of our own times, but differently distributed, some of the smaller centres having disappeared at the expense of the towns. Several of the popes, as Sixtus IV and Julius III, made unsuccessful attempts to improve the condition of the Campagna, the former making a serious attempt to revive agriculture as against pasture, while in the latter part of the 16th century a line of watch-towers was erected along the coast. In the Renaissance, it is true, falls the erection of many fine villas in the neighbourhood of Rome—not only in the hills round the Campagna, but even in certain places in the lower ground, *e.g* those of Julius II. at La Magliana and of Cardinal Trivulzio at Salone,—and these continued to be frequented until the end of the 18th century, when the French Revolution dealt a fatal blow to the prosperity of the Roman nobility The 17th and 18th centuries, however, mark the worst period of depopulation in the more malarious parts of the Campagna, which seems to have begun in the 15th century, though we hear of malaria throughout the middle ages. The most healthy portions of the territory are in the north and east, embracing the slopes of the Apennines which are watered by the Teverone and Sacco, and the most pestilential is the stretch between the Monti Lepini and the sea. The Pontine Marshes (*q.v.*) included in the latter division, were drained, according to the plan of Bolognini, by Pius VI., who restored the ancient Via Appia to traffic, but though they have returned to pasture and cultivation, their insalubrity is still notorious. The soil in many parts is very fertile and springs are plentiful and abundant the water is in some cases sulphureous or ferruginous. In summer, indeed, the vast expanse is little better than an arid steppe, but in the winter it furnishes abundant pasture to flocks of sheep from the Apennines and herds of silver-grey oxen and shaggy black horses, and sheep passing in the summer to the mountain pastures. A certain amount of horse-breeding is done, and the government has, as elsewhere in Italy, a certain number of stallions Efforts have been made since 1882 to cure the waterlogged condition of the marshy grounds. The methods employed have been three—(i) the cutting of drainage channels and clearing the marshes by pumping, the method principally employed, (ii) the system of warping, *i.e.* directing a river so that it may deposit its sedimentary matter in the lower-lying parts, thus levelling them up and consolidating them, and then leading the water away again by drainage, (iii.) the planting of firs and eucalyptus trees, *e.g.* at Tre Fontane and elsewhere. These efforts have not been without success, though it cannot be affirmed that the malarial Campagna is anything like healthy yet The regulation of the rivers, more especially of the Tiber, is probably the most efficient method for coping with the problem. Since 1884 the Italian Government have been systematically enclosing, pumping dry and generally draining the marshes of the Agro Romano, that is, the tracts around Ostia, the Isola Sacra, at the mouth of the Tiber, and Maccarese. Of the whole of the Campagna less than one-tenth comes annually under the plough In its picturesque desolation, contrasting so strongly with its prosperity in Roman times, immediately surrounding a city of over half a million inhabitants, and with lofty mountains in view from all parts of it, it is one of the most interesting districts in the world, and has a peculiar and indefinable charm The modern province of Rome (forming the *compartimento* of Lazio) includes also considerable mountain districts, extending as far N.W as the Lake of Bolsena, and being divided on the N E. from Umbria by the Tiber, while on the E. it includes a considerable part of the Sabine mountains and Apennines. The ancient district of the Hernicans, of which Alatri is regarded as the centre, is known as the Ciociaria, from a kind of sandals (*cioce*) worn by the peasants. On the S.E too a considerable proportion of the group of the Lepini belongs to the province. The land is for the most part let by the proprietors to *mercanti di Campagna*, who employ a subordinate class of factors (*fattori*) to manage their affairs on the spot

Under the commune.

Modern conditions.

[1] The commune of Rome as such seems to have been in existence in 999 at least.

The recent discovery that the malaria which has hitherto rendered parts of the Campagna almost uninhabitable during the summer is propagated by the mosquito (*Anopheles claviger*) marks a new epoch; the most diverse theories as to its origin had hitherto been propounded, but it is now possible to combat it on a definite plan, by draining the marshes, protecting the houses by fine mosquito-proof wire netting (for *Anopheles* is not active by day), improving the water supply, &c., while for those who have fever, quinine (now sold cheaply by the state) is a great specific. A great improvement is already apparent; and a law carried in 1903 for the *Bonifica dell' Agro Romano* compels the proprietors within a radius of some 6 m. of Rome to cultivate their lands in a more productive way than has often hitherto been the case, exemption from taxes for ten years and loans at 2½% from the government being granted to those who carry on improvements, and those who refuse being expropriated compulsorily. The government further resolved to open roads and schools and provide twelve additional doctors. Much is done in contending against malaria by the Italian Red Cross Society. In 1900 31% of the inhabitants of the Agro Romano had been fever-stricken; since then the figure has rapidly decreased (5·1% in 1905).

Malaria.

The wheat crop in 1906 in the Agro Romano was 8,108,500 bushels, the Indian corn 3,314,000 bushels, the wine 12,100,000 gallons and the olive oil 1,980,000 gallons,—these last two from the hill districts. The wine production had declined by one-half from the previous year, exportation having fallen off in the whole country. 1907, however, was a year of great overproduction all over Italy. The wine of the Alban hills is famous in modern as in ancient times, but will not as a rule bear exportation. The forests of the Alban hills and near the coast produce much charcoal and light timber, while the Sabin and Volscian hills have been largely deforested and are now bare limestone rocks. Much of the labour in the winter and spring is furnished by peasants who come down from the Volscian and Hernican mountains, and from Abruzzi, and occupy sometimes caves, but more often the straw or wicker huts which are so characteristic a feature of the Campagna. The fixed population of the Campagna in the narrower sense (as distinct from the hills) is less than 1000. Emigration to America, especially from the Volscian and Hernican towns, is now considerable.

Produce.

2. Latium Novum or Adjectum, as it is termed by Pliny, comprised the territories occupied in earlier times by the Volsci and Hernici. It was for the most part a rugged and mountainous country, extending at the back of Latium proper, from the frontier of the Sabines to the sea-coast between Terracina and Sinuessa. But it was not separated from the adjacent territories by any natural frontier or physical boundaries, and it is only by the enumeration of the towns in Pliny according to the division of Italy by Augustus that we can determine its limits. It included the Hernican cities of Anagnia, Ferentinum, Alatrium and Verulae—a group of mountain strongholds on the north side of the valley of the Trerus (Sacco); together with the Volscian cities on the south of the same valley, and in that of the Liris, the whole of which, with the exception of its extreme upper end, was included in the Volscian territory. Here were situated Signia, Frusino, Fabrateria, Fregellae, Sora, Arpinum, Atina, Aquinum, Casinum and Interamna; Anxur (Terracina) was the only seaport that properly belonged to the Volscians, the coast from thence to the mouth of the Liris being included in the territory of the Aurunci, or Ausones as they were termed by Greek writers; who possessed the maritime towns of Fundi, Formiae, Caieta and Minturnae, together with Suessa in the interior, which had replaced their more ancient capital of Aurunca. Sinuessa, on the sea-coast between the Liris (Garigliano) and the Vulturnus, at the foot of the Monte Massico, was the last town in Latium according to the official use of the term and was sometimes assigned to Campania, while Suessa was more assigned to Latium. On the other hand, as Nissen points out (*Italische Landeskunde*, ii. 564), the Pons Campanus, by which the Via Appia crossed the Savo some 9 m. S.E. of Sinuessa, indicates by its name the position of the old Campanian frontier. In the interior the boundary fell between Casinum and Teanum Sidicinum, at about the 100th milestone of the Via Latina—a fact which led later to the jurisdiction of the Roman courts being extended on every side to the 100th mile from the city, and to this being the limit beyond which banishment from Rome was considered to begin.

Though the Apennines comprised within the boundaries of Latium do not rise to a height approaching that of the loftiest summits of the central range, they attain to a considerable altitude, and form steep and rugged mountain masses from 4000 to 5000 ft. high. They are traversed by three principal valleys: (1) that of the Anio, now called Teverone, which descends from above Subiaco to Tivoli, where it enters the plain of the Campagna; (2) that of the Trerus (Sacco), which has its source below Palestrina (Praeneste), and flows through a comparatively broad valley that separates the main mass of the Apennines from the Volscian mountains or Monti Lepini, till it joins the Liris below Ceprano; (3) that of the Liris (Garigliano), which enters the confines of New Latium about 20 m. from its source, flows past the town of Sora, and has a very tortuous course from thence to the sea at Minturnae; its lower valley is for the most part of considerable width, and forms a fertile tract of considerable extent, bordered on both sides by hills covered with vines, olives and fruit trees, and thickly studded with towns and villages.

It may be observed that, long after the Latins had ceased to exist as a separate people we meet in Roman writers with the phrase of *nomen Latinum*, used not in an ethnical but a purely political sense, to designate the inhabitants of all those cities on which the Romans had conferred "Latin rights" (*jus Latinum*)—an inferior form of the Roman franchise, which had been granted in the first instance to certain cities of the Latins, when they became subjects of Rome, and was afterwards bestowed upon many other cities of Italy, especially the so-called Latin colonies. At a later period the same privileges were extended to places in other countries also—as for instance to most of the cities in Sicily and Spain. All persons enjoying these rights were termed in legal phraseology *Latini* or *Latinae conditionis*.

Authorities.—For the topography of Latium, and the local history of its more important cities, the reader may consult Sir W. Gell's *Topography of Rome and its Vicinity* (2nd ed., 1 vol., London, 1846); A. Nibby, *Analisi storico-topografico-antiquaria della carta dei dintorni di Roma* (3 vols., 2nd ed., 1848); J. Westphal, *Die römische Kampagne* (Berlin, 1829); A. Bormann, *Alt-lateinische Chorographie und Städte-Geschichte* (Halle, 1852); M. Zoeller, *Latium und Rom* (Leipzig, 1878); R. Burn's *Rome and the Campagna* (London, 1871); H. Dessau, *Corp. Inscr. Lat.* v. xiv. (Berlin, 1887) (Latium); Th. Mommsen, *Corp. Inscr. Lat.* vol. x. pp. 498-675 (Berlin, 1883); G. Tomassetti, "Della Campagna Romana nel medioevo," published in the *Archivio della Società Romana di Storia Patria* (Rome, 1874-1907), and separately (a work dealing with the medieval history and topography of the Campagna in great detail, containing also valuable notices of the classical period); by the same author, *La Campagna romana* (Rome, 1910 foll.); R. A. Lanciani, "I Comentari di Frontino intorno agli acquedotti," *Memorie dei Lincei* (Rome, 1880), serie iii. vol. v. p. 215 sqq. (and separately), also many articles, and *Wanderings in the Roman Campagna* (London, 1909); E. Abbate, *Guida della provincia di Roma* (Rome, 1894, 2 vols.); H. Nissen, *Italische Landeskunde*, ii. (Berlin, 1902), 557 sqq.; T. Ashby, "The Classical Topography of the Roman Campagna," in *Papers of the British School at Rome*, i., iii.-v. (London, 1902 foll.). (T. As.)

LATONA (Lat. form of Gr. Λητώ, Leto), daughter of Coeus and Phoebe, mother of Apollo and Artemis. The chief seats of her legend are Delos and Delphi, and the generally accepted tradition is a union of the legends of these two places. Leto, pregnant by Zeus, seeks for a place of refuge to be delivered. After long wandering she reaches the barren isle of Delos, which, according to Pindar (Frag. 87, 88), was a wandering rock borne about by the waves till it was fixed to the bottom of the sea for the birth of Apollo and Artemis. In the oldest forms of the legend Hera is not mentioned; but afterwards the wanderings of Leto are ascribed to the jealousy of that goddess, enraged at her amour with Zeus. The foundation of Delphi follows immediately on the birth of the god; and on the sacred way between Tempe and Delphi the giant Tityus offers violence to Leto, and is immediately slain by the arrows of Apollo and Artemis (*Odyssey*, xi. 576-581; Apollodorus i. 4). Such are the main facts of the Leto legend in its common literary form, which is due especially to the two Homeric hymns to Apollo. But Leto is a real goddess, not a mere mythological figure. The honour paid to her in Delphi and Delos might be explained as part of the cult of her son Apollo; but temples to her existed in Argos, in Mantineia and in Xanthus in Lycia; her sacred grove was on the coast of Crete. In Lycia graves are frequently placed under her protection, and she is also known as a goddess of fertility and as κουροτρόφος. It is to be observed that she appears far more conspicuously in the Apolline myths than in those which grew round the great centres of Artemis worship, the reason being that the idea of Apollo and Artemis as twins is one of later growth on Greek soil. Lycia, one of the chief seats of the cult of Apollo, where most frequent traces are found of the worship of Leto as the great goddess, was probably the earliest home of her religion.

In Greek art Leto usually appears carrying her children in her arms, pursued by the dragon sent by the jealous Hera, which is slain by the infant Apollo, in vase paintings especially she is often represented with Apollo and Artemis. The statue of Leto in the Letoon at Argos was the work of Praxiteles.

LATOUCHE, HYACINTHE JOSEPH ALEXANDRE THABAUD DE [known as HENRI] (1785–1851), French poet and novelist, was born at La Châtre (Indre) on the 2nd of February 1785. Among his works may be distinguished his comedies: *Projets de sagesse* (1811), and, in collaboration with Émile Deschamps, *Selmours de Florian* (1818), which ran for a hundred nights, also *La Reine d'Espagne* (1831), which proved too indecent for the public taste; a novel, *Fragoletta: Naples et Paris en 1799* (1829), which attained a success of notoriety; *Le Vallée aux loups* (1833), a volume of prose essays and verse; and two volumes of poems, *Les Adieux* (1843) and *Les Agrestes* (1844). Latouche's chief claim to remembrance is that he revealed to the world the genius of André Chénier, then only known to a limited few. The remains of the poet's work had passed from the hands of Daunou to Latouche, who had sufficient critical insight instantly to recognize their value. In editing the first selection of Chénier's poems (1819) he made some trifling emendations, but did not, as Béranger afterwards asserted, make radical and unnecessary changes. Latouche was guilty of more than one literary fraud. He caused a licentious story of his own to be attributed to the duchesse de Duras, the irreproachable author of *Ourika*. He made many enemies by malicious attacks on his contemporaries. The *Constitutionnel* was suppressed in 1817 by the government for an obscure political allusion in an article by Latouche. He then undertook the management of the *Mercure du XIXe siècle*, and began a bitter warfare against the monarchy. After 1830 he edited the *Figaro*, and spared neither the liberal politicians nor the romanticists who triumphed under the monarchy of July. In his turn he was violently attacked by Gustave Planche in the *Revue des deux mondes* for November 1831. But it must be remembered to the credit of Latouche that he did much to encourage George Sand at the beginning of her career. The last twenty years of his life were spent in retirement at Aulnay, where he died on the 9th of March 1851.

Sainte-Beuve, in the *Causeries du lundi*, vol. 3, gives a not too sympathetic portrait of Latouche. See also George Sand in the *Siècle* for the 18th, 19th and 20th of July 1851.

LA TOUR, MAURICE QUENTIN DE (1704–1788), French pastellist, was born at St Quentin on the 5th of September 1704. After leaving Picardy for Paris in 1727 he entered the studio of Spoède—an upright man, but a poor master, rector of the academy of St Luke, who still continued, in the teeth of the Royal Academy, the traditions of the old gild of the master painters of Paris. This possibly contributed to the adoption by La Tour of a line of work foreign to that imposed by an academical training, for pastels, though occasionally used, were not a [illegible] and distinct branch of work until 1720, when Rosalba [illegible] brought them into fashion with the Parisian world. [illegible] La Tour exhibited the first of that splendid series of a [illegible] portraits which formed the glory of the Salon [illegible] thirty-seven years. In 1746 he was received [illegible] and in 1751, the following year to that [illegible] the title of painter to the king, he was [illegible] to the grade of councillor. His work [illegible] satisfying at once both the taste of his [illegible] and the judgment of his brother artists. [illegible] his kind, achieved the task of flattering [illegible] flattery behind the just and striking [illegible] Mariette, he hardly ever missed. [illegible] of Voltaire, of Louis XV., of his queen, [illegible], are at once documents and [illegible] by his life-size portrait of [illegible] exhibited at the Salon of 1755, [illegible] cabinet of pastels in the Louvre. [illegible] a magnificent collection [illegible] in hi[illegible] La Tour [illegible] the [illegible]

18th of February 1788. The riches amassed during his long life were freely bestowed by him in great part before his death; he founded prizes at the school of fine arts in Paris and for the town of Amiens, and endowed St Quentin with a great number of useful and charitable institutions. He never married, but lived on terms of warm affection with his brother (who survived him, and left to the town the drawings now in the museum); and his relations to Mlle Marie Fel (1713–1789), the celebrated singer, were distinguished by a strength and depth of feeling not common to the loves of the 18th century.

See, in addition to the general works on French art, C. Desmaze, *M. Q. de La Tour, peintre du roi* (1854); Champfleury, *Les Peintres de Laon et de St Quentin* (1855); and "La Tour" in the *Collection des artistes célèbres* (1886); E. and J. de Goncourt, *La Tour* (1867); Guiffrey and M. Tourneux, *Correspondance inédite de M. Q. de la Tour* (1885); Tourneux, *La Tour, biographie critique* (1904); and Patoux, *L'Œuvre de M. Quentin de la Tour au musée de St Quentin* (St Quentin, 1882).

LA TOUR D'AUVERGNE, THÉOPHILE MALO (1743–1800), French soldier, was born at Carhaix in Brittany on the 23rd of December 1743, the son of an advocate named Corret. His desire for a military career being strongly marked, he was enabled, by the not uncommon device of producing a certificate of nobility signed by his friends, first to be nominally enlisted in the Maison du Roi, and soon afterwards to receive a commission in the line, under the name of Corret de Kerbaufret. Four years after joining, in 1771, he assumed by leave of the duke of Bouillon the surname of La Tour d'Auvergne, being in fact descended from an illegitimate half-brother of the great Turenne. Many years of routine service with his regiment were broken only by his participation as a volunteer in the duc de Crillon's Franco-Spanish expedition to Minorca in 1781. This led to an offer of promotion into the Spanish army, but he refused to change his allegiance. In 1748 he was promoted captain, and in 1791 he received the cross of St Louis. In the early part of the Revolution his patriotism was still more conspicuously displayed in his resolute opposition to the proposals of many of his brother officers in the Angoumois regiment to emigrate rather than to swear to the constitution. In 1792 his lifelong interest in numismatics and questions of language was shown by a work which he published on the Bretons. At this time he was serving under Montesquiou in the Alps, and although there was only outpost fighting he distinguished himself by his courage and audacity, qualities which were displayed in more serious fighting in the Pyrenees the next year. He declined well-earned promotion to colonel, and, being broken in health and compelled, owing to the loss of his teeth, to live on milk, he left the army in 1795. On his return by sea to Brittany he was captured by the English and held prisoner for two years. When released, he settled at Passy and published *Origines gauloises*, but in 1797, on the appeal of an old friend whose son had been taken as a conscript, he volunteered as the youth's substitute, and served on the Rhine (1797) and in Switzerland (1798–1799) as a captain. In recognition of his singular bravery and modesty Carnot obtained a decree from the first consul naming La Tour d'Auvergne "first grenadier of France" (27th of April 1800). This led him to volunteer again, and he was killed in action at Oberhausen, near Donauwörth, on the 27th of June 1800.

La Tour d'Auvergne's almost legendary courage had captivated the imagination of the French soldier, and his memory was not suffered to die. It was customary for the French troops and their allies of the Rhine Confederation under Napoleon to march at attention when passing his burial-place on the battlefield. His heart was long carried by the grenadier company of his regiment, the 46th; after being in the possession of Garibaldi for many years, it was finally deposited in the keeping of the city of Paris in 1883. But the most striking tribute to his memory is paid to-day as it was by order of the first consul in 1800. "His name is to be kept on the pay list and roll of his company. It will be called at all parades and a non-commissioned officer will reply, *Mort au champ d'honneur*." This custom, with little variation, is still observed in the 46th regiment on all occasions when the colour is taken on parade.

LATREILLE, PIERRE ANDRÉ (1762–1833), French naturalist, was born in humble circumstances at Brives-la-Gaillarde (Corrèze), on the 20th of November 1762. In 1778 he entered the collège Lemoine at Paris, and on his admission to priestly orders in 1786 he retired to Brives, where he devoted all the leisure which the discharge of his professional duties allowed to the study of entomology. In 1788 he returned to Paris and found means of making himself known to the leading naturalists there. His "Mémoire sur les mutilles découvertes en France," contributed to the *Proceedings* of the Society of Natural History in Paris, procured for him admission to that body. At the Revolution he was compelled to quit Paris, and as a priest of conservative sympathies suffered considerable hardship, being imprisoned for some time at Bordeaux. His *Précis des caractères génériques des insectes, disposés dans un ordre naturel*, appeared at Brives in 1796. In 1798 he became a corresponding member of the Institute, and at the same time was entrusted with the task of arranging the entomological collection at the recently organized Muséum d'Histoire Naturelle (Jardin des Plantes); in 1814 he succeeded G. A. Olivier as member of the Académie des Sciences, and in 1821 he was made a chevalier of the Legion of Honour. For some time he acted as professor of zoology in the veterinary school at Alfort near Paris, and in 1830, when the chair of zoology of invertebrates at the Muséum was divided after the death of Lamarck, Latreille was appointed professor of zoology of crustaceans, arachnids and insects, the chair of molluscs, worms and zoophytes being assigned to H. M. D. de Blainville. "On me donne du pain quand je n'ai plus de dents," said Latreille, who was then in his sixty-eighth year. He died in Paris on the 6th of February 1833.

In addition to the works already mentioned, the numerous works of Latreille include: *Histoire naturelle générale et particulière des crustacés et insectes* (14 vols., 1802–1805), forming part of C. N. S. Sonnini's edition of Buffon; *Genera crustaceorum et insectorum, secundum ordinem naturalem in familias disposita* (4 vols., 1806–1807); *Considérations générales sur l'ordre naturel des animaux composant les classes des crustacés, des arachnides, et des insectes* (1810); *Familles naturelles du règne animal, exposées succinctement et dans un ordre analytique* (1825); *Cours d'entomologie* (of which only the first volume appeared, 1831); the whole of the section "Crustacés, Arachnides, Insectes," in G. Cuvier's *Règne animal*; besides many papers in the *Annales du Muséum*, the *Encyclopédie méthodique*, the *Dictionnaire classique d'histoire naturelle* and elsewhere.

LA TRÉMOILLE, an old French family which derives its name from a village (the modern La Trimouille) in the department of Vienne. The family has been known since the middle of the 11th century, and since the 14th century its members have been conspicuous in French history. Guy, sire de la Trémoille, standard-bearer of France, was taken prisoner at the battle of Nicopolis (1396), and Georges, the favourite of King Charles VII., was captured at Agincourt (1415). Louis (2), called the *chevalier sans reproche*, defeated and captured the duke of Orleans at the battle of Saint-Aubin-du-Cormier (1488), distinguished himself in the wars in Italy, and was killed at Pavia (1525). In 1521 François (2) acquired a claim on the kingdom of Naples by his marriage with Anne de Laval, daughter of Charlotte of Aragon. Louis (3) became duke of Thouars in 1563, and his son Claude turned Protestant, was created a peer of France in 1595, and married a daughter of William the Silent in 1598. To this family belonged the lines of the counts of Joigny, the marquises of Royan and counts of Olonne, and the marquises and dukes of Noirmoutier.

LATROBE, CHARLES JOSEPH (1801–1875), Australian governor, was born in London on the 20th of March 1801. The Latrobes were of Huguenot extraction, and belonged to the Moravian community, of which the father and grandfather of C. J. Latrobe were ministers. His father, Christian Ignatius Latrobe (1758–1836), a musician of some note, did good service in the direction of popularizing classical music in England by his *Selection of Sacred Music from the Works of the most Eminent Composers of Germany and Italy* (6 vols., 1806–1825). C. J. Latrobe was an excellent mountaineer, and made some important ascents in Switzerland in 1824–1826. In 1832 he went to America with Count Albert Pourtales, and in 1834 crossed the prairies from New Orleans to Mexico with Washington Irving. In 1837 he was invested with a government commission in the West Indies, and two years later was made superintendent of the Port Philip district of New South Wales. When Port Philip was erected into a separate colony as Victoria in 1851, Latrobe became lieutenant-governor. The discovery of gold in that year attracted enormous numbers of immigrants annually. Latrobe discharged the difficult duties of government at this critical period with tact and success. He retired in 1854, became C. B. in 1858 and died in London on the 2nd of December 1875. Beside some volumes of travel he published a volume of poems, *The Solace of Song* (1837).

See *Brief Notices of the Latrobe Family* (1864), a privately printed translation of an article revised by members of the family in the Moravian *Bruderbote* (November 1864).

LATTEN (from O. Fr. *laton*, mod. Fr. *laiton*, possibly connected with Span. *lata*, Ital. *latta*, a lath), a mixed metal like brass, composed of copper and zinc, generally made in thin sheets, and used especially for monumental brasses and effigies. A fine example is in the screen of Henry VII.'s tomb in Westminster Abbey. There are three forms of latten, "black latten," unpolished and rolled, "shaven latten," of extreme thinness, and "roll latten," of the thickness either of black or shaven latten, but with both sides polished.

LATTICE LEAF PLANT, in botany, the common name for *Ouvirandra fenestralis*, an aquatic monocotyledonous plant belonging to the small natural order Aponogetonaceae and a native of Madagascar. It has a singular appearance from the structure of the leaves, which are oblong in shape, from 6 to 18 in. long and from 2 to 4 in. broad; they spread horizontally beneath the surface of the water, and are reduced to little more than a lattice-like network of veins. The tuberculate roots are edible. The plant is grown in cultivation as a stove-aquatic.

LATUDE, JEAN HENRI, often called DANRY or MASERS DE LATUDE (1725–1805), prisoner of the Bastille, was born at Montagnac in Gascony on the 23rd of March 1725. He received a military education and went to Paris in 1748 to study mathematics. He led a dissipated life and endeavoured to curry favour with the marquise de Pompadour by secretly sending her a box of poison and then informing her of the supposed plot against her life. The ruse was discovered, and Mme de Pompadour, not appreciating the humour of the situation, had Latude put in the Bastille on the 1st of May 1749. He was later transferred to Vincennes, whence he escaped in 1750. Retaken and reimprisoned in the Bastille, he made a second brief escape in 1756. He was transferred to Vincennes in 1764, and the next year made a third escape and was a third time recaptured. He was put in a madhouse by Malesherbes in 1775, and discharged in 1777 on condition that he should retire to his native town. He remained in Paris and was again imprisoned. A certain Mme Legros became interested in him through chance reading of one of his memoirs, and, by a vigorous agitation in his behalf, secured his definite release in 1784. He exploited his long captivity with considerable ability, posing as a brave officer, a son of the marquis de la Tude, and a victim of Pompadour's intrigues. He was extolled and pensioned during the Revolution, and in 1793 the convention compelled the heirs of Mme de Pompadour to pay him 60,000 francs damages. He died in obscurity at Paris on the 1st of January 1805.

The principal work of Latude is the account of his imprisonment, written in collaboration with an advocate named Thiéry, and entitled *Le Despotisme dévoilé, ou Mémoires de Henri Masers de la Tude, détenu pendant trente-cinq ans dans les diverses prisons d'état* (Amsterdam, 1787, ed. Paris, 1889). An Eng. trans. of a portion was published in 1787. The work is full of lies and misrepresentations, but had great vogue at the time of the French Revolution. Latude also wrote essays on all sorts of subjects.

See J. F. Barrière, *Mémoires de Linguet et de Latude* (1884); G. Bertin, *Notice* in edition of the *Mémoires* (1889); F. Funck-Brentano, "Latude," in the *Revue des deux mondes* (1st October 1889).

LATUKA, a tribe of negroid stock inhabiting the mountainous country E. of Gondokoro on the upper Nile. They have received a tinge of Hamitic blood from the Galla people, and have high [illegible] straight noses and thick but not pouting [illegible] by Sir H. H. Johnston to be the original [illegible] great Masai people, and are assimilated [illegible] in customs. Like their neighbours [illegible] they despise clothing, though the [illegible] adopted Arab attire. Their country is [illegible] tobacco, durra and other crops. Their [illegible] and some are of considerable size. Tar[illegible] the Kher Kohs, has upwards of three [illegible] for many thousands of cattle. The [illegible] and especially noted for skill as smiths. [illegible] the lion was so little dreaded by the [illegible] caught in a leopard trap they hastily [illegible]

[illegible] Germany in the Prussian province of [illegible] a picturesque valley, at the junction of [illegible] Görlitz and Soran, 16 m. E. of the former. [illegible] has a Roman Catholic and two Evan[illegible] [illegible] dating from 1541, a conventual [illegible] Magdalene, dating from the 14th century, [illegible] museum, two hospitals, an orphanage [illegible] Its industrial establishments comprise [illegible] linen and woollen cloth manufactories, [illegible] works, breweries and oil and flour mills. [illegible] the 10th and fortified in the 13th [illegible] it was devastated by the Hussites, [illegible] In 1761 it was the headquarters [illegible] Swedes, and in 1815 it was the last Saxon town [illegible] to Prussia.

[illegible] *der Stadt Lauban* (Lauban, 1896).

[illegible] -1884), German dramatist, novelist [illegible] Sprottau in Silesia on the [illegible] studied theology at Halle and [illegible] Leipzig in 1832. Here he [illegible] his political essays, collected [illegible], in two parts—*Polen* (1833) [illegible] with the novel *Das junge* [illegible] *Die Krieger*, *Die Bürger*— [illegible] in which, after the fashion of [illegible] Börne, he severely criticized the [illegible] together with the part he played [illegible] known as *Das junge Deutschland*, led [illegible] police surveillance and his works con[illegible] [illegible] from a journey to Italy, under[illegible] [illegible] Karl Gutzkow, Laube was expelled [illegible] for nine months in Berlin. In [illegible] of Professor Hänel of Leipzig; [illegible] he suffered a year's imprison[illegible] [illegible] In 1839 he again settled [illegible] as a playwright. Chief [illegible] activity are the tragedies *Monaldeschi* [illegible] the comedies *Rokoko, oder die alten* [illegible] *Gallore* (1847); and *Die Karls-* [illegible] Schiller is the hero. In [illegible] assembly at Frankfort [illegible] resigned in the spring [illegible] director of the Hofburg [illegible] and in this [illegible] notably the tragedies [illegible] historical romance [illegible] which graphically [illegible] In 1869 he became [illegible] returned to Vienna [illegible] of the new [illegible] he managed [illegible] retirement from [illegible] of his work [illegible] *Burgtheater* [illegible] *Das Wiener Stadt-* [illegible] retirement, [illegible] took place at [illegible]

novels *Die Böhminger* (1880), *Louison* (1881), *Der Schatten-Wilhelm* (1883), and published an interesting volume of reminiscences, *Erinnerungen, 1841–1881* (1882). Laube's dramas are not remarkable for originality or for poetical beauty; their real and great merit lies in their stage-craft. As a theatre-manager he has had no equal in Germany, and his services in this capacity have assured him a more lasting name in German literary history than his writings.

His *Gesammelte Schriften* (excluding his dramas) were published in 16 vols. (1875–1882); his *Dramatische Werke* in 13 vols. (1845–1875); a popular edition of the latter in 12 vols. (1880–1892). An edition of Laube's *Ausgewählte Werke* in 10 vols. appeared in 1906 with an introduction by H. H. Houben. See also J. Proelss, *Das junge Deutschland* (1892); and H. Bulthaupt, *Dramaturgie des Schauspiels* (vol. iii., 6th ed., 1901).

L'AUBESPINE, a French family which sprang from Claude de l'Aubespine, a lawyer of Orleans and bailiff of the abbey of St Euverte in the beginning of the 16th century, and rapidly acquired distinction in offices connected with the law. Sebastien de l'Aubespine (d. 1582), abbot of Bassefontaine, bishop of Vannes and afterwards of Limoges, fulfilled important diplomatic missions in Germany, Hungary, England, the Low Countries and Switzerland under Francis I. and his successors. Claude (*c.* 1500–1567), baron of Châteauneuf-sur-Cher, Sebastien's brother, was a secretary of finance; he had charge of negotiations with England in 1555 and 1559, and was several times commissioned to treat with the Huguenots in the king's name. His son Guillaume was a councillor of state and ambassador to England. Charles de l'Aubespine (1580–1653) was ambassador to Germany, the Low Countries, Venice and England, besides twice holding the office of keeper of the seals of France, from 1630 to 1633, and from 1650 to 1651. The family fell into poor circumstances and became extinct in the 19th century. (M.P.*)

LAUCHSTÄDT, a town of Germany in the province of Prussian Saxony, on the Laucha, 6 m. N.W. of Merseburg by the railway to Schafstadt. Pop. (1905) 2034. It contains an Evangelical church, a theatre, a hydropathic establishment and several educational institutions, among which is an agricultural school affiliated to the university of Halle. Its industries include malting, vinegar-making and brewing. Lauchstädt was a popular watering-place in the 18th century, the dukes of Saxe-Merseburg often making it their summer residence. From 1789 to 1811 the Weimar court theatrical company gave performances here of the plays of Schiller and Goethe, an attraction which greatly contributed to the well-being of the town.

See Maak, *Das Goethetheater in Lauchstädt* (Lauchstädt, 1905); and Nasemann, *Bad Lauchstadt* (Halle, 1885).

LAUD, WILLIAM (1573–1645), English archbishop, only son of William Laud, a clothier, was born at Reading on the 7th of October 1573. He was educated at Reading free school, matriculated at St John's college, Oxford, in 1589, gained a scholarship in 1590, a fellowship in 1593, and graduated B.A. in 1594, proceeding to D.D. in 1608. In 1601 he took orders, in 1603 becoming chaplain to Charles Blount, earl of Devonshire. Laud early took up a position of antagonism to the Calvinistic party in the church, and in 1604 was reproved by the authorities for maintaining in his thesis for the degree of B.D. "that there could be no true church without bishops," and again in 1606 for advocating "popish" opinions in a sermon at St Mary's. If high-church doctrines, however, met with opposition at Oxford, they were relished elsewhere, and Laud obtained rapid advancement. In 1607 he was made vicar of Stanford in Northamptonshire, and in 1608 he became chaplain to Bishop Neile, who in 1610 presented him to the living of Cuxton, when he resigned his fellowship. In 1611, in spite of the influence of Archbishop Abbot and Lord Chancellor Ellesmere, Laud was made president of St John's, and in 1614 obtained in addition the prebend of Buckden, in 1615 the archdeaconry of Huntingdon, and in 1616 the deanery of Gloucester. Here he repaired the fabric and changed the position of the communion table, a matter which aroused great religious controversy, from the centre of the choir to the east end, by a characteristic tactless exercise of power offending the bishop, who henceforth refused to enter the cathedral. In 1617 he went with the king to Scotland, and aroused hostility by wearing the surplice. In 1621 he became bishop of St David's, when he resigned the presidentship of St John's.

In April 1622 Laud, by the king's orders, took part in a controversy with Percy, a Jesuit, known as Fisher, the aim of which was to prevent the conversion of the countess of Buckingham, the favourite's mother, to Romanism, and his opinions expressed on that occasion show considerable breadth and comprehension. While refusing to acknowledge the Roman Church as *the* true church, he allowed it to be *a* true church and a branch of the Catholic body, at the same time emphasizing the perils of knowingly associating with error; and with regard to the English Church he denied that the acceptance of all its articles was necessary. The foundation of belief was the Bible, not any one branch of the Catholic church arrogating to itself infallibility, and when dispute on matters of faith arose, "a lawful and free council, determining according to Scripture, is the best judge on earth." A close and somewhat strange intimacy, considering the difference in the characters and ideals of the two men, between Laud and Buckingham now began, and proved the chief instrument of Laud's advancement. The opportunity came with the old king's death in 1625, for James, with all his pedantry, was too wise and cautious to embark in Laud's rash undertakings, and had already shown a prudent moderation, after setting up bishops in Scotland, in going no further in opposition to the religious feelings of the people. On the accession of Charles, Laud's ambitious activities were allowed free scope. A list of the clergy was immediately prepared by him for the king, in which each name was labelled with an O or a P, distinguishing the Orthodox to be promoted from the Puritans to be suppressed. Laud defended Richard Montague, who had aroused the wrath of the parliament by his pamphlet against Calvinism. His influence soon extended into the domain of the state. He supported the king's prerogative throughout the conflict with the parliament, preached in favour of it before Charles's second parliament in 1626, and assisted in Buckingham's defence. In 1626 he was nominated bishop of Bath and Wells, and in July 1628 bishop of London. On the 12th of April 1629 he was made chancellor of Oxford University.

In the patronage of learning and in the exercise of authority over the morals and education of youth Laud was in his proper sphere, many valuable reforms at Oxford being due to his activity, including the codification of the statutes, the statute by which public examinations were rendered obligatory for university degrees, and the ordinance for the election of proctors, the revival of the college system, of moral and religious discipline and order, and of academic dress. He founded or endowed various professorships, including those of Hebrew and Arabic, and the office of public orator, encouraged English and foreign scholars, such as Voss, Selden and Jeremy Taylor, founded the university printing press, procuring in 1633 the royal patent for Oxford, and obtained for the Bodleian library over 1300 MSS., adding a new wing to the building to contain his gifts. His rule at Oxford was marked by a great increase in the number of students. In his own college he erected the new buildings, and was its second founder. Of his chancellorship he himself wrote a history, and the Laudian tradition long remained the great standard of order and good government in the university. Elsewhere he showed his liberality and his zeal for reform. He was an active visitor of Eton and Winchester, and endowed the grammar school at Reading, where he was himself educated. In London he procured funds for the restoration of the dilapidated cathedral of St Paul's.

He was far less great as a ruler in the state, showing as a judge a tyrannical spirit both in the star chamber and high-commission court, threatening Felton, the assassin of Buckingham, with the rack, and showing special activity in procuring a cruel sentence in the former court against Alexander Leighton in June 1630 and against Henry Sherfield in 1634. His power was greatly increased after his return from Scotland, whither he had accompanied the king, by his promotion to the archbishopric of Canterbury in August 1633. "As for the state indeed," he wrote to Wentworth on this occasion, "I am for *Thorough*." In 1636 the privy council decided in his favour his claim of jurisdiction as visitor over both universities. Soon afterwards he was placed on the commission of the treasury and on the committee of the privy council for foreign affairs. He was all-powerful both in church and state. He proceeded to impose by authority the religious ceremonies and usages to which he attached so much importance. His vicar-general, Sir Nathaniel Brent, went through the dioceses of his province, noting every dilapidation and every irregularity. The pulpit was no longer to be the chief feature in the church, but the communion table. The Puritan lecturers were suppressed. He showed great hostility to the Puritan sabbath and supported the reissue of the *Book of Sports*, especially odious to that party, and severely reprimanded Chief Justice Richardson for his interference with the Somerset wakes. He insisted on the use of the prayer-book among the English soldiers in the service of Holland, and forced strict conformity on the church of the merchant adventurers at Delft, endeavouring even to reach the colonists in New England. He tried to compel the Dutch and French refugees in England to unite with the Church of England, advising double taxation and other forms of persecution. In 1634 the justices of the peace were ordered to enter houses to search for persons holding conventicles and bring them before the commissioners. He took pleasure in displaying his power over the great, and in punishing them in the spiritual courts for moral offences. In 1637 he took part in the sentence of the star chamber on Prynne, Bastwick and Burton, and in the same year in the prosecution of Bishop Williams. He urged Strafford in Ireland to carry out the same reforms and severities.

He was now to extend his ecclesiastical system to Scotland, where during his visits the appearance of the churches had greatly displeased him. The new prayer-book and canons were drawn up by the Scottish bishops with his assistance and enforced in the country, and, though not officially connected with the work, he was rightly regarded as its real author. The attack not only on the national religion, but on the national independence of Scotland, proved to be the point at which the system, already strained, broke and collapsed. Laud continued to support Strafford's and the king's arbitrary measures to the last, and spoke in favour of the vigorous continuation of the war on Strafford's side in the memorable meeting of the committee of eight on the 5th of May 1640, and for the employment of any means for carrying it on. "Tried all ways," so ran the notes of his speech, "and refused all ways. By the law of God and man you should have subsistence and lawful to take it." Though at first opposed to the sitting of convocation, after the dissolution of parliament, as an independent body, on account of the opposition it would arouse, he yet caused to be passed in it the new canons which both enforced his ecclesiastical system and assisted the king's divine right, resistance to his power entailing "damnation." Laud's infatuated policy could go no further, and the *etcetera* oath, according to which whole classes of men were to be forced to swear perpetual allegiance to the "government of this church by archbishops, bishops, deans and archdeacons, &c.," was long remembered and derided. His power now quickly abandoned him. He was attacked and reviled as the chief author of the troubles on all sides. In October he was ordered by Charles to suspend the *etcetera* oath. The same month, when the high commission court was sacked by the mob, he was unable to persuade the star chamber to punish the offenders. On the 18th of December he was impeached by the Long Parliament, and on the 1st of March imprisoned in the tower. On the 12th of May, at Strafford's request, the archbishop appeared at the window of his cell to give him his blessing on his way to execution, and fainted as he passed by. For some time he was left unnoticed in confinement. On the 31st of May 1643, however, Prynne received orders from the parliament to search his papers, and published a mutilated edition of his diary. The articles of impeachment were sent up to the Lords in October, the trial beginning on the 12th of March 1644, but the attempt to bring his conduct under a charge of high treason proving hopeless, an attainder was substituted and sent up to the Lords on the 22nd of November. In these proceedings there was no semblance of respect for law or justice, the Lords yielding (4th of January 1645) to the menaces of the Commons, who arrogated to themselves the right to declare any crimes they pleased high treason. Laud now tendered the king's pardon, which had been granted to him in April 1643. This was rejected, and it was with [illegible] difficulty that his petition to be executed with the axe, instead of undergoing the ordinary brutal punishment for high treason, was granted. He suffered death on the 10th of January [illegible], asserting his innocence of any offence known to [illegible] repudiating the charge of "popery," and declaring that [illegible] lived in the Protestant Church of England. He [illegible] in the chancel of All Hallows, Barking, whence his [illegible] removed on the 24th of July 1663 to the chapel of [illegible] College, Oxford.

[illegible] He is described by Fuller as "low of [illegible] cheerful in countenance (wherein gravity [illegible] compounded), of a sharp and piercing eye, [illegible] (against the influence of age) firm memory." [illegible] an account of the sharp religious antagonisms [illegible] inevitably associated, has rarely been [illegible]. His severities were the result of a [illegible] vindictive spirit, and their number [illegible] exaggerated. His career was distinguished by [illegible] by a devotion to duty, by courage and [illegible] it is clear that the charge of partiality [illegible]. At the same time the circumstances of [illegible] schemes of union with Rome [illegible] of Panzani and later of Conn were [illegible] Church of Rome numbers of members of the [illegible] Laud himself, were dissatisfied with [illegible] characterized it, the incident mentioned [illegible] his being twice offered the cardinalate, [illegible] at the court in favour of Romanism, [illegible] changes in ritual, however clearly [illegible] in his own intention, all tended towards [illegible] the suspicions and fears of his [illegible] neglect of the national sentiment [illegible] of mere power was sufficient [illegible] of his total lack of true statesmanship [illegible] "innovations in religion," it is [illegible] incentive to the rebellion [illegible] than even the violation [illegible] Laud, therefore, more than to [illegible] perhaps to Charles himself, [illegible] the catastrophe. He held [illegible] of the English Church, [illegible] it as a branch of the whole [illegible] historical continuity and [illegible] but here again his policy [illegible] not only excited [illegible] and independentism [illegible] large bodies of faithful [illegible] their church and from their [illegible] Massachusetts in 1629, which [illegible] composed of separatists [illegible] Laud grasped with one hand [illegible]

[illegible] influence of Laud on his times, [illegible] and aim which separates [illegible] imagination and idealism as [illegible] their policies may have [illegible] of Laud's administration [illegible] trivial of which he [illegible] which are uninspired by [illegible] was always essentially [illegible] which to him was all [illegible] source of his intense [illegible] conception of the [illegible] form. Hence the necessity for outward conformity, and the importance attached to ritual and ceremony, unity in which must be established at all costs, in contrast to dogma and doctrine, in which he showed himself lenient and large-minded, winning over Hales by friendly discussion, and encouraging the publication of Chillingworth's *Religion of Protestants*. He was not a bigot, but a martinet. The external form was with him the essential feature of religion, preceding the spiritual conception, and in Laud's opinion being the real foundation of it. In his last words on the scaffold he alludes to the dangers and slanders he had endured labouring to keep an uniformity in the external service of God; and Bacon's conception of a spiritual union founded on variety and liberty was one completely beyond his comprehension.

This narrow materialism was the true cause of his fatal influence both in church and state. In his own character it produced the somewhat blunted moral sense which led to the few incidents in his career which need moral defence, his performance of the marriage ceremony between his first patron Lord Devonshire and the latter's mistress, the divorced wife of Lord Rich, an act completely at variance with his principles; his strange intimacy with Buckingham; his love of power and place. Indistinguishable from his personal ambition was his passion for the aggrandisement of the church and its predominance in the state. He was greatly delighted at the foolish appointment of Bishop Juxon as lord treasurer in 1636. "No churchman had it," he cries exultingly, "since Henry VII.'s time, . . . and now if the church will not hold up themselves under God, I can do no more." Spiritual influence, in Laud's opinion, was not enough for the church. The church as the guide of the nation in duty and godliness, even extending its activity into state affairs as a mediator and a moderator, was not sufficient. Its power must be material and visible, embodied in great places of secular administration and enthroned in high offices of state. Thus the church, descending into the political arena, became identified with the doctrines of one political party in the state—doctrines odious to the majority of the nation—and at the same time became associated with acts of violence and injustice, losing at once its influence and its reputation. Equally disastrous to the state was the identification of the king's administration with one party in the church, and that with the party in an immense minority not only in the nation but even among the clergy themselves.

Bibliography.—All Laud's works are to be found in the *Library of Anglo-Catholic Theology* (7 vols.), including his sermons (of no great merit), letters, history of the chancellorship, history of his troubles and trial, and his remarkable diary, the MSS. of the last two works being the property of St John's College. Various modern opinions of Laud's career can be studied in T. Longueville's *Life of Laud, by a Romish Recusant* (1894); *Congregational Union Jubilee Lectures*, vol. i. (1882); J. B. Mozley's *Essay on Laud*; *Archbishop Laud*, by A. C. Benson (1887); *Wm. Laud*, by W. H. Hutton (1895); *Archbishop Laud Commemoration*, ed. by W. F. Collins (lectures, bibliography, catalogue of exhibits, 1895); Hook's *Lives of the Archbishops of Canterbury*; and H. Bell, *Archbishop Laud and Priestly Government* (1907). (P. C. Y.)

LAUD (Lat. *laus*), a term meaning praise, now rarely found in this sense except in poetry or hymns. Lauds is the name for the second of the offices of the canonical hours in the Roman breviary, so called from the three *laudes* or psalms of praise, cxlviii.-cl. which form part of the service (see Breviary and Hours, Canonical).

LAUDANUM, originally the name given by Paracelsus to a famous medical preparation of his own composed of gold, pearls, &c. (*Opera*, 1658, i. 492/2), but containing opium as its chief ingredient. The term is now only used for the alcoholic tincture of opium (*q.v.*). The name was either invented by Paracelsus from Lat. *laudare* to praise, or was a corrupted form of "ladanum" (Gr. λήδανον, from Pers. *lodan*), a resinous juice or gum obtained from various kinds of the *Cistus* shrub, formerly used medicinally in external applications and as a stomachic, but now only in perfumery and in making fumigating pastilles, &c.

LAUDER, SIR THOMAS DICK, Bart. (1784–1848), Scottish author, only son of Sir Andrew Lauder, 6th baronet, was born at Edinburgh in 1784. He succeeded to the baronetcy in 1820. His first contribution to *Blackwood's Magazine* in 1817, entitled

"Simon Roy, Gardener at Dunphail," was by some ascribed to Sir Walter Scott. His paper (1818) on "The Parallel Roads of Glenroy," printed in vol. ix. of the *Transactions of the Royal Society of Edinburgh*, first drew attention to the phenomenon in question. In 1825 and 1827 he published two romances, *Lochandhu* and the *Wolf of Badenoch*. He became a frequent contributor to *Blackwood* and also to *Tait's Magazine*, and in 1830 he published *An Account of the Great Floods of August 1829 in the Province of Moray and adjoining Districts*. Subsequent works were *Highland Rambles, with Long Tales to Shorten the Way* (2 vols. 8vo, 1837), *Legendary Tales of the Highlands* (3 vols. 12mo, 1841), *Tour round the Coasts of Scotland* (1842) and *Memorial of the Royal Progress in Scotland* (1843). Vol. i. of a *Miscellany of Natural History*, published in 1833, was also partly prepared by Lauder. He was a Liberal, and took an active interest in politics; he held the office of secretary to the Board of Scottish Manufactures. He died on the 29th of May 1848. An unfinished series of papers, written for *Tait's Magazine* shortly before his death, was published under the title *Scottish Rivers*, with a preface by John Brown, M.D., in 1874.

LAUDER, WILLIAM (d. 1771), Scottish literary forger, was born in the latter part of the 17th century, and was educated at Edinburgh university, where he graduated in 1695. He applied unsuccessfully for the post of professor of humanity there, in succession to Adam Watt, whose assistant he had been for a time, and also for the keepership of the university library. He was a good scholar, and in 1739, published *Poetarum Scotorum Musae Sacrae*, a collection of poems by various writers, mostly paraphrased from the Bible. In 1742 Lauder came to London. In 1747 he wrote an article for the *Gentleman's Magazine* to prove that Milton's *Paradise Lost* was largely a plagiarism from the *Adamus Exul* (1601) of Hugo Grotius, the *Sarcotis* (1654) of J. Masen (Masenius, 1606–1681), and the *Poemata Sacra* (1633) of Andrew Ramsay (1574–1659). Lauder expounded his case in a series of articles, and in a book (1753) increased the list of plundered authors to nearly a hundred. But his success was short-lived. Several scholars, who had independently studied the alleged sources of Milton's inspiration, proved conclusively that Lauder had not only garbled most of his quotations, but had even inserted amongst them extracts from a Latin rendering of *Paradise Lost*. This led to his exposure, and he was obliged to write a complete confession at the dictation of his former friend Samuel Johnson. After several vain endeavours to clear his character he emigrated to Barbadoes, where he died in 1771.

LAUDER, a royal and police burgh of Berwickshire, Scotland. Pop. (1901) 719. It is situated on the Leader, 29 m. S.E. of Edinburgh by the North British railway's branch line from Fountainhall, of which it is the terminus. The burgh is said to date from the reign of William the Lion (1165–1214); its charter was granted in 1502. In 1482 James III. with his court and army rested here on the way to raise the siege of Berwick. While the nobles were in the church considering grievances, Robert Cochrane, recently created earl of Mar, one of the king's favourites, whose "removal" was at the very moment under discussion, demanded admittance. Archibald Douglas, earl of Angus, opened the door and seized Mar, who was forthwith dragged to Lauder Bridge and there, along with six other obnoxious favourites, hanged in sight of his royal master. It was in connexion with this exploit that Angus acquired the nickname of "Bell-the-cat." The public buildings include a town-hall and a library. The parish church was built in 1673 by the earl of Lauderdale, in exchange for the older edifice, the site of which was required for the enlargement of Thirlestane castle, which, originally a fortress, was then remodelled for a residence. The town is a favourite with anglers.

LAUDERDALE, JOHN MAITLAND, DUKE OF (1616–1682), eldest surviving son of John Maitland, 2nd Lord Maitland of Thirlestane (d. 1645), who was created earl of Lauderdale in 1624, and of Lady Isabel Seton, daughter of Alexander, earl of Dunfermline, and great-grandson of Sir Richard Maitland (*q.v.*), the poet, a member of an ancient family of Berwickshire, was born on the 24th of May 1616, at Lethington. He began public life as a zealous adherent of the Presbyterian cause, took the covenant, sat as an elder in the assembly at St Andrews in July 1643, and was sent to England as a commissioner for the covenant in August, and to attend the Westminster assembly in November. In February 1644 he was a member of the committee of both kingdoms, and on the 20th of November was one of the commissioners appointed to treat with the king at Uxbridge, when he made efforts to persuade Charles to agree to the establishment of Presbyterianism. In 1645 he advised Charles to reject the proposals of the Independents, and in 1647 approved of the king's surrender to the Scots. At this period Lauderdale veered round completely to the king's cause, had several interviews with him, and engaged in various projects for his restoration, offering the aid of the Scots, on the condition of Charles's consent to the establishment of Presbyterianism, and on the 26th of December he obtained from Charles at Carisbrooke "the engagement" by which Presbyterianism was to be established for three years, schismatics were to be suppressed, and the acts of the Scottish parliament ratified, the king in addition promising to admit the Scottish nobles into public employment in England and to reside frequently in Scotland. Returning to Scotland, in the spring of 1648, Lauderdale joined the party of Hamilton in alliance with the English royalists. Their defeat at Preston postponed the arrival of the prince of Wales, but Lauderdale had an interview with the prince in the Downs in August, and from this period obtained supreme influence over the future king. He persuaded him later to accept the invitation to Scotland from the Argyll faction, accompanied him thither in 1650 and in the expedition into England, and was taken prisoner at Worcester in 1651, remaining in confinement till March 1660. He joined Charles in May 1660 at Breda, and, in spite of the opposition of Clarendon and Monk, was appointed secretary of state. From this time onwards he kept his hold upon the king, was lodged at Whitehall, was "never from the king's ear nor council,"[1] and maintained his position against his numerous adversaries by a crafty dexterity in dealing with men, a fearless unscrupulousness, and a robust strength of will, which overcame all opposition. Though a man of considerable learning and intellectual attainment, his character was exceptionally and grossly licentious, and his base and ignoble career was henceforward unrelieved by a single redeeming feature. He abandoned Argyll to his fate, permitted, if he did not assist in, the restoration of episcopacy in Scotland, and after triumphing over all his opponents in Scotland drew into his own hands the whole administration of that kingdom, and proceeded to impose upon it the absolute supremacy of the crown in church and state, restoring the nomination of the lords of the articles to the king and initiating severe measures against the Covenanters. In 1669 he was able to boast with truth that "the king is now master here in all causes and over all persons."

His own power was now at its height, and his position as the favourite of Charles, controlled by no considerations of patriotism or statesmanship, and completely independent of the English parliament, recalled the worst scandals and abuses of the Stuart administration before the Civil War. He was a member of the cabal ministry, but took little part in English affairs, and was not entrusted with the first secret treaty of Dover, but gave personal support to Charles in his degrading demands for pensions from Louis XIV. On the 2nd of May 1672 he was created duke of Lauderdale and earl of March, and on the 3rd of June knight of the garter. In 1673, on the resignation of James in consequence of the Test Act, he was appointed a commissioner for the admiralty. In October he visited Scotland to suppress the dissenters and obtain money for the Dutch War, and the intrigues organized by Shaftesbury against his power in his absence, and the attacks made upon him in the House of Commons in January 1674 and April 1675, were alike rendered futile by the steady support of Charles and James. On the 25th of June 1674 he was created earl of Guilford and Baron Petersham in the peerage of England. His ferocious measures having failed to suppress the conventicles in Scotland, he summoned to his

[1] Pepys's *Diary*, 2nd of March 1664.

[illegible]

cluded in the Prussian province of Schleswig-Holstein. It lies on the right bank of the Elbe, is bounded by the territories of Hamburg, Lübeck, Mecklenburg-Strelitz and the province of Hanover, and comprises an area of 453 sq. m. The surface is a slightly undulating plain. The soil, chiefly alluvial, though in some places arenaceous, is generally fertile and well cultivated, but a great portion is covered with forests, interspersed with lakes. By means of the Stecknitz canal, the Elbe, the principal river, is connected with the Trave. The chief agricultural products are timber, fruit, grain, hemp, flax and vegetables. Cattle-breeding affords employment for many of the inhabitants. The railroad from Hamburg to Berlin traverses the country. The capital is Ratzeburg, and there are two other towns, Mölln and Lauenburg.

The earliest inhabitants of Lauenburg were a Slav tribe, the Polabes, who were gradually replaced by colonists from Saxony. About the middle of the 12th century the country was subdued by the duke of Saxony, Henry the Lion, who founded a bishopric at Ratzeburg, and after Henry's fall in 1180 it formed part of the smaller duchy of Saxony, which was governed by Duke Bernhard. In 1203 it was conquered by Waldemar II., king of Denmark, but in 1227 it reverted to Albert, a son of its former duke. When Albert died in 1260 Saxony was divided. Lauenburg, or Saxe-Lauenburg, as it is generally called, became a separate duchy ruled by his son John, and had its own lines of dukes for over 400 years, one of them, Magnus I. (d. 1543), being responsible for the introduction of the reformed teaching into the land. The reigning family, however, became extinct when Duke Julius Francis died in September 1689, and there were at least eight claimants for his duchy, chief among them being John George III., elector of Saxony, and George William, duke of Brunswick-Lüneburg-Celle, the ancestors of both these princes having made treaties of mutual succession with former dukes of Saxe-Lauenburg. Both entered the country, but George William proved himself the stronger and occupied Ratzeburg; having paid a substantial sum of money to the elector, he was recognized by the inhabitants as their duke. When he died three years later Lauenburg passed to his nephew, George Louis, elector of Hanover, afterwards king of Great Britain as George I., whose rights were recognized by the emperor Charles VI. in 1728. In 1803 the duchy was occupied by the French, and in 1810 it was incorporated with France. It reverted to Hanover after the battle of Leipzig in 1813, and in 1816 was ceded to Prussia, the greater part of it being at once transferred by her to Denmark in exchange for Swedish Pomerania. In 1848, when Prussia made war on Denmark, Lauenburg was occupied at her own request by some Hanoverian troops, and was then administered for three years under the authority of the German confederation, being restored to Denmark in 1851. Definitely incorporated with this country in 1853, it experienced another change of fortune after the short war of 1864 between Denmark on the one side and Prussia and Austria on the other, as by the peace of Vienna (30th of October 1864) it was ceded with Schleswig and Holstein to the two German powers. By the convention of Gastein (14th of August 1865) Austria surrendered her claim to Prussia in return for the payment of nearly £300,000 and in September 1865 King William I. took formal possession of the duchy. Lauenburg entered the North German confederation in 1866 and the new German empire in 1870. It retained its constitution and its special privileges until the 1st of July 1876, when it was incorporated with the kingdom of Prussia. In 1890 Prince Bismarck received the title of duke of Lauenburg.

See P. von Kobbe, *Geschichte und Landesbeschreibung des Herzogtums Lauenburg* (Altona, 1836–1837); Duve, *Mitteilungen zur Kunde der Staatsgeschichte Lauenburgs* (Ratzeburg, 1852–1857), and the *Archiv des Vereins für die Geschichte des Herzogtums Lauenburg* (Ratzeburg, 1884 seq.).

LAUFF, JOSEF (1855–), German poet and dramatist, was born at Cologne on the 16th of November 1855, the son of a jurist. He was educated at Münster in Westphalia, and entering the army served as a lieutenant of artillery at Thorn and subsequently at Cologne, where he attained the rank of captain in 1890. In 1898 he was summoned by the German emperor,

William II., to Wiesbaden, being at the same time promoted to major's rank, in order that he might devote his great dramatic talents to the royal theatre. His literary career began with the epic poems *Jan van Calker, ein Malerlied vom Niederrhein* (1887, 3rd ed., 1892) and *Der Helfensteiner, ein Sang aus dem Bauernkriege* (3rd ed., 1896). These were followed by *Die Overstolzin* (5th ed., 1900), *Herodias* (2nd ed., 1898) and the *Geisslerin* (4th ed., 1902). He also wrote the novels *Die Hexe* (6th ed., 1900), *Regina coeli* (a story of the fall of the Dutch Republic) (7th ed., 1904), *Die Hauptmannsfrau* (8th ed., 1903) and *Marie Verwahnen* (1903). But he is best known as a dramatist. Beginning with the tragedy *Ignes de Castro* (1894), he proceeded to dramatize the great monarchs of his country, and, in a Hohenzollern tetralogy, issued *Der Burggraf* (1897, 6th ed. 1900) and *Der Eisenzahn* (1900), to be followed by *Der grosse Kurfürst* (The Great Elector) and *Friedrich der Grosse* (Frederick the Great).

See A. Schroeter, *Josef Lauff, Ein litterarisches Zeitbild* (1899), and B. Sturm, *Josef Lauff* (1903).

LAUGHTER, the visible and audible expression of mirth, pleasure or the sense of the ridiculous by movements of the facial muscles and inarticulate sounds (see COMEDY, PLAY and HUMOUR). The O. Eng. *hleahtor* is formed from *hlehhan*, to laugh, a common Teutonic word; cf. Ger. *lachen*, Goth. *hlahjan*, Icel. *hlæja*, &c. These are in origin echoic or imitative words, to be referred to a Teut. base *hlah-*, Indo-Eur. *kark-*, to make a noise; Skeat (*Etym. Dict.*, 1898) connects ultimately Gr. *κλώσσειν*, to cluck like a hen, *κρώζειν*, to croak, &c. A gentle and inaudible form of laughter expressed by a movement of the lips and by the eyes is a "smile." This is a comparatively late word in English, and is due to Scandinavian influence; cf. Swed. *smila*; it is ultimately connected with Lat. *mirari*, to wonder, and probably with Gr. *μειδᾶν*.

LAUMONT, FRANÇOIS PIERRE NICHOLAS GILLET DE (1747–1834), French mineralogist, was born in Paris on the 28th of May 1747. He was educated at a military school and served in the army from 1772–1784, when he was appointed inspector of mines. His attention in his leisure time was wholly given to mineralogy, and he assisted in organizing the new École des Mines in Paris. He was author of numerous mineralogical papers in the *Journal* and *Annales des Mines*. The mineral laumontite was named after him by Haüy. He died in Paris on the 1st of June 1834.

LAUNCESTON, a market town and municipal borough in the Launceston parliamentary division of Cornwall, England, 35½ m. N.W. of Plymouth, on branches of the Great Western and the London & South-Western railways. Pop. (1901) 4053. It lies in a hilly district by and above the river Kensey, an affluent of the Tamar, the houses standing picturesquely on the southern slope of the narrow valley, with the keep of the ancient castle crowning the summit. On the northern slope lies the parish of St Stephen. The castle, the ruins of which are in part of Norman date, was the seat of the earls of Cornwall, and was frequently besieged during the civil wars of the 17th century. In 1656 George Fox the Quaker was imprisoned in the north-east tower for disturbing the peace at St Ives by distributing tracts. Fragments of the old town walls and the south gateway, of the Decorated period, are standing. The church of St Mary Magdalen, built of granite, and richly ornamented without, was erected early in the 16th century, but possesses a detached tower dated 1380. A fine Norman doorway, now appearing as the entrance to a hotel, is preserved from an Augustinian priory founded in the reign of Henry I. The parish church of St Stephen is Early English, and later, with a Perpendicular tower. The trade of Launceston is chiefly agricultural, but there are tanneries and iron foundries. The borough is under a mayor, 4 aldermen and 12 councillors. Area, 2189 acres.

A silver penny of Æthelred II. witnesses to the fact that the privilege of coining money was exercised by Launceston (Dunheved, Lanscaveton, Lanstone) more than half a century before the Norman conquest. At the time of the Domesday survey the canons of St Stephen held Launceston, and the count of Mortain held Dunheved. The number of families settled on the former is not given, but attention is called to the market which had been removed thence by the count to the neighbouring castle of Dunheved, which had two mills, one villein and thirteen bordars. A spot more favoured by nature could not have been chosen either for settlement or for defence than the rich lands near the confluence of the Kensey and Tamar, out of which there rises abruptly the gigantic mound upon which the castle is built. It is not known when the canons settled here nor whether the count's castle, then newly erected, replaced some earlier fortification. Reginald, earl of Cornwall (1140–1175), granted to the canons rights of jurisdiction in all their lands and exemption from suit of court in the shire and hundred courts. Richard (1225–1272), king of the Romans, constituted Dunheved a free borough, and granted to the burgesses freedom from pontage, stallage and suffrage, liberty to elect their own reeves, exemption from all pleas outside the borough except pleas of the crown, and a site for a gild-hall. The farm of the borough was fixed at 100s. payable to the earl, 65s. to the prior and 100s. 10d. to the lepers of St Leonard's. In 1205 the market which had been held on Sunday was changed to Thursday. An inquisition held in 1383 discloses two markets, a merchant gild, pillory and tumbrel. In 1555 Dunheved, otherwise Launceston, received a charter of incorporation, the common council to consist of a mayor, 8 aldermen and a recorder. By its provisions the borough was governed until 1835. The parliamentary franchise which had been conferred in 1294 was confined to the corporation and a number of free burgesses. In 1832 Launceston was shorn of one of its members, and in 1885 merged in the county. Separated from it by a small bridge over the Kensey lies the hamlet of Newport which, from 1547 until 1832, also returned two members. These were swept away when the Reform Bill became law. Launceston was the assize town until Earl Richard, having built a palace at Restormel, removed the assize to Lostwithiel. In 1386 Launceston regained the privilege by royal charter. From 1715 until 1837, eleven years only excepted, the assize was held alternately here and at Bodmin. Since that time Bodmin has enjoyed the distinction. Launceston has never had a staple industry. The manufacture of serge was considerable early in the 19th century. Its market on Saturdays is well attended, and an ancient fair on the Feast of St Thomas is among those which survive.

See A. F. Robbins, *Launceston Past and Present*.

LAUNCESTON, the second city of Tasmania, in the county of Cornwall, on the river Tamar, 40 m. from the N. coast of the island, and 133 m. by rail N. by W. of Hobart. The city lies amid surroundings of great natural beauty in a valley enclosed by lofty hills. Cora Linn, about 6 m. distant, a deep gorge of the North Esk river, the Punch Bowl and Cataract Gorge, over which the South Esk falls in a magnificent cascade, joining the North Esk to form the Tamar, are spots famed throughout the Australian commonwealth for their romantic beauty. The city is the commercial capital of northern Tasmania, the river Tamar being navigable up to the town for vessels of 4000 tons. The larger ships lie in midstream and discharge into lighters, while vessels of 2000 tons can berth alongside the wharves on to which the railway runs. Launceston is a well-planned, pleasant town, lighted by electricity, with numerous parks and squares and many fine buildings. The post office, the custom house, the post office savings bank and the Launceston bank form an attractive group; the town hall is used exclusively for civic purposes, public meetings and social functions being held in an elegant building called the Albert hall. There are also a good art gallery, a theatre and a number of fine churches, one of which, the Anglican church of St John, dates from 1824. The city, which attained that rank in 1889, has two attractive suburbs, Invermay and Trevallyn; it has a racecourse at Mowbray 2 m. distant, and is the centre and port of an important fruit-growing district. Pop. of the city proper (1901) 18,022, of the city and suburbs 21,180.

LAUNCH. (1) A verb meaning originally to hurl, discharge a missile or other object, also to rush or shoot out suddenly or rapidly. It is particularly used of the setting afloat a vessel from the stocks on which she has been built. The word is an adaptation of O. Fr. *lancher*, *lancier*, to hurl, throw, Lat. *lanceare*, from *lancea*, a lance or spear. (2) The name of a particular type of boat, usually applied to one of the largest size of ships' boats, or to a large boat moved by electricity, steam or other power. The word is an adaptation of the Span. *lancha*, pinnace, which is usually connected with *lanchara*, the Portuguese name, common in 16th and 17th century histories, for a fast-moving small vessel. This word is of Malay origin and is derived from *lanchār*, quick, speedy.

LAUNDRY, a place or establishment where soiled linen, &c., is washed. The word is a contraction of an earlier form *lavendry*, from Lat. *lavanda*, things to be washed, *lavare*, to wash. "Launder," a similar contraction of *lavender*, was one (of either sex) who washes linen; from its use as a verb came the form "launderer," employed as both masculine and feminine in America, and the feminine form "laundress," which is also applied to a female caretaker of chambers in the Inns of Court, London.

Laundry-work has become an important industry, organized on a scale which requires elaborate mechanical plant very different from the simple appliances that once sufficed for domestic needs. For the actual cleansing of the articles, instead of being rubbed by the hand or trodden by the foot of the washer-woman, or stirred and beaten with a "dolly" in the wash-tub, they are very commonly treated in rotary washing machines driven by power. These machines consist of an outer casing containing an inner horizontal cylindrical cage, in which the clothes are placed. By the rotation of this cage, which is reversed by automatic gearing every few turns, they are rubbed and tumbled on each other in the soap and water which is contained in the outer casing and enters the inner cylinder through perforations. The outer casing is provided with inlet valves for hot and cold water, and with discharge valves; and often also arrangements are made for the admission of steam under pressure, so that the contents can be boiled. Thus the operations of washing, boiling, rinsing and blueing (this last being the addition of a blue colouring matter to mask the yellow tint and thus give the linen the appearance of whiteness) can be performed without removing the articles from the machine. For drying, the old methods of wringing by hand, or by machines in which the clothes were squeezed between rollers of wood or india-rubber, have been largely superseded by "hydro-extractors" or "centrifugals." In these the wet garments are placed in a perforated cage or basket, supported on vertical bearings, which is rotated at a high speed (1000 to 1500 times a minute) and in a short time as much as 85% of the moisture may thus be removed. The drying is often completed in an apartment through which dry air is forced by fans. In the process of finishing linen the old-fashioned laundress made use of the mangle, about the only piece of mechanism at her disposal. In the box-mangle the articles were pressed on a flat surface by rollers which were weighted with a box full of stones, moved to and fro by a rack and pinion. In a later and less cumbrous form of the machine they were passed between wooden rollers or "bowls" held close together by weighted levers. An important advance was marked by the introduction of machines which not only smooth and press the linen like the mangle, but also give it the glazed finish obtained by hot ironing. Machines of this kind are essentially the same as the calenders used in paper and textile manufacture. They are made in a great variety of forms, to enable them to deal with articles of different shapes, but they may be described generally as consisting either of a polished metal roller, heated by steam or gas, which works against a blanketted or felted surface in the form of another roller or a flat table, or, as in the Decoudun type, of a felted metal roller rotating against a heated concave bed of polished metal. In cases where hand-ironing is resorted to, time is economized by the employment of irons which are continuously heated by gas or electricity.

LA UNION, a seaport and the capital of the department of La Union, Salvador, 144 m. E.S.E. of San Salvador. Pop. (1905) about 4000. La Union is situated at the foot of a lofty volcano, variously known as Conchagua, Pinos and Meanguera, and on a broad indentation in the western shore of Fonseca Bay. Its harbour, the best in the republic, is secure in all weathers and affords good anchorage to large ships. La Union is the port of shipment for the exports of San Miguel and other centres of production in eastern Salvador.

LA UNION, a town of eastern Spain in the province of Murcia, 5 m. by rail E. of Cartagena and close to the Mediterranean Sea. Pop. (1900) 30,275, of whom little more than half inhabit the town itself. The rest are scattered among the numerous metal works and mines of iron, manganese, calamine, sulphur and lead, which are included within the municipal boundaries. La Union is quite a modern town, having sprung up in the second half of the 19th century. It has good modern municipal buildings, schools, hospital, town hall and large factories.

LAURAHÜTTE, a village of Germany, in the Prussian province of Silesia, 5 m. S.E. of Beuthen, on the railway Tarnowitz-Emanuelsegen. It has an Evangelical and a Roman Catholic church, but is especially noteworthy for its huge iron works, which employ about 6000 hands. Pop. (1900) 13,571.

LAUREATE (Lat. *laureatus*, from *laurea*, the laurel tree). The laurel, in ancient Greece, was sacred to Apollo, and as such was used to form a crown or wreath of honour for poets and heroes; and this usage has been widespread. The word "laureate" or "laureated" thus came in English to signify eminent, or associated with glory, literary or military. "Laureate letters" in old times meant the despatches announcing a victory; and the epithet was given, even officially (*e.g.* to John Skelton) by universities, to distinguished poets. The name of "bacca-laureate" for the university degree of bachelor shows a confusion with a supposed etymology from Lat. *bacca lauri* (the laurel berry), which though incorrect (see BACHELOR) involves the same idea. From the more general use of the term "poet laureate" arose its restriction in England to the office of the poet attached to the royal household, first held by Ben Jonson, for whom the position was, in its essentials, created by Charles I. in 1617. (Jonson's appointment does not seem to have been formally made as poet-laureate, but his position was equivalent to that). The office was really a development of the practice of earlier times, when minstrels and versifiers were part of the retinue of the King; it is recorded that Richard Cœur de Lion had a *versificator regis* (Gulielmus Peregrinus), and Henry III. had a versificator (Master Henry); in the 15th century John Kay, also a "versifier," described himself as Edward IV.'s "humble poet laureate." Moreover, the crown had shown its patronage in various ways; Chaucer had been given a pension and a perquisite of wine by Edward III., and Spenser a pension by Queen Elizabeth. W. Hamilton classes Chaucer, Gower, Kay, Andrew Bernard, Skelton, Robert Whittington, Richard Edwards, Spenser and Samuel Daniel, as "volunteer Laureates." Sir William Davenant succeeded Jonson in 1638, and the title of poet laureate was conferred by letters patent on Dryden in 1670, two years after Davenant's death, coupled with a pension of £300 and a butt of Canary wine. The post then became a regular institution, though the emoluments varied, Dryden's successors being T. Shadwell (who originated annual birthday and New Year odes), Nahum Tate, Nicholas Rowe, Laurence Eusden, Colley Cibber, William Whitehead, Thomas Warton, H. J. Pye, Southey, Wordsworth, Tennyson and, four years after Tennyson's death, Alfred Austin. The office took on a new lustre from the personal distinction of Southey, Wordsworth and Tennyson; it had fallen into contempt before Southey, and on Tennyson's death there was a considerable feeling that no possible successor was acceptable (William Morris and Swinburne being hardly court poets). Eventually, however, the undesirability of breaking with tradition for temporary reasons, and thus severing the one official link between literature and the state, prevailed over the protests against following Tennyson by any one of inferior genius. It may be noted that abolition was similarly advocated when Warton and Wordsworth died.

The poet laureate, being a court official, was considered

responsible for producing formal and appropriate verses on birthdays and state occasions; but his activity in this respect has varied, according to circumstances, and the custom ceased to be obligatory after Pye's death. Wordsworth stipulated, before accepting the honour, that no formal effusions from him should be considered a necessity; but Tennyson was generally happy in his numerous poems of this class. The emoluments of the post have varied; Ben Jonson first received a pension of 100 marks, and later an annual "terse of Canary wine." To Pye an allowance of £27 was made instead of the wine. Tennyson drew £72 a year from the lord chamberlain's department, and £27 from the lord steward's in lieu of the "butt of sack."

See Walter Hamilton's *Poets Laureate of England* (1879), and his contributions to *Notes and Queries* (Feb. 4, 1893).

LAUREL. At least four shrubs or small trees are called by this name in Great Britain, viz. the common or cherry laurel (*Prunus Laurocerasus*), the Portugal laurel (*P. lusitanica*), the bay or sweet laurel (*Laurus nobilis*) and the spurge laurel (*Daphne Laureola*). The first two belong to the rose family (*Rosaceae*), to the section *Cerasus* (to which also belongs the cherry) of the genus *Prunus*.

The common laurel is a native of the woody and sub-alpine regions of the Caucasus, of the mountains of northern Persia, of north-western Asia Minor and of the Crimea. It was received into Europe in 1576, and flowered for the first time in 1583. Ray in 1688 relates that it was first brought from Trebisonde to Constantinople, thence to Italy, France, Germany and England. Parkinson in his *Paradisus* records it as growing in a garden at Highgate in 1629; and in Johnson's edition of Gerard's *Herbal* (1633) it is recorded that the plant "is now got into many of our choice English gardens, where it is well respected for the beauty of the leaues and their lasting or continuall greennesse" (see Loudon's *Arboretum*, ii. 717). The leaves of this plant are rather large, broadly lance-shaped and of a leathery consistence, the margin being somewhat serrated. They are remarkable for their poisonous properties, giving off the odour of bitter almonds when bruised; the vapour thus issuing is sufficient to kill small insects by the prussic acid which it contains. The leaves when cut up finely and distilled yield oil of bitter almonds and hydrocyanic (prussic) acid. Sweetmeats, custards, cream, &c., are often flavoured with laurel-leaf water, as it imparts the same flavour as bitter almonds; but it should be used sparingly, as it is a dangerous poison, having several times proved fatal. The first case occurred in 1731, which induced a careful investigation to be made of its nature; Schrader in 1802 discovered it to contain hydrocyanic acid. The effects of the distilled laurel-leaf water on living vegetables is to destroy them like ordinary prussic acid; while a few drops act on animals as a powerful poison. It was introduced into the British pharmacopoeia in 1839, but is generally superseded by the use of prussic acid. The *aqua laurocerasi*, or cherry laurel water, is now standardized to contain 0·1% of hydrocyanic acid. It must not be given in doses larger than 2 drachms. It contains benzole hydrate, which is antiseptic, and is therefore suitable for hypodermic injection; but the drug is of inconsistent strength, owing to the volatility of prussic acid.

The following varieties of the common laurel are in cultivation: the Caucasian (*Prunus Laurocerasus*, var. *caucasica*), which is hardier and bears very rich dark-green glossy foliage; the Versailles laurel (var. *latifolia*), which has larger leaves; the Colchican (var. *colchica*), which is a dwarf-spreading bush with narrow sharply serrated pale-green leaves. There is also the variety *rotundifolia* with short broad leaves, the Grecian with narrow leaves and the Alexandrian with very small leaves.

The Portugal laurel is a native of Portugal and Madeira. It was introduced into England about the year 1648, when it was cultivated in the Oxford Botanic Gardens. During the first half of the 18th century this plant, the common laurel and the holly were almost the only hardy evergreen shrubs procurable in British nurseries. They are all three tender about Paris, and consequently much less seen in the neighbourhood of that city than in England, where they stand the ordinary winters but not very severe ones. There is a variety (*myrtifolia*) of compact habit with smaller narrow leaves, also a variegated variety.

The evergreen glossy foliage of the common and Portugal laurels render them well adapted for shrubberies, while the racemes of white flowers are not devoid of beauty. The former often ripens its insipid drupes, but the Portugal rarely does so. It appears to be less able to accommodate itself to the English climate, as the wood does not usually "ripen" so satisfactorily. Hence it is rather more liable to be cut by the frost. It is grown in the open air in the southern United States.

The bay or sweet laurel (*Laurus nobilis*) belongs to the family Lauraceae, which contains sassafras, benzoin, camphor and other trees remarkable for their aromatic properties. It is a large evergreen shrub, sometimes reaching the height of 60 ft., but rarely assuming a truly tree-like character. The leaves are smaller than those of the preceding laurels, possessing an aromatic and slightly bitter flavour, and are quite devoid of the poisonous properties of the cherry laurel. The small yellowish-green flowers are produced in axillary clusters, are male or female, and consist of a simple 4-leaved perianth which encloses nine stamens in the male, the anthers of which dehisce by valves which lift upwards as in the common barberry, and carry glandular processes at the base of the filament. The fruit consists of a succulent berry surrounded by the persistent base of the perianth. The bay laurel is a native of Italy, Greece and North Africa, and is abundantly grown in the British Isles as an evergreen shrub, as it stands most winters. The date of its introduction is unknown, but must have been previous to 1562, as it is mentioned in Turner's *Herbal* published in that year. A full description also occurs in Gerard's *Herball* (1597, p. 1222). It was used for strewing the floors of houses of distinguished persons in the reign of Elizabeth. Several varieties have been cultivated, differing in the character of their foliage, as the *undulata* or wave-leafed, *salicifolia* or willow-leafed, the variegated, the broad-leafed and the curled; there is also the double-flowered variety. The bay laurel was carried to North America by the early colonists.

This laurel is generally held to be the *Daphne* of the ancients, though Lindley, following Gerard (*Herball*, 1597, p. 761), asserted that the Greek *Daphne* was *Ruscus racemosus*. Among the Greeks the laurel was sacred to Apollo, especially in connexion with Tempe, in whose laurel groves the god himself obtained purification from the blood of the Python. This legend was dramatically represented at the Pythian festival once in eight years, a boy fleeing from Delphi to Tempe, and after a time being led back with song, crowned and adorned with laurel. Similar δαφνηφορίαι were known elsewhere in Greece. Apollo, himself purified, was the author of purification and atonement to other penitents, and the laurel was the symbol of this power, which came to be generally associated with his person and sanctuaries. The relation of Apollo to the laurel was expressed in the legend of Daphne (*q.v.*). The victors in the Pythian games were crowned with the laurels of Apollo, and thus the laurel became the symbol of triumph in Rome as well as in Greece. As Apollo was the god of poets, the *Laurea Apollinaris* naturally belonged to poetic merit (see LAUREATE). The various prerogatives of the laurel among the ancients are collected by Pliny (*Hist. Nat.* xv. 30). It was a sign of truce, like the olive branch; letters announcing victory and the arms of the victorious soldiery were garnished with it; it was thought that lightning could not strike it, and the emperor Tiberius always wore a laurel wreath during thunderstorms. From its association with the divine power of purification and protection, it was often set before the door of Greek houses, and among the Romans it was the guardian of the gates of the Caesars (Ovid, *Met.* i. 562 sq.). The laurel worn by Augustus and his successors had a miraculous history: the laurel grove at the imperial villa by the ninth milestone on the Flaminian way sprang from a shoot sent from heaven to Livia Drusilla (Sueton. *Galba*, i.). Like the olive, the laurel was forbidden to profane use. It was employed in divination; the crackling of its leaves in the sacred flame was a good omen (Tibull. ii. 5. 81).

and their silence unlucky (Propert. ii. 21); and the leaves when chewed excited a prophetic afflatus (δαφνηφάγοι, cf. Tibull. ii. 5. 63). There is a poem enumerating the ancient virtues of the laurel by J. Passeratius (1594).

The last of the plants mentioned above under the name of laurel is the so-called spurge laurel (*Daphne Laureola*). This and one other species (*D. Mezereum*), the mezereon, are the sole representatives of the family Thymelaeaceae in Great Britain. The spurge laurel is a small evergreen shrub, with alternate somewhat lanceolate leaves with entire margins. The green flowers are produced in early spring, and form drooping clusters at the base of the leaves. The calyx is four-cleft, and carries eight stamens in two circles of four each within the tube. The pistil forms a berry, green at first, but finally black. The mezereon differs in blossoming before the leaves are produced, while the flowers are lilac instead of green. The bark furnishes the drug *Cortex Mezerei*, for which that of the spurge laurel is often substituted. Both are powerfully acrid, but the latter is less so than the bark of mezereon. It is now only used as an ingredient of the *liquor sarsae compositus concentratus*. Of other species in cultivation there are *D. Fortunei* from China, which has lilac flowers; *D. pontica*, a native of Asia Minor; *D. alpina*, from the Italian Alps; *D. collina*, south European; and *D. Cneorum*, the garland flower or trailing daphne, the handsomest of the hardy species.

See Hemsley's *Handbook of Hardy Trees, &c.*

LAURENS, HENRY (1724–1792), American statesman, was born in Charleston, South Carolina, on the 24th of February 1724, of Huguenot ancestry. When sixteen he became a clerk in a counting-house in London, and later engaged in commercial pursuits with great success at Charleston until 1771, when he retired from active business. He spent the next three years travelling in Europe and superintending the education of his sons in England. In spite of his strong attachment to England, and although he had defended the Stamp Act, in 1774, in the hope of averting war, he united with thirty-seven other Americans in a petition to parliament against the passing of the Boston Port Bill. Becoming convinced that a peaceful settlement was impracticable, he returned to Charleston at the close of 1774, and there allied himself with the conservative element of the Whig party. He was soon made president of the South Carolina council of safety, and in 1776 vice-president of the state; in the same year he was sent as a delegate from South Carolina to the general continental congress at Philadelphia, of which body he was president from November 1777 until December 1778. In August 1780 he started on a mission to negotiate on behalf of congress a loan of ten million dollars in Holland; but he was captured on the 3rd of September off the Banks of Newfoundland by the British frigate "Vestal," taken to London and closely imprisoned in the Tower. His papers were found to contain a sketch of a treaty between the United States and Holland projected by William Lee, in the service of Congress, and Jan de Neufville, acting on behalf of Mynheer Van Berckel, pensionary of Amsterdam, and this discovery eventually led to war between Great Britain and the United Provinces. During his imprisonment his health became greatly impaired. On the 31st of December 1781 he was released on parole, and he was finally exchanged for Cornwallis. In June 1782 he was appointed one of the American commissioners for negotiating peace with Great Britain, but he did not reach Paris until the 28th of November 1782, only two days before the preliminaries of peace were signed by himself, John Adams, Franklin and Jay. On the day of signing, however, he procured the insertion of a clause prohibiting the British from "carrying away any negroes or other property of American inhabitants"; and this subsequently led to considerable friction between the British and [illegible] governments. On account of failing health he did [illegible] to the signing of the definitive treaty, but [illegible] in Charleston, where he died on the 8th of December [illegible].

[illegible] (1754–1782), American revolutionary [illegible] Charleston, South [illegible] 28th of October 1754. He was educated in England, and on his return to America in 1777, in the height of the revolutionary struggle, he joined Washington's staff. He soon gained his commander's confidence, which he reciprocated with the most devoted attachment, and was entrusted with the delicate duties of a confidential secretary, which he performed with much tact and skill. He was present in all Washington's battles, from Brandywine to Yorktown, and his gallantry on every occasion has gained him the title of "the Bayard of the Revolution." Laurens displayed bravery even to rashness in the storming of the Chew mansion at Germantown; at Monmouth, where he saved Washington's life, and was himself severely wounded; and at Coosahatchie, where, with a handful of men, he defended a pass against a large English force under General Augustine Prevost, and was again wounded. He fought a duel against General Charles Lee, and wounded him, on account of that officer's disrespectful conduct towards Washington. Laurens distinguished himself further at Savannah, and at the siege of Charleston in 1780. After the capture of Charleston by the English, he rejoined Washington, and was selected by him as a special envoy to appeal to the king of France for supplies for the relief of the American armies, which had been brought by prolonged service and scanty pay to the verge of dissolution. The more active co-operation of the French fleets with the land forces in Virginia, which was one result of his mission, brought about the disaster of Cornwallis at Yorktown. Laurens lost no time in rejoining the army, and at Yorktown was at the head of an American storming party which captured an advanced redoubt. Laurens was designated with the vicomte de Noailles to arrange the terms of the surrender, which virtually ended the war, although desultory skirmishing, especially in the South, attended the months of delay before peace was formally concluded. In one of these trifling affairs on the 27th of August 1782, on the Combahee river, Laurens exposed himself needlessly and was killed. Washington lamented deeply the death of Laurens, saying of him, "He had not a fault that I could discover, unless it were intrepidity bordering upon rashness."

The most valuable of Henry Laurens's papers and pamphlets including the important "Narrative of the Capture of Henry Laurens, of his Confinement in the Tower of London, &c., 1780, 1781, 1782," in vol. i. (Charleston, 1857) of the Society's *Collections*, have been published by the South Carolina Historical Society. John Laurens's military correspondence, with a brief memoir by W. G. Simms, was privately printed by the Bradford Club, New York, in 1867.

LAURENT, FRANÇOIS (1810–1887), Belgian historian and jurisconsult, was born at Luxemburg on the 8th of July 1810. He held a high appointment in the ministry of justice for some time before he became professor of civil law in the university of Ghent in 1836. His advocacy of liberal and anti-clerical principles both from his chair and in the press made him bitter enemies, but he retained his position until his death on the 11th of February 1887. He treated the relations of church and state in *L'Église et l'état* (Brussels, 3 vols., 1858–1862; new and revised edition, 1865); and the same subject occupied a large proportion of the eighteen volumes of his chief historical work, *Études sur l'histoire de l'humanité* (Ghent and Brussels, 1855–1870), which aroused considerable interest beyond the boundaries of Belgium. His fame as a lawyer rests on his authoritative exposition of the Code Napoléon in his *Principes de droit civil* (Brussels, 33 vols., 1869–1878), and his *Droit civil international* (Brussels, 8 vols., 1880–1881). He was charged in 1879 by the minister of justice with the preparation of a report on the proposed revision of the civil code. Besides his anti-clerical pamphlets his minor writings include much discussion of social questions, of the organization of savings banks, asylums, &c., and he founded the *Société Callier* for the encouragement of thrift among the working classes. With Gustave Callier, whose funeral in 1863 was made the occasion of a display of clerical intolerance, Laurent had much in common, and the efforts of the society were directed to the continuation of Callier's philanthropic schemes.

For a complete list of his works, see G. Koninck, *Bibliographie nationale* (Brussels, vol. ii., 1892).

LAURENTINA, VIA, an ancient road of Italy, leading southwards from Rome. The question of the nomenclature of the group of roads between the Via Ardeatina and the Via Ostiensis is somewhat difficult, and much depends on the view taken as to the site of Laurentum. It seems probable, however, that the Via Laurentina proper is that which led out of the Porta Ardeatina of the Aurelian wall and went direct to Tor Paterno, while the road branching from the Via Ostiensis at the third mile, and leading past Decimo to Lavinium (Pratica), which crosses the other road at right angles not far from its destination (the Laurentina there running S.W. and that to Lavinium S.E.) may for convenience be called Lavinatis, though this name does not occur in ancient times. On this latter road, beyond Decimo, two milestones, one of Tiberius, the other of Maxentius, each bearing the number 11, have been found; and farther on, at Capocotta, traces of ancient buildings, and an important sepulchral inscription of a Jewish ruler of a synagogue have come to light. That the Via Laurentina was near the Via Ardeatina is clear from the fact that the same contractor was responsible for both roads. Laurentum was also accessible by a branch from the Via Ostiensis at the eighth mile (at Malafede) leading past Castel Porziano, the royal hunting-lodge, which is identical with the ancient Ager Solonius (in which, Festus tells us, was situated the Pomonal or sacred grove of Pomona) and which later belonged to Marius.

See R. Lanciani in articles quoted under LAVINIUM. (T. As.)

LAURENTIUS, PAUL (1554–1624), Lutheran divine, was born on the 30th of March 1554 at Ober Wierau, where his father, of the same names, was pastor. From a school at Zwickau he entered (1573) the university of Leipzig, graduating in 1577. In 1578 he became rector of the Martin school at Halberstadt; in 1583 he was appointed town's preacher at Plauen-im-Vogtland, and in 1586 superintendent at Oelnitz. On the 20th of October 1595 he took his doctorate in theology at Jena, his thesis on the *Symbolum Athanasii* (1597), gaining him similar honours at Wittenberg and Leipzig. He was promoted (1605) to be pastor and superintendent at Dresden, and transferred (1616) to the superintendence at Meissen, where he died on the 24th of February 1624. His works consist chiefly of commentaries and expository discourses on prophetic books of the Old Testament, parts of the Psalter, the Lord's Prayer and the history of the Passion. In two orations he compared Luther to Elijah. Besides theological works he was the author of a *Spicilegium Gnomonologicum* (1612).

The main authority is C. Schlegel, the historian of the Dresden superintendents (1698), summarized by H. W. Rotermund, in the additions (1810) to Jöcher, *Gelehrten-Lexicon* (1750). (A. Go.*)

LAURIA (LURIA or LORIA) ROGER DE (d. 1305), admiral of Aragon and Sicily, was the most prominent figure in the naval war which arose directly from the Sicilian Vespers. Nothing is really known of his life before he was named admiral in 1283. His father was a supporter of the Hohenstaufen, and his mother came to Spain with Costanza, the daughter of Manfred of Beneventum, when she married Peter, the eldest son and heir of James the Conqueror of Aragon. According to one account Bella of Lauria, the admiral's mother, had been the foster mother of Costanza. Roger, who accompanied his mother, was bred at the court of Aragon and endowed with lands in the newly conquered kingdom of Valencia. When the misrule of Charles of Anjou's French followers had produced the famous revolt known as the Sicilian Vespers in 1282, Roger de Lauria accompanied King Peter III. of Aragon on the expedition which under the cover of an attack on the Moorish kingdom of Tunis was designed to be an attempt to obtain possession of all or at least part of the Hohenstaufen dominions in Naples and Sicily which the king claimed by right of his wife as the heiress of Manfred. In 1283, when the island had put itself under the protection of Peter III. and had crowned him king, he gave the command of his fleet to Roger de Lauria. The commission speaks of him in the most laudatory terms, but makes no reference to previous military services.

From this time forward till the peace of Calatabellota in 1303, Roger de Lauria was the ever victorious leader of fleets in the service of Aragon, both in the waters of southern Italy and on the coast of Catalonia. In the year of his appointment he defeated a French naval force in the service of Charles of Anjou, off Malta. The main object before him was to repel the efforts of the Angevine party to reconquer Sicily and then to carry the war into their dominions in Naples. Although Roger de Lauria did incidental fighting on shore, he was as much a naval officer as any modern admiral, and his victories were won by good manœuvring and by discipline. The Catalan squadron, on which the Sicilian was moulded, was in a state of high and intelligent efficiency. Its chiefs relied not on merely boarding, and the use of the sword, as the French forces of Charles of Anjou did, but on the use of the ram, and of the powerful cross-bows used by the Catalans either by hand or, in case of the larger ones, mounted on the bulwarks, with great skill. The conflict was in fact the equivalent on the water of the battles between the English bowmen and the disorderly chivalry of France in the Hundred Years' War. In 1284 Roger defeated the Angevine fleet in the Bay of Naples, taking prisoner the heir to the kingdom, Charles of Salerno, who remained a prisoner in the hands of the Aragonese in Sicily, and later in Spain, for years. In 1285 he fought on the coast of Catalonia one of the most brilliant campaigns in all naval history. The French king Philippe le Hardi had invaded Catalonia with a large army to which the pope gave the character of crusaders, in order to support his cousin of Anjou in his conflict with the Aragonese. The king, Peter III., had offended his nobles by his vigorous exercise of the royal authority, and received little support from them, but the outrages perpetrated by the French invaders raised the towns and country against them. The invaders advanced slowly, taking the obstinately defended towns one by one, and relying on the co-operation of a large number of allies, who were stationed in squadrons along the coast, and who brought stores and provisions from Narbonne and Aigues Mortes. They relied in fact wholly on their fleet for their existence. A successful blow struck at that would force them to retreat. King Peter was compelled to risk Sicily for a time, and he recalled Roger de Lauria from Palermo to the coast of Catalonia. The admiral reached Barcelona on the 24th of August, and was informed of the disposition of the French. He saw that if he could break the centre of their line of squadrons, stretched as it was so far that its general superiority of numbers was lost in the attempt to occupy the whole of the coast, he could then dispose of the extremities in detail. On the night of the 9th of September he fell on the central squadron of the French fleet near the Hormigas. The Catalan and Sicilian squadrons doubled on the end of the enemies' line, and by a vigorous employment of the ram, as well as by the destructive shower of bolts from the cross-bows, which cleared the decks of the French, gained a complete victory. The defeat of the enemy was followed, as usually in medieval naval wars, by a wholesale massacre. Roger then made for Rosas, and tempted out the French squadron stationed there by approaching under French colours. In the open it was beaten in its turn. The result was the capture of the town, and of the stores collected there by King Philippe for the support of his army. Within a short time he was forced to retreat amid sufferings from hunger, and the incessant attacks of the Catalan mountaineers, by which his army was nearly annihilated. This campaign, which was followed up by destructive attacks on the French coast, saved Catalonia from the invaders, and completely ruined the French naval power for the time being. No medieval admiral of any nation displayed an equal combination of intellect and energy, and none of modern times has surpassed it. The work had been so effectually done on the coast of Catalonia that Roger de Lauria was able to return to Sicily, and resume his command in the struggle of Aragonese and Angevine to gain, or to hold, the possession of Naples.

He maintained his reputation and was uniformly successful in his battles at sea, but they were not always fought for the defence of Sicily. The death of Peter III. in 1286 and of his [illegible] in the following year caused a division among [illegible] house of Aragon. The new king, James, [illegible] up Sicily to the Angevine line with which [illegible] and alliance, but his younger brother Fadrique [illegible] offered him by the Sicilians, and fought [illegible] against both the Angevines and his senior. [illegible] to force him to submission without success. [illegible] adhered for a time to Fadrique, but his arrogant [illegible] an intolerable supporter, and he appears, [illegible] thought that he was bound to obey the king [illegible] large estates in Valencia gave him a strong [illegible] offending that sovereign. He therefore left [illegible] confiscated his estates in Sicily and put one of [illegible] death as a traitor. For this Roger de Lauria [illegible] revenge in two successive victories at sea over [illegible] When the war, which had become a ravening of [illegible] at last ended by the peace of Calatabellota, [illegible] retired to Valencia, where he died on the 2nd [illegible] and was buried, by his express orders, in the [illegible] Creus, a now deserted monastery of the Cistercians [illegible] of his old master Peter III. In his ferocity, [illegible] combination of loyalty to his feudal lord with utter [illegible] to all other men, Roger belonged to his age. [illegible] he was far above his contemporaries and his [illegible] many generations.

[illegible] Guerra del Vespro Siciliano gives a general picture [illegible] but the portrait of Roger de Lauria must be sought in [illegible] Chronicle of the Catalan Ramon de Muntaner who knew him and [illegible] his school. There is a very fair and well "documented" account of the masterly campaign of 1285 in Charles de la [illegible] Histoire de la marine française, i. 189-217. (D. H.)

LAURIA, or Loria, a city of Basilicata, Italy, in the province of Potenza, situated near the borders of Calabria, 7½ m. by road [illegible] of Lagonegro. Pop. (1901) 10,470. It is a walled town on the steep side of a hill with another portion in the plain below, 1271 ft. above sea-level. The castle was the birthplace of Ruggiero di Loria, the great Italian admiral of the 13th century. It was destroyed by the French under Masséna in 1806.

LAURIER, SIR WILFRID (1841-), Canadian statesman, was born on the 20th of November 1841, at St Lin in the province of Quebec. The child of French Roman Catholic parents, he [illegible] school of his native parish and for eight [illegible] of the Protestant elementary school [illegible] English; his association with [illegible] whom he lived during this period [illegible] his mind. At twelve years of age [illegible] and was there for seven years. [illegible] schools in Quebec then available [illegible] direct ecclesiastical control. [illegible] office at Montreal and took the [illegible] At graduation he delivered [illegible] This, like so many of his [illegible] an appeal for sympathy and union [illegible] races as the secret of the future [illegible] law in Montreal, but owing to [illegible] where he opened a law [illegible] a newspaper then [illegible] the seat of one of the [illegible] the district was fairly [illegible] speaking people, and [illegible] by his constant [illegible] and his intimate [illegible] the Institut Canadien, a [illegible] owing to its liberal dis- [illegible] upon its shelves were [illegible] by the Roman [illegible] an organ of extreme [illegible] and also under [illegible] surviving copies contains [illegible] as a scheme [illegible]

of Lower Canada. The Liberals of Quebec under the leadership of Sir Antoine Dorion were hostile to confederation, or at least to the terms of union agreed upon at the Quebec conference, and Laurier in editorials and speeches maintained the position of Dorion and his allies. He was elected to the Quebec legislature in 1871, and his first speech in the provincial assembly excited great interest on account of its literary qualities and the attractive manner and logical method of the speaker. He was not less successful in the Dominion House of Commons, to which he was elected in 1874. During his first two years in the federal parliament his chief speeches were made in defence of Riel and the French halfbreeds who were concerned in the Red River rebellion, and on fiscal questions. Sir John Macdonald, then in opposition, had committed his party to a protectionist policy, and Laurier, notwithstanding that the Liberal party stood for a low tariff avowed himself to be "a moderate protectionist." He declared that if he were in Great Britain he would be a free trader, but that free trade or protection must be applied according to the necessities of a country, and that which protection necessarily involved taxation it was the price a young and vigorous nation must pay for its development. But the Liberal government, to which Laurier was admitted as minister of inland revenue in 1877, made only a slight increase in duties, raising the general tariff from 15% to 17½%; and against the political judgment of Alexander Mackenzie, Sir Richard Cartwright, George Brown, Laurier and other of the more influential leaders of the party, it adhered to a low tariff platform. In the bye-election which followed Laurier's admission to the cabinet he was defeated—the only personal defeat he ever sustained; but a few weeks later he was returned for Quebec East, a constituency which he held thenceforth by enormous majorities. In 1878 his party went out of office and Sir John Macdonald entered upon a long term of power, with protection as the chief feature of his policy, to which was afterwards added the construction of the Canadian Pacific railway

After the defeat of the Mackenzie government, Laurier sat in Parliament as the leader of the Quebec Liberals and first lieutenant to the Hon. Edward Blake, who succeeded Mackenzie in the leadership of the party. He was associated with Blake in his sustained opposition to high tariff, and to the Conservative plan for the construction of the Canadian Pacific railway, and was a conspicuous figure in the long struggle between Sir John Macdonald and the leaders of the Liberal party to settle the territorial limits of the province of Ontario and the legislative rights of the provinces under the constitution. He was forced also to maintain a long conflict with the ultramontane element of the Roman Catholic church in Quebec, which for many years had a close working alliance with the Conservative politicians of the province and even employed spiritual coercion in order to detach votes from the Liberal party. Notwithstanding that Quebec was almost solidly Roman Catholic the Rouges sternly resisted clerical pressure; they appealed to the courts and had certain elections voided on the ground of undue clerical influence, and at length persuaded the pope to send out a delegate to Canada, through whose inquiry into the circumstances the abuses were checked and the zeal of the ultramontanes restrained.

In 1887, upon the resignation of Blake on the ground of ill-health, Laurier became leader of the Liberal party, although he and many of the more influential men in the party doubted the wisdom of the proceeding. He was the first French Canadian to lead a federal party in Canada since confederation. Apart from the natural fear that he would arouse prejudice in the English-speaking provinces, the second Riel rebellion was then still fresh in the public mind, and the fierce nationalist agitation which Riel's execution had excited in Quebec had hardly subsided. Laurier could hardly have come to the leadership at a more inopportune moment, and probably he would not have accepted the office at all if he had not believed that Blake could be persuaded to resume the leadership when his health was restored. But from the first he won great popularity even in the English-speaking provinces, and showed unusual capacity for leadership. His party was beaten in the first general election held after he became leader (1891), but even with its policy of unrestricted reciprocity with the United States, and with Sir John Macdonald still at the head of the Conservative party, it was beaten by only a small majority. Five years later, with unrestricted reciprocity relegated to the background, and with a platform which demanded tariff revision so adjusted as not to endanger established interests, and which opposed the federal measure designed to restore in Manitoba the separate or Roman Catholic schools which the provincial government had abolished, Laurier carried the country, and in July 1896 he was called by Lord Aberdeen, then governor-general, to form a government.

He was the first French-Canadian to occupy the office of premier; and his personal supremacy was shown by his long continuance in power. During the years from 1896 to 1910, he came to hold a position within the British Empire which was in its way unique, and in this period he had seen Canadian prosperity advance progressively by leaps and bounds. The chief features of his administration were the fiscal preference of 33⅓% in favour of goods imported into Canada from Great Britain, the despatch of Canadian contingents to South Africa during the Boer war, the contract with the Grand Trunk railway for the construction of a second transcontinental road from ocean to ocean, the assumption by Canada of the imperial fortresses at Halifax and Esquimault, the appointment of a federal railway commission with power to regulate freight charges, express rates and telephone rates, and the relations between competing companies, the reduction of the postal rate to Great Britain from 5 cents to 2 cents and of the domestic rate from 3 cents to 2 cents, a substantial contribution to the Pacific cable, a practical and courageous policy of settlement and development in the Western territories, the division of the North-West territories into the provinces of Alberta and Saskatchewan and the enactment of the legislation necessary to give them provincial status, and finally (1910), a tariff arrangement with the United States, which, if not all that Canada might claim in the way of reciprocity, showed how entirely the course of events had changed the balance of commercial interests in North America.

Laurier made his first visit to Great Britain on the occasion of Queen Victoria's diamond jubilee (1897), when he received the grand cross of the Bath; he then secured the denunciation of the Belgian and German treaties and thus obtained for the colonies the right to make preferential trade arrangements with the mother country. His personality made a powerful impression in Great Britain and also in France, which he visited before his return to Canada. His strong facial resemblance both to Lord Beaconsfield and to Sir John Macdonald marked him out in the public eye, and he captured attention by his charm of manner, fine command of scholarly English and genuine eloquence. Some of his speeches in Great Britain, coming as they did from a French-Canadian, and revealing delicate appreciation of British sentiment and thorough comprehension of the genius of British institutions, excited great interest and enthusiasm, while one or two impassioned speeches in the Canadian parliament during the Boer war profoundly influenced opinion in Canada and had a pronounced effect throughout the empire.

A skilful party-leader, Laurier kept from the first not only the affection of his political friends but the respect of his opponents; while enforcing the orderly conduct of public business, he was careful as first minister to maintain the dignity of parliament. In office he proved more of an opportunist than his career in opposition would have indicated, but his political courage and personal integrity remained beyond suspicion. His jealousy for the political autonomy of Canada was noticeable in his attitude at the Colonial conference held at the time of King Edward's coronation, and marked all his diplomatic dealings with the mother country. But he strove for sympathetic relations between Canadian and imperial authorities, and favoured general legislative and fiscal co-operation between the two countries. He strove also for good relations between the two races in Canada, and between Canada and the United States. Although he was classed in Canada as a Liberal, his tendencies would in England have been considered strongly conservative; an individualist rather than a collectivist, he opposed the intrusion of the state into the sphere of private enterprise, and showed no sympathy with the movement for state operation of railways, telegraphs and telephones, or with any kindred proposal looking to the extension of the obligations of the central government.

Bibliography.—J. S. Willison, *Sir Wilfrid Laurier and the Liberal Party; a Political History* (Toronto, 1903); L. O. David, *Laurier et son temps* (Montreal, 1905); see also Henri Moreau, *Sir Wilfrid Laurier, Premier Ministre du Canada* (Paris, 1902); and the collection of Laurier's speeches from 1871 to 1890, compiled by Ulric Barthe (Quebec, 1890). (J. S. W.)

LAURISTON, JACQUES ALEXANDRE BERNARD LAW, Marquis de (1768–1828), French soldier and diplomatist, was the son of Jacques François Law de Lauriston (1724–1785), a general officer in the French army, and was born at Pondicherry on the 1st of February 1768. He obtained his first commission about 1786, served with the artillery and on the staff in the earlier Revolutionary campaigns, and became brigadier of artillery in 1795. Resigning in 1796, he was brought back into the service in 1800 as aide-de-camp to Napoleon, with whom as a cadet Lauriston had been on friendly terms. In the years immediately preceding the first empire Lauriston was successively director of the Le Fère artillery school and special envoy to Denmark, and he was selected to convey to England the ratification of the peace of Amiens (1802). In 1805, having risen to the rank of general of division, he took part in the war against Austria. He occupied Venice and Ragusa in 1806, was made governor-general of Venice in 1807, took part in the Erfurt negotiations of 1808, was made a count, served with the emperor in Spain in 1808–1809 and held commands under the viceroy Eugène Beauharnais in the Italian campaign and the advance to Vienna in the same year. At the battle of Wagram he commanded the guard artillery in the famous "artillery preparation" which decided the battle. In 1811 he was made ambassador to Russia; in 1812 he held a command in the *Grande Armée* and won distinction by his firmness in covering the retreat from Moscow. He commanded the V. army corps at Lützen and Bautzen and the V. and XI. in the autumn campaign, falling into the hands of the enemy in the disastrous retreat from Leipzig. He was held a prisoner of war until the fall of the empire, and then joined Louis XVIII., to whom he remained faithful in the Hundred Days. His reward was a seat in the house of peers and a command in the royal guard. In 1817 he was created marquis and in 1823 marshal of France. During the Spanish War he commanded the corps which besieged and took Pamplona. He died at Paris on the 12th of June 1828.

LAURIUM (Λαύριον, mod. Ergastiri), a mining town in Attica, Greece, famous for the silver mines which were one of the chief sources of revenue of the Athenian state, and were employed for coinage. After the battle of Marathon, Themistocles persuaded the Athenians to devote the revenue derived from the mines to shipbuilding, and thus laid the foundation of the Athenian naval power, and made possible the victory of Salamis. The mines, which were the property of the state, were usually farmed out for a certain fixed sum and a percentage on the working; slave labour was exclusively employed. Towards the end of the 5th century the output was diminished, partly owing to the Spartan occupation of Decelea. But the mines continued to be worked, though Strabo records that in his time the tailings were being worked over, and Pausanias speaks of the mines as a thing of the past. The ancient workings, consisting of shafts and galleries for excavating the ore, and pans and other arrangements for extracting the metal, may still be seen. The mines are still worked at the present day by French and Greek companies, but mainly for lead, manganese and cadmium. The population of the modern town was 10,007 in 1907.

See E. Ardaillon, "Les Mines du Laurion dans l'antiquité," No. lxxvii. of the *Bibliothèque des écoles françaises d'Athènes et de Rome.*

LAURIUM, a village of Houghton county, Michigan, U.S.A.; near the centre of Keweenaw peninsula, the northern extremity of the state. Pop. (1890) 1159; (1900) 5643, of whom 2286 were foreign-born; (1904) 7653; (1910) 8537. It is served by

usually darker and denser than lavas of acid type, and when fused they tend to flow to great distances, and may thus form far-spreading sheets, whilst the acid lavas, being more viscous, rapidly consolidate after extrusion. The lava is emitted from the volcanic vent at a high temperature, but on exposure to the air it rapidly consolidates superficially, forming a crust which in many cases is soon broken up by the continued flow of the subjacent liquid lava, so that the surface becomes rugged with clinkers. J. D. Dana introduced the term "aa" for this rough kind of lava-stream, whilst he applied the term "pahoehoe" to those flows which have a smooth surface, or are simply wrinkled and ropy; these terms being used in this sense in Hawaii, in relation to the local lavas. The different kinds of lava are more fully described in the article VOLCANO.

LAVABO (Lat. "I will wash"; the Fr. equivalent is *lavoir*), in ecclesiastical usage, the term for the washing of the priests' hands, at the celebration of the Mass, at the offertory. The words of Psalm xxvi. 6, *Lavabo inter innocentes manus meas*, are said during the rite. The word is also used for the basin employed in the ritual washing, and also for the lavatories, generally erected in the cloisters of monasteries. Those at Gloucester, Norwich and Lincoln are best known. A very curious example at Fontenay, surrounding a pillar, is given by Viollet-le-Duc. In general the lavabo is a sort of trough; in some places it has an almery for towels, &c.

LAVAGNA, a seaport of Liguria, Italy, in the province of Genoa, from which it is 25½ m. S.E. by rail. Pop. (1901) 7005. It has a small shipbuilding trade, and exports great quantities of slate (*lavagna*, taking its name from the town). It also has a large cotton-mill. It was the seat of the Fieschi family, independent counts, who, at the end of the 12th century, were obliged to recognize the supremacy of Genoa. Sinibaldo Fieschi became Pope Innocent IV. (1243–1254), and Hadrian V. (1276) was also a Fieschi.

LAVAL, ANDRÉ DE, SEIGNEUR DE LOHÉAC (*c.* 1408–1485), French soldier. In 1423 he served in the French army against England, and in 1428 was taken prisoner by John Talbot, 1st earl of Shrewsbury, after the capitulation of Laval, which he was defending. After paying his ransom he was present with Joan of Arc at the siege of Orleans, at the battle of Patay, and at the coronation of Charles VII. He was made admiral of France in 1437 and marshal in 1439. He served Charles VII. faithfully in all his wars, even against the dauphin (1456), and when the latter became king as Louis XI., Laval was dismissed from the marshal's office. After the War of the Public Weal he was restored to favour, and recovered the marshal's bâton, the king also granting him the offices of lieutenant-general to the government of Paris and governor of Picardy, and conferring upon him the collar of the order of St Michael. In 1472 Laval was successful in resisting the attacks of Charles the Bold, duke of Burgundy, on Beauvais.

LAVAL, a town of north-western France, capital of the department of Mayenne, on the Mayenne river, 188 m. W.S.W. of Paris by rail. Pop. (1906) 24,874. On the right bank of the river stands the old feudal city, with its ancient castle and its irregularly built houses whose slate roofs and pointed gables peep from the groves of trees which clothe the hill. On the left bank the regularly built new town extends far into the plain. The river, here 80 yds. broad, is crossed by the handsome railway viaduct, a beautiful stone bridge called Pont Neuf, and the Pont Vieux with three pointed arches, built in the 16th century. There is communication by steamer as far as Angers. Laval may justly claim to be one of the loveliest of French towns. Its most curious and interesting monument is the sombre old castle of the counts (now a prison) with a donjon of the 12th century, the roof of which presents a fine example of the timber-work superseded afterwards by stone machicolation. The "new castle," dating partly from the Renaissance, serves as court-house. Laval possesses several churches of different periods: in that of the Trinity, which serves as the cathedral, the transept and nave are of the 12th century while the choir is of the 16th; St Vénérand (15th century) has good stained glass; Notre-Dame des Cordeliers, which dates from the end of the 14th century or the beginning of the 15th, has some fine marble altars. Half-a-mile below the Pont Vieux is the beautiful 12th-century church of Avenières, with an ornamental spire of 1534. The finest remaining relic of the ancient fortifications is the Beucheresse gate near the cathedral. The narrow streets around the castle are bordered by many old houses of the 15th and 16th century, chief among which is that known as the "Maison du Grand Veneur." There are an art-museum, a museum of natural history and archaeology and a library. The town is embellished by fine promenades, at the entrance of one of which, facing the mairie, stands the statue of the celebrated surgeon Ambroise Paré (1517–1590). Laval is the seat of a prefect, a bishopric created in 1855, and a court of assizes, and has tribunals of first instance and of commerce, a chamber of commerce, a board of trade-arbitrators, training colleges, an ecclesiastical seminary and a lycée for boys. The principal industry of the town is the cloth manufacture, introduced from Flanders in the 14th century. The production of fabrics of linen, of cotton or of mixtures of both, occupies some 10,000 hands in the town and suburbs. Among the numerous other industries are metal-founding, flour-milling, tanning, dyeing, the making of boots and shoes, and the sawing of the marble quarried in the vicinity. There is trade in grain.

Laval is not known to have existed before the 9th century. It was taken by John Talbot, earl of Shrewsbury, in 1428, changed hands several times during the wars of the League, and played an important part at the end of the 18th century in the war of La Vendée.

SEIGNEURS AND COUNTS OF LAVAL. The castle of Laval was founded at the beginning of the 11th century by a lord of the name of Guy, and remained in the possession of his male descendants until the 13th century. In 1218 the lordship passed to the house of Montmorency by the marriage of Emma, daughter of Guy VI. of Laval, to Mathieu de Montmorency, the hero of the battle of Bouvines. Of this union was born Guy VII. seigneur of Laval, the ancestor of the second house of Laval. Anne of Laval (d. 1466), the heiress of the second family, married John de Montfort, who took the name of Guy (XIII.) of Laval. At Charles VII.'s coronation (1429) Guy XIV., who was afterwards son-in-law of John V., duke of Brittany, and father-in-law of King René of Anjou, was created count of Laval, and the countship remained in the possession of Guy's male descendants until 1547. After the Montforts, the countship of Laval passed by inheritance to the families of Rieux and Sainte Maure, to the Colignys, and finally to the La Trémoilles, who held it until the Revolution.

See Bertrand de Broussillon, *La Maison de Laval* (3 vols., 1895–1900).

LA VALLIÈRE, LOUISE FRANÇOISE DE (1644–1710), mistress of Louis XIV., was born at Tours on the 6th of August 1644, the daughter of an officer, Laurent de la Baume le Blanc, who took the name of La Vallière from a small property near Amboise. Laurent de la Vallière died in 1651; his widow, who soon married again, joined the court of Gaston d'Orléans at Blois. Louise was brought up with the younger princesses, the step-sisters of La Grande Mademoiselle. After Gaston's death his widow moved with her daughters to the palace of the Luxembourg in Paris, and with them went Louise, who was now a girl of sixteen. Through the influence of a distant kinswoman, Mme de Choisy, she was named maid of honour to Henrietta of England, who was about her own age and had just married Philip of Orleans, the king's brother. Henrietta joined the court at Fontainebleau, and was soon on the friendliest terms with her brother-in-law, so friendly indeed that there was some scandal, to avoid which it was determined that Louis should pay marked attentions elsewhere. The person selected was Madame's maid of honour, Louise. She had been only two months in Fontainebleau before she became the king's mistress. The affair, begun on Louis's part as a blind, immediately developed into real passion on both sides. It was Louis's first serious attachment, and Louise was an innocent, religious-minded girl, who brought neither coquetry nor self-interest to their relation, which was sedulously concealed. Nicolas Fouquet's curiosity in the matter was one of the causes of his disgrace. In February 1662 there was a storm when Louise refused to tell her lover the relations between Madame (Henrietta) and the comte de Guiche. She fled to an obscure convent at Chaillot, where Louis rapidly followed her. Her enemies, chief of whom was Olympe Mancini, comtesse de Soissons, Mazarin's niece, sought her downfall by bringing her liaison to the ears of Queen Maria Theresa. She was presently removed from the service of Madame, and established in a small building in the Palais Royal, where in December 1663 she gave birth to a son Charles, who was given in charge to two faithful servants of Colbert. Concealment was practically abandoned after her return to court, and within a week of Anne of Austria's death in January 1666, La Vallière appeared at mass side by side with Maria Theresa. But her favour was already waning. She had given birth to a second child in January 1665, but both children were dead before the autumn of 1666. A daughter born at Vincennes in October 1666, who received the name of Marie Anne and was known as Mlle de Blois, was publicly recognized by Louis as his daughter in letters-patent making the mother a duchess in May 1667 and conferring on her the estate of Vaujours. In October of that year she bore a son, but by this time her place in Louis's affections was definitely usurped by Athénaïs de Montespan (*q.v.*), who had long been plotting against her. She was compelled to remain at court as the king's official mistress, and even to share Mme de Montespan's apartments at the Tuileries. She made an attempt at escape in 1671, when she fled to the convent of Ste Marie de Chaillot, only to be compelled to return. In 1674 she was finally permitted to enter the Carmelite convent in the Rue d'Enfer. She took the final vows a year later, when Bossuet pronounced the allocution.

Her daughter married Armand de Bourbon, prince of Conti, in 1680. The count of Vermandois, her youngest born, died on his first campaign at Courtrai in 1683.

La Vallière's *Réflexions sur la miséricorde de Dieu*, written after her retreat, were printed by Lequeux in 1767, and in 1860 *Réflexions, lettres et sermons*, by M. P. Clement (2 vols.). Some apocryphal *Mémoires* appeared in 1829, and the *Lettres de Mme la duchesse de la Vallière* (1767) are a corrupt version of her correspondence with the maréchal de Bellefonds. Of modern works on the subject see Arsène Houssaye, *Mlle de la Vallière et Mme de Montespan* (1860); Jules Lair, *Louise de la Vallière* (3rd ed., 1902, Eng. trans., 1908); and C. Bonnet, *Documents inédits sur Mme de la Vallière* (1904).

LAVATER, JOHANN KASPAR (1741–1801), German poet and physiognomist, was born at Zürich on the 15th of November 1741. He was educated at the gymnasium of his native town, where J. J. Bodmer and J. J. Breitinger were among his teachers. When barely one-and-twenty he greatly distinguished himself by denouncing, in conjunction with his friend, the painter H. Fuseli, an iniquitous magistrate, who was compelled to make restitution of his ill-gotten gains. In 1769 Lavater took orders, and officiated till his death as deacon or pastor in various churches in his native city. His oratorical fervour and genuine depth of conviction gave him great personal influence; he was extensively consulted as a casuist, and was welcomed with demonstrative enthusiasm in his numerous journeys through Germany. His mystical writings were also widely popular. Scarcely a trace of this influence has remained, and Lavater's name would be forgotten but for his work on physiognomy, *Physiognomische Fragmente zur Beförderung der Menschenkenntnis und Menschenliebe* (1775–1778). The fame even of this book, which found enthusiastic admirers in France and England, as well as in Germany, rests to a great extent upon the handsome style of publication and the accompanying illustrations. It left, however, the study of physiognomy (*q.v.*), as desultory and unscientific as it found it. As a poet, Lavater published *Christliche Lieder* (1776–1780) and two epics, *Jesus Messias* (1780) and *Joseph von Arimathia* (1794), in the style of Klopstock. More important and characteristic of the religious temperament of Lavater's age are his introspective *Aussichten in die Ewigkeit* (4 vols., 1768–1778); *Geheimes Tagebuch von einem Beobachter seiner selbst* (2 vols., 1772–1773) and *Pontius Pilatus, oder der Mensch in allen Gestalten* (4 vols., 1782–1785). From 1774 on, Goethe was intimately acquainted with Lavater, but at a later period he became estranged from him, somewhat abruptly accusing him of superstition and hypocrisy. Lavater had a mystic's indifference to historical Christianity, and, although esteemed by himself and others a champion of orthodoxy, was in fact only an antagonist of rationalism. During the later years of his life his influence waned, and he incurred ridicule by some exhibitions of vanity. He redeemed himself by his patriotic conduct during the French occupation of Switzerland, which brought about his tragical death. On the taking of Zürich by the French in 1799, Lavater, while endeavouring to appease the soldiery, was shot through the body by an infuriated grenadier; he died after long sufferings borne with great fortitude, on the 2nd of January 1801.

Lavater himself published two collections of his writings, *Vermischte Schriften* (2 vols., 1774–1781), and *Kleinere prosaische Schriften* (3 vols., 1784–1785). His *Nachgelassene Schriften* were edited by G. Gessner (5 vols., 1801–1802); *Sämtliche Werke* (but only poems) (6 vols., 1836–1838); *Ausgewählte Schriften* (8 vols., 1841–1844). See G. Gessner, *Lavaters Lebensbeschreibung* (3 vols., 1802–1803); U. Hegner, *Beiträge zur Kenntnis Lavaters* (1836); F. W. Bodemann, *Lavater nach seinem Leben, Lehren und Wirken* (1856; 2nd ed., 1877); F. Muncker, *J. K. Lavater* (1883); H. Waser, *J. K. Lavater nach Hegners Aufzeichnungen* (1894); *J. K. Lavater, Denkschrift zum 100. Todestag* (1902).

LAVAUR, a town of south-western France, capital of an arrondissement in the department of Tarn, 37 m. S.E. of Montauban by rail. Pop. (1906), town 4069; commune 6388. Lavaur stands on the left bank of the Agout, which is here crossed by a railway-bridge and a fine stone bridge of the late 18th century. From 1317 till the Revolution Lavaur was the seat of a bishopric, and there is a cathedral dating from the 13th, 14th and 15th centuries, with an octagonal bell-tower; a second smaller square tower contains a *jaquemart* (a statue which strikes the hours with a hammer) of the 16th century. In the bishop's garden is the statue of Emmanuel Augustin, marquis de Las Cases, one of the companions of Napoleon at St Helena. The town carries on distilling and flour-milling and the manufacture of brushes, plaster and wooden shoes. There are a subprefecture and tribunal of first instance. Lavaur was taken in 1211 by Simon de Montfort during the wars of the Albigenses, and several times during the religious wars of the 16th century.

LAVEDAN, HENRI LÉON ÉMILE (1859–), French dramatist and man of letters, was born at Orleans, the son of Hubert Léon Lavedan, a well-known Catholic and liberal journalist. He contributed to various Parisian papers a series of witty tales and dialogues of Parisian life, many of which were collected in volume form. In 1891 he produced at the Théâtre Français *Une Famille*, followed at the Vaudeville in 1894 by *Le Prince d'Aurec*, a satire on the nobility, afterwards re-named *Les Descendants*. Later brilliant and witty pieces were *Les Deux noblesses* (1897), *Catherine* (1897), *Le Nouveau jeu* (1898), *Le Vieux marcheur* (1899), *Le Marquis de Priola* (1902), and *Varennes* (1904), written in collaboration with G. Lenôtre. He had a great success with *Le Duel* (Comédie Française, 1905), a powerful psychological study of the relations of two brothers. Lavedan was admitted to the French Academy in 1898.

LAVELEYE, ÉMILE LOUIS VICTOR DE (1822–1892), Belgian economist, was born at Bruges on the 5th of April 1822, and educated there and at the Collège Stanislas in Paris, a celebrated establishment in the hands of the Oratorians. He continued his studies at the Catholic university of Louvain and afterwards at Ghent, where he came under the influence of François Huet, the philosopher and Christian Socialist. In 1844 he won a prize with an essay on the language and literature of Provence. In 1847 he published *L'Histoire des rois francs*, and in 1861 a French version of the *Nibelungen*, but though he never lost his interest in literature and history, his most important work was in the domain of economics. He was one of a group of young lawyers, doctors and critics, all old pupils of Huet, who met once a week to discuss social and economic questions, and was thus led to

ker and denser than h
tend to flow to great u
ng sheets whilst the act
nsolidate after extrusion
aic vent at a high temper
idly consolidates superfi
cases is soon broken up b
liquid lavas so that the s
J. D. Dana introduced th
lava-stream whilst he ap
flows which have a smooth s
y; these terms being used
to the local lavas. The d
scribed in the article Volca
LAVABO (Lat. "I will wash"; t
esiastical usage, the term f
at the celebration of the M
of Psalm xxvi. 6, Lavabo i
id during the rite. The w
yed in the ritual washing,
ally erected in the cloisters
cester, Norwich and Lincoln
us example at Fontenay, sur
et-le-Duc. In general the l
places it has an almery for t
LAVAGNA, a seaport of Ligu
oa, from which it is 25½ m. S
as a small shipbuilding trad
late (Javagna, taking its nam
arge cotton-mill. It was t
ependent counts, who, at the
ged to recognize the suprem
ame Pope Innocent IV. (12
also a Fieschi.

LAVAL, ANDRÉ DE, SEIGNE
nch soldier. In 1423 he s
gland, and in 1428 was t
l of Shrewsbury, after paying
s defending. After the siege of Or
an of Arc at the coronation of Charles
ance in 1437 and marshal i
thfully in all his wars, ev
d when the latter became
missed from the marshal's
eal he was restored to favo
ton, the king also granting h
the government of Paris an
g upon him the collar of t
aval was successful in resisti
ke of Burgundy, on Beauv

LAVAL, a town of nort
partment of Mayenne, on t
Paris by rail. Pop. (1901
e river stands the old feudal
irregularly built houses w
ep from the groves of trees
nk the regularly built new
he river, here 80 yds. bro
llway viaduct, a beautiful s
e Pont Vieux with three
ntury. There is communica
aval may justly claim to be o
s most curious and interesti
stle of the counts (now a p
ntury, the roof of which pre
ork superseded afterwards by
stle," dating partly from the
aval possesses several church
the Trinity, which ser
ave are of the 12th
t Vénéran

of wine with the addition of the essences of musk, rose, bergamot and ambergris, but is very rarely prepared by distillation of the flowers with spirit.

In the climate of New York lavender is scarcely hardy, but in the vicinity of Philadelphia considerable quantities are grown for the market. In American gardens sweet basil (*Ocimum basilicum*) is frequently called lavender.

Lavandula Spica, a species which differs from *L. vera* chiefly in its smaller size, more crowded leaves and linear bracts, is also used for the distillation of an essential oil, which is known in England as oil of spike and in France under the name of *essence d'aspic*. It is used in painting on porcelain and in veterinary medicine. The oil met with in commerce is less fragrant than that of *L. vera*—probably because the whole plant is distilled, for the flowers of the two species are scarcely distinguishable in fragrance. *L. Spica* does not extend so far north, nor ascend the mountains beyond 2000 ft. It cannot be cultivated in Britain except in sheltered situations. A nearly allied species, *L. lanata*, a native of Spain, with broader leaves, is also very fragrant, but does not appear to be distilled for

Lavandula Stoechas, a species extending from the Canaries to Asia Minor, is distinguished from the above plants by its blackish purple flowers, and shortly stalked spikes crowned by conspicuous purplish sterile bracts. The flowers were official in the London Pharmacopoeia as late as 1746. They are still used by the Arabs as an expectorant and antispasmodic. The Stoechades (now called isles of Hyères near Toulon) owed their name to the abundance of the plant growing there.

Other species of lavender are known, some of which extend as east as to India. A few which differ from the above in having divided leaves, as *L. dentata*, *L. abrotanoides*, *L. multifolia*, *L. pinnata* and *L. viridis*, have been cultivated in greenhouses, &c., in England.

Sea lavender is a name applied in England to several species of *Statice*, a genus of littoral plants belonging to the order *Plumbaginaceae*. Lavender cotton is a species of the genus *Santolina*, small, yellow-flowered, evergreen undershrubs of the Composite order.

LAVERDY, CLÉMENT CHARLES FRANÇOIS DE (1723–1793), French statesman, was a member of the parlement of Paris when the case against the Jesuits came before that body in August 1761. He demanded the suppression of the order and acquired popularity. Louis XV. named him controller-general of the finances in December 1763, but the burden was heavy and Laverdy knew nothing of finance. Three months after his nomination he forbade anything of any kind whatever to be printed concerning his administration, thus refusing praise as well as censure. He used all sorts of expedients, sometimes dishonest, to replenish the treasury, and was even accused of having himself profited from the commerce in wheat. Court intrigue led to his sudden dismissal on the 1st of October 1768. Henceforward he lived in retirement until, during the Revolution, he was involved in the charges against the financiers of the old régime. The Revolutionary tribunal condemned him to death, and he was guillotined on the 24th of November 1793.

See A. Jobez, *La France sous Louis XV* (1869).

LAVERNA, an old Italian divinity, originally one of the spirits of the underworld. A cup found in an Etruscan tomb bears the inscription "Lavernai Pocolom," and in a fragment of Septimius Serenus Laverna is expressly mentioned in connexion with the *di inferi*. By an easy transition, she came to be regarded as the protectress of thieves, whose operations were associated with darkness. She had an altar on the Aventine hill, near the gate called after her Lavernalis, and a grove on the Via Salaria. Her aid was invoked by thieves to enable them to carry out their plans successfully without forfeiting their reputation for piety and honesty (Horace, *Ep.* i. 16, 60). Many explanations have been given of the name: (1) from *latere* (schol. on Horace, who gives *laternio* as another form of *lavernio* or robber); (2) from *lavare* (Acron on Horace, according to whom thieves were called *lavatores*, perhaps referring to bath thieves); (3) from *levare* (cf. shop-lifters). Modern etymologists connect it with *lu-crum*, and explain it as meaning the goddess of gain.

LAVERY, JOHN (1857–), British painter, was born in Belfast, and received his art training in Glasgow, London and Paris. He was elected associate of the Royal Scottish Academy in 1892 and academician in 1896, having won a considerable reputation as a painter of portraits and figure subjects, and as a facile and vigorous executant. He became also vice-president of the International Society of sculptors, painters and gravers. Many of his paintings have been acquired for public collections, and he is represented in the National Galleries at Brussels, Berlin and Edinburgh, in the Carnegie Institute at Pittsburg, the Philadelphia Gallery, the New South Wales Gallery, the Modern Gallery, Venice, the Pinakothek, Munich, the Glasgow Corporation Gallery, and the Luxembourg.

LAVIGERIE, CHARLES MARTIAL ALLEMAND (1825–1892), French divine, cardinal archbishop of Carthage and Algiers and primate of Africa, was born at Bayonne on the 31st of October 1825, and was educated at St Sulpice, Paris. He was ordained priest in 1849, and was professor of ecclesiastical history at the Sorbonne from 1854 to 1856. In 1856 he accepted the direction of the schools of the East, and was thus for the first time brought into contact with the Mahommedan world. "C'est là," he wrote, "que j'ai connu enfin ma vocation." Activity in missionary work, especially in alleviating the distresses of the victims of the Druses, soon brought him prominently into notice; he was made a chevalier of the Legion of Honour, and in October 1861, shortly after his return to Europe, was appointed French auditor at Rome. Two years later he was raised to the see of Nancy, where he remained for four years, during which the diocese became one of the best administered in France. While bishop of Nancy he met Marshal MacMahon, then governor-general of Algeria, who in 1866 offered him the see of Algiers, just raised to an archbishopric. Lavigerie landed in Africa on the 11th of May 1868, when the great famine was already making itself felt, and he began in November to collect the orphans into villages. This action, however, did not meet with the approval of MacMahon, who feared that the Arabs would resent it as an infraction of the religious peace, and thought that the Mahommedan church, being a state institution in Algeria, ought to be protected from proselytism; so it was intimated to the prelate that his sole duty was to minister to the colonists. Lavigerie, however, continued his self-imposed task, refused the archbishopric of Lyons, which was offered to him by the emperor, and won his point. Contact with the natives during the famine caused Lavigerie to entertain exaggerated hopes for their general conversion, and his enthusiasm was such that he offered to resign his archbishopric in order to devote himself entirely to the missions. Pius IX. refused this, but granted him a coadjutor, and placed the whole of equatorial Africa under his charge. In 1870 Lavigerie warmly supported papal infallibility. In 1871 he was twice a candidate for the National Assembly, but was defeated. In 1874 he founded the Sahara and Sudan mission, and sent missionaries to Tunis, Tripoli, East Africa and the Congo. The order of African missionaries thus founded, for which Lavigerie himself drew up the rule, has since become famous as the *Pères Blancs*. From 1881 to 1884 his activity in Tunisia so raised the prestige of France that it drew from Gambetta the celebrated declaration, *L'Anticléricalisme n'est pas un article d'exportation*, and led to the exemption of Algeria from the application of the decrees concerning the religious orders. On the 27th of March 1882 the dignity of cardinal was conferred upon Lavigerie, but the great object of his ambition was to restore the see of St Cyprian; and in that also he was successful, for by a bull of 10th November 1884 the metropolitan see of Carthage was re-erected, and Lavigerie received the pallium on the 25th of January 1885. The later years of his life were spent in ardent anti-slavery propaganda, and his eloquence moved large audiences in London, as well as in Paris, Brussels and other parts of the continent. He hoped, by organizing a fraternity of armed laymen as pioneers, to restore fertility to the Sahara; but this community did not succeed, and was dissolved before his death. In 1890 Lavigerie appeared in the new character of a politician, and arranged with Pope Leo XIII. to make an attempt to reconcile the church with the republic. He invited the officers of the Mediterranean squadron to lunch at Algiers, and, practically renouncing his monarchical sympathies, to which he clung as long as the comte de Chambord was alive, expressed his support of the republic.

and emphasized it by having the Marseillaise played by a band of his *Pères Blancs*. The further steps in this evolution emanated from the pope, and Lavigerie, whose health now began to fail, receded comparatively into the background. He died at Algiers on the 26th of November 1892. (G. F. B.)

LA VILLEMARQUÉ, THÉODORE CLAUDE HENRI, VICOMTE HERSART DE (1815–1895), French philologist and man of letters, was born at Keransker, near Quimperlé, on the 6th of July 1815. He was descended from an old Breton family, which counted among its members a Hersart who had followed Saint Louis to the Crusade, and another who was a companion in arms of Du Guesclin. La Villemarqué devoted himself to the elucidation of the monuments of Breton literature. Introduced in 1851 by Jacob Grimm as correspondent to the Academy of Berlin, he became in 1858 a member of the Academy of Inscriptions. His works include: *Contes populaires des anciens Bretons* (1842), to which was prefixed an essay on the origin of the romances of the Round Table; *Essai sur l'histoire de la langue bretonne* (1837); *Poèmes des bardes bretons du sixième siècle* (1850); *La Légende celtique en Irelande, en Cambrie et en Bretagne* (1859). The popular Breton songs published by him in 1839 as *Barzas Breiz* were considerably retouched. La Villemarqué's work has been superseded by the work of later scholars, but he has the merit of having done much to arouse popular interest in his subject. He died at Keransker on the 8th of December 1895.

On the subject of the doubtful authenticity of *Barzas Breiz*, see Luzel's Preface to his *Chansons populaires de la Basse-Bretagne*, and, for a list of works on the subject, the *Revue Celtique* (vol. v.).

LAVINIUM, an ancient town of Latium, on the so-called Via Lavinatis (see LAURENTINA, VIA), 19 m. S. of Rome, the modern PRATICA, situated 300 ft. above sea-level and 2½ m. N.E. from the sea-coast. Its foundation is attributed to Aeneas (whereas Laurentum was the primitive city of King Latinus), who named it after his wife Lavinia. It is rarely mentioned in Roman history and often confused with Lanuvium or Lanivium in the text both of authors and of inscriptions. The custom by which the consuls and praetors or dictators sacrificed on the Alban Mount and at Lavinium to the Penates and to Vesta, before they entered upon office or departed for their province, seems to have been one of great antiquity. There is no trace of its having continued into imperial times, but the cults of Lavinium were kept up; largely by the imperial appointment of honorary non-resident citizens to hold the priesthoods. The citizens of Lavinium were known under the empire as Laurentes Lavinates, and the place itself at a late period as Laurolavinium. It was deserted or forgotten not long after the time of Theodosius.

Lavinium was preceded by a more ancient town, LAURENTUM, the city of Latinus (Verg. *Aen.* viii.); of this the site is uncertain, but it is probably to be sought at the modern Tor Paterno, close to the sea-coast and 5 m. N. by W. of Lavinium. Here the name of Laurentum is preserved by the modern name Pantan di Lauro. Even in ancient times it was famous for its groves of bay-trees (*laurus*) from which its name was perhaps derived, and which in imperial times gave the villas of its territory a name for salubrity, so that both Vitellius and Commodus resorted there. The exact date of the abandonment of the town itself and the incorporation of its territory with that of Lavinium is uncertain, but it may be placed in the latter part of the republic. Under the empire a portion of it must have been imperial domain and forest. We hear of an imperial procurator in charge of the elephants at Laurentum; and the imperial villa may perhaps be identified with the extensive ruins at Tor Paterno itself. The remains of numerous other villas lie along the ancient coast-line (which was half a mile inland of the modern, being now marked by a row of sand-hills, and was followed by the Via Severiana), both north-west and south-east of Tor Paterno: they extended as a fact in an almost unbroken line along the low sandy coast—now entirely deserted and largely occupied by the low scrub which serves as cover for the wild boars of the king of Italy's preserves—from the mouth of the Tiber to Antium, and thence again to Astura; but there are no traces of any buildings previous to the imperial period. In one of these villas, excavated by the king of Italy in 1906, was found a fine replica of the famous discobolus of Myron. The plan of the building is interesting, as it diverges entirely from the normal type and adapts itself to the site. Some way to the N.W. was situated the village of Vicus Augustanus Laurentium, taking its name probably from Augustus himself, and probably identical with the village mentioned by Pliny the younger as separated by only one villa from his own. This village was brought to light by excavation in 1874, and its forum and curia are still visible. The remains of the villa of Pliny, too, were excavated in 1713 and in 1802–1819, and it is noteworthy that the place bears the name Villa di Pino (*sic*) on the staff map; how old the name is, is uncertain. It is impossible without further excavation to reconcile the remains—mainly of substructions—with the elaborate description of his villa given by Pliny (cf. H. Winnefeld in *Jahrbuch des Instituts*, 1891, 200 seq.).

The site of the ancient Lavinium, no less than 300 ft. above sea-level and 2½ m. inland, is far healthier than the low-lying Laurentum, where, except in the immediate vicinity of the coast, malaria must have been a dreadful scourge. It possesses considerable natural strength, and consists of a small hill, the original acropolis, occupied by the modern castle and the village surrounding it, and a larger one, now given over to cultivation, where the city stood. On the former there are now no traces of antiquity, but on the latter are scanty remains of the city walls, in small blocks of the grey-green tufa (*cappellaccio*) which is used in the earliest buildings of Rome, and traces of the streets. The necropolis, too, has been discovered, but not systematically excavated; but objects of the first Iron age, including a sword of Aegean type (thus confirming the tradition), have been found; also remains of a building with Doric columns of an archaistic type, remains of later buildings in brick, and inscriptions, some of them of considerable interest.

See R. Lanciani in *Monumenti dei Lincei*, xiii. (1903), 133 seq.; xvi. (1906), 241 seq. (T. As.)

LAVISSE, ERNEST (1842–), French historian, was born at Nouvion-en-Thiérache, Aisne, on the 17th of December 1842. In 1865 he obtained a fellowship in history, and in 1875 became a doctor of letters, he was appointed *maître de conférence* (1876) at the école normale supérieure, succeeding Fustel de Coulanges, and then professor of modern history at the Sorbonne (1888), in the place of Henri Wallon. He was an eloquent professor and very fond of young people, and played an important part in the revival of higher studies in France after 1871. His knowledge of pedagogy was displayed in his public lectures and his addresses, in his private lessons, where he taught a small number of pupils the historical method, and in his books, where he wrote *ad probandum* at least as much as *ad narrandum*: class-books, collections of articles, intermingled with personal reminiscences (*Questions d'enseignement national*, 1885; *Études et étudiants*, 1890; *À propos de nos écoles*, 1895), rough historical sketches (*Vue générale de l'histoire politique de l'Europe*, 1890), &c. Even his works of learning, written without a trace of pedantry, are remarkable for their lucidity and vividness.

After the Franco-Prussian War Lavisse studied the development of Prussia and wrote *Étude sur l'une des origines de la monarchie prussienne, ou la Marche de Brandebourg sous la dynastie ascanienne*, which was his thesis for his doctor's degree in 1875, and *Études sur l'histoire de la Prusse* (1879). In connexion with his study of the Holy Roman Empire, and the cause of its decline, he wrote a number of articles which were published in the *Revue des Deux Mondes*; and he wrote *Trois empereurs d'Allemagne* (1888), *La Jeunesse du grand Frédéric* (1891) and *Frédéric II. avant son avènement* (1893) when studying the modern German empire and the grounds for its strength. With his friend Alfred Rambaud he conceived the plan of *L'Histoire générale du IVe siècle jusqu'à nos jours*, to which, however, he contributed nothing. He edited the *Histoire de France depuis les origines jusqu'à la Révolution* (1901–), in which he carefully revised the work of his numerous assistants, reserving the greatest part of the reign of Louis XIV. for himself. This section occupies the whole of volume vii. It is a remarkable piece of work, and the sketch of absolute government in France during this period has never before been traced with an equal amount of insight and brilliance. Lavisse was admitted to the Académie Française on the death of Admiral Jurien de la Gravière in 1892, and after the death of James Darmesteter became editor of the *Revue de Paris*. He is, however, chiefly a master of pedagogy. When the école normale was joined to the university of Paris, Lavisse was appointed director of the new organization, which he had helped more than any one to bring about.

LAVOISIER, ANTOINE LAURENT (1743–1794), French chemist, was born in Paris on the 26th of August 1743. His father, an *avocat au parlement*, gave him an excellent education at the collège Mazarin, and encouraged his taste for natural science; and he studied mathematics and astronomy with N. L. de Lacaille, chemistry with the elder Rouelle and botany with Bernard de Jussieu. In 1766 he received a gold medal from the Academy of Sciences for an essay on the best means of lighting a large town; and among his early work were papers on the analysis of gypsum, on thunder, on the aurora and on congelation, and a refutation of the prevalent belief that water by repeated distillation is converted into earth. He also assisted J. E. Guettard (1715–1786) in preparing his mineralogical atlas of France. In 1768, recognized as a man who had both the ability and the means for a scientific career, he was nominated *adjoint chimiste* to the Academy, and in that capacity made numerous reports on the most diverse subjects, from the theory of colours to water-supply and from invalid chairs to mesmerism and the divining rod. The same year he obtained the position of *adjoint* to Baudon, one of the farmers-general of the revenue, subsequently becoming a full titular member of the body. This was the first of a series of posts in which his administrative abilities found full scope. Appointed *régisseur des poudres* in 1775, he not only abolished the vexatious search for saltpetre in the cellars of private houses, but increased the production of the salt and improved the manufacture of gunpowder. In 1785 he was nominated to the committee on agriculture, and as its secretary drew up reports and instructions on the cultivation of various crops, and promulgated schemes for the establishment of experimental agricultural stations, the distribution of agricultural implements and the adjustment of rights of pasturage. Seven years before he had started a model farm at Fréchine, where he demonstrated the advantages of scientific methods of cultivation and of the introduction of good breeds of cattle and sheep. Chosen a member of the provincial assembly of Orleans in 1787, he busied himself with plans for the improvement of the social and economic conditions of the community by means of savings banks, insurance societies, canals, workhouses, &c.; and he showed the sincerity of his philanthropical work by advancing money out of his own pocket, without interest, to the towns of Blois and Romorantin, for the purchase of barley during the famine of 1788. Attached in this same year to the *caisse d'escompte*, he presented the report of its operations to the national assembly in 1789, and as commissary of the treasury in 1791 he established a system of accounts of unexampled punctuality. He was also asked by the national assembly to draw up a new scheme of taxation in connexion with which he produced a report *De la richesse territoriale de la France*, and he was further associated with committees on hygiene, coinage, the casting of cannon, &c., and was secretary and treasurer of the commission appointed in 1790 to secure uniformity of weights and measures.

In 1791, when Lavoisier was in the middle of all this official activity, the suppression of the farmers-general marked the beginning of troubles which brought about his death. His membership of that body was alone sufficient to make him an object of suspicion; his administration at the *régie des poudres* was attacked; and Marat accused him in the *Ami du Peuple* of putting Paris in prison and of stopping the circulation of air in the city by the *mur d'octroi* erected at his suggestion in 1787. The Academy, of which as treasurer at the time he was a conspicuous member, was regarded by the convention with no friendly eyes as being tainted with "incivism," and in the spring of 1792 A. F. Fourcroy endeavoured to persuade it to purge itself of suspected members. The attempt was unsuccessful, but in August of the same year Lavoisier had to leave his house and laboratory at the Arsenal, and in November the Academy was forbidden until further orders to fill up the vacancies in its numbers. Next year, on the 1st of August, the convention passed a decree for the uniformity of weights and measures, and requested the Academy to take measures for carrying it out, but a week later Fourcroy persuaded the same convention to suppress the Academy together with other literary societies *patentées et dotées* by the nation. In November it ordered the arrest of the ex-farmers-general, and on the advice of the committee of public instruction, of which Guyton de Morveau and Fourcroy were members, the names of Lavoisier and others were struck off from the commission of weights and measures. The fate of the ex-farmers-general was sealed on the 2nd of May 1794, when, on the proposal of Antoine Dupin, one of their former officials, the convention sent them for trial by the Revolutionary tribunal. Within a week Lavoisier and 27 others were condemned to death. A petition in his favour addressed to Coffinhal, the president of the tribunal, is said to have been met with the reply *La République n'a pas besoin de savants*, and on the 8th of the month Lavoisier and his companions were guillotined at the Place de la Révolution. He died fourth, and was preceded by his colleague Jacques Paulze, whose daughter he had married in 1771. "*Il ne leur a fallu*," Lagrange remarked, "*qu'un moment pour faire tomber cette tête, et cent années peut-être ne suffiront pas pour en reproduire une semblable.*"

Lavoisier's name is indissolubly associated with the overthrow of the phlogistic doctrine that had dominated the development of chemistry for over a century, and with the establishment of the foundations upon which the modern science reposes. "He discovered," says Justus von Liebig (*Letters on Chemistry*, No. 3), "no new body, no new property, no natural phenomenon previously unknown; but all the facts established by him were the necessary consequences of the labours of those who preceded him. His merit, his immortal glory, consists in this—that he infused into the body of the science a new spirit; but all the members of that body were already in existence, and rightly joined together." Realizing that the total weight of all the products of a chemical reaction must be exactly equal to the total weight of the reacting substances, he made the balance the *ultima ratio* of the laboratory, and he was able to draw correct inferences from his weighings because, unlike many of the phlogistonists, he looked upon heat as imponderable. It was by weighing that in 1770 he proved that water is not converted into earth by distillation, for he showed that the total weight of a sealed glass vessel and the water it contained remained constant, however long the water was boiled, but that the glass vessel lost weight to an extent equal to the weight of earth produced, his inference being that the earth came from the glass, not from the water. On the 1st of November 1772 he deposited with the Academy a sealed note which stated that sulphur and phosphorus when burnt increased in weight because they absorbed "air," while the metallic lead formed from litharge by reduction with charcoal weighed less than the original litharge because it had lost "air." The exact nature of the airs concerned in the processes he did not explain until after the preparation of "dephlogisticated air" (oxygen) by Priestley in 1774. Then, perceiving that in combustion and the calcination of metals only a portion of a given volume of common air was used up, he concluded that Priestley's new air, *air éminemment pur*, was what was absorbed by burning phosphorus, &c., "non-vital air," azote, or nitrogen remaining behind. The gas given off in the reduction of metallic calces by charcoal he at first supposed to be merely that contained in the calx, but he soon came to understand that it was a product formed by the union of the charcoal with the "dephlogisticated air" in the calx. In a memoir presented to the Academy in 1777, but not published till 1782, he assigned to dephlogisticated air the name oxygen, or "acid-producer," on the supposition that all acids were formed by its union with a simple, usually non-metallic, body; and having verified this notion for phosphorus, sulphur, charcoal, &c., and even extended it to the vegetable acids, he naturally asked himself what was formed by the combustion of "inflammable air" (hydrogen). This problem he had attacked in 1774, and in subsequent years he made various attempts to discover the acid which, under the influence of his oxygen theory, he expected would be formed. It was not till the 25th of June 1783 that in conjunction with Laplace he announced to the Academy that water was the product formed by the combination of hydrogen and oxygen, but by that time he had been anticipated by Cavendish, to whose prior work, however, as to that of several other investigators in other matters, it is to be regretted that he did not render due acknowledgment. But a knowledge of the composition of water enabled him to storm the last defences of the phlogistonists. Hydrogen they held to be the phlogiston of metals, and they supported this view by pointing out that it was liberated when metals were dissolved in acids. Considerations of weight had long prevented Lavoisier from accepting this doctrine, but he was now able to explain the process fully, showing that the hydrogen evolved did not come from the metal itself, but was one product of the decomposition of the water of the dilute acid, the other product, oxygen, combining with the metal to form an oxide which in turn united with the acid. A little later this same knowledge led him to the beginnings of quantitative organic analysis. Knowing that the water produced by the combustion of alcohol was not pre-existent in that substance but was formed by the combination of its hydrogen with the oxygen of the air, he burnt alcohol and other combustible organic substances, such as wax and oil, in a known volume of oxygen, and, from the weight of the water and carbon dioxide produced and his knowledge of their composition, was able to calculate the amounts of carbon, hydrogen and oxygen present in the substance.

Up to about this time Lavoisier's work, mainly quantitative in character, had appealed most strongly to physicists, but it now began to win conviction from chemists also. C. L. Berthollet, L. B. Guyton de Morveau and A. F. Fourcroy, his collaborators in the reformed system of chemical terminology set forth in 1787 in the *Méthode de nomenclature chimique*, were among the earliest French converts, and they were followed by M. H. Klaproth and the German Academy, and by most English chemists except Cavendish, who rather suspended his judgment, and Priestley, who stubbornly clung to the opposite view. Indeed, though the partisans of phlogiston did not surrender without a struggle, the history of science scarcely presents a second instance of a change so fundamental accomplished with such ease. The [illegible] of Lavoisier's doctrines was greatly facilitated by the [illegible] and logical form in which he presented them in his [illegible] *élémentaire de chimie* (*présenté dans un ordre nouveau et* [illegible] *des découvertes modernes*) (1789). The list of simple [illegible] contained in the first volume of this work includes [illegible] and caloric with oxygen, azote and hydrogen. Under the [illegible] "oxidable or acidifiable" substances, the combination [illegible] with oxygen yielded acids, were placed sulphur, phos[illegible] carbon, and the muriatic, fluoric and boracic radicles. [illegible] which by combination with oxygen became oxides, [illegible] antimony, silver, arsenic, bismuth, cobalt, copper, tin, iron, [illegible] mercury, molybdenum, nickel, gold, platinum, lead, [illegible] and zinc; and the "simple earthy salifiable sub[illegible] were lime, baryta, magnesia, alumina and silica. [illegible] nature of the alkalies Lavoisier considered so doubtful [illegible] did not class them as elements, which he conceived as [illegible] which could not be further decomposed by any [illegible] process of analysis—*les molécules simples et indivisibles* [illegible] *les corps*. The union of any two of the elements [illegible] to binary compounds, such as oxides, acids, sulphides, [illegible] substance containing three elements was a binary com[illegible] the sec[illegible], the most important [illegible] of th[illegible] the union of acids and oxides, iron sulphate, for instance, being a compound of iron oxide with sulphuric acid.

In addition to his purely chemical work, Lavoisier, mostly in conjunction with Laplace, devoted considerable attention to physical problems, especially those connected with heat. The two carried out some of the earliest thermochemical investigations, devised apparatus for measuring linear and cubical expansions, and employed a modification of Joseph Black's ice calorimeter in a series of determinations of specific heats. Regarding heat (*matière de feu* or *fluide igné*) as a peculiar kind of imponderable matter, Lavoisier held that the three states of aggregation—solid, liquid and gas—were modes of matter, each depending on the amount of *matière de feu* with which the ponderable substances concerned were interpenetrated and combined; and this view enabled him correctly to anticipate that gases would be reduced to liquids and solids by the influence of cold and pressure. He also worked at fermentation, respiration and animal heat, looking upon the processes concerned as essentially chemical in nature. A paper discovered many years after his death showed that he had anticipated later thinkers in explaining the cyclical process of animal and vegetable life, for he pointed out that plants derive their food from the air, from water, and in general from the mineral kingdom, and animals in turn feed on plants or on other animals fed by plants, while the materials thus taken up by plants and animals are restored to the mineral kingdom by the breaking-down processes of fermentation, putrefaction and combustion.

A complete edition of the writings of Lavoisier, *Œuvres de Lavoisier, publiées par les soins du ministre de l'instruction publique*, was issued at Paris in six volumes from 1864-1893. This publication comprises his *Opuscules physiques et chimiques* (1774), many memoirs from the Academy volumes, and numerous letters, notes and reports relating to the various matters on which he was engaged. At the time of his death he was preparing an edition of his collected works, and the portions ready for the press were published in two volumes as *Mémoires de chimie* in 1805 by his widow (in that year married to Count Rumford), who had drawn and engraved the plates in his *Traité élémentaire de chimie* (1789).

See E. Grimaux, *Lavoisier 1743-1794, d'après sa correspondance, ses manuscripts, &c.* (1888), which gives a list of his works; P. E. M. Berthelot, *La Révolution chimique—Lavoisier* (1890), which contains an analysis of and extracts from his laboratory notebooks.

LA VOISIN. Catherine Monvoisin, known as "La Voisin" (d. 1680), French sorceress, whose maiden name was Catherine Deshayes, was one of the chief personages in the famous *affaire des poisons*, which disgraced the reign of Louis XIV. Her husband, Monvoisin, was an unsuccessful jeweller, and she practised chiromancy and face-reading to retrieve their fortunes. She gradually added the practice of witchcraft, in which she had the help of a renegade priest, Étienne Guibourg, whose part was the celebration of the "black mass," an abominable parody in which the host was compounded of the blood of a little child mixed with horrible ingredients. She practised medicine, especially midwifery, procured abortion and provided love powders and poisons. Her chief accomplice was one of her lovers, the magician Lesage, whose real name was Adam Cœuret. The great ladies of Paris flocked to La Voisin, who accumulated enormous wealth. Among her clients were Olympe Mancini, comtesse de Soissons, who sought the death of the king's mistress, Louise de la Vallière; Mme de Montespan, Mme de Gramont (*la belle* Hamilton) and others. The bones of toads, the teeth of moles, cantharides, iron filings, human blood and human dust were among the ingredients of the love powders concocted by La Voisin. Her knowledge of poisons was not apparently so thorough as that of less well-known sorcerers, or it would be difficult to account for La Vallière's immunity. The art of poisoning had become a regular science. The death of Henrietta, duchess of Orleans, was attributed, falsely it is true, to poison, and the crimes of Marie Madeleine de Brinvilliers (executed in 1676) and her accomplices were still fresh in the public mind. In April 1679 a commission appointed to inquire into the subject and to prosecute the offenders met for the first time. Its proceedings, including some suppressed in the official records, are preserved in the notes of one of the official *rapporteurs*, Gabriel Nicolas de la Reynie. The revelation of the treacherous intention of Mme de Montespan to poison Louis XIV. and of other crimes, planned by personages who could not be attacked without scandal which touched the throne, caused Louis XIV. to close the *chambre ardente*, as the court was called, on the 1st of October 1680. It was reopened on the 19th of May 1681 and sat until the 21st of July 1682. Many of the culprits escaped through private influence. Among these were Marie Anne Mancini, duchesse de Bouillon, who had sought to get rid of her husband in order to marry the duke of Vendôme, though Louis XIV. banished her to Nérac. Mme de Montespan was not openly disgraced, because the preservation of Louis's own dignity was essential, and some hundred prisoners, among them the infamous Guibourg and Lesage, escaped the scaffold through the suppression of evidence insisted on by Louis XIV. and Louvois. Some of these were imprisoned in various fortresses, with instructions from Louvois to the respective commandants to flog them if they sought to impart what they knew. Some innocent persons were imprisoned for life because they had knowledge of the facts. La Voisin herself was executed at an early stage of the proceedings, on the 20th of February 1680, after a perfunctory application of torture. The authorities had every reason to avoid further revelations. Thirty-five other prisoners were executed; five were sent to the galleys and twenty-three were banished. Their crimes had furnished one of the most extraordinary trials known to history.

See F. Ravaisson, *Archives de la Bastille*, vols. iv.-vii. (1870–1874); the notes of La Reynie, preserved in the Bibliothèque Nationale; F. Funck-Brentano, *Le Drame des poisons* (1899); A. Masson, *La Sorcellerie et la science des poisons au XVIIe siècle* (1904). Sardou made the affair a background for his *Affaire des poisons* (1907). There is a portrait of La Voisin by Antoine Coypel, which has been often reproduced.

LAW, JOHN (1671–1729), Scots economist, best known as the originator of the "Mississippi scheme," was born at Edinburgh in April 1671. His father, a goldsmith and banker, bought shortly before his death, which took place in his son's youth, the lands of Lauriston near Edinburgh. John lived at home till he was twenty, and then went to London. He had already studied mathematics, and the theory of commerce and political economy, with much interest; but he was known rather as fop than scholar. In London he gambled, drank and flirted till in April 1694 a love intrigue resulted in a duel with Beau Wilson in Bloomsbury Square. Law killed his antagonist, and was condemned to death. His life was spared, but he was detained in prison. He found means to escape to Holland, then the greatest commercial country in Europe. Here he observed with close attention the practical working of banking and financial business, and conceived the first ideas of his celebrated "system." After a few years spent in foreign travel, he returned to Scotland, then exhausted and enraged by the failure of the Darien expedition (1695–1701). He propounded plans for the relief of his country in a work[1] entitled *Money and Trade Considered, with a Proposal for supplying the Nation with Money* (1705). This attracted some notice, but had no practical effect, and Law again betook himself to travel. He visited Brussels, Paris, Vienna, Genoa, Rome, making large sums by gambling and speculation, and spending them lavishly. He was in Paris in 1708, and made some proposals to the government as to their financial difficulties, but Louis XIV. declined to treat with a "Huguenot," and d'Argenson, chief of the police, had Law expelled as a suspicious character. He had, however, become intimately acquainted with the duke of Orleans, and when in 1715 that prince became regent, Law at once returned to Paris.

The extravagant expenditure of the late monarch had plunged the kingdom into apparently inextricable financial confusion. The debt was 3000 million livres, the estimated annual expenditure, exclusive of interest payments, 148 million livres, and the income about the same. The advisability of declaring a national bankruptcy was seriously discussed, and though this plan was rejected, measures hardly less violent were carried. By a *visa*, or examination of the state liabilities by a committee with full powers of quashing claims, the debt was reduced nearly a half, the coin in circulation was ordered to be called in and reissued at the rate of 120 for 100—a measure by which foreign coiners profited greatly, and a chamber of justice was established to punish speculators, to whom the difficulties of the state were ascribed. These measures had so little success that the *billets d'état* which were issued as part security for the new debt at once sank 75% below their nominal value. At this crisis Law unfolded a vast scheme to the perplexed regent. A royal bank was to manage the trade and currency of the kingdom, to collect the taxes, and to free the country from debt. The council of finance, then under the duc de Noailles, opposed the plan, but the regent allowed Law to take some tentative steps. By an edict of 2nd May 1716, a private institution called *La Banque générale*, and managed by Law, was founded. The capital was 6 million livres, divided into 1200 shares of 5000 livres, payable in four instalments, one-fourth in cash, three-fourths in *billets d'état*. It was to perform the ordinary functions of a bank, and had power to issue notes payable at sight in the weight and value of the money mentioned at day of issue. The bank was a great and immediate success. By providing for the absorption of part of the state paper it raised the credit of the government. The notes were a most desirable medium of exchange, for they had the element of fixity of value, which, owing to the arbitrary mint decrees of the government, was wanting in the coin of the realm. They proved the most convenient instruments of remittance between the capital and the provinces, and they thus developed the industries of the latter. The rate of interest, previously enormous and uncertain, fell first to 6 and then to 4%; and when another decree (10th April 1717) ordered collectors of taxes to receive notes as payments, and to change them for coin at request, the bank so rose in favour that it soon had a note-issue of 60 million livres. Law now gained the full confidence of the regent, and was allowed to proceed with the development of the "system."

The trade of the region about the Mississippi had been granted to a speculator named Crozat. He found the undertaking too large, and was glad to give it up. By a decree of August 1717 Law was allowed to establish the *Compagnie de la Louisiane ou d'Occident*, and to endow it with privileges practically amounting to sovereignty over the most fertile region of North America. The capital was 100 million livres divided into 200,000 shares of 500 livres. The payments were to be one-fourth in coin and three-fourths in *billets d'état*. On these last the government was to pay 3 million livres interest yearly to the company. As the state paper was depreciated the shares fell much below par. The rapid rise of Law had made him many enemies, and they took advantage of this to attack the system. D'Argenson, now head of the council of finance, with the brothers Paris of Grenoble, famous tax farmers of the day, formed what was called the "anti-system." The farming of the taxes was let to them, under an assumed name, for 48½ million livres yearly. A company was formed, the exact counterpart of the Mississippi company. The capital was the same, divided in the same manner, but the payments were to be entirely in money. The returns from the public revenue were sure; those from the Mississippi scheme were not. Hence the shares of the latter were for some time out of favour. Law proceeded unmoved with the development of his plans. On the 4th of December 1718 the bank became a government institution under the name of *La Banque royale*. Law was director, and the king guaranteed the notes. The shareholders were repaid in coin, and, to widen the influence

[1] A work entitled *Proposals and Reasons for constituting a Council of Trade in Scotland* was published anonymously at Edinburgh in 1701. It was republished at Glasgow in 1751 with Law's name attached; but several references in the state papers of the time mention William Paterson (1658–1719), founder of the Bank of England, as the author of the plan therein propounded. Even if Law had nothing to do with the composition of the work, he must have read it and been influenced by it. This may explain how it contains the germs of many of the developments of the "system." Certainly the suggestion of a central board, to manage great commercial undertakings, to furnish occupation for the poor, to encourage mining, fishing and manufactures, and to bring about a reduction in the rate of interest, was largely realized in the Mississippi scheme. See Bannister's *Life of William Paterson* (ed. 1858), and *Writings of William Paterson* (2nd ed., 3 vols., 1859).

[illegible] institution, the transport of money between towns where it had branches was forbidden. The paper-issue now reached [illegible] millions. Law had such confidence in the success of his plans that he agreed to take over shares in the Mississippi company at par at a near date. The shares began rapidly to rise. The next move was to unite the companies *Des Indes Orientales* and *De Chine*, founded in 1664 and 1713 respectively, but now dwindled away to a shadow, to his company. The united association, *La Compagnie des Indes*, had a practical monopoly of the foreign trade of France. These proceedings necessitated the creation of new capital to the nominal amount of 25 million livres. The payment was spread over 20 months. Every holder of four original shares (*mères*) could purchase one of the new shares (*filles*) at a premium of 50 livres. All these 500-livre shares rapidly rose to 750, or 50% above par. Law now turned his attention to obtaining additional powers within France itself. On the 25th of July 1719 an edict was issued granting the company for nine years the management of the mint and the [illegible]. For this privilege the company paid 5 million livres, and the money was raised by a new issue of shares of the nominal value of 500 livres, but with a premium of other 500. The list [illegible] open for twenty days, and it was necessary to present [illegible] and one *fille* in order to obtain one of the new shares [illegible]. At the same time two dividends per annum of [illegible] were promised. Again there was an attempt to ruin [illegible] bank by the commonplace expedient of making a run on [illegible]; but the conspirators had to meet absolute power [illegible] with fearlessness and skill. An edict appeared reducing, [illegible] a given date, the value of money, and those who had with[illegible] coin from the bank hastened again to exchange it for the [illegible] notes. Public confidence in Law was increased, [illegible] he was enabled rapidly to proceed with the completion of [illegible] system. A decree of 27th August 1719 deprived the rival [illegible] of the farming of the revenue, and gave it to the [illegible] des Indes for nine years in return for an annual [illegible] of 52 million livres. Thus at one blow the "anti[illegible]" was crushed. One thing yet remained; Law proposed [illegible] the national debt, and manage it on terms advan[illegible] to the state. The mode of transfer was this. The debt [illegible] million livres. Notes were to be issued to that [illegible], and with these the state creditors must be paid in a [illegible]. Shares were to be issued at intervals corresponding [illegible], and it was expected that the notes would be [illegible] them. The government was to pay 3% for the [illegible] formerly been bound to pay 80 millions, it would [illegible] a clear gain of over 30. As the shares of [illegible] were almost the only medium for investment, [illegible] would be surely effected. The creditors would [illegible] the government payments and the commercial [illegible] company for their annual returns. Indeed the [illegible] not able to procure the shares, for each [illegible] was immediately seized upon, though the 500-[illegible] issued at a premium of 4500 livres. After [illegible] the end of October, the shares immediately [illegible] in the Rue Quincampoix, then used as a [illegible] on rapidly rising as new privileges were [illegible] the company. Law had now more than regal [illegible] Stuarts paid him court; the proudest [illegible] humbled themselves before him; and his [illegible] of the populace. After, as a neces[illegible] a Catholic, he was made controller-[illegible] in place of d'Argenson. Finally, in [illegible] was in name as well as in reality united [illegible]

[illegible] complete, but it had already begun to [illegible] it was at its height. The shares [illegible] livres, forty times their nominal [illegible] overcomed the nation. Men sold their [illegible] to speculate. The population of the [illegible] an enormous influx of provincials and [illegible] a vast though un[illegible] [illegible] getting richer, no[illegible] who could still reflect saw that this prosperity was not real. The whole issue of shares at the extreme market-price valued 12,000 million livres. It would require 600 million annual revenue to give a 5% dividend on this. Now, the whole income of the company as yet was hardly sufficient to pay 5% on the original capital of 1677 million livres. The receipts from the taxes, &c., could be precisely calculated, and it would be many years before the commercial undertakings of the company—with which only some trifling beginning had been made—would yield any considerable return. People began to sell their shares, and to buy coin, houses, land—anything that had a stable element of value in it. There was a rapid fall in the shares, a rapid rise in all kinds of property, and consequently a rapid depreciation of the paper money. Law met these new tendencies by a succession of the most violent edicts. The notes were to bear a premium over specie. Coin was only to be used in small payments, and only a small amount was to be kept in the possession of private parties. The use of diamonds, the fabrication of gold and silver plate, was forbidden. A dividend of 40% on the original capital was promised. By several ingenious but fallaciously reasoned pamphlets Law endeavoured to restore public confidence. The shares still fell. At last, on the 5th of March 1720, an edict appeared fixing their price at 9000 livres, and ordering the bank to buy and sell them at that price. The fall now was transferred to the notes, of which there were soon over 2500 million livres in circulation. A large proportion of the coined money was removed from the kingdom. Prices rose enormously. There was everywhere distress and complete financial confusion. Law became an object of popular hatred. He lost his court influence, and was obliged to consent to a decree (21st May 1720) by which the notes and consequently the shares were reduced to half their nominal value. This created such a commotion that its promoters were forced to recall it, but the mischief was done. What confidence could there be in the depreciated paper after such a measure? Law was removed from his office, and his enemies proceeded to demolish the "system." A vast number of shares had been deposited in the bank. These were destroyed. The notes were reconverted into government debt, but there was first a *visa* which reduced that debt to the same size as before it was taken over by the company. The rate of interest was lowered, and the government now only pledged itself to pay 37 instead of 80 millions annually. Finally the bank was abolished, and the company reduced to a mere trading association. By November the "system" had disappeared. With these last measures Law, it may well be believed, had nothing to do. He left France secretly in December 1720, resumed his wandering life, and died at Venice, poor and forgotten, on the 21st of March 1729.

Of Law's writings the most important for the comprehension of the "system" is his *Money and Trade Considered*. In this work he says that national power and wealth consist in numbers of people, and magazines of home and foreign goods. These depend on trade, and that on money, of which a greater quantity employs more people; but credit, if the credit have a circulation, has all the beneficial effects of money. To create and increase instruments of credit is the function of a bank. Let such be created then, and let its notes be only given in return for land sold or pledged. Such a currency would supply the nation with abundance of money; and it would have many advantages, which Law points out in detail, over silver. The bank or commission was to be a government institution, and its profits were to be spent in encouraging the export and manufacture of the nation. A very evident error lies at the root of the "system." Money is not the result but the cause of wealth, he thought. To increase it then must be beneficial, and the best way is by a properly secured paper currency. This is the motive force; but it is to be applied in a particular way. Law had a profound belief in the omnipotence of government. He saw the evils of minor monopolies, and of private farming of taxes. He proposed to centre foreign trade and internal finance in one huge monopoly managed by the state for the people, and carrying on business through a plentiful supply of paper money. He did not see that trade and commerce are best left to private enterprise, and that such a scheme would simply result in the profits of speculators and favourites. The "system" was never so far developed as to exhibit its inherent faults. The madness of speculators ruined the plan when only its foundations were laid. One part indeed might have been saved. The bank was not necessarily bound to the company, and had its note-issue been retrenched it might have become a permanent institution. As Thiers points out, the edict of the 5th of March 1720, which made the shares convertible into notes, ruined the bank without saving the company. The shares had risen to an unnatural height, and they should have been allowed to fall to their natural level. Perhaps Law felt this to be impossible. He had friends at court whose interests were involved in the shares, and he had enemies eager for his overthrow. It was necessary to succeed completely or not at all; so Law, a gambler to the core, risked and lost everything. Notwithstanding the faults of the "system," its author was a financial genius of the first order. He had the errors of his time; but he propounded many truths as to the nature of currency and banking then unknown to his contemporaries. The marvellous skill which he displayed in adapting the theory of the "system" to the actual condition of things in France, and in carrying out the various financial transactions rendered necessary by its development, is absolutely without parallel. His profound self-confidence and belief in the truth of his own theories were the reasons alike of his success and his ruin. He never hesitated to employ the whole force of a despotic government for the definite ends which he saw before him. He left France poorer than he entered it, yet he was not perceptibly changed by his sudden transitions of fortune. Montesquieu visited him at Venice after his fall, and has left a description of him touched with a certain pathos. Law, he tells us, was still the same in character, perpetually planning and scheming, and, though in poverty, revolving vast projects to restore himself to power, and France to commercial prosperity.

The fullest account of the Mississippi scheme is that of Thiers, *Law et son système des finances* (1826, American trans. 1859). See also Heymann, *Law und sein System* (1853); Pierre Bonnassieux, *Les Grandes Compagnies de commerce* (1892); S. Alexi, *John Law und sein System* (1885); E. Levasseur, *Recherches historiques sur le système de Law* (1854); and Jobez, *Une Préface au socialisme, ou le système de Law et la chasse aux capitalistes* (1848). Full biographical details are given in Wood's *Life of Law* (Edinburgh, 1824). All Law's later writings are to be found in Daire, *Collection des principaux économistes*, vol. i. (1843). Other works on Law are: A. W. Wiston-Glynn, *John Law of Lauriston* (1908); P. A. Cochut, *The Financier Law, his Scheme and Times* (1856); A. MacI. Davis, *An Historical Study of Law's System* (Boston, 1887); A. Beljame, *La Prononciation du nom de Jean Law le financier* (1891). See also E. A. Benians in *Camb. Mod. Hist.* vi. 6 (1909). For minor notices see Poole's *Index to Periodicals*. There is a portrait of Law by A. S. Belle in the National Portrait Gallery, London. (F. Wa.)

LAW, WILLIAM (1686–1761), English divine, was born at King's Cliffe, Northamptonshire. In 1705 he entered as a sizar at Emmanuel College, Cambridge; in 1711 he was elected fellow of his college and was ordained. He resided at Cambridge, teaching and taking occasional duty until the accession of George I., when his conscience forbade him to take the oaths of allegiance to the new government and of abjuration of the Stuarts. His Jacobitism had already been betrayed in a tripos speech which brought him into trouble; and he was now deprived of his fellowship and became a non-juror. For the next few years he is said to have been a curate in London. By 1727 he was domiciled with Edward Gibbon (1666–1736) at Putney as tutor to his son Edward, father of the historian, who says that Law became "the much honoured friend and spiritual director of the whole family." In the same year he accompanied his pupil to Cambridge, and resided with him as governor, in term time, for the next four years. His pupil then went abroad, but Law was left at Putney, where he remained in Gibbon's house for more than ten years, acting as a religious guide not only to the family but to a number of earnest-minded folk who came to consult him. The most eminent of these were the two brothers John and Charles Wesley, John Byrom the poet, George Cheyne the physician and Archibald Hutcheson, M.P. for Hastings. The household was dispersed in 1737. Law was parted from his friends, and in 1740 retired to King's Cliffe, where he had inherited from his father a house and a small property. There he was presently joined by two ladies: Mrs Hutcheson, the rich widow of his old friend, who recommended her on his death-bed to place herself under Law's spiritual guidance, and Miss Hester Gibbon, sister to his late pupil. This curious trio lived for twenty-one years a life wholly given to devotion, study and charity, until the death of Law on the 9th of April 1761.

Law was a busy writer under three heads:—

1. *Controversy.*—In this field he had no contemporary peer save perhaps Richard Bentley. The first of his controversial works was *Three Letters to the Bishop of Bangor* (1717), which were considered by friend and foe alike as one of the most powerful contributions to the Bangorian controversy on the high church side. Thomas Sherlock declared that "Mr Law was a writer so considerable that he knew but one good reason why his lordship did not answer him." Law's next controversial work was *Remarks on Mandeville's Fable of the Bees* (1723), in which he vindicates morality on the highest grounds; for pure style, caustic wit and lucid argument this work is remarkable; it was enthusiastically praised by John Sterling, and republished by F. D. Maurice. Law's *Case of Reason* (1732), in answer to Tindal's *Christianity as old as the Creation* is to a great extent an anticipation of Bishop Butler's famous argument in the *Analogy*. In this work Law shows himself at least the equal of the ablest champion of Deism. His *Letters to a Lady inclined to enter the Church of Rome* are excellent specimens of the attitude of a high Anglican towards Romanism. His controversial writings have not received due recognition, partly because they were opposed to the drift of his times, partly because of his success in other fields.

2. *Practical Divinity.*—The *Serious Call to a Devout and Holy Life* (1728), together with its predecessor, *A Treatise of Christian Perfection* (1726), deeply influenced the chief actors in the great Evangelical revival. The Wesleys, George Whitefield, Henry Venn, Thomas Scott and Thomas Adam all express their deep obligation to the author. The *Serious Call* affected others quite as deeply. Samuel Johnson, Gibbon, Lord Lyttelton and Bishop Horne all spoke enthusiastically of its merits; and it is still the only work by which its author is popularly known. It has high merits of style, being lucid and pointed to a degree. In a tract entitled *The Absolute Unlawfulness of Stage Entertainments* (1726) Law was tempted by the corruptions of the stage of the period to use unreasonable language, and incurred some effective criticism from John Dennis in *The Stage Defended*.

3. *Mysticism.*—Though the least popular, by far the most interesting, original and suggestive of all Law's works are those which he wrote in his later years, after he had become an enthusiastic admirer (not a disciple) of Jacob Boehme, the Teutonic theosophist. From his earliest years he had been deeply impressed with the piety, beauty and thoughtfulness of the writings of the Christian mystics, but it was not till after his accidental meeting with the works of Boehme, about 1734, that pronounced mysticism appeared in his works. Law's mystic tendencies divorced him from the practical-minded Wesley, but in spite of occasional wild fancies the books are worth reading. They are *A Demonstration of the Gross and Fundamental Errors of a late Book called a "Plain Account, &c., of the Lord's Supper"* (1737); *The Grounds and Reasons of the Christian Regeneration* (1739); *An Appeal to all that Doubt and Disbelieve the Truths of Revelation* (1740); *An Earnest and Serious Answer to Dr Trapp's Sermon on being Righteous Overmuch* (1740); *The Spirit of Prayer* (1749, 1752); *The Way to Divine Knowledge* (1752); *The Spirit of Love* (1752, 1754); *A Short but Sufficient Confutation of Dr Warburton's Projected Defence (as he calls it) of Christianity in his "Divine Legation of Moses"* (1757); *A Series of Letters* (1760); a *Dialogue between a Methodist and a Churchman* (1760); and *An Humble, Earnest and Affectionate Address to the Clergy* (1761).

Richard Tighe wrote a short account of Law's life in 1813. See also Christopher Walton, *Notes and Materials for a Complete Biography of W. Law* (1848); Sir Leslie Stephen, *English Thought in the 18th century*, and in the *Dict. Nat. Biog.* (xxxii. 236); W. H. Lecky, *History of England in the 18th Century*; C. J. Abbey, *The English Church in the 18th Century*; and J. H. Overton, *William Law, Nonjuror and Mystic* (1881).

LAW (O. Eng. *lagu*, M. Eng. *lawe*; from an old Teutonic root *lag*, "lie," what lies fixed or evenly; cf. Lat. *lex*, Fr. *loi*), a word used in English in two main senses—(1) as a rule prescribed by authority for human action, and (2) in scientific and philosophic phraseology, as a uniform order of sequence (*e.g.* "laws" of motion). In the first sense the word is used either in the abstract, for jurisprudence generally or for a state of things in which the laws of a country are duly observed ("law and order"), or in the concrete for some particular rule or body of rules. It is usual to distinguish further between "law" and "equity" (*q.v.*) The scientific and philosophic usage has grown out of an early conception of jurisprudence, and is really metaphorical, derived from the phrase "natural law" or "law of nature," which presumed that commands were laid on matter by God (see T. E. Holland, *Elements of Jurisprudence*, ch. ii.). The adjective "legal" is only used in the first sense, never in the second. In the case of the "moral law" (see ETHICS) the term is employed somewhat ambiguously because of its connexion with both meanings. There is also an Old English use of the word "law" in a more or less sporting sense ("to give law" or "allow so much law"), meaning a start or fair allowance in time or distance. Presumably this originated simply in the liberty-loving Briton's respect for proper legal procedure; instead of the brute exercise of tyrannous force he demanded "law," or a fair opportunity [illegible] But it may simply be an extension of the meaning of "[illegible]," or of the sense of "leave" which is found in early [illegible] of the French *loi*.

[illegible] the laws or uniformities of the physical universe [illegible] in the articles on the various sciences. The general [illegible] of law in the legal sense are discussed under JURIS-[illegible]. What may be described as "national systems" [illegible] historically and generally under ENGLISH [illegible] LAW, ROMAN LAW, GREEK LAW, MAHOMMEDAN [illegible] LAW, &c. Certain broad divisions of law are [illegible] CONSTITUTIONAL LAW, CANON [illegible] COMMON LAW, CRIMINAL LAW, ECCLESIASTICAL [illegible] INTERNATIONAL LAW, MILITARY LAW, &c. And [illegible] laws of different countries on special subjects [illegible] under the headings for those subjects (BANKRUPTCY, [illegible] (q.v.)) of law, and procedure, see JURISPRUDENCE, [illegible] KING'S BENCH, &c.

[illegible]—The various legal articles have bibliographies [illegible] here to mention such general [illegible] science of jurisprudence, as (for English [illegible] *England* (vol. i., 1907), *The Encyclo-*[illegible] ed. Wood Renton (1907), Stephen's [illegible] *England* (1908), Brett's *Commentaries* [illegible] *England* [illegible], Broom's *Commentaries on* [illegible] Brodie-Innes's *Comparative Principles* [illegible] (1903)); and, for America, [illegible] Kent's *Commentaries on American* [illegible]

[illegible] ([illegible]–1662), English musician, was born [illegible] in December 1595, and received his [illegible] from John Cooper, better known under his [illegible] Coperario (d. 1627), a famous [illegible]. In 1626 he was received as one of the [illegible] chapel royal, which place he held till the [illegible] a stop to church music. But even during [illegible] continued his work as a composer, and [illegible] his vocal pieces, *Ayres and Dialogues for* [illegible] was published in 1653, being followed [illegible] under the same title in 1655 and 1658 [illegible] the king returned, Lawes once [illegible] royal chapel, and composed an anthem for [illegible] II. He died on the 21st of October [illegible] in Westminster Abbey. Lawes's name [illegible] musical circles by his friendship with [illegible] he supplied with incidental music for the [illegible] in 1634. The poet in return im-[illegible] sonnet in which Milton, [illegible] not common amongst poets, exactly [illegible] Lawes. His careful attention to the [illegible] manner in which his music seems to grow [illegible] coincidence of the musical with the [illegible] Lawes's songs on a level with those of [illegible] modern composer. At the same time [illegible] in genuine melodic invention, and [illegible] above the learned contrapuntist.

[illegible], BART. (1814–1900), English [illegible] was born at Rothamsted on the 28th of December [illegible] Oxford, where he matriculated [illegible] himself in growing various [illegible] Rothamsted estates, which he inherited [illegible]. About 1837 he began to experi-[illegible] various manures on plants growing in [illegible] the experiments were extended to [illegible] immediate consequence was that in [illegible] by treating phosphates with [illegible] the artificial manure industry. [illegible] he enlisted the services of Sir J. H. [illegible] on for more than half a century [illegible] crops and feeding animals which [illegible] famous in the eyes of scientific [illegible] world (see AGRICULTURE). In 1854 [illegible] the Royal Society, which in 1867 [illegible] Lawes and Gilbert jointly, and in [illegible]. In the [illegible] his death, which happened on the 31st of August 1900, he took measures to ensure the continued existence of the Rothamsted experimental farm by setting aside £100,000 for that purpose and constituting the Lawes Agricultural Trust, composed of four members from the Royal Society, two from the Royal Agricultural Society, one each from the Chemical and Linnaean Societies, and the owner of Rothamsted mansion-house for the time being.

LAW MERCHANT or LEX MERCATORIA, originally a body of rules and principles relating to merchants and mercantile transactions, laid down by merchants themselves for the purpose of regulating their dealings. It was composed of such usages and customs as were common to merchants and traders in all parts of Europe, varied slightly in different localities by special peculiarities. The law merchant owed its origin to the fact that the civil law was not sufficiently responsive to the growing demands of commerce, as well as to the fact that trade in pre-medieval times was practically in the hands of those who might be termed cosmopolitan merchants, who wanted a prompt and effective jurisdiction. It was administered for the most part in special courts, such as those of the gilds in Italy, or the fair courts of Germany and France, or as in England, in courts of the staple or piepowder (see also SEA LAWS). The history of the law merchant in England is divided into three stages: the first prior to the time of Coke, when it was a special kind of law—as distinct from the common law—administered in special courts for a special class of the community (*i.e.* the mercantile); the second stage was one of transition, the law merchant being administered in the common law courts, but as a body of customs, to be proved as a fact in each individual case of doubt; the third stage, which has continued to the present day, dates from the presidency over the king's bench of Lord Mansfield (*q.v.*), under whom it was moulded into the mercantile law of to-day. To the law merchant modern English law owes the fundamental principles in the law of partnership, negotiable instruments and trade marks.

See G. Malynes, *Consuetudo vel lex mercatoria* (London, 1622); W. Mitchell, *The Early History of the Law Merchant* (Cambridge, 1904); J. W. Smith, *Mercantile Law* (ed. Hart and Simey, 1905).

LAWN, a very thin fabric made from level linen or cotton yarns. It is used for light dresses and trimmings, also for handkerchiefs. The terms lawn and cambric (*q.v.*) are often intended to indicate the same fabric. The word "lawn" was formerly derived from the French name for the fabric *linon*, from *lin*, flax, linen, but Skeat (*Etym. Dict.*, 1898, Addenda) and A. Thomas (*Romania*, xxix. 182, 1900) have shown that the real source of the word is to be found in the name of the French town Laon. Skeat quotes from Palsgrave, *Les clarcissement de la langue Françoyse* (1530), showing that the early name of the fabric was *Lawne lynen*. An early form of the word was "laund," probably due to an adaptation to "laund," lawn, glade or clearing in a forest, now used of a closely-mown expanse of grass in a garden, park, &c. (see GRASS and HORTICULTURE). This word comes from O. Fr. *launde*, mod. *lande*, wild, heathy or sandy ground, covered with scrub or brushwood, a word of Celtic origin; cf. Irish and Breton *lann*, heathy ground, also enclosure, land; Welsh *llan*, enclosure. It is cognate with "land," common to Teutonic languages. In the original sense of clearing in a forest, glade, Lat. *saltus*, "lawn," still survives in the New Forest, where it is used of the feeding-places of cattle.

LAWN-TENNIS, a game played with racquet and ball on a court traversed by a net, but without enclosing walls. It is a modern adaptation of the ancient game of tennis (*q.v.*), with which it is identical as regards the scoring of the game and "set." Lawn-tennis is essentially a summer game, played in the open air, either on courts marked with whitewash on close-cut grass like a cricket pitch, or on asphalt, cinders, gravel, wood, earth or other substance which can be so prepared as to afford a firm, level and smooth surface. In winter, however, the game is often played on the floor of gymnasiums, drill sheds or other buildings, when it is called "covered-court lawn-tennis";

but there is no difference in the game itself corresponding to these varieties of court.

The lawn-tennis court for the single-handed game, one player against one ("singles"), is shown in fig. 1, and that for the four-handed game ("doubles") in fig. 2. The net stretched across the middle of the court is attached to the tops of two posts which stand 3 ft. outside the court on each side. The height of the net is 3 ft. 6 in. at the posts and 3 ft. at the centre.

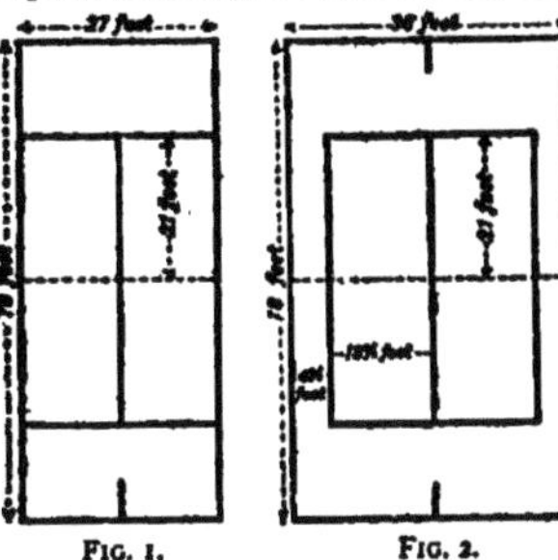

Fig. 1. Fig. 2.

The court is bisected longitudinally by the half-court-line, which, however, is marked only between the two service-lines and at the points of junction with the base-lines. The divisions of the court on each side of the half-court-line are called respectively the right-hand and left-hand courts; and the portion of these divisions between the service-lines and the net are the right-hand service-court and left-hand service-court respectively. The balls, which are made of hollow india-rubber, tightly covered with white flannel, are $2\frac{1}{2}$ in. in diameter, and from $1\frac{7}{8}$ to 2 oz. in weight. The racquets (fig. 3), for which there are no regulation dimensions, are broader and lighter than those used in tennis.

Before play begins, a racquet is spun as in tennis, and the winner of the spin elects either to take first service or to take choice of courts. If he takes choice of courts, he and his partner (if the game be doubles) take their position on the selected side of the net, one stationing himself in the right-hand court and the other in the left, which positions are retained throughout the set. If the winner of the spin takes choice of courts, his opponent has first service; and vice versa. The players change sides of the net at the end of the first, third and every subsequent alternate game, and at the end of each set; but they may agree not to change during any set except the last. Service is delivered by each player in turn, who retains it for one game irrespective of the winning or losing of points. In doubles the partner of the server in the first game serves in the third, and the partner of the server in the second game serves in the fourth; the same order being preserved till the end of the set; but each pair of partners decide for themselves before their first turn of service which of the two shall serve first. The server delivers the service from the right- and left-hand courts alternately, beginning in each of his service games from the right-hand court, even though odds be given or owed; he must stand behind (*i.e.* farther from the net than) the base-line, and must serve the ball so that it drops in the opponent's service-court diagonally opposite to the court served from, or upon one of the lines enclosing that service-court. If in a serve, otherwise good, the ball touches the net, it is a "let" whether the serve be "taken" or not by striker-out; a "let" does not annul a previous "fault." (For the meaning of "let," "rest," "striker-out" and other technical terms used in the game, see TENNIS and RACQUETS.) The serve is a fault (1) if it be not delivered by the server from the proper court, and from behind the base-line; (2) if the ball drops into the net or out-of-court, or into any part of the court other than the proper service-court. The striker-out cannot, as in racquets, "take," and thereby condone, a fault. When a fault has been served, the server must serve again from the same court, unless it was a fault because served from the wrong court, in which case the server crosses to the proper court before serving again. Two consecutive faults score a point against the side of the server. Lawn-tennis differs from tennis and racquets in that the service may not be taken on the volley by striker-out. After the serve has been returned the play proceeds until the "rest" (or "rally") ends by one side or the other failing to make a "good return"; a good return in lawn-tennis meaning a stroke by which the ball, having been hit with the racquet before its second bound, is sent over the net, even if it touches the net, so as to fall within the limits of the court on the opposite side. A point is scored by the player, or side, whose opponent fails to return the serve or to make a good return in the rest. A player also loses a point if the ball when in play touches him or his partner, or their clothes; or if he or his racquet touches the net or any of its supports while the ball is in play; or if he leaps over the net to avoid touching it; or if he volley the ball before it has passed the net.

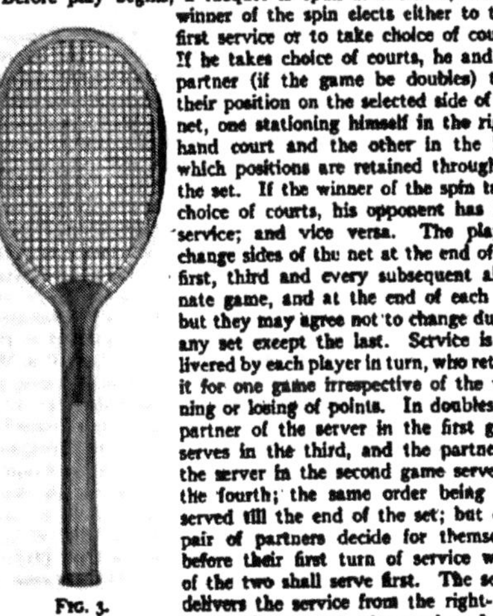

Fig. 3.

For him who would excel in lawn-tennis a strong fast service is hardly less necessary than a heavily "cut" service to the tennis player and the racquet player. High overhand service, by which alone any great pace can be obtained, was first perfected by the brothers Renshaw between 1880 and 1890, and is now universal even among players far below the first rank. The service in vogue among the best players in America, and from this circumstance known as the "American service," has less pace than the English but is "cut" in such a way that it swerves in the air and "drags" off the ground, the advantage being that it gives the server more time to "run in" after his serve, so as to volley his opponent's return from a position within a yard or two of the net. Both in singles and doubles the best players often make it their aim to get up comparatively near the net as soon as possible, whether they are serving or receiving the serve, the object being to volley the ball whenever possible before it begins to fall. The server's partner, in doubles, stands about a yard and a half from the net, and rather nearer the side-line than the half-court-line; the receiver of the service, not being allowed to volley the serve, must take his stand according to the nature of the service, which, if very fast, will require him to stand outside the base-line; the receiver's partner usually stands between the net and the service-line. All four players, if the rest lasts beyond a stroke or two, are generally found nearer to the net than the service-lines; and the game, assuming the players to be of the championship class, consists chiefly of rapid low volleying, varied by attempts on one side or the other to place the ball out of the opponents' reach by "lobbing" it over their heads into the back part of the court. Good "lobbing" demands great skill, to avoid on the one hand sending the ball out of court beyond the base-line, and on the other allowing it to drop short enough for the adversary to kill it with a "smashing" volley. Of "lobbing" it has been laid down by the brothers Doherty that "the higher it is the better, so long as the length is good"; and as regards returning lobs the same authorities say, "you must get them if you can before they drop, for it is usually fatal to let them drop when playing against a good pair." The reason for this is that if the lob be allowed to drop before being returned, so much time is given to the striker of it to gain position that he is almost certain to be able to kill the return, unless the lob be returned by an equally good and very high lob, dropping within a foot or so of the base-line in the opposite court, a stroke that requires the utmost accuracy of strength to accomplish safely. The game in the hands of first-class players consists largely in manœuvring for favourable position in the court while driving the opponent into a less favourable position on his side of the net; the player who gains the advantage of position in this way being generally able to finish the rest by a smashing volley impossible to return. Ability to play this "smash" stroke is essential to strong lawn-tennis. "To be good overhead," say the Dohertys, "is the sign of a first-class player, even if a few have managed to get on without it." The smash stroke is played very much in the same way as the overhand service, except that it is not from a defined position of known distance from the net; and therefore when making it the player must realize almost instinctively what his precise position is in relation to the net and the side-lines, for it is of the last importance that he should not take his eye off the ball "even for the hundredth part of a second." By drawing the racquet across the ball at the moment of impact spin may be imparted to it as in tennis, or as "side" is imparted to a billiard ball, and the direction of this spin and the consequent behaviour of the ball after the stroke may be greatly varied by a skilful player. Perhaps the most generally useful form of spin, though by no means the only one commonly used, is that known as "top" or "lift," a vertical rotatory motion of the ball in the same direction as its flight, which is imparted to it by an upward draw of the racquet at the moment of making the stroke, and the effect of which is to make it drop more suddenly than it would ordinarily do, and in an unexpected curve. A drive made with plenty of "top" can be hit much harder than would otherwise be possible without sending the ball out of court, and it is therefore extensively employed by the best players. While the volleying game is almost universally the practice of first-class players—A. W. Gore, M. J. G. Ritchie and S. H. Smith being almost alone among those of championship rank in modern days to use the volley comparatively little—its difficulty places it beyond the reach of the less skilful. In lawn-tennis as played at the ordinary country house or local club the real "smash" of a Renshaw or a Doherty is seldom to be seen, and the high lob is almost equally rare. Players of moderate calibre are content to take the ball on the bound and to return it with some pace along the side-lines or across the court, with the aim of placing it as artfully as possible beyond the reach of the adversary; and if now and again they venture to imitate a stroke employed with killing effect at Wimbledon, they think themselves fortunate if they occasionally succeed in making it without disaster to themselves.

Before 1890 the method of handicapping at lawn-tennis was the same as in tennis so far as it was applicable to a game played in an open court. In 1890 bisques were abolished, and in 1894 an elaborate system was introduced by which fractional parts of "fifteen" could be conceded by way of handicap, in accordance with tables inserted in the laws of the game. The system is a development of the tennis handicapping by which a finer graduation of odds may be given. "One-sixth of fifteen" is one stroke given in every six games of a set; and similarly two-sixths, three-sixths, four-sixths and five-sixths of fifteen, are respectively two, three, four and five strokes given in every six games of a set; the particular game in the set in which the stroke in each case must be given being specified in the tables.

History.—Lawn-tennis cannot be said to have existed prior to the year 1874. It is, indeed, true that outdoor games based on tennis were from time to time improvised by lovers of that game who found themselves out of reach of a tennis-court. Lord Arthur Hervey, sometime bishop of Bath and Wells, had thus devised a game which he and his friends played on the lawn of his rectory in Suffolk; and even so early as the end of the 18th century "field tennis" was mentioned by the *Sporting Magazine* as a game that rivalled the popularity of cricket. But, however much or little this game may have resembled lawn-tennis, it had long ceased to exist; and even to be remembered, when in 1874 Major Wingfield took out a patent for a game called Sphairistike, which the specification described as "a new and improved portable court for playing the ancient game of tennis." The court for this game was wider at the base-lines than at the net, giving the whole court the shape of an hour-glass; one side of the net only was divided into service-courts, service being always delivered from a fixed mark in the centre of the opposite court; and from the net-posts side-nets were fixed which tapered down to the ground at about the middle [illegible] side-lines, thus enclosing nearly half the courts on each [illegible] net. The possibilities of Sphairistike were quickly [illegible] and under the new name of lawn-tennis its popularity [illegible] that in 1875 a meeting of those interested in [illegible] was held at Lord's cricket-ground, where a committee [illegible] Club (M.C.C.) was appointed to draw up a [illegible] The hour-glass shape of the court was retained [illegible] in May 1875), and the scoring of the game [illegible] the racquets instead of the tennis model. [illegible] of J. M. Heathcote, the amateur tennis [illegible] covered with white flannel were sub- [illegible] balls used at first. In 1875, through [illegible] Jones ("Cavendish"), lawn-tennis was [illegible] of the All England Croquet Club, [illegible] the All England Croquet and Lawn- [illegible] at Wimbledon the All England [illegible] annually played since that date. [illegible] of the first championship [illegible] a committee consisting of Henry [illegible] Heathcote to revise the M.C.C. [illegible] being the introduction [illegible] scoring, the substitution [illegible] " court, and the enactment of the modern rule as regards the "fault." The height of the net, which under the M.C.C. rules had been 4 ft. in the centre, was reduced to 3 ft. 3 in.; and regulations as to the size and weight of the ball were also made. Some controversy had already taken place in the columns of the *Field* as to whether volleying the ball, at all events within a certain distance of the net, should not be prohibited. Spencer Gore, the first to win the championship in 1877, used the volley with great skill and judgment, and in principle anticipated the tactics afterwards brought to perfection by the Renshaws, which aimed at forcing the adversary back to the base-line and killing his return with a volley from a position near the net. P. F. Hadow, champion in 1878, showed how the volley might be defeated by skilful use of the lob; but the question of placing some check on the volley continued to be agitated among lovers of the game. The rapidly growing popularity of lawn-tennis was proved in 1879 by the inauguration at Oxford of the four-handed championship, and at Dublin of the Irish championship, and by the fact that there were forty-five competitors for the All England single championship at Wimbledon, won by J. T. Hartley, a player who chiefly relied on the accuracy of his return without frequent resort to the volley. It was in the autumn of the same year, in a tournament at Cheltenham, that W. Renshaw made his first successful appearance in public. The year 1880 saw the foundation of the Northern Lawn-Tennis Association, whose tournaments have long been regarded as inferior in importance only to the championship meetings at Wimbledon and Dublin, and a revision of the rules which substantially made them what they have ever since remained. This year is also memorable for the first championship doubles won by the twin brothers William and Ernest Renshaw, a success which the former followed up by winning the Irish championship, beating among others H. F. Lawford for the first time.

The Renshaws had already developed the volleying game at the net, and had shown what could be done with the "smash" stroke (which became known by their name as the "Renshaw smash"), but their service had not as yet become very severe. In 1881 the distinctive features of their style were more marked, and the brothers first established firmly the supremacy which they maintained almost without interruption for the next eight years. In the doubles they discarded the older tactics of one partner standing back and the other near the net; the two Renshaws stood about the same level, just inside the service-line, and from there volleyed with relentless severity and with an accuracy never before equalled, and seldom if ever since; while their service also acquired an immense increase of pace. Their chief rival, and the leading exponent of the non-volleying game for several years, was H. F. Lawford. After a year or two it became evident that neither the volleying tactics of Renshaw nor the strong back play of Lawford would be adopted to the exclusion of the other, and both players began to combine the two styles. Thus the permanent features of lawn-tennis may be said to have been firmly established by about the year 1885; and the players who have since then come to the front have for the most part followed the principles laid down by the Renshaws and Lawford. One of the greatest performances at lawn-tennis was in the championship competition in 1886 when W. Renshaw beat Lawford a love set in 9½ minutes. The longest rest in first-class lawn-tennis occurred in a match between Lawford and E. Lubbock in 1880, when eighty-one strokes were played. Among players in the first class who were contemporaries of the Renshaws, mention should be made of E. de S. Browne, a powerful imitator of the Renshaw style; C. W. Grinstead, R. T. Richardson, V. Goold (who played under the *nom de plume* "St Leger"), J. T. Hartley, E. W. Lewis, E. L. Williams, H. Grove and W. J. Hamilton; while among the most prominent lady players of the period were Miss M. Langrishe, Miss Bradley, Miss Maud Watson, Miss L. Dod, Miss Martin and Miss Bingley (afterwards Mrs Hillyard). In 1888 the Lawn-Tennis Association was established; and the All England Mixed Doubles Championship (four-handed matches for ladies and gentlemen in partnership) was added to the existing annual competitions. Since 1881 lawn-tennis matches between Oxford and Cambridge universities have been played annually; and almost every county in England, besides Scotland, Wales and districts such as "Midland Counties," "South of England," &c., have their own championship meetings. Tournaments are also played in winter at Nice, Monte Carlo and other Mediterranean resorts where most of the competitors are English visitors.

The results of the All England championships have been as follows:—

Year.	Gentlemen's Singles.	Year.	Gentlemen's Singles.
1877	S. W. Gore	1894	J. Pim
1878	P. F. Hadow	1895	W. Baddeley
1879	J. T. Hartley	1896	H. S. Mahony
1880	J. T. Hartley	1897	R. F. Doherty
1881	W. Renshaw	1898	R. F. Doherty
1882	W. Renshaw	1899	R. F. Doherty
1883	W. Renshaw	1900	R. F. Doherty
1884	W. Renshaw	1901	A. W. Gore
1885	W. Renshaw	1902	H. L. Doherty
1886	W. Renshaw	1903	H. L. Doherty
1887	H. F. Lawford	1904	H. L. Doherty
1888	E. Renshaw	1905	H. L. Doherty
1889	W. Renshaw	1906	H. L. Doherty
1890	W. J. Hamilton	1907	N. E. Brookes
1891	W. Baddeley	1908	A. W. Gore
1892	W. Baddeley	1909	A. W. Gore
1893	J. Pim	1910	A. F. Wilding

Year.	Gentlemen's Doubles.		
1879	L. R. Erskine	and	H. F. Lawford
1880	W. Renshaw	"	E. Renshaw
1881	W. Renshaw	"	E. Renshaw
1882	J. T. Hartley	"	R. T. Richardson
1883	C. W. Grinstead	"	C. E. Welldon
1884	W. Renshaw	"	E. Renshaw
1885	W. Renshaw	"	E. Renshaw
1886	W. Renshaw	"	E. Renshaw
1887	P. B. Lyon	"	H. W. W. Wilberforce
1888	W. Renshaw	"	E. Renshaw
1889	W. Renshaw	"	E. Renshaw
1890	J. Pim	"	F. O. Stoker
1891	W. Baddeley	"	H. Baddeley
1892	H. S. Barlow	"	E. W. Lewis
1893	J. Pim	"	F. O. Stoker
1894	W. Baddeley	"	H. Baddeley
1895	W. Baddeley	"	H. Baddeley
1896	W. Baddeley	"	H. Baddeley
1897	R. F. Doherty	"	H. L. Doherty
1898	R. F. Doherty	"	H. L. Doherty
1899	R. F. Doherty	"	H. L. Doherty
1900	R. F. Doherty	"	H. L. Doherty
1901	R. F. Doherty	"	H. L. Doherty
1902	S. H. Smith	"	F. L. Riseley
1903	R. F. Doherty	"	H. L. Doherty
1904	R. F. Doherty	"	H. L. Doherty
1905	R. F. Doherty	"	H. L. Doherty
1906	S. H. Smith	"	F. L. Riseley
1907	N. E. Brookes	"	A. F. Wilding
1908	M. J. G. Ritchie	"	A. F. Wilding
1909	A. W. Gore	"	H. Roper Barrett
1910	M. J. G. Ritchie	"	A. F. Wilding

Year.	Ladies' Singles.	Year.	Ladies' Singles.
1884	Miss M. Watson	1898	Miss C. Cooper
1885	Miss M. Watson	1899	Mrs Hillyard
1886	Miss Bingley	1900	Mrs Hillyard
1887	Miss Dod	1901	Mrs Sterry (Miss C. Cooper)
1888	Miss Dod		
1889	Mrs Hillyard (Miss Bingley)	1902	Miss M. E. Robb
		1903	Miss D. K. Douglass
1890	Miss Rice	1904	Miss D. K. Douglass
1891	Miss Dod	1905	Miss M. Sutton
1892	Miss Dod	1906	Miss D. K. Douglass
1893	Miss Dod	1907	Miss M. Sutton
1894	Mrs Hillyard	1908	Mrs Sterry
1895	Miss C. Cooper	1909	Miss D. Boothby
1896	Miss C. Cooper	1910	Mrs Lambert Chambers (Miss Douglass)
1897	Mrs Hillyard		

Year.	Ladies' and Gentlemen's Doubles.		
1888	E. Renshaw	and	Mrs Hillyard
1889	J. C. Kay	"	Miss Dod
1890	J. Baldwin	"	Miss K. Hill
1891	J. C. Kay	"	Miss Jackson
1892	A. Dod	"	Miss Dod
1893	W. Baddeley	"	Mrs Hillyard
1894	H. S. Mahony	"	Miss C. Cooper
1895	H. S. Mahony	and	Miss C. Cooper
1896	H. S. Mahony	"	Miss C. Cooper
1897	H. S. Mahony	"	Miss C. Cooper
1898	H. S. Mahony	"	Miss C. Cooper
1899	C. H. L. Cazalet	"	Miss Robb
1900	H. L. Doherty	"	Miss C. Cooper
1901	S. H. Smith	"	Miss Martin
1902	S. H. Smith	"	Miss Martin
1903	F. L. Riseley	"	Miss D. K. Douglass
1904	S. H. Smith	"	Miss E. W. Thompson
1905	S. H. Smith	"	Miss E. W. Thompson
1906	F. L. Riseley	"	Miss D. K. Douglass
1907	N. E. Brookes	"	Mrs Hillyard
1908	A. F. Wilding	"	Mrs Lambert Chambers (Miss D. K. Douglass)
1909	H. Roper Barrett	"	Miss Morton
1910	S. N. Doust	"	Mrs Lambert Chambers

In the United States lawn-tennis was played at Nahant, near Boston, within a year of its invention in England, Dr James Dwight and the brothers F. R. and R. D. Sears being mainly instrumental in making it known to their countrymen. In 1881 at a meeting in New York of representatives of thirty-three clubs the United States National Lawn-Tennis Association was formed; and the adoption of the English rules put an end to the absence of uniformity in the size of the ball and height of the net which had hindered the progress of the game. The association decided to hold matches for championship of the United States at Newport, Rhode Island; and, by a curious coincidence, in the same year in which W. Renshaw first won the English championship, R. D. Sears won the first American championship by playing a volleying game at the net which entirely disconcerted his opponents, and he successfully defended his title for the next six years, winning the doubles throughout the same period in partnership with Dwight. In 1887, Sears being unable to play through ill-health, the championship went to H. W. Slocum. Other prominent players of the period were the brothers C. M. and J. S. Clark, who in 1883 came to England and were decisively beaten at Wimbledon by the two Renshaws. To a later generation belong the strongest single players, M. D. Whitman, Holcombe Ward, W. A. Larned and Karl Behr. Holcombe Ward and Dwight Davis, who have the credit of introducing the peculiar "American twist service," were an exceedingly strong pair in doubles; but after winning the American doubles championship for three years in succession, they were defeated in 1902 by the English brothers R. F. and H. L. Doherty. The championship singles in 1904 and 1905 was won by H. Ward and B. C. Wright, the latter being one of the finest players America has produced; and these two in partnership won the doubles for three years in succession, until they were displaced by F. B. Alexander and H. H. Hackett, who in their turn held the doubles championship for a like period. In 1909 two young Californians, Long and McLoughlin, unexpectedly came to the front, and, although beaten in the final round for the championship doubles, they represented the United States in the contest for the Davis cup (see below) in Australia in that year; McLoughlin having acquired a service of extraordinary power and a smashing stroke with a reverse spin which was sufficient by itself to place him in the highest rank of lawn-tennis players.

Winners of United States Championships.

Year.	Gentlemen's Singles.	Year.	Gentlemen's Singles.
1881	R. D. Sears	1896	R. D. Wrenn
1882	R. D. Sears	1897	R. D. Wrenn
1883	R. D. Sears	1898	M. D. Whitman
1884	R. D. Sears	1899	M. D. Whitman
1885	R. D. Sears	1900	M. D. Whitman
1886	R. D. Sears	1901	W. A. Larned
1887	R. D. Sears	1902	W. A. Larned
1888	H. W. Slocum	1903	H. L. Doherty
1889	H. W. Slocum	1904	H. Ward
1890	O. S. Campbell	1905	B. C. Wright
1891	O. S. Campbell	1906	W. J. Clothier
1892	O. S. Campbell	1907	W. A. Larned
1893	R. D. Wrenn	1908	W. A. Larned
1894	R. D. Wrenn	1909	W. A. Larned
1895	F. H. Hovey	1910	W. A. Larned

Year.	Gentlemen's Doubles.		
1882	J. Dwight	and	R. D. Sears
1883	J. Dwight	,,	R. D. Sears
1884	J. Dwight	,,	R. D. Sears
1885	J. S. Clark	,,	R. D. Sears
1886	J. Dwight	,,	R. D. Sears
1887	J. Dwight	,,	R. D. Sears
1888	V. G. Hall	,,	O. S. Campbell
1889	H. W. Slocum	,,	H. A. Taylor
1890	V. G. Hall	,,	C. Hobart
1891	O. S. Campbell	,,	R. P. Huntingdon
1892	O. S. Campbell	,,	R. P. Huntingdon
1893	C. Hobart	,,	F. H. Hovey
1894	C. Hobart	,,	F. H. Hovey
1895	R. D. Wrenn	,,	M. G. Chase
1896	C. B. Neel	,,	S. R. Neel
1897	L. E. Ware	,,	G. P. Sheldon
1898	L. E. Ware	,,	G. P. Sheldon
1899	D. F. Davis	,,	H. Ward
1900	D. F. Davis	,,	H. Ward
1901	D. F. Davis	,,	H. Ward
1902	R. F. Doherty	,,	H. L. Doherty
1903	R. F. Doherty	,,	H. L. Doherty
1904	H. Ward	,,	B. C. Wright
1905	H. Ward	,,	B. C. Wright
1906	H. Ward	,,	B. C. Wright
1907	F. B. Alexander	,,	H. H. Hackett
1908	F. B. Alexander	,,	H. H. Hackett
1909	F. B. Alexander	,,	H. H Hackett
1910	F. B. Alexander	,,	H. H. Hackett

Year.	Ladies' Singles.		
1890	Miss E. C. Roosevelt	1900	Miss Myrtle McAteer
1891	Miss Mabel E. Cahill	1901	Miss Elizabeth H. Moore
[illegible]	Miss Mabel E. Cahill	1902	Miss Marion Jones
[illegible]	Miss Aline M. Terry	1903	Miss Elizabeth H. Moore
[illegible]	Miss Helen R. Helwig	1904	Miss May Sutton
[illegible]	Miss J. P. Atkinson	1905	Miss Elizabeth H. Moore
[illegible]	Miss Elizabeth H. Moore	1906	Miss Helen H. Homans
[illegible]	Miss J. P. Atkinson	1907	Miss Evelyn Sears
[illegible]	Miss J. P. Atkinson	1908	Mrs Barger Wallach
[illegible]	Miss Marion Jones	1909	Miss Hazel Hotchkiss
		1910	Miss Hazel Hotchkiss

Year.	Ladies' and Gentlemen's Doubles.		
1894	E. P. Fischer	and	Miss J. P. Atkinson
1895	E. P. Fischer	,,	Miss J. P. Atkinson
[illegible]	E. P. Fischer	,,	Miss J. P. Atkinson
[illegible]	D. L. Magruder	,,	Miss Laura Henson
[illegible]	E. P. Fischer	,,	Miss Carrie Neely
[illegible]	A. L. Hoskins	,,	Miss Edith Rastall
[illegible]	Alfred Codman	,,	Miss M. Hunnewell
[illegible]	R. D. Little	,,	Miss Marion Jones
[illegible]	W. C. Grant	,,	Miss E. H. Moore
[illegible]	Harry Allen	,,	Miss Chapman
[illegible]	W. C. Grant	,,	Miss E. H. Moore
[illegible]	Clarence Hobart	,,	Mrs Clarence Hobart
[illegible]	E. B. Dewhurst	,,	Miss Coffin
[illegible]	W. F. Johnson	,,	Miss Sayres
[illegible]	N. W. Niles	,,	Miss E. Rotch
[illegible]	W. F. Johnson	,,	Miss H. Hotchkiss
[illegible]	J. R. Carpenter	,,	Miss H. Hotchkiss

[illegible] international challenge cup was presented by the [illegible] to be competed for in the country of the [illegible] summer of that year a British team, consisting [illegible] Black and H. R. Barrett, challenged for the [illegible] by the Americans, Whitman, Larned, [illegible]. In 1902 a more representative British team, [illegible] and Pim, were again defeated by the same [illegible] United States; but in the following [illegible] brought the Davis cup to England by beating [illegible] Longwood. In 1904 the cup [illegible], when representatives of Belgium, [illegible] but failed to defeat the Dohertys [illegible] represented Great Britain. In 1905 the [illegible] Australasia, Belgium and the [illegible] countries, except Belgium, [illegible] the British players withstood the [illegible] when the contest was confined to [illegible] and Australasia, the latter was suc[illegible] which was then for the first time taken [illegible] was retained in the following year [illegible] and A. F. Wilding defeated [illegible] United States, who had previously [illegible] America. In [illegible]

was not represented in the competition, and the Australians again retained the cup, beating the Americans McLoughlin and Long both in singles and doubles.

See "The Badminton Library," *Tennis: Lawn-Tennis: Racquets: Fives*, new and revised edition (1903); R. F. and H. L. Doherty, *On Lawn-Tennis* (1903); E. H. Miles, *Lessons in Lawn-Tennis* (1899); E. de Nanteuil, *La Paume et le lawn-tennis* (1898); J. Dwight, "Form in Lawn-Tennis," in *Scribner's Magazine*, vol. vi.; A. Wallis Myers, *The Complete Lawn-Tennis Player* (1908). (R. J. M.)

LAWRENCE (Laurentius, Lorenzo), **ST**, Christian martyr, whose name appears in the canon of the mass, and whose festival is on the 10th of August. The basilica reared over his tomb at Rome is still visited by pilgrims. His legend is very popular. Deacon of the pope (St) Sixtus (Xystus) II., he was called upon by the judge to bring forth the treasures of the church which had been committed to his keeping. He thereupon produced the church's poor people. Seeing his bishop, Sixtus, being led to punishment, he cried: "Father! whither goest thou without thy son? Holy priest! whither goest thou without thy deacon?" Sixtus prophesied that Lawrence would follow him in three days. The prophecy was fulfilled, and Lawrence was sentenced to be burnt alive on a gridiron. In the midst of his torments he addressed the judge ironically with the words: *Assum est, versa et manduca* ("I am roasted enough on this side; turn me round, and eat"). All these details of the well-known legend are already related by St Ambrose (*De Offic.* i. 41, ii. 28). The punishment of the gridiron and the speech of the martyr are probably a reminiscence of the Phrygian martyrs, as related by Socrates (iii. 15) and Sozomen (v. 11). But the fact of the martyrdom is unquestionable. The date is usually put at the persecution of Valerian in 258.

The cult of St Lawrence has spread throughout Christendom, and there are numerous churches dedicated to him, especially in England, where 228 have been counted. The Escurial was built in honour of St Lawrence by Philip II. of Spain, in memory of the battle of St Quentin, which was won in 1557 on the day of the martyr's festival. The meteorites which appear annually on or about the 10th of August are popularly known as "the tears of St Lawrence."

See *Acta sanctorum*, Augusti ii. 485-532; P. Franchi de' Cavalieri, *S. Lorenzo e il supplicio della graticola* (Rome, 1900); *Analecta Bollandiana*, xix. 452 and 453; Fr. Arnold-Forster, *Studies in Church Dedications or England's Patron Saints*, i. 508-515, iii. 18, 389-390 (1899). (H. De.)

LAWRENCE, AMOS (1786–1852), American merchant and philanthropist, was born in Groton, Massachusetts, U.S.A., on the 22nd of April 1786, a descendant of John Lawrence of Wisset, Suffolk, England, who was one of the first settlers of Groton. Leaving Groton academy (founded by his father, Samuel Lawrence, and others) in 1799, he became a clerk in a country store in Groton, whence after his apprenticeship he went, with $20 in his pocket, to Boston and there set up in business for himself in December 1807. In the next year he took into his employ his brother, Abbott (see below), whom he made his partner in 1814, the firm name being at first A. & A. Lawrence, and afterwards A. & A. Lawrence & Co. In 1831 when his health failed, Amos Lawrence retired from active business, and Abbott Lawrence was thereafter the head of the firm. The firm became the greatest American mercantile house of the day, was successful even in the hard times of 1812–1815, afterwards engaged particularly in selling woollen and cotton goods on commission, and did much for the establishment of the cotton textile industry in New England: in 1830 by coming to the aid of the financially distressed mills of Lowell, Massachusetts, where in that year the Suffolk, Tremont and Lawrence companies were established, and where Luther Lawrence, the eldest brother, represented the firm's interests; and in 1845–1847 by establishing and building up Lawrence, Massachusetts, named in honour of Abbott Lawrence, who was a director of the Essex company, which controlled the water power of Lawrence, and afterwards was president of the Atlantic Cotton Mills and Pacific Mills there. In 1842 Amos Lawrence decided not to allow his property to increase any further, and in the last eleven years of his life he spent in charity at least $525,000, a large sum in those days. He gave to Williams college, to Bowdoin college, to the Bangor theological seminary, to Wabash college, to Kenyon college and to Groton academy, which was re-named Lawrence academy in honour of the family, and especially in recognition of the gifts of William Lawrence, Amos's brother; to the Boston children's infirmary, which he established, and ($10,000) to the Bunker Hill monument fund; and, besides, he gave to many good causes on a smaller scale, taking especial delight in giving books, occasionally from a bundle of books in his sleigh or carriage as he drove. He died in Boston on the 31st of December 1852.

See *Extracts from the Diary and Correspondence of the late Amos Lawrence, with a Brief Account of Some Incidents in his Life* (Boston, 1856), edited by his son William R. Lawrence.

His brother, ABBOTT LAWRENCE (1792–1855), was born in Groton, Massachusetts, on the 16th of December 1792. Besides being a partner in the firm established by his brother, and long its head, he promoted various New England railways, notably the Boston & Albany. He was a Whig representative in Congress in 1835–1837 and in 1839–1840 (resigning in September 1840 because of ill-health); and in 1842 was one of the commissioners for Massachusetts, who with commissioners from Maine and with Daniel Webster, secretary of state and plenipotentiary of the United States, settled with Lord Ashburton, the British plenipotentiary, the question of the north-eastern boundary. In 1842 he was presiding officer in the Massachusetts Whig convention; he broke with President Tyler, tacitly rebuked Daniel Webster for remaining in Tyler's cabinet after his colleagues had resigned, and recommended Henry Clay and John Davis as the nominees of the Whig party in 1844—an action that aroused Webster to make his famous Faneuil Hall address. In 1848 Lawrence was a prominent candidate for the Whig nomination for the vice-presidency, but was defeated by Webster's followers. He refused the portfolios of the navy and of the interior in President Taylor's cabinet, and in 1849–1852 was United States minister to Great Britain, where he was greatly aided by his wealth and his generous hospitality. He was an ardent protectionist, and represented Massachusetts at the Harrisburg convention in 1827. He died in Boston on the 18th of August 1855, leaving as his greatest memorial the Lawrence scientific school of Harvard university, which he had established by a gift of $50,000 in 1847 and to which he bequeathed another $50,000; in 1907–1908 this school was practically abolished as a distinct department of the university. He made large gifts to the Boston public library, and he left $50,000 for the erection of model lodging-houses, thus carrying on the work of an Association for building model lodging-houses for the poor, organized in Boston in 1857.

See Hamilton A. Hill, *Memoir of Abbott Lawrence* (Boston, 1884). Randolph Anders' *Der Weg zum Glück, oder die Kunst Millionär zu werden* (Berlin, 1856) is a pretended translation of moral maxims from a supposititious manuscript bequeathed to Abbott Lawrence by a rich uncle.

LAWRENCE, AMOS ADAMS (1814–1886), American philanthropist, son of Amos Lawrence, was born in Groton, Massachusetts, U.S.A., on the 31st of July 1814. He graduated at Harvard in 1835, went into business in Lowell, and in 1837 established in Boston his own counting-house, which from 1843 to 1858 was the firm of Lawrence & Mason, and which was a selling agent for the Cocheco mills of Dover, New Hampshire, and for other textile factories. Lawrence established a hosiery and knitting mill at Ipswich—the first of importance in the country—and was a director in many large corporations. He was greatly interested in the claims of Eleazer Williams of Green Bay, Wisconsin, and through loans to this "lost dauphin" came into possession of much land in Wisconsin; in 1849 he founded at Appleton, Wisconsin, a school named in his honour Lawrence university (now Lawrence college). He also contributed to funds for the colonization of free negroes in Liberia. In 1854 he became treasurer of the Massachusetts Emigrant Aid Company (reorganized in 1855 as the New England Emigrant Aid Company), which sent 1300 settlers to Kansas, where the city of Lawrence was named in his honour. He contributed personally for the famous Sharp rifles, which, packed as "books" and "primers," were shipped to Kansas and afterwards came into the hands of John Brown, who had been a *protégé* of Lawrence. During the contest in Kansas, Lawrence wrote frequently to President Pierce (his mother's nephew) in behalf of the free-state settlers; and when John Brown was arrested he appealed to the governor of Virginia to secure for him a lawful trial. On Robinson and others in Kansas he repeatedly urged the necessity of offering no armed resistance to the Federal government; and he deplored Brown's fanaticism. In 1858 and in 1860 he was the Whig candidate for governor of Massachusetts. Till the very outbreak of the Civil War he was a "law and order" man, and he did his best to secure the adoption of the Crittenden compromise; but he took an active part in drilling troops, and in 1862 he raised a battalion of cavalry which became the 2nd Massachusetts Regiment of Cavalry, of which Charles Russell Lowell was colonel. Lawrence was a member of the Protestant Episcopal Church and built (1873–1880) Lawrence hall, Cambridge, for the Episcopal theological school, of which he was treasurer. In 1857–1862 he was treasurer of Harvard college, and in 1879–1885 was an overseer. He died in Nahant, Mass., on the 22nd of August 1886.

See William Lawrence, *Life of Amos A. Lawrence, with Extracts from his Diary and Correspondence* (Boston, 1888).

His son, WILLIAM LAWRENCE (1850–   ), graduated in 1871 at Harvard, and in 1875 at the Episcopal theological school, where, after being rector of Grace Church, Lawrence, Mass., in 1876–1884, he was professor of homiletics and natural theology in 1884–1893 and dean in 1888–1893. In 1893 he succeeded Phillips Brooks as Protestant Episcopal bishop of Massachusetts. He wrote *A Life of Roger Wolcott, Governor of Massachusetts* (1902).

LAWRENCE, GEORGE ALFRED (1827–1876), English novelist, was born at Braxted, Essex, on the 25th of March 1827, and was educated at Rugby and at Balliol college, Oxford. He was called to the bar at the Inner Temple in 1852, but soon abandoned the law for literature. In 1857 he published, anonymously, his first novel, *Guy Livingstone, or Thorough*. The book achieved a very large sale, and had nine or ten successors of a similar type, the best perhaps being *Sword and Gown* (1859). Lawrence may be regarded as the originator in English fiction of the *beau sabreur* type of hero, great in sport and love and war. He died at Edinburgh on the 23rd of September 1876.

LAWRENCE, SIR HENRY MONTGOMERY (1806–1857), British soldier and statesman in India, brother of the 1st Lord Lawrence (*q.v.*), was born at Matara, Ceylon, on the 28th of June 1806. He inherited his father's stern devotion to duty and Celtic impulsiveness, tempered by his mother's gentleness and power of organization. Early in 1823 he joined the Bengal Artillery at the Calcutta suburb of Dum Dum, where also Henry Havelock was stationed about the same time. The two officers pursued a very similar career, and developed the same Puritan character up to the time that both died at Lucknow in 1857. In the first Burmese War Henry Lawrence and his battery formed part of the Chittagong column which General Morrison led over the jungle-covered hills of Arakan, till fever decimated the officers and men, and Lawrence found himself at home again, wasted by a disease which never left him. On his return to India with his younger brother John in 1829 he was appointed revenue surveyor by Lord William Bentinck. At Gorakhpur the wonderful personal influence which radiated from the young officer formed a school of attached friends and subordinates who were always eager to serve under him. After some years spent in camp, during which he had married his cousin Honoria Marshall, and had surveyed every village in four districts, each larger than Yorkshire, he was recalled to a brigade by the outbreak of the first Afghan War towards the close of 1838. As assistant to Sir George Clerk, he now added to his knowledge of the people political experience in the management of the district of Ferozepore; and when disaster came he was sent to Peshawar in order to push up supports for the relief of Sale and the garrison of Jalalabad. The war had been begun under the tripartite treaty signed at Lahore on the 20th of June 1838. But the Sikhs were slow to play their part after the calamities in Afghanistan. No one but Henry Lawrence could manage the disorderly contingent which they reluctantly supplied to Pollock's avenging army in 1842. He helped to force the Khyber Pass on the 5th of April, playing his guns from the heights, for 8 and 20 m. In recognition of his services Lord Ellenborough appointed him to the charge of the valley of Dehra Dun and its hill stations, Mussoorie and Landour, where he first formed the idea of asylums for the children of European soldiers. After a month's experience there it was discovered that the appointment was the legal right of the civil service, and he was transferred, as assistant to the envoy at Lahore, to Umballa, where he reduced to order the lapsed territory of Kaithal. Soon he received the office of resident at the protected court of Nepal, where, assisted by his wife, he began a series of contributions to the *Calcutta Review*, a selected volume of which forms an Anglo-Indian classic. There, too, he elaborated his plans which resulted in the erection and endowment of the noblest philanthropic establishments in the East—the Lawrence military asylums at Sanawar (on the road to Simla), at Murree in the Punjab, at Mount Abu in Rajputana, and at Lovedale on the Madras Nilgiris. From 1844 to his death he devoted all his income, above a modest pittance for his children, to this and other forms of charity.

The *Review* articles led the new governor-general, Lord Hardinge, to summon Lawrence to his side during the first Sikh War; and not these articles only. He had published the [illegible] of his experience of Sikh rule and soldiering in a vivid [illegible] the *Adventures of an Officer in the Service of Ranjit Singh* [illegible] in which he vainly attempted to disguise his own person[illegible] and exploits. After the doubtful triumphs of Moodkee [illegible] Ferozshah Lawrence was summoned from Nepal to take [illegible] place of Major George Broadfoot, who had fallen. Aliwal [illegible] the guns of Sobraon chased the demoralized Sikhs [illegible] Sutlej. All through the smoke Lawrence was at the [illegible] governor-general. He gave his voice, not for the [illegible] people from anarchy by annexation, but for the [illegible] of the Sikh government, and was himself appointed [illegible] Lahore, with power "over every department and [illegible]" as president of the council of regency till the [illegible] Dhuleep Singh should come of age. Soon disgusted [illegible] and selfish durbar" who formed his Sikh colleagues, [illegible] his side assistants like Nicholson, James Abbott [illegible] they all did too much for the people, as he [illegible] confessed. But "my chief confidence was in my [illegible] who gave me always such help as only a brother [illegible] out he went home with Lord Hardinge, and [illegible] when the second Sikh War summoned him [illegible] to see the whole edifice of Sikh "recon[illegible] It fell to Lord Dalhousie to proclaim the [illegible] British territory on the 29th of March [illegible] compromise was tried. As the best [illegible] Sikh chiefs to the inevitable, Henry Lawrence [illegible] the new board of administration with [illegible] and his brother John was entrusted [illegible] could not find the revenue necessary [illegible] of the new province so long as Henry [illegible] insist on granting life pensions and [illegible] the needy remnants of Ranjit Singh's [illegible] but firmly removed Sir Henry [illegible] the great nobles of Rajputana, and [illegible] commissioner. If resentment burned [illegible] against his younger brother, who [illegible] he said, "If you preserve the [illegible] the people high and low happy, [illegible] the field for you."

[illegible] he once more took up [illegible] and September 1856 [illegible] by conversations with [illegible] had gone as the hero [illegible] had vainly warned the home authorities against reducing below 40,000 the British garrison of India even for the Crimean War, and had sought to improve the position of the sepoys. Lawrence pointed out the latent causes of mutiny, and uttered warnings to be too soon justified. In March 1857 he yielded to Lord Canning's request that he should then take the helm at Lucknow, but it was too late. In ten days his magic rule put down administrative difficulties indeed, as he had done at Lahore. But what could even he effect with only 700 European soldiers, when the epidemic spread after the Meerut outbreak of mutiny on the 10th of May? In one week he had completed those preparations which made the defence of the Lucknow residency for ever memorable. Amid the deepening gloom Lord Canning ever wrote home of him as "a tower of strength," and he was appointed provisional governor-general. On the 30th of May mutiny burst forth in Oudh, and he was ready. On the 29th of June, pressed by fretful colleagues, and wasted by unceasing toil, he led 336 British soldiers with 11 guns and 220 natives out of Chinhat to reconnoitre the insurgents, when the natives joined the enemy and the residency was besieged. On the 2nd of July, as he lay exhausted by the day's work and the terrific heat in an exposed room, a shell struck him, and in forty-eight hours he was no more. A baronetcy was conferred on his son. A marble statue was placed in St Paul's as the national memorial of one who has been declared to be the noblest man that has lived and died for the good of India.

His biography was begun by Sir Herbert Edwardes, and completed (2 vols. 1872) by Herman Merivale. See also J. J. McLeod Innes, *Sir Henry Lawrence* ("Rulers of India" series), 1898.

LAWRENCE, JOHN LAIRD MAIR LAWRENCE, 1st Baron (1811–1879), viceroy and governor-general of India, was born at Richmond, Yorkshire, on the 24th of March 1811. His father, Colonel Alexander Lawrence, volunteered for the forlorn hope at Seringapatam in presence of Baird and of Wellington, whose friend he became. His mother, Letitia Knox, was a collateral descendant of John Knox. To this couple were born twelve children, of whom three became famous in India, Sir George St Patrick, Sir Henry (*q.v.*) and Lord Lawrence. Irish Protestants, the boys were trained at Foyle college, Derry, and at Clifton, and received Indian appointments from their mother's cousin, John Hudleston, who had been the friend of Schwartz in Tanjore. In 1829, when only seventeen, John Lawrence landed at Calcutta as a civilian; he mastered the Persian language at the college of Fort William, and was sent to Delhi, on his own application, as assistant to the collector. The position was the most dangerous and difficult to which a Bengal civilian could be appointed at that time. The titular court of the pensioner who represented the Great Mogul was the centre of that disaffection and sensuality which found their opportunity in 1857. A Mussulman rabble filled the city. The district around, stretching from the desert of Rajputana to the Jumna, was slowly recovering from the anarchy to which Lord Lake had given the first blow. When not administering justice in the city courts or under the village tree, John Lawrence was scouring the country after the marauding Meos and Mahommedan freebooters. His keen insight and sleepless energy at once detected the murderer of his official superior, William Fraser, in 1835, in the person of Shams-uddin Khan, the nawab of Loharu, whose father had been raised to the principality by Lake, and the assassin was executed. The first twenty years, from 1829 to 1849, during which John Lawrence acted as the magistrate and land revenue collector of the most turbulent and backward portion of the Indian empire as it then was, formed the period of the reforms of Lord William Bentinck. To what became the lieutenant-governorship of the North-Western (now part of the United) Provinces Lord Wellesley had promised the same permanent settlement of the land-tax which Lord Cornwallis had made with the large landholders or zemindars of Bengal. The court of directors, going to the opposite extreme, had sanctioned leases for only five years, so that agricultural progress was arrested. In 1833 Merttins Bird and James Thomason introduced the system of thirty years' leases based on a careful survey of every estate by trained civilians, and on the mapping of every village holding by native subordinates. These two revenue officers created a school of enthusiastic economists who rapidly registered and assessed an area as large as that of Great Britain, with a rural population of twenty-three millions. Of that school John Lawrence proved the most ardent and the most renowned. Intermitting his work at Delhi, he became land revenue settlement officer in the district of Etawah, and there began, by buying out or getting rid of the talukdars, to realize the ideal which he did much to create throughout the rest of his career—a country "thickly cultivated by a fat contented yeomanry, each man riding his own horse, sitting under his own fig-tree, and enjoying his rude family comforts." This and a quiet persistent hostility to the oppression of the people by their chiefs formed the two features of his administrative policy throughout life.

It was fortunate for the British power that, when the first Sikh War broke out, John Lawrence was still collector of Delhi. The critical engagements at Ferozeshah, following Moodkee, and hardly redeemed by Aliwal, left the British army somewhat exhausted at the gate of the Punjab, in front of the Sikh entrenchments on the Sutlej. For the first seven weeks of 1846 there poured into camp, day by day, the supplies and munitions of war which this one man raised and pushed forward, with all the influence acquired during fifteen years of an iron yet sympathetic rule in the land between the Jumna and the Sutlej. The crowning victory of Sobraon was the result, and at thirty-five Lawrence became commissioner of the Jullundur Doab, the fertile belt of hill and dale stretching from the Sutlej north to the Indus. The still youthful civilian did for the newly annexed territory what he had long before accomplished in and around Delhi. He restored it to order, without one regular soldier. By the fascination of his personal influence he organized levies of the Sikhs who had just been defeated, led them now against a chief in the upper hills and now to storm the fort of a raja in the lower, till he so welded the people into a loyal mass that he was ready to repeat the service of 1846 when, three years after, the second Sikh War ended in the conversion of the Punjab up to Peshawar into a British province.

Lord Dalhousie had to devise a government for a warlike population now numbering twenty-three millions, and covering an area little less than that of the United Kingdom. The first results were not hopeful; and it was not till John Lawrence became chief commissioner, and stood alone face to face with the chiefs and people and ring fence of still untamed border tribes, that there became possible the most successful experiment in the art of civilizing turbulent millions which history presents. The province was mapped out into districts, now numbering thirty-two, in addition to thirty-six tributary states, small and great. To each the thirty years' leases of the north-west settlement were applied, after a patient survey and assessment by skilled officials ever in the saddle or the tent. The revenue was raised on principles so fair to the peasantry that Ranjit Singh's exactions were reduced by a fourth, while agricultural improvements were encouraged. For the first time in its history since the earliest Aryan settlers had been overwhelmed by successive waves of invaders, the soil of the Punjab came to have a marketable value, which every year of British rule has increased. A stalwart police was organized; roads were cut through every district, and canals were constructed. Commerce followed on increasing cultivation and communications, courts brought justice to every man's door, and crime hid its head. The adventurous and warlike spirits, Sikh and Mahommedan, found a career in the new force of irregulars directed by the chief commissioner himself, while the Afghan, Dost Mahommed, kept within his own fastnesses, and the long extent of frontier at the foot of the passes was patrolled.

Seven years of such work prepared the lately hostile and always anarchic Punjab under such a pilot as John Lawrence not only to weather the storm of 1857 but to lead the older provinces into port. On the 12th of May the news of the tragedies at Meerut and Delhi reached him at Rawalpindi. The position was critical in the last degree, for of 50,000 native soldiers 38,000 were Hindustanis of the very class that had mutinied elsewhere, and the British troops were few and scattered. For five days the fate of the Punjab hung upon a thread, for the question was, "Could the 12,000 Punjabis be trusted and the 38,000 Hindustanis be disarmed?" Not an hour was lost in beginning the disarming at Lahore; and, as one by one the Hindustani corps succumbed to the epidemic of mutiny, the sepoys were deported or disappeared, or swelled the military rabble in and around the city of Delhi. The remembrance of the ten years' war which had closed only in 1849, a bountiful harvest, the old love of battle, the offer of good pay, but, above all, the personality of Lawrence and his officers, raised the Punjabi force into a new army of 59,000 men, and induced the non-combatant classes to subscribe to a 6% loan. Delhi was invested, but for three months the rebel city did not fall. Under John Nicholson, Lawrence sent on still more men to the siege, till every available European and faithful native soldier was there, while a movable column swept the country, and the border was kept by an improvised militia. At length, when even in the Punjab confidence became doubt, and doubt distrust, and that was passing into disaffection, John Lawrence was ready to consider whether we should not give up the Peshawar valley to the Afghans as a last resource, and send its garrison to recruit the force around Delhi. Another week and that alternative must have been faced. But on the 20th of September the city and palace of Delhi were again in British hands, and the chief commissioner and his officers united in ascribing "to the Lord our God all the praise due for nerving the hearts of our statesmen and the arms of our soldiers." As Sir John Lawrence, Bart., G.C.B., with the thanks of parliament, the gratitude of his country, and a life pension of £2000 a year in addition to his ordinary pension of £1000, the "saviour of India" returned home in 1859. After guarding the interests of India and its people as a member of the secretary of state's council, he was sent out again in 1864 as viceroy and governor-general on the death of Lord Elgin. If no great crisis enabled Lawrence to increase his reputation, his five years' administration of the whole Indian empire was worthy of the ruler of the Punjab. His foreign policy has become a subject of imperial interest, his name being associated with the "close border" as opposed to the "forward" policy; while his internal administration was remarkable for financial prudence, a jealous regard for the good of the masses of the people and of the British soldiers, and a generous interest in education, especially in its Christian aspects.

When in 1854 Dost Mahommed, weakened by the antagonism of his brothers in Kandahar, and by the interference of Persia, sent his son to Peshawar to make a treaty, Sir John Lawrence was opposed to any entangling relation with the Afghans after the experience of 1838–1842, but he obeyed Lord Dalhousie so far as to sign a treaty of perpetual peace and friendship. His ruling idea, the fruit of long and sad experience, was that *de facto* powers only should be recognized beyond the frontier. When in 1863 Dost Mahommed's death let loose the factions of Afghanistan he acted on this policy to such an extent that he recognized both the sons, Afzul Khan and Shere Ali, at different times, and the latter fully only when he had made himself master of all his father's kingdom. The steady advance of Russia from the north, notwithstanding the Gortchakov circular of 1864, led to severe criticism of this cautious "buffer" policy which he justified under the term of "masterly inactivity." But he was ready to receive Shere Ali in conference, and to aid him in consolidating his power after it had been established and maintained for a time, when his term of office came to an end and it fell to Lord Mayo, his successor, to hold the Umballa conference in 1869. When, nine years after, the second Afghan War was precipitated, the retired viceroy gave the last days of his life to an unsparing exposure, in the House of Lords and in the press, of a policy which he had striven to prevent in its inception, and which he did not cease to denounce in its course and consequences.

On his final return to England early in 1869, after forty years' service in and for India, "the great proconsul of our English Christian empire" was created Baron Lawrence of the Punjab, and of Grately, Hants. He assumed the same arms and crest as those of his brother Henry, with a Pathan and a Sikh trooper as supporters, and took as his motto "Be ready," his brother's being "Never give in." For ten years he gave himself to the work of the London school board, of which he was the first chairman, and of the Church missionary society. Towards the end his eyesight failed, and on the 27th of June 1879 he died at the age of sixty-eight. He was buried in the nave of Westminster Abbey, beside Clyde, Outram and Livingstone. He had married the daughter of the Rev. Richard Hamilton, Harriette-Katherine, who survived him, and he was succeeded as 2nd baron by his [illegible] son, John Hamilton Lawrence (b. 1846).

[illegible] Bosworth Smith, *Life of Lord Lawrence* (1885); Sir Charles [illegible], *Lord Lawrence* ("Rulers of India" series, 1892); L. J. [illegible], *Lord Lawrence* (1880); and F. M. Holmes, *Four Heroes of* [illegible].

LAWRENCE, STRINGER (1697–1775), English soldier, was [illegible] on the 6th of March 1697. He seems to have [illegible] 1727 and served in Gibraltar and Flanders, [illegible] part in the battle of Culloden. In 1748, [illegible] major and the reputation of an experienced [illegible] India to command the East India Com- [illegible] Dupleix's schemes for the French conquest of [illegible] on the point of taking effect, and not long [illegible] Fort St David, Stringer Lawrence was actively [illegible] foiled an attempted French surprise [illegible] subsequently was captured by a French cavalry [illegible] near Pondicherry and kept prisoner till [illegible]. In 1749 he was in command at the [illegible] this occasion Clive served under him [illegible] began. On one occasion, when Clive [illegible] the creator of the Indian army [illegible] sword of honour unless one was voted to [illegible] Lawrence returned to England, but [illegible]. Here he found Clive in command [illegible] relief of Trichinopoly. As senior [illegible] command, but was careful to allow [illegible] share in the subsequent operations, [illegible] Trichinopoly and the surrender of [illegible]. In 1752 with an inferior force [illegible] (Behoor) and in 1753 again [illegible] the next seventeen months he [illegible] of this place, finally arranging [illegible] was afterwards converted into [illegible] commanded in chief up to the [illegible] regular forces of the crown. [illegible] against Wandiwash, and in [illegible] Fort St George during the siege [illegible] failing health compelled [illegible] his command in 1761 [illegible] chief. Clive supplemented [illegible] income by settling on him an [illegible] over the board [illegible] Madras army, [illegible] in London on [illegible] Company erected a [illegible]

[illegible] English painter, [illegible] His father was an [illegible] Devizes, and at [illegible] the guests of [illegible] sketch their [illegible] In 1779 the elder [illegible] in business, [illegible] had gained a sort [illegible] the support of [illegible] painter was made [illegible] in 1782 the family [illegible] himself fully [illegible] fashionables of the place at a guinea or a guinea and a half a head. In 1784 he gained the prize and silver-gilt palette of the Society of Arts for a crayon drawing after Raphael's "Transfiguration," and presently beginning to paint in oil. Throwing aside the idea of going on the stage which he had for a short time entertained, he came to London in 1787, was kindly received by Reynolds, and entered as a student at the Royal Academy. He began to exhibit almost immediately, and his reputation increased so rapidly that he became an associate of the Academy in 1791. The death of Sir Joshua in 1792 opened the way to further successes. He was at once appointed painter to the Dilettanti society, and principal painter to the king in room of Reynolds. In 1794 he was a Royal Academician, and he became the fashionable portrait painter of the age, having as his sitters all the rank, fashion and talent of England, and ultimately most of the crowned heads of Europe. In 1815 he was knighted; in 1818 he went to Aix-la-Chapelle to paint the sovereigns and diplomatists gathered there, and visited Vienna and Rome, everywhere receiving flattering marks of distinction from princes, due as much to his courtly manners as to his merits as an artist. After eighteen months he returned to England, and on the very day of his arrival was chosen president of the Academy in room of West, who had died a few days before. This office he held from 1820 to his death on the 7th of January 1830. He was never married.

Sir Thomas Lawrence had all the qualities of personal manner and artistic style necessary to make a fashionable painter, and among English portrait painters he takes a high place, though not as high as that given to him in his lifetime. His more ambitious works, in the classical style, such as his once celebrated "Satan," are practically forgotten.

The best display of Lawrence's work is in the Waterloo Gallery of Windsor, a collection of much historical interest. "Master Lambton," painted for Lord Durham at the price of 600 guineas, is regarded as one of his best portraits, and a fine head in the National Gallery, London, shows his power to advantage. The *Life and Correspondence of Sir T. Lawrence*, by D. E. Williams, appeared in 1831.

LAWRENCE, a city and the county-seat of Douglas county, Kansas, U.S.A., situated on both banks of the Kansas river, about 40 m. W. of Kansas City. Pop. (1890) 9997, (1900) 10,862, of whom 2032 were negroes, (1910 census) 12,374. It is served by the Atchison, Topeka & Santa Fe and the Union Pacific railways, both having tributary lines extending N. and S. Lawrence is surrounded by a good farming region, and is itself a thriving educational and commercial centre. Its site slopes up from the plateau that borders the river to the heights above, from which there is a view of rare beauty. Among the city's principal public buildings are the court house and the Y.M.C.A. building. The university of Kansas, situated on Mount Oread, overlooking the city, was first opened in 1866, and in 1907–1908 had a faculty of 105 and 2063 students, including 702 women (see KANSAS). Just S. of the city of Lawrence is Haskell institute (1884), one of the largest Indian schools in the country, maintained for children of the tribal Indians by the national government. In 1907 the school had 813 students, of whom 313 were girls; it has an academic department, a business school and courses in domestic science, in farming, dairying and gardening, and in masonry, carpentry, painting, blacksmithing, waggon-making, shoemaking, steam-fitting, printing and other trades. Among the city's manufactures are flour and grist mill products, pianos and cement plaster. Lawrence, named in honour of Amos A. Lawrence, was founded by agents of the Massachusetts Emigrant Aid Company in July 1854, and during the Territorial period was the political centre of the free-state cause and the principal point against which the assaults of the pro-slavery party were directed. It was first known as Wakarusa, from the creek by which it lies. A town association was organized in September 1854 before any Territorial government had been established. In the next month some pro-slavery men presented claims to a part of the land, projected a rival town to be called Excelsior on the same site, and threatened violence; but when Lawrence had organized its "regulators" the pro-slavery men retired and later agreed to a compromise by which the town site was limited to 640 acres. In December 1855 occurred the "Wakarusa war." A free-state man having been murdered for his opinions, a friend who threatened retaliation was arrested by the pro-slavery sheriff, S. J. Jones; he was rescued and taken to Lawrence; the city disclaimed complicity, but Jones persuaded Governor Wilson Shannon that there was rebellion, and Shannon authorized a posse; Missouri responded, and a pro-slavery force marched on Lawrence. The governor found that Lawrence had not resisted and would not resist the service of writs; by a written "agreement" with the free-state leaders he therefore withdrew his sanction from the Missourians and averted battle. The retreating Missourians committed some homicides. It was during this "war" that John Brown first took up arms with the free-state men. Preparations for another attack continued, particularly after Sheriff Jones, while serving writs in Lawrence, was wounded. On the 21st of May 1856, at the head of several hundred Missourians, he occupied the city without resistance, destroyed its printing offices and the free-state headquarters and pillaged private houses. In 1855 and again in 1857 the pro-slavery Territorial legislature passed an Act giving Lawrence a charter, but the people of Lawrence would not recognize that "bogus" government, and on the 13th of July 1857, after an application to the Topeka free-state legislature for a charter had been denied, adopted a city charter of their own. Governor Walker proclaimed this rebellion against the United States, appeared before the town in command of 400 United States dragoons and declared it under martial law; as perfect order prevailed, and there was no overt resistance to Territorial law, the troops were withdrawn after a few weeks by order of President Buchanan, and in February 1858 the legislature passed an Act legalizing the city charter of July 1857. On the 21st of August 1863 William C. Quantrell and some 400 mounted Missouri bushrangers surprised the sleeping town and murdered 150 citizens. The city's arms were in storage and no resistance was possible. This was the most distressing episode in all the turbulence of territorial days and border warfare in Kansas. A monument erected in 1895 commemorates the dead. After the free-state men gained control of the Territorial legislature in 1857 the legislature regularly adjourned from Lecompton, the legal capital, to Lawrence, which was practically the capital until the choice of Topeka under the Wyandotte constitution. The first railway to reach Lawrence was the Union Pacific in 1864.

See F. W. Blackmar, "The Annals of an Historic Town," in the *Annual Report* of the American Historical Association for 1893 (Washington, 1894).

LAWRENCE, a city, and one of the three county-seats (Salem and Newburyport are the others) of Essex county, Massachusetts, U.S.A., on both sides of the Merrimac river, about 30 m. from its mouth and about 26 m. N.N.W. of Boston. Pop. (1890) 44,654, (1900) 62,559, of whom 28,577 were foreign-born (7058 being Irish, 6909 French Canadians, 5131 English, 2465 German, 1683 English Canadian), and (1910 census) 85,892. It is served by the Boston & Maine railroad and by electric railways to Andover, Boston, Lowell, Haverhill and Salem, Massachusetts, and to Nashua and Salem, New Hampshire. The city's area of 6·54 sq. m. is about equally divided by the Merrimac, which is here crossed by a great stone dam 900 ft. long, and, with a fall of 28 ft., supplies about 12,000 horse-power. Water from the river is carried to factories by a canal on each side of the river and parallel to it; the first canal was built on the north side in 1845–1847 and is 1 m. long; the canal on the south side is about ¾ m. long, and was built several years later. There are large and well-kept public parks, a common (17 acres) with a soldiers' monument, a free public library, with more than 50,000 volumes in 1907, a city hall, county and municipal court-houses, a county gaol and house of correction, a county industrial school and a state armoury.

The value of the city's factory product was $48,036,593 in 1905, $41,741,980 in 1900. The manufacture of textiles is the most important industry; in 1905 the city produced worsteds valued at $30,926,964 and cotton goods worth $5,745,611, the worsted product being greater than that of any other American city. The Wood worsted mill here is said to be the largest single mill in the world. The history of Lawrence is largely the history of its textile mills. The town was formed in 1845 from parts of Andover (S. of the Merrimac) and of Methuen (N. of the river), and it was incorporated as a town in 1847, being named in honour of Abbott Lawrence, a director of the Essex company, organized in 1845 (on the same day as the formation of the town) for the control of the water power and for the construction of the great dam across the Merrimac. The Bay State woollen mills, which in 1858 became the Washington mills, and the Atlantic cotton mills were both chartered in 1846. The Pacific mills (1853) introduced from England in 1854 Lister combs for worsted manufacture; and the Washington mills soon afterward began to make worsted dress goods. Worsted cloths for men's wear seem to have been made first about 1870 at nearly the same time in the Washington mills here, in the Hockanum mills of Rockville, Connecticut, and in Wanskuck mills, Providence, Rhode Island. The Pemberton mills, built in 1853, collapsed and afterwards took fire on the 10th of January 1860; 90 were killed and hundreds severely injured. Lawrence was chartered as a city in 1853, and annexed a small part of Methuen in 1854 and parts of Andover and North Andover in 1879.

See H. A. Wadsworth, *History of Lawrence, Massachusetts* (Lawrence, 1880).

LAWRENCEBURG, a city and the county-seat of Dearborn county, Indiana, U.S.A., on the Ohio river, in the S.E. part of the state, 22 m. (by rail) W. of Cincinnati. Pop. (1890) 4284, (1900) 4326 (413 foreign-born); (1910) 3930. Lawrenceburg is served by the Baltimore & Ohio South-Western and the Cleveland, Cincinnati, Chicago & St Louis railways, by the Cincinnati, Lawrenceburg & Aurora electric street railroad, and by river packets to Louisville and Cincinnati. The city lies along the river and on higher land rising 100 ft. above river-level. It formerly had an important river trade with New Orleans, beginning about 1820 and growing in volume after the city became the terminus of the Whitewater canal, begun in 1836. The place was laid out in 1802. In 1846 an "old" and a "new" settlement were united, and Lawrenceburg was chartered as a city. Lawrenceburg was the birthplace of James B. Eads, the famous engineer, and of John Coit Spooner (b. 1843), a prominent Republican member of the United States Senate from Wisconsin in 1885–1891 and in 1897–1907; and the Presbyterian Church of Lawrenceburg was the first charge (1837–1839) of Henry Ward Beecher.

LAWSON, CECIL GORDON (1851–1882), English landscape painter, was the youngest son of William Lawson of Edinburgh, esteemed as a portrait painter. His mother also was known for her flower pieces. He was born near Shrewsbury on the 3rd of December 1851. Two of his brothers (one of them, Malcolm, a clever musician and song-writer) were trained as artists, and Cecil was from childhood devoted to art with the intensity of a serious nature. Soon after his birth the Lawsons moved to London. Lawson's first works were studies of fruit, flowers, &c., in the manner of W. Hunt; followed by riverside Chelsea subjects. His first exhibit at the Royal Academy (1870) was "Cheyne Walk," and in 1871 he sent two other Chelsea subjects. These gained full recognition from fellow-artists, if not from the public. Among his friends were now numbered Fred Walker, G. J. Pinwell and their associates. Following them, he made a certain number of drawings for wood-engraving. Lawson's Chelsea pictures had been painted in somewhat low and sombre tones; in the "Hymn to Spring" of 1872 (rejected by the Academy) he turned to a more joyous play of colour, helped by work in more romantic scenes in North Wales and Ireland. Early in 1874 he made a short tour in Holland, Belgium and Paris; and in the summer he painted his large "Hop Gardens of England." This was much praised at the Academy of 1876. But Lawson's triumph was with the great luxuriant canvas "The Minister's Garden," exhibited in 1878 at the Grosvenor Gallery, and now in the Manchester Art Gallery. This was followed by several works conceived

[illegible]

LAY, a word of several meanings. Apart from obsolete and dialectical usages, such as the East Anglian word meaning "pond," possibly cognate with Lat. *lacus*, pool or lake, or its use in weaving for the batten of a loom, where it is a variant form of "lath," the chief uses are as follows: (1) A song or, more accurately, a short poem, lyrical or narrative, which could be sung or accompanied by music; such were the romances sung by minstrels. Such an expression as the "Lay of the Nibelungen" is due to mistaken association of the word with Ger. *Lied*, song, which appears in Anglo-Saxon as *léoð*. "Lay" comes from O. Fr. *lai*, of which the derivation is doubtful. The *New English Dictionary* rejects Celtic origins sometimes put forward, such as Ir. *laoidh*, Welsh *llais*, and takes O. Mid. and High Ger. *leich* as the probable source. (2) "Non-clerical" or "unlearned." In this sense "lay" comes directly from Fr. *lai* (*laïque*, the learned form nearer to the Latin, is now used) from Lat. *laicus*, Gr. λαϊκός, of or belonging to the people (λαός, Attic λεώς). The word is now specially applied to persons who are not in orders, and more widely to those who do not belong to other learned professions, particularly the law and medicine. The *New English Dictionary* quotes two examples from versions of the Bible. In the Douai version of 1 Sam. xxi. 4, Ahimelech tells David that he has "no lay bread at hand but only holy bread"; here the Authorized Version has "common bread," the Vulgate *laicos panes*. In Coverdale's version of Acts iv. 13, the high priest and his kindred marvel at Peter and John as being "unlearned and lay people"; the Authorized Version has "unlearned and ignorant men." In a cathedral of the Church of England "lay clerks" and "lay vicars" sing such portions of the service as may be performed by laymen and clergy in minor orders. "Lay readers" are persons who are granted a commission by the bishop to perform certain religious duties in a particular parish. The commission remains in force until it is revoked by the bishop or his successors, or till there is a new incumbent in the parish, when it has to be renewed. In a religious order a "lay brother" is freed from duties at religious services performed by the other members, and from their studies, but is bound by vows of obedience and chastity and serves the order by manual labour. For "lay impropriator" see APPROPRIATION, and for "lay rector" see RECTOR and TITHES; see further LAYMEN, HOUSES OF. (3) "Lay" as a verb means "to make to lie down," "to place upon the ground," &c. The past tense is "laid"; it is vulgarly confused with the verb "to lie," of which the past is "lay." The common root of both "lie" and "lay" is represented by O. Teut. *leg*; cf. Dutch *leggen*, Ger. *legen*, and Eng. "ledge."[1] (4) "Lay-figure" is the name commonly given to articulated figures of human beings or animals, made of wood, papier-maché or other materials; draped and posed, such figures serve as models for artists (see MODELS, ARTISTS). The word has no connexion with "to lay," to place in position, but is an adaptation of the word "layman," commonly used with this meaning in the 18th century. This was adapted from Dutch *leeman* (the older form is *ledenman*) and meant an "articulated or jointed man" from *led*, now *lid*, a joint; cf. Ger. *Gliedermann*.

LAYA, JEAN LOUIS (1761–1833), French dramatist, was born in Paris on the 4th of December 1761 and died in August 1833. He wrote his first comedy in collaboration with Gabriel M. J. B. Legouvé in 1785, but the piece, though accepted by the Comédie Française, was never represented. In 1789 he produced a plea for religious toleration in the form of a five-act tragedy in verse, *Jean Calas*; the injustice of the disgrace cast on a family by the crime of one of its members formed the theme of *Les Dangers de l'opinion* (1790); but it is by his *Ami des lois* (1793) that Laya is remembered. This energetic protest against mob-rule, with its scarcely veiled characterizations of Robespierre as Nomophage and of Marat as Duricrâne, was an act of the highest courage, for the play was produced at the Théâtre Français (temporarily Théâtre de la Nation) only

[1] The verb "to lie," to speak falsely, to tell a falsehood, is in O. Eng. *léogan*; it appears in most Teutonic languages, e.g. Dutch *liegen*, Ger. *lügen*.

nineteen days before the execution of Louis XVI. Ten days after its first production the piece was prohibited by the commune, but the public demanded its representation; the mayor of Paris was compelled to appeal to the convention, and the piece was played while some 30,000 Parisians guarded the hall. Laya went into hiding, and several persons convicted of having a copy of the obnoxious play in their possession were guillotined. At the end of the Terror Laya returned to Paris. In 1813 he replaced Delille in the Paris chair of literary history and French poetry; he was admitted to the Academy in 1817. Laya produced in 1797 *Les Deux Stuarts*, and in 1799 *Falkland*, the title-rôle of which provided Talma with one of his finest opportunities. Laya's works, which chiefly owe their interest to the circumstances attending their production, were collected in 1836–1837.

See *Notice biographique sur J. L. Laya* (1833); Ch. Nodier, *Discours de réception*, 26th December 1833); Welschinger, *Théâtre de la révolution* (1880).

LAYAMON, early English poet, was the author of a chronicle of Britain entitled *Brut*, a paraphrase of the *Brut d'Angleterre* by Wace, a native of Jersey, who is also known as the author of the *Roman de Rou*. The excellent edition of Layamon by Sir F. Madden (Society of Antiquaries, London, 1847) should be consulted. All that is known concerning Layamon is derived from two extant MSS., which present texts that often vary considerably, and it is necessary to understand their comparative value before any conclusions can be drawn. The older text (here called the A-text) lies very near the original text, which is unfortunately lost, though it now and then omits lines which are absolutely necessary to the sense. The later text (here called the B-text) represents a later recension of the original version by another writer who frequently omits couplets, and alters the language by the substitution of better-known words for such as seemed to be obsolescent; *e.g. harme* (harm) in place of *balewe* (bale), and *dead* in place of *feie* (fated to die, or dead). Hence little reliance can be placed on the B-text, its chief merit being that it sometimes preserves couplets which seem to have been accidentally omitted in A; besides which, it affords a valuable commentary on the original version.

We learn from the brief prologue that Layamon was a priest among the people, and was the son of Leovenath (a late spelling of A. S. Leofnoth); also, that he lived at Ernley, at a noble church on Severn bank, close by Radstone. This is certainly Areley Regis, or Areley Kings, close by Redstone rock and ferry, 1 m. to the S. of Stourport in Worcestershire. The B-text turns Layamon into the later form Laweman, *i.e.* Law-man, correctly answering to Chaucer's "Man of Lawe," though here apparently used as a mere name. It also turns Leovenath into Leuca, *i.e.* Leofeca, a diminutive of Leofa, which is itself a pet-name for Leofnoth; so that there is no real contradiction. But it absurdly substitutes "with the good knight," which is practically meaningless, for "at a noble church."

We know no more about Layamon except that he was a great lover of books; and that he procured three books in particular which he prized above others, "turning over the leaves, and beholding them lovingly." These were: the English book that St Beda made; another in Latin that St Albin and St Austin made; whilst the third was made by a French clerk named Wace, who (in 1155) gave a copy to the noble Eleanor, who was queen of the high king Henry (*i.e.* Henry II.).

The first of these really means the Anglo-Saxon translation of Beda's *Ecclesiastical History*, which begins with the words: "Ic Beda, Cristes theow," *i.e.* "I, Beda, Christ's servant." The second is a strange description of the original of the translation, *i.e.* Albinus Beda's own Latin book, the second paragraph of which begins with the words: "Auctor ante omnes atque adiutor opusculi huius Albinus Abba reverentissimus vir per omnia doctissimus extitit"; which Layamon evidently misunderstood. As to the share of St Augustine in this work, see Book I., chapters 23-34, and Book II., chapters 1 and 2, which are practically all concerned with him and occupy more than a tenth of the whole work. The third book was Wace's poem, *Brut d'Angleterre*. But we find that although Layamon had ready access to all three of these works, he soon settled down to the translation of the third, without troubling much about the others. His chief obligation to Beda is for the well-known story about Pope Gregory and the English captives at Rome; see Layamon, vol. iii. 180.

It is impossible to enter here upon a discussion of the numerous points of interest which a proper examination of this vast and important work would present to any careful inquirer. Only a few bare results can be here enumerated. The A-text may be dated about 1205, and the B-text (practically by another writer) about 1275. Both texts, the former especially, are remarkably free from admixture with words of French origin; the lists that have been given hitherto are inexact, but it may be said that the number of French words in the A-text can hardly exceed 100, or in the B-text 160. Layamon's work is largely original; Wace's *Brut* contains 15,300 lines, and Layamon's 32,240 lines of a similar length; and many of Layamon's additions to Wace are notable, such as his story "regarding the fairy elves at Arthur's birth, and his transportation by them after death in a boat to Avalon, the abode of Argante, their queen"; see Sir F. Madden's pref. p. xv. Wace's *Brut* is almost wholly a translation of the Latin chronicle concerning the early history of Britain by Geoffrey of Monmouth, who said that he obtained his materials from a manuscript written in Welsh. The name Brut is the French form of Brutus, who was the fabulous grandson of Ascanius, and great-grandson of Aeneas of Troy, the hero of Virgil's *Aeneid*. After many adventures, this Brutus arrived in England, founded Troynovant or New Troy (better known as London), and was the progenitor of a long line of British kings, among whom were Locrine, Bladud, Leir, Gorboduc, Ferrex and Porrex, Lud, Cymbeline, Constantine, Vortigern, Uther and Arthur; and from this mythical Brutus the name Brut was transferred so as to denote the entire chronicle of this British history. Layamon gives the whole story, from the time of Brutus to that of Cadwalader, who may be identified with the Caedwalla of the *Anglo-Saxon Chronicle*, baptized by Pope Sergius in the year 688. Both texts of Layamon are in a south-western dialect; the A-text in particular shows the Wessex dialect of earlier times (commonly called Anglo-Saxon) in a much later form, and we can hardly doubt that the author, as he intimates, could read the old version of Beda intelligently. The remarks upon the B-text in Sir F. Madden's preface are not to the point; the peculiar spellings to which he refers (such as *same* for *shame*) are by no means due to any confusion with the Northumbrian dialect, but rather to the usual vagaries of a scribe who knew French better than English, and had some difficulty in acquiring the English pronunciation and in representing it accurately. At the same time, he was not strong in English grammar, and was apt to confuse the plural form with the singular in the tenses of verbs; and this is the simple explanation of most of the examples of so-called "nunnation" in this poem (such as the use of *wolden* for *wolde*), which only existed in writing and must not be seriously considered as representing real spoken sounds. The full proof of this would occupy too much space; but it should be noticed that, in many instances, "this pleonastic *n* has been struck out or erased by a second hand." In other instances it has escaped notice, and that is all that need be said. The peculiar metre of the poem has been sufficiently treated by J. Schipper. An abstract of the poem has been given by Henry Morley; and good general criticisms of it by B. ten Brink and others.

See *Layamon's Brut, or a Chronicle of Britain; a Poetical Semi-Saxon Paraphrase of the Brut of Wace;*...by Sir F. Madden (1847); B. ten Brink, *Early English Literature*, trans. by H. M. Kennedy (in Bohn's Standard Library, 1885); H. Morley, *English Writers*, vol. iii. (1888); J. Schipper, *Englische Metrik*, i. (Bonn, 1882), E. Guest, *A History of English Rhythms* (new ed. by W. W. Skeat, 1882). Article "Layamon," in the *Dict. Nat. Biog.*; *Six Old English Chronicles*, including Gildas, Nennius and Geoffrey of Monmouth (in Bohn's Antiquarian Library); *Le Roux de Lincy, Le Roman de Brut, par Wace, avec un commentaire et des notes* (Rouen, 1836–1838). E. Mätzner, *Altenglische Sprachproben* (Berlin, 1867) (W. W. S.)

he was appointed as second [illegible] Society From Willman's [illegible] clarinet at the opera, and at [illegible] concerts. His beautiful [illegible] execution were greatly admired [illegible] at the Royal Academy of [illegible] time of his death, and was [illegible] instrument at the Military School [illegible] His last public appearance was [illegible] in St James's Hall, in June [illegible] of March 1895.

LAZARUS, MORITZ [illegible] philosopher, was born on the 15th of [illegible] Posen. The son of a rabbinical [illegible] Hebrew literature and history, and [illegible] philosophy at the university of [illegible] he was professor in the university of [illegible] returned to Berlin as professor of [illegible] Akademie (1868) and later in the [illegible] On the occasion of his seventieth [illegible] with the title of *Geheimrath*. The fundamental [illegible] philosophy was that truth must be sought [illegible] or a priori abstractions but in psychological [illegible], and further that this investigation cannot [illegible] successfully to the individual consciousness, but must be devoted primarily to society as a whole. The psychologist must study mankind from the historical or comparative standpoint, analysing the elements which constitute the fabric of society, with its customs, its conventions and the main tendencies of its evolution. This *Völkerpsychologie* (folk- or comparative psychology) is one of the chief developments of the Herbartian theory of philosophy; it is a protest not only against the so-called scientific standpoint of natural philosophers, but also against the individualism of the positivists. In support of his theory he founded, in combination with H. Steinthal, the *Zeitschrift für Völkerpsychologie und Sprachwissenschaft* (1859). His own contributions to this periodical were numerous and important. His chief work was *Das Leben der Seele* (Berlin, 1855–1857; 3rd edition, 1883). Other philosophical works were:—*Ueber den Ursprung der Sitten* (1860 and 1867), *Ueber die Ideen in der Geschichte* (1865 and 1872); *Zur Lehre von den Sinnestäuschungen* (1867); *Ideale Fragen* (1875 and 1885), *Erziehung und Geschichte* (1881); *Unser Standpunkt* (1881); *Ueber die Reize des Spiels* (1883). Apart from the great interest of his philosophical work, Lazarus was pre-eminent among the Jews of the so-called Semitic domination in Germany. Like Heine, Auerbach and Steinthal, he rose superior to the narrower ideals of the German Jews, and took a leading place in German literature and thought. He protested against the violent anti-Semitism of the time, and, in spite of the moderate tone of his publications, drew upon himself unqualified censure. He wrote in this connexion a number of articles collected in 1887 under the title *Treu und Frei. Reden und Vorträge über Juden und Judenthum*. In 1869 and 1871 he was president of the first and second Jewish Synods at Leipzig and Augsburg.

See R. Flint, *The Philosophy of History in Europe*; M. Brasch, *Gesammelte Essays und Characterköpfe zur neuen Philos. und Literatur*; E. Berliner, *Lazarus und die öffentliche Meinung*; M. Brasch, "Der Begründer de Völkerpsychologie," in *Nord et Sud* (September 1894).

LAZARUS, ST, ORDER OF, a religious and military order founded in Jerusalem about the middle of the 12th century. Its primary object was the tending of the sick, especially lepers, of whom Lazarus (see LAZAR) was regarded as the patron. From the 13th century, the order made its way into various countries of Europe—Sicily, Lower Italy and Germany (Thuringia); but its chief centre of activity was France, where Louis IX. (1253) gave the members the lands of Boigny near Orleans and a building at the gates of Paris, which they turned into a lazar house for the use of the lepers of the city. A papal confirmation was obtained from Alexander IV. in 1255. The knights were one hundred in number, and possessed the right of marrying and receiving pensions charged on ecclesiastical [illegible] An eight-pointed cross was the insignia of both the French and Italian orders. The gradual disappearance of leprosy combined with other causes to secularize the order more and more. In Savoy in 1572 it was merged by Gregory XIII. (at the instance of Emanuel Philibert, duke of Savoy) in the order of St Maurice (see KNIGHTHOOD AND CHIVALRY: *Orders of Knighthood, Italy*). The chief task of this branch was the defence of the Catholic faith, especially against the Protestantism of Geneva. It continued to exist till the second half of the 19th century. In 1608 it was in France united by Henry IV. with the order of Notre-Dame du Mont-Carmel. It was treated with especial favour by Louis XIV., and the most brilliant period of its existence was from 1673 to 1691, under the marquis de Louvois. From that time it began to decay. It was abolished at the Revolution, reintroduced during the Restoration, and formally abolished by a state decree of 1830.

See L. Mainbourg, *Hist. des croisades* (1682; Eng. trans. by Nalson, 1686); P. Hélyot, *Hist. des ordres monastiques* (1714), pp. 257, 386; J. G. Uhlhorn, *Die christliche Liebesthätigkeit im Mittelalter* (Stuttgart, 1884); articles in Herzog-Hauck's *Realencyklopädie für protestantische Theologie*, xi. (1902) and Wetzer and Welte's (Catholic) *Kirchenlexikon*, vii. (1891).

LEA, HENRY CHARLES (1825–1909), American historian, was born at Philadelphia, on the 19th of September 1825. His father was a publisher, whom in 1843 he joined in business, and he retained his connexion with the firm till 1880. Weak health, however, caused him from early days to devote himself to research, mainly on church history in the later middle ages, and his literary reputation rests on the important books he produced on this subject. These are: *Superstition and Force* (Philadelphia, 1866, new ed. 1892); *Historical Sketch of Sacerdotal Celibacy* (Philadelphia, 1867); *History of the Inquisition of the Middle Ages* (New York, 1888); *Chapters from the religious history of Spain connected with the Inquisition* (Philadelphia, 1890); *History of auricular Confession and Indulgences in the Latin Church* (3 vols., London, 1896); *The Moriscos of Spain* (Philadelphia, 1901), and *History of the Inquisition of Spain* (4 vols., New York and London, 1906–1907). He also edited a *Formulary of the Papal Penitentiary in the 13th century* (Philadelphia, 1892), and in 1908 was published his *Inquisition in the Spanish Dependencies*. As an authority on the Inquisition he stood in the highest rank of modern historians, and distinctions were conferred on him by the universities of Harvard, Princeton, Pennsylvania, Giessen and Moscow. He died at Philadelphia on the 24th of October 1909.

LEAD (pronounced *leed*), a city of Lawrence county, South Dakota, U.S.A., situated in the Black Hills, at an altitude of about 5300 ft., 3 m. S.W. of Deadwood. Pop. (1890) 2581, (1900) 6210, of whom 2145 were foreign-born, (1905) 8217, (1910) 8392. In 1905 it was second in population among the cities of the state. It is served by the Chicago, Burlington & Quincy, the Chicago & North-Western, and the Chicago, Milwaukee & St Paul railways. Lead has a hospital, the Hearst Free Library and the Hearst Free Kindergarten, and is the see of a Roman Catholic bishopric. It is the centre of the mining interests of the Black Hills, and the Homestake Gold Mine here contains perhaps the largest and most easily worked mass of low-grade ore and one of the largest mining plants (1000 stamps) in the world; it has also three cyanide mills. From 1878 to 1906 the value of the gold taken from this mine amounted to about $58,000,000, and the net value of the product of 1906 alone was approximately $5,313,516. For two months in the spring of 1907 the mine was rendered idle by a fire (March 25), which was so severe that it was necessary to flood the entire mine. Mining tools and gold jewelry are manufactured. The first settlement was made here by mining prospectors in July 1876. Lead was chartered as a city in 1890 and became a city of the first class in 1904.

LEAD, a metallic chemical element; its symbol is Pb (from the Lat. *plumbum*), and atomic weight 207·10 (O=16). This metal was known to the ancients, and is mentioned in the Old Testament. The Romans used it largely, as it is still used, for the making of water pipes, and soldered these with an alloy of lead and tin. Pliny treats of these two metals as *plumbum nigrum* and *plumbum album* respectively, which seems to show that at his time they were looked upon as being only two varieties of the same species. In regard to the ancients' knowledge of lead compounds, we may state that the substance described by Dioscorides as μολυβδαῖνα was undoubtedly litharge, that Pliny uses the word minium in its present sense of red lead, and that white lead was well known to Geber in the 8th century. The alchemists designated it by the sign of Saturn ♄.

Occurrence.—Metallic lead occurs in nature but very rarely and then only in minute amount. The chief lead ores are galena and cerussite; of minor importance are anglesite, pyromorphite and mimetesite (*qq.v.*). Galena (*q.v.*), the principal lead ore, has a world-wide distribution, and is always contaminated with silver sulphide, the proportion of noble metal varying from about 0·01 or less to 0·3%, and in rare cases coming up to ½ or 1%. Fine-grained galena is usually richer in silver than the coarse-grained. Galena occurs in veins in the Cambrian clay-slate, accompanied by copper and iron pyrites, zinc-blende, quartz, calc-spar, iron-spar, &c.; also in beds or nests within sandstones and rudimentary limestones, and in a great many other geological formations. It is pretty widely diffused throughout the earth's crust. The principal English lead mines are in Derbyshire; but there are also mines at Allandale and other parts of western Northumberland, at Alston Moor and other parts of Cumberland, in the western parts of Durham, in Swaledale and Arkendale and other parts of Yorkshire, in Salop, in Cornwall, in the Mendip Hills in Somersetshire, and in the Isle of Man. The Welsh mines are chiefly in Flint, Cardigan and Montgomery shires; the Scottish in Dumfries, Lanark and Argyll; and the Irish in Wicklow, Waterford and Down. Of continental mines we may mention those in Saxony and in the Harz, Germany; those of Carinthia, Austria; and especially those of the southern provinces of Spain. It is widely distributed in the United States, and occurs in Mexico and Brazil; it is found in Tunisia and Algeria, in the Altai Mountains and India, and in New South Wales, Queensland, and in Tasmania.

The native carbonate or cerussite (*q.v.*) occasionally occurs in the pure form, but more frequently in a state of intimate intermixture with clay ("lead earth," *Bleierde*), limestone, iron oxides, &c. (as in the ores of Nevada and Colorado), and some times also with coal ("black lead ore"). All native carbonate of lead seems to be derived from what was originally galena, which is always present in it as an admixture. This ore, metallurgically, was not reckoned of much value, until immense quantities of it were discovered in Nevada and in Colorado (U.S.). The Nevada mines are mostly grouped around the city of Eureka, where the ore occurs in "pockets" disseminated at random through limestone. The crude ore contains about 30% lead and 0·2 to 0·3% silver. The Colorado lead district is in the Rocky Mountains, a few miles from the source of the Arkansas river. It forms gigantic deposits of almost constant thickness, embedded between a floor of limestone and a roof of porphyry. Stephens's discovery of the ore in 1877 was the making of the city of Leadville, which, in 1878, within a year of its foundation, had over 10,000 inhabitants. The Leadville ore contains from 24 to 42% lead and 0·1 to 2% silver. In Nevada and Colorado the ore is worked chiefly for the sake of the silver. Deposits are also worked at Broken Hill, New South Wales.

Anglesite, or lead sulphate, $PbSO_4$, is poor in silver, and is only exceptionally mined by itself; it occurs in quantity in France, Spain, Sardinia and Australia. Of other lead minerals we may mention the basic sulphate lanarkite, $PbO\cdot PbSO_4$; leadhillite, $PbSO_4\cdot 3PbCO_3$; the basic chlorides matlockite, $PbO\cdot PbCl_2$, and mendipite, $PbCl_2\cdot 2PbO$; the chloro-phosphate pyromorphite, $PbCl_2\cdot 3Pb_3(PO_4)_2$, the chloro-arsenate mimetesite, $PbCl_2\cdot 3Pb_3(AsO_4)_2$; the molybdate wulfenite, $PbMoO_4$; the chromate crocoite or crocoisite, $PbCrO_4$; the tungstate stolzite, $PbWO_4$.

Production.—At the beginning of the 19th century the bulk of the world's supply of lead was obtained from England and Spain, the former contributing about 17,000 tons and the latter 10,000 tons annually. Germany, Austria, Hungary, France, Russia and the United States began to rank as producers during the second and third decades; Belgium entered in about 1840; Italy in the 'sixties; Mexico, Canada, Japan and Greece in the 'eighties; while Australia assumed importance in 1888 with a production of about 18,000 tons, although it had contributed small and varying amounts for many preceding decades. In 1850 England headed the list of producers with about 66,000 tons; this amount had declined in 1872 to 61,000 tons. Since this date, it has, on the whole, diminished, although large outputs occurred in isolated years, for instance, a production of 40,000 tons in 1893 was followed by 60,000 tons in 1896 and 40,000 in 1897. The output in 1900 was 35,000 tons, and in 1905, 25,000 tons. Spain ranked second in 1850 with about 47,000 tons; this was increased in 1863, 1876 and in 1888 to 84,000, 127,000 and 187,000 tons respectively; but the maximum outputs mentioned were preceded and succeeded by periods of depression. In 1900 the production was 176,000 tons, and in 1905, 179,000 tons. The United States, which ranked third with a production of 20,000 tons in 1850, maintained this annual yield, until 1870, when it began to increase; the United States now ranks as the chief producer; in 1900 the output was 253,000 tons, and in 1905, 319,744 tons. Germany has likewise made headway; an output of 12,000 tons in 1850 being increased to 120,000 tons in 1900 and to 152,590 in 1905. This country now ranks third, having passed England in 1873. Mexico increased its production from 18,000 tons in 1883 to 83,000 tons in 1900 and about 88,000 tons in 1905. The Australian production of 18,000 tons in 1888 was increased to 58,000 tons in 1891, a value maintained until 1893, when a depression set in, only 21,000 tons being produced in 1897; prosperity then returned, and in 1898 the yield was 68,000 tons, and in 1905, 120,000 tons. Canada became important in 1895 with a production of 10,000 tons; this increased to 28,654 tons in 1900; and in 1905 the yield was 25,391 tons. Italy has been a fairly steady producer; the output in 1896 was 20,000 tons, and in 1905, 25,000 tons.

Metallurgy.

The extraction of the metal from pure (or nearly pure) galena is the simplest of all metallurgical operations. The ore is roasted (*i.e.* heated in the presence of atmospheric oxygen) until all the sulphur is burned away and the lead left. This simple statement, however, correctly formulates only the final result. The first effect of the roasting is the elimination of sulphur as sulphur-dioxide, with formation of oxide and sulphate of lead. In practice this oxidation process is continued until the whole of the oxygen is as nearly as possible equal in weight to the sulphur present as sulphide or as sulphate, *i.e.* in the ratio S : O_2. The heat is then raised in (relative) absence of air, when the two elements named unite into sulphur-dioxide, while a regulus of molten lead remains. Lead ores are smelted in the reverberatory furnace, the ore-hearth, and the blast-furnace. The use of the first two is restricted, as they are suited only for galena ores or mixtures of galena and carbonate, which contain not less than 58% lead and not more than 4% silica; further, ores to be treated in the ore-hearth should run low in or be free from silver, as the loss in the fumes is excessive. In the blast-furnace all lead ores are successfully smelted. Blast-furnace treatment has therefore become more general than any other.

Three types of reverberatory practice are in vogue—the English, Carinthian and Silesian. In Wales and the south of England the process is conducted in a reverberatory furnace, the sole of which is paved with slags from previous operations, and has a depression in the middle where the metal formed collects to be let off by a tap-hole. The dressed ore is introduced through a "hopper" at the top, and exposed to a moderate oxidizing flame until a certain proportion of ore is oxidized, openings at the side enabling the workmen to stir up the ore so as to constantly renew the surface exposed to the air. At this stage as a rule some rich slags of a former operation are added and a quantity of quicklime is incorporated, the chief object of which is to diminish the fluidity of the mass in the next stage, which consists in this, that, with closed air-holes, the heat is raised so as to cause the oxide and sulphate on the one hand and the sulphide on the other to reduce each other to metal. The lead produced runs into the hollow and is tapped off. The roasting process is then resumed, to be followed by another reduction, and so on.

A similar process is used in Carinthia; only the furnaces are smaller and of a somewhat different form. They are long and narrow; the sole is plane, but slopes from the fire-bridge towards the flue, so that the metal runs to the latter end to collect in pots placed *outside* the furnace. In Carinthia the oxidizing process from the first is pushed on so far that metallic lead begins to show, and the oxygen introduced predominates over the sulphur left. The mass is then stirred to liberate the lead, which is removed as *Rührblei*. Charcoal is now added, and the heat urged on to obtain *Pressblei*, an inferior metal formed partly by the action of the charcoal on the oxide of lead. The fuel used is fir-wood.

[illegible] Silesian furnace has an oblong hearth sloping from the fire-[illegible] the flue-bridge. This causes the lead to collect at the [illegible] of the hearth, whence it is tapped, &c., as in the English [illegible]. While by the English and Carinthian processes as much [illegible] is extracted in the furnace, with the Silesian method [illegible] temperature is used, thus taking out about one-half of [illegible] and leaving very rich slags (50% lead) to be smelted in [illegible] furnace, the ultimate result being a very much higher yield [illegible] either of the other processes. The loss in lead by the [illegible] reverberatory and blast-furnace treatment is only 3·2%.

[illegible] Cumberland, Northumberland, Durham and latterly the United [illegible] the reverberatory furnace is used only for roasting the ore, [illegible] ore is then reduced by fusion in a low, square blast-[illegible] (a "Scottish hearth furnace") lined with cast iron, as is [illegible] inclined sole-plate which is made to project beyond the [illegible] the outside portion (the "work-stone") being provided with [illegible] guiding any molten metal that may be placed on the [illegible] into a cast iron pot; the "tuyère" for the introduc-[illegible] the wind was, in the earlier types, about half way down the [illegible]

[illegible] preliminary to the melting process, the "browse" left in the [illegible] operation (half-fused and imperfectly reduced ore) is [illegible] with some peat and coal, and heated with the help of [illegible]. It is then taken out on the work-stone and divided into [illegible] "grey" slag which is put aside, and a richer portion, [illegible] back into the furnace. Some of the roasted ore is strewed [illegible] after a quarter of an hour's working, the whole is taken [illegible] the work-stone, where the lead produced runs off. The [illegible] of the "grey" slag, is reintroduced, ore [illegible] after a quarter of an hour's heating, the mass again [illegible] work-stone, &c.

[illegible] form of the hearth process the blocks of cast [illegible] the sides and back of the Scottish furnace are now [illegible] the United States by water-cooled shells (water-[illegible]). In this way continuous working has been [illegible] whereas formerly operations had to be stopped [illegible] hours to allow the over-heated blocks and [illegible]. A later improvement (which somewhat [illegible] working) is that by Moffett. While he also [illegible] of the operation by means of water-jackets, [illegible] produces, besides metallic lead, large volumes [illegible] which are drawn off by fans through long cooling [illegible] through suspended bags which filter off the [illegible] powder. Thus, a mixture of lead sulphate [illegible] with some sulphide (8%), zinc and carbon-[illegible] by a heap-roast and then smelted [illegible] with grey slag from the ore-hearth. The [illegible] to the usual tuyères near the bottom, a [illegible] in order to effect a complete oxidation of [illegible]. Much fume is thus produced. This is [illegible], and forms a white paint of good body, [illegible] lead sulphate, 26% lead oxide, 6% zinc [illegible] other substances. Thus in the Moffett method it is [illegible] metal or fume is produced, as in either case it is [illegible] about the same.

[illegible] in the same blast-furnace ores of different [illegible] of separate processes of precipitation, roasting [illegible] reduction prevailing in the Harz Moun-[illegible] other places, to suit local conditions, has been [illegible] smelted raw if the fall of matte (metallic [illegible] exceed 5%); otherwise they are subjected to a [illegible] roast to expel the sulphur, unless they run too [illegible] oz. to the ton, when they are smelted raw. [illegible] furnace for roasting lead-bearing sulphide [illegible] 14-16 ft. wide and 60-80 ft. long. It puts [illegible] in twenty-four hours, reducing the percent-[illegible], and requires four to six men and about 2 [illegible] instances it has been replaced by mechanical [illegible] now common in roasting sulphide copper ores [illegible]. A modern blast-furnace is oblong in hori-[illegible] about 24 ft. high from furnace floor to feed floor. [illegible] arches supported by four cast iron columns [illegible] usually of brick, red brick on the outside, fire-[illegible] sometimes it is made of wrought iron water-[illegible] always has a bosh and a contracted [illegible] enclosed by water-jackets, which are usually [illegible] mild steel. The hearth always has an Arents [illegible] an inclined channel running through the side-[illegible] the bottom of the crucible and ending at the [illegible] where it is enlarged into a basin. The crucible [illegible] the two limbs of an inverted siphon. While [illegible] the crucible and channel remain filled with [illegible] reduced to the metallic state in smelting collects [illegible] in the channel, overflows into the basin, [illegible]. The slag and matte formed float upon the [illegible] and are tapped, usually together, at intervals [illegible] the heavy matter settles on the bottom and [illegible]. When cold they are readily separated by [illegible]. The following table gives the dimensions [illegible]

Lead Blast-Furnace.

Locality.	Year.	Tuyère Section.	Height, Tuyère to Throat.
		In.	Ft.
Leadville, Colorado	1880	33×84	14
Denver "	1880	36×100	17
Durango "	1882	36×96	12·6
Denver "	1892	42×100	16
Leadville, "	1892	42×120	18
Salt Lake City, Utah	1895	45×140	20

A furnace, 42 by 120 in. at the tuyères, with a working height of 17-20 ft., will put through in twenty-four hours, with twelve men, 12% coke and 2 lb blast-pressure, 85-100 tons average charge, *i.e.* one that is a medium coarse, contains 12-15% lead, not over 5% zinc, and makes under 5% matte. In making up a charge, the ores and fluxes, whose chemical compositions have been determined, are mixed so as to form out of the components, not to be reduced to the metallic or sulphide state, typical slags (silicates of ferrous and calcium oxides, incidentally of aluminium oxide, which have been found to do successful work). Such slags contain SiO_2 = 30-33%, Fe(Mn)O = 27-50%, Ca(Mg, Ba)O = 12-28%, and retain less than 1% lead and 1 oz. silver to the ton. The leading products of the blast-furnace are argentiferous lead (base bullion), matte, slag and flue-dust (fine particles of charge and volatilized metal carried out of the furnace by the ascending gas current). The base bullion (assaying 300 ± oz. per ton) is desilverized (see below); the matte (Pb = 8-12%, Cu = 3-4%, Ag = ½-¾ of the assay-value of the base bullion, rest Fe and S) is roasted and resmelted, when part of the argentiferous lead is recovered as base bullion, while the rest remains with the copper, which becomes concentrated in a copper-matte (60% copper) to be worked up by separate processes. The slag is a waste product, and the flue-dust, collected by special devices in dust-chambers, is briquetted by machinery, with lime as a bond, and then resmelted with the ore-charge. The yield in lead is over 90%, in silver over 97% and in gold 100%. The cost of smelting a ton of ore in Colorado in a single furnace, 42 by 120 in. at the tuyères, is about $3.

The lead produced in the reverberatory furnace and the ore-hearth is of a higher grade than that produced in the blast-furnace, as the ores treated are purer and richer, and the reducing action is less powerful. The following analysis of blast-furnace *Refining.* lead of Freiberg, Saxony, is from an exceptionally impure lead: Pb = 95·088, Ag = 0·470, Bi = 0·019, Cu = 0·225, As = 1·826, Sb = 0·958, Sn = 1·354, Fe = 0·007, Zn = 0·002, S = 0·051. Of the impurities, most of the copper, nickel and copper, considerable arsenic, some antimony and small amounts of silver are removed by liquation. The lead is melted down slowly, when the impurities separate in the form of a scum (dross), which is easily removed. The purification by liquation is assisted by poling the lead when it is below redness. A stick of green wood is forced into it, and the vapours and gases set free expose new surfaces to the air, which at this temperature has only a mildly oxidizing effect. The pole, the use of which is awkward, has been replaced by dry stream, which has a similar effect. To remove tin, arsenic and antimony, the lead has to be brought up to a bright-red heat, when the air has a strongly oxidizing effect. Tin is removed mainly as a powdery mixture of stannate of lead and lead oxide, arsenic and antimony as a slagged mixture of arsenate and antimonate of lead and lead oxide. They are readily withdrawn from the surface of the lead, and are worked up into antimony (arsenic)—tin-lead and antimony-lead alloys. Liquation, if not followed by poling, is carried on as a rule in a reverberatory furnace with an oblong, slightly trough-shaped inclined hearth; if the lead is to be poled it is usually melted down in a cast-iron kettle. If the lead is to be liquated and then brought to a bright-red heat, both operations are carried on in the same reverberatory furnace. This has an oblong, dish-shaped hearth of acid or basic fire-brick built into a wrought-iron pan, which rests on transverse rails supported by longitudinal walls. The lead is melted down at a low temperature and drossed. The temperature is then raised, and the scum which forms on the surface is withdrawn until pure litharge forms, which only takes place after all the tin, arsenic and antimony have been eliminated.

Silver is extracted from lead by means of the process of cupellation. Formerly all argentiferous lead had to be cupelled, and the resulting litharge then reduced to metallic lead. In 1833 Pattinson invented his process by means of which practically all the *Desilverizing.* silver is concentrated in 13% of the original lead to be cupelled, while the rest becomes market lead. In 1842 Karsten discovered that lead could be desilverized by means of zinc. His invention, however, only took practical form in 1850-1852 through the researches of Parkes, who showed how the zinc-silver-lead alloy formed could be worked and the desilverized lead freed from the zinc it had taken up. In the Parkes process only 5% of the original lead need be cupelled. Thus, while cupellation still furnishes the only means for the final separation of lead and silver, it has become an auxiliary process to the two methods of concentration given. Of these the Pattinson process has become subordinate to the Parkes process, as it is more expensive and leaves more silver and impurities in the market lead. It holds its own, however, when base bullion contains bismuth in appreciable amounts, as in the Pattinson process bismuth follows the lead to be cupelled, while in the Parkes process it remains with the desilverized lead which goes to market, and lead of commerce should contain little bismuth. At Freiberg, Saxony, the two processes have been combined. The base bullion is imperfectly Pattinsonized, giving lead rich in silver and bismuth, which is cupelled, and lead low in silver, and especially so in bismuth, which is further desilverized by the Parkes process.

The effect of the two processes on the purity of the market lead is clearly shown by the two following analyses by Hampe, which represent lead from Lautenthal in the Harz Mountains, where the Parkes process replaced that of Pattinson, the ores and smelting process remaining practically the same:—

Parkes process.

It is absolutely necessary for the success of the *Parkes* process that the zinc and lead should contain only a small amount of impurity. The spelter used must therefore be of a good grade, and the lead is usually first refined in a reverberatory furnace (the softening furnace). The capacity of the furnace must be 10 % greater than that of the kettle into which the softened lead is tapped, as the dross and skimmings formed amount to about 10 % of the weight of the lead charged. The kettle is spherical, and is suspended over a fire-place by a broad rim resting on a wall; it is usually of cast iron. Most kettles at present hold 30 tons of lead; some, however, have double that capacity. When zinc is placed on the lead (heated to above the melting-point of zinc), liquefied and brought into intimate contact with the lead by stirring, gold, copper, silver and lead will combine with the zinc in the order given. By beginning with a small amount

Process.	Pb.	Cu.	Sb.	As.	Bi.	Ag.	Fe.	Zn.	Ni.
Pattinson . .	99·966200	0·015000	1·010000	none	0·000600	0·002200	0·004000	0·001000	1·001000
Parkes . .	99·983139	0·001413	0·005698	none	0·005487	0·000460	0·002289	0·000834	0·000680

Cupelling.

The reverberatory furnace commonly used for cupelling goes by the name of the English cupelling furnace. It is oblong, and has a fixed roof and a movable iron hearth (test). Formerly the test was lined with bone-ash; at present the hearth material is a mixture of crushed limestone and clay (3:1) or Portland cement, either alone or mixed with crushed fire-brick; in a few instances the lining has been made of burnt magnesite. In the beginning of the operation enough argentiferous lead is charged to fill the cavity of the test. After it has been melted down and brought to a red heat, the blast, admitted at the back, oxidizes the lead and drives the litharge formed towards the front, where it is run off. At the same time small bars of argentiferous lead, inserted at the back, are slowly pushed forward, so that in melting down they may replace the oxidized lead. Thus the level of the lead is kept approximately constant, and the silver becomes concentrated in the lead. In large works the silver-lead alloy is removed when it contains 60-80 % silver, and the cupellation of the rich bullion from several concentration furnaces is finished in a second furnace. At the same time the silver is brought to the required degree of fineness, usually by the use of nitre. In small works the cupellation is finished in one furnace, and the resulting low-grade silver fined in a plumbago crucible, either by overheating in the presence of air, or by the addition of silver sulphate to the melted silver, when air or sulphur trioxide and oxygen oxidize the impurities. The lead charged contains about 1·5 % lead if it comes from a Pattinson plant, from 5·10 % if from a Parkes plant. In a test 7 ft. by 4 ft. 10 in. and 4 in. deep, about 6 tons of lead are cupelled in twenty-four hours. A furnace is served by three men, working in eight-hour shifts, and requires about 2 tons of coal, which corresponds to about 110 gallons reduced oil, air being used as atomizer. The loss in lead is about 5 %. The latest cupelling furnaces have the general form of a reverberatory copper-smelting furnace. The working door through which the litharge is run off lies under the flue which carries off the products of combustion and the lead fumes, the lead is charged and the blast is admitted near the fire-bridge.

Pattinson process.

In the *Pattinson* process the argentiferous lead is melted down in the central cast iron kettle of a series 8-15, placed one next to the other, each having a capacity of 9-15 tons and a separate fire-place. The crystals of impoverished lead which fall to the bottom, upon cooling the charge, are taken out with a skimmer and discharged into the neighbouring kettle (say to the right) until about two-thirds of the original charge has been removed: then the liquid enriched lead is ladled into the kettle on the opposite side. To the kettle, two-thirds full of crystals of lead, is now added lead of the same tenor in silver, the whole is liquefied, and the cooling, crystallizing, skimming and ladling are repeated. The same is done with the kettle one-third filled with liquid lead, and so on until the first kettle contains market lead, the last cupelling lead. The intervening kettles contain leads with silver contents ranging from above market to below cupelling lead. The original Pattinson process has been in many cases replaced by the Luce-Rozan process (1870), which does away with arduous labour and attains a more satisfactory crystallization. The plant consists of two tilting oval metal pans (capacity 7 tons), one cylindrical crystallizing pot (capacity 22 tons), with two discharging spouts and one steam inlet opening, two lead moulds (capacity 3½ tons), and a steam crane. Pans and pot are heated from separate fire-places. Supposing the pot to be filled with melted lead to be treated, the fire is withdrawn beneath and steam introduced. This cools and stirs the lead when crystals begin to form. As soon as two-thirds of the lead has separated in the form of crystals, the steam is shut off and the liquid lead drained off through the two spouts into the moulds. The fire underneath the pot is again started, the crystals are liquefied, and one of the two pans, filled with melted lead, is tilted by means of the crane and its contents poured into the pot. In the meantime the lead in the moulds, which has solidified, is removed with the crane and stacked to one side, until its turn comes to be raised and charged into one of the pans. The crystallization proper lasts one hour, the working of a charge four hours, six charges being run in twenty-four hours.

of zinc, all the gold and copper and some silver and lead will be alloyed with the zinc to a so-called gold—or copper—crust, and the residual lead saturated with zinc. By removing from the surface of the lead this first crust and working it up separately (liquating, retorting and cupelling), doré silver is obtained. By the second addition of zinc most of the silver will be collected in a saturated zinc-silver-lead crust, which, when worked up, gives fine silver. A third addition becomes necessary to remove the rest of the silver, when the lead will assay only 0·1 oz. silver per ton. As this complete desilverization is only possible by the use of an excess of zinc, the unsaturated zinc-silver-lead alloy is put aside to form part of the second zincking of the next following charge. In skimming the crust from the surface of the lead some unalloyed lead is also drawn off, and has to be separated by an additional operation (liquation), as, running lower in silver than the crust, it would otherwise reduce its silver content and increase the amount of lead to be cupelled. A zincking takes 5-6 hours; 1·5-2·5 % zinc is required for desilverizing. The liquated zinc-silver-lead crust contains 5-10 % silver, 30-40 % zinc and 65-50 % lead. Before it can be cupelled it has to be freed from most of the zinc, which is accomplished by distilling in a retort made of a mixture similar to that of the plumbago crucible. The retort is pear-shaped, and holds 1000-1500 lb of charge, consisting of liquated crust mixed with 1-3 % of charcoal. The condenser commonly used is an old retort. The distillation of 1000 lb charge lasts 5-6 hours, requires 500-600 lb coke or 30 gallons reduced oil, and yields about 10 % metallic zinc and 1 % blue powder—a mixture of finely-divided metallic zinc and zinc oxide. About 60 % of the zinc used in desilverizing is recovered in a form to be used again. One man serves 2-4 retorts. The desilverized lead, which retains 0·6-0·7 % zinc, has to be refined before it is suited for industrial use. The operation is carried on in a reverberatory furnace or in a kettle. In the reverberatory furnace, similar to the one used in softening, the lead is brought to a bright-red heat and air allowed to have free access. The zinc and some lead are oxidized; part of the zinc passes off with the fumes, part is dissolved by the litharge, forming a melted mixture which is skimmed off and reduced in a blast-furnace or a reverberatory smelting furnace. In the kettle covered with a hood the zinc is oxidized by means of dry steam, and incidentally some lead by the air which cannot be completely excluded. A yellowish powdery mixture of zinc and lead oxides collects on the lead; it is skimmed off and sold as paint. From the reverberatory furnace or the kettle the refined lead is siphoned off into a storage (market) kettle after it has cooled somewhat, and from this it is siphoned off into moulds placed in a semicircle on the floor. In the process the yield in metal, based upon the charge in the kettle, is lead 99 %, silver 100+ %, gold 98-100 %. The plus-silver is due to the fact that in assaying the base bullion by cupellation, the silver lost by volatilization and cupel-absorption is neglected. In the United States the cost of desilverizing a ton base bullion is about $6.

Properties of Lead.—Pure lead is a feebly lustrous bluish-white metal, endowed with a characteristically high degree of softness and plasticity, and almost entirely devoid of elasticity. Its breaking strain is very small: a wire $\frac{1}{12}$th in. thick is ruptured by a charge of about 30 lb. The specific gravity is 11·352 for ingot, and from 11·354 to 11·365 for sheet lead (water of 4° C. = 1). The expansion of unit-length from 0° C. to 100° C. is ·002948 (Fizeau). The conductivity for heat (Wiedemann and Franz) or electricity is 8·5, that of silver being taken as 100. It melts at 327·7° C. (H. L. Callendar); at a bright-red heat it perceptibly vapourizes, and boils at a temperature between 1450° and 1600°. The specific heat is ·0314 (Regnault). Lead exposed to ordinary air is rapidly tarnished, but the thin dark film formed is very slow in increasing. When kept fused in the presence of air lead readily takes up oxygen, with the formation [illegible] of a dark-coloured scum, and then of monoxide PbO, [illegible] with the temperature.

[illegible] pure has no action on lead, but in the [illegible] is quickly attacked, with formation [illegible] which is appreciably soluble in water [illegible]. When carbonic acid is present the [illegible] precipitated as basic carbonate, so that the [illegible] continuous. Since all soluble lead [illegible] cumulative poisons, danger is involved [illegible] pipes in the distribution of *pure* waters. [illegible] is emphasized because experience shows [illegible] water of even small proportions of calcium [illegible] prevents its action on lead. All im- [illegible] a similar way. Ammonium nitrate and [illegible] intensify the action of a water on lead. Even [illegible] however, such as that of Loch Katrine (which [illegible] supply), act so slowly, at least on such lead [illegible] been in use for some time, that there is no [illegible] lead service pipes even for them, if the taps [illegible] used. Lead cisterns must be unhesitatingly [illegible]

[illegible] carbonic acid in a water does not affect its [illegible] Aqueous non-oxidizing acids generally have [illegible] lead in the absence of air. Dilute sulphuric [illegible] H_2SO_4 or less) has no action on lead [illegible] not on boiling. Strong acid does act, the [illegible] concentration and the higher its tempera- [illegible] more readily corroded than a metal con- [illegible] even less of antimony or copper. Boiling [illegible] acid converts lead into sulphate, with [illegible] dioxide. Dilute nitric acid readily dissolves [illegible] formation of nitrate $Pb(NO_3)_2$.

[illegible] unites readily with almost all other [illegible] account of its being used for the extrac- [illegible] silver, its alchemistic name of *saturnus*. [illegible] may be named:—

[illegible] contaminated with small proportions of [illegible] proof against sulphuric acid than the pure [illegible] parts of lead and 17 of antimony is used as [illegible] are used, however, and other metals [illegible] tin, bismuth) to give the alloy certain [illegible]

[illegible] An alloy made by addition of about [illegible] for making shot.

[illegible] An alloy consisting of 9 parts of lead, [illegible] of bismuth is used for stereotype plates.

[illegible] triple alloys are noted for their low [illegible] alloy of 5 of lead, 8 of bismuth and 3 of tin [illegible] below the boiling point of water (Rose's metal). [illegible] bismuth, 8 of lead, 4 of tin and 3 of cadmium [illegible] below 70° C.

[illegible] in any proportion with slight expansion, the [illegible] temperature than either component. It is [illegible]

[illegible] be said to be substantially an alloy of the [illegible] quantities of copper, antimony and zinc [illegible]

Compounds of Lead.

[illegible] functions as a divalent element of distinctly [illegible] a definite series of salts derived [illegible] At the same time, however, it forms a [illegible] in which it is most decidedly tetravalent; [illegible] to carbon, silicon, germanium and tin. [illegible] with oxygen to form five oxides, viz. [illegible] and PbO_2. The *suboxide*, Pb_2O, is the [illegible] of lead, and is also obtained as a black [illegible] to 300° out of contact with air. [illegible] with the formation of the monoxide; [illegible] lead and lead monoxide, the latter [illegible] PbO, occurs in nature as the [illegible] is produced by heating lead in contact [illegible] of oxide as formed. It is manu- [illegible] as "massicot" and "litharge." [illegible] below, the latter at tempera- [illegible] the oxide. The liquid litharge when [illegible] mass, which, however, [illegible] up into a heap of resplendent [illegible] litharge." "Buff" or "levigated litharge" is prepared by grinding the larger pieces under water. Litharge is much used for the preparation of lead salts, for the manufacture of oil varnishes, of certain cements, and of lead plaster, and for other purposes. Massicot is the raw material for the manufacture of "red lead" or "minium."

Lead monoxide is dimorphous, occurring as cubical dodecahedra and as rhombic octahedra. Its specific gravity is about 9; it is sparingly soluble in water, but readily dissolves in acids and molten alkalis. A yellow and red modification have been described (*Zeit. anorg. Chem.*, 1906, 50, p. 265). The corresponding *hydrate*, $Pb(OH)_2$, is obtained as a white crystalline precipitate by adding ammonia to a solution of lead nitrate or acetate. It dissolves in an excess of alkali to form *plumbites* of the general formula $Pb(OM)_2$. It absorbs carbon dioxide from the air when moist. A hydrated oxide, $2PbO \cdot H_2O$, is obtained when a solution of the monoxide in potash is treated with carbon dioxide.

Lead dioxide, PbO_2, also known as "puce oxide," occurs in nature as the mineral plattnerite, and may be most conveniently prepared by heating mixed solutions of lead acetate and bleaching powder until the original precipitate blackens. The solution is filtered, the precipitate well washed, and, generally, is put up in the form of a paste in well-closed vessels. It is also obtained by passing chlorine into a suspension of lead oxide or carbonate, or of magnesia and lead sulphate, in water; or by treating the sesquioxide or red oxide with nitric acid. The formation of lead dioxide by the electrolysis of a lead solution, the anode being a lead plate coated with lead oxide or sulphate and the cathode a lead plate, is the fundamental principle of the storage cell (see ACCUMULATOR). Heating or exposure to sunlight reduces it to the red oxide; it fires when ground with sulphur, and oxidizes ammonia to nitric acid, with the simultaneous formation of ammonium nitrate. It oxidizes a manganese salt (free from chlorine) in the presence of nitric acid to a permanganate; this is a very delicate test for manganese. It forms crystallizable salts with potassium and calcium hydrates, and functions as a weak acid forming salts named plumbates. The Kassner process for the manufacture of oxygen depends upon the formation of calcium plumbate, Ca_2PbO_4, by heating a mixture of lime and litharge in a current of air, decomposing this substance into calcium carbonate and lead dioxide by heating in a current of carbon dioxide, and then decomposing these compounds with the evolution of carbon dioxide and oxygen by raising the temperature. *Plumbic acid*, $PbO(OH)_2$, is obtained as a bluish-black, lustrous body of electrolysing an alkaline solution of lead sodium tartrate.

Tetravalent Lead.—If a suspension of lead dichloride in hydrochloric acid be treated with chlorine gas, a solution of lead tetrachloride is obtained; by adding ammonium chloride ammonium plumbichloride, $(NH_4)_2PbCl_6$, is precipitated, which on treatment with strong sulphuric acid yields *lead tetrachloride*, $PbCl_4$, as a translucent, yellow, highly refractive liquid. It freezes at −15° to a yellowish crystalline mass; on heating it loses chlorine and forms lead dichloride. With water it forms a hydrate, and ultimately decomposes into lead dioxide and hydrochloric acid. It combines with alkaline chlorides—potassium, rubidium and caesium—to form crystalline *plumbichlorides*; it also forms a crystalline compound with quinoline. By dissolving red lead, Pb_3O_4, in glacial acetic acid and crystallizing the filtrate, colourless monoclinic prisms of lead tetracetate, $Pb(C_2H_3O_2)_4$, are obtained. This salt gives the corresponding chloride and fluoride with hydrochloric and hydrofluoric acids, and the phosphate, $Pb(HPO_4)_2$, with phosphoric acid.

These salts are like those of tin; and the resemblance to this metal is clearly enhanced by the study of the alkyl compounds. Here compounds of divalent lead have not yet been obtained; by acting with zinc ethide on lead chloride, *lead tetraethide*, $Pb(C_2H_5)_4$, is obtained, with the separation of metallic lead.

Lead sesquioxide, Pb_2O_3, is obtained as a reddish-yellow amorphous powder by carefully adding sodium hypochlorite to a cold potash solution of lead oxide, or by adding very dilute ammonia to a solution of red lead in acetic acid. It is decomposed by acids into a mixture of lead monoxide and dioxide, and may thus be regarded as lead metaplumbate, $PbPbO_3$. *Red lead* or *triplumbic tetroxide*, Pb_3O_4, is a scarlet crystalline powder of specific gravity 8·6–9·1, obtained by roasting very finely divided pure massicot or lead carbonate; the brightness of the colour depends in a great measure on the roasting. Pliny mentions it under the name of *minium*, but it was confused with cinnabar and the red arsenic sulphide; Dioscorides mentions its preparation from white lead or lead carbonate. On heating it assumes a finer colour, but then turns violet and finally black; regaining, however, its original colour on cooling. On ignition, it loses oxygen and forms litharge. Commercial red lead is frequently contaminated with this oxide, which may, however, be removed by repeated digestion with lead acetate. Its common adulterants are iron oxides, powdered barytes and brick dust. Acids decompose it into lead dioxide and monoxide, and the latter may or may not dissolve to form a salt; red lead may, therefore, be regarded as *lead orthoplumbate*, Pb_2PbO_4. It is chiefly used as a pigment and in the manufacture of flint glass.

Lead chloride, $PbCl_2$, occurs in nature as the mineral cotunnite, which crystallizes in the rhombic system, and is found in the neighbourhood of volcanic craters. It is artificially obtained by adding hydrochloric acid to a solution of lead salt, as a white precipitate, little soluble in cold water, less so in dilute hydrochloric acid, more so in the strong acid, and readily soluble in hot water, from which on cooling, the excess of dissolved salt separates out in silky rhombic needles. It melts at 485° and solidifies on cooling to a translucent, horn-like mass; an early name for it was *plumbum corneum*, horn lead. A basic chloride, $Pb(OH)Cl$, was introduced in 1849 by Pattinson as a substitute for white lead. Powdered galena is dissolved in hot hydrochloric acid, the solution allowed to cool and the deposit of impure lead chloride washed with cold water to remove iron and copper. The residue is then dissolved in hot water, filtered, and the clear solution is mixed with very thin milk of lime so adjusted that it takes out one-half of the chlorine of the $PbCl_2$. The oxychloride comes down as an amorphous white precipitate. Another oxychloride, $PbCl_2 \cdot 7PbO$, known as "Cassel yellow," was prepared by Vauquelin by fusing pure oxide, PbO, with one-tenth of its weight of sal ammoniac. "Turner's yellow" or "patent yellow" is another artificially prepared oxychloride, used as a pigment. Mendipite and matlockite are mineral oxychlorides.

Lead fluoride, PbF_2, is a white powder obtained by precipitating a lead salt with a soluble fluoride; it is sparingly soluble in water but readily dissolves in hydrochloric and nitric acids. A chlorofluoride, PbClF, is obtained by adding sodium fluoride to a solution of lead chloride. Lead bromide, $PbBr_2$, a white solid, and lead iodide, PbI_2, a yellow solid, are prepared by precipitating a lead salt with a soluble bromide or iodide; they resemble the chloride in solubility.

Lead carbonate, $PbCO_3$, occurs in nature as the mineral cerussite (*q.v.*). It is produced by the addition of a solution of lead salt to an excess of ammonium carbonate, as an almost insoluble white precipitate. Of greater practical importance is a basic carbonate, substantially $2PbCO_3 \cdot Pb(OH)_2$, largely used as a white pigment under the name of "white lead." This pigment is of great antiquity; Theophrastus called it ψιμύθιον, and prepared it by acting on lead with vinegar, and Pliny, who called it *cerussa*, obtained it by dissolving lead in vinegar and evaporating to dryness. It thus appears that white lead and sugar of lead were undifferentiated. Geber gave the preparation in a correct form, and T. O. Bergman proved its composition. This pigment is manufactured by several methods. In the old Dutch method, pieces of sheet lead are suspended in stoneware pots so as to occupy the upper two-thirds of the vessels. A little vinegar is poured into each pot; they are then covered with plates of sheet lead, buried in horse-dung or spent tanner's bark, and left to themselves for a considerable time. By the action of the acetic acid and atmospheric oxygen, the lead is converted superficially into a basic acetate, which is at once decomposed by the carbon dioxide, with formation of white lead and acetic acid, which latter then acts *de novo*. After a month or so the plates are converted to a more or less considerable depth into crusts of white lead. These are knocked off, ground up with water, freed from metal-particles by elutriation, and the paste of white lead is allowed to set and dry in small conical forms. The German method differs from the Dutch inasmuch as the lead is suspended in a large chamber heated by ordinary means, and there exposed to the simultaneous action of vapour of aqueous acetic acid and of carbon dioxide. Another process depends upon the formation of lead chloride by grinding together litharge with salt and water, and then treating the alkaline fluid with carbon dioxide until it is neutral. White lead is an earthy, amorphous powder. The inferior varieties of commercial "white lead" are produced by mixing the genuine article with more or less of finely powdered heavy spar or occasionally zinc-white (ZnO). Venetian white, Hamburg white and Dutch white are mixtures of one part of white lead with one, two and three parts of barium sulphate respectively.

Lead sulphide, PbS, occurs in nature as the mineral galena (*q.v.*), and constitutes the most valuable ore of lead. It may be artificially prepared by leading sulphur vapour over lead, by fusing litharge with sulphur, or, as a black precipitate, by passing sulphuretted hydrogen into a solution of a lead salt. It dissolves in strong nitric acid with the formation of the nitrate and sulphate, and also in hot concentrated hydrochloric acid.

Lead sulphate, $PbSO_4$, occurs in nature as the mineral anglesite (*q.v.*), and may be prepared by the addition of sulphuric acid to solutions of lead salts, as a white precipitate almost insoluble in water (1 in 21,739), less soluble still in dilute sulphuric acid (1 in 36,504) and insoluble in alcohol. Ammonium sulphide blackens it, and it is soluble in solution of ammonium acetate, which distinguishes it from barium sulphate. Strong sulphuric acid dissolves it, forming an acid salt, $Pb(HSO_4)_2$, which is hydrolysed by adding water, the normal sulphate being precipitated; hence the milkiness exhibited by samples of oil of vitriol on dilution.

Lead nitrate, $Pb(NO_3)_2$, is obtained by dissolving the metal or oxide in aqueous nitric acid; it forms white crystals, difficultly soluble in cold water, readily in hot water and almost insoluble in strong nitric acid. It was mentioned by Libavius, who named it *calx plumb dulcis*. It is decomposed by heat into oxide, nitrogen peroxide and oxygen; and is used for the manufacture of fusees and other deflagrating compounds, and also for preparing mordants in the dyeing and calico-printing industries. Basic nitrates, *e.g.* $Pb(NO_3)OH$, $Pb_3O(OH)_2(NO_3)_2$, $Pb_6O_5(OH)NO_3$, &c., have been described.

Lead Phosphates.—The normal ortho-phosphate, $Pb_3(PO_4)_2$, is a white precipitate obtained by adding sodium phosphate to lead acetate; the acid phosphate, $PbHPO_4$, is produced by precipitating a boiling solution of lead nitrate with phosphoric acid; the pyrophosphate and meta-phosphate are similar white precipitates.

Lead Borates.—By fusing litharge with boron trioxide, glasses of a composition varying with the proportions of the mixture are obtained; some of these are used in the manufacture of glass. The borate, $Pb_2B_6O_{11} \cdot 4H_2O$, is obtained as a white precipitate by adding borax to a lead salt; this on heating with strong ammonia gives $PbB_2O_4 \cdot H_2O$, which, in turn, when boiled with a solution of boric acid, gives $PbB_4O_7 \cdot 4H_2O$.

Lead silicates are obtained as glasses by fusing litharge with silica; they play a considerable part in the manufacture of the lead glasses (see GLASS).

Lead chromate, $PbCrO_4$, is prepared industrially as a yellow pigment, chrome yellow, by precipitating sugar of lead solution with potassium bichromate. The beautiful yellow precipitate is little soluble in dilute nitric acid, but soluble in caustic potash. The vermilion-like pigment which occurs in commerce as "chrome-red" is a basic chromate, Pb_2CrO_5, prepared by treating recently precipitated normal chromate with a properly adjusted proportion of caustic soda, or by boiling it with normal (yellow) potassium chromate.

Lead acetate, $Pb(C_2H_3O_2)_2 \cdot 3H_2O$ (called "sugar" of lead, on account of its sweetish taste), is manufactured by dissolving massicot in aqueous acetic acid. It forms colourless transparent crystals, soluble in one and a half parts of cold water and in eight parts of alcohol, which on exposure to ordinary air become opaque through absorption of carbonic acid, which forms a crust of basic carbonate. An aqueous solution readily dissolves lead oxide, with formation of a strongly alkaline solution containing basic acetates (*Acetum Plumbi* or *Saturni*). When carbon dioxide is passed into this solution the whole of the added oxide, and even part of the oxide of the normal salt, is precipitated as a basic carbonate chemically similar, but not quite equivalent as a pigment, to white lead.

Analysis.—When mixed with sodium carbonate and heated on charcoal in the reducing flame lead salts yield malleable globules of metal and a yellow oxide-ring. Solutions of lead salts (colourless in the absence of coloured acids) are characterized by their behaviour to hydrochloric acid, sulphuric acid and potassium chromate. But the most delicate precipitant for lead is sulphuretted hydrogen, which produces a black precipitate of lead sulphide, insoluble in cold dilute nitric acid, less so in cold hydrochloric, and easily decomposed by hot hydrochloric acid with formation of the characteristic chloride. The atomic weight, determined by G. P. Baxter and J. H. Wilson (*J. Amer. Chem. Soc.*, 1908, 30, p. 187) by analysing the chloride, is 270·190 (O = 16).

Pharmacology and Therapeutics.

The metal itself is not used in medicine. The chief pharmacopoeial salts are: (1) *Plumbi oxidum* (lead oxide), litharge. It is not used internally, but from it is made *Emplastrum Plumbi* (diachylon plaster), which is an oleate of lead and is contained in emplastrum hydrargeri, emplastrum plumbi iodidi, emplastrum resinae, emplastrum saponis. (2) *Plumbi Acetas* (sugar of lead), dose 1 to 5 grains. From this salt are made the following preparations: (*a*) *Pilula Plumbi cum Opio*, the strength of the opium in it being 1 in 8, dose 2 to 4 grains; (*b*) *Suppositoria Plumbi composita*, containing lead acetate, opium and oil of theobroma, there being one grain of opium in each suppository; (*c*) *Unguentum Plumbi Acetatis*; (*d*) *Liquor Plumbi Subacetatis Fortior*, Goulard's extract, strength 24% of the subacetate; this again has a sub-preparation, the *Liquor Plumbi Subacetatis Dilutis*, called Goulard's water or Goulard's lotion, containing 1 part in 80 of the strong extract; (*e*) *Glycerinum Plumbi Subacetatis*, from which is made the *Unguentum Glycerini Plumbi Subacetatis*. (3) *Plumbi Carbonas*, white lead, a mixture of the carbonate and the hydrate, a heavy white powder insoluble in water; it is not used internally, but from it is made *Unguentum Plumbi Carbonatis*, strength 1 in 10 parts of paraffin ointment. (4) *Plumbi Iodidium*, a heavy bright yellow powder not used internally. From it are made (*a*) *Emplastrum Plumbi Iodidi*, and (*b*) *Unguentum Plumbi Iodidi*. The strength of each is 1 in 10.

Applied externally lead salts have practically no action upon the unbroken skin, but applied to sores, ulcers or any exposed mucous membranes they coagulate the albumen in the tissues themselves and contract the small vessels. They are very astringent, haemostatic and sedative; the strong solution of the subacetate is powerfully caustic and is rarely used undiluted. Lead salts are applied as lotions in conditions where a sedative astringent effect is desired, as in weeping eczema; in many varieties of chronic ulceration; and as an injection for various inflammatory discharges from the vagina, ear and urethra, the Liquor Plumbi Subacetatis Dilutum being the one employed. The sedative effect of lead lotion in pruritus is well known. Internally lead has an astringent action on the mucous membranes, causing a sensation of dryness; the dilute solution of the subacetate forms an effective gargle in tonsillitis. The chief use of the preparations of lead, however, is as an astringent in acute diarrhoea, particularly if ulceration be present, when it is usefully given in combination with opium in the form of the Pilula Plumbi cum Opio. It is useful in haemorrhage from a gastric ulcer or in haemorrhage from the intestine. Lead salts usually produce constipation, and lead is an active ecbolic. Lead is said to enter the blood as an albuminate in which form it is deposited in the tissues. As a rule the soluble salts if taken in sufficient quantities produce acute poisoning, and the insoluble salts chronic plumbism. The symptoms of acute poisoning are pain and diarrhoea, owing to the setting up of an active gastro-enteritis, the foeces being black (due to the formation of a sulphide of lead), thirst, cramps in the legs and muscular twitchings, with torpor, collapse, convulsions and coma. The treatment is the prompt use of emetics, or the stomach should be washed out, and large doses of sodium or magnesium sulphate given in order to form an insoluble sulphate. Stimulants, warmth and opium may be required. For an account of chronic plumbism see Lead Poisoning.

Authorities.—For the history of lead see W. H. Pulsifer, *Notes for a History of Lead* (1888); B. Neumann, *Die Metalle* (1904); A. Rossing, *Geschichte der Metalle* (1901). For the chemistry see H. Roscoe and C. Schorlemmer, *Treatise on Inorganic Chemistry*, vol. ii. (1897); H. Moissan, *Traité de chimie minerale*; O. Dammer, *Handbuch der anorganischen Chemie*. For the metallurgy see J. Percy, *The Metallurgy of Lead* (London, 1870); H. F. Collins, *The Metallurgy of Lead and Silver* (London, 1899), part i. "Lead"; H. O. Hofmann, *The Metallurgy of Lead* (6th ed., New York, 1901); W. R. Ingalls, *Lead Smelting and Refining* (1906); A. G. Betts, *Lead Refining by Electrolysis* (1908); M. Eissler, *The Metallurgy of Argentiferous Silver*. *The Mineral Industry*, begun in 1892, annually records the progress made in lead smelting.

LEADER, BENJAMIN WILLIAMS (1831–), English painter, the son of E. Leader Williams, an engineer, received his art education first at the Worcester School of Design and later in the schools of the Royal Academy. He began to exhibit at the Academy in 1854, was elected A.R.A. in 1883 and R.A. in 1898, and became exceedingly popular as a painter of landscape. His subjects are attractive and skilfully composed. He was awarded a gold medal at the Paris Exhibition in 1889, and was made a knight of the Legion of Honour. One of his pictures, "The Valley of the Llugwy," is in the National Gallery of British Art.

See *The Life and Work of B. W. Leader, R.A.*, by Lewis Lusk, *Art Journal* Office (1901).

LEADHILLITE, a rare mineral consisting of basic lead sulphatocarbonate, $Pb_4SO_4(CO_3)_2(OH)_2$. Crystals have usually the form of six-sided plates (fig. 1) or sometimes of acute rhombohedra (fig. 2); they have a perfect basal cleavage (parallel to P in fig. 1) on which the lustre is strongly pearly; they are usually white and translucent. The hardness is 2·5 and the sp. gr. 6·26–6·44. The crystallographic and optical characters point to the existence of three distinct kinds of leadhillite, which are, however, identical in external appearance and may even occur intergrown together in the same crystal: (*a*) monoclinic with an optic axial angle of 20°; (*b*) rhombohedral (fig. 2) and optically [illegible] orthorhombic (fig. 1) with an optic axial angle of [illegible]. The [illegible] of these is the more [illegible], and the second has long been known under the name susannite. The fact that the published analyses of leadhillite vary somewhat from the formula given above suggests that these three kinds may also be chemically distinct.

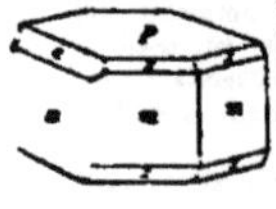

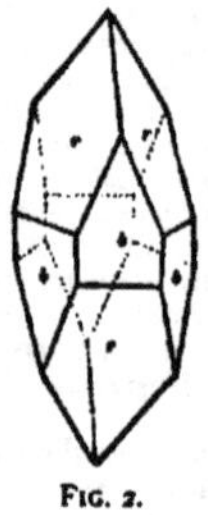

Fig. 1.

Fig. 2.

Leadhillite is a mineral of secondary origin, occurring with cerussite, anglesite, &c., in the oxidized portions of lead-bearing lodes; it has also been found in weathered lead slags left by the Romans. It has been found most abundantly in the Susanna mine at Leadhills in Scotland (hence the names leadhillite and susannite). Good crystals have also been found at Red Gill in Cumberland and at Granby in Missouri. Crystals from Sardinia have been called maxite. (L. J. S.)

LEADHILLS, a village of Lanarkshire, Scotland, 5½ m. W.S.W. of Elvanfoot station on the Caledonian Railway Company's main line from Glasgow to the south. Pop. (1901) 835. It is the highest village in Scotland, lying 1301 ft. above sea-level, near the source of Glengonner Water, an affluent of the Clyde. It is served by a light railway. Lead and silver have been mined here and at Wanlockhead, 1½ m. S.W., for many centuries—according to some authorities even in Roman days. Gold was discovered in the reign of James IV., but though it is said then to have provided employment for 300 persons, its mining has long ceased to be profitable. The village is neat and well built, and contains a masonic hall and library, the latter founded by the miners about the middle of the 18th century. Allan Ramsay, the poet, and William Symington (1763–1831), one of the earliest adaptors of the steam engine to the purposes of navigation, were born at Leadhills.

LEAD POISONING, or Plumbism, a "disease of occupations," which is itself the cause of organic disease, particularly of the nervous and urinary systems. The workpeople affected are principally those engaged in potteries where lead-glaze is used; but other industries in which health is similarly affected are file-making, house-painting and glazing, glass-making, copper-working, coach-making, plumbing and gasfitting, printing, cutlery, and generally those occupations in which lead is concerned.

The symptoms of chronic lead poisoning vary within very wide limits, from colic and constipation up to total blindness, paralysis, convulsions and death. They are thus described by Dr J. T. Arlidge (*Diseases of Occupations*):—

> The poison finds its way gradually into the whole mass of the circulating blood, and exerts its effects mainly on the nervous system, paralysing nerve-force and with it muscular power. Its victims become of a sallow-waxy hue; the functions of the stomach and bowels are deranged, appetite fails and painful colic with constipation supervenes. The loss of power is generally shown first in the fingers, hands and wrists, and the condition known as "wrist-drop" soon follows, rendering the victim useless for work. The palsy will extend to the shoulders, and after no long time to the legs also. Other organs frequently involved are the kidneys, the tissue of which becomes permanently damaged; whilst the sight is weakened or even lost.

Dr M'Aldowie, senior physician to the North Staffordshire Infirmary, has stated that "in the pottery trade lead is very slow in producing serious effects compared with certain other industries." In his experience the average period of working in lead before serious lesions manifest themselves is 18 years for females and 22½ years for males. But some individuals fall victims to the worst forms of plumbism after a few months' or even weeks' exposure to the danger. Young persons are more readily affected than those of mature age, and women more than men. In addition, there seems to be an element of personal susceptibility, the nature of which is not understood. Some persons "work in the lead" for twenty, forty or fifty years without the slightest ill effects; others have attacks whenever they are brought into contact with it. Possibly the difference is due to the general state of health; robust persons resist the poison successfully, those with impoverished blood and feeble constitution are mastered by it. Lead enters the body chiefly through the nose and mouth, being inspired in the form of dust or swallowed with food eaten with unwashed hands. It is very apt to get under the nails, and is possibly absorbed in this way through the skin. Personal care and cleanliness are therefore of the greatest importance. A factory surgeon of great experience in the English Potteries has stated that seventeen out of twenty cases of lead-poisoning in the china and earthenware industry are due to carelessness (*The Times*, 8th October 1898).

The Home Office in England has from time to time made special rules for workshops and workpeople, with the object of minimizing or preventing the occurrence of lead-poisoning; and in 1895 notification of cases was made compulsory. The health of workpeople in the Potteries was the subject of a special inquiry by a scientific committee in 1893. The committee stated that "the general truth that the potteries occupation is one fraught with injury to health and life is beyond dispute," and that "the ill effects of the trade are referable to two chief causes—namely, dust and the poison of lead." Of these the inhalation of clay and flint dust was the more important. It led to bronchitis, pulmonary tuberculosis and pneumonia, which were the most prevalent disorders among potters, and responsible for 70% of the mortality. That from lead the committee did not attempt to estimate, but they found that plumbism was less prevalent than in past times, and expressed the opinion "that a large part of the mortality from lead poisoning is avoidable; although it must always be borne in mind that no arrangements or rules, with regard to the work itself, can entirely obviate the effects of the poison to which workers are exposed, because so much depends upon the individual and the observance of personal care and cleanliness." They recommended the adoption of certain special rules in the workshops, with the objects of protecting young persons from the lead, of minimizing the evils of dust, and of promoting cleanliness, particularly in regard to meals. Some of these recommendations were adopted and applied with good results. With regard to the suggestion that "only leadless glazes should be used on earthenware," they did not "see any immediate prospect of such glazes becoming universally applicable to pottery manufacture," and therefore turned their attention to the question of "fritting" the lead.

It may be explained that lead is used in china and earthenware to give the external glaze which renders the naturally porous ware watertight. Both "white" and "red" lead are used. The lead is added to other ingredients, which have been "fritted" or fused together and then ground very fine in water, making a thick creamy liquid into which the articles are dipped. After dipping the glaze dries quickly, and on being "fired" in the kiln it becomes fused by the heat into the familiar glassy surface. In the manufacture of ware with enamelled colours, glaze is mixed with the pigment to form a flux, and such colours are used either moist or in the form of a dry powder. "Fritting" the lead means mixing it with the other ingredients of the glaze beforehand and fusing them all together under great heat into a kind of rough glass, which is then ground to make the glaze. Treated in this way the lead combines with the other ingredients and becomes less soluble, and therefore less dangerous, than when added afterwards in the raw state. The committee (1893) thought it "reasonable to suppose that the fritting of lead might ultimately be found universally practicable," but declared that though fritting "no doubt diminishes the danger of lead-poisoning," they "could not regard all fritts as equally innocuous."

In the annual report of the chief inspector of factories for 1897, it was stated that there had been "material improvement in dust conditions" in the potting industry, but "of lead-poisoning unfortunately the same could not be said, the number of grave cases reported, and particularly cases of blindness, having ominously increased of late." This appears to have been largely due to the erroneous inclusion among potting processes of "litho-transfer making," a colour industry in which girls are employed. New special rules were imposed in 1899 prohibiting the employment of persons under fifteen in the dangerous processes, ordering a monthly examination of all women and young persons working in lead by the certifying surgeon, with power to suspend those showing symptoms of poisoning, and providing for the more effectual removal of dust and the better enforcement of cleanliness. At the same time a scientific inquiry was ordered into the practicability of dispensing with lead in glazes or of substituting fritted compounds for the raw carbonate. The scientific experts reported in 1899, recommending that the use of raw lead should be absolutely prohibited, and expressing the opinion that the greater amount of earthenware could be successfully glazed without any lead. These views were in advance of the opinions held by practical potters, and met with a good deal of opposition. By certain manufacturers considerable progress had been made in diminishing the use of raw lead and towards the discovery of satisfactory leadless glazes; but it is a long step from individual experiments to the wholesale compulsory revolution of the processes of manufacture in so large and varied an industry, and in the face of foreign competitors hampered by no such regulations. The materials used by each manufacturer have been arrived at by a long process of experience, and they are such as to suit the particular goods he supplies for his particular market. It is therefore difficult to apply a uniform rule without jeopardizing the prosperity of the industry, which supports a population of 250,000 in the Potteries alone. However, the bulk of the manufacturers agreed to give up the use of raw lead, and to fritt all their glazes in future, time being allowed to effect the change of process; but they declined to be bound to any particular composition of glaze for the reasons indicated.

In 1901 the Home Office brought forward a new set of special rules. Most of these were framed to strengthen the provisions for securing cleanliness, removing dust, &c., and were accepted with a few modifications. But the question of making even more stringent regulations, even to the extent of making the use of lead-glaze illegal altogether, was still agitated; and in 1906 the Home Office again appointed an expert committee to reinvestigate the subject. They reported in 1910, and made various recommendations in detail for strengthening the existing regulations; but while encouraging the use of leadless glaze in certain sorts of common ceramic ware, they pointed out that, without the use of lead, certain other sorts could either not be made at all or only at a cost or sacrifice of quality which would entail the loss of important markets.

In 1908 Dr Collis made an inquiry into the increase of plumbism in connexion with the smelting of metals, and he considered the increase in the cases of poisoning reported to be due to the third schedule of the Workmen's Compensation Act, (1) by causing the prevalence of pre-existing plumbism to come to light, (2) by the tendency this fostered to replace men suspected of lead impregnation by new hands amongst whom the incidence is necessarily greater.

LEADVILLE, a city and the county seat of Lake county, Colorado, U.S.A., one of the highest (mean elevation *c.* 10,150 ft.) and most celebrated mining "camps" of the world. Pop. (1900) 12,455, of whom 3802 were foreign-born; (1910 census) 7508. It is served by the Denver & Rio Grande, the Colorado & Southern and the Colorado Midland railways. It lies amid towering mountains on a terrace of the western flank of the Mosquito Range at the head of the valley of the Arkansas river, where the river cuts the valley between the Mosquito and the Sawatch (Saguache) ranges. Among the peaks in the immediate environs are Mt. Massive (14,424 ft., the highest in the state) and Elbert Peak (14,421 ft.). There is a United States fish hatchery at the foot of Mt. Massive. In the spring of 1860 placer gold was discovered in California Gulch, and by July 1860 Oro City had probably 10,000 inhabitants. In five years the total yield was more than $5,000,000; then it diminished, and Oro City shrank to a few hundred inhabitants. This settlement was within the present limits of Leadville. In 1876 the output of the mines was about $20,000. During sixteen years "heavy sands" and great boulders that obstructed the placer fields had been moved thoughtlessly to one side. These boulders were from enormous lead carbonate deposits extremely rich in silver. The discovery of these deposits was made on the hills at the edge of Leadville. The first building was erected in June 1877; in December there were several hundred miners, in January the town was organized and named; at the end of 1879 there were, it is said, 35,000 inhabitants. Leadville was already a chartered city, with the usual organization and all public facilities. In 1880 it was reached by the Denver & Rio Grande railway. In early years Leadville was one of the most turbulent, picturesque and in all ways extraordinary, of the mining camps of the West. The value of the output from 1879 to 1889 totalled $147,834,186, including one-fifth of the silver production and a third of the lead consumption of the country. The decline in the price of silver, culminating with the closing of the India mints

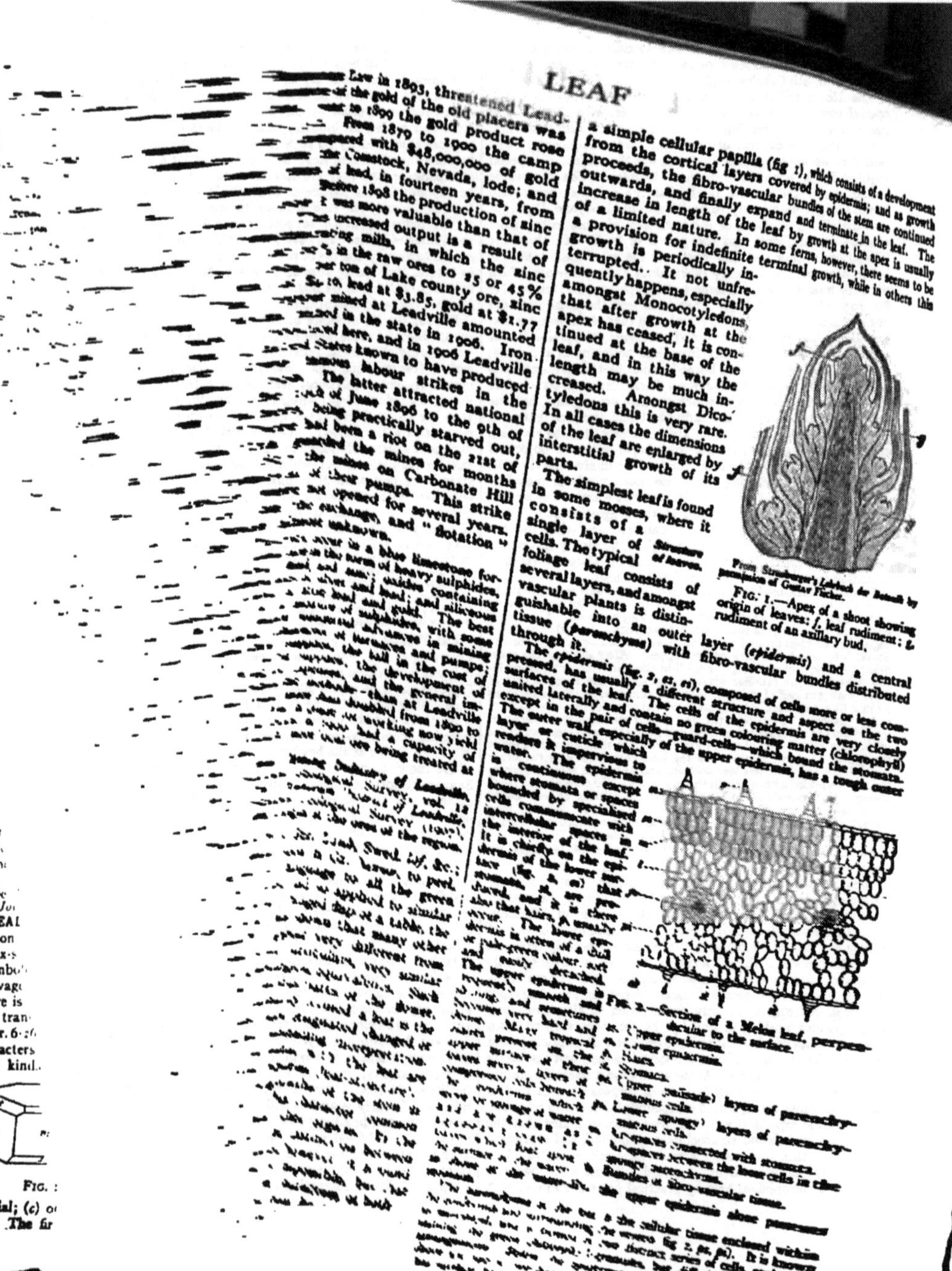

[illegible] Law in 1893, threatened Lead[illegible] [illegible] of the gold of the old placers was [illegible] to 1899 the gold product rose [illegible]. From 1879 to 1900 the camp [illegible] compared with $48,000,000 of gold [illegible] the Comstock, Nevada, lode; and [illegible] of lead, in fourteen years, from [illegible]. Before 1898 the production of zinc [illegible] it was more valuable than that of [illegible]. This increased output is a result of [illegible] concentrating mills, in which the zinc [illegible] in the raw ores to 35 or 45% [illegible] per ton of Lake county ore, zinc [illegible] $2.10, lead at $3.85, gold at $1.77 [illegible] mined at Leadville amounted [illegible] in the state in 1906. Iron [illegible] here, and in 1906 Leadville [illegible] States known to have produced [illegible] labour strikes in the [illegible]. The latter attracted national [illegible] of June 1896 to the 9th of [illegible] being practically starved out, [illegible] had been a riot on the 21st of [illegible] guarded the mines for months [illegible] the mines on Carbonate Hill [illegible] of their pumps. This strike [illegible] not opened for several years. [illegible] the exchange, and "flotation" [illegible] almost unknown.

[illegible] occur in a blue limestone for[illegible] in the form of heavy sulphides, [illegible] containing [illegible] silver and lead; and siliceous [illegible] lead and gold. The best [illegible] of sulphides, with some [illegible] advances in mining [illegible] and pumps; [illegible] the fall in the cost of [illegible] the development of [illegible] and the general im[illegible] than at Leadville [illegible] doubled from 1890 to [illegible] working now yield [illegible] had a capacity of [illegible] being treated at [illegible]

[illegible] Industry of Leadville [illegible] Survey, vol. 12 [illegible] of Leadville [illegible] of the region.

[illegible]

a simple cellular papilla (fig. 1), which consists of a development from the cortical layers covered by epidermis; and as growth proceeds, the fibro-vascular bundles of the stem are continued outwards, and finally expand and terminate in the leaf. The increase in length of the leaf by growth at the apex is usually of a limited nature. In some ferns, however, there seems to be a provision for indefinite terminal growth, while in others this growth is periodically interrupted. It not unfrequently happens, especially amongst Monocotyledons, that after growth at the apex has ceased, it is continued at the base of the leaf, and in this way the length may be much increased. Amongst Dicotyledons this is very rare. In all cases the dimensions of the leaf are enlarged by interstitial growth of its parts.

From Strasburger's *Lehrbuch der Botanik* by permission of Gustav Fischer.

FIG. 1.—Apex of a shoot showing origin of leaves; *f*, leaf rudiment; *g*, rudiment of an axillary bud.

The simplest leaf is found in some mosses, where it consists of a single layer of cells. The typical foliage leaf consists of several layers, and amongst vascular plants is distinguishable into an outer layer (*epidermis*) and a central tissue (*parenchyma*) with fibro-vascular bundles distributed through it.

Structure of leaves.

The *epidermis* (fig. 2, *es*, *ei*), composed of cells more or less compressed, has usually a different structure and aspect on the two surfaces of the leaf. The cells of the epidermis are very closely united laterally and contain no green colouring matter (chlorophyll) except in the pair of cells—guard-cells—which bound the stomata. The outer wall, especially of the upper epidermis, has a tough outer layer or cuticle which renders it impervious to water. The epidermis is continuous except where stomata or spaces bounded by specialized cells communicate with intercellular spaces in the interior of the leaf. It is chiefly on the epidermis of the lower surface (fig. 2, *ei*) that stomata, *st*, are produced, and it is there also that hairs, *p*, usually occur. The lower epidermis is often of a dull or pale-green colour, and easily detached. The upper epidermis is [illegible] smooth and [illegible] sometimes very hard and [illegible]. Many tropical [illegible] present on the upper surface of their [illegible] layers of [illegible] cells beneath [illegible] which [illegible] of water [illegible] as [illegible] the surface of the [illegible]

FIG. 2.—Section of a Melon leaf, perpendicular to the surface.
es, Upper epidermis.
ei, Lower epidermis.
p, Hairs.
st, Stomata.
pa, Upper (palisade) layers of parenchymatous cells.
pi, Lower (spongy) layers of parenchymatous cells.
m, Air-spaces connected with stomata.
i, Air-spaces between the loose cells in the spongy parenchyma.
b, Bundles of fibro-vascular tissue.

[illegible] the upper epidermis alone possesses [illegible]

The *parenchyma* of the leaf is the cellular tissue enclosed within [illegible] and surrounding the veins (fig. 2, *pa*, *pi*). It is known [illegible] two distinct series of cells, each containing the green [illegible] but differing in form and arrangement. Those [illegible] at the upper side of the leaf [illegible] cells elongated at right angles to the [illegible] closely to each other as to [illegible] only small intercellular spaces, except where stomata happen to be present (fig. 2, *m*); they form the palisade tissue. On the other side of the leaf the cells are irregular, often branched, and are arranged more or less horizontally (fig. 2, *pi*), leaving air-spaces between them, *l*, which communicate with stomata; on this account the tissue has received the name of spongy. In leaves having a very firm texture, as those of Coniferae and Cycadaceae, the cells of the parenchyma immediately beneath the epidermis are very much thickened and elongated in a direction parallel to the surface of the leaf, so as to be fibre-like. These constitute a hypodermal layer, beneath which the chlorophyll cells of the parenchyma are densely packed together, and are elongated in a direction vertical to the surface of the leaf, forming the palisade tissue. The form and arrangement of the cells, however, depend much on the nature of the plant, and its exposure to light and air. Sometimes the arrangement of the cells on both sides of the leaf is similar, as occurs in leaves which have their edges presented to the sky. In very succulent plants the cells form a compact mass, and those in the centre are often colourless. In some cases the cellular tissue is deficient at certain points, giving rise to distinct holes in the leaf, as in *Monstera Adansonii*. The fibro-vascular system in the leaf constitutes the *venation*. The fibro-vascular bundles from the stem bend out into the leaf, and are there arranged in a definite manner. In *skeleton leaves*, or leaves in which the parenchyma is removed, this arrangement is well seen. In some leaves, as in the barberry, the veins are hardened, producing spines without any parenchyma. The hardening of the extremities of the fibro-vascular tissue is the cause of the spiny margin of many leaves, such as the holly, of the sharp-pointed leaves of madder, and of mucronate leaves, or those having a blunt end with a hard projection in the centre.

The form and arrangement of the parts of a typical foliage leaf are intimately associated with the part played by the leaf in the life of the plant. The flat surface is spread to allow the maximum amount of sunlight to fall upon it, as it is by the absorption of energy from the sun's rays by means of the chlorophyll contained in the cells of the leaf that the building up of plant food is rendered possible; this process is known as photo-synthesis; the first stage is the combination of carbon dioxide, absorbed from the air taken in through the stomata into the living cells of the leaf, with water which is brought into the leaf by the wood-vessels. The wood-vessels form part of the fibro-vascular bundles or veins of the leaf and are continuous throughout the leaf-stalk and stem with the root by which water is absorbed from the soil. The palisade layers of the mesophyll contain the larger number of chlorophyll grains (or corpuscles) while the absorption of carbon dioxide is carried on chiefly through the lower epidermis which is generally much richer in stomata. The water taken up by the root from the soil contains nitrogenous and mineral salts which combine with the first product of photo-synthesis—a carbohydrate—to form more complicated nitrogen-containing food substances of a proteid nature; these are then distributed by other elements of the vascular bundles (the *phloem*) through the leaf to the stem and so throughout the plant to wherever growth or development is going on. A large proportion of the water which ascends to the leaf acts merely as a carrier for the other raw food materials and is got rid of from the leaf in the form of water vapour through the stomata—this process is known as *transpiration*. Hence the extended surface of the leaf exposing a large area to light and air is eminently adapted for the carrying out of the process of photo-synthesis and transpiration. The arrangement of the leaves on the stem and branches (see *Phyllotaxy*, below) is such as to prevent the upper leaves shading the lower, and the shape of the leaf serves towards the same end—the disposition of leaves on a branch or stem is often seen to form a "mosaic," each leaf fitting into the space between neighbouring leaves and the branch on which they are borne without overlapping.

Submerged leaves, or leaves which are developed under water, differ in structure from aerial leaves. They have usually no fibro-vascular system, but consist of a congeries of cells, which sometimes become elongated and compressed so as to resemble veins. They have a layer of compact cells on their surface, but no true epidermis, and no stomata. Their internal structure consists of cells, disposed irregularly, and sometimes leaving spaces which are filled with air for the purpose of floating the leaf. When exposed to the air these leaves easily part with their moisture, and become shrivelled and dry. In some cases there is only a network of filament-like cells, the spaces between which are not filled with parenchyma, giving a skeleton appearance to the leaf, as in *Ouvirandra fenestralis* (Lattice plant).

A leaf, whether aerial or submerged, generally consists of a flat expanded portion, called the *blade*, or *lamina*, of a narrower portion called the *petiole* or *stalk*, and sometimes of a portion at the base of the petiole, which forms a *sheath* or *vagina* (fig. 5, *s*), or is developed in the form of outgrowths, called *stipules* (fig. 24, *s*). All these portions are not always present. The sheathing or stipulary portion is frequently wanting. When a leaf has a distinct stalk it is *petiolate*; when it has none, it is *sessile*, and if in this case it embraces the stem it is said to be *amplexicaul*. The part of the leaf next the petiole or the axis is the *base*, while the opposite extremity is the *apex*. The leaf is usually flattened and expanded horizontally, *i.e.* at right angles to the longitudinal axis of the shoot, so that the upper face is directed towards the heavens, and the lower towards the earth. In some cases leaves, as in Iris, or leaf-like petioles, as in Australian acacias and eucalypti, have their plane of expansion parallel to the axis of the shoot, there is then no distinction into an upper and a lower face, but the two sides are developed alike; or the leaf may have a cylindrical or polyhedral form, as in mesembryanthemum. The upper angle formed between the leaf and the stem is called its *axil*; it is there that leaf-buds are normally developed. The leaf is sometimes articulated with the stem, and when it falls off a *scar* remains; at other times it is continuous with it, and then decays, while still attached to the axis. In their early state all leaves are continuous with the stem, and it is only in their after growth that articulations are formed. When leaves fall off annually they are called *deciduous*; when they remain for two or more years they are *persistent*, and the plant is *evergreen*. The laminar portion of a leaf is occasionally articulated with the petiole, as in the orange, and a joint at times exists between the vaginal or stipulary portion and the petiole.

Venation.

The arrangement of the fibro-vascular system in the lamina constitutes the *venation* or *nervation*. In an ordinary leaf, as that of the elm, there is observed a large central vein running from the base to the apex of the leaf, this is the *midrib* (fig. 3); it gives off veins laterally (*primary veins*). A leaf with

FIG. 3.—Leaf of Elm (*Ulmus*). Reticulated venation; primary veins going to the margin, which is serrated. Leaf unequal at the base.

FIG. 4.—Multicostate leaf of Castor-oil plant (*Ricinus communis*). It is palmately-cleft, and exhibits seven lobes at the margin. The petiole is inserted a little above the base, and hence the leaf is called peltate or shield-like.

only a single midrib is said to be *unicostate* and the venation is described as pinnate or feather-veined. In some cases, as sycamore or castor oil (fig. 4), in place of there being only a single midrib there are several large veins (*ribs*) of nearly equal size, which diverge from the point where the blade joins the petiole or stem, giving off lateral veins. The leaf in this case is *multicostate* and the venation palmate. The primary veins give off secondary veins, and these in their turn give off tertiary veins, and so on until a complete network of vessels is produced, and those veins usually project on the under surface of the leaf. To a distribution of veins such as this the name of *reticulated* or *netted* venation has been applied. In the leaves of some plants there exists a midrib with large veins running nearly parallel to it from the base to the apex of the lamina, as in grasses (fig. 5); or with veins diverging from the base of the lamina in more or less [illegible] as in fan palms (fig. 6), or with veins coming off [illegible] throughout its whole course, and running parallel to each [illegible] a straight or curved direction towards the margin of the leaf, [illegible] plantains and bananas. In these cases the veins are often united [illegible] venules, which do not, however, form an angular network. [illegible] are said to be *parallel-veined*. The leaves of Mono[illegible] venation, while reticulated [illegible] this kind of venation [illegible] occurs amongst Dicotyledons. Some plants, which in most points of their structure are monocotyledonous, yet have reticulated venation; as in *Smilax* and *Dioscorea*. In vascular acotyledonous plants there is frequently a tendency to fork exhibited by the fibro-vascular bundles in the leaf; and when this is the case we have *fork-veined* leaves. This is well seen in many ferns. The distribution of the system of vessels in the leaf is

Fig. 6.—Leaf of a Fan Palm (*Chamaerops*), showing the veins [illegible] from the base to the margin, and not forming an angular network.

[illegible] of succulent plants, as *Hoya*, [illegible] the veins are obscure. [illegible] of vessels and fibres is to [illegible] conduct liquids. [illegible] are present at some [illegible] (Dodder) (*q.v.*), however, [illegible] by leaves vary much, [illegible] same plant. It is only [illegible] Characeae, &c.— [illegible] As we pass up the [illegible] more and more variable. [illegible] segmented as leaves are [illegible] frequently spoken of [illegible] on the stem we [illegible] are always produced [illegible] their number [illegible] from the [illegible] simple and undivided; it [illegible] becomes segmented [illegible] or in both [illegible] have a leaf formed [illegible] either of these [illegible] &c., leaves [illegible] the lamina, [illegible] margins. In [illegible] (1) Simple [illegible] extends into [illegible] lamina which [illegible] and (2) [illegible] separated as [illegible] the midrib or [illegible] according to the [illegible] development of the [illegible] bundles, many [illegible]

If these divisions take place in a simple *feather-veined* leaf it becomes either *pinnatifid* (fig. 9), when the segments extend to about the middle, or *pinnatipartite*, when the divisions extend nearly to the midrib. These primary divisions may be again subdivided in a similar manner, and thus a feather-veined leaf will become *bipinnatifid* or *bipinnatipartite*; still further subdivisions give origin to *tripinnatifid* and *laciniated* leaves. The same kinds of divisions

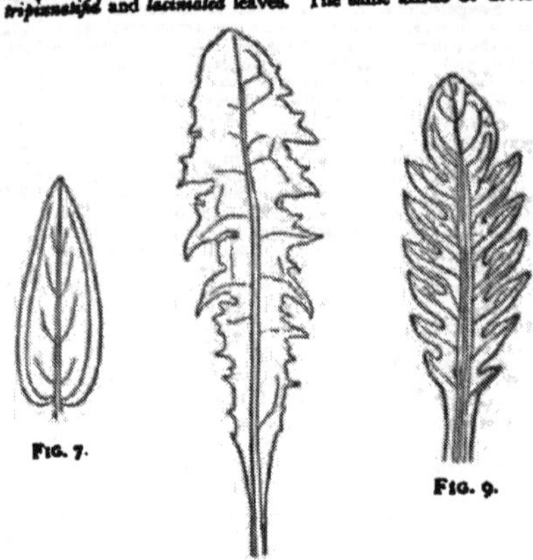

Fig. 7.—Ovate acute leaf of *Coriara myrtifolia*. Besides the midrib there are two intra-marginal ribs which converge to the apex. The leaf is therefore tricostate.

Fig. 8.—Runcinate leaf of Dandelion. It is a pinnatifid leaf, with the divisions pointing towards the petiole and a large triangular apex.

Fig. 9.—Pinnatifid leaf of *Valeriana dioica*.

taking place in a simple leaf with palmate or *radiating* venation, give origin to *lobed*, *cleft* and *partite* forms. The name *palmate* or *palmatifid* (fig. 4) is the general term applied to leaves with radiating venation, in which there are several lobes united by a broad expansion of parenchyma, like the palm of the hand, as in the sycamore, castor-oil plant, &c. The divisions of leaves with radiating venation may extend to near the base of the leaf, and the names *bipartite*, *tripartite*, *quinquepartite*, &c., are given according as the partitions are two, three, five or more. The term *dissected* is applied to leaves with radiating venation, having numerous narrow divisions, as in *Geranium dissectum*.

When in a radiating leaf there are three primary partitions, and the two lateral lobes are again cleft, as in hellebore (fig. 11), the leaf is called *pedate* or *pedatifid*, from a fancied resem-

Fig. 10.—Five-partite leaf of Aconite.

Fig. 11.—Pedate leaf of Stinking Hellebore (*Helleborus foetidus*). The venation is radiating. It is a palmately-partite leaf, in which the lateral lobes are deeply divided. When the leaf hangs down it resembles the foot of a bird, and hence the name.

blance to the claw of a bird. In all the instances already alluded to the leaves have been considered as flat expansions, in which the ribs or veins spread out on the same plane with the stalk. In some cases, however, the veins spread at right angles to the stalk, forming a *peltate* leaf as in Indian cress (fig. 12).

The form of the leaf shows a very great variety ranging from the narrow *linear* form with parallel sides, as in grasses or the needle-like leaves of pines and firs to more or less rounded or *orbicular*—descrip[illegible] of these will be found in works on descriptive botany—a few examples are illustrated here (figs. 7, 13, 14, 15). The apex also varies considerably, being rounded, or *obtuse*, sharp or *acute* (fig. 7), notched (fig. 15), &c. Similarly the shape of the base may vary, when rounded lobes are formed, as in dog-violet, the leaf is *cordate* or heart-shaped; or kidney-shaped or *reniform* (fig. 16), when the apex is rounded as in ground ivy. When the lobes are prolonged downwards and are acute, the leaf is *sagittate* (fig. 17); when they proceed at right angles, as in *Rumex Acetosella*, the leaf is *hastate* or halbert-shaped. When a simple leaf is divided at the base into two leaf-like appendages, it is called *auriculate*. When the development of parenchyma is such that it more than fills up the spaces between the veins, the margins become *wavy*, *crisp* or *undulated*, as in *Rumex crispus* and *Rheum undulatum*. By cultivation the cellular tissue is often much increased, giving rise to the *curled* leaves of greens, savoys, creases, lettuce, &c.

Compound leaves. Compound leaves are those in which the divisions extend to the midrib or petiole, and the separated portions become each articulated with it, and receive the name of *leaflets*. The midrib, or petiole, has thus the appearance of a branch with

Fig. 12.—Peltate leaves of Indian Cress (*Tropaeolum majus*).

Fig. 13.—Lanceolate leaf of a species of Senna.

separate leaves attached to it, but it is considered properly as one leaf, because in its earliest state it arises from the axis as a single piece, and its subsequent divisions in the form of leaflets are all in one plane. The leaflets are either sessile (fig. 18) or have stalks, called *petiolules* (fig. 19). Compound leaves are pinnate (fig. 19) or palmate (fig. 18) according to the arrangement of leaflets. When a pinnate leaf ends in a pair of pinnae it is *equally* or *abruptly pinnate* (paripinnate); when there is a single terminal leaflet (fig. 19), the leaf is *unequally pinnate* (imparipinnate); when the leaflets or pinnae are placed alternately on either side of the midrib, and not directly opposite to each other, the leaf is *alternately pinnate*; and when the pinnae are of different sizes, the leaf is *interruptedly pinnate*. When the division

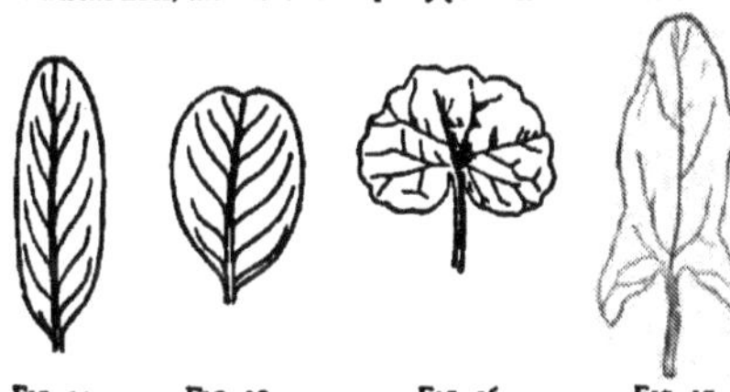

Fig. 14. Fig. 15. Fig. 16. Fig. 17.

Fig. 14.—Oblong leaf of a species of Senna.
Fig. 15.—Emarginate leaf of a species of Senna. The leaf in its contour is somewhat obovate, or inversely egg-shaped, and its base is oblique.
Fig. 16.—Reniform leaf of *Nepeta Glechoma*, margin crenate.
Fig. 17.—Sagittate leaf of Convolvulus.

is carried into the second degree, and the pinnae of a compound leaf are themselves pinnately compound, a bipinnate leaf is formed.

Petiole. The *petiole* or leaf-stalk is the part which unites the limb or blade of the leaf to the stem. It is absent in *sessile* leaves, and this is also frequently the case when a sheath is present, as in grasses (fig. 5). It consists of the fibro-vascular bundles with a varying amount of cellular tissue. When the vascular bundles reach the base of the lamina they separate and spread out in various ways, as already described under venation. The lower part of the petiole is often swollen (fig. 20, *p*), forming the *pulvinus*, formed of cellular tissue, the cells of which exhibit the phenomenon of irritability. In *Mimosa pudica* (fig. 20) a sensitiveness is located in the pulvinus which upon irritation induces a depression of the whole bipinnate leaf, a similar property exists in the pulvini at the base of the leaflets which fold upwards. The petiole varies in length, being usually shorter than the lamina, but sometimes much longer. In some palms it is 15 or 20 ft. long, and is so firm as to be used for poles or walking-sticks. In general, the petiole is more or less rounded in its form, the upper surface being flattened or grooved. Sometimes it is compressed laterally, as in the aspen, and to this peculiarity the trembling of the leaves of this tree is due. In aquatic plants the leaf-stalk is sometimes distended with air, as in *Pontederia* and *Trapa*, so as to float the leaf. At other times it is *winged*, and is either leafy, as in the orange (fig. 21, *p*), lemon and *Dionaea*, or pitcher-like, as in *Sarracenia* (fig. 22). In some Australian acacias, and in some species of *Oxalis* and *Bupleurum*, the petiole is flattened in a vertical direction, the vascular bundles separating immediately after quitting the stem and running nearly parallel from base to apex. This kind of petiole (fig. 23, *p*) has been called a *phyllode*. In these plants the laminae or blades of the leaves are pinnate or bipinnate, and are produced at the

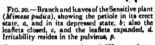

Fig. 18.—Palmately compound leaf of the Horse-chestnut (*Aesculus Hippocastanum*).

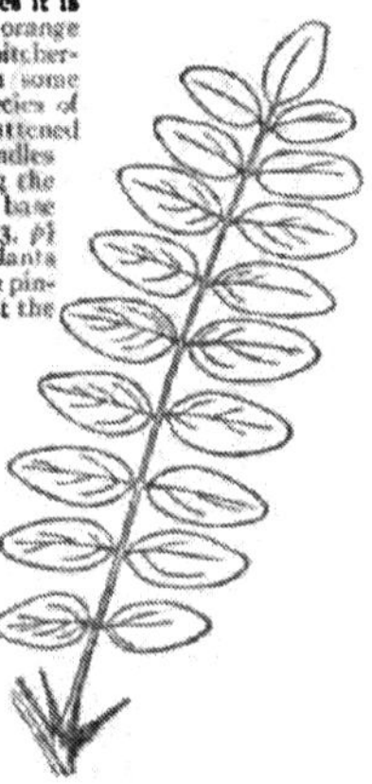

Fig. 19.—Imparipinnate (unequally pinnate) leaf of Robinia. There are nine pairs of shortly-stalked leaflets (foliola, pinnae), and an odd one at the extremity. At the base of the leaf the spiny stipules are seen.

extremities of the phyllodes in a horizontal direction; but in many instances they are not developed, and the phyllode serves the purpose of a leaf. These phyllodes, by their vertical position and their peculiar form, give a remarkable aspect to vegetation. On the same acacia there occur leaves with the petiole and lamina perfect; others having the petiole slightly expanded or winged, and the lamina imperfectly developed; and others in which there is no lamina, and the petiole becomes large and broad. Some petioles are long, slender and sensitive to contact, and function as tendrils by means of which the plant climbs; as in the nasturtiums (*Tropaeolum*), clematis and others; and in compound leaves the midrib and some of the leaflets may similarly be transformed into tendrils, as in the pea and vetch.

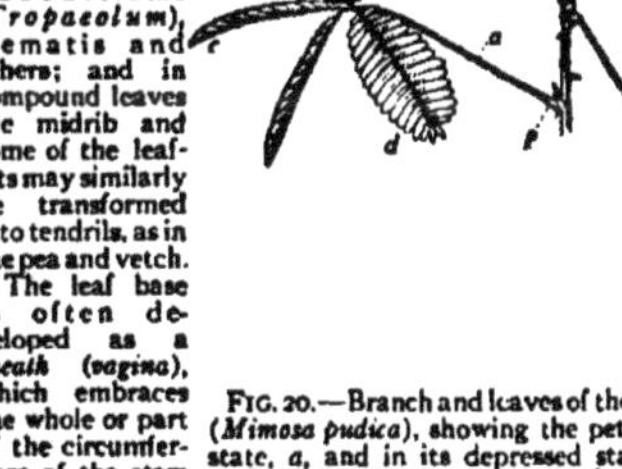

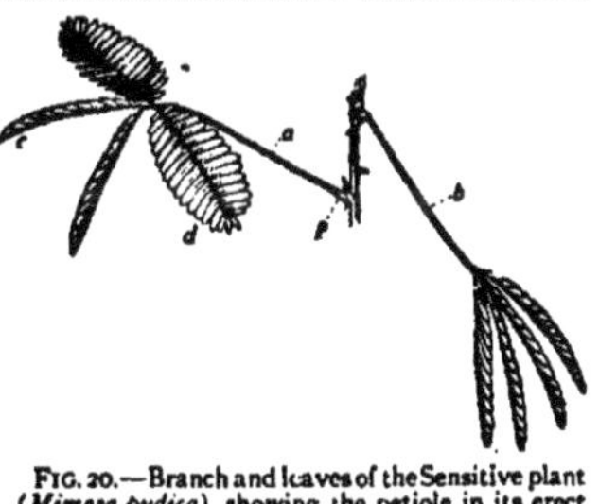

Fig. 20.—Branch and leaves of the Sensitive plant (*Mimosa pudica*), showing the petiole in its erect state, *a*, and in its depressed state, *b*; also the leaflets closed, *c*, and the leaflets expanded, *d*. Irritability resides in the pulvinus, *p*.

Leaf base. The leaf base is often developed as a *sheath* (*vagina*), which embraces the whole or part of the circumference of the stem (fig. 5). This sheath is comparatively rare in dicotyledons, but is seen in umbelliferous plants. It is much more common amongst monocotyledons. In sedges the sheath forms a complete investment of the stem, whilst in grasses it is split on one side. In the latter plants there is also a membranous outgrowth, the *ligule*, at right angles to the median plane of the leaf from the point where the sheath passes into the lamina, there being no petiole (fig. 5, *l*).

In leaves in which no sheath is produced we not infrequently find small foliar organs, *stipules*, at the base of the petiole (fig. 24, *s*). The stipules are generally two in number, and they are important as supplying characters in certain natural orders. Thus they occur in the pea and bean family, in rosaceous plants and the family Rubiaceae. They are not common in dicotyledons with opposite leaves. Plants having stipules are called *stipulate*; those having none are *exstipulate*. Stipules may be large or small, entire or divided, deciduous or persistent. They are not usually of the same form as the ordinary foliage leaves of the plant, from which they are distinguished by their lateral position at the base of the petiole. In the pansy (fig. 24) the true leaves are stalked and crenate, while the stipules *s* are large, sessile and pinnatifid. In *Lathyrus Aphaca* and some other plants the true pinnate leaves are abortive, the petiole forms a tendril, and the stipules alone are developed, performing the office of leaves. When stipulate leaves are opposite to each other, at the same height on the stem, it occasionally happens that the stipules on the two sides unite wholly or partially, so as to form an *interpetiolary* or *interfoliar* stipule, as in members of the family Rubiaceae. In the case of alternate leaves, the stipules at the base of each leaf are sometimes united to the petiole and to each other, so as to form an *adnate*, *adherent* or *petiolary* stipule, as in the [illegible], or an *axillary* stipule, as in *Houttuynia cordata*. In other instances the stipules unite together on the side of the stem opposite the leaf forming an *ocrea*, as in the dock family (fig. 25).

Fig. 21.—Leaf of Orange (*Citrus Aurantium*), showing a winged leafy petiole *p*, which is articulated to the lamina *l*.

Fig. 22.—Pitcher (*ascidium*) of a species of Side-saddle plant (*Sarracenia purpurea*). The pitcher is formed from the petiole, which is prolonged.

In the development of the leaf the stipules frequently play a most important part. They begin to be formed after the origin of the leaves, but grow much more rapidly than the leaves, and in this way they arch over the young leaves and form protective chambers wherein the parts of the leaf may develop. In the figs, magnolia and pondweeds they are very large and completely envelop the young leaf-bud. The stipules are sometimes so minute as to be scarcely distinguishable without the aid of a lens, and so fugacious as to be visible only in the very young state of the leaf. They may assume a hard and spiny character, as in *Robinia Pseud-acacia* (fig 19), or may be cirrose, as in *Smilax*, where each stipule is represented by a tendril. At the base of the leaflets of a compound leaf, small stipules (*stipels*) are occasionally produced.

[illegible] Leaf of an Acacia (*Acacia* [illegible]) showing a flattened [illegible] called a phyllode, [illegible] and a bipin-[illegible]

Modifications. Variations in the structure and forms of leaves and leaf-stalks are produced by the increased development of cellular tissue, by the abortion or degeneration of parts, by the multiplication or repetition of parts and by adhesion. When cellular tissue is developed to a great extent, leaves become succulent and occasionally assume a crisp or curled appearance. Such changes take place naturally, but they are [illegible] by the art of the gardener, and the object of [illegible] operations is to increase the bulk and suc-[illegible]. It is in this way that cabbages and savoys [illegible] delicate and nutritious. By a deficiency in [illegible]chyma and an increase in the mechanical [illegible] liable to become hardened and spinescent. [illegible] and of some species of *Astragalus*, and the stipules of the false acacia (*Robinia*) are spiny. To the same cause is due the spiny margin of the holly-leaf. When two lobes at the base of a leaf are prolonged beyond the stem and unite (fig. 26), the leaf is *perfoliate*, the stem appearing to pass through it, as in *Bupleurum perfoliatum* and *Chlora perfoliata*; when two leaves unite by their bases they become *connate* (fig. 27), as in *Lonicera Caprifolium*; and when leaves adhere to the stem, forming a sort of winged or leafy appendage, they are *decurrent*, as in thistles. The formation of peltate leaves has been traced to the union of the lobes of a cleft leaf. In the leaf of the *Victoria regia* the transformation may be traced during germination. The first leaves produced by the young plant are linear, the second are sagittate and hastate, the third are rounded-cordate and the next are orbicular. The cleft indicating the union of the lobes remains in the large leaves.

Fig. 24.—Leaf of Pansy. *s*, Stipules.

Fig. 25.—Leaf of Polygonum, with part of stem. *o*, Ocrea.

The parts of the leaf are frequently transformed into *tendrils*, with the view of enabling the plants to twine round others for support. In Leguminous plants (the pea tribe) the pinnae are frequently modified to form tendrils, as in *Lathyrus Aphaca*, in which the stipules perform the function of true leaves. In *Flagellaria indica*, *Gloriosa superba* and others, the midrib of the leaf ends in a tendril. In *Smilax* there are two stipulary tendrils.

Fig. 26.—Perfoliate leaf of a species of Hare's-ear (*Bupleurum rotundifolium*). The two lobes at the base of the leaf are united, so that the stalk appears to come through the leaf.

Fig. 27.—Connate leaves of a species of Honeysuckle (*Lonicera Caprifolium*). Two leaves are united by their bases.

The vascular bundles and cellular tissue are sometimes developed in such a way as to form a circle, with a hollow in the centre, and thus give rise to what are called *fistular* or hollow leaves, as in the onion, and to *ascidia* or *pitchers*. Pitchers are formed either by petioles or by laminae, and they are composed of one or more leaves. In *Sarracenia* (fig. 22) and *Heliamphora* the pitcher is composed of the petiole of the leaf. In the pitcher plant, *Nepenthes*, the pitcher is a modification of the lamina, the petiole often plays the part of a tendril, while the leaf base is flat and leaf-like (fig. 28).

In *Utricularia* bladder-like sacs are formed by a modification of leaflets on the submerged leaves.

In some cases the leaves are reduced to mere *scales—cataphyllary* leaves; they are produced abundantly upon underground shoots. In parasites (*Lathraea*, *Orobanche*) and in plants growing on decaying vegetable matter (*saprophytes*), in which no chlorophyll is formed, these scales are the only leaves produced. In *Pinus* the only leaves produced on the main stem and the lateral shoots are scales, the acicular leaves of the tree growing from axillary shoots. In *Cycas* whorls of scales alternate with large pinnate leaves. In many plants, as already noticed, phyllodia or stipules perform the function of leaves. The production of leaf-buds from

Fig. 28.—Pitcher of a species of pitcher-plant (*Nepenthes distillatoria*).

leaves sometimes occurs as in *Bryophyllum*, and many plants of the order Gesneraceae. The leaf of Venus's fly-trap (*Dionaea muscipula*) when cut off and placed in damp moss, with a pan of water underneath and a bell-glass for a cover, has produced buds from which young plants were obtained. Some species of saxifrage and of ferns also produce buds on their leaves and fronds. In *Nymphaea micrantha* buds appear at the upper part of the petiole.

Leaves occupy various positions on the stem and branches, and have received different names according to their situation.

Phyllotaxis.

Thus leaves arising from the crown of the root, as in the primrose, are called *radical*; those on the stem are *cauline*; on flower-stalks, *floral* leaves (see FLOWER). The first leaves developed are known as seed leaves or *cotyledons*. The arrangement of the leaves on the axis and its appendages is called *phyllotaxis*.

In their arrangement leaves follow a definite order. The points on the stem at which leaves appear are called nodes; the part of the stem between the nodes is the *internode*. When two leaves are produced at the same node, one on each side of the stem or axis, and at the same level, they are *opposite* (fig. 29); when more than two are produced they are *verticillate*, and the circle of leaves is then called a *verticil* or *whorl*. When leaves are opposite, each successive pair may be placed at right angles to the pair immediately preceding. They are then said to *decussate*, following thus a law of alternation (fig. 29). The same occurs in the verticillate arrangement, the leaves of each whorl rarely being *superposed* on those of the whorl next it, but usually alternating so that each leaf in a whorl occupies the space between two leaves of the whorl next to it. There are considerable irregularities, however, in this respect, and the number of leaves in different whorls is not always uniform, as may be seen in *Lysimachia vulgaris*. When a single leaf is produced at a node, and the nodes are separated so that each leaf is placed at a different height on the stem, the leaves are *alternate* (fig. 30). A plane passing through the point of insertion of the leaf in the node, dividing the leaf into similar halves, is the median plane of the leaf; and when the leaves are arranged alternately on an axis so that their median planes coincide they form a straight row or *orthostichy*. On every axis there are usually two or more orthostichies. In fig. 31, leaf 1 arises from a node *n*; leaf 2 is separated from it by an internode *m*, and is placed to the right or left; while leaf 3 is situated directly above leaf 1. In this case, then, there are two orthostichies, and the arrangement is said to be *distichous*. When the fourth leaf is directly above the first, the arrangement is *tristichous*. The same arrangement continues throughout the branch, so that in the latter case the 7th leaf is above the 4th, the 10th above the 7th; also the 5th above the 2nd, the 6th above the 3rd and so on. The size of the angle between the median planes of two consecutive leaves in an alternate arrangement is their *divergence*, and it is expressed in fractions of the circumference of the axis which is supposed to be a circle. In a regularly-formed straight branch covered with leaves, if a thread is passed from one to the other, turning always in the same direction, a spiral is described, and a certain number of leaves and of complete turns occur before reaching the leaf directly above that from which the enumeration commenced. If this arrangement is expressed by a fraction, the numerator of which indicates the number of turns, and the denominator the number of internodes in the spiral cycle, the fraction will be found to represent the angle of divergence of the consecutive leaves on the axis. Thus, in fig 32, *a*, *b*, the cycle consists of five leaves, the 6th leaf being placed vertically over the 1st, the 7th over the 2nd and so on; while the number of turns between the 1st and 6th leaf is two; hence this arrangement is indicated by the fraction $\frac{2}{5}$. In other words, the distance or divergence between the first and second leaf, expressed in parts of a circle, is $\frac{2}{5}$ of a circle or $360°\times\frac{2}{5}=144°$. In fig. 31, *a*, *b*, the spiral is $\frac{1}{2}$, *i.e* one turn and two leaves; the third leaf being placed vertically over the first, and the divergence between the first and second leaf being one-half the circumference of a circle, $360°\times\frac{1}{2}=180°$. Again, in a tristichous arrangement the number is $\frac{1}{3}$, or one turn and three leaves, the angular divergence being 120°.

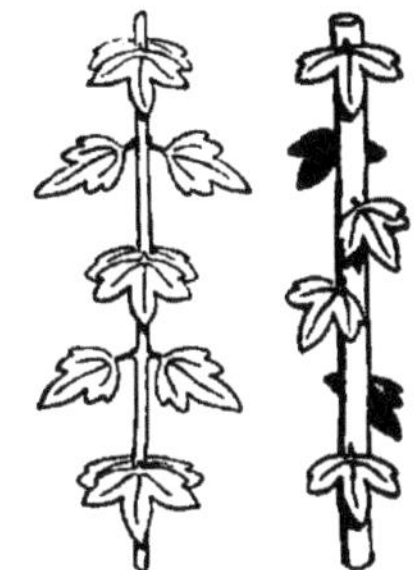

FIG. 29.—A stem with opposite leaves. The pairs are placed at right angles alternately, or in what is called a decussate manner. In the lowest pair one leaf is in front and the other at the back; in the second pair the leaves are placed laterally, and so on.

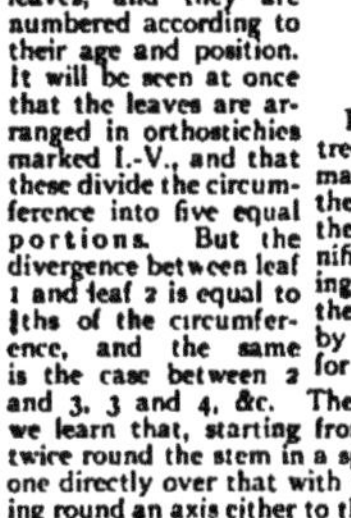

FIG. 30.—A stem with alternate leaves, arranged in a pentastichous or quincuncial manner. The sixth leaf is directly above the first, and commences the second cycle. The fraction of the circumference of the stem expressing the divergence of the leaves is two-fifths.

By this means we have a convenient mode of expressing on paper the exact position of the leaves upon an axis. And in many cases such a mode of expression is of excellent service in enabling us readily to understand the relations of the leaves. The divergences may also be represented diagrammatically on a horizontal projection of the vertical axis, as in fig. 33. Here the outermost circle represents a section of that portion of the axis bearing the lowest leaf, the innermost represents the highest. The broad dark lines represent the leaves, and they are numbered according to their age and position. It will be seen at once that the leaves are arranged in orthostichies marked I.-V., and that these divide the circumference into five equal portions. But the divergence between leaf 1 and leaf 2 is equal to $\frac{2}{5}$ths of the circumference, and the same is the case between 2 and 3, 3 and 4, &c. The divergence, then, is $\frac{2}{5}$, and from this we learn that, starting from any leaf on the axis, we must pass twice round the stem in a spiral through five leaves before reaching one directly over that with which we started. The line which, winding round an axis either to the right or to the left, passes through the points of insertion of all the leaves on the axis is termed the *genetic* or *generating spiral*; and that margin of each leaf which is towards the direction from which the spiral proceeds is the *kathodic* side, the other margin facing the point whither the spiral passes being the *anodic* side.

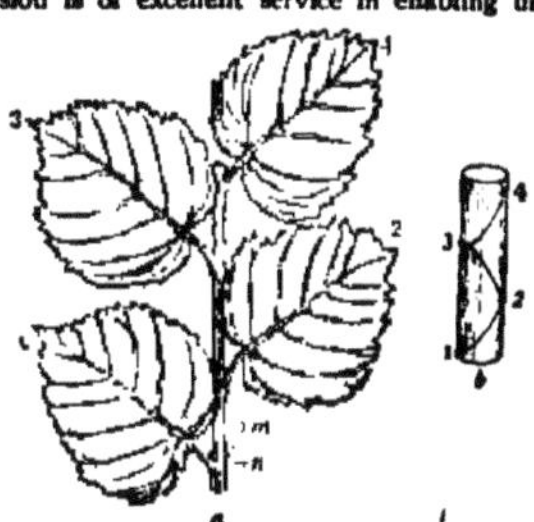

FIG. 31.—Portion of a branch of a Lime tree, with four leaves arranged in a distichous manner, or in two rows. *a*, The branch with the leaves numbered in their order, *n* being the node and *m* the internode; *b* is a magnified representation of the branch, showing the points of insertion of the leaves and their spiral arrangement, which is expressed by the fraction $\frac{1}{2}$, or one turn of the spiral for two internodes.

In cases where the internodes are very short and the leaves are closely applied to each other, as in the house-leek, it is difficult to trace the *generating spiral*. Thus, in fig. 34 there are thirteen leaves which are numbered in their order, and five turns of the spiral marked by circles in the centre ($\frac{5}{13}$ indicating the arrangement); but this could not be detected at once. So also in fir cones (fig. 35), which are composed of scales or modified leaves, the generating spiral cannot be determined easily. But in such cases a series of *secondary spirals* or *parastichies* are seen running parallel with each other both right and left, which to a certain extent conceal the genetic spiral.

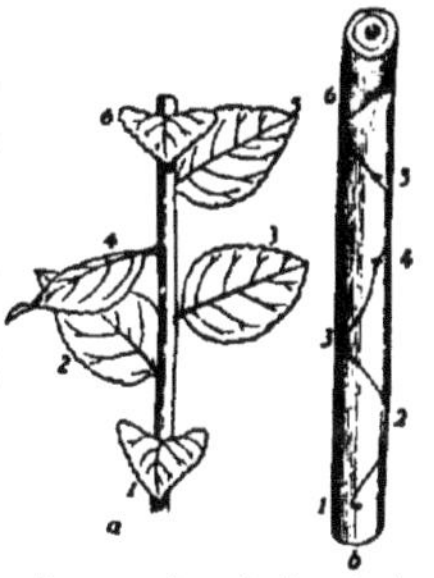

FIG. 32.—Part of a branch of a Cherry with six leaves, the sixth being placed vertically over the first, after two turns of the spiral. This is expressed by two-fifths. *a*, The branch, with the leaves numbered in order; *b*, a magnified representation of the branch, showing the points of insertion of the leaves and their spiral arrangement.

The spiral is not always constant throughout the whole length of an axis. The angle of divergence may alter either abruptly or gradually, and the phyllotaxis thus becomes very complicated. This change may be brought about by arrest of development, by increased development of parts or by a torsion of the axis. The former are exemplified in many Crassulaceae and aloes. The latter is seen well in the screw-pine (*Pandanus*). In the bud of the screw-pine the leaves are arranged in three orthostichies with the phyllotaxis $\frac{1}{3}$, but by torsion the developed leaves become arranged in three strong spiral rows running round the stem. These causes of change in phyllotaxis are also well exemplified in the alteration of an opposite or verticillate arrangement to an alternate, and vice versa; thus the effect of interruption of growth, in causing alternate leaves to become opposite and verticillate, can be distinctly shown in *Rhododendron ponticum*. The primitive or generating spiral may

in the pea and
Rubiaceae. Th
leaves. Plant
none are *exstip*
deciduous or p
ordinary folia
by their later

FIG. 21.—L
Orange (*Citrus*
tium), show
winged leafy p
which is arti
to the lamina *l*

family Rubiac
the base of each
other, so as to f
rose, or an *axil*
stances the sti
the leaf forming
In the develo

FIG. 23.—Leaf of an A
heterophylla), showing
leaf-like petiole *p*, calle
with straight venation,
nate lamina.

often increased by the
many horticultural oper
culence of leaves. It is
are rendered more deli
development of pa
tissue, leaves are
The leaves of bar

a regular law. The
...tion, as in the
...ally or laterally,
...icated in figs. 36
...ent the leaves, the
...ken individually is
...e, as in the tulip-tree,
... ircular manner
... ircinate; or folded
... has several folds
... and sycamore, and in
... mark the foldings;
... banana and apricot;
... 40), as in violet; or

FIG. 38.

FIG. 41.

... of a conduplicate leaf.
... of a plicate or plaited leaf.
... of a convolute leaf.
... of an involute leaf.
... of a revolute leaf.

... rosemary. The different divisions
... rolled up separately, as in ferns.
... either the same or a different kind of
... definite relation to each other in the
...nate or verticillate; and thus different
... Sometimes they are nearly in a
...aining flat or only slightly convex
... touch each other by their edges, thus
... At other times they are at different
... each other, so as to be *imbricated*, as in
... of sycamore; and occasionally the
... that of another, while it in its turn is
... to be *twisted*, *spiral* or *contortive*. When
... other face to face, without being folded or

FIG. 43. FIG. 44. FIG. 45.

...verse section of a bud, in which the leaves are
...itant manner.
...verse section of a bud, in which the leaves are
...ant manner.
...verse section of a bud, showing two leaves folded
...anner. Each is conduplicate, and one embraces
...ther.
...verse section of a bud, showing two leaves arranged
... manner.

... are *appressed*. When the leaves are more com-
... either touch at their extremities and are *accumbent*
... or are folded inwards by their margin and become
... a conduplicate leaf covers another similarly folded,
... covers a third, and thus the vernation is *equitant*
... over; or conduplicate leaves are placed so that the
... one covers the half of another, and thus they become
... or *obvolute* (fig. 44), as in sage. When in the case of
... one leaf is rolled up within the other, it is *super-*
... The scales of a bud sometimes exhibit one kind of
... leaves another. The same modes of arrangement
...ds.
...ning their functions for a certain time, wither
...ey frequently change colour, and hence arise
... tints of the autumnal foliage. This change

of colour is chiefly occasioned by the diminished circulation in the leaves, and the higher degree of oxidation to which their chlorophyll has been submitted.

Leaves which are articulated with the stem, as in the walnut and horse-chestnut, fall and leave a scar, while those which are continuous with it remain attached for some time after they have lost their vitality. Most of the trees of Great Britain have deciduous leaves, their duration not extending over more than a few months, while in trees of warm climates the leaves often remain for two or more years. In tropical countries, however, many trees lose their leaves in the dry season. The period of defoliation varies in different countries according to the nature of their climate. Trees which are called evergreen, as pines and evergreen-oak, are always deprived of a certain number of leaves at intervals, sufficient being left, however, to preserve their green appearance. The cause of the fall of the leaf in cold climates seems to be deficiency of light and heat in winter, which causes a cessation in the functions of the cells of the leaf. The fall is directly caused by the formation of a layer of tissue across the base of the leaf-stalk; the cells of this layer separate from one another and the leaf remains attached only by the fibres of the veins until it becomes finally detached by the wind or frost. Before its fall the leaf has become dry owing to loss of water and the removal of the protoplasm and food substances to the stem for use next season; the red and yellow colouring matters are products of decomposition of the chlorophyll. Inorganic and other waste matters are stored in the leaf-tissue and thus got rid of by the plant. The leaf scar is protected by a corky change (suberization) in the walls of the exposed cells. (A. B. R.)

LEAF-INSECT, the name given to orthopterous insects of the family Phasmidae, referred to the single genus *Phyllium* and characterized by the presence of lateral laminae upon the legs and abdomen, which, in association with an abundance of green colouring-matter, impart a broad and leaf-like appearance to the whole insect. In the female this deceptive resemblance is enhanced by the large size and foliaceous form of the front wings which, when at rest edge to edge on the abdomen, forcibly suggest in their neuration the midrib and costae of an ordinary leaf. In this sex the posterior wings are reduced and functionless so far as flight is concerned; in the male they are ample, membranous and functional, while the anterior wings are small and not leaf-like. The freshly hatched young are reddish in colour; but turn green after feeding for a short time upon leaves. Before death a specimen has been observed to pass through the various hues of a decaying leaf, and the spectrum of the green colouring matter does not differ from that of the chlorophyll of living leaves. Since leaf-insects are purely vegetable feeders and not predaceous like mantids, it is probable that their resemblance to leaves is solely for purposes of concealment from enemies. Their egg capsules are similarly protected by their likeness to various seeds. Leaf-insects range from India to the Seychelles on the one side, and to the Fiji Islands on the other. (R. I. P.)

LEAGUE. 1 (Through Fr. *ligue*, Ital. *liga*, from Lat. *ligare*, to bind), an agreement entered into by two or more parties for mutual protection or joint attack, or for the furtherance of some common object, also the body thus joined or "leagued" together. The name has been given to numerous confederations, such as the Achaean League (*q.v.*), the confederation of the ancient cities of Achaia, and especially to the various holy leagues (*ligues saintes*), of which the better known are those formed by Pope Julius II. against Venice in 1508, often known as the League of Cambrai, and against France in 1511. "The League," in French history, is that of the Catholics headed by the Guises to preserve the Catholic religion against the Huguenots and prevent the accession of Henry of Navarre to the throne (see FRANCE: *History*). "The Solemn League and Covenant" was the agreement for the establishment of Presbyterianism in both countries entered into by England and Scotland in 1643 (see COVENANTERS). Of commercial leagues the most famous is that of the Hanse towns, known as the Hanseatic League (*q.v.*). The word has been adopted by political associations, such as the Anti-Corn Law League, the Irish Land League, the Primrose League and the United Irish League, and by numerous social organizations. "League" has also been applied to a special form of competition in athletics, especially in Association football. In this system clubs "league" together in a competition, each playing every other member of the association twice, and the order of merit is decided by the points gained during the season, a win counting two and a draw one.

2. (From the late Lat. *leuga*, or *leuca*, said to be a Gallic word, the mod. Fr. *lieue* comes from the O. Fr. *liue*; the Gaelic *leac*, meaning a flat stone posted as a mark of distance on a road, has been suggested as the origin), a measure of distance, probably never in regular use in England, and now only in poetical or rhetorical language. It was the Celtic as opposed to the Teutonic unit, and was used in France, Spain, Portugal and Italy. In all the countries it varies with different localities, and the ancient distance has never been fixed. The kilometric league of France is fixed at four kilometres. The nautical league is equal to three nautical miles.

LEAKE, WILLIAM MARTIN (1777–1860), British antiquarian and topographer, was born in London on the 14th of January 1777 After completing his education at the Royal Military Academy, Woolwich, and spending four years in the West Indies as lieutenant of marine artillery, he was sent by the government to Constantinople to instruct the Turks in this branch of the service. A journey through Asia Minor in 1800 to join the British fleet at Cyprus inspired him with an interest in antiquarian topography In 1801, after travelling across the desert with the Turkish army to Egypt, he was, on the expulsion of the French, employed in surveying the valley of the Nile as far as the cataracts, but having sailed with the ship engaged to convey the Elgin marbles from Athens to England, he lost all his maps and observations when the vessel foundered off Cerigo. Shortly after his arrival in England he was sent out to survey the coast of Albania and the Morea, with the view of assisting the Turks against attacks of the French from Italy, and of this he took advantage to form a valuable collection of coins and inscriptions and to explore ancient sites. In 1807, war having broken out between Turkey and England, he was made prisoner at Salonica; but, obtaining his release the same year, he was sent on a diplomatic mission to Ali Pasha of Iannina, whose confidence he completely won, and with whom he remained for more than a year as British representative. In 1810 he was granted a yearly sum of £600 for his services in Turkey. In 1815 he retired from the army, in which he held the rank of colonel, devoting the remainder of his life to topographical and antiquarian studies, the results of which were given to the world in the following volumes: *Topography of Athens* (1821); *Journal of a Tour in Asia Minor* (1824); *Travels in the Morea* (1830), and a supplement, *Peloponnesiaca* (1846); *Travels in Northern Greece* (1835); and *Numismata Hellenica* (1854), followed by a supplement in 1859. A characteristic of the researches of Leake was their comprehensive minuteness, which was greatly aided by his mastery of technical details. His *Topography of Athens*, the first attempt at a scientific treatment of the subject, is still authoritative in regard to many important points (see ATHENS). He died at Brighton on the 6th of January 1860. The marbles collected by him in Greece were presented to the British Museum; his bronzes, vases, gems and coins were purchased by the university of Cambridge after his death, and are now in the Fitzwilliam Museum. He was elected F.R.S. and F.R.G.S., received the honorary D.C.L. at Oxford (1816), and was a member of the Berlin Academy of Sciences and correspondent of the Institute of France.

See *Memoir* by J. H. Marsden (1864); the *Architect* for the 7th of October 1876; E. Curtius in the *Preussische Jahrbucher* (Sept., 1876); J. E. Sandys, *Hist. of Classical Scholarship*, iii. (1908), p. 442.

LEAMINGTON, a municipal borough and health resort of Warwickshire, England, on the river Leam near its junction with the Avon, 98 m. N.W. from London, served by the Great Western and London & North Western railways. Pop. (1901) 26,888. The parliamentary boroughs of Leamington and Warwick were joined into one constituency in 1885, returning one member. The centres of the towns are 2 m apart, Warwick lying to the west, but they are united by the intermediate parish of New Milverton. There are three saline springs, and the principal pump-rooms, baths and pleasant gardens lie on the right bank of the river. The chief public

Albania, Corsica, &c. From 1848–1849 he explored Greece, Constantinople, the Ionian Islands, Lower Egypt, the wildest recesses of Albania, and the desert of Sinai. He returned to London, but the climate did not suit him. In 1854–1855 he wintered on the Nile, and migrated successively to Corfu, Malta and Rome, finally building himself a villa at San Remo. From Corfu Lear visited Mount Athos, Syria, Palestine, and Petra; and when over sixty, by the assistance of Lord Northbrook, then Govenor-General, he saw the cities and scenery of greatest interest within a large area of India. From first to last he was, in whatever circumstances of difficulty or ill-health, an indomitable traveller. Before visiting new lands he studied their geography and literature, and then went straight for the mark; and wherever he went he drew most indefatigably and most accurately. His sketches are not only the basis of more finished works, but an exhaustive record in themselves. Some defect of technique or eyesight occasionally left his larger oil painting, though nobly conceived, crude or deficient in harmony; but his smaller pictures and more elaborate sketches abound in beauty, delicacy, and truth. Lear modestly called himself a topographical artist; but he included in the term the perfect rendering of all characteristic graces of form, colour, and atmosphere. The last task he set himself was to prepare for popular circulation a set of some 200 drawings, illustrating from his travels the scenic touches of Tennyson's poetry; but he did not live to complete the scheme, dying at San Remo on the 30th of January 1888. Until sobered by age, his conversation was brimful of humorous fun. The paradoxical originality and ostentatiously uneducated draughtsmanship of his numerous nonsense books won him a more universal fame than his serious work. He had a true artist's sympathy with art under all forms, and might have become a skilled musician had he not been a painter. Swainson, the naturalist, praised young Lear's great red and yellow macaw as "equalling any figure ever painted by Audubon in grace of design, perspective, and anatomical accuracy." Murchison, examining his sketches, complimented them as rigorously embodying geological truth. Tennyson's lines "To E.L. on his Travels in Greece," mark the poet's genuine admiration of a cognate spirit in classical art. Ruskin placed the *Book of Nonsense* first in the list of a hundred delectable volumes of contemporary literature, a judgment endorsed by English-speaking children all over the world.

See *Letters of Edward Lear to Chichester Fortescue, Lord Carlingford, and Frances, Countess Waldegrave* (1907), edited by Lady Strachey, with an introduction by Henry Strachey. (F. L.*)

LEASE (derived through the Fr. from the Lat. *laxare*, to loosen), a certain form of tenure, or the contract embodying it, of land, houses, &c., see LANDLORD AND TENANT.

LEATHER (a word which appears in all Teutonic languages; cf. Ger. *Leder*, Dutch *leer* or *leder*, Swed. *läder*, and in such Celtic forms as Welsh *lledr*), an imputrescible substance prepared from the hides or skins of living creatures, both cold and warm blooded, by chemical and mechanical treatment. Skins in the raw and natural moist state are readily putrescible, and are easily disintegrated by bacterial or chemical action, and if dried in this condition become harsh, horny and intractable. The art of the leather manufacturer is principally directed to overcoming the tendency to putrefaction, securing suppleness in the material, rendering it impervious to and unalterable by water, and increasing the strength of the skin and its power to resist wear and tear.

Leather is made by three processes or with three classes of substances. Thus we have (1) tanned leather, in which the hides and skins are combined with tannin or tannic acid; (2) tawed leather, in which the skins are prepared with mineral salts; (3) chamoised (shamoyed) leather, in which the skins are rendered imputrescible by treatment with oils and fats, the decomposition products of which are the actual tanning agents.

Sources and Qualities of Hides and Skins.—The hides used in heavy leather manufacture may be divided into three classes: (1) ox and heifer, (2) cow, (3) bull. Oxen and heifer hides produce the best results, forming a tough, tight, solid leather. Cow hides are thin, the hide itself

Heavy leathers.

being fibrous, but still compact, and by reason of its spread or area is used chiefly for dressing purposes in the bag and portmanteau manufacture and work of a similar description. Bull hides are fibrous; they are largely used for heel lifts, and for cheap belting, the thicker hides being used in the iron and steel industry.

A second classification now presents itself, viz. the British home supply, continental (Europe), British colonial, South American, East Indian, Chinese, &c.

In the British home supply there are three chief breeds: (1) Shorthorns (Scotch breed), (2) Herefords (Midland breed), (3) Lowland, or Dutch class. From a tanner's standpoint, the shorthorns are the best hides procurable. The cattle are exposed to a variable climate in the mountainous districts of Scotland, and nature, adapting herself to circumstances, provides them with a thicker and more compact hide; they are well grown, have short necks and small heads. The Hereford class are probably the best English hide; they likewise have small heads and horns, and produce good solid sole leather. The Lowland hides come chiefly from Suffolk, Kent and Surrey; the animals have long legs, long necks and big heads. The hides are usually thin and spready. The hides of the animals killed for the Christmas season are poor. The animals being stall-fed for the beef, the hides become distended, thin and surcharged with fat, which renders them unsuitable for first-class work.

The continental supply may be divided into two classes. (1) Hides from hilly regions, (2) hides from lowlands. All animals subject to strong winds and a wide range of temperatures have a very strong hide, and for this reason those bred in hilly and mountainous districts are best. The hides coming under heading No. 1 are of this class, and include those from the Swiss and Italian Alps, Bavarian Highlands and Pyrenees, also Florence, Oporto and Lisbon hides. They are magnificent hides, thick, tightly-built, and of smooth grain. The butt is long and the legs short. A serious defect in some of these hides is a thick place on the neck caused by the yoke; this part of the hide is absolute waste. Another defect, specially noticeable in Lisbon and Oporto hides, is goad marks on the rump, barbed wire scratches and warbles, caused by the gadfly. Those hides coming under heading No. 2 are Dutch, Rhine valley, Danish, Swedish, Norwegian, Hungarian, &c. The first three hides are very similar; they are spready, poorly grown, and are best used for bag and portmanteau work. Hungarian oxen are immense animals, and supply a very heavy bend. Swedish and Norwegian hides are evenly grown and of good texture; they are well flayed, and used a great deal for manufacturing picker bands, which require an even leather.

New Zealand, Australian and Queensland hides resemble good English. A small quantity of Canadian steers are imported; these are generally branded.

Chinese hides are exported dry, and they have generally suffered more or less from peptonization in the storing and drying; this cannot be detected until they are in the pits, when they fall to pieces.

Anglos are imported as live-stock, and are killed within forty-eight hours. They come to Hull, Birkenhead, Avonmouth and Deptford from various American ports, and usually give a flatter result than English, the general quality depending largely on whether the ship has had a good voyage or not.

Among South American hides, Liebig's slaughter supply the best; they are thoroughly clean and carefully trimmed and flayed. They come to London, Antwerp and Havre, and except for being branded are of first-class quality. Second to the Liebig slaughter come the Uruguay hides.

East Indian hides are known as kips, and are supposed to be, and should be, the hides of yearling cattle. They are now dressed to a large extent in imitation of box calf, being much cheaper. They come from a small breed of ox, and have an extremely tight grain; the leather is not so soft as calf.

Calf-skins are largely supplied by the continent. They are soft and pliant, and have a characteristically fine grain, are tight in texture and quite apart from any other kind of skin.

The most valuable part of a sheep-skin is the wool, and the value of the pelt is inversely as the value of the wool. Pure Leicester and Norfolk wools are very valuable, and next is the North and South Downs, but the skins, *i.e.* the pelts, of these animals are extremely poor. Devon and Cheviot cross-bred sheep supply a fair pelt, and sometimes these sheep are so many times crossed that it is quite impossible to tell what the skin is. Welsh skins also supply a good tough pelt, though small. Indian and Persian sheep-skins are very goaty, the herds being allowed to roam about together so much. The sheep-skin is the most porous and open-textured skin in existence, as also the most greasy one; it is flabby and soft, with a tight, compact grain, but an extremely loose flesh. Still-born lambs and lambs not over a month old are worth much more than when they have lived for three months; they are used for the manufacture of best kid gloves, and must be milk skins. Once the lambs have taken to grass the skins supply a harsher leather.

Light leathers.

The best goat-skins come from the Saxon and Bavarian Highlands, Swiss Alps, Pyrenees, Turkey, Bosnia, Southern Hungary and the Urals. The goats being exposed to all winds yield fine skins. A good number come from Argentina and from Abyssinia, the Cape and other parts of Africa. Of all light leathers the goat has the toughest and tightest grain; it is, therefore, especially liked for fancy work. The grain is rather too bold for glacé work, for which the sheep is largely used.

The seal-skin, used largely for levant work, is the skin of the yellow-hair seal, found in the Northern seas, the Baltic, Norway and Sweden, &c. The skin has a large, bold, brilliant grain, and being a large skin is much used for upholstery and coach work, like the Cape goat. It is quite distinct from the fur seal.

Porpoise hide is really the hide of the white whale; it is dressed for shooting, fishing and hunting boots. Horse hide is dressed for light split and upper work; being so much stall-fed it supplies only a thin, spready leather. The skins of other Equidae, such as the ass, zebra, quagga, &c. are also dressed to some small extent, but are not important sources.

Structure of Skin.—Upon superficial inspection, the hides and skins of all mammalia appear to be unlike each other in general structure, yet, upon closer examination, it is found that the anatomical structure of most skins is so similar that for all practical purposes we may assume that there is no distinction (see SKIN AND EXOSKELETON). But from the practical point of view, as opposed to the anatomical, there are great and very important differences, such as those of texture, thickness, area, &c.; and these differences cause a great divergence in the methods of tanning used, almost necessitating a distinct tannage for nearly every class of hide or skin.

The skins of the lower animals, such as alligators, lizards, fish and snakes, differ to a large extent from those of the mammalia, chiefly in the epidermis, which is much more horny in structure and forms scales.

The skin is divided into two distinct layers: (1) the epidermis or epithelium, *i.e.* the cuticle, (2) the corium derma, or cutis, *i.e.* the true skin. These two layers are not only different in structure, but are also of entirely distinct origin. The epidermis again divides itself into two parts, viz. the "horny layer" or surface skin, and the *rete Malpighi*, named after the Italian anatomist who first drew attention to its existence. The *rete Malpighi* is composed of living, soft, nucleated cells, which multiply by division, and, as they increase, are gradually pushed to the surface of the skin, becoming flatter and drier as they near it, until they reach the surface as dried scales. The epidermis is thus of cellular structure, and more or less horny or waterproof. It must consequently be removed together with the hair, wool or bristles before tannage begins, but as it is very thin compared with the corium, this matters little.

The hair itself does not enter the corium, but is embedded in a sheath of epidermic structure, which is part of and continuous with the epidermis. It is of cellular structure, and the fibrous part is composed of long needle-shaped cells which contain the pigment with which the hair is coloured. Upon removal of the hair some of these cells remain behind and colour the skin, and this colour does not disappear until these cells are removed by scudding. Each hair is supplied with at least two fat or sebaceous glands, which discharge into the orifice of the hair sheath; these glands impart to the hair that natural glossy appearance which is characteristic of good health. The hair bulb (*b*, fig. 1) consists of living nucleated cells, which multiply rapidly, and, like the *rete Malpighi*, cause an upward pressure, getting harder at the same time, thereby lengthening the hair.

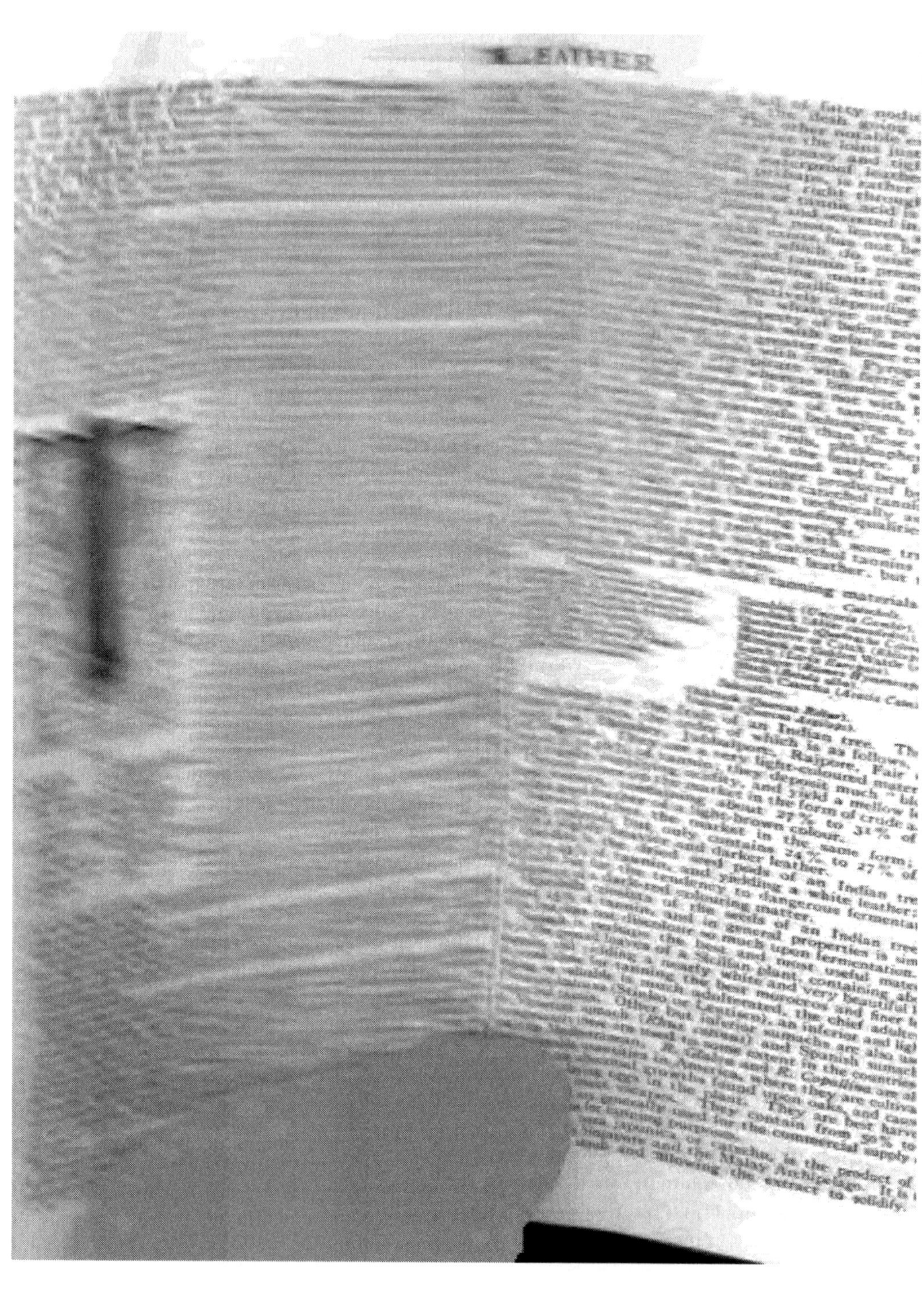

peculiar material, and may be completely washed out of a leather tanned with it. It mellows exceedingly, and keeps the leather fibre open; it may be said that it only goes in the leather to prepare and make easy the way for other tannins. Block gambier contains from 35% to 40% and cube gambier from 50% to 65% of tannin.

Hemlock generally reaches the market as extract, prepared from the bark of the American tree. It contains about 22% of tannin, has a pine-like odour, but yields a rather dark-coloured red leather.

Quebracho is imported mainly as solid extract, containing 63% to 70% of tannin; it is a harsh, light-red tannage, but darkens rapidly on exposure to light. It is used for freshening up very mellow liquors, but is rather wasteful, as it deposits an enormous amount of its tannin as phlobaphenes.

Mangrove or cutch is a solid extract prepared from the mangrove tree found in the swamps of Borneo and the Straits Settlements; it contains upwards of 60% of a red tannin.

Mimosa is the bark of the Australian golden wattle (*Acacia pycnantha*), and contains from 36% to 50% of tannin. It is a rather harsh tannage, yielding a flesh-coloured leather, and is useful for sharpening liquors. This bark is now successfully cultivated in Natal. The tannin content of this Natal bark is somewhat inferior, but the colour is superior to the Australian product.

Larch bark contains 9% to 10% of light-coloured tannin, and is used especially for tanning Scotch basils.

Canaigre is the air-dried tuberous roots of a Mexican plant, containing 25% to 30% of tannin and about 8% of starch. It yields an orange-coloured leather of considerable weight and firmness. Its cultivation did not pay well enough, so that it is little used.

Cutch, catechu or "dark catechu," is obtained from the wood of Indian acacias, and is not to be confounded with mangrove cutch. It contains 60% of tanning matter and a large proportion of catechin similar to that contained in gambier, but much redder. It is used for dyeing browns and blacks with chrome and iron mordants.

The willow and the white birch barks contain, respectively, 12% to 14% and 2% to 5% of tannin. In combination they are used to produce the famous Russia leather, whose insect-resisting odour is due to the birch bark. In America this leather is imitated with the American black birch bark (*Betula lenta*), and also with the oil obtained from its dry distillation.

In the list of materials two have been placed in a subsidiary class because they are a mixture of catechol and pyrogallol tannin. Oak bark produces the best leather known, proving that a blend of the two classes of tannins gives the best results. It is the bark of the coppice oak, and contains 12% to 14% of a reddish-yellow tannage. Valonia is the acorn cup of the Turkish and Greek oak. The Smyrna or Turkish valonia is best, and contains 32% to 36% of an almost white tannin. Greek valonia is greyer in colour, and contains 26% to 30% of tannin. It yields a tough, firm leather of great weight, due to the rapid deposition of a large amount of bloom.

Grinding and Leaching[1] *Tanning Materials.*—At first sight it would not seem possible that science could direct such a clumsy process as the grinding of tanning materials, and yet even here, the "scientific smashing" of tanning materials may mean the difference between profit and loss to the tanner. In most materials the tannin exists imprisoned in cells, and is also to some extent free, but with this latter condition the science of grinding has nothing to do. If tanning materials are simply broken by a series of clean cuts, only those cells directly on the surfaces of the cuts will be ready to yield their tannin; therefore, if materials are ground by cutting, a proportion of the total tannin is thrown away. Hence it is necessary to bruise, break and otherwise sever the walls of all the cells containing the tannin; so that the machine wanted is one which crushes, twists and cuts the material at the same time, turning it out of uniform size and with little dust.

The apparatus in most common use is built on the same principle as the coffee mill, which consists of a series of segmental cutters; as the bark works down into the smaller cutters of the mill it is twisted and cut in every direction. This is a very good form of mill, but it requires a considerable amount of power and works slowly. The teeth require constant renewal, and should, therefore, be replaceable in rows, not, as in some forms, cast on the bell. The disintegrator is another form of mill, which produces its effect by violent concussion, obtained by the revolution in opposite directions of from four to six large metal arms fitted with projecting spikes inside a drum, the faces of which are also fitted with protruding pieces of metal. The arms make from 2000 to 4000 revolutions per minute. The chief objection to this apparatus is that it forms much dust, which is caught in silken bags fitted to gratings in the drum. The myrobalans crusher, a very useful machine for such materials as myrobalans and valonia, consists of a pair of toothed rollers above and a pair of fluted rollers beneath. The material is dropped upon the toothed rollers first, where it is broken and crushed; then the crushing is finished and any sharp corners rounded off in the fluted rollers.

It must not be thought that now the material is ground it is necessarily ready for leaching. This may or may not be so, depending upon whether the tanner is making light or heavy leathers. If light leathers are being considered, it is ready for immediate leaching, *i.e.* to be infused with water in preparation of a liquor. If heavy leathers are in process of manufacture, he would be a very wasteful tanner who would extract his material raw. It must be borne in mind that when an infusion is made with fresh tanning material, the liquor begins to deposit decomposition products after standing a day or two, and the object of the heavy-leather tanner is to get this material deposited in the leather, to fill the pores, produce weight and make a firm, tough product. With this end in view he dusts his hides with this fresh material in the layers, *i.e.* he spreads a layer between each hide as it is laid down, so that the strong liquors penetrate and deposit in the hides. When most of this power to deposit has been usefully utilized in the layers, then the material (which is now, perhaps, half spent) is leached. The light-leather maker does not want a hard, firm leather, but a soft and pliable product, hence he leaches his material fresh, and does not trouble as to whether the tannin deposits in the pits or not.

Whether fresh or partially spent material is leached, the process is carried out in the same way. There are several methods in vogue; the best method only will be described, viz. the "press leach" system.

The leaching is carried out in a series of six square pits, each holding about 3 to 4 tons of material. The method depends upon the fact that when a weak liquor is forced over a stronger one they do not mix, by reason of the higher specific gravity of the stronger one; the weaker liquor, therefore, by its weight forces the stronger liquor downwards, and as the pit in which it is contained is fitted with a false bottom and side duct running over into the next pit, the stronger liquor is forced upwards through this duct on to the next stronger pit. There the process is repeated, until finally the weak liquor or water, as the case may be, is run off the last vat as a very strong infusion. As a concrete example let us take the six pits shown in the figure.

4	5	6
3	2	1

No. 6 is the last vat, and the liquor, which is very strong, is about to be run off. No. 1 is spent material, over which all six liquors have passed, the present liquor having been pumped on as fresh water. The liquor from No. 6 is run off into the pump well, and liquor No. 1 is pumped over No. 2, thus forcing all liquors one forward and leaving pit No. 1 empty; this pit is now cast and filled with clean fishings and perhaps a little new material, clean water is then pumped on No. 2, which is now the weakest pit, and all liquors are thus forced forward one pit more, making No. 1 the strongest pit. After infusing for some time this is run off to the pump well, and the process repeated. It may be noted that the hotter the water is pumped on the weakest pit, the better will the material be spent, and the nearer the water is to boiling-point the better; in fact, a well-managed tanyard should have the spent tan down to between 1% and 2% of tannin, although this material is frequently thrown away containing up to 10% and sometimes even more. There is a great saving of time and labour in this method, since the liquors are self-adjusting.

Testing Tan Liquors.—The methods by which the tanning value of any substance may be determined are many, but few are at once capable of simple application and minute accuracy. An old method of ascertaining the strength of a tan liquor is by means of a hydrometer standardized against water, and called a barkometer. It consists of a long graduated stem fixed to a hollow bulb, the opposite end of which is weighted. It is placed in the liquor, the weighted end sinks to a certain depth, and the reading is taken on the stem at that point which touches "water mark." The graduations are such that if the specific gravity is multiplied by 1000 and then 1000 is subtracted from the result, the barkometer strength of the liquor is obtained. Thus 1029 specific gravity equals 29° barkometer. This method affords no indication of the amount of tannin present, but is useful to the man who knows his liquors by frequent analysis.

A factor which governs the quality of the leather quite as much as the tannin itself is the acidity of the liquors. It is known that gallic and tannic acids form insoluble calcium salts, and all the other acids present as acetic, propionic, butyric, lactic, formic, &c., form comparatively soluble salts, so that an easy method of determining this important factor is as follows:—

Take a quantity, say 100 c.c., of tan liquor, filter till clear through paper, then pipette 10 c.c. into a small beaker (about 1½ in. diameter), place it on some printed paper and note how clear the print appears through the liquor; now gradually add from a burette a clear solution of saturated lime water until the liquor becomes just cloudy, that is until it just loses its brilliancy. Now read off the number of cubic centimetres required in the graduated stem of the burette, and either read as degrees (counting each c.c. as one degree), to which practice at once gives a useful signification, or calculate out in terms of acetic acid per 100 c.c. of liquor, reckoning saturated lime water as $\frac{1}{20}$ normal.

The methods which deal with the actual testing for tannin itself

[1] See LYE.

depend mostly upon one or other of two processes; either the precipitation of the tannin by means of gelatin, or its absorption by means of prepared hide. Sir Humphry Davy was the first to propose a method for analysing tanning materials, and he precipitated the tannin by means of gelatin in the presence of alum, then dried and weighed the precipitate, after washing free from excess of reagents. This method was improved by Stoddart, but cannot lay claim to much accuracy. Warington and Müller again modified the method, but their procedure being tedious and difficult to work could not be regarded as a great advance. Wagner then proposed precipitation by means of the alkaloids, with special regard to cinchonine sulphate in the presence of rosaniline acetate as indicator, but this method also proved useless. After this many metallic precipitants were tried, used gravimetrically and volumetrically, but without success. The weighing of precipitated tannates will never succeed, because the tannins are such a diverse class of substances that each tannin precipitates different quantities of the precipitants, and some materials contain two or three different tannins. Then there are also the difficulties of incomplete precipitation and the precipitation of colouring matter, &c. Among this class of methods may be mentioned Garland's, in which tartar emetic and sal ammoniac were employed. It was improved by Richards and Palmer.

Another class of methods depends upon the destruction of the tannin by some oxidizing agent, and the estimation of the amount required. Terreil rendered the tannin alkaline, and after agitating it with a known quantity of air, estimated the volume of oxygen absorbed. The method was slow and subject to many sources of error. Cammaille oxidized with a known quantity of iodic acid and estimated the excess of iodate. This process also was troublesome, besides oxidizing the gallic acid (as do all the oxidation processes), and entailing a separate estimation of them after the removal of the tannin. Ferdinand Jean (1877) titrated alkaline tannin solution with standard iodine, but the mixture was so dark that the end [illegible] with starch could not be seen; in addition the gallic acid had again to be estimated. Monier proposed permanganate as an oxidizing agent, and Lowenthal made a very valuable improvement by adding indigo solution to the tannin solution, which controlled the oxidation and acted as indicator. This method also required [illegible] titration because of the gallic acid present, the tanning [illegible] being removed from solution by means of gelatin and [illegible] salt.

[illegible] gravimetric hide-powder method first took form [illegible]. It was published in *Der Gerber* by Simand and Weiss, [illegible] being Eitner and Meerkatz. Hammer, Muntz and [illegible] did some earlier work on similar lines, depending upon [illegible] gravity of solutions. Professor H. R. Procter perfected [illegible] by packing a bell, similar in shape to a bottomless [illegible] (the) capacity, with the hide-powder, and siphon[illegible] up through the powder and over into a receiver. [illegible] the tan liquor of tannin, and a portion of this non-[illegible] is evaporated to dryness and weighed till constant; [illegible] of the original solution containing non-tannins [illegible] is evaporated and weighed till constant; then the [illegible] subtracted from the weight of the non-[illegible] gives the weight of tannin, which is calculated [illegible] original solutions. This method was adopted as [illegible] International Association of Leather Trades Chemists [illegible] when its faults were vividly brought before [illegible] of London and Bennett of Leeds, working [illegible] although other but not so complete work had been [illegible] to the same end. The main faults of the method [illegible] absorbed non-tannins, and therefore [illegible] and the hide-powder was partially [illegible] has now been overcome to a large extent [illegible] method of the I.A.L.T.C.

[illegible] Messrs Payne proposed a new method [illegible] which is as follows:—A definite excess [illegible] to a definite quantity of tannin solution [illegible]; the tan solution is now deprived [illegible] a soluble modification of gelatin, called [illegible] is repeated. Thus we get two sets of [illegible] and acid absorption (*i.e.* acids other [illegible] from the former gives tannin [illegible] out in percentage of original [illegible] theoretically, because a definite mole-[illegible] for tannins which are all different. [illegible] objections, but though, like the hide-[illegible], it gives exceedingly useful [illegible] are strictly adhered to.

[illegible] the I.A.L.T.C. is a modification of [illegible] which is in turn a modification of a [illegible] of the Vienna Leather Research [illegible] very slightly chrome-tanned with a [illegible] grammes of the latter being [illegible] and is then washed free from [illegible] contain 70% of moisture, and is [illegible] chroming does away with the [illegible], by rendering it quite in-[illegible] tendency to absorb non-tannins. Such a quantity of this wet powder as contains 6·5 grammes of dry hide is now taken, and water is added until this quantity contains exactly 20 grammes of moisture, *i.e.* 26·5 grammes in all; it is then agitated for 15 minutes with 100 c.c. of the prepared tannin solution, which is made up to contain tannin within certain definite limits, in a mechanical rotator, and filtered. Of this non-tannin solution 50 c.c. is then evaporated to dryness. The same thing is done with 50 c.c. of original solution containing non-tannins and tannins, and both residues are weighed. The tannin is thus determined by difference. The method does all that science can do at present. The rules for carrying out the analysis are necessarily very strict. The object in view is that all chemists should get exactly concordant results, and in this the I.A.L.T.C. has succeeded.

The work done by Wood, Trotman, Procter, Parker and others on the alkaloidal precipitation of tannin deserves mention.

Heavy Leathers.—The hides of oxen are received in the tanyard in four different conditions: (1) market or slaughter hides, which, coming direct from the local abattoirs, are soft, moist and covered with dirt and blood; (2) wet salted hides; (3) dry salted hides; (4) sun-dried or "flint" hides—the last three forms being the condition in which the imports of foreign hides are made. The first operation in the tannery is to clean the hides and bring them back as nearly as possible to the flaccid condition in which they left the animal's back. The blood and other matter on market hides must be removed as quickly as possible, the blood being of itself a cause of dark stains and bad grain, and with the other refuse a source of putrefaction. When the hides are sound they are given perhaps two changes of water.

Salted hides need a longer soaking than market hides, as it is not only essential to remove the salt from the hide, but also necessary to plump and soften the fibre which has been partially dehydrated and contracted by the salt. It must also be borne in mind that a 10% solution of salt dissolves hide substance, thereby causing an undesirable loss of weight, and a weak solution prevents plumping, especially when taken into the limes, and may also cause "buckling," which cannot easily be removed in after processes. Dried and dry salted hides require a much longer soaking than any other variety. Dried hides are always uncertain, as they may have putrefied before drying, and also may have been dried at too high a temperature; in the former case they fall to pieces in the limes, and in the latter case it is practically impossible to soak them back, unless putrefactive processes are used, and such are always dangerous and difficult to work because of the Rivers Pollution Acts. Prolonged soaking in cold water dissolves a serious amount of hide substance. Soaking in brine may be advantageous, as it prevents putrefaction to some extent. Caustic soda, sodium sulphide and sulphurous acid may also be advantageously employed on account of their softening and antiseptic action. In treating salted goods, the first wash water should always be rapidly changed, because, as mentioned, strong salt solutions dissolve hide; four changes of water should always be given to these goods.

There are other and mechanical means of softening obstinate material, viz. by stocking. The American hide mill, or double-acting stocks, shown diagrammatically in fig. 2, is a popular piece of apparatus, but the goods should never be subjected to violent mechanical treatment until soft enough to stand it, else severe grain cracking may result. Perhaps the use of sodium sulphide or caustic soda in conjunction with the American wash wheel is the safest method.

Fig. 2.—Double-acting Stocks.

Whatever means are used the ultimate object is first to swell and open up the fibres as much as possible, and secondly to remove putrefactive refuse and dirt, which if left in is fixed by the lime in the process of depilation, and causes a dirty buff.

After being thus brought as nearly as possible into a uniform condition, all hides are treated alike. The first operation to which they are subjected is *depilation*, which removes not only the hair but also the scarf skin or epidermis. When the goods are sent to the limes for depilation they are, first of all, placed in an old lime, highly charged with organic matter and bacteria. It is the common belief that the lime causes the hair to loosen and fall out, but this is not so; in fact, pure lime has the opposite effect of tightening the hair. The real cause of the loosening of the hair is that the bacteria in the old lime creep down the hair, enter the *rete Malpighi* and hair sheath, and attack and decompose the soft cellular structure of the sheath and bulb, also altering the composition of the *rete Malpighi* by means of which the scarf skin adheres to the true skin. These products of the bacterial action are soluble in lime, and immediately dissolve, leaving the scarf skin and hair unbound and in a condition to leave the skin upon scraping. In this first "green" lime the action is mainly this destructive one, but the goods have yet to be made ready to receive the tan liquor, which they must enter in a plump, open and porous condition. Consequently, the "green" lime is followed with two more, the second being less charged with bacteria, and the third being, if not actually a new one, a very near approach to it; in these two limes the bundles of fibre are gradually softened, split up and distended, causing the hide to swell, the interfibrillar substance is rendered soluble and the whole generally made suitable for transference to the tan liquors. The hide itself is only very slightly soluble; if care is taken, the grease is transformed into an insoluble calcium soap, and the hair is hardly acted upon at all.

The time the goods are in the limes and the method of making new limes depends upon the quality of the leather to be turned out. The harder and tougher the leather required the shorter and fresher the liming. For instance, for sole leather where a hard result is required, the time in the limes would be from 8 to 10 days, and a perfectly fresh top lime would be used, with the addition of sodium sulphide to hasten the process. Every tanner uses a different quantity of lime and sulphide, but a good average quantity is 7 lb lime per hide and 10-15 lb sodium sulphide per pit of 100 hides. The lime is slaked with water and the sulphide mixed in during the slaking; if it is added to the pit when the slaking is finished the greater part of its effect is lost, as it does not then enter into the same chemical combinations with the lime, forming polysulphides, as when it is added during the process of slaking.

For softer and more pliable leathers, such as are required for harness and belting, a "lower" or mellower liming is given, and the time in the limes is increased from 9 to 12 days. Some of the old mellow liquor is added to the fresh lime in the making, so as just to take off the sharpness. It would be made up as for sole leather, but with less sulphide or none at all, and then a dozen buckets of an old lime would be added. For lighter leathers from 3 to 6 weeks' liming is given, and a fresh lime is never used.

"Sweating" as a method of depilation is obsolete in England so far as heavy leathers are concerned. It consists of hanging the goods in a moist warm room until incipient putrefaction sets in. This first attacks the more mucous portions, as the *rete Malpighi*, hair bulb and sheath, and so allows the hair to be removed as before. The method pulls down the hide, and the putrefaction may go too far, with disastrous results, but there is much to recommend it for sheepskins where the wool is the main consideration, the main point being that while lime entirely destroys wool, this process leaves it intact, only loosening the roots. It is consequently still much used.

Another method of fellmongering (dewooling) sheepskins is to paint the flesh side with a cream of lime made with a 10% solution of sodium sulphide and lay the goods in pile flesh to flesh, taking care that none of the solution comes in contact with the wool, which is ready for pulling in from 4 to 8 hours. Although this process may be used for any kind of skin, it is practically only used for sheep, as if any other skin is depilated in this manner all plumping effect is lost. Since this must be obtained in some way, it is an economy of time and material to place the goods in lime in the first instance.

Sometimes, in the commoner classes of sole leather, the hair is removed by painting the hair side with cream of lime and sulphide, or the same effect is produced by drawing the hides through a strong solution of sulphide; this completely destroys the hair, actually taking it into solution. But the hair roots remain embedded in the skin, and for this reason such leather always shows a dirty buff.

Arsenic sulphide (realgar) is slaked with the lime for the production of the finer light leathers, such as glace kid and glove kid. This method produces a very smooth grain (the tendency of sodium sulphide being to make the grain harsh and bold), and is therefore very suitable for the purpose, but it is very expensive.

Sufficient proof of the fact that it is not the lime which causes skins to unhair is found in the process of chemical liming patented by Payne and Pullman. In this process the goods are first treated with caustic soda and then with calcium chloride; in this manner lime is formed in the skin by the reaction of the two salts, but still the hair remains as tight as ever. If this process is to be used for unhairing and liming effect, the goods must be first subjected to a putrid soak to loosen the hair, and afterwards limed. Experiments made by the present writer also prove this theory. A piece of calf skin was subjected to sterilized lime for several months, at the end of which time the hair was as tight as ever; then bacterial influence was introduced, and the skin unhaired in as many days.

After liming it is necessary to unhair the goods. This is done by stretching a hide over a tanner's beam (fig. 3), when with an unhairing knife (*a*, fig. 4) the beamsman partially scrapes and partially shaves off the hair and epidermis. Another workman, a "flesher," removes the flesh or "net skin" (*panniculus adiposus*), a fatty matter from the flesh side of the skin, with the fleshing knife (two-edged), seen in *b*, fig. 4. For these operations several machines have been adapted, working mostly with revolving spiral blades or vibrating cutters, under which the hides pass in a fully extended state. Among these may be mentioned the Leidgen unhairer, which works on a rubber bed, which "gives" with the irregularities of the hide, and the Wilson flesher, consisting of a series of knives attached to a revolving belt, and which also "give" in contact with irregularities.

FIG. 3.—Tanner's Beam.

At this stage the hide is divided into several parts, the process being known as "rounding." The object of the division is this: certain parts of the hide termed the "offal" are of less value than the "butt," which consists of the prime part. The grain of the butt is fine and close in texture, whereas the offal grain is loose, coarse and open, and if the offal is placed in the same superior liquors as the butt, being open and porous, it will absorb the best of the tannin first; consequently the offal goes to a set of inferior liquors, often consisting of those through which the butts have passed. The hides are "rounded" with a sharp curved butcher's knife; the divisions are seen in fig. 5. The bellies, cheeks and shoulders constitute the offal, and are tanned separately although the shoulder is not often detached from the butt until the end of the "suspenders," being of slightly better quality than the bellies. The butt is divided into two "bends." This separation is not made until the tanning of the butt is finished, when it is cut in two, and the components sold as "bends," although as often as not the butt is not divided. In America the hides are only split down the ridge of the back, from head to tail, and tanned as hides. Dressing hides are more frequently rounded after tanning, the mode depending on the purpose for which the leather is required.

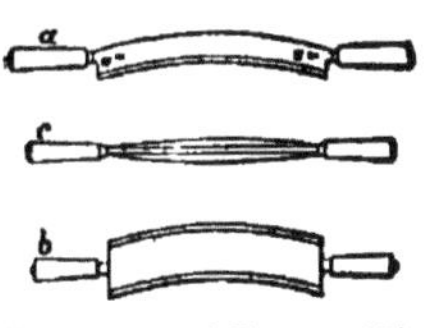

FIG. 4.—Tanner's Knives and Pin.

The next step is to remove as much "scud" and lime as possible, the degree of removal of the latter depending upon the kind of leather to be turned out. "Scudding" consists of working the already unhaired hide over the beam with an unhairing knife with increased pressure, squeezing out the dirt, which is composed of pigment cells, semi-soluble compounds of lime, and hide, hair sacks and soluble hide substance, &c. This exudes as a dirty, milky, viscid liquid, and mechanically brings the

[illegible] involves a great and undesirable loss [illegible] being sold by weight. This [illegible] giving the goods an acid bath first, [illegible] the acid fixes this soluble hide substance [illegible] alkalies, and hardens it, thus preventing [illegible] the goods may then be scudded clean with safety. [illegible] leathers must be delimed to obtain a [illegible] the demand of the present day boot [illegible] also necessary to carry this further with milder leathers than sole, such as harness and belly, &c., as excess of lime causes the leather to crack when finished. Perhaps the best material for this purpose is boracic acid, using about 10 lb per 100 butts, and suspending the goods. This acid yields a characteristic fine grain, and because of its limited solubility cannot be used in excess. Other acids are also used, such as acetic, lactic, formic, hydrochloric, with varying success. Where the water used is very [illegible] water for a few hours, when [illegible] the water is hard, the [illegible] bicarbonates it contains, in the [illegible] somewhat disastrous.

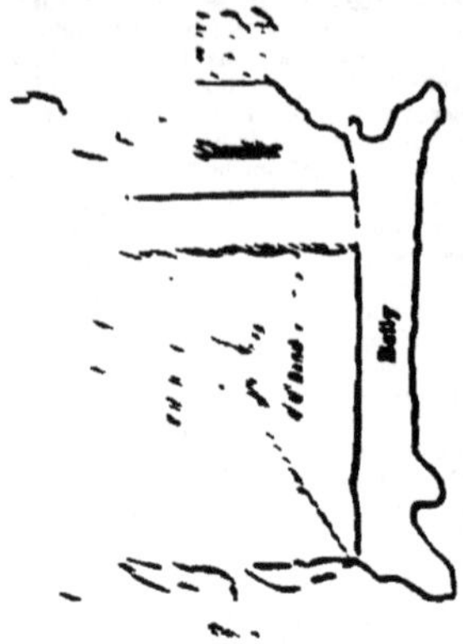

[illegible] rinsed through water [illegible] tanning proper. Any [illegible] removed by the acidity of the [illegible]

[illegible] and the operations involved [illegible] (1) colouring, (2) handling, [illegible]

[illegible] "suspenders," perhaps a series of eight [illegible] to 40° barkometer, which [illegible] but have gradually [illegible] hides through them; [illegible] and consist mainly of [illegible] the lime, plump the hide, [illegible] to receive stronger liquors. [illegible] pits on poles, which are lifted [illegible] to ensure the goods taking an [illegible] pit forward each day into [illegible] from 7 to 18 days to get [illegible]

[illegible] at this stage instead of [illegible] were adopted, the hides [illegible] marks, not being [illegible] and uneven colouring [illegible] of the top hides would [illegible] plumping, and this con- [illegible] in the after liquors. [illegible] non-technical reader is, [illegible] by placing the goods in [illegible] strong tanning solutions [illegible] i.e. contracting the [illegible] very wrinkled appearance [illegible] at the same time "case [illegible] tanned, leaving the [illegible] is case-hardened it is [illegible] the tanning. This [illegible] would thus be [illegible] [illegible]des of "handlers" or "floaters," consisting of, perhaps, a dozen pits containing liquors ranging from 30° to 55° barkometer. These liquors contain an appreciable quantity of both tannin and acid, once formed the "lay-aways," and are destined to constitute the "suspenders." In these pits the goods, having been evenly coloured off, are laid flat, handled every day in the "hinder" (weaker) liquors and shifted forward, perhaps every two days, at the tanner's convenience. The "handling" consists of lifting the butts out of the pit by means of a tanner's hook (fig. 6), piling them on the side of the pit to drain, and returning them to the pit, the top butt in the one handler being returned as the bottom in the next. This operation is continued throughout the process, only, as the hides advance, the necessity for frequent handling decreases.

Fig. 6.—Tanner's Hook (without handle).

The top two handler pits are sometimes converted into "dusters," *i.e.* when the hides have advanced to these pits, as each butt is lowered, a small quantity of tanning material is sprinkled on it.

Some tanners, now that the hides are set flat, put them in suspension again before laying away; the method has its advantages, but is not general. The goods are generally laid away immediately. The layer liquors consist of leached liquors from the fishings, strengthened with either chestnut or oakwood extract, or a mixture of the two. The first layer is made up to, say, 60° barkometer in this way, and as the hides are laid down they are sprinkled with fresh tanning material, and remain undisturbed for about one week. The second layer is a 70° barkometer liquor, the hides are again sprinkled and allowed to lie for perhaps two weeks. The third may be 80° barkometer and the fourth 90°, the goods being "dusted" as before, and lying undisturbed for perhaps three or four weeks respectively. Some tanners give more layers, and some give less, some more or less time, or greater or lesser strengths of liquor, but this tannage is a typical modern one.

As regards "dusting" material, for mellow leather, mellow materials are required, such as myrobalans being the mellowest and mimosa bark the most astringent of those used in this connexion. For harder leather, as sole leather, a much smaller quantity of myrobalans is used, if any at all, a fair quantity of mimosa bark as a medium, and much valonia, which deposits a large amount of bloom, and is of great astringency. About 3 to 4 cwt. of a judicious mixture is used for each pit, the mellower material predominating in the earlier liquors and the most astringent in the later liquors.

The tanning is now finished, and the goods are handled out of the pits, brushed free from dusting material, washed up in weak liquor, piled and allowed to drip for 2 or 3 days so that the tan may become set.

Finishing.—From this stage the treatment of sole leather differs from that of harness, belting and mellower leathers. As regards the first, it will be found on looking at the dripping pile of leather that each butt is covered with a fawn-coloured deposit, known technically as "bloom"; this disguises the under colour of the leather, just like a coat of paint. The theory of the formation of this bloom is this. Strong solutions of tannin, such as are formed between the hides from dusting materials, are not able to exist for long without decomposition, and consequently the tannin begins to condense, and forms other acids and insoluble anhydrides; this insoluble matter separates in and on the leather, giving weight, firmness, and rendering the leather waterproof. It is known technically as bloom and chemically as ellagic acid.

After dripping, the goods are scoured free from surface bloom in a Wilson scouring machine, and are then ready for bleaching. There are several methods by which this is effected, or, more correctly several materials or mixtures are used, the method of application being the same, viz. the goods are "vatted" (steeped) for some hours in the bleaching mixture at a temperature of 110° F. The mixture may consist of either sumach and a light-coloured chestnut extract made to 110° barkometer, and 110° F., or some bleaching extract made for the purpose, consisting of bisulphited liquid quebracho, which bleaches by reason of the free sulphurous acid it contains. The former method is best (though more expensive), as it removes less weight, and the light shade of colour is more permanent than that obtained by using bisulphited extracts.

After the first vatting the goods are laid up in pile to drip; meanwhile the liquor is again heated, and they are then returned for another twenty-four hours, again removed and allowed to drip for 2 to 3 days, after which they are oiled with cod oil on the grain and hung up in the sheds to dry in the dark. When they have dried to an indiarubber-like condition, they are piled and allowed to heat slightly until a greyish " bloom " rises to the surface, they are then set out and stretched in a Wilson scouring machine; using brass slickers instead of the stone ones used for scouring, " pinned " over by hand (with the three-edged instrument seen in *c*, fig. 4, and known as a " pin ") to remove any bloom not removed by the machine, oiled and dried. When of a damp even colour they are " rolled on " between two heavy rollers like a wringing machine, the pressure being applied from above, hung up in the dark sheds again until the uneven colour so produced has dried in, and then " rolled off " through the same machine, the pressure being applied from below. They are now dried right out, brushed on the grain to produce a slight gloss, and are finished.

As regards the finishing of harness leather, &c., the goods, after thorough dripping for a day or two, are brushed, lightly scoured, washed up in hot sumach and extract to improve the colour, and are again laid up in pile for two days; they are then given a good coat of cod oil, sent to the sheds, and dried right out. Only sufficient scouring is given to clean the goods, the object of the tanner being to leave as much weight in as possible, although all this superfluous tan has to be washed out by the currier before he can proceed.

Currying.—When the goods are dried from the sheds they are purchased by the currier. If, as is often the case, the tanner is his own currier, he does not tan the goods so heavily, or trouble about adding superfluous weight, but otherwise the after processes, the art of the currier, are the same.

Currying consists of working oil and grease into the leather to render it pliable and increase its strength. It was once thought that this was a mere physical effect produced by the oil, but such is not the case. Currying with animal oils is a second tannage in itself; the oils oxidize in the fibres and produce aldehydes, which are well-known tanning agents; and this double tannage renders the leather very strong. Then there is the lubricating effect, a very important physical action so far as the strength of the leather is concerned. Mineral oils are much used, but they do not oxidize to aldehydes, or, for the matter of that, to anything else, as they are not subject to decomposition. They, therefore, produce no second tannage, and their action is merely the physical one of lubrication, and this is only more or less temporary, as, except in the case of the heavier greases, they slowly evaporate. Where animal fats and oils are used, the longer the goods are left in contact with the grease the better and stronger will be the leather.

In the " Einbrennen " process (German for " burning in "), the hides are thoroughly scoured, and when dry are dipped into hot grease, which is then allowed to cool; when it is nearly set the goods are removed and set out. This process is not much used in Great Britain.

In hand-stuffing belting butts the goods are first thoroughly soaked in water to which has been added some soda, and then scoured and stretched by machine. They are then lightly shaved, to take off the loose flesh and thin the neck. The whole of the mechanically deposited tannin is removed by scouring, to make room for the grease, and they are then put into a sumach vat of 40° barkometer to brighten the colour, horsed up to drip, and set out. If any loading, to produce fictitious weight, is to be done, it is done now, by brushing the solution of either epsom salts, barium chloride or glucose, or a mixture, into the flesh, and laying away in pile for some days to allow of absorption, when, perhaps, another coat is given. Whether this is done or not, the goods are hung up until " tempered " (denoting a certain degree of dryness), and then treated with dubbin. This is manufactured by melting down tallow in a steam-jacketed pan, and adding cod oil, the mixture being stirred continually; when quite clear, it is cooled as rapidly as possible by running cold water through the steam pan, the stirring being continued until it has set. The tempered leather having been set out on a glass table, to which the flesh side adheres, is given a thin coat of the dubbin on the grain, turned, set out on the flesh, and given a thick coat of dubbin. Then it is hung up in a wind shed, and as the moisture dries out the grease goes in. After two or three days the goods are " set out in grease " with a brass slicker, given a coat of dubbin on the grain slightly thicker than the first coat, then flesh dubbined, a slightly thinner coat being applied than at first, and stoved at 70° F. The grease which is slicked off when " setting out in grease " is collected and sold. After hanging in the warm stove for 2 or 3 days the butts are laid away in grease for a month; they are then slicked out tight, flesh and grain, and buck tallowed. Hard tallow is first rubbed on the grain, when a slight polish is induced by rubbing with the smoothed rounded edge of a thick slab of glass; they are then hung up in the stove or stretched in frames to dry. A great deal of stuffing is now carried out by drumming the goods in hot hard fats in previously heated drums; and in modern times the tedious process of laying away in grease for a month is either left undone altogether or very considerably shortened.

In the tanning and dressing of the commoner varieties of kips and dried hides, the materials used are of a poorer quality, and the time taken for all processes is cut down, so that whereas the time taken to dress the better class of leather is from 7 to 10 months, and in a few cases more, these cheaper goods are turned out in from 3½ to 5 months.

A considerable quantity of the leather which reaches England, such as East India tanned kips, Australian sides, &c., is bought up and retanned, being sold then as a much better-class leather. The first operation with such goods is to " strip " them of any grease they may contain, and part of their original tannage. This is effectually carried out by first soaking them thoroughly, laying them up to drip, and drumming for half an hour in a weak solution of soda; they are then washed by drumming in plenty of water, the water is run off and replaced by very weak sulphuric acid to neutralize any remaining soda; this is in turn run off and replaced by weak tan liquor, and the goods are so tanned by drumming for some days in a liquor of gradually increasing strength. The liquor is made up as cheaply as possible with plenty of solid quebracho and other cheap extract, which is dried in with, perhaps, glucose, epsom salts, &c. to produce weight. Sometimes a better tannage is given to goods of fair quality, in which they are, perhaps, started in the drum and finished in layers, slightly better materials being used all through, and a longer time taken to complete the tannage.

The tannage of dressing hides for bag and portmanteau work is rather different from the other varieties described, in that the goods, after having had a rather longer liming, are " bated " or " puered."

Bating consists of placing the goods in a wheel or paddle with hen or pigeon excrement, and paddling for from a few hours to 2 or 3 days. In puering, dog manure is used, and this being rather more active, the process does not take so long. This bating or puering is carried out in warm liquors, and the actions involved are several. From a practical point of view the action is the removal of the lime and the solution of the hair sacs and a certain amount of interfibrillar substance. In this way the goods are pulled down to a soft flaccid condition, which allows of the removal of short hair, hair sacs and other filth by scudding with an unhairing knife upon the beam. The lime is partially taken into solution and partially removed mechanically during the scudding. A large quantity of hide substance semi-soluble and soluble, is lost by being pressed out, but this matters little, as for dressing work, area, and not weight, is the main consideration. Theoretically the action is due to bacteria and bacterial products (organized ferments and enzymes), unorganized ferments or vegetable ferments like the yeast ferment, such as pancreadine, pepsin, &c. and chemicals, such as ammonium and calcium salts and phosphates, all of which are present in the manure. The evolved gases also play their part in the action.

There are several bates upon the market as substitutes for dung bate. A most popular one was the American " Tiffany " bate, made by keeping a weak glue solution warm for some hours and then introducing a piece of blue cheese to start fermentation; when fermenting, glucose was added, and the bate was then ready for work. This and all other bates have been more or less supplanted by " erodin," discovered after years of research by Mr Wood (Nottingham) and Drs Popp and Becker (Vienna). This is an artificial bate, containing the main constituents of the dung bate. It is supplied

soft, it is
the butts
lime is fix
form of ca
After d
or weak ac
lime which
early tan li
The actu
may be divi
(3) laying av
The colour
pits, consist o
were once the
worked down,
they now con
developed aci
colour it off, an
The goods are s
up and down s
even colour; th
slightly stronger
through the susp

The reason why
being laid flat is t
would sink and tou
accessible to the ta
would thus result;
flatten the lower on
dition would be exc
Another question wh
why should not the
strong liquors? Th
have the effect of "dr
fibres, and causing the
which cannot afterwar
tanning" results, *i.e.*
centre still raw hide,
impossible for the liquor
condition being almost
rendered useless.

After the "suspender.

... two to absorb, dried out, flattened ...

... sumach liquor and drummed ... such as size, glucose, barium ... which they are piled up to drain, ... rolled to make firm, and dried

... very mellow materials are used. ... the main body of the tannage, ... extract, mimosa bark, sumach

... the head of upper leather are included ... leathers, which find their principal ... application in making the uppers ... may be taken as a type of a class of ... from such skins as East Indian kips, ... split hides, such as those described ... split rather thinner, and calf. The ... such skins and the tanning operations ... from those already described. In pro... of the skin treated, the processes are ... less complex, the tannage is a little ... such as valonia being used sparsely ... speaking, the goods have a longer and ... the time being more thoroughly ... leathers previously described, to produce ... everything must tend in this direction. ... kips are split as described under dressing ... right out.

... *Leathers.*—The duty of the currier is ... heavier leathers; he is also entrusted ... and fitting of the lighter leathers for the ... saddler, &c. He has to pare the leather ... inequalities in thickness, to impregnate it with ... render it soft and pliable, and to give it ... dressing, colour and finish as will please the eye ... of its consumers. The fact that machinery ... curriers for nearly every mechanical operation, ... adhere to the manual system, renders it almost ... a brief an outline of operations which will be ... any considerable number of curriers.

... may be taken as a typical modern dressing of ... The goods are first of all soaked down ... condition for shaving. In the better- ... is still adhered to, as it is maintained ... the shaving machine on the leather causes the ... to be coarser. Hand-shaving is carried out on a ... supporting a stout plank faced with ... or nearly so. The knife (fig. 8) is ... about 12 in. by 5 in., girded on ... length and down the centre with two ... each ... 1 in. be- ... has a straight ... and a cross ... in the ... The edges ... are first made ... are then turned ... a wire edge, ... of the ... tools shown

FIG. 8.—Currying Knife.

... The wire edge is ... drawing the thinner of the two steel tools along ... angle of the wire edge and then along the outside ... edge. The skin being thrown flesh uppermost ... vertical beam, the shaver presses his body against it, ... over the top holds the knife by its two handles almost ... angles to the leather, and proceeds to shave it by a ... downwards which the wire edge, being set at right ... knife and almost parallel with the skin, turns into a ... skin is shifted so as to bring all parts under the action of ... the shaver frequently passing a fold between his finger ... progress of his work. After shaving, the goods are ... allowed to drip, and are ready for "scouring." ... operation has for its object the removal of bloom (ellagic acid) ... other superfluous adherent matter. The scouring solution ... weak solution of soft soap and borax. This is first ... into the flesh of the leather, which is then "sleeked" ... with a steel slicker shown at S fig. 9. The upper part of the "slicker" is wooden, and into it a steel, stone, brass or vulcanite blade is forced and fastened. The wooden part is grasped in both hands, and the blade is half rubbed and half scraped over the surface of the leather in successive strokes, the angle of the slicker being a continuation of the angle which the thrust out arms of the worker form with the body, perhaps 30° to 45°, with the leather, depending upon the pressure to be applied. The soap and borax solution is continually dashed on the leather to supply a body for the removal of the bloom with the steel slicker. The hide is now turned, and the grain is scoured with a stone slicker and brush, with soap and borax solution, it is then rinsed up, and sent to dry; when sammied, it is "set" *i.e.* the grain is laid smooth with a brass or steel slicker and dried right out. It is now ready for "stuffing," which is invariably done in the drum with a mixture of stearine and "sod" oil, to which is sometimes added cod oil and wool fat; it is then set out on the grain and "canked" on the flesh, the grain side is glassed, and the leather dried right out. The goods are now "rounded," *i.e.* the lighter coloured parts of the grain are damped with a mixture of dubbin and water to bring them to even colour, and are then laid in pile for a few days to mellow, when they are ready for whitening. The goods are damped down and got to the right temper with a weak soap and water solution, and are then "whitened," an operation similar to shaving, carried out with a turned edge slicker. By this means a fine flesh surface is obtained upon which to finish by waxing; after this they are "boarded" with an arm board (R, fig. 9) to bring up the grain, or give a granular appearance to the leather and make it supple, when they may be turned flesh inwards and bruised, a similar operation to graining, essentially to soften and make them pliant. At this stage the goods are known as "finished russet," and are stored until ready for waxing.

Fig 9.—Currying Apparatus. C, pommel; R, raising board; S, slicker.

For waxing, the first operation is to black the goods. In England this is generally done by hand, but machinery is much more used in the United States. The process consists of well brushing into the flesh side of the skins a black preparation made in one of two ways. The older recipe is a mixture of lampblack, oil and perhaps a little tallow; the newer recipe consists of soap, lampblack, logwood extract and water. Either of these is brushed well into the flesh side, which is then glassed up by means of a thick slab of glass, the smooth rounded edges being used with a slicking motion, and the goods are hung up to dry. When dry they are oiled with cod oil, and are ready for sizing. Goods blacked with soap blacking are sized once, those prepared with oil blacking are sized twice. The size used for soap black skins may consist of a mixture of beeswax, pitch, linseed oil, tallow, soap, glue and logwood extract. For oil blacked skins the "bottom sizing" may be glue, soap, logwood extract and water, after the application of which the goods are dried and the "top sizing" applied; this consists of glue, cod oil, beeswax, tallow, venice turps, black dye and water. The sizings having been applied with a sponge or soft brush, thoroughly rubbed in with a glass slicker, crush marks are removed by padding with a soft leather pad, and the goods, after being dried out, are ready for the market.

In the dressing of waxed grain leathers, such as French calf, satin leather, &c., the preparatory processes are much the same as for waxed leathers described above as far as stuffing, after which the grain is prepared to take the colour by light hand scouring with weak soap and borax solution. The dye is now applied, and so that it may take well on the grain of the greasy leather, a quantity of either soap, turkey red oil or methylated spirit is added to the solution. Acid colours are preferably used, and three coats are given to the dry leather, which is then grained with an arm board, and finished by the application of hard buck tallow to the grain and brushing. The dye or stain may consist of aniline colours for coloured leathers, or, in the case of blacks, consecutive applications of logwood and iron solutions are given.

Finishing dressing Hides for Bag and Portmanteau Work.—The hides as received from the tanner are soaked down, piled sammy, and shaved, generally by machine, after which ...red, as under waxed leather, sumached and hung ...damp they are set out with a brass slicker ...is now filled by applying a solu... ...any other mucilagin... ...with a mixture of ...goods are brush... ...added linseed ...to the sammied leather. When the goods have sammied, after the last coat of stain, they are "printed" with a brass roller in a "jigger," or by means of a machine embosser. This process consists of imprinting the grain by pressure from a brass roller, on which the pattern is deeply etched. After printing, the flesh side is sponged with a weak milk solution, lightly glassed and dried, when the grain is sponged with weak linseed mucilage, almost dried, and brushed by machine. The hides are now finished, by the application either of pure buck tallow or of a mixture of carnauba wax and soap; this is rubbed up into a slight gloss with a flannel.

Light Leathers.—So far only the heavier leathers have been dealt with; we will now proceed to discuss lighter calf, goat, sheep, seal, &c.

In tanning light leathers everything must tend towards suppleness and pliability in the finished leather, in contrast to the firmness and solidity required in heavy leathers. Consequently, the liming is longer and mellower; puering, bating or some bacterial substitute always follows; the tannage is much shorter; and mellow materials are used. A deposition of bloom in the goods is not often required, so that very soon after they are struck through they are removed as tanned. The materials largely used are sumach, oak bark, gambier, myrobalans, mimosa bark, willow, birch and larch barks.

As with heavy leathers, so also with light leathers, there are various ways of tanning; and quality has much to do with the elaboration or modification of the methods employed. The tanning of all leathers will be dealt with first, dyeing and finishing operations being treated later.

The vegetable-tanned leather *de luxe* is a bottle-tanned skin. It is superior to every other class of vegetable-tanned leather in every way, but owing to competition not a great deal is now produced, as it is perhaps the most expensive leather ever put on the market. The method of preparation is as follows.

The skins are usually hard and dry when received, so they are at once soaked down, and when sufficiently soft are either milled in the stocks, drummed in a lattice drum (American dash wheel, fig. 10), or "broken down" over the beam by working on the flesh with a blunt unhairing knife. They are next mellow limed (about 3 weeks), sulphide being used if convenient, unhaired and fleshed as described under heavy leathers, and are then ready for puering. This process is carried through at about 80° F., when the goods are worked on the beam, rinsed, drenched in a bran drench, scudded, and are ready for tanning. The skins are now folded down the centre of the back from neck to butt (tail end), flesh outwards, and the edges are tightly stitched all round to form bags, leaving an aperture at one of the shanks for filling; they are now turned grain outwards and filled with strong sumach liquor and some quantity of solid sumach to fill up the interstices and prevent leakage, after which the open shank is tied up, and they are thrown into warm sumach liquor, where they float about like so many pigs, being continually pushed under the surface with a dole. When struck through they are piled on a shelf above the vat, and by their own weight the liquor is forced through the skins. The tannage takes about 24 hours, and when finished the stitching is ripped up, the skins are slicked out, "strained" on frames and dried. "Straining" consists of nailing the skins out on boards in a stretched condition, or the stretching in frames by means of strings laced in the edge of the frame and attached to the edge of the skin.

Fig. 10.—Dash Wheel.

The commoner sumach-tanned skins (but still of very good quality) are tanned in paddle wheels, a series of three being most

This latt[illegible] of an endl[illegible] with its cut[illegible] which the l[illegible] of these roll[illegible] capable of [illegible] thicknesses [illegible] to be cut is [illegible] screws *b b* wi[illegible] the cutter is [illegible] *c* as it passes [illegible] that slices of [illegible] be easily prep[illegible] hides into as m[illegible]

The dressing [illegible] the split (flesh) [illegible] grain. After s[illegible] then piled up f[illegible] with sumach mix[illegible] extract. They a[illegible] mellow the grain [illegible] and dr[illegible]

[illegible] other convenient way; the fleshes, on the other hand, go back into the limes, as it is necessary to get a large quantity of lime into leather which is to be finished as chamois.

Russia Leather was originally a speciality of Russia, where it was made from the hides of young cattle, and dressed either a brownish red or black colour for upper leather, bookbinding, dressing-cases, purses, &c. It is now made throughout Europe and America, the best qualities being obtained from Austria. The empyreumatic odour of the old genuine "Russia" leather was derived from a long-continued contact with willow and the bark of the *white* birch, which contains the odorous betulin oil. Horse hides, calf, goat, sheep skins and even splits are now dressed as "Russia leather," but most of these are of a decidedly inferior quality, and as they are merely treated with birch bark oil to give them something of the odour by which Russia leather is ordinarily recognized, they scarcely deserve the name under which they pass. The present-day genuine Russia leather is tanned like other light leathers, but properly in willow bark, although poplar and spruce fir barks are used. After tanning and setting out the goods are treated with the empyreumatic oil obtained by the dry distillation of birch bark. The red colour commonly seen in Russia leather is now produced by aniline colours, but was originally gained by the application of an infusion of Brazil wood, which was rubbed over the grain with a brush or sponge. Some time ago Russia leather got into disrepute because of its rapid decay; this was owing to its being dyed with a very acid solution of tin salts and cochineal, the acid completely destroying the leather in a year or two. The black leather is obtained by staining with logwood infusion and iron acetate. The leather, if genuine quality, is very watertight and strong, and owing to its impregnation with the empyreumatic oil, it wards off the attacks of insects.

Seal Leathers, &c.—The tannage of seal skins is now an important department of the leather industry of the United Kingdom. The skins form one of the items of the whaling industry which principally centres in Dundee, and at that port, as well as at Hull and Peterhead, they are received in large quantities from the Arctic regions. This skin is that of the white hair seal, and must not be confused with the expensive seal fur obtained from Russian and Japanese waters. These white hair seal skins are light but exceedingly close in texture, yielding a very strong tough leather of large area and fine bold grain, known as *[illegible]* [illegible]. The area of the skins renders them suitable for upholstery work, and the flesh splits are dressed in considerable quantity for "japanned" ("patent") leather and "[illegible]," which are used to grain other skins on, the raised [illegible] affording a grip on the skin being grained and thus preventing [illegible]. When the skins arrive in the tanyard (generally [illegible]) they are drummed in old drench liquors until soft, [illegible] warm water and "blubbered" with a sharp knife; they are then alternately dipped in warm water and drummed [illegible] times to remove fat, after which they are heavily limed, as they are still very greasy, and after unhairing and fleshing they are heavily [illegible] for the same reason. The tannage takes about a month, and is much the same as for other leathers, the skins being [illegible] when "struck through."

[illegible] leather is now produced to some extent both in the United States and India. The belly and flanks alone are useful. There are no special tanneries or processes for dressing the skins [illegible] not given. The leather is used mostly for small fancy [illegible] and is much imitated on sheepskin by embossing.

[illegible] and [illegible] skins are also dressed to some extent, the latter [illegible] a considerable item in the exports of Japan, they [illegible] mostly for cigar cases and pocket books. The general [illegible] is first to lime the goods and then to remove any scales [illegible] of snake skins) by scraping with an unhairing knife on [illegible], after which the skins are bated and tanned in sumach [illegible].

A considerable amount of leather is now produced in Australia from the skins of kangaroo, wallaby and other marsupials. These skins are both tanned and "tawed," the principal tanning agents being mimosa bark, mallet bark and sugar bush, which abound in [illegible]. The leather produced is of excellent quality, strong and [illegible] and rivals in texture and appearance the kid of Europe; [illegible] circumstance that the animals exist only in the wild state [illegible] a limited and insecure source of leather.

Japan and Enamel Leathers.—Japanning is usually done on flesh splits, whereas enamelling is done on the grain, and if splits are used they are printed and boarded. The leather should be mellow, soft, free from grease, with a firm grain and no inclination to stretch. It is first shaved very smooth, thoroughly scoured with a stone, sumached, washed, slicked out tight and dried; when "sammied," the grain is buffed to remove scratches and oiled, the goods are then whitened or fluffed, and if too hard, bruised by boarding; enamel goods are now grained. The skins are now tightly nailed on boards and any holes patched up with brown paper, so that the japan shall not touch the flesh when the first thick coat of japan or the "daub" is put on. This is applied so thickly that it cannot soak in, with fine-toothed slicker, and then placed in a hot stove for twenty-four hours until quite dry; the coating is then pumiced smooth and the second thinner coat, termed "blanback," is applied. This is dried and pumiced, and a fine coating of japan or copal varnish is finally given. This is dried and cooled, and if the goods are for enamel they are boarded.

English japans sometimes contain light petroleum, but no turps. The secret of successful japanning lies in the age of the oil used; the older the linseed oil is, the better the result. To prepare the ground coat, boil 10 gallons linseed oil for one hour with 2 lb litharge at 600° F. to jellify the oil, and then add 2 lb prussian blue and boil the whole for half an hour longer. Before application the mixture is thinned with 10 gallons light petroleum. For the second coat, boil 10 gallons linseed oil for 2 hours with 2 lb prussian blue and 2 lb lampblack; when of a thin jelly consistency thin with 5 gallons of benzine or light petroleum. For the finishing coat, boil 5 gallons of linseed oil for 1 hour, then add 1 lb prussian blue, and boil for another hour; thin with 10 gallons petroleum and apply with a brush in a warm room. After drying, the goods are mellowed by exposure to the sun for at least three days.

Tawing.—Wool rugs are, after the preliminary processes, sometimes tanned in oak bark liquors by paddling, but are generally "tawed," that is, dressed with alum and salt, and are therefore more suitably dealt with under that head. Tawing implies that the conversion of skins into leather is carried out by means of a mixture of which the more important constituents are mineral salts, such as alum, chrome and iron, which may or may not be supplemented with fatty and albuminous matter, both animal and vegetable.

As an example of alum tawing, calf kid may be taken as characteristic of the process; glove kid is also treated on similar lines. The goods are prepared for tawing in a manner similar to the preparation of tanned leathers, arsenical limes being used to ensure a fine grain. After being well drenched and washed the goods are ready for the tawing process. On the continent of Europe it is usual for the goods to be thrown into a tub with the tawing paste and trodden with the bare feet, although this old-fashioned method is gradually being driven out, and the drum or tumbler is being used.

The tawing paste consists of a mixture of alum, salt, flour, egg yolk and water; the quantities of each constituent diverge widely, every dresser having his own recipe. The following has been used, but cannot well be classed as typical: For 100 lb skin take 9 lb alum, 5 lb salt, dissolve in water, and mix to a thin paste with from 5 to 13 lb flour, using 4 to 6 egg yolks for every pound of flour used. Olive oil is also mixed in sometimes. The skins are drummed or trodden, at intervals, in the warm paste for some hours, removed, allowed to drain, and dried rapidly, damped down or "sammied" and "staked" by drawing them to and fro over a blunt knife fixed in the top of a post, and known as a knee stake; this process softens them very considerably. After staking, the goods are wet back and shaved smooth, either with a moon knife, *i.e.* a circular concave convex knife, the centre of which has been cut out, a piece of wood bridging the cavity forming the grip, or with an ordinary currier's shaving knife; the skins are now ready for dyeing and finishing.

Wool Rug Dressing.—Wool rugs are first thoroughly soaked, well washed and clean-fleshed, scoured well by rubbing into the wool a solution of soft soap and soda, and then leathered by rubbing into the flesh of the wet skins a mixture consisting of three parts of alum and two parts of salt until they are practically dry; they are now piled up over-night, and the mixture is again applied. After the second or third application the goods should be quite leathered. Other methods consist of stretching the skins in frames and painting the flesh with a solution of alum and salt, or, better, with a solution of basic alum and salt, the alum being made basic by the gradual addition of soda until a permanent precipitate is produced.

The goods are now bleached, for even the most vigorous scouring will not remove the yellow tint of the wool, especially at the tips. There are several methods of bleaching, viz. by hydrogen peroxide, following up with a weak vitriol bath; by potassium permanganate, following up with a bath of sulphurous acid; or by fumigating in an air-tight chamber with burning sulphur. The last-named method is the more general, the wet skins are hung in the chamber, an iron pot containing burning sulphur is introduced, and the exposure is continued for several hours.

If the goods are to be finished white, they are now given a vitriol sour, scoured, washed, retanned, dried, and when dry softened by working with a moon knife. If they are to be dyed, they must be prepared for the dye solution by "chloring," which consists of immersion in a cold solution of bleaching powder for some hours, and then souring in vitriol.

The next step is dyeing. If basic dyes are to be used, it is necessary to neutralize the acidity of the skins by careful addition of soda, and to prevent the tips from being dyed a darker colour than the roots. Glauber salts and acetic acid are added to the dye-bath. The tendency of basic colours to rub off may be overcome by passing the goods through a solution of tannin in the form of cutch, sumach, quebracho, &c.; in fact, some of the darker-coloured materials may be used as a ground colour, thus economizing dyestuff and serving two purposes. If acid colours are used, it is necessary to add sulphuric acid to the dye bath, and in either case colours which will strike below 50° C. must be used, as at that temperature alum leather perishes.

After being dyed, the goods are washed up, drained, and if necessary retanned, the glossing finish is then produced by passing them through a weak emulsion or "fat liquor" of oil, soap and water, after which they are dried, softened by working with a moon knife and beating, when they are combed out, and are ready for the market.

Blacks are dyed by immersing the goods alternately in solutions of logwood and iron, or a one-solution method is used, consisting of a mixture of these two, with, in either case, varying additions of lactic acid and sumach, copper salts, potassium bichromate, &c.; the time of immersion varies from hours to days. After striking, the goods are exposed to the air for some hours in order to oxidize to a good black; they are then well scoured, washed, drained, retanned, dried, softened and combed.

Chrome Tanning.—The first chrome tanning process was described by Professor Knapp in 1858 in a paper on "Die Natur und Wesen der Gerberie," but was first brought into commercial prominence by Dr Heinzerling about 1878, and was worked in a most persevering way by the Eglinton Chemical Company, who owned the English patents, though all their efforts failed to produce any lasting effects. Now chrome tanning is almost the most important method of light leather dressing, and has also taken a prominent place in the heavy department, more especially in curried leathers and cases where greater tensile strength is needed. The leather produced is much stronger than any other leather, and will also stand boiling water, whereas vegetable-tanned leather is completely destroyed at 70° C. and alum leather at 50° C.

The theory of chrome tanning is not perfectly understood, but in general terms it consists of a partial chemical combination between the hide fibre and the chrome salts, and a partial mechanical deposition of chromium oxide in and on the fibre. The wet work, or preparation for tanning, may be taken as much the same as for any other leather.

There are two distinct methods of chrome tanning, and several different methods of making the solutions. The "two bath process" consists of treating the skins with a bichromate in which the chromium is in the acidic state, and afterwards reducing it to the basic state by some reducing agent. The exact process is as follows: To prevent wrinkled or "drawn" grain the goods are first paddled for half an hour in a solution of vitriol and salt, when they are piled or "horsed" up over night, and then, without washing, placed in a solution consisting of 7 lb of potassium bichromate, 3½ lb of hydrochloric acid to each 100 lb of pelts, with sufficient water to conveniently paddle in; it is recommended that 5% of salt be added to this mixture. The goods are run in this for about 3 hours, or until struck through, when they are horsed up for some hours, care being taken to cover them up, and are then ready for the reducing bath. This consists of a 14% solution of plain "hypo," or hyposulphite of soda, to which, during the process of reduction, frequent additions of hydrochloric acid are made to free the sulphurous and thiosulphuric acids, which are the active reducing agents. After about 3 hours' immersion, during which time the goods will have changed in colour from bright yellow to bright green, one or two skins are cut in the thickest part, and if the green has struck right through, the pack is removed as tanned, washed up, and allowed to drain.

[illegible]

liquors of gambier alum and salt, and when tanned, washed the goods in warm water to remove excess of tanning agent, piled up to samm, and fatliquored. In making alum combinations it must be borne in mind that alum leather will not glaze, and if a glazed finish is required, a fairly heavy vegetable tannage should be first applied. For dull finishes the mineral tannage may advantageously precede the vegetable.

Very excellent chrome combination leather is also manufactured by the application of the above principles, gambier always being in great favour as the vegetable agent. The use of other materials deprives the leather of its stretch, although they may be advantageously used where the latter property is objectionable.

Oil Tanning.—Under the head of oil tanning is included "buff leather," "buck leather," "piano leather," "chamois leather," and to a greater or lesser extent, "Preller's crown or helvetia leather." The process of oil tanning dates back to antiquity, and was known as "shamoying," now spelt "chamoising." Chamoising yields an exceedingly tough, strong and durable leather, and forms an important branch of the leather industry. The theory of the process is the same as the theory of currying, which is nothing more or less than chamoising, viz. the lubrication of the fibres by the oil itself and the aldehyde tanning which takes place, due to the oxidation and decomposition of the esters of the fatty acids contained in the oil. The fact that an aldehyde tannage takes place seems to have been first discovered by Payne and Pullman, who took out a patent in 1898, covering formaldehyde and other aldehydes used in alkaline solutions. Their product, "Kaspine" leather, found considerable application in the way of military accoutrements. Chamois, buff, buck and piano leathers are all manufactured by the same process slightly modified to suit the class of hide used, the last three being heavy leathers, the first light.

As regards the process used for chamois leather, the reader will remember, from the account of the vegetable tannage of sheep skins, that after splitting from the limes, the fleshes were thrown back into the pits for another three weeks' liming (six weeks in all) preparatory to being dressed as chamois leather. It is necessary to lime the goods for oil dressing very thoroughly, and if the grain has not been removed by splitting, as in the case of sheep skins, it is "frized" off with a sharp knife over the beam. The goods are now rinsed, scudded and drenched, dried out until stiff, and stocked in the faller stocks with plenty of cod oil for 2 to 3 hours until they show signs of heating, when they are hung up in a cool shed. This process is repeated several times during a period of from 4 to 6 days, the heat driving the water out of the skins and the oil replacing it. At the end of this time the goods, which will have changed to a brown colour, are hung up and allowed to become as dry as possible, when they are hung in a warm stove for some hours, after which they are piled to heat off, thrown into tepid water and put through a wringing machine. The grease which is recovered from the wringing machine is known commercially as "degras" or "moellon," and fetches a good price, as it is unrivalled for fatliquoring and related processes, such as stuffing, producing a very soft product. They next receive a warm soda lye bath, and are again wrung; this removes more grease, which forms soap with the lye, and is recovered by treatment with vitriol, which decomposes the soap. The grease which floats on top of the liquor is sold under the name of "sod oil." This also is a valuable material for fatliquoring, &c., but not so good as degras.

After being wrung out, the goods are bleached by one of the processes mentioned in the section on wool rug dressing, the permanganate method being in general use in England. In countries where a fine climate prevails the soap bleach or "sun bleach" is adopted; this consists of dipping the goods in soap solution and exposing them to the sun's rays, the process being repeated three or more times as necessary.

The next step is fatliquoring to induce softness, after which they are dried out slowly, staked or "perched" with a moon knife, fluffed on a revolving wheel covered with fine emery to produce the fine "nap" or surface, brushed over with french chalk, fuller's earth or china clay, and finally finished on a very fine emery wheel.

Preller's Helvetia or Crown Leather.—This process of leather manufacture was discovered in 1850 by Theodor Klemm, a cabinetmaker of Württemberg, who being then in poor circumstances, sold his patent to an Englishman named Preller, who manufactured it in Southwark, and adopted a crown as his trade mark. Hence the name "crown" leather. The manufacture then spread through Switzerland and Germany, the product being used in the main for picker straps, belting and purposes where waterproof goods were required, such as [illegible] pipes and military water bags. No taste is imparted to water by this leather.

The process of manufacture is as follows: The hides are unhaired by short liming, painting with lime and sulphide, or sweating, and cleansed by scudding and washing, after which they are coloured in bark liquors, washed up through clean water, and hung up to dry partially. When in a sammied condition the goods are placed on a table and a thick layer of the tanning paste spread on the flesh side. The tanning paste varies with each manufacturer, but the following is the mixture originally used by Preller: 100 parts flour, 100 parts soft fat or horse tallow, 35 parts butter, 88 parts ox brains, 50 parts milk, 15 parts salt or saltpetre.

The hides are now rolled in bundles, placed in a warm drum and worked for 8 to 10 hours, after which they are removed and hung up until half dry, when the process is repeated. Thus they are tumbled 3 to 4 times, set out flesh and grain, rinsed through tepid water, set out, sammied, and curried by coating with glycerin, oil, tallow and degras. The table grease is now slicked off, and the goods are set out in grease, grained and dried.

Transparent Leather.—Transparent leather is a rather horny product, somewhat like raw hide, and has been used for stitching belts and picker bands. The goods to be dressed are limed, unhaired, very thoroughly delimed with acids, washed in water, scudded and clean-fleshed right to the veins; they are now stretched in frames, clean-fleshed with a moon knife, and brushed with warm water, when several coats of glycerin, to which has been added some antiseptic such as salicylic or picric acid, are applied; the goods are then dried out, and another coat is applied, and when semi-dry they are drummed in a mixture of glycerin, boracic acid, alum and salt, with the addition of a little bichromate of potash to stain them a yellow colour. After drumming for 2 to 3 hours they are removed, washed up, lightly set out, and stretched in frames to dry, when they are ready for cutting into convenient lengths for use.

Parchment.—A certain class of sheep skin known as Hampshires is generally used in the manufacture of this speciality. The skins as received are first very carefully washed to remove all dirt, dewooled, limed for 3 to 4 weeks, they are then cleanly fleshed, unhaired, rinsed up in water, and thickly split, the poorer hides being utilized for chamois; they are now re-split at the fatty strata so that all fat may be easily removed, and while the grains are dressed as skivers, the fleshes are tied in frames, watered with hot water, scraped and coated on both sides with a cream consisting of whiting, soda and water, after which they are dried out in a hot stove. In the drying the whiting mixture absorbs the grease from the skins; in fact, this method of degreasing is often employed in the manufacture of wool rugs. When dry, both sides of the skins are flooded to remove the whiting, and are then well rubbed over with a flat piece of pumice-stone, swilled, dried, re-pumiced, again swilled, and when sammied are rolled off with a wooden roller and dried out.

Tar and Peat Tanning.—Tar tanning was discovered by a French chemist named Philippi, who started with the idea that, if coal was a decomposition product of forests, it must still necessarily possess the tanning properties originally present in the trees. However far-fetched such an argument may seem, Philippi succeeded in producing a leather from wood and coal tar at a fairly cheap rate, the product being of excellent texture and strength, but rather below the average in the finish, which was inclined to be patchy, showing oily spots. His method consisted of impregnating the goods with refined tar and some organic acid, but the product does not seem to have taken any hold upon the market, and is not much heard of now.

Peat tanning was discovered by Payne, an English chemist, who was also the co-discoverer of the Payne-Pullman formaldehyde tanning process. His peat or humic acid tannage was patented by him about 1905, and is now worked on a commercial scale. The humic acid is first extracted from the peat by means of alkalis, and the hides are treated with this solution, the humic acid being afterwards precipitated in the hides by treatment with some stronger organic or mineral acid.

Dyeing, Staining and Finishing.—These operations are practised almost exclusively on the lighter leathers. Heavy leathers, except coloured and black harness and split hides for bag work, are not often dyed, and their finishing is generally considered to be part of the tannage. In light leathers a great business is done in buying up "crust" stock, *i.e.* rough tanned stock, and then dyeing and finishing to suit the needs and demands of the various markets. The carrying out of these operations is a distinct and separate business from tanning, although where possible the two businesses are carried on in the same works.

Whatever the goods are and whatever their ultimate finish, the first operation, upon receipt by the dyer of the crust stock, is sorting, an operation requiring much skill. The sorter must be familiar with the why and wherefore of all subsequent processes through which the leather must go, so as to judge of the suitability of the various qualities of leather for these processes, and to know where any flaws that may exist will be sufficiently suppressed or hidden to produce a saleable product, or will be rendered entirely unnoticeable. The points to be considered in the sorting are coarseness or fineness of texture, boldness or fineness of grain, colour, flaws including stains and scratches, substance, &c. Light-coloured and flawless goods are parcelled out for fine and delicate shades, those of darker hue and few flaws are parcelled out for the darker shades, such as maroons, greens (sage and olive), dark blues, &c., and those which are so badly stained as to be unsuitable for colours go for blacks. After sorting, the goods are soaked back to a limp condition by immersion in warm water, and are then horsed up to drip, having been given, perhaps, a preliminary slicking out.

Up to this point all goods are treated alike, but the subsequent processes now diverge according to the class of leather being treated and the finish required.

Persian goods for glacés, moroccos, &c., require special preparation for dyeing, being first re-tanned. As received, they are sorted and soaked as above, piled to samm, and shaved. Shaving consists of rendering the flesh side of the skins smooth by shaving off irregularities, the skin, which is supported on a rubber roller actuated by a foot lever, being pressed against a series of spiral blades set on a steel roller, which is caused to revolve rapidly. When shaved, the goods are stripped, washed up, soured, sweetened and re-tanned in sumach, washed up, and slicked out, and are then ready for dyeing.

There are three distinct methods of dyeing, with several minor modifications. Tray dyeing consists of immersing the goods, from 2 to 4 dozen at a time, in two separate piles, in the dye solution at 60° C., contained in a flat wooden tray about 5 ft.×4 ft.×1 ft., and keeping them constantly moving by continually turning them from one pile to the other. The disadvantages of this method are that the bath rapidly cools, thus dyeing rapidly at the beginning and slowly at the termination of the operation; hence a large excess of dye is wasted, much labour is required, and the shades obtained are not so level as those obtained by the other methods. But the goods are under observation the whole time, a very distinct advantage when matching shades, and a white flesh may be preserved. The paddle method of dyeing consists of paddling the goods in a large volume of liquor contained in a semi-circular wooden paddle for from half to three-quarters of an hour. The disadvantages are that the liquor cools fairly rapidly, more dye is wasted than in the tray method, and a white flesh cannot be preserved. But larger packs can be dyed at the one operation, the goods are under observation the whole time, and little labour is required.

The drum method of dyeing is perhaps best, a drum somewhat similar to that used by curriers being preferable. The goods are placed on the shelves inside the dry drum, the lid of which is then fastened on, and the machinery is started; when the drum is revolving at full speed, which should be about 12 to 15 revolutions per minute, the dye solution is added through the hollow axle, and the dyeing continued for half an hour, when, without stopping the drum, if desired, the goods may be fatliquored by running in the fatliquor through the hollow axle. The disadvantages are that the flesh is dyed and the goods cannot be seen. The advantages are that little labour is required, a large pack of skins may be treated, level shades are produced, heat is retained, almost complete exhaustion of the dye-bath is effected, and subsequent processes, such as fatliquoring, may be carried out without stopping the drum.

Of the great number of coal-tar dyes on the market comparatively few can be used in leather manufacture. The four chief classes are: (1) acid dyes; (2) basic or tannin dyes; (3) direct or cotton dyes; (4) mordant (alizarine) dyes.

Acid dyes are not so termed because they have acid characteristics; the name simply denotes that for the development of the full shade of colour it is necessary to add acid to the dye-bath. These dyes are generally sodium salts of sulphonic acids, and need the addition of an acid to free the dye, which is the sulphonic acid. Although theoretically any acid (stronger than the sulphonic acid present) will do for this purpose, it is found in practice that only sulphuric and formic acids may be employed, because others, such as acetic, lactic, &c., do not develop the full shade of colour. Acid sodium sulphate may also be successfully used.

The [illegible] other[illegible] usuall[illegible] there[illegible] as fol[illegible] in 9 [illegible] 1 gall[illegible] third [illegible] added [illegible] third [illegible] liquor [illegible] bichr[illegible] and [illegible] redu[illegible] whol[illegible] In y[illegible] by [illegible] solu[illegible]

Aft[illegible] more, [illegible] being [illegible] simil[illegible] when [illegible] water, [illegible] furth[illegible] meth[illegible] which [illegible] longer [illegible]

Iro[illegible] made [illegible] posit[illegible] perti[illegible] who [illegible] leath[illegible] great[illegible] bloo[illegible] made [illegible] and [illegible] nitri[illegible] is a[illegible] colo[illegible] does [illegible] skin [illegible] or [illegible] whi[illegible]

T[illegible] stu[illegible] use[illegible] leat[illegible] par[illegible] Lea[illegible] iron [illegible] alu[illegible]

C[illegible] sep[illegible] hav[illegible] leat[illegible] Stat[illegible] ness [illegible] tann[illegible] the [illegible] tann[illegible] It m[illegible] tann[illegible] will [illegible] first [illegible] tanna[illegible] manu[illegible] leather [illegible] applied [illegible] Americ[illegible] ing," a[illegible] of this [illegible] leathers.

The Sw[illegible] of alum a[illegible] were then [illegible] with [illegible]

[illegible] when [illegible] picked out and [illegible] [illegible] Germans [illegible] [illegible] grain, [illegible]

[illegible]—The goods are [illegible] soaked back, [illegible] machine, finished off by hand, [illegible] trimming in warm stomach and [illegible] washed up, struck out, [illegible] consists of laying the grain flat and [illegible] with a steel or sharp brass slicker. They [illegible] topped with linseed mucilage, and again dried.

This brushing over with linseed mucilage prevents the dye from sinking too far into the leather; gelatine, Irish moss, starch and gums are also used for the same purpose. These materials are also added to the staining solution to thicken it and further prevent its sinking in.

When dry, the goods are stained by applying a ½% (usually) solution of a suitable basic dye, thickened with linseed, with a brush. Two men are usually employed on this work; one starts at the right-hand flank and the other at the left-hand shank, and they work towards each other, staining in sections; much skill is needed to obviate markings where the sections overlap. The goods may advantageously be bottomed with an acid dye or a dye-wood extract, and then finished with basic dyes. Whichever method is used, two to three coats are given, drying between each. After the last coat of stain, and while the goods are still in a sammied condition, a mixture of linseed mucilage and French chalk is applied to the flesh and glassed off wet, to give it a white appearance, and then the goods are printed with any of the usual bag grains by machine or hand, and dried out. For a bright finish the season may consist of a solution of 15 parts carnauba wax, 10 parts curd soap and 100 parts water boiled together; this is sponged into the grain, dried and the hides are finished by either glassing or brushing. For a duller finish the grain is simply rubbed over with buck tallow and brushed. Hide bellies for small work are treated in much the same manner.

Glove Leathers.—As these goods were tanned in alum, salt, flour and egg, any undue immersion in water removes the tannage; for this reason they are generally stained like bag hides, one man only being employed on the same skin. The skins are first thoroughly soaked in warm water and then drummed for some minutes in a fresh supply, when they are re-egged to replace that which has been lost. This is best done by drumming them for about 1½ hours in 40 to 50 egg yolks and 5 ℔ of salt for every hundred skins; they are then allowed to be in pile for 24 hours, and are set out on the table ready for mordanting. The mordants universally used are ammonia or alkaline soft soap; 1 in 1000 of the former or a 1% solution of the latter. When the goods have partially dried in, bottoming follows, and usually the natural wood dyestuffs are used for this operation, such as fustic, Brazil wood, peachwood, logwood and turmeric. After application of these colours the goods are sammied and topped with a 1% solution of an acid dye, to which has been added 20% of methylated spirit to prevent frothing with the egg yolk; they are then dried out slowly, staked, pulled in shape, fluffed and brushed by machine. The season, which is sponged on, may consist of 1 part dye, 1 part albumen, 2 parts dextrine and ½ part glycerine, made up to 100 parts with water; when it has been applied, the goods are sammied, brushed and ironed with a warm flat iron such as is used in laundry work.

Bookbinding Leathers.—A committee of the Society of Arts (London) has investigated the question of leather for bookbinding, attention having been drawn to this subject by the rotten and decayed condition often observed in bindings less than fifty years old. This committee engaged in research work extending over several years, and the report in which its results were given was edited for the Society of Arts and the Leathersellers' Company (which also did much important work in connexion with it) by Lord Cobham, chairman of the committee, and Sir Henry Trueman Wood, secretary of the society. The essence of the report, so far as leather manufacture is concerned, is as follows: The goods should be soaked and limed in fresh liquors, and bating and puering should be avoided, weak organic acids or erodine being used; they should also be tanned with pyrogallol tanning materials, and preferably with sumach. In shaving, they should only be necked and backed, *i.e.* only irregularities should be removed, as further shaving has a considerable weakening effect on the fibre. The striking out should not be heavy enough to lay the fibre. In dyeing, acid dyes and a few direct colours only are permissible, and in connexion with the former the use of sulphuric acid is strongly condemned, as it absolutely disintegrates the fibre; the use of formic, acetic and lactic acids is permitted. The use of salts of mineral acids is to be avoided, and in finishing, tight setting out and damp glazing is not to be recommended; oil may be advantageously used.

Bibliography.—H. G. Bennett, *The Manufacture of Leather* (1909); S. R. Trotman, *Leather Trades Chemistry* (1908); M. C. Lamb, *Leather Dressing* (1907); A. Watt, *Leather Manufacture* (1906); H. R. Procter, *Principles of Leather Manufacture* (1903), and *Leather Industries Laboratory Book* (1908); L. A. Flemming, *Practical Tanning* (1910); A. M. Villon, *Practical Treatise on the Leather Industry* (1901); C. T. Davis, *Manufacture of Leather* (1897). German works include J. Borgman, *Die Rotlederfabrikation* (Berlin, 1904–1905), and *Feinlederfabrikation* (1901); J. Jettmar, *Handbuch der Chromgerbung* (Leipzig, 1900); J. von Schroeder, *Gerbereichemie* (Berlin, 1898). (J. G. P.*)

LEATHER, ARTIFICIAL. Under the name of artificial leather, or of American leather cloth, large quantities of a material having, more or less, a leather-like surface are used, principally for upholstery purposes, such as the covering of chairs, lining the tops of writing desks and tables, &c. There is considerable diversity in the preparation of such materials. A common variety consists of a web of calico coated with boiled linseed oil mixed with dryers and lamp-black or other pigment. Several coats of this mixture are uniformly spread, smoothed and compressed on the cotton surface by passing it between metal rollers, and when the surface is required to possess a glossy enamel-like appearance, it receives a finishing coat of copal varnish. A grained morocco surface is given to the material by passing it between suitably embossed rollers. Preparations of this kind have a close affinity to cloth waterproofed with indiarubber, and to such manufactures as ordinary waxcloth. An artificial leather which has been patented and proposed for use as soles for boots, &c., is composed of powdered scraps and cuttings of leather mixed with solution of guttapercha dried and compressed. In place of the guttapercha solution, oxidized linseed oil or dissolved resin may be used as the binding medium for the leather powder.

LEATHERHEAD, an urban district in the Epsom parliamentary division of Surrey, England, 18 m. S.S.W. of London, on the London, Brighton & South Coast and the London & South-Western railways. Pop. (1901) 4694. It lies at the foot of the North Downs in the pleasant valley of the river Mole. The church of St Mary and St Nicholas dates from the 14th century. St John's Foundation School, opened in London in 1852, is devoted to the education of sons of poor clergymen. Leatherhead has brick-making and brewing industries, and the district is largely residential.

LEATHES, STANLEY (1830–1900), English divine and Orientalist, was born at Ellesborough, Bucks, on the 21st of March 1830, and was educated at Jesus College, Cambridge, where he graduated B.A. in 1852, M.A. 1853. In 1853 he was the first Tyrwhitt's Hebrew scholar. He was ordained priest in 1857, and after serving several curacies was appointed professor of Hebrew at King's College, London, in 1863. In 1868–1870 he was Boyle lecturer (*The Witness of the Old Testament to Christ*), in 1873 Hulsean lecturer (*The Gospel its Own Witness*), in 1874 Bampton Lecturer (*The Religion of the Christ*) and from 1876 to 1880 Warburtonian lecturer. He was a member of the Old Testament revision committee from 1870 to 1885. In 1876 he was elected prebendary of St Paul's Cathedral, and he was rector of Cliffe-at-Hoo near Gravesend (1880–1889) and of Much Hadham, Hertfordshire (1889–1900). The university of Edinburgh gave him the honorary degree of D.D. in 1878, and his own college made him an honorary fellow in 1885. Besides the lectures noted he published *Studies in Genesis* (1880), *The Foundations of Morality* (1882) and some volumes of sermons. He died in May 1900.

His son, Stanley Mordaunt Leathes (b. 1861), became a fellow of Trinity, Cambridge, and lecturer on history, and was one of the editors of the *Cambridge Modern History*; he was secretary to the Civil Service Commission from 1903 to 1907, when he was appointed a Civil Service Commissioner.

LEAVEN (in Mid. Eng. *levain*, adapted from Fr. *levain*, in same sense, from Lat. *levamen*, which is only found in the sense of alleviation, comfort, *levare*, to lift up), a substance which produces fermentation, particularly in the making of bread, properly a portion of already fermented dough added to other dough for this purpose (see Bread). The word is used figuratively of any element, influence or agency which effects a subtle or secret change. These figurative usages are mainly due to the comparison of the kingdom of Heaven to leaven in Matt. xiii. 33, and to the warning against the leaven of the Pharisees in Matt. xvi. 6. In the first example the word is used of a good influence, but the more usual significance is that of an evil agency. There was among the Hebrews an association of the idea of fermentation and corruption, which may have been one source of the prohibition of the use of leavened bread in sacrificial offerings. For the usage of unleavened bread at the feasts of the Passover and of Massôth, and the connexion of the two, see Passover.

LEAVENWORTH, a city and the county-seat of Leavenworth county, Kansas, U.S.A., on the W. bank of the Missouri river.

[illegible] were foreign-born and 2925 [illegible] It is one of the most [illegible] the Missouri river, being [illegible] & Santa Fé, the Chicago, Bur- [illegible] Rock Island & Pacific, the [illegible] Missouri Pacific, the Union Pacific [illegible] railways. The city is laid out [illegible] the river, and its streets are [illegible] rolling hills surround it on three [illegible] public buildings, and contains [illegible] Leavenworth being [illegible] The public institutions [illegible] Protective Home (1880) for negroes, [illegible] Vincent's Orphans' Asylum (1886, [illegible] Angels' Home (1889), for [illegible] by the state; also St John's [illegible] and Leavenworth [illegible] training schools for nurses. There [illegible] Home for Disabled Volunteer [illegible] are the state and United States [illegible] trading centre and has various [illegible] foundry and machine [illegible] products, and furniture. The [illegible] in value from $3,251,460 in [illegible] There are valuable coal [illegible] immediate vicinity. About [illegible] about 6000 acres, is Fort [illegible] United States military post, [illegible] National Cemetery and Service [illegible] in 1881 as the U.S. Infantry [illegible] into a General Service [illegible] were three general divisions [illegible] the Line, for officers (not [illegible] regular army and for militia [illegible] their respective states [illegible] military art, engineering, law [illegible] also open to regular [illegible] of field signalling, [illegible] languages; and the Army [illegible] are the highest graduates [illegible] the course of instruction [illegible] art, engineering, law, [illegible] one year in each [illegible] bronze statue [illegible] A military prison was [illegible] it was used as a civil [illegible] as a military [illegible] various trades, but [illegible] this system was [illegible] employed in work on

[illegible] was built in 1827, [illegible]

[illegible] The both a[illegible] are best [illegible]

The [illegible] inclined [illegible] shanks t[illegible]

Coal-ta[illegible] as they d[illegible] an iron [illegible] operation [illegible] sometimes, [illegible] necessary to [illegible] and cheaply [illegible] dressed for [illegible] already desc[illegible] dye; they are [illegible] a hot solution [illegible] through a wa[illegible]

chalk or limestone which form the characteristic feature of the whole range), in its widest sense is the central mountain mass of Syria, extending for about 100 m. from N.N.E. to S.S.W. It is bounded W. by the sea, N. by the plain Jun Akkar, beyond which rise the mountains of the Ansarieh, and E. by the inland plateau of Syria, mainly steppe-land. To the south Lebanon ends about the point where the river Litany bends westward, and at Banias. A valley narrowing towards its southern end, and now called the Buka'a, divides the mountainous mass into two great parts. That lying to the west is still called Jebel Libnan; the greater part of the eastern mass now bears the name of the Eastern Mountain (Jebel el-Sharḳi). In Greek the western range was called Libanos, the eastern Antilibanos. The southern extension of the latter, Mount Hermon (*q.v.*), may in many respects be treated as a separate mountain.

Lebanon and Anti-Lebanon have many features in common; in both the southern portion is less arid and barren than the northern, the western valleys better wooded and more fertile than the eastern. In general the main elevations of the two ranges form pairs lying opposite one another; the forms of both ranges are monotonous, but the colouring is splendid, especially when viewed from a distance; when seen close at hand only a few valleys with perennial streams offer pictures of landscape beauty, their rich green contrasting pleasantly with the bare brown and yellow mountain sides. The finest scenery is found in N. Lebanon, in the Maronite districts of Kesrawan and Bsherreh, where the gorges are veritable canyons, and the villages are often very picturesquely situated. The south of the chain is more open and undulating. Anti-Lebanon is the barest and most inhospitable part of the system.

The district west of Lebanon, averaging about 20 m. in breadth, slopes in an intricate series of plateaus and terraces to the Mediterranean. The coast is for the most part abrupt and rocky, often leaving room for only a narrow path along the shore, and when viewed from the sea it does not suggest the extent of country lying between its cliffs and the lofty summits behind. Most of the mountain spurs run from east to west, but in northern Lebanon the prevailing direction of the valleys is north-westerly, and in the south some ridges run parallel with the principal chain. The valleys have for the most part been deeply excavated by mountain streams; the apparently inaccessible heights are crowned by numerous villages, castles or cloisters embosomed among trees. The chief perennial streams, beginning from the north, are the Nahr Akkar, N. Arka, N. el-Barid, N. Radisha, "the holy river" (the valley of which begins in the immediate neighbourhood of the highest summits, and rapidly descends in a series of great bends till the river reaches the sea at Tripoli), Wadi el-Joz (falling into the sea at Batrun), Wadi Fidar, Nahr Ibrahim (the ancient Adonis, having its source in a recess of the great mountain amphitheatre where the famous sanctuary Apheca, the modern Afka, lay), Nahr el-Kelb (the ancient Lycus), Nahr Beirut (the ancient Magoras, entering the sea at Beirut), Nahr Damur (ancient Tamyras), Nahr el-'Auwali (the ancient Bostrenus, which in the upper part of its course is joined by the Nahr el-Baruk). The 'Auwali and the Nahr el-Zaherani, the only other considerable streams before we reach the Litany, flow north-east to south-west, in consequence of the interposition of a ridge subordinate and parallel to the central chain. On the north, where the mountain bears the special name of Jebel Akkar, the main ridge of Lebanon rises gradually from the plain. A number of valleys run to the north and north-east, among them that of the Nahr el-Kebir, the Eleutherus of the ancients, which rises in the Jebel el-Abiaḍ on the eastern slope of Lebanon, and afterwards, skirting the district, flows westward to the sea. South of Jebel el-Abiaḍ, beneath the main ridge, which as a rule falls away suddenly towards the east, occur several small elevated terraces having a southward slope; among these are the Wadi en-Nusur ("vale of eagles"), and the basin of the lake Yammuna, with its intermittent spring Neb'a el-Arba'in. Of the streams which descend into the Buka'a, the Berdani rises in Jebel Sunnin, and enters the plain by a deep and picturesque mountain cleft at Zaḥleh.

The most elevated summits occur in the north, but even these are of very gentle gradient. The "Cedar block" consists of a double line of four and three summits respectively, ranged from north to south, with a deviation of about 35°. Those to the east are 'Uyun Urghush, Makmal, Muskiyya (or Naba' esh-Shemaila) and Ras Zahr el-Kazib; fronting the sea are Ḳarn Sauda or Timarun, Fumm el-Mizab and Zahr el-Ḳandil. The height of Zahr el-Kazib, by barometric measurement, is 10,018 ft.; that of the others does not reach 10,000 ft. South from them is the pass (8351 ft.) which leads from Baalbek to Tripoli; the great mountain amphitheatre on the west side of its summit is remarkable. Farther south is a second group of lofty summits—the snow-capped Sunnin, visible from Beirut; its height is 8482 ft. Between this group and the more southerly Jebel Keniseh (about 6700 ft.) lies the pass (4700 ft.) traversed by the French post road between Beirut and Damascus. Among the bare summits still farther south are the long ridge of Jebel el-Baruk (about 7000 ft.), the Jebel Niha, with the Tau'amat Niha (about 6100 ft.), near which is a pass to Sidon, and the Jebel Rihan (about 5400 ft.).

The Buka'a, the broad valley which separates Lebanon from Anti-Lebanon, is watered by two rivers having their watershed near Baalbek, at an elevation of about 3600 ft., and separated only by a short mile at their sources. That flowing northwards, El-'Asi, is the ancient Orontes (*q.v.*); the other is the Litany. In the lower part of its course the latter has scooped out a deep and narrow rocky bed; at Burghuz it is spanned by a great natural bridge. Not far from the point where it suddenly trends to the west lie, immediately above the romantic valley, at an elevation of 1500 ft., the imposing ruins of the old castle Kal'at esh-Shakif, near one of the passes to Sidon. In its lower part the Litany bears the name of Nahr el-Kasimiya. Neither the Orontes nor the Litany has any important affluent.

The Buka'a used to be known as Coelesyria (Strabo. xvi. 2, 21); but that word as employed by the ancients had a much more extensive application. At present its full name is Buka'a el-'Aziz (the dear Buka'a), and its northern portion is known as Sahlet Ba'albek (the plain of Baalbek). The valley is from 4 to 6 m. broad, with an undulating surface.

The Anti-Lebanon chain has been less fully explored than that of Lebanon. Apart from its southern offshoots it is 67 m. long, while its width varies from 16 to 13½ m. It rises from the plain of Hasya-Homs, and in its northern portion is very arid. The range has not so many offshoots as occur on the west side of Lebanon; under its precipitous slopes stretch table-lands and broad plateaus, which, especially on the east side looking towards the steppe, steadily increase in width. Along the western side of northern Anti-Lebanon stretches the Khasha'a, a rough red region lined with juniper trees, a succession of the hardest limestone crests and ridges, bristling with bare rock and crag that shelter tufts of vegetation, and are divided by a succession of grassy ravines. On the eastern side the parallel valley of 'Asal el-Ward deserves special mention: the descent towards the plain eastwards, as seen for example at Ma'lula, is singular—first a spacious amphitheatre and then two deep very narrow gorges. Few perennial streams take their rise in Anti-Lebanon; one of the finest and best watered valleys is that of Helbun, the ancient Chalybon, the Helbon of Ezek. xxvii. 18. The highest points of the range, reckoning from the north, are Halimat el-Kabu (8257 ft.), which has a splendid view; the Fatli block, including Tal'at Musa (8721 ft.) and the adjoining Jebel Nebi Baruh (7900 ft.); and a third group near Bludan, in which the most prominent names are Shakif, Akhyar and Abu'l-Hin (8330 ft.). Of the valleys descending westward the first to claim mention is the Wadi Yafufa; a little farther south, lying north and south, is the rich upland valley of Zebedani, where the Barada has its highest sources. Pursuing an easterly course, this stream receives the waters of the romantic 'Ain Fije (which doubles its volume), and bursts out by a rocky gateway upon the plain of Damascus, in the irrigation of which it is the chief agent. It is the Abana of 2 Kings v. 12; the portion of Anti-Lebanon traversed by it was also called by the same name (Canticles iv. 8). From the point where the southerly continuation of Anti-Lebanon begins to take a more westerly direction, a low ridge shoots out towards the south-west, trending farther and farther away from the eastern chain and narrowing the Buka'a; upon the eastern side of this ridge lies the elevated valley or hilly stretch known as Wadi et-Teim. In the north, beside 'Ain Faluj, it is connected by a low watershed with the Buka'a; from the gorge of the Litany it is separated by the ridge of Jebel ed-Dahr. At its southern end it contracts and merges into the plain of Banias, thus enclosing Mount Hermon on its north-west and west sides; eastward from the Hasbany branch of the Jordan lies the meadow-land Merj 'Iyun, the ancient Ijon (1 Kings xv. 20).

Vegetation.—The western slope of Lebanon has the common characteristics of the flora of the Mediterranean coast, but the Anti-Lebanon belongs to the poorer region of the steppes, and the Mediterranean species are met with only sporadically along the water-courses. Forest and pasture land do not properly exist: the place of the first is for the most part taken by a low brushwood; grass is not plentiful, and the higher ridges maintain alpine plants only so long as patches of snow continue to lie. The rock walls harbour some rock plants, but many absolutely barren wildernesses of stone occur. (1) On the western slope, to a height of 1600 ft., is the coast region, similar to that of Syria in general and of the south of Asia Minor. Characteristic trees are the locust tree and the stone pine; in *Melia Azedarach* and *Ficus Sycomorus* (Beirut) is an admixture of foreign and partially subtropical elements. The great mass of the vegetation, however is of the low-growing type (*maquis* or *garrigue* of the western Mediterranean), with small and stiff leaves, and frequently thorny and aromatic, as for example the ilex (*Quercus coccifera*), *Smilax*, *Cistus*, *Lentiscus*, *Calycotome*, &c. (2) Next comes, from 1600 to 6500 ft., the mountain region, which may also be called the forest region, still exhibiting sparse woods and isolated trees wherever shelter, moisture and the inhabitants have permitted their growth. From 1600 to 3200 ft. is a zone of dwarf hard-leaved oaks, amongst which occur the Oriental forms *Fontanesia phillyraeoides*, *Acer syriacum* and the beautiful red-stemmed *Arbutus Andrachne*. Higher up, between 3700 and 4200 ft., a tall pine, *Pinus Brutia*, is characteristic. Between 4200 and 6200 ft. is the region of the two most interesting forest trees of Lebanon, the cypress and the cedar. The former still grows thickly, especially in the valley of the Kadisha; the horizontal is the prevailing variety. In the upper Kadisha valley there is a cedar grove of about three hundred trees, amongst which five are of gigantic size. (See also CEDAR.) The cypress and cedar zone exhibits a variety of other leaf-bearing and coniferous trees; of the first may be mentioned several oaks—*Quercus subalpina* (Kotschy), *Q. Cerris* and the hop-hornbeam (*Ostrya*); of the second class the rare Cilician silver fir (*Abies cilicica*) may be noticed. Next come the junipers, sometimes attaining the size of trees (*Juniperus excelsa*, *J. rufescens* and, with fruit as large as plums, *J. drupacea*). But the chief ornament of Lebanon is the *Rhododendron ponticum*, with its brilliant purple flower clusters; a peculiar evergreen, *Vinca libanotica*, also adds beauty to this zone. (3) Into the alpine region (6200 to 10,400 ft.) penetrate a few very stunted oaks (*Quercus subalpina*), the junipers already mentioned and a barberry (*Berberis cretica*), which sometimes spreads into close thickets. Then follow the low, dense, prone, pillow-like dwarf bushes, thorny and grey, common to the Oriental highlands—*Astragalus* and the peculiar *Acantholimon*. They are found to within 300 ft. of the highest summits.

Upon the exposed mountain slopes a species of rhubarb (*Rheum Ribes*) is noticeable, and also a vetch (*Vicia canescens*) excellent for sheep. The spring vegetation, which lasts until July, appears to be rich, especially as regards showy plants, such as *Corydalis*, *Gagea*, *Colchicum*, *Puschkinia*, *Geranium*, *Ornithogalum*, &c. The flora of the highest ridges, along the edges of the snow patches, exhibits no forms related to the northern alpine flora, but suggestions of it are found in a *Draba*, an *Androsace*, an *Alsine* and a violet, occurring, however, only in local species. Upon the highest summits are found *Saponaria Pumilio* (resembling our *Silene acaulis*) and varieties of *Galium*, *Euphorbia*, *Astragalus*, *Veronica*, *Jurinea*, *Festuca*, *Scrophularia*, *Geranium*, *Asphodeline*, *Allium*, *Asperula*; and, on the margins of the snow fields, a *Taraxacum* and *Ranunculus demissus*. The alpine flora of Lebanon thus connects itself directly with the Oriental flora of lower altitudes, and is unrelated to the glacial flora of Europe and northern Asia.

Zoology.—There is nothing of special interest about the fauna of Lebanon. Bears are no longer numerous; the panther and the ounce are met with; the wild hog, hyaena, wolf and fox are by no means rare; jackals and gazelles are very common. The polecat and hedgehog also occur. As a rule there are not many birds, but the eagle and the vulture may occasionally be seen; of eatable kinds partridges and wild pigeons are the most abundant.

Population.—In the following sections the Lebanon proper will alone be considered, without reference to Anti-Lebanon, because the peculiar political status of the former range since 1864 has effectually differentiated it; whereas the Anti-Lebanon still forms an integral part of the Ottoman province of Syria (*q.v.*), and neither its population nor its history is readily distinguishable from those of the surrounding districts.

The total population in the Lebanon proper is about 400,000, and is increasing faster than the development of the province will admit. There is consequently much emigration, the Christian surplus going mainly to Egypt, and to America, the Druses to the latter country and to the Hauran. The emigrants to America, however, usually return after making money, build new houses and settle down. The singularly complex population is composed of Christians, Maronites, and Orthodox Eastern and Uniate; of Moslems, both Sunni and Shiah (Metawali); and of Druses.

(*a*) *Maronites* (*q.v.*) form about three-fifths of the whole and have the north of the Mountain almost to themselves, while even in the south, the old Druse stronghold, they are now numerous. Feudalism is practically extinct among them and with the decline of the Druses, and the great stake they have acquired in agriculture, they have laid aside much of their warlike habit together with their arms. Even their instinct of nationality is being sensibly impaired by their gradual assimilation to the Papal Church, whose agents exercise from Beirut an increasing influence on their ecclesiastical elections and church government. They are strong also in the Buka'a, and have colonies in most of the Syrian cities.

(*b*) *Orthodox* Eastern form a little more than one-eighth of the whole, and are strongest in S. Lebanon (Metn and Kurah districts). Syrians by race and Arab-speaking, they are descendants of those "Melkites" who took the side of the Byzantine church in the time of Justinian II. against the Moslems and eventually the Maronites. They are among the most progressive of the Lebanon elements.

(*c*) *Greek Uniats* are less numerous, forming little more than

Pop. (1900) 20
were negroes;
important rai
served by the
lington & Q
Chicago Gre
and the Lea
regularly in
named aft
sides. The
the Cathedr
the see of
include th
an Old La
open to a
negroes—
Hospital
Hospital
is also a
Soldiers
penitent
manufa
shop an
city's f
1900 to
mines
3 m. N.
Leaven
associa
School
and Ca
and St.
of thes
below t
officers
or terri
and lan
and mil
signal e
Staff Co
from the
are inclu
language
school.
of Gener
establish
prison fro
prison. 1
owing to t
discontinu
the militar
The fort
in the India
of the 3rd
the Missour
Missourians
the oldest p
in Kansas b
known as a
Territorial le
and in 1908
On the 3rd of
worth Constit
anti-slavery a
nominally app
submitted to C
War Leavenw
more inland to
gave it immu
important dep
and out of
until

... Their headquarters is ... in Metn and Jezzin, ... They sympathize with ... and, like both, are of

... strongest in Shuf and ... renegades and "Druse" ... Arab extraction and never

... and make about one ... and are strongest ... but found also in the ... Beirut to Acre. They ... but the fact is very ... as the Maronites, ... which did not ... free from those ... own a chief *sheikh*, ... like most heretical ... world, of being ex- ... undoubtedly the case ... of interference. ... Assassins (q.v.) of the ... origin, live about ... outside the limits of ... strong.

... whole and confined ... emigrate or conform ... privileged province ... to compensate for ... Christians; and ... distinctiveness. No ... the remnant of ... assimilated to the ... Maronites, whose ... was largely due to ... now reduced to low ... at their old clan ...

... the usual charac- ... previous independent ... way before strong ... century, and the ... which the purely ... of the mulberry ... many kinds of ... and the Lebanon ... in Asiatic Turkey ... through Beirut ... which crosses S. ... excellent roads and ... deposits of ... the presence of ... Manufactures ... mostly to the ... wines, of which ... beverage. ... will not bear ... is general.

... the time played ... of prehistoric ... dwelt there ... they belonged ... Bible mentions ... Lebanon ... land of Israel, ... Hebrews, by whose ... How far the ... is unknown, the ... jurisdiction ... have much ... period the district ... century, with ... of the province ... the same

independent again; its Christianization had begun with the immigration of Monothelite sectaries, flying from persecution in the Antioch district and Orontes valley. At all times Lebanon has been a place of refuge for unpopular creeds. Large part of the mountaineers took up Monothelism and initiated the national distinction of the Maronites, which begins to emerge in the history of the 7th century. The sectaries, after helping Justinian II. against the caliph Abdalmalik, turned on the emperor and his Orthodox allies, and were named Mardaites (rebels). Islam now began to penetrate S. Lebanon, chiefly by the immigration of various more or less heretical elements, Kurd, Turkoman, Persian and especially Arab, the latter largely after the break-up of the kingdom of Hira; and early in the 11th century these coalesced into a nationality (see DRUSES) under the congenial influence of the Incarnationist creed brought from Cairo by Ismael Darazi and other emissaries of the caliph Hakim and his vizier Hamza. The subsequent history of Lebanon to the middle of the 19th century will be found under DRUSES and MARONITES, and it need only be stated here that Latin influence began to be felt in N. Lebanon during the Frank period of Antioch and Palestine, the Maronites being inclined to take the part of the crusading princes against the Druses and Moslems; but they were still regarded as heretic Monothelites by Abulfaragius (Bar-Hebraeus) at the end of the 13th century; nor is their effectual reconciliation to Rome much older than 1736, the date of the mission sent by the pope Clement XII., which fixed the actual status of their church. An informal French protection had, however, been exercised over them for some time previously, and with it began the feud of Maronites and Druses, the latter incited and spasmodically supported by Ottoman pashas. The feudal organization of both, the one under the house of Khazin, the other under those of Maan and Shehab successively, was in full force during the 17th and 18th centuries; and it was the break-up of this in the first part of the 19th century which produced the anarchy that culminated after 1840 in the civil war. The Druses renounced their Shehab amirs when Beshir al-Kassim openly joined the Maronites in 1841, and the Maronites definitely revolted from the Khazin in 1858. The events of 1860 led to the formation of the privileged Lebanon province, finally constituted in 1864. It should be added, however, that among the Druses of Shuf, feudalism has tended to re-establish itself, and the power is now divided between the Jumblat and Yezbeki families, a leading member of one of which is almost always Ottoman *kaimakam* of the Druses, and locally called *amir*.

The Lebanon has now been constituted a *sanjak* or *mutessarifluk*, dependent directly on the Porte, which acts in this case in consultation with the six great powers. This province extends about 93 m. from N. to S. (from the boundary of the *sanjak* of Tripoli to that of the *casa* of Saida), and has a mean breadth of about 28 m. from one foot of the chain to the other, beginning at the edge of the littoral plain behind Beirut and ending at the W. edge of the Buka'a: but the boundaries are ill-defined, especially on the E. where the original line drawn along the crest of the ridge has not been adhered to, and the mountaineers have encroached on the Buka'a. The Lebanon is under a military governor (*mushir*) who must be a Christian in the service of the sultan, approved by the powers, and has, so far, been chosen from the Roman Catholics owing to the great preponderance of Latin Christians in the province. He resides at Deir al Kamar, an old seat of the Druse amirs. At first appointed for three years, then for ten, his term has been fixed since 1892 at five years, the longer term having aroused the fear of the Porte, lest a personal domination should become established. Under the governor are seven *kaimakams*, all Christians except a Druse in Shuf, and forty-seven *mudirs*, who all depend on the kaimakams except one in the home district of Deir al-Kamar. A central *mejliss* or Council of twelve members is composed of four Maronites, three Druses, one Turk, two Greeks (Orthodox), one Greek Uniate and one Metawali. This was the original proportion, and it has not been altered in spite of the decline of the Druses and increase of the Maronites. The members are elected by the seven cazas. In each *mudirieh* there is also a local *mejliss*. The old feudal and *mukataji* (see DRUSES) jurisdictions are abolished, *i.e.* they often persist under Ottoman forms, and three courts of First Instance, under the *mejliss*, and superior to the petty courts of the *mudirs* and the village *sheikhs*, administer justice. Judges are appointed by the governor, but *sheikhs* by the villages. Commercial cases, and litigation in which strangers are concerned, are carried to Beirut. The police is recruited locally, and no regular troops appear in the province except on special requisition. The taxes are collected directly, and must meet the needs of the province, before any sum is remitted to the Imperial Treasury. The latter has to make deficits good. Ecclesiastical jurisdiction is exercised only over the clergy, and all rights of asylum are abolished.

This constitution has worked well on the whole, the only serious hitches having been due to the tendency of governors-general and *kaimakams* to attempt to supersede the *mejliss* by autocratic action, and to impair the freedom of elections. The attention of the porte was called to these tendencies in 1892 and again in 1902, on the appointments of new governors. Since the last date there has been no complaint. Nothing now remains of the former French predominance in the Lebanon, except a certain influence exerted by the fact that the railway is French, and by the precedence in ecclesiastical functions still accorded by the Maronites to official representatives of France. In the Lebanon, as in N. Albania, the traditional claim of France to protect Roman Catholics in the Ottoman Empire has been greatly impaired by the non-religious character of the Republic. Like Italy, she is now regarded by Eastern Catholics with distrust as an enemy of the Holy Father.

See DRUSES. Also V. Cuinet, *Syrie, Liban et Palestine* (1896); N. Verney and G. Dambmann, *Puissances étrangères en Syrie*, &c. (1900); G. Young, *Corps de droit ottoman*, vol. i. (1905); G. E. Post, *Flora of Syria*, &c. (1896); M. von Oppenheim, *Vom Mittelmeer*, &c. (1899). (A. So.; D. G. H.)

LEBANON, a city of Saint Clair county, Illinois, U.S.A., on Silver Creek, about 24 m. E. of Saint Louis, Missouri. Pop. (1910) 1907. It is served by the Baltimore & Ohio South-Western railroad and by the East Saint Louis & Suburban Electric line. It is situated on a high tableland. Lebanon is the seat of McKendree College, founded by Methodists in 1828 and one of the oldest colleges in the Mississippi valley. It was called Lebanon Seminary until 1830, when the present name was adopted in honour of William McKendree (1757–1835), known as the "Father of Western Methodism," a great preacher, and a bishop of the Methodist Church in 1808–1835, who had endowed the college with 480 acres of land. In 1835 the college was chartered as the "McKendreean College," but in 1839 the present name was again adopted. There are coal mines and excellent farming lands in the vicinity of Lebanon. Among the city's manufactures are flour, planing-mill products, malt liquors, soda and farming implements. The municipality owns and operates its electric-lighting plant. Lebanon was chartered as a city in 1874.

LEBANON, a city and the county-seat of Lebanon county, Pennsylvania, U.S.A., in the fertile Lebanon Valley, about 25 m. E. by N. of Harrisburg. Pop. (1900) 17,628, of whom 618 were foreign-born, (1910 census) 19,240. It is served by the Philadelphia & Reading, the Cornwall and the Cornwall & Lebanon railways. About 5 m. S. of the city are the Cornwall (magnetite) iron mines, from which about 18,000,000 tons of iron ore were taken between 1740 and 1902, and 804,848 tons in 1906. The ore yields about 46% of iron, and contains about 2·5% of sulphur, the roasting of the ores being necessary—ore-roasting kilns are more extensively used here than in any other place in the country. The area of ore exposed is about 4000 ft. long and 400 to 800 ft. wide, and includes three hills; it has been one of the most productive magnetite deposits in the world. Limestone, brownstone and brick-clay also abound in the vicinity; and besides mines and quarries, the city has extensive manufactories of iron, steel, chains, and nuts and bolts. In 1905 its factory products were valued at $6,978,458. The municipality owns and operates its water-works.

The first settlement in the locality was made about 1730, and twenty years later a town was laid out by one of the landowners, George Steitz, and named Steitztown in his honour. About 1760 the town became known as Lebanon, and under this name it was incorporated as a borough in 1821 and chartered as a city in 1885.

LE BARGY, CHARLES GUSTAVE AUGUSTE (1858–), French actor, was born at La Chapelle (Seine). His talent both as a comedian and a serious actor was soon made evident, and he became a member of the Comédie Française, his chief successes being in such plays as *Le Duel*, *L'Énigme*, *Le Marquis de Priola*, *L'Autre Danger* and *Le Dédale*. His wife, Simone le Bargy *née* Benda, an accomplished actress, made her début at the Gymnase in 1902, and in later years had a great success in *La Rafale* and other plays. In 1910 he had differences with the authorities of the Comédie Française and ceased to be a *sociétaire*.

LE BEAU, CHARLES (1701–1778), French historical writer, was born at Paris on the 15th of October 1701, and was educated at the Collège de Sainte-Barbe and the Collège du Plessis; at the latter he remained as a teacher until he obtained the chair of rhetoric in the Collège des Grassins. In 1748 he was admitted a member of the Academy of Inscriptions, and in 1752 he was nominated professor of eloquence in the Collège de France. From 1755 he held the office of perpetual secretary to the Academy of Inscriptions, in which capacity he edited fifteen volumes (from the 25th to the 39th inclusive) of the *Histoire* of that institution. He died at Paris on the 13th of March 1778.

The only work with which the name of Le Beau continues to be associated is his *Histoire du Bas-Empire, en commençant à Constantin le Grand*, in 22 vols. 12mo (Paris, 1756–1779), being a continuation of C. Rollin's *Histoire Romaine* and J. B. L. Crevier's *Histoire des empereurs*. Its usefulness arises entirely from the fact of its being a faithful résumé of the Byzantine historians, for Le Beau had no originality or artistic power of his own. Five volumes were added by H. P. Ameilhon (1781–1811), which brought the work down to the fall of Constantinople. A later edition, under the care of M. de Saint-Martin and afterwards of Brosset, has had the benefit of careful revision throughout, and has received considerable additions from Oriental sources.

See his "Éloge" in vol. xlii. of the *Histoire de l'Académie des Inscriptions* (1786), pp. 190-207.

LEBEAU, JOSEPH (1794–1865), Belgian statesman, was born at Huy on the 3rd of January 1794. He received his early education from an uncle who was parish priest of Hannut, and became a clerk. By dint of economy he raised money to study law at Liége, and was called to the bar in 1819. At Liége he formed a fast friendship with Charles Rogier and Paul Devaux, in conjunction with whom he founded at Liége in 1824 the *Mathieu Laensbergh*, afterwards *Le politique*, a journal which helped to unite the Catholic party with the Liberals in their opposition to the ministry, without manifesting any open disaffection to the Dutch government. Lebeau had not contemplated the separation of Holland and Belgium, but his hand was forced by the revolution. He was sent by his native district to the National Congress, and became minister of foreign affairs in March 1831 during the interim regency of Surlet de Chokier. By proposing the election of Leopold of Saxe-Coburg as king of the Belgians he secured a benevolent attitude on the part of Great Britain, but the restoration to Holland of part of the duchies of Limburg and Luxemburg provoked a heated opposition to the treaty of London, and Lebeau was accused of treachery to Belgian interests. He resigned the direction of foreign affairs on the accession of King Leopold, but in the next year became minister of justice. He was elected deputy for Brussels in 1833, and retained his seat until 1848. Differences with the king led to his retirement in 1834. He was subsequently governor of the province of Namur (1838), ambassador to the Frankfort diet (1839), and in 1840 he formed a short-lived Liberal ministry. From this time he held no office of state, though he continued his energetic support of liberal and anti-clerical measures. He died at Huy on the 19th of March 1865.

Lebeau published *La Belgique depuis 1847* (Brussels, 4 vols., 1852). *Lettres aux électeurs belges* (8 vols., Brussels, 1853–1856). His *Souvenirs personnels et correspondance diplomatique 1824–1841* (Brussels, 1883) were edited by A. Fréson. See an article by A. Fréson in the *Biographie nationale de Belgique*; and T. Juste, *Joseph Lebeau* (Brussels, 1865).

LEBEL, JEAN (d. 1370), Belgian chronicler, was born near the end of the 13th century. His father, Gilles le Beal des Changes, was an alderman of Liége. Jean entered the church and became a canon of the cathedral church, but he and his brother Henri followed Jean de Beaumont to England in 1327, and took part in the border warfare against the Scots. His will is dated 1369, and his epitaph gives the date of his death as 1370. Nothing more is known of his life, but Jacques de Hemricourt, author of the *Miroir des nobles de Hesbaye*, has left a eulogy of his character, and a description of the magnificence of his attire, his retinue and his hospitality. Hemricourt asserts that he was eighty years old or more when he died. For a long time Jean Lebel (or le Bel) was only known as a chronicler through a reference by Froissart, who quotes him in the prologue of his first book as one of his authorities. A fragment of his work, [illegible] was dis- [illegible] preserved in [illegible] by L. [illegible] a desire to [illegible] the wars of [illegible] to the [illegible] the matter of style [illegible] of Froissart. [illegible] either he [illegible] from. This scrupulous- [illegible] against his imita- [illegible] to Froissart's; [illegible] or politics; and, [illegible] general notion [illegible] into a series [illegible] Froissart was considerably [illegible] from him some [illegible] Robert the Bruce, [illegible] and the devotion [illegible] in the art of [illegible] an expert,

[illegible] le Bel (1863); [illegible] de Bruges, [illegible] de Géographie nationale

[illegible] (1780–1859), French [illegible] on the 8th of [illegible] Jean of Arc (1804); [illegible] général synthétique, [illegible] M. de Gérando, then [illegible] the interior. The latter [illegible] which left him leisure [illegible] to Italy when Napoleon [illegible] the Roman states [illegible] Leber however did [illegible] attacks on the temporal [illegible]. On his return to [illegible] work. Literary recreations [illegible] a part of his time [illegible] he began to collect old [illegible] historians. His office [illegible], and Leber put his [illegible]. When the question [illegible] he wrote, as an answer [illegible] *cérémonies du sacre*, which [illegible] coronation of Charles X. To- [illegible] there was a movement [illegible] municipal liberties, [illegible] system of centraliza- [illegible], an *Histoire critique* [illegible] *de la monarchie jusqu'à* [illegible] treatise entitled *De l'état* [illegible] *François Ier jusqu'à* [illegible] an empty paradox [illegible] prove that the press had [illegible] free as under the Grand [illegible] retired (1839), and sold to [illegible] of books which he had [illegible]. The catalogue he made [illegible] he read at the Académie [illegible] dissertations, an "Essai [illegible] au moyen âge," followed by [illegible] du marc d'argent depuis [illegible] were included by the [illegible] *présentés par divers savants* [illegible] and published by Leber [illegible] work, and assure him [illegible] history of France. He [illegible] by the publication of [illegible], *notices et traités relatifs* [illegible] 1840); in the absence of [illegible], an analytical table of contents is to be found in Alfred Franklin's *Sources de l'histoire de France* (1876, pp. 342 sqq.). In consequence of the revolution of 1848, Leber decided to leave Paris. He retired to his native town, and spent his last years in collecting old engravings. He died at Orléans on the 22nd of December 1859.

In 1832 he had been elected as a member of the *Société des Antiquaires de France*, and in the *Bulletin* of this society (vol. i., 1860) is to be found the most correct and detailed account of his life's works.

LEBEUF, JEAN (1687–1760), French historian, was born on the 7th of March 1687 at Auxerre, where his father, a councillor in the parlement, was *receveur des consignations*. He began his studies in his native town, and continued them in Paris at the Collège Ste Barbe. He soon became known as one of the most cultivated minds of his time. He made himself master of practically every branch of medieval learning, and had a thorough knowledge of the sources and the bibliography of his subject. His learning was not drawn from books only; he was also an archaeologist, and frequently went on expeditions in France, always on foot, in the course of which he examined the monuments of architecture and sculpture, as well as the libraries, and collected a number of notes and sketches. He was in correspondence with all the most learned men of the day. His correspondence with Président Bouhier was published in 1885 by Ernest Petit; his other letters have been edited by the *Société des sciences historiques et naturelles de l'Yonne* (2 vols., 1866–1867). He also wrote numerous articles, and, after his election as a member of the Académie des Inscriptions et Belles-Lettres (1740), a number of *Mémoires* which appeared in the *Recueil* of this society. He died at Paris on the 10th of April 1760. His most important researches had Paris as their subject.

He published first a collection of *Dissertations sur l'histoire civile et ecclésiastique de Paris* (3 vols., 1739–1743), then an *Histoire de la ville et de tout le diocèse de Paris* (15 vols., 1745–1760), which is a mine of information, mostly taken from the original sources. In view of the advance made by scholarship in the 19th century, it was found necessary to publish a second edition. The work of reprinting it was undertaken by H. Cocheris, but was interrupted (1863) before the completion of vol. iv. Adrien Augier resumed the work, giving Lebeuf's text, though correcting the numerous typographical errors of the original edition (5 vols., 1883), and added a sixth volume containing an analytical table of contents. Finally, Fernand Bournon completed the work by a volume of *Rectifications et additions* (1890), worthy to appear side by side with the original work.

The bibliography of Lebeuf's writings is, partly, in various numbers of the *Bibliothèque des écrivains de Bourgogne* (1716–1741). His biography is given by Lebeau in the *Histoire de l'Académie royale des Inscriptions* (xxix., 372, published 1764), and by H. Cocheris, in the preface to his edition.

LE BLANC, NICOLAS (1742–1806), French chemist, was born at Issoudun, Indre, in 1742. He made medicine his profession and in 1780 became surgeon to the duke of Orleans, but he also paid much attention to chemistry. About 1787 he was attracted to the urgent problem of manufacturing carbonate of soda from ordinary sea-salt. The suggestion made in 1789 by Jean Claude de la Métherie (1743–1817), the editor of the *Journal de physique*, that this might be done by calcining with charcoal the sulphate of soda formed from salt by the action of oil of vitriol, did not succeed in practice because the product was almost entirely sulphide of soda, but it gave Le Blanc, as he himself acknowledged, a basis upon which to work. He soon made the crucial discovery—which proved the foundation of the huge industry of artificial alkali manufacture—that the desired end was to be attained by adding a proportion of chalk to the mixture of charcoal and sulphate of soda. Having had the soundness of this method tested by Jean Darcet (1725–1801), the professor of chemistry at the Collège de France, the duke of Orleans in June 1791 agreed to furnish a sum of 200,000 francs for the purpose of exploiting it. In the following September Le Blanc was granted a patent for fifteen years, and shortly afterwards a factory was started at Saint-Denis, near Paris. But it had not long been in operation when the Revolution led to the confiscation of the duke's property, including the factory, and about the same time the Committee of Public Safety called upon all citizens who possessed soda-factories to disclose their situation and capacity and the nature of the methods employed. Le Blanc had no choice but to reveal the secrets of his process, and he had the misfortune to see his factory dismantled and his stocks of raw and finished materials sold. By way of compensation for the loss of his rights, the works were handed back to him in 1800, but all his efforts to obtain money enough to restore them and resume manufacturing on a profitable scale were vain, and, worn out with disappointment, he died by his own hand at Saint-Denis on the 16th of January 1806.

Four years after his death, Michel Jean Jacques Dizé (1764–1852), who had been *préparateur* to Darcet at the time he examined the process and who was subsequently associated with Le Blanc in its exploitation, published in the *Journal de physique* a paper claiming that it was he himself who had first suggested the addition of chalk; but a committee of the French Academy, which reported fully on the question in 1856, came to the conclusion that the merit was entirely Le Blanc's (*Com. rend.*, 1856, p. 553).

LE BLANC, a town of central France, capital of an arrondissement, in the department of Indre, 44 m. W.S.W. of Châteauroux on the Orléans railway between Argenton and Poitiers. Pop. (1906) 4719. The Creuse divides it into a lower and an upper town. The church of St Génitour dates from the 12th, 13th and 15th centuries, and there is an old castle restored in modern times. It is the seat of a subprefect, and has a tribunal of first instance and a communal college. Wool-spinning, and the manufacture of linen goods and edge-tools are among the industries. There is trade in horses and in the agricultural and other products of the surrounding region.

Le Blanc, which is identified with the Roman *Oblincum*, was in the middle ages a lordship belonging to the house of Naillac and a frontier fortress of the province of Berry.

LEBŒUF, EDMOND (1809–1888), marshal of France, was born at Paris on the 5th of November 1809, passed through the École Polytechnique and the school of Metz, and distinguished himself as an artillery officer in Algerian warfare, becoming colonel in 1852. He commanded the artillery of the 1st French corps at the siege of Sebastopol, and was promoted in 1854 to the rank of general of brigade, and in 1857 to that of general of division. In the Italian War of 1859 he commanded the artillery, and by his action at Solferino materially assisted in achieving the victory. In September 1866, having in the meantime become aide-de-camp to Napoleon III., he was despatched to Venetia to hand over that province to Victor Emmanuel. In 1869, on the death of Marshal Niel, General Lebœuf became minister of war, and earned public approbation by his vigorous reorganization of the War Office and the civil departments of the service. In the spring of 1870 he received the marshal's baton. On the declaration of war with Germany Marshal Lebœuf delivered himself in the Corps Législatif of the historic saying, "So ready are we, that if the war lasts two years, not a gaiter button would be found wanting." It may be that he intended this to mean that, given time, the reorganization of the War Office would be perfected through experience, but the result inevitably caused it to be regarded as a mere boast, though it is now known that the administrative confusion on the frontier in July 1870 was far less serious than was supposed at the time. Lebœuf took part in the Lorraine campaign, at first as chief of staff (major-general) of the Army of the Rhine, and afterwards, when Bazaine became commander-in-chief, as chief of the III. corps, which he led in the battles around Metz. He distinguished himself, whenever engaged, by personal bravery and good leadership. Shut up with Bazaine in Metz, on its fall he was confined as a prisoner in Germany. On the conclusion of peace he returned to France and gave evidence before the commission of inquiry into the surrender of that stronghold, when he strongly denounced Bazaine. After this he retired into private life to the Château du Moncel near Argentan, where he died on the 7th of June 1888.

LE BON, JOSEPH (1765–1795), French politician, was born at Arras on the 29th of September 1765. He became a priest in the order of the Oratory, and professor of rhetoric at Beaune. He adopted revolutionary ideas, and became a curé of the Constitutional Church in the department of Pas-de-Calais, where he was later elected as a *député suppléant* to the Convention. He became *maire* of Arras and *administrateur* of Pas-de-Calais, and on the 2nd of July 1793 took his seat in the Convention. He was sent as a representative on missions into the departments of the Somme and Pas-de-Calais, where he showed great severity in dealing with offences against revolutionaries (8th Brumaire, year II. to 22nd Messidor, year II.; *i.e.* 29th October 1793 to 10th July 1794). In consequence, during the reaction which followed the 9th Thermidor (27th July 1794) he was arrested on the 22nd Messidor, year III. (10th July 1795). He was tried before the criminal tribunal of the Somme, condemned to death for abuse of his power during his mission, and executed at Amiens on the 24th Vendémiaire in the year IV. (10th October 1795). Whatever Le Bon's offences, his condemnation was to a great extent due to the violent attacks of one of his political enemies, Armand Guffroy; and it is only just to remember that it was owing to his courage that Cambrai was saved from falling into the hands of the Austrians.

His son, Émile le Bon, published a *Histoire de Joseph le Bon et des tribunaux révolutionnaires d'Arras et de Cambrai* (2nd ed., 2 vols., Arras, 1864).

LEBRIJA, or Lebrixa, a town of southern Spain, in the province of Seville, near the left bank of the Guadalquivir, and on the eastern edge of the marshes known as Las Marismas. Pop. (1900) 10,997. Lebrija is 44 m. S. by W. of Seville, on the Seville-Cadiz railway. Its chief buildings are a ruined Moorish castle and the parish church, an imposing structure in a variety of styles—Moorish, Gothic, Romanesque—dating from the 14th century to the 16th, and containing some early specimens of the carving of Alonso Cano (1601–1667). There are manufactures of bricks, tiles and earthenware, for which clay is found in the neighbourhood; and some trade in grain, wine and oil.

Lebrija is the *Nabrissa* or *Nebrissa*, surnamed *Veneria*, of the Romans; by Silius Italicus (iii. 393), who connects it with the worship of Dionysus, the name is derived from the Greek νεβρίς (a "fawn-skin," associated with Dionysiac ritual). *Nebriskah* was a strong and populous place during the period of Moorish domination (from 711); it was taken by St Ferdinand in 1249, but again lost, and became finally subject to the Castilian crown only under Alphonso the Wise in 1264. It was the birthplace of Elio Antonio de Lebrija or Nebrija (1444–1522), better known as Nebrissensis, one of the most important leaders in the revival of learning in Spain, the tutor of Queen Isabella, and a collaborator with Cardinal Jimenes in the preparation of the Complutensian Polyglot (see Alcala de Henares).

LE BRUN, CHARLES (1619–1690), French painter, was born at Paris on the 24th of February 1619, and attracted the notice of Chancellor Séguier, who placed him at the age of eleven in the studio of Vouet. At fifteen he received commissions from Cardinal Richelieu, in the execution of which he displayed an ability which obtained the generous commendations of Poussin, in whose company Le Brun started for Rome in 1642. In Rome he remained four years in the receipt of a pension due to the liberality of the chancellor. On his return to Paris Le Brun found numerous patrons, of whom Superintendent Fouquet was the most important. Employed at Vaux le Vicomte, Le Brun ingratiated himself with Mazarin, then secretly pitting Colbert against Fouquet. Colbert also promptly recognized Le Brun's powers of organization, and attached him to his interests. Together they founded the Academy of Painting and Sculpture (1648), and the Academy of France at Rome (1666), and gave a new development to the industrial arts. In 1660 they established the Gobelins, which at first was a great school for the manufacture, not of tapestries only, but of every class of furniture required in the royal palaces. Commanding the industrial arts through the Gobelins—of which he was director—and the whole artist world through the Academy—in which he successively held every post—Le Brun imprinted his own character on all that was produced in France during his lifetime, and gave a direction to the national tendencies which endured after his death. The nature of his emphatic and pompous talent was in harmony with the taste of the king, who, full of admiration at the decorations designed by Le Brun for his triumphal entry into Paris (1660), commissioned him to execute [illegible] from the history of Alexander. The first [illegible] Alexander and the Family of Darius," so delighted [illegible] he at once ennobled Le Brun (December, 1662), [illegible] created first painter to his majesty with a pension [illegible] the same amount as he had yearly received [illegible] the magnificent Fouquet. From this date all [illegible] the royal palaces was directed by Le Brun. [illegible] of the gallery of Apollo in the Louvre were interrupted [illegible] accompanied the king to Flanders (on his return [illegible] several compositions in the Château of [illegible] they remained unfinished at [illegible] Versailles, where he reserved [illegible] War and Peace, the Ambassadors' [illegible] other artists being forced [illegible] At the death of Colbert, [illegible] department of public works, [illegible] and in spite of the king's con[illegible] change in his position. This [illegible] of February 1690 [illegible] Besides his gigantic labours [illegible] his works for religious [illegible] enormous. He modelled [illegible] of the heaviness [illegible] his extraordinary activity [illegible] his claim to fame. [illegible] reproduced by celebrated

[illegible] duc de Plaisance (1739– [illegible] St-Sauveur-Lendelin [illegible] made his first [illegible] the posts successively [illegible] general of the domains [illegible] the chief advisers of [illegible] his struggle against the [illegible] He then devoted [illegible] at the Revolution [illegible] which [illegible] events would [illegible] he sat as deputy [illegible] the proposer [illegible] of the [illegible] a deputy [illegible] of the 18th [illegible] Lebrun was [illegible]

[illegible] fo[illegible] for[illegible] wa[illegible] wh[illegible] not[illegible] pro[illegible] Par[illegible] and[illegible] writ[illegible] essa[illegible] was [illegible] literar[illegible] of the [illegible] to Vol[illegible] was pu[illegible] wards [illegible] of publ[illegible] he und[illegible] tion, an[illegible] *du pouv*[illegible] *nos jour*[illegible] *réel de la* [illegible] *Louis XI*[illegible] of Charles [illegible] never bee[illegible] Monarch. [illegible] the library [illegible] amassed du[illegible] himself (4 v[illegible] des Inscript[illegible] sur l'apprécia[illegible] an "Examen [illegible] l'époque de S[illegible] Academy in [illegible] (vol. i., 1844). [illegible] (1847). They [illegible] a position of e[illegible] also rendered g[illegible] his *Collection des* [illegible] *à l'histoire de F*[illegible] an index, since [illegible]

author a pension of 1200 francs. Lebrun's plays, once famous, are now forgotten. They are: *Ulysse* (1814), *Marie Stuart* (1820), which obtained a great success, and *Le Cid d'Andalousie* (1825). Lebrun visited Greece in 1820, and on his return to Paris he published in 1822 an ode on the death of Napoleon which cost him his pension. In 1825 he was the guest of Sir Walter Scott at Abbotsford. The coronation of Charles X. in that year inspired the verses entitled *La Vallée de Champrosay*, which have, perhaps, done more to secure his fame than his more ambitious attempts. In 1828 appeared his most important poem, *La Grèce*, and in the same year he was elected to the Academy. The revolution of 1830 opened up for him a public career; in 1831 he was made director of the Imprimerie Royale, and subsequently filled with distinction other public offices, becoming senator in 1853. He died on the 27th of May 1873.

See Sainte-Beuve, *Portraits contemporains*, vol. ii.

LEBRUN, PONCE DENIS ÉCOUCHARD (1729–1807), French lyric poet, was born in Paris on the 11th of August 1729, in the house of the prince de Conti, to whom his father was valet. Young Lebrun had among his schoolfellows a son of Louis Racine whose disciple he became. In 1755 he published an *Ode sur les désastres de Lisbon*. In 1759 he married Marie Anne de Surcourt, addressed in his *Élégies* as Fanny. To the early years of his marriage belongs his poem *Nature*. His wife suffered much from his violent temper, and when in 1774 she brought an action against him to obtain a separation, she was supported by Lebrun's own mother and sister. He had been *secrétaire des commandements* to the prince de Conti, and on his patron's death was deprived of his occupation. He suffered a further misfortune in the loss of his capital by the bankruptcy of the prince de Guémené. To this period belongs a long poem, the *Veillées des Muses*, which remained unfinished, and his ode to Buffon, which ranks among his best works. Dependent on government pensions he changed his politics with the times. Calonne he compared to the great Sully, and Louis XVI. to Henry IV., but the Terror nevertheless found in him its official poet. He occupied rooms in the Louvre, and fulfilled his obligations by shameless attacks on the unfortunate king and queen. His excellent ode on the *Vengeur* and the *Ode nationale contre Angleterre* on the occasion of the projected invasion of England are in honour of the power of Napoleon. This "versatility" has so much injured Lebrun's reputation that it is difficult to appreciate his real merit. He had a genius for epigram, and the quatrains and dizaines directed against his many enemies have a verve generally lacking in his odes. The one directed against La Harpe is called by Sainte-Beuve the "queen of epigrams." La Harpe has said that the poet, called by his friends, perhaps with a spice of irony, Lebrun-Pindare, had written many fine strophes but not one good ode. The critic exposed mercilessly the obscurities and unlucky images which occur even in the ode to Buffon, and advised the author to imitate the simplicity and energy that adorned Buffon's prose. Lebrun died in Paris on the 31st of August 1807.

His works were published by his friend P. L. Ginguené in 1811. The best of them are included in Prosper Poitevin's "*Petits poètes français*," which forms part of the "*Panthéon littéraire*."

LE CARON, HENRI (whose real name was THOMAS MILLER BEACH) (1841–18[illegible]), British secret service agent, was born at Colchester, on the 26th of September 1841. He was of an adventurous character, and when nineteen years old went to Paris, where he found employment in business connected with America. Infected with the excitement of the American Civil War he crossed the Atlantic in 1861 and enlisted in the Northern army, taking the name of Henri Le Caron. In 1864 he married [illegible] who had helped him to escape from some Confederate [illegible] and by the end of the war he rose to be major. [illegible] through a companion in arms named O'Neill, he was [illegible] contact with Fenianism, and having learnt of the [illegible] plot against Canada, he mentioned the designs when writing home to his father. Mr Beach told his local M.P., who [illegible] told the Home Secretary, and the latter asked Mr Beach [illegible] further information. Le Caron, inspired (as all [illegible] shows) by genuinely patriotic feeling, from that time till 1889 acted for the British government as a paid military spy. He was a proficient in medicine, among other qualifications for this post, and he remained for years on intimate terms with the most extreme men in the Fenian organization under all its forms. His services enabled the British government to take measures which led to the fiasco of the Canadian invasion of 1870 and Riel's surrender in 1871, and he supplied full details concerning the various Irish-American associations, in which he himself was a prominent member. He was in the secrets of the "new departure" in 1879–1881, and in the latter year had an interview with Parnell at the House of Commons, when the Irish leader spoke sympathetically of an armed revolution in Ireland. For twenty-five years he lived at Detroit and other places in America, paying occasional visits to Europe, and all the time carrying his life in his hand. The Parnell Commission of 1889 put an end to this. Le Caron was subpoenaed by *The Times*, and in the witness-box the whole story came out, all the efforts of Sir Charles Russell in cross-examination failing to shake his testimony, or to impair the impression of iron tenacity and absolute truthfulness which his bearing conveyed. His career, however, for good or evil, was at an end. He published the story of his life, *Twenty-five Years in the Secret Service*, and it had an immense circulation. But he had to be constantly guarded, his acquaintances were hampered from seeing him, and he was the victim of a painful disease, of which he died on the 1st of April 1894. The report of the Parnell Commission is his monument.

LE CATEAU, or CATEAU-CAMBRÉSIS, a town of northern France, in the department of Nord, on the Selle, 15 m E.S.E. of Cambrai by road. Pop. (1906) 10,400. A church of the early 17th century and a town-hall in the Renaissance style are its chief buildings. Its institutions include a board of trade-arbitration and a communal college, and its most important industries are wool-spinning and weaving. Formed by the union of the two villages of Péronne and Vendelgies, under the protection of a castle built by the bishop of Cambrai, Le Cateau became the seat of an abbey in the 11th century. In the 15th it was frequently taken and retaken, and in 1556 it was burned by the French, who in 1559 signed a celebrated treaty with Spain in the town. It was finally ceded to France by the peace of Nijmwegen in 1678.

LECCE (anc. *Lupiae*), a town and archiepiscopal see of Apulia, Italy, capital of the province of Lecce, 24 m. S.E. of Brindisi by rail. Pop. (1906) 35,179. The town is remarkable for the number of buildings of the 17th century, in the rococo style, which it contains; among these are the cathedral of S. Oronzo, and the churches of S. Chiara, S. Croce, S. Domenico, &c., the Seminario, and the Prefettura (the latter contains a museum, with a collection of Greek vases, &c.). Buildings of an earlier period are not numerous, but the fine portal of the Romanesque church of SS. Nicola e Cataldo, built by Tancred in 1180, may be noted. Another old church is S. Maria di Cerrate, near the town. Lecce contains a large government tobacco factory, and is the centre of a fertile agricultural district. To the E. 7½ m. is the small harbour of S. Cataldo, reached by electric tramway. Lecce is quite close to the site of the ancient Lupiae, equidistant (25 m.) from Brundusium and Hydruntum, remains of which are mentioned as existing up to the 15th century. A colony was founded there in Roman times, and Hadrian made a harbour—no doubt at S. Cataldo. Hardly a mile west was Rudiae, the birthplace of the poet Ennius, spoken of by Silius Italicus as worthy of mention for that reason alone. Its site was marked by the now deserted village of Rugge. The name Lycea, or Lycia, begins to appear in the 6th century. The city was for some time held by counts of Norman blood, among whom the most noteworthy is Bohemond, son of Robert Guiscard. It afterwards passed to the Orsini. The rank of provincial capital was bestowed by Ferdinand of Aragon in acknowledgment of the fidelity of Lecce to his cause. (T. As.)

See M. S. Briggs, *In the Heel of Italy* (1910).

LECCO, a town of Lombardy, in the province of Como, 32 m. by rail N. by E. of Milan, and reached by steamer from Como, 673 ft. above sea-level. Pop. (1901) 10,352 It is situated near the southern extremity of the eastern branch of the Lake of Como, which is frequently distinguished as the Lake of Lecco. At Lecco begins the line (run by electricity) to Colico, whence there are branches to Chiavenna and Sondrio, and another line runs to Bergamo. To the south the Adda is crossed by a fine bridge originally constructed in 1335, and rebuilt in 1609 by Fuentes. Lecco, in spite of its antiquity, presents a modern appearance, almost the only old building being its castle, of which a part remains. Its schools are particularly good Besides iron-works, there are copper-works, brass-foundries, olive-oil mills and a manufacture of wax candles; and silk-spinning, cotton-spinning and wood-carving. In the neighbourhood is the villa of Caleotto, the residence of Alessandro Manzoni, who in his *Promessi Sposi* has left a full description of the district. A statue has been erected to him.

In the 11th century Lecco, previously the seat of a marquisate, was presented to the bishops of Como by Otto II.; but in the 12th century it passed to the archbishops of Milan, and in 1127 it assisted the Milanese in the destruction of Como. During the 13th century it was struggling for its existence with the metropolitan city; and its fate seemed to be sealed when the Visconti drove its inhabitants across the lake to Valmadrera, and forbade them to raise their town from its ashes. But in a few years the people returned; Azzone Visconti made Lecco a strong fortress, and in 1335 united it with the Milanese territory by a bridge across the Adda. During the 15th and 16th centuries the citadel of Lecco was an object of endless contention. In 1647 the town with its territory was made a countship. Morone, Charles V.'s Italian chancellor, was born in Lecco.

See A. L. Apostolo, *Lecco ed il suo territorio* (Lecco, 1855).

LECH (*Licus*), a river of Germany in the kingdom of Bavaria, 177 m. long, with a drainage basin of 2550 sq. m. It rises in the Vorarlberg Alps, at an altitude of 6120 ft. It winds out of the gloomy limestone mountains, flows in a north-north-easterly direction, and enters the plains at Füssen (2580 ft.), where it forms rapids and a fall, then pursues a northerly course past Augsburg, where it receives the Wertach, and joins the Danube from the right just below Donauwörth (1330 ft.). It is not navigable, owing to its torrential character and the gravel beds which choke its channel. More than once great historic events have been decided upon its banks. On the Lechfeld, a stony waste some miles long, between the Lech and the Wertach, the emperor Otto I. defeated the Hungarians in August 955. Tilly, in attempting to defend the passage of the stream at Rain against the forces of Gustavus Adolphus, was fatally wounded, on the 5th of April 1632. The river was formerly the boundary between Bavaria and Swabia.

LE CHAMBON, or LE CHAMBON-FEUGEROLLES, a town of east-central France in the department of Loire, 7½ m. S.W. of St Étienne by rail, on the Ondaine, a tributary of the Loire. Pop. (1906) town, 7525; commune, 12,011. Coal is mined in the neighbourhood, and there are forges, steel works, manufactures of tools and other iron goods, and silk mills. The feudal castle of Feugerolles on a hill to the south-east dates in part from the 11th century.

Between Le Chambon and St Étienne is La Ricamarie (pop. of town 5289) also of importance for its coal-mines. Many of the galleries of a number of these mines are on fire, probably from spontaneous combustion. According to popular tradition these fires date from the time of the Saracens; more authentically from the 15th century.

LE CHAPELIER, ISAAC RENÉ GUY (1754–1794), French politician, was born at Rennes on the 12th of June 1754, his father being *bâtonnier* of the corporation of lawyers in that town. He entered his father's profession, and had some success as an orator. In 1789 he was elected as a deputy to the States General by the Tiers-État of the *sénéchaussée* of Rennes. He adopted advanced opinions, and was one of the founders of the Breton Club (see JACOBIN CLUB); his influence in the Constituent Assembly was considerable, and on the 3rd of August 1789 he was elected its president. Thus he presided over the Assembly during the important period following the 4th of August, he took an active part in the debates, and was a leading member of the committee which drew up the new constitution, he further presented a report on the liberty of theatres and on literary copyright. He was also conspicuous as opposing Robespierre when he proposed that members of the Constituent Assembly should not be eligible for election to the proposed new Assembly. After the flight of the king to Varennes (20th of June 1791), his opinions became more moderate, and on the 29th of September he brought forward a motion to restrict the action of the clubs. This, together with a visit which he paid to England in 1792 made him suspect, and he was denounced on his return for conspiring with foreign nations. He went into hiding, but was discovered in consequence of a pamphlet which he published to defend himself, arrested and condemned to death by the Revolutionary Tribunal. He was executed at Paris on the 22nd of April 1794.

See A. Aulard, *Les Orateurs de la constituante* (2nd ed., Paris, 1905); R. Kerviler, *Récherches et notices sur les députés de la Bretagne aux états généraux* (2 vols., Rennes, 1888–1889); P. J. Levot, *Biographie bretonne* (2 vols., 1853–1857).

LECHLER, GOTTHARD VICTOR (1811–1888), German Lutheran theologian, was born on the 18th of April 1811 at Kloster Reichenbach in Württemberg. He studied at Tübingen under F. C. Baur, and became in 1858 pastor of the church of St Thomas, professor ordinarius of historical theology and superintendent of the Lutheran church of Leipzig. He died on the 26th of December 1888. A disciple of Neander, he belonged to the extreme right of the school of mediating theologians. He is important as the historian of early Christianity and of the pre-Reformation period. Although F. C. Baur was his teacher, he did not attach himself to the Tübingen school, in reply to the contention that there are traces of a sharp conflict between two parties, Paulinists and Petrinists, he says that "we find variety coupled with agreement, and unity with difference, between Paul and the earlier apostles; we recognize the *one* spirit in the many gifts." His *Das apostolische und das nachapostolische Zeitalter* (1851), which developed out of a prize essay (1849), passed through three editions in Germany (3rd ed., 1885), and was translated into English (2 vols., 1886). The work which in his own opinion was his greatest, *Johann von Wiclif und die Vorgeschichte der Reformation* (2 vols., 1873), appeared in English with the title *John Wiclif and his English Precursors* (1878, new ed., 1884). An earlier work, *Geschichte des engl. Deismus* (1841), is still regarded as a valuable contribution to the study of religious thought in England.

Lechler's other works include *Geschichte der Presbyterial- und Synodal-verfassung* (1854), *Urkundenfunde zur Geschichte des christl. Altertums* (1886), and biographies of Thomas Bradwardine (1862) and Robert Grosseteste (1867). He wrote part of the commentary on the Acts of the Apostles in J. P. Lange's *Bibelwerk*. From 1882 he edited with F. W. Dibelius the *Beiträge zur sächsischen Kirchengeschichte*. *Johannes Hus* (1890) was published after his death.

LECKY, WILLIAM EDWARD HARTPOLE (1838–1903), Irish historian and publicist, was born at Newtown Park, near Dublin, on the 26th of March 1838, being the eldest son of John Hartpole Lecky, whose family had for many generations been landowners in Ireland. He was educated at Kingstown, Armagh, and Cheltenham College, and at Trinity College, Dublin, where he graduated B.A. in 1859 and M.A. in 1863, and where, with a view to becoming a clergyman in the Irish Protestant Church, he went through a course of divinity. In 1860 he published anonymously a small book entitled *The Religious Tendencies of the Age*, but on leaving college he abandoned his first intention and turned to historical work. In 1861 he published *Leaders of Public Opinion in Ireland*, a brief sketch of the lives and work of Swift, Flood, Grattan and O'Connell, which gave decided promise of his later admirable work in the same field. This book, originally published anonymously, was republished in 1871; and the essay on Swift, rewritten and amplified, appeared again in 1897 as an introduction to a new edition of Swift's works. Two learned surveys of certain aspects of history followed: *A History of the Rise and Influence of Rationalism in Europe* (2 vols., 1865), and *A History of European Morals from Augustus to Charlemagne* (2 vols., 1869) Some criticism was aroused by these books, especially by the last named, with its opening dissertation on "the natural history of morals," but both have been generally accepted as acute and suggestive commentaries upon a wide range of facts. Lecky then devoted himself to the chief work of his life, *A History of England during the Eighteenth Century*, vols. i. and ii. of which appeared in 1878, and vols. vii. and viii. (completing the work) in 1890. His object was "to disengage from the great mass of facts those which relate to the permanent forces of the nation, or which indicate some of the more enduring features of national life," and in the carrying out of this task Lecky displays many of the qualities of a great historian. The work is distinguished by the lucidity of its style, but the fulness and extent of the authorities referred to, and, above all, by the judicial impartiality maintained by the author throughout. These qualities are perhaps most conspicuous and most valuable in the chapters which deal with the history of Ireland, and in the cabinet edition of 1892, in 12 vols. (frequently reprinted) this part of the work is separated from the rest, and occupies five volumes under the title of *A History of Ireland in the Eighteenth Century*. A volume of *Poems*, published in 1891, was characterized by a certain frigidity and by occasional lapses into commonplace, objections which may also be fairly urged against much of Lecky's prose-writing. In 1896 he published two volumes entitled *Democracy and Liberty*, in which he considered, with special reference to Great Britain, France and America, some of the tendencies of modern democracies. The somewhat gloomy conclusions at which he arrived provoked much criticism both in Great Britain and America, which was renewed when he published in a new edition (1899) an elaborate and very depreciatory estimate of Gladstone, then recently dead. This work, though essentially different from the author's purely historical writings, has many of their merits, though it was inevitable that other minds should take a different view of the evidence. In *The Map of Life* (1900) he discussed in a popular style some of the ethical problems which arise in everyday life. In 1903 he published a revised and greatly enlarged edition of *Leaders of Public Opinion in Ireland*, in two volumes, from which the essay on Swift was omitted and that on O'Connell was expanded into a complete biography of the great advocate of repeal of the Union. Though always a keen sympathiser with the Irish people in their misfortunes and aspirations, and though he had criticized severely the methods by which the Act of Union was passed, Lecky, who grew up as a moderate Liberal, was from the first strenuously opposed to Gladstone's policy of Home Rule, and in 1895 he was returned to parliament as Unionist member for Dublin University. In 1897 he was made a privy councillor, and among the coronation honours in 1902 he was nominated an original member of the new Order of Merit. His university honours included the degree of LL.D. from Dublin, St Andrews and Glasgow, the degree of D.C.L. from Oxford and the degree of Litt.D. from Cambridge. In 1894 he was elected corresponding member of the Institute of France. He contributed occasionally to periodical literature, and two of his addresses, *The Political Value of History* (1892) and *The Empire, its Value and its Growth* (1893), were published. He died in London on the 22nd of October 1903. He married in 1871 Elisabeth, baroness de Dedem, daughter of baron de Dedem, a general in the Dutch service, but had no children. Mrs Lecky contributed to various reviews a number of articles, chiefly on historical and political subjects. A volume of Lecky's *Historical and Political Essays* was published posthumously (London, 1908).

LE CLERC [Clericus], **JEAN** (1657–1736), French Protestant theologian, was born on the 19th of March 1657 at Geneva, where his father, Stephen Le Clerc, was professor of Greek. The family originally belonged to the neighbourhood of Beauvais in France, and several of its members acquired some name in literature. Jean Le Clerc applied himself to the study of philosophy under J. R. Chouet (1642–1731) the Cartesian, and attended the theological lectures of P. Mestrezat, Franz Turretin and Louis Tronchin (1629–1705). In 1678–1679 he spent some time at Grenoble as tutor in a private family; on his return to Geneva he passed his examinations and received ordination. Soon afterwards he went to Saumur, where in 1679 were published *Liberii de Sancto Amore Epistolae Theologicae* (Irenopoli: Typis Philalethianis), usually attributed to him; they deal with the doctrine of the Trinity, the hypostatic union of the two natures in Jesus Christ, original sin, and the like, in a manner sufficiently far removed from that of the conventional orthodoxy of the period. In 1682 he went to London, where he remained six months, preaching on alternate Sundays in the Walloon church and in the Savoy chapel. Passing to Amsterdam he was introduced to John Locke and to Philip v. Limborch, professor at the Remonstrant college; the acquaintance with Limborch soon ripened into a close friendship, which strengthened his preference for the Remonstrant theology, already favourably known to him by the writings of his grand-uncle, Stephan Curcellaeus (d. 1645) and by those of Simon Episcopius. A last attempt to live at Geneva, made at the request of relatives there, satisfied him that the theological atmosphere was uncongenial, and in 1684 he finally settled at Amsterdam, first as a moderately successful preacher, until ecclesiastical jealousy shut him out from that career, and afterwards as professor of philosophy, belles-lettres and Hebrew in the Remonstrant seminary. This appointment, which he owed to Limborch, he held from 1684, and in 1712 on the death of his friend he was called to occupy the chair of church history also. His suspected Socinianism was the cause, it is said, of his exclusion from the chair of dogmatic theology. Apart from his literary labours, Le Clerc's life at Amsterdam was uneventful. In 1691 he married a daughter of Gregorio Leti. From 1728 onward he was subject to repeated strokes of paralysis, and he died on the 8th of January 1736.

A full catalogue of the publications of Le Clerc will be found, with biographical material, in E. and E. Haag's *France Protestante* (where seventy-three works are enumerated), or in J. G. de Chauffepié's *Dictionnaire*. Only the most important of these can be mentioned here. In 1685 he published *Sentimens de quelques théologiens de Hollande sur l'histoire critique du Vieux Testament composée par le P. Richard Simon*, in which, while pointing out what he believed to be the faults of that author, he undertook to make some positive contributions towards a right understanding of the Bible. Among these last may be noted his argument against the Mosaic authorship of the Pentateuch, his views as to the manner in which the five books were composed, his opinions (singularly free for the time in which he lived) on the subject of inspiration in general, and particularly as to the inspiration of Job, Proverbs, Ecclesiastes, Canticles. Richard Simon's *Réponse* (1686) elicited from Le Clerc a *Défense des sentimens* in the same year, which was followed by a new *Réponse* (1687). In 1692 appeared his *Logica sive Ars Ratiocinandi*, and also *Ontologia et Pneumatologia*; these, with the *Physica* (1695), are incorporated with the *Opera Philosophica*, which have passed through several editions. In 1693 his series of Biblical commentaries began with that on Genesis; the series was not completed until 1731. The portion relating to the New Testament books included the paraphrase and notes of Henry Hammond (1605–1660). Le Clerc's commentary had a great influence in breaking up traditional prejudices and showing the necessity for a more scientific inquiry into the origin and meaning of the biblical books. It was on all sides hotly attacked. His *Ars Critica* appeared in 1696, and, in continuation, *Epistolae Criticae et Ecclesiasticae* in 1700. Le Clerc's new edition of the *Apostolic Fathers* of Johann Cotelerius (1627–1686), published in 1698, marked an advance in the critical study of these documents. But the greatest literary influence of Le Clerc was probably that which he exercised over his contemporaries by means of the serials, or, if one may so call them, reviews, of which he was editor. These were the *Bibliothèque universelle et historique* (Amsterdam, 25 vols. 12 mo., 1686–1693), begun with J. C. de la Croze; the *Bibliothèque choisie* (Amsterdam, 28 vols., 1703–1713); and the *Bibliothèque ancienne et moderne*, (29 vols., 1714–1726).

See Le Clerc's *Parrhasiana ou pensées sur des matières de critique, d'histoire, de morale, et de politique: avec la défense de divers ouvrages de M. L. C. par Théodore Parrhase* (Amsterdam, 1699); and *Vita et opera ad annum MDCCXI., amici ejus opusculum, philosophicis Clerici operibus subjiciendum*, also attributed to himself. The supplement to Hammond's notes was translated into English in 1699, *Parrhasiana, or Thoughts on Several Subjects*, in 1700, the *Harmony of the Gospels* in 1701, and *Twelve Dissertations out of M. Le Clerc's Genesis* in 1696.

LECOCQ, ALEXANDRE CHARLES (1832–), French musical composer, was born in Paris, on the 3rd of June 1832. He was admitted into the Conservatoire in 1849, being already an accomplished pianist. He studied under Bazin, Halévy and Benoist, winning the first prize for harmony in 1850, and the second prize for fugue in 1852. He first gained notice by dividing with Bizet the first prize for an operetta in a competition instituted by Offenbach. His operetta, *Le Docteur miracle*, was performed at the Bouffes Parisiens in 1857. After that he wrote constantly for theatres, but produced nothing worthy of mention until *Fleur de thé* (1868), which ran for more than a hundred nights. *Les Cent vierges* (1872) was favourably received also, but all his previous successes were cast into the shade by *La Fille de Madame Angot* (Paris, 1873; London, 1873), which was performed for 400 nights consecutively, and has since gained and retained enormous popularity. After 1873 Lecocq produced a large number of comic operas, though he never equalled his early triumph in *La Fille de Madame Angot*. Among the best of his pieces are *Giroflé-Girofla* (Paris and London, 1874); *Les Prés Saint-Gervais* (Paris and London, 1874); *La Petite Mariée* (Paris, 1875; London, 1876, revived as *The Scarlet Feather*, 1897); *Le Petit Duc* (Paris, 1878; London, as *The Little Duke*, 1878); *La Petite Mademoiselle* (Paris, 1879; London, 1880); *Le Jour et la Nuit* (Paris, 1881; London, as *Manola*, 1882); *Le Cœur et la main* (Paris, 1882, London, as *Incognita*, 1893); *La Princesse des Canaries* (Paris, 1883; London, as *Pepita*, 1888). In 1899 a ballet by Lecocq, entitled *Le Cygne*, was staged at the Opéra Comique, Paris; and in 1903 *Yetta* was produced at Brussels.

LECOINTE-PUYRAVEAU, MICHEL MATHIEU (1764–1827), French politician, was born at Saint-Maixent (Deux-Sèvres) on the 13th of December 1764. Deputy for his department to the Legislative Assembly in 1792, and to the Convention in the same year, he voted for "the death of the tyrant." His association with the Girondins nearly involved him in their fall, in spite of his vigorous republicanism. He took part in the revolution of Thermidor, but protested against the establishment of the Directory, and continually pressed for severer measures against the *émigrés*, and even their relations who had remained in France. He was secretary and then president of the Council of Five Hundred, and under the Consulate a member of the Tribunate. He took no part in public affairs under the Empire, but was lieutenant-general of police for south-east France during the Hundred Days. After Waterloo he took ship from Toulon, but the ship was driven back by a storm and he narrowly escaped massacre at Marseilles. After six weeks' imprisonment in the Château d'If he returned to Paris, escaping, after the proscription of the regicides, to Brussels, where he died on the 15th of January 1827.

LE CONTE, JOSEPH (1823–1901), American geologist, of Huguenot descent, was born in Liberty county, Georgia, on the 26th of February 1823. He was educated at Franklin College, Georgia, where he graduated (1841); he afterwards studied medicine and received his degree at the New York College of Physicians and Surgeons in 1845. After practising for three or four years at Macon, Georgia, he entered Harvard, and studied natural history under L. Agassiz. An excursion made with Professors J. Hall and Agassiz to the Helderberg mountains of New York developed a keen interest in geology. After graduating at Harvard, Le Conte in 1851 accompanied Agassiz on an expedition to study the Florida reefs. On his return he became professor of natural science in Oglethorpe University, Georgia, and from 1852 to 1856 professor of natural history and geology in Franklin College. From 1857 to 1869 he was professor of chemistry and geology in South Carolina College, and he was then appointed professor of geology and natural history in the university of California, a post which he held until his death. He published a series of papers on monocular and binocular vision, and also on psychology. His chief contributions, however, related to geology, and in all he wrote he was lucid and philosophical. He described the fissure-eruptions in western America, discoursed on earth-crust movements and their causes and on the great features of the earth's surface. As separate works he published *Elements of Geology* (1878, 5th ed. 1889), *Religion and Science* (1874), and *Evolution: its History, its*

Evidences, and its Relation to Religious Thought (1888). He was president of the American Association for the Advancement of Science in 1892, and of the Geological Society of America in 1896. He died in the Yosemite Valley, California, on the 6th of June 1901.

See Obituary by J. J. Stevenson, *Annals of New York Acad. of Sciences*, vol. xiv. (1902), p. 150.

LECONTE DE LISLE, CHARLES MARIE RENÉ (1818–1894), French poet, was born in the island of Réunion on the 22nd of October 1818. His father, an army surgeon, who brought him up with great severity, sent him to travel in the East Indies with a view to preparing him for a commercial life. After this voyage he went to Rennes to complete his education, studying especially Greek, Italian and history. He returned once or twice to Réunion, but in 1846 settled definitely in Paris. His first volume, *La Vénus de Milo*, attracted to him a number of friends many of whom were passionately devoted to classical literature. In 1873 he was made assistant librarian at the Luxembourg; in 1886 he was elected to the Academy in succession to Victor Hugo. His *Poèmes antiques* appeared in 1852; *Poèmes et poésies* in 1854; *Le Chemin de la croix* in 1859; the *Poèmes barbares*, in their first form, in 1862; *Les Erinnyes*, a tragedy after the Greek model, in 1872; for which occasional music was provided by Jules Massenet; the *Poèmes tragiques* in 1884; *L'Apollonide*, another classical tragedy, in 1888; and two posthumous volumes, *Derniers poèmes* in 1899, and *Premières poésies et lettres intimes* in 1902. In addition to his original work in verse, he published a series of admirable prose translations of Theocritus, Homer, Hesiod, Aeschylus, Sophocles, Euripides, Horace. He died at Voisins, near Louveciennes (Seine-et-Oise), on the 18th of July 1894.

In Leconte de Lisle the Parnassian movement seems to crystallize. His verse is clear, sonorous, dignified, deliberate in movement, classically correct in rhythm, full of exotic local colour, of savage names, of realistic rhetoric. It has its own kind of romance, in its "legend of the ages," so different from Hugo's, so much fuller of scholarship and the historic sense, yet with far less of human pity. Coldness cultivated as a kind of artistic distinction seems to turn all his poetry to marble, in spite of the fire at its heart. Most of Leconte de Lisle's poems are little chill epics, in which legend is fossilized. They have the lofty monotony of a single conception of life and of the universe. He sees the world as what Byron called it, "a glorious blunder," and desires only to stand a little apart from the throng, meditating scornfully. Hope, with him, becomes no more than this desperate certainty:—

> "Tu te tairas, ô voix sinistre des vivants!"

His only prayer is to Death, "divine Death," that it may gather its children to its breast:—

> "Affranchis-nous du temps, du nombre et de l'espace,
> Et rends-nous le repos que la vie a troublé!"

The interval which is his he accepts with something of the defiance of his own Cain, refusing to fill it with the triviality of happiness, waiting even upon beauty with a certain inflexible austerity. He listens and watches, throughout the world, for echoes and glimpses of great tragic passions, languid with fire in the East, a tumultuous conflagration in the middle ages, a sombre darkness in the heroic ages of the North. The burning [illegible] of the desert attracts him, the inexplicable melancholy [illegible] the dogs that bark at the moon; he would interpret the [illegible] dreams, the sleep of the condor. He sees nature with [illegible] wrathful impatience as man, praising it for its destruc[illegible], its haste to crush out human life before the stars [illegible] chaos, and the world with them, as one of the least [illegible] He sings the "Dies Irae" exultingly; only seeming [illegible] end of God as well as of man, universal nothingness. [illegible] that he does well to be angry, and this anger is [illegible] personal note of his pessimism; but it leaves him [illegible] apart from the philosophical poets, too fierce for [illegible] rapturous enough for poetry. (A. Sy.)

[illegible], *Leconte de Lisle intime* (1895); F. Calmette, *Un* [illegible], *Leconte de Lisle et ses amis* (1902); Paul Bourget, *Nouveaux essais de psychologie contemporaine* (1885); F. Brunetière, *L'Évolution de la poésie lyrique en France au XIXe siècle* (1894); Maurice Spronck, *Les Artistes littéraires* (1889); J. Lemaître, *Les Contemporains* (2nd series, 1886); F. Brunetière, *Nouveaux essais sur la litt. contemp.* (1895).

LE COQ, ROBERT (d. 1373), French bishop, was born at Montdidier, although he belonged to a bourgeois family of Orléans, where he first attended school before coming to Paris. In Paris he became advocate to the parlement (1347); then King John appointed him master of requests, and in 1351, a year during which he received many other honours, he became bishop of Laon. At the opening of 1354 he was sent with the cardinal of Boulogne, Pierre I., duke of Bourbon, and Jean VI., count of Vendome, to Mantes to treat with Charles the Bad, king of Navarre, who had caused the constable, Charles of Spain, to be assassinated, and from this time dates his connexion with this king. At the meeting of the estates which opened in Paris in October 1356 Le Coq played a leading rôle and was one of the most outspoken of the orators, especially when petitions were presented to the dauphin Charles, denouncing the bad government of the realm and demanding the banishment of the royal councillors. Soon, however, the credit of the estates having gone down, he withdrew to his diocese, but at the request of the bourgeois of Paris he speedily returned. The king of Navarre had succeeded in escaping from prison and had entered Paris, where his party was in the ascendant; and Robert le Coq became the most powerful person in his council. No one dared to contradict him, and he brought into it whom he pleased. He did not scruple to reveal to the king of Navarre secret deliberations, but his fortune soon turned. He ran great danger at the estates of Compiègne in May 1358, where his dismissal was demanded, and he had to flee to St Denis, where Charles the Bad and Etienne Marcel came to find him. After the death of Marcel, he tried, unsuccessfully, to deliver Laon, his episcopal town, to the king of Navarre, and he was excluded from the amnesty promised in the treaty of Calais (1360) by King John to the partisans of Charles the Bad. His temporalities had been seized, and he was obliged to flee from France. In 1363, thanks to the support of the king of Navarre, he was given the bishopric of Calahorra in the kingdom of Aragon, which he administered until his death in 1373.

See L. C. Douët d'Arcq, "Acte d'accusation contre Robert le Coq, évêque de Laon" in *Bibliothèque de l'Ecole des Chartes*, 1st series, t. ii., pp. 350-387; and R. Delachenal, "La Bibliothèque d'un avocat du XIVe siècle, inventaire estimatif des livres de Robert le Coq," in *Nouvelle revue historique de droit français et étranger* (1887), pp. 524-537.

LECOUVREUR, ADRIENNE (1692–1730), French actress, was born on the 5th of April 1692, at Damery, Marne, the daughter of a hatter, Robert Couvreur. She had an unhappy childhood in Paris. She showed a natural talent for declamation and was instructed by La Grand, *sociétaire* of the Comédie Française, and with his help she obtained a provincial engagement. It was not until 1717, after a long apprenticeship, that she made her Paris début as Electre, in Crébillon's tragedy of that name, and Angélique in Molière's *George Dandin*. Her success was so great that she was immediately received into the Comédie Française, and for thirteen years she was the queen of tragedy there, attaining a popularity never before accorded an actress. She is said to have played no fewer than 1184 times in a hundred rôles, of which she created twenty-two. She owed her success largely to her courage in abandoning the stilted style of elocution of her predecessors for a naturalness of delivery and a touching simplicity of pathos that delighted and moved her public. In Baron, who returned to the stage at the age of sixty-seven, she had an able and powerful coadjutor in changing the stage traditions of generations. The jealousy she aroused was partly due to her social successes, which were many, in spite of the notorious freedom of her manner of life. She was on visiting and dining terms with half the court, and her *salon* was frequented by Voltaire and all the other notables and men of letters. She was the mistress of Maurice de Saxe from 1721, and sold her plate and jewels to supply him with funds for his ill-starred adventures as duke of Courland. By him she had a daughter, her third, who was grandmother of the father of George Sand. Adrienne Lecouvreur died on the 20th of March 1730. She was denied the last rites of the Church, and her remains were refused burial in consecrated ground. Voltaire, in a fine poem on her death, expressed his indignation at the barbarous treatment accorded to the woman whose "friend, admirer, lover" he was.

Her life formed the subject of the well-known tragedy (1849), by Eugène Scribe and Ernest Legouvé.

LE CREUSOT, a town of east-central France in the department of Saône-et-Loire, 55 m. S.W. of Dijon on the Paris-Lyon railway. Pop. (1906), town, 22,535; commune, 33,437. Situated at the foot of lofty hills in a district rich in coal and iron, it has the most extensive iron works in France. The coal bed of Le Creusot was discovered in the 13th century; but it was not till 1774 that the first workshops were founded there. The royal crystal works were transferred from Sèvres to Le Creusot in 1787, but this industry came to an end in 1831. Meanwhile two or three enterprises for the manufacture of metal had ended in failure, and it was only in 1836 that the foundation of iron works by Adolphe and Eugène Schneider definitely inaugurated the industrial prosperity of the place. The works supplied large quantities of war material to the French armies during the Crimean and Franco-German wars. Since that time they have continuously enlarged the scope of their operations, which now embrace the manufacture of steel, armour-plate, guns, ordnance-stores, locomotives, electrical machinery and engineering material of every description. A net-work of railways about 37 m. in length connects the various branches of the works with each other and with the neighbouring Canal du Centre. Special attention is paid to the welfare of the workers who, not including the miners, number about 12,000, and good schools have been established. In 1897 the ordnance-manufacture of the Société des Forges et Chantiers de la Méditerranée at Havre was acquired by the Company, which also has important branches at Chalon-sur-Saône, where ship-building and bridge-construction is carried on, and at Cette (Hérault).

LECTERN (through O. Fr. *leitrun*, from Late Lat. *lectrum*, or *lectrinum*, *legere*, to read; the French equivalent is *lutrin*; Ital. *leggio*; Ger. *Lesepult*), in the furniture of certain Christian churches, a reading-desk, used more especially for the reading of the lessons and in the Anglican Church practically confined to that purpose. In the early Christian Church this was done from the ambo (*q.v.*), but in the 15th century, when the books were often of great size, it became necessary to provide a lectern to hold them. These were either in wood or metal, and many fine examples still exist; one at Detling in wood, in which there are shelves on all four sides to hold books, is perhaps the most elaborate. Brass lecterns, as in the colleges of Oxford and Cambridge, are common; in the usual type the book is supported on the outspread wings of an eagle or pelican, which is raised on a moulded stem, carried on three projecting ledges or feet with lions on them. In the example in Norwich cathedral, the pelican supporting the book stands on a rock enclosed with a rich cresting of Gothic tabernacle work; the central stem or pillar, on which this rests, is supported by miniature projecting buttresses, standing on a moulded base with lions on it.

LECTION, LECTIONARY. The custom of reading the books of Moses in the synagogues on the Sabbath day was a very ancient one in the Jewish Church. The addition of lections (*i.e.* readings) from the prophetic books had been made afterwards and was in existence in our Lord's time, as may be gathered from such passages as St Luke iv. 16-20, xvi. 29. This element in synagogue worship was taken over with others into the Christian divine service, additions being made to it from the writings of the apostles and evangelists. We find traces of such additions within the New Testament itself in such directions as are contained in Col. iv. 16; 1 Thess. v. 27.

From the 2nd century onwards references multiply, though the earlier references do not prove the existence of a fixed lectionary or order of lessons, but rather point the other way. Justin Martyr, describing divine worship in the middle of the 2nd century says: "On the day called Sunday all who live in cities or in the country gather together to one place, and the memoirs of the Apostles, or the writings of the Prophets are read as long as time permits" (*Apol.* i. cap. 67). Tertullian about half a century later makes frequent reference to the reading of Holy Scripture in public worship (*Apol.* 39; *De praescript.* 36; *De anima*, 9).

In the canons of Hippolytus in the first half of the 3rd century we find this direction: "Let presbyters, subdeacons and readers, and all the people assemble daily in the church at time of cock-crow, and betake themselves to prayers, to psalms and to the reading of the Scriptures, according to the command of the Apostles, until I come attend to reading" (canon xxi.).

But there are traces of fixed lessons coming into existence in the course of this century; Origen refers to the book of Job being read in Holy Week (*Commentaries on Job*, lib. i.). Allusions of a similar kind in the 4th century are frequent. John Cassian (*c.* 380) tells us that throughout Egypt the Psalms were divided into groups of twelve, and that after each group there followed two lessons, one from the Old, one from the New Testament (*De caenob. inst.* ii. 4), implying but not absolutely stating that there was a fixed order of such lessons just as there was of the Psalms. St Basil the Great mentions fixed lessons on certain occasions taken from Isaiah, Proverbs, St Matthew and Acts (Hom. xiii. *De bapt.*). From Chrysostom (Hom. lxiii. *in Act.* &c.), and Augustine (Tract. vi. *in Joann.* &c.) we learn that Genesis was read in Lent, Job and Jonah in Passion Week, the Acts of the Apostles in Eastertide, lessons on the Passion on Good Friday and on the Resurrection on Easter Day. In the *Apostolical Constitutions* (ii. 57) the following service is described and enjoined. First come two lessons from the Old Testament by a reader, the whole of the Old Testament being made use of except the books of the Apocrypha. The Psalms of David are then to be sung. Next the Acts of the Apostles and the Epistles of Paul are to be read, and finally the four Gospels by a deacon or a priest. Whether the selections were *ad libitum* or according to a fixed table of lessons we are not informed. Nothing in the shape of a lectionary is extant older than the 8th century, though there is evidence that Claudianus Mamercus made one for the church at Vienne in 450, and that Musaeus made one for the church at Marseilles *c.* 458. The *Liber comitis* formerly attributed to St Jerome must be three, or nearly three, centuries later than that saint, and the Luxeuil lectionary, or *Lectionarium Gallicanum*, which Mabillon attributed to the 7th, cannot be earlier than the 8th century; yet the oldest MSS. of the Gospels have marginal marks, and sometimes actual interpolations, which can only be accounted for as indicating the beginnings and endings of liturgical lessons. The third council of Carthage in 397 forbade anything but Holy Scripture to be read in church; this rule has been adhered to so far as the liturgical epistle and gospel, and occasional additional lessons in the Roman missal are concerned, but in the divine office, on feasts when nine lessons are read at matins, only the first three lessons are taken from Holy Scripture, the next three being taken from the sermons of ecclesiastical writers, and the last three from expositions of the day's gospel; but sometimes the lives or *Passions* of the saints, or of some particular saints, were substituted for any or all of these breviary lessons. (F. E. W.)

LECTISTERNIUM (from Lat. *lectum sternere*, "to spread a couch"; στρωμναί in Dion. Halic. xii. 9), in ancient Rome, a propitiatory ceremony, consisting of a meal offered to gods and goddesses, represented by their busts or statues, or by portable figures of wood, with heads of bronze, wax or marble, and covered with drapery. Another suggestion is that the symbols of the gods consisted of bundles of sacred herbs, tied together in the form of a head, covered by a waxen mask so as to resemble a kind of bust (cf. the straw puppets called Argei). These symbols were laid upon a couch (*lectus*), the left arm resting on a cushion (*pulvinus*, whence the couch itself was often called *pulvinar*) in the attitude of reclining. In front of the couch, which was placed in the open street, a meal was set out on a table. It is definitely stated by Livy (v. 13) that the ceremony took place "for the first time" in Rome in the year

399 B.C., after the Sibylline books had been consulted by their keepers and interpreters (*duumviri sacris faciendis*), on the occasion of a pestilence. Three couches were prepared for three pairs of gods—Apollo and Latona, Hercules and Diana, Mercury and Neptune. The feast, which on that occasion lasted for eight (or seven) days, was also celebrated by private individuals; the citizens kept open house, quarrels were forgotten, debtors and prisoners were released, and everything done to banish sorrow. Similar honours were paid to other divinities in subsequent times—Fortuna, Saturnus, Juno Regina of the Aventine, the three Capitoline deities (Jupiter, Juno, Minerva), and in 217, after the defeat of lake Trasimenus, a lectisternium was held for three days to six pairs of gods, corresponding to the twelve great gods of Olympus—Jupiter, Juno, Neptune, Minerva, Mars, Venus, Apollo, Diana, Vulcan, Vesta, Mercury, Ceres. In 205, alarmed by unfavourable prodigies, the Romans were ordered to fetch the Great Mother of the gods from Pessinus in Phrygia; in the following year the image was brought to Rome, and a lectisternium held. In later times, the lectisternium became of constant (even daily) occurrence, and was celebrated in the different temples. Such celebrations must be distinguished from those which were ordered, like the earlier lectisternia, by the Sibylline books in special emergencies. Although undoubtedly offerings of food were made to the gods in very early Roman times on such occasions as the ceremony of *confarreatio*, and the *epulum Jovis* (often confounded with the lectisternium), it is generally agreed that the lectisternia were of Greek origin. In favour of this may be mentioned: the similarity of the Greek θεοξένια, in which, however, the gods played the part of hosts; the gods associated with it were either previously unknown to Roman religion, though often concealed under Roman names, or were provided with a new cult (thus Hercules was not worshipped as at the Ara Maxima, where, according to Servius on *Aeneid*, viii. 176 and Cornelius Balbus, *ap.* Macrobius, *Sat.* iii. 6, a lectisternium was forbidden); the Sibylline books, which decided whether a lectisternium was to be held or not, were of Greek origin; the custom of reclining at meals was Greek. Some, however, assign an Etruscan origin to the ceremony, the Sibylline books themselves being looked upon as old Italian "black books." A probable explanation of the confusion between the lectisternia and genuine old Italian ceremonies is that, as the lectisternia became an almost everyday occurrence in Rome, people forgot their foreign origin and the circumstances in which they were first introduced, and then the word *pulvinar* with its associations was transferred to times in which it had no existence. In imperial times, according to Tacitus (*Annals*, xv. 44), chairs were substituted for couches in the case of goddesses, and the lectisternium in their case became a sellisternium (the reading, however, is not certain). This was in accordance with Roman custom, since in the earliest times all the members of a family sat at meals, and in later times at least the women and children. This is a point of distinction between the original practice at the lectisternium and the epulum Jovis, the goddesses at the latter being provided with chairs, whereas in the lectisternium they reclined. In Christian times the word was used for a feast in memory of the dead (Sidonius Apollinaris, *Epistulae*, iv. 15).

See article by A. Bouché-Leclercq in Daremberg and Saglio, *Dictionnaire des antiquités*; Marquardt, *Römische Staatsverwaltung*, iii. 45, 187 (1885); G. Wissowa, *Religion und Kultus der Römer*, p. 355 seq.; monograph by Wackermann (Hanau, 1888); C. Pascal, *Studii di antichità e mitologia* (1896).

LECTOR, or READER, a minor office-bearer in the Christian Church. From an early period men have been set apart, under the title of *anagnostae*, *lectores*, or readers, for the purpose of reading Holy Scripture in church. We do not know what the custom of the Church was in the first two centuries, the earliest reference to readers, as an order, occurring in the writings of Tertullian (*De praescript. haeret.* cap. 41); there are frequent allusions to them in the writings of St Cyprian and afterwards. Cornelius, bishop of Rome in A.D. 251–252, in a well-known letter mentions readers among the various church orders then existing at Rome. In the *Apostolic Church Order* (canon 19), mention is made of the qualifications and duties of a reader, but no reference is made to their method of ordination. In the *Apostolic Didascalia* there is recognition of three minor orders of men; subdeacons, readers and singers, in addition to two orders of women, deaconesses and widows. A century later, in the *Apostolic Constitutions*, we find not only a recognition of readers, but also a form of admission provided for them, consisting of the imposition of hands and prayer (lib. viii. cap. 22). In Africa the imposition of hands was not in use, but a Bible was handed to the newly appointed reader with words of commission to read it, followed by a prayer and a benediction (Fourth Council of Carthage, can. 8). This is the ritual of the Roman Church of to-day. With regard to age, the novels of Justinian (No. 123) forbade any one to be admitted to the office of reader under the age of eighteen. (F. E. W.)

LECTOURE, a town of south-western France, capital of an arrondissement in the department of Gers, 21 m. N. of Auch on the Southern railway between that city and Agen. Pop. (1906), town, 2426; commune, 4310. It stands on the right bank of the Gers, overlooking the river from the summit of a steep plateau. The church of St Gervais and St Protais was once a cathedral. The massive tower which flanks it on the north belongs to the 15th century; the rest of the church dates from the 13th, 15th, 16th and 17th centuries. The hôtel de ville, the sous-préfecture and the museum occupy the palace of the former bishops, which was once the property of Marshal Jean Lannes, a native of the town. A recess in the wall of an old house contains the Fontaine de Houndélie, a spring sheltered by a double archway of the 13th century. At the bottom of the hill a church of the 16th century marks the site of the monastery of St Gény. Lectoure has a tribunal of first instance and a communal college. Its industries include distilling, the manufacture of wooden shoes and biscuits, and market gardening; it has trade in grain, cattle, wine and brandy.

Lectoure, capital of the Iberian tribe of the *Lactorates* and for a short time of Novempopulania, became the seat of a bishopric in the 4th century. In the 11th century the counts of Lomagne made it their capital, and on the union of Lomagne with Armagnac, in 1325, it became the capital of the counts of Armagnac. In 1473 Cardinal Jean de Jouffroy besieged the town on behalf of Louis XI. and after its fall put the whole pupulation to the sword. In 1562 it again suffered severely at the hands of the Catholics under Blaise de Montluc.

LEDA, in Greek mythology, daughter of Thestius, king of Aetolia, and Eurythemis (her parentage is variously given). She was the wife of Tyndareus and mother of Castor and Pollux, Clytaemnestra and Helen (see CASTOR AND POLLUX). In another account Nemesis was the mother of Helen (*q.v.*) whom Leda adopted as her daughter. This led to the identification of Leda and Nemesis. In the usual later form of the story, Leda herself, having been visited by Zeus in the form of a swan, produced two eggs, from one of which came Helen, from the other Castor and Pollux.

See Apollodorus iii. 10; Hyginus, *Fab.* 77; Homer, *Iliad*, iii. 426, *Od.* xi. 298; Euripides, *Helena*, 17; Isocrates, *Helena*, 59; Ovid, *Heroides*, xvii. 55; Horace, *Ars poetica*, 147; Stasinus in Athenaeus viii. 334 c.; for the representations of Leda and the swan in art, J. A. Overbeck, *Kunstmythologie*, i., and Atlas to the same; also article in Roscher's *Lexikon der Mythologie*.

LE DAIM (or LE DAIN), **OLIVIER** (d. 1484), favourite of Louis XI. of France, was born of humble parentage at Thielt near Courtrai in Flanders. Seeking his fortune at Paris, he became court barber and valet to Louis XI., and so ingratiated himself with the king that in 1474 he was ennobled under the title Le Daim and in 1477 made comte de Meulant. In the latter year he was sent to Burgundy to influence the young heiress of Charles the Bold, but he was ridiculed and compelled to leave Ghent. He thereupon seized and held Tournai for the French. Le Daim had considerable talent for intrigue, and, according to his enemies, could always be depended upon to execute the baser designs of the king. He amassed a large fortune, largely by oppression and violence, and was named gentleman-in-waiting, captain of Loches, and governor of Saint-Quentin. He remained in favour until the death of Louis XI., when the rebellious lords were able to avenge the slights and insults they had suffered at the hands of the royal barber. He was arrested on charges, the nature of which is uncertain, tried before the parlement of Paris, and on the 21st of May 1484 hanged at Montfaucon without the knowledge of Charles VIII., who might have heeded his father's request and spared the favourite. Le Daim's property was given to the duke of Orleans.

See the memoirs of the time, especially those of Ph. de Commines (ed. Mandrot, 1901–1903, Eng. trans. in Bohn Library); Robt. Gaguin, *Compendium de origine et gestis Francorum* (Paris, 1586)—it was Gaguin who made the celebrated epigram concerning Le Daim: "Eras judex, lector, et exitium"; De Reiffenberg, *Olivier le Dain* (Brussels, 1829); Delanone, *Le Barbier de Louis XI.* (Paris, 1832); G. Picot, "Procès d'Olivier le Dain," in the *Comptes rendus de l'Académie des sciences morales et politiques*, viii. (1877), 485-537. The memoirs of the time are uniformly hostile to Le Daim.

LEDBURY, a market town in the Ross parliamentary division of Herefordshire, England, 14½ m. E. of Hereford by the Great Western railway, pleasantly situated on the south-western slope of the Malvern Hills. Pop. of urban district (1901) 3259. Cider and agricultural produce are the chief articles of trade, and there are limestone quarries in the neighbouring hills. The town contains many picturesque examples of timbered houses, characteristic of the district, the principal being the Market House (1633) elevated on massive pillars of oak. The fine church of St Michael exhibits all the Gothic styles, the most noteworthy features being the Norman chancel and west door, and the remarkable series of ornate Decorated windows on the north side. Among several charities is the hospital of St Catherine, founded by Foliot, bishop of Hereford, in 1232. Hope End, 2 m. N.E. of Ledbury, was the residence of Elizabeth Barrett Browning during her early life. A clock-tower in the town commemorates her.

Wall Hills Camp, supposed to be of British origin, is the earliest evidence of a settlement near Ledbury (Liedeburge, Lidebury). The manor was given to the see of Hereford in the 11th century; but in 1561–1562 became crown property. As early as 1170–1171 an episcopal castle existed in Ledbury. The town was not incorporated, but was early called a borough; and in 1295 and 1304–1305 returned two members to parliament. A fair on the day of the decollation of John the Baptist was granted to the bishop in 1249. Of fairs which survived in 1792 those of the days of St Philip and St James and St Barnabas were granted in 1584–1585; those held on the Monday before Easter and St Thomas's day were reputed ancient, but not those of the 12th of May, the 22nd of June, the 2nd of October and the 21st of December. Existing fairs are on the second Tuesday in every month and in October. A weekly market, granted to the bishop by Stephen, John and Henry III., was obsolete in 1584–1585, when the present market of Tuesday was authorized. The wool trade was considerable in the 14th century; later Ledbury was inhabited by glovers and clothiers. The town was deeply involved in the operations of the Civil Wars, being occupied both by the royalist leader Prince Rupert and by the Parliamentarian Colonel Birch.

LEDGER (from the English dialect forms *liggen* or *leggen*, to lie or lay; in sense adapted from the Dutch substantive *legger*), properly a book remaining regularly in one place, and so used of the copies of the Scriptures and service books kept in a church. The *New English Dictionary* quotes from Charles Wriothesley's *Chronicle*, 1538 (ed. *Camden Soc.*, 1875, by W. D. Hamilton), "the curates should provide a booke of the bible in Englishe, of the largest volume, to be a lidger in the same church for the parishioners to read on." It is an application of this original meaning that is found in the commercial usage of the term for the principal book of account in a business house (see BOOK-KEEPING). Apart from these applications to various forms of books, the word is used of the horizontal timbers in a scaffold (*q.v.*) lying parallel to the face of a building, which support the "put-logs"; of a flat stone to cover a grave; and of a stationary form of tackle and bait in angling. In the form "lieger" the term was formerly frequently applied to a "resident," as distinguished from an "extraordinary" ambassador.

LEDOCHOWSKI, MIECISLAUS JOHANN, COUNT (1822–1902), Polish cardinal, was born on the 29th of October 1822 in Gorki (Russian Poland), and received his early education at the gymnasium and seminary of Warsaw. After finishing his studies at the Jesuit Accademia dei Nobili Ecclesiastici in Rome, which strongly influenced his religious development and his attitude towards church affairs, he was ordained in 1845. From 1856 to 1858 he represented the Roman See in Columbia, but on the outbreak of the Columbian revolution had to return to Rome. In 1861 Pope Pius IX. made him his nuncio at Brussels, and in 1865 he was made archbishop of Gnesen-Posen. His preconization followed on the 8th of January 1866. This date marks the beginning of the second period in Ledochowski's life; for during the Prussian and German *Kulturkampf* he was one of the most declared enemies of the state. It was only during the earliest years of his appointment as archbishop that he entertained a different view, invoking, for instance, an intervention of Prussia in favour of the Roman Church, when it was oppressed by the house of Savoy. On the 12th of December 1870 he presented an effective memorandum on the subject at the headquarters at Versailles. In 1872 the archbishop protested against the demand of the government that religious teaching should be given only in the German language, and in 1873 he addressed a circular letter on this subject to the clergy of his diocese. The government thereupon demanded a statement from the teachers of religion as to whether they intended to obey it or the archbishop, and on their declaring for the archbishop, dismissed them. The count himself was called upon at the end of 1873 to lay aside his office. On his refusing to do so, he was arrested between 3 and 4 o'clock in the morning on the 3rd of February 1874 by Staudi, the director of police, and taken to the military prison of Ostrowo. The pope made him a cardinal on the 13th of March, but it was not till the 3rd of February 1876 that he was released from prison. Having been expelled from the eastern provinces of Prussia, he betook himself to Cracow, where his presence was made the pretext for anti-Prussian demonstrations. Upon this he was also expelled from Austria, and went to Rome, whence, in spite of his removal from office, which was decreed on the 15th of April 1874, he continued to direct the affairs of his diocese, for which he was on several occasions from 1877 to 1879 condemned *in absentia* by the Prussian government for "usurpation of episcopal rights." It was not till 1885 that Ledochowski resolved to resign his archbishopric, in which he was succeeded by Dinder at the end of the year. Ledochowski's return in 1884 was forbidden by the Prussian government (although the *Kulturkampf* had now abated), on account of his having stirred up anew the Polish nationalist agitation. He passed the closing years of his life in Rome. In 1892 he became prefect of the Congregation of the Propaganda, and he died in Rome on the 22nd of July 1902.

See Ograbiszewski, *Deutschlands Episkopat in Lebensbildern* (1876 and following years); Holtzmann-Zöpffel, *Lexikon für Theologie und Kirchenwesen* (2nd ed., 1888); Vapereau, *Dictionnaire universel des contemporains* (6th ed., 1893); Brück, *Geschichte der katholischen Kirche in Deutschland im neunzehnten Jahrhundert* vol. 4 (1901 and 1908); Lauchert, *Biographisches Jahrbuch*, vol. 7 (1905). (J. HN.)

LEDRU-ROLLIN, ALEXANDRE AUGUSTE (1807–1874), French politician, was the grandson of Nicolas Philippe Ledru, the celebrated quack doctor known as "Comus" under Louis XIV., and was born in a house that was once Scarron's, at Fontenay-aux-Roses (Seine), on the 2nd of February 1807. He had just begun to practise at the Parisian bar before the revolution of July, and was retained for the Republican defence in most of the great political trials of the next ten years. In 1838 he bought for 330,000 francs Desiré Dalloz's place in the Court of Cassation. He was elected deputy for Le Mans in 1841 with hardly a dissentient voice; but for the violence of his electoral speeches he was tried at Angers and sentenced to four months' imprisonment and a fine, against which he appealed successfully on a technical point. He made a rich and romantic marriage in 1843, and in 1846 disposed of his charge at the Court of Cassation to give his time entirely to politics. He was now the recognized leader of the working-men of France. He had more authority in the country than in the Chamber, where the violence of his oratory diminished its effect. He asserted that the fortifications of Paris were directed against liberty, not against foreign invasion, and he stigmatized the law of regency (1842) as an audacious usurpation. Neither from official Liberalism nor from the press did he receive support; even the Republican *National* was

[illegible] Boston, [illegible] and [illegible] Virginia, [illegible] Washington, [illegible] University Library are [illegible] *University, Bibliographical* [illegible]

[illegible] American cavalry general, was born at [illegible] in Fairfax county, Virginia, on the 19th [illegible] He was the grandson of "Light Horse [illegible] nephew of Robert E. Lee. His father, [illegible] was [illegible] under Commodore Perry [illegible] to the rank of commodore; his mother was a daughter of George Mason. Graduating from West Point in 1856, he was appointed to the 2nd Cavalry, which was commanded by Colonel Albert Sidney Johnston, and in which his uncle, Robert E. Lee, was lieutenant-colonel. As a cavalry subaltern he distinguished himself by his gallant conduct in actions with the Comanches in Texas, and was severely wounded in 1859. In May 1860 he was appointed instructor of cavalry at West Point, but resigned on the secession of Virginia. Lee was at once employed in the organization of the forces of the South, and served at first as a staff officer to General R. S. Ewell, and afterwards, from September 1861, as lieutenant-colonel, and from April 1862 as colonel of the First Virginia Cavalry in the Army of Northern Virginia. He became brigadier-general on General J. E. B. Stuart's recommendation on the 25th of July 1862, and served under that general throughout the Virginian campaigns of 1862 and 1863, becoming major-general on the 3rd of September 1863. He conducted the cavalry action of Beverly Ford (17th March 1863) with skill and success. In the Wilderness and Petersburg campaigns he was constantly employed as a divisional commander under Stuart, and, after Stuart's death, under General Wade Hampton. He took part in Early's campaign against Sheridan in the Shenandoah Valley, and at Winchester (19th Sept. 1864) three horses were shot under him and he was severely wounded. On General Hampton's being sent to assist General Joseph E. Johnston in North Carolina, the command of the whole of General Lee's cavalry devolved upon Fitzhugh Lee early in 1865, but the surrender of Appomattox followed quickly upon the opening of the campaign. Fitzhugh Lee himself led the last charge of the Confederates on the 9th of April that year at Farmville.

After the war he devoted himself to farming in Stafford county, Virginia, and was conspicuous in his efforts to reconcile the Southern people to the issue of the war, which he regarded as a final settlement of the questions at issue. In 1875 he attended the Bunker Hill centenary at Boston, Mass., and delivered a remarkable address. In 1885 he was a member of the board of visitors of West Point, and from 1886 to 1890 was governor of Virginia. In April 1896 he was appointed by President Cleveland consul-general at Havana, with duties of a diplomatic and military character added to the usual consular business. In this post (in which he was retained by President McKinley) he was from the first called upon to deal with a situation of great difficulty, which culminated with the destruction of the "Maine" (see SPANISH-AMERICAN WAR). Upon the declaration of war between Spain and the United States he re-entered the army. He was one of the three ex-Confederate general officers who were made major-generals of United States Volunteers. Fitzhugh Lee commanded the VII. army corps, but took no part in the actual operations in Cuba. He was military governor of Havana and Pinar del Rio in 1899, subsequently commanded the department of the Missouri, and retired as a brigadier-general U.S. Army in 1901. He died in Washington on the 28th of April 1905. He wrote *Robert E. Lee* (1894) in the "Great Commanders" series, and *Cuba's Struggle Against Spain* (1899).

LEE, GEORGE ALEXANDER (1802–1851), English musician, was born in London, the son of Henry Lee, a pugilist and innkeeper. He became "tiger" to Lord Barrymore, and his singing led to his being educated for the musical profession. After appearing as a tenor at the theatres in Dublin and London, he joined in producing opera at the Tottenham Street theatre in 1829, and afterwards was connected with musical productions at Drury Lane and Covent Garden. He married Mrs Waylett, a popular singer. Lee composed music for a number of plays, and also many songs, including the popular "Come where the Aspens quiver," and for a short time had a music-selling business in the Quadrant. He died on the 8th of October 1851.

LEE, HENRY (1756–1818), American general, called "Light Horse Harry," was born near Dumfries, Virginia, on the 29th of January 1756. His father was first cousin to Richard Henry Lee. With a view to a legal career he graduated (1773) at Princeton, but soon afterwards, on the outbreak of the War of Independence, he became an officer in the patriot forces. He served with great distinction under Washington, and in 1778 was promoted major and given the command of a small irregular corps, with which he won a great reputation as a leader of light troops. His services on the outpost line of the army earned for him the soubriquet of "Light Horse Harry." His greatest exploit was the brilliant surprise of Paulus Hook, N.J., on the 19th of August 1779; for this feat he received a gold medal, a reward given to no other officer below general's rank in the whole war. He was promoted lieutenant-colonel 1780, and sent with a picked corps of dragoons to the southern theatre of war. Here he rendered invaluable services in victory and defeat, notably at Guilford Court House, Camden and Eutaw Springs. He was present at Cornwallis's surrender at Yorktown, and afterwards left the army owing to ill-health. From 1786 to 1788 he was a delegate to the Confederation Congress, and in the last-named year in the Virginia convention he favoured the adoption of the Federal constitution. From 1789 to 1791 he served in the General Assembly, and from 1791 to 1794 was governor of Virginia. In 1794 Washington sent him to help in the suppression of the "Whisky Insurrection" in western Pennsylvania. A new county of Virginia was named after him during his governorship. He was a major-general in 1798–1800. From 1799 to 1801 he served in Congress. He delivered the address on the death of Washington which contained the famous phrase, "first in war, first in peace, and first in the hearts of his countrymen." Soon after the War of 1812 broke out, Lee, while helping to resist the attack of a mob on his friend, A. C. Hanson, editor of the Baltimore *Federal Republican*, which had opposed the war, received grave injuries, from which he never recovered. He died at the house of General Nathanael Greene on Cumberland Island, Georgia, on the 25th of March 1818.

Lee wrote valuable *Memoirs of the War in the Southern Department* (1812; 3rd ed., with memoir by Robert E. Lee, 1869).

LEE, JAMES PRINCE (1804–1869), English divine, was born in London on the 28th of July 1804, and was educated at St Paul's school and at Trinity College, Cambridge, where he displayed exceptional ability as a classical scholar. After taking orders in 1830 he served under Thomas Arnold at Rugby school, and in 1838 was appointed head-master of King Edward's school, Birmingham, where he had among his pupils E. W. Benson, J. B. Lightfoot and B. F. Westcott. In 1848 Lord John Russell nominated him as first bishop of the newly-constituted see of Manchester. His pedagogic manner bore somewhat irksomely on his clergy. He is best remembered for his splendid work in church extension; during his twenty-one years' tenure of the see he consecrated 130 churches. He took a foremost part in founding the Manchester free library, and bequeathed his own valuable collection of books to Owens College. He died on the 24th of December 1869.

A memorial sermon was preached by Archbishop E. W. Benson, and was published with biographical details by J. F. Wickenden and others.

LEE, NATHANIEL (*c.* 1653–1692), English dramatist, son of Dr Richard Lee, a Presbyterian divine, was born probably in 1653. His father was rector of Hatfield, and held many preferments under the Commonwealth. He was chaplain to General Monk, afterwards duke of Albemarle, and after the Restoration he conformed to the Church of England, abjuring his former opinions, especially his approval of Charles I.'s execution. Nathaniel Lee was educated at Westminster school, and at Trinity College, Cambridge, taking his B.A. degree in 1668. Coming to London under the patronage, it is said, of the duke of Buckingham, he tried to earn his living as an actor, but though he was an admirable reader, his acute stage fright made acting impossible. His earliest play, *Nero, Emperor of Rome*, was acted in 1675 at Drury Lane. Two tragedies written in rhymed heroic couplets, in imitation of Dryden, followed in 1676—*Sophonisba, or Hannibal's Overthrow* and *Gloriana, or the Court of Augustus Caesar*. Both are extravagant in design and treatment. Lee made his reputation in 1677 with a blank verse tragedy, *The Rival Queens, or the Death of Alexander the Great*. The play, which treats of the jealousy of Alexander's first wife, Roxana, for his second wife, Statira, was, in spite of much [illegible] English stage down to the days of [illegible] Faustus (acted 1678), [illegible] (acted 1680), *Caesar Borgia* [illegible] worst blood and thunder [illegible] Brutus, *Father of His* [illegible] the Great (acted 1684) [illegible] a gross adaptation of [illegible] of that name. *The* [illegible] was written about this time. [illegible] *Junius Brutus*, [illegible] representation for some [illegible] taken to be a reflection on [illegible] Dryden, who had already [illegible] an adaptation of *Oedipus*, [illegible] which directly advocated [illegible] the *Massacre of Paris* [illegible] years of age, and had [illegible] But he had lived [illegible] Rochester and his associates, [illegible] grew more disreputable, [illegible] his mind was completely [illegible] Bethlehem Hospital, and [illegible] a drunken fit in 1692, and was [illegible] on the 6th of May. [illegible] in 1784. In spite of their [illegible] of great beauty.

[illegible] 1794), American statesman [illegible] in Westmoreland county, [illegible] 1732, and was one of six dis- [illegible] 1750), a descendant of an [illegible] representative of which in America [illegible] member of the privy council, and [illegible] emigrated to Virginia. Richard [illegible] education in England, then [illegible] to Virginia in 1752, having [illegible] property left him by his father, [illegible] himself to varied studies. When [illegible] of the peace of Westmore- [illegible] was chosen a member of the [illegible] in which he served from 1758 to [illegible] during two sessions, his first [illegible] to slavery, which he proposed [illegible] to abolish, by imposing a heavy [illegible] He early allied himself with [illegible] Virginia, and in the years immedi- [illegible] Independence was conspicuous as an [illegible] measures of the British ministry. [illegible] Dickinson of Pennsylvania, he sug- [illegible] among the friends of liberty [illegible] 1773 he became a member of the [illegible] correspondence. [illegible] from Virginia to the first Con- [illegible] Philadelphia in 1774, and prepared the [illegible] America, and the second address [illegible] Britain, which are among the most [illegible] In accordance with instructions [illegible] of Burgesses, Lee introduced in [illegible] 1776, the following famous resolu- [illegible] united colonies are, and of right ought [illegible] states, that they are absolved from [illegible] crown, and that all political con- [illegible] the state of Great Britain is, and ought [illegible] "that it is expedient to take the [illegible] forming foreign alliances"; and [illegible] be prepared and transmitted [illegible] their consideration and approba- [illegible] of these resolutions for three [illegible] the further consideration of it [illegible] of July, but that a committee [illegible] a declaration of independence. [illegible] him from being a member of [illegible] was adopted on the 2nd of July, and the Declaration of Independence, prepared principally by Thomas Jefferson, was adopted two days later. Lee was in Congress from 1774 to 1780, and was especially prominent in connexion with foreign affairs. He was a member of the Virginia House of Delegates in 1777, 1780–1784 and 1786–1787; was in Congress again from 1784 to 1787, being president in 1784–1786; and was one of the first United States senators chosen from Virginia after the adoption of the Federal constitution. Though strongly opposed to the adoption of that constitution, owing to what he regarded as its dangerous infringements upon the independent power of the states, he accepted the place of senator in hope of bringing about amendments, and proposed the Tenth Amendment in substantially the form in which it was adopted. He became a warm supporter of Washington's administration, and his prejudices against the constitution were largely removed by its working in practice. He retired from public life in 1792, and died at Chantilly, in Westmoreland county, on the 19th of June 1794.

See the *Life* (Philadelphia, 1825), by his grandson, R. H. Lee; and *Letters* (New York, 1910), edited by J. C. Ballagh.

His brother, William Lee (1739–1795), was a diplomatist during the War of Independence. He accompanied his brother, Arthur Lee (*q.v.*), to England in 1766 to engage in mercantile pursuits, joined the Wilkes faction, and in 1775 was elected an alderman of London, then a life-position. In April 1777, however, he received notice of his appointment by the Committee of Secret Correspondence in America to act with Thomas Morris as commercial agent at Nantes. He went to Paris and became involved in his brother's opposition to Franklin and Deane. In May 1777 Congress chose William Lee commissioner to the courts of Vienna and Berlin, but he gained recognition at neither. In September 1778, however, while at Aix-la-Chapelle, he negotiated a plan of a treaty with Jan de Neufville, who represented Van Berckel, pensionary of Amsterdam. It was a copy of this proposed treaty which, on falling into the hands of the British on the capture of Henry Laurens, the duly appointed minister to the Netherlands, led to Great Britain's declaration of war against the Netherlands in December 1780. Lee was recalled from his mission to Vienna and Berlin in June 1779, without being required to return to America. He resigned his post as an alderman of London in January 1780, and returned to Virginia about 1784.

See *Letters of William Lee*, edited by W. C. Ford (Brooklyn, 1891).

Another brother, Francis Lightfoot Lee (1734–1797), was a member of the Virginia House of Burgesses in 1770–1775. In 1775–1779 he was a delegate to the Continental Congress, and as such signed the Declaration of Independence. He served on the committee which drafted the Articles of Confederation, and contended that there should be no treaty of peace with Great Britain which did not grant to the United States both the right to the Newfoundland fisheries and the free navigation of the Mississippi. After retiring from Congress he served in 1780–1782 in the Virginia Senate.

LEE, ROBERT EDWARD (1807–1870), American soldier, general in the Confederate States army, was the youngest son of major-general Henry Lee, called "Light Horse Harry." He was born at Stratford, Westmoreland county, Virginia, on the 19th of January 1807, and entered West Point in 1825. Graduating four years later second in his class, he was given a commission in the U.S. Engineer Corps. In 1831 he married Mary, daughter of G. W. P. Custis, the adopted son of Washington and the grandson of Mrs Washington. In 1836 he became first lieutenant, and in 1838 captain. In this rank he took part in the Mexican War, repeatedly winning distinction for conduct and bravery. He received the brevets of major for Cerro Gordo, lieut.-colonel for Contreras-Churubusco and colonel for Chapultepec. After the war he was employed in engineer work at Washington and Baltimore, during which time, as before the war, he resided on the great Arlington estate, near Washington, which had come to him through his wife. In 1852 he was appointed superintendent of West Point, and during his three years here he carried out many important changes in the academy. Under him as cadets were his son G. W. Custis Lee, his nephew, Fitzhugh Lee and J. E. B. Stuart, all of whom became general officers in the Civil War. In 1855 he was appointed as lieut.-colonel to the 2nd Cavalry, commanded by Colonel Sidney Johnston, with whom he served against the Indians of the Texas border. In 1859, while at Arlington on leave, he was summoned to command the United States troops sent to deal with the John Brown raid on Harper's Ferry. In March 1861 he was made colonel of the 1st U.S. Cavalry; but his career in the old army ended with the secession of Virginia in the following month. Lee was strongly averse to secession, but felt obliged to conform to the action of his own state. The Federal authorities offered Lee the command of the field army about to invade the South, which he refused. Resigning his commission, he made his way to Richmond and was at once made a major-general in the Virginian forces. A few weeks later he became a brigadier-general (then the highest rank) in the Confederate service.

The military operations with which the great Civil War opened in 1861 were directed by President Davis and General Lee. Lee was personally in charge of the unsuccessful West Virginian operations in the autumn, and, having been made a full general on the 31st of August, during the winter he devoted his experience as an engineer to the fortification and general defence of the Atlantic coast. Thence, when the well-drilled Army of the Potomac was about to descend upon Richmond, he was hurriedly recalled to Richmond. General Johnston was wounded at the battle of Fair Oaks (Seven Pines) on the 31st of May 1862, and General Robert E. Lee was assigned to the command of the famous Army of Northern Virginia which for the next three years "carried the rebellion on its bayonets." Little can be said of Lee's career as a commander-in-chief that is not an integral part of the history of the Civil War. His first success was the "Seven Days' Battle" (*q.v.*) in which he stopped McClellan's advance; this was quickly followed up by the crushing defeat of the Federal army under Pope, the invasion of Maryland and the sanguinary and indecisive battle of the Antietam (*q.v.*). The year ended with another great victory at Fredericksburg (*q.v.*). Chancellorsville (see Wilderness), won against odds of two to one, and the great three days' battle of Gettysburg (*q.v.*), where for the first time fortune turned decisively against the Confederates, were the chief events of 1863. In the autumn Lee fought a war of manœuvre against General Meade. The tremendous struggle of 1864 between Lee and Grant included the battles of the Wilderness (*q.v.*), Spottsylvania, North Anna, Cold Harbor and the long siege of Petersburg (*q.v.*), in which, almost invariably, Lee was locally successful. But the steady pressure of his unrelenting opponent slowly wore down his strength. At last with not more than one man to oppose to Grant's three he was compelled to break out of his Petersburg lines (April 1865). A series of heavy combats revealed his purpose, and Grant pursued the dwindling remnants of Lee's army to the westward. Headed off by the Federal cavalry, and pressed closely in rear by Grant's main body, General Lee had no alternative but to surrender. At Appomattox Court House, on the 9th of April, the career of the Army of Northern Virginia came to an end. Lee's farewell order was issued on the following day, and within a few weeks the Confederacy was at an end. For a few months Lee lived quietly in Powhatan county, making his formal submission to the Federal authorities and urging on his own people acceptance of the new conditions. In August he was offered, and accepted, the presidency of Washington College, Lexington (now Washington and Lee University), a post which he occupied until his death on the 12th of October 1870 He was buried in the college grounds.

For the events of Lee's military career briefly indicated in this notice the reader is referred to the articles American Civil War, &c. By his achievements he won a high place amongst the great generals of history. Though hampered by lack of materials and by political necessities, his strategy was daring always, and he never hesitated to take the gravest risks. On the field of battle he was as energetic in attack as he was constant in defence, and his personal influence over the men whom he led was extraordinary. No student of the American Civil War can fail to notice how the influence of Lee dominated the course of the struggle, and his surpassing ability was never more conspicuously shown than in the last hopeless stages of the contest. The personal history of Lee is lost in the history of the great crisis of America's national life; friends and foes alike acknowledged the purity of his motives, the virtues of his private life, his earnest Christianity and the unrepining loyalty with which he accepted the ruin of his party.

See A. L. Long, *Memoirs of Robert E. Lee* (New York, 1886); Fitzhugh Lee, *General Lee* (New York, 1894, "Great Commanders" series); R. A. Brock, *General Robert E. Lee* (Washington, 1904); R. E. Lee, *Recollections and Letters of General R. E. Lee* (London, 1904); H. A. White, *Lee* ("Heroes of the Nations") (1897); P. A. Bruce, *Robert E. Lee* (1907); T. N. Page, *Lee* (1909); W. H. Taylor, *Four Years with General Lee*; J. W. Jones, *Personal Reminiscences of Robert E. Lee* (1874).

LEE (or Legh) **ROWLAND** (d. 1543), English bishop, belonged to a Northumberland family and was educated at Cambridge. Having entered the Church he obtained several livings owing to the favour of Cardinal Wolsey; after Wolsey's fall he rose high in the esteem of Henry VIII. and of Thomas Cromwell, serving both king and minister in the business of suppressing the monasteries, and he is said to have celebrated Henry's secret marriage with Anne Boleyn in January 1533. Whether this be so or not, Lee took part in preparing for the divorce proceedings against Catherine of Aragon, and in January 1534 he was elected bishop of Coventry and Lichfield, or Chester as the see was often called, taking at his consecration the new oath to the king as head of the English Church and not seeking confirmation from the pope. As bishop he remained in Henry's personal service, endeavouring to establish the legality of his marriage with Anne, until May 1534, when he was appointed lord president of the council in the marches of Wales. At this time the Welsh marches were in a very disorderly condition. Lee acted in a stern and energetic fashion, holding courts, sentencing many offenders to death and overcoming the hostility of the English border lords. After some years of hard and successful work in this capacity, "the last survivor of the old martial prelates, fitter for harness than for bishops' robes, for a court of justice than a court of theology," died at Shrewsbury in June 1543. Many letters from Lee to Cromwell are preserved in the Record Office, London; these throw much light on the bishop's career and on the lawless condition of the Welsh marches in his time.

One of his contemporaries was Edward Lee (*c.* 1482–1544) archbishop of York, famous for his attack on Erasmus, who replied to him in his *Epistolae aliquot eruditorum virorum.* Like Rowland, Edward was useful to Henry VIII. in the matter of the divorce of Catherine of Aragon, and was sent by the king on embassies to the emperor Charles V. and to Pope Clement VII. In 1531 he became archbishop of York, but he came under suspicion as one who disliked the king's new position as head of the English Church. At Pontefract in 1536, during the Pilgrimage of Grace, the archbishop was compelled to join the rebels, but he did not sympathize with the rising and in 1539 he spoke in parliament in favour of the six articles of religion. Lee, who was the last archbishop of York to coin money, died on the 13th of September 1544.

LEE, SIDNEY (1859–), English man of letters, was born in London on the 5th of December 1859. He was educated at the City of London school, and at Balliol College, Oxford, where he graduated in modern history in 1882. In the next year he became assistant-editor of the *Dictionary of National Biography.* In 1890 he was made joint-editor, and on the retirement of Sir Leslie Stephen in 1891 succeeded him as editor. He was himself a voluminous contributor to the work, writing some 800 articles, mainly on Elizabethan authors or statesmen. While he was still at Balliol he wrote two articles on Shakespearian questions, which were printed in the *Gentleman's Magazine*, and in 1884 he published a book on Stratford-on-Avon. His article on Shakespeare in the fifty-first volume (1897) of the *Dictionary of National Biography* formed the basis of his *Life of William Shakespeare* (1898), which reached its fifth edition in 1905. Mr Lee edited in 1902 the Oxford facsimile edition of the first folio of *Shakespeare's Comedies, Histories and Tragedies*, followed in 1902 and 1904 by supplementary volumes giving details of extant copies, and in 1906 by a complete edition of

Shakespeare's Works. Besides editions of English classics his works include a Life of Queen Victoria (1902), *Great Englishmen of the Sixteenth Century* (1904), based on his Lowell Institute lectures at Boston, Mass., in 1903, and *Shakespeare and the Modern Stage* (1906).

LEE, SOPHIA (1750–1824), English novelist and dramatist, daughter of John Lee (d. 1781), actor and theatrical manager, was born in London. Her first piece, *The Chapter of Accidents*, a [illegible]-opera based on Diderot's *Père de famille*, was produced by George Colman at the Haymarket Theatre on the 5th of August 1780. The proceeds were spent in establishing a school at Bath, where Miss Lee made a home for her sisters. Her subsequent productions included *The Recess, or a Tale of other Times* (1785), a historical romance; and *Almeyda, Queen of Granada* (1796), a tragedy in blank verse; she also contributed to her sister's *Canterbury Tales* (1797). She died at her house near Clifton on the 13th of March 1824.

Her sister, HARRIET LEE (1757–1851), published in 1786 a novel written in letters, *The Errors of Innocence*. *Clara Lennox* followed in 1797. Her chief work is the *Canterbury Tales* (1797–1805), a series of twelve stories which became very popular. Lord Byron dramatized one of the tales, "Kruitzner," as *Werner, or the Inheritance*. She died at Clifton on the 1st of August 1851.

LEE, STEPHEN DILL (1833–1908), Confederate general in the American Civil War, came of a family distinguished in the history of South Carolina, and was born at Charleston, S.C., on the 22nd of September 1833. Graduating from West Point in 1854, he served for seven years in the United States army and resigned in 1861 on the secession of South Carolina. He was aide de camp to General Beauregard in the attack on Fort Sumter, and captain commanding a light battery in General Johnston's army later in the year 1861. Thereafter, by successive steps, each gained by distinguished conduct on the field of battle, he rose to the rank of brigadier-general in November 1862, being ordered to take command of defences at Vicksburg. He served at this place with great credit until its surrender to General Grant in July 1863, and on becoming a prisoner of war, he was immediately exchanged and promoted major-general. His regimental service had been chiefly with artillery, but he had generally worked with and at times commanded cavalry, and he was now assigned to command the troops of that arm in the south-western theatre of war. After harassing, as far as his limited numbers permitted, the advance of Sherman's column on Meridian, he took General Polk's place as commander of the department of Mississippi. In June 1864, on Hood's promotion to command the Army of Tennessee, S. D. Lee was made a lieutenant-general and assigned to command Hood's old corps in that army. He fought at Atlanta and Jonesboro and in the skirmishing and manœuvring along middle Tennessee which ended in the great crisis of Nashville and the "March to the Sea." Lee's corps accompanied Hood in the bold advance to Nashville, and fought in the battles of Franklin and Nashville, after which, in the rout of the Confederate army he kept his troops closed up and well in hand, and for three successive days formed the fighting rearguard of the otherwise disorganized army. Lee was himself wounded, but did not give up the command until an organized rearguard took over the post of danger. On recovery he joined General J. E. Johnston in North Carolina, and he surrendered with Johnston in April 1865. After the war he settled in Mississippi, which was his wife's state and during the greater part of the war his own territorial command, and devoted himself to planting. He was president of the Agricultural and Mechanical College of Mississippi from 1880 to 1899, took some part in state politics and was an active member—at the time of his death commander-in-chief of the "United Confederate Veterans" society. He died at Vicksburg on the 28th of May 1908.

LEE, a township of Berkshire county, in western Massachusetts, U.S.A. Pop. (1900) 3596; (1905) 3972; (1910) 4106. The township is traversed by the New York, New Haven & Hartford railway, covers an area of 22½ sq. m., and includes the village of Lee, 10 m. S. of Pittsfield, East Lee adjoining it on the S.E., and South Lee, about 3 m. to the S.W. Lee and South Lee are on, and East Lee is near, the Housatonic river. The eastern part of the township is generally hilly, reaching a maximum altitude of about 2200 ft., and there are two considerable bodies of water—Laurel Lake in the N.W. (partly in Lenox) and Goose Pond, in the S.E. (partly in Tyringham). The region is healthy as well as beautiful, and is much frequented as a summer resort. Memorial Hall was built in memory of the soldiers from Lee who died during the Civil War. The chief manufactures are paper and wire, and from the quarries near the village of Lee is obtained an excellent quality of marble; these quarries furnished the marble for the extension of the Capitol at Washington, for St Patrick's cathedral in New York City and for the Lee High School and the Lee Public Library (1908). Lime is quarried in the township. Lee was formerly a paper-manufacturing place of great importance. The first paper mill in the township was built in South Lee in 1806, and for a time more paper was made in Lee than in any other place in the United States; the Housatonic Mill in Lee was probably the first (1867) in the United States to manufacture paper from wood pulp.

The first settlement within the present township of Lee was made in 1760. The township was formed from parts of Great Barrington and Washington, was incorporated in 1777 and was named in honour of General Charles Lee (1731–1782). In the autumn of 1786 there was an encounter near the village of East Lee between about 250 adherents of Daniel Shays (many of them from Lee township) and a body of state troops under General John Paterson, wherein the Shays contingent paraded a bogus cannon (made of a yarn beam) with such effect that the state troops fled.

See Amory Gale, *History of the Town of Lee* (Lee, 1854), and *Lee, The Centennial Celebration and Centennial History of the Town of Lee* (Springfield, Mass., 1878), compiled by Charles M. Hyde and Alexander Hyde.

LEE. (1) (In O. Eng. *hléo*; cf. the pronunciation *lew-ward* of "leeward"; the word appears in several Teutonic languages; cf. Dutch *lij*, Dan. *læ*), properly a shelter or protection, chiefly used as a nautical term for that side of a ship, land, &c., which is farthest from the wind, hence a "lee shore," land under the lee of a ship, *i.e.* one on which the wind blows directly and which is unsheltered. A ship is said to make "leeway" when she drifts laterally away from her course. (2) A word now always used in the plural "lees," meaning dregs, sediment, particularly of wine. It comes through the O. Fr. *lie* from a Gaulish Lat. *lia*, and is probably of Celtic origin.

LEECH, JOHN (1817–1864), English caricaturist, was born in London on the 29th of August 1817. His father, a native of Ireland, was the landlord of the London Coffee House on Ludgate Hill, "a man," on the testimony of those who knew him, "of fine culture, a profound Shakespearian, and a thorough gentleman." His mother was descended from the family of the famous Richard Bentley. It was from his father that Leech inherited his skill with the pencil, which he began to use at a very early age. When he was only three, he was discovered by Flaxman, who had called on his parents, seated on his mother's knee, drawing with much gravity. The sculptor pronounced his sketch to be wonderful, adding, "Do not let him be cramped with lessons in drawing; let his genius follow its own bent; he will astonish the world"—an advice which was strictly followed. A mail-coach, done when he was six years old, is already full of surprising vigour and variety in its galloping horses. Leech was educated at Charterhouse, where Thackeray, his lifelong friend, was his schoolfellow, and at sixteen he began to study for the medical profession at St Bartholomew's Hospital, where he won praise for the accuracy and beauty of his anatomical drawings. He was then placed under a Mr Whittle, an eccentric practitioner, the original of "Rawkins" in Albert Smith's *Adventures of Mr Ledbury*, and afterwards under Dr John Cockle; but gradually the true bent of the youth's mind asserted itself, and he drifted into the artistic profession. He was eighteen when his first designs were published, a quarto of four pages, entitled *Etchings and Sketchings by A. Pen, Esq.*, comic character studies from the London streets. Then he drew some political lithographs, did rough sketches for *Bell's Life*, produced an exceedingly popular parody on Mulready's postal envelope, and, on the death of Seymour, applied unsuccessfully to illustrate the *Pickwick Papers*. In 1840 Leech began his contributions to the magazines with a series of etchings in *Bentley's Miscellany*, where Cruikshank had published his splendid plates to *Jack Sheppard* and *Oliver Twist*, and was illustrating *Guy Fawkes* in sadly feebler fashion. In company with the elder master Leech designed for the *Ingoldsby Legends* and *Stanley Thorn*, and till 1847 produced many independent series of etchings. These cannot be ranked with his best work; their technique is exceedingly imperfect; they are rudely bitten, with the light and shade out of relation; and we never feel that they express the artist's individuality, the *Richard Savage* plates, for instance, being strongly reminiscent of Cruikshank, and "The Dance at Stamford Hall" of Hablot Browne. In 1845 Leech illustrated *St Giles and St James* in Douglas Jerrold's newly started *Shilling Magazine*, with plates more vigorous and accomplished than those in *Bentley*, but it is in subjects of a somewhat later date, and especially in those lightly etched and meant to be printed with colour, that we see the artist's best powers with the needle and the acid. Among such of his designs are four charming plates to Dickens's *Christmas Carol* (1844), the broadly humorous etchings in the *Comic History of England* (1847–1848), and the still finer illustrations to the *Comic History of Rome* (1852)—which last, particularly in its minor woodcuts, shows some exquisitely graceful touches, as witness the fair faces that rise from the surging water in "Cloelia and her Companions Escaping from the Etruscan Camp." Among the other etchings which deserve very special reference are those in *Young Master Troublesome or Master Jacky's Holidays*, and the frontispiece to *Hints on Life, or How to Rise in Society* (1845)—a series of minute subjects linked gracefully together by coils of smoke, illustrating the various ranks and conditions of men, one of them—the doctor by his patient's bedside—almost equalling in vivacity and precision the best of Cruikshank's similar scenes. Then in the 'fifties we have the numerous etchings of sporting scenes, contributed, together with woodcuts, to the *Handley Cross* novels.

Turning to Leech's lithographic work, we have, in 1841, the *Portraits of the Children of the Mobility*, an important series dealing with the humorous and pathetic aspects of London street Arabs, which were afterwards so often and so effectively to employ the artist's pencil. Amid all the squalor which they depict, they are full of individual beauties in the delicate or touching expression of a face, in the graceful turn of a limb. The book is scarce in its original form, but in 1875 two reproductions of the outline sketches for the designs were published—a lithographic issue of the whole series, and a finer photographic transcript of six of the subjects, which is more valuable than even the finished illustrations of 1841, in which the added light and shade is frequently spotty and ineffective, and the lining itself has not the freedom which we find in some of Leech's other lithographs, notably in the *Fly Leaves*, published at the *Punch* office, and in the inimitable subject of the nuptial couch of the Caudles, which also appeared, in woodcut form, as a political cartoon, with Mrs Caudle, personated by Brougham, disturbing by untimely loquacity the slumbers of the lord chancellor, whose haggard cheek rests on the woolsack for pillow.

But it was in work for the wood-engravers that Leech was most prolific and individual. Among the earlier of such designs are the illustrations to the *Comic English* and *Latin Grammars* (1840), to *Written Caricatures* (1841), to Hood's *Comic Annual*, (1842), and to Albert Smith's *Wassail Bowl* (1843), subjects mainly of a small vignette size, transcribed with the best skill of such woodcutters as Orrin Smith, and not, like the larger and later *Punch* illustrations, cut at speed by several engravers working at once on the subdivided block. It was in 1841 that Leech's connexion with *Punch* began, a connexion which subsisted till his death on the 29th of October 1864, and resulted in the production of the best-known and most admirable of his designs. His first contribution appeared in the issue of the 7th of August, a full-page illustration—entitled "Foreign Affairs"—of character studies from the neighbourhood of Leicester Square. His cartoons deal at first mainly with social subjects, and are rough and imperfect in execution, but gradually their method gains in power and their subjects become more distinctly political, and by 1849 the artist is strong enough to produce the splendidly humorous national personification which appears in "Disraeli Measuring the British Lion." About 1845 we have the first of that long series of half-page and quarter-page pictures of life and manners, executed with a hand as gentle as it was skilful, containing, as Ruskin has said, "admittedly the finest definition and natural history of the classes of our society, the kindest and subtlest analysis of its foibles, the tenderest flattery of its pretty and well-bred ways," which has yet appeared. In addition to his work for the weekly issue of *Punch*, Leech contributed largely to the *Punch* almanacks and pocket-books, to *Once a Week* from 1859 till 1862, to the *Illustrated London News*, where some of his largest and best sporting scenes appeared, and to innumerable novels and miscellaneous volumes besides, of which it is only necessary to specify *A Little Tour in Ireland* (1859), which is noticeable as showing the artist's treatment of pure landscape, though it also contains some of his daintiest figure-pieces, like that of the wind-blown girl, standing on the summit of a pedestal, with the swifts darting around her and the breadth of sea beyond.

In 1862 Leech appealed to the public with a very successful exhibition of some of the most remarkable of his *Punch* drawings. These were enlarged by a mechanical process, and coloured in oils by the artist himself, with the assistance and under the direction of his friend J. E. Millais.

Leech was a singularly rapid and indefatigable worker. Dean Hole tells us, when he was his guest, "I have known him send off from my house three finished drawings on the wood, designed, traced, and rectified, without much effort as it seemed, between breakfast and dinner." The best technical qualities of Leech's art, his unerring precision, his unfailing vivacity in the use of the line, are seen most clearly in the first sketches for his woodcuts, and in the more finished drawings made on tracing-paper from these first outlines, before the chiaroscuro was added and the designs were transcribed by the engraver. Turning to the mental qualities of his art, it would be a mistaken criticism which ranked him as a comic draughtsman. Like Hogarth he was a true humorist, a student of human life, though he observed humanity mainly in its whimsical aspects,

"Hitting all he saw with shafts
With gentle satire, kin to charity,
That harmed not."

The earnestness and gravity of moral purpose which is so constant a note in the work of Hogarth is indeed far less characteristic of Leech, but there are touches of pathos and of tragedy in such of the *Punch* designs as the "Poor Man's Friend" (1845), and "General Février turned Traitor" (1855), and in "The Queen of the Arena" in the first volume of *Once a Week*, which are sufficient to prove that more solemn powers, for which his daily work afforded no scope, lay dormant in the artist. The purity and manliness of Leech's own character are impressed on his art. We find in it little of the exaggeration and grotesqueness, and none of the fierce political enthusiasm, of which the designs of Gillray are so full. Compared with that of his great contemporary George Cruikshank, his work is restricted both in compass of subject and in artistic dexterity.

Biographies of Leech have been written by John Brown (1882), and Frith (1891); see also "John Leech's Pictures of Life and Character," by Thackeray, *Quarterly Review* (December 1854), letter by John Ruskin, *Arrows of the Chace*, vol. i. p. 161; "Un Humoriste Anglais," by Ernest Chesneau, *Gazette des Beaux Arts* (1875). (J. M. G.)

LEECH, the common name of members of the Hirudinea, a division of Chaetopod worms. It is doubtful whether the medicinal leech, *Hirudo medicinalis*, which is rarer in England than on the continent of Europe, or the horse leech, *Aulastoma gulo*, often confused with it, has the best right to the original possession of this name. But at present the word "leech" is applied to every member of the group Hirudinea, for the general structure and classification of which see CHAETOPODA. There are many genera and species of leeches, the exact definitions of which are still in need of a more complete survey. They occur in all parts of the world and are mostly aquatic, though sometimes terrestrial, in habit. The aquatic forms frequent streams, ponds and marshes, and the sea. The members of this group are always

... or parasitic, and prey upon both vertebrates and ... In relation to their parasitic habit one or two ... always developed, the one at the anterior and the posterior end of the body. In one subdivision of the *Gnathobdellidae*, the mouth has three chitinous ... produce a triangular bite, though the action has been ... like that of a circular saw. Leeches without biting ... a protrusible proboscis, and generally engulf their ... the horse leech when it attacks earthworms. But ... are also ectoparasites. The leech has been used from remote antiquity as a moderate blood-letter; ... so used, though more rarely than formerly. As ... blood-letters, certain land-leeches are among the most ... parasites that can be encountered in a tropical ... species of *Haemadipsa* of Ceylon attaches itself to ... and draws blood with so little irritation that the ... to be aware of its presence only by the trickling ... wounds produced. Small leeches taken into the mouth ... water may give rise to serious symptoms by attaching ... to the fauces and neighbouring parts and thence ... The effects of these parasites have been mistaken ... disease. All leeches are very extensile and can ... body to a plump, pear-shaped form, or extend ... and worm-like shape. They frequently progress ... of a "looper" caterpillar, attaching themselves ... the anterior and the posterior sucker. Others ... curves through the water, while one land-leech, ... moves in a gliding way like a land Planarian, and ... like the Planarian, a slimy trail behind it. Leeches ... green to brown in colour, darker patches and ... scattered over a paler ground. The marine parasitic ... is of a bright green, as is also the land-leech ... [illegible]

The ... "leech," as an old English synonym for physician, ... root meaning "heal," and is etymologically ... the name (O. Eng. *lyce*) of the *Hirudo*, though ... the other has helped to assimilate the two ... (F. E. B.)

LEEDS, THOMAS OSBORNE, 1st DUKE OF (1631–1712), ... commonly known also by his earlier title of ... son of Sir Edward Osborne, Bart., of Kiveton, ... born in 1631. He was great-grandson of Sir ... lord mayor of London, who, according ... while apprentice to Sir William Hewett, ... mayor in 1559, made the fortunes of the ... London Bridge into the river and rescuing ... daughter of his employer, whom he afterwards ... the future lord treasurer, succeeded ... estates in Yorkshire on his father's death ... unsuccessfully courting his cousin Dorothy ... Bridget Bertie, daughter of the earl of ... introduced to public life and to court by his ... George, 2nd duke of Buckingham, ... in 1665, and gained the "first step ... supporting Buckingham in his attack on ... he was appointed joint treasurer ... Thomas Lyttelton, and subsequently ... succeeded Sir William Coventry as com... in 1669, and in 1673 was appointed ... He was created Viscount ... the 2nd of February 1673, ... May. On the 19th of June, ... appointed lord treasurer ... and Viscount Latimer in ... 15th of June 1674 he was ... resigned his Scottish peerage ... Peregrine Osborne. He was ... of the West Riding of ... Garter. ... different calibre from the ... [illegible] (1897) 213, quoting

leaders of the Cabal ministry, Buckingham and Arlington. His principal aim was no doubt the maintenance and increase of his own influence and party, but his ambition corresponded with definite political views. A member of the old cavalier party, a confidential friend and correspondent of the despotic Lauderdale, he desired to strengthen the executive and the royal authority. At the same time he was a keen partisan of the established church, an enemy of both Roman Catholics and dissenters, and an opponent of all toleration. In 1673 he opposed the Indulgence, supported the Test Act, and spoke against the proposal for giving relief to the dissenters. In June 1675 he signed the paper of advice drawn up by the bishops for the king, urging the rigid enforcement of the laws against the Roman Catholics, their complete banishment from the court, and the suppression of conventicles,[1] and a bill introduced by him imposing special taxes on recusants and subjecting Roman Catholic priests to imprisonment for life was only thrown out as too lenient because it secured offenders from the charge of treason. The same year he introduced a Test Oath by which all holding office or seats in either House of Parliament were to declare resistance to the royal power a crime, and promise to abstain from all attempts to alter the government of either church or state; but this extreme measure of retrograde toryism was successfully opposed by wiser statesmen. The king himself as a Roman Catholic secretly opposed and also doubted the wisdom and practicability of this "thorough" policy of repression. Danby therefore ordered a return from every diocese of the numbers of dissenters, both Romanist and Protestant, in order by a proof of their insignificance to remove the royal scruples.[2] In December 1676 he issued a proclamation for the suppression of coffee-houses because of the "defamation of His Majesty's Government" which took place in them, but this was soon withdrawn. In 1677, to secure Protestantism in case of a Roman Catholic succession, he introduced a bill by which ecclesiastical patronage and the care of the royal children were entrusted to the bishops; but this measure, like the other, was thrown out.

In foreign affairs Danby showed a stronger grasp of essentials. He desired to increase English trade, credit and power abroad. He was a determined enemy both to Roman influence and to French ascendancy. He terminated the war with Holland in 1674, and from that time maintained a friendly correspondence with William; while in 1677, after two years of tedious negotiations, he overcame all obstacles, and in spite of James's opposition, and without the knowledge of Louis XIV., effected the marriage between William and Mary that was the germ of the Revolution and the Act of Settlement. This national policy, however, could only be pursued, and the minister could only maintain himself in power, by acquiescence in the king's personal relations with the king of France settled by the disgraceful Treaty of Dover in 1670, which included Charles's acceptance of a pension, and bound him to a policy exactly opposite to Danby's, one furthering French and Roman ascendancy. Though not a number of the Cabal ministry, and in spite of his own denial, Danby must, it would seem, have known of these relations after becoming lord treasurer. In any case, in 1676, together with Lauderdale alone, he consented to a treaty between Charles and Louis according to which the foreign policy of both kings was to be conducted in union, and Charles received an annual subsidy of £100,000. In 1678 Charles, taking advantage of the growing hostility to France in the nation and parliament, raised his price, and Danby by his directions demanded through Ralph Montagu (afterwards duke of Montagu) six million livres a year (£300,000) for three years. Simultaneously Danby guided through parliament a bill for raising money for a war against France; a league was concluded with Holland, and troops were actually sent there. That Danby, in spite of these compromising transactions, remained in intention faithful to the national interests, appears clearly from the hostility with which he was still regarded by France. In 1676 he is described

[1] *Cal. of St Pap. Dom.* (1673–1675), p. 449.

[2] Letter of Morley, Bishop of Winchester, to Danby (June 10, 1676). (*Hist. MSS. Com.* xi. Rep. pt. vii. 14.)

by Ruvigny to Louis XIV. as intensely antagonistic to France and French interests, and as doing his utmost to prevent the treaty of that year.[1] In 1678, on the rupture of relations between Charles and Louis, a splendid opportunity was afforded Louis of paying off old scores by disclosing Danby's participation in the king's demands for French gold.

Every circumstance now conspired to effect his fall. Although both abroad and at home his policy had generally embodied the wishes of the ascendant party in the state, Danby had never obtained the confidence of the nation. His character inspired no respect, and he could not reckon during the whole of his long career on the support of a single individual. Charles is said to have told him when he made him treasurer that he had only two friends in the world, himself and his own merit.[2] He was described to Pepys on his acquiring office as "one of a broken sort of people that have not much to lose and therefore will venture all," and as "a beggar having £1100 or £1200 a year, but owes above £10,000." His office brought him in £20,000 a year,[3] and he was known to be making large profits by the sale of offices; he maintained his power by corruption and by jealously excluding from office men of high standing and ability. Burnet described him as "the most hated minister that had ever been about the king." Worse men had been less detested, but Danby had none of the amiable virtues which often counteract the odium incurred by serious faults. Evelyn, who knew him intimately from his youth, describes him as "a man of excellent natural parts but nothing of generous or grateful." Shaftesbury, doubtless no friendly witness, speaks of him as an inveterate liar, "proud, ambitious, revengeful, false, prodigal and covetous to the highest degree,"[4] and Burnet supports his unfavourable judgment to a great extent. His corruption, his mean submission to a tyrant wife, his greed, his pale face and lean person, which had succeeded to the handsome features and comeliness of earlier days,[5] were the subject of ridicule, from the witty sneers of Halifax to the coarse jests of the anonymous writers of innumerable lampoons. By his championship of the national policy he had raised up formidable foes abroad without securing a single friend or supporter at home,[6] and his fidelity to the national interests was now, through a very mean and ignoble act of personal spite, to be the occasion of his downfall.

Danby in appointing a new secretary of state had preferred Sir W. Temple, a strong adherent of the anti-French policy, to Montagu. The latter, after a quarrel with the duchess of Cleveland, was dismissed from the king's employment. He immediately went over to the opposition, and in concert with Louis XIV. and Barillon, the French ambassador, by whom he was supplied with a large sum of money, arranged a plan for effecting Danby's ruin. He obtained a seat in parliament; and in spite of Danby's endeavour to seize his papers by an order in council, on the 20th of December 1678 caused two of the incriminating letters written by Danby to him to be read aloud to the House of Commons by the Speaker. The House immediately resolved on Danby's impeachment. At the foot of each of the letters appeared the king's postscripts, "I approve of this letter. C.R.," in his own handwriting; but they were not read by the Speaker, and were entirely neglected in the proceedings against the minister, thus emphasizing the constitutional principle that obedience to the orders of the sovereign can be no bar to an impeachment. He was charged with having encroached to himself royal powers by treating matters of peace and war without the knowledge of the council, with having promoted the raising of a standing army on pretence of a war with France, with having obstructed the assembling of parliament, with corruption and embezzlement in the treasury. Danby, while communicating the "Popish Plot" to the parliament, had from the first expressed his disbelief in the so-called revelations of Titus Oates, and his backwardness in the matter now furnished an additional charge of having "traitorously concealed the plot." He was voted guilty by the Commons; but while the Lords were disputing whether the accused peer should have bail, and whether the charges amounted to more than a misdemeanour, parliament was prorogued on the 30th of December and dissolved three weeks later. In March 1679 a new parliament hostile to Danby was returned, and he was forced to resign the treasurership; but he received a pardon from the king under the Great Seal, and a warrant for a marquessate.[7] His proposed advancement in rank was severely reflected upon in the Lords, Halifax declaring it in the king's presence the recompense of treason, "not to be borne"; and in the Commons his retirement from office by no means appeased his antagonists. The proceedings against him were revived, a committee of privileges deciding on the 19th of March 1679 that the dissolution of parliament was no abatement of an impeachment. A motion was passed for his committal by the Lords, who, as in Clarendon's case, voted his banishment. This was, however, rejected by the Commons, who now passed an act of attainder. Danby had removed to the country, but returned on the 21st of April to avoid the threatened passing by the Lords of the attainder, and was sent to the Tower. In his written defence he now pleaded the king's pardon, but on the 5th of May 1679 it was pronounced illegal by the Commons. This declaration was again repeated by the Commons in 1689 on the occasion of another attack made upon Danby in that year, and was finally embodied in the Act of Settlement in 1701.

The Commons now demanded judgment against the prisoner from the Lords. Further proceedings, however, were stopped by the dissolution of parliament again in July; but for nearly five years Danby remained a prisoner in the Tower. A number of pamphlets asserting the complicity of the fallen minister in the Popish Plot, and even accusing him of the murder of Sir Edmund Berry Godfrey, were published in 1679 and 1680; they were answered by Danby's secretary, Edward Christian, in *Reflections*; and in May 1681 Danby was actually indicted by the Grand Jury of Middlesex for Godfrey's murder on the accusation of Edward FitzHarris. His petition to the king for a trial by his peers on this indictment was refused, and an attempt to prosecute the publishers of the false evidence in the king's bench was unsuccessful. For some time all appeals to the king, to parliament, and to the courts of justice were unavailing; but on the 12th of February 1684 his application to Chief Justice Jeffreys was at last successful, and he was set at liberty on finding bail to the amount of £40,000, to appear in the House of Lords in the following session. He visited the king at court the same day; but took no part in public affairs for the rest of the reign.

After James's accession Danby was discharged from his bail by the Lords on the 19th of May 1685, and the order declaring a dissolution of parliament to be no abatement of an impeachment was reversed. He again took his seat in the Lords as a leader of the moderate Tory party. Though a strong Tory and supporter of the hereditary principle, James's attacks on Protestantism soon drove him into opposition. He was visited by Dykvelt, William of Orange's agent; and in June 1687 he wrote to William assuring him of his support. On the 30th of June 1688 he was one of the seven leaders of the Revolution who signed the invitation to William. In November he occupied York in the prince's interest, returning to London to meet William on the 26th of December. He appears to have thought that William would not claim the crown,[8] and at first supported the theory that the throne having been vacated by James's flight the succession fell as of right to Mary; but as this met with little support, and was rejected both by William and by Mary herself, he voted against the regency and joined with

[1] *Memoirs of Great Britain and Ireland*, by Sir J. Dalrymple 1773), i. app. 104.
[2] *Letters to Sir Joseph Williamson* (Camden Soc., 1874), i. 64.
[3] Halifax note-book in Devonshire House collection, quoted in Foxcroft's *Life of Halifax*, ii. 63, note.
[4] *Life of Shaftesbury*, by W. D. Christie (1871), ii. 312.
[5] Macky's *Memoirs*, 46; Pepys's *Diary*, viii. 143.
[6] See the description of his position at this time by Sir W. Temple in *Lives of Illustrious Persons* (1714), 40.
[7] Add. MSS. 28094, f. 47.
[8] Boyer's *Annals* (1722), 433.

Halifax and the Commons in declaring the prince and princess joint sovereigns.

Danby had rendered extremely important services to William's cause. On the 20th of April 1689 he was created marquess of Carmarthen and was made lord-lieutenant of the three ridings of Yorkshire. He was, however, still greatly disliked by the Whigs, and William, instead of reinstating him in the lord treasurership, only appointed him president of the council in February 1689. He did not conceal his vexation and disappointment, which were increased by the appointment of Halifax to the office of lord privy seal. The antagonism between the "black" and the "white marquess" (the latter being the nickname given to Carmarthen in allusion to his sickly appearance), which had been forgotten in their common hatred to the French policy and to Rome, revived in all its bitterness. He retired to the country and was seldom present at the council. In June and July new motions were made in parliament for his removal; but notwithstanding his great unpopularity, on the retirement of Halifax in 1690 he again acquired the chief power in the state, which he retained till 1695 by bribery in parliament and by the support of the king and queen. In 1690, during William's absence in Ireland, he was appointed Mary's chief adviser. In 1691, desiring to compromise Halifax, he discredited himself by the patronage of an informer named Fuller, soon proved an impostor. He was absent in 1692 when the Place Bill was thrown out. In 1693 he presided in great state as lord high steward at the trial of Lord Mohun; and on the 4th of May 1694 he was created duke of Leeds.[1] The same year he supported the Triennial Bill, but opposed the new treason bill as weakening the hands of the executive. Meanwhile fresh attacks had been made upon him. He was accused unjustly of Jacobitism. In April 1695 he was impeached once more by the Commons for having received a bribe of 5000 guineas to procure the new charter for the East India Company. In his defence, whilst denying that he had received the money and appealing to his past services, he did not attempt to conceal the fact that according to his experience bribery was an acknowledged and universal custom in public business, and that he himself had been instrumental in obtaining money for others. Meanwhile his servant, who was said to have been the intermediary between the duke and the Company in the transaction, fled the country; and no evidence being obtainable to convict, the proceedings fell to the ground. In May 1695 he had been ordered to discontinue his attendance at the council. He returned in October, but was not included among the lords justices appointed regents during William's absence in this year. In November he was created D.C.L. by the university of Oxford; in December he became a commissioner of trade, and in December 1696 governor of the Royal Fishery Company. He opposed the prosecution of Sir John Fenwick, but supported the action taken by members of both Houses in defence of William's rights in the same year. On the 23rd of April 1698 he entertained the tsar, Peter the Great, at Wimbledon. He had for some time lost the real direction of affairs, and in May 1699 he was compelled to retire from office and from the lord-lieutenancy of Yorkshire.

In Queen Anne's reign, in his old age, he is described as "a gentleman of admirable natural parts, great knowledge and experience in the affairs of his own country, but of no reputation with any party. He hath not been regarded, although he took his place at the council board."[2] The veteran statesman, however, by no means acquiesced in his enforced retirement, and continued to take an active part in politics. As a zealous churchman and Protestant he still possessed a following. In 1705 he supported a motion that the church was in danger, and in 1710 in Sacheverell's case spoke in defence of hereditary right.[3] In November of this year he obtained a renewal of his pension of £3500 a year from the post office which he was holding in 1694,[4] and in 1711 at the age of eighty was a competitor for the office of lord privy seal.[5] His long and eventful career, however, terminated soon afterwards by his death on the 26th of July 1712.

In 1710 the duke had published *Copies and Extracts of some letters written to and from the Earl of Danby . . . in the years 1676, 1677 and 1678*, in defence of his conduct, and this was accompanied by *Memoirs relating to the Impeachment of Thomas, Earl of Danby*. The original letters, however, of Danby to Montagu have now been published (by the Historical MSS. Commission from the MSS. of J. Eliot Hodgkin), and are seen to have been considerably garbled by Danby for the purposes of publication, several passages being obliterated and others altered by his own hand.

See the lives, by Sidney Lee in the *Dict. Nat. Biography* (1895); by T. P. Courtenay in *Lardner's Encyclopaedia*, "Eminent British Statesmen," vol. v. (1830), in Lodge's *Portraits*, vii.; and *Lives and Characters of . . . Illustrious Persons*, by J. le Neve (1714). Further material for his biography exists in *Add. MSS.*, 26040-95 (56 vols., containing his papers); in the *Duke of Leeds MSS. at Hornby Castle*, calendered in *Hist. MSS. Comm.* 11th Rep. pt. vii. pp. 1-43; *MSS. of Earl of Lindsay and J. Eliot Hodgkin*; and *Calendars of State Papers Dom.* See also *Add. MSS. 1894–1899*, Index and Calendar; *Hist. MSS. Comm.* 11th Rep. pt. ii., *House of Lords MSS.*; *Gen. Cat. British Museum* for various pamphlets.
(P. C. Y.)

Later Dukes of Leeds.

The duke's only surviving son, Peregrine (1659–1729), who became 2nd duke of Leeds on his father's death, had been a member of the House of Lords as Baron Osborne since 1690, but he is better known as a naval officer; in this service he attained the rank of a vice-admiral. He died on the 25th of June 1729, when his son Peregrine Hyde (1691–1731) became 3rd duke. The 4th duke was the latter's son Thomas (1713–1789), who was succeeded by his son Francis.

Francis Osborne, 5th duke of Leeds (1751–1799), was born on the 29th of January 1751 and was educated at Westminster school and at Christ Church, Oxford. He was a member of parliament in 1774 and 1775; in 1776 he became a peer as Baron Osborne, and in 1777 lord chamberlain of the queen's household. In the House of Lords he was prominent as a determined foe of the prime minister, Lord North, who, after he had resigned his position as chamberlain, deprived him of the office of lord-lieutenant of the East Riding of Yorkshire in 1780. He regained this, however, two years later. Early in 1783 the marquess of Carmarthen, as he was called, was selected as ambassador to France, but he did not take up this appointment, becoming instead secretary for foreign affairs under William Pitt in December of the same year. As secretary he was little more than a cipher, and he left office in April 1791. Subsequently he took some slight part in politics, and he died in London on the 31st of January 1799. His *Political Memoranda* were edited by Oscar Browning for the Camden Society in 1884, and there are eight volumes of his official correspondence in the British Museum. His first wife was Amelia (1754–1784), daughter of Robert Darcy, 4th earl of Holdernesse, who became Baroness Conyers in her own right in 1778. Their elder son, George William Frederick (1775–1838), succeeded his father as duke of Leeds and his mother as Baron Conyers. These titles were, however, separated when his son, Francis Godolphin Darcy, the 7th Duke (1798–1859), died without sons in May 1859. The barony passed to his nephew, Sackville George Lane-Fox (1827–1888), falling into abeyance on his death in August 1888, and the dukedom passed to his cousin, George Godolphin Osborne (1802–1872), a son of Francis Godolphin Osborne (1777–1850), who was created Baron Godolphin in 1832. In 1895 George's grandson George Godolphin Osborne (b. 1862) became 10th duke of Leeds. The name of Godolphin, which is borne by many of the Osbornes, was introduced into the family through the marriage of the 4th duke with Mary (d. 1764), daughter and co-heiress of Francis Godolphin, 2nd earl of Godolphin, and grand-daughter of the great duke of Marlborough.

LEEDS, a city and municipal county and parliamentary borough in the West Riding of Yorkshire, England, 185 m.

[1] The title was taken, not from Leeds in Yorkshire, but from Leeds in Kent, 4½ m. from Maidstone, which in the 17th century was a more important place than its Yorkshire namesake.

[2] *Memoirs of Sir John Macky* (Roxburghe Club, 1895), 46.

[3] Boyer's *Annals*, 219, 433.

[4] *Harleian MSS.* 2264, No. 239.

[5] Boyer's *Annals*, 515.

N.N.W. from London. Pop. (1891) 367,505; (1901) 428,968. It is served by the Great Northern railway (Central station), the Midland (Wellington station), North-Eastern and London & North-Western (New station), and Great Central and Lancashire & Yorkshire railways (Central station). It lies nearly in the centre of the Riding, in the valley of the river Aire.

The plan of the city is in no way regular, and the numerous handsome public buildings are distributed among several streets, principally on the north side of the narrow river. The town hall is a fine building in Grecian style, well placed in a square between Park Lane and Great George Street. It is of oblong shape, with a handsome façade over which rises a domed clock-tower. The principal apartment is the Victoria Hall, a richly ornamented chamber measuring 161 ft. in length, 72 in breadth and 75 in height. It was opened in 1858 by Queen Victoria. Immediately adjacent to it are the municipal offices (1884) in Italian style. The Royal Exchange (1872) in Boar Lane is an excellent Perpendicular building. In ecclesiastical architecture Leeds is not rich. The church of St John, however, is an interesting example of the junction of Gothic traditions with Renaissance tendencies in architecture. It dates from 1634 and contains some fine contemporary woodwork. St Peter's parish church occupies an ancient site, and preserves a very early cross from the former building. The church was rebuilt in 1840 at the instance of the vicar, Dr Walter Farquhar Hook (1798–1875), afterwards dean of Chichester, whose work here in a poor and ill-educated parish brought him fame. The church of All Souls (1880) commemorates him. It may be noted that the vicarage of Leeds has in modern times commonly formed a step to the episcopal bench. There are numerous other modern churches and chapels, of which the Unitarian chapel in Park Row is noteworthy. Leeds is the seat of a Roman Catholic bishop, with a pro-cathedral dedicated to St Anne. There is a large free library in the municipal offices, and numerous branch libraries are maintained. The Leeds old library is a private institution founded in 1768 by Dr Priestley, who was then minister of the Unitarian chapel. It occupies a building in Commercial Street. The Philosophical and Literary Society, established in 1820, possesses a handsome building in Park Row, known as the Philosophical Hall, containing a laboratory, scientific library, lecture room, and museum, with excellent natural history, geological and archaeological collections. The City Art Gallery was completed in 1888, and contains a fine permanent collection, while exhibitions are also held. The University, incorporated in 1904, grew out of Yorkshire College, established in 1875 for the purpose of supplying instruction in the arts and sciences which are applicable to the manufactures, engineering, mining and agriculture of the county. In 1887 it became one of the constituent colleges of Victoria University, Manchester, and so remained until its separate incorporation. The existing building was completed in 1885, and contains a hall of residence, a central hall and library, and complete equipments in all departments of instruction. New departments have been opened in extension of the original scheme, such as the medical department (1894). A day training college is a branch of the institution. The Mechanics' Institute (1865) occupies a handsome Italian building in Cookridge Street near the town hall. It comprises a lecture room, library, reading and class rooms; and day and evening classes and an art school are maintained. The grammar school, occupying a Gothic building (1858) at Woodhouse Moor, dates its foundation from 1552. It is largely endowed, and possesses exhibitions tenable at Oxford, Cambridge and Durham universities. There is a large training college for the Wesleyan Methodist ministry in the suburb of Headingley. The Yorkshire Ladies' Council of Education has as its object the promotion of female education, and the instruction of girls and women of the artisan class in domestic economy, &c. The general infirmary in Great George Street is a Gothic building of brick with stone dressings with a highly ornamental exterior by Sir Gilbert Scott, of whose work this is by no means the only good example in Leeds. The city possesses further notable buildings in its market-halls, theatres, clubs, &c.

Among open spaces devoted by the corporation to public use that of Woodhouse Moor is the principal one within the city, but 3 m. N.E. of the centre is Roundhay Park, a tract of 700 acres, beautifully laid out and containing a picturesque lake. In 1889 there came into the possession of the corporation the ground, lying 3 m. up the river from the centre of the city, containing the celebrated ruins of Kirkstall Abbey. The remains of this great foundation, of the middle of the 12th century, are extensive, and so far typical of the usual arrangement of Cistercian houses as to be described under the heading ABBEY. The ruins are carefully preserved, and form a remarkable contrast with the surrounding industrial district. Apart from Kirkstall there are few antiquarian remains in the locality. In Guildford Street, near the town hall, is the Red Hall, where Charles I. lay during his enforced journey under the charge of the army in 1647.

For manufacturing and commercial purposes the situation of Leeds is highly advantageous. It occupies a central position in the railway system of England. It has communication with Liverpool by the Leeds and Liverpool Canal, and with Goole and the Humber by the Aire and Calder Navigation. It is moreover the centre of an important coal and iron district. Though regarded as the capital of the great manufacturing district of the West Riding, Leeds is not in its centre but on its border. Eastward and northward the country is agricultural, but westward and southward lies a mass of manufacturing towns. The characteristic industry is the woollen manufacture. The industry is carried on in a great number of neighbouring townships, but the cloth is commonly finished or dressed in the city itself, this procedure differing from that of the wool manufacturers in Gloucestershire and the west of England, who carry out the entire process in one factory. Formerly much of the business between manufacturer and merchant was transacted in the cloth halls, which formed a kind of market, but merchants now order goods directly from the manufacturers. Artificial silk is important among the textile products. Subsidiary to these leading industries is the production of machine-made clothing, hats and caps. The leather trade of Leeds is the largest in England, though no sole leather is tanned. The supply comes chiefly from British India. Boots and shoes are extensively manufactured. The iron trade in its different branches rivals the woollen trade in wealth, including the casting of metal, and the manufacture of steam engines, steam wagons, steam ploughs, machinery, tools, nails, &c. Leeds was formerly famed for the production of artistic pottery, and specimens of old Leeds ware are highly prized. The industry lapsed about the end of the 18th century, but has been revived in modern times. Minor and less specialized industries are numerous.

The parliamentary borough is divided into five divisions (North, Central, South, East and West), each returning one member. The county borough was created in 1888. Leeds was raised to the rank of a city in 1893. The municipal borough is under a lord mayor (the title was conferred in 1897 on the occasion of Queen Victoria's Diamond Jubilee), 16 aldermen and 48 councillors. Area, 21,572 acres.

Leeds (Loidis, Ledes) is mentioned by Bede as the district where the Northumbrian kings had a royal vill in 627, and where Oswy, king of Northumbria, defeated Penda, king of the Mercians, in 665. Before the Norman Conquest seven thanes held it of Edward the Confessor as seven manors, but William the Conqueror granted the whole to Ilbert de Lacy, and at the time of the Domesday Survey it was held of him by Ralph Paganel, who is said to have raised Leeds castle, possibly on the site of an earlier fortification. In 1207 Maurice Paganel constituted the inhabitants of Leeds free burgesses, granting them the same liberties as Robert de Lacy had granted to Pontefract, including the right of selling burgher land to whom they pleased except to religious houses, and freedom from toll. He also appointed as the chief officer of the town a reeve who was to be chosen by the lord of the manor, the burgesses being "more eligible if only they would pay as much as others for the office." The town was incorporated by Charles I. in 1626 under the title of an alderman, 7 principal burgesses and 24 assistants. A second charter granted by Charles II. in 1661 appointed a mayor, 12 aldermen and 24 assistants, and is still the governing charter of the borough. The woollen manufacture is said to have been introduced into Leeds in the 14th century, and owing to the facilities for trade afforded by its position on the river Aire soon became an important [illegible] Camden, writing about 1590, says, "Leeds is rendered [illegible] by its woollen manufactures," and the incorporation [illegible] states that "the inhabitants have for a long time [illegible] the art of making cloth." The cloth was then, as it is [illegible] in the neighbouring villages and only finished and sold [illegible]. A successful attempt was made in the beginning of [illegible] century by Mr William Hirst to introduce goods of a [illegible] which were made and finished in his own factory. [illegible] followed his example, but their factories are [illegible] for the finishing process. The worsted trade which [illegible] carried on to some extent has now almost disappeared. [illegible] of flax by machinery was introduced early in the 19th [illegible] by Mr John Marshall, a Holbeck manufacturer, who was [illegible] the first to apply Sir Richard Arkwright's water frame, [illegible] manufacture, to the spinning of linen yarn. [illegible] represented in parliament by one member during [illegible] but not again until by the Reform Act of 1832 [illegible] to return two members. In 1867 they were [illegible] member.

[illegible] *The Municipal History of the Borough of Leeds* [illegible] *Loidis and Elmete: or an Attempt to illustrate* [illegible] *in these words by Bede* (1816); D. H. [illegible] *the Topographer; his Town* (*Leeds*) *and* [illegible]

[illegible] town in the Leek parliamentary division of [illegible], 157 m. N.W. from London, on the [illegible] of the North Staffordshire railway. [illegible] (1901) 15,484. The town lies high in [illegible] near the head of the river Churnet. [illegible] Edward the Confessor is mainly Decorated, [illegible] commanding a beautiful view from [illegible]. There is here a curious pillar of [illegible]. An institute contains a free library, [illegible] and school of art. A grammar school [illegible]. In the vicinity are ruins of the Cistercian [illegible], or Dieulacresse, erected in 1214 [illegible] earl of Chester. The slight remains are [illegible] in a farm-house. The silk manufacture [illegible] silk buttons, &c. Cloud Hill, rising [illegible] causes a curious phenomenon in the [illegible] sinking behind one flank to reappear [illegible] appearing to set twice.

[illegible] formed part of the great estates of [illegible] to William the Conqueror [illegible] of the Domesday Survey. Later it [illegible] of Chester, remaining in their hands [illegible] earl of Chester, gave it to the abbey [illegible] to hold it until its dissolution. [illegible] which he gave to the town (*temp.* [illegible]) to his free burgesses various [illegible] toll throughout Cheshire. [illegible] Richard, abbot of Dieulacresse, [illegible] charter and failed to establish [illegible] market which is still [illegible] the earl of Chester: in the [illegible]. A fair, also granted by [illegible] before the Translation of [illegible]. The silk manufacture which [illegible] 17th century is thought [illegible] Leek of some Huguenots [illegible]. In the 17th and [illegible]. Prince Charles [illegible] march to Derby (1745) [illegible] Scotland. A story in con[illegible] to explain the expression [illegible] of a citizen, who by [illegible] sought escape on the [illegible]

[illegible], a plant now con[illegible], wild leek, [illegible] probably of Eastern [illegible] Egypt in the time [illegible]; while as regards [illegible] and Gerard—two [illegible], the former of [illegible] in the later part [illegible]

vated and used.[1] The Romans, it would appear, made great use of the leek for savouring their dishes, as seems proved by the number of recipes for its use referred to by Celsius. Hence it is more than probable that it was brought to England by the Romans. Italy was celebrated for leeks in the time of Pliny (*H.N.* xix. c. 6), according to whom they were brought into great esteem through the emperor Nero, derisively surnamed "Porrophagus," who used to eat them for several days in every month to clear his voice. The leek is very generally cultivated in Great Britain as an esculent, but more especially in Scotland and in Wales, being esteemed as an excellent and wholesome vegetable, with properties very similar to those of the onion, but of a milder character. In America it is not much cultivated except by market gardeners in the neighbourhood of large cities. The whole plant, with the exception of the fibrous roots, is used in soups and stews. The sheathing stalks of the leaves lap over each other, and form a thickish stem-like base, which is blanched, and is the part chiefly preferred. These blanched stems are much employed in French cookery. They form an important ingredient in Scotch winter broth, and particularly in the national dish *cock-a-leekie*, and are also largely used boiled, and served with toasted bread and white sauce, as in the case of asparagus. Leeks are sown in the spring, earlier or later according to the soil and the season, and are planted out for the summer, being dropped into holes made with a stout dibble and left unfilled in order to allow the stems space to swell. When they are thus planted deeply the holes gradually fill up, and the base of the stem becomes blanched and prepared for use, a process aided by drawing up the earth round about the stems as they elongate. The leek is one of the most useful vegetables the cottager can grow, as it will supply him with a large amount of produce during the winter and spring. It is extremely hardy, and presents no difficulty in its cultivation, the chief point, as with all succulent esculents, being that it should be grown quickly upon well-enriched soil. The plant is of biennial duration, flowering the second year, and perishing after perfecting its seeds. The leek is the national symbol or badge of the Welsh, who wear it in their hats on St David's Day. The origin of this custom has received various explanations, all of which are more or less speculative.

LEER, a town and river port in the Prussian province of Hanover, lying in a fertile plain on the right bank of the Leda near its confluence with the Ems, and at the junction of railways to Bremen, Emden and Münster. Pop. (1905) 12,347. The streets are broad, well paved, and adorned with many elegant buildings, among which are Roman Catholic, Lutheran and Calvinist churches, and a new town hall with a tower 165 ft. high. Among its educational establishments are a classical school and a school of navigation. Linen and woollen fabrics, hosiery, paper, cigars, soap, vinegar and earthenware are manufactured, and there are iron-foundries, distilleries, tanneries and shipbuilding yards. Many markets for horses and cattle are held. The transit trade from the regions traversed by the Westphalian and Oldenburg railways is considerable. The principal exports are cattle, horses, cheese, butter, honey, wax, flour, paper, hardware and Westphalian coal. Leer is one of the principal ports for steamboat communication with the North Sea watering-places of Borkum and Norderney. Leer is a very old place, although it only obtained municipal privileges in 1823. Near the town is the Plitenberg, formerly a heathen place of sacrifice.

LEEUWARDEN, the capital of the province of Friesland, Holland, on the canal between Harlingen and Groningen, 33 m. by rail W. of Groningen. Pop (1901) 32,203. It is one of the most prosperous towns in the country. To the name of the Frisian Hague, it is entitled as well by similarity of history as by similarity of appearance. As the Hague grew up round the court of the counts of Holland, so Leeuwarden round the

[1] The title [illegible] Leeds in K[illegible] a more impo[illegible]

[2] *Memoirs* [illegible]

[3] Boyer's [illegible]

[1] Tusser, in his verse for the month of March, writes:—

> "Now leekes are in season, for pottage ful good,
> And spareth the milck cow, and purgeth the blood.
> These hauving with peason, for pottage in Lent,
> Thou spareth both otemel and bread to be spent."

court of the Frisian stadtholders; and, like the Hague, it is an exceptionally clean and attractive town, with parks, pleasure grounds, and drives. The old gates have been somewhat ruthlessly cleared away, and the site of the town walls on the north and west competes with the park called the Prince's Garden as a public pleasure ground. The Prince's Garden was originally laid out by William Frederick of Nassau in 1648, and was presented to the town by King William I. in 1819. The royal palace, which was the seat of the Frisian court from 1603 to 1747, is now the residence of the royal commissioner for Friesland. It was restored in 1816 and contains a portrait gallery of the Frisian stadtholders. The fine mansion called the Kanselary was begun in 1502 as a residence for the chancellor of George of Saxony (1539), governor of Friesland, but was only completed in 1571 and served as a court house until 1811. It was restored at the end of the 19th century to contain the important provincial library and national archives. Other noteworthy buildings are the picturesque weigh-house (1595), the town hall (1715), the provincial courts (1850), and the great church of St Jacob, once the church of the Jacobins, and the largest monastic church in the Netherlands. The splendid tombs of the Frisian stadtholders buried here (Louis of Nassau, Anne of Orange, and others) were destroyed in the revolution 1795. The unfinished tower of Oldehove dates from 1529–1532. The museum of the Frisian Society is of modern foundation and contains a collection of provincial antiquities, including two rooms from Hindeloopen, an ancient village of Friesland, some 16th- and 17th-century portraits, some Frisian works in silver of the 17th and 18th centuries, and a collection of porcelain and faience.

Leeuwarden is the centre of a flourishing trade, being easily accessible from all parts of the province by road, rail and canal. The chief business is in stock of every kind, dairy and agricultural produce and fresh-water fish, a large quantity of which is exported to France. The industries include boat-building and timber yards, iron-foundries, copper and lead works, furniture, organ, tobacco and other factories, and the manufacture of gold and silver wares. The town is first mentioned in documents of the 13th century.

LEEUWENHOEK, or LEUWENHOEK, **ANTHONY VAN** (1632–1723), Dutch microscopist, was born at Delft on the 24th of October 1632. For a short time he was in a merchant's office in Amsterdam, but early devoted himself to the manufacture of microscopes and to the study of the minute structure of organized bodies by their aid. He appears soon to have found that single lenses of very short focus were preferable to the compound microscopes then in use; and it is clear from the discoveries he made with these that they must have been of very excellent quality. His discoveries were for the most part made public in the *Philosophical Transactions* of the Royal Society, to the notice of which body he was introduced by R. de Graaf in 1673, and of which he was elected a fellow in 1680. He was chosen a corresponding member of the Paris Academy of Sciences in 1697. He died at his native place on the 26th of August 1723. Though his researches were not conducted on any definite scientific plan, his powers of careful observation enabled him to make many interesting discoveries in the minute anatomy of man, the higher animals and insects. He confirmed and extended M. Malpighi's demonstration of the blood capillaries in 1668, and six years later he gave the first accurate description of the red blood corpuscles, which he found to be circular in man but oval in frogs and fishes. In 1677 he described and illustrated the spermatozoa in dogs and other animals, though in this discovery Stephen Hamm had anticipated him by a few months; and he investigated the structure of the teeth, crystalline lens, muscle, &c. In 1680 he noticed that yeast consists of minute globular particles, and he described the different structure of the stem in monocotyledonous and dicotyledonous plants.

His researches in the life-history of various of the lower forms of animal life were in opposition to the doctrine that they could be "produced spontaneously, or bred from corruption." Thus he showed that the weevils of granaries, in his time commonly supposed to be bred *from* wheat, as well as *in* it, are grubs hatched from eggs deposited by winged insects. His chapter on the flea, in which he not only describes its structure, but traces out the whole history of its metamorphoses from its first emergence from the egg, is full of interest—not so much for the exactness of his observations, as for its incidental revelation of the extraordinary ignorance then prevalent in regard to the origin and propagation of "this minute and despised creature," which some asserted to be produced from sand, others from dust, others from the dung of pigeons, and others from urine, but which he showed to be "endowed with as great perfection in its kind as any large animal," and proved to breed in the regular way of winged insects. He even noted the fact that the pupa of the flea is sometimes attacked and fed upon by a mite—an observation which suggested the well known lines of Swift. His attention having been drawn to the blighting of the young shoots of fruit-trees, which was commonly attributed to the ants found upon them, he was the first to find the *Aphides* that really do the mischief; and, upon searching into the history of their generation, he observed the young within the bodies of their parents. He carefully studied also the history of the ant and was the first to show that what had been commonly reputed to be "ants' eggs" are really their pupae, containing the perfect insect nearly ready for emersion, whilst the true eggs are far smaller, and give origin to "maggots" or larvae. Of the sea-mussel, again, and other shell-fish, he argued (in reply to a then recent defence of Aristotle's doctrine by F. Buonanni, a learned Jesuit of Rome) that they are not generated out of the mud or sand found in the seashore or the beds of rivers at low water, but from spawn, by the regular course of generation; and he maintained the same to be true of the fresh-water mussel (*Unio*), whose ova he examined so carefully that he saw in them the rotation of the embryo, a phenomenon supposed to have been first discovered long afterwards. In the same spirit he investigated the generation of eels, which were at that time supposed, not only by the ignorant vulgar, but by "respectable and learned men," to be produced from dew without the ordinary process of generation. Not only was he the first discoverer of the rotifers, but he showed "how wonderfully nature has provided for the preservation of their species," by their tolerance of the drying-up of the water they inhabit, and the resistance afforded to the evaporation of the fluids of their bodies by the impermeability of the casing in which they then become enclosed. "We can now easily conceive," he says, "that in all rain-water which is collected from gutters in cisterns, and in all waters exposed to the air, animalcules may be found; for they may be carried thither by the particles of dust blown about by the winds."

Leeuwenhoek's contributions to the *Philosophical Transactions* amounted to one hundred and twelve; he also published twenty-six papers in the *Memoirs of the Paris Academy of Sciences*. Two collections of his works appeared during his life, one in Dutch (Leiden and Delft, 1685–1718), and the other in Latin (*Opera omnia s. Arcana naturae ope exactissimorum microscopiorum selecta*, Leiden, 1715–1722); and a selection from them was translated by S. Hoole and published in English (London, 1798–1781).

LEEWARD ISLANDS, a group in the West Indies. They derive their name from being less exposed to the prevailing N.E. trade wind than the adjacent Windward Islands. They are the most northerly of the Lesser Antilles, and form a curved chain stretching S.W. from Puerto Rico to meet St Lucia, the most northerly of the Windward Islands. They consist of the Virgin Islands, with St Kitts, Antigua, Montserrat, Guadeloupe, Dominica, Martinique and their various dependencies. The Virgin Islands are owned by Great Britain and Denmark, Holland having St Eustatius, with Saba, and part of St Martin. France possesses Guadeloupe, Martinique, St Bartholomew and the remainder of St Martin. The rest of the islands are British, and (with the exception of Sombrero, a small island used only as a lighthouse-station) form, under one governor, a colony divided into five presidencies, namely: Antigua (with Barbuda and Redonda), St Kitts (with Nevis and Anguilla), Dominica, Montserrat and the Virgin Islands. Total pop. (1901) 127,536. There is one federal executive council nominated by the crown, and one federal legislative council—ten nominated and ten elected members. Of the latter, four are chosen by the unofficial members of the local legislative council of Antigua, two by those of Dominica, and four by the non-official members of the local legislative council of St Kitts-Nevis. The federal legislative council meets once annually, usually at St John, Antigua.

LE FANU, JOSEPH SHERIDAN (1814–1873), Irish journalist and author, was born of an old Huguenot family at Dublin on the 28th of August 1814. He entered Trinity College, Dublin, in 1833. At an early age he had given proof of literary talent, and in 1837 he joined the staff of the *Dublin University Magazine*, of which he became later editor and proprietor. In 1837 he produced the Irish ballad *Phaudhrig Croohore*, which was shortly afterwards followed by a second, *Shamus O'Brien*, successfully recited in the United States by Samuel Lover. In 1839 he became proprietor of the *Warder*, a Dublin newspaper, and, after purchasing the *Evening Packet* and a large interest in the *Dublin Evening Mail*, he combined the three papers under the title the *Evening Mail*, a weekly reprint from which was issued as the *Warder*. After the death of his wife in 1858 he lived in retirement, and his best work was produced at this period of his life. He wrote some clever novels, of a sensational order, in which his vigorous imagination and his Irish love of the supernatural have full play. He died in Dublin on the 7th of February 1873. His best-known novels are *The House by the Churchyard* (1863) and *Uncle Silas, a Tale of Bartram Haugh* (1864). *The Purcell Papers*, Irish stories dating from his college days, were edited with a memoir of the author by A. P. Graves in 1880.

LEFEBVRE, PIERRE FRANÇOIS JOSEPH, duke of Danzig (1755–1820), marshal of France, was born at Rouffach in Alsace on the 20th of October 1755. At the outbreak of the Revolution he was a sergeant in the Gardes françaises, and with many of his comrades of this regiment took the popular side. He distinguished himself by bravery and humanity in many of the street fights in Paris, and becoming an officer and again distinguishing himself—this time against foreign invaders—he was made a general of division in 1794. He took part in the Revolutionary Wars from Fleurus to Stokach, always resolute, strictly obedient and calm. At Stokach (1799) he received a severe wound and had to return to France, where he assisted Napoleon during the *coup d'état* of 18 Brumaire. He was one of the first generals of division to be made marshal at the beginning of the First Empire. He commanded the guard infantry at Jena, conducted the siege of Danzig 1806–1807 (from which town he received his title in 1808), commanded a corps in the emperor's campaign of 1808–1809 in Spain, and in 1809 was given the difficult task of commanding the Bavarian contingent, which he led in the containing engagements of Abensberg and Rohr, and at the battle of Eckmühl. He commanded the Imperial Guard in Russia, 1812, fought through the last campaign of the Empire, and won fresh glory at Montmirail, Arcis-sur-Aube and Champaubert. He was made a peer of France by Louis XVIII. but joined Napoleon during the Hundred Days, and was only amnestied and permitted to resume his seat in the upper chamber in 1819. He died at Paris on the 14th of September 1820. Marshal Lefebvre was a simple soldier, whose qualifications for high rank, great as they were, came from experience and not from native genius. He was incapable of exercising a supreme command, even of leading an important detachment, but he was absolutely trustworthy as a subordinate, as brave as he was experienced, and intensely loyal to his chief. He maintained to the end of his life a rustic simplicity of speech and demeanour. Of his wife (formerly a *blanchisseuse* to the Gardes Françaises) many stories have been told, but in so far as they are to her discredit they seem to be false, she being, like the marshal, a plain "child of the people."

LEFEBVRE, TANNEGUY (TANAQUILLUS FABER) (1615–1672), French classical scholar, was born at Caen. After completing his studies in Paris, he was appointed by Cardinal Richelieu inspector of the printing-press at the Louvre. After Richelieu's death he left Paris, joined the Reformed Church, and in 1651 obtained a professorship at the academy of Saumur, which he filled with great success for nearly twenty years. His increasing ill-health and a certain moral laxity (as shown in his judgment on Sappho) led to a quarrel with the consistory, as a result of which he resigned his professorship. Several universities were eager to obtain his services, and he had accepted a post offered him by the elector palatine at Heidelberg, when he died suddenly on the 12th of September, 1672. One of his children was the famous Madame Dacier. Lefebvre, who was by no means a typical student in dress or manners, was a highly cultivated man and a thorough classical scholar. He brought out editions of various Greek and Latin authors—Longinus, Anacreon and Sappho, Virgil, Horace, Lucretius and many others. His most important original works are: *Les Vies des poëtes Grecs* (1665); *Méthode pour commencer les humanités Grecques et Latines* (2nd ed., 1731), of which several English adaptations have appeared; *Epistolae Criticae* (1659).

In addition to the *Mémoires pour . . . la vie de Tanneguy Lefebvre*, by F. Graverol (1686), see the article in the *Nouvelle biographie générale*, based partly on the MS. registers of the Saumur Académie.

LEFEBVRE-DESNOËTTES, CHARLES, COMTE (1773–1822), French cavalry general, joined the army in 1792 and served with the armies of the North, of the Sambre-and-Meuse and Rhine-and-Moselle in the various campaigns of the Revolution. Six years later he had become captain and aide-de-camp to General Bonaparte. At Marengo he won further promotion, and at Austerlitz became colonel, serving also in the Prussian campaigns of 1806–1807. In 1808 he was made general of brigade and created a count of the Empire. Sent with the army into Spain, he conducted the first and unsuccessful siege of Saragossa. The battlefield of Tudela showed his talents to better advantage, but towards the end of 1808 he was taken prisoner in the action of Benavente by the British cavalry under Paget (later Lord Uxbridge, and subsequently Marquis of Anglesey). For over two years he remained a prisoner in England, living on parole at Cheltenham. In 1811 he escaped, and in the invasion of Russia in 1812 was again at the head of his cavalry. In 1813 and 1814 his men distinguished themselves in most of the great battles, especially La Rothière and Montmirail. He joined Napoleon in the Hundred Days and was wounded at Waterloo. For his part in these events he was condemned to death, but he escaped to the United States, and spent the next few years farming in Louisiana. His frequent appeals to Louis XVIII. eventually obtained his permission to return, but the "Albion," the vessel on which he was returning to France, went down off the coast of Ireland with all on board on the 22nd of May 1822.

LE FÈVRE, JEAN (*c.* 1395–1468), Burgundian chronicler and seigneur of Saint Remy, is also known as *Toison d'or* from his long connexion with the order of the Golden Fleece. Of noble birth, he adopted the profession of arms and with other Burgundians fought in the English ranks at Agincourt. In 1430, on the foundation of the order of the Golden Fleece by Philip III. the Good, duke of Burgundy, Le Fèvre was appointed its king of arms and he soon became a very influential person at the Burgundian court. He frequently assisted Philip in conducting negotiations with foreign powers, and he was an arbiter in tournaments and on all questions of chivalry, where his wide knowledge of heraldry was highly useful. He died at Bruges on the 16th of June 1468.

Le Fèvre wrote a *Chronique, or Histoire de Charles VI., roy de France*. The greater part of this chronicle is merely a copy of the work of Enguerrand de Monstrelet, but Le Fèvre is an original authority for the years between 1428 and 1436 and makes some valuable additions to our knowledge, especially about the chivalry of the Burgundian court. He is more concise than Monstrelet, but is equally partial to the dukes of Burgundy. The *Chronique* has been edited by F. Morand for the Société de l'histoire de France (Paris, 1876). Le Fèvre is usually regarded as the author of the *Livre des faits de Jacques de Lalaing*.

LEG (a word of Scandinavian origin, from the Old Norwegian *leggr*, cf. Swed. *lägg*, Dan. *læg*; the O. Eng. word was *sceanca*, shank), the general name for those limbs in animals which support and move the body, and in man for the lower limbs of the body (see ANATOMY, *Superficial and Artistic*; SKELETON, *Appendicular*; MUSCULAR SYSTEM). The word is in common use for many objects which resemble the leg in shape or function. As a slang term, "leg," a shortened form of "blackleg," has been in use since the end of the 18th century for a swindler, especially in connexion with racing or gambling. The term "blackleg" is now also applied by trade-unionists to a workman who, during a strike or lockout, continues working or is brought to take the place of the withdrawn workers.

LEGACY (Lat. *legatum*), in English law, some particular thing or things given or left by a testator in his will, to be paid or performed by his executor or administrator. The word is primarily applicable to gifts of personalty or gifts charged upon real estate; but if there is nothing else to which it can refer it may refer to realty, the proper word, however, for gifts of realty is *devise*

Legacies may be either specific, general or demonstrative. A *specific legacy* is "something which a testator, identifying it by a sufficient description and manifesting an intention that it should be enjoyed in the state and condition indicated by that description, separates in favour of a particular legatee from the general mass of his personal estate," *e.g.* a gift of "my portrait by X," naming the artist. A *general legacy* is a gift not so distinguished from the general mass of the personal estate, *e.g.* a gift of £100 or of a gold ring. A *demonstrative legacy* partakes of the nature of both the preceding kinds of legacies, *e.g.* a gift of £100 payable out of a named fund is a specific legacy so far as the fund named is available to pay the legacy; after the fund is exhausted the balance of the legacy is a general legacy and recourse must be had to the general estate to satisfy such balance. Sometimes a testator bequeaths two or more legacies to the same person; in such a case it is a question whether the later legacies are in substitution for, or in addition to, the earlier ones. In the latter case they are known as *cumulative* In each case the intention of the testator is the rule of construction; this can often be gathered from the terms of the will or codicil, but in the absence of such evidence the following rules are followed by the courts. Where the same specific thing is bequeathed twice to the same legatee or where two legacies of equal amount are bequeathed by the same instrument the second bequest is mere repetition; but where legacies of equal amounts are bequeathed by different instruments or of unequal amounts by the same instruments they are considered to be cumulative.

If the estate of the testator is insufficient to satisfy all the legacies these must abate, *i.e.* be reduced rateably; as to this it should be noticed that specific and demonstrative legacies have a prior claim to be paid in full out of the specific fund before general legacies, and that general legacies abate rateably *inter se* in the absence of any provision to the contrary by the testator. Specific legacies are liable to ademption where the specific thing perishes or ceases to belong to the testator, *e.g.* in the instance given above if the testator sells the portrait the legatee will get nothing by virtue of the legacy. As a general rule, legacies given to persons who predecease the testator do not take effect; they are said to lapse. This is so even if the gift be to A and his executors, administrators and assigns, but this is not so if the testator has shown a contrary intention, thus, a gift to A *or* his personal representative will be effective even though A predecease the testator; further, by the Wills Act 1837, devises of estates tail and gifts to a child or other issue of the testator will not lapse if any issue of the legatee survive the testator. Lapsed legacies fall into and form part of the residuary estate. In the absence of any indication to the contrary a legacy becomes due on the day of the death of the testator, though for the convenience of the executor it is not payable till a year after that date; this delay does not prevent the legacy vesting on the testator's death. It frequently happens, however, that a legacy is given payable at a future date; in such a case, if the legatee dies after the testator but prior to the date when the legacy is payable it is necessary to discover whether the legacy was vested or contingent, as in the former case it becomes payable to the legatee's representative; in the latter, it lapses. In this, as in other cases, the test is the intention of the testator as expressed in the will; generally it may be said that a gift "payable" or "to be paid" at a certain fixed time confers a vested interest on the legatee, while a gift to A "at" a fixed time, *e.g.* twenty-one years of age, only confers on A an interest contingent on his attaining the age of twenty-one.

Legacy Duty is a duty charged by the state upon personal property devolving upon the legatees or next of kin of a dead person, either by virtue of his will or upon his intestacy. The duty was first imposed in England in 1780, but the principal act dealing with the subject is the Legacy Duty Act 1796. The principal points as to the duty are these. The duty is charged on personalty only. It is payable only where the person on whose death the property passes was domiciled in the United Kingdom. The rate of duty varies from 1 to 10% according to the relationship between the testator and legatee. As between husband and wife no duty is payable. The duty is payable by the executors and deducted from the legacy unless the testator directs otherwise. Special provisions as to valuation are in force where the gift is of an annuity or is settled on various persons in succession, or the legacy is given in joint tenancy and other cases. In some cases the duty is payable by instalments which carry interest at 3%. In various cases legacies are exempt from duty—the more important are gifts to a member of the royal family, specific legacies under £20 (pecuniary legacies under £20 pay duty), legacies of books, prints, &c., given to a body corporate for preservation, not for sale, and legacies given out of an estate the principal value of which is less than £100. Further, by the Finance Act 1894, payment of the estate duty thereby created absorbs the 1% duty paid by lineal ancestors or descendants of the deceased[1] and the duty on a settled legacy, and, lastly, in the event of estate duty being paid on an estate the total value of which is under £1000, no legacy duty is payable. The legacy duty payable in Ireland is now for all practical purposes assimilated to that in Great Britain. The principal statute in that country is an act of 1814.

LE GALLIENNE, RICHARD (1866-), English poet and critic, was born in Liverpool on the 20th of January 1866. He started life in a business office in Liverpool, but abandoned this to turn author. *My Lady's Sonnets* appeared at Liverpool in 1887, and in 1889 he became for a short time literary secretary to Wilson Barrett In the same year he published *Volumes in Folio*, *The Book Bills of Narcissus* and *George Meredith: some Characteristics* (new ed., 1900). He joined the staff of the *Star* in 1891, and wrote for various papers over the signature of "Logroller." *English Poems* (1892), *R. L. Stevenson and other Poems* (1895), a paraphrase (1897) of the *Rubáiyát* of Omar Khayyám, and *Odes from the Divan of Hafiz* (1903), contained some light, graceful verse, but he is best known by the fantastic prose essays and sketches of *Prose Fancies* (2 series, 1894–1896), *Sleeping Beauty and other Prose Fancies* (1900), *The Religion of a Literary Man* (1893), *The Quest of the Golden Girl* (1897), *The Life Romantic* (1901), &c. His first wife, Mildred Lee, died in 1894, and in 1897 he married Julie Norregard, subsequently taking up his residence in the United States. In 1906 he translated, from the Danish, Peter Nansen's *Love's Trilogy*.

LEGARÉ, HUGH SWINTON (1797–1843), American lawyer and statesman, was born in Charleston, South Carolina, on the 2nd of January 1797, of Huguenot and Scotch stock. Partly on account of his inability to share in the amusements of his fellows by reason of a deformity due to vaccine poisoning before he was five (the poison permanently arresting the growth and development of his legs), he was an eager student, and in 1814 he graduated at the College of South Carolina with the highest rank in his class and with a reputation throughout the state for scholarship and eloquence. He studied law for three years in South Carolina, and then spent two years abroad, studying French and Italian in Paris and jurisprudence at Edinburgh. In 1820–1822 and in 1824–1830 he was a member of the South Carolina legislature. In 1827, with Stephen Elliott (1771–1830), the naturalist, he founded the *Southern Review*, of which he was the sole editor after Elliott's death until 1834, when it was discontinued, and to which he contributed articles on law, travel, and modern and classical literature. In 1830–1832 he was attorney-general of South Carolina, and, although a State's Rights man, he strongly opposed nullification. During his term of office he appeared in a case before the United States Supreme Court, where his knowledge of civil law so strongly impressed Edward Livingston, the secretary of state, who was himself an admirer of Roman Law, that he urged Legaré to devote himself to the study of this subject with the hope that he might influence American law toward the spirit and philosophy and even the forms and processes of Roman jurisprudence.

[1] The Finance Bill 1909–1910 re-imposed this duty, and extended it to husbands and wives as well as descendants and ancestors.

… was appointed American *chargé* … from 1833 to 1836 he perfected … German commentaries on civil … Democrat, he was a member of … representatives, and there ably opposed … spite of the enthusiasm in South … project. He supported Harrison … 1840, and when the cabinet was … Legaré was appointed attorney- … the 9th of May 1843 he was … secretary, after the resignation of … June 1843 he died suddenly at … studies into common law of the … accomplished; but Story says " he … his arguments before the … the principles of the Roman … the Common Law with great … argued the famous cases, the … the *United States*, and

… Legaré (2 vols., Charleston, … Mary Bullen, who contributed … J. Ramage in *The* …

… regarded as among … They occupy the upper … the Sudan frontier. The … the Negro Shangalla. They … with narrow hollow- … foreheads. The chiefs' … perceptible Negro strain. … upwards of a hundred … They are, however, … and slaves, and energetic … they came about 1900 … are pagans, but Mahom- … among them.

… English fanatic, … About the … preacher among a sect … have held unorthodox … Together with his … in 1611. Thomas … imprisonment … with him, and on … Consistory Court of … Eventually, after … imprisonment, … in February 1612, … to the secular … his opinions … 18th of March 1612. … for his religious … burned at Lichfield … in England. … R. Gardiner,

… as deputy), … of diplomatic … used, in … diplomatic agent. … of Gregory IX., … recognizes two … *datus* or *missus*. … *delegatus*, or (2) … *collateralis*). … concurrent juris- … province, have … they were alto- … of a *legatus* … It was …

… **LEFEBV**… 1672), Fre… ing his stu… inspector … death he … obtained a … filled with … ill-health an… on Sappho) … which he resi… eager to obtai… him by the elec… on the 12th of … famous Madam… typical student … man and a thorou… of various Greek … Sappho, Virgil, …

Gran, Prague, Gnesen-Posen, Cologne, Salzburg, among others. The commission of the *legatus delegatus* (generally a member of the local clergy) is of a limited nature, and relates only to some definite piece of work. The *nuncius apostolicus* (who has the privilege of red apparel, a white horse and golden spurs) possesses ordinary jurisdiction within the province to which he has been sent, but his powers otherwise are restricted by the terms of his mandate. The *legatus a latere* (almost invariably a cardinal, though the power can be conferred on other prelates) is in the fullest sense the plenipotentiary representative of the pope, and possesses the high prerogative implied in the words of Gregory VII., " nostra vice quae corrigenda sunt corrigat, quae statuend constituat." He has the power of suspending all the bishops in his province, and no judicial cases are reserved from his judgment. Without special mandate, however, he cannot depose bishops or unite or separate bishoprics. At present *legati a latere* are not sent by the holy see, but diplomatic relations, where they exist, are maintained by means of nuncios, internuncios and other agents.

The history of the office of papal legate is closely involved with that of the papacy itself. If it were proved that papal legates exercised the prerogatives of the primacy in the early councils, it would be one of the strongest points for the Roman Catholic view of the papal history. Thus it is claimed that Hosius of Cordova presided over the council of Nicaea (325) in the name of the pope. But the claim rests on slender evidence, since the first source in which Hosius is referred to as representative of the pope is Gelasius of Cyzicus in the Propontis, who wrote toward the end of the 5th century. It is even open to dispute whether Hosius was president at Nicaea, and though he certainly presided over the council of Sardica in 343, it was probably as representative of the emperors Constans and Constantius, who had summoned the council. Pope Julius I. was represented at Sardica by two presbyters. Yet the fifth canon, which provides for appeal by a bishop to Rome, sanctions the use of embassies *a latere*. If the appellant wishes the pope to send priests from his own household, the pope shall be free to do so, and to furnish them with full authority from himself (" ut de latere suo presbyteros mittat . . . habentes ejus auctoritatem a quo destinati sunt "). The decrees of Sardica, an obscure council, were later confused with those of Nicaea and thus gained weight. In the synod of Ephesus in 431, Pope Celestine I. instructed his representatives to conduct themselves not as disputants but as judges, and Cyril of Alexandria presided not only in his own name but in that of the pope (and of the bishop of Jerusalem). Instances of delegation of the papal authority in various degrees become numerous in the 5th century, especially during the pontificate of Leo I. Thus Leo writes in 444 (*Ep.* 6) to Anastasius of Thessalonica, appointing him his vicar for the province of Illyria; the same arrangement, he informs us, had been made by Pope Siricius in favour of Anysius, the predecessor of Anastasius. Similar vicarial or legatine powers had been conferred in 418 by Zosimus upon Patroclus, bishop of Arles. In 449 Leo was represented at the " Robber Synod," from which his legates hardly escaped with life; at Chalcedon, in 451, they were treated with singular honour, though the imperial commissioners presided. Again, in 453 the same pope writes to the empress Pulcheria, naming Julianus of Cos as his representative in the defence of the interests of orthodoxy and ecclesiastical discipline at Constantinople (*Ep.* 112); the instructions to Julianus are given in *Ep.* 113 (" hanc specialem curam vice mea functus assumas "). The designation of Anastasius as vicar apostolic over Illyria may be said to mark the beginning of the custom of conferring, *ex officio*, the title of *legatus* upon the holders of important sees, who ultimately came to be known as *legati nati*, with the rank of primate; the appointment of Julianus at Constantinople gradually developed into the long permanent office of *apocrisiarius* or *responsalis*. Another sort of delegation is exemplified in Leo's letter to the African bishops (*Ep.* 12), in which he sends Potentius, with instructions to inquire in his name, and to report (" vicem curae nostrae fratri et consacerdoti nostro Potentio delegantes qui de episcopis, quorum culpabilis ferebatur electio, quid veritas haberet inquireret, nobisque omnia fideliter indicaret "). Passing on to the time of Gregory the Great, we find him sending two representatives to Gaul in 599, to suppress simony, and one to Spain in 603. Augustine of Canterbury is sometimes spoken of as legate, but it does not appear that in his case this title was used in any strictly technical sense, although the archbishop of Canterbury afterwards attained the permanent dignity of a *legatus natus*. Boniface, the apostle of Germany, was in like manner constituted, according to Hincmar (*Ep.* 30), a legate of the apostolic see by Popes Gregory II. and Gregory III. According to Hefele (*Conc.* iv. 239), Rodoald of Porto and Zecharias of Anagni, who were sent by Pope Nicolas to Constantinople in 860, were the first actually called *legati a latere*. The policy of Gregory VII. naturally led to a great development of the legatine as distinguished from the ordinary episcopal function. From the creation of the medieval papal monarchy until the close of the middle ages, the papal legate played a most important rôle in national as well as church history. The further definition of his powers proceeded throughout the 12th and 13th centuries. From the 16th century legates *a latere* give way almost entirely to nuncios (*q.v.*).

See P. Hinschius, *Kirchenrecht*, i. 498 ff.; G. Phillips, *Kirchenrecht*, vol. vi. 680 ff.

LEGATION (Lat. *legatio*, a sending or mission), a diplomatic mission of the second rank. The term is also applied to the building in which the minister resides and to the area round it covered by his diplomatic immunities. See DIPLOMACY.

LEGEND (through the French from the med. Lat. *legenda*, things to be read, from *legere*, to read), in its primary meaning the history or life-story of a saint, and so applied to portions of Scripture and selections from the lives of the saints as read at divine service. The statute of 3 and 4 Edward VI. dealing with the abolition of certain books and images (1549), cap. 10, sect. 1, says that "all bookes . . . called processionalles, manuelles, *legends* . . . shall be . . . abolished." The "Golden Legend," or *Aurea Legenda*, was the name given to a book containing lives of the saints and descriptions of festivals, written by Jacobus de Voragine, archbishop of Genoa, in the 13th century. From the original application of the word to stories of the saints containing wonders and miracles, the word came to be applied to a story handed down without any foundation in history, but popularly believed to be true. "Legend" is also used of a writing, inscription, or motto on coins or medals, and in connexion with coats of arms, shields, monuments, &c.

LEGENDRE, ADRIEN MARIE (1752–1833), French mathematician, was born at Paris (or, according to some accounts, at Toulouse) in 1752. He was brought up at Paris, where he completed his studies at the *Collège Mazarin*. His first published writings consist of articles forming part of the *Traité de mécanique* (1774) of the Abbé Marie, who was his professor; Legendre's name, however, is not mentioned. Soon afterwards he was appointed professor of mathematics in the *École Militaire* at Paris, and he was afterwards professor in the *École Normale*. In 1782 he received the prize from the Berlin Academy for his "Dissertation sur la question de balistique," a memoir relating to the paths of projectiles in resisting media. He also, about this time, wrote his "Recherches sur la figure des planètes," published in the *Mémoires* of the French Academy, of which he was elected a member in succession to J. le Rond d'Alembert in 1783. He was also appointed a commissioner for connecting geodetically Paris and Greenwich, his colleagues being P. F. A. Méchain and C. F. Cassini de Thury; General William Roy conducted the operations on behalf of England. The French observations were published in 1792 (*Exposé des opérations faites en France in 1787 pour la jonction des observatoires de Paris et de Greenwich*). During the Revolution, he was one of the three members of the council established to introduce the decimal system, and he was also a member of the commission appointed to determine the length of the metre, for which purpose the calculations, &c., connected with the arc of the meridian from Barcelona to Dunkirk were revised. He was also associated with G. C. F. M. Prony (1755–1839) in the formation of the great French tables of logarithms of numbers, sines, and tangents, and natural sines, called the *Tables du Cadastre*, in which the quadrant was divided centesimally; these tables have never been published (see LOGARITHMS). He was examiner in the *École Polytechnique*, but held few important state offices. He died at Paris on the 10th of January 1833, and the discourse at his grave was pronounced by S. D. Poisson. The last of the three supplements to his *Traité des fonctions elliptiques* was published in 1832, and Poisson in his funeral oration remarked: "M. Legendre a eu cela de commun avec la plupart des géomètres qui l'ont précédé, que ses travaux n'ont fini qu'avec sa vie. Le dernier volume de nos mémoires renferme encore un mémoire de lui, sur une question difficile de la théorie des nombres; et peu de temps avant la maladie qui l'a conduit au tombeau, il se procura les observations les plus récentes des comètes à courtes périodes, dont il allait se servir pour appliquer et perfectionner ses méthodes."

It will be convenient, in giving an account of his writings, to consider them under the different subjects which are especially associated with his name.

Elliptic Functions.—This is the subject with which Legendre's name will always be most closely connected, and his researches upon it extend over a period of more than forty years. His first published writings upon the subject consist of two papers in the *Mémoires de l'Académie Française* for 1786 upon elliptic arcs. In 1792 he presented to the Academy a memoir on elliptic transcendents. The contents of these memoirs are included in the first volume of his *Exercices de calcul intégral* (1811). The third volume (1816) contains the very elaborate and now well-known tables of the elliptic integrals which were calculated by Legendre himself, with an account of the mode of their construction. In 1827 appeared the *Traité des fonctions elliptiques* (2 vols., the first dated 1825, the second 1826); a great part of the first volume agrees very closely with the contents of the *Exercices*; the tables, &c., are given in the second volume. Three supplements, relating to the researches of N. H. Abel and C. G. J. Jacobi, were published in 1828–1832, and form a third volume. Legendre had pursued the subject which would now be called elliptic integrals alone from 1786 to 1827, the results of his labours having been almost entirely neglected by his contemporaries, but his work had scarcely appeared in 1827 when the discoveries which were independently made by the two young and as yet unknown mathematicians Abel and Jacobi placed the subject on a new basis, and revolutionized it completely. The readiness with which Legendre, who was then seventy-six years of age, welcomed these important researches, that quite overshadowed his own, and included them in successive supplements to his work, does the highest honour to him (see FUNCTION).

Eulerian Integrals and Integral Calculus.—The *Exercices de calcul intégral* consist of three volumes, a great portion of the first and the whole of the third being devoted to elliptic functions. The remainder of the first volume relates to the Eulerian integrals and to quadratures. The second volume (1817) relates to the Eulerian integrals, and to various integrals and series, developments, mechanical problems, &c., connected with the integral calculus; this volume contains also a numerical table of the values of the gamma function. The latter portion of the second volume of the *Traité des fonctions elliptiques* (1826) is also devoted to the Eulerian integrals, the table being reproduced. Legendre's researches connected with the "gamma function" are of importance, and are well known; the subject was also treated by K. F. Gauss in his memoir *Disquisitiones generales circa series infinitas* (1816), but in a very different manner. The results given in the second volume of the *Exercices* are of too miscellaneous a character to admit of being briefly described. In 1788 Legendre published a memoir on double integrals, and in 1809 one on definite integrals.

Theory of Numbers.—Legendre's *Théorie des nombres* and Gauss's *Disquisitiones arithmeticae* (1801) are still standard works upon this subject. The first edition of the former appeared in 1798 under the title *Essai sur la théorie des nombres*; there was a second edition in 1808; a first supplement was published in 1816, and a second in 1825. The third edition, under the title *Théorie des nombres*, appeared in 1830 in two volumes. The fourth edition appeared in 1900. To Legendre is due the theorem known as the law of quadratic reciprocity, the most important general result in the science of numbers which has been discovered since the time of P. de Fermat, and which was called by Gauss the "gem of arithmetic." It was first given by Legendre in the *Mémoires* of the Academy for 1785, but the demonstration that accompanied it was incomplete. The symbol (a/p) which is known as Legendre's symbol, and denotes the positive or negative unit which is the remainder when $a^{\frac{1}{2}(p-1)}$ is divided by a prime number p, does not appear in this memoir, but was first used in the *Essai sur la théorie des nombres*. Legendre's formula $x: (\log x - 1\cdot08366)$ for the approximate number of forms inferior to a given number x was first given by him also in this work (2nd ed., p. 394) (see NUMBER).

Attractions of Ellipsoids.—Legendre was the author of four important memoirs on this subject. In the first of these, entitled "Recherches sur l'attraction des sphéroides homogènes," published in the *Mémoires* of the Academy for 1785, but communicated to it at an earlier period, Legendre introduces the celebrated expressions which, though frequently called Laplace's coefficients, are more correctly named after Legendre. The definition of the coefficients is that if $(1-2h\cos\phi+h^2)^{-\frac{1}{2}}$ be expanded in ascending powers of h, and if the general term be denoted by P_nh^n, then P_n is of the Legendrian coefficient of the nth order. In this memoir also the function which is now called the potential was, at the suggestion of Laplace, first introduced. Legendre shows that Maclaurin's theorem with respect to confocal ellipsoids is true for any position of the external point when the ellipsoids are solids of revolution. Of this memoir Isaac Todhunter writes: "We may affirm that no single memoir in the history of our subject can rival this in interest and importance. During forty years the resources of analysis, even in the hands of d'Alembert, Lagrange and Laplace, had not carried the theory of the attraction of ellipsoids beyond the point which the geometry of Maclaurin had reached. The introduction of the coefficients now called Laplace's, and their application, commence a new era in mathematical physics." Legendre's second memoir was communicated to the *Académie* in 1784, and relates to the conditions of equilibrium of a mass of rotating fluid in the form of a figure of revolution which does not deviate much from a sphere. The third memoir relates to Laplace's theorem respecting confocal ellipsoids. Of the fourth memoir Todhunter writes: "It occupies an important position in the history of our subject. The most striking addition which is here made to previous researches consists in the treatment of a planet supposed entirely fluid; the general equation for the form of a stratum is given for the first time and discussed. For the first time we have a correct and convenient expression for Laplace's nth coefficient." (See Todhunter's *History of the Mathematical Theories of Attraction and the Figure of the Earth* (1873), the twentieth, twenty-second, twenty-fourth, and twenty-fifth chapters of which contain a full and complete account of Legendre's four memoirs. See also SPHERICAL HARMONICS.)

Geodesy.—Besides the work upon the geodetical operations connecting Paris and Greenwich, of which Legendre was one of the [illegible], he published in the *Mémoires de l'Académie* for 1787 two papers on trigonometrical operations depending upon the figure of the earth, containing many theorems relating to this subject. The best known of these, which is called Legendre's theorem, is usually given in treatises on spherical trigonometry; by means of it a small spherical triangle may be treated as a plane triangle, certain corrections being applied to the angles. Legendre was also the author of a memoir upon triangles drawn upon a spheroid. Legendre's theorem is of fundamental use in geodesy, and his contributions to [illegible] of the greatest importance.

Method of Least Squares.—In 1806 appeared Legendre's *Nouvelles méthodes pour la détermination des orbites des comètes*, which is [illegible] the first published suggestion of the method [illegible] (see PROBABILITY). In the preface Legendre remarks [illegible] "...la plus simple et la plus générale [illegible] la somme des quarrés des erreurs, ... [illegible] méthode des moindres quarrés"; and in an appendix [illegible] of the method is explained his words are [illegible] pour cet objet, je pense [illegible] de plus exact, ni d'une application [illegible] avons fait usage dans les recherches [illegible] rendre minimum la somme des quarrés [illegible] proposed by Legendre only as a [illegible] observations, without reference to [illegible]. It has, however, been applied by Gauss [illegible] was fully explained, and the law [illegible] by him in 1809. Laplace also [illegible] of the principles of the theory of [illegible] to republish the part of his [illegible] in the *Mémoires de l'Académie* [illegible] of least squares was first [illegible] the theory and algorithm and [illegible] are due to Gauss and [illegible] supplements to his *Nouvelles* [illegible]

[illegible] Legendre's name is most widely [illegible], the most successful [illegible] to supersede Euclid [illegible] in 1794, and went [illegible] translated into almost [illegible] Sir David Brewster, [illegible] in 1823, and is [illegible] did not contain the [illegible] a proof of the [illegible] J. H. Lambert [illegible] similar in prin- [illegible] of the objections [illegible]

It will thus be seen that Legendre's works have placed him in the very foremost rank in the widely distinct subjects of elliptic functions, theory of numbers, attractions, and geodesy, and have given him a conspicuous position in connexion with the integral calculus and other branches of mathematics. He published a memoir on the integration of partial differential equations and a few others which have not been noticed above, but they relate to subjects with which his name is not especially associated. A good account of the principal works of Legendre is given in the *Bibliothèque universelle de Genève* for 1833, pp. 45-82.

See Élie de Beaumont, "Memoir de Legendre," translated by C. A. Alexander, *Smithsonian Report* (1874). (J. W. L. G.)

LEGENDRE, LOUIS (1752–1797), French revolutionist, was born at Versailles on the 22nd of May 1752. When the Revolution broke out, he kept a butcher's shop in Paris, in the rue des Boucheries St Germain. He was an ardent supporter of the ideas of the Revolution, a member of the Jacobin Club, and one of the founders of the club of the Cordeliers. In spite of the incorrectness of his diction, he was gifted with a genuine eloquence, and well knew how to carry the populace with him. He was a prominent actor in the taking of the Bastille (14th of July 1789), in the massacre of the Champ de Mars (July 1791), and in the attack on the Tuileries (10th of August 1792). Deputy from Paris to the Convention, he voted for the death of Louis XVI., and was sent on mission to Lyons (27th of February 1793) before the revolt of that town, and was on mission from August to October 1793 in Seine-Inférieure. He was a member of the *Comité de Sûreté Générale*, and contributed to the downfall of the Girondists. When Danton was arrested, Legendre at first defended him, but was soon cowed and withdrew his defence. After the fall of Robespierre, Legendre took part in the reactionary movement, undertook the closing of the Jacobin Club, was elected president of the Convention, and helped to bring about the impeachment of J. B. Carrier, the perpetrator of the *noyades* of Nantes. He was subsequently elected a member of the Council of Ancients, and died on the 13th of December 1797.

See F. A. Aulard, *Les Orateurs de la Législative et de la Convention* (2nd ed., Paris, 1906, 2 vols.); "Correspondance de Legendre" in the *Révolution française* (vol. xl., 1901).

LEGERDEMAIN (Fr. *léger-de-main*, *i.e.* light or sleight of hand), the name given specifically to that form of conjuring in which the performer relies on dexterity of manipulation rather than on mechanical apparatus. See CONJURING.

LEGGE, afterwards BILSON-LEGGE, **HENRY** (1708–1764), English statesman, fourth son of William Legge, 1st earl of Dartmouth (1672–1750), was born on the 29th of May 1708. Educated at Christ Church, Oxford, he became private secretary to Sir Robert Walpole, and in 1739 was appointed secretary of Ireland by the lord-lieutenant, the 3rd duke of Devonshire; being chosen member of parliament for the borough of East Looe in 1740, and for Orford, Suffolk, at the general election in the succeeding year. Legge only shared temporarily in the downfall of Walpole, and became in quick succession surveyor-general of woods and forests, a lord of the admiralty, and a lord of the treasury. In 1748 he was sent as envoy extraordinary to Frederick the Great, and although his conduct in Berlin was sharply censured by George II., he became treasurer of the navy soon after his return to England. In April 1754 he joined the ministry of the duke of Newcastle as chancellor of the exchequer, the king consenting to this appointment although refusing to hold any intercourse with the minister; but Legge shared the elder Pitt's dislike of the policy of paying subsidies to the landgrave of Hesse, and was dismissed from office in November 1755. Twelve months later he returned to his post at the exchequer in the administration of Pitt and the 4th duke of Devonshire, retaining office until April 1757 when he shared both the dismissal and the ensuing popularity of Pitt. When in conjunction with the duke of Newcastle Pitt returned to power in the following July, Legge became chancellor of the exchequer for the third time. He imposed new taxes upon houses and windows, and he appears to have lost to some extent the friendship of Pitt, while the king refused to make him a peer. In 1759 he obtained the insecure position of surveyor of the petty customs and subsidies [illegible] the port of London, and having in consequence to resign his [illegible] in parliament he was chosen one of the members for

Hampshire, a proceeding which greatly incensed the earl of Bute, who desired this seat for one of his friends. Having thus incurred Bute's displeasure Legge was again dismissed from the exchequer in March 1761, but he continued to take part in parliamentary debates until his death at Tunbridge Wells on the 23rd of August 1764. Legge appears to have been a capable financier, but the position of chancellor of the exchequer was not at that time a cabinet office. He took the additional name of Bilson on succeeding to the estates of a relative, Thomas Bettersworth Bilson, in 1754. Pitt called Legge, "the child, and deservedly the favourite child, of the Whigs." Horace Walpole said he was "of a creeping, underhand nature, and aspired to the lion's place by the manœuvre of the mole," but afterwards he spoke in high terms of his talents. Legge married Mary, daughter and heiress of Edward, 4th and last Baron Stawel (d. 1755). This lady, who in 1760 was created Baroness Stawel of Somerton, bore him an only child, Henry Stawel Bilson-Legge (1757–1820), who became Baron Stawel on his mother's death in 1780. When Stawel died without sons his title became extinct. His only daughter, Mary (d. 1864), married John Dutton, 2nd Baron Sherborne.

See John Butler, bishop of Hereford, *Some Account of the Character of the late Rt. Hon. H. Bilson-Legge* (1765); Horace Walpole, *Memoirs of the Reign of George II.* (London, 1847); and *Memoirs of the Reign of George III.*, edited by G. F. R. Barker (London, 1894); W. E. H. Lecky, *History of England*, vol. ii. (London, 1892); and the memoirs and collections of correspondence of the time.

LEGGE, JAMES (1815–1897), British Chinese scholar, was born at Huntly, Aberdeenshire, in 1815, and educated at King's College, Aberdeen. After studying at the Highbury Theological College, London, he went in 1839 as a missionary to the Chinese, but, as China was not yet open to Europeans, he remained at Malacca three years, in charge of the Anglo-Chinese College there. The College was subsequently moved to Hong-Kong, where Legge lived for thirty years. Impressed with the necessity of missionaries being able to comprehend the ideas and culture of the Chinese, he began in 1841 a translation in many volumes of the Chinese classics, a monumental task admirably executed and completed a few years before his death. In 1870 he was made an LL.D. of Aberdeen and in 1884 of Edinburgh University. In 1875 several gentlemen connected with the China trade suggested to the university of Oxford a Chair of Chinese Language and Literature to be occupied by Dr Legge. The university responded liberally, Corpus Christi College contributed the emoluments of a fellowship, and the chair was constituted in 1876. In addition to his other work Legge wrote *The Life and Teaching of Confucius* (1867); *The Life and Teaching of Mencius* (1875); *The Religions of China* (1880); and other books on Chinese literature and religion. He died at Oxford on the 29th of November 1897.

LEGHORN (Ital. *Livorno*, Fr. *Livourne*), a city of Tuscany, Italy, chief town of the province of the same name, which consists of the commune of Leghorn and the islands of Elba and Gorgona. The town is the seat of a bishopric and of a large naval academy—the only one in Italy—and the third largest commercial port in the kingdom, situated on the west coast, 12 m. S.W. of Pisa by rail, 10 ft. above sea-level. Pop. (1901) 78,308 (town), 96,528 (commune). It is built along the seashore upon a healthy and fertile tract of land, which forms, as it were, an oasis in a zone of Maremma. Behind is a range of hills, the most conspicuous of which, the Monte Nero, is crowned by a frequented pilgrimage church and also by villas and hotels, to which a funicular railway runs. The town itself is almost entirely modern. The 16th-century Fortezza Vecchia, guarding the harbour, is picturesque, and there is a good bronze statue of the grand duke Ferdinand I. by Pietro Tacca (1577–1640), a pupil of Giovanni da Bologna. The lofty Torre del Marzocco, erected in 1423 by the Florentines, is fine. The façade of the cathedral was designed by Inigo Jones. The old Protestant cemetery contains the tombs of Tobias Smollett (d. 1771) and Francis Horner (d. 1817). There is also a large synagogue founded in 1581. The exchange, the chamber of commerce and the clearing-house (one of the oldest in the world, dating from 1764) are united under one roof in the Palazzo del Commercio, opened in 1907. Several improvements have been carried out in the city and port, and the place is developing rapidly as an industrial centre. The naval academy, formerly established partly at Naples and partly at Genoa, has been transferred to Leghorn. Some of the navigable canals which connected the harbour with the interior of the city have been either modified or filled up. Several streets have been widened, and a road along the shore has been transformed into a fine and shady promenade. Leghorn is the principal sea-bathing resort in this part of Italy, the season lasting from the end of June to the end of August. A spa for the use of the Acque della Salute has been constructed. Leghorn is on the main line from Pisa to Rome; another line runs to Colle Salvetti. A considerable number of important steamship lines call here. The new rectilinear mole, sanctioned in 1881, has been built out into the sea for a distance of 600 yds. from the old Vegliaia lighthouse, and the docking basin has been lengthened to 490 ft. Inside the breakwater the depth varies from 10 to 26 ft. The total trade of the port increased from £3,853,593 in 1897 to £5,675,285 in 1905 and £7,009,758 in 1906 (the large increase being mainly due to a rise of over £1,000,000 in imports—mainly of coal, building materials and machinery), the average ratio of imports to exports being as three to two. The imports consist principally of machinery, coal, grain, dried fish, tobacco and hides, and the exports of hemp, hides, olive oil, soap, coral, candied fruit, wine, straw hats, boracic acid, mercury, and marble and alabaster. In 1885 the total number of vessels that entered the port was 4281 of 1,434,000 tons; of these, 1251 of 750,000 tons were foreign; 688,000 tons of merchandise were loaded and unloaded. In 1906, after considerable fluctuations during the interval, the total number that entered was 4623 vessels of 2,372,551 tons; of these, 935 of 1,002,119 tons were foreign; British ships representing about half this tonnage. In 1906 the total imports and exports amounted to 1,470,000 tons including coasting trade. A great obstacle to the development of the port is the absence of modern mechanical appliances for loading and unloading vessels, and of quay space and dock accommodation. The older shipyards have been considerably extended, and shipbuilding is actively carried on, especially by the Orlando yard which builds large ships for the Italian navy, while new industries—namely, glass-making and copper and brass-founding, electric power works, a cement factory, porcelain factories, flour-mills, oil-mills, a cotton yarn spinning factory, electric plant works, a ship-breaking yard, a motor-boat yard, &c.—have been established. Other important firms, Tuscan wine-growers, oil-growers, timber traders, colour manufacturers, &c., have their head offices and stores at Leghorn, with a view to export. The former British "factory" here was of great importance for the trade with the Levant, but was closed in 1825. The two villages of Ardenza and Antignano, which form part of the commune, have acquired considerable importance, the former in part for sea-bathing.

The earliest mention of Leghorn occurs in a document of 891, relating to the first church here; in 1017 it is called a castle. In the 13th century the Pisans tried to attract a population to the spot, but it was not till the 14th that Leghorn became a rival of Porto Pisano at the mouth of the Arno, which it was destined ultimately to supplant. It was at Leghorn that Urban V. and Gregory XI. landed on their return from Avignon. When in 1405 the king of France sold Pisa to the Florentines he kept possession of Leghorn; but he afterwards (1407) sold it for 26,000 ducats to the Genoese, and from the Genoese the Florentines purchased it in 1421. In 1496 the city showed its devotion to its new masters by a successful defence against Maximilian and his allies, but it was still a small place; in 1551 there were only 749 inhabitants. With the rise of the Medici came a rapid increase of prosperity; Cosmo, Francis and Ferdinand erected fortifications and harbour works, warehouses and churches, with equal liberality, and the last especially gave a stimulus to trade by inviting "men of the East and the West, Spanish and Portuguese, Greeks, Germans, Italians, Hebrews, Turks.

[illegible] about 25,000. In 1815 the period of service of the corps [illegible] expired when Napoleon returned from Elba, but its [illegible] voluntarily offered to prolong their service. It lost [illegible] at Waterloo, in which Baring's battalion of the light infantry distinguished itself by its gallant defence of La Haye Sainte. The [illegible] of the Legion at the time of its disbandment was 1100 [illegible] and 23,500 men. A short-lived "King's German Legion" [illegible] raised by the British government for service in the Crimean [illegible] Certain Hanoverian regiments of the German army to-day represent the units of the Legion and carry Peninsular battle-[illegible] on their standards and colours.

LEGITIM, or BAIRN'S PART, in Scots law, the legal share of the movable property of a father due on his death to his children. [illegible] a father dies leaving a widow and children, the movable property is divided into three equal parts; one-third part is divided equally among all the children who survive, although they may be of different marriages (the issue of predeceased children do not share); another third goes to the widow as her *jus relictae*, and the remaining third, called "dead's part," may be disposed of by the father by will as he pleases. If the father die intestate the dead's part goes to the children as next of kin. Should the father leave no widow, one-half of the movable estate is legitim and one-half dead's part. In claiming legitim, however, credit must be given for any advance made by the father out of his movable estate during his lifetime.

LEGITIMACY, and **LEGITIMATION**, the status derived by individuals in consequence of being born in legal wedlock, and the means by which the same status is given to persons not so born. Under the Roman or civil law a child born before the marriage of the parents was made legitimate by their subsequent marriage. This method of legitimation was accepted by the canon law, by the legal systems of the continent of Europe, of Scotland and of some of the states of the United States. The early Germanic codes, however, did not recognize such legitimation, nor among the Anglo-Saxons had the natural-born child any rights of inheritance, or possibly any right other than that of protection, even when acknowledged by its father. The principle of the civil and canon law was at one time advocated by the clergy of England, but was summarily rejected by the barons at the parliament of Merton in 1236, when they replied *Nolumus leges Angliae mutare.*

English law takes account solely of the fact that marriage precedes the birth of the child; at whatever period the birth happens after the marriage, the offspring is prima facie legitimate. The presumption of law is always in favour of the legitimacy of the child of a married woman, and at one time it was so strong that Sir Edward Coke held that "if the husband be within the four seas, *i.e.* within the jurisdiction of the king of England, and the wife hath issue, no proof shall be admitted to prove the child a bastard unless the husband hath an apparent impossibility of procreation." It is now settled, however, that the presumption of legitimacy may be rebutted by evidence showing non-access on the part of the husband, or any other circumstance showing that the husband could not in the course of nature have been the father of his wife's child. If the husband had access, or the access be not clearly negatived, even though others at the same time were carrying on an illicit intercourse with the wife, a child born under such circumstances is legitimate. If the husband had access intercourse must be presumed, unless there is irresistible evidence to the contrary. Neither husband or wife will be permitted to prove the non-access directly or indirectly. Children born after a divorce *a mensa et thoro* will, however, be presumed to be bastards unless access be proved. A child born so long after the death of a husband that he could not in the ordinary course of nature have been the father is illegitimate. The period of gestation is presumed to be *about* nine calendar months; and if there were any circumstances from which an unusually long or short period of gestation could be inferred, special medical testimony would be required.

A marriage between persons within the prohibited degrees of affinity was before 1835 not void, but only voidable, and the ecclesiastical courts were restrained from bastardizing the issue after the death of either of the parents. Lord

Lyndhurst's act (1835) declared all such existing marriages valid, but all subsequent marriages between persons within the prohibited degrees of consanguinity or affinity were made null and void and the issue illegitimate (see MARRIAGE). By the Legitimacy Declaration Act 1858, application may be made to the Probate, Divorce and Admiralty Court (in Scotland, to the Court of Session by action of declarator) for a declaration of legitimacy and of the validity of a marriage. The status of legitimacy in any country depending upon the fact of the child having been born in wedlock, it may be concluded that any question as to the legitimacy of a child turns either on the validity of the marriage or on whether the child has been born in wedlock.

Legitimation effected by the subsequent marriage of the parents of the illegitimate child is technically known as legitimation *per subsequens matrimonium*. This adoption of the Roman law principle is followed by most of the states of the continent of Europe (with distinctions, of course, as to *certain* illegitimate children, or as to the forms of acknowledgment by the parent or parents), in the Isle of Man, Guernsey, Jersey, Lower Canada, St Lucia, Trinidad, Demerara, Berbice, Cape Colony, Ceylon, Mauritius; it has been adopted in New Zealand (Legitimation Act 1894), South Australia (Legitimation Act 1898, amended 1902), Queensland (Legitimation Act 1899), New South Wales (Legitimation Act 1902), and Victoria (Registration of Births, Deaths and Marriages Act 1903). It is to be noted, however, that in these states the mere fact of the parents marrying does not legitimate the child; indeed, the parents may marry, yet the child remain illegitimate. In order to legitimate the child it is necessary for the father to make application for its registration; in South Australia, the application must be made by both parents; so also in Victoria, if the mother is living, if not, application by the father will suffice. In New Zealand, Queensland and New South Wales, registration may be made at any time after the marriage; in Victoria, within six months from the date of the marriage; in South Australia, by the act of 1898, registration was permissible only within thirty days before or after the marriage, but by the amending act of 1902 it is allowed at any time more than thirty days after the marriage, provided the applicants prove before a magistrate that they are the parents of the child. In all cases the legitimation is retrospective, taking effect from the birth of the child. Legitimation by subsequent marriage exists also in the following states of the American Union: Maine, Pennsylvania, Illinois, Michigan, Iowa, Minnesota, California, Oregon, Nevada, Washington, N. and S. Dakota, Idaho, Montana and New Mexico. In Massachusetts, Vermont, Illinois, Indiana, Wisconsin, Nebraska, Maryland, Virginia, West Virginia, Kentucky, Missouri, Arkansas, Texas, Colorado, Idaho, Wyoming, Georgia, Alabama, Mississippi and Arizona, in addition to the marriage the father must recognize or acknowledge the illegitimate child as his. In New Hampshire, Connecticut and Louisiana both parents must acknowledge the child, either by an authentic act before marriage or by the contract of marriage. In some states (California, Nevada, N. and S. Dakota and Idaho) if the father of an illegitimate child receives it into his house (with the consent of his wife, if married), and treats it as if it were legitimate, it becomes legitimate for all purposes. In other states (N. Carolina, Tennessee, Georgia and New Mexico) the putative father can legitimize the child by process in court. Those states of the United States which have not been mentioned follow the English common law, which also prevails in Ireland, some of the West Indies and part of Canada. In Scotland, on the other hand, the principle of the civil law is followed. In Scotland, bastards could be legitimized in two ways: either by the subsequent intermarriage of the mother of the child with the father, or by letters of legitimation from the sovereign. With respect to the last, however, it is to be observed that letters of legitimation, be their clauses ever so strong, could not enable the bastard to succeed to his natural father; for the sovereign could not, by any prerogative, cut off the private right of third parties. But by a special clause in the letters of legitimation, the sovereign could renounce his right to the bastard's succession, failing legitimate descendants, in favour of him who would have been the bastard's heir had he been born in lawful wedlock, such renunciation encroaching upon no right competent to any third person.

The question remains, how far, if at all, English law recognizes the legitimacy of a person born out of wedlock. Strictly speaking, English law does not recognize any such person as legitimate (though the supreme power of an act of parliament can, of course, confer the rights of legitimacy), but under certain circumstances it will recognize, for purposes of succession to property, a legitimated person as legitimate. The general maxim of law is that the status of legitimacy must be tried by the law of the country where it originates, and where the law of the father's domicile at the time of the child's birth, and of the father's domicile at the time of the subsequent marriage, taken together, legitimize the child, English law will recognize the legitimacy. For purposes of succession to real property, however, legitimacy must be determined by the *lex loci rei sitae*; so that, for example, a legitimized Scotsman would be recognized as legitimate in England, but not legitimate so far as to take lands as heir (*Birtwhistle* v. *Vardill*, 1840). The conflict of laws on the subject yields some curious results. Thus, a domiciled Scotsman had a son born in Scotland and then married the mother in Scotland. The son died possessed of land in England, and it was held that the father could not inherit from the son. On the other hand, where an unmarried woman, domiciled in England died intestate there, it was held that her brother's daughter, born before marriage, but whilst the father was domiciled in Holland, and legitimized by the parents' marriage while they were still domiciled in Holland, was entitled to succeed to the personal property of her aunt (*In re Goodman's Trusts*, 1880). *In re Grey's Trusts* (1892) decided that, where *real estate* was bequeathed to the children of a person domiciled in a foreign country and these children were legitimized by the subsequent marriage in that country of their father with their mother, that they were entitled to share as legitimate children in a devise of English realty. It is to be noted that this decision does not clash with that of *Birtwhistle* v. *Vardill*.

See J. A. Foote, *Private International Law*; A. V. Dicey, *Conflict of Laws*; L. von Bar, *Private International Law*; Story, *Conflict of Laws*; J. Westlake, *International Law*.

LEGITIMISTS (Fr. *légitimistes*, from *légitime*, lawful, legitimate), the name of the party in France which after the revolution of 1830 continued to support the claims of the elder line of the house of Bourbon as the legitimate sovereigns "by divine right." The death of the comte de Chambord in 1883 dissolved the *parti légitimiste*, only an insignificant remnant, known as the *Blancs d'Espagne*, repudiating the act of renunciation of Philip V. of Spain and upholding the rights of the Bourbons of the line of Anjou. The word *légitimiste* was not admitted by the French Academy until 1878; but meanwhile it had spread beyond France, and the English word legitimist is now applied to any supporter of monarchy by hereditary right as against a parliamentary or other title.

LEGNAGO, a fortified town of Venetia, Italy, in the province of Verona, on the Adige, 29 m. by rail E. of Mantua, 52 ft. above sea-level. Pop. (1906) 2731 (town), 17,000 (commune). Legnago is one of the famous Quadrilateral fortresses. The present fortifications were planned and made in 1815, the older defences having been destroyed by Napoleon I. in 1801. The situation is low and unhealthy, but the territory is fertile, rice, cereals and sugar being grown. Legnago is the birthplace of G. B. Cavalcaselle, the art historian (1827–1897). A branch line runs hence to Rovigo.

LEGNANO, a town of Lombardy, Italy, in the province of Milan, 17 m. N.W. of that city by rail, 682 ft. above sea-level. Pop. (1881) 7153, (1901) 18,285. The church of S. Magno, built in the style of Bramante by G. Lampugnano (1504–1529), contains an altar-piece considered one of Luini's best works. There are also remains of a castle of the Visconti. Legnano is the seat of important cotton and silk industries, with

Moors, Arm
n the city,
in 1691, Legh
by the Quadr
all the hostil
by the law of
LEGION (L
marching out
primitive stat
at once and
a unit of 4000
some light infa
who were "alli
from the
The legionaries
Roman soldier
they enjoyed
"auxiliaries."
such legions:
about A.D. 290
the number of
of the legions
They lost their
the character
important arm
A.D. In the m
been used as
employed for o
such as a co
further ROMAN

The term le
of all arms in
being the Prov
INFANTRY). N
the word to d
tained in Franc
The term "For
corps of foreig
smaller states
legions the "B
commanded by
was a regularly
is colloquially
étrangers in the
spirits of all nati
colonial campaig
The most famo
in modern times
history of the co
threatened by the
sidered possible, t
part of the Hano
by the Hanoveria
late, and it was on
the army as a unit
"King's German R
England. This enl
Germans as well, as
Major Colin Halket
of the new corps, w
arms with the title c
a dragoon and a huss
line battalions and a
increased. Its servi
of November 1805,
minor sieges and c
expedition of 1809, th
in 1808, and the cam
title to fame is its par
to last it was an ackno
whose services both o
highest value. The ex
Legion at Garcia Hern
they charged and broke
some 1400 prisoners, is
history of the cavalry
Cavalry). A general off
commanded the British L
It should be said that t
It was considered rather a
which served abroad by
portion and depot

—LEGROS

portraits to the Salon of 1857: one was rejected, and formed part of the exhibition of protest organized by Bonvin in his studio, the other, which was accepted, was a profile portrait of his father. This work was presented to the museum at Tours by the artist when his friend Cazin was curator. Champfleury saw the work in the Salon, and sought out the artist to enlist him in the small army of so-called "Realists," comprising (round ... Courbet) all those who raised protest against the ... of the degenerate Romantics. In 1859 ... "Angelus" was exhibited, the first of those quiet ... with kneeling figures of patient women, by ... is best known as a painter. "Ex Voto," a work of ... and insight, painted in 1861, now in the museum ... was received by his friends with enthusiasm, but it ... mention at the Salon. Legros came to England ... in 1864 married Miss Frances Rosetta Hodgson. ... by his etching and teaching. He then became ... at the South Kensington School of Art, and ... Professor at University College, London. He ... as an Englishman in 1881, and remained at ... College seventeen years. His influence there was ... a certain distinction, severity and truth ... the work of his pupils, with a simple technique ... traditions of the old masters, until thensome- ... English art. He would draw or paint a torso ... the students in an hour or even less, so that the ... pupils might not be dulled. As students had ... weeks and even months over a single drawing, ... the positions of the casts in the Antique School ... every week. In the painting school he ... a good outline, preserved by a thin rub in of ... the work was to be finished in a single painting. Experiments in all varieties of art work were ... whenever the professor saw a fine example in the ... a process interested him in a workshop, he ... had mastered the technique and his students ... their prentice hands at it. As he had casually ... etching by watching a comrade in Paris ... commercial engraving, so he began the making ... a walk in the British Museum, studying the ... Pisanello, and a visit to the Cabinet des Médailles ... considered the traditional journey to Italy ... part of artistic training, and in order that ... have the benefit of such study he devoted ... to augment the income available for a travel- ... His later works, after he resigned his pro- ... were more in the free and ardent manner ... imaginative landscapes, castles in Spain, ... etchings like the series of "The Triumph ... sculptured fountains for the gardens of the ... Welbeck.

... by Legros, besides those already ... seen in the following galleries and museums: ... Dead Christ, bronzes, medals and ... in the Luxembourg, Paris; "Landscape," ... and portraits of Browning, Burne-Jones, ... at the Victoria and Albert Museum, ... National Gallery of British ... other works ... the Ionides Collection, ... "Christening," "Barricade," ... and several drawings and ... "Two Priests at the Organ," ... collection of Rev. Stopford Brooke; ... Mr Vereker Hamilton; "The ... and a large collection of etchings ... collection of Mr L. W. ... collection of Mr G. F. Watts, R.A.; ... the Print Room, British Museum; ... drawings of the antique, Cambridge; ... heads and some drawings, Man- ... made before the Class," ... "Study of Heads," Peel Park

... "Alphonse Legros," *Die graphischen* ... Alphonse Legros, *Revue de* ... Cosmo Monkhouse, "Professor

LEGUMINOSAE, the second largest family of seed-plants, containing about 430 genera with 7000 species. It belongs to the series Rosales of the Dicotyledons, and contains three well-marked suborders, Papilionatae, Mimosoideae and Caesalpinioideae. The plants are trees, shrubs or herbs of very various habit. The British representatives, all of which belong to the suborder Papilionatae, include a few shrubs, such as *Ulex* (gorse, furze), *Cytisus* (broom) and *Genista*, but the majority, and this applies to the suborder as a whole, are herbs, such as the clovers, *Medicago*, *Melilotus*, &c., sometimes climbing by aid of tendrils which are modified leaf-structures, as in *Lathyrus* and the vetches (*Vicia*). Scarlet runner (*Phaseolus multiflorus*) has a herbaceous twining stem. Woody climbers (lianes) are represented by species of *Bauhinia* (Caesalpinioideae), which with their curiously flattened twisted stems are characteristic features of tropical forests, and *Entada scandens* (Mimosoideae) also common in the tropics; these two suborders, which are confined to the warmer parts of the earth, consist chiefly of trees and shrubs such as *Acacia* and *Mimosa* belonging to the Mimosoideae, and the Judas tree of southern Europe (*Cercis*) and tamarind belonging to the Caesalpinioideae. The so-called acacia of European gardens (*Robinia Pseudacacia*) and laburnum are examples of the tree habit in the Papilionatae. Water plants are rare, but are represented by *Aeschynomene* and *Neptunia*, tropical genera. The roots of many species bear nodular swellings (tubercles), the cells of which contain bacterium-like bodies which have the power of fixing the nitrogen of the atmosphere in such a form as to make it available for plant food. Hence the value of these plants as a crop on poor soil or as a member of a series of rotation of crops, since they enrich the soil by the nitrogen liberated by the decay of their roots or of the whole plant if ploughed in as green manure.

The leaves are alternate in arrangement and generally compound and stipulate. A common form is illustrated by the trefoil or clovers, which have three leaflets springing from a common point (digitately trifoliate); pinnate leaves are also frequent as in laburnum and *Robinia*. In Mimosoideae the leaves are generally bipinnate (figs. 1, 2, 3). Rarely are the leaves simple as in *Bauhinia*. Various departures from the usual leaf-type occur in association with adaptations to different functions or environments. In leaf-climbers, such as pea or vetch, the end of the rachis and one or more pairs of leaflets are changed into tendrils. In gorse the leaf is reduced to a slender spine-like structure, though the leaves of the seedling have one to three leaflets. In many Australian acacias the leaf surface in the adult plant is much reduced, the petiole being at the same time flattened and enlarged (fig. 1), frequently the leaf is reduced to a petiole flattened in the vertical plane; by this means a minimum surface is exposed to the intense sunlight. In the garden pea the stipules are large and foliaceous, replacing the leaflets, which are tendrils; in *Robinia* the stipules are spiny and persist after leaf-fall. In some acacias (*q.v.*) the thorns are hollow, and inhabited by ants as in *A. sphaerocephala*, a central American plant (fig. 2) and others. In some species of *Astragalus*, *Onobrychis* and others, the leaf-stalk persists after the fall of the leaf and becomes hard and spiny.

FIG. 1.—Leaf of an Acacia (*A. heterophylla*) showing flattened leaf-like petiole (phyllode), *p*, and bipinnate blade.

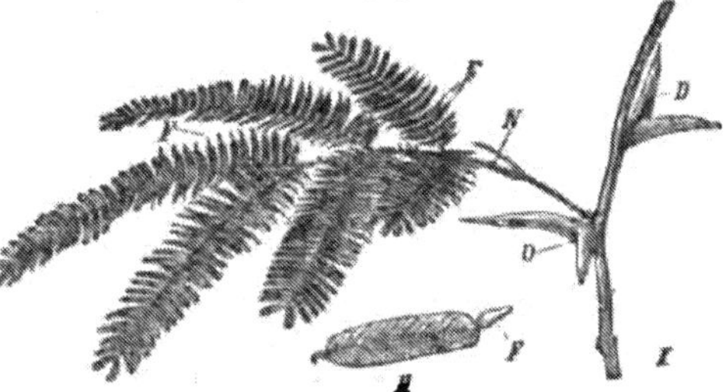

From Strasburger's *Lehrbuch der Botanik*, by permission of Gustav Fischer.

FIG. 2.—*Acacia sphaerocephala*.

I, Leaf and part of stem; *D*, hollow thorns in which the ants live; *F*, food bodies at the apices of the lower pinnules; *N*, nectary on the petiole. (Reduced.) *II*, Single pinnule with food-body, *F*. (Somewhat enlarged.)

Leaf-movements occur in many of the genera. Such are the sleep-movement in the clovers, runner bean (*Phaseolus*), *Robinia* and acacia, where the leaflets assume a vertical position at nightfall. Spontaneous movements are exemplified in the telegraph-plant (*Desmodium gyrans*), native of tropical Asia, where the small lateral leaflets move up and down every few minutes. The sensitive plant (*Mimosa pudica*) is an example of movement in response to contact, the leaves assuming a sleep-position if touched. The seat of the movement is the swollen base of the leaf-stalk, the so-called pulvinus (fig. 3).

The stem of the lianes shows some remarkable deviations from the normal in form and structure. In Papilionatae anomalous secondary thickening arises from the production of new cambium zones outside the original ring (*Mucuna*, *Wistaria*) forming concentric rings or transverse or broader strands; where, as in *Rhyncosia* the successive cambiums are active only at two opposite points, a flat ribbon-like stem is produced. The climbing Bauhinias (Caesalpinioideae) have a flattened stem with basin-like undulations; in some growth in thickness is normal, in others new cambium-zones are found concentrically, while in others new and distinct growth-centres, each with its cambium-zone, arise outside the primary zone. The climbing Mimosoideae show no anomalous growth in thickness, but in some cases the stem becomes strongly winged. Gum passages in the pith and medullary rays occur, especially in species of acacia and *Astragalus*; gum-arabic is an exudation from the branches of *Acacia Senegal*, gum-tragacanth from *Astragalus gummifer* and other species. Logwood is the coloured heartwood of *Haematoxylon campechianum*; red sandalwood of *Pterocarpus santalinus*.

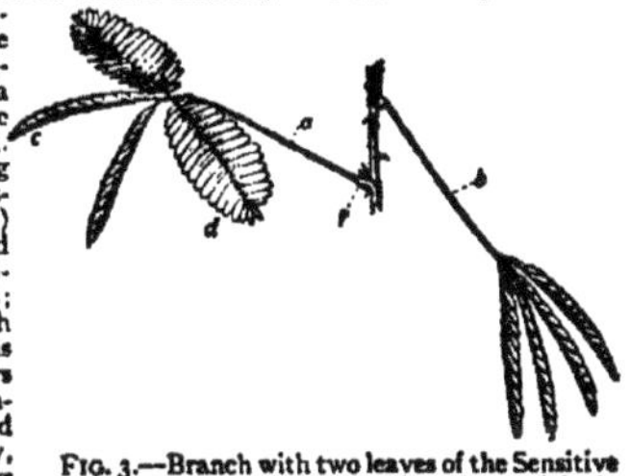

FIG. 3.—Branch with two leaves of the Sensitive Plant (*Mimosa pudica*), showing the petiole in its erect state, *a*, and in its depressed state, *b*; also the leaflets closed, *c*, and the leaflets expanded, *d*; *p*, pulvinus, the seat of the movement of the petiole.

The flowers are arranged in racemose inflorescences, such as the simple raceme (*Laburnum*, *Robinia*), which is condensed to a head in *Trifolium*; in *Acacia* and *Mimosa* the flowers are densely crowded (fig. 4). The flower is characterized by a hypogynous or slightly perigynous arrangement of parts, the anterior position of the odd sepal, the free petals, and the single median carpel with a terminal style, simple stigma and two

is often explosive, the valves separating elastically and twisting spirally, thus shooting out the seeds, as in gorse, broom and others. In Desmodium, *Entada* and others the pod is constricted between each seed, and breaks up into indehiscent one-seeded parts; it is then called a lomentum (fig. 11); in *Astragalus* it is divided by a longitudinal septum.

The pods show a very great variety in form and size. Thus in the

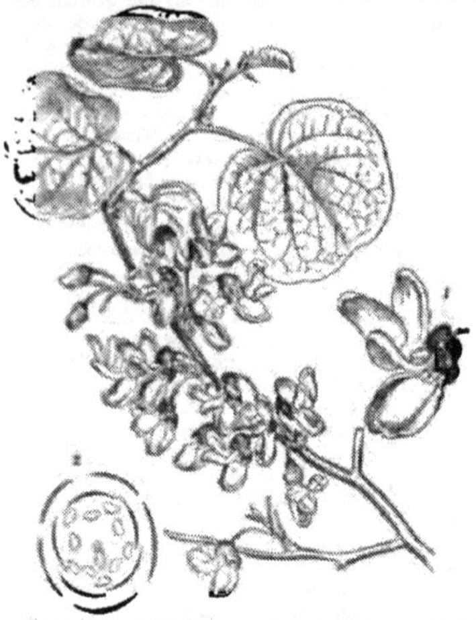

FIG. 5.—Flowering branch of Judas-tree (*Cercis siliquastrum*) reduced. 1, Flower, natural size. 2, Floral diagram.

flowers they are a small fraction of an inch, while in the common tropical climber *Entada scandens* they are woody structures more than a yard long and several inches wide. They are generally more or less flattened, but sometimes round and rod-like, as in species of Cassia, or are spirally coiled as in *Medicago*. Indehiscent one-seeded pods occur in species of clover and in *Medicago*, also in [illegible] and allied genera, where they are winged. In *Colutea*, the bladder-senna of gardens, the pod forms an inflated bladder which bursts under pressure; it often becomes detached and is blown some distance before bursting. An arillar outgrowth is often developed on the funicle, and is sometimes brightly coloured, rendering the seed conspicuous and favouring dissemination by birds; in such cases the seed-coat is hard. In other cases the hard seed-coat itself is bright-coloured as in the scarlet seeds of *Abrus precatorius*, the so-called weather-plant. Animals also act as the agents of distribution in the case of fleshy edible pods containing seeds with a hard smooth testa, which will pass uninjured through the body, as in tamarind and the fruit of the carob-tree (*Ceratonia*). In the ground-nut (*Arachis hypogaea*), *Trifolium subterraneum* and others, the flower-stalks grow downwards after fertilization of the ovules and bury the fruit in the earth. In the suborders Mimosoideae and Papilionatae the embryo fills the seed or a small quantity of endosperm occurs, chiefly round the radicle. In Caesalpinioideae endosperm is absent, or present forming a thin layer round the embryo as in the tribe *Bauhinieae*, or copious and cartilaginous as in the *Cassieae*. The embryo has generally flat leaf-like or fleshy cotyledons with a short radicle.

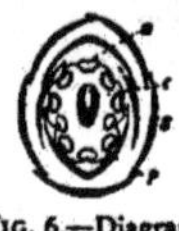

FIG. 6.—Diagram of Flower of Sweet Pea (*Lathyrus*), showing five sepals, *s*, two are superior, one inferior, and two lateral; five petals, *p*, one superior, two inferior, and two lateral; ten stamens in two rows, *a*, and one carpel, *c*.

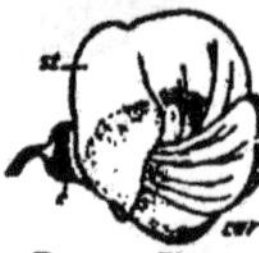

FIG. 7.—Flower of Pea (*Pisum sativum*), showing a papilionaceous corolla, with one petal superior, *st*, the standard (vexillum), two inferior, *car*, the keel (carina), and two lateral, *a*, wings (alae). The calyx is marked *c*.

Insects play an important part in the pollination of the flowers. In the two smaller suborders the stamens and stigma are freely exposed and the conspicuous coloured stamens serve as well as the petals to attract insects; in *Mimosa* and *Acacia* the flowers are crowded in conspicuous heads or spikes. The relation of insects to the flower has been carefully studied in the Papilionatae, chiefly in European species. Where honey is present it is secreted on the inside of the base of the stamens and accumulated in the base of the tube formed by the united filaments round the ovary. It is accessible only to insects with long probosces, such as bees. In these cases the posterior stamen is free, allowing access to the honey. The flowers stand more or less horizontally; the large erect white or coloured standard renders them conspicuous, the wings form a platform on which the insect rests and the keel encloses the stamens and pistil, protecting them from rain and the attacks of unbidden pollen-eating insects. In his book on the fertilization of flowers, Hermann Müller distinguishes four types of papilionaceous flowers according to the way in which the pollen is applied to the bee:

FIG. 8.—Stamens and Pistil of Sweet Pea (*Lathyrus*). The stamens are diadelphous, nine of them being united by their filaments *f*, while the uppermost one (*c*) is free; *st*, stigma, *c*, calyx.

(1) Those in which the stamens and stigma return within the carina and thus admit of repeated visits, such are the clovers, *Melilotus* and laburnum. (2) Explosive flowers where stamens and style are confined within the keel under tension and the pressure of the insect causes their sudden release and the scattering of the pollen, as in broom and *Genista*; these contain no honey but are visited for the sake of the pollen. (3) The piston-mechanism as in bird's-foot trefoil (*Lotus corniculatus*), *Anthyllis*, *Ononis* and *Lupinus*, where the pressure of the bee upon the carina while probing for honey squeezes a narrow ribbon of pollen through the opening at the tip. The pollen has been shed into the cone-like tip of the carina, and the heads of the five outer stamens form a piston beneath it, pushing it out at the tip when pressure is exerted on the keel; a further pressure causes the protrusion of the stigma, which is thus brought in contact with the insect's belly. (4) The style bears a brush of hairs which sweeps small quantities of pollen out of the tip of the carina, as in *Lathyrus*, *Pisum*, *Vicia* and *Phaseolus*.

FIG. 9.—Broom (*Cytisus scoparius*). (2-7 slightly reduced.)

1, Calyx. 2, Standard. 3, Wing. 4, Keel. 5, Monadelphous stamens and style. 6, Pistil. 7, Pod.

Leguminosae is a cosmopolitan order, and often affords a characteristic feature of the vegetation. Mimosoideae and Caesalpinioideae are richly developed in the tropical rain forests, where Papilionatae are less conspicuous and mostly herbaceous; in subtropical forests arborescent forms of all three suborders occur. In the temperate regions, tree-forms are rare—thus Mimosoideae are unrepresented in Europe; Caesalpinioideae are represented by species of *Cercis*, *Gymnocladus* and *Gleditschia*; Papilionatae by *Robinia*; but herbaceous Papilionatae abound and penetrate to the limit of growth of seed-plants in arctic and high alpine regions. Shrubs and undershrubs, such as *Ulex*, *Genista*, *Cytisus* are a characteristic feature in Europe and the Mediterranean area. Acacias are an important component of the evergreen bush-vegetation of Australia, together with genera of the tribe *Podalyrieae* of Papilionatae (*Chorizema*, *Oxylobium*, &c.). *Astragalus*, *Oxytropis*, *Hedysarum*, *Onobrychis*, and others are characteristic of the steppe-formations of eastern Europe and western Asia.

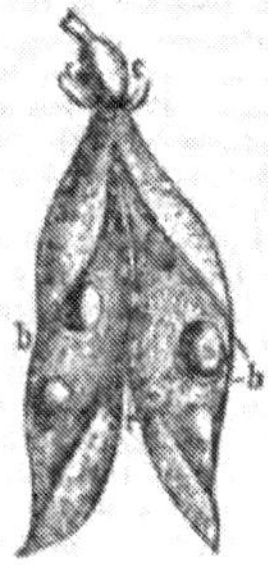

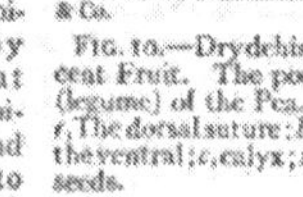

From Vines's *Students' Text-Book of Botany*, by permission of Swan, Sonnenschein & Co.

FIG. 10.—Dry dehiscent Fruit. The pod (legume) of the Pea. *r*, The dorsal suture; *b*, the ventral; *c*, calyx; *s*, seeds.

FIG. 11.—Lomentum or lomentaceous legume of a species of *Desmodium*. Each seed is contained in a separate cavity by the folding inwards of the walls of the legume at equal intervals; the legume, when ripe, separates transversely into single-seeded portions or mericarps.

The order is a most important one economically. The seeds, which are rich in starch and proteids, form valuable foods, as in pea, the various beans, vetch, lentil, ground-nut (*Arachis*) and others; seeds of *Arachis* and others yield oils; those of *Physostigma venenosum*, the Calabar ordeal bean, contain a strong poison. Many are useful fodder-plants, as the clovers (*Trifolium*) (*q.v.*), Medicago (*e.g. M. sativa*, lucerne (*q.v.*), or alfalfa); *Melilotus*, *Vicia*, *Onobrychis* (*O. sativa* is sainfoin, *q.v.*); species of *Trifolium*, lupine and others are used as green manure. Many of the tropical trees afford useful timber; *Crotalaria*, *Sesbania*, *Aeschynomene* and others yield fibre; species of *Acacia* and *Astragalus* yield gum; *Copaifera*, *Hymenaea* and others balsams and resins; dyes are obtained from *Genista* (yellow), *Indigofera* (blue) and others; *Haematoxylon campechianum* is logwood; of medicinal value are species of *Cassia* (senna leaves) and *Astragalus*; *Tamarindus indica* is tamarind, *Glycyrrhiza glabra* yields liquorice root. Well-known ornamental trees and shrubs are *Cercis* (*C. siliquastrum* is the Judas-tree), *Gleditschia*, *Genista*, *Cytisus* (broom), *Colutea* (*C. arborescens* is bladder-senna), *Robinia* and *Acacia*; *Wistaria sinensis*, a native of China, is a well-known climbing shrub; *Phaseolus multiflorus* is the scarlet runner; *Lathyrus* (sweet and everlasting peas), *Lupinus*, *Galega* (goat's-rue) and others are herbaceous garden plants. *Ceratonia Siliqua* is the carob-tree of the Mediterranean, the pods of which (algaroba or St John's bread) contain a sweet juicy pulp and are largely used for feeding stock.

The order is well represented in Britain. Thus *Genista tinctoria* is dyers' greenweed, yielding a yellow dye; *G. anglica* is needle furze; other shrubs are *Ulex* (*U. europaeus*, gorse, furze or whin, *U. nanus*, a dwarf species) and *Cytisus scoparius*, broom. Herbaceous plants are *Ononis spinosa* (rest-harrow), *Medicago* (medick), *Melilotus* (melilot), *Trifolium* (the clovers), *Anthyllis Vulneraria* (kidney-vetch), *Lotus corniculatus* (bird's-foot trefoil), *Astragalus* (milk-vetch), *Vicia* (vetch, tare) and *Lathyrus*.

LÈGYA, called by the Shans LAI-KA, a state in the central division of the southern Shan States of Burma, lying approximately between 20° 15′ and 21° 30′ N. and 97° 50′ and 98° 30′ E., with an area of 1433 sq. m. The population was estimated at 30,000 in 1881. On the downfall of King Thibaw civil war

[illegible] of Denmark (1864) went through many [illegible] posthumous works were published in 4 vols., [illegible]

[illegible] Orla Lehmann og hans samtid (Copenhagen, 1871); [illegible] J. Lehmanns Papirer (Copenhagen, 1903).

[illegible], a village and health resort of Germany, in the [illegible] province of Brandenburg, situated between two lakes, [illegible] connected by the navigable Emster with the Havel, [illegible] from Potsdam, and with a station on the main line [illegible] Magdeburg, and a branch line to Grosskreuz. Pop. (1900) [illegible] It contains the ruins of a Cistercian monastery called [illegible] am See, founded in 1180 and dissolved in 1542; [illegible] parish church, formerly the monasterial chapel, [illegible] in 1872–1877; and a fine statue of the emperor [illegible] III. Boat-building and saw-milling are the chief [illegible]

[illegible] Heffter, *Geschichte des Klosters Lehnin* (Brandenburg, 1851); [illegible] *Lehnin, Beiträge zur Geschichte von Kloster und Amt* [illegible] 1881).

[illegible] LEHNIN PROPHECY (*Lehninsche Weissagung, Vaticinium [illegible]*), a poem in 100 Leonine verses, reputed to be from [illegible] of a monk, Hermann of Lehnin, who lived about the [illegible] 1300, made its appearance about 1690 and caused much [illegible] controversy. This so-called prophecy bewails the extinction of [illegible] rulers of Brandenburg and the rise of the Hohen[illegible] dynasty to power; each successive ruler of the latter [illegible] down to the eleventh generation is described, the date of [illegible] extinction of the race fixed, and the restoration of the Roman [illegible] Church foretold. But as the narrative is only exact in [illegible] down to the death of Frederick William, the great [illegible] in 1688, and as all prophecies of the period subsequent to [illegible] were falsified by events, the poem came to be regarded [illegible] a compilation and the date of its authorship placed about [illegible] year 1684. Andreas Fromm (d. 1685), rector of St Peter's [illegible] in Berlin, an ardent Lutheran, is commonly believed to [illegible] been the forger. This cleric, resisting certain measures [illegible] by the great elector against the Lutheran pastors, fled the [illegible] in 1668 to avoid prosecution, and having been received [illegible] Prague into the Roman Catholic Church was appointed canon [illegible] Leitmeritz in Bohemia, where he died. During the earlier [illegible] of the 19th century the poem was eagerly scanned by the [illegible] of the Hohenzollerns, some of whom believed that the [illegible] would end with King Frederick William III., the repre[illegible]tive of the eleventh generation of the family.

[illegible] "Vaticinium" was first published in Lilienthal's *Gelehrtes [illegible]* (Königsberg, 1723), and has been many times reprinted. [illegible] Boost, *Die Weissagungen des Mönchs Hermann zu Lehnin* [illegible] 1848); Hilgenfeld, *Die Lehninische Weissagung* (Leipzig, [illegible]); Sabell, *Literatur der sogenannten Lehninschen Weissagung* ([illegible]ilbronn, 1879) and Kampers, *Die Lehninsche Weissagung über [illegible] Haus Hohenzollern* (Münster, 1897).

LEHRS, KARL (1802–1878), German classical scholar, was born at Königsberg on the 2nd of June 1802. He was of Jewish extraction, but in 1822 he embraced Christianity. In 1845 he was appointed professor of ancient Greek philology in Königsberg university, which post he held till his death on the 9th of June [illegible]. His most important works are: *De Aristarchi Studiis [illegible]omericis* (1833, 2nd ed. by A. Ludwich, 1882), which laid a new foundation for Homeric exegesis (on the Aristarchean lines of explaining Homer from the text itself) and textual criticism; *[illegible]stiones Epicae* (1837); *De Asclepiade Myrleano* (1845); *[illegible]rodiani Scripta Tria emendatiora* (1848); *Populäre Aufsätze [illegible] Altertum* (1856, 2nd much enlarged ed., 1875), his best-known work; *Horatius Flaccus* (1869), in which, on aesthetic grounds, he rejected many of the odes as spurious; *Die Pindar[illegible]* (1873). Lehrs was a man of very decided opinions, "one of the most masculine of German scholars"; his enthusiasm for everything Greek led him to adhere firmly to the undivided authorship of the *Iliad*; comparative mythology and the symbolical interpretation of myths he regarded as a species of sacrilege.

[illegible] the exhaustive article by L. Friedländer in *Allgemeine Deutsche Biographie*, xviii.; E. Kammer in C. Bursian's *Jahresbericht* (1879); [illegible] Jung, *Zur Erinnerung an Karl Lehrs* (progr. Meseritz, 1880); [illegible] Ludwich edited Lehrs' select correspondence (1894) and his [illegible] (1902).

LEIBNITZ (LEIBNIZ), **GOTTFRIED WILHELM** (1646–1716), German philosopher, mathematician and man of affairs, was born on the 1st of July 1646 at Leipzig, where his father was professor of moral philosophy. Though the name Leibniz, Leibnitz or Lubeniecz was originally Slavonic, his ancestors were German, and for three generations had been in the employment of the Saxon government. Young Leibnitz was sent to the Nicolai school at Leipzig, but, from 1652 when his father died, seems to have been for the most part his own teacher. From his father he had acquired a love of historical study. The German books at his command were soon read through, and with the help of two Latin books—the *Thesaurus Chronologicus* of Calvisius and an illustrated edition of Livy—he learned Latin at the age of eight. His father's library was now thrown open to him, to his great joy, with the permission, "Tolle, lege." Before he was twelve he could read Latin easily and had begun Greek; he had also remarkable facility in writing Latin verse. He next turned to the study of logic, attempting already to reform its doctrines, and zealously reading the scholastics and some of the Protestant theologians.

At the age of fifteen, he entered the university of Leipzig as a law student. His first two years were devoted to philosophy under Jakob Thomasius, a Neo-Aristotelian, who is looked upon as having founded the scientific study of the history of philosophy in Germany. It was at this time probably that he first made acquaintance with the modern thinkers who had already revolutionized science and philosophy, Francis Bacon, Cardan and Campanella, Kepler, Galileo and Descartes; and he began to consider the difference between the old and new ways of regarding nature. He resolved to study mathematics. It was not, however, till the summer of 1663, which he spent at Jena under E. Weigel, that he obtained the instructions of a mathematician of repute; nor was the deeper study of mathematics entered upon till his visit to Paris and acquaintance with Huygens many years later.

The next three years he devoted to legal studies, and in 1666 applied for the degree of doctor of law, with a view to obtaining the post of assessor. Being refused on the ground of his youth he left his native town for ever. The doctor's degree refused him there was at once (November 5, 1666) conferred on him at Altdorf—the university town of the free city of Nuremberg—where his brilliant dissertation procured him the immediate offer of a professor's chair. This, however, he declined, having, as he said, "very different things in view."

Leibnitz, not yet twenty-one years of age, was already the author of several remarkable essays. In his bachelor's dissertation *De principio individui* (1663), he defended the nominalistic doctrine that individuality is constituted by the whole entity or essence of a thing; his arithmetical tract *De complexionibus*, published in an extended form under the title *De arte combinatoria* (1666), is an essay towards his life-long project of a reformed symbolism and method of thought; and besides these there are our juridical essays, including the *Nova methodus docendi discendique juris*, written in the intervals of his journey from Leipzig to Altdorf. This last essay is remarkable, not only for the reconstruction it attempted of the *Corpus Juris*, but as containing the first clear recognition of the importance of the historical method in law. Nuremberg was a centre of the Rosicrucians, and Leibnitz, busying himself with writings of the alchemists, soon gained such a knowledge of their tenets that he was supposed to be one of the secret brotherhood, and was even elected their secretary. A more important result of his visit to Nuremberg was his acquaintance with Johann Christian von Boyneburg (1622–1672), formerly first minister to the elector of Mainz, and one of the most distinguished German statesmen of the day. By his advice Leibnitz printed his *Nova methodus* in 1667, dedicated it to the elector, and, going to Mainz, presented it to him in person. It was thus that Leibnitz entered the service of the elector of Mainz, at first as an assistant in the revision of the statute-book, afterwards on more important work.

The policy of the elector, which the pen of Leibnitz was now called upon to promote, was to maintain the security of the German empire, threatened on the west by the aggressive power of France, on the east by Turkey and Russia. Thus when in 1669 the crown of Poland became vacant, it fell to Leibnitz to support the claims of the German candidate, which he did in his first political writing, *Specimen demonstrationum politicarum pro rege Polonorum eligendo*, attempting, under the guise of a Catholic Polish nobleman, to show by mathematical demonstration that it was necessary in the interest of Poland that it should have the count palatine of Neuburg as its king. But neither the diplomatic skill of Boyneburg, who had been sent as plenipotentiary to the election at Warsaw, nor the arguments of Leibnitz were successful, and a Polish prince was elected to fill the vacant throne.

A greater danger threatened Germany in the aggressions of Louis XIV. (see FRANCE: *History*). Though Holland was in most immediate danger, the seizure of Lorraine in 1670 showed that Germany too was threatened. It was in this year that Leibnitz wrote his *Thoughts on Public Safety*,[1] in which he urged the formation of a new "Rheinbund" for the protection of Germany, and contended that the states of Europe should employ their power, not against one another, but in the conquest of the non-Christian world, in which Egypt, "one of the best situated lands in the world," would fall to France. The plan thus proposed of averting the threatened attack on Germany by a French expedition to Egypt was discussed with Boyneburg, and obtained the approval of the elector. French relations with Turkey were at the time so strained as to make a breach imminent, and at the close of 1671, about the time when the war with Holland broke out, Louis himself was approached by a letter from Boyneburg and a short memorial from the pen of Leibnitz, who attempted to show that Holland itself, as a mercantile power trading with the East, might be best attacked through Egypt, while nothing would be easier for France or would more largely increase her power than the conquest of Egypt. On February 12, 1672, a request came from the French secretary of state, Simon Arnauld de Pomponne (1618–1699), that Leibnitz should go to Paris. Louis seems still to have kept the matter in view, but never granted Leibnitz the personal interview he desired, while Pomponne wrote, "I have nothing against the plan of a holy war, but such plans, you know, since the days of St Louis, have ceased to be the fashion." Not yet discouraged, Leibnitz wrote a full account of his project for the king,[2] and a summary of the same[3] evidently intended for Boyneburg. But Boyneburg died in December 1672, before the latter could be sent to him. Nor did the former ever reach its destination. The French quarrel with the Porte was made up, and the plan of a French expedition to Egypt disappeared from practical politics till the time of Napoleon. The history of this scheme, and the reason of Leibnitz's journey to Paris, long remained hidden in the archives of the Hanoverian library. It was on his taking possession of Hanover in 1803 that Napoleon learned, through the *Consilium Aegyptiacum*, that the idea of a French conquest of Egypt had been first put forward by a German philosopher. In the same year there was published in London an account of the *Justa dissertatio*[4] of which the British Government had procured a copy in 1799. But it was only with the appearance of the edition of Leibnitz's works begun by Onno Klopp in 1864 that the full history of the scheme was made known.

Leibnitz had other than political ends in view in his visit to France. It was as the centre of literature and science that Paris chiefly attracted him. Political duties never made him lose sight of his philosophical and scientific interests. At Mainz he was still busied with the question of the relation between the old and new methods in philosophy. In a letter to Jakob

[1] *Bedenken, welchergestalt securitas publica interna et externa und status praesens jetzigen Umständen nach im Reich auf festen Fuss zu stellen.*

[2] *De expeditione Aegyptiaca regi Franciae proponenda justa dissertatio.*

[3] *Consilium Aegyptiacum.*

[4] *A Summary Account of Leibnitz's Memoir addressed to Lewis the Fourteenth*, &c. [edited by Granville Penn], (London, 1803).

made to raise the duke of Hanover to the electorate, he had to show that this did not interfere with the rights of the duke of Wurtemberg. In 1692 the duke of Hanover was made elector. Before, and with a view to this, Leibnitz had been engaged by him to write the history of the Brunswick-Lüneburg family, and, to collect material for his history, had undertaken a journey through Germany and Italy in 1687–1690, visiting and examining the records in Marburg, Frankfort-on-the-Main, Munich, Vienna (where he remained nine months), Venice, Modena and Rome. At Rome he was offered the custodianship of the Vatican library on condition of his joining the Catholic church.

About this time, too, his thoughts and energies were partly taken up with the scheme for the reunion of the Catholic and Protestant Churches. At Mainz he had joined in an attempt made by the elector and Boyneburg to bring about a reconciliation, and now, chiefly through the energy and skill of the Catholic Royas de Spinola, and from the spirit of moderation which prevailed among the theologians he met with at Hanover in 1683, it almost seemed as if some agreement might be arrived at. In 1686 Leibnitz wrote his *Systema theologicum*,[4] in which he strove to find common ground for Protestants and Catholics in the details of their creeds. But the English revolution of 1688 interfered with the scheme in Hanover, and it was soon found that the religious difficulties were greater than had at one time appeared. In the letters to Leibnitz from Bossuet, the landgrave of Hessen-Rheinfels, and Madame de Brinon, the aim is obviously to make converts to Catholicism, not to arrive at a compromise with Protestantism, and when it was found that Leibnitz refused to be converted the correspondence ceased. A further scheme of church union in which Leibnitz was engaged, that between the Reformed and Lutheran Churches, met with no better success.

Returning from Italy in 1690, Leibnitz was appointed librarian at Wolfenbüttel by Duke Anton of Brunswick-Wolfenbüttel. Some years afterwards began his connexion with Berlin through his friendship with the electress Sophie Charlotte of Brandenburg and her mother the princess Sophie of Hanover. He was invited to Berlin in 1700, and on the 11th July of that year the academy (Akademie der Wissenschaften) he had planned was founded, with himself as its president for life. In the same year he was made a privy councillor of justice by the elector of Brandenburg. Four years before he had received a like honour from the elector of Hanover, and twelve years afterwards the same distinction was conferred upon him by Peter the Great, to whom he gave a plan for an academy at St Petersburg, carried out after the czar's death. After the death of his royal pupil in 1705 his visits to Berlin became less frequent and less welcome, and in 1711 he was there for the last time. In the following year he undertook his fifth and last journey to Vienna, where he stayed till 1714. An attempt to found an academy of science there was defeated by the opposition of the Jesuits, but he now attained the honour he had coveted of an imperial privy councillorship (1712), and, either at this time or on a previous occasion (1709), was made a baron of the empire (*Reichsfreiherr*). Leibnitz returned to Hanover in September 1714, but found the elector George Louis had already gone to assume the crown of England. Leibnitz would gladly have followed him to London, but was bidden to remain at Hanover and finish his history of Brunswick.

During the last thirty years Leibnitz had been busy with many matters. Mathematics, natural science,[5] philosophy, theology, history jurisprudence, politics (particularly the French wars with Germany, and the question of the Spanish succession), economics and philology, all gained a share of his attention; almost all of them he enriched with original observations.

His genealogical researches in Italy—through which he established the common origin of the families of Brunswick and

[4] Not published till 1819. It is on this work that the assertion has been founded that Leibnitz was at heart a Catholic—a supposition clearly disproved by his correspondence.

[5] In his *Protogaea* (1691) he developed the notion of the historical genesis of the present condition of the earth's surface. Cf. O. Peschel, *Gesch. d. Erdkunde* (Munich, 1865), pp. 615 sq.

Este—were not only preceded by an immense collection of historical sources, but enabled him to publish materials for a code of international law.[1] The history of Brunswick itself was the last work of his life, and had covered the period from 768 to 1005 when death ended his labours. But the government, in whose service and at whose order the work had been carried out, left it in the archives of the Hanover library till it was published by Pertz in 1843.

It was in the years between 1690 and 1716 that Leibnitz's chief philosophical works were composed, and during the first ten of these years the accounts of his system were, for the most part, preliminary sketches. Indeed, he never gave a full and systematic account of his doctrines. His views have to be gathered from letters to friends, from occasional articles in the *Acta Eruditorum*, the *Journal des Savants*, and other journals, and from one or two more extensive works. It is evident, however, that philosophy had not been entirely neglected in the years in which his pen was almost solely occupied with other matters. A letter to the duke of Brunswick, and another to Arnauld, in 1671, show that he had already reached his new notion of substance; but it is in the correspondence with Antoine Arnauld, between 1686 and 1690, that his fundamental ideas and the reasons for them are for the first time made clear. The appearance of Locke's *Essay* in 1690 induced him (1696) to note down his objections to it, and his own ideas on the same subjects. In 1703–1704 these were worked out in detail and ready for publication, when the death of the author whom they criticized prevented their appearance (first published by Raspe, 1765). In 1710 appeared the only complete and systematic philosophical work of his life-time, *Essais de Théodicée sur la bonté de Dieu, la liberté de l'homme, et l'origine du mal*, originally undertaken at the request of the late queen of Prussia, who had wished a reply to Bayle's opposition of faith and reason. In 1714 he wrote, for Prince Eugene of Savoy, a sketch of his system under the title of *La Monadologie*, and in the same year appeared his *Principes de la nature et de la grâce*. The last few years of his life were perhaps more occupied with correspondence than any others, and, in a philosophical regard, were chiefly notable for the letters, which, through the desire of the new queen of England, he interchanged with Clarke, *sur Dieu, l'âme, l'espace, la durée*.

Leibnitz died on the 14th of November 1716, his closing years enfeebled by disease, harassed by controversy, embittered by neglect; but to the last he preserved the indomitable energy and power of work to which is largely due the position he holds as, more perhaps than any one in modern times, a man of almost universal attainments and almost universal genius. Neither at Berlin, in the academy which he had founded, nor in London, whither his sovereign had gone to rule, was any notice taken of his death. At Hanover, Eckhart, his secretary, was his only mourner; "he was buried," says an eyewitness, "more like a robber than what he really was, the ornament of his country."[2] Only in the French Academy was the loss recognized, and a worthy eulogium devoted to his memory (November 13, 1717). The 200th anniversary of his birth was celebrated in 1846, and in the same year were opened the Königlichsächsische Gesellschaft der Wissenschaften and the Kaiserliche Akademie der Wissenschaften in Leipzig and Vienna respectively. In 1883, a statue was erected to him at Leipzig.

Leibnitz possessed a wonderful power of rapid and continuous work. Even in travelling his time was employed in solving mathematical problems. He is described as moderate in his habits, quick of temper but easily appeased, charitable in his judgments of others, and tolerant of differences of opinion, though impatient of contradiction on small matters. He is also said to have been fond of money to the point of covetousness; he was certainly desirous of honour, and felt keenly the neglect in which his last years were passed.

Philosophy.—The central point in the philosophy of Leibnitz was only arrived at after many advances and corrections in his opinions. This point is his new doctrine of substance (p. 702),[3] and it is through it that unity is given to the succession of occasional writings, scattered over fifty years, in which he explained his views. More inclined to agree than to differ with what he read (p. 425), and borrowing from almost every philosophical system, his own standpoint is yet most closely related to that of Descartes, partly as consequence, partly by way of opposition. Cartesianism, Leibnitz often asserted, is the ante-room of truth, but the ante-room only. Descartes's separation of things into two heterogeneous substances only connected by the omnipotence of God, and the more logical absorption of both by Spinoza into the one divine substance, followed from an erroneous conception of what the true nature of substance is. Substance, the ultimate reality, can only be conceived as force. Hence Leibnitz's metaphysical view of the monads as simple, percipient, self-active beings, the constituent elements of all things, his physical doctrines of the reality and constancy of force at the same time that space, matter and motion are merely phenomenal, and his psychological conception of the continuity and development of consciousness. In the closest connexion with the same stand his logical principles of consistency and sufficient reason, and the method he developed from them, his ethical end of perfection, and his crowning theological conception of the universe as the best possible world, and of God both as its efficient cause and its final harmony.

The ultimate elements of the universe are, according to Leibnitz, individual centres of force or monads. Why they should be individual, and not manifestations of one world-force, he never clearly proves.[4] His doctrine of individuality seems to have been arrived at, not by strict deduction from the nature of force, but rather from the empirical observation that it is by the manifestation of its activity that the separate existence of the individual becomes evident; for his system individuality is as fundamental as activity. "The monads," he says, "are the very atoms of nature—in a word, the elements of things," but, as centres of force, they have neither parts, extension nor figure (p. 705). Hence their distinction from the atoms of Democritus and the materialists. They are metaphysical points or rather spiritual beings whose very nature it is to act. As the bent bow springs back of itself, so the monads naturally pass and are always passing into action without any aid but the absence of opposition (p. 122). Nor do they, like the atoms, act upon one another (p. 680); the action of each excludes that of every other. The activity of each is the result of its own past state, the determinator of its own future (pp. 706, 722). "The monads have no windows by which anything may go in or out" (p. 705).

Further, since all substances are of the nature of force, it follows that—"in imitation of the notion which we have of souls"—they must contain something analogous to feeling and appetite. It is the nature of the monad to represent the many in one, and this is perception, by which external events are mirrored internally (p. 438). Through their own activity the monads mirror the universe (p. 725), but each in its own way and from its own point of view, that is, with a more or less perfect perception (p. 127); for the Cartesians were wrong in ignoring the infinite grades of perception, and identifying it with the reflex cognizance of it which may be called apperception. Every monad is thus a microcosm, the universe in little,[5] and according to the degree of its activity is the distinctness of its representation of the universe (p. 709). Thus Leibnitz, borrowing the Aristotelian term, calls the monads *entelechies*, because they have a certain perfection (τὸ ἐντελές) and sufficiency (αὐτάρκεια) which make them sources of their internal actions and, so to speak, incorporeal automata (p. 706). That the monads are not pure entelechies is shown by the differences amongst them. Excluding all external limitation, they are yet limited by their own nature. All created monads contain a passive element or *materia prima* (pp. 440, 687, 725), in virtue of which their perceptions are more or less confused. As the activity of the monad consists in perception, this is inhibited by the passive principle, so that there arises in the monad an appetite or tendency to overcome the inhibition and become more perceptive, whence follows the change from one perception to another (pp. 706, 714). By the proportion of activity to passivity in it one monad is differentiated from another. The greater the amount of activity or of distinct perceptions the more perfect is the monad; the stronger the element of passivity, the more confused its perceptions, the less perfect is it (p. 709). The soul would be a divinity had it nothing but distinct perceptions (p. 520).

The monad is never without a perception; but, when it has a number of little perceptions with no means of distinction, a state similar to that of being stunned ensues, the *monade nue* being perpetually in this state (p. 707). Between this and the most distinct perception there is room for an infinite diversity of nature among the monads themselves. Thus no one monad is exactly the same as another; for, were it possible that there should be two identical, there would be no sufficient reason why God, who brings them into

[1] *Codex juris gentium diplomaticus* (1693); *Mantissa codicis juris gentium diplomatici* (1700).

[2] *Memoirs of John Ker of Kersland*, by himself (1726), i. 118.

[3] When not otherwise stated, the references are to Erdmann's edition of the *Opera philosophica*.

[4] See *Considérations sur la doctrine d'un esprit universel* (1702).

[5] Cf. *Opera*, ed. Dutens, II. ii. 20.

actua[illegible] [illegible]existence, should put one of them at one definite time and place, [illegible] rather at a different time and place. This is Leibnitz's princ[illegible] of the *identity of indiscernibles* (pp. 277, 755); by it his early [illegible] problem as to the principle of individuation is solved by the distin[illegible] between genus and individual being abolished, and every indivi[illegible] monad *sui generis*. The principle thus established is formu[illegible] in Leibnitz's law of continuity, founded, he says, on the d[illegible] of the mathematical infinite, essential to geometry, and of imp[illegible] in physics (pp. 104, 105), in accordance with which there [illegible] neither vacuum nor break in nature, but "everything takes [illegible] by degrees" (p. 392), the different species of creatures rising [illegible] insensible steps from the lowest to the most perfect form (p. 3[illegible]).

As i[illegible] every monad each succeeding state is the consequence of the [illegible] as it is of the nature of every monad to mirror or [illegible] universe, it follows (p. 774) that the perceptive con[illegible] monad is in "accord" or correspondence with that of [illegible] (cf. p. 127), though this content is represented with varying degrees of perfection. This is Leibnitz's famous [illegible] pre-established harmony, in virtue of which the infinitely [illegible] independent substances of which the world is composed [illegible] each other and form one universe. It is essential to [illegible] proceeds from the very nature of the monads as per[illegible] beings, and not from an arbitrary determination [illegible]

[illegible] of self-determining percipient units Leibnitz [illegible] the world of nature and mind. As everything that [illegible] of the nature of spiritual or metaphysical points [illegible] that space and matter in the ordinary sense can [illegible] phenomenal existence (p. 745), being dependent not on the monads themselves but on the way in which they [illegible] Considering that several things exist at the same [illegible] certain order of coexistence, and mistaking this con[illegible] as something that exists outside of them, the mind [illegible] perception of space (p. 768). But space and [illegible] relative, the former an order of coexistences, the [illegible] (pp. [illegible], 752). Hence not only the secondary [illegible] and Locke, but their so-called primary qualities [illegible] phenomenal (p. 445). The monads are really [illegible] distance from each other; but, as we perceive [illegible] there is for us an aggregate or extended [illegible] this active extension (pp. 110, 111). The unity of [illegible] entirely on our perceiving the monads com[illegible] There is no such thing as an absolute vacuum [illegible] more than there are indivisible material units [illegible] which all things are built up (pp. 126, 186, 277). [illegible] or, as Leibnitz calls it, to distinguish it from [illegible] which every monad partakes (p. 440), *materia* [illegible] a "phenomenon bene fundatum" (p. 436). [illegible] *substantiae* or *substantiatum* (p. 745). [illegible] the only view consistent with Leibnitz's [illegible] and is often clearly stated by himself, he [illegible] the *materia secunda* as itself a composite [illegible] of a real metaphysical bond between soul and body [illegible] chiefly in the letters to des Bosses, in [illegible] trying to reconcile his views with the doctrines of [illegible] Catholic church, especially with that of the real presence [illegible] referred to by him as doctrines of [illegible] especially p. 680). The true *vinculum* [illegible] the *materia secunda*, which a consistent develop[illegible] of Leibnitz's principles can only regard as phenomenal, but the [illegible] through which the monads are individualized and [illegible] rendered possible. And Leibnitz [illegible] that the opposite assumption is inconsistent [illegible] metaphysical view of the monads as the only [illegible]

[illegible] Leibnitz's doctrine of force as the ultimate reality it follows [illegible] must be throughout dynamical. And though [illegible] theory of natural philosophy, was never [illegible] of his own theory and his criticism of the [illegible] Descartes are known to us. The whole dis[illegible] in the difference between the mechanical [illegible] of nature. Descartes started from the [illegible] the nature of material substance, [illegible] figure and motion the explanation of the [illegible] he admitted the mechanical view of [illegible] phenomena (p. 438), applying [illegible] in animal organisms, even the [illegible] is phenomenal, these laws must find [illegible] thus in final causes (p. 555). [illegible] (mechanism), can be explained [illegible] but the latter method is not [illegible] though it must be applied [illegible] and explanation (p. 678). [illegible] of the quantity of motion

[illegible] an inorganic body con[illegible] even in its smallest

(*i.e.* momentum) in the world Leibnitz substitutes the principle of the conservation of *vis viva*, and contends that the Cartesian position that motion is measured by velocity should be superseded by the law that moving force (*vis motrix*) is measured by the square of the velocity (pp. 192, 193). The long controversy raised by this criticism was really caused by the ambiguity of the terms employed. The principles held by Descartes and Leibnitz were both correct, though different, and their conflict only apparent. Descartes's principle is now enunciated as the conservation of momentum, that of Leibnitz as the conservation of energy. Leibnitz further criticizes the Cartesian view that the mind can alter the direction of motion though it cannot initiate it, and contends that the quantity of "direction," estimated between the same parts, is constant (p. 108)—a position developed in his statical theorem for determining geometrically the resultant of any number of forces acting at a point.

Like the monad, body, which is its analogue, has a passive and an active element. The former is the capacity of resistance, and includes impenetrability and inertia; the latter is active force (pp. 250, 687). Bodies, too, like the monads, are self-contained activities, receiving no impulse from without—it is only by an accommodation to ordinary language that we speak of them as doing so—but moving themselves in harmony with each other (p. 250).

The psychology of Leibnitz is chiefly developed in the *Nouveaux essais sur l'entendement humain*, written in answer to Locke's famous *Essay*, and criticizing it chapter by chapter. In these essays he worked out a theory of the origin and development of knowledge in harmony with his metaphysical views, and thus without Locke's implied assumption of the mutual influence of soul and body. When one monad in an aggregate perceives the others so clearly that they are in comparison with it bare monads (*monades nues*), it is said to be the ruling monad of the aggregate, not because it actually does exert an influence over the rest, but because, being in close correspondence with them, and yet having so much clearer perception, it seems to do so (p. 683). This monad is called the entelechy or soul of the aggregate or body, and as such mirrors the aggregate in the first place and the universe through it (p. 710). Each soul or entelechy is surrounded by an infinite number of monads forming its body (p. 714); soul and body together make a living being, and as their laws are in perfect harmony—a harmony established between the whole realm of final causes and that of efficient causes (p. 714)—we have the same result as if one influenced the other. This is further explained by Leibnitz in his well-known illustration of the different ways in which two clocks may keep exactly the same time. The machinery of the one may actually move that of the other, or whenever one moves the mechanician may make a similar alteration in the other, or they may have been so perfectly constructed at first as to continue to correspond at every instant without any further influence (pp. 133, 134). The first way represents the common (Locke's) theory of mutual influence, the second the method of the occasionalists, the third that of pre-established harmony. Thus the body does not act on the soul in the production of cognition, nor the soul on the body in the production of motion. The body acts just as if it had no soul, the soul as if it had no body (p. 711). Instead, therefore, of all knowledge coming to us directly or indirectly through the bodily senses, it is all developed by the soul's own activity, and sensuous perception is itself but a confused kind of cognition. Not a certain select class of our ideas only (as Descartes held), but all our ideas, are innate, though only worked up into actual cognition in the development of knowledge (p. 212). To the aphorism made use of by Locke, "Nihil est in intellectu quod non prius fuerit in sensu," must be added the clause, "nisi intellectus ipse" (p. 223). The soul at birth is not comparable to a *tabula rasa*, but rather to an unworked block of marble, the hidden veins of which already determine the form it is to assume in the hands of the sculptor (p. 196). Nor, again, can the soul ever be without perception; for it has no other nature than that of a percipient active being (p. 246). Apparently dreamless sleep is to be accounted for by unconscious perception (p. 223); and it is by such insensible perceptions that Leibnitz explains his doctrine of pre-established harmony (p. 197).

In the human soul perception is developed into thought, and there is thus an infinite though gradual difference between it and the mere monad (p. 464). As all knowledge is implicit in the soul, it follows that its perfection depends on the efficiency of the instrument by which it is developed. Hence the importance, in Leibnitz's system, of the logical principles and method, the consideration of which occupied him at intervals throughout his whole career.

There are two kinds of truths—(1) truths of reasoning, and (2) truths of fact (pp. 83, 99, 707). The former rest on the principle of identity (or contradiction) or of possibility, in virtue of which that is false which contains a contradiction, and that true which is contradictory to the false. The latter rest on the principle of sufficient reason or of reality (*compossibilité*), according to which no fact is true unless there be a sufficient reason why it should be so and not otherwise (agreeing thus with the *principium melioris* or final cause). God alone, the purely active monad, has an *a priori* knowledge of the latter class of truths; they have their source in the human mind only in so far as it mirrors the outer world, *i.e.* its passivity, whereas the truths of reason have their source in our mind in itself or in its activity.

Both kinds of truths fall into two classes, primitive and derivative. The primitive truths of fact are, as Descartes held, those of internal experience, and the derivative truths are inferred from them in accordance with the principle of sufficient reason, by their agreement with our perception of the world as a whole. They are thus reached by probable arguments—a department of logic which Leibnitz was the first to bring into prominence (pp. 84, 164, 168, 169, 343). The primitive truths of reasoning are identical (in later terminology, analytical) propositions, the derivative truths being deduced from them by the principle of contradiction. The part of his logic on which Leibnitz laid the greatest stress was the separation of these rational cognitions into their simplest elements—for he held that the root-notions (*cogitationes primae*) would be found to be few in number (pp. 92, 93)—and the designation of them by universal characters or symbols,[1] composite notions being denoted by the formulae formed by the union of several definite characters, and judgments by the relation of aequipollence among these formulae, so as to reduce the syllogism to a calculus. This is the main idea of Leibnitz's "universal characteristic," never fully worked out by him, which he regarded as one of the greatest discoveries of the age. An incidental result of its adoption would be the introduction of a universal symbolism of thought comparable to the symbolism of mathematics and intelligible in all languages (cf. p. 356). But the great revolution it would effect would chiefly consist in this, that truth and falsehood would be no longer matters of opinion but of correctness or error in calculation,[2] (pp. 83, 84, 89, 93). The old Aristotelian analytic is not to be superseded, but it is to be supplemented by this new method, for of itself it is but the ABC of logic.

But the logic of Leibnitz is an art of discovery (p. 85) as well as of proof, and, as such, applies both to the sphere of reasoning and to that of fact. In the former it has by attention to render explicit what is otherwise only implicit, and by the intellect to introduce order into the *a priori* truths of reason, so that one may follow from another and they may constitute together a *monde intellectuel*. To this art of orderly combination Leibnitz attached the greatest importance, and to it one of his earliest writings was devoted. Similarly, in the sphere of experience, it is the business of the art of discovery to find out and classify the primitive facts or data, referring every other fact to them as its sufficient reason, so that new truths of experience may be brought to light.

As the perception of the monad when clarified becomes thought, so the appetite of which all monads partake is raised to will, their spontaneity to freedom, in man (p. 669). The will is an effort or tendency to that which one finds good (p. 251), and is free only in the sense of being exempt from external control[3] (pp. 262, 513, 521), for it must always have a sufficient reason for its action determined by what seems good to it. The end determining the will is pleasure (p. 269), and pleasure is the sense of an increase of perfection (p. 670). A will guided by reason will sacrifice transitory and pursue constant pleasures or happiness, and in this weighing of pleasures consists true wisdom. Leibnitz, like Spinoza, says that freedom consists in following reason, servitude in following the passions (p. 669), and that the passions proceed from confused perceptions (pp. 188, 269). In love one finds joy in the happiness of another; and from love follow justice and law. "Our reason," says Leibnitz,[4] "illumined by the spirit of God, reveals the law of nature," and with it positive law must not conflict. Natural law rises from the strict command to avoid offence, through the maxim of equity which gives to each his due, to that of probity or piety (*honeste vivere*),—the highest ethical perfection,—which presupposes a belief in God, providence and a future life.[5] Moral immortality—not merely the simple continuity which belongs to every monad—comes from God having provided that the changes of matter will not make man lose his individuality (pp. 126, 466).

Leibnitz thus makes the existence of God a postulate of morality as well as necessary for the realization of the monads. It is in the *Théodicée* that his theology is worked out and his view of the universe as the best possible world defended. In it he contends that faith and reason are essentially harmonious (pp. 402, 479), and that nothing can be received as an article of faith which contradicts an eternal truth, though the ordinary physical order may be superseded by a higher.[6]

The ordinary arguments for the being of God are retained by Leibnitz in a modified form (p. 375). Descartes's ontological proof is supplemented by the clause that God as the *ens a se* must either exist or be impossible (pp. 80, 177, 708), in the cosmological proof he passes from the infinite series of finite causes to their sufficient reason which contains all changes in the series necessarily in itself (pp. 147, 708); and he argues teleologically from the existence of harmony among the monads without any mutual influence to God as the author of this harmony (p. 430).

In these proofs Leibnitz seems to have in view an extramundane power to whom the monads owe their reality, though such a conception evidently breaks the continuity and harmony of his system, and can only be externally connected with it. But he also speaks in one place at any rate[7] of God as the "universal harmony", and the historians Erdmann and Zeller are of opinion that this is the only sense in which his system can be consistently theistic. Yet it would seem that to assume a purely active and therefore perfect monad as the source of all things is in accordance with the principle of continuity and with Leibnitz's conception of the gradation of existences. In this sense he sometimes speaks of God as the first or highest of the monads (p. 678), and of created substances proceeding from Him continually by "fulgurations" (p. 708) or by "a sort of emanation as we produce our thoughts."[8]

The positive properties or perfections of the monads, Leibnitz holds, exist *eminenter*, *i.e.* without the limitation that attaches to created monads (p. 716), in God—their perception as His wisdom or intellect, and their appetite as His absolute will or goodness (p. 654); while the absence of all limitation is the divine independence or power, which again consists in this, that the possibility of things depends on His intellect, their reality on His will (p. 506). The universe in its harmonious order is thus the realization of the divine end, and as such must be the best possible (p. 506). The teleology of Leibnitz becomes necessarily a *Théodicée*. God created a world to manifest and communicate His perfection (p. 524), and, in choosing this world out of the infinite number that exist in the region of ideas (p. 515), was guided by the *principium melioris* (p. 506). With this thoroughgoing optimism Leibnitz has to reconcile the existence of evil in the best of all possible worlds.[9] With this end in view he distinguishes (p. 655) between (1) metaphysical evil or imperfection, which is unconditionally willed by God as essential to created beings; (2) physical evil, such as pain, which is conditionally willed by God as punishment or as a means to greater good (cf. p. 510); and (3) moral evil, in which the great difficulty lies, and which Leibnitz makes various attempts to explain. He says that it was merely permitted not willed by God (p. 655), and, that being obviously no explanation, adds that it was permitted because it was foreseen that the world with evil would nevertheless be better than any other possible world (p. 350). He also speaks of the evil as a mere set-off to the good in the world, which it increases by contrast (p. 149), and at other times reduces moral to metaphysical evil by giving it a merely negative existence, or says that their evil actions are to be referred to men alone, while it is only the power of action that comes from God, and the power of action is good (p. 658).

The great problem of Leibnitz's *Théodicée* thus remains unsolved. The suggestion that evil consists in a mere imperfection, like his idea of the monads proceeding from God by a continual emanation, was too bold and too inconsistent with his immediate apologetic aim to be carried out by him. Had he done so his theory would have transcended the independence of the monads with which it started, and found a deeper unity in the world than that resulting from the somewhat arbitrary assertion that the monads reflect the universe.

The philosophy of Leibnitz, in the more systematic and abstract form it received at the hands of Wolf, ruled the schools of Germany for nearly a century, and largely determined the character of the critical philosophy by which it was superseded. On it Baumgarten laid the foundations of a science of aesthetic. Its treatment of theological questions heralded the German *Aufklärung*. And on many special points—in its physical doctrine of the conservation of force, its psychological hypothesis of unconscious perception, its attempt at a logical symbolism—it has suggested ideas fruitful for the progress of science.

BIBLIOGRAPHY.—(1) Editions: Up to 1900 no attempt had been made to publish the complete works. Several editions existed, but a vast mass of MSS. (letters, &c.) remained only roughly classified in the Hanover library. The chief editions were: (1) L. Dutens (Geneva, 1768), called *Opera Omnia*, but far from complete; (2) G. H. Pertz, *Leibnizens gesammelte Werke* (Berlin, 1843-1863) (1st ser. History, 4 vols.; 2nd ser. Philosophy, vol. i. correspondence with Arnauld, &c., ed. C. L. Grotefend; 3rd ser. Mathematics, 7 vols., ed. C. J. Gerhardt); (3) Foucher de Careil (planned in 20 vols., 7 published, Paris, 1859-1875), the same editor having previously published *Lettres et opuscules inédits de Leibniz* (Paris, 1854-1857); (4) Onno Klopp, *Die Werke von Leibniz gemäss seinem Handschriftlichen Nachlasse in der Königlichen Bibliothek zu Hannover* (1st series, Historico-Political and Political, 10 vols., 1864-1877). The *Œuvres de Leibnitz*, by A. Jacques (2 vols., Paris, 1846) also

[1] Different symbolic systems were proposed by Leibnitz at different periods; cf. Květ, *Leibnitzens Logik* (1857), p. 37.

[2] The places at which Leibnitz anticipated the modern theory of logic mainly due to Boole are pointed out in Mr Venn's *Symbolic Logic* (1881).

[3] Hence the difference of his determinism from that of Spinoza, though Leibnitz too says in one place that "it is difficult enough to distinguish the actions of God from those of the creatures" (*Werke*, ed. Pertz, 2nd ser. vol. i. p. 160).

[4] *Opera omnia*, ed. Dutens, IV. iii. 282.

[5] *Ibid.* IV. iii. 295. Cf. Bluntschli, *Gesch. d. allg. Staatsrechts u. Politik* (1864), pp. 143 sqq.

[6] P. 480; cf. *Werke*, ed. Pertz, 2nd ser. vol. i. pp. 158, 159.

[7] *Werke*, ed. Klopp, iii. 239; cf. *Op. phil.*, p. 716.

[8] *Werke*, ed. Pertz, 2nd ser. vol. i. p. 167.

[9] "Si c'est ici le meilleur des mondes possibles, que sont donc les autres?"—Voltaire, *Candide*, ch. vi.

[illegible] The philosophical writings had been published [illegible] and Leipzig, 1765), by J. E. Erdmann, [illegible] quae extant Latina, Gallica, Germanica, omnia [illegible], by F. [illegible] (2 vols., Paris, 1866, 2nd ed. 1900), [illegible] by C. J. Gerhardt, Die Philosophischen Schriften von [illegible] (7 vols., 1875–1890); cf. also Die kleineren philos. [illegible] with commentary, J. H. von Kirchmann, [illegible] works had also been partly published separately, [illegible] (Berlin, 1858–1840). Of the letters various collections [illegible] published up to 1900, e.g. C. J. Gerhardt (Halle, [illegible]) Der Briefwechsel von G. W. Leibniz mit Mathematikern [illegible] tra L. A. Muratori e G. Leibniz (1899), [illegible] zum Briefwechsel zwischen D. E. Jablonsky [illegible].

[illegible] it was decided by scholars in Berlin and Paris that a complete edition should be published, and with this object [illegible] and four French critics were entrusted with the preparation [illegible] the MSS. in the royal library at Hanover. [illegible] in the preparation of the Kritischer Katalog [illegible] der interakademischen [illegible] (1908), and also in certain other [illegible], e.g. L. Couturat, Opuscules et fragments [illegible]; E. Gerland, Leibnizens nachgelassene Schriften [illegible] und technischen Inhalts (1906); Jean [illegible] containing unedited MSS. and a sketch [illegible] the same author's Leibniz et l'organisation religieuse [illegible].

[illegible]—Of the Systema Theologicum (1850, C. W. Russell), [illegible] correspondence with Clarke (1717); Works, by G. M. Duncan [illegible]; of the Nouveaux Essais, by A. G. Langley [illegible]; the Monadology and other Writings, by R. Latta [illegible].

[illegible]—The materials for the life of Leibnitz, in addition [illegible] works, are the notes of Eckhart (not published till 1779), [illegible] by Fontenelle (read to the French Academy in 1717), the [illegible] by Wolf, in the Acta Eruditorum for July 1717, and [illegible] to the same by Feller, published in his [illegible] (Leipzig, 1718). The best biography is that of [illegible] G. W. Freiherr von Leibnitz (2 vols., Breslau, 1842; [illegible], Breslau, 1846). A shorter Life of G. W. von Leibnitz, on [illegible] of the German Work of Guhrauer, has been published by J. M. [illegible] (Boston, 1845). More recent works are those of L. Grote, [illegible] und seine Zeit (Hanover, 1869); E. Pfleiderer, Leibniz als [illegible], Staatsmann, und Bildungsträger (Leipzig, 1870); the [illegible] volume of F. Kirchner, G. W. Leibniz: sein Leben und Denken (Köthen, 1876); Kuno Fischer, vol. iii. in Gesch. der neuern Philosophie (4th ed., 1902).

[illegible]—The monographs and essays on Leibnitz are too numerous to mention, but reference may be made to Feuerbach, Darstellung, Entwicklung, und Kritik der Leibnitz'schen Phil. (2nd ed., Leipzig, 1844); Nourrisson, La Philosophie de Leibniz (Paris, 1860); R. Zimmermann, Leibnitz und Herbart: eine Vergleichung ihrer Monadologien (Vienna, 1849); O. Caspari, Leibniz' Philosophie beleuchtet vom Gesichtspunkt der physikalischen Grundbegriffe von Kraft und Stoff (Leipzig, 1870); G. Hartenstein, "Locke's Lehre von der menschl. Erk. in Vergl. mit Leibniz's Kritik derselben dargestellt," in the Abhandl. d. philol.-hist. Cl. d. K. Sächs. Gesells. d. Wiss., vol. iv. (Leipzig, 1865); G. Class, Die metaph. Voraussetzungen des Leibnitzischen Determinismus (Tübingen, 1874); F. B. Květ, Leibnitzens Logik (Prague, 1857); the essays on Leibnitz in Trendelenburg's Beiträge, vols. ii. and iii. (Berlin, 1855, 1867); L. Neff, Leibniz [illegible] (Heidelberg, 1870–1871); J. Schmidt, Leibniz und Baumgarten (Halle, 1875); D. Nolen, La Critique de Kant et [illegible] de Leibniz (Paris, 1875); and the exhaustive work [illegible] A. Pichler, Die Theologie des Leibniz (Munich, 1869–1870). Among [illegible] works are: C. Braig, Leibniz: sein Leben und die [illegible] Lehre (1907); E. Cassirer, Leibniz' System in seinem [illegible] Grundlagen (1902); L. Couturat, La Logique de [illegible] des documents inédits (1901); L. Davillé, Leibniz [illegible]; Kuno Fischer, G. W. Leibniz (1889); R. B. [illegible] Der Associationsbegriff bei Leibniz (1898); R. Herbertz, [illegible] vom Unbewussten im System des Leibniz (1905); H. Hoff[illegible] Leibniz'sche Religions-philosophie in ihrer geschichtlichen [illegible]; W. Kabitz, Die Philosophie des jungen Leibniz [illegible] of the development of the Leibnitzian system; [illegible] Materie und Organismus bei Leibniz (1908); G. Niel, [illegible] de Leibniz (1888); Bertrand A. W. Russell, A Critical [illegible] of the Philosophy of Leibniz (1900); F. Schmöger, Leibniz [illegible] zur tellurischen Physik (1901); A. Silberstein, [illegible] in Verhältnis zu seiner Metaphysik (1904); [illegible] und Spinoza (1890); F. Thilly, Leibnizens Streit gegen [illegible] der angeborenen Ideen (1891); R. Urbach, [illegible] des Uebels in der besten Welt (1901); W. [illegible], Der Leibnizische Substanzbegriff (1899); F. G. F. [illegible], Leibniz' Lehre von der Freiheit des menschlichen Willens [illegible] (W. R. So.)

LEICESTER, EARLS OF. The first holder of this English earldom belonged to the family of Beaumont, although a certain Saxon named Edgar has been described as the 1st earl of Leicester. Robert de Beaumont (d. 1118) is frequently but erroneously considered to have received the earldom from Henry I., about 1107, he had, however, some authority in the county of Leicester and his son Robert was undoubtedly earl of Leicester in 1131. The 3rd Beaumont earl, another Robert, was also steward of England, a dignity which was attached to the earldom of Leicester from this time until 1399. The earldom reverted to the crown when Robert de Beaumont, the 4th earl, died in January 1204.

In 1207 Simon IV., count of Montfort (*q.v.*), nephew and heir of Earl Robert, was confirmed in the possession of the earldom by King John, but it was forfeited when his son, the famous Simon de Montfort, was attainted and was killed at Evesham in August 1265. Henry III.'s son Edmund, earl of Lancaster, was also earl of Leicester and steward of England, obtaining these offices a few months after Earl Simon's death. Edmund's sons, Thomas and Henry, both earls of Lancaster, and his grandson Henry, duke of Lancaster, in turn held the earldom, which then passed to a son-in-law of Duke Henry, William V., count of Holland (*c.* 1327–1389), and then to another and more celebrated son-in-law, John of Gaunt, duke of Lancaster. When in 1399 Gaunt's son became king as Henry IV. the earldom was merged in the crown.

In 1564 Queen Elizabeth created her favourite, Lord Robert Dudley, earl of Leicester. The new earl was a son of John Dudley, duke of Northumberland; he left no children, or rather none of undoubted legitimacy, and when he died in September 1588 the title became extinct.

In 1618 the earldom of Leicester was revived in favour of Robert Sidney, Viscount Lisle, a nephew of the late earl and a brother of Sir Philip Sidney; it remained in this family until the death of Jocelyn (1682–1743), the 7th earl of this line, in July 1743. Jocelyn left no legitimate children, but a certain John Sidney claimed to be his son and consequently to be 8th earl of Leicester.

In 1744, the year after Jocelyn's death, Thomas Coke, Baron Lovel (*c.* 1695–1759), was made earl of Leicester, but the title became extinct on his death in April 1759. The next family to hold the earldom was that of Townshend, George Townshend (1755–1811) being created earl of Leicester in 1784. In 1807 George succeeded his father as 2nd marquess Townshend, and when his son George Ferrars Townshend, the 3rd marquess (1778–1855), died in December 1855 the earldom again became extinct. Before this date, however, another earldom of Leicester was in existence. This was created in 1837 in favour of Thomas William Coke, who had inherited the estates of his relative Thomas Coke, earl of Leicester. To distinguish his earldom from that held by the Townshends Coke was ennobled as earl of Leicester of Holkham; his son Thomas William Coke (1822–1909) became 2nd earl of Leicester in 1842, and the latter's son Thomas William (b. 1848) became 3rd earl.

See G. E. C(okayne), *Complete Peerage*, vol. v. (1893).

LEICESTER, ROBERT DUDLEY, Earl of (*c.* 1531–1588). This favourite of Queen Elizabeth came of an ambitious family. They were not, indeed, such mere upstarts as their enemies loved to represent them; for Leicester's grandfather—the notorious Edmund Dudley who was one of the chief instruments of Henry VII.'s extortions—was descended from a younger branch of the barons of Dudley. But the love of power was a passion which seems to have increased in them with each succeeding generation, and though the grandfather was beheaded by Henry VIII. for his too devoted services in the preceding reign, the father grew powerful enough in the days of Edward VI. to trouble the succession to the crown. This was that John Dudley, duke of Northumberland, who contrived the marriage of Lady Jane Grey with his own son Guildford Dudley, and involved both her and her husband in a common ruin with himself. Robert Dudley, the subject of this article, was an elder brother of Guildford, and shared at that time in the misfortunes of the whole family. Having taken up arms with them against Queen Mary, he was sent to the Tower, and was sentenced to death; but the queen not only pardoned and restored him to liberty, but appointed him master of the ordnance. On the accession of Elizabeth he was also made master of the horse. He was then, perhaps, about seven-and-twenty, and was evidently rising rapidly in the queen's favour. At an early age he had been married to Amy, daughter of Sir John Robsart. The match had been arranged by his father, who was very studious to provide in this way for the future fortunes of his children, and the wedding was graced by the presence of King Edward. But if it was not a love match, there seems to have been no positive estrangement between the couple. Amy visited her husband in the Tower during his imprisonment; but afterwards when, under the new queen, he was much at court, she lived a good deal apart from him. He visited her, however, at times, in different parts of the country, and his expenses show that he treated her liberally. In September 1560 she was staying at Cumnor Hall in Berkshire, the house of one Anthony Forster, when she met her death under circumstances which certainly aroused suspicions of foul play. It is quite clear that her death had been surmised some time before as a thing that would remove an obstacle to Dudley's marriage with the queen, with whom he stood in so high favour. We may take it, perhaps, from Venetian sources, that she was then in delicate health, while Spanish state papers show further that there were scandalous rumours of a design to poison her; which were all the more propagated by malice after the event. The occurrence, however, was explained as owing to a fall down stairs in which she broke her neck, and the explanation seems perfectly adequate to account for all we know about it. Certain it is that Dudley continued to rise in the queen's favour She made him a Knight of the Garter, and bestowed on him the castle of Kenilworth, the lordship of Denbigh and other lands of very great value in Warwickshire and in Wales. In September 1564 she created him baron of Denbigh, and immediately afterwards earl of Leicester. In the preceding month, when she visited Cambridge, she at his request addressed the university in Latin. The honours shown him excited jealousy, especially as it was well known that he entertained still more ambitious hopes, which the queen apparently did not altogether discourage. The earl of Sussex, in opposition to him, strongly favoured a match with the archduke Charles of Austria. The court was divided, and, while arguments were set forth on the one side against the queen's marrying a subject, the other party insisted strongly on the disadvantages of a foreign alliance. The queen, however, was so far from being foolishly in love with him that in 1564 she recommended him as a husband for Mary Queen of Scots. But this, it was believed, was only a blind, and it may be doubted how far the proposal was serious. After his creation as earl of Leicester great attention was paid to him both at home and abroad. The university of Oxford made him their chancellor, and Charles IX. of France sent him the order of St Michael. A few years later he formed an ambiguous connexion with the baroness dowager of Sheffield, which was maintained by the lady, if not with truth at least with great plausibility, to have been a valid marriage, though it was concealed from the queen. Her own subsequent conduct, however, went far to discredit her statements; for she married again during Leicester's life, when he, too, had found a new conjugal partner. Long afterwards, in the days of James I., her son, Sir Robert Dudley, a man of extraordinary talents, sought to establish his legitimacy; but his suit was suddenly brought to a stop, the witnesses discredited and the documents connected with it sealed up by an order of the Star Chamber.

In 1575 Queen Elizabeth visited the earl at Kenilworth, where she was entertained for some days with great magnificence. The picturesque account of the event given by Sir Walter Scott has made every one familiar with the general character of the scene. Next year Walter, earl of Essex, died in Ireland, and Leicester's subsequent marriage with his widow again gave rise to very serious imputations against him. For report said that he had had two children by her during her husband's absence in Ireland, and, as the feud between the two earls was notorious, Leicester's many enemies easily suggested that he had poisoned his rival. This marriage, at all events, tended to Leicester's discredit and was kept secret at first; but it was revealed to the queen in 1579 by Simier, an emissary of the duke of Alençon, to whose projected match with Elizabeth the earl seemed to be the principal obstacle. The queen showed great displeasure at the news, and had some thought, it is said, of committing Leicester to the Tower, but was dissuaded from doing so by his rival the earl of Sussex. He had not, indeed, favoured the Alençon marriage, but otherwise he had sought to promote a league with France against Spain. He and Burleigh had listened to proposals from France for the conquest and division of Flanders, and they were in the secret about the capture of Brill. When Alençon actually arrived, indeed, in August 1579, Dudley being in disgrace, showed himself for a time anti-French; but he soon returned to his former policy. He encouraged Drake's piratical expeditions against the Spaniards and had a share in the booty brought home. In February 1582 he, with a number of other noblemen and gentlemen, escorted the duke of Alençon on his return to Antwerp to be invested with the government of the Low Countries. In 1584 he inaugurated an association for the protection of Queen Elizabeth against conspirators. About this time there issued from the press the famous pamphlet, supposed to have been the work of Parsons the Jesuit, entitled *Leicester's Commonwealth*, which was intended to suggest that the English constitution was subverted and the government handed over to one who was at heart an atheist and a traitor, besides being a man of infamous life and morals. The book was ordered to be suppressed by letters from the privy council, in which it was declared that the charges against the earl were to the queen's certain knowledge untrue; nevertheless they produced a very strong impression, and were believed in by some who had no sympathy with Jesuits long after Leicester's death. In 1585 he was appointed commander of an expedition to the Low Countries in aid of the revolted provinces, and sailed with a fleet of fifty ships to Flushing, where he was received with great enthusiasm. In January following he was invested with the government of the provinces, but immediately received a strong reprimand from the queen for taking upon himself a function which she had not authorized. Both he and the states general were obliged to apologize; but the latter protested that they had no intention of giving him absolute control of their affairs, and that it would be extremely dangerous to them to revoke the appointment. Leicester accordingly was allowed to retain his dignity; but the incident was inauspicious, nor did affairs prosper greatly under his management. The most brilliant achievement of the war was the action at Zutphen, in which his nephew Sir Philip Sidney was slain. But complaints were made by the states general of the conduct of the whole campaign. He returned to England for a time, and went back in 1587, when he made an abortive effort to raise the siege of Sluys. Disagreements increasing between him and the states, he was recalled by the queen, from whom he met with a very good reception; and he continued in such favour that in the following summer (the year being that of the Armada, 1588) he was appointed lieutenant-general of the army mustered at Tilbury to resist Spanish invasion. After the crisis was past he was returning homewards from the court to Kenilworth, when he was attacked by a sudden illness and died at his house at Cornbury in Oxfordshire, on the 4th September.

Such are the main facts of Leicester's life. Of his character it is more difficult to speak with confidence, but some features of it are indisputable. Being in person tall and remarkably handsome, he improved these advantages by a very ingratiating manner. A man of no small ability and still more ambition, he was nevertheless vain, and presumed at times upon his influence with the queen to a degree that brought upon him a sharp rebuff. Yet Elizabeth stood by him. That she was ever really in love with him, as modern writers have supposed, is extremely questionable; but she saw in him some valuable qualities which marked him as the fitting recipient of high favours. He was a man of princely tastes, especially in architecture. At court he became latterly the leader of the Puritan party.

and his letters were pervaded by expressions of religious feeling which it is hard to believe were insincere. Of the darker suspicions against him it is enough to say that much was certainly reported beyond the truth; but there remain some facts sufficiently disagreeable, and others, perhaps, sufficiently mysterious, to make a just estimate of the man a rather perplexing problem.

No special biography of Leicester has yet been written except in biographical dictionaries and encyclopaedias. A general account of him will be found in the Memoirs of the Sidneys prefixed to Collins's *Letters and Memorials of State*; but the fullest yet published is Mr Sidney Lee's article in the *Dictionary of National Biography* (London, 1888) where the sources are given. Leicester's career has to be made out from documents and state papers, especially from the Hatfield MSS. and Major Hume's *Calendar* of documents from the Spanish archives bearing on the history of Queen Elizabeth. This last is the most recent source. Of others the principal are Digges's *Compleat Ambassador* (1655), John Nichols's *Progresses of Queen Elizabeth* and the *Leycester Correspondence* edited by J. Bruce for the Camden Society. The death of Dudley's first wife has been a fruitful source of literary controversy. The most recent addition to the evidences, which considerably alters their complexion, will be found in the *English Historical Review*, xiii. 83, giving the full text (in English) of De Quadra's letter of Sept. 11, 1560, on which so much has been built. (J. GA.)

LEICESTER, ROBERT SIDNEY, EARL OF (1563–1626), second son of Sir Henry Sidney (*q.v.*), was born on the 19th of November 1563, and was educated at Christ Church, Oxford, afterwards travelling on the Continent for some years between 1578 and 1583. In 1585 he was elected member of parliament for Glamorganshire; and in the same year he went with his elder brother Sir Philip Sidney (*q.v.*) to the Netherlands, where he served in the war against Spain under his uncle Robert Dudley, earl of Leicester. He was present at the engagement where Sir Philip Sidney was mortally wounded, and remained with his brother till the latter's death in October 1586. After visiting Scotland on a diplomatic mission in 1588, and France on a similar errand in 1593, he returned to the Netherlands in 1596, where he rendered distinguished service in the war for the next two years. He had been appointed governor of Flushing in 1588, and he spent much time there till 1603, when, on the accession of James I., he returned to England. James raised him at once to the peerage as Baron Sidney of Penshurst, and he was appointed chamberlain to the queen consort. In 1605 he was created Viscount Lisle, and in 1618 earl of Leicester, the latter title having become extinct in 1588 on the death of his uncle, whose property he had inherited (see LEICESTER, EARLS OF). Leicester was a man of taste and a patron of literature, whose cultured mode of life at his country seat, Penshurst, was celebrated in verse by Ben Jonson. The earl died at Penshurst on the 13th of July 1626. He was twice married; first to Barbara, daughter of John Gamage, a Glamorganshire gentleman; and secondly to Sarah, daughter of William Blount, and widow of Sir Thomas Smythe. By his first wife he had a large family. His eldest son having died unmarried in 1613, Robert, the second son (see below), succeeded to the earldom; one of his daughters married Sir John Hobart, ancestor of the earls of Buckinghamshire.

ROBERT SIDNEY, 2nd earl of Leicester of the 1618 creation (1595–1677), was born on the 1st of December 1595, and was educated at Christ Church, Oxford; he was called to the bar in 1618, having already served in the army in the Netherlands during his father's governorship of Flushing, and having entered parliament as member for Wilton in 1614. In 1616 he was given command of an English regiment in the Dutch service; and having succeeded his father as earl of Leicester in 1626, he was employed on diplomatic business in Denmark in 1632, and in France from 1636 to 1641. He was then appointed lord-lieutenant of Ireland in place of the earl of Strafford, but he waited in vain for instructions from the king, and in 1643 he was compelled to resign the office without having set foot in Ireland. He shared the literary and cultivated tastes of his family, without possessing the statesmanship of his uncle Sir Philip Sidney; his character was lacking in decision, and, as commonly befalls men of moderate views in times of acute party strife, he failed to win the confidence of either of the opposing parties. His sincere protestantism offended Laud, without being sufficiently extreme to please the puritans of the parliamentary faction; his fidelity to the king restrained him from any act tainted with rebellion, while his dislike for arbitrary government prevented him giving whole-hearted support to Charles I. When, therefore, the king summoned him to Oxford in November 1642, Leicester's conduct bore the appearance of vacillation, and his loyalty of uncertainty. Accordingly, after his resignation of the lord-lieutenancy of Ireland at the end of 1643, he retired into private life. In 1649 the younger children of the king were for a time committed to his care at Penshurst. He took no part in public affairs during the Commonwealth; and although at the Restoration he took his seat in the House of Lords and was sworn of the privy council, he continued to live for the most part in retirement at Penshurst, where he died on the 2nd of November 1677. Leicester married, in 1616, Dorothy, daughter of Henry Percy, 9th earl of Northumberland, by whom he had fifteen children. Of his nine daughters, the eldest, Dorothy, the "Sacharissa" of the poet Waller, married Robert Spencer, 2nd earl of Sunderland; and Lucy married John Pelham, by whom she was the ancestress of the 18th-century statesmen, Henry Pelham, and Thomas Pelham, duke of Newcastle. Algernon Sidney (*q.v.*), and Henry Sidney, earl of Romney (*q.v.*), were younger sons of the earl.

Leicester's eldest son, Philip, 3rd earl (1619–1698), known for most of his life as Lord Lisle, took a somewhat prominent part during the civil war. Being sent to Ireland in 1642 in command of a regiment of horse, he became lieutenant-general under Ormonde; he strongly favoured the parliamentary cause, and in 1647 he was appointed lord-lieutenant of Ireland by the parliament. Named one of Charles I.'s judges, he refused to take part in the trial; but he afterwards served in Cromwell's Council of State, and sat in the Protector's House of Lords. Lisle stood high in Cromwell's favour, but nevertheless obtained a pardon at the Restoration. He carried on the Sidney family tradition by his patronage of men of letters; and, having succeeded to the earldom on his father's death in 1677, he died in 1698, and was succeeded in the peerage by his son Robert, 4th earl of Leicester (1649–1702), whose mother was Catherine, daughter of William Cecil, 2nd earl of Salisbury.

See *Sydney Papers*, edited by A. Collins (2 vols., London, 1746); *Sydney Papers*, edited by R. W. Blencowe (London, 1825) containing the 2nd earl of Leicester's journal; Lord Clarendon *History of the Rebellion and Civil Wars in England* (8 vols. Oxford, 1826); S. R. Gardiner, *History of the Great Civil War* (3 vols., London, 1886–1891). (R. J. M.)

LEICESTER, THOMAS WILLIAM COKE, EARL OF (1754–1842), English agriculturist, known as Coke of Norfolk, was the eldest son of Wenman Roberts, who assumed the name of Coke in 1750. In 1759 Wenman Coke's maternal uncle Thomas Coke, earl of Leicester, died leaving him his estates, subject, however, to the life-interest of his widow, Margaret, Baroness de Clifford in her own right. This lady's death in 1775 was followed by that of Wenman Coke in 1776, when the latter's son, Thomas William, born on the 6th of May 1754, succeeded to his father's estates at Holkham and elsewhere From 1776 to 1784, from 1790 to 1806, and again from 1807 to 1832 Coke was member of parliament for Norfolk; he was a friend and supporter of Charles James Fox and a sturdy and aggressive Whig, acting upon the maxim taught him by his father "never to trust a Tory." Coke's chief interests, however, were in the country, and his fame is that of an agriculturist. His land around Holkham in Norfolk was poor and neglected, but he introduced many improvements, obtained the best expert advice, and in a few years wheat was grown upon his farms, and the breed of cattle, sheep and pigs greatly improved. It has been said that "his practice is really the basis of every treatise on modern agriculture." Under his direction the rental of the Holkham estate is said to have increased from £2200 to over £20,000 a year In 1837 Coke was created earl of Leicester of Holkham. Leicester, who was a strong and handsome man and a fine sportsman, died at Longford Hall in Derbyshire on the 30th of June 1842. He was twice married, and Thomas William, his son by his second marriage, succeeded to his earldom.

See A. M. W. Stirling, *Coke of Norfolk and his Friends* (1907).

LEICESTER, a municipal county and parliamentary borough, and the county town of Leicestershire, England; on the river Soar, a southern tributary of the Trent. Pop. (1891) 174,624, (1901) 211,579. It is 99 m. N.N.W. from London by the Midland railway, and is served by the Great Central and branches of the Great Northern and London and North-Western railways, and by the Leicester canal.

This was the Roman *Ratae* (*Ratae Coritanorum*), and Roman remains of high interest are preserved. They include a portion of Roman masonry known as the Jewry Wall; several pavements have been unearthed; and in the museum, among other remains, is a milestone from the Fosse Way, marking a distance of 2 m. from Ratae. St Nicholas church is a good example of early Norman work, in the building of which Roman bricks are used. St Mary de Castro church, with Norman remains, including sedilia, shows rich Early English work in the tower and elsewhere, and has a Decorated spire and later additions. All Saints church has Norman remains. St Martin's is mainly Early English, a fine cruciform structure. St Margaret's, with Early English nave, has extensive additions of beautiful Perpendicular workmanship. North of the town are slight remains of an abbey of Black Canons founded in 1143. There are a number of modern churches. Of the Castle there are parts of the Norman hall, modernized, two gateways and other remains, together with the artificial Mount on which the keep stood. The following public buildings and institutions may be mentioned—municipal buildings (1876), old town hall, formerly the gild-hall of Corpus Christi; market house, free library, opera house and other theatres and museum. The free library has several branches; there are also a valuable old library founded in the 17th century, a permanent library and a literary and philosophical society. Among several hospitals are Trinity hospital, founded in 1331 by Henry Plantagenet, earl of Lancaster and of Leicester, and Wyggeston's hospital (1513). The Wyggeston schools and Queen Elizabeth's grammar school are amalgamated, and include high schools for boys and girls; there are also Newton's greencoat school for boys, and municipal technical and art schools. A memorial clock tower was erected in 1868 to Simon de Montfort and other historical figures connected with the town. The Abbey Park is a beautiful pleasure ground; there are also Victoria Park, St Margaret's Pasture and other grounds. The staple trade is hosiery, an old-established industry; there are also manufactures of elastic webbing, cotton and lace, iron-works, maltings and brick-works. Leicester became a county borough in 1888, and the bounds were extended and constituted one civil parish in 1892. It is a suffragan bishopric in the diocese of Peterborough. The parliamentary borough returns two members. Area, 8586 acres.

The Romano-British town of *Ratae Coritanorum*, on the Fosse Way, was a municipality in A.D. 120–121. Its importance, both commercial and military, was considerable, as is attested by the many remains found here. Leicester (*Ledecestre*, *Legecestria*, *Leyrcestria*) was called a "burh" in 918, and a city in Domesday. Until 874 it was the seat of a bishopric. In 1086 both the king and Hugh de Grantmesnil had much land in Leicester; by 1101 the latter's share had passed to Robert of Meulan, to whom the rest of the town belonged before his death. Leicester thus became the largest mesne borough. Between 1103 and 1118 Robert granted his first charter to the burgesses, confirming their merchant gild. The portmanmote was confirmed by his son. In the 13th century the town developed its own form of government by a mayor and 24 jurats. In 1464 Edward IV. made the mayor and 4 of the council justices of the peace. In 1489 Henry VII. added 48 burgesses to the council for certain purposes, and made it a close body; he granted another charter in 1505. In 1589 Elizabeth incorporated the town, and gave another charter in 1599. James I. granted charters in 1605 and 1610; and Charles I. in 1630. In 1684 the charters were surrendered; a new one granted by James II. was rescinded by proclamation in 1688.

Leicester has been represented in parliament by two members since 1295. It has had a prescriptive market since the 13th century, now held on Wednesday and Saturday. Before 1228–1229 the burgesses had a fair from July 31 to August 14; changes were made in its date, which was fixed in 1360 at September 26 to October 2. It is now held on the second Thursday in October and three following days. In 1473 another fair was granted on April 27 to May 4. It is now held on the second Thursday in May and the three following days. Henry VIII. granted two three-day fairs beginning on December 8 and June 26; the first is now held on the second Friday in December; the second was held in 1888 on the last Tuesday in June. In 1307 Edward III granted a fair for seventeen days after the feast of the Holy Trinity. This would fall in May or June, and may have merged in other fairs. In 1794 the corporation sanctioned fairs on January 4, June 1, August 1, September 13 and November 2. Other fairs are now held on the second Fridays in March and July and the Saturdays next before Easter and in Easter week. Leicester has been a centre for brewing and the manufacture of woollen goods since the 13th century. Knitting frames for hosiery were introduced about 1680. Boot manufacture became important in the 19th century.

See *Victoria County History, Leicester*; M. Bateson, *Records of Borough of Leicester* (Cambridge, 1899).

LEICESTERSHIRE, a midland county of England, bounded N. by Nottinghamshire, E. by Lincolnshire and Rutland, S.E. by Northamptonshire, S.W. by Warwickshire, and N.W. by Derbyshire, also touching Staffordshire on the W. The area is 823·6 sq. m. The surface of the county is an undulating tableland, the highest eminences being the rugged hills of Charnwood Forest (*q.v.*) in the north-west, one of which, Bardon Hill, has an elevation of 912 ft. The county belongs chiefly to the basin of the Trent, which forms for a short distance its boundary with Derbyshire. The principal tributary of the Trent in Leicestershire is the Soar, from whose old designation the *Leire* the county is said to derive its name, and which rises near Hinckley in the S.E., and forms the boundary with Nottinghamshire for some distance above its junction with the Trent. The Wreak, which, under the name of the Eye, rises on the borders of Rutland, flows S.W. to the Soar. Besides the Soar the other tributaries of the Trent are the Anker, touching the boundary with Warwickshire, the Devon and the Mease. A portion of the county in the S. drains to the Avon, which forms part of the boundary with Northamptonshire, and receives the Swift. The Welland forms for some distance the boundary with Northamptonshire.

Geology.—The oldest rocks in the county belong to the Charnian System, a Pre-Cambrian series of volcanic ashes, grits and slates, into which porphyroid and syenite were afterwards intruded. These rocks emerge from the plain formed by the Keuper Marls of the Triassic System as a group of isolated hills and peaks (known as Charnwood Forest); these are the tops of an old mountain-range, the lower slopes of which are still buried under the surrounding Keuper Marls. West of this district lies the Leicestershire coalfield, where the poor state of development of the Carboniferous Limestone shows that the Charnian rocks formed shoals or islands in the Carboniferous Limestone sea. The Millstone Grit just enters the county to the north of the same region, while the Coal Measures occupy a considerable area round Ashby-de-la-Zouch and contain valuable coal-seams. The rest of the county is almost equally divided between the red Keuper Marls of the Trias on the west and the grey limestones and shales of the Lias on the east. The former were deposited in lagoons into which the land was gradually lowered after a prolonged period of desert conditions. The Rhaetic beds which follow the Keuper mark the incoming of the sea and introduce the fossiliferous Liassic deposits. On the eastern margin of the county a few small outliers of the Inferior Oolite sands and limestones are present. The Glacial Period has left boulder-clay, gravel and erratic blocks scattered over the surface, while later gravels, with remains of mammoth, reindeer, &c., border some of the present streams.

Slates, honestones, setts and roadstone from the Charnian rocks, limestone and cement from the Carboniferous and Lias, and coal from the Coal Measures are the chief mineral products.

Agriculture.—The climate is mild, and, on account of the inland position of the county, and the absence of any very high elevations, the rainfall is very moderate. The soil is of a loamy character, the richest district being that east of the Soar, which is occupied by pasture, while the corn crops are grown chiefly on a lighter soil resting above the Red Sandstone formation. About nine-tenths of the total area is under cultivation. The proportion of pasture land is large and increasing. It is especially rich along the river-banks. Dairy-farming is extensively carried on, the famous Stilton cheese being produced near Melton Mowbray. Cattle are reared in large numbers, while of sheep the New Leicester breed is well known. It was introduced by Robert Bakewell the agriculturist, who was born near Loughborough in 1725. He also improved the breed of horses by the importation of mares from Flanders.

The county is especially famed for fox-hunting, Leicester and Melton Mowbray being favourite centres, while the kennels of the Quorn hunt are located at Quorndon near Mount Sorrel. For this reason Leicestershire is rich in good riding horses.

Other Industries.—Coal is worked in the districts about Moira, Coleorton and Coalville. Limestone is worked in various parts, freestone is plentiful, gypsum is found, and a kind of granite, extensively used for paving, is obtained in the Charnwood district, as at Bardon and Mount Sorrel, and at Sapcote and Stoney Stanton in the south-west. Apart from the mining industries, the staple manufacture of Leicestershire is hosiery, for which the wool is obtained principally from home-bred sheep. Its principal seats are Leicester, Loughborough, Hinckley and Castle Donington. Cotton hose are likewise made, and other industries include the manufacture of boots and shoes, as at Market Harborough, elastic webbing, and bricks, also iron founding. Melton Mowbray gives name to a well-known manufacture of pork pies.

Communications.—The main line of the Midland railway serves Market Harborough, Leicester, and Loughborough, having an important junction at Trent (on that river) for Derby and Nottingham. Branches radiate from Leicester to Melton Mowbray, to Coalville, Ashby-de-la-Zouch, Moira and Burton-upon-Trent, with others through the mining district of the N.W., which is also served by the branch of the London & North-Western railway from Nuneaton to Market Bosworth, Coalville and Loughborough. This company serves Market Harborough from Rugby, and branches of the Great Northern serve Market Harborough, Leicester and Melton Mowbray. The main line of the Great Central railway passes through Lutterworth, Leicester and Loughborough. The principal canals are the Union and Grand Union, with which various branches are connected with the Grand Junction, and the Ashby-de-la-Zouch canal, which joins the Coventry canal at Nuneaton. The Loughborough canal serves that town, connecting with the river Soar.

Population and Administration.—The area of the ancient county is 527,123 acres, pop. (1891) 373,584, (1901) 434,019. The area of the administrative county is 532,788 acres. The county contains six hundreds. The municipal boroughs are: Leicester, the county town and a county borough (pop. 211,579), Loughborough (21,508). The urban districts are: Ashby-de-la-Zouch (4726), Ashby Woulds (2799), Coalville (15,281), Hinckley (11,304), Market Harborough (7735), Melton Mowbray (7454), Quorndon (2173), Shepshed (5293), Thurmaston (1732), Wigston Magna (8404). The county is in the Midland circuit, has one court of quarter sessions, and is divided into 9 petty sessional divisions. The county borough of Leicester has a separate court of quarter sessions and a separate commission of the peace. There are 327 civil parishes. The county is divided into four parliamentary divisions (Eastern or Melton, Mid or Loughborough, Western or Bosworth, Southern or Harborough), each returning one member; and the parliamentary borough of Leicester returns 2 members. The county is in the diocese of Peterborough, with the exception of small parts in those of Southwell and Worcester; and contains 255 ecclesiastical parishes or districts, wholly or in part.

History.—The district which is now Leicestershire was reached in the 6th century by Anglian invaders who, making their way across the Trent, penetrated Charnwood Forest as far as Leicester, the fall of which may be dated at about 556. In 679 the district formed the kingdom of the Middle Angles within the kingdom of Mercia, and on the subdivision of the Mercian see in that year was formed into a separate bishopric having its see at Leicester. In the 9th century the district was subjugated by the Danes, and Leicester became one of the five Danish boroughs. It was recovered by Æthelflaed in 918, but the Northmen regained their supremacy shortly after, and the prevalence of Scandinavian place-names in the county bears evidence of the extent of their settlement.

Leicestershire probably originated as a shire in the 10th century, and at the time of the Domesday Survey was divided into the four wapentakes of Guthlaxton, Framland, Goscote and Gartree. The Leicestershire Survey of the 12th century shows an additional grouping of the vills into small local hundreds, manorial rather than administrative divisions, which have completely disappeared. In the reign of Edward I. the divisions appear as hundreds, and in the reign of Edward III. the additional hundred of Sparkenhoe was formed out of Guthlaxton. Before the 17th century Goscote was divided into East and West Goscote, and since then the hundreds have undergone little change. Until 1566 Leicestershire and Warwickshire had a common sheriff, the shire-court for the former being held at Leicester.

Leicestershire constituted an archdeaconry within the diocese of Lincoln from 1092 until its transference to Peterborough in 1837. In 1291 it comprised the deaneries of Akeley, Leicester (now Christianity), Framland, Gartree, Goscote, Guthlaxton and Sparkenhoe. The deaneries remained unaltered until 1865. Since 1894 they have been as follows: East, South and West Akeley, Christianity, Framland (3 portions), Sparkenhoe (2 portions), Gartree (3 portions), Goscote (2 portions), Guthlaxton (3 portions).

Among the earliest historical events connected with the county were the siege and capture of Leicester by Henry II. in 1173 on the rebellion of the earl of Leicester; the surrender of Leicester to Prince Edward in 1264; and the parliament held at Leicester in 1414. During the Wars of the Roses Leicester was a great Lancastrian stronghold. In 1485 the battle of Bosworth was fought in the county. In the Civil War of the 17th century the greater part of the county favoured the parliament, though the mayor and some members of the corporation of Leicester sided with the king, and in 1642 the citizens of Leicester on a summons from Prince Rupert lent Charles £500. In 1645 Leicester was twice captured by the Royalist forces.

Before the Conquest large estates in Leicestershire were held by Earls Ralf, Morcar, Waltheof and Harold, but the Domesday Survey of 1086 reveals an almost total displacement of English by Norman landholders, only a few estates being retained by Englishmen as under-tenants. The first lay-tenant mentioned in the survey is Robert, count of Meulan, ancestor of the Beaumont family and afterwards earl of Leicester, to whose fief was afterwards annexed the vast holding of Hugh de Grantmesnil, lord high steward of England. Robert de Toeni, another Domesday tenant, founded Belvoir Castle and Priory. The fief of Robert de Buci was bestowed on Richard Basset, founder of Laund Abbey, in the reign of Henry I. Loughborough was an ancient seat of the Despenser family, and Brookesby was the seat of the Villiers and the birthplace of George Villiers, the famous duke of Buckingham. Melton Mowbray was named from its former lords, the Mowbrays, descendants of Nigel de Albini, the founder of Axholme Priory. Lady Jane Grey was born at Bradgate near Leicester, and Bishop Latimer was born at Thurcaston.

The woollen industry flourished in Leicestershire in Norman times, and in 1343 Leicestershire wool was rated at a higher value than that of most other counties. Coal was worked at Coleorton in the early 15th century and at Measham in the 17th century. The famous blue slate of Swithland has been quarried from time immemorial, and the limestone quarry at Barrow-on-Soar is also of very ancient repute, the monks of the abbey of St Mary de Pré formerly enjoying the tithe of its produce. The staple manufacture of the county, that of hosiery, originated in the 17th century, the chief centres being Leicester, Hinckley and Loughborough, and before the development of steam-driven frames in the 19th century hand framework knitting of hose and gloves was carried on in about a hundred villages. Wool-carding was also an extensive industry before 1840.

In 1290 Leicestershire returned two members to parliament, and in 1295 Leicester was also represented by two members. Under the Reform Act of 1832 the county returned four members in two divisions until the Redistribution of Seats Act of 1885, under which it returned four members in four divisions.

Antiquities.—Remains of monastic foundations are slight, though there were a considerable number of these. There are traces of Leicester Abbey and of Gracedieu near Coalville, while at Ulverscroft in Charnwood, where there was an Augustinian priory of the 12th century, there are fine Decorated remains, including a tower. The most noteworthy churches are found in the towns, as at Ashby-de-la-Zouch, Hinckley, Leicester, Loughborough, Lutterworth, Market Bosworth, Market Harborough, and Melton Mowbray (*qq.v.*). The principal old castle is that of Ashby-de-la-Zouch, while at Kirby Muxloe there is a picturesque fortified mansion of Tudor date. There are several good Elizabethan mansions, as that at Laund in the E. of the county. Among modern mansions that of the dukes of Rutland, Belvoir Castle in the extreme N.E., is a massive mansion of the early 19th century, finely placed on the summit of a hill.

See *Victoria County History, Leicestershire*; W. Burton, *Description of Leicestershire* (London, 1622; 2nd ed., Lynn, 1777); John Nicholls, *History and Antiquities of the County of Leicester* (4 vols., London, 1795–1815); John Curtis, *A Topographical History of the County of Leicester* (Ashby-de-la-Zouch, 1831).

LEIDEN or LEYDEN, a city in the province of South Holland, the kingdom of the Netherlands, on the Old Rhine, and a junction station 18 m. by rail S.S.W. of Haarlem. It is connected by steam tramway with Haarlem and The Hague respectively, and with the seaside resorts of Katwyk and Noordwyk. There is also regular steamboat connexion with Katwyk, Noordwyk, Amsterdam and Gouda. The population of Leiden which, it is estimated, reached 100,000 in 1640, had sunk to 30,000 between 1796 and 1811, and in 1904 was 56,044. The two branches of the Rhine which enter Leiden on the east unite in the centre of the town, which is further intersected by numerous small and sombre canals, with tree-bordered quays and old houses. On the south side of the town pleasant gardens extend along the old Singel, or outer canal, and there is a large open space, the Van der Werf Park, named after the burgomaster, Pieter Andriaanszoon van der Werf, who defended the town against the Spaniards in 1574. This open space was formed by the accidental explosion of a powdership in 1807, hundreds of houses being demolished, including that of the Elzevir family of printers. At the junction of the two arms of the Rhine stands the old castle (De Burcht), a circular tower built on an earthen mound. Its origin is unknown, but some connect it with Roman days and others with the Saxon Hengist. Of Leiden's old gateways only two—both dating from the end of the 17th century—are standing. Of the numerous churches the chief are the Hooglandsche Kerk, or the church of St Pancras, built in the 15th century and restored in 1885–1902, containing the monument of Pieter Andriaanszoon van der Werf, and the Pieterskerk (1315) with monuments to Scaliger, Boerhaave and other famous scholars. The most interesting buildings are the town hall (Stadhuis), a fine example of 16th-century Dutch building; the Gemeenlandshuis van Rynland (1596, restored 1878); the weight-house built by Pieter Post (1658); the former court-house, now a military storehouse; and the ancient gymnasium (1599) and the so-called city timber-house (Stads Timmerhuis) (1612), both built by Lieven de Key (c. 1560–1627).

In spite of a certain industrial activity and the periodical bustle of its cattle and dairy markets, Leiden remains essentially an academic city. The university is a flourishing institution. It was founded by William of Orange in 1575 as a reward for the heroic defence of the previous year, the tradition being that the citizens were offered the choice between a university and a certain exemption from taxes. Originally located in the convent of St Barbara, the university was removed in 1581 to the convent of the White Nuns, the site of which it still occupies, though that building was destroyed in 1616. The presence within half a century of the date of its foundation of such scholars as Justus Lipsius, Joseph Scaliger, Francis Gomarus, Hugo Grotius, Jacobus Arminius, Daniel Heinsius and Guardas Johannes Vossius, at once raised Leiden university to the highest European fame, a position which the learning and reputation of Jacobus Gronovius, Hermann Boerhaave, Tiberius Hemsterhuis and David Ruhnken, among others, enabled it to maintain down to the end of the 18th century. The portraits of many famous professors since the earliest days hang in the university *aula*, one of the most memorable places, as Niebuhr called it, in the history of science. The university library contains upwards of 190,000 volumes and 6000 MSS. and pamphlet portfolios, and is very rich in Oriental and Greek MSS. and old Dutch travels. Among the institutions connected with the university are the national institution for East Indian languages, ethnology and geography; the fine botanical gardens, founded in 1587; the observatory (1860); the natural history museum, with a very complete anatomical cabinet; the museum of antiquities (Museum van Oudheden), with specially valuable Egyptian and Indian departments; a museum of Dutch antiquities from the earliest times; and three ethnographical museums, of which the nucleus was P. F. von Siebold's Japanese collections. The anatomical and pathological laboratories of the university are modern, and the museums of geology and mineralogy have been restored. The university has now five faculties, of which those of law and medicine are the most celebrated, and is attended by about 1200 students.

The municipal museum, founded in 1869 and located in the old cloth-hall (Laeckenhalle) (1640), contains a varied collection of antiquities connected with Leiden, as well as some paintings including works by the elder van Swanenburgh, Cornelius Engelbrechtszoon, Lucas van Leiden and Jan Steen, who were all natives of Leiden. Jan van Goyen, Gabriel Metsu, Gerard Dou and Rembrandt were also natives of this town. There is also a small collection of paintings in the Meermansburg. The Thysian library occupies an old Renaissance building of the year 1655, and is especially rich in legal works and native chronicles. Noteworthy also are the collection of the Society of Dutch Literature (1766); the collections of casts and of engravings; the seamen's training school; the Remonstrant seminary, transferred hither from Amsterdam in 1873; the two hospitals (one of which is private); the house of correction; and the court-house.

Leiden is an ancient town, although it is not the *Lugdunum Batavorum* of the Romans. Its early name was Leithen, and it was governed until 1420 by burgraves, the representatives of the courts of Holland. The most celebrated event in its history is its siege by the Spaniards in 1574. Besieged from May until October, it was at length relieved by the cutting of the dikes, thus enabling ships to carry provisions to the inhabitants of the flooded town. The weaving establishments (mainly broadcloth) of Leiden at the close of the 15th century were very important, and after the expulsion of the Spaniards Leiden cloth, Leiden baize and Leiden camlet were familiar terms. These industries afterwards declined, and in the beginning of the 19th century the baize manufacture was altogether given up. Linen and woollen manufactures are now the most important industries, while there is a considerable transit trade in butter and cheese.

Katwyk, or Katwijk, 6 m. N.W. of Leiden, is a popular seaside resort and fishing village. Close by are the great locks constructed in 1807 by the engineer, F. W. Conrad (d. 1808), through which the Rhine (here called the Katwyk canal) is admitted into the sea at low tide. The shore and the entrance to the canal are strengthened by huge dikes. In 1520 an ancient Roman camp known as the Brittenburg was discovered here. It was square in shape, each side measuring 82 yds., and the remains stood about 10 ft. high. By the middle of the 18th century it had been destroyed and covered by the sea.

See P. J. Blok, *Eine hollandsche stad in de middeleeuwen* (The Hague, 1883); and for the siege see J. L. Motley, *The Rise of the Dutch Republic* (1896).

LEIDY, JOSEPH (1823–1891), American naturalist and palaeontologist, was born in Philadelphia on the 9th of September 1823. He studied mineralogy and botany without an instructor, and graduated in medicine at the university of Pennsylvania in 1844. Continuing his work in anatomy and physiology, he visited Europe in 1848, but both before and after this period of foreign study lectured and taught in American medical colleges. In 1853 he was appointed professor of anatomy in the university of Pennsylvania, paying special attention to comparative anatomy. In 1884 he promoted the establishment in the same institution of the department of biology, of which he became director, and meanwhile taught natural history in Swarthmore College, near Philadelphia. His papers on biology and palaeontology were very numerous, covering both fauna and flora, and ranging from microscopic forms of animal life to the higher vertebrates. He wrote also occasional papers on minerals. He was an active member of the Boston Society of Natural History and of the American Philosophical Society; and was the recipient of various American and foreign degrees and honours. His *Cretaceous Reptiles of the United States* (1865) and *Contributions to the Extinct Vertebrate Fauna of the Western Territories* (1873) were the most important of his larger works; the best known and most widely circulated was an *Elementary Treatise on Human* [illegible] 1860, afterwards revised in new editions). He died [illegible] on the 30th of April 1891.

[illegible] and portrait in *Amer. Geologist*, vol. ix. (Jan. 1892) [illegible] in vol. viii. (Nov. 1891) and Memoir by H. C. [illegible] *Proc. Acad. Nat. Sc.* (Philadelphia, 1891), p. 342.

[LEIF ER]ICSSON [LEIFR EIRIKSSON] (fl. 999–1000), Scandi[navian] [illegible], of Icelandic family, the first known European [illegible] "Vinland," "Vineland" or "Wineland, the Good," [illegible] America. He was a son of Eric the Red (Eirikr hinn [illegible]dsson), the founder of the earliest Scandinavian [illegible] from Iceland—in Greenland (985). In 999 he [illegible] Greenland to the court of King Olaf Tryggvason in [illegible] in the Hebrides on the way. On his departure [illegible] in 1000, the king commissioned him to proclaim [illegible] Greenland. As on his outward voyage, Leif was [illegible] far out of his course by contrary weather—this [illegible] (in America) "of which he had previously had no [illegible] where "self-sown" wheat grew, and vines, and [illegible] wood. Leif took specimens of all these, [illegible] came home safely to his father's home in [illegible] in Greenland. On his voyage from this [illegible] Greenland, Leif rescued some shipwrecked men, [illegible] and his discoveries, gained his name of "The [illegible]). On the subsequent expedition of [illegible] for the further exploration and settlement of [illegible]-country, it is recorded that certain Gaels, [illegible] of foot, who had been given to Leif by Olaf [illegible] and whom Leif had offered to Thorfinn, were put [illegible]

[illegible] of the *Saga of Eric the Red*, supported by [illegible] references in early Icelandic and other [illegible] trustworthy history of the *Flatey Book* [illegible] in 985 discover Helluland (Labrador?) [illegible] lands which he does not explore, not [illegible] to land; while Leif Ericsson follows [illegible] begins the exploration of Helluland, [illegible] and realizes some of the charms of the [illegible] winters. But this secondary authority [illegible], which till lately formed the basis [illegible] as to Vinland, abounds in contradictions [illegible] which *Eric the Red Saga* is comparatively [illegible] the grapes of Vinland are found in winter [illegible] the man who first finds them, Leif's [illegible] the German, gets drunk from eating the [illegible] themselves are spoken of as big trees afford[ing] [illegible] the record in *Eric the Red Saga*, it would [illegible] Leif's Vinland answers to some part of [illegible] See VINLAND. (As to Helluland and [illegible] KJALARNES.)

[illegible] *Saga* are Nos. 544 and 557 of the [illegible] Copenhagen; the MS. of the *Flatey* [illegible] the property of a family living on [illegible] in Breidafjord [B-eidafj-d]), on the [illegible] presented in 1662 to the Royal Lib[rary] [illegible] one of the chief treasures. Those [illegible] by Adam of Bremen, *Gesta* [illegible], chap. 38 (247 Lappenberg) [illegible] *Descriptio Insularum Aquilonis*; [illegible] to Vinland, *c.* 1070); we [illegible] *Libellus Islandorum* of Ari Frodi [illegible]; in the *Kristni Saga* (re[illegible]); in *Eyrbyggia Saga* [illegible] and in an Icelandic chorography [illegible] derived from the famous [illegible] (1150).

[illegible] Vinland Voyages," in the [illegible] *du Nord* (Copenhagen, [illegible], 1891), A. M. Reeves, [illegible] *of the Icelandic Discovery* [illegible] the original authorities [illegible], English translations [illegible] *Antiquitates Americanae* [illegible] but the editor's personal [illegible] criticism; the *Flatey* [illegible] *Flateyjar-bok*, vol. i. [illegible] of *Flatey* and *Red* [illegible] *by the Northmen* [illegible] (Boston, 1877); B. F. de Costa, *Pre-Columbian Discovery of America by the Northmen* (Albany, 1901); and *Original Narratives of Early American History; The Northmen, Columbus and Cabot*, pp. 1-66 (New York, 1906). See also C. Raymond Beazley, *Dawn of Modern Geography* ii. 48-83 (London, 1901); Josef Fischer, *Die Entdeckungen der Normannen in Amerika* (Freiburg i. B., 1902); John Fiske, *Discovery of America*, vol. i.; Juul Dieserud, "Norse Discoveries in America," in the *Bulletin of the American Geographical Society* (February, 1901); G. Vigfusson, *Origines Islandicae* (1905), which strangely expresses a preference for the *Flatey Book* "account of the first sighting of the American continent" by the Norsemen. (C. R. B.)

LEIGH, EDWARD (1602–1671), English Puritan and theologian, was born at Shawell, Leicestershire. He was educated at Magdalen Hall, Oxford, from 1616, and subsequently became a member of the Middle Temple. In 1636 he entered parliament as member for Stafford, and during the Civil War held a colonelcy in the parliamentary army. He has sometimes been confounded with John Ley (1583–1662), and so represented as having sat in the Westminster Assembly. The public career of Leigh terminated with his expulsion from parliament with the rest of the Presbyterian party in 1648. From an early age he had studied theology and produced numerous compilations, the most important being the *Critica Sacra, containing Observations on all the Radices of the Hebrew Words of the Old and the Greek of the New Testament* (1639–1644; new ed., with supplement, 1662), for which the author received the thanks of the Westminster Assembly, to whom it was dedicated. His other works include *Select and Choice Observations concerning the First Twelve Caesars* (1635); *A Treatise of Divinity* (1646–1651); *Annotations upon the New Testament* (1650), of which a Latin translation by Arnold was published at Leipzig in 1732; *A Body of Divinity* (1654); *A Treatise of Religion and Learning* (1656); *Annotations of the Five Poetical Books of the Old Testament* (1657). Leigh died in Staffordshire in June 1671.

LEIGH, a market town and municipal borough in the Leigh parliamentary division of Lancashire, England, 11 m. W. by N. from Manchester by the London & North-Western railway. Pop. (1891) 30,882, (1901) 40,001. The ancient parish church of St Mary the Virgin was, with the exception of the tower, rebuilt in 1873 in the Perpendicular style. The grammar school, the date of whose foundation is unknown, received its principal endowments in 1655, 1662 and 1681. The staple manufactures are silk and cotton; there are also glass works, foundries, breweries, and flour mills, with extensive collieries. Though the neighbourhood is principally an industrial district, several fine old houses are left near Leigh. The town was incorporated in 1899, and the corporation consists of a mayor, 8 aldermen and 24 councillors. Area, 6358 acres.

LEIGHTON, FREDERICK LEIGHTON, BARON (1830–1896), English painter and sculptor, the son of a physician, was born at Scarborough on the 3rd of December 1830. His grandfather, Sir James Leighton, also a physician, was long resident at the court of St Petersburg. Frederick Leighton was taken abroad at a very early age. In 1840 he learnt drawing at Rome under Signor Meli. The family moved to Dresden and Berlin, where he attended classes at the Academy. In 1843 he was sent to school at Frankfort, and in the winter of 1844 accompanied his family to Florence, where his future career as an artist was decided. There he studied under Bezzuoli and Segnolini at the Accademia delle Belle Arti, and attended anatomy classes under Zanetti; but he soon returned to complete his general education at Frankfort, receiving no further direct instruction in art for five years. He went to Brussels in 1848, where he met Wiertz and Gallait, and painted some pictures, including "Cimabue finding Giotto," and a portrait of himself. In 1849 he studied for a few months in Paris, where he copied Titian and Correggio in the Louvre, and then returned to Frankfort, where he settled down to serious art work under Edward Steinle, whose pupil he declared he was "in the fullest sense of the term." Though his artistic training was mainly German, and his master belonged to the same school as Cornelius and Overbeck, he loved Italian art and Italy and the first picture by which he became known to the British public was "Cimabue's Madonna carried in Procession through the

Streets of Florence," which appeared at the Royal Academy in 1855. At this time the works of the Pre-Raphaelites almost absorbed public interest in art—it was the year of Holman Hunt's "Light of the World," and the "Rescue," by Millais. Yet Leighton's picture, painted in quite a different style, created a sensation, and was purchased by Queen Victoria. Although, since his infancy, he had only visited England once (in 1851, when he came to see the Great Exhibition), he was not quite unknown in the cultured and artistic world of London, as he had made many friends during a residence in Rome of some two years or more after he left Frankfort in 1852. Amongst these were Giovanni Costa, Robert Browning, James Knowles, George Mason and Sir Edward Poynter, then a youth, whom he allowed to work in his studio. He also met Thackeray, who wrote from Rome to the young Millais: "Here is a versatile young dog, who will run you close for the presidentship one of these days." During these years he painted several Florentine subjects—"Tybalt and Romeo," "The Death of Brunelleschi," a cartoon of "The Pest in Florence according to Boccaccio," and "The Reconciliation of the Montagues and the Capulets." He now turned his attention to themes of classic legend, which at first he treated in a "Romantic spirit." His next picture, exhibited in 1856, was "The Triumph of Music: Orpheus by the Power of his Art redeems his Wife from Hades." It was not a success, and he did not again exhibit till 1858, when he sent a little picture of "The Fisherman and the Syren" to the Royal Academy, and "Samson and Delilah" to the Society of British Artists in Suffolk Street. In 1858 he visited London and made the acquaintance of the leading Pre-Raphaelites—Rossetti, Holman Hunt and Millais. In the spring of 1859 he was at Capri, always a favourite resort of his, and made many studies from nature, including a very famous drawing of a lemon tree. It was not till 1860 that he settled in London, when he took up his quarters at 2 Orme Square, Bayswater, where he stayed till, in 1866, he moved to his celebrated house in Holland Park Road, with its Arab hall decorated with Damascus tiles. There he lived till his death. He now began to fulfil the promise of his "Cimabue," and by such pictures as "Paolo e Francesca," "The Star of Bethlehem," "Jezebel and Ahab taking Possession of Naboth's Vineyard," "Michael Angelo musing over his Dying Servant," "A Girl feeding Peacocks," and "The Odalisque," all exhibited in 1861–1863, rose rapidly to the head of his profession. The two latter pictures were marked by the rhythm of line and luxury of colour which are among the most constant attributes of his art, and may be regarded as his first dreams of Oriental beauty, with which he afterwards showed so great a sympathy. In 1864 he exhibited "Dante in Exile" (the greatest of his Italian pictures), "Orpheus and Eurydice" and "Golden Hours." In the winter of the same year he was elected an Associate of the Royal Academy. After this the main effort of his life was to realize visions of beauty suggested by classic myth and history. If we add to pictures of this class a few Scriptural subjects, a few Oriental dreams, one or two of tender sentiment like "Wedded" (one of the most popular of his pictures, and well known by not only an engraving, but a statuette modelled by an Italian sculptor), a number of studies of very various types of female beauty, "Teresina," "Biondina," "Bianca," "Moretta," &c., and an occasional portrait, we shall nearly exhaust the two classes into which Lord Leighton's work (as a painter) can be divided.

Amongst the finest of his classical pictures were—"Syracusan Bride leading Wild Beasts in Procession to the Temple of Diana" (1866), "Venus disrobing for the Bath" (1867), "Electra at the Tomb of Agamemnon," and "Helios and Rhodos" (1869), "Hercules wrestling with Death for the Body of Alcestis" (1871), "Clytemnestra" (1874), "The Daphnephoria" (1876), "Nausicaa" (1878), "An Idyll" (1881), two lovers under a spreading oak listening to the piping of a shepherd and gazing on the rich plain below; "Phryne" (1882), a nude figure standing in the sun; "Cymon and Iphigenia" (1884), "Captive Andromache" (1888), now in the Manchester Art Gallery; with the "Last Watch of Hero" (1887), "The Bath of Psyche" (1890), now in the Chantrey Bequest collection; "The Garden of the Hesperides" (1892), "Perseus and Andromeda" and "The Return of Persephone," now in the Leeds Gallery (1891); and "Clytie," his last work (1896). All these pictures are characterized by nobility of conception, by almost perfect draughtsmanship, by colour which, if not of the highest quality, is always original, choice and effective. They often reach distinction and dignity of attitude and gesture, and occasionally, as in the "Hercules and Death," the "Electra" and the "Clytemnestra," a noble intensity of feeling. Perhaps, amidst the great variety of qualities which they possess, none is more universal and more characteristic than a rich elegance, combined with an almost fastidious selection of beautiful forms. It is the super-eminence of these qualities, associated with great decorative skill, that make the splendid pageant of the "Daphnephoria" the most perfect expression of his individual genius. Here we have his composition, his colour, his sense of the joy and movement of life, his love of art and nature at their purest and most spontaneous, and the result is a work without a rival of its kind in the British School.

Leighton was one of the most thorough draughtsmen of his day. His sketches and studies for his pictures are numerous and very highly esteemed. They contain the essence of his conceptions, and much of their spiritual beauty and subtlety of expression was often lost in the elaboration of the finished picture. He seldom succeeded in retaining the freshness of his first idea more completely than in his last picture—"Clytie"—which was left unfinished on his easel. He rarely painted sacred subjects. The most beautiful of his few pictures of this kind was the "David musing on the Housetop" (1865). Others were "Elijah in the Wilderness" (1879), "Elisha raising the Son of the Shunammite" (1881) and a design intended for the decoration of the dome of St Paul's Cathedral, "And the Sea gave up the Dead which were in it" (1892), now in the Tate Gallery, and the terrible "Rizpah" of 1893. His diploma picture was "St Jerome," exhibited in 1869. Besides these pictures of sacred subjects, he made some designs for Dalziel's Bible, which for force of imagination excel the paintings. The finest of these are "Cain and Abel," and "Samson with the Gates of Gaza."

Not so easily to be classed, but among the most individual and beautiful of his pictures, are a few of which the motive was purely aesthetic. Amongst these may specially be noted "The Summer Moon," two Greek girls sleeping on a marble bench, and "The Music Lesson," in which a lovely little girl is seated on her lovely young mother's lap learning to play the lute. With these, as a work produced without any literary suggestion, though very different in feeling, may be associated the "Eastern Slinger scaring Birds in the Harvest-time: Moon-rise" (1875), a nude figure standing on a raised platform in a field of wheat.

Leighton also painted a few portraits, including those of Signor Costa, the Italian landscape painter, Mr F. P. Cockerell, Mrs Sutherland Orr (his sister), Amy, Lady Coleridge, Mrs Stephen Ralli and (the finest of all) Sir Richard Burton, the traveller and Eastern scholar, which was exhibited in 1876 and is now in the National Portrait Gallery.

Like other painters of the day, notably G. F. Watts, Lord Leighton executed a few pieces of sculpture. His "Athlete struggling with a Python" was exhibited at the Royal Academy in 1877, and was purchased for the Chantrey Bequest collection. Another statue, "The Sluggard," of equal merit, was exhibited in 1886; and a charming statuette of a nude figure of a girl looking over her shoulder at a frog, called "Needless Alarms," was completed in the same year, and presented by the artist to Sir John Millais in acknowledgment of the gift by the latter of his picture, "Shelling Peas." He made the beautiful design for the reverse of the Jubilee Medal of 1887. It was also his habit to make sketch models in wax for the figures in his pictures, many of which are in the possession of the Royal Academy. As an illustrator in black and white he also deserves to be remembered, especially for the cuts to Dalziel's Bible, already mentioned, and his illustrations to George Eliot's *Romola*, which appeared in the *Cornhill Magazine*. The latter are full of the spirit of

[illegible] the name of the Elster, discharge themselves into the [illegible]. The climate, though not generally unhealthy, may be [illegible] in winter and hot in summer.

Leipzig is one of the most enterprising and prosperous of German towns, and in point of trade and industries ranks among German cities immediately after Berlin and Hamburg. It possesses the third largest German university, is the seat of the supreme tribunal of the German empire and the headquarters of the XIX. (Saxon) army corps, and forms one of the most [illegible] literary and musical centres in Europe. Its general [illegible] is imposing owing to the number of new public buildings [illegible] during the last 20 years of the 19th century. It consists [illegible] inner city, surrounded by a wide and pleasant [illegible] laid out on the site of the old fortifications, and of [illegible] more extensive inner and outer suburbs. Many [illegible] villages, such as Reudnitz, Volkmarsdorf, [illegible], Plagwitz and Lindenau, have been incorporated with the city, and with these accretions the population in [illegible]. On the north-west the town is [illegible] by the fine public park and woods of the Rosenthal, [illegible] the west by the Johanna Park and by pleasant groves [illegible] the banks of the Pleisse.

[illegible] town, with its narrow streets and numerous houses [illegible] with their high-pitched roofs, [illegible] medieval aspect. The market square, [illegible] of great interest. Upon it the four [illegible] the Grimmasche, the Peters-, the Hain- [illegible] streets, converge, and its north side is [illegible] old Rathaus, a Gothic edifice built by [illegible] Lotter in 1556, and containing [illegible] the Saxon rulers. Superseded by the new [illegible] has been restored and accommodates a municipal [illegible] the market square and the main street lie a [illegible] interconnected by covered courtyards [illegible] warehouses and cellars. The whole, [illegible] when every available place is packed [illegible] thronged with a motley crowd, presents [illegible] bazaar. Close to the old Rathaus is [illegible] and interesting as being immor- [illegible]. It has a curious old wine vault [illegible] mural paintings of the 16th [illegible] on which the play is based. [illegible] Königshaus, for several centuries [illegible] in Leipzig and in which King [illegible] prisoner by the Allies after the [illegible]. At the end of the Petersstrasse, [illegible] inner town and on the promenade, [illegible] according to tradition, [illegible] in the 13th century. Here [illegible] disputation. The round [illegible] and the building as a [illegible] of the tower, which has been [illegible] height—to 300 ft.—the [illegible] is occupied by the majestic [illegible] style with the tower as [illegible] Leipzig is chiefly concen- [illegible] of the book trade [illegible] the inner town and the [illegible] one of the most [illegible] the side of the inner [illegible] main building [illegible] a splendid hall [illegible] collections, adjoining [illegible]. The other sides [illegible] theatre, an imposing [illegible] the past [illegible] the latter faced [illegible] are compara- [illegible] is the Paul- [illegible] 1900, with a [illegible] town is the [illegible]

memorable for its association with J. Sebastian Bach, who was organist here. Among others may be mentioned the new Gothic Petrikirche, with a lofty spire, in the south suburb. On the east is the Johanniskirche, round which raged the last conflict in the battle of 1813, when it suffered severely from cannon shot. In it is the tomb of Bach, and outside that of the poet Gellert. Opposite its main entrance is the Reformation monument, with bronze statues of Luther and Melanchthon, by Johann Schilling, unveiled in 1883. In the Johanna Park is the Lutherkirche (1886), and close at hand the Roman Catholic and English churches. To the south-west of the new Rathaus, lying beyond the Pleisse and between it and the Johanna Park, is the new academic quarter. Along the fine thoroughfares, noticeable among which is the Karl Tauchnitz Strasse, are closely grouped many striking buildings. Here is the new Gewandhaus, or Konzerthaus, built in 1880–1884, in which the famous concerts called after its name are given, the old Gewandhaus, or Drapers' Hall, in the inner town having again been devoted to commercial use as a market hall during the fairs. Immediately opposite to it is the new university library, built in 1891, removed hither from the old monasterial buildings behind the Augusteum, and containing some 500,000 volumes and 5000 MSS. Behind that again is the academy of art, one wing of which accommodates the industrial art school; and close beside it are the school of technical arts and the conservatoire of music. Between the university library and the new Gewandhaus stands a monument of Mendelssohn (1892). Immediately to the east of the school of arts rises the grand pile of the supreme tribunal of the German empire, the Reichsgericht, which compares with the Reichstag building in Berlin. It was built in 1888–1895 from plans by Ludwig Hoffmann, and is distinguished for the symmetry and harmony of its proportions. It bears an imposing dome, 225 ft. high, crowned by a bronze figure of Truth by O. Lessing, 18 ft. high. Opposite, on the outer side of the Pleisse, are the district law-courts, large and substantial, though not specially imposing edifices. In the same quarter stands the Grassi Museum (1893–1896) for industrial art and ethnology, and a short distance away are the palatial buildings of the Reichs and Deutsche Banks. Farther east and lying in the centre of the book-trade quarter stand close together the Buchhändlerhaus (booksellers' exchange), the great hall decorated with allegorical pictures by Sascha Schneider, and the Buchgewerbehaus, a museum of the book trade, both handsome red brick edifices in the German Renaissance style, erected in 1886–1890. South-west of these buildings, on the other side of the Johannisthal Park, are clustered the medical institutes and hospitals of the university—the infirmary, clinical and other hospitals, the physico-chemical institute, pathological institute, physiological institute, ophthalmic hospital, pharmacological institute, the schools of anatomy, the chemical laboratory, the zoological institute, the physico-mineralogical institute, the botanical garden and also the veterinary schools, deaf and dumb asylum, agricultural college and astronomical observatory. Among other noteworthy buildings in this quarter must be noted the Johannisstift, an asylum for the relief of the aged poor, with a handsome front and slender spire. On the north side of the inner town and on the promenade are the handsome exchange with library, and the reformed church, a pleasing edifice in late Gothic.

Leipzig has some interesting monuments; the Siegesdenkmal, commemorative of the wars of 1866 and 1870, on the market square, statues of Goethe, Leibnitz, Gellert, J. Sebastian Bach, Robert Schumann, Hahnemann, the homoeopathist, and Bismarck. There are also many memorials of the battle of Leipzig, including an obelisk on the Ranstädter-Steinweg, on the site of the bridge which was prematurely blown up, when Prince Poniatowski was drowned; a monument of cannon balls collected after the battle; a "relief" to Major Friccius, who stormed the outer Grimma gate; while on the battle plain itself and close to "Napoleonstein," which commemorates Napoleon's position on the last day of the battle, a gigantic obelisk surrounded by a garden has been planned for dedication on the hundredth anniversary of the battle (October 19, 1913).

The University and Education.—The university of Leipzig, founded in 1409 by a secession of four hundred German students from Prague, is one of the most influential universities in the world. It was a few years since the most numerously attended of any university in Germany, but it has since been outstripped by those of Berlin and of Munich. Its large revenues, derived to a great extent from house property in Leipzig and estates in Saxony, enable it, in conjunction with a handsome state subvention, to provide rich endowments for the professorial chairs. To the several faculties also belong various collegiate buildings, notably, to the legal, that of the *Collegium beatae Virginis* in the Petersstrasse, and to the philosophical the *Rothe Haus* on the promenade facing the theatre. The other educational institutions of Leipzig include the Nicolai and Thomas gymnasia, several "Realschulen," a commercial academy (*Handelsschule*), high schools for girls, and a large number of public and private schools of all grades.

Art and Literature.—The city has a large number of literary, scientific and artistic institutions. One of the most important is the museum, which contains about four hundred modern paintings, a large number of casts, a few pieces of original sculpture and a well-arranged collection of drawings and engravings. The collection of the historical society and the ethnographical and art-industrial collections in the Grassi Museum are also of considerable interest. The museum was erected with part of the munificent bequest made to the city by Dominic Grassi in 1881. As a musical centre Leipzig is known all over the world for its excellent conservatorium, founded in 1843 by Mendelssohn. The series of concerts given annually in the Gewandhaus is also of world-wide reputation, and the operatic stage of Leipzig is deservedly ranked among the finest in Germany. There are numerous vocal and orchestral societies, some of which have brought their art to a very high pitch of perfection. The prominence of the publishing interest has attracted to Leipzig a large number of gifted authors, and made it a literary centre of considerable importance. Over five hundred newspapers and periodicals are published here, including several of the most widely circulated in Germany. Intellectual interests of a high order have always characterized, Leipzig, and what Karl von Holtei once said of it is true to-day: "There is only one city in Germany that represents Germany; only a single city where one can forget that he is a Hessian, a Bavarian, a Swabian, a Prussian or a Saxon; only one city where, amid the opulence of the commercial world with which science is so gloriously allied, even the man who possesses nothing but his personality is honoured and esteemed; only one city, in which, despite a few narrownesses, all the advantages of a great, I may say a world-metropolis, are conspicuous! This city is, in my opinion, and in my experience, Leipzig."

Commerce, Fairs.—The outstanding importance of Leipzig as a commercial town is mainly derived from its three great fairs, which annually attract an enormous concourse of merchants from all parts of Europe, and from Persia, Armenia and other Asiatic countries. The most important fairs are held at Easter and Michaelmas, and are said to have been founded as markets about 1170. The smaller New Year's fair was established in 1458. Under the fostering care of the margraves of Meissen, and then of the electors of Saxony they attained great popularity. In 1268 the margrave of Meissen granted a safe-conduct to all frequenters of the fairs, and in 1497 and 1507 the emperor Maximilian I. greatly increased their importance by prohibiting the holding of annual markets at any town within a wide radius of Leipzig. During the Thirty Years' War, the Seven Years' War and the troubles consequent upon the French Revolution, the trade of the Leipzig fairs considerably decreased, but it recovered after the accession of Saxony to the German Customs Union (*Zollverein*) in 1834, and for the next twenty years rapidly and steadily increased. Since then, owing to the greater facilities of communication, the transactions at the fairs have diminished in relative, though they have increased in actual, value. Wares that can be safely purchased by sample appear at the fairs in steadily diminishing quantities, while others, such as hides, furs and leather, which require to be actually examined, show as marked an increase. The value of the sales considerably exceeds £10,000,000 sterling per annum. The principal commodity is furs (chiefly American and Russian), of which about one and a quarter million pounds worth are sold annually, other articles disposed of are leather, hides, wool, cloth, linen and glass. The Leipzig wool-market, held for two days in June, is also important.

In the trades of bookselling and publishing Leipzig occupies a unique position, not only taking the first place in Germany, but even surpassing London and Paris in the number and total value of its sales. There are upwards of nine hundred publishers and booksellers in the town, and about eleven thousand firms in other parts of Europe are represented here. Several hundred booksellers assemble in Leipzig every year, and settle their accounts at their own exchange (*Buchhändler-Börse*). Leipzig also contains about two hundred printing-works, some of great extent, and a corresponding number of type-foundries, binding-shops and other kindred industries.

The book trades give employment to over 15,000 persons, and since 1878 Leipzig has grown into an industrial town of the first rank. The iron and machinery trades employ 4500 persons; the textile industries, cotton and yarn spinning and hosiery, 6000; and the making of scientific and musical instruments, including pianos, 2650. Other industries include the manufacture of artificial flowers, wax-cloth, chemicals, ethereal oils and essences, beer, mineral waters, tobacco and cigars, lace, india-rubber wares, rush-work and paper, the preparation of furs and numerous other branches. These industries are mostly carried on in the suburbs of Plagwitz, Reudnitz, Lindenau, Gohlis, Eutritzsch, Konnewitz and the neighbouring town of Markranstädt.

Communications.—Leipzig lies at the centre of a network of railways giving it direct communication with all the more important cities of Germany. There are six main line railway stations, of which the Dresden and the Magdeburg lie side by side in the north-east corner of the promenade, the Thuringian and Berlin stations further away in the northern suburb; in the eastern is the Eilenburg station (for Breslau and the east) and in the south the Bavarian station. The whole traffic of these stations is to be directed into a vast central station (the largest in the world), lying on the sites of the Dresden, Magdeburg and Thuringian stations. The estimated cost, borne by Prussia, Saxony and the city of Leipzig, is estimated at 6 million pounds sterling. The city has an extensive electric tramway system, bringing all the outlying suburbs into close connexion with the business quarters of the town.

Population.—The population of Leipzig was quintupled within the 19th century, rising from 31,887 in 1801 to 153,988 in 1881, to 455,089 in 1900 and to 502,570 in 1905.

History.—Leipzig owes its origin to a Slav settlement between the Elster and the Pleisse, which was in existence before the year 1000, and its name to the Slav word *lipa*, a lime tree. There was also a German settlement near this spot, probably round a castle erected early in the 10th century by the German king, Henry the Fowler. The district was part of the mark of Merseburg, and the bishops of Merseburg were the lords of extensive areas around the settlements. In the 11th century Leipzig is mentioned as a fortified place and in the 12th it came into the possession of the margrave of Meissen, being granted some municipal privileges by the margrave, Otto the Rich, before 1190. Its favourable situation in the midst of a plain intersected by the principal highways of central Europe, together with the fostering care of its rulers, now began the work of raising Leipzig to the position of a very important commercial town. Its earliest trade was in the salt produced at Halle, and its enterprising inhabitants constructed roads and bridges to lighten the journey of the traders and travellers whose way led to the town. Soon Leipzig was largely used as a depot by the merchants of Nuremberg, who carried on a considerable trade with Poland. Powers of self-government were acquired by the council (*Rat*) of the town, the importance of which was enhanced during the 15th century by several grants of privileges from the emperors. When Saxony was divided in 1485 Leipzig fell to the Albertine, or ducal branch of the family, whose head Duke George gave new rights to the burghers. This duke, however, at whose instigation the famous discussion between Luther and Johann von Eck took place in the Pleissenburg of Leipzig, inflicted some injury upon the town's trade and also upon its university by the harsh treatment which he meted out to the adherents of the new doctrines; but under the rule of his successor, Henry, Leipzig accepted the teaching of the reformers. In 1547 during the war of the league of Schmalkalden the town was besieged by the elector of Saxony, John Frederick I. It was not captured, although its suburbs were destroyed. These and the Pleissenburg were rebuilt by the elector Maurice, who also strengthened the fortifications. Under the elector Augustus I. emigrants from the Netherlands were encouraged to settle in Leipzig and its trade with Hamburg and with England was greatly extended.

During the Thirty Years' War Leipzig suffered six sieges and on four occasions was occupied by hostile troops, being retained by the Swedes as security for the payment of an indemnity from 1648 to 1650. After 1650 its fortifications were strengthened; its finances were put on a better footing; and its trade, especially with England, began again to prosper; important steps being taken with regard to its organization. Towards the end of the 17th century the publishing trade began to increase very rapidly, partly because the severity of the censorship at Frankfort-on-the-Main caused many booksellers to remove to Leipzig. During the Seven Years' War Frederick the Great exacted a heavy contribution from Leipzig, but this did not seriously interfere with its prosperity. In 1784 the fortifications were pulled down. The wars in the first decade of the 19th century were not on the whole unfavourable to the commerce of Leipzig, but in 1813 and 1814, owing to the presence of enormous armies in the neighbourhood, it suffered greatly. Another revival, however, set in after the peace of 1815, and this was aided by the accession of Saxony to the German Zollverein in 1834, and by the opening of the first railway a little later. In 1831 the town was provided with a new constitution, and in 1837 a scheme for the reform of the university was completed. A riot in 1845, the revolutionary movement of 1848 and the Prussian occupation of 1866 were merely passing shadows. In 1879 Leipzig acquired a new importance by becoming the seat of the supreme court of the German empire.

The immediate neighbourhood of Leipzig has been the scene of several battles, two of which are of more than ordinary importance. These are the battles of Breitenfeld, fought on the 17th of September 1631, between the Swedes under Gustavus Adolphus and the imperialists, and the great battle of Leipzig, known in Germany as the Völkerschlacht, fought in October 1813 between Napoleon and the allied forces of Russia, Prussia and Austria.

Towards the middle of the 18th century Leipzig was the seat of the most influential body of literary men in Germany, over whom Johann Christoph Gottsched, like his contemporary, Samuel Johnson, in England, exercised a kind of literary dictatorship. Then, if ever, Leipzig deserved the epithet of a "Paris in miniature" (*Klein Paris*) assigned to it by Goethe in his *Faust*. The young Lessing produced his first play in the Leipzig theatre, and the university counts Goethe, Klopstock, Jean Paul Richter, Fichte and Schelling among its alumni. Schiller and Gellert also resided for a time in Leipzig, and Sebastian Bach and Mendelssohn filled musical posts here. Among the celebrated natives of the town are the philosopher Leibnitz and the composer Wagner.

Authorities.—For the history of Leipzig see E. Hasse, *Die Stadt Leipzig und ihre Umgebung, geographisch und statistisch beschrieben* (Leipzig, 1878); K. Grosse, *Geschichte der Stadt Leipzig* (Leipzig, 1897–1898); Kachel, *Verwaltungsorganisation und Ämterwesen der Stadt Leipzig bis 1627* (Leipzig, 1902); G. Wustmann, *Aus Leipzigs Vergangenheit* (Leipzig, 1898); *Bilderbuch aus der Geschichte der Stadt Leipzig* (Leipzig, 1897); *Leipzig durch drei Jahrhunderte, Atlas zur Geschichte des Leipziger Stadtbildes* (Leipzig, 1891); *Quellen zur Geschichte Leipzigs* (Leipzig, 1889–1895); and *Geschichte der Stadt Leipzig* (Leipzig, 1905); F. Seifert, *Die Reformation in Leipzig* (Leipzig, 1883); G. Buchwald, *Reformationsgeschichte der Stadt Leipzig* (Leipzig, 1900); Geffcken and Tykocinski, *Stiftungsbuch der Stadt Leipzig* (Leipzig, 1905); the *Urkundenbuch der Stadt Leipzig*, edited by C. F. Posern-Klett and Förstemann (Leipzig, 1870–1895); and the *Schriften des Vereins für die Geschichte Leipzigs* (Leipzig, 1872–1904). For other aspects of the town's life see Hirschfeld, *Leipzigs Grossindustrie und Grosshandel* (Leipzig, 1867); Hassert, *Die geographische Lage und Entwickelung Leipzigs* (Leipzig, 1899); Helm, *Heimatkunde von Leipzig* (Leipzig, 1903); E. Friedberg, *Die Universität Leipzig in Vergangenheit und Gegenwart* (Leipzig, 1897); F. Zarncke, *Die Statutenbücher der Universität Leipzig* (Leipzig, 1861); E. Hasse, *Geschichte der Leipziger Messen* (Leipzig, 1885); Tille, *Die Anfänge der hohen Landstrasse* (Gotha, 1906); Biedermann, *Geschichte der Leipziger Kramerinnung* (Leipzig, 1881); and Moltke, *Die Leipziger Kramerinnung im 15 und 16 Jahrhundert* (Leipzig, 1901).

LEIRIA, an episcopal city and the capital of the district of Leiria, formerly included in Estremadura, Portugal; on the river Liz and on the Lisbon-Figueria da Foz railway. Pop. (1900) 4459. The principal buildings of Leiria are the ruined citadel, which dates from 1135, and the cathedral, a small Renaissance building erected in 1571 but modernized in the 18th century. The main square of the city is named after the poet Francisco Rodrigues Lobo, who was born here about 1500. Between Leiria and the Atlantic there are extensive pine woods known as the Pinhal de Leiria, which were planted by King Diniz (1279–1325) with trees imported from the Landes in France, in order to give firmness to the sandy soil. In the neighbourhood there are glass and iron foundries, oil wells and mineral springs. Leiria, the Roman Calippo, was taken from the Moors in 1135 by Alphonso I. (Affonso Henriques). King Diniz made it his capital. In 1466 the first Portuguese printing-press was established here, in 1545 the city was made an episcopal see. The administrative district of Leiria coincides with the north and north-west of the ancient province of Estremadura (*q.v.*); pop. (1900) 238,755; area 1317 sq. m.

LEISLER, JACOB (*c.* 1635–1691), American political agitator, was born probably at Frankfort-on-Main, Germany, about 1635. He went to New Netherland (New York) in 1660, married a wealthy widow, engaged in trade, and soon accumulated a fortune. The English Revolution of 1688 divided the people of New York into two well-defined factions. In general the small shop-keepers, small farmers, sailors, poor traders and artisans were arrayed against the patroons, rich fur-traders, merchants, lawyers and crown officers. The former were led by Leisler, the latter by Peter Schuyler (1657–1724), Nicholas Bayard (*c.* 1644–1707), Stephen van Cortlandt (1643–1700), William Nicolls (1657–1723) and other representatives of the aristocratic Hudson Valley families. The "Leislerians" pretended greater loyalty to the Protestant succession. When news of the imprisonment of Gov. Andros in Massachusetts was received, they took possession on the 31st of May 1689 of Fort James (at the southern end of Manhattan Island), renamed it Fort William and announced their determination to hold it until the arrival of a governor commissioned by the new sovereigns. The aristocrats also favoured the Revolution, but preferred to continue the government under authority from James II. rather than risk the danger of an interregnum. Lieutenant-Governor Francis Nicholson sailed for England on the 24th of June, a committee of safety was organized by the popular party, and Leisler was appointed commander-in-chief. Under authority of a letter from the home government addressed to Nicholson, "or in his absence, to such as for the time being takes care for preserving the peace and administering the laws in His Majesty's province of New York," he assumed the title of lieutenant-governor in December 1689, appointed a council and took charge of the government of the entire province. He summoned the first Intercolonial Congress in America, which met in New York on the 1st of May 1690 to plan concerted action against the French and Indians. Colonel Henry Sloughter was commissioned governor of the province on the 2nd of September 1689 but did not reach New York until the 19th of March 1691. In the meantime Major Richard Ingoldsby and two companies of soldiers had landed (January 28, 1691) and demanded possession of the fort. Leisler refused to surrender it, and after some controversy an attack was made on the 17th of March in which two soldiers were killed and several wounded. When Sloughter arrived two days later Leisler hastened to give over to him the fort and other evidences of authority. He and his son-in-law, Jacob Milborne, were charged with treason for refusing to submit to Ingoldsby, were convicted, and on the 16th of May 1691 were executed. There has been much controversy among historians with regard both to the facts and to the significance of Leisler's brief career as ruler in New York.

See J. R. Brodhead, *History of the State of New York* (vol. 2, New York, 1871). For the documents connected with the controversy see E. B. O'Callaghan, *Documentary History of the State of New York* (vol. 2, Albany, 1850).

LEISNIG, a town in the kingdom of Saxony, prettily situated on the Freiberger Mulde, 7 m. S. of Grimma by the railway from Leipzig to Dresden via Döbeln. Pop. (1905) 8147. On a high rock above the town lies the old castle of Mildenstein, now utilized as administrative offices. The industries include the manufacture of cloth, furniture, boots, buttons, cigars, beer, machinery and chemicals. Leisnig is a place of considerable antiquity. About 1080 it passed into the possession of the counts of Groitzsch, but was purchased in 1157 by the emperor Frederick I., who committed it to the charge of counts. It fell to Meissen in 1365, and later to Saxony.

LEITH, a municipal and police burgh, and seaport, county of Midlothian, Scotland. Pop. (1901) 77,439. It is situated on the south shore of the Firth of Forth, 1½ m. N.N.E. of Edinburgh, of which it is the port and with which it is connected by Leith Walk, practically a continuous street. It has stations on the North British and Caledonian railways, and a branch line (N.B.R.) to Portobello. Lying at the mouth of the Water of Leith, which is crossed by several bridges and divides it into the parishes of North and South Leith, it stretches for 3½ m. along the shore of the Firth from Seafield in the east to near Granton in the west. There is tramway communication with Edinburgh and Newhaven.

The town is a thriving centre of trade and commerce. St Mary's in Kirkgate, the parish church of South Leith, was founded in 1483, and was originally cruciform but, as restored in 1852, consists of an aisled nave and north-western tower. Here David Lindsay (1531–1613), its minister, James VI.'s chaplain and afterwards bishop of Ross, preached before the king the thanksgiving sermon on the Gowrie conspiracy (1600). John Logan, the hymn-writer and reputed author of "The Ode to the Cuckoo," was minister for thirteen years; and in its graveyard lies the Rev. John Home, author of *Douglas*, a native of Leith. Near it in Constitution Street is St James's Episcopal church (1862–1869), in the Early English style by Sir Gilbert Scott, with an apsidal chancel and a spire 160 ft. high. The parish church of North Leith, in Madeira Street, with a spire 158 ft high, is one of the best livings in the Established Church of Scotland. St Thomas's, at the head of Shirra Brae, in the Gothic style, was built in 1843 by Sir John Gladstone of Fasque, who—prior to his removal to Liverpool, where his son, W. E. Gladstone, was born—had been a merchant in Leith. The public buildings are wholly modern, the principal being of classic design. They include the custom house (1812) in the Grecian style; Trinity House (1817), also Grecian, containing Sir Henry Raeburn's portrait of Admiral Lord Duncan, David Scott's "Vasco da Gama Rounding the Cape" and other paintings; the markets (1818); the town hall (1828), with an Ionic façade on Constitution Street and a Doric porch on Charlotte Street; the corn exchange (1862) in the Roman style; the assembly rooms; exchange buildings; the public institute (1867) and Victoria public baths (1899). Trinity House was founded in 1555 as a home for old and disabled sailors, but on the decline of its revenues it became the licensing authority for pilots, its humane office being partly fulfilled by the sailors' home, established about 1840 in a building adjoining the Signal Tower, and re-housed in a handsome structure in the Scottish Baronial style in 1883–1884. Other charitable institutions include the hospital, John Watt's hospital and the smallpox hospital. The high school, built in 1806, for many years a familiar object on the west margin of the Links, gave way to the academy, a handsome and commodious structure, to which are drafted senior pupils from the numerous board schools for free education in the higher branches. Here also is accommodated the technical college. Secondary instruction is given also in Craighall Road school. A bronze statue of Robert Burns was unveiled in 1898. Leith Links, one of the homes of golf in Scotland, is a popular resort, on Lochend Road are situated Hawkhill recreation grounds, and Lochend Loch is used for skating and curling. There are small links at Newhaven, and in Trinity are Starbank Park and Cargilfield playing ground. The east pier (1177 yds. long) and the west pier (1041 yds.) are favourite promenades. The waterway between them is the entrance to the harbour. Leith cemetery is situated at Seafield and the Eastern cemetery in Easter Road

The oldest industry is shipbuilding, which dates from 1313. Here in 1511 James IV built the "St Michael," "ane verrie monstruous great ship, whilk tuik sae meikle timber that schee waisted all the woodis in Fyfe, except Falkland wood, besides the timber that cam out of Norroway." Other important industries are engineering, sugar-refining (established 1757), meat-preserving, flour-milling, sailcloth-making, soap-boiling, rope and twine-making, tanning, chemical manures-making, wood-sawing, hosiery, biscuit-baking, brewing, distilling and lime-juice making. Of the old trade of glass-making, which began in 1682, scarcely a trace survives. As a distributing centre, Leith occupies a prominent place. It is the headquarters of the whisky business in Great Britain, and stores also large quantities of wine from Spain, Portugal and France. This pre-eminence is due to its excellent dock and harbour accommodation and capacious warehouses. The two old docks (1801–1807) cover 10¾ acres; Victoria Dock (1852) 5 acres; Albert Dock (1863–1869) 10¾ acres; Edinburgh Dock (1874–1881) 16¾ acres; and the New Dock (1892–1901) 60 acres. There are several dry docks, of which the Prince of Wales Graving Dock (1858), the largest, measures 370 ft. by 60 ft. Space can always be had for more dock room by reclaiming the east sands, where in the 17th and 18th centuries Leith Races were held, the theme of a humorous descriptive poem by Robert Fergusson. Apart from coasting trade there are constant sailings to the leading European ports, the United States and the British colonies. In 1908 the tonnage of ships entering the harbour was (including coastwise trade) 1,975,457; that of ships clearing the harbour 1,993,227. The number of vessels registered at the port was 213 (net tonnage 146,799). The value of imports was £12,883,890, of exports £5,377,188. In summer there are frequent excursions to the Bass Rock and the Isle of May, North Berwick, Elie, Aberdour, Alloa and Stirling. Leith Fort, built in North Leith in 1779 for the defence of the harbour, is now the headquarters of the Royal Artillery in Scotland. Leith is the head of a fishery district. The town, which is governed by a provost, bailies and council, unites with Musselburgh and Portobello to send one member to parliament.

Leith figures as Inverleith in the foundation charter of Holyrood Abbey (1128). In 1329 Robert I. granted the harbour to the magistrates of Edinburgh, who did not always use their power wisely. They forbade, for example, the building of streets wide enough to admit a cart, a regulation that accounted for the number of narrow wynds and alleys in the town. Had the overlords been more considerate incorporation with Edinburgh would not have been so bitterly resisted. Several of the quaint bits of ancient Leith yet remain, and the appearance of the shore as it was in the 17th and 18th centuries, and even at a later date, was picturesque in the extreme. During the centuries of strife between Scotland and England its situation exposed the port to attack both by sea and land. At least twice (in 1313 and 1410) its shipping was burned by the English, who also sacked the town in 1544—when the 1st earl of Hertford destroyed the first wooden pier—and 1547. In the troublous times that followed the death of James V., Leith became the stronghold of the Roman Catholic and French party from 1548 to 1560, Mary of Guise, queen regent, not deeming herself secure in Edinburgh. In 1549 the town was walled and fortified by Montalembert, sieur d'Essé, the commander of the French troops, and endured an ineffectual siege in 1560 by the Scots and their English allies. A house in Coalhill is thought to be the "handsome and spacious edifice" erected for her privy council by Mary of Guise. D'Essé's wall, pierced by six gates, was partly dismantled on the death of the queen regent, but although rebuilt in 1571, not a trace of it exists. The old tolbooth, in which William Maitland of Lethington, Queen Mary's secretary, poisoned himself in 1573, to avoid execution for adhering to Mary's cause, was demolished in 1819. Charles I. is said to have received the first tidings of the Irish rebellion while playing golf on the links in 1641. Cromwell in his Scottish campaign built the Citadel in 1650 and the mounds on the links, known as "Giant's Brae" and "Lady Fife's Brae," were thrown up by the Protector as batteries. In 1698 the sailing of the first Darien expedition created great excitement. In 1715 William Mackintosh of Borlum (1662–1743) and his force of Jacobite Highlanders captured the Citadel, of which only the name of Citadel Street and the archway in Couper Street have preserved the memory.

A mile S.E. of the links lies the ancient village of Restalrig, the home of the Logans, from whom the superiority of Leith was purchased in 1553 by the queen regent. Sir Robert Logan (d. 1606) was alleged to have been one of the Gowrie conspirators and to have arranged to imprison the king in Fast Castle. This charge, however, was not made until three years after his death, when his bones were exhumed for trial. He was then found guilty of high treason and sentence of forfeiture pronounced; but there is reason to suspect that the whole case was trumped up. The old church escaped demolition at the Reformation and even the fine east

tow[illegible] wh[illegible] unc[illegible] of [illegible] kal[illegible] Fr[illegible] str[illegible] Ma[illegible] Aug[illegible] settl[illegible] was [illegible]

D[illegible] four[illegible] the [illegible] 1648 finan[illegible] Engl[illegible] with [illegible] the p[illegible] the s[illegible] many War [illegible] but t[illegible] the fo[illegible] of the comme[illegible] of eno[illegible] Anoth[illegible] was ai[illegible] 1834, a the tow[illegible] for the [illegible] the rev[illegible] of 1866 new imp[illegible] German [illegible]

The in[illegible] several b[illegible] These are[illegible] 1631, bet[illegible] perialists. Völkerschl[illegible] allied forc[illegible]

Toward[illegible] the most i[illegible] Johann Ch[illegible] in England. Leipzig des[illegible] assigned to [illegible] his first pl[illegible] Goethe, Klo[illegible] its alumni. and Sebasti[illegible] Among the [illegible] Leibnitz and [illegible]

AUTHORITI[illegible] *Stadt Leipzig* [illegible] *schrieben* (Le[illegible] (Leipzig, 1897[illegible] *wesen der Sta*[illegible] *Aus Leipzigs* [illegible] *Geschichte der* [illegible] *Jahrhunderte*, A[illegible] 1891); *Quellen* [illegible] *Geschichte der* [illegible] *formation in Le*[illegible] *geschichte der St*[illegible] cinski, *Stiftungsb*[illegible] *denbuch der Stadt* [illegible] mann (Leipzig, [illegible] *Geschichte Leipzig*[illegible] town's life see H[illegible] (Leipzig, 1887); [illegible] *Leipzigs* (Leipzig, 1903); E. Friedbe[illegible] *Gegenwart* (Leipzi[illegible] *Universität Leipzig* [illegible] *siger Messen* (Leip[illegible] *strasse* (Gotha, 1906[illegible] *nung* (Leipzig, 1881[illegible] *15 und 16 Jahrhund*[illegible]

LEIRIA, an epis[illegible] Leiria, formerly [illegible] river Lis [illegible]

[illegible] in the [illegible] repose Sir Robert and other [illegible] of the [illegible], and Lord Brougham's [illegible] the well of St Triduana, which was [illegible] wonderful [illegible] powers, vanished when the [illegible] was constructed.

[illegible] (Czech *Litoměřice*), a town and episcopal see of [illegible] of Prague by rail. Pop. (1900) 13,075, mostly [illegible] right bank of the Elbe, which becomes [illegible] and is spanned by an iron bridge [illegible] the cathedral, founded in 1057, was [illegible] some valuable paintings. The library [illegible] between 1694 and 1701, possesses the [illegible] made in [illegible] by Nicolaus Claudianus [illegible] churches that of All Saints dates [illegible] The town-hall, with its remarkable [illegible] century. Leitmeritz is situated in [illegible] country called the "Bohemian [illegible] quantities of corn, fruit, hops [illegible] enjoys a high reputation. [illegible] where the Eger discharges [illegible] (pop. [illegible]), an important [illegible] fortress, erected [illegible] named after his mother [illegible] was dismantled in 1882.

[illegible] royal count and is first [illegible] of the convent of St [illegible] charter, and was [illegible] of Ferdinand I., [illegible] royal towns where [illegible] degree of prosperity [illegible] tracts of forest. [illegible] after its [illegible] "the Chalice," [illegible] suffered in con[illegible] Thirty Years' [illegible] inhabitants left [illegible] given to German [illegible] 1855.

[illegible] Anglo-Hun[illegible] He was the son [illegible] college. [illegible] the Crimean [illegible] and in [illegible] Lahore in [illegible] was subse[illegible] He [illegible] He died [illegible]

This varied county has in general a floor of Carboniferous Limestone, which forms finely scarped hills as it reaches the sea in Donegal Bay. The underlying sandstone appears at Lough Melvin, and again on the margin of a Silurian area in the extreme south. The Upper Carboniferous series, dipping gently southward, form mountainous country round Lough Allen, where the name of Slieve Anierin records the abundance of clay-ironstone beneath the coal seams. The sandstones and shales of this series scarp boldly towards the valley of the Bonnet, across which rises, in picturesque contrast, the heather-clad ridge of ancient gneiss which forms, in Benbo, the north-east end of the Ox Mountains. The ironstone was smelted in the upland at Creevelea down to 1859, and the coal is worked in a few thin seams.

The climate is moist and unsuitable for grain crops. On the higher districts the soil is stiff and cold, and, though abounding in stones, retentive of moisture, but in the valleys there are some fertile districts. Lime, marl and similar manures are abundant, and on the coast seaweed is plentiful. The proportion of tillage to pasture is roughly as 1 to 3. Potatoes are grown, but oats, the principal grain crop, are scanty. The live stock consists chiefly of cattle, pigs and poultry. Coarse linens for domestic purposes are manufactured and coarse pottery is also made. The Sligo, Leitrim and Northern Counties railway, connecting Sligo with Enniskillen, crosses the northern part of the county, by way of Manor Hamilton; the Mullingar and Sligo line of the Midland Great Western touches the south-western boundary of the county, with a station at Carrick-on-Shannon; while connecting with this line at Dromod is the Cavan and Leitrim railway to Ballinamore and Arigna, and to Belturbet in county Cavan.

The population (78,618 in 1891; 69,343 in 1901) decreases owing to emigration, the decrease being one of the most serious shown by any Irish county. It includes nearly 90% of Roman Catholics. The only towns are Carrick-on-Shannon (pop. 1118) and Manor Hamilton (903). The county is divided into five baronies. It is within the Connaught circuit, and assizes are held at Carrick-on-Shannon, and quarter sessions at Ballinamore, Carrick-on-Shannon and Manor Hamilton. It is in the Protestant diocese of Kilmore, and the Roman Catholic dioceses of Ardagh and Kilmore. In the Irish House of Commons two members were returned for the county and two for the boroughs of Carrick-on-Shannon and Jamestown, but at the Union the boroughs were disfranchised. The county divisions are termed the North and South, each returning one member.

With the territory which afterwards became the county Cavan, Leitrim formed part of Brenny or Breffny, which was divided into two principalities, of which Leitrim, under the name of Hy Bruin-Brenny, formed the western. Being for a long time in the possession of the O'Rourkes, descendants of Roderick, king of Ireland, it was also called Brenny O'Rourke. This family long maintained its independence; even in 1579, when the other existing counties of Connaught were created, the creation of Leitrim was deferred, and did not take place until 1583. Large confiscations were made in the reigns of Elizabeth and James I., in the Cromwellian period, and after the Revolution of 1688.

There are "druidical" remains near Fenagh and at Letterman, and important monastic ruins at Creevelea near the Bonnet, with several antique monuments, and in the parish of Fenagh. There was a flourishing Franciscan friary at Jamestown. The abbeys of Mohill, Annaduff and Drumlease are converted into parish churches. Among the more notable old castles are Manor Hamilton Castle, originally very extensive, but now in ruins, and Castle John on an island in Lough Scur. There is a small village named Leitrim about 4 m. N. of Carrick-on-Shannon, which was once of enough importance to give its name to a barony and to the county, and is said to have been the seat of an early bishopric.

[illegible]ES, a seaport and harbour of refuge of northern [illegible] in 41° 9′ 10″ N., 8° 40′ 35″ W., 3 m. N. of the mouth [illegible]. Leixões is included in the parish of Matozinhos [illegible] 1900) and constitutes the main port of the city of

Oporto (*q.v.*), with which it is connected by an electric tramway. The harbour, of artificial construction, has an area of over 220 acres, and admits vessels of any size, the depth at the entrance being nearly 50 ft. The transference of cargo to and from ships lying in the Leixões basin is effected entirely by means of lighters from Oporto. In addition to wine, &c., from Oporto, large numbers of emigrants to South America are taken on board here. The trade of the port is mainly in British hands, and large numbers of British ships call at Leixões on the voyage between Lisbon and Liverpool, London or Southampton.

LEJEUNE, LOUIS FRANÇOIS, Baron (1776–1848), French general, painter, and lithographer, was born at Versailles. As aide-de-camp to General Berthier he took an active part in many of the Napoleonic campaigns, which he made the subjects of an important series of battle-pictures. The vogue he enjoyed is due to the truth and vigour of his work, which was generally executed from sketches and studies made on the battlefield. When his battle-pictures were shown at the Egyptian Hall in London, a rail had to be put up to protect them from the eager crowds of sightseers. Among his chief works are "The Entry of Charles X. into Paris, 6 June 1825" at Versailles; "Episode of the Prussian War, October 1807" at Douai Museum; "Marengo" (1801); "Lodi," "Thabor," "Aboukir" (1804); "The Pyramids" (1806); "Passage of the Rhine in 1795" (1824), and "Moskawa" (1812). The German campaign of 1806 brought him to Munich, where he visited the workshop of Senefelder, the inventor of lithography. Lejeune was so fascinated by the possibilities of the new method that he then and there made the drawing on stone of his famous "Cossack" (printed by C. and T. Senefelder, 1806). Whilst he was taking his dinner, and with his horses harnessed and waiting to take him back to Paris, one hundred proofs were printed, one of which he subsequently submitted to Napoleon. The introduction of lithography into France was greatly due to the efforts of Lejeune. Many of his battle-pictures were engraved by Coiny and Bovinet.

See Fournier-Sarlovèze, *Le Général Lejeune* (Paris, *Libraire de l'art*).

LEKAIN, the stage name of Henri Louis Cain (1728–1778), French actor, who was born in Paris on the 14th of April 1728, the son of a silversmith. He was educated at the Collège Mazarin, and joined an amateur company of players against which the Comédie Française obtained an injunction. Voltaire supported him for a time and enabled him to act in his private theatre and also before the duchess of Maine. Owing to the hostility of the actors it was only after a struggle of seventeen months that, by the command of Louis XV., he was received at the Comédie Française. His success was immediate. Among his best parts were Herod in *Mariamne*, Nero in *Britannicus* and similar tragic rôles, in spite of the fact that he was short and stout, with irregular and rather common features. His name is connected with a number of important scenic reforms. It was he who had the benches removed on which privileged spectators formerly sat encumbering the stage, Count Lauragais paying for him an excessive indemnity demanded. Lekain also protested against the method of sing-song declamation prevalent, and endeavoured to correct the costuming of the plays, although unable to obtain the historic accuracy at which Talma aimed. He died in Paris on the 8th of February 1778.

His eldest son published his *Mémoires* (1801) with his correspondence with Voltaire, Garrick and others. They were reprinted with a preface by Talma in *Mémoires sur l'art dramatique* (1825).

LELAND, CHARLES GODFREY (1824–1903), American author, son of a merchant, was born at Philadelphia on the 15th of August 1824, and graduated at Princeton in 1845. He afterwards studied at Heidelberg, Munich and Paris. He was in Paris during the revolution of 1848, and took an active part in it. He then returned to Philadelphia, and after being admitted to the bar in 1851, devoted himself to contributing to periodicals, editing various magazines and writing books. At the opening of the Civil War he started at Boston the *Continental Magazine*, which advocated emancipation. In 1868 he became known as the humorous author of *Hans Breitmann's Party and Ballads*, which was followed by other volumes of the same kind, collected in 1871 with the title of *Hans Breitmann's Ballads*. These dialect poems, burlesquing the German American, at once became popular. In 1869 he went to Europe, and till 1880 was occupied, chiefly in London, with literary work; after returning to Philadelphia for six years, he again made his home in Europe, generally at Florence, where he died on the 20th of March 1903. Though his humorous verses were most attractive to the public, Leland was a serious student of folk-lore, particularly of the gipsies, his writings on the latter (*The English Gypsies and their Language*, 1872; *The Gypsies*, 1882; *Gypsy Sorcery and Fortune-telling* . . . , 1891, &c.) being recognized as valuable contributions to the literature of the subject. He was president of the first European folk-lore congress, held in Paris in 1889.

His other publications include *Poetry and Mystery of Dreams* (1855), *Meister Karl's Sketch-book* (1855), *Pictures of Travel* (1856), *Sunshine in Thought* (1862), *Heine's Book of Songs* (1862), *The Music Lesson of Confucius* (1870), *Egyptian Sketch-book* (1873), *Abraham Lincoln* (1879), *The Minor Arts* (1880), *Algonquin Legends of New England* (1884), *Songs of the Sea and Lays of the Land* (1895), *Hans Breitmann in Tyrol* (1895), *One Hundred Profitable Acts* (1897), *Unpublished Legends of Vergil* (1899), *Kuloskap the Master, and other Algonquin Poems* (1903, with J. Dyneley Prince).

See his *Memoirs* (2 vols., 1893), and E. R. Pennell, *C. G. Leland* (1906).

LELAND (Leyland or Laylonde), **JOHN** (*c.* 1506–1552), English antiquary, was born in London on the 13th of September, probably in 1506. He owed his education at St Paul's school under William Lilly, and at Christ's College, Cambridge, to the kindness of a patron, Thomas Myles. He graduated at Cambridge in 1521, and subsequently studied at All Souls College, Oxford, and in Paris under François Dubois (Sylvius). On his return to England he took holy orders. He had been tutor to Lord Thomas Howard, son of the 3rd duke of Norfolk, and to Francis Hastings, afterwards earl of Huntingdon. Meanwhile his learning had recommended him to Henry VIII., who presented him to the rectory of Peuplingues in the marches of Calais in 1530. He was already librarian and chaplain to the king, and in 1533 he received a novel commission under the great seal as king's antiquary, with power to search for records, manuscripts and relics of antiquity in all the cathedrals, colleges and religious houses of England. Probably from 1534, and definitely from 1536 onwards to 1542, he was engaged on an antiquarian tour through England and Wales. He sought to preserve the MSS. scattered at the dissolution of the monasteries, but his powers did not extend to the actual collection of MSS. Some valuable additions, however, he did procure for the king's library, chiefly from the abbey of St Augustine at Canterbury. He had received a special dispensation permitting him to absent himself from his rectory of Peuplingues in 1536, and on his return from his itinerary he received the rectory of Haseley in Oxfordshire; his support of the church policy of Henry and Cranmer being further rewarded by a canonry and prebend of King's College (now Christ Church), Oxford, and a prebend of Salisbury. In a *Strena Henrico*[1] (pr. 1546), addressed to Henry VIII. in 1545, he proposed to execute from the materials which he had collected in his journeys a topography of England, an account of the adjacent islands, an account of the British nobility, and a great history of the antiquities of the British Isles. He toiled over his papers at his house in the parish of St Michael le Querne, Cheapside, London, but he was not destined to complete these great undertakings, for he was certified insane in March 1550, and died on the 18th of April 1552.

Leland was an exact observer, and a diligent student of local chronicles. The bulk of his work remained in MS. at the time of his death, and various copies were made, one by John Stowe in 1576. After passing through various hands the greater part of

[1] Re-edited in 1549 by John Bale as *The laboryeuse Journey and Serche of J. Leylande for Englandes Antiquitees geven of him for a New Yeares Gifte, &c.*, modern edition by W. A. Copinger (Manchester, 1895).

[illegible]

inner [illegible] about a court which is 586 by 246 ft. and is [illegible] by a [illegible] open arcade and adorned with large [illegible] of tropical plants and flowers, consists of twelve one-storey buildings and a beautiful memorial church. Of the fourteen buildings of the outer quadrangle some are two storeys high. A magnificent memorial arch (100 ft. high), adorned with a frieze [illegible] by John Evans, representing the "Progress of Civilization in America," and forming the main gateway, was destroyed by the earthquake of 1906. Outside the quadrangles are other buildings—a museum of art and archaeology, [illegible] collections made by Leland Stanford, Jr., chemical laboratories, engineering work-shops, dormitories, a mausoleum of the founders, &c. There is a fine arboretum (300 acres) and a [illegible]. The charming views, the grace and harmonious [illegible] the buildings, and the tropic vegetation make a campus of [illegible] beauty. The students in 1907–1908 numbered [illegible] of whom [illegible] were graduates, 99 special students, and [illegible] women.[1] The university library (with the library of the [illegible] department) contained in 1908 about 107,000 volumes. A marine biological laboratory, founded by Timothy Hopkins, is maintained at Pacific Grove on the Bay of Monterey. The university has an endowment from its founders estimated at [illegible] including three great estates with 85,000 acres of [illegible] and vineyard lands, and several smaller tracts; but the [illegible] was very largely in interest-bearing securities, [illegible] which was temporarily cut off in the early years of the university's life by litigation. The founders wished the university "to qualify students for personal success and direct usefulness in life, to promote the public welfare by exercising an influence in behalf of humanity and civilization, teaching the blessings of liberty regulated by law, and inculcating love and reverence for the great principles of government as derived from the inalienable rights of man to life, liberty and the pursuit of happiness." There are no inflexible entrance requirements [illegible] studies except English composition to ensure [illegible] mental maturity, the minimum amount of preparation [illegible] which should be given by four years in a secondary school, [illegible] to the applicants a wide choice of subjects (35 [illegible] ranging from ancient history to woodworking and [illegible] shop. In the curriculum, liberty perhaps even greater than at Harvard is allowed as to "electives." Work on some [illegible] major subject occupies about one-third of the undergraduate course, the remaining two-thirds (or more) is purely elective. The influence of sectarianism and politics is barred from the university by its charter, and by its private origin and private support. At the same time in its policy it is practically a state university of the most liberal type. Instruction is entirely free. The president of the university has the initiative in all appointments and in all matters of general policy. Within the university [illegible] power lies in an academic council, and, more particularly, in an advisory board of nine professors, elected by the academic council, to which all propositions of the president are submitted. The growth of the university has been steady, and its conduct [illegible]. David Starr Jordan[2] was its first president.

See [illegible] M. Elliott and O. V. Eaton, *Stanford University and thereabouts* (San Francisco, 1896), and the official publications of the university.

LELEGES, the name applied by Greek writers to an early people or peoples of which traces were believed to remain in [illegible].

[illegible] Minor.—In Homer the Leleges are allies of the [illegible], but they do not occur in the formal catalogue in *Iliad*,

[1] The number of women attending the university as students in [illegible] is limited by the founding grant to 500.

[2] [illegible] Jordan was born in 1851 at Gainesville, New York; [illegible] at Cornell, where he taught botany for a time; became [illegible] assistant to the United States fish commission in 1872; [illegible] was president of the university of Indiana, where [illegible] he had been professor of zoology; and in 1891 was [illegible] president of Leland Stanford Jr. University. An eminent [illegible] he wrote, with Barton Warren Evermann (b. 1853), [illegible] States Bureau of Fisheries, *Fishes of North and Middle* [illegible] vols., [illegible]), and *Food and Game Fishes of North* [illegible], and prepared *A Guide to the Study of Fishes* (1905).

bk. ii., and their habitat is not specified. They are distinguished from the Carians, with whom some later writers confused them; they have a king Altes, and a town Pedasus which was sacked by Achilles. The name Pedasus occurs (i.) near Cyzicus, (ii.) in the Troad on the Satnioeis river, (iii.) in Caria, as well as (iv.) in Messenia. Alcaeus (7th–6th centuries B.C.) calls Antandrus in the Troad Lelegian, but Herodotus (5th century) substitutes Pelasgian (*q.v.*). Gargara in the Troad also counted as Lelegian. Pherecydes (5th century) attributed to Leleges the coast land of Caria from Ephesus to Phocaea, with the islands of Samos and Chios, placing the "true Carians" farther south from Ephesus to Miletus. If this statement be from Pherecydes of Leros (*c.* 480) it has great weight. In the 4th century, however, Philippus of Theangela in south Caria describes Leleges still surviving as serfs of the true Carians, and Strabo, in the 1st century B.C., attributes to the Leleges a well-marked group of deserted forts, tombs and dwellings which ranged (and can still be traced) from the neighbourhood of Theangela and Halicarnassus as far north as Miletus, the southern limit of the "true Carians" of Pherecydes. Plutarch also implies the historic existence of Lelegian serfs at Tralles in the interior.

2. *In Greece and the Aegean.*—A single passage in the Hesiodic catalogue (fr. 136 Kinkel) places Leleges "in Deucalion's time," *i.e.* as a primitive people, in Locris in central Greece. Not until the 4th century B.C. does any other writer place them anywhere west of the Aegean. But the confusion of the Leleges with the Carians (immigrant conquerors akin to Lydians and Mysians, and probably to Phrygians) which first appears in a Cretan legend (quoted by Herodotus, but repudiated, as he says, by the Carians themselves) and is repeated by Callisthenes, Apollodorus and other later writers, led easily to the suggestion of Callisthenes, that Leleges joined the Carians in their (half legendary) raids on the coasts of Greece. Meanwhile other writers from the 4th century onwards claimed to discover them in Boeotia, west Acarnania (Leucas), and later again in Thessaly, Euboea, Megara, Lacedaemon and Messenia. In Messenia they were reputed immigrant founders of Pylos, and were connected with the seafaring Taphians and Teleboans of Homer, and distinguished from the Pelasgians; in Lacedaemon and in Leucas they were believed to be aboriginal. These European Leleges must be interpreted in connexion with the recurrence of place names like Pedasus, Physcus, Larymna and Abae, (*a*) in Caria, and (*b*) in the "Lelegian" parts of Greece; perhaps this is the result of some early migration; perhaps it is also the cause of these Lelegian theories.

Modern speculations (mainly corollaries of Indo-Germanic theory) add little of value to the Greek accounts quoted above. H. Kiepert ("Über den Volksstamm der Leleges," in *Monatsber. Berl. Akad.*, 1861, p. 114) makes the Leleges an aboriginal people akin to Albanians and Illyrians; K. W. Deimling, *Die Leleger* (Leipzig, 1862), starts them in south-west Asia Minor, and brings them thence to Greece (practically the Greek view); G. F. Unger, "Hellas in Thessalien," in *Philologus*, Suppl. ii. (1863), makes them Phoenician, and derives their name from λαλάζειν (cf. the names *Βάρβαροι*, *Wälsche*). E. Curtius (*History of Greece*, i.) distinguished a "Lelegian" phase of nascent Aegean culture. Most later writers follow Deimling. For Strabo's "Lelegian" monuments, cf. Paton and Myres, *Journal of Hellenic Studies*, xvi. 188-270. (J. L. M.)

LELEWEL, JOACHIM (1786–1861), Polish historian, geographer and numismatist, was born at Warsaw on the 22nd of March 1786. His family came from Prussia in the early part of the 18th century; his grandfather was appointed physician to the reigning king of Poland, and his father caused himself to be naturalized as a Polish citizen. The original form of the name appears to have been Lölhöffel. Joachim was educated at the university of Vilna, and became in 1807 a teacher in a school at Krzemieniec in Volhynia, in 1814 teacher of history at Vilna, and in 1818 professor and librarian at the university of Warsaw. He returned to Vilna in 1821. His lectures enjoyed great popularity, and enthusiasm felt for him by the students is shown in the beautiful lines addressed to him by Mickiewicz. But this very circumstance made him obnoxious to the Russian government, and at Vilna Novosiltsev was then all-powerful. Lelewel was removed from his professorship in 1824, and returned to Warsaw, where he was elected a deputy to the diet in 1829. He joined the revolutionary movement with more enthusiasm than energy, and though the emperor Nicholas I. distinguished him as one of the most dangerous rebels, did not appear to advantage as a man of action. On the suppression of the rebellion he made his way in disguise to Germany, and subsequently reached Paris in 1831. The government of Louis Philippe ordered him to quit French territory in 1833 at the request of the Russian ambassador. The cause of this expulsion is said to have been his activity in writing revolutionary proclamations. He went to Brussels, where for nearly thirty years he earned a scanty livelihood by his writings. He died on the 29th of May 1861 in Paris, whither he had removed a few days previously.

Lelewel, a man of austere character, simple tastes and the loftiest conception of honour, was a lover of learning for its own sake. His literary activity was enormous, extending from his *Edda Skandinawska* (1807) to his *Géographie des Arabes* (2 vols., Paris, 1851). One of his most important publications was *La Géographie du moyen âge* (5 vols., Brussels, 1852–1857), with an atlas (1849) of fifty plates entirely engraved by himself, for he rightly attached such importance to the accuracy of his maps that he would not allow them to be executed by any one else. His works on Polish history are based on minute and critical study of the documents; they were collected under the title *Polska, dzieje i rzeczy jej rozpatrzywane* (*Poland, her History and Affairs surveyed*), in 20 vols. (Posen, 1853–1876). He intended to write a complete history of Poland on an extensive scale, but never accomplished the task. His method is shown in the little history of Poland, first published at Warsaw in Polish in 1823, under the title *Dzieje Polski*, and afterwards almost rewritten in the *Histoire de Pologne* (2 vols., Paris, 1844). Other works on Polish history which may be especially mentioned are *La Pologne au moyen âge* (3 vols., Posen, 1846–1851), an edition of the *Chronicle of Matthew Cholewa* [1] (1811) and *Ancient Memorials of Polish Legislation* (*Ksiegi ustaw polskich i mazowieckich*). He also wrote on the trade of Carthage, on Pytheas of Marseilles, the geographer, and two important works on numismatics (*La Numismatique du moyen âge*, Paris, 2 vols., 1835; *Études numismatiques*, Brussels, 1840). While employed in the university library of Warsaw he studied bibliography, and the fruits of his labours may be seen in his *Bibliograficznych Ksiag dwoje* (*A Couple of Books on Bibliography*) (2 vols., Vilna, 1823–1826). The characteristics of Lelewel as an historian are great research and power to draw inferences from his facts; his style is too often careless, and his narrative is not picturesque, but his expressions are frequently terse and incisive.

He left valuable materials for a just comprehension of his career in the autobiography (*Adventures while Prosecuting Researches and Inquiries on Polish Matters*) printed in his *Polska*.

LELONG, JACQUES (1665–1721), French bibliographer, was born at Paris on the 19th of April 1665. He was a priest of the Oratory, and was librarian to the establishment of the Order in Paris, where he spent his life in seclusion. He died at Paris on the 13th of August 1721. He first published a *Bibliotheca sacra* (1709), an index of all the editions of the Bible, then a *Bibliothèque historique de la France* (1719), a volume of considerable size, containing 17,487 items to which Lelong sometimes appends useful notes. His work is far from complete. He vainly hoped that his friend and successor Father Desmolets, would continue it; but it was resumed by Charles-Marie Fevret de Fontette, a councillor of the parlement of Dijon, who spent fifteen years of his life and a great deal of money in rewriting the *Bibliothèque historique*. The first two volumes (1768 and 1769) contained as many as 29,143 items. Fevret de Fontette died on the 16th of February 1772, leaving the third volume almost finished. It appeared in 1772, thanks to Barbaud de La Bruyère, who later brought out the 4th and 5th volumes (1775 and 1778).

[1] *I.e.* the three first books of the *Historia Polonica* of Vincentius (Kadlbek), bishop of Cracow (d. 1223), wrongly ascribed by Lelewel to Matthaeus Cholewa, bishop of Cracow. See Potthast, *Bibliotheca hist. med. aev.*, *s.v.* "Vincentius."

a work of reference

painter, was born
... a military captain
... der Vaes;
... he was generally
... After studying
... of some note
... of Charles I. for
... There he at first
... he soon became so
... by Charles to paint
... He afterwards
... his genius and agreeable
... made him his state-
... He formed a famous
... drawings, prints and
... by auction for no less
... was Vandyck,
... he almost rivals.
... warm and clear in colour-
... posture of the heads,
... the broad folds of the
... portraits. The eyes of
... and allegory
... introduced. His most
... the ladies of the court
... formerly at Windsor
... Court Palace. Of his
... Susannah and the Elders,"
... Europa," in the duke of
... Lely was nearly
... Towards the close
... which he had bought at
... Covent Garden,
... Garden church, where a
... his memory. Pepys
... man and full of state."
... family, and left a son
... only disciples were J.
... however, allow them
... of work. (W. M. R.)

... chan-
... Sarthe. He was
... later a councillor of
... a partisan of the house
... to Isabella of Bavaria
... of July commissary
... the count of Ponthieu,
... August he bought the
... bore the title of
... by the Burgundians
... Tanguy Duchâtel
... the cause of the latter
... of John the Fearless,
... the political amnesty
... though he retained
... by the dauphin's side
... of Montereau
... the walls at the
... great influence.
... the king and the
... Jean de Langeac,
... he was shut
... When set at
... appointed
... It was he
... in December
... with an embassy
... he died
... where

See C. Bourcier, "Robert le Masson," in the *Revue historique de l'Anjou* (1873); and the *Nouvelle biographie générale*, vol. xxx. (J. V.*)

LE MAIRE DE BELGES, JEAN (1473–c. 1525), French poet and historiographer, was born at Bavai in Hainault. He was a nephew of Jean Molinet, and spent some time with him at Valenciennes, where the elder writer held a kind of academy of poetry. Le Maire in his first poems calls himself a disciple of Molinet. In certain aspects he does belong to the school of the *grands rhétoriqueurs*, but his great merit as a poet is that he emancipated himself from the affectations and puerilities of his masters. This independence of the Flemish school he owed in part perhaps to his studies at the university of Paris and to the study of the Italian poets at Lyons, a centre of the French renascence. In 1503 he was attached to the court of Margaret of Austria, duchess of Savoy, afterwards regent of the Netherlands. For this princess he undertook more than one mission to Rome; he became her librarian and a canon of Valenciennes. To her were addressed his most original poems, *Epistres de l'amand verd*, the *amant vert* being a green parrot belonging to his patroness. Le Maire gradually became more French in his sympathies, eventually entering the service of Anne of Brittany. His prose *Illustrations des Gaules et singularitez de Troye* (1510–1512), largely adapted from Benoît de Sainte More, connects the Burgundian royal house with Hector. Le Maire probably died before 1525. Étienne Pasquier, Ronsard and Du Bellay all acknowledged their indebtedness to him. In his love for antiquity, his sense of rhythm, and even the peculiarities of his vocabulary he anticipated the *Pléiade*.

His works were edited in 1882–1885 by J. Stecher, who wrote the article on him in the *Biographie nationale de Belgique*.

LEMAÎTRE, FRANÇOIS ÉLIE JULES (1853–), French critic and dramatist, was born at Vennecy (Loiret) on the 27th of April 1853. He became a professor at the university of Grenoble, but he had already become known by his literary criticisms, and in 1884 he resigned his position to devote himself entirely to literature. He succeeded J. J. Weiss as dramatic critic of the *Journal des Débats*, and subsequently filled the same office on the *Revue des Deux Mondes*. His literary studies were collected under the title of *Les Contemporains* (7 series, 1886–1899), and his dramatic *feuilletons* as *Impressions de théâtre* (10 series, 1888–1898). His sketches of modern authors are interesting for the insight displayed in them, the unexpectedness of the judgments and the gaiety and originality of their expression. He published two volumes of poetry: *Les Médaillons* (1880) and *Petites orientales* (1883); also some volumes of *contes*, among them *En marge des vieux livres* (1905). His plays are: *Révoltée* (1889), *Le député Leveau*, and *Le Mariage blanc* (1891), *Les Rois* (1893), *Le Pardon* and *L'Age difficile* (1895), *La Massière* (1905) and *Bertrade* (1906). He was admitted to the French Academy on the 16th of January 1896. His political views were defined in *La Campagne nationaliste* (1902), lectures delivered in the provinces by him and by G. Cavaignac. He conducted a nationalist campaign in the *Écho de Paris*, and was for some time president of the Ligue de la Patrie Française, but resigned in 1904, and again devoted himself to literature.

LE MANS, a town of north-western France, capital of the department of Sarthe, 77 m. S.W. of Chartres on the railway from Paris to Brest. Pop. (1906) town, 54,907, commune, 65,467. It is situated just above the confluence of the Sarthe and the Huisne, on an elevation rising from the left bank of the Sarthe. Several bridges connect the old town and the new quarters which have sprung up round it with the more extensive quarter of Pré on the right bank. Modern thoroughfares are gradually superseding the winding and narrow streets of old houses, a tunnel connects the Place des Jacobins with the river side. The cathedral, built in the highest part of the town, was originally founded by St Julian, to whom it is dedicated. The nave dates from the 11th and 12th centuries. In the 13th century the choir was enlarged in the grandest and boldest style of that period. The transepts, which are higher than the nave, were rebuilt in the 15th century, and the bell-tower of the south transept, the lower part of which is Romanesque, was rebuilt in the 15th and 16th centuries. Some of the stained glass in the nave, dating from the first half of the 12th century, is the oldest in France, the west window, representing the legend of St Julian, is especially interesting. The south lateral portal (12th century) is richly decorated, and its statuettes exhibit many costumes of the period. The austere simplicity of the older part of the building is in striking contrast with the lavish richness of the ornamentation in the choir, where the stained glass is especially fine. The rose-window (15th century) of the north transept, representing the Last Judgment, contains many historical figures. The cathedral also has curious tapestries and some remarkable tombs, including that of Berengaria, queen of Richard Cœur de Lion. Close to the western wall is a megalithic monument nearly 15 ft. in height. The church of La Couture, which belonged to an old abbey founded in the 7th century by St Bertrand, has a porch of the 13th century with fine statuary; the rest of the building is older. The church of Notre-Dame du Pré, on the right bank of the Sarthe, is Romanesque in style. The hôtel de ville was built in 1756 on the site of the former castle of the counts of Maine; the prefecture (1760) occupies the site of the monastery of La Couture, and contains the library, the communal archives, and natural history and art collections; there is also an archaeological museum. Among the old houses may be mentioned the Hôtel du Grabatoire of the Renaissance, once a hospital for the canons and the so-called house of Queen Berengaria (16th century), meeting place of the historical and archaeological society of Maine. A monument to General Chanzy commemorates the battle of Le Mans (1871). Le Mans is the seat of a bishopric dating from the 3rd century, of a prefect, and of a court of assizes, and headquarters of the IV. army corps. It has also tribunals of first instance and of commerce, a council of trade-arbitrators, a chamber of commerce, a branch of the Bank of France, an exchange, a lycée for boys, training colleges, a higher ecclesiastical seminary and a school of music. The town has a great variety of industries, carried on chiefly in the southern suburb of Pontlieue. The more important are the state manufacture of tobacco, the preparation of preserved vegetables, fish, &c., tanning, hemp-spinning, bell-founding, flour-milling, the founding of copper and other metals, and the manufacture of railway wagons, machinery and engineering material, agricultural implements, rope, cloth and stained glass. The fattening of poultry is an important local industry, and there is trade in cattle, wine, cloth, farm-produce, &c. The town is an important railway centre.

As the capital of the Aulerci Cenomanni, Le Mans was called Suindinum or Vindinum. The Romans built walls round it in the 3rd century, and traces of them are still to be seen close to the left bank of the river near the cathedral. In the same century the town was evangelized by St Julian, who became its first bishop. Ruled at first by his successors—notably St Aldric—Le Mans passed in the middle ages to the counts of Maine (*q.v.*), whose capital and residence it became. About the middle of the 11th century the citizens secured a communal charter, but in 1063 the town was seized by William the Conqueror, who deprived them of their liberties, which were recovered when the countship of Maine had passed to the Plantagenet kings of England. Le Mans was taken by Philip Augustus in 1189, recaptured by John, subsequently confiscated and later ceded to Queen Berengaria, who did much for its prosperity. It was several times besieged in the 15th and 16th centuries. In 1793 it was seized by the Vendeans, who were expelled by the Republican generals Marceau and Westermann after a stubborn battle in the streets. In 1799 it was again occupied by the Chouans.

The battle of Le Mans (10th–12th January 1871) was the culminating point of General Chanzy's fighting retreat into western France after the winter campaign in Beauce and Perche (see Franco-German War). The numerous, but ill-trained and ill-equipped, levies of the French were followed up by Prince Frederick Charles with the German II. Army, now very much weakened but consisting of soldiers who had in six months' active warfare acquired the self-confidence of veterans. The Germans advanced with three army corps in first line and one in reserve. On the 9th of January the centre corps (III.) drove an advanced division of the French from Ardenay (13 m. E. of Le Mans). On the 10th of January Chanzy's main defensive position was approached. Its right wing was east of the Sarthe and 3-5 m. from Le Mans, its centre on the heights of Anvours with the river Huisne behind it, and its left scattered along the western bank of the same river as far as Montfort (12 m. E.N.E. of Le Mans) and thence northward for some miles. On the 10th there was a severe struggle for the villages along the front of the French centre. On the 11th Chanzy attempted a counter-offensive from many points, but owing to the misbehaviour of certain of his rawest levies, the Germans were able to drive him back, and as their cavalry now began to appear beyond his extreme left flank, he retreated in the night of the 11th on Laval, the Germans occupying Le Mans after a brief rearguard fight on the 12th.

LE MARCHANT, JOHN GASPARD (1766–1812), English major-general, was the son of an officer of dragoons, John Le Marchant, a member of an old Guernsey family. After a somewhat wild youth, Le Marchant, who entered the army in 1781, attained the rank of lieutenant-colonel in 1797. Two years before this he had designed a new cavalry sword; and in 1801 his scheme for establishing at High Wycombe and Great Marlow schools for the military instruction of officers was sanctioned by Parliament, and a grant of £30,000 was voted for the "royal military college," the two original departments being afterwards combined and removed to Sandhurst. Le Marchant was the first lieutenant-governor, and during the nine years that he held this appointment he trained many officers who served with distinction under Wellington in the Peninsula. Le Marchant himself was given the command of a cavalry brigade in 1810, and greatly distinguished himself in several actions, being killed at the battle of Salamanca on the 22nd of July 1812, after the charge of his brigade had had an important share in the English victory. He wrote several treatises on cavalry tactics and other military subjects, but few of them were published. By his wife, Mary, daughter of John Carey of Guernsey, Le Marchant had four sons and six daughters.

His second son, Sir Denis le Marchant, Bart. (1795–1874), was educated at Eton and Trinity College, Cambridge, and was called to the bar in 1823. In 1830 he became secretary to Lord Chancellor Brougham, and in the Reform Bill debates made himself exceedingly useful to the ministers. Having been secretary to the board of trade from 1836 to 1841, he was created a baronet in 1841. He entered the House of Commons in 1846, and was under secretary for the home department in the government of Lord John Russell. He was chief clerk of the House of Commons from 1850 to 1871. He published a *Life* of his father in 1841, and began a *Life* of Lord Althorpe which was completed after his death by his son; he also edited Horace Walpole's *Memoirs of the Reign of George III.* (1845). Sir Denis Le Marchant died in London on the 30th of October 1874.

The third son of General Le Marchant, Sir John Gaspard Le Marchant (1803–1874), entered the English army, and saw service in Spain in the Carlist War of 1835–37. He was afterwards lieutenant-governor of Newfoundland (1847–1852) and of Nova Scotia (1852–1857); governor of Malta (1859–1864); commander-in-chief at Madras (1865–1868). He was made K.C.B. in 1865, and died on the 6th of February 1874.

See Sir Denis Le Marchant, *Memoirs of General Le Marchant* (1841); Sir William Napier, *History of the War in the Peninsula* (6 vols., 1828–1840).

LEMBERG (Pol. *Lwów*, Lat. *Leopolis*), the capital of the crownland of Galicia, Austria, 468 m. N.W. of Vienna by rail. Pop. (1900) 159,618, of whom over 80% were Poles, 10% Germans, and 8% Ruthenians; nearly 30% of the population were Jews. According to population Lemberg is the fourth city in the Austrian empire, coming after Vienna, Prague and Trieste. Lemberg is situated on the small river Peltew, an affluent of the Bug, in a valley in the Sarmatian plateau, and is surrounded by hills. It is composed of the inner town and of four suburbs.

subjects might be treated without offence. The *Pinto* (1800) was the result of a wager that no further dramatic innovations were possible after the comedies of Beaumarchais. It is a historical comedy on the subject of the Portuguese revolution of 1640. This play was construed as casting reflections on the first consul, who had hitherto been a firm friend of Lemercier. His extreme freedom of speech finally offended Napoleon, and the quarrel proved disastrous to Lemercier's fortune for the time. None of his subsequent work fulfilled the expectations raised by *Agamemnon*, with the exception perhaps of *Frédégonde et Brunéhaut* (1821). In 1810 he was elected to the Academy, where he consistently opposed the romanticists, refusing to give his vote to Victor Hugo. In spite of this, he has some pretensions to be considered the earliest of the romantic school. His *Christophe Colomb* (1809), advertised on the playbill as a *comédie shakespirienne* (*sic*), represented the interior of a ship, and showed no respect for the unities. Its numerous innovations provoked such violent disturbances in the audience that one person was killed and future representations had to be guarded by the police. Lemercier wrote four long and ambitious epi[c] poems: *Homère, Alexandre* (1801), *L'Atlantiade, ou la théogo[nie] newtonienne* (1812) and *Moïse* (1823), as well as an extraordi[nary] *Panhypocrisiade* (1819–1832), a distinctly romantic produ[ction] in twenty cantos, which has the sub-title *Spectacle infer[nal du] XVIe siècle*. In it 16th-century history, with Charles [V. and] Francis I. as principal personages, is played out on an in[fernal] stage by demons in the intervals of their sufferings. [He] died on the 7th of June 1840 in Paris.

LEMERY, NICOLAS (1645–1715), French chemist, [was born at] Rouen on the 17th of November 1645. After learning pharm[acy] in his native town he became a pupil of C Glaser's in Paris, and then went to Montpellier, where he began to lecture on chemistry. He next established a pharmacy in Paris, still continuing his lectures, but in 1683, being a Calvinist, he was obliged to retire to England. In the following year he returned to France, and turning Catholic in 1686 was able to reopen his shop and resume his lectures. He died in Paris on the 19th of June 1715. Lemery did not concern himself much with theoretical speculations, but holding chemistry to be a demonstrative science, confined himself to the straightforward exposition of facts and experiments. In consequence, his lecture-room was thronged with people of all sorts, anxious to hear a man who shunned the barren obscurities of the alchemists, and did not regard the quest of the philosopher's stone and the elixir of life as the sole end of his science. Of his *Cours de chymie* (1675) he lived to see 13 editions, and for a century it maintained its reputation as a standard work. His other publications included *Pharmacopée universelle* (1697), *Traité universel des drogues simples* (1698), *Traité de l'antimoine* (1707), together with a number of papers contributed to the French Academy, one of which offered a chemical and physical explanation of underground fires, earthquakes, lightning and thunder. He discovered that heat is evolved when iron filings and sulphur are rubbed together to a paste with water, and the artificial *volcan de Lemery* was produced by burying underground a considerable quantity of this mixture, which he regarded as a potent agent in the causation of volcanic action.

His son LOUIS (1677–1743) was appointed physician at the Hôtel Dieu in 1710, and became demonstrator of chemistry at the Jardin du Roi in 1731. He was the author of a *Traité des aliments* (1702), and of a *Dissertation sur la nature des os* (1704), as well as of a number of papers on chemical topics.

LEMERY, a town of the province of Batangas, Luzon, Philippine Islands, on the Gulf of Balayan and the Pansipit river, opposite Taal (with which it is connected by a bridge), and about 50 m. S. of Manila. Pop. of the municipality (1903) 11,150. It has a fine church and convent. Lemery is situated on a plain in a rich agricultural district, which produces rice, Indian corn, sugar and cotton, and in which horses and cattle are bred. It is also a port for coasting vessels, and has an important trade with various parts of the archipelago. The language is Tagalog.

…des, the tyrant … returned to … sion till the … les of its … Inst. but … ion

LEMGO, a town of Germany, in the … in a broad and fertile plain, 0 m. N. … the railway Hameln-Lage. Pop. (1905) … gloomy aspect, enhanced by the tortuous … by gabled houses of the 15th century, has … countryfolk the sobriquet of the "Witches' … It is replete with interest for the antiquar… Evangelical churches, two with curiously lo… spires; an old town-hall; a gymnasium; an… thropic and religious institutions. Among … Jungfrauenstift, of which a princess of the … Lippe-Detmold has always been lady superi… chief industry of Lemgo is the manufactu… pipes, which has attained here a high pitch … infusteries are weaving, brewing and the ma… and cigars. The town was a member of the l…

LEMIERRE, ANTOINE MARIN (1733–17… dist and poet, was born in Paris on the 12t… His parents were poor, but Lemierre foun… collector-general of taxes, Dupin, whose se… Lemierre gained his first success on the stage… (1758); *Térée* (1761) and *Idoménée* (1764) … the subjects. *Artaxerce*, modelled on Meta… *Tell* were produced in 1766; other succ… *La Veuve de Malabar* (1770) and *Barnav*… revived *Guillaume Tell* in 1786 with enor… the Revolution he professed great remors… of a play inculcating revolutionary princi… doubt that the horror of the excesses he witnessed … death, which took place on the 4th of July 1793. He had bee… admitted to the Academy in 1781. Lemierre published *La Peinture* (1769), based on a Latin poem by the abbé de Marsy, and a poem in six cantos, *Les Fastes, ou les usages de l'année* (1779), an unsatisfactory imitation of Ovid's *Fasti*.

His *Œuvres* (1810) contain a notice of Lemierre by R. Perrin, and his *Œuvres choisies* (1811) one by F. Fayolle.

LEMIRE, JULES AUGUSTE (1853–), French priest and social reformer, was born at Vieux-Berquin (Nord) on the 23rd of April 1853. He was educated at the college of St Francis of Assisi, Hazebrouck, where he subsequently taught philosophy and rhetoric. In 1897 he was elected deputy for Hazebrouck and was returned unopposed at the elections of 1898, 1902 and 1906. He organized a society called *La Ligue du coin de terre et du foyer*, the object of which was to secure, at the expense of the state, a piece of land for every French family desirous of possessing one. The abbé Lemire sat in the chamber of deputies as a conservative republican and Christian Socialist. He protested in 1893 against the action of the Dupuy cabinet in closing the Bourse du Travail, characterizing it as the expression of "a policy of disdain of the workers." In December 1893 he was seriously injured by the bomb thrown by the anarchist Vaillant from the gallery of the chamber.

LEMMING, the native name of a small Scandinavian rodent mammal *Lemmus norvegicus* (or *L. lemmus*), belonging to the mouse tribe, or *Muridae*, and nearly related, especially in the structure of its cheek-teeth, to the voles. Specimens vary considerably in size and colour, but the usual length is about 5 in., and the soft fur yellowish-brown, marked with spots of dark brown and black. It has a short, rounded head, obtuse muzzle, small bead-like eyes, and short rounded ears, nearly concealed by the fur. The tail is very short. The feet are small, each with five claws, those of the fore feet strongest, and fitted for scratching and digging. The usual habitat of lemmings is the high lands or fells of the great central mountain chain of Norway and Sweden, from the southern branches of the Langfjeldene in Christiansand *stift* to the North Cape and the Varangerfjord. South of the Arctic circle they are, under ordinary circumstances, confined to the plateaus covered with dwarf birch and juniper above the conifer-region, though in Tromsö *amt* and in Finmarken they occur in all suitable localities down to the level of the sea. The nest, under a tussock of grass or a stone, is constructed of short dry straws, and usually lined with hair. The number of

Études critiques et biographiques (1862). He died in Paris … the 14th of December 1892.

LEMON, MARK (1809–1870), editor of *Punch*, was born … London on the 30th of November 1809. He had a natural tale… for journalism and the stage, and, at twenty-six, retired from le… congenial business to devote himself to the writing of play… More than sixty of his melodramas, operettas and comedies we… produced in London. At the same time he contributed to … variety of magazines and newspapers, and founded and editc… *The Field*. In 1841 Lemon and Henry Mayhew conceived th… a of a humorous weekly paper to be called *Punch*, and whe… first number was issued, in July 1841, were joint-editors and … he printer and engraver, equal owners. The paper wa… time unsuccessful, Lemon keeping it alive out of th… is plays. On the sale of *Punch* Lemon became sol… new proprietors, and it remained under his contro… achieving remarkable popularity and influence … or of ability, a pleasing lecturer and a success… f Shakespearian characters. He also wrote … and lyrics, over a hundred songs, a few … eral Christmas fairy tales and a volume … ley, Sussex, on the 23rd of May 1870 … *us Limonum*, which is regarded by … *Citrus medica*. The wild stock of … ative of the valleys of Kumaon … rovinces of India, ascending … g under several forms. Si… *Products of India*, ii. 352) … the lime or citron and … form of the lemon has … to the ancient … by the Arabs …

The Norwegian Lemming (*Lemmus Norvegicus*).

and birds of prey, as bears, wolves, foxes, dogs, wild cats, … weasels, eagles, hawks and owls, and never spared by … even domestic animals, as cattle, goats and reindeer, join in … destruction, stamping them to the ground with their feet, a… even eating their bodies. Numbers also die from disea… produced apparently from overcrowding. None returns, and … onward march of the survivors never ceases until they reach … sea, into which they plunge, and swimming onwards in the sa… direction perish in the waves. These sudden appearances of … bodies of lemmings, and their singular habit of persiste… pursuing the same onward course of migration, have given … to various speculations, from the ancient belief of the Norwe… peasants, shared by Olaus Magnus, that they fall down from … clouds, to the hypothesis that they are acting in obedienc… an instinct inherited from ancient times, and still seeking … congenial home in the submerged Atlantis, to which … ancestors of the Miocene period were wont to resort when dr… from their ordinary dwelling-places by crowding or scarcit… food. The principal facts regarding these migrations seem … as follows. When any combination of circumstances has … sioned an increase of the numbers of the lemmings in … ordinary dwelling-places, impelled by the restless or migr… instinct possessed in a less developed degree by so many of … congeners, a movement takes place at the edge of the ele… plateau, and a migration towards the lower-lying land be… The whole body moves forward slowly, always advancing i…

[illegible] direction in which they originally started, but [illegible] the great valleys. They only [illegible] places for considerable [illegible] abundance of provender, notwithstanding [illegible] to which they are exposed, [illegible] during their journey, having families [illegible] their usual homes. The [illegible] years, according to the [illegible] traversed until the sea-coast [illegible] surrounded by water as the [illegible] the ultimate goal of such a [illegible] the Atlantic or the Gulf of Bothnia, [illegible] commenced from the west or the [illegible] plateau. Those that finally [illegible] what appears to be a voluntary [illegible] the same blind impulse which has [illegible] pieces of water with safety. [illegible] Asia and North America the group [illegible] *L. obensis*, and in Alaska, by *L.* [illegible] banded lemming, *Dicrostonyx* [illegible] winter, represents a second genus [illegible] claws on one of the toes of the [illegible]

[illegible] R. Collett, *Myodes lemmus, its habits* [illegible] Christiania Videnskabs-Selskabs For- [illegible]
(W. H. F.; R. L.*)

[illegible] ribbon), a quartic curve [illegible] *Acta Eruditorum*, 1694) and [illegible] Carlo Fagnano, who gave its [illegible] to effect the division of a [illegible] and $5\cdot 2^m$ equal parts. Following [illegible] the curve to be engraved on his [illegible] analytical treatment was first given [illegible] lemniscate of Bernoulli may be defined [illegible] moves so that the product of its [illegible] is constant and is equal to the [illegible] between these points. It is therefore [illegible] oval (see Oval). Its cartesian [illegible] the two fixed points is the axis [illegible] this line is the origin, is $(x^2+y^2)^2=$ [illegible] equation is $r^2=2a^2\cos 2\theta$. The curve [illegible] symmetrically placed about the [illegible] equation is $r^2=a^2p$, which shows [illegible]

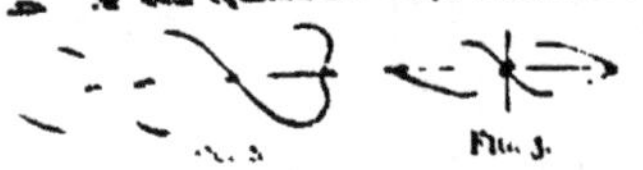

Fig. 3.

[illegible] a rectangular hyperbola with [illegible] inverse of the same curve for [illegible] circles described on the [illegible] The area of the complete [illegible] may be expressed in the [illegible] integral sometimes termed the [illegible]

[illegible] given to any unicursal quartic [illegible] which is symmetrical about [illegible] the curve resembles fig. 2, and [illegible] if it be less than b, the [illegible]

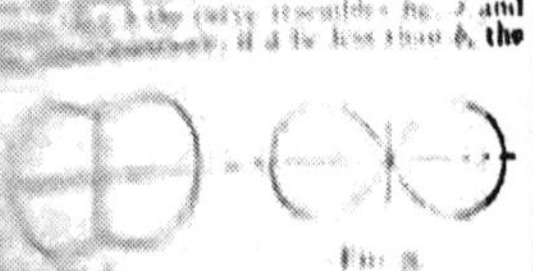

Fig. 2.

[illegible] lemniscate has for its [illegible] The [illegible] and the curve resembles [illegible]

LEMNOS (mod. *Limnos*), an island in the northern part of the Aegean Sea. The Italian form of the name, Stalimene, *i.e.* ἐς τὴν Λῆμνον, is not used in the island itself, but is commonly employed in geographical works. The island, which belongs to Turkey, is of considerable size: Pliny says that the coast-line measured 112½ Roman miles, and the area has been estimated at 150 sq m. Great part is mountainous, but some very fertile valleys exist, to cultivate which 2000 yoke of oxen are employed. The hill-sides afford pasture for 20,000 sheep. No forests exist on the island; all wood is brought from the coast of Rumelia or from Thasos. A few mulberry and fruit trees grow, but no olives. The population is estimated by some as high as 27,000, of whom 2000 are Turks and the rest Greeks, but other authorities doubt whether it reaches more than half this number. The chief towns are Kastro on the western coast, with a population of 4000 Greeks and 800 Turks, and Mudros on the southern coast. Kastro possesses an excellent harbour, and is the seat of all the trade carried on with the island. Greek, English and Dutch consuls or consular agents were formerly stationed there; but the whole trade is now in Greek hands. The archbishops of Lemnos and Ai Strati, a small neighbouring island with 2000 inhabitants, resides in Kastro. In ancient times the island was sacred to Hephaestus, who as the legend tells fell on Lemnos when his father Zeus hurled him headlong out of Olympus. This tale, as well as the name Aethaleia, sometimes applied to it, points to its volcanic character. It is said that fire occasionally blazed forth from Mosychlos, one of its mountains, and Pausanias (viii. 33) relates that a small island called Chryse, off the Lemnian coast, was swallowed up by the sea. All volcanic action is now extinct.

The most famous product of Lemnos is the medicinal earth, which is still used by the natives. At one time it was popular over western Europe under the name *terra sigillata*. This name, like the Gr. Λημνία σφραγίς, is derived from the stamp impressed on each piece of the earth; in ancient times the stamp was the head of Artemis. The Turks now believe that a vase of this earth destroys the effect of any poison drunk from it—a belief which the ancients attached rather to the earth from Cape Kolias in Attica. Galen went to see the digging up of this earth (see Kuhn, *Medic. Gr. Opera*, xii. 172 sq.); on one day in each year a priestess performed the due ceremonies, and a waggon-load of earth was dug out. At the present time the day selected is the 6th of August, the feast of Christ the Saviour. Both the Turkish *hodja* and the Greek priest are present to perform the necessary ceremonies; the whole process takes place before daybreak. The earth is sold by apothecaries in stamped cubical blocks. The hill from which the earth is dug is a dry mound, void of vegetation, beside the village of Kotschinos, and about two hours from the site of Hephaestia. The earth was considered in ancient times a cure for old festering wounds, and for the bite of poisonous snakes.

The name Lemnos is said by Hecataeus (*ap.* Steph. Byz.) to have been a title of Cybele among the Thracians, and the earliest inhabitants are said to have been a Thracian tribe, called by the Greeks Sinties, *i.e.* "the robbers." According to a famous legend the women were all deserted by their husbands, and in revenge murdered every man on the island. From this barbarous act, the expression Lemnian deeds, Λήμνια ἔργα, became proverbial. The Argonauts landing soon after found only women in the island, ruled over by Hypsipyle, daughter of the old king Thoas. From the Argonauts and the Lemnian women were descended the race called Minyae, whose king Euneus, son of Jason and Hypsipyle, sent wine and provisions to the Greeks at Troy. The Minyae were expelled by a Pelasgian tribe who came from Attica. The historical element underlying these traditions is probably that the original Thracian people were gradually brought into communication with the Greeks as navigation began to unite the scattered islands of the Aegean (see Jason); the Thracian inhabitants were barbarians in comparison with the Greek mariners. The worship of Cybele was characteristic of Thrace, whither it spread from Asia Minor at a very early period, and it deserves notice that Hypsipyle and Myrina (the name of one of the chief towns) are Amazon names, which are always connected with Asiatic Cybele-worship. Coming down to a better authenticated period, we find that Lemnos was conquered by Otanes, one of the generals of Darius

Hystaspis; but was soon reconquered by Miltiades, the tyrant of the Thracian Chersonese. Miltiades afterwards returned to Athens, and Lemnos continued an Athenian possession till the Macedonian empire absorbed it. On the vicissitudes of its history in the 3rd century B.C. see Köhler in *Mittheil. Inst. Athen.* i. 261 The Romans declared it free in 197 B.C., but gave it over in 166 to Athens, which retained nominal possession of it till the whole of Greece was made a Roman province. A colony of Attic cleruchs was established by Pericles, and many inscriptions on the island relate to Athenians. After the division of the empire, Lemnos passed under the Byzantine emperors; it shared in the vicissitudes of the eastern provinces, being alternately in the power of Greeks, Italians and Turks, till finally the Turkish sultans became supreme in the Aegean. In 1476 the Venetians successfully defended Kotschinos against a Turkish siege; but in 1657 Kastro was captured by the Turks from the Venetians after a siege of sixty-three days. Kastro was again besieged by the Russians in 1770.

Homer speaks as if there were one town in the island called Lemnos, but in historical times there was no such place. There were two towns, Myrina, now Kastro, and Hephaestia. The latter was the chief town; its coins are found in considerable number, the types being sometimes the Athenian goddess and her owl, sometimes native religious symbols, the caps of the Dioscuri, Apollo, &c. Few coins of Myrina are known. They belong to the period of Attic occupation, and bear Athenian types. A few coins are also known which bear the name, not of either city, but of the whole island. Conze was the first to discover the site of Hephaestia, at a deserted place named Palaeokastro on the east coast. It had once a splendid harbour, which is now filled up. Its situation on the east explains why Miltiades attacked it first when he came from the Chersonese. It surrendered at once, whereas Myrina, with its very strong citadel built on a perpendicular rock, sustained a siege. It is said that the shadow of Mount Athos fell at sunset on a bronze cow in the agora of Myrina. Pliny says that Athos was 87 m. to the north-west; but the real distance is about 40 English miles. One legend localized in Lemnos still requires notice. Philoctetes was left there by the Greeks on their way to Troy; and there he suffered ten years' agony from his wounded foot, until Ulysses and Neoptolemus induced him to accompany them to Troy. He is said by Sophocles to have lived beside Mount Hermaeus, which Aeschylus (*Agam.* 262) makes one of the beacon points to flash the news of Troy's downfall home to Argos.

See Rhode, *Res Lemnicae*; Conze, *Reise auf den Inseln des Thrakischen Meeres* (from which the above-mentioned facts about the present state of the island are taken); also Hunt in Walpole's *Travels*; Belon du Mans, *Observations de plusieurs singularites*, &c.; Finlay, *Greece under the Romans*; von Hammer, *Gesch. des Osman. Reiches*; *Gött. Gel. Anz.* (1837). The chief references in ancient writers are *Iliad* i. 593, v. 138, xiv. 229, &c.; Herod. iv. 145; Str. pp. 124, 330; Plin. iv. 23, xxxvi. 13.

LEMOINNE, JOHN ÉMILE (1815–1892), French journalist, was born of French parents, in London, on the 17th of October 1815. He was educated first at an English school and then in France. In 1840 he began writing for the *Journal des débats*, on English and other foreign questions, and under the empire he held up to admiration the free institutions of England by contrast with imperial methods. After 1871 he supported Thiers, but his sympathies rather tended towards a liberalized monarchy, until the comte de Chambord's policy made such a development an impossibility, and he then ranged himself with the moderate Republicans. In 1875 Lemoinne was elected to the French Academy, and in 1880 he was nominated a life senator. Distinguished though he was for a real knowledge of England among the French journalists who wrote on foreign affairs, his tone towards English policy greatly changed in later days, and though he never shared the extreme French bitterness against England as regards Egypt, he maintained a critical attitude which served to stimulate French Anglophobia. He was a frequent contributor to the *Revue des deux mondes*, and published several books, the best known of which is his *Études critiques et biographiques* (1862). He died in Paris on the 14th of December 1892.

LEMON, MARK (1809–1870), editor of *Punch*, was born in London on the 30th of November 1809. He had a natural talent for journalism and the stage, and, at twenty-six, retired from less congenial business to devote himself to the writing of plays. More than sixty of his melodramas, operettas and comedies were produced in London. At the same time he contributed to a variety of magazines and newspapers, and founded and edited the *Field*. In 1841 Lemon and Henry Mayhew conceived the idea of a humorous weekly paper to be called *Punch*, and when the first number was issued, in July 1841, were joint-editors and, with the printer and engraver, equal owners. The paper was for some time unsuccessful, Lemon keeping it alive out of the profits of his plays. On the sale of *Punch* Lemon became sole editor for the new proprietors, and it remained under his control until his death, achieving remarkable popularity and influence. Lemon was an actor of ability, a pleasing lecturer and a successful impersonator of Shakespearian characters. He also wrote a host of novelettes and lyrics, over a hundred songs, a few three-volume novels, several Christmas fairy tales and a volume of jests. He died at Crawley, Sussex, on the 23rd of May 1870.

LEMON, the fruit of *Citrus Limonum*, which is regarded by some botanists as a variety of *Citrus medica*. The wild stock of the lemon tree is said to be a native of the valleys of Kumaon and Sikkim in the North-West provinces of India, ascending to a height of 4000 ft., and occurring under several forms. Sir George Watt (*Dictionary of Economic Products of India*, ii. 352) regards the wild plants as wild forms of the lime or citron and considers it highly probable that the wild form of the lemon has not yet been discovered.

The lemon seems to have been unknown to the ancient Greeks and Romans, and to have been introduced by the Arabs

FIG. 1.—Lemon—*Citrus Limonum*.

1, Flowering shoot.
2, Flower with two petals and two bundles of stamens removed; slightly enlarged.
3, Fruit.
4, Same cut across.
5, Seed.
6, Same cut lengthwise.

into Spain between the 12th and 13th centuries. In 1494 the fruit was cultivated in the Azores, and largely shipped to England, but since 1838 the exportation has ceased. As a cultivated plant the lemon is now met with throughout the Mediterranean region, in Spain and Portugal, in California and Florida, and in almost all tropical and subtropical countries. Like the apple and pear, it varies exceedingly under cultivation. Risso and Poiteau enumerate forty-seven varieties of this fruit, although they maintain as distinct the sweet lime, *C. Limetta*, with eight varieties, and the sweet lemon, *C. Lumia*, with twelve varieties, which differ only in the fruit possessing an insipid instead of an acid juice.

The lemon is more delicate than the orange, although, according to Humboldt, both require an annual mean temperature of 62° Fahr.

[illegible] a fine clear head of deep green [illegible] or small tree, 10 to 12 ft. high, [illegible] and short angular branches with [illegible] flowers, which possess a sweet odour [illegible] are in part hermaphrodite [illegible] of the corolla having a purplish [illegible] with a nipple, consists of [illegible] more or less rough [illegible] in it, and of a white inner [illegible] the whole of the interior [illegible] parenchymatous tissue, divided [illegible] each generally containing [illegible] varies much in thickness [illegible] As lemons [illegible] oranges, on account of their [illegible] during [illegible] preferred in Italy wherever [illegible] (see orange q.v.) [illegible] leaves, and fruit [illegible] coincident with or [illegible] *Chermes hesperidum* [illegible] and are suffer [illegible] or milk [illegible] they have [illegible] this fungoid [illegible] the lemon and citron [illegible] attributes the prevalence [illegible] the growers have [illegible] vitality [illegible] the lemon on [illegible] fruit until they [illegible]

The lemon tree is [illegible] in Spain or [illegible] favourable [illegible] more or [illegible] the chief [illegible] end of [illegible] the year [illegible] The fruit is [illegible] specimens [illegible] about four [illegible] which are [illegible] paper. [illegible] fruits are [illegible] The [illegible] but those [illegible] over [illegible] The exporta- [illegible] The large [illegible] market [illegible] and are [illegible]

[illegible] a larger [illegible]

alcoholic solution of shellac—the coating thus formed being easily removed when the fruit is required for household use by gently kneading it in the hands. Besides citric acid, lemon juice contains 3 to 4% of gum and sugar, albuminoid matters, malic acid and 2·28% of inorganic salts. Cossa has determined that the ash of dried lemon juice contains 54% of potash, besides 15% of phosphoric acid. In the white portion of the peel (in common with other fruits of the genus) a bitter principle called *hesperidin* has been found. It is very slightly soluble in boiling water, but is soluble in dilute alcohol and in alkaline solutions, which it soon turns of a yellow or reddish colour. It is also darkened by tincture of perchloride of iron. Another substance named *lemonin*, crystallizing in lustrous plates, was discovered in 1879 by Palerno and Aglialoro in the seeds, in which it is present in very small quantity, 15,000 grains of seed yielding only 80 grains of it. It differs from hesperidin in dissolving in potash without alteration. It melts at 275° F.

The simplest method of preserving lemon juice in small quantities for medicinal or domestic use is to keep it covered with a layer of olive or almond oil in a closed vessel furnished with a glass tap, by which the clear liquid may be drawn off as required. Lemon juice is largely used on shipboard as a preventive of scurvy. By the Merchant Shipping Act 1867 every British ship going to other countries where lemon or lime juice cannot be obtained was required to take sufficient to give 1 oz. to every member of the crew daily. Of this juice it requires about 13,000 lemons to yield 1 pipe (108 gallons). Sicilian juice in November yields about 9 oz. of crude citric acid per gallon, but only 6 oz. if the fruit is collected in April. The crude juice was formerly exported to England, and was often adulterated with sea-water, but is now almost entirely replaced by lime juice. A concentrated lemon juice for the manufacture of citric acid is prepared in considerable quantities, chiefly at Messina and Palermo, by boiling down the crude juice in copper vessels over an open fire until its specific gravity is about 1·239, seven to ten pipes of raw making only one of concentrated lemon juice. "Lemon juice" for use on shipboard is prepared also from the fruits of limes and Bergamot oranges. It is said to be sometimes adulterated with sulphuric acid on arrival in England.

The lemon used in medicine is described in the British pharmacopoeia as being the fruit of *Citrus medica*, var. Limonum. The preparations of lemon peel are of small importance. From the fresh peel is obtained the *oleum limonis* (dose ½-3 minims), which has the characters of its class. It contains a terpene known as citrene or limonene, which also occurs in orange peel: and citral, the aldehyde of geraniol, which is the chief constituent of oil of roses. Of much importance is the *succus limonis* or lemon juice, 1 oz. of which contains about 40 grains of free citric acid, besides the citrate of potassium (·25 %) and malic acid, free and combined. Ten per cent. of alcohol must be added to lemon juice if it is to be kept. From it are prepared the *syrupus limonis* (dose ½-2 drachms), which consists of sugar, lemon juice and an alcoholic extract of lemon peel, and also citric acid itself. Lemon juice is practically impure citric acid (*q.v.*).

Essence or Essential Oil of Lemon.—The essential oil contained in the rind of the lemon occurs in commerce as a distinct article. It is manufactured chiefly in Sicily, at Reggio in Calabria, and at Mentone and Nice in France. The small and irregularly shaped fruits are employed while still green, in which state the yield of oil is greater than when they are quite ripe. In Sicily and Calabria the oil is extracted in November and December as follows. A workman cuts three longitudinal slices off each lemon, leaving a three-cornered central core having a small portion of rind at the apex and base. These pieces are then divided transversely and cast on one side, and the strips of peel are thrown in another place. Next day the pieces of peel are deprived of their oil by pressing four or five times successively the outer surface of the peel (zest or flavedo) bent into a convex shape, against a flat sponge held in the palm of the left hand and wrapped round the forefinger. The oil vesicles in the rind, which are ruptured more easily in the fresh fruit than in the state in which lemons are imported, yield up their oil to the sponge, which when saturated is squeezed into an earthen vessel furnished with a spout and capable of holding about three pints. After a time the oil separates from the watery liquid which accompanies it, and is then decanted. By this process four hundred fruits yield 9 to 14 oz. of essence. The prisms of pulp are afterwards expressed to obtain lemon juice, and then distilled to obtain the small quantity of volatile oil they contain. At Mentone and Nice a different process is adopted. The lemons are placed in an *écuelle à piquer*, a shallow basin of pewter about 8½ in. in diameter, having a lip for pouring on one side and a closed tube at the bottom about 5 in. long and 1 in. in diameter. A number of stout brass pins stand up about half an inch from the bottom of the vessel. The workman rubs a lemon over these pins, which rupture the oil vesicles, and the oil collects in the tube, which when it becomes full is emptied into another vessel that it may separate from the aqueous liquid mixed with it. When filtered it is known as *Essence de citron au zeste*, or, in the English market, as perfumers' essence of lemon, inferior [illegible] being distinguished as druggists' essence of lemon. An [illegible] product is obtained by immersing the scarified lemons in [illegible] water and separating the oil which floats off. *Essence de* [illegible] is obtained by rubbing the surface of fresh lemons (or of those which have been submitted to the action of the *écuelle à piquer*) on a coarse grater of tinned iron, and distilling the grated peel. The oil so obtained is colourless, and of inferior fragrance, and is sold at a lower price, while that obtained by the cold processes has a yellow colour and powerful odour.

Essence of lemon is chiefly brought from Messina and Palermo packed in copper bottles holding 25 to 50 kilogrammes or more, and sometimes in tinned bottles of smaller size. It is said to be rarely found in a state of purity in commerce, almost all that comes into the market being diluted with the cheaper distilled oil. This fact may be considered as proved by the price at which the essence of lemon is sold in England, this being less than it costs the manufacturer to make it. When long kept the essence deposits a white greasy stearoptene, apparently identical with the bergaptene obtained from the essential oil of the Bergamot orange. The chief constituent of oil of lemon is the terpene, $C_{10}H_{16}$, boiling at 348°·8 Fahr., which, like oil of turpentine, readily yields crystals of terpin, $C_{10}H_{16}3OH_2$, but differs in yielding the crystalline compound, $C_{10}H_{16}+2Cl$, oil of turpentine forming one having the formula $C_{10}H_{16}+HCl$. Oil of lemons also contains, according to Tilden, another hydrocarbon, $C_{10}H_{16}$, boiling at 3·20° Fahr., a small amount of *cymene*, and a compound acetic ether, $C_2H_3O{\cdot}C_{10}H_{17}O$. The natural essence of lemon not being wholly soluble in rectified spirit of wine, an essence for culinary purposes is sometimes prepared by digesting 6 oz of lemon peel in one pint of pure alcohol of 95%, and, when the rind has become brittle, which takes place in about two and a half hours, powdering it and percolating the alcohol through it This article is known as "lemon flavour."

The name lemon is also applied to some other fruits. The Java lemon is the fruit of *Citrus javanica*, the pear lemon of a variety of *C. Limetta*, and the pearl lemon of *C. margarita*. The fruit of a passion-flower, *Passiflora laurifolia*, is sometimes known as the water-lemon, and that of a Berberidaceous plant, *Podophyllum peltatum*, as the wild lemon. In France and Germany the lemon is known as the citron, and hence much confusion arises concerning the fruits referred to in different works. The essential oil known as oil of cedrat is usually a factitious article instead of being prepared, as its name implies, from the citron (Fr. *cédratier*). An essential oil is also prepared from *C. Lumia*, at Squillace in Calabria, and has an odour like that of Bergamot but less powerful.

The sour lime is *Citrus acida*, generally regarded as a var. (*acida*) of *C. medica*. It is a native of India, ascending to about 4000 ft. in the mountains, and occurring as a small, much-branched thorny bush. The small flowers are white or tinged with pink

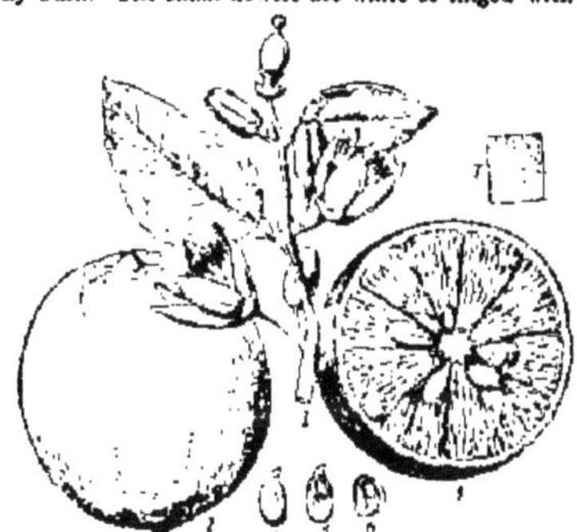

FIG. 2.—Lime—*Citrus medica*, var. *acida*.

1, Flowering shoot.
2, Fruit.
3, Same cut transversely.
4, Seed.
5, Seed cut lengthwise.
6, Seed cut transversely.
7, Superficial view of portion of rind showing oil glands.

on the outside; the fruit is small and generally round, with a thin, light green or lemon-yellow bitter rind, and a very sour, somewhat bitter juicy pulp. It is extensively cultivated throughout the West Indies, especially in Dominica, Montserrat and Jamaica, the approximate annual value of the exports from these islands being respectively £45,000, £6000 and £6000. The plants are grown from seed in nurseries and planted out about 200 to the acre. They begin to bear from about the third year, but full crops are not produced until the trees are six or seven years old. The ripe yellow fruit is gathered as it falls. The fruit is bruised by hand in a funnel-shaped vessel known as an *écuelle*, with a hollow stem; by rolling the fruit on a number of points on the side of the funnel the oil cells in the rind are broken and the oil collects in the hollow stem—this is the essential oil or essence of limes. The fruits are then taken to the mill, sorted, washed and passed through rollers and exposed to two squeezings. Two-thirds of the juice is expressed by the first squeezing, is strained at once, done up in puncheons and exported as raw juice. The product of the second squeezing, together with the juice extracted by a subsequent squeezing in a press, is strained and evaporated down to make concentrated juice; ten gallons of the raw juice yield one gallon of the concentrated juice. The raw juice is used for preparations of lime juice cordial, the concentrated for manufactures of citric acid.

On some estates citrate of lime is now manufactured in place of concentrated acid. Distilled oil of limes is prepared by distilling the juice, but its value is low in comparison with the expressed oil obtained by hand as described above. Green limes and pickled limes preserved in brine are largely exported to the United States, and more recently green limes have been exported to the United Kingdom. Limalade or preserved limes is an excellent substitute for marmalade. A spineless form of the lime appeared as a sport in Dominica in 1892, and is now grown there and elsewhere on a commercial scale. A form with seedless fruits has also recently been obtained in Dominica and Trinidad independently. The young leaves of the lime are used for perfuming the water in finger-glasses, a few being placed in the water and bruised before use.

LEMONNIER, ANTOINE LOUIS CAMILLE (1844–), Belgian poet, was born at Ixelles, Brussels, on the 24th of March 1844. He studied law, and then took a clerkship in a government office, which he resigned after three years. Lemonnier inherited Flemish blood from both parents, and with it the animal force and pictorial energy of the Flemish temperament. He published a *Salon de Bruxelles* in 1863, and again in 1866. His early friendships were chiefly with artists; and he wrote art criticisms with recognized discernment. Taking a house in the hills near Namur, he devoted himself to sport, and developed the intimate sympathy with nature which informs his best work. *Nos Flamands* (1869) and *Croquis d'automne* (1870) date from this time. *Paris-Berlin* (1870), a pamphlet pleading the cause of France, and full of the author's horror of war, had a great success. His capacity as a novelist, in the fresh, humorous description of peasant life, was revealed in *Un Coin de village* (1879). In *Un Mâle* (1881) he achieved a different kind of success. It deals with the amours of a poacher and a farmer's daughter, with the forest as a background. Cachaprès, the poacher, seems the very embodiment of the wild life around him. The rejection of *Un Mâle* by the judges for the quinquennial prize of literature in 1883 made Lemonnier the centre of a school, inaugurated at a banquet given in his honour on the 27th of May 1883. *Le Mort* (1882), which describes the remorse of two peasants for a murder they have committed, is a masterpiece in its vivid representation of terror. It was remodelled as a tragedy in five acts (Paris, 1899) by its author. *Ceux de la glèbe* (1889), dedicated to the "children of the soil," was written in 1885. He turned aside from local subjects for some time to produce a series of psychological novels, books of art criticism, &c., of considerable value, but assimilating more closely to French contemporary literature. The most striking of his later novels are: *L'Hystérique* (1885); *Happe-chair* (1886), often compared with Zola's *Germinal*; *Le Possédé* (1890); *La Fin des bourgeois* (1892); *L'Arche, journal d'une maman* (1894), a quiet book, quite different from his usual work; *La Faute de Mme Charvet* (1895); *L'Homme en amour* (1897); and, with a return to Flemish subjects, *Le Vent dans les moulins* (1901); *Petit Homme de Dieu* (1902), and *Comme va le ruisseau* (1903). In 1888 Lemonnier was prosecuted in Paris for offending against public morals by a story in *Gil Blas*, and was condemned to a fine. In a later prosecution at Brussels he was defended by Edmond Picard, and acquitted; and he was arraigned for a third time, at Bruges, for his *Homme en amour*, but again [illegible] in *Les Deux consciences* [illegible] of a trilogy to be called [illegible] under the fortunes of [illegible] sorrow and sacrifice to [illegible] In *Adam et Ève* [illegible] 1900), he preached the [illegible] of the individual but [illegible] more important works [illegible] *des Beaux-Arts* [illegible] (1888), dealing [illegible] *La Belgique* (1888), [illegible] many illustrations; *La* [illegible] (1906).

[illegible] was one of the early [illegible] He began to write at a [illegible] and with much toil, and [illegible] medium for the expression [illegible] process in a preface [illegible] *prose* (1902). His [illegible] abounds in neologisms [illegible]

[illegible] which contains [illegible] Edmond Picard, [illegible] various writers.

[illegible] (1715–1799), French [illegible] November 1715 in Paris, [illegible] at the collège [illegible] was made before [illegible] elaborate lunar map [illegible] on the 21st of [illegible] He was chosen in the [illegible] and Alexis Clairault [illegible] In 1738, shortly [illegible] read before the [illegible] mode of determining [illegible] in fact, [illegible] effectively [illegible] and constituted [illegible] He corresponded [illegible] effects of nutation [illegible] use of the transit- [illegible] visited England in [illegible] and James Short [illegible] where he observed [illegible] of Louis XV., in [illegible] with the means of [illegible] by English [illegible] be mentioned [illegible] of Jupiter by [illegible] and confirmed by [illegible] observations [illegible] researches in [illegible] in the latter [illegible] and the determina- [illegible] including twelve [illegible] and its discovery [illegible] France he first [illegible] gravitation, and [illegible] J. J. Lalande for [illegible] hasty utterances [illegible] forgive. Against [illegible] his doors" during [illegible] career was arrested [illegible] stroke terminated [illegible] 31st of May 1799. [illegible] he left three [illegible] J. L. Lagrange. [illegible] and was one of [illegible] of the Institute.

book; *Nouveau zodiaque* (1755); *Observations de la lune, du soleil, et des étoiles fixes* (1751–1775); *Lois du magnétisme* (1776–1778), &c.

See J. J. Lalande, *Bibl. astr.*, p. 819 (also in the *Journal des savants* for 1801); F. X. von Zach, *Allgemeine geog. Ephemeriden*, iii. 625; J. S. Bailly, *Hist. de l'astr. moderne*, iii.; J. B. J. Delambre, *Hist. de l'astr. au XVIIIe. siècle*, p. 179; J. Mädler, *Geschichte der Himmelskunde*, ii. 6; R. Wolf, *Geschichte der Astronomie*, p. 480.

LEMOYNE, JEAN BAPTISTE (1704–1778), French sculptor, was the pupil of his father, Jean Louis Lemoyne, and of Robert le Lorrain. He was a great figure in his day, around whose modest and kindly personality there waged opposing storms of denunciation and applause. Although his disregard of the classic tradition and of the essentials of dignified sculpture, as well as his lack of firmness and of intellectual grasp of the larger principles of his art, lay him open to stringent criticism, de Clarac's charge that he had delivered a mortal blow at sculpture is altogether exaggerated. Lemoyne's more important works have for the most part been destroyed or have disappeared. The equestrian statue of "Louis XV." for the military school, and the composition of "Mignard's daughter, Mme Feuquières, kneeling before her father's bust" (which bust was from the hand of Coysevox) were subjected to the violence by which Bouchardon's equestrian monument of Louis XIV. (*q.v.*) was destroyed. The panels only have been preserved. In his busts evidence of his riotous and florid imagination to a great extent disappears, and we have a remarkable series of important portraits, of which those of women are perhaps the best. Among Lemoyne's leading achievements in this class are "Fontenelle" (at Versailles), "Voltaire," "Latour" (all of 1748), "Duc de la Valière" (Versailles), "Comte de St Florentin," and "Crébillon" (Dijon Museum); "Mlle Chiron" and "Mlle Dangeville," both produced in 1761 and both at the Théâtre Français in Paris, and "Mme de Pompadour," the work of the same year. Of the Pompadour he also executed a statue in the costume of a nymph, very delicate and playful in its air of grace. Lemoyne was perhaps most successful in his training of pupils, one of the leaders of whom was Falconnet.

LEMPRIÈRE, JOHN (*c.* 1765–1824), English classical scholar, was born in Jersey, and educated at Winchester and Pembroke College, Oxford. He is chiefly known for his *Bibliotheca Classica* or *Classical Dictionary* (1788), which, edited by various later scholars, long remained a readable if not very trustworthy reference book in mythology and classical history. In 1792, after holding other scholastic posts, he was appointed to the head-mastership of Abingdon grammar school, and later became the vicar of that parish. While occupying this living, he published a *Universal Biography of Eminent Persons in all Ages and Countries* (1808). In 1809 he succeeded to the head-mastership of Exeter free grammar school. On retiring from this, in consequence of a disagreement with the trustees, he was given the living of Meeth in Devonshire, which, together with that of Newton Petrock, he held till his death in London on the 1st of February 1824.

LEMUR (from Lat. *lemures*, "ghosts"), the name applied by Linnaeus to certain peculiar Malagasy representatives of the order PRIMATES (*q.v.*) which do not come under the designation of either monkeys or apes, and, with allied animals from the same island and tropical Asia and Africa, constitute the sub-order *Prosimiae*, or *Lemuroidea*, the characteristics of which are given in the article just mentioned. The typical lemurs include species like *Lemur mongoz* and *L. catta*, but the English name "lemur" is often taken to include all the members of the sub-order, although the aberrant forms are often conveniently termed "lemuroids." All the Malagasy lemurs, which agree in the structure of the internal ear, are now included in the family *Lemuridae*, confined to Madagascar and the Comoro Islands, which comprises the great majority of the group. The other families are the *Nycticebidae*, common to tropical Asia and Africa, and the *Tarsiidae*, restricted to the Malay countries. In the more typical *Lemuridae* there are two pairs of upper incisor teeth, separated by a gap in the middle line; the premolars may be either two or three, but the molars, as in the lower jaw, are always three on each side. In the lower jaw the incisors and canines are directed straight forwards, and are of small size and nearly similar form; the function of the canine being discharged by the first premolar, which is larger than the other teeth of the same series. With the exception of the second toe of the hind-foot, the digits have well-formed, flattened nails as in the majority of monkeys. In the members of the typical genus *Lemur*, as well as in the allied *Hapalemur* and *Lepidolemur*, none of the toes or fingers are connected by webs, and all have the hind-limbs of moderate length, and the tail long. The maximum number of teeth is 36, there being typically two pairs of incisors and three of premolars in each jaw. In habits some of the species are nocturnal and others diurnal; but all subsist on a mixed diet, which includes birds, reptiles, eggs, insects and fruits. Most are arboreal, but the ring-tailed lemur (*L. catta*) often dwells among rocks. The species of the genus *Lemur* are diurnal, and may be recognized by the length of the muzzle, and the large tufted ears. In some cases, as in the black lemur (*L. macaco*) the two sexes are differently coloured; but in others, especially the ruffed lemur (*L. varius*), there is much individual variation in this respect, scarcely any two being alike. The gentle lemurs (*Hapalemur*) have a rounder head, with smaller ears and a shorter muzzle, and also a bare patch covered with spines on the fore-arm. The sportive lemurs (*Lepidolemur*) are smaller than the typical species of *Lemur*, and the adults generally lose their upper incisors. The head is short and conical, the ears large, round and mostly bare, and the tail shorter than the body. Like the gentle lemurs they are nocturnal. (See AVAHI, AYE-AYE, GALAGO, INDRI, LORIS, POTTO, SIFAKA and TARSIER.) (R. L.*)

LENA, a river of Siberia, rising in the Baikal Mountains, on the W. side of Lake Baikal, in 54° 10′ N. and 107° 55′ E. Wheeling round by the S., it describes a semicircle, then flows N.N.E. and N.E., being joined by the Kirenga and the Vitim, both from the right; from 113° E. it flows E.N.E as far as Yakutsk (62° N., 127° 40′ E.), where it enters the lowlands, after being joined by the Olekma, also from the right. From Yakutsk it goes N. until joined by its right-hand affluent the Aldan, which deflects it to the north-west; then, after receiving its most important left-hand tributary, the Vilyui, it makes its way nearly due N. to the Nordenskjöld Sea, a division of the Arctic, disemboguing S.W. of the New Siberian Islands by a delta 10,800 sq. m. in area, and traversed by seven principal branches, the most important being Bylov, farthest east. The total length of the river is estimated at 2860 m. The delta arms sometimes remain blocked with ice the whole year round. At Yakutsk navigation is generally practicable from the middle of May to the end of October, and at Kirensk, at the confluence of the Lena and the Kirenga, from the beginning of May to about the same time. Between these two towns there is during the season regular steamboat communication. The area of the river basin is calculated at 895,500 sq. m. Gold is washed out of the sands of the Vitim and the Olekma, and tusks of the mammoth are dug out of the delta.

See G. W. Melville, *In the Lena Delta* (1885).

LE NAIN, the name of three brothers, LOUIS, ANTOINE and MATHIEU, who occupy a peculiar position in the history of French art. Although they figure amongst the original members of the French Academy, their works show no trace of the influences which prevailed when that body was founded. Their sober execution and choice of colour recall characteristics of the Spanish school, and when the world of Paris was busy with mythological allegories, and the "heroic deeds" of the king, the three Le Nain devoted themselves chiefly to subjects of humble life such as "Boys Playing Cards," "The Forge," or "The Peasants' Meal." These three paintings are now in the Louvre; various others may be found in local collections, and some fine drawings may be seen in the British Museum; but the Le Nain signature is rare, and is never accompanied by initials which might enable us to distinguish the work of the brothers. Their lives are lost in obscurity; all that can be affirmed is that they were born at Laon in Picardy towards the close of the 16th century. About 1629 they went to Paris; in 1648 the three brothers were received into the Academy, and in the same year both Antoine and Louis died. Mathieu lived on till August 1677; he bore the title of chevalier, and painted many portraits. Mary of Medici and Mazarin were amongst his sitters, but these works seem to have disappeared.

See Champfleury, *Essai sur la vie et l'œuvre des Le Nain* (1850), and *Catalogue des tableaux des Le Nain* (1861).

LENAU, NIKOLAUS, the pseudonym of NIKOLAUS FRANZ NIEMBSCH VON STREHLENAU (1802–1850), Austrian poet, who was born at Csatád near Temesvar in Hungary, on the 15th of August 1802. His father, a government official, died at Budapest in 1807, leaving his children to the care of an affectionate, but jealous and somewhat hysterical, mother, who in 1811 married again. In 1819 the boy went to the university of Vienna; he subsequently studied Hungarian law at Pressburg and then spent the best part of four years in qualifying himself in medicine. But he was unable to settle down to any profession. He had early begun to write verses; and the disposition to sentimental melancholy acquired from his mother, stimulated by love disappointments and by the prevailing fashion of the romantic school of poetry, settled into gloom after his mother's death in 1829. Soon afterwards a legacy from his grandmother enabled him to devote himself wholly to poetry. His first published poems appeared in 1827, in J. G. Seidl's *Aurora*. In 1831 he went to Stuttgart, where he published a volume of *Gedichte* (1832) dedicated to the Swabian poet Gustav Schwab. Here he also made the acquaintance of Uhland, Justinus Kerner, Karl Mayer[1] and others; but his restless spirit longed for change, and he determined to seek for peace and freedom in America. In October 1832 he landed at Baltimore and settled on a homestead in Ohio. But the reality of life in "the primeval forest" fell lamentably short of the ideal he had pictured; he disliked the Americans with their eternal "English lisping of dollars" (*englisches Talergelispel*); and in 1833 he returned to Germany, where the appreciation of his first volume of poems revived his spirits. From now on he lived partly in Stuttgart and partly in Vienna. In 1836 appeared his *Faust*, in which he laid bare his own soul to the world; in 1837, *Savonarola*, an epic in which freedom from political and intellectual tyranny is insisted upon as essential to Christianity. In 1838 appeared his *Neuere Gedichte*, which prove that *Savonarola* had been but the result of a passing exaltation. Of these new poems, some of the finest were inspired by his hopeless passion for Sophie von Löwenthal, the wife of a friend, whose acquaintance he had made in 1833 and who "understood him as no other." In 1842 appeared *Die Albigenser*, and in 1844 he began writing his *Don Juan*, a fragment of which was published after his death. Soon afterwards his never well-balanced mind began to show signs of aberration, and in October 1844 he was placed under restraint. He died in the asylum at Oberdöbling near Vienna on the 22nd of August 1850. Lenau's fame rests mainly upon his shorter poems; even his epics are essentially lyric in quality. He is the greatest modern lyric poet of Austria, and the typical representative in German literature of that pessimistic *Weltschmerz* which, beginning with Byron, reached its culmination in the poetry of Leopardi.

Lenau's *Sämtliche Werke* were published in 4 vols. by A. Grün (1855); but there are several more modern editions, as those by M. Koch in Kürschner's *Deutsche Nationalliteratur*, vols. 154-155 (1888), and by E. Castle (2 vols., 1900). See A. Schurz, *Lenaus Leben, grossentheils aus des Dichters eigenen Briefen* (1855); L. A. Frankl, *Zu Lenaus Biographie* (1854, 2nd ed., 1885); A. Marchand, *Les Poètes lyriques de l'Autriche* (1881); L. A. Frankl, *Lenaus Tagebuch und Briefe an Sophie Löwenthal* (1891); A. Schlossar, *Lenaus Briefe an die Familie Reinbeck* (1896); L. Roustan, *Lenau et son temps* (1898); E. Castle, *Lenau und die Familie Löwenthal* (1906).

LENBACH, FRANZ VON (1836–1904), German painter, was born at Schrobenhausen, in Bavaria, on the 13th of December 1836. His father was a mason, and the boy was intended to follow his father's trade or be a builder. With this view he was sent to school at Landsberg, and then to the polytechnic at Augsburg. But after seeing Hofner, the animal painter, execut-

[1] Karl Friedrich Hartmann Mayer (1786–1870), poet, and biographer of Uhland, was by profession a lawyer and government official in Württemberg.

[illegible] at painting, which [illegible] when he had seen [illegible] he finally obtained his [illegible] and worked for a short [illegible] after this he devoted [illegible] was already accomplished in [illegible] Piloty, with whom he [illegible] interesting works remain as [illegible] Peasant seeking Shelter [illegible] Shepherd" (1860, in the [illegible] Arch of Titus" (in the [illegible] returning to Munich, he was [illegible] the appointment of professor [illegible] having made the [illegible] commissioned a great [illegible] Lenbach returned to Italy [illegible] many famous pictures. He [illegible] copied not only the famous [illegible] but also some landscapes [illegible] Alhambra (1868). In the [illegible] great exhibition at Paris [illegible] third-class medal. There- [illegible] at Munich and at Vienna, [illegible] was awarded a Grand Prix [illegible] painted many of the [illegible]

[illegible] Velhagen und Klasings Monatshefte [illegible] à l'exposition de Munich [illegible] Franz von Lenbach Bildnisse

[illegible], the daughter of a gentle- [illegible] was born in Paris in November [illegible] divides into two periods, [illegible] was the typical Frenchwoman [illegible] society of the 17th century, [illegible] of the fashion in Paris, [illegible] All that can be pleaded in [illegible] had been educated by her [illegible] and that she retained [illegible] disregard of money, which [illegible] that she was an *honnête* [illegible] distinguished lovers, among [illegible] marquis d'Estrées, La [illegible] Queen Christina [illegible] Austria was powerless [illegible] her career for a pre- [illegible] down to the social leadership [illegible] Mme de la Sablière, [illegible] Maintenon. It became the [illegible] to throng round her, and [illegible] young man who wished to [illegible] to Mlle de Lenclos. [illegible] must be briefly [illegible] had been lovers in [illegible] the wit seems to have [illegible] The few really authentic [illegible] to her old friend, and the [illegible] of their equally long lives [illegible] in the polite compliments [illegible] If Ninon owes part of [illegible] she owes at least as [illegible] to her as a promising boy [illegible] he left 2000 francs [illegible] was the chief authority of [illegible] personal appearance is, [illegible] described in *Clélie*, a novel by [illegible] as Clarisse. Her distin- [illegible] beauty nor wit, but high [illegible] according [illegible]

interesting notice of these letters in the *Causeries du Lundi*, vol. iv. The *Correspondance authentique* was edited by E. Colombey in 1886. See also Helen K. Hayes, *The Real Ninon de l'Enclos* (1908); and Mary C. Rowsell, *Ninon de l'Enclos and her century* (1910).

LENFANT, JACQUES (1661–1728), French Protestant divine, was born at Bazoche in La Beauce on the 13th of April 1661, son of Paul Lenfant, Protestant pastor at Bazoche and afterwards at Châtillon-sur-Loing until the revocation of the edict of Nantes, when he removed to Cassel. After studying at Saumur and Geneva, Lenfant completed his theological course at Heidelberg, where in 1684 he was ordained minister of the French Protestant church, and appointed chaplain to the dowager electress palatine. When the French invaded the Palatinate in 1688 Lenfant withdrew to Berlin, as in a recent book he had vigorously attacked the Jesuits. Here in 1689 he was again appointed one of the ministers of the French Protestant church; this office he continued to hold until his death, ultimately adding to it that of chaplain to the king, with the dignity of *Consistorialrath*. He visited Holland and England in 1707, preached before Queen Anne, and, it is said, was invited to become one of her chaplains. He was the author of many works, chiefly on church history. In search of materials he visited Helmstädt in 1712, and Leipzig in 1715 and 1725. He died at Berlin on the 7th of August 1728.

An exhaustive catalogue of his publications, thirty-two in all, will be found in J. G. de Chauffepié's *Dictionnaire*. See also E. and S. Haag's *France Protestante*. He is now best known by his *Histoire du concile de Constance* (Amsterdam, 1714; 2nd ed., 1728; English trans., 1730). It is of course largely dependent upon the laborious work of Hermann von der Hardt (1660–1746), but has literary merits peculiar to itself, and has been praised on all sides for its fairness. It was followed by *Histoire du concile de Pise* (1724), and (posthumously) by *Histoire de la guerre des Hussites et du concile de Basle* (Amsterdam, 1731; German translation, Vienna, 1783–1784). Lenfant was one of the chief promoters of the *Bibliothèque Germanique*, begun in 1720; and he was associated with Isaac Beausobre (1659–1738) in the preparation of the new French translation of the New Testament with original notes, published at Amsterdam in 1718.

LENKORAN, a town in Russian Transcaucasia, in the government of Baku, stands on the Caspian Sea, at the mouth of a small stream of its own name, and close to a large lagoon. The lighthouse stands in 38° 45′ 38″ N. and 48° 50′ 18″ E. Taken by storm on New Year's day 1813 by the Russians, Lenkoran was in the same year formally surrendered by Persia to Russia by the treaty of Gulistan, along with the khanate of Talysh, of which it was the capital. Pop. (1867) 15,933, (1897) 8768. The fort has been dismantled; and in trade the town is outstripped by Astara, the customs station on the Persian frontier.

The District of Lenkoran (2117 sq. m.) is a thickly wooded mountainous region, shut off from the Persian plateau by the Talysh range (7000–8000 ft. high), and with a narrow marshy strip along the coast. The climate is exceptionally moist and warm (annual rainfall 52·79 in.; mean temperature in summer 75° F., in winter 40°), and fosters the growth of even Indian species of vegetation. The iron tree (*Parrotia persica*), the silk acacia, *Carpinus betulus*, *Quercus iberica*, the box tree and the walnut flourish freely, as well as the sumach, the pomegranate, and the *Gleditschia caspica*. The Bengal tiger is not unfrequently met with, and wild boars are abundant. Of the 131,361 inhabitants in 1897 the Talyshes (35,000) form the aboriginal element, belonging to the Iranian family, and speaking an independently developed language closely related to Persian. They are of middle height and dark complexion, with generally straight nose, small round skull, small sharp chin and large full eyes, which are expressive, however, rather of cunning than intelligence. They live exclusively on rice. In the northern half of the district the Tatar element predominates (40,000) and there are a number of villages occupied by Russian Raskolniks (Nonconformists). Agriculture, bee-keeping, silkworm-rearing and fishing are the principal occupations.

LENNEP, JACOB VAN (1802–1868), Dutch poet and novelist, was born on the 24th of March 1802 at Amsterdam, where his father, David Jacob van Lennep (1774–1853), a scholar and poet, was professor of eloquence and the classical languages in the Athenaeum. Lennep took the degree of doctor of laws at Leiden, and then settled as an advocate in Amsterdam. His first poetical efforts had been translations from Byron, of whom he was an ardent admirer, and in 1826 he published a collection of original *Academische Idyllen*, which had some success. He first attained genuine popularity by the *Nederlandsche Legenden* (2 vols., 1828) which reproduced, after the manner of Sir Walter Scott, some of the more stirring incidents in the early history of his fatherland. His fame was further raised by his patriotic songs at the time of the Belgian revolt, and by his comedies *Het Dorp aan de Grenzen* (1830) and *Het Dorp over de Grenzen* (1831), which also had reference to the political events of 1830. In 1833 he broke new ground with the publication of *De Pleegzoon* (*The Adopted Son*), the first of a series of historical romances in prose, which have acquired for him in Holland a position somewhat analogous to that of Sir Walter Scott in Great Britain. The series included *De Roos van Dekama* (2 vols., 1836), *Onze Voorouders* (5 vols., 1838), *De Lotgevallen van Ferdinand Huyck* (2 vols., 1840), *Elizabeth Musch* (3 vols., 1850), and *De Lotgevallen van Klaasje Zevenster* (5 vols., 1865), several of which have been translated into German and French, and two—*The Rose of Dekama* (1847) and *The Adopted Son* (New York, 1847)—into English. His Dutch history for young people (*Voornaamste Geschiedenissen van Noord-Nederland aan mijne Kindern verhaald*, 4 vols., 1845) is attractively written. Apart from the two comedies already mentioned, Lennep was an indefatigable journalist and literary critic, the author of numerous dramatic pieces, and of an excellent edition of Vondel's works. For some years Lennep held a judicial appointment, and from 1853 to 1856 he was a member of the second chamber, in which he voted with the conservative party. He died at Oosterbeek near Arnheim on the 25th of August 1868.

There is a collective edition of his *Poetische Werken* (13 vols., 1859–1872), and also of his *Romantische Werken* (23 vols., 1855–1872). See also a bibliography by P. Knoll (1869); and Jan ten Brink, *Geschiedenis der Noord-Nederlandsche Letteren in de XIXe Eeuw* (No. iii.).

LENNEP, a town of Germany, in the Prussian Rhine province, 18 m. E. of Düsseldorf, and 9 m. S. of Barmen by rail, at a height of 1000 ft. above the level of the sea. Pop. (1905) 10,323. It lies in the heart of one of the busiest industrial districts in Germany, and carries on important manufactures of the finer kinds of cloth, wool, yarn and felt, and also of iron and steel goods. It has an Evangelical and a Protestant church, a modern school and a well-equipped hospital. Lennep, which was the residence of the counts of Berg from 1226 to 1300, owes the foundation of its prosperity to an influx of Cologne weavers during the 14th century.

LENNOX, a name given to a large district in Dumbartonshire and Stirlingshire, which was erected into an earldom in the latter half of the 12th century. It embraced the ancient sheriffdom of Dumbarton and nineteen parishes with the whole of the lands round Loch Lomond, formerly Loch Leven, and the river of that name which glides into the estuary of the Clyde at the ancient castle of Dumbarton.

On this river Leven, at Balloch, was the seat of Alwin, first earl of Lennox. It is probable that he was of Celtic descent, but the records are silent as to his part in history; that he was earl at all is only proved from the charters of his son, another Alwin, and he died some time before 1217. The second Alwin was father of ten sons, one of whom founded the clan Macfarlane, famous in the annals of the district, while another was ancestor of Walter of Farlane, who married the heiress of the 6th earl of Lennox. Maldouen, the 3rd earl, eldest of the sons of Alwin the younger, is an historical personage; he was a witness to the treaty between Alexander II., king of Scotland, and his brother-in-law the English king Henry III., at Newcastle in 1237, concerning the much disputed northern counties of England. His grandson, Malcolm, successor to the title, swore fealty to Edward I. in 1296; it was apparently his son, another Malcolm, the 5th earl, who was summoned by Edward to parliament and entrusted with the important post of guarding the fords of the river Forth. But the 5th earl soon after gave his services to the party of Bruce, the cause of that family having been embraced by his father as early as 1292. As a result the English king bestowed the earldom on Sir John Menteith, who was holding it in 1307 while the real earl was with King Robert Bruce in his wanderings in the Lennox country. For his services he was rewarded with a renewal of the earldom and the keeping of Dumbarton Castle; he fell fighting for his country at Halidon Hill in 1333. His son Donald, the 6th earl, an adherent of King David II., left a daughter, Margaret, countess of Lennox, who was married to her kinsman the above-mentioned Walter of Farlane, nearest heir male of the Lennox family.

In 1392, on the marriage of their grand-daughter Isabella, eldest daughter of Duncan, 8th earl, with Sir Murdoch Stewart, afterwards duke of Albany, the earldom was resigned into the hands of the king, who re-granted it to Earl Duncan, with remainder to the heirs male of his body, with remainder to Murdoch and Isabella and the heirs of their bodies begotten between them, with eventual remainder to Earl Duncan's nearest and lawful heirs. In 1424, when Murdoch, then duke of Albany, succeeded in ransoming the poet king James I. from his long English captivity, the aged Earl Duncan went with the Scottish party to Durham. The next year, however, he suffered the fate of Albany, being executed perhaps for no other reason than that he was his father-in-law. The earldom was not forfeited, and the widowed duchess of Albany, now also countess of Lennox, lived secure in her island castle of Inchmurrin on Loch Lomond until her death. Of her four sons, none of whom left legitimate issue, the eldest died in 1421, the two next suffered their father's fate at Stirling, while the youngest had to flee for his life to Ireland. Her daughter Isobel appears to have been the wife of Sir Walter Buchanan of that ilk.

It was from Elizabeth, sister of the countess, that the next holders of the title descended. She was married to Sir John Stewart of Darnley (distinguished in the military history of France as seigneur d'Aubigny), whose immediate ancestor was brother of James, 5th high steward of Scotland. Their grandson, another Sir John Stewart, created a lord of parliament as Lord Darnley, was served heir to his great-grandfather Duncan, earl of Lennox, in 1473, and was designated as earl of Lennox in a charter under the great seal in the same year. Thereafter followed disputes with John of Haldane, whose wife's great-grandmother had been another of the three daughters of Duncan, 8th earl of Lennox, and in her right he contested the succession. Lord Darnley, however, appears to have silenced all opposition and for the last seven years of his life maintained his right to the earldom undisputed. Three of his younger sons were greatly distinguished in the French service, one being captain of Scotsmen-at-arms, another *premier homme d'armes*, and a third *maréchal de France*. Their elder brother Matthew, 2nd earl of this line, fell on Flodden Field, leaving by his wife Elizabeth, daughter of James, earl of Arran, and niece of James III., a son and successor John, who became one of the guardians of James V. and was murdered in 1526. His son Matthew, the 4th earl, played a great part in the intrigues of his time, and by his marriage with Margaret Douglas allied himself to the royal house of England as well as strengthening the ties which bound his family to that of Scotland; because Margaret was the daughter and heir of the 6th earl of Angus by his wife, Margaret Tudor, sister of King Henry VIII. and widow of King James IV. Though his estates were forfeited in 1545, Earl Matthew in 1564 not only had them restored but had the satisfaction of getting his eldest son Henry married to Mary, queen of Scots. The murder of Lord Darnley, now created earl of Rosse, lord of Ardmanoch and duke of Albany, took place in February 1567, and in July his only son James, by Mary's abdication, became king of Scotland. The old earl of Lennox, now grandfather of his sovereign, obtained the regency in 1570, but in the next year was killed in the attack made on the parliament at Stirling, being the third earl in succession to meet with a violent death.

The title was now merged in the crown in the person of

[illegible] granimother's French [illegible], as were the [illegible] Lady Charlotte Gordon. [illegible] estates of her family [illegible] of Gordon being taken [illegible] Lennox on the death of his [illegible] In the next generation further [illegible] in the person of the 6th [illegible] great public services with the [illegible] Kinrara in the peerage [illegible]

[illegible] accounts of these peerages [illegible] Dept. H.M. Register [illegible] Grant, Rothesay Herald.

[illegible], daughter [illegible] New York, [illegible] She went to London in 1735, and, being left [illegible] death, she began to earn her [illegible] made some unsuccessful appearances [illegible] Samuel Johnson had an [illegible] "Three such women," he [illegible] Hannah More and Fanny [illegible] I know not where to find a [illegible] who is superior to them all." Her [illegible] *Adventures of* [illegible] *corrected; or the novels* [illegible] 1753–1754), [illegible] Shakespeare had spoiled the stories [illegible] unnecessary intrigues [illegible], a novel; and [illegible] Covent Garden [illegible] February [illegible] was withdrawn after the first night, after a [illegible] to the fact that its author [illegible]

[illegible], MARGARET, Countess of [illegible], daughter [illegible] Douglas, [illegible] earl of Angus, and Margaret Tudor, [illegible] of England and widow of James IV. of [illegible] was born at Harbottle Castle, Northumberland, on [illegible] 1515. On account of her nearness to the [illegible] Lady Margaret Douglas was brought up chiefly [illegible] court in close association with the Princess Mary, [illegible] her best friend throughout life. She was high [illegible] favour, but was twice disgraced; first for an [illegible] to Lord Thomas Howard, who died in the Tower [illegible] and again in 1541 for a similar affair with Sir Charles [illegible] brother of Queen Catherine Howard. In 1544 she married a Scottish exile, Matthew Stewart, 4th earl of Lennox [illegible] who was regent of Scotland in 1570–1571. During [illegible] reign the countess of Lennox had rooms in Westminster [illegible], but on Elizabeth's accession she removed to Yorkshire, where her home at Temple Newsam became a centre for Catholic intrigue. By a series of successful manœuvres she married her son Henry Stewart, Lord Darnley, to Mary, queen of Scots. In [illegible] she was sent to the Tower, but after the murder of Darnley in 1567 she was released. She was at first loud in her denunciations of Mary, but was eventually reconciled with her daughter-in-law. In 1574 she again aroused Elizabeth's anger by the marriage of her son Charles, earl of Lennox, with Elizabeth Cavendish, daughter of the earl of Shrewsbury. She was sent to the Tower with Lady Shrewsbury, and was only pardoned after her son's death in 1577. Her diplomacy largely contributed to the future succession of her grandson James to the English throne. She died on the 7th of March 1578.

The famous Lennox jewel, made for Lady Lennox as a memento of her husband, was bought by Queen Victoria in 1842.

LENO, DAN, the stage-name of George Galvin (1861–1904), English comedian, who was born at Somers Town, London, in February 1861. His parents were actors, known as Mr and Mrs Johnny Wilde. Dan Leno was trained to be an acrobat, but soon became a dancer, travelling with his brother as "the brothers Leno," and winning the world's championship in clog-dancing at Leeds in 1880. Shortly afterwards he appeared in London at the Oxford, and in 1886–1887 at the Surrey Theatre. In 1888–1889 he was engaged by Sir Augustus Harris to play the Baroness in the *Babes in the Wood*, and from that time he was a principal figure in the Drury Lane pantomimes. He was the wittiest and most popular comedian of his day, and delighted London music-hall audiences by his shop-walker, stores-proprietor, waiter, doctor, beef-eater, bathing attendant, "Mrs Kelly," and other impersonations. In 1900 he engaged to give his entire services to the Pavilion Music Hall, where he received £100 per week. In November 1901 he was summoned to Sandringham to do a "turn" before the king, and was proud from that time to call himself the "king's jester." Dan Leno's generosity endeared him to his profession, and he was the object of much sympathy during the brain failure which recurred during the last eighteen months of his life. He died on the 31st of October 1904.

LENORMANT, FRANÇOIS (1837–1883), French Assyriologist and archaeologist, was born in Paris on the 17th of January 1837. His father, Charles Lenormant, distinguished as an archaeologist, numismatist and Egyptologist, was anxious that his son should follow in his steps. He made him begin Greek at the age of six, and the child responded so well to this precocious scheme of instruction, that when he was only fourteen an essay of his, on the Greek tablets found at Memphis, appeared in the *Revue archéologique*. In 1856 he won the numismatic prize of the Académie des Inscriptions with an essay entitled *Classification des monnaies des Lagides*. In 1862 he became sub-librarian of the Institute. In 1859 he accompanied his father on a journey of exploration to Greece, during which Charles Lenormant succumbed to fever at Athens (24th November). Lenormant returned to Greece three times during the next six years, and gave up all the time he could spare from his official work to archaeological research. These peaceful labours were rudely interrupted by the war of 1870, when Lenormant served with the army and was wounded in the siege of Paris. In 1874 he was appointed professor of archaeology at the National Library, and in the following year he collaborated with Baron de Witte in founding the *Gazette archéologique*. As early as 1867 he had turned his attention to Assyrian studies; he was among the first to recognize in the cuneiform inscriptions the existence of a non-Semitic language, now known as Accadian. Lenormant's knowledge was of encyclopaedic extent, ranging over an immense number of subjects, and at the same time thorough, though somewhat lacking perhaps in the strict accuracy of the modern school. Most of his varied studies were directed towards tracing the origins of the two great civilizations of the ancient world, which were to be sought in Mesopotamia and on the shores of the Mediterranean. He had a perfect passion for exploration. Besides his early expeditions to Greece, he visited the south of Italy three times with this object, and it was while exploring in Calabria that he met with an accident which ended fatally in Paris on the 9th of December 1883, after a long illness. The amount and variety of Lenormant's work is truly amazing when it is remembered that he died at the early age of forty-six. Probably the best known of his books are *Les Origines de l'histoire d'après la Bible*, and his ancient history of the East and account of Chaldean magic. For breadth of view, combined with extraordinary subtlety of intuition, he was probably unrivalled.

LENOX, a township of Berkshire county, Massachusetts, U.S.A. Pop. (1900) 2942, (1905) 3058; (1910) 3060. Area, 19·2 sq. m. The principal village, also named Lenox (or Lenox-on-the-Heights), lies about 2 m. W. of the Housatonic river, at an altitude of about 1000 ft., and about it are high hills—Yokun Seat (2080 ft.), South Mountain (1200 ft.), Bald Head (1583 ft.), and Rattlesnake Hill (1540 ft.). New Lenox and Lenoxdale are other villages in the township. Lenox is a fashionable summer and autumn resort, much frequented by wealthy people from Washington, Newport and New York. There are innumerable lovely walks and drives in the surrounding region, which contains some of the most beautiful country of the Berkshires—hills, lakes, charming intervales and woods. As early as 1835 Lenox began to attract summer residents. In the next decade began the creation of large estates, although the great holdings of the present day, and the villas scattered over the hills, are comparatively recent features. The height of the season is in the autumn, when there are horse-shows, golf, tennis, hunts and other outdoor amusements. The Lenox library (1855) contained about 20,000 volumes in 1908. Lenox was settled about 1750, was included in Richmond township in 1765, and became an independent township in 1767. The names were those of Sir Charles Lennox, third duke of Richmond and of Lennox (1735–1806), one of the staunch friends of the American colonies during the War of Independence. Lenox was the county-seat from 1787 to 1868. It has literary associations with Catherine M. Sedgwick (1789–1867), who passed here the second half of her life; with Nathaniel Hawthorne, whose brief residence here (1850–1851) was marked by the production of the *House of the Seven Gables* and the *Wonder Book*; with Fanny Kemble, a summer resident from 1836–1853; and with Henry Ward Beecher (see his *Star Papers*). Elizabeth (Mrs Charles) Sedgwick, the sister-in-law of Catherine Sedgwick, maintained here from 1828 to 1864 a school for girls, in which Harriet Hosmer, the sculptor, and Maria S. Cummins (1827–1866), the novelist, were educated, and in Lenox academy (1803), a famous classical school (now a public high school) were educated W. L. Yancey, A. H. Stephens, Mark Hopkins and David Davis (1815–1886), a circuit judge of Illinois from 1848 to 1862, a justice (1862–1877) of the United States Supreme Court, a Republican member of the United States Senate from Illinois in 1877–1883, and president of the Senate from the 31st of October 1881, when he succeeded Chester A. Arthur, until the 3rd of March 1883. There is a statue commemorating General John Paterson (1744–1808) a soldier from Lenox in the War of Independence.

See R. de W. Mallary, *Lenox and the Berkshire Highlands* (1902); J. C. Adams, *Nature Studies in Berkshire*; C. F. Warner, *Picturesque Berkshire* (1890); and Katherine M. Abbott, *Old Paths and Legends of the New England Border* (1907).

LENS, a town of Northern France, in the department of Pas-de-Calais, 13 m. N.N.E. of Arras by rail on the Deûle and on the Lens canal. Pop. (1906) 27,692. Lens has important iron and steel foundries, and engineering works and manufactories of steel cables, and occupies a central position in the coalfields of the department. Two and a half miles W.S.W. lies Liévin (pop. 22,070), likewise a centre of the coalfield. In 1648 the neighbourhood of Lens was the scene of a celebrated victory gained by Louis II. of Bourbon, prince of Condé, over the Spaniards.

LENS (from Lat. *lens*, lentil, on account of the similarity of the form of a lens to that of a lentil seed), in optics, an instrument which refracts the luminous rays proceeding from an object in such a manner as to produce an image of the object. It may be regarded as having four principal functions: (1) to produce an image larger than the object, as in the magnifying glass, microscope, &c.; (2) to produce an image smaller than the object, as in the ordinary photographic camera; (3) to convert rays proceeding from a point or other luminous source into a definite pencil, as in light-house lenses, the engraver's globe, &c.; (4) to collect luminous and heating rays into a smaller area, as in the burning glass. A lens made up of two or more lenses cemented together or very close to each other is termed "composite" or "compound"; several lenses arranged in succession at a distance from each other form a "system of lenses," and if the axes be collinear a "centred system." This article is concerned with the general theory of lenses, and more particularly with spherical lenses. For a special part of the theory of lenses see ABERRATION; the instruments in which the lenses occur are treated under their own headings.

The most important type of lens is the spherical lens, which is a piece of transparent material bounded by two spherical surfaces, the boundary at the edge being usually cylindrical or conical. The line joining the centres, C_1, C_2 (fig. 1), of the bounding surfaces is termed the *axis*; the points S_1, S_2, at

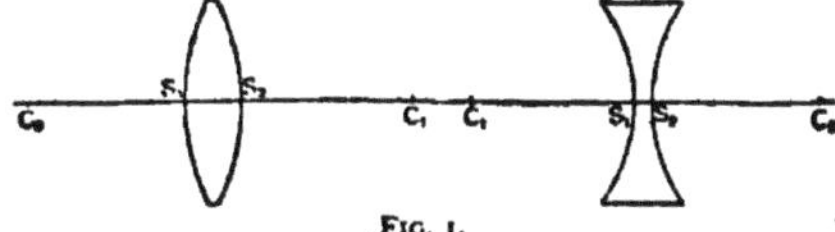

FIG. 1.

which the axis intersects the surfaces, are termed the "vertices" of the lens; and the distance between the vertices is termed the "thickness." If the edge be everywhere equidistant from the vertex, the lens is "centred."

Although light is really a wave motion in the aether, it is only necessary, in the investigation of the optical properties of systems of lenses, to trace the rectilinear path of the waves, *i.e.* the direction of the normal to the wave front, and this can be done by purely geometrical methods. It will be assumed that light, so long as it traverses the same medium, always travels in a straight line; and in following out the geometrical theory it will always be assumed that the light travels from left to right; accordingly all distances measured in this direction are positive, while those measured in the opposite direction are negative.

Theory of Optical Representation.—If a pencil of rays, *i.e.* the totality of the rays proceeding from a luminous point, falls on a lens or lens system, a section of the pencil, determined by the dimensions of the system, will be transmitted. The emergent rays will have directions differing from those of the incident rays, the alteration, however, being such that the transmitted rays are convergent in the "image-point," just as the incident rays diverge from the "object-point." With each incident ray is associated an emergent ray; such pairs are termed "conjugate ray pairs." Similarly we define an object-point and its image-point as "conjugate points"; all object-points lie in the "object-space," and all image-points lie in the "image-space."

The laws of optical representations were first deduced in their most general form by E. Abbe, who assumed (1) that an optical representation always exists, and (2) that to every point in the

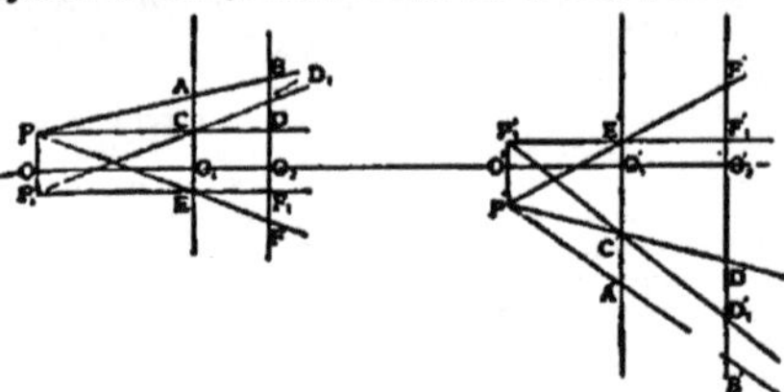

FIG. 2.

object-space there corresponds a point in the image-space, these points being mutually convertible by straight rays; in other words, with each object-point is associated one, and only one, image-point, and if the object-point be placed at the image-point, the conjugate point is the original object-point. Such a transformation is termed a "collineation," since it transforms points into points and straight lines into straight lines. Prior to Abbe, however, James Clerk Maxwell published, in 1856, a geometrical theory of optical representation, but his methods were unknown to Abbe and to his pupils until O. Eppenstein drew attention to them. Although Maxwell's theory is not so general as Abbe's, it is used here since its methods permit a simple and convenient deduction of the laws.

Maxwell assumed that two object-planes perpendicular to the axis are represented sharply and similarly in two image-planes also perpendicular to the axis (by "sharply" is meant that the assumed ideal instrument unites all the rays proceeding from an object-point in one of the two planes in its image-point, the rays being generally transmitted by the system). The symmetry of the axis being premised, it is sufficient to deduce laws for a plane containing the axis. In fig. 2 let O_1, O_2 be the two points in which the perpendicular object-planes meet the axis; and since the axis corresponds to itself, the two conjugate points O'_1, O'_2 are at the intersections of the two image-planes with the axis. We denote the four planes by the letters O_1, O_2, and O'_1, O'_2. If two points A, C be taken in the plane O_1, their images are A', C' in the plane O'_1, and since the planes are represented similarly, we have $O'_1A' : O_1A = O'_1C' : O_1C = \beta_1$, in which β_1 is easily seen to be the *linear magnification* of the planes O_1, O'_1. Similarly, if two points B, D be taken in [illegible] and their images B', D' in the plane O'_2, we have [illegible] $= \beta_2$ (say), β_2 being the linear magnification [illegible] O_2, O'_2. The joins of A and B and of C and D [illegible] P, and the joins of the conjugate points similarly [illegible] P'.

[illegible] image-point of the object-point P, then [illegible] through P must pass through [illegible] line through P intersecting the [illegible] E, F, and by means of the magnifications [illegible] E', F' in the planes O'_1, O'_2. [illegible] then AC/AE = BD/BF; and [illegible] similarly in O'_1, O'_2, then A'C'/A'E' [illegible] only possible when the straight [illegible] P was any point whatever, [illegible] space is represented in [illegible] under P and defined by the two rays CD_1, and EF_1; the conjugate point P'_1 will be determined by the intersection of the conjugate rays $C'D'_1$ and $E'F'_1$, the points D'_1, F'_1, being readily found from the magnifications β_1, β_2. Since PP_1 is parallel to CE and also to DF, then $DF = D_1F_1$. Since the plane O_2 is similarly represented in O'_2, $D'F' = D'_1F'_1$; this is impossible unless $P'P'_1$ be parallel to C'E'. Therefore every perpendicular object-plane is represented by a perpendicular image-plane.

Let O be the intersection of the line PP_1 with the axis, and let O' be its conjugate; then it may be shown that a fixed magnification β_3 exists for the planes O and O'. For $PP_1/FF_1 = OO_1/O_1O_2$, $P'P'_1/F'F'_1 = O'O'/O'_1O'_2$, and $F'F'_1 = \beta_2 FF_1$. Eliminating FF_1 and $F'F'_1$ between these ratios, we have $P'P'_1/PP_1\beta_2 = O'O'_1 \cdot O_1O_2/OO_1 . O'_1O'_2$, or $\beta_3 = \beta_2 . O'O'_1 . O_1O_2/OO_1 . O'_1O'_2$, *i.e.* $\beta_3 = \beta_2 \times$ a product of the axial distances.

The determination of the image-point of a given object-point is facilitated by means of the so-called "cardinal points" of the optical system. To determine the image-point O'_1 (fig. 3) corresponding to the object-point O_1, we begin by choosing from the ray pencil proceeding from O_1, the ray parallel with the axis, *i.e.* intersecting the axis at infinity. Since the axis is its own conjugate, the parallel ray through O_1 must intersect the axis after refraction (say at F'). Then F' is the image-point of an object-point situated at infinity on the axis, and is termed the "second principal focus" (German *der bildseitige Brennpunkt*, the image-side focus). Similarly if O'_4 be on the parallel through O_1 but in the image-space, then the conjugate ray must intersect the axis at a point (say F), which is conjugate with the point at infinity on the axis in the image-space. This point is termed the "first principal focus" (German *der objektseitige Brennpunkt*, the object-side focus).

Let H_1, H'_1 be the intersections of the focal rays through F and F' with the line $O_1O'_4$. These two points are in the position of object and image, since they are each determined by two pairs of conjugate rays (O_1H_1 being conjugate with H'_1F', and $O'_4H'_1$ with H_1F). It has already been shown that object-planes perpendicular to the axis are represented by image-planes also perpendicular to the axis. Two vertical planes through H_1 and H'_1, are related as object- and image-planes; and if these planes intersect the axis in two points H and H', these points are named the "principal," or "Gauss points" of the system, H being the "object-side" and H' the "image-side principal point." The vertical planes containing H and H' are the "principal planes." It is obvious that conjugate points in these planes are equidistant from the axis; in other words, the magnification β of the pair of planes is unity. An additional characteristic of the principal planes is that the object and image are direct and not inverted. The distances between F and H, and between F' and H' are termed the focal lengths; the former may be called the "object-side focal length" and the latter the "image-side focal length." The two focal points and the two principal points constitute the so-called four cardinal points of the system, and with their aid the image of any object can be readily determined.

Equations relating to the Focal Points.—We know that the ray proceeding from the object point O_1, parallel to the axis and intersecting the principal plane H in H_1, passes through H'_1 and F'.

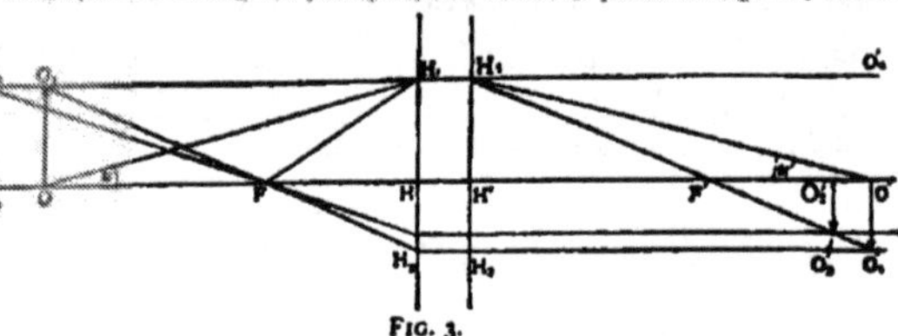

FIG. 3.

Choose from the pencil a second ray which contains F and intersects the principal plane H in H_2; then the conjugate ray must contain points corresponding to F and H_2. The conjugate of F is the point at infinity on the axis, *i.e.* on the ray parallel to the axis. The image of H_2 must be in the plane H' at the same distance from, and on the same side of, the axis, as in H'_2. The straight line passing through H'_2 parallel to the axis intersects the ray H'_1F' in the point O'_1, which must be the image of O_1. If O be the foot of the perpendicular from O_1 to the axis, then OO_1 is represented by the line $O'O'_1$ also perpendicular to the axis.

This construction is not applicable if the object or image be infinitely distant. For example, if the object OO_1 be at infinity (O being assumed to be on the axis for the sake of simplicity), so that the object appears under a constant angle w, we know that the second principal focus is conjugate with the infinitely distant axis-point. If the object is at infinity in a plane perpendicular to the axis, the image must be in the perpendicular plane through the focal point F' (fig. 4).

The size y' of the image is readily deduced. Of the parallel rays from the object subtending the angle w, there is one which passes through the first principal focus F, and intersects the principal plane H in H_1. Its conjugate ray passes through H' parallel to, and at the same distance from the axis, and intersects the image-side focal plane in O'_1; this point is the image of O_1, and y' is its magnitude. From the figure we have $\tan w = HH_1/FH = y'/f$, or $f = y'/\tan w$; this equation was used by Gauss to define the focal length.

Referring to fig. 3, we have from the similarity of the triangles OO_1F and HH_2F, $HH_2/OO_1 = FH/FO$, or $O'O'_1/OO_1 = FH/FO$. Let y be the magnitude of the object OO_1, y' that of the image $O'O'_1$, x the focal distance FO of the object, and f the object-side focal distance FH; then the above equation may be written $y'/y = f/x$. From the similar triangles $H'_1H'F'$ and $O'_1O'F'$, we obtain $O'O'_1/OO_1 = F'O'/F'H'$. Let x' be the focal distance of the image F'O', and f' the image-side focal length F'H'; then $y'/y = x'/f'$. The ratio of the size of the image to the size of the object is termed the *lateral magnification*. Denoting this by β, we have

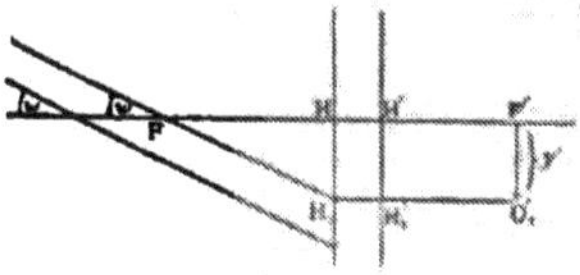

Fig. 4.

$$\beta = y'/y = f/x = x'/f'. \qquad (1)$$

and also

$$xx' = ff'. \qquad (2)$$

By differentiating equation (2) we obtain

$$dx' = -(ff'/x^2)dx \text{ or } dx'/dx = -ff'/x^2. \qquad (3)$$

The ratio of the displacement of the image dx' to the displacement of the object dx is the axial magnification, and is denoted by α. Equation (3) gives important information on the displacement of the image when the object is moved. Since f and f' always have contrary signs (as is proved below), the product $-ff'$ is invariably positive, and since x^2 is positive for all values of x, it follows that dx and dx' have the same sign, *i.e.* the object and image always move in the same direction, either both in the direction of the light, or both in the opposite direction. This is shown in fig. 3 by the object O_2O_3 and the image $O'_2O'_3$.

If two conjugate rays be drawn from two conjugate points on the axis, making angles u and u' with the axis, as for example the rays OH_3, $O'H'_3$, in fig. 3, u is termed the "angular aperture for the object," and u' the "angular aperture for the image." The ratio of the tangents of these angles is termed the "convergence" and is denoted by γ, thus $\gamma = \tan u'/\tan u$. Now $\tan u' = H'H'_3/O'H' = H'H'_3/(O'F' + F'H') = H'H'_3/(F'H' - F'O')$. Also $\tan u = HH_3/OH = HH_3/(OF + FH) = HH_3/(FH - FO)$. Consequently $\gamma = (FH - FO)/(F'H' - F'O')$, or, in our previous notation, $\gamma = (f - x)/(f' - x')$.

From equation (1) $f/x = x'/f'$, we obtain by subtracting unity from both sides $(f - x)/x = (x' - f')/f'$, and consequently

$$\frac{f - x}{f' - x'} = -\frac{x}{f'} = -\frac{f}{x'} = \gamma. \qquad (4)$$

From equations (1), (3) and (4), it is seen that a simple relation exists between the lateral magnification, the axial magnification and the convergence, viz. $\alpha\gamma = \beta$.

In addition to the four cardinal points F, H, F', H', J. B. Listing, "Beiträge aus physiologischen Optik," *Göttinger Studien* (1845) introduced the so-called "nodal points" (*Knotenpunkte*) of the system, which are the two conjugate points from which the object and image appear under the same angle. In fig. 5 let K be the nodal point from which the object y appears under the same angle as the image y' from the other nodal point K'. Then $OO_1/KO = O'O'_1/K'O'$, or $OO_1/(KF + FO) = O'O'_1/(K'F' + F'O')$, or $OO_1/(FO - FK) = O'O'_1/(F'O' - F'K')$. Calling the focal distances FK and F'K', X and X', we have $y/(x - X) = y'/(x' - X')$, and since $y'/y = \beta$, it follows that $1/(x - X) = \beta/(x' - X')$. Replace x' and X' by the values given in equation (2), and we obtain

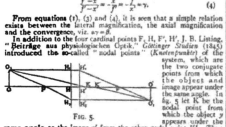

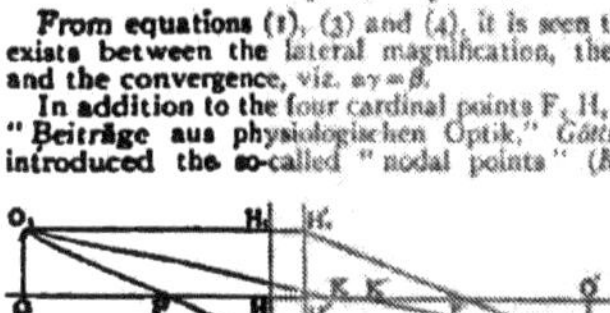

Fig. 5.

$$\frac{1}{x - X} = \beta/\left(\frac{ff'}{x} - \frac{ff'}{X}\right) \text{ or } 1 = -\beta\frac{xX}{ff'}.$$

Since $\beta = f/x = x'/f'$, we have $f' = -X$, $f = -X'$.
These equations show that to determine the nodal points, it is only necessary to measure the focal distance of the second principal focus from the first principal focus, and vice versa. In the special case when the initial and final medium is the same, as for example, a lens in air, we have $f = -f'$, and the nodal points coincide with the principal points of the system; we then speak of the "nodal point property of the principal points," meaning that the object and corresponding image subtend the same angle at the principal points.

Equations Relating to the Principal Points.—It is sometimes desirable to determine the distances of an object and its image, not from the focal points, but from the principal points. Let A (see fig. 3) be the principal point distance of the object and A' that of the image, we then have

$$A = HO = HF + FO = FO - FH = x - f,$$
$$A' = H'O' = H'F' + F'O' = F'O' - F'H' = x' - f',$$

whence $x = A + f$ and $x' = A' + f'$.
Using $xx' = ff'$, we have $(A + f)(A' + f') = ff'$, which leads to $AA' + Af' + A'f = O$, or

$$1 + \frac{f'}{A'} + \frac{f}{A} = O;$$

this becomes in the special case when $f = -f'$,

$$\frac{1}{A'} - \frac{1}{A} = \frac{1}{f'}.$$

To express the linear magnification in terms of the principal point distances, we start with equation (4) $(f - x)/(f' - x') = -x/f'$. From this we obtain $A/A' = -x/f'$, or $x = -f'A/A'$; and by using equation (1) we have $\beta = -fA'/f'A$.

In the special case of $f = -f'$, this becomes $\beta = A'/A = y'/y$, from which it follows that the ratio of the dimensions of the object and image is equal to the ratio of the distances of the object and image from the principal points.

The convergence can be determined in terms of A and A' by substituting $x = -f'A/A'$ in equation (4), when we obtain $\gamma = A/A'$.

Compound Systems.—In discussing the laws relating to compound systems, we assume that the cardinal points of the component systems are known, and also that the combinations are centred, *i.e.* that the axes of the component lenses coincide. If some object be represented by two systems arranged one behind the other, we can regard the systems as co-operating in the formation of the final image.

Let such a system be represented in fig. 6. The two single systems are denoted by the suffixes 1 and 2; for example, F_1 is the first

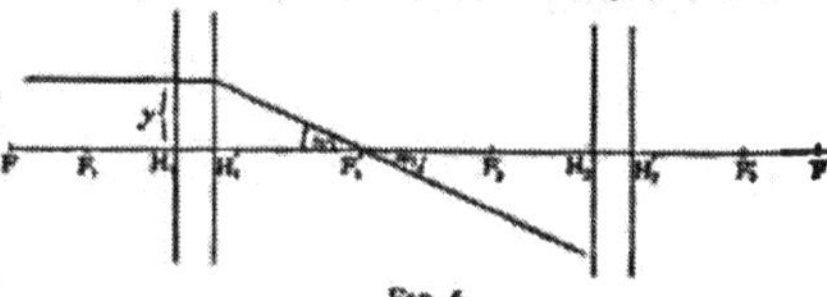

Fig. 6.

principal focus of the first, and F'_2 the second principal focus of the second system. A ray parallel to the axis at a distance y passes through the second principal focus F'_1 of the first system, intersecting the axis at an angle w'_1. The point F'_1 will be represented in the second system by the point F', which is therefore conjugate to the point at infinity for the entire system, *i.e.* it is the second principal focus of the compound system. The representation of F'_1 in F' by the second system leads to the relations $F_2F'_1 = x_2$, and $F'_2F' = x'_2$, whence $x_2x'_2 = f_2f'_2$. Denoting the distance between the adjacent focal planes F'_1, F_2 by Δ, we have $\Delta = F'_1F_2 = -F_2F'_1$, so that $x'_2 = -f_2f'_2/\Delta$. A similar ray parallel to the axis at a distance y proceeding from the image-side will intersect the axis at the focal point F_2; and by finding the image of this point in the first system, we determine the first principal focus of the compound system. Equation (2) gives $x_1x'_1 = f_1f'_1$, and since $x'_1 = F'_1F_2 = \Delta$, we have $x_1 = f_1f'_1/\Delta$ as the distance of the first principal focus F of the compound system from the first principal focus F_1 of the first system.

To determine the focal lengths f and f' of the compound system and the principal points H and H', we employ the equations defining the focal lengths, viz. $f = y'/\tan w$, and $f' = y/\tan w'$. From the construction (fig. 6) $\tan w'_1 = y/f'_1$. The variation of the angle w'_1 by the second system is deduced from the equation to the convergence, viz. $\gamma = \tan w'_2/\tan w_2 = -x_2/f'_2 = \Delta/f'_2$, and since $w_2 = w'_1$, we have $\tan w'_2 = (\Delta/f'_2)\tan w'_1$. Since $w' = w'_2$ in our system of notation, we have

$$f' = \frac{y}{\tan w'} = \frac{yf'_2}{\Delta \tan w'_1} = \frac{f'_1 \cdot f'_2}{\Delta}. \qquad (5)$$

By taking a ray proceeding from the image-side we obtain for the first principal focal distance of the combination

$$f = -f_1f_2/\Delta.$$

In the particular case in which $\Delta = O$, the two focal planes F'_1, F_2 coincide, and the focal lengths f, f' are infinite. Such a system is called a telescopic system, and this condition is realized in a telescope focused for a normal eye.

So far we have assumed that all the rays proceeding from an object-point are exactly united in an image-point after transmission through the ideal system. The question now arises so to how far this assumption is justified for spherical lenses. To investigate this it is simplest to trace the path of a ray through one spherical refracting surface. Let such a surface divide media of refractive indices n and n', the former being to the left. The point where the axis intersects the surface is the vertex S (fig. 7). Denote the distance of the axial object-point O from S by s; the distance from

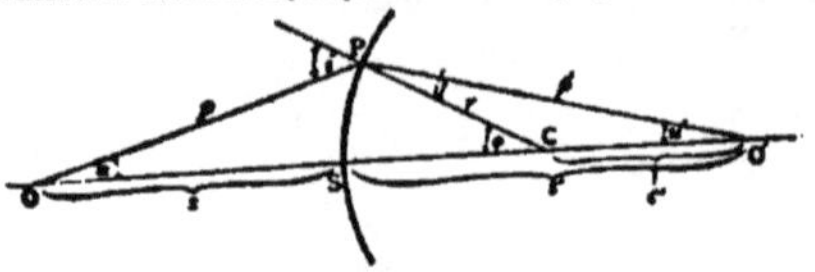

FIG. 7.

O to the point of incidence P by p; the radius of the spherical surface by r; and the distance OC by c, C being the centre of the sphere. Let u be the angle made by the ray with the axis, and i the angle of incidence, *i.e.* the angle between the ray and the normal to the sphere at the point of incidence. The corresponding quantities in the image-space are denoted by the same letters with a dash. From the triangle O'PC we have $\sin u = (r/c) \sin i$, and from the triangle O'PC we have $\sin u' = (r/c') \sin i'$. By Snell's law we have $n \sin i = n' \sin i'$, and also $\phi = u' + i'$. Consequently c' and the position of the image may be found.

To determine whether all the rays proceeding from O are reunited through O', we investigate the triangle OPO'. We have $p'/p = \sin u/\sin u'$. Substituting for $\sin u$ and $\sin u'$ the values found above, we obtain $p'/p = c' \sin i/c \sin i' = n'c'/nc$. Also $c = OC = CS + SO = -(SC + OS) = s - r$, and similarly $c' = s' - r$. Substituting these values we obtain

$$\frac{p'}{p} = \frac{n'(s'-r)}{n(s-r)}, \text{ or } \frac{n(s-r)}{p} = \frac{n'(s'-r)}{p'}. \qquad (6)$$

To obtain p and p' we use the triangles OPC and O'PC; we have $p^2 = (s-r)^2 + r^2 + 2r(s-r) \cos \phi$, $p'^2 = (s'-r)^2 + r^2 + 2r(s'-r) \cos \phi$. Hence if s, r, n and n' be constant, s' must vary as ϕ varies. The refracted rays therefore do not reunite in a point, and the deflection is termed the spherical aberration (see ABERRATION).

Developing $\cos \phi$ in powers of ϕ, we obtain

$$p^2 = (s-r)^2 + r^2 + 2r(s-r)\left\{1 - \frac{\phi^2}{2!} + \frac{\phi^4}{4!} - \frac{\phi^6}{6!} + \dots\right\},$$

and therefore for such values of ϕ for which the second and higher powers may be neglected, we have $p^2 = (s-r)^2 + r^2 + 2r(s-r)$, *i.e.* $p = s$, and similarly $p' = s'$. Equation (6) then becomes $n(s-r)/s = n'(s'-r)/s'$, or

$$\frac{n'}{s'} = \frac{n}{s} + \frac{n'-n}{r}. \qquad (7)$$

This relation shows that in a very small central aperture in which the equation $p = s$ holds, all rays proceeding from an object-point are exactly united in an image-point, and therefore the equations previously deduced are valid for this aperture. K. F. Gauss deduced the equations for thin pencils in his *Dioptrische Untersuchungen* (1840) by very elegant methods. More recently the laws relating to systems with finite aperture have been approximately realized, as for example, in well-corrected photographic objectives.

Determination of the Cardinal Points of a Lens.—Taking the case of a single spherical refracting surface, and limiting ourselves to the central aperture, it is seen that the second principal focus F' is obtained when s is infinitely great. Consequently $s' = -f'$; the negative sign is obvious, since s' is measured from S, while f' is measured from F'. The focal lengths are directly deducible from equation (7):

$$f' = -n'r/(n'-n) \qquad (8)$$
$$f = nr/(n'-n). \qquad (9)$$

[illegible] this simple refracting system with a similar one, so [illegible] surface limits the medium of refractive [illegible] we derive the spherical lens. Generally the two spherical [illegible] a glass lens, and are bounded on the outside by air [illegible]

[illegible] of the cardinal points of a spherical glass lens in [illegible] already proved is readily effected if we regard [illegible] combination of two systems each having one refracting [illegible] passing in the first system from air to glass, and [illegible] from glass to air. If we know the refractive index of [illegible] of the spherical surfaces, and the distances [illegible] (or the thickness of the lens d) we can deter-[illegible] of the lens. A biconvex lens is shown in [illegible] the first principal focus of the first system of [illegible] second principal focus; and let S_1 be its [illegible] distance F_1S_1 (the first principal focal length) [illegible] distance F'_1S_1 by f'_1. Let the corre-[illegible] in the second system be denoted by the same [illegible]

[illegible] we have

$$[illegible] \quad f_2 = -\frac{nr_2}{n-1}, \quad f'_2 = \frac{r_2}{n-1}$$

f_2 having the opposite sign to f_1. Denoting the distance F'_1F_2 by Δ, we have $\Delta = F'_1F_2 = F'_1S_1 + S_1S_2 + S_2F_2 = F'_1S_1 + S_1S_2 - F_2S_2 = f'_1 + d - f_2$. Substituting for f'_1 and f_2 we obtain

$$\Delta = -\frac{nr_1}{n-1} + d + \frac{nr_2}{n-1}.$$

Writing $R = \Delta(n-1)$, this relation becomes

$$R = n(r_2 - r_1) + d(n-1).$$

We have already shown that f (the first principal focal length of a compound system) $= -f_1f_2/\Delta$. Substituting for f_1, f_2, and Δ the values found above, we obtain

$$f = \frac{r_1r_2n}{(n-1)R} = \frac{r_1r_2n}{(n-1)[n(r_2-r_1)+d(n-1)]}, \qquad (10)$$

which is equivalent to

$$\frac{1}{f} = (n-1)\left\{\frac{1}{r_1} - \frac{1}{r_2}\right\} + \frac{(n-1)^2d}{r_1r_2n}.$$

If the lens be infinitely thin, *i.e.* if d be zero, we have for the first principal focal length,

$$\frac{1}{f} = (n-1)\left\{\frac{1}{r_1} - \frac{1}{r_2}\right\}.$$

By the same method we obtain for the second principal focal length

$$f' = \frac{f'_1f'_2}{\Delta} = -\frac{nr_1r_2}{(n-1)R} = -f.$$

The reciprocal of the focal length is termed the *power* of the lens and is denoted by ϕ. In formulae involving ϕ it is customary to

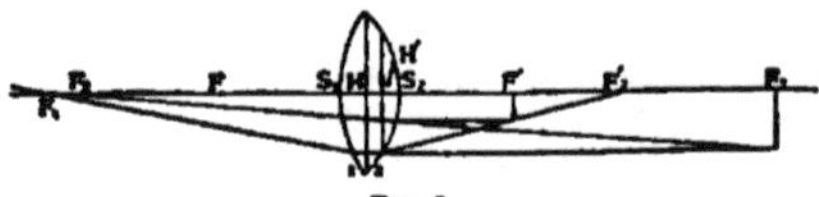

FIG. 8.

denote the reciprocal of the radii by the symbol ρ; we thus have $\phi = 1/f$, $\rho = 1/r$. Equation (10) thus becomes

$$\phi = (n-1)(\rho_1 - \rho_2) + \frac{(n-1)^2 d\rho_1\rho_2}{n}.$$

The unit of power employed by spectacle-makers is termed the *diopter* or *dioptric* (see SPECTACLES).

We proceed to determine the distances of the focal points from the vertices of the lens, *i.e.* the distances FS_1 and $F'S_2$. Since F is represented by the first system in F_2, we have by equation (2)

$$x_1 = \frac{f_1f'_1}{x'_1} = \frac{f_1f'_1}{\Delta} = -\frac{nr_1^2}{(n-1)R},$$

where $x_1 = F_1F$, and $x'_1 = F'_1F_2 = \Delta$. The distance of the first principal focus from the vertex S_1, *i.e.* S_1F, which we denote by s_F is given by $s_F = S_1F = S_1F_1 + F_1F = -F_1S_1 + F_1F$. Now F_1S_1 is the distance from the vertex of the first principal focus of the first system, *i.e.* f_1, and $F_1F = x_1$. Substituting these values, we obtain

$$s_F = -\frac{r_1}{n-1} - \frac{nr_1^2}{(n-1)R} = -\frac{r_1(nr_1 + R)}{(n-1)R}.$$

The distance F'_2F' or x'_2 is similarly determined by considering F'_1 to be represented by the second system in F'. We have

$$x'_2 = \frac{f_2f'_2}{x_2} = -\frac{f_2f'_2}{\Delta} = \frac{nr_2^2}{(n-1)R},$$

so that

$$s_{F'} = x'_2 - f'_2 = \frac{r_2(nr_2 - R)}{(n-1)R},$$

where $s_{F'}$ denotes the distance of the second principal focus from the vertex S_2.

The two focal lengths and the distances of the foci from the vertices being known, the positions of the remaining cardinal points, *i.e.* the principal points H and H', are readily determined. Let $s_H = S_1H$, *i.e.* the distance of the object-side principal point from the vertex of the first surface, and $s_{H'} = S_2H'$, *i.e.* the distance of the image-side principal point from the vertex of the second surface, then $f = FH = FS_1 + S_1H = -S_1F + S_1H = -s_F + s_H$; hence $s_H = s_F + f = -dr_1/R$. Similarly $s_{H'} = s_{F'} + f' = -dr_2/R$. It is readily seen that the distances s_H and $s_{H'}$ are in the ratio of the radii r_1 and r_2.

The distance between the two principal planes (the *interstitium*) is deduced very simply. We have $S_1S_2 = S_1H + HH' + H'S_2$, or $HH' = S_1S_2 - S_1H + S_2H'$. Substituting, we have

$$HH' = d - s_H + s_{H'} = d(n-1)(r_2 - r_1 + d)/R.$$

The interstitium becomes zero, or the two principal planes coincide, if $d = r_1 - r_2$.

We have now derived all the properties of the lens in terms of its elements, viz. the refractive index, the radii of the surfaces, and the thickness.

Forms of Lenses.—By varying the signs and relative magnitude of the radii, lenses may be divided into two groups according to their action, and into four groups according to their form.

According to their action, lenses are either collecting, convergent and condensing, or divergent and dispersing; the term positive is sometimes applied to the former, and the term negative to the latter. Convergent lenses transform a parallel pencil into a converging one, and increase the convergence, and diminish the divergence of any pencil. Divergent lenses, on the other hand, transform a parallel pencil into a diverging one, and diminish the convergence, and increase the divergence of any pencil. In convergent lenses the first principal focal distance is positive and the second principal focal distance negative; in divergent lenses the converse holds.

The four forms of lenses are interpretable by means of equation (10).

$$f = \frac{r_1 r_2 n}{(n-1)\{n(r_2-r_1)+d(n-1)\}}$$

(1) If r_1 be positive and r_2 negative. This type is called biconvex (fig. 9, 1). The first principal focus is in front of the lens, and the second principal focus behind the lens, and the two principal points

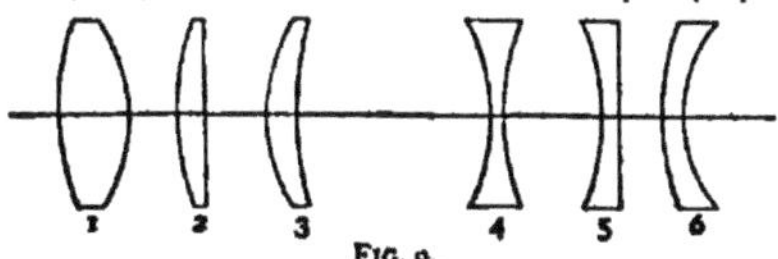

Fig. 9.

are inside the lens. The order of the cardinal points is therefore $FS_1HH'S_2F'$. The lens is convergent so long as the thickness is less than $n(r_1-r_2)/(n-1)$. The special case when one of the radii is infinite, in other words, when one of the bounding surfaces is plane is shown in fig. 9, 2. Such a collective lens is termed *plano-convex*. As d increases, F and H move to the right and F′ and H′ to the left. If $d=n(r_1-r_2)/(n-1)$, the focal length is infinite, *i.e.* the lens is *telescopic*. If the thickness be greater than $n(r_1-r_2)/(n-1)$, the lens is dispersive, and the order of the cardinal points is $HFS_1S_2F'H'$.

(2) If r_1 is negative and r_2 positive. This type is called *biconcave* (fig. 9, 4). Such lenses are dispersive for all thicknesses. If d increases, the radii remaining constant, the focal lengths diminish. It is seen from the equations giving the distances of the cardinal points from the vertices that the first principal focus F is always behind S_1, and the second principal focus F′ always in front of S_2, and that the principal points are within the lens, H′ always following H. If one of the radii becomes infinite, the lens is *plano-concave* (fig. 9, 5).

(3) If the radii are both positive. These lenses are called *convexo-concave*. Two cases occur according as $r_2 > r_1$, or $< r_1$ (*a*) If $r_2 > r_1$, we obtain the *mensicus* (fig. 9, 3). Such lenses are always collective; and the order of the cardinal points is FHH′F′ Since s_F and s_H are always negative, the object-side cardinal points are always in front of the lens. H′ can take up different positions. Since $s_{H'} = -dr_2/R = -dr_2/\{n(r_2-r_1)+d(n-1)\}$, $s_{H'}$ is greater or less than d, *i.e.* H′ is either in front of or inside the lens, according as d <or> $\{r_2-n(r_2-r_1)\}/(n-1)$. (*b*) If $r_2 < r_1$ the lens is dispersive so long as $d < n(r_1-r_2)/(n-1)$. H is always behind S_1 and H′ behind S_2, since s_H and $s_{H'}$ are always positive. The focus F is always behind S_1 and F′ in front of S_2. If the thickness be small, the order of the cardinal points is F′HH′F; a dispersive lens of this type is shown in fig. 9, 6. As the thickness increases, H, H′ and F move to the right, F more rapidly than H, and H more rapidly than H′; F′, on the other hand, moves to the left. As with biconvex lenses, a telescopic lens, having all the cardinal points at infinity, results when $d=n(r_1-r_2)/(n-1)$. If $d > n(r_1-r_2)/(n-1)$, f is positive and the lens is collective. The cardinal points are in the same order as in the mensicus, viz. FHH′F′; and the relation of the principal points to the vertices is also the same as in the mensicus.

(4) If r_1 and r_2 are both negative. This case is reduced to (3) above, by assuming a change in the direction of the light, or, in other words, by interchanging the object- and image-spaces.

The six forms shown in fig. 9 are all used in optical constructions. It may be stated fairly generally that lenses which are thicker at the middle are collective, while those which are thinnest at the middle are dispersive.

Different Positions of Object and Image.—The principal points are always near the surfaces limiting the lens, and consequently the lens divides the direct pencil containing the axis into two parts. The object can be either in front of or behind the lens as in fig. 10. If the object point be in front of the lens, and if it be realized by rays passing from it, it is called *real*. If, on the other hand, the object be behind the lens, it is called *virtual*; it does not actually exist, and can only be realized as an image.

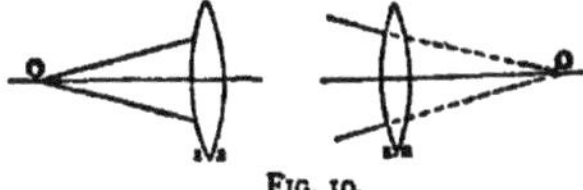

Fig. 10.

When we speak of "object-points," it is always understood that the rays from the object traverse the first surface of the lens before meeting the second. In the same way, images may be either real or virtual. If the image be behind the second surface, it is *real*, and can be intercepted on a screen. If, however, it be in front of the lens, it is visible to an eye placed behind the lens, although the rays do not actually intersect, but only appear to do so, but the image cannot be intercepted on a screen behind the lens. Such an image is said to be *virtual*. These relations are shown in fig. 11.

Fig. 11.

By referring to the equations given above, it is seen that a thin convergent lens produces both real and virtual images of real objects, but only a real image of a virtual object, whilst a divergent lens produces a virtual image of a real object and both real and virtual images of a virtual object. The construction of a real image of a

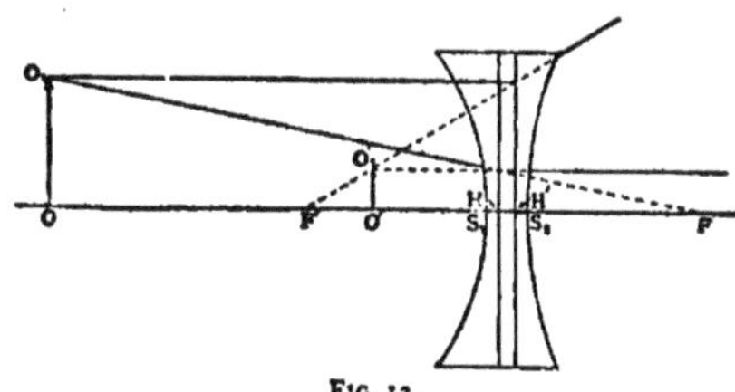

Fig. 12.

real object by a convergent lens is shown in fig. 3; and that of a virtual image of a real object by a divergent lens in fig. 12.

The optical centre of a lens is a point such that, for any ray which passes through it, the incident and emergent rays are parallel. The idea of the optical centre was originally due to J. Harris (*Treatise on Optics*, 1775); it is not properly a cardinal point, although it has several interesting properties. In fig. 13, let C_1P_1 and C_2P_2 be two parallel radii of a biconvex lens. Join P_1P_2 and let O_1P_1 and O_2P_2

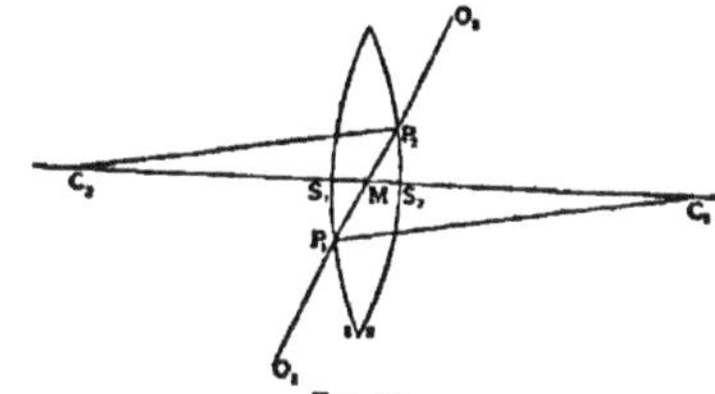

Fig. 13.

be incident and emergent rays which have P_1P_2 for the path through the lens. Then if M be the intersection of P_1P_2 with the axis, we have angle C_1P_1M = angle C_2P_2M; these two angles are—for a ray travelling in the direction $O_1P_1P_2O_2$—the angles of emergence and of incidence respectively. From the similar triangles C_2P_2M and C_1P_1M we have

$$C_1M : C_2M = C_1P_1 : C_2P_2 = r_1 : r_2. \qquad (11)$$

Such rays as P_1P_2 therefore divide the distance C_1C_2 in the ratio of the radii, *i.e.* at the fixed point M, the optical centre. Calling $S_1M = s_1$, $S_2M = s_2$, then $C_1S_1 = C_1M + MS_1 = C_1M - S_1M$, *i.e.* since $C_1S_1 = r_1$, $C_1M = r_1 + s_1$, and similarly $C_2M = r_2 + s_2$. Also $S_1S_2 = S_1M + MS_2 = S_1M - S_2M$, *i.e.* $d = s_1 - s_2$. Then by using equation (11) we have $s_1 = r_1d/(r_1-r_2)$ and $s_2 = r_2d/(r_1-r_2)$, and hence $s_1/s_2 = r_1/r_2$. The vertex distances of the optical centre are therefore in the ratio of the radii.

The values of s_1 and s_2 show that the optical centre of a biconvex or biconcave lens is in the interior of the lens, that in a plano-convex or plano-concave lens it is at the vertex of the curved surface, and in a concavo-convex lens outside the lens.

The Wave-theory Derivation of the Focal Length.—The formulae above have been derived by means of geometrical rays. We here give an account of Lord Rayleigh's wave-theory derivation of the focal length of a convex lens in terms of the aperture, thickness and refractive index (*Phil. Mag.* 1879 (5) 8, p. 480; 1885, 20, [illegible] is based on the principle that the optical [illegible] the arrangement [illegible] image is constant.

[illegible] of a convex lens of glass, let us suppose that [illegible] fall upon the lens ACB, and are [illegible]. The points D, E, G, equally distant [illegible] of the wave before it impinges upon the [illegible] at which the different parts of the wave [illegible] and that such a point can exist depends [illegible] propagation is slower in glass than in air. The ray ECF is retarded from having to pass through the thickness (d) of glass by the amount $(\mu-1)d$. The ray DAF, which traverses only the extreme edge of the lens, is retarded merely on account of the crookedness of its path, and the

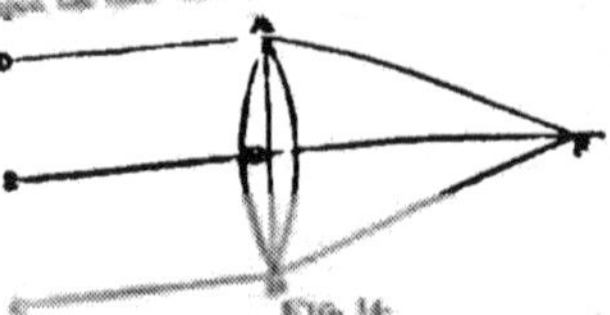

FIG. 14.

[illegible] retardation is measured by AF−CF. If F is a focus [illegible] be equal, or $AF-CF=(\mu-1)d$. Now if y [illegible] AC of the lens, and f be the focal length CF, [illegible] $=\frac{1}{2}y^2/f$ approximately, whence

$$f=\tfrac{1}{2}y^2/(\mu-1)d. \qquad (12)$$

[illegible] $(\mu-1)=\frac{1}{2}$ (nearly), and then the rule (12) [illegible] semi-aperture is a mean *proportional between* [illegible] thickness. The form (12) is in general the [illegible] as the more practically useful, but we may, [illegible] thickness in terms of the curvatures and semi- [illegible] $=\frac{1}{2}y^2(r_1^{-1}-r_2^{-1})$. In the preceding statement [illegible] simplicity that the lens comes to a sharp [illegible] case we must take as the thickness of the [illegible] thicknesses at the centre and at the circum- [illegible] statement is applicable to concave lenses, [illegible] length is positive when the lens is thickest [illegible] when the lens is thickest at the edge."

[illegible] of the Rays.

[illegible] of optical instruments can be con- [illegible] parts: (1) The relations of the [illegible] objects and their images (see above); [illegible] from an ideal image (see ABERRA- [illegible] radiation in the object- and image- [illegible] the alteration of brightness caused by [illegible] influences; and (4) the regulation [illegible]

[illegible] be treated only in systems free [illegible] gave a connected theory; and M [illegible] towards the elaboration. The [illegible] simple to construct the image of [illegible] taken of the size of the system, or [illegible] construction really assist in the [illegible]. The diverging cones of rays [illegible] only take a certain small part [illegible] consequence of the apertures of [illegible] happens that the rays used [illegible] do not pass through the system; [illegible] quite different rays. If we take a [illegible] on the axis of the system then an [illegible] sees in the instrument several [illegible] the fittings of the lenses or their [illegible] of their images. The innermost

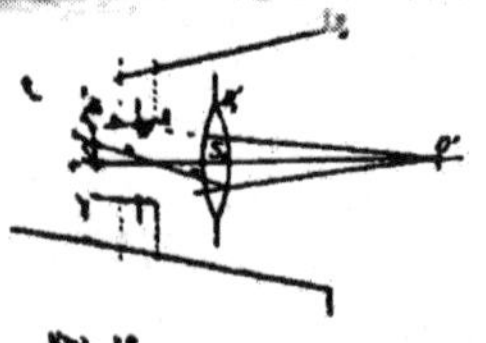

FIG. 15.

[illegible] and forms the origin of the [illegible]. Abbe called it the *exit pupil*. [illegible] smallest ring in the object- [illegible] cone of rays. This is called the [illegible] acting as a limit at any part [illegible] *diaphragm*. These diaphragms [illegible] the same for all points lying on [illegible] that one and the same diaphragm fulfils the functions of the entrance pupil and the aperture-diaphragm or the exit pupil and the aperture-diaphragm.

Fig. 15 shows the general but simplified case of the different diaphragms which are of importance for the regulation of the rays. S_1, S_2 are two centred systems. A′ is a real diaphragm lying between them. B_1 and B'_2 are the fittings of the systems. Then S_1 produces the virtual image A of the diaphragm A′ and the image B_2 of the fitting B'_2, whilst the system S_2 makes the virtual image A″ of the diaphragm A′ and the virtual image B'_1 of the fitting B_1. The object-point O is reproduced really through the whole system in the point O′. From the object-point O three diaphragms can be seen in the object-space, viz. the fitting B_1, the image of the fitting B_2 and the image A of the diaphragm A′ formed by the system S_1. The cone of rays nearest to B_2 is not received to its total extent by the fitting B_1, and the cone which has entered through B_1 is again diminished in its further course, when passing through the diaphragm A′, so that the cone of rays really used for producing the image is limited by A, the diaphragm which seen from O appears to be the smallest. A is therefore the entrance pupil. The real diaphragm A′ which limits the rays in the centre of the system is the aperture diaphragm. Similarly three diaphragms lying in the image-space are to be seen from the image-point O′—namely B′, A″, and B'_2. A″ limits the rays in the image-space, and is therefore the exit pupil. As A is conjugate to the diaphragm A′ in the system S_1, and A″ to the same diaphragm A′ in the system S_2, the entrance pupil A is conjugate to the exit pupil A″ throughout the instrument. This relation between entrance and exit pupils is general.

The apices of the cones of rays producing the image of points near the axis thus lie in the object-points, and their common base is the entrance pupil. The axis of such a cone, which connects the object point with the centre of the entrance pupil, is called the *principal ray*. Similarly, the principal rays in the image-space join the centre of the exit pupil with the image-points. The centres of the entrance and exit pupils are thus the intersections of the principal rays.

For points lying farther from the axis, the entrance pupil no longer alone limits the rays, the other diaphragms taking part. In fig. 16 only one diaphragm L is present besides the entrance pupil A, and the object-space is divided to a certain extent into four parts. The section M contains all points rendered by a system with a complete aperture; N contains all points rendered by a system with a gradually diminishing aperture; but this diminution does not attain the principal ray passing through the centre C. In the section O are those points rendered by a system with an aperture which gradually decreases to zero. No rays pass from the points of the section P through the system and no image can arise from them.

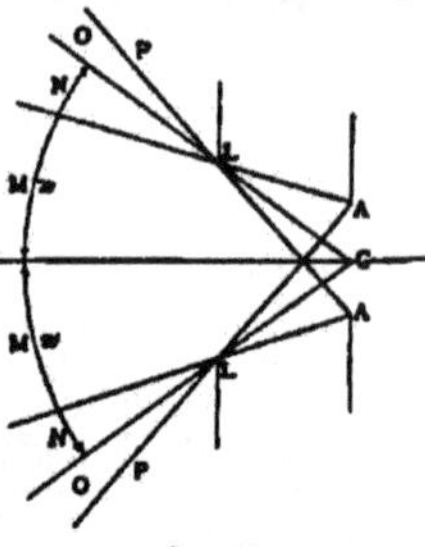

FIG. 16.

The second diaphragm L therefore limits the three-dimensional object-space containing the points which can be rendered by the optical system. From C through this diaphragm L this three-dimensional object-space can be seen as through a window. L is called by M von Rohr the *entrance luke*. If several diaphragms can be seen from C, then the entrance *luke* is the diaphragm which seen from C appears the smallest. In the sections N and O the entrance *luke* also takes part in limiting the cones of rays. This restriction is known as the "vignetting" action of the entrance *luke*. The base of the cone of rays for the points of this section of the object-space is no longer a circle but a two-cornered curve which arises from the object-point by the projection of the entrance *luke* on the entrance pupil. Fig. 17*a* shows the base of such a cone of rays. It often happens that besides the entrance *luke*, another diaphragm acts in a vignetting manner, then

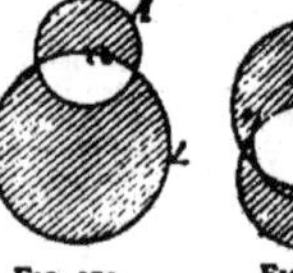

FIG. 17*a*. FIG. 17*b*.

the operating aperture of the cone of rays is a curve made up of circular arcs formed out of the entrance pupil and the two projections of the two acting diaphragms (fig. 17*b*).

If the entrance pupil is narrow, then the section NO, in which the vignetting is increasing, is diminished, and there is really only one division of the section M which can be reproduced, and of the section P which cannot be reproduced. The angle $w+w=2w$, comprising the section which can be reproduced, is called the angle of the field of view on the object-side. The field of view $2w$ retains its importance if the entrance pupil is increased. It then comprises all points reached by principal rays. The same relations apply to the image-space, in which there is an exit *luke*, which, seen from the middle of the exit pupil, appears under the smallest angle. It is the image of the entrance *luke* produced by the whole system. The image-side field of view $2w'$ is the angle comprised by the principal rays reaching the edge of the exit *luke*.

Most optical instruments are used to observe object-reliefs (three-dimensional objects), and generally an image-relief (a three-dimensional image) is conjugate to this object-relief. It is sometimes required, however, to represent by means of an optical instrument the object-relief on a plane or on a ground-glass as in the photographic camera. For simplicity we shall assume the intercepting plane as perpendicular to the axis and shall call it, after von Rohr, the "ground glass plane." All points of the image not lying in this plane produce circular spots (corresponding to the form of the pupils) on it, which are called "circles of confusion." The ground-glass plane (fig. 18) is conjugate to the object-plane E in the object-space, perpendicular to the axis, and called the "plane focused for." All points lying in this plane are reproduced exactly on the ground-glass plane as the points OO. The circle of confusion

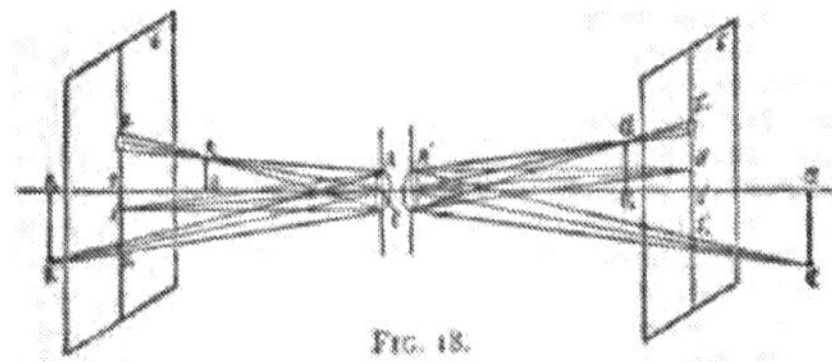

FIG. 18.

Z on the plane focused for corresponds to the circle of confusion Z' on the ground-glass plane. The figure formed on the plane focused for by the cones of rays from all of the object-points of the total object-space directed to the entrance pupil, was called "object-side representation" (*imago*) by M von Rohr. This representation is a central projection. If, for instance, the entrance pupil is imagined so small that only the principal rays pass through, then they project directly, and the intersections of the principal rays represent the projections of the points of the object lying off the plane focused for. The centre of the projection or the perspective centre is the middle point of the entrance pupil C. If the entrance pupil is opened, in place of points, circles of confusion appear, whose size depends upon the size of the entrance pupil and the position of the object-points and the plane focused for. The intersection of the principal ray is the centre of the circle of confusion. The clearness of the representation on the plane focused for is of course diminished by the circles of confusion. This central projection does not at all depend upon the instrument, but is entirely geometrical, arising when the position and the size of the entrance pupil, and the position of the plane focused for, have been fixed. The instrument then produces an image on the ground-glass plane of this perspective representation on the plane focused for, and on account of the exact likeness which this image has to the object-side representation it is called the "representation copy." By moving it round an angle of 180°, this representation can be brought into a perspective position to the objects, so that all rays coming from the middle of the entrance pupil and aiming at the object-points, would always meet the corresponding image-points. This representation is accessible to the observer in different ways in different instruments. If the observer desires a perfectly correct perspective impression of the object-relief the distance of the pivot of the eye from the representation copy must be equal to the nth part of the distance of the plane focused for from the entrance pupil, if the instrument has produced a nth diminution of the object-side representation. The pivot of the eye must coincide with the centre of the perspective, because all images are observed in direct vision. It is known that the pivot of the eye is the point of intersection of all the directions in which one can look. Thus all these points represented by circles of confusion which are less than the angular sharpness of vision appear clear to the eye; the space containing all these object-points, which appear clear to the eye, is called the *depth*. The depth of definition, therefore, is not a special property of the instrument, but depends on the size of the entrance pupil, the position of the plane focused for and on the conditions under which the representation can be observed.

If the distance of the representation from the pivot of the eye be altered from the correct distance already mentioned, the angles of vision under which various objects appear are changed; perspective errors arise, causing an incorrect idea to be given of the depth. A simple case is shown in fig. 19. A cube is the object, and if it is observed as in fig. 19*a* with the representation copy at the correct distance, a correct idea of a cube will be obtained. If, as in figs. 19*b* and 19*c*, the distance is too great, there can be two results. If it is known that the farthest section is just as high as the nearer one then the cube appears exceptionally deepened, like a long parallelepipedon. But if it is known to be as deep as it is high then the eye will see it low at the back and high at the front. The reverse occurs when the distance of observation is too short, the body then appears either too flat, or the nearer sections seem too low in relation to those farther off. These perspective errors can be seen in any telescope. In the

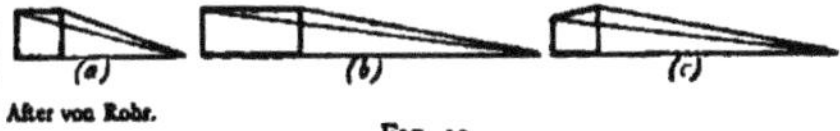

After von Rohr.

FIG. 19.

telescope ocular the representation copy has to be observed under too large an angle or at too short a distance: all objects therefore appear flattened, or the more distant objects appear too large in comparison with those nearer at hand.

From the above the importance of experience will be inferred. But it is not only necessary that the objects themselves be known to the observer but also that they are presented to his eye in the customary manner. This depends upon the way in which the principal rays pass through the system—in other words, upon the special kind of "transmission" of the principal rays. In ordinary vision the pivot of the eye is the centre of the perspective representation which arises on the very distant plane standing perpendicular to the mean direction of right. In this kind of central projection all objects lying in front of the plane focused for are diminished when projected on this plane, and those lying behind it are magnified. (The distances are always given in the direction of light.) Thus the objects near to the eye appear large and those farther from it appear small. This perspective has been called by M von Rohr[1] "entocentric transmission" (fig. 20). If the entrance pupil of the instrument lies at infinity, then all the principal rays are parallel and the

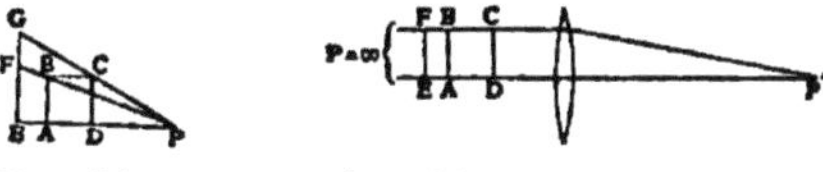

After von Rohr. FIG. 20.

After von Rohr. FIG. 21.

projections of all objects on the plane focused for are exactly as large as the objects themselves. After E. Abbe, this course of rays is called "telecentric transmission" (fig. 21). The exit pupil then lies in the image-side focus of the system. If the perspective centre lies in front of the plane focused for, then the objects lying in front of this plane are magnified and those behind it are diminished. This is just the reverse of perspective representation in ordinary sight, so that the relations of size and the arrangements for space must be quite incorrectly indicated (fig. 22); this representation is called by M von Rohr a "hypercentric transmission." (O. HR.)

After von Rohr

FIG. 22.

LENT (O. Eng. *lencten*, "spring," M. Eng. *lenten*, *lente*, *lent*; cf. Dut. *lente*, Ger. *Lenz*, "spring," O. H. Ger. *lenzin*, *lengizin*, *lenzo*, probably from the same root as "long" and referring to "the lengthening days"), in the Christian Church, the period of fasting preparatory to the festival of Easter. As this fast falls in the early part of the year, it became confused with the season, and gradually the word Lent, which originally meant spring, was confined to this use. The Latin name for the fast, *Quadragesima* (whence Ital. *quaresima*, Span. *cuaresma* and Fr. *carême*), and its Gr. equivalent τεσσαρακοστή (now superseded by the term ἡ νηστεία "the fast"), are derived from the Sunday which was the fortieth day before Easter, as *Quinquagesima* and *Sexagesima* are the fiftieth and sixtieth, Quadragesima being until the 7th century the *caput jejunii* or first day of the fast.

The length of this fast and the rigour with which it has been observed have varied greatly at different times and in different countries (see FASTING). In the time of Irenaeus the fast before Easter was very short, but very severe; thus some ate nothing for forty hours between the afternoon of Good Friday and the morning of Easter. This was the only authoritatively prescribed fast known to Tertullian (*De jejunio*, 2, 13, 14; *De oratione*, 18). In Alexandria about the middle of the 3rd century it was already

[1] M von Rohr, *Zeitschr. für Sinnesphysiologie* (1907), xli. 408-429.

(445), denouncing the contumacy of the Gallic bishop, and enacting "that nothing should be done in Gaul, contrary to ancient usage, without the authority of the bishop of Rome, and that the decree of the apostolic see should henceforth be law." In 447 Leo held the correspondence with Turribus of Astorga which led to the condemnation of the Priscillianists by the Spanish national church. In 448 he received with commendation a letter from Eutyches, the Constantinopolitan monk, complaining of the revival of the Nestorian heresy there; and in the following year Eutyches wrote his circular, appealing against the sentence which at the instance of Eusebius of Dorylaeum had been passed against him at a synod held in Constantinople under the presidency of the patriarch Flavian, and asking papal support at the oecumenical council at that time under summons to meet at Ephesus. The result of a correspondence was that Leo by his legates sent to Flavian that famous epistle in which he sets forth with great fulness of detail the doctrine ever since recognized as orthodox regarding the union of the two natures in the one person of Jesus Christ. The events at the "robber" synod at Ephesus belong to general church history rather than to the biography of Leo; his letter, though submitted, was not read by the assembled fathers, and the papal legates had some difficulty in escaping with their lives from the violence of the theologians who, not content with deposing Flavian and Eusebius, shouted for the dividing of those who divided Christ. When the news of the result of this oecumenical council (oecumenical in every circumstance except that it was not presided over by the pope) reached Rome, Leo wrote to Theodosius "with groanings and tears," requesting the emperor to sanction another council, to be held this time, however, in Italy. In this petition he was supported by Valentinian III., by the empress-mother Galla Placidia and by the empress Eudoxia, but the appeal was made in vain. A change, however, was brought about by the accession in the following year of Marcian, who three days after coming to the throne published an edict bringing within the scope of the penal laws against heretics the supporters of the dogmas of Apollinaris and Eutyches. To convoke a synod in which greater orthodoxy might reasonably be expected was in these circumstances no longer difficult, but all Leo's efforts to secure that the meeting should take place on Italian soil were unavailing. When the synod of Chalcedon assembled in 451, the papal legates were treated with great respect, and Leo's former letter to Flavian was adopted by acclamation as formulating the creed of the universal church on the subject of the person of Christ. Among the reasons urged by Leo for holding this council in Italy had been the threatening attitude of the Huns; the dreaded irruption took place in the following year (452). After Aquileia had succumbed to Attila's long siege, the conqueror set out for Rome. Near the confluence of the Mincio and the Po he was met by Leo, whose eloquence persuaded him to turn back. Legend has sought to enhance the impressiveness of the occurrence by an unnecessarily imagined miracle. The pope was less successful with Genseric when the Vandal chief arrived under the walls of Rome in 455, but he secured a promise that there should be no incendiarism or murder, and that three of the oldest basilicas should be exempt from plunder—a promise which seems to have been faithfully observed. Leo died on the 10th of November 461, the liturgical anniversary being the 11th of April. His successor was Hilarius or Hilarus, who had been one of the papal legates at the "robber" synod in 449.

The title of *doctor ecclesiae* was given to Leo by Benedict XIV. As bishop of the diocese of Rome, Leo distinguished himself above all his predecessors by his preaching, to which he devoted himself with great zeal and success. From his short and pithy *Sermones* many of the lessons now to be found in the Roman breviary have been taken. Viewed in conjunction with his voluminous correspondence, the sermons sufficiently explain the secret of his greatness, which chiefly lay in the extraordinary strength and purity of his convictions as to the primacy of the successors of St Peter at a time when the civil and ecclesiastical troubles of the civilized world made men willing enough to submit themselves to any authority whatsoever that could establish its right to exist by courage, honesty and knowledge of affairs.

The works of Leo I. were first collectively edited by Quesnel (Lyons, 1700), and again, on the basis of this, in what is now the standard edition by Ballerini (Venice, 1753–1756). Ninety-three *Sermones* and one hundred and seventy-three *Epistolae* occupy the first volume; the second contains the *Liber Sacramentorum*, usually attributed to Leo, and the *De Vocatione Omnium Gentium*, also ascribed, by Quesnel and others, to him, but more probably the production of a certain Prosper, of whom nothing further is known. The works of Hilary of Arles are appended.

Leo II., pope from August 682 to July 683, was a Sicilian by birth, and succeeded Agatho I. Agatho had been represented at the sixth oecumenical council (that of Constantinople in 681), where Pope Honorius I. was anathematized for his views in the Monothelite controversy as a favourer of heresy, and the only fact of permanent historical interest with regard to Leo is that he wrote once and again in approbation of the decision of the council and in condemnation of Honorius, whom he regarded as one who *profana proditione immaculatam fidem subvertere conatus est*. In their bearing upon the question of papal infallibility these words have excited considerable attention and controversy, and prominence is given to the circumstance that in the Greek text of the letter to the emperor in which the phrase occurs the milder expression παρεχώρησεν (*subverti permisit*) is used for *subvertere conatus est*. This Hefele in his *Conciliengeschichte* (iii. 294) regards as alone expressing the true meaning of Leo. It was during Leo's pontificate that the dependence of the see of Ravenna upon that of Rome was finally settled by imperial edict. Benedict II. succeeded him.

Leo III., whose pontificate (795–816) covered the last eighteen years of the reign of Charlemagne, was a native of Rome, and having been chosen successor of Adrian I. on the 26th of December 795, was consecrated to the office on the following day. His first act was to send to Charles as patrician the standard of Rome along with the keys of the sepulchre of St Peter and of the city; a gracious and condescending letter in reply made it still more clear where all real power at that moment lay. For more than three years his term of office was uneventful; but at the end of that period the feelings of disappointment which had secretly been rankling in the breasts of Paschalis and Campulus, nephews of Adrian I., who had received from him the offices of *primicerius* and *sacellarius* respectively, suddenly manifested themselves in an organized attack upon Leo as he was riding in procession through the city on the day of the Greater Litany (25th April 799); the object of his assailants was, by depriving him of his eyes and tongue, to disqualify him for the papal office, and, although they were unsuccessful in this attempt, he found it necessary to accept the protection of Winegis, the Frankish duke of Spoleto, who came to the rescue. Having vainly requested the presence of Charles in Rome, Leo went beyond the Alps to meet the king at Paderborn; he was received with much ceremony and respect, but his enemies having sent in serious written charges, of which the character is not now known, Charles decided to appoint both the pope and his accusers to appear as parties before him when he should have arrived in Rome. Leo returned in great state to his diocese, and was received with honour; Charles, who did not arrive until November in the following year, lost no time in assuming the office of a judge, and the result of his investigation was the acquittal of the pope, who at the same time, however, was permitted or rather required to clear himself by the oath of compurgation. The coronation of the emperor followed two days afterwards; its effect was to bring out with increased clearness the personally subordinate position of Leo. The decision of the emperor, however, secured for Leo's pontificate an external peace which was only broken after the accession of Louis the Pious. His enemies began to renew their attacks; the violent repression of a conspiracy led to an open rebellion at Rome; serious charges were once more brought against him, when he was overtaken by death in 816. It was under this pontificate that Felix of Urgel, the adoptianist, was anathematized (798) by a

Roman synod. Leo at another synod held in Rome in 810 admitted the dogmatic correctness of the *filioque*, but deprecated its introduction into the creed. On this point, however, the Frankish Church persevered in the course it had already initiated. Leo's successor was Stephen IV.

Leo IV., pope from 847 to 855, was a Roman by birth, and succeeded Sergius II. His pontificate was chiefly distinguished by his efforts to repair the damage done by the Saracens during the reign of his predecessor to various churches of the city, especially those of St Peter and St Paul. It was he who built and fortified the suburb on the right bank of the Tiber still known as the Civitas Leonina. A frightful conflagration, which he is said to have extinguished by his prayers, is the subject of Raphael's great work in the Sala dell' Incendio of the Vatican. He held three synods, one of them (in 850) distinguished by the presence of Louis II., who was crowned emperor on the occasion, but none of them otherwise of importance. The history of the papal struggle with Hincmar of Reims, which began during Leo's pontificate, belongs rather to that of Nicholas I. Benedict III. was Leo's immediate successor.

Leo V., a native of Ardea, was pope for two months in 903 after the death of Benedict IV. He was overthrown and cast into prison by the priest Christopher, who installed himself in his place.

Leo VI. succeeded John X. in 928, and reigned seven months and a few days. He was succeeded by Stephen VIII.

Leo VII., pope from 936 to 939, was preceded by John XI., and followed by Stephen IX.

Leo VIII., pope from 963 to 965, a Roman by birth, held the lay office of *protoscrinius* when he was elected to the papal chair at the instance of Otto the Great by the Roman synod which deposed John XII. in December 963. Having been hurried with unseemly haste through all the intermediate orders, he received consecration two days after his election, which was unacceptable to the people. In February 964, the emperor having withdrawn from the city, Leo found it necessary to seek safety in flight, whereupon he was deposed by a synod held under the presidency of John XII. On the sudden death of the latter, the populace chose Benedict V. as his successor; but Otto, returning and laying siege to the city, compelled their acceptance of Leo. It is usually said that, at the synod which deposed Benedict, Leo conceded to the emperor and his successors as sovereign of Italy full rights of investiture, but the genuineness of the document on which this allegation rests is more than doubtful. Leo VIII. was succeeded by John XIII.

Leo IX., pope from 1049 to 1054, was a native of Upper Alsace, where he was born on the 21st of June 1002. His proper name was Bruno; the family to which he belonged was of noble rank, and through his father he was related to the emperor Conrad II. He was educated at Toul, where he successively became canon and (1026) bishop; in the latter capacity he rendered important political services to his relative Conrad II., and afterwards to Henry III., and at the same time he became widely known as an earnest and reforming ecclesiastic by the zeal he showed in spreading the rule of the order of Cluny. On the death of Damasus II., Bruno was in December 1048, with the concurrence both of the emperor and of the Roman delegates, selected his successor by an assembly at Worms; he stipulated, however, as a condition of his acceptance that he should first proceed to Rome and be canonically elected by the voice of clergy and people. Setting out shortly after Christmas, he had a meeting with abbot Hugo of Cluny at Besançon, where he was joined by the young monk Hildebrand, who afterwards became Pope Gregory VII.; arriving in pilgrim garb at Rome in the following February, he was received with much cordiality, and at his consecration assumed the name of Leo IX. One of his first public acts was to hold the well-known Easter synod of 1049, at which celibacy of the clergy (down to the rank of subdeacon) was anew enjoined, and where he at least succeeded in making clear his own convictions against every kind of simony. The greater part of the year that followed was occupied in one of those progresses through Italy, Germany and France which form a marked feature in Leo's pontificate. After presiding over a synod at Pavia, he joined the emperor Henry III. in Saxony, and accompanied him to Cologne and Aix-la-Chapelle; to Reims he also summoned a meeting of the higher clergy, by which several important reforming decrees were passed. At Mainz also he held a council, at which the Italian and French as well as the German clergy were represented, and ambassadors of the Greek emperor were present; here too simony and the marriage of the clergy were the principal matters dealt with. After his return to Rome he held (29th April 1050) another Easter synod, which was occupied largely with the controversy about the teachings of Berengarius of Tours; in the same year he presided over provincial synods at Salerno, Siponto and Vercelli, and in September revisited Germany, returning to Rome in time for a third Easter synod, at which the question of the reordination of those who had been ordained by simonists was considered. In 1052 he joined the emperor at Pressburg, and vainly sought to secure the submission of the Hungarians; and at Regensburg, Bamberg and Worms the papal presence was marked by various ecclesiastical solemnities. After a fourth Easter synod in 1053 Leo set out against the Normans in the south with an army of Italians and German volunteers, but his forces sustained a total defeat at Astagnum near Civitella (18th June 1053); on going out, however, from the city to meet the enemy he was received with every token of submission, relief from the pressure of his ban was implored and fidelity and homage were sworn. From June 1053 to March 1054 he was nevertheless detained at Benevento in honourable captivity; he did not long survive his return to Rome, where he died on the 19th of April 1054. He was succeeded by Victor II.

Leo X. [Giovanni de' Medici] (1475–1521), pope from the 11th of March 1513 to the 1st of December 1521, was the second son of Lorenzo de' Medici, called the Magnificent, and was born at Florence on the 11th of December 1475. Destined from his birth for the church, he received the tonsure at the age of seven and was soon loaded with rich benefices and preferments. His father prevailed on Innocent VIII. to name him cardinal-deacon of Sta Maria in Dominica in March 1489, although he was not allowed to wear the insignia or share in the deliberations of the college until three years later. Meanwhile he received a careful education at Lorenzo's brilliant humanistic court under such men as Angelo Poliziano, the classical scholar, Pico della Mirandola, the philosopher and theologian, the pious Marsilio Ficino who endeavoured to unite the Platonic cult with Christianity and the poet Bernardo Dovizio Bibbiena. From 1489 to 1491 he studied theology and canon law at Pisa under Filippo Decio and Bartolomeo Sozzini. On the 23rd of March 1492 he was formally admitted into the sacred college and took up his residence at Rome, receiving a letter of advice from his father which ranks among the wisest of its kind. The death of Lorenzo on the 8th of April, however, called the seventeen-year-old cardinal to Florence. He participated in the conclave which followed the death of Innocent VIII. in July 1492 and opposed the election of Cardinal Borgia. He made his home with his elder brother Piero at Florence throughout the agitation of Savonarola and the invasion of Charles VIII. of France, until the uprising of the Florentines and the expulsion of the Medici in November 1494. While Piero found refuge at Venice and Urbino, Cardinal Giovanni travelled in Germany, in the Netherlands and in France. In May 1500 he returned to Rome, where he was received with outward cordiality by Alexander VI., and where he lived for several years immersed in art and literature. In 1503 he welcomed the accession of Julius II. to the pontificate; the death of Piero de' Medici in the same year made Giovanni head of his family. On the 1st of October 1511 he was appointed papal legate of Bologna and the Romagna, and when the Florentine republic declared in favour of the schismatic Pisans Julius II. sent him against his native city at the head of the papal army. This and other attempts to regain political control of Florence were frustrated, until a bloodless revolution permitted the return of the Medici on the 14th of September 1512. Giovanni's younger brother Giuliano was placed at the head of the republic, but the cardinal actually managed the government. Julius II. died in February 1513, and the conclave, after a stormy seven day's session, united on Cardinal de' Medici as the candidate of the younger cardinals. He was ordained to the priesthood on the 15th of March, consecrated bishop on the 17th, and enthroned with the name of Leo X. on the 19th. There is no evidence of simony in the conclave, and Leo's election was hailed with delight by the Romans on account of his reputation for liberality, kindliness and love of peace. Following the example of many of his predecessors, he promptly repudiated his election "capitulation" as an infringement on the divinely bestowed prerogatives of the Holy See.

Many problems confronted Leo X. on his accession. He must preserve the papal conquests which he had inherited from Alexander VI. and Julius II. He must minimize foreign influence, whether French, Spanish or German, in Italy. He must put an end to the Pisan schism and settle the other troubles incident to the French invasion. He must restore the French Church to Catholic unity, abolish the pragmatic sanction of Bourges, and bring to a successful close the Lateran council convoked by his predecessor. He must stay the victorious advance of the Turks. He must quiet the disagreeable wranglings of the German humanists. Other problems connected with his family interests were to complicate the situation and eventually to prevent the successful consummation of many of his plans. At the very time of Leo's accession Louis XII. of France, in alliance with Venice, was making a determined effort to regain the duchy of Milan, and the pope, after fruitless endeavours to maintain peace, joined the league of Mechlin on the 5th of April 1513 with the emperor Maximilian I., Ferdinand I. of Spain and Henry VIII. of England. The French and Venetians were at first successful, but on the 6th of June met overwhelming defeat at Novara. The Venetians continued the struggle until October. On the 19th of December the 8th Lateran council, which had been reopened by Leo in April, ratified the peace with Louis XII. and registered the conclusion of the Pisan schism. While the council was engaged in planning a crusade and in considering the reform of the clergy, a new crisis occurred between the pope and the king of France. Francis I., who succeeded Louis XII. on the 1st of January 1515, was an enthusiastic young prince, dominated by the ambition of recovering Milan and Naples. Leo at once formed a new league with the emperor and the king of Spain, and to ensure English support made Wolsey a cardinal. Francis entered Italy in August and on the 14th of September won the battle of Marignano. The pope in October signed an agreement binding him to withdraw his troops from Parma and Piacenza, which had been previously gained at the expense of the duchy of Milan, on condition of French protection at Rome and Florence. The king of Spain wrote to his ambassador at Rome "that His Holiness had hitherto played a double game and that all his zeal to drive the French from Italy had been only a mask"; this reproach seemed to receive some confirmation when Leo X. held a secret conference with Francis at Bologna in December 1515. The ostensible subjects under consideration were the establishment of peace between France, Venice and the Empire, with a view to an expedition against the Turks, and the ecclesiastical affairs of France. Precisely what was arranged is unknown. During these two or three years of incessant political intrigue and warfare it was not to be expected that the Lateran council should accomplish much. Its three main objects, the peace of Christendom, the crusade and the reform of the church, could be secured only by general agreement among the powers, and Leo or the council failed to secure such agreement. Its most important achievements were the registration at its eleventh sitting (19th December 1516) of the abolition of the pragmatic sanction, which the popes since Pius II. had unanimously condemned, and the confirmation of the concordat between Leo X. and Francis I., which was destined to regulate the relations between the French Church and the Holy See until the Revolution. Leo closed the council on the 16th of March 1517. It had ended the schism, ratified the censorship of books introduced by Alexander VI. and imposed tithes for a war against the Turks. It raised no voice against the primacy of the pope.

The year which marked the close of the Lateran council was also signalized by Leo's unholy war against the duke of Urbino. The pope was naturally proud of his family and had practised nepotism from the outset. His cousin Giulio, who subsequently became Clement VII., he had made the most influential man in the curia, naming him archbishop of Florence, cardinal and vice-chancellor of the Holy See. Leo had intended his younger brother Giuliano and his nephew Lorenzo for brilliant secular careers. He had named them Roman patricians; the latter he had placed in charge of Florence; the former, for whom he planned to carve out a kingdom in central Italy of Parma, Piacenza, Ferrara and Urbino, he had taken with himself to Rome and married to Filiberta of Savoy. The death of Giuliano in March 1516, however, caused the pope to transfer his ambitions to Lorenzo. At the very time (December 1516) that peace between France, Spain, Venice and the Empire seemed to give some promise of a Christendom united against the Turk, Leo was preparing an enterprise as unscrupulous as any of the similar exploits of Cesare Borgia. He obtained 150,000 ducats towards the expenses of the expedition from Henry VIII. of England, in return for which he entered the imperial league of Spain and England against France. The war lasted from February to September 1517 and ended with the expulsion of the duke and the triumph of Lorenzo; but it revived the nefarious policy of Alexander VI., increased brigandage and anarchy in the States of the Church, hindered the preparations for a crusade and wrecked the papal finances. Guicciardini reckoned the cost of the war to Leo at the prodigious sum of 800,000 ducats. The new duke of Urbino was the Lorenzo de' Medici to whom Machiavelli addressed *The Prince*. His marriage in March 1518 was arranged by the pope with Madeleine la Tour d'Auvergne, a royal princess of France, whose daughter was the Catherine de' Medici celebrated in French history. The war of Urbino was further marked by a crisis in the relations between pope and cardinals. The sacred college had grown especially worldly and troublesome since the time of Sixtus IV., and Leo took advantage of a plot of several of its members to poison him, not only to inflict exemplary punishments by executing one and imprisoning several others, but also to make a radical change in the college. On the 3rd of July 1517 he published the names of thirty-one new cardinals, a number almost unprecedented in the history of the papacy. Some of the nominations were excellent, such as Lorenzo Campeggio, Giambattista Pallavicini, Adrian of Utrecht, Cajetan, Cristoforo Numai and Egidio Canisio. The naming of seven members of prominent Roman families, however, reversed the wise policy of his predecessor which had kept the dangerous factions of the city out of the curia. Other promotions were for political or family considerations or to secure money for the war against Urbino. The pope was accused of having exaggerated the conspiracy of the cardinals for purposes of financial gain, but most of such accusations appear to be unsubstantiated.

Leo, meanwhile, felt the need of staying the advance of the warlike sultan, Selim I., who was threatening western Europe, and made elaborate plans for a crusade. A truce was to be proclaimed throughout Christendom; the pope was to be the arbiter of disputes; the emperor and the king of France were to lead the army; England, Spain and Portugal were to furnish the fleet; and the combined forces were to be directed against Constantinople. Papal diplomacy in the interests of peace failed, however; Cardinal Wolsey made England, not the pope, the arbiter between France and the Empire; and much of the money collected for the crusade from tithes and indulgences was spent in other ways. In 1519 Hungary concluded a three years' truce with Selim I., but the succeeding sultan, Suliman the Magnificent, renewed the war in June 1521 and on the 28th of August captured the citadel of Belgrade. The pope was greatly alarmed, and although he was then involved in war with France he sent about 30,000 ducats to the Hungarians. Leo treated the Uniate Greeks with great loyalty, and by bull of the 18th of May 1521 forbade Latin clergy to celebrate mass in Greek churches and Latin bishops to ordain Greek clergy.

These provisions were later strengthened by Clement VII. and Paul III. and went far to settle the chronic disputes between the Latins and Uniate Greeks.

Leo was disturbed throughout his pontificate by heresy and schism. The dispute between Reuchlin and Pfefferkorn relative to the Talmud and other Jewish books was referred to the pope in September 1513. He in turn referred it to the bishops of Spires and Worms, who gave decision in March 1514 in favour of Reuchlin. After the appeal of the inquisitor-general, Hochstraten, and the appearance of the *Epistolae obscurorum virorum*, however, Leo annulled the decision (June 1520) and imposed silence on Reuchlin. The pope had already authorized the extensive grant of indulgences in order to secure funds for the crusade and more particularly for the rebuilding of St Peter's at Rome. Against the attendant abuses the Augustinian monk Martin Luther (*q.v.*) posted (31st October 1517) on the church door at Wittenberg his famous ninety-five theses, which were the signal for widespread revolt against the church. Although Leo did not fully comprehend the import of the movement, he directed (3rd February 1518) the vicar-general of the Augustinians to impose silence on the monks. On the 30th of May Luther sent an explanation of his theses to the pope; on the 7th of August he was cited to appear at Rome. An arrangement was effected, however, whereby that citation was cancelled, and Luther betook himself in October 1518 to Augsburg to meet the papal legate, Cardinal Cajetan, who was attending the imperial diet convened by the emperor Maximilian to impose the tithes for the Turkish war and to elect a king of the Romans; but neither the arguments of the learned cardinal, nor the dogmatic papal bull of the 9th of November to the effect that all Christians must believe in the pope's power to grant indulgences, moved Luther to retract. A year of fruitless negotiation followed, during which the pamphlets of the reformer set all Germany on fire. A papal bull of the 15th of June 1520, which condemned forty-one propositions extracted from Luther's teachings, was taken to Germany by Eck in his capacity of apostolic nuncio, published by him and the legates Alexander and Caracciola, and burned by Luther on the 10th of December at Wittenberg. Leo then formally excommunicated Luther by bull of the 3rd of January 1521; and in a brief directed the emperor to take energetic measures against heresy. On the 26th of May 1521 the emperor signed the edict of the diet of Worms, which placed Luther under the ban of the Empire; on the 21st of the same month Henry VIII. of England sent to Leo his book against Luther on the seven sacraments. The pope, after careful consideration, conferred on the king of England the title "Defender of the Faith" by bull of the 11th of October 1521. Neither the imperial edict nor the work of Henry VIII. stayed the Lutheran movement, and Luther himself, safe in the solitude of the Wartburg, survived Leo X. It was under Leo X. also that the Protestant movement had its beginning in Scandinavia. The pope had repeatedly used the rich northern benefices to reward members of the Roman curia, and towards the close of the year 1516 he sent the grasping and impolitic Arcimboldi as papal nuncio to Denmark to collect money for St Peter's. King Christian II. took advantage of the growing dissatisfaction on the part of the native clergy toward the papal government, and of Arcimboldi's interference in the Swedish revolt, in order to expel the nuncio and summon (1520) Lutheran theologians to Copenhagen. Christian approved a plan by which a formal state church should be established in Denmark, all appeals to Rome should be abolished, and the king and diet should have final jurisdiction in ecclesiastical causes. Leo sent a new nuncio to Copenhagen (1521) in the person of the Minorite Francesco de Potentia, who readily absolved the king and received the rich bishopric of Skara. The pope or his legate, however, took no steps to remove abuses or otherwise reform the Scandinavian churches.

That Leo did not do more to check the tendency toward heresy and schism in Germany and Scandinavia is to be partially explained by the political complications of the time, and by his own preoccupation with schemes of papal and Medicean aggrandizement in Italy. The death of the emperor Maximilian on the 12th of January 1519 had seriously affected the situation. Leo vacillated between the powerful candidates for the succession, allowing it to appear at first that he favoured Francis I. while really working for the election of some minor German prince. He finally accepted Charles I. of Spain as inevitable, and the election of Charles (28th of June 1519) revealed Leo's desertion of his French alliance, a step facilitated by the death at about the same time of Lorenzo de' Medici and his French wife. Leo was now anxious to unite Ferrara, Parma and Piacenza to the States of the Church. An attempt late in 1519 to seize Ferrara failed, and the pope recognized the need of foreign aid. In May 1521 a treaty of alliance was signed at Rome between him and the emperor. Milan and Genoa were to be taken from France and restored to the Empire, and Parma and Piacenza were to be given to the Church on the expulsion of the French. The expense of enlisting 10,000 Swiss was to be borne equally by pope and emperor. Charles took Florence and the Medici family under his protection and promised to punish all enemies of the Catholic faith. Leo agreed to invest Charles with Naples, to crown him emperor, and to aid in a war against Venice. It was provided that England and the Swiss might join the league. Henry VIII. announced his adherence in August. Francis I. had already begun war with Charles in Navarre, and in Italy, too, the French made the first hostile movement (23rd June 1521). Leo at once announced that he would excommunicate the king of France and release his subjects from their allegiance unless Francis laid down his arms and surrendered Parma and Piacenza. The pope lived to hear the joyful news of the capture of Milan from the French and of the occupation by papal troops of the long-coveted provinces (November 1521). Leo X. died on the 1st of December 1521, so suddenly that the last sacraments could not be administered; but the contemporary suspicions of poison were unfounded. His successor was Adrian VI.

Several minor events of Leo's pontificate are worthy of mention. He was particularly friendly with King Emmanuel of Portugal on account of the latter's missionary enterprises in Asia and Africa. His concordat with Florence (1516) guaranteed the free election of the clergy in that city. His constitution of the 1st of March 1519 condemned the king of Spain's claim to refuse the publication of papal bulls. He maintained close relations with Poland because of the Turkish advance and the Polish contest with the Teutonic Knights. His bull of the 1st of July 1519, which regulated the discipline of the Polish Church, was later transformed into a concordat by Clement VII. Leo showed special favours to the Jews and permitted them to erect a Hebrew printing-press at Rome. He approved the formation of the Oratory of Divine Love, a group of pious men at Rome which later became the Theatine Order, and he canonized Francesco di Paola.

As patron of learning Leo X. deserves a prominent place among the popes. He raised the church to a high rank as the friend of whatever seemed to extend knowledge or to refine and embellish life. He made the capital of Christendom the centre of culture. Every Italian artist and man of letters in an age of singular intellectual brilliancy tasted or hoped to taste of his bounty. While yet a cardinal, he had restored the church of Sta Maria in Domnica after Raphael's designs; and as pope he built S. Giovanni on the Via Giulia after designs by Jacopo Sansovino and pressed forward the work on St Peter's and the Vatican under Raphael and Chigi. His constitution of the 5th of November 1513 reformed the Roman university, which had been neglected by Julius II. He restored all its faculties, gave larger salaries to the professors, and summoned distinguished teachers from afar; and, although it never attained to the importance of Padua or Bologna, it nevertheless possessed in 1514 an excellent faculty of eighty-eight professors. Leo called Theodore Lascaris to Rome to give instruction in Greek, and established a Greek printing-press from which the first Greek book printed at Rome appeared in 1515. He made Raphael custodian of the classical antiquities of Rome and the vicinity. The distinguished Latinists Pietro Bembo (1470–1547) and [illegible] were papal secretaries, as well as [illegible] (d. 1534). Writers of poetry [illegible] (1476–1530), and Bibbiena (1470– [illegible] Bandello, and a hundred other [illegible] or papal scriptors or abbreviators, [illegible] Leo's lively interest in art and [illegible] liberality, his nepotism, [illegible] and his immoderate [illegible] within two years the hard savings of [illegible] a financial crisis from which he never [illegible] was a direct cause of most of the calamities [illegible] many new offices and shamelessly [illegible] He sold membership in [illegible] He borrowed large sums from bankers, [illegible] The Venetian ambassador Gradenigo [illegible] of offices on Leo's death at 2150, [illegible] nearly 3,000,000 ducats and a yearly [illegible] Marino Giorgi reckoned the ordinary [illegible] the year 1517 at about 580,000 ducats, [illegible] the States of the Church, 100,000 [illegible] the composition tax instituted by [illegible] together with the considerable amounts [illegible] and special fees, vanished [illegible] received. Then the pope resorted to [illegible] table plate, jewels, even statues of the [illegible] and many individual creditors [illegible] the pope.

[illegible] estimates were made of the [illegible] of the pope during whose pontificate [illegible] More recent studies have served [illegible] honest opinion of Leo X. A [illegible] Marino Giorgi bearing date of [illegible] predominant characteristics:— [illegible] and extremely free-hearted man, [illegible] and above all wants peace; [illegible] himself unless his own personal [illegible] learning; of canon law and [illegible] knowledge; he is, moreover, [illegible] Leo was dignified in appearance [illegible] and writing. He enjoyed music [illegible] the masterpieces of the ancients [illegible] his contemporaries, the spiritual [illegible] It is by no means certain that [illegible] attributed to him, "Let us enjoy the [illegible] to us," but there is little doubt [illegible] of moral earnestness or deep [illegible] hand, in spite of his worldliness, [illegible] he prayed, fasted, and participated [illegible] with conscientiousness. To the [illegible] he added the Machia- [illegible] so highly esteemed [illegible] Leo was deemed fortunate by his [illegible] malady, wars, enemies, a [illegible] of all his nearest relations [illegible] in his general policy [illegible] of securing peace throughout [illegible] the Turks. He failed [illegible] within the church and [illegible] the papal monarchy; [illegible] needs of the time. [illegible] establishing the political [illegible] unquestionably supreme in [illegible] papal power in France; [illegible] history of culture.

[illegible] written shortly after his [illegible] who had known him [illegible] are the Italian [illegible] covering the period [illegible] of the Venetian [illegible] and Luigi [illegible]

edited by Joseph Cardinal Hergenröther (Freiburg-i-B., 1884 ff.); in the Turin collection of papal bulls (1859, &c.); in *Il Diario di Leone X. dai volumi manoscritti degli archivi Vaticani della S. Sede connote di M. Armellini* (Rome, 1884); and in "Documenti risguardanti Giovanni de' Medici e il pontifice Leone X.," appendix to vol. 1 of the *Archivio storico Italiano* (Florence, 1842).

See L. Pastor, *Geschichte der Päpste im Zeitalter der Renaissance u. der Glaubensspaltung von der Wahl Leos X. bis zum Tode Klemens VII.* part 1 (Freiburg-i.-B., 1906); M. Creighton, *History of the Papacy*, vol. 6 (1901); F. Gregorovius, *Rome in the Middle Ages*, trans. by Mrs G. W. Hamilton, vol. viii., part 1 (1902); L. von Ranke, *History of the Popes*, vol. i., trans. by E. Foster in the Bohn Library; *Histoire de France*, ed. by E. Lavisse, vol. 5, part 1 (1903); Walter Friedensburg, "Ein rotulus familiae Papst Leos X.," in *Quellen u. Forschungen aus italienischen Archiven u. Bibliotheken*, vol. vi. (1904); W. Roscoe, *Life and Pontificate of Leo X.* (6th ed., 2 vols., 1853), a celebrated biography but considerably out of date in spite of the valuable notes of the German and Italian translators, Henke and Bossi; F. S. Nitti, *Leone X. e la sua politica secondo documenti e carteggi inediti* (Florence, 1892); A. Schulte, *Die Fugger in Rom 1495–1523* (2 vols., Leipzig, 1906); and H. M. Vaughan, *The Medici Popes* (1908). (C. H. Ha.)

Leo XI. (Alessandro de' Medici) was elected pope on the 1st of April 1605, at the age of seventy. He had long been archbishop of Florence and nuncio to Tuscany; and was entirely pro-French in his sympathies. He died on the 27th day of his pontificate, and was succeeded by Paul V.

See the contemporary life by Vitorelli, continuator of Ciaconius, *Vitae et res gestae summorum Pontiff. Rom.*; Ranke, *Popes* (Eng. trans., Austin), ii. 330; v. Reumont, *Gesch. der Stadt Rom*, iii. 2, 604, Brosch, *Gesch. des Kirchenstaates* (1880), i. 350.

Leo XII. (Annibale della Genga), pope from 1823 to 1829, was born of a noble family, near Spoleto, on the 22nd of August 1760. Educated at the Accademia dei Nobili ecclesiastici at Rome, he was ordained priest in 1783, and in 1790 attracted favourable attention by a tactful sermon commemorative of the emperor Joseph II. In 1792 Pius VI. made him his private secretary, in 1793 creating him titular archbishop of Tyre and despatching him to Lucerne as nuncio. In 1794 he was transferred to the nunciature at Cologne, but owing to the war had to make his residence in Augsburg. During the dozen or more years he spent in Germany he was entrusted with several honourable and difficult missions, which brought him into contact with the courts of Dresden, Vienna, Munich and Württemberg, as well as with Napoleon. It is, however, charged at one time during this period that his finances were disordered, and his private life not above suspicion. After the abolition of the States of the Church, he was treated by the French as a state prisoner, and lived for some years at the abbey of Monticelli, solacing himself with music and with bird-shooting, pastimes which he did not eschew even after his election as pope. In 1814 he was chosen to carry the pope's congratulations to Louis XVIII.; in 1816 he was created cardinal-priest of Santa Maria Maggiore, and appointed to the see of Sinigaglia, which he resigned in 1818. In 1820 Pius VII. gave him the distinguished post of cardinal vicar. In the conclave of 1823, in spite of the active opposition of France, he was elected pope by the *zelanti* on the 28th of September. His election had been facilitated because he was thought to be on the edge of the grave; but he unexpectedly rallied. His foreign policy, entrusted at first to Della Somaglia and then to the more able Bernetti, moved in general along lines laid down by Consalvi; and he negotiated certain concordats very advantageous to the papacy. Personally most frugal, Leo reduced taxes, made justice less costly, and was able to find money for certain public improvements; yet he left the finances more confused than he had found them, and even the elaborate jubilee of 1825 did not really mend matters. His domestic policy was one of extreme reaction. He condemned the Bible societies, and under Jesuit influence reorganized the educational system. Severe ghetto laws led many of the Jews to emigrate. He hunted down the *Carbonari* and the Freemasons; he took the strongest measures against political agitation in theatres. A well-nigh ubiquitous system of espionage, perhaps most fruitful when directed against official corruption, sapped the foundations of public confidence Leo, temperamentally stern, hard-working in spite of bodily infirmity, died at Rome on the 10th of February

1829. The news was received by the populace with unconcealed joy. He was succeeded by Pius VIII.

AUTHORITIES.—Artaud de Montor, *Histoire du Pape Léon XII.* (2 vols., 1843; by the secretary of the French embassy in Rome); Brück, "Leo XII.," in Wetzer and Welte's *Kirchenlexikon*, vol. vii. (Freiburg, 1891); F. Nippold, *The Papacy in the 19th Century* (New York, 1900), chap. 5; Benrath, "Leo XII.," in Herzog-Hauck, *Realencyklopädie*, vol. xi. (Leipzig, 1902), 390-393, with bibliography; F. Nielsen, *The History of the Papacy in the 19th century* (1906), vol. ii. 1-30; Lady Blennerhassett, in the *Cambridge Modern History*, vol. x. (1907), 151-154. (W. W. R.*)

LEO XIII. (Gioacchino Pecci) (1810–1903), pope from 1878 to 1903, reckoned the 257th successor of St Peter, was born at Carpineto on the 2nd of March 1810. His family was Sienese in origin, and his father, Colonel Domenico Pecci, had served in the army of Napoleon. His mother, Anna Prosperi, is said to have been a descendant of Rienzi, and was a member of the third order of St Francis. He and his elder brother Giuseppe (known as Cardinal Pecci) received their earliest education from the Jesuits at Viterbo, and completed their education in Rome. In the jubilee year 1825 he was selected by his fellow-students at the Collegium Romanum to head a deputation to Pope Leo XII., whose memory he subsequently cherished and whose name he assumed in 1878. Weak health, consequent on over-study, prevented him from obtaining the highest academical honours, but he graduated as doctor in theology at the age of twenty-two, and then entered the Accademia dei Nobili ecclesiastici, a college in which clergy of aristocratic birth are trained for the diplomatic service of the Roman Church. Two years later Gregory XVI. appointed him a domestic prelate, and bestowed on him, by way of apprenticeship, various minor administrative offices. He was ordained priest on the 31st of December 1837, and a few weeks later was made apostolic delegate of the small papal territory of Benevento, where he had to deal with brigands and smugglers, who enjoyed the protection of some of the noble families of the district. His success here led to his appointment in 1841 as delegate of Perugia, which was at that time a centre of anti-papal secret societies. This post he held for eighteen months only, but in that brief period he obtained a reputation as a social and municipal reformer. In 1843 he was sent as nuncio to Brussels, being first consecrated a bishop (19th February), with the title of archbishop of Damietta. During his three years' residence at the Belgian capital he found ample scope for his gifts as a diplomatist in the education controversy then raging, and as mediator between the Jesuits and the Catholic university of Louvain. He gained the esteem of Leopold I., and was presented to Queen Victoria of England and the Prince Consort. He also made the acquaintance of many Englishmen, Archbishop Whately among them. In January 1846, at the request of the magistrates and people of Perugia, he was appointed bishop of that city with the rank of archbishop; but before returning to Italy he spent February in London, and March and April in Paris. On his arrival in Rome he would, at the request of King Leopold, have been created cardinal but for the death of Gregory XVI. Seven years later, 19th December 1853, he received the red hat from Pius IX. Meanwhile, and throughout his long episcopate of thirty-two years, he foreshadowed the zeal and the enlightened policy later to be displayed in the prolonged period of his pontificate, building and restoring many churches, striving to elevate the intellectual as well as the spiritual tone of his clergy, and showing in his pastoral letters an unusual regard for learning and for social reform. His position in Italy was similar to that of Bishop Dupanloup in France; and, as but a moderate supporter of the policy enunciated in the Syllabus, he was not altogether *persona grata* to Pius IX. But he protested energetically against the loss of the pope's temporal power in 1870, against the confiscation of the property of the religious orders, and against the law of civil marriage established by the Italian government, and he refused to welcome Victor Emmanuel in his diocese. Nevertheless, he remained in the comparative obscurity of his episcopal see until the death of Cardinal Antonelli, but in 1877, when the important papal office of *camerlengo* became vacant, Pius IX. appointed to it Cardinal Pecci, who thus returned to reside in Rome, with the prospect of having shortly responsible functions to perform during the vacancy of the Holy See, though the *camerlengo* was traditionally regarded as disqualified by his office from succeeding to the papal throne.

When Pius IX. died (7th February 1878) Cardinal Pecci was elected pope at the subsequent conclave with comparative unanimity, obtaining at the third scrutiny (20th February) forty-four out of sixty-one votes, or more than the requisite two-thirds majority. The conclave was remarkably free from political influences, the attention of Europe being at the time engrossed by the presence of a Russian army at the gates of Constantinople. It was said that the long pontificate of Pius IX. led some of the cardinals to vote for Pecci, since his age (within a few days of sixty-eight) and health warranted the expectation that his reign would be comparatively brief; but he had for years been known as one of the few "papable" cardinals; and although his long seclusion at Perugia had caused his name to be little known outside Italy, there was a general belief that the conclave had selected a man who was a prudent statesman as well as a devout churchman; and Newman (whom he created a cardinal in the year following) is reported to have said, "In the successor of Pius I recognize a depth of thought, a tenderness of heart, a winning simplicity, and a power answering to the name of Leo, which prevent me from lamenting that Pius is no longer here."

The second day after his election Pope Leo XIII. crossed the Tiber *incognito* to his former residence in the Falconieri Palace to collect his papers, returning at once to the Vatican, where he continued to regard himself as "imprisoned" so long as the Italian government occupied the city of Rome. He was crowned in the Sistine Chapel 3rd March 1878, and at once began a reform of the papal household on austere and economic lines which found little favour with the *entourage* of the former pope. To fill posts near his own person he summoned certain of the Perugian clergy who had been trained under his own eye, and from the first he was less accessible than his predecessor had been, either in public or private audience. Externally uneventful as his life henceforth necessarily was, it was marked chiefly by the reception of distinguished personages and of numerous pilgrimages, often on a large scale, from all parts of the world, and by the issue of encyclical letters. The stricter theological training of the Roman Catholic clergy throughout the world on the lines laid down by St Thomas Aquinas was his first care, and to this end he founded in Rome and endowed an academy bearing the great schoolman's name, further devoting about £12,000 to the publication of a new and splendid edition of his works, the idea being that on this basis the later teaching of Catholic theologians and many of the speculations of modern thinkers could best be harmonized and brought into line. The study of Church history was next encouraged, and in August 1883 the pope addressed a letter to Cardinals de Luca, Pitra and Hergenröther, in which he made the remarkable concession that the Vatican archives and library might be placed at the disposal of persons qualified to compile manuals of history. His belief was that the Church would not suffer by the publication of documents. A man of literary taste and culture, familiar with the classics, a facile writer of Latin verses[1] as well as of Ciceronian prose, he was as anxious that the Roman clergy should unite human science and literature with their theological studies as that the laity should be educated in the principles of religion; and to this end he established in Rome a kind of voluntary school board, with members both lay and clerical; and the rivalry of the schools thus founded ultimately obliged the state to include religious teaching in its curriculum. The numerous encyclicals by which the pontificate of Leo XIII. will always be distinguished were prepared and written by himself, but were submitted to the customary revision. The encyclical *Aeterni Patris* (4th August 1879) was

[1] *Leonis XIII. Pont. Maximi carmina*, ed. Brunelli (Udine, 1883); *Leonis XIII. carmina, inscriptiones, numismata*, ed. J. Bach (Cologne, 1903).

[illegible] in the defence of the philosophy of St Thomas Aquinas. In [illegible], working on the principle that the Christian Church should superintend and direct every form of civil life, he dealt with the Christian constitution of states (*Immortale Dei*, 1st November 1885), with human liberty (*Libertas*, 20th June 1888), and with the condition of the working classes (*Rerum novarum*, 15th May 1891). This last was slightly tinged with modern socialism; it was described as "the social Magna Carta of Catholicism," and it won for Leo the name of "the working-man's pope." Translated into the chief modern languages, many thousands of copies were circulated among the working classes in Catholic countries. Other encyclicals, such as those on Christian marriage (*Arcanum divinae sapientiae*, 10th February [illegible]), on the Rosary (*Supremi apostolatus officii*, 1st September [illegible], and *Superiore anno*, 5th September 1898), and on Free-[illegible] (*Humanum genus*, 20th April 1884), dealt with subjects [illegible] his predecessor had been accustomed to pronounce [illegible], and were on similar lines. It was the knowledge [illegible] of religious faith and practice Leo XIII. stood [illegible] Pius IX. had stood that served to render in-[illegible] of his encyclicals, in which he dealt earnestly [illegible] with matters in which orthodox Protestants had [illegible] interest with him and might otherwise have lent [illegible] counsels. Such were the letters on the study of [illegible], 18th November 1893), and on the reunion of [illegible] 20th June 1894). He showed special anxiety for [illegible] England to the Roman Catholic fold, and addressed [illegible] dated 14th April 1895. This he followed [illegible] on the unity of the Church (*Satis cognitum*, [illegible] 1896), and the question of the validity of Anglican [illegible] from the Roman Catholic point of view having been [illegible] by Viscount Halifax, with whom the abbé [illegible] and one or two other French priests were in [illegible] a commission was appointed to consider the subject, [illegible] September 1896 a condemnation of the [illegible] theologically insufficient was issued, and was [illegible] as final.

[illegible] of a diocesan hierarchy in Scotland had [illegible] before the death of Pius IX., but the actual [illegible] was made by Leo XIII. On the 25th of [illegible] to the Scottish Catholic bishops a letter, [illegible] which he said that "many of the Scottish [illegible] with us in faith sincerely love the name [illegible] to ascertain His doctrine and to imitate [illegible]." The Irish and American bishops [illegible] to confer with him on the subjects of [illegible] "Americanism" respectively. In India [illegible] hierarchy, with seven archbishoprics, [illegible] taking precedence with the rank of [illegible]

[illegible] of Italy his general policy was to be as [illegible] with his oath as pope never to [illegible] of St Peter"; but a moderate attitude [illegible] by partisans on either side in the press, [illegible] his views. In 1879, addressing [illegible] journalists in Rome, he exhorted them [illegible] of the temporal power, and to proclaim [illegible] of Italy would never prosper until [illegible] he found it necessary to deprecate [illegible] doctrine was advocated in certain [illegible] of moderation was given to the [illegible] with the Manitoba school question [illegible] conciliatory attitude towards the [illegible] in an encyclical addressed [illegible] August 1898), in which he insisted [illegible] to abstain from political life [illegible] its "painful, precarious and [illegible] And in January 1902, reversing the [illegible] in the encyclical, *Rerum novarum*, [illegible] developed ten years later in a [illegible] *Graves de communi*, the [illegible] of Extraordinary Ecclesiastical Affairs" issued instructions concerning "Christian Democracy in Italy," directing that the popular Christian movement, which embraced in its programme a number of social reforms, such as factory laws for children, old-age pensions, a minimum wage in agricultural industries, an eight-hours' day, the revival of trade gilds, and the encouragement of Sunday rest, should divert its attention from all such things as savoured of novelty and devote its energies to the restoration of the temporal power. The reactionary policy thus indicated gave the impression that a similar aim underlay the appointment about the same date of a commission to inquire into Biblical studies; and in other minor matters Leo XIII. disappointed those who had looked to him for certain reforms in the devotional system of the Church. A revision of the breviary, which would have involved the omission of some of the less credible legends, came to nothing, while the recitation of the office in honour of the Santa Casa at Loreto was imposed on all the clergy. The worship of Mary, largely developed during the reign of Pius IX., received further stimulus from Leo; nor did he do anything during his pontificate to correct the superstitions connected with popular beliefs concerning relics and indulgences.

His policy towards all governments outside Italy was to support them wherever they represented social order; and it was with difficulty that he persuaded French Catholics to be united in defence of the republic. The German *Kulturkampf* was ended by his exertions. In 1885 he successfully arbitrated between Germany and Spain in a dispute concerning the Caroline Islands. In Ireland he condemned the "Plan of Campaign" in 1888, but he conciliated the Nationalists by appointing Dr Walsh archbishop of Dublin. His hope that his support of the British government in Ireland would be followed by the establishment of formal diplomatic relations between the court of St James's and the Vatican was disappointed. But the jubilee of Queen Victoria in 1887 and the pope's priestly jubilee a few months later were the occasion of friendly intercourse between Rome and Windsor, Mgr. Ruffo Scilla coming to London as special papal envoy, and the duke of Norfolk being received at the Vatican as the bearer of the congratulations of the queen of England. Similar courtesies were exchanged during the jubilee of 1897, and again in March 1902, when Edward VII. sent the earl of Denbigh to Rome to congratulate Leo XIII. on reaching his ninety-third year and the twenty-fifth year of his pontificate. The visit of Edward VII. to Leo XIII. in April 1903 was a further proof of the friendliness between the English court and the Vatican.

The elevation of Newman to the college of Cardinals in 1879 was regarded with approval throughout the English-speaking world, both on Newman's account and also as evidence that Leo XIII. had a wider horizon than his predecessor; and his similar recognition of two of the most distinguished "inopportunist" members of the Vatican council, Haynald, archbishop of Kalocsa, and Prince Fürstenberg, archbishop of Olmütz, was even more noteworthy. Dupanloup would doubtless have received the same honour had he not died shortly after Leo's accession. Döllinger the pope attempted to reconcile, but failed. He laboured much to bring about the reunion of the Oriental Churches with the see of Rome, establishing Catholic educational centres in Athens and in Constantinople with that end in view. He used his influence with the emperor of Russia, as also with the emperors of China and Japan and with the shah of Persia, to secure the free practice of their religion for Roman Catholics within their respective dominions. Among the canonizations and beatifications of his pontificate that of Sir Thomas More, author of *Utopia*, is memorable. His encyclical issued at Easter 1902, and described by himself as a kind of will, was mainly a reiteration of earlier condemnations of the Reformation, and of modern philosophical systems, which for their atheism and materialism he makes responsible for all existing moral and political disorders. Society, he earnestly pleaded, can only find salvation by a return to Christianity and to the fold of the Roman Catholic Church.

Grave and serious in manner, speaking slowly, but with

energetic gestures, simple and abstemious in his life—his daily bill of fare being reckoned as hardly costing a couple of francs—Leo XIII. distributed large sums in charity, and at his own charges placed costly astronomical instruments in the Vatican observatory, providing also accommodation and endowment for a staff of officials. He always showed the greatest interest in science and in literature, and he would have taken a position as a statesman of the first rank had he held office in any secular government. He may be reckoned the most illustrious pope since Benedict XIV., and under him the papacy acquired a prestige unknown since the middle ages. On the 3rd of March 1903 he celebrated his jubilee in St Peter's with more than usual pomp and splendour; he died on the 20th of July following. His successor was Pius X.

See *Scelta di atti episcopali del cardinale G. Pecci* . . . (Rome, 1879); *Leonis XIII. Pont. Max. acta* (17 vols., Rome, 1881–1898); *Sanctissimi Domini N. Leonis XIII. allocutiones, epistolae, &c.* (Bruges and Lille, 1887, &c.); the encyclicals (*Samtliche Rundschreiben*) with a German translation (6 vols., Freiburg, 1878–1904); *Discorsi del Sommo Pontefice Leone XIII. 1878–1882* (Rome, 1882). There are lives of Leo XIII. by B. O'Reilly (new ed., Chicago, 1903), H. des Houx (pseudonym of Durand Morimbeau) (Paris, 1900), by W. Meynell (1887), by J. McCarthy (1896), by Boyer d'Agen, (*Jeunesse de Léon XIII.* (1896); *La Prélature*, 1900), by M. Spahn (Munich, 1905), by L. K. Goetz (Gotha, 1899), &c. A life of Leo XIII. (4 vols.) was undertaken by F. Marion Crawford, Count Edoardo Soderini and Professor Giuseppe Clementi. (A. W. Hu.; M. Br.)

LEO, the name of six emperors of the East.

Leo I., variously surnamed Thrax, Magnus and Makelles, emperor of the East, 457–474, was born in Thrace about 400. From his position as military tribune he was raised to the throne by the soldiery and recognized both by senate and clergy; his coronation by the patriarch of Constantinople is said to have been the earliest instance of such a ceremony. Leo owed his elevation mainly to Aspar, the commander of the guards, who was debarred by his Arianism from becoming emperor in his own person, but hoped to exercise a virtual autocracy through his former steward and dependant. But Leo, following the traditions of his predecessor Marcian, set himself to curtail the domination of the great nobles and repeatedly acted in defiance of Aspar. Thus he vigorously suppressed the Eutychian heresy in Egypt, and by exchanging his Germanic bodyguard for Isaurians removed the chief basis of Aspar's power. With the help of his generals Anthemius and Anagastus, he repelled invasions of the Huns into Dacia (466 and 468). In 467 Leo had Anthemius elected emperor of the West, and in concert with him equipped an armament of more than 1100 ships and 100,000 men against the pirate empire of the Vandals in Africa. Through the remissness of Leo's brother-in-law Basiliscus, who commanded the expedition, the fleet was surprised by the Vandal king, Genseric, and half of its vessels sunk or burnt (468). This failure was made a pretext by Leo for killing Aspar as a traitor (471), and Aspar's murder served the Goths in turn as an excuse for ravaging Thrace up to the walls of the capital. In 473 the emperor associated with himself his infant grandson, Leo II., who, however, survived him by only a few months. His surnames Magnus (Great) and Makelles (butcher) respectively reflect the attitude of the Orthodox and the Arians towards his religious policy.

See E. Gibbon, *The Decline and Fall of the Roman Empire* (ed. Bury, 1896), iv. 29-37; J. B. Bury, *The Later Roman Empire* (1889), i. 227-233.

Leo III. (*c.* 680–740), surnamed The Isaurian, emperor of the East, 717–740. Born about 680 in the Syrian province of Commagene, he rose to distinction in the military service, and under Anastasius II. was invested with the command of the eastern army. In 717 he revolted against the usurper Theodosius III. and, marching upon Constantinople, was elected emperor in his stead. The first year of Leo's reign saw a memorable siege of his capital by the Saracens, who had taken advantage of the civil discord in the Roman empire to bring up a force of 80,000 men to the Bosporus. By his stubborn defence the new ruler wore out the invaders who, after a twelve months' investment, withdrew their forces. An important factor in the victory of the Romans was their use of Greek fire. Having thus preserved the empire from extinction, Leo proceeded to consolidate its administration, which in the previous years of anarchy had become completely disorganized. He secured its frontiers by inviting Slavonic settlers into the depopulated districts and by restoring the army to efficiency; when the Arabs renewed their invasions in 726 and 739 they were decisively beaten. His civil reforms include the abolition of the system of prepaying taxes which had weighed heavily upon the wealthier proprietors, the elevation of the serfs into a class of free tenants, the remodelling of family and of maritime law. These measures, which were embodied in a new code published in 740, met with some opposition on the part of the nobles and higher clergy. But Leo's most striking legislative reforms dealt with religious matters. After an apparently successful attempt to enforce the baptism of all Jews and Montanists in his realm (722), he issued a series of edicts against the worship of images (726–729). This prohibition of a custom which had undoubtedly given rise to grave abuses seems to have been inspired by a genuine desire to improve public morality, and received the support of the official aristocracy and a section of the clergy. But a majority of the theologians and all the monks opposed these measures with uncompromising hostility, and in the western parts of the empire the people refused to obey the edict. A revolt which broke out in Greece, mainly on religious grounds, was crushed by the imperial fleet (727), and two years later, by deposing the patriarch of Constantinople, Leo suppressed the overt opposition of the capital. In Italy the defiant attitude of Popes Gregory II. and III. on behalf of image-worship led to a fierce quarrel with the emperor. The former summoned councils in Rome to anathematize and excommunicate the image-breakers (730, 732); Leo retaliated by transferring southern Italy and Greece from the papal diocese to that of the patriarch. The struggle was accompanied by an armed outbreak in the exarchate of Ravenna (727), which Leo finally endeavoured to subdue by means of a large fleet. But the destruction of the armament by a storm decided the issue against him; his south Italian subjects successfully defied his religious edicts, and the province of Ravenna became detached from the empire. In spite of this partial failure Leo must be reckoned as one of the greatest of the later Roman emperors. By his resolute stand against the Saracens he delivered all eastern Europe from a great danger, and by his thorough-going reforms he not only saved the empire from collapse, but invested it with a stability which enabled it to survive all further shocks for a space of five centuries.

See E. Gibbon, *The Decline and Fall of the Roman Empire* (ed. Bury, 1896), v. 185 seq., 251 seq. and appendices, vi. 6-12, J. B. Bury, *The Later Roman Empire* (1889), ii. 401-449; K. Schenk, *Kaiser Leo III.* (Halle, 1880), and in *Byzantinische Zeitschrift* (1896), v. 257-301; T. Hodgkin, *Italy and her Invaders* (1892, &c.), bk. vii., chs. 11, 12. See also Iconoclasts.

Leo IV., called Chozar, succeeded his father, Constantine V., as emperor of the East in 775. In 776 he associated his young son, Constantine, with himself in the empire, and suppressed a rising led by his five step-brothers which broke out as a result of this proceeding. Leo was largely under the influence of his wife Irene (*q.v.*), and when he died in 780 he left her as the guardian of his successor, Constantine VI.

Leo V., surnamed The Armenian, emperor of the East, 813–820, was a distinguished general of Nicephorus I. and Michael I. After rendering good service on behalf of the latter in a war with the Arabs (812), he was summoned in 813 to co-operate in a campaign against the Bulgarians. Taking advantage of the disaffection prevalent among the troops, he left Michael in the lurch at the battle of Adrianople and subsequently led a successful revolution against him. Leo justified his usurpation by repeatedly defeating the Bulgarians who had been contemplating the siege of Constantinople (814–817). By his vigorous measures of repression against the Paulicians and image-worshippers he roused considerable opposition, and after a conspiracy under his friend Michael Psellus had been foiled by the imprisonment of its leader, he was assassinated in the palace chapel on Christmas Eve, 820.

See E. Gibbon, *The Decline and Fall of the Roman Empire* (ed. Bury, 1896), v. 193-195. (M. O. B. C.)

[illegible] the writings of Hamann [illegible] direction of conservatism [illegible] a mood almost of [illegible] right wing of the [illegible] Göttingen, he had [illegible] von Haller's *Handbuch* [illegible] the constru[illegible] his teacher's [illegible] as *Privatdocent* at the [illegible] this other purpose he had [illegible] of the free Lombard cities in the [illegible] which he was destined to do most [illegible] history. His interest in it was greatly [illegible] to Italy in 1823; in 1824 he returned [illegible] the result, published in five volumes [illegible] (1829–1832). Meanwhile he had [illegible] as *Docent* at Berlin, where he came [illegible] of German thought and was somewhat [illegible] of the highest Prussian society. [illegible] Hegel's philosophy of history made a deep [illegible] It was at Halle, however, where he [illegible] (1828–1868), that he acquired his fame [illegible] His wonderful power of exposition, [illegible] memory, is attested by the most various [illegible] became ordinary professor.

[illegible] lecturing, Leo found time for much literary [illegible] He collaborated in the *Jahrbücher für* [illegible] from its foundation in 1827 until the [illegible] in 1838. As a critic of independent [illegible] the approval of Goethe; on the other hand, he [illegible] controversy with Ranke about questions con[illegible] history. Up to the revolutionary year 1830 [illegible] remained strongly tinged with rational[illegible] as guide in religion as in practical politics [illegible] history. It was not till 1838 that Leo's [illegible] *Hegelingen* proclaimed his breach with the [illegible] of the philosopher's later disciples; a [illegible] into opposition to the philosopher him[illegible] the impression of the July revolution in Paris and [illegible] influences at Halle, Leo's political [illegible] were henceforth dominated by reactionary principles. [illegible] the Prussian "Camarilla" and of King Frederick [illegible] he collaborated especially in the high conservative [illegible] *Wochenblatt*, which first appeared in 1831, as well as [illegible] *Kirchenzeitung*, the *Kreuzzeitung* and the [illegible] *Staat und Land*. In all this his critics scented an [illegible] towards Catholicism; and Leo did actually glorify [illegible] Counter-Reformation, e.g. in his *History of the Netherlands* [illegible] His other historical works also, notably [illegible] (6 vols., 1835–1844), display a very one[illegible] point of view. When, however, in connexion with the [illegible] about the archbishopric of Cologne (1837), political [illegible] raised its head menacingly, Leo turned against it [illegible] extreme violence in his open letter (1838) to Goerres, its [illegible] champion. On the other hand, he took a lively part in [illegible] religious controversies within the fold of Prussian Protestantism.

Leo was by nature highly excitable and almost insanely [illegible], though at the same time strictly honourable, unselfish, and in private intercourse even gentle. During the last year of his life his mind suffered rapid decay, of which signs had been apparent so early as 1868. He died at Halle on the 24th of April [illegible]. In addition to the works already mentioned, he left behind an account of his early life (*Meine Jugendzeit*, Gotha, 1880) which is of interest.

[illegible] Lord Acton, *English Historical Review*, i. (1886); H. Haupt, [illegible] *und die Giessener Schwarzen* (Giessen, 1907); W. Herbst, [illegible] *Blätter*, Bd. 3; P. Krägelin, *H. Leo*, vol. i. (Leipzig, 1908); P. Kraus, *Allgemeine Konservative* [illegible], Bd. 50 u. 51; R. M. Meyer, *Gestalten und Probleme* [illegible] Schrader, *Geschichte der Friedrichs-Universität zu Halle* [illegible]; C. Varrentrapp; *Historische Zeitschrift*, Bd. 92; [illegible], *Allgemeine Deutsche Biographie*, Bd. 18 (1883);

Geschichte der deutschen Historiographie (1885); G. Wolf, *Einführung in das Studium der neueren Geschichte* (1910). Leo's *Rectitudines singularum personarum nebst einer einleitenden Abhandlung über Landsiedelung, Landbau, gutsherrliche und bäuerliche Verhältnisse der Angelsachsen*, was translated into English by Lord Acton (1852). (J. Hn.)

LEO, JOHANNES (*c.* 1494–1552), in Italian GIOVANNI LEO or LEONE, usually called LEO AFRICANUS, sometimes ELIBERITANUS (*i.e.* of Granada), and properly known among the Moors as Al Hassan Ibn Mahommed Al Wezaz Al Fasi, was the author of a *Descrizione dell' Affrica*, or *Africae descriptio*, which long ranked as the best authority on Mahommedan Africa. Born probably at Granada of a noble Moorish stock (his father was a landowner; an uncle of his appears as an envoy from Fez to Timbuktu), he received a great part of his education at Fez, and while still very young began to travel widely in the Barbary States. In 1512 we trace him at Morocco, Tunis, Bugia and Constantine; in 1513 we find him returning from Tunis to Morocco; and before the close of the latter year he seems to have started on his famous Sudan and Sahara journeys (1513–1515) which brought him to Timbuktu, to many other regions of the Great Desert and the Niger basin (Guinea, Melli, Gago, Walata, Aghadez, Wangara, Katsena, &c.), and apparently to Bornu and Lake Chad. In 1516–1517 he travelled to Constantinople, probably visiting Egypt on the way; it is more uncertain when he visited the three Arabias (*Deserta*, *Felix* and *Petraea*), Armenia and "Tartary" (the last term is perhaps satisfied by his stay at Tabriz). His three Egyptian journeys, immediately after the Turkish conquest, all probably fell between 1517 and 1520; on one of these he ascended the Nile from Cairo to Assuan. As he was returning from Egypt about 1520 he was captured by pirates near the island of Gerba, and was ultimately presented as a slave to Leo X. The pope discovered his merit, assigned him a pension, and having persuaded him to profess the Christian faith, stood sponsor at his baptism, and bestowed on him (as Ramusio says) his own names, Johannes and Leo. The new convert, having made himself acquainted with Latin and Italian, taught Arabic (among his pupils was Cardinal Egidio Antonini, bishop of Viterbo); he also wrote books in both the Christian tongues he had acquired. His *Description of Africa* was first, apparently, written in Arabic, but the primary text now remaining is that of the Italian version, issued by the author at Rome, on the 10th of March 1526, three years after Pope Leo's death, though originally undertaken at the latter's suggestion. The Moor seems to have lived on Rome for some time longer, but he returned to Africa some time before his death at Tunis in 1552; according to some, he renounced his Christianity and returned to Islam; but the later part of his career is obscure.

The *Descrizione dell' Affrica* in its original Arabic MS. is said to have existed for some time in the library of Vincenzo Pinelli (1535–1601); the Italian text, though issued in 1526, was first printed by Giovanni Battista Ramusio in his *Navigationi et Viaggi* (vol. i.) of 1550. This was reprinted in 1554, 1563, 1588, &c. In 1556 Jean Temporal executed at Lyons an admirable French version from the Italian (*Historiale description de l'Afrique*); and in the same year appeared at Antwerp both Christopher Plantin's and Jean Bellere's pirated issues of Temporal's translation, and a new (very inaccurate) Latin version by Joannes Florianus, *Joannis Leonis Africani de totius Africae descriptione libri i.-ix.* The latter was reprinted in 1558, 1559 (Zürich), and 1632 (Leiden), and served as the basis of John Pory's Elizabethan English translation, made at the suggestion of Richard Hakluyt (*A Geographical Historie of Africa*, London, 1600). Pory's version was reissued, with notes, maps, &c., by Robert Brown, E. G. Ravenstein, &c. (3 vols., Hakluyt Society, London, 1896). An excellent German translation was made by Lorsbach, from the Italian, in 1805 (*Johann Leos des Afrikaners Beschreibung von Afrika*, Herborn). See also Francis Moore's *Travels into the inland parts of Africa* (1738), containing a translation of Leo's account of negro kingdoms. Heinrich Barth intended to have made a fresh version, with a commentary, but was prevented by death; as it is, his own great works on the Sudan are the best elucidation of the *Descrizione dell' Affrica*.

Leo also wrote lives of the Arab physicians and philosophers (*De viris quibusdam illustribus apud Arabes*; see J. A. Fabricius, *Bibliotheca Graeca*, Hamburg, 1726, xiii. 259–298); a Spanish-Arabic vocabulary, now lost, but noticed by Ramusio as having been consulted by the famous Hebrew physician, Jacob Mantino; a collection of Arabic epitaphs in and near Fez (the MS. of this Leo presented, it is said, to the brother of the king); and poems, also lost. It is stated, moreover, that Leo intended writing a history of the Mahommedan religion, an epitome of Mahommedan chronicles, and an account of his travels in Asia and Egypt. (C. R. B.)

LEO, LEONARDO (1694–1744), more correctly LIONARDO ORONZO SALVATORE DE LEO, Italian musical composer, was born on the 5th of August 1694 at S. Vito dei Normanni, near Brindisi. He became a student at the Conservatorio della Pietà dei Turchini at Naples in 1703, and was a pupil first of Provenzale and later of Nicola Fago. It has been supposed that he was a pupil of Pitoni and Alessandro Scarlatti, but he could not possibly have studied with either of these composers, although he was undoubtedly influenced by their compositions. His earliest known work was a sacred drama, *L'Infedeltà abbattuta*, performed by his fellow-students in 1712. In 1714 he produced, at the court theatre, an opera, *Pisistrato*, which was much admired. He held various posts at the royal chapel, and continued to write for the stage, besides teaching at the conservatorio. After adding comic scenes to Gasparini's *Bajazette* in 1722 for performance at Naples, he composed a comic opera, *La 'Mpeca scoperta*, in Neapolitan dialect, in 1723. His most famous comic opera was *Amor vuol sofferenze* (1739), better known as *La Finta Frascatana*, highly praised by Des Brosses. He was equally distinguished as a composer of serious opera, *Demofoonte* (1735), *Farnace* (1737) and *L'Olimpiade* (1737) being his most famous works in this branch, and is still better known as a composer of sacred music. He died of apoplexy on the 31st of October 1744 while engaged in the composition of new airs for a revival of *La Finta Frascatana*.

Leo was the first of the Neapolitan school to obtain a complete mastery over modern harmonic counterpoint. His sacred music is masterly and dignified, logical rather than passionate, and free from the sentimentality which disfigures the work of F. Durante and G. B. Pergolesi. His serious operas suffer from a coldness and severity of style, but in his comic operas he shows a keen sense of humour. His *ensemble* movements are spirited, but never worked up to a strong climax.

A fine and characteristic example of his sacred music is the *Dixit Dominus* in C, edited by C. V. Stanford and published by Novello. A number of songs from operas are accessible in modern editions. (E. J. D.)

LEO (THE LION), in astronomy, the fifth sign of the zodiac (*q.v.*), denoted by the symbol ♌. It is also a constellation, mentioned by Eudoxus (4th century B.C.) and Aratus (3rd century B.C.). According to Greek mythology this constellation is the Nemean lion, which, after being killed by Hercules, was raised to the heavens by Jupiter in honour of Hercules. A part of Ptolemy's Leo is now known as Coma Berenices (*q.v.*). α Leonis, also known as Cor Leonis or the Lion's Heart, Regulus, Basilicus, &c., is a very bright star of magnitude 1·23, and parallax 0·02″, and proper motion 0·27″ per annum. γ Leonis is a very fine orange-yellow binary star, of magnitudes 2 and 4, and period 400 years. ι Leonis is a binary, composed of a 4th magnitude pale yellow star, and a 7th magnitude blue star. The LEONIDS are a meteoric swarm, appearing in November and radiating from this constellation (see METEOR).

LEOBEN, a town in Styria, Austria, 44 m. N.W. of Graz by rail. Pop. (1900) 10,204. It is situated on the Mur, and part of its old walls and towers still remain. It has a well-known academy of mining and a number of technical schools. Its extensive iron-works and trade in iron are a consequence of its position on the verge of the important lignite deposits of Upper Styria and in the neighbourhood of the iron mines and furnaces of Vordernberg and Eisenerz. On the 18th of April 1797 a preliminary peace was concluded here between Austria and France, which led to the treaty of Campo-Formio.

LEOBSCHÜTZ (Bohemian *Lubczyce*), a town of Germany, in the Prussian province of Silesia, on the Zinna, about 20 m. to the N.W. of Ratibor by rail. Pop. (1905) 12,700. It has a large trade in wool, flax and grain, its markets for these commodities being very numerously attended. The principal industries are malting, carriage-building, wool-spinning and glass-making. The town contains three Roman Catholic

[illegible] and a nunnery existed here until the Conquest, when the place became a royal demesne. It was granted by Henry I. to the monks of Reading, who built in it a cell of their abbey, and under whose protection the town grew up and was exempted from the sphere of the county and hundred courts. In 1539 it reverted to the crown; and in 1554 was incorporated, by a charter renewed in 1562, 1563, 1605, 1666, 1685 and 1786. The borough returned two members to the parliament of 1295 and to other parliaments, until by the Representation Act 1867 it lost one representative, and by the Redistribution of Seats Act 188[illegible] separate representation. A fair was granted in the time of Henry II., and fairs in the seasons of Michaelmas and the feasts of St Philip and St James and of Edward the Confessor, in 1205, 1281 and 1290 respectively. Charters to the burghers authorized fairs on the days of St Peter and of St Simon and St Jude in 1554, on St Bartholomew's day in 1605, in Mid-lent week in 1665, and on the feast of the Purification and on the [illegible] of May in 1685; these fairs have modern representatives. A market was held by the abbey by a grant of Henry I.; Friday is now market day. Leominster was famous for wool from the [illegible] to the 18th century. There were gilds of mercers, tailors, drapers, dyers and glovers in the 16th century. In 1835 the wool trade was said to be dead; and that of glove-making, which had been important, was diminishing. Hops and apples were grown in 1715.

See G. Townsend, *The Town and Borough of Leominster* (1863), and John Price, *An Historical and Topographical Account of Leominster* [illegible] (Ludlow, 1715).

LEOMINSTER, a township of Worcester county, Massachusetts, U.S.A., about 45 m. N.W. of Boston and about 20 m. N. by E. of Worcester. Pop. (1890) 7269; (1900) 12,392, of whom [illegible] were foreign-born; (1910 census) 17,580. It is a broken, hilly district, 26·48 sq. m. in area, traversed by the Nashua river, crossed by the Northern Division of the New York, New Haven & Hartford railroad, and by the Fitchburg Division of the Boston & Maine, and connected with Boston, Worcester and other cities by interurban electric lines. Along the N.E. border and mostly in the township of Lunenburg are Whalom Lake and Whalom Park, popular pleasure resorts. The principal villages are Leominster, 5 m. S.E. of Fitchburg, and North Leominster; the two adjoin and are virtually one. According to the Special U.S. Census of Manufactures of 1905 the township had in that year a greater diversity of important manufacturing industries than any place of its size in the state, or, probably, in the United States; its 65 manufactories, with a capital of $[illegible] and with a product for the year valued at $[illegible] ([illegible]% more than in 1900), produced celluloid and horn work (the manufacture of which is a more important industry here than elsewhere in the United States), celluloid goods, furniture, paper, buttons, pianos and piano-cases, children's carriages and sleds, stationery, leatherboard, worsted, woollen and cotton goods, shirts, paper boxes, &c. Leominster owns and operates its water-works. The township was formed from a part of Lancaster township in 1740.

LEÓN, LUIS PONCE DE (1527–1591), Spanish poet and [illegible] was born at Belmonte de Cuenca, entered the university of Salamanca at the age of fourteen, and in 1544 joined the Augustinian order. In 1561 he obtained a theological chair at Salamanca, to which in 1571 was added that of sacred literature. He was denounced to the Inquisition for translating the book of Canticles, and for criticizing the text of the Vulgate. He was consequently imprisoned at Valladolid from March 1572 till December 1576; the charges against him were then abandoned, and he was released with an admonition. He returned to Salamanca as professor of Biblical exegesis, and was again reported to the Inquisition in 1582, but without result. In 1583–1585 he published the three books of a celebrated [illegible] treatise, *Los Nombres de Cristo*, which he had written in prison. In 1583 also appeared the most popular of his prose works, a treatise entitled *La Perfecta Casada*, for the use of a [illegible] newly married. Ten days before his death, which occurred at Madrigal on the 23rd of August 1591, he was elected vicar general of the Augustinian order. Luis de León is not only the greatest of Spanish mystics; he is among the greatest of Spanish lyrical poets. His translations of Euripides, Pindar, Virgil and Horace are singularly happy; his original pieces, whether devout like the ode *De la vida del cielo*, or secular like the ode *A Salinas*, are instinct with a serene sublimity unsurpassed in any literature, and their form is impeccable. Absorbed by less worldly interests, Fray Luis de León refrained from printing his poems, which were not issued till 1631, when Quevedo published them as a counterblast to *culteranismo*.

The best edition of Luis de León's works is that of Merino (6 vols., Madrid, 1816); the reprint (Madrid, 1885) by C. Muñoz Saenz is incorrect. The text of *La Perfecta Casada* has been well edited by Miss Elizabeth Wallace (Chicago, 1903). See *Coleccion de documentos inéditos para la historia de España*, vols. x.-xi.; F. H. Reusch, *Luis de León und die spanische Inquisition* (Bonn, 1873); M. Gutiérrez, *Fray Luis de León y la filosofía española* (Madrid, 1885); M. Menendez y Pelayo, *Estudios de crítica literaria* (Madrid, 1893), Primera série, pp. 1-72.

LEON, MOSES [Ben Shem-tob] **DE** (d. 1305), Jewish scholar, was born in Leon (Spain) in the middle of the 13th century and died at Arevalo. His fame is due to his authorship of the most influential Kabbalist work, the *Zohar* (see Kabbala), which was attributed to Simon b. Yohai, a Rabbi of the 2nd century. In modern times the discovery of the modernity of the *Zohar* has led to injustice to the author. Moses de Leon undoubtedly used old materials and out of them constructed a work of genius. The discredit into which he fell was due partly to the unedifying incidents of his personal career. He led a wandering life, and was more or less of an adventurer. But as to the greatness of his work, the profundity of his philosophy and the brilliance of his religious idealism, there can be no question.

See Graetz, *History of the Jews*, vol. iv. ch. i.; Geiger, *Leon de Modena*. (I. A.)

LEON OF MODENA (1571–1648), Jewish scholar, was born in Venice, of a notable French family which had migrated to Italy after the expulsion of the Jews from France. He was a precocious child, but, as Graetz points out, his lack of stable character prevented his gifts from maturing. "He pursued all sorts of occupations to support himself, viz. those of preacher, teacher of Jews and Christians, reader of prayers, interpreter, writer, proof-reader, bookseller, broker, merchant, rabbi, musician, matchmaker and manufacturer of amulets." Though he failed to rise to real distinction he earned a place by his criticism of the Talmud among those who prepared the way for the new learning in Judaism. One of Leon's most effective works was his attack on the Kabbala ('*Ari Nohem*, first published in 1840), for in it he demonstrated that the "Bible of the Kabbalists" (the *Zohar*) was a modern composition. He became best known, however, as the interpreter of Judaism to the Christian world. At the instance of an English nobleman he prepared an account of the religious customs of the Synagogue, *Riti Ebraici* (1637). This book was widely read by Christians; it was rendered into various languages, and in 1650 was translated into English by Edward Chilmead. At the time the Jewish question was coming to the fore in London, and Leon of Modena's book did much to stimulate popular interest. He died at Venice.

See Graetz, *History of the Jews* (Eng. trans.), vol. v. ch. iii.; *Jewish Encyclopedia*, viii. 6; Geiger, *Leon de Modena*. (I. A.)

LEÓN, or León de las Aldamas, a city of the state of Guanajuato, Mexico, 209 m. N.W. of the federal capital and 30 m. W. by N. of the city of Guanajuato. Pop. (1895) 90,978; (1900) 62,623, León ranking fourth in the latter year among the cities of Mexico. The Mexican Central gives it railway connexion with the national capital and other prominent cities of the Republic. León stands in a fertile plain on the banks of the Turbio, a tributary of the Rio Grande de Lerma, at an elevation of 5862 ft. above sea-level and in the midst of very attractive surroundings. The country about León is considered to be one of the richest cereal-producing districts of Mexico. The city itself is subject to disastrous floods, sometimes leading to loss of life as well as damage to property, as in the great flood of 1889. León is essentially a manufacturing and commercial city; it has a cathedral and a theatre, the latter one of the largest and finest in the republic. The city is regularly built, with wide streets and numerous shady parks and gardens. It manufactures saddlery and other leather work, gold and silver embroideries, cotton and woollen goods, especially *rebozos* (long shawls), soap and cutlery. There are also tanneries and flour mills. The city has a considerable trade in wheat and flour. The first settlement of León occurred in 1552, but its formal foundation was in 1576, and it did not reach the dignity of a city until 1836.

LEON, the capital of the department of Leon, Nicaragua, an episcopal see, and the largest city in the republic, situated midway between Lake Managua and the Pacific Ocean, 50 m. N.W. of Managua, on the railway from that city to the Pacific port of Corinto. Pop. (1905) about 45,000, including the Indian town of Subtiaba. Leon covers a very wide area, owing to its gardens and plantations. Its houses are usually one-storeyed, built of adobe and roofed with red tiles; its public buildings are among the finest in Central America. The massive and elaborately ornamented cathedral was built in the Renaissance style between 1746 and 1774; a Dominican church in Subtiaba is little less striking. The old (1678) and new (1873) episcopal palaces, the hospital, the university and the barracks (formerly a Franciscan monastery) are noteworthy examples of Spanish colonial architecture. Leon has a large general trade, and manufactures cotton and woollen fabrics, ice, cigars, boots, shoes and saddlery; its tanneries supply large quantities of cheap leather for export. But its population (about 60,000 in 1850) tends to decrease.

At the time of the Spanish conquest Subtiaba was the residence of the great cacique of Nagrando, and contained an important Indian temple. The city of Leon, founded by Francisco Hernandez de Cordova in 1523, was originally situated at the head of the western bay of Lake Managua, and was not removed to its present position till 1610. Thomas Gage, who visited it in 1665, describes it as a splendid city; and in 1685 it yielded rich booty to William Dampier (*q.v.*). Until 1855 Leon was the capital of Nicaragua, although its great commercial rival Granada contested its claim to that position, and the jealousy between the two cities often resulted in bloodshed. Leon was identified with the interests of the democracy of Nicaragua, Granada with the clerical and aristocratic parties.

See Nicaragua; E. G. Squier, *Central America*, vol. i. (1856); and T. Gage, *Through Mexico, &c.* (1665).

LEON, the name of a modern province and of an ancient kingdom, captaincy-general and province in north-western Spain. The modern province, founded in 1833, is bounded on the N. by Oviedo, N.E. by Santander, E. by Palencia, S. by Valladolid and Zamora, and W. by Orense and Lugo. Pop. (1900) 386,083. Area, 5986 sq. m. The boundaries of the province on the north and west, formed respectively by the central ridge and southerly offshoots of the Cantabrian Mountains (*q.v.*), are strongly marked; towards the south-east the surface merges imperceptibly into the Castilian plateau, the line of demarcation being for the most part merely conventional. León belongs partly to the river system of the Miño (see Spain), partly to that of the Duero or Douro (*q.v.*), these being separated by the Montañas de Leon, which extend in a continuous wall (with passes at Manzanal and Poncebadon) from north to south-west. To the north-west of the Montañas de Leon is the richly wooded pastoral and highland district known as the Vierzo, which in its lower valleys produces grain, fruit, and wine in abundance. The Tierra del Campo in the west of the province is fairly productive, but in need of irrigation. The whole province is sparsely peopled. Apart from agriculture, stock-raising and mining, its commerce and industries are unimportant. Cattle, mules, butter, leather, coal and iron are exported. The hills of Leon were worked for gold in the time of the Romans; iron is still obtained, and coal-mining developed considerably towards the close of the 19th century. The only towns with more than 5000 inhabitants in 1900 were Leon (15,580) and Astorga (5573) (*q.v.*). The main railway from Madrid to Corunna passes through the province, and there are branches from the city of Leon to Vierzo, Oviedo, and the Biscayan port of Gijón.

afterwards it reverted to the Spaniards. It was the seat of several ecclesiastical councils, the first of which was held under Alphonso V. in 1012 and the last in 1288.

LEONARDO DA VINCI (1452–1519), the great Italian painter, sculptor, architect, musician, mechanician, engineer and natural philosopher, was the son of a Florentine lawyer, born out of wedlock by a mother in a humble station, variously described as a peasant and as of gentle birth. The place of his birth was Vinci, a *castello* or fortified hill village in the Florentine territory near Empoli, from which his father's family derived its name. The Christian name of the father was Piero (the son of Antonio the son of Piero the son of Guido, all of whom had been men of law like their descendant). Leonardo's mother was called Catarina. Her relations with Ser Piero da Vinci seem to have come to an end almost immediately upon the birth of their son. She was soon afterwards married to one Accattabriga di Piero del Vacca, of Vinci. Ser Piero on his part was four times married, and had by his last two wives nine sons and two daughters; but he had from the first acknowledged the boy Leonardo and brought him up in his own house, principally, no doubt, at Florence. In that city Ser Piero followed his profession with success, as notary to many of the chief families in the city, including the Medici, and afterwards to the signory or governing council of the state. The son born to him before marriage grew up into a youth of shining promise. To splendid beauty and activity of person he joined a winning charm of temper and manners, a tact for all societies, and an aptitude for all accomplishments. An inexhaustible intellectual energy and curiosity lay beneath this amiable surface. Among the multifarious pursuits to which the young Leonardo set his hand, the favourites at first were music, drawing and modelling. His father showed some of his drawings to an acquaintance, Andrea del Verrocchio, who at once recognized the boy's artistic vocation, and was selected by Ser Piero to be his master.

Verrocchio, although hardly one of the great creative or inventive forces in the art of his age at Florence, was a first-rate craftsman alike as goldsmith, sculptor and painter, and particularly distinguished as a teacher. In his studio Leonardo worked for several years (about 1470–1477) in the company of Lorenzo di Credi and other less celebrated pupils. Among his contemporaries he formed special ties of friendship with the painters Sandro Botticelli and Pietro Perugino. He had soon learnt all that Verrocchio had to teach—more than all, if we are to believe the oft-told tale of the figure, or figures, executed by the pupil in the picture of Christ's Baptism designed by the master for the monks of Vallombrosa. The work in question is now in the Academy at Florence. According to Vasari the angel kneeling on the left, with a drapery over the right arm, was put in by Leonardo, and when Verrocchio saw it his sense of its superiority to his own work caused him to forswear painting for ever after. The latter part of the story is certainly false. The picture, originally painted in tempera, has suffered much from later repaints in oil, rendering exact judgment difficult. The most competent opinion inclines to acknowledge the hand of Leonardo, not only in the face of the angel, but also in parts of the drapery and of the landscape background. The work was probably done in or about 1470, when Leonardo was eighteen years old. In 1472 we find him enrolled in the lists of the painters' gild at Florence. Here he continued to live and work for ten or eleven years longer. Up till 1477 he is still spoken of as a pupil or apprentice of Verrocchio; but in that year he seems to have been taken into special favour by Lorenzo the Magnificent, and to have worked as an independent artist under his patronage until 1482–1483. In 1478 we find him receiving an important commission from the signory, and in 1480 another from the monks of San Donato in Scopeto.

Leonardo was not one of those artists of the Renaissance who sought the means of reviving the ancient glories of art mainly in the imitation of ancient models. The antiques of the Medici gardens seem to have had little influence on him beyond that of generally stimulating his passion for perfection. By his own instincts he was an exclusive student of nature.

From his earliest days he had flung himself upon that study with an unprecedented ardour of delight and curiosity. In drawing from life he had early found the way to unite precision with freedom and fire—the subtlest accuracy of expressive definition with vital movement and rhythm of line—as no draughtsman had been able to unite them before. He was the first painter to recognize the play of light and shade as among the most significant and attractive of the world's appearances, the earlier schools having with one consent subordinated light and shade to colour and outline. Nor was he a student of the broad, usual, patent appearances only of the world; its fugitive, fantastic, unaccustomed appearances attracted him most of all. Strange shapes of hills and rocks, rare plants and animals, unusual faces and figures of men, questionable smiles and expressions, whether beautiful or grotesque, far-fetched objects and curiosities, were things he loved to pore upon and keep in memory. Neither did he stop at mere appearances of any kind, but, having stamped the image of things upon his brain, went on indefatigably to probe their hidden laws and causes. He soon satisfied himself that the artist who was content to reproduce the external aspects of things without searching into the hidden workings of nature behind them, was one but half equipped for his calling. Every fresh artistic problem immediately became for him a far-reaching scientific problem as well. The laws of light and shade, the laws of "perspective," including optics and the physiology of the eye, the laws of human and animal anatomy and muscular movement, those of the growth and structure of plants and of the powers and properties of water, all these and much more furnished food almost from the beginning to his insatiable spirit of inquiry

The evidence of the young man's predilections and curiosities is contained in the legends which tell of lost works produced by him in youth. One of these was a cartoon or monochrome painting of Adam and Eve in tempera, and in this, besides the beauty of the figures, the infinite truth and elaboration of the foliage and animals in the background are celebrated in terms which bring to mind the treatment of the subject by Albrecht Dürer in his famous engraving done thirty years later Again, a peasant of Vinci having in his simplicity asked Ser Piero to get a picture painted for him on a wooden shield, the father is said to have laughingly handed on the commission to his son, who thereupon shut himself up with all the noxious insects and grotesque reptiles he could find, observed and drew and dissected them assiduously, and produced at last a picture of a dragon compounded of their various shapes and aspects, which was so fierce and so life-like as to terrify all who saw it. With equal research and no less effect he painted on another occasion the head of a snaky-haired Medusa. (A picture of this subject which long did duty at the Uffizi for Leonardo's work is in all likelihood merely the production of some later artist to whom the descriptions of that work have given the cue.) Lastly, Leonardo is related to have begun work in sculpture about this time by modelling several heads of smiling women and children.

Of certified and accepted paintings produced by the young genius, whether during his apprentice or his independent years at Florence (about 1470–1482), very few are extant, and the two most important are incomplete. A small and charming strip of an oblong "Annunciation" at the Louvre is generally accepted as his work, done soon after 1470; a very highly wrought drawing at the Uffizi, corresponding on a larger scale to the head of the Virgin in the same picture, seems rather to be a copy by a later hand. This little Louvre "Annunciation" is not very compatible in style with another and larger, much-debated "Annunciation" at the Uffizi, which manifestly came from the workshop of Verrocchio about 1473–1474, and which many critics claim confidently for the young Leonardo. It may have been joint studio-work of Verrocchio and his pupils including Leonardo, who certainly was concerned in it, since a study for the sleeve of the angel, preserved at Christ Church, Oxford, is unquestionably by his hand. The landscape, with its mysterious spiry mountains and winding waters, is very Leonardesque both in this picture and in another contemporary product of the workshop, or as some think of Leonardo's hand, namel[y] highly and coldly finished small "Madonna with a P[...] Munich. The likeness he is recorded to have painted of [...] de' Benci used to be traditionally identified with the fine [...] of a matron at the Pitti absurdly known as *La Monac[a]* lately it has been recognized in a rather dull, expre[...] Verrocchiesque portrait of a young woman with a [...] background of pine-sprays in the Liechtenstein ga[llery] Vienna. Neither attribution can be counted cor[...] Several works of sculpture, including a bas-relief at Pist[oia] small terra-cotta model of a St John at the Victoria an[d] Museum, have also been claimed, but without general co[...] the young master's handiwork. Of many brilliant early [...] by him, the first that can be dated is a study of landsc[ape] in 1473. A magnificent silver-point head of a Roman [...] at the British Museum was clearly done, from or fo[r a] relief, under the immediate influence of Verrocchio. A n[...] studies of heads in pen or silver point, with some [...] for Madonnas, including a charming series in the British [...] for a "Madonna with the Cat," may belong to the sa[...] or the first years of his independence. A sheet with tw[o] of heads bears a MS. note of 1478, saying that in one of [the] months of that year he began painting the "Two Marie[s]" of the two may have been a picture of the Virgin app[...] St Bernard, which we know he was commissioned to pain[t] year for a chapel in the Palace of the Signory, but never [...] the commission was afterwards transferred to Filippin[o] whose performance is now in the Badia. One of the two [...] this dated sheet may probably have been a study for t[...] St Bernard; it was used afterwards by some follower [...] Leonard in a stiff and vapid "Ascension of Christ," [...] attributed to the master himself in the Berlin Mus[eum] pen-drawing representing a ringleader of the Pazzi co[...] Bernardo Baroncelli, hung out of a window of the Barg[ello] his surrender by the sultan at Constantinople to the c[...] of Florence, can be dated from its subject as done in D[...] 1479. A number of his best drawings of the next [...] years are preparatory pen-studies for an altarpiece "Adoration of the Magi," undertaken early in 1481 on [...] mission of the monks of S. Donato at Scopeto. The pre[...] in monochrome for this picture, a work of extraordina[...] both of design and physiognomical expression, is [...] at the Uffizi, but the painting itself was never carried [...] after Leonardo's failure to fulfil his contract Filippi[no] had once more to be employed in his place. Of equal [...] more intense power, though of narrower scope, is an u[...] monochrome preparation for a St Jerome, found acc[...] at Rome by Cardinal Fesch and now in the Vatican [...] this also seems to belong to the first Florentine perio[d] not mentioned in documents.

The tale of completed work for these twelve or fourt[een] (1470–1483 or thereabouts) is thus very scanty. But [...] be remembered that Leonardo was already full of pr[...] mechanics, hydraulics, architecture, and military a[...] engineering, ardently feeling his way in the work of exp[...] study and observation in every branch of theoretical o[...] science in which any beginning had been made in hi[...] well as in some in which he was himself the first pioneer full of new ideas concerning both the laws and the applic[...] mechanical forces. His architectural and engineering [...] were of a daring which amazed even the fellow-citizens o[f] and Brunelleschi. History presents few figures more a[...] to the mind's eye than that of Leonardo during this [...] his all-capable and dazzling youth. He did not indee[...] calumny, and was even denounced on a charge of [...] practices, but fully and honourably acquitted. T[...] nothing about him, as there was afterwards about Mich[...] dark-tempered, secret or morose; he was open and ge[...] all men. He has indeed praised "the self-sufficing [...] solitude" in almost the same phrase as Wordsworth, [...] time to time would even in youth seclude himself for [...] in complete intellectual absorption, as when he toiled a[...]

[illegible] ful of rest and food, and in- [illegible] But we have to [illegible] and gathering about him a [illegible] with them until they were [illegible] company and [illegible] with them until they were [illegible] observing their burlesque [illegible] the society of men [illegible] generation like the mathe- [illegible] the physician, geographer [illegible] the famous Greek Aristotelian [illegible] all the youth of the [illegible] by skill in music and now [illegible]; or as stopping to buy [illegible] set them free and watch [illegible] as standing radiant [illegible] rich gold hair among the [illegible] and holding them spell- [illegible] projects in art and [illegible] his mind. Unluckily it is to [illegible] that we have to trust ex- [illegible] No portrait of Leonardo as he [illegible] has come down to us.

[illegible] period of his life has come down to us. [illegible] and studies brought him no [illegible] from the tasks by which he [illegible] For all his shining power and [illegible] Probably also his exclusive belief [illegible] and slight regard for mere authority [illegible] the intellectual atmosphere [illegible] passionate mixed cult of the [illegible] mystically blended and recon- [illegible] Christianity [illegible] to him. At any rate he was [illegible] when the chance was offered him of [illegible] Ludovico Sforza (il Moro) at Milan. [illegible] of Ludovico [illegible] established his power as nominal [illegible] Gian Galeazzo but really [illegible] of his nephew [illegible] he received a project previously [illegible] the state, he received a project previously [illegible] of an equestrian monument in honour [illegible] greatness, Francesco Sforza, and [illegible] on the choice of an artist. Lorenzo [illegible] Medici on the choice of an artist. Lorenzo [illegible] who went to Milan accord- [illegible] Leonardo [illegible] in or about 1483), taking as a gift [illegible] skill a silver lute of wondrous [illegible] of a horse's head. Hostilities [illegible] between Milan and Venice; it [illegible] that in the letter commending him- [illegible] forth his own capacities, Leonardo [illegible] chiefly on his attainments and in- [illegible] After asserting these in detail [illegible] he speaks under a tenth of his pro- [illegible] and architect, and adds lastly a brief [illegible] to what he can do in painting and [illegible] to carry out in a fitting [illegible] Sforza.

[illegible] evidence of Leonardo's em- [illegible] Some biographers have [illegible] part of it, between 1483 and that [illegible] the East. The grounds of the [illegible] among his MSS. of a [illegible] of Syria, lieutenant [illegible] according to a usage [illegible] Leonardo describes in the [illegible] traveller's strange experiences [illegible] the Cilician coasts about [illegible] the rise and persecution [illegible] of a falling mountain [illegible] by a general inunda- [illegible] to have foretold these dis- [illegible] of the Euphrates river [illegible] on the Taurus range. [illegible] of Leonardo's having the Taurus and the Caucasus; some of the phenomena he mentions are repeated from Aristotle and Ptolemy; and there seems little reason to doubt that these passages in his MSS. are merely his drafts of a projected geographical treatise or perhaps romance. He had a passion for geography and travellers' tales, for descriptions of natural wonders and ruined cities, and was himself a practised fictitious narrator and fabulist, as other passages in his MSS. prove. Neither is the gap in the account of his doings after he first went to the court of Milan really so complete as has been represented. Ludovico was vehemently denounced and attacked during the earlier years of his usurpation, especially by the partisans of his sister-in-law Bona of Savoy, the mother of the rightful duke, young Gian Galeazzo. To repel these attacks he employed the talents of a number of court poets and artists, who in public recitation and page[illegible] in emblematic picture and banner and device, proclaime[illegible] wisdom and kindness of his guardianship and the wic[illegible] of his assailants. That Leonardo was among the arti[illegible] employed is proved both by notes and projects among [illegible] and by allegoric sketches still extant. Several suc[illegible] are at Christ Church, Oxford: one shows a horned fiend urging her hounds to an attack on the state baffled by the Prudence and Justice of Il Moro [illegible] clear by easily recognizable emblems). The allu[illegible] certainly be to the attempted assassination of L[illegible] of the duchess Bona in 1484. Again, it m[illegible] pestilence decimating Milan in 1484–1485 [illegible] to the projects submitted by Leonardo to [illegible] up the city and reconstructing it on imp[illegible] ciples. To 1485–1486 also appears to belong the [illegible] elaborate though unfulfilled architectural plans for bea[illegible] and strengthening the *Castello*, the great stronghold of the ruling power in the state. Very soon afterwards he must have begun work upon his plans and models, undertaken during an acute phase of the competition which the task had called forth between German and Italian architects, for another momentous enterprise, the completion of Milan cathedral. Extant records of payments made to him in connexion with these architectural plans extend from August 1487 to May 1490: in the upshot none of them was carried out. From the beginning of his residence with Ludovico his combination of unprecedented mechanical ingenuity with apt allegoric invention and courtly charm and eloquence had made him the directing spirit in all court ceremonies and festivities. On the occasion of the marriage of the young duke Gian Galeazzo with Isabella of Aragon in 1487, we find Leonardo devising all the mechanical and spectacular part of a masque of Paradise; and presently afterwards designing a bathing pavilion of unheard-of beauty and ingenuity for the young duchess. Meanwhile he was filling his note-books as busily as ever with the results of his studies in statics and dynamics, in human anatomy, geometry and the phenomena of light and shade. It is probable that from the first he had not forgotten his great task of the Sforza monument, with its attendant researches in equine movement and anatomy, and in the science and art of bronze casting on a great scale. The many existing sketches for the work (of which the chief collection is at Windsor) cannot be distinctly dated. In 1490, the seventh year of his residence at Milan, after some expressions of impatience on the part of his patron, he had all but got his model ready for display on the occasion of the marriage of Ludovico with Beatrice d'Este, but at the last moment was dissatisfied with what he had done and determined to begin all over again.

In the same year, 1490, Leonardo enjoyed some months of uninterrupted mathematical and physical research in the libraries and among the learned men of Pavia, whither he had been called to advise on some architectural difficulties concerning the cathedral. Here also the study of an ancient equestrian monument (the so-called *Regisole*, destroyed in 1796) gave him fresh

Galeazzo) again called forth his powers as a master. For the next following years gaiety and splendour of the Milanese cou employment in similar kinds, including recitation of jests, tales, fables and "proph social satires and allegories cast in the his MSS. occur the drafts of many suc profound and pungent. Meanwhile he w the monument to Francesco Sforza, and purpose. When ambassadors from A towards the close of 1493 to escort the emperor Maximilian, Bianca Maria Sfor journey, the finished colossal model, in its place for all to see in the courtyar temporary accounts attest the magnif the enthusiasm it excited, but are not us to judge to which of the two main its design corresponded. One of these and rider in relatively tranquil marc Gattemalata monument put up fifty at Padua and the Colleoni monument now engaged at Venice. Another gr horse galloping or rearing in violent in the act of trampling a fallen enc to discriminate with certainty the Sforza monument from others whi in view of another and later commis namely, that in honour of Ludovico' Trivulzio.

-ained action of the -dle in many places the master. The -sterpiece; as to said. The the Castello. -ned, and -ks still of the -ilia

The year 1494 is a momentous one in politics. In that year the long ousted and secl Gian Galeazzo, died under circumstances more than suspicio In that year Ludovico, now duke of Milan in his own right, for the strengthening of his power against Naples, first entered into those intrigues with Charles VIII. of France which later brought upon Italy successive floods of invasion, revolution and calamity. The same year was one of special importance in the prodigiously versatile activities of Leonardo da Vinci. Documents show him, among other things, planning during an absence of several months from the city vast new engineering works for improving the irrigation and water-ways of the Lomellina and adjacent regions of the Lombard plain; ardently studying phenomena of storm and lightning, of river action and of mountain structure; co-operating with his friend, Donato Bramante, the great architect, in fresh designs for the improvement and embellishment of the Castello at Milan; and petitioning the duke to secure him proper payment for a Madonna lately executed with the help of his pupil, Ambrogio de Predis, for the brotherhood of the Conception of St Francis at Milan. (This is almost certainly the fine, slightly altered second version of the "Virgin of the Rocks," now in the National Gallery, London. The original and earlier version is one of the glories of the Louvre, and shows far more of a Florentine and less of a Milanese character than the London picture.) In the same year, 1494, or early in the next, Leonardo, if Vasari is to be trusted, paid a visit to Florence to take part in deliberations concerning the projected new council-hall to be constructed in the palace of the Signory. Lastly, recent research has proved that it was in 1494 that Leonardo got to work in earnest on what was to prove not only by far his greatest but by far his most expeditiously and steadily executed work in painting. This was the "Last Supper" undertaken for the refectory of the convent church of Sta Maria delle Grazie at Milan on the joint commission (as it would appear) of Ludovico and of the monks themselves.

This picture, the world-famous "Cenacolo" of Leonardo, has been the subject of much erroneous legend and much misdirected experiment. Having through centuries undergone cruel injury, from technical imperfections at the outset, from disastrous atmospheric conditions, from vandalism and neglect, and most of all from unskilled repair, its remains have at last (1904–1908) been treated with a mastery of scientific resource and a tenderness of conscientious skill that have revived for ourselves and for

where the same engravings were copied by Albrecht Dürer. The whole notion has been proved mistaken. There existed no such academy at Milan, with Leonardo as president. The academies of the day represented the prevailing intellectual tendency of Renaissance humanism, namely, an absorbing enthusiasm for classic letters and for the transcendental speculations of Platonic and neo-Platonic mysticism, not unmixed with the traditions and practice of medieval alchemy, astrology and necromantics. For these last pursuits Leonardo had nothing but contempt. His many-sided and far-reaching studies in experimental science were mainly his own, conceived and carried out long in advance of his time, and in communion with only -uch more or less isolated spirits as were advancing along one or -other of the same paths of knowledge. He learnt indeed on - lines eagerly wherever he could, and in learning imparted -dge to others. But he had no school in any proper sense -is studio, and his only scholars were those who painted these one or two, as we have evidence, tried their hands -g; among their engravings were these "knots," things of use for decorative craftsmen to copy, -or identification, and perhaps for protection, as Achademia Leonardi Vinci; a trifling matter -e unfit to sustain the elaborate structure -s been built on it.

-er: when he and Luca Pacioli left Milan destination was Venice. They made -re Leonardo was graciously received -nzaga, the most cultured of the -f her time, whose portrait he day; meantime he made the Louvre. Arrived at Venice, -iefly with studies in mathe- -he friends heard of the

im- il Moro, and at that of true li- moved on to Florence, restorers, Cavaliere -rnal troubles and of a competent commission, a- -lorious war with found it possible to secure to the w- altar-piece for mildewed and half-detached flakes -o had already work that yet remained, to clear the -n it in his much of the obliterating accretions due to -made with and to bring the whole to unity by touch- -ineering tempera the spots and spaces actually left -dents gain obtained through these operations has been -eas. immediately above the main subject, of a beautiful -he painted lunettes and vaultings, the lunettes filled by ... hand with inscribed scutcheons and interlaced pla- ornaments (*intrecciàmenti*), the vaultings with stars ... ground. The total result, if adequate steps can be taken counteract the effects of atmospheric change in future, remain a splendid gain for posterity and a happy refutation of D'Annunzio's despairing poem, the *Death of a Masterpiece*.

Leonardo's "Last Supper," for all its injuries, became from the first, and has ever since remained, for all Christendom the typical representation of the scene. Goethe in his famous criticism has said all that needs to be said of it. The painter has departed from precedent in grouping the disciples, with their Master in the midst, along the far side and the two ends of a long, narrow table, and in leaving the near or service side of the table towards the spectator free. The chamber is seen in a perfectly symmetrical perspective, its rear wall pierced by three plain openings which admit the sense of quiet distance and mystery from the open landscape beyond, by the central of these openings, which is the widest of the three, the head and shoulders of the Saviour are framed in. On His right and left are ranged the disciples in equal numbers. The furniture and accessories of the chamber, very simply conceived, have been rendered with scrupulous exactness and distinctness; yet they leave to the human and dramatic elements the absolute mastery of the scene. The serenity of the holy company has within a moment been broken by the words of their Master, "One of you shall betray Me." In the agitation of their consciences and affections, the disciples have started into groups [illegible] standing, some still remaining [illegible] groups, of three disciples each, [illegible] interlinked by some natural [illegible] Leonardo, though no special [illegible] perfectly carried out the Greek [illegible] variety in particulars subordinated to [illegible] all his acquired science of linear [illegible] create an almost complete illusion [illegible] that has in it nothing trivial, and in [illegible] the material reality of the scene only [illegible] spiritual impressiveness and gravity. [illegible] meditations on the psychology and [illegible] significance of the event (on which he [illegible] in written words of his own) are [illegible] of his subtlest technical calculations [illegible] of groups and arrangement of [illegible]

[illegible] studies for this work there remain [illegible] at the Louvre of much earlier date [illegible] commission for this particular picture, [illegible] sketches for the arrangement of the [illegible] farther advanced, but still probably [illegible] commission, at Venice, and a MS. [illegible] at the Victoria and Albert Museum, [illegible] has noted in writing the dramatic motives [illegible] several disciples. At Windsor and Milan [illegible] in red chalk for the heads. A highly-[illegible] chalk drawings of the same heads, [illegible] portion is at Weimar, consists of early [illegible] though having no just claim to origin-[illegible] doubtful is the celebrated unfinished and [illegible] head of Christ at the Brera, Milan.

[illegible] with his "Last Supper" encouraged him [illegible] now to the casting of the Sforza [illegible] Horse," the model of which had stood for [illegible] the admiration of all beholders, in the Corte [illegible] He had formed a new and close friend-[illegible] Pacioli of Borgo San Sepolcro, the great mathe-[illegible] *de aritmetica, geometrica*, &c., he had [illegible] Pavia on its first appearance, and who arrived [illegible] Milan about the moment of the completion of [illegible] Pacioli was equally amazed and delighted [illegible] great achievements in sculpture and painting, [illegible] the genius for mathematical, physical and [illegible] collections of MS. notes which [illegible] The two began working together [illegible] Pacioli's next book, *De divina proportione*. [illegible] Pacioli's help in calculations and measure-[illegible] of casting the bronze horse and man. [illegible] away by Ludovico to a different under-[illegible] of the interior decorations, already [illegible] and interrupted, of certain chambers [illegible] the *Saletta Negra* and the *Sala Grande* [illegible] When, in the last decade of the [illegible] thorough architectural investigation and [illegible] in that building under the superintend [illegible] Beltrami, a devoted foreign student, [illegible] leave to scrape for traces of [illegible] the replastered and white [illegible] chambers that might be identified [illegible] there was cleared a frieze [illegible] but in this, after the first [illegible] possible to acknowledge the [illegible] decorator of the school, [illegible] as by Leonardo. In another [illegible] a gigantic headless figure, [illegible] wrongly claimed at first [illegible] to all appearance rightly, for [illegible] *dell' Asse* (or *della Torre*) [illegible] hand were found, in the [illegible] cal knot or plait work [illegible], of

a kind in which Leonardo took peculiar pleasure, intermingling in cunning play and contrast with a pattern of living boughs and leaves exquisitely drawn in free and vital growth. Sufficient portions of this design were found in good preservation to enable the whole to be accurately restored—a process as legitimate in such a case as censurable in the case of a figure-painting. For these and other artistic labours Leonardo was rewarded in 1498 (ready money being with difficulty forthcoming and his salary being long in arrears) by the gift of a suburban garden outside the Porta Vercelli.

But again he could not get leave to complete the task in hand. He was called away on duty as chief military engineer (*ingegnere camerale*) with the special charge of inspecting and maintaining all the canals and waterways of the duchy. Dangers were accumulating upon Ludovico and the state of Milan. France had become Ludovico's enemy; and Louis XII., the pope and Venice had formed a league to divide his principality among them. He counted on baffling them by forming a counter league of the principalities of northern Italy, and by raising the Turks against Venice, and the Germans and Swiss against France. Germans and Swiss, however, inopportunely fell to war against each other. Ludovico travelled to Innsbruck, the better to push his interests (September 1499). In his absence Louis XII. invaded the Milanese, and the officers left in charge of the city surrendered it without striking a blow. The invading sovereign, going to Sta Maria delle Grazie with his retinue to admire the renowned painting of the "Last Supper," asked if it could not be detached from the wall and transported to France. The French lieutenant in Milan, Gian Giacomo Trivulzio, the embittered enemy of Ludovico, began exercising a vindictive tyranny over the city which had so long accepted the sway of the usurper. Great artists were usually exempt from the consequences of political revolutions, and Trivulzio, now or later, commissioned Leonardo to design an equestrian monument to himself. Leonardo, having remained unmolested at Milan for two months under the new régime, but knowing that Ludovico was preparing a great stroke for the re-establishment of his power, and that fresh convulsions must ensue, thought it best to provide for his own security. In December he left Milan with his friend Luca Pacioli, having first sent some of his modest savings to Florence for investment. His intention was to watch events. They took a turn which made him a stranger to Milan for the next seven years. Ludovico, at the head of an army of Swiss mercenaries, returned victoriously in February 1500, and was welcomed by a population disgusted with the oppression of the invaders. But in April he was once more overthrown by the French in a battle fought at Novara, his Swiss clamouring at the last moment for their overdue pay, and treacherously refusing to fight against a force of their own countrymen led by La Trémouille. Ludovico was taken prisoner and carried to France; the city, which had been strictly spared on the first entry of Louis XII., was entered and sacked; and the model of Leonardo's great statue made a butt (as eye witnesses tell) for Gascon archers. Two years later we find the duke Ercole of Ferrara begging the French king's lieutenant in Milan to let him have the model, injured as it was, for the adornment of his own city, but nothing came of the petition, and within a short time it seems to have been totally broken up.

Thus, of Leonardo's sixteen years' work at Milan (1483–1499) the results actually remaining are as follows: The Louvre "Virgin of the Rocks" possibly, *i.e.* as to its execution; the conception and style are essentially Florentine, carried out by Leonardo to a point of intense and almost glittering finish, of quintessential, almost overstrained, refinement in design and expression, and invested with a new element of romance by the landscape in which the scene is set—a strange watered country of basaltic caves and arches, with the lights and shadows striking sharply and yet mysteriously among rocks, some upright, some jutting, some pendent, all tufted here and there with exquisite growths of shrub and flower. The National Gallery "Virgin of the Rocks" certainly, with help from Ambrogio de Predis; in this the Florentine character of the original is modified by an admixture of Milanese elements, the tendency to harshness and over-elaboration of detail softened, the strained action of the angel's pointing hand altogether dropped, while in many places pupils' work seems recognizable beside that of the master. The "Last Supper" of Sta Maria delle Grazie, his masterpiece; as to its history and present condition enough has been said. The decorations of the ceiling of the Sala della Torre in the Castello. Other paintings done by him at Milan are mentioned, and attempts have been made to identify them with works still existing. He is known to have painted portraits of two of the king's mistresses, Cecilia Gallerani and Lucrezia Crivelli. Cecilia Gallerani used to be identified as a lady with ringlets and a lute, depicted in a portrait at Milan, now rightly assigned to Bartolommeo Veneto. More lately she has by some been conjecturally recognized in a doubtful, though Leonardesque, portrait of a lady with a weasel in the Czartoryski collection at Prague. Lucrezia Crivelli has, with no better reason, been identified with the famous "Belle Ferronnière" (a mere misnomer, caught from the true name of another portrait which used to hang near it) at the Louvre; this last is either a genuine Milanese portrait by Leonardo himself or an extraordinarily fine work of his pupil Boltraffio. Strong claims have also been made on behalf of a fine profile portrait resembling Beatrice d'Este in the Ambrosiana; but this the best judges are agreed in regarding as a work, done in a lucky hour, of Ambrogio de Predis. A portrait of a musician in the same gallery is in like manner contested between the master and the pupil. Mention is made of a "Nativity" painted for and sent to the emperor Maximilian, and also apparently of some picture painted for Matthias Corvinus, king of Hungary; both are lost or at least unidentified. The painters especially recorded as Leonardo's immediate pupils during this part of his life at Milan are the two before mentioned, Giovanni Antonio Boltraffio and Ambrogio Preda or de Predis, with Marco d'Oggionno and Andrea Salai, the last apparently less a fully-trained painter than a studio assistant and personal attendant, devotedly attached and faithful in both capacities. Leonardo's own native Florentine manner had at first been not a little modified by that of the Milanese school as he found it represented in the works of such men as Bramantino, Borgognone and Zenale; but his genius had in its turn reacted far more strongly upon the younger members of the school, and exercised, now or later, a transforming and dominating influence not only upon his immediate pupils, but upon men like Luini, Giampetrino, Bazzi, Cesare da Sesto and indeed the whole Lombard school in the early 15th century. Of sculpture done by him during this period we have no remains, only the tragically tantalizing history of the Sforza monument. Of drawings there are very many, including few only for the "Last Supper," many for the Sforza monument, as well as the multitude of sketches, scientific and other, which we find intermingled among the vast body of his miscellaneous MSS., notes and records. In mechanical, scientific and theoretical studies of all kinds it was a period, as these MSS. attest, of extraordinary activity and self-development. At Pavia in 1494 we find him taking up literary and grammatical studies, both in Latin and the vernacular; the former, no doubt, in order the more easily to read those among the ancients who had laboured in the fields that were his own, as Euclid, Galen, Celsus, Ptolemy, Pliny, Vitruvius and, above all, Archimedes; the latter with a growing hope of some day getting into proper form and order the mass of materials he was daily accumulating for treatises on all his manifold subjects of enquiry. He had been much helped by his opportunities of intercourse with the great architects, engineers and mathematicians who frequented the court of Milan—Bramante, Alberghetti, Andrea di Ferrara, Pietro Monti, Fazio Cardano and, above all, Luca Pacioli. The knowledge of Leonardo's position among and familiarity with such men early helped to spread the idea that he had been at the head of a regularly constituted academy of arts and sciences at Milan. The occurrence of the words "Achademia Leonardi Vinci" on certain engravings, done after his drawings, of geometric "knots" or puzzle-patterns (things for which we have already learned his partiality), helped to give currency to this impression not only in Italy but in the North, where the same engravings were copied by Albrecht Dürer. The whole notion has been proved mistaken. There existed no such academy at Milan, with Leonardo as president. The academies of the day represented the prevailing intellectual tendency of Renaissance humanism, namely, an absorbing enthusiasm for classic letters and for the transcendental speculations of Platonic and neo-Platonic mysticism, not unmixed with the traditions and practice of medieval alchemy, astrology and necromantics. For these last pursuits Leonardo had nothing but contempt. His many-sided and far-reaching studies in experimental science were mainly his own, conceived and carried out long in advance of his time, and in communion with only such more or less isolated spirits as were advancing along one or another of the same paths of knowledge. He learnt indeed on these lines eagerly wherever he could, and in learning imparted knowledge to others. But he had no school in any proper sense except his studio, and his only scholars were those who painted there. Of these one or two, as we have evidence, tried their hands at engraving; among their engravings were these "knots," which, being things of use for decorative craftsmen to copy, were inscribed for identification, and perhaps for protection, as coming from the Achademia Leonardi Vinci; a trifling matter altogether, and quite unfit to sustain the elaborate structure of conjecture which has been built on it.

To return to the master: when he and Luca Pacioli left Milan in December 1499, their destination was Venice. They made a brief stay at Mantua, where Leonardo was graciously received by the duchess Isabella Gonzaga, the most cultured of the many cultured great ladies of her time, whose portrait he promised to paint on a future day; meantime he made the fine chalk drawing of her now at the Louvre. Arrived at Venice, he seems to have occupied himself chiefly with studies in mathematics and cosmography. In April the friends heard of the second and final overthrow of Ludovico il Moro, and at that news, giving up all idea of a return to Milan, moved on to Florence, which they found depressed both by internal troubles and by the protraction of the indecisive and inglorious war with Pisa. Here Leonardo undertook to paint an altar-piece for the Church of the Annunziata, Filippino Lippi, who had already received the commission, courteously retiring from it in his favour. A year passed by, and no progress had been made with the painting. Questions of physical geography and engineering engrossed him as much as ever. He writes to correspondents making enquiries about the tides in the Euxine and Caspian Seas. He reports for the information of the *Arte de' Mercanti* on the precautions to be taken against a threatening landslip on the hill of S. Salvatore dell' Osservanza. He submits drawings and models for the canalization and control of the waters of the Arno, and propounds, with compulsive eloquence and conviction, a scheme for transporting the Baptistery of St John, the "bel San Giovanni" of Dante, to another part of the city, and elevating it on a stately basement of marble. Meantime the Servite brothers of the Annunziata were growing impatient for the completion of their altar-piece. In April 1501 Leonardo had only finished the cartoon, and this all Florence flocked to see and admire. Isabella Gonzaga, who cherished the hope that he might be induced permanently to attach himself to the court of Mantua, wrote about this time to ask news of him, and to beg for a painting from him for her study, already adorned with masterpieces by the first hands of Italy, or at least for a "small Madonna, devout and sweet as is natural to him." In reply her correspondent says that the master is wholly taken up with geometry and very impatient of the brush, but at the same time tells her all about his just completed cartoon for the Annunziata. The subject was the Virgin seated in the lap of St Anne, bending forward to hold her child who had half escaped from her embrace to play with a lamb upon the ground. The description answers exactly to the composition of the celebrated picture of the Virgin and St Anne at the Louvre. A cartoon of this composition in the Esterhazy collection at Vienna is held to be only a copy, and the original cartoon must be regarded as lost. But another of kindred though not identical motive has come down to us

[illegible] he was at last persuaded, on the initiative of [illegible] to undertake for his native city a work of painting [illegible] with which he had adorned Milan. This was [illegible] to decorate one of the walls of the new council [illegible] of the signory. He chose an episode in the [illegible] the generals of the republic in 1440 over Niccolo [illegible] at Anghiari, in the upper valley of the [illegible] young Michelangelo was presently entrusted a [illegible] to be painted on another wall of the same [illegible] chose, as is well known, a surprise of the Floren[illegible] in the act of bathing near Pisa. About the same [illegible] a part in the debate on the proper site for [illegible] newly finished colossal "David," and voted [illegible] the Loggia dei Lanzi, against a majority which [illegible] himself. Neither Leonardo's genius nor [illegible] could soften the rude and taunting temper [illegible] whose style as an artist, nevertheless, in [illegible] and terror, underwent at this time [illegible] from Leonardo's example.

[illegible] of his projected *Treatise on Painting*, [illegible] at length, and obviously from his own [illegible] aspects of a battle. His choice of [illegible] was certainly not made from any love [illegible] to its horrors. In his MSS. there [illegible] trenchant sayings on life and human [illegible] natural law; and of war he has disposed [illegible] "bestial frenzy" (*pazzia bestialissima*). In [illegible] Hall of Council he set himself to depict this [illegible]. He chose the moment of a terrific struggle [illegible] between the opposing sides; hence the work [illegible] known as the "Battle of the Standard." [illegible] those who saw it, and the fragmentary [illegible] remain, the tumultuous medley of men and [illegible] expressions of martial fury and despair, must [illegible] rendered with a mastery not less [illegible] the looks and gestures of bodeful [illegible] among the quiet company on the [illegible] Milan. The place assigned to Leonardo for [illegible] his cartoon was the Sala del Papa at Santa [illegible] worked steadily and unremittingly [illegible] the signory enable us to follow [illegible] finished the cartoon in less [illegible], and when it was exhibited along [illegible] the two rival works seemed to all [illegible] the powers of art, and served as a model [illegible] generation, as the frescoes [illegible] had served to those of two generations [illegible] whose incomparable instinct for [illegible] hitherto on subjects of [illegible] according to the traditions [illegible] Leonardo's example to apply the [illegible] violent action and strife. From [illegible] Bartolommeo and a crowd of other [illegible] risen generation took in like [illegible]. The master lost no time in proceeding [illegible] design upon the mural surface; this [illegible] method of which, after a pre[illegible] Papa, he regarded the success as [illegible] whether tempera or other remains in [illegible] on a specially prepared ground, and then [illegible] ground made secure upon the wall by the [illegible]. When the central group was done the heat [illegible] it was found to take effect unequally; the [illegible] upper part ran or scaled from the wall, and the [illegible] more or less complete. The unfinished [illegible] remained for some fifty years on the wall, [illegible] was covered over with new frescoes by Vasari. [illegible] not last so long. After doing its work as the [illegible] examples for students it seems to have been [illegible] Leonardo left Italy for good in 1516 he is recorded [illegible] the greater part of it" in deposit at the hospital [illegible], where he was accustomed also to deposit his moneys, and whence it seems before long to have disappeared. Our only existing memorials of the great work are a number of small pen-studies of fighting men and horses, three splendid studies in red chalk at Budapest for heads in the principal group, one head at Oxford copied by a contemporary of the size of the original cartoon (above life); a tiny sketch, also at Oxford, by Raphael after the principal group; an engraving done by Zacchia of Lucca in 1558 not after the original but after a copy; a 16th-century Flemish drawing of the principal group, and another, splendidly spirited, by Rubens, both copies of copies; with Edelinck's fine engraving after the Rubens drawing.

During these years, 1503–1506, Leonardo also resumed (if it is true that he had already begun it before his travels with Cesare Borgia) the portrait of Madonna Lisa, the Neapolitan wife of Zanobi del Giocondo, and finished it to the last pitch of his powers. In this lady he had found a sitter whose face and smile possessed in a singular degree the haunting, enigmatic charm in which he delighted. He worked, it is said, at her portrait during some portion of four successive years, causing music to be played during the sittings that the rapt expression might not fade from off her countenance. The picture was bought afterwards by Francis I. for four thousand gold florins, and is now one of the glories of the Louvre. The richness of colouring on which Vasari expatiates has indeed flown, partly from injury, partly because in striving for effects of light and shade the painter was accustomed to model his figures on a dark ground, and in this as in his other oil-pictures the ground has to a large extent come through. Nevertheless, in its dimmed and blackened state, the portrait casts an irresistible spell alike by subtlety of expression, by refinement and precision of drawing, and by the romantic invention of its background. It has been the theme of endless critical rhapsodies, among which that of Pater is perhaps the most imaginative as it is the best known.

In the spring of 1506 Leonardo, moved perhaps by chagrin at the failure of his work in the Hall of Council, accepted a pressing invitation to Milan, from Charles d'Amboise, Maréchal de Chaumont, the lieutenant of the French king in Lombardy. The leave of absence granted to him by the signory on the request of the French viceroy was for three months only. The period was several times extended, at first grudgingly, Soderini complaining that Leonardo had treated the republic ill in the matter of the battle picture; whereupon the painter honourably offered to refund the money paid, an offer which the signory as honourably refused. Louis XII. sent messages urgently desiring that Leonardo should await his own arrival in Milan, having seen a small Madonna by him in France (probably that painted for Robertet) and hoping to obtain from him works of the same class and perhaps a portrait. The king arrived in May 1507, and soon afterwards Leonardo's services were formally and amicably transferred from the signory of Florence to Louis, who gave him the title of painter and engineer in ordinary. In September of the same year troublesome private affairs called him to Florence. His father had died in 1504, apparently intestate. After his death Leonardo experienced unkindness from his seven half-brothers, Ser Piero's legitimate sons. They were all much younger than himself. One of them, who followed his father's profession, made himself the champion of the others in disputing Leonardo's claim to his share, first in the paternal inheritance, and then in that which had been left to be divided between the brothers and sisters by an uncle. The litigation that ensued dragged on for several years, and forced upon Leonardo frequent visits to Florence and interruptions of his work at Milan, in spite of pressing letters to the authorities of the republic from Charles d'Amboise, from the French king himself, and from others of his powerful friends and patrons, begging that the proceedings might be accelerated. There are traces of work done during these intervals of compulsory residence at Florence. A sheet of sketches drawn there in 1508 shows the beginning of a Madonna now lost except in the form of copies, one of which (known as the "Madonna Litta") is at St Petersburg, another in the Poldi-Pezzoli Museum at Milan. A letter from Leonardo to Charles d'Amboise in 1511, announcing the end of his law troubles, speaks of two Madonnas of different sizes that he means to bring with him to Milan. One was no doubt that just mentioned; can the other have been the Louvre "Virgin with St Anne and St John," now at last completed from the cartoon exhibited in 1501? Meantime the master's main home and business were at Milan. Few works of painting and none of sculpture (unless the unfulfilled commission for the Trivulzio monument belongs to this time) are recorded as occupying him during the seven years of his second residence in that city (1506–1513). He had attached to himself a new and devoted young friend and pupil of noble birth, Francesco Melzi. At the villa of the Melzi family at Vaprio, where Leonardo was a frequent visitor, a colossal Madonna on one of the walls is traditionally ascribed to him, but is rather the work of Sodoma or of Melzi himself working under the master's eye. Another painter in the service of the French king, Jehan Perréal or Jehan de Paris, visited Milan, and consultations on technical points were held between him and Leonardo. But Leonardo's chief practical employments were evidently on the continuation of his great hydraulic and irrigation works in Lombardy. His old trivial office of pageant-master and inventor of scientific toys was revived on the occasion of Louis XII.'s triumphal entry after the victory of Agnadello in 1509, and gave intense delight to the French retinue of the king. He was consulted on the construction of new choir-stalls for the cathedral. He laboured in the natural sciences as ardently as ever, especially at anatomy in company with the famous professor of Pavia, Marcantonio della Torre. To about this time, when he was approaching his sixtieth year, may belong the noble portrait-drawing of himself in red chalk at Turin. He looks too old for his years, but quite unbroken; the character of a veteran sage has fully imprinted itself on his countenance; the features are grand, clear and deeply lined, the mouth firmly set and almost stern, the eyes strong and intent beneath their bushy eyebrows, the hair flows untrimmed over his shoulders and commingles with a majestic beard.

Returning to Milan with his law-suits ended in 1511, Leonardo might have looked forward to an old age of contented labour, the chief task of which, had he had his will, would undoubtedly have been to put in order the vast mass of observations and speculations accumulated in his note-books, and to prepare some of them for publication. But as his star seemed rising that of his royal protector declined. The hold of the French on Lombardy was rudely shaken by hostile political powers, then confirmed again for a while by the victories of Gaston de Foix, and finally destroyed by the battle in which that hero fell under the walls of Ravenna. In June 1512 a coalition between Spain, Venice and the pope re-established the Sforza dynasty in power at Milan in the person of Ludovico's son Massimiliano. This prince must have been familiar with Leonardo as a child, but perhaps resented the ready transfer of his allegiance to the French, and at any rate gave him no employment. Within a few months the ageing master uprooted himself from Milan, and moved with his chattels and retinue of pupils to Rome, into the service of the house that first befriended him, the Medici. The vast enterprises of Pope Julius II. had already made Rome the chief seat and centre of Italian art. The accession of Giulio de' Medici in 1513 under the title of Leo X. raised on all hands hopes of still ampler and more sympathetic patronage. Leonardo's special friend at the papal court was the pope's youngest brother, Giuliano de' Medici, a youth who combined dissipated habits with thoughtful culture and a genuine interest in arts and sciences. By his influence Leonardo and his train were accommodated with apartments in the Belvedere of the Vatican. But the conditions of the time and place proved adverse. The young generation held the field. Michelangelo and Raphael, who had both, as we have seen, risen to greatness partly on Leonardo's shoulders, were fresh from the glory of their great achievements in the Sistine Chapel and the Stanze. Their rival factions hated each other, but both, especially the faction of Michelangelo, turned bitterly against the veteran

and is preserved
In this incomp
left hand, smil
inward sweetn
smiles down u,
blessing to t
two different
in Leonardo'
Academy ca
of the lost
painting by
the Ambro
of St Jose
the Acade
ziata in 1
of the A
Florence,
example
composit
are some
and her n
In spit
not pers
had to
death t
certain
the cor
having
was ever
time, th
a youth
for cosn
the famo
afterwar
to do w
marble o
" David.
letter, th
was put
and rep
Lorenzo
tunate e
or sculp
him to
of a ge
scope t
cording
Cesare
the rea
in cons
May 1
to Duk
with a
by way
began w
and Rin
Cesenat
and plan
hurriedly
at Imola
through
treasons,
way of Chi
to Rome,
The pope's
to be long
enough of t
has left date
we have nar
minutely wit
territory of
Apenni

Among his visitors was a fellow-countryman, Cardinal Louis of Aragon, whose secretary has left an account of the day. Leonardo, it seems, was suffering from some form of slight paralysis which impaired his power of hand. But he showed the cardinal three pictures, the portrait of a Florentine lady done for Giuliano de' Medici (the Gioconda ?), the Virgin in the lap of St Anne (the Louvre picture; finished at Florence or Milan 1507–1513?), and a youthful John the Baptist. The last, which may have been done since he settled in France, is the darkened and partly repainted, but still powerful and haunting half-length figure in the Louvre, with the smile of inward ravishment and the prophetic finger beckoning skyward like that of St Anne in the Academy cartoon. Of the " Pomona " mentioned by Lomazzo as a work of the Amboise time his visitor says nothing, nor yet of the Louvre " Bacchus," which tradition ascribes to Leonardo but which is clearly pupil's work. Besides pictures, the master seems also to have shown and explained to his visitors some of his vast store of notes and observations on anatomy and physics. He kept hoping to get some order among his papers, the accumulation of more than forty years, and perhaps to give the world some portion of the studies they contained. But his strength was nearly exhausted. On Easter Eve 1519, feeling that the end was near, he made his will. It made provision, as became a great servant of the most Christian king, for masses to be said and candles to be offered in three different churches of Amboise, first among them that of St Florentin, where he desired to be buried, as well as for sixty poor men to serve as torch-bearers at his funeral. Vasari babbles of a death-bed conversion and repentance. But Leonardo had never been either a friend or an enemy of the Church. Sometimes, indeed, he denounces fiercely enough the arts and pretensions of priests; but no one has embodied with such profound spiritual insight some of the most vital moments of the Christian story. His insatiable researches into natural fact brought upon him among the vulgar some suspicion of practising those magic arts which of all things he scouted and despised. The bent of his mind was all towards the teachings of experience and against those of authority, and laws of nature certainly occupied far more of his thoughts than dogmas of religion; but when he mentions these it is with respect as throwing light on the truth of things from a side which was not his own. His conformity at the end had in it nothing contradictory of his past. He received the sacraments of the Church and died on the 2nd of May 1519. King Francis, then at his court of St Germain-en-Laye, is said to have wept for the loss of such a servant; that he was present beside the death-bed and held the dying painter in his arms is a familiar but an untrue tale. After a temporary sepulture elsewhere his remains were transferred on the 12th of August to the cloister of St Florentin according to his wish. He left all his MSS. and apparently all the contents of his studio, with other gifts, to the devoted Melzi, whom he named executor; to Salai and to his servant Battista Vilanis a half each of his vineyard outside Milan; gifts of money and clothes to his maid Maturina; one of money to the poor in the hospital in Amboise; and to his unbrotherly half-brothers a sum of four hundred ducats lying to his credit at Florence.

History tells of no man gifted in the same degree as Leonardo was at once for art and science. In art he was an inheritor and a worker born in a day of great and many-sided endeavours on which he put the crown, surpassing both predecessors and contemporaries. In science, on the other hand, he was a pioneer, working wholly for the future, and in great part alone. That the two stupendous gifts should in some degree neutralize each other was inevitable. No imaginable strength of any single man would have sufficed to carry out a hundredth part of what Leonardo essayed. The mere attempt to conquer the kingdom of light and shade for the art of painting was destined to tax the skill of centuries, and is perhaps not wholly and finally accomplished. Leonardo sought to achieve that conquest and at the same time to carry the old Florentine excellences of linear drawing and psychological expression to a perfection of which other men had not dreamed. The result, though marvellous in quality, is in quantity lamentably meagre. Knowing and doing allured him equally, and in art, which consists in doing, his efforts were often paralysed by his strained desire to know. The thirst for knowledge had first been aroused in him by the desire of perfecting the images of beauty and power which it was his business to create.

Thence there grew upon him the passion of knowledge for its own sake. In the splendid balance of his nature the Virgilian longing, *rerum cognoscere causas*, could never indeed wholly silence the call to exercise his active powers. But the powers he cared most to exercise ceased by degree to be those of imaginative creation, and came to be those of turning to practical human use the mastery which his studies had taught him over the forces of nature. In science he was the first among modern men to set himself most of those problems which unnumbered searchers of later generations have laboured severally or in concert to solve. Florence had had other sons of comprehensive genius, artistic and mechanical, Leon Battista Alberti perhaps the chief. But the more the range and character of Leonardo's studies becomes ascertained the more his greatness dwarfs them all. A hundred years before Bacon, say those who can judge best, he showed a firmer grasp of the principles of experimental science than Bacon showed, fortified by a far wider range of actual experiment and observation. Not in his actual conclusions, though many of these point with surprising accuracy in the direction of truths established by later generations, but in the soundness, the wisdom, the tenacity of his methods lies his great title to glory. Had the Catholic reaction not fatally discouraged the pursuit of the natural sciences in Italy, had Leonardo even left behind him any one with zeal and knowledge enough to extract from the mass of his MSS. some portion of his labours in those sciences and give them to the world, an incalculable impulse would have been given to all those enquiries by which mankind has since been striving to understand the laws of its being and control the conditions of its environment,—to mathematics and astronomy, to mechanics, hydraulics, and physics generally, to geology, geography, and cosmology, to anatomy and the sciences of life. As it was, these studies of Leonardo—"studies intense of strong and stern delight"—seemed to his trivial followers and biographers merely his whims and fancies, *ghiribizzi*, things to be spoken of slightingly and with apology. The MSS., with the single exception of some of those relating to painting, lay unheeded and undivulged until the present generation; and it is only now that the true range of Leonardo's powers is beginning to be fully discerned.

So much for the intellectual side of Leonardo's character and career. As a moral being we are less able to discern what he was like. The man who carried in his brain so many images of subtle beauty, as well as so much of the hidden science of the future, must have lived spiritually, in the main, alone. Of things communicable he was at the same time, as we have said, communicative—a genial companion, a generous and loyal friend, ready and eloquent of discourse, impressing all with whom he was brought in contact by the power and the charm of genius, and inspiring fervent devotion and attachment in friends and pupils. We see him living on terms of constant affection with his father, and in disputes with his brothers not the aggressor but the sufferer from aggression. We see him full of tenderness to animals, a virtue not common in Italy in spite of the example of St Francis; open-handed in giving, not eager in getting—"poor," he says, "is the man of many wants"; not prone to resentment—"the best shield against injustice is to double the cloak of long-suffering"; zealous in labour above all men—"as a day well spent gives joyful sleep, so does a life well spent give joyful death." With these instincts and maxims, and with his strength, granting it almost more than human, spent ever tunnelling in abstruse mines of knowledge, his moral experience is not likely to have been deeply troubled. In religion, he regarded the faith of his age and country at least with imaginative sympathy and intellectual acquiescence, if no more. On the political storms which shook his country and drove him from one employment to another, he seems to have looked not with the passionate participation of a Dante or a Michelangelo but rather with the serene detachment of a Goethe. In matters of the heart, if any consoling or any disturbing passion played a great part in his life, we do not know it; we know only (apart from a few passing shadows cast by calumny and envy) of affectionate and dignified relations with friends, patrons and pupils, of public and private regard mixed in the days of his youth with dazzled admiration, and in those of his age with something of reverential awe.

The Drawings of Leonardo.—These are among the greatest treasures ever given to the world by the human spirit expressing itself in pen and pencil. Apart from the many hundreds of illustrative pen-sketches scattered through his autobiographic and scientific MSS., the principal collection is at Windsor Castle (partly derived from the Arundel collection); others of importance are in the British Museum; at Christ Church, Oxford; in the Louvre, at Chantilly, in the Uffizi, the Venice Academy, the Royal Library at Turin, the Museum of Budapest, and in the collections of M. Bonnat, Mrs Mond, and Captain Holford. Leonardo's chief implements were pen, silver-point, and red and black chalk (red chalk especially). In silver-point there are many beautiful drawings of his earlier time, and some of his later; but of the charming heads of women and young men in this material attributed to him in various collections, comparatively few are his own work, the majority being drawings in his spirit by his pupils Ambrogio Preda or Boltraffio. Leonardo appears to have been left-handed. There is some doubt on the point; but a contemporary and intimate friend, Luca Pacioli, speaks of his "ineffable left hand"; all the best of his drawings are shaded downward from left to right, which would be the readiest way for a left-handed man; and his habitual eccentric practice of writing from right to left is much more likely to have been due to natural left-handedness than to any desire of mystery or concealment. A full critical discussion and catalogue of the extant drawings of Leonardo are to be found in Berenson's *Drawings of the Florentine Painters.*

The Writings of Leonardo.—The only printed book bearing Leonardo's name until the recent issues of transcripts from his MSS. was the celebrated *Treatise on Painting* (*Trattato della pittura*, *Traité de la peinture*). This consists of brief didactic chapters, or more properly paragraphs, of practical direction or critical remark on all the branches and conditions of a painter's practice. The original MS. draft of Leonardo has been lost, though a great number of notes for it are scattered through the various extant volumes of his MSS. The work has been printed in two different forms; one of these is an abridged version consisting of 365 sections; the first edition of it was published in Paris in 1551, by Raphael Dufresne, from a MS. which he found in the Barberini library; the last, translated into English by J. F. Rigaud, in London, 1877. The other is a more extended version, in 912 sections, divided into eight books; this was printed in 1817 by Guglielmo Manzi at Rome, from two MSS. which he had discovered in the Vatican library; a German translation from the same MS. has been edited by G. H. Ludwig in Eitelberger's series of *Quellenschriften für Kunstgeschichte* (Vienna, 1882; Stuttgart, 1885). On the history of the book in general see Max Jordan, *Das Malerbuch des Leonardo da Vinci* (Leipzig, 1873). The unknown compilers of the Vatican MSS. must have had before them much more of Leonardo's original text than is now extant. Only about a quarter of the total number of paragraphs are identical with passages to be found in the master's existing autograph note-books. It is indeed doubtful whether Leonardo himself ever completed the MS. treatise (or treatises) on painting and kindred subjects mentioned by Fra Luca Pacioli and by Vasari, and probable that the form and order, and perhaps some of the substance, of the *Trattato* as we have it was due to compilers and not to the master himself.

In recent years a whole body of scholars and editors have been engaged in giving to the world the texts of Leonardo's existing MSS. The history of these is too complicated to be told here in any detail. Francesco Melzi (d. 1570) kept the greater part of his master's bequest together as a sacred trust as long as he lived, though even in his time some MSS. on the art of painting seem to have passed into other hands. But his descendants suffered the treasure to be recklessly dispersed. The chief agents in their dispersal were the Doctor Orazio Melzi who possessed them in the last quarter of the 16th century; the members of a Milanese family called Mazzenta, into whose hands they passed in Orazio Melzi's lifetime; and the sculptor Pompeo Leoni, who at one time entertained the design of procuring their presentation to Philip II. of Spain, and who cut up a number of the note-books to form the great miscellaneous single volume called the *Codice Atlantico*, now at Milan. This volume, with a large proportion of the total number of other Leonardo MSS. then existing, passed into the hands of a Count Arconati, who presented them to the Ambrosian library at Milan in 1636. In the meantime the earl of Arundel had made a vain attempt to purchase one of these volumes (the *Codice Atlantico*?) at a great price for the king of England. Some stray parts of the collection, including the MSS. now at Windsor, did evidently come into Lord Arundel's possession, and the history of some other parts can be followed, while much, it is evident, was lost or ground. In 1796 Napoleon swept away to Paris all, with the other art treasures, ... the Ambrosiana; ... the other volumes ... These also have ... by Count ... Ashburnham, ... to the Institute. ... knowledge of the MSS. ... publications ... C. Ravaisson-... J. P. Richter's ... this work ... the MSS., fac-... matter of auto-... transcripts and ... progress has ... MSS., scientific and ... or in the form of ... of the several ... anatomy, published ... 1901); partially, ... Piumati and Sabachni-... miscellaneous, ... note-books bound ... collection of Lord ... of water; published ... Gerolamo Calvi. ... published with ... (6 vols., Paris, ... Codice Atlantico, ... study of the master, ... facsimile, with trans-... Milan: collection ... and edited by ... Marmolini; *Treatise* ... Piumati and Sabach-...

... are:—"Il libro di ... Fabriczy in *Archivio* ... Leonardo da Vinci, ... Anonimo Gaddiano), ... t. xvi. (1872), trans-... by the Unicorn ... Vincii vita," in his ... *Ital.* t. vii. pt. 4, ... in his celebrated *Lives* ... 2nd ed. *ibid.* 1568; ed. ... 1878–1885); Sabba da ... Lomazzo, *Trattato dell'* ... *Idea del tempio della* ... *de Fontaine-* ... *ouvrages physico-mathé-* ... *Memorie storiche* ... a work which laid the ... Bossi, *Del Cenacolo* ... *di Leonardo da* ... 1839–1841); G. Uzielli, ... 1872; Rome, 1884; ... researches of the first ... *principali professori* ... *Histoire de L. de V.* ... biography of the pre-... London, 1872), a work ... Grothe, *L. da V.* ... Marks, the *S. Anne* ... *the Literary Works of* ... very important and ... mentioned above ... *de L. da V.* (Paris, ... *und Forschungen* ... des L. da V.," *in* ... (1897–1899), the ... high value; the whole ... of L. da V., but it ... collected by him will ... *da V.* (London, 1902); ... *Painters* (London, ... *di L. da V.* ... 1st ed. 1900, 2nd ed. ... the most complete ... which yet exists); ... of art biographies ... general estimate ... relations to ... in Bell's "Great ...

summary of the master's career as an artist; *Id., L. da V.'s Note-Books* (1908), a selection from the passages of chief general interest in the master's MSS., very well chosen, arranged, and translated, with a useful history of the MSS. prefixed, *Le Vicende del Cenacolo di L. da V. nel secolo XIX.* (Milan, 1906), an official account of the later history and vicissitudes of the "Last Supper" previous to its final repair; Luca Beltrami, *Il Castello di Milano* (1894); *Id., L. da V. et la Sala dell' Asse* (1902); *Id.*, "Il Cenacolo di Leonardo," in *Raccolta Vinciana* (Milan, 1908), the official account of the successful work of repair carried out by Signor Cavenaghi in the preceding years; Woldemar von Seidlitz, *Leonardo da Vinci, der Wendepunkt der Renaissance* (2 vols., 1909), a comprehensive and careful work by an accomplished and veteran critic, inclined to give perhaps an excessive share in the reputed works of Leonardo to a single pupil, Ambrogio Preda. It seems needless to give references to the voluminous discussion in newspapers and periodicals concerning the authenticity of a wax bust of Flora acquired in 1909 for the Berlin Museum and unfortunately ascribed to Leonardo da Vinci, its real author having been proved by external and internal evidence to be the Englishman Richard Cockle Lucas, and its date 1846. (S. C.)

LEONARDO OF PISA (LEONARDUS PISANUS or FIBONACCI), Italian mathematician of the 13th century. Of his personal history few particulars are known. His father was called Bonaccio, most probably a nickname with the ironical meaning of "a good, stupid fellow," while to Leonardo himself another nickname, Bigollone (dunce, blockhead), seems to have been given. The father was secretary in one of the numerous factories erected on the southern and eastern coasts of the Mediterranean by the warlike and enterprising merchants of Pisa. Leonardo was educated at Bugia, and afterwards toured the Mediterranean. In 1202 he was again in Italy and published his great work, *Liber abaci*, which probably procured him access to the learned and refined court of the emperor Frederick II. Leonardo certainly was in relation with some persons belonging to that circle when he published in 1220 another more extensive work, *De practica geometriae*, which he dedicated to the imperial astronomer Dominicus Hispanus. Some years afterwards (perhaps in 1228) Leonardo dedicated to the well-known astrologer Michael Scott the second edition of his *Liber abaci*, which was printed with Leonardo's other works by Prince Bald. Boncompagni (Rome, 1857–1862, 2 vols.). The other works consist of the *Practica geometriae* and some most striking papers of the greatest scientific importance, amongst which the *Liber quadratorum* may be specially signalized. It bears the notice that the author wrote it in 1225, and in the introduction Leonardo tells us the occasion of its being written. Dominicus had presented Leonardo to Frederick II. The presentation was accompanied by a kind of mathematical performance, in which Leonardo solved several hard problems proposed to him by John of Palermo, an imperial notary, whose name is met with in several documents dated between 1221 and 1240. The methods which Leonardo made use of in solving those problems fill the *Liber quadratorum*, the *Flos*, and a *Letter to Magister Theodore*. All these treatises seem to have been written nearly at the same period, and certainly before the publication of the second edition of the *Liber abaci*, in which the *Liber quadratorum* is expressly mentioned. We know nothing of Leonardo's fate after he issued that second edition.

Leonardo's works are mainly developments of the results obtained by his predecessors; the influences of Greek, Arabian, and Indian mathematicians may be clearly discerned in his methods. In his *Practica geometriae* plain traces of the use of the Roman *agrimensores* are met with; in his *Liber abaci* old Egyptian problems reveal their origin by the reappearance of the very numbers in which the problem is given, though one cannot guess through what channel they came to Leonardo's knowledge. Leonardo cannot be regarded as the inventor of that very great variety of truths for which he mentions no earlier source.

The *Liber abaci*, which fills 459 printed pages, contains the most perfect methods of calculating with whole numbers and with fractions, practice, extraction of the square and cube roots, proportion, chain rule, finding of proportional parts, averages, progressions, even compound interest, just as in the completest mercantile arithmetics of our days. They teach further the solution of problems leading to equations of the first and second degree, to determinate and indeterminate equations, not by single and double position only, but by real algebra, proved by means of geometric constructions, and including the use of letters as symbols for known numbers, the unknown quantity being called *res* and its square *census*.

The second work of Leonardo, his *Practica geometriae* (1220) requires readers already acquainted with Euclid's planimetry, who are able to follow rigorous demonstrations and feel the necessity for them. Among the contents of this book we simply mention a trigonometrical chapter, in which the words *sinus versus arcus* occur, the approximate extraction of cube roots shown more at large than in the *Liber abaci*, and a very curious problem, which nobody would search for in a geometrical work, viz.—To find a square number remaining so after the addition of 5. This problem evidently suggested the first question, viz.—To find a square number which remains a square after the addition and subtraction of 5, put to our mathematician in presence of the emperor by John of Palermo, who, perhaps, was quite enough Leonardo's friend to set him such problems only as he had himself asked for. Leonardo gave as solution the numbers $11\frac{97}{144}$, $16\frac{97}{144}$ and $6\frac{97}{144}$,—the squares of $3\frac{5}{12}$, $4\frac{1}{12}$ and $2\frac{7}{12}$; and the method of finding them is given in the *Liber quadratorum*. We observe, however, that this kind of problem was not new. Arabian authors already had found three square numbers of equal difference, but the difference itself had not been assigned in proposing the question. Leonardo's method, therefore, when the difference was a fixed condition of the problem, was necessarily very different from the Arabian, and, in all probability, was his own discovery. The *Flos* of Leonardo turns on the second question set by John of Palermo, which required the solution of the cubic equation $x^3+2x^2+10x=20$. Leonardo, making use of fractions of the sexagesimal scale, gives $x=1^{\circ}\ 22'\ 7''\ 42'''\ 33^{iv}\ 4^{v}\ 40^{vi}$, after having demonstrated, by a discussion founded on the 10th book of Euclid, that a solution by square roots is impossible. It is much to be deplored that Leonardo does not give the least intimation how he found his approximative value, outrunning by this result more than three centuries. Genocchi believes Leonardo to have been in possession of a certain method called *regula recta* by H. Cardan in the 16th century, but this is a mere hypothesis without solid foundation. In the *Flos* equations with negative values of the unknown quantity are also to be met with, and Leonardo perfectly understands the meaning of these negative solutions. In the *Letter to Magister Theodore* indeterminate problems are chiefly worked, and Leonardo hints at his being able to solve by a general method any problem of this kind not exceeding the first degree.

As for the influence he exercised on posterity, it is enough to say that Luca Pacioli, about 1500, in his celebrated *Summa*, leans so exclusively to Leonardo's works (at that time known in manuscript only) that he frankly acknowledges his dependence on them, and states that wherever no other author is quoted all belongs to Leonardus Pisanus.

Fibonacci's series is a sequence of numbers such that any term is the sum of the two preceding terms; also known as *Lamé's series*. (M. Ca.)

LEONCAVALLO, RUGGIERO (1858–), Italian operatic composer, was born at Naples and educated for music at the conservatoire. After some years spent in teaching and in ineffectual attempts to obtain the production of more than one opera, his *Pagliacci* was performed at Milan in 1892 with immediate success; and next year his *Medici* was also produced there. But neither the latter nor *Chatterton* (1896)—both early works—obtained any favour; and it was not till *La Bohème* was performed in 1897 at Venice that his talent obtained public confirmation. Subsequent operas by Leoncavallo were *Zaza* (1900), and *Der Roland* (1904). In all these operas he was his own librettist.

LEONIDAS, king of Sparta, the seventeenth of the Agiad line. He succeeded, probably in 489 or 488 B.C., his half-brother Cleomenes, whose daughter Gorgo he married. In 480 he was sent with about 7000 men to hold the pass of Thermopylae against the army of Xerxes. The smallness of the force was, according to a current story, due to the fact that he was deliberately going to his doom, an oracle having foretold that Sparta could be saved only by the death of one of its kings: in reality it seems rather that the ephors supported the scheme half-heartedly, their policy being to concentrate the Greek forces at the Isthmus. Leonidas repulsed the frontal attacks of the Persians, but when the Malian Ephialtes led the Persian general Hydarnes by a mountain track to the rear of the Greeks he divided his army, himself remaining in the pass with 300 Spartiates, 700 Thespians and 400 Thebans. Perhaps he hoped to surround Hydarnes' force: if so, the movement failed, and the little Greek army, attacked from both sides, was cut down to a man save the Thebans, who are said to have surrendered. Leonidas fell in the thickest of the fight; his head was afterwards cut off by Xerxes' order and his body crucified. Our knowledge of the circumstances is too slight to enable us to judge of Leonidas's strategy, but his heroism and devotion secured him an almost unique place in the imagination not only of his own but also of succeeding times.

See Herodotus v. 39-41, vii. 202-225, 238, ix. 10; Diodorus xi. 4-11; Plutarch, *Apophthegm. Lacon.*; *de malignitate Herodoti*, 28-33; Pausanias i. 13, iii. 3, 4; Isocrates, *Paneg.* 92; Lycurgus, *c. Leocr.* 110, 111; Strabo i. 10, ix. 429; Aelian, *Var hist.* iii. 25; Cicero, *Tusc. disput.* i. 42, 49; *de Finibus*, ii. 30; Cornelius Nepos, *Themistocles*, 3; Valerius Maximus iii. 2; Justin ii. 11. For modern criticism on the battle of Thermopylae see G. B. Grundy, *The Great Persian War* (1901); G. Grote, *History of Greece*, part ii., c. 40; E. Meyer, *Geschichte des Altertums*, iii., §§ 219, 220; G. Busolt, *Griechische Geschichte*, 2nd ed., ii. 666-688; J. B. Bury, "The Campaign of Artemisium and Thermopylae," in *British School Annual*, ii. 83 seq.; J. A. R. Munro, "Some Observations on the Persian Wars, II.," in *Journal of Hellenic Studies*, xxii. 294-332. (M. N. T.)

LEONTIASIS OSSEA, a rare disease characterized by an overgrowth of the facial and cranial bones. The common form is that in which one or other maxilla is affected, its size progressively increasing both regularly and irregularly, and thus encroaching on the cavities of the orbit, the mouth, the nose and its accessory sinuses. Exophthalmos gradually develops, going on later to a complete loss of sight due to compression of the optic nerve by the overgrowth of bone. There may also be interference with the nasal respiration and with the taking of food. In the somewhat less common form of this rare disease the overgrowth of bone affects all the cranial bones as well as those of the face, the senses being lost one by one and death finally resulting from cerebral pressure. There is no treatment other than exposing the overgrown bone, and chipping away pieces, or excising entirely, where possible.

LEONTINI (mod. *Lentini*), an ancient town in the south-east of Sicily, 22 m. N.N.W. of Syracuse direct, founded by Chalcidians from Naxos in 729 B.C. It is almost the only Greek settlement not on the coast, from which it is 6 m. distant. The site, originally held by the Sicels, was seized by the Greeks owing to its command of the fertile plain on the north. It was reduced to subjection in 498 B.C. by Hippocrates of Gela, and in 476 Hieron of Syracuse established here the inhabitants of Catana and Naxos. Later on Leontini regained its independence, but in its efforts to retain it, the intervention of Athens was more than once invoked. It was mainly the eloquence of Gorgias (*q.v.*) of Leontini which led to the abortive Athenian expedition of 427. In 422 Syracuse supported the oligarchs against the people and received them as citizens, Leontini itself being forsaken. This led to renewed Athenian intervention, at first mainly diplomatic; but the exiles of Leontini joined the envoys of Segesta in persuading Athens to undertake the great expedition of 415. After its failure, Leontini became subject to Syracuse once more (see Strabo vi. 272). Its independence was guaranteed by the treaty of 405 between Dionysius and the Carthaginians, but it very soon lost it again. It was finally stormed by M. Claudius Marcellus in 214 B.C. In Roman times it seems to have been of small importance. It was destroyed by the Saracens A.D. 848, and almost totally ruined by the earthquake of 1698. The ancient city is described by Polybius (vii. 6) as lying in a bottom between two hills, and facing north. On the western side of this bottom ran a river with a row of houses on its western bank under the hill. At each end was a gate, the northern leading to the plain, the southern, at the upper end, to Syracuse. There was an acropolis on each side of the valley, which lies between precipitous hills with flat tops, over which buildings had extended. The eastern hill[1] still has considerable remains of a strongly fortified medieval castle, in which some writers are inclined (though wrongly) to recognize portions of Greek masonry. See G. M. Columba, in *Archeologia di Leontinoi* (Palermo, 1891), reprinted from *Archivio Storico Siciliano*, xi.; P. Orsi in *Römische Mitteilungen* (1900), 61 seq. Excavations were made in 1899 in one of the ravines in a Sicel necropolis of the third period; explorations in the various Greek cemeteries resulted in the discovery of some fine bronzes, notably a fine bronze *lebes*, now in the Berlin museum. (T. As.)

[1] As a fact there are two flat valleys, up both of which the modern Lentini extends; and hence there is difficulty in fitting Polybius's account to the site.

[illegible] born at Byzantium, flourished [illegible] He is variously styled BYZANTINUS, [illegible] of the monastery of St Saba [illegible] (the first "schoolman," [illegible] definitions into theology; [illegible] as an advocate, a special meaning [illegible]. He himself states that in his early [illegible] community. Nothing else is [illegible] confused with others of the [illegible] which of the works bearing the [illegible]. Most scholars regard as [illegible] *Contra Nestorianos et Eutychianos*, [illegible] *Contra Severum* [illegible] generally called *De Sectis*. [illegible] and two homilies [illegible] to a Leontius, presbyter [illegible]

[illegible] *Patrologia Graeca*, lxxxvi.; for [illegible] with Leontius see F. Loops, *Das* [illegible] *von Byzanz* (Leipzig, [illegible] (1894); V. Ermoni, [illegible]; C. Krumbacher, *Geschichte* [illegible] P. Junglas, *Leontius von* [illegible] see Fabricius, *Biblio-* [illegible]

[illegible] *Felis pardus*), the largest [illegible] World, with the exception of the snow- [illegible] in point of size to the largest [illegible] Snow-Leopard.) Leopards, [illegible] are characterized by the rosette- [illegible] the greater part of the body, [illegible] each rosette. Towards the [illegible] spots tend to become solid, but there [illegible] to their form and arrangement. [illegible] *Felis pardus*, the spots are large [illegible] the case with the long-haired [illegible]. On the other hand the [illegible] *F. p.* [illegible] has more [illegible] again, to one of which [illegible] shew a decided tendency [illegible] West African animals being [illegible] from the east side of the con- [illegible]

[illegible] and habits, the leopard may be [illegible] representatives of the genus [illegible] the hyoid bone is loosely [illegible] ossification of its [illegible] when contracted under [illegible] as in the smaller cats. [illegible] the head and body usually [illegible] and the tail from [illegible] to 3 ft., [illegible] the Somali leopard [illegible] of them. The ground- [illegible] taking the form of an excessive breaking-up of the spots, which finally show a tendency to coalesce.

In habits the leopard resembles the other large cat-like animals, yielding to none in the ferocity of its disposition. It is exceedingly quick in its movements, but seizes its prey by waiting in ambush or stealthily approaching to within springing distance, when it suddenly rushes upon it and tears it to ground with its

The Leopard (*Felis pardus*).

powerful claws and teeth. It preys upon almost any animal it can overcome, such as antelopes, deer, sheep, goats, monkeys, peafowl, and has a special liking for dogs. It not unfrequently attacks human beings in India, chiefly children and old women, but instances have been known of a leopard becoming a regular "man-eater." When favourable opportunities occur, it often kills many more victims than it can devour at once, either to gratify its propensity for killing or for the sake of their fresh blood. It generally inhabits woody districts, and can climb trees with facility when hunted, but usually lives on or near the ground, among rocks, bushes and roots and low branches of large trees.

The geographical range of the leopard embraces practically all Africa, and Asia from Palestine to China and Manchuria, inclusive of Ceylon and the great Malay Islands as far as Java. Fossil bones and teeth, indistinguishable from those of existing leopards, have been found in cave-deposits of Pleistocene age in Spain, France, Germany and England. (R. L.*; W. H. F.)

LEOPARDI, GIACOMO, COUNT (1798–1837), Italian poet, was born at Recanati in the March of Ancona, on the 29th of June 1798. All the circumstances of his parentage and education conspired to foster his precocious and sensitive genius at the expense of his physical and mental health. His family was ancient and patrician, but so deeply embarrassed as to be only rescued from ruin by the energy of his mother, who had taken the control of business matters entirely into her own hands, and whose engrossing devotion to her undertaking seems to have almost dried up the springs of maternal tenderness. Count Monaldo Leopardi, the father, a mere nullity in his own household, secluded himself in his extensive library, to which his nervous, sickly and deformed son had free access, and which absorbed him exclusively in the absence of any intelligent sympathy from his parents, any companionship except that of his brothers and sister, or any recreation in the dullest of Italian towns. The lad spent his days over grammars and dictionaries, [illegible] Latin with little assistance, and Greek and the principal [illegible] languages with none at all. Any ordinarily clever boy [illegible] have emerged from this discipline a mere pedant and bookworm. Leopardi came forth a Hellene, not merely a consummate Greek scholar, but penetrated with the classical conception of life, and a master of antique form and style. At sixteen he composed a Latin treatise on the Roman rhetoricians of the 2nd century, a commentary on Porphyry's life of Plotinus and a history of astronomy; at seventeen he wrote on the popular errors of the ancients, citing more than four hundred authors. A little later he imposed upon the first scholars of Italy by two odes in the manner of Anacreon. At eighteen he produced a poem of considerable length, the *Appressamento alla Morte*, which, after being lost for many years, was discovered and published by Zanino Volta. It is a vision of the omnipotence of death, modelled upon Petrarch, but more truly inspired by Dante, and in its conception, machinery and general tone offering a remarkable resemblance to Shelley's *Triumph of Life* (1822), of which Leopardi probably never heard. This juvenile work was succeeded (1819) by two lyrical compositions which at once placed the author upon the height which he maintained ever afterwards. The ode to Italy, and that on the monument to Dante erected at Florence, gave voice to the dismay and affliction with which Italy, aroused by the French Revolution from the torpor of the 17th and 18th centuries, contemplated her forlorn and degraded condition, her political impotence, her degeneracy in arts and arms and the frivolity or stagnation of her intellectual life. They were the outcry of a student who had found an ideal of national existence in his books, and to whose disappointment everything in his own circumstances lent additional poignancy. But there is nothing unmanly or morbid in the expression of these sentiments, and the odes are surprisingly exempt from the failings characteristic of young poets. They are remarkably chaste in diction, close and nervous in style, sparing in fancy and almost destitute of simile and metaphor, antique in spirit, yet pervaded by modern ideas, combining Landor's dignity with a considerable infusion of the passion of Byron. These qualities continued to characterize Leopardi's poetical writings throughout his life. A third ode, on Cardinal Mai's discoveries of ancient MSS., lamented in the same spirit of indignant sorrow the decadence of Italian literature. The publication of these pieces widened the breach between Leopardi and his father, a well-meaning but apparently dull and apathetic man, who had lived into the 19th century without imbibing any of its spirit, and who provoked his son's contempt by a superstition unpardonable in a scholar of real learning. Very probably from a mistaken idea of duty to his son, very probably, too, from his own entire dependence in pecuniary matters upon his wife, he for a long time obstinately refused Leopardi funds, recreation, change of scene, everything that could have contributed to combat the growing pessimism which eventually became nothing less than monomaniacal. The affection of his brothers and sister afforded him some consolation, and he found intellectual sympathy in the eminent scholar and patriot Pietro Giordani, with whom he assiduously corresponded at this period, partly on the ways and means of escaping from "this hermitage, or rather seraglio, where the delights of civil society and the advantages of solitary life are alike wanting." This forms the keynote of numerous letters of complaint and lamentation, as touching but as effeminate in their pathos as those of the banished Ovid. It must be remembered in fairness that the weakness of Leopardi's eyesight frequently deprived him for months together of the resource of study. At length (1822) his father allowed him to repair to Rome, where, though cheered by the encouragement of C. C. J. Bunsen and Niebuhr, he found little satisfaction in the trifling pedantry that passed for philology and archaeology, while his sceptical opinions prevented his taking orders, the indispensable condition of public employment in the Papal States. Dispirited and with exhausted means, he returned to Recanati, where he spent three miserable years, brightened only by the production of several lyrical masterpieces, which appeared in 1824. The most remarkable is perhaps the *Bruto Minore*, the condensation of his philosophy of despair. In 1825 he accepted an engagement to edit Cicero and Petrarch for the publisher Stella at Milan, and took up his residence at Bologna, where his life was for a time made almost cheerful by the friendship of the countess Malvezzi. In 1827 appeared the *Operette Morali*, consisting principally of dialogues and his imaginary biography of Filippo Ottonieri, which have given Leopardi a fame as a prose writer hardly inferior to his celebrity as a poet. Modern literature has few productions so eminently classical in form and spirit, so symmetrical in construction and faultless in style. Lucian is evidently the model; but the wit and irony which were playthings to Lucian are terribly earnest with Leopardi. Leopardi's invention is equal to Lucian's and his only drawback in comparison with his exemplar is that, while the latter's campaign against pretence and imposture commands hearty sympathy, Leopardi's philosophical creed is a repulsive hedonism in the disguise of austere stoicism. The chief interlocutors in his dialogues all profess the same unmitigated pessimism, claim emancipation from every illusion that renders life tolerable to the vulgar, and assert or imply a vast moral and intellectual superiority over unenlightened mankind. When, however, we come to inquire what renders them miserable, we find it is nothing but the privation of pleasurable sensation, fame, fortune or some other external thing which a lofty code of ethics would deny to be either indefeasibly due to man or essential to his felicity. A page of *Sartor Resartus* scatters Leopardi's sophistry to the winds, and leaves nothing of his dialogues but the consummate literary skill that would render the least fragment precious. As works of art they are a possession for ever, as contributions to moral philosophy they are worthless, and apart from their literary qualities can only escape condemnation if regarded as lyrical expressions of emotion, the wail extorted from a diseased mind by a diseased body. *Filippo Ottonieri* is a portrait of an imaginary philosopher, imitated from the biography of a real sage in Lucian's *Demonax*. Lucian has shown us the philosopher he wished to copy, Leopardi has truly depicted the philosopher he was. Nothing can be more striking or more tragical than the picture of the man superior to his fellows in every quality of head and heart, and yet condemned to sterility and impotence because he has, as he imagines, gone a step too far on the road to truth, and illusions exist for him no more. The little tract is full of remarks on life and character of surprising depth and justice, manifesting what powers of observation as well as reflection were possessed by the sickly youth who had seen so little of the world.

Want of means soon drove Leopardi back to Recanati, where, deaf, half-blind, sleepless, tortured by incessant pain, at war with himself and every one around him except his sister, he spent the two most unhappy years of his unhappy life. In May 1831 he escaped to Florence, where he formed the acquaintance of a young Swiss philologist, M. de Sinner. To him he confided his unpublished philological writings, with a view to their appearance in Germany. A selection appeared under the title *Excerpta ex schedis criticis J. Leopardi* (Bonn, 1834). The remaining MSS. were purchased after Sinner's death by the Italian government, and, together with Leopardi's correspondence with the Swiss philologist, were partially edited by Aulard. In 1831 appeared a new edition of Leopardi's poems, comprising several new pieces of the highest merit. These are in general less austerely classical than his earlier compositions, and evince a greater tendency to description, and a keener interest in the works and ways of ordinary mankind. *The Resurrection*, composed on occasion of his unexpected recovery, is a model of concentrated energy of diction, and *The Song of the Wandering Shepherd in Asia* is one of the highest flights of modern lyric poetry. The range of the author's ideas is still restricted, but his style and melody are unsurpassable. Shortly after the publication of these pieces (October 1831) Leopardi was driven from Florence to Rome by an unhappy attachment. His feelings are powerfully expressed in two poems, *To Himself* and *Aspasia*, which seem to breathe wounded pride at least as much as wounded love. In 1832 Leopardi returned to Florence, and there formed acquaintance with a young Neapolitan, Antonio Ranieri, himself an author of merit, and destined to enact towards him the part performed by Severn towards Keats, an enviable title to renown [illegible] of the dialogues were translated by James Thomson, author of [illegible] originally published in the *National* [illegible] (R. G.)

[illegible] 1512), Italian sculptor, [illegible] first known work is the [illegible] Andrea Vendramini, now in [illegible] in this he had the co- [illegible] parts are Leopardo's, [illegible] and two in the Berlin [illegible] his work. He was exiled [illegible] in 1490 by the senate [illegible] of Bartolommeo Colleoni. [illegible] tomb of Cardinal Zeno [illegible] by Pietro Lombardo; [illegible] sockets for the three [illegible] the antique character of [illegible] model. (See VENICE.)

[illegible] Ger. *Leupold*, from [illegible] "bold," *i.e.* "bold [illegible] has been that of several [illegible]

[illegible] emperor, the second son of [illegible] first wife Maria Anna, [illegible] born on the 9th of June [illegible] received a good education, [illegible] death of his elder brother, [illegible] 1654, when he became [illegible] king of Hungary and [illegible] 1658, more than a year [illegible] emperor at Frankfort, [illegible]

on the imperial throne Ferdinand, elector of Bavaria, or some other prince whose elevation would break the Habsburg succession. Mazarin, however, obtained a promise from the new emperor that he would not send assistance to Spain, then at war with France, and, by joining a confederation of German princes, called the league of the Rhine, France secured a certain influence in the internal affairs of Germany. Leopold's long reign covers one of the most important periods of European history; for nearly the whole of its forty-seven years he was pitted against Louis XIV. of France, whose dominant personality completely overshadowed Leopold. The emperor was a man of peace and never led his troops in person; yet the greater part of his public life was spent in arranging and directing wars. The first was with Sweden, whose king Charles X. found a useful ally in the prince of Transylvania, George II. Rakocky, a rebellious vassal of the Hungarian crown. This war, a legacy of the last reign, was waged by Leopold as the ally of Poland until peace was made at Oliva in 1660. A more dangerous foe next entered the lists. The Turks interfered in the affairs of Transylvania, always an unruly district, and this interference brought on a war with the Empire, which after some desultory operations really began in 1663. By a personal appeal to the diet at Regensburg Leopold induced the princes to send assistance for the campaign; troops were also sent by France, and in August 1664 the great imperialist general, Montecuculli, gained a notable victory at St Gotthard. By the peace of Vasvar the emperor made a twenty years' truce with the sultan, granting more generous terms than his recent victory seemed to render necessary.

After a few years of peace began the first of three wars between France and the Empire. The aggressive policy pursued by Louis XIV. towards Holland had aroused the serious attention of Europe, and steps had been taken to check it. Although the French king had sought the alliance of several German princes and encouraged the Turks in their attacks on Austria the emperor at first took no part in this movement. He was on friendly terms with Louis, to whom he was closely related and with whom he had already discussed the partition of the lands of the Spanish monarchy; moreover, in 1671 he arranged with him a treaty of neutrality. In 1672, however, he was forced to take action. He entered into an alliance for the defence of Holland and war broke out; then, after this league had collapsed owing to the defection of the elector of Brandenburg, another and more durable alliance was formed for the same purpose, including, besides the emperor, the king of Spain and several German princes, and the war was renewed. At this time, twenty-five years after the peace of Westphalia, the Empire was virtually a confederation of independent princes, and it was very difficult for its head to conduct any war with vigour and success, some of its members being in alliance with the enemy and others being only lukewarm in their support of the imperial interests. Thus this struggle, which lasted until the end of 1678, was on the whole unfavourable to Germany, and the advantages of the treaty of Nijmwegen (February 1679) were with France.

Almost immediately after the conclusion of peace Louis renewed his aggressions on the German frontier. Engaged in a serious struggle with Turkey, the emperor was again slow to move, and although he joined a league against France in 1682 he was glad to make a truce at Regensburg two years later. In 1686 the league of Augsburg was formed by the emperor and the imperial princes, to preserve the terms of the treaties of Westphalia and of Nijmwegen. The whole European position was now bound up with events in England, and the tension lasted until 1688, when William of Orange won the English crown and Louis invaded Germany. In May 1689 the grand alliance was formed, including the emperor, the kings of England, Spain and Denmark, the elector of Brandenburg and others, and a fierce struggle against France was waged throughout almost the whole of western Europe. In general the several campaigns were favourable to the allies, and in September 1697 England and Holland made peace with Louis at Ryswick.

To this treaty Leopold refused to assent, as he considered that his allies had somewhat neglected his interests, but in the following month he came to terms and a number of places were transferred from France to Germany. The peace with France lasted for about four years and then Europe was involved in the War of the Spanish Succession. The king of Spain, Charles II., was a Habsburg by descent and was related by marriage to the Austrian branch, while a similar tie bound him to the royal house of France. He was feeble and childless, and attempts had been made by the European powers to arrange for a peaceable division of his extensive kingdom. Leopold refused to consent to any partition, and when in November 1700 Charles died, leaving his crown to Philip, duke of Anjou, a grandson of Louis XIV., all hopes of a peaceable settlement vanished. Under the guidance of William III. a powerful league, the grand alliance, was formed against France; of this the emperor was a prominent member, and in 1703 he transferred his claim on the Spanish monarchy to his second son, the archduke Charles. The early course of the war was not favourable to the imperialists, but the tide of defeat had been rolled back by the great victory of Blenheim before Leopold died on the 5th of May 1705.

In governing his own lands Leopold found his chief difficulties in Hungary, where unrest was caused partly by his desire to crush Protestantism. A rising was suppressed in 1671 and for some years Hungary was treated with great severity. In 1681, after another rising, some grievances were removed and a less repressive policy was adopted, but this did not deter the Hungarians from revolting again. Espousing the cause of the rebels the sultan sent an enormous army into Austria early in 1683; this advanced almost unchecked to Vienna, which was besieged from July to September, while Leopold took refuge at Passau. Realizing the gravity of the situation somewhat tardily, some of the German princes, among them the electors of Saxony and Bavaria, led their contingents to the imperial army which was commanded by the emperor's brother-in-law, Charles, duke of Lorraine, but the most redoubtable of Leopold's allies was the king of Poland, John Sobieski, who was already dreaded by the Turks. On the 12th of September 1683 the allied army fell upon the enemy, who was completely routed, and Vienna was saved. The imperialists, among whom Prince Eugene of Savoy was rapidly becoming prominent, followed up the victory with others, notably one near Mohacz in 1687 and another at Zenta in 1697, and in January 1699 the sultan signed the treaty of Karlowitz by which he admitted the sovereign rights of the house of Habsburg over nearly the whole of Hungary. Before the conclusion of the war, however, Leopold had taken measures to strengthen his hold upon this country. In 1687 at the diet of Pressburg the constitution was changed, the right of the Habsburgs to succeed to the throne without election was admitted and the emperor's elder son Joseph was crowned hereditary king of Hungary.

During this reign some important changes were made in the constitution of the Empire. In 1663 the imperial diet entered upon the last stage of its existence, and became a body permanently in session at Regensburg; in 1692 the duke of Hanover was raised to the rank of an elector, becoming the ninth member of the electoral college; and in 1700 Leopold, greatly in need of help for the impending war with France, granted the title of king of Prussia to the elector of Brandenburg. The net result of these and similar changes was to weaken the authority of the emperor over the members of the Empire, and to compel him to rely more and more upon his position as ruler of the Austrian archduchies and of Hungary and Bohemia, and Leopold was the first who really appears to have realized this altered state of affairs and to have acted in accordance therewith.

The emperor was married three times. His first wife was Margaret Theresa (d. 1673), daughter of Philip IV. of Spain; his second Claudia Felicitas (d. 1676), the heiress of Tirol; and his third Eleanora, a princess of the Palatinate. By his first two wives he had no sons, but his third wife bore him two, Joseph and Charles, both of whom became emperors. He had also four daughters.

Leopold was a man of industry and education, and during his later years he showed some political ability. Extremely tenacious of his rights, and regarding himself as an absolute sovereign, he was also very intolerant and was greatly influenced by the Jesuits. In person he was short, but strong and healthy. Although he had no inclination for a military life he loved exercises in the open air, such as hunting and riding; he had also a taste for music.

Leopold's letters to Marco d'Aviano from 1680 to 1699 were edited by O. Klopp and published at Graz in 1888. Other letters are found in the *Fontes rerum Austriacarum*, Bände 56 and 57 (Vienna, 1903–1904). See also F. Krones, *Handbuch der Geschichte Österreichs* (Berlin, 1876–1879); R. Baumstark, *Kaiser Leopold I.* (1873); and A. F. Pribram, *Zur Wahl Leopolds I.* (Vienna, 1888). (A. W. H.*)

LEOPOLD II. (1747–1792), Roman emperor, and grand-duke of Tuscany, son of the empress Maria Theresa and her husband, Francis I., was born in Vienna on the 5th of May 1747. He was a third son, and was at first educated for the priesthood, but the theological studies to which he was forced to apply himself are believed to have influenced his mind in a way unfavourable to the Church. On the death of his elder brother Charles in 1761 it was decided that he should succeed to his father's grand duchy of Tuscany, which was erected into a "secundogeniture" or apanage for a second son. This settlement was the condition of his marriage on the 5th of August 1764 with Maria Louisa, daughter of Charles III. of Spain, and on the death of his father Francis I. (13th August 1765) he succeeded to the grand duchy. For five years he exercised little more than nominal authority under the supervision of counsellors appointed by his mother. In 1770 he made a journey to Vienna to secure the removal of this vexatious guardianship, and returned to Florence with a free hand. During the twenty years which elapsed between his return to Florence and the death of his eldest brother Joseph II. in 1790 he was employed in reforming the administration of his small state. The reformation was carried out by the removal of the ruinous restrictions on industry and personal freedom imposed by his predecessors of the house of Medici, and left untouched during his father's life; by the introduction of a rational system of taxation; and by the execution of profitable public works, such as the drainage of the Val di Chiana. As he had no army to maintain, and as he suppressed the small naval force kept up by the Medici, the whole of his revenue was left free for the improvement of his state. Leopold was never popular with his Italian subjects. His disposition was cold and retiring. His habits were simple to the verge of sordidness, though he could display splendour on occasion, and he could not help offending those of his subjects who had profited by the abuses of the Medicean régime. But his steady, consistent and intelligent administration, which advanced step by step, making the second only when the first had been justified by results, brought the grand duchy to a high level of material prosperity. His ecclesiastical policy, which disturbed the deeply rooted convictions of his people, and brought him into collision with the pope, was not successful. He was unable to secularize the property of the religious houses, or to put the clergy entirely under the control of the lay power.

During the last few years of his rule in Tuscany Leopold had begun to be frightened by the increasing disorders in the German and Hungarian dominions of his family, which were the direct result of his brother's headlong methods. He and Joseph II. were tenderly attached to one another, and met frequently both before and after the death of their mother, while the portrait by Pompeo Batoni in which they appear together shows that they bore a strong personal resemblance to one another. But it may be said of Leopold, as of Fontenelle, that his heart was made of brains. He knew that he must succeed his childless eldest brother in Austria, and he was unwilling to inherit his unpopularity. When, therefore, in 1789 Joseph, who knew himself to be dying, asked him to come to Vienna, and become co-regent, Leopold coldly evaded the request. He was still in Florence when Joseph II. died at Vienna on the 20th of February 1790, and he did not leave his Italian capital till the [illegible] Leopold, during his government in Tuscany, [illegible] speculative tendency to grant his subjects a con- [illegible] When he succeeded to the Austrian lands he began [illegible] concessions to the interests offended by his [illegible] He recognised the Estates of his different [illegible] "the pillars of the monarchy," pacified the [illegible] divided the Belgian insurgents by concessions. [illegible] to restore order, he marched troops into the [illegible] at the same time his own authority, [illegible] of the Flemings. Yet he did not [illegible] that could be retained of what Maria Theresa [illegible] to strengthen the hands of the state. He [illegible] to insist that no papal bull could be [illegible] without his consent (*placetum regium*). [illegible] emperor, and king of Hungary and [illegible] during years of peace, it is probable [illegible] his successes as a reforming ruler [illegible] scale. But he lived for barely two [illegible] he was hard pressed by peril from [illegible] The growing revolutionary disorders in [illegible] of his sister Marie Antoinette, the [illegible] threatened his own dominions [illegible] agitation. His sister sent him [illegible] and he was pestered by the royalist [illegible] both to bring about an armed [illegible] against Louis XVI. From the east [illegible] aggressive ambition of Catherine II. [illegible] policy of Prussia. Catherine [illegible] see Austria and Prussia embark [illegible] against the Revolution. While [illegible] she would have annexed what [illegible] have made conquests in Turkey. [illegible] through the rather trans- [illegible] empress, and he refused to be [illegible] good advice and promises of help [illegible] escape from Paris. The emigrants [illegible] were refused audience, or when [illegible] were peremptorily denied all [illegible] a politician not to be secretly [illegible] the power of France and of her [illegible] internal disorders. Within six [illegible] contempt for her weakness [illegible] of alliance made by Maria [illegible] with England to impose [illegible] he was able to put pressure [illegible] part of the Low Countries [illegible] English support, he was in a [illegible] A personal appeal to [illegible] between them at [illegible] arrangement which was in fact [illegible] as king of Hungary on [illegible] by a settlement with the [illegible] position of the Magyars. [illegible] truce with the Turks [illegible] way for the termination of [illegible] of Sistova being signed [illegible] his eastern dominions [illegible] and to confirm [illegible] increasingly pre- [illegible] In January he had to [illegible] king of France, [illegible] was revolted by the [illegible] utmost to avoid [illegible] country. The insults [illegible] however, at the [illegible] in June, turned his [illegible] to the sovereigns [illegible] which [illegible] all sovereigns and [illegible]

final peace with Turkey. On the 25th of August he met the king of Prussia at Pillnitz, near Dresden, and they drew up a declaration of their readiness to intervene in France if and when their assistance was called for by the other powers. The declaration was a mere formality, for, as Leopold knew, neither Russia nor England was prepared to act, and he endeavoured to guard against the use which he foresaw the emigrants would endeavour to make of it. In face of the agitation caused by the Pillnitz declaration in France, the intrigues of the emigrants, and the attacks made by the French revolutionists on the rights of the German princes in Alsace, Leopold continued to hope that intervention might not be required. When Louis XVI. swore to observe the constitution of September 1791, the emperor professed to think that a settlement had been reached in France. The attacks on the rights of the German princes on the left bank of the Rhine, and the increasing violence of the parties in Paris which were agitating to bring about war, soon showed, however, that this hope was vain. Leopold met the threatening language of the revolutionists with dignity and temper. His sudden death on the 1st of March 1792 was an irreparable loss to Austria.

Leopold had sixteen children, the eldest of his eight sons being his successor, the emperor Francis II. Some of his other sons were prominent personages in their day. Among them were: Ferdinand III., grand duke of Tuscany; the archduke Charles, a celebrated soldier; the archduke John, also a soldier; the archduke Joseph, palatine of Hungary; and the archduke Rainer, viceroy of Lombardy-Venetia.

Several volumes containing the emperor's correspondence have been published. Among these are: *Joseph II. und Leopold von Toskana. Ihr Briefwechsel 1781–1790* (Vienna, 1872), and *Marie Antoinette, Joseph II. und Leopold II. Ihr Briefwechsel* (Vienna, 1866), both edited by A. Ritter von Arneth; *Joseph II., Leopold II. und Kaunitz. Ihr Briefwechsel* (Vienna, 1873); and *Leopold II., Franz II. und Catharina. Ihre Correspondenz nebst einer Einleitung: Zur Geschichte der Politik Leopolds II.* (Leipzig, 1874), both edited by A. Beer; and *Leopold II. und Marie Christine. Ihr Briefwechsel 1781–1792*, edited by A. Wolf (Vienna, 1867). See also H. von Sybel, *Über die Regierung Kaiser Leopolds II.* (Munich, 1860); A. Schultze, *Kaiser Leopold II. und die französische Revolution* (Leipzig, 1899); and A. Wolf and H. von Zwiedeneck-Südenhorst, *Österreich unter Maria Theresa, Joseph II. und Leopold II.* (Berlin, 1882–1884).

LEOPOLD I. (1790–1865), king of the Belgians, fourth son of Francis, duke of Saxe-Coburg-Saalfeld, and uncle of Queen Victoria of England, was born at Coburg on the 18th of December 1790. At the age of eighteen he entered the military service of Russia, and accompanied the emperor Alexander to Erfurt as a member of his staff. He was required by Napoleon to quit the Russian army, and spent some years in travelling. In 1813 he accepted from the emperor Alexander the post of a cavalry general in the army of invasion, and he took part in the whole of the campaign of that and the following year, distinguishing himself in the battles of Leipzig, Lützen and Bautzen. He entered Paris with the allied sovereigns, and accompanied them to England. He married in May 1816 Charlotte, only child of George, prince regent, afterwards George IV., heiress-presumptive to the British throne, and was created duke of Kendal in the British peerage and given an annuity of £50,000. The death of the princess in the following year was a heavy blow to his hopes, but he continued to reside in England. In 1830 he declined the offer of the crown of Greece, owing to the refusal of the powers to grant conditions which he considered essential to the welfare of the new kingdom, but was in the following year elected king of the Belgians (4th June 1831). After some hesitation he accepted the crown, having previously ascertained that he would have the support of the great powers on entering upon his difficult task, and on the 12th of July he made his entry into Brussels and took the oath to observe the constitution. During the first eight years of his reign he was confronted with the resolute hostility of King William I. of Holland, and it was not until 1839 that the differences between the two states, which until 1830 had formed the kingdom of the Netherlands, were finally settled at the conference of London by the treaty of the 24 Articles (see BELGIUM). From this date until his death, King Leopold spent all his energies in the wise administration of the affairs of the newly formed kingdom, which may be said to owe in a large measure its first consolidation and constant prosperity to the care and skill of his discreet and fatherly government. In 1848 the throne of Belgium stood unshaken amidst the revolutions which marked that year in almost every European country. On the 8th of August 1832 Leopold married, as his second wife, Louise of Orleans, daughter of Louis Philippe, king of the French. Queen Louise endeared herself to the Belgian people, and her death in 1850 was felt as a national loss. This union produced two sons and one daughter—(1) Leopold, afterwards king of the Belgians; (2) Philip, count of Flanders; (3) Marie Charlotte, who married Maximilian of Austria, the unfortunate emperor of Mexico. Leopold I. died at Laeken on the 10th of December 1865. He was a most cultured man and a great reader, and did his utmost during his reign to encourage art, science and education. His judgment was universally respected by contemporary sovereigns and statesmen, and he was frequently spoken of as "the Nestor of Europe" (see also VICTORIA, QUEEN).

See Th. Juste, *Léopold Ier, roi des Belges d'après des doc. inéd. 1790–1865* (2 vols., Brussels, 1868), and *Les Fondateurs de la monarchie Belge* (22 vols., Brussels, 1878–1880); J. J. Thonissen, *La Belgique sous le règne de Léopold Ier* (Louvain, 1862).

LEOPOLD II. [LEOPOLD LOUIS PHILIPPE MARIE VICTOR] (1835–1909), king of the Belgians, son of the preceding, was born at Brussels on the 9th of April 1835. In 1846 he was created duke of Brabant and appointed a sub-lieutenant in the army, in which he served until his accession, by which time he had reached the rank of lieutenant-general. On attaining his majority he was made a member of the senate, in whose proceedings he took a lively interest, especially in matters concerning the development of Belgium and its trade. On the 22nd of August 1853 Leopold married Marie Henriette (1836–1902), daughter of the archduke Joseph of Austria, palatine of Hungary, by his wife Marie Dorothea, duchess of Württemberg. This princess, who was a great-granddaughter of the empress Maria Theresa, and a great-niece of Marie Antoinette, endeared herself to the people by her elevated character and indefatigable benevolence, while her beauty gained for her the sobriquet of "The Rose of Brabant"; she was also an accomplished artist and musician, and a fine horsewoman. Between the years 1854 and 1865 Leopold travelled much abroad, visiting India and China as well as Egypt and the countries on the Mediterranean coast of Africa. On the 10th of December 1865 he succeeded his father. On the 28th of January 1869 he lost his only son, Leopold (b. 1859), duke of Hainaut. The king's brother Philip, count of Flanders (1837–1905), then became heir to the throne; and on his death his son Albert (b. 1875) became heir-presumptive. During the Franco-Prussian War (1870–1871) the king of the Belgians preserved neutrality in a period of unusual difficulty and danger. But the most notable event in Leopold's career was the foundation of the Congo Free State (*q.v.*). While still duke of Brabant he had been the first to call the attention of the Belgians to the need of enlarging their horizon beyond sea, and after his accession to the throne he gave the first impulse towards the development of this idea by founding in 1876 the *Association Internationale Africaine*. He enlisted the services of H. M. Stanley, who visited Brussels in 1878 after exploring the Congo river, and returned in 1879 to the Congo as agent of the *Comité d'Études du Haut Congo*, soon afterwards reorganized as the "International Association of the Congo." This association was, in 1884–1885, recognized by the powers as a sovereign state under the name of the *État Indépendant du Congo*. Leopold's exploitation of this vast territory, which he administered autocratically, and in which he associated himself personally with various financial schemes, was understood to bring him an enormous fortune; it was the subject of acutely hostile criticism, to a large extent substantiated by the report of a commission of inquiry instituted by the king himself in 1904, and followed in 1908 by the annexation of the state to Belgium (see CONGO FREE STATE: *History*). In 1880 Leopold sought an interview with General C. G. Gordon and obtained his promise, subject to the approval of the British government, to enter the Belgian service on the Congo. Three years later Leopold claimed fulfilment of the promise, and Gordon was about to proceed to the Congo when the British government required his services for the Sudan. On the 15th of November 1902 King Leopold's life was attempted in Brussels by an Italian anarchist named Rubino. Queen Marie Henriette died at Spa on the 19th of September of the same year. Besides the son already mentioned she had borne to Leopold three daughters—Louise Marie Amélie (b. 1858), who in 1875 married Philip of Saxe-Coburg and Gotha, and was divorced in 1906; Stéphanie (b. 1864), who married Rudolph, crown prince of Austria, in 1881, and after his death in 1889 married, against her father's wishes, Elemer, Count Lonyay, in 1900; and Clémentine (b. 1872). At the time of the queen's death an unseemly incident was occasioned by Leopold's refusal to see his daughter Stéphanie, who in consequence was not present at her mother's funeral. The disagreeable impression on the public mind thus created was deepened by an unfortunate litigation, lasting for two years (1904–1906), over the deceased queen's will, in which the creditors of the princess Louise, together with princess Stéphanie (Countess Lonyay), claimed that under the Belgian law the queen's estate was entitled to half of her husband's property. This claim was disallowed by the Belgian courts. The king died at Laeken, near Brussels, on the 17th of December 1909. On the 23rd of that month his nephew took the oath to observe the constitution, assuming the title of Albert I. King Leopold was personally a man of considerable attainments and much strength of character, but he was a notoriously dissolute monarch, who even to the last offended decent opinion by his indulgences at Paris and on the Riviera. The wealth he amassed from the Congo he spent, no doubt, royally not only in this way but also on public improvements in Belgium; but he had a hard heart towards the natives of his distant possession.

LEOPOLD II. (1797–1870), of Habsburg-Lorraine, grand-duke of Tuscany, was born on the 3rd of October 1797, the son of the grand-duke Ferdinand III., whom he succeeded in 1824. During the first twenty years of his reign he devoted himself to the internal development of the state. His was the mildest and least reactionary of all the Italian despotisms of the day, and although always subject to Austrian influence he refused to adopt the Austrian methods of government, allowed a fair measure of liberty to the press, and permitted many political exiles from other states to dwell in Tuscany undisturbed. But when in the early 'forties a feeling of unrest spread throughout Italy, even in Tuscany demands for a constitution and other political reforms were advanced; in 1845–1846 riots broke out in various parts of the country, and Leopold granted a number of administrative reforms. But Austrian influence prevented him from going further, even had he wished to do so. The election of Pope Pius IX. gave fresh impulse to the Liberal movement, and on the 4th of September 1847 Leopold instituted the National Guard—a first step towards the constitution; shortly after the marchese Cosimo Ridolfi was appointed prime minister. The granting of the Neapolitan and Piedmontese constitutions was followed (17th February 1848) by that of Tuscany, drawn up by Gino Capponi. The revolution in Milan and Vienna aroused a fever of patriotic enthusiasm in Tuscany, where war against Austria was demanded; Leopold, giving way to popular pressure, sent a force of regulars and volunteers to co-operate with Piedmont in the Lombard campaign. His speech on their departure was uncompromisingly Italian and Liberal. "Soldiers," he said, "the holy cause of Italian freedom is being decided to-day on the fields of Lombardy. Already the citizens of Milan have purchased their liberty with their blood and with a heroism of which history offers few examples. . . . Honour to the arms of Italy! Long live Italian independence!" The Tuscan contingent fought bravely, if unsuccessfully, at Curtatone and Montanara. On the 26th of June the first Tuscan parliament assembled, but the

c
a
su
anc
cont
publ
If
Bohen
that h
in Tusc
years, a
west and
France c
queen of
with the s
passionate
emigrants,
interventio
he was thr
of Russia, a
would have
on a crusade
they were bu
remained of i
Leopold II. h
parent "cunnir
misled. To h
If she and her
who followed i
they forced th
help. Leopold
pleased at the
influence in F
weeks of his acc
by practically t
Theresa in 1756
a check on Rus
on England by t
to France, and th
position to baffle
Frederick Willia
Reichenbach in Ju
a defeat for Prussi
the 15th of Novem
diet in which he rec
He had already m
in September, whi
the war begun by J
in August 1791.
left Leopold free to
friendly relations wi
During 1791 the
occupied with the
dismiss the count of A
in a very peremptory
folly of the French e
being entangled in t
inflicted on Louis X
time of their attempt
indignation, and he n
of Europe to take con
"immediately compro
the security of all gov
interested in the confer

[illegible] and finally rejected the proposals as derogatory to his dignity. On the 27th of April there was great excitement in Florence, Italian colours appeared everywhere, but order was maintained, and the grand-duke and his family departed for Bologna undisturbed. Thus the revolution was accomplished without a drop of blood being shed, and after a period of provisional government Tuscany was incorporated in the kingdom of Italy. On the [illegible] Leopold abdicated in favour of his son Ferdinand IV., who never reigned, but issued a protest from Dresden (26th March [illegible]). He spent his last years in Austria, and died in Rome on the [illegible] of January [illegible].

Leopold of Tuscany was a well-meaning, not unkindly man, [illegible] of his subjects than were the other Italian despots, but he was weak, and too closely bound by family ties and [illegible] ever to become a real Liberal. Had he not [illegible] at Gaeta, and, above all, had he [illegible] Austrian assistance while denying that he had [illegible] he might yet have preserved his throne, and [illegible] the whole course of Italian history. At the same [illegible] was enervating and demoralizing.

[illegible] (Florence, [illegible]), useful but [illegible] having been Leopold's minister [illegible] F. D. Guerrazzi [illegible]

[illegible]

[illegible], a lake of Central Africa in the basin of the [illegible]

[illegible]

According to Diodorus (xi. 48) Leotychides reigned twenty-two, his successor Archidamus forty-two years. The total duration of the two reigns, sixty-four years, we know to be correct, for Leotychides came to the throne in 491 and Archidamus (*q.v.*) died in 427. On this basis, then, Leotychides's exile would fall in 469 and the Thessalian expedition in that or the preceding year (so E. Meyer, *Geschichte des Altertums*, iii. § 287). But Diodorus is not consistent with himself; he attributes (xi. 48) Leotychides's death to the year 476–475 and he records (xii. 35) Archidamus's death in 434–433, though he introduces him in the following years at the head of the Peloponnesian army (xii. 42, 47, 52). Further, he says expressly that Leotychides ἐτελεύτησεν ἄρξας ἔτη εἴκοσι καὶ δύο, *i.e.* he lived twenty-two years after his accession. The twenty-two years, then, may include the time which elapsed between his exile and his death. In that case Leotychides died in 469, and 476–475 may be the year in which his reign, though not his life, ended. This date seems, from what we know of the political situation in general, to be more probable than the later one for the Thessalian campaign.

G. Busolt, *Griech. Geschichte*, iii. 83, note; J. B. Bury, *History of Greece*, p. 326; G. Grote, *History of Greece*, new edition 1888, iv. 349, note; also abridged edition 1907, p. 273, note 3. Beloch's view (*Griech. Geschichte*, i. 455, note 2) that the expedition took place in 476, the trial and flight in 469, is not generally accepted. (M. N. T.)

LEOVIGILD, or **LÖWENHELD** (d. 586), king of the Visigoths, became king in 568 after the short period of anarchy which followed the death of King Athanagild, whose widow, Goisvintha, he married. At first he ruled that part of the Visigothic kingdom which lay to the south of the Pyrenees, his brother Liuva or Leova governing the small part to the north of these mountains; but in 572 Liuva died and Leovigild became sole king. At this time the Visigoths who settled in Spain early in the 5th century were menaced by two powerful enemies, the Suevi who had a small kingdom in the north-west of the peninsula, and the Byzantines who had answered Athanagild's appeal for help by taking possession of a stretch of country in the south-east. Their kingdom, too, was divided and weakened by the fierce hostility between the orthodox Christians and those who professed Arianism. Internal and external dangers alike, however, failed to daunt Leovigild, who may fairly be called the restorer of the Visigothic kingdom. He turned first against the Byzantines, who were defeated several times; he took Cordova and chastised the Suevi; and then by stern measures he destroyed the power of those unruly and rebellious chieftains who had reduced former kings to the position of ciphers. The chronicler tells how, having given peace to his people, he, first of the Visigothic sovereigns, assumed the attire of a king and made Toledo his capital. He strengthened the position of his family and provided for the security of his kingdom by associating his two sons, Recared and Hermenegild, with himself in the kingly office and placing parts of the land under their rule. Leovigild himself was an Arian, being the last of the Visigothic kings to hold that creed; but he was not a bitter foe of the orthodox Christians, although he was obliged to punish them when they conspired against him with his external enemies. His son Hermenegild, however, was converted to the orthodox faith through the influence of his Frankish wife, Ingundis, daughter of King Sigebert I., and of Leander, metropolitan of Seville. Allying himself with the Byzantines and other enemies of the Visigoths, and supported by most of the orthodox Christians he headed a formidable insurrection. The struggle was fierce; but at length, employing persuasion as well as force, the old king triumphed. Hermenegild was captured; he refused to give up his faith and in March or April 585 he was executed. He was canonized at the request of Philip II., king of Spain, by Pope Sixtus V. About this time Leovigild put an end to the kingdom of the Suevi. During his last years he was engaged in a war with the Franks. He died at Toledo on the 21st of April 586 and was succeeded by his son Recared.

LEPANTO,[1] **BATTLE OF,** fought on the 7th of October 1571. The conquest of Cyprus by the Turks, and their aggressions on the Christian powers, frightened the states of the Mediterranean into forming a holy league for their common defence. The main promoter of the league was Pope Pius V., but the bulk of the forces was supplied by the republic of Venice and Philip II. of Spain, who was peculiarly interested in checking the Turks both because of the Moorish element in the population of Spain, and because he was also sovereign of Naples and Sicily. In compliment to King Philip, the general command of the league's fleet was given to his natural brother, Don John of Austria. It included, however, only twenty-four Spanish ships. The great majority of the two hundred galleys and eight galeasses, of which the fleet was composed, came from Venice, under the command of the proveditore Barbarigo; from Genoa, which was in close alliance with Spain, under Gianandrea Doria; and from the Pope whose squadron was commanded by Marc Antonio Colonna. The Sicilian and Neapolitan contingents were commanded by the marquess of Santa Cruz, and Cardona, Spanish officers. Eight thousand Spanish soldiers were embarked. The allied fleet was collected slowly at Messina, from whence it advanced by the passage between Ithaca and Cephalonia to Cape Marathia near Dragonera. The Turkish fleet which had come up from Cyprus and Crete anchored in the Gulf of Patras. It consisted in all of 273 galleys which were of lighter build than the Christians', and less well supplied with cannon or small arms. The Turks still relied mainly on the bow and arrow. Ali, the capitan pasha, was commander-in-chief, and he had with him Chulouk Bey of Alexandria, commonly called Scirocco, and Uluch Ali, dey of Algiers. On the 7th of October the Christian fleet advanced to the neighbourhood of Cape Scropha. It was formed in the traditional order of the galleys—a long line abreast, subdivided into the centre or "battle" commanded by Don John in person, the left wing under the proveditore Barbarigo, and the right under Gianandrea Doria. But a reserve squadron was placed behind the centre under the marquess of Santa Cruz, and the eight lumbering galeasses were stationed at intervals in front of the line to break the formation of the Turks. The capitan pasha left his anchorage in the Gulf of Patras with his fleet in a single line, without reserve or advance-guard. He was himself in the centre, with Scirocco on his right and Uluch Ali on his left. The two fleets met south of Cape Scropha, both drawn up from north to south, the land being close to the left flank of the Christians, and the right of the Turks. To the left of the Turks and the right of the Christians, there was open sea. Ali Pasha's greater numbers enabled him to outflank his enemy. The Turks charged through the intervals between the galeasses, which proved to be of no value. On their right Scirocco outflanked the Venetians of Barbarigo, but the better build of the galleys of Saint Mark and the admirable discipline of their crews gave them the victory. The Turks were almost all sunk or driven on shore. Scirocco and Barbarigo both lost their lives. On the centre Don John and the capitan pasha met prow to prow —the Christians reserving the fire of their bow guns (called *di cursia*) till the moment of impact, and then boarding. Ali Pasha was slain and his galley taken. Everywhere on the centre the Christians gained the upper hand, but their victory was almost turned into a defeat by the mistaken manœuvres of Doria. In fear lest he should be outflanked by Uluch Ali, he stood out to sea, leaving a gap between himself and the centre. The dey of Algiers, who saw the opening, reversed the order of his squadron, and fell on the right of the centre. The galleys of the Order of Malta, which were stationed at this point, suffered severely, and their flagship was taken with great slaughter. A disaster was averted by the marquess of Santa Cruz, who brought up the reserve. Uluch Ali then retreated with sail and oar, bringing most of his division off in good order.

The loss of life in the battle was enormous, being put at 30,000 for the Turks and 8000 for the Christians. The battle of Lepanto was of immense political importance. It gave the naval power of the Turks a blow from which it never recovered, and put a stop to their aggression in the Eastern Mediterranean. Historically the battle is interesting because it was the last example of an encounter on a great scale between fleets of galleys and also because it was the last crusade. The Christian powers of the Mediterranean did really combine to avert the ruin of Christendom. Hardly a noble house of Spain or Italy was not represented in the fleet, and the princes headed the boarders. Volunteers came from all parts of Europe, and it is said that

[1] For Lepanto see NAUPACTUS.

[illegible] was Sir Richard Grenville, afterwards famous for [illegible] the "Revenge" off Flores in the Azores. Cervantes [illegible] present, and had his left hand shattered by a [illegible].

[illegible] of the battle, with copious references to authorities [illegible] controversies, mostly arising out of the conduct [illegible] W. Stirling Maxwell, *Don John of Austria* (1883); [illegible] Gravière, *La Guerre de Chypre et la bataille de* [illegible] (D. H.)

[illegible] (1618–1682), French designer and en[illegible] apprenticed to a carpenter and builder and [illegible] learning mechanical and constructive work [illegible] facility with the pencil. His designs, [illegible] in quantity and exuberant in fancy, [illegible] ceilings, friezes, chimney-pieces, doorways [illegible]; he also devised fire-dogs, sideboards, [illegible] tables, mirrors and other pieces of furniture; [illegible] at the Gobelins. His work is often ex[illegible] and over-elaborate; he revelled in amorini [illegible] and cartouches. His chimney-pieces, [illegible] simple and elegant. His engraved [illegible] original, are something like 1500 in number [illegible] of himself. He became a member of the [illegible]

[illegible] of the aboriginal inhabitants of Sikkim [illegible], the Lepchas have been repeatedly [illegible] hill-tribes, and their ancient patri[illegible] yet. The total number of speakers [illegible] India in 1901, was only 19,291. Their [illegible] has been preserved from extinction [illegible] General Mainwaring and others; but their [illegible] entirely destroyed by the Tibetans, and [illegible] rapidly forgotten. Once free and [illegible] the poorest people in Sikkim, and it [illegible] class is drawn. They are above [illegible] the ways of beasts and birds, and [illegible] zoological and botanical nomenclature of [illegible]

[illegible] *Land* (1900).

[illegible], **DE SAINT-FARGEAU,** [illegible], French politician, was born on the [illegible] Paris. He belonged to a well-known family, [illegible] Michel Robert Le Peletier des Forts, [illegible] having been controller-general of finance. [illegible], and soon became president of the [illegible] he was a deputy of the *noblesse* [illegible] he shared the conservative [illegible], but by slow degrees his ideas [illegible] advanced. On the 13th of July [illegible] Necker, whose dismissal by the [illegible] in Paris; and in the Con[illegible] the abolition of the penalty [illegible] branding, and the substitution [illegible] attitude won him great [illegible] June 1790 he was made president [illegible] During the existence of the [illegible] president of the general council [illegible] and was afterwards elected [illegible] the Convention. Here he [illegible] XVI. by the assembly and [illegible] this vote, together with his [illegible] of the royalists, and on the [illegible] execution of the king, he was [illegible] Paris by a member of the [illegible] named Le Peletier by a [illegible] L. David represented [illegible] destroyed by his [illegible] had interested [illegible] his left fragments [illegible] borrowed in later [illegible] of ideas. His daughter, Suzanne Louise, was "adopted" by the French nation.

See *Œuvres de M. le Peletier de Saint-Fargeau* (Brussels, 1826) with a life by his brother Félix; E. Le Blant, "Le Peletier de St-Fargeau, et son meurtrier," in the *Correspondant* review (1874); F. Clerembray, *Épisodes de la Révolution* (Rouen, 1891); Brette, "La Réforme de la législation universelle, et le plan de Lepelletier Saint-Fargeau," in *La Révolution française*, xlii. (1902); and M. Tourneux, *Bibliog. de l'hist. de Paris* . . . (vol. i., 1890, Nos. 3896-3910, and vol. iv., 1906, *s.v.* Lepeletier).

LEPIDOLITE, or LITHIA-MICA, a mineral of the mica group (see MICA). It is a basic aluminium, potassium and lithium fluo-silicate, with the approximate formula $KLi[Al(OH,F)_2]Al(SiO_3)_3$. Lithia and fluorine are each present to the extent of about 5%; rubidium and caesium are sometimes present in small amounts. Distinctly developed monoclinic crystals or cleavage sheets of large size are of rare occurrence, the mineral being usually found as scaly aggregates, and on this account was named lepidolite (from Gr. λεπίς, scale) by M. H. Klaproth in 1792. It is usually of a lilac or peach-blossom colour, but is sometimes greyish-white, and has a pearly lustre on the cleavage surfaces. The hardness is 2½–4 and the sp. gr. 2·8–2·9, the optic axial angle measures 50°–70°. It is found in pegmatite-veins, often in association with pink tourmaline (rubellite) and sometimes intergrown in parallel position with muscovite. Scaly masses of considerable extent are found at Rozena near Bystrzitz in Moravia and at Pala in San Diego county, California. The material from Rozena has been known since 1791, and has sometimes been cut and polished for ornamental purposes: it has a pretty colour and spangled appearance and takes a good polish, but is rather soft. At Pala it has been extensively mined for the preparation of lithium and rubidium salts. Other localities for the mineral are the island of Utö in Sweden, and Auburn and Paris in Maine, U.S.A.; at Alabashka near Mursinka in the Urals large isolated crystals have been found, and from Central Australia transparent cleavage sheets of a fine lilac colour are known.

The lithium-iron mica *zinnwaldite* or *lithionite* is closely allied to lepidolite, differing from it in containing some ferrous iron in addition to the constituents mentioned above. It occurs as greyish silvery scales with hexagonal outlines in the tin-bearing granites of Zinnwald in the Erzgebirge, Bohemia and of Cornwall. (L. J. S.)

LEPIDOPTERA (Gr. λεπίς, a scale or husk, and πτερόν, a wing), a term used in zoological classification for one of the largest and best-known orders of the class Hexapoda (*q.v.*), in order that comprises the insects popularly called butterflies and moths. The term was first used by Linnaeus (1735) in the sense still accepted by modern zoologists, and there are few

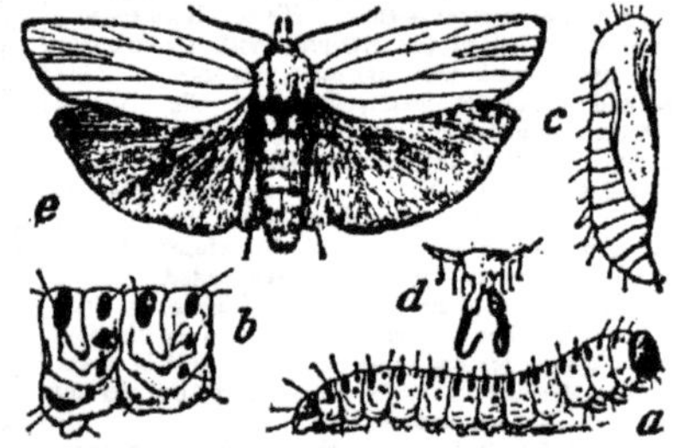

After Edwards, Riley and Howard's *Insect Life*, vol. 3 (U.S. Dept. Agr.).

FIG. 1.—*e*, *Crytophasa unipuctata*, Donov., Australia. *a*, Larva, *c*, pupa, natural size; *b*, 2nd and 3rd abdominal segments of larva, *d*, cremaster of pupa, magnified.

groups of animals as to whose limits and distinguishing characters less controversy has arisen.

Characters.—The name of the order indicates the fact that the wings (and other parts of the body) are clothed with flattened cuticular structures—the scales (fig. 7)—that may be regarded as modified arthropodan "hairs." Such scales are not peculiar to the Lepidoptera—they are found also on many of the Aptera, on the Psocidae, a family of Corrodentia, on some Coleoptera (beetles) and on the gnats (Culicidae), a family of Diptera. The most distinctive structural features of the Lepidoptera are to be found in the jaws. The mandibles are mere vestiges or entirely absent; the second maxillae are usually reduced to a narrow transverse mentum which bears the scale-covered labial palps, between which project the elongate first maxillae, grooved on their inner faces, so as to form when apposed a tubular proboscis adapted for sucking liquid food.

All Lepidoptera are hatched as the eruciform soft-bodied type of larva (fig. 1, *a*) known as the caterpillar, with biting mandibles, three pairs of thoracic legs and with a variable number (usually five pairs) of abdominal prolegs, which carry complete or incomplete circles of hooklets. The pupa in a single family only is free (*i.e.* with the appendages free from the body), and mandibulate. In the vast majority of the order it is more or less obtect (*i.e.* with the appendages fixed to the cuticle of the body) and without mandibles (fig. 1, *c*).

Structure.—The head in the Lepidoptera is sub-globular in shape with the compound eyes exceedingly well developed, and with a pair of ocelli or "simple eyes" often present on the vertex. It is connected to the thorax by a relatively broad and membranous "neck." The feelers are many-jointed, often they are complex, the segments bearing processes arranged in a comb-like manner and furnished with numerous sensory hairs (fig. 2). The complexity of the feelers is carried to its highest development in certain male moths that have a wonderful power of discovering their females by smell or some analogous sense. Often the feelers are excessively complex in male moths whose maxillae are so reduced that they take no food in the imaginal state. The nature of the jaws has already been briefly described. Functional mandibles of peculiar form (fig. 3, A) are present in the remarkable small moths of the genus *Micropteryx* (or *Eriocephala*), and there are vestiges of these jaws in other moths of low type, but the minute structures in the higher Lepidoptera that were formerly described as mandibles are now believed to belong to the labrum, the true mandibles being perhaps represented by rounded prominences, not articulated with the head-capsule. Throughout the order, as a whole, the jaws are adapted for sucking liquid food, and the suctorial proboscis (often erroneously called a "tongue") is formed as was shown by J. C. Savigny in 1816 by two elongated and flexible outgrowths of the first maxillae, usually regarded as representing the outer lobes or galeae (fig. 4, A, B, *g*). These structures are grooved along their inner faces and by means of a series of interlocking hair-like bristles can be joined together so as to form a tubular sucker (fig. 4, C). At their extremities they are beset with club-like sense-organs, whose apparent function is that of taste. The proboscis when in use is stretched out in front of the head and inserted into the corolla of a flower or elsewhere, for the absorption of liquid nourishment. When at rest, the proboscis is rolled up into a close spiral beneath the head and between the labial palps (fig. 4, A, *p*). Only in the genus *Micropteryx* mentioned above is the lacinia of the maxilla (as A. Walter has shown) developed (fig. 3, B, *c*). The maxillary palp is usually a mere vestige (fig. 4, B, *p*) though it is conspicuous in a few families of small moths. A considerable number of Lepidoptera take no food in the imaginal state; in these the maxillae are reduced or altogether atrophied. The second maxillae are intimately fused together to form the labium, which consists only of a reduced mentum, bearing sometimes vestigial lobes and always a pair of palps. These have two or three segments and are clothed with scales. The form and direction of the terminal segment of the labial palp afford valuable characters in classification.

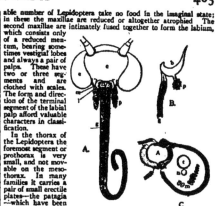

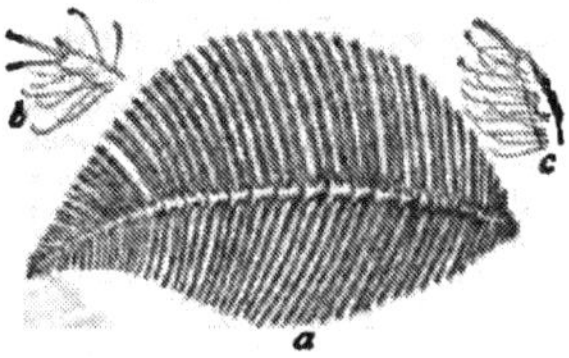

From Riley and Howard, *Insect Life*, vol. 7 (U.S. Dept. Agr.).

FIG. 2.—*a*, Feeler of Saturniid Moth (*Telea polyphemus*). *b*, *c*, Tips of branches, highly magnified.

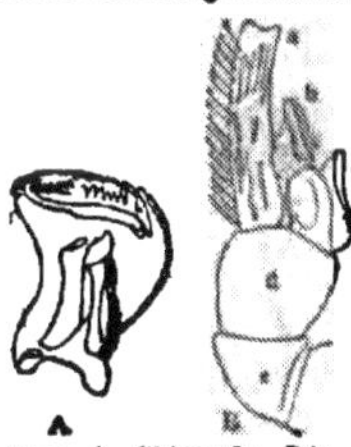

After A. Walter (*Jen. Zeits. f. Naturw.* vol. 18).

FIG. 3.—A, Mandible, and B, 1st maxilla of *Micropteryx* (*Eriocephala*). Magnified.

a, Palp. *d*, Stipes.
b, Galea. *e*, Cardo of
c, Lacinia. maxilla.

In the thorax of the Lepidoptera the foremost segment or prothorax is very small, and not movable on the mesothorax. In many families it carries a pair of small erectile plates—the patagia—which have been regarded as serially homologous with the wings. The mesothorax is extensive; its scutum forming most of the dorsal thoracic area and small plates—tegulae—are often present at the base of the forewings, as in Hymenoptera. The tegulae which are beset with long hair-like scales are often conspicuous. The metathorax is smaller than the mesothorax. The legs are of the typical hexapodan form with five-segmented feet; the shins often bear terminal and median spurs articulated at their bases and the entire limbs are clothed with scales.

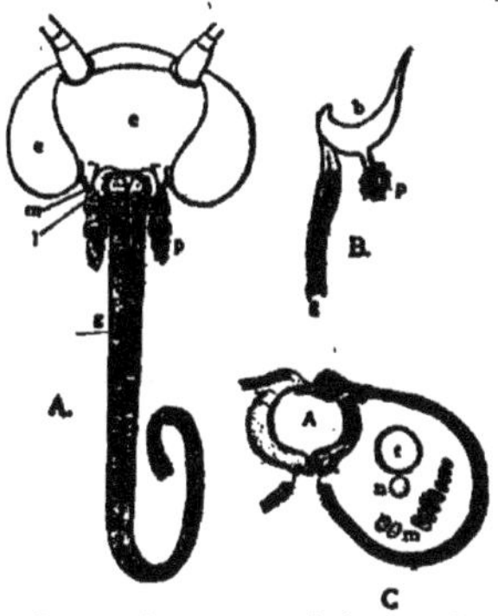

FIG. 4.—Arrangement of the jaws in a typical Moth. Somewhat diagrammatic and in part after E. Burgess and V. L. Kellogg (*Amer. Nat.* xiv. xxix.).

A, Front view of head.
c, Clypeus.
e, Compound eye.
m, Vestigial mandible.
l, Labrum.
g, Galeae of 1st maxillae.
p, Labial palp. Magnified. B.
b, Base of first maxilla dissected out of the head.
p, Vestigial palp.
g, Galea. Further magnified.
C, Part transverse section showing how the channel (A) of the proboscis is formed by the interlocking of the grooved inner faces of the flexible maxillae.
t, Air-tube.
n, Nerve.
m, Muscle-fibres. Highly magnified.

The wings of the Lepidoptera may be said to dominate the structure of the insect; only exceptionally, in certain female moths, are they vestigial or absent (fig. 17). The forewing, with its prominent apex, is longer than the hindwing, and the neuration in both (see figs. 5 and 6) is for the most part longitudinal, only a few transverse nervures, which are, in fact, branches of the median trunk, marking off a discoidal areolet or "cell" (fig. 5, *a*). The five branches of the radial nervure (figs. 5, 6, 3) (see HEXAPODA) are usually present in the forewing, but the hindwing, in most families, has only a single radial nervure; its anal area is, however, often more strongly developed than that of the forewing. The two wings of a side are usually kept together during flight by a few stout bristles—the frenulum—(fig. 5, *f*) projecting from the base of the costa of the hindwing and fitting beneath a membranous fold or a few thickened scales—the retinaculum—on the under surface of the forewing. In butterflies there is no frenulum, but a costal outgrowth of the

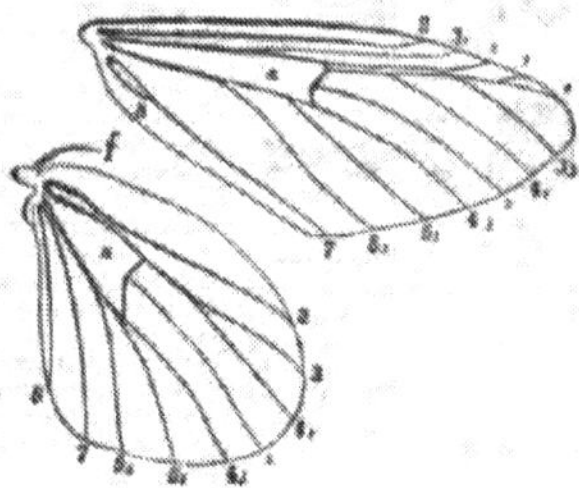

After A. S. Packard, *Mem. Nat. Acad. Sci.* vol. vii.

FIG. 5.—Wing-neuration of a Notodont Moth. 2, Subcostal; 3, radial; 4, median; 5, cubital; 7, 8, anal nervures. *a*, Discoidal areolet or "cell"; *f*, frenulum. Note that the forewing has five branches (1—5) of the radial nervure, the hindwing one only. The first anal nervure (No. 6) is absent.

amo
his f
was
Turk.
For
ities a
of Do
and J
Lepant
LE P
graver.
in add
develo
which
consiste
and mu
cabinets,
he was
cessively
and swa
however,
plates, al
and inclu
academy
LEPCHA
(*q.v.*). A
conquered
archal cus
of Lepcha
rich and
by the ci
literature
their trad
independer
is from th
all things
possessing
their own
See Flor
LE PEL
LOUIS MI
29th of M
his great-
count of Sa
He inherit
parlement
to the Stat
views of th
changed an
1789 he den
king had ar
stituent Ass
of death, of
of beheadin
popularity, a
of the Const
Legislative As
for the depart
by this depart
was in favour
voted for the d
ideas in general,
20th of January
assassinated in t
king's body-guard
magnificent funer
his death in a fam
daughter. Toward
himself in the ques
of a plan, the ideas
schemes. His assass
being discovered, he
a brother, Félix (17

... are sacred or... among ... the special ... ... made on the ... of the more ...

...Mackenzie's Goat Moth.)

... The post-embryonic develop... familiar, perhaps, than that of any ... shows great variation in ... being in some ... again erect and sub-conical ... often exhibits a ... Throughout the ... as the caterpillar (fig. 1, ...)

... (Goat Moth.) Europe.

... of three pairs of jointed and ... a variable number of pairs of abdominal ... outgrowths of the abdominal seg... a complete or incomplete circle of hooklets ...

... abdominal segments—the ninth often small and ... are usually present on the third, fourth, fifth, ... these segments. ... caterpillar (fig. 9) ... cuticle; ... simple eyes ... short feelers (fig. ... strong mandibles ... the caterpillar feeds ... other plant- ... maxillae, so highly ... imago, are in the ... inconspicuous ap- ... bearing two short ... the galea and ... The second ... plate-like labium ... projects the ... which is usually regarded ... hypopharynx (fig. 9, ... glands whose ducts ... spinneret are paired ... lying alongside ... cylindrical stomach. ... "silkworm" these ... five times as long as the caterpillar. They are re... salivary glands, ... correspondence has been doubted by some students. The caterpillar is usually cylindrical and wormlike, with the

FIG. 9.—Head of Goat Moth Caterpillar (*Cossus*) from behind. Magnified. (From Miall and Denny after Lyonnet.)
At, Feeler.
Mn, Mandible.
Mx, First maxilla.
Lm, Second maxillae (Labium) with spinneret.

segmentation well marked and the cuticle feebly chitinized and flexible. Firm chitinous plates are, however, not seldom present on the prothorax and on the hindmost abdominal segment. The segments are mostly provided with bristle or spine-bearing tubercles, whose arrangement has lately been shown by H. G. Dyar to give partially trustworthy indications of relationship. On either side of the median line we find two dorsal or trapezoidal tubercles (Nos. 1 and 2), while around the spiracle are grouped (Nos. 3, 4 and 5) supra-, post-, and pre-spiracular tubercles; below are the sub-spiraculars, of which there may be two (Nos. 6, 7). The last-named is situated on the base of the abdominal proleg, and yet another tubercle (No. 8) may be present on the inner aspect of the proleg. The spiracles are very conspicuous on the body of a caterpillar, occurring on the prothorax and on the first eight abdominal segments. Various tubercles may become coalesced or aborted (fig. 10, B); often, in conjunction with the spines that they bear, the tubercles serve as a valuable protective armature for the caterpillar. Much discussion has taken place as to whether the abdominal prolegs are or are not developed directly from the embryonic abdominal appendages. In the more lowly families of Lepidoptera, these organs are provided at the extremity with a complete circle of hooklets, but in the more highly organized families, only the inner half of this circle is retained.

The typical Lepidopteran pupa, or "chrysalis," as shown in the higher families, is an obtect pupa (fig. 11) with no trace of mandibles, the appendages being glued to the body by an exudation, and

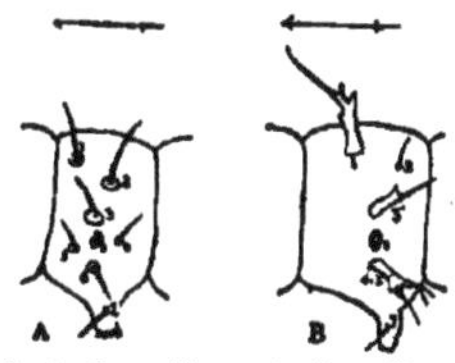

B, after Grote, *Mitt. aus dem Roemer Museum*, No. 6.

FIG. 10.—Abdominal segments of Caterpillars, to show arrangement of tubercles; the arrows point anteriorly. A, Generalized condition; B, specialized condition in the Saturniidae. *s*, Spiracle; the numbering of the tubercles is explained in the text. Note that in B No. 2 is much reduced and disappears after the first moult. 4 and 5 are coalesced, and 6 is absent.

FIG. 11.—Pupa of a Butterfly (*Amathusia phidippus*).

motion being possible only at three of the abdominal intersegmental regions, the fifth and sixth abdominal segments at most being "free." A flattened or pointed process—the cremaster—often prominent at the tail-end, may carry one or several hooks (fig. 1, *d*) which serve to anchor the pupa to its cocoon or to suspend butterfly-pupae from their pad of silk (fig. 11). In the lower families the pupa (fig. 1, *c*) is only incompletely obtect, and a greater number of abdominal segments can move on one another. The seventh abdominal segment is, in all female lepidopterous pupae, fused with those behind it; in the male "incomplete" pupa this becomes "free" and so may the segments anterior to it, in both sexes, forward to and including the third. The presence of circles of spines on the abdominal segments enables the "incomplete" pupa as a whole to work its way partly out of the cocoon when the time for the emergence of the imago draws near. In the family of the Eriocraniidae (often called the Micropterygidae) the pupa resembles that of a caddis-fly (*Trichopteron*) being active before the emergence of the imago and provided with strong mandibles by means of which it bites its way out of the cocoon. The importance of the pupa in the phylogeny and classification of the Lepidoptera has lately been demonstrated by T. A. Chapman in a valuable series of papers. Sometimes organs are present in the pupa which are undeveloped in the imago, such as the maxillary palps of the Sesiidae (clearwing moths) and the pectination on the feelers of female Saturniida. E. B. Poulton has drawn attention to the ancestral value of such characters.

Habits and Life-Relations.—The attractiveness of the Lepidoptera and the conspicuous appearance of many of them have led to numerous observations on their habits. The method of feeding of the imago by the suction of liquids has already been mentioned in connexion with the structure of the maxillae and the food-canal. Nectar from flowers is the usual food of moths and butterflies, most of which alight on a blossom before thrusting the proboscis into the corolla of the flower, while others—the hawk moths (Sphingidae) for example—remain poised in the air in front of the flower by means of excessively rapid vibration of the wings, and quickly unrolling the proboscis sip the nectar. Certain flowers with remarkably long tubular corollas seem to be specially adapted for the visits of hawk moths. Some Lepidoptera have other sources of food-supply. The juices of fruit are often sought for, and certain moths can pierce the envelope of a succulent fruit with the rough cuticular outgrowths at the tips of the maxillae, so as to reach the soft tissue within. Animal juices attract other Lepidoptera, which have been observed to suck blood from a wounded mammal; while putrid meat is a familiar "lure" for the gorgeous "purple emperor" butterfly (*Apatura iris*). The water of streams or the dew on leaves may be frequently sought by Lepidoptera desirous of quenching their thirst, possibly with fatal results, the insects being sometimes drowned in rivers in large numbers. Members of several families of the Lepidoptera—the Hepialidae, Lasiocampidae and Saturniidae, for example—have the maxillae vestigial or aborted, and take no food at all after attaining the winged condition. In such insects there is a complete "division of labour" between the larval and the imaginal instars, the former being entirely devoted to nutritive, the latter to reproductive functions.

Of much interest is the variety displayed among the Lepidoptera in the season and the duration of the various instars. The brightly coloured vanessid butterflies, for example, emerge from the pupa in the late summer and live through the winter in sheltered situations, reappearing to lay their eggs in the succeeding spring. Many species, such as the vapourer moths (*Orgyia*), lay eggs in the autumn, which remain unhatched through the winter. The eggs of the well-known magpie moths (*Abraxas*) hatch in autumn and the caterpillar hibernates while still quite small, awaiting for its growth the abundant food-supply to be afforded by the next year's foliage. The codlin moths (*Carpocapsa*) pass the winter as resting full-grown larvae, which seek shelter and spin cocoons in autumn, but do not pupate until the succeeding spring. Lastly, many of the Lepidoptera hibernate in the pupal stage; the death's head moth (*Acherontia*) and the cabbage-white butterflies (*Pieris*) are familiar examples of such. The last-named insects afford instances of the "double-brooded" condition, two complete life-cycles being passed through in the year. The flour moth (*Ephestia kühniella*) is said to have five successive generations in a twelvemonth. On the other hand, certain species whose larvae feed in wood or on roots take two or three years to reach the adult stage.

The rate of growth of the larva depends to a great extent on the nature of its food, and the feeding-habits of caterpillars afford much of interest and variety to the student. The contrast among the Lepidoptera between the suctorial mouth of the imago and the biting jaws of the caterpillar is very striking (cf. figs. 4 and 9), and the profound transformation in structure which takes place is necessarily accompanied by the change from solid to liquid food. The first meal of a young caterpillar is well known to be often its empty egg-shell; from this it turns to feed upon the leaves whereon its provident parent has laid her eggs. But in a few cases hatching takes place in winter or early spring, and the young larvae have then to find a temporary food until their own special plant is available. For example, the caterpillars of some species of *Xanthia* and other noctuid moths feed at first upon willow-catkins. On the other hand, the caterpillars of the pith moth (*Blastodacna*) hatched at midsummer, feed on leaves when young, and burrow into woody shoots in autumn. All who have tried to rear caterpillars know that, while those of some species will feed only on one particular species of plant, others will eat several species of the same genus or family, while others again are still less particular, some being able to feed on almost any green herb. It is curious to note how certain species change their food in different localities, a caterpillar confined to one plant in some localities being less particular elsewhere. Individual aberrations in food are of special interest in suggesting the starting-point for a change in the race. When we consider the vast numbers of the Lepidoptera and the structural modifications which they have undergone, their generally faithful adherence to a vegetable diet is remarkable. The vast majority

ıerves the same function. In the most primitive
lobate outgrowth—the jugum (fig. 6, j.)—from the
forewing is present, but it can be of little service in
ro wings together. A jugum may be also present on
The legs, which are generally used for clinging rather
ing, have five-segmented feet and are covered with
me families the front pair are reduced and without
ts.
inal segments are recognizable in many Lepidopt
nal segments are reduced or modified to form exter
organs of reproduction.
the male, according to
interpretation of C.
toureau, the lateral
belonging to the nin
ment form paired
beset with harpes
of ridges or teeth,
tergum of the
ment forms a
—the uncus—a
num a ventral
scaphium. In
the termin
form, in s
protrusible
the typical
positor wi
of proces
in the L
As al
the cha
the w
of th
cutic
com
tio
be

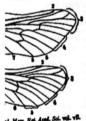

d, Mem. Nat. Acad. Sci. vol. vii.
-Wing neuration of a Swift
pialid). j, Jugum. Ner-
bered as in fig. 5. Note
are five branches to the
vure (No. 3) in both fore-
ving, and that the median
vures (No. 4) traverse the
areolet.

scales (fig. 7, B) with numerous
rthropod "hair." Either a "
a special cell of the ectoderm (
ows through the general cuti
ance of the cuticular append
ged in regular rows (fig. 7, A
ut into a narrow neck or c
he scales can be easily rubb
series of collars in which t
, c) on the wing-membra
s there are specially
)—which are formed by gl
. In some cases, the a
scales; in others they
" (see fig. 66). The adi
era are due partly to p
s, browns, reds and

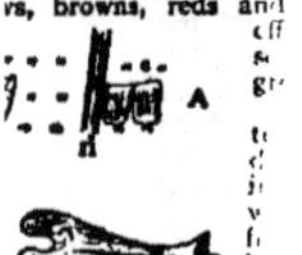

—A, Arrangement
in rows on wing
fly. n, Nervure;
-like outgrowths
Magnified. B,
le, and C, an
m more highly

horacic and four
each ovary has fo
enclosed in follicl
special bursa whic
e eighth abdomina
e and the lower T
ina, which still op
ptera, the bursa
tinct from the va
e duct of the bur-
ich opens opposit

rarum) to the densely woven ...ae and Saturniidae) or the ...ars (Lasiocampidae). Fre...ed up with the silk and serve hairs from the body of the itself, as among the "tigers") or chips of wood, as with ...er-burrowing larva of the (*Cossus*). In many families ...ptera we can trace a degenera... the cocoon. Thus, the pupae ...t owl moths (Noctuidae) and moths (Sphingidae) lie buried in ...then cell. Among the butterflies ...l that the cocoon is reduced to a ...f silk which gives attachment to ...remaster; in the Pieridae there is ...ddition a girdle of silk around the ...st-region of the pupa, but the pupae the Nymphalidae (figs. 11, 65) ...mply hang from the supporting pad the tail-end. Poulton has shown ...at the colours of some exposed ...pupae vary with the nature of the surroundings of the larva during the final stage.

When the pupal stage is complete the insect has to make its way out of ...wer families of moths it is the pupa least partially, working itself onwards abdominal segments; the pupa of the has functional mandibles with which it ...oon. In the higher Lepidoptera the pupa is ...imago, after the ecdysis of the pupal cuticle, ...mergence is in some cases facilitated by the ...r alkaline solvent discharged from the mouth ...ut, which weakens the cocoon—so that the ...reak through without injury.

...pected, the conditions to which larva and ...! have often a marked influence on the nature ...An indifferent food-supply for the larva leads ...the moth or butterfly. Many converging lines ...nd observation tend to show that cool conditions ...l stage frequently induce darkening of pigment while a warm temperature brightens the colours insect. For example, in many species of butterfly ...ble-brooded, the spring brood emerging from the ...pae are more darkly coloured than the summer ...the pupae producing the latter be subjected artifici... conditions, the winter form of imago results. It is possible, however, to produce the summer form of from wintering pupae by artificial heat. From this ...ann argued that the more stable winter form must be as representing the ancestral race of the species. examples of this "seasonal dimorphism" are afforded ...tropical butterflies which possess a darker "wet-season" brighter "dry-season" generation. So different in ...ance are often these two seasonal forms that before their ...elationship was worked out they had been naturally ...ed as independent species. The darkening of wing...rns in many species of Lepidoptera has been carefully ...ed in our own British fauna. Melanic or melanochroic ...ties are specially characteristic of western and hilly regions, some remarkable dark races (fig. 43) of certain geometrid ...ths have arisen and become perpetuated in the manufacturing ...stricts of the north of England. The production of these ...lanic forms is explained by J. W. Tutt and others as largely ...ue to the action of natural selection, the damp and sooty conditions of the districts where they occur rendering unusually dark the surfaces—such as rocks, tree-trunks and palings—on which moths habitually rest and so favouring the survival of dark, and the elimination of pale varieties, as the latter would be conspicuous to their enemies. Breeding experiments have shown that these melanic races are sometimes "dominant" to their parent-stock. An evidently adaptive connexion can be frequently traced between the resting situation and attitude of the insect and the colour and pattern of its wings. Moths that rest with the hindwings concealed beneath the forewings (fig. 34, *f*) often have the latter dull and mottled, while the former are sometimes highly coloured. Butterflies whose normal resting attitude is with the wings closed vertically over the back (fig. 63) so that the under surface is exposed to view, often have this under surface mottled and inconspicuous although the upper surface may be bright with flashing colours. Various degrees of such "protective resemblance" can be traced, culminating in the wonderful "imitation" of its surroundings shown by the tropical "leaf-butterflies" (*Kallima*), the under surfaces of whose wings, though varying greatly, yet form in every case a perfect representation of a leaf in some stage or other of decay, the butterfly at the same time disposing of the rest of its body so as to bear out the deception. How this is effected is best told by A. R. Wallace, who was the first to observe it, in his work *The Malay Archipelago*:—

> "The habit of the species is always to rest on a twig and among dead or dried leaves, and in this position, with the wings closely pressed together, their outline is exactly that of a moderately sized leaf slightly curved or shrivelled. The tail of the hindwings forms a perfect stalk and touches the stick, while the insect is supported by the middle pair of legs, which are not noticed among the twigs and fibres that surround it. The head and antennae are drawn back between the wings so as to be quite concealed, and there is a little notch hollowed out at the very base of the wings, which allows the head to be retracted sufficiently."

But the British Vanessids often rest on a bare patch of ground with the brightly coloured upper surface of their wings fully exposed to view, and even make themselves still more conspicuous by fanning their wings up and down. Some genera and families of Lepidoptera, believed to secrete noxious juices that render them distasteful, are adorned with the staring contrasts of colour usually regarded as "warning," while other genera, belonging to harmless families sought for as food by birds and lizards, are believed to obtain complete or partial immunity by their likeness to the conspicuous noxious groups. (See MIMICRY.)

Sexual dimorphism is frequent among the Lepidoptera. In many families this takes the form of more elaborate feelers in the male than in the female moth. Such complex feelers (fig. 2) bear numerous sensory (olfactory) nerve-endings and give to the males that possess them a wonderful power of discovering their mates. A single captive female of the Endromidae or Lasiocampidae often causes hundreds of males of her species to "assemble" around her prison, and this character is made use of by collectors who want to secure specimens. In many butterflies—notably the "blues" (Lycaenidae)—the male is brilliant while the female is dull, and in other groups (the Danainae for example) he is provided with scent-producing glands believed to be "alluring" in function. The apparent evidence given by the sexual differences among the Lepidoptera in favour of C. Darwin's theory of sexual selection finds no support from a study of their habits. The male indeed usually seeks the female, but she appears to exercise no choice in pairing. In some cases the female is attracted by the male, and here a modified form of sexual selection appears to be operative. The ghost swift moth (*Hepialus humuli*) affords a curious and interesting example of this condition, the female showing the usual brown and buff coloration of her genus, while the wings of the male are pure white, rendering him conspicuous in the dusky evening when pairing takes place. But in the northernmost

FIG. 17.—Vapourer Moth (*Ocneria detrita*). S. Europe. A, Male; B, Female.

[illegible]

America companies of the monarch (*Anosia archippus*) invade Canada every summer from the United States, and are believed to return southwards in autumn. This latter species has, during the last half-century, extended its range south-westwards across the Pacific and reached the Austro-Malayan islands, while several specimens have occurred in southern and western England, though it has not established itself on this side of the Atlantic. It is noteworthy that the introduction of its food-plant —*Asclepias*—into the Sandwich Islands in 1850 apparently enabled it to spread across the Pacific.

Fossil History.—Our knowledge of the geological history of the Lepidoptera is but scanty. Certain Oolitic fossil insects from the lithographic stone of Solenhofen, Bavaria, have been described as moths, but it is only in Tertiary deposits that undoubted Lepidoptera occur, and these, all referable to existing families, are very scarce. Most of them come from the Oligocene beds of Florissant, Colorado, and have been described by S. H. Scudder. The paucity of Lepidoptera among the fossils is not surprising when we consider the delicacy of their structure, and though their past history cannot be traced back beyond early Cainozoic times, we can have little doubt from the geographical distribution of some of the families that the order originated with the other higher Endopterygota in the Mesozoic epoch.

Classification.—The order Lepidoptera contains more than fifty families, the discussion of whose mutual relationships has given rise to much difference of opinion. The generally received distinction is between butterflies or *Rhopalocera* (Lepidoptera with clubbed feelers, whose habit is to fly by day) and moths or *Heterocera* (Lepidoptera with variously shaped feelers, mostly crepuscular or nocturnal in habit). This distinction is quite untenable as a zoological conception, for the relationship of butterflies to some moths is closer than that of many families of Heterocera to each other. Still more objectionable is the division of the order into *Macrolepidoptera* (including the butterflies and large moths) and the *Microlepidoptera* (comprising the smaller moths). Most of the recent suggestions for the division of the Lepidoptera into sub-orders depend upon some single character. Thus J. H. Comstock has proposed to separate the three lowest families, which have—like caddis-flies (Trichoptera) —a jugum on each forewing, as a sub-order *Jugatae*, distinct from all the rest of the Lepidoptera—the *Frenatae*, mostly possessing a frenulum on the hindwing. A. S. Packard places one family (Micropterygidae) with functional mandibles and a lacinia in the first maxilla alone in a sub-order *Laciniata*, all the rest of the order forming the sub-order *Haustellata*. T. A. Chapman divides the families with free or incompletely obtect and mobile pupae (*Incompletae*) from those with obtect pupae which never leave the cocoon (*Obtectae*), and this is probably the most natural primary division of the Lepidoptera that has as yet been suggested. Dyar puts forward a classification founded entirely on the structure of the larva, while Tutt divides the Lepidoptera into three great stirps characterized by the shape of the chorion of the egg. The primitive form of the egg is oval, globular, or flattened with the micropyle at one end; from this has apparently been derived the upright form of egg with the micropyle on top which characterizes the butterflies and the higher moths. These schemes, though helpful in pointing out important differences, are unnatural in that they lay stress on single, often adaptive, characters to the exclusion of others equally important. Although it is perhaps best to establish no division among the Lepidoptera between the order and the family, an attempt has been made in the classification adopted in this article to group the families into tribes or super-families which may indicate their probable affinities. The systematic work of G. F. Hampson, A. R. Grote and E. Meyrick has done much to place the classification of the Lepidoptera on a sound basis, so far as the characters of the imago are concerned, but attention must also be paid to the preparatory stages if a truly natural system is to be reached.

Jugatae.

hree families are included in this group having in common in primitive characters of the wings and neuration (see fig. 6).

as well as of the larva and pupa. There is a membranous lobe or jugum near the base of the wing, and the neuration of the hindwing is closely like that of the forewing, the radial nervure being five-branched in both. The pupa has four or five movable segments, and the larval prolegs have complete circles of hooklets.

The three families of the Jugatae are not very closely related to each other. The *Micropterygidae* (often known as *Eriocephalidae*), comprising a few small moths with metallic wings, are the most primitive of all Lepidoptera. They are provided with functional mandibles, while the maxillae have distinct laciniae, well-developed palps and galeae not modified for suction (see fig. 3). The larva is remarkable on account of its long feelers, the presence of pairs of jointed prolegs on the first eight abdominal segments, an anal sucker beneath the last segment and bladder-like outgrowths on the cuticle. These curious larvae feed on wet moss. The family has only a few genera scattered widely over the earth's surface (Europe, America, Australia, New Zealand).

The *Eriocraniidae* resemble the Micropterygidae in appearance, but the imago has no mandibles, and the maxillae, though short and provided with conspicuous palps, have no laciniae and form a proboscis as in Lepidoptera generally. The abdomen of the female carries a serrate piercing process, and the eggs are laid in the leaves of deciduous trees, the white larvae, with aborted legs, mining in the leaf tissue. The fully-fed larva winters in an underground cocoon and then changes into the most remarkable of all known lepidopterous pupae, with relatively enormous toothed mandibles which bite a way out of the cocoon in preparation for the final change. These pupal mandibles of the Eriocraniidae, together with the nature of the imaginal maxillae in the Micropterygidae (Eriocephalidae) and the wing-neuration in both families, point strongly to a relationship between the Lepidoptera and the Trichoptera.

The *Hepialidae* or swift moths—the third family of the Jugatae—are in some respects specialized. The moths are of large or moderate size with the maxillae in a vestigial condition, no food being taken after the attainment of the perfect state. The larvae (fig. 12) feed either on roots or in the wood of trees and shrubs, not attaining their growth in less than a year and some large exotic species living for two or three. The family is world-wide in range, and Australia possesses some almost gigantic and strangely coloured genera.

Tineides.

A large assemblage of moths, mostly of small size, are included in this group. The wings have no jugum, but there is a frenulum on the hindwing, which has, as in all the groups above the Jugatae, only a single radial nervure. Three anal nervures are present in the hindwing in those families whose wings are well developed, but in several families of small moths the wings of both pairs are very narrow and pointed, and the neuration is consequently reduced. The sub-costal nervure of the hindwing is usually present and distinct from the radial nervure. The egg is flat except in the Cossidae and Castniidae in which it is upright. The larval prolegs, with few exceptions, have a complete circle of hooklets, and the larvae usually feed in some concealed situation. The pupa is incompletely obtect, with three (in some females only two) to five free abdominal segments, and emerges partly from the cocoon before the moth appears. The cremaster serves to anchor the pupa to its cocoon at the correct degree of emergence, and thus facilitates the eclosion of the imago.

The *Cossidae* are a small family of large moths (figs. 8, 18, 19) belonging to this section, characterized by their heads with erect rough scales or hairs, the pectinate feelers of the males, their reduced maxillae so that no food is taken in the perfect state, and their

FIG. 18.—*Stygia australis.* S. Europe.

FIG. 19.—*Zeuzera scalaris.* India.

wings with the fifth radial nervure arising from the third, and the main median nervure forking in the discoidal areolet. The larvae feed in plant stems, often in the wood of trees, forming tunnels and galleries, and usually taking a year or more to reach maturity. The pupa which has three or four free segments in the male and four or five in the female, rests in a cocoon within the food plant, often strengthened by chips of wood, or in a subterranean cocoon. The family is fairly well represented in the tropics; the British fauna possesses only three species, of which the "goat" (*Cossus cossus*) and the "leopard" (*Zeuzera pyrina*) are well known, the caterpillars of both being often injurious to timber and fruit trees.

The *Tortricidae* are a large family of small moths (see fig. 1), nearly allied to the Cossidae. The fifth radial nervure does not arise from the third, the maxillae are well developed, but their palps are obsolete; the head is densely clothed with erect scales; the terminal segment of the labial palp is short and obtuse. The female pupa has three, the male four, free segments. All the larvae of these moths have some method of concealing themselves while feeding. A frequent plan is to roll up a leaf of the food-plant, fastening the twisted portion with silken threads so as to make a tubular retreat; this is the habit of the caterpillar of the green bell moth (*Tortrix viridana*) which often ravages the foliage of oak plantations. The larvae of the pine-shoot moths (*Retinia*) shelter in solidified resinous exudations from their coniferous food-plants, while the codlin-moth caterpillar (*Carpocapsa pomonella*) feeds in apples and pears, growing with the growth of the fruit which affords them both provender and home. The antics of "jumping-beans" are due to the movements of tortricid caterpillars within the substance of the seed.

The *Psychidae* are a small but widely-distributed family of moths whose males have the head, densely clothed with rough hairs, bearing complex, bipectinated feelers, but with the maxillae reduced and useless. The larvae live in portable cases made of grass, pieces of leaf or stick, with a silken lining, and these cases serve as cocoons for the pupae which agree in structure with those of the Tortricidae. But the most remarkable feature of the family is the extreme degradation of the female, which, wingless, legless and without jaws or feelers, never emerges from the cocoon.

The *Castniidae* are a small family of large, conspicuous, day-flying exotic moths (fig. 20) whose clubbed feelers and bright colours give them a resemblance to butterflies, although their wing-neuration is of the primitive tineoid type; the smooth larvae feed on the stems or roots of plants and the pupal structure agrees with that of the Tortricidae and Psychidae. The distribution of the family is confined to Tropical America and the Indo-Malayan and Australian regions.

FIG. 20.—*Castnia acraeoides.* Brazil.

The *Zygaenidae* (burnet moths) are a large family of day-flying moths (fig. 21) adorned with brilliant metallic colours. The feelers are long, stout in the middle and tapering, bearing numerous long or short pectinations. The well-developed maxillae have vestigial palps. The larvae—often very conspicuously coloured—are remarkable among the Tineides in having incomplete circles of hooks on the prolegs, and they feed exposed on the leaves of various plants. The pupa, enclosed in a silken cocoon, has four or five free segments. The *Limacodidae* are a small family of brownish nocturnal moths, allied to the Zygaenidae and agreeing with them in the structure of the pupa. The larva in this family also is an exposed feeder, but it is remarkable in form, being flattened and slug-like, without prolegs and adorned with curious spinous processes.

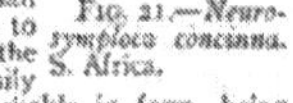

FIG. 21.—*Neurosymploca concinna.* S. Africa.

The *Sesiidae* are a large family of small, narrow-winged moths, the sub-costal nervure of the hindwing being absent and the wings being for the most part destitute of scales (fig. 22). The maxillae are developed but their palps are vestigial, while the terminal segment of the labial palp is short and pointed. Many of these insects have their bodies banded with black and yellow; this in conjunction with the transparent wings makes some of them like wasps or hornets in appearance. The larvae feed in the woody stems of various plants. The pupa, with three or four free abdominal segments, remains within its cocoon, formed with chips of wood, until the time for its final change draws near; then it works itself partly out of the tree by means of the spines on its abdominal segments.

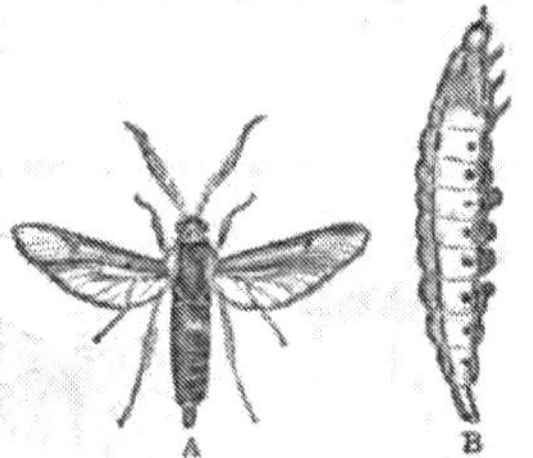

FIG. 22.—A. *Sesia asiliformis* (Gad-fly Hawk Moth). Europe. B, Larva.

The *Nepticulidae* are the smallest of all the Lepidoptera, measuring only 3-8 mm. across the outspread wings, which are all lanceolate and pointed at the tip. The sucking portions of the maxillae are vestigial, but the palps are long and jointed. The larvae, without [illegible] rudimentary [illegible] seven [illegible] and five [illegible] moths with very [illegible] larvae feed, when [illegible] devour leaves, [illegible] the Nepticulidae [illegible] has an ovipositor [illegible] plant tissues.

[illegible] are a large and important [illegible] moths (figs. 14, 24, 25) with [illegible] heads, and with the maxillae

[illegible]

FIG. 24.—*[illegible]* [illegible]. Europe.

FIG. 25.—*Tinea tapetzella* (Clothes Moth). Europe.

[illegible] usually well developed. Many of the genera have [illegible] with degraded neuration. The larvae differ [illegible] for example—mine in leaves, while [illegible] caterpillars of the clothes moth (*Tinea*) [illegible] with portable cases (fig. 14) formed by spinning [illegible]. The female pupa has three, the [illegible] segments.

[illegible]

[illegible] a few large families of small moths that are [illegible] and larval structure to the Tineidae (in [illegible] included) and by their pupal structure [illegible] but have yet to be considered. The moths [illegible] with slender pointed terminal segments, and [illegible] neuration (except in the Elachistidae) [illegible] Tineidae. The hairy covering of the [illegible] maxillary palps are usually vestigial. The [illegible] have complete circles of hooklets. [illegible] two free abdominal segments (fifth [illegible] not move out of the cocoon.

[illegible] this group. The *Plutellidae* (fig. 26) [illegible] developed in some genera, as slender [illegible] straight forward. The larvae do not [illegible] openly, keeping to the underside for protection (*Plutella*), or spinning by their united labour a mass of web over the food-plant (*Hyponomeuta*). In the other three families the maxillary palps are vestigial or obsolete. The *Elachistidae* have remarkably narrow, pointed wings [illegible] form portable cases and feed [illegible] (fig. 27) the sub-costal nervure [illegible] throughout its length, and the [illegible] leaves or seeds, or in decayed [illegible] family with similar larval habits; [illegible] sinuate termen of the hindwing [illegible] nervure with the discoidal

[illegible]

[illegible] moths of delicate build with [illegible] palps being usually well developed. The forewings have two anal nervures, the hindwings three (fig. 30, *h*, *i*); in the hindwing the sub-costal nervure bends towards and often connects with the radial, and the frenulum is usually present. The egg is flat. [illegible] five pairs of prolegs, [illegible]

[illegible]

mention. The *Pterophoridae* (plume moths, fig. 28) usually have the wings deeply cleft—a single cleft in the forewing and two in the hindwing. The hairy larvae feed openly on leaves, while the soft and hairy pupa remains attached to its cocoon by the cremaster, although it is incompletely obtect and has three or four free abdominal segments. The *Orneodidae* (multiplume moths) have all the wings six-cleft. Our British species, *Orneodes hexadactyla* (fig. 29), is an exquisite little insect, whose larva feeds on the blossoms of honeysuckle. The pupa is completely obtect, with only two free abdominal segments. The *Pyralidae* (figs. 13, 30), a large family with numerous divisions, have entire wings, and their pupae are

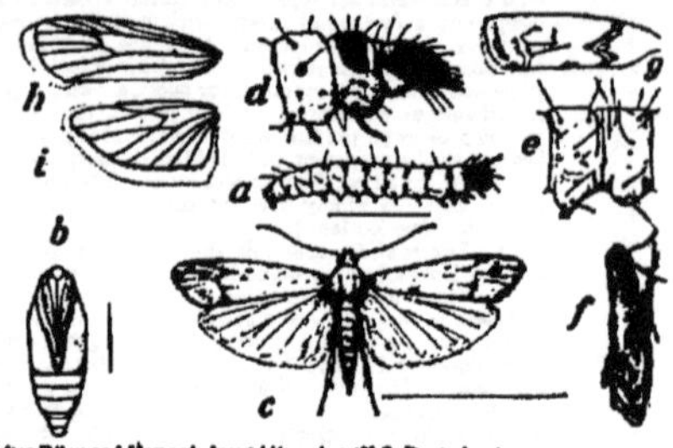

After Riley and Howard, *Insect Life*, vol. 2 (U.S. Dept. Agr.).

FIG. 30.—Flour Moth (*Ephestia kühniella*).

c, With wings spread.
f, At rest.
g, *h*, *i*, Marking and neuration of wings.
a, Larva.
b, Pupa.
d, Head and front body-segments of larva.
e, 2nd and 3rd abdominal segments.

obtect. The caterpillars feed in some kind of shelter, some spinning a loose case among the leaves of their food-plant, others burrowing into dry vegetable substances or eating the waxen cells of bees. Several species of this group, such as the Mediterranean flour moth, *Ephestia kühniella* (fig. 30), become serious pests in storehouses and granaries, their larvae devouring flour and similar food-stuffs.

Noctuides.

In this group may be included a number of families of moths with the second median nervure of the forewing arising close to the third. This feature of neuration characterizes also the Jugatae (see fig. 6), Tineides, Plutellides and Pyralides. But the Noctuides differ from these groups in having only two anal nervures in the hindwing. The maxillary palps are absent or vestigial, and a frenulum is usually present on the hindwing. The larva has usually ten prolegs, whose hooklets are arranged only along the inner edge, while the immobile pupa is always obtect with only two free abdominal segments (the fifth and sixth). The Lasiocampidae and their allies have flat eggs, but in the Noctuidae, Arctiidae and their allies the egg is upright.

The *Lasiocampidae*, together with a few small families, differ from the majority of this group in wanting a frenulum. The maxillae of the Lasiocampidae are so reduced that no food is taken in the imaginal state, and in correlation with this condition the feelers of the male are strongly (those of the female more feebly) bipectinated. The moths are stout, hairy insects, usually brown or yellow in the pattern of their wings. The caterpillars are densely hairy and many species hibernate in the larval stage. The pupa is enclosed in a hard, dense cocoon, whence the name "eggars" is often applied to the family, which has a wide distribution, but is absent from New Zealand. The *Drepanulidae* are an allied family, in which the frenulum is usually present, while the hindmost pair of larval prolegs are absent, their segment being prolonged into a pointed process which is raised up when the caterpillar is at rest. The hook-tip moths represent this family in the British fauna.

FIG. 31.—*Claterna cydonia*. India.

The *Lymantriidae* resemble the Lasiocampidae in their hairy bodies and vestigial maxillae, but the frenulum is usually present on the hindwing and the feelers are bipectinate only in the males. Some females of this family—the vapourer moths (*Orgyia* and allies, fig. 17), for example—are degenerate creatures with vestigial wings. The larvae (fig. 15) are very hairy, and often carry dense tufts on some of their segments; hence the name of "tussocks" frequently applied to them. The pupae are also often hairy (fig. 16)—an

An "e[illegible] to s[illegible] with yello[illegible] exter[illegible] in th[illegible] have condit[illegible] compar[illegible] the nur[illegible] can onl[illegible] (*Pyram*[illegible] *rameus*[illegible]

exceptional condition—and are protected by a cocoon of silk mixed with some of the larval hairs, while the female sheds some hairs from her own abdomen to cover the eggs. The family is widely distributed, its headquarters being the eastern tropics. To that part of the world is restricted the allied family of the *Hypsidae*, distinguished from the "tussocks" by the slender upturned terminal segment of the labial palps and by the development of the maxillae.

FIG. 32.—*Ophideres imperator*. Madagascar.

The *Noctuidae* are the largest and most dominant family of the Lepidoptera, comprising some 10,000 known species. They are mostly moths of dull coloration, flying at dusk or by night. The maxillae are well developed, the hindwing has a frenulum, and its sub-costal nervure touches the radial near the base. The larvae of the Noctuidae (fig. 34, *c*) are rarely hairy and the pupa (fig. 34, *d*) usually rests in an earthen cell, being often the wintering stage for the species, sometimes the pupa is enclosed in a loose cocoon of silk and leaves. In some Noctuidae (fig. 32) the hindwings are brightly coloured, but these are concealed beneath the dull, inconspicuous forewings when the insect rests (fig. 34, *f*). Nearly allied to the Noctuidae, but very different in appearance, are the gaily-coloured *Agaristidae*, a family of day-flying moths (figs. 35, 36), confined to the warmer regions of the globe and distinguished by their thickened feelers, those of the Noctuids being thread-like or slightly pectinate.

FIG. 33.—*Cyligramma fluctuosa*. W. Africa.

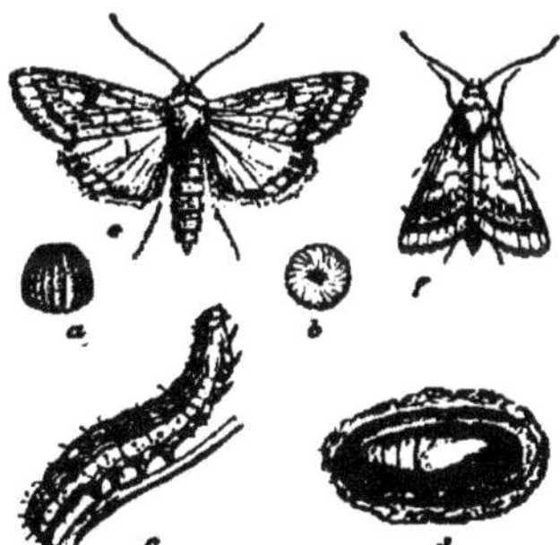

From Mally, *Bull.* 24, *Div. Ent. U.S. Dept. Agr.*
FIG. 34.—*e, f, Heliothis armigera*. Europe. *c*, Larva; *d*, pupa in cell. Natural size. *a, b*, Egg, highly magnified.

The *Arctiidae* (tiger moths, footmen, &c.) are allied to the Noctuidae, but their wing-neuration is more specialized, the sub-costal nervure of the hindwing being confluent with the radial for the basal part of its course. These moths (fig. 37) have gaily coloured wings, and the caterpillars are often densely covered with long smooth hairs. The pupae are enclosed in silken cocoons (fig. 38). The highest specialization of structure in this group of the Lepidoptera is reached by the *Syntomidae*, a family nearly allied to the Arctiidae, but with the sub-costal nervure in the hindwing absent. The Syntomidae have elongate narrow forewings and short hindwings, usually dark in colour with clear spots and dashes destitute of scales (fig. 40). The body, on the other hand, is often brilliantly adorned. The family, abundant in the tropics of the Old World, has only two European species.

FIG. 35.—*Rothia pales*. Madagascar.

Sphingides.

This group includes a series of families which agree with the Noctuides in most points, but are distinguished by the origin of the second median nervure of the forewing close to the first, or from the discocellular nervure midway between the first and third medians (see fig. 5). These neurational characters may appear somewhat insignificant, but such slight though constant distinctions in structures of no adaptational value may be safely regarded as truly significant of relationship. Several of the families in this group have lost the frenulum. In larval and pupal characters the Sphingides generally resemble the Noctuides, but in some families there is a reduction in the number of the larval prolegs. The egg is spherical or flat, upright only in the Notodontidae.

FIG. 36.—*Aegocera rectilinea*. Tropical Africa.
FIG. 37.—*Haploa Lecontei*. N. America.

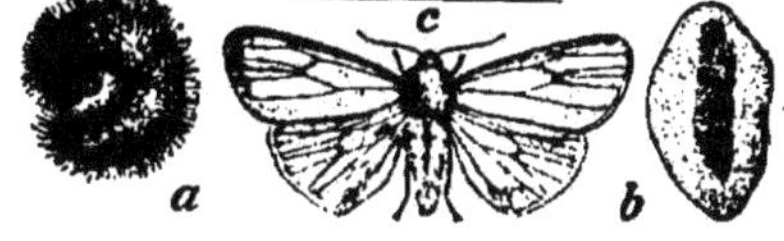

After Lugger, Riley and Howard, *Insect Life*, vol. 2 (U.S. Dept. Agr.).
FIG. 38.—*c*, Tiger Moth (*Phragmatobia fuliginosa*, Linn.). Europe. *a*, Caterpillar; *b*, cocoon with pupa. Slightly enlarged.

The *Notodontidae* are stout, hairy moths (figs. 5, 41, 42 *a*) with maxillae and frenulum developed. In the larva the prolegs on the hindmost segment are sometimes modified into pointed outgrowths which are carried erect when the caterpillar moves about. From these structures whip-like, coloured processes are protruded by the caterpillar (fig. 42 *b*) of the puss moth (*Cerura*) when alarmed; these processes are believed to help in "terrifying" the caterpillar's enemies. Allied to the Notodontidae are the *Cymatophoridae*—a family of moths agreeing with the Noctuidae in appearance and habits—and the large and important family of the *Geometridae*.

FIG. 39.—*Halias prasinana*. Europe.
FIG. 40.—*Euchromia formosa*. S. Africa.

The moths (fig. 43) of this family are distinguished from the Notodontidae by their delicate build and elongate feet, the caterpillars (fig. 43, c) by the absence or vestigial condition of the three anterior pairs of prolegs. The two hinder pairs of prolegs are therefore alone

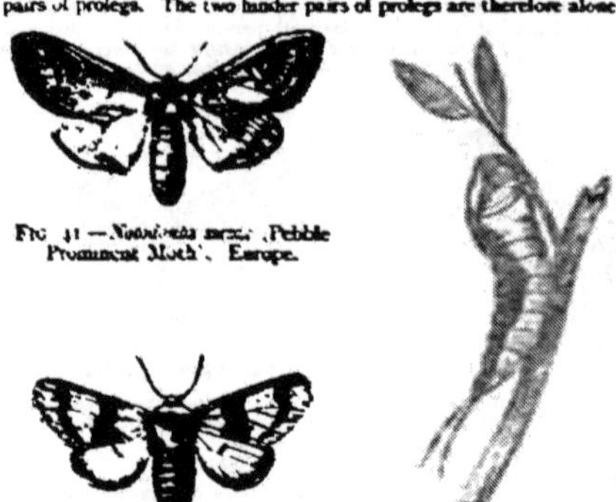

Fig. 41.—*Notodonta ziczac* (Pebble Prominent Moth). Europe.

Fig. 42a.—*Cerura borealis.* N. America.

Fig. 42b.—Larva of *Cerura* (Puss Moth).

functional and the larva progresses by "looping," i.e. bending the body so as to bring these prolegs close up to the thoracic legs, and then, taking a fresh grip on the twig whereon it walks, stretching the body straight out again. Many of these larvae have a striking

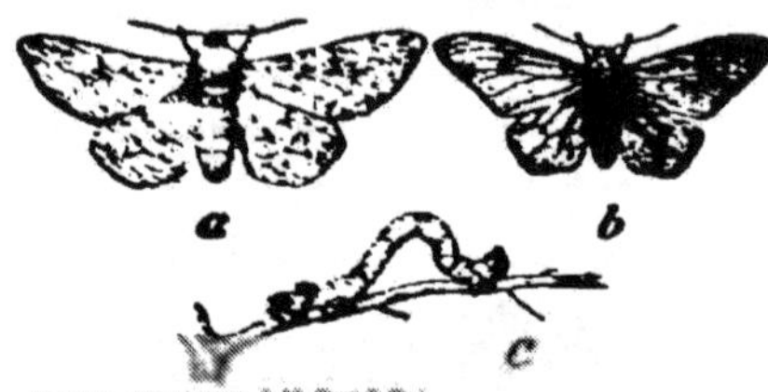

[illegible] (J. M. Dent & Co.)

[illegible] Moth (*Amphidasys betularia* Linn.), Europe. [illegible] A dark variety; c, caterpillar in looping [illegible].

[illegible] and colour to the twigs of their food-[illegible] species the female has the wings reduced to [illegible]. The family is world-wide in its range. The tropical [illegible] moths (figs. 44, 45), often with ex-

[illegible]

The Sphingidae (hawk moths) are insects often of large size (figs. 46a, 47), with spindle-shaped feelers, elongate and powerful forewings and the maxillae very well developed. The hindwing carries a frenulum and has its sub-costal nervure connected with the radial by a short bar. The caterpillars have the full number of prolegs, and, in many genera, carry a prominent dorsal horn on the eighth abdominal segment (fig. 46 b). The pupa lies in an earthen cell. On account of their powerful flight the moths of this family have a wide range; certain species—like *Acherontia atropos* and *Protoparce convolvuli*—migrate into the British Islands in numbers almost every summer.

Fig. 45.—*Urania boisduvalii* at rest, showing under surface of wings.

Fig. 46a.—*Chlaenogramma jasminearum* (Jessamine Sphinx). N. America.

A group of families in which the first maxillae are vestigial, the feelers bipectinate and the pupa enclosed in a dense silken cocoon, have been regarded as the most highly specialized of all the moths, though according to other views the whole series of the Lepidoptera culminates in the Sy[illegible]. Of these cocoon-spinning families may be specially mentioned the *Eupterotidae*, large brown or yellow moths inhabiting tropical Asia and Africa, and represented in Europe only by the "processionary moth" (*Cnethocampa processionea*). In this family the frenulum is present, and the larvae are protected with tufts of long hair. The *Bombycidae* have no frenulum, and

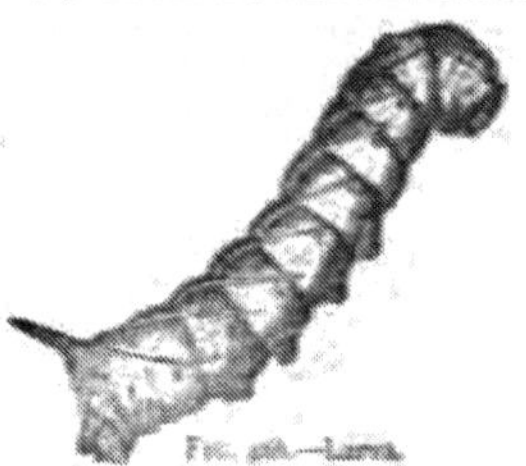

Fig. 46b.—Larva.

[illegible] 47.—*Smerinthus ocellatus* (Eyed Hawk moth). Europe.

[illegible] are smooth, with some of the segments humped and [illegible] abdominal often carrying a dorsal spine. The family

is tropical in its distribution, but the common silkworm (*Bombyx mori*, fig. 48) has become acclimatized in southern Europe and is the source of most of the silk used in manufacture and art. Of

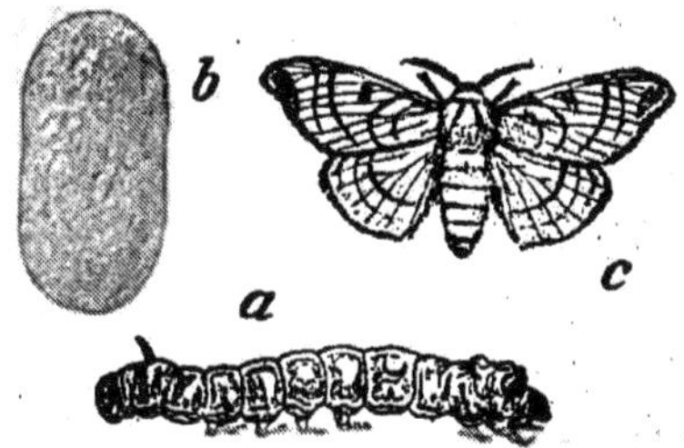

After C. V. Riley, *Bull.* 14, *Div. Ent. U.S. Dept. Agr.*

FIG. 48.—*Bombyx mori*. China. *a*, Caterpillar (the common silk-worm); *b*, cocoon; *c*, male moth.

commercial value also is the silk spun by the great moths of the family *Saturniidae*, well represented in warm countries and contributing a single species (*Saturnia pavonia-minor*) to the British fauna. These moths (fig. 49) have but a single anal nervure in the hindwing and only three radial nervures in the forewing. The wing-patterns are handsome and striking; usually an unscaled "eyespot" is conspicuous at the end of each discoidal areolet. The

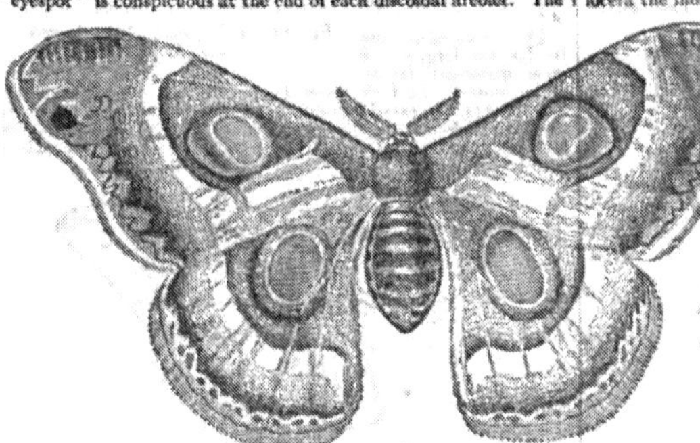

FIG. 49.—*Epiphora bouhiniae*. W. Africa.

caterpillars are protected by remarkable spine-bearing tubercles (fig. 10, B).

Grypocera.

This group stands at the base of the series of families that are usually distinguished as "butterflies." The feelers are recurved at the tip, and thickened just before the extremity. The forewing has the full number of radial nervures, distinct and evenly spaced, and two anal nervures; the frenulum is usually absent. The larvae (fig. 51) have prolegs with complete circles of hooklets, and often feed in concealed situations, while the pupa is protected by a light cocoon. The affinities of this group are clearly not with the higher groups of moths just described, but with some of the lower families. According to Meyrick they are most closely related to the Pyralidae, but Hampson and most other students would derive them (through the Castniidae) from a primitive Tineoid stock allied to the Cossidae and Zygaenidae.

FIG. 50.—*Tagiades sabadius.* S. Africa.

Three families are included in the section. The North American *Megathymidae* and the Australian *Euschemonidae* have a frenulum and are usually reckoned among the "moths." The *Hesperiidae* in which the frenulum is wanting form the large family of the skipper butterflies, represented in our own fauna by several species. They are insects with broad head—the feelers being widely separated—usually brown or grey wings (fig. 50) and a peculiar jerky flight. The family has an extensive range but is unknown in Greenland, New Zealand, and in many oceanic islands.

Rhopalocera.

This group comprises the typical butterflies which are much more highly specialized than the Grypocera, and may be readily distinguished by the knobbed or clubbed feelers and by the absence of a frenulum. Two or more of the radial nervures in the forewing arise from a common stalk or are suppressed. The egg is "upright." The larvae have hooklets only on the inner edges of the prolegs. The pupa is very highly modified, only two free abdominal segments are ever recognizable, and in some genera even these have become consolidated. The cocoon is reduced to a pad of silk, to which the pupa is attached, suspended by the cremastral hooks; in some families there is also a silken girdle around the waist-region. In correlation with the exposed condition of the pupa, we find the presence of a specially developed "head-piece" or "nose-horn" to protect the head-region of the contained imago. Their bright colours and conspicuous flight in the sunshine has made the Rhopalocera the most admired of all insects by the casual observer.

FIG. 51.—Chrysalis and Larva of *Nisoniadestages* (dingy skipper). Europe.

A modification that has taken place in several families of butterflies is the reduction of the first pair of legs. H. W. Bates arranged the families in a series depending on this character, but neurational and pupal features must be taken into account as well, and the sequence followed here is modified from that proposed by A. R. Grote and J. W. Tutt.

FIG. 52.—*Chrysophanus thoe.* N. America.

The *Lycaenidae* are a large family including the small butterflies (figs. 52, 53, 54) popularly known as blues, coppers and hairstreaks. The forelegs in the female are normal, but in the male the tarsal segments are shortened and the claws sometimes are absent. The forewing has only three or four radial nervures (fig. 55), the last two of which arise from a common stalk; the feelers are inserted close together on the head. The larva is short and hairy, somewhat like a woodlouse in shape, the broad sides concealing the legs and prolegs, while the pupa, which is also hairy or bristly, is attached by the cremaster to a silken pad and cinctured with a silken thread. The upper surfaces of the wings of these insects are usually of a bright metallic hue—blue or coppery—while beneath there are often

FIG. 53.—*Rathinda amor.* India.

FIG. 54.—*Cheritra freja.* India.

numerous dark centred "eye-spots." The family is widely distributed. Nearly related are the *Lemoniidae*, a family abundantly represented in the Neotropical Region, but scarce in the Old World and having only a single European species (*Nemeobius lucina*) which occurs also in England. In the Lemoniidae (figs. 56, 57) the forelegs of the male are reduced and useless for walking. The *Libytheidae* may be recognized by the elongate snout-like palps,

… A similar larva … or owl-butterflies—

… phidippus.

… Brazil.

… Arctic …

quisite wing-…
by the absenc…
normal ten pr…

including our native browns and the Alpine *Erebiae*, resemble the foregoing group in many respects of structure, but the sub-costal nervure is greatly thickened at the base (fig. 74). This sub-family is world-wide in its distribution. One genus (*Oeneis*, fig. 75) is found in high northern latitudes, but reappears in South America. The dark, spotted species of *Erebia* are familiar insects to travellers among the Alps; yet butterflies nearly related to these Alpine insects occur in Patagonia, in South Africa and in New Zealand. Such facts of distribution clearly show that though the Nymphalidae have attained a high degree of specialisation among the Lepidoptera, some of their genera have a history which goes back to a time when the distribution of land and water on the earth's surface must have been very different from what it is to-day.

BIBLIOGRAPHY.—The handsome Lepidoptera, with their interesting and easily observed life-histories, have naturally attracted many students, and the literature of the order is enormous. M. Malpighi's treatise on the anatomy of the silkworm (*De Bombycibus*, London, 1669) and P. Lyonnet's memoir on the Goat-caterpillar, are among the earliest and most famous of entomological writings. W. F. Kirby's *Handbook to the Order Lepidoptera* (5 vols., London, 1894–1897) should be consulted for references to the older systematic writers such as Linnaeus, J. C. Fabricius, J. Hübner, P. Cramer, E. Doubleday and W. C. Hewitson. Kirby's *Catalogues* are also invaluable for the systematist. For the jaws of the Lepidoptera see F. Darwin, *Quart. Journ. Mic. Sci.* xv. (1875); E. Burgess, *Amer. Nat.* xiv. (1880); A. Walter, *Jen. Zeits. f. Naturw.* xviii. (1885); W. Breitenbach, *Ib.* xv. (1882); V. L. Kellogg, *Amer. Nat.* xxix. (1895). The last-named deals also with wing structure, which is further described by A. Spuler, *Zeits. wiss. Zool.* liii. (1892) and *Zool. Jahrb. Anat.* viii. (1895); A. R. Grote, *Mitt. aus dem Roemer-Museum* (Hildesheim, 1896–1897); G. Enderlein, *Zool. Jahrb. Anat.* xvi. (1903), and many others. For scales see A. G. Mayer, *Bull. Mus. Comp. Zool. Harvard*, xxix. (1896). For internal anatomy W. H. Jackson, *Trans. Linn. Soc. Zool.* (2) v. (1891), and W. Petersen, *Mem. Acad. Imp. Sci. St Petersburg* (8) ix. (1900). The early stages and transformations of Lepidoptera are described by J. Gonin, *Bull. Soc. Vaud. Sci. Nat.* xxx. (1894); E. B. Poulton, *Trans. Linn. Soc. Zool.* (2) v. (1891); H. G. Dyar, *Ann. New York Acad. Sci.* viii. (1894); T. A. Chapman, *Trans. Entom. Soc. Lond.* (1893), &c. For habits and life-relations see A. Seitz, *Zool. Jahrb. Syst.* v., vii. (1890, 1894); A. Weismann, *Studies in the Theory of Descent* (London, 1882) and *Entomologist*, xxix. (1896); F. Merrifield, *Trans. Entom. Soc. Lond.* (1890, 1893, 1905); M. Standfuss, *Handbuch der paläarktischen Gross-schmetterlinge* (Jena, 1896); R. Trimen, *Proc. Ent. Soc. Lond.* (1898); E. B. Poulton, *Colours of Animals* (London, 1890); *Trans. Entom. Soc.* (1892 and 1903), and *Journ. Linn. Soc. Zool.* xxvi. (1898); F. E. Beddard, *Animal Coloration* (London, 1892). For distribution see H. J. Elwes, *Proc. Entom. Soc. Lond.* (1894); J. W. Tutt, *Migration and Dispersal of Insects* (London, 1902); Fossil Lepidoptera, S. H. Scudder, *8th Rep. U.S. Geol. Survey* (1889). Among recent general works on the Lepidoptera, most of which contain numerous references to the older literature, may be mentioned A. S. Packard's unfinished work on the Bombycine Moths of N. America, *Mem. Nat. Acad. Sci. Philadelphia*, vii. (1895), and *Mem. Acad. Sci. Washington*, ix. (1905); D. Sharp's chapter in *Cambridge Nat. Hist.* vi. (London, 1898); G. F. Hampson, *Moths of India* (4 vols., London, 1892–1896), and *Catalogue of the Lepidoptera Phalaenae* (1898) and onwards; S. H. Scudder, *Butterflies of New England* (3 vols., Cambridge, Mass., 1888–1889); W. J. Holland, *Butterfly Book* (New York, 1899). Works on the British Lepidoptera are numerous, for example, those of H. T. Stainton (1851), C. G. Barrett (1893–1907), E. Meyrick (1895), and J. W. Tutt (1899 and onwards). For recent general systematic works, the student should consult the catalogues mentioned above and the *Zoological Record*. The writings of O. Staudinger, E. Schatz, C. Oberthür, K. Jordan, C. Aurivillius and P. Mabille may be specially mentioned.

(G. H. C.)

LEPIDUS, the name of a Roman patrician family in the Aemilian gens.

1. MARCUS AEMILIUS LEPIDUS, one of the three ambassadors sent to Egypt in 201 B.C. as guardians of the infant king Ptolemy V. He was consul in 187 and 175, censor 179, *pontifex maximus* from 180 onwards, and was six times chosen by the censors *princeps senatus*. He died in 152. He distinguished himself in the war with Antiochus III. of Syria, and against the Ligurians. He made the Via Aemilia from Ariminum to Placentia, and led colonies to Mutina and Parma.

Livy xl. 42-46, *epit.* 48; Polybius xvi. 34.

2. MARCUS AEMILIUS LEPIDUS, surnamed PORCINA (probably from his personal appearance), consul 137 B.C. Being sent to Spain to conduct the Numantine war, he began against the will of the senate to attack the Vaccaei. This enterprise was so unsuccessful that he was deprived of his command in 136 and …mned to pay a fine. He was among the greatest of the Roman orators, and Cicero praises him for having

introduced the well-constructed sentence and even flow of language from Greek into Roman oratory.

Cicero, *Brutus*, 25, 27, 86, 97; Vell. Pat. ii. 10; Appian, *Hisp.* 80-83; Livy, *epit.* 56.

3. MARCUS AEMILIUS LEPIDUS, father of the triumvir. In 81 B.C. he was praetor of Sicily, where he made himself detested by oppression and extortion. In the civil wars he sided with Sulla and bought much of the confiscated property of the Marian partisans. Afterwards he became leader of the popular party, and with the help of Pompey was elected consul for 78, in spite of the opposition of Sulla. When the dictator died, Lepidus tried in vain to prevent the burial of his body in the Campus Martius, and to alter the constitution established by him. His colleague Lutatius Catulus found a tribune to place his veto on Lepidus's proposals; and the quarrel between the two parties in the state became so acute that the senate made the consuls swear not to take up arms. Lepidus was then ordered by the senate to go to his province, Transalpine Gaul; but he stopped in Etruria on his way from the city and began to levy an army. He was declared a public enemy early in 77, and forthwith marched against Rome. A battle took place in the Campus Martius, Pompey and Catulus commanding the senatorial army, and Lepidus was defeated. He sailed to Sardinia, in order to put himself into connexion with Sertorius in Spain, but here also suffered a repulse, and died shortly afterwards.

Plutarch, *Sulla*, 34, 38, *Pompey*, 15; Appian, *B.C.* i. 105, 107; Livy, *epit.* 90; Florus iii. 23; Cicero, *Balbus*, 15.

4. MARCUS AEMILIUS LEPIDUS, the triumvir. He joined the party of Julius Caesar in the civil wars, and was by the dictator thrice nominated *magister equitum* and raised to the consulship in 46 B.C. He was a man of great wealth and influence, and it was probably more on this ground than on account of his ability that Caesar raised him to such honours. In the beginning of 44 B.C he was sent to Gallia Narbonensis, but before he had left the city with his army Caesar was murdered. Lepidus, as commander of the only army near Rome, became a man of great importance in the troubles which followed. Taking part with Marcus Antonius (Mark Antony), he joined in the reconciliation which the latter effected with the senatorial party, and afterwards sided with him when open war broke out. Antony, after his defeat at Mutina, joined Lepidus in Gaul, and in August 43 Octavian (afterwards the emperor Augustus), who had forced the senate to make him consul, effected an arrangement with Antony and Lepidus, and their triumvirate was organized at Bononia. Antony and Octavian soon reduced Lepidus to an inferior position. His province of Gaul and Spain was taken from him; and, though he was included in the triumvirate when it was renewed in 37, his power was only nominal. He made an effort in the following year to regain some reality of power, conquered part of Sicily, and claimed the whole island as his province, but Octavian found means to sap the fidelity of his soldiers, and he was obliged to supplicate for his life. He was allowed to retain his fortune and the office of *pontifex maximus* to which he had been appointed in 44, but had to retire into private life. According to Suetonius (*Augustus*, 16) he died at Circeii in the year 13.

See ROME: *History* ii., "The Republic," Period C, *ad fin.*; Appian, *Bell. Civ.* ii.-v.; Dio Cassius xli.-xlix.; Vell. Pat. ii. 64, 80; Orelli's *Onomasticon* to Cicero.

LE PLAY, PIERRE GUILLAUME FRÉDÉRIC (1806-1882), French engineer and economist, was born at La Rivière-Saint-Sauveur (Calvados) on the 11th of April 1806, the son of a custom-house official. He was educated at the École Polytechnique, and from there passed into the State Department of Mines. In 1834 he was appointed head of the permanent committee of mining statistics, and in 1840 engineer-in-chief and professor of metallurgy at the school of mines, where he became inspector in 1848. For nearly a quarter of a century Le Play spent his vacations travelling in the various countries of Europe, and collected a vast quantity of material bearing upon the social condition of the working classes. In 1855 he published *Les Ouvriers européens*, which comprised a series of thirty-six monographs on the budgets of typical families selected from the most diverse industries. The Académie des Sciences conferred on him the Montyon prize. Napoleon III., who held him in high esteem, entrusted him with the organization of the Exhibition of 1855, and appointed him counsellor of state, commissioner general of the Exhibition of 1867, senator of the empire and grand officer of the Legion of Honour. He died in Paris on the 5th of April 1882.

In 1856 Le Play founded the *Société internationale des études pratiques d'Économie sociale*, which has devoted its energies principally to forwarding social studies on the lines laid down by its founder. The journal of the society, *La Réforme sociale*, founded in 1881, is published fortnightly. Other works of Le Play are *La Réforme sociale* (2 vols., 1864, 7th ed., 3 vols., 1887); *L'Organisation de la famille* (1871); *La Constitution de l'Angleterre* (in collaboration with M. Delaire, 1875). See article in *Harvard Quarterly Journal of Economics* (June 1890), by H. Higgs.

LEPROSY (*Lepra Arabum*, *Elephantiasis Graecorum*, *Aussatz*, *Spedalskhed*), the greatest disease of medieval Christendom, identified, on the one hand, with a disease endemic from the earliest historical times (1500 B.C.) in the delta and valley of the Nile, and, on the other hand, with a disease now common in Asia, Africa, South America, the West Indies, and certain isolated localities of Europe. An authentic representation of the leprosy of the middle ages exists in a picture at Munich by Holbein, painted at Augsburg in 1516; St Elizabeth gives bread and wine to a prostrate group of lepers, including a bearded man whose face is covered with large round reddish knobs, an old woman whose arm is covered with brown blotches, the leg swathed in bandages through which matter oozes, the bare knee also marked with discoloured spots, and on the head a white rag or plaster, and, thirdly, a young man whose neck and face (especially round the somewhat hairless eyebrows) are spotted with brown patches of various size. It is conjectured by Virchow that the painter had made studies of lepers from the leper-houses then existing at Augsburg. These external characters of medieval leprosy agree with the descriptions of it by the ancients, and with the pictures of modern leprosy given by Danielssen and Boeck for Norway, by various authors for sporadic European cases, by Anderson for Malacca, by Carter for India, by Wolff for Madeira and by Hillis for British Guiana. There has been some confusion in the technical naming of the disease; it is called *Elephantiasis* (*Leontiasis*, *Satyriasis*) by the Greek writers, and *Lepra* by the Arabians.

Leprosy is now included among the parasitic diseases (see PARASITIC DISEASES). The cause is believed to be infection by the bacillus leprae, a specific microbe discovered by Armauer Hansen in 1871. It is worthy of note that tuberculosis is very common among lepers, and especially attacks the serous membranes. The essential character of leprosy is a great multiplication of cells, resembling the "granulation cells" of lupus and syphilis, in the tissues affected, which become infiltrated and thickened, with degeneration and destruction of their normal elements. The new cells vary in size from ordinary leucocytes to giant cells three or four times larger. The bacilli are found in these cells, sometimes in small numbers, sometimes in masses. The structures most affected are the skin, nerves, mucous membranes and lymphatic glands.

The symptoms arise from the anatomical changes indicated, and they vary according to the parts attacked. Three types of disease are usually described—(1) nodular, (2) smooth or anaesthetic, (3) mixed. In the first the skin is chiefly affected, in the second the nerves; the third combines the features of both. It should be understood that this classification is purely a matter of convenience, and is based on the relative prominence of symptoms, which may be combined in all degrees. The incubation period of leprosy—assuming it to be due to infection—is unknown, but cases are on record which can only be explained on the hypothesis that it may be many years. The invasion is usually slow and intermittent. There are occasional feverish attacks, with the usual constitutional disturbance and other slight premonitory signs, such as changes in the colour of the skin and in its sensibility. Sometimes, but rarely, the onset is acute and the characteristic symptoms develop rapidly. These begin with [illegible] according to the type of [illegible] are red or coppery patches appear [illegible] and [illegible] on the body. [illegible] vary from the size of a shilling [illegible] and [illegible]. After a time [illegible] the skin becomes noticeable, and the [illegible] lumpy excrescences, at first pink but [illegible] thickening of the skin of the face produces [illegible] appearance, recalling the aspect of a lion. [illegible] the eye undergo degenerative changes; the [illegible] the nose and throat is thickened, impairing [illegible] the voice, the eyebrows fall off, the ears and [illegible] and enlarged. As the disease progresses [illegible] break down and ulcerate, leaving open sores. [illegible] condition is extremely wretched, gradually [illegible] and eventually succumbs to exhaustion or is [illegible] intercurrent disease, usually inflammation [illegible] tuberculosis. A severe case may end fatally [illegible], as a rule, when patients are well cared for the [illegible] years. There is often temporary improve[illegible] recovery from this form of leprosy rarely [illegible]. The smooth type is less severe and more [illegible] symptom consists of patches of dry, slightly dis[illegible] elevated above the surface. These patches [illegible] changes affecting the cutaneous nerves, [illegible] by diminished sensibility over the areas of [illegible] the same time certain nerve trunks in the [illegible] particularly the ulnar nerve, are found to be [illegible] further stages the symptoms are those of [illegible] of the nerves. Bullae form on the skin, [illegible] patches become enlarged; sensation is lost, [illegible] diminished, with wasting, contraction of tendons, [illegible] signs of impaired nutrition. The nails become hard [illegible] perforating ulcers of the feet are common; portions [illegible] the extremities, including whole fingers and toes, die and drop [illegible] paralysis becomes more marked, affecting the [illegible] the face and limbs. The disease runs a very chronic [illegible] may last twenty or thirty years. Recovery occasion[illegible]. In the mixed form, which is probably the most [illegible] the symptoms described are combined in varying [illegible]. Leprosy may be mistaken for syphilis, tuberculosis, [illegible] obscure disease affecting negroes, in which the little [illegible], and several affections of the skin. Diagnosis is [illegible] by the presence of the bacillus leprae in the nodules [illegible] by the signs of nerve degeneration exhibited in [illegible] and by the [illegible] patches of skin and the thickened nerve trunks.

[illegible] times leprosy was often confounded with other [illegible] especially psoriasis and leucoderma, the white [illegible] Testament was probably a form of the latter. [illegible] that true leprosy has existed from time [illegible] prescriptions for treating it have been found in [illegible] about 4600 B.C. is assigned. The disease [illegible] and by later Greek writers, but not [illegible] leprosy derives its name from his "lepra" [illegible] was no doubt psoriasis. In ancient [illegible] throughout Asia as well as in [illegible] Greeks and Romans. In the middle [illegible] diffused in Europe, and in some [illegible] Germany and Spain—every con[illegible] house, in which the patients were [illegible] of such houses has been reckoned [illegible] in England was established at [illegible] at Highgate in 1472. At one [illegible] hospitals for lepers in Great [illegible] James Simpson). During the 15th [illegible] a remarkable diminution. It [illegible] civilized parts of Europe, and the [illegible]. It is a singular fact that this [illegible] with the great extension of syphilis [illegible] general disappearance of leprosy [illegible] unintelligible because it did not take effect everywhere. In Scotland the disease lingered until the 18th century, and in some other parts it has never died out at all. At the present time it still exists in Norway, Iceland, along the shores of the Baltic, in South Russia, Greece, Turkey, several Mediterranean islands, the Riviera, Spain and Portugal. Isolated cases occasionally occur elsewhere, but they are usually imported. The Teutonic races seem to be especially free from the taint. Leper asylums are maintained in Norway and at two or three places in the Baltic, San Remo, Cyprus, Constantinople, Alicante and Lisbon. Except in Spain, where some increase has taken place, the disease is dying out. The number of lepers in Norway was 3000 in 1856, but has now dwindled to a few hundreds. They are no longer numerous in any part of Europe. On the other hand, leprosy prevails extensively throughout Asia, from the Mediterranean to Japan, and from Arabia to Siberia. It is also found in nearly all parts of Africa, particularly on the east and west coasts near the equator. In South Africa it has greatly increased, and attacks the Dutch as well as natives. Leper asylums have been established at Robben Island near Cape Town, and in Tembuland. In Australia, where it was introduced by Chinese, it has also spread to Europeans. In New Zealand the Maoris are affected; but the amount of leprosy is not large in either country. A much more remarkable case is that of the Hawaiian Islands, where the disease is believed to have been imported by Chinese. It was unknown before 1848, but in 1866 the number of lepers had risen to 230 and in 1882 to 4000 (Liveing). All attempts to stop it by segregating lepers in the settlement of Molokai appear to have been fruitless. In the West Indies and on the American continent, again, leprosy has a wide distribution. It is found in nearly all parts of South and Central America, and in certain parts of North America—namely, Louisiana, California (among Chinese), Minnesota, Wisconsin and North and South Dakota (Norwegians), New Brunswick (French Canadians).

It is difficult to find any explanation of the geographical distribution and behaviour of leprosy. It seems to affect islands and the sea-coast more than the interior, and to some extent this gives colour to the old belief that it is caused or fostered by a fish diet, which has been revived by Mr Jonathan Hutchinson, but is not generally accepted. Leprosy is found in interiors where fish is not an article of diet. Climate, again, has obviously little, if any, influence. The theory of heredity is equally at fault, whether it be applied to account for the spread of the disease by transmission or for its disappearance by the elimination of susceptible persons. The latter is the manner in which heredity might be expected to act, if at all, for lepers are remarkably sterile. But we see the disease persisting among the Eastern races, who have been continuously exposed to its selective influence from the earliest times, while it has disappeared among the Europeans, who were affected very much later. The opposite theory of hereditary transmission from parents to offspring is also at variance with many observed facts. Leprosy is very rarely congenital, and no cases have occurred among the descendants to the third generation of 160 Norwegian lepers settled in the United States. Again, if hereditary transmission were an effective influence, the disease could hardly have died down so rapidly as it did in Europe in the 15th century. Then we have the theory of contagion. There is no doubt that human beings are inoculable with leprosy, and that the disease may be communicated by close contact. Cases have been recorded which prove it conclusively; for instance, that of a man who had never been out of the British islands, but developed leprosy after sharing for a time the bed and clothes of his brother, who had contracted the disease in the West Indies. Some of the facts noted, such as the extensive dissemination of the disease in Europe during the middle ages, and its subsequent rapid decline, suggest the existence of some unknown epidemic factor. Poverty and insanitation are said to go with the prevalence of leprosy, but they go with every malady, and there is nothing to show that they have any special influence. Vaccination has been blamed for spreading it, and a few cases of communication by arm-to-arm inoculation are recorded. The influence of this factor, however, can only be trifling. Vaccination is a new thing, leprosy a very old one; where there is most vaccination there is no leprosy, and where there is most leprosy there is little or no vaccination. In India 78% of the lepers are unvaccinated, and in Canton since vaccination was introduced leprosy has declined (Cantlie). On the whole we must conclude that there is still much to be learnt about the conditions which govern the prevalence of leprosy.

With regard to prevention, the isolation of patients is obviously desirable, especially in the later stages, when open sores may disseminate the bacilli; but complete segregation, which has been urged, is regarded as impracticable by those who have had most experience in leprous districts. Scrupulous cleanliness should be exercised by persons attending on lepers or brought into close contact with them. In treatment the most essential thing is general care of the health, with good food and clothing. The tendency of modern therapeutics to attach increasing importance to nutrition in various morbid states, and notably in diseases of degeneration, such as tuberculosis and affections of the nervous system, is borne out by experience in leprosy, which has affinities to both; and this suggests the application to it of modern methods for improving local as well as general nutrition by physical means. A large number of internal remedies have been tried with varying results; those most recommended are chaulmoogra oil, arsenic, salicylate of soda, salol and chlorate of potash. Vergueira uses Collargol intravenously and subcutaneously, and states that in all the cases treated there was marked improvement, and hair that had been lost grew again. Calmette's Anterenene injected subcutaneously has been followed by good results. Deycke together with R. Bey isolated from a non-ulcerated leprous nodule a streptothrix which they call S. leproides. Its relation to the bacillus is uncertain. They found that injections of this organism had marked curative effects, due to a neutral fat which they named "Nastin." Injections of Nastin together with Benzoyl Chloride directly act on the lepra bacilli. Some cases were unaffected by this treatment, but with others the effect was marvellous. Dr W. A. Pusey of Chicago uses applications of carbon dioxide snow with good effect. In the later stages of the disease there is a wide field for surgery, which is able to give much relief to sufferers.

LITERATURE.—For history and geographical distribution, see Hirsch, *Handbuch der historisch-geographischen Pathologie* (1st ed., Erlangen, 1860, with exhaustive literature). For pathology, Virchow, *Die krankhaften Geschwülste* (Berlin, 1863-1867), vol. ii. For clinical histories, R. Liveing, *Elephantiasis Graecorum or True Leprosy* (London, 1873), ch. iv. For medieval leprosy—in Germany, Virchow, in *Virchow's Archiv*, five articles, vols. xviii-xx. (1860-1861); in the Netherlands, Israels, in *Nederl. Tijdschr. voor Geneeskunde*, vol. i. (1857); in Britain, J. Y. Simpson, *Edin. Med. and Surg. Journ.*, three articles, vols. lvi. and lvii. (1846-1847). Treatises on modern leprosy in particular localities: Danielssen and Boeck (Norway), *Traité de la Spédalskhed*, with atlas of twenty-four coloured plates (Paris, 1848); A. F. Anderson, *Leprosy as met with in the Straits Settlements*, coloured photographs with explanatory notes (London, 1872); H. Vandyke Carter (Bombay), *On Leprosy and Elephantiasis*, with coloured plates (London, 1874); Hillis, *Leprosy in British Guiana*, an account of West Indian leprosy, with twenty-two coloured plates (London, 1881). See also the dermatological works of Hebra, Erasmus Wilson, Bazin and Jonathan Hutchinson (also the latter's letters to *The Times* of the 11th of April and the 25th of May 1903); *British Medical Journal* (April 1, 1908); *American Journal of Dermatology* (Dec. 1907); *The Practitioner* (February 1910). An important early work is that of P. G. Hensler, *Vom abendländischen Aussatze im Mittelalter* (Hamburg, 1790).

LEPSIUS, KARL RICHARD (1810-1884), German Egyptologist, was born at Naumburg-am-Saale on the 23rd of December 1810, and in 1823 was sent to the "Schulpforta" school near Naumburg, where he came under the influence of Professor Lange. In 1829 he entered the university of Leipzig, and one year later that of Göttingen, where, under the influence of Otfried Müller, he finally decided to devote himself to the archaeological side of philology. From Göttingen he proceeded to Berlin, where he graduated in 1833 as doctor with the thesis *De tabulis Eugubinis*. In the same year he proceeded to study in Paris, and was commissioned by the duc de Luynes to collect material from the Greek and Latin writers for his work on the weapons of the ancients. In 1834 he took the Volney prize with his *Paläographie als Mittel der Sprachforschung*. Befriended by Bunsen and Humboldt, Lepsius threw himself with great ardour into Egyptological studies, which, since the death of Champollion in 1832, had attracted no scholar of eminence and weight. Here Lepsius found an ample field for his powers. After four years spent in visiting the Egyptian collections of Italy, Holland and England, he returned to Germany, where Humboldt and Bunsen united their influence to make his projected visit to Egypt a scientific expedition with royal support. For three years Lepsius and his party explored the whole of the region in which monuments of ancient Egyptian and Ethiopian occupation are found, from the Sudan above Khartum to the Syrian coast. At the end of 1845 they returned home, and the results of the expedition, consisting of casts, drawings and squeezes of inscriptions and scenes, maps and plans collected with the utmost thoroughness, as well as antiquities and papyri, far surpassed expectations. In 1846 he married Elisabeth Klein, and his appointment to a professorship in Berlin University in the following August afforded him the leisure necessary for the completion of his work. In 1859 the twelve volumes of his vast *Denkmäler aus Ägypten und Äthiopien* were finished, supplemented later by a *text* prepared from the note-books of the expedition; they comprise its entire archaeological, palaeographical and historical results. In 1866 Lepsius again went to Egypt, and discovered the famous Decree of Tanis or Table of Canopus, an inscription of the same character as the Rosetta Stone, in hieroglyphic, demotic and Greek. In 1873 he was appointed keeper of the Royal Library, Berlin, which, like the Berlin Museum, owes much to his care. About ten years later he was appointed Geheimer Oberregierungsrath. He died at Berlin on the 10th of July 1884. Besides the colossal *Denkmäler* and other publications of texts such as the *Todtenbuch der Ägypter* (*Book of the Dead*, 1842) his other works, amongst which may be specially named his *Königsbuch der Ägypter* (1858) and *Chronologie der Ägypter* (1849), are characterized by a quality of permanence that is very remarkable in a subject of such rapid development as Egyptology. In spite of his scientific training in philology Lepsius left behind few translations of inscriptions or discussions of the meanings of words: by preference he attacked historical and archaeological problems connected with the ancient texts, the alphabet, the metrology, the names of metals and minerals, the chronology, the royal names. On the other hand one of his latest works, the *Nubische Grammatik* (1880), is an elaborate grammar of the then little-known Nubian language, preceded by a linguistic sketch of the African continent. Throughout his life he profited by the gift of attaching to himself the right men, whether as patrons or, like Weidenbach and Stern, as assistants. Lepsius was a fine specimen of the best type of German scholar.

See *Richard Lepsius*, by Georg Ebers (New York, 1887), and art. EGYPT, section *Exploration and Research*.

LEPTINES, an Athenian orator, known as the proposer of a law that no Athenian, whether citizen or resident alien (with the sole exception of the descendants of Harmodius and Aristogeiton), should be exempt from the public charges (λειτουργίαι) for the state festivals. The object was to provide funds for the festivals and public spectacles at a time when both the treasury and the citizens generally were short of money. It was further asserted that many of the recipients of immunity were really unworthy of it. Against this law Demosthenes delivered (354 B.C.) his well-known speech *Against Leptines* in support of the proposal of Ctesippus that all the cases of immunity should be carefully investigated. Great stress is laid on the reputation for ingratitude and breach of faith which the abolition of immunities would bring upon the state. Besides, the law itself had been passed unconstitutionally, for an existing law confirmed these privileges, and by the constitution of Solon no law could be enacted until any existing law which it contravened had been repealed. The law was probably condemned. Nothing further is known of Leptines.

See the edition of the speech by J. E. Sandys (1890).

LEPTIS, [illegible] two towns in ancient Africa. The [illegible] the modern Lebda, was in [illegible] and Mesrata at the mouth of the [illegible] Parva ([illegible]), known also [illegible] the modern Lamta, was a [illegible] Ruspina (Monastir) and [illegible]

[illegible] one of the oldest and most flourishing [illegible] established on the coasts of the [illegible] commercial entrepot for the interior of the [illegible] was founded by the Sidonians (Sallust, [illegible] by people of Tyre (Pliny, *Hist.* [illegible] on the fertility of its territory [illegible] to Carthage to which it paid a [illegible] xxxiv. 62). After the Second [illegible] master of it (Sallust, *Jug.* [illegible] 100). During the Jugurthine [illegible] to Rome (Sallust, *Jug.* 78). [illegible] by Juba, it maintained its [illegible] the senatorial cause, received [illegible] of the Pompeian forces after [illegible] victory Julius Caesar imposed upon [illegible] measures of oil. Neverthe[illegible] free city governed by its own [illegible] It received the title of *muni*[illegible] was subsequently made a *colonia* [illegible] Septimius Severus, who was [illegible] and conferred upon it the *Jus* [illegible] of the Roman state, the [illegible]; hence, especially during [illegible] Empire, it suffered much from the [illegible] the Garamantes, the Austuriani and the [illegible] 6; Procop. *De Aedif.* vi. 4). [illegible] harbour silted up. Justinian [illegible] it (Procop. *ibid.*; Ch. Diehl, [illegible] It was the seat of a bishopric, [illegible] bishops after 462.

[illegible] which protected the commercial [illegible] Neapolis, the situation of which [illegible] Carthage at the foot of Byrsa. [illegible] remains of ramparts and docks, [illegible] buildings of the Roman period still [illegible] the current pronunciation of the [illegible] instead of Leptis, Leptitana [illegible] *d'Afrique*, ii. 219; Clermont-[illegible] *orientale*, vi. 41; *Comptes* [illegible] *B.-Lettres*, 1903, p. 333; [illegible] The coins of Leptis Magna, [illegible] the neighbourhood, present a [illegible] They are of bronze with the legend [illegible] side the head of Bacchus, [illegible] various emblems of these [illegible] have also coins bearing the [illegible] which still have the name [illegible] (Lud. Müller, *Numism. de* [illegible]

[illegible] by numerous travellers [illegible] and Henry William Beechey [illegible] Barth (*Wanderungen*, pp. [illegible] (*Géogr. comp.* ii. 219 [illegible] p. 33 (Paris, 1881, [illegible] York journal, *The Nation* [illegible] de Mathuisieulx explored [illegible] in the *Nouvelles* [illegible] See also J. Toutain, [illegible] *Bulletin archéologique* [illegible]

[illegible] Monastir, which is [illegible] Leptis Magna in their [illegible] *Géogr. comp.* ii. 169), [illegible] 18 m. south of

I
I
is
Er
is
by
or
tim
Eg
ages
count
sidera
segreg
at 19
Canter
time th
Britain
century
practicall
leper-hous
diminutio
(see PROS
at this tim

engineer, A. Daux, has discovered a probable line of ramparts. Like its neighbour Hadrumetum, Leptis Parva declared for Rome after the last Punic War. Also after the fall of Carthage in 146 it preserved its autonomy and was declared a *civitas libera et immunis* (Appian, *Punica*, 94; *C.I.L.* i. 200; *De bell. Afric.* c. xii.). Julius Caesar made it the base of his operations before the battle of Thapsus in 46 (Ch. Tissot, *Géogr. comp.* ii. 728). Under the Empire Leptis Parva became extremely prosperous; its bishops appeared in the African councils from 258 onwards. In Justinian's reorganization of Africa we find that Leptis Parva was with Capsa one of the two residences of the *Dux Byzacenae* (Tissot, *op. cit.* p. 171). The town had coins under Augustus and Tiberius. On the obverse is the imperial effigy with a Latin legend, and on the reverse the Greek legend ΛΕΠΤΙC with the bust of Mercury (Lud. Müller, *Numism. de l'anc. Afrique*, ii. 49). The ruins extend along the sea-coast to the north-west of Lemta; the remains of docks, the amphitheatre and the acropolis can be distinguished; a Christian cemetery has furnished tombs adorned with curious mosaics.

See *Comptes rendus de l'Acad. des Inscrip. et B.-Lettres* (1883), p. 189, Cagnat and Saladin, "Notes d'archéol. tunisiennes," in the *Bulletin monumental* of 1884; *Archives des missions*, xii. 111; Cagnat, *Explorations archéol. en Tunisie*, 3me fasc. pp. 9-16, and *Tour du monde* (1881), i. 292; Saladin, *Rapport sur une mission en Tunisie* (1886), pp. 9-20; *Bulletin archéol. du comité de travaux historiques* (1895), pp. 69-71 (inscriptions of Lamta); *Bulletin de la Soc. archéol. de Sousse* (1905; plan of the ruins of Lamta). (E. B.*)

LE PUY, or LE PUY EN VELAY, a town of south-eastern France, capital of the department of Haute-Loire, 90 m. S.W. of Lyons on the Paris-Lyon railway. Pop. (1906) town, 17,291; commune, 21,420. Le Puy rises in the form of an amphitheatre from a height of 2050 ft. above sea-level upon Mont Anis, a hill that divides the left bank of the Dolézon from the right bank of the Borne (a rapid stream joining the Loire 3 m. below). From the new town, which lies east and west in the valley of the Dolézon, the traveller ascends the old feudal and ecclesiastical town through narrow steep streets, paved with pebbles of lava, to the cathedral commanded by the fantastic pinnacle of Mont Corneille. Mont Corneille, which is 433 ft. above the Place de Breuil (in the lower town), is a steep rock of volcanic breccia, surmounted by an iron statue of the Virgin (53 ft. high) cast, after a model by Bonassieux, out of guns taken at Sebastopol. Another statue, that of Msgr de Morlhon, bishop of Le Puy, also sculptured by Bonassieux, faces that of the Virgin. From the platform of Mont Corneille a magnificent panoramic view is obtained of the town and of the volcanic mountains, which make this region one of the most interesting parts of France.

The Romanesque cathedral (Notre-Dame), dating chiefly from the first half of the 12th century, has a particoloured façade of white sandstone and black volcanic breccia, which is reached by a flight of sixty steps, and consists of three tiers, the lowest composed of three high arcades opening into the porch, which extends beneath the first bays of the nave; above are three windows lighting the nave; and these in turn are surmounted by three gables, two of which, those to the right and the left, are of open work. The staircase continues within the porch, where it divides, leading on the left to the cloister, on the right into the church. The doorway of the south transept is sheltered by a fine Romanesque porch. The isolated bell-tower (184 ft.), which rises behind the choir in seven storeys, is one of the most beautiful examples of the Romanesque transition period. The bays of the nave are covered in by octagonal cupolas, the central cupola forming a lantern. The choir and transepts are barrel-vaulted. Much veneration is paid to a small image of the Virgin on the high altar, a modern copy of the medieval image destroyed at the Revolution. The cloister, to the north of the choir, is striking, owing to its variously-coloured materials and elegant shafts. Viollet-le-Duc considered one of its galleries to belong to the oldest known type of cathedral cloister (8th or 9th century). Connected with the cloister are remains of fortifications of the 13th century, by which it was [se]parated from the rest of the city. Near the cathedral the baptistery of St John (11th century), built on the foundations of a Roman building, is surrounded by walls and numerous remains of the period, partly uncovered by excavations. The church of St Lawrence (14th century) contains the tomb and statue of Bertrand du Guesclin, whose ashes were afterwards carried to St Denis.

Le Puy possesses fragmentary remains of its old line of fortifications, among them a machicolated tower, which has been restored, and a few curious old houses dating from the 12th to the 17th century. In front of the hospital there is a fine medieval porch under which a street passes. Of the modern monuments the statue of Marie Joseph Paul, marquis of La Fayette, and a fountain in the Place de Breuil, executed in marble, bronze and syenite, may be specially mentioned. The museum, named after Charles Crozatier, a native sculptor and metal-worker to whose munificence it principally owes its existence, contains antiquities, engravings a collection of lace, and ethnographical and natural history collections. Among the curiosities of Le Puy should be noted the church of St Michel d'Aiguilhe, beside the gate of the town, perched on an isolated rock like Mont Corneille, the top of which is reached by a staircase of 271 steps. The church dates from the end of the 10th century and its chancel is still older. The steeple is of the same type as that of the cathedral. Three miles from Le Puy are the ruins of the Château de Polignac, one of the most important feudal strongholds of France.

Le Puy is the seat of a bishopric, a prefect and a court of assizes, and has tribunals of first instance and of commerce, a board of trade arbitration, a chamber of commerce, and a branch of the Bank of France. Its educational institutions include ecclesiastical seminaries, lycées and training colleges for both sexes and municipal industrial schools of drawing, architecture and mathematics applied to arts and industries. The principal manufacture is that of lace and guipure (in woollen, linen, cotton, silk and gold and silver threads), and distilling, leather-dressing, malting and the manufacture of chocolate and cloth are carried on. Cattle, woollens, grain and vegetables are the chief articles of trade.

It is not known whether Le Puy existed previously to the Roman invasion. Towards the end of the 4th or beginning of the 5th century it became the capital of the country of the Vellavi, at which period the bishopric, originally at Revession, now St Paulien, was transferred hither. Gregory of Tours speaks of it by the name of Anicium, because a chapel "ad Deum" had been built on the mountain, whence the name of Mont Adidon or Anis, which it still retains. In the 10th century it was called Podium Sanctae Mariae, whence Le Puy. In the middle ages there was a double enclosure, one for the cloister, the other for the town. The sanctuary of Nôtre Dame was much frequented by pilgrims, and the city grew famous and populous. Rivalries between the bishops who held directly of the see of Rome and had the right of coining money, and the lords of Polignac, revolts of the town against the royal authority, and the encroachments of the feudal superiors on municipal prerogatives often disturbed the quiet of the town. The Saracens in the 8th century, the Routiers in the 12th, the English in the 14th, the Burgundians in the 15th, successively ravaged the neighbourhood. Le Puy sent the flower of its chivalry to the Crusades in 1096, and Raymond d'Aiguille, called d'Agiles, one of its sons, was their historian. Many councils and various assemblies of the states of Languedoc met within its walls; popes and sovereigns, among the latter Charlemagne and Francis I., visited its sanctuary. Pestilence and the religious wars put an end to its prosperity. Long occupied by the Leaguers, it did not submit to Henry IV. until many years after his accession.

LERDO DE TEJADA, SEBASTIAN (1825–1889), president of Mexico, was born at Jalapa on the 25th of April 1825. He was educated as a lawyer and became a member of the supreme court. He became known as a liberal leader and a supporter of President Juarez. He was minister of foreign affairs for three months in 1857, and became president of the Chamber of Deputies in 1861. During the French intervention and the reign of the emperor Maximilian he continued loyal to the patriotic party, and had an active share in conducting the national resistance. He was minister of foreign affairs to President Juarez, and he showed an implacable resolution in carrying out the execution of Maximilian at Querétaro. When Juarez died in 1872 Lerdo succeeded him in office in the midst of a confused civil war. He achieved some success in pacifying the country and began the construction of railways. He was re-elected on the 24th of July 1876, but was expelled in January of the following year by Porfirio Diaz. He had made himself unpopular by the means he took to secure his re-election and by his disposition to limit state rights in favour of a strongly centralized government. He fled to the United States and died in obscurity at New York in 1889.

See H. H. Bancroft, *Pacific States*, vol. 9 (San Francisco, 1882–1890).

LERICI, a village of Liguria, Italy, situated on the N.E. side of the Gulf of Spezia, about 12 m. E.S.E. of Spezia, and 4 m. W.S.W. of Sarzana by road, 17 ft. above sea-level. Pop. (1901) 9316. Its small harbour is guarded by an old castle, said to have been built by Tancred; in the middle ages it was the chief place on the gulf. S. Terenzo, a hamlet belonging to Lerici, was the residence of Shelley during his last days. Farther north-west is the Bay of Pertusola, with its large lead-smelting works.

LÉRIDA, a province of northern Spain, formed in 1833 of districts previously included in the ancient province of Catalonia, and bounded on the N. by France and Andorra, E. by Gerona and Barcelona, S. by Tarragona and W. by Saragossa and Huesca. Pop. (1900) 274,590; area 4690 sq. m. The northern half of Lérida belongs entirely to the Mediterranean or eastern section of the Pyrenees, and comprises some of the finest scenery in the whole chain, including the valleys of Aran and La Cerdaña, and large tracts of forest. It is watered by many rivers, the largest of which is the Segre, a left-hand tributary of the Ebro. South of the point at which the Segre is joined on the right by the Noguera Pallaresa, the character of the country completely alters. The Llaños de Urgel, which comprise the greater part of southern Lérida, are extensive plains forming part of the Ebro valley, but redeemed by an elaborate system of canals from the sterility which characterizes so much of that region in Aragon. Lérida is traversed by the main railway from Barcelona to Saragossa, and by a line from Tarragona to the city of Lérida. In 1904 the Spanish government agreed with France to carry another line to the mouth of an international tunnel through the Pyrenees. Industries are in a more backward condition than in any other province of Catalonia, despite the abundance of water-power. There are, however, many saw-mills, flour-mills, and distilleries of alcohol and liqueurs, besides a smaller number of cotton and linen factories, paper-mills, soap-works, and oil and leather factories. Zinc, lignite and common salt are mined, but the output is small and of slight value. There is a thriving trade in wine, oil, wool, timber, cattle, mules, horses and sheep, but agriculture is far less prosperous than in the maritime provinces of Catalonia. Lérida (*q.v.*) is the capital (pop. 21,432), and the only town with more than 5000 inhabitants. Séo de Urgel, near the headwaters of the Segre, is a fortified city which has been an episcopal see since 840, and has had a close historical connexion with Andorra (*q.v.*). Solsona, on a small tributary of the Cardoner, which flows through Barcelona to the Mediterranean, is the *Setelis* of the Romans, and contains in its parish church an image of the Virgin said to possess miraculous powers, and visited every year by many hundreds of pilgrims. Cervera, on a small river of the same name, contains the buildings of a university which Philip V. established here in 1717. This university had originally been founded at Barcelona in the 15th century, and was reopened there in 1842. In character, and especially in their industry, intelligence and keen local patriotism, the inhabitants of Lérida are typical Catalans. (See CATALONIA.)

LÉRIDA, the capital of the Spanish province of Lérida, on the river Segre and the Barcelona-Saragossa and Lérida-Tarragona railways. Pop. (1900) 21,432. The older parts of the city, on the right bank of the river, are a maze of narrow and crooked streets, surrounded by ruined walls and a moat, and commanded by the ancient citadel, which stands on a height overlooking the plains of Noguera on the north and of Urgel on the south. On the left bank, connected with the older quarters by a fine [illegible] bridge and an iron railway bridge, are the suburbs, laid out [illegible] in broad and regular avenues of modern houses. The [illegible] cathedral, last used for public worship in 1707, is a very [illegible] Romanesque building, with Gothic and Mauresque [illegible]; but the interior was much defaced by its conversion [illegible] barracks after 1717. It was founded in 1203 by Pedro II. [illegible], and consecrated in 1278. The fine octagonal belfry [illegible] early in the 15th century. A second cathedral, with [illegible] façade, was completed in 1781. The church of San [illegible] (1270–1300) is noteworthy for the beautiful tracery of [illegible] windows; its nave is said to have been a Roman [illegible] converted by the Moors into a mosque and by Ramon [illegible] IV., last count of Barcelona, into a church. Other [illegible] buildings are the Romanesque town hall, founded in [illegible] century but several times restored, the bishop's palace [illegible] military hospital, formerly a convent. The museum [illegible] a good collection of Roman and Romanesque antiquities; [illegible] are a school for teachers, a theological seminary and [illegible] of literature and science. Leather, paper, glass, silk, [illegible] cloth are manufactured in the city, which has also [illegible] trade in agricultural produce.

[illegible] is the *Ilerda* of the Romans, and was the capital of the [illegible] they called *Ilerdenses* (Pliny) or *Ilergetes* (Ptolemy). [illegible] the key of Catalonia and Aragon, it was from a very [illegible] an important military station. In the Punic Wars [illegible] with the Carthaginians and suffered much from the [illegible]. In its immediate neighbourhood Hanno was [illegible] by Scipio in 216 B.C., and it afterwards became famous [illegible] of Caesar's arduous struggle with Pompey's generals [illegible] and Petreius in the first year of the civil war (49 B.C.). [illegible] a municipium in the time of Augustus, and enjoyed [illegible] prosperity under later emperors. Under the Visigoths [illegible] episcopal see, and at least one ecclesiastical council [illegible] here (in 546). Under the Moors *Lareda* [illegible] one of the principal cities of the province of Saragossa, [illegible] tributary to the Franks in 793, but was reconquered [illegible] it fell into the hands of Ramon Berenguer IV. [illegible] it has come through numerous sieges, having [illegible] by the French in November 1707 during the War of [illegible], and again in 1810. In 1300 James II. of Aragon [illegible] a university at Lérida, which achieved some repute in [illegible] suppressed in 1717, when the university of [illegible].

[illegible] DE SANDOVAL Y ROJAS, DUKE OF [illegible] Spanish minister, was born in 1552. At the [illegible] he entered the royal palace as a page. The [illegible] was ancient and powerful, but under Philip II. [illegible] the nobles, with the exception of a few who held [illegible] commanded armies abroad, had little share in [illegible]. The future duke of Lerma, who was by descent [illegible] passed his life as a courtier, and possessed [illegible] the accession of Philip III. in 1598. He had [illegible] a favourite with the prince, and was in fact [illegible] as the dying king Philip II fore- [illegible] the new sovereign. The old king's [illegible] was Philip III. king than he [illegible] his favourite, whom he created duke [illegible] whom he lavished an immense list of [illegible] Lerma lasted for twenty years, [illegible] intrigue carried out by his own [illegible] the entire direction of his [illegible] him to affix the royal [illegible] whatever presents were [illegible] ever more amply trusted, [illegible] a time when the state was [illegible] the king in extravagance, [illegible] he [illegible]

useless hostilities with England till, in 1604, Spain was forced by exhaustion to make peace, and he used all his influence against a recognition of the independence of the Low Countries. The fleet was neglected, the army reduced to a remnant, and the finances ruined beyond recovery. His only resources as a finance minister were the debasing of the coinage, and foolish edicts against luxury and the making of silver plate. Yet it is probable that he would never have lost the confidence of Philip III., who divided his life between festivals and prayers, but for the domestic treachery of his son, the duke of Uceda, who combined with the king's confessor, Aliaga, whom Lerma had introduced to the place, to turn him out. After a long intrigue in which the king was all but entirely dumb and passive, Lerma was at last compelled to leave the court, on the 4th of October 1618. As a protection, and as a means of retaining some measure of power in case he fell from favour, he had persuaded Pope Paul V. to create him cardinal, in the year of his fall. He retired to the town of Lerma in Old Castile, where he had built himself a splendid palace, and then to Valladolid. Under the reign of Philip IV., which began in 1621 he was despoiled of part of his wealth, and he died in 1625.

The history of Lerma's tenure of office is in vol. xv. of the *Historia General de España* of Modesto Lafuente (Madrid, 1855)—with references to contemporary authorities.

LERMONTOV, MIKHAIL YUREVICH (1814–1841), Russian poet and novelist, often styled the poet of the Caucasus, was born in Moscow, of Scottish descent, but belonged to a respectable family of the Tula government, and was brought up in the village of Tarkhanui (in the Penzensk government), which now preserves his dust. By his grandmother—on whom the whole care of his childhood was devolved by his mother's early death and his father's military service—no cost nor pains was spared to give him the best education she could think of. The intellectual atmosphere which he breathed in his youth differed little from that in which Pushkin had grown up, though the domination of French had begun to give way before the fancy for English, and Lamartine shared his popularity with Byron. From the academic gymnasium in Moscow Lermontov passed in 1830 to the university, but there his career came to an untimely close through the part he took in some acts of insubordination to an obnoxious teacher. From 1830 to 1834 he attended the school of cadets at St Petersburg, and in due course he became an officer in the guards. To his own and the nation's anger at the loss of Pushkin (1837) the young soldier gave vent in a passionate poem addressed to the tsar, and the very voice which proclaimed that, if Russia took no vengeance on the assassin of her poet, no second poet would be given her, was itself an intimation that a poet had come already. The tsar, however, seems to have found more impertinence than inspiration in the address, for Lermontov was forthwith sent off to the Caucasus as an officer of dragoons. He had been in the Caucasus with his grandmother as a boy of ten, and he found himself at home by yet deeper sympathies than those of childish recollection. The stern and rocky virtues of the mountaineers against whom he had to fight, no less than the scenery of the rocks and mountains themselves, proved akin to his heart, the emperor had exiled him to his native land. He was in St Petersburg in 1838 and 1839, and in the latter year wrote the novel, *A Hero of Our Time*, which is said to have been the occasion of the duel in which he lost his life in July 1841. In this contest he had purposely selected the edge of a precipice, so that if either combatant was wounded so as to fall his fate should be sealed.

Lermontov published only one small collection of poems in 1840. Three volumes, much mutilated by the censorship, were issued in 1842 by Glazounov; and there have been full editions of his works in 1860 and 1863. To Bodenstedt's German translation of his poems (*Michail Lermontow's poetischer Nachlass*, Berlin, 1842, 2 vols.), which indeed was the first satisfactory collection, he is indebted for a wide reputation outside of Russia. His novel has found several translators (August Boltz, Berlin, 1852, &c.). Among his best-known pieces are "Ismail-Bey," "Hadji Abrek," "Walerik," "The Novice," and, remarkable as an imitation of the old Russian ballad, "The song of the tsar Ivan Vasilivitch, his young bodyguard, and the bold merchant Kalashnikov."

See Taillandier, "Le Poète du Caucase," in *Revue des deux mondes*

(February 1855), reprinted in *Allemagne et Russie* (Paris, 1856); Duduishkin's "Materials for the Biography of Lermontov," prefixed to the 1863 edition of his works. *The Demon*, translated by Sir Alexander Condie Stephen (1875), is an English version of one of his longer poems. (W. R. S.-R.)

LEROUX, PIERRE (1798–1871), French philosopher and economist, was born at Bercy near Paris on the 7th of April 1798, the son of an artisan. His education was interrupted by the death of his father, which compelled him to support his mother and family. Having worked first as a mason and then as a compositor, he joined P. Dubois in the foundation of *Le Globe* which became in 1831 the official organ of the Saint-Simonian community, of which he became a prominent member. In November of the same year, when Enfantin preached the enfranchisement of women and the functions of the *couple-prêtre*, Leroux separated himself from the sect. In 1838, with J. Regnaud, who had seceded with him, he founded the *Encyclopédie nouvelle* (eds. 1838–1841). Amongst the articles which he inserted in it were *De l'égalité* and *Réfutation de l'éclectisme*, which afterwards appeared as separate works. In 1840 he published his treatise *De l'humanité* (2nd ed. 1845), which contains the fullest exposition of his system, and was regarded as the philosophical manifesto of the Humanitarians. In 1841 he established the *Revue indépendante*, with the aid of George Sand, over whom he had great influence. Her *Spiridion*, which was dedicated to him, *Sept cordes de la lyre*, *Consuelo*, and *La Comtesse de Rudolstadt*, were written under the Humanitarian inspiration. In 1843 he established at Boussac (Creuse) a printing association organized according to his systematic ideas, and founded the *Revue sociale*. After the outbreak of the revolution of 1848 he was elected to the Constituent Assembly, and in 1849 to the Legislative Assembly, but his speeches on behalf of the extreme socialist wing were of so abstract and mystical a character that they had no effect. After the *coup d'état* of 1851 he settled with his family in Jersey, where he pursued agricultural experiments and wrote his socialist poem *La Grève de Samarez*. On the definitive amnesty of 1869 he returned to Paris, where he died in April 1871, during the Commune.

The writings of Leroux have no permanent significance in the history of thought. He was the propagandist of sentiments and aspirations rather than the expounder of a systematic theory. He has, indeed, a system, but it is a singular medley of doctrines borrowed, not only from Saint-Simonian, but from Pythagorean and Buddhistic sources. In philosophy his fundamental principle is that of what he calls the "triad"—a triplicity which he finds to pervade all things, which in God is "power, intelligence and love," in man "sensation, sentiment and knowledge." His religious doctrine is Pantheistic; and, rejecting the belief in a future life as commonly conceived, he substitutes for it a theory of metempsychosis. In social economy his views are very vague; he preserves the family, country and property, but finds in all three, as they now are, a despotism which must be eliminated. He imagines certain combinations by which this triple tyranny can be abolished, but his solution seems to require the creation of families without heads, countries without governments and property without rights of possession. In politics he advocates absolute equality—a democracy pushed to anarchy.

See Raillard, *Pierre Leroux et ses œuvres* (Paris, 1899); Thomas, *Pierre Leroux: sa vie, son œuvre, sa doctrine* (Paris, 1904); L. Reybaud, *Études sur les réformateurs et socialistes modernes*; article in R. H. Inglis Palgrave's *Dictionary of Pol. Econ.*

LEROY-BEAULIEU, HENRI JEAN BAPTISTE ANATOLE (1842–), French publicist, was born at Lisieux, on the 12th of February 1842. In 1866 he published *Une troupe de comédiens*, and afterwards *Essai sur la restauration de nos monuments historiques devant l'art et devant le budget*, which deals particularly with the restoration of the cathedral of Evreux. He visited Russia in order to collect documents on the political and economic organization of the Slav nations, and on his return published in the *Revue des deux mondes* (1882–1889) a series of articles, which appeared shortly afterwards in book form under the title *L'Empire des tsars et les Russes* (4th ed., revised in 3 vols., 1897–1898). The work entitled *Un empereur, un roi, un pape, une restauration*, published in 1879, was an analysis and criticism of the politics of the Second Empire. *Un homme d'état russe* (1884) gave the history of the emancipation of the serfs by Alexander II. Other works are *Les Catholiques libéraux, l'église et le libéralisme* (1890), *La Papauté, le socialisme et la démocratie* (1892), *Les Juifs et l'antisémitisme; Israël chez les nations* (1893), *Les Arméniens et la question arménienne* (1896), *L'Antisémitisme* (1897), *Études russes et européennes* (1897). These writings, mainly collections of articles and lectures intended for the general public, display enlightened views and wide information. In 1881 Leroy-Beaulieu was elected professor of contemporary history and eastern affairs at the École Libre des Sciences Politiques, becoming director of this institution on the death of Albert Sorel in 1906, and in 1887 he became a member of the Académie des Sciences Morales et Politiques.

Two of Leroy-Beaulieu's works have been translated into English: one as the *Empire of the Tsars and the Russians*, by Z. A. Ragozin (New York, 1893–1896), and another as *Papacy, Socialism, Democracy*, by B. L. O'Donnell (1892). See W. E. H. Lecky, *Historical and Political Essays* (1908).

LEROY-BEAULIEU, PIERRE PAUL (1843–), French economist, brother of the preceding, was born at Saumur on the 9th of December 1843, and educated in Paris at the Lycée Bonaparte and the École de Droit. He afterwards studied at Bonn and Berlin, and on his return to Paris began to write for *Le Temps*, *Revue nationale* and *Revue contemporaine*. In 1867 he won a prize offered by the Academy of Moral Science with an essay entitled "L'Influence de l'état moral et intellectuel des populations ouvrières sur le taux des salaires." In 1870 he gained three prizes for essays on "La Colonization chez les peuples modernes," "L'Administration en France et en Angleterre," and "L'Impôt foncier et ses conséquences économiques." In 1872 Leroy-Beaulieu became professor of finance at the newly-founded École Libre des Sciences Politiques, and in 1880 he succeeded his father-in-law, Michel Chevalier, in the chair of political economy in the Collège de France. Several of his works have made their mark beyond the borders of his own country. Among these may be mentioned his *Recherches économiques, historiques et statistiques sur les guerres contemporaines*, a series of studies published between 1863 and 1869, in which he calculated the loss of men and capital caused by the great European conflicts. Other works by him are—*La Question ouvrière au dix-neuvième siècle* (1861), *Le Travail des femmes au dix-neuvième siècle* (1873), *Traité de la science des finances* (1877), *Essai sur la répartition des richesses* (1882), *L'Algérie et la Tunisie* (1888), *Précis d'économie politique* (1888), and *L'État moderne et ses fonctions* (1889). He also founded in 1873 the *Économiste français*, on the model of the English *Economist*. Leroy-Beaulieu may be regarded as the leading representative in France of orthodox political economy, and the most pronounced opponent of protectionist and collectivist doctrines.

LERWICK, a municipal and police burgh of Shetland, Scotland, the most northerly town in the British Isles. Pop. (1901) 4281. It is situated on Brassay Sound, a fine natural harbour, on the east coast of the island called Mainland, 115 m. N.E. of Kirkwall, in Orkney, and 340 m. from Leith by steamer. The town dates from the beginning of the 17th century, and the older part consists of a flagged causeway called Commercial Street, running for 1 m. parallel with the sea (in which the gable ends of several of the quaint-looking houses stand), and so narrow in places as not to allow of two vehicles passing each other. At right angles to this street lanes ascend the hill-side to Hillhead, where the more modern structures and villas have been built. At the north end stands Fort Charlotte, erected by Cromwell, repaired in 1665 by Charles II. and altered in 1781 by George III., after whose queen it was named. It is now used as a depôt for the Naval Reserve, for whom a large drill hall was added. The Anderson Institute, at the south end, was constructed as a secondary school in 1862 by Arthur Anderson, a native, who also presented the Widows' Asylum in the same quarter, an institution intended by preference for widows of Shetland sailors. The town-hall, built in 1881, contains several stained-glass windows, two of which were the gift of citizens of Amsterdam and Hamburg, in gratitude for services rendered by the islanders to fishermen and seamen of those ports. Lerwick's main industries are connected with the fisheries, of which it is an important centre. Docks, wharves, piers, curing stations and warehouses have been provided or enlarged to cope with the growth of the trade, and an esplanade has been constructed along the front. The town is also the chief distributing agency for the islands, and carries on some business in knitted woollen goods. One mile west of Lerwick is Clickimin Loch, separated from the sea by a narrow strip of land. On an islet in the lake stands a ruined "broch" or round tower.

LE SAGE, ALAIN RENÉ (1668–1747), French novelist and dramatist, was born at Sarzeau in the peninsula of Rhuys, between the Morbihan and the sea, on the 13th of December 1668. Rhuys was a legal district, and Claude le Sage, the father of the novelist, held the united positions of advocate, notary and registrar of its royal court. His wife's name was Jeanne Brenugat. Both father and mother died when Le Sage was very young, and his property was wasted or embezzled by his guardians. Little is known of his youth except that he went to school with the Jesuits at Vannes until he was eighteen. Conjecture has it that he continued his studies at Paris, and it is certain that he was called to the bar at the capital in 1692. In August 1694 he married the daughter of a joiner, Marie Elizabeth Huyard. She was beautiful but had no fortune, and Le Sage had little practice. About this time he met his old schoolfellow, the dramatist Danchet, and is said to have been advised by him to betake himself to literature. He began modestly as a translator, and published in 1695 a French version of the *Epistles* of Aristaenetus, which was not successful. Shortly afterwards he found a valuable patron and adviser in the abbé de Lyonne, who bestowed on him an annuity of 600 livres, and recommended him to exchange the classics for Spanish literature, of which he was himself a student and collector.

Le Sage began by translating plays chiefly from Rojas and Lope de Vega. *Le Traître puni* and *Le Point d'honneur* from the former, *Don Félix de Mendoce* from the latter, were acted or published in the first two or three years of the 18th century. In 1704 he translated the continuation of *Don Quixote* by Avellaneda, and soon afterwards adapted a play from Calderon, *Don César Ursin*, which had a divided fate, being successful at court and damned in the city. He was, however, nearly forty before he obtained anything like decided success. But in 1707 his admirable farce of *Crispin rival de son maître* was acted with great applause, and *Le Diable boiteux* was published. This latter went through several editions in the same year, and was frequently reprinted till 1725, when Le Sage altered and improved it considerably, giving it its present form. Notwithstanding the success of *Crispin*, the actors did not like Le Sage, and refused a small piece of his called *Les Étrennes* (1707). He thereupon altered it into *Turcaret*, his theatrical masterpiece, and one of the best comedies in French literature. This appeared in 1709. Some years passed before he again attempted romance writing, and then the first two parts of *Gil Blas de Santillane* appeared in 1715. Strange to say, it was not so popular as *Le Diable boiteux*. Le Sage worked at it for a long time, and did not bring out the third part till 1724, nor the fourth till 1735. For this last he had been part paid to the extent of a hundred [illegible] some years before its appearance. During these twenty years he was, however, continually busy. Notwithstanding the [illegible] and success of *Turcaret* and *Crispin*, the Théâtre [illegible] did not welcome him, and in the year of the publication [illegible] he began to write for the Théâtre de la Foire—the [illegible] held in booths at festival time. This, though not a [illegible] occupation, was followed by many writers of dis[illegible] the date, and by none more assiduously than by [illegible] to one computation he produced, either [illegible] others, about a hundred pieces, varying from [illegible] with no regular dialogues, to comediettas only [illegible] regular plays by the introduction of music. [illegible] industrious in prose fiction. Besides finishing [illegible] the *Orlando innamorato* (1721), rearranged [illegible] two more or less original [illegible] *Estévanille Gonzalez*, [illegible] *de M. de Beauchesne*, which is curiously like certain works of Defoe. Besides all this, Le Sage was also the author of *La Valise trouvée*, a collection of imaginary letters, and of some minor pieces, of which *Une journée des parques* is the most remarkable. This laborious life he continued until 1740, when he was more than seventy years of age. His eldest son had become an actor, and Le Sage had disowned him, but the second was a canon at Boulogne in comfortable circumstances. In the year just mentioned his father and mother went to live with him. At Boulogne Le Sage spent the last seven years of his life, dying on the 17th of November 1747. His last work, *Mélange amusant de saillies d'esprit et de traits historiques les plus frappants*, had appeared in 1743.

Not much is known of Le Sage's life and personality, and the foregoing paragraph contains not only the most important but almost the only facts available for it. The few anecdotes which we have of him represent him as a man of very independent temper, declining to accept the condescending patronage which in the earlier part of the century was still the portion of men of letters. Thus it is said that, on being remonstrated with, as he thought impolitely, for an unavoidable delay in appearing at the duchess of Bouillon's house to read *Turcaret*, he at once put the play in his pocket and retired, refusing absolutely to return. It may, however, be said that as in time so in position he occupies a place apart from most of the great writers of the 17th and 18th centuries respectively. He was not the object of royal patronage like the first, nor the pet of *salons* and coteries like the second. Indeed, he seems all his life to have been purely domestic in his habits, and purely literary in his interests.

The importance of Le Sage in French and in European literature is not entirely the same, and he has the rare distinction of being more important in the latter than in the former. His literary work may be divided into three parts. The first contains his Théâtre de la Foire and his few miscellaneous writings, the second his two remarkable plays *Crispin* and *Turcaret*, the third his prose fictions. In the first two he swims within the general literary current in France; he can be and must be compared with others of his own nation. But in the third he emerges altogether from merely national comparison. It is not with Frenchmen that he is to be measured. He formed no school in France; he followed no French models. His work, admirable as it is from the mere point of view of style and form, is a parenthesis in the general development of the French novel. That product works its way from Madame de la Fayette through Marivaux and Prévost, not through Le Sage. His literary ancestors are Spaniards, his literary contemporaries and successors are Englishmen. The position is almost unique; it is certainly interesting and remarkable in the highest degree.

Of Le Sage's miscellaneous work, including his numerous farce-operettas, there is not much to be said except that they are the very best kind of literary hack-work. The pure and original style of the author, his abundant wit, his cool, humoristic attitude towards human life, which wanted only greater earnestness and a wider conception of that life to turn it into true humour, are discernible throughout. But this portion of his work is practically forgotten, and its examination is incumbent only on the critic. *Crispin* and *Turcaret* show a stronger and more deeply marked genius, which, but for the ill-will of the actors, might have gone far in this direction. But Le Sage's peculiar unwillingness to attempt anything absolutely new discovered itself here. Even when he had devoted himself to the Foire theatre, it seems that he was unwilling to attempt, when occasion called for it, the absolute innovation of a piece with only one actor, a crux which Alexis Piron, a lesser but a bolder genius, accepted and carried through. *Crispin* and *Turcaret* are unquestionably Molièresque, though they are perhaps more original in their following of Molière than any other plays that can be named. For this also was part of Le Sage's idiosyncrasy that, while he was apparently unable or unwilling to strike out an entirely novel line for himself, he had no sooner entered upon the beaten path than he left it to follow his own devices. *Crispin rival de son maître* is a farce in one act and many scenes, after the earlier manner of motion. Its plot is somewhat extravagant, inasmuch as it lies in the effort of a knavish valet, not as usual to further his master's interests, but to supplant that master in love and gain. But the charm of the piece consists first in the lively bustling action of the short scenes which take each other up so promptly and smartly that the spectator has not time to cavil at the improbability of the action, and secondly in the abundant wit of the dialogue. *Turcaret* is a far more important piece of work and ranks high among comedies dealing with the actual society of their time. The only thing which prevents it from holding the very highest place is a certain want of unity in the plot. This want, however, is compensated in *Turcaret* by the most masterly profusion of character-drawing in the separate parts. Turcaret, the ruthless, dishonest and dissolute financier, his vulgar wife as dissolute as himself, the harebrained marquis, the knavish chevalier, the baroness (a coquette with the finer edge taken off her fine-ladyhood, yet by no means unlovable), are each and all finished portraits of the best comic type, while almost as much may be said of the minor characters. The style and dialogue are also worthy of the highest praise; the wit never degenerates into mere "wit-combats."

It is, however, as a novelist that the world has agreed to remember Le Sage. A great deal of unnecessary labour has been spent on the discussion of his claims to originality. What has been already said will give a sufficient clue through this thorny ground. In mere form Le Sage is not original. He does little more than adopt that of the Spanish picaroon romance of the 16th and 17th century. Often, too, he prefers merely to rearrange and adapt existing work, and still oftener to give himself a kind of start by adopting the work of a preceding writer as a basis. But it may be laid down as a positive truth that he never, in any work that pretends to originality at all, is guilty of anything that can fairly be called plagiarism. Indeed we may go further, and say that he is very fond of asserting or suggesting his indebtedness when he is really dealing with his own funds. Thus the *Diable boiteux* borrows the title, and for a chapter or two the plan and almost the words, of the *Diablo Cojuelo* of Luis Velez de Guevara. But after a few pages Le Sage leaves his predecessor alone. Even the plan of the Spanish original is entirely discarded, and the incidents, the episodes, the style, are as independent as if such a book as the *Diablo Cojuelo* had never existed. The case of *Gil Blas* is still more remarkable. It was at first alleged that Le Sage had borrowed it from the *Marcos de Obregon* of Vincent Espinel, a curiously rash assertion, inasmuch as that work exists and is easily accessible, and as the slightest consultation of it proves that, though it furnished Le Sage with separate incidents and hints for more than one of his books, *Gil Blas* as a whole is not in the least indebted to it. Afterwards Father Isla asserted that *Gil Blas* was a mere translation from an actual Spanish book—an assertion at once incapable of proof and disproof, inasmuch as there is no trace whatever of any such book. A third hypothesis is that there was some manuscript original which Le Sage may have worked up in his usual way, in the same way, for instance, as he professes himself to have worked up the *Bachelor of Salamanca*. This also is in the nature of it incapable of refutation, though the argument from the *Bachelor* is strong against it, for there could be no reason why Le Sage should be more reticent of his obligations in the one case than in the other. Except, however, for historical reasons, the controversy is one which may be safely neglected, nor is there very much importance in the more impartial indication of sources—chiefly works on the history of Olivares—which has sometimes been attempted. That Le Sage knew Spanish literature well is of course obvious; but there is as little doubt (with the limitations already laid down) of his real originality as of that of any great writer in the world. *Gil Blas* then remains his property, and it is admittedly the capital example of its own style. For Le Sage has not only the characteristic, which Homer and Shakespeare have, of absolute truth to human nature as distinguished from truth to this or that national character, but he has what has been called the quality of detachment, which they also have. He never takes sides with his characters as Fielding (whose master, with Cervantes, he certainly was) sometimes does. Asmodeus and Don Cleofas, Gil Blas and the Archbishop and Doctor Sangrado, are produced by him with exactly the same impartiality of attitude. Except that he brought into novel writing this highest quality of artistic truth, it perhaps cannot be said that he did much to advance prose fiction in itself. He invented, as has been said, no new *genre*; he did not, as Marivaux and Prévost did, help on the novel as distinguished from the romance. In form his books are undistinguishable, not merely from the Spanish romances which are, as has been said, their direct originals, but from the medieval *romans d'aventures* and the Greek prose romances. But in individual excellence they have few rivals. Nor should it be forgotten, as it sometimes is, that Le Sage was a great master of French style, the greatest unquestionably between the classics of the 17th century and the classics of the 18th. He is perhaps the last great writer before the decadence (for since the time of Paul Louis Courier it has not been denied that the *philosophe* period is in point of style a period of decadence). His style is perfectly easy at the same time that it is often admirably epigrammatic. It has plenty of colour, plenty of flexibility, and may be said to be exceptionally well fitted for general literary work.

The dates of the original editions of Le Sage's most important works have already been given. He published during his life a collection of his regular dramatic works, and also one of his pieces for the Foire, but the latter is far from exhaustive; nor is there any edition which can be called so, though the *Œuvres choisies* of 1782 and 1818 are useful, and there are so-called *Œuvres complètes* of 1821 and 1840. Besides critical articles by the chief literary critics and historians, the work of Eugène Lintilhac, in the *Grands écrivains français* (1893), should be consulted. The *Diable boiteux* and *Gil Blas* have been reprinted and translated numberless times. Both will be found conveniently printed, together with *Estévanille Gonzalez* and *Guzman d'Alfarache*, the best of the minor novels, in four volumes of Garnier's *Bibliothèque amusante* (Paris, 1865). *Turcaret* and *Crispin* are to be found in all collected editions of the French drama. There is a useful edition of them, with ample specimens of Le Sage's work for the Foire, in two volumes (Paris, 1821). (G. SA.)

LES ANDELYS, a town of northern France, capital of an arrondissement in the department of Eure about 30 m. S.E. of Rouen by rail. Pop. (1906) 3955. Les Andelys is formed by the union of Le Grand Andely and Le Petit Andely, the latter situated on the right bank of the Seine, the former about half a mile from the river. Grand Andely, founded, according to tradition, in the 6th century, has a church (13th, 14th and 15th centuries) parts of which are of fine late Gothic and Renaissance architecture. The works of art in the interior include beautiful stained glass of the latter period. Other interesting buildings are the hôtel du Grand Cerf dating from the first half of the 16th century, and the chapel of Sainte-Clotilde, close by a spring which, owing to its supposed healing powers, is the object of a pilgrimage. Grand Andely has a statue of Nicolas Poussin a native of the place. Petit Andely sprang up at the foot of the eminence on which stands the château Gaillard, now in ruins, but formerly one of the strongest fortresses in France (see FORTIFICATION AND SIEGECRAFT and CASTLE). It was built by Richard Cœur de Lion at the end of the 12th century to protect the Norman frontier, was captured by the French in 1204 and passed finally into their possession in 1449. The church of St Sauveur at Petit Andely also dates from the end of the 12th century. Les Andelys is the seat of a sub-prefect and of a tribunal of first instance, has a preparatory infantry school; it carries on silk milling, and the manufacture of leather, organs and sugar. It has trade in cattle, grain, flour, &c.

LES BAUX, a village of south-eastern France, in the department of Bouches-du-Rhône, 11 m. N.E. of Arles by road. Pop. (1906) 111. Les Baux, which in the middle ages was a flourishing town, is now almost deserted. Apart from a few inhabited dwellings, it consists of an assemblage of ruined towers, fallen walls and other débris, which cover the slope of a hill crowned by the remains of a huge château, once the seat of a celebrated "court of love." The ramparts, a medieval church, the château, parts of which date to the 11th century, and many of the dwellings are, [illegible] of the white friable limestone on [illegible]. [illegible] may be found houses preserv- [illegible] workmanship. Les Baux has [illegible] (bauxite) which is plentiful [illegible] which aluminium is obtained. [illegible] Baux was the seat of a powerful family [illegible], extensive domains in [illegible]. The decadence of the seigneurs de Baux [illegible] the power of the house of Anjou, [illegible] of their possessions. In 1632 [illegible] were dismantled.

[illegible] a [illegible] Greek sophist and rhetorician, [illegible]. According to Photius (*cod.* 74) [illegible] political speeches, of which two are [illegible] after the style of Thucydides, and a [illegible] War. In the first he exhorts the [illegible], in the second (the title of which [illegible] (edition by F. Kiehr, *Les-* [illegible] 1907). Some erotic letters are [illegible].

[illegible] Suidas as the author of a large number [illegible] of much earlier date; on the [illegible] a small treatise *Περὶ Σχημάτων* on [illegible] Müller, Leipzig, 1900), is probably [illegible].

[illegible] Turk. [illegible]), an island in the Aegean [illegible] N. of the entrance of the Gulf of [illegible] part of a sanjak in the archipelago [illegible]. It is divided into three districts, [illegible] Molyvo in the N., and Calloni in the [illegible] it has been known as Mytilene, from [illegible]. Strabo estimated the circum- [illegible] stadia, or about 138 m., and Scylax [illegible] of the islands of the Mediterranean. [illegible] channel between it and the mainland varies [illegible] The island is roughly triangular in shape; the [illegible] on the N.E., Sigrium (Sigri) on the [illegible] on the S.E. The Euripus Pyrrhaeus [illegible] on the west between Sigrium and Malea. [illegible] is very fertile, Lesbos being [illegible] for its wine, oil and grain. Homer [illegible] chief produce now is olives, which also [illegible] Soap, skins and valonea are also [illegible] cattle are extensively bred. The sardine [illegible] and antimony, marble and coal [illegible]. The surface is rugged and mountainous, [illegible] (Hagios Elias) being 3080 ft. [illegible] periodical earthquakes. The roads [illegible] is telegraphic communication on [illegible] by cable. The ports are Sigri [illegible] Calloni and Hiera or Olivieri can [illegible] of small draught.

[illegible] Mytilene, is built in amphitheatre shape [illegible] by remains of an ancient fortress. [illegible] churches, including a cathedral. [illegible] island close to the eastern coast of [illegible] the town became too large for the [illegible] by a causeway, and the city spread [illegible] was a harbour on each side of the small [illegible] to be the northern of these, [illegible] the five cities which gave the island [illegible] Mytilene, Methymna, Antissa, Eresus, [illegible] called Arisba, destroyed by an earth- [illegible] Professor Conze thinks that [illegible] Palaikastro, N.E. of Calloni. Pyrrha [illegible] also called Palaikastro. Antissa [illegible] It was destroyed by the Romans [illegible] Sigri on the E. coast. Methymna [illegible] site of Molyvo, still the second [illegible] from the wine [illegible] remains of [illegible] all these [illegible] E. Ga.)

History.—Although the position of Lesbos near the old-established trade-route to the Hellespont marks it out as an important site even in pre-historic days, no evidence on the early condition of the island is as yet obtainable, beyond the Greek tradition which represented it at the time of the Trojan War as inhabited by an original stock of Pelasgi and an immigrant population of Ionians. In historic times it was peopled by an "Aeolian" race who reckoned Boeotia as their motherland and claimed to have migrated about 1050 B.C.; its principal nobles traced their pedigree to Orestes, son of Agamemnon. Lesbos was the most prominent of Aeolian settlements, and indeed played a large part in the early development of Greek life. Its commercial activity is attested by several colonies in Thrace and the Troad, and by the participation of its traders in the settlement of Naucratis in Egypt; hence also the town of Mytilene, by virtue of its good harbour, became the political capital of the island. The climax of its prosperity was reached about 600 B.C., when a citizen named Pittacus was appointed as *aesymnetes* (dictator) to adjust the balance between the governing nobility and the insurgent commons and by his wise administration and legislation won a place among the Seven Sages of Greece. These years also constitute the golden age of Lesbian culture. The lyric poetry of Greece, which owed much to two Lesbians of the 7th century, the musician Terpander and the dithyrambist Arion, attained the standard of classical excellence under Pittacus' contemporaries Alcaeus and Sappho. In the 6th century the importance of the island declined, partly through a protracted and unsuccessful struggle with Athens for the possession of Sigeum near the Hellespont, partly through a crushing naval defeat inflicted by Polycrates of Samos (about 550). The Lesbians readily submitted to Persia after the fall of Croesus of Lydia, and although hatred of their tyrant Coës, a Persian protégé, drove them to take part in the Ionic revolt (499–493), they made little use of their large navy and displayed poor spirit at the decisive battle of Lade. In the 5th century Lesbos for a long time remained a privileged member of the Delian League (*q.v.*), with full rights of self-administration, and under the sole obligation of assisting Athens with naval contingents. Nevertheless at the beginning of the Peloponnesian War the ruling oligarchy of Mytilene forced on a revolt, which was ended after a two years' siege of that town (429–427). The Athenians, who had intended to punish the rebels by a wholesale execution, contented themselves with killing the ringleaders, confiscating the land and establishing a garrison. In the later years of the war Lesbos was repeatedly attacked by the Peloponnesians, and in 405 the harbour of Mytilene was the scene of a battle between the admirals Callicratidas and Conon. In 389 most of the island was recovered for the Athenians by Thrasybulus; in 377 it joined the Second Delian League, and remained throughout a loyal member, although in the second half of the century the dominant democracy was for a while supplanted by a tyranny. In 334 Lesbos served as a base for the Persian admiral Memnon against Alexander the Great. During the Third Macedonian War the Lesbians sided with Perseus against Rome; similarly in 88 they became eager allies of Mithradates VI. of Pontus, and Mytilene stood a protracted siege on his behalf. This town, nevertheless, was raised by Pompey to the status of a free community, thanks no doubt to his confidant Theophanes, a native of Mytilene.

Of the other towns on the island, Antissa, Eresus and Pyrrha possess no separate history. Methymna in the 5th and 4th centuries sometimes figures as a rival of Mytilene, with an independent policy. Among the distinguished Lesbians, in addition to those cited, may be mentioned the cyclic poet Lesches, the historian Hellanicus and the philosophers Theophrastus and Cratippus.

During the Byzantine age the island, which now assumes the name of Mytilene, continued to flourish. In 1091 it fell for a while into the hands of the Seljuks, and in the following century was repeatedly occupied by the Venetians. In 1224 it was recovered by the Byzantine emperors, who in 1354 gave it as a dowry to the Genoese family Gattilusio. After prospering under their administration Mytilene passed in 1462 under Turkish control, and has since had an uneventful history. The present population is about 130,000 of whom 13,000 are Turks and Moslems and 117,000 Greeks.

See Strabo xiii. pp. 617-619; Herodotus ii. 178, iii. 39, vi. 8, 14; Thucydides iii. 2-50; Xenophon, *Hellenica*, i., ii.; S. Plehn, *Lesbiacorum Liber* (Berlin, 1828); C. T. Newton, *Travels and Discoveries in the Levant* (London, 1865); B. V. Head, *Historia Numorum* (Oxford, 1887), pp. 487-488; E. L. Hicks and G. F. Hill, *Greek Historical Inscriptions* (Oxford, 1901), Nos. 61, 94, 101, 139, 164; Conze, *Reise auf der Insel Lesbos* (1865); Koldewey, *Antike Baureste auf Lesbos* (Berlin, 1890). (M. O. B. C.)

LESCHES (Lescheos in Pausanias x. 25. 5), the reputed author of the *Little Iliad* ('Ιλιὰς μικρά), one of the "cyclic" poems. According to the usually accepted tradition, he was a native of Pyrrha in Lesbos, and flourished about 660 B.C. (others place him about 50 years earlier). The *Little Iliad* took up the story of the Homeric *Iliad*, and, beginning with the contest between Ajax and Odysseus for the arms of Achilles, carried it down to the fall of Troy (Aristotle, *Poetics*, 23). According to the epitome in the *Chrestomathy* of Proclus, it ended with the admission of the wooden horse within the walls of the city. Some ancient authorities ascribe the work to a Lacedaemonian named Cinaethon, and even to Homer.

See F. G. Welcker, *Der epische Cyclus* (1865–1882); Müller and Donaldson, *Hist. of Greek Literature*, i. ch. 6; G. H. Bode, *Geschichte der hellenischen Dichtkunst*, i.

LESCURE, LOUIS MARIE JOSEPH, MARQUIS DE (1766–1793), French soldier and anti-revolutionary, was born near Bressuire. He was educated at the École Militaire, which he left at the age of sixteen. He was in command of a company of cavalry in the Régiment de Royal-Piémont, but being opposed to the ideas of the Revolution he emigrated in 1791; he soon, however, returned to France, and on the 10th of August 1792 took part in the defence of the Tuileries against the mob of Paris. The day after, he was forced to leave Paris, and took refuge in the château of Clisson near Bressuire. On the outbreak of the revolt of Vendée against the Republic, he was arrested and imprisoned with all his family, as one of the promoters of the rising. He was set at liberty by the Royalists, and became one of their leaders, fighting at Thouars, taking Fontenay and Saumur (May–June 1793), and, after an unsuccessful attack on Nantes, joining H. du Verger de la Rochejaquelein, another famous Vendean leader. Their peasant troops, opposed to the republican general F. J. Westermann, sustained various defeats, but finally gained a victory between Tiffauges and Cholet on the 19th of September 1793. The struggle was then concentrated round Chatillon, which was time after time taken and lost by the Republicans. Lescure was killed on the 15th of October 1793 near the château of La Tremblaye between Einée and Fougères.

See Marquise de la Rochejaquelein (Lescure's widow, who afterwards married La Rochejaquelein), *Mémoires* (Paris, 1817); Jullien de Courcelles, *Dictionnaire des généraux français*, tome vii. (1823); T. Muret, *Histoire des guerres de l'ouest* (Paris, 1848); and J. A. M. Crétineau-Joly, *Guerres de Vendée* (1834).

LESDIGUIÈRES, FRANÇOIS DE BONNE, DUC DE (1543–1626), constable of France, was born at Saint-Bonnet de Champsaur on the 1st of April 1543, of a family of notaries with pretensions to nobility. He was educated at Avignon under a Protestant tutor, and had begun the study of law in Paris when he enlisted as an archer. He served under the lieutenant-general of his native province of Dauphiné, Bertrand de Simiane, baron de Gordes, but when the Huguenots raised troops in Dauphiné Lesdiguières threw in his lot with them, and under his kinsman Antoine Rambaud de Furmeyer, whom he succeeded in 1570, distinguished himself in the mountain warfare that followed by his bold yet prudent handling of troops. He fought at Jarnac and Moncontour, and was a guest at the wedding of Henry IV. of Navarre. Warned of the impending massacre he retired hastily to Dauphiné, where he secretly equipped and drilled a determined body of Huguenots, and in 1575, after the execution of Montbrun, became the acknowledged leader of the Huguenot resistance in the district with the title of commandant general, confirmed in 1577 by Marshal Damville, by Condé in 1580, and by Henry of Navarre in 1582. He seized Gap by a lucky night attack on the 3rd of January 1577, re-established the reformed religion there, and fortified the town. He refused to acquiesce in the treaty of Poitiers (1578) which involved the surrender of Gap, and after two years of fighting secured better terms for the province. Nevertheless in 1580 he was compelled to hand the place over to Mayenne and to see the fortifications dismantled. He took up arms for Henry IV. in 1585, capturing Chorges, Embrun, Châteauroux and other places, and after the truce of 1588-1589 secured the complete submission of Dauphiné. In 1590 he beat down the resistance of Grenoble, and was now able to threaten the leaguers and to support the governor of Provence against the raids of Charles Emmanuel I. of Savoy. He defeated the Savoyards at Esparron in April 1591, and in 1592 began the reconquest of the marquessate of Saluzzo which had been seized by Charles Emmanuel. After his defeat of the Spanish allies of Savoy at Salebertrano in June 1593 there was a truce, during which Lesdiguières was occupied in maintaining the royal authority against Éperon in Provence. The war with Savoy proceeded intermittently until 1601, when Henry IV. concluded peace, much to the dissatisfaction of Lesdiguières. The king regarded his lieutenant's domination in Dauphiné with some distrust, although he was counted among the best of his captains. Nevertheless he made him a marshal of France in 1609, and ensured the succession to the lieutenant-generalship of Dauphiné, vested in Lesdiguières since 1597, to his son-in-law Charles de Créquy. Sincerely devoted to the throne, Lesdiguières took no part in the intrigues which disturbed the minority of Louis XIII., and he moderated the political claims made by his co-religionists under the terms of the Edict of Nantes. After the death of his first wife, Claudine de Bérenger, he married the widow of Ennemond Matel, a Grenoble shopkeeper, who was murdered in 1617. Lesdiguières was then 73, and this lady, Marie Vignon, had long been his mistress. He had two daughters, one of whom, Françoise, married Charles de Créquy. In 1622 he formally abjured the Protestant faith, his conversion being partly due to the influence of Marie Vignon. He was already a duke and peer of France; he now became constable of France, and received the order of the Saint Esprit. He had long since lost the confidence of the Huguenots, but he nevertheless helped the Vaudois against the duke of Savoy. Lesdiguières had the qualities of a great general, but circumstances limited him to the mountain warfare of Dauphiné, Provence and Savoy. He had almost unvarying success through sixty years of fighting. His last campaign, fought in alliance with Savoy to drive the Spaniards from the Valtelline, was the least successful of his enterprises. He died of fever at Valence on the 21st of September 1626.

The life of the Huguenot captain has been written in detail by Ch. Dufayard, *Le Connétable de Lesdiguières* (Paris, 1892). His first biographer was his secretary Louis Videl, *Histoire de la vie du connestable de Lesdiguières* (Paris, 1638). Much of his official correspondence, with an admirable sketch of his life, is contained in *Actes et correspondance du connétable de Lesdiguières*, edited by Comte Douglas and J. Roman in *Documents historiques inédits pour servir à l'histoire de Dauphiné* (Grenoble, 1878). Other letters are in the *Lettres et mémoires* (Paris, 1647) of Duplessis-Mornay.

LESGHIANS, or LESGHIS (from the Persian *Leksi*, called Leki by the Grusians or Georgians, Armenians and Ossetes), the collective name for a number of tribes of the eastern Caucasus, who, with their kinsfolk the Chechenzes, have inhabited Daghestan from time immemorial. They spread southward into the Transcaucasian circles Kuba, Shemakha, Nukha and Sakataly. They are mentioned as Λῆχαι by Strabo and Plutarch along with the Γῆλαι (perhaps the modern Galgai, a Chechenzian tribe), and their name occurs frequently in the chronicles of the Georgians, whose territory was exposed to their raids for centuries, until, on the surrender (1859) to Russia of the Chechenzian chieftain Shamyl, they became Russian subjects. Moses of Chorene mentions a battle in the reign of the Armenian king Baba (A.D. 370–377), in which Shagir, king of the Lekians, was slain. The most important of the Lesghian tribes are the Avars (*q.v.*), the Kasimukhians or Lakians, the Darghis and the

Kurins or Lesghians proper. Komarov[1] gives the total number of the tribes as twenty-seven, all speaking distinct dialects. Despite this, the Lesghian peoples, with the exception of the Udi and Kubatschi, are held to be ethnically identical. The Lesghians are not usually so good-looking as the Circassians or the Chechenzes. They are tall, powerfully built, and their hybrid descent is suggested by the range of colouring, some of the tribes exhibiting quite fair, others quite dark, individuals. Among some there is an obvious mongoloid strain. In disposition they are intelligent, bold and persistent, and capable of reckless bravery, as was proved in their struggle to maintain their independence. They are capable of enduring great physical fatigue. They live a semi-savage life on their mountain slopes, for the most part living by hunting and stock-breeding. Little agriculture is possible. Their industries are mainly restricted to smith-work and cutlery and the making of felt cloaks, and the women weave excellent shawls. They are for the most part fanatical Mahommedans.

See Moritz Wagner, *Schamyl* (Leipzig, 1854); von Seidlitz, "Ethnographie des Kaukasus," in *Petermann's Mitteilungen* (1880); Ernest Chantre, *Recherches anthropologiques dans le Caucase* (Lyon, 1885–1887); J. de Morgan, *Recherches sur les origines des peuples du Caucase* (Paris, 1889).

LESINA (Serbo-Croatian, *Hvar*), an island in the Adriatic Sea, forming part of Dalmatia, Austria. Lesina lies between the islands of Brazza on the north and Curzola on the south; and is divided from the peninsula of Sabbioncello by the Narenta [illegible]. Its length is 41 m.; its greatest breadth less than 4 m. It has a steep rocky coast with a chain of thinly wooded [illegible] hills. The climate is mild, and not only the grape and [illegible], but dates, figs and the carob or locust-bean flourish. The [illegible] of these fruits, boat-building, fishing and the [illegible] of rosemary essence and liqueurs are the principal [illegible] of the islanders. Lesina (*Hvar*) and Cittavecchia [illegible] are the principal towns and seaports, having respec[illegible] and 3120 inhabitants. Lesina, the capital, contains [illegible] an observatory and some interesting old buildings [illegible] century. It is a Roman Catholic bishopric, and the [illegible] administrative district, which includes Cittavecchia, [illegible] some small neighbouring islands. Pop. (1900) of island [illegible] district 27,928.

[illegible] primitive "Illyrian" race, whose stone cists and bronze [illegible] have been disinterred from barrows near the capital, [illegible] be attributed the "Cyclopean" walls at Citta[illegible] about 385 B.C., a Greek colony from Paros built a city [illegible] the present Lesina, naming it *Paros* or *Pharos*. [illegible] *Pharia* (common among Latin writers), and [illegible]. In 229 B.C. the island was betrayed to the [illegible] Demetrius, lieutenant of the Illyrian queen Teuta; [illegible] Demetrius proved false to Rome also, his capital [illegible] Lucius Aemilius Paullus. *Neos Pharos*, now [illegible] its place, and flourished until the 6th century, [illegible] was laid waste by barbarian invaders. Con[illegible]genitus mentions Lesina as a colony of pagan [illegible] century. Throughout the middle ages it [illegible] Slavonic community; and its name, which [illegible] as *Lisna*, *Lesna* or *Lyesena*, "wooded" [illegible] derived from the Slavonic *lyés*, "forest," not [illegible], "an awl." But the old form Pharia [illegible], with the curious result that the modern [illegible] is Greek, and the modern Italian name [illegible] Lesina became a bishopric in 1145, and [illegible] Venice in 1331. It was sacked by the [illegible] and 1358; ceded to Hungary in the [illegible] from 1413 to 1416; and incorporated [illegible] in 1420. During the 16th century [illegible] considerable maritime trade, and, though [illegible] by the Turks in 1571, it remained [illegible] Venice, in these waters, until 1776, [illegible] Curzola. Passing to Austria in 1797, [illegible] withstood a Russian attack in 1807, but was surrendered by the French in 1813, and finally annexed to Austria in 1815.

[illegible]

LESION (through Fr. from Lat. *laesio*, injury, *laedere*, to hurt), an injury, hurt, damage. In Scots law the term is used of damage suffered by a party in a contract sufficient to enable him to bring an action for setting it aside. In pathology, the chief use, the word is applied to any morbid change in the structure of an organ, whether shown by visible changes or by disturbance of function.

LESKOVATS (LESKOVATZ or LESKOVAC), a town in Servia, between Nish and Vranya, on the railway line from Nish to Salonica. Pop. (1901) 13,707. It is the headquarters of the Servian hemp industry, the extensive plain in which the town lies growing the best flax and hemp in all the Balkan peninsula. The plain is not only the most fertile portion of Servia, but also the best cultivated. Besides flax and hemp, excellent tobacco is grown. Five valleys converge on the plain from different directions, and the inhabitants of the villages in these valleys are all occupied in growing flax and hemp, which they send to Leskovats to be stored or manufactured into ropes. After Belgrade and Nish, Leskovats is the most prosperous town in Servia.

LESLEY, JOHN (1527–1596), Scottish bishop and historian, was born in 1527. His father was Gavin Lesley, rector of Kingussie. He was educated at the university of Aberdeen, where he took the degree of M.A. In 1538 he obtained a dispensation permitting him to hold a benefice, notwithstanding his being a natural son, and in June 1546 he was made an acolyte in the cathedral church of Aberdeen, of which he was afterwards appointed a canon and prebendary. He also studied at Poitiers, at Toulouse and at Paris, where he was made doctor of laws in 1553. In 1558 he took orders and was appointed Official of Aberdeen, and inducted into the parsonage and prebend of Oyne. At the Reformation Lesley became a champion of Catholicism. He was present at the disputation held in Edinburgh in 1561, when Knox and Willox were his antagonists. He was one of the commissioners sent the same year to bring over the young Queen Mary to take the government of Scotland. He returned in her train, and was appointed a privy councillor and professor of canon law in King's College, Aberdeen, and in 1565 one of the senators of the college of justice. Shortly afterwards he was made abbot of Lindores, and in 1565 bishop of Ross, the election to the see being confirmed in the following year. He was one of the sixteen commissioners appointed to revise the laws of Scotland, and the volume of the *Actis and Constitutiounis of the Realme of Scotland* known as the Black Acts was, chiefly owing to his care, printed in 1566.

The bishop was one of the most steadfast friends of Queen Mary. After the failure of the royal cause, and whilst Mary was a captive in England, Lesley (who had gone to her at Bolton) continued to exert himself on her behalf. He was one of the commissioners at the conference at York in 1568. He appeared as her ambassador at the court of Elizabeth to complain of the injustice done to her, and when he found he was not listened to he laid plans for her escape. He also projected a marriage for her with the duke of Norfolk, which ended in the execution of that nobleman. For this he was put under the charge of the bishop of London, and then of the bishop of Ely (in Holborn), and afterwards imprisoned in the Tower of London. During his confinement he collected materials for his history of Scotland, by which his name is now chiefly known. In 1571 he presented the latter portion of this work, written in Scots, to Queen Mary to amuse her in her captivity. He also wrote for her use his *Piae Consolationes*, and the queen devoted some of the hours of her captivity to translating a portion of it into French verse.

In 1573 he was liberated from prison, but was banished from England. For two years he attempted unsuccessfully to obtain the assistance of Continental princes in favour of Queen Mary. While at Rome in 1578 he published his Latin history *De Origine, Moribus, et Rebus Gestis Scotorum*. In 1579 he went to France, and was made suffragan and vicar-general of the archbishopric of Rouen. Whilst visiting his diocese, however, he was thrown into prison, and had to pay 3000 pistoles to prevent his being given up to Elizabeth. During the remainder of the reign of Henry III. he lived unmolested, but on the accession of the Protestant Henry IV. he again fell into trouble. In 1590 he was thrown into prison, and had to purchase his freedom at the same expense as before. In 1593 he was made bishop of Coutances in Normandy, and had licence to hold the bishopric of Ross till he should obtain peaceable possession of the former see. He retired to an Augustinian monastery near Brussels, where he died on the 31st of May 1596.

The chief works of Lesley are as follows: *A Defence of the Honour of . . . Marie, Queene of Scotland, by Eusebius Dicaeophile* (London, 1569), reprinted, with alterations, at Liége in 1571, under the title, *A Treatise concerning the Defence of the Honour of Marie, Queene of Scotland, made by Morgan Philippes, Bachelar of Divinitie*, *Piae afflicti animi consolationes, ad Mariam Scot. Reg.* (Paris, 1574); *De origine, moribus et rebus gestis Scotorum libri decem* (Rome, 1578; re-issued 1675); *De illustrium feminarum in republica administranda authoritate libellus* (Reims, 1580; a Latin version of a tract on "The Lawfulness of the Regiment of Women": cf. Knox's pamphlet); *De titulo et jure Mariae Scot. Reg., quo regni Angliae successionem sibi juste vindicat* (Reims, 1580; translated in 1584). The history of Scotland from 1436 to 1561 owes much, in its earlier chapters, to the accounts of Hector Boece (*q.v.*) and John Major (*q.v.*), though no small portion of the topographical matter is first-hand. In the later sections he gives an independent account (from the Catholic point of view) which is a valuable supplement and a corrective in many details, to the works of Buchanan and Knox. A Scots version of the history was written in 1596 by James Dalrymple of the Scottish Cloister at Regensburg. It has been printed for the Scottish Text Society (2 vols., 1888–1895) under the editorship of the Rev. E. G. Cody, O.S.B. A slight sketch by Lesley of Scottish history from 1562 to 1571 has been translated by Forbes-Leith in his *Narrative of Scottish Catholics* (1885), from the original MS. now in the Vatican.

LESLEY, J. PETER (1819–1903), American geologist, was born in Philadelphia on the 17th of September 1819. It is recorded by Sir A. Geikie that "He was christened Peter after his father and grandfather, and at first wrote his name 'Peter Lesley, Jr.,' but disliking the Christian appellation that had been given to him, he eventually transformed his signature by putting the J. of 'Junior' at the beginning." He was educated for the ministry at the university of Pennsylvania, where he graduated in 1838; but the effects of close study having told upon his health, he served for a time as sub-assistant on the first geological survey of Pennsylvania under Professor H. D. Rogers, and was afterwards engaged in a special examination of the coal regions. On the termination of the survey in 1841 he entered Princeton seminary and renewed his theological studies, at the same time giving his leisure time to assist Professor Rogers in preparing the final report and map of Pennsylvania. He was licensed to preach in 1844; he then paid a visit to Europe and entered on a short course of study at the university of Halle. Returning to America he worked during two years for the American Tract Society, and at the close of 1847 he joined Professor Rogers again in preparing geological maps and sections at Boston. He then accepted the pastorate of the Congregational church at Milton, a suburb of Boston, where he remained until 1851, when, his views having become Unitarian, he abandoned the ministry and entered into practice as a consulting geologist. In the course of his work he made elaborate surveys of the Cape Breton coalfield, and of other coal and iron regions. From 1855 to 1859 he was secretary of the American Iron Association; for twenty-seven years (1858–1885) he was secretary and librarian of the American Philosophical Society; from 1872 to 1878 he was professor of geology and dean of the faculty of science in the university of Pennsylvania, and from 1874–1893 he was in charge of the second geological survey of the state. He then retired to Milton, Mass., where he died on the 1st of June 1903. He published *Manual of Coal and its Topography* (1856); *The Iron Manufacturer's Guide to the Furnaces, Forges and Rolling Mills of the United States* (1859).

See Memoir by Sir A. Geikie in *Quart. Journ. Geol. Soc.* (May 1904); and Memoir (with portrait) by B. S. Lyman, printed in advance with portrait, and afterwards in abstract only in *Trans. Amer. Inst. Mining Engineers*, xxxiv. (1904) p. 726.

LESLIE, CHARLES (1650–1722), Anglican nonjuring divine, son of John Leslie (1571–1671), bishop of Raphoe and afterwards of Clogher, was born in July 1650 in Dublin, and was educated at Enniskillen school and Trinity College, Dublin. Going to England he read law for a time, but soon turned his attention to theology, and took orders in 1680. In 1687 he became chancellor of the cathedral of Connor and a justice of the peace, and began a long career of public controversy by responding in public disputation at Monaghan to the challenge of the Roman Catholic bishop of Clogher. Although a vigorous opponent of Roman Catholicism, Leslie was a firm supporter of the Stuart dynasty, and, having declined at the Revolution to take the oath to William and Mary, he was on this account deprived of his benefice. In 1689 the growing troubles in Ireland induced him to withdraw to England, where he employed himself for the next twenty years in writing various controversial pamphlets in favour of the nonjuring cause, and in numerous polemics against the Quakers, Jews, Socinians and Roman Catholics, and especially in that against the Deists with which his name is now most commonly associated. He had the keenest scent for every form of heresy and was especially zealous in his defence of the sacraments. A warrant having been issued against him in 1710 for his pamphlet *The Good Old Cause, or Lying in Truth*, he resolved to quit England and to accept an offer made by the Pretender (with whom he had previously been in frequent correspondence) that he should reside with him at Bar-le-Duc. After the failure of the Stuart cause in 1715, Leslie accompanied his patron into Italy, where he remained until 1721, in which year, having found his sojourn amongst Roman Catholics extremely unpleasant, he sought and obtained permission to return to his native country. He died at Glaslough, Monaghan, on the 13th of April 1722.

The *Theological Works* of Leslie were collected and published by himself in 2 vols. folio in 1721; a later edition, slightly enlarged, appeared at Oxford in 1832 (7 vols. 8vo). Though marred by persistent arguing in a circle they are written in lively style and show considerable erudition. He had the somewhat rare distinction of making several converts by his reasonings, and Johnson declared that "Leslie was a reasoner, and a reasoner who was not to be reasoned against." An historical interest in all that now attaches to his subjects and his methods, as may be seen when the promise given in the title of his best-known work is contrasted with the actual performance. The book professes to be *A Short and Easy Method with the Deists, wherein the certainty of the Christian Religion is Demonstrated by Infallible Proof from Four Rules, which are incompatible to any imposture that ever yet has been, or that can possibly be* (1697). The four rules which, according to Leslie, have only to be rigorously applied in order to establish not the probability merely but the absolute certainty of the truth of Christianity are simply these: (1) that the matter of fact be such as that men's outward senses, their eyes and ears, may be judges of it; (2) that it be done publicly, in the face of the world; (3) that not only public monuments be kept up in memory of it, but some outward actions be performed; (4) that such monuments and such actions or observances be instituted and do commence from the time that the matter of fact was done. Other publications of Leslie are *The Snake in the Grass* (1696), against the Quakers; *A Short Method with the Jews* (1689); *Gallienus Redivivus* (an attack on William III., 1695); *The Socinian Controversy Discussed* (1697); *The True Notion of the Catholic Church* (1703); and *The Case Stated between the Church of Rome and the Church of England* (1713).

LESLIE, CHARLES ROBERT (1794–1859), English genre-painter, was born in London on the 19th of October 1794. His parents were American, and when he was five years of age he returned with them to their native country. They settled in Philadelphia, where their son was educated and afterwards apprenticed to a bookseller. He was, however, mainly interested in painting and the drama, and when George Frederick Cooke visited the city he executed a portrait of the actor, from recollection of him on the stage, which was considered a work of such promise that a fund was raised to enable the young artist to study in Europe. He left for London in 1811, bearing introductions which procured for him the friendship of West, Beechey, Allston, Coleridge and Washington Irving, and was admitted as a student of the Royal Academy, where he carried off two silver medals. At first, influenced by West and Fuseli, he essayed "high art," and his earliest important subject depicted Saul and the Witch of Endor; but he soon discovered his true aptitude and became a painter of cabinet-pictures, dealing, not like those of Wilkie, with the contemporary life that surrounded him, but with scenes from the great masters of fiction, from Shakespeare and Cervantes, Addison and Molière, Swift, Sterne, Fielding and Smollett. Of individual paintings we may specify "Sir Roger de Coverley going to Church" (1819); "May-day in the Time of Queen Elizabeth" (1821); "Sancho Panza and the Duchess" (1824); "Uncle Toby and the Widow Wadman" (1831); *La Malade Imaginaire*, act iii. sc. 6 (1843); and the "Duke's Chaplain Enraged leaving the Table," from *Don Quixote* (1849). Many of his more important subjects exist in varying replicas. He possessed a sympathetic imagination, which enabled him to enter freely into the spirit of the author whom he illustrated, a delicate perception for female beauty, an unfailing eye for character and its outward manifestation in face and figure, and a genial and sunny sense of humour, guarded by an instinctive refinement which prevented it from overstepping the bounds of good taste. In 1821 Leslie was elected A.R.A., and five years later full academician. In 1833 [illegible] left for America to become teacher of drawing in the military academy at West Point, but the post proved an irksome one, and [illegible] some six months he returned to England. He died on the 5th of May 1859.

In addition to his skill as an artist, Leslie was a ready and pleasant writer. His *Life of his friend Constable*, the landscape painter, appeared in 1843, and his *Handbook for Young Painters*, a volume embodying the substance of his lectures as professor of painting to the Royal Academy, in 1855. In 1860 Tom Taylor edited his *Autobiographical Recollections*, which contain interesting reminiscences of his [illegible] friends and contemporaries.

LESLIE, FRED [FREDERICK HOBSON] (1855–1892), English actor, was born at Woolwich on the 1st of April 1855. He made his first stage appearance in London as Colonel Hardy in [illegible] in 1878. He had a good voice, and in 1882 made a [illegible] as Rip Van Winkle in Planquette's opera of that name [illegible]. In 1885 he appeared at the Gaiety as Jonathan [illegible] in [illegible] and W. Yardley's burlesque *Little Jack Sheppard*. His extraordinary success in this part determined his subsequent career, and for some years he and Nelly Farren, [illegible] played in perfect association, were the pillars of [illegible]. Leslie's "Don Caesar de Bazan" in *Ruy Blas* [illegible] was perhaps the most popular of his later [illegible] his own versatility and entertaining [illegible] formed the attraction; whether he sang, [illegible] his performance was an unending [illegible] charm. Under the pseudonym [illegible] acknowledged on the programmes as [illegible] "A. C. Torr" [illegible], and while on occasion he acted [illegible] for which he had undoubted capacity, [illegible] with them. In 1881 and 1883 [illegible]. He died on the 7th of December 1892.

[illegible] *Recollections of Fred Leslie* (1894).

LESLIE, SIR JOHN [illegible], Scottish mathematician [illegible] parentage at Largo, Fifeshire, [illegible] his early education there [illegible] year, encouraged by friends [illegible] aptitude for mathematical and [illegible] university of St Andrews. On [illegible] he nominally studied divinity [illegible] he spent rather more [illegible] family, and from 1790 [illegible] appointment at Etruria [illegible] Josiah Wedgwood, em[illegible] research and in preparing [illegible] *History of Birds*, which was [illegible] brought him some money. [illegible] in London or at Largo, [illegible] of Europe) he continued [illegible] numerous papers contri[illegible] *Journal*, and in the [illegible] *Inquiry into the Nature* [illegible]

to succeed John Playfair in the chair of mathematics at Edinburgh, not, however, without violent though unsuccessful opposition on the part of a narrow-minded clerical party who accused him of heresy in something he had said as to the "unsophisticated notions of mankind" about the relation of cause and effect. During his tenure of this chair he published two volumes of a *Course of Mathematics*—the first, entitled *Elements of Geometry, Geometrical Analysis and Plane Trigonometry*, in 1809, and the second, *Geometry of Curve Lines*, in 1813; the third volume, on *Descriptive Geometry and the Theory of Solids* was never completed. With reference to his invention (in 1810) of a process of artificial congelation, he published in 1813 *A Short Account of Experiments and Instruments depending on the relations of Air to Heat and Moisture*; and in 1818 a paper by him "On certain impressions of cold transmitted from the higher atmosphere, with an instrument (the aethrioscope) adapted to measure them," appeared in the *Transactions of the Royal Society of Edinburgh*. In 1819, on the death of Playfair, he was promoted to the more congenial chair of natural philosophy, which he continued to hold until his death, and in 1823 he published, chiefly for the use of his class, the first volume of his never-completed *Elements of Natural Philosophy*. Leslie's main contributions to physics were made by the help of the "differential thermometer," an instrument whose invention was contested with him by Count Rumford. By adapting to this instrument various ingenious devices he was enabled to employ it in a great variety of investigations, connected especially with photometry, hygroscopy and the temperature of space. In 1820 he was elected a corresponding member of the Institute of France, the only distinction of the kind which he valued, and early in 1832 he was created a knight. He died at Coates, a small property which he had acquired near Largo, on the 3rd of November 1832.

LESLIE, THOMAS EDWARD CLIFFE (1827–1882), English economist, was born in the county of Wexford in (as is believed) the year 1827. He was the second son of the Rev. Edward Leslie, prebendary of Dromore, and rector of Annahilt, in the county of Down. His family was of Scottish descent, but had been connected with Ireland since the reign of Charles I. Amongst his ancestors were that accomplished prelate, John Leslie (1571–1671), bishop first of Raphoe and afterwards of Clogher, who, when holding the former see, offered so stubborn a resistance to the Cromwellian forces, and the bishop's son Charles (see above), the nonjuror. Cliffe Leslie received his elementary education from his father, who resided in England, though holding church preferment as well as possessing some landed property in Ireland; by him he was taught Latin, Greek and Hebrew, at an unusually early age; he was afterwards for a short time under the care of a clergyman at Clapham, and was then sent to King William's College, in the Isle of Man, where he remained until, in 1842, being then only fifteen years of age, he entered Trinity College, Dublin. He was a distinguished student there, obtaining, besides other honours, a classical scholarship in 1845, and a senior moderatorship (gold medal) in mental and moral philosophy at his degree examination in 1846. He became a law student at Lincoln's Inn, was for two years a pupil in a conveyancer's chambers in London, and was called to the English bar. But his attention was soon turned from the pursuit of legal practice, for which he seems never to have had much inclination, by his appointment, in 1853, to the professorship of jurisprudence and political economy in Queen's College, Belfast. The duties of this chair requiring only short visits to Ireland in certain terms of each year, he continued to reside and prosecute his studies in London, and became a frequent writer on economic and social questions in the principal reviews and other periodicals. In 1870 he collected a number of his essays, adding several new ones, into a volume entitled *Land Systems and Industrial Economy of Ireland, England and Continental Countries*. J. S. Mill gave a full account of the contents of this work in a paper in the *Fortnightly Review*, in which he pronounced Leslie to be "one of the best living writers on applied political economy." Mill had sought his acquaintance on reading his first article in *Macmillan's Magazine*; he admired his talents and took pleasure in his society, and treated him with a respect and kindness which Leslie always gratefully acknowledged.

In the frequent visits which Leslie made to the continent, especially to Belgium and some of the less-known districts of France and Germany, he occupied himself much in economic and social observation, studying the effects of the institutions and system of life which prevailed in each region, on the material and moral condition of its inhabitants. In this way he gained an extensive and accurate acquaintance with continental rural economy, of which he made excellent use in studying parallel phenomena at home. The accounts he gave of the results of his observations were among his happiest efforts; "no one," said Mill, "was able to write narratives of foreign visits at once so instructive and so interesting." In these excursions he made the acquaintance of several distinguished persons, amongst others of M. Léonce de Lavergne and M. Émile de Laveleye. To the memory of the former of these he afterwards paid a graceful tribute in a biographical sketch (*Fortnightly Review*, February 1881); and to the close of his life there existed between him and M. de Laveleye relations of mutual esteem and cordial intimacy.

Two essays of Leslie's appeared in volumes published under the auspices of the Cobden Club, one on the "Land System of France" (2nd ed., 1870), containing an earnest defence of *la petite culture* and still more of *la petite propriété*; the other on "Financial Reform" (1871), in which he exhibited in detail the impediments to production and commerce arising from indirect taxation. Many other articles were contributed by him to reviews between 1875 and 1879, including several discussions of the history of prices and the movements of wages in Europe, and a sketch of life in Auvergne in his best manner; the most important of them, however, related to the philosophical method of political economy, notably a memorable one which appeared in the Dublin University periodical, *Hermathena*. In 1879 the provost and senior fellows of Trinity College published for him a volume in which a number of these articles were collected under the title of *Essays in Political and Moral Philosophy*. These and some later essays, together with the earlier volume on *Land Systems*, form the essential contribution of Leslie to economic literature. He had long contemplated, and had in part written, a work on English economic and legal history, which would have been his *magnum opus*—a more substantial fruit of his genius and his labours than anything he has left. But the MS. of this treatise, after much pains had already been spent on it, was unaccountably lost at Nancy in 1872; and, though he hoped to be able speedily to reproduce the missing portion and finish the work, no material was left in a state fit for publication. What the nature of it would have been may be gathered from an essay on the "History and Future of Profit" in the *Fortnightly Review* for November 1881, which is believed to have been in substance an extract from it.

That he was able to do so much may well be a subject of wonder when it is known that his labours had long been impeded by a painful and depressing malady, from which he suffered severely at intervals, whilst he never felt secure from its recurring attacks. To this disease he in the end succumbed at Belfast, on the 27th of January 1882.

Leslie's work may be distributed under two heads, that of applied political economy and that of discussion on the philosophical method of the science. The *Land Systems* belonged principally to the former division. The author perceived the great and growing importance for the social welfare of both Ireland and England of what is called "the land question," and treated it in this volume at once with breadth of view and with a rich variety of illustrative detail. His general purpose was to show that the territorial systems of both countries were so encumbered with elements of feudal origin as to be altogether unfitted to serve the purposes of a modern industrial society. The policy he recommended is summed up in the following list of requirements, "a simple jurisprudence relating to land, a law of equal intestate succession, a prohibition of entail, a legal security for tenants' improvements, an open registration of title and transfer and a considerable number of peasant properties." The volume is full of practical good sense, and exhibits a thorough knowledge of home and foreign agricultural economy; and in the handling of the subject is everywhere shown the special power which its author possessed of making what he wrote interesting as well as instructive. The way in which sagacious observation and shrewd comment are constantly intermingled in the discussion not seldom reminds us of Adam Smith, whose manner was more congenial to Leslie than the abstract and arid style of Ricardo.

But what, more than anything else, marks him as an original thinker and gives him a place apart among contemporary economists, is his exposition and defence of the historical method in political economy. Both at home and abroad there has for some time existed a profound and growing dissatisfaction with the method and many of the doctrines of the hitherto dominant school, which, it is alleged, under a "fictitious completeness, symmetry and exactness" disguises a real hollowness and discordance with fact. It is urged that the attempt to deduce the economic phenomena of a society from the so-called universal principle of "the desire of wealth" is illusory, and that they cannot be fruitfully studied apart from the general social conditions and historic development of which they are the outcome. Of this movement of thought Leslie was the principal representative, if not the originator, in England. There is no doubt, for he has himself placed it on record, that the first influence which impelled him in the direction of the historical method was that of Sir Henry Maine, by whose personal teaching of jurisprudence, as well as by the example of his writings, he was led "to look at the present economic structure and state of society as the result of a long evolution." The study of those German economists who represent similar tendencies doubtless confirmed him in the new line of thought on which he had entered, though he does not seem to have been further indebted to any of them except, perhaps, in some small degree to Roscher. And the writings of Comte, whose "prodigious genius," as exhibited in the *Philosophie Positive*, he admired and proclaimed, though he did not accept his system as a whole, must have powerfully co-operated to form in him the habit of regarding economic science as only a single branch of sociology, which should always be kept in close relation to the others. The earliest writing in which Leslie's revolt against the so-called "orthodox school" distinctly appears is his *Essay on Wages*, which was first published in 1868 and was reproduced as an appendix to the volume on *Land Tenures*. In this, after exposing the inanity of the theory of the wage-fund, and showing the utter want of agreement between its results and the observed phenomena, he concludes by declaring that "political economy must be content to take rank as an inductive, instead of a purely deductive science," and that, by this change of character, "it will gain in utility, interest and real truth far more than a full compensation for the forfeiture of a fictitious title to mathematical exactness and certainty." But it is in the essays collected in the volume of 1879 that his attitude in relation to the question of method is most decisively marked. In one of these, on "the political economy of Adam Smith," he exhibits in a very interesting way the co-existence in the *Wealth of Nations* of historical-inductive investigation in the manner of Montesquieu with a priori speculation founded on theologico-metaphysical bases, and points out the error of ignoring the former element, which is the really characteristic feature of Smith's social philosophy, and places him in strong contrast with his *soi-disant* followers of the school of Ricardo. The essay, however, which contains the most brilliant polemic against the "orthodox school," as well as the most luminous account and the most powerful vindication of the new direction, was that of which we have above spoken as having first appeared in *Hermathena*. It may be recommended as supplying the best extant presentation of one of the two contending views of economic method. On this essay mainly rests the claim of Leslie to be regarded as the founder and first head of the English historical school of political economy. Those who share his views on the philosophical constitution of the science regard the work he did, notwithstanding its unsystematic character, as in reality the most important done by any English economists in the latter half of the 19th century. But even the warmest partisans of the older school acknowledge that he did excellent service by insisting on a kind of inquiry, previously too much neglected, which was of the highest interest and value, in whatever relation it might be supposed to stand to the establishment of economic truth. The members of both groups alike recognized his great learning, his patient and conscientious habits of investigation and the large social spirit in which he treated the problems of his science. (J. K. I.)

LESLIE, a police burgh of Fifeshire, Scotland. Pop. (1901) 3587. It lies on the Leven, the vale of which is overlooked by the town, 4 m. W. of Markinch by the North British railway. The industries include paper-making, flax-spinning, bleaching and linen-weaving. The old church claims to be the "Christ's Kirk on the Green" of the ancient ballads of that name. A stone on the Green, called the Bull Stone, is said to have been used when bull-baiting was a popular pastime. Leslie House, the seat of the earl of Rothes, designed by Sir William Bruce, rivalled Holyrood in magnificence. It was noted for its tapestry and its gallery of family portraits and other pictures, including a

rendered his society charming. Whatever his cares, his work or his troubles, I have never noticed in him aught but generous impulses and a love of humanity carried even to those heroic imprudences of which they alone are capable who devote themselves to the amelioration of humanity." No doubt this eulogy requires some reservations. The striking and universal success which crowned his work on the Suez Canal gave him an absoluteness of thought which brooked no contradiction, a despotic temper before which every one must bow, and against which, when he had once taken a resolution, nothing could prevail, not even the most authoritative opposition or the most legitimate entreaties. He had resolved to construct the Panama Canal without locks, to make it an uninterrupted navigable way. All attempts to dissuade him from this resolution failed before his tenacious will. At his advanced age he went with his youngest child to Panama to see with his own eyes the field of his new enterprise. He there beheld the Culebra and the Chagres; he saw the mountain and the stream, those two greatest obstacles of nature that sought to bar his route. He paid no heed to them, but began the struggle against the Culebra and the Chagres. It was against them that was broken his invincible will, sweeping away in the defeat the work of Panama, his own fortune, his fame and almost an atom of his honour. But this atom, only grazed by calumny, has already been restored to him by posterity, for he died poor, having been the first to suffer by the disaster to his illusions. Political agitators, in order to sap the power of the Opportunist party, did not hesitate to drag in the mud one of the greatest citizens of France. But when the Panama "scandal" has been forgotten, for centuries to come the traveller in saluting the statue of Ferdinand de Lesseps at the entrance of the Suez Canal will pay homage to one of the most powerful embodiments of the creative genius of the 19th century.

See G. Barnett Smith, *The Life and Enterprises of Ferdinand de Lesseps* (London, 1893); and *Souvenirs de quarante ans*, by Ferdinand de Lesseps (trans. by C. B. Pitman). (DE B.)

LESSING, GOTTHOLD EPHRAIM (1729–1781), German critic and dramatist, was born at Kamenz in Upper Lusatia (Oberlausitz), Saxony, on the 22nd of January 1729. His father, Johann Gottfried Lessing, was a clergyman, and, a few years after his son's birth, became *pastor primarius* or chief pastor of Kamenz. After attending the Latin school of his native town, Gotthold was sent in 1741 to the famous school of St Afra at Meissen, where he made such rapid progress, especially in classics and mathematics, that, towards the end of his school career, he was described by the rector as "a steed that needed double fodder." In 1746 he entered the university of Leipzig as a theological student. The philological lectures of Johann Friedrich Christ (1700–1756) and Johann August Ernesti (1707–1781) proved, however, more attractive than those on theology, and he attended the philosophical disputations presided over by his friend A. G. Kästner, professor of mathematics and also an epigrammatist of repute. Among Lessing's chief friends in Leipzig were C. F. Weisse (1726–1804) the dramatist, and Christlob Mylius (1722–1754), who had made some name for himself as a journalist. He was particularly attracted by the theatre then directed by the talented actress Karoline Neuber (1697–1760), who had assisted Gottsched in his efforts to bring the German stage into touch with literature. Frau Neuber even accepted for performance Lessing's first comedy, *Der junge Gelehrte* (1748), which he had begun at school. His father naturally did not approve of these new interests and acquaintances, and summoned him home. He was only allowed to return to Leipzig on the condition that he would devote himself to the study of medicine. Some medical lectures he did attend, but as long as Frau Neuber's company kept together the theatre had an irresistible fascination for him.

In 1748, however, the company broke up, and Lessing, who had allowed himself to become surety for some of the actors' debts, was obliged to leave Leipzig too, in order to escape their creditors. He went to Wittenberg, and afterwards, towards the end of the year, to Berlin, where his friend Mylius had established himself as a journalist. In Berlin Lessing now spent three years, maintaining himself chiefly by literary work. He translated three volumes of Charles Rollin's *Histoire ancienne*, wrote several plays—*Der Misogyn*, *Der Freigeist*, *Die Juden*—and in association with Mylius, began the *Beiträge zur Historie und Aufnahme des Theaters* (1750), a periodical—which soon came to an end—for the discussion of matters connected with the drama. Early in 1751 he became literary critic to the *Vossische Zeitung*, and in this position laid the foundation for his reputation as a reviewer of learning, judgment and wit. At the end of 1751 he was in Wittenberg again, where he spent about a year engaged in unremitting study and research. He then returned to Berlin with a view to making literature his profession; and the next three years were among the busiest of his life. Besides translating for the booksellers, he issued several numbers of the *Theatralische Bibliothek*, a periodical similar to that which he had begun with Mylius; he also continued his work as critic to the *Vossische Zeitung*. In 1754 he gave a particularly brilliant proof of his critical powers in his *Vademecum für Herrn S. G. Lange*; as a retort to that writer's overbearing criticism, Lessing exposed with scathing satire Lange's errors in his popular translation of Horace.

By 1753 Lessing felt that his position was sufficiently assured to allow of him issuing an edition of his collected writings (*Schriften*, 6 vols., 1753–1755). They included his lyrics and epigrams, most of which had already appeared during his first residence in Berlin in a volume of *Kleinigkeiten*, published anonymously. Much more important were the papers entitled *Rettungen*, in which he undertook to vindicate the character of various writers—Horace and writers of the Reformation period, such as Cochlaeus and Cardanus—who had been misunderstood or falsely judged by preceding generations. The *Schriften* also contained Lessing's early plays, and one new one, *Miss Sara Sampson* (1755). Hitherto Lessing had, as a dramatist, followed the methods of contemporary French comedy as cultivated in Leipzig; *Miss Sara Sampson*, however, marks the beginning of a new period in the history of the German drama. This play, based more or less on Lillo's *Merchant of London*, and influenced in its character-drawing by the novels of Richardson, is the first *bürgerliches Trauerspiel*, or "tragedy of common life" in German. It was performed for the first time at Frankfort-on-Oder in the summer of 1755, and received with great favour. Among Lessing's chief friends during his second residence in Berlin were the philosopher Moses Mendelssohn (1729–1786), in association with whom he wrote in 1755 an admirable treatise, *Pope ein Metaphysiker!* tracing sharply the lines which separate the poet from the philosopher. He was also on intimate terms with C. F. Nicolai (1733–1811), a Berlin bookseller and rationalistic writer, and with the "German Horace" K. W. Ramler (1725–1798); he had also made the acquaintance of J. W. L. Gleim (1719–1803), the Halberstadt poet, and E. C. von Kleist (1715–1759), a Prussian officer, whose fine poem, *Der Frühling*, had won for him Lessing's warm esteem.

In October 1755 Lessing settled in Leipzig with a view to devoting himself more exclusively to the drama. In 1756 he accepted the invitation of Gottfried Winkler, a wealthy young merchant, to accompany him on a foreign tour for three years. They did not, however, get beyond Amsterdam, for the outbreak of the Seven Years' War made it necessary for Winkler to return home without loss of time. A disagreement with his patron shortly after resulted in Lessing's sudden dismissal; he demanded compensation and, although in the end the court decided in his favour, it was not until the case had dragged on for about six years. At this time Lessing began the study of medieval literature to which attention had been drawn by the Swiss critics, Bodmer and Breitinger, and wrote occasional criticisms for Nicolai's *Bibliothek der schönen Wissenschaften*. In Leipzig Lessing had also an opportunity of developing his friendship with Kleist who happened to be stationed there. The two men were mutually attracted, and a warm affection sprang up betweem them. In 1758 Kleist's regiment being ordered to new quarters, Lessing decided not to remain behind him and returned again to Berlin. Kleist was mortally wounded in the following year at the battle of Kunersdorf.

Lessing's third residence in Berlin was made memorable by the *Briefe, die neueste Literatur betreffend* (1759–1765), a series of critical essays—written in the form of letters to a wounded officer—on the principal books that had appeared since the beginning of the Seven Years' War. The scheme was suggested by Nicolai, by whom the *Letters* were published. In Lessing's share in this publication, his critical powers and methods are to be seen at their best. He insisted especially on the necessity of truth to nature in the imaginative presentation of the facts of life, and in one letter he boldly proclaimed the superiority of Shakespeare to Corneille, Racine and Voltaire. At the same time he marked the immutable conditions to which even genius must submit if it is to succeed in its appeal to our sympathies. While in Berlin at this time, he edited with Ramler a selection from the writings of F. von Logau, an epigrammatist of the 17th century, and introduced to the German public the *Lieder eines preussischen Grenadiers*, by J. W. L. Gleim. In 1759 he published *Philotas*, a prose tragedy in one act, and also a complete collection of his fables, preceded by an essay on the nature of the fable. The latter is one of his best essays on criticism, defining with perfect lucidity what is meant by "action" in works of the imagination, and distinguishing the action of the fable from that of the epic and the drama.

In 1760, feeling the need of some change of scene and work, Lessing went to Breslau, where he obtained the post of secretary to General Tauentzien, to whom Kleist had introduced him in Leipzig. Tauentzien was not only a general in the Prussian army, but governor of Breslau, and director of the mint. During the four years which Lessing spent in Breslau, he associated chiefly with Prussian officers, went much into society, and developed a dangerous fondness for the gaming table. He did not, however, lose sight of his true goal; he collected a large library, and, after the conclusion of the Seven Years' War, in 1763, he resumed more enthusiastically than ever the studies which had been partially interrupted. He investigated the early history of Christianity and penetrated more deeply than any contemporary thinker into the significance of Spinoza's philosophy. He also found time for the studies which were ultimately to appear in the volume entitled *Laokoon*, and in fresh spring mornings he sketched in a garden the plan of *Minna von Barnhelm*.

After resigning his Breslau appointment in 1765, he hoped for a time to obtain a congenial appointment in Dresden, but nothing came of this and he was again compelled, much against his will, to return to Berlin. His friends there exerted themselves to obtain for him the office of keeper of the royal library, but Frederick had not forgotten Lessing's quarrel with Voltaire, and declined to consider his claims. During the two years which Lessing now spent in the Prussian capital, he was restless and unhappy, yet it was during this period that he published two of his greatest works, *Laokoon, oder über die Grenzen der Malerei und Poesie* (1766) and *Minna von Barnhelm* (1767). The aim of *Laokoon*, which ranks as a classic, not only in German but in European literature, is to define by analysis the limitations of poetry and the plastic arts. Many of his conclusions have been corrected and extended by later criticism; but he indicated more decisively than any of his predecessors the fruitful principle that each art is subject to definite conditions, and that it can accomplish great results only by limiting itself to its special function. The most valuable parts of the work are those which relate to poetry, of which he had a much more intimate knowledge than of sculpture and painting. His exposition of the methods of Homer and Sophocles is especially suggestive, and he may be said to have marked an epoch in the appreciation of these writers, and of Greek literature generally. The power of *Minna von Barnhelm*, Lessing's greatest drama. was also immediately recognized. Tellheim, the hero of the comedy, is an admirable study of a manly and sensitive soldier, with somewhat exaggerated ideas of conventional honour; and Minna, the heroine, is one of the brightest and most attractive figures in German

government in or
Canal. Once this
towards those who
betta. He afterwar
offered him: for the S
In 1873 he became
and Asia by a railw
He subsequently enc
transform the Sahara
Belgians having form
Lesseps accepted the
facilitated M. de Braz
that he subsequently
These stations were
1879 a congress assem
Society at Paris, under
le Noury, and voted
Canal. Public opinion,
de Lesseps as the hea
occasion that Gambett
Grand Français. He
and notwithstanding t
undertook to carry out
CANAL and FRANCE: *H*
always avoided, was hi
winding-up of the Pa
in the month of Decem
Republic, seeking for a
ment, hoped to bring
of the Panama Comp
made that the governm
judicial proceedings ta
son Charles (b. 1849) a
Charles de Lesseps, a vi
tried to divert the sto
reaching his father. H
alone the burden of th
the consequences of the
was to oblige him to sp
England, where his pa
Suez Canal had won for
he was able to see the g
name of his father were l

Ferdinand de Lesseps
December 1894. He had
with Mlle Autard de Br
of Mauritius; and eleven
survived him. M. de L
Academy, of the Academ
societies, Grand Cross of t
of India, and had receive
According to some account
events that took place du
Others report that, feelin
gathered clouds, and aware
had the moral courage to p
he did not wish to afflict, as t
to conceal the truth from hi
surprising if we relied upon
a person who knew him i
never thinking of himself, c
supremely kind, he did not
as evil. Of a confiding nat
by himself. This naturall
every one felt in him had p
and rare devotions. He sho
what a gift he possessed for
ducted. He set duty abov
degree a reverence for honour,
at the service of everything
that nothing could
equilibrium gave

patriotism, an extravagant respect for rank, and exclusive devotion to any particular church.

Lessing's theological opinions exposed him to much petty persecution, and he was in almost constant straits for money. Nothing, however, broke his manly and generous spirit. To the end he was always ready to help those who appealed to him for aid, and he devoted himself with growing ardour to the search for truth. He formed many new plans of work, but in the course of 1780 it became evident to his friends that he would not be able much longer to continue his labours. His health had been undermined by excessive work and anxiety, and after a short illness he died at Brunswick on the 15th of February 1781. "We lose much in him," wrote Goethe after Lessing's death, "more than we think." It may be questioned whether there is any other writer to whom the Germans owe a deeper debt of gratitude. He was succeeded by poets and philosophers who gave Germany for a time the first place in the intellectual life of the world, and it was Lessing, as they themselves acknowledged, who prepared the way for their achievements. Without attaching himself to any particular system of philosophical doctrine, he fought error incessantly, and in regard to art, poetry and the drama and religion, suggested ideas which kindled the enthusiasm of aspiring minds, and stimulated their highest energies.

Bibliography.—The first edition of Lessing's collected works, edited by his brother Karl Gotthelf Lessing (1740–1812), J. J. Eschenburg and F. Nicolai, appeared in 26 vols. between 1791 and 1794, as a continuation of the *Vermischte Schriften*, edited by Lessing himself in 4 vols. (1771–1785); the *Sämtliche Schriften*, edited by Karl Lachmann, were published in 13 vols. (1825–1828), this edition being subsequently re-edited by W. von Maltzahn (1853–1857) and by F. Muncker (21 vols., 1886 ff.), the last mentioned being the standard edition of Lessing's works. Other editions are *Lessings Werke*, published by Hempel, under the editorship of various scholars (23 vols., 1868–1877); an illustrated edition published by Grote in 8 vols. (1875, new ed., 1882); *Lessings Werke*, edited by R. Boxberger and H. Blümner, in Kürschner's *Deutsche Nationalliteratur*, vols. 58–71 (1883–1890). There are also many popular editions. Lessing's correspondence is included in the Lachmann editions and in that of Hempel (edited by C. C. Redlich, 1879; *Nachträge und Berichtigungen*, 1886); his correspondence with his wife was published as early as 1789 (2 vols., new edition by A. Schöne, 1885). The chief biographies of Lessing are by K. G. Lessing (his brother), (1793–1795, a reprint in Reclam's *Universalbibliothek*); by J. F. Schink (1825); T. W. Danzel and G. E. Guhrauer (1850–1853, 2nd ed. by W. von Maltzahn and R. Boxberger, 2 vols., 1880–1881); A. Stahr (2 vols., 1859, 9th ed., 1887); J. Sime, *Lessing, his Life and Works* (2 vols., 1877); H. Zimmern, *Lessing's Life and Works* (1878); H. Düntzer, *Lessings Leben* (1882); E. Schmidt, *Lessing, Geschichte seines Lebens und seiner Schriften* (2 vols., 1884–1892, 3rd ed., 1910)—this is the most complete biography; T. W. Rolleston, *Lessing* (in "Great Writers," 1889); K. Borinski, *Lessing* (2 vols., 1900). Cf. also C. Hebler, *Lessing-Studien* (1862); A. Lehmann, *Forschungen über Lessings Sprache* (1875); W. Cosack, *Materialien zu Lessings Hamburgischer Dramaturgie* (1876, 2nd ed., 1891); H. Blümner, *Lessings Laokoon* (1876, 2nd ed., 1880); H. Blümner, *Laokoon-Studien* (2 vols., 1881–1882); K. Fischer, *Lessing als Reformator der deutschen Literatur dargestellt* (2 vols., 1881, 2nd ed., 1888); B. A. Wagner, *Lessing-Forschungen* (1881); J. W. Braun, *Lessing im Urteile seiner Zeitgenossen* (3 vols., 1884); P. Albrecht, *Lessings Plagiate* (6 vols., 1890 ff.); K. Werder, *Vorlesungen über Lessings Nathan* (1892); G. Kettner, *Lessings Dramen im Lichte ihrer und unserer Zeit* (1904). Translations of Lessing's *Dramatic Works* (2 vols., 1878), edited by E. Bell, and of *Laokoon, Dramatic Notes and the Representation of Death by the Ancients*, by E. C. Beasley and H. Zimmern (1 vol., 1879), will be found in Bohn's "Standard Library." (J. Si.; J. G. R.)

LESSON (through Fr. *leçon* from Lat. *lectio*, reading; *legere*, to read), properly a certain portion of a book appointed to be read aloud, or learnt for repetition, hence anything learnt or studied, a course of instruction or study. A specific meaning of the word is that of a portion of Scripture or other religious writings appointed to be read at divine service, in accordance with a table known as a "lectionary." In the Church of England the lectionary is so ordered that most of the Old Testament is read through during the year as the First Lesson at Morning and Evening Prayer, and as the Second Lesson the whole of the New Testament, except Revelation, of which only portions are read. (See Lection and Lectionary.)

LESTE, a desert wind, similar to the Leveche (*q.v.*), observed in Madeira. It blows from an easterly direction in autumn, winter and spring, rarely in summer, and is of intense dryness, sometimes reducing the relative humidity at Funchal to below 20%. The Leste is commonly accompanied by clouds of fine red sand.

L'ESTRANGE, SIR ROGER (1616–1704), English pamphleteer on the royalist and court side during the Restoration epoch, but principally remarkable as the first English man of letters of any distinction who made journalism a profession, was born at Hunstanton in Norfolk on the 17th of December 1616. In 1644, during the civil war, he headed a conspiracy to seize the town of Lynn for the king, under circumstances which led to his being condemned to death as a spy. The sentence, however, was not executed, and after four years' imprisonment in Newgate he escaped to the Continent. He was excluded from the Act of Indemnity, but in 1653 was pardoned by Cromwell upon his personal solicitation, and lived quietly until the Restoration, when after some delay his services and sufferings were acknowledged by his appointment as licenser of the press. This office was administered by him in the spirit which might be expected from a zealous cavalier. He made himself notorious, not merely by the severity of his literary censorship, but by his vigilance in the suppression of clandestine printing. In 1663 (see Newspapers) he commenced the publication of the *Public Intelligencer* and the *News*, from which eventually developed the famous official paper the *London Gazette* in 1665. In 1679 he again became prominent with the *Observator*, a journal specially designed to vindicate the court from the charge of a secret inclination to popery. He discredited the Popish Plot, and the suspicion he thus incurred was increased by the conversion of his daughter to Roman Catholicism, but there seems no reason to question the sincerity of his own attachment to the Church of England. In 1687 he gave a further proof of independence by discontinuing the *Observator* from his unwillingness to advocate James II.'s Edict of Toleration, although he had previously gone all lengths in support of the measures of the court. The Revolution cost him his office as licenser, and the remainder of his life was spent in obscurity. He died in 1704. It is to L'Estrange's credit that among the agitations of a busy political life he should have found time for much purely literary work as a translator of Josephus, Cicero, Seneca, Quevedo and other standard authors.

LESUEUR, DANIEL, the pseudonym of Jeanne Lapauze, *née* Loiseau (1860–), French poet and novelist, who was born in Paris in 1860. She published a volume of poems, *Fleurs d'avril* (1882), which was crowned by the Academy. She also wrote some powerful novels dealing with contemporary life: *Le Mariage de Gabrielle* (1882); *Un Mystérieux Amour* (1892), with a series of philosophical sonnets; *L'Amant de Geneviève* (1883); *Marcelle* (1885); *Une Vie tragique* (1890); *Justice de femme* (1893); *Comédienne Haine d'amour* (1894); *Honneur d'une femme* (1901); *La Force du passé* (1905). Her poems were collected in 1895. She published in 1905 a book on the economic status of women, *L'Évolution féminine*; and in 1891–1893 a translation (2 vols.) of the works of Lord Byron, which was awarded a prize by the Academy. Her *Masque d'amour*, a five-act play based on her novel (1904) of the same name, was produced at the Théâtre Sarah Bernhardt in 1905. She received the ribbon of the Legion of Honour in 1900, and the prix Vitet from the French Academy in 1905. She married in 1904 Henry Lapauze (b. 1867), a well-known writer on art.

LE SUEUR, EUSTACHE (1617–1655), one of the founders of the French Academy of painting, was born on the 19th of November 1617 at Paris, where he passed his whole life, and where he died on the 30th of April 1655. His early death and retired habits have combined to give an air of romance to his simple history, which has been decorated with as many fables as that of Claude. We are told that, persecuted by Le Brun, who was jealous of his ability, he became the intimate friend and correspondent of Poussin, and it is added that, broken-hearted at the death of his wife, Le Sueur retired to the monastery of the Chartreux and died in the arms of the prior. All this, however, is pure fiction. The facts of Le Sueur's life are these. He was

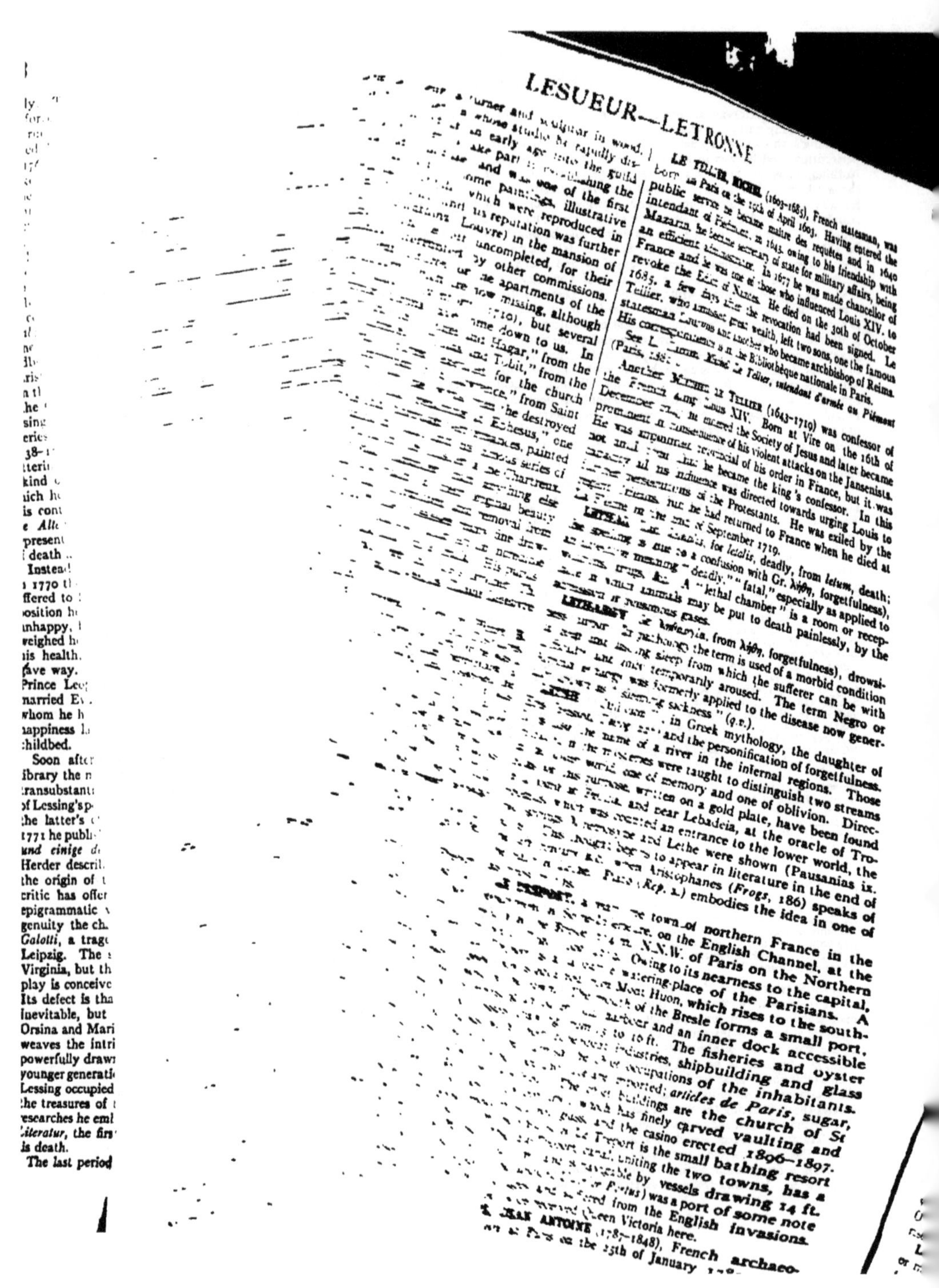

[illegible] turner and sculptor in wood, [illegible] whose studio he rapidly dis- [illegible] at an early age into the guild [illegible] take part in [illegible] the [illegible] and was one of the first [illegible] some paintings, illustrative [illegible] which were reproduced in [illegible] and his reputation was further [illegible] Louvre) in the mansion of [illegible] uncompleted, for their [illegible] by other commissions. [illegible] the apartments of the [illegible] are now missing, although [illegible] (1710), but several [illegible] come down to us. In [illegible] and Hagar," from the [illegible] and Tobit," from the [illegible] for the church [illegible] ence," from Saint [illegible] the destroyed [illegible] Ephesus," one [illegible] paintings, painted [illegible] famous series of [illegible] the Chartreux [illegible] anything else [illegible] original beauty [illegible] removal from [illegible] fine draw- [illegible]

LE TELLIER, MICHEL (1603–1685), French statesman, was born in Paris on the 19th of April 1603. Having entered the public service he became maître des requêtes and in 1640 intendant of [illegible], [illegible] 1643, owing to his friendship with Mazarin, he became secretary of state for military affairs, being an efficient [illegible]. In 1677 he was made chancellor of France and he was one of those who influenced Louis XIV. to revoke the Edict of Nantes. He died on the 30th of October 1685, a few days after the revocation had been signed. Le Tellier, who amassed great wealth, left two sons, one the famous statesman Louvois and another who became archbishop of Reims. His correspondence is in the Bibliothèque nationale in Paris.

See L. [illegible], *Michel Le Tellier, intendant d'armée au Piémont* (Paris, 188[illegible]).

Another MICHEL LE TELLIER (1643–1719) was confessor of the French king Louis XIV. Born at Vire on the 16th of December [illegible], he entered the Society of Jesus and later became prominent in consequence of his violent attacks on the Jansenists. He was [illegible] provincial of his order in France, but it was not until [illegible] that he became the king's confessor. In this capacity all his influence was directed towards urging Louis to further persecutions of the Protestants. He was exiled by the [illegible], but he had returned to France when he died at La Flèche on the [illegible] of September 1719.

LETHAL [illegible], for *letalis*, deadly, from *letum*, death; the spelling is due to a confusion with Gr. λήθη, forgetfulness), an [illegible] meaning "deadly," "fatal," especially as applied to [illegible], drugs, &c. A "lethal chamber" is a room or receptacle in which animals may be put to death painlessly, by the agency of poisonous gases.

LETHARGY (Gr. ληθαργία, from λήθη, forgetfulness), drowsi[illegible] pathology the term is used of a morbid condition [illegible] sleep from which the sufferer can be with [illegible] temporarily aroused. The term Negro or [illegible] was formerly applied to the disease now gener[illegible] "sleeping sickness" (*q.v.*).

LETHE [illegible], in Greek mythology, the daughter of [illegible] and the personification of forgetfulness. [illegible] the name of a river in the infernal regions. Those [illegible] in the mysteries were taught to distinguish two streams [illegible] one of memory and one of oblivion. Direc[illegible] this purpose, written on a gold plate, have been found [illegible] and near Lebadeia, at the oracle of Tro[illegible] which was regarded as an entrance to the lower world, the [illegible] Mnemosyne and Lethe were shown (Pausanias ix. [illegible]). This [illegible] begins to appear in literature in the end of [illegible] century B.C., when Aristophanes (*Frogs*, 186) speaks of [illegible]. Plato (*Rep.* x.) embodies the idea in one of [illegible]

LE TRÉPORT, a [illegible] town of northern France in the [illegible] on the English Channel, at the [illegible] N.N.W. of Paris on the Northern [illegible]. Owing to its nearness to the capital, [illegible] watering-place of the Parisians. A [illegible] Mont Huon, which rises to the south[illegible] of the Bresle forms a small port, [illegible] harbour and an inner dock accessible [illegible] to 16 ft. The fisheries and oyster [illegible] industries, shipbuilding and glass [illegible] occupations of the inhabitants. [illegible] imported; *articles de Paris*, sugar, [illegible] buildings are the church of St [illegible] which has finely carved vaulting and [illegible] glass and the casino erected 1896–1897. [illegible] Le Tréport is the small bathing resort [illegible] uniting the two towns, has a [illegible] navigable by vessels drawing 14 ft. [illegible] *Portus*) was a port of some note [illegible] from the English invasions. [illegible] Queen Victoria here.

LETRONNE, JEAN ANTOINE (1787–1848), French archaeo[illegible] born at Paris on the 25th of January 17[illegible] father, a poor engraver, sent him to study art under the painter David, but his own tastes were literary, and he became a student in the Collège de France, where it is said he used to exercise his already strongly developed critical faculty by correcting for his own amusement old and bad texts of Greek authors, afterwards comparing the results with the latest and most approved editions. From 1810 to 1812 he travelled in France, Switzerland and Italy, and on his return to Paris published an *Essai critique sur la topographie de Syracuse* (1812), designed to elucidate Thucydides. Two years later appeared his *Recherches géographiques et critiques* on the *De Mensura Orbis Terrae* of Dicuil. In 1815 he was commissioned by government to complete the translation of Strabo which had been begun by Laporte-Dutheil, and in March 1816 be was one of those who were admitted to the Academy of Inscriptions by royal ordinance, having previously contributed a *Mémoire*, "On the Metrical System of the Egyptians," which had been crowned. Further promotion came rapidly; in 1817 he was appointed director of the École des Chartes, in 1819 inspector-general of the university, and in 1831 professor of history in the Collège de France. This chair he exchanged in 1838 for that of archaeology, and in 1840 he succeeded Pierre C. François Daunou (1761–1840) as keeper of the national archives. Meanwhile he had published, among other works, *Considérations générales sur l'évaluation des monnaies grecques et romaines et sur la valeur de l'or et de l'argent avant la découverte de l'Amérique* (1817), *Recherches pour servir à l'histoire d'Égypte pendant la domination des Grecs et des Romains* (1823), and *Sur l'origine grecque des zodiaques prétendus égyptiens* (1837). By the last-named he finally exploded a fallacy which had up to that time vitiated the chronology of contemporary Egyptologists. His *Diplômes et chartres de l'époque Mérovingienne sur papyrus et sur vélin* were published in 1844. The most important work of Letronne is the *Recueil des inscriptions grecques et latines de l'Égypte*, of which the first volume appeared in 1842, and the second in 1848. He died at Paris on the 14th of December 1848.

LETTER (through Fr. *lettre* from Lat. *littera* or *litera*, letter of the alphabet; the origin of the Latin word is obscure; it has probably no connexion with the root of *linere*, to smear, *i.e.* with wax, for an inscription with a stilus), a character or symbol expressing any one of the elementary sounds into which a spoken word may be analysed, one of the members of an alphabet. As applied to things written, the word follows mainly the meanings of the Latin plural *litterae*, the most common meaning attaching to the word being that of a written communication from one person to another, an epistle (*q.v.*). For the means adopted to secure the transmission of letters see POST AND POSTAL SERVICE. The word is also, particularly in the plural, applied to many legal and formal written documents, as in letters patent, letters rogatory and dismissory, &c. The Latin use of the plural is also followed in the employment of "letters" in the sense of literature (*q.v.*) or learning.

LETTERKENNY, a market town of Co. Donegal, Ireland, 23 m. W. by S. of Londonderry by the Londonderry and Lough Swilly and Letterkenny railway. Pop. (1901) 2370. It has a harbour at Port Ballyrane, 1 m. distant on Lough Swilly. In the market square a considerable trade in grain, flax and provisions is prosecuted. Rope-making and shirt-making are industries. The handsome Roman Catholic cathedral for the diocese of Raphoe occupies a commanding site, and cost a large sum, as it contains carving from Rome, glass from Munich and a pulpit of Irish and Carrara marble. It was consecrated in 1901. There is a Catholic college dedicated to St Ewnan. The town, which is governed by an urban district council, is a centre for visitors to the county. Its name signifies the "hill of the O'Cannanans," a family who lorded over Tyrconnell before the rise of the O'Donnells.

LETTER OF CREDIT, a letter, open or sealed, from a banker or merchant, containing a request to some other person or firm to advance the bearer of the letter, or some other person named therein, upon the credit of the writer a particular or an unlimited sum of money. A letter of credit is either general or special. It is general when addressed to merchants or other persons in general, requesting an advance to a third person, and special when addressed to a particular person by name requesting him to make such an advance. A letter of credit is not a negotiable instrument. When a letter of credit is given for the purchase of goods, the letter of credit usually states the particulars of the merchandise against which bills are to be drawn, and shipping documents (bills of lading, invoices, insurance policies) are usually attached to the draft for acceptance.

LETTERS PATENT. It is a rule alike of common law and sound policy that grants of freehold interests, franchises, liberties, &c., by the sovereign to a subject should be made only after due consideration, and in a form readily accessible to the public. These ends are attained in England through the agency of that piece of constitutional machinery known as "letters patent." It is here proposed to consider only the characteristics of letters patent generally. The law relating to letters patent for inventions is dealt with under the heading PATENTS.

Letters patent (*litterae patentes*) are letters addressed by the sovereign "to all to whom these presents shall come," reciting the grant of some dignity, office, monopoly, franchise or other privilege to the patentee. They are not sealed up, but are left open (hence the term "patent"), and are recorded in the Patent Rolls in the Record Office, or in the case of very recent grants, in the Chancery Enrolment Office, so that all subjects of the realm may read and be bound by their contents. In this respect they differ from certain other letters of the sovereign directed to particular persons and for particular purposes, which, not being proper for public inspection, are closed up and sealed on the outside, and are thereupon called *writs close* (*litterae clausae*) and are recorded in the Close Rolls. Letters patent are used to put into commission various powers inherent in the crown—legislative powers, as when the sovereign entrusts to others the duty of opening parliament or assenting to bills; judicial powers, *e.g.* of gaol delivery; executive powers, as when the duties of Treasurer and Lord High Admiral are assigned to commissioners of the Treasury and Admiralty (Anson, *Const.* ii. 47). Letters patent are also used to incorporate bodies by charter—in the British colonies, this mode of legislation is frequently applied to joint stock companies (cf. Rev. Stats. Ontario, c. 191, s. 9)—to grant a *congé d'élire* to a dean and chapter to elect a bishop, or licence to convocation to amend canons; to grant pardon, and to confer certain offices and dignities. Among grants of offices, &c., made by letters patent the following may be enumerated: offices in the Heralds' College; the dignities of a peer, baronet and knight bachelor; the appointments of lord-lieutenant, custos rotulorum of counties, judge of the High Court and Indian and Colonial judgeships, king's counsel, crown livings; the offices of attorney- and solicitor-general, commander-in-chief, master of the horse, keeper of the privy seal, postmaster-general, king's printer; grants of separate courts of quarter-sessions. The fees payable in respect of the grant of various forms of letters patent are fixed by orders of the lord chancellor, dated 20th of June 1871, 18th of July 1871 and 11th of Aug. 1881. (These orders are set out at length in the *Statutory Rules and Orders Revised* (ed. 1904), vol. ii. *tit.* "Clerk of the Crown in Chancery," pp. i. et seq.) Formerly each colonial governor was appointed and commissioned by letters patent under the great seal of the United Kingdom. But since 1875, the practice has been to create the office of governor in each colony by letters patent, and then to make each appointment to the office by commission under the Royal Sign Manual and to give to the governor so appointed instructions in a uniform shape under the Royal Sign Manual. The letters patent, commission and instructions, are commonly described as the Governor's Commission (see Jenkyns, *British Rule and Jurisdiction beyond the Seas*, p. 100; the forms now in use are printed in Appx. iv. Also the *Statutory Rules and Codes Revised*, ed. 1904, under the title of the colony to which they relate). The Colonial Letters Patent Act 1863 provides that letters patent shall not take effect in the colonies or possessions beyond the seas until their publication there by proclamation or otherwise (s. 2), and shall

the so
who pl
tinguis
of mast
academy
twelve p
of the H
tapestry,
enhanced
Lambert d
execution
Amongst th
king and qu
they were e
works produc
the gallery of
mansion of De
Fieubet collec
of Saint Gerva
Germain de l'A
abbey of Marn
of Le Sueur's m
for the goldsmi
the "Life of St
These last hav
which Le Sueu
survives in spi
the wall to can
ings (reproduce
quantity, chiefl
who aided him
Goussé, and th
and Patel the l

Most of his
Audran, Seb. L
Le Sueur's work
charming draug
varied shades of
power to rende
always restraine
please complete
recourse to conv
colour except wi
of Vouet; yet his
show that he was
we get direct ref
series—we recogn
nomy of varied a

See Guillet de
peintres; Vitet,
Vies des peintres.

LESUEUR, JE
musical compose
1763) at Drucat-
in the cathedral
at various church
the musical dire
Paris, where he
with a full orche
after a retirement
produced *La Ca*
Feydeau in Paris.
(1795) Lesueur w
but was dismisse
Méhul. Lesueur
to Napoleon, and
also composed for
Deum. Louis XVI
appointed him (18
servatoire; and at
pupils, Hector Berli
and Charles Gounod.
composed eight op
All his works are
See Raoul

[illegible] his will, he could decide without heeding the laws, and even in a sense contrary to the laws. This was an early conception, and in early times the order in question was simply verbal; thus some letters patent of Henry III. of France in 1576 (Isambert, *Anciennes lois françaises*, xiv. 278) state that François de Montmorency was "prisoner in our castle of the Bastille in Paris by verbal command" of the late king Charles IX. But in the 14th century the principle was introduced that the order should be written, and hence arose the *lettre de cachet*. The *lettre de cachet* belonged to the class of *lettres closes*, as opposed to *lettres patentes*, which contained the expression of the legal and permanent will of the king, and had to be furnished with the seal of state affixed by the chancellor. The *lettres de cachet*, on the contrary, were signed simply by a secretary of state (formerly known as *secrétaire des commandements*) for the king; they bore merely the imprint of the king's privy seal, from which circumstance they were often called, in the 14th and 15th centuries, *lettres de petit signet* or *lettres de petit cachet*, and were entirely exempt from the control of the chancellor.

While serving the government as a silent weapon against [illegible] adversaries or dangerous writers and as a means of [illegible] of high birth without the scandal of a suit at [illegible] the *lettres de cachet* had many other uses. They were [illegible] by the police in dealing with prostitutes, and on their [illegible] were shut up in hospitals and sometimes in [illegible]. They were also often used by heads of families as a [illegible] for protecting the family honour from [illegible] conduct of sons; wives, too, took [illegible] to curb the profligacy of husbands and [illegible] versa. They were issued by the intermediary on the advice [illegible] in the provinces and of the lieutenant of police [illegible]. In reality the secretary of state issued them in a [illegible] manner, and in most cases the king was [illegible]. In the 18th century it is certain that the [illegible] containing the name [illegible] were directed; the recipient, [illegible] in order to make the letter [illegible].

[illegible] against the *lettres de cachet* were made continually [illegible] and by the provincial parlements, [illegible]. In 1648 the sovereign [illegible] momentary suppression in a kind [illegible] imposed upon the crown, [illegible]. It was not until the reign of [illegible] against this abuse became clearly [illegible] Malesherbes during [illegible] some measure of justice [illegible] the baron de Breteuil, a [illegible] addressed a circular to the [illegible] with a view to preventing [illegible] the issue of *lettres de cachet*. [illegible] demanded their suppression, [illegible] at Paris made some exceedingly [illegible] are important for the light they [illegible]. The crown, however, did [illegible] weapon, and in a declaration to the [illegible] session of the 23rd of June 1789 [illegible] it absolutely. *Lettres de cachet* [illegible] Constituent Assembly, but Napoleon re[illegible] by a political measure in the decree [illegible] on the state prisons. This was one of [illegible] against him by the *senatus-consulte* of the [illegible] pronounced his fall "considering that [illegible] constitutional laws by the decrees on the [illegible]

[illegible], *Des Lettres de cachet et des prisons d'état* [illegible] the dungeon at Vincennes into which [illegible] *lettre de cachet*, one of the ablest and [illegible] which had an immense circulation and [illegible] with a dedication to the duke of Norfolk [illegible], *Les Lettres de cachet à Paris* (Paris, [illegible], *Les Lettres de cachet sous l'ancien* [illegible]

(J. P. E.)

LETTUCE, known botanically as *Lactuca sativa* (nat. ord. Compositae), a hardy annual, highly esteemed as a salad plant. The London market-gardeners make preparation for the first main crop of Cos lettuces in the open ground early in August, a frame being set on a shallow hotbed, and, the stimulus of heat not being required, this is allowed to subside till the first week in October, when the soil, consisting of leaf-mould mixed with a little sand, is put on 6 or 7 in. thick, so that the surface is within 4½ in. of the sashes. The best time for sowing is found to be about the 11th of October, one of the best varieties being Lobjoits Green Cos. When the seeds begin to germinate the sashes are drawn quite off in favourable weather during the day, and put on, but tilted, at night in wet weather. Very little watering is required, and the aim should be to keep the plants gently moving till the days begin to lengthen. In January a more active growth is encouraged, and in mild winters a considerable extent of the planting out is done, but in private gardens the preferable time would be February. The ground should be light and rich, and well manured below, and the plants put out at 1 ft. apart each way with the dibble. Frequent stirring of the ground with the hoe greatly encourages the growth of the plants. A second sowing should be made about the 5th of November, and a third in frames about the end of January or beginning of February. In March a sowing may be made in some warm situation out of doors; successional sowings may be made in the open border about every third or fourth week till August, about the middle of which month a crop of Brown Cos, Hardy Hammersmith or Hardy White Cos should be sown, the latter being the most reliable in a severe winter. These plants may be put out early in October on the sides of ridges facing the south or at the front of a south wall, beyond the reach of drops from the copings, being planted 6 or 8 in. apart. Young lettuce plants should be thinned out in the seed-beds before they crowd or draw each other, and transplanted as soon as possible after two or three leaves are formed. Some cultivators prefer that the summer crops should not be transplanted, but sown where they are to stand, the plants being merely thinned out; but transplanting checks the running to seed, and makes the most of the ground.

For a winter supply by gentle forcing, the Hardy Hammersmith and Brown Dutch Cabbage lettuces, and the Brown Cos and Green Paris Cos lettuces, should be sown about the middle of August and in the beginning of September, in rich light soil, the plants being pricked out 3 in. apart in a prepared bed, as soon as the first two leaves are fully formed. About the middle of October the plants should be taken up carefully with balls attached to the roots, and should be placed in a mild hotbed of well-prepared dung (about 55°) covered about 1 ft. deep with a compost of sandy peat, leaf-mould and a little well-decomposed manure. The Cos and Brown Dutch varieties should be planted about 9 in. apart. Give plenty of air when the weather permits, and protect from frost. For winter work Stanstead Park Cabbage Lettuce is greatly favoured now by London market-gardeners, as it stands the winter well. Lee's Immense is another good variety, while All the Year Round may be sown for almost any season, but is better perhaps for summer crops.

There are two races of the lettuce, the Cos lettuce, with erect oblong heads, and the Cabbage lettuce, with round or spreading heads,—the former generally crisp, the latter soft and flabby in texture. Some of the best lettuces for general purposes of the two classes are the following:—

Cos: White Paris Cos, best for summer; Green Paris Cos, hardier than the white; Brown Cos, Lobjoits Green Cos, one of the hardiest and best for winter; Hardy White Cos.

Cabbage: Hammersmith Hardy Green: Stanstead Park, very hardy, good for winter; Tom Thumb; Brown Dutch; Neapolitan, best for summer; All the Year Round; Golden Ball, good for forcing in private establishments.

Lactuca virosa, the strong-scented lettuce, contains an alkaloid which has the power of dilating the pupil and may possibly be identical with hyoscyamine, though this point is as yet not determined. No variety of lettuce is now used for any medicinal purpose, though there is probably some slight foundation for the belief that the lettuce has faint narcotic properties.

LEUCADIA, the ancient name of one of the Ionian Islands, now Santa Maura (*q.v.*), and of its chief town (Hamaxichi).

LEUCIPPUS, Greek philosopher, born at Miletus (or Elea), founder of the Atomistic theory, contemporary of Zeno, Empedocles and Anaxagoras. His fame was so completely overshadowed by that of Democritus, who subsequently developed the theory into a system, that his very existence was denied by Epicurus (Diog. Laërt. x. 7), followed in modern times by E. Rohde. Epicurus, however, distinguishes Leucippus from Democritus, and Aristotle and Theophrastus expressly credit him with the invention of Atomism. There seems, therefore, no reason to doubt his existence, although nothing is known of his life, and even his birthplace is uncertain. Between Leucippus and Democritus there is an interval of at least forty years; accordingly, while the beginnings of Atomism are closely connected with the doctrines of the Eleatics, the system as developed by Democritus is conditioned by the sophistical views of his time, especially those of Protagoras. While Leucippus's notion of Being agreed generally with that of the Eleatics, he postulated its plurality (atoms) and motion, and the reality of not-Being (the void) in which his atoms moved.

See DEMOCRITUS. On the Rohde-Diels controversy as to the existence of Leucippus, see F. Lortzing in Bursian's *Jahresbericht*, vol. cxvi. (1904); also J. Burnet, *Early Greek Philosophy* (1892).

LEUCITE, a rock-forming mineral composed of potassium and aluminium metasilicate $KAl(SiO_3)_2$. Crystals have the form of cubic icositetrahedra {211}, but, as first observed by Sir David Brewster in 1821, they are not optically isotropic, and are therefore pseudo-cubic. Goniometric measurements made by G. vom Rath in 1873 led him to refer the crystals to the tetragonal system, the faces *o* being distinct from those lettered *i* in the adjoining figure. Optical investigations have since proved the crystals to be still more complex in character, and to consist of several orthorhombic or monoclinic individuals, which are optically biaxial and repeatedly twinned, giving rise to twin-lamellae and to striations on the faces. When the crystals are raised to a temperature of about 500° C. they become optically isotropic, the twin-lamellae and striations disappearing, reappearing, however, when the crystals are again cooled. This pseudo-cubic character of leucite is exactly the same as that of the mineral boracite (*q.v.*).

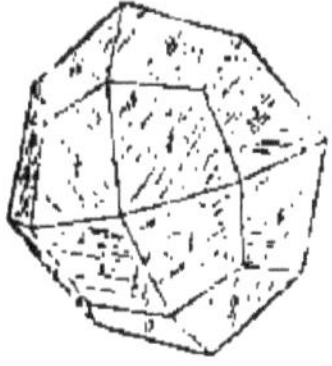

The crystals are white (hence the name suggested by A. G. Werner in 1791, from λευκός) or ash-grey in colour, and are usually dull and opaque, but sometimes transparent and glassy; they are brittle and break with a conchoidal fracture. The hardness is 5·5, and the specific gravity 2·5. Enclosures of other minerals, arranged in concentric zones, are frequently present in the crystals. On account of the colour and form of the crystals the mineral was early known as "white garnet." French authors employ R. J. Haüy's name "amphigène." (L. J. S.)

Leucite Rocks.—Although rocks containing leucite are numerically scarce, many countries such as England being entirely without them, yet they are of wide distribution, occurring in every quarter of the globe. Taken collectively, they exhibit a considerable variety of types and are of great interest petrographically. For the presence of this mineral it is necessary that the silica percentage of the rock should not be high, for leucite never occurs in presence of free quartz. It is most common in lavas of recent and Tertiary age, which have a fair amount of potash, or at any rate have potash equal to or greater than soda; if soda preponderates nepheline occurs rather than leucite. In pre-Tertiary rocks leucite is uncommon, since it readily decomposes and changes to zeolites, analcite and other secondary minerals. Leucite also is rare in plutonic rocks and dike rocks, but leucite-syenite and leucite-tinguaite bear witness to the possibility that it may occur in this manner. The rounded shape of its crystals, their white or grey colour, and rough cleavage, make the presence of leucite easily determinable in many of these rocks by simple inspection, especially when the crystals are large. "Pseudo-leucites" are rounded areas consisting of felspar, nepheline, analcite,

be void unl[illegible]
colonies east [illegible]
months in a[illegible]
offices by pa[illegible]
by a speci[illegible]
Council, sub[illegible]
(Leave of A[illegible]
see *Montagu* [illegible]
P.C. 491; [illegible]
law of conq[illegible]
by letters p[illegible]
or Order i[illegible]
3 St. Trials [illegible]

Procedure [illegible]
under the G[illegible]
and the Or[illegible]
are sealed [illegible]
tions are is[illegible]
cedure by [illegible]
warrant for [illegible]
by the lord [illegible]
the crown, [illegible]
and counte[illegible]
signature. [illegible]
filed, after i[illegible]
under the gr[illegible]
letters pate[illegible]
whose favou[illegible]

Construct[illegible]
that of oth[illegible]
contrary to [illegible]
to the gra[illegible]
although th[illegible]
is made for [illegible]
certâ scient[illegible]
of the gran[illegible]
either in [illegible]
suggestion [illegible]
grants, or [illegible]
patent are [illegible]
cancelled [illegible]
are revoke[illegible]
Patents A[illegible]
action bro[illegible]
with the fi[illegible]

As to [illegible]
rogative," [illegible]
Anson, *La*[illegible]
1907–190[illegible]

LETTR[illegible]
ments, *le*[illegible]
king of Fr[illegible]
with the [illegible]
principle, [illegible]
king, and [illegible]
lettres de c[illegible]
to assembl[illegible]
estates we[illegible]
cachet (call[illegible]
to register [illegible]
best-known [illegible]
called penal [illegible]
and without [illegible]
state prison [illegible]
hospital, tran[illegible]
place within t[illegible]

The power [illegible]
was a royal p[illegible]
traced to a [illegible]
tinian: "R[illegible]
that wh[illegible]
proper, [illegible]

[illegible] (Africa) [illegible]

[illegible] are [illegible] and [illegible] resemb[illegible] [illegible] rocks [illegible] between [illegible] [illegible] depending [illegible] [illegible] S. F

[illegible] territory of Thespiae, [illegible] neighbourhood [illegible] Spartans and their allies [illegible] which had invaded [illegible] Boeotian [illegible] In spite [illegible] Boeotian allies, [illegible] Mess[illegible] Theban [illegible] advance [illegible] centre [illegible] in which [illegible] the decisive issue was [illegible] The latter [illegible] deep formation [illegible] and were [illegible] of whom [illegible] were Spartan [illegible] their right wing [illegible] the enemy [illegible] the arrival of a Thessalian [illegible] they did not [illegible] their victory. But [illegible] significance in Greek history. [illegible] military tactics, affording the first [illegible] concentration of attack upon the [illegible] political effects were equally [illegible] strength and prestige which [illegible] deprived them for ever of their [illegible]

[illegible] *Hellenica*, vi. 4. 3-15; Diodorus xi. [illegible] Pausanias ix. [illegible] 2-10; [illegible] *the Battle of Plataea* [illegible] London, [illegible] *Geschichte der Kriegskunst* (Berlin, [illegible]

(M. O. B. C.)

[illegible] an ancient and very picturesque [illegible] of the Valais. It is built above [illegible] the Rhone, and is about 1 m. from the Leuk [illegible] east of Sion and 17½ m. west of Brieg [illegible] In 1900 it had 1592 inhabitants, all but [illegible] and Romanists. About 10½ m. by a [illegible] of Leuk, and near the head of the Dala [illegible] above the sea-level, and over[illegible] of the Gemmi Pass (7641 ft.; *q.v.*) leading [illegible] are the Baths of Leuk (*Leukerbad*, [illegible] They have only [illegible] permanent inhabitants, [illegible] in summer by visitors (largely French [illegible] the hot mineral springs. These are [illegible] The principal is that of [illegible] has a temperature of 124° F. [illegible] The village in winter [illegible] exposed to avalanches, [illegible] but it is now [illegible] from a similar catastrophe.

(W. A. B. C.)

[illegible] Silesia, 10 m. W. of Breslau, [illegible] Frederick the Great's victory over the [illegible] The high road from Breslau [illegible] Schweidnitz Water at Lissa, [illegible] the rolling country about Neumarkt.

Leuthen itself stands some 4000 paces south of the road, and a similar distance south again lies Sagschütz, while Nypern, on the northern edge of the hill country, is 5000 paces from the road. On Frederick's approach the Austrians took up a line of battle resting on the two last-named villages. Their whole position was strongly garrisoned and protected by obstacles, and their artillery was numerous though of light calibre. A strong outpost of Saxon cavalry was in Borne to the westward. Frederick had the previous day surprised the Austrian bakeries at Neumarkt, and his Prussians, 33,000 to the enemy's 82,000, moved towards Borne and Leuthen early on the 5th. The Saxon outpost was rushed at in the morning mist, and, covered by their advanced guard on the heights beyond, the Prussians wheeled to their right. Prince Charles of Lorraine, the Austrian commander-in-chief, on Leuthen Church tower, could make nothing of Frederick's movements, and the commander of his right wing (Lucchesi) sent him message after message from Nypern and Gocklerwitz asking for help, which was eventually despatched. But the real blow was to fall on the left under Nadasdy. While the Austrian commander was thus wasting time, the Prussians were marching against Nadasdy in two columns, which preserved their distances with an exactitude which has excited the wonder of modern generations of soldiers; at the due place they wheeled into line of battle obliquely to the Austrian front, and in one great *échelon*,—the cavalry of the right wing foremost, and that of the left "refused,"—Frederick advanced on Sagschütz. Nadasdy, surprised, put a bold face on the matter and made a good defence, but he was speedily routed, and, as the Prussians advanced, battalion after battalion was rolled up towards Leuthen until the Austrians faced almost due south. The fighting in Leuthen itself was furious; the Austrians stood, in places, 100 deep, but the disciplined valour of the Prussians carried the village. For a moment the victory was endangered when Lucchesi came down upon the Prussian left wing from the north, but Driesen's cavalry, till then refused, charged him in flank and scattered his troopers in wild rout. This stroke ended the battle. The retreat on Breslau became a rout almost comparable to that of Waterloo, and Prince Charles rallied, in Bohemia, barely 37,000 out of his 82,000. Ten thousand Austrians were left on the field, 21,000 taken prisoners (besides 17,000 in Breslau a little later), with 51 colours and 116 cannon. The Prussian loss in all was under 5500. It was not until 1854 that a memorial of this astonishing victory was erected on the battlefield.

See Carlyle, *Frederick*, bk. xviii. cap. x.; V. Ollech, *Friedrich der Grosse von Kolin bis Leuthen* (Berlin, 1858); Kutzen, *Schlacht bei Leuthen* (Breslau, 1851); and bibliography under SEVEN YEARS' WAR.

LEUTZE, EMANUEL (1816–1868), American artist, was born at Gmünd, Württemberg, on the 24th of May 1816, and as a child was taken by his parents to Philadelphia, where he early displayed talent as an artist. At the age of twenty-five he had earned enough to take him to Düsseldorf for a course of art study at the royal academy. Almost immediately he began the painting of historical subjects, his first work, "Columbus before the Council of Salamanca," being purchased by the Düsseldorf Art Union. In 1860 he was commissioned by the United States Congress to decorate a stairway in the Capitol at Washington, for which he painted a large composition, "Westward the Star of Empire takes its Way." His best-known work, popular through engraving, is "Washington crossing the Delaware," a large canvas containing a score of life-sized figures; it is now owned by the Metropolitan Museum of Art, New York. He became a member of the National Academy of Design in 1860, and died at Washington, D.C., on the 18th of July 1868.

LEVALLOIS-PERRET, a north-western suburb of Paris, on the right bank of the Seine, 2½ m. from the centre of the city. Pop. (1906) 61,419. It carries on the manufacture of motor-cars and accessories, carriages, groceries, liqueurs, perfumery, soap, &c., and has a port on the Seine.

LEVANT (from the French use of the participle of *lever*, to rise, for the east, the orient), the name applied widely to the coastlands of the eastern Mediterranean Sea from Greece to Egypt, or, in a more restricted and commoner sense, to the Mediterranean coastlands of Asia Minor and Syria. In the 16th and 17th centuries the term "High Levant" was used of the Far East. The phrase "to levant," meaning to abscond, especially of one who runs away leaving debts unpaid, particularly of a betting man or gambler, is taken from the Span. *levantar*, to lift or break up, in such phrases as *levantar la casa*, to break up a household, or *el campo*, to break camp.

LEVASSEUR, PIERRE EMILE (1828–), French economist, was born in Paris on the 8th of December 1828. Educated in Paris, he began to teach in the lycée at Alençon in 1852, and in 1857 was chosen professor of rhetoric at Besançon. He returned to Paris to become professor at the lycée Saint Louis, and in 1868 he was chosen a member of the academy of moral and political sciences. In 1872 he was appointed professor of geography, history and statistics in the Collège de France, and subsequently became also professor at the Conservatoire des arts et métiers and at the École libre des sciences politiques. Levasseur was one of the founders of the study of commercial geography, and became a member of the Council of Public Instruction, president of the French society of political economy and honorary president of the French geographical society.

His numerous writings include: *Histoire des classes ouvrières en France depuis la conquête de Jules César jusqu'à la Révolution* (1859); *Histoire des classes ouvrières en France depuis la Révolution jusqu'à nos jours* (1867); *L'Étude et l'enseignement de la géographie* (1871); *La Population française* (1889–1892); *L'Agriculture aux États-Unis* (1894); *L'Enseignement primaire dans les pays civilisés* (1897); *L'Ouvrier américain* (1898); *Questions ouvrières et industrielles sous la troisième République* (1907); and *Histoire des classes ouvrières et de l'industrie en France de 1789 à 1870* (1903–1904). He also published a *Grand Atlas de géographie physique et politique* (1890–1892).

LEVECHE, the name given to the dry hot sirocco wind in Spain; often incorrectly called the "solano." The direction of the Leveche is mostly from S.E., S. or S.W., and it occurs along the coast from Cabo de Gata to Cabo de Nao, and even beyond Malaga for a distance of some 10 m. inland.

LEVÉE (from Fr. *lever*, to raise), an embankment which keeps a river in its channel. A river such as the Mississippi (*q.v.*), draining a large area, carries a great amount of sediment from its swifter head-streams to the lower ground. As soon as a stream's velocity is checked, it drops a portion of its load of sediment and spreads an alluvial fan in the lower part of its course. This deposition of material takes place particularly at the sides of the stream where the velocity is least, and the banks are in consequence raised above the main channel, so that the river becomes lifted bodily upwards in its bed, and flows above the level of the surrounding country. In flood-time the muddy water flows over the river's banks, where its velocity is at once checked as it flows gently down the outer side, causing more material to be deposited there, and a long alluvial ridge, called a natural levée, to be built up on either side of the stream. These ridges may be wide or narrow, but they slope from the stream's outer banks to the plain below, and in consequence require careful watching, for if the levée is broken by a "crevasse," the whole body of the river may pour through and flood the country below. In 1890 the Mississippi near New Orleans broke through the Nita crevasse and flowed eastward with a current of 15 m. an hour, spreading destruction in its path. The Hwang-ho river in China is peculiarly liable to these inundations. The word levée is also sometimes used to denote a riverside quay or landing-place.

LEVEE (from the French substantival use of *lever*, to rise; there is no French substantival use of *levée* in the English sense), a reception or assembly held by the British sovereign or his representative, in Ireland by the lord-lieutenant, in India by the viceroy, in the forenoon or early afternoon, at which men only are present in distinction from a "drawing-room," at which ladies also are presented or received. Under the *ancien régime* in France the *lever* of the king was regulated, especially under Louis XIV., by elaborate etiquette, and the various divisions of the ceremonial followed the stages of the king's rising from bed, from which it gained its name. The *petit lever* began when the [illegible] and read his daily offices; to this were admitted [illegible] the closet, certain high officers of the household [illegible] to whom a special permit had been granted; then [illegible] the *premiere entrée*, in which came the secretaries and [illegible] and [illegible] the *entrée*; these were received [illegible]. Finally, at the *grand lever*, [illegible] the nobles and gentlemen of the [illegible] received; the king by that time was shaved, had [illegible]. In the United States the [illegible] 'levee' was formerly used of the public receptions held [illegible].

LEVELLERS, the name given to an important political party [illegible] the period of the Civil War and the Commonwealth. The germ of the Levelling movement must be sought [illegible] men of strong republican views, [illegible] appears in a letter of the 1st of [illegible], although it was undoubtedly in existence as a [illegible] (Gardiner, *Great Civil War*, iii. 380). [illegible] thus: "They have given [illegible], viz. Levellers, for they intend to [illegible], and cause a parity and community in [illegible]."

The Levellers [illegible] prominent in 1647 during the [illegible] negotiations between the king and [illegible] while the relations between the latter and [illegible] strained. Like the Agitators they were [illegible] the soldiers; they were opposed to the [illegible], and they feared that Cromwell and the [illegible] leaders were too complaisant in their dealings [illegible] they doubted their sincerity in this [illegible] John Lilburne (*q.v.*) they presented a manifesto, [illegible] to the commander-in-chief, Lord [illegible] October 1647. In this they demanded a dissolution [illegible] a year and substantial changes in the con[illegible] future parliaments, which were to be regulated by an [illegible] parliament." In a second document, *The* [illegible], they expanded these ideas, which were [illegible] by Cromwell, Ireton and other officers on the one side, [illegible] Thomas Rainsborough and Edward [illegible] on the other. But no settlement was [illegible] the Levellers clamoured for the king's death, [illegible] November 1647, just after his flight from Hampton Court [illegible], they were responsible for a mutiny which broke [illegible] at Corkbush Field, near Ware. This, [illegible] was promptly suppressed by Cromwell. During the [illegible] which immediately preceded the execution of the [illegible] the Levellers conducted a lively agitation in favour of the [illegible] in the *Agreement of the people*, and in January [illegible] Lilburne was arrested for using seditious language at a [illegible] in London. But no success attended these and similar [illegible] the only result was that the Levellers regarded [illegible] with still greater suspicion.

[illegible] after the death of the king, the Levellers [illegible]. They were both numerous and danger[illegible] says Gardiner, "for an exaggeration [illegible] supremacy." In a pamphlet, [illegible] for the dissolution of the [illegible] reformed parliament. He [illegible] *England's New Chains*; [illegible] by parliament, and in [illegible] Levellers, Richard Over[illegible] were arrested. The discontent [illegible] was fanned when certain [illegible] Ireland, and in April 1649 [illegible] was quickly put down [illegible] Robert Lockyer, was [illegible] were also suppressed [illegible] with the Levellers [illegible] less prominent, [illegible] advances to [illegible]

from England. The distinguishing mark of the Leveller was a sea-green ribbon.

Another but more harmless form of the same movement was the assembling of about fifty men on St George's Hill near Oatlands in Surrey. In April 1649 these "True Levellers" or "Diggers," as they were called, took possession of some unoccupied ground which they began to cultivate. They were, however, soon dispersed, and their leaders were arrested and brought before Fairfax, when they took the opportunity of denouncing landowners. It is interesting to note that Lilburne and his colleagues objected to being designated Levellers, as they had no desire to take away "the proper right and title that every man has to what is his own."

Cromwell attacked the Levellers in his speech to parliament in September 1654 (Carlyle, *Cromwell's Letters and Speeches*, Speech II.). He said: "A nobleman, a gentleman, a yeoman; the distinction of these; that is a good interest of the nation, and a great one. The 'natural' magistracy of the nation, was it not almost trampled under foot, under despite and contempt, by men of Levelling principles? I beseech you, for the orders of men and ranks of men, did not that Levelling principle tend to the reducing of all to an equality? Did it 'consciously' think to do so; or did it 'only unconsciously' practise towards that for property and interest? 'At all events,' what was the purport of it but to make the tenant as liberal a fortune as the landlord? Which, I think, if obtained, would not have lasted long."

In 1724 there was a rising against enclosures in Galloway, and a number of men who took part therein were called Levellers or Dykebreakers (A. Lang, *History of Scotland*, vol. iv.). The word was also used in Ireland during the 18th century to describe a secret revolutionary society similar to the Whiteboys. (A. W. H.*)

LEVEN, ALEXANDER LESLIE, 1st Earl of (*c.* 1580–1661), Scottish general, was the son of George Leslie, captain of Blair-in-Athol, and a member of the family of Leslie of Balquhain. After a scanty education he sought his fortune abroad, and became a soldier, first under Sir Horace Vere in the Low Countries, and afterwards (1605) under Charles IX. and Gustavus Adolphus of Sweden, in whose service he remained for many years and fought in many campaigns with honour. In 1626 Leslie had risen by merit to the rank of lieutenant-general, and had been knighted by Gustavus. In 1628 he distinguished himself by his constancy and energy in the defence of Stralsund against Wallenstein, and in 1630 seized the island of Rügen in the name of the king of Sweden. In the same year he returned to Scotland to assist in recruiting and organizing the corps of Scottish volunteers which James, 3rd marquis of Hamilton, brought over to Gustavus in 1631. Leslie received a severe wound in the following winter, but was able nevertheless to be present at Gustavus's last battle at Lützen. Like many others of the soldiers of fortune who served under Gustavus, Leslie cherished his old commander's memory to the day of his death, and he kept with particular care a jewel and miniature presented to him by the king. He continued as a general officer in the Swedish army for some years, was promoted in 1636 to the rank of field marshal, and continued in the field until 1638, when events recalled him to his own country. He had married long before this—in 1637 his eldest son was made a colonel in the Swedish army—and he had managed to keep in touch with Scottish affairs.

As the foremost Scottish soldier of his day he was naturally nominated to command the Scottish army in the impending war with England, a post which, resigning his Swedish command, he accepted with a glad heart, for he was an ardent Covenanter and had caused "a great number of our commanders in Germany subscryve our covenant" (Baillie's *Letters*). On leaving Sweden he brought back his arrears of pay in the form of cannon and muskets for his new army. For some months he busied himself with the organization and training of the new levies, and with inducing Scottish officers abroad to do their duty to their country by returning to lead them. Diminutive in size and somewhat deformed in person as he was, his reputation and his shrewdness and simple tact, combined with the respect for his office of lord general that he enforced on all ranks, brought even the unruly nobles to subordination. He had by now amassed a considerable fortune and was able to live in a manner befitting a commander-in-chief, even when in the field. One of his first exploits was to take the castle of Edinburgh by surprise, without the loss of a man. He commanded the Scottish army at Dunse Law in May of that year, and in 1640 he invaded England, and defeated the king's troops at Newburn on the Tyne, which gave him possession of Newcastle and of the open country as far as the Tees. At the treaty with the king at Ripon, Leslie was one of the commissioners of the Scottish parliament, and when Charles visited Edinburgh Leslie entertained him magnificently and accompanied him when he drove through the streets. His affirmations of loyalty to the crown, which later events caused to be remembered against him, were sincere enough, but the complicated politics of the time made it difficult for Leslie, the lord general of the Scottish army, to maintain a perfectly consistent attitude. However, his influence was exercised chiefly to put an end to, even to hush up, the troubles, and he is found, now giving a private warning to plotters against the king to enable them to escape, now guarding the Scottish parliament against a royalist *coup d'état*, and now securing for an old comrade of the German wars, Patrick Ruthven, Lord Ettrick, indemnity for having held Edinburgh Castle for the king against the parliament. Charles created him, by patent dated Holyrood, October 11, 1641, earl of Leven and Lord Balgonie, and made him captain of Edinburgh Castle and a privy councillor. The parliament recognized his services by a grant, and, on his resigning the lord generalship, appointed him commander of the permanent forces. A little later, Leven, who was a member of the committee of the estates which exercised executive powers during the recess of parliament, used his great influence in support of a proposal to raise a Scottish army to help the elector palatine in Germany, but the Ulster massacres gave this force, when raised, a fresh direction and Leven himself accompanied it to Ireland as lord general. He did not remain there long, for the Great Rebellion (*q.v.*) had begun in England, and negotiations were opened between the English and the Scottish parliaments for mutual armed assistance. Leven accepted the command of the new forces raised for the invasion of England, and was in consequence freely accused of having broken his personal oath to Charles, but he could hardly have acted otherwise than he did, and at that time, and so far as the Scots were concerned, to the end of the struggle, the parliaments were in arms, professedly and to some extent actually, to rescue his majesty from the influence of evil counsellors.

The military operations preceding Marston Moor are described under GREAT REBELLION, and the battle itself under its own heading. Leven's great reputation, wisdom and tact made him an ideal commander for the allied army formed by the junction of Leven's, Fairfax's and Manchester's in Yorkshire. After the battle the allied forces separated, Leven bringing the siege of Newcastle to an end by storming it. In 1645 the Scots were less successful, though their operations ranged from Westmorland to Hereford, and Leven himself had many administrative and political difficulties to contend with. These difficulties became more pronounced when in 1646 Charles took refuge with the Scottish army. The king remained with Leven until he was handed over to the English parliament in 1647, and Leven constantly urged him to take the covenant and to make peace. Presbyterians and Independents had now parted, and with no more concession than the guarantee of the covenant the Scottish and English Presbyterians were ready to lay down their arms, or to turn them against the "sectaries." Leven was now old and infirm, and though retained as nominal commander-in-chief saw no further active service. He acted with Argyll and the "godly" party in the discussions preceding the second invasion of England, and remained at his post as long as possible in the hope of preventing the Scots becoming merely a royalist instrument for the conquest of the English Independents. But he was induced in the end to resign, though he was appointed lord general of all new forces that might be raised for the defence of Scotland. The occasion soon came, for Cromwell annihilated the Scottish invaders at Preston and Uttoxeter, and thereupon Argyll assumed political and Leven military control at Edinburgh. But he was now over seventy years of age, and willingly resigned the effective command to his subordinate David Leslie (see NEWARK, LORD), in whom he had entire confidence. After the execution of Charles I. the war broke out afresh, and this time the "godly" party acted with the royalists. In the new war, and in the disastrous campaign of Dunbar, Leven took but a nominal part, though attempts were afterwards made to hold him responsible. But once more the parliament refused to accept his resignation. Leven at last fell into the hands of a party of English dragoons in August 1651, and with some others was sent to London. He remained incarcerated in the Tower for some time, till released on finding securities for £20,000, upon which he retired to his residence in Northumberland. While on a visit to London he was again arrested, for a technical breach of his engagement, but by the intercession of the queen of Sweden he obtained his liberty. He was freed from his engagements in 1654, and retired to his seat at Balgonie in Fifeshire, where he died at an advanced age in 1661. He acquired considerable landed property, particularly Inchmartin in the Carse of Gowrie, which he called Inchleslie.

See LEVEN AND MELVILLE, EARLS OF, below.

LEVEN, a police burgh of Fifeshire, Scotland. Pop. (1901) 5577. It is situated on the Firth of Forth, at the mouth of the Leven, 5¾m. E. by N. of Thornton Junction by the North British railway. The public buildings include the town hall, public hall and people's institute, in the grounds of which the old town cross has been erected. The industries are numerous, comprising flax-spinning, brewing, linen-weaving, paper-making, seed-crushing and rope-making, besides salt-works, a foundry, saw-mill and brick-works. The wet dock is not much used, owing to the constant accumulation of sand. The golf-links extending for 2 m. to Lundin are among the best in Scotland. Two miles N.E. is Lundin Mill and Drumochie, usually called LUNDIN (pop. 570), at the mouth of Kiel Burn, with a station on the Links. The three famous standing stones are supposed to be either of "Druidical" origin or to mark the site of a battle with the Danes. In the vicinity are the remains of an old house of the Lundins, dating from the reign of David II. To the N.W. of Leven lies the parish of KENNOWAY (pop. 870). In Captain Seton's house, which still stands in the village of Kennoway, Archbishop Sharp spent the night before his assassination (1679). One mile east of Lundin lies LARGO (pop. of parish 2046), consisting of Upper Largo, or Kirkton of Largo, and Lower Largo. The public buildings include Simpson institute, with a public hall, library, reading-room, bowling-green and lawn-tennis court, and John Wood's hospital, founded in 1659 for poor persons bearing his name. A statue of Alexander Selkirk, or Selcraig (1676–1721), the prototype of "Robinson Crusoe," who was born here, was erected in 1886. Sir John Leslie (1766–1832), the natural philosopher, was also a native. Largo claims two famous sailors, Admiral Sir Philip Durham (1763–1845), commander-in-chief at Portsmouth from 1836 to 1839, and Sir Andrew Wood (d. 1515), the trusted servant of James III. and James IV., who sailed the "Great Michael," the largest ship of its time. When he was past active service he had a canal cut from his house to the parish church, to which he was rowed every Sunday in an eight-oared barge. Largo House was granted to him by James III., and the tower of the original structure still exists. About 1½ m. from the coast rises the height of Largo Law (948 ft.). Kellie Law lies some 5½ m. to the east.

LEVEN, LOCH, a lake of Kinross-shire, Scotland. It has an oval shape, the longer axis running from N.W. to S.E., has a length of 3¾ m., and a breadth of 2¾ m. and is situated near the south and east boundaries of the shire. It lies at a height of 350 ft. above the sea. The mean depth is less than 15 ft., with a maximum of 83 ft., the lake being thus one of the shallowest in Scotland. Reclamation works carried on from 1826 to 1836 reduced its area by one quarter, but it still possesses a surface

king had washed
mitted the prince
hold and those t
followed the *pr*
other officials
by the king
the remainde
court were
changed his
term "lev
by the pre

LEVELL
in Englan
wealth.
for amon
and the
Novem
nicknan
This le
themsel
sett all
the kin

The
tracte
the pa
the a
mainl
existe
other
ings
matt
The (
Fairf
of pa
stitu
unal
Agr
discu
and
Sexby
made
and in
to Ca
out in
howev
twelve
king th
ideas
1648 L
meeting
efforts,
Cromw

Early
renewed
ous, and
of the d
England
council
followed
his writi
March 16
ton, Willi
which was
regiments
there was
by Fairfax
shot. Risi
without any
was practic
but under t
the exiled

[illegible] 1664. The younger Alexander's two daughters were [illegible] countesses of Leven in their own right; and after the [illegible] of the second of these two ladies in 1676 a dispute arose [illegible] the succession to the earldom between John Leslie, earl [illegible] duke) of Rothes, and David Melville, 2nd earl of [illegible] mentioned above. In 1681, however, Rothes died, [illegible], who was a great-grandson of the 1st earl of Leven, [illegible] the title, calling himself earl of Leven and Melville [illegible] he succeeded his father as earl of Melville in May 1707. [illegible] 1805 the family has borne the name of Leslie-Melville. [illegible] John David Leslie-Melville (b. 1886) became 12th earl [illegible] Leven and 11th earl of Melville.

[illegible] W. Fraser, *The Melvilles, Earls of Melville, and the Leslies, Earls of Leven* (1890); and the *Leven and Melville Papers*, edited by [illegible] W. H. Leslie-Melville for the Bannatyne Club (1843).

[illegible], CHARLES JAMES (1806–1872), Irish novelist, second [illegible] of James Lever, a Dublin architect and builder, was born [illegible] the Irish capital on the 31st of August 1806. His descent [illegible] English. He was educated in private schools, where [illegible] wore a ring, smoked, read novels, was a ringleader in every [illegible] of discipline, and behaved generally like a boy destined [illegible] the navy in one of Captain Marryat's novels. His escapades [illegible] Trinity College, Dublin (1823–1828), whence he took the [illegible] of M.B. in 1831, form the basis of that vast cellarage [illegible] anecdote from which all the best vintages in his novels are [illegible]. The inimitable Frank Webber in *Charles O'Malley* [illegible] ancestor of Foker and Mr Bouncer) was a college [illegible], Robert Boyle, later on an Irish parson. Lever and Boyle [illegible] ballads of their own composing in the streets of Dublin, [illegible] the manner of Fergusson or Goldsmith, filled their caps [illegible] coppers and played many other pranks embellished in the [illegible] of *O'Malley*, *Con Cregan* and *Lord Kilgobbin*. Before [illegible] embarking upon the medical studies for which he was [illegible]. Lever visited Canada as an unqualified surgeon on an emigrant ship, and has drawn upon some of his experiences [illegible] *Con Cregan*; *Arthur O'Leary* and *Roland Cashel*. Arrived in Canada he plunged into the backwoods, was affiliated to a tribe [illegible] and had to escape at the risk of his life, like his own [illegible] Daly.

Back in Europe, he travelled in the guise of a student from [illegible] to Weimar (where he saw Goethe), thence to Vienna; [illegible] the German student life with its beer, its fighting and [illegible], and several of his merry songs, such as "The Pope he [illegible] a merry life" (greatly envied by Titmarsh), are on [illegible] models. His medical degree admitted him to an [illegible] from the Board of Health in Co. Clare and then [illegible] doctor at Port Stewart, but the liveliness of his [illegible] as a country doctor seems to have prejudiced the [illegible] against him. In 1833 he married his first love, [illegible] Baker, and in February 1837, after varied experiences, he began running *The Confessions of Harry Lorrequer* through the pages of the recently established *Dublin University Magazine*. [illegible] the previous seven years the popular taste had declared [illegible] in favour of the service novel as exemplified by *Frank* [illegible], *Tom Cringle*, *The Subaltern*, *Cyril Thornton*, *Stories of* [illegible] and *The Bivouac*; and Lever himself [illegible] met William Hamilton Maxwell, the titular founder of the [illegible]. Before *Harry Lorrequer* appeared in volume form (1839), [illegible] on the strength of a slight diplomatic connexion [illegible] physician in Brussels (16, Rue Ducale). *Lorrequer* [illegible] a string of Irish and other stories good, bad and [illegible] but mostly rollicking, and Lever, who strung together [illegible] late at night after the serious business of the day [illegible] was astonished at its success. "If this sort of thing [illegible], I can go on for ever." Brussels was indeed a [illegible] for the observation of half-pay officers, such as [illegible] (Commissioner Meade), Captain Bubbleton and [illegible], who terrorised the *tavernes* of the place with their [illegible] stories, and of English society a little damaged, [illegible] became the specialty of Lever to depict. He sketched [illegible] hand, wrote, as he lived, from hand to mouth, and [illegible] difficulty he experienced was that of getting rid of his characters who "hung about him like those tiresome people who never can make up their minds to bid you good night." Lever had never taken part in a battle himself, but his next three books, *Charles O'Malley* (1841), *Jack Hinton* and *Tom Burke of Ours* (1843), written under the spur of the writer's chronic extravagance, contain some splendid military writing and some of the most animated battle-pieces on record. In pages of *O'Malley* and *Tom Burke* Lever anticipates not a few of the best effects of Marbot, Thiébaut, Lejeune, Griois, Seruzier, Burgoyne and the like. His account of the Douro need hardly fear comparison, it has been said, with Napier's. Condemned by the critics, Lever had completely won the general reader from the Iron Duke himself downwards.

In 1842 he returned to Dublin to edit the *Dublin University Magazine*, and gathered round him a typical coterie of Irish wits (including one or two hornets) such as the O'Sullivans, Archer Butler, W. Carleton, Sir William Wilde, Canon Hayman, D. F. McCarthy, McGlashan, Dr Kenealy and many others. In June 1842 he welcomed at Templeogue, 4 m. south-west of Dublin, the author of the *Snob Papers* on his Irish tour (the *Sketch Book* was, later, dedicated to Lever). Thackeray recognized the fund of Irish sadness beneath the surface merriment. "The author's character is not humour but sentiment. The spirits are mostly artificial, the *fond* is sadness, as appears to me to be that of most Irish writing and people." The Waterloo episode in *Vanity Fair* was in part an outcome of the talk between the two novelists. But the "Galway pace," the display he found it necessary to maintain at Templeogue, the stable full of horses, the cards, the friends to entertain, the quarrels to compose and the enormous rapidity with which he had to complete *Tom Burke*, *The O'Donoghue* and *Arthur O'Leary* (1845), made his native land an impossible place for Lever to continue in. Templeogue would soon have proved another Abbotsford. Thackeray suggested London. But Lever required a new field of literary observation and anecdote. His *sève originel* was exhausted and he decided to renew it on the continent. In 1845 he resigned his editorship and went back to Brussels, whence he started upon an unlimited tour of central Europe in a family coach. Now and again he halted for a few months, and entertained to the limit of his resources in some ducal castle or other which he hired for an off season. Thus at Riedenburg, near Bregenz, in August 1846, he entertained Charles Dickens and his wife and other well-known people. Like his own *Daltons* or *Dodd Family Abroad* he travelled continentally, from Carlsruhe to Como, from Como to Florence, from Florence to the Baths of Lucca and so on, and his letters home are the litany of the literary remittance man, his ambition now limited to driving a pair of novels abreast without a diminution of his standard price for serial work ("twenty pounds a sheet"). In the *Knight of Gwynne*, a story of the Union (1847), *Con Cregan* (1849), *Roland Cashel* (1850) and *Maurice Tiernay* (1852) we still have traces of his old manner; but he was beginning to lose his original joy in composition. His *fond* of sadness began to cloud the animal joyousness of his temperament. Formerly he had written for the happy world which is young and curly and merry; now he grew fat and bald and grave. "After 38 or so what has life to offer but one universal declension. Let the crew pump as hard as they like, the leak gains every hour." But, depressed in spirit as he was, his wit was unextinguished; he was still the delight of the *salons* with his stories, and in 1867, after a few years' experience of a similar kind at Spezia, he was cheered by a letter from Lord Derby offering him the more lucrative consulship of Trieste. "Here is six hundred a year for doing nothing, and you are just the man to do it." The six hundred could not atone to Lever for the lassitude of prolonged exile. Trieste, at first "all that I could desire," became with characteristic abruptness "detestable and damnable." "Nothing to eat, nothing to drink, no one to speak to." "Of all the dreary places it has been my lot to sojourn in this is the worst" (some references to Trieste will be found in *That Boy of Norcott's*, 1869). He could never be alone and was almost morbidly dependent upon literary encouragement. Fortunately, like Scott, he had unscrupulous friends who assured him that his last efforts were his best. They include *The Fortunes of Glencore* (1857), *Tony Butler* (1865), *Luttrell of Arran* (1865), *Sir Brooke Fosbrooke* (1866), *Lord Kilgobbin* (1872) and the table-talk of *Cornelius O'Dowd*, originally contributed to Blackwood. His depression, partly due to incipient heart disease, partly to the growing conviction that he was the victim of literary and critical conspiracy, was confirmed by the death of his wife (23rd April 1870), to whom he was tenderly attached. He visited Ireland in the following year and seemed alternately in very high and very low spirits. Death had already given him one or two runaway knocks, and, after his return to Trieste, he failed gradually, dying suddenly, however, and almost painlessly, from failure of the heart's action on the 1st of June 1872. His daughters, one of whom, Sydney, is believed to have been the real author of *The Rent in a Cloud* (1869), were well provided for.

Trollope praised Lever's novels highly when he said that they were just like his conversation. He was a born raconteur, and had in perfection that easy flow of light description which without tedium or hurry leads up to the point of the good stories of which in earlier days his supply seemed inexhaustible. With little respect for unity of action or conventional novel structure, his brightest books, such as *Lorrequer*, *O'Malley* and *Tom Burke*, are in fact little more than recitals of scenes in the life of a particular "hero," unconnected by any continuous intrigue. The type of character he depicted is for the most part elementary. His women are mostly rouées, romps or Xanthippes; his heroes have too much of the Pickle temper about them and fall an easy prey to the serious attacks of Poe or to the more playful gibes of Thackeray in *Phil Fogarty* or Bret Harte in *Terence Deuville*. This last is a perfect bit of burlesque. Terence exchanges nineteen shots with the Hon. Captain Henry Somerset in the glen. "At each fire I shot away a button from his uniform. As my last bullet shot off the last button from his sleeve, I remarked quietly, 'You seem now, my lord, to be almost as ragged as the gentry you sneered at,' and rode haughtily away." And yet these careless sketches contain such haunting creations as Frank Webber, Major Monsoon and Micky Free, "the Sam Weller of Ireland." Falstaff is alone in the literature of the world; but if ever there came a later Falstaff, Monsoon was the man. As for Baby Blake, is she not an Irish Di Vernon? The critics may praise Lever's thoughtful and careful later novels as they will, but *Charles O'Malley* will always be the pattern of a military romance.

Superior, it is sometimes claimed, in construction and style, the later books approximate it may be thought to the good *ordinary* novel of commerce, but they lack the *extraordinary* qualities, the incommunicable "go" of the early books—the élan of Lever's untamed youth. Artless and almost formless these productions may be, but they represent to us, as very few other books can, that pathetic ejaculation of Lever's own—"Give us back the wild freshness of the morning!" We know the novelist's teachers, Maxwell, Napier, the old-fashioned compilation known as *Victoires, conquêtes et désastres des Français* (1835), and the old buffers at Brussels who emptied the room by uttering the word "Badajos." But where else shall we find the equals of the military scenes in *O'Malley* and *Tom Burke*, or the military episodes in *Jack Hinton*, *Arthur O'Leary* (the story of Aubuisson) or *Maurice Tiernay* (nothing he ever did is finer than the chapter introducing "A remnant of Fontenoy")? It is here that his true genius lies, even more than in his talent for conviviality and fun, which makes an early copy of an early Lever (with Phiz's illustrations) seem literally to exhale an atmosphere of past and present entertainment. It is here that he is a true romancist, not for boys only, but also for men.

Lever's lack of artistry and of sympathy with the deeper traits of the Irish character have been stumbling-blocks to his reputation among the critics. Except to some extent in *The Martins of Cro'Martin* (1856) it may be admitted that his portraits of Irish are drawn too exclusively from the type depicted in Sir Jonah Barrington's *Memoirs* and already well known on

the English stage. I
"lowering the natio
posthumous reput
in spite of all h
endeavours to ap

The chief author
and the *Letters*, ed
which, however,
See also Dr Garn
465 and 570;
(August 1862);
Essays in Little
Literature of the
Literature (1900)
edition of the
superintendence

LEVER (thr
levare, to lift,
"simple" lev
point, termed
the piece to
(see Mechan

LEVERRIE
astronomer, w
1811. His
made great
tion gained
The distin
choice amo
pupils of t
addressing
guidance o
two pape
and oxy
(1835 and
came fro
École P
and acc
instantly
powers
were co
Septem
of Lapl
the sola
eccentri
remark
mendat
Mercury
planet.
H. A. E.
Vico a
the resu
Lexell's
1585. O
Vico's co
in 1678.
planetary
to Uranu
he advan
name. C
showed th
and on th
discerned
the spot L

This mo
of public
rolling Le
awarded him
the
of

it existed in the post-exilic age was really the work of Moses, it is inexplicable that all trace of it was so completely lost that the degradation of the non-Zadokites in Ezekiel was a new feature and a punishment, whereas in the Mosaic law the ordinary Levites, on the traditional view, was already forbidden priestly rights under penalty of death. There is in fact no clear evidence of the existence of a distinction between priests and Levites in any Hebrew writing demonstrably earlier than the Deuteronomic stage, although, even as the Pentateuch contains ordinances which have been carried back by means of a "legal convention" to the days of Moses, writers have occasionally altered earlier records of the history to agree with later standpoints.[1]

No argument in support of the traditional theory can be drawn from the account of Korah's revolt (Num. xvi. sqq., see § 3) or from the Levitical cities (Num. xxxv.; Josh. xxi.). Some of the latter were either not conquered by the Israelites until long after the invasion, or, if conquered, were not held by Levites; and names are wanting of places in which priests are actually known to have lived. Certainly the names are largely identical with ancient holy cities, which, however, are holy because they possessed noted shrines, not because the inhabitants were members of a holy tribe. Gezer and Taanach, for example, are said to have remained in the hands of Canaanites (Judges i. 27, 29; cf. 1 Kings ix. 16), and recent excavation has shown how far the cultus of these cities was removed from Mosaic religion and ritual and how long the grosser elements persisted.[2] On the other hand, the sanctuaries obviously had always their local ministers, all of whom in time could be called Levitical, and it is only in this sense, not in that of the late priestly legislation, that a place like Shechem could ever have been included. Further, instead of holding cities and pasture-grounds, the Levites are sometimes described as scattered and divided (Gen. xlix. 7; Deut. xviii. 6), and though they may naturally possess property as private individuals, they alone of all the tribes of Israel possess no tribal inheritance (Num. xviii. 23, xxvi. 62; Deut. x. 9; Josh. xiv. 3). This fluctuation finds a parallel in the age at which the Levites were to serve; for neither has any reasonable explanation been found on the traditional view. Num. iv. 3 fixes the age at thirty, although in i. 3 it has been reduced to twenty; but in 1 Chron. xxiii. 3, David is said to have numbered them from the higher limit, whereas in vv. 24, 27 the lower figure is given on the authority of "the last words (or acts) of David." In Num. viii. 23-26, the age is given as twenty-five, but twenty became usual and recurs in Ezra iii. 8 and 2 Chron. xxxi. 17. There are, however, independent grounds for believing that 1 Chron. xxiii. 24, 27, 2 Chron. xxxi. 17 belong to later insertions and that Ezr. iii. 8 is relatively late.

When, in accordance with the usual methods of Hebrew genealogical history, the Levites are defined as the descendants of Levi, the third son of Jacob by Leah (Gen. xxix. 34), a literal interpretation is unnecessary, and the only narrative wherein Levi appears as a person evidently delineates under the form of personification events in the history of the Levites (Gen. xxxiv.).[3] They take their place in Israel as the tribe set apart for sacred duties, and without entering into the large question how far the tribal schemes can be used for the earlier history of Israel, it may be observed that no adequate interpretation has yet been found of the ethnological traditions of Levi and other sons of Leah in their historical relation to one another or to the other tribes. However intelligible may be the notion of a tribe *reserved* for priestly service, the fact that it does not apply to early biblical history is apparent from the heterogeneous details of the Levitical divisions. The incorporation of singers and porters is indeed a late process, but it is typical of the tendency to co-ordinate all the religious classes (see GENEALOGY: *Biblical*). The genealogies in their complete form pay little heed to Moses, although Aaron and Moses could typify the priesthood and other Levites generally (1 Chron. xxiii. 14). Certain priesthoods in the first stage (§ 1 [*a*]) claimed descent from these prototypes, and it is interesting to observe (1) the growing importance of Aaron in the later sources of "the Exodus," and (2) the relation between Mosheh (Moses) and his two sons Gershom and Eliezer, on the one side, and the Levitical names Mushi (*i.e.* the Mosaite), Gershon and the Aaronite priest Eleazar, on the other. There are links, also, which unite Moses with Kenite, Rechabite, Calebite and Edomite families, and the Levitical names themselves are equally connected with the southern tribes of Judah and Simeon and with the Edomites.[4] It is to be inferred, therefore, that some relationship subsisted, or was thought to subsist, among (1) the Levites, (2) clans actually located in the south of Palestine, and (3) families whose names and traditions point to a southern origin. The exact meaning of these features is not clear, but if it be remembered (*a*) that the Levites of post-exilic literature represent only the result of a long and intricate development, (*b*) that the name "Levite," in the later stages at least, was extended to include all priestly servants, and (*c*) that the priesthoods, in tending to become hereditary, included priests who were Levites by adoption and not by descent, it will be recognized that the examination of the evidence for the earlier stages cannot confine itself to those narratives where the specific term alone occurs.

3. *The Traditions of the Levites.*—In the "Blessing of Moses" (Deut. xxxiii. 8-11), Levi is a collective name for the priesthood, probably that of (north) Israel. He is the guardian of the sacred oracles, knowing no kin, and enjoying his privileges for proofs of fidelity at Massah and Meribah. That these places (in the district of Kadesh) were traditionally associated with the origin of the Levites is suggested by various Levitical stories, although it is in a narrative now in a context pointing to Horeb or Sinai that the Levites are Israelites who for some cause (now lost) severed themselves from their people and took up a stand on behalf of Yahweh (Exod. xxxii.). Other evidence allows us to link together the Kenites, Calebites and Danites in a tradition of some movement into Palestine, evidently quite distinct from the great invasion of Israelite tribes which predominates in the existing records. The priesthood of Dan certainly traced its origin to Moses (Judges xvii. 9, xviii. 30); that of Shiloh claimed an equally high ancestry (1 Sam. ii. 27 seq.).[5] Some tradition of a widespread movement appears to be ascribed to the age of Jehu, whose accession, promoted by the prophet Elisha, marks the end of the conflict between Yahweh and Baal. To a Rechabite (the clan is allied to the Kenites) is definitely ascribed a hand in Jehu's sanguinary measures, and, though little is told of the obviously momentous events, one writer clearly alludes to a bloody period when reforms were to be effected by the sword (1 Kings xix. 17). Similarly the story of the original selection of the Levites in the wilderness mentions an uncompromising massacre of idolaters. Consequently, it is very noteworthy that popular tradition preserves the recollection of some attack by the "brothers" Levi and Simeon

A. van Hoonacker, *Le Sacerdoce lévitique* (1899); and J. Orr, *Problem of the O.T.* (1905). These and other apologetic writings have so far failed to produce any adequate alternative hypothesis, and while they argue for the traditional theory, later revision not being excluded, the modern critical view accepts late dates for the literary sources in their present form, and explicitly recognizes the presence of much that is ancient. Note the curious old tradition that Ezra wrote out the law which had been burnt (2 Esdr. xiv. 21 sqq.).

[1] For example, in 1 Kings viii. 4, there are many indications that the context has undergone considerable editing at a fairly late date. The Septuagint translators did not read the clause which speaks of "priests *and* Levites," and 2 Chron. v. 5 reads "the Levite priests," the phrase characteristic of the Deuteronomic identification of priestly and Levitical ministry. 1 Sam. vi. 15, too, brings in the Levites, but the verse breaks the connexion between 14 and 16. For the present disorder in the text of 2 Sam. xv. 24, see the commentaries.

[2] See Father H. Vincent, O.P., *Canaan d'après l'exploration récente* (1907), pp. 151, 200 sqq., 463 sq.

[3] So Gen. xxxiv. 7, Hamor has wrought folly "in Israel" (cf. Judges xx. 6 and often), and in v. 30 "Jacob" is not a personal but a collective idea, for he says, "I am a few men," and the capture and destruction of a considerable city is in the nature of things the work of more than two individuals. In the allusion to Levi and Simeon in Gen. xlix. the two are spoken of as "brothers" with a communal assembly. See, for other examples of personification, GENEALOGY: *Biblical*.

[4] See E. Meyer, *Israeliten u. ihre Nachbarstämme*, pp. 299 sqq. (passim); S. A. Cook, *Ency. Bib.* col. 1665 seq.; *Crit. Notes on O.T. History*, pp. 84 sqq., 122-125.

[5] The second element of the name Abiathar is connected with Jether or Jethro, the father-in-law of Moses, and even Ichabod (1 Sam. iv. 21) seems to be an intentional reshaping of Jochebed, which is elsewhere the name of the mother of Moses. Phinehas, Eli's son, becomes in later writings the name of a prominent Aaronite priest in the days of the exodus from Egypt.

Lev. xviii.–xx.; (3) the calendar of Lev. xxiii. represents an earlier stage of development than the fixed days and months of Ezek. xlv.; (4) the sin- and trespass-offerings are not mentioned in H (cf. Ezek. xl. 39, xlii. 13, xliv. 29, xlvi. 20); (5) the parallels to H, which are found especially in Ezek. xviii., xx., xxii. f., include both the paraenetic setting and the laws; and lastly, (6) a comparison of Lev. xxvi. with Ezekiel points to the greater originality of the former. Baentsch, however, who is followed by Bertholet, adopts the view that Lev. xxvi. is rather an independent hortatory discourse modelled on Ezekiel. The same writer further maintains that H consists of three separate elements, viz. chaps. xvii.; xviii.–xx., with various continuances in chaps. xxiii.–xxv.; and xxii., xxiii., of which the last is certainly later than Ezekiel, while the second is in the main prior to that author. But the arguments which he adduces in favour of the threefold origin of H are not sufficient to outweigh the general impression of unity which the code presents.

Chap. xvii. comprises four main sections which are clearly marked off by similar introductory and closing formulae: (1) vv. 3-7, prohibition of the slaughter of domestic animals, unless they are presented to Yahweh; (2) vv. 8, 9, sacrifices to be offered to Yahweh alone; (3) vv. 10-12, prohibition of the eating of blood; (4) vv. 13, 14, the blood of animals not used in sacrifice to be poured on the ground. The chapter as a whole is to be assigned to H. At the same time it exhibits many marks of affinity with P, a phenomenon most easily explained by the supposition that older laws of H have been expanded and modified by later hands in the spirit of P. Clear instances of such revision may be seen in the references to "the door of the tent of meeting" (vv. 4, 5, 6, 9) and "the camp" (v. 3), as well as in vv. 6, 11, 12-14; vv. 15, 16 (prohibiting the eating of animals that die a natural death or are torn by beasts) differ formally from the preceding paragraphs, and are to be assigned to P. What remains after the excision of later additions, however, is not entirely uniform, and points to earlier editorial work on the part of the compiler of H. Thus vv. 3-7 reflect two points of view, vv. 3, 4 drawing a contrast between profane slaughter and sacrifice, while vv. 5-7 distinguish between sacrifices offered to Yahweh and those offered to demons.

Chap. xviii. contains laws on prohibited marriages (vv. 6-18) and various acts of unchastity (vv. 19-23) embedded in a paraenetic setting (vv. 1-5 and 24-30), the laws being given in the 2nd pers. sing., while the framework employs the 2nd pers. plural. With the exception of v. 21 (on Molech worship), which is here out of place, and has possibly been introduced from xx. 2-5, the chapter displays all the characteristics of H.

Chap. xix. is a collection of miscellaneous laws, partly moral, partly religious, of which the fundamental principle is stated in v. 2 ("Ye shall be holy"). The various laws are clearly defined by the formula "I am Yahweh," or "I am Yahweh your God," phrases which are especially characteristic of chaps. xviii.–xx. The first group of laws (vv. 3 f.) corresponds to the first table of the decalogue, while vv. 11-18 are analogous to the second table; vv. 5-8 (on peace-offerings) are obviously out of place here, and are possibly to be referred to the cognate passage xxii. 29 f., while the humanitarian provisions of vv. 9 and 10 (cf. xxiii. 22) have no connexion with the immediate context; similarly v. 20 (to which a later redactor has added vv. 21, 22, in accordance with vi. 6 f.) appears to be a fragment from a penal code; the passage resembles Exod. xx. [illegible] the offence is clearly one against property, the omission of the punishment being possibly due to the redactor who added [illegible]

[illegible] xx. Prohibitions against Molech worship, vv. 2-5, witchcraft [illegible] unlawful marriages and acts of unchastity, vv. [illegible] chap. xviii., the main body of laws is provided with a paraenetic setting, vv. 7, 8 and 22-24; it differs from that chapter, [illegible] the death penalty in each case for disobedience [illegible] the close resemblance between the two chapters, [illegible] assumed that they are derived from the same [illegible] the later chapter was added for the purpose of [illegible] This view, however, is not borne out by [illegible] two chapters, for four of the cases mentioned [illegible] are ignored in chap. xx., while the [illegible] are also different; further, it is [illegible] the two chapters are separated [illegible] explanation is that the compiler [illegible] but independent, sources. Signs [illegible] especially in vv. 2-5, where vv. 4 f. are a [illegible] the inconsistency of v. 2 with [illegible] connected with xix. 31, appears to [illegible] be ascribed to the same hand [illegible] context—it would be more [illegible] setting (vv. 7, 8 and 22-24) [illegible] who doubtless prefaced the [illegible] vv. 2-6. Verses 25, 26 [illegible] on clean and unclean [illegible] probably mark the place [illegible] mood.

[illegible] the priests and offerings [illegible] of (4) ordinary [illegible]

vv. 16-24; (3) the enjoyment of sacred offerings limited to (a) priests, if they are ceremonially clean, xxii. 1-9, and (b) members of a priestly family, vv. 10-16; (4) animals offered in sacrifice must be without blemish, vv. 17-25; (5) further regulations with regard to sacrifices, vv. 26-30, with a paraenetic conclusion, vv. 31-33.

These chapters present considerable difficulty to the literary critic; for while they clearly illustrate the application of the principle of "holiness," and in the main exhibit the characteristic phraseology of H, they also display many striking points of contact with P and the later strata of P, which have been closely interwoven into the original laws. These phenomena can be best explained by the supposition that we have here a body of old laws which have been subjected to more than one revision. The nature of the subjects with which they deal is one that naturally appealed to the priestly schools, and owing to this fact the laws were especially liable to modification and expansion at the hands of later legislators who wished to bring them into conformity with later usage. Signs of such revision may be traced back to the compiler of H, but the evidence shows that the process must have been continued down to the latest period of editorial activity in connexion with P. To redactors of the school of P belong such phrases as "the sons of Aaron" (xxi. 1, 24, xxii. 2, 18), "the seed of Aaron" (xxi. 21, xxii. 4 and "thy seed," v. 17; cf. xxii. 3), "the offerings of the Lord made by fire" (xxi. 6, 21, xxii. 22, 27), "the most holy things" (xxi. 22; cf. xxii. 3 ff. "holy things" only), "throughout their (or your) generations" (xxi. 7, xxii. 3), the references to the anointing of Aaron (xxi. 10, 12) and the Veil (xxi. 23), the introductory formulae (xxi. 1, 16 f., xxii. 1 f., 17 f., 26) and the subscription (xxi. 24). Apart from these redactional additions, chap. xxi. is to be ascribed to H, vv. 6 and 8 being possibly the work of R_s. Most critics detect a stronger influence of P in chap. xxii., more especially in vv. 3-7 and 17-25, 29, 30; most probably these verses have been largely recast and expanded by later editors, but it is noticeable that they contain no mention of either sin- or trespass-offerings.

Chap. xxiii. A calendar of sacred seasons. The chapter consists of two main elements which can easily be distinguished from one another, the one being derived from P and the other from H. To the former belongs the fuller and more elaborate description of vv. 4-8, 21, 23-38; to the latter, vv. 9-20, 22, 39-44. Characteristic of the priestly calendar are (1) the enumeration of "holy convocations," (2) the prohibition of all work, (3) the careful determination of the date by the day and month, (4) the mention of "the offerings made by fire to Yahweh," and (5) the stereotyped form of the regulations. The older calendar, on the other hand, knows nothing of "holy convocations," nor of abstinence from work; the time of the feasts, which are clearly connected with agriculture, is only roughly defined with reference to the harvest (cf. Exod. xxiii. 14 ff., xxxiv. 22; Deut. xvi. 9 ff.).

The calendar of P comprises (a) the Feast of Passover and the Unleavened Cakes, vv. 4-8; (b) a fragment of Pentecost, v. 21; (c) the Feast of Trumpets, vv. 23-25; (d) the Day of Atonement, vv. 26-32; and (e) the Feast of Tabernacles, vv. 33-36, with a subscription in vv. 37, 38. With these have been incorporated the older regulations of H on the Feast of Weeks, or Pentecost, vv. 9-20, which have been retained in place of P's account (cf. v. 21), and on the Feast of Tabernacles, vv. 39-44, the latter being clearly intended to supplement vv. 33-36. The hand of the redactor who combined the two elements may be seen partly in additions designed to accommodate the regulations of H to P (e.g. v. 39a, "on the fifteenth day of the seventh month," and 39b, "and on the eighth day shall be a solemn rest"), partly in the later expansions corresponding to later usage, vv. 12 f., 18, 19a, 21b, 41. Further, vv. 26-32 (on the Day of Atonement, cf. xvi.) are a later addition to the P sections.

Chap. xxiv. affords an interesting illustration of the manner in which the redactor of P has added later elements to the original code of H. For the first part of the chapter, with its regulations as to (a) the lamps in the Tabernacle, vv. 1-4, and (b) the Shewbread, vv. 5-9, is admittedly derived from P, vv. 1-4, forming a supplement to Exod. xxv. 31-40 (cf. xxvii. 20 f.) and Num. viii. 1-4, and vv. 5-9 to Exod. xxv. 30. The rest of the chapter contains old laws (vv. 15b-22) derived from H on blasphemy, manslaughter and injuries to the person, to which the redactor has added an historical setting (vv. 10-14, 23) as well as a few glosses.

Chap. xxv. lays down regulations for the observance of (a) the Sabbatical year, vv. 1-7, 19-22, and (b) the year of Jubilees, vv. 8-18, 23, and then applies the principle of redemption to (1) land and house property, vv. 24-34, and (2) persons, vv. 35-55. The rules for the Sabbatical year (vv. 1-7) are admittedly derived from H, and vv. 19-22 are also from the same source. Their present position after vv. 8-18 is due to the redactor who wished to apply the same rules to the year of Jubilee. But though the former of the two sections on the year of Jubilee (vv. 8-18, 23) exhibits undoubted signs of P, the traces of H are also sufficiently marked to warrant the conclusion that the latter code included laws relating to the year of Jubilee, and that these have been modified by R_p and then connected with the regulations for the Sabbatical year. Signs of the redactor's handiwork may be seen in vv. 9, 11-13 (the year of Jubilee treated as a fallow year) and 15, 16 (cf. the repetition of "ye shall not wrong one another," vv. 14 and 17). Both on historical and on critical grounds, however, it is improbable that the principle of restitution underlying the regulations for the year of Jubilee was originally extended to *persons* in the earlier code. For it is difficult to harmonize the laws as to the release of Hebrew slaves with the other legislation on the same subject (Exod. xxi. 2-6; Deut. xv.), while both the secondary position which they occupy in this chapter and their more elaborate and formal character point to a later origin for *vv.* 35-55. Hence these verses in the main must be assigned to R_p. In this connexion it is noticeable that *vv.* 35-38, 39-40*a*, 43, 47, 53, 55, which show the characteristic marks of H, bear no special relation to the year of Jubilee, but merely inculcate a more humane treatment of those Israelites who are compelled by circumstances to sell themselves either to their brethren or to strangers. It is probable, therefore, that they form no part of the original legislation of the year of Jubilee, but were incorporated at a later period. The present form of *vv.* 24-34 is largely due to R_p, who has certainly added *vv.* 32-34 (cities of the Levites) and probably *vv.* 29-31.

Chap. xxvi. The concluding exhortation. After reiterating commands to abstain from idolatry and to observe the Sabbath, *vv.* 1, 2, the chapter sets forth (*a*) the rewards of obedience, *vv.* 3-13, and (*b*) the penalties incurred by disobedience to the preceding laws, *vv.* 14-46. The discourse, which is spoken throughout in the name of Yahweh, is similar in character to Exod. xxiii. 20-33 and Deut. xxviii., more especially to the latter. That it forms an integral part of H is shown both by the recurrence of the same distinctive phraseology and by the emphasis laid on the same motives. At the same time it is hardly doubtful that the original discourse has been modified and expanded by later hands, especially in the concluding paragraphs. Thus *vv.* 34, 35, which refer back to xxv. 2 ff., interrupt the connexion and must be assigned to the priestly redactor, while *vv.* 40-45 display obvious signs of interpolation. With regard to the literary relation of this chapter with Ezekiel, it must be admitted that Ezekiel presents many striking parallels, and in particular makes use, in common with chap. xxvi., of several expressions which do not occur elsewhere in the Old Testament. But there are also points of difference both as regards phraseology and subject-matter, and in view of these latter it is impossible to hold that Ezekiel was either the author or compiler of this chapter.

Chap. xxvii. On the commutation of vows and tithes. The chapter as a whole must be assigned to a later stratum of P, for while *vv.* 2-25 (on vows) presuppose the year of Jubilee, the section on tithes, *vv.* 30-33, marks a later stage of development than Num. xviii. 21 ff. (P); *vv.* 26-29 (on firstlings and devoted things) are supplementary restrictions to *vv.* 2-25.

Literature.—*Commentaries*: Dillmann-Ryssel, *Die Bücher Exodus und Leviticus* (1897); Driver and White, *SBOT. Leviticus* (English, 1898); B. Baentsch, *Exod. Lev. u. Num.* (HK, 1900) Bertholet, *Leviticus* (KHC, 1901). *Criticism*: The Introductions to the Old Testament by Kuenen, Holzinger, Driver, Cornill, König and the archaeological works of Benzinger and Nowack. Wellhausen, *Die Composition des Hexateuchs*, &c. (1899); Kayser, *Das vorexilische Buch der Urgeschichte Isr.* (1874); Klostermann, *Zeitschrift für Luth. Theologie* (1877); Horst, *Lev. xvii.-xxvi. und Hezekiel* (1881); Wurster, *ZATW* (1884); Baentsch, *Das Heiligkeitsgesetz* (1893); L. P. Paton, "The Relation of Lev. 20 to Lev. 17-19," *Hebraica* (1894); "The Original Form of Leviticus," *JBL* (1897, 1898); "The Holiness Code and Ezekiel," *Pres. and Ref. Review* (1896); Carpenter, *Composition of the Hexateuch* (1902). Articles on Leviticus by G. F. Moore, Hastings's *Dict. Bib.*, and G. Harford Battersby, *Ency. Bib.* (J. F. St.)

LEVY, AMY (1861–1889), English poetess and novelist, second daughter of Lewis Levy, was born at Clapham on the 10th of November 1861, and was educated at Newnham College, Cambridge. She showed a precocious aptitude for writing verse of exceptional merit, and in 1884 she published a volume of poems, *A Minor Poet and Other Verse*, some of the pieces in which had already been printed at Cambridge with the title *Xantippe and Other Poems*. The high level of this first publication was maintained in *A London Plane Tree and Other Poems*, a collection of lyrics published in 1889, in which the prevailing pessimism of the writer's temperament was conspicuous. She had already in 1888 tried her hand at prose fiction in *The Romance of a Shop*, which was followed by *Reuben Sachs*, a powerful novel. She committed suicide on the 10th of September 1889.

LEVY, AUGUSTE MICHEL (1844–), French geologist, was born in Paris on the 7th of August 1844. He became inspector-general of mines, and director of the Geological Survey of France. He was distinguished for his researches on eruptive rocks, their microscopic structure and origin; and he early employed the polarizing microscope for the determination of minerals. In his many contributions to scientific journals he described the granulite group, and dealt with pegmatites, variolites, eurites, the ophites of the Pyrenees, the extinct volcanoes of Central France, gneisses, and the origin of crystalline schists. He wrote *Structures et classification des roches éruptives* (1889), but his more elaborate studies were carried on with F. Fouqué. Together they wrote on the artificial production of felspar, nepheline and other minerals, and also of meteorites, and produced *Minéralogie micrographique* (1879) and *Synthèse des minéraux et des roches* (1882). Levy also collaborated with A. Lacroix in *Les Minéraux des roches* (1888) and *Tableau des minéraux des roches* (1889).

LEVY (Fr. *levée*, from *lever*, Lat. *levare*, to lift, raise), the raising of money by the collection of an assessment, &c., a tax or compulsory contribution; also the collection of a body of men for military or other purposes. When all the able-bodied men of a nation are enrolled for service, the French term *levée en masse*, levy in mass, is frequently used.

LEWALD, FANNY (1811–1889), German author, was born at Königsberg in East Prussia on the 24th of March 1811, of Jewish parentage. When seventeen years of age she embraced Christianity, and after travelling in Germany, France and Italy, settled in 1845 at Berlin. Here, in 1854, she married the author, Adolf Wilhelm Theodor Stahr (1805–1876), and removed after his death in 1876 to Dresden, where she resided, engaged in literary work, until her death on the 5th of August 1889. Fanny Lewald is less remarkable for her writings, which are mostly sober, matter-of-fact works, though displaying considerable talent and culture, than for her championship of "women's rights," a question which she was practically the first German woman to take up, and for her scathing satire on the sentimentalism of the Gräfin Hahn Hahn. This authoress she ruthlessly attacked in the exquisite parody (*Diogena, Roman von Iduna Gräfin H . . . . H. . . .* (2nd ed., 1847). Among the best known of her novels are *Klementine* (1842); *Prinz Louis Ferdinand* (1849; 2nd ed., 1859); *Das Mädchen von Hela* (1860); *Von Geschlecht zu Geschlecht* (8 vols., 1863–1865); *Benvenuto* (1875), and *Stella* (1883; English by B. Marshall, 1884). Of her writings in defence of the emancipation of women *Osterbriefe für die Frauen* (1863) and *Für und wider die Frauen* (1870) are conspicuous. Her autobiography, *Meine Lebensgeschichte* (6 vols., 1861–1862), is brightly written and affords interesting glimpses of the literary life of her time.

A selection of her works was published under the title *Gesammelte Schriften* in 12 vols. (1870–1874). Cf. K. Frenzel, *Erinnerungen und Strömungen* (1890).

LEWANIKA (*c.* 1860–), paramount chief of the Barotse and subject tribes occupying the greater part of the upper Zambezi basin, was the twenty-second of a long line of rulers, whose founder invaded the Barotse valley about the beginning of the 17th century, and according to tradition was the son of a woman named Buya Mamboa by a god. The graves of successive ruling chiefs are to this day respected and objects of pilgrimage for purposes of ancestor worship. Lewanika was born on the upper Kabompo in troublous times, where his father—Letia, a son of a former ruler—lived in exile during the interregnum of a foreign dynasty (Makololo), which remained in possession from about 1830 to 1865, when the Makololo were practically exterminated in a night by a well-organized revolt. Once more masters of their own country, the Barotse invited Sepopa, an uncle of Lewanika, to rule over them. Eleven years of brutality and licence resulted in the tyrant's expulsion and subsequent assassination, his place being taken by Ngwana-Wina, a nephew. Within a year abuse of power brought about this chief's downfall (1877), and he was succeeded by Lobosi, who assumed the name of Lewanika in 1885. The early years of his reign were also stained by many acts of blood, until in 1884 the torture and murder of his own brother led to open rebellion, and it was only through extreme presence of mind that the chief escaped with his life into exile. His cousin, Akufuna or Tatela, was then proclaimed chief. It was during his brief reign that François Coillard, the eminent missionary, arrived at Lialui, the capital. The following year Lewanika, having collected his partisans, deposed the usurper and re-established his power. Ruthless revenge not unmixed with treachery characterized his return to power, but gradually the strong

Lev xviii.-xx.; (3) the calendar of
stage of development than the fixed
(4) the sin- and trespass-offerings are
xl. 39, xlii. 13, xliv. 29, xlvi. 20);
found especially in Ezek. xviii., xx
netic setting and the laws; and la
with Ezekiel points to the greater or
however, who is followed by Bert
xxvi. is rather an independent
Ezekiel. The same writer further
separate elements, viz. chaps. xvii.;
in chaps. xxiii.-xxv.; and xxii., xx
later than Ezekiel, while the sec
author. But the arguments wh
threefold origin of H are not
impression of unity which the cod

Chap. xvii. comprises four
marked off by similar introduct
3-7, prohibition of the slaughter
presented to Yahweh; (2) vv. 8, 9,
alone; (3) vv. 10-12, prohibition
14, the blood of animals not
ground. The chapter as a whole
same time it exhibits many mar
most easily explained by the sug
been expanded and modified by
instances of such revision may
door of the tent of meeting"
as well as in vv. 6, 11, 12-14;
animals that die a natural death
from the preceding paragraph
remains after the excision of
uniform, and points to earl
compiler of H. Thus vv. 3-7
drawing a contrast between
vv. 5-7 distinguish between
offered to demons.

Chap. xviii. contains law
and various acts of uncha
setting (vv. 1-5 and 24-30),
sing., while the framework
exception of v. 21 (on Mol
and has possibly been intr
all the characteristics of H

Chap. xix. is a collect
partly religious, of which
("Ye shall be holy"). T
formula "I am Yahweh,"
which are especially ch
group of laws (vv. 3 f.)
while vv. 11-18 are an
peace-offerings) are ob
to be restored to the
tarian provisions of
with the immediate
redactor has added
to be a fragment from
xxi. 7 ff., and the offe
of the punishment
vv. 21, 22.

Chap. xx. Prohi
craft, vv. 6 and 27,
10-21. Like chap.
paraenetic setting.
however, in prese
ence. Owing to
many critics hav
source and that
supplying the pe
a comparison of
in chap. xviii. (
order and in par
difficult on this
by chap. xix. A
of H has drawn
of revision are no
later addition in
v. 3 (Rr); v. 6,
be less original th
as v. 3; v. 9 can
suitable after xxi
is to be assigned
parallel version w
apparently forme
animals similar to
where H's regulati

Chaps. xxi., xxii.
ings, viz. (1) regu
priests, xxi. 1-9, an
physical defects wh

in themselves is a futile question that belongs to the sterile region of "metempirics." But philosophical questions may be so stated as to be susceptible of a precise solution by scientific method. Thus, since the relation of subject to object falls within our experience, it is a proper matter for philosophic investigation. It may be questioned whether Lewes is right in thus identifying the methods of science and philosophy. Philosophy is not a mere extension of scientific knowledge; it is an investigation of the nature and validity of the knowing process itself. In any case Lewes cannot be said to have done much to aid in the settlement of properly philosophical questions. His whole treatment of the question of the relation of subject to object is vitiated by a confusion between the scientific truth that mind and body coexist in the living organism and the philosophic truth that all knowledge of objects implies a knowing subject. In other words, to use Shadworth Hodgson's phrase, he mixes up the question of the *genesis* of mental forms with the question of their *nature* (see *Philosophy of Reflexion*, ii. 40–58). Thus he reaches the "monistic" doctrine that mind and matter are two aspects of the same existence by attending simply to the parallelism between psychical and physical processes given as a fact (or a probable fact) of our experience, and by leaving out of account their relation as subject and object in the cognitive act. His identification of the two as phases of one existence is open to criticism, not only from the point of view of philosophy, but from that of science. In his treatment of such ideas as "sensibility," "sentience" and the like, he does not always show whether he is speaking of physical or of psychical phenomena. Among the other properly philosophic questions discussed in these two volumes the nature of the casual relation is perhaps the one which is handled with most freshness and suggestiveness. The third volume, *The Physical Basis of Mind*, further develops the writer's views on organic activities as a whole. He insists strongly on the radical distinction between organic and inorganic processes, and on the impossibility of ever explaining the former by purely mechanical principles. With respect to the nervous system, he holds that all its parts have one and the same elementary property, namely, sensibility. Thus sensibility belongs as much to the lower centres of the spinal cord as to the brain, contributing in this more elementary form elements to the "subconscious" region of mental life. The higher functions of the nervous system, which make up our conscious mental life, are merely more complex modifications of this fundamental property of nerve substance. Closely related to this doctrine is the view that the nervous organism acts as a whole, that particular mental operations cannot be referred to definitely circumscribed regions of the brain, and that the hypothesis of nervous activity passing in the centre by an isolated pathway from one nerve-cell to another is altogether illusory. By insisting on the complete coincidence between the regions of nerve-action and sentience, and by holding that these are but different aspects of one thing, he is able to attack the doctrine of animal and human automatism, which affirms that feeling or consciousness is merely an incidental concomitant of nerve-action and in no way essential to the chain of physical events. Lewes's views in psychology, partly opened up in the earlier volumes of the *Problems*, are more fully worked out in the last two volumes (3rd series). He discusses the method of psychology with much insight. He claims against Comte and his followers a place for introspection in psychological research. In addition to this subjective method there must be an objective, which consists partly in a reference to nervous conditions and partly in the employment of sociological and historical data. Biological knowledge, or a consideration of the organic conditions, would only help us to explain mental *functions*, as feeling and thinking; it would not assist us to understand differences of mental *faculty* as manifested in different races and stages of human development. The organic conditions of these differences will probably for ever escape detection. Hence they can be explained only as the products of the social environment. This idea of dealing with mental phenomena in their relation to social and historical conditions is probably Lewes's most important contribution to psychology. Among other points which he emphasizes is the complexity of mental phenomena. Every mental state is regarded as compounded of three factors in different proportions—namely, a process of sensible affection, of logical grouping and of motor impulse. But Lewes's work in psychology consists less in any definite discoveries than in the inculcation of a sound and just method. His biological training prepared him to view mind as a complex unity, in which the various functions interact one on the other, and of which the highest processes are identical with and evolved out of the lower. Thus the operations of thought, "or the logic of signs," are merely a more complicated form of the elementary operations of sensation and instinct or "the logic of feeling." The whole of the last volume of the *Problems* may be said to be an illustration of this position. It is a valuable repository of psychological facts, many of them drawn from the more obscure regions of mental life and from abnormal experience, and is throughout suggestive and stimulating. To suggest and to stimulate the mind, rather than to supply it with any complete system of knowledge, may be said to be Lewes's service in philosophy. The exceptional rapidity and versatility of his intelligence seems to account at once for the freshness in his way of envisaging the subject-matter of philosophy and psychology, and for the want of satisfactory elaboration and of systematic co-ordination. (J. S.; X.)

LEWES, a market-town and municipal borough and the county town of Sussex, England, in the Lewes parliamentary division, 50 m. S. from London by the London, Brighton & South Coast railway. Pop. (1901) 11,249. It is picturesquely situated on the slope of a chalk down falling to the river Ouse. Ruins of the old castle, supposed to have been founded by King Alfred and rebuilt by William de Warenne shortly after the Conquest, rise from the height. There are two mounds which bore keeps, an uncommon feature. The castle guarded the pass through the downs formed by the valley of the Ouse. In one of the towers is the collection of the Sussex Archaeological Society. St Michael's church is without architectural merit, but contains old brasses and monuments; St Anne's church is a transitional Norman structure; St Thomas-at-Cliffe is Perpendicular; St John's, Southover, of mixed architecture, preserves some early Norman portions, and has some relics of the Warenne family. In the grounds of the Cluniac priory of St Pancras, founded in 1078, the leaden coffins of William de Warenne and Gundrada his wife were dug up during an excavation for the railway in 1845. There is a free grammar school dating from 1512, and among the other public buildings are the town hall and corn exchange, county hall, prison, and the Fitzroy memorial library. The industries include the manufacture of agricultural implements, brewing, tanning, and iron and brass founding. The municipal borough is under a mayor, 6 aldermen and 18 councillors. Area, 1042 acres.

The many neolithic and bronze implements that have been discovered, and the numerous tumuli and earthworks which surround Lewes, indicate its remote origin. The town Lewes (Loewas, Loewen, Leswa, Laquis, Latisaquensis) was in the royal demesne of the Saxon kings, from whom it received the privilege of a market. Æthelstan established two royal mints there, and by the reign of Edward the Confessor, and probably before, Lewes was certainly a borough. William I. granted the whole barony of Lewes, including the revenue arising from the town, to William de Warenne, who converted an already existing fortification into a place of residence. His descendants continued to hold the barony until the beginning of the 14th century. In default of male issue, it then passed to the earl of Arundel, with whose descendants it remained until 1439, when it was divided between the Norfolks, Dorsets and Abergavennys. By 1086 the borough had increased 30% in value since the beginning of the reign, and its importance as a port and market-town is evident from Domesday. A gild merchant seems to have existed at an early date. The first mention of it is in a charter of Reginald de Warenne, about 1148, by which he restored to the burgesses the privileges they had enjoyed in the time of his grandfather and father, but of which they had been deprived. In 1595 a "Fellowship" took the place of the old gild and in conjunction with two constables governed the town until the beginning of the 18th century. The borough seal probably dates from the 14th century. Lewes was incorporated by royal charter in 1881. The town returned two representatives to parliament from 1295 until deprived of one member in 1867. It was disfranchised in 1885. Earl Warenne and his descendants held the fairs and markets from 1066. In 1792 the fair-days were the 6th of May, Whit-Tuesday, the 26th of July (for wool), and the 2nd of October. The market-day was Saturday. Fairs are now held on the 6th of May for horses and cattle, the 20th of July for wool, and the 21st and 28th of September for Southdown sheep. A corn-market is held every Tuesday, and a stock-market every alternate Monday. The trade in wool has been important since the 14th century.

Lewes was the scene of the battle fought on the 14th of May 1264 between Henry III. and Simon de Montfort, earl of Leicester. Led by the king and by his son, the future king Edward I., the royalists left Oxford, took Northampton and drove Montfort from Rochester into London. Then, harassed on the route by their foes, they marched through Kent into Sussex and took up their quarters at Lewes, a stronghold of the royalist Earl Warenne. Meanwhile, reinforced by a number of Londoners, Earl Simon left London and reached Fletching, about 9 m. north of Lewes,

a baronet in 1846. Young Lewis was educated at Eton and at Christ Church, Oxford, where in 1828 he took a first-class in classics and a second-class in mathematics. He then entered the Middle Temple, and was called to the bar in 1831. In 1833 he undertook his first public work as one of the commissioners to inquire into the condition of the poor Irish residents in the United Kingdom.[1] In 1834 Lord Althorp included him in the commission to inquire into the state of church property and church affairs generally in Ireland. To this fact we owe his work on *Local Disturbances in Ireland, and the Irish Church Question* (London, 1836), in which he condemned the existing connexion between church and state, proposed a state provision for the Catholic clergy, and maintained the necessity of an efficient workhouse organization. During this period Lewis's mind was much occupied with the study of language. Before leaving college he had published some observations on Whately's doctrine of the predicables, and soon afterwards he assisted Thirlwall and Hare in starting the *Philological Museum*. Its successor, the *Classical Museum*, he also supported by occasional contributions. In 1835 he published an *Essay on the Origin and Formation of the Romance Languages* (re-edited in 1862), the first effective criticism in England of Raynouard's theory of a uniform romance tongue, represented by the poetry of the troubadours. He also compiled a glossary of provincial words used in Herefordshire and the adjoining counties. But the most important work of this earlier period was one to which his logical and philological tastes contributed. The *Remarks on the Use and Abuse of some Political Terms* (London, 1832) may have been suggested by Bentham's *Book of Parliamentary Fallacies*, but it shows all that power of clear sober original thinking which marks his larger and later political works. Moreover, he translated Boeckh's *Public Economy of Athens* and Müller's *History of Greek Literature*, and he assisted Tufnell in the translation of Müller's *Dorians*. Some time afterwards he edited a text of the *Fables* of Babrius. While his friend Hayward conducted the *Law Magazine*, he wrote in it frequently on such subjects as secondary punishments and the penitentiary system. In 1836, at the request of Lord Glenelg, he accompanied John Austin to Malta, where they spent nearly two years reporting on the condition of the island and framing a new code of laws. One leading object of both commissioners was to associate the Maltese in the responsible government of the island. On his return to England Lewis succeeded his father as one of the principal poor-law commissioners. In 1841 appeared the *Essay on the Government of Dependencies*, a systematic statement and discussion of the various relations in which colonies may stand towards the mother country. In 1844 Lewis married Lady Maria Theresa Lister, sister of Lord Clarendon, and a lady of literary tastes. Much of their married life was spent in Kent House, Knightsbridge. They had no children. In 1847 Lewis resigned his office. He was then returned for the county of Hereford, and Lord John Russell appointed him secretary to the Board of Control, but a few months afterwards he became under-secretary to the Home Office. In this capacity he introduced two important bills, one for the abolition of turnpike trusts and the management of highways by a mixed county board, the other for the purpose of defining and regulating the law of parochial assessment. In 1850 he succeeded Hayter as financial secretary to the treasury. About this time, also, appeared his *Essay on the Influence of Authority in Matters of Opinion*. On the dissolution of parliament which followed the resignation of Lord John Russell's ministry in 1852, Lewis was defeated for Herefordshire and then for Peterborough. Excluded from parliament he accepted the editorship of the *Edinburgh Review*, and remained editor until 1855. During this period he served on the Oxford commission, and on the commission to inquire into the government of London. But its chief fruits were the *Treatise on the Methods of Observation and Reasoning in Politics*, and the *Enquiry into the Credibility of the Early Roman History*,[2] in which he vigorously attacked

[1] See the *Abstract of Final Report of Commissioners of Irish Poor Enquiry*, &c., by G. C. Lewis and N. Senior (1837).

[2] Translated into German by Liebrecht (Hanover, 1858).

the theory of epic lays and other theories on which Niebuhr's reconstruction of that history had proceeded. In 1855 Lewis succeeded his father in the baronetcy. He was at once elected member for the Radnor boroughs, and Lord Palmerston made him chancellor of the exchequer. He had a war loan to contract and heavy additional taxation to impose, but his industry, method and clear vision carried him safely through. After the change of ministry in 1859 Sir George became home secretary under Lord Palmerston, and in 1861, much against his wish, he succeeded Sidney Herbert (Lord Herbert of Lea) at the War Office. The closing years of his life were marked by increasing intellectual vigour. In 1859 he published an able *Essay on Foreign Jurisdiction and the Extradition of Criminals*, a subject to which the attempt on Napoleon's life, the discussions on the Conspiracy Bill, and the trial of Bernard, had drawn general attention. He advocated the extension of extradition treaties, and condemned the principal idea of *Weltrechtsordnung* which Mohl of Heidelberg had proposed. His two latest works were the *Survey of the Astronomy of the Ancients*, in which, without professing any knowledge of Oriental languages, he applied a sceptical analysis to the ambitious Egyptology of Bunsen; and the *Dialogue on the Best Form of Government*, in which, under the name of Crito, the author points out to the supporters of the various systems that there is no one abstract government which is the best possible for all times and places. An essay on the *Characteristics of Federal, National, Provincial and Municipal Government* does not seem to have been published. Sir George died in April 1863. A marble bust by Weekes stands in Westminster Abbey.

Lewis was a man of mild and affectionate disposition, much beloved by a large circle of friends, among whom were Sir E. Head, the Grotes, the Austins, Lord Stanhope, J. S. Mill, Dean Milman, the Duff Gordons. In public life he was distinguished, as Lord Aberdeen said, "for candour, moderation, love of truth." He had a passion for the systematic acquirement of knowledge, and a keen and sound critical faculty. His name has gone down to history as that of a many-sided man, sound in judgment, unselfish in political life, and abounding in practical good sense.

A reprint from the *Edinburgh Review* of his long series of papers on the *Administration of Great Britain* appeared in 1864, and his *Letters to various Friends* (1870) were edited by his brother Gilbert, who succeeded him in the baronetcy.

LEWIS, HENRY CARVILL (1853-1888), American geologist, was born in Philadelphia on the 16th of November 1853. Educated in the university of Pennsylvania he took the degree of M.A. in 1876. He became attached to the Geological Survey of Pennsylvania in 1879, serving for three years as a volunteer member, and during this term he became greatly interested in the study of glacial phenomena. In 1880 he was chosen professor of mineralogy in the Philadelphia academy of natural sciences, and in 1883 he was appointed to the chair of geology in Haverford College, Pennsylvania. During the winters of 1885 to 1887 he studied petrology under H. F. Rosenbusch at Heidelberg, and during the summers he investigated the glacial geology of northern Europe and the British Islands. His observations in North America, where he had studied under Professor G. F. Wright, Professor T. C. Chamberlin and Warren Upham, had demonstrated the former extension of land-ice, and the existence of great terminal moraines. In 1884 his *Report on the Terminal Moraine in Pennsylvania and New York* was published: a work containing much information on the limits of the North American ice-sheet. In Britain he sought to trace in like manner the southern extent of the terminal moraines formed by British ice-sheets, but before his conclusions were matured he died at Manchester on the 21st of July 1888. The results of his observations were published in 1894 entitled *Papers and Notes on the Glacial Geology of Great Britain and Ireland*, edited by Dr H. W. Crosskey.

See "Prof. Henry Carvill Lewis and his Work in Glacial Geology," by Warren Upham, *Amer. Geol.* vol. ii. (Dec. 1888) p. 371, with portrait.

LEWIS, JOHN FREDERICK (1805-1876), British painter, son of F. C. Lewis, engraver, was born in London. He was elected in 1827 associate of the Society of Painters in Water Colours, of which he became full member in 1829 and president in 1855; he resigned in 1858, and was made associate of the Royal Academy in 1859 and academician in 1865. Much of his earlier life was spent in Spain, Italy and the East, but he returned to England in 1851 and for the remainder of his career devoted himself almost exclusively to Eastern subjects, which he treated with extraordinary care and minuteness of finish, and with much beauty of technical method. He is represented by a picture, "Edfou: Upper Egypt," in the National Gallery of British Art. He achieved equal eminence in both oil and water-colour painting.

LEWIS, MATTHEW GREGORY (1775-1818), English romance-writer and dramatist, often referred to as "Monk" Lewis, was born in London on the 9th of July 1775. He was educated for a diplomatic career at Westminster school and at Christ Church, Oxford, spending most of his vacations abroad in the study of modern languages; and in 1794 he proceeded to the Hague as attaché to the British embassy. His stay there lasted only a few months, but was marked by the composition, in ten weeks, of his romance *Ambrosio, or the Monk*, which was published in the summer of the following year. It immediately achieved celebrity; but some passages it contained were of such a nature that about a year after its appearance an injunction to restrain its sale was moved for and a rule *nisi* obtained. Lewis published a second edition from which he had expunged, as he thought, all the objectionable passages, but the work still remains of such a character as almost to justify the severe language in which Byron in *English Bards and Scotch Reviewers* addresses—

> "Wonder-working Lewis, Monk or Bard,
> Who fain would'st make Parnassus a churchyard;
> Even Satan's self with thee might dread to dwell,
> And in thy skull discern a deeper hell."

Whatever its demerits, ethical or aesthetic, may have been, *The Monk* did not interfere with the reception of Lewis into the best English society; he was favourably noticed at court, and almost as soon as he came of age he obtained a seat in the House of Commons as member for Hindon, Wilts. After some years, however, during which he never addressed the House, he finally withdrew from a parliamentary career. His tastes lay wholly in the direction of literature, and *The Castle Spectre* (1796, a musical drama of no great literary merit, but which enjoyed a long popularity on the stage), *The Minister* (a translation from Schiller's *Kabale u. Liebe*), *Rolla* (1797, a translation from Kotzebue), with numerous other operatic and tragic pieces, appeared in rapid succession. *The Bravo of Venice*, a romance translated from the German, was published in 1804; next to *The Monk* it is the best known work of Lewis. By the death of his father he succeeded to a large fortune, and in 1815 embarked for the West Indies to visit his estates; in the course of this tour, which lasted four months, the *Journal of a West Indian Proprietor*, published posthumously in 1833, was written. A second visit to Jamaica was undertaken in 1817, in order that he might become further acquainted with, and able to ameliorate, the condition of the slave population; the fatigues to which he exposed himself in the tropical climate brought on a fever which terminated fatally on the homeward voyage on the 14th of May 1818.

The Life and Correspondence of M. G. Lewis, in two volumes, was published in 1839.

LEWIS, MERIWETHER (1774-1809), American explorer, was born near Charlottesville, Virginia, on the 18th of August 1774. In 1794 he volunteered with the Virginia troops called out to suppress the "Whisky Insurrection," was commissioned as ensign in the regular United States army in 1795, served with distinction under General Anthony Wayne in the campaigns against the Indians, and attained the rank of captain in 1797. From 1801 to 1803 he was the private secretary of President Jefferson. On the 18th of January 1803 Jefferson sent a confidential message to Congress urging the development of trade with the Indians of the Missouri Valley and recommending that an exploring party be sent into this region, notwithstanding

on the 13th of May. Efforts at reconciliation h... led his army against the town, which he hoped to on the following day. His plan was to direct his m against the priory of St Pancras, which sheltered th his brother Richard, earl of Cornwall, king of the while causing the enemy to believe that his princip... was the castle, where Prince Edward was. But ... was not complete and the royalists rushed from the meet the enemy in the open field. Edward led h against the Londoners, who were gathered around th of Montfort, put them to flight, pursued them for ... and killed a great number of them. Montfort's ru... had been successful. He was not with his standard thought, but with the pick of his men he attack... followers and took prisoner both the king and ... Before Edward returned from his chase the earl was i... of the town. In its streets the prince strove to r fortunes, but in vain. Many of his men perished but others escaped, one band, consisting of Earl W others, taking refuge in Pevensey Castle. Edward sanctuary and on the following day peace was n the king and the earl.

LEWES, a town in Sussex county, Delaware, U S.E. part of the state, on Delaware Bay. Pop. (Lewes is served by the Philadelphia, Baltimore & (Pennsylvania System), and the Maryland, Delaw... railways. Its harbour is formed by the Delaware built by the national government and complete... 2½ m. above it another breakwater was complete... 1901 by the government. The cove between ... harbour of refuge of about 550 acres. At the mout Bay, about 2 m. below Lewes, is the Henlopen the oldest lighthouses in America. The Delaw... make their headquarters at Lewes. Lewes has a ... northern cities in fruits and vegetables, and is a s... of the Wilmington Customs District. The first Delaware soil by Europeans was made near h Dutch colonists, sent by a company organiz... the previous year by Samuel Blommaert, Killian David Pieterszen de Vries and others. The s... place Zwaanendael, valley of swans. The sett... entirely destroyed by the Indians, and a second ... whom de Vries, who had been made director brought in 1632 remained for only two years. ... settlement is important; because of it the Engl... the Delaware country with Maryland, for the ... of 1632 restricted colonization to land with... boundaries, uncultivated and either uninhab... only by Indians. In 1658 the Dutch estab... trading post, and in 1659 erected a fort at Zw... the annexation of the Delaware counties to Pe... its name was changed to Lewes, after the to... Sussex, England. It was pillaged by Frenc... One of the last naval battles of the War of fought in the bay near Lewes on the 8th of Ap... American privateer "Hyder Ally" (16), comm... Joshua Barnes (1750–1818), defeated and ca... sloop "General Monk" (20), which had ... privateer, the "General Washington," had Admiral Arbuthnot's squadron in 1780, ... chased by the United States government an... Washington," was commanded by Capta... 1784. In March 1813 the town was bomb... frigate.

See the "History of Lewes" in the Papers of ... of Delaware, No. xxxviii. (Wilmington, ... *History of Delaware* (2 vols., Philadelphia, ...

LEWIS, SIR GEORGE C... English statesman and ... the 21st of April ... Court, ... adv...

as a condition of membership. There are no secret fraternities. From the beginning women have been admitted on the same terms as men. The Cobb Divinity School (Free Baptist), which was founded at Parsonfield, Maine, in 1840 as a department of Parsonfield Seminary, and was situated in 1842–1844 at Dracut, Massachusetts, in 1844–1854 at Whitestown, New York, and in 1854–1870 at New Hampton, New Hampshire, was moved to Lewiston in 1870 and became a department (known as Bates Theological Seminary until 1888) of Bates College, with which it was merged in 1908. Lewiston has a fine city hall, a Carnegie library and a public park of 10½ acres, with a bronze soldiers' monument by Franklin Simmons, who was born in 1839 at Webster near Lewiston, and is known for his statues of Roger Williams, William King, Francis H. Pierpont and U. S. Grant in the national Capitol, and for "Grief" and "History" on the Peace Monument at Washington. In Lewiston are the Central Maine General Hospital (1888), the Sisters' Hospital (1888), under the charge of the French Catholic Sisters of Charity, a home for aged women, a young women's home and the Healey Asylum for boys. The Shrine Building (Kora Temple), dedicated in 1909, is the headquarters of the Shriners of the state. The river at Lewiston breaks over a ledge of mica-schist and gneiss, the natural fall of 40 ft. having been increased to more than 50 ft. by a strong granite dam, and 3 m. above the city at Deer Rips a cement dam furnishes 10,000 horse-power. The water-power thus obtained is distributed by canals from the nearer dam and transmitted by wire from the upper dam. The manufacture of cotton goods is the principal industry, and in 1905 the product of the city's cotton mills was valued at about one-third of that of the mills of the whole state. Among other industries are the manufacture of woollen goods, shirts, dry-plates, carriages, spools and bobbins, and boots and shoes, and the dyeing and finishing of textiles. The total factory product in 1905 was valued at $8,527,649. The municipality owns its water works and electric lighting plant. Lewiston was settled in 1770, incorporated as a township in 1795 and chartered as a city in 1861. It was the home of Nelson Dingley (1832–1899), who from 1856 until his death controlled the Lewiston *Journal*. He was governor of the state in 1874–1876, Republican representative in Congress in 1881–1899, and the drafter of the Dingley Tariff Bill (1897).

LEWIS-WITH-HARRIS, the most northerly island of the Outer Hebrides, Scotland. It is sometimes called the Long Island and is 24 m. from the nearest point of the mainland, from which it is separated by the strait called The Minch. It is 60 m. long and has an extreme breadth of 30 m., its average breadth being 15 m. It is divided into two portions by a line roughly drawn between Loch Resort on the west and Loch Seaforth on the east, of which the larger or more northerly portion, known as Lewis (pron. *Lews*), belongs to the county of Ross and Cromarty and the lesser, known as Harris, to Inverness-shire. The area of the whole island is 492,800 acres, or 770 sq. m., of which 368,000 acres belong to Lewis. In 1891 the population of Lewis was 27,045, of Harris 3681; in 1901 the population of Lewis was 28,357, of Harris 3803, or 32,160 for the island, of whom 17,175 were females, 11,209 spoke Gaelic only, and 17,685 both Gaelic and English. There is communication with certain ports of the Western Highlands by steamer via Stornoway every week—oftener during the tourist and special seasons—the steamers frequently calling at Loch Erisort, Loch Sealg, Ardvourlie, Tarbert, Ardvey, Rodel and The Obe. The coast is indented to a remarkable degree, the principal sea-lochs in Harris being East and West Loch Tarbert; and in Lewis, Loch Seaforth, Loch Erisort and Broad Bay (or Loch a Tuath) on the east coast and Loch Roag and Loch Resort on the west. The mainland is dotted with innumerable fresh-water lakes. The island is composed of gneiss rocks, excepting a patch of granite near Carloway, small bands of intrusive basalt at Gress and in Eye Peninsula and some Torridonian sandstone at Stornoway, Tong, Vatskir and Carloway. Most of Harris is mountainous, there being more than thirty peaks above 1000 ft. high. Lewis is comparatively flat, save in the south-east, where Ben More reaches 1874 ft., and in the south-west, where Mealasbhal (1885) is the highest point; but in this division there are only eleven peaks exceeding 1000 ft. in height. The rivers are small and unimportant. The principal capes are the Butt of Lewis, in the extreme north, where the cliffs are nearly 150 ft. high and crowned with a lighthouse, the light of which is visible for 19 m., Tolsta Head, Tiumpan Head and Cabag Head, on the east; Renish Point, in the extreme south; and, on the west, Toe Head and Gallon Head. The following inhabited islands in the Inverness-shire division belong to the parish of Harris: off the S.W. coast, Bernera (pop. 524), Ensay, Killigray and Pabbay; off the W. coast, Scarp (160), Soay and Tarrensay (72); off the E. coast, Scalpa (587) and Scotasay. Belonging to the county of Ross and Cromarty are Great Bernera (580) to the W. of Lewis, in the parish of Uig, and the Shiant Isles, about 21 m. S. of Stornoway, in the parish of Lochs, so named from the number of its sea lochs and fresh-water lakes. The south-eastern base of Broad Bay is furnished by the peninsula of Eye, attached to the main mass by so slender a neck as seemingly to be on the point of becoming itself an island. Much of the surface of both Lewis and Harris is composed of peat and swamp; there are scanty fragments of an ancient forest. The rainfall for the year averages 41·7 in., autumn and winter being very wet. Owing to the influence of the Gulf Stream, however, the temperature is fairly high, averaging for the year 46·6° F., for January 39·5° F. and for August 56·5° F.

The economic conditions of the island correspond with its physical conditions. The amount of cultivable land is small and poor. Sir James Matheson (1796–1878), who purchased the island in 1844, is said to have spent nearly £350,000 in reclamation and improvements. Barley and potatoes are the chief crops. A large number of black cattle are reared and some sheep-farming is carried on in Harris. Kelp-making, once important, has been extinct for many years. Harris has obtained great reputation for tweeds. The cloth has an aroma of heather and peat, and is made in the dwellings of the cotters, who use dyes of long-established excellence. The fisheries are the principal mainstay of the people. In spite of the very considerable reductions in rent effected by the Crofters' Commission (appointed in 1886) and the sums expended by government, most of the crofters still live in poor huts amid dismal surroundings. The island affords good sporting facilities. Many of the streams abound with salmon and trout; otters and seals are plentiful, and deer and hares common; while bird life includes grouse, ptarmigan, woodcock, snipe, heron, widgeon, teal, eider duck, swan and varieties of geese and gulls. There are many antiquarian remains, including duns, megaliths, ruined towers and chapels and the like. At Rodel, in the extreme south of Harris, is a church, all that is left of an Augustinian monastery. The foundation is Norman and the superstructure Early English. On the towers are curious carved figures and in the interior several tombs of the Macleods, the most remarkable being that of Alastair (Alexander), son of William Macleod of Dunvegan, dated 1528. The monument, a full-length recumbent effigy of a knight in armour, lies at the base of a tablet in the shape of an arch divided into compartments, in which are carved in bas-relief, besides the armorial bearings of the deceased and a rendering of Dunvegan castle, several symbolical scenes, one of which exhibits Satan weighing in the balance the good and evil deeds of Alastair Macleod, the good obviously preponderating. Stornoway, the chief town (pop. 3852) is treated under a separate heading. At Callernish, 13 m. due W. of Stornoway, are several stone circles, one of which is probably the most perfect example of so-called "Druidical" structures in the British Isles. In this specimen the stones are huge, moss-covered, undressed blocks of gneiss. Twelve of such monoliths constitute the circle, in the centre of which stands a pillar 17 ft. high. From the circle there runs northwards an avenue of stones, comprising on the right-hand side nine blocks and on the left-hand ten. There also branch off from the circle, on the east and west, a single line of four stones and, on the south, a single line of five stones. From the extreme point of the south file to the farther

[illegible] Cupes of Christ, which gave [illegible] ogetown, [illegible] iversity, and was incor[illegible] Lexington it was a [illegible] sylvania well-known institution [illegible] Transylvania Seminary [illegible] was removed [illegible] Transylvania University [illegible] Transylvania University. [illegible] College of Law, a preparatory [illegible] Female College [illegible] College [illegible] colleges of the University [illegible] of the Bible [illegible] Transylvania [illegible] University [illegible] students. [illegible] College and Sayre College [illegible] Roman Catholic [illegible] College, and St [illegible] has a public library. The [illegible] under the Federal Land Grant [illegible] the State Agricultural and Mechanical [illegible] and was a college of [illegible] the college received [illegible] Kentucky [illegible] it received various grants from the [illegible] imposed a state tax of one-half of [illegible] support. In connexion with it an Agricultural [illegible] was established in 1885 [illegible] Legislature, the State University. In 1908 its title [illegible] College of Agriculture, a College of Arts and [illegible] of Law, a School of Civil Engineering, a School [illegible] and Electrical Engineering, and a School of mining [illegible] The university campus is the former City Park, [illegible] part of the city. In 1907–1908 the university [illegible] students. The city is the see of a Protestant Episcopal [illegible]

[illegible] the home of Henry Clay from 1797 until his [illegible] in his memory a monument has been erected, [illegible] magnesian-limestone column (about 120 ft.) in [illegible] style and surmounted by a statue of Clay, the [illegible] torn off in 1902 by a thunderbolt. Clay's [illegible] is now one of the best known of the stock-[illegible] vicinity; the present house is a replica of Clay's [illegible] and most extensive of these stock-farms, and [illegible] the world, is "Elmendorf," 6 m. from the [illegible] many famous trotting and running horses [illegible] There are two race-tracks in Lexington, and [illegible] trotting race meetings attract large crowds. [illegible] consist chiefly in a large trade in tobacco, [illegible] stock—there are large semi-annual horse [illegible] manufacture of "Bourbon" whisky, tobacco, [illegible] hemp, carriages, harness and saddles. [illegible] city's factory products in 1905 was [illegible] more than in 1900).

Lexington was named from Lexington, Massachusetts, in 1775 by a party of hunters who were encamped here when they received the news of the battle of Lexington; the permanent settlement dates from 1779. It was laid out in 1781, incorporated as a town in 1782, and chartered as a city in 1832. The first newspaper published west of the Alleghany Mountains, the *Kentucky Gazette*, was established here in 1787, to promote the separation of Kentucky from Virginia. The first state legislature met here in 1792, but later in the same year Frankfort became the state capital. Until 1907, when the city was enlarged by [illegible], its limits remained as they were first laid out, a [illegible] with a radius of 1 m., the court house being its centre.

[illegible] G. W. Ranck, *History of Lexington, Kentucky* (Cincinnati, 1872). [illegible] Robert Peter, *Transylvania University: Its Origin, Rise, [illegible] and Fall* (Louisville, 1896), and his *History of the Medical [illegible] of Transylvania University* (Louisville, 1905).

LEXINGTON, a township of Middlesex county, Massachusetts, U.S.A., about 11 m. N.W. of Boston. Pop. (1900) 3831, (1910 U.S. census) 4918. It is traversed by the Boston & Maine railroad and by the Lowell & Boston electric railway. Its area is about 17 sq. m., and it contains three villages—Lexington, East Lexington and North Lexington. Agriculture is virtually the only industry. Owing to its historic interest the village of Lexington is visited by thousands of persons annually, for it was on the green or common of this village that the first armed conflict of the American War of Independence occurred. On the green stand a monument erected by the state in 1799 to the memory of the minute-men who fell in that engagement, a drinking fountain surmounted by a bronze statue (1900, by Henry Hudson Kitson) of Captain John Parker, who was in command of the minute-men, and a large boulder, which marks the position of the minute-men when they were fired upon by the British. Near the green, in the old burying-ground, are the graves of Captain Parker and other American patriots—the oldest gravestone is dated 1690. The Hancock-Clarke House (built in part in 1698) is now owned by the Lexington Historical Society and contains a museum of revolutionary and other relics, which were formerly exhibited in the Town Hall. The Buckman Tavern (built about 1690), the rendezvous of the minute-men, and the Munroe Tavern (1695), the headquarters of the British, are still standing, and two other houses, on the common, antedate the War of Independence. The Cary Library in this village, with 25,000 volumes (1908), was founded in 1868, and was housed in the Town Hall from 1871 until 1906, when it was removed to the Cary Memorial Library building. In the library are portraits of Paul Revere, William Dawes and Lord Percy. The Town Hall (1871) contains statues of John Hancock (by Thomas R. Gould) and Samuel Adams (by Martin Millmore), of the "Minute-Man of 1775," and the "Soldier of 1861," and a painting by Henry Sandham, "The Battle of Lexington."

Lexington was settled as a part of Cambridge as early as 1642. It was organized as a parish in 1691 and was made a township (probably named in honour of Lord Lexington) in 1713. In the evening of the 18th of April 1775 a British force of about 800 men under Lieut.-Colonel Francis Smith and Major John Pitcairn was sent by General Thomas Gage from Boston to destroy military stores collected by the colonists at Concord, and to seize John Hancock and Samuel Adams, then at Parson Clarke's house (now known as the Hancock-Clarke House) in Lexington. Although the British had tried to keep this movement a secret, Dr Joseph Warren discovered their plans and sent out Paul Revere and William Dawes to give warning of their approach. The expedition had not proceeded far when Smith, discovering that the country was aroused, despatched an express to Boston for reinforcements and ordered Pitcairn to hasten forward with a detachment of light infantry. Early in the morning of the 19th Pitcairn arrived at the green in the village of Lexington, and there found between sixty and seventy minute-men under Captain John Parker drawn up in line of battle. Pitcairn ordered them to disperse, and on their refusal to do so his men fired a volley. Whether a stray shot preceded the first volley, and from which side it came, are questions which have never been determined. After a second volley from the British, Parker ordered his men to withdraw. The engagement lasted only a few minutes, but eight Americans were killed and nine were wounded; not more than two or three of the British were wounded. Hancock and Adams had escaped before the British troops reached Lexington. The British proceeded from Lexington to Concord (*q.v.*) On their return they were continually fired upon by Americans from behind trees, rocks, buildings and other defences, and were threatened with complete destruction until they were rescued at Lexington by a force of 1000 men under Lord Hugh Percy (later, 1786, duke of Northumberland). Percy received the fugitives within a hollow square, checked the onslaught for a time with two field-pieces, used the Munroe Tavern for a hospital, and later in the day carried his command with little further injury back to Boston. The British losses for the entire day were 73 killed, 174 wounded and 26 missing; the American losses were 49 killed, 39 wounded and 5 missing.

In 1839 a state normal school for women (the first in Massachusetts and the first public training school for teachers in the United States) was opened at Lexington; it was transferred to West Newton in 1844 and to Framingham in 1853.

See Charles Hudson, *History of the Town of Lexington* (Boston, 1868), and the publications of the Lexington Historical Society, (1890 seq.).

LEXINGTON, a city and the county-seat of Lafayette county, Missouri, U.S.A., situated on the S. bank of the Missouri river, about 40 m. E. of Kansas City. Pop. (1900) 4190, including 1170 negroes and 283 foreign-born; (1910) 5242. It is served by the Atchison, Topeka & Santa Fé, the Wabash (at Lexington Junction, 4 m. N.W.), and the Missouri Pacific railway systems. The city lies for the most part on high broken ground at the summit of the river bluffs, but in part upon their face. Lexington is the seat of the Lexington College for Young Women (Baptist, established 1855), the Central College for Women (Methodist Episcopal, South; opened 1869), and the Wentworth Military Academy (1880). There are steam flour mills, furniture factories and various other small manufactories; but the main economic interest of the city is in brickyards and coal-mines in its immediate vicinity. It is one of the principal coal centres of the state, Higginsville (pop. in 1910, 2628), about 12 m. S. E., in the same county, also being important. Lexington was founded in 1819, was laid out in 1832, and, with various additions, was chartered as a city in 1845. A new charter was received in 1870. Lexington succeeded Sibley as the eastern terminus of the Santa Fé trade, and was in turn displaced by Independence; it long owed its prosperity to the freighting trade up the Missouri, and at the opening of the Civil War it was the most important river town between St Louis and St Joseph and commanded the approach by water to Fort Leavenworth.

After the Confederate success at Wilson's Creek (Aug. 10, 1861), General Sterling Price advanced northward, and with about 15,000 men arrived in the vicinity of Lexington on the 12th of September. Here he found a Federal force of about 2800 men under Colonel James A. Mulligan (1830–1864) throwing up intrenchments on Masonic College Hill, an eminence adjoining Lexington on the N.E. An attack was made on the same day and the Federals were driven within their defences, but at night General Price withdrew to the Fair-grounds not far away and remained there five days waiting for his wagon train and for reinforcements. On the 18th the assault was renewed, and on the 20th the Confederates, advancing behind movable breastworks of water-soaked bales of hemp, forced the besieged, now long without water, to surrender. The losses were: Confederate, 25 killed and 75 wounded; Federal, 39 killed and 120 wounded. At the end of September General Price withdrew, leaving a guard of only a few hundred in the town, and on the 16th of the next month a party of 220 Federal scouts under Major Frank J. White (1842–1875) surprised this guard, released about 15 prisoners, and captured 60 or more Confederates. Another Federal raid on the town was made in December of the same year by General John Pope's cavalry. Again, during General Price's Missouri expedition in 1864, a Federal force entered Lexington on the 16th of October, and three days later there was some fighting about 4 m. S. of the town.

LEXINGTON, a town and the county-seat of Rockbridge county, Virginia, U.S.A., on the North river (a branch of the James), about 30 m. N.N.W. of Lynchburg. Pop. (1900) 3203 (1252 negroes); (1910) 2931. It is served by the Chesapeake & Ohio and the Baltimore & Ohio railways. The famous Natural Bridge is about 16 m. S.W., and there are mineral springs in the vicinity—at Rockbridge Baths, 10 m. N., at Wilson's Springs, 12 m. N, and at Rockbridge Alum Springs, 17 m. N.W. Lexington is best known as the seat of Washington and Lee University, and of the Virginia Military Institute. The former grew out of Augusta Academy, which was established in 1749 in Augusta county, about 15 m. S.W. of what is now the city of Staunton, was renamed Liberty Hall and was established near

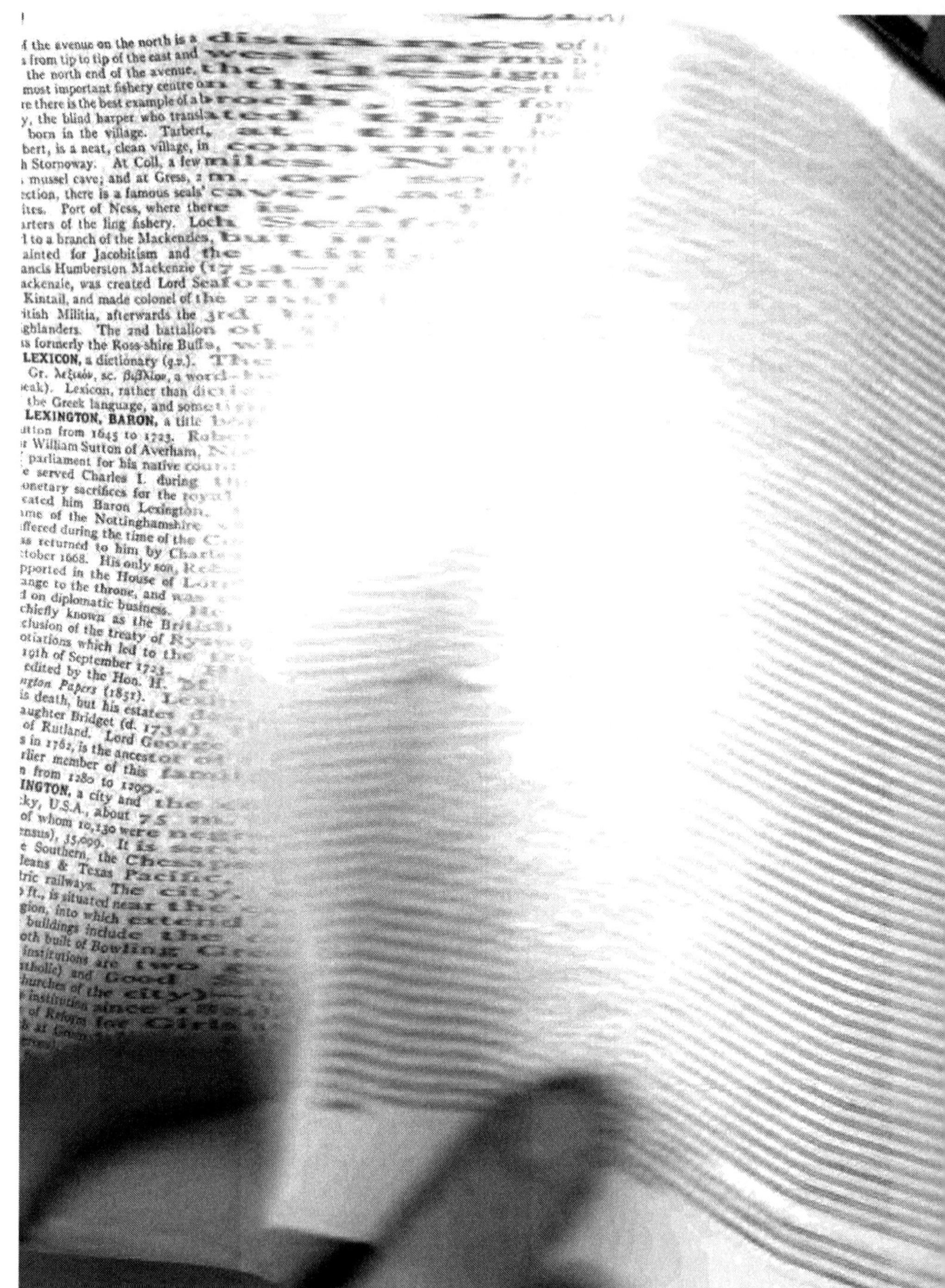
f the avenue on the north is a
a from tip to tip of the east and
the north end of the avenue.
most important fishery centre on
re there is the best example of a
y, the blind harper who transl
born in the village. Tarbert,
bert, is a neat, clean village, in
h Stornoway. At Coll, a few
mussel cave; and at Gress,
ection, there is a famous seals'
ites. Port of Ness, where there
arters of the ling fishery. Loch
d to a branch of the Mackenzies,
ainted for Jacobitism and the
ancis Humberston Mackenzie
ackenzie, was created Lord Seaforth
Kintail, and made colonel of the
itish Militia, afterwards the
ighlanders. The 2nd battalion
as formerly the Ross-shire Buffs,
LEXICON, a dictionary (q.v.).
Lexicon, rather than dict
the Greek language, and somet
LEXINGTON, BARON, a title
utton from 1645 to 1723.
r William Sutton of Averham,
parliament for his native coun
e served Charles I. during
onetary sacrifices for the royal
eated him Baron Lexington.
me of the Nottinghamshire
ffered during the time of the
as returned to him by Charles
tober 1668. His only son,
pported in the House of Lords
ange to the throne, and was
d on diplomatic business.
chiefly known as the British
clusion of the treaty of Ryswick
otiations which led to the
19th of September 1723.
edited by the Hon. H.
ngton Papers (1851).
is death, but his estates
aughter Bridget (d. 1734)
of Rutland. Lord George
s in 1782, is the ancestor of
rlier member of this family
n from 1280 to 1290.
INGTON, a city and the
cky, U.S.A., about 75
of whom 10,130 were negroes
ensus), 35,099. It is served
e Southern, the Chesapeake
leans & Texas Pacific,
tric railways. The city,
ion, into which extend
buildings include the
oth built of Bowling Green
institutions are two
tholic) and Good
urches of the city
institution since 1854
of Reform for Girls

half the outside and half the inside : with tin foil, and the remainder of e is painted with shellac varnish. A loses the mouth of the jar, and through sses which terminates in a chain, or elastic brass springs, which make good ating. The rod terminates externally nal. The jar has a certain capacity C n microfarads or electrostatic units (see , determined by the surface of the tin quality of the glass. The jar can be in potential difference V, reckoned in he two coatings. If a certain critical the glass gives way under the electric The safe voltage for most glass jars is or glass $\frac{1}{8}$th in. in thickness; this corre- . spark of about 7 millimetres in length. ed, it is usually discharged through a discharging tongs, and this discharge is illatory current (see ELECTROKINETICS). the jar in joules is expressed by the value he capacity measured in farads and V the the coatings in volts. If the capacity C arads then the energy storage is equal to $0{\cdot}737\ CV^2/2\times10^6$ foot-pounds. The size wn as a quart size may have a capacity of a microfarad, and if charged to 20,000 y from a quarter to half a joule or from t-pound.

now much employed for the production of lectric currents used in wireless telegraphy WIRELESS). For this purpose they are made form of glass tubes partly coated by silver l on the glass on the inner and outer surfaces. lls thicker at the ends than in the middle, puncture the glass is greatest at the edges of other cases, Leyden jars or condensers take . of mica or micanite or ebonite partly coated lver leaf on both sides; or a pile of sheets of nd mica may be built up, the tin foil sheets ting out first on one side and then on the other. ne side are connected together, and so also are he other side, and the two sets of tin foils separ- of mica constitute the two metallic surfaces of - condenser. For the purposes of wireless tele- rge condensers are required, the ordinary Leyden cupies too much space in comparison with its ical capacity, and hence the best form of con- r consists of a number of sheets of crown glass, partly coated on both sides with tin foil. The have lugs attached which project beyond the glass. placed in a vessel full of insulating oil which pre- or brush discharge taking place over their edges. ls on one side of the glass plates are connected all the tin foils on the opposite sides, so as to con- lenser of any required capacity. The box should toneware or other non-conducting material. When re used it is better to employ tubes thicker at the the middle, as it has been found that when the safe ceeded and the glass gives way under electric strain, of the glass nearly always takes place at the edges oil.

still commonly used as a dielectric because of its high dielectric strength or resistance to electric puncture, and its high dielectric constant (see ELECTROSTATICS). It has been found, however, that very efficient condensers can be made with compressed air as dielectric. If a number of metal plates separated by ance pieces are enclosed in an iron box which is pumped to a pressure, say, of 100 lb. to 1 sq. in., the dielectric of the air is greatly increased, and the plates may there- rought very near to one another without causing a spark to pass under such voltage as would cause discharge in air at normal pressure. Condensers of this kind have been employed by R. A. Fessenden in wireless telegraphy, and they form a very excellent arrangement for standard condensers with which to compare the capacity of other Leyden jars. Owing to the variation in the value of the dielectric constant of glass with the temperature and with the frequency of the applied electromotive force, and also owing to electric glow discharge from the edges of the tin foil coatings, the capacity of an ordinary Leyden jar is not an absolutely fixed quantity, but its numerical value varies somewhat with the method by which it is measured, and with the other circumstances above mentioned. For the purpose of a standard condenser a number of concentric metal tubes may be arranged on an insulating stand, alternate tubes being connected together. One coating of the condenser is formed by one set of tubes and the other by the other set, the air between being the dielectric. Paraffin oil or any liquid dielectric of constant inductivity may replace the air.

See J. A. Fleming, *Electric Wave Telegraphy* (London, 1906); R. A. Fessenden, "Compressed Air for Condensers," *Electrician*, 1905, 55, p. 795; Moscicki, "Construction of High Tension Condensers," *L'Éclairage électrique*, 1904, 41, p. 14, or *Engineering*, 1904, p. 865. (J. A. F.)

LEYS, HENDRIK, BARON (1815–1869), Belgian painter, was born at Antwerp on the 18th of February 1815. He studied under Wappers at the Antwerp Academy. In 1833 he painted "Combat d'un grenadier et d'un cosaque," and in the following year "Combat de Bourguignons et Flamands." In 1835 he went to Paris where he was influenced by the Romantic movement. Examples of this period of his painting are "Massacre des échevins de Louvain," "Mariage flamand," "Le Roi des arbalétriers" and other works. Leys was an imitative painter in whose works may rapidly be detected the schools which he had been studying before he painted them. Thus after his visit to Holland in 1839 he reproduced many of the characteristics of the Dutch genre painters in such works as "Franz Floris se rendant à une fête" (1845) and "Service divin en Hollande" (1850). So too the methods of Quentin Matsys impressed themselves upon him after he had travelled in Germany in 1852. In 1862 Leys was created a baron. At the time of his death, which occurred in August 1869, he was engaged in decorating with fresco the large hall of the Antwerp Hôtel de Ville.

LEYTON, an urban district forming one of the north-eastern suburbs of London, England, in the Walthamstow (S.W.) parliamentary division of Essex. Pop. (1891) 63,106; (1901) 98,912. It lies on the east (left) bank of the Lea, along the flat open valley of which runs the boundary between Essex and the county of London. The church of St Mary, mainly a brick reconstruction, contains several interesting memorials; including one to William Bowyer the printer (d. 1737), erected by his son and namesake, more famous in the same trade. Here is also buried John Strype the historian and biographer (d. 1737), who held the position of curate and lecturer at this church. Leyton is in the main a residential as distinct from a manufacturing locality. Its name is properly Low Leyton, and the parish includes the district of Leytonstone to the east. Roman remains have been discovered here, but no identification with a Roman station by name has been made with certainty. The ground of the Essex County Cricket Club is at Leyton.

LHASA (LHASSA, LASSA, "God's ground"), the capital of Tibet. It lies in 29° 39′ N., 91° 5′ E., 11,830 ft. above sea-level. Owing to the inaccessibility of Tibet and the political and religious exclusiveness of the lamas, Lhasa was long closed to European travellers, all of whom during the latter half of the 19th century were stopped in their attempts to reach it. It was popularly known as the "Forbidden City." But its chief features were known by the accounts of the earlier Romish missionaries who visited it and by the investigations, in modern times, of native Indian secret explorers, and others, and the British armed mission of 1904 (see TIBET).

Site and General Aspect.—The city stands in a tolerably level plain, which is surrounded on all sides by hills. Along its southern side, about ½ m. south of Lhasa, runs a considerable river called the Kyichu (Ki-chu) or Kyi, flowing here from E.N.E., and joining the great Tsangpo (or upper course of the Brahmaputra) some 38 m. to the south-west. The hills round the city are barren. The plain, however, is fertile, though in parts marshy. There are gardens scattered over it round the city, and these are planted with fine trees. The city is screened from view from the west by a rocky ridge, lofty and narrow, with summits at the north and south, the one flanked and crowned by the majestic buildings of Potala, the chief residence of the Dalai lama, the other by the temple of medicine. Groves, gardens and open ground intervene between this ridge and the city itself for a distance of about 1 m. A gate through the centre of the ridge gives access from the west; the road thence to the north part of the city throws off a branch to the Yutok sampa or turquoise-tiled covered bridge, one of the noted features of Lhasa, which crosses a former channel of the Kyi, and carries the road to the centre of the town.

The city is nearly circular in form, and less than 1 m. in diameter. It was walled in the latter part of the 17th century, but the walls were destroyed during the Chinese occupation in 1722. The chief streets are fairly straight, but generally of no great width. There is no paving or metal, nor any drainage system, so that the streets are dirty and in parts often flooded. The inferior quarters are unspeakably filthy, and are rife with evil smells and large mangy dogs and pigs. Many of the houses are of clay and sun-dried brick, but those of the richer people are of stone and brick. All are frequently white-washed, the doors and windows being framed in bands of red and yellow. In the suburbs there are houses entirely built of the horns of sheep and oxen set in clay mortar. This construction is in some cases very roughly carried out, but in others it is solid and highly picturesque. Some of the inferior huts of this type are inhabited by the Ragyaba or scavengers, whose chief occupation is that of disposing of corpses according to the practice of cutting and exposing them to the dogs and birds of prey. The houses generally are of two or three storeys. Externally the lower part generally presents dead walls (the ground floor being occupied by stables and similar apartments); above these rise tiers of large windows with or without projecting balconies, and over all flat broad-eaved roofs at varying levels. In the better houses there are often spacious and well-finished apartments, and the principal halls, the verandahs and terraces are often highly ornamented in brilliant colours. In every house there is a kind of chapel or shrine, carved and gilt, on which are set images and sacred books.

Temples and Monasteries.—In the centre of the city is an open square which forms the chief market-place. Here is the great temple of the "Jo" or Lord Buddha, called the Jokhang,[1] regarded as the centre of all Tibet, from which all the main roads are considered to radiate. This is the great metropolitan sanctuary and church-centre of Tibet, the St Peter's or Lateran of Lamaism. It is believed to have been founded by the Tibetan Constantine, Srong-tsan-gampo, in 652, as the shrine of one of those two very sacred Buddhist images which were associated with his conversion and with the foundation of the civilized monarchy in Tibet. The exterior of the building is not impressive; it rises little above the level of other buildings which closely surround it, and the effect of its characteristic gilt roof, though conspicuous and striking from afar, is lost close at hand.

The Jokhang.

The main building of the Jokhang is three storeys high. The entrance consists of a portico supported on timber columns, carved and gilt, while the walls are engraved with Chinese, Mongolian and Tibetan characters, and a great prayer-wheel stands on one side. Massive folding doors, ornamented with scrollwork in iron, lead to an antehall, and from this a second gate opens into a courtyard surrounded by a verandah with many pillars and chapels, and frescoes on its walls. On the left is the throne of the grand lama, laid with cushions, together with the seats of other ecclesiastical dignitaries, variously elevated according to the rank of their occupants. An inner door with enclosed vestibule gives access to the quadrangular choir or chancel, as it may be called, though its centre is open to the sky. On either side of it are three chapels, and at the extremity is the rectangular "holy of holies," flanked by two gilded images of the coming Buddha, and screened by lattice-work. In it is the shrine on which sits the great image of Śakya, set about with small figures, lamps and a variety of offerings, and richly jewelled, though the workmanship of the whole is crude. In the second and third storeys of the temple are shrines and representations of a number of gods and goddesses. The temple contains a vast accumulation of images, gold and silver vessels, lamps, reliquaries and precious bric-à-brac of every kind. The daily offices are attended by crowds of worshippers, and a sacred way which leads round the main building is constantly traversed by devotees who perform the circuit as a work of merit, always in a particular direction. The temple was found by the members of the British mission who visited it to be exceedingly dirty, and the atmosphere was foul with the fumes of butter-lamps.

Besides the convent-cells, halls of study and magazines of precious lumber, buildings grouped about the Jokhang are occupied by the civil administration, *e.g.* as treasuries, customs office, courts of justice, &c., and there are also private apartments for the grand lama and other high functionaries. No woman is permitted to pass the night within the precinct.

In front of the main entrance to the Jokhang, in the shadow of a sacred willow tree, stands a famous monument, the Doring monolith, which bears the inscribed record of a treaty of peace concluded in 822 (or, according to another view, in 783) between the king of Tibet and the emperor of China. Before this monument the apostate from Lamaism, Langdharma, brother and successor of the last-named king, is said to have been standing when a fanatic recluse, who had been stirred by a vision to avenge his persecuted faith, assassinated him.

Potala.

The famous Potala hill, covered by the palace of the Dalai lama, forms a majestic mountain of building; with its vast inward-sloping walls broken only in the upper parts by straight rows of many windows, and its flat roofs at various levels, it is not unlike a fortress in appearance. At the south base of the rock is a large space enclosed by walls and gates, with great porticoes on the inner side. This swarms with lamas and with beggars. A series of tolerably easy staircases, broken by intervals of gentle ascent, leads to the summit of the rock. The whole width of this is occupied by the palace. The central part of this group of buildings (for the component parts of Potala are of different dates) rises in a vast quadrangular mass above its satellites to a great height, terminating in gilt canopies similar to those on the Jokhang. Here on the lofty terrace is the grand lama's promenade, and from this great height he looks down upon the crowds of his votaries far below. This central member of Potala is called the red palace from its crimson colour, which distinguishes it from the rest. It contains the principal halls and chapels and shrines of past Dalai lamas. There is in these much rich decorative painting, with jewelled work, carving and other ornament, but the interior of Potala as a whole cannot compare in magnificence with the exterior. Among the numerous other buildings of note on or near Potala hill, one is distinguished by the Chinese as one of the principal beauties of Lhasa. This is a temple not far from the base of the hill, in the middle of a lake which is surrounded by trees and shrubberies. This temple, called Lu-kang, is circular in form, with a *loggia* or portico running all round and adorned with paintings. Its name, "the serpent house," comes from the tradition of a serpent or dragon, which dwelt here and must be propitiated lest it should cause the waters to rise and flood Lhasa.

Another great and famous temple is Ramo-ché, at the north side of the city. This is also regarded as a foundation of Srong-tsangampo, and is said to contain the body of his Chinese wife and the second of the primeval palladia, the image that she brought with her to the Snow-land; whence it is known as the "small Jokhang." This temple is noted for the practice of magical arts. Its buildings are in a neglected condition.

Another monastery within the city is that of Moru, also on the north side, remarkable for its external order and cleanliness. Though famous as a school of orthodox magic, it is noted also for the printing-house in the convent garden. This convent was the temporary residence of the regent during the visit of the British mission in 1904. Other monasteries in or near the city are the Tsamo Ling or Chomoling at the north-west corner; the Tangyä Ling or Tengyeling at the west of the city; the Kundü Ling or Kundeling about 1 m. west of the city, at the foot of a low isolated hill called Chapochi. Three miles south, beyond the river, is the Tsemchog Ling or Tsecholing. These four convents are known as "The Four Ling." From their inmates the Dalai lama's regent, during his minority, was formerly chosen. The temple of medicine, as already stated, crowns the summit (Chagpa) at the end of the ridge west of the city, opposite to that on which stands the Potala. It is natural that in a country possessing a religious system like that of Tibet the medical profession should form a branch of the priesthood. "The treatment of disease, though based in some measure upon a judicious use of the commoner simple drugs of the country, is, as was inevitable amongst so superstitious a people, saturated with absurdity" (Waddell, *Lhasa and its Mysteries*).

The three great monasteries in the vicinity of Lhasa, all claiming to be foundations of Tsongkhapa (1356–1418), the medieval reformer and organizer of the modern orthodox Lama Church, "the yellow caps," are the following:—

1. *Debung* (written *'Bras spungs*) is 6 m. west of Lhasa at the foot

[1] The name given by Köppen (*Die lamaische Kirche*, Berlin, 1859, p. 74) is "La Brang," by which it is sometimes known.

of the hills which flank the plain on the north. It is one of the largest monasteries in the world, having some 8000 monks. In the middle of the convent buildings rises a kind of pavilion, brilliant with colour and gilding, which is occupied by the Dalai Lama when he visits Debung once a year and expounds to the inmates. The place is frequented by the Mongol students who come to Lhasa to graduate, and is known in the country as the Mongol convent; it has also been notorious as a centre of political intrigue. Near it is the seat of the chief magician of Tibet, the Nachung Chos-kyong, a building picturesque in itself and in situation.

2. *Sera* is 3 m. north of the city on the acclivity of the hills and close to the road by which pilgrims enter from Mongolia. From a distance the crowd of buildings and temples, rising in amphitheatre against a background of rocky mountains, forms a pleasing picture. In the recesses of the hill, high above the convent, are scattered cells of lamas adopting the solitary life. The chief temple of Sera, a highly ornate building, has a special reputation as the resting-place of a famous *Dorji*, *i.e.* the *Vajra* or Thunderbolt of Jupiter, the symbol of the strong and indestructible, which the priest grasps and manipulates in various ways during prayer. The emblem is a bronze instrument, shaped much like a dumbbell with pointed ends, and it is carried solemnly in procession to the Jokhang during the New Year's festival.

The hill adjoining Sera is believed to be rich in silver ore, but it is not allowed to be worked. On the summit is a spring and a holy place of the Lhasa Mahommedans, who resort thither. Near the monastery there is said to be gold, which is worked by the monks. "Should they . . . discover a nugget of large size, it is immediately replaced in the earth, under the impression that the large nuggets . . . germinate in time, producing the small lumps which they are privileged to search for" (Nain Singh).

3. *Galdan.*—This great convent is some 25 m. east of Lhasa, on the other side of the Kyichu. It is the oldest monastery of the "Yellow" sect, having been founded by Tsongkhapa and having had him for its first superior. Here his body is said to be preserved with miraculous circumstances; here is his tomb, of marble and malachite, with a great shrine said to be of gold, and here are other relics of him, such as the impression of his hands and feet.

Samyé is another famous convent intimately connected with Lhasa, being said to be used as a treasury by the government, but it lies some 36 m. south-east on the left bank of the great Tsangpo. It was founded in 770, and is the oldest extant monastery in Tibet. It is surrounded by a very high circular stone wall, 1½ m. in circumference, with gates facing the four points of the compass. On this wall Nain Singh, who was here on his journey in 1874, counted 1030 votive piles of brick. One very large temple occupies the centre, and round it are four smaller but still large temples. Many of the idols are said to be of pure gold, and the wealth is very great. The interiors of the temples are covered with beautiful writing in enormous characters, which the vulgar believe to be the writing of Ṣakya himself.

Population and Trade.—The total population of Lhasa, including the lamas in the city and vicinity, is probably about 30,000; a census in 1854 made the figure 42,000, but it is known to have greatly decreased since. There are only some 1500 resident Tibetan laymen and about 5500 Tibetan women. The permanent population embraces, besides Tibetans, settled families of Chinese (about 2000 persons), as well as people from Nepal, from Ladak, and a few from Bhotan and Mongolia. The Ladakis and some of the other foreigners are Mahommedans, and much of the trade is in their hands. Desideri (1716) speaks also of Armenians and even "Muscovites." The Chinese have a crowded burial-ground at Lhasa, tended carefully after their manner. The Nepalese (about 800) supply the mechanics and metal-workers. There are among them excellent gold- and silversmiths; and they make the elaborate gilded canopies crowning the temples. The chief industries are the weaving of a great variety of stuffs from the fine Tibetan wool; the making of earthenware and of the wooden porringers (varying immensely in elaboration and price) of which every Tibetan carries one about with him; also the making of certain fragrant sticks of incense much valued in China and elsewhere.

As Lhasa is not only the nucleus of a cluster of vast monastic establishments, which attract students and aspirants to the religious life from all parts of Tibet and Mongolia, but is also a great place of pilgrimage, the streets and public places swarm with visitors from every part of the Himalayan plateau,[1] and from all the steppes of Asia between Manchuria and the Balkhash Lake., Naturally a great traffic arises quite apart from the pilgrimage. The city thus swarms with crowds attracted by devotion and the love of gain, and presents a great diversity of language, costume and physiognomy; though, in regard to the last point, varieties of the broad face and narrow eye greatly predominate. Much of the retail trade of the place is in the hands of the women. The curious practice of the women in plastering their faces with a dark-coloured pigment is less common in Lhasa than in the provinces.

[1] Among articles sold in the Lhasa bazaars are fossil bones, called by the people "lightning bones," and believed to have healing virtues.

During December especially traders arrive from western China by way of Tachienlu bringing every variety of silk-stuffs, carpets, china-ware and tea; from Siningfu come silk, gold lace, Russian goods, carpets of a superior kind, semi-precious stones, horse furniture, horses and a very large breed of fat-tailed sheep; from eastern Tibet, musk in large quantities, which eventually finds its way to Europe through Nepal; from Bhotan and Sikkim, rice; from Sikkim also tobacco; besides a variety of Indian and European goods from Nepal and Darjeeling, and *charas* (resinous exudation of hemp) and saffron from Ladakh and Kashmir. The merchants leave Lhasa in March, before the setting in of the rains renders the rivers impassable.

The tea importation from China is considerable, for tea is an absolute necessary to the Tibetan. The tea is of various qualities, from the coarsest, used only for "buttered" tea (a sort of broth), to the fine quality drunk by the wealthy. This is pressed into bricks or cakes weighing about 5½ lb, and often passes as currency. The quantity that pays duty at Tachienlu is about 10,000,000 lb, besides some amount smuggled. No doubt a large part of this comes to Lhasa.

Lhasa Festivities.—The greatest of these is at the new year. This lasts fifteen days, and is a kind of lamaic carnival, in which masks and mummings, wherein the Tibetans take especial delight, play a great part. The celebration commences at midnight, with shouts and clangour of bells, gongs, chank-shells, drums and all the noisy repertory of Tibetan music; whilst friends exchange early visits and administer coarse sweetmeats and buttered tea. On the second day the Dalai Lama gives a grand banquet, at which the Chinese and native authorities are present, whilst in the public spaces and in front of the great convents all sorts of shows and jugglers' performances go on. Next day a regular Tibetan exhibition takes place. A long cable, twisted of leather thongs, is stretched from a high point in the battlements of Potala slanting down to the plain, where it is strongly moored. Two men slide from top to bottom of this huge hypothenuse, sometimes lying on the chest (which is protected by a breast-plate of strong leather), spreading their arms as if to swim, and descending with the rapidity of an arrow-flight. Occasionally fatal accidents occur in this performance, which is called "the dance of the gods"; but the survivors are rewarded by the court, and the Grand Lama himself is always a witness of it. This practice occurs more or less over the Himalayan plateau, and is known in the neighbourhood of the Ganges as *Barat*. It is employed as a kind of expiatory rite in cases of pestilence and the like. Exactly the same performance is described as having been exhibited in St Paul's Churchyard before King Edward VI., and again before Philip of Spain, as well as, about 1750, at Hertford and other places in England (see Strutt's *Sports*, &c., 2nd ed., p. 198).

The most remarkable celebration of the new year's festivities is the great jubilee of the *Monlam* (*sMon-lam*, "prayer"), instituted by Tsongkhapa himself in 1408. Lamas from all parts of Tibet, but chiefly from the great convents in the neighbourhood, flock to Lhasa, and every road leading thither is thronged with troops of monks on foot or horseback, on yaks or donkeys, carrying with them their breviaries and their cooking-pots. Those who cannot find lodging bivouac in the streets and squares, or pitch their little black tents in the plain. The festival lasts six days, during which there reigns a kind of saturnalia. Unspeakable confusion and disorder reign, while gangs of lamas parade the streets, shouting, singing and coming to blows. The object of this gathering is, however, supposed to be devotional. Vast processions take place, with mystic offerings and lama-music, to the Jokhang and Moru convents; the Grand Lama himself assists at the festival, and from an elevated throne beside the Jokhang receives the offerings of the multitude and bestows his benediction.

On the 15th of the first month multitudes of torches are kept ablaze, which lighten up the city to a great distance, whilst the interior of the Jokhang is illuminated throughout the night by innumerable lanterns shedding light on coloured figures in bas-relief, framed in arabesques of animals, birds and flowers, and representing the history of Buddha and other subjects, all modelled in butter. The figures are executed on a large scale, and, as described by Huc, who witnessed the festival at Kunbum on the frontier of China, with extraordinary truth and skill. These singular works of art occupy some months in preparation, and on the morrow are thrown

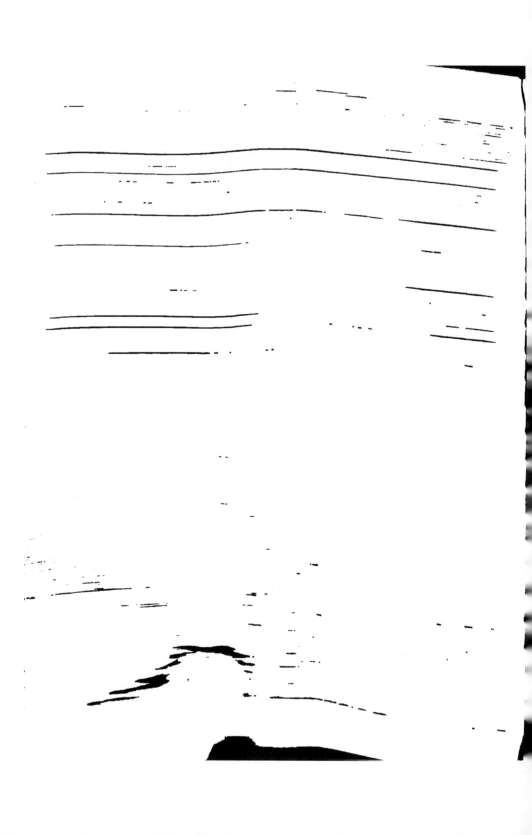

2 m. S. of the town until a canal was dug through the peninsula in 1697; it is now deepened to 23 ft., and is mostly free from ice throughout the year. Since being brought, in 1872, into railway connexion with Moscow, Orel and Kharkov, Libau has become an important port. New Libau possesses large factories for colours, explosives, machinery belts, sails and ropes, tobacco, furniture, matches, as well as iron works, agricultural machinery works, tin-plate works, soap works, saw-mills, breweries, oil-mills, cork and linoleum factories and flour-mills. The exports reach the annual value of £3,250,000 to £5,500,000, oats being the chief export, with flour, wheat, rye, butter, eggs, spirits, flax, linseed, oilcake, pork, timber, horses and petroleum. The imports average £1,500,000 to £2,000,000 annually. Shipbuilding, including steamers for open-sea navigation, is on the increase. North of the commercial harbour and enclosing it the Russian government made (1893–1906) a very extensive fortified naval port, protected by moles and breakwaters. Libau is visited for sea-bathing in summer.

The port of Libau, *Lyra portus*, is mentioned as early as 1263; it then belonged to the Livonian Order or Brothers of the Sword. In 1418 it was burnt by the Lithuanians, and in 1560 it was mortgaged by the grandmaster of the Teutonic Order, to which it had passed, to the Prussian duke Albert. In 1701 it was captured by Charles XII. of Sweden, and was annexed to Russia in 1795.

See Wegner, *Geschichte der Stadt Libau* (Libau, 1898).

LIBEL and **SLANDER**, the terms employed in English law to denote injurious attacks upon a man's reputation or character by words written or spoken, or by equivalent signs. In most early systems of law verbal injuries are treated as a criminal or quasi-criminal offence, the essence of the injury lying not in pecuniary loss, which may be compensated by damages, but in the personal insult which must be atoned for—a vindictive penalty coming in the place of personal revenge. By the law of the XII. Tables, the composition of scurrilous songs and gross noisy public affronts were punished by death. Minor offences of the same class seem to have found their place under the general conception of *injuria*, which included ultimately every form of direct personal aggression which involved contumely or insult. In the later Roman jurisprudence, which has, on this point, exercised considerable influence over modern systems of law, verbal injuries are dealt with in the edict under two heads. The first comprehended defamatory and injurious statements made in a public manner (*convicium contra bonos mores*). In this case the essence of the offence lay in the unwarrantable public proclamation. In such a case the truth of the statements was no justification for the unnecessarily public and insulting manner in which they had been made. The second head included defamatory statements made in private, and in this case the offence lay in the imputation itself, not in the manner of its publication. The truth was therefore a sufficient defence, for no man had a right to demand legal protection for a false reputation. Even belief in the truth was enough, because it took away the intention which was essential to the notion of *injuria*. The law thus aimed at giving sufficient scope for the discussion of a man's character, while it protected him from needless insult and pain. The remedy for verbal injuries was long confined to a civil action for a money penalty, which was estimated according to the gravity of the case, and which, although vindictive in its character, doubtless included practically the element of compensation. But a new remedy was introduced with the extension of the criminal law, under which many kinds of defamation were punished with great severity. At the same time increased importance attached to the publication of defamatory books and writings, the *libri* or *libelli famosi*, from which we derive our modern use of the word libel; and under the later emperors the latter term came to be specially applied to anonymous accusations or pasquils, the dissemination of which was regarded as peculiarly dangerous, and visited with very severe punishment, whether the matter contained in them were true or false.

The earlier history of the English law of defamation is somewhat obscure. Civil actions for damages seem to have been tolerably frequent so far back as the reign of Edward I. There was no distinction drawn between words written and spoken. When no pecuniary penalty was involved such cases fell within the old jurisdiction of the ecclesiastical courts, which was only finally abolished in the 19th century. It seems, to say the least, uncertain whether any generally applicable criminal process was in use. The crime of *scandalum magnatum*, spreading false reports about the magnates of the realm, was established by statutes, but the first fully reported case in which libel is affirmed generally to be punishable at common law is one tried in the star chamber in the reign of James I. In that case no English authorities are cited except a previous case of the same nature before the same tribunal; the law and terminology appear to be taken directly from Roman sources, with the insertion that libels tended to a breach of the peace; and it seems probable that that not very scrupulous tribunal had simply found it convenient to adopt the very stringent Roman provisions regarding the *libelli famosi* without paying any regard to the Roman limitations. From that time we find both the criminal and civil remedies in full operation, and the law with regard to each at the present time may now be considered.

Civil Law.—The first important distinction encountered is that between slander and libel, between the oral and written promulgation of defamatory statements. In the former case the remedy is limited. The law will not take notice of every kind of abusive or defamatory language. It must be shown either that the plaintiff has suffered actual damage as a direct consequence of the slander, or that the imputation is of such a nature that we are entitled to infer damage as a necessary consequence. The special damage on which an action is founded for slanderous words must be of the nature of pecuniary loss. Loss of reputation or of position in society, or even illness, however clearly it may be traced to the slander, is insufficient. When we cannot prove special damage, the action for slander is only allowed upon certain strictly defined grounds. These are the imputation of a crime or misdemeanour which is punishable corporeally, *e.g.* by imprisonment; the imputation of a contagious or infectious disease; statements which tend to the disherison of an apparent heir (other cases of slander of title when the party is in possession requiring the allegation of special damage); the accusing a woman of unchastity (Slander of Women Act 1891); and, lastly, slanders directed against a man's professional or business character, which tend directly to prejudice him in his trade, profession, or means of livelihood. In the latter case the words must either be directly aimed at a man in his business or official character, or they must be such as necessarily to imply unfitness for his particular office or occupation. Thus words which merely reflect generally upon the moral character of a tradesman or professional man are not actionable, but they are actionable if directed against his dealings in the course of his trade or profession. But, in the case of a merchant or trader, an allegation which affects his credit generally is enough, and it has been held that statements are actionable which affect the ability or moral characters of persons who hold offices, or exercise occupation which require a high degree of ability, or infer peculiar confidence. In every case the plaintiff must have been at the time of the slander in the actual exercise of the occupation or enjoyment of the office with reference to which the slander is supposed to have affected him.

The action for libel is not restricted in the same way as that for slander. Originally there appears to have been no essential distinction between them, but the establishment of libel as a criminal offence had probably considerable influence, and it soon became settled that written defamatory statements, or pictures and other signs which bore a defamatory meaning, implied greater malice and deliberation, and were generally fraught with greater injury than those made by word of mouth. The result has been that the action for libel is not limited to special grounds, or by the necessity of proving special damage. It may be founded on any statement which disparages a man's private or professional character, or which tends to hold him up to hatred,

[illegible] for example. [illegible]

Act 1888. The reports must, however, be published in a newspaper as defined in the Newspaper Libel and Registration Act 1881. Under this act a newspaper must be published "at intervals not exceeding twenty-six days."

By s. 3 of the act of 1888 fair and accurate reports of judicial proceedings are absolutely privileged provided that the report is published contemporaneously with the proceedings and no blasphemous or indecent matter is contained therein. By s. 4 a limited privilege is given to fair and accurate reports (1) of the proceedings of a *bona fide* public meeting lawfully held for a lawful purpose and for the furtherance and discussion of any matter of public concern, even when the admission thereto is restricted; (2) of any meeting, open either to the public or to a reporter, of a vestry, town council, school board, board of guardians, board of local authority, formed or constituted under the provisions of any act of parliament, or of any committee appointed by any of these bodies; or of any meeting of any commissioners authorized to act by letters patent, act of parliament, warrant under royal sign manual, or other lawful warrant or authority, select committees of either House of parliament, justices of the peace in quarter sessions assembled for administrative or [illegible] purposes; (3) of the publication of any notice or report issued for the information of the public by any government office or department, officer of state, commissioner of police or chief constable, and published at their request. But the privilege given in s. 4 does not authorize the publication of any blasphemous or [illegible] matter; nor is the protection available as a defence if it be [illegible] that the reports or notices were published maliciously, in the legal sense of the word, or the defendant has been requested to insert in the newspaper in which the report was issued a reasonable letter or statement [illegible] contradiction or explanation, and has refused or neglected [illegible]. Moreover, nothing in s. 4 is to interfere with any [illegible] existing, or to protect the publication of any matter not of public concern, or in cases where publication is not for the public benefit. Consequently no criminal prosecution should be commenced where the interests of the public are not affected. By the Law of Libel Amendment Act 1888, s. 8, no criminal prosecution [illegible] be commenced against any newspaper proprietor, publisher or editor unless the order of a judge at chambers has been first obtained. This protection does not cover the actual writer of the [illegible].

In private life a large number of statements are privileged so long as they remain matters of strictly private communication. It is difficult to define the limits of private privilege without extensive reference to concrete cases; but generally it may be said that it includes all communications made in performance of a duty not merely legal but moral or social, answers to *bona fide* inquiries, communications made by persons in confidential [illegible] regarding matters in which one or both are interested, and even statements made within proper limits by persons in [illegible] prosecution of their own interest. Common examples of this kind of privilege are to be found in answer to inquiries as to the character of servants or the solvency of a [illegible], warnings to a friend, communications between persons who are jointly interested in some matters of business. But in every case care must be taken not to exceed the limits of [illegible] required by the occasion, or otherwise the privilege is lost. Thus defamatory statements may be privileged when made to a meeting of shareholders, but not when published to persons who have no immediate concern in the business.

In a few instances in which an action cannot be maintained even by the averment of malice, the plaintiff may maintain an action by averring not only malice but also want of reasonable and probable cause. The most common instances of this kind are [illegible] charges made in the ordinary course of justice and [illegible] prosecutions. In such cases it would be contrary to [illegible] to punish or prevent every charge which was made [illegible] motive, but there is no reason for protecting accusations which are not only malicious, but destitute [illegible] reasonable probability.

[illegible]—Publications which are blasphemous, immoral or seditious are frequently termed libels, and are punishable both at common law and by various statutes. The matter, however, which constitutes the offence in these publications lies beyond our present scope. Libels upon individuals may be [illegible] by criminal information or indictment, but there can be no criminal prosecution for slander. So far as concerns the [illegible] of libel, and its limitation by the necessity of proving [illegible] cases express malice, there is no substantial difference between the rules which apply to criminal prosecutions and to

civil actions, with the one important exception (now considerably modified) that the falsity of a libel is not in criminal law an essential element of the offence. If the matter alleged were in itself defamatory, the court would not permit inquiry into its truth. The sweeping application of this rule seems chiefly due to the indiscriminate use, in earlier cases, of a rule in Roman law which was only applicable to certain modes of publication, but has been supported by various reasons of general policy, and especially by the view that one main reason for punishing a libel was its tendency to provoke a breach of the peace.

An important dispute about the powers of the jury in cases of libel arose during the 19th century in connexion with some well-known trials for seditious libels. The point is familiar to readers of Macaulay in connexion with the trial of the seven bishops, but the cases in which it was brought most prominently forward, and which led to its final settlement, were those against Woodfall (the printer of *Junius*), Wilkes and others, and especially the case against Shipley, the dean of St Asaph (21 St. Tr. 925), in which the question was fought by Lord Erskine with extraordinary energy and ability. The controversy turned upon the question whether the jury were to be strictly confined to matters of fact which required to be proved by evidence, or whether in every case they were entitled to form their own opinion upon the libellous character of the publication and the intention of the author. The jury, if they pleased, had it in their power to return a general verdict of guilty or not guilty, but both in theory and practice they were subject in law to the directions of the court, and had to be informed by it as to what they were to take into consideration in determining upon their verdict. There is no difficulty about the general application of this principle in criminal trials. If the crime is one which is inferred by law from certain facts, the jury are only concerned with these facts, and must accept the construction put upon them by law. Applying these principles to the case of libel, juries were directed that it was for the court to determine whether the publication fell within the definition of libel, and whether the case was one in which malice was to be inferred by construction of law. If the case were one in which malice was inferred by law, the only facts left to the jury were the fact of publication and the meaning averred by innuendoes; they could not go into the question of intention, unless the case were one of privilege, in which express malice had to be proved. In general principle, therefore, the decisions of the court were in accordance with the ordinary principles of criminal law. But there were undoubtedly some peculiarities in the case of libel. The sense of words, the inferences to be drawn from them, and the effect which they produce are not so easily defined as gross matters of fact. They seem to belong to those cases in which the impression made upon a jury is more to be trusted than the decision of a judge. Further, owing to the mode of procedure, the defendant was often punished before the question of law was determined. But, nevertheless, the question would scarcely have been raised had the libels related merely to private matters. The real ground of dispute was the liberty to be accorded to political discussion. Had the judges taken as wide a view of privilege in discussing matters of public interest as they do now, the question could scarcely have arisen; for Erskine's whole contention really amounted to this, that the jury were entitled to take into consideration the good or bad intent of the authors, which is precisely the question which would now be put before them in any matter which concerned the public. But at that time the notion of a special privilege attaching to political discussion had scarcely arisen, or was confined within very narrow limits, and the cause of free political discussion seemed to be more safely entrusted to juries than to courts. The question was finally settled by the Libel Act 1792, by which the jury were entitled to give a general verdict on the whole matter put in issue.

Scots Law.—In Scots law there were originally three remedies for defamation. It might be prosecuted by or with the concurrence of the lord advocate before the court of justiciary; or, secondly, a criminal remedy might be obtained in the commissary (ecclesiastical) courts, which originally dealt with the defender by public retractation or penance, but subsequently made use of fines payable to their own procurator or to the party injured, these latter being regarded as solatium to his feelings; or, lastly, an action of damages was competent before the court of session, which was strictly civil in its character and aimed at the reparation of patrimonial loss. The first remedy has fallen into disuse; the second and third (the commissary courts being now abolished) are represented by the present action for damages or solatium. Originally the action before the court of session was strictly for damages—founded, not upon the *animus injuriandi*, but upon culpa, and could be defended by proving the truth of the statements. But in time the court of session began to assume the original jurisdiction of the commissary courts, and entertained actions for solatium in which the *animus injuriandi* was a necessary element, and to which, as in Roman law, the truth was not necessarily a defence. Ultimately the two actions got very much confused. We find continual disputes as to the necessity for the *animus injuriandi* and the applicability of the plea of *veritas convicii*, which arose from the fact that the courts were not always conscious that they were dealing with two actions, to one of which these notions were applicable, and to the other not. On the introduction of the jury court, presided over by an English lawyer, it was quite natural that he, finding no very clear distinction maintained between damage and solatium, applied the English plea of truth as a justification to every case, and retained the *animus injuriandi* both in ordinary cases and cases of privilege in the same shape as the English conception of malice. The leading and almost only differences between the English and Scots law now are that the latter makes no essential distinction between oral and written defamation, that it practically gives an action for every case of defamation, oral or written, upon which in England a civil action might be maintained for libel, and that it possesses no criminal remedy. In consequence of the latter defect and the indiscriminate application of the plea of veritas to every case both of damages and solatium, there appears to be no remedy in Scotland even for the widest and most needless publication of offensive statements if only they are true.

American Law.—American law scarcely if at all differs from that of England. In so far indeed as the common law is concerned, they may be said to be substantially identical. The principal statutes which have altered the English criminal law are represented by equivalent legislation in most American states.

See generally W. B. Odgers, *Libel and Slander*; Fraser, *Law of Libel and Slander*.

LIBELLATICI, the name given to a class of persons who, during the persecution of Decius, A.D. 250, evaded the consequences of their Christian belief by procuring documents (*libelli*) which certified that they had satisfied the authorities of their submission to the edict requiring them to offer incense or sacrifice to the imperial gods. As thirty-eight years had elapsed since the last period of persecution, the churches had become in many ways lax, and the number of those who failed to hold out under the persecution was very great. The procedure of the courts which had cognizance of the matter was, however, by no means strict, and the judges and subordinate officials were often not ill-disposed towards Christians, so that evasion was fairly easy. Many of those who could not hold out were able to secure certificates which gave them immunity from punishment without actually renouncing the faith, just as "parliamentary certificates" of conformity used to be given in England without any pretext of fact. It is to the persons who received such certificates that the name *libellatici* belonged (those who actually fulfilled the edict being called *thurificati* or *sacrificati*). To calculate their number would be impossible, but we know from the writings of Cyprian, Dionysius of Alexandria and other contemporaries, that they were a numerous class, and that they were to be found in Italy, in Egypt and in Africa, and among both clergy and laity. Archbishop Benson is probably right in thinking that "there was no systematic and regular procedure in the matter," and that the *libelli* may have been of very different kinds. They must, however, as a general rule, have consisted of a certificate *from the authorities* to the effect that the accused person had satisfied them. [The name *libellus* has also been applied to another kind of document—to the letters given by confessors, or by those who were about to suffer martyrdom, to persons who had fallen, to be used to secure forgiveness for them from the authorities of the Church. With such *libelli* we are not here concerned.] The subject has acquired a fresh interest from the fact that two of these actual *libelli* have been recovered, in 1893 and 1894 respectively, both from Egypt; one is now in the Brugsch Pasha collection in the Berlin Museum; the other is in the collection of papyri belonging to the Archduke Rainer. The former is on a papyrus leaf about [illegible] by 3 in. [illegible] fragments of papyrus which have been [illegible] former was first deciphered and [illegible] the latter by Dr K. Wessely: [illegible] upon by Dr Benson. There is a [illegible] in each the form is that N. [illegible] to the gods"; and that he now, in [illegible] of the sacrifices [illegible] drunk [or has poured libations], [illegible] a witness whereof he begs them to [illegible] follows the signature, with attesta- [illegible] is dated, and the date must fall [illegible] impossible to prove that either of the [illegible] Christians: they may have been [illegible] accused and had cleared them- [illegible] Christians who had apostatized. But no [illegible] were delivered, in Egypt at least, [illegible] immunity without actual apostasy; [illegible] Africa probably did not differ widely [illegible] gave rise to complicated problems of [illegible] which are reflected in the correspondence [illegible] in the Novatian controversy.

[illegible] (London, 1897); *Theol. Literatur-* [illegible] and 17th of March 1894. (W. E. Co.)

[illegible], in Roman mythology, deities, male [illegible] with the Greek Dionysus and Persephone. [illegible] called Liber Pater and Bacchus) two [illegible]. In the country feast of the vintage, [illegible] gathering of the grapes, and the city [illegible] called *Liberalia* (Ovid, *Fasti*, iii. 711) [illegible] unaffected by Greek religion. [illegible] was a great merry-making, where the first- [illegible] offered to the gods. It was char- [illegible] symbolism, in honour of the fertility of [illegible] growing civilization had impressed [illegible] religion, and connected it with [illegible]. At this time the youths laid aside [illegible] assumed the man's *toga libera* or [illegible] of meal, honey and oil were [illegible] this festival. Liber was originally [illegible] activity of nature, especially of the [illegible] the unrestrained character of his [illegible] period, the Hellenic religion of [illegible] and Libera were identified [illegible] and associated with another [illegible] identified with Demeter. By [illegible] temple was built to these three [illegible] the whole cultus was borrowed [illegible] terminology, and priestesses [illegible]

[illegible] the name given to and [illegible] party (see WHIG AND [illegible] opposed to Toryism or [illegible] originators and champions [illegible] legislation. The term came [illegible] of one of the two great [illegible] became its leader, but [illegible] current coin, as a political [illegible] with the use of such [illegible] of "favourable to [illegible] freedom and democracy." [illegible] the French Revolution, [illegible] society the term was used [illegible] made about the "British [illegible] the work of Bentham and [illegible]. In Leigh Hunt's [illegible] and more thorough- [illegible] Radicals . . . since [illegible] (from his own [illegible] forward for [illegible] The [illegible] al

Conservatism," describing the position of the later Peelites; and Mr Gladstone's own career is the best instance of its changing signification; moreover the adjective "liberal" came meanwhile into common use in other spheres than that of parliamentary politics, *e.g.* in religion, as meaning "intellectually advanced" and free from the trammels of tradition. Broadly speaking, the Liberal party stands for progressive legislation in accordance with freedom of social development and advanced ethical ideas. It claims to represent government by the people, by means of trust in the people, in a sense which denies genuine popular sympathy to its opponents. Being largely composed of dissenters, it has identified itself with opposition to the vested interests of the Church of England; and, being apt to be thwarted by the House of Lords, with attempts to override the veto of that house. Its old watchword, "Peace, retrenchment and reform," indicated its tendency to avoidance of a "spirited" foreign policy, and to parsimony in expenditure. But throughout its career the Liberal party has always been pushed forward by its extrême Radical wing, and economy in the spending of public money is no longer cherished by those who chiefly represent the non-taxpaying classes. The party organization lends itself to the influence of new forces. In 1861 a central organization was started in the "Liberal Registration Association," composed "of gentlemen of known Liberal opinions"; and a number of "Liberal Associations" soon rose throughout the country. Of these, that at Birmingham became, under Mr J. Chamberlain and his active supporter Mr Schnadhorst, particularly active in the 'seventies; and it was due to Mr Schnadhorst that in 1877 a conference was held at Birmingham which resulted in the formation of the "National Federation of Liberal Associations," or "National Liberal Federation," representing a system of organization which was dubbed by Lord Beaconsfield "the Caucus." The Birmingham Caucus and the Central Liberal Association thus coexisted, the first as an independent democratic institution, the second as the official body representing the whips of the party, the first more advanced and "Radical," the second inclined to Whiggishness. Friction naturally resulted, but the 1880 elections confirmed the success of the Caucus and consolidated its power. And in spite of the Home Rule crisis in 1886, resulting in the splitting off of the Liberal Unionists—"dissentient Liberals," as Mr Gladstone called them—from the Liberal party, the organization of the National Liberal Federation remained, in the dark days of the party, its main support. Its headquarters were, however, removed to London, and under Mr Schnadhorst it was practically amalgamated with the old Central Association.

It is impossible here to write in detail the later history of the Liberal party, but the salient facts will be found in such articles as those on Mr Gladstone, Mr J. Chamberlain, Lord Rosebery, Sir Henry Campbell-Bannerman, Mr H. H. Asquith and Mr David Lloyd George.

See, apart from general histories of the period, M. Ostrogorski's *Democracy and the Organization of Political Parties* (Eng. trans. 1902).

LIBER DIURNUS ROMANORUM PONTIFICUM, or "Journal of the Roman Pontiffs," the name given to a collection of formulae used in the papal chancellery in preparing official documents, such as the installation of a pope, the bestowal of the pallium and the grant of papal privileges. It was compiled between 685 and 751, and was constantly employed until the 11th century, when, owing to the changed circumstances of the Church, it fell into disuse, and was soon forgotten and lost. During the 17th century a manuscript of the *Liber* was discovered in Rome by the humanist, Lucas Holstenius, who prepared an edition for publication; for politic reasons, however, the papal authorities would not allow this to appear, as the book asserted the superiority of a general council over the pope. It was, however, published in France by the Jesuit, Jean Garnier, in 1680, and other editions quickly followed.

The best modern editions are one by Eugène de Rozière (Paris, 1869) and another by T. E. von Sichel (Vienna, 1889), both of which contain critical introductions. The two existing manuscripts of the *Liber* are in the Vatican library, Rome, and in the library of St Ambrose at Milan.

LIBERIA, a negro republic in West Africa, extending along the coast of northern Guinea about 300 m., between the British colony of Sierra Leone on the N.W. and the French colony of the Ivory Coast on the S.E. The westernmost point of Liberia (at the mouth of the river Mano) lies in about 6° 55′ N. and 11° 32′ W. The southernmost point of Liberia, and at the same time almost its most eastern extension, is at the mouth of the Cavalla, beyond Cape Palmas, only 4° 22′ N. of the equator, and in about 7° 33′ W. The width of Liberia inland varies very considerably; it is greatest, about 200 m., from N.E. to S.W. The Liberia-Sierra Leone boundary was determined by a frontier commission in 1903. Commencing at the mouth of the river Mano, it follows the Mano up stream till that river cuts 10° 40′ W. It then followed this line of longitude to its intersection with N. latitude 9° 6′, but by the Franco-Liberian understanding of 1907 the frontier on this side was withdrawn to 8° 25′ N., where the river Makona crosses 10° 40′ W. The Liberian frontier with the adjacent French possessions was defined by the Franco-Liberian treaty of 1892, but as the definition therein given was found to be very difficult of reconciliation with geographical features (for in 1892 the whole of the Liberian interior was unmapped) further negotiations were set on foot. In 1905 Liberia proposed to France that the boundary line should follow the river Moa from the British frontier of Sierra Leone up stream to near the source of the Moa (or Makona), and that from this point the boundary should run eastwards along the line of water-parting between the system of the Niger on the north and that of the coast rivers (Moa, Lofa, St Paul's) on the south, until the 8th degree of N. latitude was reached, thence following this 8th degree eastwards to where it cuts the head stream of the Cavalla river. From this point the boundary between France and Liberia would be the course of the Cavalla river from near its source to the sea. Within the limits above described Liberia would possess a total area of about 43,000 to 45,000 sq. m. But after deliberation and as the result of certain "frontier incidents" France modified her counter-proposals in 1907, and the actual definition of the northern and eastern frontiers of Liberia is as follows:—

Starting from the point on the frontier of the British colony of Sierra Leone where the river Moa or Makona crosses that frontier, the Franco-Liberian frontier shall follow the left bank of the river Makona up stream to a point 5 kilometres to the south of the town of Bofosso. From this point the frontier shall leave the line of the Makona and be carried in a south-easterly direction to the source of the most north-westerly affluent of the Nuon river or Western Cavalla. This line shall be so drawn as to leave on the French side of the boundary the following towns: Kutumai, Kisi Kurumai, Sundibú, Zuapa, Nzibila, Koiama, Bangwedu and Lola. From the north-westernmost source of the Nuon the boundary shall follow the right bank of the said Nuon river down stream to its presumed confluence with the Cavalla, and thenceforward the right bank of the river Cavalla down to the sea. If the ultimate destination of the Nuon is not the Cavalla river, then the boundary shall follow the right bank of the Nuon down stream as far as the town of Tuleplan. A line shall then be drawn from the southern outskirts of the town of Tuleplan due E. to the Cavalla river, and thence shall follow the right bank of the Cavalla river to the sea.

(The delimitation commission proved that the Nuon does not flow into the Cavalla, but about 6° 30′ N. it flows very near the north-westernmost bend of that river. Tuleplan is in about lat. 6° 50′ N. The river Makona takes a much more northerly course than had been estimated. The river Nuon also is situated 20 or 30 m. farther to the east than had been supposed. Consequently the territory of Liberia as thus demarcated is rather larger than it would appear on the uncorrected English maps of 1907—about 41,000 sq. m.)

It is at the southern extremity of Liberia, Cape Palmas, that the West African coast from Morocco to the southernmost extremity of Guinea turns somewhat abruptly eastwards and northwards and faces the Gulf of Guinea. As the whole coastline of Liberia thus fronts the sea route from Europe to South Africa it is always likely to possess a certain degree of strategical importance. The coast, however, is unprovided with a single good harbour. The anchorage at Monrovia is safe, and with some expenditure of money a smooth harbour could be made in front of Grand Basa.

Coast Features.—The coast is a good deal indented, almost all the headlands projecting from north-east to south-west. A good deal of the seaboard is dangerous by reason of the sharp rocks which lie near the surface. As most of the rivers have rapids or falls actually at the sea coast or close to it, they are, with the exception of the Cavalla, useless for penetrating far inland, and the whole of this part of Africa from Cape Palmas north-west to the Senegal suggests a sunken land. In all probability the western projection of Africa was connected by a land bridge with the opposite land of Brazil as late as the Eocene period of the Tertiary epoch. The Liberian coast has few lagoons compared with the adjoining littoral of Sierra Leone or that of the Ivory Coast. The coast, in fact, rises in some places rather abruptly from the sea. Cape Mount (on the northern side of which is a large lagoon—Fisherman Lake) at its highest point is 1050 ft. above sea level. Cape Mesurado is about 350 ft., Cape Palmas about 200 ft. above the sea. There is a salt lake or lagoon between the Cape Palmas river and the vicinity of the Cavalla. Although very little of the coast belt is actually swampy, a kind of natural canalization connects many of the rivers at their mouths with each other, though some of these connecting creeks are as yet unmarked on maps.

Mountains.—Although there are patches of marsh—generally the swampy bottoms of valleys—the whole surface of Liberia inclines to be hilly or even mountainous at a short distance inland from the coast. In the north-east, French explorers have computed the altitudes of some mountains at figures which would make them the highest land surfaces of the western projection of Africa—from 6000 to 9000 ft. But these altitudes are largely matters of conjecture. The same mountains have been sighted by English explorers coming up from the south and are pronounced to be "very high." It is possible that they may reach to 6000 ft. in some places. Between the western bend of the Cavalla river and the coast there is a somewhat broken mountain range with altitudes of from 2000 to 5000 ft. (approximate). The Pö range to the west of the St Paul's river may reach in places to 3000 ft.

Rivers.—The work of the Franco-Liberian delimitation commission in 1908–1909 cleared up many points connected with the hydrography of the country. Notably it traced the upper Cavalla, proving that that river was not connected either with the Nuon on the west or the Ko or Zo on the east. The upper river and the left bank of the lower river of the Cavalla are in French territory. It rises in about 7° 50′ N., 8° 30′ W. in the Nimba mountains, where also rise the Nuon, St John's and Dukwia rivers. After flowing S.E. the Cavalla, between 7° and 6° N., under the name of Dugu, makes a very considerable elbow to the west, thereafter resuming its south-easterly course. It is navigable from the sea for some 80 m. from its mouth and after a long series of rapids is again navigable. Unfortunately the Cavalla does not afford a means of easy penetration into the rich hinterland of Liberia on account of the bad bar at its mouth. The Nuon (or Nipwe), which up to 1908 was described sometimes as the western Cavalla and sometimes as the upper course of the St John's river, has been shown to be the upper course of the Cestos. About 6° 30′ N. it approaches within 16 m. of the Cavalla. It rises in the Nimba mountains some 10 m. S. of the source of the Cavalla, and like all the Liberian rivers (except the Cavalla) it has a general S.W. flow. The St Paul, though inferior to the Cavalla in length, is a large river with a considerable volume of water. The main branch rises in the Bella country nearly as far north as 9° N. under the name of Diani. Between 8° and 7° N. it is joined by the Wë from the west and the Walë from the east. The important river Lofa flows nearly parallel with the St Paul's river and enters the sea about 40 m. to the west, under the name of Little Cape Mount river. The Mano or Bewa river rises in the dense Gora forest, but is of no great importance until it becomes the frontier between Liberia and Sierra Leone. The Dukwia and Farmington are tortuous rivers entering the sea under the name of the river Junk (Portuguese, *Junco*). The Farmington is a short stream, but the Dukwia is believed to be the lower course of the Mani, which rises as the Tigney (Tige), north of the source of the Cavalla, just south of 8° N. The St John's river of the Basa country appears to be of considerable importance and volume. The Sino river rises in the Niete mountains and brings down a great volume of water to the sea, though it is not a river of considerable length. The Duobe rises at the back of the Satro Mountains and flows nearly parallel with the Cavalla, which it joins. The Moa or Makona river is a fine stream of considerable volume, but its course is perpetually interrupted by rocks and rapids. Its lower course is through the territory of Sierra Leone, and it enters the sea as the Sulima.

Climate and Rainfall.—Liberia is almost everywhere well watered. The climate and rainfall over the whole of the coast region for about 120 m. inland are equatorial, the rainfall in the western half of the country being about 150 in. per annum and in the eastern half about 100 in. North of a distance of about 120 m. inland the climate is not quite so rainy, and the weather is much cooler during the dry season. This region beyond the hundred-miles coast belt is far more agreeable and healthy to Europeans.

Forests.—Outside a coast belt of about 20 m. and south of 8° N. the country is one vast forest, except where the natives have cleared the land for cultivation. In many districts the land has been cleared and cultivated and then abandoned, and has relapsed into scrub and jungle which is gradually returning to the condition of forest. The densest forest of all would seem to be that known as Gora, [illegible] entirely uninhabited and occupies an area of about [illegible] between the Pō hills and the British frontier. There is [illegible] forest stretching with little interruption from the [illegible] the St Paul's river nearly to the Cavalla. The Nidi [illegible] for its magnificent growth of *Funtumia* rubber [illegible] between the Duobe and the Cavalla rivers. The [illegible] Liberia is still for the most part a very well-watered [illegible] with a rich vegetation, but there are said to be a [illegible] are rather stony and that have a very well-marked [illegible] the vegetation is a good deal burnt up. In the [illegible] the forest country par excellence of West Africa, [illegible] the region of dense forests overlaps the political [illegible] Sierra Leone and the Ivory Coast, it is a feature of [illegible] so nearly coincident with the actual frontiers [illegible] give this country special characteristics clearly [illegible] fauna.

[illegible] of Liberia is sufficiently peculiar, at any rate [illegible] vertebrates, to make it very nearly identical with a [illegible] sub-province of the West African province, though [illegible] "district" would not include the northern-[illegible] the country and would overlap on the east and west [illegible] and the French Ivory Coast. It is probable that [illegible] may offer one or more distinct varieties; [illegible] local development of the Diana monkey, [illegible] the bay-thighed monkey (*Cercopithecus diana* [illegible] of its brilliant orange-red thighs. One or more [illegible] are peculiar to the country—*Vespertilio stampflii*, [illegible] *büttikoferi*; two species of shrew (*Crocidura*), [illegible] *sagiglasii*); the pygmy hippopotamus [illegible] from the common hippopotamus by its [illegible] by the reduction of the incisor teeth to a [illegible] or occasionally to the odd number of three; [illegible] *Cephalophus* antelopes peculiar to this region [illegible] are the white-shouldered duiker, *Cephalo-*[illegible] the zebra antelope, *C. doriae*, a creature the size [illegible] bright bay brown, with broad black zebra-like [illegible] interesting mammals are four species of the [illegible] monkeys (black, black and white, greenish-[illegible] the Potto lemur, fruit bats of large size [illegible] *Hypsignathus monstrosus*); the brush-[illegible] several very brightly coloured squirrels; [illegible]; the common porcupine; the [illegible] (*Felis celidogaster*) in two varieties, the [illegible] grey, possibly the same animal at different [illegible] spotted hyenas (beyond the forest region); [illegible] the hyrax, elephant and manati; the red [illegible] *porcus*); the West African chevrotain [illegible] buffalo; Bongo antelope (*Boocercus*); [illegible] *Cephalophus sylvicultrix*), black duiker, [illegible] beyond the forest), pygmy antelope [illegible] of *Manis* or pangolin (*M. gigantea*, [illegible]).

[illegible] not quite so peculiar as the mammals. [illegible] guineafowl, *Agelastes* (which is [illegible] and elsewhere west of the lower Niger); [illegible] eagle owl (*Bubo lettii*) and a very [illegible] *büttikoferi*); a few sun-birds, [illegible] to the region. The other birds [illegible] and of the West African forest region [illegible] handsome bird is the blue plantain-eater [illegible] vulture (*Gypohierax*) is found in all the [illegible] are almost entirely absent except [illegible] brown *Percnopterus* makes its [illegible]) visits Fisherman Lake, [illegible] of herons. Cuckoos are abundant, [illegible] also rollers, kingfishers and horn-[illegible] represented, especially by the three [illegible] and black hornbill (*Ceratogymna*), [illegible] hornbill (*Ortholophus leucolophus*), [illegible], a brightly coloured ground [illegible] and barbets; glossy starlings, [illegible] and a great variety of brilliantly [illegible] and sun-birds.

[illegible] at least seven poisonous snakes—[illegible]. The brilliantly coloured [illegible] is found in the coast region [illegible] species of crocodile, at least two [illegible] forest is further explored), the [illegible] and a rare Boine snake (*Cala-*[illegible] leathery turtle (*Dermochelis*) [illegible] in the rivers and swamps there [illegible]). The land tor-[illegible]. The fresh-water fish [illegible] to those of the Niger and [illegible] and it is probable that the [illegible] though its existence has [illegible]. As regards invertebrates, [illegible] Liberia so far as is yet [illegible] of local [illegible] 6 in.

long—are a common feature in the forest. One noteworthy feature in Liberia, however, is the relative absence of mosquitoes, and the white ants and some other insect pests are not so troublesome here as in other parts of West Africa. The absence or extreme paucity of mosquitoes no doubt accounts for the infrequency of malarial fever in the interior.

Flora.—Nowhere, perhaps, does the flora of West Africa attain a more wonderful development than in the republic of Liberia and in the adjoining regions of Sierra Leone and the Ivory Coast. This is partly due to the equatorial position and the heavy rainfall. The region of dense forest, however, does not cover the whole of Liberia; the Makona river and the northern tributaries of the Lofa and St Paul's flow through a mountainous country covered with grass and thinly scattered trees, while the ravines and watercourses are still richly forested. A good deal of this absence of forest is directly due to the action of man. Year by year the influence of the Mahommedan tribes on the north leads to the cutting down of the forest, the extension of both planting and pasture and the introduction of cattle and even horses. In the regions bordering the coast also a good deal of the forest has disappeared, its place being taken (where the land is not actually cultivated) by very dense scrub. The most striking trees in the forest region are, in the basin of the Cavalla, the giant *Funtumia elastica*, which grows to an altitude of 200 ft.; various kinds of *Parinarium*, *Oldfieldia* and *Khaya*; the bombax or cotton tree, giant dracaenas, many kinds of fig; *Borassus* palms, oil palms, the climbing *Calamus* palms, and on the coast the coconut. The most important palm of the country perhaps is the *Raphia vinifera*, which produces the piassava fibre of commerce. There are about twenty-two different trees, shrubs and vines producing rubber of more or less good quality. These belong chiefly to the Apocynaceous order. In this order is the genus *Strophanthus*, which is represented in Liberia by several species, amongst others *S. gratus*. This *Strophanthus* is not remarkable for its rubber—which is mere bird lime—but for the powerful poison of its seeds, often used for poisoning arrows, but of late much in use as a drug for treating diseases of the heart. Coffee of several species is indigenous and grows wild. The best known is the celebrated *Coffea liberica*. The kola tree is also indigenous. Large edible nuts are derived from *Coula edulis* of the order Olacineae. The country is exceedingly rich in Aroids, many of which are epiphytic, festooning the trunks of tall trees with a magnificent drapery of abundant foliage. A genus much represented is *Culcasia*, and swampy localities are thickly set with the giant *Cyrtosperma* arum, with flower spathes that are blotched with deep purple. Ground orchids and tree orchids are well represented; *Polystachya liberica*, an epiphytic orchid with sprays of exquisite small flowers of purple and gold, might well be introduced into horticulture for its beauty. The same might be said of the magnificent *Lissochilus roseus*, a terrestrial orchid, growing to 7 ft. in height, with rose-coloured flowers nearly 1 in. long; there are other orchids of fantastic design in their green and white flowers, some of which have spurs (nectaries) nearly 7 in. long.

Many trees offer magnificent displays of flowers at certain seasons of the year; perhaps the loveliest effect is derived from the bushes and trailing creepers of the *Combretum* genus, which, during the "winter" months from December to March, cover the scrub and the forest with mantles of rose colour. *Smeathmannia* trees are thickly set at this season with large blossoms of waxen white. Very beautiful also are the red velvet or white velvet sepals of the *Mussaenda* genus. Bamboos of the genus *Oxytenanthera* are indigenous. Tree ferns are found on the mountains above 4000 ft. The bracken grows in low sandy tracts near the coast. The country in general is a fern paradise, and the iridescent creeping *Selaginella* (akin to *Lycopodium*) festoons the undergrowth by the wayside. The cultivated trees and plants of importance are, besides rubber, the manioc or cassada, the orange tree, lime, cacao, coffee, pineapple (which now runs wild over the whole of Liberia), sour sop, ginger, papaw, alligator apple, avocado pear, okro, cotton (*Gossypium peruvianum*—the kidney cotton), indigo, sweet potato, capsicum (chillie), bread-fruit, arrow-root (*Maranta*), banana, yam, "coco"-yam (*Colocasia antiquorum*, var. *esculenta*), maize, sorghum, sugar cane, rice and eleusine (*Eleusine*), besides gourds, pumpkins, cabbages and onions.

Minerals.—The hinterland of Liberia has been but slightly explored for mineral wealth. In a general way it is supposed that the lands lying between the lower St Paul's river and the Sierra Leone frontier are not much mineralized, except that in the vicinity of river mouths there are indications of bitumen. The sand of nearly all the rivers contains a varying proportion of gold. Garnets and mica are everywhere found. There have been repeated stories of diamonds obtained from the Finley Mountains (which are volcanic) in the central province, but all specimens sent home, except one, have hitherto proved to be quartz crystals. There are indications of sapphires and other forms of corundum. Corundum indeed is abundantly met with in the eastern half of Liberia. The sand of the rivers contains monazite. Graphite has been discovered in the Pō Hills. Lead has been reported from the Nidi or Niete Mountains. Gold is present in some abundance in the river sand of central Liberia, and native reports speak of the far interior as being rich in gold. Iron—haematite—is present almost everywhere. There are other indications of bitumen, besides those mentioned, in the coast region of eastern Liberia.

History and Population.—Tradition asserts that the Liberian coast was first visited by Europeans when it was reached by the Dieppois merchant-adventurers in the 14th century. The French in the 17th century claimed that but for the loss of the archives of Dieppe they would be able to prove that vessels from this Norman port had established settlements at Grand Basa, Cape Mount, and other points on the coast of Liberia. No proof has yet been forthcoming, however, that the Portuguese were not the first white men to reach this coast. The first Portuguese pioneer was Pedro de Sintra, who discovered and noted in 1461 the remarkable promontory of Cape Mount, Cape Mesurado (where the capital, Monrovia, is now situated) and the mouth of the Junk river. In 1462 de Sintra returned with another Portuguese captain, Sueiro da Costa, and penetrated as far as Cape Palmas and the Cavalla river. Subsequently the Portuguese mapped the whole coast of Liberia, and nearly all the prominent features—capes, rivers, islets—off that coast still bear Portuguese names. From the 16th century onwards, English, Dutch, German, French and other European traders contested the commerce of this coast with the Portuguese, and finally drove them away. In the 18th century France once or twice thought of establishing colonies here. At the end of the 18th century, when the tide was rising in favour of the abolition of slavery and the repatriation of slaves, the Grain Coast [so called from the old trade in the "Grains of Paradise" or *Amomum* pepper] was suggested once or twice as a suitable home for repatriated negroes. Sierra Leone, however, was chosen first on account of its possessing an admirable harbour. But in 1821 Cape Mesurado was selected by the American Colonization Society as an appropriate site for the first detachment of American freed negroes, whom difficulties in regard to extending the suffrage in the United States were driving away from a still slave-holding America. From that date, 1821, onwards to the present day, negroes and mulattos—freed slaves or the descendants of such—have been crossing the Atlantic in small numbers to settle on the Liberian coast. The great migrations took place during the first half of the 19th century. Only two or three thousand American emigrants—at most—have come to Liberia since 1860.

The colony was really founded by Jehudi Ashmun, a white American, between 1822 and 1828. The name "Liberia" was invented by the Rev. R. R. Gurley in 1824. In 1847 the American colonists declared their country to be an independent republic, and its status in this capacity was recognized in 1848–1849 by most of the great powers with the exception of the United States. Until 1857 Liberia consisted of two republics—Liberia and Maryland. These American settlements were dotted at intervals along the coast from the mouth of the Sewa river on the west to the San Pedro river on the east (some 60 m. beyond Cape Palmas). Some tracts of territory, such as the greater part of the Kru coast, still, however, remain without foreign—American—settlers, and in a state of quasi-independence. The uncertainty of Liberian occupation led to frontier troubles with Great Britain and disputes with France. Finally, by the English and French treaties of 1885 and 1892 Liberian territory on the coast was made continuous, but was limited to the strip of about 300 m. between the Mano river on the west and the Cavalla river on the east. The Sierra Leone-Liberia frontier was demarcated in 1903; then followed the negotiations with France for the exact delimitation of the Ivory Coast-Liberia frontier, with the result that Liberia lost part of the hinterland she had claimed. Reports of territorial encroachments aroused much sympathy with Liberia in America and led in February 1909 to the appointment by President Roosevelt of a commission which visited Liberia in the summer of that year to investigate the condition of the country. As a result of the commissioners' report negotiations were set on foot for the adjustment of the Liberian debt and the placing of United States officials in charge of the Liberian customs. In July 1910 it was announced that the American government, acting in general agreement with Great Britain, France and Germany, would take charge of the finances, military organization, agriculture and boundary questions of the republic. A loan for £400,000 was also arranged. Meantime the attempts of the Liberian government to control the Kru coast led to various troubles, such as the fining or firing upon foreign steamships for alleged contraventions of regulations. During 1910 the natives in the Cape Palmas district were at open warfare with the Liberian authorities.

One of the most notable of the Liberian presidents was J. J. Roberts, who was nearly white, with only a small proportion of negro blood in his veins. But perhaps the ablest statesman that this American-Negro republic has as yet produced is a pure-blooded negro—President Arthur Barclay, a native of Barbados in the West Indies, who came to Liberia with his parents in the middle of the 19th century, and received all his education there. President Barclay was of unmixed negro descent, but came of a Dahomey stock of superior type.[1] Until the accession to power of President Barclay in 1904 (he was re-elected in 1907), the Americo-Liberian government on the coast had very uncertain relations with the indigenous population, which is well armed and tenacious of local independence. But of late Liberian influence has been extending, more especially in the counties of Maryland and Montserrado.

The president is now elected for a term of four years. There is a legislature of eight senators and thirteen representatives. The type of the constitution is very like that of the United States. Increasing attention is being given to education, to deal with which there are several colleges and a number of schools. The judicial functions are discharged by four grades of officials—the local magistrates, the courts of common pleas, the quarterly courts (five in number) and the supreme court. The customs service includes British customs officers lent to the Liberian service. A gunboat for preventive service purchased from the British government and commanded by an Englishman, with native petty officers and crew, is employed by the Liberian government. The language of government and trade is English, which is understood far and wide throughout Liberia. As the origin of the Sierra Leonis and the Americo-Liberian settlers was very much the same, an increasing intimacy is growing up between the English-speaking populations of these adjoining countries. Order is maintained in Liberia to some extent by a militia.

The population of Americo-Liberian origin in the coast regions is estimated at from 12,000 to 15,000. To these must be added about 40,000 civilized and Christianized negroes who make common cause with the Liberians in most matters, and have gradually been filling the position of Liberian citizens.

For administrative purposes the country is divided into four counties, Montserrado, Basa, Sino and Maryland, but Cape Mount in the far west and the district round it has almost the status of a fifth county. The approximate revenue for 1906 was £65,000, and the expenditure about £60,000, but some of the revenue was still collected in paper of uncertain value. There are three custom-houses, or ports of entry on the Sierra Leone land frontier between the Moa river on the north and the Mano on the south, and nine ports of entry along the coast. At all of these Europeans are allowed to settle and trade, and with very slight restrictions they may now trade almost anywhere in Liberia. The rubber trade is controlled by the Liberian Rubber Corporation, which holds a special concession from the Liberian government for a number of years, and is charged with the preservation of the forests. Another English company has constructed motor roads in the Liberian hinterland to connect centres of trade with the St Paul's river. The trade is done almost entirely with Great Britain, Germany and Holland, but friendly relations are maintained with Spain, as the Spanish plantations in Fernando Pô are to a great extent worked by Liberian labour.

The indigenous population must be considered one of the assets of Liberia. The native population—apart from the American element—is estimated at as much as 2,000,000; for

[1] Amongst other remarkable negroes that Liberian education produced was Dr E. W. Blyden (b. 1832), the author of many works dealing with negro questions.

[illegible] the Oriental bishops; but the document is now held to be spurious [illegible] Hefele, *Conciliengesch.* i. 648 seq. Three other letters, though [illegible] by Hefele, seem to have b[illegible] written by Liberius at the time of his submission to the emperor. (L. D.*)

LIBER PONTIFICALIS, or Gesta Pontificum Romanorum [illegible] book of the popes), consists of the lives of the bishops of Rome from the time of St Peter to the death of Nicholas I. in [illegible]67. A supplement continues the series of lives almost to the close of the 9th century, and several other continuations were written later. During the 16th century there was some discussion about the authorship of the *Liber*, and for some time it was thought to be the work of an Italian monk, Anastasius Bibliothecarius (d. 886). It is now, however, practically certain that it was of composite authorship and that the earlier part of it was compiled about 530, three centuries before the time of Anastasius. This is the view taken by Louis Duchesne and substantially by G. Waitz and T. Mommsen, although these scholars think that it was written about a century later. The *Liber* contains much information about papal affairs in general, and about endowments, martyrdoms and the like, but a considerable part of it is obviously legendary. It assumes that the bishops of Rome exercised authority over the Christian Church from its earliest days.

The *Liber*, which was used by Bede for his *Historia Ecclesiastica*, was first printed at Mainz in 1602. Among other editions is the one [illegible] by T. Mommsen for the *Monumenta Germaniae historica*. [illegible] *Romanorum pontificum*, Band i., but the best is the one by [illegible] Duchesne, *Le Liber pontificalis: texte, introduction, commentaire* ([illegible]). See also the same writer's *Étude sur le Liber* [illegible] (Paris, 1877); and the article by A. Brackmann in [illegible]-Hauck's *Realencyklopädie*, Band xi. (Leipzig, 1902).

LIBERTAD, or La Libertad, a coast department of Peru, bounded N. by Lambayeque and Cajamarca, E. by San Martin, S. [illegible] Ancachs, S.W. and W. by the Pacific. Pop. (1906 estimate [illegible]); area 10,209 sq. m. Libertad formerly included [illegible] present department of Lambayeque. The Western Cordillera [illegible] it into two nearly equal parts; the western consisting [illegible] a narrow, arid, sandy coast zone and the western slopes [illegible] the Cordillera broken into valleys by short mountain spurs, and the eastern a high inter-Andine valley lying between the Western and Central Cordilleras and traversed by the upper Marañon or Amazon, which at one point is less than 90 m. in a straight line from the Pacific coast. The coast region is [illegible] by several short streams, which are fed by the melting snows of the Cordillera and are extensively used for irrigation. These are ([illegible] names also applying to their valleys) the Jequetepeque or Pacasmayo, in whose valley rice is an important product, the Chicama, in whose valley the sugar plantations are among the largest and best in Peru, the Moche, Viru, Chao and Santa; the last, with its northern tributary, the Tablachaca, forming the southern boundary line of the department. The Santa Valley [illegible] noted for its sugar plantations. Cotton is produced in several of these valleys, coffee in the Pacasmayo district, and [illegible] on the mountain slopes about Huamachuco and Otuzco, at elevations of 3000 to 6000 ft. above sea-level. The upland regions, which have a moderate rainfall and a cool, healthy climate, are partly devoted to agriculture on a small scale (producing wheat, Indian corn, barley, potatoes, quinua, alfalfa, [illegible] and vegetables), partly to grazing and partly to mining. Cattle and sheep have been raised on the upland pastures of Libertad and Ancachs since early colonial times, and the llama and alpaca were reared throughout this "sierra" country long before the Spanish conquest. Gold and silver mines are worked in the districts of Huamachuco, Otuzco and Pataz, and coal has been found in the first two. The department had 169 m. of railway in 1000, viz.: from Pacasmayo to Yonán (in Cajamarca) with a branch to Guadalupe, 60 m.; from Salaverry to Trujillo with its extension to Ascope, 47 m.; from Trujillo to Laredo, [illegible] and Menocucho, 18½ m.; from Huanchaco to Roma, 15 m., and from Chicama to Pampas, 18½ m. The principal [illegible] are Pacasmayo and Salaverry, which have long iron piers [illegible] by the national government; Malabrigo, Huanchuco, [illegible] and Chao are open roadsteads. The capital of the [illegible]ment is Trujillo. The other principal towns are San

Pedro, Otuzco, Huamachuco, Santiago de Chuco and Tuyabamba—all provincial capitals and important only through their mining interests, except San Pedro, which stands in the fertile district of the Jequetepeque. The population of Otuzco (35 m. N.E. of Trujillo) was estimated to be about 4000 in 1896, that of Huamachuco (65 m. N.E. of Trujillo) being perhaps slightly less.

LIBERTARIANISM (from Lat. *libertas*, freedom), in ethics, the doctrine which maintains the freedom of the will, as opposed to necessitarianism or determinism. It has been held in various forms. In its extreme form it maintains that the individual is absolutely free to chose this or that action indifferently (the *liberum arbitrium indifferentiae*), but most libertarians admit that acquired tendencies, environment and the like, exercise control in a greater or less degree.

LIBERTINES, the nickname, rather than the name, given to various political and social parties. It is futile to deduce the name from the Libertines of Acts vi. 9; these were "sons of freedmen," for it is vain to make them citizens of an imaginary Libertum, or to substitute (with Beza) Libustines, in the sense of inhabitants of Libya. In a sense akin to the modern use of the term "libertine," *i.e* a person who sets the rules of morality, &c., at defiance, the word seems first to have been applied, as a stigma, to Anabaptists in the Low Countries (Mark Pattison, *Essays*, ii. 38). It has become especially attached to the liberal party in Geneva, opposed to Calvin and carrying on the tradition of the Liberators in that city; but the term was never applied to them till after Calvin's death (F. W. Kampschulte, *Johann Calvin*). Calvin, who wrote against the "Libertins qui se nomment Spirituelz" (1545), never confused them with his political antagonists in Geneva, called Perrinistes from their leader Amadeo Perrin. The objects of Calvin's polemic were the Anabaptists above mentioned, whose first obscure leader was Coppin of Lisle, followed by Quintin of Hennegau, by whom and his disciples, Bertram des Moulins and Claude Perseval, the principles of the sect were disseminated in France. Quintin was put to death as a heretic at Tournai in 1546. His most notable follower was Antoine Pocquet, a native of Enghien, Belgium, priest and almoner (1540–1549), afterwards pensioner of the queen of Navarre, who was a guest of Bucer at Strassburg (1543–1544) and died some time after 1560. Calvin (who had met Quintin in Paris) describes the doctrines he impugns as pantheistic and antinomian.

See Choisy in Herzog-Hauck's *Realencyklopädie* (1902).

(A. Go.*)

LIBERTINES, SYNAGOGUE OF THE, a section of the Hellenistic Jews who attacked Stephen (Acts vi. 9). The passage reads, *τίνες τῶν ἐκ τῆς συναγωγῆς τῆς λεγομένης Λιβερτίνων, καὶ Κυρηναίων καὶ Ἀλεξανδρέων, καὶ τῶν ἀπὸ Κιλικίας καὶ Ἀσίας*, and opinion is divided as to the number of synagogues here named. The probability is that there are three, corresponding to the geographical regions involved, (1) Rome and Italy, (2) N.E. Africa, (3) Asia Minor. In this case "the Synagogue of the Libertines" is the assembly of "the Freedmen" from Rome, descendants of the Jews enslaved by Pompey after his conquest of Judaea 63 B.C. If, however, we take *Λιβερτίνων καὶ Κυρηναίων καὶ Ἀλεξανδρέων* closely together, the first name must denote the people of some city or district. The obscure town Libertum (inferred from the title Episcopus Libertinensis in connexion with the synod of Carthage, A.D. 411) is less likely than the reading (*Λιβύων* or) *Λιβυστίνων* underlying certain Armenian versions and Syriac commentaries. The Greek towns lying west from Cyrene would naturally be called Libyan. In any case the interesting point is that these returned Jews, instead of being liberalized by their residence abroad, were more tenacious of Judaism and more bitter against Stephen than those who had never left Judaea.

LIBERTY (Lat. *libertas*, from *liber*, free), generally the state of freedom, especially opposed to subjection, imprisonment or slavery, or with such restricted or figurative meaning as the circumstances imply. The history of political liberty is in modern days identified practically with the progress of civilization. In a more particular sense, "a liberty" is the term for a franchise, a privilege or branch of the crown's prerogative granted to a subject, as, for example, that of executing legal process; hence the district over which the privilege extends. Such liberties are exempt from the jurisdiction of the sheriff and have separate commissions of the peace, but for purposes of local government form part of the county in which they are situated. The exemption from the jurisdiction of the sheriff was recognized in England by the Sheriffs Act 1887, which provides that the sheriff of a county shall appoint a deputy at the expense of the lord of the liberty, such deputy to reside in or near the liberty. The deputy receives and opens in the sheriff's name all writs, the return or execution of which belongs to the bailiff of the liberty, and issues to the bailiff the warrant required for the due execution of such writs. The bailiff then becomes liable for non-execution, mis-execution or insufficient return of any writs, and in the case of non-return of any writ, if the sheriff returns that he has delivered the writ to a bailiff of a liberty, the sheriff will be ordered to execute the writ notwithstanding the liberty, and must cause the bailiff to attend before the high court of justice and answer why he did not execute the writ.

In nautical phraseology various usages of the term are derived from its association with a sailor's leave on shore, *e.g.* liberty-man, liberty-day, liberty-ticket.

A History of Modern Liberty, in eight volumes, of which the third appeared in 1906, has been written by James Mackinnon; see also Lord Acton's lectures, and such works as J. S. Mill's *On Liberty* and Sir John Seeley's *Introduction to Political Science*.

LIBERTY PARTY, the first political party organized in the United States to oppose the spread and restrict the political power of slavery, and the lineal precursor of the Free Soil and Republican parties. It originated in the Old North-west. Its organization was preceded there by a long anti-slavery religious movement. James G. Birney (*q.v.*), to whom more than to any other man belongs the honour of founding and leading the party, began to define the political duties of so-called "abolitionists" about 1836; but for several years thereafter he, in common with other leaders, continued to disclaim all idea of forming a political party. In state and local campaigns, however, non-partisan political action was attempted through the questioning of Whig and Democratic candidates. The utter futility of seeking to obtain in this way any satisfactory concessions to anti-slavery sentiment was speedily and abundantly proved. There arose, consequently, a division in the American Anti-slavery Society between those who were led by W. L. Garrison (*q.v.*), and advocated political non-resistance—and, besides, had loaded down their anti-slavery views with a variety of religious and social vagaries, unpalatable to all but a small number—and those who were led by Birney, and advocated independent political action. The sentiment of the great majority of "abolitionists" was, by 1838, strongly for such action; and it was clearly sanctioned and implied in the constitution and declared principles of the Anti-slavery Society; but the capture of that organization by the Garrisonians, in a "packed" convention in 1830, made it unavailable as a party nucleus—even if it had not been already outgrown—and hastened a separate party organization. A convention of abolitionists at Warsaw, New York, in November 1839 had resolved that abolitionists were bound by every consideration of duty and expediency to organize an independent political party. Accordingly, the political abolitionists, in another convention at Albany, in April 1840, containing delegates from six states but not one from the North-west, launched the "Liberty Party," and nominated Birney for the presidency. In the November election he received 7069 votes.[1]

The political "abolitionists" were abolitionists only as they were restrictionists. they wished to use the federal government to exclude (or abolish) slavery from the federal Territories and the District of Columbia, but they saw no opportunity to attack slavery in the states—*i.e.* to attack the institution *per se*; also

[1] Mr T. C Smith estimates that probably not one in ten of even professed abolitionists supported Birney; only in Massachusetts did he receive as much as 1% of the total vote cast.

although | parts are | fertility o | the follo | eastward | (the Va | tribes | the d | river i | (3) I | Ca | lang | &c. | Ce | all | pro | sh | of I | pr | still | spr | race | are | have | Som | with | are I | Mand. | Au | d'un | Libera | 1906), | compar. | et dans l. | to deal | relations

LIBER | was con | 22nd of | been held | Arles (353 | with refer. | Vincentius | ciliabulum | demnation | Liberius wa | Dionysius o | condemnati | Milan by in | consequence | (antipope) b | haud episcop | exile of more | formula givin | and to accep | mistake, with | mission led t | Roman see wa | Liberius was s | Liberius shoul | the arrival of L | Neither Liberiu | (359). After t | Liberius annulle | concurrence of S | who had signed | Liberius gave a | Eastern episcopat | moderate of the | September 366.

... division ... supplied an ... ordinary ... the ... of ... the ... men. ... little known ... promis- ... campaigns ... in 1843 ... convince the ... question in ... slavery ... Until ... Liberty ... that the ... As the ... Liberty ... But the ... and ... had ... resist ... such as ... again ... more ... and the ... support. The ... Democratic ... apart from ... though ... were ... own ... progress. ... ablest ... accident ... was in a ... though ... antecedents ... above ... Whigs, for ... anti-slavery ... union. ... who had ... Whigs ... the issue ... Mexico ... men ... Party ... state ... in ... the ... to be

Liberty men with other anti-slavery men in state politics—was nominated for the presidency. But the nomination by the Democrats of Lewis Cass shattered the Democratic organization in New York and the North-west; and when the Whigs nominated General Taylor, adopted a non-committal platform, and showed hostility to the Wilmot Proviso, the way was cleared for a union of all anti-slavery men. The Liberty Party, abandoning therefore its independent nominations, joined in the first convention and nominations of the Free Soil Party (*q.v.*), thereby practically losing its identity, although it continued until after the organization of the Republican Party to maintain something of a semi-independent organization. The Liberty Party has the unique honour among third-parties in the United States of seeing its principles rapidly adopted and realized.

See T. C. Smith, *History of the Liberty and Free Soil Parties in the Northwest* (Harvard University Historical Studies, New York, 1897), and lives and writings of all the public men mentioned above; also of G. W. Julian, J. R. Giddings and S. P. Chase.

LIBITINA, an old Roman goddess of funerals. She had a sanctuary in a sacred grove (perhaps on the Esquiline), where, by an ordinance of Servius Tullius, a piece of money (*lucar Libitinae*) was deposited whenever a death took place. Here the undertakers (*libitinarii*), who carried out all funeral arrangements by contract, had their offices, and everything necessary was kept for sale or hire; here all deaths were registered for statistical purposes. The word *Libitina* then came to be used for the business of an undertaker, funeral requisites, and (in the poets) for death itself. By later antiquarians Libitina was sometimes identified with Persephone, but more commonly (partly or completely) with Venus Lubentia or Lubentina, an Italian goddess of gardens. The similarity of name and the fact that Venus Lubentia had a sanctuary in the grove of Libitina favoured this idea. Further, Plutarch (*Quaest. Rom.* 23) mentions a small statue at Delphi of Aphrodite Epitymbia (A. of tombs = Venus Libitina), to which the spirits of the dead were summoned. The inconsistency of selling funeral requisites in the temple of Libitina, seeing that she is identified with Venus, is explained by him as indicating that one and the same goddess presides over birth and death; or the association of such things with the goddess of love and pleasure is intended to show that death is not a calamity, but rather a consummation to be desired. Libitina may, however, have been originally an earth goddess, connected with luxuriant nature and the enjoyments of life (cf. *lub-et, lib-ido*); then, all such deities being connected with the underworld, she also became the goddess of death, and that side of her character predominated in the later conceptions.

See Plutarch, *Numa*, 12; Dion. Halic. iv. 15; Festus xvi., s.v. "Rustica Vinalia"; Juvenal xii. 121, with Mayor's note; G. Wissowa in Roscher's *Lexicon der Mythologie*, s.v.

LIBMANAN, a town of the province of Ambos Camarines, Luzon, Philippine Islands, on the Libmanan river, 11 m. N.W. of Nueva Cáceres, the capital. Pop. (1903) 17,416. It is about 4½ m. N.E. of the Bay of San Miguel. Rice, coco-nuts, hemp, Indian corn, sugarcane, bejuco, arica nuts and camotes, are grown in the vicinity, and the manufactures include hemp goods, alcohol (from coco-nut-palm sap), copra, and baskets, chairs, hammocks and hats of bejuco and bamboo. The Libmanan river, a tributary of the Bicol, into which it empties 2 m. below the town, is famous for its clear cold water and for its sulphur springs. The language is Bicol.

LIBO, in ancient Rome, the name of a family belonging to the Scribonian gens. It is chiefly interesting for its connexion with the Puteal Scribonianum or Puteal Libonis in the forum at Rome,[1] dedicated or restored by one of its members, perhaps the praetor of 204 B.C., or the tribune of the people in 149. In its vicinity the praetor's tribunal, removed from the comitium in the 2nd century B.C., held its sittings, which led to the place becoming the haunt of litigants, money-lenders and business people. According to ancient authorities, the Puteal Libonis

... was the name given to an erection (or enclosure) on a ... ad been struck by lightning; it was so called from its ... o the stone kerb or low enclosure round a well (*puteus*).

was between the temples of Castor and Vesta, near the Porticus Julia and the Arcus Fabiorum, but no remains have been discovered. The idea that an irregular circle of travertine blocks, found near the temple of Castor, formed part of the puteal is now abandoned.

See Horace, *Sat.* ii. 6. 35, *Epp.* i. 19. 8; Cicero, *Pro Sestio*, 8; for the well-known coin of L. Scribonius Libo, representing the puteal of Libo, which rather resembles a *cippus* (sepulchral monument) or an altar, with laurel wreaths, two lyres and a pair of pincers or tongs below the wreaths (perhaps symbolical of Vulcanus as forger of lightning), see C. Hülsen, *The Roman Forum* (Eng. trans. by J. B. Carter, 1906), p. 150, where a marble imitation found at Veii is also given.

LIBON, a Greek architect, born at Elis, who was employed to build the great temple of Zeus at Olympia (*q.v.*) about 460 B.C. (Pausanias v. 10. 3).

LIBOURNE, a town of south-western France, capital of an arrondissement of the department of Gironde, situated at the confluence of the Isle with the Dordogne, 22 m. E.N.E. of Bordeaux on the railway to Angoulême. Pop. (1906) town, 15,280; commune, 19,323. The sea is 56 m. distant, but the tide affects the river so as to admit of vessels drawing 14 ft. reaching the town at the highest tides. The Dordogne is here crossed by a stone bridge 492 ft. long, and a suspension bridge across the Isle connects Libourne with Fronsac, built on a hill on which in feudal times stood a powerful fortress. Libourne is regularly built. The Gothic church, restored in the 19th century, has a stone spire 232 ft. high. On the quay there is a machicolated clock-tower which is a survival of the ramparts of the 14th century; and the town-house, containing a small museum and a library, is a quaint relic of the 16th century. There is a statue of the Duc Decazes, who was born in the neighbourhood. The sub-prefecture, tribunals of first instance and of commerce, and a communal college are among the public institutions. The principal articles of commerce are the wines and brandies of the district. Printing and cooperage are among the industries.

Like other sites at the confluence of important rivers, that of Libourne was appropriated at an early period. Under the Romans *Condate* stood rather more than a mile to the south of the present Libourne; it was destroyed during the troubles of the 5th century. Resuscitated by Charlemagne, it was rebuilt in 1269, under its present name and on the site and plan it still retains, by Roger de Leybourne (of Leybourne in Kent), seneschal of Guienne, acting under the authority of King Edward I. of England. It suffered considerably in the struggles of the French and English for the possession of Guienne in the 14th century.

See R. Guinodie, *Hist. de Libourne* (2nd ed., 2 vols., Libourne, 1876-1877).

LIBRA ("THE BALANCE"), in astronomy, the 7th sign of the zodiac (*q.v.*), denoted by the symbol ♎, resembling a pair of scales, probably in allusion to the fact that when the sun enters this part of the ecliptic, at the autumnal equinox, the days and nights are equal. It is also a constellation, not mentioned by Eudoxus or Aratus, but by Manetho (3rd century B.C.) and Geminus (1st century B.C.), and included by Ptolemy in his 48 asterisms; Ptolemy catalogued 17 stars, Tycho Brahe 10, and Hevelius 20. *δ Librae* is an Algol (*q.v.*) variable, the range of magnitude being 5·0 to 6·2, and the period 2 days 7 hrs. 51 min.; and the cluster *M. 5 Librae* is a faint globular cluster of which only about one star in eleven is variable.

LIBRARIES. A library (from Lat. *liber*, book), in the modern sense, is a collection of printed or written literature. As such, it implies an advanced and elaborate civilization. If the term be extended to any considerable collection of written documents, it must be nearly as old as civilization itself. The earliest use to which the invention of inscribed or written signs was put was probably to record important religious and political transactions. These records would naturally be preserved in sacred places, and accordingly the earliest libraries of the world were probably temples, and the earliest librarians priests. And indeed before the extension of the arts of writing and reading the priests were the only persons who could perform such work as, *e.g.* the compilation of the *Annales Maximi*, which was the duty of the pontifices in ancient Rome. The beginnings of literature proper in the shape of ballads and songs may have continued to be conveyed orally only from one generation to another, long after the record of important religious or civil events was regularly committed to writing. The earliest collections of which we know anything, therefore, were collections of archives. Of this character appear to have been such famous collections as that of the Medians at Ecbatana, the Persians at Susa or the hieroglyphic archives of Knossos discovered by A. J. Evans (*Scripta Minoa*, 1909) of a date synchronizing with the XIIth Egyptian dynasty. It is not until the development of arts and sciences, and the growth of a considerable written literature, and even of a distinct literary class, that we find collections of books which can be called libraries in our modern sense. It is of libraries in the modern sense, and not, except incidentally, of archives that we are to speak.

ANCIENT LIBRARIES

Assyria.

The researches which have followed the discoveries of P. E. Botta and Sir H. Layard have thrown unexpected light not only upon the history but upon the arts, the sciences and the literatures of the ancient civilizations of Babylonia and Assyria. In all these wondrous revelations no facts are more interesting than those which show the existence of extensive libraries so many ages ago, and none are more eloquent of the elaborateness of these forgotten civilizations. In the course of his excavations at Nineveh in 1850, Layard came upon some chambers in the south-west palace, the floor of which, as well as the adjoining rooms, was covered to the depth of a foot with tablets of clay, covered with cuneiform characters, in many cases so small as to require a magnifying glass. These varied in size from 1 to 12 in. square. A great number of them were broken, as Layard supposed by the falling in of the roof, but as George Smith thought by having fallen from the upper storey, upon which he believed the collection to have been placed. These tablets formed the library of the great monarch Assur-bani-pal—the Sardanapalus of the Greeks—the greatest patron of literature amongst the Assyrians. It is estimated that this library consisted of some ten thousand distinct works and documents, some of the works extending over several tablets. The tablets appear to have been methodically arranged and catalogued, and the library seems to have been thrown open for the general use of the king's subjects.[1] A great portion of this library has already been brought to England and deposited in the British museum, but it is calculated that there still remain some 20,000 fragments to be gathered up. For further details as to Assyrian libraries, and the still earlier Babylonian libraries at Tello, the ancient Lagash, and at Niffer, the ancient Nippur, from which the Assyrians drew their science and literature, see BABYLONIA and NIPPUR.

Ancient Egyptian Libraries.

Of the libraries of ancient Egypt our knowledge is scattered and imperfect, but at a time extending to more than 6000 years ago we find numerous scribes of many classes who recorded official events in the life of their royal masters or details of their domestic affairs and business transactions. Besides this official literature we possess examples of many commentaries on the sacerdotal books, as well as historical treatises, works on moral philosophy and proverbial wisdom, science, collections of medical receipts as well as a great variety of popular novels and humoristic pieces. At an early date Heliopolis was a literary centre of great importance with culture akin to the Babylonian. Attached to every temple were professional scribes whose function was partly religious and partly scientific. The sacred books of Thoth constituted as it were a complete encyclopaedia of religion and science, and on these books was gradually accumulated an immense mass of exposition and commentary. We possess a record relating to "the land of the collected works [library] of Khufu," a monarch of the IVth dynasty, and a similar inscription relating to the library of Khafra, the builder of the second pyramid. At Edfu

[1] See Menant, *Bibliothèque du palais de Ninive* (Paris, 1880).

they declared there should be "absolute and unqualified division of the General Government from slavery"—which implied an amendment of the constitution. They proposed to use ordinary moral and political means to attain their ends—not, like the Garrisonians, to abstain from voting, or favour the dissolution of the Union.

After 1840 the attempt began in earnest to organize the Liberty Party thoroughly, and unite all anti-slavery men. The North-west, where "there was, after 1840, very little known of Garrison and his methods" (T. C. Smith), was the most promising field, but though the contest of state and local campaigns gave morale to the party, it made scant political gains (in 1843 it cast hardly 10% of the total vote); it could not convince the people that slavery should be made the paramount question in politics. In 1844, however, the Texas question gave slavery precisely this pre-eminence in the presidential campaign. Until then, neither Whigs nor Democrats had regarded the Liberty Party seriously; now, however, each party charged that the Liberty movement was corruptly auxiliary to the other. As the campaign progressed, the Whigs alternately abused the Liberty men and made frantic appeals for their support. But the Liberty men were strongly opposed to Clay personally; and even if his equivocal campaign letters (see CLAY, HENRY) had not left exceedingly small ground for belief that he would resist the annexation of Texas, still the Liberty men were not such as to admit that an end justifies the means; therefore they again nominated Birney. He received 62,263 votes[1]—many mor than enough in New York to have carried that state and th presidency for Clay, had they been thrown to his support. Th Whigs, therefore, blamed the Liberty Party for Democr success and the annexation of Texas; but—quite apart fr the issue of political ethics—it is almost certain that th Clay's chances were injured by the Liberty ticket, they injured much more outside the Liberty ranks, by h quibbles.[2] After 1844 the Liberty Party made little pr Its leaders were never very strong as politicians, and it organizer, Birney, was about this time compelled by an to abandon public life. Moreover, the election of 184 way fatal to the party; for it seemed to prove th "abolition" was not the party programme, still its a and personnel were too radical to unite the North; all it could not, after 1844, draw the disaffected though their party was steadily moving toward their dislike of the Liberty Party effectually prev Indeed, no party of one idea could hope to satisfy been Whigs or Democrats. At the same time, anti- and Democrats were segregating in state politics, of excluding slavery from the new territory acquir afforded a golden opportunity to unite all anti-sl the principle of the Wilmot Proviso (1846). The reached its greatest strength (casting 74,017 vot elections of 1846. Thereafter, though growin New England, it rapidly became ineffective in North. Many, including Birney, thought it sho an isolated party of one idea—striving for n power between Whigs and Democrats, welcomi sions from them, almost dependent upon them to revivify it by making it a party of general ref was the secession and formation of the Liberty L 1847 nominated Gerrit Smith for the presidency effort was made to take advantage of the disint parties. In October 1847, at Buffalo, was held t national convention. John P. Hale—whose United States Senate had justified the first suc

Liberty me nominated Democrat in New Yo General T hostility of all a fore it and no losing tion indep hon prin

[1] Birney's vote was reduced by a disgraceful the Whigs (the circulation of a forged letter on the e a trick to which he had exposed himself by an in reception of Democratic advances in a matter of lo ment in Michigan.

[2] *E.g.* Horace Greeley made the Wh repeatedly attributed Clay's defeat and for Millard Fillmore's impo NOTHING PARTY.

'.e acropolis of Pergamum between 1878 rooms which had originally been appro- .e library (Alex. Conze, *Die pergamen.* 54). Despite the obstacles presented by placed by the Ptolemies upon the export -y of the Attali attained considerable e have seen, when it was transported . o,000 vols. We learn from a notice in Antiochus the Great summoned the poet 'orion of Chalcis to be his librarian.

re far too warlike and practical a people on to literature, and it is not until the of the republic that we hear of libraries The collections of Carthage, which fell into ipio sacked that city (146 B.C.), had no and with the exception of the writings of re, which the senate reserved for translation stowed all the books upon the kinglets of . xviii. 5). It is in accordance with the of the Romans that the first considerable we hear in Rome were brought there as the first of these was that brought by Aemilius nia after the conquest of Perseus (167 B.C.). onquered monarch was all that he reserved ctory for himself and his sons, who were fond ne the library of Apellicon the Teian, brought lla (86 B.C.). This passed at his death into on, but of its later history nothing is known. literature brought home by Lucullus from his (about 67 B.C.) were freely thrown open to his en of letters. Accordingly his library and the lks were much resorted to, especially by Greeks. oming fashionable for rich men to furnish their and the fashion prevailed until it became the eca's scorn and Lucian's wit. The zeal of Cicero n adding to their collections is well known to every lassics. Tyrannion is said to have had 30,000 vols. and that M. Terentius Varro had large collections r from Cicero's writing to him. "Si hortum in habes, nihil deerit." Not to prolong the list of ctors, Serenus Sammonicus is said to have left to young Gordian no less than 62,000 vols. Amongst us projects entertained by Caesar was that of pre- ne with public libraries, though it is doubtful whether were actually taken towards its execution. The task .g and arranging the books was entrusted to Varro. ission, as well as his own fondness for books, may arro to write the book upon libraries of which a few have come down to us, preserved by a grammarian. ur of being the first actually to dedicate a library to is said by Pliny and Ovid to have fallen to G. Asinius ho erected a library in the Atrium Libertatis on Mount , defraying the cost from the spoils of his Illyrian n. The library of Pollio was followed by the public established by Augustus. That emperor, who did so or the embellishment of the city, erected two libraries, tavian and the Palatine. The former was founded .) in honour of his sister, and was placed in the Porticus ae, a magnificent structure, the lower part of which served promenade, while the upper part contained the library. harge of the books was committed to C. Melissus. The library formed by Augustus was attached to the temple of o on the Palatine hill, and appears from inscriptions to consisted of two departments, a Greek and a Latin one, h seem to have been separately administered. The charge he Palatine collections was given to Pompeius Macer, who succeeded by Julius Hyginus, the grammarian and friend of d. The Octavian library perished in the fire which raged three days in the reign of Titus. The Palatine was, n great part, destroyed by fire in the reign of he story that its collections were destroyed by Gregory the Great in the 6th century is now generally rejected. The successors of Augustus, though they did not equal him in their patronage of learning, maintained the tradition of forming libraries. Tiberius, his immediate successor, established one in his splendid house on the Palatine, to which Gellius refers as the "Tiberian library," and Suetonius relates that he caused the writings and images of his favourite Greek poets to be placed in the public libraries. Vespasian established a library in the Temple of Peace erected after the burning of the city under Nero. Domitian restored the libraries which had been destroyed in the same conflagration, procuring books from every quarter, and even sending to Alexandria to have copies made. He is also said to have founded the Capitoline library, though others give the credit to Hadrian. The most famous and important of the imperial libraries, however, was that created by Ulpius Trajanus, known as the Ulpian library, which was first established in the Forum of Trajan, but was afterwards removed to the baths of Diocletian. In this library were deposited by Trajan the "libri lintei" and "libri elephantini," upon which the senatus consulta and other transactions relating to the emperors were written. The library of Domitian, which had been destroyed by fire in the reign of Commodus, was restored by Gordian, who added to it the books bequeathed to him by Serenus Sammonicus. Altogether in the 4th century there are said to have been twenty-eight public libraries in Rome.

Roman provincial libraries.

Nor were public libraries confined to Rome. We possess records of at least 24 places in Italy, the Grecian provinces, Asia Minor, Cyprus and Africa in which libraries had been established, most of them attached to temples, usually through the liberality of generous individuals. The library which the younger Pliny dedicated to his townsmen at Comum cost a million sesterces and he contributed a large sum to the support of a library at Milan. Hadrian established one at Athens, described by Pausanias, and recently identified with a building called the Stoa of Hadrian, which shows a striking similarity with the precinct of Athena at Pergamum. Strabo mentions a library at Smyrna; Aulus Gellius one at Patrae and another at Tibur from which books could be borrowed. Recent discoveries at Ephesus in Asia Minor and Timegad in Algeria have furnished precise information as to the structural plan of these buildings. The library at Ephesus was founded by T. Julius Aquila Polemaeanus in memory of his father, pro-consul of Asia in the time of Trajan, about A.D. 106–107. The library at Timegad was established at a cost of 400,000 sesterces by M. Julius Quintianus Flavius Rogatianus, who probably lived in the 3rd century (R. Cagnat, "Les Bibliothèques municipales dans l'Empire Romain," 1906, *Mém. de l'Acad. des Insc.*, tom. xxxviii. pt. 1). At Ephesus the light came through a circular opening in the roof; the library at Timegad greatly resembles that discovered at Pompeii and possesses a system of book stores. All these buildings followed the same general plan, consisting of a reading-room and more or less ample book stores; the former was either rectangular or semi-circular in shape and was approached under a stately portico and colonnade. In a niche facing the entrance a statue was always erected; that formerly at Pergamum—a figure of Minerva—is now preserved at Berlin. From a well-known line of Juvenal (*Sat.* iii. 219) we may assume that a statue of the goddess was usually placed in libraries. The reading-room was also ornamented with busts or life-sized images of celebrated writers. The portraits or authors were also painted on medallions on the presses (*armaria*) in which the books or rolls were preserved as in the library of Isidore of Seville; sometimes these medallions decorated the walls, as in a private library discovered by Lanciani in 1883 at Rome (*Ancient Rome*, 1888, p. 193). Movable seats, known to us by pictorial representations, were in use. The books were classified, and the presses (framed of precious woods and highly ornamented) were numbered to facilitate reference from the catalogues. A private library discovered at Herculaneum contained 1756 MSS. placed on shelves round the room to a height of about 6 ft. with a central press. In the public rooms some of the books were arranged

[illegible]

soon swept the old learning and libraries alike from the soil of Italy. With the close of the Western empire in 476 the ancient history of libraries may be said to cease.

Medieval Period

During the first few centuries after the fall of the Western empire, literary activity at Constantinople had fallen to its lowest ebb. In the West, amidst the general neglect of learning and literature, the collecting of books, though not wholly forgotten, was cared for by few. Sidonius Apollinaris tells us of the libraries of several private collectors in Gaul. Publius Consentius possessed a library at his villa near Narbonne which was due to the labour of three generations. The most notable of these appears to have been the prefect Tonantius Ferreolus, who had formed in his villa of Prusiana, near Nîmes, a collection which his friend playfully compares to that of Alexandria. The Goths, who had been introduced to the Scriptures in their own language by Ulfilas in the 4th century, began to pay some attention to Latin literature. Cassiodorus, the favourite minister of Theodoric, was a collector as well as an author, and on giving up the cares of government retired to a monastery which he founded in Calabria, where he employed his monks in the transcription of books.

Gaul.

Henceforward the charge of books as well as of education fell more and more exclusively into the hands of the church. While the old schools of the rhetoricians died out new monasteries arose everywhere. Knowledge was no longer pursued for its own sake, but became subsidiary to religious and theological teaching. The proscription of the old classical literature, which is symbolized in the fable of the destruction of the Palatine library by Gregory the Great, was only too effectual. The Gregorian tradition of opposition to pagan learning long continued to dominate the literary pursuits of the monastic orders and the labours of the scriptorium.

During the 6th and 7th centuries the learning which had been driven from the Continent took refuge in the British Islands, where it was removed from the political disturbances of the mainland. In the Irish monasteries during this period there appear to have been many books, and the Venerable Bede was superior to any scholar of his age. Theodore of Tarsus brought a considerable number of books to Canterbury from Rome in the 7th century, including several Greek authors. The library of York, which was founded by Archbishop Egbert, was [illegible] more famous than that of Canterbury. The verses are well known in which Alcuin describes the extensive library under his charge, and the long list of authors whom he enumerates is superior to that of any other library possessed by either England or France in the 12th century, when it was unhappily burnt. The inroads of the Northmen in the 9th and 10th centuries had been fatal to the monastic libraries on both sides of the channel. It was from York that Alcuin came to Charlemagne to superintend the school attached to his palace; and it was doubtless inspired by Alcuin that Charles issued the memorable document which enjoined that in the bishoprics and monasteries within his realm care should be taken that there should be not only a regular manner of life, but also the study of letters. When Alcuin finally retired from the court to the abbacy of Tours, there to carry out his own theory of monastic discipline and instruction, he wrote to Charles for leave to send to York for copies of the books of which they had so much need at Tours. While Alcuin thus increased the library at Tours, Charlemagne enlarged that at Fulda, which had been founded in 744 and which all through the middle ages stood in great respect. Lupus Servatus, a pupil of Rhabanus Maurus at Fulda, and afterwards abbot of Ferrières, was a devoted student of the classics and a great collector of books. His correspondence illustrates the difficulties which then attended the study of literature through the paucity and dearness of books, the declining care for learning, and the increasing troubles of the time. Nor were private collections of books altogether wanting during the period in which Charlemagne and his successors laboured to restore the lost traditions of

Alcuin.

Charlemagne.

liberal education and literature. Pepin le Bref had indeed met with scanty response to the request for books which he addressed to the pontiff Paul I. Charlemagne, however, collected a considerable number of choice books for his private use in two places. Although these collections were dispersed at his death, his son Louis formed a library which continued to exist under Charles the Bald. About the same time Everard, count of Friuli, formed a considerable collection which he bequeathed to a monastery. But the greatest private collector of the middle ages was doubtless Gerbert, Pope Sylvester II., who showed the utmost zeal and spent large sums in collecting books, not only in Rome and Italy, but from Germany, Belgium and even from Spain.

The hopes of a revival of secular literature fell with the decline of the schools established by Charles and his successors. The knowledge of letters remained the prerogative of the church, and for the next four or five centuries the collecting and multiplication of books were almost entirely confined to the monasteries. Several of the greater orders made these an express duty; this was especially the case with the Benedictines. It was the first care of St Benedict, we are told, that in each newly founded monastery there should be a library, "et velut curia quaedam illustrium auctorum." Monte Cassino became the starting-point of a long line of institutions which were destined to be the centres of religion and of literature. It must indeed be remembered that literature in the sense of St Benedict meant Biblical and theological works, the lives of the saints and martyrs, and the lives and writings of the fathers. Of the reformed Benedictine orders the Carthusians and the Cistercians were those most devoted to literary pursuits. The abbeys of Fleury, of Melk and of St Gall were remarkable for the splendour of their libraries. In a later age the labours of the congregation of St Maur form one of the most striking chapters in the history of learning. The Augustinians and the Dominicans rank next to the Benedictines in their care for literature. The libraries of St Geneviève and St Victor, belonging to the former, were amongst the largest of the monastic collections. Although their poverty might seem to put them at a disadvantage as collectors, the mendicant orders cultivated literature with much assiduity, and were closely connected with the intellectual movement to which the universities owed their rise. In England Richard of Bury praises them for their extraordinary diligence in collecting books. Sir Richard Whittington built a large library for the Grey Friars in London, and they possessed considerable libraries at Oxford.

St Benedict.

It would be impossible to attempt here an account of all the libraries established by the monastic orders. We must be content to enumerate a few of the most eminent.

In Italy Monte Cassino is a striking example of the dangers and vicissitudes to which monastic collections were exposed. Ruined by the Lombards in the 6th century, the monastery was rebuilt and a library established, to fall a prey to Saracens and to fire in the 9th. The collection then reformed survived many other chances and changes, and still exists. Boccaccio gives a melancholy description of its condition in his day. It affords a conspicuous example of monastic industry in the transcription not only of theological but also of classical works. The library of Bobbio, which owed its existence to Irish monks, was famous for its palimpsests. The collection, of which a catalogue of the 10th century is given by Muratori (*Antiq. Ital. Med. Aev.* iii. 817–824), was mainly transferred to the Ambrosian library at Milan. Of the library of Pomposia, near Ravenna, Montfaucon has printed a catalogue dating from the 11th century (*Diarium Italicum*, chap. xxii.).

Monastic libraries.

Of the monastic libraries of France the principal were those of Fleury, of Cluny, of St Riquier and of Corbie. At Fleury Abbot Macharius in 1146 imposed a contribution for library purposes upon the officers of the community and its dependencies, an example which was followed elsewhere. After many vicissitudes, its MSS., numbering 238, were deposited in 1793 in the town library of Orleans. The library of St Riquier in the time of Louis the Pious contained 256 MSS., with over 500 works. Of the collection at Corbie in Picardy we have also catalogues dating from the 12th and from the 17th centuries. Corbie was famous for the industry of its transcribers, and appears to have stood in active literary intercourse with other monasteries. In 1638, 400 of its choicest manuscripts were removed to St Germain-des-Prés. The remainder were removed after 1794, partly to the national library at Paris, partly to the town library of Amiens.

The chief monastic libraries of Germany were at Fulda, Corvey, Reichenau and Sponheim. The library at Fulda owed much to Charlemagne and to its abbot Hrabanus Maurus. Under Abbot Sturmius four hundred monks were hired as copyists. In 1561 the collection numbered 774 volumes. The library of Corvey on the Weser, after being despoiled of some of its treasures in the Reformation age, was presented to the university of Marburg in 1811. It then contained 109 vols., with 400 or 500 titles. The library of Reichenau, of which several catalogues are extant, fell a prey to fire and neglect, and its ruin was consummated by the Thirty Years' War. The library of Sponheim owes its great renown to John Tritheim, who was abbot at the close of the 15th century. He found it reduced to 10 vols., and left it with upwards of 2000 at his retirement. The library at St Gall, formed as early as 816 by Gozbert, its second abbot, still exists.

In England the principal collections were those of Canterbury, York, Wearmouth, Jarrow, Whitby, Glastonbury, Croyland, Peterborough and Durham. Of the library of the monastery of Christ Church, Canterbury, originally founded by Augustine and Theodore, and restored by Lanfranc and Anselm, a catalogue has been preserved dating from the 13th or 14th century, and containing 698 volumes, with about 3000 works. Bennet Biscop, the first abbot of Wearmouth, made five journeys to Rome, and on each occasion returned with a store of books for the library. It was destroyed by the Danes about 867. Of the library at Whitby there is a catalogue dating from the 12th century. The catalogue of Glastonbury has been printed by Hearne in his edition of John of Glastonbury. When the library of Croyland perished by fire in 1091 it contained about 700 vols. The library at Peterborough was also rich; from a catalogue of about the end of the 14th century it had 344 vols., with nearly 1700 titles. The catalogues of the library at the monastery of Durham have been printed by the Surtees Society, and form an interesting series. These catalogues with many others[1] afford abundant evidence of the limited character of the monkish collections, whether we look at the number of their volumes or at the nature of their contents. The scriptoria were manufactories of books and not centres of learning. That in spite of the labours of so many transcribers the costliness and scarcity of books remained so great may have been partly, but cannot have been wholly, due to the scarcity of writing materials. It may be suspected that indolence and carelessness were the rule in most monasteries, and that but few of the monks keenly realized the whole force of the sentiment expressed by one of their number in the 12th century—"Claustrum sine armario quasi castrum sine armamentario." Nevertheless it must be

England.

[1] The oldest catalogue of a western library is that of the monastery of Fontanelle in Normandy compiled in the 8th century. Many catalogues may be found in the collections of D'Achery, Martène and Durand, and Pez, in the bibliographical periodicals of Naumann and Petzholdt and the *Centralblatt f. Bibliothekswissenschaft*. The Rev. Joseph Hunter has collected some particulars as to the contents of the English monastic libraries, and Ed. Edwards has printed a list of the catalogues (*Libraries and Founders of Libraries*, 1865, pp. 448–454). See also G. Becker, *Catalogi Bibliothecarum Antiqui* (1885). There are said to be over six hundred such catalogues in the Royal Library at Munich. In the 13th century the Franciscans compiled a general catalogue of the MSS. in 160 English libraries and about the year 1400 John Boston, a Benedictine monk of Bury, travelled over England and a part of Scotland and examined the libraries of 195 religious houses (Tanner, *Bibliotheca Brit. Hibern.* 1748). Leland's list of the books he found during his visitation of the houses in 1539–1545 is printed in his *Collectanea* (ed. Hearne, 1715, 6 vols.). T. W. Williams has treated Gloucestershire and Bristol medieval libraries and their catalogues in a paper in the Bristol and Gloucestershire *Arch. Soc.* vol. xxxi.

[illegible] that to the labours of the monastic transcribers we are [illegible] for the preservation of Latin literature.

The subject of the evolution of the arrangement of library [illegible] and fittings as gradually developed throughout medieval Europe should not be passed over.[1] The real origin of library organization in the Christian world, one may almost say the origin of modern library methods, began with the rule of St Benedict early in the 6th century. In the 48th chapter the monks were ordered to borrow a book apiece and to read it straight through. There was no special apartment for the books in the primitive [illegible] house. After the books became too numerous to [illegible] in the church they were preserved in *armaria*, or chests, [illegible] the cloister, hence the word *armarius*, the Benedictine [illegible] who at first joined with it the office of precentor. The [illegible] regulations were developed in the stricter obser[illegible] which provided for a kind of annual report [illegible] The Carthusians were perhaps the first to lend [illegible] the convent; and the Cistercians to possess a [illegible] library official as well as a room specially devoted to [illegible] The [illegible] of the Augustinians contained rules for [illegible] cataloguing and arranging the books by [illegible] as well as a prescription of the exact kind of chest [illegible] the Premonstratensians or Reformed [illegible] was one of the duties of the librarian to provide [illegible] books elsewhere for the use of the monks. [illegible] books so necessary that at last [illegible] with some exaggeration that their [illegible] Many volumes still exist which [illegible] the parent house of the Francis[illegible] was drawn up in 1381. No authentic [illegible] be found; the doubtful example [illegible] contained ecclesiastical utensils. [illegible] at Barnwell the presses were lined [illegible] damp and were partitioned off both [illegible] Sometimes there were recesses in [illegible] with shelves and closed with a [illegible] into a small windowless room [illegible] At Clairvaux, Kirkstall, Fountains, [illegible] this small chamber was placed [illegible] and the transept of the church. At [illegible] books were lodged on shelves against [illegible] of such a chamber. In many [illegible] contained two classes of books [illegible] others more closely guarded. A [illegible] books used by the reader in [illegible] of the 15th century the larger [illegible] of many volumes and found [illegible] books, hitherto placed in various [illegible] apartment. We now find [illegible] Canterbury, Durham, Citeaux, [illegible] with this specialization there grew [illegible] of books and learned strangers [illegible] date students were permitted [illegible] St Germain-des-Prés at Paris, [illegible] in 1513 a noble library [illegible] and enlarged and made [illegible] in the 17th and 18th centuries. [illegible] libraries of early foundation [illegible] monastic libraries. There was [illegible] inspection of what we would [illegible] students; while the books, [illegible] department kept in the [illegible] of the fellows—followed a [illegible] By the 15th century [illegible] on the same plan, with [illegible] placed on their sides on [illegible] attached by chains to a horizontal bar. As the books increased the accommodation was augmented by one or two shelves erected above the desks. The library at Cesena in North Italy may still be seen in its original condition. The Laurentian library at Florence was designed by Michelangelo on the monastic model. Another good example of the old form may be seen in the library of Merton College at Oxford, a long narrow room with bookcases standing between the windows at right angles to the walls. In the chaining system one end was attached to the wooden cover of the book while the other ran freely on a bar fixed by a method of double locks to the front of the shelf or desk on which the book rested. The fore edges of the volumes faced the reader. The seat and shelf were sometimes combined. Low cases were subsequently introduced between the higher cases, and the seat replaced by a step. Shelf lists were placed at the end of each case. There were no chains in the library of the Escorial, erected in 1584, which showed for the first time bookcases placed against the walls. Although chains were no longer part of the appliances in the newly erected libraries they continued to be used and were ordered in bequests in England down to the early part of the 18th century. Triple desks and revolving lecterns, raised by a wooden screw, formed part of the library furniture. The English cathedral libraries were fashioned after the same principle. The old methods were fully reproduced in the fittings at Westminster, erected at a late date. Here we may see books on shelves against the walls as well as in cases at right angles to the walls; the desk-like shelves for the chained volumes (no longer in existence) have a slot in which the chains could be suspended, and are hinged to allow access to shelves below. An ornamental wooden tablet at the end of each case is a survival of the old shelf list. By the end of the 17th century the type of the public library developed from collegiate and monastic prototypes, became fixed as it were throughout Europe (H. R. Tedder, "Evolution of the Public Library," in *Trans. of 2nd Int. Library Conference*, 1897, 1898).

Arabians. The first conquests of the Arabians, as we have already seen, threatened hostility to literature. But, as soon as their conquests were secured, the caliphs became the patrons of learning and science. Greek manuscripts were eagerly sought for and translated into Arabic, and colleges and libraries everywhere arose. Baghdad in the east and Cordova in the west became the seats of a rich development of letters and science during the age when the civilization of Europe was most obscured. Cairo and Tripoli were also distinguished for their libraries. The royal library of the Fatimites in Africa is said to have numbered 100,000 manuscripts, while that collected by the Omayyads of Spain is reported to have contained six times as many. It is said that there were no less than seventy libraries opened in the cities of Andalusia. Whether these figures be exaggerated or not—and they are much below those given by some Arabian writers, which are undoubtedly so—it is certain that the libraries of the Arabians and the Moors of Spain offer a very remarkable contrast to those of the Christian nations during the same period.[2]

Renaissance. The literary and scientific activity of the Arabians appears to have been the cause of a revival of letters amongst the Greeks of the Byzantine empire in the 9th century. Under Leo the Philosopher and Constantine Porphyrogenitus the libraries of Constantinople awoke into renewed life. The compilations of such writers as Stobaeus, Photius and Suidas, as well as the labours of innumerable critics and commentators, bear witness to the activity, if not to the lofty character of the pursuits, of the Byzantine scholars. The labours of transcription were industriously pursued in the libraries and in the monasteries of Mount Athos and the Aegean, and it was from these quarters that the restorers of learning brought into Italy so many Greek manuscripts. In this way many of the treasures of ancient literature had been already

[1] [illegible] by J. Willis Clark in [illegible] volume, *The Care of* [illegible] On Medieval Monastic [illegible]

[2] Among the Arabs, however, as among the Christians, theological bigotry did not always approve of non-theological literature, and the great library of Cordova was sacrificed by Almanzor to his reputation for orthodoxy, 978 A.D.

conveyed to the West before the fate which overtook the libraries of Constantinople on the fall of the city in 1453.

Meanwhile in the West, with the reviving interest in literature which already marks the 14th century, we find arising outside the monasteries a taste for collecting books. St Louis of France and his successors had formed small collections, none of which survived its possessor. It was reserved for Charles V. to form a considerable library which he intended to be permanent. In 1373 he had amassed 910 volumes, and had a catalogue of them prepared, from which we see that it included a good deal of the new sort of literature. In England Guy, earl of Warwick, formed a curious collection of French romances, which he bequeathed to Bordesley Abbey on his death in 1315. Richard d'Aungervyle of Bury, the author of the *Philobiblon*, amassed a noble collection of books; and had special opportunities of doing so as Edward III.'s chancellor and ambassador. He founded Durham College at Oxford, and equipped it with a library a hundred years before Humphrey, duke of Gloucester, made his benefaction of books to the university. The taste for secular literature, and the enthusiasm for the ancient classics, gave a fresh direction to the researches of collectors. A disposition to encourage literature began to show itself amongst the great. This was most notable amongst the Italian princes. Cosimo de' Medici formed a library at Venice while living there in exile in 1433, and on his return to Florence laid the foundation of the great Medicean library. The honour of establishing the first modern public library in Italy had been already secured by Niccolo Niccoli, who left his library of over 800 volumes for the use of the public on his death in 1436. Frederick, duke of Urbino, collected all the writings in Greek and Latin which he could procure, and we have an interesting account of his collection written by his first librarian, Vespasiano. The ardour for classical studies led to those active researches for the Latin writers who were buried in the monastic libraries which are especially identified with the name of Poggio. For some time before the fall of Constantinople, the perilous state of the Eastern empire had driven many Greek scholars from that capital into western Europe, where they had directed the studies and formed the taste of the zealous students of the Greek language and literature. The enthusiasm of the Italian princes extended itself beyond the Alps. Matthias Corvinus, king of Hungary, amassed a collection of splendidly executed and magnificently bound manuscripts, which at his death are said to have reached the almost incredible number of 50,000 vols. The library was not destined long to survive its founder. There is reason to believe that it had been very seriously despoiled even before it perished at the hands of the Turks on the fall of Buda in 1527. A few of its treasures are still preserved in some of the libraries of Europe. While these munificent patrons of learning were thus taking pains to recover and multiply the treasures of ancient literature by the patient labour of transcribers and calligraphers, an art was being elaborated which was destined to revolutionize the whole condition of literature and libraries. With the invention of printing, so happily coinciding with the revival of true learning and sound science, the modern history of libraries may be said to begin.

Modern Libraries

In most of the European countries and in the United States libraries of all kinds have during the last twenty years been undergoing a process of development and improvement which has greatly altered their policy and methods. At one time libraries were regarded almost entirely as repositories for the storage of books to be used by the learned alone, but now they are coming to be regarded more and more as workshops or as places for intellectual recreation adapted for every department of life. This is particularly to be found as the ideal in the public libraries of the Anglo-Saxon races throughout the world.

The following details comprise the chief points in the history, equipment and methods of the various libraries and systems noticed.

The United Kingdom.

State Libraries.—The British Museum ranks in importance before all the great libraries of the world, and excels in the arrangement and accessibility of its contents. The library consists of over 2,000,000 printed volumes and 56,000 manuscripts, but this large total does not include pamphlets and other small publications which are usually counted in other libraries. Adding these together it is probable that over 5,000,000 items are comprised in the collections. This extraordinary opulence is principally due to the enlightened energy of Sir Anthony Panizzi (*q.v.*). The number of volumes in the printed book department, when he took the keepership in 1837, was only 240,000; and during the nineteen years he held that office about 400,000 were added, mostly by purchase, under his advice and direction. It was Panizzi likewise who first seriously set to work to see that the national library reaped all the benefits bestowed upon it by the Copyright Act.

British Museum.

The foundation of the British Museum dates from 1753, when effect was given to the bequest (in exchange for £20,000 to be paid to his executors) by Sir Hans Sloane, of his books, manuscripts, curiosities, &c., to be held by trustees for the use of the nation. A bill was passed through parliament for the purchase of the Sloane collections and of the Harleian MSS., costing £10,000. To these, with the Cottonian MSS., acquired by the country in 1700, was added by George II., in 1757, the royal library of the former kings of England, coupled with the privilege, which that library had for many years enjoyed, of obtaining a copy of every publication entered at Stationers' Hall. This addition was of the highest importance, as it enriched the museum with the old collections of Archbishop Cranmer, Henry prince of Wales, and other patrons of literature, while the transfer of the privilege with regard to the acquisition of new books, a right which has been maintained by successive Copyright Acts, secured a large and continuous augmentation. A lottery having been authorized to defray the expenses of purchases, as well as for providing suitable accommodation, the museum and library were established in Montague House, and opened to the public 15th January 1759. In 1763 George III. presented the well-known Thomason collection (in 2220 volumes) of books and pamphlets issued in England between 1640 and 1662, embracing all the controversial literature which appeared during that period. The Rev. C. M. Cracherode, one of the trustees, bequeathed his collection of choice books in 1799; and in 1820 Sir Joseph Banks left to the nation his important library of 16,000 vols. Many other libraries have since then been incorporated in the museum, the most valuable being George III.'s royal collection (15,000 vols. of tracts, and 65,259 vols. of printed books, including many of the utmost rarity, which had cost the king about £130,000), which was presented (for a pecuniary consideration, it has been said) by George IV. in 1823, and that of the Right Honourable Thomas Grenville (20,240 vols. of rare books, all in fine condition and binding), which was acquired under bequest in 1846. The Cracherode, Banksian, King's and Grenville libraries are still preserved as separate collections. Other libraries of minor note have also been absorbed in a similar way, while, at least since the time of Panizzi, no opportunity has been neglected of making useful purchases at all the British and Continental book auctions.

The collection of English books is far from approaching completeness, but, apart from the enormous number of volumes, the library contains an extraordinary quantity of rarities. Few libraries in the United States equal either in number or value the American books in the museum. The collection of Slavonic literature, due to the initiative of Thomas Watts, is also a remarkable feature. Indeed, in cosmopolitan interest the museum is without a rival in the world, possessing as it does the best library in any European language out of the territory in which the language is vernacular. The Hebrew, the Chinese, and printed books in other Oriental languages are important and represented in large numbers. Periodical literature has not been ad[illegible] ind[illegible] [illegible] roo[illegible]

The deve[illegible] men[illegible] libr[illegible] arra[illegible] bee[illegible]

Th[illegible] Be[illegible] be[illegible] in [illegible] lib[illegible] Th[illegible] va[illegible] an[illegible] bo[illegible] sep[illegible] boo[illegible] the [illegible] the [illegible] to [illegible] Aug[illegible] for [illegible] The [illegible] Rich[illegible] libr[illegible] belo[illegible] cans[illegible] mon[illegible] show[illegible] At t[illegible] with [illegible] vert[illegible] the [illegible] door. [illegible] in th[illegible] Tinte[illegible] betwe[illegible] Meau[illegible] the w[illegible] houses [illegible] —one [illegible] press r[illegible] the re[illegible] monas[illegible] themse[illegible] parts of [illegible] libraries [illegible] Clairvau[illegible] up incre[illegible] were adm[illegible] to borrow[illegible] of which [illegible] erected ov[illegible] very acces[illegible] The metho[illegible] closely res[illegible] in both the [illegible] now call the [illegible] fastened by [illegible] library cham[illegible] similar syste[illegible] collegiate an[illegible] the separate [illegible] desks or lecte[illegible]

[1] This subject [illegible] several works [illegible] Books [illegible] Libraries [illegible]

[illegible] department of printed [illegible]

[illegible] reading at the British Museum, [illegible] recommendation [illegible] librarian.

[illegible] the Library has [illegible] the existing [illegible] Natural History Museum, [illegible] the British Museum under [illegible] books on the natural sciences [illegible]

[illegible] to the British Museum, and superior to [illegible] the library of the Patent Office in South[illegible] [illegible]. This is a department of [illegible] primarily intended [illegible] a public library [illegible]. The only formality required from [illegible] the entrance hall. After [illegible] complete access to the shelves. The library [illegible] and possesses complete [illegible] of all countries, and a remark[illegible] of the [illegible] and scientific periodicals of all [illegible]. The library was first opened in 18[illegible], in somewhat [illegible] it was transferred to a handsome [illegible]

[illegible] with two galleries and the majority [illegible] without the need for [illegible] in author-alphabetical form [illegible] In addition, separate subject [illegible] the most complete libraries of [illegible] its collection of scientific transactions [illegible]

Patent Office.

[illegible] is the National Art Library, [illegible] to South Kensington in 1856. [illegible] books, prints, drawings [illegible] used mostly by the students [illegible] though the general public [illegible] of sixpence per week. [illegible] library on the science side is the

Other state libraries.

cience Library of the Victoria and Albert Museum, South :ensington, which was founded in 1857. It is a general science ollection and incorporates most of the books which at one time /ere in the Museum of Practical Geology.

The only other state library which is open to the public is hat of the Board of Education in Whitehall, which was opened 1 a new building in 1908. It contains a large collection of /orks on educational subjects for which a special classification as been devised and printed.

The other state libraries in London may be briefly noted as ollows: Admiralty (1700), 40,000 vols.; College of Arms, or leralds College, 15,000 vols.; Colonial Office, c. 15,000 vols.; 'oreign Office, c. 80,000 vols.; Home Office (1800) c. 10,000 vols.; louse of Commons (1818), c. 50,000 vols.; House of Lords (1834), o,000 vols.; India Office (1800), c. 86,000 vols.; Kew, Royal lotanic Gardens (1853), 22,000 vols.; and Royal Observatory Greenwich), c. 20,000 vols.

Outside London the most important state library is the National .ibrary of Ireland, Dublin, founded in 1877 and incorporating the ibrary of the Royal Dublin Society. It is housed in a handsome uilding (1890) and contains about 200,000 vols., classified on the Decimal system, and catalogued in various forms. The library of the Museum of Science and Art at Edinburgh, containing over 20,000 /ols., was opened to the public in 1890. Practically every department of the state has a reference library of some kind for the use of the staff, and provision is also made for lending libraries and reading-rooms in connexion with garrisons, naval depots and other services of the army and navy.

No professional qualifications are required for positions in British state libraries, most of the assistants being merely second-division clerks who have passed the Civil Service examinations. It would be an advantage from an administrative point of view if the professional certificates of the Library Association were adopted by the Civil Service Commissioners as compulsory requirements in addition to their own examination. The official recognition of a grade of properly trained librarians would tend to improve the methods and efficiency of the state libraries, which are generally behind the municipal libraries in organization and administration.

University and Collegiate Libraries.—The Bodleian Library, Oxford, though it had been preceded by various efforts towards a university library, owed its origin to Sir Thomas Bodley (*q.v.*). Contributing largely himself, and procuring contributions from others, he opened the library with upwards of 2000 vols. in 1602. In 1610 he obtained a grant from the Stationers' Company of a copy of every work printed in the country, a privilege still enjoyed under the provisions of the various copyright acts. The additions made to the library soon surpassed the capacity of the room, and the founder proceeded to enlarge it. By his will he left considerable property to the university for the maintenance and increase of the library. The example set by Bodley found many noble imitators. Amongst the chief benefactors have been Archbishop Laud, the executors of Sir Kenelm Digby, John Selden, Sir Thomas (Lord) Fairfax, Richard Gough, Francis Douce, Richard Rawlinson, and the Rev. Robert Mason. The library now contains almost 800,000 printed vols., and about 41,000 manuscripts. But the number of volumes, as bound up, conveys a very inadequate idea of the size or value of the collection. In the department of Oriental manuscripts it is perhaps superior to any other European library; and it is exceedingly rich in other manuscript treasures. It possesses a splendid series of Greek and Latin *editiones principes* and of the earliest productions of English presses. Its historical manuscripts contain most valuable materials for the general and literary history of the country.

Oxford.

The last general catalogue of the printed books was printed in 4 vols. folio (1843–1851). In 1859 it was decided to prepare a new manuscript catalogue on the plan of that then in use at the British Museum, and this has been completed in duplicate. In 1910 it was being amended with a view to printing. It is an alphabetical author-catalogue; and the Bodleian, like the British Museum, has no complete subject-index. A slip-catalogue on subjects was, however, in course of preparation in 1910, and there are classified hand-lists of accessions since 1883. There are also printed catalogues of the books belonging to several of the separate collections. The MSS. are in general catalogued according to the collections to which they belong, and they are all indexed. A number of the catalogues of manuscripts have been printed.

In 1860 the beautiful Oxford building known as the "Radcliffe Library," now called the "Radcliffe Camera," was offered to the curators of the Bodleian by the Radcliffe trustees. The Radcliffe Library was founded by the famous physician Dr John Radcliffe, who died in 1714, and bequeathed, besides a permanent endowment of £350 a year, the sum of £40,000 for a building. The library was opened in 1749. Many years ago the trustees resolved to confine their purchases of books to works on medicine and natural science. When the university museum and laboratories were built in 1860, the trustees allowed the books to be transferred to the museum. It is used as a storehouse for the more modern books, and it also serves as a reading-room. It is the only room open after the hour when the older building is closed owing to the rule as to the exclusion of artificial light. In 1889 the gallery of the Radcliffe Camera was opened as an addition to the reading-room.

A *Staff Kalendar* has been issued since 1902, which with a *Supplement* contains a complete list of cataloguing rules, routine work of the libraries and staff, and useful information of many kinds concerning the library methods.

The Bodleian Library is open by right to all graduate members of the university, and to others upon producing a satisfactory recommendation. No books are allowed to be sent out of the library except by special leave of the curators and convocation of the university. The administration and control of the library are committed to a librarian and board of thirteen curators. The permanent endowment is comparatively small; the ordinary expenditure, chiefly defrayed from the university chest, is about £10,000. Within recent years the use of wheeling metal bookcases has been greatly extended, and a large repository has been arranged for economical book storage underground.

The Taylor Institution is due to the benefaction of Sir Robert Taylor, an architect, who died in 1788, leaving his property to found an establishment for the teaching of modern languages. The library was established in 1848, and is devoted to the literature of the modern European languages. It contains a fair collection of works on European philology, with a special Dante collection, about 1000 Mazarinades and 400 Luther pamphlets. The Finch collection, left to the university in 1830, is also kept with the Taylor Library. Books are lent out to members of the university and to others on a proper introduction. The endowment affords an income of £800 to £1000 for library purposes.

The libraries of the several colleges vary considerably in extent and character, although, owing chiefly to limited funds, the changes and growth of all are insignificant. That of All Souls was established in 1443 by Archbishop Chichele, and enlarged in 1710 by the munificent bequest of Christopher Codrington. It devotes special attention to jurisprudence, of which it has a large collection. It possesses 40,000 printed volumes and 300 MSS., and fills a splendid hall 200 ft. long. The library of Brasenose College has a special endowment fund, so that it has, for a college library, the unusually large income of £200. The library of Christ Church is rich in divinity and topography. It embraces the valuable library bequeathed by Charles Boyle, 4th earl of Orrery, amounting to 10,000 volumes, the books and MSS. of Archbishop Wake, and the Morris collection of Oriental books. The building was finished in 1761, and closely resembles the basilica of Antoninus at Rome, now the Dogana. Corpus possesses a fine collection of Aldines, many of them presented by its founder, Bishop Fox, and a collection of 17th-century tracts catalogued by Mr Edwards, with about 400 MSS. Exeter College Library has 25,000 volumes, with special collections of classical dissertations and English theological and political tracts. The library of Jesus College has few books of later date than the early part of the last century. Many of them are from the bequest of Sir Leoline Jenkins, who built the existing library. There are also some valuable Welsh MSS. The library of Keble College consists largely of theology, including the MSS. of many of Keble's works. The library of Magdalen College has about 22,500 volumes (including many volumes of pamphlets) and 250 MSS. It has scientific and topographical collections. The library of Merton College has of late devoted itself to foreign modern history. New College Library has about 17,000 printed volumes and about 350 MSS., several of which were presented by its founder, William of Wykeham. Oriel College Library, besides its other possessions, has a special collection of books on comparative philology and mythology, with a printed catalogue. The fine library of Queen's College is strong in theology, in English and modern European history, and in English county histories. St John's College Library is largely composed of the literature of theology and jurisprudence before 1750, and possesses a collection of medical books of the 16th and 17th centuries. The newer half of the library building was [illegible] the expense of Laud, who also gave many [illegible]. The room used as a library at [illegible] Durham College, the library of which [illegible] at Bury. Wadham College Library [illegible] books bequeathed by Richard [illegible] of books, relating chiefly to the [illegible] by the executors of Benjamin Wiffen. [illegible] has of late specially devoted itself to [illegible] rich in old plays. [illegible] have not been used to the extent they [illegible] done before they can be said to be [illegible] might be.

[illegible] Library at Cambridge dates [illegible] century. Two early lists of [illegible] preserved, the first embracing 52 vols. [illegible] the second a shelf-list, ap- [illegible] drawn up by the outgoing proctors [illegible] was Thomas Scott of Rother- [illegible] erected in 1475 the building in [illegible] 1755. He also gave more than [illegible] the library, some of which still [illegible] other benefactions, but neverthe- [illegible] John Evelyn when he visited [illegible] Rustat presented a sum of [illegible] choicest and most useful books. [illegible] library of Bishop Moore, which [illegible] printed books, forming over [illegible] manuscripts. The funds [illegible] John Manistre, together with [illegible] about £1500 a year. The [illegible] appropriated to library purposes [illegible] the library is entitled to [illegible]. The number of printed [illegible] exactly stated, as no recent [illegible] it has been estimated at half [illegible] *principes* of the [illegible] of the English press. The [illegible] are included a considerable [illegible] with MS. notes, which [illegible]. The most famous of [illegible] gospels and the Acts [illegible] Beza, and which was [illegible].

[illegible] 4 vols. (1856–1861), [illegible] of a number of [illegible], Chinese, &c., MSS. [illegible] although the catalogue [illegible] up and arranged in [illegible] 1040 is in course of [illegible] with regard to the [illegible] ten volumes being [illegible]. The annual income

[illegible] Fitzwilliam Museum, be- [illegible] consists of the entire [illegible] of an archaeological [illegible] Leake, and a small [illegible] art, since added by [illegible] of engravings of [illegible] and MS., and a [illegible] and Flemish, of [illegible] are not allowed to be [illegible] of the music and [illegible]

[illegible] in a magnificent [illegible] printed and [illegible] theology, classics and [illegible] the possession [illegible]. Amongst these [illegible] early dramatic and [illegible] German theology [illegible] Hare, and the Grylls [illegible] early printed books. [illegible] and other Oriental [illegible] of the incunabula by [illegible]

is that of Trinity Hall, in which the original bookcases and benches are preserved, and many books are seen chained to the cases, as used formerly to be the practice.

None of the other college libraries rivals Trinity in the number of books. The library of Christ's College received its first books from the foundress. Clare College Library includes a number of Italian and Spanish plays of the end of the 16th century left by George Ruggle. The library of Corpus Christi College first became notable through the bequest of books and MSS. made by Archbishop Parker in 1575. The printed books are less than 5000 in number, and the additions now made are chiefly in such branches as throw light on the extremely valuable collection of ancient MSS., which attracts scholars from all parts of Europe. There is a printed catalogue of these MSS. Gonville and Caius College Library is of early foundation. A catalogue of the MSS. was printed in 1849, with pictorial illustrations, and a list of the incunabula in 1850. The printed books of King's College includes the fine collection bequeathed by Jacob Bryant in 1804. The MSS. are almost wholly Oriental, chiefly Persian and Arabic, and a catalogue of them has been printed. Magdalene College possesses the curious library formed by Pepys and bequeathed by him to the college, together with his collections of prints and drawings and of rare British portraits. It is remarkable for its treasures of popular literature and English ballads, as well as for the Scottish manuscript poetry collected by Sir Richard Maitland. The books are kept in Pepys's own cases, and remain just as he arranged them himself. The library of Peterhouse is the oldest library in Cambridge, and possesses a catalogue of some 600 or 700 books dating from 1418, in which year it was completed. It is chiefly theological, though it possesses a valuable collection of modern works on geology and natural science, and a unique collection of MS. music. Queen's College Library contains about 30,000 vols. mainly in theology, classics and Semitic literature, and has a printed class-catalogue. The library of St John's College is rich in early printed books, and possesses a large collection of English historical tracts. Of the MSS. and rare books there is a printed catalogue.

London.

The library of the university of London, founded in 1837, has over 60,000 vols. and includes the Goldsmith Library of economic literature, numbering 30,000 vols. Other collections are De Morgan's collection of mathematical books, Grote's classical library, &c. There is a printed catalogue of 1897, with supplements. Since its removal to South Kensington, this library has been greatly improved and extended. University College Library, Gower Street, established in 1829, has close upon 120,000 vols. made up chiefly of separate collections which have been acquired from time to time. Many of these collections overlap, and much duplicating results, leading to congestion. These collections include Jeremy Bentham's library, Morrison's Chinese library, Barlow's Dante library, collections of law, mathematical, Icelandic, theological, art, oriental and other books, some of them of great value.

King's College Library, founded in 1828, has over 30,000 vols. chiefly of a scientific character. In close association with the university of London is the London School of Economics and Political Science in Clare Market, in which is housed the British Library of Political Science with 50,000 vols. and a large number of official reports and pamphlets.

The collegiate library at Dulwich dates from 1619, and a list of its earliest accessions, in the handwriting of the founder, may still be seen. There are now about 17,000 vols. of miscellaneous works of the 17th and 18th centuries, with a few rare books. A catalogue of them was printed in 1880; and one describing the MSS. (567) and the muniments (606) was issued during the succeeding year. The last two classes are very important, and include the well-known "Alleyn Papers" and the theatrical diary of Philip Henslow. Sion College is a gild of the parochial clergy of the city and suburbs of London, and the library was founded in 1629 for their use; laymen may also read (but not borrow) the books when recommended by some beneficed metropolitan clergyman. The library is especially rich in liturgies, Port-Royal authors, pamphlets, &c., and contains about 100,000 vols. classified on a modification of the Decimal system. The copyright privilege was commuted in 1835 for an annual sum of £363, 15s. 2d. The present building was opened in 1886 and is one of the striking buildings of the Victoria Embankment.

Most of the London collegiate or teaching institutions have libraries attached to them, and it will only be necessary to mention a few of the more important to get an idea of their variety: Baptist College (1810), 13,000 vols.; Bedford College (for women), 17,000 vols.; Birkbeck College (1823), 12,000 vols.; Congregational Library (1832–1893), 14,000 vols.; the Royal College of Music, containing the library of the defunct Sacred Harmonic Society; Royal Naval College (Greenwich, 1873), 7000 vols.; St Bartholomew's Hospital (1422), 15,000 vols.; St Paul's School (1509), 10,000 vols.; the Working Men's College (1854), 5000 vols.; and all the Polytechnic schools in the Metropolitan area.

English provinces.

The university library of Durham (1832) contains about 35,000 vols., and all the modern English universities—Birmingham, Mason University College (1880), 27,000 vols.; Leeds, Liverpool (1882), 56,000 vols.; Manchester, Victoria University, which absorbed Owens College (1851), 115,000 vols.; Newcastle-upon-Tyne; Sheffield (1907), &c. —have collections of books. The libraries in connexion with theological colleges and public schools throughout England are often quite extensive, and reference may be made to Eton College (1441), 25,000 vols.; Haileybury (1862), 12,000 vols.; Harrow (Vaughan Library), 12,000 vols.; Mill Hill; Oscott College, Erdington (1838), 36,000 vols.; Rugby (1878), 8000 vols.; Stonyhurst College (1794), *c.* 40,000 vols., &c. The new building for the university of Wales at Bangor has ample accommodation for an adequate library, and the University College at Aberystwith is also equipped with a library.

Scotland.

The origin of the University Library of Edinburgh is to be found in a bequest of his books of theology and law made to the town in 1580 by Clement Little, advocate. This was two years before the foundation of the university, and in 1584 the town council caused the collection to be removed to the college, of which they were the patrons. As it was the only library in the town, it continued to grow and received many benefactions, so that in 1615 it became necessary to erect a library building. Stimulated perhaps by the example of Bodley at Oxford, Drummond of Hawthornden made a large donation of books, of which he printed a catalogue in 1627, and circulated an appeal for assistance from others. In 1678 the library received a bequest of 2000 vols. from the Rev. James Nairne. In 1709 the library became entitled to the copy privilege, which has since been commuted for a payment of £575 per annum. In 1831 the books were removed to the present library buildings, for which a parliamentary grant had been obtained. The main library hall (190 ft. in length) is one of the most splendid apartments in Scotland. One of the rooms is set apart as a memorial to General Reid, by whose benefaction the library has greatly benefited. Amongst the more recent accessions have been the Halliwell-Phillips Shakespeare collection, the Laing collection of Scottish MSS., the Baillie collection of Oriental MSS. (some of which are of great value), and the Hodgson collection of works on political economy. The library now consists of about 210,000 vols. of printed books with over 2000 MSS. Recently it has been found necessary to make considerable additions to the shelving. The library of the university of Glasgow dates from the 15th century, and numbers George Buchanan and many other distinguished men amongst its early benefactors. A classified subject-catalogue has been printed, and there is also a printed dictionary catalogue. The annual accessions are about 1500, and the commutation-grant £707. Connected with the university, which is trustee for the public, is the library of the Hunterian Museum, formed by the eminent anatomist Dr William Hunter. It is a collection of great bibliographical interest, as it is rich in MSS. and in fine specimens of early printing, especially in Greek and Latin classics. There are about 200,000 vols. in the library.

The first mention of a library at St Andrews is as early as 1456. The three colleges were provided with libraries of their own about the time of their foundation—St Salvator's 1455, St Leonard's 1512, St Mary's 1537. The University Library was established about 1610 by King James VI., and in the course of the 18th century the college libraries were merged in it. The copyright privilege was commuted in 1837. The collection numbers 120,000 vols. exclusive of pamphlets, with about 200 MSS., chiefly of local interest. A library is supposed to have existed at Aberdeen since the foundation of King's College by Bishop Elphinstone in 1494. The present collection combines the libraries of King's College and Marischal College, now incorporated in the university. The latter had its origin in a collection of books formed by the town authorities at the time of the Reformation, and for some time kept in one of the churches. The library has benefited by the Melvin bequest, chiefly of classical books, and those of Henderson and Wilson, and contains some very valuable books. The general library is located in Old Aberdeen in a room of imposing design, while the medical and law books are in the New Town in Marischal College. The library has a grant, in lieu of the copyright privilege, of £320. The annual income of the library is £2500, and it contains over 180,000 vols. The books are classified on a modification of the decimal system, and there are printed author and MS. subject-catalogues. By arrangement with the municipal library authority, books are lent to non students. All the technical schools, public schools, and theological and other colleges in Scotland are well equipped with libraries as the following list will show:—Aberdeen: Free Church College, 17,000 vols. Edinburgh: Fettes College, *c.* 5000 vols.; Heriot's Hospital (1762), *c.* 5000 vols.; New College (1843), 50,000 vols. Glasgow: Anderson's College (containing the valuable Euing music library), 16,000 vols.; United Free Church Theological College, 33,000 vols. Trinity College, Glenalmond, 5000 vols.

Ireland.

The establishment of the library of Trinity College, Dublin, is contemporaneous with that of the Bodleian at Oxford, and it is an interesting circumstance that, when Challoner and Ussher (afterwards the archbishop) were in London purchasing books to form the library, they met Bodley there, and entered into friendly intercourse and co-operation with him to procure the choicest and best books. The commission was given to Ussher and Challoner as trustees of the singular donation which laid the foundation of the library. In the year 1601 the English army determined to commemorate their victory over the Spanish troops at Kinsale by some permanent monument. Accordingly they subscribed the sum of £1800 to establish a library in the university of Dublin. For Ussher's own collection, consisting of 10,000 vols. and many valuable MSS., the college was also indebted to military generosity. On his death in 1655 the officers and soldiers of the English army then in Ireland purchased the whole collection for £22,000 with the design of presenting it to the college. Cromwell, however, interfered, alleging that he proposed to found a new college, where the books might more conveniently be preserved. They were deposited therefore in Dublin Castle, and the college only obtained them after the Restoration. In 1674 Sir Jerome Alexander left his law books with some valuable MSS. to the college. In 1726 Dr Palliser, archbishop of Cashel, bequeathed over 4000 vols. to the library; and ten years later Dr Gilbert gave the library nearly 13,000 vols. which he had himself collected and arranged. In 1745 the library received a valuable collection of MSS. as a bequest from Dr Stearne. In 1802 the collection formed by the pensionary Fagel, which had been removed to England on the French invasion of Holland, was acquired for £10,000. It consisted of over 20,000 vols. In 1805 Mr Quin bequeathed a choice collection of classical and Italian books. There have been many other smaller donations, in addition to which the library is continually increased by the books received under the Copyright Act. The library now contains 300,000 vols. and over 2000 MSS. There is no permanent endowment, and purchases are made by grants from the board. The whole collections are contained in one building, erected in 1732, consisting of eight rooms. The great library hall is a magnificent apartment over 200 ft. long. A new reading-room was opened in 1848. A catalogue of the books acquired before 1872 has been printed (1887). There is a printed catalogue of the MSS. and Incunabula (1890). Graduates of Dublin, Oxford, and Cambridge are admitted to read permanently, and temporary admission is granted by the board to any fit person who makes application.

The library of Queen's College, Belfast (1849), contains about 60,000 vols., while Queen's College, Cork (1849), has over 32,000 vols. St Patrick's College, Maynooth (1795), has about 60,000, and other collegiate libraries are well supplied with books.

Cathedral and church libraries.

With one or two exceptions, libraries are attached to the cathedrals of England and Wales. Though they are of course intended for the use of the cathedral or diocesan clergy, they are in most cases open to any respectable person who may be properly introduced. They seldom contain very much modern literature, chiefly consisting of older theology, with more or less addition of classical and historical literature. They vary in extent from a few volumes, as at Llandaff or St David's, to 20,000 vols., as at

erected by Inigo Jones at the
printed and manuscript bo
Trinity College formed part o
was established by Richard
includes a collection of bo
Warner in 1775 and a coll
Spanish Reformers, presented
Worcester College Library
classical archaeology. It is
The college libraries as a
deserve, and a good deal m
as useful and efficient as th

The history of the Uni
from the earlier part of t

Cambridge.

its contents are
dating from a
parently of 330
in 1473. Its first great b
ham, archbishop of York
which the library contin
200 books and manuscr
remain. The library re
less appeared "but m
Cambridge in 1654. In
money to be invested to
In 1715 George I. prese
was very rich in early
30,000 vols. of printed
bequeathed by William
that of Rustat, produ
share of university
amounts to £3000 a ye
new books under the
volumes in the library
calculation on the su
a million. It includ
classics and of the e
MSS. number over
number of adversa
form a leading fea
the MSS. is the cel
of the Apostles, wh
presented to the u
A catalogue of th
and this has been
separate catalogu
There is no publi
is in print, the a
volumes. A cata
publication. Th
lending of book
allowed out to
is about £7000.

There is a
queathed to
library of Lo
library boug
number of
purchase or
old master
collection
the 14th t
taken out.
other colle

The libra
hall built
1918 MS.
bibliograph
of a great
special coll
especially S
and philos
bequest in
There are
MSS. by Dr
the late
of the colle
property

The most important endowed library in Scotland is the Mitchell Library in Glasgow, founded by Stephen Mitchell, tobacco-manufacturer (1874), who left £70,000 for the purpose. It was opened in 1877 in temporary premises, and after various changes will soon be transferred to a very fine new building specially erected. It contains some very valuable special collections, among which may be mentioned Scottish poetry, Burns' works, Glasgow books and printing, and a choice collection of fine books on art and other subjects given by Robert Jeffrey. It contains nearly 200,000 vols. and is the reference library for the Glasgow public library system. Another older Glasgow public library, also founded by a tobacco merchant, is Stirling's and Glasgow Public Library (1791), which was endowed by Walter Stirling, and amalgamated with an existing subscription library. It contains 60,000 vols. and is free to reference readers, but a subscription is charged for borrowing privileges. Still another Glasgow institution is Baillie's Institution Free Reference Library, established under the bequest of George Baillie (1863), but not opened till 1887. It contains over 24,000 vols. Other Scottish endowed libraries are the Anderson Library, Woodside, Aberdeen (1883); the Taylor Free Library, Crieff (1890), the Elder Free Library, Govan (1900); and the Chambers Institution, Peebles (1859), founded by William Chambers, the well-known publisher. The public library of Armagh, Ireland, was founded by Lord Primate Robinson in 1770, who gave a considerable number of books and an endowment. The books are freely available, either on the spot, or by loan on deposit of double the value of the work applied for

Libraries of societies and learned bodies.

There are many libraries belonging to societies devoted to the study of every kind of subject, and it is only necessary to mention a few of the principal. Full particulars of most of them will be found in Reginald A. Rye's *Libraries of London: a Guide for Students* (1910), a work of accuracy and value.

Of the law libraries, that at Lincoln's Inn, London, is the oldest and the largest. It dates from 1497, when John Nethersale, a member of the society, made a bequest of forty marks, part of which was to be devoted to the building of a library for the benefit of the students of the laws of England. A catalogue of the printed books was published in 1859 and since supplemented, and the MSS. were catalogued by the Rev. Joseph Hunter in 1837. There are about 72,000 vols. The library of the Inner Temple is known to have existed in 1540. In the middle of the 17th century it received a considerable benefaction from William Petyt, the well-known keeper of the Tower records. There are now about 60,000 vols., including the pamphlets collected by John Adolphus for his *History of England*, books on crime and prisons brought together by Mr Crawford, and a selection of works on jurisprudence made by John Austin. A library in connexion with the Middle Temple was in existence during the reign of Henry VIII., but the date usually assigned to its foundation is 1641, when Robert Ashley left his books to the Inn of which he had been a member. There are now about 50,000 vols. Gray's Inn Library (21,000 vols.) was perhaps established before 1555. In 1669 was made the first catalogue of the books, and the next, still extant, in 1689. The Law Society (1828) has a good law and general library (50,000 vols.), including the best collection of private acts of parliament in England. The library of the Royal Society (1667), now housed in Burlington House, contains over 80,000 vols., of which many are the transactions and other publications of scientific bodies. The Royal Institution of Great Britain (1803) possesses a reference library of 60,000 vols. Some of its early catalogues were in classified form. The London Institution (1805), in the City, is a general library of reference and lending books open to members only. There are about 150,000 vols., and lectures are given in connexion with the institution. The Royal Society of Arts has a library numbering about 11,000 vols., chiefly the publications of other learned bodies.

The best library of archaeology and kindred subjects is that of the Society of Antiquaries, Burlington House, consisting of nearly 40,000 printed vols. and many MSS. It is rich in early printed books, topography, heraldry and numismatics, and includes a curious collection of books on pageants presented by Mr Fairholt, and the remarkable assemblage of lexicographical works formerly belonging to Albert Way.

Of libraries devoted to the natural sciences may be mentioned those of the Geological Society of London (1807), with over 30,000 vols. and maps; the Linnean Society (1788), 35,000 vols.; the Zoological Society (1829), about 31,000 vols. Of libraries associated with medicine there are those of the Royal Society of Medicine (1907), incorporating a number of medical societies, over 95,000 vols., about to be housed in a new building; the Royal College of Physicians (1525), 26,000 vols.; the British Medical Association, 20,000 vols.; the Royal College of Surgeons of England (1800), 60,000 vols., with a MS. catalogue on cards; the Chemical Society (1841), over 25,000 vols.; and the Pharmaceutical Society of Great Britain (1841), about 15,000 vols. Other important London society libraries are—the Royal Geographical Society (1830), 50,000 vols., and numerous maps in a special room, open to the public for reference; the Royal Colonial Institute (1868), 70,000 vols. of British colonial literature; the Royal United Service Institution, Whitehall (1831), has 32,000 works on military and naval subjects and a museum. Large and interesting collections of books are owned by the British and Foreign Bible Society, the Institution of Civil Engineers, the Institution of Electrical Engineers (containing the Ronalds Library), the Royal Academy, the Royal Institute of British Architects, and practically every other working society in London.

The English provincial libraries connected with societies or learned bodies are mostly attached to those concerned with law, medicine, and various antiquarian, literary and scientific subjects. The headquarters of most national societies being in London to some extent accounts for the comparatively small number of these special libraries in the provinces.

The most important libraries of this description outside London are situated in Scotland and Ireland, and one at least is practically a national collection.

The principal library in Scotland is that of the Faculty of Advocates at Edinburgh, who in 1680 appointed a committee of their number, which reported that "it was fitt that, seeing if the recusants could be made pay their entire money, there wold be betwixt three thousand and four thousand pounds in cash; that the same be imployed on the best and fynest lawers and other law bookes, conforme to a catalogue to be condescended upon by the Facultie, that the samen may be a fonde for ane Bibliothecque whereto many lawers and others may leave their books." In 1682 the active carrying out of the scheme was committed to the Dean of Faculty, Sir George Mackenzie of Rosehaugh, who may be regarded as the founder of the library. In 1684 the first librarian was appointed, and the library appears to have made rapid progress, since it appears from the treasurer's accounts that in 1686 the books and furniture were valued at upwards of £11,000 Scots, exclusive of donations. In the year 1700, the rooms in the Exchange Stairs, Parliament Close, in which the library was kept, being nearly destroyed by fire the collection was removed to the ground floor of the Parliament House, where it has ever since remained. The library retains the copyright privilege conferred upon it in 1709. Of the special collections the most important are the Astorga collection of old Spanish books, purchased by the faculty in 1824 for £4000; the Thorkelin collection, consisting of about 1200 vols., relating chiefly to the history and antiquities of the northern nations, and including some rare books on old Scottish poetry; the Dietrich collection of over 100,000 German pamphlets and dissertations, including many of the writings of Luther and Melanchthon, purchased for the small sum of £80; and the Combe collection.

The faculty appear early to have turned their attention to the collection of MSS., and this department of the library now numbers about 3000 vols. Many of them are of great interest and value, especially for the civil and ecclesiastical history of Scotland before and after the Reformation. There are thirteen monastic chartularies which escaped the destruction of the religious houses to which they belonged. The MSS. relating to Scottish church history include the collections of Spottiswoode, Wodrow and Calderwood. The Wodrow collection consists of 154 vols., and includes his correspondence, extending from 1694 to 1726. Sir James Balfour's collection and the Balcarres papers consist largely of original state papers, and include many interesting royal letters of the times of James V., Queen Mary and James VI. The Sibbald papers, numbering over 30 vols., are largely topographical. The Riddel notebooks, numbering 156 vols., contain collections to illustrate the genealogy of Scottish families. There are about one hundred volumes of Icelandic MSS., purchased in 1825 from Professor Finn Magnusson, and some Persian and Sanskrit, with a few classical, manuscripts. The department has some interesting treasures of old poetry, extending to 73 vols. The most important are the Bannatyne MS., in 2 vols. folio, written by George Bannatyne in 1568, and the Auchinleck MS., a collection of ancient English poetry, named after Alexander Boswell of Auchinleck, who presented it in 1774.

The first catalogue of the printed books was compiled in 1692, and contains a preface by Sir George Mackenzie. Another was prepared under the care of Ruddiman in 1742. In 1853 the late Mr Halkett commenced a catalogue, which has been printed in 6 vols. 4to, with a supplement, and includes all the printed books in the library at the end of 1871, containing about 260,000 entries. The library, managed by a keeper and staff, under a board of six curators, is easily accessible to all persons engaged in literary work, and now contains about 500,000 vols.

The library of the Writers to the Signet was established by the Society at Edinburgh in 1755. At first it consisted of law books exclusively, but in 1788 they began to collect the best editions of works in other departments of literature. During the librarianship of Macvey Napier (1805-1837) the number of volumes was more than sextupled, and in 1812 the library was removed to the new hall adjoining the Parliament House. In 1834 the upper hall was devoted to the collection. This is a magnificent apartment 142 ft. long, with a beautiful cupola painted by Stothard. The library now contains over 110,000 vols. and includes some fine specimens of early printing, as well as many other rare and costly works. It is especially rich in county histories and British topography and antiquities. A catalogue of the law books was printed in 1856. The late David Laing, who became librarian in 1837, published the first volume of a new catalogue in 1871, and in 1891 this was completed with a subject

libraries use the card, sheaf and other systems which allow constant and infinite intercalation coupled with economy and ease in making additions.

The idea of using separate slips or cards for cataloguing books, in order to obtain complete powers of arrangement and revision is not new, having been applied during the French revolutionary period to the cataloguing of libraries. More recently the system has been applied to various commercial purposes, such as book-keeping by what is known as the "loose-leaf ledger," and in this way greater public attention has been directed to the possibilities of adjustable methods both in libraries and for business. The card system is perhaps the most generally used at present, but many improvements in the adjustable binders, called by librarians the "sheaf system," will probably result in this latter form becoming a serious rival. The card method consists of a series of cards in alphabetical or other order kept on edge in trays or drawers, to which projecting guides are added in order to facilitate reference. Entries are usually made on one side of the card, and one card serves for a single entry. The sheaf method provides for slips of an uniform size being kept in book form in volumes capable of being opened by means of a screw or other fastening, for the purpose of adding or withdrawing slips. In addition to the advantage of being in book-form the sheaf system allows both sides of a slip to be used, while in many cases from two to twelve entries may be made on one slip. This is a great economy and leads to considerable saving of space. A great advantage resulting from the use of an adjustable manuscript catalogue, in whatever form adopted, is the simplicity with which it can be kept up-to-date. This is an advantage which in the view of many librarians outweighs the undoubted valuable qualities of comparative safety and multiplication of copies possessed by the printed form. There are many different forms of both card and sheaf systems, and practically every library now uses one or other of them for cataloguing or indexing purposes.

One other modification in connexion with the complete printed catalogue has been tried with success, and seems worthy of brief mention. After a complete manuscript catalogue has been provided in sheaf form, a select or eclectic catalogue is printed, comprising all the most important books in the library and those that represent special subjects. This, when supplemented by a printed list or bulletin of additions, seems to supply every need.

The most striking tendency of the modern library movement is the great increase in the freedom allowed to readers both in reference and lending departments. Although access to the shelves was quite a common feature in the older subscription libraries, and in state libraries like the British Museum and Patent Office, it is only within comparatively recent years that lending library borrowers were granted a similar privilege. Most municipal reference libraries grant access to a large or small collection of books, and at Cambridge, Birmingham and elsewhere in the United Kingdom, the practice is of long standing. So also in the United States, practically every library has its open shelf collection. On the continent of Europe, however, this method is not at all general, and books are guarded with a jealousy which in many cases must militate against their utility. The first "safe-guarded" open access municipal lending library was opened at Clerkenwell (now Finsbury), London, in 1893, and since then over one hundred cities and districts of all sizes in Britain have adopted the system. The British municipal libraries differ considerably from those of the United States in the safeguards against abuse which are employed, and the result is that their losses are insignificant, whilst in America they are sometimes enormous. Pawtucket and Cleveland in America were pioneers to some extent of the open shelf system for lending libraries, but the methods employed had little resemblance to the safe-guarded system of British libraries. The main features of the British plan are: exact classification, ... shelf and book [illegible] provision of automatic ... wickets to [illegible] and exit of borrowers, ... the rule that [illegible] tered before they can obtain admission. This last rule is not always current in America, and in consequence abuses are liable to take place. The great majority of British and American libraries, whether allowing open access or not, use cards for charging or registering books loaned to borrowers. In the United Kingdom a considerable number of places still use indicators for this purpose, although this mechanical method is gradually being restricted to fiction, save in very small places.

Other activities of modern libraries which are common to both Britain and America are courses of lectures, book exhibitions, work with children, provision of books for the blind and for foreign residents, travelling libraries and the education of library assistants. In many of the recent buildings, especially in those erected from the gifts of Mr Andrew Carnegie, special rooms for lectures and exhibitions and children are provided. Courses of lectures in connexion with the Liverpool and Manchester public libraries date from 1860, but during the years 1900–1910 there was a very great extension of this work. As a rule these courses are intended to direct attention to the literature of the subjects treated, as represented in the libraries, and in this way a certain amount of mutual advantage is secured. In some districts the libraries work in association with the education authorities, and thus it is rendered possible to keep schools supplied with books, over which the teachers are able to exercise supervision. This connexion between libraries and schools is much less common in the United Kingdom than in the British colonies and the United States, where the libraries are regarded as part of the national system of education. Excellent work has been accomplished within recent years by the Library Association in the training of librarians, and it is usual for about 300 candidates to come forward annually for examination in literary history, bibliography, classification, cataloguing, library history and library routine for which subjects certificates and diplomas are awarded. The profession of municipal librarian is not by any means remunerative as compared with employment in teaching or in the Civil Service, and until the library rate is increased there is little hope of improvement.

The usefulness of public libraries has been greatly increased by the work of the Library Association, founded in 1877, during the first International Library Conference held in London in October 1877. A charter of incorporation was granted to the association in 1898. It holds monthly and annual meetings, publishes a journal, conducts examinations, issues certificates, holds classes for instruction, and has greatly helped to improve the public library law. The Library Assistants Association (1895) publishes a journal. A second International Library Conference was held at London in 1897, and a third at Brussels in 1910. Library associations have been started in most of the countries of Europe, and the American Library Association, the largest and most important in existence, was established in 1876. These associations are giving substantial aid in the development and improvement of library methods and the status of librarians, and it is certain that their influence will in time produce a more scientific and valuable type of library than at present generally exists.

British Colonies and India

The majority of the British Colonies and Dependencies have permissive library laws on lines very similar to those in force in the mother country. There are, however, several points of difference which are worth mention. The rate limit is not so strict in every case, and an effort is made to bring the libraries into closer relations with the educational machinery of each colony. There is, for example, no rate limit in Tasmania; and South Australia may raise a library rate equivalent to 3d. in the £, although, in both cases, owing to the absence of large towns, the legislation existing has not been adopted. In Africa, Australia and Canada the governments make grants to public libraries up to a certain amount, on condition that the reading-rooms are open to the public, and some of the legislatures are even in closer touch with the libraries. The Canadian and Australian libraries are administered more or less on American lines, whilst those of South Africa, India, &c., are managed on the plan followed in England.

Africa.

There are several important libraries in South Africa, and many small town libraries which used to receive a government grant equal to the subscriptions of the members, but in no case did such grants exceed £150 for any one library in one year. These grants fluctuate considerably owing to the changes and temper of successive governments, and since the last war they have been considerably reduced everywhere. One of the oldest libraries is the South African Public Library at Cape Town established in 1818, which enjoys the copyright-privilege of receiving a free copy of every publication issued in Cape Colony. This library contains the great collection of colonial books bequeathed by Sir George Grey. The libraries of the various legislatures are perhaps the best supported and most important, but mention should be made of the public libraries of Port Elizabeth, Cape Colony, which published an excellent catalogue, and the public libraries at Kimberley; Durban, Natal; Bloemfontein, Orange River Colony; Bulawayo, Rhodesia; Johannesburg, Transvaal; and the public and university libraries at Pretoria. None of the libraries of North Africa are specially notable, although there are considerable collections at Cairo and Algiers.

Australasia.

All the public libraries, mechanics' institutes, schools of arts and similar institutes receive aid from the government, either in the form of grants of money or boxes of books sent from some centre. The public library of New South Wales, Sydney (1869), which includes the Mitchell Library of over 50,000 vols., now possesses a total of nearly 250,000 vols., and circulates books to country libraries, lighthouses and teachers' associations to the number of about 20,000 vols. per annum. The public library of Victoria, Melbourne (1853), with about 220,000 vols., also sends books to 443 country libraries of various kinds, which among them possess 750,000 vols., and circulate annually considerably over 2½ million vols. The university library at Melbourne (1855) has over 20,000 vols., and the libraries connected with the parliament and various learned societies are important. The public library of South Australia, Adelaide, has about 75,000 vols., and is the centre for the distribution of books to the institutes throughout the colony. These institutes possess over 325,000 vols. There is a good public library at Brisbane, Queensland, and there are a number of state-aided schools of arts with libraries attached. The Library of Parliament in Brisbane possesses over 40,000, and the Rockhampton School of Arts has 10,000 vols. Western Australia has a public library at Perth, which was established in 1887, and the small town institutes are assisted as in the other colonies.

Tasmania has several good libraries in the larger towns, but none of them had in 1910 taken advantage of the act passed in 1867 which gives municipalities practically unlimited powers and means as far as the establishment and maintenance of public libraries are concerned. At Hobart the Tasmanian Public Library (1849) is one of the most important, with 25,000 vols.

New Zealand is well equipped with public libraries established under acts dating from 1869 to 1877, as well as subscription, college and government libraries. At Auckland the Free Public Library (1880) has 50,000 vols., including Sir George Grey's Australasian collection; the Canterbury Public Library, Christchurch (1874), has 40,000 vols.; the University of Otago Library, Dunedin (1872), 10,000 vols.; and the public library at Wellington (1893) contains 20,000 vols.

India and the East.

Apart from government and royal libraries, there are many college, society, subscription and others, both English and oriental. It is impossible to do more than name a few of the most notable. Lists of many of the libraries in private hands including descriptions of their MS. contents have been issued by the Indian government. At Calcutta the Sanskrit college has 1652 printed Sanskrit volumes and 2769 Sanskrit MSS., some as old as the 14th century; there is also a large collection of Jain MSS. The Arabic library attached to the Arabic department of the Madrasa was founded about 1781, and now includes 731 printed volumes, 143 original MSS. and 151 copies; the English library of the Anglo-Persian department dates from 1854, and extends to 3254 vols. The library of the Asiatic Society of Bengal was founded in 1784, and now contains 15,000 printed vols., chiefly on eastern and philological subjects, with a valuable collection of 9500 Arabic and Persian MSS.

At Bombay the library of the Bombay branch of the Royal Asiatic Society, established in 1804 as the Literary Society of Bengal, is now an excellent general and oriental collection of 75,000 printed vols. and MSS., described in printed catalogues. The Moolla Feroze Library was bequeathed for public use by Moolla Feroze, head priest of the Parsis of the Kudmi sect in 1831, and consisted chiefly of MSS., in Arabic and Persian on history, philosophy and astronomy; some additions of English and Gujarati works have been made, as well as of European books on Zoroastrianism. The Native General Library (1845) has 11,000 vols., and there are libraries attached to Elphinstone College and the university of Bombay.

The library of Tippoo Sahib, consisting of 2000 MSS., fell into the hands of the British, and a descriptive catalogue of them by Charles Stewart was published at Cambridge in 1809, 4to. A few were presented to public libraries in England, but the majority were placed in the college of Fort William, then recently established. The first volume, containing Persian and Hindustani poetry, of the *Catalogue of the Libraries of the King of Oudh*, by A. Sprenger, was published at Calcutta in 1854. The compiler shortly afterwards left the Indian service, and no measures were taken to complete the work. On the annexation of the kingdom in 1856 the ex-king is believed to have taken some of the most valuable MSS. to Calcutta, but the largest portion was left behind at Lucknow. During the siege the books were used to block up windows, &c., and those which were not destroyed were abandoned and plundered by the soldiers. Many were burnt for fuel; a few, however, were rescued and sold by auction, and of these some were purchased for the Asiatic Society of Bengal.

Perhaps the most remarkable library in India is that of the rājā of Tanjore, which dates from the end of the 16th or beginning of the 17th century, when Tanjore was under the rule of the Telugu Nāiks, who collected Sanskrit MSS. written in the Telugu character. In the 18th century the Mahrattas conquered the country, and since that date the library increased but slowly. By far the greater portion of the store was acquired by Sharabhojī Rājā during a visit to Benares in 1820–1830; his successor Sivajī added a few, but of inferior value. There are now about 18,000 MSS. written in Devanāgarī, Nandināgarī, Telugu, Kannada, Granthī, Malayālam, Bengalī, Panjābī or Kashmirī, and Uriya; 8000 are on palm leaves. Dr Burnell's printed catalogue describes 12,375 articles.

The Royal Asiatic Society has branches with libraries attached in many of the large cities of India, the Straits Settlements, Ceylon, China, Japan, &c. At Rangoon in Burma there are several good libraries. The Raffles Library at Singapore was established as a proprietary institution in 1844, taken over by the government in 1874, and given legal status by an ordinance passed in 1878. It now contains about 35,000 vols. in general literature, but books relating to the Malayan peninsula and archipelago have been made a special feature, and since the acquisition of the collection of J. R. Logan in 1879 the library has become remarkably rich in this department. In Ceylon there is the Museum Library at Colombo (1877), which is maintained by the government, and there are many subscription and a few oriental libraries.

Canada.

The public libraries of the various provinces of Canada have grown rapidly in importance and activity, and, assisted as they are by government and municipal grants, they promise to rival those of the United States in generous equipment. Most of the library work in Canada is on the same lines as that of the United States, and there are no special points of difference worth mention. The library laws of the Dominion are embodied in a series of acts dating from 1854, by which much the same powers are conferred on local authorities as by the legislation of Britain and the United States. An important feature of the Canadian library law is the close association maintained between schools and libraries, and in some provinces the school libraries are established by the school and not the library laws. There is also an important extension of libraries to the rural districts, so that in every direction full provision is being made for the after-school education and recreation of the people.

The province of Ontario has a very large and widespread library system of which full particulars are given in the annual reports of the minister of education. The library portion has been printed separately, and with its illustrations and special articles forms quite a handbook of Canadian library practice. There are now 413 public libraries described as free and not free, and of these 131 free and 234 not free reported in 1909. The free libraries possessed 775,976 vols. and issued 2,421,049 vols. The not free libraries, most of which receive legislative or municipal grants, possessed 502,879 vols. and issued 650,826 vols. This makes a grand total of 1,278,855 vols. in municipal and assisted subscription libraries without counting the university and other libraries in the province. The most important other libraries in Ontario are—Queen's University, Kingston (1841), 40,000 vols.; Library of Parliament, Ottawa, about 250,000 vols.; university of Ottawa, 35,000 vols.; Legislative Library of Ontario, Toronto, about 100,000 vols.; university of Toronto (1856), 50,000 vols. The Public (municipal) Library of Toronto has now over 152,000 vols.

In the province of Quebec, in addition to the state-aided libraries there are several large and important libraries, among which may be mentioned the Fraser Institute, Montreal, 40,000 vols.; McGill University, Montreal (1855), 125,000 vols., comprising many important collections; the Seminary of St Sulpice, Montreal, about 80,000 vols.; Laval University, Quebec, 125,000 vols.; and the library of the Legislature (1792), about 100,000 vols. In the western provinces several large public, government and college libraries have been formed, but none of them are as old and important as those in the eastern provinces.

In Nova Scotia there are now 279 cases of books circulating among the school libraries, containing about 40,000 vols., and in addition 2800 vols. were stocked for the use of rural school libraries. The rural school libraries of Nova Scotia are regulated by a special law, and a little handbook has been printed, somewhat similar to that published by the French educational authorities for the communale libraries. The Legislative Library at Halifax contains nearly 35,000 vols., and the Dalhousie University (1868), in the same town, contains about 20,000 vols. The Legislative Library of Prince Edward Island, Charlottetown, containing the Dodd Library, issues books for home use. The school law of New Brunswick provides for grants being made in aid of school libraries by the Board of Education equal to one half the amount raised by a district, and a series of rules has been published. The only other British libraries in America of much consequence are those in the West Indian Islands. The Institute of Jamaica, Kingston (1879) has about 15,000 vols.; the Trinidad Public Library (1841), recently revised and catalogued, 23,000 vols.; and there are a few small legislative and college libraries in addition.

AUTHORITIES.—For the history of British libraries see H. B. Adams, *Public Libraries and Popular Education* (Albany, N.Y., 1900); J. D. Brown, *Guide to Librarianship* (1909); G. F. Chambers and H. W. Fovargue, *The Law relating to Public Libraries* (4th ed., 1899); J. W. Clark, *The Care of Books* (1909); E. Edwards, *Memoirs of Libraries* (1859); T. Greenwood, *Edward Edwards* (1901) and *Public Libraries* (4th ed., revised, 1891); J. J. Ogle, *The Free Library* (1897); Maurice Pellisson, *Les Bibliothèques populaires à l'étranger et en France* (Paris, 1906); R. A. Rye, *The Libraries of London* (1910); E. A. Savage, *The Story of Libraries and Book-Collectors* (1909).

For library economy consult J. D. Brown, *Manual of Library Economy* (1907); F. J. Burgoyne, *Library Construction, &c.* (1897); A. L. Champneys, *Public Libraries: a Treatise on their Design* (1907); J. C. Dana, *A Library Primer* (Chicago, 1910); Arnim Graesel, *Handbuch der Bibliothekslehre* (Leipzig, 1902); Albert Maire, *Manuel pratique du bibliothécaire* (Paris, 1896). On the subject of classification consult J. D. Brown, *Manual of Library Classification* (1898) and *Subject Classification* (1906); C. A. Cutter, *Expansive Classification* (1891–1893) (not yet completed); M. Dewey, *Decimal Classification* (6th ed., 1899), and *Institut International de Bibliographie: Classification bibliographique décimale* (Brussels, 1905); E. C. Richardson, *Classification: Theoretical and Practical* (1901).

Various methods of cataloguing books are treated in *Cataloguing Rules, author and title entries, compiled by the Committees of the American Library Association and the Library Association* (1908); C. A. Cutter, *Rules for a Printed Dictionary Catalogue* (Washington, 1904); M. Dewey, *Rules for Author and Classed Catalogues* (1892); T. Hitchler, *Cataloguing for Small Libraries* (Boston, 1905); K. A. Linderfelt, *Eclectic Card Catalog Rules* (Boston, 1890); J. H. Quinn, *Manual of Library Cataloguing* (1899); E. A. Savage, *Manual of Descriptive Annotation* (1906); J. D. Stewart, *The Sheaf Catalogue* (1909); H. B. Wheatley, *How to Catalogue a Library* (1889).

United States of America.

The libraries of the United States are remarkable for their number, size, variety, liberal endowment and good administration. The total number of libraries with over 1000 vols. was 5383 in 1900, including those attached to schools and institutions, and in 1910 there were probably at least 10,000 libraries having 1000 vols. and over. It is impossible to do more than glance at the principal libraries and activities, where the field is so immense, and a brief sketch of some of the chief federal, state, university, endowed and municipal libraries will therefore be presented.

Federal libraries.

The Library of Congress was first established in 1800 at Washington, and was burned together with the Capitol by the British army in 1814. President Jefferson's books were purchased to form the foundation of a new library, which continued to increase slowly until 1851, when all but 20,000 vols. were destroyed by fire. From this time the collection has grown rapidly, and now consists of about 1,800,000 vols. In 1866 the library of the Smithsonian Institution, consisting of 40,000 vols., chiefly in natural science, was transferred to the Library of Congress. The library is specially well provided in history, jurisprudence, the political sciences and Americana. Since 1832 the law collections have been constituted into a special department. This is the national library. In 1870 the registry of copyrights was transferred to it under the charge of the librarian of Congress, and two copies of every publication which claims copyright are required to be deposited. Cards for these are now printed and copies are sold to other libraries for an annual subscription fixed according to the number taken. The building in which the library is now housed was opened in 1897. It covers 3½ acres of ground, contains 10,000,000 cub. ft. of space, and has possible accommodation for over 4 million vols. Its cost was $6,500,000, or including the land, $7,000,000. It is the largest, most ornate and most costly building in the world yet erected for library purposes. Within recent years the appropriation has been largely increased, and the bibliographical department has been able to publish many valuable books on special subjects. The *A.L.A. Catalog* (1904) and *A.L.A. Portrait Index* (1906), may be mentioned as of especial value. The classification of the library is being gradually completed, and in every respect this is the most active government library in existence.

Other important federal libraries are those attached to the following departments at Washington: Bureau of Education (1868); Geological Survey (1882); House of Representatives; Patent Office (1836); Senate (1868); Surgeon General's Office (1870), with an elaborate analytical printed catalogue of world-wide fame.

State libraries.

Although the state libraries of Pennsylvania and New Hampshire are known to have been established as early as 1777, it was not until some time after the revolution that any general tendency was shown to form official libraries in connexion with the state system. It is especially within the last thirty years that the number of these libraries has so increased that now every state and territory possesses a collection of books and documents for official and public purposes. These collections depend for their increase upon annual appropriations by the several states, and upon a systematic exchange of the official publications of the general government and of the several states and territories. The largest is that of the state of New York at Albany, which contains nearly 500,000 vols., and is composed of a general and a law library. Printed and MS. card catalogues have been issued. The state libraries are libraries of reference, and only members of the official classes are allowed to borrow books, although any well-behaved person is admitted to read in the libraries.

University libraries.

The earliest libraries formed were in connexion with educational institutions, and the oldest is that of Harvard (1638). It was destroyed by fire in 1764, but active steps were at once taken for its restoration. From that time to the present, private donations have been the great resource of the library. In 1840 the collection was removed to Gore Hall, erected for the purpose with a noble bequest from Christopher Gore (1758–1829), formerly governor of Massachusetts. There are also ten special libraries connected with the different departments of the university. The total numbers of vols. in all these collections is over 800,000. There is a MS. card-catalogue in two parts, by authors and subjects, which is accessible to the readers. The only condition of admission to use the books in Gore Hall is respectability; but only members of the university and privileged persons may borrow books. The library of Yale College, New Haven, was founded in 1701, but grew so slowly that, even with the 1000 vols. received from Bishop Berkeley in 1733, it had only increased to 4000 vols. in 1766, and some of these were lost in the revolutionary war. During the 19th century the collection grew more speedily, and now the library numbers over 550,000 vols.

Other important university and college libraries are Amherst College, Mass. (1821), 93,000 vols.; Brown University, R.I. (1767), 156,000 vols.; Columbia University, N.Y. (1763), 430,000 vols.; Cornell University, N.Y. (1868), 355,000 vols.; Dartmouth College, N.H. (1769), 106,000 vols.; Johns Hopkins University, Baltimore (1876), 220,000 vols.; Lehigh University, Pa. (1877), 150,000 vols.; Leland Stanford University, Cal. (1891), 113,000 vols.; Princeton University, N.J. (1746), 260,000 vols.; University of California (1868), 240,000 vols.; University of Chicago, Ill. (1892), 480,000 vols.; University of Michigan (1837), 252,000 vols.; University of Pennsylvania (1749), 285,000 vols. There are numerous other college libraries, several of them even larger than some of those named above.

Subscription and Endowed Libraries.

The establishment of proprietary or subscription libraries runs back into the first half of the 18th century, and is connected with the name of Benjamin Franklin. It was at Philadelphia, in the year 1731, that he set on foot what he called "his first project of a public nature, that for a subscription library. . . . The institution soon manifested its ability, was imitated by other towns and in other provinces." The Library Company of Philadelphia was soon regularly incorporated, and gradually drew to itself other collections of books, including the Loganian Library, which was vested in the company by the state legislature in 1792 in trust for public use. Hence the collection combines the character of a public and of a proprietary library, being freely open for reference purposes, while the books circulate only among the subscribing members. It numbers at present 226,000 vols., of which 11,000 belong to the Loganian Library, and may be freely ent. In 1869 Dr James Rush left a bequest of over one million dollars for the purpose of erecting a building to be called the Ridgeway branch of the library. The building is very handsome, and has been very highly spoken of as a library structure. Philadelphia has another large proprietary library—that of the Mercantile Library Company, which was established in 1821. It possesses 200,000 vols., and its members have always enjoyed direct access to the shelves. The library of the Boston Athenaeum was established in 1807, and numbers 235,000 vols. It has published an admirable dictionary-catalogue. The collection is especially rich in art and in history, and possesses a part of the library of George Washington. The Mercantile Library Association of New York, which was founded in 1820, has over 240,000 vols. New York possesses two other large proprietary libraries, one of which claims to have been formed as early as 1700 as the "public" library of New York. It was organized as the New York Society Library in 1754, and has been especially the library of the old Knickerbocker families and their descendants, its contents bearing witness to its history. It contains about 100,000 vols. The Apprentices' Library (1820) has about 100,000 vols., and makes a special feature of works on trades and useful arts.

The Astor Library in New York was founded by a bequest of John Jacob Astor, whose example was followed successively by his son and grandson. The library was opened to the public in 1854, and consists of a careful selection of the most valuable books upon all subjects. It is a library of reference, for which purpose it is freely open, and books are not lent out. It is "a working library for studious persons." The Lenox Library was established by James Lenox in 1870, when a body of trustees was incorporated by an act of the legislature. In addition to the funds intended for the library building and endowment, amounting to $1,247,000, the private collection of books which Mr Lenox had long been accumulating is extremely valuable. Though it does not rank high in point of mere numbers, it is exceedingly rich in early books on America, in Bibles, in Shakespeariana and in Elizabethan poetry. Both those libraries are now merged in the New York Public Library. The Peabody Institute at Baltimore was established by George Peabody in 1857, and contains a reference library open to all comers. The institute has an endowment of $1,000,000, which, however, has to support, besides the library, a conservatoire of music, an art gallery, and courses of popular lectures. It has a very fine printed dictionary catalogue and now contains nearly 200,000 vols. In the same city is the Enoch Pratt Free Library (1882) with 257,000 vols. In the city of Chicago are two very important endowed libraries, the Newberry Library (1887) with over 200,000 vols., and the John Crerar Library (1894), with 235,000 vols. Both of these are reference libraries of great value, and the John Crerar Library specializes in science, for which purpose its founder left $3,000,000.

It will be sufficient to name a few of the other endowed libraries to give an idea of the large number of donors who have given money to libraries. Silas Bronson (Waterbury), Annie T. Howard (New Orleans), Joshua Bates (Boston), Charles E. Forbes (Northampton, Mass.), Mortimer F. Reynolds (Rochester, N.Y.), Leonard Case (Cleveland), I. Osterhout (Wilkes-Barré, Pa.), and above all Andrew Carnegie, whose library benefactions exceed $53,000,000.

It remains to mention another group of proprietary and society libraries.

Since the organization of the government in 1789, no less than one hundred and sixty historical societies have been formed in the United States, most of which still continue to exist. Many of them have formed considerable libraries, and possess extensive and valuable manuscript collections. The oldest of them is the Massachusetts Historical Society, which dates from 1791.

The earliest of the scientific societies, the American Philosophical Society (1743), has 73,000 vols. The most extensive collection is that of the Academy of Natural Sciences of Philadelphia, which consists of 60,000 vols. and pamphlets. For information as to the numerous professional libraries of the United States—theological, legal and medical—the reader may be referred to the authorities quoted below.

Municipal Libraries.

In no country has the movement for the development of municipal libraries made such progress as in the United States; these institutions called free or public as the case may be are distinguished for their work, enterprise and the liberality with which they are supported. They are established under laws passed by the different states, the first to pass such an enactment being Massachusetts, which in 1848 empowered the city of Boston to establish a free public library. This was subsequently extended to the whole state in 1851. Other states followed, all with more or less variation in the provisions, till practically every state in the Union now has a body of library laws. In general the American library law is much on the same lines as the English. In most states the acts are permissive. In New Hampshire aid is granted by the state to any library for which a township contracts to make a definite annual appropriation. A limit is imposed in most states on the library tax which may be levied, although there are some, like Massachusetts and New Hampshire, which fix no limit. In every American town the amount derived from the library tax usually exceeds by double or more the same rate raised in Britain in towns of similar size. For example, East Orange, N.J., with a population of 35,000, expends £2400, while Dumfries in Scotland, with 23,000 pop. expends £500. Cincinnati, 345,000 pop., expenditure £26,000; Islington (London), 350,000 pop., expenditure £8200, is another example. In the smaller towns the difference is not so marked, but generally the average American municipal library income is considerably in excess of the British one. Many American municipal libraries have also endowments which add to their incomes.

American Library Administration.

In one respect the American libraries differ from those of the United Kingdom. They are usually managed by a small committee or body of trustees, about five or more in number, who administer the library independent of the city council. This is akin to the practice in Scotland, although there, the committees are larger. In addition to the legislation authorizing town libraries to be established, thirty-two states have formed state library commissions. These are small bodies of three or five trained persons appointed by the different states which, acting on behalf of the state, encourage the formation of local libraries, particularly in towns and villages, and in many cases have authority to aid [illegible] the state funds of a [illegible] the purchase of books, upon [illegible] sum by the local authorities. [illegible] to aid further with select lists [illegible] suggestions or advice in the [illegible] and maintenance. Such commissions [illegible] California, Colorado, Connecticut, [illegible] Illinois, Indiana, Iowa, Kansas, [illegible] Michigan, Minnesota, Missouri, [illegible] New Jersey, New York, North [illegible] Oregon, Pennsylvania, Tennessee, [illegible] Washington and Wisconsin.

[illegible] documents issued by some of these [illegible] interesting and valuable, especially as [illegible] on the working of the travelling [illegible] These to some extent are a [illegible] library idea of Samuel Brown of [illegible] who from 1817 to 1836 carried on [illegible] subscription libraries in that country. [illegible] there were 3850 vols. in 47 libraries. [illegible] often under state supervision, [illegible] and the books are circu- [illegible] was the pioneer in this movement which [illegible] states which have established [illegible] There are also town travelling libraries [illegible] to branches, so that every [illegible] people in outlying districts into touch [illegible]

[illegible] of the United States work in con- [illegible] and it is generally considered that [illegible] machinery of the country. [illegible] the state libraries have been put under [illegible] university of the state of New York, which [illegible] libraries. Work with the schools [illegible] cultivated in the libraries of the [illegible] In some cases the libraries send [illegible] the schools; in others provision is made [illegible] and lending departments at the [illegible] At Cleveland (Ohio), Pittsburg (Pa.), New [illegible] other places, elaborate arrangements are in [illegible] and amusement of children. There [illegible] Carnegie Library training school for [illegible] at Pittsburg, and within recent years the [illegible] the art of telling stories to children at [illegible] "story-hour" idea has been the cause of [illegible] in the United States, librarians and [illegible] as to the value of the service. [illegible] work in American libraries, often [illegible] the number of non-English reading [illegible] of children of foreign origin. The [illegible] to any large extent, but the [illegible] at the schools, are brought into [illegible] departments of the libraries. In [illegible] obliged to undertake special work [illegible] is performed in a sane, practical [illegible] The preponderance of women librarians [illegible] regard for children has tended [illegible] in some quarters, but with [illegible] behalf of children is justified [illegible] all, it is manifest that a rapidly [illegible] for thousands of foreigners and [illegible] use every means of rapidly [illegible] and the public library is one of the [illegible] of accomplishing this great

[illegible] American libraries are working [illegible] of the United Kingdom. They [illegible] universally, and there is much [illegible] matters. [illegible] on the [illegible] largest [illegible] world, is that of New York City, which, after struggling with a series of Free Circulating Libraries, blossomed out in 1895 into the series of combinations which resulted in the present great establishment. In that year, the Astor and Lenox libraries (see above) were taken over by the city, and in addition, $2,000,000 was given by one of the heirs of Mr S. J. Tilden, who had bequeathed about $4,000,000 for library purposes in New York but whose will had been upset in the law courts. In 1901 Mr Andrew Carnegie gave about £1,500,000 for the purpose of providing 65 branches, and these are now nearly all erected. A very fine central library building has been erected, and when the organization is completed there will be no system of municipal libraries to equal that of New York. It possesses about 1,400,000 vols. in the consolidated libraries. Brooklyn, although forming part of Greater New York, has an independent library system, and possesses about 560,000 vols. distributed among 26 branches and including the old Brooklyn Library which has been absorbed in the municipal library system. At Boston (Mass.) is one of the most renowned public libraries in the United States, and also the oldest established by act of legislature. It was first opened to the public in 1854, and is now housed in a very magnificently decorated building which was completed in 1895. The central library contains many fine special collections, and there are 28 branch and numerous school libraries in connexion. It possesses about 1,000,000 vols. altogether, its annual circulation is about 1,500,000 vols., and its annual expenditure is nearly £70,000.

Other notable municipal libraries are those of Philadelphia (1891), Chicago (1872); Los Angeles (Cal.), 1872; Indianapolis (1868), Detroit (1865), Minneapolis (1885), St Louis (1865), Newark, N.J. (1889), Cincinnati (1856), Cleveland (1869), Allegheny (1890), Pittsburg (1895), Providence, R.I. (1878), Milwaukee (1875), Washington, D.C. (1898), Worcester, Mass. (1859), Buffalo (1837).

AUTHORITIES.—*The Annual Library Index* (New York, 1908)—contains a select list of libraries in the United States; Arthur E. Bostwick, *The American Public Library*, illust. (New York, 1910)—the most comprehensive general book; Bureau of Ed cation, *Statistics of Public Libraries in the United States and Canada* (1893)—this has been succeeded by a list of "Public, Society and School Libraries," reprinted at irregular intervals from the Report of the Commissioner of Education and giving a list of libraries containing over 5000 vols. with various other particulars; Clegg, *International Directory of Booksellers* (1910) and earlier issues—contains a list of American libraries with brief particulars; John C. Dana, *A Library Primer* (Chicago, 1910)—the standard manual of American library practice; *Directory of Libraries in the United States and Canada* (6th ed., Minneapolis, 1908)—a brief list of 4500 libraries, with indication of the annual income of each; Wm. I. Fletcher, *Public Libraries in America* (2nd ed., Boston, 1899), illust.; T. W. Koch, *Portfolio of Carnegie Libraries* (1908); Cornelia Marvin, *Small Library Buildings* (Boston, 1908); A. R. Spofford, *A Book for all Readers. . . the Formation of Public and Private Libraries* (1905).

France.

French libraries (other than those in private hands) belong either to the state, to the departments, to the communes or to learned societies, educational establishments and other public institutions; the libraries of judicial or administrative bodies are not considered to be owned by them, but to be state property. Besides the unrivalled library accommodation of the capital, France possesses a remarkable assemblage of provincial libraries. The communal and school libraries also form striking features of the French free library system. Taking as a basis for comparison the *Tableau statistique des bibliothèques publiques* (1857), there were at that date 340 departmental libraries, with a total of 3,734,260 vols., and 44,436 MSS. In 1908 the number of volumes in all the public libraries; communal, university, learned societies, educational and departmental, was more than 10,060,148 vols., 93,986 MSS. and 15,530 incunabula. Paris alone now possesses over 10,570,000 printed vols., 147,543 MSS., 5000 incunabula, 609,439 maps and plans, 2,000,000 prints (designs and reproductions).

Paris. The Bibliothèque Nationale (one of the most extensive libraries in the world) has had an advantage over others in the length of time during which its contents have been accumulating, and in the great zeal shown for it by several kings and other eminent men. Enthusiastic writers find the original of this library in the MS. collections of Charlemagne and Charles the Bald, but these were dispersed in course of time, and the few precious relics of them which the national library now possesses have been acquired at a much later date. Of the library which St Louis formed in the 13th century (in imitation of what he had seen in the East) nothing has fallen into the possession of the Bibliothèque Nationale, but much has remained of the royal collections made by kings of the later dynasties. The real foundation of the institution (formerly known as the Bibliothèque du Roi) may be said to date from the reign of King John, the Black Prince's captive, who had a considerable taste for books, and bequeathed his "royal library" of MSS. to his successor Charles V. Charles V. organized his library in a very effective manner, removing it from the Palais de la Cité to the Louvre, where it was arranged on desks in a large hall of three storeys, and placed under the management of the first librarian and cataloguer, Claude Mallet, the king's valet-de-chambre. His catalogue was a mere shelf-list, entitled *Inventaire des Livres du Roy nostre Seigneur estans au chastel du Louvre*; it is still extant, as well as the further inventories made by Jean Blanchet in 1380, and by Jean le Bègue in 1411 and 1424. Charles V. was very liberal in his patronage of literature, and many of the early monuments of the French language are due to his having employed Nicholas Oresme, Raoul de Presle and other scholars to make translations from ancient texts. Charles VI added some hundreds of MSS. to the royal library, which, however, was sold to the regent, duke of Bedford, after a valuation had been established by the inventory of 1424. The regent transferred it to England, and it was finally dispersed at his death in 1435. Charles VII. and Louis XI. did little to repair the loss of the precious Louvre library, but the news of the invention of printing served as a stimulus to the creation of another one, of which the first librarian was Laurent Paulmier. The famous miniaturist, Jean Foucquet of Tours, was named the king's *enlumineur*, and although Louis XI. neglected to avail himself of many precious opportunities that occurred in his reign, still the new library developed gradually with the help of confiscation. Charles VIII. enriched it with many fine MSS. executed by his order, and also with most of the books that had formed the library of the kings of Aragon, seized by him at Naples. Louis XII., on coming to the throne, incorporated the Bibliothèque du Roi with the fine Orleans library at Blois, which he had inherited. The Blois library, thus augmented, and further enriched by plunder from the palaces of Pavia, and by the purchase of the famous Gruthuyse collection, was described at the time as one of the four marvels of France. Francis I. removed it to Fontainebleau in 1534, enlarged by the addition of his private library. He was the first to set the fashion of fine artistic bindings, which was still more cultivated by Henry II., and which has never died out in France. During the librarianship of Amyot (the translator of Plutarch) the library was transferred from Fontainebleau to Paris, not without the loss of several books coveted by powerful thieves. Henry IV. removed it to the Collége de Clermont, but in 1604 another change was made, and in 1622 it was installed in the Rue de la Harpe. Under the librarianship of J. A. de Thou it acquired the library of Catherine de' Medici, and the glorious Bible of Charles the Bald. In 1617 a decree was passed that two copies of every new publication should be deposited in the library, but this was not rigidly enforced till Louis XIV.'s time. The first catalogue worthy of the name was finished in 1622, and contains a description of some 6000 vols., chiefly MSS. Many additions were made during Louis XIII.'s reign, notably that of the Dupuy collection, but a new era dawned for the Bibliothèque du Roi under the patronage of Louis XIV. The enlightened activity of Colbert, one of the greatest of collectors, so enriched the library that it became necessary for want of space to make another removal. It was therefore in 1666 installed in the Rue Vivien (now Vivienne) not far from its present habitat. The departments of engravings and medals were now created, and before long rose to nearly equal importance with that of books. Marolles's prints, Foucquet's books, and many from the Mazarin library were added to the collection, and, in short, the Bibliothèque du Roi had its future pre-eminence undoubtedly secured. Nic. Clément made a catalogue in 1684 according to an arrangement which has been followed ever since (that is, in twenty-three classes, each one designated by a letter of the alphabet), with an alphabetical index to it. After Colbert's death Louvois emulated his predecessor's labours, and employed Mabillon, Thevenot and others to procure fresh accessions from all parts of the world. A new catalogue was compiled in 1688 in 8 vols. by several distinguished scholars. The Abbé Louvois, the minister's son, became head of the library in 1691, and opened it to all students—a privilege which although soon withdrawn was afterwards restored. Towards the end of Louis XIV.'s reign it contained over 70,000 vols. Under the management of the Abbé Bignon numerous additions were made in all departments, and the library was removed to its present home in the Rue Richelieu. Among the more important acquisitions were 6000 MSS. from the private library of the Colbert family, Bishop Huet's forfeited collection, and a large number of Oriental books imported by missionaries from the farther East, and by special agents from the Levant. Between 1739 and 1753 a catalogue in 11 vols. was printed, which enabled the administration to discover and to sell its duplicates. In Louis XVI.'s reign the sale of the La Vallière library furnished a valuable increase both in MSS. and printed books. A few years before the Revolution broke out the latter department contained over 300,000 vols. and opuscules. The Revolution was serviceable to the library, now called the Bibliothèque Nationale, by increasing it with the forfeited collections of the *émigrés*, as well as of the suppressed religious communities. In the midst of the difficulties of placing and cataloguing these numerous acquisitions, the name of Van Praet appears as an administrator of the first order. Napoleon increased the amount of the government grant; and by the strict enforcement of the law concerning new publications, as well as by the acquisition of several special collections, the Bibliothèque made considerable progress during his reign towards realizing his idea that it should be universal in character. At the beginning of last century the recorded numbers were 250,000 printed vols., 83,000 MSS., and 1,500,000 engravings. After Napoleon's downfall the MSS. which he had transferred from Berlin, Hanover, Florence, Venice, Rome, the Hague and other places had to be returned to their proper owners. The MacCarthy sale in 1817 brought a rich store of MSS. and incunabula. From that time onwards to the present, under the enlightened administration of MM. Taschereau and Delisle and Marcel, the accessions have been very extensive.

According to the statistics for 1908 the riches of the Bibliothèque Nationale may be enumerated as follows: (1) Département des Imprimés: more than 3,000,000 vols.; Maps and plans, 500,000 in 28,000 vols. (2) Département des Manuscrits: 110,000 MSS. thus divided: Greek 4960, Latin 21,544, French 44,913, Oriental and miscellaneous 38,583. (3) Département des Estampes: 1,000,000 pieces. (4) Département des Médailles: 207,096 pieces.

Admittance to the "salle de travail" is obtained through a card procured from the secretarial office; the "salle publique" contains 344 places for readers, who are able to consult more than 50,000 vols. of books of reference. Great improvements have lately been introduced into the service. A "salle de lecture publique" is free to all readers and is much used. New buildings are in process of construction. The slip catalogue bound in volumes dates from 1882 and gives a list of all accessions since that date; it is divided into two parts, one for the names of authors and the other for subjects. There is not yet, as at the British Museum, an alphabetical catalogue of all the printed works and kept up by periodical supplements, but since 1897 a *Catalogue général des livres imprimés* has been begun. In 1909 the 38th vol. containing letters A to Delp had appeared. Some volumes are published each year, but the earlier volumes only contain a selection of the books; this inconvenience has now been remedied. Among the other catalogues published by the Printed Book Department, the following may be mentioned: *Répertoire alphabétique des livres mis à la disposition des lecteurs dans la salle de travail* (1896, 8vo), *Liste des périodiques français et étrangers mis à la disposition des lecteurs* (1907, 4to, autogr.), *Liste des périodiques étrangers* (new ed., 1896, 8vo) and *Supplément* (1902, 8vo), *Bulletin des récentes publications françaises* (from 1882, 8vo), *Catalogue des dissertations et écrits académiques provenant des échanges avec les universités étrangères* (from 1882, 8vo). The other extensive catalogues apart from those of the 18th century are: *Catalogue de l'histoire de France* (1855–1889, 4to, 11 vols.); *Table des auteurs*,

[illegible]

comte d'Artois, who had bought it from the marquis de Paulmy in his lifetime. It contains at the present time about 600,000 vols., 10,000 manuscripts, 120,000 prints and the Bastille collection (2500 portfolios) of which the inventory is complete; it is the richest library for the literary history of France and has more than 30,000 theatrical pieces.

L'Inventaire des manuscrits was made by H. Martin (1885–1899, t. i.–viii.), the other catalogues and lists are: *Extrait du catalogue des journaux conservés à la Bibliothèque de l'Arsenal* ("Bulletin des biblioth. et des archives," t. i.), *Archives de la Bastille*, par F. Funck-Brentano (1892–1894, 3 vols. 8vo); *Notice sur les dépôts littéraires* par J. B. Labiche (1880, 8vo); *Catalogue des estampes, dessins et cartes composant le cabinet des estampes de la bibliothèque de l'Arsenal*, par G. Schefer (1894–1905, 8 pts. 8vo).

The Bibliothèque Mazarine owes its origin to the great cardinal, who confided the direction to Gabriel Naudé; it was open to the public in 1643, and was transferred to Rue de Richelieu in 1648. Dispersed during the Fronde in the lifetime of Mazarin, it was reconstituted after the death of the cardinal in 1661, when it contained 40,000 vols. which were left to the Collège des Quatre-Nations, which in 1691 made it again public. It now has 250,000 vols.; with excellent manuscript catalogues.

The catalogues of incunabula and manuscripts are printed: P. Marais et A. Dufresne de Saint-Léon, *Catalogue des incunables de la bibliothèque Mazarine* (1893, 8vo); *Supplément, additions et corrections* (1898, 4 vols. 8vo); *Catalogue des MSS.*, par A. Molinier (1885–1892, 4 vols. 8vo); *Inventaire sommaire des MSS. grecs*, par H. Omont.

The first library of the Genovéfains had nearly disappeared owing to bad administration when Cardinal François de la Rochefoucauld, who had charge of the reformation of that religious order, constituted in 1642 a new library with his own books. The Bibliothèque Ste-Geneviève in 1716 possessed 45,000 vols.; important gifts were made by Letellier and the duc d'Orléans increased it still more. It became national property in 1791, and was called the Bibliothèque du Panthéon and added to the Lycée Henri IV. under the empire. In 1908 the library contained 350,000 printed vols., 1225 incunabula, 3510 manuscripts, 10,000 prints (including 7357 portraits and 3000 maps and plans).

The printed catalogues at present comprise: Poirée et Lamoureux, *Catalogue abrégé de la bibliothèque Ste-Geneviève* (1891, 8vo); 3 supplements (1890–1896, 1897–1899, 1900–1902); *Catalogue des incunables de la bibliothèque Ste-Geneviève, rédigé par Daunou*, publié par M. Pellechet (1892, 8vo); *Catalogue général des MSS.*, par Ch. Kohler (1893–1896, 2 vols. 8vo); *Inventaire sommaire des MSS. grecs*, par H. Omont; *Notices sur quelques MSS. normands*, par E. Deville (1904–1906, 10 pts. 8vo), &c.

The Bibliothèque des Archives nationales, founded in 1808 by Daunou, contains 30,000 vols. on sciences auxiliary to history. It is only accessible to the officials.

It would be impossible to describe all the official, municipal and academic libraries of Paris more or less open to the public, which are about 200 in number, and in the following survey we deal only with those having 10,000 vols. and over.

The Bibliothèque du Ministère des affaires étrangères was founded by the marquis de Torcy, minister for foreign affairs under Louis XIV.; it contains 80,000 vols. and is for official use only. The Bibliothèque du Ministère de l'Agriculture dates from 1882 and has only 4000 vols. At the Ministry for the Colonies the library (of 10,000 vols.) dates from 1897; the catalogue was published in 1905; the library of the Colonial office is attached to this ministry; suppressed in 1896, it was re-established in 1899, and now contains 6000 vols., 2400 periodicals and 5000 photographs; it is open to the public. There are 30,000 vols. in the Bibliothèque du Ministère du commerce et de l'industrie; the Bibliothèque du Ministère des finances was burnt at the Commune, but has been reconstituted and now contains 35,000 vols.; connected with it are the libraries of the following offices: Contributions directes, Contributions indirectes, Enregistrement et inspection des finances; the contents of these four libraries make a total of 13,500 vols. [illegible]

Cour d'appel (12,000 vols.); Ordre des avocats, dating from 1871 (56,000 vols., with a catalogue printed in 1880-1881); the Bibliothèque des avocats de la cour de Cassation (20,000 vols.); that of the Cour de Cassation (40,000 vols.). The Bibliothèque du Ministère de la Marine is of old formation (catalogue 1838-1843); it contains 100,000 vols. and 356 MSS.; the catalogue of manuscripts was compiled in 1907. The Bibliothèque du service hydrographique de la Marine has 65,000 vols. and 250 MSS. The Ministère des Travaux publics possesses 12,000 vols., and the Sous-Secrétariat des postes et télégraphes a further 30,000 vols. The Bibliothèque de la Chambre des députés (1796) possesses 250,000 printed books and 1546 MSS. (*Catalogue des manuscrits*, by E. Coyecque et H. Debray, 1907; *Catalogue des livres de jurisprudence, d'économie politique, de finances, et d'administration*, 1883). The Bibliothèque du Sénat (1818) contains 150,000 vols. and 1343 MSS. The Bibliothèque du Conseil d'État has 30,000 vols. All these libraries are only accessible to officials except by special permission.

The Bibliothèque Historique de la ville de Paris was destroyed in 1871, but Jules Cousin reconstituted it in 1872; it possesses 400,000 vols., 3500 MSS. and 14,000 prints; the principal printed catalogues are *Catalogue des imprimés de la Réserve* by M. Poëte (1910), *Catalogue des manuscrits*, by F. Bournon (1893); a *Bulletin* has been issued periodically since 1906. The Bibliothèque administrative de la préfecture de la Seine is divided into two sections; French (40,000 vols.) and foreign (22,000 vols.); it is only accessible to officials and to persons having a card of introduction; the catalogues are printed.

The other libraries connected with the city of Paris are that of the Conseil municipal (20,000 vols.), the Bibliothèques Municipales Populaires, 82 in number with a total of 590,000 books; those of the 22 Hospitals (92,887 vols.), the Préfecture de police (10,000 vols.), the Bibliothèque Forney (10,000 vols. and 80,000 prints), the five Écoles municipales supérieures (19,700 vols.), the six professional schools (14,200 vols.).

The libraries of the university and the institutions dealing with higher education in Paris are well organized and their catalogues generally printed.

The Bibliothèque de l'Université, although at present grouped as a system in four sections in different places, historically considered is the library of the Sorbonne. This was founded in 1762 by Montempuis and only included the faculties of Arts and Theology. It changed its name several times, in 1800 it was the Bibliothèque du Prytanée, in 1808 Bibliothèque des Quatre Lycées and in 1812 Bibliothèque de l'Université de France. The sections into which the Bibliothèque de l'Université is now divided are: (1) Facultés de Sciences et des Lettres à la Sorbonne, (2) Faculté de Médecine, (3) Faculté de droit, (4) École supérieure de pharmacie. Before the separation of Church and State there was a fifth section, that of Protestant theology. After the Bibliothèque nationale it is the richest in special collections, and above all as regards classical philology, archaeology, French and foreign literature and literary criticism, just as the library of the Faculté des Sciences et des Lettres is notable for philosophy, mathematics and chemico-physical sciences. The great development which has taken place during the last thirty years, especially under the administration of M. J. de Chantepie du Dézert, its installation since 1897 in the buildings of the New Sorbonne, have made it a library of the very first rank. The reading-room only seats about 300 persons. The average attendance per day is 1200, the number of books consulted varies from 1500 to 3000 vols. a day, and the loans amount to 14,000 vols. per year. The store-rooms, although they contain more than 1200 mètres of shelves and comprise two buildings of five storeys each, are insufficient for the annual accessions, which reach nearly 10,000 vols. by purchase and presentation. Amongst the latter the most important are the bequests of Leclerc, Peccot, Lavisse, Derenbourg and Beljame; the last-named bequeathed more than 3000 vols., including an important Shakespearean library. The first section contains more than 550,000 vols., 2800 periodicals which include over 70,000 vols., 320 incunabula, 2106 MSS., more than 2000 maps and plans and some prints. The alphabetical catalogues are kept up day by day on slips. The classified catalogues were in 1910 almost ready for printing, and some had already been published: *Périodiques* (1905); *Cartulaires* (1907); *Mélanges jubilaires et publications commémoratives* (1908); *Inventaires des MSS.*, by E. Chatelain (1892); *Incunables*, by E. Chatelain (1902); and *Supplément*, *Réserve de la bibliothèque 1501-1540*, by Ch. Beaulieux (1909); *Nouvelles acquisitions* (1905-1908); *Catalogue des livres de G. Duplessis donnés à l'Université de Paris* (1907), *Catalogue collectif des bibliothèques universitaires* by Fécamp (1898-1901). For French thèses, of which the library possesses a rich collection, the catalogues are as follows: Mourier et Deltour, *Catalogue des thèses de lettres* (1809, &c.); A. Maire, *Répertoire des thèses de lettres* (1809-1900), A. Maire, *Catalogue des thèses de sciences* (1809-1890) with *Supplément* to 1900 by Estanave, *Catalogue des thèses publié par le Ministère de l'Instruction publique* (1882, &c.).

At the Sorbonne are also to be found the libraries of A. Dumont and V. Cousin (15,000 vols.), and those of the laboratories, of which the richest is the geological (30,000 specimens and books). The section relating to medicine, housed since 1891 in the new buildings of the Faculté de Médecine, includes 180,000 vols. and 88 MSS. (catalogue 1910). The Bibliothèque de la faculté de droit dates from 1772 and contains 80,000 vols., 239 MSS. The fourth section, l'École supérieure de pharmacie, greatly developed since 1882, now contains 50,000 vols.

The other libraries connected with higher education include that of the École des Beaux-Arts (40,000 vols., 100,000 reproductions, 14,000 drawings). The library of the École normale supérieure (1794), established in the Rue d'Ulm in 1846, has received legacies from Verdet (1867), Caboche (1887), Lerambert-Whitcomb (1890), and a portion of Cuvier's library; the system of classification in use is practically the same as that of the Sorbonne, being devised by Philippe Lebas (librarian of the Sorbonne) about 1845; there are 200,000 vols. The library of the Muséum d'histoire naturelle dates from the 18th century, and contains 220,000 vols., 2000 MSS., 8000 original drawings on vellum beginning in 1631. The Bibliothèque de l'Office et Musée de l'Instruction publique (formerly Musée pédagogique), founded only in 1880, has 75,000 vols. In 1760 was founded the Bibliothèque de l'Institut de France, which is very rich; its acquisitions come particularly from gifts and exchanges (400,000 vols., numerous and scarce; valuable MSS., especially modern ones).

The following may be briefly mentioned: Conservatoire national de musique (1775), which receives everything published in France relating to music (200,000 vols.); the Bibliothèque du théâtre de l'Opéra (25,000 vols., 5000 songs, 20,000 romances, and a dramatic library of 12,000 vols. and 20,000 prints); the Théâtre français (40,000 vols.); the Académie de médecine (15,000 vols., 10,000 vols. of periodicals, 5000 portraits), l'Observatoire (18,400 vols.); the Bureau des Longitudes (15,000 vols. and 850 MSS.). The scholastic libraries are: L'École centrale des arts et manufactures (16,000 vols.), l'École coloniale (11,000 vols.); l'École d'application du service de santé militaire (23,000 vols.); l'École d'application du génie maritime (14,000 vols.); l'École libre des sciences politiques (25,000 vols., 250 periodicals); l'École normale d'instituteurs de la Seine (10,000 vols.); l'École normale israélite (30,000 vols., 250 MSS.); l'École nationale des ponts-et-chaussées (9000 vols., 5000 MSS., 5000 photographs), Bibliothèque de l'Institut catholique (160,000 vols.); l'Institut national agronomique (25,000 vols.); Faculté libre de théologie protestante (36,000 vols.); Conservatoire des arts et métiers (46,000 vols., 2500 maps and plans); Bibliothèque polonaise, administered by the Académie des Sciences de Cracovie (80,000 vols., 30,000 prints); Séminaire des Missions étrangères (25,000 vols.); l'Association Valentin Haüy, established 1885 (2000 vols. printed in relief) which lends out 40,000 books per annum; l'Association générale des Étudiants (22,000 vols.), which lends and allows reference on the premises to books by students; Bibliothèque de la Chambre de Commerce (40,000 vols.), the catalogues of which were printed in 1879, 1889 and 1902; the Société nationale d'agriculture (20,000 vols.); the Société d'anthropologie (25,000 vols.); the Société asiatique (12,000 vols., 200 MSS.); the Société chimique de France (10,000 vols.), the catalogue of which was published in 1907; the Société de chirurgie, dating from 1843 (20,000 vols.); the Société entomologique (30,000 vols.); the Société de géographie founded 1821 (60,000 vols., 6000 maps, 22,000 photographs, 2200 portraits, 80 MSS. of which the catalogue was printed in 1901); the Société géologique de France (15,000 vols., 30,000 specimens, 800 periodicals); the Société de l'histoire du protestantisme français, founded in 1852 (50,000 vols., 1000 MSS.; income 25,000 frs.); the Société d'encouragement pour l'industrie nationale (50,000 vols., income 8000 frs.), the Société des Ingénieurs civils (47,000 vols.; catalogue made in 1894); the Société de legislation comparée (15,000 vols., 4500 pamphlets); and lastly the Bibliothèque de la Société de Statistique de Paris, founded in 1860 (60,000 vols., with a printed catalogue).

Before the Revolution there were in Paris alone 1100 libraries containing altogether 2,000,000 vols. After the suppression of the religious orders the libraries were confiscated, and in 1791 more than 800,000 vols. were seized in 162 religious houses and transferred to eight literary foundations in accordance with a decree of November 14, 1789. In the provinces 6,000,000 vols. were seized and transferred to local depositories. The organization of the central libraries under the decree of 3 Brumaire An IV. (October 25, 1795) came to nothing, but the consular edict of January 28, 1803 gave definitive organization to the books in the local depositories. From that time the library system was reconstituted, alike in Paris and the provinces. Unfortunately many precious books and MSS. were burnt, since by the decree of 4 Brumaire An II. (October 25, 1793) the Committee of Instruction ordered, on the proposition of its president the deputy Romme, the destruction or modification of books and objects of art, under the pretext that they recalled the outward signs of feudalism.

The books in the provincial libraries, not including those in private hands or belonging to societies, number over 9,200,000 vols., 15,540 incunabula and 93,986 MSS. The number in the colonies and protected states outside France is uncertain, but it extends to more than 200,000 vols.; to this number must be added the 2,428,954 vols. contained in the university libraries. There are over 300 departmental libraries, and as many belong to learned societies. The increase in the provincial libraries is slower than that of the Parisian collections. With the exception of 26 libraries connected specially with the state, the others are municipal and are administered under state control by municipal librarians. The original foundation of most of the libraries dates but a short time before the Revolution, but there are a few exceptions. Thus the Bibliothèque d'Angers owes its first collection to Alain de la Rue about 1376; it now contains 72,485 vols., 134 incunabula and 2039 MSS. That of Bourges dates from 1466 (36,856 vols., 325 incunabula, 741 MSS.). The library of Carpentras was established by Michel Anglici between 1452 and 1474 (50,000 vols., 2154 MSS.). Mathieu de la Porte is said to be the founder of the library at Clermont-Ferrand at the end of the 15th century; it contained rather more than 49,000 vols. at the time of its [illegible] with the Bibliothèque Universitaire.

Libraries of the Departments.

[illegible] the libraries which date from the 16th century must be [illegible] that at Lyons founded by François I. in 1527; it possesses [illegible] vols., 870 incunabula and 5243 MSS. That of the Palais des [illegible] has 58,[illegible] vols., 64 incunabula and 311 MSS.

[illegible] 17th century were established the following libraries: [illegible] by Charles Sanson in 1685 (46,929 vols., 42 incunabula, [illegible] MSS.); Besançon by Abbé Boisot in 1696 (93,580 vols., 1000 [illegible] 2247 MSS.). In 1604 the Consistoire réformé de la [illegible] established a library which possesses to-day 58,900 vols., [illegible] incunabula, 1715 MSS. St Étienne, founded by Cardinal de [illegible] vols., 8 incunabula, 343 MSS.

[illegible] libraries founded during the 18th century are the [illegible] Aix-en-Provence, established by Tournon and Méjane in [illegible] vols., 300 incunabula, 1351 MSS.); Bordeaux, 1738 [illegible] MSS.); Chambéry, 1736 (64,200 vols., 47 in[illegible] MSS.); Dijon, 1701, founded by P. Fevret (125,000 [illegible] incunabula, [illegible] MSS.); Grenoble, 1772 (260,772 vols., [illegible] MSS.); Marseilles, 1799 (111,672 vols., 143 [illegible] MSS.); Nancy, founded in 1750 by Stanislas [illegible] incunabula, 1625 MSS.); Nantes, 1753 (103,328 [illegible] 2750 MSS.); Nice, founded in 1786 by Abbé [illegible] vols., 300 incunabula, 150 MSS.); Nîmes, founded by [illegible] in 1778 (80,000 vols., 61 incunabula, 675 MSS.); [illegible] and R. Bion in 1771 (40,413 vols., 67 incunabula [illegible] Perpignan, by Maréchal de Mailly in 1759 (27,200 [illegible] 127 MSS.); Rennes, 1733 (110,000 vols., 116 [illegible] MSS., income 6950 frs.); Toulouse, by archbishop [illegible] (213,000 vols., 859 incunabula, 1020 MSS.).

[illegible] municipal libraries date from the Revolution, [illegible] period of the redistribution of the books in 1803. [illegible] libraries possess more than 100,000 vols.: [illegible] vols., [illegible] incunabula, 4152 MSS.), of which the first [illegible] of Calvet in 1810; Caen (122,000 vols., 109 [illegible] MSS.); Montpellier (130,300 vols., 40 incunabula, [illegible] vols., 400 incunabula, 4000 MSS.); [illegible] incunabula, 1999 MSS.); Versailles (161,000 [illegible] MSS.).

[illegible] libraries with more than 50,000 volumes: [illegible] Brest, Douai, le Hâvre, Lille, le Mans, [illegible] and Verdun.

[illegible] greater part of the municipal libraries are [illegible] in the *Catalogues des MSS. des biblio-* [illegible], which began to appear in 1885; [illegible] volumes, and those of the provinces [illegible]

[illegible] provincial universities, thanks to their re[illegible] the care exhibited by the general in[illegible]. Aix has 74,058 vols.; Alger 160,489; [illegible] 216,278; Caen 127,542; Clermont [illegible] 127,400; Lille 215,427; Lyons [illegible] Montpellier 210,938; Nancy 139,036; [illegible] Toulouse 232,000.

[illegible] libraries have largely developed; in [illegible] in 1907 they were 44,021, con[illegible] purely scholastic libraries have de[illegible] libraries with 1,034,132 vols., [illegible] (Circulaire of March 14, 1904) there [illegible]. The Société Franklin pour la [illegible] populaires et militaires distributed [illegible] 55,185 vols., between the years [illegible]

The [illegible] been given for this account by [illegible] de Paris [illegible]. See also the following [illegible] received [illegible] organisation, [illegible] its con[illegible] [illegible] par [illegible] Départe[illegible] [illegible] des manuscrits, par Paul Marchal et Camille Couderc (Paris, 1907, 2 vols.); Félix Chambon, *Notes sur la bibliothèque de l'Université de Paris de 1763 à 1905* (Ganat, 1905); Fosseyeux, *La Bibliothèque des hôpitaux de Paris* (Revue des bibliothèques, t. 18, 1908); Alfred Franklin, *Guide des savants, des littérateurs et des artistes dans les bibliothèques de Paris* (Paris, 1908); *Instruction du 7 Mars 1809 sur l'organisation des bibliothèques militaires* (Paris, 1899); Henri Jadart, *Les Anciennes bibliothèques de Reims, leur sort en 1790–1791 et la formation de la bibliothèque publique* (Reims, 1891); Henry Marcel, *Rapport adressé au Ministre de l'Instruction Publique, sur l'ensemble des services de la bibliothèque nationale en 1905* (Journal Officiel, 1906); Henry Martin, *Histoire de la bibliothèque de l'Arsenal* (Paris, 1899); E. Morel, *Le Développement des bibliothèques publiques* (Paris, 1909); Théod. Mortreuil, *La Bibliothèque nationale, son origine et ses accroissements; notice historique* (Paris, 1878); Abbé L. V. Pécheur, *Histoire des bibliothèques publiques du département de l'Aisne existant à Soissons, Laon et Saint-Quentin* (Soissons, 1884); M. Poëte, E. Beaurepaire and E. Clouzot, *Une visite à la bibliothèque de la ville de Paris* (Paris, 1907); E. de Saint-Albin, *Les Bibliothèques municipales de la ville de Paris* (Paris, 1896); B. Subercaze, *Les Bibliothèques populaires, scolaires et pédagogiques* (Paris, 1892).

Germany (with Austria-Hungary and Switzerland).

Germany is emphatically the home of large libraries; her former want of political unity and consequent multiplicity of capitals have had the effect of giving her many large state libraries, and the number of her universities has tended to multiply considerable collections; 1617 libraries were registered by P. Schwenke in 1891. As to the conditions, hours of opening, &c., of 200 of the most important of them, there is a yearly statement in the *Jahrbuch der deutschen Bibliotheken*, published by the Verein deutscher Bibliothekare.

Germany.

The public libraries of the German empire are of four distinct types: state libraries, university libraries, town libraries and popular libraries. The administration and financial affairs of the state and university libraries are under state control. The earlier distinction between these two classes has become less and less marked. Thus the university libraries are no longer restricted to professors and students, but they are widely used by scientific workers, and books are borrowed extensively, especially in Prussia. In Prussia, as a link between the state and the libraries, there has been since 1907 a special office which deals with library matters at the Ministry of Public Instruction. Generally the state does not concern itself with the town libraries and the popular libraries, but there is much in common between these two classes. Sometimes popular libraries are under the supervision of a scientifically administered town library as in Berlin, Dantzig, &c.; elsewhere, as at Magdeburg, we see an ancient foundation take up the obligations of a public library. Only in Prussia and Bavaria are regulations in force as to the professional education of librarians. Since 1904 the librarians of the Prussian state libraries have been obliged to complete their university courses and take up their doctorate, after which they have to work two years in a library as volunteers and then undergo a technical examination. The secretarial officials since 1909 have to reach a certain educational standard and must pass an examination. This regulation has been in force as regards librarians in Bavaria from 1905.

Berlin is well supplied with libraries, 268 being registered by P. Schwenke and A. Hortzschansky in 1906, with about 5,000,000 printed vols. The largest of them is the Royal Library, which was founded by the "Great Elector" Frederick William, and opened as a public library in a wing of the electoral palace in 1661. From 1699 the library became entitled to a copy of every book published within the royal territories, and it has received many valuable accessions by purchase and otherwise. It now includes 1,230,000 printed vols. and over 30,000 MSS. The amount yearly expended upon binding and the acquisition of books, &c., is £11,326. The catalogues are in manuscript, and include two general alphabetical catalogues, the one in volumes, the other on slips, as well as a systematic catalogue in volumes. The following annual printed catalogues are issued: *Verzeichnis der aus der neu erschienenen Literatur von der K. Bibliothek und den Preussischen Universitäts-Bibliotheken erworbenen Druckschriften* (since 1892); *Jahresverzeichnis der an den Deutschen Universitäten erschienenen Schriften* (since 1887); *Jahresverzeichnis der an den Deutschen Schulanstalten erschienenen Abhandlungen* (since 1889). There is besides a printed *Verzeichnis der im grossen Lesesaal aufgestellten Handbibliothek* (4th ed. 1909), the alphabetical *Verzeichnis der laufenden Zeitschriften* (last ed., 1908), and the classified *Verzeichnis der laufenden Zeitschriften*

Berlin.

(1908). The catalogue of MSS. are mostly in print, vols. 1–13, 16–23 (1853–1905). The library is specially rich in oriental MSS., chiefly due to purchases of private collections. The musical MSS. are very remarkable and form the richest collection in the world as regards autographs. The building, erected about 1780 by Frederick the Great, has long been too small, and a new one was completed in 1909. The building occupies the whole space between the four streets: Unter den Linden, Dorotheenstrasse, Universitätsstrasse and Charlottenstrasse, and besides the Royal Library, houses the University Library and the Academy of Sciences. The conditions as to the use of the collections are, as in most German libraries, very liberal. Any adult person is allowed to have books in the reading-room. Books are lent out to all higher officials, including those holding educational offices in the university, &c., and by guarantee to almost any one recommended by persons of standing; borrowing under pecuniary security is also permitted. By special leave of the librarian, books and MSS. may be sent to a scholar at a distance, or, if especially valuable, may be deposited in some public library where he can conveniently use them. In 1908–1909 264,000 vols. were used in the reading-rooms, 312,000 were lent inside Berlin, and 32,000 outside. There is a regular system of exchange between the Royal Library and a great number of Prussian libraries. It is the same in Bavaria, Württemberg and Baden; the oldest system is that between Darmstadt and Giessen (dating from 1837). There is either no charge for carriage to the borrower or the cost is very small. The reading-room and magazine hall are, with the exception of Sundays and holidays, open daily from 9 to 9, the borrowing counter from 9 to 6.

Associated with the Royal Library are the following undertakings: the *Gesamtkatalog der Preussischen wissenschaftlichen Bibliotheken* (describing the printed books in the Royal Library and the Prussian University Libraries in one general catalogue upon slips), the Auskunftsbureau der Deutschen Bibliotheken (bureau to give information where any particular book may be consulted), and the Kommission für den Gesamtkatalog der Wiegendrucke (to draw up a complete catalogue of books printed before 1500).

The University Library (1831) numbers 220,000 vols. together with 250,000 academical and school dissertations. The number of volumes lent out in 1908–1909 was 104,000. The library possesses the right to receive a copy of every work published in the province of Brandenburg.

Some of the governmental libraries are important, especially those of the Statistisches Landesamt (184,000 vols.); Reichstag (181,000 vols.); Patent-Amt (118,000 vols.); Haus der Abgeordneten (100,000 vols.); Auswärtiges-Amt (118,000 vols.).

The public library of Berlin contains 102,000 vols.; connected therewith 28 municipal Volksbibliotheken and 14 municipal reading-rooms. The 28 Volksbibliotheken contain (1908) 194,000 vols.

The Prussian university libraries outside Berlin include Bonn (332,000 printed vols., 1500 MSS.); Breslau (330,000 printed vols., 3700 MSS.); Göttingen, from its foundation in 1736/7 the best administered library of the 18th century (552,000 printed vols., 6800 MSS.); Greifswald (200,000 printed vols., 800 MSS.), Halle (261,000 printed vols., 2000 MSS.); Kiel (278,000 printed vols., 2400 MSS.); Königsberg (287,000 printed vols., 1500 MSS.); Marburg (231,000 printed vols. and about 800 MSS.); Münster (191,000 printed vols., 800 MSS.). Under provincial administration are the Königliche and Provinzialbibliothek at Hanover (203,000 printed vols., 4000 MSS.); the Landesbibliothek at Cassel (230,000 printed vols., 4400 MSS.); and the Kaiser-Wilhelm-Bibliothek at Posen (163,000 printed vols.). A number of the larger towns possess excellent municipal libraries; Aix-la-Chapelle (112,000 vols.), Breslau (164,000 vols., 4000 MSS.); Dantzig (145,600 vols., 2900 MSS.); Frankfort a/M (342,000 vols. besides MSS.); Cassel Murhardsche Bibliothek (141,000 vols., 6300 MSS.); Cologne (235,000 vols.); Treves (100,000 vols., 2260 MSS.); Wiesbaden (158,000 vols.).

Munich. The libraries of Munich, though not so numerous as those of Berlin, include two of great importance. The Royal Library, for a long time the largest collection of books in Germany, was founded by Duke Albrecht V. of Bavaria (1550–1579), who made numerous purchases from Italy, and incorporated the libraries of the Nuremberg physician and historian Schedel, of Widmannstadt, and of J. J. Fugger. The number of printed vols. is estimated at about 1,100,000 and about 50,000 MSS. The library is especially rich in incunabula, many of them being derived from the libraries of over 150 monasteries closed in 1803. The oriental MSS. are numerous and valuable, and include the library of Martin Haug. The amount annually spent upon books and binding is £5000. The catalogues of the printed books are in manuscript, and include (1) a general alphabetical catalogue, (2) an alphabetical repertorium of each of the 195 subdivisions of the library, (3) biographical and other subject catalogues. A printed catalogue of MSS. in 8 vols. was in 1910 nearly complete; the first was published in 1858. The library is open on weekdays from 8 to 1 (November to March 8.30 to 1), and on Monday to Friday (except from August 1 to September 15) also from 3 to 8. The regulations for the use of the library are very similar to those of the Royal Library at Berlin. The building was erected for this collection under King Louis I in 1832–1843. The archives are bestowed on the ground floor, and the two upper floors are devoted to the library, which occupies seventy-seven apartments. The University Library was originally founded at Ingolstadt in 1472, and removed with the university to Munich in 1826. At present the number of vols. amounts to 550,000; the MSS. number 2000. Forty-six Munich libraries are described in Schwenke's *Adressbuch*, 15 of which possessed in 1909 about 2,000,000 printed vols. and about 60,000 MSS. After the two mentioned above the most noteworthy is the Königlich Bayrische Armee-Bibliothek (100,000 printed vols., 1000 MSS.).

The chief Bavarian libraries outside Munich are the Royal Library at Bamberg (350,000 vols., 4300 MSS.) and the University Library at Würzburg (390,000 vols., 1500 MSS.); both include rich monastic libraries. The University Library at Erlangen has 237,000 vols. The Staats-Kreis and Stadtbibliothek at Augsburg owns 200,000 vols. and 3000 MSS.; Nuremberg has two great collections, the Bibliothek des Germanischen National-museums (250,000 vols., 3550 MSS.) and the Stadtbibliothek (104,000 vols., 2500 MSS.).

Dresden. In 1906 there were in Dresden 78 public libraries with about 1,495,000 vols. The Royal Public Library in the Japanese Palace was founded in the 16th century. Among its numerous acquisitions have been the library of Count Bünau in 1764, and the MSS. of Ebert. Special attention is devoted to history and literature. The library possesses more than 520,000 vols. (1909); the MSS. number 6000. Admission to the reading-room is granted to any respectable adult on giving his name, and books are lent out to persons qualified by their position or by a suitable guarantee. Here, as at other large libraries in Germany, works of belles-lettres are only supplied for a literary purpose. The number of persons using the reading-room in a year is about 14,000, and about 23,000 vols. are lent. The second largest library in Dresden, the Bibliothek des Statistischen Landes-Amtes, has 120,000 vols.

Leipzig is well equipped with libraries; that of the University has 550,000 vols. and 6500 MSS. The Bibliothek des Reichsgerichts has 151,000 vols., the Pädagogische Central-Bibliothek der Comenius-Stiftung 150,000 vols., and the Stadtbibliothek 125,000 vols., with 1500 MSS.

Stuttgart. The Royal Public Library of Stuttgart, although only established in 1765, has grown so rapidly that it now possesses about 374,000 vols. of printed works and 5300 MSS. There is a famous collection of Bibles, containing over 7200 vols. The annual expenditure devoted to books and binding is £2475. The library also enjoys the copy-privilege in Württemberg. The annual number of borrowers is over 2600, who use nearly 29,000 vols. The number issued in the reading-room is 41,000. The number of parcels despatched from Stuttgart is nearly 23,000. Admission is also gladly granted to the Royal Private Library, founded in 1810, which contains about 137,000 vols.

Of the other libraries of Württemberg the University Library of Tübingen (500,000 vols. and 4100 MSS.) need only be noted.

Darmstadt. The Grand-ducal Library of Darmstadt was established by the grand-duke Louis I. in 1819, on the basis of the still older library formed in the 17th century, and includes 510,000 vols. and about 3600 MSS. (1909). The number of vols. used in the course of the year is about 90,000, of which 14,000 are lent out.

Among the other libraries of the Grand Duchy of Hesse the most remarkable are the University Library at Giessen (230,000 vols., 1500 MSS.), and the Stadtbibliothek at Mainz (220,000 vols., 1200 MSS.) to which is attached the Gutenberg Museum.

In the Grand Duchy of Baden are the Hof- and Landes-bibliothek at Carlsruhe (202,000 vols., 3800 MSS.), the University Library at Freiburg i/B (300,000 vols., 700 MSS.), and the University Library at Heidelberg. This, the oldest of the German University libraries, was founded in 1386. In 1623 the whole collection, described by Joseph Scaliger in 1608 as "locupletior et meliorum librorum quam Vaticana," was carried as a gift to the pope and only the German MSS. were afterwards returned. The library was re-established in 1703, and after 1800 enriched with monastic spoils; it now contains about 400,000 vols. and 3500 MSS. for the most part of great value.

Among the State or University libraries of other German states should be mentioned Detmold (110,000 vols.); Jena (264,000 vols.); Neustrelitz (130,000 vols.); Oldenburg (126,000 vols.); Rostock (275,000 vols.); Schwerin (225,000 vols.); and Weimar (270,000), all possessing rich collections of MSS.

Gotha. The Ducal Library of Gotha was established by Duke Ernest the Pious in the 17th century, and contains many valuable books and MSS. from monastic collections. It numbers about 192,000 vols., with 7400 MSS. The catalogue of the oriental MSS., chiefly collected by Seetzen, and forming one-half of the collection, is one of the best in existence.

The Ducal Library at Wolfenbüttel, founded in the second half of the 16th century by Duke Julius, was made over to the university of Helmstedt in 1614, whence the most important treasures were returned to Wolfenbüttel in the 19th century; it now numbers 300,000 vols., 7400 MSS.

The chief libraries of the Hanse towns are: Bremen (Stadtbibliothek, 141,000 vols.), and Lübeck (Stadtbibliothek, 121,000 vols.); the most important being the Stadtbibliothek at Hamburg, made public since 1648 (383,000 vols., 7300 MSS., among them many Mexican). Hamburg has also in the Kommerzbibliothek (120,000 vols.) a valuable trade collection, and the largest Volksbibliothek [illegible] vols.) after that at Berlin. Alsace-Lorraine has the [illegible] formed of the great German collections—the University [illegible] at Strassburg, which, though [illegible] in 1871 to replace that which had been destroyed in the [illegible] ranks amongst the largest libraries of the empire. [illegible] amount to 922,000 vols., the number of MSS. is 5900.

The *Adressbuch der Bibliotheken der Oesterreich-ungarischen Monarchie* by Bohatta and Holzmann (1900) describes 1014 libraries in Austria, 656 in Hungary, and 23 in Bosnia and Herzegovina. Included in this list, however, are private lending libraries.

Austria.

The largest library in Austria, and one of the most important collections in Europe, is the Imperial Public Library at Vienna, apparently founded by the emperor Frederick III. in 1440, although its illustrious librarian Lambecius, in the well-known inscription over the entrance to the library which summarizes its history attributes this honour to Frederick's son Maximilian. However this may be, the munificence of succeeding emperors greatly added to the wealth of the collection, including a not inconsiderable portion of the dispersed library of Corvinus. Since 1808 the library has also been entitled to the copy-privilege in respect of all books published in the empire. The sum devoted to the purchase and binding of books is £6068 annually. The number of printed vols. is 1,000,000; 8000 incunabula. The MSS. amount to 27,000, with 100,000 papyri of the collection of archduke Rainer. The main library apartment is one of the most splendid halls in Europe. Admission to the reading-room is free to everybody, and books are also lent out under stricter [illegible]. The University Library of Vienna was established by Maria Theresa. The reading-room is open to all comers, and the library is open from 1st Oct. to 30th June from 9 a.m. to [illegible] p.m.; in the other months for shorter hours. In 1909 [illegible] vols. were used in the library, 45,000 vols. lent out in Vienna, and 6529 vols. sent carriage free to borrowers outside Vienna. The number of printed vols. is 757,000. For the purchase of books and binding the Vienna University Library has annually [illegible] crowns from the state as well as 44,000 crowns from matriculation fees and contributions from the students.

The [illegible] number of libraries in Vienna enumerated by Bohatta and Holzmann is [illegible], and many of them are of considerable extent. [illegible] the oldest and most important libraries of the monarchy is the [illegible] at Cracow, with 380,000 vols. and 8169 MSS.

The number of monastic libraries in Austria is very considerable. [illegible] altogether more than 2,500,000 printed vols., 25,000 [illegible] and [illegible] MSS. The oldest of them, and the oldest in [illegible] was at the monastery of St Peter at Salzburg, which was [illegible] archbishop Arno (785–821). It includes 70,000 vols., [illegible] incunabula. The three next in point of antiquity are [illegible]), Admont (86,000) and Melk (70,000), all of [illegible] the 11th century. Many of the librarians of [illegible] libraries are trained in the great Vienna libraries [illegible] training as in Prussia and Bavaria.

[illegible] income, administration, accessions, &c., of [illegible] the Hungarian kingdom, are given in the [illegible] *Year Book* annually. The largest [illegible] Hungary is the Széchenyi-Nationalbibliothek [illegible] by the gift of the library of Count [illegible] 400,000 printed vols., 16,000 MSS., [illegible] of Hungarica. The University [illegible] 273,000 printed books and more [illegible] there has been in Hungary a Chief [illegible] Libraries whose duty is to watch [illegible] which are administered by [illegible] religious bodies and societies. He [illegible] organizing a general catalogue [illegible] books in Hungary.

[illegible] and other institutions of the [illegible] but not so numerous as in [illegible] library of the Benedictines at [illegible] the order in Hungary and [illegible] constituted in 1802 after the [illegible] principal treasures of this abbey [illegible] of the monasteries under [illegible] libraries in Budapest.

[illegible] numbered 2096 in 1868; [illegible] [illegible] 100,000 [illegible] he

Cantonal Library at Lausanne, and the Stadtbibliothek at Berne, which since 1905 is united to the University Library of that city. One great advantage of the Swiss libraries is that they nearly all possess printed catalogues, which greatly further the plan of compiling a great general catalogue of all the libraries of the republic. A valuable co-operative work is their treatment of Helvetiana. All the literature since 1848 is collected by the Landes-Bibliothek at Berne, established in 1895 for this special object. The older literature is brought together in the Bürgerbibliothek at Lucerne, for which it has a government grant. The monastic libraries of St Gall and Einsiedeln date respectively from the years 830 and 946, and are of great historical and literary interest.

Switzerland.

AUTHORITIES.—Information has been supplied for this account by Professor Dr A. Hortzschansky, librarian of the Royal Library, Berlin. See also *Adressbuch der deutschen Bibliotheken* by Paul Schwenke (Leipzig, 1893); *Jahrbuch der deutschen Bibliotheken* (Leipzig, 1902–1910); *Berliner Bibliothekenführer*, by P. Schwenke and A. Hortzschansky (Berlin, 1906); A. Hortzschansky, *Die K. Bibliothek zu Berlin* (Berlin, 1908); Ed. Zarncke, *Leipziger Bibliothekenführer* (Leipzig, 1909); J. Bohatta and M. Holzmann, *Adressbuch der Bibliotheken der österreich-ungarischen Monarchie* (Vienna, 1900); Ri. Kukula, *Die österreichischen Studienbibliotheken* (1905); A. Hittl, *Die österreichischen Klosterbibliotheken in den Jahren 1848–1908* (1908); P. Gulyas, *Das ungarische Oberinspektorat der Museen und Bibliotheken* (1909); *Die über 10,000 Bände zählenden öffentlichen Bibliotheken Ungarns, im Jahre 1908* (Budapest, 1910); H. Escher, "Bibliothekswesen" in *Handbuch der Schweizer Volkswirtschaft*, vol. i. (1903).

Italy.

As the former centre of civilization, Italy is, of course, the country in which the oldest existing libraries must be looked for, and in which the rarest and most valuable MSS. are preserved. The Vatican at Rome and the Laurentian Library at Florence are sufficient in themselves to entitle Italy to rank before most other states in that respect, and the venerable relics at Vercelli, Monte Cassino and La Cava bear witness to the enlightenment of the peninsula while other nations were slowly taking their places in the circle of Christian polity. The local rights and interests which so long helped to impede the unification of Italy were useful in creating and preserving at numerous minor centres many libraries which otherwise would probably have been lost during the progress of absorption that results from such centralization as exists in England. In spite of long centuries of suffering and of the aggression of foreign swords and foreign gold, Italy is still rich in books and MSS. The latest official statistics (1896) give particulars of 1831 libraries, of which 419 are provincial and communal. In 1893 there were 542 libraries of a popular character and including circulating libraries.

The governmental libraries (*biblioteche governative*) number 36 and are under the authority of the minister of public instruction. The *Regolamento* controlling them was issued in the *Bolletino Ufficiale*, 5 Dec. 1907. They consist of the national central libraries of Rome (Vittorio Emanuele) and Florence, of the national libraries of Milan (Braidense), Naples, Palermo, Turin and Venice (Marciana); the Biblioteca governativa at Cremona; the Marucelliana, the Mediceo-Laurenziana and the Riccardiana at Florence; the governativa at Lucca; the Estense at Modena; the Brancacciana and that of San Giacomo at Naples; the Palatina at Parma; the Angelica, the Casanatense, and the Lancisiana at Rome; the university libraries of Bologna, Cagliari, Catania, Genoa, Messina, Modena, Naples, Padua, Pavia, Pisa, Rome and Sassari; the Ventimiliana at Catania (joined to the university library for administrative purposes); the Vallicelliana and the musical library of the R. Accad. of St Cecilia at Rome; the musical section of the Palatine at Parma; and the Lucchesi-Palli (added to the national library at Naples). There are provisions whereby small collections can be united to larger libraries in the same place and where there are several government libraries in one city a kind of corporate administration can be arranged. The libraries belonging to bodies concerned with higher education, to the royal scientific and literary academies, fine art galleries, museums and scholastic institutions are ruled by special regulations. The minister of public instruction is assisted by a technical board.

Governmental libraries.

The librarians and subordinates are divided into (1) librarians, or keepers of MSS.; (2) sub-librarians, or sub-keepers of MSS.; (3) attendants, or book distributors; (4) ushers, &c. Those of class 1 constitute the "board of direction," which is presided over by the librarian, and meets from time to time to consider important measures connected with the administration of the library. Each library is to possess, alike for books and MSS., a general inventory, an accessions register, an alphabetical author-catalogue and a subject-catalogue. When they are ready, catalogues of the special collections are to be compiled, and these the government intends to print. A general catalogue of the MSS. was in 1910 being issued together with catalogues of oriental codices and incunabula. Various other small registers are provided for. The sums granted by the state for library purposes must be applied to (1) salaries and the catalogues of the MSS.; (2) maintenance and other expenses; (3) purchase of books, binding and repairs, &c. Books are chosen by the librarians. In the university libraries part of the expenditure is decided by the librarians, and part by a council formed by the professors of the different faculties. The rules (*Boll. Ufficiale*, Sept. 17, 1908) for lending books and MSS. allow them to be sent to other countries under special circumstances.

The 36 *biblioteche governative* annually spend about 300,000 lire in books. From the three sources of gifts, copyright and purchases, their accessions in 1908 were 142,930, being 21,122 more than the previous year. The number of readers is increasing. In 1908 there were 1,176,934, who made use of 1,650,542 vols., showing an increase of 30,456 readers and 67,579 books as contrasted with the statistics of the previous year. Two monthly publications catalogue the accessions of these libraries, one dealing with copyright additions of Italian literature, the other with all foreign books.

The minister of public instruction has kept a watchful eye upon the literary treasures of the suppressed monastic bodies. In 1875 there were 1700 of these confiscated libraries, containing two millions and a half of volumes. About 650 of the collections were added to the contents of the public libraries already in existence; the remaining 1050 were handed over to the different local authorities, and served to form 371 new communal libraries, and in 1876 the number of new libraries so composed was 415.

The Biblioteca Vaticana stands in the very first rank among European libraries as regards antiquity and wealth of MSS.

Vatican. We can trace back the history of the Biblioteca Vaticana to the earliest records of the *Scrinium Sedis Apostolicae*, which was enshrined in safe custody at the Lateran, and later on partly in the Turris Chartularia, but of all the things that used to be stored there, the only survival, and that is a dubious example, is the celebrated Codex Amiatinus now in the Laurentian Library at Florence. Of the new period inaugurated by Innocent III. there but remains to us the inventory made under Boniface VIII. The library shared in the removal of the Papal court to Avignon, where the collection was renewed and increased, but the Pontifical Library at Avignon has only in part, and in later times, been taken into the Library of the Vatican. This latter is a new creation of the great humanist popes of the 15th century. Eugenius IV. planted the first seed, but Nicholas V. must be looked upon as the real founder of the library, to which Sixtus IV. consecrated a definite abode, ornate and splendid, in the Court of the Pappagallo. Sixtus V. erected the present magnificent building in 1588, and greatly augmented the collection. The library increased under various popes and librarians, among the most noteworthy of whom were Marcello Cervini, the first *Cardinale Bibliotecario*, later Pope Marcel II., Sirleto and A. Carafa. In 1600 it was further enriched by the acquisition of the valuable library of Fulvio Orsini, which contained the pick of the most precious libraries. Pope Paul V. (1605–1621) separated the library from the archives, fixed the progressive numeration of the Greek and Latin MSS., and added two great halls, called the Pauline, for the new codices. Under him and under Urban VIII. a number of MSS. were purchased from the Convento of Assisi, of the Minerva at Rome, of the Capranica College, &c. Especially noteworthy are the ancient and beautiful MSS. of the monastery of Bobbio, and those which were acquired in various ways from the monastery of Rossano. Gregory XV. (1622) received from Maximilian I., duke of Bavaria, by way of compensation for the money supplied by him for the war, the valuable library of the Elector Palatine, which was seized by Count Tilly at the capture of Heidelberg. Alexander VII. (1658), having purchased the large and beautiful collection formerly belonging to the dukes of Urbino, added the MSS. of it to the Vatican library. The *Libreria della Regina*, *i.e.* of Christina, queen of Sweden, composed of very precious manuscripts from ancient French monasteries, from St Gall in Switzerland, and others—also of the MSS. of Alexandre Petau, of great importance for their history and French literature, was purchased and in great part presented to the Vatican library by Pope Alexander VIII. (Ottoboni) in 1689, while other MSS. came in later with the Ottoboni library. Under Clement XI. there was the noteworthy purchase of the 54 Greek MSS. which had belonged to Pius II., and also the increase of the collection of Oriental MSS. Under Benedict XIV. there came into the Vatican library, as a legacy, the library of the Marchese Capponi, very rich in rare and valuable Italian editions, besides 285 MSS.; and by a purchase, the Biblioteca Ottoboniana, which, from its wealth in Greek, Latin, and even Hebrew MSS., was, after that of the Vatican, the richest in all Rome. Clement XIII. in 1758, Clement XIV. in 1769, and Pius VI. in 1775 were also benefactors. During three centuries the vast and monumental library grew with uninterrupted prosperity, but it was to undergo a severe blow at the end of the 18th century. In 1798, as a sequel to the Treaty of Tolentino, 500 MSS. picked from the most valuable of the different collections were sent to Paris by the victorious French to enrich the Bibliothèque Nationale and other libraries. These, however, were chiefly restored in 1815. Most of the Palatine MSS., which formed part of the plunder, found their way back to the university of Heidelberg. Pius VII. acquired for the Vatican the library of Cardinal Zelada in 1800, and among other purchases of the 19th century must be especially noted the splendid Cicognara collection of archaeology and art (1823); as well as the library in 40,000 vols. of Cardinal Angelo Mai (1856). Recent more important purchases, during the Pontificate of Leo XIII., have been the Borghese MSS., about 300 in number, representing part of the ancient library of the popes at Avignon; the entire precious library of the Barberini; the Borgia collection *De Propaganda Fide*, containing Latin and Oriental MSS., and 500 incunabula.

Few libraries are so magnificently housed as the Biblioteca Vaticana. The famous *Codici Vaticani* are placed in the *salone* or great double hall, which is decorated with frescoes depicting ancient libraries and councils of the church. At the end of the great hall an immense gallery, also richly decorated, and extending to 1200 ft., opens out from right to left. Here are preserved in different rooms the codici Palatini, Regin., Ottoboniani, Capponiani, &c. The printed books only are on open shelves, the MSS. being preserved in closed cases. The printed books that were at first stored in the Borgia Apartment, now with the library of Cardinal Mai, constitute in great part the *Nuova Sala di Consultazione*, which was opened to students under the Pontificate of Leo XIII. Other books, on the other hand, are still divided into 1ª and 2ª raccolta, according to the ancient denomination, and are stored in adjacent halls.

Well-reasoned calculations place the total number of printed books at 400,000 vols.; of incunabula about 4000, with many vellum copies; 500 Aldines and a great number of bibliographical rarities. The Latin manuscripts number 31,373; the Greek amount to 4148; the Oriental MSS., of which the computation is not complete, amount to about 4000. Among the Greek and Latin MSS. are some of the most valuable in the world, alike for antiquity and intrinsic importance. It is sufficient to mention the famous biblical *Codex Vaticanus* of the 4th century, the two Virgils of the 4th and 5th centuries, the Bembo Terence, the palimpsest *De Republica* of Cicero, conjectured to be of the 4th century, discovered by Cardinal Mai, and an extraordinary

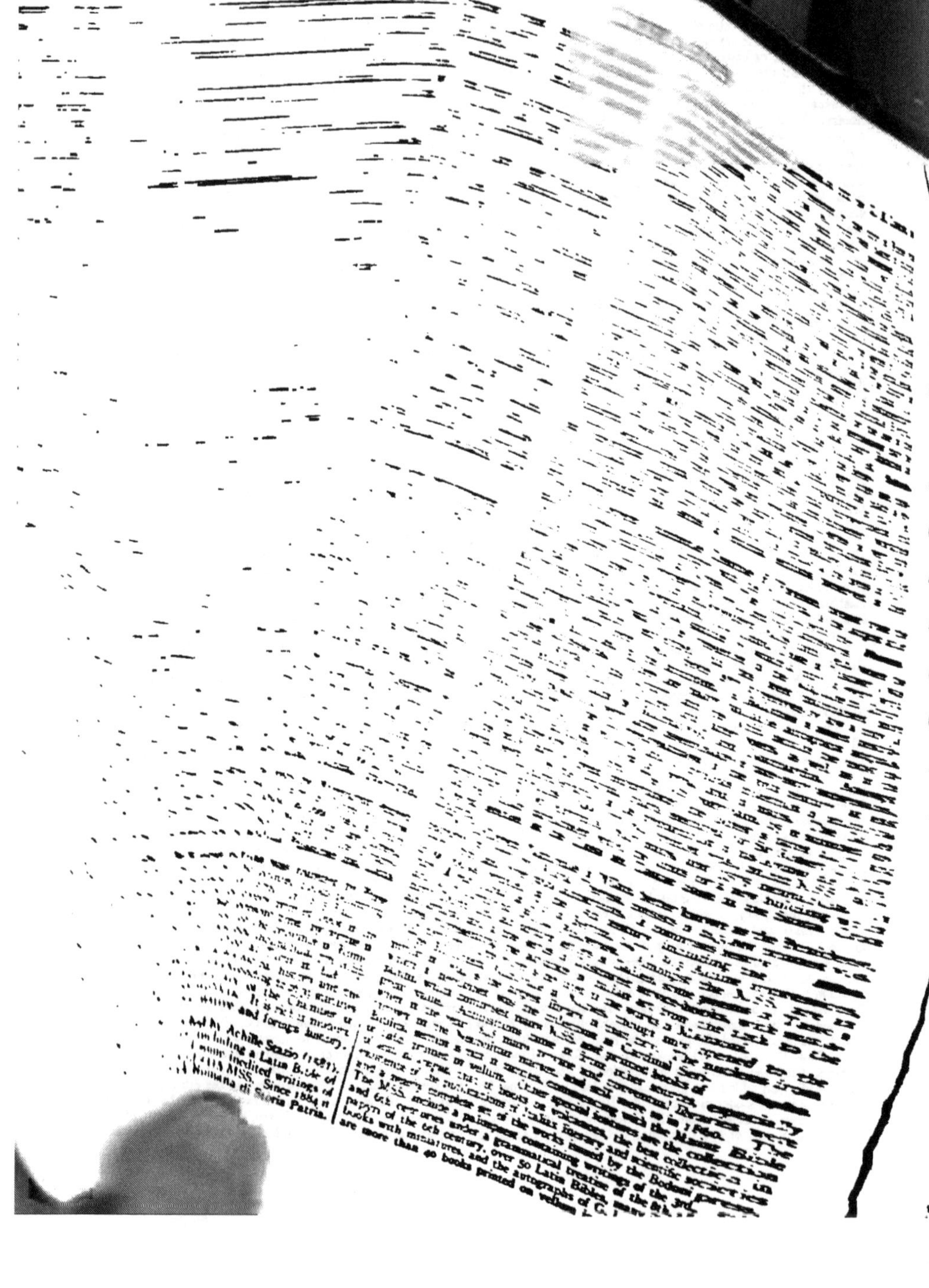
and foreign history.
Achille Sazio (1881),
including a Latin Bible of
inedited writings of
MSS. Since 1884
Romana di Storia Patria.
The MSS. include a palimpsest
works literary and scientific
over 50 Latin Bibles
are more than 40 books printed on vellum

centuries, including a fine first Homer; and several MS. maps and portolani, one dating from the end of the 14th century. The library contains about 389,100 printed vols., 7990 MSS. and 4217 incunabula.

Palermo.

The Biblioteca Nazionale of Palermo, founded from the Collegio Massimo of the Jesuits, with additions from other libraries of that suppressed order, is rich in 15th-century books, which have been elaborately described in a catalogue printed in 1875, and in Aldines and bibliographical curiosities of the 16th and following centuries, and a very complete series of the Sicilian publications of the 16th century, many being unique. The library contains 167,898 printed vols., 2550 incunabula, 1537 MSS.

Turin.

The Biblioteca Nazionale Universitatis of Turin took its origin in the donation of the private library of the House of Savoy, which in 1720 was made to the University by Vittorio Amedeo II. The disastrous fire of January 1904 destroyed about 24,000 out of the 300,000 vols. which the library possessed, and of the MSS., the number of which was 4138, there survive now but 1500 in a more or less deteriorated condition. Among those that perished were the palimpsests of Cicero, Cassidorus, the Codex Theodosianus and the famous *Livre d'Heures*. What escaped the fire entirely was the valuable collection of 1095 incunabula, the most ancient of which is the *Rationale Divinarum Officiorum* of 1459. Since the fire the library has been enriched by new gifts, the most conspicuous of which is the collection of 30,000 vols. presented by Baron Alberto Lumbroso, principally relating to the French Revolution and empire. The library was in 1910 about to be transferred to the premises of the Palazzo of the Debito Publico.

Venice.

The Biblioteca Marciana, or library of St Mark at Venice, was traditionally founded in 1362 by a donation of MSS. from the famous Petrarch (all of them now lost) and instituted as a library by Cardinal Bessarione in 1468. The printed vols. number 417,314. The precious contents include 12,106 MSS. of great value, of which more than 1000 Greek codices were given by Cardinal Bessarione, important MS. collections of works on Venetian history, music and theatre, rare incunabula, and a great number of volumes, unique or exceedingly rare, on the subject of early geographical research. Amongst the MSS. is a Latin Homer, an invaluable codex of the laws of the Lombards, and the autograph MS. of Sarpi's *History of the Council of Trent*. Since the fall of the republic and the suppression of the monasteries a great many private and conventual libraries have been incorporated with the Marciana, which had its first abode in the Libreria del Sansovino, from which in turn it was transferred in 1812 to the Palazzo Ducale, and from this again in 1904 to the Palazzo della Zecca (The Mint).

University Libraries.

Among the university libraries under government control some deserve special notice. First in historical importance comes the Biblioteca della Università at Bologna, founded by the naturalist U. Aldrovandi, who bequeathed by his will in 1605 to the senate of Bologna his collection of 3800 printed books and 360 MSS. Count Luigi F. Marsili increased the library by a splendid gift in 1712 and established an Istituto delle Scienze, reconstituted as a public library by Benedict XIV. in 1756. The printed books number 255,000 vols., and the MSS. 5000. The last comprise a rich Oriental collection of 547 MSS. in Arabic, 173 in Turkish, and several in Persian, Armenian and Hebrew. Amongst the Latin codices is a Lactantius of the 6th or 7th century. The other noteworthy articles include a copy of the Armenian gospels (12th century), the Avicenna, with miniatures dated 1194, described in Montfaucon's *Diarium Italicum*, and some unpublished Greek texts. Amongst the Italian MSS. is a rich assemblage of municipal histories. Mezzofanti was for a long time the custodian here, and his own collection of books has been incorporated in the library, which is remarkable likewise for the number of early editions and Aldines which it contains. A collection of drawings by Agostino Caracci is another special feature of worth. The grand hall with its fine furniture in walnut wood merits particular attention. The Biblioteca della Università at Naples was established by Joachim Murat in 1812 in the buildings of Monte Oliveto, and has thence been sometimes called the "Biblioteca Gioacchino." Later it was transferred to the Royal University of studies, and was opened to the public in 1827. It was increased by the libraries of several monastic bodies. The most copious collections relate to the study of medicine and natural science. It possesses about 300,000 printed books, 404 incunabula, 203 Aldines, and 196 Bodoni editions, but the more important incunabula and MSS. about the middle of the 19th century went to enrich the Biblioteca Nazionale. Other important university libraries are those of Catania (1755), 130,000 vols.; Genoa (1773), 132,000 vols., 1588 MSS.; Pavia (1763), 250,000 vols., 1100 MSS.; Padua (200,000 vols., 2356 MSS.), which in 1910 was housed in a new building; Cagliari (90,000 vols.); Sassari (74,000 vols.). Messina, destroyed in the earthquake of 1908, preserved, however, beneath its ruins the more important part of its furniture and fittings, and in 1910 was already restored to active work, as regards the portion serving for the reawakened Faculty of Law in the University.

Medicео-Laurenziana.

Chief among the remaining government libraries comes the world-famed Biblioteca Mediceo-Laurenziana at Florence, formed from the collections of Cosimo the Elder, Pietro de' Medici, and Lorenzo the Magnificent (which, however, passed away from the family after the expulsion of the Medici from Florence, and were repurchased in 1508 by Cardinal Giovanni, afterwards Leo X.). It was first constituted as a public library in Florence by Clement VII., who charged Michelangelo to construct a suitable edifice for its reception. It was opened to the public by Cosimo I. in 1571, and has ever since gone on increasing in value, the accessions in the 18th century alone being enough to double its former importance. The printed books it contains are probably no more than 11,000 in number, but are almost all of the highest rarity and interest, including 242 incunabula of which 151 *editiones principes*. It is, however, the precious collection of MSS., amounting to 9603 articles, which gives its chief importance to this library. They comprise more than 700 of dates earlier than the 11th century. Some of them are the most valuable codices in the world—the famous Virgil of the 4th or 5th century, Justinian's *Pandects* of the 6th, a Homer of the 10th, and several other very early Greek and Latin classical and Biblical texts, as well as copies in the handwriting of Petrarch, about 100 codices of Dante, a *Decameron* copied by a contemporary from Boccaccio's own MS., and Cellini's MS. of his autobiography. Bandini's catalogue of the MSS. occupies 13 vols. folio, printed in 1764–1778. Administratively united to the Laurentian is the Riccardiana rich in MSS. of Italian literature, especially the Florentine (33,000 vols., 3905 MSS.). At Florence the Biblioteca Marucelliana, founded in 1703, remarkable for its artistic wealth of early woodcuts and metal engravings, was opened to the public in 1753. The number of these and of original drawings by the old masters amounts to 80,000 pieces; the printed volumes number 200,000, the incunabula 620, and the MSS. 1500.

Modena.

At Modena is the famous Biblioteca Estense, so called from having been founded by the Este family at Ferrara in 1393; it was transferred to Modena by Cesare D'Este in 1598. Muratori, Zaccaria and Tiraboschi were librarians here, and made good use of the treasures of the library. It is particularly rich in early printed literature and valuable codices. Between 1859 and 1867 it was known as the Biblioteca Palatina. The printed vols. number 150,570, the incunabula 1600, the MSS. 3336, besides the 4958 MSS. and the 100,000 autographs of the Campori collection.

Parma.

The oldest library at Naples is the Biblioteca Brancacciana, with many valuable MSS. relating to the history of Naples. Two planispheres by Coronelli are preserved here. It was founded in 1673 by Cardinal F. M. Brancaccio, and opened by his heirs in 1675; 150,000 vols. and 3000 MSS. The Regia Biblioteca di Parma, founded definitively in 1779, owes its origin to the grand-duke Philip, who employed the famous scholar Paciaudi to organize it. It is now a public library containing 308,770 vols. and 4890 MSS. Amongst its treasures is De Rossi's magnificent collection of Biblical and rabbinical MSS. Also worthy of note are the Bibl. Pubblica or governation of Lucca (1600) with 214,000 vols., 725 incunabula and 3091 MSS. and that of Cremona (1774), united to that of the Museo Civico.

Ambrosiana.

Among the great libraries not under government control, the most important is the famous Biblioteca Ambrosiana at Milan, founded in 1609 by Cardinal Fed. Borromeo. It contains 230,000 printed vols. and 8400 MSS. Amongst the MSS. are a Greek Pentateuch of the 5th century, the famous Peshito and Syro-Hexaplar from the Nitrian convent of St Maria Deipara, a Josephus written on papyrus, supposed to be of the 5th century, several palimpsest texts, including an early Plautus, and St Jerome's commentary on the Psalms in a volume of 7th-century execution, full of contemporary glosses in Irish, Gothic fragments of Ulfilas, and a Virgil with notes in Petrarch's handwriting. Cardinal Mai was formerly custodian here. In 1879 Professor C. Mensinger presented his "Biblioteca Europea," consisting of 2500 vols., 300 maps and 5000 pieces, all relating to the literature and linguistics of European countries. The Melzi and Trivulzio libraries should not pass without mention here, although they are private and inaccessible without special permission. The former is remarkable for its collection of early editions with engravings, including the Dante of 1481, with twenty designs by Baccio Bandinelli. The latter is rich in MSS. with miniatures of the finest and rarest kind, and in printed books of which many are unique or nearly so. It consists of 70,000 printed vols. At Genoa the Biblioteca Franzoniana, founded about 1770 for the instruction of the poorer classes, is noteworthy as being the first European library lighted up at night for the use of readers.

Monte Cassino.

The foundation of the monastery of Monte Cassino is due to St Benedict, who arrived there in the year 529, and established the prototype of all similar institutions in western Europe. The library of printed books now extends to about 20,000 vols., chiefly relating to the theological sciences, but including some rare editions. A collection of the books belonging to the monks contains about the same number of volumes. But the chief glory of Monte Cassino consists of the *archivio*, which is quite apart; and this includes more than 30,000 bulls, diplomas, charters and other documents, besides 1000 MSS. dating from the 6th century downwards. The latter comprehend some very early Bibles and important codices of patristic and other medieval writings. There are good written catalogues, and descriptions with extracts are published in the *Bibliotheca Casinensis*. The monastery was declared a national monument in 1866. At Ravenna the Biblioteca Classense [illegible] codex of Aristophanes and two 14th-century [illegible]. At Vercelli the Biblioteca dell' Archivio Capitolare, [illegible] foundation of which can be assigned to no certain date, [illegible] cannot be referred to the early days when the barbarian [illegible] finally had become christianized, comprises nothing but [illegible] of great antiquity and value. Amongst them is an Evangel[illegible] in Latin, supposed to be of the 4th century; also [illegible] containing the Anglo-Saxon homilies which have [illegible] by the Ælfric Society.

The Biblioteca del Monastero della S. Trinità, at La Cava dei Tirreni [illegible] of Salerno, is said to date from the foundation of the abbey itself (beginning of the 11th century). It [illegible] only some 40,000 vols., but these include a [illegible] MSS. of very great rarity and value, ranging from the [illegible] century. Amongst these is the celebrated Codex [illegible], dated 1023, besides a well-known geographi[illegible] 14th century, over 100 Greek MSS., and about 1000 [illegible] with the year 840, more than 200 of which belong [illegible] and Norman periods. The library is now national [illegible] holding the office of Keeper of the Archives.

[illegible] of the communal and municipal libraries are of great [illegible]: Bologna (1801), 191,000 vols., 5060 MSS.; [illegible], 125,000 vols., 1500 MSS.; Ferrara (1753), [illegible] MSS., many Ferrarese rarities; Macerata, the [illegible] (1855), 50,000 vols.; Mantua, [illegible] MSS.; Novara, Negroni e Civica (1847 and 1890), [illegible], 30,000 vols., 1600 MSS.; Palermo (1760), [illegible] MSS., coins and Sicilian collection; Perugia [illegible] by F. Podiani, 70,000 vols., 915 MSS.; Siena [illegible] by S. Bandini, fine art collection, 83,250 vols., 5070 [illegible] Museo Civico Correr, 50,000 vols., 11,000 MSS.; [illegible] (1868), 180,000 vols., 2650 MSS.; Vicenza, [illegible] local literature, archives of religious corporations, [illegible] MSS.

[illegible] have now been largely developed in Italy, chiefly [illegible] or municipal enterprise; they enjoy a small state [illegible]. The government report for 1908 stated that [illegible] *biblioteche popolari* numbering altogether [illegible] 353 were established by municipalities, 113 by [illegible], 80 by working men's societies and [illegible] of religion; 225 are open to the public, 358 lend [illegible], and 127 on payment of a small fee. In order [illegible] throughout the kingdom, a *Bollettino* [illegible] at Milan since 1907, and a National Congress was [illegible] in December 1908.

[illegible] has been given for this account by Dr G. Staderini [illegible] Biblioteca Casanatense, Rome. See also F. Bluhme, *Iter* [illegible] 1824–1836); *Notizie sulle biblioteche governative* [illegible] (Roma, 1893); *Le biblioteche governative Italiane* [illegible] (Roma, 1900); *Statistica delle biblioteche* (Roma, 1893–[illegible]); *Le biblioteche popolari in Italia, relazione al Ministro* [illegible] (Roma, 1898); *Bollettino delle biblioteche* [illegible] (Milano, 1907, in progress); E. Fabietti, *Manuale per le biblioteche popolari* ([illegible] edit., Milano); *Le biblioteche pop. al 1° Congresso* [illegible] 1908 (Milano, 1910).

Latin America.

Much interest in libraries has not been shown in south, central and other parts of Latin America. Most of the libraries which exist are national or legislative libraries.

As the libraries of the republic of Cuba are more Spanish than [illegible] in character, it will be convenient to consider them here. The chief libraries are in Havana, and the best are the Biblioteca Publica and the University Library. The [illegible] Publica has within recent years been completely over[illegible] and is now one of the most actively-managed libraries in [illegible].

[illegible] of the twenty-nine states and territories of the Mexican [illegible] about half have public libraries, and only a small proportion [illegible] of the contents consists of modern literature. Many [illegible] possess rare and valuable books, of interest to the biblio[illegible], which have come from the libraries of the sup[illegible]. There is a large number of scientific and [illegible] in the republic, each possessing books. The Society [illegible] and Statistics, founded in 1851 in Mexico City, [illegible] of them, and owns a fine museum and excellent [illegible] of the Liberal party the cathedral, uni[illegible] libraries of the city of Mexico came into the [illegible], and steps were taken to form them into [illegible]. No definite system was organized, however, [illegible] when the church of San Augustin was taken and fitted up [illegible]. In 1884 it was opened as the Biblioteca Nacional, [illegible] some 200,000 vols. Two copies of every book [illegible] must be presented to this library. Most of the [illegible], city or provincial, are subscription, and belong [illegible] of various kinds.

Argentina.

The importance of public libraries has been fully recognized in Argentina, and more than two hundred of these are in the country. They are due to benefactions, but the government in every case adds an equal sum to any endowment. A central commission exists for the purpose of facilitating the acquisition of books and to promote a uniform excellence of administration. The most considerable is the Biblioteca Nacional at Buenos Aires, which is peculiarly rich in MSS., some of great interest, concerning the early history of the Spanish colonies. There is also the Biblioteca Municipal with about 25,000 vols. There are libraries attached to colleges, churches and clubs, and most of the larger towns possess public libraries.

Brazil.

The chief library in Brazil is the Bibliotheca Publica Nacional at Rio de Janeiro (1807) now comprising over 250,000 printed vols. with many MSS. National literature and works connected with South America are special features of this collection. A handsome new building has been erected which has been fitted up in the most modern manner. Among other libraries of the capital may be mentioned those of the Faculty of Medicine, Marine Library, National Museum, Portuguese Literary Club, Bibliotheca Fluminense, Benedictine Monastery, and the Bibliotheca Municipal. There are various provincial and public libraries throughout Brazil, doing good work, and a typical example is the public library of Maranhão.

Chile.

The Biblioteca Nacional at Santiago is the chief library in Chile. The catalogue is printed, and is kept up by annual supplements. It possesses about 100,000 vols. There is also a University Library at Santiago, and a fairly good Biblioteca Publica at Valparaiso.

Peru.

The Biblioteca Nacional at Lima was founded by a decree of the liberator San Martin on the 28th of August 1821, and placed in the house of the old convent of San Pedro. The nucleus of the library consisted of those of the university of San Marcos and of several monasteries, and a large present of books was also made by San Martin. The library is chiefly interesting from containing so many MSS. and rare books relating to the history of Peru in vice-regal times.

Spain and Portugal.

Most of the royal, state and university libraries of Spain and Portugal have government control and support. In Portugal the work of the universities is to a certain extent connected up, and an official bulletin is published in which the laws and accessions of the libraries are contained.

The chief library in Spain is the Biblioteca Nacional (formerly the Biblioteca Reall at Madrid. The printed volumes number 600,000 with 200,000 pamphlets. Spanish literature is of course well represented, and, in consequence of the numerous accessions from the libraries of the suppressed convents, the classes of theology, canon law, history, &c., are particularly complete. There are 30,000 MSS., including some finely illuminated codices, historical documents, and many valuable autographs. The collection of prints extends to 120,000 pieces, and was principally formed from the important series bought from Don Valentin Carderera in 1865. The printed books have one catalogue arranged under authors' names, and one under titles; the departments of music, maps and charts, and prints have subject-catalogues as well. There is a general index of the MSS., with special catalogues of the Greek and Latin codices and genealogical documents. The cabinet of medals is most valuable and well arranged. Of the other Madrid libraries it is enough to mention the Biblioteca de la Real Academia de la Historia, 1758 (20,000 vols. and 1500 MSS.), which contains some printed and MS. Spanish books of great value, including the well-known Salazar collection. The history of the library of the Escorial (*q.v.*) has been given elsewhere. In 1808, before the invasion, the Escorial is estimated to have contained 30,000 printed vols. and 3400 MSS.; Joseph removed the collection to Madrid, but when it was returned by Ferdinand 10,000 vols. were missing. There are now about 40,000 printed vols. The Arabic MSS. have been described by M. Casiri, 1760–1770; and a catalogue of the Greek codices by Müller was issued at the expense of the French government in 1848. There is a MS. catalogue of the printed books. Permission to study at the Escorial, which is one of the royal private libraries, must be obtained by special application. The Biblioteca Provincial y Universitaria of Barcelona (1841) contains about 155,000 vols., and that of Seville (1767) has 82,000 vols. Other cities in Spain possess provincial or university libraries open to students under various restrictions, among them may be mentioned the Biblioteca Universitaria of Salamanca (1254) with over 80,000 vols.

Portugal.

Among the libraries of Portugal the Bibliotheca Nacional at Lisbon (1796) naturally takes the first place. In 1841 it was largely increased from the monastic collections, which, however, seem to have been little cared for according to a report prepared by the principal librarian three years later. There are now said to be 400,000 vols. of printed books, among which theology, canon law, history and Portuguese and Spanish literature largely predominate. The MSS. number 16,000 including many of great value. There is also a cabinet of 40,000 coins and medals. The Bibliotheca da Academia, founded in 1780, is preserved in the suppressed convent of the Ordem Terceira da Penitencia. In 1836 the Academy acquired the library of that convent, numbering 30,000 vols., which have since been kept apart. The Archivo Nacional, in the same building, contains the archives of the kingdom, brought here after the destruction of the Torre do Castello during the great earthquake.

The Biblioteca Publica Municipal at Oporto is the second largest in Portugal, although only dating from the 9th of July 1833, the anniversary of the debarcation of D. Pedro, and when the memorable siege was still in progress; from that date to 1874 it was styled the Real Biblioteca do Porto. The regent (ex-emperor of Brazil) gave to the town the libraries of the suppressed convents in the northern provinces, the municipality undertaking to defray the expense of keeping up the collection. Recent accessions consist mainly of Portuguese and French books. The important Camoens collection is described in a printed catalogue (Oporto, 1880). A notice of the MSS. may be found in *Catalogo dos MSS. da B. Publica Eborense*, by H. da Cunha Rivara (Lisbon, 1850–1870), 3 vols. folio, and the first part of an *Indice preparatorio do Catalogo dos Manuscriptos* was produced in 1880. The University Library of Coimbra (1591) contains about 100,000 vols., and other colleges possess libraries.

Netherlands.

Since 1900 there has been considerable progress made in both Belgium and Holland in the development of public libraries, and several towns in the latter country have established popular libraries after the fashion of the municipal libraries of the United Kingdom and America.

Belgium.

The national library of Belgium is the Bibliothèque Royale at Brussels, of which the basis may be said to consist of the famous Bibliothèque des ducs de Bourgogne, the library of the Austrian sovereigns of the Low Countries, which had gradually accumulated during three centuries. After suffering many losses from thieves and fire, in 1772 the Bibliothèque de Bourgogne received considerable augmentations from the libraries of the suppressed order of Jesuits, and was thrown open to the public. On the occupation of Brussels by the French in 1794 a number of books and MSS. were confiscated and transferred to Paris (whence the majority were returned in 1815); in 1795 the remainder were formed into a public library under the care of La Serna Santander, who was also town librarian, and who was followed by van Hulthem. At the end of the administration of van Hulthem a large part of the precious collections of the Bollandists was acquired. In 1830 the Bibliothèque de Bourgogne was added to the state archives, and the whole made available for students. Van Hulthem died in 1832, leaving one of the most important private libraries in Europe, described by Voisin in *Bibliotheca Hulthemiana* (Brussels, 1836), 5 vols., and extending to 60,000 printed vols. and 1016 MSS., mostly relating to Belgian history. The collection was purchased by the government in 1837, and, having been added to the Bibliothèque de Bourgogne (open since 1772) and the Bibliothèque de la Ville (open since 1794), formed what has since been known as the Bibliotheque Royale de Belgique. The printed volumes now number over 600,000 with 30,000 MSS., 105,000 prints and 80,000 coins and medals. The special collections, each with a printed catalogue, consist of the Fonds van Hulthem, for national history; the Fonds Fétis, for music; the Fonds Goethals, for genealogy; and the Fonds Müller, for physiology. The catalogue of the MSS. has been partly printed, and catalogues of accessions and other departments are also in course of publication. There are libraries attached to most of the departments of the government, the ministry of war having 120,000 vols. and the ministry of the interior, 15,000 vols. An interesting library is the Bibliothèque Collective des Sociétés Savantes founded in 1906 to assemble in one place the libraries of all the learned societies of Brussels. It contains about 40,000 vols. which have been catalogued on cards. The Bibliothèque du Conservatoire royal de Musique (1832) contains 12,000 vols. and 6000 dramatic works. The popular or communal libraries of Brussels contain about 30,000 vols. and those of the adjoining suburbs about 50,000 vols., most of which are distributed through the primary and secondary schools. At Antwerp the Stadt Bibliothek (1805) has now 70,000 vols., and is partly supported by subscriptions and endowments. The valuable collection of books in the Musée Plantin-Moretus (1640) should also be mentioned. It contains 11,000 MSS. and 15,000 printed books, comprising the works issued by the Plantin family and many 15th-century books.

The University Library of Ghent, known successively as the Bibliothèque de l'École Centrale and Bibliothèque Publique de la Ville, was founded upon the old libraries of the Conseil de Flandres, of the College des Échevins, and of many suppressed religious communities. It was declared public in 1797, and formally opened in 1798. On the foundation of the university in 1817 the town placed the collection at its disposal, and the library has since remained under state control. The printed volumes now amount to 353,000. There are important special collections on archaeology, Netherlands literature, national history, books printed in Flanders, and 23,000 historical pamphlets of the 16th and 17th centuries. The main catalogue is in MS. on cards. There are printed catalogues of the works on jurisprudence (1839), and of the MSS. (1852). The Bibliothèque de l'Université Catholique of Louvain is based upon the collection of Beyerlinck, who bequeathed it to his alma mater in 1627; this example was followed by Jacques Romain, professor of medicine, but the proper organization of the library began in 1636. There are now said to be 211,000 vols. The Bibliothèque de l'Université of Liége dates from 1817, when on the foundation of the university the old Bibliothèque de la Ville was added to it. There are now 350,000 printed vols., pamphlets, MSS., &c. The Liége collection (of which a printed catalogue appeared in 3 vols. 8vo., 1872), bequeathed by M. Ulysse Capitaine, extends to 12,061 vols. and pamphlets. There are various printed catalogues. The Bibliothèques Populaires of Liége established in 1862, now number five, and contain among them 50,000 vols. which are circulated to the extent of 130,000 per annum among the school children. The Bibliothèque publique of Bruges (1798) contains 145,600 printed books and MSS., housed in a very artistic building, once the Tonlieu or douane, 1477. There are communal libraries at Alost, Arlon (1842), Ath (1842), Courtrai, Malines (1864), Mons (1797), Namur (1800), Ostend (1861), Tournai (1794, housed in the Hôtel des Anciens Prêtres, 1755), Ypres (1839) and elsewhere, all conducted on the same system as the French communal libraries. Most of them range in size from 5000 to 40,000 vols. and they are open as a rule only part of the day. Every small town has a similar library, and a complete list of them, together with much other information, will be found in the *Annuaire de la Belgique, scientifique, artistique et littéraire* (Brussels 1908 and later issues).

Holland.

The national library of Holland is the Koninklijke Bibliotheek at Hague, which was established in 1798, when it was decided to join the library of the princes of Orange with those of the defunct government bodies in order to form a library for the States-General, to be called the National Bibliotheek. In 1805 the present name was adopted; and since 1815 it has become the national library. In 1848 the Baron W. Y. H. van Westreenen van Tiellandt bequeathed his valuable books, MSS., coins and antiquities to the country, and directed that they should be preserved in his former residence as a branch of the royal library. There are now upwards of 500,000 vols. of printed books, and the MSS. number 6000, chiefly historical, but including many fine books of hours with miniatures. Books are lent all over the country. The library boasts of the richest collection in the world of books on chess, Dutch incunabula, Elzevirs and Spinozana. There is one general written catalogue arranged in classes, with alphabetical indexes. In 1800 a printed catalogue was issued, with four supplements down to 1811; and since 1866 a yearly list of additions has been published. Special mention should be made of the excellent catalogue of the incunabula published in 1856.

The next library in numerical importance is the famous Bibliotheca Academiae Lugduno-Batavae, which dates from the foundation of the university of Leiden by William I., prince of Orange, on the 8th of February 1575. It has acquired many valuable additions from the books and MSS. of the distinguished scholars, Golius, Joseph Scaliger, Isaac Voss, Ruhnken and Hemsterhuis. The MSS. comprehend many of great intrinsic importance. The library of the Society of Netherland Literature has been placed here since 1877; this is rich in the national history and literature. The Arabic and Oriental MSS. known as the Legatum Warnerianum are of great value and interest; and the collection of maps bequeathed in 1870 by J. J. Bodel Nyenhuis is also noteworthy. The library is contained in a building which was formerly a church of the Béguines, adapted in 1860 somewhat after the style of the British Museum. The catalogues (one alphabetical and one classified) are on slips, the titles being printed. A catalogue of books and MSS. was printed in 1716, one of books added between 1814 and 1847 and a supplementary part of MSS. only in 1850. A catalogue of the Oriental MSS. was published in 6 vols. (1851–1877). The Bibliotheek der Rijks Universiteit (1575) at Leiden contains over 190,000 vols.

The University Library at Utrecht dates from 1582, when certain conventual collections were brought together in order to form a public library, which was shortly afterwards enriched by the books bequeathed by Hub. Buchelius and Ev. Pollio. Upon the foundation of the university in 1636, the town library passed into its charge. Among the MSS. are some interesting cloister MSS. and the famous "Utrecht Psalter," which contains the oldest text of the Athanasian creed. The last edition of the catalogue was in 2 vols. folio, 1834, with supplement in 1845, index from 1845–1855 in 8vo., and additions 1856–1870, 2 vols. 8vo. A catalogue of the MSS. was issued in 1887. The titles of accessions are now printed in sheets and pasted down for insertion. There are now about 250,000 vols. in the library.

The basis of the University Library at Amsterdam consists of a collection of books brought together in the 15th century and preserved in the Nieuwe Kerk. At the time of the Reformation in 1578 they became the property of the city, but remained in the Nieuwe Kerk for the use of the public till 1632, when they were transferred to the Athenaeum. Since 1877 the collection has been known as the University Library, and in 1881 it was removed to a building designed upon the plan of the new library and reading-room of the British Museum. The library includes the best collection of medical works in Holland, and the Bibliotheca Rosenthaliana of Hebrew and Talmudic literature is of great fame and value; a catalogue of the last was printed in 1875. The libraries of the Dutch Geographical, and other societies are preserved here. A general printed catalogue was issued in 6 vols. 8vo., Amsterdam (1856–1877); one describing the bequests of J. de Bosch Kemper, E. J. Potgieter and F. W. Rive, in 3 vols., 8vo. (1878–1879); a catalogue of the MSS. of Professor [illegible] was published in 1880, and one of those of P. Camper in 1881. Other catalogues have been published up to 1902, including one of the MSS. The library contains about half a million volumes. There are popular subscription libraries with reading-rooms in all parts of Holland, and in Rotterdam there is a society for the encouragement of social culture which has a large library as part of its equipment. [illegible] Hague, Leiden, Haarlem, Dordrecht and other towns popular libraries have been established, and there is a movement of recent growth in favour of training librarians on advanced English lines.

The library of the Genootschap van Kunsten en Wetenschappen at Batavia contains books printed in Netherlandish India, works relating to the Indian Archipelago and adjacent countries, and the history of the Dutch in the East. There are 20,000 printed vols. and [illegible] MSS., of which 243 are Arabic, 445 Malay, 303 Javanese, 60 Batak and 517 on lontar leaves, in the ancient Kawi, Javanese and Bali languages, &c. Printed catalogues of the Arabic, Malay, Javanese and Kawi MSS. have been issued.

Scandinavia.

Owing largely to so many Scandinavian librarians having been trained and employed in American libraries, a greater approach has been made to Anglo-American library ideals in Norway, Sweden and Denmark than anywhere else on the continent of Europe.

Denmark. The beginning of the admirably managed national library of Denmark, the great Royal Library at Copenhagen (Det Store Kongelige Bibliothek) may be said to have taken place during the reign of Christian III. (1533–1559), who took pride in importing foreign books and choice MSS.; but the true founder was Frederick III. (1648–1670); to him is mainly due the [illegible] collection of Icelandic literature and the acquisition of Tycho Brahe's MSS. The present building (in the Christiansborg castle) was begun in [illegible]. Among notable accessions may be mentioned the collections of C. Reitzer, the count of Danneskjöld (8000 vols. [illegible] MSS.) and Count de Thott; the last bequeathed 6039 vols. printed before 1531, and the remainder of his books, over 100,000 vols., [illegible] purchased. In 1793 the library was opened to the public, [illegible] remained under state control. Two copies [illegible] published within the kingdom must be deposited here. [illegible] and block books form an important series. There is [illegible] catalogue in writing for the use of readers; and [illegible] arranged in boxes for the officials. A [illegible] de Thott collection was printed in 12 vols. 8vo. [illegible] catalogue of the French MSS. appeared in 1844; [illegible] of the Danish collection, 1875, 8vo. Annual [illegible] notable MSS. have been published since 1864. [illegible] over 750,000 vols.

[illegible] founded in 1482, was destroyed by fire [illegible] shortly afterwards. A copy of every [illegible] be deposited here. The MSS. include the [illegible] collection. There are now about 400,000 [illegible] The Statsbiblioteket of Aarhus (1902) possesses [illegible] and the Landsbókasafn Islands (National [illegible] Iceland, has about 50,000 printed books and [illegible] there are 11 popular libraries supported [illegible] are at least 50 towns in the provinces [illegible] some cases reading-rooms. An associa[illegible] libraries was formed in 1905, and in 1909 [illegible] appointed a special adviser in [illegible] the towns and villages are aided by the [illegible] state and local authorities, and it is [illegible] them 500,000 vols., and circulate [illegible]

[illegible] the University Library at Christiania, [illegible] the university, September 2nd, 1811, [illegible] donation from the king of many [illegible] from the Royal Library at [illegible] by important bequests. Annual [illegible] now over 420,000 vols. in the [illegible] in Christiania was founded [illegible] library. In 1898 it was reorgan[illegible] was installed by Haakon [illegible] trained in the United States. [illegible] partly by grants from [illegible] vols., and is a typical [illegible] Library at Bergen (1872) [illegible] been re-housed in a new [illegible] has also been opened at [illegible] the Kongelige Videns[illegible] about 120,000 vols. [illegible] in Norway, most of [illegible]

Gustavus II., that formed by Christina is at the Vatican, and the library brought together by Charles X. was destroyed by fire in 1697. The present library was organized shortly afterwards. The Benzelstjerna-Engeström Library (14,500 printed vols. and 1200 MSS.) rich in materials for Swedish history) is now annexed to it. Natural history, medicine and mathematics are left to other libraries. Among the MSS. the *Codex Aureus* of the 6th or 7th century, with its interesting Anglo-Saxon inscription, is particularly noteworthy. The catalogues are in writing, and are both alphabetical and classified; printed catalogues have been issued of portions of the MSS. The present building was opened in 1882. The library now contains about 320,000 printed books and over 11,000 MSS. The Karolinska Institutet in Stockholm, contains a library of medical books numbering over 40,000. **Sweden.**

The University Library at Upsala was founded by Gustavus Adolphus in 1620, from the remains of several convent libraries; he also provided an endowment. The MSS. chiefly relate to the history of the country, but include the *Codex Argenteus*, containing the Gothic gospels of Ulfilas. The general catalogue is in writing. A catalogue was printed in 1814; special lists of the foreign accessions have been published each year from 1850; the Arabic, Persian and Turkish MSS. are described by C. J. Tornberg, 1846. It now contains about 340,000 printed books and MSS. The library at Lund dates from the foundation of the university in 1668, and was based upon the old cathedral library. The MSS. include the de la Gardie archives, acquired in 1848. There are about 200,000 vols. in the library. The Stadsbibliotek of Gothenburg contains about 100,000 vols., and has a printed catalogue.

Russia.

The imperial Public Library at St Petersburg is one of the largest libraries in the world, and now possesses about 1,800,000 printed vols. and 34,000 MSS., as well as large collections of maps, autographs, photographs, &c. The beginning of this magnificent collection may be said to have been the books seized by the Czar Peter during his invasion of Courland in 1714; the library did not receive any notable augmentation, however, till the year 1795, when, by the acquisition of the famous Zaluski collection, the Imperial Library suddenly attained a place in the first rank among great European libraries. The Zaluski Library was formed by the Polish count Joseph Zaluski, who collected at his own expense during forty-three years no less than 200,000 vols., which were added to by his brother Andrew, bishop of Cracow, by whom in 1747 the library was thrown open to the public. At his death it was left under the control of the Jesuit College at Warsaw; on the suppression of the order it was taken care of by the Commission of Education; and finally in 1795 it was transferred by Suwaroff to St Petersburg as a trophy of war. It then extended to 260,000 printed vols. and 10,000 MSS., but in consequence of the withdrawal of many medical and illustrated works to enrich other institutions, hardly 238,000 vols. remained in 1810. Literature, history and theology formed the main features of the Zaluski Library; the last class alone amounted to one-fourth of the whole number. Since the beginning of the 19th century, through the liberality of the sovereigns, the gifts of individuals, careful purchases, and the application of the law of 1810, whereby two copies of every Russian publication must be deposited here, the Imperial Library has attained its present extensive dimensions. Nearly one hundred different collections, some of them very valuable and extensive, have been added from time to time. They include, for example, the Tolstoi Sclavonic collection (1830), Tischendorf's MSS. (1858), the Dolgorousky Oriental MSS. (1859), and the Firkowitsch Hebrew (Karaite) collection (1862–1863), the libraries of Adelung (1858) and Tobler (1877), that of the Slavonic scholar Jungmann (1856), and the national MSS. of Karamzin (1867). This system of acquiring books, while it has made some departments exceedingly rich, has left others comparatively meagre. The library was not regularly opened to the public until 1814; it is under the control of the minister of public instruction. There are fine collections of Aldines and Elzevirs, and the numerous incunabula are instructively arranged.

The manuscripts include 26,000 codices, 41,320 autographs, 4689 charters and 576 maps. The glory of this department is the celebrated *Codex Sinaiticus* of the Greek Bible, brought from the convent of St Catherine on Mount Sinai by Tischendorf in 1859. Other important Biblical and patristic codices are to be found among the Greek and Latin MSS.; the Hebrew MSS.

include some of the most ancient that exist, and ... collection is one of the largest in Europe; the ... comprehend many valuable texts, and among the ... some of great historical value. The general catalo... writing, but many special catalogues of the MSS. a... books have been published.

The nucleus of the library at the Hermitage Palace was the empress Catherine II., who purchased the books an... Voltaire and Diderot. In the year 1861 the collection am... 150,000 vols., of which nearly all not relating to the histo... were then transferred to the Imperial Library. There a... large and valuable libraries attached to the government dep... in St Petersburg, and most of the academies and colle... learned societies are provided with libraries.

The second largest library in Russia is contained in the Museum at Moscow. The class of history is particularly ri... Russian early printed books are well represented. The MSS. ... 5000, including many ancient Sclavonic codices and historica... ments of value. One room is devoted to a collection of M... MSS., which comprehend the archives of the lodges in Russia b... 1816 and 1821. There is a general alphabetical catalogue in wr... the catalogue of the MSS. has been printed, as well as those of of the special collections. This large and valuable library contains close upon 1,000,000 printed books and MSS. The Im... University at Moscow (1755) has a library of over 310,000 vols.. the Duchovnaja Academy has 120,000 vols. The Imperial Ru... Historical Museum (1875–1883) in Moscow contains nearly 200... vols. and most of the state institutions and schools are supp... with libraries. All the Russian universities have libraries, som... them being both large and valuable—Dorpat (1802) 400,000 v... Charkov (1804) 180,000 vols.; Helsingfors (1640–1827) 193... vols.; Kasan (1804) 242,000 vols.; Kiev (1832) 125,000 vols.; Odessa (1865) 250,000 vols.; and Warsaw (1817) 550,000 vols. There are also communal or public libraries at Charkov (1886) 110,000 vols.; Odessa (1830) 130,000 vols.; Reval (1825) 40,000 vols.; Riga, 90,000 vols.; Vilna (1856) 210,000 vols. and many other towns. A text-book on library economy, based on Graesel and Brown, was issued at St Petersburg in 1904.

Eastern Europe.

At Athens the National Library (1842) possesses about 260,000 vols., and there is also a considerable library at the university. The Public Library at Corfu has about 40,000 vols. Belgrade University Library has 60,000 vols. and the University Library of Sofia has 30,000 vols. Constantinople University in 1910 had a library in process of formation, and there are libraries at the Greek Literary Society (20,000 vols.) and Theological School (11,000 vols.).

China.

Chinese books were first written on thin slips of bamboo, which were replaced by silk or cloth scrolls in the 3rd century B.C., paper coming into use in the beginning of the 2nd century. These methods were customary down to the 10th or 11th century. There were no public libraries in the western sense.

The practice of forming national collections of the native literature originated in the attempts to recover the works destroyed in the "burning of the books" by the "First Emperor" (220 B.C.). In 190 B.C. the law for the suppression of literary works was repealed, but towards the close of the 1st century B.C. many works were still missing. Hsiao Wu (139–86 B.C.) formed the plan of Repositories, in which books might be stored, with officers to transcribe them. Liu Hsiang (80–9 B.C.) was specially appointed to classify the literature and form a library. His task was completed by his son, and the *resumé* of their labours is a detailed catalogue with valuable notes describing 11,332 "sections" (volumes) by 625 authors. Similar national collections were formed by nearly every succeeding dynasty. The high estimation in which literature has always been held has led to the formation of very large imperial, official and private collections of books. Large numbers of works, chiefly relating to Buddhism and Taoism, are also stored in many of the temples. Chinese books are usually in several, and frequently in many volumes. The histories and encyclopaedias are mostly of vast dimensions. Collections of books are kept in wooden cupboards or on open shelves, placed on their sides, each set (*t'ao*) of volumes (*pên*) being protected and held together by two thin wooden or card boards, one forming the front cover (in a European book) and the other the back cover, joined by two cords or tapes running round the whole. By untying and tying these tapes the *t'ao* is opened and closed. The titles of the whole work and of each section are written on the edge (either the top or bottom in a European book) and so face outwards as it lies on the shelf. Catalogues are simple lists with comments on the books, not the systematic and scientific productions used in Western countries. There are circulating libraries in large numbers in Peking, Canton and other cities.

Gonidia.—It has been made clear above that the gonidia are nothing more than algal cells, which have been ensnared by fungal hyphae and made to develop in captivity (fig. 1). Funfstuck gives ten free living algae which have been identified as the gonidia of lichens. *Pleurococcus* (*Cystococcus*) *humicola* in the majority of lichens, *e.g.* *Usnea*, *Cladonia*, *Physcia*, *Parmelia*, *Calicium*, many species of *Lecidea*, &c., *Trentepohlia* (*Chroolepus*) *umbrina* in many species of *Verrucaria*, *Graphidieae* and *Lecidea*; *Palmella botryoides* in *Epigloea*; *Pleurococcus vulgaris* in Acarospora, Dermatocarpon, Catillaria; *Dactylococcus infusionum* in *Solorina*, *Nephromia*;

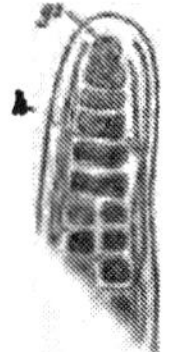

The first ... librarianship was the Americ... Library Association of the United Kingdom ... as an outcome of the first International Library Con... held at London, and in 1898 it received a royal char... publishes a *Year Book*, the monthly *Library Association Record*, and a number of professional handbooks. It also holds examinations in Literary History, Bibliography and Library Economy, and issues certificates and diplomas. There are also English and Scottish district library associations. The Library Assistants Association was formed in 1895 and has branches in different parts of England, Wales and Ireland. It issues a monthly magazine entitled *The Library Assistant*. There is an important Library Association in Germany which issues a year-book giving information concerning the libraries of the country, and a similar organization in Austria-Hungary which issues a magazine at irregular intervals. An Association of Archivists and Librarians was formed at Brussels in 1907, and there are similar societies in France, Italy, Holland and elsewhere. In every country there is now some kind of association for the study of librarianship, archives or bibliography. International conferences have been held at London, 1877; London, 1897; Paris (at Exhibition), 1903; St Louis, 1904; Brussels (preliminary), 1908; and Brussels, 1910.

Library Periodicals.—The following is a list of the current periodicals which deal with library matters, with the dates of their establishment and place of publication: *The Library Journal* (New York, 1876); *The Library* (London, 1889); *Public Libraries* (Chicago, 1896); *The Library World* (London, 1898); *The Library Assistant* (1898); *The Library Association Record* (1899); *Library Work* (Minneapolis, U.S., 1906); *Bulletin of the American Library Association* (Boston, 1907); *Revue des bibliothèques* (Paris, 1891); *Bulletin des bibliothèques populaires* (Paris, 1906); *Courrier des Bibliothèques* (Paris); *Bulletin de l'institut international de bibliographie* (Brussels, 1895); *Revue des bibliothèques et archives de Belgique* (Brussels, 1903); *Tijdschrift voor boekund bibliotheekwezen* (Hague, 1903); *De Boekzaal* (Hague, 1907); *Bogsamlingsbladet* (Copenhagen, 1906); *For Folke-og Barnboksamlinger* (Christiania, 1906); *Folkebibliotheksbladet* (Stockholm, 1903); *Zentralblatt fur Bibliothekswesen* (Leipzig, 1884); *Blätter fur Volksbibliotheken und Lesehallen* (1899; occasional supplement to the above); *Bibliographie des Bibliotheks- and Buchwesens* (ed. by Adalbert Hortzschansky, 1904; issued in the *Zentralblatt*); *Jahrbuch der Deutschen Bibliotheken* (Leipzig, 1902); *Minerva. Jahrbuch der gelehrten Welt* (Strassburg, 1890); *Mitteilungen des österreichischen Vereins für Bibliothekswesen* (Vienna, 1896); *Ceská Osvěta* (Novy Bydzov, Bohemia, 1905); *Revista delle biblioteche e degli archivi* (Florence, 1890); *Bollettino delle biblioteche popolari* (Milan, 1907); *Revista de Archivos, Bibliotecas y Museos Madrid* (1907); *The Gakuto* (Tokio, Japan, 1897).

(H. R. T.; J. D. Br.)

[illegible] (Lat. *libra*, a balance), a slow oscillation, as of a balance, in astronomy especially the seeming oscillation of the moon around her axis, by which portions of her surface near the edge of the disk are alternately brought into sight and swung out of sight.

LIBYA, the Greek name for the northern part of Africa, with which ancient Greek and Roman history are concerned. It is mentioned as a land of great fertility in Homer (*Odyssey*, iv. 85), but no indication of its extent is given. It did not originally include Egypt, which was considered part of Asia, and first assigned to Africa by Ptolemy, who made the isthmus of Suez and the Red Sea the boundary between the two continents. The name Africa came into general use through the Romans. In the early empire, North Africa (excluding Egypt) was divided into Mauretania, Numidia, Africa Propria and Cyrenaica. The old name was reintroduced by Diocletian, by whom Cyrenaica (detached from Crete) was divided into Marmarica (Libya inferior) in the east, and Cyrenaica (Libya superior) in the west. A further distinction into Libya interior and exterior is also known. The former (ἡ ἐντὸς) included the interior (known and unknown) of the continent, as contrasted with the N. and N.E. portion; the latter (ἡ ἔξω, called also simply Libya, or [illegible] [illegible]), between Egypt and Marmarica, was so called as having once formed an Egyptian "nome." See AFRICA, ROMAN.

LICATA, a seaport of Sicily, in the province of Girgenti, 24 m. S.E. of Girgenti direct and 54 m. by rail. Pop. (1901) [illegible]. It occupies the site of the town which Phintias of Akragas (Agrigentum) erected after the destruction of Gela, about 280 B.C., by the Mamertines, and named after himself. The river Salso, which flows into the sea on the east of the town, is the ancient *Himera Meridionalis*. The promontory at the foot of which the town is situated, the *Poggio di Sant' Angelo*, is the Ecnomus (*Ἔκνομος*) of the Greeks, and upon its slopes are scanty traces of ancient structures and rock tombs. It was off this promontory that the Romans gained their famous naval victory over the Carthaginians in the spring of 256 B.C., while the plain to the north was the scene of the defeat of Agathocles by Hamilcar in 310 B.C. The modern town is mainly important as a shipping port for [illegible]

[illegible] (through the French from Lat. *licentia*, *licere*, to be lawful), permission, leave, liberty, hence an abuse of liberty, [illegible]; in particular, a formal authority to do some [illegible]. Such authority may be either verbal or written; [illegible] the document containing the authority is called [illegible]. [illegible] acts, lawful in themselves, are regulated [illegible] and licences must be obtained. For the [illegible] see LIQUOR LAWS.

[illegible] [illegible] in medical terminology, a papular [illegible] of the skin, consisting of an eruption in small [illegible] red points, more or less widely [illegible] the body, and accompanied by slight febrile [illegible]

[illegible], [illegible] compound or dual organisms each [illegible] of a higher fungus, with a usually [illegible] filamentous, alga. The fungal part of [illegible] consists of a number of the *Disco*-[illegible] while the algal portion is a member [illegible] Cyanophyceae or Blue-green Algae) or [illegible] in a very few cases is the fungus a [illegible]. The special fungi which [illegible] are, with rare exceptions, not [illegible] with the algal forms are constantly [illegible] organs of the lichen are of a [illegible] are apothecia or perithecia [illegible]. The algal cells are never [illegible] of the lichen-thallus, but [illegible] it and growing [illegible] in the [illegible] live

in situations where neither the alga nor fungus could exist alone. The enclosed alga is protected by the threads (hyphae) of the fungus, and supplied with water and salts and, possibly, organic nitrogenous substances; in its turn the alga by means of its green or blue-green colouring matter and the sun's energy manufactures carbohydrates which are used in part by the fungus. An association of two organisms to their mutual advantage is known as *symbiosis*, and the lichen in botanical language is described as a symbiotic union of an alga and a fungus. This form of relationship is now known in other groups of plants (see BACTERIOLOGY and FUNGI), but it was first discovered in the lichens. The lichens are characterized by their excessively slow growth and their great length of life.

Until comparatively recent times the lichens were considered as a group of simple organisms on a level with algae and fungi. The green (or blue-green) cells were termed gonidia by Wallroth, who looked upon them as asexual reproductive cells, but when it was later realized that they were not reproductive elements they were considered as mere outgrowths of the hyphae of the thallus which had developed chlorophyll. In 1865 De Bary suggested the possibility that such lichens as *Collema*, *Ephebe*, &c., arose as a result of the attack of parasitic Ascomycetes upon the algae, Nostoc, Chroococcus, &c. In 1867 the observations of Famintzin and Baranetzky showed that the gonidia, in certain cases, were able to live outside the lichen-thallus, and in the case of Physcia, Evernia and Cladonia were able to form zoospores. Baranetzky therefore concluded that a certain number, if not all of the so-called algae were nothing more than free living lichen-gonidia. In 1869 Schwendener put forward the really illuminating view—exactly opposite to that of Baranetzky—that the gonidia in all cases were algae which had been attacked by parasitic fungi. Although Schwendener supported this view of the "dual" nature of lichens by very strong evidence and identified the more common lichen-gonidia with known free-living algae, yet the theory was received with a storm of opposition by nearly all lichenologists. These workers were unable to consider with equanimity the loss of the autonomy of their group and its reduction to the level of a special division of the fungi. The observations of Schwendener, however, received ample support from Bornet's (1873) examination of 60 genera. He investigated the exact relation of fungus and alga and showed that the same alga is able to combine with a number of different fungi to form lichens; thus *Chroolepus umbrinus* is found as the gonidia of 13 different lichen genera.

The view of the dual nature of lichens had hitherto been based on analysis; the final proof of this view was now supplied by the actual *synthesis* of a lichen from fungal and algal constituents. Rees in 1871 produced the sterile thallus of a *Collema* from its constituents; later Stahl did the same for three species. Later Bonnier (1886) succeeded in producing fertile thalli by sowing lichen spores and the appropriate algae upon sterile glass plates or portions of bark, and growing them in sterilized air (fig. 1). Möller also in 1887 succeeded in growing small lichen-thalli without their algal constituent (gonidia) on nutritive solutions; in the case of *Calicium* pycnidia were actually produced under these conditions.

The thallus or body of the lichen is of very different form in different genera. In the simplest filamentous lichens (*e.g.* *Ephebe pubescens*) the form of thallus is the form of the filamentous alga which is merely surrounded by the fungal hyphae (fig. 2). The next simplest forms are gelatinous lichens (*e.g.* *Collemaceae*); in these the algae are Chroococcaceae and Nostocaceae, and the fungus makes its way into the gelatinous membranes of the algal cells and ramifies there (fig. 3). We can distinguish this class of forms as lichens with a *homoiomerous* thallus, *i.e.* one in which the alga and fungus are equally distributed. The majority of the lichens, however, possess a stratified thallus in which the gonidia are found as a definite layer or layers embedded in a pseudo-parenchymatous mass of fungal hyphae, *i.e.* they are *heteromerous* (figs. 5 and 9). Obviously these two conditions may merge into one another, and the distinction is not of classificatory value.

In external form the heteromerous thallus presents the following modifications. (*a*) The *foliaceous* (leaf-like) thallus, which may be either peltate, *i.e.* rounded and entire, as in *Umbilicaria*, &c., or variously lobed and laciniated, as in *Sticta*, *Parmelia*, *Cetraria* (fig. 4), &c. This is the highest type of its development, and is sometimes very considerably expanded. (*b*) The *fruticose* thallus may be either erect, becoming pendulous, as in *Usnea* (fig. 5), *Ramalina*, &c., or prostrate, as in *Alectoria jubata*, var. *chalybeiformis*. It is usually divided into branches and branchlets, bearing some resemblance to a miniature shrub. An erect cylindrical thallus terminated by the fruit is termed a *podetium*, as in *Cladonia* (fig. 7). (*c*) The *crustaceous* thallus, which is the most common of all, forms a mere crust on the substratum, varying in thickness, and may be squamose (in *Squamaria*), radiate (in *Placodium*), areolate, granulose or pulverulent (in various *Lecanorae* and *Lecideae*). (*d*) The *hypophloeodal* thallus is often concealed beneath the bark of trees (as in some *Verrucariae* and *Arthoniae*), or enters into the fibres of wood (as in *Xylographa* and

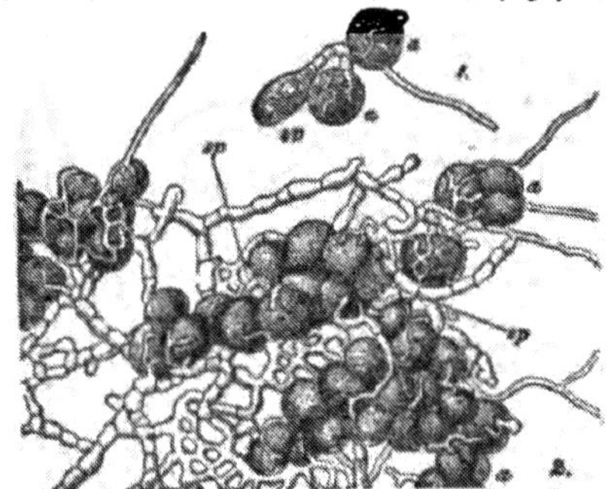

After Bonnier, from v. Tavel. From Strasburger's *Lehrbuch der Botanik*, by permission of Gustav Fischer.

FIG. 1.—*Xanthoria parietina*. By the fusion of the hyphae in the middle of the mycelium a pseudo-parenchymatous cortical layer has begun to form.

1, Germinating ascospore (*sp*) with branching germ-tube applied to the *Cystococcus* cells (*a*).
2, Thallus in process of formation.
sp, Two ascospores.
p, *Cystococcus* cells.

Agyrium), being indicated externally only by a very thin film (figs. 3, 4, 5, 6, 7 and 8). In colour also the thallus externally is very variable. In the dry and more typical state it is most frequently white or whitish, and almost as often greyish or greyish glaucous. Less commonly it is of different shades of brown, red, yellow and black. In the moist state of the thallus these colours are much less apparent, as the textures then become more or less translucent, and the thallus usually prevents the greenish colour of the gonidia (*e.g.* *Parmelia Borreri*, *Peltidea aphthosa*, *Umbilicaria pustulata* and pulverulent *Lecideae*).

The thallus may be free upon the surface of the substratum (*e.g.* *Collema*) or may be fixed more or less closely to it by special hyphae or rhizoids. These may penetrate but slightly into the substratum, but the connexion established may be so close that it is impossible to remove the thallus from the substratum without injury (*e.g.* *Physcia*, *Placodium*). In some cases the rhizoids are united together into larger strands, the *rhizines*.

The typical heteromerous thallus shows on section a peripheral, thin and therefore transparent, layer, the *cortical layer*, and centrally a mass of denser tissue the so-called *medullary layer*, between these two layers is the algal zone or gonidial layer (figs. 8 and 9).

The term *epithallus* is sometimes applied to the superficial dense portion of the cortical layer and the term *hypothallus* to the layer, when specially modified, in immediate contact with the substratum: the hypothallus is usually dark or blackish. The cylindrical branches of the fruticose forms are usually radially symmetrical, but the flattened branches of these forms and also the thalli of the foliaceous form show a difference in the cortex of the upper and lower side. The cortical layer is usually more developed on the side towards the light, while in many lichens this is the only side provided with a cortical layer. The podetia of some species of Cladonia possess no cortical layer at all. The surface of the thallus often exhibits outgrowths in the form of warts, hairs, &c. The medullary layer, which usually forms the main part of the thallus, is distinguished from the cortical layer by its looser consistence and the presence in it of numerous, large, air-containing spaces.

Gonidia.—It has been made clear above that the gonidia are nothing more than algal cells, which have been ensnared by fungal hyphae and made to develop in captivity (fig. 1). Funfstuck gives ten free living algae which have been identified as the gonidia of lichens. *Pleurococcus* (*Cystococcus*) *humicola* in the majority of lichens, *e.g.* *Usnea*, *Cladonia*, *Physcia*, *Parmelia*, *Calicium*, many species of *Lecidea*, &c., *Trentepohlia* (*Chroolepus*) *umbrina* in many species of *Verrucaria*, *Graphidieae* and *Lecidea*; *Palmella botryoides* in *Epigloea*; *Pleurococcus vulgaris* in Acarospora, Dermatocarpon, Catillaria; *Dactylococcus infusionum* in *Solorina*, *Nephromia*;

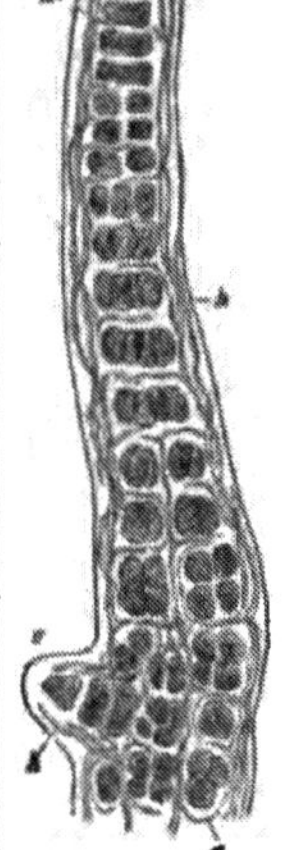

After Sachs, from De Bary's *Vergleichende Morphologie und Biologie der Pilze, Mycetozoen und Bacterien*, by permission of Wilhelm Engelmann.

FIG. 2.—*Ephebe pubescens*, Fr. A branched filiform thallus of *Stigonema* with the hyphae of the fungus growing through its gelatinous membranes. Extremity of a branch of the thallus with a young lateral branch *a*; *h*, hyphae; *g*, cells of the alga; *gs*, the apex of the thallus.

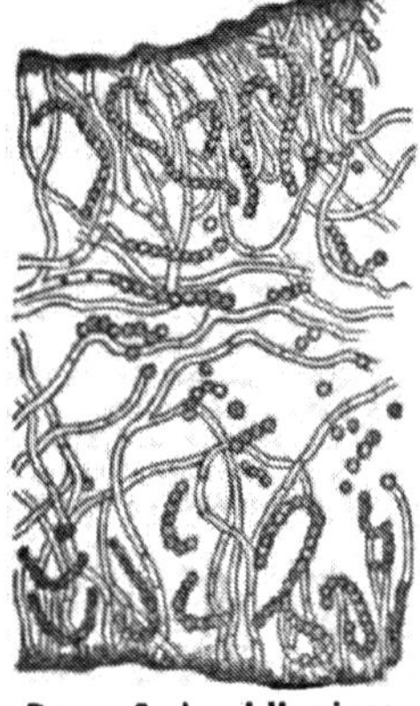

FIG. 3.—Section of Homoiomerous Thallus of *Collema conglomeratum*, with *Nostoc* threads scattered among the hyphae.

Nostoc lichenoides in most of the Collemaceae; *Rivularia rutida* in *Omphalaria*; *Lichina*, &c., *Polycoccus punctiformis* in *Peltigera*, *Pannaria* and *Stictina*; *Gloeocapsa polydermatica* in *Baeomyces* and *Omphalaria*; *Sirosiphon pulvinatus* in *Ephebe pubescens*. The majority of lichens are confined to one particular kind of gonidium (*i.e.* species of alga) but a few forms are known (*Lecanora granatina*, *Solorina crocea*) which make use of more than one kind in their development. In the case of *Solorina*, for example, the principal alga is a green alga, one of the Palmellaceae, but *Nostoc* (a blue-green alga) is also found playing a subsidiary part as

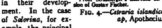

From Strasburger's *Lehrbuch der Botanik*, by permission of Gustav Fischer.

FIG. 4.—*Cetraria islandica*. (Nat. size.) *ap*, Apothecium.

[illegible] In *L.* [illegible] the primary alga is *Pleurococcus*, the [illegible]

[illegible]—In about 100 species of lichens peculiar growths are [illegible] in the interior of the thallus which cause a slight projection of the upper or lower surface. These structures are known as *cephalodia* and they usually occupy a definite position in the thallus. They are distinguished by possessing as gonidia algae foreign to the ordinary part of the thallus. The foreign algae are always members of the Cyanophyceae and on the same individual and even in the same cephalodium more than one type of gonidium may be found. The function of these peculiar structures is unknown. Zukal has suggested that they may play the part of water-absorbing organs.

From Strasburger's *Lehrbuch der Botanik*, by permission of Gustav Fischer.

FIG. 5.—*Usnea barbata*. (Nat. size.) *ap*, Apothecium.

The exact relation of gonidia and hyphae has been investigated especially by Bornet and also by Hedlund, and very considerable differences have been shown to exist in different genera. In *Physma*, *Arnoldia*, [illegible] and other genera the gonidia are killed sooner or later by special hyphal branches, *haustoria*, which pierce the membrane of the algal cell, penetrate the protoplasm and absorb the contents (fig. 11, C). In other cases, e.g. *Synalissa*, *Micarea*, the haustoria pierce the membrane, but do not penetrate the protoplasm (fig. 11, D). In many other cases, especially those algae possessing *Pleurococcus* as their gonidia, there are no penetrating hyphae, but merely

From Strasburger's *Lehrbuch der Botanik*, by permission of Gustav Fischer.

FIG. 7.—*Cladonia coccifera*. Podetia bearing apothecia. (Nat. size.)

t, Scales of primary thallus.

[illegible] *Lehrbuch der Botanik*. [illegible]

[illegible] branches which are in close contact with [illegible] fig. 3).

[illegible]

[illegible] reproduction of the lichen: by [illegible] formation of fungal spores. [illegible] containing gonidia may [illegible] start new plants. The [illegible] of fragmentation. The [illegible] of lichens, and consist [illegible] gonidia, surrounded by a [illegible] in the gonidial layer [illegible] and the development around them of the hyphal investment; their increase in number leads to the rupture of the enclosing cortical layer and the soredia escape from the thallus as a powdery mass (fig. 12). Since they are provided with both fungal and algal elements, they are able to develop directly, under suitable conditions, into a new thallus. The soredia are the most successful method of reproduction in lichens, for not only are some forms nearly always without spore-formation and in others the spores laregly abortive, but in all cases the spore represents only the fungal component of the thallus, and its success in the development of a new lichen-thallus depends on the chance meeting, at the time of germination, with the appropriate algal component.

Conidia.—Contrary to the behaviour of the non-lichen forming Ascomycetes the lichen-fungi show very few cases of ordinary conidial formation. Bornet describes free conidia in *Arnoldia minitula*, and *Placodium decipiens* and *Conidia*-formation has been described by Neubner in the Caliciae.

Spermatia.—In the majority of genera of lichens small flask-shaped structures are found embedded in the thallus (fig. 13). These were investigated by Tulasne in 1853, who gave them the name *spermogonia*. The lower, ventral portion of the spermogonium is lined by delicate hyphae, the *sterigmata*, which give origin to minute colourless cells, the *spermatia*. The sterigmata are either simple (fig. 13, C) or septate—the so-called arthrosterigmata (fig. 13, B). The spermogonia open by a small pore at the apex, towards which the sterigmata converge and through which the spermatia escape (fig. 13). There are two views as to the nature of the spermatia. In one view they are mere asexual conidia, and the term *pycnoconidia* is accordingly applied since they are borne in structures like the non-sexual *pycnidia* of other fungi. In the other view the spermatia are the male sexual cells and thus are rightly named; it should, however, be pointed out that this was not the view of Tulasne, though we owe to him the designation which carries with it the sexual significance. The question is one very difficult to settle owing to the fact that the majority of spermatia appear to be functionless. In favour of the conidial view is the fact that in the case of *Collema* and a few other forms the spermatia have been made to germinate in artificial cultures, and in the case of *Calicium parietinum* Möller succeeded in producing a spermogonia bearing thallus from a spermatium. For the germination of the spermatia in nature there is only the observation of Hedlund, that in *Catillaria denigrata* and *C. prasena* a thallus may be derived from the spermatia under natural conditions. In relation to the view that the spermatia are sexual cells, or at least were primitively so, it must be pointed out that although the actual fusion of the spermatial nucleus with a female nucleus has not been observed, yet in a few cases the spermatia have been seen to fuse with a projecting portion (trichogyne) of the ascogonium, as in *Collema* and *Physcia*, and there is very strong circumstantial evidence that fertilization takes place (see later in section on development of ascocarp). The resemblance of the spermatia and spermogonia to those of Uredineae should be pointed out, where also there is considerable evidence for their original sexual nature, though they appear in that group to be functionless in all cases. The observations of Möller, &c., on the germination cannot be assumed to negative the sexual hypothesis for the sexual cells of *Ulothrix* and *Ectocarpus*, for example

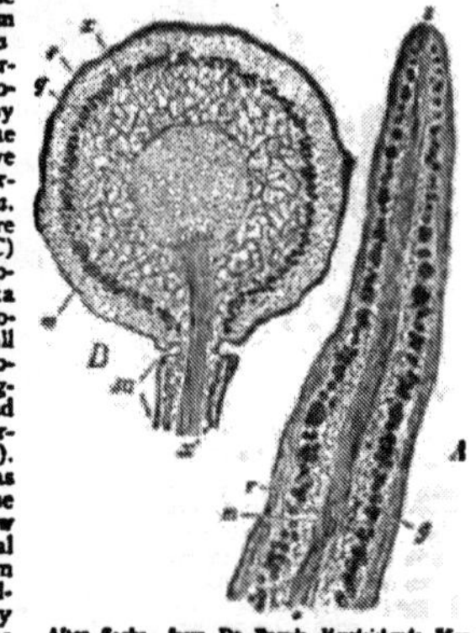

After Sachs, from De Bary's *Vergleichende Morphologie und Biologie der Pilze, Mycetozoen und Bacterien*, by permission of Wilhelm Engelmann.

FIG. 8.—*Usnea barbata*. (Mag. nearly 100 times.)

A, Optical longitudinal section of the extremity of a thin branch of the thallus which has become transparent in solution of potash.
B, Transverse section through a stronger branch with the point of origin of an adventitious branch (*sa*).
r, Cortical layer.
m, Medullary layer.
x, Stout axile strand.
g, The algal zone (*Cystococcus*).
s, Apex of the branch.

are able to develop with or without fusion. The most satisfactory view in the present state of our knowledge seems to be that the spermatia are male cells which, while retaining their fertilizing action in a few cases are now mainly functionless. The female sexual organs, the ascogonia, would thus in the majority of cases develop by the aid of some reduced sexual process or the ascocarps be developed without relation to sexual organs. A further argument in support of this view is that it is in complete agreement with what we know of the sexuality of the ordinary, free-living ascomycetes, where we find both normal and reduced forms (see FUNGI).

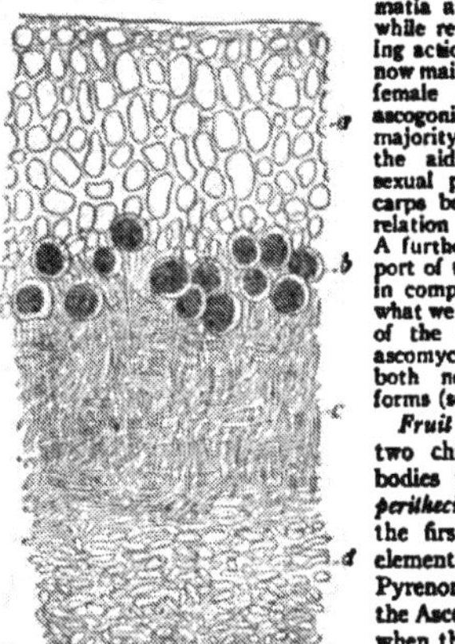

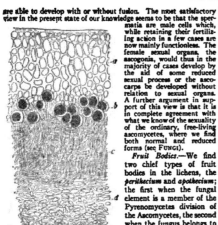

From *Beiträge zur Wissenschaftlichen Botanik*.

FIG. 9.—Section of Heteromerous Lichen Thallus.
a, Upper cortical layer.
d, Lower cortical layer.
c, Medullary layer.
b, Gonidial layer.

Fruit Bodies.—We find two chief types of fruit bodies in the lichens, the ***perithecium*** and ***apothecium***; the first when the fungal element is a member of the Pyrenomycetes division of the Ascomycetes, the second when the fungus belongs to the Discomycetes division. In the two genera of lichens—the ***Basidiolichens***—in which the fungus is a member of the Basidiomycetes, we have the fructification characteristic of that class of fungi: these are dealt with separately. The perithecium is very constant in form and since the gonidia take no part in the formation of this organ or that of the apothecium it has the general structure characteristic of that division of fungi. The apothecia, though of the normal fungal type and usually disk-shaped, are somewhat more variable, and since the variations are of value in classification some more details may be added.

After Bornet, from De Bary's *Vergleichende Morphologie und Biologie der Pilze, Mycetozoen und Bacterien*, by permission of Wilhelm Engelmann.

FIG. 11.—Lichen-forming Algae. (A, C, D, E mag. 950, B 650 times.) The alga is in all cases indicated by the letter *g*, the assailing hyphae by *h*.

A, *Pleurococcus*, Ag. (*Cystococcus*, Näg.) attacked by the germ-tube from a spore of *Physica parietina*.
B, *Scytonema* from the thallus of *Stereocaulon ramulosum*.
C, *Nostoc* from the thallus of *Physma chalazanum*.
D, *Gloeocapsa* from the thallus of *Synalissa Symphorea*.
E, *Pleurococcus* Sp. (*Cystococcus*) from the thallus of *Cladonia furcata*.

They present various shapes, of which the following are the principal: (*a*) ***peltate***, which are large, rounded, without any distinct thalline margin[1] (*e.g. Usnea, Peltigera*); (*b*) ***lecanorine***, or scutelliform, which are orbicular and surrounded by a distinct, more or less prominent thalline margin (*e.g. Parmelia, Lecanora*), having sometimes also in addition a proper one[1] (*e.g. Thelotrema, Urceolaria*); (*c*) ***lecideine***, or patelliform, which are typically orbicular, with only a proper margin (*e.g. Lecidea*), sometimes obsolete, and which are occasionally irregular in shape, angular or flexuose (*e.g. Lecidea jurana, L. myrmecina*), or complicated and gyrose (*e.g. Gyrophora*), and even stipitate (*e.g. Baeomyces*); (*d*) ***lirelliform***, which are of very irregular figure, elongated, branched or flexuose, with only a proper margin (*e.g. Xylographa, Graphis*, &c.) or none (*e.g.* some *Arthoniae*), and often very variable even in the same species. In colour the apothecia are extremely variable, and it is but rarely that they are the same colour as the thallus (*e.g. Usnea, Ramalina*). Usually they are of a different colour, and may be black, brown, yellowish, or also less frequently rose-coloured, rusty-red, orange-reddish, saffron, or of various intermediate shades. Occasionally in the same species their colour is very variable (*e.g. Lecanora metaboloides, Lecidea decolorans*), while sometimes they are white or glaucous, rarely greenish, pruinose. Lecideine apothecia, which are not black, but otherwise variously coloured, are termed *biatorine*.

After Schwendener, from De Bary's *Vergleichende Morphologie und Biologie der Pilze, Mycetozoen und Bacterien*, by permission of Wilhelm Engelmann.

FIG. 12.—*Usnea barbata*. (Mag. more than 500 times.)
c, An isolated mature soredium, with an algal cell (*Pleurococcus*) in the envelope or hyphae.
d, Another with several algal cells in optical longitudinal section.
e, *f*, Two soredia in the act of germinating; the hyphal envelope has grown out below into rhizoid branches, and above shows already the structure of the apex of the thallus (see fig. 9).

The two principal parts of which an apothecium consists are the ***hypothecium*** and the hymenium, or thecium. The ***hypothecium*** is the basal part of the apothecium on which the ***hymenium*** is borne; the latter consists of asci (thecae) with ascospores, and paraphyses. The paraphyses (which may be absent entirely in the Pyrenolichens) are erect, colourless filaments which are usually dilated and coloured at the apex; the apices are usually cemented together into a definite layer, the ***epithecium*** (fig. 14). The spores themselves may be unicellular without a septum or multicellular with one or more septa. Sometimes the two cavities are restricted to the two ends of the spore, the ***polari-bilocular*** type and the two loculi may be united

After Tulasne, from De-Bary's *Vergleichende Morphologie und Biologie der Pilze, Mycetozoen und Bacterien*, by permission of Wilhelm Engelmann.

FIG. 13.—*A*, *B*, *Gyrophora cylindrica*. (A mag. 90, B 390 times, C highly magnified.)
A, A vertical median section through a spermogonium imbedded in the thallus.
o, Upper rind.
u, Under rind.
m, Medullary layer of the thallus.
B, Portion of a very thin section from the base of the spermogonium.
w, Its wall from which proceed sterigmata with rod-like spermatia (*s*).
m, Medullary hyphae of the thallus.
C, *Cladonia novae Angliae*, Delise; sterigmata with spermatia from the spermogonium.

[1] The ***thalline margin*** (margo thallinus) is the projecting edge of a special layer of thallus, the amphithecium, round the actual apothecium; the ***proper margin*** (margo proprius) is the projecting edge of the apothecium itself

by a narrow channel (fig. 15). At other times the spores are divided by both transverse and longitudinal septa producing the muriform (murali-divided) spore so called from the resemblance of the individual chambers to the stones in a wall. The very large single spores of *Pertusaria* have been shown to contain numerous nuclei and when thev germinate develop a large number of germ tubes.

Development of the Ascocarps.—As the remarks on the nature of the spermatia show, the question of the sexuality of the lichens has been hotly disputed in common with that of the rest of the Ascomycetes. As indicated above, the weight of evidence seems to favour what has been put forward in the case of the non-lichen-forming fungi (see FUNGI), that in some cases the ascogonia develop as a result of a previous fertilization by spermatia, in other cases the ascogonia develop without such a union, while in still other cases the reduction goes still farther and the ascogenous hyphae instead of developing from the ascogonia are derived directly from the vegetative hyphae.

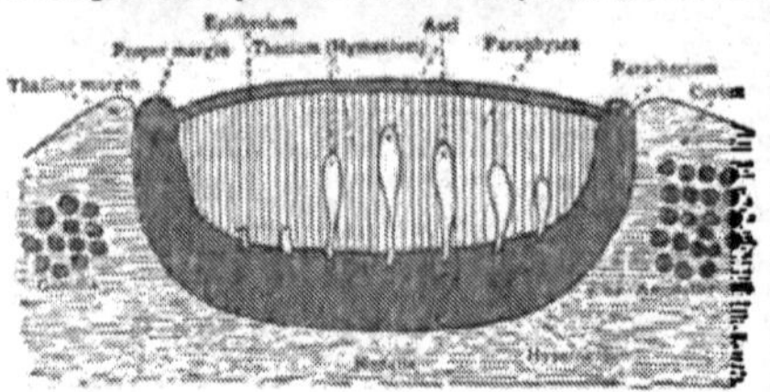

After Darbishire, from *Berichte der deutschen botanischen Gesellschaft*, by permission of Borntraeger & Co.

FIG. 14.—Diagram showing Apothecium in Section and surrounding Portion of Thallus, and special terms used to designate these parts.

The first exact knowledge as to the origin of the ascocarp was the work of Stahl on *Collema* in 1877. He showed that the archicarp consisted of two parts, a lower coiled portion, the ascogonium, and an upper portion, the trichogyne, which projected from the thallus. Only when a spermatium was found attached to the trichogyne did the further development of the ascogonium take place. From these observations he drew the natural conclusion that the spermatium was a male, sexual cell. This view was hotly contested by many workers and it was sought to explain the trichogyne—without much success—as a respiratory organ, or as a boring organ which made a way for the developing apothecium. It was not till 1898, however, that Stahl's work received confirmation and addition at the hands of Baur (fig. 16). The latter showed that in *Collema crispum* there are two kinds of thalli, one with numerous apothecia, the other quite sterile or bearing only a few. The sterile thalli possessed no spermogonia, but were found to show sometimes as many as 1000 archicarps with trichogynes; yet none or very few came to maturity. The fertile thalli were shown to bear either spermogonia or to be in immediate connexion with spermogonia-bearing thalli. Furthermore Baur showed that after the fusion of the spermatium with the trichogyne the transverse walls of that organ became perforated. There was thus very strong circumstantial evidence in favour of fertilization, although the male nucleus was not traced. The further work of Baur, and that of Darbishire, Funfstuck and Lindau, have shown that in a number of other cases trichogynes are present. Thus ascogonia with trichogynes have been observed in *Endocarpon*, *Collema*, *Pertusaria*, *Lecanora*, *Gyrophora*, *Parmelia*, *Ramalina*, *Physcia*, *Anaptychia* and *Cladonia*. In *Nephroma*, *Peltigera*, *Peltidea* and *Solorina* a cogonia without trichogynes have been observed. In *Collema* and a form like *Xanthoria parietina* it is probable that actual fertilization takes place, and possibly also in some of the other forms. It is probable, however, that in the majority of cases the ascogonia develop without normal fertilization, as is necessarily the case where the ascogonia have no trichogynes or the spermatia are absent. In these cases we should expect to find some reduced process of fertilization similar to that of *Humaria granulata* among the ordinary Ascomycetes, where in the absence of the antheridia the female nuclei fuse in pairs. In other lichens we should expect to find the ascogenous hyphae arising directly from the vegetative hyphae as in *Humaria rutilans* among the ordinary fungi, where the process is associated with the fusion of vegetative nuclei. It is possible that *Solorina saccata* belongs to this class. Cytological details of nuclear behaviour among the lichens are, however, difficult to obtain owing to the slow growth of these forms and the often refractory nature of the material in the matter of preparation for microscopical examination.

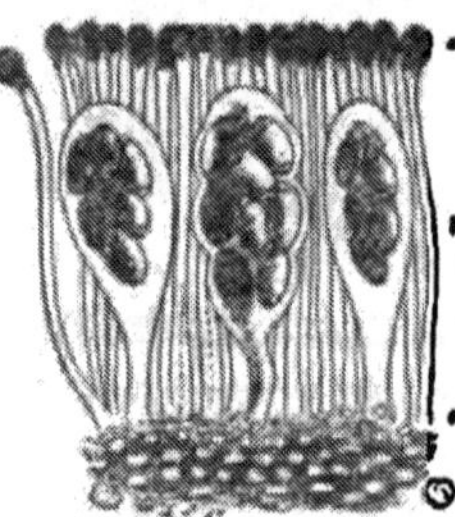

FIG. 15.—Vertical Section of Apothecium of *Xanthoria parietina*.

a, Paraphyses.
b, Asci (thecae) with bilocular spores.
c, Hypothecium.

Ejection of Spores.—The spores are ejected from the apothecia and perithecia as in the fungi by forcible ejaculation from the asci. In the majority of forms it is clear that the soredia rather than the ascospore must play the more important part in lichen distribution as the development of the ordinary spores is dependent on their finding the proper alga on the substratum on which they happen to fall. In a number of forms (*Endocarpon pusillum*, *Stigmatomma cataleptum*, various species of *Staurothele*), however, there is a special arrangement by which the spores are, on ejection, associated with gonidia. In these forms gonidia are found in connexion with the young fruit; such algal cells undergo numerous divisions becoming very small in size and penetrating into the hymenium among the asci and paraphyses. When the spores are thrown out some of these hymenial gonidia, as they are called, are carried with them. When the spores germinate the germ-tubes surround the algal cells, which now increase in size and become the normal gonidia of the thallus.

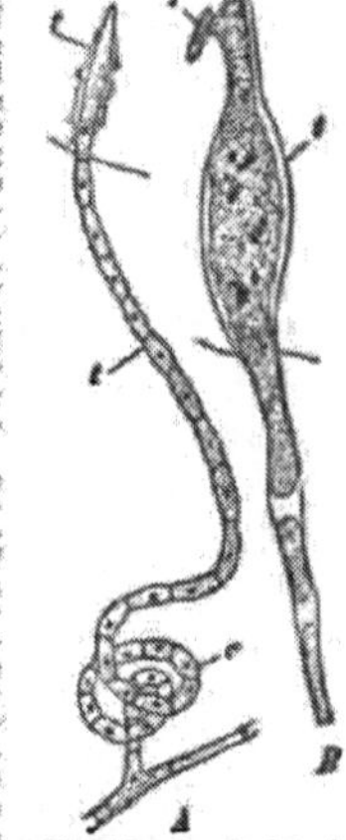

After E. Baur, from Strasburger's *Lehrbuch der Botanik*, by permission of Gustav Fischer.

FIG. 16.—*Collema crispum*.
A, Carpogonium, *c*, with its trichogyne *t*.
B, Apex of the trichogyne with the spermatium, *s*, attached.

Basidiolichens.

As is clear from the above, nearly all the lichens are produced by the association of an ascomycetous fungus with algae. For some obscure reason the Basidiomycetes do not readily form lichens, so that only a few forms are known in which the fungal element is a member of this family. The two best-known genera are *Cora* and *Dictyonema*; *Corella*, whose hymenium is unknown, is also placed here by Wainio. The so-called Gasterolichens, *Trichocoma* and *Emericella*, have been shown to be merely ascomycetous fungi. *Clavaria mucida*, however, has apparently some claims to be considered as a Basidiolichen, since the base of the fruit body and the thallus from which it arises, according to Coker, always shows a mixture of hyphae and algae.

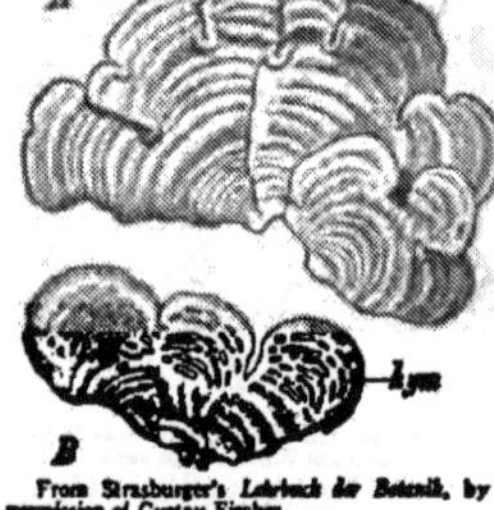

From Strasburger's *Lehrbuch der Botanik*, by permission of Gustav Fischer.

FIG. 17.—*Cora pavonia*. A, Viewed from above; B, From below; *hym*, hymenium. (Nat. size.)

The best-known species is *Cora pavonia*, which is found in tropical regions growing on the bare earth and on trees; the gonidia belong to the genus *Chroococcus* while the fungus belongs, apparently, to the Thelephoreae (see FUNGI). This lichen seems unique in the fact that the fungal element is also found growing and fruiting entirely devoid of algae, while in the ascolichens the fungus portion seems to have become so specialized to its symbiotic mode of life that it is never found growing independently.

The genus *Dictyonema* has gonidia belonging to the blue-green alga, *Scytonema*. When the fungus predominates in the thallus it has a bracket-like mode of growth and is found projecting from the branches of trees with the hymenium on the under side. When the alga is predominant it forms felted patches on the bark of trees, the *Laudatea* form. It is said that the fungus of *Cora pavonia* and of *Dictyonema* is identical, the difference being in the nature of the alga.

Mode of Life.

Lichens are found growing in various situations such as bare earth, the bark of trees, dead wood, the surface of stones and rocks, where they have little competition to fear from ordinary plants. As is well known, the lichens are often found in the most exposed and arid situations; in the extreme polar regions these plants are practically the only vegetable forms of life. They owe their capacity to live under the most inhospitable conditions to the dual nature of the organism, and to their capacity to withstand extremes of heat, cold and drought without destruction. On a bare rocky surface a fungus would die from want of organic substance and an alga from drought and want of mineral substances. The lichen, however, is able to grow as the alga supplies organic food material and the fungus has developed a battery of acids (see below) which enable it actually to dissolve the most resistant rocks. It is owing to the power of disintegrating by both mechanical and chemical means the rocks on which they are growing that lichens play such an important part in soil-production. The resistance of lichens is extraordinary; they may be cooled to very low temperatures and heated to high temperatures without being killed. They may be dried so thoroughly that they can easily be reduced to powder yet their vitality is not destroyed but only suspended; on being supplied with water they absorb it rapidly by their general surface and renew their activity. The life of many lichens thus consists of alternating periods of activity when moisture is plentiful, and completely suspended animation under conditions of dryness. Though so little sensitive to drought and extremes of temperature lichens appear to be very easily affected by the presence in the air of noxious substances such as are found in large cities or manufacturing towns. In such districts lichen vegetation is entirely or almost entirely absent. The growth of lichens is extremely slow and many of them take years before they arrive at a spore-bearing stage. *Xanthoria parietina* has been known to grow for forty-five years before bearing apothecia. This slowness of growth is associated with great length of life and it is probable that individuals found growing on hard mountain rocks or on the trunks of aged trees are many hundreds of years old. It is possible that specimens of such long-lived species as *Lecidea geographica* actually outrival in longevity the oldest trees.

Relation of Fungus and Alga.

The relation of the two constituents of the lichen have been briefly stated in the beginning of this article. The relation of the fungus to the alga, though it may be described in general terms as one of symbiosis, partakes also somewhat of the nature of parasitism. The algal cells are usually controlled in their growth by the hyphae and are prevented from forming zoospores, and in some cases, as already described, the algal cells are killed sooner or later by the fungus. The fungus seems, on the other hand, to stimulate the algal cells to special development, for those in the lichen are larger than those in the free state, but this is not necessarily adverse to the idea of parasitism, for it is well known that an increase in the size of the cells of the host is often the result of the attacks of parasitic fungi. It must be borne in mind that the exact nutritive relations of the two constituents of the lichen have not been completely elucidated, and that it is very difficult to draw the line between symbiosis and parasitism. The lichen algae are not alone in their specialization to the symbiotic (or parasitic) mode of life, for, as stated earlier, the fungus appear in the majority of cases to have completely lost the power of independent development since with very rare exceptions they are not found alone. They also differ very markedly from free living fungi in their chemical reactions.

Chemistry of Lichens.

The chemistry of lichens is very complex, not yet fully investigated and can only be very briefly dealt with here. The wall of the hyphae of the fungus give in the young state the ordinary reactions of cellulose but older material shows somewhat different reactions, similar to those of the so-called fungus-cellulose. In many lichen-fungi the wall shows various chemical modifications. In numerous lichens, *e.g. Cetraria islandica*, the wall contains Lichenin ($C_6H_{10}O_5$), a gummy substance which swells in cold water and dissolves in hot. Besides this substance, a very similar one, Isolichenin, is also found which is distinguished from lichenin by the fact that it dissolves in cold water and turns blue under the reaction of iodine. Calcium oxalate is a very common substance, especially in crustaceous lichens; fatty oil in the form of drops or as an infiltration in the membrane is also common; it sometimes occurs in special cells and in extreme cases may represent 90% of the dry substance as in *Verrucaria calciseda*, *Biatora immersa*.

Colouring Matters.—Many lichens, as is well known, exhibit a vivid colouring which is usually due to the incrustation of the hyphae with crystalline excretory products. These excretory products have usually an acid nature and hence are generally known as lichen-acids. A large number of these acids, which are mostly benzene derivatives, have been isolated and more or less closely investigated. They are characterized by their insolubility or very slight solubility in water; as examples may be mentioned erythrinic acid in *Roccella* and *Lecanora*; evernic acid in species of *Evernia*, *Ramalina* and *Cladonia*; lecanoric acid in *Lecanora*, *Gyrophora*. The so-called chrysophanic acid found in *Xanthoria* (Physcia) *parietina* is not an acid but a quinone and is better termed physcion.

Colour Reactions of Lichens.—The classification of lichens is unique in the fact that chemical colour reactions are used by many lichenologists in the discrimination of species, and these reactions are included in the specific diagnoses. The substances used as tests in these reactions are caustic potash and calcium hypochlorite; the former being the substance dissolved in an equal weight of water and the latter a saturated extract of bleaching powder in water. These substances are represented by lichenologists by the signs K and CaCl respectively, and the presence or absence of the colour reactions are represented thus, K+, CaCl+, or K−, CaCl−. If the cortical layer should exhibit positive reaction and the medulla of the same species a negative reaction with both reagents, the result is represented thus, K±CaCl±. If a reaction is only produced after the consecutive addition of the two reagents, this is symbolized by K(CaCl)+. A solution of iodine is also used as a test owing to the blue or wine-red colour which the thallus, hymenium or spores may give with this reagent. The objection to the case of these colour reactions is due to the indefinite nature of the reaction and the doubt as to the constant presence of a definite chemical compound in a given species. A yellow colour with caustic potash solution is produced not only by atranoric acid but also by evernic acid, thamnolic acid, &c. Again in the case of *Xanthoria parietina* vulpinic acid is only to be found in young thalli growing on sandstone; in older forms or in those growing on another substratum it is not to be detected. A similar relation between oil formation and the nature of the substratum has been observed in many lichens. Considerations such as these should make one very wary in placing reliance on these colour reactions for the purposes of classification.

Economic Uses of Lichens.

In the arts, as food and as medicine, many lichens have been highly esteemed, though others are not now employed for the same purposes as formerly.

1. *Lichens Used in the Arts.*—Of these the most important are such as yield, by maceration in ammonia, the dyes known in commerce as archil, cudbear and litmus. These, however, may with propriety be regarded as but different names for the same pigmentary substance, the variations in the character of which are attributable to the different modes in which the pigments are manufactured. Archil proper is derived from several species of *Roccella* (*e.g. R. Montaguei*, *R. tinctoria*), which yield a rich purple dye; it once fetched a high price in the market. Of considerable value is the "perelle" prepared from *Lecanora parella*, and used in the preparation of a red or crimson dye. Inferior to this is "cudbear," derived from *Lecanora tartarea*, which was formerly very extensively employed by the peasantry of north Europe for giving a scarlet or purple colour to woollen cloths. By adding certain alkalies to the other ingredients used

in the preparation of these pigments, the colour becomes indigo-blue, in which case it is the litmus of the Dutch manufacturers. Amongst other lichens affording red, purple or brown dyes may be mentioned *Ramalina scopulorum*, *Parmelia, saxatilis* and *P. omphalodes*, *Umbilicaria pustulata* and several species of *Gyrophora*, *Urceolaria scruposa*, all of which are more or less employed as domestic dyes. Yellow dyes, again, are derived from *Chlorea vulpina*, *Platysma juniperinum*, *Parmelia caperata* and *P. conspersa*, *Physcia flavicans*, *Ph. parietina* and *Ph. lychnea*, though like the preceding they do not form articles of commerce, being merely used locally by the natives of the regions in which they occur most plentifully. In addition to these, many exotic lichens, belonging especially to *Parmelia* and *Sticta* (*e.g. Parmelia tinctorum*, *Sticta argyracea*), are rich in colouring matter, and, if obtained in sufficient quantity, would yield a dye in every way equal to archil. These pigments primarily depend upon special acids contained in the thalli of lichens, and their presence may readily be detected by means of the reagents already noticed. In the process of manufacture, however, they undergo various changes, of which the chemistry is still but little understood. At one time also some species were used in the arts for supplying a gum as a substitute for gum-arabic. These were chiefly *Ramalina fraxinea*, *Evernia prunastri* and *Parmelia physodes*, all of which contain a considerable proportion of gummy matter (of a much inferior quality, however, to gum-arabic), and were employed in the process of calico-printing and in the making of parchment and cardboard. In the 17th century some filamentose and fruticulose lichens, viz. species of *Usnea* and *Ramalina*, also *Evernia furfuracea* and *Cladonia rangiferina*, were used in the art of perfumery. From their supposed aptitude to imbibe and retain odours, their powder was the basis of various perfumes, such as the celebrated "Poudre de Cypre" of the hairdressers, but their employment in this respect has long since been abandoned.

2. *Nutritive Lichens.*—Of still greater importance is the capacity of many species for supplying food for man and beast. This results from their containing starchy substances, and in some cases a small quantity of saccharine matter of the nature of mannite. One of the most useful nutritious species is *Cetraria islandica*, "Iceland moss," which, after being deprived of its bitterness by boiling in water, is reduced to a powder and made into cakes, or is boiled and eaten with milk by the poor Icelander, whose sole food it often constitutes. Similarly *Cladonia rangiferina* and *Cl. sylvatica*, the familiar "reindeer moss," are frequently eaten by man in times of scarcity, after being powdered and mixed with flour. Their chief importance, however, is that in Lapland and other northern countries they supply the winter food of the reindeer and other animals, who scrape away the snow and eagerly feed upon them. Another nutritious lichen is the "[illegible] de Roche" of the arctic regions, consisting of several [illegible] of the *Gyrophorei*, which when boiled is often eaten by [illegible] hunters and Red Indians when pressed by hunger. [illegible] singular esculent lichen of all is the "manna lichen," [illegible] drought and famine has served as food for large [illegible] cattle in the arid steppes of various countries [illegible] Algiers to Tartary. This is derived chiefly [illegible], which grows unattached on the ground [illegible] thick over large tracts of country in [illegible] lumps of a greyish or white colour. [illegible] as food we may observe that of [illegible] and Russia an alcoholic spirit has [illegible] *rangiferina* and extensively con[illegible] when potatoes were scarce and [illegible] *pulmonaria* was much employed in [illegible] that a Siberian monastery [illegible] which was flavoured with the [illegible]

[illegible] during the middle ages, and even in [illegible] period, lichens were extensively [illegible] countries. Many species [illegible] febrifuges, astringents, tonics, [illegible] The chief of those employed for one or other, and in some cases for several, of these purposes were *Cladonia pyxidata*, *Usnea barbata*, *Ramalina farinacea*, *Evernia prunastri*, *Cetraria islandica*, *Sticta pulmonaria*, *Parmelia saxatilis*, *Xanthoria parietina* and *Pertusaria amara*. Others again were believed to be endowed with specific virtues, *e.g. Peltigera canina*, which formed the basis of the celebrated "pulvis antilyssus" of Dr Mead, long regarded as a sovereign cure for hydrophobia; *Platysma juniperinum*, lauded as a specific in jaundice, no doubt on the *similia similibus* principle from a resemblance between its yellow colour and that of the jaundiced skin; *Peltidea aphthosa*, which on the same principle was regarded by the Swedes, when boiled in milk, as an effectual remedy for the *aphthae* or rash on their children. Almost all of these virtues, general or specific, were imaginary; and at the present day, except perhaps in some remoter districts of northern Europe, only one of them is employed as a remedial agent. This is the "Iceland moss" of the druggists' shops, which is undoubtedly an excellent demulcent in various dyspeptic and chest complaints. No lichen is known to be possessed of any poisonous properties to man, although *Chlorea vulpina* is believed by the Swedes to be so. Zukal has considered that the lichen acids protect the lichen from the attacks of animals; the experiments of Zopf, however, have cast doubt on this; certainly lichens containing very bitter acids are eaten by mites though some of the acids appear to be poisonous to frogs.

Classification.

The dual nature of the lichen thallus introduces at the outset a classificatory difficulty. Theoretically the lichens may be classified on the basis of their algal constituent, on the basis of their fungal constituent, or they may be classified as if they were homogeneous organisms. The first of these systems is impracticable owing to the absence of algal reproductive organs and the similarity of the algal cells (gonidia) in a large number of different forms. The second system is the most obvious one, since the fungus is the dominant partner and produces reproductive organs. The third system was that of Nylander and his followers, who did not accept the Schwenderian doctrine of duality. In actual practice the difference between the second and third methods is not very great since the fungus is the producer of the reproductive organs and generally the main constituent. Most systems agree in deriving the major divisions from the characters of the reproductive organs (perithecia, apothecia, or basidiospore bearing fructification), while the characters of the algal cells and those of the thallus generally are used for the minor divisions. The difference between the various systems lies in the relative importance given to the reproductive characters on the one hand and the vegetative characters on the other. In the system (1854–1855) of Nylander the greater weight is given to the latter, while in more modern systems the former characters receive the more attention.

A brief outline of a system of classification, mainly that of Zahlbruckner as given in Engler and Prantl's *Pflanzenfamilien*, is outlined below.

There are two main divisions of lichens, *Ascolichenes* and *Basidiolichenes*, according to the nature of the fungal element, whether an ascomycete or basidiomycete. The Ascolichenes are again divided into *Pyrenocarpeae* or *Pyrenolichenes* and *Gymnocarpeae* or *Discolichenes*; the first having an ascocarp of the nature of a perithecium, the second bearing their ascospores in an open apothecium.

Pyrenolichenes

Series I. Perithecium simple not divided.
- *a.* With *Pleurococcus* or *Palmella* gonidia.
  Moriolaceae, Verrucariaceae, Pyrenothamnaceae.
- *b.* With *Chroolepus* gonidia.
  Pyrenulaceae, Paratheliaceae.
- *c.* With *Phyllactidium* or *Cephaleurus* gonidia.
  Strigulaceae.
- *d.* With *Nostoc* or *Scytonema* gonidia.
  Pyrenidiaceae.

Series II. Perithecia divided or imperfectly divided by cross-walls.
Mycoporaceae with *Palmella* or *Chroolepus* gonidia.

Discolichenes

Series I. Coniocarpineae. The paraphyses branch and form a network (capillitium) over the asci, the capillitium and ejected spores forming a long persistent powdery mass (mazaedium).
 Caliciaceae, Cypheliaceae, Sphaerophoraceae.

Series II. Graphidineae. Apothecia seldom round, usually elongated-ellipsoidal, no capillitium.
 Arthoniaceae, Graphidiaceae, Roccellaceae.

Series III. Cyclocarpineae, Apothecium usually circular, no capillitium.

A. Spores usually two-celled, either with a strongly thickened cross-wall often perforated by a narrow canal or with cross-wall only slightly thickened. In the first case the spores are usually colourless, the second case always brown.
 Buelliaceae, Physciaceae.

B. Spores unicellular, parallel-multicellular or muriform, usually colourless, cross-walls usually thin.
 α Thallus in moist state more or less gelatinous.
  Gonidia always belonging to the Cyanophyceae. Lichinaceae, Ephebaceae, Collemaceae, Pyrenopsidaceae.
 β Thallus not gelatinous.
  Coenogoniaceae, Lecideaceae, Cladoniaceae, Lecanoraceae, Pertusariaceae, Peltigeraceae, Stictaceae, Pannariaceae, Gyrophoraceae, Parmeliaceae, Cladoniaceae, Usneaceae.

Basidiolichenes (Hymenolichenes)

Cora, *Dictyonema* (incl. Laudatea), *Corella* (doubtfully placed here as the hymenium is unknown).

Habitats and Distribution of Lichens.

1. *Habitats.*—These are extremely varied, and comprise a great number of very different substrata. Chiefly, however, they are the bark of trees, rocks, the ground, mosses and, rarely, perennial leaves. (*a*) With respect to *corticolous* lichens, some prefer the rugged bark of old trees (*e.g. Ramalina, Parmelia, Sticlei*) and others the smooth bark of young trees and shrubs (*e.g. Graphidei* and some *Lecideae*). Many are found principally in large forests (*e.g. Usnea, Alectoria jubata*); while a few occur more especially on trees by roadsides (*e.g. Physcia parietina* and *Ph. pulverulenta*). In connexion with corticolous lichens may be mentioned those *lignicole* species which grow on decayed, or decaying wood of trees and on old pales (*e.g. Caliciei*, various *Lecideae, Xylographa*). (*b*) As to *saxicolous* lichens, which occur on rocks and stones, they may be divided into two sections, viz. *calcicolous* and *calcifugous*. To the former belong such as are found on calcareous and cretaceous rocks, and the mortar of walls (*e.g. Lecanora calcarea, Lecidea calcivora* and several *Verrucariae*), while all other saxicolous lichens may be regarded as belonging to the latter, whatever may be the mineralogical character of the substratum. It is here worthy of notice that the apothecia of several calcicolous lichens (*e.g. Lecanora Prevostii, Lecidea calcivora*) have the power of forming minute cavities in the rock, in which they are partially buried. (*c*) With respect to terrestrial species, some prefer peaty soil (*e.g. Cladonia, Lecidea decolorans*), others calcareous soil (*e.g. Lecanora crassa, Lecidea decipiens*), others sandy soil or hardened mud (*e.g. Collema limosum, Peltidea venosa*); while many may be found growing on all kinds of soil, from the sands of the sea-shore to the granitic detritus of lofty mountains, with the exception of course of cultivated ground, there being no agrarian lichens. (*d*) *Muscicolous* lichens again are such as are most frequently met with on decayed mosses and *Jungermannia*, whether on the ground, trees or rocks (*e.g. Leptogium muscicola, Gomphillus calicioides*). (*e*) The *epiphyllous* species are very peculiar as occurring upon perennial leaves of certain trees and shrubs, whose vitality is not at all affected by their presence as it is by that of fungi. In so far, however, as is known, they are very limited in number (*e.g. Lecidea, Bouteillei, Strigula*).

Sometimes various lichens occur abnormally in such unexpected habitats as dried dung of sheep, bleached bones of reindeer and whales, old leather, iron and glass, in districts where the species are abundant. It is apparent that in many cases lichens are quite indifferent to the substrata on which they occur, whence we infer that the preference of several for certain substrata depends upon the temperature of the locality or that of the special habitat. Thus in the case of saxicolous lichens the mineralogical character of the rock has of itself little or no influence upon lichen growth, which is influenced more especially and directly by their physical properties, such as their capacity for retaining heat and moisture. As a rule lichens grow commonly in open exposed habitats, though some are found only or chiefly in shady situations; while, as already observed, scarcely any occur where the atmosphere is impregnated with smoke. Many species also prefer growing in moist places by streams, lakes and the sea, though very few are normally and probably none entirely, *aquatic*, being always at certain seasons exposed for a longer or shorter period to the atmosphere (*e.g. Lichina, Leptogium rivulare, Endocarpon fluviatile, Verrucaria maura*). Some species are entirely parasitical on other lichens (*e.g.* various *Lecideae* and *Pyrenocarpei*), and may be peculiar to one (*e.g. Lecidea vitellinaria*) or common to several species (*e.g. Habrothallus parmeliarum*). A few, generally known as *erratic* species, have been met with growing unattached to any substratum (*e.g. Parmelia revoluta*, var. *concentrica, Lecanora esculenta*); but it can hardly be that these are really free *ab initio* (*vide* Crombie in *Journ. Bot.*, 1872, p. 306). It is to the different characters of the stations they occupy with respect to exposure, moisture, &c., that the variability observed in many types of lichens is to be attributed.

2. *Distribution.*—From what has now been said it will readily be inferred that the distribution of lichens over the surface of the globe is regulated, not only by the presence of suitable substrata, but more especially by climatic conditions. At the same time it may safely be affirmed that their geographical range is more extended than that of any other class of plants, occurring as they do in the coldest and warmest regions—on the dreary shores of arctic and antarctic seas and in the torrid valleys of tropical climes, as well as on the greatest mountain elevations yet attained by man, on projecting rocks even far above the snow-line (*e.g. Lecidea geographica*). In arctic regions lichens form by far the largest portion of the vegetation, occurring everywhere on the ground and on rocks, and fruiting freely; while terrestrial species of *Cladonia* and *Stereocaulon* are seen in the greatest luxuriance and abundance spreading over extensive tracts almost to the entire exclusion of other vegetation. The lichen flora of temperate regions again is essentially distinguished from the preceding by the frequency of corticolous species belonging to *Lecanora, Lecidea* and *Graphidei*. In intertropical regions lichens attain their maximum development (and beauty) in the foliaceous *Sticlei* and *Parmeliei*, while they are especially characterized by epiphyllous species, as *Strigula*, and by many peculiar corticole *Thelotremei, Graphidei* and *Pyrenocarpei*. Some lichens, especially saxicolous ones, seem to be cosmopolitan (*e.g. Lecanora subfusca, Cladonia pyxidata*); and others, not strictly cosmopolitan, have been observed in regions widely apart. A considerable number of species, European and exotic, seem to be *endemic*, but further research will no doubt show that most of them occur in other climatic regions similar to those in which they have hitherto alone been detected. To give any detailed account, however, of the distribution of the different genera (not to speak of that of individual species) of lichens would necessarily far exceed available limits.

Bibliography.—General: Engler and Prantl, *Die natürlichen Pflanzenfamilien*, Teil 1, Abt. 1 * where full literature will be found up to 1898. M. Funfstuck, "Der gegenwärtige Stand der Flechtenkunde," *Refer. Generalvers. d. deut. bot. Ges.* (1902). Dual Nature: J. Baranetzky, "Beiträge zur Kenntnis des selbstständigen Lebens der Flechtengonidien," *Prings. Jahrb. f. wiss. Bot.* vii. (1869); E. Bornet, "Recherches sur les gonidies des lichens," *Ann. de sci. nat. bot.*, 5 sér. n. 17 (1873); G. Bonnier, "Recherches sur la synthèse des lichens," *Ann. de sci. nat. bot.*, 7 sér. n. 9 (1889); A. Famintzin and J. Baranetzky, "Zur Entwickelungsgeschichte der Gonidien u. Zoosporenbildung der Lichenen," *Bot. Zeit.* (1867, p. 189, 1868, p. 169); S. Schwendener, *Die Algentypen der Flechtengonidien* (Basel, 1869); A. Möller, *Über die Kultur flechtenbildender Ascomyceten ohne Algen.* (Münster, 1887). Sexuality: E. Stahl, *Beiträge zur Entwickelungsgeschichte der Flechten* (Leipzig, 1877); G. Lindau, *Über Anlage und Entwickelung einiger Flechtenapothecien* (Flora, 1888); E. Baur, "Zur Frage nach der Sexualität der Collemaceae," *Ber. d. deut. bot. Ges.* (1898); "Über Anlage und

Entwickelung einiger Flechtenapothecien" (*Flora*, Bd. 88, 1901); "Untersuchungen über die Entwickelungsgeschichte der Flechtenapothecien," *Bot. Zeit.* (1904); O. V. Darbishire, "Über die Apothecium-entwickelung der Flechte, Physcia pulverulenta," *Nyl. Prings. Jahrb.* (Bd. 34, 1900). Chemistry.—W. Zopf, "Vergleichende Produkte," *Beitr. z. bot. Centralbl.* (Bd. 14, 1903); *Die Flechtenstoffe* (Jena, 1907). (J. M. C.; V. H. B.)

LICHFIELD, a city, county of a city, and municipal borough in the Lichfield parliamentary division of Staffordshire, England, 118 m. N.W. from London. Pop. (1901) 7902. The London and North-Western railway has stations at Trent Valley Junction on the main line, and in the city on a branch westward. The town lies in a pleasant country, on a small stream draining eastward to the Trent, with low hills to the E. and S. The cathedral is small (the full internal length is only 370 ft., and the breadth of the nave 68 ft.), but beautiful in both situation and style. It stands near a picturesque sheet of water named Minster Pool. The present building dates from various periods in the 13th and early 14th centuries, but the various portions cannot be allocated to fixed years, as the old archives were destroyed during the Civil Wars of the 17th century. The earlier records of the church are equally doubtful. A Saxon church founded by St Chad, who was subsequently enshrined here, occupied the site from the close of the 7th century; of its Norman successor portions of the foundations have been excavated, but no record exists either of its date or of its builders. The fine exterior of the cathedral exhibits the feature, unique in England, of a lofty central and two lesser western spires, of which the central, 252 ft. high, is a restoration attributed to Sir Christopher Wren after its destruction during the Civil Wars. The west front is composed of three stages of ornate arcading, with niches containing statues, of which most are modern. Within, the south transept shows simple Early English work, the north transept and chapter house more ornate work of a later period in that style, the nave, with its geometrical ornament, marks the transition to the Decorated style, while the Lady chapel is a [illegible] specimen of fully developed Decorated work with an [illegible] east end. The west front probably falls in date between the nave and the Lady chapel. Among numerous monuments [illegible] memorials to Samuel Johnson, a native of Lichfield, and [illegible] Garrick, who spent his early life and was educated here; [illegible] monument to Major Hodson, who fell in the Indian mutiny, [illegible] whose father was canon of Lichfield; the tomb of Bishop [illegible], who restored the cathedral after the Civil Wars; and a [illegible] effigy of Perpendicular date displaying Sir John [illegible] stripped to the waist and awaiting chastisement. Here [illegible] the "Sleeping Children," a masterpiece by Chantrey (1817). [illegible] bishop's palace (1687) and a theological college [illegible] are adjacent to the cathedral. The diocese covers the [illegible] part of Staffordshire and about half the parishes in [illegible], with small portions of Cheshire and Derbyshire. [illegible] church of St Chad is ancient though extensively restored; [illegible] St Chad is said to have occupied a hermit's cell. The [illegible] schools are those of King Edward and St Chad. There [illegible] picturesque half-timbered and other old houses, among [illegible] that in which Johnson was born, which stands in the [illegible], and is the property of the corporation and opened [illegible]. There is also in the market place a statue to [illegible] fair is held annually on Whit-Monday, accompanied [illegible] of ancient origin. Brewing is the principal industry, [illegible] neighbourhood are large market gardens. The city [illegible] by a mayor, 6 aldermen and 18 councillors. Area, [illegible]

[illegible] a tradition that "Christianfield" near Lichfield was [illegible] the martyrdom of a thousand Christians during the [illegible] of Maximian about 286, but there is no evidence in [illegible] the tradition. At Wall, 3 m. from the present city, [illegible] a Romano-British village called Letocetum ("grey [illegible] which the first half of the name Lichfield is [illegible] first authentic notice of Lichfield (*Lyccidfelth*, [illegible]) occurs in Bede's history where it is mentioned [illegible] St Chad fixed the episcopal see of the Mercians. [illegible] of the see by St Chad in 669, it was raised in 786 by Pope Adrian through the influence of Offa, King of Mercia, to the dignity of an archbishopric, but in 803 the primacy was restored to Canterbury. In 1075 the see of Lichfield was removed to Chester, and thence a few years later to Coventry, but it was restored in 1148. At the time of the Domesday Survey Lichfield was held by the bishop of Chester: it is not called a borough, and it was a small village, whence, on account of its insignificance, the see had been moved. The lordship and manor of the town were held by the bishop until the reign of Edward VI., when they were leased to the corporation. There is evidence that a castle existed here in the time of Bishop Roger Clinton (*temp.* Henry I.), and a footpath near the grammar-school retains the name of Castle-ditch. Richard II. gave a charter (1387) for the foundation of the gild of St Mary and St John the Baptist; this gild obtained the whole local government, which it exercised until its dissolution by Edward VI., who incorporated the town (1548), vesting the government in two bailiffs and twenty-four burgesses; further charters were given by Mary, James I. and Charles II. (1664), the last, incorporating it under the title of the "bailiffs and citizens of the city of Lichfield," was the governing charter until 1835; under this charter the governing body consisted of two bailiffs and twenty-four brethren. Lichfield sent two members to the parliament of 1304 and to a few succeeding parliaments, but the representation did not become regular until 1552; in 1867 it lost one member, and in 1885 its representation was merged in that of the county. By the charter of James I. the market day was changed from Wednesday to Tuesday and Friday; the Tuesday market disappeared during the 19th century; the only existing fair is a small pleasure fair of ancient origin held on Ash-Wednesday; the annual fête on Whit-Monday claims to date from the time of Alfred. In the Civil Wars Lichfield was divided. The cathedral authorities with a certain following were for the king, but the townsfolk generally sided with the parliament, and this led to the fortification of the close in 1643. Lord Brooke, notorious for his hostility to the church, came against it, but was killed by a deflected bullet on St Chad's day, an accident welcomed as a miracle by the Royalists. The close yielded and was retaken by Prince Rupert in this year; but on the breakdown of the king's cause in 1646 it again surrendered. The cathedral suffered terrible damage in these years.

See Rev. T Harwood, *Hist. and Antiquities of Church and City of Lichfield* (1806), *Victoria County History, Stafford.*

LICH-GATE, or LYCH-GATE (from O. Eng. *lic* "a body, a corpse"; cf Ger. *Leiche*), the roofed-in gateway or porch-entrance to churchyards. Lich-gates existed in England certainly thirteen centuries ago, but comparatively few early ones survive, as they were almost always of wood. One at Bray, Berkshire, is dated 1448. Here the clergy meet the corpse and some portion of the service is read. The gateway was really part of the church; it also served to shelter the pall-bearers while the bier was brought from the church. In some lich-gates there stood large flat stones called lich-stones upon which the corpse, usually uncoffined, was laid. The most common form of lich-gate is a simple shed composed of a roof with two gabled ends, covered with tiles or thatch. At Berrynarbor, Devon, there is a lich-gate in the form of a cross, while at Troutbeck, Westmorland, there are three lich-gates to one churchyard. Some elaborate gates have chambers over them. The word *lich* entered into composition constantly in old English, thus, lich-bell, the hand-bell rung before a corpse; lich-way, the path along which a corpse was carried to burial (this in some districts was supposed to establish a right-of-way); lich-owl, the screech-owl, because its cry was a portent of death; and lyke-wake, a night watch over a corpse.

LICHTENBERG, GEORG CHRISTOPH (1742–1799), German physicist and satirical writer, was born at Oberramstadt, near Darmstadt, on the 1st of July 1742. In 1763 he entered Göttingen university, where in 1769 he became extraordinary professor of physics, and six years later ordinary professor. This post he held till his death on the 24th of February 1799. As a physicist he is best known for his investigations in electricity, more especially as to the so-called Lichtenberg figures, which are fully described in two memoirs *Super nova methodo motum ac naturam fluidi electrici investigandi* (Göttingen, 1777–1778). These figures, originally studied on account of the light they were supposed to throw on the nature of the electric fluid or fluids, have reference to the distribution of electricity over the surface of non-conductors. They are produced as follows: A sharp-pointed needle is placed perpendicular to a non-conducting plate, such as of resin, ebonite or glass, with its point very near to or in contact with the plate, and a Leyden jar is discharged into the needle. The electrification of the plate is now tested by sifting over it a mixture of flowers of sulphur and red lead. The negatively electrified sulphur is seen to attach itself to the positively electrified parts of the plate, and the positively electrified red lead to the negatively electrified parts. In addition to the distribution of colour thereby produced, there is a marked difference in the *form* of the figure, according to the nature of the electricity originally communicated to the plate. If it be positive, a widely extending patch is seen on the plate, consisting of a dense nucleus, from which branches radiate in all directions; if negative the patch is much smaller and has a sharp circular boundary entirely devoid of branches. If the plate receives a mixed charge, as, for example, from an induction coil, a "mixed" figure results, consisting of a large red central nucleus, corresponding to the negative charge, surrounded by yellow rays, corresponding to the positive charge. The difference between the positive and negative figures seems to depend on the presence of the air; for the difference tends to disappear when the experiment is conducted in vacuo. Riess explains it by the negative electrification of the plate caused by the friction of the water vapour, &c., driven along the surface by the explosion which accompanies the disruptive discharge at the point. This electrification would favour the spread of a positive, but hinder that of a negative discharge. There is, in all probability, a connexion between this phenomenon and the peculiarities of positive and negative brush and other discharge in air.

As a satirist and humorist Lichtenberg takes high rank among the German writers of the 18th century. His biting wit involved him in many controversies with well-known contemporaries, such as Lavater, whose science of physiognomy he ridiculed, and Voss, whose views on Greek pronunciation called forth a powerful satire, *Über die Pronunciation der Schöpse des alten Griechenlandes* (1782). In 1769 and again in 1774 he resided for some time in England and his *Briefe aus England* (1776–1778), with admirable descriptions of Garrick's acting, are the most attractive of his writings. He contributed to the *Göttinger Taschenkalender* from 1778 onwards, and to the *Göttingisches Magazin der Literatur und Wissenschaft*, which he edited for three years (1780–1782) with J. G. A. Forster. He also published in 1794–1799 an *Ausführliche Erklärung der Hogarthschen Kupferstiche.*

Lichtenberg's *Vermischte Schriften* were published by F. Kries in 9 vols. (1800–1805); new editions in 8 vols. (1844–1846 and 1867). Selections by E. Grisebach, *Lichtenbergs Gedanken und Maximen* (1871); by F. Robertag (in Kürschner's *Deutsche Nationalliteratur* (vol. 141, 1886); and by A. Wilbrandt (1893). Lichtenberg's *Briefe* have been published in 3 vols. by C. Schüddekopf and A. Leitzmann (1900–1902); his *Aphorismen* by A. Leitzmann (3 vols., 1902–1906). See also R. M. Meyer, *Swift und Lichtenberg* (1886); F. Lauchert, *Lichtenbergs schriftstellerische Tätigkeit* (1893); and A. Leitzmann, *Aus Lichtenbergs Nachlass* (1899).

LICHTENBERG, formerly a small German principality on the west bank of the Rhine, enclosed by the Nahe, the Blies and the Glan, now belonging to the government district of Trier, Prussian Rhine province. The principality was constructed of parts of the electorate of Trier, of Nassau-Saarbrücken and other districts, and lay between Rhenish Bavaria and the old Prussian province of the Rhine. Originally called the lordship of Baumholder, it owed the name of Lichtenberg and its elevation in 1819 to a principality to Ernest, duke of Saxe-Coburg, to whom it was ceded by Prussia, in 1816, in accordance with terms agreed upon at the congress of Vienna. The duke, however, restored it to Prussia in 1834, in return for an annual pension of £12,000 sterling. The area is about 210 sq. m.

LICINIANUS, GRANIUS, Roman annalist, probably lived in the age of the Antonines (2nd century A.D.). He was the author of a brief epitome of Roman history based upon Livy, which he utilised as a means of displaying his antiquarian lore. Accounts of omens, portents, prodigies and other remarkable things apparently took up a considerable portion of the work. Some fragments of the books relating to the years 163–178 B.C. are preserved in a British Museum MS.

EDITIONS.—C. A. Pertz (1857); seven Bonn students (1858); M. Flemisch (1904); see also J. N. Madvig, *Kleine philologische Schriften* (1875), and the list of articles in periodicals in Flemisch's edition (p. iv.).

LICINIUS [FLAVIUS GALERIUS VALERIUS LICINIANUS], Roman emperor, A.D. 307–324, of Illyrian peasant origin, was born probably about 250. After the death of Flavius Valerius Severus he was elevated to the rank of Augustus by Galerius, his former friend and companion in arms, on the 11th of November 307, receiving as his immediate command the provinces of Illyricum. On the death of Galerius, in May 311, he shared the entire empire with Maximinus, the Hellespont and the Thracian Bosporus being the dividing line. In March 313 he married Constantia, half-sister of Constantine, at Mediolanum (Milan), in the following month inflicted a decisive defeat on Maximinus at Heraclea Pontica, and established himself master of the East, while his brother-in-law, Constantine, was supreme in the West. In 314 his jealousy led him to encourage a treasonable enterprise on the part of Bassianus against Constantine. When his perfidy became known a civil war ensued, in which he was twice severely defeated—first near Cibalae in Pannonia (October 8th, 314), and next in the plain of Mardia in Thrace; the outward reconciliation, which was effected in the following December, left Licinius in possession of Thrace, Asia Minor, Syria and Egypt, but added numerous provinces to the Western empire. In 323 Constantine, tempted by the "advanced age and unpopular vices" of his colleague, again declared war against him, and, having defeated his army at Adrianople (3rd of July 323), succeeded in shutting him up within the walls of Byzantium. The defeat of the superior fleet of Licinius by Flavius Julius Crispus, Constantine's eldest son, compelled his withdrawal to Bithynia, where a last stand was made; the battle of Chrysopolis, near Chalcedon (18th of September), finally resulted in his submission. He was interned at Thessalonica and executed in the following year on a charge of treasonable correspondence with the barbarians.

See Zosimus ii. 7–28; Zonaras xiii. 1; Victor, *Caes.* 40, 41; Eutropius x. 3; Orosius vii. 28.

LICINIUS CALVUS STOLO, GAIUS, Roman statesman, the chief representative of the plebeian Licinian gens, was tribune in 377 B.C., consul in 361. His name is associated with the Licinian or Licinio-Sextian laws (proposed 377, passed 367), which practically ended the struggle between patricians and plebeians. He was himself fined for possessing a larger share of the public land than his own law allowed.

See ROME: *History*, II. "The Republic."

LICINIUS MACER CALVUS, GAIUS (82–47 B.C.), Roman poet and orator, was the son of the annalist Licinius Macer. As a poet he is associated with his friend Catullus, whom he followed in style and choice of subjects. As an orator he was the leader of the opponents of the florid Asiatic school, who took the simplest Attic orators as their model and attacked even Cicero as wordy and artificial. Calvus held a correspondence on questions connected with rhetoric, perhaps (if the reading be correct) the *commentarii* alluded to by Tacitus (*Dialogus*, 23; compare also Cicero, *Ad Fam.* xv. 21) Twenty-one speeches by him are mentioned, amongst which the most famous were those delivered against Publius Vatinius. Calvus was very short of stature, and is alluded to by Catullus (Ode 53) as *Salaputium disertum* (eloquent Lilliputian).

For Cicero's opinion see *Brutus*, 82; Quintilian x. 1. 115; Tacitus, *Dialogus*, 18. 21; the monograph by F. Plessis (Paris, 1896) contains a collection of the fragments (verse and prose).

[illegible] province of Catania, [illegible] Catania by rail. Pop. [illegible] the place in 1872 [illegible] Greek city of Euboea, [illegible] early in the 6th century [illegible] the site of an [illegible] have been explored. [illegible] but practically all [illegible] the fourth period (700- [illegible] Hellenization among [illegible]

[illegible] *Notizie degli scavi*, [illegible] (T. As.)

[illegible] a class of the [illegible] Roman and provincial [illegible] supposed by some to have [illegible] back to the regal period [illegible] The majority of the [illegible] formed a corporation divided [illegible] the magistrates in office [illegible] the nomination of their [illegible] perhaps girded up; on a [illegible] the red military [illegible] representatives of magis- [illegible] they carried the fasces and [illegible] They were exempt from [illegible] theoretically they were [illegible] They were the constant [illegible] of the magistrate to [illegible] before him in Indian [illegible] through the crowd, [illegible] the marks of respect due to [illegible] when he took his seat on the [illegible] against the wall of [illegible] offenders before him, [illegible] (in earlier times) carried [illegible] should be noted that directly a [illegible] state, he was obliged [illegible] The king had twelve lictors; each [illegible] their institution) twelve, [illegible] consul, although [illegible] original arrangement; the [illegible] twenty-four; the emperors [illegible] who had twenty-four. The [illegible] the *magister vicorum* (over- [illegible] city was divided) were also [illegible] were probably supplied [illegible] in number, whose functions were [illegible] in attendance on the [illegible] summoned the comitia [illegible] merely a formality, acted [illegible] assembly. Lictors were also [illegible] the celebration of funeral [illegible] games provided by them and [illegible] their supervision.

[illegible] see Mommsen, *Römisches* [illegible]

[illegible] (1811–1898), English scholar [illegible] Henry George Liddell, younger [illegible] was born at Binchester, [illegible] of February 1811. He was [illegible] Christ Church, Oxford. Gaining [illegible] became a college tutor, and was [illegible] Dean Gaisford appointed [illegible] and in 1846 he was appointed to the headmastership of Westminster School. Meanwhile his life work, the great *Lexicon* (based on the German work of F. Passow), which he and Robert Scott began as early as 1834, had made good progress, and the first edition appeared in 1843. It immediately became the standard Greek-English dictionary and still maintains this rank, although, notwithstanding the great additions made of late to our Greek vocabulary from inscriptions, papyri and other sources, scarcely any enlargement has been made since about 1880. The 8th edition was published in 1897. As headmaster of Westminster Liddell enjoyed a period of great success, followed by trouble due to the outbreak of fever and cholera in the school. In 1855 he accepted the deanery of Christ Church, then vacant by the death of Gaisford. In the same year he brought out a *History of Ancient Rome* (much used in an abridged form as the *Student's History of Rome*) and took a very active part in the first Oxford University Commission. His tall figure, fine presence and aristocratic mien were for many years associated with all that was characteristic of Oxford life. Coming just at the transition period when the "old Christ Church," which Pusey strove so hard to preserve, was inevitably becoming broader and more liberal, it was chiefly due to Liddell that necessary changes were effected with the minimum of friction. In 1859 Liddell welcomed the then prince of Wales when he matriculated at Christ Church, being the first holder of that title who had matriculated since Henry V. In conjunction with Sir Henry Acland, Liddell did much to encourage the study of art at Oxford, and his taste and judgment gained him the admiration and friendship of Ruskin. In 1891, owing to advancing years, he resigned the deanery. The last years of his life were spent at Ascot, where he died on the 18th of January 1898. Dean Liddell married in July 1846 Miss Lorina Reeve (d. 1910), by whom he had a numerous family.

See memoir by H. L. Thompson, *Henry George Liddell* (1899).

[illegible] are ῥαβδοῦχοι, ῥαβδοφόροι, [illegible] word is variously derived [illegible] (*b*) *licere*, to summon, [illegible] before the magistrate; [illegible] (according to some) their toga [illegible] assuming an [illegible] one

LIDDESDALE, the valley of Liddel Water, Roxburghshire, Scotland, extending in a south-westerly direction from the vicinity of Peel Fell to the Esk, a distance of 21 m. The Waverley route of the North British railway runs down the dale, and the Catrail, or Picts' Dyke, crosses its head. At one period the points of vantage on the river and its affluents were occupied with freebooters' peel-towers, but many of them have disappeared and the remainder are in decay. Larriston Tower belonged to the Elliots, Mangerton to the Armstrongs and Park to "little Jock Elliot," the outlaw who nearly killed Bothwell in an encounter in 1566. The chief point of interest in the valley, however, is Hermitage Castle, a vast, massive H-shaped fortress of enormous strength, one of the oldest baronial buildings in Scotland. It stands on a hill overlooking Hermitage Water, a tributary of the Liddel. It was built in 1244 by Nicholas de Soulis and was captured by the English in David II.'s reign. It was retaken by Sir William Douglas, who received a grant of it from the king. In 1492 Archibald Douglas, 5th earl of Angus, exchanged it for Bothwell Castle on the Clyde with Patrick Hepburn, 1st earl of Bothwell. It finally passed to the duke of Buccleuch, under whose care further ruin has been arrested. It was here that Sir Alexander Ramsay of Dalhousie was starved to death by Sir William Douglas in 1342, and that James Hepburn, 4th earl of Bothwell, was visited by Mary, queen of Scots, after the assault referred to.

To the east of the castle is Ninestane Rig, a hill 943 ft. high, 4 m. long and 1 m. broad, where it is said that William de Soulis, hated for oppression and cruelty, was (in 1320) boiled by his own vassals in a copper cauldron, which was supported on two of the nine stones which composed the "Druidical" circle that gave the ridge its name. Only five of the stones remain. James Telfer (1802–1862), the writer of ballads, who was born in the parish of Southdean (pronounced Soudan), was for several years schoolmaster of Saughtree, near the head of the valley. The castle of the lairds of Liddesdale stood near the junction of Hermitage Water and the Liddel and around it grew up the village of Castleton.

LIDDON, HENRY PARRY (1829–1890), English divine, was the son of a naval captain and was born at North Stoneham, Hampshire, on the 20th of August 1829. He was educated at King's College School, London, and at Christ Church, Oxford, where he graduated, taking a second class, in 1850. As vice-principal of the theological college at Cuddesdon (1854–1859) he wielded considerable influence, and, on returning to Oxford as vice-principal of St Edmund's Hall, became a growing force among the undergraduates, exercising his influence in strong opposition to the liberal reaction against Tractarianism, which had set in after Newman's secession in 1845. In 1864 the bishop of Salisbury (W. K. Hamilton), whose examining chaplain he had been, appointed him prebendary of Salisbury cathedral. In 1866 he delivered his Bampton Lectures on the doctrine of the divinity of Christ. From that time his fame as a preacher, which had been steadily growing, may be considered established. In 1870 he was made canon of St Paul's Cathedral, London. He had before this published *Some Words for God*, in which, with great power and eloquence, he combated the scepticism of the day. His preaching at St Paul's soon attracted vast crowds. The afternoon sermon, which fell to the lot of the canon in residence, had usually been delivered in the choir, but soon after Liddon's appointment it became necessary to preach the sermon under the dome, where from 3000 to 4000 persons used to gather to hear the preacher. Few orators belonging to the Church of England have acquired so great a reputation as Liddon. Others may have surpassed him in originality, learning or reasoning power, but for grasp of his subject, clearness of language, lucidity of arrangement, felicity of illustration, vividness of imagination, elegance of diction, and above all, for sympathy with the intellectual position of those whom he addressed, he has hardly been rivalled. In the elaborate arrangement of his matter he is thought to have imitated the great French preachers of the age of Louis XIV. In 1870 he had also been made Ireland professor of exegesis at Oxford. The combination of the two appointments gave him extensive influence over the Church of England. With Dean Church he may be said to have restored the waning influence of the Tractarian school, and he succeeded in popularizing the opinions which, in the hands of Pusey and Keble, had appealed to thinkers and scholars. His forceful spirit was equally conspicuous in his opposition to the Church Discipline Act of 1874, and in his denunciation of the Bulgarian atrocities of 1876. In 1882 he resigned his professorship and utilized his thus increased leisure by travelling in Palestine and Egypt, and showed his interest in the Old Catholic movement by visiting Döllinger at Munich. In 1886 he became chancellor of St Paul's, and it is said that he declined more than one offer of a bishopric. He died on the 9th of September 1890, in the full vigour of his intellect and at the zenith of his reputation. He had undertaken and nearly completed an elaborate life of Dr Pusey, for whom his admiration was unbounded; and this work was completed after his death by Messrs Johnston and Wilson. Liddon's great influence during his life was due to his personal fascination and the beauty of his pulpit oratory rather than to any high qualities of intellect. As a theologian his outlook was that of the 16th rather than the 19th century; and, reading his Bampton Lectures now, it is difficult to realize how they can ever have been hailed as a great contribution to Christian apologetics. To the last he maintained the narrow standpoint of Pusey and Keble, in defiance of all the developments of modern thought and modern scholarship; and his latter years were embittered by the consciousness that the younger generation of the disciples of his school were beginning to make friends of the Mammon of scientific unrighteousness. The publication in 1889 of *Lux Mundi*, a series of essays attempting to harmonize Anglican Catholic doctrine with modern thought, was a severe blow to him, for it showed that even at the Pusey House, established as the citadel of Puseyism at Oxford, the principles of Pusey were being departed from. Liddon's importance is now mainly historical. He was the last of the classical pulpit orators of the English Church, the last great popular exponent of the traditional Anglican orthodoxy. Besides the works mentioned, Liddon published several volumes of *Sermons*, a volume of Lent lectures entitled *Some Elements of Religion* (1870), and a collection of *Essays and Addresses* on such themes as Buddhism, Dante, &c.

See *Life and Letters*, by J. O. Johnston (1904); G. W. E. Russell, *H. P. Liddon* (1903); A. B. Donaldson, *Five Great Oxford Leaders* (1900), from which the life of Liddon was reprinted separately in 1905.

LIE, JONAS LAURITZ EDEMIL (1833–1908), Norwegian novelist, was born on the 6th of November 1833 close to Hougsund (Eker), near Drammen. In 1838, his father being appointed sheriff of Tromsö, the family removed to that Arctic town. Here the future novelist enjoyed an untrammelled childhood among the shipping of the little Nordland capital, and gained acquaintance with the wild seafaring life which he was afterwards to describe. In 1846 he was sent to the naval school at Frederiksvaern, but his extreme near-sight unfitted him for the service, and he was transferred to the Latin school at Bergen. In 1851 he went to the university of Christiania, where Ibsen and Björnson were among his fellow-students. Jonas Lie, however, showed at this time no inclination to literature. He pursued his studies as a lawyer, took his degrees in law in 1858, and settled down to practice as a solicitor in the little town of Kongsvinger. In 1860 he married his cousin, Thomasine Lie, whose collaboration in his work he acknowledged in 1893 in a graceful article in the *Samtiden* entitled "Min hustru." In 1866 he published his first book, a volume of poems. He made unlucky speculations in wood, and the consequent financial embarrassment induced him to return to Christiania to try his luck as a man of letters. As a journalist he had no success, but in 1870 he published a melancholy little romance, *Den Fremsynte* (Eng. trans., *The Visionary*, 1894), which made him famous. Lie proceeded to Rome, and published *Tales* in 1871 and *Tremasteren "Fremtiden"* (Eng. trans., *The Barque "Future,"* Chicago, 1879), a novel, in 1872. His first great book, however, was *Lodsen og hans Hustru* (*The Pilot and his Wife*, 1874), which placed him at the head of Norwegian novelists; it was written in the little town of Rocca di Papa in the Albano mountains. From that time Lie enjoyed, with Björnson and Ibsen, a stipend as poet from the Norwegian government. Lie spent the next few years partly in Dresden, partly in Stuttgart, with frequent summer excursions to Berchtesgaden in the Bavarian highlands. During his exile he produced the drama in verse called *Faustina Strozzi* (1876). Returning to Norway, Lie began a series of romances of modern life in Christiania, of which *Thomas Ross* (1878) and *Adam Schrader* (1879) were the earliest. He returned to Germany, and settled first in Dresden again, then in Hamburg, until 1882, when he took up his abode in Paris, where he lived in close retirement in the society of Scandinavian friends. His summers were spent at Berchtesgaden in Tirol. The novels of his German period are *Rutland* (1881) and *Gaa paa* ("*Go Ahead!*" 1882), tales of life in the Norwegian merchant navy. His subsequent works, produced with great regularity, enjoyed an immense reputation in Norway. Among the best of them are: *Livsslaven* (1883, Eng. trans., "*One of Life's Slaves,*" 1895); *Familjen paa Gilje* ("*The Family of Gilje,*" 1883); *Malstroem* (1885), describing the gradual ruin of a Norwegian family; *Et Samliv* ("*Life in Common,*" 1887), describing a marriage of convenience. Two of the most successful of his novels were *The Commodore's Daughters* (1886) and *Niobe* (1894), both of which were presented to English readers in the International library, edited by Mr Gosse. In 1891–1892 he wrote, under the influence of the new romantic impulse, twenty-four folk-tales, printed in two volumes entitled *Trold*. Some of these were translated by R. N. Bain in *Weird Tales* (1893), illustrated by L. Housman. Among his later works were the romance *Naar Sol gaar ned* ("*When the Sun goes down,*" 1895), the powerful novel of *Dyre Rein* (1896), the fairy drama of *Lindelin* (1897), *Faste Forland* (1899), a romance which contains much which is autobiographical, *When the Iron Curtain falls* (1901), and *The Consul* (1904). His *Samlede Vaerker* were published at Copenhagen in 14 vols. (1902–1904). Jonas Lie left Paris in 1891, and, after spending a year in Rome, returned to Norway, establishing himself at Holskogen, near Christiansand. He died at Christiania on the 5th of July 1908. As a novelist he stands with those minute and unobtrusive

[illegible] of great value to the government. He was one of the first to [illegible] secession, and was active in upholding [illegible] the Union. He prepared, upon the requisition of the president, [illegible] *War for the Government of the Armies [illegible] the Field*, which was promulgated by [illegible] General Orders No. 100 of the war department. [illegible] suggested to Bluntschli his codification of the law [illegible] in the preface to his *Droit International* [illegible] period also Lieber wrote his *Guerilla* [illegible] *the Laws and Usages of War*. At the [illegible] he was the umpire of the commission for the [illegible] claims. He died on the 2nd of October [illegible] were acquired by the University of California, [illegible] placed in the Johns Hopkins University.

[illegible] *Writings* were published by D. C. Gilman [illegible] See T. S. Perry, *Life and Letters* (1882), and [illegible].

[illegible], MAX (1849–), German painter and [illegible], was born in Berlin. After studying under Steffeck, [illegible] the school of art at Weimar in 1869. Though the [illegible] of his first exhibited picture, "Women [illegible]," presented already a striking contrast [illegible] art then in vogue, it was heavy and [illegible] like all the artist's paintings before his [illegible]. A summer spent at Barbizon [illegible] personally acquainted with Millet [illegible] the works of Corot, Troyon, and [illegible] the clearing and brightening of his palette, [illegible] the example of Munkacsy, under whose [illegible] his first pictures in Paris. He sub[illegible] where the example of Israels con[illegible] he had adopted at Barbizon but on [illegible] he caused much unfavourable [illegible] painting of "Christ in the Temple," [illegible] by the clergy as irreverent and [illegible] scriptural subject. Henceforth he [illegible] the study of free-light and [illegible]. He found his best subjects [illegible] the old [illegible] Amsterdam, among the [illegible] and village streets of Holland, and [illegible] and workrooms [illegible] however [illegible] admitting [illegible]

[illegible] He became a member [illegible] of the Société [illegible] the Cercle des Aquarellistes [illegible] represented in most of the [illegible] galleries. The Berlin National [illegible] "[illegible]-Spinners"; the Munich Pinakothek [illegible] Goats"; the Hamburg Gallery, "The [illegible] the Hanover Gallery, the "Village Street [illegible] "The Seamstress" is at the Dresden Gallery; [illegible] in the Dunes" at Leipzig; "Dutch Orphan Girls" [illegible]; "Beer-cellar at Brandenburg" at the Luxembourg Museum in Paris, and the "Knöpflerinnen" in Venice. [illegible] etchings are to be found in the leading print cabinets of Europe.

LIEBIG, JUSTUS VON, BARON (1803–1873), German chemist, was born at Darmstadt, according to his baptismal certificate, on the 12th of May 1803 (4th of May, according to his mother). His father, a drysalter and dealer in colours, used sometimes to make experiments in the hope of finding improved processes for the production of his wares, and thus his son early acquired familiarity with practical chemistry. For the theoretical side he read all the text-books which he could find, somewhat to the detriment of his ordinary school studies. Having determined to make chemistry his profession, at the age of fifteen he entered the shop of an apothecary at Appenheim, near Darmstadt; but he soon found how great is the difference between practical pharmacy and scientific chemistry, and the explosions and other incidents that accompanied his private efforts to increase his chemical knowledge disposed his master to view without regret his departure at the end of ten months. He next entered the university of Bonn, but migrated to Erlangen when the professor of chemistry, K. W. G. Kastner (1783–1857), was appointed in 1821 to the chair of physics and chemistry at the latter university. He followed this professor to learn how to analyse certain minerals, but in the end he found that the teacher himself was ignorant of the process. Indeed, as he himself said afterwards, it was a wretched time for chemistry in Germany. No laboratories were accessible to ordinary students, who had to content themselves with what the universities could give in the lecture-room and the library, and though both at Bonn and Erlangen Liebig endeavoured to make up for the deficiencies of the official instruction by founding a students' physical and chemical society for the discussion of new discoveries and speculations, he felt that he could never become a chemist in his own country. Therefore, having graduated as Ph.D. in 1822, he left Erlangen—where he subsequently complained that the contagion of the "greatest philosopher and metaphysician of the century" (Schelling), in a period "rich in words and ideas, but poor in true knowledge and genuine studies," had cost him two precious years of his life—and by the liberality of Louis I., grand-duke of Hesse-Darmstadt, was enabled to go to Paris. By the help of L. J. Thénard he gained admission to the private laboratory of H. F. Gaultier de Claubry (1792–1873), professor of chemistry at the École de Pharmacie, and soon afterwards, by the influence of A. von Humboldt, to that of Gay-Lussac, where in 1824 he concluded his investigations on the composition of the fulminates. It was on Humboldt's advice that he determined to become a teacher of chemistry, but difficulties stood in his way. As a native of Hesse-Darmstadt he ought, according to the academical rules of the time, to have studied and graduated at the university of Giessen, and it was only through the influence of Humboldt that the authorities forgave him for straying to the foreign university of Erlangen. After examination his Erlangen degree was recognized, and in 1824 he was appointed extraordinary professor of chemistry at Giessen, becoming ordinary professor two years later. In this small town his most important work was accomplished. His first care was to persuade the Darmstadt government to provide a chemical laboratory in which the students might obtain a proper practical training. This laboratory, unique of its kind at the time, in conjunction with Liebig's unrivalled gifts as a teacher, soon rendered Giessen the most famous chemical school in the world; men flocked from every country to enjoy its advantages, and many of the most accomplished chemists of the 19th century had to thank it for their early training. Further, it gave a great impetus to the progress of chemical education throughout Germany, for the continued admonitions of Liebig combined with the influence of his pupils induced many other universities to build laboratories modelled on the same plan. He remained at Giessen for twenty-eight years, until in 1852 he accepted the invitation of the Bavarian government to the ordinary chair of chemistry at Munich university, and this office he held, although he was offered the chair at Berlin in 1865, until his death, which occurred at Munich on the 18th of April 1873.

Apart from Liebig's labours for the improvement of chemical teaching, the influence of his experimental researches and of his contributions to chemical thought was felt in every branch of the science. In regard to methods and apparatus, mention should be made of his improvements in the technique of organic analysis, his plan for determining the natural alkaloids and for ascertaining the molecular weights of organic bases by means of their chloroplatinates, his process for determining the quantity of urea in a solution—the first step towards the introduction of precise chemical methods into practical medicine—and his invention of the simple form of condenser known in every laboratory. His contributions to inorganic chemistry were numerous, including investigations on the compounds of antimony, aluminium, silicon, &c., on the separation of nickel and cobalt, and on the analysis of mineral waters, but they are outweighed in importance by his work on organic substances. In this domain his first research was on the fulminates of mercury and silver, and his study of these bodies led him to the discovery of the isomerism of cyanic and fulminic acids, for the composition of fulminic acid as found by him was the same as that of cyanic acid, as found by F. Wöhler, and it became necessary to admit them to be two bodies which differed in properties, though of the same percentage composition. Further work on cyanogen and connected substances yielded a great number of interesting derivatives, and he described an improved method for the manufacture of potassium cyanide, an agent which has since proved of enormous value in metallurgy and the arts. In 1832 he published, jointly with Wöhler, one of the most famous papers in the history of chemistry, that on the oil of bitter almonds (benzaldehyde), wherein it was shown that the radicle benzoyl might be regarded as forming an unchanging constituent of a long series of compounds obtained from oil of bitter almonds, throughout which it behaved like an element. Berzelius hailed this discovery as marking the dawn of a new era in organic chemistry, and proposed for benzoyl the names "Proin" or "Orthrin" (from πρωΐ and ὄρθρος). A continuation of their work on bitter almond oil by Liebig and Wöhler, who remained firm friends for the rest of their lives, resulted in the elucidation of the mode of formation of that substance and in the discovery of the ferment emulsin as well as the recognition of the first glucoside, amygdalin, while another and not less important and far-reaching inquiry in which they collaborated was that on uric acid, published in 1837. About 1832 he began his investigations into the constitution of ether and alcohol and their derivatives. These on the one hand resulted in the enunciation of his ethyl theory, by the light of which he looked upon those substances as compounds of the radicle ethyl (C_2H_5), in opposition to the view of J. B. A. Dumas, who regarded them as hydrates of olefiant gas (ethylene); on the other they yielded chloroform, chloral and aldehyde, as well as other compounds of less general interest, and also the method of forming mirrors by depositing silver from a slightly ammoniacal solution by acet aldehyde. In 1837 with Dumas he published a note on the constitution of organic acids, and in the following year an elaborate paper on the same subject appeared under his own name alone; by this work T. Graham's doctrine of polybasicity was extended to the organic acids. Liebig also did much to further the hydrogen theory of acids.

These and other studies in pure chemistry mainly occupied his attention until about 1838, but the last thirty-five years of his life were devoted more particularly to the chemistry of the processes of life, both animal and vegetable. In animal physiology he set himself to trace out the operation of determinate chemical and physical laws in the maintenance of life and health. To this end he examined such immediate vital products as blood, bile and urine; he analysed the juices of flesh, establishing the composition of creatin and investigating its decomposition products, creatinin and sarcosin; he classified the various articles of food in accordance with the special function performed by each in the animal economy, and expounded the philosophy of cooking; and in opposition to many of the medical opinions of his time taught that the heat of the body is the result of the processes of combustion and oxidation performed within the organism. A secondary result of this line of study was the preparation of his food for infants and of his extract of meat. Vegetable physiology he pursued with special reference to agriculture, which he held to be the foundation of all trade and industry, but which could not be rationally practised without the guidance of chemical principles. His first publication on this subject was *Die Chemie in ihrer Anwendung auf Agricultur und Physiologie* in 1840, which was at once translated into English by Lyon Playfair. Rejecting the old notion that plants derive their nourishment from humus, he taught that they get carbon and nitrogen from the carbon dioxide and ammonia present in the atmosphere, these compounds being returned by them to the atmosphere by the processes of putrefaction and fermentation—which latter he regarded as essentially chemical in nature—while their potash, soda, lime, sulphur, phosphorus, &c., come from the soil. Of the carbon dioxide and ammonia no exhaustion can take place, but of the mineral constitutents the supply is limited because the soil cannot afford an indefinite amount of them; hence the chief care of the farmer, and the function of manures, is to restore to the soil those minerals which each crop is found, by the analysis of its ashes, to take up in its growth. On this theory he prepared artificial manures containing the essential mineral substances together with a small quantity of ammoniacal salts, because he held that the air does not supply ammonia fast enough in certain cases, and carried out systematic experiments on ten acres of poor sandy land which he obtained from the town of Giessen in 1845. But in practice the results were not wholly satisfactory, and it was a long time before he recognized one important reason for the failure in the fact that to prevent the alkalis from being washed away by the rain he had taken pains to add them in an insoluble form, whereas, as was ultimately suggested to him by experiments performed by J. T. Way about 1850, this precaution was not only superfluous but harmful, because the soil possesses a power of absorbing the soluble saline matters required by plants and of retaining them, in spite of rain, for assimilation by the roots.

Liebig's literary activity was very great. The Royal Society's *Catalogue of Scientific Papers* enumerates 318 memoirs under his name, exclusive of many others published in collaboration with other investigators. A certain impetuousness of character which disposed him to rush into controversy whenever doubt was cast upon the views he supported accounted for a great deal of writing, and he also carried on an extensive correspondence with Wöhler and other scientific men. In 1832 he founded the *Annalen der Pharmazie*, which became the *Annalen der Chemie und Pharmazie* in 1840 when Wöhler became joint-editor with himself, and in 1837 with Wöhler and Poggendorff he established the *Handwörterbuch der reinen und angewandten Chemie*. After the death of Berzelius he continued the *Jahresbericht* with H. F. M. Kopp. The following are his most important separate publications, many of which were translated into English and French almost as soon as they appeared: *Anleitung zur Analyse der organischen Körper* (1837); *Die Chemie in ihrer Anwendung auf Agrikultur und Physiologie* (1840); *Die Thier-Chemie oder die organische Chemie in ihrer Anwendung auf Physiologie und Pathologie* (1842); *Handbuch der organischen Chemie mit Rücksicht auf Pharmazie* (1843); *Chemische Briefe* (1844); *Chemische Untersuchungen über das Fleisch und seine Zubereitung zum Nahrungsmittel* (1847); *Die Grundsätze der Agrikultur-Chemie* (1855); *Über Theorie und Praxis in der Landwirthschaft* (1856); *Naturwissenschaftliche Briefe über die moderne Landwirthschaft* (1859). A posthumous collection of his miscellaneous addresses and publications appeared in 1874 as *Reden und Abhandlungen*, edited by his son George (b. 1827). His criticism of Bacon, *Über Francis von Verulam*, was first published in 1863 in the *Augsburger allgemeine Zeitung*, where also most of his letters on chemistry made their first appearance.

See *The Life Work of Liebig* (London, 1876), by his pupil A. W. von Hofmann, which is the Faraday lecture delivered before the London Chemical Society in March 1875, and is reprinted in Hofmann's *Zur Erinnerung an vorangegangene Freunde*; also W. A. Shenstone, *Justus von Liebig, his Life and Work* (1895).

LIEBKNECHT, WILHELM (1826–1900), German socialist, was born at Giessen on the 29th of March 1826. Left an orphan at an early age, he was educated at the gymnasium in his native town, and attended the universities of Giessen, Bonn and Marburg. Before he left school he had become affected by the political discontent then general in Germany; he had already studied the writings of St Simon, from which he gained his first interest in communism, and had been converted to the extreme republican theories of which Giessen was a centre. He soon came into conflict with the authorities, and was expelled from Berlin apparently in consequence of the strong sympathy he displayed for some Poles, who were being tried for high treason. He proposed in 1846 to migrate to America, but went instead to Switzerland, where he earned his living as a teacher. As soon as the revolution of 1848 broke out he hastened to Paris, but the attempt to organize a republican corps for the invasion of Germany was prevented by the government. In September, however, in concert with Gustav von Struve, he crossed the Rhine from Switzerland at the head of a band of volunteers, and proclaimed a republic in Baden. The attempt collapsed; he was captured, and, after suffering eight months' imprisonment, was brought to trial. Fortunately for him, a new rising had just broken out; the mob burst into the court, and he was acquitted. During the short duration of the revolutionary government he was an active member of the most extreme party, but on the arrival of the Prussian troops he succeeded in escaping to France. Thence he went to Geneva, where he came into intercourse with Mazzini; but, unlike most of the German exiles, he was already an adherent of the socialist creed, which at that time was more strongly held in France. Expelled from Switzerland he went to London, where he lived for thirteen years in close association with Karl Marx. He endured great hardships, but secured a livelihood by teaching and writing; he was a correspondent of the *Augsburger Allgemeine Zeitung*. The amnesty of 1861 opened for him the way back to Germany, and in 1862 he accepted the post of editor of the *Norddeutsche Allgemeine Zeitung*, the founder of which was an old revolutionist. Only a few months elapsed before the paper passed under Bismarck's influence. There is no more curious episode in German history than the success with which Bismarck acquired the services of many of the men of 1848, but Liebknecht remained faithful to his principles and resigned his editorship. He became a member of the Arbeiterverein, and after the death of Ferdinand Lassalle he was the chief mouthpiece in Germany of Karl Marx, and was instrumental in spreading the influence of the newly-founded *International*. Expelled from Prussia in 1865, he settled at Leipzig, and it is primarily to his activity in Saxony among the newly-formed unions of workers that the modern social democrat party owes its origin. Here he conducted the *Demokratisches Wochenblatt*. In 1867 he was elected a member of the North German Reichstag, but in opposition to Lassalle's followers he refused all compromise with the "capitalists," and avowedly used his position merely for purposes of agitation whilst taking every opportunity for making the parliament ridiculous. He was strongly influenced by the "great German" traditions of the democrats of 1848, and, violently anti-Prussian, he distinguished himself by his attacks on the policy of 1866 and the "revolution from above," and by his opposition to every form of militarism. His adherence to the traditions of 1848 are also seen in his dread of Russia, which he maintained to his death. His opposition to the war of 1870 exposed him to insults and violence, and in 1872 he was condemned to two years' imprisonment in a fortress for treasonable intentions. The union of the German Socialists in 1874 at the congress of Gotha was really a triumph of his influence, and from that time he was regarded as founder and leader of the party. From 1874 till his death he was a member of the German Reichstag, and for many years also of the Saxon diet. He was one of the chief spokesmen of the party, and he took a very important part in directing its policy. In 1881 he was expelled from Leipzig, but took up his residence in a neighbouring village. After the lapse of the Socialist law (1890) he became chief editor of the *Vorwärts*, and settled in Berlin. If he did not always find it easy in his later years to follow the new developments, he preserved to his death the idealism of his youth, the hatred both of Liberalism and of State Socialism; and though he was to some extent overshadowed by Bebel's greater oratorical power, he was the chief support of the orthodox Marxian tradition. Liebknecht was the author of numerous pamphlets and books, of which the most important were: *Robert Blum und seine Zeit* (Nuremberg, 1892); *Geschichte der Französischen Revolution* (Dresden, 1890); *Die Emser Depesche* (Nuremberg, 1899) and *Robert Owen* (Nuremberg, 1892). He died at Charlottenburg on the 6th of August 1900.

See Kurt Eisner, *Wilhelm Liebknecht, sein Leben und Wirken* (Berlin, 1900).

LIECHTENSTEIN, the smallest independent state in Europe, save San Marino and Monaco. It lies some way S. of the Lake of Constance, and extends along the right bank of the Rhine, opposite Swiss territory, between Sargans and Sennwald, while on the E. it also comprises the upper portion of the Samina glen that joins the Ill valley at Frastanz, above Feldkirch. It is about 12 m. in length, and covers an area of 61·4 or 68·8 sq. m. (according to different estimates). Its loftiest point rises at the S.E. angle of the state, in the Rhätikon range, and is named to Naafkopf or the Rothe Wand (8445 ft.); on its summit the Swiss, Vorarlberg, and Liechtenstein frontiers join. In 1901 the population was 9477 (of whom 4890 were women and 4587 men). The capital is Vaduz (1523 ft.), with about 1100 inhabitants, and 2 m. S. of the Schaan railway station, which is 2 m. from Buchs (Switz.). Even in the 17th century the Romonsch language was not extinguished in the state, and many Romonsch place-names still linger, *e.g.* Vaduz, Samina, Gavadura, &c. Now the population is German-speaking and Romanist. The constitution of 1862 was amended in 1878, 1895 and 1901. All males of 24 years of age are primary electors, while the diet consists of 12 members, holding their seats for 4 years and elected indirectly, together with 3 members nominated by the prince. The prince has a lieutenant resident at Vaduz, whence there is an appeal to the prince's court at Vienna, with a final appeal (since 1884) to the supreme district court at Innsbruck. Compulsory military service was abolished in 1868, the army having till then been 91 strong. The principality forms ecclesiastically part of the diocese of Coire, while as regards customs duties it is joined with the Vorarlberg, and as regards postal and coinage arrangements with Austria, which (according to the agreement of 1852, renewed in 1876, by which the principality entered the Austrian customs union) must pay it at least 40,000 crowns annually. In 1904 the revenues of the principality amounted to 888,931 crowns, and its expenditure to 802,163 crowns. There is no public debt.

The county of Vaduz and the lordship of Schellenberg passed through many hands before they were bought in 1613 by the count of Hohenems (to the N. of Feldkirch) In consequence of financial embarrassments, that family had to sell both (the lordship in 1699, the county in 1713) to the Liechtenstein family, which had since the 12th century owned two castles of that name (both now ruined), one in Styria and the other a little S.W. of Vienna. In 1719 these new acquisitions were raised by the emperor into a principality under the name of Liechtenstein, which formed part successively of the Holy Roman Empire (till 1806) and of the German Confederation (1815–1866), having been sovereign 1806–1815 as well as since 1866.

See J. Falke's *Geschichte d. fürstlichen Hauses Liechtenstein* (3 vols., Vienna, 1868–1883); J. C. Heer, *Vorarlberg und Liechtenstein* (Feldkirch, 1906); P. Kaiser, *Geschichte d. Furstenthums Liechtenstein* (Coire, 1847); F. Umlauft, *Das Fürstenthum Liechtenstein* (Vienna, 1891); E. Walder, *Aus den Bergen* (Zürich, 1896); A. Waltenberger, *Algäu, Vorarlberg, und Westtirol* (Rtes. 25 and 26) (10th ed., Innsbruck, 1906). (W. A. B. C.)

LIÉGE, one of the nine provinces of Belgium, touching on the east the Dutch province of Limburg and the German district of Rhenish Prussia. To a certain extent it may be assumed to represent the old prince-bishopric. Besides the city of Liége it contains the towns of Verviers, Dolhain, Seraing, Huy, &c. The Meuse flows through the centre of the province, and its valley from Huy down to Herstal is one of the most productive mineral districts in Belgium. Much has been done of late years to develop the agricultural resources of the Condroz district south of the Meuse. The area of the province is 723,470 acres, or 1130 sq. m. The population in 1904 was 863,254, showing an average of 763 per sq. m.

LIÉGE (Walloon, *Lige*, Flemish, *Luik*, Ger. *Lüttich*), the capital of the Belgian province that bears its name. It is finely situated on the Meuse, and was long the seat of a prince-bishopric. It is the centre of the Walloon country, and Scott commits a curious mistake in *Quentin Durward* in making its people talk Flemish. The Liége Walloon is the nearest existing approach to the old Romance language. The importance of the city to-day arises from its being the chief manufacturing centre in Belgium, and owing to its large output of arms it has been called the Birmingham of the Netherlands. The productive coal-mines of the Meuse valley, extending from its western suburb of Seraing to its northern faubourg of Herstal, constitute its chief wealth. At Seraing is established the famous manufacturing firm of Cockerill, whose offices are in the old summer palace of the prince-bishops.

The great cathedral of St Lambert was destroyed and sacked by the French in 1794, and in 1802 the church of St Paul, dating from the 10th century but rebuilt in the 13th, was declared the cathedral. The law courts are installed in the old palace of the prince-bishops, a building which was constructed by Bishop Everard de la Marck between 1508 and 1540. The new boulevards are well laid out, especially those flanking the river, and the views of the city and surrounding country are very fine. The university, which has separate schools for mines and arts and manufactures, is one of the largest in the country, and enjoys a high reputation for teaching in its special line.

Liége is a fortified position of far greater strength than is generally appreciated. In the wars of the 18th century Liége played but a small part. It was then defended only by the citadel and a detached fort on the right side of the Meuse, but at a short distance from the river, called the Chartreuse. Marlborough captured these forts in 1703 in preparation for his advance in the following year into Germany which resulted in the victory of Blenheim. The citadel and the Chartreuse were still the only defences of Liége in 1888 when, after long discussions, the Belgian authorities decided on adequately fortifying the two important passages of the Meuse at Liége and Namur. A similar plan was adopted at each place, viz. the construction of a number of detached forts along a perimeter drawn at a distance varying from 4 to 6 m. of the town, so as to shelter it so far as possible from bombardment. At Liége twelve forts were constructed, six on the right bank and six on the left. Those on the right bank beginning at the north and following an eastern curve are Barchon, Evegnée, Fléron, Chaudfontaine, Embourg and Boncelles. The average distance between each fort is 4 m., but Fléron and Chaudfontaine are separated by little over 1 m. in a direct line as they defend the main line of railway from Germany. The six forts on the left bank also commencing at the north, but following a western curve, are Pontisse, Liers, Lantin, Loncin, Hollogne and Flemalle. These forts were constructed under the personal direction of General Brialmont, and are on exactly the same principle as those he designed for the formidable defences of Bucarest. All the forts are constructed in concrete with casemates, and the heavy guns are raised and lowered automatically. Communication is maintained between the different forts by military roads in all cases, and by steam tramways in some. It is estimated that 25,000 troops would be required for the defence of the twelve forts, but the number is inadequate for the defence of so important and extensive a position. The population of Liége, which in 1875 was only 117,600, had risen by 1900 to 157,760, and in 1905 it was 168,532.

History.—Liége first appears in history about the year 558, at which date St Monulph, bishop of Tongres, built a chapel near the confluence of the Meuse and the Legia. A century later the town, which had grown up round this chapel, became the favourite abode of St Lambert, bishop of Tongres, and here he was assassinated. His successor St Hubert raised a splendid church over the tomb of the martyred bishop about 720 and made Liége his residence. It was not, however, until about 930 that the title bishop of Tongres was abandoned for that of bishop of Liége. The episcopate of Notger (972–1008) was marked by large territorial acquisitions, and the see obtained recognition as an independent principality of the Empire. The popular saying was "Liége owes Notger to God, and everything else to Notger." By the munificent encouragement of successive bishops Liége became famous during the 11th century as a centre of learning, but the history of the town for centuries records little else than the continuous struggles of the citizens to free themselves from the exactions of their episcopal sovereigns; the aid of the emperor and of the dukes of Brabant being frequently called in to repress the popular risings. In 1316 the citizens compelled Bishop Adolph de la Marck to sign a charter, which made large concessions to the popular demands. It was, however, a triumph of short duration, and the troubles continued, the insurgent subjects now and again obtaining a fleeting success, only to be crushed by the armies of the powerful relatives of the bishops, the houses of Brabant or of Burgundy. During the episcopate of Louis de Bourbon (1456–1484) the Liégeois, having expelled the bishop, had the temerity to declare war on Philip V., duke of Burgundy. Philip's son, Charles the Bold, utterly defeated them in 1467, and razed the walls of the town to the ground. In the following year the citizens again revolted, and Charles being once more successful delivered up the city to sack and pillage for three days, and deprived the remnant of the citizens of all their privileges. This incident is narrated in *Quentin Durward*. The long episcopate of Eberhard de la Marck (1505–1538) was a time of good administration and of quiet, during which the town regained something of its former prosperity. The outbreak of civil war between two factions, named the *Chiroux* and the *Grignoux*, marked the opening of the 17th century. Bishop Maximilian Henry of Bavaria (1650–1688) at last put an end to the internal strife and imposed a regulation (*règlement*) which abolished all the free institutions of the citizens and the power of the gilds. Between this date and the outbreak of the French Revolution the chief efforts of the prince-bishops were directed to maintaining neutrality in the various wars, and preserving their territory from being ravaged by invading armies. They were only in part successful. Liége was taken by Marlborough in 1702, and the fortress was garrisoned by the Dutch until 1718. The French revolutionary armies overran the principality in 1792, and from 1794 to the fall of Napoleon it was annexed to France, and was known as the department of the Ourthe. The Congress of Vienna in 1815 decreed that Liége with the other provinces of the southern Netherlands should form part of the new kingdom of the Netherlands under the rule of William I., of the house of Orange. The town of Liége took an active part in the Belgian revolt of 1830, and since that date the ancient principality has been incorporated in the kingdom of Belgium.

The see, which at first bore the name of the bishopric of Tongres, was under the metropolitan jurisdiction of the archbishops of Cologne. The principality comprised besides the town of Liége and its district, the counties of Looz and Hoorn, the marquessate of Franchimont, and the duchy of Bouillon.

AUTHORITIES.—Théodore Bouille, *Histoire de la ville et du pays de Liége* (3 vols., Liége, 1725–1732); A. Borgnet, *Histoire de la révolution liégeoise* (2 vols., Liége, 1865), Baron B. C. de Gerlache, *Histoire de Liége* (Brussels, 1843); J. Daris, *Histoire du diocèse et de la principauté de Liége* (10 vols., Liége, 1868–1885); Ferdinand Henaux, *Histoire du pays de Liége* (2 vols., Liége, 1857); L. Polain, *Histoire de l'ancien pays de Liége* (2 vols., Liége, 1844–1847). For full bibliography see Ulysse Chevalier, *Répertoire des sources historiques. Topo-bibliographie*, s.v. (Montbéliard, 1900).

LIEGE, an adjective implying the mutual relationship of a feudal superior and his vassal; the word is used as a substantive of the feudal superior, more usually in this sense, however, in the form "liege lord," and also of the vassals, his "lieges." Hence the word is often used of the loyal subjects of a sovereign, with no reference to feudal ties. It appears [illegible] *ligeitas* or *ligentia*, the medieval Latin term for this relation[illegible] was restricted to a particular form of homage. According [illegible] Brussel (*Nouvel examen de l'usage général des fiefs en France*, 1727) the homage of a "liege" was a stronger form [illegible] ordinary homage, the especial distinction being that [illegible] ordinary vassal only undertook forty days' military [illegible] the liege promised to serve as long as the war might [illegible] which his superior was engaged (cf. Ducange, *Glossarium*, [illegible] *ligius*").

[illegible] etymology of the word has been much discussed. It [illegible] English through the O. Fr. *lige* or *liege*, Med. [illegible] This was early connected with the Lat. *ligatus*, [illegible] to bind, from the sense of the obligation of the [illegible] lord, but this has been generally abandoned. [illegible] the Med. Lat. *liga*, i.e., *foedus*, *confederatio*, [illegible] "league," as the origin. Ducange connects it with [illegible] which appears in a gloss of the Salic law, and [illegible] *adscriptitius*, *servus glebae*. The more usually [illegible] is now from the Old High Ger. *ledic*, or [illegible] "free" (Mod. Ger. *ledig* means unoccupied, [illegible] confirmed by the occurrence in a charter of [illegible] 1253, of a word "ledigh-man" (quoted in [illegible] s.v.), *Preinde affecti sumus ligius homo*, [illegible] *Ledighman*. Skeat, in explaining the [illegible] "free" to such a relationship as that subsisting [illegible] superior and his vassal, says "'a *liege* lord' [illegible] the lord of a free band; and his *lieges*, [illegible] him, were privileged men, free from all [illegible] their name being due to their *freedom*, not [illegible] *Dict.*, ed. 1898). A. Luchaire (*Manuel* [illegible] 1892, p. 180, n. 1) considers it difficult [illegible] who is under a strict obligation to another; [illegible] " was not free from all obligation to a [illegible] charters prove without doubt that the [illegible] to more than one lord.

[illegible] Germany, in the Prussian province [illegible] Katzbach, just above its junction with the Schwarzwasser, and 40 m. W.N.W. of Breslau, on the main line of railway to Berlin via Sommerfeld. Pop. (1885) 43,347, (1905) 59,710. It consists of an old town, surrounded by pleasant, shady promenades, and several well-built suburbs. The most prominent building is the palace, formerly the residence of the dukes of Liegnitz, rebuilt after a fire in 1835 and now used as the administrative offices of the district. The Ritter Akademie, founded by the emperor Joseph I. in 1708 for the education of the young Silesian nobles, was reconstructed as a gymnasium in 1810. The Roman Catholic church of St John, with two fine towers, contains the burial vault of the dukes. The principal Lutheran church, that of SS. Peter and Paul (restored in 1892–1894), dates from the 14th century. The manufactures are considerable, the chief articles made being cloth, wool, leather, tobacco, pianos and machinery. Its trade in grain and its cattle-markets are likewise important. The large market gardens in the suburbs grow vegetables of considerable annual value.

Liegnitz is first mentioned in an historical document in the year 1004. In 1163 it became the seat of the dukes of Liegnitz, who greatly improved and enlarged it. The dukes were members of the illustrious Piast family, which gave many kings to Poland. During the Thirty Years' War Liegnitz was taken by the Swedes, but was soon recaptured by the Imperialists. The Saxon army also defeated the imperial troops near Liegnitz in 1634. On the death of the last duke of Liegnitz in 1675, the duchy came into the possession of the Empire, which retained it until the Prussian conquest of Silesia in 1742. On the 15th of August 1760 Frederick the Great gained a decisive victory near Liegnitz over the Austrians, and in August 1813 Blücher defeated the French in the neighbourhood at the battle of the Katzbach. During the 19th century Liegnitz rapidly increased in population and prosperity. In 1906 the German autumn manœuvres were held over the terrain formerly the scene of the great battles already mentioned.

See Schuchard, *Die Stadt Liegnitz* (Berlin, 1868); Sammter and Kraffert, *Chronik von Liegnitz* (Liegnitz, 1861–1873); Jander, *Liegnitz in seinem Entwickelungsgange* (Liegnitz, 1905); and *Führer für Liegnitz und seine Umgebung* (Liegnitz, 1897); and the *Urkundenbuch der Stadt Liegnitz bis 1455*, edited by Schirrmacher (Liegnitz, 1866).

LIEN, in law. The word *lien* is literally the French for a band, cord or chain, and keeping in mind that meaning we see in what respect it differs from a pledge on the one hand and a mortgage on the other. It is the bond which attaches a creditor's right to a debtor's property, but which gives no right *ad rem*, *i.e.* to property in the thing; if the property is in the possession of the creditor he may retain it, but in the absence of statute he cannot sell to recover what is due to him without the ordinary legal process against the debtor; and if it is not in possession, the law would indeed assist him to seize the property, and will hold it for him, and enable him to sell it in due course and pay himself out of the proceeds, but does not give him the property itself. It is difficult to say at what period the term lien made its appearance in English law; it probably came from more than one source. In fact, it was used as a convenient phrase for any right against the owner of property in regard to the property not specially defined by other better recognized species of title.

The possessory lien of a tradesman for work done on the thing, of a carrier for his hire, and of an innkeeper for his bill, would seem to be an inherent right which must have been in existence from the dawn, or before the dawn, of civilization. Probably the man who made or repaired weapons in the Stone Age was careful not to deliver them until he received what was stipulated for, but it is also probable that the term itself resulted from the infusion of the civil law of Rome into the common law of England which the Norman Conquest brought about, and that it represents the "tacit pledge" of the civil law. As might be expected, so far as the possessory lien is concerned the common law and civil law, and probably the laws of all countries, whether civilized or not, coincide; but there are many differences with respect to other species of lien. For instance, by the common law—in this respect a legacy of the feudal system—a landlord has a lien over his tenant's furniture and effects for rent due, which can be enforced without the assistance of the law simply by the landlord taking possession, personally or by his agent, and selling enough to satisfy his claim; whereas the maritime lien is more distinctly the product of the civil law, and is only found and used in admiralty proceedings, the high court of admiralty having been founded upon the civil law, and still (except so far as restrained by the common-law courts prior to the amalgamation and co-ordination of the various courts by the Judicature Acts, and as affected by statute law) acting upon it. The peculiar effects of this maritime lien are discussed below. There is also a class of liens, usually called equitable liens (*e.g.* that of an unpaid vendor of real property over the property sold), which are akin to the nature of the civil law rather than of the common law. The word lien does not frequently occur in statute law, but it is found in the extension of the common-law "carriers' or shipowners' lien" in the Merchant Shipping Act 1894; in the definition, extension and limitation of the vendor's lien; in the Factors Act 1877, and the Sale of Goods Act 1893; in granting a maritime lien to a shipmaster for his wages and disbursements, and in regulating that of the seamen in the Merchant Shipping Act 1894, and in the equity jurisdiction of the county courts 1888.

Common-Law Liens.—These may be either particular, *i.e.* a right over one or more specified articles for a particular debt, or general, *i.e.* for all debts owing to the creditor by the debtor

The requisites for a particular lien are, firstly, that the creditor should be in possession of the article; secondly, that the debt should be incurred with reference to the article; and thirdly, that the amount of the debt should be certain. It may be created by express contract, by implied contract (such as the usage of a particular trade or business), or as a consequence of the legal relation existing between the parties. As an example of the first, a shipowner at common law has a lien on the cargo for the freight; but though the shipper agrees to pay dead freight in addition, *i.e.* to pay freight on any space in the ship which he fails to occupy with his cargo, the shipowner has no lien on the cargo for such dead freight except by express agreement. The most usual form of the second is that which is termed a possessory lien—the right a ship-repairer has to retain a ship in his yard till he is paid for the repairs executed upon her,[1] and the right a cobbler has to retain a pair of shoes till he is paid for the repairs done to them. But this lien is only in respect of the work done on, and consequent benefit received by, the subject of the lien. Hence an agistor of cattle has no lien at common law upon them for the value of the pasturage consumed, though he may have one by agreement; nor a conveyancer upon deeds which he has not drawn, but which are in his possession for reference. The most common example of the third is that of a carrier, who is bound by law to carry for all persons, and has, therefore, a lien for the price of the carriage on the goods carried It has been held that even if the goods are stolen, and entrusted to the carrier by the thief, the carrier can hold them for the price of the carriage against the rightful owner. Of the same nature is the common-law lien of an innkeeper on the baggage of his customer for the amount of his account, he being under a legal obligation to entertain travellers generally. Another instance of the same class is where a person has obtained possession of certain things over which he claims to hold a lien in the exercise of a legal right For example, when a lord of a manor has seized cattle as estrays, he has a lien upon them for the expense of their keep as against the real owner; but the holder's claim must be specific, otherwise a general tender of compensation releases the lien.

A general lien is a right of a creditor to retain property, not merely for charges relating to it specifically, but for debts due on a general account. This not being a common-law right, is viewed by the English courts with the greatest jealousy, and to be enforced must be strictly proved. This can be done by proof either of an express or implied contract or of a general usage of trade. The first of these is established by the ordinary methods or by previous dealings between the parties on such terms; the second is recognized in certain businesses; it would probably be exceedingly difficult, if not impossible, to extend it at the present time to any other trades. When, however, a lien by general usage has once been judicially established, it becomes part of the Law Merchant, and the courts are bound to recognize and enforce it. The best known and most important instance is the right of a solicitor to retain papers in his hands belonging to his client until his account is settled. The solicitor's lien, though probably more commonly enforced than any other, is of no great antiquity in English law, the earliest reported case of it being in the reign of James II.; but it is now of a twofold nature. In the first place there is the retaining lien. This is similar in kind to other possessory liens, but of a general nature attaching to all papers of the client, and even to his money, up to the amount of the solicitor's bill, in the hands of the solicitor in the ordinary course of business. There are certain exceptions which seem to have crept in for the same reason as the solicitor's lien itself, *i.e.* general convenience of litigation; such exceptions are the will of the client after his decease, and proceedings in bankruptcy. In this latter case the actual possessory lien is given up, the solicitor's interests and priorities being protected by the courts, and it may be said that the giving up the papers is really only a means of enforcing the lien they give in the bankruptcy proceedings. In the second place there is what is called a charging lien—more correctly classed under the head of equitable lien, since it does not require possession, but is a lien the solicitor holds over property recovered or preserved for his client. He had the lien on an order by the court upon a fund in court by the common law, but as to property generally it was only given by 23 & 24 Vict. c. 127, § 28; and it has been held to attach to property recovered in a probate action (*ex parte Tweed*, C.A. 1899, 2 Q.B. 167). A banker's lien is the right of a banker to retain securities belonging to his customer for money due on a general balance. Other general liens, judicially established, are those of wharfingers, brokers and factors (which are in their nature akin to those of solicitors and bankers), and of calico printers, packers of goods, fullers (at all events at Exeter), dyers and millers, but in all these special trades it is probable that the true reason is that the account due was for one continuous transaction. The calico would come to be printed, the goods to be packed, the cloth to be bleached, the silk to be dyed, and the corn to be ground, in separate parcels, and at different times, but all as one undertaking; and they are therefore, though spoken of as instances of general lien, only adaptations by the courts of the doctrine of particular lien to special peculiarities of business. In none of these cases would the lien exist, in the absence of special agreement, for other matters of account, such as money lent or goods sold.

Equitable Liens.—"Where equity has jurisdiction to enforce rights and obligations growing out of an executory contract," *e.g.* in a suit for specific performance, "this equitable theory of remedies cannot be carried out unless the notion is admitted that the contract creates some right or interest in or over specific property, which the decree of the court can lay hold of, and by means of which the equitable relief can be made efficient. The doctrine of equitable liens supplies this necessary element; and it was introduced for the sole purpose of furnishing a ground for these specific remedies which equity confers, operating upon particular identified property instead of the general pecuniary recoveries granted by courts of common law. It follows, therefore, that in a large class of executory contracts express and implied, which the common law regards as creating no property, right nor interest analogous to property, but only a mere personal right to obligation, equity recognizes in addition to the personal obligation a particular right over the thing with which the contract deals, which it calls a *lien*, and which though not property is analogous to property, and by means of which the plaintiff is enabled to follow the identical thing and to enforce the defendant's obligation by a remedy which operates directly on the thing.

[1] This right, however, is not absolute, but depends on the custom of the port (*Raitt* v. *Mitchell*, 1815, 4 Camp. 146).

The theory of equitable liens has its ultimate foundation, therefore, in contracts express or implied which either deal or in some manner relate to specific property, such as a tract of land, particular chattels or securities, a certain fund and the like. It is necessary to divest oneself of the purely legal notion concerning the effects of such contracts, and to recognize the fact that equity regards them as creating a charge upon, or hypothecation of, the specific thing, by means of which the personal obligation arising from the agreement may be more effectively enforced than by a mere pecuniary recovery at law" (Pomeroy, 2 Eq. Jur. 232).

This description from an American text-book seems to give [illegible] the fullest and most concise definition and description [illegible] equitable lien. It differs essentially from a common-law [illegible] inasmuch as in the latter possession or occupation is as a [illegible] necessary, whereas in the equitable lien the person claiming [illegible] in possession or occupation of the property, [illegible] to obtain the possession wholly or partially. [illegible] instance of such a lien is that claimed by a publisher [illegible] copyright of a book which he has agreed to publish [illegible] which are not complied with—for example, the author [illegible] to get the book published elsewhere. It cannot [illegible] that this has been absolutely decided to exist, [illegible] of the English court of exchequer towards [illegible] the 18th century was expressed in its favour (*Brook* [illegible], 3 Anstruther 881). Other instances are the [illegible] a solicitor, and the lien of a person on improve- [illegible] by him on the property of another who "lies [illegible] work to be done before claiming the property. [illegible] for expenses lawfully incurred about the [illegible]. The power of a limited liability company to [illegible] its own shares was in 1901 established (*Allen* [illegible] C.A. 1900, 1 Ch. 656)

[illegible]—Maritime lien differs from all the others [illegible] more elastic nature. Where a maritime [illegible] to property—and it may and generally [illegible] possession—it will continue to attach, [illegible] as long as the thing to which it attaches [illegible] changes in the possession of and pro- [illegible] notwithstanding that the new possessor [illegible] ignorant of its existence; and even [illegible] owner's personal liability for any balance [illegible] "1899, P. 285). So far as England [illegible] in mind that the courts of admiralty [illegible] with the principles of civil law, [illegible] with possession and the hypothe- [illegible] were well recognized. The extreme [illegible] as the latter with regard to such [illegible] as ships is apparent. Strictly [illegible] confined to cases arising in those [illegible] of admiralty had original juris- [illegible] seamen's wages, salvage and [illegible] the appropriate remedy is a [illegible] court. In the first of these— [illegible] no maritime lien there would [illegible] When two ships have collided [illegible] innocent ship knows neither the [illegible] the wrongdoer, and the vessel [illegible] and not have to make a port [illegible] Months afterwards it is ascer- [illegible] and in the interval she has [illegible] not a fact that a maritime [illegible] nevertheless attaches itself to [illegible] and continues to attach, [illegible] innocent ship would have no [illegible] of pursuing the former owner [illegible] own country in a personal [illegible] which is by no means [illegible] The same reasons apply, [illegible] same force, to the other [illegible] miralty

court was largely extended. At the latter date it was merged in the probate, divorce and admiralty division of the High Court of Justice. Since the merger questions have arisen as to how far the enlargement of jurisdiction has extended the principle of maritime lien. An interesting article on this subject by J. Mansfield, barrister-at-law, will be found in the *Law Quarterly Review*, vol. iv., October 1888. It must be sufficient to state here that where legislation has extended the already existing jurisdiction to which a maritime lien pertained, the maritime lien is extended to the subject matter, but that where a new jurisdiction is given, or where a jurisdiction formerly existing without a maritime lien is extended, no maritime lien is given, though even then the extended jurisdiction can be enforced by proceedings *in rem*. Of the first class of extended jurisdictions are collisions, salvage and seamen's wages. Prior to 1840 the court of admiralty only had jurisdiction over these when occurring or earned on the high seas. The jurisdiction, and with it the maritime lien, is extended to places within the body of a county in collision or salvage; and as to seamen's wages, whereas they were dependent on the earning of freight, they are now free from any such limitation, and also, whereas the remedy *in rem* was limited to seamen's wages not earned under a special contract, it is now extended to all seamen's wages, and also to a master's wages and disbursements, and the maritime lien covers all these. The new jurisdiction given over claims for damage to cargo carried into any port in England or Wales, and on appeal from the county courts over all claims for damage to cargo under £300, though it may be prosecuted by proceedings *in rem*, *i.e.* by arrest of the ship, yet confers no maritime lien; and so also in the case of claims by material men (builders and fitters-out of ships) and for necessaries. Even though in the latter case the admiralty court had jurisdiction previously to 1840 where the necessaries were supplied on the high seas, yet as it could not be shown that such jurisdiction had ever been held to confer a maritime lien, no such lien is given. Even now there is much doubt as to whether towage confers a maritime lien or not, the services rendered being pursuant to contract, and frequently to a contract made verbally or in writing on the high seas, and being rendered also to a great extent on the high seas. In these cases and to that extent the high court of admiralty would have had original jurisdiction. But prior to 1840 towage, as now rendered by steam tugs expressly employed for the service, was practically unknown, and therefore there was no established catena of precedent to show the exercise of a maritime lien. It may be argued on the one hand that towage is only a modified form of salvage, and therefore entitled to a maritime lien, and on the other that it is only a form of necessary power supplied like a new sail or mast to a ship to enable her to complete her voyage expeditiously, and therefore of the nature of necessaries, and as such not entitled to a maritime lien. The matter is not of academical interest only, for though in the case of an inward-bound ship the tug owner can make use of his statutory right of proceeding *in rem*, and so obtain much of the benefit of a maritime lien, yet in the case of an outward-bound ship, if she once gets away without payment, and the agent or other authorized person refuses or is unable to pay, the tug owner's claim may, on the return of the ship to a British port, be met by an allegation of a change of ownership, which defeats his right of proceeding at all if he has no maritime lien; whereas if he has a maritime lien he can still proceed against the ship and recover his claim, if he has not been guilty of laches.

A convenient division of the special liens other than possessory on ships may be made by classifying them as maritime, statutory-maritime or quasi-maritime, and statutory. The first attach only in the case of damage done by collision between ships on the high seas, salvage on the high seas, bottomry and seamen's wages so far as freight has been earned; the second attach in cases of damage by collision within the body of a county, salvage within the body of a county, life salvage everywhere, seamen's wages even if no freight has been earned, master's wages and disbursements. These two classes continue to attach notwithstanding a change of ownership without notice of the lien, if there have been no laches in enforcing it (the "*Bold Buccleuch*," 1852, 7 Moo. P.C. 267; the "*Kong Magnus*," 1891, P. 223). The third class, which only give a right to proceed *in rem*, *i.e.* against the ship itself, attach, so long as there is no *bona fide* change of ownership, without citing the owners, in all cases of claims for damage to ship and of claims for damage to cargo where no owner is domiciled in England or Wales. Irrespective of this limitation, they attach in all cases not only of damage to cargo, but also of breaches of contract to carry where the damage does not exceed £300, when the suit must be commenced in a county court having admiralty jurisdiction; and in cases of claims for necessaries supplied elsewhere than in the ship's home port, for wages earned even under a special contract by masters and mariners, and of claims for towage. In all three classes the lien also exists over cargo where the suit from its nature extends to it, as in salvage and in some cases of bottomry or respondentia, and in cases where proceedings are taken against cargo by the shipowner for a breach of contract (cargo *ex* "*Argos*" and the "*Hewsons*," 1873, L.R. 5 P.C. 134; the "*Aline*," 1880, 5 Ex. D. 227).

Elsewhere than in England, and those countries such as the United States which have adopted her jurisprudence in maritime matters generally, the doctrine of maritime lien, or that which is substituted for it, is very differently treated. Speaking generally, those states which have adopted the Napoleonic codes or modifications of them—France, Italy, Spain, Holland, Portugal, Belgium, Greece, Turkey, and to some extent Russia—have instead of a maritime lien the civil-law principle of privileged debts. Amongst these in all cases are found claims for salvage, wages, bottomry under certain restrictions, and necessaries. Each of these has a privileged claim against the ship, and in some cases against freight and cargo as well, but it is a matter of very great importance that, except in Belgium, a claim for collision damage (which as we have seen confers a maritime lien, and one of a very high order, in Great Britain) confers no privilege against the wrong-doing ship, whilst in all these countries an owner can get rid of his personal liability by abandoning the ship and freight to his creditor, and so, if the ship is sunk, escape all liability whilst retaining any insurance there may be. This, indeed, was at one time the law of Great Britain; the measure of damage was limited by the value of the *res*; and in the United States at the present time a shipowner can get rid of his liability for damage by abandoning the ship and freight. A different rule prevails in Germany and the Scandinavian states. There claims relating to the ship, unless the owner has specially rendered himself liable, confer no personal claim at all against him. The claim is limited *ab initio* to ship and freight, except in the case of seamen's wages, which do confer a personal claim so far as they have been earned on a voyage or passage completed prior to the loss of the ship. In all maritime states, however, except Spain, a provisional arrest of the ship is allowed, and thus between the privilege accorded to the debt and the power to arrest till bail is given or the ship abandoned to creditors, a condition of things analogous to the maritime lien is established; especially as these claims when the proper legal steps have been taken to render them valid—usually by endorsement on the ship's papers on board, or by registration at her port of registry—attach to the ship and follow her into the hands of a purchaser. They are in fact notice to him of the incumbrance.

Duration of Lien.—So long as the party claiming the lien at common law retains the property, the lien continues, notwithstanding the debt in respect of which it is claimed becoming barred by the Statute of Limitations (*Higgins* v. *Scott*, 1831, 2 B. & Ald. 413). But if he takes proceedings at law to recover the debt, and on a sale of the goods to satisfy the judgment purchases them himself, he so alters the nature of the possession that he loses his lien (*Jacobs* v. *Latour*, 5 Bing. 130). An equitable lien probably in all cases continues, provided the purchaser of the subject matter has notice of the lien at the time of his purchase. A maritime lien is in no respect subject to the Statute of Limitations, and continues in force notwithstanding a change in the ownership of the property without notice, and is only terminated when it has once attached, by laches on the part of the person claiming it (the "*Kong Magnus*," 1891, P. 223). There is an exception in the case of seamen's wages, where by 4 Anne c. 16 (*Stat. Rev.* 4 & 5 Anne c. 3) all suits for seamen's wages in the Admiralty must be brought within six years.

Ranking of Maritime Liens.—There may be several claimants holding maritime and other liens on the same vessel. For example, a foreign vessel comes into collision by her own fault and is damaged and her cargo also; she is assisted into port by salvors and ultimately under a towage agreement, and put into the hands of a shipwright who does necessary repairs. The innocent party to the collision has a maritime lien for his damage, and the seamen for their wages; the cargo owner has a suit *in rem* or a statutory lien for damage, and the shipwright a possessory lien for the value of his repairs, while the tugs certainly have a right *in rem* and possibly a maritime lien also in the nature of salvage. The value of the property may be insufficient to pay all claims, and it becomes a matter of great consequence to settle whether any, and if so which, have priority over the others, or whether all rank alike and have to divide the proceeds of the property *pro rata* amongst them. The following general rules apply: liens for benefits conferred rank against the fund in the inverse, and those for the reparation of damage sustained in the direct order of their attaching to the *res*; as between the two classes those last mentioned rank before those first mentioned of earlier date; as between liens of the same class and the same date, the first claimant has priority over others who have not taken action. The courts of admiralty, however, allow equitable considerations, and enter into the question of marshalling assets. For example, if one claimant has a lien on two funds, or an effective right of action in addition to his lien, and another claimant has only a lien upon one fund, the first claimant will be obliged to exhaust his second remedy before coming into competition with the second. As regards possessory liens, the shipwright takes the ship as she stands, *i.e.* with her incumbrances, and it appears that the lien for seaman's wages takes precedence of a solicitor's lien for costs, under a charging order made in pursuance of the Solicitors Act 1860, § 28.

Subject to equitable considerations, the true principle appears to be that services rendered under an actual or implied contract, which confer a maritime lien, make the holder of the lien in some sort a proprietor of the vessel, and therefore liable for damage done by her—hence the priority of the damage lien—but, directly it has attached, benefits conferred on the property by enabling it to reach port in safety benefit the holder of the damage lien in common with all other prior holders of maritime liens. It is less easy to see why of two damage liens the earlier should take precedence of the later, except on the principle that the *res* which came into collision the second time is depreciated in value by the amount of the existing lien upon her for the first collision, and where there was more than one damage lien, and also liens for benefits conferred prior to the first collision between the two collisions and subsequent to the second, the court would have to make a special order to meet the peculiar circumstances. The claim of a mortgagee naturally is deferred to all maritime liens, whether they are for benefits conferred on the property in which he is interested or for damage done by it, and also for the same reason to the possessory lien of the shipwright, but both the possessory lien of the shipwright and the claim of the mortgagee take precedence over a claim for necessaries, which only confers a statutory lien or a right to proceed *in rem* in certain cases. In other maritime states possessing codes of commercial law, the privileged debts are all set out in order of priority in these codes, though, as has been already pointed out, the lien for damage by collision—the most important in English law—has no counterpart in most of the foreign codes.

Stoppage in Transitu.—This is a lien held by an unpaid vendor in certain cases over goods sold after they have passed out of his actual possession. It has been much discussed whether it is an equitable or common-law right or lien. The fact appears to be that it has always been a part of the Law Merchant, which, properly speaking, is itself a part of the common law of England unless inconsistent with it. This particular right was, in the first instance, held by a court of equity to be equitable and not contrary to English law, and by that decision this particular part of the Law Merchant was approved and became part of the common law of England (see per Lord Abinger in *Gibson* v. *Carruthers*, 8 M. & W., p. 336 et seq.). It may be described as a lien by the Law Merchant, decided by equity to be part of the common law, but in its nature partaking rather of the character of an equitable lien than one at common law. "It is a right which arises solely upon the insolvency of the buyer, and is based on the plain reason of justice and equity that one man's goods shall not be applied to the payment of another man's debts. If, therefore, after the vendor has delivered the goods out of his own possession and put them in the hands of a carrier for delivery to the buyer, he discovers that the buyer is insolvent, he may re-take the goods if he can before they reach the buyer's possession, and thus avoid having his property applied to paying debts due by the buyer to other people" (*Benjamin on Sales*, 2nd ed., 289). This right, though only recognized by English law in 1690, is highly favoured by the courts on account of its intrinsic justice, and extends to quasi-vendors, or persons in the same position, such as consignors who have bought on behalf of a principal and forwarded the goods. It is, however, defeated by a lawful transfer of the document of title to the goods by the vendor to a third person, who takes it *bonâ fide* and for valuable consideration (Factors Act 1889; Sale of Goods Act 1893).

Assignment or Transfer of Lien.—A lien being a personal right acquired in respect of personal services, it cannot, as a rule, be assigned or transferred; but here again there are exceptions. The personal representative of the holder of a possessory lien on his decease would probably in all cases be held entitled to it; and it has been held that the lien over a client's papers remains with the firm of solicitors notwithstanding changes in the constitution of the firm (*Gregory* v. *Cresswell*, 14 L.J. Ch. 300). So also where a solicitor, having a lien on documents for his costs, assigned the debt to his bankers with the benefit of the lien, it was held that the bankers might enforce such lien in equity. But though a tradesman has a lien on the property of his customer for his charges for work done upon it, where the property is delivered to him by a servant acting within the scope of his employment, such lien cannot be transferred to the servant, even if he has paid the money himself; and the lien does not exist at all if the servant was acting without authority in delivering the goods, except where (as in the case of a common carrier) he is bound to receive the goods, in which case he retains his lien for the carriage against the rightful owner. Where, however, there is a lien on property of any sort not in possession, a person acquiring the property with knowledge of the lien takes it subject to such lien. This applies to equitable liens, and cannot apply to those common-law liens in which possession is necessary. It is, however, true that by statute certain common-law liens can be transferred, *e.g.* under the Merchant Shipping Act a master of a ship having a lien upon cargo for his freight can transfer the possession of the cargo to a wharfinger, and with it the lien (Merchant Shipping Act 1894, § 494). In this case, however, though the matter is simplified by the statute, if the wharfinger was constituted the agent or servant of the shipmaster, his possession would be the possession of the shipmaster, and there would be no real transfer of the lien; therefore the common-law doctrine is not altered, only greater facilities for the furtherance of trade are given by the statute, enabling the wharfinger to act in his own name without reference to his principal, who may be at the other side of the world. So also a lien may be retained, notwithstanding that the property passes out of possession, where it has to be deposited in some special place (such as the Custom-House) to comply with the law. Seamen cannot sell or assign or in any way part with their maritime lien for wages (Merchant Shipping Act 1894, § [illegible]), but, nevertheless, with the sanction of the court, a person who pays seamen their wages is entitled to stand in their place and exercise their rights (the *Cornelia Henrietta*, 1866, L.R. [illegible] Ec. 51).

[illegible]—Any parting with the possession of goods is in [illegible] waiver of the lien upon them; for example, when a [illegible] a lien on the goods of his principal gives them to a [illegible] carried at the expense of his principal, even if [illegible] waives his lien, and has no right to stop the goods [illegible] it; so also where a coach-builder who has [illegible] repairs allows the owner from time to [illegible] without expressly reserving his lien, [illegible] a lien for the standage of the carriage [illegible], as mere standage does not give a [illegible] been held that where a portion of [illegible] lump sum has been taken away and [illegible] conversion has taken place and the [illegible] unpaid purchase-money has gone [illegible] Ex. 309). Again, an acceptance [illegible] with the existence of a lien, [illegible] guarantee [illegible]. For the same reason even an agreement to take security is a waiver of the lien, though the security is not, in fact, given (*Alliance Bank* v. *Broom*, 11 L.T. 332).

Sale of Goods under Lien.—At common law the lien only gives a right to retain the goods, and ultimately to sell by legal process, against the owner; but in certain cases a right has been given by statute to sell without the intervention of legal process, such as the right of an innkeeper to sell the goods of his customer for his unpaid account (Innkeepers Act 1878, § 1), the right of a wharfinger to sell goods entrusted to him by a shipowner with a lien upon them for freight, and also for their own charges (Merchant Shipping Act 1894, §§ 497, 498), and of a railway company to sell goods for their charges (Railway Clauses Act 1845, § 97). Property affected by an equitable lien or a maritime lien cannot be sold by the holder of the lien without the interposition of the court to enforce an order, or judgment of the court. In Admiralty cases, where a sale is necessary, no bail having been given and the property being under arrest, the sale is usually made by the marshal in London, but may be elsewhere on the parties concerned showing that a better price is likely to be obtained.

American Law.—In the United States, speaking very generally, the law relating to liens is that of England, but there are some considerable differences occasioned by three principal causes. (1) Some of the Southern States, notably Louisiana, have never adopted the common law of England. When that state became one of the United States of North America it had (and still preserves) its own system of law. In this respect the law is practically identical with the Code Napoleon, which, again speaking generally, substitutes privileges for liens, *i.e.* gives certain claims a prior right to others against particular property. These privileges being *strictissimae interpretationis*, cannot be extended by any principle analogous to the English doctrine of equitable liens. (2) Probably in consequence of the United States and the several states composing it having had a more democratic government than Great Britain, in their earlier years at all events, certain liens have been created by statute in several states in the interest of the working classes which have no parallel in Great Britain, *e.g.* in some states workmen employed in building a house or a ship have a lien upon the building or structure itself for their unpaid wages. This statutory lien partakes rather of the nature of an equitable than of a common-law lien, as the property is not in the possession of the workman, and it may be doubted whether the right thus conferred is more beneficial to the workman than the priority his wages have in bankruptcy proceedings in England. Some of the states have also practically extended the maritime lien to matters over which it was never contended for in England. (3) By the constitution of the United States the admiralty and inter-state jurisdiction is vested in the federal as distinguished from the state courts, and these federal courts have not been liable to have their jurisdiction curtailed by prohibition from courts of common law, as the court of admiralty had in England up to the time of the Judicature Acts; consequently the maritime lien in the United States extends further than it does in England, even after recent enlargements; it covers claims for necessaries and by material men (see *Maritime Lien*), as well as collision, salvage, wages, bottomry and damage to cargo.

Difficulties connected with lien occasionally arise in the federal courts in admiralty cases, from a conflict on the subject between the municipal law of the state where the court happens to sit and the admiralty law; but as there is no power to prohibit the federal court, its view of the admiralty law based on the civil law prevails. More serious difficulties arise where a federal court has to try inter-state questions, where the two states have different laws on the subject of lien; one for example, like Louisiana, following the civil law, and the other the common law and equitable practice of Great Britain. The question as to which law is to govern in such a case can hardly be said to be decided. "The question whether equitable liens can exist to be enforced in Louisiana by the federal courts, notwithstanding its restrictive law of privileges, is still an open one" (Derris,

Contracts of Pledge, 517; and see *Burdon Sugar Refining Co.* v. *Payne*, 167 U.S. 127).

British Colonies.—In those colonies which before the Canadian federation were known as Upper Canada and the Maritime Provinces of British North America, and in the several Australasian states where the English common law is enforced except as modified by colonial statute, the principles of lien, whether by common law or equitable or maritime, discussed above with reference to England, will prevail; but questions not dissimilar to those treated of in reference to the United States may arise where colonies have come to the crown of Great Britain by cession, and where different systems of municipal law are enforced. For example, in Lower Canada the law of France prior to the Revolution occupies the place of the common law in England, but is generally regulated by a code very similar to the Code Napoleon; in Mauritius and its dependencies the Code Napoleon itself is in force except so far as modified by subsequent ordinances. In South Africa, and to some extent in Ceylon and Guiana, Roman-Dutch law is in force; in the island of Trinidad old Spanish law, prior to the introduction of the present civil code of Spain, is the basis of jurisprudence. Each several system of law requires to be studied on the point; but, speaking generally, apart from the possessory lien of workmen and the maritime lien of the vice-admiralty courts, it may be assumed that the rules of the civil law, giving a privilege or priority in certain specified cases rather than a lien as understood in English law, prevail in those colonies where the English law is not in force. (F. W. Ra.)

LIERRE (Flemish, *Lier*), a town in the province of Antwerp, Belgium; 9 m. S.E. of Antwerp. Pop. (1904) 24,229. It carries on a brisk industry in silk fabrics. Its church of St Gommaire was finished in 1557 and contains three fine glass windows, the gift of the archduke Maximilian, to celebrate his wedding with Mary of Burgundy.

LIESTAL, the capital (since 1833) of the half canton of Basel-Stadt in Switzerland. It is a well-built but uninteresting industrial town, situated on the left bank of the Ergolz stream, and is the most populous town in the entire canton of Basel, after Basel itself. By rail it is 9½ m. S.E. of Basel, and 15¾ m. N.W. of Olten. In the 15th-century town hall (*Rathaus*) is preserved the golden drinking cup of Charles the Bold, duke of Burgundy, which was taken at the battle of Nancy in 1477. In 1900 the population was 5403, all German-speaking and mainly Protestants. The town was sold in 1302 by its lord to the bishop of Basel who, in 1400, sold it to the city of Basel, at whose hands it suffered much in the Peasants' War of 1653, and so consented gladly to the separation of 1833.

LIEUTENANT, one who takes the place, office and duty of and acts on behalf of a superior or other person. The word in English preserves the form of the French original (from *lieu*, place, *tenant*, holding), which is the equivalent of the Lat. *locum tenens*, one holding the place of another. The usual English pronunciation appears early, the word being frequently spelled *lieftenant*, *lyeftenant* or *luftenant* in the 14th and 15th centuries. The modern American pronunciation is *lewtenant*, while the German is represented by the present form of the word *Leutnant*. In French history, *lieutenant du roi* (*locum tenens regis*) was a title borne by the officer sent with military powers to represent the king in certain provinces. With wider powers and functions, both civil as well as military, and holding authority throughout an entire province, such a representative of the king was called *lieutenant général du roi*. The first appointment of these officials dates from the reign of Philip IV. the Fair (see Constable). In the 16th century the administration of the provinces was in the hands of *gouverneurs*, to whom the *lieutenants du roi* became subordinates. The titles *lieutenant civil* or *criminel* and *lieutenant général de police* have been borne by certain judicial officers in France (see Châtelet and Bailiff: *Bailli*). As the title of the representative of the sovereign, "lieutenant" in English usage appears in the title of the lord lieutenant of Ireland, and of the lords lieutenant of the counties of the United Kingdom (see below).

The most general use of the word is as the name of a grade of naval and military officer. It is common in this application to nearly every navy and army of the present day. In Italy and Spain the first part of the word is omitted, and an Italian and Spanish officer bearing this rank are called *tenente* or *teniente* respectively. In the British and most other navies the lieutenants are the commissioned officers next in rank to commanders, or second class of captains. Originally the lieutenant was a soldier who aided, and in case of need replaced, the captain, who, until the latter half of the 17th century, was not necessarily a seaman in any navy. At first one lieutenant was carried, and only in the largest ships. The number was gradually increased, and the lieutenants formed a numerous corps. At the close of the Napoleonic War in 1815 there were 3211 lieutenants in the British navy. Lieutenants now often qualify for special duties such as navigation, or gunnery, or the management of torpedoes. In the British army a lieutenant is a subaltern officer ranking next below a captain and above a second lieutenant. In the United States of America subalterns are classified as first lieutenants and second lieutenants. In France the two grades are *lieutenant* and *sous-lieutenant*, while in Germany the *Leutnant* is the lower of the two ranks, the higher being *Ober-leutnant* (formerly *Premier-leutnant*). A "captain lieutenant" in the British army was formerly the senior subaltern who virtually commanded the colonel's company or troop, and ranked as junior captain, or "puny captain," as he was called by Cromwell's soldiers.

The lord lieutenant of a county, in England and Wales and in Ireland, is the principal officer of a county. His creation dates from the reign of Henry VIII. (or, according to some, Edward VI.), when the military functions of the sheriff were handed over to him. He was responsible for the efficiency of the militia of the county, and afterwards of the yeomanry and volunteers. He was commander of these forces, whose officers he appointed. By the Regulation of the Forces Act 1871, the jurisdiction, duties and command exercised by the lord lieutenant were revested in the crown, but the power of recommending for first appointments was reserved to the lord lieutenant. By the Territorial and Reserve Forces Act 1907, the lord lieutenant of a county was constituted president of the county association. The office of lord lieutenant is honorary, and is held during the royal pleasure, but virtually for life. Appointment to the office is by letters patent under the great seal. Usually, though not necessarily, the person appointed lord lieutenant is also appointed custos rotulorum (*q.v.*). Appointments to the county bench of magistrates are usually made on the recommendation of the lord lieutenant (see Justice of the Peace).

A deputy lieutenant (denoted frequently by the addition of the letters D.L. after a person's name) is a deputy of a lord lieutenant of a county. His appointment and qualifications previous to 1908 were regulated by the Militia Act 1882. By s. 30 of that act the lieutenant of each county was required from time to time to appoint such properly qualified persons as he thought fit, living within the county, to be deputy lieutenants. At least twenty had to be appointed for each county, if there were so many qualified; if less than that number were qualified, then all the duly qualified persons in the county were to be appointed. The appointments were subject to the sovereign's approval, and a return of all appointments to, and removals from, the office had to be laid before parliament annually. To qualify for the appointment of deputy lieutenant a person had to be (*a*) a peer of the realm, or the heir-apparent of such a peer, having a place of residence within the county; or (*b*) have in possession an estate in land in the United Kingdom of the yearly value of not less than £200; or (*c*) be the heir-apparent of such a person; or (*d*) have a clear yearly income from personalty within the United Kingdom of not less than £200 (s. 33). If the lieutenant were absent from the United Kingdom, or through illness or other cause were unable to act, the sovereign might authorize any three deputy lieutenants to act as lieutenant (s. 31), or might appoint a deputy lieutenant to act as vice-lieutenant. Otherwise, the duties of the office were practically nominal, except that a deputy lieutenant might attest militia recruits and administer the oath of allegiance to them. The reorganization in 1907 of the forces of the British crown, and the formation of county associations to administer the territorial army, placed increased duties on deputy lieutenants, and it was publicly announced that the king's approval of appointments to that position would only be given in the case of gentlemen who had served for ten years in some force of the crown, or had rendered eminent service in connexion with a county association.

The lord lieutenant of Ireland is the head of the executive in that country. He represents his sovereign and maintains the formalities of government, the business of government being entrusted to the [illegible] of his chief secretary, who represents the Irish government in the House of Commons, and may have a seat in the cabinet. The chief secretary occupies an important position, and in every cabinet either the lord lieutenant or he has a seat.

Lieutenant-governor is the title of the governor of an Indian province, in direct subordination to the governor-general in council. The lieutenant-governor comes midway in dignity between the governors of Madras and Bombay, who are appointed from England, and the chief commissioners of smaller provinces. In the Dominion of Canada the governors of provinces also have the title of lieutenant-governor. The representatives of the sovereign in the Isle of Man and the Channel Islands are likewise styled lieutenant-governors.

LIFE, the popular name for the activity peculiar to protoplasm (q.v.). This conception has been extended by analogy to phenomena different in kind, such as the activities of masses of water or of air, or of machinery, or by another analogy, to the [illegible] of a composite structure, and by imagination to real or supposed phenomena such as the manifestations of incorporeal [illegible]. From the point of view of exact science life is associated with matter, is displayed only by living bodies, by all living bodies, and is what distinguishes living bodies from bodies that are not alive. Herbert Spencer's formula that life is "the [illegible] adjustment of internal relations to external relations" was the result of a profound and subtle analysis, but omits the [illegible] consideration that we know life only as a quality [illegible] association with living matter.

In developing our conception we must discard from consideration the complexities that arise from the organization of the higher living bodies, the differences between one living animal and another, or between plant and animal. Such differentiations [illegible] of living bodies are the subject-matter of [illegible] evolution; some will see in the play of circum-[illegible], natural or supernatural, on the simplest forms [illegible] sufficient explanation of the development of [illegible] the highest forms of living organisms; others [illegible] of such living matter so to develop as a [illegible] peculiar quality that must be added to the [illegible]. Choice amongst these alternatives need not [illegible] of the nature of life. The explanation [illegible] of living matter, the vehicle of life, [illegible] of life. What we have to deal with [illegible] form.

[illegible] must really be a description of the [illegible], and we must set out with an investigation [illegible] living substance with the special object [illegible] between organisms and unorganized [illegible] between dead and living organized [illegible]

[illegible] (see PROTOPLASM), as it now exists in all [illegible] particulate, consisting of elementary [illegible], or grouped in communities, [illegible] the bodies of the higher animals and [illegible] or larger communities are subject [illegible], which destroy them, immedi-[illegible] cease; or they may wear out, [illegible] products of their own activity. There [illegible] mortality of protoplasm and the [illegible] of life as more than the necessary [illegible] character of living matter (see [illegible]

[illegible] contains only a few elements, [illegible] and none of which is peculiar [illegible] form compounds characteristic [illegible] part peculiar to it. Proteid, [illegible] hydrogen, nitrogen, oxygen and [illegible], is the most complex of all [illegible] only from organic bodies. [illegible] organic compounds, of which [illegible] known, occur in different [illegible] proportions, and are much less [illegible] they may be stages in the [illegible] though they [illegible] living

matter, are gradually being conquered by the synthetic chemist. Finally, protoplasm contains various inorganic substances, such as salts and water, the latter giving it its varying degrees of liquid consistency.

We attain, therefore, our first generalized description of life as the property or peculiar quality of a substance composed of none but the more common elements, but of these elements grouped in various ways to form compounds ranging from proteid, the most complex of known substances to the simplest salts. The living substance, moreover, has its mixture of elaborate and simple compounds associated in a fashion that is peculiar. The older writers have spoken of protoplasm or the cell as being in a sense "manufactured articles"; in the more modern view such a conception is replaced by the statement that protoplasm and the cell have behind them a long historical architecture Both ideas, or both modes of expressing what is fundamentally the same idea, have this in common, that life is not a sum of the qualities of the chemical elements contained in protoplasm, but a function first of the peculiar architecture of the mixture, and then of the high complexity of the compounds contained in the mixture. The qualities of water are no sum of the qualities of oxygen and hydrogen, and still less can we expect to explain the qualities of life without regard to the immense complexity of the living substance.

We must now examine in more detail the differences which exist or have been alleged to exist between living organisms and inorganic bodies. There is no essential difference in structure. Confusion has arisen in regard to this point from attempts to compare organized bodies with crystals, the comparison having been suggested by the view that as crystals present the highest type of inorganic structure, it was reasonable to compare them with organic matter. Differences between crystals and organized bodies have no bearing on the problem of life, for organic substance must be compared with a liquid rather than with a crystal, and differs in structure no more from inorganic liquids than these do amongst themselves, and less than they differ from crystals. Living matter is a mixture of substances chiefly dissolved in water; the comparison with the crystals has led to a supposed distinction in the mode of growth, crystals growing by the superficial apposition of new particles and living substance by intussusception. But inorganic liquids also grow in the latter mode, as when a soluble substance is added to them.

The phenomena of movement do not supply any absolute distinction. Although these are the most obvious characters of life, they cannot be detected in quiescent seeds, which we know to be alive, and they are displayed in a fashion very like life by inorganic foams brought in contact with liquids of different composition. Irritability, again, although a notable quality of living substance, is not peculiar to it, for many inorganic substances respond to external stimulation by definite changes. Instability, again, which lies at the root of Spencer's definition "continuous adjustment of internal relations to external relations" is displayed by living matter in very varying degrees from the apparent absolute quiescence of frozen seeds to the activity of the central nervous system, whilst there is a similar range amongst inorganic substances.

The phenomena of reproduction present no fundamental distinction. Most living bodies, it is true, are capable of reproduction, but there are many without this capacity, whilst, on the other hand, it would be difficult to draw an effective distinction between that reproduction of simple organisms which consists of a sub-division of their substance with consequent resumption of symmetry by the separate pieces, and the breaking up of a drop of mercury into a number of droplets.

Consideration of the mode of origin reveals a more real if not an absolute distinction. All living substance so far as is known at present (see BIOGENESIS) arises only from already existing living substance. It is to be noticed, however, that green plants have the power of building up living substance from inorganic material, and there is a certain analogy between the building up of new living material only in association with pre-existing living material, and the greater readiness with which certain inorganic reactions take place if there already be present some trace of the result of the reaction.

The real distinction between living matter and inorganic matter is chemical. Living substance always contains proteid, and although we know that proteid contains only common inorganic elements, we know neither how these are combined to form proteid, nor any way in which proteid can be brought into existence except in the presence of previously existing proteid. The central position of the problem of life lies in the chemistry of proteid, and until that has been fully explored, we are unable to say that there is any problem of life behind the problem of proteid.

Comparison of living and lifeless organic matter presents the initial difficulty that we cannot draw an exact line between a living and a dead organism. The higher "warm-blooded" creatures appear to present the simplest case and in their life-history there seems to be a point at which we can say "that which was alive is now dead." We judge from some major arrest of activity, as when the heart ceases to beat. Long after this, however, various tissues remain alive and active, and the event to which we give the name of death is no more than a superficially visible stage in a series of changes. In less highly integrated organisms, such as "cold-blooded" vertebrates, the point of death is less conspicuous, and when we carry our observations further down the scale of animal life, there ceases to be any salient phase in the slow transition from life to death.

The distinction between life and death is made more difficult by a consideration of cases of so-called "arrested vitality." If credit can be given to the stories of Indian fakirs, it appears that human beings can pass voluntarily into a state of suspended animation that may last for weeks. The state of involuntary trance, sometimes mistaken for death, is a similar occurrence. A. Leeuwenhoek, in 1719, made the remarkable discovery, since abundantly confirmed, that many animalculae, notably tardigrades and rotifers, may be completely desiccated and remain in that condition for long periods without losing the power of awaking to active life when moistened with water. W. Preyer has more recently investigated the matter and has given it the name "anabiosis." Later observers have found similar occurrences in the cases of small nematodes, rotifers and bacteria. The capacity of plant seeds to remain dry and inactive for very long periods is still better known. It has been supposed that in the case of the plant seeds and still more in that of the animals, the condition of anabiosis was merely one in which the metabolism was too faint to be perceptible by ordinary methods of observation, but the elaborate experiments of W. Kochs would seem to show that a complete arrest of vital activity is compatible with viability. The categories, "alive" and "dead," are not sufficiently distinct for us to add to our conception of life by comparing them. A living organism usually displays active metabolism of proteid, but the metabolism may slow down, actually cease and yet reawaken; a dead organism is one in which the metabolism has ceased and does not reawaken.

Origin of Life.—It is plain that we cannot discuss adequately the origin of life or the possibility of the artificial construction of living matter (see ABIOGENESIS and BIOGENESIS) until the chemistry of protoplasm and specially of proteid is more advanced. The investigations of O. Bütschli have shown how a model of protoplasm can be manufactured. Very finely triturated soluble particles are rubbed into a smooth paste with an oil of the requisite consistency. A fragment of such a paste brought into a liquid in which the solid particles are soluble, slowly expands into a honeycomb like foam, the walls of the minute vesicles being films of oil, and the contents being the soluble particles dissolved in droplets of the circumambient liquid. Such a model, properly constructed, that is to say, with the vesicles of the foam microscopic in size, is a marvellous imitation of the appearance of protoplasm, being distinguishable from it only by a greater symmetry. The nicely balanced conditions of solution produce a state of unstable equilibrium, with the result that internal streaming movements and changes of shape and changes of position in the model simulate closely the corresponding manifestations in real protoplasm. The model has no power of recuperation; in a comparatively short time equilibrium is restored and the resemblance with protoplasm disappears. But it suggests a method by which, when the chemistry of protoplasm and proteid is better known, the proper substances which compose protoplasm may be brought together to form a simple kind of protoplasm.

It has been suggested from time to time that conditions very unlike those now existing were necessary for the first appearance of life, and must be repeated if living matter is to be constructed artificially. No support for such a view can be derived from observations of the existing conditions of life. The chemical elements involved are abundant; the physical conditions of temperature pressure and so forth at which living matter is most active, and within the limits of which it is confined, are familiar and almost constant in the world around us. On the other hand, it may be that the initial conditions for the synthesis of proteid are different from those under which proteid and living matter display their activities. E. Pflüger has argued that the analogies between living proteid and the compounds of cyanogen are so numerous that they suggest cyanogen as the starting-point of protoplasm. Cyanogen and its compounds, so far as we know, arise only in a state of incandescent heat. Pflüger suggests that such compounds arose when the surface of the earth was incandescent, and that in the long process of cooling, compounds of cyanogen and hydrocarbons passed into living protoplasm by such processes of transformation and polymerization as are familiar in the chemical groups in question, and by the acquisition of water and oxygen. His theory is in consonance with the interpretation of the structure of protoplasm as having behind it a long historical architecture and leads to the obvious conclusion that if protoplasm be constructed artificially it will be by a series of stages and that the product will be simpler than any of the existing animals or plants.

Until greater knowledge of protoplasm and particularly of proteid has been acquired, there is no scientific room for the suggestion that there is a mysterious factor differentiating living matter from other matter and life from other activities. We have to scale the walls, open the windows, and explore the castle before crying out that it is so marvellous that it must contain ghosts.

As may be supposed, theories of the origin of life apart from doctrines of special creation or of a primitive and slow spontaneous generation are mere fantastic speculations. The most striking of these suggests an extra-terrestrial origin. H. E. Richter appears to have been the first to propound the idea that life came to this planet as cosmic dust or in meteorites thrown off from stars and planets. Towards the end of the 19th century Lord Kelvin (then Sir W. Thomson) and H. von Helmholtz independently raised and discussed the possibility of such an origin of terrestrial life, laying stress on the presence of hydrocarbons in meteoric stones and on the indications of their presence revealed by the spectra of the tails of comets. W. Preyer has criticized such views, grouping them under the phrase "theory of cosmozoa," and has suggested that living matter preceded inorganic matter. Preyer's view, however, enlarges the conception of life until it can be applied to the phenomena of incandescent gases and has no relation to ideas of life derived from observation of the living matter we know.

REFERENCES.—O. Bütschli, *Investigations on Microscopic Foams and Protoplasm* (Eng. trans. by E. A. Minchin, 1894), with a useful list of references; H. von Helmholtz, *Vorträge und Reden*, ii. (1884); W. Kochs, *Allgemeine Naturkunde*, x. 673 (1890); A. Leeuwenhoek, *Epistolae ad Societatem regiam Anglicam* (1719); E. Pflüger, "Über einige Gesetze des Eiweissstoffwechsels," in *Archiv. Ges. Physiol.* liv. 333 (1893); W. Preyer, *Die Hypothesen über den Ursprung des Lebens* (1880); H. E. Richter, *Zur Darwinischen Lehre* (1865); Herbert Spencer, *Principles of Biology*; Max Verworn, *General Physiology* (English trans. by F. S. Lee, 1899), with a very full literature. (P. C. M.)

LIFE-BOAT, AND LIFE-SAVING SERVICE

[illegible] and [illegible]-SAVING SERVICE. The article on [illegible] (*q.v.*) deals generally with the [illegible] but under this heading it is convenient [illegible] connected specially with the life-boat [illegible] boat is unsuited for life-saving in [illegible] contrivances, in regard to which [illegible] England, have been made for securing the [illegible]

[illegible] was conceived and designed by Lionel [illegible] coachbuilder, in 1785. Encouraged by the [illegible] George IV.), Lukin fitted up a Norway yawl [illegible] a patent for it, and wrote a pamphlet [illegible] "Unimmergible Boat." Buoyancy he obtained [illegible] gunwale of cork and air-chambers inside [illegible] at the bow, another at the stern. Stability [illegible] iron keel. The self-righting and self-empty- [illegible] not to have thought of; at all events he [illegible] Despite the patronage of the prince, [illegible] grave a neglected and disappointed man. [illegible] altogether unsuccessful, for, at the request of the [illegible] fitted up a coble as an "unimmergible" [illegible] launched at Bamborough, saved several [illegible] and afterwards saved many lives and much [illegible]

[illegible] in regard to shipwreck was temporally swept [illegible] the "Adventure" of Newcastle in 1789. [illegible] only 300 yds. from the shore, and her [illegible] into the raging breakers in presence [illegible] none of whom dared to put off in [illegible] the rescue. An excited meeting among the [illegible] followed; a committee was formed, [illegible] the best models of a life-boat. [illegible] of which those of William Would- [illegible] Henry Greathead, a boatbuilder, of South [illegible] The committee awarded the prize to [illegible] the good points of both models, gave [illegible] of their boat to Greathead. This [illegible] by nearly 7 cwts. of cork, and had [illegible] posts, with great curvature of keel. [illegible] Greathead was well rewarded; neverthe- [illegible] launched till 1798, when the duke of [illegible] Greathead to build him a life-boat which [illegible] also did good service, and its owner [illegible] Oporto. In the same year Mr Cath- [illegible] for St Andrews, where, two years [illegible] Thus the value of life-boats began [illegible] the end of 1803 Greathead had built [illegible] for England, five for Scotland and [illegible] Nevertheless, public interest in life-boats [illegible] till 1823.

[illegible] Hillary, Bart., stood forth to champion [illegible] dwelt in the Isle of Man, and had [illegible] in the saving of three hundred and [illegible] with two members of parliament— [illegible] Mr George Hibbert—Hillary founded [illegible] Institution for the Preservation of Life [illegible] perhaps the grandest of England's [illegible] now named the "Royal National [illegible] founded on the 4th of March 1824. [illegible] archbishop of Canterbury presided [illegible] men in the land—among them [illegible] nevertheless, the institution [illegible] of only £9826. In the first year [illegible] and placed at different stations, [illegible] had been stationed on the [illegible] individuals and by independent [illegible] institution exercised no control [illegible] In its early years the institution [illegible] Captain Manby at many stations, [illegible] sailors and others saved from [illegible] discharged by the "Ship- [illegible] Royal Benevolent Society."

At the date of the institution's second report it had contributed to the saving of three hundred and forty-two lives, either by its own life-saving apparatus or by other means for which it had granted rewards. With fluctuating success, both as regards means and results, the institution continued its good work—saving many lives, and occasionally losing a few brave men in its tremendous battles with the sea. Since the adoption of the self-righting boats, loss of life in the service has been comparatively small and infrequent.

Towards the middle of the 19th century the life-boat cause appeared to lose interest with the British public, though the life-saving work was prosecuted with unremitting zeal, but the increasing loss of life by shipwreck, and a few unusually severe disasters to life-boats, brought about the reorganization of the society in 1850. The Prince Consort became vice-patron of the institution in conjunction with the king of the Belgians, and Queen Victoria, who had been its patron since her accession, became an annual contributor to its funds. In 1851 the duke of Northumberland became president, and from that time forward a tide of prosperity set in, unprecedented in the history of benevolent institutions, both in regard to the great work accomplished and the pecuniary aid received. In 1850 its committee undertook the immediate superintendence of all the life-boat work on the coasts, with the aid of local committees. Periodical inspections, quarterly exercise of crews, fixed rates of payments to coxswains and men, and quarterly reports were instituted, at the time when the self-righting self-emptying boat came into being. This boat was the result of a hundred-guinea prize, offered by the president, for the best model of a life-boat, with another hundred to defray the cost of a boat built on the model chosen. In reply to the offer no fewer than two hundred and eighty models were sent in, not only from all parts of the United Kingdom, but from France, Germany, Holland and the United States of America. The prize was gained by Mr James Beeching of Great Yarmouth, whose model, slightly modified by Mr James Peake, one of the committee of inspection, was still further improved as time and experience suggested (see below).

The necessity of maintaining a thoroughly efficient life-boat service is now generally recognized by the people not only of Great Britain, but also of those other countries on the European Continent and America which have a sea-board, and of the British colonies, and numerous life-boat services have been founded more or less on the lines of the Royal National Life-boat Institution. The British Institution was again reorganized in 1883; it has since greatly developed both in its life-saving efficiency and financially, and has been spoken of in the highest terms as regards its management by successive governments—a Select Committee of the House of Commons in 1897 reporting to the House that the thanks of the whole community were due to the Institution for its energy and good management. On the death of Queen Victoria in January 1901 she was succeeded as patron of the Institution by Edward VII., who as prince of Wales had been its president for several years. At the close of 1908 the Institution's fleet consisted of 280 life-boats, and the total number of lives for the saving of which the committee of management had granted rewards since the establishment of the Institution in 1824 was 47,983. At this time there were only seventeen life-boats on the coast of the United Kingdom which did not belong to the Institution. In 1882 the total amount of money received by the Institution from all sources was £57,797, whereas in 1901 the total amount received had increased to £107,293. In 1908 the receipts were £115,303, the expenditure £90,335.

In 1882 the Institution undertook, with the view of diminishing the loss of life among the coast fishermen, to provide the masters and owners of fishing-vessels with trustworthy aneroid barometers, at about a third of the retail price, and in 1883 the privilege was extended to the masters and owners of coasters under 100 tons burden. At the end of 1901 as many as 4417 of these valuable instruments had been supplied. In 1889 the committee of management secured the passing of the Removal of Wrecks Act 1877 Amendment Act, which provides for the removal of wrecks in non-navigable waters which might prove dangerous to life-boat crews and others. Under its provisions numerous highly dangerous wrecks have been removed.

In 1893 the chairman of the Institution moved a resolution in the House of Commons that, in order to decrease the serious loss of life from shipwreck on the coast, the British Government should provide either telephonic or telegraphic communication between all the coast-guard stations and signal stations on the coast of the United Kingdom; and that where there are no coast-guard stations the post offices nearest to the life-boat stations should be electrically connected, the object being to give the earliest possible information to the life-boat authorities at all times, by day and night, when the life-boats are required for service; and further, that a Royal Commission should be appointed to consider the desirability of electrically connecting the rock lighthouses, light-ships, &c., with the shore. The resolution was agreed to without a division, and its intention has been practically carried out, the results obtained having proved most valuable in the saving of life.

On the 1st of January 1898 a pension and gratuity scheme was introduced by the committee of management, under which life-boat coxswains, bowmen and signalmen of long and meritorious service, retiring on account of old age, accident, ill-health or abolition of office, receive special allowances as a reward for their good services. While these payments act as an incentive to the men to discharge their duties satisfactorily, they at the same time assist the committee of management in their effort to obtain the best men for the work. For many years the Institution has given compensation to any who may have received injury while employed in the service, besides granting liberal help to the widows and dependent relatives of any in the service who lose their own lives when endeavouring to rescue others.

A very marked advance in improvement in design and suitability for service has been made in the life-boat since the re-organization of the Institution in 1883, but principally since

Fig. 1.—The 33-ft., Double-banked, Ten-oared, Self-righting and Self-emptying Life-boat (1881) of the Institution on its Transporting Carriage, ready for launching.

1887, when, as the result of an accident in December 1886 to two self-righting life-boats in Lancashire, twenty-seven out of twenty-nine of the men who manned them were drowned. At this time a permanent technical sub-committee was appointed by the Institution, whose object was, with the assistance of an eminent consulting naval architect—a new post created—and the Institution's official experts, to give its careful attention to the designing of improvements in the life-boat and its equipment, and to the scientific consideration of any inventions or proposals submitted by the public, with a view to adopting them if of practical utility. Whereas in 1881 the self-righting life-boat of that time was looked upon as the Institution's special life-boat, and there were very few life-boats in the Institution's fleet not of that type, at the close of 1901 the life-boats of the Institution included 60 non-self-righting boats of various types, known by the following designations: Steam life-boats 4, Cromer 3, Lamb and White 1, Liverpool 14, Norfolk and Suffolk 19, tubular 1, Watson 18. In 1901 a steam-tug was placed at Padstow for use solely in conjunction with the life-boats on the north coast of Cornwall. The self-righting life-boat of 1901 was a very different boat from that of 1881 The Institution's present policy is to allow the men who man the life-boats, after having seen and tried by deputation the various types, to select that in which they have the most confidence.

The present life-boat of the self-righting type (fig 2) differs materially from its predecessor, the stability being increased and the righting power greatly improved The test of efficiency in this last quality was formerly considered sufficient if the boat would quickly right herself in smooth water without her crew and gear, but every self-righting life-boat now built by the Institution will right with her full crew and gear on board, with her sails set and the anchor down. Most of the larger self-righting boats are furnished with "centre-boards" or

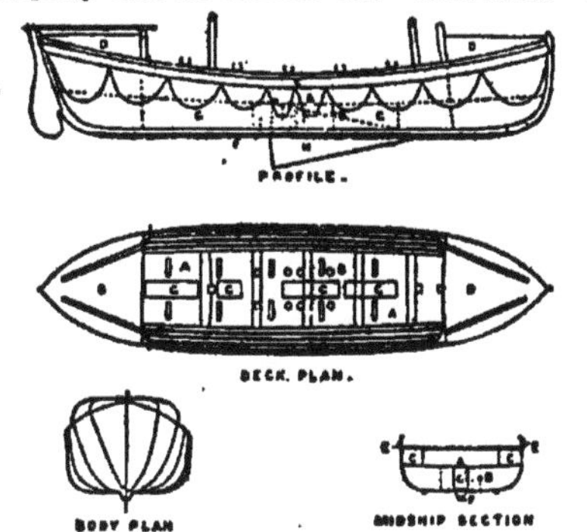

Fig. 2.—Plans, Profile and Section of Modern English Self-righting Life-boat.

A, Deck.
B, Relieving valves for automatic discharge of water off deck.
C, Side air-cases above deck.
D, End air compartments, usually called "end-boxes," an important factor in self-righting.
E, Wale, or fender.
F, Iron keel ballast, important in general stability and self-righting.
G, Water-ballast tanks.
H, Drop-keel.

"drop-keels" of varying size and weight, which can be used at pleasure, and materially add to their weather qualities. The drop-keel was for the first time placed in a life-boat in 1885.

Steam was first introduced into a life-boat in 1890, when the Institution, after very full inquiry and consideration,

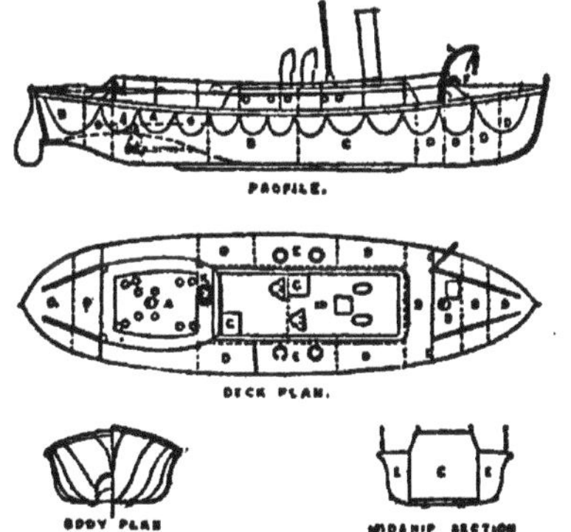

Fig. 3.—Plans, Profile and Section of English Steam Life-boat.

A, Cockpit.
a, Deck
b, Propeller hatch.
c, Relief valves.
B, Engine-room.
C, Boiler-room.
D, Water-tight compartments.
E, Coal-bunkers.
F, Capstan.
G, Hatches to engine-and boiler-rooms.
H, Cable reel.
I, Anchor davit.

stationed on the coast a steel life-boat, 50 ft. long and 12 ft. beam, and a depth of 3 ft. 6 in., propelled by a turbine wheel driven by engines developing 170 horse-power. It had been [illegible] held by all competent judges that a mechanically-[illegible] life-boat, suitable for service in heavy weather, was a [illegible] surrounded by so many and great difficulties that even the most sanguine experts dared not hope for an early [illegible] of it. This type of boat (fig. 3) has proved very useful. It is, however, fully recognized that boats of this description can [illegible] be used at only a very limited number of stations, and where there is a harbour which never dries out. The highest [illegible] attained by the first hydraulic steam life-boat was rather [illegible] than 9 knots, and that secured in the latest 9½ knots. In [illegible] the fleet of the Institution included 4 steam life-boats and 5 motor life-boats. The experiments with motor life-boats [illegible] years had proved successful.

The other types of pulling and sailing life-boats are all non-self-righting, and are specially suitable for the requirements of the different parts of the coast on which they are placed. Their various qualities will be understood by a glance at the illustrations (figs. 4, 5, 6, 7 and 8).

The Institution continues to build life-boats of different sizes according to the requirements of the various points of the coast at which they are placed, but of late years the tendency has been generally to increase the dimensions of the boats. The change of policy is mainly due to the fact that the small

[illegible] Profile and Section of Cromer Type of Life-boat.
[illegible] C, Side air-cases above deck.
[illegible] valves for auto- E, Wale, or fender.
[illegible] discharge of water off G, Water-ballast tanks.

[illegible] boats have in great measure disappeared, [illegible] taken by steamers and steam trawlers. The [illegible] and equipping of pulling and sailing life-[illegible] increased, more especially since 1898, [illegible] due to improvements and the seriously [illegible] materials and labour. In 1881 the [illegible] fully-equipped life-boat and carriage was [illegible] end of 1901 it amounted to £1000, the [illegible] of maintaining a station having risen

[illegible] continues to be a most important [illegible] life-boats, generally of the self-righting [illegible] where it is necessary to launch the [illegible] the immediate vicinity of the boat-[illegible] usual to supply carriages to boats [illegible] ft. in length by 9 ft. beam, those [illegible] and beam being either launched [illegible] or kept afloat. The transporting-[illegible] rendered particularly useful at [illegible] sandy or shingly, by the intro-[illegible] sand-plates. They are composed of an endless plateway or jointed wheel tyre fitted to the main wheels of the carriage, thereby enabling the boat to be transferred with rapidity and with greatly decreased labour over beach and soft sand. Further efficiency in launching has also been attained at many stations by the introduction in 1890 of pushing-poles, attached to the transporting-carriages, and

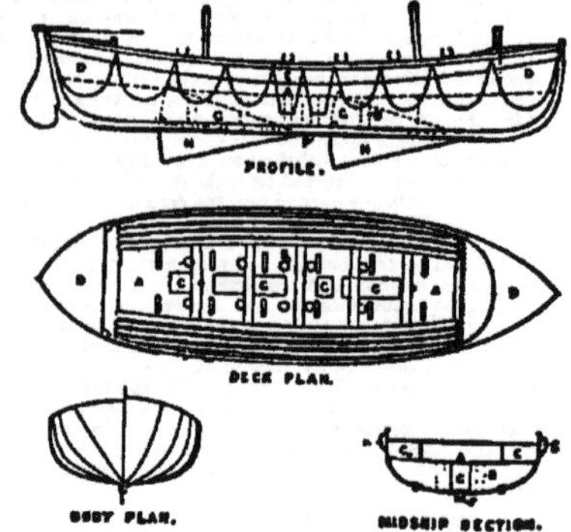

Fig. 5.—Plans, Profile and Section of Liverpool Type of Life-boat. A, B, C, E, G, as in fig. 3; D, end air-compartments; F, iron keel; H, drop-keels.

of horse launching-poles, first used in 1892. Fig. 9 gives a view of the modern transporting-carriage fitted with Tipping's sand- or wheel-plates.

The *life-belt* has since 1898 been considerably improved, being now less cumbersome than formerly, and more comfortable. The feature of the principal improvement is the reduction in length of the corks under the arms of the wearer and the rounding-off of the upper portions, the result being that considerably more freedom is provided for the arms. The maximum extra buoyancy has thereby been reduced from 25 lb to 22 lb, which is more than sufficient to support a man heavily clothed with his head and shoulders above the water, or to enable him to

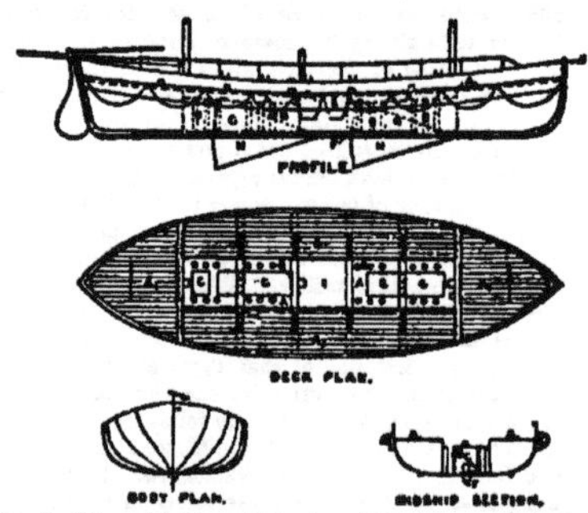

Fig. 6.—Plans, Profile and Section of Norfolk and Suffolk Type of Life-boat. A, B, E, F, G, H, as in fig. 4, A, side deck; I, cable-well.

support another person besides himself. Numerous life-belts of very varied descriptions, and made of all sorts of materials, have been patented, but it is generally agreed that for life-boat work the cork life-belt of the Institution has not yet been equalled.

Life-saving rafts, seats for ships' decks, dresses, buoys, belts, &c.,

have been produced in all shapes and sizes, but apparently nothing indispensable has as yet been brought out. Those interested in life-saving appliances were hopeful that the Paris

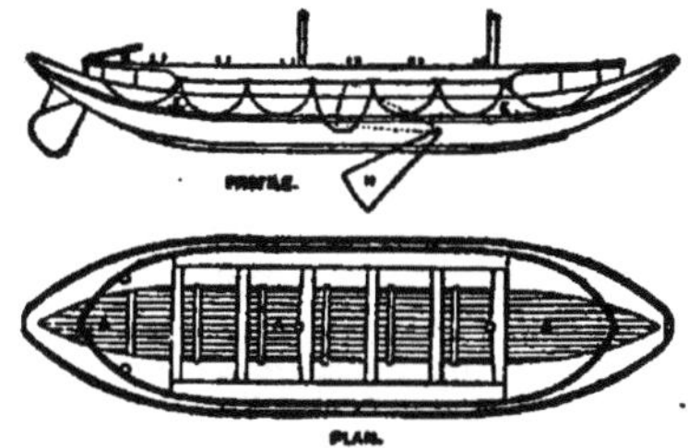

FIG. 7.—Plan, Profile and Section of Tubular Type of Life-boat. A, deck; E, wale, or fender; H, drop-keel.

Exhibition of 1900 would have produced some life-saving invention which might prove a benefit to the civilized world, but so lacking in real merit were the life-saving exhibits that the jury of experts were unable to award to any of the 435 competitors the Andrew Pollok prize of £4000 for the best method or device for saving life from shipwreck.

The *rocket apparatus*, which in the United Kingdom is under the management of the coast-guard, renders excellent service in life-saving. This, next to the life-boat, is the most important and successful means by which shipwrecked persons are rescued

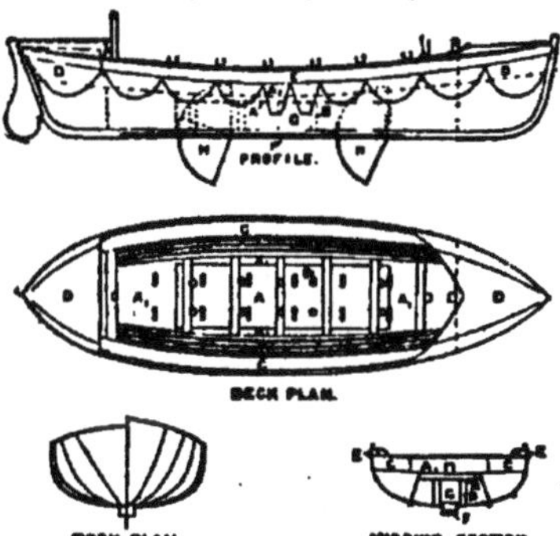

FIG. 8.—Plans, Profile and Section of Watson Type of Life-boat. Lettering as in fig. 5, but C, side air-cases above deck and thwarts.

on the British shores. Many vessels are cast every year on the rocky parts of the coasts, under cliffs, where no life-boat could be of service. In such places the rocket alone is available.

The rocket apparatus consists of five principal parts, viz. the rocket, the rocket-line, the whip, the hawser and the sling life-buoy. The mode of working it is as follows. A rocket, having a light line attached to it, is fired over the wreck. By means of this line the wrecked crew haul out the whip, which is a double or endless line, rove through a block with a tail attached to it. The tail-block, having been detached from the rocket-line, is fastened to a mast, or other portion of the wreck, high above the water. By means of the whip the rescuers haul off the hawser, to which is hung the travelling or sling life-buoy. When one end of the hawser has been made fast to the mast, about 18 in. *above* the whip, and its other end to tackle fixed to an anchor on shore, the life-buoy is run out by the rescuers, and the shipwrecked persons, getting into it one at a time, are hauled ashore. Sometimes, in cases of urgency, the life-buoy is worked by means of the whip alone, without the hawser. Captain G. W. Manby, F.R.S., in 1807 invented, or at least introduced, the mortar apparatus, on which the system of the rocket apparatus, which superseded it in England, is founded. Previously, however, in 1791, the idea of throwing a rope from a wreck to the shore by means of a shell from a mortar had occurred to Serjeant Bell of the Royal Artillery, and about the same time, to a Frenchman named La Fère, both of whom made successful experiments with their apparatus. In the same year (1807) a rocket was proposed by Mr Trengrouse of Helston in Cornwall, also a hand and lead line as means of communicating with vessels in distress. The *heaving cane* was a fruit of the latter suggestion. In 1814 forty-five mortar stations were established, and Manby received £2000, in addition to previous grants, in acknowledgment of the good service rendered by his invention. Mr John Dennett of Newport, Isle of Wight, introduced the rocket, which was afterwards extensively used. In 1826 four places in the Isle of Wight were supplied with Dennett's rockets, but it was not till after government had taken the apparatus

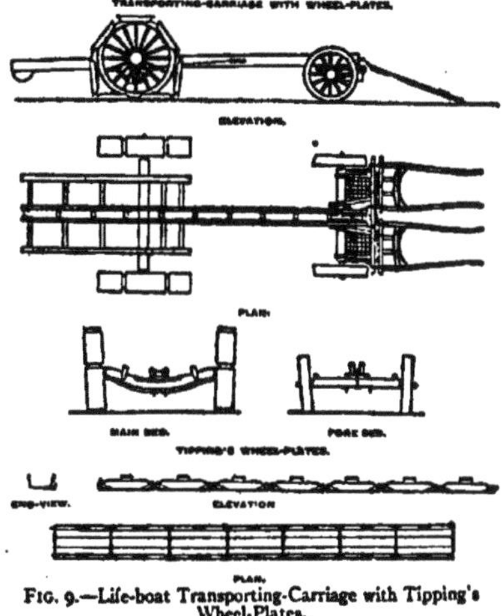

FIG. 9.—Life-boat Transporting-Carriage with Tipping's Wheel-Plates.

under its own control, in 1855, that the rocket invented by Colonel Boxer was adopted. Its peculiar characteristic lies in the combination of two rockets in one case, one being a continuation of the other, so that, after the first compartment has carried the machine to its full elevation, the second gives it an additional impetus whereby a great increase of range is obtained. (R. M. B.; C. Dr.)

UNITED STATES.—In the extent of coast line covered, magnitude of operations and the extraordinary success which has crowned its efforts, the life-saving service of the United States is not surpassed by any other institution of its kind in the world. Notwithstanding the exposed and dangerous nature of the coasts flanking and stretching between the approaches to the principal seaports, and the immense amount of shipping concentrating upon them, the loss of life among a total of 121,459 persons imperilled by marine casualty within the scope of the operations of the service from its organization in 1871 to the 30th of June 1907, was less than 1%, and even this small proportion is made up largely of persons washed overboard immediately upon the striking of vessels and before any assistance could reach them, or lost in attempts to land in their own boats, and people thrown into the sea by the capsizing of small craft. In the scheme of the service, next in importance to the saving of life is the saving of property from marine disaster, for which no salvage or reward is allowed. During the period named vessels and cargoes to the value of nearly two hundred million dollars were saved, while only about a quarter as much was lost.

[illegible]

yachts rendezvous and many accidents occur, which, with the one at Louisville are believed to be the only floating life-saving stations in the world, is manned from May 1st to November 15th. Its equipment includes a steam tug and two gasoline launches, the latter being harboured in a slip cut into the after-part of the station and extending from the stern to nearly amidships. The Louisville stations guard the falls of the Ohio river, where life is much endangered from accidents to vessels passing over the falls and small craft which are liable to be drawn into the chutes while attempting to cross the river. Its equipment includes two river skiffs which can be instantly launched directly from the ways at one end of the station. These skiffs are small boats modelled much like surf-boats, designed to be rowed by one or two men. Other equipments are provided for the salvage of property. The stations, located as near as practicable to a launching place, contain as a rule convenient quarters for the residence of the keeper and crew and a boat and apparatus room. In some instances the dwelling- and boat-house are built separately. Each station has a look-out tower for the day watch.

The principal apparatus consists of surf- and life-boats, Lyle gun and breeches-buoy apparatus and life-car. The Hunt gun and Cunningham line-carrying rocket are available at selected stations on account of their greater range, but their use is rarely necessary. The crews are drilled daily in some portion of rescue work, as practice in manœuvring, upsetting and righting boats, with the breeches-buoy, in the resuscitation of the apparently drowned and in signalling. The district officers upon their quarterly visits examine the crews orally and by drill, recording the proficiency of each member, including the keeper, which record accompanies their report to the general superintendent. For watch and patrol the day of twenty-four hours is divided into periods of four or five hours each. Day watches are stood by one man in the look-out tower or at some other point of vantage, while two men are assigned to each night watch between sunset and sunrise. One of the men remains on watch at the station, dividing his time between the beach look-out and visits to the telephone at specified intervals to receive messages, the service telephone system being extended from station to station nearly throughout the service, with watch telephones at half-way points. The other man patrols the beach to the end of his beat and returns, when he takes the look-out and his watchmate patrols in the opposite direction. A like patrol and watch is maintained in thick or stormy weather in the daytime. Between adjacent stations a record of the patrol is made by the exchange of brass checks; elsewhere the patrolman carries a watchman's clock, on the dial of which he records the time of his arrival at the keypost which marks the end of his beat. On discovering a vessel standing into danger the patrolman burns a Coston signal, which emits a brilliant red flare, to warn the vessel of her danger. The number of vessels thus warned averages about two hundred in each year, whereby great losses are averted, the extent of which can never be known. When a stranded vessel is discovered, the patrolman's Coston signal apprises the crew that they are seen and assistance is at hand. He then notifies his station, by telephone if possible. When such notice is received at the station, the keeper determines the means with which to attempt a rescue, whether by boat or beach-apparatus. If the beach-apparatus is chosen, the apparatus cart is hauled to a point directly opposite the wreck by horses, kept at most of the stations during the inclement months, or by the members of the crew. The gear is unloaded, and while being set up—the members of the crew performing their several allotted parts simultaneously—the keeper fires a line over the wreck with the Lyle gun, a small bronze cannon weighing, with its 18 lb elongated iron projectile to which the line is attached, slightly more than 200 lb, and having an extreme range of about 700 yds., though seldom available at wrecks for more than 400 yds. This gun was the invention of Lieutenant (afterwards Colonel) David A. Lyle, U.S. Army. Shotlines are of three sizes, [illegible], [illegible] and [illegible] of an inch diameter, designated respectively Nos. 4, 7 and 9. The two larger are ordinarily used, the No. 4 for extreme range. A line having been fired within reach of the persons on the wreck, an endless rope rove through a tail-block is sent out by it with instructions, printed in English and French on a tally-board, to make the tail fast to a mast or other elevated portion of the wreck. This done, a 3-in. hawser is bent on to the whip and hauled off to the wreck, to be made fast a little above the tail-block, after which the shore end is hauled taut over a crotch by means of tackle attached to a sand anchor. From this hawser the breeches-buoy or life-car is suspended and drawn between the ship and shore of the endless whip-line. The life-car can also be drawn like a boat between ship and shore without the use of a hawser. The breeches-buoy is a cork life-buoy to which is attached a pair of short canvas breeches, the whole suspended from a traveller block by suitable lanyards. It usually carries one person at a time, although two have frequently been brought ashore together. The life-car, first introduced in 1848, is a boat of corrugated iron with a convex iron cover, having a hatch in the top for the admission of passengers, which can be fastened either from within or without, and a few perforations to admit air, with raised edges to exclude water. At wreck operations during the night the shore is illuminated by powerful acetylene (calcium carbide) lights. If any of the rescued persons are frozen, as often happens, or are injured or sick, first aid and simple remedies are furnished them. Dry clothing, supplied by the Women's National Relief Association, is also furnished to survivors, which the destitute are allowed to keep.

Several types of light open surf-boats are used, adapted to the special requirements of the different localities and occasions. They are built of cedar, from 23 to 27 ft. long, and are provided with end air chambers and longitudinal air cases on each side under the thwarts.

Self-righting and self-bailing life-boats, patterned after those used in England and other countries, have heretofore been used at most of the Lake stations and at points on the ocean coast where they can be readily launched from ways. Most of these boats, however, have now been transformed into power boats without the sacrifice of any of their essential qualities. The installation of power is effected by introducing a 25 H.P. four-cycle gasoline motor, weighing with its fittings, tanks, &c., about 800 lb. The engine is installed in the after air chamber, with the starting crank, reversing clutches, &c., recessed into the bulkhead to protect them from accidents. These boats attain a speed of from 7 to 9 m. an hour, and have proved extremely efficient. A new power life-boat (fig. 10) on somewhat improved lines, 36 ft. in length, and equipped with a 35-40 H.P. gasoline engine, promises to prove still more efficient. A number of surf-boats have also been equipped with gasoline engines of from 5 to 7 H.P., for light and quick work, with very satisfactory results.

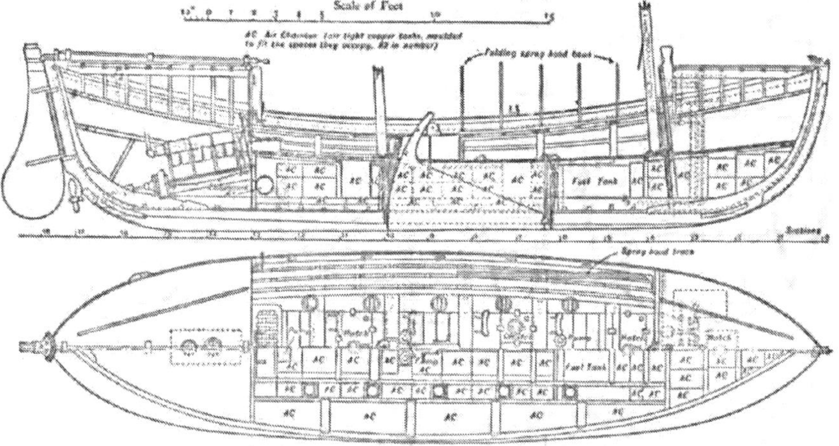

FIG. 10.—American Power Life-boat.

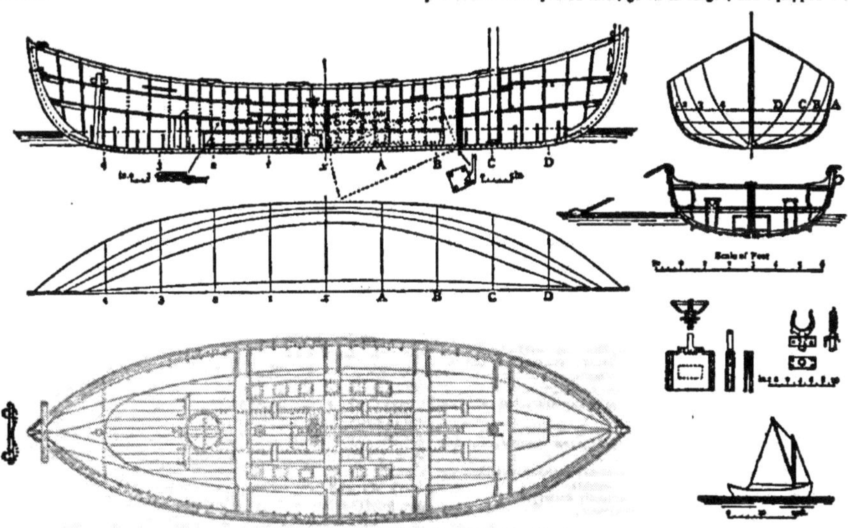

FIG. 11.—Beebe-McLellan Self-bailing Boat.

numerous branches with local committees. The Imperial government contributes an annual subsidy of 20,000 yen (£2000). The members of the Institution consist of three classes—honorary, ordinary and sub-ordinary, the amount contributed by the member determining the class in which he is placed. The chairman and council are not, as in Great Britain, appointed by the subscribers, but by the president, who must always be a member of the imperial family. The Institution bestows three medals: (a) the medal of

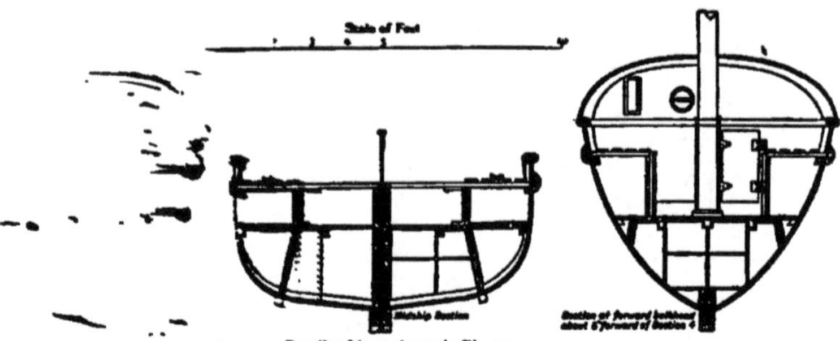

Fig. 11.—Details of boat shown in Fig. 10.

merit, to be awarded to persons rendering distinguished service to the Institution; (b) the medal of membership, to be held by honorary and ordinary members or subscribers; and (c) the medal of praise, which is bestowed on those distinguishing themselves by special service in the work of rescue.

LIFFORD, the county town of Co. Donegal, Ireland, on the left bank of the Foyle. Pop. (1901) 446. The county gaol, court house and infirmary are here, but the town is practically a suburb of Strabane, across the river, in Co. Londonderry. Lifford, formerly called Ballyduff, was a chief stronghold of the O'Donnells of Tyrconnell. It was incorporated as a borough (under the name of Liffer) in the reign of James I. It returned two members to the Irish parliament until the union in 1800.

LIGAMENT (Lat. *ligamentum*, from *ligare*, to bind), anything which binds or connects two or more parts; in anatomy a piece of tissue connecting different parts of an organism (see Connective Tissues and Joints).

LIGAO, a town near the centre of the province of Albay, Luzon, Philippine Islands, close to the left bank of a tributary of the Bicol river, and on the main road through the valley. Pop. (1903) 17,687. East of the town rises Mayón, an active volcano, and the rich volcanic soil in this region produces hemp, rice and coco-nuts. Agriculture is the sole occupation of the inhabitants. Their language is Bicol.

LIGHT. *Introduction.*—§ 1 "Light" may be defined subjectively as the sense-impression formed by the eye. This is the most familiar connotation of the term, and suffices for the discussion of optical subjects which do not require an objective definition, and, in particular for the treatment of physiological optics and vision. The objective definition, or the "nature of light," is the *ultima Thule* of optical research. "Emission theories," based on the supposition that light was a stream of corpuscles, were at first accepted. These gave place during the opening decades of the 19th century to the "undulatory or wave theory," which may be regarded as culminating in the "elastic solid theory"—so named from the lines along which the mathematical investigation proceeded—and according to which light is a transverse vibratory motion propagated longitudinally though the aether. The mathematical researches of James Clerk Maxwell have led to the rejection of this theory, and it is now held that light is identical with electromagnetic disturbances, such as are generated by oscillating electric currents or moving magnets. Beyond this point we cannot go at present. To quote Arthur Schuster (*Theory of Optics*, 1904), "So long as the character of the displacements which constitute the waves remains [un]defined we cannot pretend to have established a theory of light." It will thus be seen that optical and electrical phenomena are co-ordinated as a phase of the physics of the "aether," and that the investigation of these sciences culminates in the derivation of the properties of this conceptual medium, the existence of which was called into being as an instrument of research.[1] The methods of the elastic-solid theory can still be used with advantage in treating many optical phenomena, more especially so long as we remain ignorant of fundamental matters concerning the origin of electric and magnetic strains and stresses; in addition, the treatment is more intelligible, the researches on the electromagnetic theory leading in many cases to the derivation of differential equations which express quantitative relations between diverse phenomena, although no precise meaning can be attached to the symbols employed. The school following Clerk Maxwell and Heinrich Hertz has certainly laid the foundations of a complete theory of light and electricity, but the methods must be adopted with caution, lest one be constrained to say with Ludwig Boltzmann as in the introduction to his *Vorlesungen über Maxwell's Theorie der Elektricität und des Lichtes*:—

> "So soll ich denn mit saurem Schweiss
> Euch lehren, was ich selbst nicht weiss."
>
> GOETHE, *Faust*.

The essential distinctions between optical and electromagnetic phenomena may be traced to differences in the lengths of light-waves and of electromagnetic waves. The aether can probably transmit waves of any wave-length, the velocity of longitudinal propagation being about $3 \cdot 10^{10}$ cms. per second. The shortest waves, discovered by Schumann and accurately measured by Lyman, have a wave-length of 0·0001 mm.; the ultra-violet, recognized by their action on the photographic plate or by their promoting fluorescence, have a wave-length of 0·0002 mm.; the eye recognizes vibrations of a wave-length ranging from about 0·0004 mm. (violet) to about 0·0007 (red); the infra-red rays, recognized by their heating power or by their action on phosphorescent bodies, have a wave-length of 0·001 mm.; and the longest waves present in the radiations of a luminous source are the residual rays ("*Rest-strahlen*") obtained by repeated reflections from quartz (·0085 mm.), from fluorite (0·056 mm.), and from sylvite (0·06 mm.). The research-field of optics includes the investigation of the rays which we have just enumerated. A delimitation may then be made, inasmuch as luminous sources yield no other radiations, and also since the next series of waves, the electromagnetic waves, have a minimum wave-length of 6 mm.

§ 2. The commonest subjective phenomena of light are colour and visibility, *i.e.* why are some bodies visible and others not, or, in other words, what is the physical significance of the words "transparency," "colour" and "visibility." What is ordinarily understood by a *transparent* substance is one which transmits all the rays of white light without appreciable absorption—that some absorption does occur is perceived when the substance is viewed through a sufficient thickness. *Colour* is due to the absorption of certain rays of the spectrum, the unabsorbed rays being transmitted to the eye, where they occasion the sensation of colour (see COLOUR; ABSORPTION OF LIGHT). Transparent bodies are seen partly by reflected and partly by transmitted light, and opaque bodies by absorption. Refraction also influences visibility. Objects immersed in a liquid of the same refractive index and dispersion would be invisible; for example, a glass rod can hardly be seen when immersed in Canada balsam; other instances occur in the petrological examination of rock-sections under the microscope. In a complex rock-section the boldness with which the constituents stand out are measures of the difference between their refractive indices and the refractive index of the mounting medium, and the more nearly the indices coincide the less defined become the boundaries, while the interior of the mineral may be most advantageously explored. Lord Rayleigh has shown that transparent objects can only be seen when non-uniformly illuminated, the differences in the refractive indices of the substance and the surrounding medium becoming inoperative when the illumination is uniform on all sides. R. W. Wood has performed experiments which confirm this view.

The analysis of white light into the spectrum colours, and the re-formation of the original light by transmitting the spectrum through a reversed prism, proved, to the satisfaction of Newton and subsequent physicists until late in the 19th century, that the various coloured rays were present in white light, and that the action of the prism was merely to sort out the rays. This view, which suffices for the explanation of most phenomena, has now been given up, and the modern view is that the prism or grating really does *manufacture* the colours, as was held previously to Newton. It appears that white light is a sequence of irregular wave trains which are analysed into series of more regular trains by the prism or grating in a manner comparable with the analytical resolution presented by Fourier's theorem. The modern view points to the *mathematical* existence of waves of all wave-lengths in white light, the Newtonian view to the *physical* existence. Strictly, the term "monochromatic" light is only applicable to light of a single wave-length (which can have no actual existence), but it is commonly used to denote light which cannot be analysed by the instruments at our disposal; for example, with low-power instruments the light emitted by sodium vapour would be regarded as homogeneous or monochromatic, but higher power instruments resolve this light into two components of different wave-lengths, each of which is of a higher degree of homogeneity, and it is not impossible that these rays may be capable of further analysis.

§ 3. *Divisions of the Subject.*—In the early history of the science of light or optics a twofold division was adopted: *Catoptrics* (from Gr. κάτοπτρον, a mirror), embracing the phenomena of reflection, *i.e.* the formation of images by mirrors; and *Dioptrics* (Gr. διά, through), embracing the phenomena of refraction, *i.e.* the bending of a ray of light when passing obliquely through the surface dividing two media.[2] A third element, *Chromatics* (Gr. χρῶμα, colour), was subsequently introduced to include phenomena involving colour transformations, such as the iridescence of mother-of-pearl, feathers, soap-bubbles, oil floating on water, &c. This classification has been discarded (although the terms, particularly "dioptric" and "chromatic," have survived as adjectives) in favour of a twofold division: geometrical optics and physical optics. *Geometrical optics* is a mathematical development (mainly effected by geometrical methods) of three laws assumed to be rigorously true: (1) the law of rectilinear propagation, viz. that light travels in straight lines or *rays* in any homogeneous medium; (2) the law of reflection, viz. that the incident and reflected rays at any point of a surface are equally inclined to, and coplanar with, the normal to the surface at the point of incidence; and (3) the law of refraction, viz. that the incident and refracted rays at a surface dividing two media make angles with the normal to the surface at the point of incidence whose sines are in a ratio (termed the "refractive index") which is constant for every particular pair of media, and that the incident and refracted rays are coplanar with the normal. *Physical optics*, on the other hand, has for its ultimate object the elucidation of the question: what is light? It investigates the nature of the rays themselves, and, in addition to determining the validity of the axioms of geometrical optics, embraces phenomena for the explanation of which an expansion of these assumptions is necessary.

Of the subordinate phases of the science, "physiological optics" is concerned with the phenomena of vision, with the eye as an optical instrument, with colour-perception, and

[1] The invention of "aethers" is to be carried back, at least, to the Greek philosophers, and with the growth of knowledge they were empirically postulated to explain many diverse phenomena. Only one "aether" has survived in modern science—that associated with light and electricity, and of which Lord Salisbury, in his presidential address to the British Association in 1894, said, "For more than two generations the main, if not the only, function of the word 'aether' has been to furnish a nominative case to the verb 'to undulate.'" (See AETHER.)

[2] With the Greeks the word "Optics" or Ὀπτικά (from ὄπτομαι, the obsolete present of ὁρῶ, I see) was restricted to questions concerning vision, &c., and the nature of light.

… appearance of the eyes of a cat … meteoro- … by the atmo- … twinkling of … the effects of atmospheric … as were seen after … investigates … optical properties; … development … of light in effect- … "applied optics" may … experimental investiga- … e.g. the study of … glass of specified optical … such matters as the … and of quartz for … hand, the application … to the construction

… following three divisions … of the science of light; … velocity of light; but a … scientific precision) may … the inter-relation of … phenomena which are … in larger type.

… of light are COLOUR … the latter being named … a medium, it may be re- … ABSORPTION; or it may … and, if the light … the case of oil films on … which is due to INTER- … transmitted in two directions, … refraction" (see REFRACTION, … rays have undergone … light falling on an opaque … involves the phenomenon … have the property of trans- … the phenomena of … and PHOSPHORESCENCE. An … number of MIRRORS or LENSES, … system be not brought to a … be not concurrent, we are … ABERRATION. An optical … up of an optical system, the … optical LANTERN, … and the KALEIDOSCOPE … suitable for simultaneous vision … BINOCULAR INSTRUMENTS; the … this category; the optical … its modern development the … the physiological persistence … phenomena comprise the … colour of SKY and TWILIGHT, … (see REFRACTION, ASTRO- … the corona involves DIFFRAC- … plays a part in this group

HISTORY

… that the ancients were more … any other branch of physics; … for a knowledge of external … of vision in a far greater … that light travels in straight … object is seen in the direction … been realized in very remote … points to some acquaintance … and Layard's discovery … among the ruins of the palace … the burning and magnifying powers of this instrument. The Greeks were acquainted with the fundamental law of reflection, viz. the equality of the angles of incidence and reflection; and it was Hero of Alexandria who proved that the path of the ray is the least possible. The lens, as an instrument for magnifying objects or for concentrating rays to effect combustion, was also known. Aristophanes, in the *Clouds* (c. 424 B.C.), mentions the use of the burning-glass to destroy the writing on a waxed tablet; much later, Pliny describes such glasses as solid balls of rock-crystal or glass, or hollow glass balls filled with water, and Seneca mentions their use by engravers. A treatise on optics (Κατοπτρικά), assigned to Euclid by Proclus and Marinus, shows that the Greeks were acquainted with the production of images by plane, cylindrical and concave and convex spherical mirrors, but it is doubtful whether Euclid was the author, since neither this work nor the 'Οπτικά, a work treating of vision and also assigned to him by Proclus and Marinus, is mentioned by Pappus, and more particularly since the demonstrations do not exhibit the precision of his other writings.

Reflection, or catoptrics, was the key-note of their explanations of optical phenomena; it is to the reflection of solar rays by the air that Aristotle ascribed twilight, and from his observation of the colours formed by light falling on spray, he attributes the rainbow to reflection from drops of rain. Although certain elementary phenomena of refraction had also been noted—such as the apparent bending of an oar at the point where it met the water, and the apparent elevation of a coin in a basin by filling the basin with water—the quantitative law of refraction was unknown; in fact, it was not formulated until the beginning of the 17th century. The analysis of white light into the continuous spectrum of rainbow colours by transmission through a prism was observed by Seneca, who regarded the colours as fictitious, placing them in the same category as the iridescent appearance of the feathers on a pigeon's neck.

§ 2. The aversion of the Greek thinkers to detailed experimental inquiry stultified the progress of the science; instead of acquiring facts necessary for formulating scientific laws and correcting hypotheses, the Greeks devoted their intellectual energies to philosophizing on the nature of light itself. In their search for a theory the Greeks were mainly concerned with vision—in other words, they sought to determine how an object was seen, and to what its colour was due. Emission theories, involving the conception that light was a stream of concrete particles, were formulated. The Pythagoreans assumed that vision and colour were caused by the bombardment of the eye by minute particles projected from the surface of the object seen. The Platonists subsequently introduced three elements—a stream of particles emitted by the eye (their "divine fire"), which united with the solar rays, and, after the combination had met a stream from the object, returned to the eye and excited vision.

In some form or other the emission theory—that light was a longitudinal propulsion of material particles—dominated optical thought until the beginning of the 19th century. The authority of the Platonists was strong enough to overcome Aristotle's theory that light was an activity (ἐνέργεια) of a medium which he termed the *pellucid* (διαφανές); about two thousand years later Newton's exposition of his corpuscular theory overcame the undulatory hypotheses of Descartes and Huygens; and it was only after the acquisition of new experimental facts that the labours of Thomas Young and Augustin Fresnel indubitably established the wave-theory.

§ 3. The experimental study of refraction, which had been almost entirely neglected by the early Greeks, received more attention during the opening centuries of the Christian era. Cleomedes, in his *Cyclical Theory of Meteors*, c. A.D. 50, alludes to the apparent bending of a stick partially immersed in water, and to the rendering visible of coins in basins by filling up with water; and also remarks that the air may refract the sun's rays so as to render that luminary visible, although actually it may be below the horizon. The most celebrated of the early writers on optics is the Alexandrian Ptolemy (2nd century). His writings on light are believed to be preserved in two imperfect Latin manuscripts, themselves translations from the Arabic. The subjects discussed include the nature of light and colour; the formation of images by various types of mirrors, refractions at the surface of glass and of water, with tables of the angle of refraction corresponding to given angles of incidence for rays passing from air to glass and from air to water; and also astronomical refractions, *i.e.* the apparent displacement of a heavenly body due to the refraction of light in its passage through the atmosphere. The authenticity of these manuscripts has been contested: the *Almagest* contains no mention of the *Optics*, nor is the subject of astronomical refractions noticed, but the strongest objection, according to A. de Morgan, is the fact that their author was a poor geometer.

§ 4. One of the results of the decadence of the Roman empire was the suppression of the academies, and few additions were made to scientific knowledge on European soil until the 13th century. Extinguished in the West, the spirit of research was kindled in the East. The accession of the Arabs to power and territory in the 7th century was followed by the acquisition of the literary stores of Greece, and during the following five centuries the Arabs, both by their preservation of existing works and by their original discoveries (which, however, were but few), took a permanent place in the history of science. Pre-eminent among Arabian scientists is Alhazen, who flourished in the 11th century. Primarily a mathematician and astronomer, he also investigated a wide range of optical phenomena. He examined the anatomy of the eye, and the functions of its several parts in promoting vision; and explained how it is that we see one object with two eyes, and then not by a single ray or beam as had been previously held, but by two cones of rays proceeding from the object, one to each eye. He attributed vision to emanations from the body seen; and on his authority the Platonic theory fell into disrepute. He also discussed the magnifying powers of lenses; and it may be that his writings on this subject inspired the subsequent invention of spectacles. Astronomical observations led to the investigation of refraction by the atmosphere, in particular, astronomical refraction; he explained the phenomenon of twilight, and showed a connexion between its duration and the height of the atmosphere. He also treated *optical deceptions*, both in direct vision and in vision by reflected and refracted light, including the phenomenon known as the *horizontal moon*, *i.e.* the apparent increase in the diameter of the sun or moon when near the horizon. This appearance had been explained by Ptolemy on the supposition that the diameter was actually increased by refraction, and his commentator Theon endeavoured to explain why an object appears larger when viewed under water. But actual experiment showed that the diameter did not increase. Alhazen gave the correct explanation, which, however, Friar Bacon attributes to Ptolemy. We judge of distance by comparing the angle under which an object is seen with its supposed distance, so that if two objects be seen under nearly equal angles and one be supposed to be more distant than the other, then the former will be supposed to be the larger. When near the horizon the sun or moon, conceived as very distant, are intuitively compared with terrestrial objects, and therefore they appear larger than when viewed at elevations.

§ 5. While the Arabs were acting as the custodians of scientific knowledge, the institutions and civilizations of Europe were gradually crystallizing. Attacked by the Mongols and by the Crusaders, the Bagdad caliphate disappeared in the 13th century. At that period the Arabic commentaries, which had already been brought to Europe, were beginning to exert great influence on scientific thought; and it is probable that their rarity and the increasing demand for the originals and translations led to those forgeries which are of frequent occurrence in the literature of the middle ages. The first treatise on optics written in Europe was admitted by its author Vitello or Vitellio, a native of Poland, to be based on the works of Ptolemy and Alhazen. It was written in about 1270, and first published in 1572, with a Latin translation of Alhazen's treatise, by F. Risner, under the title *Thesaurus opticae*. Its tables of refraction are more accurate than Ptolemy's; the author follows Alhazen in his investigation of lenses, but his determinations of the foci and magnifying powers of spheres are inaccurate. He attributed the twinkling of stars to refraction by moving air, and observed that the scintillation was increased by viewing through water in gentle motion; he also recognized that both reflection and refraction were instrumental in producing the rainbow, but he gave no explanation of the colours.

The *Perspectiva Communis* of John Peckham, archbishop of Canterbury, being no more than a collection of elementary propositions containing nothing new, we have next to consider the voluminous works of Vitellio's illustrious contemporary, Roger Bacon. His writings on light, *Perspectiva* and *Specula mathematica*, are included in his *Opus majus*. It is conceivable that he was acquainted with the nature of the images formed by light traversing a small orifice—a phenomenon noticed by Aristotle, and applied at a later date to the construction of the camera obscura. The invention of the magic lantern has been ascribed to Bacon, and his statements concerning spectacles, the telescope, and the microscope, if not based on an experimental realization of these instruments, must be regarded as masterly conceptions of the applications of lenses. As to the nature of light, Bacon adhered to the theory that objects are rendered visible by emanations from the eye.

The history of science, and more particularly the history of inventions, constantly confronts us with the problem presented by such writings as Friar Bacon's. Rarely has it been given to one man to promote an entirely new theory or to devise an original instrument; it is more generally the case that, in the evolution of a single idea, there comes some stage which arrests our attention, and to which we assign the dignity of an "invention." Furthermore, the obscurity that surrounds the early history of spectacles, the magic lantern, the telescope and the microscope, may find a partial solution in the spirit of the middle ages. The natural philosopher who was bold enough to present to a prince a pair of spectacles or a telescope would be in imminent danger of being regarded in the eyes of the church as a powerful and dangerous magician; and it is conceivable that the maker of such an instrument would jealously guard the secret of its actual construction, however much he might advertise its potentialities.[1]

§ 6. The awakening of Europe, which first manifested itself in Italy, England and France, was followed in the 16th century by a period of increasing intellectual activity. The need for experimental inquiry was realized, and a tendency to dispute the dogmatism of the church and to question the theories of the established schools of philosophy became apparent. In the science of optics, Italy led the van, the foremost pioneers being Franciscus Maurolycus (1494–1575) of Messina, and Giambattista della Porta (1538–1615) of Naples. A treatise by Maurolycus entitled *Photismi de Lumine et Umbra prospectivum radiorum incidentium facientes* (1575), contains a discussion of the measurement of the intensity of light—an early essay in photometry; the formation of circular patches of light by small holes of any shape, with a correct explanation of the phenomenon; and the optical relations of the parts of the eye, maintaining that the crystalline humour acts as a lens which focuses images on the retina, explaining short- and long-sight (myopia and hypermetropia), with the suggestion that the former may be corrected by concave, and the latter by convex, lenses. He observed the spherical aberration due to elements beyond the axis of a lens, and also the caustics of refraction (diacaustics) by a sphere (seen as the bright boundaries of the luminous patches formed by receiving the transmitted light on a screen), which he correctly

[1] It seems probable that spectacles were in use towards the end of the 13th century. The Italian dictionary of the *Accademici della Crusca* (1612) mentions a sermon of Jordan de Rivalto, published in 1305, which refers to the invention as "not twenty years since"; and Muschenbroek states that the tomb of Salvinus Armatus, a Florentine nobleman who died in 1317, bears an inscription assigning the invention to him. (See the articles TELESCOPE and CAMERA OBSCURA for the history of these instruments.)

regarded as determined by the intersections of the refracted rays. His researches on refraction were less fruitful; he assumed the angles of incidence and refraction to be in the constant ratio of 8 to 5, and the rainbow, in which he recognized four colours, orange, green, blue and purple, to be formed by rays reflected in the drops along the sides of an octagon. Porta's fame rests chiefly on his *Magia naturalis sive de miraculis rerum naturalium*, of which four books were published in 1558, the complete work of twenty books appearing in 1589. It attained great popularity, perhaps by reason of its astonishing medley of subjects—pyrotechnics and perfumery, animal reproduction and hunting, alchemy and optics,—and it was several times reprinted, and translated into English (with the title *Natural Magick*, 1658), German, French, Spanish, Hebrew and Arabic. The work contains an account of the camera obscura, with the invention of which the author has sometimes been credited; but, whoever the inventor, Porta was undoubtedly responsible for improving and popularizing that instrument, and also the magic lantern. In the same work practical applications of lenses are suggested, combinations comparable with telescopes are vaguely treated and spectacles are discussed. His *De Refractione, optices parte* (1593) contains an account of binocular vision, in which are found indications of the principle of the stereoscope.

§ 7. The empirical study of lenses led, in the opening decade of the 17th century, to the emergence of the telescope from its former obscurity. The first form, known as the Dutch or Galileo telescope, consisted of a convex and a concave lens, a combination which gave erect images; the later form, now known as the "Keplerian" or "astronomical" telescope (in contrast with the earlier or "terrestrial" telescope) consisted of two convex lenses, which gave inverted images. With the microscope, too, advances were made, and it seems probable that the compound type came into common use about this time. These single instruments were followed by the invention of binoculars, *i.e.* instruments which permitted simultaneous vision with both eyes. There is little doubt that the experimental realization of the telescope, opening up as it did such immense fields for astronomical research, stimulated the study of lenses and optical systems. The investigations of Maurolycus were insufficient to explain the theory of the telescope, and it was Kepler who first determined the principle of the Galilean telescope in his *Dioptrice* (1611), which also contains the first description of the astronomical or Keplerian telescope, and the demonstration that rays parallel to the axis of a plano-convex lens come to a focus at a point on the axis distant twice the radius of the curved surface of the lens, and, in the case of an equally convex lens, at an axial point distant only once the radius. He failed, however, to determine accurately the case for unequally convex lenses, a problem which was solved by Bonaventura Cavalieri, a pupil of Galileo.

Early in the 17th century great efforts were made to determine the law of refraction. Kepler, in his *Prolegomena ad Vitellionem* (1604), assiduously, but unsuccessfully, searched for the law, and can only be credited with twenty-seven empirical rules, really of the nature of approximations, which he employed in his theory of lenses. The true law—that the ratio of the sines of the angles of incidence and refraction is constant—was discovered in 1621 by Willebrord Snell (1591–1626); but was published for the first time after his death, and with no mention of his name, by Descartes. Whereas in Snell's manuscript the law was stated in the form of the ratio of certain lines, trigonometrically interpretable as a ratio of cosecants, Descartes expressed the law in its modern trigonometrical form, viz. as the ratio of the sines. It may be observed that the modern form was independently obtained by James Gregory and published in his *Optica promota* (1663). Armed with the law of refraction, Descartes determined the geometrical theory of the primary and secondary rainbows, but did not mention how far he was indebted to the explanation of the primary bow by Antonio de Dominis in 1611; and, similarly, in his additions to the knowledge of the telescope the influence of Galileo is not recorded.

§ 8. In his metaphysical speculations on the system of nature, Descartes formulated a theory of light at variance with the generally accepted emission theory and showing some resemblance to the earlier views of Aristotle, and, in a smaller measure, to the modern undulatory theory. He imagined light to be a pressure transmitted by an infinitely elastic medium which pervades space, and colour to be due to rotatory motions of the particles of this medium. He attempted a mechanical explanation of the law of refraction, and came to the conclusion that light passed more readily through a more highly refractive medium. This view was combated by Pierre de Fermat (1601–1665), who, from the principle known as the "law of least time," deduced the converse to be the case, *i.e.* that the velocity varied inversely with the refractive index. In brief, Fermat's argument was as follows: Since nature performs her operations by the most direct routes or shortest paths, then the path of a ray of light between any two points must be such that the time occupied in the passage is a minimum. The rectilinear propagation and the law of reflection obviously agree with this principle, and it remained to be proved whether the law of refraction tallied.

Although Fermat's premiss is useless, his inference is invaluable, and the most notable application of it was made in about 1824 by Sir William Rowan Hamilton, who merged it into his conception of the "characteristic function," by the help of which all optical problems, whether on the corpuscular or on the undulatory theory, are solved by one common process. Hamilton was in possession of the germs of this grand theory some years before 1824, but it was first communicated to the Royal Irish Academy in that year, and published in imperfect instalments some years later. The following is his own description of it. It is of interest as exhibiting the origin of Fermat's deduction, its relation to contemporary and subsequent knowledge, and its connexion with other analytical principles. Moreover, it is important as showing Hamilton's views on a very singular part of the more modern history of the science to which he contributed so much.

"Those who have meditated on the beauty and utility, in theoretical mechanics, of the general method of Lagrange, who have felt the power and dignity of that central dynamical theorem which he deduced, in the *Mécanique analytique* . . ., must feel that mathematical optics can only *then* attain a coordinate rank with mathematical mechanics . . ., when it shall possess an appropriate method, and become the unfolding of a central idea. . . . It appears that if a general method in deductive optics can be attained at all, it must flow from some law or principle, itself of the highest generality, and among the highest results of induction. . . . [This] must be the principle, or law, called usually the Law of Least Action; suggested by questionable views, but established on the widest induction, and embracing every known combination of media, and every straight, or bent, or curved line, ordinary or extraordinary, along which light (whatever light may be) extends its influence successively in space and time: namely, that this linear path of light, from one point to another, is always found to be such that, if it be compared with the other infinitely various lines by which in thought and in geometry the same two points might be connected, a certain integral or sum, called often *Action*, and depending by fixed rules on the length, and shape, and position of the path, and on the media which are traversed by it, is less than all the similar integrals for the other neighbouring lines, or, at least, possesses, with respect to them, a certain *stationary* property. From this Law, then, which may, perhaps, be named the Law of Stationary Action, it seems that we may most fitly and with best hope set out, in the synthetic or deductive process and in the search of a mathematical method.

"Accordingly, from this known law of least or stationary action I deduced (long since) another connected and coextensive principle, which may be called by analogy the Law of Varying Action, and which seems to offer naturally a method such as we are seeking; the one law being as it were the last step in the ascending scale of induction, respecting linear paths of light, while the other law may usefully be made the first in the descending and deductive way.

"The former of these two laws was discovered in the following manner. The elementary principle of straight rays showed that light, under the most simple and usual circumstances, employs the direct, and therefore the shortest, course to pass from one point to another. Again, it was a very early discovery (attributed by Laplace to Ptolemy), that, in the case of a plane mirror, the bent line formed by the incident and reflected rays is shorter than any other bent line having the same extremities, and having its point of bending on the mirror. These facts were thought by some to be instances and results of the simplicity and economy of nature; and Fermat, whose researches on maxima and minima are claimed by the Continental mathematicians as the germ of the differential calculus, sought anxiously to trace some similar economy in the more complex case of refraction. He believed that by a metaphysical or cosmological necessity, arising from the simplicity of the universe, light always takes the course which it can traverse in the shortest time. To reconcile this metaphysical opinion with the law of refraction, discovered experimentally by Snellius, Fermat was led to suppose that the two lengths, or *indices*, which Snellius had measured on the incident ray prolonged and on the refracted ray, and had observed to have one common projection on a refracting plane, are inversely proportional to the two successive velocities of the light before and after refraction, and therefore that the velocity of light is diminished on entering those denser media in which it is observed to approach the perpendicular: for Fermat believed that the time of propagation of light along a line bent by refraction was represented by the sum of the two products, of the incident portion multiplied by the index of the first medium and of the refracted portion multiplied by the index of the second medium; because he found, by his mathematical method, that this sum was less, in the case of a plane refractor, than if light went by any other than its actual path from one given point to another, and because he perceived that the supposition of a velocity inversely as the index reconciled his mathematical discovery of the minimum of the foregoing sum with his cosmological principle of least time. Descartes attacked Fermat's opinions respecting light, but Leibnitz zealously defended them; and Huygens was led, by reasonings of a very different kind, to adopt Fermat's conclusions of a velocity inversely as the index, and of a *minimum time* of propagation of light, in passing from one given point to another through an ordinary refracting plane. Newton, however, by his theory of emission and attraction, was led to conclude that the velocity of light was *directly*, not *inversely*, as the index, and that it was *increased* instead of being *diminished* on entering a denser medium; a result incompatible with the theorem of the shortest time in refraction. This theorem of shortest time was accordingly abandoned by many, and among the rest by Maupertuis, who, however, proposed in its stead, as a new cosmological principle, that *celebrated law of least action* which has since acquired so high a rank in mathematical physics, by the improvements of Euler and Lagrange."

§ 9. The second half of the 17th century witnessed developments in the practice and theory of optics which equal in importance the mathematical, chemical and astronomical acquisitions of the period. Original observations were made which led to the discovery, in an embryonic form, of new properties of light, and the development of mathematical analysis facilitated the quantitative and theoretical investigation of these properties. Indeed, mathematical and physical optics may justly be dated from this time. The phenomenon of *diffraction*, so named by Grimaldi, and by Newton *inflection*, which may be described briefly as the spreading out, or deviation, from the strictly rectilinear path of light passing through a small aperture or beyond the edge of an opaque object, was discovered by the Italian Jesuit, Francis Maria Grimaldi (1619–1663), and published in his *Physico-Mathesis de Lumine* (1665); at about the same time Newton made his classical investigation of the spectrum or the band of colours formed when light is transmitted through a prism,[1] and studied *interference* phenomena in the form of the colours of thin and thick plates, and in the form now termed *Newton's rings*; *double refraction*, in the form of the dual images of a single object formed by a rhomb of Iceland spar, was discovered by Bartholinus in 1670; Huygens's examination of the transmitted beams led to the discovery of an absence of symmetry now called *polarisation*; and the finite velocity of light was deduced in 1676 by Ole Roemer from the comparison of the observed and computed times of the eclipses of the moons of Jupiter.

These discoveries had a far-reaching influence upon the theoretical views which had been previously held: for instance, Newton's recombination of the spectrum by means of a second (inverted) prism caused the rejection of the earlier view that the prism actually manufactured the colours, and led to the acceptance of the theory that the colours were physically present in the white light, the function of the prism being merely to separate the physical mixture; and Roemer's discovery of the finite velocity of light introduced the necessity of considering the momentum of the particles which, on the accepted emission theory, composed the light. Of greater moment was the controversy concerning the emission or corpuscular theory championed by Newton and the undulatory theory presented by Huygens (see section II. of this article). In order to explain the colours of thin plates Newton was forced to abandon some of the original simplicity of his theory; and we may observe that by postulating certain motions for the Newtonian corpuscles all the phenomena of light can be explained, these motions aggregating to a transverse displacement translated longitudinally, and the corpuscles, at the same time, becoming otiose and being replaced by a medium in which the vibration is transmitted. In this way the Newtonian theory may be merged into the undulatory theory. Newton's results are collected in his *Opticks*, the first edition of which appeared in 1704. Huygens published his theory in his *Traité de lumière* (1690), where he explained reflection, refraction and double refraction, but did not elucidate the formation of shadows (which was readily explicable on the Newtonian hypothesis) or polarization; and it was this inability to explain polarization which led to Newton's rejection of the wave theory. The authority of Newton and his masterly exposition of the corpuscular theory sustained that theory until the beginning of the 19th century, when it succumbed to the assiduous skill of Young and Fresnel.

§ 10. Simultaneously with this remarkable development of theoretical and experimental optics, notable progress was made in the construction of optical instruments. The increased demand for telescopes, occasioned by the interest in observational astronomy, led to improvements in the grinding of lenses (the primary aim being to obtain forms in which spherical aberration was a minimum), and also to the study of achromatism, the principles of which followed from Newton's analysis and synthesis of white light. Kepler's supposition that lenses having the form of surfaces of revolution of the conic sections would bring rays to a focus without spherical aberration was investigated by Descartes, and the success of the latter's demonstration led to the grinding of ellipsoidal and hyperboloidal lenses, but with disappointing results.[2] The grinding of spherical lenses was greatly improved by Huygens, who also attempted to reduce chromatic aberration in the refracting telescope by introducing a stop (*i.e.* by restricting the aperture of the rays); to the same experimenter are due compound eye-pieces, the invention of which had been previously suggested by Eustachio Divini. The so-called Huygenian eye-piece is composed of two plano-convex lenses with their plane faces towards the eye; the field-glass has a focal length three times that of the eye-glass, and the distance between them is twice the focal length of the eye-glass. Huygens observed that spherical aberration was diminished by making the deviations of the rays at the two lenses equal, and Ruggiero Giuseppe Boscovich subsequently pointed out that the combination was achromatic. The true development, however, of the achromatic refracting telescope, which followed from the introduction of compound object-glasses giving no dispersion, dates from about the middle of the 18th century.

[1] Newton's observation that a second refraction did not change the colours had been anticipated in 1648 by Marci de Kronland (1595–1667), professor of medicine at the university of Prague, in his *Thaumantias*, who studied the spectrum under the name of *Iris trigonia*. There is no evidence that Newton knew of this, although he mentions de Dominic's experiment with the glass globe containing water.

[2] The geometrical determination of the form of the surface which will reflect, or of the surface dividing two media which will refract, rays from one point to another, is very easily effected by using the "characteristic function" of Hamilton, which for the problems under consideration may be stated in the form that "the optical paths of all rays must be the same." In the case of reflection, if A and B be the diverging and converging points, and P a point on the reflecting surface, then the locus of P is such that AP+PB is constant. Therefore the surface is an ellipsoid of revolution having A and B as foci. If the rays be parallel, *i.e.* if A be at infinity, the surface is a paraboloid of revolution having B as focus and the axis parallel to the direction of the rays. In refraction if A be in the medium of index μ, and B in the medium of index μ', the characteristic function shows that $\mu AP+\mu' PB$, where P is a point on the surface, must be constant. Plane sections through A and B of such surfaces were originally investigated by Descartes, and are named Cartesian ovals. If the rays be parallel, *i.e.* A be at infinity, the surface becomes an ellipsoid of revolution having B for one focus, μ'/μ for eccentricity, and the axis parallel to the direction of the rays.

[illegible] difficulty of obtaining lens [illegible] in which aberrations [illegible], and the theory of Newton that colour production [illegible] attended refraction, led [illegible] the manufacture of im[illegible] specula which [illegible] the [illegible] of reflecting telescopes. The idea of [illegible] but the first reflector occurred to Marin Mersenne [illegible] James Gregory in his *Optica* [illegible] of note was [illegible] Newton, and a *promota*; a [illegible] were made third in [illegible] type did in the [illegible] years after John [illegible] of the achromatic [illegible] TELESCOPE, MICROSCOPE, BINO[illegible]

[illegible] by Ehrenfried Walther [illegible] produced by reflection [illegible] with large reflectors and [illegible] which he established glass[illegible] Bradley's discovery in 1728 of the [illegible] the subsequent derivation of the [illegible] well with Roemer's [illegible] photometry by Pierre [illegible] and expanded in 1760 [illegible] *de la lumière*; the [illegible] treatise on the same subject, [illegible] *Gradibus Luminis*, [illegible] the development of the telescope [illegible] at the closing decades [illegible] the sixty years 1780 to 1820 the [illegible] marked by the names of Thomas [illegible] and in a lesser degree by Arago, [illegible] Fraunhofer, Wollaston, Biot and

[illegible] theory had been disputed by [illegible] and others, the authority [illegible] general acceptance until [illegible], when Young and Fresnel [illegible]. Basing his views on [illegible] diffraction phenomena of [illegible] the Huygenian theory, [illegible] sound waves, that the wave[illegible] ignoring the suggestion [illegible] direction of the vibration might [illegible] to the direction of the rays. [illegible] unable to explain diffraction [illegible] assumption enabled him to [illegible]ence,[1] one of the most fertile [illegible] The undulatory theory was [illegible] perceiving the inadequacy of the [illegible] showed in 1818 by an analysis [illegible] an objection, that, by assuming [illegible] surface could act as a source of [illegible] the diffraction bands were due [illegible] waves formed by each element [illegible] edge of an obstacle or aperture. [illegible] theory was that the bands were [illegible] the diffracting edge—a fact confirmed [illegible] invalidating Young's theory that [illegible] by the interference between the [illegible] reflected from the edge of the [illegible], which was first mathematically [illegible] subsequently confirmed by experi[illegible] phenomenon that a small circular [illegible] point source casts a shadow having a

[illegible] theory reached its zenith when Fresnel [illegible] phenomena of polarization, by adopting [illegible] that the vibrations were transverse, and not longitudinal.[2] Polarization by double refraction had been investigated by Huygens, and the researches of Wollaston and, more especially, of Young, gave such an impetus to the study that the Institute of France made double refraction the subject of a prize essay in 1812. E. L. Malus (1775–1812) discovered the phenomenon of polarization by reflection about 1808 and investigated metallic reflection; Arago discovered circular polarization in quartz in 1811, and, with Fresnel, made many experimental investigations, which aided the establishment of the Fresnel-Arago laws of the interference of polarized beams; Biot introduced a reflecting polariscope, investigated the colours of crystalline plates and made many careful researches on the rotation of the plane of polarization; Sir David Brewster made investigations over a wide range, and formulated the law connecting the angle of polarization with the refractive index of the reflecting medium. Fresnel's theory was developed in a strikingly original manner by Sir William Rowan Hamilton, who interpreted from Fresnel's analytical determination of the geometrical form of the wave-surface in biaxal crystals the existence of two hitherto unrecorded phenomena. At Hamilton's instigation Humphrey Lloyd undertook the experimental search, and brought to light the phenomena of external and internal conical refraction.

The undulatory vibration postulated by Fresnel having been generally accepted as explaining most optical phenomena, it became necessary to determine the mechanical properties of the aether which transmits this motion. Fresnel, Neumann, Cauchy, MacCullagh, and, especially, Green and Stokes, developed the "elastic-solid theory." By applying the theory of elasticity they endeavoured to determine the constants of a medium which could transmit waves of the nature of light. Many different allocations were suggested (of which one of the most recent is Lord Kelvin's "contractile aether," which, however, was afterwards discarded by its author), and the theory as left by Green and Stokes has merits other than purely historical. At a later date theories involving an action between the aether and material atoms were proposed, the first of any moment being J. Boussinesq's (1867). C. Christiansen's investigation of anomalous dispersion in 1870, and the failure of Cauchy's formula (founded on the elastic-solid theory) to explain this phenomenon, led to the theories of W. Sellmeier (1872), H. von Helmholtz (1875), E. Ketteler (1878), E. Lommel (1878) and W. Voigt (1883). A third class of theory, to which the present-day theory belongs, followed from Clerk Maxwell's analytical investigations in electromagnetics. Of the greatest exponents of this theory we may mention H. A. Lorentz, P. Drude and J. Larmor, while Lord Rayleigh has, with conspicuous brilliancy, explained several phenomena (*e.g.* the colour of the sky) on this hypothesis.

For a critical examination of these theories see section II. of this article; reference may also be made to the *British Association Reports*: "On Physical Optics," by Humphrey Lloyd (1834), p. 35; "On Double Refraction," by Sir G. G. Stokes (1862), p. 253; "On Optical Theories," by R. T. Glazebrook (1885), p. 157.

§ 13. *Recent Developments.*—The determination of the velocity of light (see section III. of this article) may be regarded as definitely settled, a result contributed to by A. H. L. Fizeau (1849), J. B. L. Foucault (1850, 1862), A. Cornu (1874), A. A. Michelson (1880), James Young and George Forbes (1882), Simon Newcomb (1880–1882) and Cornu (1900). The velocity in moving media was investigated theoretically by Fresnel; and Fizeau (1859), and Michelson and Morley (1886) showed experimentally that the velocity was increased in running water by an amount agreeing with Fresnel's formula, which was based on the hypothesis of a stationary aether. The optics of moving media have also been investigated by Lord Rayleigh, and more especially by H. A. Lorentz, who also assumed a stationary aether. The relative motion of the earth and the aether has an

[illegible] of light, which he formulated as [illegible] given *in extenso* in the article [illegible] "Chromatics" in the supple[illegible] *Encyclopaedia Britannica*.

[2] A crucial test of the emission and undulatory theories, which was realized by Descartes, Newton, Fermat and others, consisted in determining the velocity of light in two differently refracting media. This experiment was conducted in 1850 by Foucault, who showed that the velocity was less in water than in air, thereby confirming the undulatory and invalidating the emission theory.

important connexion with the phenomenon of the aberration of light, and has been treated with masterly skill by Joseph Larmor and others (see AETHER). The relation of the earth's motion to the intensities of terrestrial sources of light was investigated theoretically by Fizeau, but no experimental inquiry was made until 1903, when Nordmeyer obtained negative results, which were confirmed by the theoretical investigations of A. A. Bucherer and H. A. Lorentz.

Experimental photometry has been greatly developed since the pioneer work of Bouguer and Lambert and the subsequent introduction of the photometers of Ritchie, Rumford, Bunsen and Wheatstone, followed by Swan's in 1859, and O. R. Lummer and E. Brodhun's instrument (essentially the same as Swan's) in 1889. This expansion may largely be attributed to the increase in the number of artificial illuminants—especially the many types of filament- and arc-electric lights, and the incandescent gas light. Colour photometry has also been notably developed, especially since the enunciation of the "Purkinje phenomenon" in 1825. Sir William Abney has contributed much to this subject, and A. M. Meyer has designed a photometer in which advantage is taken of the phenomenon of contrast colours. "Flicker photometry" may be dated from O. N. Rood's investigations in 1893, and the same principle has been applied by Haycraft and Whitman. These questions—colour and flicker photometry—have important affinities to colour perception and the persistence of vision (see VISION). The spectrophotometer, devised by De Witt Bristol Brace in 1899, which permits the comparison of similarly coloured portions of the spectra from two different sources, has done much valuable work in the determination of absorptive powers and extinction coefficients. Much attention has also been given to the preparation of a standard of intensity, and many different sources have been introduced (see PHOTOMETRY). Stellar photometry, which was first investigated instrumentally with success by Sir John Herschel, was greatly improved by the introduction of Zöllner's photometer, E. C. Pickering's meridian photometer and C. Pritchard's wedge photometer. Other methods of research in this field are by photography—photographic photometry—and radiometric method (see PHOTOMETRY, CELESTIAL).

The earlier methods for the experimental determination of refractive indices by measuring the deviation through a solid prism of the substance in question or, in the case of liquids, through a hollow prism containing the liquid, have been replaced in most accurate work by other methods. The method of total reflection, due originally to Wollaston, has been put into a very convenient form, applicable to both solids and liquids, in the Pulfrich refractometer (see REFRACTION). Still more accurate methods, based on interference phenomena, have been devised. Jamin's interference refractometer is one of the earlier forms of such apparatus; and Michelson's interferometer is one of the best of later types (see INTERFERENCE). The variation of refractive index with density has been the subject of much experimental and theoretical inquiry. The empirical rule of Gladstone and Dale was often at variance with experiment, and the mathematical investigations of H. A. Lorentz of Leiden and L. Lorenz of Copenhagen on the electromagnetic theory led to a more consistent formula. The experimental work has been chiefly associated with the names of H. H. Landolt and J. W. Brühl, whose results, in addition to verifying the Lorenz-Lorentz formula, have established that this function of the refractive index and density is a colligative property of the molecule, *i.e.* it is calculable additively from the values of this function for the component atoms, allowance being made for the mode in which they are mutually combined (see CHEMISTRY, PHYSICAL). The preparation of lenses, in which the refractive index decreases with the distance from the axis, by K. F. J. Exner, H. F. L. Matthiessen and Schott, and the curious results of refraction by non-homogeneous media, as realized by R. Wood may be mentioned (see MIRAGE).

The spectrum of white light produced by prismatic refraction has engaged many investigators. The infra-red or heat waves were discovered by Sir William Herschel, and experiments on the actinic effects of the different parts of the spectrum on silver salts by Scheele, Senebier, Ritter, Seebeck and others, proved the increased activity as one passed from the red to the violet and the ultra-violet. Wollaston also made many investigations in this field, noticing the dark lines—the "Fraunhofer lines"—which cross the solar spectrum, which were further discussed by Brewster and Fraunhofer, who thereby laid the foundations of modern spectroscopy. Mention may also be made of the investigations of Lord Rayleigh and Arthur Schuster on the resolving power of prisms (see DIFFRACTION), and also of the modern view of the function of the prism in analysing white light. The infra-red and ultra-violet rays are of especial interest since, although not affecting vision after the manner of ordinary light, they possess very remarkable properties. Theoretical investigation on the undulatory theory of the law of reflection shows that a surface, too rough to give any trace of regular reflection with ordinary light, may regularly reflect the long waves, a phenomenon experimentally realized by Lord Rayleigh. Long waves—the so-called "residual rays" or "*Rest-strahlen*"—have also been isolated by repeated reflections from quartz surfaces of the light from zirconia raised to incandescence by the oxyhydrogen flame (E. F. Nichols and H. Rubens); far longer waves were isolated by similar reflections from fluorite (56 μ) and sylvite (61 μ) surfaces in 1899 by Rubens and E. Aschkinass. The short waves—ultra-violet rays—have also been studied, the researches of E. F. Nichols on the transparency of quartz to these rays, which are especially present in the radiations of the mercury arc, having led to the introduction of lamps made of fused quartz, thus permitting the convenient study of these rays, which, it is to be noted, are absorbed by ordinary clear glass. Recent researches at the works of Schott and Genossen, Jena, however, have resulted in the production of a glass transparent to the ultra-violet.

Dispersion, *i.e.* that property of a substance which consists in having a different refractive index for rays of different wavelengths, was first studied in the form known as "ordinary dispersion" in which the refrangibility of the ray increased with the wave-length. Cases had been observed by Fox Talbot, Le Roux, and especially by Christiansen (1870) and A. Kundt (1871–1872) where this normal rule did not hold; to such phenomena the name "anomalous dispersion" was given, but really there is nothing anomalous about it at all, ordinary dispersion being merely a particular case of the general phenomenon. The Cauchy formula, which was founded on the elastic-solid theory, did not agree with the experimental facts, and the germs of the modern theory, as was pointed out by Lord Rayleigh in 1900, were embodied in a question proposed by Clerk Maxwell for the Mathematical Tripos examination for 1869. The principle, which occurred simultaneously to W. Sellmeier (who is regarded as the founder of the modern theory) and had been employed about 1850 by Sir G. G. Stokes to explain absorption lines, involves an action between the aether and the molecules of the dispersing substance. The mathematical investigation is associated with the names of Sellmeier, Hermann Helmholtz, Eduard Ketteler, P. Drude, H. A. Lorentz and Lord Rayleigh, and the experimental side with many observers—F. Paschen, Rubens and others; absorbing media have been investigated by A. W. Pflüger, a great many aniline dyes by K. Stöckl, and sodium vapour by R. W. Wood. Mention may also be made of the beautiful experiments of Christiansen (1884) and Lord Rayleigh on the colours transmitted by white powders suspended in liquids of the same refractive index. If, for instance, benzol be gradually added to finely powdered quartz, a succession of beautiful colours—red, yellow, green and finally blue—is transmitted, or, under certain conditions, the colours may appear at once, causing the mixture to flash like a fiery opal. Absorption, too, has received much attention; the theory has been especially elaborated by M. Planck, and the experimental investigation has been prosecuted from the purely physical standpoint, and also from the standpoint of the physical chemist, with a view to correlating absorption with constitution.

Interference phenomena have been assiduously studied. The

experiments of Young, Fresnel, Lloyd, Fizeau and Foucault, of Fresnel and Arago on the measurement of refractive indices by the shift of the interference bands, of H. F. Talbot on the "Talbot bands" (which he insufficiently explained on the principle of interference, it being shown by Sir G. B. Airy that diffraction phenomena supervene), of Baden-Powell on the "Powell bands," of David Brewster on "Brewster's bands," have been developed, together with many other phenomena—Newton's rings, the colours of thin, thick and mixed plates, &c.—in a striking manner, one of the most important results being the construction of interferometers applicable to the determination of refractive indices and wave-lengths, with which the names of Jamin, Michelson, Fabry and Perot, and of Lummer and E. Gehrcke are chiefly associated. The mathematical investigations of Fresnel may be regarded as being completed by the analysis chiefly due to Airy, Stokes and Lord Rayleigh. [illegible] may be made of Sir G. G. Stokes' attribution of the [illegible] of iridescent crystals to periodic twinning; this view [illegible] been confirmed by Lord Rayleigh (*Phil. Mag.*, 1888) who, [illegible] the purity of the reflected light, concluded that the laminae [illegible] equidistant by the order of a wave-length. Prior to 1891 [illegible] interference between waves proceeding in the same direction [illegible] been studied. In that year Otto H. Wiener obtained, on a [illegible] of a wave-length in thickness, photographic impressions [illegible] stationary waves formed by the interference of waves [illegible] in opposite directions, and in 1892 Drude and Nernst [illegible] a fluorescent film to record the same phenomenon. [illegible] principle is applied in the Lippmann colour photography, [illegible] was suggested by W. Zenker, realized by Gabriel Lippmann, [illegible] investigated by R. G. Neuhauss, O. H. Wiener, [illegible] and others.

[illegible] progress has been made in the study of diffraction, [illegible] department of optics is precisely the one in which [illegible] theory has secured its greatest triumphs" (Lord [illegible]). The mathematical investigations of Fresnel and [illegible] were placed on a dynamical basis by Sir G. G. Stokes; [illegible] gained more ready interpretation by the introduc[illegible] "[illegible] principle" in 1837, and Cornu's graphic [illegible]. The theory also gained by the researches [illegible], Airy, Schwerd, E. Lommel and others. The [illegible] of the concave grating, which resulted from H. A. Row[illegible] methods of ruling lines of the necessary nature [illegible] on curved surfaces, was worked out by Rowland, [illegible] C. Runge and others. The resolving power and the [illegible] of the spectra have been treated by Lord Rayleigh [illegible] Schuster, and more recently (1905), the distribution [illegible] treated by A. B. Porter. The theory of diffrac[illegible] of great importance in designing optical instruments, [illegible] which has been more especially treated by Ernst [illegible] theory of microscopic vision dates from about [illegible] staff at the Zeiss works, Jena, by Rayleigh [illegible]. The theory of coronae (as diffraction phenomena) [illegible] due to Young, who, from the principle involved, [illegible] for measuring the diameters of very small [illegible] and Sir G. G. Stokes subsequently explained the [illegible] by minute opaque particles borne on a [illegible]. The polarization of the light diffracted at a [illegible] by Fizeau, whose researches were extended [illegible] and, for the case of gratings, by Du Bois [illegible]. The diffraction of light by small particles [illegible] of very fine chemical precipitates by [illegible] noticed the polarization of the beautiful [illegible] which was transmitted. This subject—one form [illegible] in the blue colour of the sky—has been [illegible] treated by Lord Rayleigh on both the elastic-[illegible] theories. Mention may be made of [illegible] on thin metal films which, under [illegible] colour phenomena inexplicable by [illegible]. These colours have been assigned [illegible] resonance, and have been treated by [illegible] [illegible] Garnett (*Phil.* [illegible] coloured glasses are due to ultra-microscopic particles, which have been directly studied by H. Siedentopf and R. Zsigmondy under limiting oblique illumination.

Polarization phenomena may, with great justification, be regarded as the most engrossing subject of optical research during the 19th century; the assiduity with which it was cultivated in the opening decades of that century received a great stimulus when James Nicol devised in 1828 the famous "Nicol prism," which greatly facilitated the determination of the plane of vibration of polarized light, and the facts that light is polarized by reflection, repeated refractions, double refraction and by diffraction also contributed to the interest which the subject excited. The rotation of the plane of polarization by quartz was discovered in 1811 by Arago; if white light be used the colours change as the Nicol rotates—a phenomenon termed by Biot "rotatory dispersion." Fresnel regarded rotatory polarization as compounded from right- and left-handed (dextro- and laevo-) circular polarizations; and Fresnel, Cornu, Dove and Cotton effected their experimental separation. Legrand des Cloizeaux discovered the enormously enhanced rotatory polarization of cinnabar, a property also possessed—but in a lesser degree—by the sulphates of strychnine and ethylene diamine. The rotatory power of certain liquids was discovered by Biot in 1815; and at a later date it was found that many solutions behaved similarly. A. Schuster distinguishes substances with regard to their action on polarized light as follows: substances which act in the isotropic state are termed *photogyric*; if the rotation be associated with crystal structure, *crystallogyric*; if the rotation be due to a magnetic field, *magnetogyric*; for cases not hitherto included the term *allogyric* is employed, while optically inactive substances are called *isogyric*. The theory of photogyric and crystallogyric rotation has been worked out on the elastic-solid (MacCullagh and others) and on the electromagnetic hypotheses (P. Drude, Cotton, &c.). Allogyrism is due to a symmetry of the molecule, and is a subject of the greatest importance in modern (and, more especially, organic) chemistry (see STEREOISOMERISM).

The optical properties of metals have been the subject of much experimental and theoretical inquiry. The explanations of MacCullagh and Cauchy were followed by those of Beer, Eisenlohr, Lundquist, Ketteler and others; the refractive indices were determined both directly (by Kundt) and indirectly by means of Brewster's law; and the reflecting powers from $\lambda = 251\mu\mu$ to $\lambda = 1500\mu\mu$ were determined in 1900–1902 by Rubens and Hagen. The correlation of the optical and electrical constants of many metals has been especially studied by P. Drude (1900) and by Rubens and Hagen (1903).

The transformations of luminous radiations have also been studied. John Tyndall discovered calorescence. Fluorescence was treated by John Herschel in 1845, and by David Brewster in 1846, the theory being due to Sir G. G. Stokes (1852). More recent studies have been made by Lommel, E. L. Nichols and Merritt (*Phys. Rev.*, 1904), and by Millikan who discovered polarized fluorescence in 1895. Our knowledge of phosphorescence was greatly improved by Becquerel, and Sir James Dewar obtained interesting results in the course of his low temperature researches (see LIQUID GASES). In the theoretical and experimental study of radiation enormous progress has been recorded. The pressure of radiation, the necessity of which was demonstrated by Clerk Maxwell on the electromagnetic theory, and, in a simpler manner, by Joseph Larmor in his article RADIATION in these volumes, has been experimentally determined by E. F. Nichols and Hull, and the tangential component by J. H. Poynting. With the theoretical and practical investigation the names of Balfour Stewart, Kirchhoff, Stefan, Bartoli, Boltzmann, W. Wien and Larmor are chiefly associated. Magneto-optics, too, has been greatly developed since Faraday's discovery of the rotation of the plane of polarization by the magnetic field. The rotation for many substances was measured by Sir William H Perkin, who attempted a correlation between rotation and composition. Brace effected the analysis of the beam into its two circularly polarised components, and in 1904 Mills measured their velocities. The Kerr effect, discovered in 1877, and the Zeeman effect (1896) widened the field of research, which, from its intimate connexion with the nature of light and electromagnetics, has resulted in discoveries of the greatest importance.

§ 14. *Optical Instruments.*—Important developments have been made in the construction and applications of optical instruments. To these three factors have contributed. The mathematician has quantitatively analysed the phenomena observed by the physicist, and has inductively shown what results are to be expected from certain optical systems. A consequence of this was the detailed study, and also the preparation, of glasses of diverse properties; to this the chemist largely contributed, and the manufacture of the so-called *optical glass* (see GLASS) is possibly the most scientific department of glass manufacture. The mathematical investigations of lenses owe much to Gauss, Helmholtz and others, but far more to Abbe, who introduced the method of studying the aberrations separately, and applied his results with conspicuous skill to the construction of optical systems. The development of Abbe's methods constitutes the main subject of research of the present day optician, and has brought about the production of telescopes, microscopes, photographic lenses and other optical apparatus to an unprecedented pitch of excellence. Great improvements have been effected in the stereoscope. Binocular instruments with enhanced stereoscopic vision, an effect achieved by increasing the distance between the object glasses, have been introduced. In the study of diffraction phenomena, which led to the technical preparation of gratings, the early attempts of Fraunhofer, Nobert and Lewis Morris Rutherfurd, were followed by H. A. Rowland's ruling of plane and concave gratings which revolutionized spectroscopic research, and, in 1898, by Michelson's invention of the echelon grating. Of great importance are interferometers, which permit extremely accurate determinations of refractive indices and wave-lengths, and Michelson, from his classical evaluation of the standard metre in terms of the wave-lengths of certain of the cadmium rays, has suggested the adoption of the wave-length of one such ray as a standard with which national standards of length should be compared. Polarization phenomena, and particularly the rotation of the plane of polarization by such substances as sugar solutions, have led to the invention and improvements of polarimeters. The polarized light employed in such instruments is invariably obtained by transmission through a fixed Nicol prism—the polarizer—and the deviation is measured by the rotation of a second Nicol—the analyser. The early forms, which were termed "light and shade" polarimeters, have been generally replaced by "half-shade" instruments. Mention may also be made of the microscopic examination of objects in polarized light, the importance of which as a method of crystallographic and petrological research was suggested by Nicol, developed by Sorby and greatly expanded by Zirkel, Rosenbusch and others.

BIBLIOGRAPHY.—There are numerous text-books which give elementary expositions of light and optical phenomena. More advanced works, which deal with the subject experimentally and mathematically, are A. B. Bassett, *Treatise on Physical Optics* (1892); Thomas Preston, *Theory of Light*, 2nd ed. by C. F. Joly (1901); R. W. Wood, *Physical Optics* (1905), which contains expositions on the electromagnetic theory, and treats "dispersion" in great detail. Treatises more particularly theoretical are James Walker, *Analytical Theory of Light* (1904); A. Schuster, *Theory of Optics* (1904); P. Drude, *Theory of Optics*, Eng. trans. by C. R. Mann and R. A. Millikan (1902). General treatises of exceptional merit are A. Winkelmann, *Handbuch der Physik*, vol. vi. "Optik" (1904); and E. Mascart, *Traité d'optique* (1889–1893); M. E. Verdet, *Leçons d'optique physique* (1869, 1872) is also a valuable work. Geometrical optics is treated in R. S. Heath, *Geometrical Optics* (2nd ed., 1898); H. A. Herman, *Treatise on Geometrical Optics* (1900). Applied optics, particularly with regard to the theory of optical instruments, is treated in H. D. Taylor, *A System of Applied Optics* (1906); E. T. Whittaker, *The Theory of Optical Instruments* (1907); in the publications of the scientific staff of the Zeiss works at Jena: *Die Theorie der optischen Instrumente*, vol. i. "Die Bilderzeugung in optischen Instrumenten" (1904); in S. Czapski, *Theorie der optischen Instrumente*, 2nd ed. by O. Eppenstein (1904); and in A. Steinheil and E. Voit, *Handbuch der angewandten Optik* (1901). The mathematical theory of general optics receives historical and modern treatment in the *Encyklopädie der mathematischen Wissenschaften* (Leipzig). Meteorological optics is fully treated in J. Pernter, *Meteorologische Optik*, and physiological optics in H. v. Helmholtz, *Handbuch der physiologischen Optik* (1896) and in A. Koenig, *Gesammelte Abhandlungen zur physiologischen Optik* (1903).

The history of the subject may be studied in J. C. Poggendorff, *Geschichte der Physik* (1879); F. Rosenberger, *Die Geschichte der Physik* (1882–1890); E. Gerland and F. Traumüller, *Geschichte der physikalischen Experimentierkunst* (1899); reference may also be made to Joseph Priestley, *History and Present State of Discoveries relating to Vision, Light and Colours* (1772), German translation by G. S. Klugel (Leipzig, 1775). Original memoirs are available in many cases in their author's "collected works," *e.g.* Huygens, Young, Fresnel, Hamilton, Cauchy, Rowland, Clerk Maxwell, Stokes (and also his *Burnett Lectures on Light*), Kelvin (and also his *Baltimore Lectures*, 1904) and Lord Rayleigh. Newton's *Opticks* forms volumes 96 and 97 of Ostwald's *Klassiker*, Huygens' *Über d. Licht* (1678) vol. 20, and Kepler's *Dioptrice* (1611), vol. 144 of the same series.

Contemporary progress is reported in current scientific journals, *e.g.* the *Transactions* and *Proceedings* of the Royal Society, and of the Physical Society (London), the *Philosophical Magazine* (London), the *Physical Review* (New York, 1893 seq.) and in the *British Association Reports*, in the *Annales de chimie et de physique* and *Journal de physique* (Paris); and in the *Physikalische Zeitschrift* (Leipzig) and the *Annalen der Physik und Chemie* (since 1900: *Annalen der Physik*) (Leipzig). (C. E.*)

II NATURE OF LIGHT

1. *Newton's Corpuscular Theory.*—Until the beginning of the 19th century physicists were divided between two different views concerning the nature of optical phenomena. According to the one, luminous bodies emit extremely small corpuscles which can freely pass through transparent substances and produce the sensation of light by their impact against the retina. This *emission* or *corpuscular theory* of light was supported by the authority of Isaac Newton,[1] and, though it has been entirely superseded by its rival, the *wave-theory*, it remains of considerable historical interest.

2. *Explanation of Reflection and Refraction.*—Newton supposed the light-corpuscles to be subjected to attractive and repulsive forces exerted at very small distances by the particles of matter. In the interior of a homogeneous body a corpuscle moves in a straight line as it is equally acted on from all sides, but it changes its course at the boundary of two bodies, because, in a thin layer near the surface there is a resultant force in the direction of the normal. In modern language we may say that a corpuscle has at every point a definite potential energy, the value of which is constant throughout the interior of a homogeneous body, and is even equal in all bodies of the same kind, but changes from one substance to another. If, originally, while moving in air, the corpuscles had a definite velocity v_0, their velocity v in the interior of any other substance is quite determinate. It is given by the equation $\frac{1}{2}mv^2 - \frac{1}{2}mv_0^2 = A$, in which m denotes the mass of a corpuscle, and A the excess of its potential energy in air over that in the substance considered.

A ray of light falling on the surface of separation of two bodies is reflected according to the well-known simple law, if the corpuscles are acted on by a sufficiently large force directed towards the first medium. On the contrary, whenever the field of force near the surface is such that the corpuscles can penetrate into the interior of the second body, the ray is refracted. In this case the law of Snellius can be deduced from the consideration that the projection w of the velocity on the surface of separation is not altered, either in direction or in magnitude. This obviously requires that the plane passing through the incident and the refracted rays be normal to the surface, and that, if α_1 and α_2 are the angles of incidence and of refraction, v_1 and v_2 the velocities of light in the two media,

$$\sin \alpha_1 / \sin \alpha_2 = w/v_1 : w/v_2 = v_2/v_1. \quad (1)$$

The ratio is constant, because, as has already been observed, v_1 and v_2 have definite values.

As to the unequal refrangibility of differently coloured light, Newton accounted for it by imagining different kinds of corpuscles. He further carefully examined the phenomenon of total reflection, and described an interesting experiment connected with it. If one of the faces of a glass prism receives on the inside a beam of light of such obliquity that it is totally reflected under ordinary circumstances,

[1] Newton, *Opticks* (London, 1704).

a marked change is observed when a second piece of glass is made to approach the reflecting face, so as to be separated from it only by a very thin layer of air. The reflection is then found no longer to be total, part of the light finding its way into the second piece of glass. Newton concluded from this that the corpuscles are attracted by the glass even at a certain small measurable distance.

3. *New Hypotheses in the Corpuscular Theory.*—The preceding explanation of reflection and refraction is open to a very serious objection. If the particles in a beam of light all moved with the same velocity and were acted on by the same forces, they all ought to follow exactly the same path. In order to understand that part of the incident light is reflected and part of it transmitted, Newton imagined that each corpuscle undergoes certain alternating changes; he assumed that in some of its different "phases" it is more apt to be reflected, and in others more apt to be transmitted. The same idea was applied by him to the phenomena presented by very thin layers. He had observed that a gradual increase of the thickness of a layer produces periodic changes in the intensity of the reflected light, and he very ingeniously explained these by his theory. It is clear that the intensity of the transmitted light will be a minimum if the corpuscles that have traversed the front surface of the layer, having reached that surface while in their phase of easy transmission, have passed to the opposite phase the moment they arrive at the back surface. As to the nature of the alternating phases, Newton (*Opticks*, 3rd ed., 1721, p. 347) expresses himself as follows:—"Nothing more is requisite for putting the Rays of Light into Fits of easy Reflexion and easy Transmission than that they be small Bodies which by their attractive Powers, or some other Force, stir up Vibrations in what they act upon, which Vibrations being swifter than the Rays, overtake them successively, and agitate them so as by turns to increase and decrease their Velocities, and thereby put them into those Fits."

4. *The Corpuscular Theory and the Wave-Theory compared.*—Though Newton introduced the notion of periodic changes, which was to play so prominent a part in the later development of the wave-theory, he rejected this theory in the form in which it had been set forth shortly before by Christiaan Huygens in his *Traité de la lumière* (1690), his chief objections being: (1) that the rectilinear propagation had not been satisfactorily accounted for; (2) that the motions of heavenly bodies show no sign of a resistance due to a medium filling all space; and (3) that Huygens had not sufficiently explained the peculiar properties of the rays produced by the double refraction in Iceland spar. In Newton's days these objections were of much weight.

Yet his own theory had many weaknesses. It explained the propagation in straight lines, but it could assign no cause for the equality of the speed of propagation of all rays. It adapted itself to a large variety of phenomena, even to that of double refraction (Newton says [*ibid.*]:—"... the unusual Refraction of Island Crystal looks very much as if it were perform'd by some kind of attractive virtue lodged in certain Sides both of the Rays, and of the Particles of the Crystal."), but it could do so only at the price of losing much of its original simplicity. In the earlier part of the 19th century, the corpuscular theory broke down under the weight of experimental evidence, and it received the final blow when J. B. L. Foucault proved by direct experiment that the velocity of light in water is not greater than that in air, as it should be according to the formula (1), but less [illegible] by the wave-theory.

[illegible] *Rays of Light.*—With the aid of [illegible] the Newtonian theory can accurately [illegible] of a ray of light in any system of isotropic [illegible]eous or otherwise; the problem being [illegible] determining the motion of a material [illegible] potential energy is given as a function [illegible] application of the dynamical principles [illegible] action" to this latter problem leads [illegible] theorems which William Rowan [illegible] his exhaustive treatment of systems [illegible] of a [illegible]posed to have [illegible] [illegible]cience," p. 4

a given value, so that, since the potential energy is considered as known at every point, the velocity v is so likewise.

(*a*) The path along which light travels from a point A to a point B is determined by the condition that for this line the integral $\int \mu ds$, in which ds is an element of the line, be a minimum (provided A and B be not too near each other). Therefore, since $v = \mu v_0$, if v_0 is the velocity of light *in vacuo* and μ the index of refraction, we have for every variation of the path the points A and B remaining fixed,

$$\delta \int \mu ds = 0. \tag{2}$$

(*b*) Let the point A be kept fixed, but let B undergo an infinitely small displacement BB′ $(= q)$ in a direction making an angle θ with the last element of the ray AB. Then, comparing the new ray AB′ with the original one, it follows that

$$\delta \int \mu ds = \mu_B q \cos \theta, \tag{3}$$

where μ_B is the value of μ at the point B.

6. *General Considerations on the Propagation of Waves.*—"Waves," *i.e.* local disturbances of equilibrium travelling onward with a certain speed, can exist in a large variety of systems. In a theory of these phenomena, the state of things at a definite point may in general be defined by a certain directed or vector quantity **P**,[1] which is zero in the state of equilibrium, and may be called the disturbance (for example, the velocity of the air in the case of sound vibrations, or the displacement of the particles of an elastic body from their positions of equilibrium). The components P_x, P_y, P_z of the disturbance in the directions of the axes of coordinates are to be considered as functions of the coordinates x, y, z and the time t, determined by a set of partial differential equations, whose form depends on the nature of the problem considered. If the equations are homogeneous and linear, as they always are for sufficiently small disturbances, the following theorems hold.

(*a*) Values of P_x, P_y, P_z (expressed in terms of x, y, z, t) which satisfy the equations will do so still after multiplication by a common arbitrary constant.

(*b*) Two or more solutions of the equations may be combined into a new solution by addition of the values of P_x, those of P_y, &c., *i.e.* by compounding the vectors **P**, such as they are in each of the particular solutions.

In the application to light, the first proposition means that the phenomena of propagation, reflection, refraction, &c., can be produced in the same way with strong as with weak light. The second proposition contains the principle of the "superposition" of different states, on which the explanation of all phenomena of interference is made to depend.

In the simplest cases (monochromatic or homogeneous light) the disturbance is a simple harmonic function of the time ("simple harmonic vibrations"), so that its components can be represented by

$$P_x = a_1 \cos(nt + f_1),\ P_y = a_2 \cos(nt + f_2),\ P_z = a_3 \cos(nt + f_3).$$

The "phases" of these vibrations are determined by the angles $nt + f_1$, &c., or by the times $t + f_1/n$, &c. The "frequency" n is constant throughout the system, while the quantities f_1, f_2, f_3 and perhaps the "amplitudes" a_1, a_2, a_3 change from point to point. It may be shown that the end of a straight line representing the vector **P**, and drawn from the point considered, in general describes a certain ellipse, which becomes a straight line, if $f_1 = f_2 = f_3$. In this latter case, to which the larger part of this article will be confined, we can write in vector notation

$$\mathbf{P} = \mathbf{A} \cos(nt + f), \tag{4}$$

where **A** itself is to be regarded as a vector.

We have next to consider the way in which the disturbance changes from point to point. The most important case is that of plane waves with constant amplitude **A**. Here f is the same at all points of a plane ("wave-front") of a definite direction, but changes as a linear function as we pass from one such wave-front to the next. The axis of x being drawn at right angles to the wave-fronts, we may write $f = f_0 - kx$, where f_0 and k are constants, so that (4) becomes

$$\mathbf{P} = \mathbf{A} \cos(nt - kx + f_0). \tag{5}$$

This expression has the period $2\pi/n$ with respect to the time and the period $2\pi/k$ with respect to x, so that the "time of vibration" and the "wave-length" are given by $T = 2\pi/n$, $\lambda = 2\pi/k$. Further, it is easily seen that the phase belonging to certain values of x and t is equal to that which corresponds to $x + \Delta x$ and $t + \Delta t$ provided $\Delta x = (n/k)\Delta t$. Therefore the phase, or the disturbance itself, may be said to be propagated in the direction normal to the wave-fronts with a velocity (velocity of the waves) $v = n/k$, which is connected with the time of vibration and the wave-length by the relation

$$\lambda = vT. \tag{6}$$

[1] This kind of type will always be used in this article to denote vectors.

In isotropic bodies the propagation can go on in all directions with the same velocity. In anisotropic bodies (crystals), with which the theory of light is largely concerned, the problem is more complicated. As a general rule we can say that, for a given direction of the wave-fronts, the vibrations must have a determinate direction, if the propagation is to take place according to the simple formula given above. It is to be understood that for a given direction of the waves there may be two or even more directions of vibration of the kind, and that in such a case there are as many different velocities, each belonging to one particular direction of vibration.

7. *Wave-surface.*—After having found the values of v for a particular frequency and different directions of the wave-normal, a very instructive graphical representation can be employed.

Let ON be a line in any direction, drawn from a fixed point O, OA a length along this line equal to the velocity v of waves having ON for their normal, or, more generally, OA, OA′, &c., lengths equal to the velocities v, v', &c., which such waves have according to their direction of vibration, Q, Q′, &c., planes perpendicular to ON through A, A′, &c. Let this construction be repeated for all directions of ON, and let W be the surface that is touched by all the planes Q, Q′, &c. It is clear that if this surface, which is called the "wave-surface," is known, the velocity of propagation of plane waves of any chosen direction is given by the length of the perpendicular from the centre O on a tangent plane in the given direction. It must be kept in mind that, in general, each tangent plane corresponds to one definite direction of vibration. If this direction is assigned in each point of the wave-surface, the diagram contains all the information which we can desire concerning the propagation of plane waves of the frequency that has been chosen.

The plane Q employed in the above construction is the position after unit of time of a wave-front perpendicular to ON and originally passing through the point O. The surface W itself is often considered as the locus of all points that are reached in unit of time by a disturbance starting from O and spreading towards all sides. Admitting the validity of this view, we can determine in a similar way the locus of the points reached in some infinitely short time dt, the wave-surface, as we may say, or the "elementary wave," corresponding to this time. It is similar to W, all dimensions of the latter surface being multiplied by dt. It may be noticed that in a heterogeneous medium a wave of this kind has the same form as if the properties of matter existing at its centre extended over a finite space.

8. *Theory of Huygens.*—Huygens was the first to show that the explanation of optical phenomena may be made to depend on the wave-surface, not only in isotropic bodies, in which it has a spherical form, but also in crystals, for one of which (Iceland spar) he deduced the form of the surface from the observed double refraction. In his argument Huygens availed himself of the following principle that is justly named after him: Any point that is reached by a wave of light becomes a new centre of radiation from which the disturbance is propagated towards all sides. On this basis he determined the progress of light-waves by a construction which, under a restriction to be mentioned in §13, applied to waves of any form and to all kinds of transparent media. Let σ be the surface (wave-front) to which a definite phase of vibration has advanced at a certain time t, dt an infinitely small increment of time, and let an elementary wave corresponding to this interval be described around each point P of σ. Then the envelope σ' of all these elementary waves is the surface reached by the phase in question at the time $t+dt$, and by repeating the construction all successive positions of the wave-front can be found.

Huygens also considered the propagation of waves that are laterally limited, by having passed, for example, through an opening in an opaque screen. If, in the first wave-front σ, the disturbance exists only in a certain part bounded by the contour s, we can confine ourselves to the elementary waves around the points of that part, and to a portion of the new wave-front σ' whose boundary passes through the points where σ' touches the elementary waves having their centres on s. Taking for granted Huygens's assumption that a sensible disturbance is only found in those places where the elementary waves are touched by the new wave-front, it may be inferred that the lateral limits of the beam of light are determined by lines, each element of which joins the centre P of an elementary wave with its point of contact P′ with the next wave-front. To lines of this kind, whose course can be made visible by using narrow pencils of light, the name of "rays" is to be given in the wave-theory. The disturbance may be conceived to travel along them with a velocity $u = PP'/dt$, which is therefore called the "ray-velocity."

The construction shows that, corresponding to each direction of the wave-front (with a determinate direction of vibration), there is a definite direction and a definite velocity of the ray. Both are given by a line drawn from the centre of the wave-surface to its point of contact with a tangent plane of the given direction. It will be convenient to say that this line and the plane are conjugate with each other. The rays of light, curved in non-homogeneous bodies, are always straight lines in homogeneous substances. In an isotropic medium, whether homogeneous or otherwise, they are normal to the wave-fronts, and their velocity is equal to that of the waves.

By applying his construction to the reflection and refraction of light, Huygens accounted for these phenomena in isotropic bodies as well as in Iceland spar. It was afterwards shown by Augustin Fresnel that the double refraction in biaxal crystals can be explained in the same way, provided the proper form be assigned to the wave-surface.

In any point of a bounding surface the normals to the reflected and refracted waves, whatever be their number, always lie in the plane passing through the normal to the incident waves and that to the surface itself. Moreover, if α_1 is the angle between these two latter normals, and α_2 the angle between the normal to the boundary and that to any one of the reflected and refracted waves, and v_1, v_2 the corresponding wave-velocities, the relation

$$\sin\alpha_1/\sin\alpha_2 = v_1/v_2 \qquad (7)$$

is found to hold in all cases. These important theorems may be proved independently of Huygens's construction by simply observing that, at each point of the surface of separation, there must be a certain connexion between the disturbances existing in the incident, the reflected, and the refracted waves, and that, therefore, the lines of intersection of the surface with the positions of an incident wave-front, succeeding each other at equal intervals of time dt, must coincide with the lines in which the surface is intersected by a similar series of reflected or refracted wave-fronts.

In the case of isotropic media, the ratio (7) is constant, so that we are led to the law of Snellius, the index of refraction being given by

$$\mu = v_1/v_2 \qquad (8)$$

(cf. equation 1).

9. *General Theorems on Rays, deduced from Huygens's Construction.*—(*a*) Let A and B be two points arbitrarily chosen in a system of transparent bodies, ds an element of a line drawn from A to B, u the velocity of a ray of light coinciding with ds. Then the integral $\int u^{-1}ds$, which represents the time required for a motion along the line with the velocity u, is a minimum for the course actually taken by a ray of light (unless A and B be too far apart). This is the "principle of least time" first formulated by Pierre de Fermat for the case of two isotropic substances. It shows that the course of a ray of light can always be inverted.

(*b*) Rays of light starting in all directions from a point A and travelling onward for a definite length of time, reach a surface σ, whose tangent plane at a point B is conjugate, in the medium surrounding B, with the last element of the ray AB.

(*c*) If all rays issuing from A are concentrated at a point B, the integral $\int u^{-1}ds$ has the same value for each of them.

(*d*) In case (*b*) the variation of the integral caused by an infinitely small displacement q of B, the point A remaining fixed, is given by $\delta\int u^{-1}ds = q\cos\theta/v_2$. Here θ is the angle between the displacement q and the normal to the surface σ, in the direction of propagation, v_2 the velocity of a plane wave tangent to this surface.

In the case of isotropic bodies, for which the relation (8) holds, we recover the theorems concerning the integral $\int\mu ds$ which we have deduced from the emission theory (§ 5).

10. *Further General Theorems.*—(*a*) Let V_1 and V_2 be two planes in a system of isotropic bodies, let rectangular axes of coordinates be chosen in each of these planes, and let x_1, y_1 be the coordinates of a point A in V_1, and x_2, y_2 those of a point B in V_2. The integral $\int\mu ds$, taken for the ray between A and B, is a function of x_1, y_1, x_2, y_2 and, if ξ_1 denotes either x_1 or y_1, and ξ_2 either x_2 or y_2, we shall have

$$\frac{\partial^2}{\partial\xi_1\,\partial\xi_2}\int\mu ds = \frac{\partial^2}{\partial\xi_2\,\partial\xi_1}\int\mu ds.$$

On both sides of this equation the first differentiation may be performed by means of the formula (3). The second differentiation admits of a geometrical interpretation, and the formula may finally be employed for proving the following theorem:

Let ω_1 be the solid angle of an infinitely thin pencil of rays issuing from A and intersecting the plane V_2 in an element σ_2 at the point B. Similarly, let ω_2 be the solid angle of a pencil starting from B and falling on the element σ_1 of the plane V_1 at the point A. Then, denoting by μ_1 and μ_2 the indices of refraction of the matter at the points A and B, by θ_1 and θ_2 the sharp angles which the ray AB at its extremities makes with the normals to V_1 and V_2, we have

$$\mu_1^2\,\sigma_1\,\omega_1\cos\theta_1 = \mu_2^2\,\sigma_2\,\omega_2\cos\theta_2.$$

(*b*) There is a second theorem that is expressed by exactly the same formula, if we understand by σ_1 and σ_2 elements of surface that are related to each other as an object and its optical image—by ω_1, ω_2 the infinitely small openings, at the beginning and the end of its course, of a pencil of rays issuing from a point A of σ_1 and coming together at the corresponding point B of σ_2, and by θ_1, θ_2 the sharp angles which one of the rays makes with the normals to σ_1 and σ_2. The proof may be based upon the first theorem. I. suffices to

a marked change is o
to approach the refle
by a very thin layer o
to be total, part of the
glass. Newton conclud
by the glass even at a

3. *New Hypotheses*
explanation of reflectio
objection. If the part
the same velocity and
all ought to follow exact
that part of the incident
mitted, Newton imagined
alternating changes; he
"phases," it is more apt
apt to be transmitted.
the phenomena presented
that a gradual increase
periodic changes in the int
very ingeniously explained
the intensity of the transm
corpuscles that have trave
having reached that surface
mission, have passed to the
arrive at the back surface.
phases, Newton (*Opticks*, 3rd
as follows:—"Nothing more
of Light into Fits of easy Re
that they be small Bodies w
some other Force, stir up V
which Vibrations being swift
successively, and agitate the
decrease their Velocities, and

4. *The Corpuscular Theory*
Though Newton introduced
which was to play so promine
of the wave-theory, he rejecte
it had been set forth shortly
his *Traité de la lumière* (1690),
the rectilinear propagation ha
for; (2) that the motions of
resistance due to a medium fil
had not sufficiently explain
rays produced by the doubl
Newton's days these objection

Yet his own theory had ma
propagation in straight lines,
the equality of the speed of pr
itself to a large variety of p
refraction (Newton says [*ibid.*]
of Iceland Crystal looks very
some kind of attractive virtue
the Rays, and of the Particles
do so only at the price of losin

In the earlier part of the 19th
broke down under the weight
received the final blow when J.
experiment that the velocity of
that in air, as it should be accor
than it, as is required by the wav

5. *General Theorems on R*
suitable assumptions the Ne
trace the course of a ray of
bodies, whether homogeneou
equivalent to that of
point in a space in
of the coordinates
of "least
to the
Huygens

... ressed in the terms of some
... then apply to other forms

... that the theory of diffraction
... what sense light may be said to
... an opening *whose width is very*
... *length* the limits between the
... of space are approximately
... the borders.

... arrived at by a mode of reasoning that
... diffraction.[1] If linear differential
... form (5) with A constant, they can
... function of the coordinates, such
... very little over a distance equal
... constant along each line conjugate
... of this kind the disturbance may
... of the said direction, and at
... lengths of the order of λ, and who
... dimensions, may very well have
... with a sharp boundary.
... curved waves. If the additional
... radii of curvature be very much
... Huygens's construction may com-
... amplitudes all along a ray are determined
... amplitude at one of its points.

... the theorems used in the explanation
... are true for all kinds of vibratory
... can give us no clue to the special
... waves. Further information, however,
... experiments on plane polarized light. The
... this kind are completely known when
... plane passing through the direction
... which the beam is said to be polarized, is
... polarization," as it is called, coincides
... in those cases where the light has been
... on a glass surface under an angle of
... is equal to the index of refraction

... Fresnel and Arago left no doubt as to the
... in polarized light with respect to that
... In isotropic bodies at least, the vibra-
... transverse, *i.e.* perpendicular to the rays,
... polarization or at right angles to it. The
... also applies to unpolarized light, as
... resolved into polarized components.
... work has been done on the production
... double refraction and on the reflection of
... by isotropic or by anisotropic transparent
... inquiry being in the latter case to determine
... plane of polarization of the reflected rays and

... large amount of evidence has been gathered by
... possible to test different theories concerning
... and that of the medium through which it
... common feature of nearly all these theories
... supposed to exist not only in spaces void
... in the interior of ponderable bodies.
... Theory.—Fresnel and his immediate successors
... either as an elastic solid, so that the velocity
... of transverse vibrations could be determined
... when K denotes the modulus of
... density. According to this equation the
... various isotropic transparent bodies
... different values of K, or of ρ, or of both. It has,
... that ... K and ρ are supposed to change
... it is impossible to obtain the
... assuming the constancy of K Fresnel
... agree with the observed properties
... the further assumption (to be
... Fresnel's assumption") that the
... are perpendicular to the plane

[1] ... *Vorlesungen über theoretische Physik*, 1 (1907).

Let the indices p and n relate to the two principal cases in which the incident (and, consequently, the reflected) light is polarized in the plane of incidence, or normally to it, and let positive directions h and h' be chosen for the disturbance (at the surface itself) in the incident and for that in the reflected beam, in such a manner that, by a common rotation, h and the incident ray prolonged may be made to coincide with h' and the reflected ray. Then, if a_1 and a_2 are the angles of incidence and refraction, Fresnel shows that, in order to get the reflected disturbance, the incident one must be multiplied by

$$a_p = -\sin(a_1 - a_2)/\sin(a_1 + a_2) \quad (9)$$

in the first, and by

$$a_n = \tan(a_1 - a_2)/\tan(a_1 + a_2) \quad (10)$$

in the second principal case.

As to double refraction, Fresnel made it depend on the unequal elasticity of the aether in different directions. He came to the conclusion that, for a given direction of the waves, there are two possible directions of vibration (§ 6), lying in the wave-front, at right angles to each other, and he determined the form of the wave-surface, both in uniaxal and in biaxal crystals.

Though objections may be urged against the dynamic part of Fresnel's theory, he admirably succeeded in adapting it to the facts.

16. *Electromagnetic Theory.*—We here leave the historical order and pass on to Maxwell's theory of light.

James Clerk Maxwell, who had set himself the task of mathematically working out Michael Faraday's views, and who, both by doing so and by introducing many new ideas of his own, became the founder of the modern science of electricity,[1] recognized that, at every point of an electromagnetic field, the state of things can be defined by two vector quantities, the "electric force" **E** and the "magnetic force" **H**, the former of which is the force acting on unit of electricity and the latter that which acts on a magnetic pole of unit strength. In a non-conductor (dielectric) the force **E** produces a state that may be described as a displacement of electricity from its position of equilibrium. This state is represented by a vector **D** ("dielectric displacement") whose magnitude is measured by the quantity of electricity reckoned per unit area which has traversed an element of surface perpendicular to **D** itself. Similarly, there is a vector quantity **B** (the "magnetic induction") intimately connected with the magnetic force **H**. Changes of the dielectric displacement constitute an electric current measured by the rate of change of **D**, and represented in vector notation by

$$\mathbf{C} = \dot{\mathbf{D}} \quad (11)$$

Periodic changes of **D** and **B** may be called "electric" and "magnetic vibrations." Properly choosing the units, the axes of coordinates (in the first proposition also the positive direction of s and n), and denoting components of vectors by suitable indices, we can express in the following way the fundamental propositions of the theory.

(*a*) Let s be a closed line, σ a surface bounded by it, n the normal to σ. Then, for all bodies,

$$\int H_s ds = \frac{1}{c}\int C_n d\sigma, \qquad \int E_s ds = -\frac{1}{c}\frac{d}{dt}\int B_n d\sigma,$$

where the constant c means the ratio between the electro-magnet and the electrostatic unit of electricity.

From these equations we can deduce:

(α) For the interior of a body, the equations

$$\frac{\partial H_z}{\partial y} - \frac{\partial H_y}{\partial z} = \frac{1}{c}C_x, \quad \frac{\partial H_x}{\partial z} - \frac{\partial H_z}{\partial x} = \frac{1}{c}C_y, \quad \frac{\partial H_y}{\partial x} - \frac{\partial H_x}{\partial y} = \frac{1}{c}C_z \quad (12)$$

$$\frac{\partial E_z}{\partial y} - \frac{\partial E_y}{\partial z} = -\frac{1}{c}\frac{\partial B_x}{\partial t}, \quad \frac{\partial E_x}{\partial z} - \frac{\partial E_z}{\partial x} = -\frac{1}{c}\frac{\partial B_y}{\partial t}, \quad \frac{\partial E_y}{\partial x} - \frac{\partial E_x}{\partial y} = -\frac{1}{c}\frac{\partial B_z}{\partial t}; \quad (13)$$

(β) For a surface of separation, the continuity of the tangential components of **E** and **H**;

(γ) The solenoidal distribution of **C** and **B**, and in a dielectric that of **D**. A solenoidal distribution of a vector is one corresponding to that of the velocity in an incompressible fluid. It involves the continuity, at a surface, of the normal component of the vector.

(*b*) The relation between the electric force and the dielectric displacement is expressed by

$$D_x = \epsilon_1 E_x, \quad D_y = \epsilon_2 E_y, \quad D_z = \epsilon_3 E_z, \quad (14)$$

the constants $\epsilon_1, \epsilon_2, \epsilon_3$ (dielectric constants) depending on the properties of the body considered. In an isotropic medium they have a common value ϵ, which is equal to unity for the free aether, so that for this medium **D** = **E**.

(*c*) There is a relation similar to (14) between the magnetic force and the magnetic induction. For the aether, however, and for all ponderable bodies with which this article is concerned, we may write **B** = **H**.

[1] Clerk Maxwell, *A Treatise on Electricity and Magnetism* (Oxford, 1st ed., 1873).

It follows from these principles that, in an isotropic dialectric, transverse electric vibrations can be propagated with a velocity

$$v = c/\sqrt{\epsilon}. \quad (15)$$

Indeed, all conditions are satisfied if we put

$$\left.\begin{array}{l} D_x = 0,\ D_y = a\cos n(t - xv^{-1} + l),\ D_z = 0, \\ H_x = 0,\ H_y = 0 \qquad\qquad\qquad,\ H_z = avc^{-1}\cos n(t - xv^{-1} + l) \end{array}\right\} \quad (16)$$

For the free aether the velocity has the value c. Now it had been found that the ratio c between the two units of electricity agrees within the limits of experimental errors with the numerical value of the velocity of light in aether. (The mean result of the most exact determinations[2] of c is $3{,}001\cdot 10^{10}$ cm./sec., the largest deviations being about $0{,}008\cdot 10^{10}$, and Cornu[3] gives $3{,}001\cdot 10^{10} \pm 0{,}003\cdot 10^{10}$ as the most probable value of the velocity of light.) By this Maxwell was led to suppose that light consists of transverse electromagnetic disturbances. On this assumption, the equations (16) represent a beam of plane polarized light. They show that, in such a beam, there are at the same time electric and magnetic vibrations, both transverse, and at right angles to each other.

It must be added that the electromagnetic field is the seat of two kinds of energy distinguished by the names of electric and magnetic energy, and that, according to a beautiful theorem due to J. H. Poynting,[4] the energy may be conceived to flow in a direction perpendicular both to the electric and to the magnetic force. The amounts per unit of volume of the electric and the magnetic energy are given by the expressions

$$\tfrac{1}{2}(E_x D_x + E_y D_y + E_z D_z), \quad (17)$$

and

$$\tfrac{1}{2}(H_x B_x + H_y B_y + H_z B_z) = \tfrac{1}{2}H^2, \quad (18)$$

whose mean values for a full period are equal in every beam of light.

The formula (15) shows that the index of refraction of a body is given by $\sqrt{\epsilon}$, a result that has been verified by Ludwig Boltzmann's measurements[5] of the dielectric constants of gases. Thus Maxwell's theory can assign the true cause of the different optical properties of various transparent bodies. It also leads to the reflection formulae (9) and (10), provided the electric vibrations of polarized light be supposed to be perpendicular to the plane of polarization, which implies that the magnetic vibrations are parallel to that plane.

Following the same assumption Maxwell deduced the laws of double refraction, which he ascribes to the unequality of $\epsilon_1, \epsilon_2, \epsilon_3$. His results agree with those of Fresnel and the theory has been confirmed by Boltzmann,[6] who measured the three coefficients in the case of crystallized sulphur, and compared them with the principal indices of refraction. Subsequently the problem of crystalline reflection has been completely solved and it has been shown that, in a crystal, Poynting's flow of energy has the direction of the rays as determined by Huygens's construction.

Two further verifications must here be mentioned. In the first place, though we shall speak almost exclusively of the propagation of light in transparent dielectrics, a few words may be said about the optical properties of conductors. The simplest assumption concerning the electric current **C** in a metallic body is expressed by the equation $\mathbf{C} = \sigma\mathbf{E}$, where σ is the coefficient of conductivity. Combining this with his other formulae (we may say with (12) and (13)), Maxwell found that there must be an absorption of light, a result that can be readily understood since the motion of electricity in a conductor gives rise to a development of heat. But, though Maxwell accounted in this way for the fundamental fact that metals are opaque bodies, there remained a wide divergence between the values of the coefficient of absorption as directly measured and as calculated from the electrical conductivity; but in 1903 it was shown by E. Hagen and H. Rubens[7] that the agreement is very satisfactory in the case of the extreme infra-red rays.

In the second place, the electromagnetic theory requires that a surface struck by a beam of light shall experience a certain pressure. If the beam falls normally on a plane disk, the pressure is normal too; its total amount is given by $c^{-1}(\epsilon_1 + \epsilon_2 - \epsilon_3)$, if ϵ_1, ϵ_2 and ϵ_3 are the quantities of energy that are carried forward per unit of time by the incident, the reflected, and the transmitted light. This result has been quantitatively verified by E. F. Nichols and G. F. Hull.[8]

Maxwell's predictions have been splendidly confirmed by the experiments of Heinrich Hertz[9] and others on electromagnetic waves; by diminishing the length of these to the utmost, some physicists have been able to reproduce with them all phenomena of reflection, refraction (single and double), interference, and polarization.[10] A table of the wave-lengths observed in the aether now has

[2] H. Abraham, *Rapports présentés au congrès de physique de 1900* (Paris), 2, p. 247.
[3] *Ibid.*, p. 225.
[4] *Phil. Trans.*, 175 (1884), p. 343.
[5] *Ann. d. Phys. u. Chem.* 155 (1875), p. 403.
[6] *Ibid.* 153 (1874), p. 525.
[7] *Ann. d. Phys.* 11 (1903), p. 873.
[8] *Phys. Review*, 13 (1901), p. 293.
[9] Hertz, *Untersuchungen über die Ausbreitung der elektrischen Kraft* (Leipzig, 1892).
[10] A. Righi, *L'Ottica delle oscillazioni elettriche* (Bologna, 1897); P. Lebedew, *Ann. d. Phys. u. Chem.*, 56 (1895), p. 1.

[illegible] given in § 11, the lengths of the [illegible] and extending from [illegible] to about 0·6 cm.

[illegible] *Electromagnetic Medium.*—From [illegible] a clear idea can be formed of [illegible] encountered in the older form of [illegible] Maxwell's theory, longitudinal [illegible] by the solenoidal distribution [illegible] theory had to take them [illegible] one made them disappear [illegible] a very great velocity of propagation. [illegible] be practically incompressible. [illegible] however, much in Fresnel's theory [illegible] George Green,[1] who was the first [illegible] in an unobjectionable manner, [illegible] at a formula for the reflection [illegible] differing from (20).

[illegible] the difficulties are no less [illegible] in an anisotropic elastic [illegible] of vibration (§ 6), at right angles [illegible] of the waves, but none of these [illegible] to make two of them do so and [illegible] wave-surface, new hypotheses are [illegible] it is even necessary, as was [illegible] that in the absence of all vibra- [illegible] state of pressure in the medium.

[illegible] it is indeed scarcely possible [illegible] the electromagnetic medium. It [illegible] of the particles in the model [illegible] force H, which, of course, implies [illegible] are parallel to the plane of [illegible] energy is represented by the [illegible] further that, in the case [illegible] other, there is continuity of H [illegible] continuity of the velocity of the [illegible] clear that the representation of [illegible] the same scale in all substances, so [illegible] of a particle and g a universal

[illegible] (19)

[illegible] per unit of volume becomes

[illegible]

[illegible] energy of the elastic medium, the [illegible] equal to g^2, so that it must be

[illegible] what value we have to assign to the [illegible] must correspond to the electric [illegible] Now, on account of (11) and [illegible] by putting $D_x = gc\left(\frac{\partial\zeta}{\partial y} - \frac{\partial\eta}{\partial z}\right)$, [illegible] per unit of volume becomes

[illegible]

[illegible] energy in the model. [illegible] the aether has a uniform constant [illegible] in any system, whether homo- [illegible] per unit of volume can be

[illegible] (20)

[illegible] depending on the physical properties [illegible] equations of motion will exactly [illegible] electromagnetic field.

[illegible] *and MacCullagh.*—A theory [illegible] has a uniform density, and in [illegible] to be parallel to the plane [illegible] Ernst Neumann,[2] who [illegible] for crystalline reflection. [illegible] obliged to introduce some [illegible] Here again Green

[1] [illegible] *Camb. Phil. Soc.* 7, p. 1 [illegible]

[2] [illegible] 8; [illegible]

By specializing the formula for the potential energy of an anisotropic body he arrives at an expression which, if some of his coefficients are made to vanish and if the medium is supposed to be incompressible, differs from (20) only by the additional terms

$$2\left\{L\left(\frac{\partial\zeta}{\partial y}\frac{\partial\eta}{\partial z}-\frac{\partial\eta}{\partial y}\frac{\partial\zeta}{\partial z}\right)+M\left(\frac{\partial\xi}{\partial z}\frac{\partial\zeta}{\partial x}-\frac{\partial\zeta}{\partial z}\frac{\partial\xi}{\partial x}\right)+N\left(\frac{\partial\eta}{\partial x}\frac{\partial\xi}{\partial y}-\frac{\partial\xi}{\partial x}\frac{\partial\eta}{\partial y}\right)\right\}. \quad (21)$$

If ξ, η, ζ vanish at infinite distance the integral of this expression over all space is zero, when L, M, N are constants, and the same will be true when these coefficients change from point to point, provided we add to (21) certain terms containing the differential coefficients of L, M, N, the physical meaning of these terms being that, besides the ordinary elastic forces, there is some extraneous force (called into play by the displacement) acting on all those elements of volume where L, M, N are not constant. We may conclude from this that all phenomena can be explained if we admit the existence of this latter force, which, in the case of two contingent bodies, reduces to a surface-action on their common boundary.

James MacCullagh[3] avoided this complication by simply assuming an expression of the form (20) for the potential energy. He thus established a theory that is perfectly consistent in itself, and may be said to have foreshadowed the electromagnetic theory as regards the form of the equations for transparent bodies. Lord Kelvin afterwards interpreted MacCullagh's assumption by supposing the only action which is called forth by a displacement to consist in certain couples acting on the elements of volume and proportional to the components $\frac{1}{2}\{(\partial\zeta/\partial y)-(\partial\eta/\partial z)\}$, &c., of their rotation from the natural position. He also showed[4] that this "rotational elasticity" can be produced by certain hidden rotations going on in the medium.

We cannot dwell here upon other models that have been proposed, and most of which are of rather limited applicability. A mechanism of a more general kind ought, of course, to be adapted to what is known of the molecular constitution of bodies, and to the highly probable assumption of the perfect permeability for the aether of all ponderable matter, an assumption by which it has been possible to escape from one of the objections raised by Newton (§ 4) (see AETHER).

The possibility of a truly satisfactory model certainly cannot be denied. But it would, in all probability, be extremely complicated. For this reason many physicists rest content, as regards the free aether, with some such general form of the electromagnetic theory as has been sketched in § 16.

19. *Optical Properties of Ponderable Bodies. Theory of Electrons.*—If we want to form an adequate representation of optical phenomena in ponderable bodies, the conceptions of the molecular and atomistic theories naturally suggest themselves. Already, in the elastic theory, it had been imagined that certain material particles are set vibrating by incident waves of light. These particles had been supposed to be acted on by an elastic force by which they are drawn back towards their positions of equilibrium, so that they can perform free vibrations of their own, and by a resistance that can be represented by terms proportional to the velocity in the equations of motion, and may be physically understood if the vibrations are supposed to be converted in one way or another into a disorderly heat-motion. In this way it had been found possible to explain the phenomena of dispersion and (selective) absorption, and the connexion between them (anomalous dispersion).[5] These ideas have been also embodied into the electromagnetic theory. In its more recent development the extremely small, electrically charged particles, to which the name of "electrons" has been given, and which are supposed to exist in the interior of all bodies, are considered as forming the connecting links between aether and matter, and as determining by their arrangement and their motion all optical phenomena that are not confined to the free aether.[6]

It has thus become clear why the relations that had been established between optical and electrical properties have been found to hold only in some simple cases (§16). In fact it cannot be doubted that, for rapidly alternating electric fields, the formulae expressing the connexion between the motion of electricity and the electric force take a form that is less simple than the one previously admitted, and is to be determined in each case by

[3] *Trans. Irish Acad.* 21, "Science," p. 17 (1839).

[4] *Math. and Phys. Papers* (London, 1890), 3, p. 466.

[5] Helmholtz, *Ann. d. Phys. u. Chem.*, 154 (1875), p. 582.

[6] H. A. Lorentz, *Versuch einer Theorie der elektrischen u. optischen Erscheinungen in bewegten Körpern* (1895) (Leipzig, 1906); J. Larmor, *Aether and Matter* (Cambridge, 1900).

elaborate investigation. However, the general boundary conditions given in § 16 seem to require no alteration. For this reason it has been possible, for example, to establish a satisfactory theory of metallic reflection, though the propagation of light in the interior of a metal is only imperfectly understood.

One of the fundamental propositions of the theory of electrons is that an electron becomes a centre of radiation whenever its velocity changes either in direction or in magnitude. Thus the production of Röntgen rays, regarded as consisting of very short and irregular electromagnetic impulses, is traced to the impacts of the electrons of the cathode-rays against the anticathode, and the lines of an emission spectrum indicate the existence in the radiating body of as many kinds of regular vibrations, the knowledge of which is the ultimate object of our investigations about the structure of the spectra. The shifting of the lines caused, according to Doppler's law, by a motion of the source of light, may easily be accounted for, as only general principles are involved in the explanation. To a certain extent we can also elucidate the changes in the emission that are observed when the radiating source is exposed to external magnetic forces ("Zeeman-effect"; see MAGNETO-OPTICS).

20. *Various Kinds of Light-motion.*—(*a*) If the disturbance is represented by

$$P_x = 0, P_y = a\cos(nt - kx + f), \; P_z = a'\cos(nt - kx + f'),$$

so that the end of the vector P describes an ellipse in a plane perpendicular to the direction of propagation, the light is said to be elliptically, or in special cases circularly, polarized. Light of this kind can be dissolved in many different ways into plane polarized components.

There are cases in which plane waves must be elliptically or circularly polarized in order to show the simple propagation of phase that is expressed by formulae like (5). Instances of this kind occur in bodies having the property of rotating the plane of polarization, either on account of their constitution, or under the influence of a magnetic field. For a given direction of the wave-front there are in general two kinds of elliptic vibrations, each having a definite form, orientation, and direction of motion, and a determinate velocity of propagation. All that has been said about Huygens's construction applies to these cases.

(*b*) In a perfect spectroscope a sharp line would only be observed if an endless regular succession of simple harmonic vibrations were admitted into the instrument. In any other case the light will occupy a certain extent in the spectrum, and in order to determine its distribution we have to decompose into simple harmonic functions of the time the components of the disturbance, at a point of the slit for instance. This may be done by means of Fourier's theorem.

An extreme case is that of the unpolarized light emitted by incandescent solid bodies, consisting of disturbances whose variations are highly irregular, and giving a continuous spectrum. But even with what is commonly called homogeneous light, no perfectly sharp line will be seen. There is no source of light in which the vibrations of the particles remain for ever undisturbed, and a particle will never emit an endless succession of uninterrupted vibrations, but at best a series of vibrations whose form, phase and intensity are changed at irregular intervals. The result must be a broadening of the spectral line.

In cases of this kind one must distinguish between the velocity of propagation of the phase of regular vibrations and the velocity with which the said changes travel onward (see below, iii. *Velocity of Light*).

(*c*) In a train of plane waves of definite frequency the disturbance is represented by means of goniometric functions of the time and the coordinates. Since the fundamental equations are linear, there are also solutions in which one or more of the coordinates occur in an exponential function. These solutions are of interest because the motions corresponding to them are widely different from those of which we have thus far spoken. If, for example, the formulae contain the factor

$$e^{-rx}\cos(nt - sy + f)$$

with the positive constant r, the disturbance is no longer periodic with respect to x, but steadily diminishes as x increases. A state of things of this kind, in which the vibrations rapidly die away as we leave the surface, exists in the air adjacent to the face of a glass prism by which a beam of light is totally reflected. It furnishes us an explanation of Newton's experiment mentioned in § 2.

(H. A. L.)

III. VELOCITY OF LIGHT

The fact that light is propagated with a definite speed was first brought out by Ole Roemer at Paris, in 1676, through observations of the eclipses of Jupiter's satellites, made in different relative positions of the Earth and Jupiter in their respective orbits. It is possible in this way to determine the time required for light to pass across the orbit of the earth. The dimensions of this orbit, or the distance of the sun, being taken as known, the actual speed of light could be computed. Since this computation requires a knowledge of the sun's distance, which has not yet been acquired with certainty, the actual speed is now determined by experiments made on the earth's surface. Were it possible by any system of signals to compare with absolute precision the times at two different stations, the speed could be determined by finding how long was required for light to pass from one station to another at the greatest visible distance. But this is impracticable, because no natural agent is under our control by which a signal could be communicated with a greater velocity than that of light. It is therefore necessary to reflect a ray back to the point of observation and to determine the time which the light requires to go and come. Two systems have been devised for this purpose. One is that of Fizeau, in which the vital appliance is a rapidly revolving toothed wheel; the other is that of Foucault, in which the corresponding appliance is a mirror revolving on an axis in, or parallel to, its own plane.

Fizeau. The principle underlying Fizeau's method is shown in the accompanying figs. 1 and 2. Fig. 1 shows the course of a ray of light which, emanating from a luminous point L, strikes the plane surface of a plate of glass M at an angle of about 45°. A fraction of the light is reflected from the two surfaces of the glass to a distant reflector R, the plane of which is at right angles to the course of the ray. The latter is thus reflected back on its own course and, passing through the glass M on its return, reaches a point E behind the glass. An observer with his eye at E looking through the glass sees the return ray as a distant luminous point in the reflector R, after the light has passed over the course in both directions. In actual practice it is necessary to interpose the object glass of a telescope at a point O, at a distance from M nearly equal to its focal length. The function of this appliance is to render the diverging rays, shown by the dotted lines, nearly parallel, in order that more light may reach R and be thrown back again. But the principle may be conceived without respect to the telescope, all the rays being ignored except the central one, which passes over the course we have described.

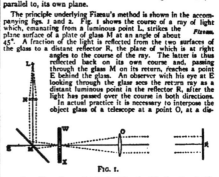

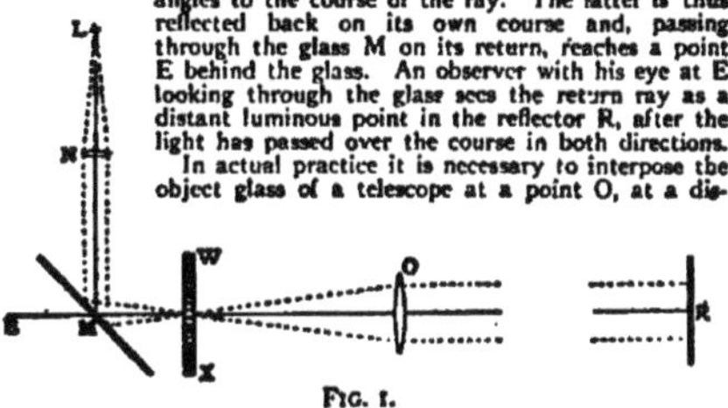

FIG. 1.

Conceiving the apparatus arranged in such a way that the observer sees the light reflected from the distant mirror R, a fine toothed wheel WX is placed immediately in front of the glass M, with its plane perpendicular to the course of the ray, in such a way that the ray goes out and returns through an opening between two adjacent teeth. This wheel is represented in section by WX in fig. 1, and a part of its circumference, with the teeth as viewed by the observer, is shown in fig. 2. We conceive that the latter sees the luminous point between two of the teeth at K. Now, conceive that the wheel is set in revolution. The ray is then interrupted as every tooth passes, so that what is sent out is a succession of flashes. Conceive that the speed of the mirror is such that while the flash is going to the distant mirror and returning again, each tooth of the wheel takes the place of an opening between the teeth. Then each flash sent out will, on its return, be intercepted by the adjacent tooth, and will therefore become invisible. If the speed be now doubled, so that the teeth pass at intervals equal to the time required for the light to go and come, each flash sent through an opening will return through the adjacent opening, and will therefore be seen with full brightness. If the speed be continuously increased the result will be successive disappearances and reappearances of the light, according as a tooth is or is not interposed when the ray reaches the apparatus on its return. The computation of the time of passage and return is then very simple. The speed of the wheel being known, the number of teeth passing in one second can be computed. The order of the disappearance, or the number of teeth which have passed while the light is going and coming, being also determined in each case, the interval of time is computed by a simple formula.

FIG. 2.

The most elaborate determination yet made by Fizeau's method was that of Cornu. The station of observation was at the Paris Observatory. The distant reflector, a telescope with a reflector at its focus, was at Montlhéry, distant 22,910 metres from the toothed wheel. Of the wheels most used one had 150 teeth, and was 35 millimetres in diameter; the other had 200 teeth, with a diameter of 45 mm. The highest speed attained was about 900 revolutions per second. At this speed, 135,000 (or 180,000) teeth would pass per second, and about 20 (or 28) would pass while the light was going and coming. But the actual speed attained was generally less than this. The definitive result derived by Cornu from the entire series of experiments was 300,400 kilometres per second. Further details of this work need not be set forth because the method is in several ways deficient in precision. The eclipses and subsequent reappearances of the light taking place gradually, it is impossible to fix with entire precision upon the moment of complete eclipse. The speed of the wheel is continually varying, and it is impossible to determine with precision what it was at the instant of an eclipse.

Cornu.

The defect would be lessened were the speed of the toothed wheel placed under control of the observer who, by action in one direction or the other, could continually check or accelerate it, so as to keep the return point of light at the required phase of brightness. If the phase of complete extinction is chosen for this purpose a definite result cannot be reached; but by choosing the moment when the light is of a certain definite brightness, before or after an eclipse, the observer will know at each instant whether the speed should be accelerated or retarded, and can act accordingly. The nearly constant speed through as long a period as is deemed necessary would then be found by dividing the entire number of revolutions of the wheel by the time through which the light was kept constant. But even with these improvements, which were not actually tried by Cornu, the estimate of the brightness on which the whole result depends would necessarily be uncertain. The outcome is that, although Cornu's discussion of his experiments is a model in the care taken to determine so far as practicable every source of error, his definitive result is shown by other determinations to have been too great by about $\frac{1}{1000}$ part of its whole amount.

An important improvement on the Fizeau method was made in 1880 by James Young and George Forbes at Glasgow. This consisted in using two distant reflectors which were placed nearly in the same straight line, and at unequal distances. The ratio of the distances was nearly 12 : 13. The phase observed was not that of complete extinction of either light, but that when the two lights appeared equal in intensity. But it does not appear that the very necessary device of placing the speed of the toothed wheel under control of the observer was adopted. The accordance between the different measures was far from satisfactory, and it will suffice to mention the result which was

Young and Forbes.

Velocity in vacuo = 301,382 km. per second.

These experimenters also found a difference of 2% between the speed of red and blue light, a result which can only be attributed to some unexplained source of error.

The Foucault system is much more precise, because it rests upon the measurement of an angle, which can be made with great precision.

The vital appliance is a rapidly revolving mirror. Let AB (fig. 3) be a section of this mirror, which we shall first suppose at rest. A ray of light LM emanating from a source at L, is reflected in the direction MQR to a distant mirror R, from which it is perpendicularly reflected back upon its original course. This mirror R should be slightly concave, with the centre of curvature near M, so that the ray shall always be reflected back to M on whatever point of R it may fall. Conceiving the revolving mirror M as at rest, the return ray will after three reflections, at M, R and M again, be returned along its original course to the point L from which it emanated. An important point is that the return ray will always follow the fixed line ML no matter what the position of the revolving mirror M, provided there is a distant reflector to send the ray back. Now, suppose that, while the ray is going and coming, the mirror M, being set in revolution, has turned from the position in which the ray was reflected to that shown by the dotted line. If α be the angle through which the surface has turned, the course of the return ray, after reflection, will then deviate from ML by the angle 2α, and so be thrown to a point E, such that the angle LME = 2α. If the mirror is in rapid rotation the ray reflected from it will reach the distant mirror as a series of flashes, each formed by the ray reflected when the mirror was in the position AB. If the speed of rotation is uniform, the reflected rays from the successive flashes when the mirror is in the dotted position will thus all follow the same line ME after their second reflection from the mirror. If the motion is sufficiently rapid an eye observing the reflected [illegible] the flashes [illegible] point of light so long as the speed of revolution remains constant. The time required for the light to go and come is then equal to that required by the mirror to turn through half the angle LME, which is therefore to be measured.

Foucault.

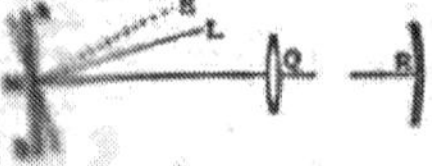

Fig. 3.

In practice it is necessary on this system, as well as on that of Fizeau, to condense the light by means of a lens, Q, so placed that L and R shall be at conjugate foci. The position of the lens may be either between the luminous point L and the mirror M, or between M and R, the latter being the only one shown in the figure. This position has the advantage that more light can be concentrated, but it has the disadvantage that, with a given magnifying power, the effect of atmospheric undulation, when the concave reflector is situated at a great distance, is increased in the ratio of the focal length of the lens to the distance LM from the light to the mirror. To state the fact in another form, the amplitude of the disturbances produced by the air in linear measure are proportional to the focal distance of the lens, while the magnification required increases in the inverse ratio of the distance LM. Another difficulty associated with the Foucault system in the form in which its originator used it is that if the axis of the mirror is at right angles to the course of the ray, the light from the source L will be flashed directly into the eye of the observer, on every passage of the revolving mirror through the position in which its normal bisects the two courses of the ray. This may be avoided by inclining the axis of the mirror.

In Foucault's determination the measures were not made upon a luminous point, but upon a reticule, the image of which could not be seen unless the reflector was quite near the revolving mirror. Indeed the whole apparatus was contained in his laboratory. The effective distance was increased by using several reflectors; but the entire course of the ray measured only 20 metres. The result reached by Foucault for the velocity of light was 298,000 kilometres per second.

The first marked advance on Foucault's determination was made by Albert A. Michelson, then a young officer on duty at the U.S. Naval Academy, Annapolis. The improvement consisted in using the image of a slit through which the rays of the sun passed after reflection from a heliostat. In this way it was found possible to see the image of the slit reflected from the distant mirror when the latter was nearly 600 metres from the station of observation. The essentials of the arrangement are those we have used in fig. 3, L being the slit. It will be seen that the revolving mirror is here interposed between the lens and its focus. It was driven by an air turbine, the blast of which was under the control of the observer, so that it could be kept at any required speed. The speed was determined by the vibrations of two tuning forks. One of these was an electric fork, making about 120 vibrations per second, with which the mirror was kept in unison by a system of rays reflected from it and the fork. The speed of this fork was determined by comparison with a freely vibrating fork from time to time. The speed of the revolving mirror was generally about 275 turns per second, and the deflection of the image of the slit about 112·5 mm. The mean result of nearly 100 fairly accordant determinations was:—

Michelson.

Velocity of light in air	299,828 km. per sec.
Reduction to a vacuum	+82
Velocity of light in a vacuum	299,910 ± 50

While this work was in progress Simon Newcomb obtained the official support necessary to make a determination on a yet larger scale. The most important modifications made in the Foucault-Michelson system were the following:—

Newcomb.

1. Placing the reflector at the much greater distance of several kilometres.

2. In order that the disturbances of the return image due to the passage of the ray through more than 7 km. of air might be reduced to a minimum, an ordinary telescope of the "broken back" form was used to send the ray to the revolving mirror.

3. The speed of the mirror was, as in Michelson's experiments, completely under con rol of the observer, so that by drawing one or the other of two cords held in the hand the return image could be kept in any required position. In making each measure the receiving telescope hereafter described was placed in a fixed position and during the "run" the image was kept as nearly as practicable upon a vertical thread passing through its focus. A "run" generally lasted about two minutes, during which time the mirror commonly made between 25,000 and 30,000 revolutions. The speed per second was found by dividing the entire number of revolutions by the number of seconds in the "run." The extreme deviations between the times of transmission of the light, as derived from any two runs, never approached to the thousandth part of its entire amount. The average deviation from the mean was indeed less than [illegible] part of the whole.

To avoid the injurious effect of the directly reflected flash, as well as to render unnecessary a comparison between the directions of the outgoing and the return ray a second telescope, turning horizontally on an axis coincident with that of the revolving mirror, was used to receive the return ray after reflection. This required the use of an elongated mirror of which the upper half of the surface reflected the outgoing ray and the lower other half received and reflected the ray on its return. On this system it was not necessary to incline the mirror in order to avoid the direct reflection of the return ray. The greatest advantage of this system was that the revolving mirror could be turned in either direction without break of continuity, so that the angular measures were made between the directions of the return ray after reflection when the mirror moved in opposite directions. In this way the speed of the mirror was as good as doubled, and the possible constant errors inherent in the reference to a fixed direction for the sending telescope were eliminated. The essentials of the apparatus are shown in fig. 4. The revolving mirror was a rectangular prism M of steel, 3 in. high and $1\frac{1}{2}$ in. on a side in cross section, which was driven by a blast of air acting on two fan-wheels, not shown in the fig., one at the top, the other at the bottom of the mirror. NPO is the object-end of the fixed sending telescope the rays passing through it being reflected to the mirror by a prism P.

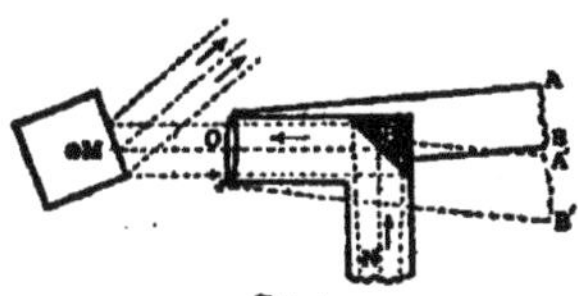

Fig. 4.

The receiving telescope ABO is straight, and has its objective under O. It was attached to a frame which could turn around the same axis as the mirror. The angle through which it moved was measured by a divided arc immediately below its eye-piece, which is not shown in the figure. The position AB is that for receiving the ray during a rotation of the mirror in the anti-clockwise direction; the position A'B' that for a clockwise rotation.

In these measures the observing station was at Fort Myer, on a hill above the west bank of the Potomac river. The distant reflector was first placed in the grounds of the Naval Observatory, at a distance of 2551 metres. But the definitive measures were made with the reflector at the base of the Washington monument, 3721 metres distant. The revolving mirror was of nickel-plated steel, polished on all four vertical sides. Thus four reflections of the ray were received during each turn of the mirror, which would be coincident were the form of the mirror invariable. During the preliminary series of measures it was found that two images of the return ray were sometimes formed, which would result in two different conclusions as to the velocity of light, according as one or the other was observed. The only explanation of this defect which presented itself was a tortional vibration of the revolving mirror, coinciding in period with that of revolution, but it was first thought that the effect was only occasional.

In the summer of 1881 the distant reflector was removed from the Observatory to the Monument station. Six measures made in August and September showed a systematic deviation of +67 km. per second from the result of the Observatory series. This difference led to measures for eliminating the defect from which it was supposed to arise. The pivots of the mirror were reground, and a change made in the arrangement, which would permit of the effect of the vibration being determined and eliminated. This consisted in making the relative position of the sending and receiving telescopes interchangeable. In this way, if the measured deflection was too great in one position of the telescopes, it would be too small by an equal amount in the reverse position. As a matter of fact, when the definitive measures were made, it was found that with the improved pivots the mean result was the same in the two positions. But the new result differed systematically from both the former ones. Thirteen measures were made from the Monument in the summer of 1882, the results of which will first be stated in the form of the time required by the ray to go and come. Expressed in millionths of a second this was:—

Least result of the 13 measures . .	24·819
Greatest result	24·831
Double distance between mirrors .	7·44242 km.

Applying a correction of +12 km. for a slight convexity in the face of the revolving mirror, this gives as the mean result for the speed of light in air, 299,778 km. per second. The mean results for the three series were:—

Observatory, 1880–1881 .	V in air = 299,627
Monument, 1881 . . .	V „ = 299,694
Monument, 1882 . . .	V „ = 299,778

The last result being the only one from which the effect of distortion was completely eliminated, has been adopted as definitive. For reduction to a vacuum it requires a correction of +82 km. Thus the final result was concluded to be

Velocity of light in vacuo = 299,860 km. per second.

This result being less by 50 km. than that of Michelson, the latter made another determination with improved apparatus and arrangements at the Case School of Applied Science in Cleveland. The result was

Velocity in vacuo = 299,853 km. per second.

So far as could be determined from the discordance of the separate measures, the mean error of Newcomb's result would be less than ±10 km. But making allowance for the various sources of systematic error the actual probable error was estimated at ±30 km.

It seems remarkable that since these determinations were made, a period during which great improvements have become possible in every part of the apparatus, no complete redetermination of this fundamental physical constant has been carried out.

The experimental measures thus far cited have been primarily those of the velocity of light in air, the reduction to a vacuum being derived from theory alone. The fundamental constant at the basis of the whole theory is the speed of light in a vacuum, such as the celestial spaces. The question of the relation between the velocity in vacuo, and in a transparent medium of any sort, belongs to the domain of physical optics. Referring to the preceding section for the principles at play we shall in the present part of the article confine ourselves to the experimental results. With the theory of the effect of a transparent medium is associated that of the possible differences in the speed of light of different colours.

Velocity and wave-length.

The question whether the speed of light in vacuo varies with its wave-length seems to be settled with entire certainty by observations of variable stars. These are situated at different distances, some being so far that light must be several centuries in reaching us from them. Were there any difference in the speed of light of various colours it would be shown by a change in the colour of the star as its light waxed and waned. The light of greatest speed preceding that of lesser speed would, when emanated during the rising phase, impress its own colour on that which it overtook. The slower light would predominate during the falling phase. If there were a difference of 10 minutes in the time at which light from the two ends of the visible spectrum arrived, it would be shown by this test. As not the slightest effect of the kind has ever been seen, it seems certain that the difference, if any, cannot approximate to $\frac{1}{1,000,000}$ part of the entire speed. The case is different when light passes through a refracting medium. It is a theoretical result of the undulatory theory of light that its velocity in such a medium is inversely proportional to the refractive index of the medium. This being different for different colours, we must expect a corresponding difference in the velocity.

Foucault and Michelson have tested these results of the undulatory theory by comparing the time required for a ray of light to pass through a tube filled with a refracting medium, and through air. Foucault thus found, in a general way, that there actually was a retardation; but his observations took account only of the mean retardation of light of all the wave-lengths, which he found to correspond with the undulatory theory. Michelson went further by determining the retardation of light of various wave-lengths in carbon bisulphide. He made two series of experiments, one with light near the brightest part of the spectrum; the other with red and blue light. Putting V for the speed in a vacuum and V_1 for that in the medium, his result was

Yellow light	$V : V_1 = 1{\cdot}758$
Refractive index for yellow . .	1·64
Difference from theory . .	+0·12

The estimated uncertainty was only 0·02, or $\frac{1}{6}$ of the difference between observation and theory.

The comparison of red and blue light was made differentially. The colours selected were of wave-length about 0·62 for red and 0·49 for blue. Putting V_r and V_b for the speeds of red and blue light respectively in bisulphide of carbon, the mean result compares with theory as follows:—

Observed value of the ratio V_r, V_b .	1·0245
Theoretical value (Verdet) . .	1·025

This agreement may be regarded as perfect. It shows that the divergence of the speed of yellow light in the medium from theory, as found above, holds through the entire spectrum.

The excess of the retardation above that resulting from theory is probably due to a difference between "wave-speed" and "group-speed" pointed out by Rayleigh. Let fig. 5 represent a short series of progressive undulations of constant period and wave-length. The wave-speed is that required to carry a wave crest A to the position of the crest B in the wave time.

[illegible] a flash of light like that measured passes through [illegible] medium, the front waves of the flash are continually [illegible] as shown at the end of the figure, and the place of [illegible] by the wave following. A familiar case of this sort [illegible] a stone is thrown into a pond. The front waves [illegible] a time, to be followed by others, each of which [illegible] than its predecessor, while new waves are formed [illegible] the group, as represented in the figure by the

Fig. 5.

[illegible] the middle, moves as a whole more slowly than [illegible] waves. When the speed of light is measured [illegible] the wave-speed as above defined, but something [illegible] depends on the time of the group passing [illegible] medium. This lower speed is called the group-[illegible]. In a vacuum there is no dying out of the [illegible] group-speed and the wave-speed are identical. [illegible] it would follow that the retarda-[illegible] the whole speed. This would indicate [illegible] each individual light wave forming [illegible] dies out in a space of about 15 wave-[illegible]

[illegible] Foucault's descriptions of his experiments [illegible] 22 and November 24, 1862), and [illegible] *de Léon Foucault* (2 vols., 4to, [illegible] information is found in *Annales de l'Ob-*[illegible] vol. xiii. The works of Michelson and [illegible] in the *Astronomical Papers of the* [illegible] (S. N.)

[illegible] (1602–1675), English divine and rab-[illegible] the son of Thomas Lightfoot, vicar of [illegible] and was born at Stoke-upon-Trent [illegible]. His education was received at [illegible] Cheshire, and at Christ's College, [illegible] he was reckoned the best orator among [illegible] taking his degree he became assistant [illegible] Derbyshire; after taking orders he was [illegible] Norton-under-Hales in Shropshire. There [illegible] Sir Rowland Cotton, an amateur [illegible] who made him his domestic [illegible] after the removal of Sir Rowland [illegible] an intention to go abroad, [illegible] Staffordshire, where he continued [illegible] he removed to Hornsey, near [illegible] in the library of Sion College. [illegible] *Erubhin, or Miscellanies,* [illegible] *for recreation at vacant hours,* [illegible] appeared at London in 1629. [illegible] by Sir R. Cotton to the [illegible] where he remained until [illegible] London, probably to superintend [illegible] *A Few and New Observations* [illegible] *therein; the rest,* [illegible] *of before,* [illegible] his arrival [illegible] Bartholomew's church, [illegible] to preach [illegible] occasion of the [illegible] published under the [illegible] it a parallel [illegible] work of reforma-[illegible] incumbent on the [illegible] of the West-[illegible] dings of the [illegible] December 31, [illegible] the 8vo edition [illegible] the brief period [illegible] attendance, and, [illegible], especially in the Erastian controversy, he exercised a material influence on the result of the discussions of the Assembly. In 1643 Lightfoot published *A Handful of Gleanings out of the Book of Exodus*, and in the same year he was made master of Catharine Hall by the parliamentary visitors of Cambridge, and also, on the recommendation of the Assembly, was promoted to the rectory of Much Munden in Hertfordshire; both appointments he retained until his death. In 1644 was published in London the first instalment of the laborious but never completed work of which the full title runs *The Harmony of the Four Evangelists among themselves, and with the Old Testament, with an explanation of the chiefest difficulties both in Language and Sense: Part I. From the beginning of the Gospels to the Baptism of our Saviour.* The second part *From the Baptism of our Saviour to the first Passover after* followed in 1647, and the third *From the first Passover after our Saviour's Baptism to the second* in 1650. On the 26th of August 1645 he again preached before the House of Commons on the day of their monthly fast. His text was Rev. xx. 1, 2. After controverting the doctrine of the Millenaries, he urged various practical suggestions for the repression with a strong hand of current blasphemies, for a thorough revision of the authorized version of the Scriptures, for the encouragement of a learned ministry, and for a speedy settlement of the church. In the same year appeared *A Commentary upon the Acts of the Apostles, chronical and critical; the Difficulties of the text explained, and the times of the Story cast into annals. From the beginning of the Book to the end of the Twelfth Chapter. With a brief survey of the contemporary Story of the Jews and Romans* (down to the third year of Claudius). In 1647 he published *The Harmony, Chronicle, and Order of the Old Testament*, which was followed in 1655 by *The Harmony, Chronicle, and Order of the New Testament*, inscribed to Cromwell. In 1654 Lightfoot had been chosen vice-chancellor of the university of Cambridge, but continued to reside by preference at Munden, in the rectory of which, as well as in the mastership of Catharine Hall, he was confirmed at the Restoration. The remainder of his life was devoted to helping Brian Walton with the Polyglot Bible (1657) and to his own best-known work, the *Horae Hebraicae et Talmudicae*, in which the volume relating to Matthew appeared in 1658, that relating to Mark in 1663, and those relating to 1 Corinthians, John and Luke, in 1664, 1671 and 1674 respectively. While travelling from Cambridge to Ely where he had been collated in 1668 by Sir Orlando Bridgman to a prebendal stall), he caught a severe cold, and died at Ely on the 6th of December 1675. The *Horae Hebraicae et Talmudicae impensae in Acta Apostolorum et in Ep. S. Pauli ad Romanos* were published posthumously.

The *Works* of Lightfoot were first edited, in 2 vols. fol., by G. Bright and Strype in 1684; the *Opera Omnia, cura Joh. Texelii*, appeared at Rotterdam in 1686 (2 vols. fol.), and again, edited by J. Leusden, at Franeker in 1699 (3 vols. fol.). A volume of *Remains* was published at London in 1700. The *Hor. Hebr. et Talm.* were also edited in Latin by Carpzov (Leipzig, 1675–1679), and again, in English, by Gandell (Oxford, 1859). The most complete edition is that of the *Whole Works*, in 13 vols. 8vo. edited, with a life, by R. Pitman (London, 1822–1825). It includes, besides the works already noticed, numerous sermons, letters and miscellaneous writings; and also *The Temple, especially as it stood in the Days of our Saviour* (London, 1650).

See D. M. Welton, *John Lightfoot, the Hebraist* (Leipzig, 1878).

LIGHTFOOT, JOSEPH BARBER (1828–1889), English theologian and bishop of Durham, was born at Liverpool on the 13th of April 1828. His father was a Liverpool accountant. He was educated at King Edward's school, Birmingham, under James Prince Lee, afterwards bishop of Manchester, and had as contemporaries B. F. Westcott and E. W. Benson. In 1847 Lightfoot went up to Trinity College, Cambridge, and there read for his degree with Westcott. He graduated senior classic and 30th wrangler, and was elected a fellow of his college. From 1854 to 1859 he edited the *Journal of Classical and Sacred Philology*. In 1857 he became tutor and his fame as a scholar grew rapidly. He was made Hulsean professor in 1861, and shortly afterwards chaplain to the Prince Consort and honorary chaplain in ordinary to the queen. In 1866 he was Whitehall preacher, and in 1871 he became canon of St Paul's. His sermons were not remarkable for eloquence, but a certain solidity and balance of judgment, an absence of partisanship, a sobriety of expression combined with clearness and force of diction, attracted hearers and inspired them with confidence. As was written of him in *The Times* after his death, "his personal character carried immense weight, but his great position depended still more on the universally recognized fact that his belief in Christian truth and his defence of it were supported by learning as solid and comprehensive as could be found anywhere in Europe, and by a temper not only of the utmost candour but of the highest scientific capacity. The days in which his university influence was asserted were a time of much shaking of old beliefs. The disintegrating speculations of an influential school of criticism in Germany were making their way among English men of culture just about the time, as is usually the case, when the tide was turning against them in their own country. The peculiar service which was rendered at this juncture by the 'Cambridge School' was that, instead of opposing a mere dogmatic opposition to the Tübingen critics, they met them frankly on their own ground; and instead of arguing that their conclusions ought not to be and could not be true, they simply proved that their facts and their premisses were wrong. It was a characteristic of equal importance that Dr Lightfoot, like Dr Westcott, never discussed these subjects in the mere spirit of controversy. It was always patent that what he was chiefly concerned with was the substance and the life of Christian truth, and that his whole energies were employed in this inquiry because his whole heart was engaged in the truths and facts which were at stake. He was not diverted by controversy to side-issues; and his labour was devoted to the positive elucidation of the sacred documents in which the Christian truth is enshrined."

In 1872 the anonymous publication of *Supernatural Religion* created considerable sensation. In a series of masterly papers in the *Contemporary Review*, between December 1874 and May 1877, Lightfoot successfully undertook the defence of the New Testament canon. The articles were published in collected form in 1889. About the same time he was engaged in contributions to W. Smith's *Dictionary of Christian Biography* and *Dictionary of the Bible*, and he also joined the committee for revising the translation of the New Testament. In 1875 he became Lady Margaret professor of divinity in succession to William Selwyn. He had previously written his commentaries on the epistles to the Galatians (1865), Philippians (1868) and Colossians (1875), the notes to which were distinguished by sound judgment and enriched from his large store of patristic and classical learning. These commentaries may be described as to a certain extent a new departure in New Testament exegesis. Before Lightfoot's time commentaries, especially on the epistles, had not infrequently consisted either of short homilies on particular portions of the text, or of endeavours to enforce foregone conclusions, or of attempts to decide with infinite industry and ingenuity between the interpretations of former commentators. Lightfoot, on the contrary, endeavoured to make his author interpret himself, and by considering the general drift of his argument to discover his meaning where it appeared doubtful. Thus he was able often to recover the meaning of a passage which had long been buried under a heap of contradictory glosses, and he founded a school in which sobriety and common sense were added to the industry and ingenuity of former commentators. In 1879 Lightfoot was consecrated bishop of Durham in succession to C. Baring. His moderation, good sense, wisdom, temper, firmness and erudition made him as successful in this position as he had been when professor of theology, and he speedily surrounded himself with a band of scholarly young men. He endeavoured to combine his habits of theological study with the practical work of administration. He exercised a large liberality and did much to further the work of temperance and purity organizations. He continued to work at his editions of the *Apostolic Fathers*, and in 1885 published an edition of the Epistles of Ignatius and Polycarp, collecting also a large store of valuable materials for a second edition of Clement of Rome, which was published after his death (1st ed., 1869). His defence of the authenticity of the Epistles of Ignatius is one of the most important contributions to that very difficult controversy. His unremitting labours impaired his health and shortened his splendid career at Durham. He was never married. He died at Bournemouth on the 21st of December 1889, and was succeeded in the episcopate by Westcott, his schoolfellow and lifelong friend.

Four volumes of his *Sermons* were published in 1890.

LIGHTHOUSE, a form of building erected to carry a light for the purpose of warning or guidance, especially at sea.

1. Early History.—The earliest lighthouses, of which records exist, were the towers built by the Libyans and Cushites in Lower Egypt, beacon fires being maintained in some of them by the priests. Lesches, a Greek poet (*c.*660 B.C.) mentions a lighthouse at Sigeum (now Cape Incihisari) in the Troad. This appears to have been the first light regularly maintained for the guidance of mariners. The famous Pharos[1] of Alexandria, built by Sostratus of Cnidus in the reign of Ptolemy II. (283–247 B.C.) was regarded as one of the wonders of the world. The tower, which took its name from that of the small island on which it was built, is said to have been 600 ft. in height, but the evidence in support of this statement is doubtful. It was destroyed by an earthquake in the 13th century, but remains are said to have been visible as late as 1350. The name Pharos became the general term for all lighthouses, and the term "pharology" has been used for the science of lighthouse construction.

The tower at Ostia was built by the emperor Claudius (A.D. 50). Other famous Roman lighthouses were those at Ravenna, Pozzuoli and Messina. The ancient Pharos at Dover and that at Boulogne, later known as *la Tour d'Ordre*, were built by the Romans and were probably the earliest lighthouses erected in western Europe. Both are now demolished.

The light of Cordouan, on a rock in the sea at the mouth of the Gironde, is the earliest example now existing of a wave-swept tower. Earlier towers on the same rock are attributed the first to Louis le Debonnaire (*c.* A.D. 805) and the second to Edward the Black Prince. The existing structure was begun in 1584 during the reign of Henri II. of France and completed in 1611. The upper part of the beautiful Renaissance building was removed towards the end of the 18th century and replaced by a loftier cylindrical structure rising to a height of 207 ft. above the rock and with the focal plane of the light 196 ft. above high water (fig. 1). Until the 18th century the light exhibited from the tower was from an oak log fire, and subsequently a coal fire was in use for many years. The ancient tower at Corunna, known as the Pillar of Hercules, is supposed to have been a Roman Pharos. The Torre del Capo at Genoa originally stood on the promontory of San Berrique. It was built in 1139 and first used as a lighthouse in 1326. It was rebuilt on its present site in 1643. This beautiful tower rises 236 ft. above the cliff, the light being elevated 384 ft. above sea-level. A lens light was first installed in 1841. The Pharos of Meloria was constructed by the Pisans in 1154 and was several times rebuilt until finally destroyed in 1290. On the abandonment of Meloria by the Pisans, they erected the still existing tower at Leghorn in 1304.

In the 17th and 18th centuries numerous towers, on which were erected braziers or grates containing wood or coal fires, were established in various positions on the coasts of Europe. Among such stations in the United Kingdom were Tynemouth (*c.* 1608), the Isle of May (1636), St Agnes (1680), St Bees (1718) and the Lizard (1751). The oldest lighthouse in the United States is believed to be the Boston light situated on Little Brewster Island on the south side of the main entrance to Boston Harbour, Mass. It was established in 1716, the present structure dating from 1859. During the American War of Independence the lighthouse suffered many vicissitudes and was successively destroyed and rebuilt three times by the American or British

[1] A full account is given in Hermann Thiersch, *Pharos Antike, Islam und Occident* (1909). See also Minaret.

[illegible] At the third rebuilding in 1783 a stone tower 68 ft. in [illegible] was erected, the illuminant consisting of four oil lamps. [illegible] structures on the New England coast [illegible] near the entrance to Newport Harbour [illegible] the entrance to Nantucket Harbour [illegible] and beacon appear to have been erected [illegible] Island as well as on Point Allerton [illegible] 1673, but these structures would seem [illegible] of look-out stations in time of war [illegible] for the guidance of mariners.

[illegible] Structures.—The structures of lighthouses may be divided into two classes, (*a*) those on rocks, shoals or [illegible] other situations exposed to the force of the sea, and (*b*) the [illegible] of land structures.

Wave-swept Towers.—In determining the design of a lighthouse [illegible] in a wave-swept position consideration must

Fig. 1.—[illegible] Lighthouse.

[illegible] of the site and its surroundings. [illegible] classified as follows: (1) Masonry [illegible] (2) Openwork steel and iron-framed [illegible] (3) Cast iron plated towers; [illegible] foundations.

[illegible] towers are generally [illegible] rocks affording good [illegible] constructed in other situations [illegible] made by sinking caissons [illegible] on the Eddystone Rock is [illegible] of masonry towers have [illegible] in detail have since [illegible] exposure the following [illegible] observed: (*a*) The centre [illegible] be as low as possible. [illegible] at any horizontal [illegible] displacement by the [illegible] the [illegible]

(*d*) The lower portion of the tower exposed to the direct horizontal stroke of the waves should, for preference, be constructed with vertical face. The upper portion to be either straight with uniform batter or continuously curved in the vertical plane. External projections from the face of the tower, except in the case of a gallery under the lantern, should be avoided, the surface throughout being smooth. (*e*) The height from sea-level to the top of the tower should be sufficient to avoid the obscuration of the light by broken water or dense spray driving over the lantern. (*f*) The foundation of the tower should be carried well into the solid rock. (*g*) The materials of which the tower is built should be of high density and of resistant nature. (*h*) The stones used in the construction of the tower, at any rate those on the outer face, should be dovetailed or joggled one to the other in order to prevent their being dislodged by the sea during the process of construction and as an additional safeguard of stability. Of late years, cement concrete has been used to a considerable extent for maritime structures, including lighthouses, either alone or faced with masonry.

(2) *Openwork Structures.*—Many examples of openwork steel and iron lighthouses exist. Some typical examples are described hereafter. This form of design is suitable for situations where the tower has to be carried on a foundation of iron or steel piles driven or screwed into an insecure or sandy bottom, such as on shoals, coral reefs and sand banks or in places where other materials of construction are exceptionally costly and where facility of erection is a desideratum.

(3) *Cast iron Towers.*—Cast iron plated towers have been erected in many situations where the cost of stone or scarcity of labour would have made the erection of a masonry tower excessively expensive.

(4) *Caisson Foundations.*—Cylinder or caisson foundations have been used for lighthouse towers in numerous cases where such structures have been erected on sand banks or shoals. A remarkable instance is the Rothersand Tower. Two attempts have been made to sink a caisson in the outer Diamond Shoal off Cape Hatteras on the Atlantic coast of the United States, but these have proved futile.

The following are brief descriptions of the more important wave-swept towers in various parts of the world.

Eddystone (Winstanley's Tower).—The Eddystone rocks, which lie about 14 m. off Plymouth, are fully exposed to south-west seas. The reef is submerged at high water of spring tides. Four towers have been constructed on the reef. The first lighthouse (fig. 2 was polygonal in plan and highly ornamented with galleries and projections which offered considerable resistance to the sea stroke. The work was begun by Henry Winstanley, a gentleman of Essex, in 1695. In 1698 it was finished to a height of 80 ft. to the wind vane and the light exhibited, but in the following year, in consequence of damage by storms, the tower was increased in diameter from 16 ft. to 24 ft. by the addition of an outer ring of masonry and made solid to a height of 20 ft. above the rock, the tower being raised to nearly 120 ft. The work was completed in the year 1700. The lower part of the structure appears to have been of stone, the upper part and lantern of timber. During the great storm of the 20th of November 1703 the tower was swept away, those in it at the time, including the builder, being drowned.

Eddystone (Rudyerd's Tower, fig. 3).—This structure was begun in 1706 and completed in 1709. It was a frustum of a cone 22 ft. 8 in. in diameter at the base and 14 ft. 3 in. at the top. The tower was 92 ft. in height to the top of the lantern. The work consisted principally of oak timbers securely bolted and cramped together, the lower part being filled in solid with stone to add weight to the structure. The simplicity of the design and the absence of projections from the outer face rendered the tower very suitable to withstand the onslaught of the waves. The lighthouse was destroyed by fire in 1755.

Eddystone (Smeaton's Tower, fig. 4).—This famous work, which consisted entirely of stone, was begun in 1756, the light being first exhibited in 1759. John Smeaton was the first engineer to use dovetailed joints for the stones in a lighthouse structure. The stones, which averaged 1 ton in weight, were fastened to each other by means of dovetailed vertical joint faces, oak key wedges, and by oak tree-nails wedged top and bottom, extending vertically from every course into the stones beneath it. During the 19th century the tower was strengthened on two occasions by the addition of heavy wrought iron ties, and the overhanging cornice was reduced in diameter to prevent the waves from lifting the stones from their beds. In 1877, owing partly to the undermining of the rock on which the tower was built and the insufficient height of the structure, the Corporation of Trinity House determined on the erection of a new lighthouse in place of Smeaton's tower.

Eddystone, New Lighthouse (*J. N. Douglass*).—The site selected for the new tower is 120 ft. S.S.E. from Smeaton's lighthouse, where a suitable foundation was found, although a considerable section of the lower courses had to be laid below the level of low water. The vertical base is 44 ft. in diameter and 22 ft. in height. The tower (figs. 5 and 6) is a concave elliptic frustum, and is solid, with the exception of a fresh-water tank, to a height of 25 ft. 6 in. above high-water level. The walls above this level vary in thickness from 8 ft. 6 in. to 2 ft. 3 in. under the gallery. All the stones are dovetailed, both horizontally and vertically, on all joint faces, the stones of the foundation course being secured to the rock by Muntz metal bolts. The tower contains 62,133 cub. ft. of granite, weighing 4668 tons. The height of the structure from low water ordinary spring tides to the mean focal plane is 149 ft. and it stands 133 ft. above high water. The lantern is a cylindrical helically framed structure with domed roof. The astragals are of gunmetal and the pedestal of cast iron. The optical apparatus consists of two superposed tiers of refracting lens panels, 12 in each tier of 920 mm. focal distance. The lenses subtend an angle of 92° vertically. The 12 lens panels are arranged in groups of two, thus producing a group flashing light showing 2 flashes of 1½ seconds' duration every half minute, the apparatus revolving once in 3 minutes. The burners originally fitted in the apparatus were of 6-wick pattern, but these were replaced in 1904 by incandescent oil vapour burners. The intensity of the combined beam of light from the two apparatus is 292,000 candles. At the time of the completion of the lighthouse two bells, weighing 2 tons each and struck by mechanical power, were installed for fog-signalling purposes. Since that date an explosive gun-cotton fog signal has been erected, the bells being removed. At a lower level in the tower are installed 2 21-in. parabolic silvered reflectors with 2-wick burners, throwing a fixed light of 8000 candle-power over a danger known as the Hand Deeps. The work of preparing the foundation was begun on the 17th of July 1878, the foundation stone being laid by the late duke of Edinburgh on the 19th of August 1879. The last stone was laid on the 1st of June 1881, and the light was exhibited for the first time on the 18th of May 1882. The upper portion of Smeaton's tower, which was removed on completion of the new lighthouse, was re-erected on Plymouth Hoe, where it replaced the old Trinity House sea mark. One of the principal features in the design of the new Eddystone lighthouse tower is the solid vertical base. This construction was much criticized at the time, but experience has proved that heavy seas striking the massive cylindrical structure are immediately broken up and rush round to the opposite side, spray alone ascending to the height of the lantern gallery. On the other hand, the waves striking the old tower at its foundation ran up the surface, which presented a curved face to the waves, and, unimpeded by any projection until arriving at the lantern gallery, were partially broken up by the cornice and then spent themselves in heavy spray over the lantern. The shock to which the cornice of the gallery was exposed was so great that stones were sometimes lifted from their beds. The new Eddystone tower presents another point of dissimilarity from Smeaton's structure, in that the stones forming the floors consist of single corbels built into the wall and constituting solid portions thereof. In Smeaton's tower the floors consisted of stone arches, the thrust being taken by the walls of the tower itself, which were strengthened for the purpose by building in chains in the form of hoops (fig. 7). The system of constructing corbelled stone floors was first adopted by R. Stevenson in the Bell Rock lighthouse (fig. 8).

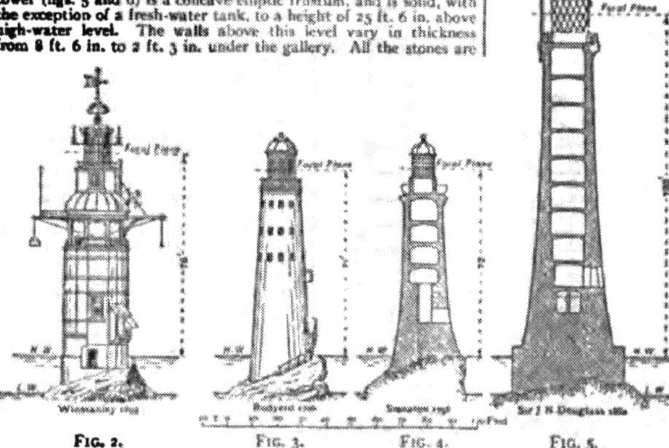

Fig. 2. Fig. 3. Fig. 4.

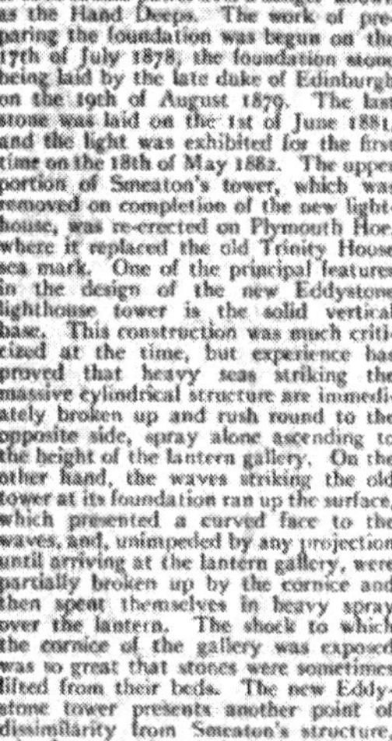

Fig. 5.

Lighthouses on the Eddystone.

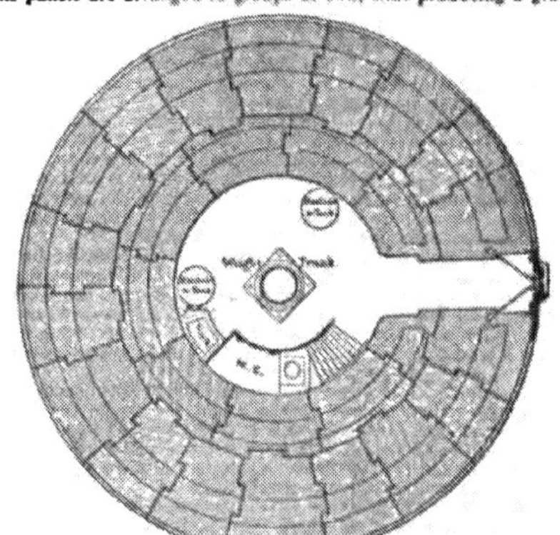

Fig. 6.—Plan of Entrance Floor, Eddystone Lighthouse.

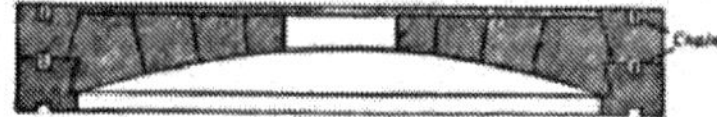

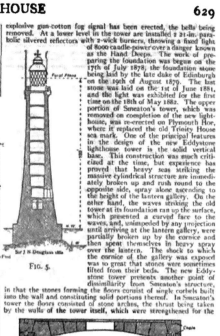

Fig. 7.—Floor, Smeaton's Eddystone Lighthouse.

Bell Rock Lighthouse (fig. 9).—The Bell Rock, which lies 12 m. off the coast of Forfarshire, is exposed to a considerable extent at low water. The tower is submerged to a depth of about 16 ft. at high water of spring tides. The rock is of hard sandstone. The lighthouse was constructed by Robert Stevenson and is 100 ft. in height, the solid portion being carried to a height of 21 ft. above high water. The work of construction was begun in 1807, and finished in 1810, the light being first exhibited in 1811. The total weight of the tower is 2076 tons. A new lantern and dioptric apparatus were erected on the tower in 1902. The focal plane of the light is elevated 93 ft. above high water.

Skerryvore Lighthouse (fig. 10).—The Skerryvore Rocks, 12 m. off the island of Tyree in Argyllshire, are wholly open to the Atlantic. The work, designed by Alan Stevenson, was begun in 1838 and finished in 1844. The tower, the profile of which is a hyperbolic curve, is 138 ft. high to the lantern base, 42 ft. diameter at the base, and 16 ft. at the top. Its weight is 4308 tons. The structure contains 9 rooms in addition to the lantern chamber. It is solid to a height of 26 ft. above the base.

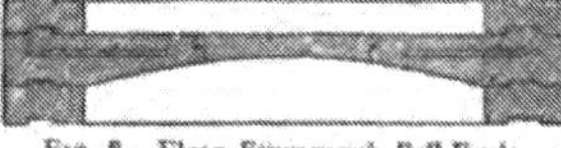

Fig. 8.—Floor, Stevenson's Bell Rock Lighthouse.

Heaux de Brehat Lighthouse.—The reef on which this tower is constructed lies off the coast of Brittany, and is submerged at high tide. The work was carried out in 1836–1839. The tower is circular in plan with a gallery at a height of about 70 ft. above the base. The tower is 156 ft. in height from base to lantern floor.

Haut Banc du Nord Lighthouse.—This tower is placed on a reef at the north-west extremity of the Île de Ré, and was constructed in 1849–1853. It is 86 ft. in height to the lantern floor.

Bishop Rock Lighthouse.—The lighthouse on the Bishop Rock, which is the westernmost landfall rock of the Scilly Islands, occupies perhaps a more exposed situation than any other in the world.

The first lighthouse erected there was begun in 1847 under the direction of N. Douglass. The tower consisted of a cast and wrought iron open-work structure having the columns deeply sunk into the rock. On the 5th of February 1850, when the tower was ready for the erection of the lantern and illuminating apparatus, a heavy storm swept away the whole of the structure. This tower was designed for an elevation of 94 ft. to the focal plane. In 1851 the

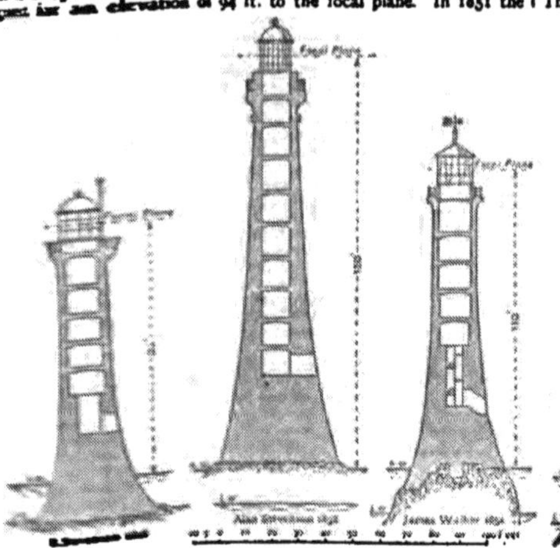

Fig. 9.—Bell Rock. Fig. 10.—Skerryvore. Fig. 11.—Bishop Rock. Fig. 12.—Bishop Rock.

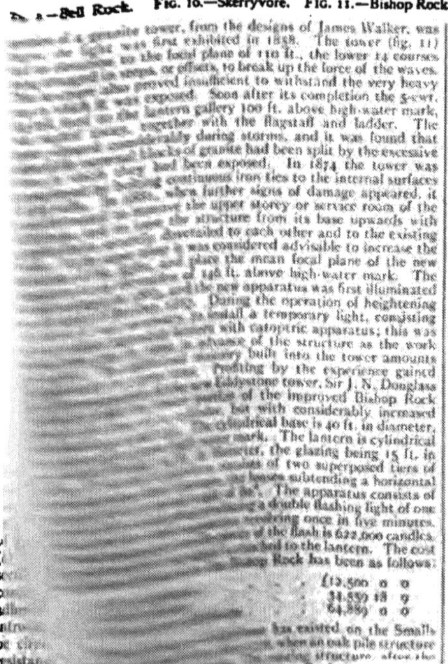

tower, from the designs of James Walker, was
first exhibited in 1858. The tower (fig. 11)
to the focal plane of 110 ft., the lower 14 courses
steps, or offsets, to break up the force of the waves.
proved insufficient to withstand the very heavy
exposed. Soon after its completion the 5-cwt.
lantern gallery 100 ft. above high-water mark,
together with the flagstaff and ladder. The
during storms, and it was found that
blocks of granite had been split by the excessive
had been exposed. In 1874 the tower was
continuous iron ties to the internal surfaces
when further signs of damage appeared, it
the upper storey or service room of the
the structure from its base upwards with
dovetailed to each other and to the existing
was considered advisable to increase the
place the mean focal plane of the new
of 146 ft. above high-water mark. The
the new apparatus was first illuminated
During the operation of heightening
install a temporary light, consisting
with catoptric apparatus; this was
advance of the structure as the work
built into the tower amounts
Profiting by the experience gained
Eddystone tower, Sir J. N. Douglass
of the improved Bishop Rock
but with considerably increased
cylindrical base is 40 ft. in diameter,
mark. The lantern is cylindrical
the glazing being 15 ft. in
of two superposed tiers of
subtending a horizontal
The apparatus consists of
a double flashing light of one
once in five minutes.
of the flash is 622,000 candles.
to the lantern. The cost
Rock has been as follows:

£12,500 0 0
34,559 18 9
64,889 0 0

has existed on the Smalls
an oak pile structure

1856–1861 by the Trinity House and is 114 ft. in height from the foundation to the lantern floor. A new optical apparatus was installed in 1907.

Minot's Ledge Lighthouse.—The tower, which is 89 ft. in height, is built of granite upon a reef off Boston Harbor, Mass., and occupied five years in construction, being completed in 1860 at a cost of £62,500. The rock just bares at low water. The stones are dovetailed vertically but not on their horizontal beds in the case of the lower 40 ft. or solid portion of the tower, bonding bolts being substituted for the horizontal dovetailed joints used in the case of the Wolf and other English towers. The shape of the tower is a conical frustum.

Wolf Rock Lighthouse.—This much exposed rock lies midway between the Scilly Isles and the Lizard Point, and is submerged to the depth of about 6 ft. at high water. The tower was erected in 1862–1869 (fig. 14). It is 116 ft. 6 in. high, 41 ft. 8 in. diameter at the base, decreasing to 17 ft. at the top. The walls are 7 ft. 9½ in. thick, decreasing to 2 ft. 3 in. The shaft is a concave elliptic frustum, and contains 3296 tons. The lower part of the tower has projecting scarcements in order to break up the sea.

Dhu Heartach Rock Lighthouse.—The Dhu Heartach Rock, 35 ft. above high water, is 14 m. from the island of Mull, which is the nearest shore. The maximum diameter of the tower (fig. 15), which is of parabolic outline, is 36 ft., decreasing to 16 ft.; the shaft is solid for 32 ft above the rock; the masonry weighs 3115 tons, of which 1810 are contained in the solid part. This tower occupied six years in erection, and was completed in 1872.

Great Basses Lighthouse, Ceylon.—The Great Basses lighthouse lies 6 m. from the nearest land. The cylindrical base is 32 ft. in diameter, above which is a tower 67 ft. 5 in. high and 23 ft. in diameter. The walls vary in thickness from 5 ft. to 2 ft. The tower, including the base, contains about 2768 tons. The work was finished in three years, 1870–1873.

Spectacle Reef Lighthouse, Lake Huron.—This is a structure similar to that on Minot's ledge, standing on a limestone reef at the northern end of the lake. The tower (fig. 16) was constructed with a view to withstanding the effects of ice massing in solid fields thousands of acres in extent and travelling at considerable velocity. The tower is in shape the frustum of a cone, 32 ft. in diameter at the base and 93 ft. in height to the coping of the gallery. The focal plane is at a level of 97 ft. above the base. The lower 34 ft. of the tower is solid. The work was completed in 1874, having occupied four years. The cost amounted to approximately £78,000.

Chicken Rock Lighthouse.—The Chicken Rock lies 1 m. off the Calf of Man. The curve of the tower, which is 123 ft. 4 in. high, is hyperbolic, the diameter varying from 42 ft. to 16 ft. The tower is submerged 5 ft. at high-water springs. The solid part is 32 ft. 6 in. in height, weighing 2050 tons, the whole weight of the tower being 3557 tons. The walls decrease from 9 ft. 3 in. to 2 ft. 3 in. in thickness. The work was begun in 1869 and completed in 1874.

Ar'men Lighthouse.—The masonry tower, erected by the French Lighthouse Service, on the Ar'men Rock off the western extremity of the Île de Sein, Finistère, occupied fifteen years in construction (1867–1881). The rock is of small area, barely uncovered at low water, and it was therefore found impossible to construct a tower having a base diameter greater than 24 ft. The focal plane of the light is 94 ft. above high water (fig. 17).

St George's Reef Lighthouse, California.—This structure consists of a square pyramidal stone tower rising from the easterly end of an oval masonry pier, built on a rock to a height of 60 ft. above the water. The focal plane is at an elevation of 146 ft. above high water. The site is an exceedingly dangerous one, and the work, which was completed in 1891, cost approximately £144,000.

Rattray Head Lighthouse.—This lighthouse was constructed between the years 1892 and 1895 by the Northern Lighthouse Commissioners upon the Ron Rock, lying about one-fifth of a mile off Rattray Head, Aberdeenshire. The focal plane is 91 ft. above high water, the building being approximately 113 ft. in height. In the tower there is a fog-horn worked by compressed air.

Fastnet Lighthouse.—In the year 1895 it was reported to the Irish Lights Commissioners that the then existing lighthouse on the Fastnet Rock off the south-west coast of Ireland, which was completed in 1854 and consisted of a circular cast iron tower 86 ft. in height on the summit of the rock, was considerably undermined. It was subsequently determined to proceed with the erection of a granite structure of increased height and founded upon a sound ledge of rock on one side of the higher, but now considerably undermined.

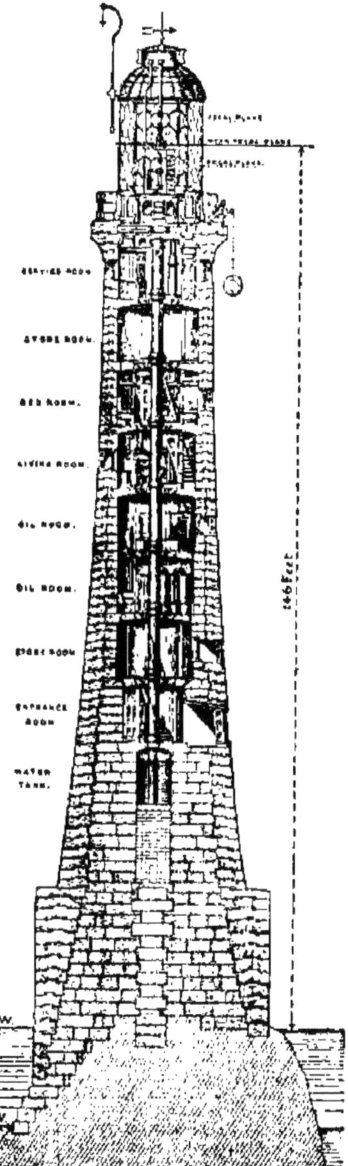

Fig. 13.—Bishop Rock Lighthouse.

portion of the reef. This lighthouse tower has its foundation laid near high-water level. The focal plane is at a level of 158 ft. above high-water mark. The cost of the structure, which was commenced in 1899 and completed in 1904, was £79,000.

Beachy Head Lighthouse.—A lighthouse has been erected upon the foreshore at the foot of Beachy Head, near Eastbourne, to replace the old structure on the cliff having an elevation of 284 ft. above high-water mark. Experience proved that the light of the latter was frequently obscured by banks of mist or fog, while at the lower level the transparency of the atmosphere was considerably less impaired. The Trinity House therefore decided in the year 1899 to proceed with the construction of a granite tower upon the foreshore at a distance of some 570 ft. from the base of the cliff (fig. 18). The foreshore at this point consists of chalk, and the selected site just bares at low water ordinary spring tides. The foundation course was laid at a depth of 10 ft. below the surface, the area being excavated within a coffer-dam. The tower, which is 47 ft. in diameter at the base, has an elevation to the focal plane above high water of 103 ft., or a total height from foundation course to gallery coping of 123 ft. 6 in. The lower or solid portion of the tower has its face stones constructed in vertical offsets or steps in a similar manner to that adopted at the Wolf Rock and elsewhere. The tower is constructed with a facing of granite, all the stones being dovetailed in the usual manner. The hearting of the base is largely composed of concrete. The work was completed in 1902 and cost £56,000.

Maplin Lighthouse.—The screw pile lighthouse erected on the Maplin Sand in the estuary of the river Thames in 1838 is the earliest of its kind and served as a model for numerous similar structures in various parts of the world. The piles are nine in number, 5 in. diameter of solid wrought iron with screws 4 ft. diameter (fig. 19).

Fowey Rocks Lighthouse, Florida.—This iron structure, which was begun in 1875 and completed in 1878, stands on the extreme northern point of the Florida reefs. The height of the tower, which is founded on wrought iron piles driven 10 ft. into the coral rock, is 110 ft. from high water to focal plane. The iron openwork pyramidal structure encloses a plated iron dwelling for the accommodation of the keepers. The cost of construction amounted to £32,600.

Alligator Reef Lighthouse, Florida.—This tower is one of the finest iron sea-swept lighthouse structures in the world. It consists of a pyramidal iron framework 135 ft. 6 in. in height, standing on the Florida Reef in 5 ft. of water. The cost of the structure, which is similar to the Fowey Rocks tower, was £37,000.

American Shoal Lighthouse, Florida.—This tower (fig. 20) is typical of the openwork pile structures on the Florida reefs, and was completed in 1880. The focal plane of the light is at an elevation of 109 ft. above high water.

Wolf Trap Lighthouse.—This building was erected during the years 1893 and 1894 on Wolf Trap Spit in Chesapeake Bay, near the site of the old openwork structure which was swept away by ice early in 1893. The new tower is formed upon a cast iron caisson 30 ft. in diameter sunk 18 ft. into the sandy bottom. The depth of water on the shoal is 16 ft. at low water. The caisson was filled with concrete, and is surmounted by a brick superstructure 52 ft. in height from low water to the focal plane of the light. A somewhat similar structure was erected in 1885–1887 on the Fourteen Foot Bank in Delaware Bay, at a cost of £24,700. The foundation in this case was, however, shifting sand, and the caisson was carried to a greater depth.

Rothersand Lighthouse.—This lighthouse, off the entrance to the river Weser (Germany), is a structure of great interest on account of the difficulties met with in its construction. The tower had to be founded on a bottom of shifting sand 20 ft. below low water and in a very exposed situation. Work was begun in May 1881, when attempts were made to sink an iron caisson under pneumatic pressure. Owing to the enormous scour removing the sand from one side of the caisson it tilted to an alarming angle, but eventually it was sunk to a level of 70 ft. below low-water mark. In October of the same year the whole structure collapsed. Another attempt, made in May 1883, to sink a caisson of bi-convex shape in plan 47 ft. long, 37 ft. wide and 62 ft. in height, met with success, and after many difficulties the structure was sunk to a depth of 73 ft. below low water, the sides being raised by the addition of iron plating as the caisson sank. The sand was removed from the interior by suction. Around the caisson foundation were placed 74,000 cub. yds. of mattress work and stones, the interior being filled with concrete. Towards the end of 1885 the lighthouse was completed, at a total cost, including the first attempt, of over £65,000. The tower is an iron structure in the shape of a concave elliptic frustum, its base being founded upon the caisson foundation at about half-tide level (fig. 21). The light is electric, the current being supplied by cable from the shore. The focal plane is 78 ft. above high water or 109 ft. from the sand level. The total height from the foundation of the caisson to the top of the vane is 185 ft.

Other famous wave-swept towers are those at **Haulbowline Rock** (Carlingford Lough, Ireland, 1823); **Horsburgh** (Singapore, 1851); **Baves d'Olonne** (Bay of Biscay, 1861); **Hanois** (Alderney, 1862), **Daedalus Reef**, iron tower (Red Sea, 1863); **Alguada Reef** (Bay of Bengal, 1864), **Longships** (Land's End, 1872); the **Prongs** (Bombay, 1874); **Little Basses** (Ceylon, 1878); the **Graves** (Boston, U.S.A.,

FIG. 17.—Ar'men. FIG. 18.—P

... and Roche Bonne

... Various methods of jointing ... The great ... successive engineers ... is that, in the ... together both ... by metal or wooden ... This dove- ... Rock at the sugges- ... one side and at ... On the under ... dovetailed

effect of waves on the Bishop Rock and I been noted above.

Land Structures for Lighthouses.—The towers and other buildings on land pr construction, and such buildings are o character. It will therefore be unnecessar in detail. Attention is directed to the Phare Penmarc'h (Finistère), completed in 1897. The cos magnificent structure, 207 ft. in height from the ground, largely defrayed by a bequest of £12,000 left by the marquis de Blocqueville. It is constructed entirely of granite, and is octagonal in plan. The total cost of the tower and other lighthouse buildings amounted to £16,000.

... Cost of Exposed Rock Towers.

Total Cost.			Cub. ft.	Cost per cub. ft. of Masonry		
[illegible]	0	0	13,343	£2	19	11½
[illegible]	12	1	28,530	1	19	0
[illegible]	11	6	58,580	1	4	7½
[illegible]	18	9	35,209	0	19	7½
[illegible]	11	8	46,386	1	1	7½
[illegible]	0	0	24,542	1	0	7½
[illegible]	0	0	59,070	1	1	3
[illegible]	9	7	42,050	1	14	6
[illegible]	8	11	47,610	0	18	5
[illegible]	0	0	65,198	0	18	2
[illegible]	0	0	45,080	1	8	9
[illegible]	0	0	47,819	1	6	7
[illegible]	0	0	36,323	1	17	2
[illegible]	0	0	42,742	1	16	2
[illegible]	0	0	32,400	1	3	3
[illegible]	0	0	62,000	1	5	5½

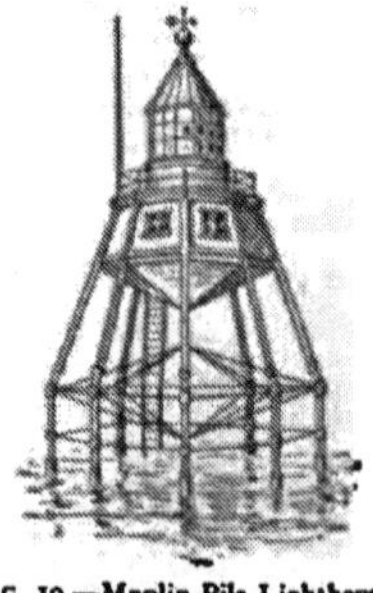

FIG. 19.—Maplin Pile Lighthouse.

The tower at Île Vierge (Finistère), completed in 1902, has an elevation of 247 ft. from the ground level to the focal plane, and is probably the highest structure of its kind in the world.

The brick tower, constructed at Spurn Point, at the entrance to the Humber and completed in 1895, replaced an earlier structure erected by Smeaton at the end of the 18th century. The existing tower is constructed on a foundation consisting of concrete cylinders sunk in the shingle beach. The focal plane of the light is elevated 120 ft. above high water.

Besides being built of stone or brick, land towers are frequently constructed of cast iron plates … to economy. Fine examples of … many British colonies and e… (Cape of Good Hope), 105 ft. … typical (fig. 25). Many op… height have been built. Rec… at Cape San Thomé (Brazil… Mocha (Red Sea) in 1903, … 1906, 165 ft. in height to th…

3. Optical Apparatus … is required for one or oth… concentration of the ray… belt of light distributed e… in the vertical plane onl… of the rays both vertic…

…at improvement in lighthouse … dioptric spherical mirror by … The zones or prisms are …led into segments. This … and 37). … to 1850 all apparatus … every azimuth either …tantly or periodic- … The only excep- …s where a light …uated on a … coast where … could be …hind the …lize the … would … land- …hem …gh …

Fig. 20.—American Shoal Lighthouse, Florida.

Appa… the second … usually employed … produce flashing lights, but sometimes the dual condensation is taken advantage of to produce a fixed pencil of rays thrown towards the horizon for the purpose of marking an isolated danger or the limits of a narrow channel. Such lights are best described by the French term *feux de direction*. Catoptric apparatus, by which dual condensation is produced, are moreover sometimes used for fixed lights, the light pencils overlapping each other in azimuth. Apparatus of the third class are employed for sector lights or those throwing a beam of light over a wider azimuth than can be conveniently covered by an apparatus of the second class, and for reinforcing the beam of light emergent from a fixed apparatus in any required direction.

The above classification of apparatus depends on the resultant effect of the optical elements. Another classification divides the instruments themselves into three classes: (*a*) catoptric, (*b*) dioptric and (*c*) catadioptric.

Catoptric apparatus are those by which the light rays are reflected only from the faces of incidence, such as silvered mirrors of plane, spherical, parabolic or other profile. *Dioptric* elements are those in which the light rays pass through the optical glass, suffering refraction at the incident and emergent faces (fig. 27). *Catadioptric* elements are combined of the two foregoing and consist of optical prisms in which the light rays suffer refraction at the incident face, total internal reflexion at a second face and again refraction on emergence at the third face (fig. 28).

The object of these several forms of optical apparatus is not

intervals. The cam-wheel is actuated by means of a weight or spring clock. Varying characteristics may be procured by means of such a contrivance—single, double, triple or other systems of occultation. The eclipses or periods of darkness bear much the same relation to the times of illumination as do the flashes to the eclipses in a revolving or flashing light. In the case of a first-order fixed light the cost of conversion to an occulting characteristic does not exceed £250 to £300. With apparatus illuminated by gas the occultations may be produced by successively raising and lowering the gas at stated intervals. Another form of occulting mechanism employed consists of a series of vertical screens mounted on … carriage and revolving …ind the burner. The car…e is rotated on rollers or …earings or carried upon …l mercury float. The …riving mechanism is a spring clock. …reens are used in …it is desired to …nt periods of … two or more …ith in order …ors mark- … screens …blacked … some … the …nd …

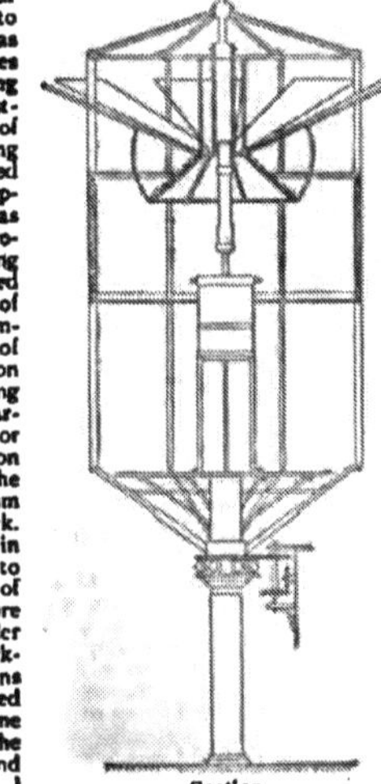

… Marstrand… Similar appa… were installed at Cordouan (1790), Flamborough Head (1806) and at the Bell Rock (1811). To produce a revolving or flashing light the reflectors were fixed on a revolving carriage having several faces. Three or more reflectors in a face were set with their axes parallel.

Fig. 21.—Rothersand Lighthouse.

A type of parabolic reflector now in use is shown in fig. 30. The sizes in general use vary from 21 in. to 24 in. diameter. These instruments are still largely used for light-vessel illumination, and a few important land lights are at the present time of catoptric type, including those at St Agnes (Scilly Islands), Cromer and St Anthony (Falmouth).

Dioptric System.—The first adaptation of dioptric lenses to lighthouses is probably due to T. Rogers, who used lenses at one of the Portland lighthouses between 1786 and 1790. Subsequently lenses by the same maker were used at Howth, Waterford and the North Foreland. Count Buffon had in 1748 proposed to grind out of a solid piece of glass a lens in steps or concentric zones in order to reduce the thickness to a minimum (fig. 31). Condorcet in 1773 and Sir D. Brewster in 1811 designed built-up lenses consisting of stepped annular rings. Neither of these proposals, however, was intended to apply to lighthouse purposes. In 1822 Augustin Fresnel constructed a built-up annular lens in which the centres of curvature of the different rings receded from the axis according to their distances from the centre, so as practically to eliminate spherical aberration; the only spherical surface being the small central part or "bull's eye" (fig. 32). These lenses were intended for revolving lights only. Fresnel next produced his cylindric refractor or lens belt, consisting of a zone of glass generated by the revolution round a vertical axis of a medial section of the annular lens (fig. 33). The lens belt condensed and parallelized the light rays in the vertical plane only, while the annular lens does so in every plane. The first revolving light constructed from Fresnel's designs was erected at the Cordouan lighthouse in 1823. It consisted of 8 panels of annular lenses placed round the lamp at a focal distance of 920 mm. To utilize the light,

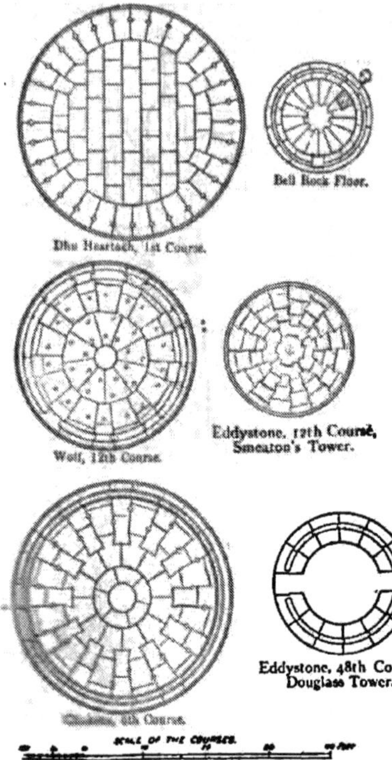

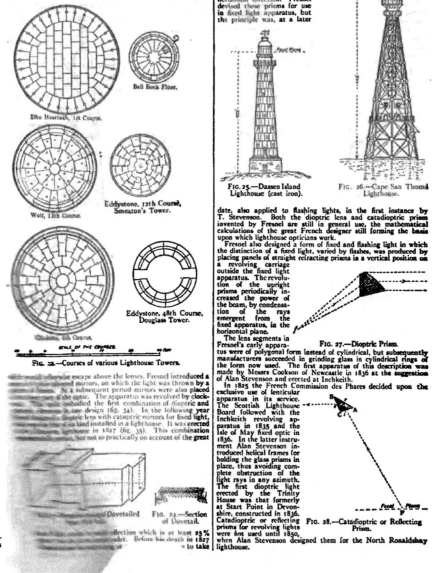

FIG. 22.—Courses of various Lighthouse Towers.

[illegible] escape above the lenses. Fresnel introduced a [illegible] mirrors, on which the light was thrown by a [illegible]. At a subsequent period mirrors were also placed [illegible] the optic. The apparatus was revolved by clock-[illegible] embodied the first combination of dioptric and [illegible] design (fig. 34). In the following year [illegible] lens with catoptric mirrors for fixed light, [illegible] installed in a lighthouse. It was erected [illegible] in 1827 (fig. 35). This combination [illegible] not so practically on account of the great

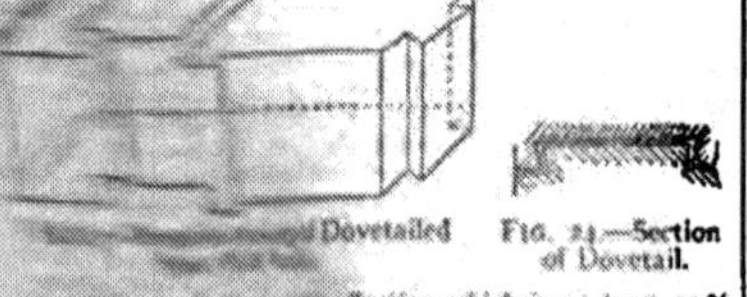

[illegible] Dovetailed [illegible]

FIG. 24.—Section of Dovetail.

[illegible] reflection which is at least 25% [illegible]. Before his death in 1827 [illegible] to take the place of the silvered reflectors previously used above and below the lens elements (fig. 28). The ray *Fi* falling on the prismoidal ring ABC is refracted in the direction *i r* and meeting the face AB at an angle of incidence greater than the critical, is totally reflected in the direction *r e* emerging after second refraction in a horizontal direction. Fresnel devised these prisms for use in fixed light apparatus, but the principle was, at a later date, also applied to flashing lights, in the first instance by T. Stevenson. Both the dioptric lens and catadioptric prism invented by Fresnel are still in general use, the mathematical calculations of the great French designer still forming the basis upon which lighthouse opticians work.

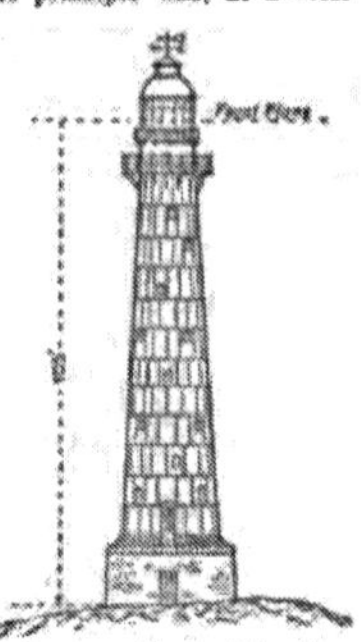

FIG. 25.—Dassen Island Lighthouse (cast iron).

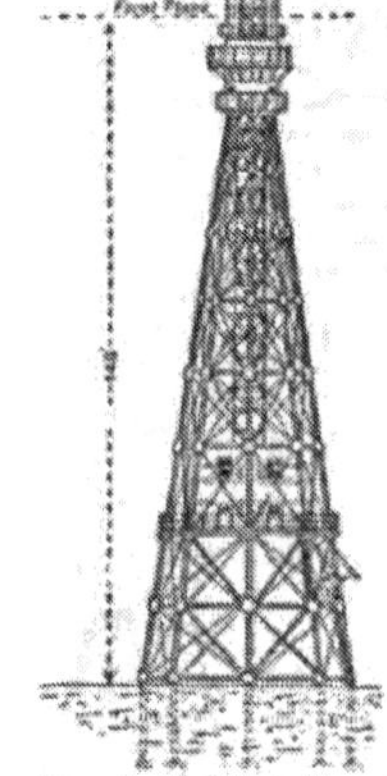

FIG. 26.—Cape San Thomé Lighthouse.

Fresnel also designed a form of fixed and flashing light in which the distinction of a fixed light, varied by flashes, was produced by placing panels of straight refracting prisms in a vertical position on a revolving carriage outside the fixed light apparatus. The revolution of the upright prisms periodically increased the power of the beam, by condensation of the rays emergent from the fixed apparatus, in the horizontal plane.

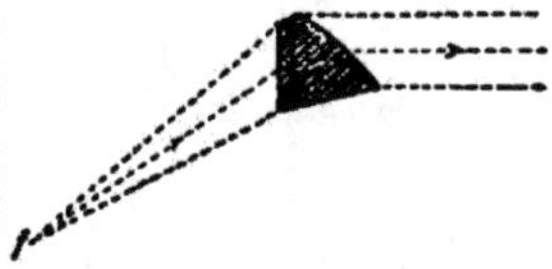

FIG. 27.—Dioptric Prism.

The lens segments in Fresnel's early apparatus were of polygonal form instead of cylindrical, but subsequently manufacturers succeeded in grinding glass in cylindrical rings of the form now used. The first apparatus of this description was made by Messrs Cookson of Newcastle in 1836 at the suggestion of Alan Stevenson and erected at Inchkeith.

In 1825 the French Commission des Phares decided upon the exclusive use of lenticular apparatus in its service. The Scottish Lighthouse Board followed with the Inchkeith revolving apparatus in 1835 and the Isle of May fixed optic in 1836. In the latter instrument Alan Stevenson introduced helical frames for holding the glass prisms in place, thus avoiding complete obstruction of the light rays in any azimuth. The first dioptric light erected by the Trinity House was that formerly at Start Point in Devonshire, constructed in 1836. Catadioptric or reflecting prisms for revolving lights were not used until 1850, when Alan Stevenson designed them for the North Ronaldshay lighthouse.

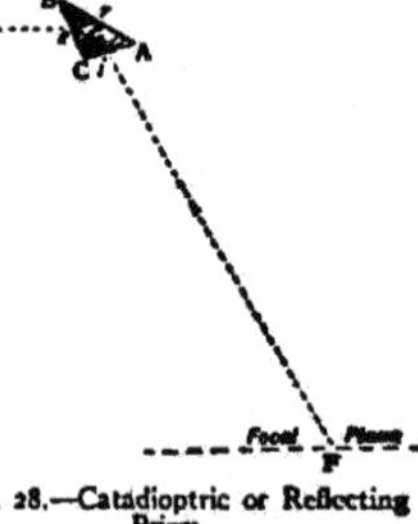

FIG. 28.—Catadioptric or Reflecting Prism.

Dioptric Mirror.—The next important improvement in lighthouse optical work was the invention of the dioptric spherical mirror by Mr (afterwards Sir) J. T. Chance in 1862. The zones or prisms are generated round a vertical axis and divided into segments. This form of mirror is still in general use (figs. 36 and 37).

Azimuthal Condensing Prisms.—Previous to 1850 all apparatus were designed to emit light of equal power in every azimuth either constantly or periodically. The only exception was where a light was situated on a stretch of coast where a mirror could be placed behind the flame to utilize the rays, which would otherwise pass landward, and reflect them back, passing through the flame and lens in a seaward direction. In order to increase the intensity of lights in certain azimuths T. Stevenson devised his azimuthal condensing prisms which, in various forms and methods of application, have been largely used for the purpose of strengthening the light rays in required directions as, for instance, where coloured sectors are provided. Applications of this system will be referred to subsequently.

Fig. 29.—Early Reflector and Lamp (1763).

Optical Glass for Lighthouses.—In the early days of lens lights the only glass used for the prisms was made in France at the St Gobain and Premontré works, which have long been celebrated for the high quality of optical glass produced. The early dioptric lights erected in the United Kingdom, some 13 in all, were made by Messrs Cookson of South Shields, who were instructed by Léonor Fresnel the brother of Augustin. At first they tried to mould the lens and then to grind it out of one thick sheet of glass. The successors of the Cookson firm abandoned the manufacture of lenses in 1845, and the firm of Letourneau & Lepaute of Paris again became the monopolists. In 1850 Messrs Chance Bros. & Co. of Birmingham began the manufacture of optical glass, assisted by M. Tabouret, a French expert who had been a colleague of Augustin Fresnel himself. The first light made by the firm was shown at the Great Exhibition of 1851, since when numerous dioptric apparatus have been constructed by Messrs Chance, who are, at this time, the only manufacturers of lighthouse glass in the United Kingdom. Most of the glass used for apparatus constructed in France is manufactured at St Gobain. Some of the glass used by German constructors is made at Rathenow in Prussia and Goslar in the Harz.

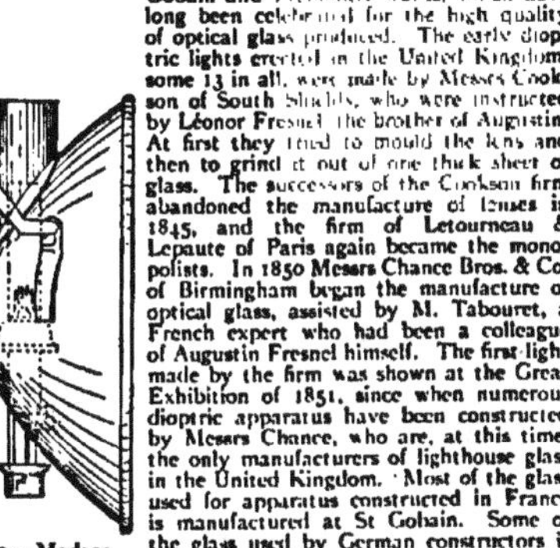

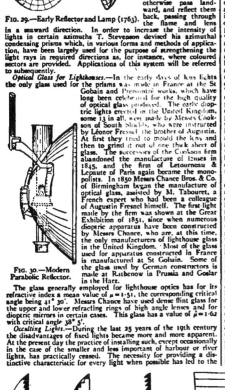

Fig. 30.—Modern Parabolic Reflector.

The glass generally employed for lighthouse optics has for its refractive index a mean value of $\mu = 1{\cdot}51$, the corresponding critical angle being 41° 30′. Messrs Chance have used dense flint glass for the upper and lower refracting rings of high angle lenses and for dioptric mirrors in certain cases. This glass has a value of $\mu = 1{\cdot}62$ with critical angle 38° 5′.

Occulting Lights.—During the last 25 years of the 19th century the disadvantages of fixed lights became more and more apparent. At the present day the practice of installing such, except occasionally in the case of the smaller and less important of harbour or river lights, has practically ceased. The necessity for providing a distinctive characteristic for every light when possible has led to the conversion of many of the fixed-light apparatus of earlier years into occulting lights, and often to their supersession by more modern and powerful flashing apparatus. An occulting apparatus in general use consists of a cylindrical screen, fitting over the burner, rapidly lowered and raised by means of a cam-wheel at stated intervals. The cam-wheel is actuated by means of a weight or spring clock. Varying characteristics may be procured by means of such a contrivance—single, double, triple or other systems of occultation. The eclipses or periods of darkness bear much the same relation to the times of illumination as do the flashes to the eclipses in a revolving or flashing light. In the case of a first-order fixed light the cost of conversion to an occulting characteristic does not exceed £250 to £300. With apparatus illuminated by gas the occultations may be produced by successively raising and lowering the gas at stated intervals. Another form of occulting mechanism employed consists of a series of vertical screens mounted on a carriage and revolving round the burner. The carriage is rotated on rollers or ball bearings or carried upon a small mercury float. The usual driving mechanism employed is a spring clock. "Otter" screens are used in cases when it is desired to produce different periods of occultations in two or more positions in azimuth in order to differentiate sectors marking shoals, &c. The screens are of sheet metal blacked and arranged vertically, somewhat in the manner of the laths of a venetian blind, and operated by mechanical means.

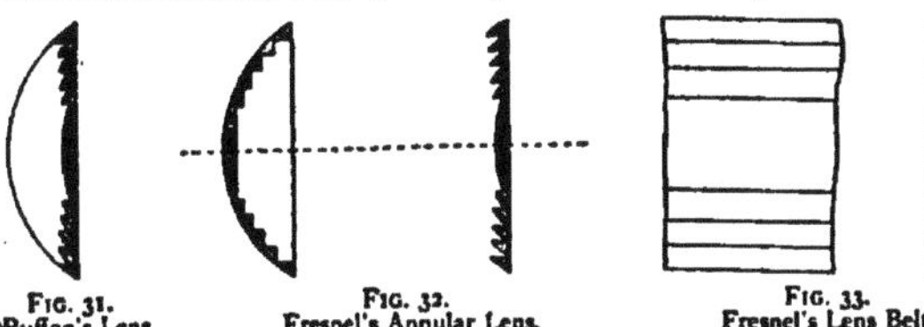

Fig. 31. Buffon's Lens. Fig. 32. Fresnel's Annular Lens. Fig. 33. Fresnel's Lens Belt.

Leading Lights.—In the case of lights designed to act as a lead through a narrow channel or as direction lights, it is undesirable to employ a flashing apparatus. Fixed-light optics are employed to meet such cases, and are generally fitted with occulting mechanism. A typical apparatus of this description is that at Gage Roads, Fremantle, West Australia (fig. 38). The occulting bright light covers the fairway, and is flanked by sectors of occulting red and green light marking dangers and intensified by vertical condensing prisms. A good example of a holophotal direction light was exhibited at the 1900 Paris Exhibition, and afterwards erected at Suzac lighthouse (France). The light consists of an annular lens 500 mm. focal distance, of 180° horizontal angle and 157° vertical, with a mirror of 180° at the back. The lens throws a red beam of about 4½° amplitude in azimuth, and 50,000 candle-power over a narrow channel. The illuminant is an incandescent petroleum vapour burner. Holophotal direction lenses of this type can only be applied where the sector to be marked is of comparatively small angle. Silvered metallic mirrors of parabolic form are also used for the purpose. The use of single direction lights frequently renders the construction of separate towers for leading lights unnecessary.

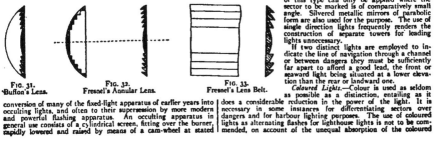

Section

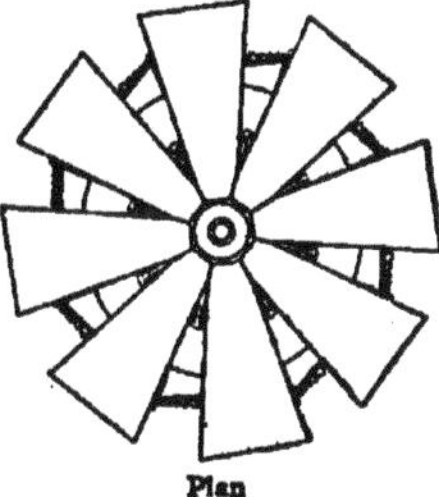

Plan

Fig. 34.—Fresnel's Revolving Apparatus at Cordouan Lighthouse.

If two distinct lights are employed to indicate the line of navigation through a channel or between dangers they must be sufficiently far apart to afford a good lead, the front or seaward light being situated at a lower elevation than the rear or landward one.

Coloured Lights.—Colour is used as seldom as possible as a distinction, entailing as it does a considerable reduction in the power of the light. It is necessary in some instances for differentiating sectors over dangers and for harbour lighting purposes. The use of coloured lights as alternating flashes for lighthouse lights is not to be commended, on account of the unequal absorption of the coloured the atmosphere. When such distinction ... employed, as in the Wolf Rock apparatus, the red and ... be approximately equalized in initial intensity by ... the lens and prism panels for the red light of larger ... the white beams. Owing to the absorption by

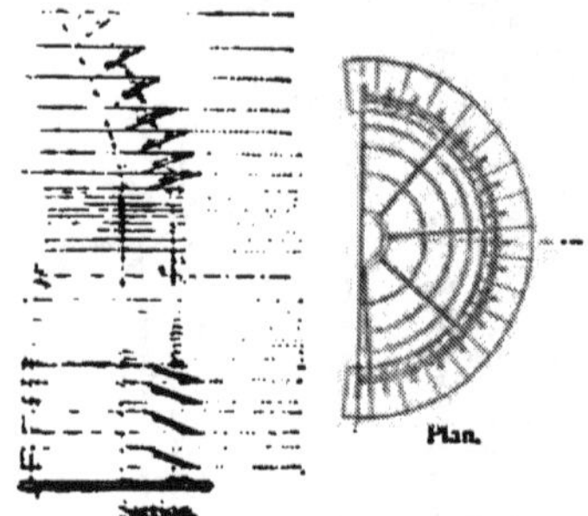

Fig. 35.—... Apparatus at Chassiron Lighthouse (1827).

the ... the power of a red beam is only 40% of the ... corresponding white light. The corresponding ... light is 25%. When red or green sectors are ... invariably be reinforced by mirrors, azimuthal ... or other means to raise the coloured beam to ... same intensity as the white light. With the ... group-flashing characteristics the necessity for using ... distinction disappeared.

... *Lenses*.—Messrs Chance of Birmingham have ... having 97° of vertical amplitude, but this result was only attained by using dense flint glass of high refractive index for the upper and lower elements. It is doubtful, however, whether the use of refracting elements for a

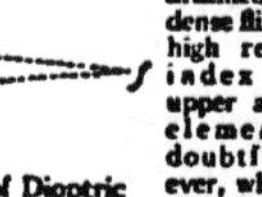

... Prism of Dioptric ... Mirror.

... is attended by any material

... One of the most useful distinctions ... more flashes separated by short ... being succeeded by a longer eclipse. ... say, half second duration or less ... about 2 seconds and are succeeded ... the sequence being completed in a ... Dr John Hopkinson introduced ... dividing the lenses of a dioptric

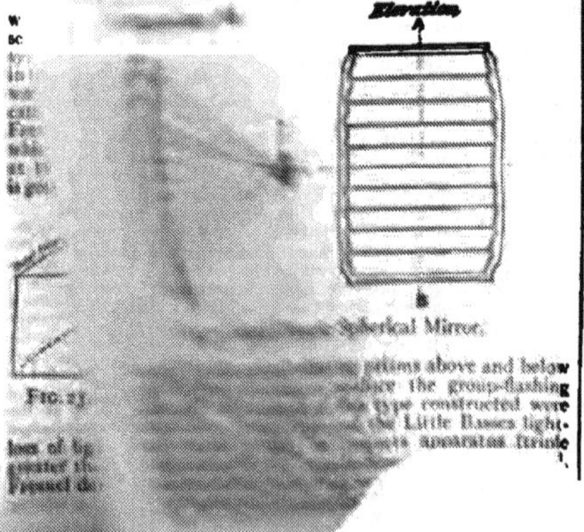

Spherical Mirror.

... prisms above and below ... the group-flashing ... type constructed were ... the Little Basses light- ... apparatus ...

at Pendeen in Cornwall is shown in fig. 39; and fig. 55 (Plate I.) illustrates a double flashing first order light at Pachena Point in British Columbia. Hopkinson's system has been very extensively used, most of the group-flashing lights shown in the accompanying tables, being designed upon the general lines he introduced. A modification of the system consists in grouping two or more lenses

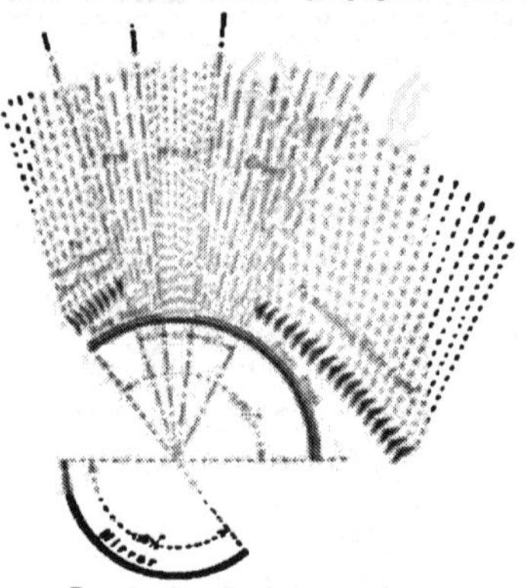

Fig. 38.—Gage Roads Direction Light

together separated by equal angles, and filling the ... in azimuth by a reinforcing mirror or screen. ... distinction was proposed for gas lights by J. R. W... who obtained it in the case of a revolving apparat... raising and lowering the flame. The first apparatus in w... method was employed was erected at Galley Head, Co. Cork (18...). At this lighthouse 4 of Wigham's large gas burners with four tiers of first-order revolving lenses, eight in each tier, were adopted. By successive lowering and raising of the gas flame at the focus of each tier of lenses he produced the group-flashing distinction. The light showed, instead of one prolonged flash at intervals of one minute, as would be produced by the apparatus in the absence of a gas occulter, a group of short flashes varying in number between six and seven. The uncertainty, however, in the number of flashes contained in each group is found to be an objection to the arrangement. This device was adopted at other gas-illuminated stations in Ireland at subsequent dates. The quadriform apparatus and gas installation at Galley Head were superseded in 1907 by a first order biform apparatus with incandescent oil vapour burner showing five flashes every 20 seconds.

Flashing Lights indicating Numbers.—Captain F. A. Mahan, late engineer secretary to the United States Lighthouse Board, devised for that service a system of flashing lights to indicate certain numbers. The apparatus installed at Minot's Ledge lighthouse near Boston Harbour, Massachusetts, has a flash indicating the number 143, thus: - ---- ---, the dashes indicating short flashes. Each group is separated by a longer period of darkness than that between successive members of a group. The flashes in a group indicating a figure are about 1½ seconds apart, the groups being 3 seconds apart, an interval of 16 seconds' darkness occurring between each repetition. Thus the number is repeated every half minute. Two examples of this system were exhibited by the United States Lighthouse Board at the Chicago Exhibition in 1893, viz. the second-order apparatus just mentioned and a similar light of the first order for Cape Charles on the Virginian coast. The lenses are arranged in a somewhat

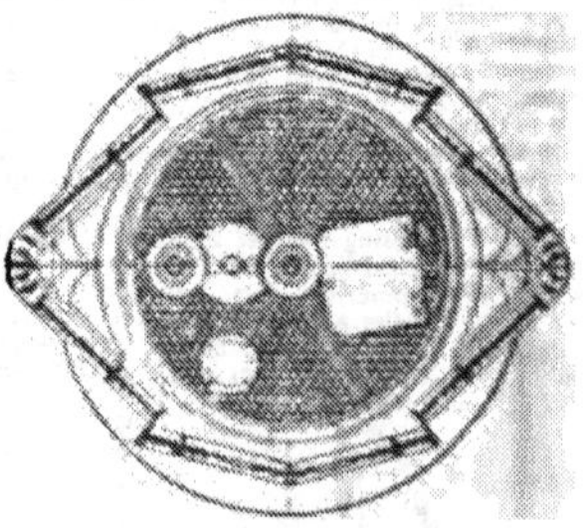

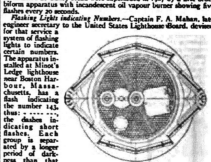

Fig. 39.—Pendeen Apparatus. Plan at Focal Plane.

similar manner to an ordinary grow... lenses being placed on one side of th... vided with a catadioptric mirror. Th... for lighthouses has been frequentl... notably by Lord Kelvin. The instal... however, the first practical applicat... important coast lights. The great c... the lights of any country to compl... numerical system is one of the object...

Hyper-radial Apparatus.—In 1885 ... structed the first hyper-radial appar... to the design of Messrs D. and C. St... 1812 mm. It was tested during the ... comparison with other lenses, and ... with burners of large focal diamete... distance (1330 mm.) were subseq... Island, Bishop Rock, and Spurn P... Sule Skerry (fig. 40) in Scotland, I...

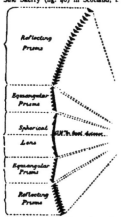

...he several sizes in use:—

...ngles of Optics. ...Dimensions.)	
...hotal Optics.	
	Upper Prisms.
	48° 8°

Reflecting Prisms

Equiangular Prisms

Spherical Lens

Equiangular Prisms

Reflecting Prisms

Fig. 40.—Sule Skerry Apparatus.

Manora ... India, in 1908 (fig. 41).

The introduction of incandescent and other burners of focal compactness and high intensity has rendered the use of optics of such large dimensions as the above, intended for burners of great focal diameter, unnecessary. It is now possible to obtain with a second-order optic (or one of 700 mm. focal distance), having a powerful incandescent petroleum burner in focus, a beam of equal intensity to that which would be obtained from the apparatus having a 10-wick oil burner or 108-jet gas burner at its focus.

Stephenson's Spherical Lenses and Equiangular Prisms.—Mr C. A. Stephenson in 1888 designed a form of lens spherical in the horizontal and vertical sections. This admitted of the construction of lenses of long focal distance without the otherwise corresponding necessity of increased diameter of lantern. A lens of this type and of 1330 mm. focal distance was constructed in 1890 for Fair Isle lighthouse. The spherical form loses in efficiency if carried beyond an angle subtending 20° at the focus, and to obviate this loss Mr Stephenson designed his equiangular prisms, which have an inclination outwards. It is claimed by the designer that the use of equiangular prisms results in less loss of light and less divergence than is the case when either the spherical or Fresnel form is adopted. An example of this design is seen (fig. 40) in the Sule Skerry apparatus (1895).

Fixed and Flashing Lights.—The use of these lights, which show a fixed beam varied at intervals by more powerful flashes, is not to be recommended, though a large number were constructed in the earlier years of dioptric illumination and many are still in existence. The distinction can be produced in one or other of three ways: (*a*) by the revolution of detached panels of straight condensing lens prisms placed vertically around a fixed light optic, (*b*) by utilizing revolving lens panels in the middle portion of the optic to produce the flashing light, the upper and lower sections of the apparatus being fixed zones of catadioptric or reflecting elements emitting a fixed belt of light, and (*c*) by interposing panels of fixed light section between the flashing light panels of a revolving apparatus. In certain conditions of the atmosphere it is possible for the fixed light of low power to be entirely obscured while the flashes are visible, thus vitiating the true characteristic of the light. Cases have frequently occurred of such lights being mistaken for, and even described in lists of light as, revolving or flashing lights.

"*Cute*" *and Screens.*—Screens of coloured glass, intended to distinguish the light in particular azimuths, and of sheet iron, when it is desired to "cut off" the light sharply on any angle, should be

Light Intensities.—The powers of lighthouse lights in the British Empire are expressed in terms of standard candles or in "lighthouse units" (one lighthouse unit = 1000 standard candles). In France the unit is the "Carcel" = 9.52 standard candle. The powers of burners and optical apparatus, then in use in the United Kingdom, were carefully determined by actual photometric measurement in 1892 by a committee consisting of the engineers of the three general lighthouse boards, and the values so obtained are used as the basis for calculating the intensities of all British lights. It was

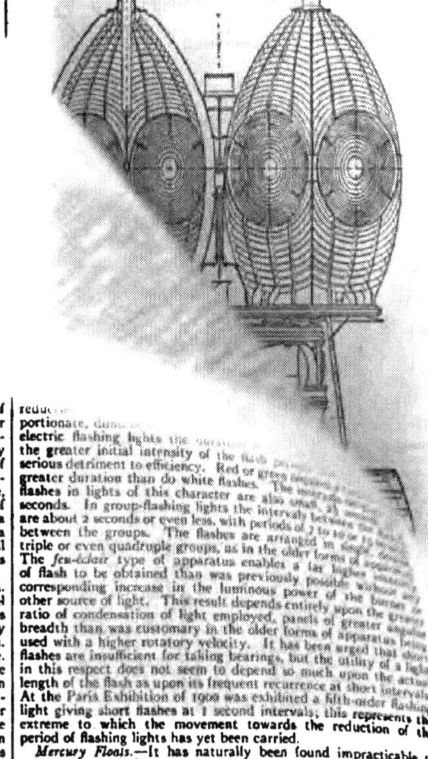

reduc... portionate, ... electric flashing lights the ... the greater initial intensity of the flash ... serious detriment to efficiency. Red or green ... greater duration than do white flashes. The ... flashes in lights of this character are also ... seconds. In group-flashing lights the intervals ... are about 2 seconds or even less, with periods of ... between the groups. The flashes are arranged in ... triple or even quadruple groups, as in the older forms ... The *feu-éclair* type of apparatus enables a far higher ... of flash to be obtained than was previously possible without ... corresponding increase in the luminous power of the burner ... other source of light. This result depends entirely upon the ... ratio of condensation of light employed, panels of greater ... breadth than was customary in the older forms of apparatus being used with a higher rotatory velocity. It has been urged that ... flashes are insufficient for taking bearings, but the utility of a light in this respect does not seem to depend so much upon the actual length of the flash as upon its frequent recurrence at short intervals. At the Paris Exhibition of 1900 was exhibited a fifth-order flashing light giving short flashes at 1 second intervals; this represents the extreme to which the movement towards the reduction of the period of flashing lights has yet been carried.

Mercury Floats.—It has naturally been found impracticable to revolve the optical apparatus of a light with its mountings, sometimes weighing over 7 tons, at the high rate of speed required for *feux-éclairs* by means of the old system of roller carriages, though for some small quick-revolving lights ball bearings have been successfully adopted. It has therefore become almost the universal practice to carry the rotating portions of the apparatus upon a mercury float. This beautiful application of mercury rotation was the invention of Bourdelles, and is now utilized not only for the high-speed apparatus, but also generally for the few examples of the older type still being constructed. The arrangement consists of an annular cast iron bath or trough of such dimensions that a similar but slightly smaller annular float immersed in the bath and surrounded by mercury displaces a volume of the liquid metal whose weight is equal to that of the apparatus supported. Thus a comparatively insignificant quantity of mercury, say 2 cwt., serves to ensure the flotation of a mass of over 3 tons. Certain differences exist between the type of float usually constructed in France and those generally designed by English engineers. In all cases provision is made for lowering the mercury bath or raising the float and apparatus for examination. Examples of mercury floats are shown in figs. 41, 42, 43 and Plate I., figs. 54 an 55.

of mean horizontal divergence, and C = constant varying between ·9 and ·75 according to the description of apparatus. The factor H/h must be eliminated in the case of fixed lights. Deduction must also be made in the case of coloured lights. It should, however, be pointed out that photometric measurements alone can be relied upon to give accurate values for lighthouse intensities. The values

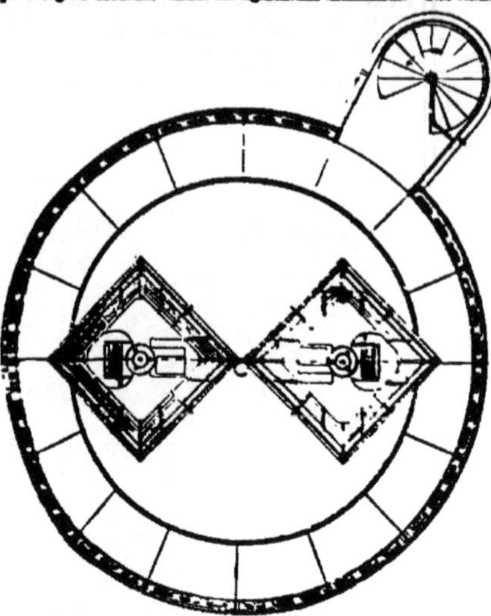

FIG. 43a.—Île Vierge Apparatus and Lantern. Plan at focal plane.

[illegible] the use of Allard's formulae, which were largely used [illegible] for actual photometric measurements came to [illegible] considerably in excess of the true intensities.

[illegible]—The mathematical theory of optical apparatus [illegible] and formulae for the calculations of profiles will [illegible] works of the Stevensons, Chance, Allard, Reynaud, [illegible] Particulars of typical lighthouse apparatus [illegible] in tables VI. and VII.

4. ILLUMINANTS.—The earliest form of illuminant used for [illegible] was a fire of coal or wood set in a brazier or grate [illegible] on top of the lighthouse tower. Until the end of the 18th [illegible] the 19th century this primitive illuminant continued [illegible] the only one in use. The coal fire at the Isle of [illegible] until 1810 and that at St Bees lighthouse [illegible] till 1823. Fires are stated to have been used [illegible] of Nidingen, in the Kattegat, until 1846. [illegible] the first to use any form of illuminant other than [illegible] within the lantern of his Eddystone light- [illegible] holding 24 tallow candles each of which [illegible] and emitted a light of 2·8 candle power. [illegible] power was 67·2 candles and the [illegible] at the rate of 3·4 lb per hour.

[illegible] were used in the Liverpool light- [illegible] between 1780 and 1783, perfected [illegible] provides a central current of air [illegible] the more perfect combustion of [illegible] in the diameter of [illegible] is due to Lange, and the [illegible] by Count Rumford. [illegible] three and four concentric [illegible] was used in English [illegible] colza oil was employed [illegible] Olive oil, lard oil and [illegible] purposes in various [illegible]

[illegible] ing a [illegible] olu- [illegible] hat [illegible] ion [illegible] ty.

The invention was quickly taken advantage of by lighthouse authorities, and the "Doty" burner, and other patterns involving the same principle, remained practically the only oil burners in lighthouse use until the last few years of the 19th century.

The lamps used for supplying oil to the burner are of two general types, viz. those in which the oil is maintained under pressure by mechanical action and constant level lamps. In the case of single wick, and some 2-wick burners, oil is supplied to the burner by the capillary action of the wick alone.

The mineral oils ordinarily in use are petroleum, which for lighthouse purposes should have a specific gravity of from ·820 to ·830 at 60° F. and flashing point of not less than 230° F. (Abel close test), and Scottish shale oil or paraffin with a specific gravity of about ·810 at 60° F. and flash point of 140° to 165° F. Both these varieties may be obtained in England at a cost of about 6½d. per gallon in bulk.

Coal Gas had been introduced in 1837 at the inner pier light of Troon (Ayrshire) and in 1847 it was in use at the Heugh lighthouse (West Hartlepool). In 1878 cannel coal gas was adopted for the Galley Head lighthouse, with 108-jet Wigham burners. Sir James Douglass introduced gas burners consisting of concentric rings, two to ten in number, perforated on the upper edges. These give excellent results and high intensity, 2600 candles in the case of the 10-ring burner with a flame diameter at the focal plane of 5½ in. They are still in use at certain stations. The use of multiple ring and jet gas burners is not being further extended. Gas for lighthouse purposes generally requires to be specially made; the erection of gas works at the station is thus necessitated and a considerable outlay entailed which is avoided by the use of oil as an illuminant.

Incandescent Coal Gas Burners.—The invention of the Welsbach mantle placed at the disposal of the lighthouse authorities the means of producing a light of high intensity combined with great focal compactness. For lighthouse purposes other gaseous illuminants than coal gas are as a rule more convenient and economical, and give better results with incandescent mantles. Mantles have, however, been used with ordinary coal gas in many instances where a local supply is available.

Incandescent Mineral Oil Burners.—Incandescent lighting with high-flash mineral oil was first introduced by the French Lighthouse Service in 1898 at L'Île Penfret lighthouse. The burners employed are all made on the same principle, but differ slightly in details according to the type of lighting apparatus for which they are intended. The principle consists in injecting the liquid petroleum in the form of spray mixed with air into a vaporizer heated by the mantle flame or by a subsidiary heating burner. A small reservoir of compressed air is used—charged by means of a hand pump—for providing the necessary pressure for injection. On first ignition the vaporizer is heated by a spirit flame to the required temperature. A reservoir air pressure of 125 lb per sq. in. is employed, a reducing valve supplying air to the oil at from 60 to 65 lb per sq. in. Small reservoirs containing liquefied carbon dioxide have also been employed for supplying the requisite pressure to the oil vessel.

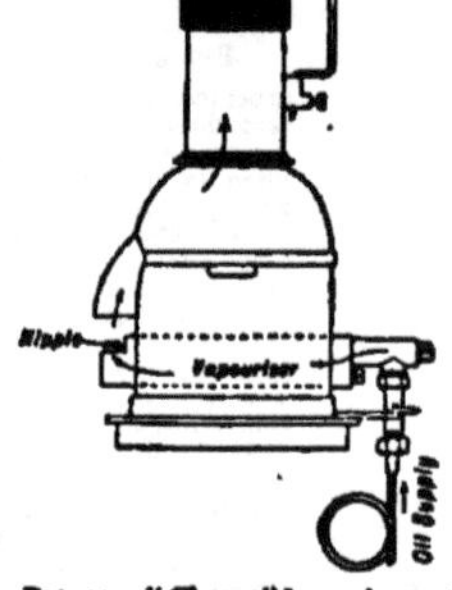

FIG. 44.—"Chance" Incandescent Oil Burner, with 85 mm. diameter mantle.

The candle-power of apparatus in which ordinary multiple wick burners were formerly employed is increased by over 300% by the substitution of suitable incandescent oil burners. In 1902 incandescent oil burners were adopted by the general lighthouse authorities in the United Kingdom. The burners used in the Trinity House Service and some of those made in France have the vaporizers placed over the flame. In other forms, of which the "Chance" burner (fig. 44) is a type, the vaporization is effected by means of a subsidiary burner placed under the main flame.

Particulars of the sizes of burner in ordinary use are given in the following table.

Diameter of Mantle.	Service Intensity.	Consumption of oil. Pints per hour.
35 mm.	600 candles.	·50
55 mm.	1200 „	1·00
85 mm.	2150 „	2·25
Triple mantle 50 mm.	3300 „	3·00

Fig. 54.—Fastnet Lighthouse—First Order Single-Flashing Biform Apparatus.

Fig. 55.—Pachena Point Lighthouse, B.C.—First Order Double-Flashing Apparatus.

LIGHTHOUSE

Fig. 56.—Old Eddystone Lighthouse.

Fig. 57 —Eddystone Lighthouse.

Fig. 58.—Il[illegible]e.

Fig. 59.—Minot's Ledge Lighthouse.

The intrinsic brightness of incandescent burners generally may be taken as being equivalent to from 30 candles to 40 candles per sq. cm. of the vertical section of the incandescent mantle.

In the case of wick burners, the intrinsic brightness varies, according to the number of wicks and the type of burner from about 3·5 candles to about 12 candles per sq. cm., the value being at its maximum with the larger type of burner. The luminous intensity of a beam from a dioptric apparatus is, *cæteris paribus*, proportional to the intrinsic brightness of the luminous source of flame, and not of the total luminous intensity. The intrinsic brightness of the flame of oil burners increases only slightly with their focal diameter, consequently while the consumption of oil increases the efficiency of the burner for a given apparatus decreases. The illuminating power of the condensed beam can only be improved to a slight extent, and, in fact, is occasionally decreased, by increasing the number of wicks in the burner. The same argument applies to the case of multiple ring and multiple jet gas burners which, notwithstanding their large total intensity, have comparatively small intrinsic brightness. The economy of the new system is instanced by the case of the Eddystone bi-form apparatus, which with the concentric 6-wick burner consuming 2500 gals. of oil per annum, gave a total intensity of 79,250 candles. Under the new régime the intensity is 292,000 candles, the oil consumption being practically halved.

Incandescent Oil Gas Burners.—It has been mentioned that incandescence with low-pressure coal gas produces flames of comparatively small intrinsic brightness. Coal gas cannot be compressed beyond a small extent without considerable injurious condensation and other accompanying evils. Recourse has therefore been had to compressed oil gas, which is capable of undergoing compression to 10 or 12 atmospheres with little detriment, and can conveniently be stored in portable reservoirs. The burner employed resembles the ordinary Bunsen burner with incandescent mantle, and the rate of consumption of gas is 27·5 cub. in. per hour per candle. A reducing valve is used for supplying the gas to the burner at constant pressure. The burners can be left unattended for considerable periods. The system was first adopted in France, where it is installed at eight lighthouses, among others the Ar'men Rock light, and has been extended to other parts of the world including several stations in Scotland and England. The mantles used in France are of 35 mm. diameter. The 35 mm. mantle gives a candle-power of 400, with an intrinsic brightness of 20 candles per sq. cm.

The use of oil gas necessitates the erection of gas works at the lighthouse or its periodical supply in portable reservoirs from a neighbouring station. A complete gas works plant costs about £800. The annual expenditure for gas lighting in France does not exceed £72 per light where works are installed, or £32 where gas is supplied from elsewhere. In the case of petroleum vapour lighting the annual cost of oil amounts to about £26 per station.

Acetylene.—The high illuminating power and intrinsic brightness of the flame of acetylene makes it a very suitable illuminant for lighthouses and beacons, providing certain difficulties attending its use can be overcome. At Grangemouth an unattended 21-day beacon has been illuminated by an acetylene flame for some years with considerable success, and a beacon light designed to run unattended for six months was established on Bedout Island in Western Australia in 1910. Acetylene has also been used in the United States, Germany, the Argentine, China, Canada, &c., for lighthouse and beacon illumination. Many buoys and beacons on the German and Dutch coasts have been supplied with oil gas mixed with 20% of acetylene, thereby obtaining an increase of over 100% in illuminating intensity. In France an incandescent burner consuming acetylene gas mixed with air has been installed at the Chassiron lighthouse (1902). The French Lighthouse Service has perfected an incandescent acetylene burner with a 55 mm. mantle having an intensity of over 2000 candle-power, with intrinsic brightness of 60 candles per sq. cm.

Electricity.—The first installation of electric light for lighthouse purposes in England took place in 1858 at the South Foreland, where the Trinity House established a temporary plant for experimental purposes. This installation was followed in 1862 by the adoption of the illuminant at the Dungeness lighthouse, where it remained in service until the year 1874 when oil was substituted for electricity. The earliest of the permanent installations now existing in England is that at Souter Point which was illuminated in 1871. There are in England four important coast lights illuminated by electricity, and one, viz. Isle of May, in Scotland. Of the former St Catherine's, in the Isle of Wight, and the Lizard are the most powerful. Elctricity was substituted as an illuminant for the then existing oil light at St Catherine's in 1888. The optical apparatus consisted of a second-order 16-sided revolving lens, which was transferred to the South Foreland station in 1904, and a new second order (700 mm.) four-sided optic with a vertical angle of 139°, exhibiting a flash of ·21 second duration every 5 seconds substituted for it. A fixed holophote is placed inside the optic in the dark or landward arc, and at the focal plane of the lamp. This holophote condenses the rays from the arc falling upon it into a pencil of small angle, which is directed horizontally upon a series of reflecting prisms which again bend the light and throw it downwards through an aperture in the lantern floor on to another series of prisms, which latter direct the rays seaward in the form of a sector of fixed red light at a lower level in the tower. A somewhat similar arrangement exists at Souter Point lighthouse.

The apparatus installed at the Lizard in 1903 is similar to that at St Catherine's, but has no arrangement for producing a subsidiary sector light. The flash is of ·13 seconds duration every 3 seconds. The apparatus replaced the two fixed electric lights erected in 1878.

The Isle of May lighthouse, at the mouth of the Firth of Forth, was first illuminated by electricity in 1886. The optical apparatus consists of a second-order fixed-light lens with reflecting prisms, and is surrounded by a revolving system of vertical condensing prisms which split up the vertically condensed beam of light into 8 separate beams of 3° in azimuth. The prisms are so arranged that the apparatus, making one complete revolution in the minute, produces a group characteristic of 4 flashes in quick succession every 30 seconds (fig. 45). The fixed light is not of the ordinary Fresnel

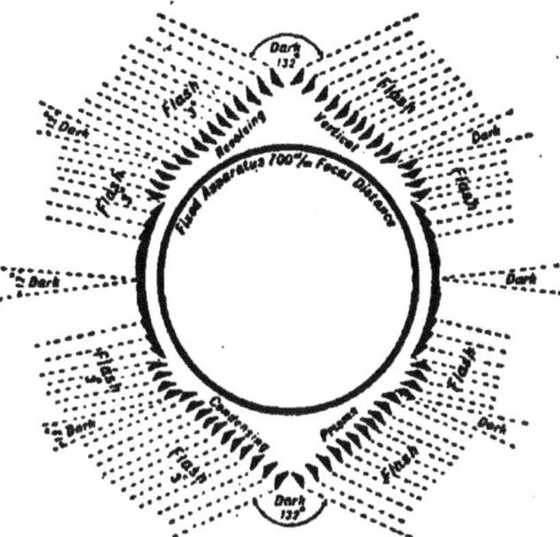

FIG. 45.—Isle of May Apparatus.

section, the refracting portion being confined to an angle of 10°, and the remainder of the vertical section consisting of reflecting prisms.

In France the old south lighthouse at La Hève was lit by electricity in 1863. This installation was followed in 1865 by a similar one at the north lighthouse. In 1910 there were thirteen important coast lights in France illuminated by electricity. In other parts of the world, Macquarie lighthouse, Sydney, was lit by electricity in 1883; Tino, in the gulf of Spezia, in 1885; and Navesink lighthouse, near the entrance to New York Bay, in 1898. Electric apparatus were also installed at the lighthouse at Port Said in 1869, on the opening of the canal; Odessa in 1871; and at the Rothersand, North Sea, in 1885. There are several other lights in various parts of the world illuminated by this agency.

Incandescent electric lighting has been adopted for the illumination of certain light-vessels in the United States, and a few small harbour and port lights, beacons and buoys.

Table VI. gives particulars of some of the more important electric lighthouses of the world.

Electric Lighthouse Installations in France.—A list of the thirteen lighthouses on the French coast equipped with electric light installations will be found in table VI. It has been already mentioned that the two lighthouses at La Hève were lit by electric light in 1863 and 1865. These installations were followed within a few years by the establishment of electricity as illuminant at Gris-Nez. In 1882 M. Allard, the then director-general of the French Lighthouse Service, prepared a scheme for the electric lighting of the French littoral by means of 46 lights distributed more or less uniformly along the coast-line. All the apparatus were to be of the same general type, the optics consisting of a fixed belt of 300 mm. focal distance, around the outside of which revolved a system of 24 faces of vertical lenses. These vertical panels condensed the belt of fixed light into beams of 3° amplitude in azimuth, producing flashes of about ⅛ sec. duration. To illuminate the near sea the vertical divergence of the lower prisms of the fixed belt was artificially increased. These optics are very similar to that in use at the Souter Point lighthouse, Sunderland. The intensities obtained were 120,000 candles in the case of fixed lights and 900,000 candles with flashing lights. As a result of a nautical inquiry held in 1886, at which date the lights of Dunkerque, Calais, Gris-Nez, La Canche, Baleines and

Planier had been lighted, in addition to the old apparatus at La Hève, it was decided to limit the installation of electrical apparatus to important landfall lights—a decision which the Trinity House had already arrived at in the case of the English coast—and to establish new apparatus at six stations only. These were Créac'h d'Ouessant (Ushant), Belle- Île, La Coubre at the mouth of the river Gironde, Barfleur, Île d'Yeu and Penmarc'h. At the same time it was determined to increase the powers of the existing electric lights. The scheme as amended in 1886 was completed in 1902.[1]

All the electrically lit apparatus, in common with other optics established in France since 1893, have been provided with mercury rotation. The most recent electric lights have been constructed in the form of twin apparatus, two complete and distinct optics being mounted side by side upon the same revolving table and with corresponding faces parallel. It is found that a far larger aggregate candle-power is obtained from two lamps with 16 mm. to 23 mm. diameter carbons and currents of 60 to 120 amperes than with carbons and currents of larger dimensions in conjunction with single optics of greater focal distance. A somewhat similar circumstance led to the choice of the twin form for the two very powerful non-electric apparatus at Île Vierge (figs. 43 and 43A) and Ailly, particulars of which will be seen in table VII.

Several of the de Meritens magneto-electric machines of 5·5 K.W., laid down many years ago at French electric lighthouse stations, are still in use. All these machines have five induction coils, which, upon the installation of the twin optics, were separated into two distinct circuits, each consisting of 24 coils. This modification has enabled the old plants to be used with success under the altered conditions of lighting entailed by the use of two lamps. The generators adopted in the French service for use at the later stations differ materially from the old type of de Meritens machine. The Phare d'Eckmühl (Penmarc'h) installation serves as a type of the more modern machinery. The dynamos are alternating current two-phase machines, and are installed in duplicate. The two lamps are supplied with current from the same machine, the second dynamo being held in reserve. The speed is 810 to 820 revolutions per minute.

The lamp generally adopted is a combination of the Serrin and Berjot principles, with certain modifications. Clockwork mechanism with a regulating electro-magnet moves the rods simultaneously and controls the movements of the carbons so that they are displaced at the same rate as they are consumed. It is usual to employ currents of varying power with carbons of corresponding dimensions according to the atmospheric conditions. In the French service two variations are used in the case of twin apparatus produced by currents of 60 and 120 amperes at 45 volts with carbons 14 mm. and 18 mm. diameter, while in single optic apparatus currents of 25, 50 and 100 amperes are utilized with carbon of 11 mm., 16 mm. and 23 mm. diameter. In England fluted carbons of larger diameter are employed with correspondingly increased current. Alternating currents have given the most successful results in all respects. Attempts to utilize continuous current for lighthouse arc lights have, up to the present, met with little success.

The cost of a first-class electric lighthouse installation of the most recent type in France, including optical apparatus, lantern, dynamos, engines, air compressor, siren, &c., but not buildings, amounts approximately to £5900.

Efficiency of the Electric Light.—In 1883 the lighthouse authorities of Great Britain determined that an exhaustive series of experiments should be carried out at the South Foreland with a view to ascertaining the relative suitability of electricity, gas and oil as lighthouse illuminants. The experiments extended over a period of more than twelve months, and were attended by representatives of the chief lighthouse authorities of the world. The results of the trials tended to show that the rays of oil and gas lights suffered to about equal extent by atmospheric absorption, but that oil had the advantage over gas by reason of its greater economy in cost of maintenance and in initial outlay on installation. The electric light was found to suffer to a much larger extent than either oil or gas light per unit of power by atmospheric absorption, but the infinitely greater total intensity of the beam obtainable by its use, both by reason of the high luminous intensity of the electric arc and its focal compactness, more than outweighed the higher percentage of loss in fog. The final conclusion of the committee on the relative merits of electricity, gas or oil as lighthouse illuminants is given in the following words: "That for ordinary necessities of lighthouse illumination, mineral oil is the most suitable and economical illuminant, and that for salient headlands, important landfalls, and places where a very powerful light is required electricity offers the greater advantages."

5. Miscellaneous Lighthouse Equipment. *Lanterns.*—Modern lighthouse lanterns usually consist of a cast iron or steel pedestal, cylindrical in plan, on which is erected the lantern glazing, surmounted by a domed roof and ventilator (fig. 41). Adequate ventilation is of great importance, and is provided by means of ventilators in the pedestal and a large ventilating dome or cowl in the roof. The astragals carrying the glazing are of wrought steel or gun-metal. The astragals are frequently arranged helically or diagonally, thus causing a minimum of obstruction to the light rays in any vertical section and affording greater rigidity to the structure. The glazing is usually ¼-in. thick plate-glass curved to the radius of the lantern. In situations of great exposure the thickness is increased. Lantern roofs are of sheet steel or copper secured to steel or cast-iron rafter frames. In certain instances it is found necessary to erect a grille or network outside the lantern to prevent the numerous sea birds, attracted by the light, from breaking the glazing by impact. Lanterns vary in diameter from 5 ft. to 16 ft. or more, according to the size of the optical apparatus. For first order apparatus a diameter of 12 ft. or 14 ft. is usual.

Lightning Conductors.—The lantern and principal metallic structures in a lighthouse are usually connected to a lightning conductor carried either to a point below low water or terminating in an earth plate embedded in wet ground. Conductors may be of copper tape or copper-wire rope.

Rotating Machinery.—Flashing-light apparatus are rotated by clockwork mechanism actuated by weights. The clocks are fitted with speed governors and electric warning apparatus to indicate variation in speed and when rewinding is required. For occulting apparatus either weight clocks or spring clocks are employed.

Accommodation for Keepers, &c.—At rock and other isolated stations, accommodation for the keepers is usually provided in the towers. In the case of land lighthouses, dwellings are provided in close proximity to the tower. The service or watch room should be situated immediately under the lantern floor. Oil is usually stored in galvanized steel tanks. A force pump is sometimes used for pumping oil from the storage tanks to a service tank in the watch-room or lantern.

6. Unattended Lights and Beacons.—Until recent years no unattended lights were in existence. The introduction of Pintsch's gas system in the early 'seventies provided a means of illumination for beacons and buoys of which large use has been made. Other illuminants are also in use to a considerable extent.

Unattended Electric Lights.—In 1884 an iron beacon lighted by an incandescent lamp supplied with current from a secondary battery was erected on a tidal rock near Cadiz. A 28-day clock was arranged for eclipsing the light between sunrise and sunset and automatically cutting off the current at intervals to produce an occulting characteristic. Several small dioptric apparatus illuminated with incandescent electric lamps have been made by the firm of Barbier Bénard et Turenne of Paris, and supplied with current from batteries of Daniell cells, with electric clockwork mechanism for occulting the light. These apparatus have been fitted to beacons and buoys, and are generally arranged to automatically switch off the current during the day-time. They run unattended for periods up to two months. Two separate lenses and lamps are usually provided, with lamp changer, only one lamp being in circuit at a time. In the event of failure in the upper lamp of the two the current automatically passes to the lower lamp.

Oil-gas Beacons.—In 1881 a beacon automatically lighted by Pintsch's compressed oil gas was erected on the river Clyde, and large numbers of these structures have since been installed in all parts of the world. The gas is contained in an iron or steel reservoir placed within the beacon structure, refilled by means of a flexible hose on the occasions of the periodical visits of the tender. The beacons, which remain illuminated for periods up to three months are charged to 7 atmospheres. Many lights are provided with occulting apparatus actuated by the gas passing from the reservoir to the burner automatically cutting off and turning on the supply. The Garvel beacon (1899) on the Clyde is shown in fig. 46. The burner has 7 jets, and the light is occulting. Since 1907 incandescent mantle burners for oil gas have been largely used for beacon illumination, both for fixed and occulting lights.

Acetylene has also been used for the illumination of beacons and other unattended lights.

Lindberg Lights.—In 1881–1882 several beacons lighted automatically by volatile petroleum spirit on the Lindberg-Lyth and Lindberg-Trotter systems were established in Sweden. Many lights of this type have subsequently been placed in different parts of the world. The volatile spirit lamp burns day and night. Occultations are produced by a screen or series of screens rotated round the light by the ascending current of heated air and gases from the lamp

Fig. 46.—Garvel Beacon.

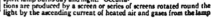

[1] In 1901 one of the lights decided upon in 1886 and installed in 1888—Créac'h d'Ouessant—was replaced by a still more powerful twin apparatus exhibited at the 1900 Paris Exhibition. Subsequently similar apparatus to that at Créac'h were installed at Gris-Nez, La Canche, Planier, Barfleur, Belle-Île and La Coubre, and the old Dunkerque optic has been replaced by that removed from Belle-Île.

acting upon a horizontal fan. The speed of rotation of the fan cannot be accurately adjusted, and the times of occultation therefore are liable to slight variation. The lights run unattended for periods up to twenty-one days.

Benson-Lee Lamps.—An improvement upon the foregoing is the Benson-Lee lamp, in which a similar occulting arrangement is often used, but the illuminant is paraffin consumed in a special burner having carbon-tipped wicks which require no trimming. The flame intensity of the light is greater than that of the burner consuming light spirit. The introduction of paraffin also avoids the danger attending the use of the more volatile spirit. Many of these lights are in use on the Scottish coast. They are also used in other parts of the United Kingdom, and in the United States, Canada and other countries.

Permanent Wick Lights.—About 1891 the French Lighthouse Service introduced petroleum lamps consuming ordinary high-flash lighthouse oil, and burning without attention for periods of several months. The burners are of special construction, provided with a very thick wick which is in the first instance treated in such a manner as to cause the formation of a deposit of carbonized tar on its exposed upper surface. This crust prevents further charring of the wick after ignition, the oil becoming vaporized from the under side of the crust. Many fixed, occulting and flashing lights fitted with these burners are established in France and other countries. In the case of the occulting types a revolving screen is placed around the burner and carried upon a miniature mercury float. The rotation is effected by means of a small Gramme motor on a vertical axis, fitted with a speed governor, and supplied with current from a battery of primary cells. The oil reservoir is placed in the upper part of the lantern and connected with the burner by a tube, to which is fitted a constant level regulator for maintaining the burning level of the oil at a fixed height. In the flashing or revolving light types the arrangement is generally similar, the lenses being revolved upon a mercury float which is rotated by the electric motor. The flashing apparatus established at St Marcouf in 1901 has a beam intensity of 1000 candle-power, and is capable of running unattended for three months. The electric current employed for rotating the apparatus is supplied by four Lalande and Chaperon primary cells, coupled in series, each giving about 0·15 ampere at a voltage of 0·65. The power required to work the apparatus is at the maximum about 0·165 ampere at 0·75 volt, the large surplus of power which is provided for the sake of safety being absorbed by a brake or governor connected with the motor.

Wigham Beacon Lights.—Wigham introduced an oil lamp for beacon and buoy purposes consisting of a vertical container filled with ordinary mineral oil or paraffin, and carrying a roller immediately under the burner case over which a long flat wick passes. One end of the wick is attached to a float which falls in the container as the oil is consumed, automatically drawing a fresh portion of the wick over the roller. The other end of the wick is attached to a free counterweight which serves to keep it stretched. The oil burns from the convex surface of the wick as it passes over the roller, a fresh portion being constantly passed under the action of the flame. The light is capable of burning without attention for thirty days. These lights are also fitted with occulting screens on the Lindberg system. The candle-power of the flame is small.

7. LIGHT-VESSELS.—The earliest light-vessel placed in English waters was that at the Nore in 1732. The early light-ships were of small size and carried lanterns of primitive construction and small size suspended from the yard-arms. Modern light-vessels are of steel, wood or composite construction. Steel is now generally employed in new ships. The wood and composite ships are sheathed with Muntz metal. The dimensions of English light-vessels vary. The following may be taken as the usual limits:

Length	80 ft. to 114 ft.
Beam	20 ft. to 24 ft.
Depth moulded . .	13 ft. to 15 ft. 6 in.
Tonnage	155 to 280.

The larger vessels are employed at outside and exposed stations, the smaller ships being stationed in sheltered positions and in estuaries. The moorings usually consist of 3-ton mushroom anchors and 1⅜ open link cables. The lanterns in common use are 8 ft. in diameter, circular in form, with glazing 4 ft. in height. They are annular in plan, surrounding the mast of the vessel upon which they are hoisted for illumination, and are lowered to the deck level during the day. Fixed lanterns mounted on hollow steel masts are now being used in many services, and are gradually displacing the older type. The first English light-vessel so equipped was constructed in 1904. Of the 87 light-vessels in British waters, including unattended light-vessels, eleven are in Ireland and six in Scotland. At the present time there are over 750 light-vessels in service throughout the world.

Until about 1895 the illuminating apparatus used in light-vessels was exclusively of catoptric form, usually consisting of 21 in. or 24 in. silvered parabolic reflectors, having 1, 2 or 3-wick mineral oil burners in focus. The reflectors and lamps are hung in gimbals to preserve the horizontal direction of the beams.

The following table gives the intensity of beam obtained by means of a type of reflector in general use:

21-in. Trinity House Parabolic Reflector

	Service Intensity of Beam.
Burners 1 wick "Douglass" . . .	2715 candles
" 2 " (Catoptric) .	4004 "
" 2 " (Dioptric). .	6722 "
" 3 " . . .	7528 "

In revolving flashing lights two or more reflectors are arranged in parallel in each face. Three, four or more faces or groups of reflectors are arranged around the lantern in which they revolve, and are carried upon a turn-table rotated by clockwork. The intensity of the flashing beam is therefore equivalent to the combined intensities of the beams emitted by the several reflectors in each face. The first light-vessel with revolving light was placed at the Swin Middle at the entrance to the Thames in 1837. Group-flashing characteristics can be produced by special arrangements of the reflectors. Dioptric apparatus is now being introduced in many new vessels, the first to be so fitted in England being that stationed at the Swin Middle in 1905, the apparatus of which is gas illuminated and gives a flash of 25,000 candle-power.

Fog signals, when provided on board light-vessels are generally in the form of reed-horns or sirens, worked by compressed air. The compressors are driven from steam or oil engines. The cost of a modern type of English light-vessel, with power-driven compressed air siren, is approximately £16,000.

In the United States service, the more recently constructed vessels have a displacement of 600 tons, each costing £18,000. They are provided with self-propelling power and steam whistle fog signals. The illuminating apparatus is usually in the form of small dioptric lens lanterns suspended at the mast-head—3 or more to each mast, but a few of the ships, built since 1907, are provided with fourth-order revolving dioptric lights in fixed lanterns. There are 53 light-vessels in service on the coasts of the United States with 13 reserve ships.

Electrical Illumination.—An experimental installation of the electric light placed on board a Mersey light-vessel in 1886 by the Mersey Docks and Harbour Board proved unsuccessful. The United States Lighthouse Board in 1892 constructed a light-vessel provided with a powerful electric light, and moored her on the Cornfield Point station in Long Island Sound. This vessel was subsequently placed off Sandy Hook (1894) and transferred to the Ambrose Channel Station in 1907. Five other light-vessels in the United States have since been provided with incandescent electric lights—either with fixed or occulting characteristics—including Nantucket Shoals (1896), Fire Island (1897), Diamond Shoals (1898), Overfalls Shoal (1901) and San Francisco (1902).

Gas Illumination.—In 1896 the French Lighthouse Service completed the construction of a steel light-vessel (Talais), which was ultimately placed at the mouth of the Gironde. The construction of this vessel was the outcome of experiments carried out with a view to produce an efficient light-vessel at moderate cost, lit by a dioptric flashing light with incandescent oil-gas burner. The construction of the Talais was followed by that of a second and larger vessel, the Snouw, on similar lines, having a length of 65 ft. 6 in., beam 20 ft. and a draught of 12 ft., with a displacement of 130 tons. The cost of this vessel complete with optical apparatus and gas-holders, with accommodation for three men, was approximately £5000. The vessel was built in 1898–1899.[1] A third vessel was constructed in 1901–1902 for the Sandettié Bank on the general lines adopted for the preceding examples of her class, but of the following increased dimensions: length 115 ft.; width at water-line 20 ft. 6 in.; and draught 15 ft., with a displacement of 342 tons (fig. 47). Accommodation is provided for a crew of eight men. The optical apparatus (fig. 48) is dioptric, consisting of 4 panels of 250 mm. focal distance, carried upon a "Cardan" joint below the lens table, and counterbalanced by a heavy pendulum weight. The apparatus is revolved by clockwork and illuminated by compressed oil gas with incandescent mantle. The candle-power of the beam is 35,000. The gas is contained in three reservoirs placed in the hold. The apparatus is contained in a 6-ft. lantern constructed at the head of a tubular mast 2 ft. 6 in. diameter. A powerful siren is provided with steam engine and boiler for working the air compressors. The total cost of the vessel, including fog signal and optical apparatus, was £13,600. A vessel of similar construction to the Talais was placed by the Trinity House in 1905 on the Swin Middle station. The illuminant is oil gas. Gas illuminated light-vessels have also been constructed for the German and Chinese Lighthouse Service.

Unattended Light-vessels.—In 1881 an unattended light-vessel, illuminated with Pintsch's oil gas, was constructed for the Clyde, and is still in use at the Garvel Point. The light is occulting, and is shown from a dioptric lens fitted at the head of a braced iron lattice tower 30 ft. above water-level. The vessel is of iron, 40 ft. long, 12 ft. beam and 8 ft. deep, and has a storeholder on board containing oil gas under a pressure of six atmospheres capable of maintaining a light for three months. A similar vessel is placed off Calshot Spit in Southampton Water, and several have been constructed for the

[1] Both the Talais and Snouw light-vessels have since been converted into unattended light-vessels.

French and other Lighthouse Services. The French boats are provided with deep main and bilge keels similar to those adopted in the larger gas illuminated vessels. In 1901 a light-vessel 60 ft. in length was placed off the Otter Rock on the west coast of Scotland; it is constructed of steel, 24 ft. beam, 12 ft. deep and draws 9 ft. of water (fig. 49). The focal plane is elevated 25 ft. above the water-line, and the lantern is 6 ft. in diameter. The optical apparatus is of 500 mm. focal distance and hung in gimbals with a pendulum balance and "Cardan" joint as in the Sandettié light-vessel. The illuminant is oil gas, with an occulting characteristic. The store-holder contains 10,500 cub. ft. of gas at eight atmospheres, sufficient to supply the light for ninety days and nights. A bell is provided, struck by clappers moved by the roll of the vessel. The cost of the vessel complete was £2979. The Northern Lighthouse Commissioners have four similar vessels in service, and others have been stationed in the Hugli estuary, at Bombay, off the Chinese coasts and elsewhere. In 1909 an unattended gas illuminated light-vessel provided with a dioptric flashing apparatus was placed at the Lune Deep in Morecambe Bay. It is also fitted with a fog bell struck automatically by a gas operated mechanism.

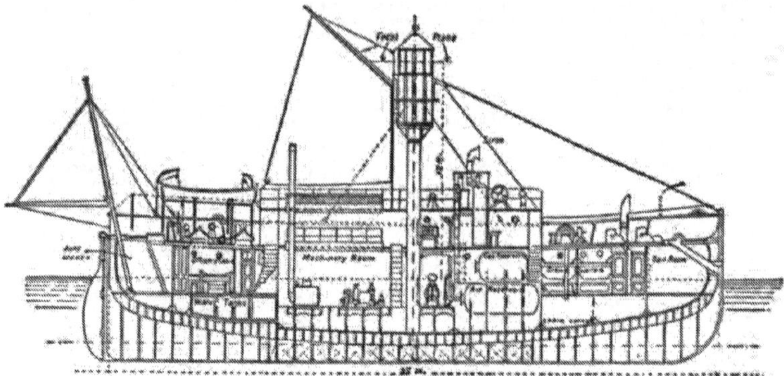

Fig. 47.—Sandettié Lightship.

Fig. 48.—Lantern of Sandettié Lightship.

Electrical Communication of Light-vessels with the Shore.—Experiments were instituted in 1886 at the Sunk light-vessel off the Essex coast with the view to maintaining telephonic communication with the shore by means of a submarine cable 9 m. in length. Great difficulties were experienced in maintaining communication during stormy weather, breakages in the cable being frequent. These difficulties were subsequently partially overcome by the employment of larger vessels and special moorings. Wireless telegraphic installations have now (1910) superseded the cable communications with light-vessels in English waters except in four cases. Seven light-vessels, including the four off the Goodwin Sands, are now fitted for wireless electrical communication with the shore.

In addition many pile lighthouses and isolated rock and island stations have been placed in electrical communication with the shore by means of cables or wireless telegraphy. The Fastnet lighthouse was, in 1894, electrically connected with the shore by means of a non-continuous cable, it being found impossible to maintain a continuous cable in shallow water near the rock owing to the heavy wash of the sea. A copper conductor, carried down from the tower to below low-water mark, was separated from the cable proper, laid on the bed of the sea in a depth of 13 fathoms, by a distance of about 100 ft. The lighthouse was similarly connected to earth on the opposite side of the rock. The conductor terminated in a large copper plate, and to the cable end was attached a copper mushroom. Weak currents were induced in the lighthouse conductor by the main current in the cable, and messages received in the tower by the help of electrical relays. On the completion of the new tower on the Fastnet Rock in 1906 this installation was superseded by a wireless telegraphic installation.

8. Distribution and Distinction of Lights, &c.—*Methods of Distinction.*—The following are the various light characteristics which may be exhibited to the mariner:—

Fixed.—Showing a continuous or steady light. Seldom used in modern lighthouses and generally restricted to small port or harbour lights. A fixed light is liable to be confused with lights of shipping or other shore lights.

Flashing.[1]—Showing a single flash, the duration of darkness always being greater than that of light. This characteristic or that immediately following is generally adopted for important lights. The French authorities have given the name *Feux-Eclair* to flashing lights of short duration.

Group-Flashing.—Showing groups of two or more flashes in quick succession (not necessarily of the same colour) separated by eclipses with a larger interval of darkness between the groups.

Fixed and Flashing.—Fixed light varied by a single white or coloured flash, which may be preceded and followed by a short eclipse. This type of light, in consequence of the unequal intensities of the beams, is unreliable, and examples are now seldom installed although many are still in service.

Fixed and Group-Flashing.—Similar to the preceding and open to the same objections.

Revolving.—This term is still retained in the "Lists of Lights" issued by the Admiralty and some other authorities to denote a light gradually increasing to full effect, then decreasing to eclipse. At short distances and in clear weather a faint continuous light may be observed. There is no essential difference between revolving and flashing lights, the distinction being merely due to the speed of rotation, and the term might well be abandoned as in the United States lighthouse list.

Occulting.—A continuous light with, at regular intervals, one sudden and total eclipse, the duration of light always being equal to or greater than that of darkness. This characteristic is usually exhibited by fixed dioptric apparatus fitted with some form of occulting mechanism. Many lights formerly of fixed characteristic have been converted to occulting.

[1] For the purposes of the mariner a light is classed as flashing or occulting solely according to the duration of light and darkness and without any reference to the apparatus employed. Thus, an occulting apparatus, in which the period of darkness is greater than that of light, is classed in the Admiralty "List of Lights" as a "flashing" light.

Group Occulting.—A continuous light with, at regular intervals, groups of two or more sudden and total eclipses.

Alternating.—Lights of different colours (generally red and white) alternately without any intervening eclipse. This characteristic is not to be recommended for reasons which have already been referred to. Many of the permanent and unwatched lights on the coasts of Norway and Sweden are of this description.

Colour.—The colours usually adopted for lights are white, red and green. White is to be preferred whenever possible, owing to the great absorption of light by the use of red or green glass screens.

Sectors.—Coloured lights are often requisite to distinguish cuts or sectors, and should be shown from fixed or occulting light apparatus and not from flashing apparatus. In marking the passage through a channel, or between sandbanks or other dangers, coloured light sectors are arranged to cover the dangers, white light being shown over the fairway with sufficient margin of safety between the edges of the coloured sectors next the fairway and the dangers.

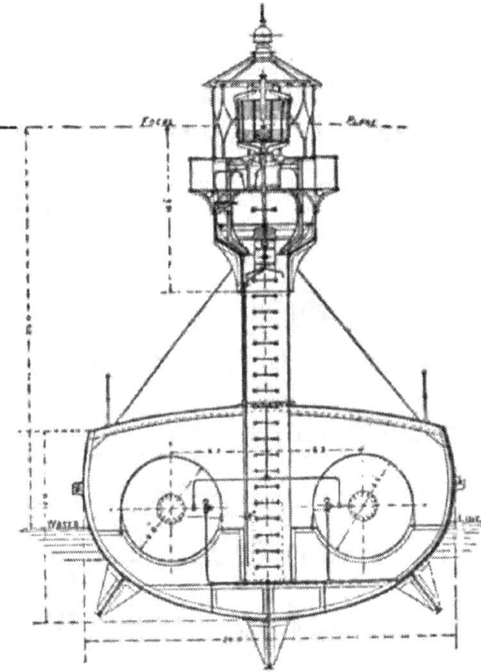

Fig. 49.—Otter Rock Light-vessel.

Choice of Characteristic and Description of Apparatus.—In determining the choice of characteristic for a light due regard must be paid to existing lights in the vicinity. No light should be placed on a coast line having a characteristic the same as, or similar to, another in its neighbourhood unless one or more lights of dissimilar characteristic, and at least as high power and range, intervene. In the case of "landfall lights" the characteristic should differ from any other within a range of 100 m. In narrow seas the distance between lights of similar characteristic may be less. Landfall lights are, in a sense, the most important of all and the most powerful apparatus available should be installed at such stations. The distinctive characteristic of a light should be such that it may be readily determined by a mariner without the necessity of accurately timing the period or duration of flashes. For landfall and other important coast stations flashing dioptric apparatus of the first order (920 mm. focal distance) with powerful burners are required. In countries where the atmosphere is generally clear and fogs are less prevalent than on the coasts of the United Kingdom, second or third order lights suffice for landfalls having regard to the high intensities available by the use of improved illuminants. Secondary coast lights may be of second, third or fourth order of flashing character, and important harbour lights of third or fourth order. Less important harbours and places where considerable range is not required, as in estuaries and narrow seas, may be lighted by flashing lights of fourth order or smaller size. Where sectors are requisite, occulting apparatus should be adopted for the main light: or subsidiary lights, fixed or occulting, may be exhibited from the same tower as the main light but at a lower level. In such cases the vertical distance between the high and the low light must be sufficient to avoid commingling of the two beams at any range at which both lights are visible. Such commingling or blending is due to atmospheric aberration.

Range of Lights.—The range of a light depends first on its elevation above sea-level and secondly on its intensity. Most important lights are of sufficient power to render them visible at the full geographical range in clear weather. On the other hand there are many harbour and other lights which do not meet this condition.

The distances given in lists of lights from which lights are visible—except in the cases of lights of low power for the reason given above—are usually calculated in nautical miles as seen from a height of 15 ft. above sea-level, the elevation of the lights being taken as above high water. Under certain atmospheric conditions, and especially with the more powerful lights, the *glare* of the light may be visible considerably beyond the calculated range.

Table III.—*Distances at which Objects can be seen at Sea, according to their Respective Elevations and the Elevation of the Eye of the Observer.* (A. Stevenson.)

Heights in Feet.	Distances in Geographical or Nautical Miles.	Heights in Feet.	Distances in Geographical or Nautical Miles.
5	2·565	110	12·03
10	3·628	120	12·56
15	4·443	130	13·08
20	5·130	140	13·57
25	5·736	150	14·02
30	6·283	200	16·22
35	6·787	250	18·14
40	7·255	300	19·87
45	7·696	350	21·46
50	8·112	400	22·94
55	8·509	450	24·33
60	8·886	500	25·65
65	9·249	550	26·90
70	9·598	600	28·10
75	9·935	650	29·25
80	10·26	700	30·28
85	10·57	800	32·45
90	10·88	900	34·54
95	11·18	1000	36·28
100	11·47		

Example: A tower 200 ft. high will be visible 20·66 nautical miles to an observer, whose eye is elevated 15 ft. above the water; thus, from the table:

15 ft. elevation, distance visible 4·44 nautical miles
200 " " 16·22 "
20·66 "

Elevation of Lights.—The elevation of the light above sea-level need not, in the case of landfall lights, exceed 200 ft., which is sufficient to give a range of over 20 nautical miles. One hundred and fifty feet is usually sufficient for coast lights. Lights placed on high headlands are liable to be enveloped in banks of fog at times when at a lower level the atmosphere is comparatively clear (*e.g.* Beachy Head). No definite rule can, however, be laid down, and local circumstances, such as configuration of the coast line, must be taken into consideration in every case.

Choice of Site.—"Landfall" stations should receive first consideration and the choice of location for such a light ought never to be made subservient to the lighting of the approaches to a port. Subsidiary lights are available for the latter purpose. Lights installed to guard shoals, reefs or other dangers should, when practicable, be placed seaward of the danger itself, as it is desirable that seamen should be able to "make" the light with confidence. Sectors marking dangers [illegible] should not be employed except when the danger [illegible] clockwork [illegible] require marking [illegible] by a floating light in its vicinity. [illegible] Oil gas has been [illegible] In 1884 an automatic [illegible] the gas passing from the reservoir [illegible] [illegible] and [illegible] are made in [illegible] may be adopted for [illegible] currents pre- [illegible] fitted to [illegible] and bell buoys. [illegible] gas buoy lantern [illegible] the 8 single-jet, [illegible] type. Incan- [illegible] a good to buoy [illegible] results. Since [illegible] the same system of [illegible] adopted in England [illegible] The lenses employed [illegible] fixed-light form, [illegible] diameter. Some [illegible] gas buoy in use on the [illegible] an elevation from water [illegible] over 26 ft. with a [illegible] more than 1000 candles. [illegible] with an elevation of 34 ft. [illegible] was placed at the entrance [illegible] in 1907. It has an incan- [illegible] and exhibits a light of over [illegible] Oil gas forms the most trust- [illegible] efficient illuminant for buoy pur- [illegible] introduced, and the system has been largely adopted by lighthouse and [illegible] authorities.

There are now over 2000 buoys fitted with [illegible] apparatus, in addition to 600 beacons, light vessels and boats.

Electric Lit Buoys.—Buoys have been fitted with electric light, both fixed and [illegible] Six electrically lit spar-buoys were laid down in the Gedney channel, New York lower bay, in 1888. These were illuminated by 100 candle-power Swan lamps with continuous current supplied by cable from a power station on shore. The wear and tear of the cables caused considerable trouble and expense. In 1895 alternating current was introduced. The installation was superseded by gas lit buoys in 1904.

Acetylene and Oil Lighted Buoys.—Acetylene has been extensively employed for the lighting of buoys in Canada and in the United States; to a less extent it has also been adopted in other countries. Both the low pressure system, by which the acetylene gas is produced by an automatic generator, and the so-called high pressure system in which purified acetylene is held in solution in a high pressure gasholder filled with asbestos composition saturated with acetone, have been employed for illuminating buoys and beacons. [illegible] oil lamps are also used to a limited extent for buoy lighting.

Bell Buoys.—One form of clapper actuated by the roll of the buoy (shown in fig. 52) consists of a hardened steel ball placed in a hori- zontal phosphor bronze cylinder provided with rubber buffers. Three of these cylinders are arranged around the mouth of the fixed bell, which is struck by the balls rolling backwards and forwards as the buoy moves. Another form of bell [illegible] a fixed bell with three or more [illegible] externally which strike the [illegible]

[illegible] introduction of coast fog [illegible] date. They were, until [illegible], practically unknown [illegible] bells and guns were [illegible] of navigation, and the application [illegible] of ships resulting in an increase [illegible] providing suitable [illegible] mist. In times [illegible] from even the most efficient system of coast lighting, since the beams of light from the most powerful electric lighthouse are frequently entirely dispersed and absorbed by the particles of moisture, forming a sea fog of even moderate density, at a distance of less than a ½ m. from the shore. The careful experiments and scientific research which have been devoted to the subject of coast fog-signalling have produced much that is useful and valuable to the mariner, but unfortunately the practical results so far have not been so satisfactory as might be desired, owing to (1) the very short range of the most powerful signals yet produced under certain unfavourable acoustic conditions of the atmosphere, (2) the difficulty experienced by the mariner in judging at any time how far the atmospheric conditions are against him in listening for the expected signal, and (3) the difficulty in locating the position of a sound signal by phonic observations.

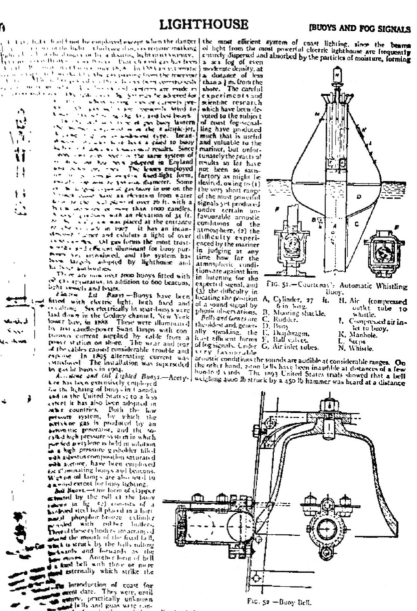

FIG. 51.—Courtenay's Automatic Whistling Buoy.

A, Cylinder, 27 ft. 6 in. long.
B, Mooring shackle.
C, Rudder.
D, Buoy.
E, Diaphragm.
F, Ball valves.
G, Air inlet tubes.
H, Air (compressed) outlet tube to whistle.
I, Compressed air inlet to buoy.
K, Manhole.
L, Steps.
N, Whistle.

Bells and Gongs are the oldest and, generally speaking, the least efficient forms of fog signals. Under very favourable acoustic conditions the sounds are audible at considerable ranges. On the other hand, 2-ton bells have been inaudible at distances of a few hundred yards. The 1893 United States trials showed that a bell weighing 4000 lb struck by a 450 lb hammer was heard at a distance of 13 m. across a gentle breeze and at over 9 m. against a 20-knot breeze. Bells are frequently used for beacon and buoy signals, and in some cases at isolated rock and other stations where there is insufficient accommodation for sirens and horns, but their use is being gradually discontinued in this country for situations where a

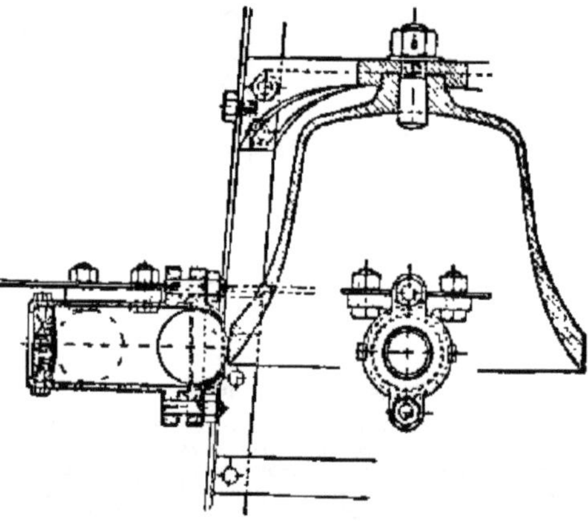

FIG. 52.—Buoy Bell.

powerful signal is required. Gongs, usually of Chinese manufacture, were formerly in use on board English lightships and are still used to some extent abroad. These are being superseded by more powerful sound instruments.

Explosive Signals.—Guns were long used at many lighthouse and light-vessel stations in England, and are still in use in Ireland and at some foreign stations. These are being gradually displaced by other explosive or compressed air signals. No explosive signals are in use on the coasts of the United States. In 1878 sound rockets charged with gun-cotton were first used at Flamborough Head and were afterwards supplied to many other stations.[1] The nitrated gun-cotton or tonite signals now in general use are made up in 4 oz. charges. These are hung at the end of an iron jib or pole attached to the lighthouse lantern or other structure, and fired by means of a detonator and electric battery. The discharge may take place within 12 ft. of a structure without danger. The cartridges are stored for a considerable period without deterioration and with safety. This form of signal is now very generally adopted for rock and other stations in Great Britain, Canada, Newfoundland, northern Europe and other parts of the world. An example will be noticed in the illustration of the Bishop Rock lighthouse, attached to the lantern (fig. 13). Automatic hoisting and firing appliances are also in use.

Whistles.—Whistles, whether sounded by air or steam, are not used in Great Britain, except in two instances of harbour signals under local control. It has been objected that their sound has too great a resemblance to steamers' whistles, and they are wasteful of power. In the United States and Canada they are largely used. The whistle usually employed consists of a metallic dome or bell against which the high-pressure steam impinges. Rapid vibrations are set up both in the metal of the bell and in the internal air, producing a shrill note. The Courtenay buoy whistle, already referred to, is an American invention and finds favour in the United States, France, Germany and elsewhere.

Reed-Horns.—These instruments in their original form were the invention of C. L. Daboll, an experimental horn of his manufacture being tried in 1851 by the United States Lighthouse Board. In 1862 the Trinity House adopted the instrument for seven land and light-vessel stations. For compressing air for the reed-horns as well as sirens, caloric, steam, gas and oil engines have been variously used, according to local circumstances. The reed-horn was improved by Professor Holmes, and many examples from his designs are now in use in England and America. At the Trinity House experiments with fog signals at St Catherine's (1901) several types of reed-horn were experimented with. The Trinity House service horn uses air at 15 lb pressure with a consumption of ·67 cub. ft. per second and 397 vibrations. A small manual horn of the Trinity House type consumes ·67 cub. ft. of air at 5 lb pressure. The trumpets of the latter are of brass.

Sirens.—The most powerful and efficient of all compressed air fog signals is the siren. The principle of this instrument may be briefly explained as follows:—It is well known that if the tympanic membrane is struck periodically and with sufficient rapidity by air impulses or waves a musical sound is produced. Robinson was the first to construct an instrument by which successive puffs of air under pressure were ejected from the mouth of a pipe. He obtained this effect by using a stop-cock revolving at high speed in such a manner that 720 pulsations per second were produced by the intermittent escape of air through the valves or ports, a smooth musical note being given. Cagniard de la Tour first gave such an instrument the name of siren, and constructed it in the form of an air chamber with perforated lid or cover, the perforations being successively closed and opened by means of a similarly perforated disk fitted to the cover and revolving at high speed. The perforations being cut at an angle, the disk was self-rotated by the oblique pressure of the air in escaping through the slots. H. W. Dove and Helmholtz introduced many improvements, and Brown of New York patented, about 1870, a steam siren with two disks having radial perforations or slots. The cylindrical form of the siren now generally adopted is due to Slight, who used two concentric cylinders, one revolving within the other, the sides being perforated with vertical slots. To him is also due the centrifugal governor largely used to regulate the speed of rotation of the siren. Over the siren mouth is placed a conical trumpet to collect and direct the sound in the desired direction. In the English service these trumpets are generally of considerable length and placed vertically, with bent top and bell mouth. Those at St Catherine's are of cast-iron with copper bell mouth, and have a total axial length of 22 ft. They are 5 in. in diameter at the siren mouth, the bell mouth being 6 ft. in diameter. At St Catherine's the sirens are two in number, 5 in. in diameter, being sounded simultaneously and in unison (fig. 53). Each siren is provided with ports for producing a high note as well as a low note, the two notes being sounded in quick succession once every minute. The trumpet mouths are separated by an angle of 120° between their axes. This double form has been adopted in certain instances where the angle desired to be covered by the sound is comparatively wide. In Scotland the cylindrical form is used generally, either automatically or motor driven. By the latter means the admission of air to the siren can be delayed until the cylinder is rotating at full speed, and a much sharper sound is produced than in the case of the automatic type. The Scottish trumpets are frequently constructed so that the greater portion of the length is horizontal. The Girdleness trumpet has an axial length of 16 ft., 11 ft. 6 in. being horizontal. The trumpet is capable of being rotated through an angle as well as dipped below the horizon. It is of cast-iron, no bell mouth is used, and the conical mouth is 4 ft. in diameter. In France the sirens are cylindrical and very similar to the English self-driven type. The trumpets have a short axial length, 4 ft. 6 in., and are of brass, with bent bell mouth. The Trinity House has in recent years reintroduced the use of disk sirens, with which experiments are still being carried out both in the United Kingdom and abroad. For light-vessels and rock stations where it is desired to distribute the sound equally in all directions the mushroom-head trumpet is occasionally used. The Casquets trumpet of this type is 22 ft. in length, of cast-iron, with a mushroom top 6 ft. in diameter. In cases where neither the mushroom trumpet nor the twin siren is used the single bent trumpet is arranged to rotate through a considerable angle. Table IV. gives particulars of a few typical sirens of the most recent form.

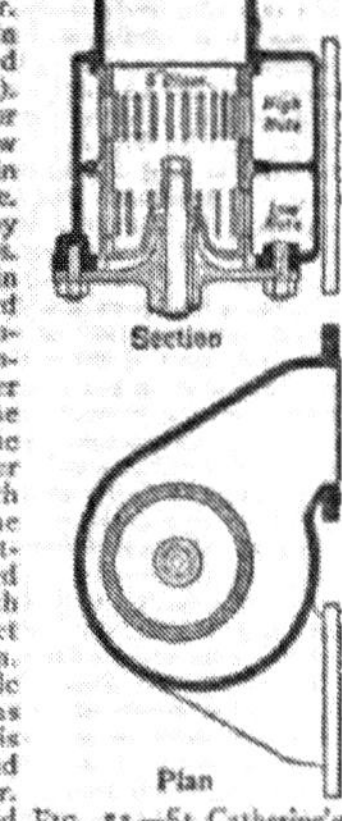

FIG. 53.—St Catherine's Double-noted Siren.

Since the first trial of the siren at the South Foreland in 1873 a very large number of these instruments have been established both at lighthouse stations and on board light-vessels. In all cases in Great Britain and France they are now supplied with air compressed by steam or other mechanical power. In the United States and some other countries steam, as well as compressed air, sirens are in use.

Diaphones.—The diaphone is a modification of the siren, which has been largely used in Canada since 1903 in place of the siren. It is claimed that the instrument emits a note of more constant pitch than does the siren. The distinction between the two instruments is that in the siren a revolving drum or disk alternately opens and closes elongated air apertures, while in the diaphone a piston pulsating at high velocity serves to alternately cover and uncover air slots in a cylinder.

The St Catherine's Experiments.—Extensive trials were carried out during 1901 by the Trinity House at St Catherine's lighthouse, Isle of Wight, with several types of sirens and reed-horns. Experiments

TABLE IV.

Station.	Description.	Vibrations per sec.		Sounding Pressure in lb per sq. in.	Cub. ft. of air used per sec. of blast reduced to atmospheric pressure.		Remarks.
		High.	Low.		High.	Low.	
St Catherine's (Trinity House)	Two 5-in. cylindrical, automatically driven sirens	295	182	25	32	16	The air consumption is for 2 sirens.
Girdleness (N.L.C.)	7-in. cylindrical siren, motor driven	234	100	30	130	26	
Casquets (Trinity House)	7-in. disk siren, motor driven	..	98	25	..	36	
French pattern siren	6-in. cylindrical siren, automatically driven	326	.	28	14	..	A uniform note of 326 vibrations per sec. has now been adopted generally in France.

[1] The Flamborough Head rocket was superseded by a siren fog signal in 1908.

[illegible] portions of trumpets, including forms [illegible] the long axis being placed vertically. [illegible] may be briefly summarized as [illegible] to be guarded two fixed [illegible] more effective than one large trumpet [illegible]. When the arc to be guarded is larger [illegible] two trumpets, the mushroom-head [illegible] instrument for the purpose. (3) A siren [illegible] better results than when self- [illegible] with the additional power [illegible] at a higher pressure than 25 lb [illegible] number of vibrations per second produced by [illegible] with the proper note of the [illegible]. When two notes of different pitch are [illegible] these should, if possible, be an [illegible] a low note is more suitable than a [illegible] against the wind and with a rough and [illegible] the greater range. (8) From causes which [illegible] at the time or predicted beforehand, areas [illegible] the sounds of fog signals may be greatly [illegible] altogether. This effect was more frequently [illegible] calm weather and at no great distance [illegible]. (It has often been observed that the sound [illegible] lost within a short distance of the source, [illegible] at a greater distance and at the same time.) [illegible] the most effective signal experimented with; the [illegible] in power, is suitable for situations of [illegible]. No explosive signals were under trial [illegible]. A fog signal, owing to the uncertainty [illegible], must be regarded only as an auxiliary aid [illegible] at all times be relied upon.

[illegible].—As early as 1841 J. D. Colladon con- [illegible] the lake of Geneva to test the suitability of [illegible] transmission of sound signals and was able [illegible] sounds through water for a distance of [illegible] not until 1904 that any successful practical [illegible] of signalling was made in connexion with [illegible] at present (1910) over 120 submarine bells [illegible] in connexion with light-vessels, off the coasts [illegible] United States, Canada, Germany, France [illegible]. These bells are struck by clappers actuated by [illegible]. Other submerged bells have been [illegible] structures, or placed on the sea bed; in [illegible] actuated by the motion of the buoy and [illegible] transmitted by cable from the shore. [illegible] bells are associated with gas buoys or [illegible] is employed to actuate the bell striking [illegible] advantage of the signals thus provided [illegible] them to be fitted with special [illegible] character installed below the [illegible] with the hull plating. The signals are [illegible] similar to ordinary telephone receivers. [illegible] be heard at considerable distances— [illegible] in all conditions of weather, but the [illegible] to the moving ship can be determined [illegible] is likely to be widely extended and [illegible] war ships have been fitted with signal [illegible].

[illegible] gives the total numbers of fog signals of [illegible] of January 1910 in certain countries.

TABLE V.

	Sirens.	Diaphones.	Horns, Trumpets, &c.		Whistles.	Explosive Signals (cotton, &c.)	Guns.	Bells.	Gongs.	Submarine Bells.	Totals.
			Power.	Manual.							
[illegible]	44	..	27	31	2	13	..	48	10	16	193
[illegible]	33	..	6	2		3	..	16	3	..	67
[illegible]	13		8	6		11	3	11	..	3	48
[illegible]	14		7	1		1	..	25	..	2	48
[illegible]	43	..	35	18	39	..	..	218	1	36	407
[illegible]	6	66	5	70	16	8	..	24	..	11	215

[illegible] employed at any one station, one being [illegible] from the enumeration. Buoy and [illegible] are also omitted, but local [illegible] under the immediate jurisdiction of the [illegible] included, more especially in Great [illegible].

[illegible]. The principal countries [illegible] central authorities responsible [illegible] and fog [illegible] House.

or according to its original charter, "The Master Wardens, and Assistants of the Guild Fraternity or Brotherhood of the most glorious and undivided Trinity and of St Clement, in the Parish of Deptford Strond, in the county of Kent," existed in the reign of Henry VII. as a religious house with certain duties connected with pilotage, and was incorporated during the reign of Henry VIII. In 1565 it was given certain rights to maintain beacons, &c., but not until 1680 did it own any lighthouses. Since that date it has gradually purchased most of the ancient privately owned lighthouses and has erected many new ones. The act of 1836 gave the corporation control of English coast lights with certain supervisory powers over the numerous local lighting authorities, including the Irish and Scottish Boards. The corporation now consists of a Master, Deputy-master, and 22 Elder Brethren (10 of whom are honorary), together with an unlimited number of Younger Brethren, who, however, perform no executive duties. In Scotland and the Isle of Man the lights are under the control of the Commissioners of Northern Lighthouses constituted in 1786 and incorporated in 1798. The lighting of the Irish coast is in the hands of the Commissioners of Irish Lights formed in 1867 in succession to the old Dublin Ballast Board. The principal local light boards in the United Kingdom are the Mersey Docks and Harbour Board, and the Clyde Lighthouse Trustees. The three general lighthouse boards of the United Kingdom, by the provision of the Mercantile Marine Act of 1854, are subordinate to the Board of Trade, which controls all finances.

On the 1st of January 1910 the lights, fog signals and submarine bells in service under the control of the several authorities in the United Kingdom were as follows:

	Light-houses.	Light-vessels.	Fog Signals.	Sub-marine Bells.
Trinity House	116	51	97	12
Northern Lighthouse Commissioners	138	5	44	..
Irish Lights Commissioners	93	11	35	3
Mersey Docks and Harbour Board	16	6	13	2
Admiralty	31	2	6	..
Clyde Lighthouse Trustees	14	1	5	..
Other local lighting authorities	809	11	89	2
Totals	1217	87	289	19

Some small harbour and river lights of subsidiary character are not included in the above total.

United States.—The United States Lighthouse Board was constituted by act of Congress in 1852. The Secretary of Commerce and Labor is the ex-officio president. The board consists of two officers of the navy, two engineer officers of the army, and two civilian scientific members, with two secretaries, one a naval officer, the other an officer of engineers in the army. The members are appointed by the president of the United States. The coast-line of the states, with the lakes and rivers and Porto Rico, is divided into 16 executive districts for purposes of administration.

The following table shows the distribution of lighthouses, light-vessels, &c., maintained by the lighthouse board in the United States in June 1909. In addition there are a few small lights and buoys privately maintained.

Lighthouses and beacon lights	1333
Light-vessels in position	53
Light-vessels for relief	13
Gas lighted buoys in position	94
Fog signals operated by steam or oil engines	228
Fog signals operated by clockwork, &c.	205
Submarine signals	43
Post lights	2333
Day or unlighted beacons	1157
Bell buoys in position	169
Whistling buoys in position	94
Other buoys	5760
Steam tenders	51
Constructional Staff	318
Light keepers; and light attendants	3137
Officers and crews of light-vessels and tenders	1693

France.—The lighthouse board of France is known as the Commission des Phares, dating from 1792 and remodelled in 1811, and is under the direction of the minister of public works. It consists of four engineers, two naval officers and one member of the Institute, one inspector-general of marine engineers, and one hydrographic engineer. The chief executive officers are an Inspecteur Général des Ponts et Chaussées, who is director of the board, and another engineer of the same corps, who is engineer-in-chief and secretary. The board has control of about 750 lights, including those of

TABLE VI.—*Electric Lighthouse Apparatus.*

Name.	Characteristic.	Period.	Duration of Flash.	Candle-power (Service Intensity).	Focal Distance of Lens.	Ratio of Angular Breadth of Panel to Whole Circle.	Current.	Voltage.	Carbons.	Electric Generators.	Lamps.	Engines.	Elevation above High Water.	Year Established.	Remarks.
		Secs.	Secs.	Standard Candles.	mm.		Amps.		mm.				Feet.		
UNITED KINGDOM— Souter Point (Durham)	Single flash	30	5		500	1 : 8	.	40	17	Holmes machines, alternating (400 revs.)	Serrin	Steam	150	1871	Fixed light apparatus, with revolving vertical condensing lenses in eight panels
South Foreland (Kent)	Single flash	2.5	.33	Candle-power not officially determined.	700	1 : 16	..	40	26	do.	Serrin[1]	Steam	374	1904	Lens elements only; 97° vertical angle. (This apparatus was in use at St Catherine's, 1888 to 1904, and replaced the two fixed electric lights established in 1872.)
Lizard (Cornwall)	Single flash	3	.13		700	1 : 4	145 for 50 mm. carbons	40	50 and 60 fluted	De Meritens alternators (600 revs.)	Modified Berjot-Serrin	Oil engines	230	1903	Mercury rotation, vertical angle, 139°. Replaced the two fixed electric lights erected in 1878.
St Catherine's (Isle of Wight)	Single flash	5	.21		700	1 : 4	145 for 50 mm. carbons	40	50 and 60 fluted	do.	do.	2 Steam, each 50 h.p.	136	1904	Mercury rotation; vertical angle, 130°.
Isle of May (Firth of Forth)	4 flash	30	.4		700 (Fixed apparatus)	1 : 8	220	40	40	do.	Berjot-Serrin	Steam	240	1886	Fixed light apparatus, with revolving vertical condensing lenses.
FRANCE— Dunkerque (Strait of Dover)	2 flash	10	.2 to .4	3,500,000 to 6,500,000	300	1 : 12	30 and 60	45	14 and 18	2 De Meritens alternators, each of 5.5 k.w. (550 revs.)	Improved Serrin	2 Semi-portable steam, each 30 i.h.p.	193	1902	Twelve panels in groups of two. (This apparatus was in use at Barfleur, 1893 to 1902.)
Calais (Strait of Dover) [Les Baleines (1882) similar]	4 flash	15	.75	900,000	300	1 : 24	60	45	18	do.	French Service pattern (1902)	do.	190	1883	Fixed light apparatus, with revolving vertical condensing prisms.
Cap Gris-nez (Strait of Dover)	Single flash	5	.10 to .14	15,000,000 to 30,000,000	300	1 : 4	60 to 120	45	18 and 28	do.	do.	Steam	233	1899	Twin optic, mercury rotation. (This light superseded a triple-flashing electric light, with intermediate red flash, of the Calais type, established in 1885. The first installation of the electric light at this station was in 1869.)
La Canche (Strait of Dover)	2 flash	10	.10 to .14	15,000,000 to 30,000,000	300	1 : 4	30 to 60	45	14 and 18	do.	do.	do.	174	1900	Twin optic, mercury rotation. (This light superseded a fixed electric light established in 1884.)
Cap de la Hève (Havre, English Channel) [Île d'Yeu in the Bay of Biscay (1895) similar]	Single flash	5	.10 to .14	10,000,000 to 20,000,000	300	1 : 4	60 to 120	45	18 and 28	De Meritens alternators (550 revs.)	Improved Serrin	do.	397	1893	Mercury rotation. (The first installation of electric light at this lighthouse was in 1863.)
Créac'h d'Ouessant (Ushant) [Barfleur (English Channel) 1903, La Coubre (Bay of Biscay) 1905, and Belle Île (Bay of Biscay) 1903, similar]	2 flash	10	.10 to .14	15,000,000 to 30,000,000	300	1 : 4	60 to 120	45	18 and 28	2 De Meritens alternators, each of 5.5 k.w. (550 revs.)	French Service pattern (1902)	do.	225	1901	Twin optic, mercury rotation. (This light superseded a double-flashing electric light, similar to that now at Dunkerque, established in 1888.)
Penmarc'h (Phare d'Eckmühl) (Finistère)	Single flash	5	.10 to .14	15,000,000 to 30,000,000	300	1 : 4	30 and 60	45	14 and 18	Two-phase Labour alternators (810 to 820 revs.)	do.	do.	197	1897	Twin optic, mercury rotation.
Planier (near Marseilles)	Single flash	5	.10 to .14	15,000,000 to 30,000,000	300	1 : 4	30 to 60	45	14 to 18	De Meritens alternators (550 revs.)	do.	do.	207	1902	Twin optic, mercury rotation. (This light superseded an electric light established in 1881, showing a group of three white flashes separated by one red flash of the Calais type.)
ITALY— Tino (Gulf of Spezia)	3 flash	30	1.25	Undetermined.	700	1 : 24	50 110 200	50	15 25 35	do. (830 revs.)	Berjot-Serrin	do.	384	1885	Eight panels of three lenses each, no mirror.
AMERICA— Navesink (Entrance to New York Bay)	Single flash	5	.08	About 60,000,000	700	Nearly 1 : 2	Max. 100	50	23	Alternating dynamos (800 revs.)	Modified Serrin (Clolina)	Oil, each 25 h.p.	246	1898	Mercury rotation. Bivalve of 165°.
AUSTRALIA— Macquarie (Sydney, N.S.W.)	Single flash	60	8	5,000,000	920	1 : 16	55 110	50	15 25	De Meritens alternators (600 revs.)	Serrin	Gas	345	1883	16-panel revolving apparatus, with 180° fixed mirror.

[illegible]	[illegible]	[illegible]	[illegible]	[illegible]	[illegible]	[illegible]	[illegible]	[illegible]	[illegible]	[illegible]	[illegible]	[illegible]	[illegible]
[illegible]	[illegible]	[illegible]	[illegible]	[illegible]	[illegible]	[illegible]	[illegible]	[illegible]	[illegible]	[illegible]	[illegible]	1877	[illegible]
[illegible]	[illegible]	[illegible]	[illegible]	[illegible]	[illegible]	[illegible]	[illegible]	do.	do.	3300	133	1882	Biform apparatus, lens elements only, 90° vertical angle, 6 sides of 2 panels each.
[illegible]	[illegible]	[illegible]	[illegible]	[illegible]	[illegible]	[illegible]	[illegible]	do.	do.	3300	134	1886	Biform apparatus, lens elements only, 80° vertical angle, 5 sides of 2 panels each.
Spurn Point	Yorkshire	Single flash	20	1.5	529,000	1330	1 : 6	do.	do.	3300	120	1895	Lens elements only, 80° vertical angle.
Lundy Island	Bristol Channel	2 flash	20	.33	374,000	920	Nearly 1 : 4	do.	do.	3300	165	1897	Mercury rotation, 4 panel bivalve. [St. Mary's Isle, Northumberland (1898), is similar.]
Pendeen	Cornwall	4 flash	15	.25	190,000	920	1 : 8	do.	do.	3300	195	1900	80° vertical angle lens, 2 sides of 4 panels each, mercury rotation.
Roker Pier	Sunderland	Single flash	5	.10	175,000	500	Nearly 1 : 2	do.	"Chance" 55 mm. dia. mantle	1200	83	1903	Mercury rotation; univalve 184° in azimuth, with 184° dioptric mirror in rear.
Bell Rock	Near Firth of Tay	Red and white flashes alternately every 30 secs.	60	.50	392,000	920 and 1330	White about 1 : 0 red about 1 : 2.2	do.	"Chance" 55 mm dia. mantle	1200	93	1902	Combined hyper-radial and first-order light with back prisms in white and mirrors in red. Revolves in 60 secs. [Holy Island, 1905 (Lamlash), similar, flash every 15 secs.]
Kinnaird's Head	Aberdeenshire	Single flash	15	.50	881,000	920 and 1330	1 : 2.2	do.	do.	2150	120	1905	Composite apparatus; panels of 1330 mm. and 920 mm. focal distance; 2 faces.
Tarbet Ness	Dornoch Firth	6 flash	30	.50	89,000	700	1 : 12	do.	"Chance" 55 mm. dia. mantle	1200	175	1892	6 panels (lens) of 30° with 180° mirror. [Douglas Head (Isle of Man) similar.]
Sule Skerry	West of Orkneys	3 flash	30	1.0	378,000	1330	1 : 9	do.	"Chance" 85 mm. dia. mantle	2150	113	1895	Equiangular lenses.
Pladda	South end of Arran Island	3 flash	30	.50	597,000	1330	1 : 6	do.	do.	2150	130	1901	3 equiangular lens panels with mirror in rear; side panels eccentric. [Hyskeir Rocks (1904) similar.]
Tory Island	Co. Donegal	3 flash	60	3.0	17 000 to 326,000	1330	1 : 6	Coal Gas	Wigham, 108 jets (maximum)	2300 (max.)	130	1887	Triform apparatus, vertical angle of lenses [illegible] 8 sides, one revolution in [illegible] minutes. The group flash from lens is divided by eclipsing burner into 3 flashes.
Fastnet	Co. Cork	Single flash	5	.17	750,000	920	1 : 4	Incandescent petroleum vapour	Irish pattern 50 mm. mantle	1200	160	1904	Biform apparatus; 4 panels of 90° vertical angle and 90° in azimuth; mercury rotation.
Kinsale	do.	2 flash	10	.25	460,000	920	1 : 6	do.	do.	1200	236	1907	Biform apparatus, 3 sides each of 2 panels; vertical angle 90°; mercury rotation [St. John's Point, Co. Down (1908) similar, period 7.5 secs.]
Howth Bailey	Dublin Bay	Single flash	30	1.0	950,000	920	13 : 32	do.	Irish pattern 3-50 mm. dia. mantles	3300	134	1902	Bivalve apparatus; panels of 147° in azimuth and 122° vertical angle; mercury rotation.
Chassiron	Bay of Biscay	Single flash	10	1.0 .50 .70	70 000 180,000 360,000	920 920 920	1 : 8 1 : 8 1 : 8	Oil Incandescent oil gas Incandescent acetylene	6 wick 30 mm dia. mantle 55 mm dia. mantle	480 400 1300	164 164 164	1891 1895 1902	The old first-order apparatus has been utilized in all cases.
Cap d'Antifer	English Channel	Single flash	20	1.0	400,000	1330	1 : 6	Incandescent petroleum vapour	French pattern 85 mm. mantle	2150	304	1894	Mercury rotation; hyper-radial apparatus with reflecting prisms. This is the only apparatus of this focal distance on the French coast.
Ile de Bats	Finistère	4 flash	25	.37	200,000	920	1 : 8	do.	do.	2150	225	1900	Group-flashing apparatus, 4 panels of 45°, with 180° mirror in rear; mercury rotation.
Ar'men	do.	3 flash	20	.38	200 000	700	1 : 5	do.	do.	2150	94	1897	Mercury rotation; 3 panels, mirror in rear.
Villefranche	Mediterranean	Single flash	5	.38	150,000	700	1 : 4	do.	do.	2150	229	1902	Mercury rotation.
Ile Vierge	Finistère	Single flash	5	.38	500,000	700	1 : 4	do.	do.	2150	252	1902	Twin optic; mercury rotation.
Kennery Island	Bombay	2 flash	10	.25	250,000	920	Nearly 1 : 4	do.	70 mm. dia. mantle	1400	153	1902	Mercury rotation, bivalve apparatus; 2 double-flashing [illegible] panels.
Cape Race	Newfoundland	Single flash	7.5	.30	1,100,000	1330	1 : 4	do.	"Chance" 85 mm. dia. mantle	2150	165	1907	4 panels, vertical angle 121½°; mercury rotation. [Manora Point, Karachi (1909), similar.]
Pachena Point	British Columbia	2 flash	7.5	.41	220,000	920	1 : 8	do.	do.	2150		1908	Mercury rotation, 4 sides of 2 panels each.
Cape Hermes	Cape Colony	Single flash	3	.31	30,000	250	1 : 3	do.	"Chance" 55 mm. dia. mantle	1200	175	1904	3 panels, vertical angle 130°; mercury rotation.
Hood Point	do.	4 flash	40	.58	200,000	920	1 : 8	do.	"Chance" 85 mm. dia. mantle	2150	180	1895	Mercury rotation; 4 panels of 45° in azimuth and 80° vertical angle, with catadioptric mirror in rear.
Cape Naturaliste	West Australia	2 flash	10	.15	450,000	920	About 1 : 5	do.	do.	2150	404	1904	Mercury rotation; 2 lenses of 126½° in azimuth, with mirror of 107°.
Point Cloates	do.	Single flash	5	.30	300,000	700	1 : 5	do.	do.	2150	190	1909	Mercury rotation; 3 panels, each 120° in azimuth and 133⅓° vertical angle.
Pecks Ledge	Connecticut, U.S.A	2 flash	30	.50	10,000	250	1 : 4	do.	35 mm. dia. mantle	300	54	1906	Rotated on ball bearings. 2 lenses of 90° each and mirror.
Fire Island	New York, U.S.A	Single flash	60	4.0	250,000	920	1 : 8	do.	55 mm. dia. mantle	1000	167	1858	Rotated on roller bearings.
Gray's Harbor	Washington, Pacific Coast, U.S.A.	Alternating red and white flashes	5	.20	White 10,000 red 8,000	500	..	Oil	3 wick	160	123	1898	Mercury rotation; one (red) lens of 170° in azimuth, reinforced by two 80° mirrors; one (white) lens of 80° in azimuth.

[1] The dates given are of the establishment of the optical apparatus. In many cases incandescent burners have been installed at later dates.

Corsica, Algeria, &c. A similar system has been established in Spain.

English Colonies.—In Canada the coast lighting is in the hands of the minister of marine, and in most other colonies the public works departments have control of lighthouse matters.

Other Countries.—In Denmark, Austria, Holland, Russia, Sweden, Norway and many other countries the minister of marine has charge of the lighting and buoying of coasts; in Belgium the public works department controls the service.

In the Trinity House Service at shore lighthouse stations there are usually two keepers, at rock stations three or four, one being ashore on leave. When there is a fog signal at a station there is usually an additional keeper, and at electric light stations a mechanical engineer is also employed as principal keeper. The crews of light-vessels as a rule consist of 11 men, three of them and the master or mate going on shore in rotation.

The average annual cost of maintenance of an English shore lighthouse, with two keepers, is £275. For shore lighthouses with three keepers and a siren fog signal the average cost is £444. The maintenance of a rock lighthouse with four keepers and an explosive fog signal is about £760, and an electric light station costs about £1100 annually to maintain.

A light-vessel of the ordinary type in use in the United Kingdom entails an annual expenditure on maintenance of approximately £1320, excluding the cost of periodical overhaul.

AUTHORITIES.—Smeaton, *Eddystone Lighthouse* (London, 1793); A. Fresnel, *Mémoire sur un nouveau système d'éclairage des phares* (Paris, 1822); R. Stevenson, *Bell Rock Lighthouse* (Edinburgh, 1824); Alan Stevenson, *Skerryvore Lighthouse* (1847); Renaud, *Mémoire sur l'éclairage et le balisage des côtes de France* (Paris, 1864); Allard, *Mémoire sur l'intensité et la portée des phares* (Paris, 1876); T. Stevenson, *Lighthouse Construction and Illumination* (London, 1881); Allard, *Mémoire sur les phares électriques* (Paris, 1881); Renaud, *Les Phares* (Paris, 1881); Edwards, *Our Sea Marks* (London, 1884); D. P. Heap, *Ancient and Modern Lighthouses* (Boston, 1889); Allard, *Les Phares* (Paris, 1889); Rey, *Les Progrès d'éclairage des côtes* (Paris, 1898); Williams, *Life of Sir J. N. Douglass* (London, 1900); J. F. Chance, *The Lighthouse Work of Sir Jas. Chance* (London, 1902); de Rochemont and Deprez, *Cours des travaux maritimes*, vol. ii. (Paris, 1902); Ribière, *Phares et Signaux maritimes* (Paris, 1908); Stevenson, "Isle of May Lighthouse," *Proc. Inst. Mech. Engineers* (1887); J. N. Douglass, "Beacon Lights and Fog Signals," *Proc. Roy. Inst.* (1889); Ribière, "Propriétés optiques des appareils des phares," *Annales des ponts et chaussées* (1894); Preller, "Coast Lighthouse Illumination in France," *Engineering* (1896); "Lighthouse Engineering at the Paris Exhibition," *Engineer* (1901–1902); N. G. Gedye, "Coast Fog Signals," *Engineer* (1902); *Trans. Int. Nav. Congress* (Paris, 1900, Milan, 1905); *Proc. Int. Eng. Congress* (Glasgow, 1901, St Louis, 1904); *Proc. Int. Maritime Congress* (London, 1893); J. T. Chance, "On Optical Apparatus used in Lighthouses," *Proc. Inst. C.E.* vol. xxvi.; J. N. Douglass, "The Wolf Rock Lighthouse," *ibid.* vol. xxx.; W. Douglass, "Great Basses Lighthouse," *ibid.* vol. xxxviii.; J. T. Chance, "Dioptric Apparatus in Lighthouses," *ibid.* vol. lii.; J. N. Douglass, "Electric Light applied to Lighthouse Illumination," *ibid.* vol. lvii.; W. T. Douglass, "The New Eddystone Lighthouse," *ibid.* vol. lxxv.; Hopkinson, "Electric Lighthouses at Macquarie and Tino," *ibid.* vol. lxxxvii.; Stevenson, "Ailsa Craig Lighthouse and Fog Signals," *ibid.* vol. lxxxix.; W. T. Douglass, "The Bishop Rock Lighthouses," *ibid.* vol. cviii.; Brebner, "Lighthouse Lenses," *ibid.* vol. cxi.; Stevenson, "Lighthouse Refractors," *ibid.* vol. cxvii.; Case, "Beachy Head Lighthouse," *ibid.* vol. clix.; *Notice sur les appareils d'éclairage* (French Lighthouse Service exhibits at Chicago and Paris) (Paris, 1893 and 1900); *Report on U.S. Lighthouse Board Exhibit at Chicago* (Washington, 1894); *Reports of the Lighthouse Board of the United States* (Washington, 1852, et seq.); British parliamentary reports, *Lighthouse Illuminants* (1883, et seq.), *Light Dues* (1896), *Trinity House Fog Signal Committee* (1901), *Royal Commission on Lighthouse Administration* (1908); *Mémoires de la Société des Ingénieurs Civils de France*, *Annales des ponts et chaussées* (Paris); *Proc. Inst. C.E.*; *The Engineer*; *Engineering* (*passim*). (W. T. D.; N. G. G.)

LIGHTING. Artificial light is generally produced by raising some body to a high temperature. If the temperature of a solid body be greater than that of surrounding bodies it parts with some of its energy in the form of radiation. Whilst the temperature is low these radiations are not of a kind to which the eye is sensitive; they are exclusively radiations less refrangible and of greater wave-length than red light, and may be called infra-red. As the temperature is increased the infra-red radiations increase, but presently there are added radiations which the eye perceives as red light. As the temperature is further increased, the red light increases, and yellow, green and blue rays are successively thrown off. On raising the temperature to a still higher point, radiations of a wave-length shorter even than violet light are produced, to which the eye is insensitive, but which act strongly on certain chemical substances; these may be called ultra-violet rays. Thus a very hot body in general throws out rays of various wave-length; the hotter the body the more of every kind of radiation will it throw out, but the proportion of short waves to long waves becomes vastly greater as the temperature is increased. Our eyes are only sensitive to certain of these waves, viz. those not very long and not very short. The problem of the artificial production of light with economy of energy is the same as that of raising some body to such a temperature that it shall give as large a proportion as possible of those rays which the eye is capable of feeling. For practical purposes this temperature is the highest temperature we can produce. As an illustration of the luminous effect of the high temperature produced by converting other forms of energy into heat within a small space, consider the following statements. If burned in ordinary gas burners, 120 cub. ft. of 15 candle gas will give a light of 360 standard candles for one hour. The heat produced by the combustion is equivalent to about 60 million foot-pounds. If this gas be burned in a modern gas-engine, about 8 million foot-pounds of useful work will be done outside the engine, or about 4 horse-power for one hour. If this be used to drive a dynamo for one hour, even if the machine has an efficiency of only 80%, the energy of the current will be about 6,400,000 foot-pounds per hour, about half of which, or only 3,200,000 foot-pounds, is converted into radiant energy in the electric arc. But this electric arc will radiate a light of 2000 candles when viewed horizontally, and two or three times as much when viewed from below. Hence 3 million foot-pounds changed to heat in the electric arc may be said roughly to affect our eyes six times as much as 60 million foot-pounds changed to heat in an ordinary gas burner.

Owing to the high temperature at which it remains solid, and to its great emissive power, the radiant body used for artificial illumination is usually some form of carbon. In an oil or ordinary coal-gas flame this carbon is present in minute particles derived from the organic substances with which the flame is supplied and heated to incandescence by the heat liberated in their decomposition, while in the electric light the incandescence is the effect of the heat developed by the electric current passed through a resisting rod or filament of carbon. In some cases, however, other substances replace carbon as the radiating body; in the incandescent gas light certain earthy oxides are utilized, and in metallic filament electric lamps such metals as tungsten or tantalum.

1. Oil Lighting

From the earliest times the burning of oil has been a source of light, but until the middle of the 19th century only oils of vegetable and animal origin were employed in indoor lamps for this purpose. Although many kinds were used locally, only colza and sperm oils had any very extended use, and they have been practically supplanted by mineral oil, which was introduced as an illuminant in 1853. *Vegetable and animal oils.* Up to the latter half of the 18th century the lamps were shallow vessels into which a short length of wick dipped; the flame was smoky and discharged acrid vapours, giving the minimum of light with the maximum of smell. The first notable improvement was made by Ami Argand in 1784. His burner consisted of two concentric tubes between which the tubular wick was placed; the open inner tube led a current of air to play upon the inner surface of the circular flame, whilst the combustion was materially improved by placing around the flame a chimney which rested on a perforated gallery a short distance below the burner. Argand's original burner is the parent form of innumerable modifications, all more or less complex, such as the Carcel and the moderator.

A typical example of the Argand burner and chimney is represented in fig. 1, in which the burner is composed of three tubes, *d*, *f*, *g*. The tube *g* is soldered to the bottom of the tube *d*, just above *e*, and the interval between the outer surface of the tube *g* and the inner surface of the tube *d* is an annular cylindrical cavity closed at the bottom, containing the cylindrical cotton wick immersed in oil. The wick is fixed to the wick tube *hi*, which is capable

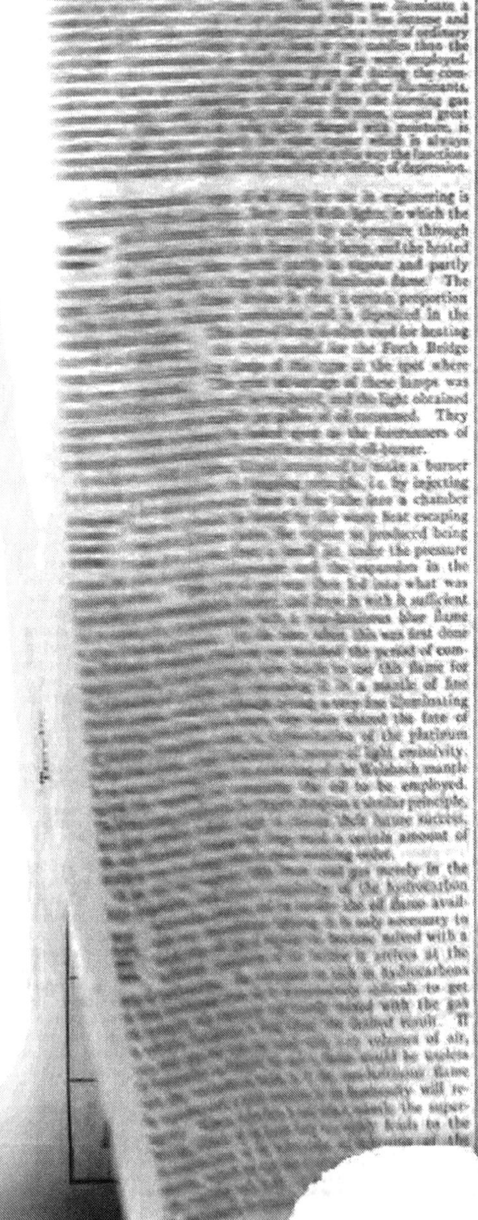

altered, and the hydrocarbon molecules being burnt up before impact with the heated surface of the mantle, all chance of blackening is avoided.

On the first attempts to construct a satisfactory oil lamp which could be used with the incandescent mantle, this trouble showed itself to be a most serious one, as although it was comparatively easy so to regulate a circular-wicked flame fed by an excess of air as to make it non-luminous, the moment the mantle was put upon this, blackening quickly appeared, while when methods for obtaining a further air supply were devised, the difficulty of producing a flame which would burn for a considerable time without constant necessity for regulation proved a serious drawback. This trouble has militated against most of the incandescent oil lamps placed upon the market.

It soon became evident that if a wick were employed the difficulty of getting it perfectly symmetrical was a serious matter, and that it could only be utilized in drawing the oil up to a heating chamber where it could be volatilized to produce the oil gas, which on then being mixed with air would give the non-luminous flame. In the earlier forms of incandescent oil lamps the general idea was to suck the oil up by the capillarity of a circular wick to a point a short distance below the opening of the burner at which the flame was formed, and here the oil was vaporized or gasified by the heat of the head of the burner. An air supply was then drawn up through a tube passing through the centre of the wick-tube, while a second air current was so arranged as to discharge itself almost horizontally upon the burning gas below the cap, in this way giving a non-luminous and very hot flame, which if kept very carefully adjusted afforded excellent results with an incandescent mantle. It was an arrangement somewhat of this character that was introduced by the Welsbach Company. The lamps, however, required such careful attention, and were moreover so irregular in their performance, that they never proved very successful. Many other forms have reached a certain degree of perfection, but have not so far attained sufficient regularity of action to make them commercial successes. One of the most successful was devised by F. Altmann, in which an ingenious arrangement caused the vaporization of oil and water by the heat of a little oil lamp in a lower and separate chamber, and the mixture of oil gas and steam was then burnt in a burner-head with a special arrangement of air supply, heating a mantle suspended above the burner-head.

The perfect petroleum incandescent lamp has not yet been made, but the results thus obtained show that when the right system has been found a very great increase in the amount of light developed from the petroleum may be expected. In one lamp experimented with for some time it was easy to obtain 3500 candle hours per gallon of oil, or three times the amount of light obtainable from the oil when burnt under ordinary conditions.

Air-gas. Before the manufacture of coal-gas had become so universal as it is at present, a favourite illuminant for country mansions and even villages where no coal-gas was available was a mixture of air with the vapour of very volatile hydrocarbons, which is generally known as "air-gas." This was produced by passing a current of dry air through or over petroleum spirit or the light hydrocarbons distilled from tar, when sufficient of the hydrocarbon was taken up to give a luminous flame in flat flame and Argand burners in the same way as coal-gas, the trouble being that it was difficult to regulate the amount of hydrocarbon held in suspension by the air, as this varied very widely with the temperature. As coal-gas spread to the smaller villages and electric lighting became utilized in large houses, the use of air-gas died out, but with the general introduction of the incandescent mantle it again came to the front. In the earlier days of this revival, air-gas rich in hydrocarbon vapour was made and was further aerated to give a non-luminous flame by burning it in an atmospheric burner.

One of the best illustrations of this system was the Aerogene gas introduced by A. I. van Vriesland, which was utilized for lighting a number of villages and railway stations on the continent of Europe. In this arrangement a revolving coil of pipes continually dips into petroleum spirit contained in a cylinder, and the air passed into the cylinder through the coil of pipes becomes highly carburetted by the time it reaches the outlet at the far end of the cylinder. The resulting gas when burnt in an ordinary burner gives a luminous flame; it can be used in atmospheric burners differing little from those of the ordinary type. With an ordinary Welsbach "C" burner it gives a duty of about 30 candles per foot of gas consumed, the high illuminating power being due to the fact that the gas is under a pressure of from 6 to 8 in. With such a gas, containing a considerable percentage of hydrocarbon vapour, any leakage into the air of a room would give rise to an explosive mixture, in the same way that coal gas would do, but inasmuch as mixtures of the vapour of petroleum spirit and air are only explosive for a very narrow range, that is, from 1·25 to 5·3%, some systems have been introduced in which by keeping the amount of petroleum vapour at 2% and burning the gas under pressure in a specially constructed non-aerating mantle burner, not only has it been found possible to produce a very large volume of gas per gallon of spirit employed, but the gas is itself non-explosive, increase in the amount of air taking it farther away from the explosive limit. The Hooker, De Laitte and several other systems have been based upon this principle.

2 Gas Lighting

In all measurements of illuminating value the standard of comparison used in England is the light yielded by a sperm candle of the size known as "sixes," *i.e.* six to the pound, consuming 120 grains of sperm per hour, and although in photometric work slight inequalities in burning have led to the candle being discarded in practice, the standard lamps burning pentane vapour which have replaced them are arranged to yield a light of ten candles, and the photometric results are expressed as before in terms of candles.

When William Murdoch first used coal-gas at his Redruth home in 1779, he burnt the gas as it escaped from the open end of a small iron tube, but soon realizing that this plan entailed very large consumption of gas and gave a very small amount of light, he welded up the end of his tube and bored three small holes in it, so arranged that they formed three divergent jets of flame. From the shape of the flame so produced this burner received the name of the "cockspur" burner, and it was the one used by Murdoch when in 1807 he fitted up an installation of gas lighting at Phillips & Lee's works in Manchester. This—the earliest form of gas burner—gave an illuminating value of a little under one candle per cubic foot of gas consumed, and this duty was slightly increased when the burner was improved by flattening up the welded end of the tube and making a series of small holes in line and close together, the jets of flame from which gave the burner the name of the "cockscomb." It did not need much inventive faculty to replace the line of holes by a saw-cut, the gas issuing from which burnt in a sheet, the shape of which led to the burner being called the "batswing." This was followed in 1820 by the discovery of J. B. Neilson, of Glasgow, whose name is remembered in connexion with the use of the hot-air blast in iron-smelting, that, by allowing two flames to impinge upon one another so as to form a flat flame, a slight increase in luminosity was obtained, and after several preliminary stages the union jet or "fishtail" burner was produced. In this form of burner two holes, bored at the necessary angle in the same nipple, caused two streams of gas to impinge upon each other so that they flattened themselves out into a sheet of flame. The flames given by the batswing and fishtail burners differed in shape, the former being wide and of but little height, whilst the latter was much higher and more narrow. This factor ensured for the fishtail a greater amount of popularity than the batswing burner had obtained, as the flame was less affected by draughts and could be used with a globe, although the illuminating efficiency of the two burners differed little.

Regenerative burner.

In a lecture at the Royal Institution on the 20th of May 1853, Sir Edward Frankland showed a burner he had devised for utilizing the heat of the flame to raise the temperature of the air supply necessary for the combustion of the gas. The burner was an Argand of the type then in use, consisting of a metal ring pierced with holes so as to give a circle of small jets, the ring of flame being surrounded by a chimney. But in addition to this chimney, Frankland added a second external one, extending some distance below the first and closed at the bottom by a glass plate fitted air-tight to the pillar carrying the burner. In this way the air needed for the combustion of the gas had to pass down the space between the two chimneys, and in so doing became highly heated, partly by contact with the hot glass, and partly by radiation. Sir Edward Frankland estimated that the temperature of the air reaching the flame was about 500° F. In 1854 a very similar arrangement was brought forward by the Rev. W. R. Bowditch, and, as a large amount of publicity was given to it, the inception of the regenerative burner was generally ascribed to Bowditch, although undoubtedly due to Frankland.

The principle of regeneration was adopted in a number of lamps, the best of which was brought out by Friedrich Siemens in 1879. Although originally made for heating purposes, the light given by the burner was so effective and superior to anything obtained up to that time that it was with some slight alterations adapted for illuminating purposes.

Improvements followed in the construction and design of the regenerative lamp, and when used as an overhead burner it was found that not only was an excellent duty obtained per cubic foot of gas consumed, but that the lamp could be made a most efficient engine of ventilation, as an enormous amount of vitiated air could be withdrawn from the upper part of a room through a flue in the ceiling space. So marked was the increase in light due to the regeneration that a considerable number of burners working on this principle were introduced, some of them like the Wenham and Cromartie coming into extensive use. They were, however, costly to instal, so that the flat flame burner retained its popularity in spite of the fact that its duty was comparatively low, owing to the flame being drawn out into a thin sheet and so exposed to the cooling influence of the atmosphere. Almost at the same time that Murdoch was introducing the cockscomb and cockspur burners, he also made rough forms of Argand burner, consisting of two concentric pipes between which the gas was led and burnt with a circular flame. This form was soon improved by filling in the space between the tubes with a ring of metal, bored with fine holes so close together that the jets coalesced in burning and gave a more satisfactory flame, the air necessary to keep the flame steady and ensure complete combustion being obtained by the draught created by a chimney placed around it. When it began to be recognized that the temperature of the flame had a great effect upon the amount of light emitted, the iron tips, which had been universally employed, both in flat flame and Argand burners, were replaced by steatite or other non-conducting material of similar character, to prevent as far as possible heat from being withdrawn from the flame by conduction.

In 1880 the burners in use for coal-gas therefore consisted of flat flame, Argand, and regenerative burners, and the duty given by them with a 16-candle gas was as follows:—

Burner.	Candle units per cub. ft. of gas.
Union jet flat flame, No. 0	0·59
" " 1	0·85
" " 2	1·22
" " 3	1·63
" " 4	1·74
" " 5	1·87
" " 6	2·15
" " 7	2·44
Ordinary Argand	2·90
Standard Argand	3·20
Regenerative	7 to 10

The luminosity of a coal-gas flame depends upon the number of carbon particles liberated within it, and the temperature to which they can be heated. Hence the light given by a flame of coal-gas can be augmented by (1) increasing the number of the carbon particles, and (2) raising the temperature to which they are exposed. The first process is carried out by enrichment (see Gas: *Manufacture*), the second is best obtained by regeneration, the action of which is limited by the power possessed by the material of which burners are composed to withstand the superheating. Although with a perfectly made regenerative burner it might be possible for a short time to get a duty as high as 16 candles per cubic foot from ordinary coal-gas, such a burner constructed of the ordinary materials would last only a few hours, so that for practical use and a reasonable life for the burner 10 candles per cubic foot was about the highest commercial duty that could be reckoned on. This limitation naturally caused inventors to search for methods by which the emission of light could be obtained from coal-gas otherwise than by the incandescence of the carbon particles contained within the

in the process by which the saturated fabric can be so prepared as to be easily burnt off by the consumer on the burner on which it is to be used, in this way doing away with the initial cost of burning off, shaping, hardening and collodionizing.

Intensifying systems.

Since 1897 inventions have been patented for methods of intensifying the light produced by burning gas under a mantle and increasing the light generated per unit volume of gas. The systems have either been self-intensifying or have depended on supplying the gas (or gas and air) under an increased pressure. Of the self-intensifying systems those of Lucas and Scott-Snell have been the most successful. A careful study has been made by the inventor of the Lucas light of the influence of various sizes and shapes of chimneys in the production of draught. The specially formed chimney used exerts a suction on the gas flame and air, and the burner and mantle are so constructed as to take full advantage of the increased air supply, with the result that the candle power given by the mantle is considerably augmented. With the Scott-Snell system the results obtained are about the same as those given by the Lucas light, but in this case the waste heat from the burner is caused to operate a plunger working in the crown of the lamp which sucks and delivers gas to the burner. Both these systems are widely used for public lighting in many large towns of the United Kingdom and the continent of Europe.

The other method of obtaining high light-power from incandescent gas burners necessitates the use of some form of motive power in order to place the gas, or both gas and air, under an increased pressure. The gas compressor is worked by a water motor, hot air or gas engine; a low pressure water motor may be efficiently driven by water from the main, but with large installations it is more economical to drive the compressor by a gas engine. To overcome the intermittent flow of gas caused by the stroke of the engine, a regulator on the floating bell principle is placed after the compressor; the pressure of gas in the apparatus governs automatically the flow of gas to the engine. With the Sugg apparatus for high power lighting the gas is brought from the district pressure, which is equal to about 1½ in. of water, to an average of 12 in. water pressure. The light obtained by this system when the gas pressure is 9½ in. is 300 candle power with an hourly consumption of 10 cub. ft. of gas, equivalent to 30 candles per cubic foot, and with a gas pressure equal to 14 in. of water 400 candles are obtained with an hourly consumption of 12½ cub. ft., which represents a duty of 32 candles per cubic foot of gas consumed. High pressure incandescent lighting makes it possible to burn a far larger volume of gas in a given time under a mantle than is the case with low pressure lighting, so as to create centres of high total illuminating value to compete with arc lighting in the illumination of large spaces, and the Lucas, Keith, Scott-Snell, Millennium, [illegible], and many other pressure systems answer most admirably for this purpose.

Inverted burners.

The light given by the ordinary incandescent mantle burning in an upright position tends rather to the upward direction, because owing to the slightly conical shape of the mantle the maximum light is emitted at an angle a little above the horizontal. Inasmuch as for working purposes the surface that a mantle illuminates is at angles below 45° from the horizontal, it is evident that a considerable loss of effective lighting is brought about, whilst directly under the light the burner and fittings throw a strong shadow. To avoid this trouble attempts have from time to time been made to produce inverted burners which should heat a mantle suspended below the mouth of the burner. As early as 1882 Clamond made what was practically an inverted gas and air blowpipe to use with his incandescent basket, but it was not until [illegible] the inverted mantle became a possibility. Although there was a strong prejudice against it at first, as soon as a really satisfactory burner was introduced, its success was [illegible]. The inverted mantle has now [illegible] lators in the enormous success [illegible] illumination

given by it is far more efficient than with the upright mantle, and it also lends itself well to ornamental treatment.

Burners.

When the incandescent mantle was first introduced in 1886 an ordinary laboratory Bunsen burner was experimentally employed, but unless a very narrow mantle just fitting the top of the tube was used the flame could not be got to fit the mantle, and it was only the extreme outer edge of the flame which endowed the mantle fabric with the high incandescent. A wide burner top was then placed on the Bunsen tube so as to spread the flame, and a larger mantle became possible, but it was then found that the slowing down of the rate of flow at the mouth of the burner owing to its enlargement caused flashing or firing back, and to prevent this a wire gauze covering was fitted to the burner head; and in this way the 1886–1887 commercial Welsbach burner was produced. The length of the Bunsen tube, however, made an unsightly fitting, so it was shortened, and the burner head made to slip over it, whilst an external lighting back plate was added. The form of the "C" burner thus arrived at has undergone no important further change. When later on it was desired to make incandescent mantle burners that should not need the aid of a chimney to increase the air supply, the long Bunsen tube was reverted to, and the Kern, Bandsept, and other burners of this class all have a greater total length than the ordinary burners. To secure proper mixing of the air and gas, and to prevent flashing back, they all have heads fitted with baffles, perforations, gauze, and other devices which oppose considerable resistance to the flow of the stream of air and gas.

In 1900, therefore, two classes of burner were in commercial existence for incandescent lighting—(1) the short burner with chimney, and (2) the long burner without chimney. Both classes had the burner mouth closed with gauze or similar device, and both needed as an essential that the mantle should fit closely to the burner head.

Prior to 1900 attempts had been made to construct a burner in which an incandescent mantle should be suspended head downwards. Inventors all turned to the overhead regenerative gas lamps of the Wenham type, or the inverted blowpipe used by Clamond, and in attempting to make an inverted Bunsen employed either artificial pressure to the gas or the air, or to both, or else enclosed the burner and mantle in a globe, and by means of a long chimney created a strong draught. These burners also were all regenerative and aimed at heating the air or gas or mixture of the two, and they had the further drawback of being complicated and costly. Regeneration is a valuable adjunct in ordinary gas lighting as it increases the actions that liberate the carbon particles upon which the luminosity of a flame is dependent, and also increases the temperature; but with the mixture of air and gas in a Bunsen regeneration is not a great gain when low and is a drawback when intense, because incipient combination is induced between the oxygen of the air and the coal-gas before the burner head is reached, the proportions of air and gas are disturbed, and the flame instead of being non-luminous shows slight luminosity and tends to blacken the mantle. The only early attempt to burn a mantle in an inverted position without regeneration or artificial pressure or draught was made by H. A. Kent in 1897, and he used, not an inverted Bunsen, but one with the top elongated and turned over to form a siphon, so that the point of admixture of air and gas was below the level of the burner head, and was therefore kept cool and away from the products of combustion.

In 1900 J. Bernt and E. Cérvenka set themselves to solve the problem of making a Bunsen burner which should consume gas under ordinary gas pressure in an inverted mantle. They took the short Bunsen burner, as found in the most commonly used upright incandescent burners, and fitted to it a long tube, preferably of non-conducting material, which they called an isolator, and which is designed to keep the flame at a distance from the Bunsen. They found that it burnt fairly well, and that the tendency of the flame to burn or lap back was lessened, but that the hot up-current of heated air and products of combustion streamed up to the air holes of the Bunsen, and by contaminating the air supply caused the flame to pulsate. They then fixed an inverted cone on the isolator to throw the products of combustion outwards and away from the air holes, and found that the addition of this "deflecting cone" steadied the flame. Having obtained a satisfactory flame, they attacked the problem of the burner head. Experiments showed that the burner head must be not only open but also of the same size or smaller than the burner tube, and that by projecting it downwards into the mantle and leaving a space between the mantle and the burner head the maximum mantle surface heated to incandescence was obtained. It was also found that the distance which the burner head projects into the mantle is equivalent to the same amount of extra water pressure on the gas, and with a long mantle it was found useful under certain conditions to add a cylinder or sleeve with perforated sides to carry the gas still lower into the mantle. The principles thus set forth by Kent, Bernt and Cérvenka form the basis of construction of all the types of inverted mantle burners which so greatly increased the popularity of incandescent gas lighting at the beginning of the 20th century, whilst improvements in the shape of the mantle for inverted lighting and the methods of attachment to the burner have added to the success achieved.

The wonderful increase in the amount of light that can be obtained from gas by the aid of the incandescent gas mantle is realized when one compares the 1 to 3·2 candles per cubic foot given by the burners used in the middle of the 19th century with the duty of incandescent burners, as shown in the following table:—

Light yielded per cubic foot of Gas.

Burner.	Candle power.
Low pressure upright incandescent burners	15 to 20 candles
Inverted burners	14 to 21 ,,
Kern burners	20 to 24 ,,
High pressure burners	22 to 36 ,,

(V. B. L.)

3. Electric Lighting.

Electric lamps are of two varieties: (1) *Arc Lamps* and (2) *Incandescent* or *Glow Lamps*. Under these headings we may briefly consider the history, physical principles, and present practice of the art of electric lighting.

1. *Arc Lamps.*—If a voltaic battery of a large number of cells has its terminal wires provided with rods of electrically-conducting carbon, and these are brought in contact and then slightly separated, a form of electric discharge takes place between them called the *electric arc*. It is not quite certain who first observed this effect of the electric current. The statement that Sir Humphry Davy, in 1801, first produced and studied the phenomenon is probably correct. In 1808 Davy had provided for him at the Royal Institution a battery of 2000 cells, with which he exhibited the electric arc on a large scale.

The electric arc may be produced between any conducting materials maintained at different potentials, provided that the source of electric supply is able to furnish a sufficiently large current; but for illuminating purposes pieces of hard graphitic carbon are most convenient. If some source of continuous electric current is connected to rods of such carbon, first brought into contact and then slightly separated, the following facts may be noticed: With a low electromotive force of about 50 or 60 volts no discharge takes place until the carbons are in actual contact, unless the insulation of the air is broken down by the passage of a small electric spark. When this occurs, the space between the carbons is filled at once with a flame or luminous vapour, and the carbons themselves become highly incandescent at their extremities. If they are horizontal the flame takes the form of an arch springing between their tips, hence the name *arc*. This varies somewhat in appearance according to the nature of the current, whether continuous or alternating, and according as it is formed in the open air or in an enclosed space to which free access of oxygen is prevented. Electric arcs between metal surfaces differ greatly in colour according to the nature of the metal When formed by an alternating current of high electromotive force they resemble a lambent flame, flickering and producing a somewhat shrill humming sound.

Electric arcs may be classified into continuous or alternating current arcs, and open or enclosed arcs, carbon arcs with pure or chemically impregnated carbons, or so-called flame arcs, and arcs formed with metallic or oxide electrodes, such as magnetite. A continuous current arc is formed with an electric current flowing always in the same direction; an alternating current arc is formed with a periodically reversed current. An open arc is one in which the carbons or other material forming the arc are freely exposed to the air; an enclosed arc is one in which they are included in a glass vessel. If carbons impregnated with various salts are used to colour or increase the light, the arc is called a chemical or flame arc. The carbons or electrodes may be arranged in line one above the other, or they may be inclined so as to project the light downwards or more in one direction. In a carbon arc if the current is continuous the positive carbon becomes much hotter at the end than the negative, and in the open air it is worn away, partly by combustion, becoming hollowed out at the extremity into a *crater*. At the same time the negative carbon gradually becomes pointed, and also wears away, though much less quickly than the positive. In the continuous-current open arc the greater part of the light proceeds from the highly incandescent positive crater. When the arc is examined through dark glasses, or by the optical projection of its image upon a screen, a violet band or stream of vapour is seen to extend between the two carbons, surrounded by a nebulous golden flame or aureole. If the carbons are maintained at the right distance apart the arc remains steady and silent, but if the carbons are impure, or the distance between them too great, the true electric arc rapidly changes its place, flickering about and frequently becoming extinguished; when this happens it can only be restored by bringing the carbons once more into contact. If the current is alternating, then the arc is symmetrical, and both carbons possess nearly the same appearance. If it is enclosed in a vessel nearly air-tight, the rate at which the carbons are burnt away is greatly reduced, and if the current is continuous the positive carbon is no longer cratered out and the negative no longer so much pointed as in the case of the open arc.

Carbons. Davy used for his first experiments rods of wood charcoal which had been heated and plunged into mercury to make them better conductors. Not until 1843 was it proposed by J. B. L. Foucault to employ pencils cut from the hard graphitic carbon deposited in the interior of gas retorts. In 1846 W. Greener and W. E. Staite patented a process for manufacturing carbons for this purpose, but only after the invention of the Gramme dynamo in 1870 any great demand arose for them. F. P. E. Carré in France in 1876 began to manufacture arc lamp carbons of high quality from coke, lampblack and syrup. Now they are made by taking some specially refined form of finely divided carbon, such as the soot or lampblack formed by cooling the smoke of burning paraffin or tar, or by the carbonization of organic matter, and making it into a paste with gum or syrup. This carbon paste is forced through dies by means of a hydraulic press, the rods thus formed being subsequently baked with such precautions as to preserve them perfectly straight In some cases they are *cored*, that is to say, have a longitudinal hole down them, filled in with a softer carbon. Sometimes they are covered with a thin layer of copper by electro-deposition. They are supplied for the market in sizes varying from 4 or 5 to 30 or 40 millimetres in diameter, and from 8 to 16 in. in length. The value of carbons for arc lighting greatly depends on their purity and freedom from ash in burning, and on perfect uniformity of structure. For ordinary purposes they are generally round in section, but for certain special uses, such as lighthouse work, they are made fluted or with a star-shaped section. The positive carbon is usually of larger section than the negative. For continuous-current arcs a cored carbon is generally used as a positive, and a smaller solid carbon as a negative. For flame arc lamps the carbons are specially prepared by impregnating them with salts of calcium, magnesium and sodium. The calcium gives the best results. The rod is usually of a composite type. The outer zone is pure carbon to give strength, the next zone contains carbon mixed with the metallic salts, and the inner core

in the process by as to be easily bur it is to be used, burning off, shapi

Since 1897 in intensifying the and ir of gas. or hav under systems those successful. A the Lucas ligh chimneys in t chimney used burner and m of the increas given by the Snell system given by th the burner of the lamp these syste large towns Europe.

Intensifying systems.

The oth descent ga power in c increased motor, h be efficie installati a gas eng by the principle in the a engine. gas is br $2\frac{1}{2}$ in. light ol is 300 c of gas, pressure an hour of 32 ca incandes volume with low illumina tion of la Selas, and for this p.

The ligi in an upr

Inverted burners.

purposes t below 45° loss of effici the light th avoid this to produce pended belo Clamond ma blowpipe to u 1900–1901 tha though there as a really sat quickly placed proved [illegible]

the carbons (the arc P.D.) decreases as the current increases. Up to a certain current strength the arc is silent, but at a particular critical value P.D. suddenly drops about 10 volts, the current at the same time rising 2 or 3 amperes. At that moment the arc begins to *hiss*, and in this hissing condition, if the current is still further increased, P.D. remains constant over wide limits. This drop in voltage on hissing was first noticed by A. Niaudet (*La Lumière électrique*, 1881, 3, p. 287). It has been shown by Mrs Ayrton (*Journ. Inst. Elec. Eng.* 28, 1899, p. 400) that the hissing is mainly due to the oxygen which gains access from the air to the crater, when the latter becomes so large by reason of the increase of the current as to overspread the end of the positive carbon. According to A. E. Blondel and Hans Luggin, hissing takes place whenever the current density becomes greater than about 0·3 or 0·5 ampere per square millimetre of crater area.

The relation between the current, the carbon P.D., and the length of arc in the case of the direct-current arc has been investigated by many observers with the object of giving it mathematical expression.

Let V stand for the potential difference of the carbons in volts, A for the current through the arc in amperes, L for the length of the arc in millimetres, R for the resistance of the arc; and let a, b, c, d, &c., be constants. Erik Edlund in 1867, and other workers after him, considered that their experiments showed that the relation between V and L could be expressed by a simple linear equation,

$$V=a+bL.$$

Later researches by Mrs Ayrton (*Electrician*, 1898, 41, p. 720), however, showed that for a direct-current arc of given size with solid carbons, the observed values of V can be better represented as a function both of A and of L in the form

$$V=a+bL+\frac{c+dL}{A}.$$

In the case of direct-current arcs formed with solid carbons, Edlund and other observers agree that the arc resistance R may be expressed by a simple straight line law, $R=e+fL$. If the arc is formed with cored carbons, Mrs Ayrton demonstrated that the lines representing resistance as a function of arc length are no longer straight, but that there is a rather sudden dip down when the length of the arc is less than 3 mm.

The constants in the above equation for the potential difference of the carbons were determined by Mrs Ayrton in the case of solid carbons to be—

$$V=38·9+2·07L+\frac{11·7+10·5L}{A}.$$

There has been much debate as to the meaning to be given to the constant a in the above equation, which has a value apparently not far from forty volts for a direct-current arc with solid carbons. The suggestion made in 1867 by Edlund (*Phil. Mag.*, 1868, 36, p. 358), that it implied the existence of a counter-electromotive force in the arc, was opposed by Luggin in 1889 (*Wien. Ber.* 98, p. [illegible]), Ernst Lecher in 1888 (*Wied. Ann.*, 1888, 33, p. 609), and by Franz Stenger in 1892 (*Id.* 45, p. 33); whereas Victor von Lang and W. Arons in [illegible] (*Id.* 30, p. 95), concluded that experiment indicated the presence of a counter-electromotive force of 20 volts. A. E. Blondel concludes, from experiments made by him in 1897 (*The Electrician*, 1897, 39, p. 615), that there is no counter-electromotive force in the arc greater than a fraction of a volt. Subsequently W. Duddell (*Proc. Roy. Soc.*, 1901, 68, p. 512) described experiments tending to prove the real existence of a counter-electromotive force in the arc, probably having a thermo-electric origin, residing near the positive electrode, and of an associated lesser back E.M.F. near the negative carbon.

The fall in voltage between the carbons and the arc is not uniformly distributed. In 1898 Mrs Ayrton described the results of experiments showing that if V_1 is the potential difference between the positive carbon and the arc, then

$$V_1=31·28+\frac{9+3·1L}{A};$$

and if V_2 is the potential difference between the arc and the negative carbon, then

$$V_2=7·6+\frac{13·6}{A},$$

where A is the current through the arc in amperes and L is the length of the arc in millimetres.

The total potential difference between the carbons, minus the fall in potential down the arc, is therefore equal to the sum of $V_1+V_2=V_3$.

$$\text{Hence } V_3=38·88+\frac{22·6+3·1L}{A}.$$

The difference between this value and the value of V, the total potential difference between the carbons, gives the loss in potential due to the true arc. These laws are simple consequences of straight-line laws connecting the work spent in the arc at the two electrodes with the other quantities. If W be the work spent in the arc on either carbon, measured by the product of the current and the potential drop in passing from the carbon to the arc, or vice versa, then for the positive carbon $W=a+bA$, if the length of arc is constant, $W=c+dL$, if the current through the arc is constant, and for the negative carbon $W=e+fA$.

In the above experiments the potential difference between the carbons and the arc was measured by using a third exploring carbon as an electrode immersed in the arc. This method, adopted by Lecher, F. Uppenborn, S. P. Thompson, and J. A. Fleming, is open to the objection that the introduction of the third carbon may to a considerable extent disturb the distribution of potential.

The total work spent in the continuous-current arc with solid carbons may, according to Mrs Ayrton, be expressed by the equation

$$W=11{\cdot}7+10{\cdot}5L+(38{\cdot}9+2{\cdot}07L)A.$$

It will thus be seen that the arc, considered as a conductor, has the property that if the current through it is increased, the difference of potential between the carbons is decreased, and in one sense, therefore, the arc may be said to act as if it were a *negative resistance*. Frith and Rodgers (*Electrician*, 1896, 38, p. 75) have suggested that the resistance of the arc should be measured by the ratio between a small increment of carbon potential difference and the resulting small increment of current; in other words, by the equation dV/dA, and not by the ratio simply of V:A. Considerable discussion has taken place whether an electrical resistance can have a negative value, belonging as it does to the class of scalar mathematical quantities. Simply considered as an electrical conductor, the arc resembles an intensely heated rod of magnesia or other refractory oxide, the true resistance of which is decreased by rise of temperature. Hence an increase of current through such a rod of refractory oxide is accompanied by a decrease in the potential difference of the ends. This, however, does not imply a negative resistance, but merely the presence of a resistance with a negative temperature coefficient. If we plot a curve such that the ordinates are the difference of potential of the carbons and the abscissae the current through the arc for constant length of arc, this curve is now called a *characteristic curve* of the arc and its slope at any point the instantaneous resistance of the arc.

Other physical investigations have been concerned with the intrinsic brightness of the crater. It has been asserted by many observers, such as Blondel, Sir W. de W. Abney, S. P. Thompson, Trotter, L. J. G. Violle and others, that this is practically independent of the current passing, but great differences of opinion exist as to its value. Abney's values lie between 39 and 116, Trotter's between 80 and 170 candles per square millimetre. Blondel in 1893 made careful determinations of the brightness of the arc crater, and came to the conclusion that it was 160 candles per square millimetre. Subsequently J. E. Petavel found a value of 147 candles per square millimetre for current densities varying from ·06 to ·26 amperes per square millimetre (*Proc. Roy. Soc.*, 1899, 65, p. 469). Violle also, in 1893, supported the opinion that the brightness of the crater per square millimetre was independent of the current density, and from certain experiments and assumptions as to the specific heat of carbon, he asserted the temperature of the crater was about 3500° C. It has been concluded that this constancy of temperature, and therefore of brightness, is due to the fact that the crater is at the temperature of the boiling-point of carbon, and in that case its temperature should be raised by increasing the pressure under which the arc works. W. E. Wilson in 1895 attempted to measure the brightness of the crater under various pressures, and found that under five atmospheres the resistance of the arc appeared to increase and the temperature of the crater to fall, until at a pressure of 20 atmospheres the brightness of the crater had fallen to a dull red. In a later paper Wilson and G. F. Fitzgerald stated that these preliminary experiments were not confirmed, and their later researches throw considerable doubt on the suggestion that it is the boiling-point of carbon which determines the temperature of the crater. (See *Electrician*, 1895, 35, p. 260, and 1897, 38, p. 343.)

Alternating current arc.

The study of the alternating-current arc has suggested a number of new experimental problems for investigators. In this case all the factors, namely, current, carbon P.D., resistance, and illuminating power, are periodically varying; and as the electromotive force reverses itself periodically, at certain instants the current through the arc is zero. As the current can be interrupted for a moment without extinguishing the arc, it is possible to work the electric arc from an alternating current generator without apparent intermission in the light, provided that the frequency is not much below 50. During the moment that the current is zero the carbon continues to glow. Each carbon in turn becomes, so to speak, the crater carbon, and the illuminating power is therefore symmetrically distributed. The curve of illumination is as shown in fig. 3. The nature of the variation of the current and arc P.D. can be examined by one of two methods, or their modifications, originally due to Jules Joubert and A. E. Blondel. Joubert's method, which has been perfected by many observers, consists in attaching to the shaft of the alternator a contact which closes a circuit at an assigned instant during the phase. This contact is made to complete connexion either with a voltmeter or with a galvanometer placed as a shunt across the carbons or in series with the arc. By this arrangement these instruments do not read, as usual, the root-mean-square value of the arc P.D. or current, but give a constant indication determined by, and indicating, the instantaneous values of these quantities at some assigned instant. By progressive variation of the phase-instant at which the contact is made, the successive instantaneous values of the electric quantities can be measured and plotted out in the form of curves. This method has been much employed by Blondel, Fleming, C. P. Steinmetz, Tobey and Walbridge, Frith, H. Görges and many others. The second method, due to Blondel, depends on the use of the *Oscillograph*, which is a galvanometer having a needle or coil of very small periodic time of vibration, say $\frac{1}{10000}$th part of a second or less, so that its deflections can follow the variations of current passing through the galvanometer. An improved form of oscillograph, devised by Duddell, consists of two fine wires, which are strained transversely to the lines of flux of a strong magnetic field (see OSCILLOGRAPH). The current to be examined is made to pass up one wire and down the other, and these wires are then slightly displaced in opposite directions. A small mirror attached to the wires is thus deflected rapidly to and fro in synchronism with the variations of the current. From the mirror a ray of light is reflected which falls upon a photographic plate made to move across the field with a uniform motion. In this manner a photographic trace can be obtained of the wave form. By this method the variations of electric quantities in an alternating-current arc can be watched. The variation of illuminating power can be followed by examining and measuring the light of the arc through slits in a revolving stroboscopic disk, which is driven by a motor synchronously with the variation of current through the arc.

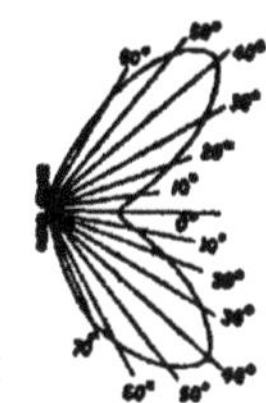

FIG. 6.

The general phenomena of the alternating-current arc are as follow:—

If the arc is supplied by an alternator of low inductance, and soft or cored carbons are employed to produce a steady and silent arc, the potential difference of the carbons periodically varies in a manner not very different from that of the alternator on open circuit. If, however, hard carbons are used, the alternating-current arc deforms the shape of the alternator electromotive force curve; the carbon P.D. curve may then have a very different form, and becomes, in general, more rectangular in shape, usually having a high peak at the front. The arc also impresses the deformation on the current curve. Blondel in 1893 (*Electrician*, 32, p. 161) gave a number of potential and current curves for alternating-current arcs, obtained by the Joubert contact method, using two movable coil galvanometers of high resistance to measure respectively potential difference and current. Blondel's deductions were that the shape of the current and volt curves is greatly affected by the nature of the carbons, and also by the amount of inductance and resistance in the circuit of the alternator. Blondel, W. E. Ayrton, W. E. Sumpner and Steinmetz have all observed that the alternating-current arc, when hissing or when formed with uncored carbons, acts like an inductive resistance, and that there is a lag between the current curves and the potential difference curves. Hence the *power-factor*, or ratio between the true power and the product of the root-mean-square values of arc current and carbon potential

If a continuous-current electric arc is formed in the open air with a positive carbon having a diameter of about 15 millimetres, and a negative carbon having a diameter of about 9 millimetres, and if a current of 10 amperes is employed, the potential difference between the carbons is generally from 40 to 50 volts. Such a lamp is therefore called a 500-watt arc. Under these conditions the carbons each burn away at the rate of about 1 in. per hour, actual combustion taking place in the air which gains access to the highly-heated crater and negative tip; hence the most obvious means of preventing this disappearance is to enclose the arc in an air-tight glass vessel. Such a device was tried very early in the history of arc lighting. The result of using a completely air-tight globe, however, is that the contained oxygen is removed by combustion with the carbon, and carbon vapour or hydrocarbon compounds diffuse through the enclosed space and deposit themselves on the cool sides of the glass, which is thereby obscured. It was, however, shown by L. B. Marks (*Electrician* 31, p. 502, and 38, p. 646) in 1893, that if the arc is an arc formed with a small current and relatively high voltage, namely, 80 to 85 volts, it is possible to admit air in such small amount that though the rate of combustion of the carbons is reduced, yet the air destroys by oxidation the carbon vapour escaping from the arc. An arc lamp operated in this way is called an enclosed arc lamp (fig. 8). The top of the enclosing bulb is closed by a gas check plug which admits through a small hole a limited supply of air. The peculiarity of an enclosed arc lamp operated with a continuous current is that the carbons do not burn to a crater on the positive, and a sharp tip or mushroom on the negative, but preserve nearly flat surfaces. This feature affects the distribution of the light. The illuminating curve of the enclosed arc, therefore, has not such a strongly marked maximum value as that of the open arc, but on the other hand the true arc or column of incandescent carbon vapour is less steady in position, wandering round from place to place on the surface of the carbons. As a compensation for this defect, the combustion of the carbons per hour in commercial forms of enclosed arc lamps is about one-twentieth part of that of an open arc lamp taking the same current.

Enclosed arc lamps.

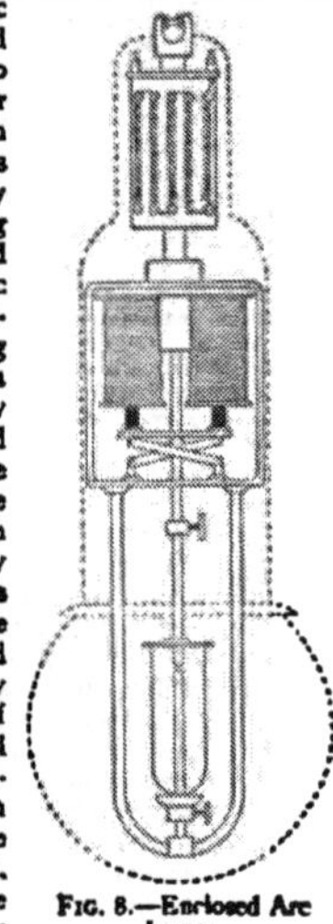

Fig. 8.—Enclosed Arc Lamp.

It was shown by Fleming in 1890 that the column of incandescent carbon vapour constituting the true arc possesses a unilateral conductivity (*Proc. Roy. Inst.* 13, p. 47). If a third carbon is dipped into the arc so as to constitute a third pole, and if a small voltaic battery of a few cells, with a galvanometer in circuit, is connected in between the middle pole and the negative carbon, it is found that when the negative pole of the battery is in connexion with the negative carbon the galvanometer indicates a current, but does not when the positive pole of the battery is in connexion with the negative carbon of the arc.

Turning next to the consideration of the electric arc as a source of light, we have already noticed that the illuminating power in different directions is not the same. If we imagine an electric arc, formed between a pair of vertical carbons, to be placed in the centre of a hollow sphere painted white on the interior, then it would be found that the various zones of this sphere are unequally illuminated. If the points in which the carbons when prolonged would intercept the sphere are called the poles, and the line where the horizontal plane through the arc would intercept the sphere

The arc as an illuminant.

is called the equator, we might consider the sphere divided up by lines of latitude into zones, each of which would be differently illuminated. The total quantity of light or the total illumination of each zone is the product of the area of the zone and the intensity of the light falling on the zone measured in candle-power. We might regard the sphere as uniformly illuminated with an intensity of light such that the product of this intensity and the total surface of the sphere was numerically equal to the surface integral obtained by summing up the products of the areas of all the elementary zones and the intensity of the light falling on each. This mean intensity is called the *mean spherical candle-power* of the arc. If the distribution of the illuminating power is known and given by an illumination curve, the mean spherical candle-power can be at once deduced (*La Lumière électrique*, 1890, 37, p. 415).

Let BMC (fig. 9) be a semicircle which by revolution round the diameter BC sweeps out a sphere. Let an arc be situated at A, and let the element of the circumference $PQ = ds$ sweep out a zone of the sphere. Let the intensity of light falling on this zone be I. Then if θ = the angle MAP and $d\theta$ the incremental angle PAQ, and if R is the radius of the sphere, we have

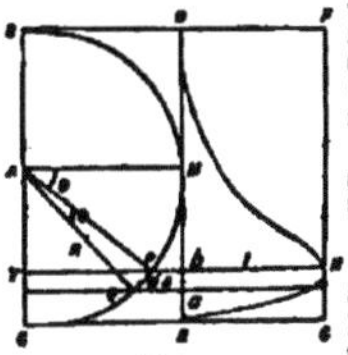

$$ds = Rd\theta;$$

also, if we project the element PQ on the line DE we have

$$ab = ds \cos\theta,$$

$$\therefore ab = R \cos\theta d\theta$$

and $$Iab = IR \cos\theta d\theta.$$

Let r denote the radius PT of the zone of the sphere, then

FIG. 9

$$r = R \cos\theta.$$

Hence the area of the zone swept out by PQ is equal to

$$2\pi R \cos\theta\, ds = 2\pi R^2 \cos\theta d\theta$$

in the limit, and the total quantity of light falling on the zone is equal to the product of the mean intensity or candle-power I in the direction AP and the area of the zone, and therefore to

$$2\pi I R^2 \cos\theta d\theta.$$

Let I_0 stand for the mean spherical candle-power, that is, let I_0 be defined by the equation

$$4\pi R^2 I_0 = 2\pi R \Sigma(Iab)$$

where $\Sigma(Iab)$ is the sum of all the light actually falling on the sphere surface, then

$$I_0 = \frac{1}{2R}\Sigma(Iab)$$

$$= \frac{\Sigma(Iab)}{2RI_{max}} I_{max}$$

where I_{max} stands for the maximum candle-power of the arc. If, then, we set off at b a line bH perpendicular to DE and in length proportional to the candle-power of the arc in the direction AP, and carry out the same construction for a number of different observed candle-power readings at known angles above and below the horizon, the summits of all ordinates such as bH will define a curve DHE. The mean spherical candle-power of the arc is equal to the product of the maximum candle-power (I_{max}), and a fraction equal to the ratio of the area included by the curve DHE to its circumscribing rectangle DFGE. The area of the curve DHE multiplied by $2\pi/R$ gives us the *total flux of light* from the arc.

Owing to the inequality in the distribution of light from an electric arc, it is impossible to define the illuminating power by a single number in any other way than by stating the mean spherical candle-power. All such commonly used expressions as "an arc lamp of 2000 candle-power" are, therefore, perfectly meaningless.

Photometry of arcs. The photometry of arc lamps presents particular difficulties, owing to the great difference in quality between the light radiated by the arc and that given by any of the ordinarily used light standards. (For standards of light and photometers, see PHOTOMETER.) All photometry depends on the principle that if we illuminate two white surfaces respectively and exclusively by two separate sources of light, we can by moving the lights bring the two surfaces into such a condition that their *illumination* or *brightness* is the same without regard to any small colour difference. The quantitative measurement depends on the fact that the illumination produced upon a surface by a source of light is inversely as the square of the distance of the source. The trained eye is capable of making a comparison between two surfaces illuminated by different sources of light, and pronouncing upon their equality or otherwise in respect of brightness, apart from a certain colour difference; but for this to be done with accuracy the two illuminated surfaces, the brightness of which is to be compared, must be absolutely contiguous and not separated by any harsh line. The process of comparing the light from the arc directly with that of a candle or other similar flame standard is exceedingly difficult, owing to the much greater proportion and intensity of the violet rays in the arc. The most convenient practical working standard is an incandescent lamp run at a high temperature, that is, at an efficiency of about 2½ watts per candle. If it has a sufficiently large bulb, and has been *aged* by being worked for some time previously, it will at a constant voltage preserve a constancy in illuminating power sufficiently long to make the necessary photometric comparisons, and it can itself be compared at intervals with another standard incandescent lamp, or with a flame standard such as a Harcourt pentane lamp.

In measuring the candle-power of arc lamps it is necessary to have some arrangement by which the brightness of the rays proceeding from the arc in different directions can be measured. For this purpose the lamp may be suspended from a support, and a radial arm arranged to carry three mirrors, so that in whatever position the arm may be placed, it gathers light proceeding at one particular angle above or below the horizon from the arc, and this light is reflected out finally in a constant horizontal direction. An easily-arranged experiment enables us to determine the constant loss of light by reflection at all the mirrors, since that reflection always takes place at 45°. The ray thrown out horizontally can then be compared with that from any standard source of light by means of a fixed photometer, and by sweeping round the radial arm the photometric or illuminating curve of the arc lamp can be obtained. From this we can at once determine the nature of the illumination which would be produced on a horizontal surface if the arc lamp were suspended at a given distance above it. Let A (fig. 10) be an arc lamp placed at a height h(= AB) above a horizontal plane. Let ACD be the illuminating power curve of the arc, and hence AC the candle-power in a direction AP. The illumination (I) or brightness on the horizontal plane at P is equal to

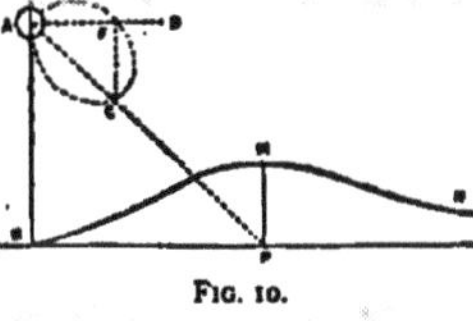

FIG. 10.

$$AC \cos APM/(AP)^2 = FC/(h^2+x^2), \text{ where } x = BP.$$

Hence if the candle-power curve of the arc and its height above the surface are known, we can describe a curve BMN, whose ordinate PM will denote the brightness on the horizontal surface at any point P. It is easily seen that this ordinate must have a maximum value at some point. This brightness is best expressed in *candle-feet*, taking the unit of illumination to be that given by a standard candle on a white surface at a distance of 1 ft. If any number of arc lamps are placed above a horizontal plane, the brightness at any point can be calculated by adding together the illuminations due to each respectively.

The process of delineating the photometric or polar curve of intensity for an arc lamp is somewhat tedious, but the curve has the advantage of showing exactly the distribution of light in different directions. When only the mean spherical or mean hemispherical candle-power is required the process can be shortened by employing an integrating photometer such as that of C. P. Matthews (*Trans. Amer. Inst. Elec. Eng.*, 1903, 19, p. 1465), or the lumen-meter of A. E. Blondel which enables us to determine at one observation the total flux of light from the arc and therefore the mean spherical candle-power per watt.

Street arc lighting. In the use of arc lamps for street and public lighting, the question of the distribution of light on the horizontal surface is all-important. In order that street surfaces may be well lighted, the minimum illumination should not fall below 0·1 candle-foot, and in general, in well-lighted streets, the maximum illumination will be 1 candle-foot and upwards. By means of an illumination photometer, such as that of W. H. Preece and A. P. Trotter, it is easy to measure the illumination in candle-feet at any point in a street surface, and to plot out a number of contour lines of equal illumination. Experience has shown that to obtain satisfactory results the lamps must be placed on a high mast 20 or 25 ft. above the roadway surface. These posts are now generally made of cast iron in various ornamental forms (fig. 11), the necessary conductors for conveying the current up to the lamp being taken

difference, in this
power-factors lyi
values such as o
factor may be as
the deformation
the electromotive
circuit a simple ha
and Walbridge in
taken with comme
which the same def
to the conclusion t
carbon P.D. curves
material of the core,
circuit. Hard carbor
worked on a low indu

The periodic varia
has also been the sub
applied a stroboscopic
ing power. Fleming a
driving the stroboscop
1896, 41). The light p
in one particular perioc
be taken from any des
carbons. The light so s
value of the horizontal
variations were thus eli
any part is periodic, bu
never quite zero, the
than the zero value o
particular carbon when it
maximum value as whe
made experiments whic
penditure of power in
general gives less mean
current one.

The effect of the wav
current arc has engaged
Wedding in 1894 gave a
current arcs produced
curves of very different
ency or mean spherical
was greatest for the flat
Burnie in 1897 gave th
His conclusion was, th
the temperature, that
maintains the temper
period. Hence, gener
after its commencemer
at that value, during
greater when the curr
important contribution
current arc phenomena
Marchant, in a paper
their improved oscillo
alternating-current arc
cored carbons, and with
with solid carbons the
and begins with a peak,

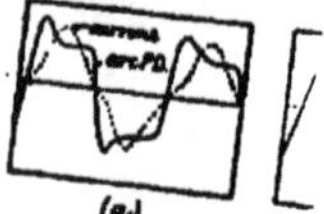

(a.)

Fig. 7.

portance of selecting a sui
current arcs. The same
able fact that if the arc
rod, say a zinc rod, there
over half a period corres
carbon is positive; this
metal facilitates the flow
flow of current to it. The
curve form in the case of a
Duddell and Marchant sh
arc is intermittent, and
have a frequency of 100
enclosing the arc increase
potential curve becoming
the arc reduced.

[1] Journ. Inst. Elec. Eng.
numerous instructive curve
be form of the arc P.D. ar
lternating-c

[illegible]

[illegible] a very usual practice is to place [illegible] or six to ten times their height above [illegible] (Electrician, 35, p. 846) gives the [illegible] of the arc to afford the maximum [illegible] from the foot of the lamp-post, [illegible] being employed:—

[illegible]	. .	$h=0{\cdot}95\,d$.
[illegible] globe	. .	$h=0{\cdot}85\,d$.
[illegible]	. .	$h=$ „
[illegible]	. .	$h=0{\cdot}5\,d$.
[illegible] globe	. .	$h=0{\cdot}5\,d$.

[illegible] distribution of light on the hori[illegible] affected by the nature of the enclosing [illegible] naked arcs, although some[illegible] factory yards, are entirely un[illegible] the eye by the bright [illegible] of the retina and contract [illegible] less sensitive when directed [illegible] Accordingly, diffusing globes [illegible] the arc in the interior [illegible] diameter. This may be made [illegible] dioptric globe such as the [illegible] are strongly absorptive, as may [illegible] experiments by Guthrie and Redhead. [illegible] the astonishing loss of light due to [illegible]

	Naked Arc.	Arc in Clear Globe.	Arc in Rough Glass Globe.	Arc in Opal Globe.
[illegible]	319	235	160	144
[illegible]	450	326	215	138
[illegible]	100	53	23	19
[illegible]	0	47	77	81

[illegible] Trudureau's or the holophane globe, [illegible] that the whole globe appears uni[illegible] not more than 20% of the light is [illegible] absorption of an ordinary opal globe [illegible] arc does not usually give more than [illegible] candle-power. Even with a naked [illegible] mean spherical candle-power is not generally [illegible] the rate of 1 c.p. per watt. The maxi[illegible] of a given electrical power is, however, [illegible] the current density in the carbon, and [illegible] current density the carbons must be as [illegible] See T. Hesketh, "Notes on the Electric [illegible] p. 707.)

[illegible] arcs of various kinds, expressed by the [illegible] candle power per ampere and per watt [illegible] the following figures were given by L. [illegible] Arc Lamps," *Journal Inst. Elec. Eng.*, [illegible]

	Candle-power per ampere.	Candle-power per watt.
[illegible] open arc . . .	82	1·54
[illegible] . . .	55	0·77
[illegible] flame arc . .	259	5·80
[illegible] carbon arc . .	200	2·24

[illegible] the flame arc lamp has an enormous advantage [illegible] the light yielded for a given electric power [illegible]

[illegible] employment of the electric arc as a means [illegible] upon mechanism for automatically [illegible] carbon rods in the proper position, [illegible] enable a steady arc to be [illegible] be provided for holding [illegible] the lamp is not in opera[illegible] come together when the current [illegible] the arc. As soon as the current [illegible] slightly apart, and gripped in [illegible] reaches its right value, being

Arc lamp mechanism.

moved farther apart if the current increases in strength, and brought together if it decreases. Moreover, it must be possible for a considerable length of carbon to be fed through the lamp as required.

One early devised form of arc-lamp mechanism was a system of clock-work driven by a spring or weight, which was started and stopped by the action of an electromagnet; in modern lighthouse lamps a similar mechanism is still employed. W. E. Staite (1847), J. B. L. Foucault (1849), V. L. M. Serrin (1857), J. Duboscq (1858), and a host of later inventors, devised numerous forms of mechanical and clock-work lamps. The modern self-regulating type may be said to have been initiated in 1878 by the differential lamp of F. von Hefner-Alteneck, and the clutch lamp of C. F. Brush. The general principle of the former may be explained as follows: There are two solenoids, placed one above the other. The lower one, of thick wire, is in series with the two carbon rods forming the arc, and is hence called the *series coil*. Above this there is placed another solenoid of fine wire, which is called the *shunt coil*. Suppose an iron rod to be placed so as to be partly in one coil and partly in another; then when the coils are traversed by currents, the iron core will be acted upon by forces tending to pull it into these solenoids. If the iron core be attached to one end of a lever, the other end of which carries the upper carbon, it will be seen that if the carbons are in contact and the current is switched on, the series coil alone will be traversed by the current, and its magnetic action will draw down the iron core, and therefore pull the carbons apart and strike the arc. The moment the carbons separate, there will be a difference of potential between them, and the shunt coil will then come into action, and will act on the core so as to draw the carbons together. Hence the two solenoids act in opposition to each other, one increasing and the other diminishing the length of the arc, and maintaining the carbons in the proper position. In the lamp of this type the upper carbon is in reality attached to a rod having a side-rack gearing, with a train of wheels governed by a pendulum. The action of the series coil on the mechanism is to first lock or stop the train, and then lift it as a whole slightly. This strikes the arc. When the arc is too long, the series coil lowers the gear and finally releases the upper carbon, so that it can run down by its own weight. The principle of a shunt and series coil operating on an iron core in opposition is the basis of the mechanism of a number of arc lamps. Thus the lamp invented by F. Krizik and L. Piette, called from its place of origin the Pilsen lamp, comprises an iron core made in the shape of a double cone or spindle (fig. 13), which is so arranged in a brass tube that it can move into or out of a shunt and series coil, wound the one with fine and the other with thick insulated wire, and hence regulate the position of the carbon attached to it. The movement of this core is made to feed the carbons directly without the intervention of any clock-work, as in the case of the Hefner-Alteneck lamp. In the clutch-lamp mechanism the lower carbon is fixed, and the upper carbon rests upon it by its own weight and that of its holder. The latter consists of a long rod passing through guides, and is embraced somewhere by a ring capable of being tilted or lifted by a finger attached to the armature of an electromagnet the coils of which are in series with the arc. When the current passes through the magnet it attracts the armature, and by tilting the ring lifts the upper carbon-holder and hence strikes the arc. If the current diminishes in value, the upper carbon drops a little by its own weight, and the feed of the lamp is thus effected by a series of small lifts and drops of the upper carbon (fig. 14). Another element sometimes employed in arc-lamp mechanism is the brake-wheel regulator. This is a feature of one form of the Brockie and of the Crompton-Pochin lamps. In these the movement of the carbons is effected by a cord or chain which passes over a wheel, or by a rack geared with the brake wheel. When no current is passing through the lamp, the wheel is free to move, and the carbons fall together; but when the current is switched on, the chain or cord passing over the brake wheel, or the brake wheel itself is gripped in some way, and at the same time the brake wheel is lifted so that the arc is struck.

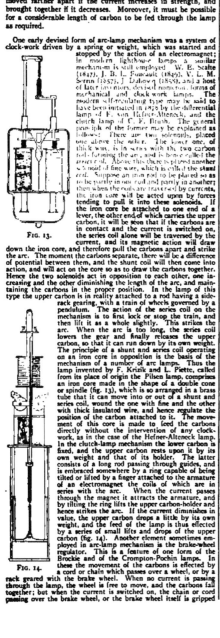

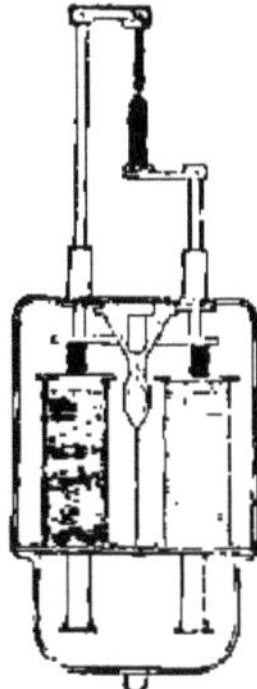

Fig. 13.

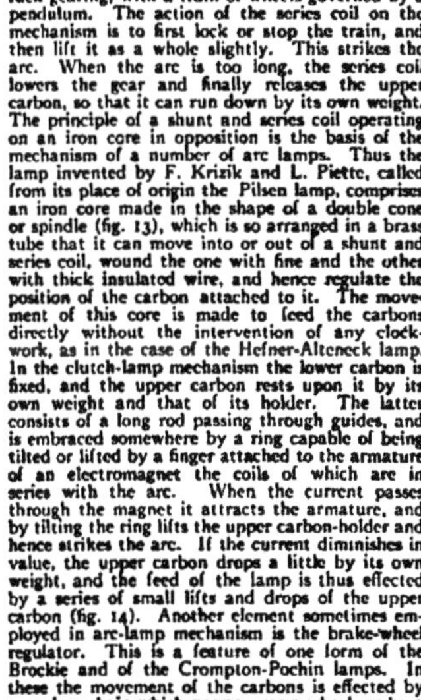

Fig. 14.

Although countless forms of self-regulating device have been invented for arc lamps, nothing has survived the test of time so well as the typical mechanisms which work with carbon rods in one line, one or both rods being moved by a controlling apparatus as required. The early forms of semi-incandescent arc lamp, such as those of R. Werdermann and others, have dropped out of existence. These were not really true arc lamps, the light being produced by the incandescence of the extremity of a thin carbon rod pressed against a larger rod or block. The once famous Jablochkoff candle, invented in 1876, consisted of two carbon rods about 4 mm. in diameter, placed parallel to each other and separated by a partition of kaolin, steatite or other refractory non-conductor. Alternating currents were employed, and the candle was set in operation by a match or starter of high-resistance carbon paste which connected the tips of the rods. When this burned off, a true arc was formed between the parallel carbons, the separator volatilizing as the carbons burned away. Although much ingenuity was expended on this system of lighting between 1877 and 1881, it no longer exists. One cause of its disappearance was its relative inefficiency in light-giving power compared with other forms of carbon arc taking the same amount of power, and a second equally important reason was the waste in carbons. If the arc of the electric candle was accidentally blown out, no means of relighting existed; hence the great waste in half-burnt candles. H. Wilde, J. C. Jamin, J. Rapieff and others endeavoured to provide a remedy, but without success.

It is impossible to give here detailed descriptions of a fraction of the arc-lamp mechanisms devised, and it must suffice to indicate the broad distinctions between various types. (1) Arc lamps may be either *continuous-current* or *alternating-current* lamps. For outdoor public illumination the former are greatly preferable, as owing to the form of the illuminating power-curve they send the light down on the road surface, provided the upper carbon is the positive one. For indoor, public room or factory lighting, *inverted arc* lamps are sometimes employed. In this case the positive carbon is the lower one, and the lamp is carried in an inverted metallic reflector shield, so that the light is chiefly thrown up on the ceiling, whence it is diffused all round. The alternating-current arc is not only less efficient in mean spherical candle-power per watt of electric power absorbed, but its distribution of light is disadvantageous for street purposes. Hence when arc lamps have to be worked off an alternating-current circuit for public lighting it is now usual to make use of a *rectifier*, which rectifies the alternating current into a unidirectional though pulsating current. (2.) Arc lamps may be also classified, as above described, into *open* or *enclosed arcs*. The enclosed arc can be made to burn for 200 hours with one pair of carbons, whereas open-arc lamps are usually only able to work, 8, 16 or 32 hours without recarboning, even when fitted with double carbons. (3) Arc lamps are further divided into *focussing* and *non-focussing* lamps. In the former the lower carbon is made to move up as the upper carbon moves down, and the arc is therefore maintained at the same level. This is advisable for arcs included in a globe, and absolutely necessary in the case of lighthouse lamps and lamps for optical purposes. (4) Another subdivision is into *hand-regulated* and *self-regulating* lamps. In the hand-regulated arcs the carbons are moved by a screw attachment as required, as in some forms of search-light lamp and lamps for optical lanterns. The carbons in large search-light lamps are usually placed horizontally. The self-regulating lamps may be classified into groups depending upon the nature of the regulating appliances. In some cases the regulation is controlled only by a *series coil*, and in others only by a *shunt coil*. Examples of the former are the original Gulcher and Brush clutch lamp, and some modern enclosed arc lamps; and of the latter, the Siemens "band" lamp, and the Jackson-Mensing lamp. In series coil lamps the variation of the current in the coil throws into or out of action the carbon-moving mechanism; in shunt coil lamps the variation in voltage between the carbons is caused to effect the same changes. Other types of lamp involve the use both of shunt and series coils acting against each other. A further classification of the self-regulating lamps may be found in the nature of the carbon-moving mechanism. This may be some modification of the Brush ring clutch, hence called *clutch* lamps; or some variety of *brake wheel*, as employed in Brockie and Crompton lamps; or else some form of *electric motor* is thrown into or out of action and effects the necessary changes. In many cases the arc-lamp mechanism is provided with a *dash-pot*, or contrivance in which a piston moving nearly air-tight in a cylinder prevents sudden jerks in the motion of the mechanism, and thus does away with the "hunting" or rapid up-and-down movements to which some varieties of clutch mechanism are liable. One very [illegible] form is illustrated in the Thomson lamp and Brush-Vienna [illegible] this mechanism a shunt and series coil are placed side by [illegible] iron cores suspended to the ends of a rocking arm [illegible] within them. Hence, according as the magnetic action [illegible] or series coil prevails, the rocking arm is tilted back[illegible] wards. When the series coil is not in action the *motion* [illegible] the upper carbon-holder slides down, or the lower one [illegible] and starts the arc. The series coil comes into action to [illegible] carbons, and at the same time locks the mechanism. [illegible] then operates against the series coil, and between them [illegible] fed forwards as required. The control to be obtained [illegible] the arc shall never become so long as to flicker and [illegible] extinguished, when the carbons would come together again [illegible] But the feed should be smooth and steady, the position [illegible] responding quickly to each change in the current.

[illegible] duction of enclosed arc lamps was a great improvement, [illegible] of the economy effected in the consumption of [illegible] in the cost of labour for trimming. A well-known and [illegible] form of enclosed arc lamp is the Jandus lamp, which in [illegible] form can be made to burn for two hundred hours [illegible] carboning, and in small or midget form to burn for forty [illegible] a current of two amperes at 100 volts. Such lamps [illegible] conveniently replace large sizes of incandescent [illegible] tally for shop lighting, as they give a whiter light. [illegible] ments have also been made in inclined carbon arc [illegible] reason for the relatively low efficiency of the usual [illegible] arrangement is that the crater can only radiate laterally, [illegible] the position of the negative carbon no crater light is [illegible] downwards. If, however, the carbons are placed [illegible] slanting position at a small angle like the letter V [illegible] formed at the bottom tips, then the crater can emit [illegible] all the light it produces. It is found, however, that [illegible] unsteady unless a suitable magnetic field is employed to [illegible] in position at the carbon tips. This method has been [illegible] Carbone arc, which, by the employment of inclined [illegible] a suitable electromagnet to keep the true arc steady [illegible] the carbons, has achieved considerable success. One [illegible] Carbone arc is the use of a relatively high voltage [illegible] carbons, their potential difference being as much as [illegible]

[illegible] may be arranged either (i.) in series, (ii.) in parallel [illegible] series parallel. In the first case a number, say 20, [illegible] be traversed by the same current, in that case [illegible] at a pressure of 1000 volts. Each must have [illegible] tic cut-out, so that if the carbons stick together [illegible] current to the other lamps is not interrupted, [illegible] a cut-out being to close the main circuit [illegible] one lamp ceases to pass current. Arc lamps [illegible] are generally supplied with a current from [illegible] dynamo, which maintains an invariable [illegible] amperes, independently of the number of [illegible] external circuit. If the lamps, however, are [illegible] constant potential circuit, such as one [illegible] incandescent lamps, provision must [illegible] resistance coil can be substituted for [illegible] removed or short-circuited. When lamps are [illegible] each lamp is independent, but it is then [illegible] a resistance in series with the lamp. By [illegible] lamps can be worked in series of 100 volt [illegible] current arc lamps can be worked off a [illegible] in parallel by providing each lamp with a [illegible] In some cases the alternating high-tension [illegible] and supplied as a unidirectional current to [illegible] alternating-current lamps have to be [illegible] alternating-circuit, each lamp must have [illegible] choking coil or economy coil, to reduce the [illegible] that required for one lamp. Alternating-[illegible] a larger *effective* current, and work with a [illegible] carbon P.D., than continuous current [illegible]

[illegible] public arc lamps is made up of several [illegible] cost of supplying the necessary electric [illegible] the cost of carbons and the labour of [illegible] and, lastly, an item due to depreciation [illegible] An ordinary type of open 10 ampere [illegible] 15 and 9 mm. in diameter for the [illegible] working every night of the year [illegible] about 600 ft. of carbons per annum. [illegible] mm. and the negative 12 mm., the consumption of each size of carbon is about 70 ft. per 1000 hours of burning. It may be roughly stated that at the present prices of plain open arc-lamp carbons the cost is about 15s. per 1000 hours of burning; hence if such a lamp is burnt every night from dusk to midnight the annual cost in that respect is about £1, 10s. The annual cost of labour per lamp for trimming is in Great Britain from £2 to £3; hence, approximately speaking, the cost per annum of maintenance of a public arc lamp burning every night from dusk to midnight is about £4 to £5, or perhaps £6, per annum, depreciation and repairs included. Since such a 10 ampere lamp uses half a Board of Trade unit of electric energy every hour, it will take 1000 Board of Trade units per annum, burning every night from dusk to midnight; and if this energy is supplied, say at 1½d. per unit, the annual cost of energy will be about £6, and the upkeep of the lamp, including carbons, labour for trimming and repairs, will be about £10 to £11 per annum. The cost for labour and carbons is considerably reduced by the employment of the enclosed arc lamp, but owing to the absorption of light produced by the inner enclosing globe, and the necessity for generally employing a second outer globe, there is a lower resultant candle-power per watt expended in the arc. Enclosed arc lamps are made to burn without attention for 200 hours, singly on 100 volt circuits, or two in series on 200 volt circuits, and in addition to the cost of carbons per hour being only about one-twentieth of that of the open arc, they have another advantage in the fact that there is a more uniform distribution of light on the road surface, because a greater proportion of light is thrown out horizontally.

It has been found by experience that the ordinary type of open arc lamp with vertical carbons included in an opalescent globe cannot compete in point of cost with modern improvements in gas lighting as a means of street illumination. The violet colour of the light and the sharp shadows, and particularly the non-illuminated area just beneath the lamp, are grave disadvantages. The high-pressure flame arc lamp with inclined chemically treated carbons has, however, put a different complexion on matters. Although the treated carbons cost more than the plain carbons, yet there is a great increase of emitted light, and a 9-ampere flame arc lamp supplied with electric energy at 1½d. per unit can be used for 1000 hours at an inclusive cost of about £5 to £6, the mean emitted illumination being at the rate of 4 c.p. per watt absorbed. In the Carbone arc lamp, the carbons are worked at an angle of 15° or 20° to each other and the arc is formed at the lower ends. If the potential difference of the carbons is low, say only 50-60 volts, the crater forms between the tips of the carbons and is therefore more or less hidden. If, however, the voltage is increased to 90-100 then the true flame of the arc is longer and is curved, and the crater forms at the exteme tip of the carbons and throws all its light downwards. Hence results a far greater mean hemispherical candle power (M.H.S.C.P.), so that whereas a 10-ampere 60 volt open arc gives at most 1200 M.H.S.C.P., a Carbone 10-ampere 85 volt arc will give 2700 M.H.S.C.P. Better results still can be obtained with impregnated carbons. But the flame arcs with impregnated carbons cannot be enclosed, so the consumption of carbon is greater, and the carbons themselves are more costly, and leave a greater ash on burning; hence more trimming is required. They give a more pleasing effect for street lighting, and their golden yellow globe of light is more useful than an equally costly plain arc of the open type. This improvement in efficiency is, however, accompanied by some disadvantages. The flame arc is very sensitive to currents of air and therefore has to be shielded from draughts by putting it under an "economizer" or chamber of highly refractory material which surrounds the upper carbon, or both carbon tips, if the arc is formed with inclined carbons. (For additional information on flame arc lamps see a paper by L. B. Marks and H. E. Clifford, *Electrician*, 1906, 57, p. 975.)

2. *Incandescent Lamps.*—Incandescent electric lighting, although not the first, is yet in one sense the most obvious method of utilizing electric energy for illumination. It was evolved from the early observed fact that a conductor is heated

when traversed by an electric current, and that if it has a high resistance and a high melting-point it may be rendered incandescent, and therefore become a source of light. Naturally every inventor turned his attention to the employment of wires of refractory metals, such as platinum or alloys of platinum-iridium, &c., for the purpose of making an incandescent lamp. F. de Moleyns experimented in 1841, E. A. King and J. W. Starr in 1845, J. J. W. Watson in 1853, and W. E. Staite in 1848, but these inventors achieved no satisfactory result. Part of their want of success is attributable to the fact that the problem of the economical production of electric current by the dynamo machine had not then been solved. In 1878 T. A. Edison devised lamps in which a platinum wire was employed as the light-giving agent, carbon being made to adhere round it by pressure. Abandoning this, he next directed his attention to the construction of an "electric candle," consisting of a thin cylinder or rod formed of finely-divided metals, platinum, iridium, &c., mixed with refractory oxides, such as magnesia, or zirconia, lime, &c. This refractory body was placed in a closed vessel and heated by being traversed by an electric current. In a further improvement he proposed to use a block of refractory oxide, round which a bobbin of fine platinum or platinum-iridium wire was coiled. Every other inventor who worked at the problem of incandescent lighting seems to have followed nearly the same path of invention. Long before this date, however, the notion of employing carbon as a substance to be heated by the current had entered the minds of inventors; even in 1845 King had employed a small rod of plumbago as the substance to be heated. It was obvious, however, that carbon could only be so heated when in a space destitute of oxygen, and accordingly King placed his plumbago rod in a barometric vacuum. S. W. Konn in 1872, and S. A. Kosloff in 1875, followed in the same direction.

Carbon filament lamp.

No real success attended the efforts of inventors until it was finally recognized, as the outcome of the work by J. W. Swan, T. A. Edison, and, in a lesser degree, St. G. Lane Fox and W. E. Sawyer and A. Man, that the conditions of success were as follow: First, the substance to be heated must be carbon in the form of a thin wire rod or thread, technically termed a *filament*; second, this must be supported and enclosed in a vessel formed entirely of glass; third, the vessel must be exhausted as perfectly as possible; and fourth, the current must be conveyed into and out of the carbon filament by means of platinum wires hermetically sealed through the glass.

One great difficulty was the production of the carbon filament. King, Sawyer, Man and others had attempted to cut out a suitably shaped piece of carbon from a solid block; but Edison and Swan were the first to show that the proper solution of the difficulty was to carbonize an organic substance to which the necessary form had been previously given. For this purpose cardboard, paper and ordinary thread were originally employed, and even, according to Edison, a mixture of lampblack and tar rolled out into a fine wire and bent into a spiral. At one time Edison employed a filament of bamboo, carbonized after being bent into a horse-shoe shape. Swan used a material formed by treating ordinary crochet cotton-thread with dilute sulphuric acid, the "parchmentized thread" thus produced being afterwards carbonized. In the modern incandescent lamp the filament is generally constructed by preparing first of all a form of soluble cellulose. Carefully purified cotton-wool is dissolved in some solvent, such as a solution of zinc chloride, and the viscous material so formed is forced by hydraulic pressure through a die. The long thread thus obtained, when hardened, is a semi-transparent substance resembling cat-gut, and when carefully carbonized at a high temperature gives a very dense and elastic form of carbon filament. It is cut into appropriate lengths, which after being bent into horse-shoes, double-loops, or any other shape desired, are tied or folded round carbon formers and immersed in plumbago crucibles, packed in with finely divided plumbago. The crucibles are then heated to a high temperature in an ordinary combustion or electric furnace, whereby the organic matter is destroyed, and a skeleton of carbon remains. The higher the temperature at which this carbonization is conducted, the denser is the resulting product. The filaments so prepared are sorted and measured, and short leading-in wires of platinum are attached to their ends by a carbon cement or by a carbon depositing process, carried out by heating electrically the junction of the carbon and platinum under the surface of a hydrocarbon liquid. They are then mounted in bulbs of lead glass having the same coefficient of expansion as platinum, through the walls of which, therefore, the platinum wires can be hermetically sealed. The bulbs pass into the exhausting-room, where they are exhausted by some form of mechanical or mercury pump. During this process an electric current is sent through the filament to heat it, in order to disengage the gases occluded in the carbon, and exhaustion must be so perfect that no luminous glow appears within the bulb when held in the hand and touched against one terminal of an induction coil in operation.

In the course of manufacture a process is generally applied to the carbon which is technically termed "treating." The carbon filament is placed in a vessel surrounded by an atmosphere of hydrocarbon, such as coal gas or vapour of benzol. If current is then passed through the filament the hydrocarbon vapour is decomposed, and carbon is thrown down upon the filament in the form of a lustrous and dense deposit having an appearance like steel when seen under the miscroscope. This deposited carbon is not only much more dense than ordinary carbonized organic material, but it has a much lower specific electric resistance. An untreated carbon filament is generally termed the primary carbon, and a deposited carbon the secondary carbon. In the process of treating, the greatest amount of deposit is at any places of high resistance in the primary carbon, and hence it tends to cover up or remedy the defects which may exist. The bright steely surface of a well-treated filament is a worse radiator than the rougher black surface of an untreated one; hence it does not require the expenditure of so much electric power to bring it to the same temperature, and probably on account of its greater density it ages much less rapidly.

Finally, the lamp is provided with a collar having two sole plates on it, to which the terminal wires are attached, or else the terminal

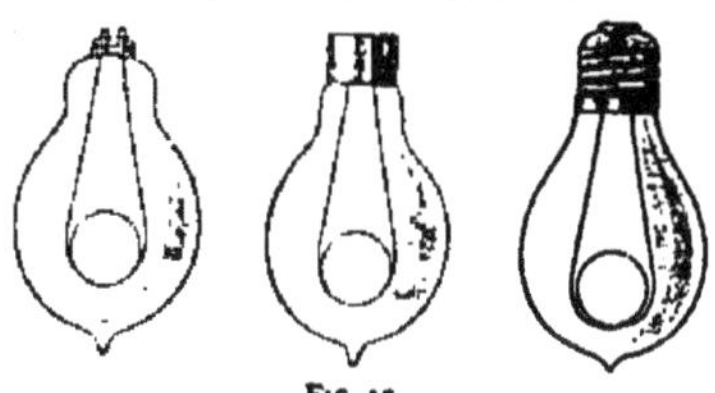

FIG. 15.

wires are simply bent into two loops; in a third form, the Edison screw terminal, it is provided with a central metal plate, to which one end of the filament is connected, the other end being joined to a screw collar. The collars and screws are formed of thin brass embedded in plaster of Paris, or in some material like vitrite or black glass (fig. 15). To put the lamp into connexion with the circuit supplying the current, it has to be fitted into a socket or holder. Three of the principal types of holder in use are the bottom contact (B.C.) or Dornfeld socket, the Edison screw-collar socket and the Swan or loop socket. In the socket of C. Dornfeld (fig. 16, *a* and *a'*) two spring pistons, in contact with the two sides of the circuit, are fitted into the bottom of a short metallic tube having bayonet joint slots cut in the top. The brass collar on the lamp has two pins, by means of which a bayonet connexion is made between it and the socket; and when this is done, the spring pins are pressed against the sole plates on the lamp. In the Edison socket (fig. 16, *b*) a short metal tube with an insulating lining has on its interior a screw sleeve, which is in connexion with one wire of the circuit; at the bottom of the tube, and insulated from the screw sleeve, is a central metal button, which is in connexion with the other side of the circuit. On screwing the lamp into the socket, the screw collar of the lamp and the boss or plate at the base of the lamp make contact with the corresponding parts of the socket, and complete the connexion. In some cases a form of switch is included in the socket, which is then termed the key-holder. For loop lamps the socket consists of an insulated block, having on it two little hooks, which engage with the eyes of the lamp. This insulating block also carries some form of spiral spring or pair of spring loops, by means of which the lamp is pressed away from the socket, and the eyes kept tight by the hooks. This spring or Swan socket (fig. 16, *c*) is found useful in places where the lamps are subject to vibration, for in such cases the Edison screw collar cannot well be used, because the vibration loosens the contact of the lamp in the socket. The sockets may be fitted with appliances for holding ornamental shades or conical reflectors.

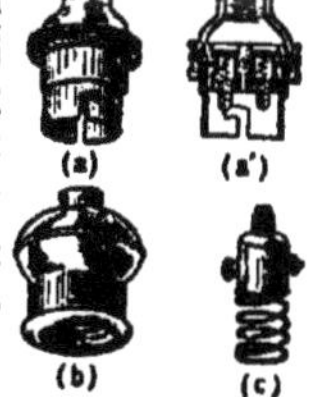

FIG. 16.—Incandescent Lamp Sockets.

The incandescent filament being a very brilliant line of light, various devices are adopted for moderating its brilliancy and distributing the light. A simple method is to sand-blast the exterior of the bulb; this [illegible] an appearance similar to that of ground glass. [illegible] the bare lamp may be enclosed in a suitable glass shade. [illegible] however, if made of opalescent or semi-opaque glass [illegible] 30 to 50% of the light. Hence various forms of [illegible] have been invented, consisting of clear glass ruled with [illegible] grooves in such a manner as to diffuse the light without any very great absorption. Invention has been fertile in devising [illegible], coloured, opalescent, frosted and ornamental shades for decorative purposes, and in constructing special forms for use in situations, such as mines and factories for explosives, where the globe containing the lamp must be air-tight. High candle-power lamps, 500, 1000 and upwards, are made by placing in one large glass bulb a number of carbon filaments arranged in parallel between two rings, which are connected with the main leading-in wires. When incandescent lamps are used for optical purposes it is necessary to compress the filament into a small space, so as to bring it into the focus of a lens or mirror. The filament is then coiled or crumpled up into a spiral or zigzag form. Such lamps are called *focus lamps*.

Incandescent lamps are technically divided into high and low voltage lamps, high and low efficiency lamps, standard and fancy lamps. The difference between high and low efficiency lamps is based upon the relation of the power absorbed by the lamp to the candle-power emitted. Every lamp when manufactured is marked with a certain figure, called the *marked volts*. This is understood to be the electromotive force in volts which must be applied to the lamp terminals to produce through the filament a current of such magnitude that the lamp will have a practically satisfactory [illegible] and give in a horizontal direction a certain candle-power which is also marked upon the glass. The numerical product of the current in amperes passing through the lamp, and the difference in potential of the terminals measured in volts gives the total power taken up by the lamp in watts; and this number divided by the candle-power of the lamp (taken generally in a horizontal direction) gives the *watts per candle-power*. This is an important figure, because it is determined by the temperature; it therefore determines the quality of the light emitted by the lamp, and also fixes the average [illegible] of the filament when rendered incandescent by a current. Even in a good vacuum the filament is not permanent. [illegible] from accidental defects, the carbon is slowly [illegible], and carbon molecules are also projected in straight [illegible] different portions of the filament. This process not [illegible] a change in the nature of the surface of the filament, [illegible] of carbon on the interior of the bulb, whereby [illegible] and the candle-power of the lamp reduced. [illegible] very rapidly as the temperature [illegible] of high resistance in the filament, more [illegible] a higher temperature is attained, and the [illegible] of the carbon becomes very rapid; in such cases the [illegible] cut through at the point of high [illegible] incandescent lighting may be practi[illegible] that the lamps shall have a certain [illegible]; and this useful duration is fixed [illegible] of passing a current through the [illegible] which the candle-power diminishes. [illegible] is called the *ageing* of the lamp, [illegible] may be said to be that period [illegible] deteriorated to a point when it gives [illegible] candle-power. It is found that in [illegible] as at present made, if worked [illegible] watts per candle-power, exhibit [illegible] power and an abbreviated life. [illegible] lamps into various classes, [illegible] and 4 watts per candle. A 2½ [illegible] called a *high-efficiency lamp*, [illegible] would be called a *low-efficiency* [illegible] the low-efficiency lamp [illegible] [illegible]ld be less [illegible] colour [illegible] [illegible]pends

greatly on the uniformity of the electric pressure of the supply. If the voltage is exceedingly uniform, then high-efficiency lamps can be satisfactorily employed; but they are not adapted for standing the variations in pressure which are liable to occur with public supply-stations, since, other things being equal, their filaments are less substantial. The classification into high and low voltage lamps is based upon the watts per candle-power corresponding to the marked volts. When incandescent lamps were first introduced, the ordinary working voltage was 50 or 100, but now a large number of public supply-stations furnish current to consumers at a pressure of 200 or 250 volts. This increase was necessitated by the enlarging area of supply in towns, and therefore the necessity for conveying through the same subterranean copper cables a large supply of electric energy without increasing the maximum current value and the size of the cables. This can only be done by employing a higher working electromotive force; hence arose a demand for incandescent lamps having marked volts of 200 and upwards, technically termed high-voltage lamps. The employment of higher pressures in public supply-stations has necessitated greater care in the selection of the lamp fittings, and in the manner of carrying out the wiring work. The advantages, however, of higher supply pressures, from the point of view of supply-stations, are undoubted. At the same time the consumer desired a lamp of a higher efficiency than the ordinary carbon filament lamp. The demand for this stimulated efforts to produce improved carbon lamps, and it was found that if the filament were exposed to a very high temperature, 3000° C. in an electric furnace, it became more refractory and was capable of burning in a lamp at an efficiency of 2½ watts per c.p. Inventors also turned their attention to substances other than carbon which can be rendered incandescent by the electric current.

The luminous efficiency of any source of light, that is to say, the percentage of rays emitted which affect the eye as light compared with the total radiation, is dependent upon its temperature. In an ordinary oil lamp the luminous rays do not form much more than 3% of the total radiation. In the carbon-filament incandescent lamp, when worked at about 3 watts per candle, the luminous efficiency is about 5%; and in the arc lamp the radiation from the crater contains about 10 to 15% of eye-affecting radiation. The temperature of a carbon filament working at about 3 watts per candle is not far from the melting-point of platinum, that is to say, is nearly 1775° C. If it is worked at a higher efficiency, say 2·5 watts per candle-power, the temperature rises rapidly, and at the same time the volatilization and molecular scattering of the carbon is rapidly increased, so that the average duration of the lamp is very much shortened. An improvement, therefore, in the efficiency of the incandescent lamp can only be obtained by finding some substance which will endure heating to a higher temperature than the carbon filament. Inventors turned their attention many years ago, with this aim, to the refractory oxides and similar substances. Paul Jablochkoff in 1877 described and made a lamp consisting of a piece of kaolin, which was brought to a state of incandescence first by passing over it an electric spark, and afterwards maintained in a state of incandescence by a current of lower electromotive force. Lane Fox and Edison, in 1878, proposed to employ platinum wires covered with films of lime, magnesia, steatite, or with the rarer oxides, zirconia, thoria, &c.; and Lane Fox, in 1879, suggested as an incandescent substance a mixture of particles of carbon with the earthy oxides. These earthy oxides—magnesia, lime and the oxides of the rare earths, such as thoria, zirconia, erbia, yttria, &c.—possess the peculiarity that at ordinary temperatures they are practically non-conductors, but at very high temperatures their resistance at a certain point rapidly falls, and they become fairly good conductors. Hence if they can once be brought into a state of incandescence a current can pass through them and maintain them in that state. But at this temperature they give up oxygen to carbon; hence no mixtures of earthy oxides with carbon are permanent when heated, and failure has attended all attempts to use a carbon filament covered with such substances as thoria, zirconia or other of the rare oxides.

Nernst lamp.

H. W. Nernst in 1897, however, patented an incandescent lamp in which the incandescent body consists entirely of a slender rod or filament of magnesia. If such a rod is heated by the oxyhydrogen blowpipe to a high temperature it becomes conductive, and can then be maintained in an intensely luminous condition by passing a current through it after the flame is withdrawn. Nernst found that by mixing together, in suitable proportions, oxides of the rare earths, he was able to prepare a material which can be formed into slender rods and threads, and which is rendered sufficiently conductive to pass a current with an electromotive force as low as 100 volts, merely by being heated for a few moments with a spirit lamp, or even by the radiation from a neighbouring platinum spiral brought to a state of incandescence.

The Nernst lamp, therefore (fig. 17), consists of a slender rod of the mixed oxides attached to platinum wires by an oxide paste. Oxide filaments of this description are not enclosed in an exhausted glass vessel, and they can be brought, without risk of destruction, to a temperature considerably higher than a carbon filament; hence the lamp has a higher luminous efficiency. The material now used for the oxide rod or "glower" of Nernst lamps is a mixture of zirconia and yttria, made into a paste and squirted or pressed into slender rods. This material is non-conductive when cold, but when slightly heated it becomes conductive and then falls considerably in resistance. The glower, which is straight in some types of the lamp but curved in others, is generally about 3 or 4 cm. long and 1 or 2 mm. in diameter. It is held in suitable terminals, and close to it, or round it, but not touching it, is a loose coil of platinum wire, also covered with oxide and called the "heater" (fig. 18). In series with it is a spiral of iron wire, enclosed in a bulb full of hydrogen, which is called the "ballast resistance." The socket also contains a switch controlled by an electromagnet. When the current is first switched on it passes through the heater coil which, becoming incandescent, by radiation heats the glower until it becomes conductive. The glower then takes current, becoming itself brilliantly incandescent, and the electromagnet becoming energized switches the heater coil out of circuit. The iron ballast wire increases in resistance with increase of current, and so operates to keep the total current through the glower constant in spite of small variations of circuit voltage. The disadvantages of the lamp are (1) that it does not light immediately after the current is switched on and is therefore not convenient for domestic use; (2) that it cannot be made in small light units such as 5 c.p.; (3) that the socket and fixture are large and more complicated than for the carbon filament lamp. But owing to the higher temperature, the light is whiter than that of the carbon glow lamp, and the efficiency or candle power per watt is greater. Since, however, the lamp must be included in an opal globe, some considerable part of this last advantage is lost. On the whole the lamp has found its field of operation rather in external than in domestic lighting.

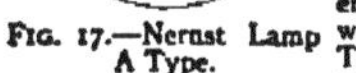

FIG. 17.—Nernst Lamp A Type.

FIG. 18.—Nernst Lamp, Burners for B Type. *a*, low voltage; *b*, high voltage.

Metallic filament lamps.

Great efforts were made in the latter part of the 19th century and the first decade of the 20th to find a material for the filament of an incandescent lamp which could replace carbon and yet not require a preliminary heating like the oxide glowers. This resulted in the production of refractory metallic filament lamps made of osmium, tantalum, tungsten and other rare metals. Auer von Welsbach suggested the use of osmium. This metal cannot be drawn into wire on account of its brittleness, but it can be made into a filament by mixing the finely divided metal with an organic binding material which is carbonized in the usual way at a high temperature, the osmium particles then cohering. The difficulty has hitherto been to construct in this way metallic filament lamps of low candle power (16 c.p.) for 220 volt circuits, but this is being overcome. When used on modern supply circuits of 220 volts a number of lamps may be run in series, or a step-down transformer employed.

The next great improvement came when W. von Bolton produced the tantalum lamp in 1904. There are certain metals known to have a melting point about 2000° C. or upwards, and of these tantalum is one. It can be produced from the potassium tantalo-fluoride in a pulverulent form. By carefully melting it *in vacuo* it can then be converted into the reguline form and drawn into wire. In this condition it has a density of 16·6 (water = 1), is harder than platinum and has greater tensile strength than steel, viz. 95 kilograms per sq. mm., the value for good steel being 70 to 80 kilograms per sq. mm. The electrical resistance at 15° C. is 0·146 ohms per metre with section of 1 sq. mm. after annealing at 1900° C. *in vacuo* and therefore about 6 times that of mercury; the temperature coefficient is 0·3 per degree C. At the temperature assumed in an incandescent lamp when working at 1·5 watts per c.p. the resistance is 0·830 ohms per metre with a section of 1 sq. mm. The specific heat is 0·0365. Bolton invented methods of producing tantalum in the form of a long fine wire 0·05 mm. in diameter. To make a 25 c.p. lamp 650 mm., or about 2 ft., of this wire are wound backwards and forwards zigzag on metallic supports carried on a glass frame, which is sealed into an exhausted glass bulb. The tantalum lamp so made (fig. 19), working on a 110 volt circuit takes 0·36 amperes or 39 watts, and hence has an efficiency of about 1·6 watts per c.p. The useful life, that is the time in which it loses 20% of its initial candle power, is about 400-500 hours, but in general a life of 800-1000 hours can be obtained. The bulb blackens little in use, but the life is said to be shorter with alternating than with direct current. When worked on alternating current circuits the filament after a time breaks up into sections which become curiously sheared with respect to each other but still maintain electrical contact. The resistance of tantalum increases with the temperature; hence the temperature coefficient is positive, and sudden rises in working voltage do not cause such variations in candle-power as in the case of the carbon lamp.

FIG. 19.—Tantalum Lamp.

Patents have also been taken out for lamps made with filaments of such infusible metals as tungsten and molybdenum, and Siemens and Halske, Sanders and others, have protected methods for employing zirconium and other rare metals. According to the patents of Sanders (German patents Nos. 133701, 137568, 137569) zirconium filaments are manufactured from the hydrogen or nitrogen compounds of the rare earths by the aid of some organic binding material. H. Kuzel of Vienna (British Patent No. 28154 of 1904) described methods of making metallic filaments from any metal. He employs the metals in a colloidal condition, either as hydrosol, organosol, gel, or colloidal suspension. The metals are thus obtained in a gelatinous form, and can be squirted into filaments which are dried and reduced to the metallic form by passing an electric current through them (*Electrician*, 57, 894). This process has a wide field of application, and enables the most refractory and infusible metals to be obtained in a metallic wire form. The zirconium and tungsten wire lamps are equal to or surpass the tantalum lamp in efficiency

The i[illegible]

[illegible] d[illegible] al[illegible] for wh[illegible] can in [illegible] para[illegible] leadi[illegible] purp[illegible] space[illegible] ment[illegible] Such l[illegible]

Inca[illegible] low vo[illegible]

Classification of lamps.

with a c[illegible] to be th[illegible] to the la[illegible] of such n[illegible] factory li[illegible] power, w[illegible] product o[illegible] and the [illegible] volts, giv[illegible] and this [illegible] (taking ge[illegible] *candle-pow*[illegible] mined by [illegible] of the light[illegible] duration of[illegible] current. E[illegible] Apart altog[illegible] volatilized, a[illegible] lines from d[illegible] only causes a[illegible] but also a de[illegible] the glass is bl[illegible] The volatiliz[illegible] rises. Hence [illegible] heat being gen[illegible] scattering of t[illegible] filament is soo[illegible] resistance. In[illegible] cally possible, [illegible] *average life*, tha[illegible] not merely by [illegible] lamp at all, but [illegible] The decay of [illegible] and the useful l[illegible] of its existence l[illegible] only 75% of i[illegible] practice carbon [illegible] at a higher effic[illegible] a rapid deterior[illegible] Hence lamp ma[illegible] marked for use s[illegible] watt per candle[illegible] and a 4 watt per[illegible] lamp. In ordin[illegible] would probably l[illegible] suitable for man[illegible] discrimination is [illegible]

The possib[illegible]

[illegible]

[illegible]mum candle-power, and a, b, c, &c., constants, it has been [illegible] A and c.p. are connected by an exponential law such that

$$c.p. = aA^x$$

[illegible] filament lamps x is a number lying between 5 and [illegible] 5·5 or 5·6. Also it has been found that c.p. = [illegible] and that

$$c.p. = cV^y \text{ nearly}$$

[illegible] some other constant, and for carbon filaments y is [illegible] equal to 6. It is obvious that if the candle-power [illegible] varies very nearly as the 6th power of the current and [illegible] voltage, the candle-power must vary as the cube of the [illegible]

[illegible] W. Abney and E. R. Festing have also given a formula [illegible] candle-power and watts equivalent to c.p. = [illegible] a constant.

[illegible] case of the tantalum lamp the exponent x has a value near [illegible] exponent y is a number near to 4, and the same [illegible] current. Hence for these metallic glowers a certain [illegible] variation of voltage does not create so great a variation in [illegible] power as in the case of the carbon lamp.

[illegible] indicating the relation of these variables for any incandescent lamp are called its [illegible]-curves. The life or average [illegible] is a function of [illegible] c.p., or of the watts per candle-power, [illegible] the voltage at which the lamp [illegible] from the above relation that the watts per candle-power [illegible] as the fourth power of the voltage. [illegible] It [illegible] observations it seems that the average life of a [illegible] lamp varies as the fifth or sixth power of the watts [illegible]. If V is the voltage at which the lamp is worked [illegible] average life, then L varies roughly as the [illegible] power of the reciprocal of the voltage, or

$$L = aV^{-n}.$$

[illegible] approximation to experience is given by the formula

$$\log_{10} L = 13.5 - \frac{V}{10} - \frac{V^2}{20{,}000}.$$

See [illegible] A. Fleming "Characteristic Curves of Incandescent [illegible]" Phil. Mag. May 1885.

[illegible] forms of incandescent or glow lamps are found to deteriorate [illegible] lighting power with use. In the case of carbon filaments [illegible] is due to two causes. As already [illegible] [illegible] is scattered from the filament and [illegible] [illegible] the glass, and changes also take place in the [illegible] [illegible]

Ageing of lamps.

[illegible]

figures show the results of some tests on typical 3·1 watt lamps run at voltages above the normal, taking the average life when worked at the marked volts (namely, 100) as 1000 hours:

At 101 volts the life was	818 hours.
„ 102	„ „	681	„
„ 103	„ „	662	„
„ 104	„ „	452	„
„ 105	„ „	374	„
„ 106	„ „	310	„

Voltage regulators.

Self-acting regulators have been devised by which the voltage at the points of consumption is kept constant, even although it varies at the point of generation. If, however, such a device is to be effective, it must operate very quickly, as even the momentary effect of increased pressure is felt by the lamp. It is only therefore where the working pressure can be kept exceedingly constant that high-efficiency lamps can be advantageously employed, otherwise the cost of lamp renewals more than counterbalances the economy in the cost of power. The slow changes that occur in the resistance of the filament make themselves evident by an increase in the watts per candle-power. The following table shows some typical figures indicating the results of ageing in a 16 candle-power carbon-filament glow lamp:—

Hours run.	Candle-Power	Watts per Candle-Power
0	16·0	3·16
100	15 8	3·26
200	15 86	3·13
300	15·68	3·37
400	15·41	3·53
500	15 17	3·51
600	14·96	3·54
700	14 74	3 74

The gradual increase in watts per candle-power shown by this table does not imply necessarily an increase in the total power taken by the lamp, but is the consequence of the decay in candle-power produced by the blackening of the lamp. Therefore, to estimate the value of an incandescent lamp the user must take into account not merely the price of the lamp and the initial watts per candle-power, but the rate of decay of the lamp.

Edison effect.

The scattering of carbon from the filament to the glass bulb produces interesting physical effects, which have been studied by T A. Edison, W. H. Preece and J. A. Fleming. If into an ordinary carbon-filament glow lamp a platinum plate is sealed, not connected to the filament but attached to a third terminal, then it is found that when the lamp is worked with continuous current a galvanometer connected in between the middle plate and the positive terminal of the lamp indicates a current, but not when connected in between the negative terminal of the lamp and the middle plate. If the middle plate is placed between the legs of a horse-shoe-shaped filament, it becomes blackened most quickly on the side facing the negative leg This effect, commonly called the *Edison effect*, is connected with an electric discharge and convection of carbon which takes place between the two extreme ends of the filament, and, as experiment seems to show, consists in the conveyance of an electric charge, either by carbon molecules or by bodies smaller than molecules. There is, however, an electric discharge between the ends of the filament, which rapidly increases with the temperature of the filament and the terminal voltage, hence one of the difficulties of manufacturing high-voltage glow lamps, that is to say, glow lamps for use on circuits having an electromotive force of 200 volts and upwards, is the discharge from one leg of the filament to the other

Domestic use.

A brief allusion may be made to the mode of use of incandescent lamps for interior and private lighting. At the present time hardly any other method of distribution is adopted than that of an arrangement *in parallel*; that is to say, each lamp on the circuit has one terminal connected to a wire which finally terminates at one pole of the generator, and its other terminal connected to a wire leading to the other pole. The lamp filaments are thus arranged between the conductors like the rungs of a ladder. In series with each lamp is placed a switch and a fuse or cut-out. The lamps themselves are attached to some variety of ornamental fitting, or in many cases suspended by a simple pendant, consisting of an insulated double flexible wire attached at its upper end to a ceiling rose, and carrying at the lower end a shade and socket in which the lamp is placed. Lamps thus hung head downwards are disadvantageously used because their *end-on candle-power* is not generally more than 60% of their maximum candle-power. In interior lighting one of the great objects to be attained is uniformity of illumination with avoidance of harsh shadows. This can only be achieved by a proper distribution of the lamps. It is impossible to give any hard and fast rules as to what number must be employed in the illumination of any room, as a great deal depends upon the nature of the reflecting surfaces, such as the walls, ceilings, &c. As a rough guide, it may be stated that for every 100 sq. ft. of floor surface one 16 candle-power lamp placed about 8 ft. above the floor will give a dull illumination, two will give a good illumination and four will give a brilliant illumination. We generally judge of the nature of the illumination in a room by our ability to read comfortably in any position. That this may be done, the horizontal illumination on the book should not be less than one candle-foot. The following table shows approximately the illuminations in candle-feet, in various situations, derived from actual experiments:—

In a well-lighted room on the floor or tables	1·0 to 3·0 c.f.
On a theatre stage	3·0 to 4·0 c.f.
On a railway platform	·05 to ·5 c.f.
In a picture gallery	·65 to 3·5 c.f.
The mean daylight in May in the interior of a room	30·0 to 40·0 c.f.
In full sunlight	7000 to 10,000 c.f.
In full moonlight	1/60th to 1/100th c.f.

From an artistic point of view, one of the worst methods of lighting a room is by pendant lamps, collected in single centres in large numbers. The lights ought to be distributed in different portions of the room, and so shaded that the light is received only by reflection from surrounding objects. Ornamental effects are frequently produced by means of candle lamps in which a small incandescent lamp, imitating the flame of a candle, is placed upon a white porcelain tube as a holder, and these small units are distributed and arranged in electroliers and brackets. For details as to the various modes of placing conducting wires in houses, and the various precautions for safe usage, the reader is referred to the article ELECTRICITY SUPPLY. In the case of low voltage metallic filament lamps when the supply is by alternating current there is no difficulty in reducing the service voltage to any lower value by means of a transformer. In the case of direct current the only method available for working such low voltage lamps off higher supply voltages is to arrange the lamps in series.

Additional information on the subjects treated above may be found in the following books and original papers:—

Mrs Ayrton, *The Electric Arc* (London, 1900); Houston and Kennelly, *Electric Arc Lighting and Electric Incandescent Lighting*; S. P. Thompson, *The Arc Light*, Cantor Lectures, Society of Arts (1895); H. Nakano, "The Efficiency of the Arc Lamp," *Proc. American Inst. Elec. Eng.* (1889), A. Blondel, "Public and Street Lighting by Arc Lamps," *Electrician*, vols. xxxv and xxxvi, (1895); T. Heskett, "Notes on the Electric Arc," *Electrician*, vol. xxxix, (1897). G. S. Ram, *The Incandescent Lamp and its Manufacture* (London, 1895). J. A. Fleming, *Electric Lamps and Electric Lighting* (London, 1899); J. A. Fleming, "The Photometry of Electric Lamps," *Jour. Inst. Elec. Eng.* (1903), 32, p. 1 (in this paper a copious bibliography of the subject of photometry is given); J. Dredge, *Electric Illumination* (2 vols., London, 1882, 1885); A. P. Trotter, "The Distribution and Measurement of Illumination," *Proc. Inst C E* vol cx. (1892); E. L. Nichols, "The Efficiency of Methods of Artificial Illumination," *Trans. American Inst. Elec. Eng.* vol. vi. (1889); Sir W de W. Abney, *Photometry*, Cantor Lectures, Society of Arts (1894) A. Blondel, "Photometric Magnitudes and Units," *Electrician* (1894); J. E. Petavel, "An Experimental Research on some Standards of Light," *Proc. Roy. Soc.* lxv. 469 (1899); F. Jehl *Carbon-Making for all Electrical Purposes* (London, 1906); G. B. Dyke, "On the Practical Determination of the Mean Spherical

Candle Power of Incandescent and Arc Lamps," *Phil. Mag.* (1905); the *Preliminary Report of the Sub-Committee of the American Institute of Electrical Engineers* on "Standards of Light"; Clifford C. Paterson, "Investigations on Light Standards and the Present Condition of the High Voltage Glow Lamp," *Jour. Inst. Elec. Eng.* (January 24, 1907); J. Swinburne, "New Incandescent Lamps," *Jour. Inst. Elec. Eng.* (1907); L. Andrews, "Long Flame Arc Lamps," *Jour. Inst. Elec. Eng.* (1906); W. von Bolton and O. Feuerlein, "The Tantalum Lamp," *The Electrician* (Jan. 27, 1905). Also the current issues of *The Illuminating Engineer*. (J. A. F.)

Commercial Aspects.—The cost of supplying electricity depends more upon the rate of supply than upon the quantity supplied; or, as John Hopkinson put it, "the cost of supplying electricity for 1000 lamps for ten hours is very much less than ten times the cost of supplying the same number of lamps for one hour." Efforts have therefore been made to devise a system of charge which shall in each case bear some relation to the cost of the service. Consumers vary largely both in respect to the quantity and to the period of their demands, but the cost of supplying any one of them with a given amount of electricity is chiefly governed by the amount of his maximum demand at any one time. The reason for this is that it is not generally found expedient to store electricity in large quantities. Electricity supply works generate the electricity for the most part at the moment it is used by the consumer. Electric lamps are normally in use on an average for only about four hours per day, and therefore the plant and organization, if employed for a lighting load only, are idle and unremunerative for about 20 hours out of the 24. It is necessary to have in readiness machinery capable of supplying the maximum possible requirements of all the consumers at any hour, and this accounts for a very large proportion of the total cost. The cost of raw material, viz. coal, water and stores consumed in the generation of electricity sold, forms relatively only a small part of the total cost, the major part of which is made up of the fixed charges attributable to the time during which the works are unproductive. This makes it very desirable to secure demands possessing high "load" and "diversity" factors. The correct way to charge for electricity is to give liberal rebates to those consumers who make prolonged and regular use of the plant, that is to say, the lower the "peak" demand and the more continuous the consumption, the better should be the discount. The consumer must be discouraged from making sudden large demands on the plant, and must be encouraged, while not reducing his total consumption, to spread his use of the plant over a large number of hours during the year. Mr Arthur Wright has devised a tariff which gives effect to this principle. The system necessitates the use of a special indicator—not to measure the quantity of electricity consumed, which is done by the ordinary meter—but to show the maximum amount of current taken by the consumer at any one time during the period for which he is to be charged. In effect it shows the proportion of plant which has had to be kept on hand for his use. If the indicator shows that say twenty lamps is the greatest number which the consumer has turned on simultaneously, then he gets a large discount on all the current which his ordinary meter shows that he has taken beyond the equivalent of one hour's daily use of those twenty lamps. Generally the rate charged under this system is [illegible] per unit for the equivalent of one hour's daily use of the maximum demand and [illegible] per unit for all surplus. It is on this [illegible] that it pays to supply current for tramway and other purposes at a price which prima facie is below the cost of production, [illegible] in comparison with the cost of [illegible] electricity for lighting purposes. In the case of [illegible] the electricity is required for 15 or 16 hours per day. [illegible] lamp would cost on the basis of this [illegible] system for 15 hours per day [illegible] a system of further discounts [illegible] with the Wright system. [illegible] the Wright system in favour [illegible] any failure of the [illegible]

Methods of charging.

able to give the supply at a fair profit, and the proportion of possible new customers being small the undertakers find it a simplification to dispense with the maximum demand indicator. But in some cases a mistake has been made by offering the unprofitable early-closing consumers the option of obtaining electricity at a flat rate much lower than their load-factor would warrant and below cost price. The effect of this is to nullify the Wright system of charging, for a consumer will not elect to pay for his electricity on the Wright system if he can obtain a lower rate by means of a flat rate system. Thus the long-hour profitable consumer is made to pay a much higher price than he need be charged, in order that the unprofitable short-hour consumer may be retained and be made actually still more unprofitable. It is not improbable that ultimately the supply will be charged for on the basis of a rate determined by the size and character of the consumer's premises, or the number and dimensions of the electrical points, much in the same way as water is charged for by a water rate determined by the rent of the consumer's house and the number of water taps.

Most new houses within an electricity supply area are wired for electricity during construction, but in several towns means have to be taken to encourage small shopkeepers and tenants of small houses to use electricity by removing the obstacle of the first outlay on wiring. The cost of wiring may be taken at 15s. to £2 per lamp installed including all necessary wire, switches, fuses, lamps, holders, casing, but not electroliers or shades. Many undertakers carry out wiring on the easy payment or hire-purchase system. Parliament has sanctioned the adoption of these systems by some local authorities and even authorized them to do the work by direct employment of labour. The usual arrangement is to make an additional charge of ½d. per unit on all current used, with a minimum payment of 1s. per 8 c.p. lamp, consumers having the option of purchasing the installation at any time on specified conditions. The consumer has to enter into an agreement, and if he is only a tenant the landlord has to sign a memorandum to the effect that the wiring and fittings belong to the supply undertakers. Several undertakers have adopted a system of maintenance and renewal of lamps, and at least one local authority undertakes to supply consumers with lamps free of charge.

Wiring of houses.

There is still considerable scope for increasing the business of electricity supply by judicious advertising and other methods. Comparisons of the kilowatt hour consumption per capita in various towns show that where an energetic policy has been pursued the profits have improved by reason of additional output combined with increased load factor. The average number of equivalent 8 c.p. lamps connected per capita in the average of English towns is about 1·2. The average number of units consumed per capita per annum is about 23, and the average income per capita per annum is about 5s. In a number of American cities 20s. per capita per annum is obtained. In the United States a co-operative electrical development association canvasses both the general public and the electricity supply undertakers. Funds are provided by the manufacturing companies acting in concert with the supply authorities and contractors, and the spirit underlying the work is to advertise the merits of electricity—not any particular company or interest. Their efforts are directed to securing new consumers and stimulating the increased and more varied use of electricity among actual consumers.

Consumption.

All supply undertakers are anxious to develop the consumption of electricity for power purposes even more than for lighting, but the first cost of installing electric motors is a deterrent to the adoption of electricity in small factories and shops, and most undertakers are therefore prepared to let out motors, &c., on hire or purchase on varying terms according to circumstances.

A board of trade unit will supply one 8 c.p. carbon lamp of 30 hours or 30 such lamps for one hour. In average use an incandescent lamp will last about 800 hours, which is equal about 12 months normal use; a good lamp will frequently t more than double this time before it breaks down.

A large number of towns have adopted electricity for street lighting. Frank Bailey has furnished particulars of photometric tests which he has made on new and old street lamps in the city of London. From these tests the following comparative figures are deduced:—

	Average total Cost per c.p. per annum.
Gas—	
Double burner ordinary low pressure incandescent (mean of six tests)	11·1d.
Single burner high-pressure gas	9·0
Double burner high-pressure gas	11·7
Arc lamp—	
Old type of lantern	8
Flame arc	5

From these tests of candle-power the illumination at a distance of 100 ft. from the source is estimated as follows:—

	Candle Ft.		Ratio.
Double ordinary incandescent gas lamp illumination	0·013	=	1·0
Single high pressure ordinary incandescent gas lamp illumination	0·016	=	1·24
Double high pressure ordinary incandescent gas lamp illumination	0·027	=	2·10
Ordinary arc lamp	0·060	=	4·50
Flame arc lamp	0·120	=	9·00

The cost of electricity, light for light, is very much less than that of gas. The following comparative figures relating to street lighting at Croydon have been issued by the lighting committee of that corporation:—

Type of Lamp.	Number of Lamps.	Distance apart (yds.)	Total Cost.	Average c.p. per Mile.	Cost per c.p. per annum.
Incandescent gas	2,137	80	£7,062	839	15·80d.
Incandescent electric	90	66	288	1,373	13·71
Electric arcs	428	65	7,212	10,537	11·32

Apart from cheaper methods of generation there are two main sources of economy in electric lighting. One is the improved arrangement and use of electrical installations, and the other is the employment of lamps of higher efficiency. As regards the first, increased attention has been given to the position, candle-power and shading of electric lamps so as to give the most effective illumination in varying circumstances and to avoid excess of light. The ease with which electric lamps may be switched on and off from a distance has lent itself to arrangements whereby current may be saved by switching off lights not in use and by controlling the number of lamps required to be alight at one time on an electrolier. Appreciable economies are brought about by the scientific disposition of lights and the avoidance of waste in use. As regards the other source of economy, the Nernst, the tantalum, the osram, and the metallized carbon filament lamp, although costing more in the first instance than carbon lamps, have become popular owing to their economy in current consumption. Where adopted largely they have had a distinct effect in reducing the rate of increase of output from supply undertakings, but their use has been generally encouraged as tending towards the greater popularity of electric light and an ultimately wider demand. Mercury vapour lamps for indoor and outdoor lighting have also proved their high efficiency, and the use of flame arc lamps has greatly increased the cheapness of outdoor electric lighting.

The existence of a "daylight load" tends to reduce the all-round cost of generating and distributing electricity. This daylight load is partly supplied by power for industrial purposes and partly by the demand for electricity in many domestic operations. The use of electric heating and cooking apparatus (including radiators, ovens, grills, chafing dishes, hot plates, kettles, flat-irons, curling irons, &c.) has greatly developed, and provides a load which extends intermittently throughout the greater part of the twenty-four hours. Electric fans for home ventilation are also used, and in the domestic operations where a small amount of power is required (as in driving sewing machines, boot cleaners, washing machines, mangles, knife cleaners, "vacuum" cleaners, &c.) the electric motor is being largely adopted. The trend of affairs points to a time when the total demand from such domestic sources will greatly exceed the demand for lighting only. The usual charges for current to be used in domestic heating or power operations vary from 1d. to 2d. per unit. As the demand increases the charges will undergo reduction, and there will also be a reflex action in bringing down the cost of electricity for lighting owing to the improved load factor resulting from an increase in the day demand. In the cooking and heating and motor departments also there has been improvement in the efficiency of the apparatus, and its economy is enhanced by the fact that current may be switched on and off as required.

Testing meters. The Board of Trade are now prepared to receive electric measuring instruments for examination or testing at their electrical standardizing laboratory, where they have a battery power admitting of a maximum current of 7000 amperes to be dealt with. The London county council and some other corporations are prepared upon requisition to appoint inspectors to test meters on consumers' premises.

Wiring rules. All supply undertakers now issue rules and regulations for the efficient wiring of electric installations. The rules and regulations issued by the institution of electrical engineers have been accepted by many local authorities and companies, and also by many of the fire insurance companies. The Phoenix fire office rules were the first to be drawn up, and are adopted by many of the fire offices, but some other leading insurance offices have their own rules under which risks are accepted without extra premium. In the opinion of the insurance companies "the electric light is the safest of all illuminants and is preferable to any others when the installation has been thoroughly well put up." Regulations have also been issued by the London county council in regard to theatres, &c., by the national board of fire underwriters of America (known as the "National Electrical Code"), by the fire underwriters association of Victoria (Commonwealth of Australia), by the Calcutta fire insurance agents association and under the Canadian Electric Light Inspection Act. In Germany rules have been issued by the Verband Deutscher Elektrotechniker and by the union of private fire insurance companies of Germany, in Switzerland by the Association Suisse des électriciens, in Austria by the Elektrotechnischer Verein of Vienna, in France by ministerial decree and by the syndicat professionnel des industries électriques. (For reprints of these regulations see *Electrical Trades Directory.*) (E. Ga.)

LIGHTNING, the visible flash that accompanies an electric discharge in the sky. In certain electrical conditions of the atmosphere a cloud becomes highly charged by the coalescence of drops of vapour. A large drop formed by the fusion of many smaller ones contains the same amount of electricity upon a smaller superficial area, and the electric potential of each drop, and of the whole cloud, rises. When the cloud passes near another cloud stratum or near a hilltop, tower or tree, a discharge takes place from the cloud in the form of lightning. The discharge sometimes takes place from the earth to the cloud, or from a lower to a higher stratum, and sometimes from conductors silently. Rain discharges the electricity quietly to earth, and lightning frequently ceases with rain (see Atmospheric Electricity).

LIGHTNING CONDUCTOR, or Lightning Rod (Franklin), the name usually given to apparatus designed to protect buildings or ships from the destructive effects of lightning (Fr. *paratonnerre*, Ger. *Blitzableiter*). The upper regions of the atmosphere being at a different electrical potential from the earth, the thick dense clouds which are the usual prelude to a thunder storm serve to conduct the electricity of the upper air down towards the earth, and an electrical discharge takes place across the air space when the pressure is sufficient. Lightning discharges were distinguished by Sir Oliver Lodge into two distinct types—the *A* and the *B* flashes. The *A* flash is of the simple type which arises when an electrically charged cloud approaches the earth without an intermediate cloud intervening. In the second type *B*, where another cloud intervenes between the cloud carrying the primary charge and the earth, the two clouds practically form a condenser; and when a discharge from the first takes place into the second the free charge on the earth side of the lower cloud is suddenly relieved, and the disruptive discharge

LIGHTNING CONDUCTOR
FIG. 2.
B
FIG. 3.—Aigrett
stack or other prominence should ha
conductors should run in the most direc
earth, and be kept away from the walls by
the manner shown by A (fig. 2); the usu
B (fig. 2), where the tape follows the con
and causes side flash. A building
roof should also be fitted with
conductor along the ridge, and
aigrettes (fig. 3) should be attached; a
method is to support the cable by
armed with a spike (fig. 4). Joints
be held together mechanically as well
electrically, and should be protected from
action of the air. At Westminster Abbey
cables are spliced and inserted in a box
which is filled with lead run in when molten.
Earth Connexion.—A copper plate not less
than 3 sq. ft. in area may be used as an
earth connexion if buried in permanently
damp ground. Instead of a plate there are
using the tubular earth shown in fig. 5.
in carbon descends to the bottom of the perfo
is driven into the ground, a connexion
being made to the nearest rain-water
pipe to secure the necessary moisture.
No further attention is required. Plate
earths should be tested every year. The

next best is to arrange the conductors so that they surround it like a bird cage.

Bibliography.—The literature, although extensive, contains so many descriptions of ludicrous devices, that the student, after reading Benjamin Franklin's *Experiments and Observations on Electricity made at Philadelphia* (1769), may turn to the *Report* of the Lightning Rod Conference of December 1881. In the latter work there are abstracts of many valuable papers, especially the reports made to the French Academy, among others by Coulomb, Laplace, Gay-Lussac, Fresnel, Regnault, &c. In 1876 J. Clerk Maxwell read a paper before the British Association in which he brought forward the idea (based on Faraday's experiments) of protecting a building from the effects of lightning by surrounding it with a sort of cage of rods or stout wire. It was not, however, until the Bath meeting of the British Association in 1888 that the subject was fully discussed by the physical and engineering sections. Sir Oliver Lodge showed the futility of single conductors, and advised the interconnexion of all the metal work on a building to a number of conductors buried in the earth. The action of lightning flashes was also demonstrated by him in lectures delivered before the Society of Arts (1888). The Clerk Maxwell system was adopted to a large extent in Germany, and in July 1901 a sub-committee of the Berlin Electrotechnical Association was formed, which published rules. In 1900 a paper entitled "The Protection of Public Buildings from Lightning," by Killingworth Hedges, led to the formation, by the Royal Institute of British Architects and the Surveyors' Institution, of the Lightning Research Committee, on which the Royal Society and the Meteorological Society were represented. The *Report*, edited by Sir Oliver Lodge, Sir John Gavey and Killingworth Hedges (Hon. Sec.), was published in April 1905. An illustrated supplement, compiled by K. Hedges and entitled *Modern Lightning Conductors* (1905), contains particulars of the independent reports of the German committee, the Dutch Academy of Science, and the Royal Joseph university, Budapest. A description is also given of the author's modified Clerk Maxwell system, in which the metal work of the roofs of a building form the upper part, the rain-water pipes taking the place of the usual lightning-rods. See also Sir Oliver Lodge, *Lightning Conductors* (London, 1902). (K. H.)

LIGHTS, CEREMONIAL USE OF. The ceremonial use of lights in the Christian Church, with which this article is mainly concerned, probably has a double origin: in a very natural symbolism, and in the adaptation of certain pagan and Jewish rites and customs of which the symbolic meaning was Christianized. Light is everywhere the symbol of joy and of life-giving power, as darkness is of death and destruction. Fire, the most mysterious and impressive of the elements, the giver of light and of all the good things of life, is a thing sacred and adorable in primitive religions, and fire-worship still has its place in two at least of the great religions of the world. The Parsis adore fire as the visible expression of Ahura-Mazda, the eternal principle of light and righteousness; the Brahmans worship it as divine and omniscient.[1] The Hindu festival of Dewali (Diyawali, from *diya*, light), when temples and houses are illuminated with countless lamps, is held every November to celebrate Lakhshmi, the goddess of prosperity. In the ritual of the Jewish temple fire and light played a conspicuous part. In the Holy of Holies was a "cloud of light" (*shekinah*), symbolical of the presence of Yahweh, and before it stood the candlestick with six branches, on each of which and on the central stem was a lamp eternally burning; while in the forecourt was an altar on which the sacred fire was never allowed to go out. Similarly the Jewish synagogues have each their eternal lamp; while in the religion of Islam lighted lamps mark things and places specially holy; thus the Ka'ba at Mecca is illuminated by thousands of lamps hanging from the gold and silver rods that connect the columns of the surrounding colonnade.

Non-Christian religions.

The Greeks and Romans, too, had their sacred fire and their ceremonial lights. In Greece the *Lampadedromia* or *Lampadephoria* (torch-race) had its origin in ceremonies connected with the relighting of the sacred fire. Pausanias (i. 26, § 6) mentions the golden lamp made by Callimachus which burned night and day in the sanctuary of Athena Polias on the Acropolis, and (vii. 22, §§ 2 and 3) tells of a statue of Hermes Agoraios, in the market-place of Pharae in Achaea, before which lamps were lighted. Among the Romans lighted candles and lamps formed part of the cult of the domestic tutelary deities; on all festivals doors were garlanded and lamps lighted (Juvenal, *Sat.* xii. 92; Tertullian, *Apol.* xxxv.). In the cult of Isis lamps were lighted by day. In the ordinary temples were candelabra, *e.g.* that in the temple of Apollo Palatinus at Rome, originally taken by Alexander from Thebes, which was in the form of a tree from the branches of which lights hung like fruit. In comparing pagan with Christian usage it is important to remember that the lamps in the pagan temples were not symbolical, but votive offerings to the gods. Torches and lamps were also carried in religious processions.

Greece and Rome.

The pagan custom of burying lamps with the dead conveyed no such symbolical meaning as was implied in the late Christian custom of placing lights on and about the tombs of martyrs and saints. Its object was to provide the dead with the means of obtaining light in the next world, a wholly material conception; and the lamps were for the most part unlighted. It was of Asiatic origin, traces of it having been observed in Phoenicia and in the Punic colonies, but not in Egypt or Greece. In Europe it was confined to the countries under the domination of Rome.[2]

Funeral lamps.

In Christianity, from the very first, fire and light are conceived as symbols, if not as visible manifestations, of the divine nature and the divine presence. Christ is "the true Light" (John i. 9), and at his transfiguration "the fashion of his countenance was altered, and his raiment was white and glistering" (Luke ix. 29); when the Holy Ghost descended upon the apostles, "there appeared unto them cloven tongues of fire, and it sat upon each of them" (Acts ii. 3); at the conversion of St Paul "there shined round him a great light from heaven" (Acts ix. 3); while the glorified Christ is represented as standing "in the midst of seven candlesticks . . . his head and hairs white like wool, as white as snow; and his eyes as a flame of fire" (Rev. i. 14, 15). Christians are "children of Light" at perpetual war with "the powers of darkness."

Christian symbolism of light.

All this might very early, without the incentive of Jewish and pagan example, have affected the symbolic ritual of the primitive Church. There is, however, no evidence of any ceremonial use of lights in Christian worship during the first two centuries. It is recorded, indeed (Acts xx. 7, 8), that on the occasion of St Paul's preaching at Alexandria in Troas "there were many lights in the upper chamber"; but this was at night, and the most that can be hazarded is that a specially large number were lighted as a festive illumination, as in modern Church festivals (Martigny, *Dict. des antiqu. Chrét.*). As to a purely ceremonial use, such early evidence as exists is all the other way. A single sentence of Tertullian (*Apol.* xxxv.) sufficiently illuminates Christian practice during the 2nd century. "On days of rejoicing," he says, "we do not shade our door-posts with laurels nor encroach upon the day-light with lamps" (*die laeto non laureis postes obumbramus nec lucernis diem infringimus*). Lactantius, writing early in the 4th century, is even more sarcastic in his references to the heathen practice. "They kindle lights," he says, "as though to one who is in darkness. Can he be thought sane who offers the light of lamps and candles to the Author and Giver of all light?" (*Div. Inst.* vi. *de vero cultu*, cap. 2, in Migne, *Patr lat.* vi. 637).[3] This is primarily an attack on votive lights, and does not necessarily exclude their ceremonial use in other ways. There is, indeed, evidence that they were so used before Lactantius wrote. The 34th canon of the synod of Elvira (305), which was contemporary with him, forbade candles to be lighted in cemeteries during the daytime, which points to an established custom as well as to an objection to it; and in the Roman catacombs lamps have been found of the 2nd and 3rd centuries which seem to have

The early Church.

Tertullian and Lactantius.

[1] "O Fire, thou knowest all things!" See A. Bourquin, "Brahmakarma, ou rites sacrés des Brahmans," in the *Annales du Musée Guimet* (Paris, 1884, t. vii.).

[2] J. Toutain, in Daremberg and Saglio, *Dictionnaire*, *s.v.* "Lucerna."

[3] This is quoted with approval by Bishop Jewel in the homily *Against Peril of Idolatry* (see below).

As to the blessing of candles, according to the *Liber pontificalis* Pope Zosimus in 417 ordered these to be blessed,[8] and the Gallican and Mozarabic rituals also provided for this ceremony.[9] The Feast of the Purification of the Virgin, known as Candlemas (*q.v.*), because on this day the candles for the whole year are blessed, was established—according to some authorities—by Pope Gelasius I. about 492. As to the question of "altar lights," however, it must be borne in mind that these were not placed upon the altar, or on a retable behind it, until the 12th century. These were originally the candles carried by the deacons, according to the *Ordo Romanus* (i. 8; ii. 5; iii. 7) seven in number, which were set down either on the steps of the altar, or, later, behind it. In the Eastern Church, to this day, there are no lights on the high altar; the lighted candles stand on a small altar beside it, and at various parts of the service are carried by the lectors or acolytes before the officiating priest or deacon. The "crowd of lights" described by Paulinus as crowning the altar were either grouped round it or suspended in front of it; they are represented by the sanctuary lamps of the Latin Church and by the crown of lights suspended in front of the altar in the Greek.

Eastern Church.

To trace the gradual elaboration of the symbolism and use of ceremonial lights in the Church, until its full development and systematization in the middle ages, would be impossible here. It must suffice to note a few stages in the process. The burning of lights before the tombs of martyrs led naturally to their being burned also before relics and lastly before images and pictures. This latter practice, hotly denounced as idolatry during the iconoclastic controversy (see ICONOCLASM), was finally established as orthodox by the second general council of Nicaea (787), which restored the worship of images. A later development, however, by which certain lights themselves came to be regarded as objects of worship and to have other lights burned before *them*, was condemned as idolatrous by the synod of Noyon in 1344.[10] The passion for symbolism extracted ever new meanings out of the candles and their use. Early in the 6th century Ennodius, bishop of Pavia, pointed out the three-fold elements of a wax-candle (*Opusc.* ix. and x.), each of which would make it an offering acceptable to God; the rush-wick is the product of pure water, the wax is the offspring of virgin bees,[11] the flame is sent from heaven.[12] Clearly, wax was a symbol of the Blessed Virgin and the holy humanity of Christ. The later middle ages developed the idea. Durandus, in his *Rationale*, interprets the wax as the body of Christ, the wick as his soul, the flame as his divine nature; and the consuming candle as symbolizing his passion and death.

Development of the use.

[8] This may be the paschal candle only. In some codices the text runs: "Per parochias concessit licentiam benedicendi Cereum Paschalem" (Du Cange, *Glossarium*, *s.v.* "Cereum Paschale"). In the three variants of the notice of Zosimus given in Duchesne's edition of the *Lib. pontif.* (1886–1892) the word *cera* is, however, alone used. Nor does the text imply that he gave to the suburbican churches a privilege hitherto exercised by the metropolitan church. The passage runs: "Hic constituit ut diaconi leva tecta haberent de palleis linostimis per parrochias et ut cera benedicatur," &c. *Per parrochias* here obviously refers to the head-gear of the deacons, not to the candles.

[9] See also the *Peregrinatio Sylviae* (386), 86, &c., for the use of lights at Jerusalem, and Isidore of Seville (*Etym.* vii. 12; xx. 10) for the usage in the West. That even in the 7th century the blessing of candles was by no means universal is proved by the 9th canon of the council of Toledo (671), "De benedicendo cereo et lucerna in privilegiis Paschae." This canon states that candles and lamps are not blessed in some churches, and that inquiries have been made why we do it. In reply, the council decides that it should be done to celebrate the mystery of Christ's resurrection. See Isidore of Seville, *Conc.*, in Migne, *Pat. lat.* lxxxiv. 369.

[10] Du Cange, *Glossarium*, *s.v.* "Candela."

[11] Bees were believed, like fish, to be sexless.

[12] "Venerandis compactam elementis facem tibi, Domine, mancipamus: in qua trium copula munerum primum de impari numero complacebit: quae quod gratis Deo veniat auctoribus, non habetur incertum: unum quod de fetibus fluminum accedunt nutrimenta [illegible]arum: aliud quod apum tribuit intemerata fecunditas, in partibus nulla partitur damna virginitas: ignis etiam [illegible]sus adhibetur" (*Opusc.* x. in Migne, *Patr. lat.* t. lxiii.).

In the Roman Catholic Church.

In the completed ritual system of the medieval Church, as still preserved in the Roman Catholic communion, the use of ceremonial lights falls under three heads. (1) They may be symbolical of the light of God's presence, of Christ as "Light of Light," or of "the children of Light" in conflict with the powers of darkness; they may even be no more than expressions of joy on the occasion of great festivals. (2) They may be votive, *i.e.* offered as an act of worship (*latria*) to God. (3) They are, in virtue of their benediction by the Church, *sacramentalia*, *i.e.* efficacious for the good of men's souls and bodies, and for the confusion of the powers of darkness.[1] With one or more of these implications, they are employed in all the public functions of the Church. At the consecration of a church twelve lights are placed round the walls at the twelve spots where these are anointed by the bishop with holy oil, and on every anniversary these are relighted: at the dedication of an altar tapers are lighted and censed at each place where the table is anointed (*Pontificale Rom.* p. ii. *De eccl. dedicat. seu consecrat.*). At every liturgical service, and especially at Mass and at choir services, there must be at least two lighted tapers on the altar,[2] as symbols of the presence of God and tributes of adoration. For the Mass the rule is that there are six lights at High Mass, four at a *missa cantata*, and two at private masses. At a Pontifical High Mass (*i.e.* when the bishop celebrates) the lights are seven, because seven golden candlesticks surround the risen Saviour, the chief bishop of the Church (see Rev. i. 12). At most pontifical functions, moreover, the bishop—as the representative of Christ—is preceded by an acolyte with a burning candle (*bugia*) on a candlestick. The *Ceremoniale Episcoporum* (i. 12) further orders that a burning lamp is to hang at all times before each altar, three in front of the high altar, and five before the reserved Sacrament, as symbols of the eternal Presence. In practice, however, it is usual to have only one lamp lighted before the tabernacle in which the Host is reserved. The special symbol of the real presence of Christ is the *Sanctus* candle, which is lighted at the moment of consecration and kept burning until the communion. The same symbolism is intended by the lighted tapers which must accompany the Host whenever it is carried in procession, or to the sick and dying.

Dedication of a church. *At Mass and choir services.* *Sanctuary lamps.* *Symbol of the Real Presence.*

As symbols of light and joy a candle is held on each side of the deacon when reading the Gospel at Mass; and the same symbolism underlies the multiplication of lights on festivals, their number varying with the importance of the occasion. As to the number of these latter no rule is laid down. They differ from liturgical lights in that, whereas these must be tapers of pure beeswax or lamps fed with pure olive oil (except by special dispensation under certain circumstances), those used merely to add splendour to the celebration may be of any material; the only exception being, that in the decoration of the altar gas-lights are forbidden.

Tenebrae.

In general the ceremonial use of lights in the Roman Catholic Church is conceived as a dramatic representation in fire of the life of Christ and of the whole scheme of salvation. On Easter Eve the new fire, symbol of the light of the newly risen Christ, is produced, and from this are kindled all the lights used throughout the Christian year until, in the gathering darkness (*tenebrae*) of the Passion, they are gradually extinguished. This quenching of the light of the world is symbolized at the service of *Tenebrae* in Holy Week by the placing on a stand before the altar of thirteen lighted tapers arranged pyramidally, the rest of the church being in darkness. The penitential psalms are sung, and at the end of each a candle is extinguished. When only the central one is left it is taken down and carried behind the altar, thus symbolizing the betrayal and the death and burial of Christ. This ceremony can be traced to the 8th century at Rome.

The Paschal Candle.

On Easter Eve new fire is made[3] with a flint and steel, and blessed; from this three candles are lighted, the *lumen Christi*, and from these again the Paschal Candle.[4] This is the symbol of the risen and victorious Christ, and burns at every solemn service until Ascension Day, when it is extinguished and removed after the reading of the Gospel at High Mass. This, of course, symbolizes the Ascension; but meanwhile the other lamps in the church have received their light from the Paschal Candle, and so symbolize throughout the year the continued presence of the light of Christ.

Baptism.

At the consecration of the baptismal water the burning Paschal Candle is dipped into the font "so that the power of the Holy Ghost may descend into it and make it an effective instrument of regeneration." This is the symbol of baptism as rebirth as children of Light. Lighted tapers are also placed in the hands of the newly-baptized, or of their god-parents, with the admonition "to preserve their baptism inviolate, so that they may go to meet the Lord when he comes to the wedding." Thus, too, as "children of Light," candidates for ordination and novices about to take the vows carry lights when they come before the bishop; and the same idea underlies the custom of carrying lights at weddings, at the first communion, and by priests going to their first mass, though none of these are liturgically prescribed. Finally, lights are placed round the bodies of the dead and carried beside them to the grave, partly as symbols that they still live in the light of Christ, partly to frighten away the powers of darkness.

Ordinations, etc. *Funeral lights.* *Excommunication.*

Conversely, the extinction of lights is part of the ceremony of excommunication (*Pontificale Rom.* pars iii.). Regino, abbot of Prum, describes the ceremony as it was carried out in his day, when its terrors were yet unabated (*De eccles. disciplina*, ii. 409). "Twelve priests should stand about the bishop, holding in their hands lighted torches, which at the conclusion of the anathema or excommunication they should cast down and trample under foot." When the excommunication is removed, the symbol of reconciliation is the handing to the penitent of a burning taper.

Protestant Churches.

As a result of the Reformation the use of ceremonial lights was either greatly modified, or totally abolished in the Protestant Churches. In the Reformed (Calvinistic) Churches altar lights were, with the rest, done away with entirely as popish and superstitious. In the Lutheran Churches they were retained, and in Evangelical Germany have even survived most of the other medieval rites and ceremonies (*e.g.* the use of vestments) which were not abolished at the Reformation itself.

Church of England.

In the Church of England the practice has been less consistent. The first Prayer-book of Edward VI. directed two lights to be placed on the altar. This direction was omitted in the second Prayer-book; but the "Ornaments Rubric" of Queen Elizabeth's Prayer-book seemed again to make them obligatory. The question of how far this did so is a much-disputed one and is connected with the whole problem of the meaning and scope of the rubric (see VESTMENTS). An equal uncertainty reigns with regard to the actual usage of the Church of England from the Reformation onwards. Lighted candles certainly continued to decorate the holy table in Queen Elizabeth's chapel, to the scandal of Protestant zealots. They also seem to have been retained, at least for a while, in certain cathedral and collegiate churches. There is, however, no mention of ceremonial candles in the detailed account of the services of the Church of England given by William Harrison (*Description of England*, 1570); and the attitude of the Church towards their use, until the ritualistic movement of the 17th century, would seem to be authoritatively expressed in the *Third Part of the Sermon against Peril of Idolatry*, which quotes with approval the views of Lactantius and compares "our Candle Religion"

[1] All three conceptions are brought out in the prayers for the blessing of candles on the Feast of the Purification of the B.V.M. (Candlemas, *q.v.*). (1) "O holy Lord, . . . who . . . by the command didst cause this liquid to come by the labour of bees to the perfection of wax, . . . we beseech thee . . . to bless and sanctify these candles for the use of men, and the health of bodies and souls. . . ." (2) ". . . these candles, which we thy servants desire to carry lighted to magnify thy name; that by offering them to thee, being worthily inflamed with the holy fire of thy most sweet charity, we may deserve," &c. (3) "O Lord Jesus Christ, the true light, . . . mercifully grant, that as these lights enkindled with visible fire dispel nocturnal darkness, so our hearts illumined by invisible fire," &c. (*Missale Rom.*). In the form for the blessing of candles *extra diem Purificationis B. Mariae Virg.* the virtue of the consecrated candles in discomfiting demons is specially brought out: "that in whatever places they may be lighted, or placed, the princes of darkness may depart, and tremble, and may fly terror-stricken with all their ministers from those habitations, nor presume further to disquiet and molest those who serve thee, Almighty God" (*Rituale Rom.*).

[2] Altar candlesticks consist of five parts: the foot, stem, knob in the centre, bowl to catch the drippings, and pricket (a sharp point on which the candle is fixed). It is permissible to use a long tube, pointed to imitate a candle, in which is a small taper forced to the top by a spring (*Cong. Rit.*, 11th May 1878).

[3] This is common to the Eastern Church also. Pilgrims from all parts of the East flock to Jerusalem to obtain the "new fire" on Easter Eve at the Church of the Holy Sepulchre. Here the fire is supposed to be miraculously sent from heaven. The rush of the pilgrims to kindle their lights at it is so great, that order is maintained with difficulty by Mahommedan soldiers.

[4] The origin of the Paschal Candle is lost in the mists of antiquity. According to the abbé Châtelain (quoted in Diderot's *Encyclopédie*, *s.v.* "Cierge") the Paschal Candle was not originally a candle at all, but a wax column on which the dates of the movable feasts were inscribed. These were later written on paper and fixed to the Paschal Candle, a custom which in his day survived in the Cluniac churches.

[illegible] "[illegible] Idolatry." This pronouncement, indeed, [illegible] the use of ceremonial lights in [illegible], and especially the conception [illegible] whether to God or to the saints, [illegible] though it undoubtedly discourages, [illegible] use.[1] In this connexion it is worth [illegible] against idolatry was reprinted, [illegible] king's authority, long after altar [illegible] under the influence of the high church [illegible] Legal under the Act of Uniformity [illegible]. The use of "wax lights and [illegible] indictments brought by P. Smart, [illegible] of Durham, against Dr Burgoyne, Cosin [illegible] "superstitious ceremonies" in the [illegible] the Act of Uniformity." The indict- [illegible] by Sir James Whitelocke, chief [illegible] judge of the King's Bench, and in 1629 [illegible] a judge of Common Pleas and himself [illegible] *Hierurgia Anglicana*, ii. pp. 230 seq.). The [illegible] among the indictments in the [illegible] other bishops by the House of [illegible] based on the Act of Uniformity. [illegible] the use of ceremonial lights, [illegible] was not unusual in cathedrals and [illegible]. It was not, however, till the ritual revival [illegible] their use was at all widely extended [illegible] growing custom met with fierce opposi- [illegible], and in 1872 the Privy Council [illegible] illegal (*Martin* v. *Mackonochie*). [illegible] was afterwards admitted on insufficient [illegible] effect; and, in the absence of any [illegible], advantage was taken of the [illegible] Ornaments Rubric to introduce [illegible] the whole ceremonial use of [illegible] pre-Reformation Church. The matter [illegible] *Read and others* v. *the Bishop* [illegible], one of the counts of the [illegible] bishop had, during the celebration [illegible] two candles to be alight on a shelf [illegible] communion table when they were not [illegible] light. The archbishop of Canter- [illegible] the case was heard (1889), decided [illegible] of two candles on the table, [illegible] service but lit before it began, [illegible] Prayer Book of Edward VI. and had [illegible] the case being appealed to the [illegible] was dismissed on the [illegible] bishop, was responsible for the [illegible] general question of the legality of [illegible] candles round the bodies [illegible] in state," has never wholly [illegible] though their significance [illegible] the 13th century, moreover, [illegible] to accompany a funeral with [illegible] gives a plate representing [illegible] by boys, each carry- [illegible] candlestick. There [illegible] having been carried in other [illegible] Reformation. The usage [illegible] churches is a revival of

[illegible] Fontain in Daremberg and [illegible] (Paris, [illegible]); [illegible] Becker's [illegible] largely founded on [illegible] (1528, [illegible] and Religious [illegible] vi. pt. 1, [illegible] Paul's, [illegible] two

Röm. Alterthümer), ii. 238-301; article "Cierges et lampes," in the Abbé J. A. Martigny's *Dict. des Antiquités Chrétiennes* (Paris, 1865); the articles "Lichter" and "Koimetarien" (pp. 834 seq.) in Herzog-Hauck's *Realencyklopädie* (3rd ed., Leipzig, 1901); the article "Licht" in Wetzer and Welte's *Kirchenlexikon* (Freiburg-i.-B., 1882–1901), an excellent exposition of the symbolism from the Catholic point of view, also "Kerze" and "Lichter"; W. Smith and S. Cheetham, *Dict. of Chr. Antiquities* (London, 1875–1880), i. 939 seq.; in all these numerous further references will be found. See also Mühlbauer, *Gesch. u. Bedeutung der Wachslichter bei den kirchlichen Funktionen* (Augsburg, 1874); V. Thalhofer, *Handbuch der Katholischen Liturgik* (Freiburg-i.-B., 1887), i. 666 seq.; and, for the post-Reformation use in the Church of England, *Hierurgia Anglicana*, new ed. by Vernon Staley (London, 1903). (W. A. P.)

LIGNE, CHARLES JOSEPH, Prince de (1735–1814), soldier and writer, came of a princely family of Hainaut, and was born at Brussels in 1735. As an Austrian subject he entered the imperial army at an early age. He distinguished himself by his valour in the Seven Years' War, notably at Breslau, Leuthen, Hochkirch and Maxen, and after the war rose rapidly to the rank of lieutenant field marshal. He became the intimate friend and counsellor of the emperor Joseph II., and, inheriting his father's vast estates, lived in the greatest splendour and luxury till the War of the Bavarian Succession brought him again into active service. This war was short and uneventful, and the prince then travelled in England, Germany, Italy, Switzerland and France, devoting himself impartially to the courts, the camps, the salons and the learned assemblies of philosophers and scientists in each country. In 1784 he was again employed in military work, and was promoted to Feldzeugmeister. In 1787 he was with Catherine II. in Russia, accompanied her in her journey to the Crimea, and was made a Russian field marshal by the empress. In 1788 he was present at the siege of Belgrade. Shortly after this he was invited to place himself at the head of the Belgian revolutionary movement, in which one of his sons and many of his relatives were prominent, but declined with great courtesy, saying that "he never revolted in the winter." Though suspected by Joseph of collusion with the rebels, the two friends were not long estranged, and after the death of the emperor the prince remained in Vienna. His Brabant estates were overrun by the French in 1792–1793, and his eldest son killed in action at La Croix-du-Bois in the Argonne (September 14, 1792). He was given the rank of field marshal (1809) and an honorary command at court, living in spite of the loss of his estates in comparative luxury and devoting himself to literary work. He lived long enough to characterize the proceedings of the congress of Vienna with the famous *mot*: "Le Congrès danse mais ne marche pas." He died at Vienna on the 13th of December 1814. His grandson, Eugene Lamoral de Ligne (1804–1880), was a distinguished Belgian statesman.

His collected works appeared in thirty-four volumes at Vienna during the last years of his life (*Mélanges militaires, littéraires, sentimentaires*), and he bequeathed his manuscripts to the emperor's Trabant Guard, of which he was captain (*Œuvres posthumes*, Dresden and Vienna, 1817). Selections were published in French and German (*Œuvres choisies de M. le prince de Ligne* (Paris, 1809); *Lettres et pensées du Maréchal Prince de Ligne*, ed. by Madame de Staël (1809); *Œuvres historiques, littéraires . . . correspondance et poésies diverses* (Brussels, 1859); *Des Prinzen Karl von Ligne militärische Werke*, ed. Count Pappenheim (Sulzbach, 1814). The most important of his numerous works on all military subjects is the *Fantaisies et préjugés militaires*, which originally appeared in 1780. A modern edition is that published by J. Dumaine (Paris, 1879). A German version (*Militärische Vorurtheile und Phantasien*, &c.) appeared as early as 1783. This work, though it deals lightly and cavalierly with the most important subjects (the prince even proposes to found an international academy of the art of war, wherein the reputation of generals could be impartially weighed), is a military classic, and indispensable to the students of the post-Frederician period. On the whole, it may be said that the prince adhered to the school of Guibert (*q.v.*), and a full discussion will be found in Max Jähns' *Gesch. d. Kriegswissenschaften*, iii. 2091 et seq. Another very celebrated work by the prince is the mock autobiography of Prince Eugene (1809).

See *Revue de Bruxelles* (October 1839); Reiffenberg, "Le Feld-maréchal Prince Charles Joseph de Ligne," *Mémoires de l'académie de Bruxelles*, vol. xix.; Peetermans, *Le Prince de Ligne, ou un écrivain grand seigneur* (Liège, 1857), *Études et notices historiques concernant l'histoire des Pays Bas*, vol. iii. (Brussels, 1890); *Mémoires et publications de la Société des Sciences, &c du Hainault*, vol. iii., 5th series; Dublet *Le Prince de Ligne et ses contemporains* (Paris, 1889), Wurzbach, *Biogr. Lexikon d. Kaiserth. Österr* (Vienna, 1858); Hirtenfeld, *Der Militär-Maria-Theresien-Orden*, vol. i. (Vienna, 1857); Ritter von Rettersberg, *Biogr. d ausgezeichnetsten Feldherren* (Prague, 1829); Schweigerd, *Österr. Helden*, vol. iii. (Vienna, 1854); Thürheim, *F. M. Karl Joseph Furst de Ligne* (Vienna, 1877).

LIGNITE (Lat. *lignum*, wood), an imperfectly formed coal, usually brownish in colour, and always showing the structure of the wood from which it was derived (see COAL).

LIGONIER, JOHN (JEAN LOUIS) **LIGONIER, EARL** (1680–1770), British Field Marshal, came of a Huguenot family of Castres in the south of France, members of which emigrated to England at the close of the 17th century. He entered the army as a volunteer under Marlborough. From 1702 to 1710 he was engaged, with distinction, in nearly every important battle and siege of the war. He was one of the first to mount the breach at the siege of Liége, commanded a company at the Schellenberg and at Blenheim, and was present at Menin (where he led the storming of the covered way), Ramillies, Oudenarde and Malplaquet (where he received twenty-three bullets through his clothing and remained unhurt). In 1712 he became governor of Fort St Philip, Minorca, and in 1718 was adjutant-general of the troops employed in the Vigo expedition, where he led the stormers of Fort Maria. Two years later he became colonel of the "Black Horse" (now 7th Dragoon Guards), a command which he retained for 29 years. His regiment soon attained an extraordinary degree of efficiency. He was made brigadier-general in 1735, major-general in 1739, and accompanied Lord Stair in the Rhine Campaign of 1742–1743. George II. made him a Knight of the Bath on the field of Dettingen. At Fontenoy Ligonier commanded the British foot, and acted throughout the battle as adviser to the duke of Cumberland. During the "Forty-Five" he was called home to command the British army in the Midlands, but in January 1746 was placed at the head of the British and British-paid contingents of the Allied army in the Low Countries. He was present at Roucoux (11th Oct. 1746), and, as general of horse, at Val (1st July 1747), where he led the last charge of the British cavalry. In this encounter his horse was killed, and he was taken prisoner, but was exchanged in a few days. With the close of the campaign ended Ligonier's active career, but (with a brief interval in 1756–1757) he occupied various high civil and military posts to the close of his life. In 1757 he was made, in rapid succession, commander-in-chief, colonel of the 1st Foot Guards (now Grenadier Guards), and a peer of Ireland under the title of Viscount Ligonier of Enniskillen, a title changed in 1762 for that of Clonmell. From 1759 to 1762 he was master-general of the Ordnance, and in 1763 he became Baron, and in 1766 Earl, in the English peerage. In the latter year he became field marshal. He died in 1770. His younger brother, Francis, was also a distinguished soldier; and his son succeeded to the Irish peerage of Lord Ligonier.

See Combes, *J. L. Ligonier, une étude* (Castres, 1866), and the histories of the 7th Dragoon Guards and Grenadier Guards.

LIGUORI, ALFONSO MARIA DEI (1696–1787), saint and doctor of the Church of Rome, was born at Marianella, near Naples, on the 27th of September 1696, being the son of Giuseppe dei Liguori, a Neapolitan noble. He began life at the bar, where he obtained considerable practice; but the loss of an important suit, in which he was counsel for a Neapolitan noble against the grand duke of Tuscany, and in which he had entirely mistaken the force of a leading document, so mortified him that he withdrew from the legal world. In 1726 he entered the Congregation of Missions as a novice, and became a priest in 1726. In 1732 he founded the "Congregation of the Most Holy Redeemer" at Scala, near Salerno; the headquarters of the Order were afterwards transferred to Nocera dei Pagani. Its members, popularly called Liguorians or Redemptorists, devote themselves to the religious instruction of the poor, more especially in country districts; Liguori specially forbade them to undertake secular educational work. In 1750 appeared his celebrated devotional book on the *Glories of Mary*; three years later came his still more celebrated treatise on moral theology. In 1755 this was much enlarged and translated into Latin under the title of *Homo Apostolicus*. In 1762, at the express desire of the pope, he accepted the bishopric of Sant' Agata dei Goti, a small town in the province of Benevent; though he had previously refused the archbishopric of Palermo. Here he worked diligently at practical reforms, being specially anxious to raise the standard of clerical life and work. In 1775 he resigned his bishopric on the plea of enfeebled health; he retired to his Redemptorists at Nocera, and died there in 1787. In 1796 Pius VI. declared him "venerable"; he was beatified by Pius VII. in 1816, canonized by Gregory XVI. in 1839, and finally declared one of the nineteen "Doctors of the Church" by Pius IX. in 1871.

Liguori is the chief representative of a school of casuistry and devotional theology still abundantly represented within the Roman Church. Not that he was in any sense its founder. He was simply a fair representative of the Italian piety of his day—amiable, ascetic in his personal habits, indefatigable in many forms of activity, and of more than respectable abilities; though the emotional side of his character had the predominance over his intellect. He was learned, as learning was understood among the Italian clergy of the 18th century; but he was destitute of critical faculty, and the inaccuracy of his quotations is proverbial. In his casuistical works he was a diligent compiler, whose avowed design was to take a middle course between the two current extremes of severity and laxity. In practice, he leant constantly towards laxity. Eighteenth-century Italy looked on religion with apathetic indifference, and Liguori convinced himself that only the gentlest and most lenient treatment could win back the alienated laity; hence he was always willing to excuse errors on the side of laxity as due to an excess of zeal in winning over penitents. Severity, on the other hand, seemed to him not only inexpedient, but positively wrong. By making religion hard it made it odious, and thus prepared the way for unbelief. Like all casuists, he took for granted that morality was a recondite science, beyond the reach of all but the learned. When a layman found himself in doubt, his duty was not to consult his conscience, but to take the advice of his confessor; while the confessor himself was bound to follow the rules laid down by the casuistical experts, who delivered themselves of a kind of "counsel's opinion" on all knotty points of practical morality. But experts proverbially differ: what was to be done when they disagreed? Suppose, for instance, that some casuists held it wrong to dance on Sunday, while others held it perfectly lawful. In Liguori's time there were four ways of answering the question. Strict moralists—called rigorists, or "tutiorists"—maintained that the austerer opinion ought always to be followed; dancing on Sundays was certainly wrong, if any good authorities had declared it to be so. Probabiliorists maintained that the more general opinion ought to prevail, irrespectively of whether it was the stricter or the laxer; dancing on Sunday was perfectly lawful, if the majority of casuists approved it. Probabilists argued that any opinion might be followed, if it could show good authority on its side, even if there was still better authority against it; dancing on Sunday must be innocent, if it could show a fair sprinkling of eminent names in its favour. The fourth and last school—the "laxists"—carried this principle a step farther, and held that a practice must be unobjectionable, if it could prove that any one "grave Doctor" had defended it, even if dancing on Sunday had hitherto lain under the ban of the church, a single casuist could legitimate it by one stroke of his pen. Liguori's great achievement lay in steering a middle course between these various extremes. The gist of his system, which is known as "equi-probabilism," is that the more indulgent opinion may always be followed, whenever the authorities in its favour are as good, or nearly as good, as those on the other side. In this way he claimed that he had secured liberty in its rights without allowing it to degenerate into licence. However much they might personally disapprove, zealous priests could not forbid their parishioners to dance on Sunday, if the practice had won wide-spread toleration; on the other hand, they could not relax the usual discipline of the church on the strength of a few unguarded opinions of too indulgent casuists. Thus the Liguorian system surpassed all its predecessors in securing uniformity in the confessional on a basis of established usage, two advantages amply sufficient to ensure its speedy general adoption within the Church of Rome.

Lives by A. M. Tannoja, a pupil of Liguori's (3 vols., Naples, 1798–1802), new ed., Turin, 1857, French trans., Paris, 1842); P. v. A. Giattini (Rome, 1815; Ger. trans., Vienna, 1835); F. W. Faber (4 vols., London, 1848–1849); M. A. Hugues (Münster, 1857); O. Gisler (Einsiedeln, 1887); K. Dilgskron (2 vols., Regensburg, 1887), perhaps the best; A. Capecelatro (2 vols., Rome, 1893); A. des Retours (Paris, 1903); A. C. Berthe (St Louis, 1906).

Works: (a) Collected editions. Italian: (Monza, 1819, 1828; Venice, 1830; Naples, 1840 ff.; Turin, 1887 ff.). French: (Tournai, 1855 ff., new ed., 1895 ff.). German: (Regensburg, 1842–1847). English: (22 vols., New York, 1887–1895). Editions of the *Theologia Moralis* and other separate works are very numerous. (b) *Letters*: (2 vols., Monza, 1831; 3 vols., Rome, 1887 ff.). See also Meyrick, *Moral and Devotional Theology of the Church of Rome, according to the Teaching of S. Alfonso de Liguori* (London, 1857), and art. Casuistry. (St. C.)

LIGURES BAEBIANI, in ancient geography, a settlement of Ligurians in Samnium, Italy. The towns of Taurasia and Cisauna in Samnium had been captured in 298 B.C. by the consul L. Cornelius Scipio Barbatus, and the territory of the former remained Roman state domain. In 180 B.C. 47,000 Ligurians from the neighbourhood of Luna (Ligures Apuani), with women and children, were transferred to this district, and two settlements were formed taking their names from the consuls of 181 B.C., the Ligures Baebiani and the Ligures Corneliani. The site of the former town lies 15 m. N. of Beneventum, on the road to Saepinum and Aesernia. In its ruins several inscriptions have been found, notably a large bronze tablet discovered in a public building in the Forum bearing the date A.D. 101, and relating to the alimentary institution founded by Trajan here (see Veleia). A sum of money was lent to landed proprietors of the district (whose names and estates are specified in the inscription), and the interest which it produced formed the income of the institution, which, on the model of that of Veleia, would have served to support a little over one hundred children. The capital was 401,800 sesterces, and the annual interest probably at 5%, *i.e.* 20,090 sesterces (£4018 and £201 respectively). The site of the other settlement—that of the Ligures Corneliani—is unknown.

See T. Mommsen in *Corp. Inscr. Lat.* ix. (Berlin, 1883), 125 sqq. (T. As.)

LIGURIA, a modern territorial division of Italy, lying between the Ligurian Alps and the Apennines on the N., and the Mediterranean on the S. and extending from the frontier of France on the W. to the Gulf of Spezia on the E. Its northern limits touch Piedmont and Lombardy, while Emilia and Tuscany fringe its eastern borders, the dividing line following as a rule the summits of the mountains. Its area is 2037 sq. m. The railway from Pisa skirts the entire coast of the territory, throwing off lines to Parma from Sarzana and Spezia, to Milan and Turin from Genoa, and to Turin from Savona, and there is a line from Ventimiglia to Cuneo and Turin by the Col di Tenda. Liguria embraces the two provinces of Genoa and Porto Maurizio (Liguria), which once formed the republic of Genoa. Its sparsely-peopled mountains slope gently northward towards the Po, descending, however, abruptly into the sea at several points, the narrow coast district, famous under the name of the Riviera (*q.v.*), is divided at Genoa into the Riviera di Ponente towards France, and the Riviera di Levante towards the east. Its principal products are wheat, maize, wine, oranges, lemons, fruits, olives and potatoes, though the olive groves are being rapidly supplanted by flower-gardens, which grow flowers for export. Copper and iron pyrites are mined. The principal industries are iron-works, foundries, iron shipbuilding, engineering, and boiler works (Genoa, Spezia, Sampierdarena, Sestri Ponente, &c.), the production of [illegible] manufacture of cottons and woollens. Owing to the sheltered situation and the mildness of their climate, many of the coast towns are chosen by thousands of foreigners for winter residence, while the Italians frequent them in summer for sea-bathing. The inhabitants have always been adventurous seamen—Columbus and Amerigo Vespucci were Genoese,—and the coast has several good harbours, Genoa, Spezia and Savona being the best. In educational and general development, Liguria stands high among the regions of Italy. The populations of the respective provinces and their chief towns are, according to the census of 1901 (*popolazione residente* or *legale*)—province of Genoa, pop. 931,156; number of communes 197; chief towns—Genoa (219,507), Spezia (66,263), Savona (38,648), Sampierdarena (34,084), Sestri Ponente (17,225). Province of Porto Maurizio, pop. 144,604, number of communes 106; chief towns—Porto Maurizio (7207), S. Remo (20,027), Ventimiglia (11,468), Oneglia (8252). Total for Liguria, 1,075,760.

The Ligurian coast became gradually subject to the Romans, and the road along it must have been correspondingly prolonged: up to the end of the Hannibalic war the regular starting-point for Spain by sea was Pisae, in 195 B.C. it was the harbour of Luna (Gulf of Spezia),[1] though Genua must have become Roman a little before this time, while, in 137 B.C., C. Hostilius Mancinus marched as far as Portus Herculis (Villafranca), and in 121 B.C. the province of Gallia Narbonensis was formed and the coast-road prolonged to the Pyrenees. In 14 B.C. Augustus restored the whole road from Placentia to Dertona (Via Postumia), and thence to Vada Sabatia (Via Aemilia [2]) and the River Varus (Var), so that it thenceforth took the name of Via Julia Augusta (see Aemilia, Via [2]). The other chief roads of Liguria were the portion of the Via Postumia from Dertona to Genua, a road from above Vada through Augusta Bagiennorum and Pollentia to Augusta Taurinorum, and another from Augusta Taurinorum to Hasta and Valentia. The names of the villages—Quarto, Quinto, &c.—on the south-east side and Pontedecimo on the north of Genoa allude to their distance along the Roman roads. The Roman Liguria, forming the ninth region of Augustus, was thus far more extensive than the modern, including the country on the north slopes of the Apennines and Maritime Alps between the Trebia and the Po, and extending a little beyond Albintimilium. On the west Augustus formed the provinces of the Alpes Maritimae and the Alpes Cottiae. Towns of importance were few, owing to the nature of the country. Dertona was the only colony, and Alba Pompeia, Augusta Bagiennorum, Pollentia, Hasta, Aquae Statiellae, and Genua may also be mentioned; but the Ligurians dwelt entirely in villages, and were organized as tribes. The mountainous character of Liguria made the spread of culture difficult; it remained a forest district, producing timber, cattle, ponies, mules, sheep, &c. Oil and wine had to be imported, and when the cultivation of the olive began is not known.

The arrangement made by Augustus lasted until the time of Diocletian, when the two Alpine provinces were abolished, and the watershed became the boundary between Italy and Gaul. At this time we find the name Liguria extended as far as Milan, while in the 6th century the old Liguria was separated from it, and under the Lombards formed the fifth Italian province under the name of Alpes Cottiae. In the middle ages the ancient Liguria north of the Apennines fell to Piedmont and Lombardy, while that to the south, with the coast strip, belonged to the republic of Genoa. (T. As.)

Archaeology and Philology.—It is clear that in earlier times the Ligurians occupied a much more extensive area than the Augustan region; for instance Strabo (i. 2, 92; iv. 1, 7) gives earlier authorities for their possession of the land on which the Greek colony of Massalia (Marseilles) was founded; and Thucydides (vi. 2) speaks of a settlement of Ligurians in Spain who expelled the Sicani thence. Southward their domain extended as far as Pisa on the coast of Etruria and Arretium inland in the

[1] The dividing line between Liguria and Etruria was the lower course of the river Macra (Magra), so that, while the harbour of Luna was in the former, Luna itself was in the latter.

time of Polybius (ii. 6), and a somewhat vague reference in Lycophron (line 1351) to the Ligurians as enemies of the founders of Agylla (*i.e.* Caere) suggests that they once occupied even a larger tract to the south. Seneca (*Cons ad Helv.* vii. 9) states that the population of Corsica was partly Ligurian. By combining traditions recorded by Dionysius (i. 22; xiv. 37) and others (*e.g.* Serv. *ad. Aen.* xi. 317) as having been held by Cato the Censor and by Philistus of Syracuse (385 B.C.) respectively, Professor Ridgeway (*Who were the Romans?* London, 1908, p. 3) decides in favour of identifying the Ligurians with a tribe called the Aborigines who occupy a large place in the early traditions of Italy (see Dionysius i. cc. 10 ff.); and who may at all events be regarded with reasonable certainty as constituting an early pre-Roman and pre-Tuscan stratum in the population of Central Italy (see LATIUM). For a discussion of this question see VOLSCI. Ridgeway holds that the language of the Ligurians, as well as their antiquities, was identical with that of the early Latins, and with that of the Plebeians of Rome (as contrasted with that of the Patrician or Sabine element), see ROME: *History* (*ad. init.*). The archaeological side of this important question is difficult. Although great progress has been made with the study of the different strata of remains in prehistoric Italy and of those of Liguria itself (see for instance the excellent *Introduction à l'histoire romaine* by Basile Modestov (Paris, 1907, p. 122 ff.) and W. Ridgeway's *Early Age of Greece*, p. 240 ff.) no general agreement has been reached among archaeologists as to the particular races who are to be identified as the authors of the early strata, earlier, that is, than that stratum which represents the Etruscans.

On the linguistic side some fairly certain conclusions have been reached. D'Arbois de Jubainville (*Les Premiers habitants de l'Europe*, ed. 2, Paris, 1889–1894) pointed out the great frequency of the suffix *-asco-* (and *-usco-*) both in ancient and in modern Ligurian districts, and as far north as *Caranusca* near Metz, and also in the eastern Alps and in Spain. He pointed out also, what can scarcely be doubted, that the great mass of the Ligurian proper names (*e.g.* the streams *Vinelasca*, *Porcobera*, *Comberanea*; *mons Tuledo*; *Venascum*), have a definite Indo-European character. Farther Karl Müllenhof in vol. iii. of his *Deutsche Alterthumskunde* (Berlin, 1898) made a careful collection of the proper names reserved in Latin inscriptions of the Ligurian districts, such as the *Tabula Genuatium* (*C.I.L.* i. 99) of 117 B.C. A complete collection of all Ligurian place and personal names known has been made by S. Elizabeth Jackson, B.A., and the collection is to be combined with the inscriptional remains of the district in *The Pre-Italic Dialects*, edited by R. S. Conway (see *The Proceedings of the British Academy*). Following Kretschmer *Kuhn's Zeitschrift* (xxxviii. 97), who discussed several inscriptions found near Ornavasso (Lago Maggiore) and concluded that they showed an Indo-European language, Conway, though holding that the inscriptions are more Celtic than Ligurian, pointed out strong evidence in the ancient place names of Liguria that the language spoken there in the period which preceded the Roman conquest was Indo-European, and belonged to a definite group, namely, languages which preserved the original *q* as Latin did, and did not convert it into *p* as did the Umbro-Safine tribes. The same is probably true of Venetia (see VENETI), and of an Indo-European language preserved on inscriptions found at Coligny and commonly referred to the Sequani (see *Comptes Rendus de l'Ac. d'Insc.*, Paris, 1897, 703; E. B. Nicholson, *Sequanian*, London, 1898; Thurneysen, *Zeitschr. f. Kelt. Phil.*, 1899, 523). Typically Ligurian names are *Quiamelius*, which contains the characteristic Ligurian word *melo-* "stone" as in *mons Blustiemelus* (*C.I.L.* v. 7749), *Intimelium* and the modern *Vintimiglia*. The tribal names *Soliceli*, *Stoniceli*, clearly contain the same element as Lat. *aequi-coli* (dwellers on the plain), *sati-cola*, &c., namely *quel-*, cf. Lat. *in-quil-inus*, *colo*, Gr. πολεῖν, τέλλεσθαι. And it should be added that the Ligurian ethnica show the prevailing use of the two suffixes *-co-* and *-ati-*, which there is reason to refer to the pre-Roman stratum of population in Italy (see VOLSCI).

Besides the authorities already cited the student may be referred to C. Pauli, *Altitalische Studien*, vol. i., especially for the alphabet of the insc.; W. Ridgeway, *Who were the Romans?* (followed by the abstract of a paper by the present writer) in *The Proceedings of the British Academy*, vol. iii. p. 42; and to W. H. Hall's, *The Romans on the Riviera and the Rhone* (London, 1898); Issel's *La Liguria geologica e preistorica* (Genoa, 1892). A further batch of Celto-Ligurian inscriptions from Giubiasco near Bellinzona (Canton Ticino) is published by G. Herbig, in the *Anzeiger f. Schweizer. Altertumskunde*, vii. (1905–1906), p. 187; and one of the same class by Elia Lattes, *Di un' Iscriz. ante-Romana trovata a Carcegna sul Lago d' Orta* (*Atti d. r. Accad. d. Scienze di Torino*, xxxix., Feb. 1904). (R. S. C.)

LI HUNG CHANG (1823–1901), Chinese statesman, was born on the 16th of February 1823 at Hofei, in Ngan-hui. From his earliest youth he showed marked ability, and when quite young he took his bachelor degree. In 1847 he became a Tsin-shi, or graduate of the highest order, and two years later was admitted into the imperial Hanlin college. Shortly after this the central provinces of the empire were invaded by the Taiping rebels, and in defence of his native district he raised a regiment of militia, with which he did such good service to the imperial cause that he attracted the attention of Tsêng Kuo-fan, the generalissimo in command. In 1859 he was transferred to the province of Fu-kien, where he was given the rank of taotai, or intendant of circuit. But Tsêng had not forgotten him, and at his request Li was recalled to take part against the rebels. He found his cause supported by the "Ever Victorious Army," which, after having been raised by an American named Ward, was finally placed under the command of Charles George Gordon. With this support Li gained numerous victories leading to the surrender of Suchow and the capture of Nanking. For these exploits he was made governor of Kiangsu, was decorated with a yellow jacket, and was created an earl. An incident connected with the surrender of Suchow, however, left a lasting stain upon his character. By an arrangement with Gordon the rebel wangs, or princes, yielded Nanking on condition that their lives should be spared. In spite of the assurance given them by Gordon, Li ordered their instant execution. This breach of faith so aroused Gordon's indignation that he seized a rifle, intending to shoot the falsifier of his word, and would have done so had not Li saved himself by flight. On the suppression of the rebellion (1864) Li took up his duties as governor, but was not long allowed to remain in civil life. On the outbreak of the rebellion of the Nienfei, a remnant of the Taipings, in Ho-nan and Shan-tung (1866) he was ordered again to take the field, and after some misadventures he succeeded in suppressing the movement. A year later he was appointed viceroy of Hukwang, where he remained until 1870, when the Tientsin massacre necessitated his transfer to the scene of the outrage. He was, as a natural consequence, appointed to the viceroyalty of the metropolitan province of Chihli, and justified his appointment by the energy with which he suppressed all attempts to keep alive the anti-foreign sentiment among the people. For his services he was made imperial tutor and member of the grand council of the empire, and was decorated with many-eyed peacocks' feathers.

To his duties as viceroy were added those of the superintendent of trade, and from that time until his death, with a few intervals of retirement, he practically conducted the foreign policy of China. He concluded the Chifu convention with Sir Thomas Wade (1876), and thus ended the difficulty caused by the murder of Mr Margary in Yunnan; he arranged treaties with Peru and Japan, and he actively directed the Chinese policy in Korea. On the death of the emperor T'ungchi in 1875 he, by suddenly introducing a large armed force into the capital, effected a *coup d'état* by which the emperor Kwang Sü was put on the throne under the tutelage of the two dowager empresses; and in 1886, on the conclusion of the Franco-Chinese war, he arranged a treaty with France. Li was always strongly impressed with the necessity of strengthening the empire, and when viceroy of Chihli he raised a large well-drilled and well-armed force, and spent vast sums both in fortifying Port Arthur and the Taku forts and in increasing the navy. For years he had watched the successful reforms effected in Japan and had a well-founded dread of coming into conflict with that empire. But in 1894 events forced his hand, and in consequence of a dispute as to the relative influence of China and Japan in Korea, war broke out. The result proved the wisdom of Li's fears. Both on land and at sea the Chinese forces were ignominiously routed, and in 1895, on the fall of Wei-hai-wei, the emperor sued for peace. With characteristic subterfuge his advisers suggested as peace envoys persons whom the mikado very properly and promptly refused to accept, and finally Li was sent to represent his imperial master at the council assembled at Shimonoseki. With great diplomatic skill Li pleaded the cause of his country, but finally had to agree to the cession of Formosa, the Pescadores, and the Liaotung peninsula to the conquerors, and to the payment of an indemnity of 200,000,000 taels. By a subsequent arrangement the Liaotung peninsula was restored to China, in exchange for an increased indemnity. During the peace discussions at Shimonoseki, as Li was being borne through the narrow streets of the town, a would-be assassin fired a pistol point-blank in his face. The wound inflicted was not serious, and after a few days' rest Li was able to take up again the suspended negotiations. In 1896 he represented the emperor at the coronation of the tsar, and visited Germany, Belgium, France, England, and the United States of America. For some time after his return to China his services were demanded at Peking, where he was virtually constituted minister for foreign affairs; but in 1900 he was transferred to Canton as viceroy of the two Kwangs. The Boxer movement, however, induced the emperor to recall him to the capital, and it was mainly owing to his exertions that, at the conclusion of the outbreak, a protocol of peace was signed in September 1901. For many months his health had been failing, and he died on the 7th of November 1901. He left three sons and one daughter. (R. K. D.)

LILAC,[1] or Pipe Tree (*Syringa vulgaris*), a tree of the olive family, Oleaceae. The genus contains about ten species of ornamental hardy deciduous shrubs native in eastern Europe and temperate Asia. They have opposite, generally entire leaves and large panicles of small regular flowers, with a bell-shaped calyx and a 4-lobed cylindrical corolla, with the two stamens characteristic of the order attached at the mouth of the tube. The common lilac is said to have come from Persia in the 16th century, but is doubtfully indigenous in Hungary, the borders of Moldavia, &c. Two kinds of *Syringa*, viz. *alba* and *caerulea*, are figured and described by Gerard (*Herball*, 1597), which he calls the white and the blue pipe privets. The former is the common privet, *Ligustrum vulgare*, which, and the ash tree, *Fraxinus excelsior*, are the only members of the family native in Great Britain. The latter is the lilac, as both figure and description agree accurately with it. It was carried by the European colonists to north-east America, and is still grown in gardens of the northern and middle states. There are many fine varieties of lilac, both with single and double [illegible] are among the commonest and most beautiful of flowering shrubs. The so-called Persian lilac of gardens [illegible] var. *Rothomagensis*), also known as the [illegible] lilac, a small shrub 4 to 6 ft. high with intense [illegible] appearing in May and June, is considered to be a [illegible] *S. vulgaris* and *S. persica*—the true Persian lilac, [illegible] Persia and Afghanistan, a shrub 4 to 7 ft. high with [illegible] white flowers. Of other species, *S. Josikaea*, from [illegible] scentless bluish-purple flowers; *S. Emodi*, a [illegible] Himalayas, is a handsome shrub with large ovate leaves [illegible] of purple or white strongly scented flowers. [illegible] and flower profusely in almost any soil and [illegible] neglected are apt to become choked with suckers [illegible] great numbers from the base. They are readily [illegible] of these suckers.

[illegible] common name for the mock-orange *Philadelphus* [illegible]), a handsome shrub 2 to 10 ft. [illegible] leaves and clusters of white flowers which [illegible] scent. It is a native of western Asia, and [illegible] southern Europe.

[illegible] (1614–1657), English political agitator, [illegible] of a gentleman of good family in the county [illegible] the age of twelve he was apprenticed to a [illegible] he appears to have early addicted himself [illegible] novelties, opposition of government, and violent and bitter expressions" for which he afterwards became so conspicuous as to provoke the saying of Harry Marten (the regicide) that, "if the world was emptied of all but John Lilburn, Lilburn would quarrel with John, and John with Lilburn." He appears at one time to have been law-clerk to William Prynne. In February 1638, for the part he had taken in importing and circulating *The Litany* and other publications of John Bastwick and Prynne, offensive to the bishops, he was sentenced by the Star Chamber to be publicly whipped from the Fleet prison to Palace Yard, Westminster, there to stand for two hours in the pillory, and afterwards to be kept in gaol until a fine of £500 had been paid. He devoted his enforced leisure to his favourite form of literary activity, and did not regain his liberty until November 1640, one of the earliest recorded speeches of Oliver Cromwell being made in support of his petition to the House of Commons (Nov. 9, 1640). In 1641 he received an indemnity of £3000. He now entered the army, and in 1642 was taken prisoner at Brentford and tried for his life; sentence would no doubt have been executed had not the parliament by threatening reprisals forced his exchange. He soon rose to the rank of lieutenant-colonel, but in April 1645, having become dissatisfied with the predominance of Presbyterianism, and refusing to take the covenant, he resigned his commission, presenting at the same time to the Commons a petition for considerable arrears of pay. His violent language in Westminster Hall about the speaker and other public men led in the following July to his arrest and committal to Newgate, whence he was discharged, however, without trial, by order of the House, in October. In January 1647 he was committed to the Tower for accusations against Cromwell, but was again set at liberty in time to become a disappointed spectator of the failure of the "Levellers" or ultrademocratic party in the army at the Ware rendezvous in the following November. The scene produced a deep impression on his mind, and in February 1649 he along with other petitioners presented to the House of Commons a paper entitled *The Serious Apprehensions of a part of the People on behalf of the Commonwealth*, which he followed up with a pamphlet, *England's New Chains Discovered*, criticizing Ireton, and another exposing the conduct of Cromwell, Ireton and other leaders of the army since June 1647 (*The Hunting of the Foxes from Newmarket and Triploe Heath to Whitehall by Five Small Beagles*, the "beagles" being Lilburne, Richard Overton, William Walwyn, Prince and another). Finally, the *Second Part of England's New Chains Discovered*, a violent outburst against "the dominion of a council of state, and a constitution of a new and unexperienced nature," became the subject of discussion in the House, and led anew to the imprisonment of its author in the Tower on the 11th of April. His trial in the following October, on a charge of seditious and scandalous practices against the state, resulted in his unanimous acquittal, followed by his release in November. In 1650 he was advocating the release of trade from the restrictions of chartered companies and monopolists.

In January 1652, for printing and publishing a petition against Sir Arthur Hesilrige and the Haberdashers' Hall for what he conceived to have been an injury done to his uncle George Lilburne in 1649, he was sentenced to pay fines amounting to £7000, and to be banished the Commonwealth, with prohibition of return under the pain of death. In June 1653 he nevertheless came back from the Low Countries, where he had busied himself in pamphleteering and such other agitation as was possible, and was immediately arrested; the trial, which was protracted from the 13th of July to the 20th of August, issued in his acquittal, to the great joy of London, but it was nevertheless thought proper to keep him in captivity for "the peace of the nation." He was detained successively in the Tower, in Jersey, in Guernsey and in Dover Castle. At Dover he came under Quaker influence, and signified his readiness at last to be done with "carnal sword fightings and fleshly bustlings and contests"; and in 1655, on giving security for his good behaviour, he was set free. He now settled at Eltham in Kent, frequently preaching at Quaker meetings in the neighbourhood during the brief remainder of his troubled life. He died on the 29th of August 1657.

[1] [illegible] mod. [illegible] from Arab. *lilak*, [illegible] indigo-plant.

His brother, Colonel Robert Lilburne, was among those who signed the death-warrant of Charles I. In 1656 he was M.P. for the East Riding of Yorkshire, and at the restoration was sentenced to lifelong imprisonment.

See D. Masson, *Life of Milton* (iv. 120); Clement Walker (*History of Independency*, ii. 247); W. Godwin (*Commonwealth*, iii. 163-177), and Robert Bisset (*Omitted Chapters of the History of England*, 191-251).

LILIACEAE, in botany, a natural order of Monocotyledons belonging to the series Lilliflorae, and generally regarded as representing the typical order of Monocotyledons. The plants are generally perennial herbs growing from a bulb or rhizome, sometimes shrubby as in butcher's broom (*Ruscus*) or tree-like as in species of *Dracaena*, *Yucca* or *Aloe*. The flowers are with few exceptions hermaphrodite, and regular with parts in threes (fig. 5), the perianth which is generally petaloid occupying the two outer whorls, followed by two whorls of stamens, with a superior ovary of three carpels in the centre of the flower; the ovary is generally three-chambered and contains an indefinite number of anatropous ovules on axile placentas (see fig. 2). The fruit is a capsule splitting along the septa (septicidal) (fig. 1), or between them (loculicidal), or a berry (fig. 6, 3); the seeds contain a small embryo in a copious fleshy or cartilaginous endosperm. Liliaceae is one of the larger orders of flowering plants containing about 2500 species in 200 genera; it is of world-wide distribution. The plants show great diversity in vegetative structure, which together with the character and mode of dehiscence of the fruit afford a basis for the subdivision of the order into tribes, eleven of which are recognized. The following are the most important tribes.

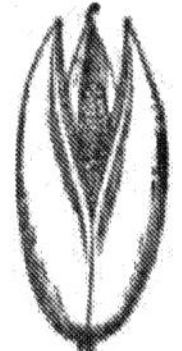

FIG. 1.—Fruit or Capsule of Meadow Saffron (*Colchicum autumnale*) dehiscing along the septa.

FIG. 2.—Same cut across showing the three chambers with the seeds attached along the middle line—axile placentation.

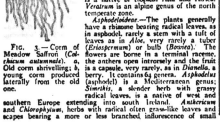

Melanthoideae.—The plants have a rhizome or corm, and the fruit is a capsule. It contains 36 genera, many of which are north temperate and three are represented in Britain, viz. *Tofieldia*, an arctic and alpine genus of small herbs with a slender scape springing from a tuft of narrow ensiform leaves and bearing a raceme of small green flowers; *Narthecium* (bog-asphodel), herbs with a habit similar to *Tofieldia*, but with larger golden-yellow flowers; and *Colchicum*, a genus with about 30 species including the meadow saffron or autumn crocus (*C. autumnale*). *Colchicum* illustrates the corm-development which is rare in Liliaceae though common in the allied order Iridaceae; a corm is formed by swelling at the base of the axis (figs. 3, 4) and persists after the flowers and leaves, bearing next season's plant as a lateral shoot in the axil of a scale-leaf at its base. *Gloriosa*, well known in cultivation, climbs by means of its tendril-like leaf-tips; it has handsome flowers with decurved orange-red or yellow petals; it is a native of tropical Asia and Africa. *Veratrum* is an alpine genus of the north temperate zone.

FIG. 3.—Corm of Meadow Saffron (*Colchicum autumnale*). *a*, Old corm shrivelling; *b*, young corm produced laterally from the old one.

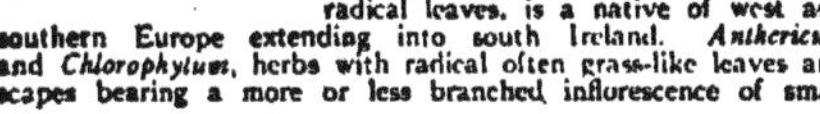

Asphodeloideae.—The plants generally have a rhizome bearing radical leaves, as in asphodel, rarely a stem with a tuft of leaves as in *Aloe*, very rarely a tuber (*Eriospermum*) or bulb (*Bowiea*). The flowers are borne in a terminal raceme, the anthers open introrsely and the fruit is a capsule, very rarely, as in *Dianella*, a berry. It contains 64 genera. *Asphodelus* (asphodel) is a Mediterranean genus; *Simethis*, a slender herb with grassy radical leaves, is a native of west and southern Europe extending into south Ireland. *Anthericum* and *Chlorophytum*, herbs with radical often grass-like leaves and scapes bearing a more or less branched inflorescence of small generally white flowers, are widely spread in the tropics. Other genera are *Funkia*, native of China and Japan, cultivated in the open air in Britain; *Hemerocallis*, a small genus of central Europe and temperate Asia—*H. flava* is known in gardens as the day lily; *Phormium*, a New Zealand genus to which belongs New Zealand flax, *P. tenax*, a useful fibre-plant; *Kniphofia*, South and East Africa, several species of which are cultivated; and *Aloe*. A small group of Australian genera closely approach the order Juncaceae in having small crowded flowers with a scarious or membranous perianth; they include *Xanthorrhoea* (grass-tree or black-boy) and *Kingia*, arborescent plants with an erect woody stem crowned with a tuft of long stiff narrow leaves, from the centre of which rises a tall dense flower-spike or a number of stalked flower-heads; this group has been included in Juncaceae, from which it is doubtfully distinguished only by the absence of the long twisted stigmas which characterize the true rushes.

Allioideae.—The plants grow from a bulb or short rhizome; the inflorescence is an apparent umbel formed of several shortened monochasial cymes and subtended by a pair of large bracts. It contains 22 genera, the largest of which *Allium* has about 250 species—7 are British; *Agapanthus* or African lily is a well-known garden plant; in *Gagea*, a genus of small bulbous herbs found in most parts of Europe, the inflorescence is reduced to a few flowers or a single flower; *G. lutea* is a local and rare British plant.

Lilioideae.—Bulbous plants with a terminal racemose inflorescence; the anthers open introrsely and the capsule is loculicidal. It contains 28 genera, several being represented in Britain. The typical genus *Lilium* and *Fritillaria* are widely distributed in the temperate regions of the northern hemisphere; *F. meleagris*, snake's head, is found in moist meadows in some of the southern and central English counties; *Tulipa* contains more than 50 species in Europe and temperate Asia, and is specially abundant in the dry districts of central Asia; *Lloydia*, a small slender alpine plant, widely distributed in the northern hemisphere, occurs on Snowdon in Wales; *Scilla* (squill) is a large genus, chiefly in Europe and Asia—*S. nutans* is the blue-bell or wild hyacinth; *Ornithogalum* (Europe, Africa and west Asia) is closely allied to *Scilla*—*O. umbellatum*, star of Bethlehem, is naturalized in Britain; *Hyacinthus* and *Muscari* are chiefly Mediterranean; *M. racemosum*, grape hyacinth, occurs in sandy pastures in the eastern counties of England. To this group belong a number of tropical and especially South African genera such as *Albuca*, *Urginea*, *Drimia*, *Lachenalia* and others.

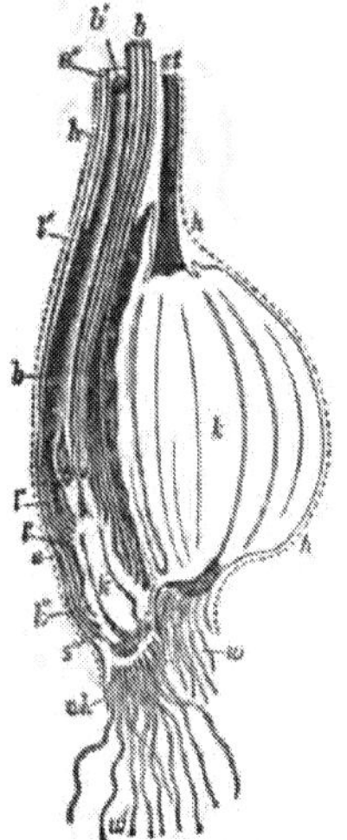

FIG. 4.—Corm of *Colchicum autumnale* in autumn when the plant is in flower.

k, Present corm.
h, *h*, Brown scales covering it.
w, Its roots.
st, Its withered flowering stem.
k', Younger corm produced from *k*.
wk, Roots from *k'*, which grows at expense of *k*.
s, *s'*, *s"*, Sheathing leaves.
l', *l"*, Foliage leaves.
b, *b'*, Flowers.
k", Young corm produced from *k'*, in autumn, which in succeeding autumn will produce flowers.

Dracaenoideae.—The plants generally have an erect stem with a crown of leaves which are often leathery; the anthers open introrsely and the fruit is a berry or capsule. It contains 9 genera, several of which, such as *Yucca* (fig. 5), *Dracaena* and *Cordyline* include arborescent species in which the stem increases in thickness continually by a centrifugal formation of new tissue; an extreme case is afforded by *Dracaena Draco*, the dragon-tree of Teneriffe. *Yucca* and several allied genera are natives of the dry country of the southern and western United States and of Central America. *Dracaena* and the allied genus *Cordyline* occur in the warmer regions of the Old World. There is a close relation between the pollination of many yuccas and the life of a moth (*Pronuba yuccasella*); the flowers are open and scented at night when the female moth becomes active; first collecting a load of pollen and then depositing her eggs, generally in a different flower from that which has supplied the pollen. The eggs are deposited in the ovary-wall, usually just below an ovule; after each deposition the moth runs to the top of the pistil and thrusts some pollen into the opening of the stigma.

... and grow together, a few of the seeds ... which when mature eats through the ... remaining dormant in its cocoon ... when it emerges as a moth.

... from a rhizome; fruit a berry. ... in the dryer warmer parts ...

... Floral diagram.

... from which ... branched, ... are flattened ... leaves being ... hard more or ... 's broom, an ...

... slightly ... enlarged; b, berry. ...

stout column on which are seated the diverging cells of the anthers; in the female the ovary is enveloped by a fleshy staminal tube on which are borne three barren anthers. *Polygonatum* and *Maianthemum* are allied genera with a herbaceous leafy stem and, in the former axillary flowers, in the latter flowers in a terminal raceme; both occur rarely in woods in Britain; *P. multiflorum* is the well-known Solomon's seal of gardens (fig. 7), so called from the seal-like scars on the rhizome of stems of previous seasons, the hanging flowers of which contain no honey, but are visited by bees for the pollen. *Convallaria* is lily of the valley; *Aspidistra*, native of the Himalayas, China and Japan, is a well-known pot plant; its flowers depart from the normal arrangement of the order in having the parts in fours (tetramerous). *Paris*, including the British Herb Paris (*P. quadrifolia*), has solitary tetra- to poly-merous flowers terminating the short annual shoot which bears a whorl of four or more leaves below the flower; in this and in some species of the nearly allied genus *Trillium* (chiefly temperate North America) the flowers have a fetid smell, which together with the dark purple of the ovary and stigmas and frequently also of the stamens and petals, attracts carrion-loving flies, which alight on the stigma and then climb the anthers and become dusted with pollen; the pollen is then carried to the stigmas of another flower.

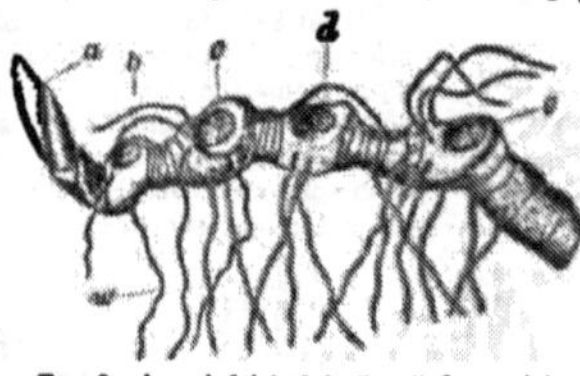

From Strasburger's *Lehrbuch der Botanik*, by permission of Gustav Fischer.

FIG. 7.—Rhizome of *Polygonatum multiflorum*.

a, Bud of next year's aerial shoot.
b, Scar of this year's, and *c*, *d*, *e*, scars of three preceding years' aerial shoots.
w, Roots.

Luzuriagoideae are shrubs or undershrubs with erect or climbing branches and fruit a berry. *Lapageria*, a native of Chile, is a favourite greenhouse climber with fine bell-shaped flowers.

Smilacoideae are climbing shrubs with broad net-veined leaves and small dioecious flowers in umbels springing from the leaf-axils; the fruit is a berry. They climb by means of tendrils, which are stipular structures arising from the leaf-sheath. *Smilax* is a characteristic tropical genus containing about 200 species; the dried roots of some species are the drug sarsaparilla.

The two tribes *Ophiopogonoideae* and *Aletroideae* are often included in a distinct order, Haemodoraceae. The plants have a short rhizome and narrow or lanceolate basal leaves; and they are characterized by the ovary being often half-inferior. They contain a few genera chiefly old world tropical and subtropical. The leaves of species of *Sansevieria* yield a valuable fibre.

Liliaceae may be regarded as the typical order of the series Liliiflorae. It resembles Juncaceae in the general plan of the flower, which, however, has become much more elaborate and varied in the form and colour of its perianth in association with transmission of pollen by insect agency; a link between the two orders is found in the group of Australian genera referred to above under Asphodeloideae. The tribe Ophiopogonoideae, with its tendency to an inferior ovary, suggests an affinity with the Amaryllidaceae which resemble Liliaceae in habit and in the horizontal plan of the flower, but have an inferior ovary. The tribe Smilacoideae, shrubby climbers with net-veined leaves and small unisexual flowers, bears much the same relationship to the order as a whole as does the order Dioscoreaceae, which have a similar habit, but flowers with an inferior ovary, to the Amaryllidaceae.

LILIENCRON, DETLEV VON (1844–1909), German poet and novelist, was born at Kiel on the 3rd of June 1844. He entered the army and took part in the campaigns of 1866 and 1870–71, in both of which he was wounded. He retired with the rank of captain and spent some time in America, afterwards settling at Kellinghusen in Holstein, where he remained till 1887. After some time at Munich, he settled in Altona and then at Altrahlstedt, near Hamburg. He died in July 1909. He first attracted attention by the volume of poems, *Adjutantenritte und andere Gedichte* (1883), which was followed by several unsuccessful dramas, a volume of short stories, *Eine Sommerschlacht* (1886), and a novel *Breide Hummelsbüttel* (1887). Other collections of short stories appeared under the titles *Unter flatternden Fahnen* (1888), *Der Mäcen* (1889), *Krieg und Frieden* (1891); of lyric poetry in 1889, 1890 (*Der Heidegänger und andere Gedichte*), 1893, and 1903 (*Bunte Beute*). Interesting, too, is the humorous epic *Poggfred* (1896; 2nd ed. 1904). Liliencron is one of the most eminent of recent German lyric poets; his *Adjutantenritte*, with its fresh original note, broke with the well-worn literary conventions which had been handed down from the middle of the century. Liliencron's work is, however, somewhat unequal, and he lacks the sustained power which makes the successful prose writer.

Liliencron's *Sämtliche Werke* have been published in 14 vols. (1904–1905); his *Gedichte* having been previously collected in four volumes under the titles *Kampf und Spiele*, *Kämpfe und Ziele*, *Nebel und Sonne* and *Bunte Beute* (1897–1903). See O. J. Bierbaum, *D. von Liliencron* (1892); H. Greinz, *Liliencron, eine literarhistorische Würdigung* (1896); F. Oppenheimer, *D. von Liliencron* (1898).

LILITH (Heb. *lîlîth*, "night"; hence "night-monster"), a female demon of Jewish folk-lore, equivalent to the English vampire. The personality and name are derived from a Babylonian-Assyrian demon Lilit or Lilu. Lilith was believed to have a special power for evil over children. The superstition was extended to a cult surviving among some Jews even as late as the 7th century A.D. In the Rabbinical literature Lilith becomes the first wife of Adam, but flies away from him and becomes a demon.

LILLE, a city of northern France, capital of the department of Nord, 154 m. N. by E. of Paris on the Northern railway. Pop. (1906) 196,624. Lille is situated in a low fertile plain on the right bank of the Deûle in a rich agricultural and industrial region of which it is the centre. It is a first-class fortress and headquarters of the I. army corps, and has an enceinte and a pentagonal citadel, one of Vauban's finest works, situated to the west of the town, from which it is divided by the Deûle. The modern fortifications comprise over twenty detached forts and batteries, the perimeter of the defences being about 20 m. Before 1858 the town, fortified by Vauban about 1668, occupied an elliptical area of about 2500 yds. by 1300, with the church of Notre-Dame de la Treille in the centre, but the ramparts on the south side have been demolished and the ditches filled up, their place being now occupied by the great Boulevard de la Liberté, which extends in a straight line from the goods station of the railway to the citadel. At the S.E. end of this boulevard are grouped the majority of the numerous educational establishments of the city. The new enceinte encloses the old communes of Esquermes, Wazemmes and Moulins-Lille, the area of the town being thus more than doubled. In the new quarters fine boulevards and handsome squares, such as the Place de la République, have been laid out in pleasant contrast with the sombre aspect of the old town. The district of St André to the north, the only elegant part of the old town, is the residence of the aristocracy. Outside the enceinte populous suburbs surround the city on every side. The demolition of the fortifications on the north and east of the city, which is continued in those directions by the great suburbs of La Madeleine, St Maurice and Fives, must accelerate its expansion towards Roubaix and Tourcoing. At the demolition of the southern fortifications, the Paris gate, a triumphal arch erected in 1682 in honour of Louis XIV., after the conquest of Flanders, was preserved. On the east the Ghent and Roubaix gates, built in the Renaissance style, with bricks of different colours, date from 1617 and 1622, the time of the Spanish domination. On the same side the Noble-Tour is a relic of the medieval ramparts. The present enceinte is pierced by numerous gates, including water gates for the canal of the Deûle and for the Arbonnoise, which extends into a marsh in the south-west corner of the town. The citadel, which contains the barracks and arsenal, is surrounded by public gardens. The more interesting buildings are in the old town, where, in the Grande Place and Rue Faidherbe, its animation is concentrated. St Maurice, a church in the late Gothic style, dates in its oldest portions from the 15th century, and was restored in 1872; Ste Catherine belongs to the 15th, 16th and 18th centuries, St André to the first years of the 18th century, and Ste Madeleine to the last half of the 17th century; all possess valuable pictures, but St Maurice alone, with nave and double aisles, and elegant modern spire, is architecturally notable. Notre-Dame de la Treille, begun in 1855, in the style of the 15th century, possesses an ancient statue of the Virgin which is the object of a well-known pilgrimage. Of the civil buildings the Bourse (17th century) built round a courtyard in which stands a bronze statue of Napoleon I., the Hôtel d'Aigremont, the Hôtel Gentil and other houses are in the Flemish style; the Hôtel de Ville, dating in the main from the middle of the 19th century, preserves a portion of a palace built by Philip the Good, duke of Burgundy, in the 15th century. The prefecture, the Palais des Beaux-Arts, the law-courts, the school of arts and crafts, and the Lycée Faidherbe are imposing modern buildings. In the middle of the Grande Place stands a column, erected in 1848, commemorating the defence of the town in 1792 (see below), and there are also statues to Generals L. L. C. Faidherbe and F. O. de Négrier, and busts of Louis Pasteur and the popular poet and singer A. Desrousseaux. The Palais des Beaux-Arts contains a museum and picture galleries, among the richest in France, as well as a unique collection of original designs of the great masters bequeathed to Lille by J. B. Wicar, and including a celebrated wax model of a girl's head usually attributed to some Italian artist of the 16th century. The city also possesses a commercial and colonial museum, an industrial museum, a fine collection of departmental and municipal archives, the museum of the Institute of Natural Sciences and a library containing many valuable manuscripts, housed at the Hôtel de Ville. The large military hospital, once a Jesuit college, is one of several similar institutions.

Lille is the seat of a prefect and has tribunals of first instance and of commerce, a board of trade arbitrators, a chamber of commerce and a branch of the Bank of France. It is the centre of an académie (educational division) and has a university with faculties of laws, letters, science and medicine and pharmacy, together with a Catholic institute comprising faculties of theology, law, medicine and pharmacy, letters, science, a technical school, and a department of social and political science. Secondary education is given at the Lycée Faidherbe, and the Lycée Fénelon (for girls), a higher school of commerce, a national technical school and other establishments; to these must be added schools of music and fine arts, and the Industrial and Pasteur Institutes.

The industries, which are carried on in the new quarters of the town and in the suburbs, are of great variety and importance. In the first rank comes the spinning of flax and the weaving of cloth, table-linen, damask, ticking and flax velvet. The spinning of flax thread for sewing and lace-making is specially connected with Lille. The manufacture of woollen fabrics and cotton-spinning and the making of cotton-twist of fine quality are also carried on. There are important printing establishments, state factories for the manufacture of tobacco and the refining of saltpetre and very numerous breweries, while chemical, oil, white lead and sugar-works, distilleries, bleaching-grounds, dye-works, machinery and boiler works and cabinet-making occupy many thousands of workmen. Plant for sugar-works and distilleries, military stores, steam-engines, locomotives, and bridges of all kinds are produced by the company of Fives-Lille. Lille is one of the most important junctions of the Northern railway, and the Deûle canal affords communication with neighbouring ports and with Belgium. Trade is chiefly in the raw material and machinery for its industries, in the products thereof, and in the wheat and other agricultural products of the surrounding district.

Lille (l'Île) is said to date its origin from the time of Count Baldwin IV. of Flanders, who in 1030 surrounded with walls a little town which had arisen around the castle of Buc. In the first half of the 13th century, the town, which had developed rapidly, obtained communal privileges. Destroyed by Philip Augustus in 1213, it was rebuilt by Joanna of Constantinople, countess of Flanders, but besieged and retaken by Philip the Fair in 1297. After having taken part with the Flemings against the king of France, it was ceded to the latter in 1312. In 1369 Charles V., king of France, gave it to Louis de Male, who transmitted his rights to his daughter Margaret, wife of Philip the Bold, duke of Burgundy. Under the Burgundian rule Lille enjoyed great prosperity; its merchants were at the head of the London Hansa. Philip the Good made it his residence, and within its walls held the first chapters of the order of the Golden Fleece. With the rest of Flanders it passed from the dukes of Burgundy to Austria and then to Spain. After the death of Philip IV. of Spain, Louis XIV. reclaimed the territory and besieged Lille in 1667. He forced it to capitulate, but preserved all its laws, customs, privileges and liberties. In 1708, after an heroic resistance, it surrendered to Prince Eugène and the duke of Marlborough. The treaty of Utrecht restored it to France. In 1792 the Austrians bombarded it for nine days and nights without intermission, but had ultimately to raise the siege.

See É. Vanhende, *Lille et ses institutions communales de 620 à 1804* (Lille, 1888).

LILLEBONNE, a town of France in the department of Seine-Inférieure, 3½ m. N. of the Seine and 24 m. E. of Havre by the Western railway. Pop. (1906) 5370. It lies in the valley of the Bolbec at the foot of wooded hills. The church of Notre-Dame, partly modern, preserves a Gothic portal of the 16th century and a graceful tower of the same period. The park contains a fine cylindrical donjon and other remains of a castle founded by William the Conqueror and rebuilt in the 13th century. The principal industries are cotton-spinning and the manufacture of calico and candles.

Lillebonne under the Romans, *Juliobona*, was the capital of the Caletes, or inhabitants of the Pays de Caux, in the time of Caesar, by whom it was destroyed. It was afterwards rebuilt by Augustus, and before it was again ruined by the barbarian invasions it had become an important centre whence Roman roads branched out in all directions. The remains of ancient baths and of a theatre capable of holding 3000 persons have been brought to light. Many Roman and Gallic relics, notably a bronze statue of a woman and two fine mosaics, have been found and transported to the museum at Rouen. In the middle ages the fortifications of the town were constructed out of materials supplied by the theatre. The town recovered some of its old importance under William the Conqueror.

LILLIBULLERO, or LILLIBURLERO, the name of a song popular at the end of the 17th century, especially among the army and supporters of William III. in the war in Ireland during the revolution of 1688. The tune appears to have been much older, and was sung to an Irish nursery song at the beginning of the 17th century, and the attribution of Henry Purcell is based on the very slight ground that it was published in *Music's Handmaid*, 1689, as "A new Irish Tune" by Henry Purcell. It was also a marching tune familiar to soldiers. The doggerel verses have generally been assigned to Thomas Wharton, and deal with the [illegible] of Talbot, earl of Tyrconnel, appointed by James [illegible] in Ireland in 1687. The refrain of the song [illegible] a la gave the title of the song. Macaulay says [illegible] "The verses and the tune caught the fancy of the [illegible] from one end of England to the other all classes were [illegible] the rhyme." Though Wharton claimed he had [illegible] of three kingdoms" and Burnet says "perhaps [illegible] slight a thing so great an effect" the success of [illegible] the effect, and not the cause of that excited state [illegible] which produced the revolution" (Macaulay, [illegible] ix.).

[illegible] (1693–1739), English dramatist, son of a [illegible] was born in London on the 4th of February [illegible] brought up to his father's trade and was for [illegible] in the business. His first piece, *Silvia*, [illegible] was a ballad opera produced at Lincoln's [illegible] 1730. On the 22nd of June 1731 [illegible] The [illegible] named later *The London* [illegible] was produced by [illegible] Lane. The piece [illegible] passages which are [illegible] excellent ballad of George Barnwell, an apprentice of London who . . . thrice robbed his master, and murdered his uncle in Ludlow." In breaking through the tradition that the characters of every tragedy must necessarily be drawn from people of high rank and fortune he went back to the Elizabethan domestic drama of passion of which the *Yorkshire Tragedy* is a type. The obtrusively moral purpose of this play places it in the same literary category as the novels of Richardson. Scoffing critics called it, with reason, a "Newgate tragedy," but it proved extremely popular on the stage. It was regularly acted for many years at holiday seasons for the moral benefit of the apprentices. The last act contained a scene, generally omitted on the London stage, in which the gallows actually figured. In 1734 Lillo celebrated the marriage of the Princess Anne with William IV. of Orange in *Britannia and Batavia*, a masque. A second tragedy, *The Christian Hero*, was produced at Drury Lane on the 13th of January 1735. It is based on the story of Scanderbeg, the Albanian chieftain, a life of whom is printed with the play. Thomas Whincop (d. 1730) wrote a piece on the same subject, printed posthumously in 1747. Both Lillo and William Havard, who also wrote a dramatic version of the story, were accused of plagiarizing Whincop's *Scanderbeg*. Another murder-drama, *Fatal Curiosity*, in which an old couple murder an unknown guest, who proves to be their own son, was based on a tragedy at Bohelland Farm near Penryn in 1618. It was produced by Henry Fielding at the Little Theatre in the Haymarket in 1736, but with small success. In the next year Fielding tacked it on to his own *Historical Register for 1736*, and it was received more kindly. It was revised by George Colman the elder in 1782, by Henry Mackenzie in 1784, &c. Lillo also wrote an adaptation of the Shakespearean play of *Pericles, Prince of Tyre*, with the title *Marina* (Covent Garden, August 1st, 1738); and a tragedy, *Elmerick, or Justice Triumphant* (produced posthumously, Drury Lane, February 23rd, 1740). The statement made in the prologue to this play that Lillo died in poverty seems unfounded. His death took place on the 3rd of September 1739. He left an unfinished version of *Arden of Feversham*, which was completed by Dr John Hoadly and produced in 1759. Lillo's reputation proved short-lived. He has nevertheless a certain cosmopolitan importance, for the influence of *George Barnwell* can be traced in the sentimental drama of both France and Germany.

See *Lillo's Dramatic Works with Memoirs of the Author by Thomas Davies* (reprint by Lowndes, 1810); Cibber's *Lives of the Poets*, v.; Genest, *Some Account of the English Stage*; Alois Brandl, "Zu Lillo's Kaufmann in London," in *Vierteljahrschrift für Litteraturgeschichte* (Weimar, 1890, vol. iii.); Leopold Hoffmann, *George Lillo* (Marburg, 1888); Paul von Hofmann-Wellenhof, *Shakspere's Pericles und George Lillo's Marina* (Vienna, 1885). There is a novel founded on Lillo's play, *Barnwell* (1807), by T. S. Surr, and in "George de Barnwell" (*Novels by Eminent Hands*) Thackeray parodies Bulwer-Lytton's *Eugene Aram*.

LILLY, WILLIAM (1602–1681), English astrologer, was born in 1602 at Diseworth in Leicestershire, his family having been settled as yeomen in the place for "many ages." He received a tolerably good classical education at the school of Ashby-de-la-Zouche, but he naïvely tells us what may perhaps have some significance in reference to his after career, that his master "never taught logic." In his eighteenth year, his father having fallen into great poverty, he went to London and was employed in attendance on an old citizen and his wife. His master, at his death in 1627, left him an annuity of £20; and, Lilly having soon afterwards married the widow, she, dying in 1633, left him property to the value of about £1000. He now began to dabble in astrology, reading all the books on the subject he could fall in with, and occasionally trying his hand at unravelling mysteries by means of his art. The years 1642 and 1643 were devoted to a careful revision of all his previous reading, and in particular having lighted on Valentine Naibod's *Commentary on Alchabitius*, he "seriously studied him and found him to be the profoundest author he ever met with." About the same time he tells us that he "did carefully take notice of every grand action betwixt king and parliament, and did first then incline to believe that as all sublunary affairs depend on superior causes, so there was a possibility of discovering them by the configurations of the superior bodies." And, having thereupon "made some essays," he "found encouragement to proceed further, and ultimately framed to himself that method which he ever afterwards followed." He then began to issue his prophetical almanacs and other works, which met with serious attention from some of the most prominent members of the Long Parliament. If we may believe himself, Lilly lived on friendly and almost intimate terms with Bulstrode Whitlock, Lenthall the speaker, Sir Philip Stapleton, Elias Ashmole and others. Even Selden seems to have given him some countenance, and probably the chief difference between him and the mass of the community at the time was that, while others believed in the general truth of astrology, he ventured to specify the future events to which its calculations pointed. Even from his own account of himself, however, it is evident that he did not trust implicitly to the indications given by the aspects of the heavens, but like more vulgar fortune-tellers kept his eyes and ears open for any information which might make his predictions safe. It appears that he had correspondents both at home and in foreign parts to keep him conversant with the probable current of affairs. Not a few of his exploits indicate rather the quality of a clever police detective than of a profound astrologer. After the Restoration he very quickly fell into disrepute. His sympathy with the parliament, which his predictions had generally shown, was not calculated to bring him into royal favour. He came under the lash of Butler, who, making allowance for some satiric exaggeration, has given in the character of Sidrophel a probably not very incorrect picture of the man; and, having by this time amassed a tolerable fortune, he bought a small estate at Hersham in Surrey, to which he retired, and where he diverted the exercise of his peculiar talents to the practice of medicine. He died in 1681.

Lilly's life of himself, published after his death, is still worth looking into as a remarkable record of credulity. So lately as 1852 a prominent London publisher put forth a new edition of Lilly's *Introduction to Astrology*, "with numerous emendations adapted to the improved state of the science."

LILOAN, a town of the province of Cebú, Philippine Islands, on the E. coast, 10 m. N.E. of Cebú, the capital of the province. Pop. (1903), after the annexation of Compostela, 15,626. There are seventeen villages or *barrios* in the town, and eight of them had in 1903 a population exceeding 1000. The language is Visayan. Fishing is the principal industry. Liloan has one of the principal coal beds on the island; and rice, Indian corn, sugar-cane and coffee are cultivated. Coconuts and other tropical fruits are important products.

LILY, *Lilium*, the typical genus of the botanical order Liliaceae, embracing nearly eighty species, all confined to the northern hemisphere, and widely distributed throughout the north temperate zone. The earliest in cultivation were described in 1597 by Gerard (*Herball*, p. 146), who figures eight kinds of true lilies, which include *L. album* (*L. candidum*) and a variety, *bisantinum*, two umbellate forms of the type *L. bulbiferum*, named *L. aureum* and *L. cruentum latifolium*, and three with pendulous flowers, apparently forms of the martagon lily. Parkinson, in his *Paradisus* (1629), described five varieties of martagon, six of umbellate kinds—two white ones, and *L. pomponium*, *L. chalcedonicum*, *L. carniolicum* and *L. pyrenaicum*—together with one American, *L. canadense*, which had been introduced in 1629. For the ancient and medieval history of the lily, see M. de Cannart d'Hamale's *Monographie historique et littéraire des lis* (Malines, 1870). Since that period many new species have been added. The latest authorities for description and classification of the genus are J. G. Baker ("Revision of the Genera and Species of Tulipeae," *Journ. of Linn. Soc.* xiv. p. 211, 1874), and J. H. Elwes (*Monograph of the Genus* Lilium, 1880), who first tested all the species under cultivation, and has published every one beautifully figured by W. H. Fitch, and some hybrids. With respect to the production of hybrids, the genus is remarkable for its power of resisting the influence of foreign pollen, for the seedlings of any species, when crossed, generally resemble that which bears them. A good account of the new species and principal varieties discovered since 1880, with much information on the cultivation of lilies and the diseases to which they are subject, will be found in the report of the Conference on Lilies, in the *Journal of the Royal Horticultural Society*, 1901. The new species include a number discovered in central and western China by Dr Augustine Henry and other collectors; also several from Japan and California.

The structure of the flower represents the simple type of monocotyledons, consisting of two whorls of petals, of three free parts each, six free stamens, and a consolidated pistil of three carpels, ripening into a three-valved capsule containing many winged seeds. In form, the flower assumes three types: trumpet-shaped, with a more or less elongated tube, *e.g. L. longiflorum* and *L. candidum*; an open form with spreading perianth leaves, *e.g. L. auratum*; or assuming a pendulous habit, with the tips strongly reflexed, *e.g.* the martagon type. All have scaly bulbs, which in three west American species, as *L. Humboldti*, are remarkable for being somewhat intermediate between a bulb and a creeping rhizome. *L. bulbiferum* and its allies produce aerial reproductive bulbils in the axils of the leaves. The bulbs of several species are eaten, such as of *L. avenaceum* in Kamchatka, of *L. Martagon* by the Cossacks, and of *L. tigrinum*, the "tiger lily," in China and Japan. Medicinal uses were ascribed to the species, but none appear to have any marked properties in this respect.

The white lily, *L. candidum*, the λείριον of the Greeks, was one of the commonest garden flowers of antiquity, appearing in the poets from Homer downwards side by side with the rose and the violet. According to Hehn, roses and lilies entered Greece from the east by way of Phrygia, Thrace and Macedonia (*Kulturpflanzen und Hausthiere*, 3rd ed., p. 217). The word λείριον itself, from which *lilium* is derived by assimilation of consonants, appears to be Eranian (*Ibid.* p. 527), and according to ancient etymologists (Lagarde, *Ges. Abh.* p. 227) the town of Susa was connected with the Persian name of the lily *sûsan* (Gr. σοῦσον, Heb. *shôshan*). Mythologically the white lily, *Rosa Junonis*, was fabled to have sprung from the milk of Hera. As the plant of purity it was contrasted with the rose of Aphrodite. The word κρίνον, on the other hand, included red and purple lilies, Plin. *H.N.* xxi. 5 (11, 12), the red lily being best known in Syria and Judaea (Phaselis). This perhaps is the "red lily of Constantinople" of Gerard, *L. chalcedonicum*. The lily of the Old Testament (shôshan) may be conjectured to be a red lily from the simile in Cant. v. 13, unless the allusion is to the fragrance rather than the colour of the lips, in which case the white lily must be thought of. The "lilies of the field," Matt. vi. 28, are κρίνα, and the comparison of their beauty with royal robes suggests their identification with the red Syrian lily of Pliny. Lilies, however, are not a conspicuous feature in the flora of Palestine, and the red anemone (*Anemone coronaria*), with which all the hill-sides of Galilee are dotted in the spring, is perhaps more likely to have suggested the figure. For the lily in the pharmacopoeia of the ancients see Adams's *Paul. Aegineta*, iii. 196. It was used in unguents and against the bites of snakes, &c. In the middle ages the flower continued to be common and was taken as the symbol of heavenly purity. The three golden lilies of France are said to have been originally three lance-heads.

Madonna or White Lily (*Lilium candidum*). About ⅓ nat. size.

Lily of the valley, *Convallaria majalis*, belongs to a different tribe (*Asparagoideae*) of the same order. It grows wild in woods in some parts of England, and in Europe, northern Asia and the Alleghany Mountains of North America. The leaves and flower-scapes spring from an underground creeping stem. The small pendulous bell-shaped flowers contain no honey but are visited by bees for the pollen.

The word "lily" is loosely used in connexion with many plants which are not really liliums at all, but belong to genera which are

convent of San Francisco, near the Plaza Mayor, is the largest monastic establishment in Lima and contains some very fine carvings. Its church is the finest in the city after the cathedral. Other noteworthy churches are those of the convents of Santo Domingo, La Merced and San Augustine. There are a number of conventual establishments (for both sexes), which, with their chapels, and with the smaller churches, retreats, sanctuaries, &c., make up a total of 66 institutions devoted to religious observ[illegible]. An attractive, and perhaps the most popular public [illegible] in Lima is the Exposition palace on the plaza and in the public gardens of the same name, on the south side of the [illegible]. It dates from 1872; its halls are used for important public [illegible] and its upper floor is occupied by the National [illegible] Institute, its museum and the gallery of historical [illegible]. Other noteworthy edifices and institutions are the [illegible] Library, the Lima Geographical Society, founded in [illegible] the Mint, which dates from 1565 and is considered to be the best in South America; the great bull-ring of the Plaza [illegible] which dates from 1768 and can seat 8000 spectators, [illegible] market; a modern penitentiary; and various [illegible]. In addition to the old university on the [illegible] which has been modernized and greatly improved, [illegible] of engineers and mines (founded 1876), the [illegible] of San Carlos, a normal school (founded 1905), a [illegible] of agriculture (situated outside the city limits and founded [illegible]) [illegible] schools for girls under the direction of religious [illegible] seminary called the Seminario Conciliar [illegible] and a school of arts and trades in which [illegible] instruction is given. Under the old régime, [illegible] was almost wholly neglected, but the 20th [illegible] about important changes in this respect. [illegible] to the primary schools, the government maintains [illegible] schools for workmen.

The [illegible] of the city are for the most part of one storey [illegible] walls supported by a wooden framework which [illegible] open spaces, called *patios*, around which the living rooms [illegible]. The better class of dwellings have two floors and [illegible] built of brick. A projecting, lattice-enclosed [illegible] for the use of women is a prominent feature of the larger [illegible] and gives a picturesque effect to the streets.

Manufacturing has had some considerable development since the closing years of the 19th century; the most important [illegible] are established outside the city limits; they produce [illegible] and woollen textiles, the products of the sugar estates, [illegible] cocaine, cigars and cigarettes, beer, artificial liquors, [illegible] oil, hats, macaroni, matches, paper, soap and candles. The commercial interests of the city are important, a large part of the interior being supplied from this point. With its port Callao the city is connected by two steam railways, one of which was built as early as 1848; one railway runs northward to Ancon, and another, the famous Oroya line, runs inland 130 m., crossing the Western Cordillera at an elevation of 15,645 ft. above sea-[illegible], with branches to Cerro de Pasco and Huari. The export trade properly belongs to Callao, though often credited to Lima. The [illegible] are an intelligent, hospitable, pleasure-loving [illegible], and the many attractive features of their city make it a [illegible] place of residence for foreigners.

Lima was founded on the 18th of January 1535 by Francisco [illegible], who named it Ciudad de los Reyes (City of the Kings) in [illegible] of the emperor Charles V. and Doña Juana his mother, [illegible] to some authorities, in commemoration of the [illegible] Epiphany (6th January) when its site is said to have [illegible]. The name soon after gave place to that of Lima, [illegible] corruption of the Quichua word Rimac. In 1541 [illegible] made an episcopal see, which in 1545 was raised to a [illegible]. Under Spanish rule, Lima was the principal [illegible] America, and for a time was the entrepôt for all the [illegible] south of Panama. It became very prosperous [illegible], though often visited by destructive earth-[illegible] disastrous of which was that of the 28th of [illegible]ed the greater part of the [illegible] were lost, and the port of Callao was destroyed. Lima was not materially affected by the military operations of the war of independence until 1821, when a small army of Argentines and Chileans under General San Martin invested the city, and took possession of it on the 12th of July upon the withdrawal of the Spanish forces. San Martin was proclaimed the protector of Peru as a free state on the 28th of July, but resigned that office on the 20th of September 1822 to avoid a fratricidal struggle with Bolívar. In March 1828 Lima was again visited by a destructive earthquake, and in 1854–1855 an epidemic of yellow fever carried off a great number of its inhabitants. In November 1864, when a hostile Spanish fleet was on the coast, a congress of South American plenipotentiaries was held here to concert measures of mutual defence. Lima has been the principal sufferer in the many revolutions and disorders which have convulsed Peru under the republic, and many of them originated in the city itself. During the earlier part of this period the capital twice fell into the hands of foreigners, once in 1836 when the Bolivian general Santa Cruz made himself the chief of a Bolivian-Peruvian confederation, and again in 1837 when an invading force of Chileans and Peruvian refugees landed at Ancon and defeated the Peruvian forces under President Orbegoso. The city prospered greatly under the two administrations of President Ramon Castilla, who gave Peru its first taste of peace and good government, and under those of Presidents Balta and Pardo, during which many important public improvements were made. The greatest calamity in the history of Lima was its occupation by a Chilean army under the command of General Baquedano after the bloody defeat of the Peruvians at Miraflores on the 15th of January 1881. Chorrillos and Miraflores with their handsome country residences had already been sacked and burned and their helpless residents murdered. Lima escaped this fate, thanks to the intervention of foreign powers, but during the two years and nine months of this occupation the Chileans systematically pillaged the public edifices, turned the old university of San Marcos into barracks, destroyed the public library, and carried away the valuable contents of the Exposition palace, the models and apparatus of the medical school and other educational institutions, and many of the monuments and art treasures with which the city had been enriched. A forced contribution of $1,000,000 a month was imposed upon the population in addition to the revenues of the custom house. When the Chilean garrison under Captain Lynch was withdrawn on the 22nd of October 1883, it took 3000 wagons to carry away the plunder which had not already been shipped. Of the government palace and other public buildings nothing remained but the bare walls. The buoyant character of the people, and the sympathy and assistance generously offered by many civilized nations, contributed to a remarkably speedy recovery from so great a misfortune. Under the direction of its keeper, Don Ricardo Palma, 8315 volumes of the public library were recovered, to which were added valuable contributions from other countries. The portraits of the Spanish viceroys were also recovered, except five, and are now in the portrait gallery of the Exposition palace. The poverty of the country after the war made recovery difficult, but years of peace have assisted it.

See Mariano F. Paz Soldan, *Diccionario geográfico-estadístico del Perú* (Lima, 1877); Mateo Paz Soldan and M. F. Paz Soldan, *Geografía del Perú* (Paris, 1862); Manuel A. Fuentes, *Lima, or Sketches of the Capital of Peru* (London, 1866); C. R. Markham, *Cuzo and Lima* (London, 1856), and *History of Peru* (Chicago, 1892); Alexandre Garland, *Peru in 1906* (Lima, 1907); and C. R. Enock, *Peru* (London, 1908). For earlier descriptions see works referred to under PERU. (A. J. L.)

LIMAÇON (from the Lat. *limax*, a slug), a curve invented by Blaise Pascal and further investigated and named by Gilles Personne de Roberval. It is generated by the extremities of a rod which is constrained to move so that its middle point traces out a circle, the rod always passing through a fixed point on the circumference. The polar equation is $r=a+b\cos\theta$, where $2a$ = length of the rod, and b = diameter of the circle. The curve may be regarded as an epitrochoid (see EPICYCLOID) in which the rolling and fixed circles have equal radii. It is the inverse of a central conic for the focus, and the first positive pedal of a circle for any point. The form of the limaçon depends on the ratio of the two constants; if a be greater than b, the curve lies entirely outside the circle; if a equals b, it is known as a cardioid (*q.v.*); if a is less than b, the curve has a node within the circle; the particular case when $b=2a$ is known as the trisectrix (*q.v.*). In the figure (1) is a limaçon, (2) the cardioid, (3) the trisectrix.

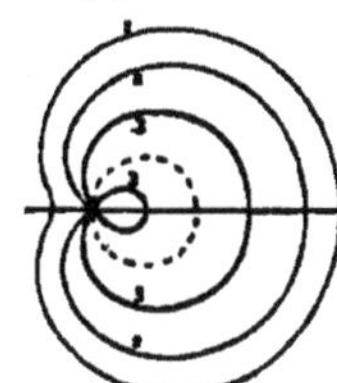

Properties of the limaçon may be deduced from its mechanical construction; thus the length of a focal chord is constant and the normals at the extremities of a focal chord intersect on a fixed circle. The area is $(b^2+a^2/2)\pi$, and the length is expressible as an elliptic integral.

LIMASOL, a seaport of Cyprus, on Akrotiri Bay of the south coast. Pop: (1901) 8298. Excepting a fort attributed to the close of the 12th century the town is without antiquities of interest, but in the neighbourhood are the ancient sites of Amathus and Curium. Limasol has a considerable trade in wine and carobs. The town was the scene of the marriage of Richard I., king of England, with Berengaria, in 1191.

LIMB. (1) (In O. Eng. *lim*, cognate with the O. Nor. and Icel. *limr*, Swed. and Dan. *lem*; probably the word is to be referred to a root *li-* seen in an obsolete English word "lith," a limb, and in the Ger. *Glied*), originally any portion or member of the body, but now restricted in meaning to the external members of the body of an animal apart from the head and trunk, the legs and arms, or, in a bird, the wings. It is sometimes used of the lower limbs only, and is synonymous with "leg." The word is also used of the main branches of a tree, of the projecting spurs of a range of mountains, of the arms of a cross, &c. As a translation of the Lat. *membrum*, and with special reference to the church as the "body of Christ," "limb" was frequently used by ecclesiastical writers of the 16th and 17th centuries of a person as being a component part of the church; cf. such expressions as "limb of Satan," "limb of the law," &c. From the use of *membrum* in medieval Latin for an estate dependent on another, the name "limb" is given to an outlying portion of another, or to the subordinate members of the Cinque Ports, attached to one of the principal towns; Pevensey was thus a "limb" of Hastings. (2) An edge or border, frequently used in scientific language for the boundary of a surface. It is thus used of the edge of the disk of the sun or moon, of the expanded part of a petal or sepal in botany, &c. This word is a shortened form of "limbo" or "limbus," Lat. for an edge, for the theological use of which see LIMBUS.

LIMBACH, a town in the kingdom of Saxony, in the manufacturing district of Chemnitz, 6 m. N.W. of that city. Pop. (1905) 13,723. It has a public park and a monument to the composer Pache. Its industries include the making of worsteds, cloth, silk and sewing-machines, and dyeing and bleaching.

LIMBER, an homonymous word, having three meanings. (1) A two-wheeled carriage forming a detachable part of the equipment of all guns on travelling carriages and having on it a framework to contain ammunition boxes, and, in most cases, seats for two or three gunners. The French equivalent is *avant-train*, the Ger. *Protz* (see ARTILLERY and ORDNANCE). (2) An adjective meaning pliant or flexible and so used with reference to a person's mental or bodily qualities, quick, nimble, adroit. (3) A nautical term for the holes cut in the flooring in a ship above the keelson, to allow water to drain to the pumps.

The etymology of these words is obscure. According to the *New English Dictionary* the origin of (1) is to be found in the Fr. *limonière*, a derivative of *limon*, the shaft of a vehicle, a meaning which appears in English from the 15th century but is now obsolete, except apparently among the miners of the north of England. The earlier English forms of the word are *lymor* or *limmer*. Skeat suggests that (2) is connected with "limp," which he refers to a Teutonic base *lap-*, meaning to hang down. The *New English Dictionary* points out that while "limp" does not occur till the beginning of the 18th century, "limber" in this sense is found as early as the 16th. In Thomas Cooper's (1517?–1594) *Thesaurus Linguae Romanae et Britannicae* (1565), it appears as the English equivalent of the Latin *lentus*. A possible derivation connects it with "limb."

LIMBORCH, PHILIPP VAN (1633–1712), Dutch Remonstrant theologian, was born on the 19th of June 1633, at Amsterdam, where his father was a lawyer. He received his education at Utrecht, at Leiden, in his native city, and finally at Utrecht University, which he entered in 1652. In 1657 he became a Remonstrant pastor at Gouda, and in 1667 he was transferred to Amsterdam, where, in the following year, the office of professor of theology in the Remonstrant seminary was added to his pastoral charge. He was a friend of John Locke. He died at Amsterdam on the 30th of April 1712.

His most important work, *Institutiones theologiae christianae, ad praxin pietatis et promotionem pacis christianae unice directae* (Amsterdam, 1686, 5th ed., 1735), is a full and clear exposition of the system of Simon Episcopius and Stephan Curcellaeus. The fourth edition (1715) included a posthumous "Relatio historica de origine et progressu controversiarum in foederato Belgio de praedestinatione." Limborch also wrote *De veritate religionis Christianae amica collatio cum erudito Judaeo* (Gouda, 1687); *Historia Inquisitionis* (1692), in four books prefixed to the "Liber Sententiarum Inquisitionis Tolosanae" (1307–1323); and *Commentarius in Acta Apostolorum et in Epistolas ad Romanos et ad Hebraeos* (Rotterdam, 1711). His editorial labours included the publication of various works of his predecessors, and of *Epistolae ecclesiasticae praestantium ac eruditorum virorum* (Amsterdam, 1684), chiefly by Jakobus Arminius, Joannes Uytenbogardus, Konrad Vorstius (1569–1622), Gerhard Vossius (1577–1649), Hugo Grotius, Simon Episcopius (his grand-uncle) and Gaspar Barlaeus; they are of great value for the history of Arminianism. An English translation of the *Theologia* was published in 1702 by William Jones (*A Complete System or Body of Divinity, both Speculative and Practical, founded on Scripture and Reason*, London, 1702); and a translation of the *Historia Inquisitionis*, by Samuel Chandler, with "a large introduction concerning the rise and progress of persecution and the real and pretended causes of it" prefixed, appeared in 1731. See Herzog-Hauck, *Realencyklopädie*.

LIMBURG, one of the many small feudal states into which the duchy of Lower Lorraine was split up in the second half of the 11th century. The first count, Walram of Arlon, married Judith the daughter of Frederick of Luxemburg, duke of Lower Lorraine (d. 1065), who bestowed upon him a portion of his possessions lying upon both sides of the river Meuse. It received its name from the strong castle built by Count Walram on the river Vesdre, where the town of Limburg now stands. Henry, Walram's son (d. 1119), was turbulent and ambitious. On the death of Godfrey of Bouillon (1089) he forced the emperor Henry IV. to recognize him as duke of Lower Lorraine. He was afterwards deposed and imprisoned by Count Godfrey of Louvain on whom the ducal title had been bestowed by the emperor Henry V. (1106). For three generations the possession of the ducal title was disputed between the rival houses of Limburg and Louvain. At length a reconciliation took place (1155); the name of duke of Lower Lorraine henceforth disappears, the rulers of the territory on the Meuse become dukes of Limburg, those of the larger territory to the west dukes of Brabant. With the death of Duke Walram IV. (1280) the succession passed to his daughter, Irmingardis, who was married to Reinald I., count of Guelders. Irmingardis died without issue (1282), and her cousin, Count Adolph of Berg, laid claim to the duchy. His rights were disputed by Reinald, who was in possession and was recognized by the emperor. Too weak to assert his claim by force of arms Adolph sold his rights (1283) to John, duke of Brabant (*q.v.*). This led to a long and desolating war for five years, at the end of which (1288), finding the power of Brabant superior to his own Reinald in his turn sold his rights to count Henry III. of Luxemburg. Henry and Reinald, supported by the archbishop of Cologne and other allies, now raised a great army. The rival forces met at Woeringen (5th of June 1288) and John of Brabant (*q.v.*) gained a complete victory. It proved decisive, the duchies of Limburg and Brabant passing under the rule of a common sovereign. The duchy comprised during this period the bailiwicks of Hervé, Montzen, Baelen, Sprimont and Wallhorn, and the counties of Rolduc, Daelhem and Falkenberg, to which was added in 1530 the town of

Maastricht. The provisions and privileges of the famous Charter of Brabant, the *Joyeuse Entrée* (*q.v.*), were from the 15th century extended to Limburg and remained in force until the French Revolution. By the treaty of Westphalia (1648) the duchy was divided into two portions, the counties of Daelhem and Falkenberg with the town of Maastricht being ceded by Spain to the United Provinces, where they formed what was known as a "Generality-Land." At the peace of Rastatt (1714) the southern portion passed under the dominion of the Austrian Habsburgs and formed part of the Austrian Netherlands until the French conquest in 1794. During the period of French rule (1794–1814) Limburg was included in the two French departments of Ourthe and Meuse Inférieure. In 1814 the old name of Limburg was restored to one of the provinces of the newly created kingdom of the Netherlands, but the new Limburg comprised besides the ancient duchy, a piece of Gelderland and the county of Looz. At the revolution of 1830 Limburg, with the exception of Maastricht, threw in its lot with the Belgians, and during the nine years that King William refused to recognize the existence of the kingdom of Belgium the Limburgers sent representatives to the legislature at Brussels and were treated as Belgians. When in 1839 the Dutch king suddenly announced his intention of accepting the terms of the settlement proposed by the treaty of London, as drawn up by representatives of the great powers in 1831, Belgium found herself compelled to relinquish portions of Limburg and Luxemburg. The part of Limburg that lay on the right bank of the Meuse, together with the town of Maastricht and a number of communes—Weert, Haelen, Kepel, Horst, &c.—on the left bank of the river, became a sovereign duchy under the rule of the king of Holland. In exchange for the cession of the rights of the Germanic confederation over the portion of Luxemburg, which was annexed by the treaty to Belgium, the duchy of Limburg (excepting the communes of Maastricht and Venloo) was declared to belong to the Germanic confederation. This somewhat unsatisfactory condition of affairs continued until 1866, when at a conference of the great powers, held in London to consider the Luxemburg question (see LUXEMBURG), it was agreed that Limburg should be freed from every political tie with Germany. Limburg became henceforth an integral part of Dutch territory.

See P. S. Ernst, *Histoire du Limbourg* (7 vols., Liége, 1837–1852); [illegible] Lunac, *De Landen van Overmaze in Zonderheid 1662* (Leiden, [illegible]); M. J. de Poully, *Histoire de Maastricht et de ses environs* ([illegible]), *Diplomaticke bescheiden betreffends de Limburg-Luxem-[illegible] aangelegenheden 1866–1867* (The Hague, 1868); and R. [illegible], *Geschied. der Staats-Instellingen in Nederland* (The Hague, [illegible]). (G. E.)

LIMBURG, or LIMBOURG, the smallest of the nine provinces [of] Belgium, occupying the north-east corner of the kingdom. [illegible] only a portion of the ancient duchy of Limburg [illegible]. The part east of the Meuse was transferred to [illegible] by the London conference, and a further portion was [illegible] the province of Liége including the old capital now [illegible]. Much of the province is represented by the wild [illegible] called the Campine, recently discovered to form [illegible] coal-field. The operations for working it were only [illegible]. North-west of Hasselt is Beverloo, where all the [illegible] go through a course of instruction annually. [illegible] are Hasselt, the capital, St Trond and Looz. [illegible] named is derived the title of the family known as [illegible] Looz, whose antiquity equals that of the extinct [illegible] of Limburg itself. The title of duc de Looz is one [illegible] ducal titles in the Netherlands, the other [illegible] Croy and d'Ursel. Limburg contains [illegible] sq. m. In 1904 the population was 255,359, [illegible] per sq. m.

[illegible] a town of Germany, in the Prussian province of [illegible] the Lahn, here crossed by a bridge dating [illegible] the main line of railway from Coblenz to [illegible] with a branch to Frankfort-on-Main. Pop. [illegible] the seat of a Roman Catholic bishop. The [illegible] cathedr[illegible] St George the [illegible] overhanging the river. This was founded by Conrad Kurzbold, count of Niederlahngau, early in the 10th century, and was consecrated in 1235. It was restored in 1872–1878. Limburg has a castle, a new town hall and a seminary for the education of priests; its industries include the manufacture of cloth, tobacco, soap, machinery, pottery and leather. Limburg, which was a flourishing place during the middle ages, had its own line of counts until 1414, when it was purchased by the elector of Trier. It passed to Nassau in 1803. In September 1796 it was the scene of a victory gained by the Austrians under the archduke Charles over the French.

See Hillebrand, *Limburg an der Lahn unter Pfandherrschaft 1344–1624* (Wiesbaden, 1899).

LIMBURG, the south-easternmost and smallest province of Holland, bounded N. by Gelderland, N.W. by North Brabant, S.W. by the Belgian province of Limburg, and S. by that of Liége, and E. by Germany. Its area is 850 sq. m., and its population in 1900 was 281,934. It is watered by the Meuse (Maas) which forms part of its south-western boundary (with Belgium) and then flows through its northern portion, and by such tributaries as the Geul and Roer (Ruhr). Its capital is Maastricht, which gives name to one of the two administrative districts into which it is divided, the other being Roermond.

LIMBURG CHRONICLE, or FASTI LIMPURGENSES, the name of a German chronicle written most probably by Tileman Elhen von Wolfhagen after 1402. It is a source for the history of the Rhineland between 1336 and 1398, but is perhaps more valuable for the information about German manners and customs, and the old German folk-songs and stories which it contains. It has also a certain philological interest.

The chronicle was first published by J. F. Faust in 1617, and has been edited by A. Wyss for the *Monumenta Germaniae historica. Deutsche Chroniken*, Band iv. (Hanover, 1883). See A. Wyss, *Die Limburger Chronik untersucht* (Marburg, 1875).

LIMBURGITE, in petrology, a dark-coloured volcanic rock resembling basalt in appearance, but containing normally no felspar. The name is taken from Limburg (Germany), where they occur in the well-known rock of the Kaiserstuhl. They consist essentially of olivine and augite with a brownish glassy ground mass. The augite may be green, but more commonly is brown or violet; the olivine is usually pale green or colourless, but is sometimes yellow (hyalosiderite). In the ground mass a second generation of small eumorphic augites frequently occurs; more rarely olivine is present also as an ingredient of the matrix. The principal accessory minerals are titaniferous iron oxides and apatite. Felspar though sometimes present is never abundant, and nepheline also is unusual. In some limburgites large phenocysts of dark brown hornblende and biotite are found, mostly with irregular borders blackened by resorption; in others there are large crystals of soda orthoclase or anorthoclase. Hauyne is an ingredient of some of the limburgites of the Cape Verde Islands. Rocks of this group occur in considerable numbers in Germany (Rhine district) and in Bohemia, also in Scotland, Auvergne, Spain, Africa (Kilimanjaro), Brazil, &c. They are associated principally with basalts, nepheline and leucite basalts and monchiquites. From the last-named rocks the limburgites are not easily separated as the two classes bear a very close resemblance in structure and in mineral composition, though many authorities believe that the ground mass of the monchiquites is not a glass but crystalline analcite. Limburgites may occur as flows, as sills or dykes, and are sometimes highly vesicular. Closely allied to them are the *augitites*, which are distinguished only by the absence of olivine; examples are known from Bohemia, Auvergne, the Canary Islands, Ireland, &c.

LIMBUS (Lat. for "edge," "fringe," *e.g.* of a garment), a theological term denoting the border of hell, where dwell those who, while not condemned to torture, yet are deprived of the joy of heaven. The more common form in English is "limbo," which is used both in the technical theological sense and derivatively in the sense of "prison," or for the condition of being lost, deserted, obsolete. In theology there are (1) the *Limbus Infantum*, and (2) the *Limbus Patrum*.

1. The *Limbus Infantum* or *Puerorum* is the abode to which

human beings dying without actual sin, but with their original sin unwashed away by baptism, were held to be consigned; the category included, not unbaptized infants merely, but also idiots, cretins and the like. The word "limbus," in the theological application, occurs first in the *Summa* of Thomas Aquinas; for its extensive currency it is perhaps most indebted to the *Commedia* of Dante (*Inf.* c. 4). The question as to the destiny of infants dying unbaptized presented itself to theologians at a comparatively early period. Generally speaking it may be said that the Greek fathers inclined to a cheerful and the Latin fathers to a gloomy view. Thus Gregory of Nazianzus (*Orat.* 40) says "that such children as die unbaptized without their own fault shall neither be glorified nor punished by the righteous Judge, as having done no wickedness, though they die unbaptized, and as rather suffering loss than being the authors of it." Similar opinions were expressed by Gregory of Nyssa, Severus of Antioch and others—opinions which it is almost impossible to distinguish from the Pelagian view that children dying unbaptized might be admitted to eternal life, though not to the kingdom of God. In his recoil from Pelagian heresy, Augustine was compelled to sharpen the antithesis between the state of the saved and that of the lost, and taught that there are only two alternatives—to be with Christ or with the devil, to be with Him or against Him. Following up, as he thought, his master's teaching, Fulgentius declared that it is to be believed as an indubitable truth that, "not only men who have come to the use of reason, but infants dying, whether in their mother's womb or after birth, without baptism in the name of the Father, Son and Holy Ghost, are punished with everlasting punishment in eternal fire." Later theologians and schoolmen followed Augustine in rejecting the notion of any final position intermediate between heaven and hell, but otherwise inclined to take the mildest possible view of the destiny of the irresponsible and unbaptized. Thus the proposition of Innocent III. that "the punishment of original sin is deprivation of the vision of God" is practically repeated by Aquinas, Scotus, and all the other great theologians of the scholastic period, the only outstanding exception being that of Gregory of Rimini, who on this account was afterwards called "tortor infantum." The first authoritative declaration of the Latin Church upon this subject was that made by the second council of Lyons (1274), and confirmed by the council of Florence (1439), with the concurrence of the representatives of the Greek Church, to the effect that "the souls of those who die in mortal sin or in original sin only forthwith descend into hell, but to be punished with unequal punishments." Perrone remarks (*Prael. Theol.* pt. iii. chap. 6, art. 4) that the damnation of infants and also the comparative lightness of the punishment involved in this are thus *de fide*; but nothing is determined as to the place which they occupy in hell, as to what constitutes the disparity of their punishment, or as to their condition after the day of judgment. In the council of Trent there was considerable difference of opinion as to what was implied in deprivation of the vision of God, and no definition was attempted, the Dominicans maintaining the severer view that the "limbus infantum" was a dark subterranean fireless chamber, while the Franciscans placed it in a region of light above the earth. Some theologians continue to maintain with Bellarmine that the infants "in limbo" are affected with some degree of sadness on account of a felt privation; others, following the *Nodus praedestinationis* of Celestine Sfrondati (1649–1696), hold that they enjoy every kind of natural felicity, as regards their souls now, and as regards their bodies after the resurrection, just as if Adam had not sinned. In the condemnation (1794) of the synod of Pistoia (1786), the twenty-sixth article declares it to be false, rash and injurious to treat as Pelagian the doctrine that those dying in original sin are not punished with fire, as if that meant that there is an intermediate place, free from fault and punishment, between the kingdom of God and everlasting damnation.

2. The *Limbus Patrum*, *Limbus Inferni* or *Sinus Abrahae* ("Abraham's Bosom"), is defined in Roman Catholic theology as the place in the underworld where the saints of the Old Testament were confined until liberated by Christ on his "descent into hell." Regarding the locality and its pleasantness or painfulness nothing has been taught as *de fide*. It is sometimes regarded as having been closed and empty since Christ's descent, but other authors do not think of it as separate in place from the *limbus infantum*. The whole idea, in the Latin Church, has been justly described as the mere *caput mortuum* of the old catholic doctrine of Hades, which was gradually superseded in the West by that of purgatory.

LIME (O. Eng. *lim*, Lat. *limus*, mud, from *linere*, to smear), the name given to a viscous exudation of the holly-tree, used for snaring birds and known as "bird-lime." In chemistry, it is the popular name of calcium oxide, CaO, a substance employed in very early times as a component of mortars and cementing materials. It is prepared by the burning of limestone (a process described by Dioscorides and Pliny) in kilns similar to those described under CEMENT. The value and subsequent treatment of the product depend on the purity of the limestone; a pure stone yields a "fat" lime which readily slakes; an impure stone, especially if magnesia be present, yields an almost unslakable "poor" lime. See CEMENT, CONCRETE and MORTAR, for details.

Pure calcium oxide "quick-lime," obtained by heating the pure carbonate, is a white amorphous substance, which can be readily melted and boiled in the electric furnace, cubic and acicular crystals being deposited on cooling the vapour. It combines with water, evolving much heat and crumbling to pieces; this operation is termed "slaking" and the resulting product "slaked lime"; it is chemically equivalent to the conversion of the oxide into hydrate. A solution of the hydrate in water, known as lime-water, has a weakly alkaline reaction; it is employed in the detection of carbonic acid. "Milk of lime" consists of a cream of the hydrate and water. Dry lime has no action upon chlorine, carbon dioxide and sulphur dioxide, although in the presence of water combination ensues.

In medicine lime-water, applied externally, is an astringent and desiccative, and it enters into the preparation of linamentum calcis and carron oil which are employed to heal burns, eczema, &c. Applied internally, lime-water is an antacid: it prevents the curdling of milk in large lumps (hence its prescription for infants); it also acts as a gastric sedative. Calcium phosphate is much employed in treating rickets, and calcium chloride in haemoptysis and haemophylia. It is an antidote for mineral and oxalic acid poisoning.

LIME,[1] or LINDEN. The lime trees, species of *Tilia*, are familiar timber trees with sweet-scented, honeyed flowers, which are borne on a common peduncle proceeding from the middle of a long bract. The genus, which gives the name to the natural order Tiliaceae, contains about ten species of trees, natives of the north temperate zone. The general name *Tilia europaea*, the name given by Linnaeus to the European lime, includes several well-marked sub-species, often regarded as distinct species. These are: (1) the small-leaved lime, *T. parvifolia* (or *T. cordata*), probably wild in woods in England and also wild throughout Europe, except in the extreme south-east, and Russian Asia. (2) *T. intermedia*, the common lime, which is widely planted in Britain but not wild there, has a less northerly distribution than *T. cordata*, from which it differs in its somewhat larger leaves and downy fruit. (3) The large-leaved lime, *T. platyphyllos* (or *T. grandifolia*), occurs only as an introduction in Britain, and is wild in Europe south of Denmark. It differs from the other two limes in its larger leaves, often 4 in. across, which are downy beneath, its downy twigs and its prominently ribbed fruit. The lime sometimes acquires a great size; one is recorded in Norfolk as being 16 yds. in circumference, and Ray mentions one of the same girth. The famous linden tree which gave the town of Neuenstadt in Württemberg the name of "*Neuenstadt an der grossen Linden*" was 9 ft. in diameter.

The lime is a very favourite tree. It is an object of beauty in

[1] This is an altered form of O. Eng. and M. Eng. *lind*; cf. Ger. *Linde*, cognate with Gr. ἐλάτη, the silver fir. "Linden" in English means properly "made of lime—or lind—wood," and the transference to the tree is due to the Ger. *Lindenbaum*.

the spring when the delicately transparent green leaves are bursting from the protection of the pink and white stipules, which have formed the bud-scales, and retains its fresh green during early summer. Later, the fragrance of its flowers, rich in honey, attracts innumerable bees; in the autumn the foliage becomes a clear yellow but soon falls. Among the many famous avenues of limes may be mentioned that which gave the name to one of the best-known ways in Berlin, "Unter den Linden," and the avenue at Trinity College, Cambridge.

The economic value of the tree chiefly lies in the inner bark or liber (Lat. for bark), called bast, and the wood. The former was used for paper and mats and for tying garlands by the ancients ([illegible] i. 38; Pliny xvi. 14. 25, xxiv. 8. 33). Bast mats are now made chiefly in Russia, the bark being cut in long strips, when the liber is easily separable from the corky superficial layer. It is then plaited into mats about 2 yds. square; 14,000,000 come to Britain annually, chiefly from Archangel. The wood is used by carvers, being soft and light, and by architects in framing the models of buildings. Turners use it for light bowls, &c. *T. americana* (bass-wood) is one of the most common trees in the forests of Canada and extends into the eastern and southern United States. It is sawn into lumber and under the name of white-wood used in the manufacture of wooden ware, cheap furniture, &c., and also for paper pulp (C. S. Sargent, *Silva of North America*). It was cultivated by Philip Miller at Chelsea in 1752.

The common lime was well known to the ancients. Theophrastus says the leaves are sweet and used for fodder for most kinds of [illegible]. Pliny alludes to the use of the liber and wood, and describes the tree as growing in the mountain-valleys of Italy (xvi. 30). See also [illegible] *Geo.* i. 173, &c.; Ov. *Met.* viii. 621, x. 92. Allusion to the [illegible] of the wood is made in Aristoph. *Birds*, 1378.

For the sweet lime (*Citrus Limetta* or *Citrus acida*) and lime-juice, see [illegible].

LIMERICK, a western county of Ireland, in the province of Munster, bounded N. by the estuary of the Shannon and the counties of Clare and Tipperary, E. by Tipperary, S. by Cork and W. by Kerry. The area is 680,842 acres, or about 1064 sq. m. The greater part of the county is comparatively level, but in the [illegible] the picturesque Galtees, which extend into Tipperary, [illegible] more a height of 3015 ft., and on the west, stretch[illegible] Kerry, there is a circular amphitheatre of less elevated [illegible]. The Shannon is navigable for large vessels to [illegible] which are the rapids of Doonas and Castleroy, [illegible]. The Shannon is widely famous as a sporting river, [illegible] is a well-known centre. The Maigue, which [illegible] Galtees and flows into the Shannon, is navigable [illegible] town of Adare.

[illegible] a Carboniferous Limestone county, with fairly [illegible] by ridges of Old Red Sandstone. On the north-[illegible] rises on Slievefelim, round a Silurian core, to [illegible], Old Red Sandstone rises above an enclosed [illegible] at Ballylanders, the opposite scarp of Old Red [illegible] the Ballyhoura Hills on the Cork border. Vol[illegible] basalts and intrusive sheets of basic rock, [illegible] in the Carboniferous Limestone. These [illegible]gunnell Castle, and in a ring of hills round [illegible], Upper Carboniferous beds occur, as [illegible] that links the west of the county with the [illegible] in the west are not of commercial value. [illegible] in places in the limestone.

[illegible] greater part of the Golden Vale, the most [illegible] which stretches from Cashel in Tipperary [illegible]. Along the banks of the Shannon [illegible] flat meadow land formed of deposits of [illegible], exceedingly fertile. The soil in the [illegible] the most part thin and poor, and in[illegible]. The large farms occupy the low grounds, [illegible] to grazing. The acreage under [illegible] to pasturage being as one to nearly [illegible] oats and potatoes are the principal) [illegible] a growing acreage of meadow land. [illegible] other hand, are on the whole well [illegible], goats and poultry are all ex[illegible] are employed chiefly in agri[illegible] manufactured, and also paper, [illegible] mills. Formerly there were [illegible] the industry is now practically [illegible] of an important salmon-[illegible] communications are entirely [illegible] Western system, whose main [illegible] county, with two branches [illegible]rleville, [illegible] Kerry, [illegible] by a line from the north through county Tipperary. The port of Limerick, at the head of the estuary, is the most important on the west coast.

The county includes 14 baronies. The number of members returned to the Irish parliament was eight, two being returned for each of the boroughs of Askeaton and Kilmallock, in addition to two returned for the county, and two for the county of the city of Limerick. The present county parliamentary divisions are the east and west, each returning one member. The population (158,912 in 1891, 146,098 in 1901) shows a decrease somewhat under the average of the Irish counties generally, emigration being, however, extensive; of the total about 94% are Roman Catholics, and about 73% are rural. The chief towns are Limerick (pop. 38,151), Rathkeale (1749) and Newcastle or Newcastle West (2599). The city of Limerick constitutes a county in itself. Assizes are held at Limerick, and quarter-sessions at Bruff, Limerick, Newcastle and Rathkeale. The county is divided between the Protestant dioceses of Cashel, Killaloe and Limerick; and between the Roman Catholic dioceses of the same names.

Limerick was included in the kingdom of Thomond. Afterwards it had a separate existence under the name of Aine-Cliach. From the 8th to the 11th century it was partly occupied by the Danes (see LIMERICK, City). As a county, Limerick is one of the twelve generally considered to owe their formation to King John. By Henry II. it was granted to Henry Fitzherbert, but his claim was afterwards resigned, and subsequently various Anglo-Norman settlements were made. About 100,000 acres of the estates of the earl of Desmond, which were forfeited in 1586, were situated in the county, and other extensive confiscations took place after the Cromwellian wars. In 1709 a German colony from the Palatinate was settled by Lord Southwell near Bruff, Rathkeale and Adare.

There are only slight remains of the round tower at Ardpatrick, but that at Dysert is much better preserved; another at Kilmallock is in great part a reconstruction. There are important remains of stone circles, pillar stones and altars at Loch Gur. In several places there are remains of old moats and tumuli. Besides the monasteries in the city of Limerick, the most important monastic ruins are those of Adare abbey, Askeaton abbey, Galbally friary, Kilflin monastery, Kilmallock and Monaster-Nenagh abbey.

LIMERICK, a city, county of a city, parliamentary borough, port and the chief town of Co. Limerick, Ireland, occupying both banks and an island (King's Island) of the river Shannon, at the head of its estuary, 129 m. W.S.W. of Dublin by the Great Southern and Western railway. Pop. (1901) 38,151. The situation is striking, for the Shannon is here a broad and noble stream, and the immediately surrounding country consists of the rich lowlands of its valley, while beyond rise the hills of the counties Clare and Tipperary. The city is divided into English Town (on King's Island), Irish Town and Newtown Pery, the first including the ancient nucleus of the city, and the last the principal modern streets. The main stream of the Shannon is crossed by Thomond Bridge and Sarsfield or Wellesley Bridge. The first is commanded by King John's Castle, on King's Island, a fine Norman fortress fronting the river, and used as barracks. At the west end of the bridge is preserved the Treaty Stone, on which the Treaty of Limerick was signed in 1691. The cathedral of St Mary, also on King's Island, was originally built in 1142–1180, and exhibits some Early English work, though largely altered at dates subsequent to that period. The Roman Catholic cathedral of St John is a modern building (1860) in early pointed style. The churches of St Munchin (to whom is attributed the foundation of the see in the 6th century) and St John, Whitamore's Castle and a Dominican priory, are other remains of antiquarian interest; while the principal city and county buildings are a chamber of commerce, a custom house commanding the river, and court house, town hall and barracks. A picturesque public park adjoins the railway station in Newtown Pery.

The port is the most important on the west coast, and accommodates vessels of 3000 tons in a floating dock; there is also a graving dock. Communication with the Atlantic is open and secure, while a vast network of inland navigation is opened up by a canal avoiding the rapids above the city. Quays extend for about 1600 yds. on each side of the river, and vessels of 600 tons can moor alongside at spring tides. The principal imports are grain, sugar, timber and coal. The exports consist mainly of agricultural produce. The principal industrial establishments include flour-mills (Limerick supplying most of the west of Ireland with flour), factories for bacon-curing and for condensed milk and creameries. Some brewing, distilling and tanning are carried on, and the manufacture of very beautiful lace is maintained at the Convent of the Good Shepherd; but a formerly important textile industry has lapsed. The salmon fisheries of the Shannon, for which Limerick is the headquarters of a district, are the most valuable in Ireland. The city is governed by a corporation, and the parliamentary borough returns one member.

Limerick is said to have been the *Regia* of Ptolemy and the *Rosse-de-Nailleagh* of the Annals of Multifernan. There is a tradition that it was visited by St Patrick in the 5th century, but it is first authentically known as a settlement of the Danes, who sacked it in 812 and afterwards made it the principal town of their kingdom of Limerick, but were expelled from it towards the close of the 10th century by Brian Boroimhe. From 1106 till its conquest by the English in 1174 it was the seat of the kings of Thomond or North Munster, and, although in 1179 the kingdom of Limerick was given by Henry II. to Herbert Fitzherbert, the city was frequently in the possession of the Irish chieftains till 1195. Richard I. granted it a charter in 1197. By King John it was committed to the care of William de Burgo, who founded English Town, and for its defence erected a strong castle. The city was frequently besieged in the 13th and 14th centuries. In the 15th century its fortifications were extended to include Irish Town, and until their demolition in 1760 it was one of the strongest fortresses of the kingdom. In 1651 it was taken by General Ireton, and after an unsuccessful siege by William III. in 1690 its resistance was terminated on the 3rd of October of the following year by the treaty of Limerick. The dismantling of its fortifications began in 1760, but fragments of the old walls remain. The original municipal rights of the city had been confirmed and extended by a succession of sovereigns, and in 1609 it received a charter constituting it a county of a city, and also incorporating a society of merchants of the staple, with the same privileges as the merchants of the staple of Dublin and Waterford. The powers of the corporation were remodelled by the Limerick Regulation Act of 1823. The prosperity of the city dates chiefly from the foundation of Newtown Pery in 1769 by Edmund Sexton Pery (d. 1806), speaker of the Irish House of Commons, whose family subsequently received the title of the earldom of Limerick. Under the Local Government Act of 1898 Limerick became one of the six county boroughs having a separate county council.

LIMERICK, a name which has been adopted to distinguish a certain form of verse which began to be cultivated in the middle of the 19th century. A limerick is a kind of burlesque epigram, written in five lines. In its earlier form it had two rhymes, the word which closed the first or second line being usually employed at the end of the fifth, but in later varieties different rhyming words are employed. There is much uncertainty as to the meaning of the name, and as to the time when it became attached to a particular species of nonsense verses. According to the *New Eng. Dict.* "a song has existed in Ireland for a very considerable time, the construction of the verse of which is identical with that of Lear's" (see below), and in which the invitation is repeated, "Will you come up to Limerick?" Unfortunately, the specimen quoted in the *New Eng. Dict.* is not only not identical with, but does not resemble Lear's. Whatever be the derivation of the name, however, it is now universally used to describe a set of verses formed on this model, with the variations in rhyme noted above:—

> "There was an old man who said 'Hush!
> I perceive a young bird in that bush!'
> When they said, 'Is it small?'
> He replied, 'Not at all!
> It is five times the size of the bush.'"

The invention, or at least the earliest general use of this form, is attributed to Edward Lear, who, when a tutor in the family of the earl of Derby at Knowsley, composed, about 1834, a large number of nonsense-limericks to amuse the little grandchildren of the house. Many of these he published, with illustrations, in 1846, and they enjoyed and still enjoy an extreme popularity. Lear preferred to give a geographical colour to his absurdities, as in:—

> "There was an old person of Tartary
> Who cut through his jugular artery,
> When up came his wife,
> And exclaimed, 'O my Life,
> How your loss will be felt through all Tartary!'"

but this is by no means essential. The neatness of the form has led to a very extensive use of the limerick for all sorts of mock-serious purposes, political, social and sarcastic, and a good many specimens have achieved a popularity which has been all the wider because they have, perforce, been confined to verbal transmission. In recent years competitions of the "missing word" type have had considerable vogue, the competitor, for instance, having to supply the last line of the limerick.

LIMES GERMANICUS. The Latin noun *limes* denoted generally a path, sometimes a boundary path (possibly its original sense) or boundary, and hence it was utilized by Latin writers occasionally to denote frontiers definitely delimited and marked in some distinct fashion. This latter sense has been adapted and extended by modern historians concerned with the frontiers of the Roman Empire. Thus the Wall of Hadrian in north England (see Britain: *Roman*) is now sometimes styled the *Limes Britannicus*, the frontier of the Roman province of Arabia facing the desert the *Limes Arabicus* and so forth. In particular the remarkable frontier lines which bounded the Roman provinces of Upper (southern) Germany and Raetia, and which at their greatest development stretched from near Bonn on the Rhine to near Regensburg on the Danube, are often called the *Limes Germanicus*. The history of these lines is the subject of the following paragraphs. They have in the last fifteen years become much better known through systematic excavations financed by the German empire and through other researches connected therewith, and though many important details are still doubtful, their general development can be traced.

From the death of Augustus (A.D. 14) till after A.D. 70 Rome accepted as her German frontier the water-boundary of the Rhine and upper Danube. Beyond these rivers she held only the fertile plain of Frankfort, opposite the Roman border fortress of Moguntiacum (Mainz), the southernmost slopes of the Black Forest and a few scattered têtes-du-pont. The northern section of this frontier, where the Rhine is deep and broad, remained the Roman boundary till the empire fell. The southern part was different. The upper Rhine and upper Danube are easily crossed. The frontier which they form is inconveniently long, enclosing an acute-angled wedge of foreign territory—the modern Baden and Württemberg. The German populations of these lands seem in Roman times to have been scanty, and Roman subjects from the modern Alsace and Lorraine had drifted across the river eastwards. The motives alike of geographical convenience and of the advantages to be gained by recognizing these movements of Roman subjects combined to urge a forward policy at Rome, and when the vigorous Vespasian had succeeded the fool-criminal Nero, a series of advances began which gradually closed up the acute angle, or at least rendered it obtuse.

The first advance came about 74, when what is now Baden was invaded and in part annexed and a road carried from the Roman base on the upper Rhine, Strassburg, to the Danube just above Ulm. The point of the angle was broken off. The second advance was made by Domitian about A.D. 83. He pushed out from Moguntiacum, extended the Roman territory east of it and enclosed the whole within a systematically delimited and defended frontier with numerous blockhouses along it and larger forts in the rear. Among the blockhouses was one which by various enlargements and refoundations grew into the well-known Saalburg fort on the Taunus near Homburg. This

… the construction of a … of A.D. 74 and 83. We … from the Main across … of the Neckar and was … We do not, however, know its … it was carried out soon … frontier thus constituted was … with a continuous wooden … The angle between … But there remained further … Either Hadrian or, more … from the Odenwald and … frontier roughly parallel to … though sometimes, as on the … This is the frontier … by the curious. It consists, … frontier works, one, known … mound and ditch, best seen … but once extending from … Germany. The other, … is a wall, though not … the Teufelsmauer; it runs … the Danube, which it finally … The Pfahlgraben is remark- … of its southern part, which … straight and points almost … It is a clear case of an ancient … This frontier remained … in that long period much was … precise dates. We cannot … the frontier laid out by Pius … and Teufelsmauer. But … barbarians began to be felt … century, and after long … district east of Rhine … all within one short

… in H. F. Pelham's essay in … reprinted in his *Collected* … the German authorities (F. J. H.)

… rock consisting essentially of … many varieties, some of … whole group has certain … the chemical composition … All limestones dissolve … bubbles of carbonic acid. … though the mineral … limestones, when pure, … knife-blade or the edge … they are earthy or … do not disintegrate by … scratched with the finger … are white, but they … minerals than calcite … are yellowish or … little iron oxide, iron … the presence of iron … grey and black from … substances. Red … green limestones … crystalline limestones … varied colours, … and garnet … and grey); epidote, … of limestones ranges

… are often recognizable … they may have

insoluble impurities of the limestone have been deposited by the rain. The less pure rocks have often eroded or pitted surfaces, showing bands or patches rendered more resistant to the action of the weather by the presence of insoluble materials such as sand, clay or chert. These surfaces are often known from the crust of hydrous oxides of iron produced by the action of the atmosphere on any ferriferous ingredients of the rock; they are sometimes black when the limestone is carbonaceous; a thin layer of gritty sand grains may be left on the surface of limestones which are slightly arenaceous. Most limestones which contain fossils show these most clearly on weathered surfaces, and the appearance of fragments of corals, crinoids and shells on the exposed parts of a rock indicate a strong probability that that rock is a limestone. The interior usually shows the organic structures very imperfectly or not at all.

Another characteristic of pure limestones, where they occur in large masses occupying considerable areas, is the frequency with which they produce bare rocky ground, especially at high elevations, or yield only a thin scanty soil covered with short grass. In mountainous districts limestones are often recognizable by these peculiarities. The chalk downs are celebrated for the close green sward which they furnish. More impure limestones, like those of the Lias and Oolites, contain enough insoluble mineral matter to yield soils of great thickness and value, *e.g.* the Cornbrash. In limestone regions all waters tend to be hard, on account of the abundant carbonate of lime dissolved by percolating waters, and caves, swallow holes, sinks, pot-holes and underground rivers may occur in abundance. Some elevated tracts of limestone are very barren (*e.g.* the Causses), because the rain which falls in them sinks at once into the earth and passes underground. To a large extent this is true of the chalk downs, where surface waters are notably scarce, though at considerable depths the rocks hold large supplies of water.

The great majority of limestones are of organic formation, consisting of the debris of the skeletons of animals. Some are foraminiferal, others are crinoidal, shelly or coral limestones according to the nature of the creatures whose remains they contain. Of foraminiferal limestones chalk is probably the best known; it is fine, white and rather soft, and is very largely made up of the shells of globigerina and other foraminifera (see CHALK). Almost equally important are the nummulitic limestones so well developed in Mediterranean countries (Spain, France, the Alps, Greece, Algeria, Egypt, Asia Minor, &c.). The pyramids of Egypt are built mainly of nummulitic limestone. Nummulites are large cone-shaped foraminifera with many chambers arranged in spiral order. In Britain the small globular shells of *Saccamina* are important constituents of some Carboniferous limestones; but the upper portion of that formation in Russia, eastern Asia and North America is characterized by the occurrence of limestones filled with the spindle-shaped shells of *Fusulina*, a genus of foraminifera now extinct.

Coral limestones are being formed at the present day over a large extent of the tropical seas; many existing coral reefs must be of great thickness. The same process has been going on actively since a very early period of the earth's history, for similar rocks are found in great abundance in many geological formations. Some Silurian limestones are rich in corals; in the Devonian there are deposits which have been described as coral reefs (Devonshire, Germany). The Carboniferous limestone, or mountain limestone, of England and North America, is sometimes nearly entirely coralline, and the great dolomite masses of the Trias in the eastern Alps are believed by many to be merely altered coral reefs. A special feature of coral limestones is that, although they may be to a considerable extent dolomitized, they are generally very free from silt and mechanical impurities.

Crinoidal limestones, though abundant among the older rocks, are not in course of formation on any great scale at the present time, as crinoids, formerly abundant, are now rare. Many Carboniferous and Silurian limestones consist mainly of the little cylindrical joints of these animals. They are easily recognized by their shape, and by the fact that many of them show a tube along their axes, which is often filled up by carbonate of lime; under the microscope they have a punctate or fenestrate structure and each joint behaves as a simple crystalline plate with uniform optical properties in polarized light. Remains of other echinoderms (starfishes and sea urchins) are often found in plenty in Secondary and Tertiary limestones, but very seldom make up the greater part of the rock. Shelly limestones may consist of mollusca or of brachiopoda, the former being common in limestones of all ages while the latter attained their principal development in the Palaeozoic epoch. The shells are often broken and may have been reduced to shell sand before the rock consolidated. Many rocks of this class are impure and pass into marls and shelly sandstones which were deposited in shallow waters, where land-derived sediment mingled with remains of the creatures which inhabited the water. Fresh-water limestones are mostly of this class and contain shells of those varieties of mollusca which inhabit lakes. Brackish water limestones also are usually shelly. Corallines (bryozoa, polyzoa, &c.), cephalopods (*e.g.* ammonites, belemnites), crustaceans and sponges occur frequently in limestones. It should be understood that it is not usual for a rock to be built up entirely of one kind of organism though it is classified according to its most abundant or most conspicuous ingredients.

In the organic limestones there usually occurs much finely granular calcareous matter which has been described as limestone mud or limestone paste. It is the finely ground substance which results from the breaking down of shells, &c., by the waves and currents, and by the decay which takes place in the sea bottom before the fragments are compacted into hard rock. The skeletal parts of marine animals are not always converted into limestone in the place where they were formed. In shallow waters, such as are the favourite haunts of mollusca, corals, &c., the tides and storms are frequently sufficiently powerful to shift the loose material on the sea bottom. A large part of a coral reef consists of broken coral rock dislodged from the growing mass and carried upwards to the beach or into the lagoon. Large fragments also fall over the steep outward slopes of the reef and build up a talus at their base. Coral muds and coral sands produced by the waves acting in these detached blocks, are believed to cover two and a half millions of square miles of the ocean floor. Owing to the fragile nature of the shells of foraminifera they readily become disintegrated, especially at considerable depths, largely by the solvent action of carbonic acid in sea water as they sink to the bottom. The chalk in very great part consists not of entire shells but of debris of foraminifera, and mollusca (such as *Inoceramus*, &c.). The Globigerina ooze is the most widespread of modern calcareous formations. It occupies nearly fifty millions of square miles of the sea bottom, at an average depth of two thousand fathoms. Pteropod ooze, consisting mainly of the shells of pteropods (mollusca) also has a wide distribution, especially in northern latitudes.

Consolidation may to a considerable extent be produced by pressure, but more commonly cementation and crystallization play a large part in the process. Recent shell sands on beaches and in dunes are not unfrequently converted into a soft, semi-coherent rock by rain water filtering downwards, dissolving and redepositing carbonate of lime between the sand grains. In coral reefs also the mass soon has its cavities more or less obliterated by a deposit of calcite from solution. The fine interstitial mud or paste presents a large surface to the solvents, and is more readily attacked than the larger and more compact shell fragments. In fresh-water marls considerable masses of crystalline calcite may be produced in this way, enclosing well-preserved molluscan shells. Many calcareous fragments consist of aragonite, wholly or principally, and this mineral tends to be replaced by calcite. The aragonite, as seen in sections under the microscope, is usually fibrous or prismatic, the calcite is more commonly granular with a well-marked network of rhombohedral cleavage cracks. The replacement of aragonite by calcite goes on even in shells lying on modern sea shores, and is often very complete in rocks belonging to the older geological periods. By the recrystallization of the finer paste and the introduction of calcite in solution the interior of shells, corals, foraminifera, &c., becomes occupied by crystalline calcite, sometimes in comparatively large grains, while the original organic structures may be very well-preserved.

Some limestones are exceedingly pure, *e.g.* the chalk and some varieties of mountain limestone, and these are especially suited for making lime. The majority, however, contain admixture of other substances, of which the commonest are clay and sand. Clayey or argillaceous limestones frequently occur in thin or thick beds alternating with shales, as in the Lias of England (the marlstone series). Friable argillaceous fresh-water limestones are called "marls," and are used in many districts for top dressing soils, but the name "marl" is loosely applied and is often given to beds which are not of this nature (*e.g.* the red marls of the Trias). The "cement stones" of the Lothians in Scotland are argillaceous limestones of Lower Carboniferous age, which when burnt yield cement. The gault (Upper Cretaceous) is a calcareous clay, often containing well-preserved fossils, which lies below the chalk and attains considerable importance in the south-east of England. Arenaceous limestones pass by gradual transitions into shelly sandstones; in the latter the shells are often dissolved leaving cavities, which may be occupied by casts. Some of the Old Red Sandstone is calcareous. In other cases the calcareous matter has recrystallized in large plates which have shining cleavage surfaces dotted over with grains of sand (Lincolnshire limestone). The Fontainebleau sandstone has large calcite rhombohedra filled with sand grains. Limestones sometimes contain much plant matter which has been converted into a dark coaly substance, in which the original woody structures may be preserved or may not. The calcareous petrified plants of Fifeshire occur in such a limestone, and much has been learned from a microscopic study of them regarding the anatomy of the plants of the Carboniferous period. Volcanic ashes occur in some limestones, a good example being the calcareous schalsteins or tuffs of Devonshire, which are usually much crushed by earth movements. In the Globigerina ooze of the present day there is always a slight admixture of volcanic materials derived either from wind-blown dust, from submarine eruptions or from floating pieces of pumice. Other limestones contain organic matter in the shape of asphalt, bitumen or petroleum, presumably derived from plant remains. The well-known *Val de Travers* is a bituminous limestone of lower Neocomian age found in the valley of that name near Neuchâtel. Some of the oil beds of North America are porous limestones, in the cavities of which the oil is stored up. Siliceous limestones, where their silica is original and of organic origin, have contained skeletons of sponges or radiolaria. In the chalk the silica has usually been dissolved and redeposited as flint nodules, and in the Carboniferous limestone as chert bands. It may also be deposited in the corals and other organic remains, silicifying them, with preservation of the original structures (*e.g.* some Jurassic and Carboniferous limestones).

The oolitic limestones form a special group distinguished by their consisting of small rounded or elliptical grains resembling fish roe; when coarse they are called pisolites. Many of them are very pure and highly fossiliferous. The oolitic grains in section may have a nucleus, *e.g.* a fragment of a shell, quartz grain, &c., around which concentric layers have been deposited. In many cases there is also a radiating structure. They consist of calcite or aragonite, and between the grains there is usually a cementing material of limestone mud or granular calcite crystals. Deposits of silica, carbonate of iron or small rhombohedra of dolomite are often found in the interior of the spheroids, and oolites may be entirely silicified (Pennsylvania, Cambrian rocks of Scotland). Oolitic ironstones are very abundant in the Cleveland district of Yorkshire and form an important iron ore. They are often impure, and their iron may be present as haematite or as chalybite. Oolitic limestones are known from many geological formations, *e.g.* the Cambrian and Silurian of Scotland and Wales, Carboniferous limestone (Bristol), Jurassic, Tertiary and Recent limestones. They are forming at the present day in some coral reefs and in certain petrifying springs like those of Carlsbad. Their chief development in England is in the Jurassic rocks where they occur in large masses excellently adapted for building purposes, and yield the well-known freestones of Portland and Bath. Some hold that they are chemical precipitates and that the concentric oolitic structure is produced by successive layers of calcareous deposit laid down on fragments of shells, &c., in highly calcareous waters. An alternative hypothesis is that minute cellular plants (*Girvanella*, &c.), have extracted the carbonate of lime from the water, and have been the principal agents in producing the successive calcareous crusts. Such plants can live even in hot waters, and there seems much reason for regarding them as of importance in this connexion.

Another group of limestones is of inorganic or chemical origin, having been deposited from solution in water without the intervention of living organisms. A good example of these is the "stalactite" which forms pendent masses on the roofs of caves in limestone districts, the calcareous waters exposed to evaporation in the air of the cave laying down successive layers of stalactite in the places from which they drip. At the same time and in the same way "stalagmite" gathers on the floor below, and often accumulates in thick masses which contain bones of animals and the weapons of primitive cave-dwelling man. Calc sinters are porous limestones deposited by the evaporation of calcareous springs; travertine is a well-known Italian rock of this kind. At Carlsbad oolitic limestones are forming, but it seems probable that minute algae assist in this process. Chemical deposits of carbonate of lime may be produced by the evaporation of sea water in some upraised coral lagoons and similar situations, but it is unlikely that this takes place to any extent in the open sea, as sea water contains very little carbonate of lime, apparently because marine organisms so readily abstract it; still some writers believe that a considerable part of the chalk is really a chemical precipitate. Onyx marbles are banded limestones of chemical origin with variegated colours such as white, yellow, green and red. They are used for ornamental work and are obtained in Persia, France, the United States, Mexico, &c.

Limestones are exceedingly susceptible to chemical changes of a metasomatic kind. They are readily dissolved by carbonated waters and acid solutions, and their place may then be occupied by deposits of a different kind. The silification of oolites and coral rocks and their replacement by iron ores above mentioned are examples of this process. Many extensive hematite deposits are in this way formed in limestone districts. Phosphatization sometimes takes place, amorphous phosphate of lime being substituted for carbonate of lime, and these replacement products often have great value as sources of natural fertilizers. On ocean rocks in dry climates the droppings of birds (guano) which contain much phosphate, percolating into the underlying limestones change them into a hard white or yellow phosphate rock (*e.g.* Sombrero, Christmas Island, &c.), sometimes known as rock-guano or mineral guano. In the north of France beds of phosphate are found in the chalk; they occur also in England on a smaller scale. All limestones, especially those laid down in deep waters contain some lime phosphate, derived from shells of certain brachiopods, fish bones, teeth, whale bones, &c.

[illegible] solution and be redeposited in certain horizons, [illegible] the formation of flints. On the sea bottom at [illegible] phosphatic nodules are found which have gathered [illegible] of fishes and other animals. As in flint the [illegible] of the original limestone may be well preserved [illegible] mass is phosphatized.

[illegible] heated waters carrying mineral solutions are [illegible] deep seated masses of igneous rocks they often [illegible] their contents in limestone beds. At Leadville, [illegible] example, great quantities of rich silver lead ore, [illegible] not a little gold, have been obtained from the [illegible] rocks, though apparently equally favourably [illegible]. The lead and fluorspar deposits of the north [illegible] (Derbyshire) occur in limestone. In the [illegible] have been impregnated with tin oxide. [illegible] frequently associated with beds of limestone, as [illegible] Belgium, and copper ores are found in great [illegible] rocks of this kind. Apart from ore deposits [illegible] great number of different minerals, often well [illegible] observed in limestones. [illegible] occur among metamorphic schists or in the [illegible] masses (such as granite), they are usually [illegible] and their organic structures. They are then [illegible] or marbles (*q.v.*). (J. S. F.)

[illegible], an ecclesiastical term used to denote [illegible] church of St Peter and St Paul. A [illegible] undertaken *ex voto* or *ex lege*. The [illegible] accordance with a vow, were very frequent [illegible] were under the special protection of the [illegible] upon any who should molest pilgrims [illegible] sake." The question of granting [illegible] a vow gave rise to much canonical [illegible] had finally to give in to the [illegible] by law were of more importance. [illegible] decreed that all bishops subject to the [illegible] should meet personally every year in [illegible] the state of their dioceses. [illegible] all metropolitans of the [illegible] the bull *Romanus Pontifex*, [illegible] bishops of Italy, Dalmatia and [illegible] three years; those of France, Ger- [illegible] Belgium, Hungary, Bohemia and the [illegible] those from the rest of Europe [illegible] from other continents every ten [illegible] extended the summons to all [illegible] territorial jurisdiction.

[illegible] the name given to acts of [illegible] actions are limited in the United [illegible] the occurrence of the events [illegible]. This is one of the devices by [illegible] disputed claims. There [illegible] may be effected. We may [illegible] of a right or possession for a [illegible] title against all the world. [illegible] as PRESCRIPTION (*q.v.*). [illegible] during which the defendant in a [illegible] of enjoyment of the matter [illegible] statutes of limitation is to [illegible] which the plaintiff has been out [illegible] which he might first have [illegible] the lapse of the [illegible] from bringing his [illegible] the law is expressed by the [illegible] adopted in English law in [illegible] for the recovery of real [illegible] and no action could [illegible] before that date. [illegible] the [illegible] as the date of [illegible] "period of [illegible] in a different class [illegible]

A period absolutely fixed became in time useless for the purposes of limitation, and the method of counting back a certain number of years from the date of the writs was adopted in the Statute 32 Henry VIII. c. 2, which fixed periods of thirty, fifty and sixty years for various classes of actions named therein. A large number of statutes since that time have established periods of limitation for different kinds of actions. Of those now in force the most important are the Limitation Act 1623 for personal actions in general, and the Real Property Limitation Act 1833 relating to actions for the recovery of land. The latter statute has been repealed and virtually re-enacted by the Real Property Limitation Act 1874, which reduced the period of limitation from twenty years to twelve, for all actions brought after the 1st January 1879. The principal section of the act of 1833 will show the *modus operandi*: "After the 31st December 1833, no person shall make an entry or distress, or bring an action to recover any land or rent *but within twenty years next after the time* at which the right to make such entry or distress or to bring such action shall have first accrued to some person through whom he claims, or shall have first accrued to the person making or bringing the same." Another section defines the times at which the right of action or entry shall be deemed to have accrued in particular cases; *e.g.* when the estate claimed shall have been an estate or interest in reversion, such right shall be deemed to have first accrued at the time at which such estate or interest became an estate or interest in possession. Thus suppose lands to be let by A to B from 1830 for a period of fifty years, and that a portion of such lands is occupied by C from 1831 without any colour of title from B or A—C's long possession would be of no avail against an action brought by A for the recovery of the land after the determination of B's lease. A would have twelve years after the determination of the lease within which to bring his action, and might thus, by an action brought in 1891, disestablish a person who had been in quiet possession since 1831. What the law looks to is not the length of time during which C has enjoyed the property, but the length of time which A has suffered to elapse since he might first have brought his action. It is to be observed, however, that the Real Property Limitation Act does more than bar the remedy. It extinguishes the right, differing in this respect from the other Limitation Acts, which, while barring the remedy, preserve the right, so that it may possibly become available in some other way than by action.

By section 14 of the act of 1833, when any acknowledgment of the title of the person entitled shall have been given to him or his agent in writing signed by the person in possession, or in receipt of the profits or rent, then the right of the person (to whom such acknowledgment shall have been given) to make an entry or distress or bring an action shall be deemed to have first accrued at the time at which such acknowledgment, or the last of such acknowledgments, was given. By section 25, persons under the disability of infancy, lunacy or coverture, or beyond seas, and their representatives, are to be allowed ten years from the termination of this disability, or death (which shall have first happened), notwithstanding that the ordinary period of limitation shall have expired.

By the act of 1623 actions of trespass, detinue, trover, replevin or account, actions on the case (except for slander), actions of debt arising out of a simple contract and actions for arrears of rent not due upon specialty shall be limited to six years from the date of the cause of action. Actions for assault, menace, battery, wounds and imprisonment are limited to four years, and actions for slander to two years. Persons labouring under the disabilities of infancy, lunacy or unsoundness of mind are allowed the same time after the removal of the disability. When the defendant was "beyond seas" (*i.e.* outside the United Kingdom and the adjacent islands) an extension of time was allowed, but by the Real Property Limitation Act of 1874 such an allowance is excluded as to real property, and as to other matters by the Mercantile Law Amendment Act 1856.

An acknowledgment, whether by payment on account or by mere spoken words, was formerly sufficient to take the case out of the statute. The Act 9 Geo. IV. c. 14 (Lord Tenterden's act) requires any promise or admission of liability to be in writing and signed by the party to be charged, otherwise it will not bar the statute.

Contracts under seal are governed as to limitation by the act of 1883, which provides that actions for rent upon any indenture of demise, or of covenant, or debt or any bond or other specialty, and on recognizances, must be brought within twenty years after cause of action. Actions of debt on an award (the submission being not under seal), or for a copyhold fine, or for money levied on a writ of *fieri facias*, must be brought within six years. With regard to the rights of the crown, the principle obtains that *nullum tempus occurrit regi*, so that no statute of limitation affects the crown without express mention. But by the Crown Suits Act 1769, as amended by the Crown Suits Act 1861, in suits relating to land, the claims of the crown to recover are barred after the lapse of sixty years. For the prosecution of criminal offences generally there is no period of limitation, except where they are punishable on summary conviction. In such case the period is six months by the Summary Jurisdiction Act 1848. But there are various miscellaneous limitations fixed by various acts, of which the following may be noticed. Suits and indictments under penal statutes are limited to two years if the forfeiture is to the crown, to one year if the forfeiture is to the common informer. Penal actions by persons aggrieved are limited to two years by the act of 1833. Prosecutions under the Riot Act can only be sued upon within twelve months after the offence has been committed, and offences against the Customs Acts within three years. By the Public Authorities Protection Act 1893, a prosecution against any person acting in execution of statutory or other public duty must be commenced within six months. Prosecutions under the Criminal Law Amendment Act, as amended by the Prevention of Cruelty to Children Act 1904, must be commenced within six months after the commission of the offence.

Trustees are expressly empowered to plead statutes of limitation by the Trustees Act 1888; indeed, a defence under the statutes of limitations must in general be specially pleaded. Limitation is regarded strictly as a law of procedure. The English courts will therefore apply their own rules to all actions, although the cause of action may have arisen in a country in which different rules of limitation exist. This is also a recognized principle of private international law (see J. A. Foote, *Private International Law*, 3rd ed., 1904, p. 516 seq.).

United States.—The principle of the statute of limitations has passed with some modification into the statute-books of every state in the Union except Louisiana, whose laws of limitation are essentially the prescriptions of the civil law drawn from the *Partidas*, or "Spanish Code." As to personal actions, it is generally provided that they shall be brought within a certain specified time—usually six years or less—from the time when the cause of action accrues, and not after, while for land the "general if not universal limitation of the right to bring action or to make entry is to twenty years after the right to enter or to bring the action accrues" (Bouvier's *Law Dictionary*, art. "Limitations"). The constitutional provision prohibiting states from passing laws impairing the obligation of contracts is not infringed by a law of limitations, unless it bars a right of action already accrued without giving a reasonable term within which to bring the action.

See Darby and Bosanquet, *Statutes of Limitations* (1899); Hewitt, *Statutes of Limitations* (1893).

LIMOGES, a town of west-central France, capital of the department of Haute-Vienne, formerly capital of the old province of Limousin, 176 m. S. by W. of Orleans on the railway to Toulouse. Pop. (1906) town, 75,906; commune, 88,597. The station is a junction for Poitiers, Angoulême, Périgueux and Clermont-Ferrand. The town occupies a hill on the right bank of the Vienne, and comprises two parts originally distinct, the *Cité* with narrow streets and old houses occupying the lower slope, and the town proper the summit. In the latter a street known as the Rue de la Boucherie is occupied by a powerful and ancient corporation of butchers. The site of the fortifications which formerly surrounded both quarters is occupied by boulevards, outside which are suburbs with wide streets and spacious squares. The cathedral, the most remarkable building in the Limousin, was begun in 1273. In 1327 the choir was completed, and before the middle of the 16th century the transept, with its fine north portal and the first two bays of the nave; from 1875 to 1890 the construction of the nave was continued, and it was united with the west tower (203 ft. high), the base of which belongs to a previous Romanesque church. In the interior there are a magnificent rood loft of the Renaissance, and the tombs of Jean de Langeac (d. 1541) and other bishops. Of the other churches of Limoges, St Michel des Lions (14th and 15th centuries) and St Pierre du Queyroix (12th and 13th centuries) both contain interesting stained glass. The principal modern buildings are the town hall and the law-courts. The Vienne is crossed by a railway viaduct and four bridges, two of which, the Pont St Étienne and the Pont St Martial, date from the 13th century. Among the chief squares are the Place d'Orsay on the site of a Roman amphitheatre, the Place Jourdan with the statue of Marshal J. B. Jourdan, born at Limoges, and the Place d'Aine with the statue of J. L. Gay-Lussac. President Carnot and Denis Dussoubs, both of whom have statues, were also natives of the town. The museum has a rich ceramic collection and art, numismatic and natural history collections.

Limoges is the headquarters of the XII. army corps and the seat of a bishop, a prefect, a court of appeal and a court of assizes, and has tribunals of first instance and of commerce, a board of trade arbitration, a chamber of commerce and a branch of the Bank of France. The educational institutions include a *lycée* for boys, a preparatory school of medicine and pharmacy, a higher theological seminary, a training college, a national school of decorative art and a commercial and industrial school. The manufacture and decoration of porcelain give employment to about 13,000 persons in the town and its vicinity. Shoemaking and the manufacture of clogs occupy over 2000. Other industries are liqueur-distilling, the spinning of wool and cloth-weaving, printing and the manufacture of paper from straw. Enamelling, which flourished at Limoges in the middle ages and during the Renaissance (see ENAMEL), but subsequently died out, was revived at the end of the 19th century. There is an extensive trade in wine and spirits, cattle, cereals and wood. The Vienne is navigable for rafts above Limoges, and the logs brought down by the current are stopped at the entrance of the town by the inhabitants of the Naveix quarter, who form a special gild for this purpose.

Limoges was a place of importance at the time of the Roman conquest, and sent a large force to the defence of Alesia. In 11 B.C. it took the name of Augustus (*Augustoritum*); but in the 4th century it was anew called by the name of the *Lemovices*, whose capital it was. It then contained palaces and baths, had its own senate and the right of coinage. Christianity was introduced by St Martial. In the 5th century Limoges was devastated by the Vandals and the Visigoths, and afterwards suffered in the wars between the Franks and Aquitanians and in the invasions of the Normans. Under the Merovingian kings Limoges was celebrated for its mints and its goldsmiths' work. In the middle ages the town was divided into two distinct parts, each surrounded by walls, forming separate fiefs with a separate system of administration, an arrangement which survived till 1792. Of these the more important, known as the *Château*, which grew up round the tomb of St Martial in the 9th century, and was surrounded with walls in the 10th and again in the 12th, was under the jurisdiction of the viscounts of Limoges, and contained their castle and the monastery of St Martial; the other, the *Cité*, which was under the jurisdiction of the bishop, had but a sparse population, the habitable ground being practically covered by the cathedral, the episcopal palace and other churches and religious buildings. In the Hundred Years' War the bishops sided with the French, while the viscounts were unwilling vassals of the English. In 1370 the *Cité*, which had opened its gates to the French, was taken by the Black Prince and given over to fire and sword.

[illegible] pestilence and famine desolated Limoges [illegible] plague of 1630-1631 carried off more than [illegible]. The [illegible] administrations of Henri d'Aguesseau, [illegible], and of Turgot enabled Limoges to [illegible] prosperity. There have been several great [illegible] whole quarters of the city, built, as it then was, [illegible] lasted for two months, and destroyed [illegible] and that of 1864 laid under ashes a large area. [illegible] every seven years a curious religious festival [illegible], during which the relics of St Martial are [illegible] weeks, attracting large numbers of visitors. [illegible] the 10th century, and commemorates a pestilence [illegible] which, after destroying 40,000 persons, is [illegible] have been stayed by the intercession of the saint.

[illegible] the scene of two ecclesiastical councils, in 1029 [illegible] proclaimed the title of St Martial as "apostle [illegible] the second insisted on the observance of the [illegible]." In 1095 Pope Urban II. held a synod of [illegible] in connexion with his efforts to organize a crusade, [illegible] consecrated the basilica of St Martial [illegible] 1794).

[illegible] Limoges, in Joanne's guides, *De Paris à Agen* [illegible] *Limoges d'après ses anciens plans* [illegible] (3rd ed., 1894). A very full list of works [illegible] the town, viscounty, bishopric, &c., is given by U. [illegible] *des sources hist. du moyen âge. Topo-bibliogr.* [illegible]

[illegible] LIMON, the chief Atlantic port of Costa Rica, [illegible] and the capital of a district also named Limon, [illegible] Caribbean Sea, 103 m. E. by N. of San José. [illegible] Limon was founded in 1871, and is the [illegible] interoceanic railway to Puntarenas which [illegible] the same year. The swamps behind the town, [illegible] coral lagoon in front of it, have been filled in. [illegible] protected by a sea-wall built along the low-water [illegible] port affords accommodation for large vessels. [illegible] from the harbour to the island of Uvita, about [illegible] would render Limon a first-class port. There is [illegible] water supply from the hills above the harbour. [illegible] coffee and banana crops of Costa Rica are sent [illegible] at Limon to Europe and the United States. [illegible] of Limon comprises the whole Atlantic [illegible] including the Talamanca country inhabited by [illegible] Indians, the richest banana-growing territories in [illegible], and the valuable forests of the San Juan valley. [illegible] visited by Indians from the Mosquito coast of [illegible] who come in canoes to fish for turtle. Its chief towns, [illegible] are Reventazon and Matina, both with fewer than [illegible] inhabitants.

[illegible] or **Brown Iron Ore**, a natural ferric hydrate [illegible] (Gr. λειμών (meadow), in allusion to its occurrence [illegible] in meadows and marshes. It is never crystallized, [illegible] have a fibrous or microcrystalline structure, and [illegible] in concretionary forms or in compact and [illegible] sometimes mammillated, botryoidal, reniform [illegible]. The colour presents various shades of brown and [illegible] the streak is always brownish, a character which [illegible] from haematite with a red, or from magnetite [illegible] streak. It is sometimes called brown haematite. [illegible] a ferric hydrate, conforming typically with the [illegible] of $2Fe_2O_3 \cdot 3H_2O$. Its hardness is rather [illegible] and its specific gravity varies from 3·5 to 4. In many [illegible] it has been formed from other iron oxides, like haematite [illegible] by the alteration of pyrites or chalybite. [illegible] iron pyrites readily pass [illegible] and the masses [illegible] mineral-veins [illegible] associated with [illegible] been found, on [illegible] carbonate; and [illegible] limonite are well [illegible] ferrous silicate, [illegible]. The ferric [illegible] waters, often [illegible] iron ore of great economic value occur in many sedimentary rocks, such as the Lias, Oolites and Lower Greensand of various parts of England. They appear in some cases to be altered limestones and in others altered glauconitic sandstones. An oolitic structure is sometimes present, and the ores are generally phosphatic, and may contain perhaps 30% of iron. The oolitic brown ores of Lorraine and Luxembourg are known as "minette," a diminutive of the French mine (ore), in allusion to their low content of metal. Granular and concretionary limonite accumulates by organic action on the floor of certain lakes in Sweden, forming the curious "lake ore." Larger concretions formed under other conditions are known as "bean ore." Limonite often forms a cementing medium in ferruginous sands and gravels, forming "pan"; and in like manner it is the agglomerating agent in many conglomerates, like the South African "banket," where it is auriferous. In iron-shot sands the limonite may form hollow concretions, known in some cases as "boxes." The "eagle stones" of older writers were generally concretions of this kind, containing some substance, like sand, which rattled when the hollow nodule was shaken. Bog iron ore is an impure limonite, usually formed by the influence of micro-organisms, and containing silica, phosphoric acid and organic matter, sometimes with manganese. The various kinds of brown and yellow ochre are mixtures of limonite with clay and other impurities; whilst in umber much manganese oxide is present. Argillaceous brown iron ore is often known in Germany as *Thoneisenstein*; but the corresponding term in English (clay iron stone) is applied to nodular forms of impure chalybite. J. C. Ullmann's name of stilpnosiderite, from the Greek στιλπνός (shining), is sometimes applied to such kinds of limonite as have a pitchy lustre. Deposits of limonite in cavities may have a rounded surface or even a stalactitic form, and may present a brilliant lustre, of blackish colour, forming what is called in Germany *Glaskopf* (glass head). It often happens that analyses of brown iron ores reveal a larger proportion of water than required by the typical formula of limonite, and hence new species have been recognized. Thus the yellowish brown ore called by E. Schmidt xanthosiderite, from ξανθός (yellow) and σίδηρος (iron), contains $Fe_2O(OH)_4$, or $Fe_2O_3 \cdot 2H_2O$; whilst the bog ore known as limnite, from λίμνη (marsh) has the formula $Fe(OH)_3$ or $Fe_2O_3 \cdot 3H_2O$. On the other hand there are certain forms of ferric hydrate containing less water than limonite and approaching to haematite in their red colour and streak: such is the mineral which was called hydrohaematite by A. Breithaupt, and is now generally known under R. Hermann's name of turgite, from the mines of Turginsk, near Bogoslovsk in the Ural Mountains. This has the formula $Fe_4O_5(OH)_2$, or $2Fe_2O_3 \cdot H_2O$. It probably represents the partial dehydration of limonite, and by further loss of water may pass into haematite or red iron ore. When limonite is dehydrated and deoxidized in the presence of carbonic acid, it may give rise to chalybite.

LIMOUSIN (or Limosin), **LÉONARD** (c. 1505–c. 1577), French painter, the most famous of a family of seven Limoges enamel painters, was the son of a Limoges innkeeper. He is supposed to have studied under Nardon Pénicaud. He was certainly at the beginning of his career influenced by the German school—indeed, his earliest authenticated work, signed L. L. and dated 1532, is a series of eighteen plaques of the "Passion of the Lord," after Albrecht Dürer, but this influence was counterbalanced by that of the Italian masters of the school of Fontainebleau, Primaticcio, Rosso, Giulio Romano and Solario, from whom he acquired his taste for arabesque ornament and for mythological subjects. Nevertheless the French tradition was sufficiently ingrained in him to save him from becoming an imitator and from losing his personal style. In 1530 he entered the service of Francis I. as painter and *varlet de chambre*, a position which he retained under Henry II. For both these monarchs he executed many portraits in enamel—among them quite a number of plaques depicting Diane de Poitiers in various characters,—plates, vases, ewers, and cups, besides decorative works for the royal palaces, for, though he is best known as an enameller distinguished for rich colour, and for graceful designs in grisaille on black or bright blue backgrounds, he also enjoyed a great reputation as an oil-painter. His last signed works bear the date 1574, but the date of his death is uncertain, though it could not have been later than the beginning of 1577. It is on record that he executed close upon two thousand enamels. He is best represented at the Louvre, which owns his two famous votive tablets for the Sainte Chapelle, each consisting of twenty-three plaques, signed L. L. and dated 1553; "La Chasse," depicting Henry II. on a white horse, Diane de Poitiers behind him on horseback; and many portraits, including the kings by whom he was employed, Marguerite de Valois, the duc de Guise, and the cardinal de Lorraine. Other representative examples are at the Cluny and Limoges museums. In England some magnificent examples of his work are to be found at the Victoria and Albert Museum, the British Museum, and the Wallace Collection. In the collection of Signor Rocchi, in Rome, is an exceptionally interesting plaque representing Frances I. consulting a fortune-teller.

See *Léonard Limousin: peintre de portraits* (*L'Œuvre des peintres émailleurs*), by L. Boudery and E. Lachenaud (Paris, 1897)—a careful study, with an elaborate catalogue of the known existing examples of the artist's work. The book deals almost exclusively with the portraits illustrated. See also Alleaume and Duplessis, *Les Douze Apôtres—émaux de Léonard Limousin*, &c. (Paris, 1865); L. Boudery, *Exposition retrospective de Limoges en 1886* (Limoges, 1886); L. Boudery, *Léonard Limousin et son œuvre* (Limoges, 1895); *Limoges et le Limousin* (Limoges, 1865); A. Meyer, *L'Art de l'émail de Limoges, ancien et moderne* (Paris, 1896); Émile Molinier, *L'Émaillerie* (Paris, 1891).

LIMOUSIN (Lat. *Pagus Lemovicinus*, *ager Lemovicensis*, *regio Lemovicum*, *Lemosinum*, *Limosinium*, &c.), a former province of France. In the time of Julius Caesar the *pagus Lemovicinus* covered the county now comprised in the departments of Haute-Vienne, Corrèze and Creuse, with the *arrondissements* of Confolens in Charente and Nontron in Dordogne. These limits it retained until the 10th century, and they survived in those of the diocese of Limoges (except a small part cut off in 1317 to form that of Tulle) until 1790. The break-up into great fiefs in the 10th century, however, tended rapidly to disintegrate the province, until at the close of the 12th century Limousin embraced only the viscounties of Limoges, Turenne and Comborn, with a few ecclesiastical lordships, corresponding roughly to the present *arrondissements* of Limoges and Saint Yrien in Haute-Vienne and part of the *arrondissements* of Brive, Tulle and Ussel in Corrèze. In the 17th century Limousin, thus constituted, had become no more than a small *gouvernement*.

Limousin takes its name from the *Lemovices*, a Gallic tribe whose county was included by Augustus in the province of *Aquitanic Magna*. Politically its history has little of separate interest; it shared in general the vicissitudes of Aquitaine, whose dukes from 918 onwards were its over-lords at least till 1264, after which it was sometimes under them, sometimes under the counts of Poitiers, until the French kings succeeded in asserting their direct over-lordship. It was, however, until the 14th century, the centre of a civilization of which the enamelling industry (see Enamel) was only one expression. The Limousin dialect, now a mere *patois*, was regarded by the troubadours as the purest form of Provençal.

See A. Leroux, *Géographie et histoire du Limousin* (Limoges, 1892). Detailed bibliography in Chevalier, *Répertoire des sources. Topo-bibliogr.* (Montbéliard, 1902), t. ii. *s.v.*

LIMPOPO, or Crocodile, a river of S.E. Africa over 1000 m. in length, next to the Zambezi the largest river of Africa entering the Indian Ocean. Its head streams rise on the northern slopes of the Witwatersrand less than 300 m. due W. of the sea, but the river makes a great semicircular sweep across the high plateau first N.W., then N.E. and finally S.E. It is joined early in its course by the Marico and Notwani, streams which rise along the westward continuation of the Witwatersrand, the ridge forming the water-parting between the Vaal and the Limpopo basins. For a great part of its course the Limpopo forms the north-west and north frontiers of the Transvaal. Its banks are well wooded and present many picturesque views. In descending the escarpment of the plateau the river passes through rocky ravines, piercing the Zoutpansberg near the north-east corner of the Transvaal at the Toli Azimé Falls. In the low country it receives its chief affluent, the Olifants river (450 m. long), which, rising in the high veld of the Transvaal east of the sources of the Limpopo, takes a more direct N.E. course than the main stream. The Limpopo enters the ocean in 25° 15′ S. The mouth, about 1000 ft. wide, is obstructed by sand-banks. In the rainy season the Limpopo loses a good deal of its water in the swampy region along its lower course. High-water level is 24 ft. above low-water level, when the depth in the shallowest part does not exceed 3 ft. The river is navigable all the year round by shallow-draught vessels from its mouth for about 100 m., to a spot known as Gungunyana's Ford. In flood time there is water communication south with the river Komati (*q.v.*). At this season stretches of the Limpopo above Gungunyana's Ford are navigable. The river valley is generally unhealthy.

The basin of the Limpopo includes the northern part of the Transvaal, the eastern portion of Bechuanaland, southern Matabeleland and a large area of Portuguese territory north of Delagoa Bay. Its chief tributary, the Olifants, has been mentioned. Of its many other affluents, the Macloutsie, the Shashi and the Tuli are the most distant north-west feeders. In this direction the Matoppos and other hills of Matabeleland separate the Limpopo basin from the valley of the Zambezi. A little above the Tuli confluence is Rhodes's Drift, the usual crossing-place from the northern Transvaal into Matabeleland. Among the streams which, flowing north through the Transvaal, join the Limpopo is the Nylstroom, so named by Boers trekking from the south in the belief that they had reached the river Nile. In the coast region the river has one considerable affluent from the north, the Chengane, which is navigable for some distance.

The Limpopo is a river of many names. In its upper course called the Crocodile that name is also applied to the whole river, which figures on old Portuguese maps as the Oori (or Oira) and Bembe. Though claiming the territory through which it ran the Portuguese made no attempt to trace the river. This was first done by Captain J. F. Elton, who in 1870 travelling from the Tati goldfields sought to open a road to the sea via the Limpopo. He voyaged down the river from the Shashi confluence to the Toli Azimé Falls, which he discovered, following the stream thence on foot to the low country. The lower course of the river had been explored 1868–1869 by another British traveller—St Vincent Whitshed Erskine. It was first navigated by a sea-going craft in 1884, when G. A. Chaddock of the British mercantile service succeeded in crossing the bar, while its lower course was accurately surveyed by Portuguese officers in 1895–1896. At the junction of the Lotsani, one of the Bechuanaland affluents, with the Limpopo, are ruins of the period of the Zimbabwes.

LINACRE (or Lynaker), **THOMAS** (*c.* 1460–1524), English humanist and physician, was probably born at Canterbury. Of his parentage or descent nothing certain is known. He received his early education at the cathedral school of Canterbury, then under the direction of William Celling (William Tilly of Selling), who became prior of Canterbury in 1472. Celling was an ardent scholar, and one of the earliest in England who cultivated Greek learning. From him Linacre must have received his first incentive to this study. Linacre entered Oxford about the year 1480, and in 1484 was elected a fellow of All Souls' College. Shortly afterwards he visited Italy in the train of Celling, who was sent by Henry VIII. as an envoy to the papal court, and he accompanied his patron as far as Bologna. There he became the pupil of Angelo Polisiano, and afterwards shared the instruction which that great scholar imparted at Florence to the sons of Lorenzo de' Medici. The younger of these princes became Pope Leo X., and was in after years mindful of his old companionship with Linacre. Among his other teachers and friends in Italy were Demetrius Chalcondylas, Hermolaus Barbarus, Aldus Romanus the printer of Venice, and Nicolaus Leonicenus of Vicenza. Linacre took the degree of doctor of medicine with great distinction at Padua. On his return to Oxford, full of the learning and imbued with the spirit of the Italian Renaissance, he formed one of the brilliant circle of Oxford scholars, including John Colet, William Grocyn and William Latimer, who are mentioned with so much warm eulogy in the letters of Erasmus.

Linacre does not appear to have practised or taught medicine in Oxford. About the year 1501 he was called to court as tutor of the young prince Arthur. On the accession of Henry VIII. he was appointed the king's physician, an office at that time of considerable influence and importance, and practised medicine in London, having among his patients most of the great statesmen and prelates of the time, as Cardinal Wolsey, Archbishop Warham and Bishop Fox.

After some years of professional activity, and when in advanced life, Linacre received priest's orders in 1520, though he had for some years previously held several clerical benefices. There is no doubt that his ordination was connected with his retirement from active life. Literary labours, and the cares of the foundation which owed its existence chiefly to him, the Royal College of Physicians, occupied Linacre's remaining years till his death on the 20th of October 1524.

Linacre was more of a scholar than a man of letters, and rather a man of learning than a scientific investigator. It is difficult now to judge of his practical skill in his profession, but it was evidently highly esteemed in his own day. He took no part in political or theological questions, and died too soon to have to declare himself on either side in the formidable controversies which were even in his lifetime beginning to arise. But his career as a scholar was one eminently characteristic of the critical period in the history of learning through which he lived. He was one of the first Englishmen who studied Greek in Italy, whence he brought back to his native country and his own university the lessons of the "New Learning." His teachers were some of the greatest scholars of the day. Among his pupils was one—Erasmus—whose name alone would suffice to preserve the memory of his instructor in Greek, and others of note in letters and politics, such as Sir Thomas More, Prince Arthur and Queen Mary. Colet, Grocyn, William Lilye and other eminent scholars were his intimate friends, and he was esteemed by a still wider circle of literary correspondents in all parts of Europe.

Linacre's literary activity was displayed in two directions, in pure scholarship and in translation from the Greek. In the domain of scholarship he was known by the rudiments of (Latin) grammar (*Progymnasmata Grammatices vulgaria*), composed in English, a revised version of which was made for the use of the Princess Mary, and afterwards translated into Latin by Robert Buchanan. He also wrote a work on Latin composition, *De emendata structura Latini sermonis*, which was published in London in 1524 and many times reprinted on the continent of Europe.

Linacre's only medical works were his translations. He desired to make the works of Galen (and indeed those of Aristotle also) accessible to all readers of Latin. What he effected in the case of the first, though not trifling in itself, is inconsiderable as compared with the whole mass of Galen's writings; and of his translations from Aristotle, some of which are known to have been completed, nothing has survived. The following are the works of Galen translated by Linacre: (1) *De sanitate tuenda*, printed at Paris in 1517; (2) *Methodus medendi* (Paris, 1519); (3) *De temperamentis et de Inaequali Intemperie* (Cambridge, 1521); (4) *De naturalibus facultatibus* (London, 1523); (5) *De symptomatum differentiis et causis* (London, 1524); (6) *De pulsuum Usu* (London, without date). He also translated for the use of Prince Arthur an astronomical treatise of Proclus, *De sphaera*, which was printed at Venice by Aldus in 1499. The accuracy of these translations and their elegance of style were universally admitted. They have been generally accepted as the standard versions of those parts of Galen's writings, and frequently reprinted, either as a part of the collected works or separately.

But the most important service which Linacre conferred upon his own profession and science was not by his writings. To him was chiefly owing the foundation by royal charter of the College of Physicians in London, and he was the first president of the new college, which he further aided by conveying to it his own house, and by the gift of his library. Shortly before his death Linacre obtained from the king letters patent for the establishment of readerships in medicine at Oxford and Cambridge, and placed valuable estates in the hands of trustees for their endowment. Two readerships were founded in Merton College, Oxford, and one in St John's College, Cambridge, but owing to neglect and bad management of the funds, they fell into uselessness and obscurity. The Oxford foundation was revived by the university commission [illegible] in the form of the Linacre professorship of anatomy. [illegible] justice to the generosity and public spirit which [illegible] foundations; and it is impossible not to recognize [illegible] in the scheme of the College of Physicians, [illegible] not only first organized the medical profession in [illegible] upon it for some centuries the stamp of his [illegible]

The [illegible] fastidiousness of Linacre, and his habits of minute [illegible] Erasmus suggests, the chief cause why he left [illegible] literary memorials. It will be found, perhaps, [illegible] extant work the extremely high reputation [illegible] the scholars of his time. His Latin style [illegible] according to the flattering eulogium of [illegible] Latin in the version of Linacre than [illegible]; and even Aristotle displayed a grace [illegible] his native tongue. Erasmus praises [illegible] ("vir non exacti tantum sed severi [illegible] it was hard to say whether he were [illegible]an. Of Greek [illegible] was equally [illegible] works of the [illegible]y have been some exaggeration; but all have acknowledged the elevation of Linacre's character, and the fine moral qualities summed up in the epitaph written by John Caius: "Fraudes dolosque mire perosus; fidus amicis; omnibus ordinibus juxta carus."

The materials for Linacre's biography are to a large extent contained in the older biographical collections of George Lilly (in Paulus Jovius, *Descriptio Britanniae*), Bale, Leland and Pits, in Wood's *Athenae Oxonienses* and in the *Biographia Britannica*; but all are completely collected in the *Life of Thomas Linacre*, by Dr Noble Johnson (London, 1835). Reference may also be made to Dr Munk's *Roll of the Royal College of Physicians* (2nd ed., London, 1878); and the Introduction, by Dr J. F. Payne, to a facsimile reproduction of Linacre's version of *Galen de temperamentis* (Cambridge, 1881). With the exception of this treatise, none of Linacre's works or translations has been reprinted in modern times.

LINARES, an inland province of central Chile, between Talca on the N. and Ñuble on the S., bounded E. by Argentina and W. by the province of Maule. Pop. (1895) 101,858; area, 3942 sq. m. The river Maule forms its northern boundary and drains its northern and north-eastern regions. The province belongs partly to the great central valley of Chile and partly to the western slopes of the Andes, the S. Pedro volcano rising to a height of 11,800 ft. not far from the sources of the Maule. The northern part is fertile, as are the valleys of the Andean foothills, but arid conditions prevail throughout the central districts, and irrigation is necessary for the production of crops. The vine is cultivated to some extent, and good pasturage is found on the Andean slopes. The province is traversed from N. to S. by the Chilean Central railway, and the river Maule gives access to the small port of Constitucion, at its mouth. From Parral, near the southern boundary, a branch railway extends westward to Cauquenes, the capital of Maule. The capital, Linares, is centrally situated, on an open plain, about 20 m. S. of the river Maule. It had a population of 7331 in 1895 (which an official estimate of 1902 reduced to 7256). Parral (pop. 8586 in 1895; est. 10,219 in 1902) is a railway junction and manufacturing town.

LINARES, a town of southern Spain, in the province of Jaen, among the southern foothills of the Sierra Morena, 1375 ft. above sea-level and 3 m. N.W. of the river Guadalimar. Pop. (1900) 38,245. It is connected by four branch railways with the important argentiferous lead mines on the north-west, and with the main railways from Madrid to Seville, Granada and the principal ports on the south coast. The town was greatly improved in the second half of the 19th century, when the town hall, bull-ring, theatre and many other handsome buildings were erected; it contains little of antiquarian interest save a fine fountain of Roman origin. Its population is chiefly engaged in the lead-mines, and in such allied industries as the manufacture of gunpowder, dynamite, match for blasting purposes, rope and the like. The mining plant is entirely imported, principally from England; and smelting, desilverizing and the manufacture of lead sheets, pipes, &c., are carried on by British firms, which also purchase most of the ore raised. Linares lead is unsurpassed in quality, but the output tends to decrease. There is a thriving local trade in grain, wine and oil. About 2 m. S. is the village of Cazlona, which shows some remains of the ancient *Castulo*. The ancient mines some 5 m. N., which are now known as Los Pozos de Anibal, may possibly date from the 3rd century B.C., when this part of Spain was ruled by the Carthaginians.

LINCOLN, EARLS OF. The first earl of Lincoln was probably William de Roumare (*c.* 1095–*c.* 1155), who was created earl about 1140, although it is possible that William de Albini, earl of Arundel, had previously held the earldom. Roumare's grandson, another William de Roumare (*c.* 1150–*c.* 1198), is sometimes called earl of Lincoln, but he was never recognized as such, and about 1148 King Stephen granted the earldom to one of his supporters, Gilbert de Gand (d. 1156), who was related to the former earl. After Gilbert's death the earldom was dormant for about sixty years; then in 1216 it was given to another Gilbert de Gand, and later it was claimed by the great earl of Chester, Ranulf, or Randulph, de Blundevill (d. 1232). From Ranulf the title to the earldom passed through his sister Hawise to the family of Lacy, John de Lacy (d. 1240) being made earl of Lincoln in 1232. He was son of Roger de Lacy (d. 1212), justiciar of England and constable of Chester. It was held by the Lacys until the death of Henry, the 3rd earl. Henry served Edward I. in Wales, France and Scotland, both as a soldier and a diplomatist. He went to France with Edmund, earl of Lancaster, in 1296, and when Edmund died in June of this year, succeeded him as commander of the English forces in Gascony; but he did not experience any great success in this capacity and returned to England early in 1298. The earl fought at the battle of Falkirk in July 1298, and took some part in the subsequent conquest of Scotland. He was then employed by Edward to negotiate successively with popes Boniface VIII. and Clement V., and also with Philip IV. of France; and was present at the death of the English king in July 1307. For a short time Lincoln was friendly with the new king, Edward II., and his favourite, Piers Gaveston; but quickly changing his attitude, he joined earl Thomas of Lancaster and the baronial party, was one of the "ordainers" appointed in 1310 and was regent of the kingdom during the king's absence in Scotland in the same year. He died in London on the 5th of February 1311, and was buried in St Paul's Cathedral. He married Margaret (d. 1309), granddaughter and heiress of William Longsword, 2nd earl of Salisbury, and his only surviving child, Alice (1283–1348), became the wife of Thomas, earl of Lancaster, who thus inherited his father-in-law's earldoms of Lincoln and Salisbury. Lincoln's Inn in London gets its name from the earl, whose London residence occupied this site. He founded Whalley Abbey in Lancashire, and built Denbigh Castle.

In 1349 Henry Plantagenet, earl (afterwards duke) of Lancaster, a nephew of Earl Thomas, was created earl of Lincoln; and when his grandson Henry became king of England as Henry IV. in 1399 the title merged in the crown. In 1467 John de la Pole (*c.* 1464–1487), a nephew of Edward IV., was made earl of Lincoln, and the same dignity was conferred in 1525 upon Henry Brandon (1516–1545), son of Charles Brandon, duke of Suffolk. Both died without sons, and the next family to hold the earldom was that of Clinton.

Edward Fiennes Clinton, 9th Lord Clinton (1512–1585), lord high admiral and the husband of Henry VIII.'s mistress, Elizabeth Blount, was created earl of Lincoln in 1572. Before his elevation he had rendered very valuable services both on sea and land to Edward VI., to Mary and to Elizabeth, and he was in the confidence of the leading men of these reigns, including William Cecil, Lord Burghley. From 1572 until the present day the title has been held by Clinton's descendants. In 1768 Henry Clinton, the 9th earl (1720–1794), succeeded his uncle Thomas Pelham as 2nd duke of Newcastle-under-Lyne, and since this date the title of earl of Lincoln has been the courtesy title of the eldest son of the duke of Newcastle.

See G. E. C.(okayne), *Complete Peerage*, vol. v. (1893).

LINCOLN, ABRAHAM (1809–1865), sixteenth president of the United States of America, was born on "Rock Spring" farm, 3 m. from Hodgenville, in Hardin (now Larue) county, Kentucky, on the 12th of February 1809.[1] His grandfather,[2] Abraham Lincoln, settled in Kentucky about 1780 and was killed by Indians in 1784. His father, Thomas (1778–1851), was born in Rockingham (then Augusta) county, Virginia; he was hospitable, shiftless, restless and unsuccessful, working now as a carpenter and now as a farmer, and could not read or write before his marriage, in Washington county, Kentucky, on the 12th of June 1806, to Nancy Hanks (1783–1818), who was a native of Virginia, who is said to have been the illegitimate daughter of one Lucy Hanks, and who seems to have been, in intellect and character, distinctly above the social class in which she was born. The Lincolns had removed from Elizabethtown, Hardin county, their first home, to the Rock Spring farm, only a short time before Abraham's birth; about 1813 they removed to a farm of 238 acres on Knob Creek, about 6 m. from Hodgenville; and in 1816 they crossed the Ohio river and settled on a quarter-section, 1½ m. E. of the present village of Gentryville, in Spencer county, Indiana. There Abraham's mother died on the 5th of October 1818. In December 1819 his father married, at his old home, Elizabethtown, Mrs Sarah (Bush) Johnston (d. 1869), whom he had courted years before, whose thrift greatly improved conditions in the home, and who exerted a great influence over her stepson. Spencer county was still a wilderness, and the boy grew up in pioneer surroundings, living in a rude log-cabin, enduring many hardships and knowing only the primitive manners, conversation and ambitions of sparsely settled backwoods communities. Schools were rare, and teachers qualified only to impart the merest rudiments. "Of course when I came of age I did not know much," wrote he years afterward, "still somehow I could read, write and cipher to the rule of three, but that was all. I have not been to school since. The little advance I now have upon this store of education I have picked up from time to time under the pressure of necessity." His entire schooling, in five different schools, amounted to less than a twelvemonth; but he became a good speller and an excellent penman. His own mother taught him to read, and his stepmother urged him to study. He read and re-read in early boyhood the Bible, Aesop, *Robinson Crusoe*, *Pilgrim's Progress*, Weems's *Life of Washington* and a history of the United States; and later read every book he could borrow from the neighbours, Burns and Shakespeare becoming favourites. He wrote rude, coarse satires, crude verse, and compositions on the American government, temperance, &c. At the age of seventeen he had attained his full height, and began to be known as a wrestler, runner and lifter of great weights. When nineteen he made a journey as a hired hand on a flatboat to New Orleans.

In March 1830 his father emigrated to Macon county, Illinois (near the present Decatur), and soon afterward removed to Coles county. Being now twenty-one years of age, Abraham hired himself to Denton Offutt, a migratory trader and storekeeper then of Sangamon county, and he helped Offutt to build a flatboat and float it down the Sangamon, Illinois and Mississippi rivers to New Orleans. In 1831 Offutt made him clerk of his country store at New Salem, a small and unsuccessful settlement in Menard county; this gave him moments of leisure to devote to self-education. He borrowed a grammar and other books, sought explanations from the village schoolmaster and began to read law. In this frontier community law and politics claimed a large proportion of the stronger and the more ambitious men; the law early appealed to Lincoln and his general popularity encouraged him as early as 1832 to enter politics. In this year Offutt failed and Lincoln was thus left without employment. He became a candidate for the Illinois House of Representatives; and on the 9th of March 1832 issued an address "To the people of Sangamon county" which betokens talent and education far beyond mere ability to "read, write and cipher," though in its preparation he seems to have had the help of a friend. Before the election the Black Hawk Indian War broke out; Lincoln volunteered in one of the Sangamon county companies on the 21st of April and was elected captain by the members of the company. It is said that the oath of allegiance was administered to Lincoln at this time by Lieut. Jefferson Davis. The company, a part of the 4th Illinois, was mustered out after the five weeks' service for which it volunteered, and Lincoln re-enlisted as a private on the 29th of May, and was finally mustered out on the 16th of June by Lieut. Robert Anderson, who in 1861 commanded the Union troops at Fort Sumter. As captain Lincoln was twice in disgrace, once for firing a pistol near camp and again because nearly his entire company was intoxicated. He was in no battle, and always spoke lightly of his military record. He was defeated in his campaign for the legislature in

[1] Lincoln's birthday is a legal holiday in California, Colorado, Connecticut, Delaware, Florida, Illinois, Indiana, Iowa, Kansas, Michigan, Minnesota, Montana, Nevada, New Jersey, New York, North Dakota, Pennsylvania, South Dakota, Utah, Washington, West Virginia and Wyoming.

[2] Samuel Lincoln (*c.* 1619–1690), the president's first American ancestor, son of Edward Lincoln, gent., of Hingham, Norfolk, emigrated to Massachusetts in 1637 as apprentice to a weaver and settled with two older brothers in Hingham, Mass. His son and grandson were iron founders; the grandson Mordecai (1686–1736) moved to Chester county, Pennsylvania. Mordecai's son John (1711–*c.* 1773), a weaver, settled in what is now Rockingham county, Va., and was the president's great-grandfather.

amendment, and official proclamation made by President Johnson on the 18th of December 1865, declared it duly adopted.

The foreign policy of President Lincoln, while subordinate in importance to the great questions of the Civil War, nevertheless presented several difficult and critical problems for his decision. The arrest (8th of November 1861) by Captain Charles Wilkes of two Confederate envoys proceeding to Europe in the British steamer "Trent" seriously threatened peace with England. Public opinion in America almost unanimously sustained the act; but Lincoln, convinced that the rights of Great Britain as a neutral had been violated, promptly, upon the demand of England, ordered the liberation of the prisoners (26th of December). Later friendly relations between the United States and Great Britain, where, among the upper classes, there was a strong sentiment in favour of the Confederacy, were seriously threatened by the fitting out of Confederate privateers in British ports, and the Administration owed much to the skilful diplomacy of the American minister in London, Charles Francis Adams. A still broader foreign question grew out of Mexican affairs, when events culminating in the setting up of Maximilian of Austria as emperor under protection of French troops demanded the constant watchfulness of the United States. Lincoln's course was one of prudent moderation. France voluntarily declared that she sought in Mexico only to satisfy injuries done her and not to overthrow or establish local government or to appropriate territory. The United States Government replied that, relying on these assurances, it would maintain strict non-intervention, at the same time openly avowing the general sympathy of its people with a Mexican republic, and that "their own safety and the cheerful destiny to which they aspire are intimately dependent on the continuance of free republican institutions throughout America." In the early part of 1863 the French Government proposed a mediation between the North and the South. This offer President Lincoln (on the 6th of February) declined to consider, Seward replying for him that it would only be entering into diplomatic discussion with the rebels whether the authority of the government should be renounced, and the country delivered over to disunion and anarchy.

The Civil War gradually grew to dimensions beyond all expectation. By January 1863 the Union armies numbered near a million men, and were kept up to this strength till the end of the struggle. The Federal war debt eventually reached the sum of $2,700,000,000. The fortunes of battle were somewhat fluctuating during the first half of 1863, but the beginning of July brought the Union forces decisive victories. The reduction of Vicksburg (4th of July) and Port Hudson (9th of July), with other operations, restored complete control of the Mississippi, severing the Southern Confederacy. In the east Lee had the second time marched his army into Pennsylvania to suffer a disastrous defeat at Gettysburg, on the 1st, 2nd and 3rd of July, though he was able to withdraw his shattered forces south of the Potomac. At the dedication of this battlefield as a soldiers' cemetery in November, President Lincoln made the following oration, which has taken permanent place as a classic in American literature:—

"Fourscore and seven years ago our fathers brought forth on this continent a new nation, conceived in liberty, and dedicated to the proposition that all men are created equal. Now we are engaged in a great civil war, testing whether that nation, or any nation so conceived and so dedicated, can long endure. We are met on a great battlefield of that war. We have come to dedicate a portion of that field as a final resting place for those who here gave their lives that that nation might live. It is altogether fitting and proper that we should do this. But, in a larger sense, we cannot dedicate, we cannot consecrate, we cannot hallow this ground. The brave men, living and dead, who struggled here have consecrated it far above our poor power to add or detract. The world will little note nor long remember what we say here, but it can never forget what they did here. It is for us the living, rather, to be dedicated here to the unfinished work which they who fought here have thus far so nobly advanced. It is rather for us to be here dedicated to the great task remaining before us—[illegible] honoured dead [illegible] increased devotion [illegible] y gave the last full measure of devotion [illegible] that these dead shall not have died in vain, that this nation under God shall have a new birth of freedom, and that government of the people, by the people, for the people, shall not perish from the earth."

In the unexpected prolongation of the war, volunteer enlistments became too slow to replenish the waste of armies, and in 1863 the government was forced to resort to a draft. The enforcement of the conscription created much opposition in various parts of the country, and led to a serious riot in the city of New York on the 13th–16th of July. President Lincoln executed the draft with all possible justice and forbearance, but refused every importunity to postpone it. It was made a special subject of criticism by the Democratic party of the North, which was now organizing itself on the basis of a discontinuance of the war, to endeavour to win the presidential election of the following year. Clement L. Vallandigham of Ohio, having made a violent public speech at Mt. Vernon, Ohio, on the 1st of May against the war and military proceedings, was arrested on the 5th of May by General Burnside, tried by military commission, and sentenced on the 16th to imprisonment; a writ of *habeas corpus* had been refused, and the sentence was changed by the president to transportation beyond the military lines. By way of political defiance the Democrats of Ohio nominated Vallandigham for governor on the 11th of June. Prominent Democrats and a committee of the Convention having appealed for his release, Lincoln wrote two long letters in reply discussing the constitutional question, and declaring that in his judgment the president as commander-in-chief in time of rebellion or invasion holds the power and responsibility of suspending the privilege of the writ of *habeas corpus*, but offering to release Vallandigham if the committee would sign a declaration that rebellion exists, that an army and navy are constitutional means to suppress it, and that each of them would use his personal power and influence to prosecute the war. This liberal offer and their refusal to accept it counteracted all the political capital they hoped to make out of the case; and public opinion was still more powerfully influenced in behalf of the president's action, by the pathos of the query which he propounded in one of his letters: "Must I shoot the simple-minded soldier boy who deserts, while I must not touch a hair of a wily agitator who induces him to desert?" When the election took place in Ohio, Vallandigham was defeated by a majority of more than a hundred thousand.

Many unfounded rumours of a willingness on the part of the Confederate States to make peace were circulated to weaken the Union war spirit. To all such suggestions, up to the time of issuing his emancipation proclamation, Lincoln announced his readiness to stop fighting and grant amnesty, whenever they would submit to and maintain the national authority under the Constitution of the United States. Certain agents in Canada having in 1864 intimated that they were empowered to treat for peace, Lincoln, through Greeley, tendered them safe conduct to Washington. They were by this forced to confess that they possessed no authority to negotiate. The president thereupon sent them, and made public, the following standing offer:—

"To whom it may concern:

"Any proposition which embraces the restoration of peace, the integrity of the whole Union, and the abandonment of slavery, and which comes by and with an authority that can control the armies now at war against the United States, will be received and considered by the Executive Government of the United States, and will be met by liberal terms on substantial and collateral points, and the bearer or bearers thereof shall have safe conduct both ways.

"July 18, 1864." "ABRAHAM LINCOLN."

A noteworthy conference on this question took place near the close of the Civil War, when the strength of the Confederacy was almost exhausted. F. P. Blair, senior, a personal friend of Jefferson Davis, acting solely on his own responsibility, was permitted to go from Washington to Richmond, where, on the 12th of January 1865, after a private and unofficial interview, Davis in writing declared his willingness to enter a conference "to secure peace to the two countries." Report being duly made to President Lincoln, he wrote a note (dated 18th January) consenting to receive any agent sent informally "with the view of securing peace to the people of our common country." Upon the basis of this latter proposition three Confederate commissioners (A. H. Stevens, J. A. C. Campbell and R. M. T. Hunter) finally came to Hampton Roads, where President Lincoln and Secretary Seward met them on the U.S. steam transport "River Queen," and on the 3rd of February 1865 an informal conference of four hours' duration was held. Private reports of the interview agree substantially in the statement that the Confederates proposed a cessation of the Civil War, and postponement of its issues for future adjustment, while for the present the belligerents should unite in a campaign to expel the French from Mexico, and to enforce the Monroe doctrine. President Lincoln, however, although he offered to use his influence to secure compensation by the Federal government to slave-owners for their slaves, if there should be "voluntary abolition of slavery by the states," a liberal and generous administration of the Confiscation Act, and the immediate representation of the southern states in Congress, refused to consider any alliance against the French in Mexico, and adhered to the instructions he had given Seward before deciding to personally accompany him. These formulated three indispensable conditions to adjustment: first, the restoration of the national authority throughout all the states; second, no receding by the executive of the United States on the slavery question; third, no cessation of hostilities short of an end of the war, and the disbanding of all forces hostile to the government. These terms the commissioners were not authorized to accept, and the interview ended without result.

As Lincoln's first presidential term of four years neared its end, the Democratic party gathered itself for a supreme effort to regain the ascendancy lost in 1860. The slow progress of the war, the severe sacrifice of life in campaign and battle, the enormous accumulation of public debt, arbitrary arrests and suspension of *habeas corpus*, the rigour of the draft, and the proclamation of military emancipation furnished ample subjects of bitter and vindictive campaign oratory. A partisan coterie which surrounded M'Clellan loudly charged the failure of his Richmond campaign to official interference in his plans. Vallandigham had returned to his home in defiance of his banishment beyond military lines, and was leniently suffered to remain. The aggressive spirit of the party, however, pushed it to a fatal extreme. The Democratic National Convention adopted (August 29, 1864) a resolution (drafted by Vallandigham) declaring the war a failure, and demanding a cessation of hostilities; it nominated M'Clellan for president, and instead of adjourning *sine die* as usual, remained organized, and subject to be convened at any time and place by the executive national committee. This threatening attitude, in conjunction with alarming indications of a conspiracy to resist the draft, had the effect to thoroughly consolidate the war party, which had on the 8th of June unanimously renominated Lincoln, and had nominated Andrew Johnson of Tennessee for the vice-presidency. At the election held on the 8th of November 1864, Lincoln received 2,216,076 of the popular votes, and M'Clellan (who had openly disapproved of the resolution declaring the war a failure) but 1,808,725; while of the presidential electors 212 voted for Lincoln and 21 for M'Clellan. Lincoln's second term of office began on the 4th of March 1865.

While this political contest was going on the Civil War was being brought to a decisive close. Grant, at the head of the Army of the Potomac, followed Lee to Richmond and Petersburg, and held him in siege to within a few days of final surrender. General W. T. Sherman, commanding the bulk of the Union forces in the Mississippi Valley, swept in a victorious march through the heart of the Confederacy to Savannah on the coast, and thence northward to North Carolina. Lee evacuated Richmond on the 2nd of April, and was overtaken by Grant and compelled to surrender his entire army on the 9th of April 1865. Sherman pushed Johnston to a surrender on the 26th of April. This ended the war.

Lincoln being at the time on a visit to the army, entered Richmond the day after its surrender. Returning to Washington, he made his last public address on the evening of the 11th of April, devoted mainly to the question of reconstructing loyal governments in the conquered states. On the evening of the 14th of April he attended Ford's theatre in Washington. While seated with his family and friends absorbed in the play, John Wilkes Booth, an actor, who with others had prepared a plot to assassinate the several heads of government, went into the little corridor leading to the upper stage-box, and secured it against ingress by a wooden bar. Then stealthily entering the box, he discharged a pistol at the head of the president from behind, the ball penetrating the brain. Brandishing a huge knife, with which he wounded Colonel Rathbone who attempted to hold him, the assassin rushed through the stage-box to the front and leaped down upon the stage, escaping behind the scenes and from the rear of the building, but was pursued, and twelve days afterwards shot in a barn where he had concealed himself. The wounded president was borne to a house across the street, where he breathed his last at 7 A.M. on the 15th of April 1865.

President Lincoln was of unusual stature, 6 ft. 4 in., and of spare but muscular build; he had been in youth remarkably strong and skilful in the athletic games of the frontier, where, however, his popularity and recognized impartiality oftener made him an umpire than a champion. He had regular and prepossessing features, dark complexion, broad high forehead, prominent cheek bones, grey deep-set eyes, and bushy black hair, turning to grey at the time of his death. Abstemious in his habits, he possessed great physical endurance. He was almost as tender-hearted as a woman. "I have not willingly planted a thorn in any man's bosom," he was able to say. His patience was inexhaustible. He had naturally a most cheerful and sunny temper, was highly social and sympathetic, loved pleasant conversation, wit, anecdote and laughter. Beneath this, however, ran an undercurrent of sadness; he was occasionally subject to hours of deep silence and introspection that approached a condition of trance. In manner he was simple, direct, void of the least affectation, and entirely free from awkwardness, oddity or eccentricity. His mental qualities were—a quick analytic perception, strong logical powers, a tenacious memory, a liberal estimate and tolerance of the opinions of others, ready intuition of human nature; and perhaps his most valuable faculty was rare ability to divest himself of all feeling or passion in weighing motives of persons or problems of state. His speech and diction were plain, terse, forcible. Relating anecdotes with appreciative humour and fascinating dramatic skill, he used them freely and effectively in conversation and argument. He loved manliness, truth and justice. He despised all trickery and selfish greed. In arguments at the bar he was so fair to his opponent that he frequently appeared to concede away his client's case. He was ever ready to take blame on himself and bestow praise on others. "I claim not to have controlled events," he said, "but confess plainly that events have controlled me." The Declaration of Independence was his political chart and inspiration. He acknowledged a universal equality of human rights. "Certainly the negro is not our equal in colour," he said, "perhaps not in many other respects; still, in the right to put into his mouth the bread that his own hands have earned, he is the equal of every other man white or black." He had unchanging faith in self-government. "The people," he said, "are the rightful masters of both congresses and courts, not to overthrow the constitution, but to overthrow the men who pervert the constitution." Yielding and accommodating in non-essentials, he was inflexibly firm in a principle or position deliberately taken. "Let us have faith that right makes might," he said, "and in that faith let us to the end dare to do our duty as we understand it." The emancipation proclamation once issued, he reiterated his purpose never to retract or modify it. "There have been men base enough," he said, "to propose to me to return to slavery our black warriors of Port Hudson and Olustee, and thus win the respect of the masters they fought. Should I do so I should deserve to be damned in time and eternity. Come what will, I will keep my faith with friend and foe." Benevolence and forgiveness were the very basis of his character; his world-wide humanity is aptly embodied in a phrase of his second inaugural: "With malice toward none, with charity for all." His nature was deeply religious, but he belonged to no denomination.

Lincoln married in Springfield on the 4th of November 1842, Mary Todd (1818–1882), also a native of Kentucky, who bore him four sons, of whom the only one to grow up was the eldest, Robert Todd Lincoln (b. 1843), who graduated at Harvard in 1864, served as a captain on the staff of General Grant in 1865, was admitted to the Illinois bar in 1867, was secretary of war in the cabinets of Presidents Garfield and Arthur in 1881–1885, and United States Minister to Great Britain in 1889–1893, and was prominently connected with many large corporations, becoming in 1897 president of the Pullman Co.

Of the many statues of President Lincoln in American cities, the best known is that, in Chicago, by St Gaudens. Among the [illegible] two by Thomas Ball, one in statuary hall in the Capitol at Washington, and one in Boston; two—one in Rochester, N.Y., and one in Springfield, Ill.—by Leonard W. Volk, who made a life-mask and a bust of Lincoln in 1860; and one by [illegible] Ward, in Lincoln Park, Washington. Francis B. Carpenter painted in 1864 "Lincoln signing the Emancipation Proclamation," now in the Capitol at Washington.

See *The Complete Works of Abraham Lincoln* (12 vols., New York, [illegible]; enlarged from the 2-volume edition of 1894 by John G. Nicolay and John Hay). There are various editions of the Lincoln-Douglas debates of 1858; perhaps the best is that edited by E. E. Sparks (1908). There are numerous biographies, and biographical [illegible], including: John G. Nicolay and John Hay, *Abraham Lincoln: A History* (10 vols., New York, 1890), a monumental work by his [illegible] who treat primarily his official life; John G. Nicolay, *A Short Life of Abraham Lincoln* (New York, 1904), con[illegible] from the preceding; John T. Morse, Jr., *Abraham Lincoln* (2 vols., Boston, 1893), in the "American Statesmen" series, an [illegible] biography, dealing chiefly with Lincoln's political [illegible] Tarbell, *The Early Life of Lincoln* (New York, 1896) and *Life of Abraham Lincoln* (2 vols., New York, 1900), containing [illegible] to which too great prominence and credence is some[illegible] Carl Schurz, *Abraham Lincoln: An Essay* (Boston, [illegible] able estimate; Ward H. Lamon, *The Life of Abraham Lincoln from his Birth to his Inauguration as President* [illegible] supplemented by *Recollections of Abraham Lincoln* [illegible] Chicago, 1895), compiled by Dorothy Lamon, valuable [illegible] recollections, but tactless, uncritical, and marred [illegible] the writer, who as marshal of the District of Columbia, [illegible] to prove that Lincoln's melancholy was [illegible] belief of the orthodox sort; William H. [illegible] W. Weik, *Abraham Lincoln, the True Story of a* [illegible] Chicago, 1889; revised, 2 vols., New York, [illegible] and ill-proportioned biography by Lincoln's law [illegible] the importance of the petty incidents of [illegible]; Isaac N. Arnold, *History of Abraham Lincoln and the Overthrow of Slavery* (Chicago, 1867), revised and [illegible] *Abraham Lincoln* (Chicago, 1885), valuable for [illegible] Gideon Welles, *Lincoln and Seward* (New [illegible] of Lincoln's secretary of the navy to Charles [illegible] delivered in Albany in April 1873) on [illegible] W. H. Seward, in which Adams claimed [illegible] of Lincoln's administration; F. B. [illegible] *White House* (New York, 1866), an [illegible] daily life while president; Robert T. [illegible] New York, 1906); A. Rothschild, *Lincoln*, [illegible] 1906); J. Eaton and E. O. Mason, [illegible] (New York, 1907); R. W. Gilder, [illegible] *Genius for Expression* (New York, [illegible] *Lincoln: An American Migration* [illegible] study of the Lincoln family in America; [illegible] *Problem: Abraham Lincoln's Solution* [illegible] Lea and J. R. Hutchinson, *The* [illegible] (Boston, 1909), a careful genealogical [illegible] *Lincoln's Plan of Reconstruction* [illegible] account of Lincoln as president [illegible] *United States from the Compromise of* [illegible]

(J. G. N.; C. C. W.)

[illegible] of a city, municipal, county and [illegible] the county town of Lincolnshire, [illegible] It is picturesquely situated on [illegible] the limestone ridge of the Cliff [illegible] the north bank of the river [illegible] the Foss Dyke, to an altitude of [illegible] cathedral rises majestically from [illegible] landmark for many miles. Lincoln [illegible] the Great Northern railway; [illegible] Great Eastern, Great Central [illegible]

[illegible] cities in England. The [illegible] of the hill beyond the [illegible] town consisted of two [illegible] extending west from [illegible] west of the castle keep. [illegible] the town increased in size [illegible] this point down the [illegible]

north wall in a line with the Newport gate. This is the oldest part of the town, and is named "above hill." After the departure of the Romans, the city walls were extended still farther in a south direction across the Witham as far as the great bar gate, the south entrance to the High Street of the city; the junction of these walls with the later Roman one was effected immediately behind Broad Street. The "above hill" portion of the city consists of narrow irregular streets, some of which are too steep to admit of being ascended by carriages. The south portion, which is named "below hill," is much more commodious, and contains the principal business premises. Here also are the railway stations.

The glory of Lincoln is the noble cathedral of the Blessed Virgin Mary, commonly known as the Minster. As a study to the architect and antiquary this stands unrivalled, not only as embodying the earliest purely Gothic work extant, but as containing within its compass every variety of style from the simple massive Norman of the central west front, and the later and more ornate examples of that style in the west doorways and towers; onward through all the Gothic styles, of each of which both early and late examples appear. The building material is the oolite and calcareous stone of Lincoln Heath and Haydor, which has the peculiarity of becoming hardened on the surface when tooled. Formerly the cathedral had three spires, all of wood or leaded timber. The spire on the central tower, which would appear to have been the highest in the world, was blown down in 1547. Those on the two western towers were removed in 1808.

The ground plan of the first church, adopted from that of Rouen, was laid by Bishop Remigius in 1086, and the church was consecrated three days after his death, on the 6th of May 1092. The west front consists of an Early English screen (*c.* 1225) thrown over the Norman front, the west towers rising behind it. The earliest Norman work is part of that of Remigius; the great portals and the west towers up to the third storey are Norman *c.* 1148. The upper parts of them date from 1365. Perpendicular windows (*c.* 1450) are inserted. The nave and aisles were completed *c.* 1220. The transepts mainly built between 1186 and 1235 have two fine rose windows, that in the N. is Early English, and that in the S. Decorated. The first has beautiful contemporary stained glass. These are called respectively the Dean's Eye and Bishop's Eye. A Galilee of rich Early English work forms the entrance of the S. transept. Of the choir the western portion known as St Hugh's (1186–1204) is the famous first example of pointed work; the eastern, called the Angel Choir, is a magnificently ornate work completed in 1280. Fine Perpendicular canopied stalls fill the western part. The great east window, 57 ft. in height, is an example of transition from Early English to Decorated *c.* 1288. Other noteworthy features of the interior are the Easter sepulchre (*c.* 1300), the foliage ornamentation of which is beautifully natural; and the organ screen of a somewhat earlier date. The great central tower is Early English as far as the first storey, the continuation dates from 1307. The total height is 271 ft.; and the tower contains the bell, Great Tom of Lincoln, weighing over 5 tons. The dimensions of the cathedral internally are—nave, 252×79·6×80 ft.; choir, 158×82×72 ft.; angel choir, which includes presbytery and lady chapel, 166×44×72 ft.; main transept, 220×63×74 ft.; choir transept, 166×44×72 ft. The west towers are 206 ft. high.

The buildings of the close that call for notice are the chapter-house of ten sides, 60 ft. diameter, 42 ft. high, with a fine vestibule of the same height, built *c.* 1225, and therefore the earliest of English polygonal chapter-houses, and the library, a building of 1675, which contains a small museum. The picturesque episcopal palace contains work of the date of St Hugh, and the great hall is mainly Early English. There is some Decorated work, and much Perpendicular, including the gateway. It fell into disuse after the Reformation, but by extensive restoration was brought back to its proper use at the end of the 19th century. Among the most famous bishops were St Hugh of Avalon (1186–1200); Robert Grosseteste (1235–1253); Richard Flemming (1420–1431), founder of Lincoln College, Oxford; William Smith (1495–1514), founder of Brasenose College, Oxford; William Wake (1705–1716); and Edmund Gibson (1716–1723). Every stall has produced a prelate or cardinal. The see covers almost the whole of the county, with very small portions of Norfolk and Yorkshire, and it included Nottinghamshire until the formation of the bishopric of Southwell in 1884. At its earliest formation, when Remigius, almoner of the abbey of Fécamp, removed the seat of the bishopric here from Dorchester in Oxfordshire shortly after the Conquest, it extended from the Humber to the Thames, eastward beyond Cambridge, and westward beyond Leicester. It was reduced, however, by the formation of the sees of Ely, Peterborough and Oxford, and by the rearrangement of diocesan boundaries in 1837.

The remains of Roman Lincoln are of the highest interest. The Newport Arch or northern gate of *Lindum* is one of the most perfect specimens of Roman architecture in England. It consists of a great arch flanked by two smaller arches, of which one remains. The Roman Ermine Street runs through it, leading northward almost in a straight line to the Humber. Fragments of the town wall remain at various points; a large quantity of coins and other relics have been discovered; and remains of a burial-place and buildings unearthed. Of these last the most important is the series of column-bases, probably belonging to a Basilica, beneath a house in the street called Bail Gate, adjacent to the Newport Arch. A villa in Greetwell; a tesselated pavement, a milestone and other relics in the cloister; an altar unearthed at the church of St Swithin, are among many other discoveries. Among churches, apart from the minster, two of outstanding interest are those of St Mary-le-Wigford and St Peter-at-Gowts (*i.e.* sluice-gates), both in the lower part of High Street. Their towers, closely similar, are fine examples of perhaps very early Norman work, though they actually possess the characteristics of pre-Conquest workmanship. Bracebridge church shows similar early work; but as a whole the churches of Lincoln show plainly the results of the siege of 1644, and such buildings as St Botolph's, St Peter's-at-Arches and St Martin's are of the period 1720–1740. Several churches are modern buildings on ancient sites. There were formerly three small priories, five friaries and four hospitals in or near Lincoln. The preponderance of friaries over priories of monks is explained by the fact that the cathedral was served by secular canons. Bishop Grosseteste was the devoted patron of the friars, particularly the Franciscans, who were always in their day the town missionaries. The Greyfriars, near St Swithin's church, is a picturesque two-storied building of the 13th century. Lincoln is rich in early domestic architecture. The building known as John of Gaunt's stables, actually St Mary's Guild Hall, is of tw storeys, with rich Norman doorway and moulding. The Jews' House is another fine example of 12th-century building; and Norman remains appear in several other houses, such as Deloraine Court and the House of Aaron the Jew. Lincoln Castle, lying W. of the cathedral, was newly founded by William the Conqueror when Remigius decided to found his minster under its protection. The site, with its artificial mounds, is of much earlier, probably British, date. There are Norman remains in the Gateway Tower; parts of the walls are of this period, and the keep dates from the middle of the 12th century. Among medieval gateways, the Exchequer Gate, serving as the finance-office of the chapter, is a fine specimen of 13th-century work. Pottergate is of the 14th century, and Stonebow in High Street of the 15th, with the Guildhall above it. St Dunstan's Lock is the name, corrupted from Dunestall, now applied to the entrance to the street where a Jewish quarter was situated: here lived the Christian boy afterwards known as "little St Hugh," who was asserted to have been crucified by the Jews in 1255. His shrine remains in the S. choir aisle of the minster. Other antiquities are the Perpendicular conduit of St Mary in High Street and the High Bridge, carrying High Street over the Witham, which is almost unique in England as retaining some of the old houses upon it.

Among modern public buildings are the county hall, old and new corn exchanges and public library. Educational establishments include a grammar school, a girls' high school, a science and art school and a theological college. The arboretum in Monks Road is the principal pleasure-ground; and there is a race-course. The principal industry is the manufacture of agricultural machinery and implements; there are also iron foundries and maltings, and a large trade in corn and agricultural produce. The parliamentary borough, returning one member, falls between the Gainsborough division of the county on the N., and that of Sleaford on the S. Area, 3755 acres.

History.—The British Lindun, which, according to the geography of Claudius Ptolemaeus, was the chief town of the Coritani, was probably the nucleus of the Roman town of Lindum. This was at first a Roman legionary fortress, and on the removal of the troops northward was converted into a municipality with the title of *colonia*. Such important structural remains as have been described attest the rank and importance of the place, which, however, did not attain a very great size. Its bishop attended the council of Arles in 314, and Lincoln (*Lindocolina*, *Lincolle*, *Nicole*) is mentioned in the Itinerary of Antoninus written about 320. Although said to have been captured by Hengest in 475 and recovered by Ambrosius in the following year, the next authentic mention of the city is Bede's record that Paulinus preached in Lindsey in 628 and built a stone church at Lincoln in which he consecrated Honorius archbishop of Canterbury. During their inroads into Mercia, the Danes in 877 established themselves at Lincoln, which was one of the five boroughs recovered by King Edmund in 941. A mint established here in the reign of Alfred was maintained until the reign of Edward I. (Mint Street turning from High Street near the Stonebow recalls its existence.) At the time of the Domesday Survey Lincoln was governed by twelve Lawmen, relics of Danish rule, each with hereditable franchises of sac and soc. Whereas it had rendered £20 annually to King Edward, and £10 to the earl, it then rendered £100. There had been 1150 houses, but 240 had been destroyed since the time of King Edward. Of these 166 had suffered by the raising of the castle by William I. in 1068 partly on the site of the Roman camp. The strength of the position of the castle brought much fighting on Lincoln. In 1141 King Stephen regained both castle and city from the empress Maud, but was attacked and captured in the same year at the "Joust of Lincoln." In 1144 he besieged the castle, held by the earl of Chester, and recovered it as a pledge in 1146. In 1191 it was held by Gerard de Camville for Prince John and was besieged by William Longchamp, Richard's chancellor, in vain; in 1216 it stood a siege by the partisans of the French prince Louis, who were defeated at the battle called Lincoln Fair on the 19th of May 1217. Granted by Henry III. to William Longepée, earl of Salisbury, in 1224, the castle descended by the marriage of his descendant Alice to Thomas Plantagenet, and became part of the duchy of Lancaster.

In 1157 Henry II. gave the citizens their first charter, granting them the city at a fee-farm rent and all the liberties which they had had under William II., with their gild merchant for themselves and the men of the county as they had then. In 1200 the citizens obtained release from all but pleas of the Crown without the walls, and pleas of external tenure, and were given the pleas of the Crown within the city according to the customs of the city of London, on which those of Lincoln were modelled. The charter also gave them quittance of toll and lastage throughout the kingdom, and of certain other dues. In 1210 the citizens owed the exchequer £100 for the privilege of having a mayor, but the office was abolished by Henry III. and by Edward I. in 1290, though restored by the charter of 1300. In 1275 the citizens claimed the return of writs, assize of bread and ale and other royal rights, and in 1301 Edward I., when confirming the previous charters, gave them quittance of murage, pannage, pontage and other dues. The mayor and citizens were given criminal jurisdiction in 1327, when the burghmanmot held weekly in the gildhall since 1272 by the mayor and bailiffs was ordered to hear all local pleas which led to friction with the judges of assize. The city became a separate county by charter of 1409, when it was decreed that the bailiffs should henceforth be sheriffs and the mayor the king's escheator, and the mayor and sheriffs with four others justices of the peace with defined jurisdiction. As the result of numerous complaints of inability to pay the fee-farm rent of £180 Edward IV. enlarged the bounds of the city in 1466, while Henry VIII. in 1546 gave the citizens four advowsons, and possibly also in consequence of declining trade the city markets were made free of tolls in 1554. Incorporated by Charles I. in 1628 under a common council with 13 aldermen, 4 coroners and other officers, Lincoln surrendered its charters in 1684, but the first charter was restored after the Revolution, and was in force till 1834.

Parliaments were held at Lincoln in 1301, 1316 and 1327, and the city returned two burgesses from 1295 to 1885, when it lost one member. After the 13th century the chief interests [illegible] of Lincoln were ecclesiastical and commercial. As early as 1103 [illegible] that a rich citizen of Lincoln kept the treasure of King Magnus of Norway, supplying him with all he [illegible], and there is other evidence of intercourse with Scandinavia. There was an important Jewish colony, Aaron of Lincoln being one of the most influential financiers in the kingdom between 1166 and 1186. It was probably jealousy of their wealth that brought the charge of the crucifixion of "little St Hugh" in 1255 upon the Jewish community. Made a staple [illegible] wool, leather and skins in 1291, famous for its scarlet cloth [illegible] the 14th century, Lincoln had a few years of great prosperity, [illegible] with the transference of the staple to Boston early in the [illegible] of Edward III., its trade began to decrease. The craft [illegible] important until after the Reformation, a pageant [illegible] held in 1564. The fair now held during the last whole [illegible] April would seem to be identical with that granted by [illegible] 1284. Edward III. authorized a fair from St [illegible] day to the feast of SS Peter and Paul in 1327, and [illegible] gave one for the first Wednesday in September [illegible] the present November fair is, perhaps, a survival [illegible] by Henry IV. in 1409 for fifteen days before the [illegible] of St Hugh.

[illegible] *Manuscripts Commission, Report*, xiv., appendix [illegible] *Lincolina, from its municipal and other* [illegible] G. Williams, "Lincoln Civic Insignia," [illegible], vols. vi.-viii. (Horncastle, 1901– [illegible] *County History, Lincolnshire*.

[illegible] [illegible] and the county-seat of Logan county, [illegible] the N. central part of the state, 156 m. S.W. [illegible] m. N.E. of Springfield. Pop. (1900) [illegible] were foreign-born; (1910 census) 10,892. [illegible] the Illinois Central and the Chicago & Alton [illegible] Illinois Traction Interurban Electric line. [illegible] the state asylum for feeble-minded [illegible] Jacksonville in 1865 and removed to [illegible] Lincoln College (Presbyterian) founded [illegible] an orphans' home, supported by the [illegible] Odd Fellows, and a Carnegie library. [illegible] which Abraham Lincoln often practised [illegible] situated in a productive grain region, [illegible]. The value of the factory products [illegible] in 1900 to $784,248 in 1905, or 109%. [illegible] the site of Lincoln was made in 1835, [illegible] chartered in 1857.

[illegible] [illegible] Nebraska, U.S.A., county-seat of [illegible] of the state. Pop. (1900) 40,169 [illegible] census) 43,973. It is served by [illegible] Quincy, the Chicago, Rock Island & [illegible] the Missouri Pacific and the Chicago & [illegible]. Lincoln is one of the most attractive [illegible]. Salt Creek, an affluent of the [illegible] this side the city has repeatedly [illegible] buildings include a state [illegible] hall, formerly the U.S. govern- [illegible] a county court-house; a federal [illegible] library (1902); a hospital [illegible] a home for the friendless, [illegible] a state penitentiary and asylum [illegible]; and the university of [illegible] are three denominational [illegible] University (Methodist Episcopal, [illegible] College (Seventh Day Ad- [illegible] Cotner University (Disciples [illegible] the Nebraska Christian Uni- [illegible] the city limits are the state [illegible] held annually. Lincoln is the [illegible]. The surrounding country is [illegible] immediate W. environs [illegible] Lincoln's [illegible] to [illegible]

The salt-springs attracted the first permanent settlers to the site of Lincoln in 1856, and settlers and freighters came long distances to reduce the brine or to scrape up the dry-weather surface deposits. In 1886–1887 the state sank a test-well 2463 ft. deep, which discredited any hope of a great underground flow or deposit. Scarcely any use is made of the salt waters locally. Lancaster county was organized extra-legally in 1859, and under legislative act in 1864; Lancaster village was platted and became the county-seat in 1864 (never being incorporated); and in 1867, when it contained five or six houses, its site was selected for the state capital after a hard-fought struggle between different sections of the state (see NEBRASKA).[1] The new city was incorporated as Lincoln (and formally declared the county-seat by the legislature) in 1869, and was chartered for the first time as a city of the second class in 1871; since then its charter has been repeatedly altered. After 1887 it was a city of the first class, and after 1889 the only member of the highest subdivision in that class. After a "reform" political campaign, the ousting in 1887 of a corrupt police judge by the mayor and city council, in defiance of an injunction of a federal court, led to a decision of the U.S. Supreme Court, favourable to the city authorities and important in questions of American municipal government.

LINCOLN JUDGMENT, THE. In this celebrated English ecclesiastical suit, the bishop of Lincoln (Edward King, *q.v.*) was cited before his metropolitan, the archbishop of Canterbury (Dr Benson), to answer charges of various ritual offences committed at the administration of Holy Communion in the church of St Peter at Gowts, in the diocese of Lincoln, on the 4th of December 1887, and in Lincoln cathedral on the 18th of December 1887. The promoters were Ernest de Lacy Read, William Brown, Felix Thomas Wilson and John Marshall, all inhabitants of the diocese of Lincoln, and the last two parishioners of St Peter at Gowts. The case has a permanent importance in two respects. First, certain disputed questions of ritual were legally decided. Secondly, the jurisdiction of the archbishop of Canterbury alone to try one of his suffragan bishops for alleged ecclesiastical offences was considered and judicially declared to be well founded both by the judicial committee of privy council and by the archbishop of Canterbury with the concurrence of his assessors. The proceedings were begun on the 2nd of June 1888 by a petition presented by the promoters to the archbishop, praying that a citation to the bishop of Lincoln might issue calling on him to answer certain ritual charges. On the 26th of June 1888 the archbishop, by letter, declined to issue citation, on the ground that until instructed by a competent court as to his jurisdiction, he was not clear that he had it. The promoters appealed to the judicial committee of the privy council, to which an appeal lies under 25 Henry VIII. c. 19 for "lack of justice" in the archbishop's court. The matter was heard on the 20th of July 1888, and on the 8th of August 1888 the committee decided (i.) that an appeal lay from the refusal of the archbishop to the judicial committee, and (ii.) that the archbishop had jurisdiction to issue a citation to the bishop of Lincoln and to hear the promoters' complaint, but they abstained from expressing an opinion as to whether the archbishop had a discretion to refuse citation—whether, in fact, he had any power of "veto" over the prosecution. The case being thus remitted to the archbishop, he decided to entertain it, and on the 4th of January 1889 issued a citation to the bishop of Lincoln.

On the 12th of February 1889 the archbishop of Canterbury sat in Lambeth Palace Library, accompanied by the bishops of London (Dr Temple), Winchester (Dr Harold Browne), Oxford (Dr Stubbs) and Salisbury (Dr Wordsworth), and the vicar-general (Sir J. Parker Deane) as assessors. The bishop of Lincoln appeared in person and read a "Protest" to the archbishop's jurisdiction to try him except in a court composed of the archbishop and all the bishops of the province as judges. The court adjourned in order that the question of jurisdiction might be argued. On the 11th of May the archbishop gave judgment to

[1] Lincoln was about equally distant from Pawnee City and the Kansas border, the leading Missouri river towns, and the important towns of Fremont and Columbus on the N. side of the Platte.

the effect that whether sitting alone or with assessors he had jurisdiction to entertain the charge. On the 23rd and 24th of July 1889 a further preliminary objection raised by the bishop of Lincoln's counsel was argued. The offences alleged against the bishop of Lincoln were largely breaches of various rubrics in the communion service of the Prayer Book which give directions to the "minister." These rubrics are by the Acts of Uniformity (1 Elizabeth c. 2, and 13 & 14 Car. II. c. 4) made legally binding. But it was argued that a bishop is not a "minister" so as to be bound by the rubrics. The archbishop, however, held otherwise, and the assessors (except the bishop of Salisbury, who dissented) concurred in this decision. At this and subsequent hearings the bishop of Hereford (Dr Atlay) took the place of the bishop of Winchester as an assessor, and the bishop of Rochester (Dr Thorold), originally appointed an assessor, but absent from England at the outset, was present.

The case was heard on its merits in February 1890, before the archbishop and all the assessors, and the archbishop delivered his judgment on the 21st of November 1890. The alleged offences were eight in number. No facts were in dispute, but only the legality of the various matters complained of. I. The bishop was charged with having mixed water with wine in the chalice during the communion service, and II. with having administered the chalice so mixed to the communicants. It was decided that the mixing of the water with the wine during service was illegal, because an additional ceremony not enjoined in the Prayer Book, but that the administration of the mixed chalice, the mixing having been effected before service, was in accordance with primitive practice and not forbidden in the Church of England. III. The bishop was charged with the ceremonial washing of the vessels used for the holy communion, and with drinking the water used for these ablutions. It was decided that the bishop had committed no offence, and that what he had done was a reasonable compliance with the requirement of the rubric that any of the consecrated elements left over at the end of the celebration should be then and there consumed. IV. The bishop was charged with taking the eastward position (*i.e.* standing at the west side of the holy table with his face to the east and his back to the congregation) during the ante-communion service (*i.e.* the part of the communion service prior to the consecration prayer). The rubric requires the celebrant to stand at the north side of the table. A vast amount of research convinced the archbishop that this is an intentionally ambiguous phrase which may with equal accuracy be applied to the north end of the table as now arranged in churches, and to the long side of the table, which, in Edward VI.'s reign, was often placed lengthwise down the church, so that the long sides would face north and south. It was therefore decided (one of the assessors dissenting) that both positions are legal, and that the bishop had not offended in adopting the eastward position. V. The bishop was charged with so standing during the consecration prayer that the "Manual Acts" of consecration were invisible to the people gathered round. It should be stated that the courts (see *Ridsdale* v. *Clifton*, L.R. 1 P.D. 316; 2 P.D. 276) had already decided that the eastward position during the consecration prayer was legal, but that it must not be so used by the celebrant as to conceal the "Manual Acts." The archbishop held that the bishop of Lincoln had transgressed the law in this particular. VI. The bishop was charged with having, during the celebration of holy communion, allowed two candles to be alight on a shelf or retable behind the altar when they were not necessary for giving light. The archbishop decided that the mere presence of two altar candles burning during the service, but lit before it began, was lawful under the First Prayer Book of Edward VI., and has never been made unlawful, and, therefore, that the bishop was justified in what he had done. VII. The bishop was charged with having permitted the hymn known as *Agnus Dei* to be sung immediately after the consecration of the elements at a celebration of the holy communion. The archbishop decided that the use of hymns in divine service was too firmly established to be legally questioned, and that there was nothing to differentiate the use of this particular hymn at this point of the service from the use of other hymns on other occasions in public worship. VIII. The bishop was charged with making the sign of the Cross in the air with his hand in the benediction and at other times during divine service. The archbishop held that these crossings were ceremonies not enjoined and, therefore, illegal. The judgment confined itself to the legal declarations here summarized, and pronounced no monition or other sentence on the bishop of Lincoln in respect of the matters in which he appeared to have committed breaches of the ecclesiastical law.

Charges and decisions.

The promoters appealed to the judicial committee. The bishop did not appear on the appeal, which was therefore argued on the side of the promoters only. The appeal was heard in June and July 1891, before Lords Halsbury, Hobhouse, Esher, Herschell, Hannen and Shand and Sir Richard Couch, with the bishop of Chichester (Dr Durnford), the bishop of St Davids (Dr Basil Jones) and the bishop of Lichfield (Dr Maclagan) as episcopal assessors. The points appealed were those above numbered II., III., IV., VI., VII. Judgment was given on the 2nd of August 1892, and the appeal failed on all points. As to II., III., IV., and VII. the Committee agreed with the archbishop. As to VI. (altar lights) they held that, as it was not shown that the bishop was responsible for the presence of lighted candles, the charge could not be sustained against him, and so dismissed it without considering the general question of the lawfulness of altar lights. They also held that the archbishop was within his right in pronouncing no sentence against the bishop, who, it should be added, conformed his practice to the judgment from the date of its delivery. (L. T. D.)

LINCOLNSHIRE, an eastern county of England, bounded N. by the Humber, E. by the German Ocean and the Wash, S.E. for 3 m. by Norfolk, S. by Cambridgeshire and Northamptonshire, S.W. by Rutland, W. by Leicestershire and Nottinghamshire and N.W. by Yorkshire. The area is 2646 sq. m., the county being second to Yorkshire of the English counties in size.

The coast-line, about 110 m. in length, including the Humber shore, is generally low and marshy, and artificial banks for guarding against the inroads of the sea are to be found, in places, all along the coast. From Grimsby to Skegness traces of a submarine forest are visible; but while the sea is encroaching upon some parts of the coast it is receding from others, as shown by Holbeach, which is now 6 m. from the sea. Several thousand acres have been reclaimed from this part of the Wash, and round the mouth of the Nene on the south-east. The deep bay between the coasts of Lincolnshire and Norfolk, called the Wash, is full of dangerous sandbanks and silt; the navigable portion off the Lincolnshire coast is known as the Boston Deeps. The rapidity of the tides in this inlet, and the lowness of its shores, which are generally indistinct on account of mist from a moderate offing, render this the most difficult portion of the navigation of the east coast of England. On some parts of the coast there are fine stretches of sand, and Cleethorpes, Skegness, Mablethorpe and Sutton-on-Sea are favourite resorts for visitors.

The surface of Lincolnshire is generally a large plain, small portions of which are slightly below the level of the sea. The south-east parts are perfectly flat; and about one-third of the county consists of fens and marshes, intersected in all directions by artificial drains, called locally dykes, delphs, drains, becks, leams and eaux. This flat surface is broken by two ranges of calcareous hills running north and south through the county, and known as the Lincoln Edge or Heights, or the Cliff, and the Wolds. The former range, on the west, runs nearly due north from Grantham to Lincoln, and thence to the Humber, traversing the Heaths of Lincolnshire, which were formerly open moors, rabbit warrens and sheep walks, but are now enclosed and brought into high cultivation. The Wolds form a ridge of bold hills extending from Spilsby to Barton-on-Humber for about 40 m., with an average breadth of about 8 m. The Humber separates Lincolnshire from Yorkshire. Its ports on the Lincolnshire side are the small ferry-ports of Barton and New Holland, and the important harbour of Grimsby. The Trent forms part of the boundary with Nottinghamshire, divides the Isle of Axholme (q.v.) from the district of Lindsey, and falls into the Humber about 50 m. below Gainsborough. The Witham rises on the S.W. border of the county, flows north past Grantham to Lincoln, and thence E. and S.E. to Boston, after a course of about 80 m. The Welland rises in north-west Northamptonshire, enters the county at Stamford, and, after receiving the Glen, flows through an artificial channel into the Fosdyke Wash. The Nene in the south-east has but a small portion of its course in Lincolnshire. It flows due north through an artificial outfall, called the Wisbech Cut. Between the Wolds and the sea lie the Marshes, a level tract of rich alluvial soil extending from Barton-on-Humber to Wainfleet, varying in breadth from 5 to 10 m. Between the Welland and the Nene in the south-east of the county are Gedney Marsh, Holbeach Marsh, Moulton Marsh and Sutton Marsh.

The Fens (q.v.), the soil of which has been formed partly by marine deposits and partly by the decay of forests, occupy the Isle of Axholme on the north-west, the vale of Ancholme on the north, and much of the country south-east of Lincoln. The chief of them are the Holland, Wildmore, West and East Fens draining into the Witham, and the Deeping, Bourn, Great Porsand, and Spalding Fens draining into the Welland.

Much of the lands adjoining the tidal reaches of the Trent and the Ancholme and part of those around the Wash have been raised above the natural level and enriched by the process of warping, which consists in letting the tide run over the land, and retaining it there a sufficient time to permit the deposit of the sand and mud held in solution by the waters.

[illegible] The geological formations for the most part extend in [illegible] the line of the length of the county, from [illegible] and succeed one another in ascending order from [illegible] The lowest is the Triassic Keuper found in the Isle of [illegible] the valley of the Trent in the form of marls, sand-[illegible] Fish scales and teeth, with bones and foot-[illegible], are met with in the sandstone. The [illegible] dug for brick-making. The beds dip gently [illegible] At the junction between the Trias and Lias are [illegible] Rhaetics, which seem to mark a transition from [illegible] These beds are in part exposed in pits near [illegible] north by Gainsborough to where the Trent [illegible] Humber, passing thence into Yorkshire. The char-[illegible] found at Lea, 2 m. south of Gainsborough, with [illegible] of fish teeth and scales. The Lower Lias comes [illegible] a valuable bed of ironstone now largely worked. [illegible] 25 ft. in thickness, and crops out at Scunthorpe [illegible] where the workings are open and shallow. The [illegible] enters the county near Woolsthorpe, is about [illegible] and is very variable both in thickness and mineral-[illegible] the iron ores of Denton and Caythorpe belong to [illegible] Lias enters the county at Stainby, passing [illegible] Lincoln where it is worked for bricks. The Lias [illegible] about 8 or 10 m. in width in the south, narrowing [illegible] it is about a mile in width. To this succeed the [illegible] The Inferior Oolite, somewhat narrower than [illegible] the boundary with Rutland due north past [illegible] of the Humber; it forms the Cliff of Lincoln-[illegible] escarpment facing westward. At Lincoln the [illegible] the river Witham. The principal member of [illegible] the Lincolnshire limestone, which is an important [illegible] is quarried at Lincoln, Ponton, Ancaster, and [illegible] building stone. Eastward of the Inferior Oolite [illegible] of the Great Oolite and Cornbrash. The [illegible] clay and Corallian is very narrow in the [illegible] widening gradually about Sleaford. It then [illegible] Lincoln with decreasing width to the vicinity [illegible] Upper Oolite, Kimeridge clay, starts from the [illegible] and after attaining its greatest width near [illegible] north-west to the Humber. The Kimeridge [illegible] the Spilsby sandstone, Tealby limestone, [illegible] stone which represent the highest Jurassic [illegible] rocks. In the Cretaceous system of the [illegible] and runs nearly parallel with the Upper [illegible] to the Humber. The Upper Green-[illegible] in Lincolnshire by the Red Chalk, run [illegible] widening out as far as Kelstern on the east. [illegible] The Chalk formation, about equal in [illegible] extends from Burgh across the [illegible] county, comprising all its south-east [illegible] Oolite belt and the sea, all its north-[illegible] the sea, and a narrow [illegible] consists of alluvial deposits or of reclaimed marsh. In the northern part boulder clay and glacial sands cover considerable tracts of the older rocks. Bunter, Permian, and Coal Measure strata have been revealed by boring to underlie the Keuper near Haxey.

Gypsum is dug in the Isle of Axholme, whiting is made from the chalk near the shores of the Humber, and lime is made on the Wolds. Freestone is quarried around Ancaster, and good oolite building stone is quarried near Lincoln and other places. Ironstone is worked at several places and there are some blast furnaces.

At Woodhall Spa on the Horncastle branch railway there is a much-frequented bromine and iodine spring.

Climate, Soil and Agriculture.—The climate of the higher grounds is healthy, and meteorological observation does not justify the reputation for cold and damp often given to the county as a whole. The soils vary considerably, according to the geological formations; ten or twelve different kinds may be found in going across the country from east to west. A good sandy loam is common in the Heath division; a sandy loam with chalk, or a flinty loam on chalk marl, abounds on portions of the Wolds; an argillaceous sand, merging into rich loam, lies on other portions of the Wolds; a black loam and a rich vegetable mould cover most of the Isle of Axholme on the north-west; a well-reclaimed marine marsh, a rich brown loam, and a stiff cold clay variously occupy the low tracts along the Humber, and between the north Wolds and the sea; a peat earth, a deep sandy loam, and a rich soapy blue clay occupy most of the east and south Fens; and an artificial soil, obtained by "warping," occupies considerable low strips of land along the tidal reaches of the rivers.

Lincolnshire is one of the principal agricultural, especially grain-producing, counties in England. Nearly nine-tenths of the total area is under cultivation. The wide grazing lands have long been famous, and the arable lands are specially adapted for the growth of wheat and beans. The largest individual grain-crop, however, is barley. Both cattle and sheep are bred in great numbers. The cattle raised are the Shorthorns and improved Lincolnshire breeds. The dairy, except in the vicinity of large towns, receives little attention. The sheep are chiefly of the Lincolnshire and large Leicestershire breeds, and go to the markets of Yorkshire and London. Lincolnshire has long been famous for a fine breed of horses both for the saddle and draught. Horse fairs are held every year at Horncastle and Lincoln. Large flocks of geese were formerly kept in the Fens, but their number has been diminished since the drainage of these parts. Where a large number of them were bred, nests were constructed for them one above another; they were daily taken down by the gooseherd, driven to the water, and then reinstated in their nests, without a single bird being misplaced. Decoys were once numerous in the undrained state of the Fens.

Industries and Communications.—Manufactures are few and, relatively to the agricultural industry, small. The mineral industries, however, are of value, and there are considerable agricultural machine and implement factories at Lincoln, Boston, Gainsborough, Grantham and Louth. At Little Bytham a very hard brick, called adamantine clinker, is made of the siliceous clay that the Romans used for similar works. Bone-crushing, tanning, the manufacture of oil-cake for cattle, and rope-making are carried on in various places. Grimsby is an important port both for continental traffic and especially for fisheries; Boston is second to it in the county; and Gainsborough has a considerable traffic on the Trent. Sutton Bridge is a lesser port on the Wash.

The principal railway is the Great Northern, its main line touching the county in the S.W. and serving Grantham. Its principal branches are from Peterborough to Spalding, Boston, Louth and Grimsby; and from Grantham to Sleaford and Boston, and to Lincoln, and Boston to Lincoln. This company works jointly with the Great Eastern the line from March to Spalding, Lincoln, Gainsborough and Doncaster, and with the Midland that from Saxby to Bourn, Spalding, Holbeach, Sutton Bridge and King's Lynn. The Midland company has a branch from Newark to Lincoln, and the Lancashire, Derbyshire, and East Coast line terminates at Lincoln. The Great Central railway connects the west, Sheffield and Doncaster with Grimsby, and with Hull by ferry from New Holland. Canals connect Louth with the Humber, Sleaford with the Witham, and Grantham with the Trent near Nottingham; but the greater rivers and many of the drainage cuts are navigable, being artificially deepened and embanked.

Population and Administration.—The area of the ancient county is 1,693,550 acres, with a population in 1891 of 472,878 and in 1901 of 498,847. The primary divisions are three trithings or Ridings (q.v.). The north division is called the Parts of Lindsey, the south-west the Parts of Kesteven, and the south-east the Parts of Holland. Each of these divisions had in early times its own reeve or gerefa. Each constitutes an administrative county, the Parts of Lindsey having an area of 967,689 acres; Kesteven, 465,877 acres; and Holland, 262,766 acres. The Parts of Lindsey contain 17 wapentakes; Kesteven, exclusive of the soke and borough of Grantham and the borough of Stamford, 9 wapentakes; and Holland, 3 wapentakes. The municipal boroughs and urban districts are as follows:—

1. Parts of Lindsey.—Municipal boroughs—Grimsby, a county borough (pop. 63,138), Lincoln, a city and county borough and the county town (48,784). Louth (9518). Urban districts—Alford

(2478), Barton-upon-Humber (5671), Brigg (3137), Broughton (1300), Brumby and Frodingham (2273), Cleethorpes with Thrunscoe (12,578), Crowle (2769), Gainsborough (17,660), Horncastle (4038), Mablethorpe (934), Market Rasen (2188), Roxby-cum-Risby (389), Scunthorpe (6750), Skegness (2140), Winterton (1361), Woodhall Spa (988).

2. Parts of Kesteven.—Municipal boroughs—Grantham (17,593), Stamford (8229). Urban districts—Bourne (4361), Bracebridge (1752), Ruskington (1196), Sleaford (5468).

3. Parts of Holland.—Municipal borough—Boston (15,667). Urban districts—Holbeach (4755), Long Sutton (2524), Spalding (9385), Sutton Bridge (2105). In the Parts of Holland the borough of Boston has a separate commission of the peace and there are two petty sessional divisions. Lincolnshire is in the Midland circuit. In the Parts of Kesteven the boroughs of Grantham and Stamford have each a separate commission of the peace and separate courts of quarter sessions, and there are 4 petty sessional divisions. In the Parts of Lindsey the county boroughs of Grimsby and Lincoln have each a separate commission of the peace and a separate court of quarter sessions, while the municipal borough of Louth has a separate commission of the peace, and there are 14 petty sessional divisions. The three administrative counties and the county boroughs contain together 761 civil parishes. The ancient county contains 580 ecclesiastical parishes and districts, wholly or in part. It is mostly in the diocese of Lincoln, but in part also in the dioceses of Southwell and York. For parliamentary purposes the county is divided into seven divisions, namely, West Lindsey or Gainsborough, North Lindsey or Brigg, East Lindsey or Louth, South Lindsey or Horncastle, North Kesteven or Sleaford, South Kesteven or Stamford, and Holland or Spalding, and the parliamentary boroughs of Boston, Grantham, Grimsby and Lincoln, each returning one member.

History.—Of the details of the English conquest of the district which is now Lincolnshire little is known, but at some time in the 6th century Engle and Frisian invaders appear to have settled in the country north of the Witham, where they became known as the Lindiswaras, the southern districts from Boston to the Trent basin being at this time dense woodland. In the 7th century the supremacy over Lindsey alternated between Mercia and Northumbria, but few historical references to the district are extant until the time of Alfred, whose marriage with Ealswitha was celebrated at Gainsborough three years before his accession. At this period the Danish inroads upon the coast of Lindsey had already begun, and in 873 Healfdene wintered at Torksey, while in 878 Lincoln and Stamford were included among the five Danish boroughs, and the organization of the districts dependent upon them probably resulted about this time in the grouping of Lindsey, Kesteven and Holland to form the shire of Lincoln. The extent and permanence of the Danish influence in Lincolnshire is still observable in the names of its towns and villages and in the local dialect, and, though about 918 the confederate boroughs were recaptured by Edward the Elder, in 993 a Viking fleet again entered the Humber and ravaged Lindsey, and in 1013 the district of the five boroughs acknowledged the supremacy of Sweyn. The county offered no active resistance to the Conqueror, and though Hereward appears in the Domesday Survey as a dispossessed under-tenant of the abbot of Peterborough at Witham-on-the-Hill, the legends surrounding his name do not belong to this county. In his northward march in 1068 the Conqueror built a castle at Lincoln, and portioned out the principal estates among his Norman followers, but the Domesday Survey shows that the county on the whole was leniently treated, and a considerable number of Englishmen retained their lands as subtenants.

The origin of the three main divisions of Lincolnshire is anterior to that of the county itself, and the outcome of purely natural conditions, Lindsey being in Roman times practically an island bounded by the swamps of the Trent and the Witham on the west and south and on the east by the North Sea, while Kesteven and Holland were respectively the regions of forest and of fen. Lindsey in Norman times was divided into three ridings—North, West and South—comprising respectively five, five and seven wapentakes; while, apart from their division into wapentakes, the Domesday Survey exhibits a unique planning out of the ridings into approximately equal numbers of 12-carucate hundreds, the term hundred possessing here no administrative or local significance, but serving merely as a unit of area for purposes of assessment. The Norman division of Holland into the three wapentakes of Elloe, Kirton and Skirbeck has remained unchanged to the present day. In Kesteven the wapentakes of Aswardhurn, Aveland, Beltisloe, Haxwell, Langoe, Loveden, Ness, Winnibriggs, and Grantham Soke have been practically unchanged, but the Domesday wapentakes of Boothby and Graffo now form the wapentake of Boothby Graffo. In Northriding Bradley and Haverstoe have been combined to form Bradley Haverstoe wapentake, and the Domesday wapentake of Epworth in Westriding has been absorbed in that of Manley. Wall wapentake in Westriding was a liberty of the bishop of Lincoln, and as late as 1515 the dean and chapter of Lincoln claimed delivery and return of writs in the manor and hundred of Navenby. In the 13th century Baldwin Wake claimed return of writs and a market in Aveland. William de Vesci claimed liberties and exemptions in Caythorpe, of which he was summoned to render account at the sheriff's tourn at Halton. The abbot of Peterborough, the abbot of Tupholme, the abbot of Bardney, the prior of Catleigh, the prior of Sixhills, the abbot of St Mary's, York, the prioress of Stixwould and several lay owners claimed liberties and jurisdiction in their Lincolnshire estates in the 13th century.

The shire court for Lincolnshire was held at Lincoln every forty days, the lords of the manor attending with their stewards, or in their absence the reeve and four men of the vill. The ridings were each presided over by a riding-reeve, and wapentake courts were held in the reign of Henry I. twelve times a year, and in the reign of Henry III. every three weeks, while twice a year all the freemen of the wapentake were summoned to the view of frankpledge or tourn held by the sheriff. The boundaries between Kesteven and Holland were a matter of dispute as early as 1389 and were not finally settled until 1816.

Lincolnshire was originally included in the Mercian diocese of Lichfield, but, on the subdivision of the latter by Theodore in 680, the fen-district was included in the diocese of Lichfield, while the see for the northern parts of the county was placed at "Sidnacester," generally identified with Stow. Subsequently both dioceses were merged in the vast West-Saxon bishopric of Dorchester, the see of which was afterwards transferred to Winchester, and by Bishop Remigius in 1072 to Lincoln. The archdeaconry of Lincoln was among those instituted by Remigius, and the division into rural deaneries also dates from this period. Stow archdeaconry is first mentioned in 1138, and in 1291 included four deaneries, while the archdeaconry of Lincoln included twenty-three. In 1536 the additional deaneries of Hill, Holland, Loveden and Graffoe had been formed within the archdeaconry of Lincoln, and the only deaneries created since that date are East and West Elloe and North and South Grantham in Lincoln archdeaconry. The deaneries of Gartree, Grimsby, Hill, Horncastle, Louthesk, Ludborough, Walshcroft, Wraggoe and Yarborough have been transferred from the archdeaconry of Lincoln to that of Stow. Benedictine foundations existed at Ikanho, Barrow, Bardney, Partney and Crowland as early as the 7th century, but all were destroyed in the Danish wars, and only Bardney and Crowland were ever rebuilt. The revival of monasticism after the Conquest resulted in the erection of ten Benedictine monasteries, and a Benedictine nunnery at Stainfield. The Cistercian abbeys at Kirkstead, Louth Park, Revesby, Vaudey and Swineshead, and the Cistercian nunnery at Stixwould were founded in the reign of Stephen, and at the time of the Dissolution there were upwards of a hundred religious houses in the county.

In the struggles of the reign of Stephen, castles at Newark and Sleaford were raised by Alexander, bishop of Lincoln, against the king, while Ranulf "Gernons," earl of Chester, in 1140 garrisoned Lincoln for the empress. The seizure of Lincoln by Stephen in 1141 was accompanied with fearful butchery and devastation, and by an accord at Stamford William of Roumare received Kirton in Lindsey, and his tenure of Gainsborough Castle was confirmed. In the baronial outbreak of 1173 Roger Mowbray, who had inherited the Isle of Axholme from Nigel d'Albini, garrisoned Ferry East, or Kinnard's Ferry, and Axholme against the king, and, after the destruction of their more northern fortresses in this campaign, Epworth in Axholme became the

principal seat of t
and his barons Li
rendering hostag
after the landing
then earl of Lin
Abbey, John jo
died, and in th
captured and
Roses the cou
Lancastrian,
and Stamford
recovered
defeat of th
near Stafo
for the n
was warml
Sir Perc
Thorold
mentary
manry
won a
at Lyn
howeve
were
1646.
shire
flourish
Henry
whom
and lat
Survey
the Ma
Despens

At the
and 500
quantiti
St Mary
centres of
Louth, O
early ma
woollen t
13th cent
sprang up
brought l
marked b
especially
Barton, S
towns suf
counties
steadily i
districts c
over 330,0
including
resulted in
trade in g
markets, a
of Englan
sometimes
of Lincoln
snaring; t
was worke

As early
the shire of
and Stamf
several tim
councils, th
while at Sta
barons, Pier
representatio
Grantham w
the act of

[illegible]

revolutionist, was born at Bernay (Eure). Before the Revolution he was an *avocat* at Bernay He acted as *procureur-syndic* of the district of Bernay during the session of the Constituent Assembly Appointed deputy to the Legislative Assembly and subsequently to the Convention, he attained considerable prominence. He was very hostile to the king, furnished a *Rapport sur les crimes imputés à Louis Capet* (10th of December 1792), and voted for the death of Louis without appeal or respite. He was instrumental in the establishment of the Revolutionary Tribunal and contributed to the downfall of the Girondists. As member of the Committee of Public Safety, he devoted himself particularly to the question of food-supplies, and it was only by dint of dogged perseverance and great administrative talent that he was successful in coping with this difficult problem. He had meanwhile been sent to suppress revolts in the districts of Rhône, Eure, Calvados and Finistère, where he had been able to pursue a conciliatory policy. Without being formally opposed to Robespierre, he did not support him, and he was the only member of the Committee of Public Safety who did not sign the order for the execution of Danton and his party. In a like spirit of moderation he opposed the Thermidorian reaction, and defended Barère, Billaud-Varenne the Collot d'Herbois from the accusations launched against them on the 22nd of March 1795. Himself denounced on the 20th of May 1795, he was defended by his brother Thomas, but only escaped condemnation by the vote of amnesty of the 4th of Brumaire, year IV (26th of October 1795) He was minister of finance from the 18th of June to the 9th of November 1799, but refused office under the Consulate and the Empire. In 1816 he was proscribed by the Restoration government as a regicide, and did not return to France until just before his death on the 17th of February 1825. His brother Thomas made some mark as a Constitutional bishop and member of the Convention.

See Amand Montier, *Robert Lindet* (Paris, 1899); H. Turpin, *Thomas Lindet* (Bernay, 1886); A. Montier, *Correspondance de Thomas Lindet* (Paris, 1899).

LINDLEY, JOHN (1799–1865), English botanist, was born on the 5th of February 1799 at Catton, near Norwich, where his father, George Lindley, author of *A Guide to the Orchard and Kitchen Garden*, owned a nursery garden. He was educated at Norwich grammar school. His first publication, in 1819, a translation of the *Analyse du fruit* of L. C. M. Richard, was followed in 1820 by an original *Monographia Rosarum*, with descriptions of new species, and drawings executed by himself, and in 1821 by *Monographia Digitalium*, and by "Observations on Pomaceae," contributed to the Linnean Society. Shortly afterwards he went to London, where he was engaged by J. C. Loudon to write the descriptive portion of the *Encyclopaedia of Plants*. In his labours on this undertaking, which was completed in 1829, he became convinced of the superiority of the "natural" system of A. L. de Jussieu, as distinguished from the "artificial" system of Linnaeus followed in the *Encyclopaedia*; the conviction found expression in *A Synopsis of British Flora, arranged according to the Natural Order* (1829) and in *An Introduction to the Natural System of Botany* (1830). In 1829 Lindley, who since 1822 had been assistant secretary to the Horticultural Society, was appointed to the chair of botany in University College, London, which he retained till 1860; he lectured also on botany from 1831 at the Royal Institution, and from 1836 at the Botanic Gardens, Chelsea. During his professoriate he wrote many scientific and popular works, besides contributing largely to the *Botanical Register*, of which he was editor for many years, and to the *Gardener's Chronicle*, in which he had charge of the horticultural department from 1841. He was a fellow of the Royal, Linnean and Geological Societies. He died at Turnham Green on the 1st of November 1865.

Besides those already mentioned, his works include *An Outline of the First Principles of Horticulture* (1832), *An Outline of the Structure and Physiology of Plants* (1832), *A Natural System of Botany* (1836), *The Fossil Flora of Great Britain* (with William Hutton, 1831–1837), *Flora Medica* (1838), *Theory of Horticulture* (1840), *The Vegetable Kingdom* (1846), *Folia Orchidacea* (1852), *Descriptive Botany* (1858).

LINDLEY, NATHANIEL LINDLEY, Baron (1828–), English judge, son of John Lindley (*q.v.*), was born at Acton Green, Middlesex, on the 29th of November 1828. He was educated at University College School, and studied for a time at University College, London. He was called to the bar at the Middle Temple in 1850, and began practice in the Court of Chancery. In 1855 he published *An Introduction to the Study of Jurisprudence*, consisting of a translation of the general part of Thibaut's *System des Pandekten Rechts*, with copious notes. In 1860 he published in two volumes his *Treatise on the Law of Partnership, including its Application to Joint Stock and other Companies*, and in 1862 a supplement including the Companies Act of 1862. This work has since been developed into two text-books well known to lawyers as *Lindley on Companies* and *Lindley on Partnership*. He became a Q.C. in January 1872. In 1874 he was elected a bencher of the Middle Temple, of which he was treasurer in 1894. In 1875 he was appointed a justice of common pleas, the appointment of a chancery barrister to a common-law court being justified by the fusion of law and equity then shortly to be brought about, in theory at all events, by the Judicature Acts. In pursuance of the changes now made he became a justice of the common pleas division of the High Court of Justice, and in 1880 of the queen's bench division. In 1881 he was raised to the Court of Appeal and made a privy councillor. In 1897, Lord Justice Lindley succeeded Lord Esher as master of the rolls, and in 1900 he was made a lord of appeal in ordinary with a life peerage and the title of Baron Lindley. He resigned the judicial post in 1905. Lord Lindley was the last serjeant-at-law appointed, and the last judge to wear the serjeant's coif, or rather the black patch representing it, on the judicial wig. He married in 1858 Sarah Katherine, daughter of Edward John Teale of Leeds.

LINDLEY, WILLIAM (1808–1900), English engineer, was born in London on the 7th of September 1808, and became a pupil under Francis Giles, whom he assisted in designing the Newcastle and Carlisle and the London and Southampton railways. Leaving England about 1837, he was engaged for a time in railway work in various parts of Europe, and then returned, as engineer-in-chief to the Hamburg-Bergedorf railway, to Hamburg, near which city he had received his early education, and to which he was destined to stand in much the same relation as Baron Haussmann to Paris. His first achievement was to drain the Hammerbrook marshes, and so add some 1400 acres to the available area of the city. His real opportunity, however, came with the great fire which broke out on the 5th of May 1842 and burned for three days. He was entrusted with the direction of the operations to check its spread, and the strong measures he adopted, including the blowing-up of the town hall, brought his life into danger with the mob, who professed to see in him an English agent charged with the destruction of the port of Hamburg. After the extinction of the fire he was appointed consulting engineer to the senate and town council, to the Water Board and to the Board of Works. He began with the construction of a complete sewerage system on principles which did not escape criticism, but which experience showed to be good. Between 1844 and 1848 water-works were established from his designs, the intake from the Elbe being at Rothenburgsort. Subsidence tanks were used for clarification, but in 1853, when he designed large extensions, he urged the substitution of sand-filtration, which, however, was not adopted until the cholera epidemic of 1892–1893 had shown the folly of the opposition directed against it. In 1846 he erected the Hamburg gas-works; public baths and wash-houses were built, and large extensions to the port executed according to his plans in 1854; and he supervised the construction of the Altona gas and water works in 1855. Among other services he rendered to the city may be mentioned the trigonometrical survey executed between 1848 and 1860, and the conduct of the negotiations which in 1852 resulted in the sale of the "Steelyard" on the banks of the Thames belonging to it jointly with the two other Hanseatic towns, Bremen and Lübeck. In 1860 he left Hamburg, and during the remaining nineteen years of his professional practice he was responsible for many engineering works in various European cities, among them being Frankfort-on-the-Main, Warsaw, Pesth, Düsseldorf, Galatz and Basel. In Frankfort he constructed sewerage works on the same principles as those he followed in Hamburg, and the system was widely imitated not only in Europe, but also in America. He was also consulted in regard to water-works at Berlin, Kiel, Stralsund, Stettin and Leipzig; he advised the New River Company of London on the adoption of the constant supply system in 1851; and he was commissioned by the British Government to carry out various works in Heligoland, including the big retaining wall "Am Falm." He died at Blackheath, London, on the 22nd of May 1900.

LINDO, MARK PRAGER (1819–1879), Dutch prose writer, of English-Jewish descent, was born in London on the 18th of September 1819. He went to Holland when nineteen years of age, and once established there as a private teacher of the English language, he soon made up his mind to remain. In 1842 he passed his examination at Arnhem, qualifying him as a professor of English in Holland, subsequently becoming a teacher of the English language and literature at the gymnasium in that town. In 1853 he was appointed in a similar capacity at the Royal Military Academy in Breda. Meanwhile Lindo had obtained a thorough grasp of the Dutch language, partly during his student years at Utrecht University, where in 1854 he gained the degree of doctor of literature. His proficiency in the two languages led him to translate into Dutch several of the works of Dickens, Thackeray and others, and afterwards also of Fielding, Sterne and Walter Scott. Some of Lindo's translations bore the imprint of hasty and careless work, and all were very unequal in quality. His name is much more likely to endure as the writer of humorous original sketches and novelettes in Dutch, which he published under the pseudonym of De Oude Herr Smits ("Old Mr Smits"). Among the most popular are: *Brieven en Ontboezemingen* ("Letters and Confessions," 1853, with three "Continuations"); *Familie van Ons* ("Family of Ours," 1855); *Bekentenissen eener Jonge Dame* ("Confessions of a Young Lady," 1858); *Uittreksels uit het Dagboek van Wijlen den Heer Janus Snor* ("Extracts from the Diary of the late Mr Janus Snor," 1865); *Typen* ("Types," 1871); and, particularly, *Afdrukken van Indrukken* ("Impressions from Impressions," 1854, reprinted many times). The last-named was written in collaboration with Lodewyk Mulder, who contributed some of its drollest whimsicalities of Dutch life and character, which, for that reason, are almost untranslatable. Lodewyk Mulder and Lindo also founded together, and carried on, for a considerable time alone, the *Nederlandsche Spectator* ("The Dutch Spectator"), a literary weekly, still published at The Hague, which bears little resemblance to its English prototype, and which perhaps reached its greatest popularity and influence when Vosmaer contributed to it a brilliant weekly letter under the fanciful title of Vlugmaren ("Swifts"). Lindo's serious original Dutch writings he published under his own name, the principal one being *De Opkomst en Ontwikkeling van het Engelsche Volk* ("The Rise and Development of the British People," 2 vols. 1868–1874)—a valuable history. Lodewyk Mulder published in 1877–1879 a collected edition of Lindo's writings in five volumes, and there has since been a popular reissue. Lindo was appointed an inspector of primary schools in the province of South Holland in 1865, a post he held until his death at The Hague on the 9th of March 1879.

LINDSAY, the family name of the earls of Crawford. The family is one of great antiquity in Scotland, the earliest to settle in that country being Sir Walter de Lindesia, who attended David, earl of Huntingdon, afterwards King David I., in his colonization of the Lowlands early in the 12th century. The descendants of Sir Walter divided into three branches, one of which held the baronies of Lamberton in Scotland, and Kendal and Molesworth in England; another held Luffness and Crawford in Scotland and half Limesi in England; and a third held Breneville and Byres in Scotland and certain lands, not by baronial tenure, in England. The heads of all these branches sat as barons in the Scottish parliament for more than two hundred years before the elevation of the chief of the house to an earldom in 1398. The [illegible] held the great mountain district of Crawford in Clydesdale, [illegible] the title of the earldom is derived, from the 12th [illegible] till the close of the 15th, when it passed to the Douglas [illegible] of Angus. See CRAWFORD, EARLS OF.

See A. W. C. Lindsay, afterwards earl of Crawford, *Lives of the* [illegible] *Memoir of the Houses of Crawford and Balcarres* (3 vols., [illegible]).

LINDSAY, a town and port of entry of Ontario, Canada, and [illegible] of Victoria county, on the Scugog river, 57 m. N.E. of [illegible] by rail, on the Canadian Pacific railway, and at the [illegible] of the Port Hope and Haliburton branches and the [illegible] of the Grand Trunk railway. Pop. (1901) 7003. [illegible] communication, by way of the Trent canal, [illegible] Scugog and the ports on the Trent system. It contains [illegible] mills, agricultural implement and other factories.

LINDSEY, THEOPHILUS (1723–1808), English theologian, [illegible] born in Middlewich, Cheshire, on the 20th of June 1723, [illegible] educated at the Leeds Free School and at St John's [illegible] Cambridge, where in 1747 he became a fellow. For [illegible] he held a curacy in Spitalfields, London, and from [illegible] he travelled on the continent of Europe as tutor [illegible] duke of Northumberland. He was then presented [illegible] of Kirkby Wiske in Yorkshire, and after exchanging [illegible] Piddletown in Dorsetshire, he removed in 1763 to [illegible] in Yorkshire. Here about 1764 he founded one of the [illegible] Sunday schools in England. Meanwhile he had begun to [illegible] Unitarian views, and to be troubled in conscience [illegible] with the Anglican belief; since 1769 [illegible] of Joseph Priestley had served to foster [illegible] and in 1771 he united with Francis Blackburne, [illegible] of Cleveland (his father-in-law), John Jebb (1736 [illegible]) (1740–1822) and Edmund Law 1703– [illegible] in preparing a petition to parliament [illegible] of the church and graduates of [illegible] relieved from the burden of subscribing [illegible] and "restored to their undoubted [illegible] of interpreting Scripture for themselves." [illegible] signatures were obtained, but in February [illegible] declined even to receive the petition [illegible] the adverse vote was repeated in the [illegible] end of 1773, seeing no prospect of [illegible] the church the relief which his conscience [illegible] resigned his vicarage. In April 1774 he [illegible] Unitarian services in a room in Essex Street, [illegible] first a church, and afterwards the Uni- [illegible] established. Here he remained till 1793, [illegible] his charge in favour of John Disney (1746– [illegible]) had left the established church and had [illegible]. He died on the 3rd of November 1808.

[illegible] *An Historical View of the State of the* [illegible] *Worship from the Reformation to our own* [illegible] amongst others, Burnet, Tillotson, [illegible] Newton for the Unitarian view. His [illegible] *Apology on Resigning the Vicarage of* [illegible] *the Apology* (1776); *The Book of* [illegible] *according to the plan of the late Dr Samuel* [illegible] *on the Preface to St John's Gospel and* [illegible] *Vindiciae Priestleianae* (1788); [illegible] *Idolatry* (1792); and *Conversations on* [illegible] *that everything is from God, and for* [illegible] *of Sermons, with appropriate prayers* [illegible] posthumously in 1810; and a volume of [illegible] appeared in 1812.

[illegible] GUSTAF ([illegible]), Swedish palaeontologist, [illegible] Gotland on the 27th of August 1829. In [illegible] university at Upsala, and in 1854 he took [illegible] Having attended a course of lectures in [illegible] he became interested in the zoology [illegible] published several papers on the invertebrate [illegible] on the fishes. In 1856 he became a [illegible] a master in the grammar school at [illegible] devoted to researches on the fossils of [illegible] Gotland, including the corals, brachiopods, [illegible] cephalopods and crustacea. He described also remains of the fish *Cyathaspis* from Wenlock Beds, and (with T. Thorell) a scorpion *Palaeophonus* from Ludlow Beds at Wisby. He determined the true nature of the operculated coral *Calceola*; and while he described organic remains from other parts of northern Europe, he worked especially at the Palaeozoic fossils of Sweden. He was awarded the Murchison medal by the Geological Society of London in 1895. In 1876 he was appointed keeper of the fossil Invertebrata in the State Museum at Stockholm, where he died on the 16th of May 1901.

See obituary (with portrait), by F. A. Bather, in *Geol. Mag* (July 1901), p. 333.

LINDUS, one of the three chief cities of the island of Rhodes before their synoecism in the city of Rhodes. It is situated on the E. side of the island, and has a finely placed acropolis on a precipitous hill, and a good natural harbour just N. of it. Recent excavations have discovered the early temple of Athena Lindia on the Acropolis, and splendid Propylaea and a staircase, resembling those at Athens. The sculptors of the Laocoon are among the priests of Athena Lindia, whose names are recorded by inscriptions. Some early temples have also been found, and inscriptions cut on the rock recording the sacrifices known as *Βουκάτια*. There are also traces of a theatre and rock-cut tombs. On the Acropolis is a castle, built by the knights in the 14th century, and many houses in the town show work of the same date.

See RHODES; also Chr. Blinkenberg and K. F. Kinch, *Exploration arch. de Rhodes* (Copenhagen, 1904–1907).

LINE, a word of which the numerous meanings may be deduced from the primary ones of thread or cord, a succession of objects in a row, a mark or stroke, a course or route in any particular direction. The word is derived from the Lat. *linea*, where all these meanings may be found, but some applications are due more directly to the Fr. *ligne*. *Linea*, in Latin, meant originally "something made of hemp or flax," hence a cord or thread, from *linum*, flax. "Line" in English was formerly used in the sense of flax, but the use now only survives in the technical name for the fibres of flax when separated by heckling from the tow (see LINEN). The ultimate origin is also seen in the verb "to line," to cover something on the inside, originally used of the "lining" of a garment with linen.

In mathematics several definitions of the line may be framed according to the aspect from which it is viewed. The synthetical genesis of a line from the notion of a point is the basis of Euclid's definition, *γραμμὴ, δὲ μῆκος ἀπλατές* ("a line is widthless length"), and in a subsequent definition he affirms that the boundaries of a line are points, *γραμμῆς δὲ πέρατα σημεῖα*. The line appears in definition 6 as the boundary of a surface: *ἐπιφανείας δὲ πέρατα γραμμαί* ("the boundaries of a surface are lines"). Another synthetical definition, also treated by the ancient Greeks, but not by Euclid, regards the line as generated by the motion of a point (*ῥύσις σημείου*), and, in a similar manner, the "surface" was regarded as the flux of a line, and a "solid" as the flux of a surface. Proclus adopts this view, styling the line *ἀρχή* in respect of this capacity. Analytical definitions, although not finding a place in the Euclidean treatment, have advantages over the synthetical derivation. Thus the boundaries of a solid may define a plane, the edges a line, and the corners a point, or a section of a solid may define the surface, a section of a surface the line, and the section of a line the "point." The notion of dimensions follows readily from either system of definitions. The solid extends three ways, *i.e.* it has length, breadth and thickness, and is therefore three-dimensional; the surface has breadth and length and is therefore two-dimensional; the line has only extension and is unidimensional; and the point, having neither length, breadth nor thickness but only position, has no dimensions.

The definition of a "straight" line is a matter of much complexity. Euclid defines it as the line which lies evenly with respect to the points on itself—*εὐθεῖα γραμμή ἐστιν ἥτις ἐξ ἴσου τοῖς ἐφ' ἑαυτῆς σημείοις κεῖται*. Plato defined it as the line having its middle point hidden by the ends, a definition of no purpose since it only defines the line by the path of a ray of light. Archimedes defines a straight line as the shortest distance between two points.

A better criterion of rectilinearity is that of Simplicius, an Arabian commentator of the 5th century: *Linea recta est quaecumque super duas ipsius extremitates rotata non movetur de loco suo ad alium locum* ("a straight line is one which when rotated about its two extremities does not change its position"). This idea was employed by Leibnitz, and most auspiciously by Gierolamo Saccheri in 1733.

The drawing of a straight line between any two given points forms the subject of Euclid's first postulate—*ᾐτήσθω ἀπὸ παντὸς σημείου ἐπὶ πᾶν σημεῖον εὐθεῖαν γραμμὴν ἀγαγεῖν*, and the producing of a straight line continuously in a straight line is treated in the second postulate—*καὶ πεπερασμένην εὐθεῖαν κατὰ τὸ συνεχὲς ἐπ' εὐθείας ἐκβαλεῖν*.

For a detailed analysis of the geometrical notion of the line and rectilinearity, see W. B. Frankland, *Euclid's Elements* (1905). In analytical geometry the right line is always representable by an equation or equations of the first degree; thus in Cartesian co-ordinates of two dimensions the equation is of the form $Ax+By+C=0$, in triangular coordinates $Ax+By+Cz=0$. In three-dimensional coordinates, the line is represented by two linear equations. (See GEOMETRY, ANALYTICAL.) *Line geometry* is a branch of analytical geometry in which the line is the element, and not the point as with ordinary analytical geometry (see GEOMETRY, LINE).

LINE ENGRAVING, on plates of copper or steel, the method of engraving (*q.v.*), in which the line itself is hollowed, whereas in the woodcut when the line is to print black it is left in relief, and only white spaces and white lines are hollowed.

The art of line engraving has been practised from the earliest ages. The prehistoric Aztec hatchet given to Humboldt in Mexico was just as truly *engraved* as a modern copper-plate which may convey a design by Flaxman; the Aztec engraving is ruder than the European, but it is the same art. The important discovery which made line engraving one of the multiplying arts was the discovery how to print an incised line, which was hit upon at last by accident, and known for some time before its real utility was suspected. Line engraving in Europe does not owe its origin to the woodcut, but to the chasing on goldsmiths' work. The goldsmiths of Florence in the middle of the 15th century were in the habit of ornamenting their works by means of engraving, after which they filled up the hollows produced by the burin with a black enamel made of silver, lead and sulphur, the result being that the design was rendered much more visible by the opposition of the enamel and the metal. An engraved design filled up in this manner was called a *niello*. Whilst a niello was in progress the artist could not see it so well as if the enamel were already in the lines, yet he did not like to put in the hard enamel prematurely, as when once it was set it could not easily be got out again. He therefore took a sulphur cast of his niello in progress, on a matrix of fine clay, and filled up the lines in the sulphur with lampblack, thus enabling himself to judge of the state of his engraving. At a later period it was discovered that a proof could be taken on damped paper by filling the engraved lines with a certain ink and wiping it off the surface of the plate, sufficient pressure being applied to make the paper go into the hollowed lines and fetch the ink out of them. This was the beginning of plate printing. The niello engravers thought it a convenient way of proving their work—the metal itself—as it saved the trouble of the sulphur cast, but they saw no further into the future. They went on engraving nielli just the same to ornament plate and furniture; nor was it until the 16th century that the new method of printing was carried out to its great and wonderful results. There are, however, certain differences between plate-printing and block-printing which affect the essentials of art. When paper is driven *into* a line so as to fetch the ink out of it, the line may be of unimaginable fineness, it will print all the same; but when the paper is only pressed *upon* a raised line, the line must have some appreciable thickness; the wood engraving, therefore, can never —except in a *tour de force*—be so delicate as plate engraving. Again, not only does plate-printing excel block-printing in delicacy; it excels it also in force and depth. There never was, and there will never be, a woodcut line having the power of a deep line in a plate, for in block-printing the line is only a blackened surface of paper slightly impressed, whereas in plate-printing it is a *cast* with an additional thickness of printing ink.

The most important of the tools used in line-engraving is the burin, which is a bar of steel with one end fixed in a handle rather like a mushroom with one side cut away, the burin itself being shaped so that the cutting end when sharpened takes the form of a lozenge, point downwards. The burin acts exactly like a plough; it makes a furrow and turns out a shaving of metal as the plough turns the soil of a field. The burin, however, is pushed while the plough is pulled, and this peculiar character of the burin, or graver, as a pushed instrument at once establishes a wide separation between it and all the other instruments employed in the arts of design, such as pencils, brushes, pens and etching needles.

The elements of engraving with the burin upon metal will be best understood by an example of a very simple kind, as in the engraving of letters. The capital letter B contains in itself the rudiments of an engraver's education. As at first drawn, before the blacks are inserted, this letter consists of two perpendicular straight lines and four curves, all the curves differing from each other. Suppose, then, that the engraver has to make a B, he will scratch these lines, reversed, very lightly with a sharp point or style. The next thing is to cut out the blacks (not the whites, as in wood engraving), and this would be done with two different burins. The engraver would get his vertical black line by a powerful ploughing with the burin between his two preparatory first lines, and then take out some copper in the thickest parts of the two curves. This done, he would then take a finer burin and work out the gradation from the thick line in the midst of the curve to the thin extremities which touch the perpendicular. When there is much gradation in a line the darker parts of it are often gradually ploughed out by returning to it over and over again. The hollows so produced are afterwards filled with printing ink, just as the hollows in a niello were filled with black enamel; the surplus printing ink is wiped from the smooth surface of the copper, damped paper is laid upon it, and driven into the hollowed letter by the pressure of a revolving cylinder; it fetches the ink out, and you have your letter B in intense black upon a white ground.

When the surface of a metal plate is sufficiently polished to be used for engraving, the slightest scratch upon it will print as a black line, the degree of blackness being proportioned to the depth of the scratch. An engraved plate from which visiting cards are printed is a good example of some elementary principles of engraving. It contains thin lines and thick ones, and a considerable variety of curves. An elaborate line engraving, if it is a pure line engraving and nothing else, will contain only these simple elements in different combinations. The real line engraver is always engraving a line more or less broad and deep in one direction or another; he has no other business than this.

In the early Italian and early German prints, the line is used with such perfect simplicity of purpose that the methods of the artists are as obvious as if we saw them actually at work.

The student may soon understand the spirit and technical quality of the earliest Italian engraving by giving his attention to a few of the series which used erroneously to be called the "Playing Cards of Mantegna," but which have been shown by Mr Sidney Colvin to represent "a kind of encyclopaedia of knowledge."

The history of these engravings is obscure. They are supposed to be Florentine; they are certainly Italian; and their technical manner is called that of Baccio Baldini. But their style is as clear as a style can be, as clear as the artist's conception of his art. In all these figures the outline is the main thing, and next to that the lines which mark the leading folds of the drapery, lines quite classical in purity of form and severity of selection, and especially characteristic in this, that they are always really engraver's lines, such as may naturally be done with the burin, and they never imitate the freer line of the pencil or etching needle. Shading is used in the greatest moderation with thin straight strokes of the burin, that never overpower the stronger organic lines of the design. Of chiaroscuro, in any complete sense, there is none. The sky behind the figures is represented by white paper, and the foreground is sometimes occupied by flat decorative engraving, much nearer in feeling to calligraphy than to modern painting. Sometimes there is a cast shadow, but it is not studied, and is only used to give relief. In this

[illegible] crossed in the shading,
[illegible] are not; the reason being
[illegible] easily be crossed as not,
[illegible] crossing involves much
[illegible] Here, then, we have pure line-
[illegible] the engraving of the pure
[illegible] and exhibited in an
[illegible] form combined with
[illegible] Even the forms are idealized,
[illegible] for the express purpose of
[illegible] Such are the character-
[illegible] which were attributed
[illegible] When we come to Mantegna himself
[illegible] and shading were for
[illegible] He did not draw and shade
[illegible] would, but he first
[illegible] all very accurate,
[illegible] shading, a very peculiar
[illegible] straight and all the shading
[illegible] its peculiarities being
[illegible] combination of natural
[illegible] made the early Italians
[illegible] simplest and easiest methods.
[illegible] straight lines the Germans
[illegible] the Italians saw good
[illegible] burins something of

[illegible] engraving in Germany are
[illegible] and Albert Dürer,
[illegible] many points in common.
[illegible] of Dürer's death is
[illegible] whole generation before
[illegible] in the use of the burin,
[illegible] due in great measure
[illegible] Schongauer is the first
[illegible] but he was preceded
[illegible] "the Master of 1466,"
[illegible] contrast to the classicism
[illegible] skilfully, conceiving of
[illegible] yet shading with an
[illegible] shaded, and with
[illegible] art is a great stride
[illegible] pleasure in the bold
[illegible] Schongauer, are not
[illegible] and the shading,
[illegible] masterly than the straight
[illegible] Schongauer's curved
[illegible] and skill; and as he
[illegible] the burin which amused
[illegible] his plates with
[illegible] each of which he
[illegible] were the most important
[illegible] of those days had no
[illegible] one part of their
[illegible] first one object
[illegible] the plate was furnished
[illegible] Here,
[illegible] is denied
[illegible] same plane.
[illegible]") of
[illegible] back, with
[illegible] as if he
[illegible] to have per-
[illegible] between us
[illegible] back
[illegible] visible
[illegible] distances,
[illegible]" [illegible]

[illegible] made him
[illegible] saw and
[illegible] the same

intensity of study to everything. Though a thorough student of the nude—witness his Adam and Eve (1504) and other plates—he would pay just as much attention to the creases of a gaiter as to the development of a muscle; and though man was his main subject, he would study dogs with equal care (see the five dogs in the "St Hubert"), as well as pigs (see the "Prodigal Son," *c.* 1495); and at a time when landscape painting was unknown he studied every clump of trees, every visible trunk and branch, nay, every foreground plant, and each leaf of it separately. In his buildings he saw every brick like a bricklayer, and every joint in the woodwork like a carpenter. The immense variety of the objects which he engraved was a training in suppleness of hand. His lines go in every direction, and are made to render both the undulations of surfaces (see the plane in the Melencolia, 1514) and their texture (see the granular texture of the stones in the same print).

From Dürer we come to Italy again, through Marcantonio, who copied Dürer, translating more than sixty of his woodcuts upon metal. It is one of the most remarkable things in the history of art, that a man who had trained himself by copying northern work, little removed from pure Gothicism, should have become soon afterwards the great engraver of Raphael, who was much pleased with his work and aided him by personal advice. Yet, although Raphael was a painter, and Marcantonio his interpreter, the reader is not to infer that engraving had as yet subordinated itself to painting. Raphael himself evidently considered engraving a distinct art, for he never once set Marcantonio to work from a picture, but always (much more judiciously) gave him drawings, which the engraver might interpret without going outside his own art; consequently Marcantonio's works are always genuine engravings, and are never pictorial. Marcantonio was an engraver of remarkable power. In him the real pure art of line-engraving reached its maturity. He retained much of the early Italian manner in his backgrounds, where its simplicity gives a desirable sobriety; but his figures are boldly modelled in curved lines, crossing each other in the darker shades, but left single in the passages from dark to light, and breaking away in fine dots as they approach the light itself, which is of pure white paper. A school of engraving was thus founded by Raphael, through Marcantonio, which cast aside the minute details of the early schools for a broad, harmonious treatment.

The group known as the engravers of Rubens marked a new development. Rubens understood the importance of engraving as a means of increasing his fame and wealth, and directed Vorsterman and others. The theory of engraving at that time was that it ought not to render accurately the local colour of painting, which would appear wanting in harmony when dissociated from the hues of the picture; and it was one of the anxieties of Rubens so to direct his engravers that the result might be a fine plate independently of what he had painted. To this end he helped his engravers by drawings, in which he sometimes indicated what he thought the best direction for the lines. Rubens liked Vorsterman's work, and scarcely corrected it, a plate he especially approved being "Susannah and the Elders," which is a learned piece of work well modelled, and shaded everywhere on the figures and costumes with fine curved lines, the straight line being reserved for the masonry. Vorsterman quitted Rubens after executing fourteen important plates, and was succeeded by Paul Pontius, then a youth of twenty, who went on engraving from Rubens with increasing skill until the painter's death. Boetius a Bolswert engraved from Rubens towards the close of his life, and his brother Schelte a Bolswert engraved more than sixty compositions of Rubens, of the most varied character, including hunting scenes and landscapes. This brings us to the engraving of landscape as a separate study. Rubens treated landscape in a broad comprehensive manner, and Schelte's way of engraving it was also broad and comprehensive. The lines are long and often undulating, the cross-hatchings bold and rather obtrusive, for they often substitute unpleasant reticulations for the refinement and mystery of nature, but it was a beginning, and a vigorous beginning. The technical developments of engraving under the influence of

Rubens may be summed up briefly as follows: (1) The Italian outline had been discarded as the chief subject of attention, and modelling had been substituted for it; (2) broad masses had been substituted for the minutely finished detail of the northern schools; (3) a system of light and dark had been adopted which was not pictorial, but belonged especially to engraving, which it rendered (in the opinion of Rubens) more harmonious.

The history of line-engraving, from the time of Rubens to the beginning of the 19th century, is rather that of the vigorous and energetic application of principles already accepted than any new development. From the two sources already indicated, the school of Raphael and the school of Rubens, a double tradition flowed to England and France, where it mingled and directed English and French practice. The first influence on English line-engraving was Flemish, and came from Rubens through Vandyck, Vorsterman, and others; but the English engravers soon underwent French and Italian influences, for although Payne learned from a Fleming, Faithorne studied in France under Philippe de Champagne the painter and Robert Nanteuil the engraver. Sir Robert Strange studied in France under Philippe Lebas, and then five years in Italy, where he saturated his mind with Italian art. French engravers came to England as they went to Italy, so that the art of engraving became in the 18th century cosmopolitan. In figure-engraving the outline was less and less insisted upon. Strange made it his study to soften and lose the outline. Meanwhile, the great classical Renaissance school, with Gérard Audran at its head, had carried forward the art of modelling with the burin, and had arrived at great perfection of a sober and dignified kind. Audran was very productive in the latter half of the 17th century, and died in 1703, after a life of severe self-direction in labour, the best external influence he underwent being that of the painter Nicolas Poussin. He made his work more rapid by the use of etching, but kept it entirely subordinate to the work of the burin. One of the finest of his large plates is "St John Baptizing," from Poussin, with groups of dignified figures in the foreground and a background of grand classical landscape, all executed with the most thorough knowledge according to the ideas of that time. The influence of Claude Lorrain on the engraving of landscape was exercised less through his etchings than his pictures, which compelled the engravers to study delicate distinctions in the values of light and dark. Through Woollett and Vivarès, Claude exercised an influence on landscape engraving almost equal to that of Raphael and Rubens on the engraving of the figure, though he did not direct his engravers personally.

In the 19th century line-engraving received first an impulse and finally a check. The impulse came from the growth of public wealth, the increasing interest in art and the increase in the commerce of art, which, by means of engraving, fostered in England mainly by John Boydell, penetrated into the homes of the middle classes, as well as from the growing demand for illustrated books, which gave employment to engravers of first-rate ability. The check to line-engraving came from the desire for cheaper and more rapid methods, a desire satisfied in various ways, but especially by etching and by the various kinds of photography. Nevertheless, the 19th century produced most highly accomplished work in line-engraving, both in the figure and in landscape. Its characteristics, in comparison with the work of other centuries, were chiefly a more thorough and delicate rendering of local colour, light and shade, and texture. The elder engravers could draw as correctly as the moderns, but they either neglected these elements or admitted them sparingly, as opposed to the spirit of their art. In a modern engraving from Landseer may be seen the blackness of a man's boots (local colour), the soft roughness of his coat (texture), and the exact value in light and dark of his face and costume against the cloudy sky. Nay more, there is to be found every sparkle on bit, boot and stirrup. Modern painting pays more attention to texture and chiaroscuro than classical painting did, and engraving necessarily followed in the same directions. But there is a certain sameness in pure line-engraving more favourable to some forms and textures than to others. This sameness of line-engraving and its costliness, led to the adoption of mixed methods, extremely prevalent in commercial prints from popular artists. In the well-known prints from Rosa Bonheur, for example, by T. Landseer, H. T. Ryall, and C. G. Lewis, the tone of the skies is got by machine-ruling, and so is much undertone in the landscape; the fur of the animals is all etched, and so are the foreground plants, the real burin work being used sparingly where most favourable to texture. Even in the exquisite engravings after Turner, by Cooke, Goodall, Wallis, Miller, Willmore, and others, who reached a degree of delicacy in light and shade far surpassing the work of the old masters, the engravers had recourse to etching, finishing with the burin and dry point. Turner's name may be added to those of Raphael, Rubens and Claude in the list of painters who have had a special influence upon engraving. The speciality of Turner's influence was in the direction of delicacy of tone. In this respect the Turner vignettes to Roger's poems were a high-water mark of human attainment, not likely ever to be surpassed.

The record of the art of line-engraving during the last quarter of the 19th century is one of continued decay. Technical improvements, it was hoped, might save the art; it was thought by some that the slight revival resultant on the turning back of the burin's cutting-point—whereby the operator pulled the tool towards him instead of pushing it from him—might effect much, in virtue of the time and labour saved by the device. But by the beginning of the 20th century pictorial line-engraving in England was practically non-existent, and, with the passing of Jeens and Stacpoole, the spasmodic demand by publishers for engravers to engrave new plates remained unanswered. Mr C. W. Sherborn, the exquisite and facile designer and engraver of book-plates, has scarcely been surpassed in his own line, but his art is mainly heraldic. There are now no men capable of such work as that with which Doo, J. H. Robinson, and their fellows maintained the credit of the English School. Line-engraving has been killed by etching, mezzotint and the "mixed method." The disappearance of the art is due not so much to the artistic objection that the personality of the line-engraver stands obtrusively between the painter and the public; it is rather that the public refuse to wait for several years for the proofs for which they have subscribed, when by another method they can obtain their plates more quickly. An important line plate may occupy a prodigious time in the engraving; J. H. Robinson's "Napoleon and the Pope" took about twelve years. The invention of steel-facing a copper plate would now enable the engraver to proceed more expeditiously; but even in this case he can no more compete with the etcher than the mezzotint-engraver can keep pace with the photogravure manufacturer.

The Art Union of London in the past gave what encouragement it could; but with the death of J. Stephenson (1886) and F. Bacon (1887) it was evident that all hope was gone. John Saddler at the end was driven, in spite of his capacity to do original work, to spend most of his time in assisting Thomas Landseer to rule the skies on his plates, simply because there was not enough line-engraving to do. Since then there was some promise of a revival, and Mr Bourne engraved a few of the pictures by Gustave Doré. But little followed. The last of the line-engravers of Turner's pictures died in the person of Sir Daniel Wilson (d. 1892), who, recognizing the hopelessness of his early profession, laid his graver aside, and left Europe for Canada and eventually became president of the university of Toronto.

If line-engraving still flourishes in France, it is due not a little to official encouragement and to intelligent fostering by collectors and connoisseurs. The prizes offered by the École des Beaux Arts would probably not suffice to give vitality to the art but for the employment afforded to the finished artist by the "Chalcographie du Musée du Louvre," in the name of which commissions are judiciously distributed. At the same time, it must be recognized that not only are French engravers less busy than they were in days when line-engraving was the only "important" method of picture-translation, but they work for the most part for much smaller rewards. Moreover, the class of the work has entirely changed, partly through the [illegible] of prices paid for it, partly through the change of [illegible], and partly, again, through the necessities [illegible]. That is to say, that public impatience is but [illegible] the abandonment of the fine broad sweeping [illegible] into the copper which was characteristic of the [illegible], either simply cut or crossed diagonally so as [illegible] of "lozenges" typical of engraving at its [illegible] period. That method was slow; but [illegible] was the shallower work rendered possible by [illegible] of the much greater degree of elabora[illegible] such pieces were capable, and which the public [illegible] by Finden—to expect. The French [illegible] were therefore driven at last to simplify their work [illegible] to satisfy the public and live by the burin. To [illegible] the art developed in the direc[illegible]. Gaillard (d. 1887), Blanchard, [illegible] (d. 1888) were perhaps the earliest [illegible], the characteristics of which are the [illegible] greys or the rich blacks of old, sim[illegible] extremely high elaboration. [illegible] engraver has always been, while [illegible] his own art to the farthermost limit, [illegible] and personal qualities of [illegible] on the plate. The height [illegible] is seen in the triptych [illegible] to whom may perhaps [illegible] among several engravers of the front [illegible] three pictures in the Louvre [illegible] of the San Zeno altarpiece [illegible] sentiment, and colour [illegible] in rendering the peculiar lumin[illegible] who gained the *Prix de Rome* [illegible] of Sir Joshua Reynolds, [illegible] Paul Dubois, Cabanel, [illegible]. The freedom of much [illegible] with etching and dry-point; [illegible] the etching-needle and acid [illegible] and outlines. Léopold Flameng's [illegible] "Virgin with the Donor," in [illegible] admirable works of its kind, [illegible] of the master, extreme [illegible] notwithstanding. Jules Jacquet [illegible] Meissonier (especially the "Fried[illegible] Didier for his plates after [illegible]), Raphael, and Paul Veronese, [illegible], Bouguereau, and Roybet [illegible] (Botticelli's "Primavera"), Sulpis [illegible] Moreau), Patricot (Gustave Moreau), [illegible] (d. 1901), have been among the [illegible]. Their object is to secure the faith[illegible] painter they reproduce, while readily [illegible] of the old method, which, whatever its [illegible] by mediocre artists of [illegible] unable to appreciate [illegible] excellence.

[illegible] is not without vitality. [illegible] portraiture and subject [illegible] Doré, among his best [illegible] after leading painters, [illegible] method" of graver[illegible] has engraved a number [illegible] is hardly sufficient in [illegible] a state of prosperous [illegible]

[illegible], line-engraving retains [illegible] orthodox form. The [illegible] freedom and lightness [illegible] the fine lines, employed [illegible] a supposed advantage [illegible] appreciation. But the more [illegible] supported, and many [illegible]. Friedrich Zimmermann (d. 1887) began his career by engraving such prints as Guido Reni's "Ecce Homo" in Dresden, and then devoted himself to the translation of modern German painters. Rudolph Pfnor was an ornamentist representative of his class; and Joseph Kohlschein, of Düsseldorf, a typical exponent of the intelligent conservative manner. His "Marriage at Cana" after Paul Veronese, "The Sistine Madonna" after Raphael, and "St Cecilia" after the same master, are all plates of a high order.

In Italy the art is well-nigh as moribund as in England. When Vittorio Pica (of Naples) and Conconi (of Milan) have been named, it is difficult to mention other successors to the fine school of the 19th century which followed Piranesi and Volpato. A few of the pupils of Rosaspina and Paolo Toschi lived into the last quarter of the century, but to the present generation Asiolo, Jesi, C. Raimondi, L. Bigola, and Antonio Isac are remembered rather for their efforts than for their success in supporting their art against the combined opposition of etching, "process" and public indifference.

Outside Europe line-engraving can no longer be said to exist. Here and there a spasmodic attempt may be made to appeal to the artistic appreciation of a limited public; but no general attention is paid to such efforts, nor, it may be added, are these inherently worthy of much notice. There are still a few who can engrave a head from a photograph or drawing, or a small engraving for book-illustration or for book-plates; there are more who are highly proficient in mechanical engraving for decorative purposes; but the engraving-machine is fast superseding this class. In short, the art of worthily translating a fine painting beyond the borders of France, Belgium, Germany and perhaps Italy can scarcely be said to survive, and even in those countries it appears to exist on sufferance and by hot-house encouragement.

AUTHORITIES.—P. G. Hamerton, *Drawing and Engraving* (Edinburgh, 1892); H. W. Singer and W. Strang, *Etching, Engraving, and other methods of Printing Pictures* (London, 1897); A. de Lostalot, *Les Procédés de la gravure* (Paris, 1882); Le Comte Henri Delaborde, *La Gravure* (Paris, English trans., with a chapter on English engraving methods, by William Walker, London, 1886); H. W. Singer, *Geschichte des Kupferstichs* (Magdeburg and Leipzig, 1895), and *Der Kupferstich* (Bielefeld and Leipzig, 1904); Alex. Waldow, *Illustrierte Encyklopadie der Graphischen Künste* (Leipzig, 1881–1884), Lippmann, *Engraving and Engraving*, translated by Martin Hardie (London, 1906); and for those who desire books of gossip on the subject, Arthur Hayden, *Chats on Old Prints* (London, 1906), and Malcolm C. Salaman, *The Old Engravers of England* (London, 1906). (P. G. H.; M. H. S.)

LINEN and LINEN MANUFACTURES. Under the name of linen are comprehended all yarns spun and fabrics woven from flax fibre (see FLAX).

From the earliest periods of human history till almost the close of the 18th century the linen manufacture was one of the most extensive and widely disseminated of the domestic industries of European countries. The industry was most largely developed in Russia, Austria, Germany, Holland, Belgium, the northern provinces of France, and certain parts of England, in the north of Ireland, and throughout Scotland; and in these countries its importance was generally recognized by the enactment of special laws, having for their object the protection and extension of the trade. The inventions of Arkwright, Hargreaves and Crompton in the later part of the 18th century, benefiting almost exclusively the art of cotton-spinning, and the unparalleled development of that branch of textile manufactures, largely due to the ingenuity of these inventors, gave the linen trade as it then existed a fatal blow. Domestic spinning, and with it hand-loom weaving, immediately began to shrink; the trade which had supported whole villages and provinces entirely disappeared, and the linen manufacture, in attenuated dimensions and changed conditions, took refuge in special localities, where it resisted, not unsuccessfully, the further assaults of cotton, and, with varying fortunes, rearranged its relations in the community of textile industries. The linen industries of the United Kingdom were the first to suffer from the aggression of cotton; more slowly the influence of the rival textile reached other countries.

In 1810 Napoleon I. offered a reward of one million francs to any inventor who should devise the best machinery for the spinning of flax yarn. Within a few weeks thereafter Philippe de Girard patented in France important inventions for flax spinning by both dry and wet methods. His inventions, however, did not receive the promised reward and were neglected in his native country. In 1815 he was invited by the Austrian government to establish a spinning mill at Hirtenberg near Vienna, which was run with his machinery for a number of years, but it failed to prove a commercial success. In the meantime English inventors had applied themselves to the task of adapting machines to the preparation and spinning of flax. The foundation of machine spinning of flax was laid by John Kendrew and Thomas Porthouse of Darlington, who, in 1787, secured a patent for "a mill or machine upon new principles for spinning yarn from hemp, tow, flax or wool." By innumerable successive improvements and modifications, the invention of Kendrew and Porthouse developed into the perfect system of machinery with which, at the present day, spinning-mills are furnished; but progress in adapting flax fibres for mechanical spinning, and linen yarn for weaving cloth by power-loom was much slower than in the corresponding case of cotton.

Till comparatively recent times, the sole spinning implements were the spindle and distaff. The spindle, which is the fundamental apparatus in all spinning machinery, was a round stick or rod of wood about 12 in. in length, tapering towards each extremity, and having at its upper end a notch or slit into which the yarn might be caught or fixed. In general, a ring or "whorl" of stone or clay was passed round the upper part of the spindle to give it momentum and steadiness when in rotation, while in some few cases an ordinary potato served the purpose of a whorl. The distaff, or rock, was a rather longer and stronger bar or stick, around one end of which, in a loose coil or ball, the fibrous material to be spun was wound. The other extremity of the distaff was carried under the left arm, or fixed in the girdle at the left side, so as to have the coil of flax in a convenient position for drawing out to form the yarn. A prepared end of yarn being fixed into the notch, the spinster, by a smart rolling motion of the spindle with the right hand against the right leg, threw it out from her, spinning in the air, while, with the left hand, she drew from the rock an additional supply of fibre which was formed into a uniform and equal strand with the right. The yarn being sufficiently twisted was released from the notch, wound around the lower part of the spindle, and again fixed in the notch at the point insufficiently twisted; and so the rotating, twisting and drawing out operations went on till the spindle was full. So persistent is an ancient and primitive art of this description that in remote districts of Scotland—a country where machine spinning has attained a high standard—spinning with rock and spindle is still practised,[1] and yarn of extraordinary delicacy, beauty and tenacity has been spun by their agency. The first improvement on the primitive spindle was found in the construction of the hand-wheel, in which the spindle, mounted in a frame, was fixed horizontally, and rotated by a band passing round it and a large wheel, set in the same framework. Such a wheel became known in Europe about the middle of the 16th century, but it appears to have been in use for cotton spinning in the East from time immemorial. At a later date, which cannot be fixed, the treadle motion was attached to the spinning wheel, enabling the spinster to sit at work with both hands free; and the introduction of the two-handed or double-spindle wheel, with flyers or twisting arms on the spindles, completed the series of mechanical improvements effected on flax spinning till the end of the 18th century. The common use of the two-handed wheel throughout the rural districts of Ireland and Scotland is a matter still within the recollection of some people; but spinning wheels are now seldom seen.

The modern manufacture of linen divides itself into two branches, spinning and weaving, to which may be added the bleaching and various finishing processes, which, in the case of many linen textures, are laborious undertakings and important branches of industry. The flax fibre is received in bundles from the scutch mill, and after having been classed into various grades, according to the quality of the material, it is labelled and placed in the store ready for the flax mill. The whole operations in yarn manufacture comprise (1) hackling, (2) preparing and (3) spinning.

Hackling.—This first preparatory process consists not only in combing out, disentangling and laying smooth and parallel the separate fibres, but also serves to split up and separate into their ultimate filaments the strands of fibre which, up to this point, have been agglutinated together. The hackling process was originally performed by hand, and it was one of fundamental importance, requiring the exercise of much dexterity and judgment. The broken, ravelled and short fibres, which separate out in the hackling process, form tow, an article of much inferior value to the spinner. A good deal of hand-hackling is still practised, especially in Irish and continental mills; and it has not been found practicable, in any case, to dispense entirely with a rough preparation of the fibre by hand labour. In hackling by hand, the hackler takes a handful or "strick" of rough flax, winds the top end around his hands, and then, spreading out the root end as broad and flat as possible, by a swinging motion dashes the fibre into the hackle teeth or needles of the rougher or "ruffer." The rougher is a board plated with tin, and studded with spikes or teeth of steel about 7 in. in length, which taper to a fine sharp point. The hackler draws his strick several times through this tool, working gradually up from the roots to near his hand, till in his judgment the fibres at the root end are sufficiently combed out and smoothed. He then seizes the root end and similarly treats the top end of the strick. The same process is again repeated on a similar tool, the teeth of which are 5 in. long, and much more closely studded together; and for the finer counts of yarn a third and a fourth hackle may be used, of still increasing fineness and closeness of teeth. In dealing with certain varieties of the fibre, for fine spinning especially, the flax is, after roughing, broken or cut into three lengths—the top, middle and root ends. Of these the middle cut is most valuable, being uniform in length, strength and quality. The root end is more woody and harsh, while the top, though fine in quality, is uneven and variable in strength. From some flax of extra length it is possible to take two short middle cuts; and, again, the fibre is occasionally only broken into two cuts. Flax so prepared is known as "cut line" in contradistinction to "long line" flax, which is the fibre unbroken. The subsequent treatment of line, whether long or cut, does not present sufficient variation to require further reference to these distinctions.

In the case of hackling by machinery, the flax is first roughed and arranged in stricks, as above described under hand hackling. In the construction of hackling machines, the general principles of those now most commonly adopted are identical. The machines are known as vertical sheet hackling machines, their essential features being a set of endless leather bands or sheets revolving over a pair of rollers in a vertical direction. These sheets are crossed by iron bars, to which hackle stocks, furnished with teeth, are screwed. The hackle stocks on each separate sheet are of one size and gauge, but each successive sheet in the length of the machine is furnished with stocks of increasing fineness, so that the hackling tool at the end where the flax is entered is the coarsest, say about four pins per inch, while that to which the fibre is last submitted has the smallest and most closely set teeth. The finest tools may contain from 45 to 60 pins per inch. Thus the whole of the endless vertical revolving sheet presents a continuous series of hackle teeth, and the machines are furnished with a double set of such sheets revolving face to face, so close together that the pins of one set of sheets intersect those on the opposite stocks. Overhead, and exactly centred between these revolving sheets, is the head or holder channel, from which the flax hangs down while it is undergoing the hackling process on both sides. The flax is fastened in a holder consisting of two heavy flat plates of iron, between which it is spread and tightly screwed up. The holder is 11 in. in length, and the holder channel is fitted to contain a line of six, eight or twelve such holders, according to the number of separate bands of hackling stocks in the machine. The head or holder channel has a falling and rising motion, by which it first presents the ends and gradually more and more of the length of the fibre to the hackle teeth, and, after dipping down the full length of the fibre exposed, it slowly rises and lifts the flax clear of the hackle stocks. By a reciprocal motion all the holders are then moved forward one length; that at the last and finest set of stocks is thrown out, and place is made for filling in an additional holder at the beginning of the series. Thus with a six-tool hackle, or set of stocks, each holder full of flax from beginning to end descends into and rises from the hackle teeth six times in travelling from end to end of the machine. The root ends being thus first hackled, the holders are shot back along an inclined plane, the iron plates unclamped, the flax reversed, and the top ends are then submitted to the same hackling operation. The tow made during the hackling

[1] See Sir Arthur Mitchell's *The Past in the Present* (Edinburgh, 1880).

[illegible]

LING[1] (*Molva vulgaris*), a fish of the family Gadidae, which is readily recognized by its long body, two dorsal fins (of which the anterior is much shorter than the posterior), single long anal fin, separate caudal fin, a barbel on the chin and large teeth in the lower jaw and on the palate. Its usual length is from 3 to 4 ft., but individuals of 5 or 6 ft. in length, and some 70 lb in weight, have been taken. The ling is found in the North Atlantic, from Spitzbergen and Iceland southwards to the coast of Portugal. Its proper home is the North Sea, especially on the coasts of Norway, Denmark, Great Britain and Ireland, it occurs in great abundance, generally at some distance from the land, in depths varying between 50 and 100 fathoms. During the winter months it approaches the shores, when great numbers are caught by means of long lines. On the American side of the Atlantic it is less common, although generally distributed along the south coast of Greenland and on the banks of Newfoundland. Ling is one of the most valuable species of the cod-fish family; a certain number are consumed fresh, but by far the greater portion are prepared for exportation to various countries (Germany, Spain, Italy). They are either salted and sold as "salt-fish," or split from head to tail and dried, forming, with similarly prepared cod and coal-fish, the article of which during Lent immense quantities are consumed in Germany and elsewhere under the name of "stock-fish." The oil is frequently extracted from the liver and used by the poorer classes of the coast population for the lamp or as medicine.

LINGARD, JOHN (1771–1851), English historian, was born on the 5th of February 1771 at Winchester, where his father, of an ancient Lincolnshire peasant stock, had established himself as a carpenter. The boy's talents attracted attention, and in 1782 he was sent to the English college at Douai, where he continued until shortly after the declaration of war by England (1793). He then lived as tutor in the family of Lord Stourton, but in October 1794 he settled along with seven other former members of the old Douai college at Crook Hall near Durham, where on the completion of his theological course he became vice-president of the reorganized seminary. In 1795 he was ordained priest, and soon afterwards undertook the charge of the chairs of natural and moral philosophy. In 1808 he accompanied the community of Crook Hall to the new college at Ushaw, Durham, but in 1811, after declining the presidency of the college at Maynooth, he withdrew to the secluded mission at Hornby in Lancashire, where for the rest of his life he devoted himself to literary pursuits. In 1817 he visited Rome, where he made researches in the Vatican Library. In 1821 Pope Pius VII. created him doctor of divinity and of canon and civil law; and in 1825 Leo XII. is said to have made him cardinal *in petto*. He died at Hornby on the 17th of July 1851.

Lingard wrote *The Antiquities of the Anglo-Saxon Church* (1806), of which a third and greatly enlarged addition appeared in 1845 under the title *The History and Antiquities of the Anglo-Saxon Church, containing an account of its origin, government, doctrines, worship, revenues, and clerical and monastic institutions*; but the work with which his name is chiefly associated is *A History of England, from the first invasion by the Romans to the commencement of the reign of William III.*, which appeared originally in 8 vols. at intervals between 1819 and 1830. Three successive subsequent editions had the benefit of extensive revision by the author; a fifth edition in 10 vols. 8vo appeared in 1849, and a sixth, with life of the author by Tierney prefixed to vol. x., in 1854–1855. Soon after its appearance it was translated into French, German and Italian. It is a work of ability and research; and, though Cardinal Wiseman's claim for its author that he was "the only impartial historian of our country" may be disregarded, the book remains interesting as representing the view taken of certain events in English history by a devout, but able and learned, Roman Catholic in the earlier part of the 19th century.

LINGAYAT (from *linga*, the emblem of Siva), the name of a peculiar sect of Siva worshippers in southern India, who call themselves *Vira-Saivas* (see HINDUISM). They carry on the person a stone *linga* (phallus) in a silver casket. The founder of

[1] As the name of the fish, "ling" is found in other Teut. languages; cf. Dutch and Ger. *Leng*, Norw. *longa*, &c. It is generally connected in origin with "long," from the length of its body. As the name of the common heather, *Calluna vulgaris* (see HEATH) the word is Scandinavian; cf. Dutch and Dan. *lyng*, Swed. *ljung*.

the sect is said to have been Basava, a Brahman prime minister of a Jain king in the 12th century. The Lingayats are specially numerous in the Kanarese country, and to them the Kanarese language owes its cultivation as literature. Their priests are called Jangamas. In 1901 the total number of Lingayats in all India was returned as more than 2½ millions, mostly in Mysore and the adjoining districts of Bombay, Madras and Hyderabad.

LINGAYEN, a town and the capital of the province of Pangasinán, Luzon, Philippine Islands, about 110 m. N. by W. of Manila, on the S. shore of the Gulf of Lingayen, and on a low and fertile island in the delta of the Agno river. Pop. (1903) 21,529. It has good government buildings, a fine church and plaza, the provincial high school and a girls' school conducted by Spanish Dominican friars. The climate is cool and healthy. The chief industries are the cultivation of rice (the most important crop of the surrounding country), fishing and the making of nipa-wine from the juice of the nipa palm, which grows abundantly in the neighbouring swamps. The principal language is Pangasinán; Ilocano is also spoken.

LINGEN, RALPH ROBERT WHEELER LINGEN, Baron (1819–1905), English civil servant, was born in February 1819 at Birmingham, where his father, who came of an old Hertfordshire family, with Royalist traditions, was in business. He became a scholar of Trinity College, Oxford, in 1837; won the Ireland (1838) and Hertford (1839) scholarships; and after taking a first-class in *Literae Humaniores* (1840), was elected a fellow of Balliol (1841). He subsequently won the Chancellor's Latin Essay (1843) and the Eldon Law scholarship (1846). After taking his degree in 1840, he became a student of Lincoln's Inn, and was called to the bar in 1847; but instead of practising as a barrister, he accepted an appointment in the Education Office, and after a short period was chosen in 1849 to succeed Sir J. Kay Shuttleworth as its secretary or chief permanent official. He retained this position till 1869. The Education Office of that day had to administer a somewhat chaotic system of government grants to local schools, and Lingen was conspicuous for his fearless discrimination and rigid economy, qualities which characterized his whole career. When Robert Lowe (Lord Sherbrooke) became, as vice-president of the council, his parliamentary chief, Lingen worked congenially with him in producing the Revised Code of 1862 which incorporated "payment by results"; but the education department encountered adverse criticism, and in 1864 the vote of censure in parliament which caused Lowe's resignation, founded (but erroneously) on an alleged "editing" of the school inspectors' reports, was inspired by a certain antagonism to Lingen's as well as to Lowe's methods. Shortly before the introduction of Forster's Education Act of 1870, he was transferred to the post of permanent secretary of the treasury. In this office, which he held till 1885, he proved a most efficient guardian of the public purse, and he was a tower of strength to successive chancellors of the exchequer. It used to be said that the best recommendation for a secretary of the treasury was to be able to say "No" so disagreeably that nobody would court a repetition. Lingen was at all events a most successful resister of importunate claims, and his undoubted talents as a financier were most prominently displayed in the direction of parsimony. In 1885 he retired. He had been made a C.B. in 1869 and a K.C.B. in 1878, and on his retirement he was created Baron Lingen. In 1889 he was made one of the first aldermen of the new London County Council, but he resigned in 1892. He died on the 22nd of July 1905. He had married in 1852, but left no issue.

LINGEN, a town in the Prussian province of Hanover, on the Ems canal, 43 m. N.N.W. of Münster by rail. Pop. 7500. It has iron foundries, machinery factories, railway workshops and a considerable trade in cattle, and among its other industries are weaving and malting and the manufacture of cloth. Lingen was the seat of a university from 1685 to 1819.

The county of Lingen, of which this town was the capital, was united in the middle ages with the county of Treklenburg. In 1508, however, it was separated from this and was divided into an upper and a lower county, but the two were united in 1541. A little later Lingen was sold to the emperor Charles V., from whom it passed to his son, Philip II. of Spain, who ceded it in 1597 to Maurice, prince of Orange. After the death of the English king, William III., in 1702, it passed to Frederick I., king of Prussia, and in 1815 the lower county was transferred to Hanover, only to be united again with Prussia in 1866.

See Möller, *Geschichte der vormaligen Grafschaft Lingen* (Lingen, 1874); Herrmann, *Die Erwerbung der Stadt und Grafschaft Lingen durch die Krone Preussen* (Lingen, 1902); and Schriever, *Geschichte des Kreises Lingen* (Lingen, 1905).

LINGUET, SIMON NICHOLAS HENRI (1736–1794), French journalist and advocate, was born on the 14th of July 1736, at Reims, whither his father, the assistant principal in the Collège de Beauvais of Paris, had recently been exiled by *lettre de cachet* for engaging in the Jansenist controversy. He attended the Collège de Beauvais and won the three highest prizes there in 1751. He accompanied the count palatine of Zweibrücken to Poland, and on his return to Paris he devoted himself to writing. He published partial French translations of Calderon and Lope de Vega, and wrote parodies for the *Opéra Comique* and pamphlets in favour of the Jesuits. Received at first in the ranks of the *philosophes*, he soon went over to their opponents, possibly more from contempt than from conviction, the immediate occasion for his change being a quarrel with d'Alembert in 1762. Thenceforth he violently attacked whatever was considered modern and enlightened, and while he delighted society with his numerous sensational pamphlets, he aroused the fear and hatred of his opponents by his stinging wit. He was admitted to the bar in 1764, and soon became one of the most famous pleaders of his century. But in spite of his brilliant ability and his record of having lost but two cases, the bitter attacks which he directed against his fellow advocates, especially against Gerbier (1725–1788), caused his dismissal from the bar in 1775. He then turned to journalism and began the *Journal de politique et de littérature*, which he employed for two years in literary, philosophical and legal criticisms. But a sarcastic article on the French Academy compelled him to turn over the *Journal* to La Harpe and seek refuge abroad. Linguet, however, continued his career of free lance, now attacking and now supporting the government, in the *Annales politiques, civiles et littéraires*, published from 1777 to 1792, first at London, then at Brussels and finally at Paris. Attempting to return to France in 1780 he was arrested for a caustic attack on the duc de Duras (1715–1789), an academician and marshal of France, and imprisoned nearly two years in the Bastille. He then went to London, and thence to Brussels, where, for his support of the reforms of Joseph II., he was ennobled and granted an honorarium of one thousand ducats. In 1786 he was permitted by Vergennes to return to France as an Austrian counsellor of state, and to sue the duc d'Aiguillon (1730–1798), the former minister of Louis XV., for fees due him for legal services rendered some fifteen years earlier. He obtained judgment to the amount of 24,000 livres. Linguet received the support of Marie Antoinette; his fame at the time surpassed that of his rival Beaumarchais, and almost excelled that of Voltaire. Shortly afterwards he visited the emperor at Vienna to plead the case of Van der Noot and the rebels of Brabant. During the early years of the Revolution he issued several pamphlets against Mirabeau, who returned his ill-will with interest, calling him "the ignorant and bombastic M. Linguet, advocate of Neros, sultans and viziers." On his return to Paris in 1791 he defended the rights of San Domingo before the National Assembly. His last work was a defence of Louis XVI. He retired to Marnes near Ville d'Avray to escape the Terror, but was sought out and summarily condemned to death "for having flattered the despots of Vienna and London." He was guillotined at Paris on the 27th of June 1794.

Linguet was a prolific writer in many fields. Examples of his attempted historical writing are *Histoire du siècle d'Alexandre le Grand* (Amsterdam, 1762), and *Histoire impartiale des Jésuites* (Madrid, 1768), the latter condemned to be burned. His opposition to the *philosophes* had its strongest expressions in *Fanatisme des philosophes* (Geneva and Paris, 1764) and *Histoire des révolutions de l'empire romain* (Paris, 1766–1768). His *Théorie des lois civiles* (London, 1767) is a vigorous defence of absolutism and attack on the politics of Montesquieu. His best legal treatise is *Mémoire pour le comte de Morangies* (Paris, 1772); Linguet's imprisonment in the Bastille afforded him the opportunity of writing his *Mémoires sur la Bastille*, first published in London in 1789; it has been translated into English (Dublin, 1783, and Edinburgh, 1884–1887), and is the best of his works, though untrustworthy.

See A. Devérité, *Notice pour servir à l'histoire de la vie et des écrits de S. N. H. Linguet* (Liége, 1782); Gardoz, *Essai historique sur la vie et les ouvrages de Linguet* (Lyon, 1808); J. F. Barrière, *Mémoire de Linguet et de Latude* (Paris, 1884); Ch. Monselet, *Les Oubliés et les dédaignés* (Paris, 1885), pp. 1-41; H. Monin, "Notice sur Linguet," in the 1889 edition of *Mémoires sur la Bastille*; J. Cruppi, *Un avocat journaliste au 18ᵉ siècle, Linguet* (Paris, 1895); A. Philipp, *Linguet, ein Nationalökonom des XVIII Jahrhunderts in seinen rechtlichen, socialen und volkswirtschaftlichen Anschauungen* (Zürich, 1896); A. Lichtenberger, *Le Socialisme utopique* (1898), pp. 77-131.

LINK. (1) (Of Scandinavian origin; cf. Swed. *länk*, Dan. *laenke*; cognate with "flank," and Ger. *Gelenk*, joint), one of the loops of which a chain is composed; used as a measure of length in surveying, being $\frac{1}{100}$th part of a "chain." In Gunter's chain, a "link" = 7·92 in.; the chain used by American engineers consists of 100 links of a foot each in length (for "link work" and "link motions" see MECHANICS: § *Applied*, and STEAM ENGINE). The term is also applied to anything used for connecting or binding together, metaphorically or absolutely. (2) (O. Eng. *hlinc*, possibly from the root which appears in "to lean"), a bank or ridge of rising ground; in Scots dialect, in the plural, applied to the ground bordering on the sea-shore, characterized by sand and coarse grass; hence a course for playing golf. (3) A torch made of pitch or tow formerly carried in the streets to light passengers, by men or boys called "link-boys" who plied for hire with them. Iron link-stands supporting a ring in which the link might be placed may still be seen at the doorways of old London houses. The word is of doubtful origin. It has been referred to a Med. Lat. *lichinus*, which occurs in the form *linchinus* (see Du Cange, *Glossarium*); this, according to a 15th-century glossary, meant a wick or match. It is an adaptation of Gr. λύχνος, lamp. Another suggestion connects it with a supposed derivation of "linstock," from "lint." The *New English Dictionary* thinks the likeliest suggestion is to identify the word with the "link" of a chain. The tow and pitch may have been manufactured in lengths, and then cut into sections or "links."

LINKÖPING, a city of Sweden, the seat of a bishop, and chief town of the district (*län*) of Östergötland. Pop. (1900) 14,552. It is situated in a fertile plain 142 m. by rail S.W. of Stockholm, and communicates with Lake Roxen (½ m. to the north) and the Göta and Kinda canals by means of the navigable Stångå. The cathedral (1150–1499), a Romanesque building with a beautiful south portal and a Gothic choir, is, next to the cathedral of Upsala, the largest church in Sweden. It contains an altar-piece by Martin Heemskerck (d. 1574), which is said to have been bought by John II. for twelve hundred measures of wheat. In the church of St Lars are some paintings by Per Horberg (1746–1816), the Swedish peasant artist. Other buildings of note are the massive episcopal palace (1470–1500), afterwards [illegible] palace, and the old gymnasium founded by Gustavus [illegible] in 1627, which contains the valuable library of old [illegible] manuscripts belonging to the diocese and state college, [illegible] of coins and antiquities. There is also the [illegible] Museum, with an art collection. The town has [illegible] of tobacco, cloth and hosiery. It is the head[illegible] the second army division.

[illegible] early became a place of mark, and was already a [illegible]. It was at a council held in the town in [illegible] payment of Peter's pence was agreed to at the [illegible] Nicholas Breakspeare, afterwards Adrian IV. [illegible] Birger Jarlsson Valdemar took place in the [illegible] and in the reign of Gustavus Vasa several [illegible] held in the town. At Stångåbro (Stångå [illegible] obelisk (1898) commemorates the battle of [illegible] (Protestant) defeated [illegible] stones in the Iron Market of Linköping marks the spot where Sigismund's adherents were beheaded in 1600.

LINLEY, THOMAS (1732–1795), English musician, was born at Wells, Somerset, and studied music at Bath, where he settled as a singing-master and conductor of the concerts. From 1774 he was engaged in the management at Drury Lane theatre, London, composing or compiling the music of many of the pieces produced there, besides songs and madrigals, which rank high among English compositions. He died in London on the 19th of November 1795. His eldest son THOMAS (1756–1778) was a remarkable violinist, and also a composer, who assisted his father; and he became a warm friend of Mozart. His works, with some of his father's, were published in two volumes, and these contain some lovely madrigals and songs. Another son, WILLIAM (1771–1835), who held a writership at Madras, was devoted to literature and music and composed glees and songs. Three daughters were similarly gifted, and were remarkable both for singing and beauty; the eldest of them ELIZABETH ANN (1754–1792), married Richard Brinsley Sheridan in 1773, and thus linked the fortunes of her family with his career.

LINLITHGOW, JOHN ADRIAN LOUIS HOPE, 1ST MARQUESS OF (1860–1908), British administrator, was the son of the 6th earl of Hopetoun. The Hope family traced their descent to John de Hope, who accompanied James V.'s queen Madeleine of Valois from France to Scotland in 1537, and of whose great-grand-children Sir Thomas Hope (d. 1646), lord advocate of Scotland, was ancestor of the earls of Hopetoun, while Henry Hope settled in Amsterdam, and was the ancestor of the famous Dutch bankers of that name, and of the later Hopes of Bedgebury, Kent. Sir Thomas's son, Sir James Hope of Hopetoun (1614–1661), Scottish lord of session, was grandfather of Charles, 1st earl of Hopetoun in the Scots peerage (1681–1742), who was created earl in 1703; and his grandson, the 3rd earl, was in 1809 made a baron of the United Kingdom. John, the 4th earl (1765–1823), brother of the 3rd earl, was a distinguished soldier, who for his services in the Peninsular War was created Baron Niddry in 1814 before succeeding to the earldom. The marquessate of Linlithgow was bestowed on the 7th earl of Hopetoun in 1902, in recognition of his success as first governor (1900–1902) of the commonwealth of Australia; he died on the 1st of March 1908, being succeeded as 2nd marquess by his eldest son (b. 1887).

An earldom of Linlithgow was in existence from 1600 to 1716, this being held by the Livingstones, a Scottish family descended from Sir William Livingstone. Sir William obtained the barony of Callendar in 1346, and his descendant, Sir Alexander Livingstone (d. c. 1450), and other members of this family were specially prominent during the minority of King James II. Alexander Livingstone, 7th Lord Livingstone (d. 1623), the eldest son of William, the 6th lord (d. c. 1580), a supporter of Mary, queen of Scots, was a leading Scottish noble during the reign of James VI. and was created earl of Linlithgow in 1600. Alexander's grandson, George, 3rd earl of Linlithgow (1616–1690), and the latter's son, George, the 4th earl (c. 1652–1695), were both engaged against the Covenanters during the reign of Charles II. When the 4th earl died without sons in August 1695 the earldom passed to his nephew, James Livingstone, 4th earl of Callendar. James, who then became the 5th earl of Linlithgow, joined the Stuart rising in 1715; in 1716 he was attainted, being thus deprived of all his honours, and he died without sons in Rome in April 1723.

The earldom of Callendar, which was thus united with that of Linlithgow, was bestowed in 1641 upon James Livingstone, the third son of the 1st earl of Linlithgow. Having seen military service in Germany and the Netherlands, James was created Lord Livingstone of Almond in 1633 by Charles I., and eight years later the king wished to make him lord high treasurer of Scotland. Before this, however, Almond had acted with the Covenanters, and during the short war between England and Scotland in 1640 he served under General Alexander Leslie, afterwards earl of Leven. But the trust reposed in him by the Covenanters did not prevent him in 1640 from signing the "band of Cumbernauld," an association for defence against Argyll, or from being in some way mixed up with the "Incident," a plot for the seizure of the Covenanting leaders, Hamilton and Argyll. In 1641 Almond became an earl, and, having declined the offer of a high position in the army raised by Charles I., he led a division of the Scottish forces into England in 1644 and helped Leven to capture Newcastle. In 1645 Callendar, who often imagined himself slighted, left the army, and in 1647 he was one of the promoters of the "engagement" for the release of the king. In 1648, when the Scots marched into England, he served as lieutenant-general under the duke of Hamilton, but the duke found him as difficult to work with as Leven had done previously, and his advice was mainly responsible for the defeat at Preston. After this battle he escaped to Holland. In 1650 he was allowed to return to Scotland, but in 1654 his estates were seized and he was imprisoned; he came into prominence once more at the Restoration. Callendar died on March 1674, leaving no children, and, according to a special remainder, he was succeeded in the earldom by his nephew Alexander (d. 1685), the second son of the 2nd earl of Linlithgow; and he again was succeeded by his nephew Alexander (d. 1692), the second son of the 3rd earl of Linlithgow. The 3rd earl's son, James, the 4th earl, then became 5th earl of Linlithgow (see *supra*).

LINLITHGOW, a royal, municipal and police burgh and county town of Linlithgowshire, Scotland. Pop. (1901) 4279. It lies in a valley on the south side of a loch, 17½ m. W. of Edinburgh by the North British railway. It long preserved an antique and picturesque appearance, with gardens running down to the lake, or climbing the lower slopes of the rising ground, but in the 19th century much of it was rebuilt. About 4 m. S. by W. lies the old village of Torphichen (pop. 540), where the Knights of St John of Jerusalem had their chief Scottish preceptory. The parish kirk is built on the site of the nave of the church of the establishment, but the ruins of the transept and of part of the choir still exist. Linlithgow belongs to the Falkirk district group of parliamentary burghs with Falkirk, Airdrie, Hamilton and Lanark. The industries include shoe-making, tanning and currying, manufactures of paper, glue and soap, and distilling. An old tower-like structure near the railway station is traditionally regarded as a mansion of the Knights Templar. Other public buildings are the first town house (erected in 1668 and restored in 1848 after a fire); the town hall, built in 1888; the county buildings and the burgh school, dating from the pre-Reformation period. There are some fine fountains. The Cross Well in front of the town house, a striking piece of grotesque work carved in stone, originally built in the reign of James V., was rebuilt in 1807. Another fountain is surmounted by the figure of St Michael, the patron-saint of the burgh. Linlithgow Palace is perhaps the finest ruin of its kind in Scotland. Heavy but effective, the sombre walls rise above the green knolls of the promontory which divides the lake into two nearly equal portions. In plan it is almost square (168 ft. by 174 ft.), enclosing a court (91 ft. by 88 ft.), in the centre of which stands the ruined fountain of which an exquisite copy was erected in front of Holyrood Palace by the Prince Consort. At each corner there is a tower with an internal spiral staircase, that of the north-west angle being crowned by a little octagonal turret known as "Queen Margaret's Bower," from the tradition that it was there that the consort of James IV. watched and waited for his return from Flodden. The west side, whose massive masonry, hardly broken by a single window, is supposed to date in part from the time of James III., who later took refuge in one of its vaults from his disloyal nobles; but the larger part of the south and east side belongs to the period of James V., about 1535; and the north side was rebuilt in 1619–1620 by James VI. Of James V.'s portion, architecturally the richest, the main apartments are the Lyon chamber or parliament hall and the chapel royal. The grand entrance, approached by a drawbridge, was on the east side; above the gateway are still some weather-worn remains of rich allegorical designs. The palace was reduced to ruins by General Hawley's dragoons, who set fire to it in 1746. Government grants have stayed further dilapidation. A few yards to the south of the palace is the church of St Michael, a Gothic (Scottish Decorated) building (180 ft. long internally excluding the apse, by 62 ft. in breadth excluding the transepts), probably founded by David I. in 1242, but mainly built by George Crichton, bishop of Dunkeld (1528–1536). The central west front steeple was till 1821 topped by a crown like that of St Giles', Edinburgh. The chief features of the church are the embattled and pinnacled tower, with the fine doorway below, the nave, the north porch and the flamboyant window in the south transept. The church contains some fine stained glass, including a window to the memory of Sir Charles Wyville Thomson (1830–1882), the naturalist, who was born in the parish.

Linlithgow (wrongly identified with the Roman *Lindum*) was made a royal burgh by David I. Edward I. encamped here the night before the battle of Falkirk (1298), wintered here in 1301, and next year built "a pele [castle] mekill and strong," which in 1313 was captured by the Scots through the assistance of William Bunnock, or Binning, and his hay-cart. In 1369 the customs of Linlithgow yielded more than those of any other town in Scotland, except Edinburgh; and the burgh was taken with Lanark to supply the place of Berwick and Roxburgh in the court of the Four Burghs (1368). Robert II. granted it a charter of immunities in 1384. The palace became a favourite residence of the kings of Scotland, and often formed part of the marriage settlement of their consorts (Mary of Guelders, 1449; Margaret of Denmark, 1468; Margaret of England, 1503). James V. was born within its walls in 1512, and his daughter Mary on the 7th of December 1542. In 1570 the Regent Moray was assassinated in the High Street by James Hamilton of Bothwellhaugh. The university of Edinburgh took refuge at Linlithgow from the plague in 1645–1646; in the same year the national parliament, which had often sat in the palace, was held there for the last time. In 1661 the Covenant was publicly burned here, and in 1745 Prince Charles Edward passed through the town. In 1859 the burgh was deprived by the House of Lords of its claim to levy bridge toll and custom from the railway company.

LINLITHGOWSHIRE, or West Lothian, a south-eastern county of Scotland, bounded N. by the Firth of Forth, E. and S.E. by Edinburghshire, S.W. by Lanarkshire and N.W. by Stirlingshire. It has an area of 76,861 acres, or 120 sq. m., and a coast line of 17 m. The surface rises very gradually from the Firth to the hilly district in the south. A few miles from the Forth a valley stretches from east to west. Between the county town and Bathgate are several hills, the chief being Knock (1017 ft.), Cairnpapple, or Cairnnaple (1000), Cocklerue (said to be a corruption of Cuckold-le-Roi, 912), Riccarton Hills (832) terminating eastwards in Binny Craig, a striking eminence similar to those of Stirling and Edinburgh, Torphichen Hills (777) and Bowden (749). In the coast district a few bold rocks are found, such as Dalmeny, Dundas (well wooded and with a precipitous front), the Binns and a rounded eminence of 559 ft. named Glower-o'er-'em or Bonnytoun, bearing on its summit a monument to General Adrian Hope, who fell in the Indian Mutiny. The river Almond, rising in Lanarkshire and pursuing a north-easterly direction, enters the Firth at Cramond after a course of 24 m., during a great part of which it forms the boundary between West and Mid Lothian. Its right-hand tributary, Breich Water, constitutes another portion of the line dividing the same counties. The Avon, rising in the detached portion of Dumbartonshire, flows eastwards across south Stirlingshire and then, following in the main a northerly direction, passes the county town on the west and reaches the Firth about midway between Grangemouth and Bo'ness, having served as the boundary of Stirlingshire, during rather more than the latter half of its course. The only loch is Linlithgow Lake (102 acres), immediately adjoining the county town on the north, a favourite resort of curlers and skaters. It is 10 ft. deep at the east end and 48 ft. at the west. Eels, perch and braise (a species of roach) are abundant.

Geology.—The rocks of Linlithgowshire belong almost without exception to the Carboniferous system. At the base is the Calciferous Sandstone series, most of which lies between the Bathgate Hills and the eastern boundary of the county. In this series are the Queensferry limestone, the equivalent of the Burdiehouse limestone of Edinburgh, and the Binny sandstone group with shales and clays and the Houston coal bed. At more than one horizon in this series oil shales are found. The Bathgate Hills are formed of basaltic lavas and tuffs—an interbedded volcanic group possibly 2000 ft. thick in the Calciferous Sandstone and Carboniferous Limestone series. A peculiar serpentinous variety of the prevailing rock is quarried at Blackburn for oven floors; it is known as "lakestone." Binns Hill is the site of one of the volcanic cones of the period. The Carboniferous Limestone series consists of an upper and lower limestone group—including the Petershill, Index, Dykeneuk and Craigenbuck limestones—and a middle group of shales, ironstones and coals; the Smithy, Easter Main, Foul, Red and Splint coals belong to this horizon. Above the Carboniferous Limestone the

Millstone grit series crops in a belt which may be traced from the mouth of the Avon southwards to Whitburn. This is followed by the true coal-measures with the Boghead or Torbanehill coal, the Colinburn, Main, Ball, Mill and Upper Cannel or Shotts gas coals of Armadale, Torbanehill and Fauldhouse.

Climate and Agriculture.—The average rainfall for the year is 29·9 in., and the average temperature 47·5° F. (January 38° F.; July 59·5° F.). More than three-fourths of the county, the agriculture of which is highly developed, is under cultivation. The best land is found along the coast, as at Carriden and Dalmeny. The farming is mostly arable, permanent pasture being practically stationary (at about 22,000 acres). Oats is the principal grain crop, but barley and wheat are also cultivated. Farms between 100 and 300 acres are the most common. Turnips and potatoes are the leading green crops. Much land has been reclaimed; the parish of Livingston, for example, which in the beginning of the 18th century was covered with heath and juniper, is now under rotation. In Torphichen and Bathgate, however, patches of peat moss and swamp occur, and in the south there are extensive moors at Fauldhouse and Polkemmet. Live stock does not count for so much in West Lothian as in other Scottish counties, though a considerable number of cattle are fattened and dairy farming is followed successfully, the fresh butter and milk finding a market in Edinburgh. There is some sheep-farming, and horses and pigs are reared. The wooded land occurs principally in the parks and "policies" surrounding the many noblemen's mansions and private estates.

Other Industries.—The shale-oil trade flourishes at Bathgate, Broxburn, Armadale, Uphall, Winchburgh, Philpstoun and Dalmeny. There are important iron-works with blast furnaces at Bo'ness, Kinneil, Whitburn and Bathgate, and coal is also largely mined at these places. Coal-mining is supposed to have been followed since Roman times, and the earliest document extant regarding coalpits in Scotland is a charter granted about the end of the 12th century to William Oldbridge of Carriden. Fire-clay is extensively worked in connexion with the coal, and ironstone employs many hands. Limestone, freestone and whinstone are all quarried. Binny freestone was used for the Royal Institution and the National Gallery in Edinburgh, and many important buildings in Glasgow. Some fishing is carried on from Queensferry, and Bo'ness is the principal port.

Communications.—The North British Railway Company's line from Edinburgh to Glasgow runs across the north of the county, it controls the approaches to the Forth Bridge, and serves the rich mineral district around Airdrie and Coatbridge in Lanarkshire via Bathgate. The Caledonian Railway Company's line from Glasgow to Edinburgh touches the extreme south of the shire. The Union Canal, constructed in 1818–1822 to connect Edinburgh with the Forth and Clyde Canal near Camelon in Stirlingshire, crosses the county, roughly following the N.B.R. line to Falkirk. The Union Canal, which is 31 m. long and belongs to the North British railway, is carried across the Almond and Avon on aqueducts designed by Thomas Telford, and near Falkirk is conveyed through a tunnel 2100 ft. long.

Population and Administration.—In 1891 the population amounted to 52,808, and in 1901 to 65,708, showing an increase of 24·43% in the decennial period, the highest of any Scottish county for that decade, and a density of 547 persons to the sq. m. In 1901 five persons spoke Gaelic only, and 575 Gaelic and English. The chief towns, with populations in 1901, are Bathgate (7549), Borrowstounness (9306), Broxburn (7099) [illegible] Linlithgow (4279). The shire returns one member to parlia[illegible]. Linlithgowshire is part of the sheriffdom of the Lothians [illegible] [illegible], and a resident sheriff-substitute sits at Linlithgow [illegible] [illegible]gate. The county is under school-board jurisdiction, [illegible] are academies at Linlithgow, Bathgate and Bo'ness. [illegible] authorities entrust the bulk of the "residue" grant [illegible] County Secondary Education Committee, which subsidizes [illegible] technical classes (cookery, laundry and dairy) [illegible] and art and technological classes, including their [illegible]

[illegible]—Traces of the Pictish inhabitants still exist. Near [illegible] an accumulation of shells—mostly oysters, which [illegible] used to be found so far up the Forth—considered [illegible] be a natural bed, but pronounced by antiquaries [illegible] midden. Stone cists have been discovered at [illegible], Newliston and elsewhere; on Cairnnaple [illegible] structure of remote but unknown date; and at [illegible] that was once surrounded by stones. The [illegible] lies for several miles in the shire. The [illegible] fine legionary tablet at Bridgeness in 1868 is [illegible] be coa[illegible] [illegible] the great rampart [illegible] [illegible]. Roman camps can be distinguished at several spots. On the hill of Bowden is an earthwork, which J. Stuart Glennie and others connect with the struggle of the ancient Britons against the Saxons of Northumbria. The historical associations of the county mainly cluster round the town of Linlithgow (*q.v.*). Kingscavil (pop. 629) disputes with Stonehouse in Lanarkshire the honour of being the birthplace of Patrick Hamilton, the martyr (1504–1528).

See Sir R. Sibbald, *History of the Sheriffdoms of Linlithgow and Stirlingshire* (Edinburgh, 1710); G. Waldie, *Walks along the Northern Roman Wall* (Linlithgow, 1883); R. J. H. Cunningham, *Geology of the Lothians* (Edinburgh, 1838).

LINNAEUS, the name usually given to Carl von Linné (1707–1778), Swedish botanist, who was born on the 13th of May, O.S. (May 23, N.S.) 1707 at Råshult, in the province of Småland, Sweden, and was the eldest child of Nils Linnaeus the comminister, afterwards pastor, of the parish, and Christina Brodersonia, the daughter of the previous incumbent. In 1717 he was sent to the primary school at Wexiö, and in 1724 he passed to the gymnasium. His interests were centred on botany, and his progress in the studies considered necessary for admission to holy orders, for which he was intended, was so slight that in 1726 his father was recommended to apprentice him to a tailor or shoemaker. He was saved from this fate through Dr Rothman, a physician in the town, who expressed the belief that he would yet distinguish himself in medicine and natural history, and who further instructed him in physiology. In 1727 he entered the university of Lund, but removed in the following year to that of Upsala. There, through lack of means, he had a hard struggle until, in 1729, he made the acquaintance of Dr Olaf Celsius (1670–1756), professor of theology, at that time working at his *Hierobotanicon*, which saw the light nearly twenty years later. Celsius, impressed with Linnaeus's knowledge and botanical collections, and finding him necessitous, offered him board and lodging.

During this period, he came upon a critique which ultimately led to the establishment of his artificial system of plant classification. This was a review of Sébastien Vaillant's *Sermo de Structura Florum* (Leiden, 1718), a thin quarto in French and Latin; it set him upon examining the stamens and pistils of flowers, and, becoming convinced of the paramount importance of these organs, he formed the idea of basing a system of arrangement upon them. Another work by Wallin, *Γάμος φυτῶν, sive Nuptiae Arborum Dissertatio* (Upsala, 1729), having fallen into his hands, he drew up a short treatise on the sexes of plants, which was placed in the hands of the younger Olaf Rudbeck (1660–1740), the professor of botany in the university. In the following year Rudbeck, whose advanced age compelled him to lecture by deputy, appointed Linnaeus his adjunctus; in the spring of 1730, therefore, the latter began his lectures. The academic garden was entirely remodelled under his auspices, and furnished with many rare species. In the preceding year he had solicited appointment to the vacant post of gardener, which was refused him on the ground of his capacity for better things.

In 1732 he undertook to explore Lapland, at the cost of the Academy of Sciences of Upsala; he traversed upwards of 4600 m., and the cost of the journey is given at 530 copper dollars, or about £25 sterling. His own account was published in English by Sir J. E. Smith, under the title *Lachesis Lapponica*, in 1811; the scientific results were published in his *Flora Lapponica* (Amsterdam, 1737). In 1733 Linnaeus was engaged at Upsala in teaching the methods of assaying ores, but was prevented from delivering lectures on botany for academic reasons. At this juncture the governor of Dalecarlia invited him to travel through his province, as he had done through Lapland. Whilst on this journey, he lectured at Fahlun to large audiences; and J. Browallius (1707–1755), the chaplain there, afterwards bishop of Abo, strongly urged him to go abroad and take his degree of M.D. at a foreign university, by which means he could afterwards settle where he pleased. Accordingly he left Sweden in 1735. Travelling by Lübeck and Hamburg, he proceeded to Harderwijk; where he went through the requisite examinations, and defended his thesis on the cause of intermittent fever. His scanty funds were now nearly spent, but he passed on through Haarlem to Leiden, there he called on Jan Fredrik Gronovius (1690–1762), who, returning the visit, was shown the *Systema naturae* in MS., and was so greatly astonished at it that he sent it to press at his own expense. This famous system, which, artificial as it was, substituted order for confusion, largely made its way on account of the lucid and admirable laws, and comments on them, which were issued almost at the same time (see BOTANY). H. Boerhaave, whom Linnaeus saw after waiting eight days for admission, recommended him to J. Burman (1707–1780), the professor of botany at Amsterdam, with whom he stayed a twelvemonth. While there he issued his ***Fundamenta Botanica***, an unassuming small octavo, which exercised immense influence. For some time also he lived with the wealthy banker, G. Clifford (1685–1750), who had a magnificent garden at Hartecamp, near Haarlem.

In 1736 Linnaeus visited England. He was warmly recommended by Boerhaave to Sir Hans Sloane, who seems to have received him coldly. At Oxford Dr Thomas Shaw welcomed him cordially; J. J. Dillenius, the professor of botany, was cold at first, but afterwards changed completely, kept him a month, and even offered to share the emoluments of the chair with him. He saw Philip Miller (1691–1771), the ***Hortulanorum Princeps***, at Chelsea Physic Garden, and took some plants thence to Clifford; but certain other stories which are current about his visit to England are of very doubtful authenticity.

On his return to the Netherlands he completed the printing of his *Genera Plantarum*, a volume which must be considered the starting-point of modern systematic botany. During the same year, 1737, he finished arranging Clifford's collection of plants, living and dried, described in the *Hortus Cliffortianus*. During the compilation he used to "amuse" himself with drawing up the *Critica Botanica*, also printed in the Netherlands. But this strenuous and unremitting labour told upon him; the atmosphere of the Low Countries seemed to oppress him beyond endurance; and, resisting all Clifford's entreaties to remain with him, he started homewards, yet on the way he remained a year at Leiden, and published his *Classes Plantarum* (1738). He then visited Paris, where he saw Antoine and Bernard de Jussieu, and finally sailed for Sweden from Rouen. In September 1738 he established himself as a physician in Stockholm, but, being unknown as a medical man, no one at first cared to consult him; by degrees, however, he found patients, was appointed naval physician at Stockholm, with minor appointments, and in June 1739 married Sara Moraea. In 1741 he was appointed to the chair of medicine at Upsala, but soon exchanged it for that of botany. In the same year, previous to this exchange, he travelled through Öland and Gothland, by command of the state, publishing his results in *Oländska och Gothländska Resa* (1745). The index to this volume shows the first employment of specific names in nomenclature.

Henceforward his time was taken up by teaching and the preparation of other works. In 1745 he issued his *Flora Suecica* and *Fauna Suecica*, the latter having occupied his attention during fifteen years; afterwards, two volumes of observations made during journeys in Sweden, *Wästgöta Resa* (Stockholm, 1747), and *Skånska Resa* (Stockholm, 1751). In 1748 he brought out his *Hortus Upsaliensis*, showing that he had added eleven hundred species to those formerly in cultivation in that garden. In 1750 his *Philosophia Botanica* was given to the world; it consists of a commentary on the various axioms he had published in 1735 in his *Fundamenta Botanica*, and was dictated to his pupil P. Löfling (1729–1756), while the professor was confined to his bed by an attack of gout. But the most important work of this period was his *Species Plantarum* (Stockholm, 1753), in which the specific names are fully set forth. In the same year he was created knight of the Polar Star, the first time a scientific man had been raised to that honour in Sweden. In 1755 he was invited by the king of Spain to settle in that country, with a liberal salary, and full liberty of conscience, but he declined on the ground that whatever merits he possessed should be devoted to his country's service, and Löfling was sent instead. He was enabled now to purchase the estates of Säfja and Hammarby; at the latter he built his museum of stone, to guard against loss by fire. His lectures at the university drew men from all parts of the world; the normal number of students at Upsala was five hundred, but while he occupied the chair of botany there it rose to fifteen hundred. In 1761 he was granted a patent of nobility, antedated to 1757, from which time he was styled Carl von Linné. To his great delight the tea-plant was introduced alive into Europe in 1763; in the same year his surviving son Carl (1741–1783) was allowed to assist his father in his professorial duties, and to be trained as his successor. At the age of sixty his memory began to fail; an apoplectic attack in 1774 greatly weakened him; two years after he lost the use of his right side; and he died on the 10th of January 1778 at Upsala, in the cathedral of which he was buried.

With Linnaeus arrangement seems to have been a passion; he delighted in devising classifications, and not only did he systematize the three kingdoms of nature, but even drew up a treatise on the *Genera Morborum*. When he appeared upon the scene, new plants and animals were in course of daily discovery in increasing numbers, due to the increase of trading facilities; he devised schemes of arrangement by which these acquisitions might be sorted provisionally, until their natural affinities should have become clearer. He made many mistakes; but the honour due to him for having first enunciated the principles for defining genera and species, and his uniform use of specific names, is enduring. His style is terse and laconic; he methodically treated of each organ in its proper turn, and had a special term for each, the meaning of which did not vary. The reader cannot doubt the author's intention; his sentences are business-like and to the point. The omission of the verb in his descriptions was an innovation, and gave an abruptness to his language which was foreign to the writing of his time; but it probably by its succinctness added to the popularity of his works.

No modern naturalist has impressed his own character with greater force upon his pupils than did Linnaeus. He imbued them with his own intense acquisitiveness, reared them in an atmosphere of enthusiasm, trained them to close and accurate observation, and then despatched them to various parts of the globe.

His published works amount to more than one hundred and eighty, including the *Amoenitates Academicae*, for which he provided the material, revising them also for press; corrections in his handwriting may be seen in the Banksian and Linnean Society's libraries. Many of his works were not published during his lifetime; those which were are enumerated by Dr Richard Pulteney in his *General View of the Writings of Linnaeus* (1781). His widow sold his collections and books to Sir J. E. Smith, the first president of the Linnean Society of London. When Smith died in 1828, a subscription was raised to purchase the herbarium and library for the Society, whose property they became. The manuscripts of many of Linnaeus's publications, and the letters he received from his contemporaries, also came into the possession of the Society. (B. D. J.)

LINNELL, JOHN (1792–1882), English painter, was born in London on the 16th of June 1792. His father being a carver and gilder, Linnell was early brought into contact with artists, and when he was ten years old he was drawing and selling his portraits in chalk and pencil. His first artistic instruction was received from Benjamin West, and he spent a year in the house of John Varley the water-colour painter, where he had William Hunt and Mulready as fellow-pupils, and made the acquaintance of Shelley, Godwin and other men of mark. In 1805 he was admitted a student of the Royal Academy, where he obtained medals for drawing, modelling and sculpture. He was also trained as an engraver, and executed a transcript of Varley's "Burial of Saul." In after life he frequently occupied himself with the burin, publishing, in 1834, a series of outlines from Michelangelo's frescoes in the Sistine chapel, and, in 1840, superintending the issue of a selection of plates from the pictures in Buckingham Palace, one of them, a Titian landscape, being mezzotinted by himself. At first he supported himself mainly by miniature painting, and by the execution of larger portraits, such as the likenesses of Mulready, Whately, Peel and Carlyle. Several of his portraits he engraved with his own hand in line and mezzotint. He also painted many subjects like the "St John Preaching," the "Covenant of Abraham," and the "Journey to Emmaus," in which, while the landscape is usually prominent the figures are yet of sufficient importance to supply the title

... paintings
... commonly
... landscape,
... or sunset.
... and glowing
... prices for
... at Redhill,
... of January
... last few years
... a study of
... several pamphlets
... was one of
... Blake. He
... received for
... engravings
... sum for those

... seems to have
... the modern
... generalized
... cannabina
... ornithologists.
... the whole of
... to Turkestan.
... Abyssinia, and
... the Canaries
... for the seeds
... its common
... largely, if not
... Compositae.
... As these
... the plough,
... and means
... and hence
... throughout
... of the year.
... by the earlier

less with that colour. In Great Britain in the breeding-season it seems to affect exclusively hilly and moorland districts from Herefordshire northward, in which it partly or wholly replaces the common linnet, but is very much more local in its distribution, and, except in the British Islands and some parts of Scandinavia, it only appears as an irregular visitant in winter. At that season it may, however, be found in large flocks in the low-lying countries, and as regards England even on the sea-shore. In Asia it seems to be represented by a kindred form *L. brevirostris*.

The redpolls form a little group placed by many authorities in the genus *Linota*, to which they are unquestionably closely allied, and, as stated elsewhere (see FINCH), the linnets seem to be related to the birds of the genus *Leucosticte*, the species of which inhabit the northern parts of North-West America and of Asia. *L. tephrocotis* is generally of a chocolate colour, tinged on some parts with pale crimson or pink, and has the crown of the head silvery-grey. Another species, *L. arctoa*, was formerly said to have occurred in North America, but its proper home is in the Kurile Islands or Kamchatka. This has no red in its plumage. The birds of the genus *Leucosticte* seem to be more terrestrial in their habit than those of *Linota*, perhaps from their having been chiefly observed where trees are scarce; but it is possible that the mutual relationship of the two groups is more apparent than real. Allied to *Leucosticte* is *Montifringilla*, to which belongs the snow-finch of the Alps, *M. nivalis*, often mistaken by travellers for the snow-bunting, *Plectrophanes nivalis*. (A. N.)

LINSANG, the native name of one of the members of the viverrine genus *Linsanga*. There are four species of the genus, from the Indo-Malay countries. Linsangs are civet-like creatures, with the body and tail greatly elongated; and the ground colour fulvous marked with bold black patches, which in one species (*L. pardicolor*) are oblong. In West Africa the group is represented by the smaller and spotted *Poiana richardsoni* which has a genet-like hind-foot. (See CARNIVORA.)

LINSEED, the seed of the common flax (*q.v.*) or lint, *Linum usitatissimum*. These seeds, the linseed of commerce, are of a lustrous brown colour externally, and a compressed and elongated oval form, with a slight beak or projection at one extremity. The brown testa contains, in the outer of the four coats into which it is microscopically distinguishable, an abundant secretion of mucilaginous matter; and it has within it a thin layer of albumen, enclosing a pair of large oily cotyledons. The seeds when placed in water for some time become coated with glutinous matter from the exudation of the mucilage in the external layer of the epidermis; and by boiling in sixteen parts of water they exude sufficient mucilage to form with the water a thick pasty decoction. The cotyledons contain the valuable linseed oil referred to below. Linseed grown in tropical countries is much larger and more plump than that obtained in temperate climes, but the seed from the colder countries yields a finer quality of oil.

Linseed formed an article of food among the Greeks and Romans, and it is said that the Abyssinians at the present day eat it roasted. The oil is to some extent used as food in Russia and in parts of Poland and Hungary. The still prevalent use of linseed in poultices for open wounds is entirely to be reprobated. It has now been abandoned by practitioners. The principal objections to this use of linseed is that it specially favours the growth of micro-organisms. There are numerous clean and efficient substitutes which have all its supposed advantages and none of its disadvantages. There are now no medicinal uses of this substance. Linseed cake, the marc left after the expression of the oil, is a most valuable feeding substance for cattle.

Linseed is subject to extensive and detrimental adulterations, resulting not only from careless harvesting and cleaning, whereby seeds of the flax dodder, and other weeds and grasses are mixed with it, but also from the direct admixture of cheaper and inferior oil-seeds, such as wild rape, mustard, sesame, poppy, &c., the latter adulterations being known in trade under the generic name of "buffum." In 1864, owing to the serious aspect of the prevalent adulteration, a union of traders was formed under the name of the "Linseed Association." This body samples all linseed oil arriving in England and reports on its value.

Linseed oil, the most valuable drying oil, is obtained by expression from the seeds, with or without the aid of heat. Preliminary to the operation of pressing, the seeds are crushed and ground to a fine meal. Cold pressing of the seeds yields a golden-yellow oil, which is often used as an edible oil. Larger quantities are obtained by heating the crushed seeds to 160° F. (71° C.), and then expressing the oil. So obtained, it is somewhat turbid and yellowish-brown in colour. On storing, moisture and mucilaginous matter gradually settle out. After storing several years it is known commercially as "tanked oil," and has a high value in varnish-making. The delay attendant on this method of purification is avoided by treating the crude oil with 1 to 2% of a somewhat strong sulphuric acid, which chars and carries down the bulk of the impurities. For the preparation of "artist's oil," the finest form of linseed oil, the refined oil is placed in shallow trays covered with glass, and exposed to the action of the sun's rays. Numerous other methods of purification, some based on the oxidizing action of ozone, have been suggested. The yield of oil from different classes of seed varies, but from 23 to 28% of the weight of the seed operated on should be obtained. A good average quality of seed weighing about 392 lb per quarter has been found in practice to give out 109 lb of oil.

Commercial linseed oil has a peculiar, rather disagreeable sharp taste and smell; its specific gravity is given as varying from 0.928 to 0.953, and it solidifies at about −27°. By saponification it yields a number of fatty acids—palmitic, myristic, oleic, linolic, linolenic and isolinolenic. Exposed to the air in thin films, linseed oil absorbs oxygen and forms "linoxyn," a resinous semi-elastic, caoutchouc-like mass, of uncertain composition. The oil, when boiled with small proportions of litharge and minium, undergoes the process of resinification in the air with greatly increased rapidity.

Its most important use is in the preparation of oil paints and varnishes. By painters both raw and boiled oil are used, the latter forming the principal medium in oil painting, and also serving separately as the basis of all oil varnishes. Boiled oil is prepared in a variety of ways—that most common being by heating the raw oil in an iron or copper boiler, which, to allow for frothing, must only be about three-fourths filled. The boiler is heated by a furnace, and the oil is brought gradually to the point of ebullition, at which it is maintained for two hours, during which time moisture is driven off, and the scum and froth which accumulate on the surface are ladled out. Then by slow degrees a proportion of "dryers" is added—usually equal weights of litharge and minium being used to the extent of 3% of the charge of oil; and with these a small proportion of umber is generally thrown in. After the addition of the dryers the boiling is continued two or three hours; the fire is then suddenly withdrawn, and the oil is left covered up in the boiler for ten hours or more. Before sending out, it is usually stored in settling tanks for a few weeks, during which time the uncombined dryers settle at the bottom as "foots." Besides the dryers already mentioned, lead acetate, manganese borate, manganese dioxide, zinc sulphate and other bodies are used.

Linseed oil is also the principal ingredient in printing and lithographic inks. The oil for ink-making is prepared by heating it in an iron pot up to the point where it either takes fire spontaneously or can be ignited with any flaming substance. After the oil has been allowed to burn for some time according to the consistence of the varnish desired, the pot is covered over, and the product when cooled forms a viscid tenacious substance which in its most concentrated form may be drawn into threads. By boiling this varnish with dilute nitric acid vapours of acrolein are given off, and the substance gradually becomes a solid non-adhesive mass the same as the ultimate oxidation product of both raw and boiled oil.

Linseed oil is subject to various falsifications, chiefly through the addition of cotton-seed, niger-seed and hemp-seed oils; and rosin oil and mineral oils also are not infrequently added. Except by smell, by change of specific gravity, and by deterioration of drying properties, these adulterations are difficult to detect.

LINSTOCK (adapted from the Dutch *lontstok*, *i.e.* "match-stick," from *lont*, a match, *stok*, a stick, the word is sometimes erroneously spelled "lintstock" from a supposed derivation from "lint" in the sense of tinder), a kind of torch made of a stout stick a yard in length, with a fork at one end to hold a lighted match, and a point at the other to stick in the ground. "Linstocks" were used for discharging cannon in the early days of artillery.

LINT (in M. Eng. *linnet*, probably through Fr. *linette*, from *lin*, the flax-plant; cf. "line"), properly the flax-plant, now only in Scots dialect; hence the application of such expressions as "lint-haired," "lint white locks" to flaxen hair. It is also the term applied to the flax when prepared for spinning, and to the waste material left over which was used for tinder. "Lint" is still the name given to a specially prepared material for dressing wounds, made soft and fluffy by scraping or ravelling linen cloth.

LINTEL (O. Fr. *lintel*, mod. *linteau*, from Late Lat. *limitellum*, *limes*, boundary, confused in sense with *limen*, threshold; the Latin name is *supercilium*, Ital. *soprasogli*, and Ger. *Sturz*), in architecture, a horizontal piece of stone or timber over a doorway or opening, provided to carry the superstructure. In order to relieve the lintel from too great a pressure a "discharging arch" is generally built over it.

LINTH, or LIMMAT, a river of Switzerland, one of the tributaries of the Aar. It rises in the glaciers of the Tödi range, and has cut out a deep bed which forms the Grossthal that comprises the greater portion of the canton of Glarus. A little below the town of Glarus the river, keeping its northerly direction, runs through the alluvial plain which it has formed, towards the Walensee and the Lake of Zürich. But between the Lake of Zürich and the Walensee the huge desolate alluvial plain grew ever in size, while great damage was done by the river, which overflowed its bed and the dykes built to protect the region near it. The Swiss diet decided in 1804 to undertake the "correction" of this turbulent stream. The necessary works were begun in 1807 under the supervision of Hans Conrad Escher of Zürich (1767–1823). The first portion of the undertaking was completed in 1811, and received the name of the "Escher canal," the river being thus diverted into the Walensee. The second portion, known as the "Linth canal," regulated the course of the river between the Walensee and the Lake of Zürich and was completed in 1816. Many improvements and extra protective works were carried out after 1816, and it was estimated that the total cost of this great engineering undertaking from 1807 to 1902 amounted to about £200,000, the date for the completion of the work being 1911. To commemorate the efforts of Escher, the Swiss diet in 1823 (after his death) decided that his male descendants should bear the name of "Escher von der Linth." On issuing from the Lake of Zürich the Linth alters its name to that of "Limmat," it does not appear wherefore, and, keeping the north-westerly direction it had taken from the Walensee, joins the Aar a little way below Brugg, and just below the junction of the Reuss with the Aar. (W. A. B. C.)

LINTON, ELIZA LYNN (1822–1898), English novelist, daughter of the Rev. J. Lynn, vicar of Crosthwaite, in Cumberland, was born at Keswick on the 10th of February 1822. She early manifested great independence of character, and in great measure educated herself from the stores of her father's library. Coming to London about 1845 with a large stock of miscellaneous erudition, she turned this to account in her first novels, *Azeth the Egyptian* (1846) and *Amymone* (1848), a romance of the days of Pericles. Her next story, *Realities*, a tale of modern life (1851), was not successful, and for several years she seemed to have abandoned fiction. When, in 1865, she reappeared with *Grasp your Nettle*, it was as an expert in a new style of novel-writing—stirring, fluent, ably-constructed stories, retaining the attention throughout, but affording little to reflect upon or to remember. Measured by their immediate success, they gave her an honourable position among the writers of her day, and secure of an audience, she continued to write with vigour nearly until her death. *Lizzie Lorton of Greyrigg* (1866), *Patricia Kemball* (1874), *The Atonement of Leam Dundas* (1877) are among the best examples of this more mechanical side of her talent, to which there were notable exceptions in *Joshua Davidson* (1872), a bold but not irreverent adaptation of the story of the Carpenter of Nazareth to that of the French Commune; and *Christopher Kirkland*, a veiled autobiography (1885). Mrs Linton was a practised and constant writer in the journals of the day, her articles on the "Girl of the Period" in the *Saturday Review* produced a great sensation, and she was a constant contributor to the *St James's Gazette*, the *Daily News* and other leading newspapers. Many of her detached essays have been collected. In 1858 she married W. J. Linton, the engraver, but the union was soon terminated by mutual consent; she nevertheless brought up one of Mr Linton's daughters by a former marriage. A few years before her death she retired to Malvern. She died in London on the 14th of July 1898.

Her reminiscences appeared after her death under the title of *My Literary Life* (1899) and her life has been written by G. S. Layard (1901).

LINTON, WILLIAM JAMES (1812–1897), English wood-engraver, republican and author, was born in London. He was educated at Stratford, and in his sixteenth year was apprenticed to the wood-engraver G. W. Bonner. His earliest known work is to be found in Martin and Westall's *Pictorial Illustrations of the Bible* (1833). He rapidly rose to a place amongst the foremost wood-engravers of the time. After working as a journeyman engraver with two or three firms, losing his money over a cheap political library called the "National," and writing a life of Thomas Paine, he went into partnership (1842) with John Orrin Smith. The firm was immediately employed on the *Illustrated London News*, just then projected. The following year Orrin Smith died, and Linton, who had married a sister of Thomas Wade, editor of *Bell's Weekly Messenger*, found himself in sole charge of a business upon which two families were dependent. For years he had concerned himself with the social and European political problems of the time, and was now actively engaged in the republican propaganda. In 1844 he took a prominent part in exposing the violation by the English post-office of Mazzini's correspondence. This led to a friendship with the Italian revolutionist, and Linton threw himself with ardour into European politics. He carried the first congratulatory address of English workmen to the French Provisional Government in 1848. He edited a twopenny weekly paper, *The Cause of the People*, published in the Isle of Man, and he wrote political verses for the Dublin *Nation*, signed "Spartacus." He helped to found the "International League" of patriots, and, in 1850, with G. H. Lewes and Thornton Hunt, started *The Leader*, an organ which, however, did not satisfy his advanced republicanism, and from which he soon withdrew. The same year he wrote a series of [illegible] propounding the views of Mazzini in *The Red Republican*. In [illegible] he took up his residence at Brantwood, which he afterwards sold to John Ruskin, and from there issued *The English* [illegible], first in the form of weekly tracts and afterwards as a [illegible] magazine—"a useful exponent of republican principles, [illegible] record of republican progress throughout the world, [illegible] of propagandism and a medium of communication for [illegible] republicans in England." Most of the paper, which [illegible] its way and was abandoned in 1855, was written by [illegible] In 1852 he also printed for private circulation an [illegible] volume of poems entitled *The Plaint of Freedom*. [illegible] failure of his paper he returned to his proper work of [illegible] In 1857 his wife died, and in the following year [illegible] Lynn (afterwards known as Mrs Lynn Linton) [illegible] to London. In 1864 he retired to Brantwood, his [illegible] in London. In 1867, pressed by financial diffi[illegible] to try his fortune in America, and finally [illegible] his wife, with whom, however, he always corre[illegible] With his children he settled at Appledore, [illegible], where he set up a printing-press. Here [illegible] *Hints on Wood-Engraving* (1879), *James* [illegible] *Chartist Times* (1879), *A History of Wood-* [illegible]), *Wood-Engraving, a Manual of* [illegible] *Masters of Wood-Engraving*, for which [illegible] England (1890), *The Life of Whittier* [illegible] autobiography (1895). He died at [illegible] December 1897. Linton was a singu[illegible] the words of his wife, if he had not [illegible] impracticable politics, would have [illegible] with art and letters. As an engraver [illegible] point of execution in his own line. [illegible] Bewick, fought for intelligent as [illegible] excellence in the use of the graver, [illegible] the "white line" as well as of the [illegible] that the former was the truer and more telling basis of aesthetic expression in the wood-block printed upon paper.

See W. J. Linton, *Memories*; F. G. Kitton, article on "Linton" in *English Illustrated Magazine* (April 1891); G. S. Layard, *Life of Mrs Lynn Linton* (1901). (G. S. L.)

LINTOT, BARNABY BERNARD (1675–1736), English publisher, was born at Southwater, Sussex, on the 1st of December 1675, and started business as a publisher in London about 1698. He published for many of the leading writers of the day, notably Vanbrugh, Steele, Gay and Pope. The latter's *Rape of the Lock* in its original form was first published in *Lintot's Miscellany*, and Lintot subsequently issued Pope's translation of the *Iliad* and the joint translation of the *Odyssey* by Pope, Fenton and Broome. Pope quarrelled with Lintot with regard to the supply of free copies of the latter translation to the author's subscribers, and in 1728 satirized the publisher in the *Dunciad*, and in 1735 in the *Prologue to the Satires*, though he does not appear to have had any serious grievance. Lintot died on the 3rd of February 1736.

LINUS, one of the saints of the Gregorian canon, whose festival is celebrated on the 23rd of September. All that can be said with certainty about him is that his name appears at the head of all the lists of the bishops of Rome. Irenaeus (*Adv. Haer.* iii. 3. 3) identifies him with the Linus mentioned by St Paul in 2 Tim. iv. 21. According to the *Liber Pontificalis*, Linus suffered martyrdom, and was buried in the Vatican. In the 17th century an inscription was found near the confession of St Peter, which was believed to contain the name Linus; but it is not certain that this epitaph has been read correctly or completely. The apocryphal Latin account of the death of the apostles Peter and Paul is falsely attributed to Linus.

See *Acta Sanctorum*, Septembris, vi. 539-545; C de Smedt, *Dissertationes selectae in primam aetatem hist. eccl.* pp. 300-312 (Ghent, 1876), L. Duchesne's edition of the *Liber Pontificalis*, i. 121 (Paris, 1886), R. A. Lipsius, *Die apokryphen Apostelgeschichten*, ii. 85-96 (Brunswick, 1883–1890); J. B. de Rossi, *Bullettino di archeologia cristiana*, p. 50 (1864). (H. De.)

LINUS, one of a numerous class of heroic figures in Greek legend, of which other examples are found in Hyacinthus and Adonis. The connected legend is always of the same character: a beautiful youth, fond of hunting and rural life, the favourite of some god or goddess, suddenly perishes by a terrible death. In many cases the religious background of the legend is preserved by the annual ceremonial that commemorated it. At Argos this religious character of the Linus myth was best preserved: the secret child of Psamathe by the god Apollo, Linus is exposed, nursed by sheep and torn in pieces by sheep-dogs. Every year at the festival Arnis or Cynophontis, the women of Argos mourned for Linus and propitiated Apollo, who in revenge for his child's death had sent a female monster (Poinê), which tore the children from their mothers' arms. Lambs were sacrificed, all dogs found running loose were killed, and women and children raised a lament for Linus and Psamathe (Pausanias i. 43. 7; Conon, *Narrat.* 19) In the Theban version, Linus, the son of Amphimarus and the muse Urania, was a famous musician, inventor of the Linus song, who was said to have been slain by Apollo, because he had challenged him to a contest (Pausanias ix. 29. 6) A later story makes him the teacher of Heracles, by whom he was killed because he had rebuked his pupil for stupidity (Apollodorus ii. 4. 9) On Mount Helicon there was a grotto containing his statue, to which sacrifice was offered every year before the sacrifices to the Muses. From being the inventor of musical methods, he was finally transformed by later writers into a composer of prophecies and legends. He was also said to have adapted the Phoenician letters introduced by Cadmus to the Greek language. It is generally agreed that Linus and Ailinus are of Semitic origin, derived from the words *ai lanu* (woe to us), which formed the burden of the Adonis and similar songs popular in the East. The Linus song is mentioned in Homer, the tragedians often use the word αἴλινος as the refrain in mournful songs, and Euripides calls the custom a Phrygian one. Linus, originally the personification of the song of lamentation, becomes, like Adonis, Maneros, Narcissus, the representative of the tender life of nature and of the vegetation destroyed by the fiery heat of the dog-star.

The chief work on the subject is H. Brugsch, *Die Adonisklage und das Linoslied* (1852); see also article in Roscher's *Lexikon der Mythologie*; J. G. Frazer, *Golden Bough* (ii. 224, 253), where, the identity of Linus with Adonis (possibly a corn-spirit) being assumed, the lament is explained as the lamentation of the reapers over the dead corn-spirit; W. Mannhardt, *Wald- und Feldculte*, ii. 281.

LINZ, capital of the Austrian duchy and crownland of Upper Austria, and see of a bishop, 117 m. W. of Vienna by rail. Pop. (1900) 58,778. It lies on the right bank of the Danube and is connected by an iron bridge, 308 yds. long, with the market-town of Urfahr (pop. 12,827) on the opposite bank. Linz possesses two cathedrals, one built in 1669–1682 in rococo style, and another in early Gothic style, begun in 1862. In the Capuchin church is the tomb of Count Raimondo Montecucculi, who died at Linz in 1680. The museum Francisco-Carolinum, founded in 1833 and reconstructed in 1895, contains several important collections relating to the history of Upper Austria. In the Franz Josef-Platz stands a marble monument, known as Trinity Column, erected by the emperor Charles VI. in 1723, commemorating the triple deliverance of Linz from war, fire, and pestilence. The principal manufactories are of tobacco, boat-building, agricultural implements, foundries and cloth factories. Being an important railway junction and a port of the Danube, Linz has a very active transit trade.

Linz is believed to stand on the site of the Roman station *Lentia*. The name of Linz appears in documents for the first time in 799 and it received municipal rights in 1324. In 1490 it became the capital of the province above the Enns. It successfully resisted the attacks of the insurgent peasants under Stephen Fadinger on the 21st and 22nd of July 1626, but its suburbs were laid in ashes. During the siege of Vienna in 1683, the castle of Linz was the residence of Leopold I. In 1741, during the War of the Austrian Succession, Linz was taken by the Bavarians, but was recovered by the Austrians in the following year. The bishopric was established in 1784.

See F. Krackowitzer, *Die Donaustadt Linz* (Linz, 1901).

LION (Lat. *leo, leonis*; Gr. λέων). From the earliest historic times few animals have been better known to man than the lion. Its habitat made it familiar to all the races among whom human civilization took its origin. The literature of the ancient Hebrews abounds in allusions to the lion; and the almost incredible numbers stated to have been provided for exhibition and destruction in the Roman amphitheatres (as many as six hundred on a single occasion by Pompey, for example) show how abundant these animals must have been within accessible distance of Rome.

Even within the historic period the geographical range of the lion covered the whole of Africa, the south of Asia, including Syria, Arabia, Asia Minor, Persia and the greater part of northern and central India. Professor A. B. Meyer, director of the zoological museum at Dresden, has published an article on the alleged existence of the lion in historical times in Greece, a translation of which appears in the *Report* of the Smithsonian Institution for 1905. Meyer is of opinion that the writer of the *Iliad* was probably acquainted with the lion, but this does not prove its former existence in Greece. The accounts given by Herodotus and Aristotle merely go to show that about 500 B.C. lions existed in some part of eastern Europe. The Greek name for the lion is very ancient, and this suggests, although by no means demonstrates, that it refers to an animal indigenous to the country. Although the evidence is not decisive, it seems probable that lions did exist in Greece at the time of Herodotus; and it is quite possible that the representation of a lion-chase incised on a Mycenean dagger may have been taken from life. In prehistoric times the lion was spread over the greater part of Europe; and if, as is very probable, the so-called *Felis atrox* be inseparable, its range also included the greater part of North America.

At the present day the lion is found throughout Africa (save in places where it has been exterminated by man) and in Mesopotamia, Persia, and some parts of north-west India. According to Dr W. T. Blanford, lions are still numerous in the reedy swamps, bordering the Tigris and Euphrates, and also occur on the west flanks of the Zagros mountains and the oak-clad ranges near Shiraz, to which they are attracted by the herds of swine which feed on the acorns. The lion nowhere exists in the table-land of Persia, nor is it found in Balūchistān. In India it is confined to the province of Kathiawar in Gujerat, though within the 19th century it extended through the north-west parts of Hindustan, from Bahāwalpur and Sind to at least the Jumna (about Delhi) southward as far as Khāndesh, and in central India through the Sagur and Narbuda territories, Bundelkund, and as far east as Palamau. It was extirpated in Hariāna about 1824. One was killed at Rhyli, in the Dumaoh district, Sagur and Narbuda territories, so late as in the cold season of 1847–1848; and about the same time a few still remained in the valley of the Sind river in Kotah, central India.

The variations in external characters which lions present, especially in the colour and the amount of mane, as well as in the general colour of the fur, indicate local races, to which

After a Drawing by Wolf in Elliot's Monograph of the *Felidae*.

Fig. 1.—Lion and Lioness (*Felis leo*).

special names have been given; the Indian lion being *F. leo gujratensis*. It is noteworthy, however, that, according to Mr F. C. Selous, in South Africa the black-maned lion and others with yellow scanty manes are found, not only in the same locality, but even among individuals of the same parentage.

The lion belongs to the genus *Felis* of Linnaeus (for the characters and position of which see Carnivora), and differs from the tiger and leopard in its uniform colouring, and from all the other *Felidae* in the hair of the top of the head, chin and neck, as far back as the shoulder, being not only much longer, but also differently disposed from the hair elsewhere, being erect or directed forwards, and so constituting the characteristic ornament called the mane. There is also a tuft of elongated hairs at the end of the tail, one upon each elbow, and in most lions a copious fringe along the middle line of the under surface of the body, wanting, however, in some examples. These characters are, however, peculiar to the adults of the male sex; and even as regards coloration young lions show indications of the darker stripes and mottlings so characteristic of the greater number of the members of the genus. The usual colour of the adult is yellowish-brown, but it may vary from a deep red or chestnut brown to an almost silvery grey. The mane, as well as the long hair of the other parts of the body, sometimes scarcely differs from the general colour, but is usually darker and not

S. of Lipari, contains a still smoking crater. Sulphur works were started in 1874, but have since been abandoned.

See Archduke Ludwig Salvator of Austria, *Die Liparischen Inseln*, 8 vols. (for private circulation) (Prague, 1893 seqq.).

LIPETSK, a town of Russia, in the government of Tambov, 108 m. by rail W. of the city of Tambov, on the right bank of the river Voronezh. Pop. (1897) 16,353. The town is built of wood and the streets are unpaved. There are sugar, tallow, and leather works, and distilleries, and an active trade in horses, cattle, tallow, skins, honey and timber. The Lipetsk mineral springs (chalybeate) came into repute in the time of Peter the Great and attract a good many visitors.

LIPPE, a river of Germany, a right-bank tributary of the Rhine. It rises near Lippspringe under the western declivity of the Teutoburger Wald, and, after being joined by the Alme, the Pader and the Ahse on the left, and by the Stever on the right, flows into the Rhine near Wesel, after a course of 154 m. It is navigable downwards from Lippstadt, for boats and barges, by the aid of twelve locks, drawing less than 4 ft. of water. The river is important for the transport facilities it affords to the rich agricultural districts of Westphalia.

LIPPE, a principality of Germany and constituent state of the German empire, bounded N.W., W. and S. by the Prussian province of Westphalia and N.E. and E. by the Prussian provinces of Hanover and Hesse-Nassau and the principality of Waldeck-Pyrmont. It also possesses three small enclaves—Kappel and Lipperode in Westphalia and Grevenhagen near Höxter. The area is 469 sq. m., and the population (1905) 145,610, showing a density of 125 to the sq. m. The greater part of the surface is hilly, and in the S. and W., where the Teutoburger Wald practically forms its physical boundary, mountainous. The chief rivers are the Weser, which crosses the north extremity of the principality, and its affluents, the Werre, Exter, Kalle and Emmer. The Lippe, which gives its name to the country, is a purely Westphalian river and does not touch the principality at any point. The forests of Lippe, among the finest in Germany, produce abundance of excellent timber. They occupy 28% of the whole area, and consist mostly of deciduous trees, beech preponderating. The valleys contain a considerable amount of good arable land, the tillage of which employs the greater part of the inhabitants. Small farms, the larger proportion of which are under 2½ acres, are numerous, and their yield shows a high degree of prosperity among the peasant farmers. The principal crops are potatoes, beetroot (for sugar), hay, rye, oats, wheat and barley. Cattle, sheep and swine are also reared, and the "Senner" breed of horses, in the stud farm at Lopshorn, is celebrated. The industries are small and consist mainly in the manufacture of starch, paper, sugar, tobacco, and in weaving and brewing. Lemgo is famous for its meerschaum pipes and Salzuflen for its brine-springs, producing annually about 1500 tons of salt, which is mostly exported. Each year, in spring, about 15,000 brickmakers leave the principality and journey to other countries, Hungary, Sweden and Russia, to return home in the late autumn.

The roads are well laid and kept in good repair. A railway intersects the country from Herford (on the Cologne-Hanover main line) to Altenbeken; and another from Bielefeld to Hameln traverses it from W. to E. More than 95% of the population in 1905 were Protestants. Education is provided for by two gymnasia and numerous other efficient schools. The principality contains seven small towns, the chief of which are Detmold, the seat of government, Lemgo, Horn and Blomberg. The present constitution was granted in 1836, but it was altered in 1867 and again in 1876. It provides for a representative chamber of twenty-one members, whose functions are mainly consultative. For electoral purposes the population is divided into three classes, rated according to taxation, each of which returns seven members. The courts of law are centred at Detmold, whence an appeal lies to the court of appeal at Celle in the Prussian province of Hanover. The estimated revenue in [illegible] was £113,000 and the expenditure £116,000. The public debt in 1908 was £64,000. Lippe has one vote in the German Reichstag, and also one vote in the Bundesrat, or federal council. Its military forces form a battalion of the 6th Westphalian infantry.

History.—The present principality of Lippe was inhabited in early times by the Cherusii, whose leader Arminius (Hermann) annihilated in A.D. 9 the legions of Varus in the Teutoburger Wald. It was afterwards occupied by the Saxons and was subdued by Charlemagne. The founder of the present reigning family, one of the most ancient in Germany, was Bernard I. (1113–1144), who received a grant of the territory from the emperor Lothair, and assumed the title of lord of Lippe (*edler Herr von Lippe*). He was descended from a certain Hoold who flourished about 950. Bernard's successors inherited or obtained several counties, and one of them, Simon III. (d. 1410), introduced the principles of primogeniture. Under Simon V. (d. 1536), who was the first to style himself count, the Reformation was introduced into the country. His grandson, Simon VI. (1555–1613), is the ancestor of both lines of the princes of Lippe. In 1613 the country, as it then existed, was divided among his three sons, the lines founded by two of whom still exist, while the third (Brake) became extinct in 1709. Lippe proper was the patrimony of the eldest son, Simon VII. (1587–1627), upon whose descendant Frederick William Leopold (d. 1802) the title of prince of the empire was bestowed in 1789, a dignity already conferred, though not confirmed, in 1720. Philip, the youngest son of Simon VI., received but a scanty part of his father's possessions, but in 1640 he inherited a large part of the countship of Schaumburg, including Bückeburg, and adopted the title of count of Schaumburg-Lippe. The ruler of this territory became a sovereign prince in 1807. Simon VII. had a younger son, Jobst Hermann (d. 1678), who founded the line of counts of Lippe-Biesterfeld, and a cadet branch of this family were the counts of Lippe-Weissenfeld. In 1762 these two counties—Biesterfeld and Weissenfeld—passed by arrangement into the possession of the senior and ruling branch of the family. Under the prudent government of the princess Pauline (from 1802 to 1820), widow of Frederick William Leopold, the little state enjoyed great prosperity. In 1807 it joined the Confederation of the Rhine and in 1813 the German Confederation. Pauline's son, Paul Alexander Leopold, who reigned from 1820 to 1851, also ruled in a wise and liberal spirit, and in 1836 granted the charter of rights upon which the constitution is based. In 1842 Lippe entered the German Customs Union (*Zollverein*), and in 1866 threw in its lot with Prussia and joined the North German Confederation.

The Lippe succession dispute.

The line of rulers in Lippe dates back, as already mentioned, to Simon VI. But besides this, the senior line, the two collateral lines of counts, Lippe-Biesterfeld and Lippe-Weissenfeld and the princely line of Schaumburg-Lippe, also trace their descent to the same ancestor, and these three lines stand in the above order as regards their rights to the Lippe succession, the counts being descended from Simon's eldest son and the princes from his youngest son. These facts were not in dispute when in March 1895 the death of Prince Woldemar, who had reigned since 1875, raised a dispute as to the succession. Woldemar's brother Alexander, the last of the senior line, was hopelessly insane and had been declared incapable of ruling. On the death of Woldemar, Prince Adolph of Schaumburg-Lippe, fourth son of Prince Adolph George of that country and brother-in-law of the German emperor, took over the regency by virtue of a decree issued by Prince Woldemar, but which had until the latter's death been kept secret. The Lippe house of representatives consequently passed a special law confirming the regency in the person of Prince Adolph, but with the proviso that the regency should be at an end as soon as the disputes touching the succession were adjusted; and with a further proviso that, should this dispute not have been settled before the death of Prince Alexander, then, if a competent court of law had been secured before that event happened, the regency of Prince Adolph should continue until such court had given its decision. The dispute in question had arisen because the heads of the two collateral countly lines had entered a *caveat*. In order to adjust matters the Lippe government moved the *Bundesrat*, on the 5th of July 1895, to pass an imperial law declaring the *Reichsgericht* (the supreme tribunal of the empire) a competent court to adjudicate upon the claims of the rival lines to the succession. In consequence the Bundesrat passed a resolution on the 1st of February 1896, requesting the chancellor of the empire to bring about a compromise for the appointment of a court of arbitration between the parties. Owing to the mediation of the chancellor a compact was on the 3rd of July 1896 concluded between the heads of the three collateral lines of the whole house of Lippe, binding "both on themselves and on the lines of which they were the heads." By clause 2 of this compact, a court of arbitration was to be appointed, consisting of the king of Saxony and six members selected by him from among the members of the supreme court of law of the empire. This court was duly constituted, and on the 22nd of June 1897 delivered judgment to the effect that Count Ernest of Lippe-Biesterfeld, head of the line of Lippe-Biesterfeld, was entitled to succeed to the throne of Lippe on the death of Prince Alexander. In consequence of this judgment Prince Adolph resigned the regency and Count Ernest became regent in his stead. On the 26th of September 1904 Count Ernest died and his eldest son, Count Leopold, succeeded to the regency; but the question of the succession was again raised by the prince of Schaumburg-Lippe, who urged that the marriage of Count William Ernest, father of Count Ernest, with Modeste von Unruh, and that of the count regent Ernest himself with Countess Carline von Wartensleben were not *ebenbürtig* (equal birth), and that the issue of these marriages were therefore excluded from the succession. Prince George of Schaumburg-Lippe and the count regent, Leopold, thereupon entered into a compact, again referring the matter to the Bundesrat, which requested the chancellor of the empire to agree to the appointment of a court of arbitration consisting of two civil senates of the supreme court, sitting at Leipzig, to decide finally the matter in dispute. It was further provided in the compact that Leopold should remain as regent, even after the death of Alexander, until the decision of the court had been given. Prince Alexander died on the 13th of January 1905; Count Leopold remained as regent, and on the 25th of October the court of arbitration issued its award, declaring the marriages in question (which were, as proved by document, contracted with the consent of the head of the house in each case) *ebenbürtig*, and that in pursuance of the award of the king of Saxony the family of Lippe-Biesterfeld, together with the collateral lines sprung from Count William Ernest (father of the regent, Count Ernest) were in the order of nearest agnates called to the succession. Leopold (b. 1871) thus became prince of Lippe.

See A. Falkmann, *Beiträge zur Geschichte des Fürstenthums Lippe* (Detmold, 1857–1892; 6 vols.); Schwanold, *Das Fürstentum Lippe, das Land und seine Bewohner* (Detmold, 1899); Piderit, *Die lippischen Edelherrn im Mittelalter* (Detmold, 1876); A. Falkmann and O. Preuss, *Lippische Regenten* (Detmold, 1860–1868); H. Triepel, *Der Streit um die Thronfolge im Fürstentum Lippe* (Leipzig, 1903); and P. Laband, *Die Thronfolge im Fürstentum Lippe* (Freiburg, 1891); and *Schiedsspruch in dem Rechtstreit über die Thronfolge im Fürstentum Lippe vom 25 Okt. 1905* (Leipzig, 1906).

LIPPI, the name of three celebrated Italian painters.

I. Fra Filippo Lippi (1406–1469), commonly called Lippo Lippi, one of the most renowned painters of the Italian quattrocento, was born in Florence—his father, Tommaso, being a butcher. His mother died in his childhood, and his father survived his wife only two years. His aunt, a poor woman named Monna Lapaccia, then took charge of the boy; and in 1420, when fourteen years of age, he was registered in the community of the Carmelite friars of the Carmine in Florence. Here he remained till 1432, and his early faculty for fine arts was probably developed by studying the works of Masaccio in the neighbouring chapel of the Brancacci. Between 1430 and 1432 he executed some works in the monastery, which were destroyed by a fire in 1771; they are specified by Vasari, and one of them was particularly marked by its resemblance to Masaccio's style. Eventually Fra Filippo quitted his convent, but it appears that he was not relieved from some sort of religious vow; in a letter dated in 1439 he speaks of himself as the poorest friar of Florence, and says he is charged with the maintenance of six marriageable nieces. In 1452 he was appointed chaplain to the convent of S. Giovannino in Florence, and in 1457 rector (*Rettore Commendatario*) of S. Quirico at Legania, and his gains were considerable and uncommonly large from time to time; but his poverty seems to have been chronic, the money being spent, according to one account, in frequently recurring amours.

Vasari relates some curious and romantic adventures of Fra Filippo, which modern biographers are not inclined to believe. Except through Vasari, nothing is known of his visits to Ancona and Naples, and his intermediate capture by Barbary pirates and enslavement in Barbary, whence his skill in portrait-sketching availed to release him. This relates to a period, 1431–1437, when his career is not otherwise clearly accounted for. The doubts thrown upon his semi-marital relations with a Florentine lady appear, however, to be somewhat arbitrary; Vasari's account is circumstantial, and in itself not greatly improbable. Towards June 1456 Fra Filippo was settled in Prato (near Florence) for the purpose of fulfilling a commission to paint frescoes in the choir of the cathedral. Before actually undertaking this work he set about painting, in 1458, a picture for the convent chapel of S. Margherita of Prato, and there saw Lucrezia Buti, the beautiful daughter of a Florentine, Francesco Buti; she was either a novice or a young lady placed under the nuns' guardianship. Lippi asked that she might be permitted to sit to him for the figure of the Madonna (or it might rather appear of S. Margherita); he made passionate love to her, abducted her to his own house, and kept her there spite of the utmost efforts the nuns could make to reclaim her The fruit of their loves was a boy, who became the painter, not less celebrated than his father, Filippino Lippi (noticed below). Such is substantially Vasari's narrative, published less than a century after the alleged events; it is not refuted by saying, more than three centuries later, that perhaps Lippo had nothing to do with any such Lucrezia, and perhaps Lippino was his adopted son, or only an ordinary relative and scholar. The argument that two reputed portraits of Lucrezia in paintings by Lippo are not alike, one as a Madonna in a very fine picture in the Pitti gallery, and the other in the same character in a Nativity in the Louvre, comes to very little; and it is reduced to nothing when the disputant adds that the Louvre painting is probably not done by Lippi at all. Besides, it appears more likely that not the Madonna in the Louvre but a S. Margaret in a picture now in the Gallery of Prato is the original portrait (according to the tradition) of Lucrezia Buti.

The frescoes in the choir of Prato cathedral, being the stories of the Baptist and of St Stephen, represented on the two opposite wall spaces, are the most important and monumental works which Fra Filippo has left, more especially the figure of Salome dancing, and the last of the series, showing the ceremonial mourning over Stephen's corpse. This contains a portrait of the painter, but which is the proper figure is a question that has raised some diversity of opinion. At the end wall of the choir are S. Giovanni Gualberto and S. Alberto, and on the ceiling the four evangelists.

The close of Lippi's life was spent at Spoleto, where he had been commissioned to paint, for the apse of the cathedral, some scenes from the life of the Virgin. In the semidome of the apse is Christ crowning the Madonna, with angels, sibyls and prophets. This series, which is not wholly equal to the one at Prato, was completed by Fra Diamante after Lippi's death. That Lippi died in Spoleto, on or about the 8th of October 1469, is an undoubted fact; the mode of his death is again a matter of dispute. It has been said that the pope granted Lippi a dispensation for marrying Lucrezia, but that, before the permission arrived, he had been poisoned by the indignant relatives either of Lucrezia herself, or of some lady who had replaced her in the inconstant painter's affections. This is now generally regarded as a fable; and indeed a vendetta upon a man aged sixty-three for a

... mature age of fifty-two ... lies buried in Spoleto, with ... the Magnificent; he had ... the Medici family, beginning ... Francesco di Pesello (called Pesel- ... among his most distinguished

... altarpiece for the nuns of S. Ambrogio ... in the Academy of Florence, ... well-known poem. It re- ... among angels and saints, of ... One of these, placed to the ... pointed out by an inscription ... The price paid for this ... which seems surprisingly ... he painted the "Death of ... His principal altarpiece ... of S. Domenico—the Infant ... Joseph, between Sts George ... with the shepherds playing and ... the Virgin adoring the infant ... National Gallery, London, a ... the "Virgin and Infant with ... ascribed to Lippi, is disputable. ... as those of Lippo Lippi; ... redundant in lively and ... approaches religious art from ... to a phase of Catholic ... and technical adept ... naturalist, with less ... temporaries, and with much ... semi-humorous incidents ... perspective and none ... pilasters and other ... was wont to hide the ... His career was one of ... variation in style or ... proportions are larger than

... amusing, and possibly not ... the work of Crowe and ... S. C. Strutt, *Fra Lippo ... Painters* (1881); ... (1902). It should be ... 1412 as the date of the ... considerable difference in ... have preferred to follow ... 1441 looks like a

... 1505), was the natural ... born in Florence and ... he had completed ... education as a painter, ... probably under Fra ... to a great extent ... manner both of Lippo ... first, more realistic ... developed early; ... when he painted ... now in the Badia of ... same force as oil ... 1482 to 1490, he ... completed the decoration ... commenced by Masolino ... finished Masaccio's ... the sole author of ... the "Liberation of ... and the "Cruci- ... prove that Lippino ... The dignified ... named subject ... appears to have ... Paul at Athens." ... Lippino himself and ... executed the great ... other figures, ... works in the

and a thronged distance. In 1489 Lippino was in Rome, painting in the church of the Minerva, having first passed through Spoleto to design the monument for his father in the cathedral of that city. Some of his principal frescoes in the Minerva are still extant, the subjects being in celebration of St Thomas Aquinas. In one picture the saint is miraculously commended by a crucifix; in another, triumphing over heretics. In 1496 Lippino painted the "Adoration of the Magi" now in the Uffizi, a very striking picture, with numerous figures. This was succeeded by his last important undertaking, the frescoes in the Strozzi chapel, in the church of S. Maria Novella in Florence—"Drusiana Restored to Life by St John, the Evangelist," "St John in the Cauldron of Boiling Oil" and two subjects from the legend of St Philip. These are conspicuous and attractive works, yet somewhat grotesque and exaggerated—full of ornate architecture, showy colour and the distinctive peculiarities of the master. Filippino, who had married in 1497, died in 1505. The best reputed of his scholars was Raffaellino del Garbo.

Like his father, Filippino had a most marked original genius for painting, and he was hardly less a chief among the artists of his time than Fra Filippo had been in his; it may be said that in all the annals of the art a rival instance is not to be found of a father and son each of whom had such pre-eminent natural gifts and leadership. The father displayed more of sentiment and candid sweetness of motive; the son more of richness, variety and lively pictorial combination. He was admirable in all matters of decorative adjunct and presentment, such as draperies, landscape backgrounds and accessories; and he was the first Florentine to introduce a taste for antique details of costume, &c. He formed a large collection of objects of this kind, and left his designs of them to his son. In his later works there is a tendency to a mannered development of the extremities, and generally to facile overdoing. The National Gallery, London, possesses a good and characteristic though not exactly a first-rate specimen of Lippino, the "Virgin and Child between Sts Jerome and Dominic"; also an "Adoration of the Magi," of which recent criticism contests the authenticity. Crowe and Cavalcaselle, supplemented by the writings of Berenson, should be consulted as to this painter. An album of his works is in Newnes' Art-library.

III. Lorenzo Lippi (1606–1664), painter and poet, was born in Florence. He studied painting under Matteo Rosselli, the influence of whose style, and more especially of that of Santi di Tito, is to be traced in Lippi's works, which are marked by taste, delicacy and a strong turn for portrait-like naturalism. His maxim was "to poetize as he spoke, and to paint as he saw." After exercising his art for some time in Florence, and having married at the age of forty the daughter of a rich sculptor named Susini, Lippi went as court painter to Innsbruck, where he has left many excellent portraits. There he wrote his humorous poem named *Malmantile Racquistato*, which was published under the anagrammatic pseudonym of "Perlone Zipoli." Lippi was somewhat self-sufficient, and, when visiting Parma, would not look at the famous Correggios there, saying that they could teach him nothing. He died of pleurisy in 1664, in Florence.

The most esteemed works of Lippi as a painter are a "Crucifixion" in the Uffizi gallery at Florence, and a "Triumph of David" which he executed for the saloon of Angiolo Galli, introducing into it portraits of the seventeen children of the owner. The *Malmantile Racquistato* is a burlesque romance, mostly compounded out of a variety of popular tales; its principal subject-matter is an expedition for the recovery of a fortress and territory whose queen had been expelled by a female usurper. It is full of graceful or racy Florentine idioms, and is counted by Italians as a "testo di lingua." Lippi is more generally or more advantageously remembered by this poem than by anything which he has left in the art of painting. It was not published until 1688, several years after his death. Lanzi as to Lorenzo Lippi's pictorial work, and Tiraboschi and other literary historians as to his writings, are among the best authorities. (W. M. R.)

LIPPSPRINGE, a town and watering-place in the Prussian province of Westphalia, lying under the western slope of the Teutoburger Wald, 5 m. N. of Paderborn. Pop. (1905) 3100. The springs, the Arminius Quelle and the Liborius Quelle, for which it is famous, are saline waters of a temperature of 70° F., and are utilized both for bathing and drinking in cases of pulmonary consumption and chronic diseases of the respiratory organs. The annual number of visitors amounts to about 6000. Lippspringe is mentioned in chronicles as early as the 9th century, and here in the 13th century the order of the Templars established a stronghold. It received civic rights about 1400.

See Dammann, *Der Kurort Lippspringe* (Paderborn, 1900); Königer, *Lippspringe* (Berlin, 1893); and Frey, *Lippspringe, Kurort für Lungenkranke* (Paderborn, 1899).

LIPPSTADT, a town in the Prussian province of Westphalia, on the river Lippe, 20 m. by rail W. by S. of Paderborn, on the main line to Düsseldorf. Pop. (1905) 15,436. The Marien Kirche is a large edifice in the Transitional style, dating from the 13th century. It has several schools, among them being one which was originally founded as a nunnery in 1185. The manufactures include cigar-making, distilling, carriage-building and metal-working.

Lippstadt was founded in 1168 by the lords of Lippe, the rights over one half of the town passing subsequently by purchase to the counts of the Mark, which in 1614 was incorporated with Brandenburg. In 1850 the prince of Lippe-Detmold sold his share to Prussia when this joint lordship ceased. In 1620 Lippstadt was occupied by the Spaniards and in 1757 by the French.

See Chalybäus, *Lippstadt, ein Beitrag zur deutschen Städtegeschichte* (Lippstadt, 1876).

LIPSIUS, JUSTUS (1547–1606), the Latinized name of Joest (Juste or Josse) Lips, Belgian scholar, born on the 18th of October (15th of November, according to Amiel) 1547 at Overyssche, a small village in Brabant, near Brussels. Sent early to the Jesuit college in Cologne, he was removed at the age of sixteen to the university of Louvain by his parents, who feared that he might be induced to become a member of the Society of Jesus. The publication of his *Variarum Lectionum Libri Tres* (1567), dedicated to Cardinal Granvella, procured him an appointment as Latin secretary and a visit to Rome in the retinue of the cardinal. Here Lipsius remained two years, devoting his spare time to the study of the Latin classics, collecting inscriptions and examining MSS. in the Vatican. A second volume of miscellaneous criticism (*Antiquarum Lectionum Libri Quinque*, 1575), published after his return from Rome, compared with the *Variae Lectiones* of eight years earlier, shows that he had advanced from the notion of purely conjectural emendation to that of emending by collation. In 1570 he wandered over Burgundy, Germany, Austria, Bohemia, and was engaged for more than a year as teacher in the university of Jena, a position which implied an outward conformity to the Lutheran Church. On his way back to Louvain, he stopped some time at Cologne, where he must have comported himself as a Catholic. He then returned to Louvian, but was soon driven by the Civil War to take refuge in Antwerp, where he received, in 1579, a call to the newly founded university of Leiden, as professor of history. At Leiden, where he must have passed as a Calvinist, Lipsius remained eleven years, the period of his greatest productivity. It was now that he prepared his *Seneca*, perfected, in successive editions, his *Tacitus* and brought out a series of works, some of pure scholarship, others collections from classical authors, others again of general interest. Of this latter class was a treatise on politics (*Politicorum Libri Sex*, 1589), in which he showed that, though a public teacher in a country which professed toleration, he had not departed from the state maxims of Alva and Philip II. He lays it down that a government should recognize only one religion, and that dissent should be extirpated by fire and sword. From the attacks to which this avowal exposed him, he was saved by the prudence of the authorities of Leiden, who prevailed upon him to publish a declaration that his expression, *Ure, seca*, was a metaphor for a vigorous treatment. In the spring of 1590, leaving Leiden under pretext of taking the waters at Spa, he went to Mainz, where he was reconciled to the Roman Catholic Church. The event deeply interested the Catholic world, and invitations poured in on Lipsius from the courts and universities of Italy, Austria and Spain. But he preferred to remain in his own country, and finally settled at Louvain, as professor of Latin in the Collegium Buslidianum. He was not expected to teach, and his trifling stipend was eked out by the appointments of privy councillor and historiographer to the king of Spain. He continued to publish dissertations as before, the chief being his *De militia romana* (Antwerp, 1595) and *Lovanium* (Antwerp, 1605; 4th ed., Wesel, 1671), intended as an introduction to a general history of Brabant. He died at Louvian on the 23rd of March (some give 24th of April) 1606.

Lipsius's knowledge of classical antiquity was extremely limited. He had but slight acquaintance with Greek, and in Latin literature the poets and Cicero lay outside his range. His greatest work was his edition of Tacitus. This author he had so completely made his own that he could repeat the whole, and offered to be tested in any part of the text, with a poniard held to his breast, to be used against him if he should fail. His *Tacitus* first appeared in 1575, and was five times revised and corrected—the last time in 1606, shortly before his death. His *Opera Omnia* appeared in 8 vols. at Antwerp (1585, 2nd ed., 1637).

A full list of his publications will be found in van der Aa, *Biographisch Woordenboek der Nederlanden* (1865), and in *Bibliographie Lipsienne* (Ghent, 1886–1888). In addition to the biography by A. le Mire (Aubertus Miraeus) (1609), the only original account of his life, see M. E. C. Nisard, *Le Triumvirat littéraire au XVIe siècle* (1852); A. Räss, *Die Convertiten seit der Reformation* (1867); P. Bergman's *Autobiographie de J. Lipse* (1889); L. Galesloot, *Particularités sur la vie de J. Lipse* (1877); E. Amiel, *Un Publiciste du XVIe siècle: Juste Lipse* (1884), and L. Müller, *Geschichte der klassischen Philologie in den Niederlanden*. The articles by J. J. Thonissen of Louvain in the *Nouvelle Biographie générale*, and L. Roersch in *Biographie nationale de Belgique*, may also be consulted.

LIPSIUS, RICHARD ADELBERT (1830–1892), German Protestant theologian, son of K. H. A. Lipsius (d. 1861), who was rector of the school of St Thomas at Leipzig, was born at Gera on the 14th of February 1830. He studied at Leipzig, and eventually (1871) settled at Jena as professor ordinarius. He helped to found the "Evangelical Protestant Missionary Union" and the "Evangelical Alliance," and from 1874 took an active part in their management. He died at Jena on the 19th of August 1892. Lipsius wrote principally on dogmatics and the history of early Christianity from a liberal and critical standpoint. A Neo-Kantian, he was to some extent an opponent of Albrecht Ritschl, demanding "a connected and consistent theory of the universe, which shall comprehend the entire realm of our experience as a whole. He rejects the doctrine of dualism in a truth, one division of which would be confined to 'judgments of value,' and be unconnected with our theoretical knowledge of the external world. The possibility of combining the results of our scientific knowledge with the declarations of our ethico-religious experience, so as to form a consistent philosophy, is based, according to Lipsius, upon the unity of the personal ego, which on the one hand knows the world scientifically, and on the other regards it as the means of realizing the ethico-religious object of its life" (Otto Pfleiderer). This, in part, is his attitude in *Philosophie und Religion* (1885). In his *Lehrbuch der evang.-prot. Dogmatik* (1876; 3rd ed., 1893) he deals in detail with the doctrines of "God," "Christ," "Justification" and the "Church." From 1875 he assisted K. Hase, O. Pfleiderer and E. Schrader in editing the *Jahrbücher für prot. Theologie*, and from 1885 till 1891 he edited the *Theol. Jahresbericht*.

His other works include *Die Pilatusakten* (1871, new ed., 1886), *Dogmatische Beiträge* (1878), *Die Quellen der ältesten Ketzergeschichte* (1875), *Die apokryphen Apostelgeschichten* (1883–1890), *Hauptpunkte der christl. Glaubenslehre im Umriss dargestellt* (1889), and commentaries on the Epistles to the Galatians, Romans and Philippians in H. J. Holtzmann's *Handkommentar zum Neuen Testament* (1891–1892).

LIPTON, SIR THOMAS JOHNSTONE, Bart. (1850–), British merchant, was born at Glasgow in 1850, of Irish parents. At a very early age he was employed as errand boy to a Glasgow stationer; at fifteen he emigrated to America, where at first he worked in a grocery store, and afterwards as a tram-car driver in New Orleans, as a traveller for a portrait firm, and on a plantation in South Carolina. Eventually, having saved some money, he returned to Glasgow and opened a small provision shop. Business gradually increased, and by degrees Lipton had provision shops first all over Scotland and then all over the United Kingdom. To supply his retail shops on the most favourable terms, he purchased extensive tea, coffee and cocoa plantations in Ceylon, and provided his own packing-house for hogs in Chicago, and fruit farms, jam factories, bakeries and bacon-curing establishments in England. In 1898 his business was converted into a limited liability company. At Queen Victoria's diamond jubilee in 1897 he gave £20,000 for providing dinners for a large number of the London poor. In 1898 he was knighted, and in 1902 was made a baronet. In the world of yacht-racing he became well known from his repeated attempts to win the America Cup.

LIQUEURS, the general term applied to perfumed or flavoured potable spirits, sweetened by the addition of sugar. The term "liqueur" is also used for certain wines and unsweetened spirits of very superior quality, or remarkable for their bouquet, such as tokay or fine old brandy or whisky. The basis of all the "liqueurs" proper consists of (*a*) relatively strong alcohol or spirit, which must be as pure and neutral as possible; (*b*) sugar or syrup; and (*c*) flavouring matters. There are three distinct main methods of manufacturing liqueurs. The first, by which liqueurs of the highest class are prepared, is the "distillation" or "alcoholate" process. This consists in macerating various aromatic substances such as seeds, leaves, roots and barks of plants, &c., with strong spirit and subsequently distilling the infusion so obtained generally in the presence of a whole or a part of the solid matter. The mixture of spirit, water and flavouring matters which distils over is termed the "alcoholate." To this is added a solution of sugar or syrup, and frequently colouring matter in the shape of harmless vegetable extracts or burnt sugar, and a further quantity of flavouring matter in the shape of essential oils or clear spirituous vegetable extracts. The second method of making liqueurs is that known as the "essence" process. It is employed, as a rule, for cheap and inferior articles; the process resolving itself into the addition of various essential oils, either natural or artificially prepared, and of spirituous extracts to strong spirit, filtering and adding the saccharine matter to the clear filtrate. The third method of manufacturing liqueurs is the "infusion" process, in which alcohol and sugar are added to various fresh fruit juices. Liqueurs prepared by this method are frequently called "cordials." It has been suggested that "cordials" are articles of home manufacture, and that liqueurs are necessarily of foreign origin, but it is at least doubtful whether this is entirely correct. The French, who excel in the preparation of liqueurs, grade their products, according to their sweetness and alcoholic strength, into *crèmes*, *huiles* or *baumes*, which have a thick, oily consistency; and *eaux*, *extraits* or *élixirs*, which, being less sweetened, are relatively limpid. Liqueurs are also classed, according to their commercial quality and composition, as *ordinaires*, *demi-fines*, *fines* and *sur-fines*. Certain liqueurs, containing only a single flavouring ingredient, or having a prevailing flavour of a particular substance, are named after that body, for instance, *crème de vanille*, *anisette*, *kümmel*, *crème de menthe*, &c. On the other hand, many well-known liqueurs are compounded of very numerous aromatic principles. The nature and quantities of the flavouring agents employed in the preparation of liqueurs of this kind are kept strictly secret, but numerous "recipes" are given in works dealing with this subject. Among the substances frequently used as flavouring agents are aniseed, coriander, fennel, wormwood, gentian, sassafras, amber, hyssop, mint, thyme, angelica, citron, lemon and orange peel, peppermint, cinnamon, cloves, iris, caraway, tea, coffee and so on. The alcoholic strength of liqueurs ranges from close on 80% of alcohol by volume in some kinds of absinthe, to 27% in anisette. The liqueur industry is a very considerable one, there being in France some 25,000 factories. Most of these are small, but [illegible] gallons are annually exported from France alone. [illegible] absinthe, benedictine, chartreuse, curaçoa, kirsch and [illegible] under separate headings. Among other well-[illegible] liqueurs may be mentioned maraschino, which takes [illegible] a variety of cherry—the marasca—grown in [illegible] centre of the trade being at Zara; kümmel, the [illegible] is largely due to caraway seeds; allasch, [illegible] variety of kümmel; and cherry and other "fruit" brandies and whiskies, the latter being perhaps more properly termed cordials.

See Duplais, *La Fabrication des liqueurs*; and Rocques, *Les Eaux-de-vie et liqueurs*.

LIQUIDAMBAR, Liquid Amber or Sweet Gum, a product of *Liquidambar styraciflua* (order Hamamelideae), a deciduous tree of from 80 to 140 ft. high, with a straight trunk 4 or 5 ft. in diameter, a native of the United States, Mexico and Central America. It bears palmately-lobed leaves, somewhat resembling those of the maple, but larger. The male and female inflorescences are on different branches of the same tree, the globular heads of fruit resembling those of the plane. This species is nearly allied to *L. orientalis*, a native of a very restricted portion of the south-west coast of Asia Minor, where it forms forests. The earliest record of the tree appears to be in a Spanish work by F. Hernandez, published in 1651, in which he describes it as a large tree producing a fragrant gum resembling liquid amber, whence the name (*Nov. Plant.*, &c., p. 56). In Ray's *Historia Plantarum* (1686) it is called *Styrax liquida*. It was introduced into Europe in 1681 by John Banister, the missionary collector sent out by Bishop Compton, who planted it in the palace gardens at Fulham. The wood is very compact and fine-grained—the heart-wood being reddish, and, when cut into planks, marked transversely with blackish belts. It is employed for veneering in America. Being readily dyed black, it is sometimes used instead of ebony for picture frames, balusters, &c.; but it is too liable to decay for out-door work.

The gum resin yielded by this tree has no special medicinal virtues, being inferior in therapeutic properties to many others of its class. Mixed with tobacco, the gum was used for smoking at the court of the Mexican emperors (Humboldt iv. 10). It has long been used in France as a perfume for gloves, &c. It is mainly produced in Mexico, little being obtained from trees growing in higher latitudes of North America, or in England.

LIQUIDATION (*i.e.* making "liquid" or clear), in law, the clearing off or settling of a debt. The word was more especially used in bankruptcy law to define the method by which, under the Bankruptcy Act 1869, the affairs of an insolvent debtor were arranged and a composition accepted by his creditors without actual bankruptcy. It was abolished by the Bankruptcy Act 1883 (see Bankruptcy). In a general sense, liquidation is used for the act of adjusting debts, as the Egyptian Law of Liquidation, July 1880, for a general settlement of the liabilities of Egypt. In company law, liquidation is the winding up and dissolving a company. The winding up may be either voluntary or compulsory, and an officer, termed a liquidator, is appointed, who takes into his custody all the property of the company and performs such duties as are necessary on its behalf (see Company).

LIQUID GASES.[1] Though Lavoisier remarked that if the earth were removed to very cold regions of space, such as those of Jupiter or Saturn, its atmosphere, or at least a portion of its aeriform constituents, would return to the state of liquid (*Œuvres*, ii. 805), the history of the liquefaction of gases may be said to begin with the observation made by John Dalton in his essay "On the Force of Steam or Vapour from Water and various other Liquids" (1801): "There can scarcely be a doubt entertained respecting the reducibility of all elastic fluids of whatever kind into liquids; and we ought not to despair of effecting it in low temperatures and by strong pressures exerted on the unmixed gases." It was not, however, till 1823 that the question was investigated by systematic experiment. In that year Faraday, at the suggestion of Sir Humphry Davy, exposed hydrate of chlorine to heat under pressure in the laboratories of the Royal Institution. He placed the substance at the end of one arm of a bent glass tube, which was then hermetically sealed, and decomposing it by heating to 100° F., he saw a yellow liquid distil to the end of the other arm. This liquid he surmised to be chlorine separated from the water by the heat and "condensed into a dry fluid by the mere pressure of its own abundant vapour," and he verified his surmise by compressing chlorine gas, freed

[1] Figs. 1, 5, 6, 7, 10, 11, 12, 13 in this article are from *Proc. Roy. Inst.*, by permission.

from water by exposure to sulphuric acid, to a pressure of about four atmospheres, when the same yellow fluid was produced (*Phil. Trans.*, 1823, 113, pp. 160-165). He proceeded to experiment with a number of other gases subjected in sealed tubes to the pressure caused by their own continuous production by chemical action, and in the course of a few weeks liquefied sulphurous acid, sulphuretted hydrogen, carbonic acid, euchlorine, nitrous acid, cyanogen, ammonia and muriatic acid, the last of which, however, had previously been obtained by Davy. But he failed with hydrogen, oxygen, fluoboric, fluosilicic and phosphuretted hydrogen gases (*Phil. Trans.*, *ib.* pp. 189-198). Early in the following year he published an "Historical statement respecting the liquefaction of gases" (*Quart. Journ. Sci.*, 1824, 16, pp. 229-240), in which he detailed several recorded cases in which previous experimenters had reduced certain gases to their liquid state.

In 1835 Thilorier, by acting on bicarbonate of soda with sulphuric acid in a closed vessel and evacuating the gas thus obtained under pressure into a second vessel, was able to accumulate large quantities of liquid carbonic acid, and found that when the liquid was suddenly ejected into the air a portion of it was solidified into a snow-like substance (*Ann. chim. phys.*, 1835, 60, pp. 427-432). Four years later J. K. Mitchell in America, by mixing this snow with ether and exhausting it under an air pump, attained a minimum temperature of 146° below zero F., by the aid of which he froze sulphurous acid gas to a solid.

Stimulated by Thilorier's results and by considerations arising out of the work of J. C. Cagniard de la Tour (*Ann. chim phys.*, 1822, 21, pp. 127 and 178, and 1823, 22, p. 410), which appeared to him to indicate that gases would pass by some simple law into the liquid state, Faraday returned to the subject about 1844, in the "hope of seeing nitrogen, oxygen and hydrogen either as liquid or solid bodies, and the latter probably as a metal" (*Phil. Trans.*, 1845, 135, pp. 155-157) On the basis of Cagniard de la Tour's observation that at a certain temperature a liquid under sufficient pressure becomes a vapour or gas having the same bulk as the liquid, he inferred that "at this temperature or one a little higher, it is not likely that any increase of pressure, except perhaps one exceedingly great, would convert the gas into a liquid." He further surmised that the Cagniard de la Tour condition might have its point of temperature for oxygen, nitrogen, hydrogen, &c., below that belonging to the bath of solid carbonic acid and ether, and he realised that in that case no pressure which any apparatus would be able to bear would be able to bring those gases into the liquid or solid state, which would require a still greater degree of cold. To fulfil this condition he immersed the tubes containing his gases in a bath of solid carbonic acid and ether, the temperature of which was reduced by exhaustion under the air pump to −166° F., or a little lower, and at the same time he subjected the gases to pressures up to 50 atmospheres by the use of two pumps working in series. In this way he added six substances, usually gaseous, to the list of those that could be obtained in the liquid state, and reduced seven, including ammonia, nitrous oxide and sulphuretted hydrogen, into the solid form, at the same time effecting a number of valuable determinations of vapour tensions. But he failed to condense oxygen, nitrogen and hydrogen, the original objects of his pursuit, though he found reason to think that "further diminution of temperature and improved apparatus for pressure may very well be expected to give us these bodies in the liquid or solid state." His surmise that increased pressure alone would not suffice to bring about change of state in these gases was confirmed by subsequent investigators, such as M. P. E. Berthelot, who in 1850 compressed oxygen to 780 atmospheres (*Ann. chim. phys.*, 1850, 30, p. 237), and Natterer, who a few years later subjected the permanent gases to a pressure of 2790 atmospheres, without result; and in 1869 Thomas Andrews (*Phil. Trans.*, 11) by his researches on carbonic acid finally established the conception of the "critical temperature" as that temperature, differing for different bodies, above which no gas can be made to assume the liquid state, no matter what pressure it be subjected to (see CONDENSATION OF GASES).

About 1877 the problem of liquefying the permanent gases was taken up by L. P. Cailletet and R. P Pictet, working almost simultaneously though independently. The former relied on the cold produced by the sudden expansion of the gases at high compression. By means of a specially designed pump he compressed about 100 cc. of oxygen in a narrow glass tube to about 200 atmospheres, at the same time cooling it to about −29° C., and on suddenly releasing the pressure he saw momentarily in the interior of the tube a mist (*brouillard*), from which he inferred the presence of a vapour very near its point of liquefaction. A few days later he repeated the experiment with hydrogen, using a pressure of nearly 300 atmospheres, and observed in his tube an exceedingly fine and subtle fog which vanished almost instantaneously. At the time when these experiments were carried out it was generally accepted that the mist or fog consisted of minute drops of the liquefied gases. Even had this been the case, the problem would not have been completely solved, for Cailletet was unable to collect the drops in the form of a true stable liquid, and at the best obtained a "dynamic" not a "static" liquid, the gas being reduced to a form that bears the same relation to a true liquid that the partially condensed steam issuing from the funnel of a locomotive bears to water standing in a tumbler. But subsequent knowledge showed that even this proximate liquefaction could not have taken place, and that the fog could not have consisted of drops of liquid hydrogen, because the cooling produced by the adiabatic expansion would give a temperature of only 44° abs., which is certainly above the critical temperature of hydrogen. Pictet again announced that on opening the tap of a vessel containing hydrogen at a pressure of 650 atmospheres and cooled by the cascade method (see CONDENSATION OF GASES) to −140° C., he saw issuing from the orifice an opaque jet which he assumed to consist of hydrogen in the liquid form or in the liquid and solid forms mixed. But he was no more successful than Cailletet in collecting any of the liquid, which—whatever else it may have been, whether ordinary air or impurities associated with the hydrogen—cannot have been hydrogen because the means he employed were insufficient to reduce the gas to what has subsequently been ascertained to be its critical point, below which of course liquefaction is impossible. It need scarcely be added that if the liquefaction of hydrogen be rejected a fortiori Pictet's claim to have effected its solidification falls to the ground.

After Cailletet and Pictet, the next important names in the history of the liquefaction of gases are those of Z. F. Wroblewski and K. S. Olszewski, who for some years worked together at Cracow In April 1883 the former announced to the French Academy that he had obtained oxygen in a completely liquid state and (a few days later) that nitrogen at a temperature of −136° C, reduced suddenly from a pressure of 150 atmospheres to one of 50, had been seen as a liquid which showed a true meniscus, but disappeared in a few seconds. But with hydrogen treated in the same way he failed to obtain even the mist reported by Cailletet. At the beginning of 1884 he performed a more satisfactory experiment. Cooling hydrogen in a capillary glass tube to the temperature of liquid oxygen, he expanded it quickly from 100 atmospheres to one, and obtained the appearance of an instantaneous ebullition. Olszewski confirmed this result by expanding from a pressure of 190 atmospheres the gas cooled by liquid oxygen and nitrogen boiling under reduced pressure, and even announced that he saw it running down the walls of the tube as a colourless liquid.

Wroblewski, however, was unable to observe this phenomenon, and Olszewski himself, when seven years later he repeated the experiment in the more favourable conditions afforded by a larger apparatus, was unable to produce again the colourless drops he had previously reported: the phenomenon of the appearance of sudden ebullition indeed lasted longer, but he failed to perceive any meniscus such as would have been a certain indication of the presence of a true liquid. Still, though neither of these investigators succeeded in reaching the goal at which they aimed, their work was of great value in elucidating the conditions of the problem and in perfecting the details of the

LIQUID GASES

. . . n particular devoted the
. . . itable investigation of the
. . . mperatures. From the data
. . . der Waals equation which
. . . temperature, pressure and
. . . greater certainty than had
. . . xygen, liquid nitrogen and
. . . Wroblewski in 1885—
. . . osities of the laboratory,
. . . such quantities as to be
. . . research. Still, nothing
. . . upon which the work of
. . . the "cascade" method,
. . . high compression (see
. . . only means of procedure
. . . branch of physics.
. . . doubt appears to have
. . . methods for the liquefaction
. . . 1895 pointed out
. . . liquefiable gases necessary
. . . between nitrogen and
. . . hydrogen not having been
. . . the non-existence of
. . . those two. By 1894
. . . Institution laboratories
. . . by adding a small
. . . get a mixture with a
. . . such a mixture was
. . . from a high degree of
. . . result was a white mass
. . . of very low density.
. . . the true liquid state,
. . . owing to its extreme
. . . might ultimately have
. . . open vessels we can-
. . . abandoned in favour of
. . . attained success.
. . . in the liquefaction
. . . In the first place, the
. . . that the change to
. . . second, means had
. . . from the influx
. . . heat is transferred
. . . with the difference
. . . heat insula-
. . . in proportion
. . . of the problem
. . . with non-conducting
. . . was not necessary
. . . visible to the eye,
. . . not the case such
. . . were made to
. . . that contained
. . . vessels, through
. . . the interior one.
. . . in the arrange-
. . . very efficient,
. . . of London,
. . . occurred to
. . . had used nearly
. . . experiments on the
. . . natural deduc-
. . . might be
. . . substances
. . . the effect
. . . space
. . . showed that
. . . the space
. . . only one
. . . with

to the vacuum. But in addition these vessels lent themselves to an arrangement by which radiant heat could still further be cut off, since it was found that when the inner wall was coated with a bright deposit of silver, the influx of heat was diminished to one-sixth of the amount existing without the metallic coating. The total effect, therefore, of the high vacuum and silvering is to reduce the in-going heat to one-thirtieth part. In making such vessels a mercurial vacuum has been found very satisfactory. The vessel in which the vacuum is to be produced is provided with a small subsidiary vessel joined by a narrow tube with the main vessel, and connected with a powerful air-pump. A quantity of mercury having been placed in it, it is heated in an oil- or air-bath to about 200° C., so as to volatilize the mercury, the vapour of which is removed by the pump. After the process has gone on for some time, the pipe leading to the pump is sealed off, the vessel immediately removed from the bath, and the small subsidiary part immersed in some cooling agent such as solid carbonic acid or liquid air, whereby the mercury vapour is condensed in the small vessel and a vacuum of enormous tenuity left in the large one. The final step is to seal off the tube connecting the two. In this way a vacuum may be produced having a vapour pressure of about the hundred-millionth of an atmosphere at 0° C. If, however, some liquid mercury be left in the space in which the vacuum is produced, and the containing part of the vessel be filled with liquid air, the bright mirror of mercury which is deposited on the inside wall of the bulb is still more effective than silver in protecting the chamber from the influx of heat, owing to the high refractive index, which involves great reflecting power, and the bad heat-conducting powers of mercury.

With the discovery of the remarkable power of gas absorption possessed by charcoal cooled to a low temperature (see below), it became possible to make these vessels of metal. Previously this could not be done with success, because gas occluded in the metal gradually escaped and vitiated the vacuum, but now any stray gas may be absorbed by means of charcoal so placed in a pocket within the vacuous space that it is cooled by the liquid in the interior of the vessel. Metal vacuum vessels (fig. 1), of a capacity of from 2 to 20 litres, may be formed of brass, copper, nickel or tinned iron, with necks of some alloy that is a bad conductor of heat, silvered glass vacuum cylinders being fitted as stoppers. Such flasks, when properly constructed, have an efficiency equal to that of the chemically-silvered glass vacuum vessels now commonly used in low temperature investigations, and they are obviously better adapted for transport. The principle of the Dewar vessel is utilized in the Thermos flasks which are now extensively manufactured and employed for keeping liquids warm in hospitals, &c.

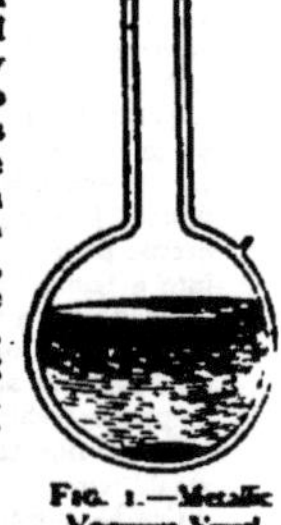

FIG. 1.—Metallic Vacuum Vessel.

Thermal Transparency at Low Temperatures.—The proposition, once enunciated by Pictet, that at low temperatures all substances have practically the same thermal transparency, and are equally ineffective as non-conductors of heat, is based on erroneous observations. It is true that if the space between the two walls of a double-walled vessel is packed with substances like carbon, magnesia, or silica, liquid air placed in the interior will boil off even more quickly than it will when the space merely contains air at atmospheric pressure; but in such cases it is not so much the carbon, &c., that bring about the transference of heat, as the air contained in their interstices. If this air be pumped out such substances are seen to exert a very considerable influence in stopping the influx of heat, and a vacuum vessel which has the space between its two walls filled with a non-conducting material of this kind preserves a liquid gas even better than one in which that space is simply exhausted of air. In experiments on this point double-walled glass tubes, as nearly identical in shape and size as possible, were mounted in sets of three on a common stem which communicated with an air-pump, so that the degree of exhaustion in each was equal. In two of each three the space between the double walls was filled with the powdered material it was desired to test, the third being left empty and used as the standard. The time required for a certain quantity of liquid air to evaporate from the interior of this empty bulb being called 1, in each of the eight sets of triple tubes, the times required for the same quantity to boil off from the other pairs of tubes were as follows:—

Charcoal	5	Lampblack	5
Magnesia	2	Silica	4
Graphite	1·3	Lampblack	4
Alumina	3·3	Lycopodium	2·5
Calcium carbonate	2·5	Barium carbonate	1·3
Calcium fluoride	1·25	Calcium phosphate	2·7
Phosphorus (amorphous)	1	Lead oxide	2
Mercuric iodide	1·5	Bismuth oxide	6

Other experiments of the same kind made—(*a*) with similar vacuum vessels, but with the powders replaced by metallic and other septa; and (*b*) with vacuum vessels having their walls silvered, yielded the following results:—

(*a*) Vacuum space empty	1	Vacuum space empty	1
Three turns silver paper, bright surface inside	4	Three turns black paper, black outside	3
Three turns silver paper, bright surface outside	4	Three turns black paper, black inside	3
Vacuum space empty	1	Vacuum space empty	1
Three turns gold paper, gold outside	4	Three turns, not touching, of sheet lead	4
Some pieces of gold-leaf put in so as to make contact between walls of vacuum-tube	0·3	Three turns, not touching, of sheet aluminium	4
(*b*) Vacuum space empty, silvered on inside surfaces	1	Empty silvered vacuum	1
Silica in silvered vacuum space	1·1	Charcoal in silvered vacuum	1·25

It appears from these experiments that silica, charcoal, lampblack, and oxide of bismuth all increase the heat insulations to four, five and six times that of the empty vacuum space. As the chief communication of heat through an exhausted space is by molecular bombardment, the fine powders must shorten the free path of the gaseous molecules, and the slow conduction of heat through the porous mass must make the conveyance of heat-energy more difficult than when the gas molecules can impinge upon the relatively hot outer glass surface, and then directly on the cold one without interruption. (See *Proc. Roy. Inst.* xv. 821-826.)

Density of Solids and Coefficients of Expansion at Low Temperatures.—The facility with which liquid gases, like oxygen or nitrogen, can be guarded from evaporation by the proper use of vacuum vessels (now called Dewar vessels), naturally suggests that the specific gravities of solid bodies can be got by direct weighing when immersed in such fluids. If the density of the liquid gas is accurately known, then the loss of weight by fluid displacement gives the specific gravity compared to water. The metals and alloys, or substances that can be got in large crystals, are the easiest to manipulate. If the body is only to be had in small crystals, then it must be compressed under strong hydraulic pressure into coherent blocks weighing about 40 to 50 grammes. Such an amount of material gives a very accurate density of the body about the boiling point of air, and a similar density taken in a suitable liquid at the ordinary temperature enables the mean coefficient of expansion between +15° C. and −185° C. to be determined. One of the most interesting results is that the density of ice at the boiling point of air is not more than 0·93, the mean coefficient of expansion being therefore 0·000081. As the value of the same coefficient between 0° C. and −27° C. is 0·000155, it is clear the rate of contraction is diminished to about one-half of what it was above the melting-point of the ice. This suggests that by no possible cooling at our command is it likely we could ever make ice as dense as water at 0°C., far less 4° C. In other words, the volume of ice at the zero of temperature would not be the minimum volume of the water molecule, though we have every reason to believe it would be so in the case of the majority of known substances. Another substance of special interest is solid carbonic acid. This body has a density of 1·53 at −78° C. and 1·633 at −185° C., thus giving a mean coefficient of expansion between these temperatures of 0·00057. This value is only about ⅛ of the coefficient of expansion of the liquid carbonic acid gas just above its melting point, but it is still much greater at the low temperature than that of highly expansive solids like sulphur, which at 40° C. has a value of 0·00019. The following table gives the densities at the temperature of boiling liquid air (−185°C.) and at ordinary temperatures (17° C.), together with the mean coefficient of expansion between those temperatures, in the case of a number of hydrated salts and other substances:

TABLE I.

	Density at −185° C.	Density at +17° C.	Mean coefficient of expansion between −185° C. and +17° C.
Aluminium sulphate (18)[1]	1·7194	1·6913	0·0000811
Sodium biborate (10)	1·7284	1·6937	0·0001000
Calcium chloride (6)	1·7187	1·6775	0·0001191
Magnesium chloride (6)	1·6039	1·5693	0·0001072
Potash alum (24)	1·6414	1·6144	0·0000813
Chrome alum (24)	1·7842	1·7669	0·0000478
Sodium carbonate (10)	1·4926	1·4460	0·0001563
Sodium phosphate (12)	1·5446	1·5200	0·0000787
Sodium thiosulphate (5)	1·7635	1·7290	0·0000969
Potassium ferrocyanide (3)	1·8688	1·8533	0·0001195
Potassium ferricyanide	1·8944	1·8109	0·0002244
Sodium nitro-prusside (4)	1·7196	1·6803	0·0001138
Ammonium chloride	1·5757	1·5188	0·0001820
Oxalic acid (2)	1·7024	1·6145	0·0002643
Methyl oxalate	1·5278	1·4260	0·0003482
Paraffin	0·9770	0·9103	0·0003567
Naphthalene	1·2355	1·1589	0·0003200
Chloral hydrate	1·9744	1·9151	0·0001482
Urea	1·3617	1·3190	0·0001579
Iodoform	4·4459	4·1955	0·0002930
Iodine	4·8943	4·6631	0·0002510
Sulphur	2·0989	2·0522	0·0001152
Mercury	14·382	..	0·0000881[2]
Sodium	1·0056	0·972	0·0001810
Graphite (Cumberland)	2·1302	2·0990	0·0000733

[1] The figures within parentheses refer to the number of molecules of water of crystallization.

[2] −189° to −38·85° C.

It will be seen from this table that, with the exception of carbonate of soda and chrome alum, the hydrated salts have a coefficient of expansion that does not differ greatly from that of ice at low temperatures. Iodoform is a highly expansive body like iodine, and oxalate of methyl has nearly as great a coefficient as paraffin, which is a very expansive solid, as are naphthalene and oxalic acid. The coefficient of solid mercury is about half that of the liquid metal, while that of sodium is about the value of mercury at ordinary temperatures. Further details on the subject can be found in the *Proc. Roy. Inst.* (1895), and *Proc. Roy. Soc.* (1902).

Density of Gases at Low Temperatures.—The ordinary mode of determining the density of gases may be followed, provided that the glass flask, with its carefully ground stop-cock sealed on, can stand an internal pressure of about five atmospheres, and that all the necessary corrections for change of volume are made. All that is necessary is to immerse the exhausted flask in boiling oxygen, and then to allow the second gas to enter from a gasometer by opening the stop-cock until the pressure is equalized. The stop-cock being closed, the flask is now taken out of the liquid oxygen and left in the balance-room until its temperature is equalized. It is then weighed against a similar flask used as a counterpoise. Following such a method, it has been found that the weight of 1 litre of oxygen vapour at its boiling point of 90·5° absolute is 4·420 grammes, and therefore the specific volume is 226·25 cc. According to the ordinary gaseous laws, the litre ought to weigh 4·313 grammes, and the specific volume should be 231·82 cc. In other words, the product of pressure and volume at the boiling point is diminished by 2·46%. In a similar way the weight of a litre of nitrogen vapour at the boiling point of oxygen was found to be 3·90, and the inferred value for 78° absolute, or its own boiling point, would be 4·51, giving a specific volume of 221·3.

Regenerative Cooling.—One part of the problem being thus solved and a satisfactory device discovered for warding off heat in such vacuum vessels, it remained to arrange some practically efficient method for reducing hydrogen to a temperature sufficiently low for liquefaction. To gain that end, the idea naturally occurred of using adiabatic expansion, not intermittently, as when gas is allowed to expand suddenly from a high compression, but in a continuous process, and an obvious way of attempting to carry out this condition was to enclose the orifice at which expansion takes place in a tube, so as to obtain a constant stream of cooled gas passing over it. But further consideration of this plan showed that although the gas jet would be cooled near the point of expansion owing to the conversion of a portion of its sensible heat into dynamical energy of the moving gas, yet the heat it thus lost would be restored to it almost

[illegible] showing by reflection all [illegible] it is remarkable that the same [illegible] gas. Dewar gives the [illegible] the density at the boiling-point [illegible] index of the liquid for the [illegible]

[illegible] by the use of liquid air. The [illegible] allowing the temperature [illegible] C. About this temperature [illegible] to a faint blue solution. [illegible] than liquid oxygen. [illegible] liquid, having a density [illegible] 195·5° C. The refractive [illegible] Evaporated under diminished [illegible] at a temperature of −215° C., [illegible] The density of the solid at [illegible]

[illegible] of nitrogen and oxygen are [illegible] liquefaction of atmospheric [illegible] as two separate liquids. Such, [illegible] down simultaneously as one [illegible] a large scale, liquid air may [illegible] collected in open vacuum- [illegible] it boils off first, and [illegible] oxygen the temperature [illegible] C. to about −182° C [illegible] of about 0·910. It is a [illegible] protected from external [illegible] air becomes a stiff [illegible] nitrogen containing [illegible] from it by means of [illegible] vacuum vessel in imitation [illegible] this solid under a [illegible] lower temperatures [illegible] becomes a white solid. [illegible] The refractive index

[illegible] Moissan's method of [illegible] anhydrous hydro- [illegible] the Royal Institution, [illegible] temperature of quietly-boiling [illegible] though it lost much [illegible] But a very small [illegible] to determine lique- [illegible] the gas to the [illegible] boiling at atmospheric [illegible] at about −187° C. The [illegible] Its density [illegible] liquid oxygen. The [illegible] does not show any [illegible] by a magnet. Cooled in [illegible] melting at about 40° abs. [illegible] liquid known to the [illegible] [illegible]

as those which hold good higher up the thermometric scale. The same remarks apply to the use of thermo-electric junctions at such exceptional temperatures. Recourse was therefore had to a constant-volume hydrogen thermometer, working under reduced pressure, experiments having shown that such a thermometer, filled with either a simple or a compound gas (*e.g.* oxygen or carbonic acid) at an initial pressure somewhat less than one atmosphere, may be relied upon to determine temperatures down to the respective boiling-points of the gases with which they are filled. The result obtained was −252° C. Subsequently various other determinations were carried out in thermometers filled with hydrogen derived from different sources, and also with helium, the average value given by the experiments being −252·5° C. (See "The Boiling Point of Liquid Hydrogen determined by Hydrogen and Helium Gas Thermometers," *Proc. Roy. Soc.*, 7th February 1901.) The critical temperature is about 30° absolute (−243° C.), and the critical pressure about 15 atmospheres. Hydrogen has not only the lowest critical temperature of all the old permanent gases, but it has the lowest critical pressure. Given a sufficiently low temperature, therefore, it is the easiest gas to liquefy so far as pressure is concerned. . Solid hydrogen has a temperature about 4° less. By exhaustion under reduced pressure a still lower depth of cold may be attained, and a steady temperature reached less than 16° above the zero of absolute temperature. By the use of high exhaustion, and the most stringent precautions to prevent the influx of heat, a temperature of 13° absolute (−260° C.) may be reached. This is the lowest steady temperature which can be maintained by the evaporation of solid hydrogen. At this temperature the solid has a density of about 0·077. Solid hydrogen presents no metallic characteristics, such as were predicted for it by Faraday, Dumas, Graham and other chemists and neither it nor the liquid is magnetic.

The Approach to the Absolute Zero.—The achievement of Kamerlingh Onnes has brought about the realization of a temperature removed only 3° from the absolute zero, and the question naturally suggests itself whether there is any probability of a still closer approach to that point. The answer is that if, as is not impossible, there exists a gas, as yet unisolated, which has an atomic weight one-half that of helium, that gas, liquefied in turn by the aid of liquid helium, would render that approach possible, though the experimental difficulties of the operation would be enormous and perhaps prohibitive. The results of experiments bearing on this question and of theory based on them are shown in table II. The third column shows the critical temperature of the gas which can be liquefied by continuous expansion through a regenerative cooling apparatus, the operation being started from the initial temperature shown in the second column, while the fourth column gives the temperature of the resulting liquid. It will be seen that by the use of liquid or solid hydrogen as a cooling agent, it should be possible to liquefy a body having a critical temperature of about 6° to 8° on the absolute scale, and a boiling point of about 4° or 5°, while with the aid of liquid helium at an initial temperature of 5° we could liquefy a body having a critical temperature of 2° and a boiling point of 1°.

TABLE II.

Substance.	Initial Temperature Abs. Degrees.	Critical Temperature. Abs. Degrees.	Boiling Point Abs. Degrees
(Low red heat)	760	304	195 (CO₂)
[illegible]	325	130	80 (Air)
[illegible]	75	30	20 (H)
[illegible]	20	8	5 (He)
[illegible]	15	6	4
[illegible]	5	2	1

It is to be remarked, however, that even so the physicist would not have attained the absolute zero, and he can scarcely hope ever to do so. It is true he would only be a very short distance from it, but it must be remembered that in a thermodynamic sense one degree low down the scale, say at 10° absolute, is equivalent to [illegible] the ordinary temperature, and as the [illegible] goes to lower and lower temperatures, the difficulties [illegible] advance increase, not in arithmetical but in geometrical progression. Thus the step between the liquefaction of air and that of hydrogen is thermodynamically and practically greater than that between the liquefaction of chlorine and that of air [illegible] of degrees of temperature that separates the boiling-points of the first pair of substances is less than half what it is in the case of the second pair. But the ratio of the absolute boiling-points in the first pair of substances is as 1 to 4, whereas in the second pair it is only 1 to 3, and it is this value that expresses the difficulty of the transition.

But though Ultima Thule may continue to mock the physicist's efforts, he will long find ample scope for his energies in the investigation of the properties of matter at the temperatures placed at his command by liquid air and liquid and solid hydrogen. Indeed, great as is the sentimental interest attached to the liquefaction of these refractory gases, the importance of the achievement lies rather in the fact that it opens out new fields of research and enormously widens the horizon of physical science, enabling the natural philosopher to study the properties and behaviour of matter under entirely novel conditions. We propose to indicate briefly the general directions in which such inquiries have so far been carried on, but before doing so will call attention to the power of absorbing gases possessed by cooled charcoal, which has on that account proved itself a most valuable agent in low temperature research.

Gas Absorption by Charcoal.—Felix Fontana was apparently the first to discover that hot charcoal has the power of absorbing gases, and his observations were confirmed about 1770 by Joseph Priestley, to whom he had communicated them. A generation later Theodore de Saussure made a number of experiments on the subject, and noted that at ordinary temperatures the absorption is accompanied with considerable evolution of heat. Among subsequent investigators were Thomas Graham and Stenhouse, Faure and Silberman, and Hunter, the last-named showing that charcoal made from coco-nut exhibits greater absorptive powers than other varieties. In 1874 Tait and Dewar for the first time employed charcoal for the production of high vacua, by using it, heated to a red heat, to absorb the mercury vapour in a tube exhausted by a mercury pump; and thirty years afterwards it occurred to the latter investigator to try how its absorbing powers are affected by cooling it, with the result that he found them to be greatly enhanced. Some of his earlier observations are given in table III., but it must be pointed out that much larger absorptions were obtained subsequently when it was found that the quality of the charcoal was greatly influenced by the mode in which it was prepared, the absorptive power being increased by carbonizing the coco-nut shell slowly at a gradually increasing temperature. The results in the table were all obtained with the same specimen of charcoal, and the volumes of the gases absorbed, both at ordinary and at low temperatures, were measured under standard conditions—at 0° C., and 760 mm. pressure. It appears that at the lower temperature there is a remarkable increase of absorption for every gas, but that the increase is in general smaller as the boiling-points of the various gases are lower. Helium is conspicuous for the fact that it is absorbed to a comparatively slight extent at both the higher and the lower temperature, but in this connexion it must be remembered that, being the most volatile gas known, it is being treated at a temperature which is relatively much higher than the other gases. At −185° (=88° abs.), while hydrogen is at about 4½ times its boiling-point (20° abs.), helium is at about 20 times its boiling-point (4·5° abs.), and it might, therefore, be expected that if it were taken at a temperature corresponding to that of the hydrogen, *i.e.* at 4 or 5 times its boiling-point, or say 20° abs., it would undergo much greater absorption. This expectation is borne out by the results shown in table IV., and it may be inferred that charcoal cooled in liquid helium would absorb helium as freely as charcoal cooled in liquid hydrogen absorbs hydrogen. It is found that a given specimen of charcoal cooled in liquid oxygen, nitrogen and hydrogen absorbs about equal volumes of those three gases (about 260 cc. per gramme; and, as the relation between volume and temperature is nearly lineal at the lowest portions of either the hydrogen or the helium absorption, it is a legitimate inference that at a temperature of 5° to 6° abs. helium would be as freely absorbed by charcoal as hydrogen is at its boiling-point and that the boiling-point of helium lies at about 5° abs.

TABLE III.—*Gas Absorption by Charcoal.*

	Volume absorbed at 0° Cent.	Volume absorbed at −185° Cent.
Helium	2 cc.	15 cc.
Hydrogen	4	135
Electrolytic gas	12	150
Argon	12	175
Nitrogen	15	155
Oxygen	18	230
Carbonic oxide	21	190
Carbonic oxide and oxygen	30	195

TABLE IV.—*Gas Absorption by Charcoal at Low Temperatures.*

Temperature.	Helium. Vols. of Carbon.	Hydrogen. Vols. of Carbon.
−185° C. (boiling-point of liquid air)	2½	137
−210° C. (liquid air under exhaustion)	5	180
−252° C. (boiling-point of liquid hydrogen)	160	258
−258° C. (solid hydrogen)	195	.

The rapidity with which air is absorbed by charcoal at −185° C. and under small pressures is illustrated by table V., which shows the reductions of pressure effected in a tube of 2000 cc. capacity by means of 20 grammes of charcoal cooled in liquid air.

TABLE V.—*Velocity of Absorption.*

Time of Exhaustion.	Pressure in mm.	Time of Exhaustion.	Pressure in mm.
0 sec.	2·190	60 sec.	0·347
10 „	1·271	2 min.	0·153
20 „	0·869	5 „	0·0274
30 „	0·632	10 „	0·00205
40 „	0·543	19 „	0·00025
50 „	0·435		

Charcoal Occlusion Pressures.—For measuring the gas concentration, pressure and temperature, use may be made of an apparatus of the type shown in fig. 5. A mass of charcoal, E, immersed in liquid air, is employed for the preliminary exhaustion of the McLeod gauge G and of the charcoal C, which is to be used in the actual experiments, and is then sealed off at S. The bulb C is then placed in a large spherical vacuum vessel containing liquid oxygen which can be made to boil at any definite temperature under diminished pressure which is measured by the manometer R. The volume of gas admitted into the charcoal is determined by the burette D and the pipette P, and the corresponding occlusion pressure at any concentration and any temperature below 90° abs. by the gauge G. In presence of charcoal, and for small concentrations, great variations are shown in the relation between the pressure and the concentration of different gases, all at the same temperature. Table VI. gives the comparison between hydrogen and nitrogen at the temperature of liquid air, 25 grammes of charcoal being employed. It is seen that 15 cc. of hydrogen produce nearly the same pressure (0·0645 mm.) as 2500 cc. of nitrogen (0·06172 mm.). This result shows how

TABLE VI.

Volume of Gas absorbed.	Occlusion Hydrogen Pressure.	Occlusion Nitrogen Pressure.
cc.	mm.	mm.
0	0·00003	0·00005
5	0·0228	..
10	0·0455	..
15	0·0645	..
20	0·0861	..
25	0·1105	.
30	0·1339	0·00031
35	0·1623	..
40	0·1870	
130	..	0·00110
500	..	0·00314
1000	..	0·01756
1500	..	0·02920
2500	..	0·06172

enormously greater, at the temperature of liquid air, is the volatility of hydrogen as compared with that of nitrogen. In the same way the concentrations, for the same pressure, vary greatly with tempera-

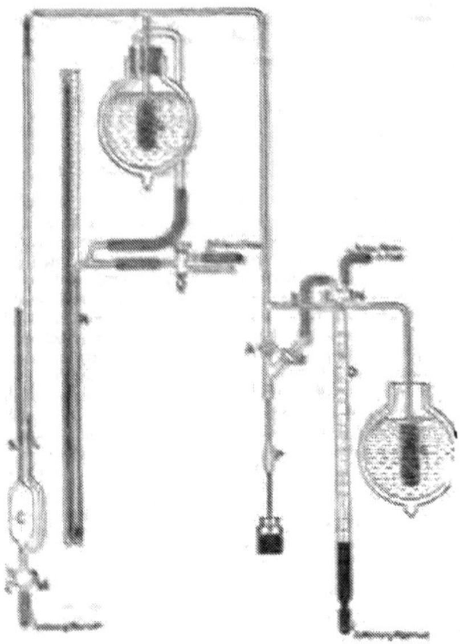

Fig. 5.

[illegible] is exemplified by table VII., even though the pressures are [illegible] quite constant. The temperatures employed were the boiling-[illegible] of hydrogen, oxygen and carbon dioxide.

Table VII.

[illegible]	Concentration in cc. per grm. of Charcoal.	Pressure in mm.	Temperature Absolute.
[illegible]	97	2·2	20°
[illegible]	397	2·2	20°
[illegible]	15	2·1	90°
[illegible]	250	1·6	90°
[illegible]	300	1·0	90°
[illegible]	90	3·6	195°

[illegible] in every case when gases are condensed to the [illegible] evolution of heat, and during the absorption of [illegible] other occluding body, as hydrogen in [illegible] heat evolved exceeds that of direct lique- [illegible] between occlusion-pressure and tempera- [illegible] on, the reaction being reversible, it is [illegible] heat evolution. Table VIII. gives the [illegible]

Table VIII.

[illegible]	[illegible]	Molecular Latent Heat.	Mean Temperature Absolute.
[illegible]	[illegible]	483·0	18°
[illegible]	[illegible]	574·4	18°
[illegible]	[illegible]	2005·6	78°
[illegible]	[illegible]	3059·0	82°
[illegible]	[illegible]	3146·4	82°
[illegible]	[illegible]	6099·6	180°

[illegible] resulting from Dewar's [illegible] concentrations in the [illegible]

Production of High Vacua.—Exceedingly high vacua can be obtained by the aid of liquid gases, with or without charcoal. If a vessel containing liquid hydrogen be freely exposed to the atmosphere, a rain of snow (solid air) at once begins to fall upon the surface of the liquid; similarly, if one end of a sealed tube containing ordinary air be immersed in the liquid, the same thing happens, but since there is now no new supply to take the place of the air that has been solidified and has accumulated in the cooled portion of the tube, the pressure is quickly reduced to something like one-millionth of an atmosphere, and a vacuum is formed of such tenuity that the electric discharge can be made to pass only with difficulty. Liquid air can be employed in the same manner if the tube, before sealing, is filled with some less volatile gas or vapour, such as sulphurous acid, benzol or water vapour. But if a charcoal condenser be used in conjunction with the liquid air it becomes possible to obtain a high vacuum when the tube contains air initially. For instance, in one experiment, with a bulb having a capacity of 300 cc. and filled with air at a pressure of about 1·7 mm. and at a temperature of 15° C., when an attached condenser with 5 grammes of charcoal was cooled in liquid air, the pressure was reduced to 0·0545 mm. of mercury in five minutes, to 0·01032 mm. in ten minutes, to 0·000139 mm. in thirty minutes, and to 0·000047 mm. in sixty minutes. The condenser then being cooled in liquid hydrogen the pressure fell to 0·0000154 mm. in ten minutes and to 0·0000058 mm. in a further ten minutes when solid hydrogen was employed as the cooling agent, and no doubt, had it not been for the presence of hydrogen and helium in the air, an even greater reduction could have been effected. Another illustration of the power of cooled charcoal to produce high vacua is afforded by a Crookes radiometer. If the instrument be filled with helium at atmospheric pressure and a charcoal bulb attached to it be cooled in liquid air, the vanes remain motionless even when exposed to the concentrated beam of an electric arc lamp; but if liquid hydrogen be substituted for the liquid air rapid rotation at once sets in. When a similar radiometer was filled with hydrogen and the attached charcoal bulb was cooled in liquid air rotation took place, because sufficient of the gas was absorbed to permit motion. But when the charcoal was cooled in liquid hydrogen instead of in liquid air, the absorption increased and consequently the rarefaction became so high that there was no motion when the light from the arc was directed on the vanes. These experiments again permit of an inference as to the boiling-point of helium. A fall of 75°, in the temperature of the charcoal bulb, from the boiling-point of air to the boiling-point of hydrogen, reduced the vanes to rest in the case of the radiometer filled with hydrogen; hence it might be inferred that a fall of like amount from the boiling-point of hydrogen would reduce the vanes of the helium radiometer to rest, and consequently that the boiling-point of helium would be about 5° abs.

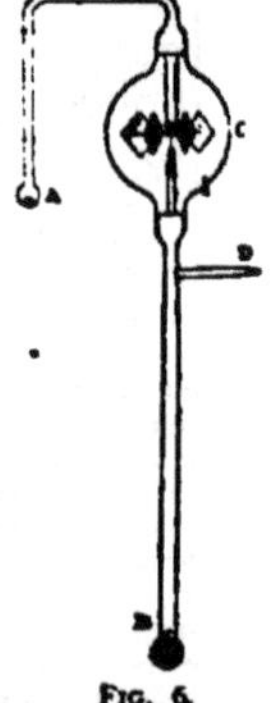

Fig. 6.

The vacua obtainable by means of cooled charcoal are so high that it is difficult to determine the pressures by the McLeod gauge, and the radiometer experiments referred to above suggested the possibility of another means of ascertaining such pressures, by determining the pressures below which the radiometer would not spin. The following experiment shows how the limit of pressure can be ascertained by reference to the pressures of mercury vapour which have been very accurately determined through a wide range of temperature. To a radiometer (fig. 6) with attached charcoal bulb B was sealed a tube ending in a small bulb A containing a globule of mercury. The radiometer and bulb B were heated, exhausted and repeatedly washed out with pure oxygen gas, and then the mercury was allowed to distil for some time into the charcoal cooled in liquid air. On exposure to the electric beam the vanes began to spin, but soon ceased when the bulb A was cooled in liquid air. When, however, the mercury was warmed by placing the bulb in liquid water, the vanes began to move again, and in the particular radiometer used this was found to happen when the temperature of the mercury had risen to −23° C. corresponding to a pressure of about one fifty-millionth of an atmosphere.

For washing out the radiometer with oxygen the arrangement shown in fig. 7 is convenient Here A is a bulb containing perchlorate of potash, which when heated gives off pure oxygen; C is again the radiometer and B the charcoal bulb. The side tube E is for the purpose of examining the gas given off by minerals like thorianite or the gaseous products of the transformation of radioactive bodies.

Analytic Uses.—Another important use of liquid gases is an analytic agents, and for this purpose liquid air is becoming an almost essential laboratory reagent. It is one of the most convenient agents for drying gases and for their purification. If a mixture of gases be subjected to the temperature of liquid air, it is obvious that all the constituents that are more condensable than air will be reduced to liquid, while those that are less condensable will either remain as a gaseous residue or be dissolved in the liquid obtained. The bodies present in the latter may be separated by fractional distillation, while the contents of the gaseous residue may be further differentiated by the air of still lower temperatures, such as are obtainable by liquid hydrogen. An apparatus such as the following can be used to separate both the less and the more volatile gases of the atmosphere, the former being obtained from their solution in liquid air by fractional distillation at low pressure and separation of the condensable part of the distillate by cooling in liquid hydrogen, while the latter are extracted from the residue of liquid air, after the distillation of the first fraction, by allowing it to evaporate gradually at a temperature rising only very slowly.

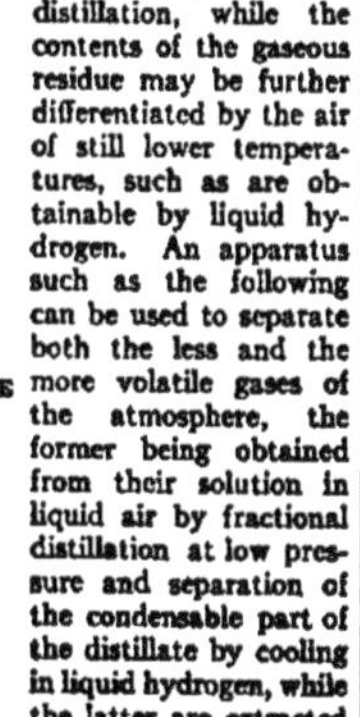

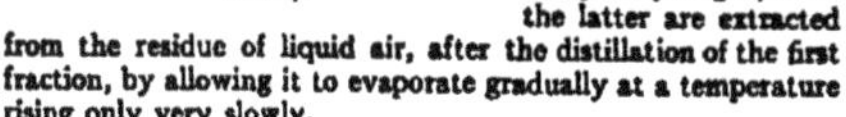

Fig. 7.

In fig. 8, A represents a vacuum-jacketed vessel, containing liquid air; this can be made to boil at reduced pressure and therefore be lowered in temperature by means of an air-pump, which is in communication with the vessel through the pipe *s*. The liquid boiled away is replenished when necessary from the reservoir C, *p* being a valve, worked by handle *q*, by which the flow along *r* is regulated. The vessel B, immersed in the liquid air of A, communicates with the atmosphere by *a*; hence when the temperature of A falls under exhaustion below that of liquid air, the contents of B condense, and if the stop-cock *m* is kept open, and *n* shut, air from the outside is continuously sucked in until B is full of liquid, which contains in solution the whole of the most volatile gases of the atmosphere which have passed in through *a*. At this stage of the operation *m* is closed and *n* opened, a passage thus being opened along *b* from A to the remainder of the apparatus seen on the left side of the figure. Here E is a vacuum vessel containing liquid hydrogen, and *d* a three-way cock by which communication can be established either btween *b* and D, between *b* and *e*, the tube leading to the sparking-tube *g*, or between D and *e*. If now *d* is arranged so that there is a free passage from *b* to D, and the stop-cock *n* also opened, the gas dissolved in the liquid in B, together with some of the most volatile part of that liquid, quickly distils over into D, which is at a much lower temperature than B, and some of it condenses there in the solid state. When a small fraction of the contents of B has thus distilled over, *d* is turned so as to close the passage between D and *b* and open that between D and *e*, with the result that the gas in D is pumped out by the mercury-pump, shown diagrammatically at *F*, along the tube *e* (which is immersed in the

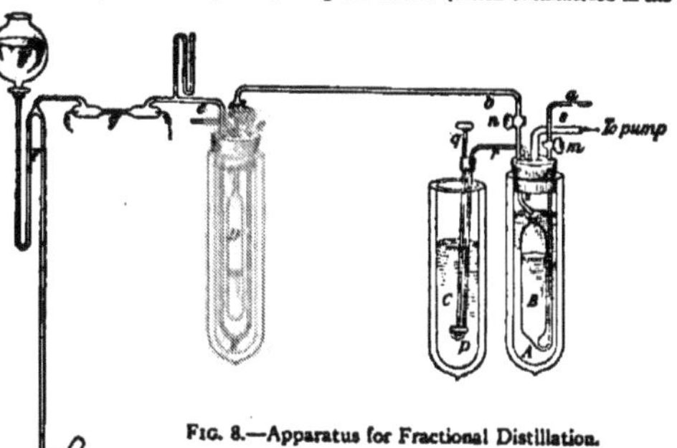

Fig. 8.—Apparatus for Fractional Distillation.

liquid hydrogen in order that any more condensable gas carried along by the current may be frozen out) to the sparking-tube or tubes *g*, where it can be examined spectroscopically. When the apparatus is used to separate the least volatile part of the gases in the atmosphere, the vessel E and its contents are omitted, and the tube *b* made to communicate with the pump through a number of sparking-tubes which can be sealed off successively. The nitrogen and oxygen which make up the bulk of the liquid in B are allowed to evaporate gradually, the temperature being kept low so as to check the evaporation of gases less volatile than oxygen. When most of the oxygen and nitrogen have thus been removed, the stop-cock *n* is closed, and the tubes partially exhausted by the pump; spectroscopic examination is made of the gases they contain, and repeated from time to time as more gas is allowed to evaporate from B. The general sequence of spectra, apart from those of nitrogen, oxygen and carbon compounds, which are never eliminated by the process of distillation alone, is as follows: The spectrum of argon first appears, followed by the brightest (green and yellow) rays of krypton. Then the intensity of the argon spectrum wanes and it gives way to that of krypton, until, as Runge observed, when a Leyden jar is in the circuit, the capillary part of the sparking-tube has a magnificent blue colour, while the wide ends are bright pale yellow. Without a jar the tube is nearly white in the middle and yellow about the poles. As distillation proceeds, the temperature of the vessel containing the residue of liquid air being allowed to rise slowly, the brightest (green) rays of xenon begin to appear, and the krypton rays soon die out, being superseded by those of xenon. At this stage the capillary part of the sparking-tube is, with a jar in circuit, a brilliant green, and it remains green, though less brilliant, if the jar is removed.

An improved form of apparatus for the fractionation is represented in fig. 9. The gases to be separated, that is, the least volatile part of atmospheric air, enter the bulb B from a gasholder by the tube *a* with stop-cock *c*. B, which is maintained at a low temperature by being immersed in liquid hydrogen, A, boiling under reduced pressure, in turn communicates through the tube *b* and stop-cock *d* with a sparking-tube or tubes *f*, and so on through *e* with a mercurial pump. To

Fig. 9.—Apparatus for continuous Spectroscopic Examination.

[illegible] condenser D along with some portion of air. The condenser E is then taken out of the liquid air, heated quickly to 15° C. to expel the occluded air and replaced. More air is then passed in, and by repeating the operation several times 50 litres of air can be treated in a short time, supplying sparking-tubes which will show the complete spectra of the volatile constituents of the air.

The less volatile constituents of the atmosphere, krypton and xenon, may be obtained by leading a current of air, purified by passage through a series of tubes cooled in liquid air, through a charcoal condenser also cooled in liquid air. The condenser is then removed and placed in solid carbon dioxide at −78° C. The gas that comes off is allowed to escape, but what remains in the charcoal is got out by heating and exhaustion, the carbon compounds and oxygen are removed and the residue, consisting of nitrogen with krypton and xenon, is separated into its constituents by condensation and fractionation. Another method [illegible] a few hundred grammes of charcoal with old liquid air, which is allowed to evaporate slowly in a silvered vacuum vessel; the gases remaining in the charcoal are then treated in the manner described above.

Charcoal enables a mixture containing a high percentage of oxygen to be extracted from the atmosphere. In one experiment [illegible] grammes of [illegible] after being heated and exhausted were allowed to absorb air at −185° C.; some 5 or 6 litres were taken up in [illegible] minutes, and it then presumably contained air of the composition of the atmosphere, *i.e.* 20% oxygen and 80% nitrogen, as shown in fig. 11. But when more air was passed over it the portion that was not absorbed was found to [illegible] of about 98%, nitrogen, showing that excess of [illegible] was being absorbed, and in the course of a few [illegible] the occluded gas [illegible] a new and apparently definite composition exhibited [illegible]. When the charcoal containing this mixture was [illegible] to a vacuum vessel and allowed to warm up [illegible] the successive litres of gas when collected and analyzed separately showed the following composition:—

[illegible]	18·5% oxygen
[illegible]	20·6% „
[illegible]	53·0% „
[illegible]	72·0% „
[illegible]	79·0% „
[illegible]	84·0% „

FIG. 11.

FIG. 12.

[illegible].—Certain liquid gases lend themselves conveniently [illegible] the construction of a calorimeter, in which the heat in [illegible] quantities of any substance with which it is desired [illegible] may be measured by the quantity of liquid gas [illegible] to evaporate. One advantage of this method is [illegible] range of temperature is available when liquid air, [illegible] or hydrogen is employed as the calorimetric [illegible]. Another is the relatively large quantity of gas [illegible] by the evaporation, as may be seen from table IX.

TABLE IX.

[illegible]	Boiling Point.	Liquid Volume of 1 gram at Boiling Point in c.c.	Latent Heat in gram Calories.	Volume of Gas at 0° C and 760 mm. per gram Calorie in c.c.
[illegible]	[illegible]	0·7	97·0	3·6
[illegible]	[illegible]	0·05 (solid)	142·4	3·6
[illegible]	[illegible]	1·7	119·0	7·0
[illegible]	[illegible]	0·9	53·0	13·2
[illegible]	[illegible]	1·3	50·0	15·9
[illegible]	[illegible]	14·3	125·0	88·9
[illegible]	[illegible]	7·0	13·0	450·0

[illegible] the special physical constants of the various gases [illegible] in calorimetry. In consequence it is [illegible] calorie with liquid air and so little as [illegible] liquid hydrogen.

The apparatus (fig. 13) consists of a large vacuum vessel A, of 2 or 3 litres' capacity, containing liquid air, in which is inserted a smaller vacuum vessel B, of 25-30 c.c. capacity, having sealed to it a long narrow tube G that projects above the mouth of A and is held in place by some loosely packed cotton wool. To the top of this tube the test tube C, containing the material under investigation, is connected by a piece of flexible rubber tubing D; this enables C to be tilted so as to throw a piece or pieces of the contained material

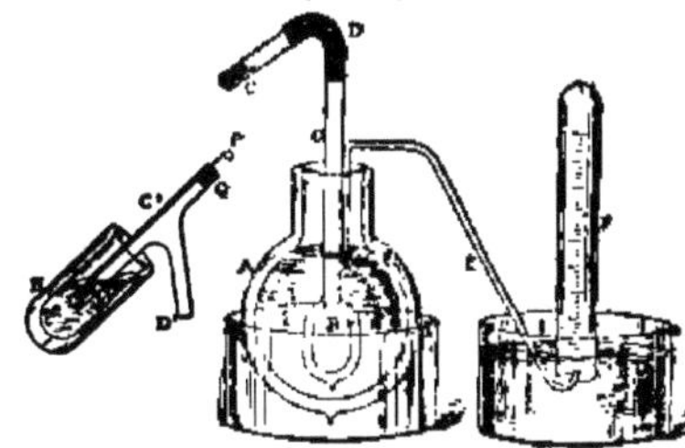

Fig. 13.—Calorimetric Apparatus.

into the calorimeter. An improved form of this receptacle, attached to B by a flexible tube at D', is shown at C'. In this P is a wire movable through a cork Q and having at its end a hook by which a piece of the substance under examination can be pulled up and dropped into B. In the absence of other arrangements the substance is at the temperature of the room, but when lower initial temperatures are desired a vacuum vessel H containing solid carbonic acid, liquid ethylene, air or other gas, can be placed to envelop C or C', or higher temperatures may be obtained by filling the surrounding vessel with vapour of water or other liquids. The gas volatilized in B is conveyed by a side tube E to be collected in a graduated receiver F over water, oil or other liquid. If liquid hydrogen is to be used as the calorimetric substance the instrument must be so modified as to prevent the ordinary atmosphere from entering G, and to that end a current of hydrogen supplied from a Kipp apparatus is arranged to flow continuously through D and E until the moment of making the experiment, when it is cut off by a suitable stop-cock. In this case the outer vessel must contain liquid hydrogen instead of liquid air.

Dewar used pure metallic lead for the purpose of conveying definite amounts of heat to liquid gas calorimeters of this kind, that metal being selected on the ground of the small variation in its specific heat at low temperatures. He was thus able to determine the latent heats of evaporation of liquid oxygen, nitrogen and hydrogen directly at their boiling points, and he also ascertained the specific heats of a large number of inorganic and organic bodies, and of some gases in the solid state, such as carbon dioxide, sulphurous acid and ammonia. Perhaps his most interesting results were those which showed the variation in the specific heats of diamond, graphite and ice as typical bodies (table X.). With Professor Curie he used both the liquid

Table X.

Substance.	18° to −78° C., or, at −30° C.	−78° to −188° C., or, at −133° C.	−188° to −252° C., or, at −220° C.
Diamond . .	0·0794	0·0190	0·0043
Graphite . .	0·1341	0·0599	0·0133
Ice	0·463*	0·285	0·146

*This is from −18° to −78° in the ice experiment.

oxygen and the liquid hydrogen calorimeter for preliminary measurements of the rate at which radium bromide gives out energy at low temperatures. The quantity of the salt available was 0·42 gram, and the thermal evolutions were as follows:—

	Gas evolved per minute.	Calories per hour.	
Liquid oxygen . .	5·5 c.c.	22·8	Crystals.
Liquid hydrogen .	51·0 "	31·6	
Melting ice . . .	..	24·1	
Liquid oxygen . .	2·0 "	8·3	After fusion
Liquid oxygen . .	2·5 "	10·3	Emanation condensed.

The apparent increase of heat evolution at the temperature of liquid hydrogen was probably due to the calorimeter being too small; hydrogen spray was thus carried away with the gas, making the volume of gas too great and inferentially also the heat evolved.

Liquid air and liquid hydrogen calorimeters open up an almost unlimited field of research in the determination of specific heats and other thermal constants, and are certain to become common laboratory instruments for such purposes.

Chemical Action.—By extreme cold chemical action is enormously reduced, though it may not in all cases be entirely abolished even at the lowest temperatures yet attained; one reason for this diminution of activity may doubtless be sought in the fact that in such conditions most substances are solid, that is, in the state least favourable to chemical combination. Thus an electric pile of sodium and carbon ceases to yield a current when immersed in liquid oxygen. Sulphur, iron and other substances can be made to burn under the surface of liquid oxygen if the combustion is properly established before the sample is immersed, and the same is true of a fragment of diamond. Nitric oxide in the gaseous condition combines instantly with free oxygen, producing the highly-coloured gas, nitric peroxide, but in the solid condition it may be placed in contact with liquid oxygen without showing any signs of chemical action. If the combination of a portion of the mixture is started by elevation of temperature, then detonation may take place throughout the cooled mass. The stability of endothermic bodies like nitric oxide and ozone at low temperatures requires further investigation. The behaviour of fluorine, which may be regarded as the most active of the elements, is instructive in this respect. As a gas, cooled to −180° C. it loses the power of attacking glass; similarly silicon, borax, carbon, sulphur and phosphorus at the same temperature do not become incandescent in an atmosphere of the gas. Passed into liquid oxygen, the gas dissolves and imparts a yellowish tint to the liquid; if the oxygen has been exposed to the air for some hours, the fluorine produces a white flocculent precipitate, which if separated by filtering deflagrates with violence as the temperature rises. It appears to be a hydrate of fluorine. As a liquid at −210° fluorine attacks turpentine also cooled to that temperature with explosive force and the evolution of light, while the direction of a jet of hydrogen upon its surface is immediately followed by combination and a flash of flame. Even when the point of a tube containing solid fluorine is broken off under liquid hydrogen, a violent explosion ensues.

Photographic Action.—The action of light on photographic plates, though greatly diminished at −180°, is far from being in abeyance; an Eastman film, for instance, remains fairly sensitive at −210°. At the still lower temperature of liquid hydrogen the photographic activity is reduced to about half what it is at that of liquid air; in other words, about 10% of the original sensitivity remains. Experiments carried out with an incandescent lamp, a Röntgen bulb and the ultra-violet spark from magnesium and cadmium, to discover at what distances from the source of light the plates must be placed in order to receive an equal photographic impression, yielded the results shown in table XI.

Table XI.

Source of Light.	Cooled Plate.	Uncooled Plate.	Ratio of Intensities at Balance.
16 C.P. lamp . .	20 in.	50 in.	1 to 6
Röntgen bulb . .	10 in.	24¾ in.	1 to 6
Ultra-violet spark	22½ in.	90 in.	1 to 16

It appears that the photographic action of both the incandescent lamp and the Röntgen rays is reduced by the temperature of liquid air to 17% of that exerted at ordinary temperatures, while ultra-violet radiation retains only 6%. It is possible that the greater dissipation of the latter by the photographic film at low temperatures than at ordinary ones is due to its

TABLE XIV.

Metals.	Platinum.	Platinum-rhodium Alloy.	Gold.	Silver.	Copper.	Iron.
Resistance at 100° C.	39·655	36·87	16·10	8·336	11·572	4·290
" 0° C.	28·851	31·93	11·58	5·990	8·117	2·765
" carbonic acid	19·620	..	..	..	..	..
" liquid oxygen	7·002	22·17	3·380	1·669	1·589	0·633
" " nitrogen		..	..	..	1·149	..
" " oxygen under exhaustion	4·634	20·73	..	..	..	..
" " hydrogen	0·826	18·96	0·381	0·244	0·077	0·356
" " hydrogen under exhaustion	0·705	18·90	0·298	0·226	0·071	..
Resistance coefficients	0·003745	0·003607	0·003903	0·003917	0·004257	0·005515
Vanishing temperatures (Centigrade)	−244·50°	−543·39°	−257·90°	−252·26°	−225·62°	−258·40° C.
	−244·15°	−530·32°	−257·8°	−252·25°	−226·04°	−246·80° D.

[illegible] their resistivity steadily increases with cold. The thermo-electric properties of metals at low temperatures are discussed in the article THERMOELECTRICITY.

Magnetic Phenomena.—Low temperatures have very marked effects upon the magnetic properties of various substances. Oxygen, long known to be slightly magnetic in the gaseous state, is powerfully attracted in the liquid condition by a magnet, and the same is true, though to a less extent, of liquid air, owing to the proportion of liquid oxygen it contains. A magnet of ordinary carbon steel has its magnetic moment temporarily increased by cooling, that is, after it has been brought to a permanent magnetic condition ("aged"). The effect of the first immersion of such a magnet in liquid air is a large diminution in its magnetic moment, which decreases still further when it is allowed to warm up to ordinary temperatures. A second cooling, however, increases the magnetic moment, which is again decreased by warming, and after a few repetitions of this cycle of cooling and heating the steel is brought into a condition such that its magnetic moment at the temperature of liquid air is greater by a constant percentage than it is at the ordinary temperature of [illegible]. The increase of magnetic moment seems then to have reached a limit, because on further cooling to the temperature of liquid hydrogen hardly any further increase is observed. The [illegible] differs with the composition of the steel and with its [illegible]. It is greater, for example, with a specimen [illegible] soft than it is with another specimen of the same [illegible] glass hard. Aluminium steels show the same kind [illegible] carbon ones, and the same may be said of chrome [illegible] permanent condition, though the effect of the [illegible] them is a slight increase of magnetic moment. [illegible] some curious phenomena. When containing [illegible] nickel (*e.g.* 0·84 or 3·82), they behave under [illegible] much like carbon steel. With a sample [illegible] the phenomena after the permanent state [illegible] similar, but the first cooling produced [illegible] magnetic moment. But steels containing [illegible] nickel behaved very differently. The result [illegible] was a reduction of the magnetic moment, [illegible] in the case of the former. Warming [illegible] increase, and the final condition was that [illegible] liquid air the magnetic moment was always [illegible] temperatures. This anomaly is all the more [illegible] behaviour of pure nickel is normal, as [illegible] the case with soft and hard iron. [illegible] steels are also substantially [illegible] although there are considerable [illegible] of the variations they display [illegible] also "The Effect of Liquid [illegible] Mechanical and other Properties [illegible] James Dewar and Sir Robert [illegible]

[illegible] the permeability of iron, *i.e.* the [illegible] capable of acquiring under the [illegible] With fine Swedish iron, [illegible] is slightly reduced by [illegible] in the same circum- [illegible] steel pianoforte wire, again, behaves like soft annealed iron. As to hysteresis, low temperatures appear to produce no appreciable effect in soft iron; for hard iron the observations are undecisive.

Biological Research.—The effect of cold upon the life of living organisms is a matter of great intrinsic interest as well as of wide theoretical importance. Experiment indicates that moderately high temperatures are much more fatal, at least to the lower forms of life, than are exceedingly low ones. Professor M'Kendrick froze for an hour at a temperature of −182° C. samples of meat, milk, &c., in sealed tubes; when these were opened, after being kept at blood-heat for a few days, their contents were found to be quite putrid. More recently some more elaborate tests were carried out at the Jenner (now Lister) Institute of Preventive Medicine on a series of typical bacteria. These were exposed to the temperature of liquid air for twenty hours, but their vitality was not affected, their functional activities remained unimpaired and the cultures which they yielded were normal in every respect. The same result was obtained when liquid hydrogen was substituted for air. A similar persistence of life has been demonstrated in seeds, even at the lowest temperatures; they were frozen for over 100 hours in liquid air at the instance of Messrs Brown and Escombe, with no other effect than to afflict their protoplasm with a certain inertness, from which it recovered with warmth. Subsequently commercial samples of barley, peas and vegetable-marrow and mustard seeds were literally steeped for six hours in liquid hydrogen at the Royal Institution, yet when they were sown by Sir W. T. Thiselton Dyer at Kew in the ordinary way, the proportion in which germination occurred was no smaller than with other batches of the same seeds which had suffered no abnormal treatment. Mr Harold Swithinbank has found that exposure to liquid air has little or no effect on the vitality of the tubercle bacillus, although by very prolonged exposures its virulence is modified to some extent; but alternate exposures to normal and very cold temperatures do have a decided effect both upon its vitality and its virulence. The suggestion once put forward by Lord Kelvin, that life may in the first instance have been conveyed to this planet on a meteorite, has been objected to on the ground that any living organism would have been killed before reaching the earth by its passage through the intense cold of interstellar space; the above experiments on the resistance to cold offered by seeds and bacteria show that this objection at least is not fatal to Lord Kelvin's idea.

At the Lister Institute of Preventive Medicine liquid air has been brought into use as an agent in biological research. An inquiry into the intracellular constituents of the typhoid bacillus, initiated under the direction of Dr Allan Macfadyen, necessitated the separation of the cell-plasma of the organism. The method at first adopted for the disintegration of the bacteria was to mix them with silver-sand and churn the whole up in a closed vessel in which a series of horizontal vanes revolved at a high speed. But certain disadvantages attached to this procedure, and accordingly some means was sought to do away with the sand and triturate the bacilli *per se*. This was found in liquid air, which, as had long before been shown at the Royal Institution, has the power of reducing materials like grass or the leaves of plants to such a state of brittleness that they can easily be powdered in a mortar. By its aid a complete trituration of the typhoid bacilli has been accomplished at the Jenner Institute, and the same process, already applied with success also to yeast cells and animal cells, is being extended in other directions.

Industrial Applications.—While liquid air and liquid hydrogen are being used in scientific research to an extent which increases every day, their applications to industrial purposes are not so numerous. The temperatures they give used as simple refrigerants are much lower than are generally required industrially, and such cooling as is needed can be obtained quite satisfactorily, and far more cheaply, by refrigerating machinery employing more easily condensable gases. Their use as a source of motive power, again, is impracticable for any ordinary purposes, on the score of inconvenience and expense. Cases may be conceived of in which for special reasons it might prove advantageous to use liquid air, vaporized by heat derived from the surrounding atmosphere, to drive compressed-air engines, but any advantage so gained would certainly not be one of cheapness. No doubt the power of a waterfall running to waste might be temporarily conserved in the shape of liquid air, and thereby turned to useful effect. But the reduction of air to the liquid state is a process which involves the expenditure of a very large amount of energy, and it is not possible even to recover all that expended energy during the transition of the material back to the gaseous state. Hence to suggest that by using liquid air in a motor more power can be developed than was expended in producing the liquid air by which the motor is worked, is to propound a fallacy worse than perpetual motion, since such a process would have an efficiency of more than 100%. Still, in conditions where economy is of no account, liquid air might perhaps, with effectively isolated storage, be utilized as a motive power, *e.g.* to drive the engines of submarine boats and at the same time provide a supply of oxygen for the crew; even without being used in the engines, liquid air or oxygen might be found a convenient form in which to store the air necessary for respiration in such vessels. But a use to which liquid air machines have already been put to a large extent is for obtaining oxygen from the atmosphere. Although when air is liquefied the oxygen and nitrogen are condensed simultaneously, yet owing to its greater volatility the latter boils off the more quickly of the two, so that the remaining liquid becomes gradually richer and richer in oxygen. The fractional distillation of liquid air is the method now universally adopted for the preparation of oxygen on a commercial scale, while the nitrogen simultaneously obtained is used for the production of cyanamide, by its action on carbide of calcium. An interesting though minor application of liquid oxygen, or liquid air from which most of the nitrogen has evaporated, depends on the fact that if it be mixed with powdered charcoal, or finely divided organic bodies, it can be made by the aid of a detonator to explode with a violence comparable to that of dynamite. This explosive, which might properly be called an emergency one, has the disadvantage that it must be prepared on the spot where it is to be used and must be fired without delay, since the liquid evaporates in a short time and the explosive power is lost; but, on the other hand, if a charge fails to go off it has only to be left a few minutes, when it can be withdrawn without any danger of accidental explosion.

For further information the reader may consult W. L. Hardin, *Rise and Development of the Liquefaction of Gases* (New York, 1899), and Lefèvre, *La Liquéfaction des gaz et ses applications*; also the article CONDENSATION OF GASES. But the literature of liquid gases is mostly contained in scientific periodicals and the proceedings of learned societies. Papers by Wroblewski and Olszewski on the liquefaction of oxygen and nitrogen may be found in the *Comptes rendus*, vols. xcvi.-cii., and there are important memoirs by the former on the relations between the gaseous and liquid states and on the compressibility of hydrogen in *Wien Akad. Sitzber.* vols. xciv. and xcvii.; his pamphlet *Comme l'air a été liquéfié* (Paris, 1885) should also be referred to. For Dewar's work, see *Proc. Roy Inst.* from 1878 onwards, including "Solid Hydrogen" (1900); "Liquid Hydrogen Calorimetry" (1904); "New Low Temperature Phenomena" (1905); "Liquid Air and Charcoal at Low Temperatures" (1906); "Studies in High Vacua and Helium at Low Temperatures" (1907); also "The Nadir of Temperature and Allied Problems" (Bakerian Lecture), *Proc. Roy. Soc.* (1901), and the Presidential Address to the British Association (1902). The researches of Fleming and Dewar on the electrical and magnetic properties of substances at low temperatures are described in *Proc. Roy. Soc.* vol. lx., and *Proc. Roy. Inst.* (1896); see also "Electrical Resistance of Pure Metals, Alloys and Non-Metals at the Boiling-point of Oxygen," *Phil. Mag.* vol. xxxiv. (1892); "Electrical Resistance of Metals and Alloys at Temperatures approaching the Absolute Zero," *ibid.* vol. xxxvi. (1893); "Thermoelectric Powers of Metals and Alloys between the Temperatures of the Boiling-point of Water and the Boiling-point of Liquid Air," *ibid.* vol. xl. (1895); and papers on the dielectric constants of various substances at low temperatures in *Proc. Roy. Soc.* vols. lxi. and lxii. Optical and spectroscopic work by Liveing and Dewar on liquid gases is described in *Phil. Mag.* vols. xxxiv. (1892), xxxvi. (1893), xxxviii. (1894) and xl. (1895); for papers by the same authors on the separation and spectroscopic examination of the most volatile and least volatile constituents of atmospheric air, see *Proc. Roy. Soc.* vols. lxiv., lxvii. and lxviii. An account of the influence of very low temperatures on the germinative power of seeds is given by H. T. Brown and F. Escombe in *Proc. Roy. Soc.* vol. lxii., and by Sir W. Thiselton Dyer, *ibid.* vol. lxv., and their effect on bacteria is discussed by A. Macfadyen, *ibid.* vols. lxvi. and lxxi. (J. De.)

LIQUORICE. The hard and semi-vitreous sticks of paste, black in colour and possessed of a sweet somewhat astringent taste, known as liquorice paste or black sugar, are the inspissated juice of the roots of a leguminous plant, *Glycyrrhiza glabra*, the *radix glycyrrhizae* of the pharmacopoeia. The plant is cultivated throughout the warmer parts of Europe, especially on the Mediterranean shores, and to some extent in Louisiana and California. The roots for use are obtained in lengths of 3 or 4 ft., varying in diameter from ¼ to 1 in.; they are soft, flexible and fibrous, and internally of a bright yellow colour, with a characteristic, sweet pleasant taste. To this sweet taste of its root the plant owes its generic name *Glycyrrhiza* (γλυκύῤῥιζα, the sweet-root), of which the word liquorice is a corruption. The roots contain grape-sugar, starch, resin, asparagine, malic acid and the glucoside glycyrrhizin, $C_{24}H_{36}O_9$, a yellow amorphous powder with an acid reaction and a distinctive bitter-sweet taste. On hydrolysis, glycyrrhizin yields glucose and glycyrrhetin.

Stick liquorice is made by crushing and grinding the roots to a pulp, which is boiled in water over an open fire, and the decoction separated from the solid residue of the root is evaporated till a sufficient degree of concentration is attained, after which, on cooling, it is rolled into the form of sticks or other shapes for the market. The preparation of the juice is a widely extended industry along the Mediterranean coasts; but the quality best appreciated in the United Kingdom is made in Calabria, and sold under the names of Solazzi and Corigliano juice. Liquorice enters into the composition of many cough lozenges and other demulcent preparations; and in the form of aromatic syrups and elixirs it has a remarkable effect in masking the taste of nauseous medicines.

LIQUOR LAWS. In most Western countries the sale of alcoholic liquor is regulated by law. The original and principal object is to check the evils arising from the immoderate use of such liquor, in the interest of public order, morality and health; a secondary object is to raise revenue from the traffic. The form and the stringency of the laws passed for these purposes vary very widely in different countries according to the habits of the people and the state of public opinion. The evils which it is desired to check are much greater in some countries than in others. Generally speaking they are greater in northern countries and cold and damp climates than in southern and more sunny ones. Climate has a marked influence on diet for physiological reasons over which we have no control. The fact is attested by universal experience and is perfectly natural and inevitable, though usually ignored in those international comparisons of economic conditions and popular customs which have become so common. It holds good both of food and drink. The inhabitants of south Europe are much less given to alcoholic excess than those of central Europe, who again are more temperate than those of the north. There is even a difference between localities so near together as the east and west of Scotland. The chairman of the Prison Commissioners pointed out before a British royal commission in the year 1897 the greater prevalence of drunkenness in the western half, and attributed it in part to the dampness of the climate on the western coast. But race also has an influence. The British carry the habit of drinking wherever they go, and their colonial descendants retain it even in hot and dry climates. The Slav peoples and the Magyars in central Europe are much more intemperate than the Teutonic and Latin peoples living under similar climatic conditions. These natural differences lead, in accordance with the principle discerned and enunciated by Montesquieu, to the adoption of different laws, which vary with the local conditions. But social laws of this character also vary with the state of public opinion, not only in different countries but in the same country at different times. The result is that the subject is in a state of incessant flux. There are not only many varieties of liquor laws, but also frequent changes in them, and new experiments are constantly being tried. The general tendency is towards increased stringency, not so much because the evils increase, though that happens in particular places at particular times, as because public opinion moves broadly towards increasing condemnation of excess and increasing reliance on legislative interference. The first is due partly to a general process of refining manners, partly to medical influence and the growing attention paid to health; the second to a universal tendency which seems inherent in democracy.

Liquor laws may be classified in several ways, but the most useful way for the present purpose will be to take the principal methods of conducting the traffic as they exist, under four main headings, and after a brief explanation give some account of the laws in the principal countries which have adopted them. The four methods are: (1) licensing or commercial sale for private profit under a legal permit; (2) sale by authorized bodies not for private profit, commonly known as the Scandinavian or company system; (3) state monopoly; (4) prohibition. It is not a scientific classification, because the company system is a form of licensing and prohibition is no sale at all; but it follows the lines of popular discussion and is more intelligible than one of a more technical character would be. All forms of liquor legislation deal mainly with retail sale, and particularly with the sale for immediate consumption on the spot.

1. *Licensing*.—This is by far the oldest and the most widely adopted method; it is the one which first suggests itself in the natural course of things. Men begin by making and selling a thing without let or hindrance to please themselves. Then objections are raised, and when they are strong or general enough the law interferes in the public interest, at first mildly; it says in effect—This must not go on in this way or to this extent; there must be some control, and permission will only be given to duly authorized persons. Such persons are licensed or permitted to carry on the traffic under conditions, and there is obviously room for infinite gradations of strictness in granting permission and infinite variety in the conditions imposed. The procedure may vary from mere notification of the intention to open an establishment up to a rigid and minutely detailed system of annual licensing laid down by the law. But in all cases, even when mere notification is required, the governing authority has the right to refuse permission or to withdraw it for reasons given, and so it retains the power of control. At the same time holders of the permission may be compelled to pay for the privilege and so contribute to the public revenue. The great merit of the licensing system is its perfect elasticity, which permits adjustment to all sorts of conditions and to the varying demands of public opinion. It is in force in the United Kingdom, which first adopted it, in most European countries, in the greater part of North America, including both the United States and Canada, in the other British dominions and elsewhere.

2. *The Scandinavian or Company System*.—The principle of this method is the elimination of private profit on the ground that it removes an incentive to the encouragement of excessive drinking. A monopoly of the sale of liquor is entrusted to a body of citizens who have, or are supposed to have, no personal interest in it, and the profits are applied to public purposes. The system, which is also called "disinterested management," is adopted in Sweden and Norway; and the principle has been applied in a modified form in England and Finland by the operation of philanthropic societies which, however, have no monopoly but are on the same legal footing as ordinary traders.

3. *State Monopoly*.—As the name implies, this system consists in retaining the liquor trade in the hands of the state, which thus secures all the profit and is at the same time able to exercise complete control. It is adopted in Russia, in certain parts of the United States and, in regard to the wholesale trade, in Switzerland.

4. *Prohibition*.—This may be general or local; in the latter case it is called "local option" or "local veto." The sale of liquor is made illegal in the hope of preventing drinking altogether or of diminishing it by making it more difficult. General prohibition has been tried in some American states, and is still in force in a few; it is also applied to native races, under civilized rule, both in Africa and North America. Local prohibition is widely in force in the United States, Canada and Australasia, Sweden and Norway. In certain areas in other countries, including the United Kingdom, the sale of liquor is in a sense prohibited, not by the law, but by the owners of the property who refuse to allow any public-houses. Such cases have nothing to do with the law, but they are mentioned here because reference is often made to them by advocates of legal prohibition.

THE UNITED KINGDOM

England has had a very much longer experience of liquor legislation than any other country, and the story forms an introduction necessary to the intelligent comprehension of liquor legislation in general. England adopted a licensing system in 1551, and has retained it, with innumerable modifications, ever since. The English were notorious for hard drinking for centuries before licensing was adopted, and from time to time sundry efforts had been made to check it, but what eventually compelled the interference of the law was the growth of crime and disorder associated with the public-houses towards the end of the 15th century. Numbers of men who had previously been engaged in the civil wars or on the establishment of feudal houses were thrown on the world and betook themselves to the towns, particularly London, where they frequented the ale-houses, "dicing and drinking," and lived largely on violence and crime. An act was passed in 1495 against vagabonds and unlawful games, whereby justices of the peace were empowered to "put away common ale-selling in towns and places where they should think convenient and to take sureties of keepers of ale-houses in their good behaviour." That was the beginning of statutory control of the trade. The act clearly recognized a connexion between public disorder and public-houses. The latter were ale-houses, for at that time ale was the drink of the people; spirits had not yet come into common use, and wine, the consumption of which on the premises was prohibited in 1552, was only drunk by the wealthier classes.

Early History of Licensing.—The act of 1551–1552, which introduced licensing, was on the same lines but went further. It confirmed the power of suppressing common ale-selling, and enacted that no one should be allowed to keep a common ale-house or "tippling" house without obtaining the permission of the justices in open session or of two of their number. It further "directed that the justices should take from the persons whom they licensed such bond and surety by recognisance as they should think convenient, and empowered them in quarter session to inquire into and try breaches by licensed persons of the conditions of their recognisances and cases of persons keeping ale-houses without licences and to punish the offenders" (Bonham Carter, Royal Commission on Liquor Licensing Laws, vol. iii.). This act embodied the whole principle of licensing, and the object was clearly stated in the preamble: "For as much as intolerable hurts and troubles to the commonwealth of this realm doth daily grow and increase through such abuses and disorders as are had and used in common ale-houses and other places called tippling houses." The evil was not due merely to the use of alcoholic liquor but to the fact that these houses, being public-houses, were the resort of idle and disorderly characters. The distinction should be borne in mind.

The act seems to have been of some effect, for no further legislation was attempted for half a century, though there is abundant evidence of the intemperate habits of all classes. Mr Bonham Carter (*loc. cit.*) observes:—

"The recognisances referred to in the act were valuable instruments for controlling the conduct of ale-house keepers. The justices, in exercise of their discretion, required the recognisances to contain such conditions for the management and good order of the business as they thought suitable. In this way a set of regulations came into existence, many of which were subsequently embodied in acts of Parliament. In some counties general rules were drawn up, which every ale-house keeper was bound to observe."

It is interesting to note that among the conditions laid down about this time were the following: Closing at 9 P.M. and during divine service on Sunday; in some cases complete closing on Sunday except to travellers; the licence-holder to notify to the constable all strangers staying for more than a night and not to permit persons to continue drinking or tippling; prohibition of unlawful games, receiving stolen goods and harbouring bad characters; the use of standard measures and prices fixed by law. There was, however, no uniformity of practice in these respects until the 17th century, when an attempt was made to establish stricter and more uniform control by a whole series of acts passed between 1603 and 1627. The evils which it was sought to remedy by these measures were the existence of unlicensed houses, the use of ale-houses for mere drinking and the prevalence of disorder. It was declared that the ancient and proper use of inns and ale-houses was the refreshment and lodging of travellers, and that they were not meant for "entertainment and harbouring of lewd and idle people to spend and consume their money and their time in lewd and drunken manner." Regulations were strengthened for the suppression of unlicensed houses, licences were made annual, and the justices were directed to hold a special licensing meeting once a year (1618). Penalties were imposed on innkeepers for permitting tippling, and also on tipplers and drunkards (1625). In 1634 licensing was first applied to Ireland. Later in the century heavy penalties were imposed for adulteration.

The next chapter in the history of licensing has to do with spirits, and is very instructive. Spirits were not a native product like beer; brandy was introduced from France, gin from the Netherlands and whisky from Ireland; but down to the year 1690 the consumption was small. The home manufacture was strictly limited, and high duties on imported spirits rendered them too dear for the general public unless smuggled. Consequently the people had not acquired the taste for them. But in 1690 distilling was thrown open to any one on the payment of very trifling duties, spirits became extremely cheap and the consumption increased with great rapidity. Regulation of the retail traffic was soon found to be necessary, and by an act passed in 1700–1701, the licensing requirements already existing for ale-house keepers were extended to persons selling distilled liquors for consumption on the premises. A new class of public-houses in the shape of spirit bars grew up. In the year 1732 a complete and detailed survey of all the streets and houses in London was carried out by William Maitland, F.R.S. Out of a total of 95,968 houses he found the following: brew-houses 171, inns 207, taverns 447, ale-houses 5975, brandy-shops 8659; total number of licensed houses for the retail sale of liquor 15,288, of which considerably more than one-half were spirit bars. The population was about three-quarters of a million. About one house in every six was licensed at this time, and that in spite of attempts made to check the traffic by restrictive acts passed in 1728–1729. The physical and moral evils caused by the excessive consumption of spirits were fully recognized; an additional duty of 5s. a gallon was placed on the distiller, and retailers were compelled to take out an excise licence of £20 per annum. The object was to make spirits dearer and therefore less accessible. At the same time, with a view to lessening the number of houses, the licensing procedure of the justices was amended by the provision that licences should only be granted at a general meeting of the justices acting in the division where the applicant resided, thus abolishing the power conferred by the original licensing act, of any two justices to grant a licence. This change, effected in 1729, was a permanent improvement, though it did not prevent the existence of the prodigious numbers of houses recorded by Maitland in 1732. The attempt to make spirits dearer by high excise duties, on the other hand, was adjudged a failure because it led to illicit trade, and the act of 1728 was repealed in 1732. But the evil was so glaring that another and more drastic attempt in the same direction was made in 1736, when the famous Gin Act was passed in response to a petition presented to parliament by the Middlesex magistrates, declaring "that the drinking of geneva and other distilled waters had for some years past greatly increased; that the constant and excessive use thereof had destroyed thousands of His Majesty's subjects; that great numbers of others were by its use rendered unfit for useful labour, debauched in morals and drawn into all manner of vice and wickedness. . . ." The retailing of spirits in quantities of less than 2 gallons was made subject to a licence costing £50 and the retailer had also to pay a duty of 20s. on every gallon sold. This experiment in "high licensing" was a disastrous failure, though energetic attempts were made to enforce it by wholesale prosecutions and by strengthening the regulations against evasion. Public opinion was inflamed against it, and the only results were corruptions of the executive and an enormous increase of consumption through illicit channels. The consumption of spirits in England and Wales nearly doubled between 1733 and 1742, and the state of things was so intolerable that after much controversy the high duties were repealed in 1742 with the object of bringing the trade back into authorized channels; the cost of a licence was reduced from £50 to £1 and the retail duty from 20s. to 1d. a gallon.

This period witnessed the high-water mark of intemperance in England. From various contemporary descriptions it is abundantly clear that the state of things was incomparably worse than anything in modern times, and that women, whose participation in the practice of drinking and frequenting public-houses is recorded by writers in the previous century, were affected as well as men. The experience is particularly instructive because it includes examples of excess and deficiency of opportunities and the ill effects of both on a people naturally inclined to indulgence in drink. It was followed by more judicious action, which showed the adaptability of the licensing system and the advantages of a mean between laxity and severity. Between 1743 and 1753 acts were passed which increased control in a moderate way and proved much more successful than the previous measures. The retail licence duty was moderately raised and the regulations were amended and made stricter. The class of houses eligible for licensing was for the first time taken into account, and the retailing of spirits was only permitted on premises assessed for rates and, in London, of the annual value of £10; justices having an interest in the trade were excluded from licensing functions. Another measure which had an excellent effect made "tippling" debts—that is, small public-houses debts incurred for spirits—irrecoverable at law. The result of these measures was that consumption diminished and the class of houses improved. At the same time (1753) the general licensing provisions were strengthened and extended. The distinction between new licences and the renewal of old ones was for the first time recognized; applicants for new licences in country districts were required to produce a certificate of character from the clergy, overseers and church-wardens or from three or four householders. The annual licensing sessions were made statutory, and the consent of a justice was required for the transfer of a licence from one person to another during the term for which it was granted. Penalties for infringing the law were increased, and the licensing system was extended to Scotland (1755–1756). With regard to wine, it has already been stated that consumption on the premises was forbidden in 1552, and at the same time the retail sale was restricted to towns of some importance and the number of retailers, who had to obtain an appointment from the corporation or the justices, was strictly limited. In 1660 consumption on the premises was permitted under a Crown (excise) licence, good for a variable term of years; in 1756 this was changed to an annual excise licence of fixed [illegible], [illegible] wine was brought under the same jurisdiction [illegible] as other liquors.

[illegible] from the foregoing that a great deal of legislation [illegible] century, and that by successive enact[illegible] about the middle of the century, the licensing [illegible] became adjusted to the requirements of the [illegible] shape. The acts then passed still form [illegible]. In the early part of the 19th century another [illegible] activity set in. A parliamentary inquiry [illegible] took place in 1821, and in 1828 important [illegible] amending and consolidating the laws for [illegible]; in 1833 a general Licensing Act was [illegible]. These are still the principal acts, though they [illegible] innumerable amendments and additions. The [illegible] introduced certain important changes. A [illegible] was no longer required for the sale of [illegible] off the premises, and the power of the [illegible] public-houses at their discretion (apart [illegible]), which they had possessed since 1495, [illegible]. The removal of this power, which had long [illegible] the natural corollary of the development [illegible], its greater stringency and efficiency [illegible] imposed on the trade. Men on whom [illegible] were laid, and who were freshly authorized [illegible] every year, could not remain liable to [illegible] the privileges thus granted and paid for. [illegible] discretion to withhold licences from [illegible] new or old; but an appeal was allowed [illegible] refusal and also against conviction [illegible]. The main points in the law at this [illegible]. The sale of alcoholic liquors for con[illegible] was forbidden under penalties except [illegible] according to law by the justices. Licences [illegible] year and had to be renewed annually. [illegible] general meeting each year at a specified [illegible] of granting licences; those peculiarly [illegible] liquor trade were disqualified. The licence [illegible] for regulating the conduct of the [illegible], but closing was only required during [illegible] on Sunday. Applicants for new [illegible] of old ones (granted at a special [illegible]) were required to give notice to the local [illegible] up notices at the parish church and on [illegible]

[illegible] It will be convenient at this point to explain [illegible] part of the licensing system which [illegible] of the traffic and lies in the juris[illegible] part which has to do with taxation [illegible] the earlier and more important [illegible]; we have traced its history [illegible]. Its object from the beginning was [illegible] order and good conduct, which were [illegible] public-houses; and all the successive [illegible] to that end. They were attempts [illegible] the evils arising from the traffic by [illegible] system has nothing to do with [illegible] of the traffic; its object is simply [illegible] long time the two systems were quite [illegible] change gradually brought them into [illegible] to form two aspects of one [illegible] revenue was first introduced in [illegible] on the manufacture of beer and [illegible] irregular character and was only [illegible] then under the jurisdiction of [illegible]. In 1710 a small annual tax was [illegible] and ale and collected by means [illegible]. In 1728 an annual excise [illegible] retailers of spirits, and in 1736 [illegible]. The object of these particular [illegible] check the sale, as previously [illegible]. In 1756 the previous tax [illegible] [illegible]ption on the premises was changed to an annual excise licence, which was in the next year extended to "made wines" and "sweets" (British wines). Similar licences, in place of the previous stamps, were temporarily required for beer and ale between 1725 and 1742 and permanently imposed in 1808. Thus the system of annual excise licences became gradually applied to all kinds of liquor. In 1825 the laws relating to them were consolidated and brought into direct relation with the other licensing laws. It was enacted that excise licences for the retail of liquor should only be granted to persons holding a justices' licence or—to use the more correct term—certificate. The actual permission to sell was obtained on payment of the proper dues from the excise authorities, but they had no power to withhold it from persons authorized by the justices. And that was still the system in 1910.

Licensing since 1828.—There was no change in the form of the British licensing system between the consolidation of the law in 1825–1828 and the time (1910) at which we write; but there were a great many changes in administrative detail and some changes in principle. Only the most important can be mentioned. In 1830 a bold experiment was tried in exempting the sale of beer from the requirement of a justice's licence. Any householder rated to the parish was entitled, under a bond with sureties, to take out an excise licence for the sale of beer for consumption on or off the premises. This measure, which applied to England and was commonly known as the Duke of Wellington's Act, had two objects; one was to encourage the consumption of beer in the hope of weaning the people from spirits; the other was to counteract the practice of "tieing" public-houses to breweries by creating free ones. With regard to the first, it was believed that spirit-drinking was increasing again at the time and was doing a great deal of harm. The reason appears to have been a great rise in the returns of consumption, which followed a lowering of the duty on spirits from 11s. 8¼d. to 7s. a gallon in 1825. The latter step was taken because of the prevalence of illicit distillation. In 1823 the duty had been lowered for the same reason in Scotland from 6s. 2d. and in Ireland from 5s. 7d. to a uniform rate of 2s. 4¾d. a gallon, with so much success in turning the trade from illegal to legal channels that a similar change was thought advisable in England, as stated. The legal or apparent consumption rose at once from 7 to nearly 13 million gallons; but it is doubtful if there was much or any real increase. According to an official statement, more than half the spirits consumed in 1820 were illicit. The facts are of much interest in showing what had already been shown in the 18th century, that the liquor trade will not bear unlimited taxation; the traffic is driven underground. It is highly probable that this accounts for part of the great fall in consumption which followed the raising of the spirit duty from 11s. to 14s. 9d. under Mr Lloyd George's Budget in 1909. With regard to "tied" houses, this is the original form of public-house. When beer was first brewed for sale a "tap" for retail purposes was attached to the brewery, and public-houses may still be found bearing the name "The Brewery Tap." At the beginning of the 19th century complaints were made of the increasing number of houses owned or controlled by breweries and of the dependence of the licence-holders, and in 1817 a Select Committee inquired into the subject. The Beerhouse Act does not appear to have checked the practice or to have diminished the consumption of spirits; but it led to a great increase in the number of beer-houses. It was modified in 1834 and 1840, but not repealed until 1869, when beer-houses were again brought under the justices.

Most of the other very numerous changes in the law were concerned with conditions imposed on licence-holders. The hours of closing are the most important of these. Apart from the ancient regulations of closing during divine service on Sunday, there were no restrictions in 1828; but after that at least a dozen successive acts dealt with the point. The first important measure was applied in London under a Police Act in 1839; it ordered licensed houses to be closed from midnight on Saturday to mid-day on Sunday, and produced a wonderful effect on public order. In 1853 a very important act (Forbes Mackenzie) was passed for Scotland, by which sale on Sunday was wholly forbidden, except to travellers and lodgers, and was restricted on week days to the hours between 8 A.M. and 11 P.M. This act also introduced a distinction between hotels, public-houses and grocers licensed to sell liquor, and forbade the sale to children under 14 years, except as messengers, and to intoxicated persons. In England, after a series of enactments in the direction of progressive restriction, uniform regulations as to the hours of opening and closing for licensed premises were applied in 1874, and are still in force (see below). In 1878 complete Sunday closing, as in Scotland, was applied in Ireland, with the exemption of the five largest towns, Dublin, Belfast, Cork, Limerick and Waterford; and in 1881 the same provision was extended to Wales.

Other changes worthy of note are the following. In 1860 the free sale of wine for consumption off the premises was introduced by the Wine and Refreshment Houses Act, which authorized any shopkeeper to take out an excise licence for this purpose; the licences so created were subsequently known as grocers' licences. By the same act refreshment houses were placed under certain restrictions, but were permitted to sell wine for consumption on the premises under an excise licence. In 1861 spirit dealers were similarly authorized to sell spirits by the bottle. The effect of these measures was to exempt a good deal of the wine and spirit trade from the control of the justices, and the idea was to wean people from public-house drinking by encouraging them to take what they wanted at home and in eating-houses.

In 1869 this policy of directing the habits of the people into channels thought to be preferable, which had been inaugurated in 1830, was abandoned for one of greater stringency all round, which has since been maintained. All the beer and wine retail licences were brought under the discretion of the justices, but they might only refuse "off" licences and the renewal of previously existing beer-house "on" licences upon specified grounds, namely (1) unsatisfactory character, (2) disorder, (3) previous misconduct, (4) insufficient qualification of applicant or premises. In 1872 an important act further extended the policy of restriction; new licences had to be confirmed, and the right of appeal in case of refusal was taken away; penalties for offences were increased and extended, particularly for public drunkenness, and for permitting drunkenness; the sale of spirits to persons under 16 was prohibited. In 1876 many of these provisions were extended to Scotland. In 1886 the sale of liquor for consumption on the premises was forbidden to persons under 13 years. In 1901 the sale for "off" consumption was prohibited to persons under 14, except in sealed vessels; this is known as the Child Messenger Act. These measures for the protection of children were extended in 1908 by an act which came into operation in April 1909, excluding children under 14 from the public-house bars altogether. The progressive protection of children by the law well illustrates the influence of changing public opinion. The successive measures enumerated were not due to increasing contamination of children caused by their frequenting the public-house, but to recognition of the harm they sustain thereby. The practice of taking and sending children to the public-house, and of serving them with drink, is an old one in England. A great deal of evidence on the subject was given before a Select Committee of the House of Commons in 1834; but it is only in recent years, when the general concern for children has undergone a remarkable development in all directions, that attempts have been made to stop it. In 1902 clubs, which had been increasing, and habitual drunkards, were brought under the law.

In 1904 a new principle was introduced into the licensing system in England, and this, too, was due to change in public opinion. Between 1830 and 1869, under the influence of the legislation described above, a continuous increase in the number of public-houses took place in England; but after 1869 they began to diminish through stricter control, and this process has gone on continuously ever since. Reduction of numbers became a prime object with many licensing benches; they were reluctant to grant new licences, and made a point of extinguishing old ones year by year. At first this was easily effected under the new and stringent provisions of the legislation of 1869–1872, but it gradually became more difficult as the worst houses disappeared and the remaining ones were better conducted, and gave less and less excuse for interference. But the desire for reduction still gained ground, and a new principle was adopted. Houses against which no ill-conduct was alleged were said to be "superfluous," and on that ground licences were taken away. But this, again, offended the general sense of justice; it was felt that to take away a man's living or a valuable property for no fault of his own was to inflict a great hardship. To meet the difficulty the principle of compensation was introduced by the act of 1904. It provides that compensation shall be paid to a licence-holder (also to the owner of the premises) whose licence is withdrawn on grounds other than misconduct of the house or unsuitability of premises or of character. The compensation is paid out of a fund raised by an annual charge on the remaining licensed houses. This act has been followed by a large reduction of licences.

State of the Law in 1910.—In consequence of the long history and evolution of legislation in the United Kingdom and of the innumerable minor changes introduced, only a few of which have been mentioned above, the law has become excessively complicated. The differences between the English, Scottish and Irish codes, the distinction between the several kinds of liquor, between consumption on and off the premises, between new licences and the renewal of old ones, between premises licensed before 1869 and those licensed since, between excise and justices' licences—all these and many other points make the subject exceedingly intricate; and it is further complicated by the uncertainty of the courts and a vast body of case-made law. Only a summary of the chief provisions can be given here.

1. The open sale of intoxicating liquor (spirits, wine, sweets, beer, cider) by retail is confined to persons holding an excise licence, with a few unimportant exceptions, including medicine.

2. A condition precedent to obtaining such a licence is permission granted by the justices who are the licensing authority and called a justices' licence or certificate. Theatres, passenger boats and canteens are exempted from this condition; also certain dealers in spirits and wine.

3. Justices' licences are granted at special annual meetings of the local justices, called Brewster Sessions. Justices having a pecuniary interest in the liquor trade of the district, except as railway shareholders, are disqualified from acting; "bias" due to other interests may also be a disqualification.

4. Justices' licences are only granted for one year and must be renewed annually, with the exception of a particular class, created by the act of 1904 and valid for a term of years. Distinctions are made between granting a new licence and renewing an old one. The proceedings are stricter and more summary in the case of a new licence; notice of application must be given to the local authorites; the premises must be of a certain annual value; a plan of the premises must be deposited beforehand in the case of an "on" licence; the justices may impose conditions and have full discretion to refuse without any right of appeal; the licence, if granted, must be confirmed by a higher authority. In the case of old licences on the other hand, no notice is required; they are renewed to the former holders on application, as a matter of right; unless there is opposition or objection, which may come from the police or from outside parties or from the justices themselves. If there is objection the renewal may be refused, but only on specified grounds—namely misconduct, unfitness of premises or character, disqualification; otherwise compensation is payable on the plan explained above. There is a right of appeal to a higher court against refusal. In all cases, whether the justices have full discretion or not, they must exercise their discretion in a judicial manner and not arbitrarily.

5. Licences may be transferred from one person to another in case of death, sickness, bankruptcy, change of tenancy, wilful omission to apply for renewal, forfeiture or disqualification. Licences may also be transferred from one house to another in certain circumstances.

6. A licence may be forfeited through the conviction of the holder of certain specified serious offences.

[illegible] disqualified from holding a
[illegible] the premises specified in the
[illegible] hours:—week-days; London,
[illegible] midnight); large towns 6 A.M.
[illegible] to 10 P.M.—Sundays; London,
[illegible] P.M.; other places 12.30 P.M. (or
[illegible] P.M. to 10 P.M.; Christmas Day
[illegible] as Sunday. In Scotland, Wales
[illegible] towns, no sale is permitted on
[illegible] during prohibited hours to
[illegible] travellers, who must
[illegible] slept in on the previous
[illegible] may be granted for special
[illegible] early markets).
[illegible] are prohibited in licensed
[illegible] 14 to be in a bar, selling
[illegible] consumption on the premises,
[illegible] messengers except in corked
[illegible] consumption on the premises
[illegible] persons and to habitual
[illegible] permitting disorder,
[illegible] constables, supplying liquor
[illegible] constables, permitting betting
[illegible] premises to be used as a
[illegible] seditious meetings;
[illegible] premises; permitting
[illegible] committee rooms. In and
[illegible] are prohibited on
[illegible]
[illegible] to licensed premises
[illegible] or detecting offences.
[illegible] liquor is prohibited;
[illegible] spirits is not unlawful
[illegible] the fact.
[illegible] liquor is sold must be
[illegible] property of the members
[illegible] liquor can be sold for
[illegible]

licensed premises; penalty, fine up to 10s. for first conviction, up to 20s. for second, and up to 40s. for third. Riotous or disorderly conduct while drunk; fine up to 40s. Falsely pretending to be a traveller or lodger; fine up to £5. Causing children to be in a bar or sending them for liquor contrary to the law; fine up to £2 for first and up to £5 for second offence. Attempt to obtain liquor by a person notified to the police as an habitual drunkard; fine up to 20s. for first offence, up to 40s. for subsequent ones. Giving drunken persons liquor or helping them to get it on licensed premises; fine up to 40s. or imprisonment for a month. Causing children under 11 to sing or otherwise perform on licensed premises, and causing boys under 14 or girls under 16 to do so between 9 P.M. and 6 A.M.; fine up to £25 or three months' imprisonment.

The foregoing statement of the law does not in all respects apply to Scotland and Ireland, where the administration differs somewhat from that of England. In Scotland the provost and bailies are the licensing authority in royal and parliamentary burghs, and elsewhere the justices. They hold two sessions annually for granting licences and have considerably more power in some respects than in England. The hours of opening are from 8 A.M. to 11 P.M. (week days only), but there is a discretionary power to close at 10 P.M. In Ireland the licensing authority is divided between quarter sessions and petty sessions. Public-house licences are granted and transferred at quarter sessions; renewals and other licences are dealt with at petty sessions. In Dublin, Belfast, Cork, Londonderry and Galway the licensing jurisdiction of quarter sessions is exercised by the recorder, elsewhere by the justices assembled and presided over by the county court judge. The licensing jurisdiction of petty sessions is exercised by two or more justices, but in Dublin by one divisional justice.

Excise Licences and Taxation.—The excise licences may be divided into four classes, (1) manufacturers', (2) wholesale dealers', (3) retail dealers' for "on" consumption, (4) retail dealers' for "off" consumption. Only the two last classes come under the jurisdiction of the justices, as explained above. The total number of different excise licences is between 30 and 40, but

Licence.	Old Duty.	New Duty 1909–1910.
Manufacturers' Licences—		
Distiller (spirits)	£10, 10s.	£10 for first 50,000 gallons, £10 for every additional 25,000 gallons.
Rectifier (spirits)	£10, 10s.	£15, 15s.
Brewer	£1	£1 for first 100 barrels, 12s. for every additional 50 barrels.
Sweets (British wines)	£1	£5, 5s.
Wholesale Dealers' Licences—		
Spirits	£10, 10s.	£15, 15s.
Beer	£3, 6s. 1d.	£10, 10s.
Wine	£10, 10s.	No change.
Sweets	£5, 5s.	No change.
Retail Licences On—		
Full or Publican's (spirits, beer, wine and cider)	£4, 10s. to £60 according to annual value of premises.	Half the annual value of premises, with a fixed minimum ranging from £5 in places with less than 2000 inhabitants to £35 in towns having over 100,000 inhabitants.
Beer-house	£3, 10s.	One-third of annual value of premises, with a minimum as above ranging from £3, 10s. to £23, 10s.
Wine (confectioners')	£3, 10s.	From £4, 10s. to £12 according to annual value.
Cider	£1, 5s.	From £2, 5s. to £6.
Sweets	£1, 5s.	From £2, 5s. to £6.
Retail Licences Off—		
Spirits	£3, 3s.	From £10 to £50 according to annual value.
Spirits (grocers', Scotland)	£4, 4s. to £13, 13s. 6d.	
Spirits (grocers', Ireland)	£9, 18s. 5d. to £14, 6s. 7d	
Beer (England)	£1, 5s.	£1, 10s. to £10.
[illegible] Scotland)	£2, 10s. and £4, 4s.	£1, 10s. to £10.
[illegible]	£2, 10s. 0d.	£2, 10s. to £10.

[illegible]

several of them are subvarieties and unimportant or are peculiar to Scotland or Ireland. The duties charged on them were greatly changed and increased by the Finance Act of 1909–1910, and it seems desirable to state the changes thus introduced. The table on the previous page gives the principal kinds of licence with the old and the new duties.

There are in addition "occasional" licences valid for one or more days, which come under the jurisdiction of the justices; the duty is 2s. 6d. a day for the full licence (raised to 10s.) and 1s. for beer or wine only (raised to 5s.).

The total amount raised by the excise licences in the United Kingdom for the financial year ending 31st March 1909 was £2,209,928. Of this amount £1,712,160, or nearly four-fifths, was derived from the full or publicans' licence, £126,053 from the wholesale spirit licence and £88,167 from the beer-house licence; the rest are comparatively unimportant. But the licences only represent a small part of the revenue derived from liquor. The great bulk of it is collected by means of duties on manufacture and importation. The total amount for the year ending March 1909 was £37,428,189, or nearly 30% of the total taxation revenue of the country. The excise duties on the manufacture of spirits yielded £17,456,366 and those on beer £12,691,332; customs duties on importation yielded £5,046,949. The excise duty on spirits was at the rate of 11s. a gallon, raised at the end of April 1909 to 14s. 9d.; the corresponding duty on beer is 7s. 9d. a barrel (36 gallons). The relative taxation of the liquor trade in the United States, which has become important as a political argument, is discussed below.

Effects of Legislation.—The only effects which can be stated with precision and ascribed with certainty to legislation are the increase or diminution of the number of licences or licensed premises; secondary effects, such as increase or diminution of consumption and of drunkenness, are affected by so many causes that only by a very careful, well-informed and dispassionate examination of the facts can positive conclusions be drawn with regard to the influence of legislation (see TEMPERANCE). There is no more prolific ground for fallacious statements and arguments, whether unconscious or deliberate. The course of legislation traced above, however, does permit the broad conclusion that great laxity and the multiplication of facilities tend to increase drinking and disorder in a country like the United Kingdom, and that extreme severity produces the same or worse effects by driving the trade into illicit channels, which escape control, and thus really increasing facilities while apparently diminishing them. The most successful course has always been a mean between these extremes in the form of restraint judiciously applied and adjusted to circumstances. The most salient feature of the situation as influenced by the law in recent years is the progressive reduction in the number of licensed houses since 1869. Previously they had been increasing in England.

The number of public-houses, including beer-houses for "on" consumption, in 1831 was 82,466; in 1869 it had risen to 118,602; in 1909 it had fallen again to 94,794. But if the proportion of public-houses to population be taken there has been a continuous fall since 1831, as the following table shows:—

England and Wales.

Year.	No. of "on" Licences.	Proportion per 10,000 of Population.
1831	82,466	59
1871	112,886	49
1901	101,940	31
1909	94,794	26

The change may be put in another way. In 1831 there was one public-house to 168 persons; in 1909 the proportion was 1 to 375. The proportional reduction goes back to the 18th century. In 1732 there was in London one public-house to every 50 persons (see above).

In Scotland the number of public-houses has been diminishing since 1829, when there were 17,713; in 1909 there were only 7065, while the population had more than doubled. The number in proportion to population has therefore fallen far more rapidly than in England, thus—1831, 1 to 134 persons; 1909, 1 to 690 persons. In Ireland the story is different. There has been a fall in the number of public-houses since 1829, when there were 20,548; but it has not been large or continuous and the population has been steadily diminishing during the time, so that the proportion to population has actually increased, thus—1831, 1 to 395 persons; 1909, 1 to 249 persons. As a whole, however, the United Kingdom shows a large and progressive diminution of public-houses to population; nor is this counterbalanced by an increase of "off" licences. If we take the whole number of licences we get the following movement in recent years:—

No. of Retail Licences ("on" and "off") per 10,000 of Population.

	1893.	1903.	1909.
England and Wales	46	42	37
Scotland	37	33	30
Ireland	41	46	45
United Kingdom	45	42	37

The diminution in the number of public-houses in England was markedly accelerated by the act of 1904, which introduced the principle of compensation. The average annual rate of reduction in the ten years 1894–1904 before the act was 359; in the four years 1905–1908; after the act it rose to 1388. The average annual number of licences suppressed with compensation was 1137, and the average annual amount of compensation paid was £1,096,946, contributed by the trade as explained above.

The reduction of public-houses has been accompanied in recent years by a constant increase in the number of clubs. By the act of 1902, which imposed registration, they were brought under some control and the number of legal clubs was accurately ascertained. Previously the number was only estimated from certain *data* with approximate accuracy. The following table gives the official figures:—

Clubs: England and Wales.

	1887.	1896.	1904.	1905.	1906.	1907.	1908.	1909.
Number	1982	3655	6371	6589	6721	6907	7133	7353
Proportion per 10,000	0·7	1·1	1·89	1·93	1·95	1·98	2·02	2·08

Clubs represent alternative channels to the licensed trade and they are under much less stringent control; they have no prohibited hours and the police have not the same right of entry. In so far, therefore, as clubs replace public-houses the reduction of the latter does not mean diminished facilities for drinking, but the contrary. In the years 1903–1908 the average number of clubs proceeded against for offences was 74 and the average number struck off the register was 52. The increase of clubs and the large proportion struck off the register suggest the need of caution in dealing with the licensed trade; over-stringent measures defeat their own end.

Persistent attempts have for many years been made to effect radical changes in the British system of licensing by the introduction of some of the methods adopted in other countries, and particularly those in the United States. But it is difficult to engraft new and alien methods, involving violent change, upon an ancient system consolidated by successive statutory enactments and confirmed by time and usage. The course of the law and administration since 1869 has made it particularly difficult. The stringent conditions imposed on licence-holders have given those who fulfil them a claim to consideration, and the reduction of licences, by limiting the market, has enhanced their value. An expectation of renewal, in the absence of misconduct, has grown up by usage and been confirmed by the law, which recognizes the distinction between granting a new licence and renewing an old one, by the treasury which levies death duties on the assumption that a licence is an enduring property, by local authorities which assess upon the same assumption, and by the High Courts of Justice, whose decisions have repeatedly turned on this point. The consequence of all this is that very large sums

[illegible]

and that the constitution of the United States is not thereby violated. Use has been made of this power in Kansas, and it appears therefore that persons who engage in the liquor trade do so at their own risk. There is in fact no stability at all except in a few states which have incorporated some principle in their constitutions, and even that does not ensure continuity of practice, as means are easily found for evading the law or substituting some other system which amounts to the same thing. As a whole the control of the liquor traffic oscillates violently between attempted suppression and great freedom combined with heavy taxation of licensed houses.

In the great majority of the states some form of licensing exists; it is the prevailing system and was adopted, no doubt from England, at an early period. It is exercised in various ways. The licensing authority may be the municipality or a specially constituted body or the police or a judicial body. The last, which is the method in Pennsylvania, seems to be exceptional. According to Mr Fanshawe there is a general tendency, due to the prevailing corruption, to withdraw from municipal authorities power over the licensing, and to place this function in the hands of commissioners, who may be elected or nominated. In New York state the licensing commissioners used to be nominated in cities by the mayors and elected elsewhere; but by the Raines law of 1896 the whole administration was placed under a state commissioner appointed by the governor with the consent of the Senate. A similar plan is in force in some important cities in other states. In Boston the licensing is in the hands of a police board appointed by the governor; in Baltimore and St Louis the authority is vested in commissioners similarly appointed; and in Washington the licensing commissioners are appointed by the president. In Pennsylvania, where the court of quarter sessions is the authority, the vesting of licensing in a judicial body dates back to 1676 and bears the stamp of English influence. It is noteworthy that in Philadelphia and Pittsburg (Allegheny county) the judicial court was for a time given up in favour of commissioners, but the change was a great failure and abandoned in 1888. The powers of the licensing authority vary widely; in some cases the only grounds of refusal are conduct and character, and licences are virtually granted to every applicant; in others the discretion to refuse is absolute. In Massachusetts the number of licences allowed bears a fixed ratio to the population, namely 1 to 1000, except in Boston, where it is 1 to 500, but as a rule where licences are given they are given freely. They are valid for a year and granted on conditions. The first and most general condition is the payment of a fee or tax, which varies in amount in different states. Under the "high licence" system (see below) it generally varies according to the size of the locality and the class of licence where different classes are recognized. In Massachusetts there are six licences; three for consumption on the premises—namely (1) full licence for all liquors, (2) beer, cider, and light wine, (3) beer and cider; two for consumption off the premises—namely (1) spirits, (2) other liquors; the sixth is for druggists. In New York state also there are six classes of licence, though they are not quite the same; but in many states there appears to be only one licence, and no distinction between on and off sale, wholesale or retail. Another condition generally imposed in addition to the tax is a heavy bond with sureties; it varies in amount but is usually not less than 2000 dollars (£400) and may be as high as 6000 dollars (£1200). A condition precedent to the granting of a licence imposed in some states is the deposit of a petition or application some time beforehand, which may have to be backed by a certain number of local residents or tax-payers. In Pennsylvania the required number is 12, and this is the common practice elsewhere; in Missouri a majority of tax-payers is required, and the licence may even then be refused, but if the petition is signed by two-thirds of the tax-payers the licensing authority is bound to grant it. This seems to be a sort of genuine local option. Provision is also generally made for hearing objectors. Another condition sometimes required (Massachusetts and Iowa) is the consent of owners of adjoining property. In some states no licences are permitted within a stated distance of certain institutions; *e.g.* public parks (Missouri) and schools (Massachusetts). Regulations imposed on the licensed trade nearly always include prohibition of sale to minors under 18 and to drunkards, on Sundays, public holidays and election days, and prohibition of the employment of barmaids. Sunday closing, which is universal, dates at least from 1816 (Indiana) and is probably much older. The hours of closing on week days vary considerably but are usually 10 P.M. or 11 P.M. Other things are often prohibited including indecent pictures, games and music.

State Prohibition.—In a few states no licences are allowed. State prohibition was first introduced in 1846 under the influence of a strong agitation in Maine, and within a few years the example was followed by the other New England states; by Vermont in 1852, Connecticut in 1854, New Hampshire in 1855 and later by Massachusetts and Rhode Island. They have all now after a more or less prolonged trial given it up except Maine. Other states which have tried and abandoned it are Illinois (1851–1853), Indiana (1855–1858), Michigan, Iowa, Nebraska, South Dakota. The great Middle states have either never tried it, as in the case of New York (where it was enacted in 1855 but declared unconstitutional), Pennsylvania and New Jersey, or only gave it a nominal trial, as with Illinois and Indiana. A curious position came about in Ohio,[1] one of the great industrial states. It did not adopt prohibition, which forbids the manufacture and sale of liquor; but in 1851 it abandoned licensing, which had been in force since 1792, and incorporated a provision in the constitution declaring that no licence should thereafter be granted in the state. The position then was that retail sale without a licence was illegal and that no licence could be granted. This singular state of things was changed in 1886 by the "Dow law," which authorized a tax on the trade and rendered it legal without expressly sanctioning or licensing it. There were therefore no licences and no licensing machinery, but the traffic was taxed and conditions imposed. In effect the Dow law amounted to repeal of prohibition and its replacement by the freest possible form of licensing. In Iowa, which early adopted a prohibitory law, still nominally in force, a law, known as the "mulct law," was passed in 1894 for taxing the trade and practically legalizing it under conditions. The story of the forty years' struggle in this state between the prohibition agitation and the natural appetites of mankind is exceedingly instructive; it is an extraordinary revelation of political intrigue and tortuous proceedings, and an impressive warning against the folly of trying to coerce the personal habits of a large section of the population against their will. It ended in a sort of compromise, in which the coercive principle is preserved in one law and personal liberty vindicated by another contradictory one. The result may be satisfactory, but it might be attained in a less expensive manner. What suffers is the principle of law itself, which is brought into disrepute.

State prohibition, abandoned by the populous New England and central states, has in recent years found a home in more remote regions. In 1907 it was in force in five states—Maine, Kansas, North Dakota, Georgia and Oklahoma; in January, 1909, it came into operation in Alabama, Mississippi, and North Carolina; and in July 1909 in Tennessee.

Local Prohibition.—The limited form of prohibition known as local veto is much more extensively applied. It is an older plan than state prohibition, having been adopted by the legislature of Indiana in 1832. Georgia followed in the next year, and then other states took it up for several years until the rise of state prohibition in the middle of the century caused it to fall into neglect for a time. But the states which adopted and then abandoned general prohibition fell back on the local form, and a great many others have also adopted it. In 1907 it was in force in over 30 states, including all the most populous and important, with one or two exceptions. But the extent to which it is applied varies very widely and is constantly changing, as different places take it up and drop it again. Some alternate in an almost regular manner every two or three years, or even every year; and periodical oscillations of a general character occur in favour of the plan or against it as the result of organized agitation followed by reaction. The wide discrepancies between the practice of different states are shown by some statistics collected in 1907, when the movement was running favourably to the adoption of no licence. In Tennessee the whole state was under prohibition with the exception of 5 municipalities; Arkansas, 56 out of 75 counties; Florida, 35 out of 46 counties; Mississippi, 56 out of 77 counties; North Carolina, 70 out of 97 counties; Vermont, 3 out of 6 cities and 208 out of 241 towns. These appear to be the most prohibitive states, and they are all of a rural character. At the other end of the scale were Pennsylvania with 1 county and a few towns ("town" in America is generally equivalent to "village" in England); Michigan, 1 county and a few towns; California, parts of 8 or 10 counties. New York had 308 out of 933 towns, Ohio, 480 out of 768 towns, Massachusetts, 19 out of 33 cities and 249 out of 321 towns. At the end of 1909 a strong reaction against the prohibition policy set in, notably in Massachusetts.

There is no more uniformity in the mode of procedure than in the extent of application. At least five methods are distinguished. In the most complete and regular form a vote is taken every year in all localities whether there shall be licences or not in the ensuing year and is decided by a bare majority. A second method of applying the general vote is to take it at any time, but not oftener than once in four years, on the demand of one-tenth of the electorate. A third plan is to apply this principle locally and put the question to the vote, when demanded, in any locality. A fourth and entirely different system is to invest the local authority with powers to decide whether there shall be licences or not; and a fifth is to give residents power to prevent licences by means of protest or petition. The first two methods are those most widely in force; but the third plan of taking a local vote by itself is adopted in some important states, including New York, Ohio and Illinois. Opinions differ widely with regard to the success of local veto, but all independent observers agree that it is more successful than state prohibition, and the preference accorded to it by so many states after prolonged experience proves that public opinion broadly endorses that view. Its advantage lies in its adaptability to local circumstances and local opinion. It prevails mainly in rural districts and small towns; in the larger towns it is best tolerated where they are in close proximity to "safety valves" or licensed areas in which liquor can be obtained; the large cities do not adopt it. On the other hand, it has some serious disadvantages. The perpetually renewed struggle between the advocates and opponents of prohibition is a constant cause of social and political strife; and the alternate shutting up and opening of public houses in many places makes continuity of administration impossible, prevents the executive from getting the traffic properly in hand, upsets the habits of the people, demoralizes the trade and stands in the way of steady improvement.

Public Dispensaries.—This entirely different system of controlling the traffic has been in general operation in one state only, South Carolina; but it was also applied to certain areas in the neighbouring states of North Carolina, Georgia and Alabama. The coloured element is very strong in these states, especially in South Carolina, where the coloured far exceeds the white population. The dispensary system was inaugurated there in 1893. It had been preceded by a licensing system with local veto (adopted in 1882), but a strong agitation for state prohibition brought matters to a crisis in 1891. The usual violent political struggle, which is the only constant feature of liquor legislation in the United States, took place, partly on temperance and partly on economic grounds; and a way out was found by adopting an idea from the town of Athens in Georgia, where the liquor trade was run by the municipality through a public dispensary. A law was passed in 1892 embodying this principle but applying it to the whole state. The measure was fiercely contested in the courts and the legislature for years and it underwent numerous amendments, but it survived. Under it the state became the sole purveyor of liquor, buying wholesale from the manufacturers

[1] In 1908 local option was adopted in Ohio.

[illegible] selling retail through [illegible] under public management [illegible] only [illegible] Many changes were [illegible] introduced from [illegible] the principle, but in 1907 the [illegible] replaced by one of county [illegible] and thus the localities have the choice [illegible] or no sale at all. The regulations are very [illegible] are few and only open on week days [illegible] time; they close at sunset. Liquor is only [illegible] and in not less quantities than half a pint of spirits [illegible] of beer, and it must be taken away; bars are [illegible] There is a general consensus of testimony to the effect of the system in improving public [illegible] especially among the coloured population, who are very susceptible to drink. The [illegible] seems to be well carried out in [illegible], but Charleston and [illegible], the only two considerable [illegible] are honeycombed with illicit drink-shops, as the writer has [illegible] by personal experience. Columbia is the capital and [illegible] of cotton [illegible], as are all the larger towns, [illegible] exception of Charleston, which is the port and business [illegible]. The population of the state is predominantly rural, and [illegible] obtains in 18 out of 41 counties.

[illegible] statistical comparison, extracted from the United [illegible] Revenue Returns by Mr W. O. [illegible] Reform) and here presented in [illegible] It shows the population and [illegible] paying the United States tax in two prohi- [illegible] what is considered the best licensing [illegible]

[illegible]	Population.	Wholesale Liquor Dealers.	Retail Liquor Dealers.
[illegible]	644,466	51	1366
[illegible]	1,470,495	129	3125
[illegible]	2,805,346	617	5092
[illegible]	1,340,316	13	534

[illegible] the results of the United States [illegible] examples of three different [illegible] liquor sellers to population is— [illegible] and 1 to 475; under licence and [illegible] dispensary and local prohibition, [illegible] is the enormous amount of [illegible] systems. It is incomparably [illegible] because the whole of the [illegible] Carolina one of the whole- [illegible] dealers were illicit. In Massa- [illegible], but it is very large. If the [illegible] legal number of licences, [illegible] (see above), would be [illegible] 1700 illicit retailers. But [illegible] than half, is under local [illegible] retail dealers must be [illegible] not exceptional, reveal [illegible]; only partial or spas- [illegible] and to a great extent [illegible] illegal trade is carried [illegible] have no difficulty [illegible] state of things, [illegible] would care to imitate.

[illegible] of the federal and [illegible] former is uniform; [illegible] which have adopted [illegible] two purposes; [illegible] and to pro- [illegible] 1881, when a tax [illegible] houses) in large [illegible] practice gradually [illegible] number of states, [illegible] and central [illegible] adopted in [illegible] prohibition, [illegible] licensed on [illegible] average tax [illegible] (£30) in [illegible] in Penn- [illegible] hand, it [illegible] in Rh[illegible]

[illegible] cont[illegible] ing [illegible] syste[illegible] a who[illegible] and s[illegible] not sui[illegible] several [illegible] what la[illegible] over-ride [illegible] in regard [illegible] to speak [illegible] country. [illegible] the traffic [illegible] liquor to In[illegible] whether in [illegible] —to a unifo[illegible] every one [illegible] tion, controls [illegible] has decided [illegible] a railway or o[illegible] point within its [illegible] out liquor or pr[illegible] may make what [illegible] the manufacture [illegible] It may go furthe[illegible] Supreme Court o[illegible] cretionary power [illegible] morals even by th[illegible]

source is distributed in many ways, but is generally divided in varying proportions between the state, the county and the municipality; sometimes a proportion goes to the relief of the poor, to road-making or some other public purpose. The amount levied in the great cities is very large. It will be seen from the foregoing that the taxation of licences is much heavier in the United States than in the United Kingdom. The total yield was ascertained by a special inquiry in 1896 and found to be rather less than 12 millions sterling; in the same year the yield from the same source in the United Kingdom was just under 2 millions. Allowing for difference of population the American rate of taxation was 3½ times as great as the British. It has been inferred that the liquor trade is much more highly taxed in the United States and that it would bear largely increased taxation in the United Kingdom; that argument was brought forward in support of Mr Lloyd George's budget of 1909. But it only takes account of the tax on licences and leaves out of account the tax on liquor which is the great source of revenue in the United Kingdom, as has been shown above. The scales are much lower in the United States, especially on spirits, which are only taxed at the average rate of 5s. 8d. a gallon against 11s. (raised to 14s. 9d. in 1909) in the United Kingdom. Mr Frederic Thompson has calculated out the effect of the two sets of rates and shown that if British rates were applied to the United States the average yield in the three years ending 1908 would be raised from 44 millions to 76 millions; and conversely if American rates were applied to the United Kingdom the average yield would be lowered from 36 millions to 23 millions. Taking licences and liquor taxation together he finds that the application of the British standards for both would still raise the total yield in the United States by 39%; and that even the exceptionally high rates prevailing in Massachusetts would, if applied to the United Kingdom, produce some 4 millions less revenue than the existing taxation. Other calculations based on the consumption and taxation per head lead to the same conclusion that the trade is actually taxed at a considerably higher rate in the United Kingdom. In the three years ending 1908 the average amount paid per head in taxation was 13s. 8½d. in the United States and 17s. 6½d. in the United Kingdom. It may be added that the method of taxing licences heavily has certain disadvantages; it stimulates that illicit trade which is the most outstanding feature of the traffic in the United States, and combined with the extreme insecurity of tenure involved in local option it gives licence-holders additional inducements to make as much money as possible by any means available, while they have the opportunity, for no compensation is ever paid for sudden dispossession. The notion that the trade will stand an indefinite amount of taxation is a dangerous and oft-proved fallacy.

European Countries.

With the exception of Sweden, Norway and Russia, which have special systems of their own, the continental countries of Europe have as yet paid comparatively little legislative attention to the subject of the liquor traffic, which is recognized by the law but for the most part freely permitted with a minimum of interference. Differences exist, but, generally speaking, establishments may be opened under a very simple procedure, which amounts to an elementary form of licensing, and the permission is only withdrawn for some definite and serious offence. Regulations and conditions are for the most part left to the discretion of the local authority and the police and are not burdensome. The reason for such freedom as compared with the elaborate and stringent codes of the United Kingdom and the United States is not less concern for public welfare but the simple fact that the traffic gives less trouble and causes less harm through the abuse of drink; the habits of the people are different in regard to the character of the drinks consumed, the mode of consumption and the type of establishment. Cafés, restaurants and beer-gardens are much more common, and mere pot-houses less so than in the English-speaking countries. Where trouble arises and engages the attention of the authorities and the legislature, it is almost invariably found to be associated with the consumption of spirits. In several of the wine-producing countries, which are generally marked by the temperate habits of the people, the widespread havoc among the vines caused some years ago by the phylloxera led to an increased consumption of spirits which had a bad effect and aroused considerable anxiety. This was notably the case in France, where an anti-alcohol congress, held in 1903, marked the rise of public and scientific [illegible] on the subject. Temperance societies have become [illegible] in some countries there is a movement towards [illegible]ations or at least a demand for it; but in others [illegible]w is a relaxation of earlier ones.

France.—The present law governing the licensing of establishments where liquor is sold for consumption on the premises was passed in 1880; it abrogated the previous decree of 1851, by which full discretion was vested in the local authorities, and freed the traffic from arbitrary restrictions. It provides that any person desiring to open a café, cabaret or other place for retailing liquor must give notice to the authorities, with details concerning himself, the establishment and the proprietor, at least 15 days beforehand; the authority in Paris is the préfecture of police and elsewhere the mairie. Transfers of proprietorship or management must be notified within 15 days, and intended transference of location 8 days beforehand. The penalty for infraction is a fine of 16 francs to 100 francs. Legal minors and persons convicted of certain crimes and offences—theft, receiving stolen goods, various forms of swindling, offences against morality, the sale of adulterated articles—are prohibited; in the case of crimes, for ever; in the case of offences, for five years. Otherwise permission cannot be refused, subject to conditions which the local authority has power to lay down regulating the distance of such establishments from churches, cemeteries, hospitals, schools and colleges. But persons engaged in the trade, who are convicted of the offences mentioned above and of infraction of the law for the suppression of public drunkenness, are disabled, as above. The law practically amounts to free trade and the number of houses has increased under it; in 1900 there was one to every 81 persons. This proportion is only exceeded by Belgium. Under the Local Government Act of 1884 municipal authorities are empowered, for the maintenance of public order, to fix hours of closing, regulate dancing, forbid the employment of girls and the harbouring of prostitutes and make other regulations. The hours of closing differ considerably but usually they are 11 P.M., midnight or 1 A.M. The trade is lightly taxed; retailers pay from 15 to 50 francs a year; wholesale dealers, 125 francs; breweries the same in most departments, distilleries 25 francs. The excise revenue from liquor amounted to £20,000,000 in 1900.

Germany.—The German law and practice are broadly similar to the French, but the several states vary somewhat in detail. Under the imperial law of 1879 inns or hotels and retail trade in spirits for on or off consumption may not be carried on without a permit or licence from the local authority which, however, can only be refused on the ground of character or of unsuitability of premises. This is the general law of the empire; but the state governments are empowered to make the granting of a licence for retailing spirits dependent on proof that it is locally required, and also to impose the same condition on inn-keeping and the retailing of other drinks in places with less than 15,000 inhabitants and in larger ones which obtain a local statute to that effect. Before a licence is granted the opinion of the police and other executive officers is to be taken. The licensing authority is the mayor in towns and the chairman of the district council in rural areas. The provisions with regard to the dependence of a licence on local requirements have been adopted by Prussia and other states, but apparently little or no use is made of them. Permits are very freely granted, and the number of licensed houses, though not so great as in France, is very high in proportion to population. Three classes of establishment are recognized—(1) *Gast-wirthschaft*, (2) *Schank-wirthschaft*, (3) *Klein-handel*. *Gast-wirthschaft* is inn-keeping, or the lodging of strangers in an open house for profit, and includes "pensions" of a public character; the imperial law provides that a licence may be limited to this function and need not include the retailing of liquor. *Schank-wirthschaft* is the retailing for profit of all sorts of drinks, including coffee and mineral waters; it corresponds to café in France and refreshment house in England; but the mere serving of food does not come under the law with which we are here concerned. *Klein-handel* is retail sale either for on or off consumption, and the liquor for which a licence is required in this connexion is described as *branntwein* or *spiritus*, and is defined as distilled alcoholic liquor, whether by itself or in combination. A licence for *Schank-wirthschaft* includes *Klein-handel*, but not vice-versa; none is required for the retail sale of wine which is the seller's own produce. Licences may be withdrawn for offences against the law. Licensed houses are under the supervision of the police, who fix the hours of closing; it is usually 10 P.M., but is commonly extended to 11 P.M. or midnight in the larger towns and still later in the case of particular establishments. Some cafés in Berlin do not close till 3 A.M. and some never close at all. Persons remaining on the premises in forbidden hours after being ordered to leave by the landlord are liable to punishment. Serving drunkards and persons of school age is forbidden. Drunkards, in addition to fines or imprisonment for disorderly conduct, are liable to be deprived of control of their affairs and placed under guardianship. For music and dancing special permits are required. With regard to taxation, in Prussia all business establishments beyond a certain value pay an annual tax and licensed houses are on the same footing as the rest. Businesses producing less than £75 a year or of less than £150 capital value are free; the rest are arranged in four classes on a rising scale. In the three lower classes the tax ranges from a minimum of 4s. to a maximum of £24; in the highest class, which represents businesses producing £2500 and upwards (or a capital value of £50,000 and upwards) the tax is 1% of the profits. There is also a stamp duty on the licence ranging from 1s. 6d. to £5. The latter goes to the local revenue, the business tax to the government. Beer and spirits are also subject to an excise tax, from which the imperial revenue derived £7,700,000 in 1901; but the total taxation of the liquor trade could only be calculated from the returns of all the federated states.

The laws of France and Germany are fairly representative of the European states, with some minor variations. In *Holland* the number of licensed spirit retailers is limited in proportion to population (1 to 500), and the taxation, which is both national and local, ranges from 10 to 25% of the annual value.

In *Austria-Hungary* and *Rumania* the licence duty is graduated according to the population of the place, as used to be the case in Prussia. In 1877 a severe police law was applied to Galicia in order to check the excesses of spirit-drinking. The Poles, it may be observed, are spirit-drinkers, and the exceptional treatment of this part of the Austrian empire is one more illustration of the trouble arising from that habit, which forces special attempts to restrain it. The law, just mentioned, in Holland is another instance; and the particular cases of Russia and Scandinavia, described below, enforce the same lesson. Where the drink of the people is confined to wine and beer there is comparatively little trouble. In *Switzerland* the manufacture and wholesale sale of spirits has been a federal monopoly since 1887, but the retailing is a licensed trade, as elsewhere, and is less restricted than formerly. Before federation in 1874 the cantons used to direct local authorities to restrict the number of licences in proportion to population; but under the new constitution the general principle of free trade was laid down, and the Federal Council intimated to the cantonal authorities that it was no longer lawful to refuse a licence on the ground that it was not needed.

Russia.—In 1895 Russia entered upon an experiment in regard to the spirit traffic and began to convert the previously existing licence system into a state monopoly. The experiment was held to be successful and was gradually extended to the whole country. Under this system, which to some extent resembles that of South Carolina but is much less rigid, the distilleries remain in private hands but their output is under government control. The retail sale is confined to government shops, which sell only in sealed bottles for consumption off the premises, and to commercial establishments which sell on commission for the government. Spirit bars are abolished and only in a few high class restaurants are spirits sold by the glass; in ordinary eating-houses and at railway refreshment rooms they are sold in sealed government bottles but may be consumed on the premises. The primary object was to check the excesses of spirit-drinking which were very great in Russia among the mass of the people. The effect has been a very large reduction in the number of liquor shops, which has extended also to the licensed beer-houses though they are not directly affected as such. Presumably when they could no longer sell spirits it did not pay them to take out a licence for beer.

Sweden and Norway.—In these countries the celebrated "Gothenburg" or company system is in force together with licensing and local veto. Like the Russian state monopoly the company system applies only to spirits, and for the same reason; spirits are or were the common drink of the people and excessive facilities in the early part of the 19th century produced the usual result. The story is very similar to that of England in the 18th century, given above. From 1774 to 1788 distilling in Sweden was a crown monopoly, but popular opposition and illicit trade compelled the abandonment of this plan in favour of general permission granted to farmers, innkeepers and landowners. At the beginning of the 19th century the right to distil belonged to every owner and cultivator of land on payment of a trifling licence duty, and it was further extended to occupiers. In 1829 the number of stills paying licence duty was 173,124 or 1 to every 16 persons; the practice was in fact universal and the whole population was debauched with spirits. The physical and moral results were the same as those recorded in England a hundred years before. The supply was somewhat restricted by royal ordinance in 1835, but the traffic was not effectively dealt with until 1855 when a law was passed which practically abolished domestic distilling by fixing a minimum daily output of 200 gallons, with a tax of about 10d. a gallon. This turned the business into a manufacture and speedily reduced the number of stills. At the same time the retail sale was subjected to drastic regulations. A licensing system was introduced which gave the local authority power to fix the number of licences and put them up to auction or to hand over the retail traffic altogether to a company formed for the purpose of carrying it on. The latter idea, which is the Gothenburg system, was taken from the example of Falun and Jönköping which had a few years ago voluntarily adopted the plan. The law of 1855 further gave rural districts the power of local veto. Four-fifths of the population live in rural districts, and the great majority of them immediately took advantage of the provision. The company system, on the other hand, was not applied by the towns until 1865, when Gothenburg adopted it.

In Norway the course of events was very similar. There, too, distilling and spirit-drinking were practically universal in the early part of the century under the laws of 1816, but were checked by legislation a few years sooner than in Sweden. In 1845 a special licensing system was introduced, giving the local authority power to fix the number of licences, and in 1848 the small and domestic

and selling retail through dispensaries under r
and only for consumption off the premises
introduced from time to time without abando
but in 1907 the system of state control was t
county administration. Local veto is also in
localities have the choice of a dispensary or no
regulations are very strict. The dispensaries
open on week-days and during the day-time
sunset. Liquor is only sold in bottles and in
than half a pint of spirits and a pint of beer,
taken away; bars are abolished. There is a g
of testimony to the effect of the system in i
order especially among the coloured population
susceptible to drink. The law seems to be w
general, but Charleston and Columbia, the only
towns, are honeycombed with illicit drink-sho
has proved by personal experience. Columbia i
the seat of cotton manufactures, as are all th
with the exception of Charleston, which is the p
centre. The population of the state is predomi
local prohibition obtains in 18 out of 41 counti

The following statistical comparison, extracted
States Census of 1900 and the Inland Revenue R
Tatum (*New Encyclopedia of Social Reform*) and t
tabular form, is highly instructive. It shows the
number of liquor dealers paying the United State
bition states, one state under what is considered
system, and South Carolina.

State.	Population.	Wh Lq D
Maine (Prohibition) . .	694,466	51
Kansas (Prohibition) . .	1,470,495	129
Massachusetts (Licence) .	2,805,346	617
S. Carolina (Dispensary) .	1,340,316	13

This table may be said to epitomize the results of th
restrictive liquor laws. It presents examples of
systems; the proportion of retail liquor sellers to
under complete prohibition, 1 to 508 and 1 to 475,
local prohibition, 1 to 530; under dispensary and
1 to 2509. But the remarkable thing is the enor
illicit traffic existing under all three systems. It i
greatest under complete prohibition because the
traffic in these states is illicit. In South Carolina o
sale dealers and 388 of the 534 retailers were ill
chusetts the number cannot be stated, but it is ver
whole state were under licence the total legal num
which is limited in proportion to population (see
3400; and in that case there would be some 1700 illic
a large part of the state, probably more than hal
prohibition, so that the majority of the 5000 retail
illicit. These facts, which are typical and not ex
the failure of the laws to control the traffic; only
modic attempts are made to enforce them and to
they are ignored by common consent. The illegal t
on so openly that the United States revenue officers
in collecting the federal tax. It is not a satisfactory
or one which countries where law is respected would
The example is a good lesson in what to avoid.

Taxation.—Mention has been made above of th
state taxation imposed on the liquor trade. The fe
the latter varies greatly, even in those states which
the "high licence." This system is intended to fulfil
to act as an automatic check on the number of licen
duce revenue. It was introduced in Nebraska in 18
of 1000 dollars (£200) was placed on saloons (public
towns, and half that amount in smaller ones. The pr
spread and has now been adopted by a large nu
noticeably the populous and industrial north-east
states. In Massachusetts, where the high licence w
1874 when the state returned to licensing after a trial
the fees are exceptionally high, the minimum for a f
and off house being 1300 dollars (£260); in Boston
is £310. In New York state it ranges from 150
sparsely populated districts to 1200 dollars (£240
sylvania it is much the same. In New Jersey, on t
ranges from £20 to £60; in Connecticut from
Island from £40 to £80. In Missouri, which
of its own and a sort of sliding scale, great
some cases the tax exceeds £
The mean for the large ci

u$_9$Al$_4$(OH)$_{15}$(AsO$_4$)$_5$.20H$_2$O. It crystallizes in the monoclinic stem, forming flattened octahedra almost lenticular in shape ce the German name *Linsenkupfer*). Characteristic is the ht sky-blue colour, though sometimes, possibly owing to rences in chemical composition, it is verdigris-green. The ur of the streak or powder is rather paler; hence the name ite, from the Gr. λειρός, pale, and κονία, powder. The s is 2½, and the specific gravity 2·95. The mineral und at the beginning of the 19th century in the copper near Gwennap in Cornwall, where it was associated with copper arsenates in the upper, oxidized portions of the (L. J. S.)

BON (*Lisboa*), the capital of the kingdom of Portugal the department of Lisbon; on the right bank of the agus, near its entrance into the Atlantic Ocean, in 24′ N. and 9° 11′ 10″ W. Pop. (1900) 356,009. Lisbon, ternmost of European capitals, is built in a succession es up the sides of a range of low hills, backed by the mountains of Cintra. It fronts the Tagus, and the view river of its white houses, and its numerous parks and is comparable in beauty with the approach to Naples tantinople by sea. The lower reaches of the estuary channel (Entrada do Tejo) about 2 m. wide and 8 m. nich is partially closed at its mouth by a bar of silt. the reclamation of the foreshore on the right, and equent narrowing of the waterway, the current flows itly down this channel, which is the sole outlet for mense volume of water accumulated in the Rada de a tidal lake formed by the broadening of the estuary per part to fill a basin 11 m. long with an average breadth y 7 m. The southern or left shore of the channel rises from the water's edge in a line of almost unbroken not lofty cliffs; the margin of the lake is flat, marshy gular. Lisbon extends for more than 5 m. along the f both channel and lake, and for more than 3 m. inland. urbs, which generally terminate in a belt of vineyards, r gardens, interspersed with villas and farms, stretch cases beyond the Estrada Militar, or Estrada da Nova allação, an inner line of defence 25 m. long supplementary rts and other military works at the mouth of the Tagus, heights of Cintra and Alverca, and at Caxias, Sacavem, to and Ameixoeira. The climate of Lisbon is mild and though somewhat oppressive in summer. Extreme so rare that in the twenty years 1856–1876 snow fell ice; and in the 18th and early 19th centuries Lisbon tly esteemed as a winter health-resort. The mean emperature is 60·1° F., the mean for winter 50·9°, the rainfall 29·45 in. As in 1906, when no rain fell between d September, long periods of drought are not uncommon, the proximity of the Atlantic and the frequency of keep the atmosphere humid; the mean atmospheric is nearly 71 (100 = saturation). There is a good water conveyed to the city by two vast aqueducts. The older is the Aqueducto das Aguas Livres, which was built st half of the 18th century and starts from a point near 5 m. W.N.W. Its conduits, which are partly under- are conveyed across the Alcantara valley through a nt viaduct of thirty-five arches, exceeding 200 ft. in At the Lisbon end of the aqueduct is the Mae d'Agua ther of Water"), containing a huge stone hall in the which is the reservoir. The Alviella aqueduct, opened brings water from Alviella near Pernes, 70 m. N.N.E. s fountains are among the means of distribution. s discharged into the Tagus, and the sanitation of the d, except in the older quarters.

s of the City.—The four municipal districts (*bairros*) h Lisbon is divided are the *Alfama*, or old town, in the *Cidade Baixa*, or lower town, which extends om the naval arsenal and custom house; the *Bairro* mprising all the high ground west of the Cidade Baixa; *Alcantara*, or westernmost district, named after the er Alcantara, which flows down into the Tagus. Other names commonly used, though unofficial, are "Lisboa Oriental" as an alternative for Alfama; "Lisboa Occidental" for the slopes which lead from the Cidade Baixa to the Bairro Alto; "Buenos Ayres" (originally so named from the number of its South American residents) for the Bairro Alto S.W. of the Estrella Gardens and E. of the Necessidades Park; "Campo de Ourique" and "Rato" for the suburbs respectively N.W. and N.E. of Buenos Ayres.

The Alfama.—The Alfama, which represents Roman and Moorish Lisbon, is less rich in archaeological interest than its great antiquity might suggest, although parts of a Roman temple, baths, &c., have been disinterred. But as the earthquake of 1755 did comparatively little damage to this quarter, many of its narrow, steep and winding alleys retain the medieval aspect which all other parts of the city have lost; and almost rival the slums of Oporto in picturesque squalor. The most conspicuous feature of the Alfama is the rocky hill surmounted by the Castello de São Jorge, a Moorish citadel which has been converted into a fort and barracks. The Sé Patriarchal, a cathedral founded in 1150 by Alphonso I., is said by tradition to have been a Moorish mosque. It was wrecked by an earthquake in 1344 and rebuilt in 1380, but the earthquake of 1755 shattered the dome, the roof and belfry were subsequently burned, and after the work of restoration was completed the choir and façade were the only parts of the 14th-century Gothic church unspoiled. In one of the side chapels is the tomb of St Vincent (d. 304), patron saint of Lisbon; a pair of ravens kept within the cathedral precincts are popularly believed to be the same birds which, according to the legend, miraculously guided the saint's vessel to the city. The armorial bearings of Lisbon, representing a ship and two ravens, commemorate the legend. Other noteworthy buildings in the Alfama are the 12th-century church of São Vicente de Fóra, originally, as its name implies, "outside" the city; the 13th-century chapel of Nossa Senhora do Monte; the 16th-century church of Nossa Senhora da Graça, which contains a reputed wonder-working statue of Christ and the tomb of Alphonso d'Albuquerque (1453–1515); and a secularized Augustinian monastery, used as the archbishop's palace.

Modern Lisbon.—West of the Alfama the city dates chiefly from the period after the great earthquake. Its lofty houses, arranged in long straight streets, its gardens and open spaces, a few of its public buildings, and almost all its numerous statues and fountains, will bear comparison with those of any European capital. The centre of social and commercial activity is the district which comprises the Praça do Commercio, Rua Augusta, Rocio, and Avenida da Liberdade, streets and squares occupying the valley of a vanished tributary of the Tagus. The Praça do Commercio is a spacious square, one side of which faces the river, while the other three sides are occupied by the arcaded buildings of the custom house, post office and other government property. In the midst is a bronze equestrian statue of Joseph I., by J. M. de Castro, which was erected in 1775 and gives point to the name of "Black Horse Square" commonly applied to the Praça by the British. A triumphal arch on the north side leads to Rua Augusta, originally intended to be the cloth-merchants' street; for the plan upon which Lisbon was rebuilt after 1755 involved the restriction of each industry to a specified area. This plan succeeded in the neighbouring Rua Aurea and Rua da Prata, still, as their names indicate, famous for goldsmiths' and silversmiths' shops. Rua Augusta terminates on the north in the Rocio or Praça de Dom Pedro Quarto, a square paved with mosaic of a curious undulatory pattern and containing two bronze fountains, a lofty pillar surmounted by a statue of Pedro IV., and the royal national theatre (Theatro de Dona Maria Segunda), erected on the site which the Inquisition buildings occupied from 1520 to 1836. The narrow Rua do Principe, leading past the central railway station, a handsome Mauresque building, connects the Rocio with the Avenida da Liberdade, one of the finest avenues in Europe. The central part of the Avenida, a favourite open-air resort of Lisbon society, is used for riding and driving; on each side of it are paved double avenues of trees, with flower-beds, statues, ponds, fountains, &c., and

. . . are two roadways for
. . . Avenida has the appearance
. . . avenues of trees instead of
. . . its name to an obelisk
. . . northern end, to commemorate
. . . rule (December, 1640).
. . . are the Avenida Park,
. . . memory of a visit paid to
. . . Campo Grande, with its
. . . with the bull-ring.
. . . the Passeio da Estrella,
. . . city and river, the Largo
. . . and other tropical
. . . especially the park of one
. . . Gardens of the poly-
. . . and collections of
. . . surpassed in Europe.
. . . east and west of Lisbon,
. . . cemetery, known also as
. . . This was laid
. . . and Dutch residents
. . . Fielding (1707–1754),
. . . (1702–1751), the Non-

. . . since 1716 has borne
. . . he presides over the
. . . arsenal. The churches
. . . Italian style of the
. . . heavy ornament.
. . . its white marble
. . . above the city.
. . . two beautiful
. . . is inlaid with
. . . Rome of coloured
. . . being shipped to
. . . exceptionally fine.
. . . shattered by the
. . . and outer walls
. . . converted into an
. . . Nossa Senhora da
. . .

. . . of Parliament
. . . for its present
. . . archives, better
. . . in 1375 the
. . . The royal
. . . Ayres, is a
. . . of a chapel
. . . "Our Lady

. . . west of Lisbon,
. . . "), beside
. . . de Belem,
. . . royal palace
. . . the foreshore,
. . . the protection
. . . Portugal except
. . . the river.
. . . convent and
. . . of the sea-
. . . limestone
. . . archi-
. . . surrounded
. . . is covered
. . . restored,
. . . unspoiled.
. . . Catherine
. . . The
. . . interred
. . . its build-
. . . Maria I.
. . . of
. . . palace,
. . . its
. . . ").
. . . coach-
. . . cars

upon which figures of saints are borne in procession, sedan chairs, old cabriolets and other curious vehicles.

The Environs of Lisbon.—The administrative district of Lisboa has an area of 3065 sq. m., with a population of 709,509 in 1900. It comprises the lower parts of the Tagus and Sado; the sea-coast from 5 m. S. of Cape Carvoeiro to within 3 m. of the bluff called the Escarpa do Rojo; and a strip of territory extending inland for a mean distance of 30 m. This region corresponds with the southern part of Estremadura (*q.v.*). Its more important towns, Setubal, Cintra, Torres Vedras and Mafra, are described in separate articles. Sines, a small seaport on Cape Sines, was the birthplace of Vasco da Gama. On the left bank of the Tagus, opposite Lisboa, are the small towns of Almada, Barreiro, Aldeia Gallega and Seixal, and the hamlet of Trafaria, inhabited by fishermen. The beautiful strip of coast west of Oeiras and south of Cape Roca is often called the "Portuguese Riviera." Its fine climate, mineral springs and sea-bathing attract visitors at all seasons to the picturesque fortified bay of Cascaes, or to Estoril, Mont' Estoril and São João do Estoril, modern towns consisting chiefly of villas, hotels and gardens. The Boca do Inferno ("Mouth of Hell") is a cavity in the rocks at Cascaes resembling the Bufador at Peñiscola (*q.v.*). The villages of Carcavellos, Bucellas, Lumiar and Collares produce excellent wines; at Carcavellos is the receiving station for cables, with a large British staff, and a club and grounds where social and athletic meetings are held by the British colony. Alhandra, on the right bank of the Tagus, above Lisbon, was the birthplace of Albuquerque; fighting bulls for the Lisbon arena are bred in the adjacent pastures.

Railways, Shipping and Commerce.—Lisbon has five railway stations—the central (Lisboa-Rocio), for the lines to Cintra, northern and central Portugal, and Madrid via Valencia de Alcántara; the Santa Apolonia or Caes dos Soldados, at the eastern extremity of the quays, for the same lines (excluding Cintra) and for southern Portugal and Andalusia; the Caes do Sodré and Santos, farther west along the quays, for Cascaes; and the Barreiro, on the left bank of the Tagus, for southern Portugal. In 1902 the railways north and south of the Tagus were connected near Lisbon by a bridge. In the previous year an extensive system of electric tramways replaced the old-fashioned cable cars and mule trams. Electric and hydraulic lifts are used where the streets are too steep for trams. Lisbon is lighted by both electricity and gas; it has an admirable telephone service, and is connected by the Carcavellos cable-station with Cornwall (England), Vigo in Galicia, Gibraltar, the Azores and Madeira.

Ships of the largest size can enter the Tagus, and the Barreiro inlet is navigable at low water by vessels drawing 16 ft. There are extensive quays along the right bank, with hydraulic cranes, two graving docks, a slipway, warehouses and lines of railway. The government and private docks are on the left bank. Loading and discharging are principally effected by means of lighters. The exports are wines, oil, fruit, tinned fish, salt, colonial produce, cork, pitwood, leather and wool. The imports include cotton and woollen goods, linen, ale and porter, butter, tea, hardware, tin plates, coal, iron, machinery, chemical manure, &c., from Great Britain; grain and petroleum from the United States; dried codfish from Norway and Newfoundland; silks, perfumery and fancy goods from France; hemp, flax, grain, petroleum and cloth from Russia; linen, machinery, hardware, sugar, &c., from Germany and Holland; iron, steel, timber, pitch and salt fish from the Baltic; cocoa, coffee, wax and rubber from the Portuguese colonies. Towards the close of the 19th century the tourist traffic from Great Britain and Germany attained considerable importance, and Lisbon has long been one of the principal ports of debarcation for passengers from Brazil and of embarcation for emigrants to South America. Shipbuilding, including the construction of vessels for the national navy, is a growing industry. The fisheries have always been important, and in no European fishmarket is the produce more varied. Sardines and tunny are cured and tinned for export. In addition to a fleet of about 600 sailing boats, the Tagus is the headquarters of a small fleet of steam trawlers. The industries of Lisbon include dyeing, distillation of spirits and manufactures of woollen, cotton, silk and linen fabrics, of pottery, soap, paper, chemicals, cement, corks, tobacco, preserved foods and biscuits.

Education and Charity.—Although the seat of the only university in Portugal was fixed at Coimbra in 1527, Lisbon is the educational centre of the Portuguese world, including Brazil.

Its chief learned societies are the Society of Medical Sciences, the Geographical Society, the Royal Academy of Sciences, the Academy of Fine Arts, the Royal Conservatory of Music and the Propaganda de Portugal. The museum of the Academy of Fine Arts contains the largest collection of pictures and statues by native and foreign artists in Portugal The Geographical Society has gained an international reputation; it possesses a valuable library and museum. The National Library, founded in 1796, contains over 400,000 printed books, and upwards of 9000 MSS. There are also colonial, naval, artillery, natural history and commercial museums, meteorological and astronomical observatories, zoological gardens and an aquarium. Purely educational institutions include the medical, polytechnic, military and naval schools, commercial, agricultural and industrial institutes, a school of art, a central lyceum, a school for teachers, &c. The English college for British Roman Catholics dates from 1628. The Irish Dominicans have a seminary, and Portuguese ecclesiastical schools are numerous. There are hospitals for women, and for contagious diseases, almshouses, orphanages, a foundling hospital and a very large quarantine station on the south bank of the Tagus, founded in 1857 after an outbreak of yellow fever had devastated the city. Foremost among the theatres, circuses and other places of amusement is the royal opera-house of São Carlos, built in 1792–1793 on the model of the Scala at Milan.

Population.—The population of Lisbon, 187,404[1] in 1878, rose to 301,206 in 1890 and 356,009 in 1900. It includes a large foreign colony, composed chiefly of Spaniards, British, Germans, French, Brazilians and immigrants from the Portuguese colonies, among whom are many half-castes. The majority of the Spaniards are domestic servants and labourers from Galicia, whose industry and easily gained knowledge of the kindred Portuguese language enables them to earn a better livelihood here than in their own homes. The British, German and French communities control a large share of the foreign trade. The Brazilians and colonial immigrants are often merchants and landowners who come to the mother-country to spend their fortunes in a congenial social environment.

The street life of the city is full of interest. The bare-footed, ungainly fishwives, dressed in black and bearing flat trays of fish on their heads; the Galician water-carriers, with their casks; the bakers, bending beneath a hundredweight of bread slung in a huge basket from their shoulders; the countrymen, with their sombreros, sashes and hardwood quarter-staves, give colour and animation to their surroundings; while the bag-pipes played by peasants from the north, the whistles of the knife-grinders, and the distinctive calls of the vendors of fruit, lottery tickets, or oil and vinegar, contribute a babel of sound. For church festivals and holidays the country-folk come to town, the women riding on pillions behind the men, adorned in shawls, aprons and handkerchiefs of scarlet or other vivid hues, and wearing the strings of coins and ornaments of exquisite gold and silver filigree which represent their savings or dowries. The costumes and manners of all classes may be seen at their best in the great bull-ring of Campo Pequeno, a Mauresque building which holds many thousands of spectators. A Lisbon bull-fight is a really brilliant exhibition of athletic skill and horsemanship, in which amateurs often take part, and neither horses nor bulls are killed. There is a Tauromachic Club solely for amateurs.

History.—The name Lisbon is a modification of the ancient name *Olisipo*, also written *Ulyssippo* under the influence of a mythical story of a city founded by Odysseus (Ulysses) in Iberia, which, however, according to Strabo, was placed by ancient tradition rather in the mountains of Turdetania (the extreme south of Spain). Under the Romans Olisipo became a *municipium* with the epithet of *Felicitas Julia*, but was inferior in importance to the less ancient *Emerita Augusta* (Mérida). From 407 to 585 it was occupied by Alaric, and thenceforward by the Visigoths until 711, when it was taken by the Moors. Under the Moors the town bore in Arabic the name of *Al Oshbūna* or *Lashbūna*. It was the first point of Moslem Spain attacked by the Normans in 844. When Alphonso I. of Portugal took advantage of the decline and fall of the Almoravid dynasty to incorporate the provinces of Estremadura and Alemtejo in his new kingdom, Lisbon was the last city of Portugal to fall into his hands, and yielded only after a siege of several months (21st October 1147), in which he was aided by English and Flemish crusaders on their way to Syria. In 1184 the city was again attacked by the Moslems under the powerful caliph Abu Yakub, but the enterprise failed. In the reign of Ferdinand I., the greater part of the town was burned by the Castilian army under Henry II. (1373), and in 1384 the Castilians again besieged Lisbon, but without success. Lisbon became the seat of an archbishop in 1390, the seat of government in 1422. During the 16th century it gained much in wealth and splendour from the establishment of a Portuguese empire in India and Africa. From 1580 to 1640 Lisbon was a provincial town under Spanish rule, and it was from this port that the Spanish Armada sailed in 1588. In 1640 the town was captured by the duke of Braganza, and the independence of the kingdom restored.

[1] This figure represents the population of a smaller area than that of modern Lisbon, for the civic boundaries were extended by a decree dated the 23rd of December 1886.

For many centuries the city had suffered from earthquakes, and on the 1st of November 1755 the greater part of it was reduced almost in an instant to a heap of ruins. A tidal wave at the same time broke over the quays and wrecked the shipping in the Tagus; fire broke out to complete the work of destruction; between 30,000 and 40,000 persons lost their lives; and the value of the property destroyed was about £20,000,000. The shock was felt from Scotland to Asia Minor. Careful investigation by Daniel Sharpe, an English geologist, has delimited the area in and near Lisbon to which its full force was confined. Lisbon is built in a geological basin of Tertiary formation, the upper portion of which is loose sand and gravel destitute of organic remains, while below these are the so-called Almada beds of yellow sand, calcareous sandstone and blue clay rich in organic remains. The Tertiary deposits, which altogether cover an area of more than 2000 sq. m., are separated near Lisbon from rocks of the Secondary epoch by a great sheet of basalt. The uppermost of these Secondary rocks is the hippurite limestone. It was found that no building on the blue clay escaped destruction, none on any of the Tertiary deposits escaped serious injury, and all on the hippurite limestone and basalt were undamaged. The line at which the earthquake ceased to be destructive thus corresponded exactly with the boundary of the Tertiary deposits.

At the beginning of the 19th century the French invasion, followed by the removal of the court to Rio de Janeiro, the Peninsular War, the loss of Brazil and a period of revolution and dynastic trouble, resulted in the utter decadence of Lisbon, from which the city only recovered after 1850 (see PORTUGAL: *History*).

BIBLIOGRAPHY.—Every book which deals with the topography, trade or history of Portugal as a whole necessarily devotes a portion of its space to the capital; see PORTUGAL: *Bibliography*. The following treat more exclusively of Lisbon: A. Dayot, *Lisbonne* (No. ix. of the "*Capitales du monde*" series) (Paris, 1892); Freire de Oliveira, *Elementos para a historia do municipio de Lisboa* (9 vols., Lisbon, 1885-1898); J. de Castilho, *Lisboa antiga* (7 vols., Lisbon, 1890), and (by the same author) *A Ribeira de Lisboa* (Lisbon, 1893).

LISBURN, a market town, and cathedral city of Co. Antrim, Ireland, situated in a beautiful and fertile district on the Lagan, and on the Great Northern railway, 8 m. S.S.W. of Belfast. Pop. (1901) 11,461. Christ Church (1622) which possesses a fine octagonal spire, is the cathedral church of the united Protestant dioceses of Down, Connor and Dromore, and contains a monument to Jeremy Taylor, who was bishop of the see. The public park was presented to the town by Sir Richard Wallace (d. 1890), and after his death the castle gardens were also given to the town. The staple manufacture is linen, especially damasks and muslins, originally introduced by Huguenots. There are also bleaching and dyeing works, and a considerable agricultural trade. The town is governed by an urban district council. The ruins of Castle Robin, 2 m. N. of the town, stand on a summit of the White Mountains, and the building dates from the time of Queen Elizabeth. At Drumbo, 3½ m. E. of Lisburn, is one of the finest examples of early fortification in Ireland, known as the Giant's Ring, with a cromlech in the centre. Here are also a round tower and the remains of a church ascribed to St Patrick.

between these and the broad
trams and heavy tra
of three paral
house

tl
Li
finc
Oth
comn
do Pr
trees,
of the r
technic
tropical
There are
a German
Os Cypresies
out in 1717
and contains
the novelist, a
conformist divi

Lisbon is the
ex officio the hon
House of Peers and
of modern Lisbon
18th century; the
Perhaps the finest is
dome and twin tow
The late Renaissance
chapels dating from th
painted tiles, while the
marbles, and consecrat
Lisbon. Its mosaics and
The 14th-century Gothic
great earthquake. Only
remain standing, and the
archaeological museum.
Conceição has a magnific

The Palacio das Cortes,
sit, is a 16th-century Ben
purpose since 1834. It co
known as the Torre do To
archives were first stored in
palace, or Paço das Necessi
vast 18th-century mansion
dedicated to Nossa Senhora
who helps at need").

The Suburbs of Ajuda and Be
beyond the Alcantara valley,
the Tagus, and Ajuda, on the
built in 1700 for the counts of
under John V. (1706–1750). T
is a small tower of beautiful
of shipping. The finest eccl
the monasteries of Alcobaça
It is the Convento dos Jero
church, founded in 1499 to co
route to India by Vasco da G
by João de Castilho (d. 1581), p
tects. Its cloisters form a squ
by a two-storeyed arcade, every
with exquisite sculptures. Part
but the cloisters and the beautif
The interior contains many roya
of Braganza (d. 1705), the wi
supposed remains of Camoens a
here in 1880. In 1834, when the
ings were assigned to the Casa Pia
Since 1903 they have contained
the Portuguese Ethnological Mu
begun (1816–1826) by John VI.
name from the chapel of N. S. d
It contains some fine pictures and
house there is an

n those gardens, Dr Joh
er Pindar, was educated
mining centre. Its manu
woollen goods, and there are iron
under a mayor, 4 aldermen and
ares.

the time of the Domesday Survey as
rendering 12d. yearly and a market
queror it had been given to the count
was held in demesne. Ever since that
e earldom or duchy of Cornwall. The
the river Looe probably led to early
Richard, king of the Romans, recognized
and built the manor house or castle
sonally. In 1240 he constituted Liskeard
s burgesses freemen with all the liberties
rgesses of Launceston and Helston. In
rs at the Feasts of the Assumption and St
Edmund earl of Cornwall in 1275 granted
r a yearly rent of £18 (sold by William III.
he borough in fee farm with its mills, tolls,
pleas of the crown excepted. Liskeard was
own for tin in 1304. Edward the Black Prince
burgesses in 1355 immunity from pleas outside
for trespass done within the borough. Queen
ted a charter of incorporation in 1580 under
ere to be a mayor, recorder and eight councillors.
was surrendered to Charles II. in 1680 and a new
by his brother under which the corporation became
body. From 1295 to 1832 Liskeard sent two
he House of Commons. The parliamentary franchise,
cised by the burgesses, was vested by James' charter
rporation and freemen. By determining to admit
emen the voters became reduced to between 30 and
dward Coke was returned for this borough in 1620,
ard Gibbon the historian in 1774. In 1832 Liskeard
ived of one of its members and in 1885 it became
n the county.

the fairs already mentioned a third was added by Eliza
arter to be held on Ascension Day. These are still among
considerable cattle fairs in the county. The same charter
a market on Mondays and provided for another on Saturdays.
tter is now held weekly, the former twice a month. The
ill at Lamellion mentioned in the charter of 1275, and pro
dentical with the mill of the Domesday Survey, is still driven
ater.

LISLE, ALICE (*c.* 1614–1685), commonly known as Lady
ce Lisle, was born about 1614. Her father, Sir White
ckenshaw, was descended from an old Hampshire family;
husband, John Lisle (d. 1664), had been one of the judges
the trial of Charles I., and was subsequently a member of
romwell's House of Lords—hence his wife's courtesy title.
dy Lisle seems to have leaned to Royalism, but with this
ttitude she combined a decided sympathy with religious
issent. On the 20th of July 1685, a fortnight after the battle
of Sedgemoor, the old lady consented to shelter John Hickes,
a well-known Nonconformist minister, at her residence, Moyles
Court, near Ringwood. Hickes, who was a fugitive from
Monmouth's army, brought with him Richard Nelthorpe, also
a partizan of Monmouth, and under sentence of outlawry.
The two men passed the night at Moyles Court, and on the following morning were arrested, and their hostess, who had denied
their presence in the house, was charged with harbouring traitors.
Her case was tried by Judge Jeffreys at the opening of the "Bloody
Assizes" at Winchester. She pleaded that she had no knowledge
that Hickes's offence was anything more serious than illegal
preaching, that she had known nothing previously of Nelthorpe
(whose name was not included in the indictment, but was,
nevertheless, mentioned to strengthen the case for the Crown),
she had no sympathy with the rebellion. The jury
found her guilty, and, the law recognizing no distinc
principals and accessories in treason, she was
be burned. Jeffreys ordered that the sentence

should be carried out that same afternoon, but a few days' respite was subsequently granted, and James II. allowed beheading to be substituted for burning. Lady Lisle was executed in Winchester market-place on the 2nd of September 1685. By many writers her death has been termed a judicial murder, and one of the first acts of parliament of William and Mary reversed the attainder on the ground that the prosecution was irregular and the verdict injuriously extorted by "the menaces and violences and other illegal practices" of Jeffreys. It is, however, extremely doubtful whether Jeffreys, for all his gross brutality, exceeded the strict letter of the existing law.

See Howell, *State Trials*; H. B. Irving, *Life of Judge Jeffreys*; Stephen, *History of the Criminal Law of England*.

LISMORE, an island in the entrance to Loch Linnhe, Argyllshire, Scotland, 5 m. N.W. of Oban. Pop. (1901) 500. It lies S.W. and N.E., is 9½ m. long and 1½ m. broad, and has an area of 9600 acres. It divides the lower end of the loch into two channels, the Lynn of Morvern on the W. and the Lynn of Lorne on the E. The name is derived from the Gaelic *lios mòr*, "great garden." Several ruined castles stand on the coast, and the highest point of the island is 500 ft. above the sea. The inhabitants raise potatoes, oats, cattle and horses, and these, with dairy produce, form the bulk of the trade. Steamers call at Auchnacrosan. A Columban monastery was founded in Lismore by St Moluag about 592. About 1200 the see of Argyll was separated from Dunkeld by Bishop John, "the Englishman," and Lismore soon afterwards became the seat of the bishop of Argyll, sometimes called "Episcopus Lismoriensis," quite distinct from the bishop of the Isles (Sudreys and Isle of Man), called "Episcopus Sodoriensis" or "Insularum," whose see was divided in the 14th century into the English bishopric of Sodor and Man and the Scottish bishopric of the Isles. The Rev. John Macaulay (d. 1789), grandfather of Lord Macaulay, the historian, and the Rev. Donald M'Nicol (1735–1802), who took up the defence of the Highlands against Dr Johnson, were ministers of Lismore.

For the *Book of the Dean of Lismore* see CELT: *Scottish Gaelic Literature*.

LISMORE, a town of Rous county, New South Wales, Australia, 320 m. direct N. by E. of Sydney. Pop. (1901) 4378. It is the principal town of the north coast district, and the seat of a Roman Catholic bishop. The surrounding country is partly pastoral, and partly agricultural, the soil being very fertile. The town has a cathedral, school of art, and other public buildings, while its industrial establishments include saw-mills, sugar-mills, butter factories and an iron foundry Standing at the head of navigation of the Richmond river, Lismore has a large export trade in dairy produce, poultry, pigs, and pine and cedar timber.

LISMORE, a market town and seat of a diocese in Co. Waterford, Ireland, 43 m. W.S.W. of Waterford by the Waterford and Mallow branch of the Great Southern & Western Railway. Pop. (1901) 1583. It is beautifully situated on a steep eminence rising abruptly from the Blackwater. At the verge of the rock on the western side is the old baronial castle, erected by King John in 1185, which was the residence of the bishops till the 14th century. It was besieged in 1641 and 1643, and in 1645 it was partly destroyed by fire. The present fabric is largely modern; while the portico was designed by Inigo Jones. To the east, on the summit of the height, is the cathedral of St Carthagh, of various dates. There are portions probably of the 12th and 13th centuries, but the bulk of the building is of the 17th century, and considerable additions, including the tower and spire, were made in the 19th. There are a grammar school, a free school and a number of charities. Some trade is carried on by means of the river, and the town is the centre of a salmon fishery district.

The original name of Lismore was Maghsciath. A monastery founded here by St Carthagh in 633 became so celebrated as a seat of learning that it is said no fewer than twenty churches were erected in its vicinity. The bishopric, which is said to have originated with this foundation, was united to that of Waterford in 1363. In the 9th and beginning of the 10th centuries the town was repeatedly plundered by the Danes, and in 978 the town and abbey were burned by the men of Ossory. Henry II., after landing at Waterford, received in Lismore castle the allegiance of the archbishops and bishops of Ireland. In 1518 the manor was granted to Sir Walter Raleigh, from whom it passed to Sir Richard Boyle, afterwards earl of Cork. From the earls of Cork it descended by marriage to the dukes of Devonshire. It was incorporated as a municipal borough in the time of Charles I., when it also received the privilege of returning members to parliament, but at the Union in 1800 it was disfranchised and also ceased to exercise its municipal functions.

LISSA (Serbo-Croatian *Vis*; Lat. *Issa*), an island in the Adriatic sea, forming part of Dalmatia, Austria. Lissa lies 31 m. S. by W. of Spalato, and is the outermost island of the Dalmatian Archipelago. Its greatest length is 10½ m.; its greatest breadth 4½ m. In shape it is a long, roughly drawn parallelogram, surrounded by a wall of rock, which incloses the fertile central plain, and is broken, on the north, west and east by natural harbours. Its culminating point is Mount Hum (1942 ft.), on the south-west. The island, which belongs to the administrative district of Lesina, is divided between two communes, named after the chief towns, Lissa (*Vis*), on the north, and Comisa (*Komiža*), on the west. Lissa, the capital, has a strongly fortified harbour. It contains the palace of the old Venetian counts Gariboldi, the former residence of the English governor, the monastery of the Minorites and at a little distance to the west the ruins of the ancient city of Issa. The islanders gain their livelihood by viticulture, for which Issa was once famous, by sardine fishing and by the distillation of rosemary oil. Pop. (1900) 9918, of whom 5261 belonged to the town and commune of Lissa, and 4657 to Comisa.

Issa is said to have been settled by people from Lesbos, the Issa of the Aegean. The Parians, assisted by Dionysius the Elder of Syracuse, introduced a colony in the 4th century B.C. During the First Punic War (265–241 B.C.) the Issaeans with their beaked ships helped the Roman Duilius; and the great republic, having defended their island against the attacks of Agron of Illyria and his queen Teuta, again found them serviceable allies in the war with Philip of Macedon (*c.* 215–211). As early as 996 the Venetians ruled the island, and, though they retired for a time before the Ragusans, their power was effectually established in 1278. Velo Selo, then the chief settlement, was destroyed by Ferdinand of Naples in 1483 and by the Turks in 1571. The present city arose shortly afterwards. During the Napoleonic wars, the French held Lissa until 1811, and during this period the island prospered greatly, its population increasing from 4000 to 12,000 between 1808 and 1811. In the latter year the French squadron was defeated by the British (see below); though in the same year a French fleet, flying British colours, entered Lissa, and only retired after burning 64 merchantmen. Thenceforward the island gained a valuable trade in British goods, which, being excluded from every port under French control, were smuggled into Dalmatia. In 1812 the British established an administrative system, under native officials, in Lissa and the adjoining islands of Curzola and Lagosta. All three were ceded to Austria in 1815.

Battles of Lissa.—Two naval actions have been fought in modern times near this island. The first took place on the 13th of March 1811, and was fought between a Franco-Venetian squadron, under the command of an officer named Dubourdieu (of whom little or nothing else is known), and Captain (afterwards Sir) William Hoste with a small British force. The Franco-Venetian squadron (Venice was then part of the dominions of the emperor Napoleon) consisted of six frigates, of which four were of forty guns, and of five corvettes or small craft. The British squadron was composed of three frigates, the "Amphion," 32 (Captain William Hoste), the "Cerberus" (Captain Henry Whitby) and the "Active," 38 (Captain James A. Gordon). With them was the "Volage," 22 (Captain Phipps Hornby). The action has a peculiar interest because the French captain imitated the method of attack employed by Nelson at Trafalgar. He came down from windward in two lines parallel to one another, and at an angle to the British squadron. Captain Hoste was not compelled to lie still as the allies did at Trafalgar. He stood on, and as the two French lines had to overtake him as he slipped away at an angle to their course, one of them got in the way of the other. Captain Hoste materially forwarded the success of his manœuvre by leading the foremost French ship, the "Favorite," 40, on to a reef, which was known to himself, but not to the enemy. Both squadrons then turned, and the Franco-Venetians falling into great confusion were defeated in spite of the gallant fighting of the individual ships. Two prizes were taken and Dubourdieu was killed.

The second naval battle of Lissa was fought between the Austrian and Italian navies on the 20th of July 1866. The island, then in possession of the Austrians, was attacked by an Italian squadron from Ancona of 12 ironclads and 22 wooden vessels. One of the ironclads was damaged in a bombardment of the forts, and two were detached on other service, when an Austrian squadron of 7 ironclads, one unarmoured warship the "Kaiser" and a number of small craft which had left Fasano under the command of Admiral Tegethoff came to interrupt their operations. The Italian admiral Persano arranged his ships in a single long line ahead, which allowing for the necessary space between them meant that the Italian formation stretched for more than 2 m. Just before the action began Admiral Persano shifted his flag from the "Ré d'Italia," the fourth ship in order from the van, to the ram "Affondatore," the fifth. This made it necessary for the "Affondatore" and the ships astern to shorten speed, and, as the leading vessels stood on, a gap was created in the Italian line. Admiral Tegethoff, who was on the port bow of the Italians, attacked with his squadron in three divisions formed in obtuse angles. The Italians opened a very rapid and ill-directed fire at a distance of 1000 yds. The Austrians did not reply till they were at a distance of 300 yds. Under Tegethoff's vigorous leadership, and aided by the disorder in the Italian line, the Austrians brought on a brief, but to the Italians destructive, mêlée. They broke through an interval between the third and fourth Italian ships. The unarmed Austrian ships headed to attack the unarmed Italians in the rear. At this point an incident occurred to which an exaggerated importance was given. The Italian ironclad "Ré di Portogallo" of 5600 tons, in the rear of the line, stood out to cover the unarmoured squadron by ramming the Austrians. She was herself rammed by the wooden "Kaiser" (5000 tons), but received little injury, while the Austrian was much injured. The "Kaiser" and the wooden vessels then made for the protection of fort San Giorgio on Lissa unpursued. In the centre, where the action was hottest, the Austrian flagship "Ferdinand Max" of 5200 tons rammed and sank the "Ré d'Italia." The Italian "Palestro" of 2000 tons was fired by a shell and blew up. By midday the Italians were in retreat, and Tegethoff anchored at San Giorgio. His squadron had suffered very little from the wild fire of the Italians. The battle of the 20th July was the first fought at sea by modern ironclad steam fleets, and therefore attracted a great deal of attention. The sinking of the "Ré d'Italia" and the ramming of the "Portogallo" by the "Kaiser" gave an immense impulse to the then popular theory that the ram would be a leading, if not the principal, weapon in modern sea warfare. This calculation has not been borne out by more recent experience, and indeed was not justified by the battle itself, in which the attempts to ram were many and the successes very few. The "Ré d'Italia" was struck only because she was suddenly and most injudiciously backed, so that she had no way on when charged by the "Ferdinand Max."

For the first battle of Lissa see James's *Naval History*, vol. v. (1837). A clear account of the second battle will be found in Sir S. Eardley-Wilmot's *Development of Navies* (London, 1892); see also H. W. Wilson's *Ironclads in Action* (London, 1896). (D. H.)

LISSA (Polish *Leszno*), a town in the Prussian province of Posen, 25 m. N.E. from Glogau by rail and at the junction of lines to Breslau, Posen and Landsberg. Pop. (1905) 16,021. The chief buildings are the handsome palace, the medieval town-hall, the four churches and the synagogue. Its manuf[illegible] chiefly of shoes, machinery, liqueurs and tobacco; it also possesses a large steam flour-mill, and carries on a brisk trade in grain and cattle.

Lissa owes its rise to a number of Moravian Brothers who were banished from Bohemia by the emperor Ferdinand I. in the 16th century and found a refuge in a village on the estate of the Polish family of Leszczynski. Their settlement received municipal rights in 1561. During the Thirty Years' War the population was reinforced by other refugees, and Lissa became an important commercial town and the chief seat of the Moravian Brothers in Poland. Johann Amos Comenius was long rector of the celebrated Moravian school here. In 1656 and 1707 Lissa was burned down.

See Voigt, *Aus Lissas erster Blütezeit* (Lissa, 1905), and Sanden, *Geschichte der Lissaer Schule* (Lissa, 1905).

LIST, FRIEDRICH (1789–1846), German economist, was born at Reutlingen, Württemberg, on the 6th of August 1789. Unwilling to follow the occupation of his father, who was a prosperous tanner, he became a clerk in the public service, and by 1816 had risen to the post of ministerial under-secretary. In 1817 he was appointed professor of administration and politics at the university of Tübingen, but the fall of the ministry in 1819 compelled him to resign. As a deputy to the Württemberg chamber, he was active in advocating administrative reforms. He was eventually expelled from the chamber and in April 1822 sentenced to ten months' imprisonment with hard labour in the fortress of Asperg. He escaped to Alsace, and after visiting France and England returned in 1824 to finish his sentence, and was released on undertaking to emigrate to America. There he resided from 1825 to 1832, first engaging in farming and afterwards in journalism. It was in America that he gathered from a study of Alexander Hamilton's work the inspiration which made him an economist of his pronounced "National" views. The discovery of coal on some land which he had acquired made him financially independent, and he became United States consul at Leipzig in 1832. He strongly advocated the extension of the railway system in Germany, and the establishment of the *Zollverein* was due largely to his enthusiasm and ardour. His latter days were darkened by many misfortunes; he lost much of his American property in a financial crisis, ill-health also overtook him, and he brought his life to an end by his own hand on the 30th of November 1846.

List holds historically one of the highest places in economic thought as applied to practical objects. His principal work is entitled *Das Nationale System der Politischen Ökonomie* (1841). Though his practical conclusions were different from those of Adam Müller (1779–1829), he was largely influenced not only by Hamilton but also by the general mode of thinking of that writer, and by his strictures on the doctrine of Adam Smith. It was particularly against the cosmopolitan principle in the modern economical system that he protested, and against the absolute doctrine of free trade, which was in harmony with that principle. He gave prominence to the national idea, and insisted on the special requirements of each nation according to its circumstances and especially to the degree of its development.

He refused to Smith's system the title of the industrial, which he thought more appropriate to the mercantile system, and designated the former as "the exchange-value system." He denied the parallelism asserted by Smith between the economic conduct proper to an individual and to a nation, and held that the immediate private interest of the separate members of the community would not lead to the highest good of the whole. That the nation was an existence, standing between the individual and humanity, and formed into a unity by its language, manners, historical development, culture and constitution. That this unity must be the first condition of the security, wellbeing, progress and civilization of the individual; and private economic interests, like all others, must be subordinated to the maintenance, completion and strengthening of the nationality. The nation having a continuous life, its true wealth must consist—and this is List's fundamental doctrine—not in the quantity of exchange-values which it possesses, but in the full and many-sided development of its productive powers. Its economic education should be more important than the immediate production of values, and it might be right that one generation should sacrifice its gain and enjoyment to secure the strength and skill of the future. In the sound and normal condition of a nation which has attained economic maturity, the three productive powers of agriculture, manufactures and commerce should be alike developed. But the two latter factors are superior in importance, as exercising a more effective and fruitful influence on the whole culture of the nation, as well as on its independence. Navigation, railways, all higher technical arts, connect themselves specially with these factors; whilst in a purely agricultural state there is a tendency to stagnation. But for the growth of the higher forms of industry all countries are not adapted—only those of the temperate zones, whilst the torrid regions have a natural monopoly in the production of certain raw materials; and thus between these two groups of countries a division of labour and confederation of powers spontaneously takes place.

List then goes on to explain his theory of the stages of economic development through which the nations of the temperate zone, which are furnished with all the necessary conditions, naturally pass, in advancing to their normal economic state. These are (1) pastoral life, (2) agriculture, (3) agriculture united with manufactures; whilst in the final stage agriculture, manufactures and commerce are combined. The economic task of the state is to bring into existence through legislative and administrative action the conditions required for the progress of the nation through these stages. Out of this view arises List's scheme of industrial politics. Every nation, according to him, should begin with free trade, stimulating and improving its agriculture by intercourse with richer and more cultivated nations, importing foreign manufactures and exporting raw products. When it is economically so far advanced that it can manufacture for itself, then a system of protection should be employed to allow the home industries to develop themselves fully, and save them from being overpowered in their earlier efforts by the competition of more matured foreign industries in the home market. When the national industries have grown strong enough no longer to dread this competition, then the highest stage of progress has been reached, free trade should again become the rule, and the nation be thus thoroughly incorporated with the universal industrial union. What a nation loses for a time in exchange values during the protective period she much more than gains in the long run in productive power—the temporary expenditure being strictly analogous, when we place ourselves at the point of view of the life of the nation, to the cost of the industrial education of the individual. The practical conclusion which List drew for Germany was that she needed for her economic progress an extended and conveniently bounded territory reaching to the sea-coast both on north and south, and a vigorous expansion of manufactures and commerce, and that the way to the latter lay through judicious protective legislation with a customs union comprising all German lands, and a German marine with a Navigation Act. The national German spirit, striving after independence and power through union, and the national industry, awaking from its lethargy and eager to recover lost ground, were favourable to the success of List's book, and it produced a great sensation. He ably represented the tendencies and demands of his time in his own country; his work had the effect of fixing the attention, not merely of the speculative and official classes, but of practical men generally, on questions of political economy; and his ideas were undoubtedly the economic foundation of modern Germany, as applied by the practical genius of Bismarck.

See biographies of List by Goldschmidt (Berlin, 1878) and Jentsch (Berlin, 1901), also *Fr List, ein Vorlaufer und ein Opfer fur das Vaterland* (Anon., 2 vols., Stuttgart, 1877), M. E. Hirst's *Life of Friedrich List* (London, 1909) contains a bibliography and a reprint of List's *Outlines of American Political Economy* (1827).

LIST (O.E. *liste*, a Teutonic word, cf. Dut. *lijst*, Ger. *Leiste*, adapted in Ital *lista* and Fr. *liste*), properly a border or edging. The word was thus formerly used of a geographical boundary or frontier and of the lobe of the ear. In current usage "list" is the term applied to the "selvage" of a piece of cloth, the edging, *i.e.* of a web left in an unfinished state or of different material from the rest of the fabric, to be torn or cut off when it is made up, or used for forming a seam. A similar edging prevents unravelling The material, cut off and collected, is known as "list," and is used as a soft cheap material for making slippers, padding cushions, &c. Until the employment of rubber, list was used to stuff the cushions of billiard tables. The same word probably appears, in a plural form "lists," applied to the barriers or palisades enclosing a space of ground set apart for tilting (see TOURNAMENT) It is thus used of any place of contest, and the phrase "to enter the lists" is frequently used in the sense of "to challenge." The word in this application was taken directly from the O Fr. *lisse*, modern *lice*, in Med. Lat. *liciae*. This word is usually taken to be a Romanic adaptation of the Teutonic word. In medieval fortifications the *lices* were the palisades forming an outwork in front of the main walls of a castle or other fortified place, and the word was also used of the space enclosed between the palisades and the enceinte; this was used for exercising troops, &c. From a transference of "list," meaning edge or border, to a "strip" of paper, parchment, &c., containing a "list" of names, numbers, &c., comes the use of the word for an enumeration of a series of names of persons or things arranged in order for some specific purpose. It is the most general word for such an enumeration, other words, such as "register," "schedule," "inventory," "catalogue," having usually some particular connotation. The chief early use of list in this meaning was of the roll containing the names of soldiers; hence to "list a soldier" meant to enter a recruit's name for service, in modern usage "to enlist" him. There are numerous particular applications of "list," as in "civil list" (*q.v.*), "active or retired list" in the navy or army. The term "free list" is used of an enumeration of such commodities as may at a particular time be exempt from the revenue laws imposing an import duty.

The verb "to list," most commonly found in the imperative, meaning "hark!" is another form of "listen," and is to be referred, as to its ultimate origin, to an Indo-European root *klu-*, seen in Gr. κλύειν, to hear, κλέος, glory, renown, and in the English "loud." The same root is seen in Welsh *clûst* and Irish *clûas*, ear. Another word "list," meaning pleasure, delight, or, as a verb, meaning "to please, choose," is chiefly found in such phrases as "the wind bloweth where it listeth." This is from the O.E. *lystan*, cf. Dut. *lusten*, Ger. *lusten*, to take pleasure in, and is also found in the English doublet "lust," now always used in the sense of an evil or more particularly sexual desire. It is probably an application of this word, in the sense of "inclination," that has given rise to the nautical term "list," for the turning over of a ship on to its side.

LISTA Y ARAGON, ALBERTO (1775–1848), Spanish poet and educationalist, was born at Seville on the 15th of October 1775. He began teaching at the age of fifteen, and when little over twenty was made professor of elocution and poetry at Seville university. In 1813 he was exiled, on political grounds, but pardoned in 1817. He then returned to Spain and, after teaching for three years at Bilbao, started a critical review at Madrid. Shortly afterwards he founded the celebrated college of San Mateo in that city. The liberal character of the San Mateo educational system was not favoured by the government, and in 1823 the college was closed. Lista after some time spent in Bayonne, Paris and London was recalled to Spain in 1833 to edit the official *Madrid Gazette*. He was one of the founders of the Ateneo, the free university of Madrid, and up till 1840 was director of a college at Cadiz. All the leading spirits of the young generation of Spaniards, statesmen, writers, soldiers and diplomatists came under his influence. He died at Seville on the 5th of October 1848.

LISTER, JOSEPH LISTER, 1st BARON (1827–), English surgeon, was born at Upton, in Essex, on the 5th of April 1827 His father, Joseph Jackson Lister, F.R.S., was eminent in science, especially in optical science; his chief claim to remembrance being that by certain improvements in lenses he raised the compound microscope from the position of a scientific toy, "distorting as much as it magnified," to its present place as a powerful engine of research. Other members of Lord Lister's family were eminent in natural science. In his boyhood Joseph Lister was educated at Quaker schools; first at Hitchin in Hertfordshire, and afterwards at Tottenham, near London. In 1844 he entered University College, London, as a student in arts, and took his B.A. degree at the University of London in 1847. He continued at University College as a medical student, and became M.B and F.R.C.S. in 1852. The keen young student was not long in bringing his faculties to bear upon pathology and the practice of medicine. While house-surgeon at University College Hospital, he had charge of certain cases during an outbreak of hospital gangrene, and carefully observed the phenomena of the disease and the effects of treatment upon it. He was thus early led to suspect the parasitic nature of the disorder, and searched with the microscope the material of the spreading sore, in the hope of discovering in it some invading fungus, he soon convinced himself of the cardinal truth that its causes were purely local. He also minutely investigated cases of pyaemia, another terrible scourge of hospitals at that time,

Transactions. His principal works were *Historiae animalium Angliae tres tractatus* (1678); *Historiae Conchyliorum* (1685–1692), and *Conchyliorum Bivalvium* (1696). As a conchologist he was held in high esteem, but while he recognized the similarity of fossil mollusca to living forms, he regarded them as inorganic imitations produced in the rocks. In 1683 he communicated to the Royal Society (*Phil. Trans.*, 1684), *An ingenious proposal for a new sort of maps of countries; together with tables of sands and clays, such as are chiefly found in the north parts of England*. In this essay he suggested the preparation of a soil or mineral map of the country, and thereby is justly credited with being the first to realize the importance of a geological survey. He died at Epsom on the 2nd of February 1712.

LISTON, JOHN (*c.* 1776–1846), English comedian, was born in London. He made his public *début* on the stage at Weymouth as Lord Duberley in *The Heir-at-law*. After several dismal failures in tragic parts, some of them in support of Mrs Siddons, he discovered accidentally that his *forte* was comedy, especially in the personation of old men and country boys, in which he displayed a fund of drollery and broad humour. An introduction to Charles Kemble led to his appearance at the Haymarket on the 10th of June 1805 as Sheepface in the *Village Lawyer*, and his association with this theatre continued with few interruptions until 1830. *Paul Pry*, the most famous of all his impersonations, was first presented on the 13th of September 1825, and soon became, thanks to his creative genius, a real personage. Liston remained on the stage till 1837; during his last years his mind failed, and he died on the 22nd of March 1846. He had married in 1807 Miss Tyrer (d. 1854), a singer and actress. Several pictures of Liston in character are in the Garrick Club, London, and one as Paul Pry in the South Kensington Museum.

LISTON, ROBERT (1794–1847), Scottish surgeon, was born on the 28th of October 1794 at Ecclesmachan, Linlithgow, where his father was parish minister. He began the study of anatomy under Dr John Barclay (1758–1826) at Edinburgh in 1810, and soon became a skilful anatomist. After eight years' study, he became a lecturer on anatomy and surgery in the Edinburgh School of Medicine; and in 1827 he was elected one of the surgeons to the Royal Infirmary. In 1835 he was chosen professor of clinical surgery in University College, London, and this appointment he held until his death, which occurred in London on the 7th of December 1847. Liston was a teacher more by what he did than by what he said. He taught simplicity in all operative procedures; fertile in expedients, of great nerve and of powerful frame, he is remembered as an extraordinarily [illegible] and rapid operator. He was the author of *The* [illegible] *Surgery* (1831–1832) and *Practical Surgery* (1837), [illegible] several improvements in methods of amputation, and [illegible] dressing of wounds.

LISZT, FRANZ (1811–1886), Hungarian pianist and composer, [illegible] on the 22nd of October 1811, at Raiding, in Hungary. [illegible] musicians was made in a threefold capacity, and [illegible] to deal with Liszt the unrivalled pianoforte [illegible]; Liszt the conductor of the "music of [illegible] Weimar, the teacher of Tausig, Bülow and a host [illegible] the eloquent writer on music and musicians, [illegible] Berlioz and Wagner (1848–1861); and Liszt [illegible], who for some five-and-thirty years con[illegible] pieces, songs, symphonic orchestral [illegible] psalms and oratorios (1847–1882). As [illegible] during which he [illegible] conductor and [illegible] the composer's [illegible] the agent of the [illegible] some attainment, [illegible] her an Austrian- [illegible] tion of certain [illegible] en annually for [illegible] Vienna and Paris. [illegible] from Carl Czerny [illegible] harmony and analysis [illegible] in public there and Beethoven came to his second concert in April 1823. During the three years following he played in Paris, the French provinces and Switzerland, and paid three visits to England. In Paris he had composition lessons from Paër, and a six months' course of lessons in counterpoint from Reicha. In the autumn of 1825 the handsome and fascinating *enfant gâté* of the salons and ateliers —"La Neuvième Merveille du monde"—had the luck to get an operetta (*Don Sancho*) performed three times at the Académie Royale. The score was accidentally destroyed by fire, but a set of studies *à la* Czerny and Cramer, belonging to 1826 and published at Marseilles as 12 Études, op. i., is extant, and shows remarkable precocity. After the death of his father in 1828 young Liszt led the life of a teacher of the pianoforte in Paris, got through a good deal of miscellaneous reading, and felt the influence of the religious, literary and political aspirations of the time. He attended the meetings of the Saint-Simonists, lent an ear to the romantic mysticism of Père Enfantin and later to the teaching of Abbé Lamennais. He also played Beethoven and Weber in public—a very courageous thing in those days. The appearance of the violinist Paganini in Paris, 1831, marks the starting-point of the supreme eminence Liszt ultimately attained as a virtuoso. Paganini's marvellous technique inspired him to practise as no pianist had ever practised before. He tried to find equivalents for Paganini's effects, transcribed his violin caprices for the piano, and perfected his own technique to an extraordinary degree. After Paganini he received a fresh impulse from the playing and the compositions of Chopin, who arrived in 1831, and yet another impulse of equal force from a performance of Berlioz's "Symphonie Fantastique, épisode de la vie d'un artiste," in 1832. Liszt transcribed this work, and its influence ultimately led him to the composition of his "Poèmes symphoniques" and other examples of orchestral programme-music.

From 1833 to 1848—when he gave up playing in public—he was greeted with frantic applause as the prince of pianists. Five years (1835–1840) were spent in Switzerland and Italy, in semi-retirement in the company of Madame la comtesse d'Agoult (George Sand's friend and would-be rival, known in literary circles as "Daniel Stern," by whom Liszt had three children, one of them afterwards Frau Cosima Wagner): these years were devoted to further study in playing and composition, and were interrupted only by occasional appearances at Geneva, Milan, Florence and Rome, and by annual visits to Paris, when a famous contest with Thalberg took place in 1837. The enthusiasm aroused by Liszt's playing and his personality—the two are inseparable—reached a climax at Vienna and Budapest in 1839–1840, when he received a patent of nobility from the emperor of Austria, and a sword of honour from the magnates of Hungary in the name of the nation. During the eight years following he was heard at all the principal centres—including London, Leipzig, Berlin, Copenhagen, St Petersburg, Moscow, Warsaw, Constantinople, Lisbon and Madrid. He gained much money, and gave large sums in charity. His munificence with regard to the Beethoven statue at Bonn made a great stir. The subscriptions having come in but sparsely, Liszt took the matter in hand, and the monument was completed at his expense, and unveiled at a musical festival conducted by Spohr and himself in 1845. In 1848 he settled at Weimar with Princess Sayn-Wittgenstein (d. 1887), and remained there till 1861. During this period he acted as conductor at court concerts and on special occasions at the theatre, gave lessons to a number of pianists, wrote articles of permanent value on certain works of Berlioz and the early operas of Wagner, and produced those orchestral and choral pieces upon which his reputation as a composer mainly depends. His ambition to found a school of composers as well as a school of pianists met with complete success on the one hand and partial failure on the other. His efforts on behalf of Wagner, who was then an exile in Switzerland, culminated in the first performance of *Lohengrin* on the 28th of August 1850, before a special audience assembled from far and near. Among the works produced for the first time or rehearsed with a view to the furtherance of musical art were

Wagner's *Tannhäuser*, *Der fliegende Holländer*, *Das Liebesmahl der Apostel*, and *Eine Faust Ouvertüre*, Berlioz's *Benvenuto Cellini*, the *Symphonie Fantastique*, *Harold en Italie*, *Roméo et Juliette*, *La Damnation de Faust*, and *L'Enfance du Christ*—the last two conducted by the composer—Schumann's *Genoveva*, *Paradise and the Peri*, the music to *Manfred* and to *Faust*, Weber's *Euryanthe*, Schubert's *Alfonso und Estrella*, Raff's *König Alfred*, Cornelius's *Der Barbier von Baghdad* and many more. It was Liszt's habit to recommend novelties to the public by explanatory articles or essays, which were written in French (some for the *Journal des débats* and the *Gazette musicale* of Paris) and translated for the journals of Weimar and Leipzig—thus his two masterpieces of sympathetic criticism, the essays *Lohengrin et Tannhäuser à Weimar* and *Harold en Italie*, found many readers and proved very effective. They are now included, together with articles on Schumann and Schubert, and the elaborate and rather high-flown essays on Chopin and *Des Bohémiens et de leur musique en Hongrie* (the latter certainly, and the former probably, written in collaboration with Madame de Wittgenstein), in his *Gesammelte Schriften* (6 vols., Leipzig). The compositions belonging to the period of his residence at Weimar comprise two pianoforte concertos, in E flat and in A, the "Todtentanz," the "Concerto pathétique" for two pianos, the solo sonata "An Robert Schumann," sundry "Études," fifteen "Rhapsodies Hongroises," twelve orchestral "Poèmes symphoniques," "Eine Faust Symphonie," and "Eine Symphonie zu Dante's 'Divina Commedia,'" the "13th Psalm" for tenor solo, chorus and orchestra, the choruses to Herder's dramatic scenes "Prometheus," and the "Missa solennis" known as the "Graner Fest Messe." Liszt retired to Rome in 1861, and joined the Franciscan order in 1865.[1] From 1869 onwards Abbé Liszt divided his time between Rome and Weimar, where during the summer months he received pupils—gratis as formerly—and, from 1876 up to his death at Bayreuth on the 31st of July 1886, he also taught for several months every year at the Hungarian Conservatoire of Budapest.

About Liszt's pianoforte technique in general it may be said that it derives its efficiency from the teaching of Czerny, who brought up his pupil on Mozart, a little Bach and Beethoven, a good deal of Clementi and Hummel, and a good deal of his (Czerny's) own work. Classicism in the shape of solid, respectable Hummel on the one hand, and Carl Czerny, a trifle flippant, perhaps, and inclined to appeal to the gallery, on the other, these gave the musical parentage of young Liszt. Then appears the Parisian Incroyable and grand seigneur—"Monsieur Lits," as the Parisians called him. Later, we find him imitating Paganini and Chopin, and at the same time making a really passionate and deep study of Beethoven, Weber, Schubert, Berlioz. Thus gradually was formed the master of style—whose command of the instrument was supreme, and who played like an inspired poet. Liszt's strange musical nature was long in maturing its fruits. At the pianoforte his achievements culminate in the two books of studies, twice rewritten, and finally published in 1852 as *Études d'exécution transcendante*, the *Études de concert* and the *Paganini Studies*; the two concertos and the *Todtentans*, the *Sonata in B minor*, the *Hungarian Rhapsodies* and the fine transcriptions of Beethoven's symphonies (the 9th for two pianofortes as well as solo), and of Berlioz's *Symphonie fantastique*, and the symphony, *Harold en Italie*. In his orchestral pieces Liszt appears—next to Berlioz—as the most conspicuous and most thorough-going representative of programme music, *i.e.* instrumental music expresly contrived to illustrate in detail some poem or some succession of ideas or pictures. It was Liszt's aim to bring about a direct alliance or amalgamation of instrumental music with poetry. To effect this he made use of the means of musical expression for purposes of illustration, and relied on points of support outside the pale of music proper. There is always danger of failure when an attempt is thus made to connect instrumental music with conceptions not in themselves musical, for the order of the ideas that serve as a programme is apt to interfere with the order which the musical exposition naturally assumes—and the result in most cases is but an amalgam of irreconcilable materials. In pieces such as Liszt's "Poèmes symphoniques," *Ce qu'on entend sur la montagne* (1848–1856), after a poem by Victor Hugo, and *Die Ideale* (1853–1857), after a poem by Schiller, the hearer is bewildered by a series of startling orchestral effects which succeed one another apparently without rhyme or reason. The music does not conform to any sufficiently definite musical plan—it is hardly intelligible as music without reference to the programme. Liszt's masterpiece in orchestral music is the *Dante Symphony* (1847–1855), the subject of which was particularly well suited to his temperament, and offered good chances for the display of his peculiar powers as a master of instrumental effect. By the side of it ranks the *Faust Symphony* (1854–1857), in which the moods of Goethe's characters—Faust, Gretchen and Mephistopheles—are depicted in three instrumental movements, with a chorus of male voices, supplying a kind of comment, by way of close. The method of presentation in both symphonies is by means of representative themes (*Leitmotif*), and their combination and interaction. Incidents of the poem or the play are illustrated or alluded to as may be convenient, and the exigencies of musical form are not unfrequently disregarded for the sake of special effects. Of the twelve Poèmes symphoniques, *Orphée* is the most consistent from a musical point of view, and is exquisitely scored. Melodious, effective, readily intelligible, with a dash of the commonplace, *Les Préludes*, *Tasso*, *Mazeppa* and *Fest-Klänge* bid for popularity. In these pieces, as in almost every production of his, in lieu of melody Liszt offers fragments of melody—touching and beautiful, it may be, or passionate, or tinged with triviality; in lieu of a rational distribution of centres of harmony in accordance with some definite plan, he presents clever combinations of chords and ingenious modulations from point to point; in lieu of musical logic and consistency of design, he is content with rhapsodical improvisation. The power of persistence seems wanting. The musical growth is spoilt, the development of the themes is stopped, or prevented, by some reference to extraneous ideas. Everywhere the programme stands in the way. In much of Liszt's vocal music, particularly in the songs and choral pieces written to German words, an annoying discrepancy is felt to exist between the true sound of the words and the musical accents. The music is generally emotional, the expression direct and passionate; there is no lack of melodic charm and originality, yet the total effect is frequently disappointing. In the choral numbers of the five masses, and in the oratorios *Die Heilige Elisabeth* and *Christus*, the rarity of fugal polyphony acts as a drawback. Its almost complete absence in some of these works makes for monotony and produces a sense of dullness, which may not be inherent in all the details of the music, but is none the less distinctly present.

Omitting trifles and all publications that have been cancelled, the following list of compositions may be taken as fairly comprehensive:—

Pianoforte Pieces.—Études d'exécution transcendante; Études de concert; Zwei Etuden, Waldesrauschen, Gnomentanz; Ab Irato; Paganini Studies; Années de Pélerinage, 3 sets; Harmonies poétiques et religieuses, 1-10; Consolations, 1-6; Ave Maria in E; Sonata in B minor; Konzert-Solo in E minor; Scherzo und Marsch; Ballades, I. II.; Polonaises, I. II.; Apparitions, 1-3; Berceuse; Valse impromptu; Mazurka brillant; 3 Caprices Valses; Galop chromatique; Mephisto-Walser, I., II., III. and Polka; Zwei Legenden, "Die Vogelpredigt," "Der heilige Franciscus auf den Wogen schreitend"; "Der Weihnachtsbaum," 1-12; Sarabande und Chaconne ("Almira"); Elegies, I., II. and III.; La lugubre Gondola; Dem Andenken Petöfi's; Mosonyi's Grabgeleit; Romance oubliée; Valses oubliées, 1-3; Liebesträume, 1-3 (originally songs); Hexameron; Rhapsodies Hongroises, 1-18.

Pieces for Two Pianos.—Concerto pathétique (identical with the Konzert-Solo in E minor); Dante symphony; Faust symphony; Poèmes symphoniques, 1-12; Beethoven's 9th symphony.

Pianoforte with Orchestra.—Concertos I. in E flat, II. in A; Todtentanz; Fantasie ueber Motif aus Beethoven's "Ruinen von Athen"; Fantasie ueber Ungarische National Melodien; Schubert's Fantasia in C; Weber's Polacca in E.

[1] It is understood that, in point of fact, the Princess Wittgenstein was determined to marry Liszt; and as neither he nor her family wished their connexion to take this form, Cardinal Hohenlohe quietly had him ordained.—[Ed. *E.B.*].

[illegible] *de Concert for Piano Solo.*—Don Juan; Norma; Son-[illegible] I Puritani; Lucia, I., II.; Lucrezia, I., II.; La Juive; [illegible] le Diable; Les Huguenots; Le Prophète, 1-4. *Paraphrases,* [illegible] di bravura (Masaniello); Verdi, Rigoletto, Ernani, [illegible]; Mendelssohn, "Hochzeitsmarsch und Elfenreigen"; [illegible] Valse de Faust, Les Adieux de Roméo et Juliette; Tschai-[illegible] Polonaise; Dargomiyski, Tarantelle; Cui, Tarantella; [illegible] Danse macabre; Schubert, Soirées de Vienne, Valses [illegible]

[illegible]—Beethoven's Nine Symphonies; Berlioz's "Sym-[illegible]"; "Harold en Italie"; Bénédiction et Serment [illegible]; Danse des Sylphes (Damnation de Faust); [illegible] Der Freischütz, Euryanthe, Oberon, Jubilee; [illegible] Hummel's Septets; Schubert's Divertissement à [illegible] Beethoven's Concertos in C minor, G and E flat [illegible] second piano); Wagner's Tannhäuser overture, [illegible] chorus of pilgrims; Lohengrin, Festzug und [illegible] Elsa's Traum, Lohengrin's Verweiss an [illegible] Spinnlied; Rienzi, Gebet; Rheingold, [illegible] "Am stillen Herd"; Tristan, Isolde's [illegible] six Chants Polonais; Meyerbeer's Schiller-[illegible] Preludes and Fugues; Prelude and Fugue [illegible]; 6 miscellaneous and 6 Geistliche [illegible] Les Soirées musicales; Schubert, [illegible] songs; Mendelssohn, 8 songs; Robert [illegible]

[illegible] Fantasia and Fugue, "Ad nos, [illegible] B-A-C-H Fugue; Variations on Bach's [illegible] Klagen"; Bach's Introduction and [illegible]"; Bach's Choral Fugue, [illegible] Kirchliche Festouvertüre, "Ein feste [illegible] Mozart's Ave Verum; Arcadelt's Ave [illegible]

[illegible] zu Dante's "Divina Com-[illegible] Poèmes symphoniques: 1. "Ce [illegible] 2. Tasso; 3. Les Préludes; 4. [illegible]; 7. Fest-Klänge; 8. Héroïde [illegible]; 11. Hunnenschlacht; 12. Die [illegible] Faust: 1. Der nächtliche Zug, [illegible] Marches, Rakoczy, Goethe, Hul-[illegible] military band); Ungarischer, [illegible] Le Triomphe funèbre du Tasse; [illegible] Hungarian rhapsodies; four [illegible] by Schubert.

[illegible] Legende von der Heiligen Elisa-[illegible] (unfinished). Masses: Missa [illegible] cathedral at Gran; Ungarische [illegible] organ); Missa and Requiem [illegible] 13, 137, 23 and 18; 12 [illegible] Cantatas; Prometheus-chöre; [illegible]"; Die Glocken des [illegible] Männergesang; Songs, 8 [illegible]

[illegible] with *Pianoforte Accompani-*[illegible] Mönch (Lenau); Des tod-[illegible] (Tolstoy).

[illegible] Sonatas; Weber's Con-[illegible] Sonatas, Impromptus, [illegible]

[illegible] *Künstler und Mensch* (1880-[illegible] vol. vi. (1905).

(E. Da.)

[illegible] (both from Mommsen), [illegible] commonly in the plural, in a [illegible] of any sort, whether [illegible] in the law of Arcadius [illegible] forbids heretics to hold [illegible]." But some trace [illegible] in the epistle (*Ep.* 63) of [illegible] which he argues, against [illegible], that neither [illegible] Gregory Thaumaturgus, [illegible], which must be [illegible] in Basil's day, [illegible] had many points in [illegible] according to Sidonius [illegible] in France about [illegible] when rain or fine [illegible] bad days before [illegible] for one particular [illegible] (A.D. c. 450) [illegible]

manner of making litanies was to some extent regulated for the entire Eastern empire by one of the *Novels* of Justinian, which forbade their celebration without the presence of the bishops and clergy, and ordered that the crosses which were carried in procession should not be deposited elsewhere than in churches, nor be carried by any but duly appointed persons. The first synod of Orleans (A.D. 511) enjoins for all Gaul that the "litanies" before Ascension be celebrated for three days; on these days all menials are to be exempt from work, so that every one may be free to attend divine service. The diet is to be the same as in Quadragesima; clerks not observing these rogations are to be punished by the bishop. In A.D. 517 the synod of Gerunda provided for two sets of "litanies"; the first were to be observed for three days (from Thursday to Saturday) in the week after Pentecost with fasting, the second for three days from November 1. The second council of Vaison (529), consisting of twelve bishops, ordered the *Kyrie eleison*—now first introduced from the Eastern Church—to be sung at matins, mass and vespers.

A synod of Paris (573) ordered litanies to be held for three days at the beginning of Lent, and the fifth synod of Toledo (636) appointed litanies to be observed throughout the kingdom for three days from December 14. The first mention of the word litany in connexion with the Roman Church goes back to the pontificate of Pelagius I. (555), but implies that the thing was at that time already old. In 590 Gregory I., moved by the pestilence which had followed an inundation, ordered a "litania septiformis," sometimes called *litania major*, that is to say, a sevenfold procession of clergy, laity, monks, virgins, matrons, widows, poor and children. It must not be confused with the *litania septena* used in church on Easter Even. He is said also to have appointed the processions or litanies of April 25 (St Mark's day), which seem to have come in the place of the ceremonies of the old Robigalia. In 747 the synod of Cloveshoe ordered the litanies or rogations to be gone about on April 25 "after the manner of the Roman Church," and on the three days before Ascension "after the manner of our ancestors." The latter are still known in the English Church as Rogation Days. Games, horse racing, junkettings were forbidden; and in the litanies the name of Augustine was to be inserted after that of Gregory. The reforming synod of Mainz in 813 ordered the major litany to be observed by all for three days in sackcloth and ashes, and barefoot. The sick only were exempted.

As regards the form of words prescribed for use in these "litanies" or "supplications," documentary evidence is defective. Sometimes it would appear that the "procession" or "litany" did nothing else but chant *Kyrie eleison* without variation. There is no reason to doubt that from an early period the special written litanies of the various churches all showed the common features which are now regarded as essential to a litany, in as far as they consisted of (1) invocations, (2) deprecations, (3) intercessions, (4) supplications. But in details they must have varied immensely. The offices of the Roman Catholic Church at present recognize two litanies, the "Litaniae majores" and the "Litaniae breves," which differ from one another chiefly in respect of the fulness with which details are entered upon under the heads mentioned above. It is said that in the time of Charlemagne the angels Orihel, Raguhel, Tobihel were invoked, but the names were removed by Pope Zacharias as really belonging to demons. In some medieval litanies there were special invocations of S. Fides, S. Spes, S. Charitas. The litanies, as given in the Breviary, are at present appointed to be recited on bended knee, along with the penitential psalms, in all the six week-days of Lent when ordinary service is held. Without the psalms they are said on the feast of Saint Mark and on the three rogation days. A litany is chanted in procession before mass on Holy Saturday. The "litany" or "general supplication" of the Church of England, which is appointed "to be sung or said after morning prayer upon Sundays, Wednesdays and Fridays, and at other times when it shall be commanded by the ordinary," closely follows the "Litaniae majores" of the Breviary, the invocations of saints being of course omitted. [illegible] similar German litany will be found in the works of Luther.

In the Roman Church there are a number of special litanies peculiar to particular localities or orders, such as the "Litanies of Mary" or the "Litanies of the Sacred Name of Jesus."

There was originally a close connexion between the litany and the liturgy (*q.v.*). The ninefold *Kyrie eleison* at the beginning of the Roman Mass is a relic of a longer litany of which a specimen may still be seen in the Stowe missal. In the Ambrosian liturgy, the threefold *Kyrie eleison* or Lesser Litany occurs thrice, after the *Gloria in excelsis*, after the gospel and at the end of Mass; and on the first five Sundays in Lent a missal litany is placed before the *Oratio super populum*, and on the same five Sundays in the Mozarabic rite before the epistle. In Eastern liturgies litanies are a prominent feature, as in the case of the deacon's litany at the beginning of the *Missa fidelium* in the Clementine liturgy, immediately before the *Anaphora* in the Greek liturgy of St James, &c. (F. E. W.)

LITCHFIELD, a township and the county-seat of Litchfield county, Connecticut, U.S.A., about 28 m. W. of Hartford, and including the borough of the same name. Pop. of the township (1890) 3304; (1900) 3214; (1910) 3005; of the borough (1890) 1058; (1900) 1120; (1910) 903. Area of the township, 48.6 sq. m. The borough is served by the New York, New Haven & Hartford railroad. It is situated on elevated land, and is one of the most attractive of southern New England summer resorts. The principal elevation in the township is Mt. Prospect, at the base of which there is a vein of pyrrhotite, with small quantities of nickel and copper. On the southern border of the borough is Lake Bantam (about 900 acres, the largest lake in the state) whose falls, at its outlet, provide water power for factories of carriages and electrical appliances. Dairying is the most important industry, and in 1899 the county ranked first among the counties of the state in the value of its dairy products—$1,373,957, from 3465 farms, the value of the product for the entire state being $7,090,188.

The lands included in the township of Litchfield (originally called Bantam) were bought from the Indians in 1715–1716 for £15, the Indians reserving a certain part for hunting. The township was incorporated in 1719, was named Litchfield, after Lichfield in England, and was settled by immigrants from Hartford, Windsor, Wethersfield, Farmington and Lebanon (all within the state) in 1720–1721. In 1751 it became the county-seat of Litchfield county, and at the same time the borough of Litchfield (incorporated in 1879) was laid out. From 1776 to 1780 two depôts for military stores and a workshop for the Continental army were maintained, and the leaden statue of George III., erected in Bowling Green, New York City, in 1770, and torn down by citizens on the 9th of July 1776, was cut up and taken to Litchfield, where, in the house (still standing) of Oliver Wolcott it was melted into bullets for the American army by Wolcott's daughter and sister. Aaron Burr, whose only sister married Tapping Reeve (1744–1823), lived in Litchfield with Reeve in 1774–1775. In 1784 Reeve established here the Litchfield Law School, the first institution of its kind in America. In 1798 he associated with himself James Gould (1770–1838), who, after Reeve's retirement in 1820, continued the work, with the assistance of Jabez W. Huntington (1788–1847), until 1833. The school was never incorporated, it had no buildings, and the lectures were delivered in the law offices of its instructors, but among its 1000 or more students were many who afterwards became famous, including John C. Calhoun; Levi Woodbury (1789–1851), United States senator from New Hampshire in 1825–1831 and in 1841–1845, secretary of the navy in 1831–1834 and of the treasury in 1834–1841, and a justice of the United States Supreme Court from 1845; John Y. Mason; John M. Clayton; and Henry Baldwin (1780–1844), a justice of the United States Supreme Court from 1830. In 1792 Mrs Sarah Pierce made one of the first efforts toward the higher education of women in the United States by opening in Litchfield her Female Seminary, which had an influential career of about forty years, and numbered among its alumnae Harriet Beecher Stowe, Mrs Marshall O. Roberts, Mrs Cyrus W. Field and Mrs Hugh McCulloch. Litchfield was the birthplace of Ethan Allen; of Henry Ward Beecher; of Harriet Beecher Stowe, whose novel, *Poganuc People*, presents a picture of social conditions in Litchfield during her girlhood; of Oliver Wolcott, Jr. (1760–1833); of John Pierpont (1785–1866), the poet, preacher and lecturer; and of Charles Loring Brace, the philanthropist. It was also the home, during his last years, of Oliver Wolcott (1726–1797); of Colonel Benjamin Tallmadge (1774–1835), an officer on the American side in the War of Independence and later (from 1801 to 1817) a Federalist member of Congress; and of Lyman Beecher, who was pastor of the First Congregational church of Litchfield from 1810 to 1826.

See Payne K. Kilbourne, *Sketches and Chronicles of the Town of Litchfield, Connecticut* (Hartford, Conn., 1859); George C. Boswell, *The Litchfield Book of Days* (Litchfield, 1900); and for an account of the Litchfield Female Seminary, Emily N. Vanderpoel, *Chronicles of a Pioneer School* (Cambridge, Mass., 1903).

LITCHFIELD, a city of Montgomery county, Illinois, U. S. A., about 50 m. N.E. of St Louis, Missouri. Pop. (1900) 5918; (1910) 5971. Its principal importance is as a railway and manufacturing centre; it is served by the Chicago, Burlington & Quincy, the Chicago & Alton, the Cleveland, Cincinnati, Chicago & St Louis, the Illinois Central, the Wabash, and the Litchfield & Madison railways, and by electric lines connecting with St Louis and the neighbouring towns. In the vicinity are deposits of bituminous coal, fire-clay and moulding sand. There are various manufactures in the city. Litchfield was incorporated as a town in 1856, and was first chartered as a city in 1859.

LITCHI, or **Lee-Chee**, the fruit of *Nephelium Litchi*, a small tree, native of southern China and one of the most important indigenous fruits. It is also cultivated in India. The tree bears large compound leaves with two to four pairs of leathery lanceolate pointed leaflets about 3 in. long, and panicles of small flowers without petals. The fruits are commonly roundish, about 1½ in. in diameter, with a thin, brittle, red shell which bears rough protuberances. In the fresh state they are filled with a sweet white pulp which envelops a large brown seed, but in the dried condition the pulp forms a blackish fleshy substance. The pulp is of the nature of an aril, that is, an additional seed-coat.

Nephelium Longana, the longan tree, also a native of southern China, is cultivated in that country, in the Malay Peninsula, India and Ceylon for its fruit, which is smaller than that of the litchi, being half an inch to an inch in diameter with a nearly smooth yellowish-brown brittle skin, and containing a pulpy aril resembling that of the litchi in flavour. Another species, *N. lappaceum*, a tall tree native of the Malay Peninsula, where it is known under the names Rambutan or Ramboosteen, is also cultivated for its pleasantly acid pulpy aril. The fruit is oval, bright red in colour, about 2 in. long and covered with long fleshy hairs.

Nephelium belongs to the natural order Sapindaceae, and contains about twenty-two species.

LITERATURE, a general term which, in default of precise definition, may stand for the best expression of the best thought reduced to writing. Its various forms are the result of race peculiarities, or of diverse individual temperaments, or of political circumstances securing the predominance of one social class which is thus enabled to propagate its ideas and sentiments. In early stages of society, the classes which first attain a distinct literary utterance are priests who compile the chronicles of tribal religious development, or rhapsodes who celebrate the prowess of tribal chiefs. As man feels before he reasons, so poetry generally precedes prose. It embodies more poignantly the sentiment of unsophisticated man. Hence sacred books and war-songs are everywhere the earliest literary monuments, and both are essentially poetic compositions which have received a religious or quasi-religious sanction. The recitation of the Homeric poems at the Panathenaea corresponds to the recitation elsewhere of the sacred texts in the temple; the statement of Phemios (*Odyssey*, xxii. 347) that a god inspired his soul with all the varied ways of song expresses the ordinary belief of early historical times. Versicles of the sacred chronicles, or fragments of epic poems, were learned by heart and supplied a standard of popular literary taste. The public declamation of long chosen passages by priests, and still more by contending rhapsodes, served to evoke the

secular theatre. She never again dominated the literatures of Europe so absolutely.

The literary sceptre passed from France to Italy during the 13th century. Brunetto Latini, who wrote in French as well as in Italian, is the connecting link between the literatures of the two countries; but Italy owes its eminence not so much to a general diffusion of literary accomplishment as to the emergence of three great personalities. Dante, Boccacio and Petrarch created a new art of poetry and of prose. England yielded to the fascination in the person of Chaucer, Spain in the person of her chancellor López de Ayala, and France in the person of Charles d'Orléans, the son of an Italian mother. Petrarch, once ambassador in France, alleged that there were no poets out of Italy, and indeed there were no living poets to compare with him elsewhere. But in all countries he raised up rivals—Chaucer, Marot, Garcilaso de la Vega—as Sannazaro did a century and a half later. Sannazaro's *Arcadia* captured the Portuguese Montemôr, whose pastoral novel the *Diana*, written in Spanish, inspired d'Urfé no less than Sidney, and, as d'Urfé's *Astrée* is considered the starting-point of the modern French novel, the historical importance of the Italian original cannot be exaggerated. Spain never obtained any intellectual predominance corresponding to that exercised by France and Italy, or to her political authority during the 16th and 17th centuries. This may be attributed partly to her geographical position which lies off the main roads of Europe, and partly to the fact that her literature is essentially local. Cervantes, indeed, may be said to have influenced all subsequent writers of fiction, and the influence of Spanish literature is visible in the body of European picaresque tales; but, apart from Corneille and a few other dramatists who preceded Molière in France, and apart from the Restoration drama in England, the influence of the Spanish drama was relatively small. In some respects it was too original to be imitated with success. Much the same may be said of England as of Spain. Like Spain, she lies outside the sphere of continental influence; like Spain, she has innumerable great names in every province of literature, and, in both cases, to Europe at large these long remained names and nothing more; like Spain, she is prone to reproduce borrowed materials in shapes so transformed and rigid as to be unrecognizable and unadaptable. Moreover, the Reformation isolated England from literary commerce with the Latin races, and till the 18th century Germany was little more than a geographical expression. Even when Germany recovered her literary independence, Lessing first heard of Shakespeare through Voltaire. Neither Shakespeare nor Milton was read in France before the 18th century—the first translated by Ducis, the second by Dupré de Saint-Maur—and they were read with curiosity rather than with rapture. On the other hand, Boileau, Rapin and Le Bossu were regarded as oracles in England, and through them French literature produced the "correctness" of Queen Anne's reign. Horace Walpole is half a Frenchman, Hume imitates Montesquieu's cold lucidity, Gibbon adapts Bossuet's majestic periods to other purposes. On the other hand Voltaire takes ideas from Locke, but his form is always intensely personal and inimitably French. After the 16th century English literature, as a whole, is refractory to external influence. Waves of enthusiasm pass over England—for Rousseau, for Goethe—but leave no abiding trace on English literature. During the latter half of the 18th century France resumed something of her old literary supremacy; the literatures of Italy and Spain at this period are purely derivative, and French influence was extended still further on the continent as the result of the Romantic movement. Since that impulse was exhausted, literature everywhere has been in a state of flux; it is less national, and yet fails to be cosmopolitan. All writers of importance, and many of no importance, are translated into other European languages; the quick succession of diverse and violent impressions has confused the scheme of literature. Literature suffers likewise from the competition [illegible] newspaper press, and as the press has multiplied it has [illegible] less literary. The diversities of modern interests, the [illegible] leisure for concentrated thought, suggest that literature may become once more the pleasure of a small caste. But the desire for the one just form which always inspires the literary artist visits most men sometimes, and it cannot be doubted that literature will continue to accommodate itself to new conditions. (J. F. K.)

LITERNUM, an ancient town of Campania, Italy, on the low sandy coast between Cumae and the mouth of the Volturnus. It was probably once dependent on Cumae. In 194 B.C. it became a Roman colony It is mainly famous as the residence of the elder Scipio, who withdrew from Rome and died here. His tomb and villa are described by Seneca. Augustus is said to have conducted here a colony of veterans,[1] but the place never had any great importance, and the lagoons behind it made it unhealthy, though the construction of the Via Domitiana through it must have made it a posting station. It ceased to exist in the 8th century. No remains are visible.

See J. Beloch, *Campanien*, ed. ii. (Breslau, 1890), 377.

LITHGOW, WILLIAM (1582–? 1650), Scottish traveller and writer, was born and educated in Lanark. He was caught in a love-adventure, mutilated of his ears by the brothers of the lady (hence the sobriquet "Cut-lugged Willie"), and forced to leave Scotland. For nineteen years he travelled, mostly on foot, through Europe, the Levant, Egypt and northern Africa, covering, according to his estimate, over 36,000 m. The story of his adventures may be drawn from *The Totall Discourse of the Rare Adventures and painfull Peregrinations of long nineteene Yeares* (London, 1614; fuller edition, 1632, &c.); *A True and Experimentall Discourse upon the last siege of Breda* (London, 1637); and a similar book giving an account of the siege of Newcastle and the battle of Marston Moor (Edinburgh, 1645). He is the author of a *Present Surveigh of London* (London, 1643). He left six poems, written between 1618 and 1640 (reprinted by Maidment, Edinburgh, 1863). Of these "Scotland's Welcome to King Charles, 1633" has considerable antiquarian interest. His writing has no literary merit; but its excessively aureate style deserves notice.

The best account of Lithgow and his works is by F. Hindes Groome in the *Dict. Nat. Biog.* The piece entitled *Scotland's Paraenesis to King Charles II.* (1660), ascribed to him in the catalogue of the Advocates' Library, Edinburgh, cannot, from internal evidence, be his.

LITHGOW, a town of Cook county, New South Wales, Australia, 96 m. W.N.W. of Sydney by rail. Pop. (1901) 5268. The town is situated at an altitude of 3000 ft., in a valley of the Blue Mountains. It has pottery and terra-cotta works, breweries, a tweed factory, iron-works, saw-mills, soap-works and brickfields. Coal, kerosene shale, iron ore and building stone are found in the district.

LITHIUM [symbol Li, atomic weight 7·00 (O=16)], an alkali metal, discovered in 1817 by J. A. Arfvedson (*Ann. chim. phys.* 10, p. 82). It is only found in combination, and is a constituent of the minerals petalite, triphyline, spodumene and lepidolite or lithia mica. It occurs in small quantities in sea, river and spring water, and is also widely but very sparingly distributed throughout the vegetable kingdom. It may be obtained (in the form of its chloride) by fusing lepidolite with a mixture of barium carbonate and sulphate, and potassium sulphate (L. Troost, *Comptes rendus*, 1856, 43, p. 921). The fused mass separates into two layers, the upper of which contains a mixture of potassium and lithium sulphates; this is lixiviated with water and converted into the mixed chlorides by adding barium chloride, the solution evaporated and the lithium chloride extracted by a mixture of dry alcohol and ether. The metal may be obtained by heating dry lithium hydroxide with magnesium (H. N. Warren, *Chem. News*, 1896, 74, p. 6). L. Kahlenberg (*Jour. phys. Chem.*, 3, p. 601) obtained it by electrolysing the chloride in pyridine solution, a carbon anode and an iron or platinum cathode being used. O. Ruff and O. Johannsen (*Zeit. elektrochem.*, 1906, 55, p. 537) electrolyse a mixture of bromide and chloride which melts at 520°. It is a soft, silvery-white metal, which readily tarnishes on exposure. Its specific gravity is 0·59, and it melts at 180° C. It burns on ignition in air, and when strongly heated in an atmosphere of nitrogen it forms lithium nitride, Li_3N. It decomposes water at ordinary temperature, liberating hydrogen and forming lithium hydroxide.

Lithium hydride, LiH, obtained by heating the metal in a current of hydrogen at a red heat, or by heating the metal with ethylene to 700° C. (M. Guntz, *Comptes rendus*, 1896, 122, p. 244; 123, p. 1273), is a white solid which inflames when heated in chlorine. With alcohol it forms lithium ethylate, $LiOC_2H_5$, with liberation of hydrogen. *Lithium oxide*, Li_2O, is obtained by burning the metal in oxygen, or by ignition of the nitrate. It is a white powder which readily dissolves in water to form the *hydroxide*, LiOH, which is also obtained by boiling the carbonate with milk of lime. It forms a white caustic mass, resembling sodium hydroxide in appearance. It absorbs carbon dioxide, but is not deliquescent. *Lithium chloride* LiCl, prepared by heating the metal in chlorine, or by dissolving the oxide or carbonate in hydrochloric acid, is exceedingly deliquescent, melts below a red heat, and is very soluble in alcohol. *Lithium carbonate*, Li_2CO_3, obtained as a white amorphous precipitate by adding sodium carbonate to a solution of lithium chloride, is sparingly soluble in water. *Lithium phosphate*, Li_3PO_4, obtained by the addition of sodium phosphate to a soluble lithium salt in the presence of sodium hydroxide, is almost insoluble in water. *Lithium ammonium*, $LiNH_3$, is obtained by passing ammonia gas over lithium, the product being heated to 70° C. in order to expel any excess of ammonia. It turns brown-red on exposure to air, and is inflammable. It is decomposed by water evolving hydrogen, and when heated *in vacuo* at 50°–60° C. it gives lithium and ammonia. With ammonia solution it gives hydrogen and *lithiamide*, $LiNH_2$ (H. Moissan, *ibid.*, 1898, 127, p. 685). *Lithium carbide*, Li_2C_2, obtained by heating lithium carbonate and carbon in the electric furnace, forms a transparent crystalline mass of specific gravity 1·65, and is readily decomposed by cold water giving acetylene (H. Moissan, *ibid.*, 1896, 122, p. 362).

Lithium is detected by the faint yellow line of wave-length 6104, and the bright red line of wave-length 6708, shown in its flame spectrum. It may be distinguished from sodium and potassium by the sparing solubility of its carbonate and phosphate. The atomic weight of lithium was determined by J. S. Stas from the analysis of the chloride, and also by conversion of the chloride into the nitrate, the value obtained being 7·03 (O=16).

The preparations of lithium used in medicine are: *Lithii Carbonis*, dose 2 to 5 grs.; *Lithii Citras*, dose 5 to 10 grs.; and *Lithii Citras effervescens*, a mixture of citric acid, lithium citrate, tartaric acid and sodium bicarbonate, dose 60 to 120 grs. Lithium salts render the urine alkaline and are in virtue of their action diuretic. They are much prescribed for acute or chronic gout, and as a solvent to uric acid calculi or gravel, but their action as a solvent of uric acid has been certainly overrated, as it has been shown that the addition of medicinal doses of lithium to the blood serum does not increase the solubility of uric acid in it. In concentrated or large doses lithium salts cause vomiting and diarrhoea, due to a gastro-enteritis set up by their action. In medicinal use they should therefore be always freely diluted.

LITHOGRAPHY (Gr. λίθος, a stone, and γράφειν, to write), the process of drawing or laying down a design or transfer, on a specially prepared stone or other suitable surface, in such a way that impressions may be taken therefrom. The principle on which lithography is based is the antagonism of grease and water. A chemically pure surface having been secured on some substance that has an equal affinity for both grease and water, in a method hereafter to be described, the parts intended to print are covered with an unctuous composition and the rest of the surface is moistened, so that when a greasy roller is applied, the portion that is wet resists the grease and that in which an affinity for grease has been set up readily accepts it; and from the surface thus treated it will be seen that it is an easy thing to secure an impression on paper or other material by applying suitable pressure.

The inventor of lithography was Alois Senefelder (1771–1834); and it is remarkable what a grip he at once seemed to get of his invention, for whereas the invention of printing seems almost a matter of evolution, lithography seems to come upon the scene fully equipped for the battle of life, so that it would be a bold craftsman at the present day who would affirm that he knew more of the principles underlying his trade than Senefelder (*q.v.*) did within thirty years of its invention. Of course practice has led to dexterity, and the great volume of trade has induced many mechanical improvements and facilities, but the principles have not been taken any further, while some valuable methods

[1] Mommsen in *C.I.L.* x. 343 does not accept this statement, but an inscription found in 1885 confirms it.

have been allowed to fall into desuetude and would well repay greater experimental diligence tending to revive.

Lithography may be divided into two main branches—that which is drawn with a greasy crayon (rather illogically called "chalk") on a grained stone, and that which is drawn in ink on a polished stone. Whatever may be thought in respect of the original work of the artists of various countries who have used lithography as a means of expression, there is no doubt that in the former method the English professional lithographer has always held the pre-eminence, while in the latter French and American artists have surpassed them in skill.

Chalk lithography subdivides itself into work in which the black is predominant, although it may be supported by 5 or 6 tints of a subdued colour—this branch is known as "black and tint" work, and that in which the black is only used exactly like any other colour. Frequently this latter class of work will require a dozen or more colours, while some of the finest examples have had some twenty to thirty stones employed on them. Work of this description is known as chromo-lithography. Each colour requires a separate stone, and work of the highest quality may want two or three blues with yellows, pinks, greens and browns in proportion, if it is desired to secure a result that is an approximate rendering of the original painting or drawing. The question may perhaps be asked: "If the well-known three-colour process" (see PROCESS) "can give the full result of the artist's palette, why should it take so many more colours in lithography to secure the same result?" The answer is that the stone practically gives but three gradations—the solid, the half tint and the quarter tint, so that the combination of three very carefully prepared stones will give a very limited number of combinations, while a moderate estimate of the shades on a toned block would be six; so that a very simple mathematical problem will show the far greater number of combinations that the three blocks will give. Beyond this, the chromo-lithographer has to exercise very great powers of colour analysis; but the human mind is quite unable to settle offhand the exact proportion of red, blue and yellow necessary to produce some particular class say of grey, and this the camera with the aid of colour filters does with almost perfect precision.

Notwithstanding these disadvantages, lithography has these strong points. (1) its utility for small editions on account of its, at present, smaller prime cost; (2) its suitability for subjects of large size, (3) its superiority for subjects with outlines, for in such cases the outline can be done in one colour, whereas to secure this effect by the admixture of the three colours requires marvellously good registration, the absence of which would produce a very large proportion of "waste" or faulty copies; (4) capacity for printing on almost any paper, whereas, at the time of writing, the tri-colour process is almost entirely limited to printing on coated papers that are very heavy and not very enduring.

With regard to the two branches of chalk lithography, the firms that maintained the English supremacy for black and tint work in the early days were Hulemandel, Day and Haghe and Maclure, while the best chromo-lithographic work in the same period was done by Vincent Brooks, the brothers Hanhart, Thomas Kell and F. Kell. In reference to the personal work of professed lithographers during the same period, the names of Louis Haghe, J. D. Harding, J. Needham, C. Baugniet, L. Ghemar, William Simpson, R. J. Lane, J. H. Lynch, A. Maclure and Rimanozcy stand for black and tint work; while in chromo-lithography J. M. Carrick, C. Risdon, William Bunney, W. Long, Samuel Hodson, Edwin Buckman and J. Lewis have been conspicuous among those who have maintained the standard of their craft. In the foregoing list will be recognized the names of several who have had admirable works on the walls of the Royal Academy and other exhibitions; Mr Lane, who exhibited lithographs from 1824 to 1872, was for many years the doyen of lithographers, and the only one of their number to attain academic rank, but Lynch and John Cardwell Bacon were his pupils, and Bacon's son, the painter John H. F. Bacon, was elected to the Royal Academy in 1903. In the first decade of the 20th century the number of firms doing high-class work, and the artists who aided them in doing it, were more numerous than ever, and scarcely less able, but it would be outside the present purpose to differentiate between them.

The *raison d'être* of "stipple" work is its capacity for re-transferring without serious loss of quality, for it can scarcely be contended that it is as artistic as the methods just described. Retransferring is the process of pulling impressions from the original stones with a view to making up a large sheet of one or more small subjects, or where it is desired to print a very large number without deterioration of the original or matrix stone. The higher class work in this direction has been done in France, Germany and the United States, where for many years superiority has been shown in regard to the excellence and rapidity of retransferring. To this cause may be attributed the fact that the box tops and Christmas cards on the English market were so largely done abroad until quite recent times. The work of producing even a small face in the finest hand stipple is a lengthy and tedious affair, and the English craftsman has seldom shown the patience necessary for this work; but since the American invention known as Ben Day's shading medium was introduced into England the trade has largely taken it up, and thereby much of the tedium has been avoided, so that it has been found possible by its means to introduce a freedom into stipple work that had not before been found possible, and a very much better class of work has since been produced in this department.

About the year 1868 grained paper was invented by Maclure, Macdonald & Co. This method consists in impressing on ordinary Scotch transfer or other suitable paper a grain closely allied to that of the lithographic stone. It appears to have been rather an improvement than a new invention, for drawing paper and even canvas had been coated previously with a material that adhered to a stone and left on the stone the greasy drawing that had been placed thereon; but still from this to the beautifully prepared paper that was placed on the market by the firm of which the late Andrew Maclure was the head was a great advance, and although the first use was by the ordinary craftsman it was not long before artists of eminence saw that a new and convenient mode of expression was opened up to them.

On the first introduction of lithography the artists of every nation hastened to avail themselves of it, but soon the cumbrous character of the stone, and the fact that their subjects had to be drawn backwards in order that they might appear correctly on the paper, wore down their newly-born zeal, and it was only when the grained paper system was perfected, by which they could make their drawings in the comfort of their studios without reversing, that any serious revival took place. Although excellent work on grained paper had been done by Andrew Maclure, Rimanozcy, John Cardwell Bacon, Rudofsky and other craftsmen, the credit for its furtherance among artists must be given to Thomas Way and his son T. R. Way, who did much valuable pioneer work in this direction. The adhesion of such artists of eminence as Whistler, Legros, Frank Short, Charles Shannon, Fantin Latour, William Strang, Will Rothenstein, Herbert Railton and Joseph Pennell, did not a little to aid lithography in resisting the encroachments of other methods into what may still be considered its sphere. As a means of reproducing effects which an artist would otherwise get by pencil or crayon, it remains entirely unequalled, and it is of obvious advantage to art that twenty-five or fifty copies of an original work should exist, which, without the aid of lithography, might have only been represented by a single sketch, perhaps stowed away among the possessions of one private collector.

In regard to grained paper work, undue stress has often been placed upon the rapid deterioration of the stone, some contending that only a few dozen first-class proofs can be taken; this has led to the feeling that it is unsuited to book illustration, and damage has been done to the trade of lithography thereby. It may be mentioned that quite recently about 100 auto-lithographs in black and three colours, the combined work of Mr and

Mrs Herbert Railton, have been treated by the Eberle system of etching described below, and although an infinitesimal loss of quality may have arisen, such as occurs when a copper etching is steel faced, some 2000 to 3000 copies were printed without further deterioration, and an edition of vignetted sketches was secured, far in advance of anything that could have been attained from the usual screen or half-toned blocks.

Grained paper is much used in the ordinary lithographic studio for work such as the hill shading of maps that can be done without much working up, but the velvety effects that in the hands of Louis Haghe and his contemporaries were so conspicuous, cannot be secured by this method. The effects referred to were obtained by much patient work of a "tinter," who practically laid a ground on which the more experienced and artistic craftsman did his work either by scraping or accentuation Where fine rich blacks are needed, artists will do well to read the notes on the "aquatint" and "wash" methods described by Senefelder in his well-known treatise, and afterwards practised with great skill by Hulemandel

Lithography is of great service in educational matters, as its use for diagrams, wall pictures and maps is very general, nor does the influence end with schooldays, for in the form of pictures at a moderate price it brings art into homes and lives that need brightening, and even in the form of posters on the much-abused hoardings does something for those who have to spend much of their time in the streets of great cities

According to the census of 1901, 14,686 people in the United Kingdom found their occupation within the trade, while according to a Home Office return (1906), 20,367 persons other than lithographic printers were employed by the firms carrying on the business. As it may be assumed that an equal number are employed in France, Germany, the United States of America and the world at large, it is clear that a vast industrial army is employed in a trade that, like letterpress printing, has a very beneficial influence upon those engaged in it.

Technical Details.—The following description of the various methods of lithography is such as may be considered of interest to the general reader, but the serious student who will require formulas and more precise directions will do well to consult one of the numerous text-books on the subject.

Stone and Stone Substitutes.—The quality of stone first used by Alois Senefelder, and discovered by him at the village of Solenhofen in Bavaria, still remains unsurpassed. This deposit, which covers a very large area and underlies the villages of Solenhofen, Moernsheim and Langenaltheim, has often been described, sometimes for interested motives, as nearly exhausted; but a visit in 1906 revealed that the output—considerable as it had been during a period little short of a century—was very unimportant when compared to the great mass of carbonaceous limestone existing in the neighbourhood. The strong point in favour of this source of supply, in addition to its unrivalled quality, is the evenness of its stratification, and the fact that after the removal of the surface deposits, which are very thin, the stones come out of large size, in thickness of 3 to 5 in., and thus just suited for lithographic purposes and needing only to be wrought in the vertical direction. Other deposits of suitable stone have been found in France, Spain, Italy and Greece, but transit and the absence of suitable stratification have restricted them to little more than local use. Beyond this, few of the deposits other than in the neighbourhood of Solenhofen have been of the exact degree of density necessary, and the heavier varieties do not receive the grease with sufficient readiness. The desire to find other sources of supply has been stimulated by the social conditions existing in southern Bavaria, for the quarries are largely owned by peasant proprietors, who have very well-defined business habits of their own which make transactions difficult. Among other things, they will seldom supply the highest grades and the largest sizes to those who will not take their proportion of lower quality and smaller sizes; and this, in view of the very expensive transit down the Rhine to Rotterdam, with a railway journey at one end and a sea journey at the other, is a source of difficulty to the importer in other countries.

The earliest substitute for lithographic stone was zinc, which has been used from early days and is now more in demand than ever; it requires very careful printing as the grease only penetrates the material to a very slight extent, and the same must be said in regard to the water. From this cause, when not in experienced hands, trouble is likely to arise; and when this has occurred, remedial methods are much more difficult than with stones. When put away for storage, a dry place is very essential, as corrosion is easily set up. At first the plates were quite thick, and almost invariably grained by a zinc "muller" and acid; now a bath of acid is more generally used, and the operation is known as "passing," while the plates are quite thin, which renders them suitable for bending round the cylinders of rotary machines.

So far we have been dealing with plain zinc, but variations are caused, either by the oxidization of the surface or by coating the plate with a composition closely allied to lithographic stone and applied in a form of semi-solution This class of plate was first invented by Messrs C & E. Layton, and a modification was invented by Messrs Wezel and Naumann of Leipzig, who brought its use to a high pitch of perfection for transferred work such as Christmas cards. A treatment of iron plates by exposing them to a high temperature has recently been patented, and has had some measure of success, while the Parker printing plate, which is practically a sheet of zinc so treated as to secure greater porosity and freedom from oxidization, is rapidly securing a good position as a stone substitute.

Preparation of the Stones.—In this department the cleanliness so necessary right through the lithographic process must be carefully observed, and a leading point is to secure a level surface and to ensure that the front and back of the stone are strictly parallel, *i.e.* that the stones stand the test of both the straight edge and the callipers. A good plan to ensure evenness on the surface is to mark the front with two diagonal lines of some non-greasy substance till the top stone (which should not be too small, and should be constantly revolved on the larger one) has entirely removed them. The application of the straight edge from time to time will end in securing the desired flatness, on which so much of the future printing quality depends. The usual method is to rub out with sand, and then rub with pumice and polish with water of Ayr or snake stone. For chalk work, the further work of graining has to be done by revolving a small stone muller on the surface with exceedingly fine sand or powdered glass. Many appliances (some very expensive) have been devised for doing the principal part of this work by machine—none more effective than those methods by which a disk of about 12 in. is kept revolving on a rod attached to the ceiling, guided by hand over all parts of the stone but for large surfaces the ceiling needs to be rather high so as to allow of a long expanding rod reaching the surface at a moderate angle When this machine is fitted with friction disk driving, very wide variations of speed are possible, and the machine can be driven so slowly and evenly as to secure a very fair (but not first class) grain, in addition to speedy rubbing out, which is the chief aim of the apparatus.

Preparing a Subject in Chalk or Chalk and Tints.—This branch of work is much less in demand than formerly. A grey stone having been selected and finely grained with sand or powdered glass passed through a sieve of 80 to 120 meshes to the lineal inch, and the artist having made his tracing, this tracing is reversed upon the stone with the interposition of a piece of paper coated with red chalk, and the chalk side towards the surface; the lines on the tracing are then gone over with a tracing point, so that a reproduction in red chalk is left upon the stone It will then be desirable to secure a stock of pointed Lemercier chalks of at least two grades, hard and soft: the pointing is a matter that requires experience, and is done by the worker drawing a sharp pen-knife towards him in a slicing manner as though trying to put a point upon a piece of cheese. Care should be taken that the falling pieces are gathered into a box, or they may do irreparable mischief to the work. The work of outlining is done with No. 1 or hard chalk, and until experience is gained it will be well to depend chiefly on this grade, securing rich dark effects by tinting or going over the stone in various directions and then finishing with lithographic ink where absolute blacks are required. This ink (Vanhymbeck's or Lemercier's are two good makes) needs careful preparation, the method being to warm a saucer and rub the ink dry upon it, then add a little distilled water and incorporate with the finger It is of great importance not to use any ink left over for the next day, but always to have a fresh daily supply.

When the drawing is thus completed, it will require what is termed etching, by which the parts intended to receive the printing ink, and already protected by an acid-resisting grease, will be left above the unprotected surface. The acid and gum mixture varies in accordance with the quality of the work and the character of the stone. A patiently executed specimen will, for instance, stand more etching than a hastily drawn one; while a grey stone will require more of the nitric acid than a yellow one. This is one of the most important tasks that a lithographer has to perform. A proportion of 1·5 parts of acid to 100 parts of a strong solution of gum arabic will be found to be approximately what is required, but the exact proportion must be settled by experience, a safe course being to watch the action that occurs when a small quantity is placed on the unused margin of the stone. Many put the etching mixture on with a flat camel-hair brush, which should be of good width to avoid streaks. The present writer's own preference is to pour the mixture on to the stone when it is in a slanting position; or it is perhaps better to have an etching trough, a strong box lined with pitch, with bearers at the bottom to prevent the stone coming in contact with it, and a hole through which the diluted acid may pass away for subsequent use. The etching is then done with acid and water poured over the stone while in a sloping position, and the subsequent pouring of a solution of gum arabic completes the preparation. The late Mr William Simpson, whose Crimean lithographs are well known, once stated at the Society of Arts that in his opinion Mr Louis Haghe's reproduction [illegible] of "The Taking of Jerusalem" was [illegible] lithographs ever executed, and [illegible] two years to execute it. And [illegible] Messrs Day & Haghe's establishment [illegible] that, notwithstanding every [illegible] and that after half a dozen [illegible] of the work had departed [illegible] the [illegible] nature of this part of

[illegible] tints it will be necessary to make [illegible] colours to be used, in this class [illegible] warm or sandy shade and [illegible] with the black and the neutral [illegible] of the two shades, give an [illegible] in Belgium may be taken

[illegible] printing in the [illegible] of a good "rag" quality, free [illegible]. To secure accuracy of [illegible] both to prevent the edges [illegible] suitable for each of the [illegible] the printing may be com[illegible] might be printed of [illegible] rendering the prints

[illegible] this purpose the proceedings [illegible] the black and tint work, [illegible] in lithographic ink on [illegible] completion, the lines being [illegible] and will be used as a "key," [illegible] and the number of stones [illegible] or four. The natural point [illegible] the outline printed from it, [illegible] proving and before printing. [illegible] or posters will be [illegible] handbills or labels, [illegible] stones. For the former class [illegible] but many of these are [illegible] that arises makes it de[illegible] is contemplated. There[illegible] stumping, wash, air brush, are [illegible] work that has to be transferred [illegible] on a polished stone with the [illegible] and ink "spluttered" on to [illegible]. It should be mentioned that work [illegible] for retransfer than ordinary [illegible] when a chalk effect is desired [illegible] opaque colours will be got on [illegible] plan to put the black on early, [illegible] and the strength [illegible] should generally be used sparingly [illegible] opaque colours which should [illegible] pull impressions of each colour on [illegible] this in important work there [illegible] that will show how the work [illegible] were on. For this may at the [illegible] error has crept in, and in any [illegible]

[illegible] made of rag or rag and esparto [illegible] grained stones, but for work in ink [illegible] stone a good coated paper with [illegible] desirable, this paper is generally

[illegible] very little encouragement for the high [illegible] was so much in evidence from 1885 [illegible] that the work could be done equally [illegible] the demand revived. Belonging [illegible] examples of chromo litho[illegible] after Turner, by Carrick, "Spanish [illegible] portrait of Shakespeare, by Risdon, [illegible]" by W. Bunney, after John [illegible] after John Leech, produced [illegible] Vincent Brooks. A small proportion [illegible] were executed in England, but [illegible] after Birket Foster, Richardson, [illegible] by Samuel Hodson, James [illegible] most consistently good work of [illegible] of Pellegrini's and [illegible] which from 1870 to 1900 were [illegible] by the firm of Vincent Brooks,

[illegible] work is got on to the stone [illegible] important part of the business [illegible] is so much original litho[illegible] of entirety, the trans[illegible] most important. The stone [illegible] neither a grey nor a light [illegible] between the two, it should be [illegible] free from scratches and [illegible] heated in an iron cupboard prepared with the necessary apparatus. The methods that sometimes prevail of pouring boiling water over the stone, heating with the flame of an ordinary plumber's lamp, or even heating the surface in front of a fire, are ineffective substitutes, for the surface may thus become unduly hot and spread the work, and there is no increased tendency for the chalk to enter into the stone and thus give the work a long life. If there are no colours or registration trouble to be considered, it is well to place the transfer in a damping book till the composition adheres firmly to the finger, before placing it on the stone, it should then be pulled through twice, after which it should be damped on the back and pulled through several times, after this has again been well damped the paper will be found to peel easily off the stone, leaving the work and nearly all the composition attached, the latter should then be very gently washed away.

In cases where the work for some reason must not stretch, such as the hills on a map, it will be necessary to keep the transfer dry and put it on a wet stone but a piece of the margin of the paper should be tested to see that it is of a class that will adhere to the stone the first time it is pulled through. Unless the adhesion is very complete it may not be safe to pull it through more than once. For a small number of copies a very moderate "etch" is desirable, but for a long run, where the object is to secure a good edition rather than a few good proofs, the Eberle system may be adopted. This method consists in protecting the work with finely powdered resin and then applying the flame of an ordinary plumber's lamp, this will melt the protecting medium round the base of each grain of work and allow of a very vigorous "etch" being applied. As before stated it is not unusual to secure 2000 to 3000 good copies in the machine after this treatment, but the rollers, the ink and the superintendence must be of the best.

When the artist who is not a professed lithographer desires to make tints to his work, a reversed offset on grained paper should be made for each colour, this is done by pulling an impression in the usual way on a hard piece of paper, and while it is yet wet this should be faced with a piece of grained paper and pulled through again, when the grained paper will be found to have received the greater portion of the ink, this should be immediately dusted with offset powder of a red shade to prevent the grease passing into the paper and the drawing of the tints should then be proceeded with in the usual way. Another method of transfer work is to pull impressions from copper or steel plates in transfer ink, it is in such way that simple etchings like those of Cruikshank, Phiz and others are produced, and nearly all commercial work such as maps, bill heads, &c., are prepared in the same manner.

Beyond this, much work is done in lithographic ink on what is called writing transfer paper, such as circulars, law writing for abstracts, specifications and plans.

Machinery.—The chief items are the hand presses and the machines, whether flat bed or rotary, the principal places of manufacture being Leeds, Otley and Edinburgh. Stimulated by American competition the standard of excellence in the United Kingdom has been very considerably raised of late years. The rotary machines have only been possible since the more frequent use of aluminium and zinc, but these materials are more suitable to receive transfer than for the general use of an office, the chief reason being that corrections on stone are more easily accomplished and more lasting when done. Preliminary work is therefore frequently done on the stone and transferred to plates for the machine.

The question is very frequently asked as to how the necessary registration of the colours is secured; it may be stated for the benefit of the amateur that in hand printing this is generally done by pricking with a pair of needles through printed marks present on each stone, but in the machine this has been done in different ways, although in quite early days "pointing" or "needling" was done even on the machine. On modern machines the registration depends on the accurate cutting of the edge of the paper, of which at least one corner must be an absolute right angle. The paper is then laid on a sloping board in such a way that the longest of the two true edges gravitates into the gripper of the machine, the stops of which move slightly forward as the gripper closes; simultaneously what is called the "side lay" moves forward automatically to a given extent, and in this way at the critical moment the sheet is always in the same position in regard to the stone, which has already been firmly secured in the bed of the machine.

Quite recently a new method has come into use that is probably destined to be a great aid to the craft in its competition with other methods. This is known as offset printing, it is more a matter of evolution than invention, and proceeds from the method adopted in tin plate decoration so much used for box-making and lasting forms of advertisement. It consists in bringing a sheet of rubber into contact with the charged stone and then setting-off the impression so obtained upon card, paper, pegamoid, cloth or other material, the elasticity of the rubber making it possible to print upon rough surfaces that have been previously unsuited to lithographic printing. Both flat bed and rotary machines are available for this system, the latter being restricted to zinc or aluminium plates, but giving a high speed, while the former can use both stones and metal plates and may be more effective for the highest grade of colour work; by both classes of machines the finest embossed note headings can be printed on rough paper, and colour work that has for so long been confined to coated or burnished papers will be available on surfaces such as the artists themselves use.

The following treatises may be referred to with advantage by those in search of more detailed information: *A Complete Course of Lithography*, by Alois Senefelder (R. Ackermann, London, 1819); *The Grammar of Lithography*, by W. D. Richmond (13th edition, E. Menken, London); *Handbook of Lithography*, by David Cumming (London, A. & C. Black). The first of these will only be found in libraries of importance; the others are present-day text-books.

(F. V. B.)

LITHOSPHERE (Gr. λίθος, a stone, and *σφαῖρα*, a sphere), the crust of the earth surrounding the earth's nucleus. The superficial soil, a layer of loose earthy material from a few feet to a few hundreds of feet in thickness, lies upon a zone of hard rock many thousands of feet in thickness but varying in character, and composed mainly of sandstones, shales, clays, limestones and metamorphic rocks. These two layers form the lithosphere. All the tectonic movements of the solid nucleus produce changes in the mobile lithosphere. Volcanic and seismic activity is manifested, mountains are folded, levels change, fresh surfaces are exposed to denudation, erosion and deposition. The crust is thus subject to constant change while retaining its more or less permanent character.

LITHUANIANS and **LETTS**, two kindred peoples of Indo-European origin, which inhabit several western provinces of Russia and the north-eastern parts of Poland and Prussia, on the shores of the Baltic Sea, and in the basins of the Niemen and of the Duna. Large colonies of Lithuanian and Lettic emigrants have been established in the United States. The two races number about 3,500,000, of whom 1,300,000 are Letts. Little is known about their origin, and nothing about the time of their appearance in the country they now inhabit. Ptolemy mentions (iii. 5) two clans, the Galindae and Sudeni, who probably belonged to the western subdivision of this racial group, the Borussians. In the 10th century the Lithuanians were already known under the name of Litva, and, together with two other branches of the same stem—the Borussians and the Letts—they occupied the south-eastern coast of the Baltic Sea from the Vistula to the Duna, extending north-east towards the Lakes Vierzi-järvi and Peipus, south-east to the watershed between the affluents of the Baltic and those of the Black Sea, and south to the middle course of the Vistula (Brest Litovsk)—a tract bounded by Finnish tribes in the north, and by Slavs elsewhere.

Inhabiting a forested, marshy country the Lithuanians have been able to maintain their national character, notwithstanding the vicissitudes of their history. Their chief priest, *Krive-Kriveyto* (the judge of the judges), under whom were seventeen classes of priests and elders, worshipped in the forests; the Waidelots brought their offerings to the divinities at the foot of oaks; even now, the veneration of great oaks is a widely spread custom in the villages of the Lithuanians, and even of the Letts.

Even in the 10th century the Lithuanian stem was divided into three main branches:—the *Borussians* or *Prussians*; the *Letts* (who call themselves *Latvis*, whilst the name under which they are known in Russian chronicles, *Letygola*, is an abbreviation of *Latvin-galas*, "the confines of Lithuania"); and the *Lithuanians*, or rather *Lituanians*, *Litva* or *Letuvininkai*,—these last being subdivided into Lithuanians proper, and *Zhmud'* (*Zmuds*, *Samogitians* or *Zemailey*), the "Lowlanders." To these main branches must be added the *Yatvyags*, or *Yadsvings*, a warlike, black-haired people who inhabited the forests at the upper tributaries of the Niemen and Bug, and the survivors of whom are easily distinguishable as a mixture with White-Russians and Mazurs in some parts of Grodno, Plotsk, Lomza and Warsaw. Nestor's chronicle distinguishes also the *Zhemgala*, who later became known under the name of *Semigallia*, and in the 10th century inhabited the left bank of the Duna. Several authors consider also as Lithuanians the *Kors* of Russian chronicles, or *Courons* of Western authors, who inhabited the peninsula of Courland, and the *Golad*, a clan settled on the banks of the Porotva, tributary of the Moskva river, which seems to have been thrown far from the main stem during its migration to the north. The *Krivichi*, who inhabited what is now the government of Smolensk, seem to belong to the same stem. Their name recalls the Krive-Kriveyto, and their ethnological features recall the Lithuanians; but they are now as much Slavonic as Lithuanian.

All these peoples are only ethnographical subdivisions, and each of them was subdivided into numerous independent clans and villages, separated from one another by forests and marshes; they had no towns or fortified places. The Lithuanian territory thus lay open to foreign invasions, and the Russians as well as the German crusaders availed themselves of the opportunity. The Borussians soon fell under the dominion of Germans, and ceased to constitute a separate nationality, leaving only their name to the state which later became Prussia. The Letts were driven farther to the north, mixing there with Livs and Ehsts, and fell under the dominion of the Livonian order. Only the Lithuanians proper, together with Samogitians, succeeded in forming an independent state. The early history of this state is imperfectly known. During the continuous petty war carried on against Slavonic invasions, the military chief of one of the clans, Ryngold, acquired, in the first half of the 13th century, a certain preponderance over other clans of Lithuania and Black Russia (Yatvyags), as well as over the republics of Red Russia. At this time, the invasions of the Livonian order becoming more frequent, and always extending southward, there was a general feeling of the necessity of some organization to resist them, and Ryngold's son, Mendowg, availed himself of this opportunity to pursue the policy of his father. He made different concessions to the order, ceded to it several parts of Lithuania, and even agreed to be baptized, in 1250, at Novograd Litovsk, receiving in exchange a crown from Innocent IV., with which he was crowned king of Lithuanians. He also ceded the whole of Lithuania to the order in case he should die without leaving offspring. But he had accepted Christianity only to increase his influence among other clans; and, as soon as he had consolidated a union between Lithuanians, Samogitians and Cours, he relapsed, proclaiming, in 1260, a general uprising of the Lithuanian people against the Livonian order. The yoke was shaken off, but internal wars followed, and three years later Mendowg was killed. About the end of the 13th century a new dynasty of rulers of Lithuania was founded by Lutuwer, whose second son, Gedymin (1316–1341), with the aid of fresh forces he organized through his relations with Red Russia, established something like regular government; he at the same time extended his dominions over Russian countries—over Black Russia (Novogrodok, Zditov, Grodno, Slonim and Volkovysk) and the principalities of Polotsk, Tourovsk, Pinsk, Vitebsk and Volhynia. He named himself *Rex Lethowinorum et multorum Ruthenorum*. In 1325 he concluded a treaty with Poland against the Livonian order, which treaty was the first step towards the union of both countries realized two centuries later. The seven sons of Gedymin considered themselves as quite independent; but two of them, Olgierd and Keistut, soon became the more powerful. They represented two different tendencies which existed at that time in Lithuania. Olgierd, whose family relations attracted him towards the south, was the advocate of union with Russia; rather politician than warrior, he increased his influence by diplomacy and by organization. His wife and sons being Christians, he also soon agreed to be baptized in the Greek Church. Keistut represented the revival of the Lithuanian nationality. Continually engaged in wars with Livonia, and remaining true to the national religion, he became the national legendary hero. In 1345 both brothers agreed to re-establish the great principality of Lithuania, and, after having taken Vilna, the old sanctuary of the country, all the brothers recognized the supremacy of Olgierd. His son, Jagiello, who married the queen of Poland, Yadviga, after having been baptized in the Latin Church, was crowned, on the 14th of February 1386, king of Poland. At the beginning of the 15th century Lithuania extended her dominions as far east as Vyazmà on the banks of the Moskva river, the present government of Kaluga, and Poutivl, and south-east as far as Poltava, the shores of the Sea of Azov, and Haji-bey (Odessa), thus including Kiev and Lutsk. The union with [illegible] but nominal until 1569, when Sigis- [illegible] Poland. In the 16th century [illegible] power so far east and south-east [illegible] it constituted a compact state, [illegible] Minsk, Grodno, Kovno, Vilna, Brest, [illegible] as Chernigov. From the union [illegible] Lithuania becomes a part of Poland's [illegible] White-Russians partaking of the fate [illegible] Poland: *History*). After its three [illegible] the dominion of the Russian empire. [illegible] provinces of Moghilev and Polotsk, and [illegible] Troki, Novgorod-Syeversk, Brest and [illegible] provinces were united together, con- [illegible] government" (Litovskaya Gubernia). [illegible] provinces was usually given [illegible] of Vilna and Kovno, and, though [illegible] the use of this name, it is still used, even [illegible] In Russia all the White-Russian popula- [illegible] Polish Lithuania are usually considered as [illegible] being restricted to Lithuanians [illegible]

[illegible] of the Lithuanians are undefined, and [illegible] estimated. The Letts occupy a part [illegible] Livonia and of Vitebsk, a few other [illegible] also in the governments of Kovno, [illegible] The Lithuanians proper inhabit the [illegible] Vilna, Suvalki and Grodno; while the [illegible] the governments of Kovno and [illegible] about 200,000 Borussians, the [illegible] and Letts in Russia being, according [illegible] They are slowly extending [illegible] the Letts; numerous emigrants [illegible] lands as far as the government of [illegible]

[illegible] the face is mostly elongated, the [illegible] blue eyes and delicate skin dis- [illegible] Their dress is usually plain [illegible] and the predominance in it of [illegible] noticed. Their chief occupation [illegible] are generally carried on by men [illegible] Jews or Poles. The only [illegible] by the Letts. The Samogitians [illegible] are given to apiculture and [illegible] as well in the Baltic provinces [illegible] the most recent time proprietors [illegible] a few families to the Russian [illegible] the people became serfs of foreign [illegible] who reduced them to the greatest [illegible] of 1863, the Russian govern- [illegible] the land of the Polish proprietors [illegible] Russia; but the allotments of [illegible] very unequally distributed; and [illegible] (the *chinshevniki*) were even [illegible] for centuries considered their own. [illegible] before, and are restrained from [illegible] measures.

[illegible] exception of about 50,000 who [illegible] Lutherans. Nearly all can read. [illegible] who were under Polish dominion, [illegible] Lithuanians proper, a part of [illegible] Greek Church, in which they [illegible] The Samogitians are Roman [illegible] Lithuanians have conserved their [illegible] have maintained much of [illegible] the names of pagan divinities, [illegible] are continually mentioned [illegible]

[illegible] *Polen und Livland bis ins* [illegible] S. Daukantas, [illegible] de Brye, *Étude historique* [illegible] *Istoriya Litovskago* [illegible] (P. A. K.)

[illegible] Lithuanian, Lettic or Lettish [illegible] together constitute a [illegible] called the Baltic [illegible] family. They have [illegible] and are sometimes [illegible] group, the Balto-Slavic. [illegible] in their structure the Baltic languages appear to be more primitive than the Slavonic. Lithuanian, for example, retains the archaic diphthongs which disappear in Slavonic—Lith. *veidas*, "face," Gr. *εἶδος*, O.S. *vidŭ*. Among other noteworthy phonological characteristics of Lithuanian are the conversion of *k* into a sibilant, the loss of *h* and change of all aspirates into tenues and the retention of primitive consonantal noun-terminations, *e.g.* the final *s* in Sans. *Vṛkás*, Lith. *vilkas*, O.S. *vlŭkŭ*. Lettic is phonologically less archaic than Lithuanian, although in a few cases it has preserved Indo-European forms which have been changed in Lithuanian, *e.g.* the *s* and *z* which have become Lith. *sz* (*sh*) and *ž* (*zh*). The accent in Lithuanian is free; in Lettic, and apparently in Old Prussian, it ultimately became fixed on the first syllable.

In its morphology Lettic represents a later stage of development than Lithuanian, their mutual relationship being analogous to that between Old High German and Gothic. Both languages have preserved seven out of the eight Indo-European cases; Lithuanian has three numbers, but Lettic has lost the dual (except in *divi*, "two" and *abbi*, "both"); the neuter gender, which still appears in Lithuanian pronouns, has also been entirely lost in Lettic; in Lithuanian there are four simple tenses (present, future, imperfect, preterite), but in Lettic the imperfect is wanting. In both languages the number of periphrastic verb-forms and of diminutives is large; in both there are traces of a suffix article; and both have enriched their vocabularies with many words of foreign, especially German, Russian and Polish origin. The numerous Lithuanian dialects are commonly divided into High or Southern, which changes *ty* and *dy* into *cz*, *dz*, and Low or Northern, which retains *ty*, *dy*. Lettic is divided into High (the eastern dialects), Low (spoken in N.W. Courland) and Middle (the literary language). Old Prussian ceased to be a spoken language in the 17th century; its literary remains, consisting chiefly of three catechisms and two brief vocabularies, date almost entirely from the period 1517–1561 and are insufficient to permit of any thorough reconstruction of the grammar.

The literary history of the Lithuanians and Letts dates from the Reformation and comprises three clearly defined periods. (1) Up to 1700 the chief printed books were of a liturgical character. (2) During the 18th century a vigorous educational movement began; dictionaries, grammars and other instructive works were compiled, and written poems began to take the place of songs preserved by oral tradition. (3) The revival of national sentiment at the beginning of the 19th century resulted in the establishment of newspapers and the collection and publication of the national folk-poetry. In both literatures, works of a religious character predominate, and both are rich in popular ballads, folk-tales and fables.

The first book printed in Lithuanian was a translation of Luther's shorter Catechism (Königsberg, 1547); other translations of devotional or liturgical works followed, and by 1701 59 Lithuanian books had appeared, the most noteworthy being those of the preacher J. Bretkun (1535–1602). The spread of Calvinism led to the publication, in 1701, of a Lithuanian New Testament. The first dictionary was printed in 1749. But perhaps the most remarkable work of the second period was *The Four Seasons*, a pastoral poem in hexameters by Christian Donalitius (1714–1780), which was edited by Nesselmann (Königsberg, 1869) with a German translation and notes. In the 19th century various collections of fables and folk-tales were published, and an epic, the *Onikshta Grove*, was written by Bishop Baranoski. But it was in journalism that the chief original work of the third period was done. F. Kelch (1801–1877) founded the first Lithuanian newspaper, and between 1834 and 1895 no fewer than 34 Lithuanian periodicals were published in the United States alone.

Luther's Catechism (Königsberg, 1586) was the first book printed in Lettic, as in the sister speech. In the 17th century various translations of psalms, hymns and other religious works were published, the majority being Calvinistic in tone. The educational movement of the 18th century was inaugurated by G. F. Stender (1714–1796), author of a Lettic dictionary and grammar, of poems, tales and of a *Book of Wisdom* which treats of elementary science and history. Much educational work was subsequently done by the Lettic Literary Society, which publishes a magazine (*Magazin*, Mitau, from 1827), and by the "Young Letts," who published various periodicals and translations of foreign classics, and endeavoured to free their language and thought from German influences. Somewhat similar tasks were undertaken by the "Young Lithuanians," whose first magazine the *Ausra* ("Dawn") was founded in 1883. From 1890 to 1910 the literature of both peoples was marked by an ever-increasing nationalism; among the names most prominent during this period may be mentioned those of the dramatist Steperman and the poet Martin Lap, both of whom wrote in Lettic.

Bibliography.—Lithuanian dictionaries: Nesselmann, *Wörterbuch der litauischen Sprache* (Königsberg, 1851); Kurschat, *Wörterbuch der litauischen Sprache* (Halle, 1870–1883); A. Juszkiewicz, *Litovskiy Slovar* (St Petersburg, 1897, &c.); P. Saurusaitis, *An Abridged Dictionary of the English-Lithuanian Languages*, 2 pts. (Waterbury, Conn., 1899–1900); A. Lalis, *Dictionary of the Lithuanian and English Languages* (Chicago, 1903, &c.). Grammar and Linguistic: Schleicher, *Handbuch der litauischen Sprache* (Prague, 1856–1857); O. Wiedemann, *Handbuch der litauischen Sprache* (Strassburg, 1897); A. Bezzenberger, *Beiträge zur Geschichte der litauischen Sprache* (Göttingen, 1877); J. Schlekopp, *Gramatyka litewska pocsątkowa* (Cracow, 1902). Literature: Nesselmann, *Litauische Volkslieder* (Berlin, 1853); A. Juszkiewicz, *Lietuviszkos Dajnos Užrašytos*, &c. (Kazan, 1881); A. Leskien and C. Brugman, *Litauische Volkslieder* (Strassburg, 1882); C. Bartsch, *Melodien litauischer Volkslieder* (Heidelberg, 1886); A. Juszkiewicz, *Melodje ludowe litewskie* (Cracow, 1900, &c.); E. A. Vol'ter, *Litovskaya Khrestomatiya* (St Petersburg, 1901, &c.).

Lettic dictionaries and grammars: Bielenstein, *Die Lettische Sprache* (Berlin, 1863–1864); id., *Lettische Grammatik* (Mitau, 1863); Ulmann and Brasche, *Lettisches Wörterbuch* (Riga, 1872–1880); A. Bezzenberger, *Über die Sprache der preussischen Letten* and *lettische Dialekt-Studien* (Göttingen, 1885); Bielenstein, *Grenzen des lettischen Volksstammes und der lettischen Sprache* (St Petersburg, 1892); Literature: Bielenstein *Tausend lettische Räthsel* (Mitau, 1881); T. Treuland, *Latyshskiya Narodnyya Skaski* (Moscow, 1887, &c.); K. Baron and H. Wissendorff, *Latwju dainas* (Mitau 1894, &c.); V. Andreyanov, *Lettische Volkslieder und Mythen* (Halle, 1896).

Old Prussian: Nesselmann, *Die Sprache der alten Preussen* (Berlin, 1845); id., *Thesaurus linguae prussicae* (Berlin, 1873); Berneker, *Die preussische Sprache* (Strassburg, 1896); M. Schultze, *Grammatik der altpreussischen Sprache* (Leipzig, 1897).

LITMUS (apparently a corruption of *lacmus*, Dutch *lacmoes*, *lac*, lac, and *moes*, pulp, due to association with "lit," an obsolete word for dye, colour; the Ger. equivalent is *Lackmus*, Fr. *tournesol*), a colouring matter which occurs in commerce in the form of small blue tablets, which, however, consist mostly, not of the pigment proper, but of calcium carbonate and sulphate and other matter devoid of tinctorial value. Litmus is extensively employed by chemists as an indicator for the detection of free acids and free alkalis. An aqueous infusion of litmus, when exactly neutralized by an acid, exhibits a violet colour, which by the least trace of free acid is changed to red, while free alkali turns it to blue. The reagent is generally used in the form of test paper—bibulous paper dyed red, purple or blue by the respective kind of infusion. Litmus is manufactured in Holland from the same kinds of lichens (species of *Roccella* and *Lecanora*) as are used for the preparation of archil (*q.v.*).

LITOPTERNA, a suborder of South American Tertiary ungulate mammals typified by *Macrauchenia*, and taking their name ("smooth-heel") from the presence of a flat facet on the heel-bone, or calcaneum for the articulation of the fibula. The more typical members of the group were digitigrade animals, recalling in general build the llamas and horses; they have small brains, and a facet on the calcaneum for the fibula. The cheek-dentition approximates more or less to the perissodactyle type. Both the terminal faces of the cervical vertebrae are flat, the femur carries a third trochanter, the bones of both the carpus and tarsus are arranged in linear series, and the number of toes, although commonly three, varies between one and five, the third or middle digit being invariably the largest.

Of the two families, the first is the *Proterotheriidae*, which exhibits, in respect of the reduction of the digits, a curious parallelism to the equine line among the Perissodactyla; in this feature, as well as in the reduction of the teeth, it is more specialized than the second family.

The molar teeth approximate to the *Palaeotherium* type, but have a more or less strongly developed median longitudinal cleft. The three-toed type is represented by *Diadiaphorus*, in which the dental formula is $i.\frac{1}{2}$, $c.\frac{0}{1}$, $p.\frac{4}{4}$, $m.\frac{3}{3}$, and the feet are very like those of *Hipparion*. The cervical vertebrae are of normal form, the orbit (as in the second family) is encircled by bone, the last molar has a third lobe, the single pair of upper incisors are somewhat elongated, and have a gap between and behind them, while the outer lower incisors are larger than the inner pair, the canines being small. The skull has a short muzzle, with elongated nasals. Remains of this and the other representatives of the group are found in the Patagonian Miocene. In *Proterotherium*, which includes smaller forms having the same, or nearly the same, dental formula, the molar teeth differ from those of *Diadiaphorus* by the deeper median longitudinal cleft, which completely divides the crown into an inner and an outer moiety, the two cones of the inner half being united. According to the description given by Argentine palaeontologists, this genus is also three-toed, the single-toed representative of the family being *Thoatherium*, in which the lateral metapodials, or splint-bones, are even more reduced than in the *Equidae*.

In the second family—*Macraucheniidae*—the dentition is complete (forty-four) and without a gap, the crowns of nearly all the teeth being of nearly uniform height, while the upper molars are distinguished from those of the *Proterotheriidae* by a peculiar arrangement of their two inner cones, and the elevation of the antero-posterior portion of the cingulum so as to form an extra pit on the crown. To describe this arrangement in detail is impossible here, but it may be stated that the two inner cones are closely approximated, and separated by a narrow V-shaped notch on the inner side of the crown. The elongated cervical vertebrae are peculiar in that the arch is perforated by the artery in the same manner as in the llamas.

In the Santa Cruz beds of Patagonia the family is represented by the generalized genus *Oxyodontotherium* (in which *Theosodon* may apparently be included). It comprises animals ranging up to the size of a tapir, in which the nostrils were more or less in the normal anterior position, and the cheek-teeth short-crowned, with the inner cones of the upper molars well developed and separated by a notch, and the pits of moderate depth. The last upper premolar is simpler than the molars, and the canine, which may be double-rooted, is like the earlier premolars. The radius and ulna, like the tibia and fibula, are distinct, and the metapodials rudimentary. On the other hand, in *Macrauchenia*, which was a much larger llama-like animal, the skull is elongated and narrow, with rudimentary nasals, and the aperture of the nose placed nearly on the line of the eyes and directed upwards, the muzzle not improbably terminating in a short trunk. Deep pits on the forehead probably served for the attachment of special muscles connected with the latter. Very curious is the structure of the cheek-teeth, which are high-crowned, with the two inner cones reduced to mere points, and the pits on the crown-surface large and funnel-shaped. In fact, the perissodactyle type is almost lost. The cervical vertebrae and limb-bones are very long, the radius and ulna being completely, and the tibia and fibula partially, united. The typical *M. patagonica* is a Pleistocene form as large as a camel, ranging from Patagonia to Brazil, but remains of smaller species have been found in the Pliocene (?) of Bolivia and Argentina.

The imperfectly known *Scalabrinia* of the Argentine Pliocene appears to occupy a position intermediate between *Oxyodontotherium* and *Macrauchenia*, having the nasal aperture situated in the middle of the length of the skull, and the crowns of the cheek-teeth nearly as tall as in the latter, but the lower molars furnished with a projecting process in the hinder valley, similar to one occurring in those of the former.

In this place may be mentioned another strange ungulate from the Santa Cruz beds of Patagonia, namely, *Astrapotherium*, sometimes regarded as typifying a suborder by itself. This huge ungulate had cheek-teeth singularly like those of a rhinoceros, and an enormous pair of tusk-like upper incisors, recalling the upper canines of *Machaerodus* on an enlarged scale. In the lower jaw are two large tusk-like canines between which are three pairs of curiously-formed spatulate incisors, and in both jaws there is a long diastema. The dental formula appears to be $i.\frac{1}{3}$, $c.\frac{1}{1}$, $p.\frac{2}{1}$, $m.\frac{3}{3}$.

Next *Astrapotherium* may be provisionally placed the genus *Homalodontotherium*, of which the teeth have much lower crowns, and are of a less decidedly rhinocerotic type than in *Astrapotherium*, and the whole dentition forms an even and unbroken series. The bodies of the cervical vertebrae are short, with flattened articular [illegible] the humerus has an enormous deltoid crest, suggestive of [illegible] and the femur is flattened, with a third trochanter. According to the Argentine palaeontologists, the carpus is of the [illegible] type, and the terminal phalanges of the pentadactyle [illegible] and very like those of Edentata. Indeed, this type [illegible] many edentate resemblances. The astragalus is [illegible] and flattened, articulating directly with the navicular, [illegible] with the cuboid, and having a slightly convex facet [illegible]. From the structure of the above-mentioned type of [illegible] which is stated to have been found in association with the skull, [illegible] been suggested that *Homalodontotherium* should be placed in [illegible] but, to say nothing of the different form of the [illegible] all the other South American Santa Cruz ungulates are [illegible] from those of other countries that this seems unlikely. [illegible] suggested that we have rather to deal with an instance of [illegible]—a view supported by the parallelism to the *Equidae* [illegible] by certain members of the *Proterotheriidae*. (R. L.*)

[illegible] (Gr. λιτότης, plainness, λιτός, plain, simple, smooth), a [illegible] figure in which emphasis is secured for a statement [illegible] a denial of the contrary, *e.g.* "a citizen of no [illegible]," i.e. a citizen of a famous city, "A. is not a man [illegible]." Litotes is sometimes used for what should be [illegible] called "meiosis" (Gr. μείωσις, lessening, diminution), where the expressions used apparently are [illegible], but the effect is to intensify.

[illegible] (through O. Fr. *litere* or *litiere*, mod. *litière* from [illegible] classical *lectica*, *lectus*, bed, couch), a word [illegible] a portable couch, shut in by curtains and borne [illegible] bearers, and of a bed of straw or other suitable [illegible] animals, hence applied to the number of young [illegible] an animal at one birth, and also to any disordered [illegible] rubbish, &c. In ancient Greece, prior [illegible] Asiatic luxury after the Macedonian conquest, [illegible] was only used by invalids or by women. [illegible] was introduced, probably about [illegible] when the [illegible] (Gellius x. 3), used it only [illegible]. Like the Greek or Asiatic litter, it had [illegible] and side curtains (*vela, plagae*). Juvenal [illegible] (*latis specularibus*). The slaves [illegible] shoulders (*succollare*) were termed [illegible] luxury and wealth to employ six [illegible]. Under the Empire the litter began to be [illegible] and its use was restricted and [illegible] (Suet. *Claudius*). The travelling *lectica* [illegible] the much earlier *lectica funebris* [illegible] on which the dead were carried to [illegible]

[illegible] a city and the county-seat of Morrison [illegible] U.S.A., on both banks of the Mississippi [illegible] N.W. of Minneapolis. Pop. (1890) 2354; [illegible] were foreign-born, chiefly Germans [illegible] (1910) 6078. It is served by the [illegible]. The city is situated in a prosperous [illegible] excellent water-power and various [illegible] was settled about 1850, was chartered [illegible] adopted a new charter in 1902. Here [illegible] Hole-in-the-Day (*c.* 1827–1868), [illegible] his father, also named Hole-[illegible] of the Chippewas in 1846. Like his [illegible] the-Day led his tribe against the [illegible] prevented the Chippewas from [illegible]. His body was subsequently [illegible]

[illegible] Herkimer county, New York, [illegible] m. E.S.E. of Utica. Pop. [illegible] of whom [illegible] were foreign-born; [illegible] served by the New York Central [illegible] the Utica & Mohawk Valley [illegible] Dolgeville railways (the last [illegible] only to Salisbury Center [illegible] river falls here by a series [illegible] furnishing water power. [illegible] hosiery and knit goods, [illegible] products were valued [illegible] of the largest cheese markets in the United States. The manufacture of flour and grist-mill products was formerly an important industry; a mill burned in 1782 by Tories and Indians had supplied almost the entire Mohawk Valley, and particularly Forts Herkimer and Dayton. Near the city is the grave of General Nicholas Herkimer, to whom a monument was erected in 1896. Little Falls was settled by Germans in 1782, and was almost immediately destroyed by Indians and Tories. It was resettled in 1790, and was incorporated as a village in 1811 and as a city in 1895.

See George A. Hardin, *History of Herkimer County* (Syracuse, 1893).

LITTLEHAMPTON, a seaport and watering-place in the Chichester parliamentary division of Sussex, England, at the mouth of the Arun, 62 m. S. by W. from London by the London, Brighton & South Coast railway. Pop. of urban district (1901) 7363. There is a beach of firm sand. The harbour is easily accessible in all weathers, and has a small general trade.

LITTLE ROCK, the capital of Arkansas, U.S.A., and the county-seat of Pulaski county, situated near the centre of the state and on the S. bank of the Arkansas river, at the E. edge of the Ozark foothills. Pop. (1890) 25,874; (1900) 38,307, of whom 14,694 were of negro blood, and 2099 were foreign-born; (1910 census) 45,941. Little Rock is served by the Chicago, Rock Island & Pacific, the St Louis South Western, and the St Louis, Iron Mountain & Southern railways and by river boats. It occupies a comparatively level site of 11 sq. m. at an altitude of 250 to 400 ft. above sea-level and 50 ft. or more above the river, which is crossed here by three railway bridges and by a county bridge. The city derived its name (originally "le Petit Roche" and "The Little Rock") from a rocky peninsula in the Arkansas, distinguished from the "Big Rock" (the site of the army post, Fort Logan H. Roots), 1 m. W. of the city, across the river. The Big Rock is said to have been first discovered and named "Le Rocher Français" in 1722 by Sieur Bernard de la Harpe, who was in search of an emerald mountain; the Little Rock is now used as an abutment for a railway bridge. The state capitol, the state insane asylum, the state deaf mute institute, the state school for the blind, a state reform school, the penitentiary, the state library and the medical and law departments of the state university are at Little Rock; and the city is also the seat of the United States court for the eastern district of Arkansas, of a United States land office, of Little Rock College, of the St Mary's Academy, of a Roman Catholic orphanage and a Roman Catholic convent, and of two schools for negroes—the Philander Smith College (Methodist Episcopal, 1877), co-educational, and the Arkansas Baptist College. The city is the seat of Protestant Episcopal and Roman Catholic bishops. Little Rock has a Carnegie library (1908), an old ladies' home, a Florence Crittenton rescue home, a children's home, St Vincent's infirmary, a city hospital, a Catholic hospital, a physicians' and surgeons' hospital and the Arkansas hospital for nervous diseases. A municipal park system includes City, Forest, Wonderland and West End parks. Immigration from the northern states has been encouraged, and northern men control much of the business of the city. In 1905 the value of factory products was $4,689,787, being 38·8% greater than the value in 1900. Cotton and lumber industries are the leading interests; the value of cotton-seed oil and cake manufactured in 1905 was $967,043, of planing mill products $835,049, and of lumber and timber products $342,134. Printing and publishing and the manufacture of foundry and machine shop products and of furniture are other important industries. Valuable deposits of bauxite are found in Pulaski county, and the mines are the most important in the United States.

Originally the site of the city was occupied by the Quapaw Indians. The earliest permanent settlement by the whites was about 1813–1814; the county was organized in 1818 while still a part of Missouri Territory; Little Rock was surveyed in 1821, was incorporated as a town and became the capital of Arkansas in 1821, and was chartered as a city in 1836. In 1850 its population was only 2167, and in 1860 3727; but in 1870 it was 12,380. Little Rock was enthusiastically anti-Union at the outbreak of the Civil War. In February 1861, the United States Arsenal was seized by the state authorities. In September 1863 the Federal generals William Steele (1819–1885) and John W. Davidson (1824–1881), operating against General Sterling Price, captured the city, and it remained throughout the rest of the war under Federal control. Constitutional conventions met at Little Rock in 1836, 1864, 1868 and 1874, and also the Secession Convention of 1861. The *Arkansas Gazette*, established at Arkansas Post in 1819 and soon afterwards removed to the new capital, was the first newspaper published in Arkansas and one of the first published west of the Mississippi

LITTLETON (or Lyttelton), **EDWARD**, Baron (1589–1645), son of Sir Edward Littleton (d. 1621) chief-justice of North Wales, was born at Munslow in Shropshire; he was educated at Oxford and became a lawyer, succeeding his father as chief-justice of North Wales. In 1625 he became a member of parliament and acted in 1628 as chairman of the committee of grievances upon whose report the Petition of Right was based. As a member of the party opposed to the arbitrary measures of Charles I. Littleton had shown more moderation than some of his colleagues, and in 1634, three years after he had been chosen recorder of London, the king attached him to his own side by appointing him solicitor-general. In the famous case about ship-money Sir Edward argued against Hampden. In 1640 he was made chief-justice of the common pleas and in 1641 lord keeper of the great seal, being created a peer as Baron Lyttelton. About this time, the lord keeper began to display a certain amount of indifference to the royal cause. In January 1642 he refused to put the great seal to the proclamation for the arrest of the five members and he also incurred the displeasure of Charles by voting for the militia ordinance. However, he assured his friend Edward Hyde, afterwards earl of Clarendon, that he had only taken this step to allay the suspicions of the parliamentary party who contemplated depriving him of the seal, and he undertook to send this to the king. He fulfilled his promise, and in May 1642 he himself joined Charles at York, but it was some time before he regained the favour of the king and the custody of the seal. Littleton died at Oxford on the 27th of August 1645; he left no sons and his barony became extinct. His only daughter, Anne, married her cousin Sir Thomas Littleton, Bart. (d. 1681), and their son Sir Thomas Littleton (*c.* 1647–1710), was speaker of the House of Commons from 1698 to 1700, and treasurer of the navy from 1700 to 1710. Macaulay thus sums up the character of Speaker Littleton and his relations to the Whigs: "He was one of their ablest, most zealous and most steadfast friends; and had been, both in the House of Commons and at the board of treasury, an invaluable second to Montague" (the earl of Halifax).

LITTLETON, SIR THOMAS DE (*c.* 1407–1481), English judge and legal author, was born, it is supposed, at Frankley Manor House, Worcestershire, about 1407. Littleton's surname was that of his mother, who was the sole daughter and heiress of Thomas de Littleton, lord of Frankley. She married one Thomas Westcote. Thomas was the eldest of four sons of the marriage, and took the name of Littleton, or, as it seems to have been more commonly spelt, Luttelton. The date of his birth is uncertain; a MS. pedigree gives 1422, but it was probably earlier than this. If, as is generally accepted, he was born at Frankley Manor, it could not have been before 1407, in which year Littleton's grandfather recovered the manor from a distant branch of the family. He is said by Sir E. Coke to have "attended one of the universities," but there is no corroboration of this statement. He was probably a member of the Inner Temple, and lectured there on the statute of Westminster II., *De Donis Conditionalibus*. His name occurs in the Paston Letters (ed. J. Gairdner, i. 60) about 1445 as that of a well-known counsel and in 1481/2 he received a grant of the manor of Sheriff Hales, Shropshire, from a Sir William Trussel as a reward for his services as counsel. He appears to have been recorder of Coventry in 1450; he was made escheator of Worcestershire, and in 1447/8 was under-sheriff of the same county, he became serjeant-at-law in 1453 and was afterwards a justice of assize on the northern circuit. In 1466 he was made a judge of the common pleas, and in 1475 a knight of the Bath. He died, according to the inscription on his tomb in Worcester cathedral, on the 23rd of August 1481. He married, about 1444, Joan, widow of Sir Philip Chetwind of Ingestre in Staffordshire, and by her had three sons, through whom he became ancestor of the families holding the peerages of Cobham (formerly Lyttelton, *q.v.*) and Hatherton.

His *Treatise on Tenures* was probably written after he had been appointed to the bench. It is addressed to his second son Richard, who went to the bar, and whose name occurs in the year books of the reign of Henry VII. The book, both historically and from its intrinsic merit, may be characterized as the first text-book upon the English law of property. The law of property in Littleton's time was mainly concerned with rights over land, and it was the law relating to this class of rights which Littleton set himself to digest and classify. The time was ripe for the task. Ever since the Conquest regular courts of justice had been at work administering a law which had grown out of an admixture of Teutonic custom and of Norman feudalism. Under Henry II. the courts had been organized, and the practice of keeping regular records of the proceedings had been carefully observed. The centralizing influence of the royal courts and of the justices of assize, working steadily through three centuries, had made the rules governing the law of property uniform throughout the land; local customs were confined within certain prescribed limits, and were only recognized as giving rise to certain well-defined classes of rights, such, for instance, as the security of tenure acquired by villeins by virtue of the custom of the manor, and the rights of freeholders, in some towns, to dispose of their land by will. Thus, by the time of Littleton (Henry VI. and Edward IV.), an immense mass of material had been acquired and preserved in the rolls of the various courts. Reports of important cases were published in the "year books." A glance at Statham's *Abridgment*, the earliest digest of decided cases, published nearly at the same time as Littleton's *Tenures*, is sufficient to show the enormous bulk which reported cases had already attained as materials for the knowledge of English law.

Littleton's treatise was written in that peculiar dialect compounded of Norman-French and English phrases called law French. Although it had been provided by a statute of 36 Edward III. that *viva voce* proceedings in court should no longer be conducted in the French tongue, "which was much unknown in the realm," the practice of reporting proceedings in that language, and of using it in legal treatises, lingered till a much later period, and was at length prohibited by a statute passed in the time of the Commonwealth in 1650. Unlike the preceding writers on English law, Glanville, Bracton and the authors of the treatises known by the names of Britton and Fleta, Littleton borrows nothing from the sources of Roman law or the commentators. He deals exclusively with English law.

The book is written on a definite system, and is the first attempt at a scientific classification of rights over land. Littleton's method is to begin with a definition, usually clearly and briefly expressed, of the class of rights with which he is dealing. He then proceeds to illustrate the various characteristics and incidents of the class by stating particular instances, some of which refer to decisions which had actually occurred, but more commonly they are hypothetical cases put by way of illustration of his principles. He occasionally refers to reported cases. His book is thus much more than a mere digest of judicial decisions; to some extent he pursues the method which gave to Roman law its breadth and consistency of principle. In Roman law this result was attained through the practice of putting to jurisconsults hypothetical cases to be solved by them. Littleton, in like manner, is constantly stating and solving by reference to principles of law cases which may or may not have occurred in actual practice.

In dealing with freehold estates Littleton adopts a classification which has been followed by all writers who have attempted to [illegible] the English [illegible] Sir [illegible] [illegible] Littleton [illegible] which first [illegible] [illegible] with [illegible] a tenant [illegible] [illegible] discussing [illegible] [illegible] With the [illegible] a tenant [illegible] to us [illegible] which was a [illegible] of a date later than the time of Littleton, the first book is a complete statement of the principles of the common law as then [illegible] the most [illegible] [illegible] exact [illegible] the [illegible] the [illegible] by the growth of the [illegible] system, acquired security of tenure.

The second book relates to the reciprocal rights and duties of lord and tenant [illegible] [illegible] to the modern lawyer. It contains a complete statement of the law as it stood in Littleton's time relating to [illegible] and escuage, the money commutation to be paid to the lord in [illegible] service to be rendered to the king, a peculiar characteristic of English as distinguished from Continental feudalism.

Littleton then proceeds to notice the important features of tenure by knight's service with its distinguishing incidents of the right of wardship of the lands and person of the infant heir or heiress and the right of disposing of the ward in marriage. The [illegible] tenures are next dealt with; we have an account of socage tenure [illegible] into which all military tenures were subsequently converted by a now unrecognized act of the Long Parliament in 1656, afterwards re-enacted by the [illegible] statute of Charles II. [illegible] and of "frankalmoign" or the [illegible] tenure by which church lands were held. In the description of [illegible] tenure and tenure in [illegible], the life of which consists in the [illegible] of ancient customs recognized by law, we recognize survivals of a time before the iron rule of feudalism had moulded the law of land in the interests of the king and the great lords. Finally he deals with the law of rents, discussing the various kinds of rents which may be reserved to the grantor upon a grant of lands and the remedies for recovery of rent, especially the remedy by distress.[1]

The third and concluding book of Littleton's treatise deals mainly with the various ways in which rights over land can be acquired and terminated in the case of a single possessor or several possessors. This leads him to discuss the various modes in which several persons may simultaneously have rights over the same land, as parceners:—daughters who are co-heiresses, or sons in gavelkind; joint tenants and tenants in common. Next follows an elaborate discussion upon what are called estates upon condition—a class of interests which occupied a large space in the early common law, giving rise on one side to estates tail, on another to mortgages. In Littleton's time a mortgage, which he carefully describes, was merely a conveyance of land by the tenant to the mortgagee, with a condition that, if the tenant paid to the mortgagee a certain sum on a certain day, he might re-enter and have the land again. If the condition was not fulfilled, the interest of the mortgagee became absolute, and Littleton gives no indication of any mitigation of this strict rule, such as was introduced by courts of equity, permitting the debtor to redeem his land by payment of all that was due to the mortgagee although the day of payment had passed, and his interest had become at law indefeasible. The remainder of the work is occupied with an exposition of a miscellaneous class of modes of acquiring rights of property, the analysis of which would occupy too large a space.

The work is thus a complete summary of the common law as it stood at the time. It is nearly silent as to the remarkable class of rights which had already assumed vast practical importance—equitable interests in lands. These are only noticed incidentally in the chapter on "Releases." But it was already clear in Littleton's time that this class of rights would become the most important of all. Littleton's own will, which has been preserved, may be adduced in proof of this assertion. Although nothing was more opposed to the spirit of Norman feudalism than that a tenant of lands should [illegible] of them by will, we find Littleton directing by his will the [illegible] of certain manors to make estates to the persons named in his will. In other words, in order to acquire over lands powers [illegible] in the common law, the lands had been conveyed to "feoffees" who had full right over them according to the common law, but who were under a conscientious obligation to exercise those rights at the direction and for the exclusive benefit of the person to whose "use" the lands were held. This conscientious obligation was recognized and enforced by the chancellor, and thus arose the [illegible] of equitable interests in lands. Littleton is the first writer on English law after these rights had risen into a prominent position, and it is curious to find to what extent they are ignored by him.

BIBLIOGRAPHY.—The work of Littleton occupies a place in the history of typography as well as of law. The earliest printed edition seems to be that by John Lettou and William de Machlinia, two printers who probably came from the Continent, and carried on their business in partnership, as their note to the edition of Littleton states, "in civitate Londoniarum, juxta ecclesiam omnium sanctorum." The date of this edition is uncertain, but the most probable conjecture, based on typographical grounds, places it about the latter part of 1481. The next edition is one by Machlinia alone, printed about two or three years later than the former. Machlinia was then in business alone "juxta pontem quae vulgo dicitur Fleta brigge." Next came the Rohan or Rouen edition, erroneously stated by Sir E. Coke to be the earliest, and to have been printed about 1553. It was, however, of a much earlier date. Tomlins, the latest editor of Littleton, gives reasons for thinking that it cannot have been later than 1490. It is stated in a note to have been printed at Rouen by William le Talleur "ad instantiam Richardi Pynson." Copies of all these editions are in the British Museum. In all these editions the work is styled Tenores Novelli, probably to distinguish it from the "Old Tenures."

There are three early MSS. of Littleton in the University Library at Cambridge. One of these formerly contained a note on its first page to the effect that it was bought in St Paul's Churchyard on July 20, 1480. It was therefore in circulation in Littleton's lifetime. The other two MSS. are of a somewhat later date; but one of them contains what seems to be the earliest English translation of the Tenures and is probably not later than 1500.

In the 16th century editions of Littleton followed in rapid succession from the presses of [illegible], Redmayne, Berthelet, Tottyl and others. The practice of annotating the text caused several additions to be introduced, which, however, are easily detected by comparison of the earlier copies. In 1581 West divided the text into 746 sections, which have ever since been preserved. Many of these editions were printed with large margins for purposes of annotation, specimens of which may be seen in Lincoln's Inn Library.

The practice of annotating Littleton was very general, and was adopted by many eminent lawyers besides Sir E. Coke, amongst others by Sir M. Hale. One commentary of this kind, by an unknown hand of earlier date than Sir E. Coke's, was edited by Cary in 1829. Following the general practice of dealing with Littleton as the great authority on the law of England, "the most perfect and absolute work that ever was written in any human science," Sir E. Coke made it in 1628 the text of that portion of his work which he calls the first part of the institutes of the law of England, in other words, the law of property.

The first printed English translation of Littleton was by Rastell, who seems to have combined the professions of author, printer and serjeant-at-law, between 1514 and 1533. Many English editions by various editors followed, the best of which is Tottyl's in 1556. Sir E. Coke adopted some translation earlier than this, which has since gone by the name of Sir E. Coke's translation. He, however, throughout comments not on the translation but on the French text; and the reputation of the commentary has to some extent obscured the intrinsic merit of the original.

See E. Wambaugh, *Littleton's Tenures in English* (Washington, D.C., 1903).

LITTRÉ, MAXIMILIEN PAUL ÉMILE (1801–1881), French lexicographer and philosopher, was born in Paris on the 1st of February 1801. His father had been a gunner, and afterwards sergeant-major of marine artillery, in the French navy, and was deeply imbued with the revolutionary ideas of the day. Settling down as a collector of taxes, he married Sophie Johannot, a free-thinker like himself, and devoted himself to the education of his son Émile. The boy was sent to the Lycée Louis-le-Grand, where he had for friends Hachette and Eugène Burnouf. After he had completed his course at school, he hesitated for a time as to what profession he should adopt, and meanwhile made himself master, not only of the English and German languages, but of the classical and Sanskrit literature and philology. At last he determined to study medicine, and in 1822 entered his name as a student of medicine. He passed all his examinations in due course, and had only his thesis to prepare in order to obtain

[1] These two books are stated, in a note to the table at the conclusion of the work, to have been made for the better understanding of certain chapters of the *Antient Book of Tenures*. This refers to a tract called *The Old Tenures*, said to have been written in the reign of Edward III. By way of distinguishing it from this work, Littleton's book is called in all the [illegible] "Tenores Novelli."

his degree as doctor when in 1827 his father died, leaving his mother absolutely without resources. He at once renounced his degree, and, while attending the lectures of P. F. O. Rayer and taking a keen interest in medicine, began teaching Latin and Greek for a livelihood. He carried a musket on the popular side in the revolution of February 1830, and was one of the national guards who followed Charles X. to Rambouillet. In 1831 he obtained an introduction to Armand Carrel, the editor of the *National*, who gave him the task of reading the English and German papers for excerpts. Carrel by chance, in 1835, discovered the ability of his reader, who from that time became a constant contributor, and eventually director of the paper. In 1836 Littré began to contribute articles on all sorts of subjects to the *Revue des deux mondes*; in 1837 he married; and in 1839 appeared the first volume of his edition of the works of Hippocrates. The value of this work was recognized by his election the same year into the Académie des Inscriptions et Belles-Lettres. At this epoch he came across the works of Auguste Comte, the reading of which formed, as he himself said, "the cardinal point of his life," and from this time onward appears the influence of positivism on his own life, and, what is of more importance, his influence on positivism, for he gave as much to positivism as he received from it. He soon became a friend of Comte, and popularized his ideas in numerous works on the positivist philosophy. At the same time he continued his edition of Hippocrates, which was not completed till 1862, published a similar edition of Pliny's *Natural History*, and after 1844 took Fauriel's place on the committee engaged on the *Histoire littéraire de la France*, where his knowledge of the early French language and literature was invaluable.

It was about 1844 that he started working on his great *Dictionnaire de la langue française*, which was, however, not to be completed till thirty years after. In the revolution of July 1848 he took part in the repression of the extreme republican party in June 1849. His essays, contributed during this period to the *National*, were collected together and published under the title of *Conservation, révolution et positivisme* in 1852, and show a thorough acceptance of all the doctrines propounded by Comte. However, during the later years of his master's life, he began to perceive that he could not wholly accept all the dogmas or the more mystic ideas of his friend and master, but he concealed his differences of opinion, and Comte failed to perceive that his pupil had outgrown him, as he himself had outgrown his master Saint-Simon. Comte's death in 1858 freed Littré from any fear of embittering his master's later years, and he published his own ideas in his *Paroles de la philosophie positive* in 1859, and at still greater length in his work in *Auguste Comte et la philosophie positive* in 1863. In this book he traces the origin of Comte's ideas through Turgot, Kant and Saint-Simon, then eulogizes Comte's own life, his method of philosophy, his great services to the cause and the effect of his works, and finally proceeds to show where he himself differs from him. He approved wholly of Comte's philosophy, his great laws of society and his philosophical method, which indeed he defended warmly against J. S. Mill, but declared that, while he believed in a positivist philosophy, he did not believe in a religion of humanity. About 1863, after completing his Hippocrates and his Pliny, he set to work in earnest on his French dictionary. In the same year he was proposed for the Académie Française, but rejected, owing to the opposition of Mgr. Dupanloup, bishop of Orleans, who denounced him in his *Avertissement aux pères de famille* as the chief of the French materialists. He also at this time started with G. Wyrouboff the *Philosophie Positive*, a review which was to embody the views of modern positivists. His life was thus absorbed in literary work till the overthrow of the empire called on him to take a part in politics. He felt himself too old to undergo the privations of the siege of Paris, and retired with his family to Britanny, whence he was summoned by M. Gambetta to Bordeaux, to lecture on history, and thence to Versailles to take his seat in the senate to which he had been chosen by the department of the Seine. In December 1871 he was elected a member of the Académie Française in spite of the renewed opposition of Mgr. Dupanloup, who resigned his seat rather than receive him. Littré's *Dictionary* was completed in 1873. An authoritative interpretation is given of the use of each word, based on the various meanings it had held in the past. In 1875 Littré was elected a life senator. The most notable of his productions in these years were his political papers attacking and unveiling the confederacy of the Orleanists and legitimists, and in favour of the republic, his republication of many of his old articles and books, among others the *Conservation, révolution et positivisme* of 1852 (which he reprinted word for word, appending a formal, categorical renunciation of many of the Comtist doctrines therein contained), and a little tract *Pour la dernière fois*, in which he maintained his unalterable belief in materialism. When it became obvious that the old man could not live much longer, his wife and daughter, who had always been fervent Catholics, strove to convert him to their religion. He had long interviews with Père Milleriot, a celebrated controversialist, and was much grieved at his death; but it is hardly probable he would have ever been really converted. Nevertheless, when on the point of death, his wife had him baptized, and his funeral was conducted with the rites of the Catholic Church. He died on the 2nd of June 1881.

The following are his most important works: his editions of Hippocrates (1839–1861), and of Pliny's *Natural History* (1848–1850); his translation of Strauss's *Vie de Jésus* (1839–1840), and Muller's *Manuel de physiologie* (1851); his edition of the works of Armand Carrel, with notes (1854–1858); the *Histoire de la langue française*, a collection of magazine articles (1862); and his *Dictionnaire de la langue française* (1863–1872). In the domain of science must be noted his edition, with Charles Robin, of Nysten's *Dictionnaire de médecine, de chirurgie, &c.* (1855); in that of philosophy, his *Analyse raisonnée du cours de philosophie positive de M. A. Comte* (1845); *Application de la philosophie positive au gouvernement* (1849); *Conservation, révolution et positivisme* (1852, 2nd ed., with supplement, 1879); *Paroles de la philosophie positive* (1859); *Auguste Comte et la philosophie positive* (1863); *La Science au point de vue philosophique* (1873); *Fragments de philosophie et de sociologie contemporaine* (1876); and his most interesting miscellaneous works, his *Études et glanures* (1880); *La Vérité sur la mort d'Alexandre le grand* (1865); *Études sur les barbares et le moyen âge* (1867); *Médecine et médecins* (1871); *Littérature et histoire* (1875); and *Discours de réception à l'Académie française* (1873).

For his life consult C. A. Sainte-Beuve, *Notice sur M. Littré, sa vie et ses travaux* (1863); and *Nouveaux Lundis*, vol. v.; also the notice by M. Durand-Gréville in the *Nouvelle Revue* of August 1881, L. Caro, *Littré et le positivisme* (1883); Pasteur, *Discours de réception* at the Academy, where he succeeded Littré, and a reply by E. Renan. (H. M. S.)

LITURGY (Low Lat. *liturgia*; Gr. λεῖτος, public, and ἔργον, work; λειτουργός, a public servant), in the technical language of the Christian Church, the order for the celebration and administration of the Eucharist. In Eastern Christendom the Greek word λειτουργία is used in this sense exclusively. But in English-speaking countries the word "liturgy" has come to be used in a more popular sense to denote any or all of the various services of the Church, whether contained in separate volumes or bound up together in the form of a Book of Common Prayer. In this article the liturgy is treated in the former and stricter sense (For the ancient Athenian λειτουργίαι, as forms of taxation, see FINANCE.)

In order to understand terms and references it will be convenient to give the tabular form the chief component parts of a liturgy, selecting the Liturgy of Rome as characteristic of Western, and that of Constantinople as characteristic of Eastern, Christendom; at the same time appending an explanation of some of the technical words which must be employed in enumerating those parts.

ORDER OF THE ROMAN LITURGY

Ordinary of the Mass.

1. Introit, or as it is always called in the Sarum rite, "Office," a Psalm or part of a Psalm sung at the entry of the priest, or clergy and choir
2. Kyrie eleison, ninefold, and sometimes lengthily farsed representing an older, now obsolete, litany
3. Collect, *i.e.* the collect for the day.
4. Prophetic lection, now obsolete, except on the Wednesday and Saturday Ember Days, Good Friday and Easter Even, and Wednesday after fourth and sixth Sundays in Lent.
5. Epistle.

[illegible] few verses from the Psalms, the shrunken remains of the [illegible] Psalm.
[illegible] now obsolete except on Feast of the Seven [illegible] Pentecost, Corpus Christi and at Masses for the dead.
[illegible]
[illegible], though the unanswered invitation, [illegible]
[illegible] or verses from the Psalms sung at the [illegible]
[illegible] or prayers said at the conclusion of the [illegible]
[illegible] "Lift up your hearts" with following [illegible]
[illegible] There are now ten proper or special prefaces and [illegible] In older missals they were extremely numerous, [illegible] and Holy-day having one assigned to it. Many [illegible] beautiful. In older missals, Nos. 13, 14 and 15 [illegible] arranged not as the concluding part of the Ordinary, [illegible] part of the Canon of the mass.
[illegible] Tersanctus, or Triumphal Hymn, "Holy, Holy, [illegible] with the Benedictus, "Blessed is he that cometh," [illegible]

Canon of the Mass.

[illegible] Te igitur, &c.
[illegible] Memento, Domine famulorum, &c.
[illegible] martyrs. Communicantes et [illegible]
[illegible] consecration of offering. Hanc [illegible]
[illegible] Qui pridie quam pateretur, &c.
[illegible]
[illegible] difficult of interpretation, but apparently [illegible] the Eastern Epiklesis or invocation of [illegible] &c.
[illegible] Memento etiam, Domine, famul[illegible]
[illegible] short introduction and the expansion of [illegible] known as the "Embolismus."
[illegible] breaking of the host into three parts, to [illegible] Christ.
[illegible] placing a small portion of the consecrated [illegible] symbolizing the reunion of Christ's body and [illegible]
[illegible] threefold petition to the Lamb of God.
[illegible] peace. The ancient ritual of the Pax has [illegible]
[illegible] accompanying the Pax and preliminary to [illegible]
[illegible] priest and people (if any), a short anthem [illegible] being sung meanwhile.
[illegible]
[illegible] concluding prayer.
[illegible] with No. 9; Nos. 10-18 being [illegible]

LITURGY OF CONSTANTINOPLE

Mass of the Catechumens. After preparation and vesting

1. The Deacon's Litany.
2. [illegible] Anthems with accompanying prayers.
3. [illegible] Entrance, *i.e.* ceremonial bringing in of the Book of the [illegible]
4. [illegible] Trisagion, *i.e.* an anthem with an accompanying prayer [illegible] the Latin Sanctus or Tersanctus
5. [illegible]
6. [illegible] with a prayer preceding it
7. [illegible] prayer
8. [illegible] catechumens.
9. [illegible] of catechumens.
10. [illegible] of the corporal.

Mass of the Faithful.

11. [illegible] of the faithful.
12. [illegible] Hymn, "Let us who mystically represent the [illegible]" not represented in the Latin liturgy.
13. [illegible] Entrance, *i.e.* of the unconsecrated elements with incense
14. [illegible] and intercessions.
15. [illegible] peace
16. [illegible]
17. [illegible] Salutation, *i.e.* 2 Cor. xiii. 14.
18. [illegible]
19. [illegible]
20. [illegible] Tersanctus, or "Triumphal Hymn."
21. [illegible] Words of Institution, prefaced by recital of the [illegible] [illegible]
22. The invocation or Epiklesis.
23. Intercession for the dead.
24. Intercession for the living.
25. The Lord's Prayer.
26. Prayer of humble access (*a*) for people (*b*) for priest.
27. Elevation with the invitation "Holy things to holy people."
28. Fraction.
29. Commixture.
30. Thanksgiving.
31. Benediction.

In both these lists many interesting features of ceremonial, the use of incense the infusion of warm water (Byzantine only), &c., have not been referred to. The lists must be regarded as skeletons only.

There are six main families or groups of liturgies, four of them being of Eastern and two of them of Western origin and use. They are known either by the names of the apostles with whom they are traditionally connected, or by the names of the countries or cities in which they have been or are still in use.

Group I. *The Syrian Rite* (St James).—The principal liturgies to be enumerated under this group are the Clementine liturgy, so called from being found in the eighth book of the Apostolic Constitutions, which claim in their title, though erroneously, to have been compiled by St Clement, the 1st-century bishop of Rome; the Greek liturgy of St James; the Syriac liturgy of St James. Sixty-four more liturgies of this group have existed, the majority being still in existence. Their titles are given in F. E. Brightman's *Liturgies, Eastern and Western* (1896), pp. lviii.-lxi.

Group II. *The Egyptian Rite* (St Mark).—This group includes the Greek liturgies of St Mark, St Basil and St Gregory, and the Coptic liturgies of St Basil, St Gregory, St Cyril or St Mark; together with certain less known liturgies the titles of which are enumerated by Brightman (*op. cit.* pp. lxxiii. lxxiv.). The liturgy of the Ethiopian church ordinances and the liturgy of the Abyssinian Jacobites, known as that of the Apostles, fall under this group.

Group III. *The Persian Rite* (SS. Adaeus and Maris).—This Nestorian rite is represented by the liturgy which bears the names of SS. Adaeus and Maris together with two others named after Theodore of Mopsuestia and Nestorius. This group has sometimes been called "East-Syrian." The titles of three more of its now lost liturgies have been preserved, namely those of Narses, Barsumas and Diodorus of Tarsus. The liturgy of the Christians of St Thomas, on the Malabar coast of India, formerly belonged to this group, but it was almost completely assimilated to the Roman liturgy by Portuguese Jesuits at the synod of Diamper in 1599.

Group IV. *The Byzantine Rite.*—The Greek liturgies of St Chrysostom, St Basil and St Gregory Dialogus, or The Presanctified, also extant in other languages, are the living representatives of this rite. The Greek liturgy of St Peter is classified under this group, but it is merely the Roman canon of the Mass &c., inserted in a Byzantine framework, and seems to have been used at one time by some Greek communities in Italy. To this group also belongs the Armenian liturgy, of which ten different forms have existed in addition to the liturgy now in general use named after St Athanasius.

We now come to the two western groups of liturgies, which more nearly concern the Latin-speaking nations of Europe, and which, therefore, must be treated of more fully.

Group V. *The Hispano-Gallican Rite* (St John).—This group of Latin liturgies, which once prevailed very widely in Western Europe, has been almost universally superseded by the liturgy of the Church of Rome. Where it survives, it has been more or less assimilated to the Roman pattern. It prevailed once throughout Spain, France, northern Italy, Great Britain and Ireland. The term "Ephesine" has been applied to this group or family of liturgies, chiefly by English liturgiologists, and the names of St John and of Ephesus, his place of residence, have been pressed into service in support of a theory of Ephesine origin, which, however, lacks proof and may now be regarded as a discarded hypothesis. Other theories represent the Gallican to be a survival of the original Roman liturgy, or as an importation into Western Europe from the east through a Milanese channel. The latter is Duchesne's theory (*Christian Worship*, London, 1904, 2nd ed., p. 94).

We must be content with mentioning these theories without attempting to discuss them.

The chief traces of oriental influence and affinity lie in the following points:—(1) various proclamations made by the deacon, including that of "Silentium facite" before the epistle (Migne, *Pat. Lat.* tom. lxxxv. col. 534); (2) the presence of a third lesson preceding the epistle, taken from the Old Testament; (3) the occasional presence of "preces" a series of short intercessions resembling the Greek "Ektené" or deacon's litany; (4) the position of the kiss of peace at an early point in the service, before the canon, instead of the Roman position after consecration; (5) the exclamation "Sancta sanctis" occurring in the Mozarabic rite, being the counterpart of the Eastern "Τὰ ἅγια τοῖς ἁγίοις," that is "holy things to holy people"; (6) traces of the presence of the "Epiklesis," that is to say, the invocation of the Holy Spirit, in its Eastern position after the words of institution, as in the prayer styled the Post-pridie in the Mozarabic service for the second Sunday after the octave of the Epiphany: "We beseech thee that thou wouldest sanctify this oblation with the permixture of thy Spirit, and conform it with full transformation into the body and blood of our Lord Jesus Christ" (Migne, *Pat. Lat.* tom. lxxxv. col. 250). On the other hand the great variableness of its parts, and the immense number of its proper prefaces, ally it to the Western family of liturgies.

We proceed now to give a more detailed account of the chief liturgies of this group.

1. *The Mozarabic Liturgy.*—This was the national liturgy of the Spanish church till the close of the 11th century, when the Roman liturgy was forced upon it. Its use, however, lingered on, till in the 16th century Cardinal Jimenes, anxious to prevent its becoming quite obsolete, had its books restored and printed, and founded a college of priests at Toledo to perpetuate its use. It survives now only in several churches in Toledo and in a chapel at Salamanca, and even there not without certain Roman modifications of its original text and ritual.

Its date and origin, like the date and origin of all existing liturgies, are uncertain, and enveloped in the mists of antiquity. It is not derived from the present Roman liturgy. Its whole structure, as well as separate details disprove such a parentage, and therefore it is strange to find St Isidore of Seville (*Lib. de Eccles. Offic.* i. 15) attributing it to St Peter. No proof is adduced, and the only value which can be placed upon such an unsupported assertion is that it shows that a very high and even apostolic antiquity was claimed for it. A theory, originating with Pinius, that it may have been brought by the Goths from Constantinople when they invaded Spain, is as improbable as it is unproven. It may have been derived from Gaul. The Gallican sister stood to it in the relation of twin-sister, if it could not claim that of mother. The resemblance was so great that when Charles the Bald (843–877) wished to get some idea of the character of the already obsolete Gallican rite, he sent to Toledo for some Spanish priests to perform Mass according to the Mozarabic rite in his presence. But there is no record of the conversion of Spain by Gallican missionaries. Christianity existed in Spain from the earliest times. Probably St Paul travelled there (Rom. xv. 24). It may be at least conjectured that its liturgy was Pauline rather than Petrine or Johannine.

2. *Gallican Liturgy.*—This was the ancient and national liturgy of the church in France till the commencement of the 9th century, when it was suppressed by order of Charlemagne, who directed the Roman missal to be everywhere substituted in its place. All traces of it seemed for some time to have been lost until three Gallican sacramentaries were discovered and published by Thomasius in 1680 under the titles of *Missale Gothicum*, *Missale Gallicum* and *Missale Francorum*, and a fourth was discovered and published by Mabillon in 1687 under the title of *Missale Gallicanum*. Fragmentary discoveries have been made since. Mone discovered fragments of eleven Gallican masses and published them at Carlsruhe in 1850. Other fragments from the library at St Gall have been published by Bunsen (*Analecta Ante-Nicaena*, iii. 263–266), and from the Ambrosian library at Milan by Cardinal Mai (*Scriptt. Vet. Vat. Coll.* iii. 2. 247). A single page was discovered in Gonville and Caius College, Cambridge, published in *Zeitschrift für Kath. Theologie*, vi. 370.

These documents, illustrated by early Gallican canons, and by allusions in the writings of Sulpicius Severus, Caesarius of Arles, Gregory of Tours, Germanus of Paris and other authors, enable us to reconstruct the greater part of this liturgy. The previously enumerated signs of Eastern origin and influence are found here as well as in the Mozarabic liturgy, together with certain other more or less minute peculiarities, which would be of interest to professed liturgiologists, but which we must not pause to specify here. They are the origin of the Ephesine theory that the Gallican liturgy was introduced into use by Irenaeus, bishop of Lyons (*c.* 130-200) who had learned it in the East from St Polycarp, the disciple of the apostle St John.

3. *Ambrosian Liturgy.*—Considerable variety of opinion has existed among liturgical writers as to the proper classification of the "Ambrosian" or "Milanese" liturgy. If we are to accept it in its present form and to make the present position of the great intercession for quick and dead the test of its *genus*, then we must classify it as "Petrine" and consider it as a branch of the Roman family. If, on the other hand, we consider the important variations from the Roman liturgy which yet exist, and the traces of still more marked variation which confront us in the older printed and MS. copies of the Ambrosian rite, we shall detect in it an original member of the Hispano-Gallican group of liturgies, which for centuries underwent a gradual but ever-increasing assimilation to Rome. We know this as a matter of history, as well as a matter of inference from changes in the text itself. Charlemagne adopted the same policy towards the Milanese as towards the Gallican church. He carried off all the Ambrosian church books which he could obtain, with the view of substituting Roman books in their place, but the completion of his intentions failed, partly through the attachment of the Lombards to their own rites, partly through the intercession of a Gallican bishop named Eugenius (Mabillon, *Mus. Ital.* tom. i. Pars. ii. p. 106). It has been asserted by Joseph Vicecomes that this is an originally independent liturgy drawn up by St Barnabas, who first preached the Gospel at Milan (*De Missae* Rit. 1 capp. xi. xii.), and this tradition is preserved in the title and proper preface for St Barnabas Day in the Ambrosian missal (Pamelius, *Liturgicon*, i. 385, 386), but it has never been proved.

We can trace the following points in which the Ambrosian differs from the Roman liturgy, many of them exhibiting traces of Eastern influence. Some of them are no longer found in recent Ambrosian missals and only survive in earlier MSS. such as those published by Pamelius (*Liturgicon*, tom. i. p. 293), Muratori (*Lit. Rom. Vet.* i. 132) and Ceriani (in his edition, 1881, of an ancient MS. at Milan). (*a*) The prayer entitled "oratio super sindonem" corresponding to the prayer after the spreading of the corporal; (*b*) the proclamation of silence by the deacon before the epistle; (*c*) the litanies said after the Ingressa (Introit) on Sundays in Lent, closely resembling the Greek Ektené; (*d*) varying forms of introduction to the Lord's Prayer, in Coena Domini (Ceriani p. 116) in Pascha (*Ib.* p. 129); (*e*) the presence of passages in the prayer of consecration which are not part of the Roman canon and one of which at least corresponds in import and position though not in words to the Greek Invocation: *Tuum vero, est, omnipotens Pater, mittere*, &c. (*Ib.* p. 116); (*f*) the survival of a distinctly Gallican formula of consecration in the Post-sanctus "in Sabbato Sancto." *Vere sanctus, vere benedictus Dominus noster*, &c. (*Ib.* p. 125); (*g*) the varying nomenclature of the Sundays after Pentecost; (*h*) the position of the fraction or ritual breaking of bread before the Lord's Prayer; (*i*) the omission of the second oblation after the words of institution (Muratori, *Lit. Rom. Vet.* i. 133); (*k*) a third lection or *Prophetia* from the Old Testament preceding the epistle and gospel; (*l*) the lay offering of the oblations and the formulae accompanying their reception (Pamelius, *Liturgicon*, i. 297); (*m*) the position of the ablution of the hands in the middle of the canon just before the words of institution; (*n*) the position of the "oratio super populum," which corresponds in matter but not in name to the collect for the day, before the Gloria in Excelsis.

4. *Celtic Liturgy.*—We postpone the consideration of this liturgy till after we have treated of the next main group.

VI. *The Roman Rite* (St Peter).—There is only one liturgy to be enumerated under this group, viz. the present liturgy of the Church of Rome, which, though originally local in character and circumscribed in use, has come to be nearly co-extensive with the Roman Catholic Church, sometimes superseding earlier national liturgies, as in Gaul and Spain, sometimes incorporating more or less of the ancient ritual of a country into itself and producing from such incorporation a sub-class of distinct Uses, as in England, France and elsewhere. Even these subordinate Uses have for the most part become, or are rapidly becoming, obsolete.

The date, origin and early history of the Roman liturgy are obscure. The first Christians at Rome were a Greek-speaking community, and their liturgy must have been Greek, and is possibly represented in the so-called Clementine liturgy. But the date when such a state of things ceased, when and by whom the present Latin liturgy was composed, whether it is an original composition, or, as its structure seems to imply, a survival of some intermediate form of liturgy—all these are questions which are waiting for solution.

One MS. exists which has been claimed to represent the Roman liturgy as it existed in the time of Leo I., 440–461. It was discovered at Verona by Bianchini in 1735 and assigned by him to the 6th century and published under the title of *Sacramentarium Leonianum*, but this title was from the first conjectural, and is in the teeth of the internal evidence which the MS. itself affords. The question is discussed at some length by Muratori (*Lit. Rom. Vet.* tom. i. cap. i. col. 16). Assemani published it under the title of *Sacramentarium Veronense* in tom. vi. of his *Codex Liturg. Eccles. Univ.*

A MS. of the 7th or 8th century was found at Rome by Thomasius and published by him in 1680 under the title of *Sacramentarium Gelasianum*. But it was written in France and is certainly not a pure Gelasian codex; and although there is historical evidence of Pope Gelasius I. (492–496) having made some changes in the Roman liturgy, and although MSS. have been published by Gerbertus and others, claiming the title of Gelasian, we neither have nor are likely to have genuine and contemporary MS. evidence of the real state of the liturgy in that pope's time. The most modern and the best edition of the Gelasian Sacramentary is that by H. A. Wilson (Oxford, 1894).

The larger number of MSS. of this group are copies of the Gregorian Sacramentary, that is to say, MSS. representing or purporting to represent, the state of Roman liturgy in the days of Pope Gregory the Great. But they cannot be accepted as certain evidence for the following reasons: not one of them was written earlier than the 9th century, not one of them was written in Italy, but every one north of the Alps; every one contains internal evidence of a post-Gregorian date in the shape of masses for the repose or for the intercession of St Gregory and in various other ways.

The Roman liturgy seems to have been introduced into England in the 7th, into France in the 9th and into Spain in the 11th century, though no doubt it was known in both France and Spain to some extent before these dates. In France certain features of the service and certain points in the ritual of the ancient national liturgy became interwoven with its text and formed those many varying medieval Gallican Uses which are associated with the names of different French sees.

The chief distinguishing characteristics of the Roman rite are these: (*a*) the position of the great intercession for quick and dead within the canon, the commemoration of the living being placed just before and the commemoration of the departed just after the words of institution; (*b*) the absence of an "Epiklesis" or invocation of the Holy Ghost upon the elements; (*c*) the position of the "Pax" or "Kiss of Peace after the consecration" and before the communion, whereas in other liturgies it occurs at a much earlier point in the service.

Liturgies of the British Islands.

Period I. *The Celtic Church.*—Until recently almost nothing was known of the character of the liturgical service of the Celtic church which existed in these islands before the Anglo-Saxon Conquest, and continued to exist in Ireland, Scotland, Wales and Cornwall for considerable though varying periods of time after that event. But in recent times a good deal of light has been thrown on the subject, partly by the publication or republication of the few genuine works of Patrick, Columba, Columbanus, Adamnan and other Celtic saints; partly by the discovery of liturgical remains in the Scottish *Book of Deer* and in the Irish *Books of Dimma and Mulling* and the *Stowe Missal*, &c., partly by the publication of medieval Irish compilations, such as the *Lebar Brecc*, *Liber Hymnorum*, *Martyrology of Oengus*, &c., which contain ecclesiastical kalendars, legends, treatises, &c., of considerable but very varying antiquity. The evidence collected from these sources is sufficient to prove that the liturgy [illegible] Celtic church was of the Gallican type. In central England [illegible] churches, with everything belonging to them, were destroyed [illegible] heathen invaders at the close of the 5th century; but [illegible] church in the rem[illegible]land, as well as in the neighbouring kingdoms of Scotland and Ireland, retained its independence for centuries afterwards.

An examination of its few extant service-books and fragments of service-books yields the following evidence of the Gallican origin and character of the Celtic liturgy: (*a*) the presence of collects and anthems which occur in the Gallican or Mozarabic but not in the Roman liturgy; (*b*) various formulae of thanksgiving after communion, (*c*) frequent biddings or addresses to the people in the form of Gallican *Praefationes*, (*d*) the Gallican form of consecration, being a prayer called "Post-Sanctus" leading up to the words of institution; (*e*) the complicated rite of "fraction" or "the breaking of bread," as described in the Irish treatise at the end of the *Stowe Missal*, finds its only counterpart in the elaborate ceremonial of the Mozarabic church; (*f*) the presence of the Gallican ceremonial of *Pedilavium* or "Washing of feet" in the earliest Irish baptismal office.

For a further description of these and other features which are characteristic of or peculiar to the Celtic liturgy the reader is referred to F. E. Warren's *Liturgy and Ritual of the Celtic Church* (Oxford, 1881).

Period II. *The Anglo-Saxon Church.*—We find ourselves here on firmer ground, and can speak with certainty as to the nature of the liturgy of the English church after the beginning of the 7th century. Information is drawn from liturgical allusions in the extant canons of numerous councils, from the voluminous writings of Bede, Alcuin and many other ecclesiastical authors of the Anglo-Saxon period, and above all from a considerable number of service-books written in England before the Norman Conquest. Three of these books are missals of more or less completeness: (1) the *Leofric Missal*, a composite 10th- to 11th-century MS. presented to the cathedral of Exeter by Leofric, the first bishop of that see (1046–1072), now in the Bodleian library at Oxford; edited by F. E. Warren (Oxford, 1883); (2) the missal of Robert of Jumièges, archbishop of Canterbury (1051–1052), written probably at Winchester and presented by Archbishop Robert to his old monastery of Jumièges in the neighbourhood of Rouen, in the public library of which it now lies; edited by H. A. Wilson (London, 1896); (3) the *Red Book of Derby*, a MS. missal of the second half of the 11th century, now in the library of Corpus Christi College, Cambridge.

A perusal of these volumes proves what we should have expected a priori, that the Roman liturgy was in use in the Anglo-Saxon church. This was the case from the very first. That church owed its foundation to a Roman pontiff, and to Roman missionaries, who brought, as we are told by Bede, their native liturgical codices with them (*Hist. Eccles.* lib. ii. cap. 28). Accordingly, when we speak of an Anglo-Saxon missal, we mean a Roman missal only exhibiting one or more of the following features, which would differentiate it from an Italian missal of the same century. (*a*) Rubrics and other entries of a miscellaneous character written in the vernacular language of the country. (*b*) The commemoration of national or local saints in the kalendar, in the canon of the mass and in the litanies which occur for use on Easter Even and in the baptismal offices. (*c*) The presence of a few special masses in honour of those local saints, together with a certain number of collects of a necessarily local character, for the rulers of the country, for its natural produce, &c. (*d*) The addition of certain peculiarities of liturgical structure and arrangement interpolated into the otherwise purely Roman service from an extraneous source. There are two noteworthy examples of this in Anglo-Saxon service-books. Every Sunday and festival and almost every votive mass has its proper preface, although the number of such prefaces in the Gregorian sacramentary of the same period had been reduced to eight. There was a large but not quite equal number of triple episcopal benedictions to be pronounced by the bishop after the Lord's Prayer and before the communion. This custom must either have been perpetuated from the old Celtic liturgy or directly derived from a Gallican source.

Period III. *Anglo-Norman Church.*—The influx of numerous foreigners, especially from Normandy and Lorraine, which preceded, accompanied and followed the Conquest, and the occupation by them of the highest posts in church as well as state had a distinct effect on the liturgy of the English church. These foreign ecclesiastics brought over with them a preference for and a habit of using certain features of the Gallican liturgy and ritual, which they succeeded in incorporating into the service-books of the church of England. One of the Norman prelates, Osmund, count of Sées, earl of Dorset, chancellor of England, and bishop of Salisbury (1078–1099), is credited with having undertaken the revision of the English service-books; and the missal which we know as the *Sarum Missal*, or the *Missal according to the Use of Sarum*, practically became the liturgy of the English church. It was not only received into use in the province of Canterbury, but was largely adopted beyond those limits—in Ireland in the 12th and in various Scottish dioceses in the 12th and 13th centuries.

It would be beyond our scope here to give a complete list of the numerous and frequently minute differences between a medieval Sarum and the earlier Anglo-Saxon or contemporaneous Roman liturgy. They lie mainly in differences of collects and lections, variations of ritual on Candlemass, Ash Wednesday and throughout Holy Week; the introduction into the canon of the mass of certain clauses and usages of Gallican character or origin; the wording of rubrics in the subjunctive or imperative tense; the peculiar "Preces in prostratione"; the procession of Corpus Christi on Palm Sunday; the forms of ejection and reconciliation of penitents, &c. The varying episcopal benedictions as used in the Anglo-Saxon church were retained, but the numerous proper prefaces were discarded, the number being reduced to ten.

Besides the famous and far-spreading Use of Sarum, other Uses, more local and less known, grew up in various English dioceses. In virtue of a recognized diocesan independence, bishops were able to regulate or alter their ritual, and to add special masses or commemorations for use within the limits of their jurisdiction. The better known and the more distinctive of these Uses were those of York and Hereford, but we also find traces of or allusions to the Uses of Bangor, Lichfield, Lincoln, Ripon, St Asaph, St Paul's, Wells and Winchester.

Service-books.—The Eucharistic service was contained in the volume called the Missal (*q.v.*), as the ordinary choir offices were contained in the volume known as the Breviary (*q.v.*). But besides these two volumes there were a large number of other service-books. Mr W. Maskell has enumerated and described ninety-one such volumes employed by the Western Church only. It must be understood, however, that many of these ninety-one names are synonyms (*Mon. Rit. Eccles. Anglic.*, 1882, vol. i. p. ccxxx.). The list might be increased, but it will be possible here only to name and briefly describe a few of the more important of them. (1) The *Agenda* is the same as the Manual, for which see below. (2) The *Antiphonary* contained the antiphons or anthems, sung at the canonical hours, and certain other minor parts of the service. (3) The *Benedictional* contained those triple episcopal benedictions previously described as used on Sundays and on the chief festivals throughout the year. (4) The *Collectarium* contained the collects for the season, together with a few other parts of the day offices. It was an inchoate breviary. (5) The *Epistolarium* contained the epistles, and the *Evangelistarium* the gospels for the year. (7) The *Gradual* contained the introit, gradual, sequences, and the other portions of the communion service which were sung by the choir at high mass. (8) *The Legenda* contained the lections which were read at matins and at other times, and may be taken as a generic term to include the *Homiliarium*, *Passional* and other volumes. (9) The *Manual* was the name usually employed in England to denote the *Ritual*, which contained the baptismal, matrimonial and other offices which might be performed by the parish priest. (10) The *Pontifical* contained the orders of consecration, ordination, and such other rites as could, ordinarily, only be performed by a bishop. To these we must add a book which was not strictly a church office book, but a handy book for the use of the laity, and which was in very popular use and often very highly embellished from the 14th to the 16th century, the *Book of Hours*, or *Horae Beatae Mariae Virginis*, also known as the *Prymer* or *Primer*. It contained portions of the canonical hours, litanies, the penitential Psalms, and other devotions of a miscellaneous and private character. Detailed information about all these and other books is to be found in C. Wordsworth and H. Littlehales', *The Old Service Books of the English Church*.

The Eastern Church too possessed and still possesses numerous and voluminous service-books, of which the chief are the following: (1) The *Euchologian*, containing the liturgy itself with the remaining sacramental offices bound up in the same volume. (2) The *Horologion*, containing the unvarying portion of the Breviary. (3) The *Menaea*, being equivalent to a complete Breviary. (4) The *Menologion* or Martyrology. (5) The *Octoechus* and (6) The *Paracletice*, containing Troparia and answering to the Western antiphonary. (7) The *Pentecostarion*, containing the services from Easter Day to All Saints' Sunday. (8) The *Triodion*, containing those from Septuagesima Sunday to Easter Even. (9) The *Typicum* is a general book of rubrics corresponding to the Ordinale or the Pie of Western Christendom.

Period IV. *The Reformed Church.*—The Anglican liturgy of Reformation and post-Reformation times is described under the heading of PRAYER, BOOK OF COMMON, but a brief description may be added here of the liturgies of other reformed churches.

The Liturgy of the Scottish Episcopal Church.—This liturgy in nearly its present form was compiled by Scottish bishops in 1636 and imposed—or, to speak more accurately, attempted to be imposed—upon the Scottish people by the royal authority of Charles I. in 1637. The prelates chiefly concerned in it were Spottiswood, bishop of Glasgow; Maxwell, bishop of Ross; Wedderburn, bishop of Dunblane; and Forbes, bishop of Edinburgh. Their work was approved and revised by certain members of the English episcopate, especially Laud, archbishop of Canterbury; Juxon, bishop of London; and Wren, bishop of Ely. This liturgy has met with varied fortune and has passed through several editions. The present Scottish office dates from 1764. It is now used as an alternative form with the English communion office in the Scottish Episcopal Church.

The general arrangements of its parts approximates more closely to that of the first book of Edward VI. than to the present Anglican Book of Common Prayer. Among its noteworthy features are (*a*) the retention in its integrity and in its primitive position after the words of institution of the invocation of the Holy Spirit. That invocation runs thus: "And we most humbly beseech thee, O merciful Father, to hear us and of thy almighty goodness vouchsafe to bless and sanctify with thy word and Holy Spirit these thy gifts and creatures of bread and wine that they may become the body and blood of thy most dearly beloved Son" (edit. 1764). This kind of petition thus placed is found in the Eastern but not in the Roman or Anglican liturgies. (*b*) The reservation of the sacrament is permitted, by traditional usage, for the purpose of communicating the absent or the sick. (*c*) The minimum number of communicants is fixed at one or two instead of three or four.

For fuller information see Bishop J. Dowden, *The Annotated Scottish Communion Service* (Edinburgh, 1884).

American Liturgy.—The Prayer Book of "the Protestant Episcopal Church" in America was adopted by the general convention of the American church in 1789. It is substantially the same as the English Book of Common Prayer, but among important variations we may name the following: (*a*) The arrangement and wording of the order for Holy Communion rather resembles that of the Scottish than that of the English liturgy, especially in the position of the oblation and invocation immediately after the words of institution. (*b*) The Magnificat, Nunc dimittis and greater part of Benedictus were disused; but these were reinstated among the changes made in the Prayer Book in 1892. (*c*) Ten selections of Psalms are appointed for use as alternatives for the Psalms of the day. (*d*) *Gloria in excelsis* is allowed as a substitute for *Gloria Patri* at the end of the Psalms at morning and evening prayer. In addition to these there are many more both important and unimportant variations from the English Book of Common Prayer.

The Irish Prayer Book.—The Prayer Book in use in the Irish portion of the United Church of England and Ireland was the Anglican Book of Common Prayer, but after the disestablishment of the Irish church several changes were introduced into it by a synod held at Dublin in 1870. These changes included such important points as: (*a*) the excision of all lessons from the Apocrypha, (*b*) of the rubric ordering the recitation of the Athanasian Creed, (*c*) of the rubric ordering the vestments of the second year of Edward VI., (*d*) of the form of absolution in the office for the visitation of the sick, (*e*) the addition to the

Catechism of a question and answer bringing out more clearly the spiritual character of the real presence.

The Presbyterian Church.—The Presbyterian churches of Scotland at present possess no liturgy properly so called. Certain general rules for the conduct of divine service are contained in the "Directory for the Public Worship of God" agreed upon by the assembly of divines at Westminster, with the assistance of commissioners from the Church of Scotland, approved and established by an act of the general assembly, and by an act of parliament, both in 1645. In 1554 John Knox had drawn up an order of liturgy closely modelled on the Genevan pattern for the use of the English congregation to which he was then ministering at Frankfort. On his return to Scotland this form of liturgy was adopted by an act of the general assembly in 1560 and became the established form of worship in the Presbyterian church until the year 1645, when the Directory of Public Worship took its place. Herein regulations are laid down for the conduct of public worship, for the reading of Scripture and for extempore prayer before and after the sermon, and in the administration of the sacrament of baptism and the Lord's Supper, for the solemnization of marriage, visitation of the sick and burial of the dead, for the observance of days of public fasting and public thanksgiving, together with a form of ordination and a directory for family worship. In all these cases, though the general terms [illegible] the prayer are frequently indicated, the wording of it is left [illegible] the discretion of the minister, with these exceptions: At [illegible] the [illegible] of baptism this formula must be used—"I baptize thee [illegible] the name of the Father, and of the Son, and of the Holy [illegible]"; and for the Lord's Supper these forms are suggested, [illegible] liberty to the minister to use "other the like, used by [illegible] his apostles upon this occasion"—"According to the [illegible]ution, command, and example of our blessed Saviour, [illegible], I take this bread, and having given thanks, break it, [illegible] unto you. Take ye, eat ye; this is the body of Christ [illegible] broken for you; do this in remembrance of him." [illegible] "According to the institution, command and example [illegible] Jesus Christ, I take this cup and give it unto you; [illegible] the New Testament in the blood of Christ, which is [illegible] the remission of the sins of many; drink ye all of it." [illegible] an unvarying form of words directed to be used [illegible] by the man to the woman, and by the woman [illegible] the case of the solemnization of matrimony. The [illegible] on all other occasions, including ordination, is [illegible] discretion of the officiating minister or of the [illegible]

[illegible] Churches. *The Calvinistic Churches.*—Rather [illegible] element in the shape of a set form of words [illegible] service of the French and German Calvinistic [illegible] Sunday morning service as drawn up by Calvin [illegible] portion of Holy Scripture and the recitation of the [illegible]. Afterwards the minister, inviting the people [illegible] proceeded to a confession of sins and supplication [illegible] of the Psalms of David was sung. Then came [illegible] by an extempore prayer and concluding with [illegible] and benediction. The communion service [illegible] leading up to the apostles' creed; then [illegible], after which the bread and wine were [illegible], who advanced in reverence and order, while [illegible] or a suitable passage of Scripture was being [illegible] communicated a set form of thanksgiving was [illegible]. Then the Song of Simeon was sung by the [illegible] then dismissed with the blessing. This form [illegible] in various ways from time to time, but [illegible] the type of service in use among the reformed [illegible] Germany, Switzerland and France.

[illegible]—Luther was far more conservative than [illegible] reformers and his conservatism appeared [illegible] service-books which he drew up for the use [illegible] his name. In 1523 he published a treatise [illegible] in the *Congregation* and in 1526 he [illegible]. Except that the vernacular was [illegible] language, the old framework and order [illegible] closely followed, beginning with the [illegible], still always sung in Greek, Gloria [illegible] this and o[illegible] services is given [illegible] Bekenntnisse[illegible] [illegible]lerant and [illegible] an church would from time to time make such changes or adaptations in the order of service as might be found convenient. The Lutheran churches of northern Europe have not been slow to avail themselves of this advice and permission. Most of them have drawn up liturgies for themselves, sometimes following very closely, sometimes differing considerably from the original service composed by Luther himself. In 1822, on the union of the Lutheran and Reformed (Calvinistic) churches of Prussia, a new liturgy was published at Berlin. It is used in its entirety in the chapel royal, but great liberty as to its use was allowed to the parochical clergy, and considerable variations of text appear in the more recent editions of this service-book.

The Church of the New Jerusalem (Swedenborgians) and the Catholic Apostolic Church (Irvingites) and other Protestant bodies have drawn up liturgies for themselves, but they are hardly of sufficient historical importance to be described at length here.

The Old Catholics, lastly, published a *Rituale* in 1875 containing the occasional offices for baptism, matrimony, burial, &c., and a form for reception of Holy Communion, in the German language. This latter is for use in the otherwise unaltered service of the mass, corresponding in purpose to the order of Communion in English published the 8th of March 1548 and in use till Whitsunday 1549.

(F. E. W.)

LITUUS, the cavalry trumpet of the Romans, said by Macrobius (*Saturn.* lib. vi.) to have resembled the crooked staff borne by the Augurs. The lituus consisted of a cylindrical tube 4 or 5 ft. long, having a narrow bore, and terminating in a conical bell joint turned up in such a manner as to give the instrument the outline of the letter "J." Unlike the buccina, cornu and tuba, the other military service instruments of the Romans, the lituus has not been traced during the middle ages, the medieval instrument most nearly resembling it being the cromorne or tournebout, which, however, had lateral holes and was played by means of a reed mouthpiece. A lituus found in a Roman warrior's tomb at Cervetri (Etruria) in 1827 is preserved in the Vatican. Victor Mahillon gives its length as 1 m. 60, and its scale as in unison with that of the trumpet in G (*Catalogue descriptif*, 1896, pp. 29-30). (K. S.)

LIUDPRAND (Liutprand, Luitprand) (*c.* 922–972), Italian historian and author, bishop of Cremona, was born towards the beginning of the 10th century, of a good Lombard family. In 931 he entered the service of King Hugo of Italy as page; he afterwards rose to a high position at the court of Hugo's successor Berengar, having become chancellor, and having been sent (949) on an embassy to the Byzantine court. Falling into disgrace with Berengar on his return, he attached himself to the emperor Otto I., whom in 961 he accompanied into Italy, and by whom in 962 he was made bishop of Cremona. He was frequently employed in missions to the pope, and in 968 to Constantinople to demand for the younger Otto (afterwards Otto II.) the hand of Theophano, daughter of the emperor Nicephorus Phocas. His account of this embassy in the *Relatio de Legatione Constantinopolitana* is perhaps the most graphic and lively piece of writing which has come down to us from the 10th century. The detailed description of Constantinople and the Byzantine court is a document of rare value—though highly coloured by his ill reception and offended dignity. Whether he returned in 971 with the embassy to bring Theophano or not is uncertain. Liudprand died in 972.

He wrote (1) *Antapodoseos, seu rerum per Europam gestarum, Libri VI*, an historical narrative, relating to the events from 887 to 949, compiled with the object of avenging himself upon Berengar and Willa his queen; (2) *Historia Ottonis*, a work of greater impartiality and merit, unfortunately covering only the years from 960 to 964; and (3) the *Relatio de Legatione Constantinopolitana* (968–969). All are to be found in the *Monum. Germ. Hist.* of Pertz, and in the *Rer. Ital. Script.* of Muratori; there is an edition by E. Dümmler (1877), and a partial translation into German, with an introduction by W. Wattenbach, is given in the second volume of the *Geschichtsschreiber der deutschen Vorzeit* (1853). Compare Wattenbach, *Deutschlands Geschichtsquellen im Mittelalter*. Three other works, entitled *Adversaria*, *Chronicon, 606-960*, and *Opusculum de vitis Romanorum pontificum*, are usually, but wrongly, assigned to Liudprand. An English translation of the embassy to Constantinople is in Ernest Henderson's *Select Documents of the Middle Ages* (Bohn series, 1896). A complete bibliography is in A. Potthast's *Bibl. Hist. Medii Aevi* (Berlin, 1896).

LIVE OAK, a city and the county-seat of Suwannee county, Florida, U.S.A., 81 m. by rail W. of Jacksonville. Pop. (1890) 687; (1900) 1659; (1905) 7200; (1910) 3450. Live Oak is served by the Atlantic Coast Line, the Seaboard Air Line, the Live Oak, Perry & Gulf and the Florida railways. There are extensive areas of pine lands in the vicinity, and large quantities of sea-island cotton are produced in the county. Lumber and naval stores are also important products. The first settlement on the site of the city was made in 1865 by John Parshley, of Massachusetts, who erected a large saw-mill here. Live Oak was first incorporated as a town in 1874, and in 1903 was chartered as a city.

LIVER (O. Eng. *lifer*; cf. cognate forms, Dutch *lever*, Ger. *Leber*, Swed. *lefver*, &c.; the O. H. Ger forms are *libara*, *lipora*, &c.; the Teut. word has been connected with Gr. ἧπαρ and Lat. *jecur*), in anatomy, a large reddish-brown digestive gland situated in the upper and right part of the abdominal cavity. When hardened *in situ* its shape is that of a right-angled, triangular prism showing five surfaces—superior, anterior, inferior, posterior and right lateral which represents the base of the prism. It weighs about three pounds or one-fortieth of the body weight.

Although the liver is a fairly solid organ, it is plastic, and moulds itself to even hollow neighbouring viscera rather than they to it. The superior surface is in contact with the diaphragm, but has peritoneum between (see COELOM AND SEROUS MEMBRANES). At its posterior margin the peritoneum of the great sac is reflected on to the diaphragm to form the anterior layer of the *coronary ligament*. Near the mid line of the body, and at right angles to the last, another reflection, the *falciform ligament*, runs forward, and the line of attachment of this indicates the junction of the *right* and *left lobes* of the liver. The anterior surface is in contact with the diaphragm and the anterior abdominal wall. The attachment of the falciform ligament is continued down it. The posterior surface is more complicated (see fig. 1); starting from the right and working toward the left, a large triangular area, uncovered by peritoneum and in direct contact with the diaphragm, is seen. This is bounded on the left by the inferior vena cava, which is sunk into a deep groove in the liver, and into the upper part of this the *hepatic veins* open. Just to the right of this and at the lower part of the bare area is a triangular depression for the right suprarenal body. To the left of the vena cava is the *Spigelian lobe*, which lies in front of the bodies of the tenth and eleventh thoracic vertebrae, the lesser sac of peritoneum, diaphragm and thoracic aorta intervening. To the left of this is the fissure for the *ductus venosus*, and to the left of this again, the left lobe, in which a broad shallow groove for the oesophagus may usually be seen. Sometimes the left lobe stretches as far as the left abdominal wall, but more often it ends below the apex of the heart, which is 3½ in. to the left of the mid line of the body. The relations of the lower surface can only be understood if it is realized that it looks backward and to the left as well as downward (see fig. 1). Again starting from the right side, two impressions are seen; the anterior one is for the hepatic flexure of the colon, and the posterior for the upper part of the right kidney. To the left of the colic impression is a smaller one for the second part of the duodenum. Next comes the *gall bladder*, a pear-shaped bag, the fundus of which is in front and below, the neck behind and above. From the neck passes the *cystic duct*, which is often twisted into the form of an S. To the left of the gall bladder is the *quadrate lobe*, which is in contact with the pylorus of the stomach. To the left of this is the *left lobe* of the liver, separated from the quadrate lobe by the umbilical fissure in which lies the *round ligament* of the liver, the remains of the umbilical vein of the foetus. Sometimes this fissure is partly turned into a tunnel by a bridge of liver substance known as the *pons hepatis*.

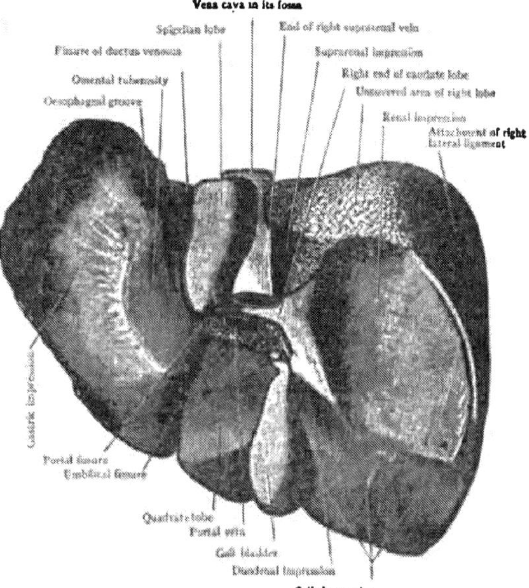

From A. Birmingham Cunningham's *Text-book of Anatomy*.

FIG. 1.—The Liver from below and behind, showing the whole of the visceral surface and the posterior area of the parietal surface. The portal fissure has been slightly opened up to show the vessels passing through it; the other fissures are represented in their natural condition—closed. In this liver, which was hardened *in situ*, the impressions of the sacculations of the colon are distinctly visible at the colic impression. The round ligament and the remains of the ductus venosus are hidden in the depths of their fissures.

The under surface of the left lobe is concave for the interior surface of the stomach (see ALIMENTARY CANAL: *Stomach Chamber*), while a convexity, known as the *tuber omentale*, fits into the lesser curvature of that organ. The posterior boundary of the quadrate lobe is the *transverse fissure*, which is little more than an inch long and more than half an inch wide. This fissure represents the hilum of the liver, and contains the right and left hepatic ducts and the right and left branches of the hepatic artery and portal vein, together with nerves and lymphatics, the whole being enclosed in some condensed subperitoneal tissue known as *Glisson's capsule*. Behind the transverse fissure the lower end of the Spigelian lobe is seen as a knob called the *tuber papillare*, and from the right of this a narrow bridge runs forward and to the right to join the Spigelian lobe to the right lobe and to shut off the transverse fissure from that for the vena cava. This is the *caudate lobe*. The right surface of the liver is covered with peritoneum and is in contact with the diaphragm, outside which are the pleura and lower ribs. From its lower margin the *right lateral ligament* is reflected on to the diaphragm. A similar fold passes from the tip of the left lobe as the *left lateral ligament*, and both these are the lateral margins of the coronary ligament. Sometimes, especially in women, a tongue-shaped projection downward of the right lobe is found, known as *Riedel's lobe*; it is of clinical interest as it may be mistaken for a tumour or floating kidney (see C. H. Leaf, *Proc. Anat. Soc.*, February 1899; *Journ. Anat. and Phys.* vol. 33, p. ix.). The right and left *hepatic ducts*, while still in the transverse fissure, unite into a single duct which joins the cystic duct from the gall bladder at an acute angle. When these have united the duct is known as the *common bile duct*, and runs down to the second part of the duodenum (see ALIMENTARY CANAL).

Minute Structure of the Liver.—The liver is made up of an enormous number of *lobules* of a conical form (see fig. 3). If the portal vein is followed from the transverse fissure, it will be seen to branch and re-branch until minute twigs called *interlobular veins* (fig. 2, i) ramify around the lobules. From these *intralobular capillaries* run toward the centre of the lobule, forming a network among the polygonal hepatic cells. On reaching the core of the conical lobule they are collected into a central or *intralobular vein* (fig. 2, c) which unites with other similar ones to form a *sublobular vein* (fig. 3, s). These eventually reach the hepatic radicles, and so the blood is conducted into the vena cava. In man the lobules are not distinctly separated one from the other, but in some animals, *e.g.* the pig, each one has a fibrous sheath derived from Glisson's capsule (fig. 3, *cl.*).

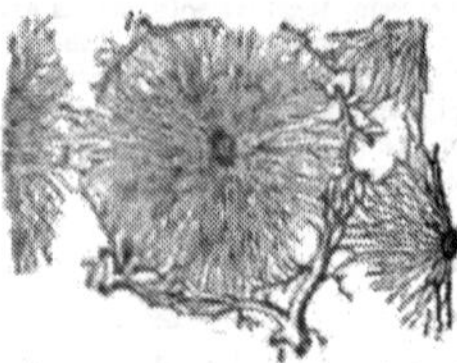

FIG. 2.—Transverse section through the hepatic lobules.
i, i, i, Interlobular veins ending in the intralobular capillaries.
c, c, Central veins joined by the intralobular capillaries. At a, a the capillaries of one lobule communicate with those adjacent to it.

Embryology.—The liver first appears as an entodermal hollow longitudinal outgrowth from the duodenum into the ventral mesentery. The upper part of this forms the future liver, and grows up into the *septum transversum* from which the central part of the diaphragm is formed (see DIAPHRAGM). From the cephalic part of this primary diverticulum solid rods of cells called the *hepatic cylinders* grow out, and these branch again and again until a cellular network is formed surrounding and breaking up the umbilical and vitelline veins. The liver cells, therefore, are entodermal, but the supporting connective tissue mesodermal from the septum transversum. The lower (caudal) part of the furrow-like outgrowth remains hollow and forms the gall bladder. At first the liver is embedded in the septum transversum, but later the diaphragm and it are constricted off one from the other, and soon the liver becomes very large and fills the greater part of the abdomen. At birth it is proportionately much larger than in the adult, and forms one-eighteenth instead of one-fortieth of the body weight, the right and left lobes being nearly equal in size.

FIG. 3.—[illegible] through two [illegible] a pig. [illegible] the intra- [illegible] tissue [illegible] of the [illegible]

Comparative Anatomy.—In the Acrania (Amphioxus) the liver is probably represented by a single ventral diverticulum from the anterior end of the intestine, which has a hepatic portal circulation and secretes digestive fluid. In all the Craniata a solid liver is developed. In the adult lamprey among the Cyclostomata the liver undergoes retrogression, and the bile ducts and gall bladder disappear, though they are present in the larval form (Ammocoetes). In fishes and amphibians the organ consists of right and left lobes, and a gall-bladder is present. The same description applies to the reptiles, but a curious network of cystic ducts is found [illegible] in crocodiles. In the Varanidae [illegible] also retiform (see F. E. Beddard, [illegible] In birds two lobes are also present, [illegible], there is no gall-bladder.

[illegible] pointed out that a generalized [illegible] of any mammal may be derived [illegible]. The accompanying diagram of [illegible] mammalian liver. It will be seen [illegible] the organ into right and left [illegible] that the ventral part of each [illegible] lobe. Passing from right to [illegible] (rl), right central (rc), left [illegible] when it is [illegible] (c) [illegible] shaped lobe attached by its stalk to the Spigelian, and having its blade flattened between the right lateral lobe and the right kidney. The vena cava (vc) is always found to the right of the Spigelian lobe and dorsal to the stalk of the caudate. In tracing the lobulation of man's liver back to this generalized type, it is evident at once that his quadrate lobe does not correspond to any one generalized lobe, but is merely that part of the right central which lies between the gall bladder and the umbilical fissure. From a careful study of human variations (see A. Thomson, *Journ. Anat. and Phys.* vol. 33, p. 546) compared with an Anthropoid liver, such as that of the gorilla, depicted by W. H. L. Duckworth (*Morphology and Anthropology*, Cambridge, 1904, p. 98), it is fairly clear that the human liver is formed, not by a suppression of any of the lobes of the generalized type, but by a fusion of those lobes and obliteration of certain fissures. This fusion is, probably correctly, attributed by Keith to the effect of pressure following the assumption of the erect position (Keith, *Proc. Anat. Soc. of Gt. Britain, Journ. Anat. and Phys.* vol. 33, p. xii.).

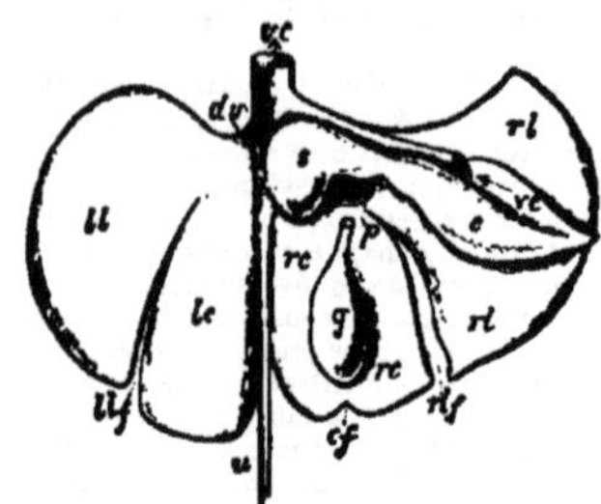

FIG. 4.—Diagrammatic Plan of the Inferior Surface of a Multi-lobed Liver of a Mammal. The posterior or attached border is uppermost.

u, Umbilical vein of the foetus, represented by the round ligament in the adult, lying in the umbilical fissure.
dv, The ductus venosus.
vc, The inferior vena cava.
p, The vena portae entering the transverse fissure.
llf, The left lateral fissure.
rlf, The right lateral fissure.
cf, The cystic fissure.
ll, The left lateral lobe.
lc, The left central lobe.
rc, The right central lobe.
rl, The right lateral lobe.
s, The Spigelian lobe.
c, The caudate lobe.
g, The gall bladder.

The accompanying diagram (fig. 5) shows an abnormal human liver in the Anatomical Department of St Thomas's Hospital which reproduces the generalized type. In its lobulation it is singularly like, in many details, that of the baboon (*Papio maimon*) figured by G. Ruge (*Morph. Jahrb.*, Bd. 35, p. 197); see F. G. Parsons, *Proc. Anat. Soc.*, Feb. 1904, *Journ. Anat. and Phys.* vol. 33, p. xxiii. Georg Ruge "Die äusseren Formverhältnisse der Leber bei den Primaten," (*Morph. Jahrb.*, Bd. 29 and 35) gives a critical study of the primate liver, and among other things suggests the recognition of the Spigelian and caudate lobes as parts of a single lobe, for which he proposes the name of lobus venae cavae. This doubtless would be an advantage morphologically, though for human descriptive anatomy the present nomenclature is not likely to be altered.

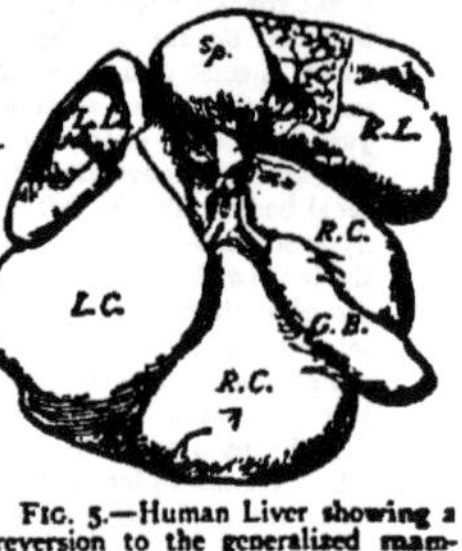

FIG. 5.—Human Liver showing a reversion to the generalized mammalian type.

The gall-bladder is usually present in mammals, but is wanting in the odd-toed ungulates (Perissodactyla) and Procavia (Hyrax). In the giraffe it may be absent or present. The cetacea and a few rodents are also without it. In the otter the same curious network of bile ducts already recorded in the reptiles is seen (see P. H. Burne, *Proc. Anat. Soc., Journ. Anat. and Phys.* vol. 33, p. xi.). (F. G. P.)

SURGERY OF LIVER AND GALL-BLADDER.—Exposed as it is in the upper part of the abdomen, and being somewhat friable, the human liver is often torn or ruptured by blows or kicks, and, the large blood-vessels being thus laid open, fatal haemorrhage into the belly-cavity may take place. The individual becomes faint, and the faintness keeps on increasing; and there are pain and tenderness in the liver-region. The right thing to do is to open the belly in the middle line, search for a wound in the liver and treat it by deep sutures, or by plugging it with gauze.

Cirrhosis of the Liver.—As the result of chronic irritation of the liver increased supplies of blood pass to it, and if the irritation is unduly prolonged inflammation is the result. The commonest causes of this chronic hepatitis are alcoholism and syphilis. The new fibrous tissue which is developed throughout the liver, as the result of the chronic inflammation, causes general enlargement of the liver with, perhaps, nausea, vomiting and jaundice. Later the new fibrous tissue undergoes contraction and the liver becomes smaller than natural. Blood then finds difficulty in passing through it, and, as a result, dropsy occurs in the belly (ascites). This may be relieved by tapping the cavity with a small hollow needle (Southey's trocar), or by passing into it a large sharp-pointed tube. This relieves the dropsy, but it does not cure the condition on which the dropsy depends. A surgical operation is sometimes undertaken with success for enabling the engorged veins to empty themselves into the blood-stream in a manner so as to avoid the liver-route.

Inflammation of the Liver (hepatitis) may also be caused by an attack of micro-organisms which have reached it through the veins coming from the large intestine, or through the main arteries. There are, of course, as the result, pain and tenderness, and there is often jaundice. The case should be treated by rest in bed, fomentations, calomel and saline aperients. But when the hepatitis is of septic origin, suppuration is likely to occur, the result being an hepatic abscess.

Hepatic Abscess is especially common in persons from the East who have recently undergone an attack of dysentery. In addition to the local pain and tenderness, there is a high temperature accompanied with shiverings or occasional rigors, the patient becoming daily more thin and miserable. Sometimes the abscess declares itself by a bulging at the surface, but if not an incision should be made through the belly-wall over the most tender spot, and a direct examination of the surface of the liver made. A bulging having been found, that part of the liver which apparently overlies the abscess should be stitched up to the sides of the opening made in belly-wall, and should then be explored by a hollow needle. Pus being found, the abscess should be freely opened and drained. It is inadvisable to explore for a suspected abscess with a hollow needle without first opening the abdomen, as septic fluid might thus be enabled to leak out, and infect the general peritoneal cavity. If an hepatic abscess is injudiciously left to itself it may eventually discharge into the chest, lungs or belly, or it may establish a communication with a piece of intestine. The only safe way for an abscess to evacuate itself is on to the surface of the body.

Hydatic Cysts are often met with in the liver. They are due to a peculiar development of the eggs of the tape-worm of the dog, which have been received into the alimentary canal with infected water or uncooked vegetables, such as watercress. The embryo of the taenia echinococcus finds its way from the stomach or intestine into a vein passing to the liver, and, settling itself in the liver, causes so much disturbance there that a capsule of inflammatory material forms around it. Inside this wall is the special covering of the embryo which shortly becomes distended with clear hydatid fluid. The cyst should be treated like a liver-abscess, by incision through the abdominal or thoracic wall, by circumferential suturing and by exploration and drainage.

Tumours of the Liver may be innocent or malignant. The most important of the former is the *gumma* of tertiary syphilis; this may steadily and completely disappear under the influence of iodide of potassium. The commonest form of malignant tumour is the result of the growth of cancerous elements which have been brought to the liver by the veins coming up from a primary focus of the large intestine. Active surgical treatment of such a tumour is out of the question. Fortunately it is, as a rule, painless.

The Gall-bladder may be ruptured by external violence, and if bile escapes from the rent in considerable quantities peritonitis will be set up, whether the bile contains septic germs or not. If, on opening the abdomen to find out what serious effects some severe injury has caused, the gall-bladder be found torn, the rent may be sewn up, or, if thought better, the gall-bladder may be removed. The peritoneal surfaces in the region of the liver should then be wiped clean, and the abdominal wound closed, except for the passage through it of a gauze drain.

Biliary concretions, known as *gall stones*, are apt to form in the gall-bladder. They are composed of crystals of bile-fat, cholesterine. Sometimes in the course of a *post-mortem* examination a gall-bladder is found packed full of gall-stones which during life had caused no inconvenience and had given rise to no suspicion of their presence. In other cases gall-stones set up irritation in the gall-bladder which runs on to inflammation, and the gall-bladder being infected by septic germs from the intestine (*bacilli coli*) an abscess forms.

Abscess of the Gall-bladder gives rise to a painful, tender swelling near the cartilage of the ninth rib of the right side. If the abscess is allowed to take its course, adhesions may form around it and it may burst into the intestine or on to the surface of the abdomen, a *biliary fistula* remaining. Abscess in the gall-bladder being suspected, an incision should be made down to it, and, its covering having been stitched to the abdominal wall, the gall-bladder should be opened and drained. The presence of concretions in the gall-bladder may not only lead to the formation of abscess but also to invasion of the gall-bladder by cancer.

Stones in the gall-bladder should be removed by operation, as, if left, there is a great risk of their trying to escape with the bile into the intestine and thus causing a blockage of the common bile-duct, and perhaps a fatal leakage of bile into the peritoneum through a perforating ulcer of the duct. If before opening the gall-bladder the surface is stitched to the deepest part of the abdominal wound, the biliary fistula left as the result of the opening of the abscess will close in due course.

"Biliary colic" is the name given to the distressing symptoms associated with the passage of a stone through the narrow bile-duct. The individual is doubled up with acute pains which, starting from the hepatic region, spread through the abdomen and radiate to the right shoulder blade. Inasmuch as the stone is blocking the duct, the bile is unable to flow into the intestine; so, being absorbed by the blood-vessels, it gives rise to jaundice. The distress is due to spasmodic muscular contraction, and it comes on at intervals, each attack increasing the patient's misery. He breaks out into profuse sweats and may vomit. If the stone happily finds its way into the intestine the distress suddenly ceases. In the meanwhile relief may be afforded by fomentations, and by morphia or chloroform, but if no prospect of the stone escaping into the intestine appears likely, the surgeon will be called upon to remove it by an incision through the gall-bladder, or the bile-duct, or through the intestine at the spot where it is trying to make its escape. Sometimes a gall-stone which has found its way into the intestine is large enough to block the bowel and give rise to intestinal obstruction which demands abdominal section.

A person who is of what used to be called a "biliary nature" should live sparingly and take plenty of exercise. He should avoid fat and rich food, butter, pastry and sauces, and should drink no beer or wine—unless it be some very light French wine or Moselle. He should keep his bowels regular, or even loose, taking every morning a dose of sulphate of soda in a glass of hot water. A course at Carlsbad, Vichy or Contrexéville, may be helpful. It is doubtful if drugs have any direct influence upon gall-stones, such as sulphate of soda, olive oil or oleate of soda. No reliance can be placed upon massage in producing the onward passage of a gall-stone from the gall-bladder towards the intestine. Indeed this treatment might be not only distressing but harmful. (E. O.*)

LIVERMORE, MARY ASHTON [RICE] (1821–1905), American reformer, was born in Boston, Massachusetts, on the 19th of December 1821. She studied at the female seminary at Charlestown, Mass.; taught French and Latin there; taught in a

du [illegible]
sc [illegible]

[illegible]

FIG. [illegible]

c, c, [illegible]

s, S[illegible]
d, I[illegible]

i, i, In[illegible]

in snak[illegible] (Monito[illegible] *Proc. Zo*[illegible] but in so[illegible]

In mar[illegible] type of liv[illegible] [illegible] suppre[illegible] lower (fig[illegible] that the [illegible] lves, as in [illegible] lf is divide[illegible] t there ar[illegible] tral (*lc*), [illegible] sent, in al[illegible] the [illegible]

[illegible]

Italian art numbering altogether about 180 pictures, collected at the beginning of the 19th century by William Roscoe, were deposited in the gallery. The Picton circular reading-room, and the rotunda lecture-room were built by the corporation and opened in 1879. Alterations in the museum were completed in 1902 by which its size was practically doubled. The literary and philosophical society was established in 1812. The Royal Institution, established mainly through the efforts of Roscoe in 1817, possessed a fine gallery of early art in the Walker Art Gallery, and is the centre of the literary institutions of the town.

Education.—Sunday schools were founded for poor children in 1784, as the result of a town's meeting. These were soon followed by day-schools supplied by the various denominations. The first were the Old Church schools in Moorfields (1789), the Unitarian schools in Mount Pleasant (1790) and Manesty Lane (1792) and the Wesleyan Brunswick school (1790). In 1826 the corporation founded two elementary schools, one of which, the North Corporation school, was erected in part substitution for the grammar school founded by John Crosse, rector of St Nicholas Fleshshambles, London, a native of Liverpool, in 1515, and carried on by the Corporation until 1815. From this date onward the number rapidly increased until the beginning of the School Board in 1870, and afterwards. Mention should be made of the training ship "Indefatigable" moored in the Mersey for the sons and orphans of sailors, and the reformatory institution at Heswall, Co. Chester, which has recently replaced the training ship "Akbar" formerly moored in the Mersey. Semi-private schools were founded by public subscription—the Royal Institution school (1819), the Liverpool Institute (1825) and the Liverpool College (1840). The first has ceased to exist. The Institute was a development of the Mechanics' Institute and was managed by a council of subscribers. It was divided into a high school and a commercial school. Under a scheme of the Board of Education under the Charitable Trusts Act this school, together with the Blackburne House high school for girls, became a public secondary school and was handed over to the corporation in 1905. Liverpool College was formerly divided into three schools, upper, middle and lower, for different classes of the community. The middle and lower schools passed into the control of the corporation in 1907. The Sefton Park elementary school and the Pupil Teachers' College in Clarence Street were transformed into municipal secondary schools for boys and girls in 1907 the corporation has also a secondary school for girls at Aigburth. There are several schools maintained by the Roman Catholics, two schools of the Girls' Public Day School Company and a large number of private schools. A cadet ship, the "Conway," for the training of boys intending to become officers in the mercantile marine, is moored in the Mersey. There are two training colleges for women, one undenominational, and the other conducted by the sisters of Notre Dame for Roman Catholic women. The central municipal technical school is in the Museum Buildings, and there are three branch technical schools. There are also a nautical college, a school of cookery and a school of art controlled by the Education Committee.

Liverpool University, as University College, received its charter of incorporation in 1881, and in 1884 was admitted as a college of the Victoria University. In the same year the medical school of the Royal Infirmary became part of the University College. In 1900 a supplemental charter extended the powers of self-government and brought the college into closer relations with the authorities of the city and with local institutions by providing for their fuller representation on the court of governors. In 1903 the charter of incorporation of the university of Liverpool was received, thus constituting it an independent university. The university is governed by the king as visitor, by a chancellor, two pro-chancellors, a vice-chancellor and a treasurer, by a court of over 300 members representing donors and public bodies, a council, senate, faculties and convocation. The fine group of buildings is situated on Brownlow Hill.

Trade and Commerce.—In 1800 the tonnage of ships entering the port was 450,060; in 1908 it reached 17,111,814 tons. In 1800 4746 vessels entered, averaging 94 tons; in 1908 there were 25,739, averaging 665 tons. The commerce of Liverpool extends to every part of the world, but probably the intercourse with North America stands pre-eminent, there being lines of steamers to New York, Philadelphia, Boston, Baltimore, Galveston, New Orleans and the Canadian ports. Cotton is the great staple import. Grain comes next, American (North and South) and Australian wheat and oats occupying a large proportion of the market. An enormous trade in American provisions, including live cattle, is carried on. Tobacco has always been a leading article of import into Liverpool, along with the sugar and rum from the West Indies. Timber forms an important part of the imports, the stacking yards extending for miles along the northern docks. In regard to exports, Liverpool possesses decided advantages; lying so near the great manufacturing districts of Lancashire and the West Riding of Yorkshire, this port is the natural channel of transmission for their goods, although the Manchester ship canal diverts a certain proportion of the traffic, while coal and salt are also largely exported.

Manufactures.—The manufactures of Liverpool are not extensive. Attempts have been repeatedly made to establish cotton mills in and near the city, but have resulted in failure. Engineering works, especially connected with marine navigation, have grown up on a large scale. Shipbuilding, in the early part of the 19th century, was active and prosperous, but has practically ceased. During the latter half of the 18th century and the beginning of the 19th, pottery and china manufacture flourished in Liverpool. John Sadler, a Liverpool manufacturer, was the inventor of printing on pottery, and during the early period of Josiah Wedgwood's career all his goods which required printing had to be sent to Liverpool. A large establishment, called the Herculaneum Pottery, was founded in a suburb on the bank of the Mersey, but the trade has long disappeared. Litherland, the inventor of the lever watch, was a Liverpool manufacturer, and Liverpool-made watches have always been held in high estimation. There are several extensive sugar refineries and corn mills. The confectionery trade has developed during recent years, several large works having been built, induced by the prospect of obtaining cheap sugar directly from the Liverpool quays. The cutting, blending and preparing of crude tobacco have led to the erection of factories employing some thousands of hands. There are also large mills for oil-pressing and making cattle-cake.

Docks.—The docks of the port of Liverpool on both sides of the Mersey are owned and managed by the same public trust, the Mersey Docks and Harbour Board. On the Liverpool side they extend along the margin of the estuary 6½ m., of which 1¼ m. is in the borough of Bootle. The Birkenhead docks have not such a frontage, but they extend a long way backward. The water area of the Liverpool docks and basins is 418 acres, with a lineal quayage of 27 m. The Birkenhead docks, including the great float of 120 acres, contain a water area of 165 acres, with a lineal quayage of 9½ m. The system of enclosed docks was begun by the corporation in 1709. They constituted from the first a public trust, the corporation never having derived any direct revenue from them, though the common council of the borough were the trustees, and in the first instance formed the committee of management. Gradually the payers of dock rates on ships and goods acquired influence, and were introduced into the governing body, and ultimately, by an act of 1857, the corporation was superseded. The management is vested in the Mersey Docks and Harbour Board, consisting of twenty-eight members, four of whom are nominated by the Mersey Conservancy commissioners, who consist of the first lord of the Admiralty, the chancellor of the duchy of Lancaster and the president of the Board of Trade, and the rest elected by the payers of rates on ships and goods, of whom a register is kept and annually revised. The revenue is derived from tonnage rates on ships, dock rates on goods, town dues on goods, with various minor sources of income.

Down to 1843 the docks were confined to the Liverpool side of the Mersey. Several attempts made to establish docks in Cheshire had been frustrated by the Liverpool corporation, who bought up the land and kept it in their own hands. In 1843, however, a scheme for docks in Birkenhead was carried through which ultimately proved unsuccessful, and the enterprise was acquired in 1855 by Liverpool. The Birkenhead docks were for many years only partially used, but are now an important centre for corn-milling, the importation of foreign cattle and export trade to the East. In addition to the wet docks, there are in Liverpool fourteen graving docks and three in Birkenhead, besides a gridiron on the Liverpool side.

The first portion of the great landing stage, known as the Georges' stage, was constructed in 1847, from the plans of Mr (afterwards Sir) William Cubitt, F.R.S. This was 500 ft. long. In 1857 the Prince's stage, 1000 ft. long, was built to the north of the Georges' stage and distant from it 500 ft. In 1874 the intervening space was filled up and the Georges' stage reconstructed. The fabric had just been completed, and was waiting to be inaugurated, when on the 28th of July 1874 it was destroyed by fire. It was again constructed with improvements. In 1896 it was farther extended to the north, and its length is now 2478 ft. and its breadth 80 ft. It is supported on floating pontoons about 200 in number, connected with the river wall by eight bridges, besides a floating bridge for heavy traffic 550 ft. in length and 35 ft. in width. The southern half is devoted to the traffic of the Mersey ferries, of which there are seven—New Brighton, Egremont, Seacombe, Birkenhead, Rock Ferry, New Ferry and Eastham. The northern half is used by ocean-going steamers and their tenders. The warehouses for storing produce form a prominent feature in the commercial part of the city. Down to 1841

and was the means of identifying his body after his death. To a house, mainly built by himself at Mabotsa, Livingstone in 1844 brought home his wife, Mary Moffat, the daughter of Moffat of Kuruman. Here he laboured till 1846, when he removed to Chonuane, 40 m. farther north, the chief place of the Bakwain or Bakwena tribe under Sechele. In 1847 he again removed to Kolobeng, about 40 m. westwards, the whole tribe following their missionary. With the aid and in the company of two English sportsmen, William C. Oswell and Mungo Murray, he was able to undertake a journey to Lake Ngami, which had never yet been seen by a white man. Crossing the Kalahari Desert, of which Livingstone gave the first detailed account, they reached the lake on the 1st of August 1849. In April next year he made an attempt to reach Sebituane, who lived 200 m. beyond the lake, this time in company with his wife and children, but again got no farther than the lake, as the children were seized with fever. A year later, April 1851, Livingstone, again accompanied by his family and Oswell, set out, this time with the intention of settling among the Makololo for a period. At last he succeeded, and reached the Chobe (Kwando), a southern tributary of the Zambezi, and in the end of June reached the Zambezi itself at the town of Sesheke. Leaving the Chobe on the 13th of August the party reached Cape Town in April 1852. Livingstone may now be said to have completed the first period of his career in Africa, the period in which the work of the missionary had the greatest prominence. Henceforth he appears more in the character of an explorer, but it must be remembered that he regarded himself to the last as a pioneer missionary, whose work was to open up the country to others.

Having seen his family off to England, Livingstone left Cape Town on the 8th of June 1852, and turning north again reached Linyante, the capital of the Makololo, on the Chobe, on the 23rd of May 1853, being cordially received by Sekeletu and his people. His first object was to seek for some healthy high land in which to plant a station. Ascending the Zambezi, he, however, found no place free from the tsetse fly, and therefore resolved to discover a route to the interior from either the west or east coast. To accompany Livingstone twenty-seven men were selected from the various tribes under Sekeletu, partly with a view to open up a trade route between their own country and the coast. The start was made from Linyante on the 11th of November 1853, and, by ascending the Liba, Lake Dilolo was reached on the 20th of February 1854. On the 4th of April the Kwango was crossed, and on the 31st of May the town of Loanda was entered, Livingstone, however, being all but dead from fever, semi-starvation and dysentery. From Loanda Livingstone sent his astronomical observations to Sir Thomas Maclear at the Cape, and an account of his journey to the Royal Geographical Society, which in May 1855 awarded him its patron's medal. Loanda was left on the 20th of September 1854, but Livingstone lingered long about the Portuguese settlements. Making a slight détour to the north to Kabango, the party reached Lake Dilolo on the 13th of June 1855. Here Livingstone made a careful study of the hydrography of the country. He "now for the first time apprehended the true form of the river systems and the continent," and the conclusions he came to have been essentially confirmed by subsequent observations. The return journey from Lake Dilolo was by the same route as that by which the party came, Linyante being reached in the beginning of September.

For Livingstone's purposes the route to the west was unavailable, and he decided to follow the Zambezi to its mouth. With a numerous following, he left Linyante on the 8th of November 1855. A fortnight afterwards he discovered the famous "Victoria" falls of the Zambezi. He had already formed a true idea of the configuration of the continent as a great hollow or basin-shaped plateau, surrounded by a ring of mountains. Livingstone reached the Portuguese settlement of Tete on the 2nd of March 1856, in a very emaciated condition. There he left his men and proceeded to Quilimane, where he arrived on the 20th of May, thus having completed in two years and six months one of the most remarkable and fruitful journeys on record. The results in geography and in natural science in all its departments were abundant and accurate; his observations necessitated a reconstruction of the map of Central Africa. When Livingstone began his work in Africa the map was virtually a blank from Kuruman to Timbuktu, and nothing but envy or ignorance can throw any doubt on the originality of his discoveries.

On the 12th of December he arrived in England, after an absence of sixteen years, and met everywhere the welcome of a hero. He told his story in his *Missionary Travels and Researches in South Africa* (1857) with straightforward simplicity, and with no effort after literary style, and no apparent consciousness that he had done anything extraordinary. Its publication brought what he would have considered a competency had he felt himself at liberty to settle down for life. In 1857 he severed his connexion with the London Missionary Society, with whom, however, he always remained on the best of terms, and in February 1858 he accepted the appointment of "Her Majesty's consul at Quilimane for the eastern coast and the independent districts in the interior, and commander of an expedition for exploring eastern and central Africa." The Zambezi expedition, of which Livingstone thus became commander, sailed from Liverpool in H.M.S. "Pearl" on the 10th of March 1858, and reached the mouth of the Zambezi on the 14th of May. The party, which included Dr (afterwards Sir) John Kirk and Livingstone's brother Charles, ascended the river from the Kongone mouth in a steam launch, the "Ma-Robert"; reaching Tete on the 8th of September. The remainder of the year was devoted to an examination of the river above Tete, and especially the Kebrabasa rapids. Most of the year 1859 was spent in the exploration of the river Shiré and Lake Nyasa, which was discovered in September; and during a great part of the year 1860 Livingstone was engaged in fulfilling his promise to take such of the Makololo home as cared to go. In January of next year arrived Bishop C. F. Mackenzie and a party of missionaries sent out by the Universities Mission to establish a station on the upper Shiré.

After exploring the river Rovuma for 30 m. in his new vessel the "Pioneer," Livingstone and the missionaries proceeded up the Shiré to Chibisa's; there they found the slave trade rampant. On the 15th of July Livingstone, accompanied by several native carriers, started to show the bishop the country. Several bands of slaves whom they met were liberated, and after seeing the missionary party settled in the highlands to the south of Lake Chilwa (Shirwa) Livingstone spent from August to November in exploring Lake Nyasa. While the boat sailed up the west side of the lake to near the north end, the explorer marched along the shore. He returned more resolved than ever to do his utmost to rouse the civilized world to put down the desolating slave-trade. On the 30th of January 1862, at the Zambezi mouth, Livingstone welcomed his wife and the ladies of the mission, with whom were the sections of the "Lady Nyassa," a river steamer which Livingstone had had built at his own expense. When the mission ladies reached the mouth of the Ruo tributary of the Shiré, they were stunned to hear of the death of the bishop and one of his companions. This was a sad blow to Livingstone, seeming to have rendered all his efforts to establish a mission futile. A still greater loss to him was that of his wife at Shupanga, on the 27th of April 1862.

The "Lady Nyassa" was taken to the Rovuma. Up this river Livingstone managed to steam 156 m., but farther progress was arrested by rocks. Returning to the Zambezi in the beginning of 1863, he found that the desolation caused by the slave trade was more horrible and widespread than ever. It was clear that the Portuguese officials were themselves at the bottom of the traffic. Kirk and Charles Livingstone being compelled to return to England on account of their health, the doctor resolved once more to visit the lake, and proceeded some distance up the west side and then north-west as far as the watershed that separates the Loangwa from the rivers that run into the lake.

Meanwhile a letter was received from Earl Russell recalling the expedition by the end of the year. In the end of April 1864 Livingstone reached Zanzibar in the "Lady Nyassa," and on the 23rd of July Livingstone arrived in England. He was naturally disappointed with the comparative failure of this expedition. Still the geographical results, though not in extent to be compared to those of his first and his final expeditions, were of high importance, as were those in various departments of science, and he had unknowingly laid the foundations of the British protectorate of Nyasaland. Details will be found in his *Narrative of an Expedition to the Zambesi and its Tributaries*, published in 1865.

By Sir Roderick Murchison and his other staunch friends Livingstone was as warmly welcomed as ever. When Murchison proposed to him that he should go out again, although he seems to have had a desire to spend the remainder of his days at home, the prospect was too tempting to be rejected. He was appointed British consul to Central Africa without a salary, and government contributed only £500 to the expedition. The chief help came from private friends. During the latter part of the expedition government granted him £1000, but that, when he learned of it, was devoted to his great undertaking. The Geographical Society contributed £500. The two main objects of the expedition were the suppression of slavery by means of civilizing influences, and the ascertainment of the watershed in the region between Nyasa and Tanganyika. At first Livingstone thought the Nile problem had been all but solved by Speke, Baker and Burton, but the idea grew upon him that the Nile sources must be sought farther south, and his last journey became in the end a forlorn hope in search of the "fountains" of Herodotus. Leaving England in the middle of August 1865, via Bombay, Livingstone arrived at Zanzibar on the 28th of January 1866. He was landed at the mouth of the Rovuma on the 22nd of March, and started for the interior on the 4th of April. His company consisted of thirteen sepoys, ten Johanna men, nine African boys from Nasik school, Bombay, and four boys from the Shiré region, besides camels, buffaloes, mules and donkeys. This imposing outfit soon melted away to four or five boys. Rounding the south end of Lake Nyasa, Livingstone struck in a north-north-west direction for the south end of Lake Tanganyika, over country much of which had not previously been explored. The Loangwa was crossed on the 15th of December 1866. On Christmas day Livingstone lost his four goats, a loss which he felt very keenly, and the medicine chest was stolen in January 1867. Fever came upon him, and for a time was his almost constant companion; this, with other serious ailments which subsequently attacked him, and which he had no medicine to counteract, told on even his iron frame. The Chambezi was crossed on the 28th of January, and the south end of Tanganyika reached on the 31st of March. Here, much to his vexation, he got into the company of Arab slave dealers (among them being Tippoo-Tib) by whom his movements were hampered; but he succeeded in reaching Lake Mweru (Nov. 1867). After visiting Lake Mofwa and the Lualaba, which he believed was the upper part of the Nile, he, on the 18th of July 1868, discovered Lake Bangweulu. Proceeding up the west coast of Tanganyika, he reached Ujiji on the 14th of March 1869, "a ruckle of bones." Livingstone recrossed Tanganyika in July, and passed through the country of the Manyema, but baffled partly by the natives, partly by the slave hunters, and partly by his long illnesses it was not till the 29th of March 1871 that he succeeded in reaching the Lualaba, at the town of Nyangwe, where he stayed four months, vainly trying to get a canoe to take him across. It was here that a party of Arab slavers, without warning or provocation, assembled one day when the market was busiest and commenced shooting the women, hundreds being killed or drowned in trying to escape. Livingstone had "the impression that he was in hell," but was helpless, though his "first impulse was to pistol the murderers." The account of this scene which he sent home roused indignation in England to such a degree as to lead to determined and to a considerable extent successful efforts to get the sultan of Zanzibar to suppress the trade. In sickened disgust the wea[...] which he reached on th[...] arrival in Ujiji he wa[...] arrival of H. M. Stanl[...] Bennett, of the *New* [...] explored the north en[...] that the Rusizi runs i[...] the two started east [...] Livingstone with an [...] Stanley left on the [...] had waited wearily [...] fifty-seven men a[...] the whole, select[...] started on the 15 [...] along the east side of [...] soon found him out. In January [...] endless spongy jungle on the east of Lake [...] stone's object being to go round by the south and away [...] find the "fountains." The doctor got worse and worse, and in the middle of April he had unwillingly to submit to be carried in a rude litter. On the 29th of April Chitambo's village on the Lulimala, in Ilala, on the south shore of the lake, was reached. The last entry in the journal is on the 27th of April: "Knocked up quite, and remain—recover—sent to buy milch goats. We are on the banks of the Molilamo." On the 30th of April he with difficulty wound up his watch, and early on the morning of the 1st of May the boys found "the great master," as they called him, kneeling by the side of his bed, dead. His faithful men preserved the body in the sun as well as they could, and, wrapping it carefully up, carried it and all his papers, instruments and other things across Africa to Zanzibar. It was borne to England with all honour, and on the 18th of April 1874, was deposited in Westminster Abbey. His faithfully kept journals during these seven years' wanderings were published under the title of the *Last Journals of David Livingstone in Central Africa*, in 1874, edited by his old friend the Rev. Horace Waller. In Old Chitambo's the time and place of his death are commemorated by a permanent monument, which replaced in 1902 the tree on which his native followers had recorded the event.

In spite of his sufferings and the many compulsory delays, Livingstone's discoveries during these last years were both extensive and of prime importance as leading to a solution of African hydrography. No single African explorer has ever done so much for African geography as Livingstone during his thirty years' work. His travels covered one-third of the continent, extending from the Cape to near the equator, and from the Atlantic to the Indian Ocean. Livingstone was no hurried traveller; he did his journeying leisurely, carefully observing and recording all that was worthy of note, with rare geographical instinct and the eye of a trained scientific observer, studying the ways of the people, eating their food, living in their huts, and sympathizing with their joys and sorrows. In all the countries through which he travelled his memory is cherished by the native tribes who, almost without exception, treated Livingstone as a superior being; his treatment of them was always tender, gentle and gentlemanly. By the Arab slavers whom he opposed he was also greatly admired, and was by them styled "the very great doctor." "In the annals of exploration of the Dark Continent," wrote Stanley many years after the death of the missionary explorer, "we look in vain among other nationalities for a name such as Livingstone's. He stands pre-eminent above all; he unites in himself all the best qualities of other explorers. . . . Britain . . . excelled herself even when she produced the strong and perseverant Scotchman, Livingstone." But the direct gains to geography and science are perhaps not the greatest results of Livingstone's journeys. His example and his death acted like an inspiration, filling Africa with an army of explorers and missionaries, and raising in Europe so powerful a feeling against the slave trade that through him it may be considered as having received its death-blow. Personally Livingstone was a pure and tender-hearted man, full of humanity and sympathy, simple-minded as a child.

[illegible] as the advice he gave to some school and was the means of [illegible] "Fear God, and work hard." a house, mainly built [illegible] narratives and W. G. Blaikie's *Life* (1880). 1844 brought home [illegible] the London Missionary Society from 1840, Moffat of Kuruman [illegible] *Proceedings of the Royal Geographical Society*, removed to Chon[illegible] the Foreign Office sent home by Livingstone the Bakwain or [illegible] expeditions, and Stanley's *Autobiography* (1909) [illegible] *and Livingstone* (1872). (J. S. K.)

removed to Ko[illegible] [LIVINGSTONE] **MOUNTAINS**, a band of highlands in German following the[illegible] forming the eastern border of the rift-valley of of two Engli[illegible] at the northern end of the lake. In parts these he was ab[illegible] known also under their native name of Kinga, present never y[illegible] character of a plateau than of a true mountain range, Desert [illegible] name may be justified by the fact that they form they [illegible] very narrow belt of country, which falls considerably yes [illegible] as well as to the west. The northern end is well b[illegible] by an escarpment falling to the Ruaha valley, [illegible] regarded as a north-eastern branch of the main rift- [illegible] towards the Livingstone range terminates in the [illegible] of the Ruhuhu in 10° 30′ S., the first decided break [illegible] that is reached from the north, on the east [illegible]. Geologically the range is formed on the side [illegible] by a zone of gneiss running in a series of ridges and [illegible] roughly parallel to its axis. The ridge nearest the lake [illegible] Jamimbi or Chamembe, 9° 41′ S., rises to an [illegible] of 7870 ft., or 6200 ft. above Nyasa) falls almost [illegible] water, the same steep slope being continued beneath [illegible]. Towards the south the range appears to have a [illegible] 20 m. only, but northwards it widens out to about [illegible] broken here by the depression, drained towards [illegible] of Bozzyi, on the south side of which is the highest [illegible] of the range (9600 ft.). North and east of [illegible] the eastern half of the range generally, table-topped [illegible] composed above of horizontally bedded [illegible] sandstones and conglomerates. The uplands are [illegible] in rich grass, forest occurring principally in [illegible] while the slopes towards the lake are covered with [illegible]. Native settlements are scattered over the whole [illegible] mission stations have been established at [illegible] Mwandala, a little north of the north end of [illegible] is here healthy, and night frosts occur in [illegible]. European crops are raised with success. At [illegible] mountains on Lake Nyasa are the ports of Wied- [illegible] of the Ruhuhu, and Old Langenburg, at [illegible] of the lake. (E. He.)

[illegible] (c. 284–204 B.C.), the founder of Roman [illegible]. His name, in which the Greek 'Ανδρόνικος [illegible] the gentile name of one of the great Roman [illegible] indicative of his own position as a manumitted [illegible] of the influences by which Roman [illegible] viz. the culture of men who were [illegible] "semi-Graeci" by birth and education, and [illegible] favour bestowed upon them by the more [illegible] of the Roman aristocracy. He is supposed [illegible] of Tarentum, and to have been brought, [illegible] after the capture of that town in 272, as a [illegible] in the household of a member of the [illegible] Livius Salinator. He determined the [illegible] literature followed for more than a century [illegible] imitation of Greek comedy, tragedy and [illegible] great results in the hands of Naevius, [illegible], received its first impulse [illegible], from the insignificant remains [illegible] the opinions of Cicero and Horace, [illegible] either to original genius or to [illegible] real claim to distinction was [illegible] schoolmaster of the Roman people. [illegible] Livius after him, he obtained [illegible] and Latin; and it was probably [illegible] a work of literary pretension, [illegible] Odyssey into Latin Saturnian [illegible] was still used in schools in the [illegible], although [illegible] executed,

(p ı rr p: Li co. forr clus sequ was being For availa With Noven famous formed great ho mountair of Tete o: Here he arrived on

satisfied a real want by introducing the Romans to a knowledge of Greek. Such knowledge became essential to men in a high position as a means of intercourse with Greeks, while Greek literature stimulated the minds of leading Romans. Moreover, southern Italy and Sicily afforded many opportunities for witnessing representations of Greek comedies and tragedies. The Romans and Italians had an indigenous drama of their own, known by the name of *Satura*, which prepared them for the reception of the more regular Greek drama. The distinction between this *Satura* and the plays of Euripides or Menander was that it had no regular plot. This the Latin drama first received from Livius Andronicus; but it did so at the cost of its originality. In 240, the year after the end of the first Punic War, he produced at the ludi Romani a translation of a Greek play (it is uncertain whether a comedy or tragedy or both), and this representation marks the beginning of Roman literature (Livy vii. 2). Livius himself took part in his plays, and in order to spare his voice he introduced the custom of having the solos (*cantica*) sung by a boy, while he himself represented the action of the song by dumb show. In his translation he discarded the native Saturnian metre, and adopted the iambic, trochaic and cretic metres, to which Latin more easily adapted itself than either to the hexameter or to the lyrical measures of a later time. He continued to produce plays for more than thirty years after this time. The titles of his tragedies—*Achilles, Aegisthus, Equus Trojanus, Hermione, Tereus*—are all suggestive of subjects which were treated by the later tragic poets of Rome. In the year 207, when he must have been of a great age, he was appointed to compose a hymn of thanksgiving, sung by maidens, for the victory of the Metaurus and an intercessory hymn to the Aventine Juno. As a further tribute of national recognition the "college" or "gild" of poets and actors was granted a place of meeting in the temple of Minerva on the Aventine.

See fragments in L. Müller, *Livi Andronici et Cn. Naevi Fabularum Reliquiae* (1885); also J. Wordsworth, *Fragments and Specimens of Early Latin* (1874); Mommsen, *Hist. of Rome*, bk. iii. ch. 14.

LIVNO, a town of Bosnia, situated on the eastern side of the fertile plain of Livno, at the foot of Mount Krug (6581 ft.). Pop. about 5000. The Dalmatian border is 7 m. W. Livno had a trade in grain, live-stock and silver filigree-work up to 1904, when a fire swept away more than 500 of the old Turkish houses, together with the Roman citadel. Remains prove that Livno occupies the site of a Roman settlement, the name of which is uncertain. The Roman Catholic convent of Gurići is 6 m. S.

LIVONIA, or LIVLAND (Russian, *Liflandia*), one of the three Baltic provinces of Russia, bounded W. by the Gulf of Riga, N. by Esthonia, E. by the governments of St Petersburg, Pskov and Vitebsk, and S. by Courland. A group of islands (1110 sq. m.) at the entrance of the Gulf of Riga, of which Oesel, Mohn, Runo and Paternoster are the largest, belong to this government. It covers an area of 18,160 sq. m., but of this the part of Lake Peipus which belongs to it occupies 1090. Its surface is diversified by several plateaus, those of Haanhof and of the Livonian Aa having an average elevation of 400 to 700 ft., while several summits reach 800 to 1000 ft. or more. The edges of the plateaus are gapped by deep valleys; the hilly tract between the Dvina and its tributary the Livonian Aa has received, from its picturesque narrow valleys, thick forests and numerous lakes, the name of "Livonian Switzerland." The plateau of Odenpäh, drained by tributaries of the Embach river, which flows for 93 m. from Lake Virz-yärvi into Lake Peipus, occupies an area of 2830 sq. m., and has an average elevation of 500 ft. More than a thousand lakes are scattered over Livonia, of which that of Virz-yärvi, having a surface of 106 sq. m. (115 ft. above sea-level), is the largest. Marshes and peat-bogs occupy one-tenth of the province. Of the numerous rivers, the Dvina, which flows for 90 m. along its frontier, the Pernau, Salis, Livonian Aa and Embach are navigable.

The Silurian formation which covers Esthonia, appears in the northern part of Livonia, the remainder of the province consisting of Devonian strata. The whole is overlaid with glacial deposits, sometimes 400 ft. thick. The typical bottom moraine, with erratics from Finland, extends all over the country. Glacial furrows, striae and elongated troughs are met with everywhere, running mostly from north-west to south-east, as well as *äsar* or *eskers*, which have the same direction. Sand-dunes cover large tracts on the shores of the Baltic. No traces of marine deposits are found higher than 100 or 190 ft. above the present sea-level. The soil is not very fertile. Forests cover about two-fifths of the surface. The climate is rather severe. The mean temperatures are 43° F. at Riga (winter 23°, summer 63°) and 40° at Yuriev. The winds are very variable; the average number of rainy and snowy days is 146 at Riga (rainfall 24·1 in.). Fogs are not uncommon.

The population of Livonia, which was 621,600 in 1826, reached 1,000,876 in 1870, and 1,295,231 in 1897, of whom 43·4% were Letts, 39·9% Ehsts, 7·6% Germans, 5·4% Russians, 2% Jews and 1·2% Poles. The estimated pop. in 1906 was 1,411,000. The Livs, who formerly extended east into the government of Vitebsk, have nearly all passed away. Their native language, of Finnish origin, is rapidly disappearing, their present language being a Lettish patois. In 1846 a grammar and dictionary of it were made with difficulty from the mouths of old people. The Ehsts, who resemble the Finns of Tavastland, have maintained their ethnic features, their customs, national traditions, songs and poetry, and their harmonious language. There is a marked revival of national feeling, favoured by "Young Esthonia." The prevailing religion is the Lutheran (79·8%); 14·3% belong to the Orthodox Greek Church; of the Russians, however, a considerable proportion are Raskolniks (Nonconformists); the Roman Catholics amount to 2·3%, and the Jews to 2%. The Russian civil code was introduced in the Baltic provinces in 1835, and the use of Russian, instead of German, in official correspondence and in law courts was ordered in 1867, but not generally brought into practice.

Nearly all the soil belongs to the nobility, the extent of the peasants' estates being only 15% of the entire area of the government. Serfdom was abolished in 1819, but the peasants remained under the jurisdiction of their landlords. The class of peasant proprietors being restricted to a small number of wealthy peasants, the bulk have remained tenants at will; they are very miserable, and about one-fourth of them are continually wandering in search of work. From time to time the emigration takes the shape of a mass movement, which the government stops by forcible measures. The average size of the landed estates is 9500 to 11,000 acres, far above the general average for Russia. Agriculture has reached a high degree of perfection on the estates of the landlords. The principal crops are rye, oats, barley, flax and potatoes, with some wheat, hemp and buckwheat. Dairy-farming and gardening are on the increase. Fishing in Lake Peipus gives occupation to nearly 100,000 persons, and is also carried on in the Gulf of Riga and in the rivers. Woollen, cloth, cotton and flax mills, steam flour and saw mills, distilleries and breweries, machinery works, paper mills, furniture, tobacco, soap, candle and hardware works are among the chief industrial establishments. Livonia carries on a large export trade, especially through Riga and Pernau, in petroleum, wool, oilcake, flax, linseed, hemp, grain, timber and wooden wares; the Dvina is the chief channel for this trade.

Education stands on a much higher level than elsewhere in Russia, no less than 87% of the children receiving regular instruction. The higher educational institutions include Yuriev (Dorpat) University, Riga polytechnic and a high school for the clergy.

The government is divided into nine districts, the chief towns of which, with their populations in 1897, are: Riga, capital of the government (282,943); Arensburg, in the island of Oesel (4621); Yuriev or Dorpat (42,421); Fellin (7659); Pernau (12,856); Walk (10,139); Wenden (6327); Werro (4154); and Wolmar (5124). The capital of the government is Riga.

Coins of the time of Alexander the Great, found on the island of Oesel, show that the coasts of the Baltic were at an early period in commercial relation with the civilized world. The chronicle of Nestor mentions as inhabitants of the Baltic coast the Chudes, the Livs, the Narova, Letgola, Semigallians and Kors. It was probably about the 9th century that the Chudes became tributary to the Varangian-Russian states. As they reacquired their independence, Yaroslav I. undertook in 1030 a campaign against them, and founded Yuriev (Dorpat). The Germans first penetrated into Livonia in the 11th century, and in 1158 several Lübeck and Visby merchants landed at the mouth of the Dvina. In 1186 the emissaries of the archbishop of Bremen began to preach Christianity among the Ehsts and Letts, and in 1201 the bishop of Livonia established his residence at Riga. In 1202 or 1204 Innocent III. recognized the order of Brothers of the Sword, the residence of its grand master being at Wenden; and the order, spreading the Christian religion by the sword among the natives, carried on from that time a series of uninterrupted wars against the Russian republics and Lithuania, as well as a struggle against the archbishop of Riga, Riga having become a centre for trade, intermediate between the Hanseatic towns and those of Novgorod, Pskov and Polotsk. The first active interference of Lithuania in the affairs of Livonia took place immediately after the great outbreak of the peasants on Oesel; Olgierd then devastated all southern Livonia. The order, having purchased the Danish part of Esthonia, in 1347, began a war against the bishop of Riga, as well as against Lithuania, Poland and Russia. The wars against those powers were terminated respectively in 1435, 1466 and 1483. About the end of the 15th century the master of the order, Plettenberg, acquired a position of great importance, and in 1527 he was recognized as a prince of the empire by Charles V. On the other hand, the authority of the bishops of Riga was soon completely destroyed (1566). The war of the order with Ivan IV. of Russia in 1558 led to a division of Livonia, its northern part, Dorpat included, being taken by Russia, and the southern part falling under the dominion of Poland. From that time (1561) Livonia formed a subject of dispute between Poland and Russia, the latter only formally abdicating its rights to the country in 1582. In 1621 it was the theatre of a war between Poland and Sweden, and was conquered by the latter power, enjoying thus for twenty-five years a milder rule. In 1654, and again at the beginning of the 18th century, it became the theatre of war between Poland, Russia and Sweden, and was finally conquered by Russia. The official concession was confirmed by the treaty of Nystad in 1721.

See E. Seraphim, *Geschichte Liv-, Esth-, und Kurlands* (2nd ed., Revel, 1897–1904) and *Geschichte von Livland* (Gotha, 1905, &c.).

(P. A. K.; J. T. Be.)

LIVY [Titus Livius] (59 B.C.–A.D. 17), Roman historian, was born at Patavium (Padua). The ancient connexion between his native city and Rome helped to turn his attention to the study which became the work of his life. For Padua claimed, like Rome, a Trojan origin, and Livy is careful to place its founder Antenor side by side with Aeneas. A more real bond of union was found in the dangers to which both had been exposed from the assaults of the Celts (Livy x. 2), and Padua must have been drawn to Rome as the conqueror of her hereditary foes. Moreover, at the time of Livy's birth, Padua had long been in possession of the full Roman franchise, and the historian's family name may have been taken by one of his ancestors out of compliment to the great Livian gens at Rome, whose connexion with Cisalpine Gaul is well-established (Suet. *Tib.* 3), and by one of whom his family may have been enfranchized.

Livy's easy independent life at Rome, and his aristocratic leanings in politics seem to show that he was the son of well-born and opulent parents; he was certainly well educated, being widely read in Greek literature, and a student both of rhetoric and philosophy. We have also evidence in his writings that he had prepared himself for his great work by researches into the history of his native town. His youth and early manhood, spent perhaps chiefly at Padua, were cast in stormy times, and the impression which they left upon his mind was ineffaceable. In the Civil War his personal sympathies were with Pompey and the republican party (Tac. *Ann.* iv. 34); but far more lasting in its effects was his experience of the licence, anarchy and confusion of these dark days. The rule of Augustus he seems to have accepted as a necessity, but he could not, like Horace and Virgil, welcome it as inaugurating a new and glorious era. He writes of it with despondency as a degenerate and declining age; and, instead of triumphant prophecies of world-wide rule, such as we find in Horace, Livy contents himself with pointing out the dangers which already threatened Rome, and exhorting his [illegible] to learn, in good time, the lessons which the past [illegible] the state had to teach.

[illegible] about the time of the battle of Actium that [illegible] himself in Rome, and there he seems chiefly [illegible] until his retirement to Padua shortly before his [illegible] We have no evidence that he travelled much, though [illegible] paid at least one visit to Campania (xxxviii. 56), [illegible] so far as we know, took any part in political life. [illegible] he enjoyed the personal friendship and patronage [illegible] (Tac. *Ann.* iv. 34) and stimulated the historical [illegible] emperor Claudius (Suet. *Claud.* xli.), can we [illegible] anything of the courtier. There is not in his history [illegible] rather gross adulation in which even Virgil does [illegible] indulge. His republican sympathies were freely [illegible] freely pardoned by Augustus. We must [illegible] devoted to the great task which he had set himself [illegible] a mind free from all disturbing cares, and in the [illegible] the facilities for study afforded by the Rome [illegible] its liberal encouragement of letters, its newly- [illegible] and its brilliant literary circles. As his work [illegible] which he had never coveted came to him in [illegible] He is said to have declared in one volume of his [illegible] already won glory enough, and the younger [illegible] relates that a Spaniard came all the way [illegible] to see him, and, this accomplished, at once [illegible] The accession of Tiberius (A.D. 14) [illegible] for the worse the prospects of literature in [illegible] retired to Padua, where he died. He had at [illegible] x. 1. 39), who also was possibly an author [illegible]), and a daughter married to a certain [illegible] of no great merit (Seneca, *Controv.* x. [illegible] is known of his personal history.

[illegible] *History.*—For us the interest of Livy's life [illegible] to which the greater part of it was devoted, [illegible] from its foundation down to the death [illegible] Its proper title was *Ab urbe condita libri* [illegible] and *annales*). Various indications point [illegible] to 20 B.C., as that during which the first [illegible] In the first book (19. 3) the emperor is [illegible] which he assumed early in 27 B.C., and [illegible] of all reference to the restoration, in [illegible] taken at Carrhae seems to justify the [illegible] passage was written before that date. In [illegible] there is a reference to a law of Augustus [illegible] B.C. The books dealing with the civil [illegible] written during Augustus's lifetime, as [illegible] (Tac. *Ann.* iv. 34), while there is some [illegible] part, from book cxxi. onwards, was [illegible] A.D. 14.

[illegible] the landing of Aeneas in Italy, and [illegible] 9 B.C., though it is possible [illegible] continue it as far as the death of [illegible] is certainly not due to the [illegible] at the end of the 5th century; [illegible] into *libri* or *volumina* seems to [illegible] were grouped and possibly pub- [illegible] both by the prefaces which [illegible] work (vi. 1, xxi. 1, xxxi. 1) and [illegible] books cix.-cxvi. as "bellorum [illegible] and publication in parts [illegible] authors, and in the case [illegible] necessity.

[illegible] the history, the first 15 carry [illegible] struggle with Carthage, a period, [illegible] (xxxi. 1); 15 more (xvi–xxx.) [illegible] Punic wars. With the close [illegible] of Macedonia in 167 B.C. [illegible] Tiberius Gracchus, 133 B.C. [illegible] dictatorship of Sulla (81 B.C.), [illegible] B.C.), in cix.-cxvi. the civil [illegible] B.C.), in cxxiv. the defeat of [illegible] and cxxxiv. the battle of Actium and the accession of Augustus. The remaining eight books give the history of the first twenty years of Augustus's reign.

Of this vast work only a small portion has come down to modern times; only thirty-five books are now extant (i.-x., xxi.-xlv.), and of these xli. and xliii. are incomplete. The lost books seem to have disappeared between the 7th century and the revival of letters in the 15th— a fact sufficiently accounted for by the difficulty of transmitting so voluminous a work in times when printing was unknown, for the story that Pope Gregory I. burnt all the copies of Livy he could lay his hands on rests on no good evidence. Only one important fragment has since been recovered—the portion of book xci. discovered in the Vatican in 1772, and edited by Niebuhr in 1820. Very much no doubt of the substance of the lost books has been preserved both by such writers as Plutarch and Dio Cassius, and by epitomizers like Florus and Eutropius. But our knowledge of their contents is chiefly derived from the so-called *periochae* or epitomes, of which we have fortunately a nearly complete series, the epitomes of books cxxxvi. and cxxxvii. being the only ones missing.[1] These epitomes have been ascribed without sufficient reason to Florus (2nd century); but, though they are probably of even later date, and are disappointingly meagre, they may be taken as giving, so far as they go, a fairly authentic description of the original. They have been expanded with great ingenuity and learning by Freinsheim in Drakenborch's edition of Livy.[2] The *Prodigia* of Julius Obsequens and the list of consuls in the *Chronica* of Cassiodorus are taken directly from Livy, and to that extent reproduce the contents of the lost books. It is probable that Obsequens, Cassiodorus and the compiler of the epitomes did not use the original work but an abridgment.

Historical Standpoint.—If we are to form a correct judgment on the merits of Livy's history, we must, above all things, bear in mind what his aim was in writing it, and this he has told us himself in the celebrated preface. He set himself the task of recording the history of the Roman people, "the first in the world," from the beginning. The task was a great one, and the fame to be won by it uncertain, yet it would be something to have made the attempt, and the labour itself would bring a welcome relief from the contemplation of present evils; for his readers, too, this record will, he says, be full of instruction; they are invited to note especially the moral lessons taught by the story of Rome, to observe how Rome rose to greatness by the simple virtues and unselfish devotion of her citizens, and how on the decay of these qualities followed degeneracy and decline.

He does not, therefore, write, as Polybius wrote, for students of history. With Polybius the greatness of Rome is a phenomenon to be critically studied and scientifically explained; the rise of Rome forms an important chapter in universal history, and must be dealt with, not as an isolated fact, but in connexion with the general march of events in the civilized world. Still less has Livy anything in common with the naïve anxiety of Dionysius of Halicarnassus to make it clear to his fellow Greeks that the irresistible people who had mastered them was in origin, in race and in language Hellenic like themselves.

Livy writes as a Roman, to raise a monument worthy of the greatness of Rome, and to keep alive, for the guidance and the warning of Romans, the recollection alike of the virtues which had made Rome great and of the vices which had threatened her with destruction. In so writing he was in close agreement with the traditions of Roman literature, as well as with the conception of the nature and objects of history current in his time. To a large extent Roman literature grew out of

[1] For the fragments of an epitome discovered at Oxyrhynchus see J. S. Reid in *Classical Review* (July, 1904); E. Kornemann, *Die neue Livius-Epitome aus Oxyrhynchus*, with text and commentary (Leipzig, 1904); C. H. Moore, "The Oxyrhynchus Epitome of Livy in relation to Obsequens and Cassiodorus," in *American Journal of Philology* (1904), 241.

[2] The various rumours once current of complete copies of Livy at Constantinople, Chios and elsewhere, are noticed by B. G. Niebuhr, *Lectures on the History of Rome from the first Punic War* (ed. L. Schmitz, 1844), i. 65.

pride in Rome, for, though her earliest authors took the form and often the language of their writings from Greece, it was the greatness of Rome that inspired the best of them, and it was from the annals of Rome that their themes were taken. And this is naturally true in an especial sense of the Roman historians; the long list of annalists begins at the moment when the great struggle with Carthage had for the first time brought Rome into direct connexion with the historic peoples of the ancient world, and when Romans themselves awoke to the importance of the part reserved for Rome to play in universal history. To write the annals of Rome became at once a task worthy of the best of her citizens. Though other forms of literature might be thought unbecoming to the dignity of a free-born citizen, this was never so with history. On the contrary, men of high rank and tried statesmanship were on that very account thought all the fitter to write the chronicles of the state they had served. And history in Rome never lost either its social prestige or its intimate and exclusive connexion with the fortunes of the Roman people. It was well enough for Greeks to busy themselves with the manners, institutions and deeds of the "peoples outside." The Roman historians, from Fabius Pictor to Tacitus, cared for none of these things. This exclusive interest in Rome was doubtless encouraged by the peculiar characteristics of the history of the state. The Roman annalist had not, like the Greek, to deal with the varying fortunes and separate doings of a number of petty communities, but with the continuous life of a single city. Nor was his attention drawn from the main lines of political history by the claims of art, literature and philosophy, for just as the tie which bound Romans together was that of citizenship, not of race or culture, so the history of Rome is that of the state, of its political constitution, its wars and conquests, its military and administrative system.

Livy's own circumstances were all such as to render these views natural to him. He began to write at a time when, after a century of disturbance, the mass of men had been contented to purchase peace at the price of liberty The present was at least inglorious, the future doubtful, and many turned gladly to the past for consolation. This retrospective tendency was favourably regarded by the government. It was the policy of Augustus to obliterate all traces of recent revolution, and to connect the new imperial régime as closely as possible with the ancient traditions and institutions of Rome and Italy. The *Aeneid* of Virgil, the *Fasti* of Ovid, suited well with his own restoration of the ancient temples, his revival of such ancient ceremonies as the Ludi Saeculares, his efforts to check the un-Roman luxury of the day, and his jealous regard for the purity of the Roman stock. And, though we are nowhere told that Livy undertook his history at the emperor's suggestion, it is certain that Augustus read parts of it with pleasure, and even honoured the writer with his assistance and friendship.

Livy was deeply penetrated with a sense of the greatness of Rome. From first to last its majesty and high destiny are present to his mind. Aeneas is led to Italy by the Fates that he may be the founder of Rome. Romulus after his ascension declares it to be the will of heaven that Rome should be mistress of the world; and Hannibal marches into Italy, that he may "set free the world" from Roman rule. But, if this ever-present consciousness often gives dignity and elevation to his narrative, it is also responsible for some of its defects. It leads him occasionally into exaggerated language (*e.g.* xxii. 33, "nullius usquam terrarum rei cura Romanos effugiebat"), or into such misstatements as his explanation of the course taken by the Romans in renewing war with Carthage, that "it seemed more suitable to the dignity of the Roman people." Often his jealousy for the honour of Rome makes him unfair and one-sided. In all her wars not only success but justice is with Rome To the same general attitude is also due the omission by Livy of all that has no direct bearing on the fortunes of the Roman people. "I have resolved," he says (xxxix. 48), "only to touch on foreign affairs so far as they are bound up with those of Rome." As the result, we get from Livy very defective accounts even of the Italic peoples most closely connected with Rome. Of the past history and the internal condition of the more distant nations she encountered he tells us little or nothing, even when he found such details carefully given by Polybius.

Scarcely less strong than his interest in Rome is his interest in the moral lessons which her history seemed to him so well qualified to teach. This didactic view of history was a prevalent one in antiquity, and it was confirmed no doubt by those rhetorical studies which in Rome as in Greece formed the chief part of education, and which taught men to look on history as little more than a storehouse of illustrations and themes for declamation. But it suited also the practical bent of the Roman mind, with its comparative indifference to abstract speculation or purely scientific research. It is in the highest degree natural that Livy should have sought for the secret of the rise of Rome, not in any large historical causes, but in the moral qualities of the people themselves, and that he should have looked upon the contemplation of these as the best remedy for the vices of his own degenerate days. He dwells with delight on the unselfish patriotism of the old heroes of the republic. In those times children obeyed their parents, the gods were still sincerely worshipped, poverty was no disgrace, sceptical philosophies and foreign fashions in religion and in daily life were unknown. But this ethical interest is closely bound up with his Roman sympathies. His moral ideal is no abstract one, and the virtues he praises are those which in his view made up the truly Roman type of character. The prominence thus given to the moral aspects of the history tends to obscure in some degree the true relations and real importance of the events narrated, but it does so in Livy to a far less extent than in some other writers. He is much too skilful an artist either to resolve his history into a mere bundle of examples, or to overload it, as Tacitus is sometimes inclined to do, with reflections and axioms. The moral he wishes to enforce is usually either conveyed by the story itself, with the aid perhaps of a single sentence of comment, or put as a speech into the mouth of one of his characters (*e.g.* xxiii. 49; the devotion of Decius, viii. 10, cf vii. 40; and the speech of Camillus, v. 54); and what little his narrative thus loses in accuracy it gains in dignity and warmth of feeling. In his portraits of the typical Romans of the old style, such as Q. Fabius Maximus, in his descriptions of the unshaken firmness and calm courage shown by the fathers of the state in the hour of trial, Livy is at his best; and he is so largely in virtue of his genuine appreciation of character as a powerful force in the affairs of men.

This enthusiasm for Rome and for Roman virtues is, moreover, saved from degenerating into gross partiality by the genuine candour of Livy's mind and by his wide sympathies with every thing great and good. Seneca (*Suasoriae* vi. 22) and Quintilian (x. 1. 101) bear witness to his impartiality. Thus, Hasdrubal's devotion and valour at the battle on the Metaurus are described in terms of eloquent praise; and even in Hannibal, the lifelong enemy of Rome, he frankly recognizes the great qualities that balanced his faults. Nor, though his sympathies are unmistakably with the aristocratic party, does he scruple to censure the pride, cruelty and selfishness which too often marked their conduct (ii. 54; the speech of Canuleius, iv. 3; of Sextius and Licinius, vi. 36); and, though he feels acutely that the times are out of joint, and has apparently little hope of the future, he still believes in justice and goodness. He is often righteously indignant, but never satirical, and such a pessimism as that of Tacitus and Juvenal is wholly foreign to his nature.

Though he studied and even wrote on philosophy (Seneca, *Ep.* 100. 9), Livy is by no means a philosophic historian. We learn indeed from incidental notices that he inclined to Stoicism and disliked the Epicurean system. With the scepticism that despised the gods (x. 40) and denied that they meddled with the affairs of men (xliii. 13) he has no sympathy. The immortal gods are everywhere the same; they govern the world (xxxvii. 45) and reveal the future to men by signs and wonders (xliii. 13), but only a debased superstition will look for their hand in every petty incident, or abandon itself to an indiscriminate belief in the portents and miracles in which popular credulity

[illegible] ies, rarely exceeding a score, and some like the [illegible] geckos deposit only one or two. The parents [illegible] to hatch where they are deposited, in sand or in [illegible] lizards, however, retain the eggs in the oviducts [illegible] embryo is fully developed; these species then bring [illegible] young and are called ovo-viviparous by purists. [illegible] possess a considerable amount of intelligence; they [illegible] other, become very tame, and act deliberately [illegible] circumstances. As a rule the Iguanids and Varans [illegible] as the Agamas are dull. Many have the power of [illegible], a faculty which they share only with various [illegible] fishes. Lizards are not poisonous, with the [illegible] of *Heloderma*.

[illegible] or lizards in the wider sense, fall easily into three [illegible] geckos (*q.v.*), chameleons (*q.v.*) and lizards.

[illegible] GECKONES. Pleurodont lizards with well-developed [illegible] temporal bony arches; postthoracic ribs united [illegible] abdomen. Tongue, thick and broad, slightly nicked [illegible] a few exceptions they have amphicoelous vertebrae, [illegible] remain separate and they have no eyelids, with [illegible].

[illegible] *Geckonidae*.—Amphicoelous; parietals separate; [illegible] and with a perforation near the ventral end. Cosmo[illegible] mainly tropical, with about 270 species (see [illegible]

[illegible] geckos are nocturnal and the pupil contracts into a [illegible] in a few diurnal kinds, *e.g.* *Phelsuma* of islands [illegible], and *Lygodactylus* of Africa. *Aeluronurus* of [illegible], and *Ptenopus* of South Africa, have upper [illegible] eyelids. Whilst the skin is mostly soft on the [illegible] granular tubercles, scales (except on the belly) are [illegible] are present in *Homopholis*, in *Geckolepis* of Mada[illegible] fully developed in *Teratoscincus scincus*. This [illegible] inhabitant of the steppes and desert regions of [illegible] peculiar [illegible] by rubbing the imbricating scales upon each other, [illegible] a shrill cricket-like noise, whilst sitting at night in front of [illegible] on the ground. Furthermore it is so thoroughly adapted [illegible] upon the desert sand that its digits are devoid of adhesive lamellae. The same beautiful adaptation to the surround[illegible] exists also in *Ptenopus* (with fringed toes) and *Stenodactylus*, which are likewise [illegible]. *Aeluronyx* of Madagascar and Seychelles [illegible] retractile claws. *Naultinus elegans* of New Zealand [illegible] viviparous; the others lay but one rather large egg at a time. Many species have a feeble voice which resembles a repeated click of the tongue, and their name "gecko" is supposed to be an Indian imitation of the sound.

2. Family. *Uroplatidae*.—Amphicoelous; parietals separate; but the nasal bones are fused together, and the clavicles are not dilated. Genus *Uroplatus*, with a few species, *e.g.* *U. fimbriatus* in Madagascar.

3. Family. *Eublepharidae*.—Procoelous; parietals united; eye[illegible] functional; clavicles expanded as in the true geckos which they resemble in other respects. The few genera and species are undoubtedly a heterogeneous assembly, as indicated by their very scattered distribution, but they all agree in their decidedly handsome colour pattern, bands of dark brown to maroon upon a light ground. *Eublepharis*, with one species each in Panama, Mexico, Texas and California; two in India. *Coleonyx elegans* in forests of Central America and Mexico. *Psilodactylus* in West Africa.

II. Suborder. CHAMAELEONTES. Acrodont, Old World lizards, with laterally compressed body, prehensile tail and well developed limbs with the digits arranged in opposing, grasping bundles of two and three respectively. The chameleons (*q.v.*) have many structural peculiarities.

III. Suborder. LACERTAE. Procoelous vertebrae; ventral portions of the clavicles not dilated; parietal bones fused into one.

The general appearance is too misleading for the classification of the Lacertae. E. D. Cope (*Proc. Ac. Philad.*, 1864, pp. 224 et seq. and *Proc. Amer.* [illegible]) therefore relied upon more fundamental [illegible] presence or absence of osteoderms, [illegible] the teeth and the tongue. G. A. Boulenger [illegible] p. 117, &c.) has further improved upon [illegible], and has elaborated a classification [illegible] the three volumes of the catalogue of [illegible] is followed in the present [illegible] treatment of the families. [illegible] preference is given to such [illegible]

The [illegible] into 4 or 5 main groups. Presumably the [illegible] complete cranial arches are more [illegible] us to conclude that limbless forms [illegible] groups possessed of fully de[illegible] [illegible] a cranial po[illegible] [illegible] [illegible]

latter is perhaps *Aniella* of California, whilst *Heloderma* and *Lanthanotus* are also specialized and isolated offshoots. A second group is formed by the few American *Xantusiidae*, the numerous American *Tejidae*, and the burrowing, degraded American and African *Amphisbaenidae*. A third group comprises the cosmopolitan *Scincidae*, the African and Malagasy *Gerrhosauridae* which in various features remind us of the *Anguidae*, and the African and Eurasian *Lacertidae* which are the highest members of this group. *Anelytropidae* and perhaps also *Dibamidae* may be degraded Scincoids. The *Varanidae* stand quite alone, in many respects the highest of all lizards, with some, quite superficial, Crocodilian resemblances. Lastly there are the few *Pygopodidae* of the Australian region, with still quite obscure relationship.

Family 1. *Agamidae*.—Acrodont; tongue broad and thick, not protractile; no osteoderms. Old World.

The agamas have always two pairs of well-developed limbs. The teeth are usually differentiated into incisors, canines and molars. The skin is devoid of ossifications, but large and numerous cutaneous spines are often present, especially on the head and on the tail. The family, comprising some 200 species, with about 30 genera, shows great diversity of form; the terrestrial members are mostly flat-bodied, the arboreal more laterally compressed and often with a very long tail. Most of them are insectivorous, but a few are almost entirely vegetable feeders. They are an exclusively Old World family; they are most numerous in Australia (except New Zealand) and the Indian and Malay countries; comparatively few live in Africa (none in Madagascar) and in the countries from Asia Minor to India.

The majority of the ground-agamas, and the most common species of the plains, deserts or rocky districts of Africa and Asia, belong to the genera *Stellio* and *Agama*. Their scales are mixed with larger prominent spines, which in some species are particularly developed on the tail, and disposed in whorls. Nearly all travellers in the north of Africa mention the *Hardûn* of the Arabs (*Agama stellio*), which is extremely common, and has drawn upon itself the hatred of the Mahommedans by its habit of nodding its head, which they interpret as a mockery of their own movements whilst engaged in prayer. In some of the Grecian islands they are still called *korkordilos*, just as they were in the time of Herodotus. *Uromastix* is one of the largest of ground-agamas, and likewise found in Africa and Asia. The body is uniformly covered with granular scales, whilst the short, strong tail is armed with powerful spines disposed in whorls. The Indian species (*U. hardwicki*) is mainly herbivorous; the African *U. acanthinurus* and *U. spinipes*, the *Dob* of the Arabs, take mixed food. *Phrynocephalus* is typical of the steppes and deserts of Asia. *Ceratophora* and *Lyriocephalus scutatus*, the latter remarkable for its chameleon-like appearance, are Ceylonese. *Calotes*, peculiar to Indian countries, comprises many species, *e.g.* *C. ophiomachus*, generally known as the "bloodsucker" on account of the red colour on the head and neck displayed during excitement. *Draco* (see DRAGON) is Indo-Malayan. *Physignathus* is known from Australia to Cochin China.

Of the Australian agamas no other genus is so numerously represented and widely distributed as *Grammatophora*, the species of which grow to a length of from 8 to 18 in. Their scales are generally rough and spinous; but otherwise they possess no strikingly distinguishing peculiarity, unless the loose skin of their throat, which is transversely folded and capable of inflation, be regarded as such. On the other hand, two other Australian agamoids have attained some celebrity by their grotesque appearance, due to the extraordinary development of their integuments. One (fig. 1) is the frilled lizard (*Chlamydosaurus kingi*), which is restricted to Queensland and the north coast, and grows to a length of 3 ft., including the long tapering tail. It is provided with a frill-like fold of the skin round the neck, which, when erected, resembles a broad collar. This lizard when startled rises with the fore-legs off the ground and squats and runs on its hind-legs. The other lizard is one which most appropriately has been called *Moloch horridus*. It is covered with large and small spine-bearing tubercules; the head is small and the tail short. It is sluggish in its movements, and so harmless that its armature and (to a casual observer) repulsive appearance are its sole means of defence. It grows only to a length of 10 in., and is not uncommon in the flats of South and West Australia.

Family 2. *Iguanidae*.—Pleurodont; tongue broad and thick, not protractile; no osteoderms. America, Madagascar and Fiji Islands.

According to the very varied habits, their external appearance varies within wide limits, there being amongst the 300 species, with 50 genera, arboreal, terrestrial, burrowing and semi-aquatic forms, and even one semi-marine kind. All have well-developed limbs. In their general structure the *Iguanidae* closely resemble the *Agamidae*, from which they differ mainly by the pleurodont dentition. Most of them are insectivorous. Some, especially *Anolis* and *Polychrus*, can change colour to a remarkable extent. The family [illegible]ll through the neotropical region, inclusive of the Galapagos [illegible] Antilles, into the southern and western states of North [illegible] Remarkable cases of discontinuous distribution are [illegible] and *Hoplodon* in Madagascar, and *Brachylophus fasciatus* [illegible] Islands. *Conolophus subcristatus* and *Amblyrhynchus* [illegible]abit the Galapagos; the former feeds upon cactus and leaves, the latter is semi-marine, diving for the algae which grow below tide-marks. For *Basiliscus* see BASILISK; IGUANA is dealt with under its own heading; allied is *Metopoceros cornutus* of Hayti. *Polychrus*, the "chameleon," and *Liolaemus* are South American; *Ctenosaura* of Central America and Mexico resembles the agamoid *Uromastix*. *Corythophanes* and *Laemanctus*, with only a few species, are rare inhabitants of the tropical forests of Central America and Mexico. *Sauromalus*, *Crotaphytus*, *Callisaurus*, *Holbrookia*, *Uma*, *Uta* are typical Sonoran genera, some ranging from Oregon through Mexico. Allied is *Sceloporus*, with about 34 species, the most characteristic genus of Mexican lizards; only 4 species live in the United States, and only 3 or 4 are found south of the Isthmus of Tehuantepec and are restricted to Central America. The majority are humivagous, while others are truly arboreal, *e.g.* *S. microlepidotus*, a species which, moreover, has the greatest possible altitudinal range, from the hot country of southern Oaxaca to the upper tree-line of Citlaltepetl, about 13,500 ft. elevation; many species are viviparous. *Phrynosoma*, with about a dozen species, the "horned toads" of California to Texas, and through Mexico. Some of these comical-looking little creatures are viviparous, others deposit their eggs in the ground. They are well concealed by the colour of their upper parts, which in most cases agrees with the prevailing tone of their surroundings, mostly arid, stony or sandy localities; the large spikes

FIG. 1.—Frilled Lizard (*Chlamydosaurus kingi*).

on the head protect them from being swallowed by snakes. The enlarged spiny scales scattered over the back look as if it were sprinkled with the dried husks of seeds. They are entirely insectivorous, bask on the broiling hot sand and then can run fast enough; otherwise they are sluggish, dig themselves into the sand by a peculiar shuffling motion of the fringed edges of their flattened bodies, and when surprised they feign death. The statement, persistently repeated (O. P. Hay, *Proc. U.S. Nat. Mus.* xv., 1892, pp. 375-378), that some, *e.g.* *P. blainvillei* of California, have the power of squirting a blood-red fluid from the corner of the eye, still requires renewed investigation.

The smallest lizards of this family belong to the genus *Anolis*, extremely numerous as regards species (more than 100) and individuals on bushes and trees of tropical America, and especially of the West Indies. They offer many points of analogy to the humming birds in their distribution, colours and even disposition. Hundreds may be seen on a bright day, disporting themselves on trees and fences, and entering houses. Like the iguanas, they (at least the males) are provided with a large, expansible dewlap at the throat, which is brilliantly coloured, and which they display on the slightest provocation. This appendage is merely a fold of the skin, ornamental and sexual; it has no cavity in its interior, and has no communication with the mouth or with the respiratory organs; it is supported by the posterior horns of the hyoid bone, and can be erected and spread at the will of the animal. The presence of such dewlaps in lizards is always a sign of an excitable temper. Many, *e.g.* *A. carolinensis*, the "chameleon," can change colour to an extraordinary degree. They are much fed upon by birds and snakes, and have a fragile tail, easily reproduced. They bring forth only one large egg at a time, but probably breed several times during the season.

Family 3. *Xenosauridae*.—Pleurodont; solid teeth; anterior part of tongue slightly emarginate and retractile, and covered with flat papillae; no osteoderms. Mexico.

The only representative of this family is *Xenosaurus grandis*, recorded from the mountains of Orizaba, Cordoba and Oaxaca. The four-footed creature is less than 1 ft. in length; the body is depressed, covered above with minute granules and tubercles; a distinct fold of skin extends from the axilla to the groin, reminding of the similar fold of some *Anguidae*, to which this singular genus seems to be allied.

Family 4. *Anguidae*.—Pleurodont; teeth solid, sometimes (*Ophiosaurus*) grooved; anterior part of tongue emarginate and retractile into the posterior portion; osteoderms on the body, and especially on the head where they are roofing over the temporal fossa; entirely zoophagous and ovo-viviparous. America, Europe and India.

Gerrhonotus, 8 species, in mountainous countries, from British Columbia to Costa Rica; like *Diploglossus* s. *Celestus* of Mexico, the Antilles and Central America, with well-developed limbs, but with a lateral fold. *Anguis fragilis* and two species of *Ophiosaurus* are the only members of this family which are not American, and even the third species of *Ophiosaurus*, *O. ventralis*, lives in the United States. *Ophiosaurus* s. *Pseudopus*, the glass-snake, from Morocco and the Balkan peninsula to Burma and Fokien; also in the U.S.A., with the limbs reduced to a pair of tiny spikes near the vent, and a lateral fold along the snake-like body. *Anguis*, with its sole species *fragilis*, the slow-worm or blind-worm, is devoid of a lateral fold, and the limbs are entirely absent. Europe, Algeria and western Asia.

Family 5. *Helodermatidae*, with *Heloderma* of Arizona and Mexico, and *Lanthanotus* of Borneo.—The teeth of *Heloderma* are recurved, with slightly swollen bases, loosely attached to the inner edge of the jaws; each tooth is grooved, and those of the lower jaw are in close vicinity of the series of labial glands which secrete a poison; the only instance among lizards.[1] Limbs well developed. Tongue resembling that of the *Anguidae*. The skin of the upper surface is granular, with many irregular bony tubercles which give it an ugly warty look. *H. horridum* in Mexico, and *H. suspectum*, the gila monster, in the hot and sandy lowlands of the Gila basin. The animal, which reaches a length of more than 2 ft., is blackish-brown and yellow or orange, and on the thick tail these "warning colours" are arranged in alternate rings. Small animals are probably paralyzed or killed by the bite, the poison being effective enough to produce severe symptoms even in man. The Zapotecs, who call the creature Talachini, and other tribes of Mexico have endowed it with fabulous properties and fear it more than the most poisonous snakes. *Lanthanotus corneensis*, of which only a few specimens are known, is apparently closely allied to *Heloderma*, although the teeth are not grooved, osteoderms are absent and probably also the poison glands.

Family 6. *Aniellidae*.—One genus, *Aniella*, with a few worm- or snake-shaped species in California, which seem to be degraded forms of *Anguidae*. The eyes and ears are concealed, the limbs are entirely absent, body and tail covered with soft, imbricating scales. The tongue is villose, smooth, bifid anteriorly. The few teeth are recurved, with swollen bases. The skull is much reduced. Total length of *A. pulchra* up to 8 in.

Family 7. *Zonuridae*.—Pleurodont; tongue short, villose, scarcely protractile, feebly nicked at the tip. With osteoderms at least upon the skull, where they roof in the temporal region. Africa and Madagascar.

Only 4 genera, with about 15 species. *Zonurus* of South Africa and Madagascar has the whole head, neck, back and tail covered with strong bony scales, the horny covering of which forms sharp spikes, especially on the tail. They defend themselves by jerking head and tail sidewards. *Z. giganteus* reaches 15 in. in length, and is, like the other members of the family, zoophagous. The other genera live in southern and in tropical Africa: *Pseudocordylus*, *Platysaurus* and *Chamaesaura*; the latter closely approaches the *Anguidae* by its snake-shaped body, very long tail and much reduced limbs, which in *C. macrolepis* are altogether absent.

Family 8. *Xantusiidae*.—Pleurodont; tongue very short and scaly; no osteoderms; supratemporal fossa roofed over by the cranial bones; eyes devoid of movable lids; tympanum exposed; femoral pores present; limbs and tail well developed. American.

Xantusia (so named after Xantus, a Hungarian collector), *e.g.* *X. vigilis* and a few other species from the desert tracts of Nevada and California to Lower California. *Lepidophyma flavomaculatum*, Central America; and *Cricosaura typica* in Cuba.

Family 9. *Tejidae*.—Teeth solid, almost acrodont; tongue long and narrow, deeply bifid, beset with papillae; no osteoderms; scales of the back very small or quite granular; limbs sometimes reduced. America.

This large, typically American family comprises more than 100 species which have been arranged in many genera. Some are entirely arboreal, dwellers in forests, while others, like *Cnemidophorus* and *Ameiva*, are strictly terrestrial, with great running powers; a few dwell below the surface and are transformed into almost limbless

[1] For anatomical detail and experiments, see R. W. Shufeldt, *P.Z.S.* (1890), p. 178; G. A. Boulenger, *ibid.* (1891), p. 109, and C. Stewart, *ibid.* (1891), p. 119.

ḍlights. The ancient state religion of Rome, with its temples, priests and auguries, he not only reverences as an integral part of the Roman constitution, with a sympathy which grows as he studies it, but, like Varro, and in true Stoic fashion, he regards it as a valuable instrument of government (i. 19. 21), indispensable in a well-ordered community. As distinctly Stoical is the doctrine of a fate to which even the gods must yield (ix. 4), which disposes the plans of men (i. 42) and blinds their minds (v 37), yet leaves their wills free (xxxvii. 45).

But we find no trace in Livy of any systematic application of philosophy to the facts of history. He is as innocent of the leading ideas which shaped the work of Polybius as he is of the cheap theorizing which wearies us in the pages of Dionysius. The events are graphically, if not always accurately, described; but of the larger causes at work in producing them, of their subtle action and reaction upon each other, and of the general conditions amid which the history worked itself out, he takes no thought at all. Nor has Livy much acquaintance with either the theory or the practice of politics. He exhibits, it is true, political sympathies and antipathies. He is on the whole for the nobles and against the commons; and, though the unfavourable colours in which he paints the leaders of the latter are possibly reflected from the authorities he followed, it is evident that he despised and disliked the multitude. Of monarchy he speaks with a genuine Roman hatred, and we know that in the last days of the republic his sympathies were wholly with those who strove in vain to save it. He betrays, too, an insight into the evils which were destined finally to undermine the imposing fabric of Roman empire. The decline of the free population, the spread of slavery (vi. 12, vii. 25), the universal craving for wealth (iii. 26), the employment of foreign mercenaries (xxv. 33), the corruption of Roman race and Roman manners by mixture with aliens (xxxix. 3), are all noticed in tones of solemn warning. But his retired life had given him no wide experience of men and things. It is not surprising, therefore, to find that he fails altogether to present a clear and coherent picture of the history and working of the Roman constitution, or that his handling of intricate questions of policy is weak and inadequate.

Sources.—If from the general aim and spirit of Livy's history we pass to consider his method of workmanship, we are struck at once by the very different measure of success attained by him in the two great departments of an historian's labour. He is a consummate artist, but an unskilled and often careless investigator and critic. The materials which lay ready to his hand may be roughly classed under two heads: (1) the original evidence of monuments, inscriptions, &c., (2) the written tradition as found in the works of previous authors. It is on the second of these two kinds of evidence that Livy almost exclusively relies. Yet that even for the very early times a certain amount of original evidence still existed is proved by the use which was made of it by Dionysius, who mentions at least three important inscriptions, two dating from the regal period and one from the first years of the republic (iv. 26, iv. 58, x. 32). We know from Livy himself (iv. 20) that the breastplate dedicated by Aulus Cornelius Cossus (428 B.C.) was to be seen in his own day in the temple of Jupiter Feretrius, nor is there any reason to suppose that the *libri lintei*, quoted by Licinius Macer, were not extant when Livy wrote. For more recent times the materials were plentiful, and a rich field of research lay open to the student in the long series of laws, decrees of the senate, and official registers, reaching back, as it probably did, at least to the beginning of the 3rd century B.C. Nevertheless it seems certain that Livy never realized the duty of consulting these relics of the past, even in order to verify the statements of his authorities. Many of them he never mentions; the others (*e.g.* the *libri lintei*) he evidently describes at second hand. Antiquarian studies were popular in his day, but the instances are very few in which he has turned their results to account. There is no
t he had ever read Varro; and he never alludes to Verrius
The haziness and inaccuracy of his topography make
at he did not attempt to familiarize himself with the actual scenes of events even that took place in Italy. Not only does he confuse Thermon, the capital of Aetolia, with Thermopylae (xxxiii. 35), but his accounts of the Roman campaigns against Volsci, Aequi and Samnites swarm with confusions and difficulties, nor are even his descriptions of Hannibal's movements free from an occasional vagueness which betrays the absence of an exact knowledge of localities.

The consequence of this indifference to original research and patient verification might have been less serious had the written tradition on which Livy preferred to rely been more trustworthy. But neither the materials out of which it was composed, nor the manner in which it had been put together, were such as to make it a safe guide. It was indeed represented by a long line of respectable names. The majority of the Roman annalists were men of high birth and education, with a long experience of affairs, and their defects did not arise from seclusion of life or ignorance of letters. It is rather in the conditions under which they wrote and in the rules and traditions of their craft that the causes of their shortcomings must be sought.

The Annalists.

It was not until the 6th century from the foundation of the city that historical writing began in Rome. The father of Roman history, Q. Fabius Pictor, a patrician and a senator, can scarcely have published his annals before the close of the Second Punic War, but these annals covered the whole period from the arrival of Evander in Italy down at least to the battle by Lake Trasimene (217 B.C.). Out of what materials, then, did he put together his account of the earlier history? Recent criticism has succeeded in answering this question with some degree of certainty. A careful examination of the fragments of Fabius (see H. Peter, *Historicorum Romanorum Relliquiae*, Leipzig, 1870; and C. W. Nitzsch, *Röm. Annalistik*, Berlin, 1873) reveals in the first place a marked difference between the kingly period and that which followed the establishment of the republic. The history of the former stretches back into the regions of pure mythology. It is little more than a collection of fables told with scarcely any attempt at criticism, and with no more regard to chronological sequence than was necessary to make the tale run smoothly or to fill up such gaps as that between the flight of Aeneas from Troy and the supposed year of the foundation of Rome. But from its very commencement the history of the republic wears a different aspect. The mass of floating tradition, which had come down from early days, with its tales of border raids and forays, of valiant chiefs and deeds of patriotism, is now rudely fitted into a framework of a wholly different kind. This framework consists of short notices of important events, wars, prodigies, consecration of temples, &c., all recorded with extreme brevity, precisely dated, and couched in a somewhat archaic style. They were taken probably from one or more of the state registers, such as the annals of the pontiffs, or those kept by the aediles in the temple of Ceres. This bare official outline of the past history of his city was by Fabius filled in from the rich store of tradition that lay ready to his hand. The manner and spirit in which he effected this combination were no doubt wholly uncritical. Usually he seems to have transferred both annalistic notices and popular traditions to his pages much in the shape in which he found them. But he unquestionably gave undue prominence to the tales of the prowess and glory of the Fabii, and probably also allowed his own strong aristocratic sympathies to colour his version of the early political controversies. This fault of partiality was, according to Polybius, a conspicuous blot in Fabius's account of his own times, which was, we are told, full and in the main accurate, and, like the earlier portions, consisted of official annalistic notices, supplemented, however, not from tradition, but from his own experience and from contemporary sources. But even here Polybius charges him with favouring Rome at the expense of Carthage, and with the undue exaltation of the great head of his house, Q. Fabius Cunctator.

Nevertheless the comparative fidelity with which Fabius seems to have reproduced his materials might have made his annals the starting point of a critical history. But unfortunately intelligent criticism was exactly what they never received. It is true that in some respects a decided advance upon Fabius was made by subsequent annalists. M. Porcius Cato (234–149 B.C.) widened the scope of Roman history so as to include that of the chief Italian cities, and made the first serious attempt to settle the chronology. In his history of the Punic wars Caelius Antipater (*c.* 130 B.C.) added fresh material, drawn probably from the works of the Sicilian Greek Silenus, while Licinius Macer (70 B.C.) distinguished himself by the use he made of the ancient "linen books." No doubt, too, the later annalists, at any rate from Caelius Antipater onwards, improved upon Fabius in treatment and style. But in more essential points we can discern no progress. One annalist after another quietly adopted the established tradition, as it had been left by his predecessors, without any serious alterations of its main outlines. Of independent research and critical analysis we find no trace, and the general agreement upon main facts is to be attributed simply to the regularity with which each writer copied the one before him. But had the later annalists contented themselves with simply reproducing the earlier ones, we should at least have had the old tradition before us in a simple and tolerably genuine form. As it was, while they slavishly clung to its substance, they succeeded, as a rule, in destroying all traces of its original form and colouring. L. Calpurnius Piso, tribune in 149 B.C. and consul in 133 B.C., prided himself on reducing the old legends to the level of common sense, and importing into them valuable moral lessons for his own generation. By Caelius Antipater the methods of rhetoric were first applied to history, a disastrous precedent enough. He inserted speeches, enlivened his pages with chance tales, and aimed, as Cicero tells us, at not merely narrating facts but also at beautifying them. His successors carried still farther the practice of dressing up the rather bald chronicles of earlier writers with all the ornaments of rhetoric. The old traditions were altered, almost beyond the possibility of recognition, by exaggerations, interpolations and additions. Fresh incidents were inserted, new motives suggested and speeches composed in order to infuse the required life and freshness into these dry bones of history. At the same time the political bias of the writers, and the political ideas of their day were allowed, in some cases perhaps half unconsciously, to affect their representations of past events. Annalists of the Gracchan age imported into the early struggles of patricians and plebeians the economic controversies of their own day, and painted the first tribunes in the colours of the two Gracchi or of Saturninus. In the next generation they dexterously forced the venerable records of the early republic to pronounce in favour of the ascendancy of the senate, as established by Sulla. To political bias was added family pride, for the gratification of which the archives of the great houses, the funeral panegyrics, or the imagination of the writer himself supplied an ample store of doubtful material. Pedigrees were invented, imaginary consulships and fictitious triumphs inserted, and family traditions and family honours were formally incorporated with the history of the state.

Things were not much better even where the annalists were dealing with recent or contemporary events. Here, indeed, their materials were naturally fuller and more trustworthy, and less room was left for fanciful decoration and capricious alteration of the facts. But their methods are in the main unchanged. What they found written they copied; the gaps they supplied, where personal experience failed, by imagination. No better proof of this can be given than a comparison of the annalist's version of history with that of Polybius. In the fourth and fifth decades of Livy the two appear side by side, and the contrast between them is striking. Polybius, for instance, gives the number of the slain at Cynoscephalae as 8000; the annalists raise it as high as 40,000 (Livy xxxiii. 10). In another case (xxxii. 6) Valerius Antias, the chief of sinners in this respect, inserts a decisive Roman victory over the Macedonians, in which 12,000 of the latter were slain and 2200 taken prisoner, an achievement recorded by no other authority.

Such was the written tradition on which Livy mainly relied. We have next to examine the manner in which he used it, and here we are met at the outset by the difficulty of determining with exactness what authorities he is following at any one time; for of the importance of full and accurate references he has no idea, and often for chapters together he gives us no clue at all. More often still he contents himself with such vague phrases as "they say," "the story goes," "some think," or speaks in general terms of "ancient writers" or "my authorities." Even where be mentions a writer by name, it is frequently clear that the writer named is not the one whose lead he is following at the moment, but that he is noticed incidentally as differing from Livy's guide for the time being on some point of detail (compare the references to Piso in the first decade, i. 55, ii. 32, &c.). It is very rarely that Livy explicitly tells us whom he has selected as his chief source (*e.g.* Fabius xxii. 7; Polybius xxxiii. 10). By a careful analysis, however, of those portions of his work which admit of a comparison with the text of his acknowledged authorities (*e.g.* fourth and fifth decades, see H. Nissen, *Untersuchungen*, Berlin, 1863), and elsewhere by comparing his version with the known fragments of the various annalists, and with what we are told of their style and method of treatment, we are able to form a general idea of his plan of procedure. As to the first decade, it is generally agreed that in the first and second books, at any rate, he follows such older and simpler writers as Fabius Pictor and Calpurnius Piso (the only ones whom he there refers to by name), to whom, so far as the first book is concerned, Niebuhr (*Lectures*, p. 33) would add the poet Ennius. With the close of the second book or the opening of the third we come upon the first traces of the use of later authors. Valerius Antias[1] is first quoted in iii. 5, and signs of his handiwork are visible here and there throughout the rest of the decade (vii. 36, ix. 27, x. 3-5). In the fourth book the principal authority is apparently Licinius Macer, and for the period following the sack of Rome by the Gauls Q. Claudius Quadrigarius, whose annals began at this point in the history. We have besides a single reference (vii. 3) to the antiquarian Cincius, and two (iv. 23, x. 9) to Q. Aelius Tubero, one of the last in the list of annalists. Passing to the third decade, we find ourselves at once confronted by a question which has been long and fully discussed—the relation between Livy and Polybius. Did Livy use Polybius at all, and, if so, to what extent?

Polybius.

It is conceded on all hands that Livy in this decade makes considerable use of other authorities than Polybius (*e.g.* Fabius xxii. 7; Caelius Antipater xxi. 38, 46, 47, xxii. 31, &c.), that he only once mentions Polybius (xxx. 45), and that, if he used him, he did so to a much less extent than in the fourth and fifth decades, and in a very different manner. It is also agreed that we can detect in Livy's account of the Hannibalic war two distinct elements, derived originally, the one from a Roman, the other from a non-Roman source. But from these generally accepted premises two opposite conclusions have been drawn. On the one hand, it is maintained (*e.g.* by Lachmann, C. Peter, H. Peter, *Hist. Rom. Reliq.*) that those parts of Livy's narrative which point to a non-Roman authority (*e.g.* Hannibal's movements prior to his invasion of Italy) are taken by Livy directly from Polybius, with occasional reference of course to other writers, and with the omission (as in the later decades) of all matters uninteresting to Livy or his Roman readers, and the addition of rhetorical touches and occasional comments. It is urged that Livy, who in the fourth and fifth decades shows himself so sensible of the great merits of Polybius, is not likely to have ignored him in the third, and that his more limited use of him in the latter case is fully accounted for by the closer connexion of the history with Rome and Roman affairs, and the comparative excellence of the available Roman authorities, and, lastly, that the points of agreement with Polybius, not only in matter but in expression, can only be explained on the theory that Livy is directly following the great Greek historian. On the other hand, it is maintained (especially by Schwegler, Nitzsch, and K. Böttcher) that the extent and nature of Livy's agreement with Polybius in this part of his work point rather to the use by both of a common original authority. It is argued that Livy's mode of using his authorities is tolerably uniform, and that his mode of using Polybius in particular is known with certainty from the later decades. Consequently the theory that he used Polybius in the third decade requires us to assume that in this one instance he departed widely, and without sufficient reason, from his usual course of procedure. Moreover, even in the passages where the agreement with Polybius is most apparent, there are so many discrepancies and divergencies in detail, and so many unaccountable omissions and additions, as to render it inconceivable that he had the text of Polybius before him. But all these are made intelligible if we suppose Livy to have been here following directly or indirectly the same original sources that were used by Polybius. The earliest of these original sources was probably Silenus, with whom may possibly be placed, for books xxi. xxii., Fabius Pictor. The latter Livy certainly used directly for some parts of the decade. The former he almost as certainly knew only at second hand, the intermediate authority being probably Caelius Antipater. This writer, who confined himself to a history of the Second Punic War, in seven books, is expressly referred to by Livy eleven times in the third decade; and in other passages where his name is not mentioned Livy can be shown to have followed him (*e.g.* xxii. 5, 49, 50, 51, xxiv. 9). In the latter books of the decade his chief authority is possibly Valerius Antias.

In the fourth and fifth decades the question of Livy's authorities presents no great difficulties, and the conclusions arrived at by Nissen in his masterly *Untersuchungen* have met with general acceptance. These may be shortly stated as follows. In the portions of the history which deal with Greece and the East, Livy follows Polybius, and these portions are easily distinguishable from the rest by their superior clearness, accuracy and fulness. On the other hand, for the history of Italy and western Europe he falls back on Roman annalists, especially, it seems, on Claudius Quadrigarius and Valerius Antias—a most unfortunate choice—and from them too he takes the annalistic mould into which his matter is cast.

Critical method.

Livy's general method of using these authorities was certainly not such as would be deemed satisfactory in a modern historian. He is indeed free from the grosser faults of deliberate injustice and falsification, and he resists that temptation to invent, to which "the minds of authors are only too much inclined" (xxii. 7). Nor is he unconscious of the necessity for some kind of criticism. He distinguishes between rumour and the precise statements of recognized authorities (cf. xxi. 46, v. 21, vii. 6). The latter he reproduced in the main faithfully, but with a certain exercise of discretion. Where they disagreed, he calls attention to the fact, occasionally pronouncing in favour of one version rather than another (ii. 41, xxi. 46) though often on no adequate grounds, or attempting to reconcile and explain discrepancies (vi. 12, 38). Where he detects or suspects the insertion of fabulous matter he has no scruple in saying so. Gross exaggerations, such as those in which Valerius Antias indulged, he roundly denounces, and with equal plainness of speech he condemns the family vanity which had so constantly corrupted and distorted the truth. "I suppose," he says (viii. 40), "that the record and memorial of these matters hath been depraved and corrupted by these funeral orations of praises, . . while every house and family draweth to it the honour and renown of noble exploits, martial feats and dignities by any untruth and lie, so it be colourable." The legendary character of the earliest traditions he frankly admits. "Such things as are reported either before or at the foundation of the city, more beautiful and set out with poets' fables than grounded upon pure and faithful records, I mean neither to aver nor disprove" (*Praef.*); and of the whole history previous

[1] For Livy's debt to Valerius Antias, see A. A. Howard in *Harvard Studies in Classical Philology*, xvii. (1906), pp. 161 sqq.

to the sack of Rome by the Gauls (390 B.C.) he writes that it was obscure "both in regard of exceeding antiquity, and also for that in those days there were very few writings and monuments, the only faithful safeguard and true remembrancers of deeds past; and, besides, whatsoever was registered in the commentaries of the priests and in other public or private records, the same for the most part, when the city was burned, perished withal." Further than this, however, Livy's criticism does not go. Where his written authorities are not palpably inconsistent with each other or with probability he accepts and transcribes their record without any further inquiry, nor does he ever attempt to get behind this record in order to discover the original evidence on which it rested. His acceptance in any particular case of the version given by an annalist by no means implies that he has by careful inquiry satisfied himself of its truth. At the most it only presupposes a comparison with other versions, equally second-hand, but either less generally accepted or less in harmony with his own views of the situation; and in many cases the reasons he gives for his preference of one account over another are eminently unscientific. Livy's history, then, rests on no foundation of original research or even of careful verification. It is a compilation, and even as such it leaves much to be desired. For we cannot credit Livy with having made such a preliminary survey of his authorities as would enable him to determine their relations to each other, and fuse their various narratives into a consistent whole. It is clear, on the contrary, that his circle of authorities for any one decade was a comparatively small one, that of these he selected one, and transcribed him with the necessary embellishments and other slight modifications until impelled by various reasons to drop him. He then, without warning, takes up another, whom he follows in the same way. The result is a curious mosaic, in which pieces of all colours and dates are found side by side, and in which even the great artistic skill displayed throughout fails to conceal the lack of internal unity. Thus many of Livy's inconsistencies are due to his having pieced together two versions, each of which gave a differently coloured account of the same event. Mommsen (*Röm. Forschungen*, ii.) has clearly shown that this is what has happened in his relation of the legal proceedings against the elder Africanus in book xxxviii.; and in the story of the first secession, as he tells it, the older version which represented it as due to political and the later which explained it by economical grievances are found side by side. Similarly a change from one authority to another leads him not unfrequently to copy from the latter statements inconsistent with those he took from the former, to forget what he has previously said, or to treat as known a fact which has not been mentioned before (cf. ii. 1, xxxiv. 6, and Weissenborn's *Introduction*, p. 37). In other cases where the same event has been placed by different annalists in different years, or where their versions of it varied, it reappears in Livy as two events. Thus the four campaigns against the Volsci (ii. 17 seq.) are, as Schwegler (*R.G.* i. 13) rightly says, simply variations of one single expedition. Other instances of such "doublettes" are the two single combats described in xxiii. 46 and xxv. 18, and the two battles at Baecula in Spain (xxvii. 18 and xxviii. 13). Without doubt, too, much of the chronological confusion observable throughout Livy is due to the fact that he follows now one now another authority, heedless of their differences on this head. Thus he vacillates between the Catonian and Varronian reckoning of the years of the city, and between the chronologies of Polybius and the Roman annalists.

To these defects in his method must be added the fact that he does not always succeed even in accurately reproducing the authority he is for the time following. In the case of Polybius, for instance, he allows himself great freedom in omitting what strikes him as irrelevant, or tedious, or uninteresting to his Roman readers, a process in which much valuable matter disappears. In other cases his desire to give a vividness and point to what he doubtless considered the [illegible] bald and dry style of Polybius leads him into absurdities and inaccuracies. Thus by the treaty with Antiochus (188 B.C.) it was provided that the Greek communities of Asia Minor "shall settle their mutual differences by arbitration," and so far Livy correctly [illegible] Polybius, but he adds with a rhetorical flourish, "or, if both parties prefer it, by war" (xxxviii. 38). Elsewhere his blunders are apparently due to haste, or ignorance or sheer carelessness; thus, for instance, when Polybius speaks of the Aetolians assembling at their capital Thermon, Livy (xxxiii. 35) not only substitutes [illegible] but gratuitously informs his readers that here the [illegible] assemblies were held. Thanks partly to carelessness, partly [illegible]ation, he makes sad havoc (xxxv. 5 seq.) of Polybius's [illegible] of the battle of Cynoscephalae. Finally, Livy cannot be [illegible] acquitted on the charge of having here and there modified [illegible] the interests of Rome.

[illegible] serious as these defects in Livy's method appear if viewed [illegible] of modern criticism, it is probable that they were easily [illegible] indeed they were ever discovered, by his contempor[illegible] was on the artistic rather than on the critical side of [illegible] stress was almost universally laid in antiquity, and the [illegible] expected from the historian was not [illegible] and accurate exposition of the [illegible] such a form as would charm and [illegible] standard, Livy deservedly won [illegible] Asinius Pollio sneered at his Patavinity, and the emperor Caligula denounced him as verbose, but with these exceptions the opinion of antiquity was unanimous in pronouncing him a consummate literary workman. The classical purity of his style, the eloquence of his speeches, the skill with which he depicted the play of emotion, and his masterly portraiture of great men, are all in turn warmly commended, and in our own day we question if any ancient historian is either more readable or more widely read. It is true that for us his artistic treatment of history is not without its drawbacks. The more trained historical sense of modern times is continually shocked by the obvious untruth of his colouring, especially in the earlier parts of his history, by the palpable unreality of many of the speeches, and by the naïveté with which he omits everything, however important, which he thinks will weary his readers. But in spite of all this we are forced to acknowledge that, as a master of what we may perhaps call "narrative history," he has no superior in antiquity; for, inferior as he is to Thucydides, to Polybius, and even to Tacitus in philosophic power and breadth of view, he is at least their equal in the skill with which he tells his story. He is indeed the prince of chroniclers, and in this respect not unworthy to be classed even with Herodotus (Quintilian, x. 1. 101). Nor is anything more remarkable than the way in which Livy's fine taste and sense of proportion, his true poetic feeling and genuine enthusiasm, saved him from the besetting faults of the mode of treatment which he adopted. The most superficial comparison of his account of the earliest days of Rome with that given by Dionysius shows from what depths of tediousness he was preserved by these qualities. Instead of the wearisome prolixity and the misplaced pedantry which make the latter almost unreadable, we find the old tales briefly and simply told. Their primitive beauty is not marred by any attempt to force them into an historical mould, or disguised beneath an accumulation of the insipid inventions of later times. At the same time they are not treated as mere tales for children, for Livy never forgets the dignity that belongs to them as the prelude to the great epic of Rome, and as consecrated by the faith of generations. Perhaps an even stronger proof of the skill which enabled Livy to avoid dangers which were fatal to weaker men is to be found in his speeches. We cannot indeed regard them, with the ancients, as the best part of his history, for the majority of them are obviously unhistorical, and nearly all savour somewhat too much of the rhetorical schools to be perfectly agreeable to modern taste. To appreciate them we must take them for what they are, pieces of declamation, intended either to enliven the course of the narrative, to place vividly before the reader the feelings and aims of the chief actors, or more frequently still to enforce some lesson which the author himself has at heart. The substance, no doubt, of many of them Livy took from his authorities, but their form is his own, and, in throwing into them all his own eloquence and enthusiasm, he not only acted in conformity with the established traditions of his art, but found a welcome outlet for feelings and ideas which the fall of the republic had deprived of all other means of expression. To us, therefore, they are valuable not only for their eloquence, but still more as giving us our clearest insight into Livy's own sentiments, his lofty sense of the greatness of Rome, his appreciation of Roman courage and firmness, and his reverence for the simple virtues of older times. But, freely as Livy uses this privilege of speechmaking, his correct taste keeps his rhetoric within reasonable limits. With a very few exceptions the speeches are dignified in tone, full of life and have at least a dramatic propriety, while of such incongruous and laboured absurdities as the speech which Dionysius puts into the mouth of Romulus, after the rape of the Sabine women, there are no instances in Livy.

Speeches.

But, if our estimate of the merits of his speeches is moderated by doubts as to his right to introduce them at all, no such scruples interfere with our admiration for the skill with which he has drawn the portraits of the great men who figure in his pages. We may indeed doubt whether in all cases they are drawn with perfect accuracy and impartiality, but of their life-like vigour and clearness there can be no question. With Livy this portrait-painting was a labour of love. "To all great men," says Seneca, "he gave their due ungrudgingly," but he is at his best in dealing with those who, like Q. Fabius Maximus, "the Delayer," were in his eyes the most perfect types of the true Roman.

The general effect of Livy's narrative is no doubt a little spoilt by the awkward arrangement, adopted from his authorities, which obliges him to group the events by years, and thus to disturb their natural relations and continuity. As the result his history has the appearance of being rather a series of brilliant pictures loosely strung together than a coherent narrative. But it is impossible not to admire the copious variety of thought and language, and the evenly flowing style which carried him safely through the dreariest periods of his history; and still more remarkable is the dramatic power he displays when some great crisis or thrilling episode stirs his blood, such as the sack of Rome by the Gauls, the battle by the Metaurus and the death of Hasdrubal.

In style and language Livy represents the best period of Latin prose writing. He has passed far beyond the bald and meagre diction of the early chroniclers. In his hands Latin acquired a flexibility and a richness of vocabulary unknown to it before. If he writes with less finish and a less perfect rhythm than his favourite model Cicero, he excels him in the varied structure of his periods, and their adaptation to the subject-matter. It is true that here and there the "creamy richness" of his style becomes verbosity, and that he occasionally draws too freely on his inexhaustible store of epithets, metaphors and turns of speech; but these faults, which did not escape the censure even of friendly critics like Quintilian, are comparatively rare in the extant parts of his work. From the tendency to use a poetic diction in prose, which was so conspicuous a fault in the writers of the silver age, Livy is not wholly free. In his earlier books especially there are numerous phrases and sentences which have an unmistakably poetic ring, recalling sometimes Ennius and more often his contemporary Virgil. But in Livy this poetic element is kept within bounds, and serves only to give warmth and vividness to the narrative. Similarly, though the influence of rhetoric upon his language, as well as upon his general treatment, is clearly perceptible, he has not the perverted love of antithesis, paradox and laboured word-painting which offends us in Tacitus; and, in spite of the Venetian richness of his colouring, and the copious flow of his words, he is on the whole wonderfully natural and simple.

These merits, not less than the high tone and easy grace of his narrative and the eloquence of his speeches, gave Livy a hold on Roman readers such as only Cicero and Virgil besides him ever obtained. His history formed the groundwork of nearly all that was afterwards written on the subject. Plutarch, writers on rhetoric like the elder Seneca, moralists like Valerius Maximus, went to Livy for their stock examples. Florus and Eutropius abridged him; Orosius extracted from him his proofs of the sinful blindness of the pagan world; and in every school Livy was firmly established as a textbook for the Roman youth.

Text.—The received text of the extant thirty-five books of Livy is taken from different sources, and no one of our MSS. contains them all. The MSS. of the first decade, some thirty in number, are with one exception derived, more or less directly, from a single archetype, viz., the recension made in the 4th century by the two Nicomachi, Flavianus and Dexter, and by Victorianus. This is proved in the case of the older MSS. by written subscriptions to that effect, and in the case of the rest by internal evidence. Of all these descendants of the Nicomachean recension, the oldest is the Codex Parisinus of the 10th century, and the best the Codex Mediceus or Florentinus of the 11th. An independent value attaches to the ancient palimpsest of Verona, of which the first complete account was given by Mommsen in *Abhandl. der preussischen Akad. der Wissenschaften* (1868). It contains the third, fourth, fifth and fragments of the sixth book, and, according to Mommsen, whose conclusions are accepted by Madvig (*Emend. Livianae*, 2nd ed., 1877, p. 37), it is derived, not from the Nicomachean recension, but from an older archetype common to both.

For the third decade our chief authority is the Codex Puteanus, an uncial MS. of the 5th century, now at Paris. For the fourth we have two leading MSS.—Codex Bambergensis, 11th century, and the slightly older Codex Moguntinus, now lost and only known through the Mainz edition of 1518–1519. What remains of the fifth decade depends on the 5th century Laurishamensis or Vindobonensis from the monastery of Lorsch, edited at Basel in 1531.

A bibliography of the various editions of Livy, or of all that has been written upon him, cannot be attempted here. The following may be consulted for purposes of reference; W. Engelmann, *Scriptores Latini* (8th ed., by E. Preuss, 1882); J. E. B. Mayor, *Bibliographical Clue to Latin Literature* (1875); Teuffel-Schwabe, *History of Roman Literature* (Eng. trans.), 256, 257; M. Schanz, *Geschichte der römischen Litteratur* ii. 1 (2nd ed., 1899). The best editions of the complete text are those of W. Weissenborn (1858–1862, containing an introductory essay on Livy's life and writings; new edition by M. Müller, 1902), and J. N. Madvig and J. L. Ussing (1863–1873). The only English translation of any merit is by Philemon Holland (1600). (H. F. P.; X.)

LIZARD (Lat. *lacerta*[1]), a name originally referred only to the small European species of four-legged reptiles, but now applied to a whole order (*Lacertilia*), which is represented by numerous species in all temperate and tropical regions. Lizards are reptiles which have a transverse external anal opening (instead of a longitudinal slit as in Crocodilians and tortoises) and which have the right and left halves of the mandibles connected by a sutural symphysis. The majority are distinguished from snakes by the possession of two pairs of limbs, of external ear-openings and movable eyelids, but since in not a few of the burrowing, snake-shaped lizards these characters give way entirely, it is well-nigh impossible to find a diagnosis which should be absolutely sufficient for the distinction between lizards and snakes. In such doubtful cases a number of characters have to be resorted to, and, while each of these may fail when taken singly, their combination decides the question. It is certain that the snakes have been evolved as a specialized branch from some Lacertilian stock, and that both "orders" are intimately related, but it is significant that it is only through the degraded members of the lizards that recent representatives of the two great groups seem to run into each other. Such critical characters are:—

	Lizards.	Snakes.
Limbs	2 pairs, 1 or 0.	0 or vestigial hind-limbs.
Ear-opening	Usually present.	Always absent.
Eyelids	Mostly movable.	No movable lids.
Tongue.	Often not retractile.	Always bifid and retractile into itself.
Teeth	Pleuro- or acrodont, not anchylosed.	Acrodont, anchylosed.
Mandibles	Mostly firmly united suturally.	Never with suture, mostly ligamentous.
Columella cranii	Mostly present.	Absent.
	Mostly with bony arches across the temporal region.	No bony arches.
	Osteoderms common.	No osteoderms.

The lizards and snakes are the two dominant reptilian orders which are still on the increase in species, though certainly not in size. As a moderate estimate, the number of recent species of lizards is about 1700. As a group they are cosmopolitan, their northern limit approaching that of the permanently frozen subsoil, while in the southern hemisphere the southern point of Patagonia forms the farthest limit. As we approach the tropics, the variety of forms and the number of individuals increase, the most specialized and developed forms, and also the most degraded, being found in the tropics. In the temperate regions they hibernate. The majority live on broken ground, with or without much vegetation; many are arboreal and many are true desert animals, while a few are more or less aquatic; one, the leguan of the Galapagos, *Amblyrhynchus*, even enters the sea. Some, like the majority of the geckos, are nocturnal. In adaptation to these varied surroundings they exhibit great variety in shape, size and structure. Most of these modifications are restricted to the skin, limbs, tail or tongue. Most lizards live on animal food, varying from tiny insects and worms to lizards, snakes, birds and mammals, while others prefer a mixed or an entirely vegetable diet. Accordingly, the teeth and the whole digestive tract are modified. But swiftness, the apparatus necessary for climbing, running and digging, the mechanism of the tongue, the muscles of the jaws (hence modifications of the cranial arches) stand also in correlation with the kind of food and with the way in which it has to be procured. Generally the teeth are conical or pointed, more rarely blunt, grooved or serrated. They are inserted either on the inner side of the margin of the jaws (*pleurodonta*) or on the edge of the bones (*acrodonta*). The tongue is generally beset with more or less scaly or velvety papillae and has always a well-marked posterior margin, while the anterior portion may or may not be more or less retractile into the posterior part.

In many lizards the muscles of the segments of the tail are so loosely connected and the vertebrae are so weak that the tail easily breaks off. The severed part retains its muscular irritability for a short time, wriggling as if it were a living creature. A lizard thus mutilated does not seem to be much affected, and the lost part is slowly reproduced. This faculty is of advantage to those lizards which lack other means of escape when pursued by some other animal, which is satisfied with capturing the detached member.

The motions of most lizards are executed with great but not enduring rapidity. With the exception of the chameleon, all drag their body over the ground, the limbs being wide apart, turned outwards and relatively to the bulk of the body generally weak. But the limbs show with regard to development great variation, and an uninterrupted transition from the most perfect condition of two pairs with five separate clawed toes to their total disappearance; yet even limbless lizards retain bony vestiges beneath the skin. The motions of these limbless lizards are similar to those of snakes, which they resemble in their elongate body.

The eggs are elliptical in shape, both poles being equal, and are covered with a shell which may be thin and leathery or hard and calcareous. The number of eggs laid is small

[1] For the etymology of this word, see CROCODILE.

[illegible] EDWARD (1845–), English tenor vocalist, [illegible] in London on the 7th of March 1845, his father, Richard [illegible] vicar choralist at Westminster Abbey. From [illegible] he sang in the abbey choir, and was thoroughly [illegible] music, eventually becoming solo tenor at the Chapel [illegible] He began singing at concerts in 1867, and in 1871 [illegible] the Gloucester Musical Festival. His fine evenly-[illegible] voice and pure style at once brought him into notice, [illegible] he gradually took the place of Sims Reeves as the leading [illegible] of the day, his singing of classical music, and [illegible] Handel, being particularly admired. At the [illegible] after 1888 he was the principal tenor, and even [illegible] at the Crystal Palace he triumphed over [illegible]. In 1888, 1890 and 1892 he paid successful [illegible] the United States; but by degrees he appeared less [illegible], and in 1900 he formally retired from the [illegible]

[illegible] (1627–1717), English divine, successively [illegible] of Lichfield and Coventry, and of Worcester, [illegible] Berkshire, in 1627, and was educated at [illegible] College, Oxford. He graduated M.A. in 1646. [illegible] of Ripon, in 1667 prebendary of [illegible] archdeacon of Merioneth, in 1672 dean of [illegible] of St Paul's, London, in 1680 bishop of [illegible], in 1692 bishop of Lichfield and [illegible] bishop of Worcester. Lloyd was an [illegible] of the Roman Catholic tendencies of [illegible] of the seven bishops who for refusing to [illegible] Indulgence read in his diocese was charged [illegible] libel against the king and acquitted [illegible] Burnet to write *The History of the* [illegible] *England* and provided him with [illegible] was a good scholar and a keen student [illegible] literature and himself "prophesied" [illegible] Harley, earl of Oxford, William Whiston, [illegible]. Lloyd was a stanch supporter [illegible] chief publication was *An Historical* [illegible] *as it was in Great Britain and* [illegible] *the Christian Religion* (London, [illegible]). He died at Hartlebury castle [illegible]

[illegible] WATKISS (1813–1843), English man of [illegible], Middlesex, on the 11th of March [illegible] education at Newcastle-under-[illegible] the age of fifteen entered a family [illegible] which he was connected for thirty-[illegible] to the study of art, architecture, [illegible] and modern languages and [illegible] on the 22nd of December 1843 [illegible] known is *The Age of* [illegible] of scholarship, great learning [illegible] of the period with which it deals [illegible] difficult and at times obscure [illegible]

[illegible]

teacher there, and afterwards in Liverpool and Haverfordwest, and then headmaster of an elementary school at Pwllheli, Carnarvonshire, where he married the daughter of David Lloyd, a neighbouring Baptist minister. Soon afterwards William George became headmaster of an elementary school in Manchester, but after the birth of his eldest son David his health failed, and he gave up his post and took a small farm near Haverfordwest. Two years later he died, leaving his widow in poor circumstances; a second child, another son, was posthumously born. Mrs George's brother, Richard Lloyd, a shoemaker at Llanystumdwy, and pastor of the Campbellite Baptists there, now became her chief support; it was from him that young David obtained his earliest views of practical and political life, and also the means of starting, at the age of fourteen, on the career of a solicitor.

Having passed his law preliminary, he was articled to a firm in Portmadoc, and in 1884 obtained his final qualifications. In 1888 he married Margaret, daughter of Richard Owen of Criccieth. From the first he managed to combine his solicitor's work with politics, becoming secretary of the South Carnarvonshire Anti-tithe League; and his local reputation was made by a successful fight, carried to the High Court, in defence of the right of Nonconformists to burial in the parish churchyard. In the first county council elections for Carnarvonshire he played a strenuous part on the Radical side, and was chosen an alderman; and in 1890, at a by-election for Carnarvon Boroughs, he was returned to parliament by a majority of 18 over a strong Conservative opponent. He held his seat successfully at the contests in 1892, 1895 and 1900, his reputation as a champion of Welsh nationalism, Welsh nonconformity and extreme Radicalism becoming thoroughly established both in parliament and in the country. In the House of Commons he was one of the most prominent guerrilla fighters, conspicuous for his audacity and pungency of utterance, and his capacity for obstruction while the Conservatives were in office. During the South African crisis of 1899–1902 he was specially vehement in opposition to Mr Chamberlain, and took the "pro-Boer" side so bitterly that he was mobbed in Birmingham during the 1900 election when he attempted to address a meeting at the Town Hall. But he was again returned for Carnarvon Boroughs, and in the ensuing parliament he came still more to the front by his resistance to the Education Act of 1902.

As the leader of the Welsh party, and one of the most daring parliamentarians on the Radical side, his appointment to office when Sir H. Campbell-Bannerman became premier at the end of 1905 was generally expected; but his elevation direct to the cabinet as president of the Board of Trade was somewhat a surprise. The responsibilities of administration have, however, often converted a political free-lance into a steady-going official, and the Unionist press did its best to encourage such a tendency by continual praise of the departmental action of the new minister. His settlement of the railway dispute in 1907 was universally applauded, and the bills he introduced and passed for reorganizing the port of London, dealing with Merchant Shipping, and enforcing the working in England of patents granted there, and so increasing the employment of British labour, were greeted with satisfaction by the tariff-reformers, who congratulated themselves that a Radical free-trader [illegible] thus threw over the policy of laissez faire. The [illegible] Board of Trade was the chief success of the [illegible] Mr Asquith became premier in 1908 and [illegible] Mr Lloyd George to the chancellorship of the exchequer, the appointment was well received even in the City of London. For that year the budget was already settled, and it was introduced by Mr Asquith himself, the ex-chancellor; but Mr Lloyd George [illegible] golden opinions, both at the Treasury and in parliament, by his industry and his handling of the Finance Bill, [illegible] for its inclusion of Old Age Pensions, [illegible] stages.

[illegible]

chancellor of the exchequer aroused misgivings by alluding in a speech to the difficulty he had in deciding what "hen roost" to "rob." The government had been losing ground in the country, and Mr Lloyd George and Mr Winston Churchill were conspicuously in alliance in advocating the use of the budget for introducing drastic reforms in regard to licensing and land, which the resistance of the House of Lords prevented the Radical party from effecting by ordinary legislation. The well-established doctrine that the House of Lords could not amend, though it might reject, a money-bill, coupled with the fact that it never had gone so far as to reject a budget, was relied on by the extremists as dictating the obvious party tactics, and before the year 1909 opened, the possibility of the Lords being driven to compel a dissolution by standing on their extreme rights as regards the financial provision for the year was already canvassed in political circles, though it was hardly credited that the government would precipitate a constitutional crisis of such magnitude. When Mr Lloyd George, on the 29th of April, introduced his budget, its revolutionary character, however, created widespread dismay in the City and among the propertied classes. In a very lengthy speech, which had to be interrupted for half an hour while he recovered his voice, he ended by describing it as a "war budget" against poverty, which he hoped, in the result, would become "as remote to the people of this country as the wolves which once infested its forests." Some of the original proposals, which were much criticized, were subsequently dropped, including the permanent diversion of the Old Sinking Fund to a National Development Fund (created by a separate bill), and a tax on "ungotten minerals," for which was substituted a tax on mineral rights. But the main features of the budget were adhered to, and eventually passed the House of Commons on the 4th of November, in spite of the persistent opposition of the scanty Unionist minority. Apart from certain non-contentious provisions, such as a tax on motor-cars, the main features of the measure were large increases in the spirit and tobacco duties, license duties, estate, legacy and succession duties, and income tax, and an elaborate and novel system of duties on land-values ("increment duty," "reversion duty," "undeveloped land duty"), depending on the setting up of arrangements for valuation of a highly complicated kind. The discussions on the budget entirely monopolized public attention for the year, and while the measure was defended by Mr Lloyd George in parliament with much suavity, and by Mr Asquith, Sir Edward Grey and Mr Haldane outside the House of Commons with tact and moderation, the feelings of its opponents were exasperated by a series of inflammatory public speeches at Limehouse and elsewhere from the chancellor of the exchequer, who took these opportunities to rouse the passions of the working-classes against the landed classes and the peers. When the Finance Bill went up to the House of Lords, Lord Lansdowne gave notice that on the second reading he would move "that this House is not justified in giving its consent to this bill until it has been submitted to the judgment of the country," and on the last day of November this motion was carried by an overwhelming majority of peers. The government passed a solemn resolution of protest in the House of Commons and appealed to the country; and the general election of January 1910 took place amid unexampled excitement. The Unionists gained a hundred seats over their previous numbers, but the constitutional issue undoubtedly helped the government to win a victory, depending indeed solely on the votes of the Labour members and Irish Nationalists, which a year before had seemed improbable.

Events had now made Mr Lloyd George and his financial policy the centre of the Liberal party programme; but party tactics for the moment prevented the ministry, who remained in office, from simply sending the budget up again to the Lords and allowing them to pass it. There was no majority in the Commons for the budget as such, since the Irish Nationalists only supported it as an engine for destroying the veto of the Lords and thus preparing the way for Irish Home Rule. Instead, therefore, of proceeding with the budget, the government allowed the financial year to end without one, and brought forward resolutions for curtailing the powers of the Lords, on which, if rejected by them, another appeal could be made to the people (see PARLIAMENT). Hardly, however, had the battle been arrayed when the King's death in May upset all calculations. An immediate continuance of hostilities between the two Houses was impossible. A truce was called, and a conference arranged between four leaders from each side—Mr Lloyd George being one—to consider whether compromise on the constitutional question was not feasible. The budget for 1909–10 went quietly through, and before the August adjournment the chancellor introduced his budget for 1910–11, discussion being postponed till the autumn. It imposed no new taxation, and left matters precisely as they were. (H. CH.)

LLOYD'S, an association of merchants, shipowners, underwriters, and ship and insurance brokers, having its headquarters in a suite of rooms in the north-east corner of the Royal Exchange, London. Originally a mere gathering of merchants for business or gossip in a coffee-house kept by one Edward Lloyd in Tower Street, London, the earliest notice of which occurs in the *London Gazette* of the 18th of February 1688, this institution has gradually become one of the greatest organizations in the world in connexion with commerce. The establishment existed in Tower Street up to 1692, in which year it was removed by the proprietor to Lombard Street, in the centre of that portion of the city most frequented by merchants of the highest class. Shortly after this event Mr Lloyd established a weekly newspaper furnishing commercial and shipping news, in those days an undertaking of no small difficulty. This paper took the name of *Lloyd's News*, and, though its life was not long, it was the precursor of the now ubiquitous *Lloyd's List*, the oldest existing paper, the *London Gazette* excepted. In Lombard Street the business transacted at Lloyd's coffee-house steadily grew, but it does not appear that throughout the greater part of the 18th century the merchants and underwriters frequenting the rooms were bound together by any rules, or acted under any organization. By and by, however, the increase of marine insurance business made a change of system and improved accommodation necessary, and after finding a temporary resting-place in Pope's Head Alley, the underwriters and brokers settled in the Royal Exchange in March 1774. One of the first improvements in the mode of effecting marine insurance was the introduction of a printed form of policy. Hitherto various forms had been in use; and, to avoid numerous disputes the committee of Lloyd's proposed a general form, which was adopted by the members on the 12th of January 1779, and remains in use, with a few slight alterations, to this day. The two most important events in the history of Lloyd's during the 19th century were the reorganization of the association in 1811, and the passing of an act in 1871 granting to Lloyd's all the rights and privileges of a corporation sanctioned by parliament. According to this act of incorporation, the three main objects for which the society exists are—first, the carrying out of the business of marine insurance; secondly, the protection of the interests of the members of the association; and thirdly, the collection, publication and diffusion of intelligence and information with respect to shipping. In the promotion of the last-named object an intelligence department has been developed which for wideness of range and efficient working has no parallel among private enterprises. By Lloyd's Signal Station Act 1888, powers were conferred on Lloyd's to establish signal stations with telegraphic communications, and by the Derelict Vessels (Report) Act 1896, masters of British ships are required to give notice to Lloyd's agents of derelict vessels, which information is published by Lloyd's.

The rooms at Lloyd's are available only to subscribers and members. The former pay an annual subscription of five guineas without entrance fee, but have no voice in the management of the institution. The latter consist of non-underwriting members, who pay an entrance fee of twelve guineas, and of underwriting members who pay a fee of £100. Underwriting members are also required to deposit securities to the value of £5000 to £10,000, according to circumstances, as a guarantee for their

L... b... fi... ar... lit... The... (18... and... but... style. *Essay*... *Carlo*... from t... *The H*... *their*... "now ... the aut... blank ve... the most... British ... *Greece*; *Th*...

See Men... published) ... a list of pub...

LLOYD G... was born at... father, Willia... Pembrokeshi...

... of the establishment is delegated ... of their number selected as a "com- ... of Lloyd's." With this body lies ... officials and agents of the institution, ... being entrusted to a secretary and a ... assistants. The mode employed ... Lloyd's is simple. The business is ... write upon a slip of paper the ... the nature of the voyage, the ... amount at which it is valued. ... underwriter subscribes his name ... or underwrite, the insurance ... value is made up.

... *Lloyd's and of Marine Insurance in* ...

... British naturalist and ... in 1660. He was educated ... not graduate; he received the ... In 1690, after serving for six ... keeper of the Ashmolean ... until 1709. In 1699 he ... in which he ... personally collected or ... were arranged in cabinets in ... many parts of England, ... Oxford. A second edition ... until 1760. He issued ... *Britannica* (afterwards ... in 1708. He died at ...

... *Cobitinae*) form a very ... and are even regarded ... Characters: Barbels, ... one row, in moderate ... divided into a right ... and enclosed in a ... They are more ... and naked or covered ... are small, the largest ... *fossilis*), 13 (the ... Central Asian *Nemachilus* ... streams and ponds, and ... entirely confined ... *abyssinicus*) ... About 120 species ... Eastern Asia. Only ... common *Nemachilus* ... *taenia*. The latter ... Many of these fishes ... which they move ... appears to be ... accessory breathing ... to lose its hydro- ... sensory organ, its ... skin by a meatus ... the thermo- ... Loaches are ...

... both these words ... conveyance," and ... is also seen ... "to lead." ... by a sup- ... word common ... the sense ... the placing ... emptying ... from the ... or con- ...

than in "lode," a vein of metal ore, in which the original meaning of "way" is clearly marked. A "load" was originally a "carriage," and its Latin equivalent in the *Promptorium Parvulorum* is *vectura*. From that it passed to that which is laid on an animal or vehicle, and so, as an amount usually carried, the word was used of a specific quantity of anything, a unit of weight, varying with the locality and the commodity. A "load" of wheat = 40 bushels, of hay = 36 trusses. Other meanings of "load" are: in electricity, the power which an engine or dynamo has to furnish; and in engineering, the weight to be supported by a structure, the "permanent load" being the weight of the structure itself, the "external load" that of anything which may be placed upon it.

LOAF, properly the mass of bread made at one baking, hence the smaller portions into which the bread is divided for retailing. These are of uniform size (see BAKING) and are named according to shape ("tin loaf," "cottage loaf," &c.), weight ("quartern loaf," &c.), or quality of flour ("brown loaf," &c.). "Loaf," O.E. *hláf*, is a word common to Teutonic languages; cf. Ger. *Laib*, or *Leib*, Dan. *lev*, Goth. *hlaifs*; similar words with the same meaning are found in Russian, Finnish and Lettish, but these may have been adapted from Teutonic. The ultimate origin is unknown, and it is uncertain whether "bread" (*q.v.*) or "loaf" is the earlier in usage. The O.E. *hláf* is seen in "Lammas" and in "lord," *i.e. hlaford* for *hlafweard*, the loaf-keeper, or "bread-warder"; cf. the O.E. word for a household servant *hláf-æta*, loaf-eater. The Late Lat. *companio*, one who shares, *panis*, bread, Eng. "companion," was probably an adaptation of the Goth. *gahlaiba*, O.H. Ger. *gileipo*, messmate, comrade. The word "loaf" is also used in sugar manufacture, and is applied to sugar shaped in a mass like a cone, a "sugar-loaf," and to the small knobs into which refined sugar is cut, or "loaf-sugar."

The etymology of the verb "to loaf," *i.e.* to idle, lounge about, and the substantive "loafer," an idler, a lazy vagabond, has been much discussed. R. H. Dana (*Two Years before the Mast*, 1840) called the word "a newly invented Yankee word." J. R. Lowell (*Biglow Papers*, 2nd series, Introd.) explains it as German in origin, and connects it with *laufen*, to run, and states that the dialectical form *lofen* is used in the sense of "saunter up and down." This explanation has been generally accepted. The *New English Dictionary* rejects it, however, and states that *laufen* is not used in this sense, but points out that the German *Landläufer*, the English obsolete word "landlouper," or "landloper," one who wanders about the country, a vagrant or vagabond, has a resemblance in meaning. J. S. Farmer and W. E. Henley's *Dictionary of Slang and its Analogues* gives as French synonyms of "loafer," *chevalier de la loupe* and *loupeur*.

LOAM (O.E. *lám*; the word appears in Dut. *leem* and Ger. *Lehm*; the ultimate origin is the root *lei-*, meaning "to be sticky," which is seen in the cognate "lime," Lat. *limus*, mud, clay), a fertile soil composed of a mixture of sand, clay, and decomposed vegetable matter, the quantity of sand being sufficient to prevent the clay massing together. The word is also used of a mixture of sand, clay and straw, used for making casting-moulds and bricks, and for plastering walls, &c. (see SOIL).

LOAN (adapted from the Scandinavian form of a word common to Teutonic languages, cf. Swed. *lån*, Icel. *lán*, Dut. *leen*; the O.E. *lǽn* appears in "lend," the ultimate source is seen in the root of Gr. λείπειν and Lat. *linquere*, to leave), that which is lent; a sum of money or something of value lent for a specific or indefinite period when it or its equivalent is to be repaid or returned, usually at a specified rate of interest (see USURY and MONEY-LENDING). For public loans see FINANCE, NATIONAL DEBT, and the various sections on finance under the names of the various countries.

LOANDA (*São Paulo de Loanda*), a seaport of West Africa, capital of the Portuguese province of Angola, situated in 8° 48′ S., 13° 7′ E., on a bay between the rivers Bengo and Kwanza. The bay, protected from the surf by a long narrow island of sand, is backed by a low sandy cliff which at its southern end sweeps out ... curve and terminates in a bold point crowned by ... guel. The depth of water at the entrance to the bay ... or more. The bay has silted up considerably, but there is a good anchorage about 1½ m. from the shore in 7 to 14 fathoms, besides cranage accommodation and a floating dock. Vessels discharge into lighters, and are rarely delayed on account of the weather. A part of the town lies on the foreshore, but the more important buildings—the government offices, the governor's residence, the palace of the bishop of Angola, and the hospital—are situated on higher ground. Most of the European houses are large stone buildings of one storey with red tile roofs. Loanda possesses a meteorological observatory, public garden, tramways, gas-works, statues to Salvador Correia de Sá, who wrested Angola from the Dutch, and to Pedro Alexandrino, a former governor, and is the starting-point of the railway to Ambaca and Malanje.

Loanda was founded in 1576, and except between 1640 and 1648, when it was occupied by the Dutch, has always been in Portuguese possession. It was for over two centuries the chief centre of the slave trade between Portuguese West Africa and Brazil. During that time the traffic of the port was of no small account, and after a period of great depression consequent on the suppression of that trade, more legitimate commerce was developed. There is a regular service of steamers between the port and Lisbon, Liverpool and Hamburg. The town has some 15,000 inhabitants, including a larger European population than any other place on the west coast of Africa. It is connected by submarine cables with Europe and South Africa. Fully half the imports and export trade of Angola (*q.v.*) passes through Loanda.

LOANGO, a region on the west coast of Africa, extending from the mouth of the Congo river in 6° S. northwards through about two degrees. At one time included in the "kingdom of Congo" (see ANGOLA, *History*), Loango became independent about the close of the 16th century, and was still of considerable importance in the middle of the 18th century. Buali, the capital, was situated on the banks of a small river not far from the port of Loango, where were several European "factories." The country afterwards became divided into a large number of petty states, while Portugal and France exercised an intermittent sovereignty over the coast. Here the slave trade was longer maintained than anywhere else on the West African seaboard, since its extirpation, palm oil and india-rubber have been the main objects of commerce. The Loango coast is now divided between French Congo and the Portuguese district of Kabinda (see those articles). The natives, mainly members of the Ba-Kongo group of Bantu negroes, and often called Ba-Fiot, are in general well-built, strongly dolichocephalous and very thick of skull, the skin of various shades of warm brown with the faintest suggestion of purple. Baldness is unknown, and many of the men wear beards. Physical deformity is extremely rare. In religious beliefs and in the use of fetishes they resemble the negroes of Upper Guinea.

LOBACHEVSKIY, NICOLAS IVANOVICH (1793–1856), Russian mathematician, was born at Makariev, Nizhniy-Novgorod, on the 2nd of November (N.S.) 1793. His father died about 1800, and his mother, who was left in poor circumstances, removed to Kazan with her three sons. In 1807 Nicolas, the second boy, entered as a student in the University of Kazan, then recently established. Five years later, having completed the curriculum, he began to take part in the teaching, becoming assistant professor in 1814 and extraordinary professor two years afterwards. In 1823 he succeeded to the ordinary professorship of mathematics, and retained the chair until about 1846, when he seems to have fallen into official disfavour. At that time his connexion with the university to which he had devoted his life practically came to an end, except that in 1855, at the celebration of his jubilee, he brought it as a last tribute his *Pangéométrie*, in which he summarized the results of his geometrical studies. This work was translated into German by H. Liebmann in 1902. He died at Kazan on the 24th of February (N.S.) 1856. Lobachevskiy was one of the first thinkers to apply a critical treatment to the fundamental axioms of geometry, and he thus became a pioneer of the modern geometries which deal with space other than as treated by Euclid. His first contribution to non-Euclidian geometry is believed to have been given in a lecture at Kazan in 1826, but the subject is treated in many of his subsequent memoirs, among which may be mentioned the *Geometrische Untersuchungen zur Theorie der Parallellinien* (Berlin, 1840, and a new edition in 1887), and the *Pangéométrie* already referred to, which in the subtitle is described as a précis of geometry founded on a general and rigorous theory of parallels. (See GEOMETRY, § *Non-Euclidean*, and GEOMETRY, § *Axioms of*.) In addition to his geometrical studies, he made various contributions to other branches of mathematical science, among them being an elaborate treatise on algebra (Kazan, 1834). Besides being a geometer of power and originality, Lobachevskiy was an excellent man of business. Under his administration the University of Kazan prospered as it had never done before; and he not only organized the teaching staff to a high degree of efficiency, but arranged and enriched its library, furnished instruments for its observatory, collected specimens for its museums and provided it with proper buildings. In order to be able to supervise the erection of the last, he studied architecture, with such effect, it is said, that he was able to carry out the plans at a cost considerably below the original estimates.

See F. Engel, *N. I. Lobatschewsky* (Leipzig, 1899).

LOBANOV-ROSTOVSKI, ALEXIS BORISOVICH, PRINCE (1824–1896), Russian statesman, was born on the 30th of December 1824, and educated, like Prince Gorchakov and so many other eminent Russians, at the lyceum of Tsarskoe Selo. At the age of twenty he entered the diplomatic service, and became minister at Constantinople in 1859. In 1863 a regrettable incident in his private life made him retire temporarily from the public service, but four years later he re-entered it and served for ten years as *adlatus* to the minister of the interior. At the close of the Russo-Turkish war in 1878 he was selected by the emperor to fill the post of ambassador at Constantinople, and for more than a year he carried out with great ability the policy of his government, which aimed at re-establishing tranquillity in the Eastern Question, after the disturbances produced by the reckless action of his predecessor, Count Ignatiev. In 1879 he was transferred to London, and in 1882 to Vienna; and in March 1895 he was appointed minister of foreign affairs in succession to M. de Giers. In this position he displayed much of the caution of his predecessor, but adopted a more energetic policy in European affairs generally and especially in the Balkan Peninsula. At the time of his appointment the attitude of the Russian government towards the Slav nationalities had been for several years one of extreme reserve, and he had seemed as ambassador to sympathize with this attitude. But as soon as he became minister of foreign affairs, Russian influence in the Balkan Peninsula suddenly revived. Servia received financial assistance; a large consignment of arms was sent openly from St Petersburg to the prince of Montenegro; Prince Ferdinand of Bulgaria became ostensibly reconciled with the Russian emperor, and his son Boris was received into the Eastern Orthodox Church; the Russian embassy at Constantinople tried to bring about a reconciliation between the Bulgarian exarch and the oecumenical patriarch; Bulgarians and Servians professed, at the bidding of Russia, to lay aside their mutual hostility. All this seemed to foreshadow the creation of a Balkan confederation hostile to Turkey, and the sultan had reason to feel alarmed. In reality Prince Lobanov was merely trying to establish a strong Russian hegemony among these nationalities, and he had not the slightest intention of provoking a new crisis in the Eastern Question so long as the general European situation did not afford Russia a convenient opportunity for solving it in her own interest without serious intervention from other powers. Meanwhile he considered that the integrity and independence of the Ottoman empire must be maintained so far as these other powers were concerned. Accordingly, when Lord Salisbury proposed energetic action to protect the Armenians, the cabinet of St Petersburg suddenly assumed the rôle of protector of the sultan and vetoed the proposal. At the same time efforts were made to weaken the Triple Alliance, the principal instrument employed being the *entente* with France, which Prince Lobanov helped to convert into a formal alliance between the two powers. In the Far East he was not less active, and became the protector of China in the same sense as he had shown himself the protector of Turkey. Japan was compelled to give up her conquests on the Chinese mainland, so as not to interfere with the future action of Russia in Manchuria, and the financial and other schemes for increasing Russian influence in that part of the world were vigorously supported. All this activity, though combined with a haughty tone towards foreign governments and diplomatists, did not produce much general apprehension, probably because there was a widespread conviction that he desired to maintain peace, and that his great ability and strength of character would enable him to control the dangerous forces which he boldly set in motion. However this may be, before he had time to mature his schemes, and when he had been the director of Russian policy for only eighteen months, he died suddenly of heart disease when travelling with the emperor on the 30th of August 1896. Personally Prince Lobanov was a *grand seigneur* of the Russian type, proud of being descended from the independent princes of Rostov, and at the same time an amiable man of wide culture, deeply versed in Russian history and genealogy, and perhaps the first authority of his time in all that related to the reign of the emperor Paul. (D. M. W.)

LÖBAU, a town of Germany, in the kingdom of Saxony, on the Löbau water, 12 m. S.E. of the town of Bautzen, on the Dresden-Görlitz railway. Pop. (1905) 10,683. There is a spa, König Albert-Bad, largely frequented during the summer season. The town has agricultural implement, pianoforte, sugar, machine-building and button works, and trade in grain, yarn, linen and stockings. Other industries are spinning, weaving, dyeing, bleaching and brewing.

Löbau is first mentioned as a town in 1221; it received civic rights early in the 14th century and, in 1346, became one of the six allied towns of Lusatia. It suffered severely during the Hussite war and was deprived of its rights in 1547.

See Bergmann, *Geschichte der Oberlausitzer Sechsstadt Löbau* (Bischofswerda, 1896); and Kretschmer, *Die Stadt Löbau* (Chemnitz, 1904).

LOBBY, a corridor or passage, also any apartment serving as an ante-room, waiting room or entrance hall in a building. The Med. Lat. *lobia*, *laubia* or *lobium*, from which the word was directly adapted, was used in the sense of a cloister, gallery or covered place for walking attached to a house, as defined by Du Cange (*Gloss. Med. et Inf. Lat.*, s.v. *Lobia*), *porticus aperta ad spatiandum idonea, aedibus adjuncta*. The French form of *lobia* was *loge*, cf. Ital. *loggia*, and this gave the Eng. "lodge," which is thus a doublet of "lobby." The ultimate derivation is given under Lodge. Other familiar uses of the term "lobby" are its application (1) to the entrance hall of a parliament house, and (2) to the two corridors known as "division-lobbies," into which the members of the House of Commons and other legislative bodies pass on a division, their votes being recorded according to which "lobby," "aye" or "no," they enter. The entrance lobby to a legislative building is open to the public, and thus is a convenient place for interviews between members and their constituents or with representatives of public bodies, associations and interests, and the press. The influence and pressure thus brought to bear upon members of legislative bodies has given rise to the use of "to lobby," "lobbying," "lobbyist," &c., with this special significance. The practice, though not unknown in the British parliament, is most prevalent in the United States of America, where the use of the term first arose (see below).

LOBBYING, in America, a general term used to designate the efforts of persons who are not members of a legislative body to influence the course of legislation. In addition to the large number of American private bills which are constantly being introduced in Congress and the various state legislatures, there are many general measures, such as proposed changes in the tariff or in the railway or banking laws, which seriously affect special interests. The people who are most intimately concerned naturally have a right to ap[illegible]ature or its representative, the committee in charge of the bill, and present their side of the case. Lobbying in this sense is legitimate, and may almost be regarded as a necessity. Unfortunately, however, all lobbying is not of this innocent character. The great industrial corporations, insurance companies, and railway and traction monopolies which have developed in comparatively recent years are constantly in need of legislative favours; they are also compelled to protect themselves against legislation which is unreasonably severe, and against what are known in the slang of politics as *strikes* or *hold-ups*.[1] In order that these objects may be accomplished there are kept at Washington and at the various state capitals paid agents whose influence is so well recognized that they are popularly called "the third house." Methods of the most reprehensible kind have often been employed by them.

Attempts have been made to remedy the evil by constitutional prohibition, by statute law and by the action of the governor of the state supported by public opinion. Improper lobbying has been declared a felony in California, Georgia, Utah, Tennessee, Oregon, Montana and Arizona, and the constitutions of practically all of the states impose restrictions upon the enactment of special and private legislation. The Massachusetts anti-lobbying act of 1890, which has served as a model for the legislation of Maryland (1900), Wisconsin (1905) and a few of the other states, is based upon the publicity principle. Counsel and other legislative agents must register with the sergeant-at-arms giving the names and addresses of their employers and the date, term and character of their employment. In 1907 alone laws regulating lobbying were passed in nine states—Alabama, Connecticut, Florida, Idaho, Missouri, Nebraska, North Dakota, South Dakota and Texas.

See James Bryce, *American Commonwealth* (New York, ed. 1889), i. 673-678; Paul S. Reinsch, *American Legislatures and Legislative Methods* (New York, 1907), chaps. viii., ix.; Margaret A. Schaffner, "Lobbying," in *Wisconsin Comparative Legislation Bulletins*, No. 2; and G. M. Gregory, *The Corrupt Use of Money in Politics and Laws for its Prevention* (Madison, Wis., 1893).

LOBE, any round projecting part, specifically the lower part of the external ear, one of the parts into which the liver is divided, also one of several parts of the brain, divided by marked fissures (see Liver and Brain). The Greek λοβός, from which "lobe" is derived, was applied to the lobe of the ear and of the liver, and to the pod of a leguminous plant.

LOBECK, CHRISTIAN AUGUST (1781–1860), German classical scholar, was born at Naumburg on the 5th of June 1781. After having studied at Jena and Leipzig, he settled at Wittenberg in 1802 as privat-docent, and in 1810 was appointed to a professorship in the university. Four years later, he accepted the chair of rhetoric and ancient literature at Königsberg, which he occupied till within two years of his death (25th of August 1860). His literary activities were devoted to the history of Greek religion and to the Greek language and literature. His greatest work, *Aglaophamus* (1829), is still valuable to students. In this he maintains, against the views put forward by G. F. Creuzer in his *Symbolik* (1810–1823), that the religion of the Greek mysteries (especially those of Eleusis) did not essentially differ from the national religion; that it was not esoteric; that the priests as such neither taught nor possessed any higher knowledge of God; that the Oriental elements were a later importation. His edition of the *Ajax* of Sophocles (1809) had gained him the reputation of a sound scholar and critic; his *Phrynichus* (1820) and *Paralipomena grammaticae graecae* (1837) exhibit the widest acquaintance with Greek literature. He had little sympathy with comparative philology, holding that it needed a lifetime to acquire a thorough knowledge of a single language.

See the article by L. Friedländer in *Allgemeine deutsche Biographie*; C. Bursian's *Geschichte der klassischen Philologie in Deutschland* (1883); Lehrs, *Populäre Aufsätze aus dem Altertum* (2nd ed., Leipzig, 1875); Ludwich, *Ausgewählte Briefe von und an Chr. Aug. Lobeck und K. Lehrs* (1894); also J. E. Sandys, *History of Classical Scholarship*, i. (1908), 103.

[1] Bills introduced for purposes of blackmail.

LOBEIRA, JOÃO (*c.* 1233–1285), a Portuguese troubadour of the time of King Alphonso III., who is supposed to have been the first to reduce into prose the story of *Amadis de Gaula* (*q.v.*). D. Carolina Michaelis de Vasconcellos, in her masterly edition of the *Cancioneiro de Ajuda* (Halle, 1904, vol. i. pp. 523–524), gives some biographical notes on João Lobeira, who is represented in the Colocci Brancuti *Canzoniere* (Halle, 1880) by five poems (Nos. 230–235). In number 230, João Lobeira uses the same *ritournelle* that Oriana sings in *Amadis de Gaula*, and this has led to his being generally considered by modern supporters of the Portuguese case to have been the author of the romance, in preference to Vasco de Lobeira, to whom the prose original was formerly ascribed. The folklorist A. Thomas Pires (in his *Vasco de Lobeira*, Elvas, 1905), following the old tradition, would identify the novelist with a man of that name who flourished in Elvas at the close of the 14th and beginning of the 15th century, but the documents he publishes contain no reference to this Lobeira being a man of letters.

LOBELIA, the typical genus of the tribe *Lobelieae*, of the order Campanulaceae, named after Matthias de Lobel, a native of Lille, botanist and physician to James I. It numbers about two hundred species, natives of nearly all the temperate and warmer regions of the world, excepting central and eastern Europe as well as western Asia. They are annual or perennial herbs or under-shrubs, rarely shrubby; remarkable arborescent forms are the tree-lobelias found at high elevations on the mountains of tropical Africa. Two species are British, *L. Dortmanna* (named by Linnaeus after Dortmann, a Dutch druggist), which occurs in gravelly mountain lakes; and *L. urens*, which is only found on heaths, &c., in Dorset and Cornwall. The genus is distinguished from *Campanula* by the irregular corona and completely united anthers, and by the excessive acridity of the milky juice. The species earliest described and figured appears to be *L. cardinalis*, under the name *Trachelium americanum sive cardinalis planta*, "the rich crimson cardinal's flower"; Parkinson (*Paradisus*, 1629, p. 357) says, "it groweth neere the riuer of Canada, where the French plantation in America is seated." It is a native of the eastern United States. This and several other species are in cultivation as ornamental garden plants, *e.g.* the dwarf blue *L. Erinus*, from the Cape, which, with its numerous varieties, forms a familiar bedding plant. *L. splendens* and *L. fulgens*, growing from 1 to 2 ft. high, from Mexico, have scarlet flowers; *L. Tupa*, a Chilean perennial 6 to 8 ft. high, has reddish or scarlet flowers; *L. tenuior* with blue flowers is a recent acquisition to the greenhouse section, while *L. amaena*, from North America, as well as *L. syphilitica* and its hybrids, from Virginia, have also blue flowers. The last-named was introduced in 1665. The hybrids raised by crossing *cardinalis*, *fulgens*, *splendens* and *syphilitica*, constitute a fine group of fairly hardy and showy garden plants. Queen Victoria is a well-known variety, but there are now many others.

The *Lobelia* is familiar in gardens under two very different forms, that of the dwarf-tufted plants used for summer bedding, and that of the tall showy perennials. Of the former the best type is *L. Erinus*, growing from 4 to 6 in. high, with many slender stems, bearing through a long period a profusion of small but bright blue two-lipped flowers. The variety *speciosa* offers the best strain of the dwarf lobelias; but the varieties are being constantly superseded by new sorts. A good variety will reproduce itself sufficiently true from seed for ordinary flower borders, but to secure exact uniformity it is necessary to propagate from cuttings.

The herbaceous lobelias, of which *L. fulgens* may be taken as the type, may be called hardy except in so far as they suffer from damp in winter; they throw up a series of short rosette-like suckers round the base of the old flowering stem, and these sometimes, despite all the care taken of them, rot off during winter. The roots should either be taken up in autumn, and planted closely side by side in boxes of dry earth or ashes, these being set for the time they are dormant either in a cold frame or in any airy place in the greenhouse; or they may be left in the ground, in which case a brick or two should be put beside the plants, some coal ashes being first placed round them, and slates to protect the plants being laid over the bricks, one end resting on the earth beyond. About February they should be placed in a warm pit, and after a few days shaken out and the suckers parted, and potted singly into small pots of light rich earth. After being kept in the forcing pit until well established, they should be moved to a more airy greenhouse pit, and eventually to a cold frame preparatory to planting out. In the more favoured parts of the United Kingdom it is unnecessary to go to this trouble, as the plants are perfectly hardy; even in the suburbs of London they live for several years without protection except in very severe winters. They should have a loamy soil, well enriched with manure; and require copious waterings when they start into free growth. They may be raised from seeds, which, being very fine, require to be sown carefully; but they do not flower usually till the second year unless they are sown very early in heat.

The species *Lobelia inflata*, the "Indian tobacco" of North America, is used in medicine, the entire herb, dried and in flower, being employed. The species derives its specific name from its characteristic inflated capsules. It is somewhat irritant to the nostrils, and is possessed of a burning, acrid taste. The chief constituent is a volatile liquid alkaloid (cf. nicotine) named lobeline, which occurs to the extent of about 30%. This is a very pungent body, with a tobacco-like odour. It occurs in combination with lobelic acid and forms solid crystalline salts. The single preparation of this plant in the British Pharmacopeia is the *Tinctura Lobeliae Ethereae*, composed of five parts of spirits of ether to one of lobelia. The dose is 5 to 15 minims. The ether is employed in order to add to the efficacy of the drug in asthma, but a simple alcoholic tincture would be really preferable.

Lobelia has certain pharmacological resemblances to tobacco. It has no action upon the unbroken skin, but may be absorbed by it under suitable conditions. Taken internally in small doses, *e.g.* 5 minims of the tincture, it stimulates the peristaltic movements of the coecum and colon. In large doses it is a powerful gastro-intestinal irritant, closely resembling tobacco, and causing giddiness, headache, nausea, vomiting, purging and extreme prostration, with clammy sweats and faltering rapid pulse. Its action on the circulation is very decided. The cardiac terminals of the vagus nerves are paralysed, the pulse being thus accelerated by loss of the normal inhibitory influence, and the blood-vessels being relaxed owing to paresis of the vasomotor centre. The blood-pressure thus falls very markedly. The respiratory centre is similarly depressed, death ensuing from this action. Lobelia is thus a typical respiratory poison. In less than toxic doses the motor terminals of the vagi in the bronchi and bronchioles are paralysed, thus causing relaxation of the bronchial muscles. It is doubtful whether lobelia affects the cerebrum directly. It is excreted by the kidneys and the skin, both of which it stimulates in its passage. In general terms the drug may be said to stimulate non-striped muscular fibres in small, and paralyse them in toxic doses.

Five minims of the tincture may be usefully prescribed to be taken night and morning in chronic constipation due to inertia of the lower part of the alimentary canal. In spasmodic (neurotic) asthma, and also in bronchitis accompanied by asthmatic spasm of the bronchioles, the tincture may be given in comparatively large doses (*e.g.* one drachm) every fifteen minutes until nausea is produced. Thereafter, whether successful or not in relieving the spasm, the administration of the drug must be stopped.

LOBENSTEIN, a town of Germany, in the principality of Reuss, on the Lemnitz, situated in a pleasant and fertile country, 25 m. N.W. from Hof by railway. Pop. (1905) 2990. The town, grouped round a rock, upon which stand the ruins of the old castle, is exceedingly picturesque. It contains a spacious parish church, a palace, until 1824 the residence of the princes of Reuss-Lobenstein-Ebersdorf, and a hydropathic establishment. The manufactures include dyeing, brewing and cigar-making.

See Zedler and Schott, *Führer durch Lobenstein und Umgebung* (2nd ed., Lobenstein, 1903).

LOBO, FRANCISCO RODRIGUES (?1575–?1627), Portuguese bucolic writer, a lineal descendant in the family of letters of Bernardim Ribeiro and Christovam Falcão. All we know of his life is that he was born of rich and noble parents at Leiria, and lived at ease in its picturesque neighbourhood, reading philosophy and poetry and writing of shepherds and shepherdesses by the rivers Liz and Lena. He studied at the university of Coimbra and took the degree of licentiate about 1600. He visited Lisbon from time to time, and tradition has it that he died by drowning on his way thither as he was descending the Tagus from Santarem. Though his first book, a little volume of verses (Romances) published in 1596, and his last, a rhymed welcome to King Philip III., published in 1623, are written in Spanish, he composed his eclogues and prose pastorals entirely in Portuguese, and thereby did a rare service to his country at a time when, owing to the Spanish domination, Castilian was the language preferred by polite society and by men of letters. His *Primavera*, a book that may be compared to the *Diana* of Jorge de Montemôr (Montemayor), appeared in 1601, its second part, the *Pastor Peregrino*, in 1608, and its third, the *Desenganado*, in 1614. The dullness of these lengthy collections of episodes without plan, thread or ideas, is relieved by charming and ingenious pastoral songs named *serranilhas*. His eclogues in endecasyllables are an echo of those of Camoens, but like his other verses they are inferior to his *redondilhas*, which show the traditional fount of his inspiration. In his *Corte na Aldeia* (1619), a man of letters, a young nobleman, a student and an old man of easy means, beguile the winter evenings at Cintra by a series of philosophic and literary discussions in dialogue which may still be read with pleasure. Lobo is also the author of an insipid epic in twenty cantos in *ottava rima* on the Constable D. Nuno Alvares Pereira, the hero of the war of independence against Spain at the end of the 14th century. The characteristics of his prose style are harmony, purity and elegance, and he ranks as one of Portugal's leading writers. A disciple of the Italian school, his verses are yet free from imitations of classical models, his descriptions of natural scenery are unsurpassed in the Portuguese language, and generally his writings strike a true note and show a sincerity that was rare at the time. Their popularity may be seen by the fact that the *Primavera* went through seven editions in the 17th century and nine in all, a large number for so limited a market as that of Portugal, while six editions exist of the *Pastor Peregrino* and four of the epic poem. An edition of his collected works was published in one volume in Lisbon in 1723, and another in four volumes, but less complete, appeared there in 1774.

See Costa e Silva, *Ensaio biographico critico*, v. 5-112, for a critical examination of Lobo's writings; also Bouterwek's *History of Portuguese Literature*. (E. Pr.)

LOBO, JERONIMO (1593–1678), Jesuit missionary, was born in Lisbon, and entered the Order of Jesus at the age of sixteen. In 1621 he was ordered as a missionary to India, and in 1622 he arrived at Goa. With the intention of proceeding to Abyssinia, whose Negus (emperor) Segued had been converted to Roman Catholicism by Pedro Paez, he left India in 1624. He disembarked on the coast of Mombasa, and attempted to reach his destination through the Galla country, but was forced to return. In 1625 he set out again, accompanied by Mendez, the patriarch of Ethiopia, and eight missionaries. The party landed on the coast of the Red Sea, and Lobo settled in Abyssinia as superintendent of the missions in Tigré. He remained there until death deprived the Catholics of their protector, the emperor Segued. Forced by persecution to leave the kingdom, in 1634 Lobo and his companions fell into the hands of the Turks at Massawa, who sent him to India to procure a ransom for his imprisoned fellow-missionaries. In this he was successful, but could not induce the Portuguese viceroy to send an armament against Abyssinia. Intent upon accomplishing this cherished project, he embarked for Portugal, and after he had been shipwrecked on the coast of Natal, and captured by pirates, arrived at Lisbon. Neither at this city, however, nor at Madrid and Rome, was any countenance given to Lobo's plan. He accordingly returned to India in 1640, and was elected rector, and afterwards provincial, of the Jesuits at Goa. After some years he returned to his native city, and died there on the 29th of January 1678.

Lobo wrote an account of his travels in Portuguese, which appears never to have been printed, but is deposited in the monastery of St Roque, Lisbon. Balthazar Telles made large use of the information therein in his *Historia geral da Ethiopia a Alta* (Coimbra, 1660), often erroneously attributed to Lobo (see Machado's *Bibliotheca Lusitana*). Lobo's own narrative was translated from a MS. copy into French in 1728 by the Abbé Joachim le Grand, under the title of *Voyage historique d'Abissinie*. In 1669 a translation by Sir Peter Wyche of several passages from a MS. account of Lobo's travels was published by the Royal Society (translated in M. Thévenot's *Relation des voyages* in 1673). An English abridgment of Le Grand's edition by Dr Johnson was published in 1735 (reprinted 1789). In a *Mémoire justificatif en réhabilitation des pères Pierre Paez et Jérôme Lobo*, Dr C. T. Beke maintains against Bruce the accuracy of Lobo's statements as to the source of the Abai branch of the Nile. See A. de Backer, *Bibliothèque de la Compagnie de Jésus* (ed. C. Sommervogel, iv., 1893).

LOBSTER (O.E. *lopustre, lopystre*, a corruption of Lat. *locusta*, lobster or other marine shell-fish; also a locust), an edible crustacean found on the c[illegible]rth Atlantic and Mediterranean. The nam[illegible]ely applied to any of the larger Crustacea of the order Macrura, especially to such as are used for food.

The true lobsters, forming the family *Homaridae*, are distinguished from the other Macrura by having the first three pairs of legs terminating in chelae or pincers. The first pair are large and massive and are composed of six segments, while the remaining legs are each composed of seven segments. The sternum of the last thoracic somite is immovably united with the preceding. This last character, together with some peculiarities of the branchial system, distinguish the lobsters from the freshwater crayfishes. The common lobster (*Homarus gammarus* or *vulgaris*) is found on the European coasts from Norway to the Mediterranean. The American lobster (*Homarus americanus*), which should perhaps be ranked as a variety rather than as a distinct species, is found on the Atlantic coast of North America from Labrador to Cape Hatteras. A third species, found at the Cape of Good Hope, is of small size and of no economic importance.

Both in Europe and in America the lobster is the object of an important fishery. It lives in shallow water, in rocky places, and is usually captured in traps known as lobster-pots, or creels, made of wickerwork or of hoops covered with netting, and having funnel-shaped openings permitting entrance but preventing escape. These traps are baited with pieces of fish, preferably stale, and are sunk on ground frequented by lobsters, the place of each being marked by a buoy. In Europe the lobsters are generally sent to market in the fresh state, but in America, especially in the northern New England states and in the maritime provinces of Canada, the canning of lobsters is an important industry. The European lobster rarely reaches 10 pounds in weight, though individuals of 14 pounds have been found, and in America there are authentic records of lobsters weighing 20 to 23 pounds.

The effects of over-fishing have become apparent, especially in America, rather in the reduced average size of the lobsters caught than in any diminution of the total yield. The imposition of a close time to protect the spawning lobsters has been often tried, but as the female carries the spawn attached to her body for nearly twelve months after spawning it is impossible to give any effective protection by this means. The prohibition of the capture of females carrying spawn, or, as it is termed, "in berry," is difficult to enforce. A minimum size, below which it is illegal to sell lobsters, is fixed by law in most lobster-fishing districts, but the value of the protection so given has also been questioned.

The Norway lobster (*Nephrops norvegicus*) is found, like the common lobster, from Norway to the Mediterranean. It is a smaller species, with long and slender claws and is of an orange colour, often beautifully marked with red and blue. It is found in deeper water and is generally captured by trawling. It is a curious and unexplained fact that nearly all the individuals so captured are males. It is less esteemed for food than the common species. In London it is sold under the name of "Dublin prawn."

The rock lobster, spiny lobster, or sea-crawfish (*Palinurus vulgaris*) belongs to the family *Palinuridae*, distinguished from the *Homaridae* by the fact that the first legs are not provided with chelae or pincers, and that all the legs possess only six segments. The antennae are very long and thick. It is found on the southern and western coasts of the British Islands and extends to the Mediterranean. It is highly esteemed for the table, especially in France, where it goes by the name of *Langouste*. Other species of the same family are used for food in various parts of the world, especially on the Pacific coast of North America and in Australia and New Zealand.

In Melbourne and Sydney the name of "Murray lobster" is given to a large species of crayfish (*Astacopsis spinifer*, formerly known as *Astacus*, or *Potamobius serratus*) which is much used for food. (W. T. Ca.)

LOCAL GOVERNMENT, a phrase specially adopted in English usage for the decentralized or deconcentrated administration, within a state or national and central government, of local affairs by local authorities. It is restricted not only in respect of area but also in respect of the character and extent of the duties assigned to them. It is not to be confused with local self-government in the wider sense in which the words are sometimes employed, *e.g.* for the granting by the crown of self-government to a colony; the expression, in a general way, may mean this, but "local government" as technically used in England refers more narrowly to the system of county or municipal administration, and English usage transfers it to denote the similar institutions in other countries. The growth and persistence of this kind of subordinate government is due practically to the need of relieving the central authority in the state, and to experience of the failure of a completely centralized bureaucracy. The degree to which local government is adopted varies considerably in different countries, and those which are the best examples of it in modern times—the United Kingdom, the United States, France and Germany—differ very much in their local institutions, partly through historical, partly through temperamental, causes. A certain shifting of ideas from time to time, as to what is local and what is central, is inevitable, and the same view is not possible in countries of different configuration, history or political system. The history and present state of the local government in the various countries are dealt with in the separate articles on them (ENGLAND, GERMANY, &c.), in the sections dealing with government and administration, or political institutions.

The best recent comparative study of local government is Percy Ashley's *Local and Central Government* (Murray, 1906), an admirable account of the evolution and working of the systems in England, France, Prussia and United States. Other important works, in addition to general works on constitutional law, are J. A. Fairlie's *Municipal Administration*, Shaw's *Municipal Government in Continental Europe*, Redlich and Hirst's *Local Government in England*, Mr and Mrs Sidney Webb's elaborate historical inquiry into English local government (1906), and for Germany, Bornhak's *Geschichte des preussischen Verwaltungsrechts*.

LOCAL GOVERNMENT BOARD, a department of the administration of the United Kingdom, constituted in 1871. It is the successor of the General Board of Health, established in 1848 pursuant to the Public Health Act of that year. The General Board of Health continued in existence until 1854, when it was reconstituted. Its existence under its new constitution was originally limited to one year, but was extended from year to year until 1858, when it was allowed to expire, its powers under the various acts for the prevention of diseases being transferred to the privy council, while those which related to the control of local authorities passed to the secretary of state for the home department, to whose department the staff of officers and clerks belonging to the board was transferred. This state of affairs continued until 1871, when the Local Government Board was created by the Local Government Board Act 1871. It consists of the lord president of the council, the five principal secretaries of state, the lord privy seal, the chancellor of the exchequer and a president appointed by the sovereign. The board itself seldom meets, and the duties of the department are discharged by the president assisted by a parliamentary and a permanent secretary and a permanent staff. The president and one of the secretaries usually have seats in parliament, and the president is generally a member of the cabinet. The salary of the president, formerly £2000, was raised in 1910 to £5000 a year. The board has all the powers of the secretary of state under the Public Health Act 1848, and the numerous subsequent acts relating to sanitary matters and the government of sanitary districts; together with all the powers and duties of the privy council under the acts relating to the prevention of epidemic disease and to vaccination. The powers and duties of the board have been largely added to by legislation since its creation; it may be said that the board exercises a general supervision over the numerous authorities to whom local government has been entrusted (see ENGLAND: *Local Government*). A committee presided over by Lord Jersey in 1904 inquired into the constitution and duties of the board, but made no recommendation as to any change therein. It recommended, however, an increase in the salaries of the president and of the parliamentary and permanent secretaries.

LOCARNO (Ger. *Luggarus*), a small town of Italian appearance in the Swiss canton of Tessin or Ticino, of which till 1881 it was one of the three capitals (the others being Bellinzona, *q.v.*, and Lugano, *q.v.*). It is built at the north or Swiss end of the Lago Maggiore, not far from the point at which the Maggia enters that lake, and is by rail 14 m. S.W. of Bellinzona. Its height above the sea-level is only 682 ft., so that it is said to be the lowest spot in Switzerland. In 1900 its population was 3603, mainly Italian-speaking and Romanists. It was taken from the Milanese in 1512 by the Swiss who ruled it till 1798, when it became part of the canton of Lugano in the Helvetic Republic, and in 1803 part of that of Tessin or Ticino, then first erected. In 1555 a number of Protestant inhabitants were expelled for religious reasons, and going to Zürich founded the silk industry there. Above Locarno is the romantically situated sanctuary of the Madonna del Sasso (now rendered easily accessible by a funicular railway) that commands a glorious view over the lake and the surrounding country. (W. A. B. C.)

LOCH, HENRY BROUGHAM LOCH, 1st BARON (1827–1900), British colonial administrator, son of James Loch, M.P., of Drylaw, Midlothian, was born on the 23rd of May 1827. He entered the navy, but at the end of two years quitted it for the East India Company's military service, and in 1842 obtained a commission in the Bengal Light Cavalry. In the Sikh war in 1845 he was given an appointment on the staff of Sir Hugh Gough, and served throughout the Sutlej campaign. In 1852 he became second in command of Skinner's Horse. At the outbreak of the Crimean war in 1854, Loch severed his connexion with India, and obtained leave to raise a body of irregular Bulgarian cavalry, which he commanded throughout the war. In 1857 he was appointed attaché to Lord Elgin's mission to the East, was present at the taking of Canton, and in 1858 brought home the treaty of Yedo. In April 1860 he again accompanied Lord Elgin to China, as secretary of the new embassy sent to secure the execution by China of her treaty engagements. The embassy was backed up by an allied Anglo-French force. With Harry S. Parkes he negotiated the surrender of the Taku forts. During the advance on Peking Loch was chosen with Parkes to complete the preliminary negotiations for peace at Tungchow. They were accompanied by a small party of officers and Sikhs. It having been discovered that the Chinese were planning a treacherous attack on the British force, Loch rode back and warned the outposts. He then returned to Parkes and his party under a flag of truce hoping to secure their safety. They were all, however, made prisoners and taken to Peking, where the majority died from torture or disease. Parkes and Loch, after enduring irons and all the horrors of a Chinese prison, were afterwards more leniently treated. After three weeks' time the negotiations for their release were successful, but they had only been liberated ten minutes when orders were received from the Chinese emperor, then a fugitive in Mongolia, for their immediate execution. Loch never entirely recovered his health after this experience in a Chinese dungeon. Returning home he was made C.B., and for a while was private secretary to Sir George Grey, then at the Home Office. In 1863 he was appointed lieutenant-governor of the Isle of Man. During his governorship the House of Keys was transformed into an elective assembly, the first line of railway was opened, and the influx of tourists began to bring fresh prosperity to the island. In 1882 Loch, who had become K.C.B. in 1880, accepted a commissionership of woods and forests, and two years later was made governor of Victoria, where he won the esteem of all classes. In June 1889 he succeeded Sir Hercules Robinson as governor of Cape Colony and high commissioner of South Africa.

As high commissioner his duties called for the exercise of great judgment and firmness. The Boers were at the same time striving to frustrate Cecil Rhodes's schemes of northern expansion and planning to occupy Mashonaland, to secure control of Swaziland and Zululand and to acquire the adjacent lands up to the ocean. Loch firmly supported Rhodes, and, by informing President Kruger that troops would be sent to prevent any invasion of territory under British protection, he effectually [illegible] across the Limpopo (1890–91). [illegible] the approval of the imperial government, [illegible] a convention with President [illegible] by which, while the Boers withdrew [illegible] north of the Transvaal, they were granted [illegible] at Kosi Bay on condition that the republic [illegible] Customs Union. This convention was [illegible] conducted with President Kruger [illegible] behalf of the high commissioner, and was [illegible] the British and Bond parties in Cape [illegible] harmony. The Transvaal did not, [illegible] necessary condition, and in view of the [illegible] attitude of the Pretoria administration to [illegible] became a strong advocate of the annexation [illegible] country east of Swaziland, through which the [illegible] would have passed. He at length induced [illegible] to adopt his view and on the 15th of [illegible] announced that these territories (Amatonga- [illegible] be annexed by Britain, an announcement [illegible] Kruger "with the greatest astonishment and [illegible] Loch had been forced to intervene in another [illegible] commandeering difficulty of 1894 had roused [illegible] Transvaal to a dangerous pitch of excite- [illegible] Pretoria to use his personal influence with [illegible] obtained the withdrawal of the obnoxious [illegible]. In the following year he entered a [illegible] the new Transvaal franchise law. Mean- [illegible] administration in South Africa was assuming [illegible] threatening aspect. Cecil Rhodes, then [illegible] Cape Colony, was strongly in favour of a more [illegible] was supported by the Imperial government, [illegible] March 1895 the high commissioner, finding [illegible] out of touch with his ministers, returned [illegible] before the expiry of his term of office. In [illegible] raised to the peerage. When the Anglo- [illegible] in 1899 Loch took a leading part in [illegible] a body of mounted men, named after [illegible]. He died in London on the 20th of [illegible] succeeded as 2nd baron by his son Edward [illegible]

[illegible] district of southern Inverness-shire, Scotland, [illegible] Linnhe, the river and loch Lochy, N. by [illegible] and adjoining hills, N.E. and E. by the [illegible] S.E. by the district of Rannoch and S. by [illegible]. It measures 32 m. from N.E. to S.W. [illegible] m., and is remarkable for wild and romantic [illegible] being the chief mountain. The district has [illegible] peculiar type of axe, consisting of a long [illegible] a blade and a large hook behind it, which, [illegible] was introduced into the Highlands [illegible]. It was the weapon of the old City [illegible]. The pathetic song of "Lochaber no more" [illegible]

[illegible] capital of an arrondissement in [illegible] 25 m. S.E. of Tours by rail, [illegible] Pop. (1906) 3751. The town, one [illegible] France, lies at the foot of the [illegible] the castle of the Anjou family, [illegible] m. in circumference, and con- [illegible] church of St Ours, the royal lodge [illegible] St Ours dates from the 10th to [illegible] distinguishing features are the [illegible] the nave and the beautiful [illegible] royal lodge, built by Charles VII. [illegible] contains the tomb of Agnes Sorel [illegible] Brittany. The donjon includes, [illegible] the Martelet, celebrated [illegible] there [illegible] taining [illegible] ling— [illegible] rdinal [illegible] veral houses of the Renaissance period. It has a tribunal of first instance, a communal college and a training college. Liqueur-distilling and tanning are carried on together with trade in farm-produce, wine, wood and live-stock.

On the right bank of the Loire, opposite the town and practically its suburb, is the village of Beaulieu-lès-Loches, once the seat of a barony. Besides the parish church of St Laurent, a beautiful specimen of 12th-century architecture, it contains the remains of the great abbey church of the Holy Sepulchre founded in the 11th century by Fulk Nerra, count of Anjou, who is buried in the chancel. This chancel, which with one of the older transepts now constitutes the church, dates from the 15th century. The Romanesque nave is in ruins, but of the two towers one survives intact; it is square, crowned with an octagonal steeple of stone, and is one of the finest extant monuments of Romanesque architecture.

Loches (the Roman *Leucae*) grew up round a monastery founded about 500 by St Ours and belonged to the counts of Anjou from 886 till 1205. In the latter year it was seized from King John of England by Philip Augustus, and from the middle of the 13th century till after the time of Charles IX. the castle was a residence of the kings of France.

LOCHGELLY, a police burgh of Fifeshire, Scotland, 7½ m. N.E. of Dunfermline by the North British railway. Pop. (1901) 5472. The town is modern and owes its prosperity to the iron-works and collieries in its immediate vicinity. Loch Gelly, from which the town takes its name, situated ½ m. S. E., measures ¾ m. in length by ½ m. in breadth, contains some trout and pike, and has on its west banks Lochgelly House, a seat of the earl of Minto. The Romans are said to have had a station at Loch Ore in the parish of Ballingry, 2½ m. N. by W., which was drained about the end of the 18th century and then cultivated. To the N.E. rises the hill of Benarty (1131 ft.). Hallyards, about 2 m. S.E. of Lochgelly, is a ruined house that once belonged to Sir William Kirkaldy of Grange, who held Edinburgh Castle for Queen Mary. Here James V. was received after his defeat at Solway Moss in 1542, and here a few Jacobites used to meet in 1715.

LOCHGILPHEAD, a municipal and police burgh of Argyllshire, Scotland, at the head of Loch Gilp, a small arm on the western side of Loch Fyne. Pop. (1901) 1313. The herring-fishery is the chief industry, but there is some weaving of woollens and, in summer, a considerable influx of visitors. Ardrishaig (pop. 1285), a seaport on the west of the mouth of Loch Gilp, is the east terminus of the Crinan Canal. It is the place of transhipment from the large Glasgow passenger steamers to the small craft built for the navigation of the canal. It is an important harbour in connexion with the Loch Fyne herring-fishery, and there is also a distillery. During the summer there is a coach service to Ford at the lower end of Loch Awe.

LOCHMABEN, a royal and police burgh of Dumfriesshire, Scotland, 8 m. N.E. of Dumfries, with a station on the Caledonian railway company's branch from Dumfries to Lockerbie. Pop. (1901) 1328. It is delightfully situated, there being eight lakes in the immediate neighbourhood, while the river Annan, and the Waters of Ae, Kinnel and Dryfe are in the vicinity. The town hall is a handsome edifice with clock tower. At the south end of Castle Loch, the chief lake, stand the ruins, a mere shell, of Lochmaben Castle, dating from the 13th century, where local tradition declares that Robert Bruce was born—an honour which is also claimed, however, for Turnberry Castle on the coast of Ayrshire. In the parish church is a bell said to have been presented to King Robert by the pope after reconciliation with him. A statue of the king stands in front of the town hall. Whether it were his birthplace or not, the associations of Bruce with Lochmaben were intimate. He exempted his followers in the district from feudal service and their descendants—the "kindly tenants of Lochmaben"—were confirmed in their tenure by the court of session in 1824. The Castle Loch is the only fresh water in Scotland, and possibly in the British Isles, where the vendace (*coregonus vandesius*) occurs. This fish, which is believed to be growing scarcer, is alleged on doubtful authority to have been introduced by Queen Mary. It is captured by the sweep-net in August, and is esteemed as a delicacy. The lakes adjoining the town afford the inhabitants exceptional advantages for the game of curling. There was once a team of Lochmaben Curlers entirely composed of shoemakers (souters) who held their own against all comers, and their prowess added the phrase "to souter" to the vocabulary of the sport, the word indicating a match in which the winners scored "game" to their opponents' "love." Lochmaben unites with Annan, Dumfries, Kirkcudbright and Sanquhar (the Dumfries burghs) in returning one member to parliament.

LOCK, MATTHIAS, English 18th-century furniture designer and cabinet-maker. The dates of his birth and death are unknown; but he was a disciple of Chippendale, and subsequently of the Adams, and was possibly in partnership with Henry Copeland (*q.v.*). During the greater part of his life he belonged to that flamboyant school which derived its inspiration from Louis XV. models; but when he fell under the influence of Robert Adam he absorbed his manner so completely that it is often difficult to distinguish between them, just as it is sometimes easy to confound Lock's work with the weaker efforts of Chippendale. Thus from being extravagantly rococo he progressed to a simple ordered classicism. His published designs are not equal to his original drawings, many of which are preserved in the Victoria and Albert Museum, South Kensington, while the pieces themselves are often bolder and more solid than is suggested by the author's representations of them. He was a clever craftsman and holds a distinct place among the minor furniture designers of the second half of the 18th century.

Among his works, some of which were issued in conjunction with Copeland, are: *A New Drawing Book of Ornaments* (n. d.); *A New Book of Ornaments* (1768); *A New Book of Pier Frames, Ovals, Girandoles, Tables, &c.* (1769); and *A New Book of Foliage* (1769).

LOCK (from the O. Eng. *loc.*; the word appears, in different forms, in many Teutonic languages, but with such various meanings as "hole," Ger. *Loch*, "lid," Swed. *lock*, &c.; probably the original was a root meaning "to enclose"), a fastening, particularly one which consists of a bolt held in a certain position by one or more movable parts which require to be placed in definite positions by the aid of a key or of a secret arrangement of letters, figures or signs, before the bolt can be moved. It is with such fastenings that the present article chiefly deals.

The word is also used, in the original sense of an enclosure or barrier, for a length of water in a river or canal, or at the entrance of a dock, enclosed at both ends by gates, the "lock-gates," and fitted with sluices, to enable vessels to be raised from a lower to a higher level or vice versa (see CANAL and DOCK). In guns and rifles the lock is the mechanism which effects the firing of the charge; it thus appears in the names of old types of weapons, such as wheel-lock, match-lock, flint-lock (see ARMS AND ARMOUR, § *Firearms*; also GUN and RIFLE). Lock (Ger. *Locke*) in the sense of a curl or tuft of hair, the separate groups in which the hair naturally grows, may be, in ultimate origin, connected with the root of the main word. Lock-jaw is the popular name of the disease known as tetanus (*q.v.*). The name "Lock Hospital" is frequently used in English for a hospital for patients suffering from venereal diseases. According to the *New English Dictionary* there was in Southwark as early as 1453 a leper-hospital, known as the Lock Lazar House, which later was used for the treatment of venereal diseases. The name appears to have become used in the present sense as early as the end of the 17th century. Lock hospitals were established in London in 1745–1747 and in Dublin in 1754–1755.

The forms in which locks are manufactured, such as padlock, rim-lock, mortise-lock, one-sided or two-sided, &c., are necessarily extremely numerous; and the variations in the details of construction of any one of these forms are still more numerous, so that it is impossible to do more here than describe the main types which have been or are in common use. Probably the earliest locks were of Chinese origin. Specimens of these still extant are quite as secure as any locks manufactured in Europe up to the 18th century, but it is impossible to ascertain the date of their manufacture. With the exception, in all probability, of these Chinese examples, the earliest lock of which the construction is known is the Egyptian, which was used four thousand years ago. In fig. 1, *aa* is the body of the lock, *bb* the bolt and *cc* the key. The three pins *p*, *p*, *p* drop into three holes in the bolt when it is pushed in, and so hold it fast; and they are raised again by putting in the key through the large hole in the bolt and raising it a little, so that the pins in the key push the locking pins up out of the way of the bolt. It was evidently to locks and keys of this nature that the prophet alluded: "And the key of the house of David will I lay upon his shoulder" (Isaiah xxii. 22), the word *maftah* used in this passage being the common word for key to this day.

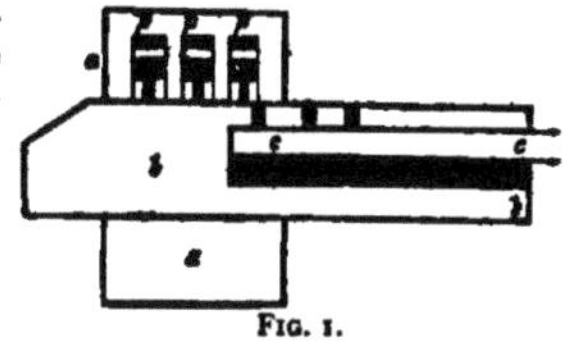
Fig. 1.

In the 18th century the European lock was nothing better than a mere bolt, held in its place, either shut or open, by a spring *b* (fig. 2), which pressed it down, and so held it at either one end or the other of the convex notch *aa*; and the only impediment to opening it was the wards which the key had to pass before it could turn in the keyhole. But it was always possible to find the shape of the wards by merely putting in a blank key covered with wax, and pressing it against them;

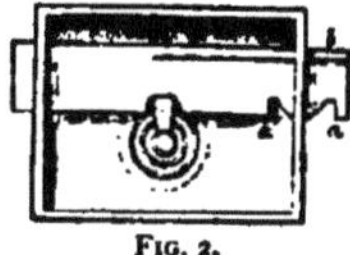
Fig. 2.

Fig. 3.

and when this had been done it was unnecessary to cut out the key into the complicated form of the wards (such as fig. 3), because no part of that key does any work except the edge *bc* farthest from the pipe *a*; and so a key of the form fig. 4 would do just as well. Thus a small collection of skeleton keys, as they are called, of a few different patterns, was all the stock in trade that a lock-picker required.

The common single-tumbler lock (fig. 5) requires two operations instead of one to open it. The tumbler *at* turns on a pivot at *t*, and has a square pin at *a*, which drops into a notch in the bolt *bb*, when it is either quite open or quite shut, and the tumbler

Fig. 4.

Fig. 5

must be lifted by the key before the bolt can be moved again. The tumbler offered little resistance to picking, as the height to which it might be lifted was not limited and the bolt would operate provided only that this height was sufficient; the improvement which formed the foundation of the modern key lock was the substitution of what is known as the "lever" for the tumbler, the difference being that the lever must be lifted to *exactly* the right height to allow the bolt to pass. This improvement, together with the obvious one of using more than one lever, was introduced in 1778 by Robert Barron, and is illustrated in figs. 6 and 7. Unless the square pin *a* (fig. 6) is lifted by the key to the proper height and no higher, the bolt cannot move. Fig. 8 illustrates the key of such a lock with four levers, the different distances between the centre of the key barrel and the edge of the bit being adapted to lift the levers to the respective heights required. This lock differs from the

Lever locks

the bolt is partly shot by the correct key, the screw which binds the sliders together as it comes opposite an opening in the back of the case is loosened, the key is removed and altered—or a fresh key substituted—and is inserted so as to lift the levers to their correct height and expose the clamping screw at the back, which is then tightened. This lock is now commonly used for safe deposits, combined with a small lever lock of which the custodian carries the key, and which either blocks the bolt of the main lock or covers the keyhole.

Fig. 15.

In connexion with changeable key locks requiring key steps of definite lengths, much ingenuity has been displayed in designing keys with movable bits or steps, as fig. 15, which are useful chiefly as duplicates, being built up to match the key from time to time in use, and then deposited in some bank or other secure place to be used in case of emergency.

Combination locks. From the very earliest times secret devices, either to hide keyholes or to take the place of locks proper, have been in use; these are to-day only seriously represented by "combination" locks which, whilst following the same general principles as key locks, differ entirely in construction. Locks in which the arranging of the internal parts in their proper positions was secured by the manipulation of external parts marked with letters or numbers were common in China in very early times, but their history is unfortunately lost. This form of lock has been developed to a very high degree of perfection and is, for safes, in almost universal use to-day in America.

The American lock consists of a series of disks mounted upon one spindle, only one, however—the bolt disk—being fixed thereto, and provided each with a gating into which a stump connected with the bolt can drop when all the gatings lie upon a given line parallel to the axis of the spindle. Each disk is provided with a driving pin so arranged that it can impinge on and drive a similar pin in its next neighbour; the gating in the bolt disk and the portion of the stump which enters it are so formed that the disk can draw the bolt back. The spindle is provided on the outside with a knob and graduated disk—usually with 100 divisions—surrounded by an annulus on which a fixed position is denoted. Each disk, including the bolt disk, is provided with a pin projecting from its surface in such a way that the pin of one disk comes into contact with that of the next disk and drives it round. If, then, the bolt disk being at the back, there are three letter disks and the spindle is rotated to the left, the bolt disk will in the course of one revolution pick up letter disk No. 1—counting from the bolt disk—in the second revolution it will pick up No. 2, and in the third No. 3, the revolution being continued for part of a turn till the number corresponding to the correct position of No. 3 is reached. The revolution of the spindle is now reversed. The bolt disk leaves No. 1 in the first revolution and picks it up again, and the second revolution picks up No. 2. The motion is continued for part of a revolution till No. 2 is brought to the correct position (No. 3 obviously not being disturbed) and is then reversed. No. 1 is again left behind and picked up in the first revolution to the left, the motion being continued till the correct position of No. 1 is reached, when, on reversal, the gating in the bolt disk comes into the correct position, the stump falls and a continuance of the motion to the right draws back the bolt. A lock constructed in this way would be of little utility, as the combination would have to be determined once for all by the maker. The difficulty is got over by making the letter disks in two parts, the inner part carrying the driving pin and the outer the gating; these two parts are locked together by small [illegible] devices which come into such a position that they can be released with the help of a square key when the lock is unlocked. The combination is set by altering the position of the inner disks and the driving pins in relation to the outer part carrying the gating [illegible] held steady by the square key.

[illegible] of the combination lock is that there is no key [illegible] the means adopted by burglars, especially [illegible] are such that even this is not a perfect [illegible] having occurred in which a person [illegible] disclose the combination. With [illegible] the safe door forms a distinct [illegible] locks the spindle passing [illegible] by explosives. To obviate [illegible] introduced in America and have [illegible] the time lock consists of a [illegible] movement [illegible] get [illegible] be [illegible]

two, three or four chronometers are used, any one of which can release the lock.

The Yale time lock contains two chronometer movements which revolve two dial plates studded with twenty-four pins to represent the twenty-four hours of the day. These pins, when pushed in, form a track on which run rollers supporting the lever which secures the bolt or locking agency, but when they are drawn out the track is broken, the rollers fall down and the bolt is released. By pulling out the day pins, say from 9 till 4, the door is automatically prepared for opening between these hours, and at 4 it again of itself locks up. For keeping the repository closed over Sundays and holidays, a subsidiary segment or track is brought into play by which a period of twenty-four hours is added to the locked interval. Careful provision is made against the eventuality of running down or accidental stoppage of the clock motion, by which the rightful owner might be as seriously incommoded as the burglar. In the Yale lock, just before the chronometers run out, a trigger is released which depresses the lever by which the bolt is held in position. (A. B. Ch.)

LOCKE, JOHN (1632–1704), English philosopher, was born at Wrington, 10 m. W. of Belluton, in Somersetshire, on the 29th of August 1632, six years after the death of Bacon, and three months before the birth of Spinoza. His father was a small landowner and attorney at Pensford, near the northern boundary of the county, to which neighbourhood the family had migrated from Dorsetshire early in that century. The elder Locke, a strict but genial Puritan, by whom the son was carefully educated at home, was engaged in the military service of the parliamentary party. "From the time that I knew anything," Locke wrote in 1660, "I found myself in a storm, which has continued to this time." For fourteen years his education, more or less interrupted, went on in the rural home at Belluton, on his father's little estate, half a mile from Pensford, and 6 m. from Bristol. In 1646 he entered Westminster School and remained there for six years. Westminster was uncongenial to him. Its memories perhaps encouraged the bias against public schools which afterwards disturbed his philosophic calm in his *Thoughts on Education*. In 1652 he entered Christ Church, Oxford, then under John Owen, the Puritan dean and vice-chancellor of the university. Christ Church was Locke's occasional home for thirty years. For some years after he entered, Oxford was ruled by the Independents, who, largely through Owen, unlike the Presbyterians, were among the first in England to advocate genuine religious toleration. But Locke's hereditary sympathy with the Puritans was gradually lessened by the intolerance of the Presbyterians and the fanaticism of the Independents. He had found in his youth, he says, that "what was called general freedom was general bondage, and that the popular assertors of liberty were the greatest engrossers of it too, and not unfitly called its *keepers*." And the influence of the liberal divines of the Church of England afterwards showed itself in his spiritual development.

Under Owen scholastic studies were maintained with a formality and dogmatism unsuited to Locke's free inquisitive temper. The aversion to them which he expressed showed thus early an innate disposition to rebel against empty verbal reasoning. He was not, according to his own account of himself to Lady Masham, a hard student at first. He sought the company of pleasant and witty men, and thus gained knowledge of life. He took the ordinary bachelor's degree in 1656, and the master's in 1658. In December 1660 he was serving as tutor of Christ Church, lecturing in Greek, rhetoric and philosophy.

At Oxford Locke was nevertheless within reach of liberal intellectual influence tending to promote self-education and strong individuality. The metaphysical works of Descartes had appeared a few years before he went to Oxford, and the *Human Nature* and *Leviathan* of Hobbes during his undergraduate years. It does not seem that Locke read extensively, but he was attracted by Descartes. The first books, he told Lady Masham, which gave him a relish for philosophy, were those of this philosopher, although he very often differed from him. At the Restoration potent influences were drawing Oxford and England into experimental inquiries. Experiment in physics became the fashion. The Royal Society was then founded, and we find Locke experimenting in chemistry in 1663, also in meteorology, in which he was particularly interested all his life.

The restraints of a professional career were not suited to Locke. There is a surmise that early in his Oxford career he contemplated taking orders in the Church of England. His religious disposition attracted him to theology. Revulsion from the dogmatic temper of the Presbyterians, and the unreasoning enthusiasm of the Independents favoured sympathy afterwards with Cambridge Platonists and other liberal Anglican churchmen. Whichcote was his favourite preacher, and close intimacy with the Cudworth family cheered his later years. But, though he has a place among lay theologians, dread of ecclesiastical impediment to free inquiry, added to strong inclination for scientific investigation, made him look to medicine as his profession, and before 1666 we find him practising as a physician in Oxford. Nevertheless, although known among his friends as "Doctor Locke," he never graduated in medicine. His health was uncertain, for he suffered through life from chronic consumption and asthma. A fortunate event soon withdrew him from the medical profession.

Locke early showed an inclination to politics, as well as to theology and medicine. As early as 1665 he diverged for a short time from medical pursuits at Oxford, and was engaged as secretary to Sir Walter Vane on his mission to the Elector of Brandenburg. Soon after his return in 1666 the incident occurred which determined his career. Lord Ashley, afterwards first earl of Shaftesbury, had come to Oxford for his health. Locke was introduced to him by his physician, Dr Thomas. This was the beginning of a lasting friendship, sustained by common sympathy with liberty—civil, religious and philosophical. In 1667 Locke moved from Christ Church to Exeter House, Lord Ashley's London residence, to become his confidential secretary. Although he retained his studentship at Christ Church, and occasionally visited Oxford, as well as his patrimony at Belluton, he found a home and shared fortune with Shaftesbury for fifteen years.

Locke's commonplace books throw welcome light on the history of his mind in early life. A paper on the "Roman Commonwealth" which belongs to this period, expresses convictions about religious liberty and the relations of religion to the state that were modified and deepened afterwards; objections to the sacerdotal conception of Christianity appear in another article; short work is made of ecclesiastical claims to infallibility in the interpretation of Scripture in a third; a scheme of utilitarian ethics, wider than that of Hobbes, is suggested in a fourth. The most significant of those early revelations is the *Essay concerning Toleration* (1666), which anticipates conclusions more fully argued nearly thirty years later.

The Shaftesbury connexion must have helped to save Locke from those idols of the "Den" to which professional life and narrow experience is exposed. It brought him into contact with public men, the springs of political action and the duties of high office. The place he held as Shaftesbury's adviser is indeed the outstanding circumstance in his middle life. Exeter House afforded every opportunity for society. He became intimate among others with the illustrious Sydenham; he joined the Royal Society and served on its council. The foundation of the monumental work of his life was laid when he was at Exeter House. He was led to it in this way. It was his habit to encourage informal reunions of his intimates, to discuss debatable questions in science and theology. One of these, in the winter of 1670, is historically memorable. "Five or six friends," he says, met in his rooms and were discussing "principles of morality and religion. They found themselves quickly at a stand by the difficulties that arose on every side." Locke proposed some criticism of the necessary "limits of human understanding" as likely to open a way out of their difficulties. He undertook to attempt this, and fancied that what he had to say might find sufficient space on "one sheet of paper." What was thus "begun by chance, was continued by entreaty, written by incoherent parcels, and after long intervals of neglect resumed again as humour and occasions permitted." At the end of nearly twenty years the issue was given to the world as Locke's now famous *Essay Concerning Human Understanding*.

The fall of Shaftesbury in 1675 enabled Locke to escape from English politics. He found a retreat in France, where he could unite calm reflection upon the legitimate operations of "human understanding" with attention to his health. He spent three years partly at Montpellier and partly in Paris. His journals and commonplace books in these years show the *Essay* in preparation. At Paris he met men of science and letters—Peter Guenellon, the well-known Amsterdam physician; Ole Römer, the Danish astronomer; Thoynard, the critic; Melchisédech Thévenot, the traveller; Henri Justel, the jurist; and François Bernier, the expositor of Gassendi. But there is no mention of Malebranche, whose *Recherche de la vérité* had appeared three years before, nor of Arnauld, the illustrious rival of Malebranche.

Locke returned to London in 1679. Reaction against the court party had restored Shaftesbury to power. Locke resumed his old confidential relations, now at Thanet House in Aldersgate. A period of often interrupted leisure for study followed. It was a time of plots and counterplots, when England seemed on the brink of another civil war. In the end Shaftesbury was committed to the Tower, tried and acquitted. More insurrectionary plots followed in the summer of 1682, after which, suspected at home, the versatile statesman escaped to Holland, and died at Amsterdam in January 1683. In these two years Locke was much at Oxford and in Somerset, for the later movements of Shaftesbury did not commend themselves to him. Yet the government had their eyes upon him. "John Locke lives a very cunning unintelligible life here," Prideaux reported from Oxford in 1682. "I may confidently affirm," wrote John Fell, the dean of Christ Church, to Lord Sunderland, "there is not any one in the college who has heard him speak a word against, or so much as censuring, the government; and, although very frequently, both in public and private, discourses have been purposely introduced to the disparagement of his master, the earl of Shaftesbury, he could never be provoked to take any notice, or discover in word or look the least concern; so that I believe there is not in the world such a master of taciturnity and passion." Unpublished correspondence with his Somerset friend, Edward Clarke of Chipley, describes Locke's life in those troubled years. It also reveals the opening of his intimate intercourse with the Cudworth family, who were friends of the Clarkes, and connected by birth with Somerset. The letters allude to toleration in the state and comprehension in the church, while they show an indifference to theological dogma hardly consistent with an exclusive connexion with any sect.

In his fifty-second year, in the gloomy autumn of 1683, Locke retired to Holland, then the asylum of eminent persons who were elsewhere denied liberty of thought. Descartes and Spinoza had speculated there; it had been the home of Erasmus and Grotius; it was now the refuge of Bayle. Locke spent more than five years there; but his (unpublished) letters show that exile sat heavily upon him. Amsterdam was his first Dutch home, where he lived in the house of Dr Keen, under the assumed name of Dr Van der Linden. For a time he was in danger of arrest at the instance of the English government. After months of concealment he escaped; but he was deprived of his studentship at Christ Church by order of the king, and Oxford was thus closed against him. Holland introduced him to new friends. The chief of these was Limborch, the successor of Episcopius as Remonstrant professor of theology, lucid, learned and tolerant, the friend of Cudworth, Whichcote and More. By Limborch he was introduced to Le Clerc, the youthful representative of letters and philosophy in Limborch's college, who had escaped from Geneva and Calvinism to the milder atmosphere of Holland and the Remonstrants. The *Bibliothèque universelle* of Le Clerc was then the chief organ in Europe of men of letters. Locke contributed several articles. It was his first appearance as an author, although he was now fifty-four years of age. This tardiness in authorship is a significant fact in his life, in harmony with his tempered wisdom.

In the next fourteen years the world received through his books the thoughts which had been gradually forming, and were taking final shape while he was in Holland. The *Essay* was finished there, and a French epitome appeared in 1688 in Le [illegible] of the larger work. Locke was then [illegible] lived for a year in the house of a Quaker [illegible] Furly, a wealthy merchant and [illegible] he was a confidant of political [illegible] and the famous earl of Peterborough, [illegible] William, prince of Orange. William [illegible] November 1688; Locke followed in [illegible] which carried the princess Mary.

[illegible] England in 1689 Locke emerged through [illegible] fame. Within a month after he [illegible] declined an offer of the embassy to [illegible] accepted the modest office of commissioner of [illegible] following years, during which he lived at [illegible], were memorable for the publication of [illegible] social polity, and of the epoch-making [illegible] which reveals the main principles [illegible] of these to appear was his defence of [illegible] the *Epistola de Tolerantia*, addressed to [illegible] at Gouda in the spring of 1689, and trans[illegible] by William Popple, a Unitarian [illegible]. *Two Treatises on Government*, in defence [illegible] sovereignty in the people, followed a [illegible] *Essay concerning Human Under*[illegible] in the spring of 1690. He received £30 [illegible] the same as Kant got in 1781 for his [illegible]. In the *Essay* Locke was the critic [illegible] of human experience: Kant, as the critic [illegible] and moral presuppositions of experience, [illegible] to the incomplete and ambiguous [illegible] question that was given in Locke's [illegible] the first book in which its author's name [illegible] *de Tolerantia* and the *Treatises on* [illegible]

[illegible] aggravated by the air of London; and the [illegible] disappointed him, for the settlement at [illegible] of his ideal. In spring, 1691, he took [illegible] house of Otes in Essex, the country [illegible], between Ongar and Harlow. Lady [illegible] daughter of Ralph Cudworth, [illegible] he went to Holland. She told Le Clerc [illegible] from exile, "by some considerably long [illegible] of the air of Otes, which is some 20 m. [illegible] thought that none would be so suitable [illegible]," she adds, "could not but be very [illegible] all the assurances we could give him [illegible]; but, to make him easy in living with [illegible] should do so on his own terms, which [illegible] to, he then believed himself at home [illegible] pleased God, here to end his days as [illegible] for fourteen years as much domestic [illegible] as was consistent with broken health, [illegible] visits to London on public affairs, in [illegible] adviser. Otes was in every way his [illegible] otherwise we have pleasant pictures of [illegible] life and the occasional visits of his [illegible] Peterborough, Lord Shaftesbury of [illegible] Newton, William Molyneux and [illegible]

[illegible] with his pen. The *Letter on Toleration* [illegible] An *Answer* by Jonas Proast of [illegible] drawn forth in 1690 a *Second* [illegible] was followed by Locke's elaborate [illegible] the summer of the following year. [illegible] were much in his thoughts, and in [illegible] an important letter to Sir John [illegible] *of the Lowering of Interest and* [illegible] When he was in Holland he had [illegible] of Chipley about the education [illegible] the substance of the little [illegible] (1693), which still holds [illegible] department. Nor were the [illegible]'s theo-logical controversies of the 17th century made him anxious to show how simple after all fundamental Christianity is. In the *Reasonableness of Christianity as delivered in the Scriptures* (anonymous, 1695), Locke sought to separate the divine essence of Christ's religion from later accretions of dogma, and from reasonings due to oversight of the necessary limits of human thought. This intended Eirenicon involved him in controversies that lasted for years. Angry polemics assailed the book. A certain John Edwards was conspicuous. Locke's *Vindication*, followed by a *Second Vindication* in 1697, added fuel to this fire. Above all, the great *Essay* was assailed and often misinterpreted by philosophers and divines. Notes of opposition had been heard almost as soon as it appeared. John Norris, the metaphysical rector of Bemerton and English disciple of Malebranche, criticized it in 1690. Locke took no notice at the time, but his second winter at Otes was partly employed in *An Examination of Malebranche's Opinion of Seeing all Things in God*, and in *Remarks upon some of Mr Norris's Books*, tracts which throw light upon his own ambiguous theory of perception through the senses. These were published after his death. A second edition of the *Essay*, with a chapter added on "Personal Identity," and numerous alterations in the chapter on "Power," appeared in 1694. The third, which was only a reprint, was published in 1695. Wynne's well-known abridgment helped to make the book known in Oxford, and his friend William Molyneux introduced it in Dublin. In 1695 a revival of controversy about the currency diverted Locke's attention. Events in that year occasioned his *Observations on Silver Money* and *Further Considerations on Raising the Value of Money*.

In 1696 Locke was induced to accept a commissionership on the Board of Trade. This required frequent visits to London. Meantime the *Essay on Human Understanding* and the *Reasonableness of Christianity* were becoming more involved in a wordy warfare between dogmatists and latitudinarians, trinitarians and unitarians. The controversy with Edwards was followed by a more memorable one with Stillingfleet, bishop of Worcester. John Toland, in his *Christianity not Mysterious*, had exaggerated doctrines in the *Essay*, and then adopted them as his own. In the autumn of 1696, Stillingfleet, an argumentative ecclesiastic more than a religious philosopher, in his *Vindication of the Doctrine of the Trinity*, charged Locke with disallowing mystery in human knowledge, especially in his account of the metaphysical idea of "substance." Locke replied in January 1697. Stillingfleet's rejoinder appeared in May, followed by a *Second Letter* from Locke in August, to which the bishop replied in the following year. Locke's *Third Letter*, in which the ramifications of this controversy are pursued with a copious expenditure of acute reasoning and polished irony, was delayed till 1699, in which year Stillingfleet died. Other critics of the *Essay* entered the lists. One of the ablest was John Sergeant, a priest of the Roman Church, in *Solid Philosophy Asserted Against the Fancies of the Ideists* (1697). He was followed by Thomas Burnet and Dean Sherlock. Henry Lee, rector of Tichmarch, criticized the *Essay*, chapter by chapter in a folio volume entitled *Anti-Scepticism* (1702); John Broughton dealt another blow in his *Psychologia* (1703); and John Norris returned to the attack, in his *Theory of the Ideal or Intelligible World* (1701–1704). On the other hand Locke was defended with vigour by Samuel Bolde, a Dorsetshire clergyman. The *Essay* itself was meanwhile spreading over Europe, impelled by the name of its author as the chief philosophical defender of civil and religious liberty. The fourth edition (the last while Locke was alive) appeared in 1700, with important additional chapters on "Association of Ideas" and "Enthusiasm." What was originally meant to form another chapter was withheld. It appeared among Locke's posthumous writings as *The Conduct of the Understanding*, one of the most characteristic of his works. The French translation of the *Essay* by Pierre Coste, Locke's amanuensis at Otes, was issued almost simultaneously with the fourth edition. The Latin version by Richard Burridge of Dublin followed a year after, reprinted in due time at Amsterdam and at Leipzig.

In 1700 Locke resigned his commission at the Board of Trade, and devoted himself to Biblical studies and religious meditation. The Gospels had been carefully studied when he was preparing his *Reasonableness of Christianity*. He now turned to the Epistles of St Paul, and applied the spirit of the *Essay* and the ordinary rules of critical interpretation to a literature which he venerated as infallible, like the pious Puritans who surrounded his youth. The work was ready when he died, and was published two years after. A tract on *Miracles*, written in 1702, also appeared posthumously. Fresh adverse criticism of the *Essay* was reported to him in his last year, and the book was formally condemned by the authorities at Oxford. "I take what has been done rather as a recommendation of the book," he wrote to his young friend Anthony Collins, "and when you and I next meet we shall be merry on the subject." One attack only moved him. In 1704 his adversary, Jonas Proast, revived their old controversy. Locke in consequence began a *Fourth Letter on Toleration*. A few pages, ending in an unfinished paragraph, exhausted his remaining strength; but the theme which had employed him at Oxford more than forty years before, and had been a ruling idea throughout the long interval, was still dominant in the last days of his life.

All the summer of 1704 he continued to decline, tenderly nursed by Lady Masham and her step-daughter Esther. On the 28th of October he died, according to his last recorded words, "in perfect charity with all men, and in sincere communion with the whole church of Christ, by whatever names Christ's followers call themselves." His grave is on the south side of the parish church of High Laver, in which he often worshipped, near the tombs of the Mashams, and of Damaris, the widow of Cudworth. At the distance of 1 m. are the garden and park where the manor house of Otes once stood.

Locke's writings have made his intellectual and moral features familiar. The reasonableness of taking probability as our guide in life was in the essence of his philosophy. The desire to see for himself what is true in the light of reasonable evidence, and that others should do the same, was his ruling passion, if the term can be applied to one so calm and judicial. "I can no more know anything by another man's understanding," he would say, "than I can see by another man's eyes." This repugnance to believe blindly what rested on arbitrary authority, as distinguished from what was seen to be sustained by self-evident reason, or by demonstration, or by good probable evidence, runs through his life. He is typically English in his reverence for facts, whether facts of sense or of living consciousness, in his aversion from abstract speculation and verbal reasoning, in his suspicion of mysticism, in his calm reasonableness, and in his ready submission to truth, even when truth was incapable of being fully reduced to system by man. The delight he took in exercising reason in regard to everything he did was what his friend Pierre Coste remarked in Locke's daily life at Otes. "He went about the most trifling things always with some good reason. Above all things he loved order; and he had got the way of observing it in everything with wonderful exactness. As he always kept the useful in his eye in all his disquisitions, he esteemed the employments of men only in proportion to the good they were capable of producing; for which cause he had no great value for the critics who waste their lives in composing words and phrases in coming to the choice of a various reading, in a passage that has after all nothing important in it. He cared yet less for those professed disputants, who, being taken up with the desire of coming off with victory, justify themselves behind the ambiguity of a word, to give their adversaries the more trouble. And whenever he had to deal with this sort of folks, if he did not beforehand take a strong resolution of keeping his temper, he quickly fell into a passion; for he was naturally choleric, but his anger never lasted long. If he retained any resentment it was against himself, for having given way to so ridiculous a passion; which, as he used to say, "may do a great deal of harm, but never yet did anyone the least good." Large, "round-about" common sense, intellectual strength directed by a virtuous purpose, not subtle or daring speculation sustained by an idealizing faculty, in which he was deficient, is what we find in Locke. Defect in speculative imagination appears when he encounters the vast and complex final problem of the universe in its organic unity.

Locke is apt to be forgotten now, because in his own generation he so well discharged the intellectual mission of initiating criticism of human knowledge, and of diffusing the spirit of free inquiry and universal toleration which has since profoundly affected the civilized world. He has not bequeathed an imposing system, hardly even a striking discovery in metaphysics, but he is a signal example in the Anglo-Saxon world of the love of attainable truth for the sake of truth and goodness. "If Locke made few discoveries, Socrates made none." But both are memorable in the record of human progress.

In the inscription on his tomb, prepared by himself, Locke refers to his books as a true representation of what he was. They are concerned with *Social Economy*, *Christianity*, *Education* and *Philosophy*, besides *Miscellaneous* writings.

I. SOCIAL ECONOMY.—(1) *Epistola de Tolerantia* (1689, translated into English in the same year). (2) *Two Treatises on Government* (1690) (the *Patriarcha* of Filmer, to which the *First Treatise* was a reply, appeared in 1680). (3) *A Second Letter concerning Toleration* (1690). (4) *Some Considerations on the Consequence of Lowering the Rate of Interest and Raising the Value of Money* (1691). (5) *A Third Letter for Toleration* (1692). (6) *Short Observations on a printed paper entitled, "For encouraging the Coining of Silver Money in England, and after for Keeping it here"* (1695). (7) *Further Considerations concerning Raising the Value of Money* (1695) (occasioned by a *Report* containing an "Essay for the Amendment of Silver Coins," published that year by William Lowndes, secretary for the Treasury). (8) *A Fourth Letter for Toleration* (1706, posthumous).

II. CHRISTIANITY.—(1) *The Reasonableness of Christianity as delivered in the Scriptures* (1695). (2) *A Vindication of the Reasonableness of Christianity from Mr Edwards's Reflections* (1695). (3) *A Second Vindication of the Reasonableness of Christianity* (1697). (4) *A Paraphrase and Notes on the Epistles of St Paul to the Galatians, First and Second Corinthians, Romans and Ephesians. To which is prefixed an Essay for the understanding of St Paul's Epistles by consulting St Paul himself* (1705–1707, posthumous). (5) *A Discourse of Miracles* (1716, posthumous).

III. EDUCATION.—(1) *Some Thoughts concerning Education* (1693). (2) *The Conduct of the Understanding* (1706, posthumous). (3) *Some Thoughts concerning Reading and Study for a Gentleman* (1706, posthumous). (4) *Instructions for the Conduct of a Young Gentleman* (1706, posthumous). (5) *Of Study* (written in France in Locke's journal, and published in L. King's *Life of Locke* in 1830).

IV. PHILOSOPHY.—(1) *An Essay concerning Human Understanding*, in four books (1690). (2) *A Letter to the Bishop of Worcester concerning some passages relating to Mr Locke's Essay of Human Understanding in a late Discourse of his Lordship's in Vindication of the Trinity* (1697). (3) *Mr Locke's Reply to the Bishop of Worcester's Answer to his Letter* (1697). (4) *Mr Locke's Reply to the Bishop of Worcester's Answer to his Second Letter* (1699). (5) *An Examination of Father Malebranche's Opinion of Seeing all Things in God* (1706, posthumous). (6) *Remarks upon Some of Mr Norris's Books, wherein he asserts Father Malebranche's Opinion of Seeing all Things in God* (1720, posthumous).

MISCELLANEOUS.—(1) *A New Method of a Common Place Book* (1686). This was Locke's first article in the *Bibliothèque* of Le Clerc; his other contributions to it are uncertain, except the *Epitome of the Essay*, in 1688). (2) *The Fundamental Constitutions of Carolina* (prepared in 1673 when Locke was Lord Shaftesbury's secretary at Exeter House, remarkable for recognition of the principle of toleration, published in 1706, in the posthumous collection). (3) *Memoirs relating to the Life of Anthony, First Earl of Shaftesbury* (1706). (4) *Elements of Natural Philosophy* (1706). (5) *Observations upon the Growth and Culture of Vines and Olives* (1706). (6) *Rules of a Society which met once a Week, for their improvement in Useful Knowledge, and for the Promotion of Truth and Christian Charity* (1706). (7) *A Letter from a Person of Quality to his Friend in the Country*, published in 1875 (included by Des Maizeaux in his *Collection of Several Pieces of Mr John Locke's*, 1720), and soon afterwards burned by the common hangman by orders from the House of Lords, was disavowed by Locke himself. It may have been dictated by Shaftesbury. There are also miscellaneous writings of Locke first published in the biographies of Lord King (1830) and of Mr Fox Bourne (1876).

Letters from Locke to Thoynard, Limborch, Le Clerc, Guenellon, Molyneux, Collins, Sir Isaac Newton, the first and the third Lord Shaftesbury, Lords Peterborough and Pembroke, Clarke of Chipley and others are preserved, many of them unpublished, most of them in the keeping of Lord Lovelace at Horsley Towers, and of Mr Sanford at Nynehead in Somerset, or in the British Museum. They express the gracious courtesy and playful humour which were natural to him, and his varied interests in human life.

I. *Social Economy*.—It has been truly said that all Locke's writings, even the *Essay on Human Understanding* itself, were occasional, and "intended directly to counteract the enemies of reason and freedom

belief is legitimately formed only by discernment of sufficient evidence; apart from evidence, a man has no right to control the understanding; he cannot determine arbitrarily what his neighbours must believe. Thus Locke's pleas for religious toleration resolve at last into his philosophical view of the foundation and limits of human knowledge.

II. *The Reasonableness of Christianity.*—The principles that governed Locke's social polity largely determined his attitude to Christianity. His "latitudinarianism" was the result of extraordinary reverence for truth, and a perception that knowledge may be sufficient for the purposes of human life while it falls infinitely short of speculative completeness. He never loses sight of essential reasonableness as the only ground on which Christian faith can ultimately rest. But Locke accepted Holy Scripture as infallible with the reverence of a Puritan. "It has God for its author, salvation for its end, and truth without any mixture of error for its matter." Yet he did not, like many Puritans, mean Scripture as interpreted by himself or by his sect. And faith in its infallibility was combined in Locke with deep distrust in "enthusiasm." This predisposed him to regard physical miracles as the solid criterion for distinguishing reasonable religious conviction from "inclinations, fancies and strong assurances." Assent in religion as in everything else he could justify only on the ground of its harmony with reason; professed "illumination without search, and certainty without proof" was to him a sign of absence of the divine spirit in the professor. Confidence that we are right, he would say, is in itself no proof that we are right: when God asks assent to the truth of a proposition in religion, he either shows us its intrinsic rationality by ordinary means, or he offers miraculous proof of the reality of which we need reasonable evidence. But we must know what we mean by miracle. Reasonableness, in short, must always at last be our guide. His own faith in Christianity rested on its moral excellence when it is received in its primitive simplicity, combined with the miracles which accompanied its original promulgation. But "even for those books which have the attestation of miracles to confirm their being from God, the miracles," he says, "are to be judged by the doctrine, and not the doctrine by the miracles." Miracles alone cannot vindicate the divinity of immoral doctrine. Locke's *Reasonableness of Christianity* was an attempt to recall religion from the crude speculations of theological sects, destructive of peace among Christians, to its original simplicity; but this is apt to conceal its transcendent mystery. Those who practically acknowledge the supremacy of Jesus as Messiah accept all that is essential to the Christianity of Locke. His own Christian belief, sincere and earnest, was more the outcome of the common sense which, largely through him, moulded the prudential theology of England in the 18th century, than of the nobler elements present in More, Cudworth and other religious thinkers of the preceding age, or afterwards in Law and Berkeley, Coleridge and Schleiermacher.

III. *Education.*—Locke has his place among classic writers on the theory and art of Education. His contribution may be taken as either an introduction to or an application of the *Essay on Human Understanding*. In the *Thoughts on Education* imaginative sentiment is never allowed to weigh against utility; information is subordinate to the formation of useful character; the part which habit plays in individuals is always kept in view; the dependence of intelligence and character, which it is the purpose of education to improve, upon health of body is steadily inculcated; to make children happy in undergoing education is a favourite precept; accumulating facts without exercising thought, and without accustoming the youthful mind to look for evidence, is always referred to as a cardinal vice. Wisdom more than much learning is what he requires in the teacher. In instruction he gives the first place to "that which may direct us to heaven," and the second to "the study of prudence, or discreet conduct, and management of ourselves in the several occurrences of our lives, which most assists our quiet prosperous passage through this present life." The infinity of real existence, in contrast with the necessary finitude of human understanding and experience, is always in his thoughts. This "disproportionateness" between the human mind and the universe of reality imposes deliberation in the selection of studies and disregard for those which lie out of the way of a wise man. Knowledge of what other men have thought is perhaps of too little account with Locke. "It is an idle and useless thing to make it one's business to study what have been other men's sentiments in matters where only reason is to be judge." In his *Conduct of the Understanding* the pupil is invited to occupy the point at which "a full view of all that relates to a question" is to be had, and at which alone a rational discernment of truth is possible. The uneducated mass of mankind, he complains, either "seldom reason at all," or "put passion in the place of reason," or "for want of large, sound, roundabout sense" they direct their minds only to one part of the evidence, "converse with one sort of men, read but one sort of books, and will not come in the hearing of but one sort of notions, and so carve out to themselves a little Goshen in the intellectual world, where light shines, and, as they conclude, day blesses them; but the rest of the vast expansion they give up to night and darkness, and avoid coming near it." Hasty judgment, bias, absence of an equal "indifference" to what the evidence may in the end require us to conclude, undue regard for authority, excessive love for custom and antiquity, indolence and sceptical despair are among the states of mind marked by him as most apt to interfere with the formation of beliefs in harmony with the Universal Reason that is active in the universe.

IV. *Philosophy.*—The *Essay Concerning Human Understanding* embodies Locke's philosophy. It was the first attempt on a great scale, and in the Baconian spirit, to estimate critically the certainty and the adequacy of human knowledge, when confronted with God and the universe.

The "Introduction" to the *Essay* is the keynote to the whole. The ill-fortune of men in their past endeavours to comprehend themselves and their environment is attributed in a great measure to their disposition to extend their inquiries into matters beyond the reach of human understanding. To inquire with critical care into "the original, certainty and extent of human knowledge, together with the grounds and degrees of belief, opinion and assent," is accordingly Locke's design in this *Essay*. Excluding from his enquiry "the physical consideration of the mind," he sought to make a faithful report, based on an introspective study of consciousness, as to how far a human understanding of the universe can reach. Although his report might show that our knowledge at its highest must be far short of a "universal or perfect comprehension of whatsoever is," it might still be "sufficient" for us, because "suited to our individual state." The "light of reason," the "candle of the Lord," that is set up in us may be found to shine bright enough for all *our* purposes. If human understanding cannot fully solve the infinite problem of the universe, man may at least see that at no stage of his finite experience is he necessarily the sport of chance, and that he can practically secure his own wellbeing.

The last book of the *Essay*, which treats of Knowledge and Probability, is concerned more directly than the three preceding ones with Locke's professed design. It has been suggested that Locke may have begun with this book. It contains few references to the foregoing parts of the *Essay*, and it might have appeared separately without being much less intelligible than it is. The other books, concerned chiefly with ideas and words, are more abstract, and may have opened gradually on his mind as he studied more closely the subject treated in the fourth book. For Locke saw that the ultimate questions about our knowledge and its extent *presuppose* questions about ideas. Without ideas knowledge is impossible. "Idea" is thus a leading term in the *Essay*. It is used in a way peculiar to himself—"the term which, I think, stands best for whatsoever is the object of the understanding when a man thinks" or "whatever it is which the mind can be employed about." But ideas themselves are, he reminds us, "neither true nor false, being nothing but bare appearances," phenomena as we might call them. Truth and falsehood belong only to assertions or denials concerning ideas, that is, to our interpretations of our ideas according to their mutual relations.

Innate ideas.

That none of our ideas are "innate" is the argument contained in the first book. This means that the human mind, before any ideas are present to it, is a *tabula rasa*: it needs the quickening of ideas to become intellectually alive. The inward purpose of this famous argument is apt to be overlooked. It has been criticized as if it was a speculative controversy between empiricism and intellectualism. For this Locke himself is partly to blame. It is not easy to determine the antagonist he had in view. Lord Herbert is referred to as a defender of innateness. Locke was perhaps too little read in the literature of philosophy to do full justice to those more subtle thinkers who, from Plato downwards, have recognised the need for categories of the understanding and presuppositions of reason in the constitution of knowledge. "Innate," Lord Shaftesbury says, "is a word Mr Locke poorly plays on." For the real question is not about the *time* when ideas entered the mind, but "whether the constitution of man be such that, being adult and grown up, the ideas of order and administration of a God will not infallibly and necessarily spring up in him." This Locke himself sometimes seems to allow. "That there are certain propositions," we find him saying, "which, though the soul from the beginning, or when a man is born, does not know, yet, by assistance from the outward senses, and the help of some previous cultivation, it may afterwards come certainly to know the truth of, is no more than what I have affirmed in my first book" ("Epistle to Reader," in second edition). And much of our knowledge, as he shows in the fourth book, is rational insight, immediate or else demonstrable, and thus intellectually necessary in its constitution.

What Locke really objects to is, that any of our supposed knowledge should claim immunity from free criticism. He argues in the first book against the innateness of our knowledge of God and of morality; yet in the fourth book he finds that the existence of God is demonstrable, being supported by causal necessity, without which there can be no knowledge; and he also maintains that morality is as demonstrable as pure mathematics. The positions are not inconsistent. The demonstrable rational necessity, instead of being innate, or conscious from our birth, may lie latent or subconscious in the individual mind; but for all that, when we gradually become more awake intellectually, such truths are seen to "carry their own evidence along with them." Even in the first book he appeals to the common reason, which he calls "common sense." "He would be thought void of common sense who asked, on the one side, or, on the other, went to give a reason, why 'it is impossible for the same thing to be and not to be.' It carries its own light and evidence with it, and needs no other proof. he that understands the terms assents to it for its own sake, or else nothing else will ever be able to prevail with him to do it" (bk. i. chap. 3. § 4).

The truth is that neither Locke, on the one hand, nor the intellectualists of the 17th century, on the other, expressed their meaning with enough of precision; if they had, Locke's argument would probably have taken a form less open to the charge of mere empiricism. Locke believed that in attacking "innate principles" he was pleading for universal reasonableness instead of blind reliance on authority, and was thus, as he says, not "pulling up the foundations of knowledge," but "laying those foundations surer." When men heard that there were propositions that could not be doubted, it was a short and easy way to assume that what are only arbitrary prejudices are "innate" certainties, and therefore must be accepted unconditionally. This "eased the lazy from the pains of search, stopped the inquiry of the doubtful, concerning all that was once styled innate. It was no small advantage to those who affected to be masters and teachers to make this the principle of principles—that principles must not be questioned." The assumption that they were "innate" was enough "to take men off the use of their own reason and judgment, and to put them upon believing and taking upon trust without further examination. . . . Nor is it a small power it gives one man over another to have the authority to make a man swallow that for an innate principle which may serve his purpose who teacheth them" (bk. i. chap. 4, § 24).

Genesis of ideas.

The second book proposes a hypothesis regarding the genesis of our ideas and closes after an elaborate endeavour to verify it. The hypothesis is, that all human ideas, even the most complex and abstract and sublime, ultimately depend upon "experience." Otherwise, what we take to be ideas are only empty words. Here the important point is what human "experience" involves. Locke says that our "ideas" all come, either from the five senses or from reflective consciousness; and he proposes to show that even those concerned with the Infinite depend at last on one or other of these two sources: our "complex ideas" are all made up of "simple ideas," either from without or from within. The "verification" of this hypothesis, offered in the thirteenth and following chapters of the second book, goes to show in detail that even those ideas which are "most abstruse," how remote soever they may seem from original data of outward sense, or of inner consciousness, "are only such as the understanding frames to itself by repeating and joining together simple ideas that it had at first, either from perceiving objects of sense, or from reflection upon its own operations."

To prove this, our thoughts of space, time, infinity, power, substance, personal identity, causality, and others which "seem most remote from the supposed original" are examined in a "plain historical method," and shown to depend either on (*a*) perception of things external, through the five senses, or on (*b*) reflection upon operations of the mind within. Reflection, "though it be not sense, as having nothing to do with external objects," is yet, he says, "very like it, and might properly enough be called internal sense." But the suggestion that "sense" might designate *both* the springs of experience is misleading, when we find in the sequel how much Locke tacitly credits "reflection" with. The ambiguity of his language makes opposite interpretations of this cardinal part of the *Essay* possible; the best we can do is to compare one part with another, and in doubtful cases to give him the benefit of the doubt.

Although the second book is a sort of inventory of our ideas, as distinguished from the certainty and boundaries of our knowledge, Locke even here makes the assumption that the "simple ideas" of the five senses are practically qualities of things which exist without us, and that the mental "operations" discovered by "reflection" are those of a person continuously existing. He thus relieves himself of the difficulty of having at the outset to explain *how* the immediate data of outward sense and reflection are accepted as "qualities" of things and persons. He takes this as a fact.

Such, according to Locke, are the only simple ideas which can appear even in the sublimest human speculations. But the mind, in becoming gradually stored with its "simple ideas" is able to elaborate them in numberless modes and relations; although it is not in the power of the most exalted wit or enlarged understanding to invent or frame any new simple idea, not taken in in one or the other of these two ways. All that man can imagine about the universe or about God is necessarily confined to them. For proof of this Locke would have any one try to fancy a taste which had never affected his palate, or to frame the idea of a scent he had never felt, or an operation of mind, divine or human, foreign to all human consciousness.

Qualities of matter.

The contrast and correlation of these two data of experience is suggested in the chapter on the "qualities of matter" in which we are introduced to a noteworthy vein of speculation (bk. ii. chap. 8). This chapter, on "things and their qualities," looks like an interpolation in an analysis of mere "ideas." Locke here treats simple ideas of the five senses as qualities of outward things. And the sense data are, he finds, partly (*a*) revelations of external things themselves in their mathematical relations, and partly (*b*) sensations, boundless in variety, which are somehow awakened in us through contact and collision with things relatively to their mathematical relations. Locke calls the former sort "primary, original or essential qualities [illegible]" and the others "secondary or derived qualities." The [illegible] which are quantities rather than qualities, are inseparable [illegible] and virtually identical with the ideas we have of them. [illegible], there is nothing perceived in the mathematical [illegible] which in the least resembles their secondary [illegible] there were no sentient beings in existence, the secondary [illegible] would cease to exist, "except perhaps as unknown modes [illegible] or, if not, as something still more obscure." On the [illegible], extension, figure and motion would," he [illegible] in the world as they are, whether there were any [illegible] to perceive them or not."

[illegible] of what Locke teaches about matter is, that [illegible] capable of being expressed in terms of mathematical [illegible] and also in terms of our own sensations. A [illegible] step was to suggest the ultimate dependence of the [illegible] bodies upon "the bulk, figures, number, [illegible] of the solid parts of which the bodies consist," [illegible] primary qualities "existing as we think of [illegible] they are perceived." This Locke proposes in a [illegible] "not knowing what particular size, figure [illegible] they are on which depend, and from which result, [illegible] make our complex idea, for example, of gold, it [illegible] know what other qualities result from, or [illegible] the same constitution of the insensible parts [illegible] consequently must always coexist with that com[illegible] else are inconsistent with it."

[illegible] remarkable chapters in the second book concern [illegible] instances" in verification of its funda[illegible] dependence of human knowledge upon the [illegible] our dual experience (bk. ii. ch. 13-28). [illegible] the ultimate mysteries which attract medi[illegible], that even our most profound and [illegible] all limited to data of the senses and of [illegible] the "modes" and "substances" and [illegible] in various degrees of complexity, we [illegible] to conceive those simple phenomena [illegible] space, and time and number, under [illegible] ourselves mentally impelled towards [illegible] innumerable—in a word, towards [illegible] quantity; then there is the [illegible] to which we find ourselves mysteri[illegible] phenomena of the senses come to be [illegible]; again there is the obscure [illegible], notwithstanding their constant [illegible] above all, the inevitable tendency we [illegible] into what we call its "Cause," [illegible] power. Locke begins with our [illegible] of Time, and Number. [illegible]

negative" idea. So for him the word substance means "only an uncertain supposition of we know not what." If one were to ask him what the substance is in which this colour and that taste or smell inhere, "he would find himself in a difficulty like that of the Indian, who, after saying that the world rested on an elephant, and the elephant on a broad-backed tortoise, could only suppose the tortoise to rest on 'Something, I know not what.'" The attempt to conceive it is like the attempt positively to conceive immensity or eternity: we are involved in an endless, ultimately incomprehensible, regress. We fail when we try either positively to phenomenalize substance or to dispense with the superphenomenal abstraction. Our only positive idea is of an aggregate of phenomena. And it is only thus, he says, that we can approach a positive conception of God, namely by "enlarging indefinitely some of the simple ideas we received from reflection." Why man must remain in this mental predicament, Locke did not inquire. He only reported the fact. He likewise struggled bravely to be faithful to fact in his report of the state in which we find ourselves when we try to conceive continued personal identity. The paradoxes in which he here gets involved illustrate this (bk. ii. ch. 27).

Causality.

Locke's thoughts about Causality and Active Power are especially noteworthy, for he rests our knowledge of God and of the external universe on those ultimate ideas. The intellectual demand for "the cause" of an event is what we find we cannot help having; yet it is a demand for what in the end the mind cannot fully grasp. Locke is content to trace the idea of "cause and effect," as far as mere natural science goes, to our "constant observation" that "qualities and finite substances begin to exist, and receive their existence from other beings which produce them." We find that this connexion is what gives intelligibility to countless and what seemed chaotic changes, converting them into the divinely concatenated system which we call the universe." Locke seems hardly to realize all that is implied in scientific prevision or expectation of change. Anything, as far as "constant observation" tells us, might a priori have been the natural cause of anything; and no finite number of "observed" sequences, *per se*, can guarantee universality and necessity. The idea of power, or active causation, on the other hand, "is got," he acknowledges, not through the senses, but "through our consciousness of our own voluntary agency, and therefore through reflection" (bk. ii. ch. 21). In bodies we observe no active agency, only a sustained natural order in the succession of passive sensuous phenomena. The true source of change in the material world must be analogous to what we are conscious of when we exert volition. Locke here unconsciously approaches the spiritual view of active power in the physical universe afterwards taken by Berkeley, forming the constructive principle of his philosophy.

Ideas and words.

Locke's book about Ideas leads naturally to his Third Book which is concerned with Words, or the sensible signs of ideas. Here he analyses "abstract ideas," and instructively illustrates the confusion apt to be produced in them by the inevitable imperfection of words. He unfolds the relations between verbal signs and the several sorts of ideas; words being the means for enabling us to treat ideas as typical, abstract and general. "Some parts of this third book," concerning Words, Locke tells his friend Molyneux, "though the thoughts were easy and clear enough, yet cost me more pains to express than all the rest of my *Essay*. And therefore I should not much wonder, if there be in some places of it obscurity and doubtfulness."

Theory of knowledge.

The Fourth Book, about Knowledge proper and Probability, closes the *Essay*. Knowledge, he says, is perception of relations among ideas; it is expressed in our affirmations and negations; and real knowledge is discernment of the relations of ideas to what is real. In the foregoing part of the *Essay* he had dealt with "ideas" and "simple apprehension," here he is concerned with intuitive "judgment" and demonstrative "reasoning," also with judgments and reasonings about matters of fact. At the end of this patient search among notions, he supposes the reader apt to complain that he has been "all this while only building a castle in the air," and to ask what the purpose of all this stir is, if we are not thereby carried beyond mere ideas. "[illegible] be true that knowledge lies only in the agreement or disagreement of ideas, the visions of an enthusiast and the reasonings of a sober man will be equally certain. [illegible] (bk. iv. 4.) [illegible]

[illegible]

reminding us. As regards kinds of knowledge, he finds that "all knowledge we are capable of" must be assertion or denial of some one of three sorts of relation among our ideas themselves, or else of relations between our ideas and reality that exists independently of us and our ideas. Accordingly, knowledge is concerned either with (*a*) relations of identity and difference among ideas, as when we say that "blue is not yellow"; or (*b*) with mathematical relations, as that "two triangles upon equal bases between two parallels must be equal"; or (*c*) in assertions that one quality does or does not coexist with another in the same substance, as that "iron is susceptible of magnetical impressions, or that ice is not hot"; or (*d*) with ontological reality, independent of our perceptions, as that "God exists" or "I exist" or "the universe exists." The first sort is analytical; mathematical and ethical knowledge represents the second; physical science forms the third; real knowledge of self, God and the world constitutes the fourth.

Four sorts of knowable relations.

Intuition and demonstration.

Locke found important differences in the way in which knowledge of any sort is reached. In some instances the known relation is self-evident, as when we judge intuitively that a circle cannot be a triangle, or that three must be more than two. In other cases the known relation is perceived to be intellectually necessary through the medium of premisses, as in a mathematical demonstration. All that is strictly knowledge is reached in these two ways. But there is a third sort, namely sense-perception, which hardly deserves the name. For "our perceptions of the particular existence of finite beings without us" go beyond mere probability, yet they are not purely rational. There is nothing self-contradictory in the supposition that our perceptions of things external are illusions, although we are somehow unable to doubt them We find ourselves inevitably "conscious of a different sort of perception," when we actually see the sun by day and when we only imagine the sun at night.

Locke next inquired to what extent knowledge—in the way either of intuitive certainty, demonstrative certainty, or sense perception—is possible, in regard to each of the four (already mentioned) sorts of knowable relation. There is only one of the four in which our knowledge is coextensive with our ideas. It is that of "identity and diversity", we cannot be conscious at all without distinguishing, and every affirmation necessarily implies negation. The second sort of knowable relation is sometimes intuitively and sometimes demonstrably discernible. Morality, Locke thinks, as well as mathematical quantity, is capable of being demonstrated. "Where there is no property there is no injustice," is an example of a proposition "as certain as any demonstration in Euclid." Only we are more apt to be biassed, and thus to leave reason in abeyance, in dealing with questions of morality than in dealing with problems in mathematics.

Turning from abstract mathematical and moral relations to concrete relations of coexistence and succession among phenomena—the third sort of knowable relation—Locke finds the light of pure reason disappear; although these relations form "the greatest and most important part of what we desire to know" Of these, including as they do all inductive science, he reports that demonstrable knowledge "is very short, if indeed we have any at all"; and are not thrown wholly on presumptions of probability, or else left in ignorance. Man cannot attain perfect and infallible science of bodies For natural science depends, he thinks, on knowledge of the relations between their secondary qualities on the one hand, and the mathematical qualities of their atoms on the other, or else "on something yet more remote from our comprehension." Now, as perception of these atoms and their relations is beyond us, we must be satisfied with inductive presumptions, for which "experimental verification" affords, after all, only conclusions that wider experience may prove to be inadequate. But this moral venture Locke accepts as "sufficient for our purposes."

Real existence.

Our knowledge under Locke's fourth category of relations—real existence—includes (*a*) intuitive perceptions of our own existence; (*b*) demonstrable certainty of the existence of God; and (*c*) actual perception of the existence of surrounding things, as long as, but only as long as the things are present to sense. "If I doubt all other things, that very doubt makes me perceive my own existence, and will not suffer me to doubt of that" (iv. 9. 3). Faith in the existence of God is virtually with Locke an expression of faith in the principle of active causality in its ultimate universality. Each person knows that he now exists, and is convinced that he had a beginning; with not less intuitive certainty he knows that "*nothing* can no more produce any real being than it can be equal to two right angles." His final conclusion is that there must be eternally "a most powerful and most knowing Being, in which, as the origin of all, must be contained all the perfections that can ever after exist," and out of which can come only what it has already in itself: so that as the cause of my mind, it must be Mind. There is thus causal necessity for Eternal Mind, or what we call "God" This is cautiously qualified thus in a letter to Anthony Collins, written by Locke a few months before he died: "Though I call the thinking faculty in me 'mind,' yet I cannot, because of that name, equal it in anything to that infinite and incomprehensible Being, which, for want of right and distinct conceptions, is called 'Mind' also." But the immanence of God in the things and persons that compose the universal order, with what this implies, is a conception foreign to Locke, whose habitual conception was of an extra-mundane deity, the dominant conception in the 18th century.

Knowledge of the external world.

Turning from our knowledge of Spirit to our knowledge of Matter, nearly all that one can affirm or deny about "things external is," according to Locke, not knowledge but venture or presumptive trust. We have, strictly speaking, no "knowledge" of real beings beyond our own self-conscious existence, the existence of God, and the existence of objects of sense as long as they are actually present to sense. "When I see an external object at a distance, a man for instance, I cannot but be satisfied of his existence while I am looking at him. (Locke might have added that when one only 'sees a man' it is merely his *visible* qualities that are perceived; his other qualities are as little 'actual present sensations' as if he were out of the range of sense.) But when the man leaves me alone, I cannot be certain that he still exists." "There is no necessary connexion between his existence a minute since (when he was present to any sense of sight) and his existence now (when he is absent from all my senses); by a thousand ways he may have ceased to be. I have not that certainty of his continued existence which we call knowledge; though the great likelihood of it puts it past doubt. But this is but probability and not knowledge" (chap. 11, § 9). Accordingly, purely rational science of external Nature is, according to Locke, impossible. All our "interpretations of nature" are inadequate; only reasonable probabilities, not final rational certainties. This boundless region affords at the best probabilities, ultimately grounded on moral faith, all beyond lies within the veil. Such is Locke's "plain, matter-of-fact" account of the knowledge of the Real that is open to man.

The rationale of probability.

We learn little from Locke as to the rationale of the probabilities on which man thus depends when he deals with the past, the distant or the future. The concluding chapters of the fourth book contain wise advice to those whose lives are passed in an ever-changing environment, for avoiding the frequent risk of error in their conclusions, with or without the help of syllogism, the office of which, as a means of discovery, is here critically considered.

Locke and Hume.

Investigation of the foundation of inductive inference was resumed by Hume where Locke left it. With a still humbler view of human reason than Locke's, Hume proposed as "a subject worthy of curiosity," to inquire into "the nature of that evidence which assures us of any real existence and matter of fact, *beyond* the present testimony of our senses and the records of our memory; a part of philosophy that has been little cultivated either by the ancients or the moderns." Hume argues that custom is a sufficient practical explanation of this gradual enlargement of our objective experience, and that no deeper explanation is open to man. All beyond each present transitory "impression" and the stores of memory is therefore reached blindly, through custom or habitual association. Associative tendency, individual or inherited, has since been the favourite constructive factor of human experience in Empirical Philosophy. This factor is not prominent in Locke's *Essay* A short chapter on "association of ideas" was added to the second book in the fourth edition. And the tendency to associate is there presented, not as the fundamental factor of human knowledge, but as a chief cause of human error.

Locke and Kant.

Kant's critical analysis of pure reason is more foreign to Locke than the attempts of 18th- and 19th-century associationists and evolutionists to explain experience and science. Kant's aim was to show the necessary rational constitution of experience. Locke's design was less profound. It was his distinction to present to the modern world, in his own "historical plain method," perhaps the largest assortment ever made by any individual of facts characteristic of human understanding. Criticism of the presuppositions implied in those facts—by Kant and his successors, and in Britain more unpretentiously by Reid, all under the stimulus of Hume's sceptical criticism—has employed philosophers since the author of the *Essay on Human Understanding* collected materials that raised deeper philosophical problems than he tried to solve. Locke's mission was to initiate modern criticism of the foundation and limits of our knowledge. Hume negatively, and the German and Scottish schools constructively, continued what it was Locke's glory to have begun.

Bibliography.—The *Essay concerning Human Understanding* has passed through more editions than any classic in modern philosophical literature. Before the middle of the 18th century it had reached thirteen, and it has now passed through some forty editions, besides being translated into Latin, French, Dutch, German and modern Greek. There are also several abridgments. In addition to those criticisms which appeared when Locke was alive, among the most important are Leibnitz's *Nouveaux Essais sur l'entendement humain*—written about 1700 and published in 1765, in which each chapter of the *Essay* of Locke is examined in a corresponding chapter by Leibnitz; Cousin's "École sensualiste: système de Locke," in his *Histoire de la philosophie au XVIIIe siècle* (1829); and the criticisms in T. H. Green's Introduction to the *Philosophical Works of Hume* (1874). The *Essay, with Prolegomena, biographical, critical and historical*, edited by Professor Campbell Fraser and published by the Oxford Clarendon Press in 1894, is the only annotated edition, unless the *Nouveaux Essais* of Leibnitz may be reduced to this category.

The *Letters on Toleration*, *Thoughts on Education* and *The*

Reasonableness of Christianity have also gone through many editions, and been translated into different languages.

The first collected edition of Locke's *Works* was in 1714, in three folio volumes. The best is that by Bishop Law, in four quartos (1777). The one most commonly known is in ten volumes (1812).

The *Eloge* of Jean le Clerc (*Bibliothèque choisie*, 1705) has been the basis of the memoirs of Locke prefixed to the successive editions of his *Works*, or contained in biographical dictionaries. In 1829 a *Life of Locke* (2nd ed. in two volumes, with considerable additions, 1830), was produced by Peter, 7th Baron King, a descendant of Locke's cousin, Anne Locke. This adds a good deal to what was previously known, as Lord King was able to draw from the mass of correspondence, journals and commonplace books of Locke in his possession. In the same year Dr Thomas Foster published some interesting letters from Locke to Benjamin Furly. The most copious account of the life is contained in the two volumes by H. R. Fox-Bourne (1876), the results of laborious research among the Shaftesbury Papers, Locke MSS. in the British Museum, the Public Record Office, the Lambeth, Christ Church and Bodleian libraries, and in the Remonstrants' library at Amsterdam. Monographs on Locke by T. H. Fowler in 1880, in "English Men of Letters," and by Fraser, in 1890, in Blackwood's "Philosophical Classics" may be mentioned; also addresses by Sir F. Pollock and Fraser at the bicentenary commemoration by the British Academy of Locke's death, published in the *Proceedings* of the Academy (1904). See also C. Bastide, *John Locke: ses théories politiques et leur influence en Angleterre* (Paris, 1907); H. Ollion, *La Philosophie générale de J. L.* (1909). (A. C. F.)

LOCKE, MATTHEW (*c.* 1630–1677), English musician, perhaps the earliest English writer for the stage, was born at Exeter, where he became a chorister in the cathedral. His music, written with Christopher Gibbons (son of Orlando Gibbons), for Shirley's masque *Cupid and Death*, was performed in London in 1653. He wrote some music for Davenant's *Siege of Rhodes* in 1656; and in 1661 was appointed composer in ordinary to Charles II. During the following years he wrote a number of anthems for the Chapel Royal, and excited some criticism on the score of novelty, to which he replied with considerable heat (*Modern Church Music; pre-accused, censured and obstructed in its Performance before His Majesty, April 1st, 1666*, [illegible] copies in the Fitzwilliam Museum, Cambridge, and the Royal College of Music). A good deal of music for the theatre followed, the most important being for Davenant's productions of *The Tempest* (1667) and of *Macbeth* (1672), but some doubt as to this latter has arisen, Purcell, Eccles or Leveridge, being [illegible] credited with it. He also composed various songs and [illegible] pieces, and published some curious works on musical [illegible]. He died in August 1677, an elegy being written by Purcell.

[illegible], a municipal and police burgh of Dumfriesshire, [illegible] the district of Annandale, 14½ m. E.N.E. of Dumfries [illegible] railway. Pop. (1901) 2358. It has long been [illegible] cattle and sheep sales, but more particularly [illegible] lamb fair, the largest in Scotland, at which [illegible] lambs have been sold. The town hall and [illegible] are in the Scottish Baronial style. The police [illegible] accommodated in an ancient square tower, [illegible] of the Johnstones, for a long period the [illegible] whose protection the town gradually grew [illegible] about 2 m. to the W., a bloody encounter [illegible] between the Johnstones and Maxwells, [illegible] pursued into Lockerbie and almost exter[illegible] "Lockerbie Lick" became a proverbial [illegible] an overwhelming defeat.

[illegible] FREDERICK (1821–1895), English man [illegible] on the 29th of May 1821, at Greenwich [illegible] who was Civil Commissioner of the [illegible] Hawke Locker, youngest son of that [illegible] who gave Nelson the memorable [illegible] and beat him." His mother, [illegible] was a daughter of the Rev. [illegible] and friend of George Washing[illegible] Frederick Locker began life [illegible] deserting this uncongenial [illegible] Somerset House, whence he [illegible] private [illegible] at the [illegible] of Lady Augusta Stanley. After his marriage he left the Civil Service, in consequence of ill-health. In 1857 he published *London Lyrics*, a slender volume of 90 pages, which, with subsequent extensions, constitutes his poetical legacy. *Lyra Elegantiarum* (1867), an anthology of light and familiar verse, and *Patchwork* (1879), a book of extracts, were his only other publications. In 1872 Lady Charlotte Locker died. Two years later Locker married Miss Hannah Jane Lampson, the only daughter of Sir Curtis Miranda Lampson, Bart., of Rowfant, Sussex, and in 1885 took his wife's surname. At Rowfant he died on the 30th of May 1895. Chronic ill-health debarred Locker from any active part in life, but it did not prevent his delighting a wide circle of friends by his gifts as a host and *raconteur*, and from accumulating many treasures as a connoisseur. His books are catalogued in the volume called the *Rowfant Library* (1886), to which an appendix (1900) was added, after his death, under the superintendence of his eldest son. As a poet, Locker belongs to the choir who deal with the gay rather than the grave in verse—with the polished and witty rather than the lofty or emotional. His good taste kept him as far from the broadly comic on the one side as his kind heart saved him from the purely cynical on the other. To something of Prior, of Praed and of Hood he added qualities of his own which lent his work distinction—a distinction in no wise diminished by his unwearied endeavour after directness and simplicity.

A posthumous volume of Memoirs, entitled *My Confidences* (1896), and edited by his son-in-law, Mr Augustine Birrell, gives an interesting idea of his personality and a too modest estimate of his gifts as a poet. (A. D.)

LOCKHART, GEORGE (1673–1731), of Carnwath, Scottish writer and politician, was a member of a Lanarkshire family tracing descent from Sir Simon Locard (the name being originally territorial, de Loch Ard), who is said to have accompanied Sir James Douglas on his expedition to the East with the heart of Bruce, which relic, according to Froissart, Locard brought home from Spain when Douglas fell in battle against the Moors, and buried in Melrose Abbey; this incident was the origin of the "man's heart within a fetterlock" borne on the Lockhart shield, which in turn perhaps led to the altered spelling of the surname. George Lockhart's grandfather was Sir James Lockhart of Lee (d. 1674), a lord of the court of session with the title of Lord Lee, who commanded a regiment at the battle of Preston. Lord Lee's eldest son, Sir William Lockhart of Lee (1621–1675), after fighting on the king's side in the Civil War, attached himself to Oliver Cromwell, whose niece he married, and by whom he was appointed commissioner for the administration of justice in Scotland in 1652, and English ambassador at the French court in 1656, where he greatly distinguished himself by his successful diplomacy. Lord Lee's second son, Sir George Lockhart (*c.* 1630–1689), was lord-advocate in Cromwell's time, and was celebrated for his persuasive eloquence; in 1674, when he was disbarred for alleged disrespect to the court of session in advising an appeal to parliament, fifty barristers showed their sympathy for him by withdrawing from practice. Lockhart was readmitted in 1676, and became the leading advocate in political trials, in which he usually appeared for the defence. He was appointed lord-president of the court of session in 1685; and was shot in the streets of Edinburgh on the 31st of March 1689 by John Chiesley, against whom the lord-president had adjudicated a cause. Sir George Lockhart purchased the extensive estates of the earls of Carnwath in Lanarkshire, which were inherited by his eldest son, George, whose mother was Philadelphia, daughter of Lord Wharton.

George Lockhart, who was member for the city of Edinburgh in the Scottish parliament, was appointed a commissioner for arranging the union with England in 1705. After the union he continued to represent Edinburgh, and later the Wigton burghs. His sympathies were with the Jacobites, whom he kept informed of all the negotiations for the union; in 1713 he took part in an abortive movement aiming at the repeal of the union. He was deeply implicated in the rising of 1715, the preparations for which he assisted at Carnwath and at Dryden, his Edinburgh residence. He was imprisoned in Edinburgh castle, but probably, through the favour of the duke of Argyll, he was released without being brought to trial; but his brother Philip was taken prisoner at the battle of Preston and condemned to be shot, the sentence being executed on the 2nd of December 1715. After his liberation Lockhart became a secret agent of the Pretender; but his correspondence with the prince fell into the hands of the government in 1727, compelling him to go into concealment at Durham until he was able to escape abroad. Argyll's influence was again exerted in Lockhart's behalf, and in 1728 he was permitted to return to Scotland, where he lived in retirement till his death in a duel on the 17th of December 1731. Lockhart was the author of *Memoirs of the Affairs of Scotland*, dealing with the reign of Queen Anne till the union with England, first published in 1714. These *Memoirs*, together with Lockhart's correspondence with the Pretender, and one or two papers of minor importance, were published in two volumes in 1817, forming the well-known "Lockhart Papers," which are a valuable authority for the history of the Jacobites.

Lockhart married Eupheme Montgomerie, daughter of Alexander, 9th earl of Eglinton, by whom he had a large family. His grandson James, who assumed his mother's name of Wishart in addition to that of Lockhart, was in the Austrian service during the Seven Years' War, and was created a baron and count of the Holy Roman Empire. He succeeded to the estates of Lee as well as of Carnwath, both of which properties passed, on the death of his son Charles without issue in 1802, to his nephew Alexander, who was created a baronet in 1806.

See *The Lockhart Papers* (2 vols., London, 1817); Andrew Lang, *History of Scotland* (4 vols., London, 1900). For the story of Sir Simon Lockhart's adventures with the heart of the Bruce, see Sir Walter Scott's *The Talisman*. (R. J. M.)

LOCKHART, JOHN GIBSON (1794–1854), Scottish writer and editor, was born on the 14th of July 1794 in the manse of Cambusnethan in Lanarkshire, where his father, Dr John Lockhart, transferred in 1796 to Glasgow, was minister. His mother, who was the daughter of the Rev. John Gibson, of Edinburgh, was a woman of considerable intellectual gifts. He was sent to the Glasgow high school, where he showed himself clever rather than industrious. He fell into ill-health, and had to be removed from school before he was twelve; but on his recovery he was sent at this early age to Glasgow University, and displayed so much precocious learning, especially in Greek, that he was offered a Snell exhibition at Oxford. He was not fourteen when he entered Balliol College, where he acquired a great store of knowledge outside the regular curriculum. He read French, Italian, German and Spanish, was interested in classical and British antiquities, and became versed in heraldic and genealogical lore. In 1813 he took a first class in classics in the final schools. For two years after leaving Oxford he lived chiefly in Glasgow before settling to the study of Scottish law in Edinburgh, where he was called to the bar in 1816. A tour on the continent in 1817, when he visited Goethe at Weimar, was made possible by the kindness of the publisher Blackwood, who advanced money for a promised translation of Schlegel's *Lectures on the History of Literature*, which was not published until 1838. Edinburgh was then the stronghold of the Whig party, whose organ was the *Edinburgh Review*, and it was not till 1817 that the Scottish Tories found a means of expression in *Blackwood's Magazine*. After a somewhat hum-drum opening, *Blackwood* suddenly electrified the Edinburgh world by an outburst of brilliant criticism. John Wilson (Christopher North) and Lockhart had joined its staff in 1817. Lockhart no doubt took his share in the caustic and aggressive articles which marked the early years of *Blackwood*; but his biographer, Mr Andrew Lang, brings evidence to show that he was not responsible for the virulent articles on Coleridge and on "The Cockney School of Poetry," that is on Leigh Hunt, Keats and their friends. He has been persistently accused of the later *Blackwood* article (August 1818) on Keats, but he showed at any rate a real appreciation of Coleridge and Wordsworth. He contributed to *Blackwood* many spirited translations of Spanish ballads, which in 1823 were published separately. In 1818 the brilliant and handsome young man attracted the notice of Sir Walter Scott, and the acquaintance soon ripened into an intimacy which resulted in a marriage between Lockhart and Scott's eldest daughter Sophia, in April 1820. Five years of domestic happiness followed, with winters spent in Edinburgh and summers at a cottage at Chiefswood, near Abbotsford, where Lockhart's two eldest children, John Hugh and Charlotte, were born; a second son, Walter, was born later at Brighton. In 1820 John Scott, the editor of the *London Magazine*, wrote a series of articles attacking the conduct of *Blackwood's Magazine*, and making Lockhart chiefly responsible for its extravagances. A correspondence followed, in which a meeting between Lockhart and John Scott was proposed, with Jonathan Henry Christie and Horace Smith as seconds. A series of delays and complicated negotiations resulted early in 1821 in a duel between Christie and John Scott, in which Scott was killed. This unhappy affair, which has been the subject of much misrepresentation, is fully discussed in Mr Lang's book on Lockhart.

Between 1818 and 1825 Lockhart worked indefatigably. In 1819 *Peter's Letters to his Kinsfolk* appeared, and in 1822 he edited Peter Motteux's edition of *Don Quixote*, to which he prefixed a life of Cervantes. Four novels followed: *Valerius* in 1821, *Some Passages in the Life of Adam Blair, Minister of Gospel at Cross Meikle* in 1822, *Reginald Dalton* in 1823 and *Matthew Wald* in 1824. But his strength did not lie in novel writing, although the vigorous quality of *Adam Blair* has been recognized by modern critics. In 1825 Lockhart accepted the editorship of the *Quarterly Review*, which had been in the hands of Sir John Taylor Coleridge since Gifford's resignation in 1824. He had now established his literary position, and, as the next heir to his unmarried half-brother's property in Scotland, Milton Lockhart, he was sufficiently independent, though he had abandoned the legal profession. In London he had great social success, and was recognized as a brilliant editor. He contributed largely to the *Quarterly Review* himself, his biographical articles being especially admirable. He showed the old railing spirit in an amusing but violent article in the *Quarterly* on Tennyson's *Poems* of 1833, in which he failed to discover the mark of genius. He continued to write for *Blackwood*; he produced for *Constable's Miscellany* in 1828 what remains the most charming of the biographies of Burns; and he undertook the superintendence of the series called "Murray's Family Library," which he opened in 1829 with a *History of Napoleon*. But his chief work was the *Life of Sir Walter Scott* (7 vols., 1837–1838; 2nd ed., 10 vols., 1839). There were not wanting those in Scotland who taxed Lockhart with ungenerous exposure of his subject, but to most healthy minds the impression conveyed by the biography was, and is, quite the opposite. Carlyle did justice to many of its excellencies in a criticism contributed to the *London and Westminster Review* (1837). Lockhart's account of the transactions between Scott and the Ballantynes and Constable caused great outcry; and in the discussion that followed he showed unfortunate bitterness by his pamphlet, "The Ballantyne Humbug handled." The *Life of Scott* has been called, after Boswell's *Johnson*, the most admirable biography in the English language. The proceeds, which were considerable, Lockhart resigned for the benefit of Scott's creditors.

The close of Lockhart's life was saddened by family bereavement, resulting in his own breakdown in health and spirits. His eldest boy (the suffering "Hugh Littlejohn" of Scott's *Tales of a Grandfather*) died in 1831; Scott himself in 1832; Mrs Lockhart in 1837; and the surviving son, Walter Lockhart, in 1852. Resigning the editorship of the *Quarterly Review* in 1853, he spent the next winter in Rome, but returned to England without recovering his health; and being taken to Abbotsford by his daughter Charlotte, who had become Mrs James Robert Hope-Scott, he died there on the 25th of November 1854. He was buried in Dryburgh Abbey, near Sir Walter Scott.

Lockhart's *Life* (2 vols., London and New York, 1897) was written by Andrew Lang. A. W. Pollard's edition of the *Life of Scott* (1900) is the best.

[illegible], SIR WILLIAM STEPHEN ALEXANDER (1841– [illegible]), [illegible] general, was born in Scotland on the [illegible] of [illegible] 1841, his father being a Lanarkshire clergyman. He entered the Indian army in 1858, in the Bengal native infantry. He served in the Indian Mutiny, the Bhutan campaign (1864–66), the [illegible] expedition (1867–68, mentioned in despatches), the Hazara Black Mountain expedition (1868–69, mentioned in despatches). From 1869 to 1879 he acted as deputy-assistant and assistant quartermaster-general in Bengal. In 1877 he was [illegible] with the Dutch army in Acheen. He served in the Afghan War of 1878–80, was mentioned in despatches and made a C.B., and from 1880 to 1885 was D.Q.G. in the intelligence branch at headquarters. He commanded a brigade in the [illegible] Burmese War (1886–87), and was made K.C.B., C.S.I., and [illegible] the thanks of the government. An attack of fever brought him to England, where he was employed as assistant military secretary for Indian affairs, but in 1890 he returned to India in the command of the Punjab frontier force, and for five years was engaged in various expeditions against the hill tribes. After the Waziristan campaign in 1894–95 he was made K.C.S.I. He became [illegible] general in 1896, and in 1897 he was given the command against the Afridis and Mohmands, and conducted the difficult Tirah campaign with great skill. He was made [illegible] and in 1898 became commander-in-chief in India. He died on the 18th of March 1900. Sir William Lockhart was not only a first-rate soldier, but also had a great gift for dealing with the native tribesmen. Among the latter he had the [illegible] of [illegible] on account of their respect and affection for him.

LOCK HAVEN, a city and the county-seat of Clinton county, Pennsylvania, U.S.A., on the west branch of the Susquehanna river, near the mouth of Bald Eagle Creek, about 70 m. N.N.W. of Harrisburg. Pop. [illegible] [illegible] foreign-born and 122 negroes; [illegible] [illegible] is served by branches of the Pennsylvania and the New York Central & Hudson River railways and by electric interurban railways. The city is pleasantly situated in an agricultural region, and there are large deposits of cement and of fire-brick clay in the vicinity. Lock Haven is the seat of the Central State Normal School (opened 1877), and has a public library and a hospital. There are various manufactures. The municipality owns and operates the water-works. The locality was settled in [illegible]. A town was founded in 1833, the Pennsylvania Canal [illegible] was completed to this point in 1834, and the name of the place was suggested by two canal locks and the harbour, or haven, for rafts in the river. Lock Haven was made the county-seat immediately after the erection of Clinton county in [illegible], was incorporated as a borough in [illegible], and was chartered as a city in 1870.

LOCKPORT, a city of [illegible] county, Illinois, U.S.A., on the Des Plaines river and the Illinois & Michigan Canal, and the [illegible] of the Chicago Sanitary [illegible] Drainage Canal, about [illegible] m. S.W. of Chicago and [illegible] m. N.N.E. of Joliet. Pop. (1900) [illegible] foreign-born and [illegible] negroes); (1910) 2555. [illegible] is served by the Chicago & Alton, and the Atchison, Topeka & Santa Fe railways, and by the Chicago & Joliet Electric [illegible] [illegible] country, and there are [illegible] of the Des Plaines river. [illegible] trade, especially in grain. [illegible] in 1837 the site was [illegible] Illinois & Michigan Canal and a [illegible] in 1853, and was [illegible] work was begun on the [illegible] works are here and [illegible] the 40 ft. fall between [illegible] with cheap power and has [illegible] commercial city.

LOCKPORT, a city [illegible] seat of Niagara county, [illegible] N. by E. of [illegible] 1881, of [illegible] (1910 [illegible] & [illegible] ay (electric interurban), and by the Erie Canal. The city owes its name to the five double locks of the canal, which here falls 66 ft. (over a continuation of the Niagara escarpment locally known as "Mountain Ridge") from the level of Lake Erie to that of the Genesee river. In 1909 a scheme was on foot to replace these five locks by a huge lift lock and to construct a large harbour immediately W. of the city. The surplus water from Tonawanda Creek, long claimed both by the Canal and by the Lockport manufacturers, after supplying the canal furnishes water-power, and electric power is derived from Niagara. The factory products, mostly paper and wood-pulp, flour and cereal foods, and foundry and machine-shop products, were valued in 1905 at $5,807,980. Lockport lies in a rich farming and fruit (especially apple and pear) country, containing extensive sandstone and Niagara limestone quarries, and is a shipping point for the fruits and grains and the limestone and sandstone of the surrounding country. Many buildings in the business part of the city are heated by the Holly distributing system, which pipes steam from a central station or plant, and originated in Lockport. The city owns and operates the water-works, long operated under the Holly system, which, as well as the Holly distributing system, was devised by Birdsill Holly, a civil engineer of Lockport. In 1909 a new system was virtually completed, water being taken from the Niagara river at Tonawanda and pumped thence to a stand-pipe in Lockport.

The site, that of the most easterly village in New York state held by the Neutral Nation of Indians, was part of the tract bought by the Holland Company in 1792–1793. Subsequently most of the land on which the city stands was bought from the Holland Company by Esek Brown, the proprietor of a local tavern, and fourteen others, but there were few settlers until after 1820. In 1822 the place was made the county-seat, and in 1823 it was much enlarged by the settlement here of workmen on the Erie Canal, and was the headquarters for a time of the canal contractors. It was incorporated as a village in 1829; was reached by the Erie railway in 1852, and in 1865 was chartered as a city.

LOCKROY, ÉDOUARD (1838–), French politician, son of Joseph Philippe Simon (1803–1891), an actor and dramatist who took the name of Lockroy, was born in Paris on the 18th of July 1838. He had begun by studying art, but in 1860 enlisted as a volunteer under Garibaldi. The next three years were spent in Syria as secretary to Ernest Renan, and on his return to Paris he embarked in militant journalism against the second empire in the *Figaro*, the *Diable à quatre*, and eventually in the *Rappel*, with which his name was thenceforward intimately connected. He commanded a battalion during the siege of Paris, and in February 1871 was elected deputy to the National Assembly where he sat on the extreme left and protested against the preliminaries of peace. In March he signed the proclamation for the election of the Commune, and resigned his seat as deputy. Arrested at Vanves he remained a prisoner at Versailles and Chartres until June when he was released without being tried. He was more than once imprisoned for violent articles in the press, and in 1872 for a duel with Paul de Cassagnac. He was returned to the Chamber in 1873 as Radical deputy for Bouches-du-Rhône in 1876, 1877 and 1881 for Aix, and in 1881 he was also elected in the 11th arrondissement of Paris. He elected to sit for Paris, and was repeatedly re-elected. During the elections of 1893 he was shot at by a cab-driver poet named Moore, but was not seriously injured. For the first ten years of his parliamentary life he voted consistently with the extreme left, but then adopted a more opportunist policy, and gave his unreserved support to the Brisson ministry of 1885. In the new Freycinet cabinet formed in January he held the portfolio of commerce and industry, which he retained in the Goblet ministry of 1886–1887. In 1885 he had been returned at the head of the poll for Paris, and his inclusion in the Freycinet ministry was taken to indicate a prospect of reconciliation between Parisian Radicalism and official Republicanism. During his tenure of the portfolio of commerce and industry he made the preliminary arrangements for the Exposition of 1889, and in a witty letter he defended the erection of the Tour Eiffel against artistic Paris. After the Panama and Boulangist scandals he became one of the leading politicians of the Radical party. He was vice-president of the Chamber in 1894 and in 1895, when he became minister of marine under Léon Bourgeois. His drastic measures of reform alarmed moderate politicians, but he had the confidence of the country, and held the same portfolio under Henri Brisson (1898) and Charles Dupuy (1898–1899). He gave his support to the Waldeck-Rousseau Administration, but actively criticized the marine policy of Camille Pelletan in the Combes ministry of 1902–1905, during which period he was again vice-president of the Chamber. M. Lockroy was a persistent and successful advocate of a strong naval policy, in defence of which he published *La Marine de Guerre* (1890), *Six mois rue Royale* (1897), *La Défense navale* (1900), *Du Weser à la Vistula* (1901), *Les Marines française et allemande* (1904), *Le Programme naval* (1906). His other works include *M. de Moltke et la guerre future* (1891) and *Journal d'une bourgeoise pendant la Révolution* (1881) derived from the letters of his great-grandmother. M. Lockroy married in 1877 Madame Charles Hugo, the daughter-in-law of the poet.

LOCKWOOD, SIR FRANK (1846–1897), English lawyer, was born at Doncaster. His grandfather and great-grandfather were mayors of Doncaster, and the former for some years filled the office of judge on the racecourse. He was educated at a private school, at Manchester grammar school, and Caius College, Cambridge. Called to the bar at Lincoln's Inn in 1872, he joined the old midland circuit, afterwards going to the north-eastern, making in his first year 120 guineas and in the next 265 guineas. From that time he had a career of uninterrupted success. In 1882 he was made a queen's counsel, in 1884 he was made recorder of Sheffield, and in 1894 he became solicitor-general in Lord Rosebery's ministry, and was knighted, having first entered parliament as Liberal member for York in 1885, after two unsuccessful attempts, the one at King's Lynn in 1880, the other at York in 1883. He was solicitor-general for less than a year. In 1896 Lord Chief Justice Coleridge, Mr Montague Crackanthorpe and Sir Frank Lockwood went to the United States to attend, as specially invited representatives of the English bar, the nineteenth meeting of the American Bar Association. On this trip Sir Frank Lockwood sustained the reputation which he enjoyed in England as a humorous after-dinner speaker, and helped to strengthen the bond of friendship which unites the bench and bar of the United States with the bench and bar of England. He died in London on the 18th of December 1897. Lockwood had considerable talent for drawing, inherited from his father, which he employed, chiefly for the amusement of himself and his friends, in the making of admirable caricatures in pen and ink, and of sketches of humorous incidents, real or imaginary, relating to the topic nearest at hand. An exhibition of them was held soon after his death.

See Augustine Birrell's biography of Lockwood and *The Frank Lockwood Sketch-Book* (1898).

LOCKWOOD, WILTON (1861–), American artist, was born at Wilton, Connecticut, on the 12th of September 1861. He was a pupil and an assistant of John La Farge, and also studied in Paris, becoming a well-known portrait and flower painter. He became a member of the Society of American Artists (1898), and of the Copley Society, Boston, and an associate of the National Academy of Design, New York.

LOCKYER, SIR JOSEPH NORMAN (1836–), English astronomer, was born at Rugby on the 17th of May 1836. After completing his education on the Continent of Europe, he obtained a clerkship in the War Office in 1857. His leisure was devoted to the study of astronomy, and he was appointed in 1870 secretary to the duke of Devonshire's royal commission on science. In 1875 he was transferred to the Science and Art Department at South Kensington, and on the foundation of the Royal College of Science he became director of the solar physics observatory and professor of astronomical physics. Eight British government expeditions for observing total solar eclipses were conducted by him between 1870 and 1905. On the 26th of October 1868 he communicated to the Paris Academy of Sciences, almost simultaneously with Dr P. J. C. Janssen, a spectroscopic method for observing the solar prominences in daylight, and the names of both astronomers appear on a medal which was struck by the French government in 1872 to commemorate the discovery. Lockyer was elected a fellow of the Royal Society in 1869, and received the Rumford medal in 1874. He initiated in 1866 the spectroscopic observation of sunspots; applied Doppler's principle in 1869 to determine the radial velocities of the chromospheric gases; and successfully investigated the chemistry of the sun from 1872 onward. Besides numerous contributions to the *Proceedings* of the Royal and the Royal Astronomical Societies, he published several books, both explanatory and speculative. The *Chemistry of the Sun* (1887) is an elaborate treatise on solar spectroscopy based on the hypothesis of elemental dissociation through the intensity of solar heat. The *Meteoritic Hypothesis* (1890) propounds a comprehensive scheme of cosmical evolution, which has evoked more dissent than approval, while the *Sun's Place in Nature* (1897) lays down the lines of a classification of the stars, depending upon their supposed temperature-relations. Among Lockyer's other works are—*The Dawn of Astronomy* (1894), to which *Stonehenge and other British Stone Monuments astronomically considered* (1906) may be considered a sequel; *Recent and coming Eclipses* (1897); and *Inorganic Evolution* (1900). He was created K.C.B. in 1897, and acted as president of the British Association in 1903–1904. His fifth son, William James Stewart Lockyer (b. 1868), devoted himself to solar research, and became chief assistant in the Solar Physics Observatory, South Kensington.

LOCLE, LE, a town in the Swiss canton of Neuchâtel, 24 m. by rail N. of Neuchâtel, and 5 m. S.W. of La Chaux de Fonds. It is built (3035 ft. above the sea-level) on the Bied stream in a valley of the Jura, and is about 1 m. from the French frontier. In 1681 Daniel Jean Richard introduced watch-making here, which soon drove out all other industries. In 1900 the population was 12,559, mainly Protestants and French-speaking. The church tower dates from 1521, but the old town was destroyed by fire in 1833. The valley in which the town is situated used to be subject to inundations, but in 1805 a tunnel was constructed by means of which the surplus waters of the Bied are carried into the Doubs. About 1 m. W. of the town the Bied plunged into a deep chasm, on the steep rock face of which were formerly the subterranean mills of the Col des Roches, situated one above another; but the stream is now diverted by the above-mentioned tunnel, while another serves the railway line from Le Locle to Morteau in France (8 m.). (W. A. B. C.)

LOCMARIAQUER, a village of western France, on the W. shore of the Gulf of Morbihan, in the department of Morbihan, 8½ m. S. of Auray by road. Pop. (1906) 756. Locmariaquer has a small port, and oyster culture is carried on close to it. Roman remains are to be seen, but the place owes its celebrity to the megalithic monuments in the vicinity, some of which are among the largest extant. The menhir of Men-er-H'roeck (Fairy stone), which was broken into four pieces by lightning in the 18th century, previously measured about 67 ft. in height, and from 9 to 13 ft. in thickness.

LOCOMOTOR ATAXIA (Gr. ἀ, priv., and τάξις, order; synonyms, *Tabes dorsalis, posterior spinal sclerosis*), a progressive degeneration of the nervous system, involving the posterior columns of the spinal cord with other structures, and causing muscular incoordination and disorder of gait and station. The essential symptoms of the disease—stamping gait, and swaying with the eyes shut, the occurrence of blindness and of small fixed pupils—were recognized by Romberg (1851), but it was the clinical genius of Duchenne and his masterly description of the symptoms which led to its acceptance as a definite disease (1858), and he named it locomotor ataxia after its most striking symptom. In 1869 Argyll Robertson discovered that the eye-pupil is inactive to light but acts upon accommodation in the great majority of cases. This most important sign is named the "Argyll Robertson pupil." With an ever-increasing knowledge of the widespread character of this disease and its manifold variation-in the complex of symptoms, the tendency among neurologists is to revert to the term employed by Romberg—*tabes dorsalis*. "Locomotor ataxia," although it expresses a very characteristic feature of the disease, has this objection: it is a symptom which does not occur in the first (preataxic) stage of the disease; indeed a great number of years may elapse before ataxy comes on, and sometimes the patient, after suffering a very long time from the disease, may die from some intercurrent complication, having never been ataxic.

It is generally recognized by neurologists that persons who are not the subjects of acquired or hereditary syphilis do not suffer from this disease; and the average time of onset after infection is ten years (see NEUROPATHOLOGY). There are three stages: (1) The preataxic, (2) the ataxic, (3) the bed-ridden paralytic. The duration of the first stage may be from one or two years, up to twenty years or even longer. In this stage various symptoms may arise. The patient usually complains of shooting, lightning-like pains in the legs, which he may attribute to rheumatism. If a physician examines him he will almost certainly find the knee-jerks absent and Argyll Robertson pupils present; probably on inquiry he will ascertain that the patient has had some difficulty in starting urination, or that he is unable to retain his water or to empty his bladder completely. In other cases, temporary or permanent paralysis of one or more muscles of the eyeball (which causes squint and double vision), a failure of sight ending in blindness, attacks of vomiting (or gastric crises), painless spontaneous fractures of bones and dislocations of joints, failing sexual power and impotence, may lead the patient to consult a physician, when this disease will be diagnosed, although the patient may not as yet have had locomotor ataxy. All cases, however, if they live long enough, pass into the second ataxic stage. The sufferer complains now of difficulty of walking in the dark; he sways with his eyes shut and feels as if he would fall (Romberg's symptom); he has the sensation of walking on wool, numbness and formication of the skin, and many sensory disturbances in the form of partial or complete loss of sensibility to pain, touch and temperature. These disturbances affect especially the feet and legs, and around the trunk at the level of the fourth to the seventh ribs, giving rise to a "girdle sensation." There may be a numbed feeling on the inner side of the arm, and muscular incoordination may affect the upper limb as well as the lower, although there is no wasting or any electrical change. The ataxic gait is very characteristic, owing to the loss of reflex tonus in the muscles, and the absence of guiding sensations from all the deep structures of the limbs, muscles, joints, bones, tendons and ligaments, as well as from the skin of the soles of the feet; therefore the sufferer has to be guided by vision as to where and how to place his feet. This necessitates the bending forward of the body, extension of the knees and broadening of the basis of support; he generally uses a walking stick or even two, and he jerks the leg forward as if he were on wires, bringing the sole of the foot down on the ground with a wide stamping action. If the arm be affected, he is unable to touch the tip of his nose with the eyes shut. Sooner or later he passes into the *third* bed-ridden stage, with muscles wasted and their tonus so much lost that he is in a perfectly helpless condition.

The complications which may arise in this disease are intercurrent affections due to septic conditions of the bladder, bed-sores, pneumonia, vascular and heart affections. About 10% of the cases, at least, develop general paralysis of the insane. This is not surprising seeing that it is due to the same cause, and the etiology of the two diseases is such as to lead many neurologists to consider them one and the same disease affecting different parts of the nervous system. *Tabes dorsalis* occurs with much greater frequency in men than in women (see NEUROPATHOLOGY).

The avoidance of all stress of the nervous system, whether physical, emotional or intellectual, is indicated, and a simple regular life, without stimulants or indulgence of the sexual passion, is the best means of delaying the progress of the disease. Great attention should be paid to micturition, so as to avoid retention and infection of the bladder. Drugs, even anti-syphilitic remedies, appear to have but little influence upon the course of the disease.

LOCO-WEEDS, or CRAZY-WEEDS, leguminous plants, chiefly species of *Astragalus* and *Lupinus*, which produce a disease in cattle known as "loco-disease." The name is apparently taken from the Spanish *loco*, mad. The disease affects the nervous system of the animals eating the plants, and is accompanied by exhaustion and wasting.

LOCRI, a people of ancient Greece, inhabiting two distinct districts, one extending from the north-east of Parnassus to the northern half of the Euboean channel, between Boeotia and Malis, the other south-west of Parnassus, on the north shore of the Corinthian Gulf, between Phocis and Aetolia. The former were divided into the northern Locri Epicnemidii, situated on the spurs of Mount Cnemis, and the southern Locri Opuntii, so named from their chief town Opus (*q.v.*): and the name Opuntia is often applied to the whole of this easterly district. Homer mentions only these eastern Locrians: their national hero in the Trojan War is Ajax Oileus, who often appears afterwards on Locrian coins. From Hesiod's time onwards, the Opuntians were thought by some to be of "Lelegian" origin (see LELEGES), but they were Hellenised early (though matriarchal customs survived among them)—, and Deucalion, the father of Hellen himself, is described as the first king of Opus. The westerly Locri "in Ozolae" on the Corinthian Gulf, a rude and barbarous people, make no appearance in Greek history till the Peloponnesian War. It was believed that they had separated from the eastern Locrians four generations before the Trojan War; yet Homer has no hint of their existence. Probably the Locrians were once a single people, extending from sea to sea, till subsequent immigrations forced them apart into two separate districts. The Locrian dialect of Greek is little known, but resembles that of Elis: it has *στ* for *σθ*; uses *α*; and has *οις* in dat. plur. 3rd decl. A colony of Locrians (whether from Opus or Ozolae was disputed in antiquity) settled, about the end of the 8th century B.C., at the south-west extremity of Italy. They are often called Locri Epizephyrii from Cape Zephyrion 15 m. S. of the city. Their founder's name was Euanthes. Their social organization resembled that of the Opuntian Locri, and like them they venerated Ajax Oileus and Persephone. Aristotle (ap. Polyb. xii. 5 sqq.) records a tradition that these Western Locrians were base-born, like the Parthenians of Tarentum; but this was disputed by his contemporary Timaeus. See LOCRI (town) below. (J. L. M.)

LOCRI, an ancient city of Magna Graecia, Italy. The original settlers took possession of the Zephyrian promontory (Capo Bruzzano some 12 m. N. of Capo Spartivento), and though after three or four years they transplanted themselves to a site 12 m. farther north, still near the coast, 2 m. S. of Gerace Marina below the modern Gerace, they still retained the name of Locri Epizephyrii (Λοκροὶ οἱ Ἐπιζεφύριοι), which served to distinguish them from the Ozolian and Opuntian Locri of Greece itself (see preceding article). The foundation of Locri goes back to about 683 B.C. It was the first of all Greek communities to have a written code of laws given by Zaleucus in 664 B.C. From Locri were founded the colonies of Meisma and Hipponium (Hipponium). It succeeded in repelling the attacks of Croton (battle on the river Sagras, perhaps sometime in the 6th century), and found in Syracuse a support against Rhegium: it was thus an active adversary or Athenian aggrandisement in the west. Pindar extolls its uprightness and love of the heroic muse of beauty, of wisdom, and of war, in the 10th and 11th Olympian Odes. Stesichorus (*q.v.*) was indeed of Locrian origin. But it owed its greatest external prosperity to the fact that Dionysius I. of Syracuse selected his wife from Locri: its territory was then increased, and the circuit of its walls was doubled, but it lost its freedom. In 356 B.C. it was ruled by Dionysius II. From the battle of Heraclea to the year 205 (when it was captured by P. Cornelius Scipio Africanus Maior, and placed under the control of his legate Q. Pleminius), Locri was continually changing its allegiance between Rome and her enemies; but it remained an ally, and was only obliged like other Greek coast towns to furnish ships. In later Roman times it is often mentioned, but was apparently of no great importance. It is mentioned incidentally until the 6th century A.D., but was destroyed by the Saracens in 915.

Excavations in 1889–1890 led to the discovery of an Ionic temple (the Doric style being usual in Magna Graecia) at the north-west angle of the town—originally a cella with two naves, a closed pronaos on the E. and an adytum at the back (W.), later converted into a hexastyle peripheral temple with 34 painted terra-cotta columns. This was then destroyed about 400 B.C. and a new temple built on the ruins, heptastyle peripteral, with no intermediate columns in the cella and opisthodomos, and with 44 columns in all. The figures from the pediment of the twin Dioscuri, who according to the legend assisted Locri against Crotona, are in the Naples museum (see R. Koldewey and O. Puchstein, *Griechische Tempel in Unteritalien und Sicilien*, Berlin, 1899, pp. 1 sqq.). Subsequent excavations in 1890–1891 were of the greatest importance, but the results remained unpublished up to 1908. From a short account by P. Orsi in *Atti del Congresso Storico*, vol. v. (Archeologia) Rome, 1904, p. 201, we learn that the exploration of the environs of the temple led to the discovery of a large number of archaic terra-cottas, and of some large trenches, covered with tiles, containing some 14,000 scyphoi arranged in rows. The plan of the city was also traced; the walls, the length of which was nearly 5 m., consisted of three parts—the fortified castles (φρούρια) with large towers, on three different hills, the city proper, and the lower town—the latter enclosed by long walls running down to the sea. In the Roman period the city was restricted to the plain near the sea. Since these excavations, a certain amount of unauthorized work has gone on, and some of the remains have been destroyed. In the course of these excavations some prehistoric objects have been discovered, which confirm the accounts of Thucydides and Polybius that the Greek settlers found the Siculi here before them. (T. As.)

LÖCSE (Ger. *Leutschau*), the capital of the county of Szepes, in Hungary, 230 m. N.E. of Budapest by rail. Pop. (1900) 6845, mostly Germans and Slovaks. The county of Szepes is the highest part of Hungary, and its north-western portion is occupied by the Tátra Mountains. Löcse lies in an elevated position surrounded by mountains, and is one of the oldest towns of Hungary. The church of St James is a Gothic structure of the 13th century, with richly carved altar, several monuments, and a celebrated organ erected in 1623, and long reputed the largest in Hungary. The old town-hall, restored in 1894, contains a Protestant upper gymnasium, founded in 1544, and one of the oldest printing establishments in Hungary, founded in 1585. Bee-keeping and the raising of garden produce are the chief industries.

Founded by Saxon colonists in 1245, Löcse had by the early part of the 16th century attained a position of great relative importance. In 1599 a fire destroyed the greater part of the town, and during the 17th century it suffered repeatedly at the hands of the Transylvanian princes and leaders.

LOCUS (Lat. for "place"; in Gr. τόπος), a geometrical term, the invention of the notion of which is attributed to Plato. It occurs in such statements as these: the locus of the points which are at the same distance from a fixed point, or of a point which moves so as to be always at the same distance from a fixed point, is a circle; conversely a circle is the locus of the points at the same distance from a fixed point, or of a point moving so as to be always at the same distance from a fixed point; and so in general a curve of any given kind is the locus of the points which satisfy, or of a point moving so as always to satisfy, a given condition. The theory of loci is thus identical with that of curves (see CURVE and GEOMETRY: § *Analytical*). The notion of a locus applies also to solid geometry. Here the locus of the points satisfying a single (or onefold) condition is a surface; the locus of the points satisfying two conditions (or a twofold condition) is a curve in space, which is in general a twisted curve or curve of double curvature.

LOCUST.[1] In its general acceptation this term is applied only to certain insects of the order *Orthoptera*, family *Acridiidae*. The family *Locustidae* is now viewed zoologically in a sense that does not admit of the species best known as "locusts" being included therein. The idea of a very destructive insect is universally associated with the term; therefore many orthopterous species that cannot be considered true locusts have been so-called; in North America it has even embraced certain *Hemiptera-Homoptera*, belonging to the *Cicadidae*, and in some parts of England cockchafers are so designated. In a more narrow definition the attribute of migration is associated with the destructive propensities, and it therefore becomes necessary that a true locust should be a migratory species of the family *Acridiidae*. Moreover, the term has yet a slightly different signification as viewed from the Old or New World. In Europe by a locust is meant an insect of large size, the smaller allied species being ordinarily known as "grasshoppers," hence the "Rocky Mountain locust" of North America is to Eastern ideas rather a grasshopper than a locust.

In Europe, and a greater part of the Old World, the best known migratory locust is that which is scientifically termed *Pachytylus cinerascens* with which an allied species *P. migratorius* has been often confounded. Another locust found in Europe and neighbouring districts is *Caloptenus italicus*, and still another, *Acridium peregrinum*, has once or twice occurred in Europe, though its home (even in a migratory sense) is more properly Africa and Asia. These practically include all the locusts of the Old World, though a migratory species of South Africa known as *Pachytylus pardalinus* (presumed to be distinct from *P. migratorius*) should be mentioned. The Rocky Mountain locust of North America is *Caloptenus spretus*, and in that continent there occurs an *Acridium* (*A. americanum*) so closely allied to *A. peregrinum* as to be scarcely distinct therefrom, though there it does not manifest migratory tendencies. In the West Indies and Central America *A. peregrinum* is also reported to occur.

The females excavate holes in the earth in which the eggs are deposited in a long cylindrical mass enveloped in a glutinous secretion. The young larvae hatch and immediately commence their destructive career. As these insects are "hemimetabolic" there is no quiescent stage; they go on increasing rapidly in size, and as they approach the perfect state the rudiments of the wings begin to appear. Even in this stage their locomotive powers are extensive and their voracity great. Once winged and perfect these powers become infinitely more disastrous, redoubled by the development of the migratory instinct. The laws regulating this instinct are not perfectly understood. Food and temperature have a great deal to do with it, and there is a tendency for the flights to take a particular direction, varied by the physical circumstances of the breeding districts. So likewise each species has its area of constant location, and its area of extraordinary migration. Perhaps the most feasible of the suggestions as to the causes of the migratory impulse is that locusts naturally breed in dry sandy districts in which food is scarce, and are impelled to wander to procure the necessaries of life; but against this it has been argued that swarms bred in a highly productive district in which they have temporarily settled will seek the barren home of their ancestors. Another ingenious suggestion is that migration is intimately connected with a dry condition of the atmosphere, urging them to move on until compelled to stop for food or procreative purposes. Swarms travel considerable distances, though probably generally fewer than 1000 m., though sometimes very much more. As a rule the progress is only gradual, and this adds vastly to the devastating effects. When an extensive swarm temporarily settles in a district, all vegetation rapidly disappears, and then hunger urges it on another stage. The large Old World species, although undoubtedly phytophagous, when compelled by hunger sometimes attack at least dry animal substances, and even cannibalism has been asserted as an outcome of the failure of all other kinds of food. The length of a single flight must depend upon

[1] The Lat. *locusta* was first applied to a lobster or other marine shell-fish and then, from its resemblance, to the insect.

circumstances. From peculiarities in the examples of *Acridium peregrinum* taken in England in 1869, it has been asserted that they must have come direct by sea from the west coast of Africa; and what is probably the same species has been seen in the Atlantic at least 1200 m. from land, in swarms completely covering the ship; thus, in certain cases flight must be sustained for several days and nights together. The height at which swarms fly, when their horizontal course is not liable to be altered by mountains, has been very variously estimated at from 40 to 200 ft., or even in a particular case to 500 ft. The extent of swarms and the number of individuals in a swarm cannot be accurately ascertained. They come sometimes in such numbers as to completely obscure the sun, when the noise made by the rustling of the wings is deafening. Nevertheless some idea on this point may be formed from the ascertained fact that in Cyprus in 1881, at the close of the season, 1,600,000,000 egg-cases, each containing a considerable number of eggs, had been destroyed; the estimated weight exceeding 1300 tons. Yet two years later, it is believed that not fewer than 5,076,000,000 egg-cases were again deposited in the island.

In Europe the best known and ordinarily most destructive species is *Pachytylus cinerascens*, and it is to it that most of the numerous records of devastations in Europe mainly refer, but it is probably not less destructive in many parts of Africa and Asia. That the arid steppes of central Asia are the home of this insect appears probable; still much on this point is enveloped in uncertainty. In any case the area of permanent distribution is enormous, and that of occasional distribution is still greater. The former area extends from the parallel of 40° N. in Portugal, rising to 48° in France and Switzerland, and passing into Russia at 55°, thence continuing across the middle of Siberia, north of China to Japan; thence south to the Fiji Islands, to New Zealand and North Australia; thence again to Mauritius

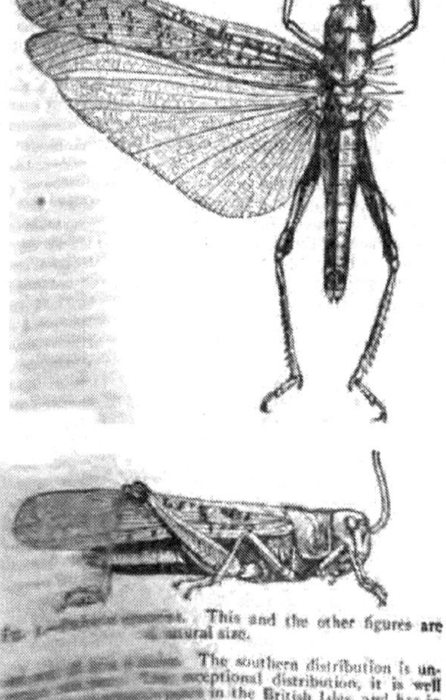

Fig. 1.—[illegible]. This and the other figures are [illegible] natural size.

[illegible] The southern distribution is un[illegible] exceptional distribution, it is well [illegible] in the British Isles, and has in [illegible] far north as Edinburgh; so also [illegible] [illegible]ably been [illegible] easy to [illegible] with [illegible] Europe

especially is this the case, because there exists a distinct species known as *P. migratorius*, the migratory area of which appears to be confined to Turkestan and eastern Europe.

P. cinerascens is certainly the most common of the "locusts" occasionally found in the British Isles, and E. de Selys-Longchamps is of opinion that it breeds regularly in Belgium, whereas the true *P. migratorius* is only accidental in that country.

A South African species allied to the preceding and provisionally identified as *Pachytylus sulcicollis* is noteworthy from the manifesta-

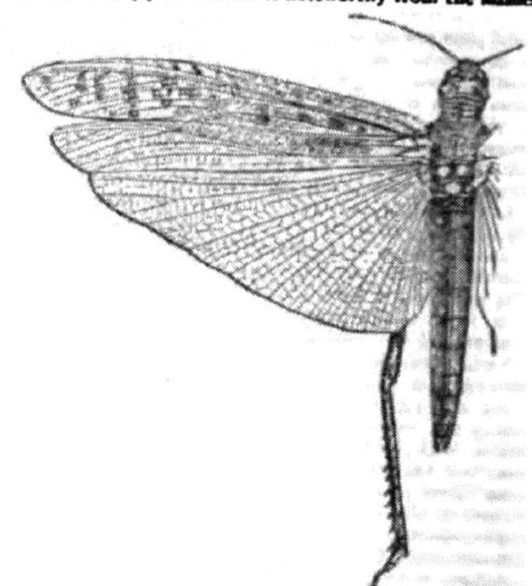

Fig. 2.—*Acridium peregrinum*.

tion of the migratory instinct in immature wingless individuals. The families of young, after destroying the vegetation of a district, unite in a vast army and move away in search of fresh pastures, devastating the country as they go and proceeding of necessity on foot, hence they are known to the Dutch as "voetgangers." Travelling northwards towards the centre of the continent, the home of their parents before migration, they are diverted from their course by no obstacles. Upon reaching a river or stream they search the bank for a likely spot to cross, then fearlessly cast themselves upon the water where they form floating islands of insects, most of which usually succeed in gaining the opposite bank, though many perish in the attempt.

Acridium peregrinum (fig. 2) can scarcely be considered even an accidental visitor to Europe; yet it has been seen in the south of Spain, and in many examples spread over a large part of England in the year 1869. It is a larger insect than *P. migratorius*. There is every reason to believe that it is the most destructive locust throughout Africa and in India and other parts of tropical Asia, and its ravages are as great as those of *P. migratorius*. Presumably it is the species occasionally noticed in a vast swarm in the Atlantic, very far from land, and presumably also it occurs in the West Indies and some parts of Central America. In the Argentine Republic a (possibly) distinct species (*A. paranense*) is the migratory locust.

Caloptenus italicus (fig. 3) is a smaller insect, with a less extended area of migration; the destruction occasioned in the districts to which it is limited is often scarce less than that of its more terrible allies. It is essentially a species of the Mediterranean district, and especially of the European side of that sea, yet it is also found in North Africa, and appears to extend far into southern Russia.

Caloptenus spretus (fig. 4) is the "Rocky Mountain locust" or "hateful grasshopper" of the North American continent. Though a comparatively small insect, not so large as some of the grasshoppers of English fields, its destructiveness has procured for it great notoriety. By early travellers and settlers the species was not recognized as distinct from some of its non-migratory congeners. But in 1877, Congress appointed a United States Entomological Commission to investigate the subject. The report of the commissioners (C.V Riley, A. S. Packard and C. Thomas) deals with the whole subject of locusts both in America and the Old World. *C. spretus* has its home or permanent area in the arid plains of the central region east of the Rocky Mountains, extending slightly into the southern portion of Canada; outside this is a wide fringe to which the term sub-permanent is applied, and this is again bounded by the limits of only occasional distribution, the whole occupying a large portion of the North American continent; but it is not known to have crossed the

Rocky Mountains westward, or to have extended into the eastern states.

As to remedial or preventive measures tending to check the ravages of locusts, little unfortunately can be said; but anything that will apply to one species may be used with practically all. Something can be done (as is now done in Cyprus) by offering a price for all the egg-tubes collected, which is the most direct manner of attacking them. Some little can be done by destroying the larvae while in an

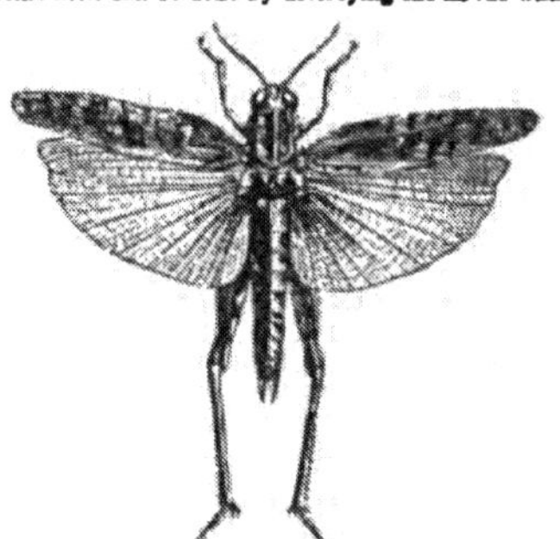

FIG. 3.—*Caloptenus italicus.*

unwinged condition, and by digging trenches in the line of march into which they can fall and be drowned or otherwise put an end to. Little can be done with the winged hordes; starvation, the outcome of their own work, probably here does much. In South Africa some success has attended the spraying of the swarms with arsenic. It has been shown that with all migratory locusts the breeding-places, or true homes, are comparatively barren districts (mostly elevated plateaus); hence the progress of colonization, and the conversion of those heretofore barren plains into areas of fertility, may (and probably will) gradually lessen the evil.

Locusts have many enemies besides man. Many birds greedily devour them, and it has many times been remarked that migratory swarms of the insects were closely followed by myriads of birds.

FIG. 4.—Rocky Mountain Locust (*Caloptenus spretus*). (After Riley.)

a, a, a, Female in different positions, ovipositing
b, Egg-pod extracted from ground, with the end broken open.
c, A few eggs lying loose on the ground
d, e show the earth partially removed, to illustrate an egg-mass already in place, and one being placed.
f, shows where such a mass has been covered up.

Predatory insects of other orders also attack them, especially when they are in the unwinged condition. Moreover, they have still more deadly insect foes as parasites. Some attack the fully developed winged insect. But the greater part attack the eggs. To such belong certain beetles, chiefly of the family *Cantharidae*, and especially certain two-winged flies of the family *Bombyliidae*. These latter, both in the Old and New World, must prevent vast quantities of eggs from producing larvae.

The larger Old World species form articles of food with certain semi-civilized and savage races, by whom they are considered as delicacies, or as part of ordinary diet, according to the race and the method of preparation. (R. M'L.; R. I. P.)

LOCUST-TREE, or CAROB-TREE (*Ceratonia siliqua*), a member of the tribe *Cassieae* of the order Leguminosae, the sole species of its genus, and widely diffused spontaneously and by cultivation from Spain to the eastern Mediterranean regions. The name of the genus is derived from the often curved pod (Gr. κεράτιον, a little horn). The flowers have no petals and are polygamous or dioecious (male, female and hermaphrodite flowers occur). The seed-pod is compressed, often curved, indehiscent and coriaceous, but with sweet pulpy divisions between the seeds, which, as in other genera of the *Cassieae*, are albuminous. The pods are eaten by men and animals, and in Sicily a spirit and a syrup are made from them. These husks being often used for swine are called swine's bread, and are probably referred to in the parable of the Prodigal Son. It is also called St John's bread, from a misunderstanding of Matt. iii. 4. The carob-tree was regarded by Sprengel as the tree with which Moses sweetened the bitter waters of Marah (Exod. xv. 25), as the *kharrûb*, according to Avicenna (p. 205), has the property of sweetening salt and bitter waters. Gerard (*Herball*, p. 1241) cultivated it in 1597, it having been introduced in 1570.

LODÈVE, a town of southern France, capital of an arrondissement of the department of Hérault, 36 m. W.N.W. of Montpellier by rail. Pop. (1906), 6142. It is situated in the southern Cévennes at the foot of steep hills in a small valley where the Soulondres joins the Lergue, a tributary of the Hérault. Two bridges over the Lergue connect the town with the faubourg of Carmes on the left bank of the river, and two others over the Soulondres lead to the extensive ruins of the château de Montbrun (13th century). The old fortified cathedral of St Fulcran, founded by him in 950, dates in its present condition from the 13th, 14th and 16th centuries; the cloister, dating from the 15th and 17th centuries, is in ruins. In the picturesque environs of the town stands the well-preserved monastery of St Michel de Grammont, dating from the 12th century and now used as farm buildings. In the neighbourhood are three fine dolmens. The manufacture of woollens for army clothing is the chief industry. Wool is imported in large quantities from the neighbouring departments, and from Morocco; the exports are cloth to Italy and the Levant, wine, brandy and wood. The town has tribunals of first instance and of commerce, a board of trade-arbitrators, a chamber of arts and manufactures, and a communal college.

Lodève (Luteva) existed before the invasion of the Romans, who for some time called it *Forum Neronis*. The inhabitants were converted to Christianity by St Flour, first bishop of the city, about 323. After passing successively into the hands of the Visigoths, the Franks, the Ostrogoths, the Arabs and the Carolingians, it became in the 9th century a separate countship, and afterwards the domain of its bishops. During the religious wars it suffered much, especially in 1573, when it was sacked. It ceased to be an episcopal see at the Revolution.

LODGE, EDMUND (1756–1839), English writer on heraldry, was born in London on the 13th of June 1756, son of Edmund Lodge, rector of Carshalton, Surrey. He held a cornet's commission in the army, which he resigned in 1773. In 1782 he became Bluemantle pursuivant-at-arms in the College of Arms. He subsequently became Lancaster herald, Norroy king-at-arms, Clarencieux king-at-arms, and, in 1832, knight of the order of the Guelphs of Hanover. He died in London on the 16th of January 1839. He wrote *Illustrations of British History, Biography and Manners in the reigns of Henry VIII., Edward VI., Mary, Elizabeth and James I....* (3 vols. 1791), consisting of selections from the MSS. of the Howard, Talbot and Cecil families preserved at the College of Arms, *Life of Sir Julius Caesar...* (2nd ed., 1827). He contributed the literary matter to *Portraits of Illustrious Personages of Great Britain* (1814, &c.), an elaborate work of which a popular edition is included in Bohn's "Illustrated Library." His most important work on heraldry was *The Genealogy of the existing British Peerage*. (1832, enlarged edition, 1859). In *The Annual Peerage and Baronetage* (1827–1829), reissued after 1832 as *Peerage of the British Empire*, and generally known as Lodge's Peerage, his share did not go beyond the title-page.

[illegible] merican political … sachusetts, on the … College in 1871 … admitted to the … 1870–1879 was … He was a member … in 1880–1881, … in 1887–1893; … States Senator from … 1905 was re-elected … most prominent of … supporter of President … Boundary Com- … Immigration Commis- … convention of 1896 … the gold standard … was the permanent … convention of 1900, and … the North American … 1884, with John T. … In 1884–1890 he … doctoral thesis at … Henry Adams, J. L. … Essays on Anglo- … Letters of George … Webster (1883) … American States- … in America … in the "His- … Essays (1892); … American History … Story of the … War with Spain … Towns (1900); … States (4 vols. … Hamilton (9 vols.

… also became … (1898), Poems, … Drama

… English physicist, … of June 1851, … school. He was … to science he … graduating D.Sc. at … appointed reader in … and in 1879 he … at University … to the chair of … he remained till … Birmingham … original work in … electromotive … and the … telegraphy, … application of … invented over … Association … in 1900 … in 1901 1904 … among other … and the … a units-

… and

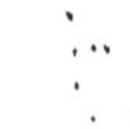

FIG. 1.—Po[illegible]

and over all A[illegible] certain and oc[illegible] known that it [illegible] them apparent. does it occasion[illegible] seen up to the[illegible] conceive th[illegible] regard to[illegible]

Inn, where, as in the other Inns of Court, a love of letters and a crop of debts and difficulties were alike wont to spring up in a kindly soil. Lodge, apparently in disregard of the wishes of his family, speedily showed his inclination towards the looser ways of life and the lighter aspects of literature. When the penitent Stephen Gosson had (in 1579) published his *Schoole of Abuse*, Lodge took up the glove in his *Defence of Poetry, Music and Stage Plays* (1579 or 1580; reprinted for the Shakespeare Society, 1853), which shows a certain restraint, though neither deficient in force of invective nor backward in display of erudition. The pamphlet was prohibited, but appears to have been circulated privately. It was answered by Gosson in his *Playes Confuted in Five Actions*; and Lodge retorted with his *Alarum Against Usurers* (1584, reprinted *ib.*)—a "tract for the times" which no doubt was in some measure indebted to the author's personal experience. In the same year he produced the first tale written by him on his own account in prose and verse, *The Delectable History of Forbonius and Priscilla*, both published and reprinted with the *Alarum*. From 1587 onwards he seems to have made a series of attempts as a playwright, though most of those attributed to him are mainly conjectural. That he ever became an actor is improbable in itself, and Collier's conclusion to that effect rested on the two assumptions that the "Lodge" of Henslowe's M.S. was a player and that his name was Thomas, neither of which is supported by the text (see C. M. Ingleby, *Was Thomas Lodge an Actor?* 1868). Having, in the spirit of his age, "tried the waves" with Captain Clarke in his expedition to Terceira and the Canaries, Lodge in 1591 made a voyage with Thomas Cavendish to Brazil and the Straits of Magellan, returning home by 1593. During the Canaries expedition, to beguile the tedium of his voyage, he composed his prose tale of *Rosalynde, Euphues Golden Legacie*, which, printed in 1590, afterwards furnished the story of Shakespeare's *As You Like It*. The novel, which in its turn owes some, though no very considerable, debt to the medieval *Tale of Gamelyn* (unwarrantably appended to the fragmentary *Cookes Tale* in certain MSS. of Chaucer's works), is written in the euphuistic manner, but decidedly attractive both by its plot and by the situations arising from it. It has been frequently reprinted. Before starting on his second expedition he had published an historical romance, *The History of Robert, Second Duke of Normandy, surnamed Robert the Devil*, and he left behind him for publication *Catharos, Diogenes in his Singularity*, a discourse on the immorality of Athens (London). Both appeared in 1591. Another romance in the manner of Lyly, *Euphues Shadow, the Battaile of the Sences* (1592), appeared while Lodge was still on his travels. His second historical romance, the *Life and Death of William Longbeard* (1593), was more successful than the first. Lodge also brought back with him from the new world *A Margarite of America* (published 1596), a romance of the same description interspersed with many lyrics. Already in 1589 Lodge had given to the world a volume of poems bearing the title of the chief among them, *Scillaes Metamorphosis, Enterlaced with the Unfortunate Love of Glaucus*, more briefly known as *Glaucus and Scilla* (reprinted with preface by S. W. Singer in 1819). To this tale Shakespeare was possibly indebted for the idea of *Venus and Adonis*. Some readers would perhaps be prepared to give up this and much else of Lodge's sugared verse, fine though much of it is in quality, largely borrowed from other writers, French and Italian in particular, in exchange for the lost *Sailor's Kalendar*, in which he must in one way or another have recounted his sea adventures. If Lodge, as has been supposed, was the Alcon in *Colin Clout's come Home Again*, it may have been the influence of Spenser which led to the composition of *Phillis*, a volume of sonnets, in which the voice of nature seems only now and then to become audible, published with the narrative poem, *The Complaynte of Elstred*, in 1593. *A Fig for Momus*, on the strength of which he has been called [illegible]he earliest English satirist, and which contains eclogues addressed [illegible] Daniel and others, an epistle addressed to Drayton, and other [illegible]es, appeared in 1595. Lodge's ascertained dramatic work [illegible] nall in quantity. In conjunction with Greene he, probably [illegible] 590, produced in a popular vein the odd but far from feeble play of *A Looking Glasse for London and England* (printed in 1594). He had already written *The Wounds of Civile War. Lively set forth in the Tragedies of Marius and Scilla* (produced perhaps as early as 1587, and published in 1594), a good second-rate piece in the half-chronicle fashion of its age. Mr F. G. Fleay thinks there were grounds for assigning to Lodge *Mucedorus and Amadine*, played by the Queen's Men about 1588, a share with Robert Greene in *George a Greene, the Pinner of Wakefield*, and in Shakespeare's 2nd part of *Henry VI.*; he also regards him as at least part-author of *The True Chronicle of King Leir and his three Daughters* (1594); and *The Troublesome Raigne of John, King of England* (c. 1588); in the case of two other plays he allowed the assignation to Lodge to be purely conjectural. That Lodge is the "Young Juvenal" of Greene's *Groatsworth of Wit* is no longer a generally accepted hypothesis. In the latter part of his life—possibly about 1596, when he published his *Wits Miserie* and the *World's Madnesse*, which is dated from Low Leyton in Essex, and the religious tract *Prosopopeia* (if, as seems probable, it was his), in which he repents him of his "lewd lines" of other days—he became a Catholic and engaged in the practice of medicine, for which Wood says he qualified himself by a degree at Avignon in 1600. Two years afterwards he received the degree of M.D. from Oxford University. His works henceforth have a sober cast, comprising translations of Josephus (1602), of Seneca (1614), a *Learned Summary* of Du Bartas's *Divine Sepmaine* (1625 and 1637), besides a *Treatise of the Plague* (1603), and a popular manual, which remained unpublished, on *Domestic Medicine*. Early in 1606 he seems to have left England, to escape the persecution then directed against the Catholics; and a letter from him dated 1610 thanks the English ambassador in Paris for enabling him to return in safety. He was abroad on urgent private affairs of one kind and another in 1616. From this time to his death in 1625 nothing further concerning him remains to be noted.

Lodge's works, with the exception of his translations, have been reprinted for the Hunterian Club with an introductory essay by Mr Edmund Gosse. This preface was reprinted in Mr Gosse's *Seventeenth Century Studies* (1883). Of *Rosalynde* there are numerous modern editions. See also J. J. Jusserand, *English Novel in the Time of Shakespeare* (Eng. trans., 1890); F. G. Fleay, *Biographical Chronicle of the English Drama* (vol. ii., 1891). (A. W. W.)

LODGE, a dwelling-place, small and usually temporary, a hut, booth or tent. The word was in M. Eng. *logge*, from Fr. *loge*, arbour, in modern French a hut; also box in a theatre; the French word, like the Italian *loggia*, came from the Med. Lat. *laubia* or *lobia*, the sheltered promenade in a cloister, from which English "lobby" is derived. The Latin is of Teutonic origin from the word which survives in the Mod. Ger. *Laube*, an arbour, but which earlier was used for any hut, booth, &c. The word is probably ultimately from the root which appears in "leaf," meaning a rough shelter of foliage or boughs. The word is especially used of a house built either in a forest or away from habitation, where people stay for the purpose of sport, as a "hunting lodge," "shooting lodge," &c. The most frequent use of the word is of a small building, usually placed at the entrance to an estate or park and inhabited by a dependant of the owner. In the same sense the word means the room or box inhabited by the porter of a college, factory or public institution. Among Freemasons and other societies the "lodge" is the name given to the meeting-place of the members of the branch or district, and is applied to the members collectively as "a meeting of the lodge." The governing body of the Freemasons presided over by the grand master is called the "Grand Lodge." At the university of Cambridge the house where the head of a college lives is called the "lodge." Formerly the word was used of the den or lair of an animal, but is now only applied to that of the beaver and the otter. It is also applied to the tent of a North American Indian, a wigwam or tepee, and to the number of inhabitants of such a tent. In mining the term is used of a subterraneous reservoir made at the bottom of the pit, or at different levels in the shaft for the purpose of draining the mine. It is used also of a room or landing-place next to the shaft, for discharging ore, &c.

LODGER AND LODGINGS. The term "lodger" (Fr. *loger*, to lodge) is used in English law in several slightly different senses. It is applied (i.) most frequently and properly to a person who takes furnished rooms in a house, the landlord also residing on the premises, and supplying him with attendance; (ii.) sometimes to a person, who takes unfurnished rooms in a house finding his own attendance; (iii.) to a boarder in a boarding-house (*q.v.*). It is with (i.) and (ii.) alone that this article is concerned.

Where furnished apartments are let for immediate use, the law implies an undertaking on the part of the landlord that they are fit for habitation, and, if this condition is broken, the tenant may refuse to occupy the premises or to pay any rent But there is no implied contract that the apartments shall *continue* fit for habitation; and the rule has no application in the case of unfurnished lodgings. In the absence of express agreement to the contrary, a lodger has a right to the use of everything necessary to the enjoyment of the premises, such as the door bell and knocker and the skylight of a staircase. Whether the rent of apartments can be distrained for by the immediate landlord where he resides on the premises and supplies attendance is a question the answer to which is involved in some uncertainty. The weight of authority seems to support the negative view (see Foa, *Landlord and Tenant*, 3rd ed. p. 434). To make good a right to distrain it is necessary to show that the terms of the letting create a tenancy or exclusive occupation and not a mere licence. Where the owner, although residing on the premises, does not supply attendance, the question depends on whether there is a real tenancy, giving the lodger an exclusive right of occupation as against the owner. The ordinary test is whether the lodger has the control of the outer door. But the whole circumstances of each case have to be taken account of. A lodger is rateable to the poor-rate where he is in exclusive occupation of the apartments let to him, and the landlord does not retain the control and dominion of the whole structure. As to distress on a lodger's goods for rent due by an immediate to a superior landlord, see Rent. As to the termination of short tenancies, as of apartments, see Landlord and Tenant. The landlord has no lien on the goods of the lodger for rent or charges. Overcrowding lodging-houses may be dealt with as a nuisance under the Public Health Acts 1875 and 1891 and the Housing of the Working Classes Acts. As to the lodger franchise, see Registration of Voters. It has been held in England that keepers of lodging-houses do not come within the category of those persons (see Carrier; Innkeeper) who hold themselves out to the public generally as trustworthy in certain employments; but that they are under an obligation to take reasonable care for the safety of their lodgers' goods; see *Scarborough* v. *Cosgrove*, 1905, 2 K.B. 805. As to Scots Law see Bell's *Prin.* s. 236 (4).

In the United States, the English doctrine of an implied warranty of fitness for habitation on a letting of furnished apartments has only met with partial acceptance; it was repudiated, *e.g.* in the District of Columbia, but has been accepted in Massachusetts. In the French *Code Civil*, there are some special rules with regard to furnished apartments. The letting is reputed to be made for a year, a month or a day, according as the rent is so much per year, per month or per day; if that test is inapplicable, the letting is deemed to be made according to the custom of the place (art. 1758). There are similar provisions in the Civil Codes of Belgium (art. 1758), Holland (art. 1622) and Spain (Civil Code, art. 1581).

See also the articles, Boarding House, and Flat; and the bibliographies to Flat and Landlord and Tenant. (A. W. R.)

LODI, a town and episcopal see of Piedmont, Italy, in the province of Milan, 20½ m. by rail S.E. of that city, on a hill above the right bank of the Adda, 230 ft. above sea-level. Pop. (1901) 19,970 (town), 26,827 (commune). The site of the city is an eminence rising very gradually from the Lombard plain, and the surrounding country is one of the richest dairy districts in Italy. The cathedral (1158), with a Gothic façade and a 16th-century lateral tower, has a restored interior. The church of the Incoronata was erected by Battaggio (1488) in the Bramantesque style. It is an elegant octagonal domed structure, and is

female line; and it is now held by the marquis of Ely in conjunction with other family titles.

See Richard Mant, *History of the Church of Ireland* (2 vols., London, 1840); J. R. O'Flanagan, *Lives of the Lord Chancellors of Ireland* (2 vols., London, 1870); John D'Alton, *Memoirs of the Archbishops of Dublin* (Dublin, 1838); Henry Cotton, *Fasti Ecclesiae Hibernicae* (5 vols., Dublin, 1848-1878); William Monck Mason, *History and Antiquities of the College and Cathedral Church of St Patrick, near Dublin* (Dublin, 1819); G. E. C., *Complete Peerage* vol. iii., sub. "Ely" (London, 1890).

LOG (a word of uncertain etymological origin, possibly onomatopoeic; the *New English Dictionary* rejects the derivation from Norwegian *låg*, a fallen tree), a large piece of, generally unhewn, wood. The word is also used in various figurative senses, and more particularly for the "nautical log," an apparatus for ascertaining the speed of ships. Its employment in this sense depends on the fact that a piece of wood attached to a line was thrown overboard to lie like a log in a fixed position, motionless, the vessel's speed being calculated by observing what length of line ran out in a given time ("common log"); and the word has been retained for the modern "patent" or "continuous" log, though it works in an entirely different manner.

The origin of the "common log" is obscure, but the beginnings of the "continuous log" may be traced back to the 16th century. By an invention probably due to Humfray Cole and published in 1578 by William Bourne in his *Inventions and Devices*, it was proposed to register a ship's speed by means of a "little small close boat," with a wheel, or wheels, and an axle-tree to turn clockwork in the little boat, with dials and pointers indicating fathoms, leagues, scores of leagues and hundreds of leagues. About 1668 Dr R. Hooke showed some members of the Royal Society an instrument for the same purpose, depending on a vane or fly which rotated as the vessel progressed (Birch, *History of the Royal Society*, iv. 231), and Sir Isaac Newton in 1715 reported unfavourably on the "marine surveyor" of Henry de Saumarez, which also depended on a rotator. Conradus Mel in his *Antiquarius Sacer* (1719) described a "pantometron nauticum" which he claimed would show without calculation the distance sailed by the ship; and J. Smeaton in 1754 published improvements on the apparatus of Saumarez. William Foxon of Deptford in 1772, James Guerimand of Middlesex in 1776 (by his "marine perambulator"), and R. H. Gower in 1772, practically demonstrated the registration of a vessel's speed by mechanical means. Viscount de Vaux in 1807 made use of water-pressure, as did the Rev. E. L. Berthon in 1849, and C. E. Kelway invented an electrical log in 1876.

Common Log.—To ascertain the ship's speed by the common log four articles are necessary—a log-ship or log-chip, log-reel, log-line and log-glass. The log-ship (fig. 1) is a wooden quadrant ½ in. thick, with a radius of 5 or 6 in., the circumference of which is weighted with lead to keep it upright and retard its passage through the water. Two holes are made near its lower angles. One end of a short piece of thin line is passed through one of these holes, and knotted; the other end has spliced to it a hard bone peg which is inserted in the other hole. The holes are so placed that the log-ship will hang square from the span thus formed. The log-line is secured to this span and consists of two parts. The portion nearest the log-ship is known as the "stray line"; its length varies from 10 to 20 fathoms, but should be sufficient to ensure that the log-ship shall be outside the disturbing element of the ship's wake. The point where it joins the other part is marked by a piece of bunting, and the line from this point towards its other end is marked at known intervals with "knots," which consist of pieces of cord worked in between the strands. A mean degree of the meridian being assumed to [illegible] value of 5280 ft., the nautical mile ($\frac{1}{60}$ degree) [illegible] which is a sufficiently close approximation [illegible] and the distances between the knots [illegible] the same relation to [illegible] to

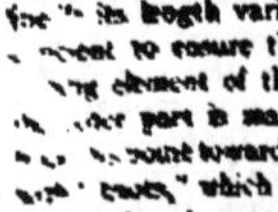

FIG. 1.

an hour (3600 seconds); that is, they are placed at intervals of 47 ft. 3 in. The end of the first interval of this length (counting from the piece of bunting) is marked by a bit of leather, the second by a cord with two knots, the third by one with three knots, and so on; the middle of each of these lengths (half-knot) is also marked by a cord with one knot. It follows that, if, say, five knots of the line run out in 28 seconds, the ship has gone 5×47¼ ft. in that time, or is moving at the rate of 5×6080 ft. (=five nautical miles) an hour; hence the common use of knot as equivalent to a nautical mile. In the log-glass the time is measured by running sand, which, however, is apt to be affected by the humidity of the atmosphere. Sometimes a 30-second glass is used instead of a 28-second one, and the intervals between the knots on the log-line are then made 50 ft. 7 in. instead of 47 ft. 3 in. For speeds over six knots a 14-second glass is employed, and the speed indicated by the log-line is doubled.

The log-line, after being well soaked, stretched and marked with knots, is wound uniformly on the log-reel, to which its inner end is securely fastened. To "heave the log," a man holds the log-reel over his head (at high speeds the man and portable reel are superseded by a fixed reel and a winch fitted with a brake), and the officer places the peg in the log-ship, which he then throws clear and to windward of the ship, allowing the line to run freely out. When the bunting at the end of the stray line passes his hand, he calls to his assistant to turn the glass, and allows the line to pay out freely. When all the sand has run through, the assistant calls "Stop!" when the log-line is quickly nipped, the knots counted, and the intermediate portion estimated. The strain on the log-ship when the log-line is nipped, causes the peg to be withdrawn from it, and the log-ship is readily hauled in. In normal circumstances the log is hove every hour. In a steam vessel running at high speed on an ocean route, with engines working smoothly and uniformly, a careful officer with correct line and glass can obtain very accurate results with the common log.

Ground Log.—In the deltas of shoal rivers, with a strong tide or current and no land visible, a 5 lb lead is substituted for the log-ship, the lead rests on the bottom, and the speed is obtained in a manner similar to that previously described. Such a "ground-log" indicates the actual speed over the ground, and in addition, when the log-line is being hauled in, it will show the real course the ship is making over the ground.

Patent Log.—The screw or rotatory log of Edward Massey, invented in 1802, came into general use in 1836 and continued until 1861. The registering wheel-work was contained in a shallow rectangular box (fig. 2), with a float plate on its upper side, carrying three indicating dials, recording respectively fractions, units and tens of miles (up to a hundred). The rotator was connected to the log by a rope 6 ft. in length, actuating a universal joint on the first spindle of the register; it consisted of an air-tight thin metal tube with a coned fore-end, carrying flat metal vanes set at an angle. Alexander Bain in 1846 suggested enclosing the wheelwork in the rotator. In Thomas Walker's harpoon or frictionless log, introduced in 1861, the wheelwork was enclosed in a cylindrical case of the same diameter as the body of the rotator or fan, and the latter was brought close up to the register, forming a compact machine and avoiding the use of the 6-ft. line. Two years later a heart-shaped float plate was attached to the case, and the log called the A1 Harpoon ship log (fig. 3). The log should be washed in fresh water when practicable, to prevent oxidization of the wheels, and be lubricated with suitable oil through a hole in the case.

FIG. 2.

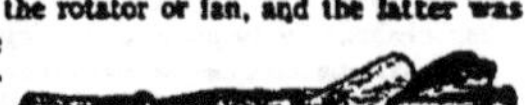

FIG. 3.—The A1 Harpoon Ship Log.

These logs were towed from the ship, but with quick passages and well surveyed coasts, the need arose for a patent log which could be readily consulted from the deck, and from which the distance run under varying speeds could be quickly ascertained. To meet this requirement, Walker in 1878 introduced the Cherub log (fig. 4), a taffrail one, which, however, is not as a rule used for speeds over 18 knots. Owing to the increased friction produced by a rotator making approximately 900 revolutions per mile, towed at the end of a line varying from 40 fathoms for a 12-knot

Fig. 4.—The Cherub Log.

speed to 60 fathoms for 20 knots, the pull of the line and rotator is borne by coned rollers, having their outlines tapering to a common point in their rotation, thus giving a broad rolling surface. Strong worms and wheels are substituted for the light clockwork. In fig. 4 the shoe H is secured to the taffrail, and the rotator in the water is hooked to the eye of the spindle M by the hook D. The case A contains the registering wheelwork and a sounding bell. The half gimbal B pivoting in the socket of the base C allows the register to receive the strain in the direct line. The bearings and rollers are lubricated with castor oil every twelve hours through holes in the sliding case E, and can be examined by unscrewing the case E and the eye M. When not in use, the register is removed from the shoe by lifting a small screw button near C. The tow line is usually plaited, and to avoid a knot close to the rotator, the latter is secured to the former by a knot inside an egg-shaped shell (fig. 5, Neptune pattern).

Fig. 5.—Neptune Pattern for securing Rotator.

Walker's Neptune log (fig. 6) is used for vessels of high speed. Case A contains the wheelwork, and case E the spindle and steel ball

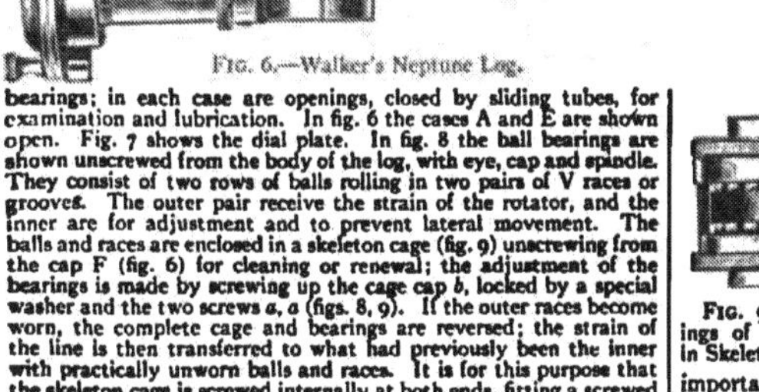

Fig. 6.—Walker's Neptune Log.

bearings; in each case are openings, closed by sliding tubes, for examination and lubrication. In fig. 6 the cases A and E are shown open. Fig. 7 shows the dial plate. In fig. 8 the ball bearings are shown unscrewed from the body of the log, with eye, cap and spindle. They consist of two rows of balls rolling in two pairs of V races or grooves. The outer pair receive the strain of the rotator, and the inner are for adjustment and to prevent lateral movement. The balls and races are enclosed in a skeleton cage (fig. 9) unscrewing from the cap F (fig. 6) for cleaning or renewal; the adjustment of the bearings is made by screwing up the cage cap *b*, locked by a special washer and the two screws *a*, *a* (figs. 8, 9). If the outer races become worn, the complete cage and bearings are reversed; the strain of the line is then transferred to what had previously been the inner with practically unworn balls and races. It is for this purpose that the skeleton cage is screwed internally at both ends, fitting a screwed ring inside the cap F (fig. 6). To enable the indications of the log register on the taffrail to be recorded in the chart room or any other part of the vessel as desired, a chart room electric register has been introduced. By means of an electric installation between the log register aft and the electric register in the chart room, every tenth of a mile indicated by the former is recorded by the latter.

Walker's Rocket log (fig. 10) is a taffrail one, with bearings of hardened steel, and is intended to be slung or secured to the taffrail by a line; the gimbal pattern has a fitting for the deck. In taffrail logs, the movement of the line owing to its length becomes spasmodic and jerky, increasing the vibration and friction; to obviate this a governor or fly-wheel is introduced, the hook of the tow line K (fig. 11) and the eye of the register M being attached to the governor. Fig. 11 represents the arrangement fitted to the Neptune log; with the Cherub log, a small piece of line is introduced between the governor and the eye of the register. The two principal American taffrail logs are the Negus and Bliss (Messrs Norie and Wilson). The former bears a general resemblance to the Cherub log, but the dial plate is horizontal and the faces turn upwards. The main shaft bearings are in two sets and composed of steel balls running in steel cones and cups; the governor is an iron rod about 16 in. long, with 1 in. balls at the extremities. The Bliss resembles the Rocket log in shape, and is secured to the taffrail by a rope or slung. A governor is not employed. The blades of the rotator are adjustable, being fitted into its tube or body by slits and holes and then soldered. The outer ends of the blades are slit (fig. 12) to form two tongues, and with the wrench (fig. 12) the angle of the pitch can be altered.

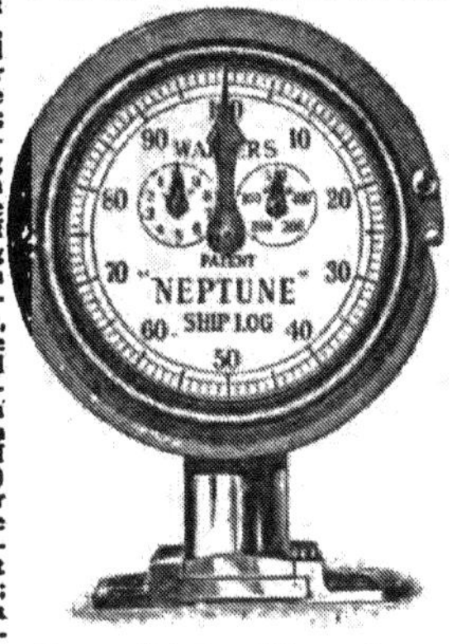

Fig. 7.—Dial-plate of Neptune Log.

All patent logs have errors, the amounts of which should be ascertained by shore observations when passing a well surveyed coast in tideless waters on a calm day. Constant use, increased friction (more especially at high speeds), and damage to the rotator will alter an ascertained log error; head or following seas, strong winds, currents and tidal streams also affect the correctness.

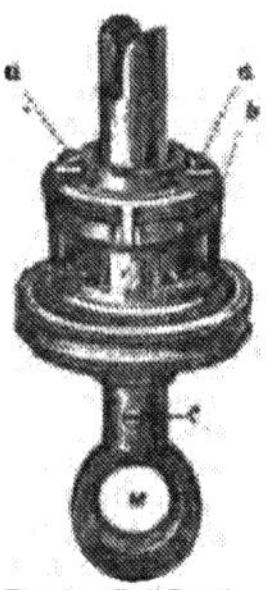

Fig. 8.—Ball Bearings of Neptune Log.

A *Log Book* is a marine or sea journal, containing, in the British navy, the speed, course, leeway, direction and force of the wind, state of the weather, and barometric and thermometric observations. Under the heading "Remarks" are noted (for vessels with sail power) making, shortening and trimming sails; and (for all ships) employment of crew, times of passing prominent landmarks, altering of course, and any subject of interest and importance. The deck log book, kept by the officers of the watch, is copied into the ship's log book by the navigating

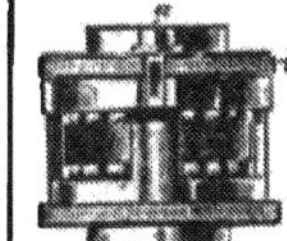

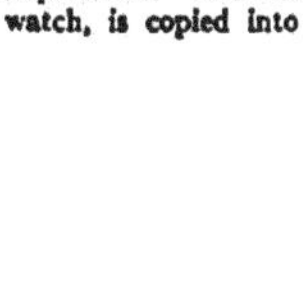

Fig. 9.—Ball Bearings of Neptune Log in Skeleton Case.

Fig. 10.—Rocket Log.

officer, and the latter is an official journal. In steam vessels a rough and fair engine room register are kept,

Fig. [illegible] Neptune Log fitted with Governor.

[illegible] with regard to the engines and boilers. [illegible] marine all ships (except those employed exclusively in trading between ports on the coasts of Scotland) are compelled to keep an official log book in a form approved by the Board of Trade. A mate's log book and engine room

Fig. [illegible] Bass Log.

[illegible], but are usually kept. (J. W. D.)

[illegible] 1780), also known as TAHGAHJUTÉ, [illegible] a Cayuga by birth, was the son of Shikel[illegible] who had been captured when a child by the [illegible] among them, and had become chief of the [illegible] Shamokin Creek in what is now Northumber[illegible]. The name Logan was given to the [illegible] Logan (1674–1751), secretary of William [illegible] friend of the Indians. John Logan lived [illegible] Reedsville, Penn., and removed to the [illegible] about 1770. He was not technically [illegible] influence among the Shawnees, into [illegible] He was on good terms with the whites [illegible] friction having arisen between the [illegible] a band of marauders, led by one Great[illegible] murdered several Indians, including, it [illegible] and possibly one or more other relatives. [illegible] Michael Cresap was responsible for this [illegible] declaration of hostilities, the result [illegible] known as Lord Dunmore's War. [illegible] Shawnee chief, Cornstalk, in meeting [illegible] council after the battle of Point [illegible] message which has become famous as [illegible]. The message seems to have [illegible] John Gibson, by whom it was [illegible] Thomas Jefferson first called [illegible] *Notes on Virginia* (1787), where he [illegible] challenge the whole orations of [illegible] of any more eminent orator, if [illegible], to produce a single passage [illegible] a victim of drink, and in 1780 [illegible] nephew whom he had attacked. [illegible] Hill Cemetery, near Auburn.

[illegible] *the Indian and Captain* [illegible] ed., Albany, 1867 defends [illegible] and also questions the [illegible] which there has been con[illegible] seems to be that of

[illegible] poet, was born at Soutra, [illegible] George Logan, was a farmer [illegible] Secession church. John [illegible] school, and in 1762 [illegible] 1769 he [illegible] John, afterwards Sir John, Sinclair, at Ulbster, Caithness, and in 1770, having left the Secession church, he was licensed as a preacher by the presbytery of Haddington. In 1771 he was presented to the charge of South Leith, but was not ordained till two years later. On the death of Michael Bruce (*q.v.*) he obtained that poet's MSS. with a view to publication. In 1770 he published *Poems on Several Occasions, by Michael Bruce* with a preface, in which, after eulogizing Bruce, who had been a fellow student of his, he remarked that "to make up a miscellany some poems wrote by different authors are inserted, all of them originals, and none of them destitute of merit. The reader of taste will easily distinguish them from those of Mr Bruce, without their being particularized by any mark." Logan was an active member of the committee of the General Assembly of the Church of Scotland which worked from 1775 to 1781 at revising the "Translations and Paraphrases" for public worship, in which many of his hymns are printed. In 1779–1781 he delivered a course of lectures on the philosophy of history at St Mary's Chapel, Edinburgh. An analysis of these lectures, *Elements of the Philosophy of History* (1781), bears striking resemblance to *A View of Ancient History* (1787), printed as the work of Dr W. Rutherford, but thought by Logan's friends to be his. In 1781 he published his own *Poems*, including the "Ode to the Cuckoo" and some other poems which had appeared in his volume of Michael Bruce's poems, and also his own contributions to the Paraphrases. His other publications were *An Essay on the Manners and Governments of Asia* (1782), *Runnamede, a tragedy* (1783), and *A Review of the Principal Charges against Warren Hastings* (1788). His connexion with the theatre gave offence to his congregation at South Leith; he was intemperate in his habits, and there was some local scandal attached to his name. He resigned his charge in 1786, retaining part of his stipend, and proceeded to London, where he became a writer for the *English Review*. He died on the 28th of December 1788. Two posthumous volumes of sermons appeared in 1790 and 1791. They were very popular, and were reprinted in 1810. His *Poetical Works* were printed in Dr Robert Anderson's *British Poets* (vol. xi., 1795), with a life of the author. They were reprinted in similar collections, and separately in 1805.

Logan was accused of having appropriated in his *Poems* (1781) verses written by Michael Bruce. The statements of John Birrell and David Pearson on behalf of Bruce were included in Dr Anderson's *Life of Logan*. The charge of plagiarism has been revived from time to time, notably by Dr W. Mackelvie (1837) and Mr James Mackenzie (1905). The whole controversy has been marked by strong partisanship. The chief points against Logan are the suppression of the major portion of Bruce's MSS. and some proved cases of plagiarism in his sermons and hymns. Even in the beautiful "Braes of Yarrow" one of the verses is borrowed direct from an old border ballad. The traditional evidence in favour of Bruce's authorship of the "Ode to the Cuckoo" can hardly be set aside, but Dr Robertson of Dalmeny, who was Logan's literary executor, stated that he had gone over the MSS. procured at Kinnesswood with Logan.

Logan's authorship of the poems in dispute is defended by David Laing, *Ode to the Cuckoo with remarks on its authorship, in a letter to J. C. Sharp, LL.D.* (1873); by John Small in the *British and Foreign Evangelical Review* (Jan. 1877, April and October, 1879); and by R. Small in two papers (Edin., 1878). See also BRUCE, MICHAEL.

LOGAN, JOHN ALEXANDER (1826–1886), American soldier and political leader, was born in what is now Murphysborough, Jackson county, Illinois, on the 9th of February 1826. He had no schooling until he was fourteen; he then studied for three years in Shiloh College, served in the Mexican War as a lieutenant of volunteers, studied law in the office of an uncle, graduated from the Law Department of Louisville University in 1851, and practised law with success. He entered politics as a Douglas Democrat, was elected county clerk in 1849, served in the State House of Representatives in 1853–1854 and in 1857, and for a time, during the interval, was prosecuting attorney of the Third Judicial District of Illinois. In 1858 and 1860 he was elected as a Democrat to the National House of Representatives. Though unattached and unenlisted, he fought at Bull Run, and then returned to Washington, resigned his seat, and entered the Union army as colonel of the 31st Illinois Volunteers, which he organized. He was regarded as one of the ablest officers who entered the army from civil life. In Grant's campaigns terminating in the capture of Vicksburg, which city Logan's division was the first to enter and of which he was military governor, he rose to the rank of major-general of volunteers; in November 1863 he succeeded Sherman in command of the XV. Army Corps; and after the death of McPherson he was in command of the Army of the Tennessee at the battle of Atlanta. When the war closed, Logan resumed his political career as a Republican, and was a member of the National House of Representatives from 1867 to 1871, and of the United States Senate from 1871 until 1877 and again from 1879 until his death, which took place at Washington, D.C., on the 26th of December 1886. He was always a violent partisan, and was identified with the radical wing of the Republican party. In 1868 he was one of the managers in the impeachment of President Johnson. His war record and his great personal following, especially in the Grand Army of the Republic, contributed to his nomination for Vice-President in 1884 on the ticket with James G. Blaine, but he was not elected. His impetuous oratory, popular on the platform, was less adapted to the halls of legislation. He was commander-in-chief of the Grand Army of the Republic from 1868 to 1871, and in this position successfully urged the observance of Memorial or Decoration Day, an idea which probably originated with him. He was the author of *The Great Conspiracy: Its Origin and History* (1886), a partisan account of the Civil War, and of *The Volunteer Soldier of America* (1887). There is a fine statue of him by St Gaudens in Chicago.

The best biography is that by George F. Dawson, *The Life and Services of Gen. John A. Logan, as Soldier and Statesman* (Chicago and New York, 1887).

LOGAN, SIR WILLIAM EDMOND (1798–1875), British geologist, was born in Montreal on the 20th of April 1798, of Scottish parents. He was educated partly in Montreal, and subsequently at the High School and university of Edinburgh, where Robert Jameson did much to excite his interest in geology. He was in a business house in London from 1817 to 1830. In 1831 he settled in Swansea to take charge of a colliery and some copper-smelting works, and here his interest in geology found abundant scope. He collected a great amount of information respecting the South Wales coal-field; and his data, which he had depicted on the 1-in. ordnance survey map, were generously placed at the disposal of the geological survey under Sir H. T. de la Beche and fully utilized. In 1840 Logan brought before the Geological Society of London his celebrated paper "On the character of the beds of clay lying immediately below the coal-seams of South Wales, and on the occurrence of coal-boulders in the Pennant Grit of that district." He then pointed out that each coal-seam rests on an under-clay with rootlets of *Stigmaria*, and he expressed his opinion that the under-clay was the old soil in which grew the plants from which the coal was formed. To confirm this observation he visited America in 1841 and examined the coal-fields of Pennsylvania and Nova Scotia, where he found the under-clay almost invariably present beneath the seams of coal. In 1842 he was appointed to take charge of the newly established geological survey in Canada, and he continued as director until 1869. During the earlier years of the survey he had many difficulties to surmount and privations to undergo, but the work was carried on with great tact and energy, and he spared no pains to make his reports trustworthy. He described the Laurentian rocks of the Laurentian mountains in Canada and of the Adirondacks in the state of New York, pointing out that they comprised an immense series of crystalline rocks, gneiss, mica-schist, quartzite and limestone, more than 30,000 ft. in thickness. The series was rightly recognized as representing the oldest type of rocks on the globe, but it is now known to be a complex of highly altered sedimentary and intrusive rocks; and the supposed oldest known fossil, the *Eozoon* described by Sir J. W. Dawson, is now regarded as a mineral structure. Logan was elected F.R.S. in 1851, and in 1856 was knighted. In the same year he was awarded the Wollaston medal by the Geological Society of London for his researches on the coal-strata, and for his excellent geological map of Canada. After his retirement in 1869, he returned to England, and eventually settled in South Wales. He died at Castle Malgwyn in Pembrokeshire, on the 22nd of June 1875.

See the *Life*, by B. J. Harrington (1883). (H. B. Wo.)

LOGAN, a city and the county-seat of Cache county, Utah, U.S.A., on the Logan river, about 70 m. N. of Salt Lake City. Pop. (1900) 5451 (1440 foreign-born); (1910) 7522. It is served by the Oregon Short Line railroad. It lies at the mouth of Logan Cañon, about 4500 ft. above the sea, and commands magnificent views of the Wasatch Mountains and the fertile Cache Valley. At Logan is a temple of the Latter-Day Saints (or Mormons), built in 1883, and the city is the seat of the Agricultural College of Utah, of Brigham Young College, and of New Jersey Academy (1878), erected by the women of the Synod of New Jersey and managed by the Woman's Board of Home Missions of the Presbyterian Church. The Agricultural College was founded in 1888 and opened in 1890; an agricultural experiment station is connected with it and the institution comprises schools of agriculture, domestic science and arts, commerce, mechanic arts and general science. Six experiment stations in different parts of the state and a central experimental farm near St George, Washington county, were in 1908 under the direction of the experiment station in Logan. Brigham Young College was endowed by Brigham Young in 1877 and was opened in 1878; it offers courses in the arts, theology, civil engineering, music, physical culture, domestic science, nurse training and manual training. Logan has various manufactures, and is the trade centre for a fertile farming region. The municipality owns and operates its water works and its electric lighting plant. Logan was settled in 1859 and first incorporated in 1866.

LOGANSPORT, a city and the county-seat of Cass county, Indiana, U.S.A., on the Wabash river, at the mouth of the Eel river, about 67 m. N. by W. of Indianapolis and 117 m. S. by E. of Chicago. Pop. (1900) 16,204, of whom 1432 were foreign-born, (1910 census) 19,050. It is served by six divisions of the Pittsburg, Cincinnati, Chicago & St Louis, two divisions of the Vandalia (Pennsylvania Lines), and the Wabash railways, and by electric interurban lines. The city is the seat of the Northern Indiana Hospital for the Insane (1888), and has a public library, and a hospital (conducted by the Sisters of St Joseph). Among the principal buildings are the court house, a Masonic temple, an Odd Fellows' temple, and buildings of the Order of Elks, of the Knights of Pythias, and of the fraternal order of Eagles. Situated in the centre of a rich agricultural region, Logansport is one of the most important grain and produce markets in the state. The Wabash and the Eel rivers provide good water power, and the city has various manufactures, besides the railway repair shops of the Vandalia and of the Pittsburg, Cincinnati, Chicago & St Louis railways. The value of the city's factory product increased from $2,100,394 in 1900 to $2,955,921 in 1905, or 40·7%. Limestone, for use in the manufacture of iron, is quarried in the vicinity. The city owns and operates the water works and the electric-lighting plant. Logansport was platted in 1828, was probably named in honour of a Shawnee chief, Captain Logan (d. 1812), became the county-seat of Cass county in 1829, and was chartered as a city in 1838.

LOGAR, a river and valley of Afghanistan. The Logar river drains a wide tract of country, rising in the southern slopes of the Sanglakh range and receiving affluents from the Kharwar hills, N.E. of Ghazni. It joins the Kabul river a few miles below the city of Kabul. The Logar valley, which is watered by its southern affluents, is rich and beautiful, about 40 m. long by 12 wide, and highly irrigated throughout. Lying in the vicinity of the capital, the district contributes largely to its food-supply. The valley was traversed in 1879 by a brigade under Sir F. (afterwards Lord) Roberts.

[illegible] (from Gr. λόγος, word, ratio, and ἀριθμός, [illegible]), a word invented by John Napier to [illegible] of function discovered by him, and [illegible] as follows: if a, x, m are any three [illegible] the equation $a^x = m$, then a is called the base, [illegible] logarithm of m to the base a. This relation [illegible] expressed also by the equation $x = \log_a m$.

[illegible]—The principal properties of logarithms are given [illegible]

$$\log_a(m/n) = \log_a m - \log_a n,$$
$$\log_a \sqrt[r]{m} = (1/r) \log_a m,$$

[illegible] deduced from the definition of a logarithm. [illegible] that the logarithm of the product [illegible] is equal to the sum of the logarithms [illegible] the logarithm of the quotient of two [illegible] the logarithm of the numerator diminished [illegible] denominator, that the logarithm of the [illegible] is equal to r times the logarithm of the [illegible] the logarithm of the rth root of a quantity [illegible] the logarithm of the quantity.

[illegible] originally invented for the sake of abbreviat[illegible], as by their means the operations [illegible] may be replaced by those of [illegible] and the operations of raising to powers [illegible] those of multiplication and division. [illegible] simplifying the operations of arith[illegible] and use is made of tables of [illegible] the values of x, the logarithm, corre[illegible] the number, are tabulated. The [illegible] frequent occurrence in analysis, [illegible] recognized function like sin x or [illegible] investigations the base generally [illegible] quantity usually denoted by the [illegible]

[illegible] if the base is not expressed [illegible] that log m denotes $\log_{10} m$; but in [illegible] understood to be e.

[illegible] the first twelve numbers to 7 [illegible]

[illegible]	log 9 = 0·9542425
[illegible]	log 10 = 1·0000000
[illegible]	log 11 = 1·0413927
[illegible]	log 12 = 1·0791812

[illegible] so that

[illegible]

[illegible] is called the index or char[illegible] the mantissa. When the base [illegible] in which the digits are the [illegible] point may be, have the same [illegible]

[illegible] log 2561300 = [illegible]

[illegible] (i.e. numbers in which the [illegible] still kept positive, so that,

[illegible] &c.

[illegible] over the characteristic, [illegible] the characteristic only, and [illegible]

[illegible] the mantissa of the logarithm [illegible] decimal point in the number [illegible] of 10 as base. The ex[illegible] is evident, for a change [illegible] amounts to multiplication [illegible] this corresponds to the [illegible] of the [illegible] should be mentioned that in most tables of trigonometrical functions, the number 10 is added to all the logarithms in the table in order to avoid the use of negative characteristics, so that the characteristic 9 denotes in reality $\bar{1}$, 8 denotes $\bar{2}$, 10 denotes 0, &c. Logarithms thus increased are frequently referred to for the sake of distinction as *tabular logarithms*, so that the tabular logarithm = the true logarithm + 10.

In tables of logarithms of numbers to base 10 the mantissa only is in general tabulated, as the characteristic of the logarithm of a number can always be written down at sight, the rule being that, if the number is greater than unity, the characteristic is less by unity than the number of digits in the integral portion of it, and that if the number is less than unity the characteristic is negative, and is greater by unity than the number of ciphers between the decimal point and the first significant figure.

It follows very simply from the definition of a logarithm that

$$\log_a b \times \log_b a = 1, \quad \log_b m = \log_a m \times (1/\log_a b).$$

The second of these relations is an important one, as it shows that from a table of logarithms to base a, the corresponding table of logarithms to base b may be deduced by multiplying all the logarithms in the former by the constant multiplier $1/\log_a b$ which is called the *modulus* of the system whose base is b with respect to the system whose base is a.

The two systems of logarithms for which extensive tables have been calculated are the Napierian, or hyperbolic, or natural system, of which the base is e, and the Briggian, or decimal, or common system, of which the base is 10; and we see that the logarithms in the latter system may be deduced from those in the former by multiplication by the constant multiplier $1/\log_e 10$, which is called the modulus of the common system of logarithms. The numerical value of this modulus is 0·43429 44819 03251 82765 11289 . . ., and the value of its reciprocal, $\log_e 10$ (by multiplication by which Briggian logarithms may be converted into Napierian logarithms) is 2·30258 50929 94045 68401 79914 . . . .

The quantity denoted by e is the series,

$$1 + \frac{1}{1} + \frac{1}{1.2} + \frac{1}{1.2.3} + \frac{1}{1.2.3.4} + \cdots$$

the numerical value of which is,

2·71828 18284 59045 23536 02874 . . .

The logarithmic Function.—The mathematical function log x or $\log_e x$ is one of the small group of transcendental functions, consisting only of the circular functions (direct and inverse) sin x, cos x, &c., arc sin x or $\sin^{-1} x$, &c., log x and e^x which are universally treated in analysis as known functions. The notation log x is generally employed in English and American works, but on the continent of Europe writers usually denote the function by lx or lg x. The logarithmic function is most naturally introduced into analysis by the equation

$$\log x = \int_1^x \frac{dt}{t}, \ (x > 0).$$

This equation defines log x for positive values of x; if $x \leq 0$ the formula ceases to have any meaning. Thus log x is the integral function of $1/x$, and it can be shown that log x is a genuinely new transcendent, not expressible in finite terms by means of functions such as algebraical or circular functions. A connexion with the circular functions, however, appears later when the definition of log x is extended to complex values of x.

A relation which is of historical interest connects the logarithmic function with the quadrature of the hyperbola, for, by considering the equation of the hyperbola in the form xy = const., it is evident that the area included between the arc of a hyperbola, its nearest asymptote, and two ordinates drawn parallel to the other asymptote from points on the first asymptote distant a and b from their point of intersection, is proportional to log b/a.

The following fundamental properties of log x are readily deducible from the definition

(i.) $\log xy = \log x + \log y$.

(ii.) Limit of $(x^h - 1)/h = \log x$, when h is indefinitely diminished.

Either of these properties might be taken as itself the definition of log x.

There is no series for log x proceeding either by ascending or descending powers of x, but there is an expansion for log $(1 + x)$, viz.

$$\log(1+x) = x - \tfrac{1}{2}x^2 + \tfrac{1}{3}x^3 - \tfrac{1}{4}x^4 + \ldots ;$$

the series, however, is convergent for real values of x only when x lies between +1 and −1. Other formulae which are deducible from the equation are given in the portion of this article relating to the calculation of logarithms.

The function log x as x increases from o towards ∞ steadily increases from $-\infty$ towards $+\infty$. It has the important property that it tends to infinity with x, but more slowly than any power of x, *i.e.* that $x^{-m} \log x$ tends to zero as x tends to ∞ for every positive value of m however small.

The exponential function, exp x, may be defined as the inverse of the logarithm: thus $x = \exp y$ if $y = \log x$. It is positive for all values of y and increases steadily from o toward ∞ as y increases from $-\infty$ towards $+\infty$. As y tends towards ∞, exp y tends towards ∞ more rapidly than any power of y.

The exponential function possesses the properties

$$\text{(i.) } \exp(x+y) = \exp x \times \exp y.$$

$$\text{(ii.) } \frac{d}{dx}\exp x = \exp x.$$

$$\text{(iii.) } \exp x = 1 + x + x^2/2! + x^3/3! + \ldots$$

From (i.) and (ii.) it may be deduced that

$$\exp x = (1 + 1 + 1/2! + 1/3! + \ldots)^x,$$

where the right-hand side denotes the positive xth power of the number $1+1+1/2!+1/3!+\ldots$ usually denoted by e. It is customary, therefore, to denote the exponential function by e^x, and the result

$$e^x = 1 + x + x^2/2! + x^3/3! \ldots$$

is known as the *exponential theorem*.

The definitions of the logarithmic and exponential functions may be extended to complex values of x. Thus if $x = \xi + i\eta$,

$$\log x = \int_1^x \frac{dt}{t}$$

where the path of integration in the plane of the complex variable t is any curve which does not pass through the origin; but now log x is not a uniform function, that is to say, if x describes a closed curve it does not follow that log x also describes a closed curve: in fact we have

$$\log(\xi + i\eta) = \log\sqrt{(\xi^2+\eta^2)} + i(\alpha + 2n\pi),$$

where α is the numerically least angle whose cosine and sine are $\xi/\sqrt{(\xi^2+\eta^2)}$ and $\eta/\sqrt{(\xi^2+\eta^2)}$, and n denotes any integer. Thus even when the argument is real log x has an infinite number of values; for putting $\eta = 0$ and taking ξ positive, in which case $\alpha = 0$, we obtain for log ξ the infinite system of values $\log \xi + 2n\pi i$. It follows from this property of the function that we cannot have for log x a series which shall be convergent for all values of x, as is the case with sin x and cos x, for such a series could only represent a uniform function, and in fact the equation

$$\log(1+x) = x - \tfrac{1}{2}x^2 + \tfrac{1}{3}x^3 - \tfrac{1}{4}x^4 + \ldots$$

is true only when the analytical modulus of x is less than unity. The exponential function, which may still be defined as the inverse of the logarithmic function, is, on the other hand, a uniform function of x, and its fundamental properties may be stated in the same form as for real values of x. Also

$$\exp(\xi + i\eta) = e^\xi(\cos\eta + i\sin\eta).$$

An alternative method of developing the theory of the exponential function is to start from the definition

$$\exp x = 1 + x + x^2/2! + x^3/3! + \ldots,$$

the series on the right-hand being convergent for all values of x and therefore defining an analytical function of x which is uniform and regular all over the plane.

Invention and Early History of Logarithms.—The invention of logarithms has been accorded to John Napier, baron of Merchiston in Scotland, with a unanimity which is rare with regard to important scientific discoveries: in fact, with the exception of the tables of Justus Byrgius, which will be referred to further on, there seems to have been no other mathematician of the time whose mind had conceived the principle on which logarithms depend, and no partial anticipations of the discovery are met with in previous writers.

The first announcement of the invention was made in Napier's *Mirifici Logarithmorum Canonis Descriptio* . . . (Edinburgh, 1614). The work is a small quarto containing fifty-seven pages of explanatory matter and a table of ninety pages (see Napier, John). The nature of logarithms is explained by reference to the motion of points in a straight line, and the principle upon which they are based is that of the correspondence of a geometrical and an arithmetical series of numbers. The table gives the logarithms of sines for every minute of seven figures; it is arranged semi-quadrantally, so that the *differentiae*, which are the differences of the two logarithms in the same line, are the logarithms of the tangents. Napier's logarithms are not the logarithms now termed Napierian or hyperbolic, that is to say, logarithms to the base e where $e = 2{\cdot}7182818\ldots$; the relation between N (a sine) and L its logarithm, as defined in the *Canonis Descriptio*, being $N = 10^7 e^{-L/10^7}$, so that (ignoring the factors 10^7, the effect of which is to render sines and logarithms integral to 7 figures), the base is e^{-1}. Napier's logarithms decrease as the sines increase. If l denotes the logarithm to base e (that is, the so-called "Napierian" or hyperbolic logarithm) and L denotes, as above, "Napier's" logarithm, the connexion between l and L is expressed by

$$L = 10^7 \log_e 10^7 - 10^7 l \text{ or } e^l = 10^7 e^{-L/10^7}$$

Napier's work (which will henceforth in this article be referred to as the *Descriptio*) immediately on its appearance in 1614 attracted the attention of perhaps the two most eminent English mathematicians then living—Edward Wright and Henry Briggs. The former translated the work into English; the latter was concerned with Napier in the change of the logarithms from those originally invented to decimal or common logarithms, and it is to him that the original calculation of the logarithmic tables now in use is mainly due. Both Napier and Wright died soon after the publication of the *Descriptio*, the date of Wright's death being 1615 and that of Napier 1617, but Briggs lived until 1631. Edward Wright, who was a fellow of Caius College, Cambridge, occupies a conspicuous place in the history of navigation. In 1599 he published *Certaine errors in Navigation detected and corrected*, and he was the author of other works; to him also is chiefly due the invention of the method known as Mercator's sailing. He at once saw the value of logarithms as an aid to navigation, and lost no time in preparing a translation, which he submitted to Napier himself. The preface to Wright's edition consists of a translation of the preface to the *Descriptio*, together with the addition of the following sentences written by Napier himself: "But now some of our countreymen in this Island well affected to these studies, and the more publique good, procured a most learned Mathematician to translate the same into our vulgar English tongue, who after he had finished it, sent the Coppy of it to me, to bee seene and considered on by myselfe. I having most willingly and gladly done the same, finde it to bee most exact and precisely conformable to my minde and the originall. Therefore it may please you who are inclined to these studies, to receive it from me and the Translator, with as much good will as we recommend it unto you." There is a short "preface to the reader" by Briggs, and a description of a triangular diagram invented by Wright for finding the proportional parts. The table is printed to one figure less than in the *Descriptio*. Edward Wright died, as has been mentioned, in 1615, and his son, Samuel Wright, in the preface states that his father "gave much commendation of this work (and often in my hearing) as of very great use to mariners"; and with respect to the translation he says that "shortly after he had it returned out of Scotland, it pleased God to call him away afore he could publish it." The translation was published in 1616. It was also reissued with a new title-page in 1618.

Henry Briggs, then professor of geometry at Gresham College, London, and afterwards Savilian professor of geometry at Oxford, welcomed the *Descriptio* with enthusiasm. In a letter to Archbishop Usher, dated Gresham House, March 10, 1615, he wrote, Napper, lord of Markinston, hath set my head and hands a work with his new and admirable logarithms. I hope to see him this summer, if it please God, for I never saw book which pleased me better, or made me more wonder.[1] I purpose to discourse with him concerning eclipses, for what is there which we may not hope for at his hands," and he also states "that he was wholly taken up and employed about the noble invention of logarithms lately discovered." Briggs accordingly visited Napier in 1615, and stayed with him a whole month.[2] He brought with him some

[1] Dr Thomas Smith thus describes the ardour with which Briggs studied the *Descriptio*: "Hunc in deliciis habuit, in sinu, in manibus, in pectore gestavit, oculisque avidissimis, et mente attentissima, iterum iterumque perlegit, . . ." *Vitae quorundam eruditissimorum et illustrium virorum* (London, 1707).

[2] William Lilly's account of the meeting of Napier and Briggs at Merchiston is quoted in the article Napier.

calculations he had made, and suggested to Napier the advantages that would result from the choice of 10 as a base, an improvement which he had explained in his lectures at Gresham College, and on which he had written to Napier. Napier said that he had already thought of the change, and pointed out a further improvement, viz., that the characteristics of numbers greater than unity should be positive and not negative, as suggested by Briggs. In 1616 Briggs again visited Napier and showed him the work he had accomplished, and, he says, he would gladly have paid him a third visit in 1617 had Napier's life been spared.

Briggs's *Logarithmorum chilias prima*, which contains the first published table of decimal or common logarithms, is only a small octavo tract of sixteen pages, and gives the logarithms of numbers from unity to 1000 to 14 places of decimals. It was [illegible], probably privately, in 1617, after Napier's death,[1] and [illegible] no author's name, place or date. The date of publication [illegible] however, fixed as 1617 by a letter from Sir Henry Bourchier [illegible], dated December 6, 1617, containing the passage—"[illegible] friend, Mr Briggs, hath lately published a supplement [illegible] most excellent tables of logarithms, which I presume he [illegible] to you." Briggs's tract of 1617 is extremely rare, and [illegible] been ignored or incorrectly described. Hutton [illegible] states that it contains the logarithms to 8 places, [illegible] account has been followed by most writers. There is a [illegible] British Museum.

[illegible] continued to labour assiduously at the calculation of [illegible] and in 1624 published his *Arithmetica logarithmica*, [illegible] containing the logarithms of the numbers from 1 [illegible] and from 90,000 to 100,000 (and in some copies to [illegible] places of decimals. The table occupies 300 pages, [illegible] an introduction of 88 pages relating to the mode of [illegible] and the applications of logarithms.

[illegible] thus left a gap between 20,000 and 90,000, which [illegible] by Adrian Vlacq (or Ulaccus), who published at [illegible], in 1628, a table containing the logarithms [illegible] from unity to 100,000 to 10 places of decimals. [illegible] 70,000 logarithms and copied only 30,000, [illegible] have been quite entitled to have called his a new [illegible] designates it, however, only a second edition of [illegible] *logarithmica*, the title running *Arithmetica [illegible] Logarithmorum Chiliades centum, . . . editio [illegible] Adrianum Vlacq, Goudanum.* This table of [illegible] published, with an English explanation prefixed, [illegible] under the title *Logarithmicall Arithmetike* . . . [illegible] by George Miller, 1631. There are also copies [illegible] and introduction in French and in Dutch [illegible]

[illegible] been engaged in filling up the gap, and in [illegible] written after the publication of Vlacq's [illegible] October 25, 1628, he says:—

"[illegible] those chiliades that are wantinge betwixt [illegible] printed, and I had done them all almost by [illegible] whom my rules had sufficiently in- [illegible] the busines was conveniently parted [illegible] of that charge and care by one Adrian [illegible] who hathe done all the whole hundred [illegible] in Latin, Dutche and Frenche, 1000 [illegible] and hathe sould them almost all. But [illegible] throughout; and hathe left out my [illegible] and two chapters the 12 and 13, in the [illegible] at all."

The [illegible] of the logarithms of numbers from [illegible] and [illegible] by Briggs and Vlacq between [illegible] not [illegible] is that from which all the hundreds [illegible] have subsequently appeared have [illegible] many errors, which were [illegible] in the course of the next [illegible]

The fa[illegible] is indep[illegible] affords [illegible] of Briggian or common [illegible] planatio[illegible] was made in 1620 by [illegible] in the p[illegible] colleague as professor of [illegible] or divisi[illegible] Briggs [illegible] addition [illegible] as the [illegible] logarithms, [illegible]

astronomy in Gresham College. The title of Gunter's book, which is very scarce, is *Canon triangulorum*, and it contains logarithmic sines and tangents for every minute of the quadrant to 7 places of decimals.

The next publication was due to Vlacq, who appended to his logarithms of numbers in the *Arithmetica logarithmica* of 1628 a table giving log sines, tangents and secants for every minute of the quadrant to 10 places; there were obtained by calculating the logarithms of the natural sines, &c. given in the *Thesaurus mathematicus* of Pitiscus (1613).

During the last years of his life Briggs devoted himself to the calculation of logarithmic sines, &c. and at the time of his death in 1631 he had all but completed a logarithmic canon to every hundredth of a degree. This work was published by Vlacq at his own expense at Gouda in 1633, under the title *Trigonometria Britannica*. It contains log sines (to 14 places) and tangents (to 10 places), besides natural sines, tangents and secants, at intervals of a hundredth of a degree. In the same year Vlacq published at Gouda his *Trigonometria artificialis*, giving log sines and tangents to every 10 seconds of the quadrant to 10 places. This work also contains the logarithms of numbers from unity to 20,000 taken from the *Arithmetica logarithmica* of 1628. Briggs appreciated clearly the advantages of a centesimal division of the quadrant, and by dividing the degree into hundredth parts instead of into minutes, made a step towards a reformation in this respect, and but for the appearance of Vlacq's work the decimal division of the degree might have become recognized, as is now the case with the corresponding division of the second. The calculation of the logarithms not only of numbers but also of the trigonometrical functions is therefore due to Briggs and Vlacq; and the results contained in their four fundamental works—*Arithmetica logarithmica* (Briggs), 1624; *Arithmetica logarithmica* (Vlacq), 1628; *Trigonometria Britannica* (Briggs), 1633; *Trigonometria artificialis* (Vlacq), 1633—have not been superseded by any subsequent calculations.

In the preceding paragraphs an account has been given of the actual announcement of the invention of logarithms and of the calculation of the tables. It now remains to refer in more detail to the invention itself and to examine the claims of Napier and Briggs to the capital improvement involved in the change from Napier's original logarithms to logarithms to the base 10.

The *Descriptio* contained only an explanation of the use of the logarithms without any account of the manner in which the canon was constructed. In an "Admonitio" on the seventh page Napier states that, although in that place the mode of construction should be explained, he proceeds at once to the use of the logarithms, "ut praelibatis prius usu, et rei utilitate, caetera aut magis placeant posthac edenda, aut minus saltem displiceant silentio sepulta." He awaits therefore the judgment and censure of the learned "priusquam caetera in lucem temerè prolata lividorum detrectationi exponantur"; and in an "Admonitio" on the last page of the book he states that he will publish the mode of construction of the canon "si huius inventi usum eruditis gratum fore intellexero." Napier, however, did not live to keep this promise. In 1617 he published a small work entitled *Rabdologia* relating to mechanical methods of performing multiplications and divisions, and in the same year he died.

The proposed work was published in 1619 by Robert Napier, his second son by his second marriage, under the title *Mirifici logarithmorum canonis constructio. . . .* It consists of two pages of preface followed by sixty-seven pages of text. In the preface Robert Napier says that he has been assured from undoubted authority that the new invention is much thought of by the ablest mathematicians, and that nothing would delight them more than the publication of the mode of construction of the canon. He therefore issues the work to satisfy their desires, although, he states, it is manifest that it would have seen the light in a far more perfect state if his father could have put the finishing touches to it; and he mentions that, in the opinion of the best judges, his father possessed, among other most excellent gifts, in the highest degree the power of explaining the most difficult matters by a certain and easy method in the fewest possible words.

It is important to notice that in the *Constructio* logarithms are called artificial numbers; and Robert Napier states that the work was composed several years (*aliquot annos*) before Napier had invented the name logarithm. The *Constructio* therefore may have been written a good many years previous to the publication of the *Descriptio* in 1614.

Passing now to the invention of common or decimal logarithms, that is, to the transition from the logarithms originally invented by Napier to logarithms to the base 10, the first allusion to a change of system occurs in the "Admonitio" on the last page of the *Descriptio* (1614), the concluding paragraph of which is "Verùm si huius inventi usum eruditis gratum fore intellexero, dabo fortasse brevi (Deo aspirante) rationem ac methodum aut hunc canonem emendandi, aut emendatiorem de novo condendi, ut ita plurium Logistarum diligentia, limatior tandem et accuratior, quàm unius opera fieri potuit, in lucem prodeat. Nihil in ortu perfectum." In some copies, however, this "Admonitio" is absent. In Wright's translation of 1616 Napier has added the sentence—"But because the addition and subtraction of these former numbers may seeme somewhat painfull, I intend (if it shall please God) in a second Edition, to set out such Logarithmes as shall make those numbers above written to fall upon decimal numbers, such as 100,000,000, 200,000,000, 300,000,000, &c., which are easie to be added or abated to or from any other number" (p. 19); and in the dedication of the *Rabdologia* (1617) he wrote "Quorum quidem Logarithmorum speciem aliam multò praestantiorem nunc etiam invenimus, & creandi methodum, unà cum eorum usu (si Deus longiorem vitae & valetudinis usuram concesserit) evulgare statuimus; ipsam autem novi canonis supputationem, ob infirmam corporis nostri valetudinem, viris in hoc studii genere versatis relinquimus: imprimis verò doctissimo viro D. Henrico Briggio Londini publico Geometriae Professori, et amico mihi longè charissimo."

Briggs in the short preface to his *Logarithmorum chilias* (1617) states that the reason why his logarithms are different from those introduced by Napier "sperandum, ejus librum posthumum, abunde nobis propediem satisfacturum." The "liber posthumus" was the *Constructio* (1619), in the preface to which Robert Napier states that he has added an appendix relating to another and more excellent species of logarithms, referred to by the inventor himself in the *Rabdologia*, and in which the logarithm of unity is 0. He also mentions that he has published some remarks upon the propositions in spherical trigonometry and upon the new species of logarithms by Henry Briggs, "qui novi hujus Canonis supputandi laborem gravissimum, pro singulari amicitiâ quae illi cum Patre meo L. M. intercessit, animo libentissimo in se suscepit; creandi methodo, et usuum explanatione Inventori relictis. Nunc autem ipso ex hâc vitâ evocato, totius negotii onus doctissimi Briggii humeris incumbere, et Sparta haec ornanda illi sorte quadam obtigisse videtur."

In the address prefixed to the *Arithmetica Logarithmica* (1625) Briggs bids the reader not to be surprised that these logarithms are different from those published in the *Descriptio*:—

"Ego enim, cum meis auditoribus Londini, publice in Collegio Greshamensi horum doctrinam explicarem; animadverti multo futurum commodius, si Logarithmus sinus totius servaretur 0 (ut in Canone mirifico), Logarithmus autem partis decimae ejusdem sinus totius, nempe sinus 5 graduum, 44, m. 21, s., esset 1000000000. atque ea de re scripsi statim ad ipsum authorem, et quamprimum per anni tempus, et vacationem a publico docendi munere licuit, profectus sum Edinburgum; ubi humanissime ab eo acceptus haesi per integrum mensem. Cum autem inter nos de horum mutatione sermo haberetur; ille se idem dudum sensisse, et cupivisse dicebat: veruntamen istos, quos jam paraverat edendos curasse, donec alios, si per negotia et valetudinem liceret, magis commodos confecisset. Istam autem mutationem ita faciendam censebat, ut 0 esset Logarithmus unitatis, et 10000000000 sinus totius: quod ego longe commodissimum esse non potui non agnoscere. Coepi igitur, ejus hortatu, rejectis illis quos anteà paraveram, de horum calculo serio cogitare; et sequenti aestate iterum profectus Edinburgum, horum quos hic exhibeo praecipuos, illi ostendi, idem etiam tertia aestate libentissime facturus, si Deus illum nobis tamdiu superstitem esse voluisset."

There is also a reference to the change of the logarithms on the title-page of the work.

These extracts contain all the original statements made by Napier, Robert Napier and Briggs which have reference to the origin of decimal logarithms. It will be seen that they are all in perfect agreement. Briggs pointed out in his lectures at Gresham College that it would be more convenient that 0 should stand for the logarithm of the whole sine as in the *Descriptio*, but that the logarithm of the tenth part of the whole sine should be 10,000,000,000. He wrote also to Napier at once; and as soon as he could he went to Edinburgh to visit him, where, as he was most hospitably received by him, he remained for a whole month. When they conversed about the change of system, Napier said that he had perceived and desired the same thing, but that he had published the tables which he had already prepared, so that they might be used until he could construct others more convenient. But he considered that the change ought to be so made that 0 should be the logarithm of unity and 10,000,000,000 that of the whole sine, which Briggs could not but admit was by far the most convenient of all. Rejecting therefore, those which he had prepared already, Briggs began, at Napier's advice, to consider seriously the question of the calculation of new tables. In the following summer he went to Edinburgh and showed Napier the principal portion of the logarithms which he published in 1624. These probably included the logarithms of the first chiliad which he published in 1617.

It has been thought necessary to give in detail the facts relating to the conversion of the logarithms, as unfortunately Charles Hutton in his history of logarithms, which was prefixed to the early editions of his *Mathematical Tables*, and was also published as one of his *Mathematical Tracts*, has charged Napier with want of candour in not telling the world of Briggs's share in the change of system, and he expresses the suspicion that "Napier was desirous that the world should ascribe to him alone the merit of this very useful improvement of the logarithms." According to Hutton's view, the words, "*it is to be hoped* that his posthumous work" . . . which occur in the preface to the *Chilias*, were a modest hint that the share Briggs had had in changing the logarithms should be mentioned, and that, as no attention was paid to it, he himself gave the account which appears in the *Arithmetica* of 1624. There seems, however, no ground whatever for supposing that Briggs meant to express anything beyond his hope that the reason for the alteration would be explained in the posthumous work; and in his own account, written seven years after Napier's death and five years after the appearance of the work itself, he shows no injured feeling whatever, but even goes out of his way to explain that he abandoned his own proposed alteration in favour of Napier's, and, rejecting the tables he had already constructed, began to consider the calculation of new ones. The facts, as stated by Napier and Briggs, are in complete accordance, and the friendship existing between them was perfect and unbroken to the last. Briggs assisted Robert Napier in the editing of the "posthumous work," the *Constructio*, and in the account he gives of the alteration of the logarithms in the *Arithmetica* of 1624 he seems to have been more anxious that justice should be done to Napier than to himself; while on the other hand Napier received Briggs most hospitably and refers to him as "amico mihi longè charissimo."

Hutton's suggestions are all the more to be regretted as they occur as a history which is the result of a good deal of investigation and which for years was referred to as an authority by many writers. His prejudice against Napier naturally produced retaliation, and Mark Napier in defending his ancestor has fallen into the opposite extreme of attempting to reduce Briggs to the level of a mere computer. In connexion with this controversy it should be noticed that the "Admonitio" on the last page of the *Descriptio*, containing the reference to the new logarithms, does not occur in all the copies. It is printed on the back of the last page of the table itself, and so cannot have been torn out from the copies that are without it. As there could have been no reason for omitting it after it had once appeared, we may assume that the copies which do not have it are those which were first issued. It is probable, therefore, that Briggs's copy contained no reference to the change, and it is even possible that the "Admonitio" may have been added after Briggs had communicated with Napier. As special attention has not been drawn to the fact that some copies have the "Admonitio" and some have not, different writers have assumed that Briggs did or did not know of the promise contained in the "Admonitio" according as it was present or absent in the copies they had themselves referred to, and this has given rise to some confusion. It may also be remarked that the date frequently assigned to Briggs's first visit to Napier is 1616, and not 1615 as stated above, the reason being that Napier was generally supposed to have died in 1618 until Mark Napier showed that the true date was 1617. When the *Descriptio* was published Briggs was fifty-seven years of age, and the remaining seventeen years of his life were devoted with steady enthusiasm to extend the utility of Napier's great invention.

The only other mathematician besides Napier who grasped the idea on which the use of logarithm depends and applied it to the construction of a table is Justus Byrgius (Jobst Bürgi), whose work *Arithmetische und geometrische Progress-Tabulen* ... was published at Prague in 1620, six years after the publication of the *Descriptio* of Napier. This table distinctly involves the principle of logarithms and may be described as a modified table of antilogarithms. It consists of two series of numbers, the one being an arithmetical and the other a geometrical progression: thus

0, 1,0000 0000
10, 1,0001 0000
20, 1,0002 0001.
. . . .
990, 1,0099 4967
. . . .

In the arithmetical column the numbers increase by 10, in the geometrical column each number is derived from its predecessor by multiplication by 1·0001. Thus the number $10x$ in the arithmetical column corresponds to $10^8 (1\cdot0001)^x$ in the geometrical column; the intermediate numbers being obtained by interpolation. If we divide the numbers in the geometrical column by 10^8 the correspondence is between $10x$ and $(1\cdot0001)^x$, and the table then becomes one of antilogarithms, the base being $(1\cdot0001)^{1/10}$, viz. for example $(1\cdot0001)^{\frac{1}{10}\cdot 990} = 1\cdot00994967$. The table extends to 230270 in the arithmetical column, and it is shown that 230270·022 corresponds to 9·9999 9999 or 109 in the geometrical column; this last result showing that $(1\cdot0001)^{23027\cdot022} = 10$. The first contemporary mention of Byrgius's table occurs on page 11 of the "Praecepta" prefixed to Kepler's *Tabulae Rudolphinae* (1627); his words are: "apices logistici J. Byrgio multis annis ante editionem Neperianam viam praeiverent ad hos ipsissimos logarithmos. Etsi homo cunctator et secretorum suorum custos foetum in partu destituit, non ad usus publicos educavit." Another reference to Byrgius occurs in a work by Benjamin Bramer, the brother-in-law and pupil of Byrgius, who, writing in 1630, says that the latter constructed his table twenty years ago or more.[1]

As regards priority of publication, Napier has the advantage by six years, and even fully accepting Bramer's statement, there are grounds for believing that Napier's work dates from a still earlier period.

The power of 10, which occurs as a factor in the tables of both Napier and Byrgius, was rendered necessary by the fact that the decimal point was not yet in use. Omitting this factor in the case of both tables, the connexion between N a number and L its "logarithm" is

$$N = (e^{-1})^L \text{ (Napier)}, \quad L = (1\cdot0001)^{\frac{1}{10}N} \text{ (Byrgius)},$$

viz. Napier gives logarithms to base e^{-1}, Byrgius gives antilogarithms to base $(1\cdot0001)^{\frac{1}{10}}$.

There is indirect evidence that Napier was occupied with logarithms as early as 1594, for in a letter to P. Crügerus from Kepler, dated September 9, 1624 (Frisch's *Kepler*, vi. 47), there occurs the sentence: "Nihil autem supra Neperianam rationem esse puto: etsi quidem Scotus quidam literis ad Tychonem 1594 scriptis jam spem fecit Canonis illius Mirifici." It is here distinctly stated that some Scotsman in the year 1594, in a letter to Tycho Brahe, gave him some hope of the logarithms; and as Kepler joined Tycho after his expulsion from the island of Huen, and had been so closely associated with him in his work, he would be likely to be correct in any assertion of this kind. In connexion with Kepler's statement the following story, told by Anthony Wood in the *Athenae Oxonienses*, is of some importance:—

> "It must be now known, that one Dr Craig, a Scotchman ... coming out of Denmark into his own country, called upon Joh. Neper, Baron of Mercheston, near Edinburgh, and told him, among other discourses, of a new invention in Denmark (by Longomontanus, as 'tis said), to save the tedious multiplication and division in astronomical calculations. Neper being solicitous to know farther of him concerning this matter, he could give no other account of it than that it was by proportional numbers. Which hint Neper taking, he desired him at his return to call upon him again. Craig, after some weeks had passed, did so, and Neper then showed him a rude draught of what he called *Canon mirabilis logarithmorum*. Which draught, with some alterations, he printing in 1614, it came forthwith into the hands of our author Briggs, and into those of Will. Oughtred, from whom the relation of this matter came."

This story, though obviously untrue in some respects, gives valuable information by connecting Dr Craig with Napier and Longomontanus, who was Tycho Brahe's assistant. Dr Craig was John Craig, the third son of Thomas Craig, who was one of the colleagues of Sir Archibald Napier, John Napier's father, in the office of justice-depute. Between John Craig and John Napier a friendship sprang up which may have been due to their common taste for mathematics. There are extant three letters from Dr John Craig to Tycho Brahe, which show that he was on the most friendly terms with him. In the first letter, of which the date is not given, Craig says that Sir William Stuart has safely delivered to him, "about the beginning of last winter," the book which he sent him. Now Mark Napier found in the library of the university of Edinburgh a mathematical work bearing a sentence in Latin which he translates, "To Doctor John Craig of Edinburgh, in Scotland, a most illustrious man, highly gifted with various and excellent learning, professor of medicine, and exceedingly skilled in the mathematics, Tycho Brahe hath sent this gift, and with his own hand written this at Uraniburg, 2d November 1588." As Sir William Stuart was sent to Denmark to arrange the preliminaries of King James's marriage, and returned to Edinburgh on the 15th of November 1588, it would seem probable that this was the volume referred to by Craig. It appears from Craig's letter, to which we may therefore assign the date 1589, that, five years before, he had made an attempt to reach Uranienburg, but had been baffled by the storms and rocks of Norway, and that ever since then he had been longing to visit Tycho. Now John Craig was physician to the king, and in 1590 James VI. spent some days at Uranienburg, before returning to Scotland from his matrimonial expedition. It seems not unlikely therefore that Craig may have accompanied the king in his visit to Uranienburg.[2] In any case it is certain that Craig was a friend and correspondent of Tycho's, and it is probable that he was the "Scotus quidam."

We may infer therefore that as early as 1594 Napier had communicated to some one, probably John Craig, his hope of being able to effect a simplification in the processes of arithmetic. Everything tends to show that the invention of logarithms

[1] [illegible] *Kepleri opera omnia*, ii. 834. Frisch thinks Bramer [illegible] relied on Kepler's statement quoted in the text ("Quibus [illegible] Kepleri verbis Benj. Bramer ..."). See also vol. vii.
[illegible] of Byrgius are discussed in Kästner's *Geschichte der* [illegible], ii. 375, and iii. 14; Montucla's *Histoire des mathé*[illegible] 10; Delambre's *Histoire de l'astronomie moderne*, [illegible] Morgan's article on "Tables" in the *English* [illegible]. Mark Napier's *Memoirs of John Napier of Merchiston* [illegible] and Cantor's *Geschichte der Mathematik*, ii. (1892), [illegible]wald, *Justus Byrg als Mathematiker und dessen* [illegible] *Logarithmen* (Danzig, 1856).

[2] See Mark Napier's *Memoirs of John Napier of Merchiston* (1834), p. 362.

was the result of many years of labour and thought,[1] undertaken with this special object, and it would seem that Napier had seen some prospect of success nearly twenty years before the publication of the *Descriptio*. It is very evident that no mere hint with regard to the use of proportional numbers could have been of any service to him, but it is possible that the news brought by Craig of the difficulties placed in the progress of astronomy by the labour of the calculations may have stimulated him to persevere in his efforts.

The "new invention in Denmark" to which Anthony Wood refers as having given the hint to Napier was probably the method of calculation called prosthaphaeresis (often written in Greek letters προσθαφαίρεσις), which had its origin in the solution of spherical triangles.[2] The method consists in the use of the formula

$$\sin a \sin b = \tfrac{1}{2}\{\cos(a-b) - \cos(a+b)\},$$

by means of which the multiplication of two sines is reduced to the addition or subtraction of two tabular results taken from a table of sines; and, as such products occur in the solution of spherical triangles, the method affords the solution of spherical triangles in certain cases by addition and subtraction only. It seems to be due to Wittich of Breslau, who was assistant for a short time to Tycho Brahe; and it was used by them in their calculations in 1582. Wittich in 1584 made known at Cassel the calculation of one case by this prosthaphaeresis; and Justus Byrgius proved it in such a manner that from his proof the extension to the solution of all triangles could be deduced.[3] Clavius generalized the method in his treatise *De astrolabio* (1593), lib. i. lemma liii. The lemma is enunciated as follows:—

"Quaestiones omnes, quae per sinus, tangentes, atque secantes absolvi solent, per solam prosthaphaeresim, id est, per solam additionem, subtractionem, sine laboriosa numerorum multiplicatione divisioneque expedire."

Clavius then refers to a work of Raymarus Ursus Dithmarsus as containing an account of a particular case. The work is probably the *Fundamentum astronomicum* (1588). Longomontanus, in his *Astronomia Danica* (1622), gives an account of the method, stating that it is not to be found in the writings of the Arabs or Regiomontanus. As Longomontanus is mentioned in Anthony Wood's anecdote, and as Wittich as well as Longomontanus were assistants of Tycho, we may infer that Wittich's prosthaphaeresis is the method referred to by Wood.

It is evident that Wittich's prosthaphaeresis could not be a good method of practically effecting multiplications unless the quantities to be multiplied were sines, on account of the labour of the interpolations. It satisfies the condition, however, equally with logarithms, of enabling multiplication to be performed by the aid of a table of single entry; and, analytically considered, it is not so different in principle from the logarithmic method. In fact, if we put $xy = \phi(X+Y)$, X being a function of x only and Y a function of y only, we can show that we must have $X = Ae^{ax}$, $y = Be^{aY}$; and if we put $xy = \phi(X+Y) - \phi(X-Y)$, the solutions are $\phi(X+Y) = \tfrac{1}{4}(x+y)^2$, and $x = \sin X$, $y = \sin Y$, $\phi(X+Y) = -\tfrac{1}{2}\cos(X+Y)$. The former solution gives a method known as that of quarter-squares; the latter gives the method of prosthaphaeresis.

An account has now been given of Napier's invention and its publication, the transition to decimal logarithms, the calculation of the tables by Briggs, Vlacq and Gunter, as well as of the claims of Byrgius and the method of prosthaphaeresis. To complete the early history of logarithms it is necessary to return to Napier's *Descriptio* in order to describe its reception on the continent, and to mention the other logarithmic tables which were published while Briggs was occupied with his calculations.

John Kepler, who has been already quoted in connexion with Craig's visit to Tycho Brahe, received the invention of logarithms almost as enthusiastically as Briggs. His first mention of the subject occurs in a letter to Schikhart dated the 11th of March 1618, in which he writes—"Extitit Scotus Baro, cujus nomen mihi excidit, qui praeclari quid praestitit, necessitate omni multiplicationum et divisionum in meras additiones et subtractiones commutata, nec sinibus utitur: at tamen opus est ipsi tangentium canone: et varietas, crebritas, difficultasque additionum subtractionumque alicubi laborem multiplicandi et dividendi superat." This erroneous estimate was formed when he had seen the *Descriptio* but had not read it; and his opinion was very different when he became acquainted with the nature of logarithms. The dedication of his *Ephemeris* for 1620 consists of a letter to Napier dated the 28th of July 1619, and he there congratulates him warmly on his invention and on the benefit he has conferred upon astronomy generally and upon Kepler's own Rudolphine tables. He says that, although Napier's book had been published five years, he first saw it at Prague two years before; he was then unable to read it, but last year he had met with a little work by Benjamin Ursinus[4] containing the substance of the method, and he at once recognized the importance of what had been effected. He then explains how he verified the canon, and so found that there were no essential errors in it, although there were a few inaccuracies near the beginning of the quadrant, and he proceeds, "Haec te obiter scire volui, ut quibus tu methodis incesseris, quas non dubito et plurimas et ingeniosissimas tibi in promptu esse, eas publici juris fieri, mihi saltem (puto et caeteris) scires fore gratissimum; eoque percepto, tua promissa folio 57, in debitum cecidisse intelligeres." This letter was written two years after Napier's death (of which Kepler was unaware), and in the same year as that in which the *Constructio* was published. In the same year (1620) Napier's *Descriptio* (1614) and *Constructio* (1619) were reprinted by Bartholomew Vincent at Lyons and issued together.[5]

Napier calculated no logarithms of numbers, and, as already stated, the logarithms invented by him were not to base e. The first logarithms to the base e were published by John Speidell in his *New Logarithmes* (London, 1619), which contains hyperbolic log sines, tangents and secants for every minute of the quadrant to 5 places of decimals.

In 1624 Benjamin Ursinus published at Cologne a canon of logarithms exactly similar to Napier's in the *Descriptio* of 1614, only much enlarged. The interval of the arguments is 10″, and the results are given to 8 places; in Napier's canon the interval is 1′, and the number of places is 7. The logarithms are strictly Napierian, and the arrangement is identical with that in the canon of 1614. This is the largest Napierian canon that has ever been published.

In the same year (1624) Kepler published at Marburg a table of Napierian logarithms of sines with certain additional columns to facilitate special calculations.

The first publication of Briggian logarithms on the continent is due to Wingate, who published at Paris in 1625 his *Arithmétique logarithmétique*, containing seven-figure logarithms of

[1] In the *Rabdologia* (1617) he speaks of the canon of logarithms as "a me longo tempore elaboratum."

[2] A careful examination of the history of the method is given by Scheibel in his *Einleitung zur mathematischen Bucherkenntniss*, Stück vii. (Breslau, 1775), pp. 13-20; and there is also an account in Kästner's *Geschichte der Mathematik*, i. 566-569 (1796); in Montucla's *Histoire des mathématiques*, i. 583-585 and 617-619; and in Klügel's *Wörterbuch* (1808), article "Prosthaphaeresis."

[3] Besides his connexion with logarithms and improvements in the method of prosthaphaeresis, Byrgius has a share in the invention of decimal fractions. See Cantor, *Geschichte*, ii. 567. Cantor attributes to him (in the use of his prosthaphaeresis) the first introduction of a subsidiary angle into trigonometry (vol. ii. 590).

[4] The title of this work is—*Benjaminis Ursini . . . cursus mathematici practici volumen primum continens illustr. & generosi Dn. Dn. Johannis Neperi Baronis Merchistonij &c. Scoti trigonometriam logarithmicam usibus discentium accommodatam . . . Coloniae . . . CIƆ IƆC XIX.* At the end, Napier's table is reprinted, but to two figures less. This work forms the earliest publication of logarithms on the continent.

[5] The title is *Logarithmorum canonis descriptio, seu arithmeticarum supputationum mirabilis abbreviatio. Ejusque usus in utraque trigonometria ut etiam in omni logistica mathematica, amplissimi, facillimi & expeditissimi explicatio. Authore ac inventore Ioanne Nepero, Barone Merchistonii, &c. Scoto. Lugduni . . .* It will be seen that this title is different from that of Napier's work of 1614; many writers have, however, erroneously given it as the title of the latter.

[illegible] up to 1000, and log sines and tangents from Gunter's [illegible] (1620). In the following year, 1626, Denis Henrion [illegible]ublished at Paris a *Traicté des Logarithmes*, containing Briggs's [illegible]rithms of numbers up to 20,001 to 10 places, and Gunter's [illegible] sines and tangents to 7 places for every minute. In the same [illegible] de Decker also published at Gouda a work entitled *Nieuwe [illegible], inhoudende de Logarithmi voor de Ghetallen beginnende [illegible] 1 tot 10,000*, which contained logarithms of numbers up to [illegible] to 10 places, taken from Briggs's *Arithmetica* of 1624, and [illegible]'s log sines and tangents to 7 places for every minute.[1] [illegible] rendered assistance in the publication of this work, and [illegible] privilege is made out to him.

[illegible] invention of logarithms and the calculation of the earlier [illegible] form a very striking episode in the history of exact science, [illegible] with the exception of the *Principia* of Newton, there is [illegible] mathematical work published in the country which has pro[illegible] such important consequences, or to which so much interest [illegible] as to Napier's *Descriptio*. The calculation of tables [illegible] natural trigonometrical functions may be said to have [illegible] the work of the last half of the 16th century, and the great [illegible] of natural sines for every 10 seconds to 15 places which [illegible] calculated by Rheticus was published by Pitiscus only [illegible] the year before that in which the *Descriptio* appeared. [illegible] construction of the natural trigonometrical tables Great [illegible] had taken no part, and it is remarkable that the discovery [illegible] principles and the formation of the tables that were to [illegible] or supersede all the methods of calculation then [illegible] have been so rapidly effected and developed in a [illegible] which so little attention had been previously devoted [illegible].

[illegible] detailed information relating to Napier, Briggs and [illegible] invention of logarithms, the reader is referred to the [illegible] *Lives of the Professors of Gresham College* [illegible] Smith's *Vitae quorundam eruditissimorum* [illegible]ta Henrici Briggii) (London, 1707); Mark [illegible] *Napier* already referred to, and the same [illegible] *supersunt* (1839); Hutton's *History*; de [illegible] referred to; Delambre's *Histoire de l'Astro*[illegible] [illegible]rt on mathematical tables in the *Report of* [illegible] 1873; and the *Philosophical Magazine* for [illegible] 1872 and May 1873. It may be remarked [illegible] assigned to Briggs's first visit to Napier is 1616 [illegible] above, the reason being that Napier was [illegible] have died in 1618; but it was shown by Mark [illegible] in 1617.

[illegible] Francis Maseres published at London, [illegible] "Scriptores Logarithmici, or a collection [illegible] tracts on the nature and construction of [illegible] Dr Hutton's historical introduction [illegible] mathematical tables . . .," [illegible] *Descriptio* of 1614. Kepler's [illegible] In 1889 a translation [illegible] was published by Walter Rae [illegible] are added by the translator, [illegible] the method employed [illegible] of a small [illegible] Appended to the Catalogue [illegible] of all Napier's writings, with [illegible] British and foreign, which possess [illegible] reproduction of Bartholomew [illegible] of the [illegible] was issued in [illegible] (this imprint occurs on page 62 [illegible]

[illegible] a few of the more important [illegible] tables subsequent to the [illegible]

[illegible] of Numbers.—Nathaniel Roe's [illegible] the first complete seven-figure [illegible]

[illegible] the language [illegible] so that for [illegible] as a table to 7 [illegible] spoken of as [illegible] Briggs, [illegible] of con[illegible]

[illegible]

table that was published. It contains seven-figure logarithms of numbers from 1 to 100,000, with characteristics unseparated from the mantissae, and was formed from Vlacq's table (1628) by leaving out the last three figures. All the figures of the number are given at the head of the columns, except the last two, which run down the extreme columns—1 to 50 on the left-hand side, and 50 to 100 on the right-hand side. The first four figures of the logarithms are printed at the top of the columns. There is thus an advance half way towards the arrangement now universal in seven-figure tables. The final step was made by John Newton in his *Trigonometria Britannica* (1658), a work which is also noticeable as being the only extensive eight-figure table that until recently had been published; it contains logarithms of sines, &c., as well as logarithms of numbers.

In 1705 appeared the original edition of Sherwin's tables, the first of the series of ordinary seven-figure tables of logarithms of numbers and trigonometrical functions such as are in general use now. The work went through several editions during the 18th century, and was at length superseded in 1785 by Hutton's tables, which continued in successive editions to maintain their position for a century.

In 1717 Abraham Sharp published in his *Geometry Improv'd* the Briggian logarithms of numbers from 1 to 100, and of primes from 100 to 1100, to 61 places; these were copied into the later editions of Sherwin and other works.

In 1742 a seven-figure table was published in quarto form by Gardiner, which is celebrated on account of its accuracy and of the elegance of the printing. A French edition, which closely resembles the original, was published at Avignon in 1770.

In 1783 appeared at Paris the first edition of François Callet's tables, which correspond to those of Hutton in England. These tables, which form perhaps the most complete and practically useful collection of logarithms for the general computer that has been published, passed through many editions.

In 1794 Vega published his *Thesaurus logarithmorum completus*, a folio volume containing a reprint of the logarithms of numbers from Vlacq's *Arithmetica logarithmica* of 1628, and *Trigonometria artificialis* of 1633. The logarithms of numbers are arranged as in an ordinary seven-figure table. In addition to the logarithms reprinted from the *Trigonometria*, there are given logarithms for every second of the first two degrees, which were the result of an original calculation. Vega devoted great attention to the detection and correction of the errors in Vlacq's work of 1628. Vega's *Thesaurus* has been reproduced photographically by the Italian government. Vega also published in 1797, in 2 vols. 8vo, a collection of logarithmic and trigonometrical tables which has passed through many editions, a very useful one volume stereotype edition having been published in 1840 by Hülsse. The tables in this work may be regarded as to some extent supplementary to those in Callet.

If we consider only the logarithms of numbers, the main line of descent from the original calculation of Briggs and Vlacq is Roe, John Newton, Sherwin, Gardiner; there are then two branches, viz. Hutton founded on Sherwin and Callet on Gardiner, and the editions of Vega form a separate offshoot from the original tables. Among the most useful and accessible of modern ordinary seven-figure tables of logarithms of numbers and trigonometrical functions may be mentioned those of Bremiker, Schrön and Bruhns. For logarithms of numbers only perhaps Babbage's table is the most convenient.[2]

In 1871 Edward Sang published a seven-figure table of logarithms of numbers from 20,000 to 200,000, the logarithms between 100,000 and 200,000 being the result of a new calculation. By beginning the table at 20,000 instead of at 10,000 the differences are halved in magnitude, while the number of them in a page is quartered. In this table multiples of the differences, instead of proportional parts, are given.[3] John Thomson of Greenock (1782–1855) made an independent calculation of logarithms of numbers up to 120,000 to 12 places of decimals, and his table has been used to verify the errata already found in Vlacq and Briggs by Lefort (see *Monthly Not. R.A.S.* vol. 34, p. 447). A table of ten-figure logarithms of numbers up to 100,009 was calculated by W. W. Duffield and published in the *Report of the U.S. Coast and Geodetic Survey for 1895–1896* as Appendix 12, pp. 395-722. The results were compared with Vega's *Thesaurus* (1794) before publication.

Common or Briggian Logarithms of Trigonometrical Functions.—The next great advance on the *Trigonometria artificialis* took place more than a century and a half afterwards, when Michael Taylor published in 1792 his seven-decimal table of log sines and tangents to every second of the quadrant; it was calculated by interpolation from the *Trigonometria* to 10 places and then contracted to 7. On account of the great size of this table, and for other reasons, it never

---

[2] The smallest number of entries which are necessary in a table of logarithms in order that the intermediate logarithms may be calculable by proportional parts has been investigated by J. E. A. Steggall in the *Proc. Edin. Math. Soc.*, 1892, 10, p. 35. This number is 1700 in the case of a seven-figure table extending to 100,000.

[3] Accounts of Sang's calculations are given in the *Trans. Roy. Soc. Edin.*, 1872, 26, p. 521, and in subsequent papers in the *Proceedings* of the same society.

came into very general use, Bagay's *Nouvelles tables astronomiques* (1829), which also contains log sines and tangents to every second, being preferred; this latter work, which for many years was difficult to procure, has been reprinted with the original title-page and date unchanged. The only other logarithmic canon to every second that has been published forms the second volume of Shortrede's *Logarithmic Tables* (1849). In 1784 the French government decided that new tables of sines, tangents, &c., and their logarithms, should be calculated in relation to the centesimal division of the quadrant. Prony was charged with the direction of the work, and was expressly required "non seulement à composer des tables qui ne laissassent rien à désirer quant à l'exactitude, mais à en faire le monument de calcul le plus vaste et le plus imposant qui eût jamais été exécuté ou même conçu." Those engaged upon the work were divided into three sections: the first consisted of five or six mathematicians, including Legendre, who were engaged in the purely analytical work, or the calculation of the fundamental numbers; the second section consisted of seven or eight calculators possessing some mathematical knowledge; and the third comprised seventy or eighty ordinary computers. The work, which was performed wholly in duplicate, and independently by two divisions of computers, occupied two years. As a consequence of the double calculation, there are two manuscripts, one deposited at the Observatory, and the other in the library of the Institute, at Paris. Each of the two manuscripts consists essentially of seventeen large folio volumes, the contents being as follows:—

Logarithms of numbers up to 200,000	8 vols.
Natural sines	1 „
Logarithms of the ratios of arcs to sines from 0^{q}·00000 to 0^{q}·05000, and log sines throughout the quadrant	4 „
Logarithms of the ratios of arcs to tangents from 0^{q}·00000 to 0^{q}·05000, and log tangents throughout the quadrant	4 „

The trigonometrical results are given for every hundred-thousandth of the quadrant (10″ centesimal or 3″·24 sexagesimal). The tables were all calculated to 14 places, with the intention that only 12 should be published, but the twelfth figure is not to be relied upon. The tables have never been published, and are generally known as the *Tables du Cadastre*, or, in England, as the great French manuscript tables.

A very full account of these tables, with an explanation of the methods of calculation, formulae employed, &c., was published by Lefort in vol. iv. of the *Annales de l'observatoire de Paris*. The printing of the table of natural sines was once begun, and Lefort states that he has seen six copies, all incomplete, although including the last page. Babbage compared his table with the *Tables du Cadastre*, and Lefort has given in his paper just referred to most important lists of errors in Vlacq's and Briggs's logarithms of numbers which were obtained by comparing the manuscript tables with those contained in the *Arithmetica logarithmica* of 1624 and of 1628.

As the *Tables du Cadastre* remained unpublished, other tables appeared in which the quadrant was divided centesimally, the most important of these being Hobert and Ideler's *Nouvelles tables trigonométriques* (1799), and Borda and Delambre's *Tables trigonométriques décimales* (1800–1801), both of which are seven-figure tables. The latter work, which was much used, being difficult to procure, and greater accuracy being required, the French government in 1891 published an eight figure centesimal table, for every ten seconds, derived from the *Tables du Cadastre*.

Decimal or Briggian Antilogarithms.—In the ordinary tables of logarithms the natural numbers are all integers, while the logarithms tabulated are incommensurable. In an antilogarithmic table, the logarithms are exact quantities such as ·00001, ·00002, &c., and the numbers are incommensurable. The earliest and largest table of this kind that has been constructed is Dodson's *Antilogarithmic canon* (1742), which gives the numbers to 11 places, corresponding to the logarithms from ·00001 to 1·00000 at intervals of ·00001. Antilogarithmic tables are few in number, the only other extensive tables of the same kind that have been published occurring in Shortrede's *Logarithmic tables* already referred to, and in Filipowski's *Table of antilogarithms* (1849). Both are similar to Dodson's tables, from which they were derived, but they only give numbers to 7 places.

Hyperbolic or Napierian logarithms (i.e. to base *e*).—The most elaborate table of hyperbolic logarithms that exists is due to Wolfram, a Dutch lieutenant of artillery. His table gives the logarithms of all numbers up to 2200, and of primes (and also of a great many composite numbers) from 2200 to 10,000, to 48 decimal places. The table appeared in Schulze's *Neue und erweiterte Sammlung logarithmischer Tafeln* (1778), and was reprinted in Vega's *Thesaurus* (1794), already referred to. Six logarithms omitted in Schulze's work, and which Wolfram had been prevented from computing by a serious illness, were published subsequently, and the table as given by Vega is complete. The largest hyperbolic table as regards range was published by Zacharias Dase at Vienna in 1850 under the title *Tafel der natürlichen Logarithmen der Zahlen*.

Hyperbolic antilogarithms are simple exponentials, *i.e.* the hyperbolic antilogarithm of *x* is e^x. Such tables can scarcely be said to come under the head of logarithmic tables. See TABLES, MATHEMATICAL: *Exponential Functions*.

Logistic or Proportional Logarithms.—The old name for what are now called ratios or fractions are *logistic numbers*, so that a table of log (a/x) where *x* is the argument and *a* a constant is called a table of logistic or proportional logarithms; and since $\log (a/x) = \log a - \log x$ it is clear that the tabular results differ from those given in an ordinary table of logarithms only by the subtraction of a constant and a change of sign. The first table of this kind appeared in Kepler's work of 1624 which has been already referred to. The object of a table of log (a/x) is to facilitate the working out of proportions in which the third term is a constant quantity *a*. In most collections of tables of logarithms, and especially those intended for use in connexion with navigation, there occurs a small table of logistic logarithms in which $a = 3600''$ ($=1°$ or 1^h), the table giving log 3600 − log *x*, and *x* being expressed in minutes and seconds. It is also common to find tables in which $a = 10800''$ ($=3°$ or 3^h), and *x* is expressed in degrees (or hours), minutes and seconds. Such tables are generally given to 4 or 5 places. The usual practice in books seems to be to call logarithms logistic when *a* is 3600″, and proportional when *a* has any other value.

Addition and Subtraction, or Gaussian Logarithms.—*Gaussian logarithms* are intended to facilitate the finding of the logarithms of the sum and difference of two numbers whose logarithms are known, the numbers themselves being unknown; and on this account they are frequently called addition and subtraction logarithms. The object of the table is in fact to give $\log (a \pm b)$ by only one entry when log *a* and log *b* are given. The utility of such logarithms was first pointed out by Leonelli in a book entitled *Supplément logarithmique*, printed at Bordeaux in the year XI. (1802/3); he calculated a table to 14 places, but only a specimen of it which appeared in the *Supplément* was printed. The first table that was actually published is due to Gauss, and was printed in Zach's *Monatliche Correspondenz*, xxvi. 498 (1812). Corresponding to the argument log *x* it gives the values of $\log (1+x^{-1})$ and $\log (1+x)$.

Dual Logarithms.—This term was used by Oliver Byrne in a series of works published between 1860 and 1870. Dual numbers and logarithms depend upon the expression of a number as a product of 1·1, 1·01, 1·001 . . . or of ·9, ·99, ·999 . . . .

In the preceding *résumé* only those publications have been mentioned which are of historic importance or interest.[1] For fuller details with respect to some of these works, for an account of tables published in the latter part of the 19th century, and for those which would now be used in actual calculation, reference should be made to the article TABLES, MATHEMATICAL.

Calculation of Logarithms.—The name logarithm is derived from the words λόγων ἀριθμός, the number of the ratios, and the way of regarding a logarithm which justifies the name may be explained as follows. Suppose that the ratio of 10, or any other particular number, to 1 is compounded of a very great number of equal ratios, as, for example, 1,000,000, then it can be shown that the ratio of 2 to 1 is very nearly equal to a ratio compounded of 301,030 of these small ratios, or *ratiunculae*, that the ratio of 3 to 1 is very nearly equal to a ratio compounded of 477,121 of them, and so on. The small ratio, or *ratiuncula*, is in fact that of the millionth root of 10 to unity, and if we denote it by the ratio of *a* to 1, then the ratio of 2 to 1 will be nearly the same as that of a^{301030} to 1, and so on; or, in other words, if *a* denotes the millionth root of 10, then 2 will be nearly equal to a^{301030}, 3 will be nearly equal to a^{477121}, and so on.

Napier's original work, the *Descriptio Canonis* of 1614, contained, not logarithms of numbers, but logarithms of sines, and the relations between the sines and the logarithms were explained by the motions of points in lines, in a manner not unlike that afterwards employed by Newton in the method of fluxions. An account of the processes by which Napier constructed his table was given in the *Constructio Canonis* of 1619. These methods apply, however, specially to Napier's own kind of logarithms, and are different from those actually used by Briggs in the construction of the tables in the *Arithmetica Logarithmica*, although some of the latter are the same in principle as the processes described in an appendix to the *Constructio*.

The processes used by Briggs are explained by him in the preface to the *Arithmetica Logarithmica* (1624). His method of finding the logarithms of the small primes, which consists in taking a great number of continued geometric means between unity and the given primes, may be described as follows. He first formed the table of numbers and their logarithms:—

Numbers.	Logarithms.
10	1
3·162277 . . .	0·5
1·778279 . . .	0·25
1·333521 . . .	0·125
1·154781 . . .	0·0625

each quantity in the left-hand column being the square root of the one above it, and each quantity in the right-hand column being the half

[1] In vol. xv. (1875) of the *Verhandelingen* of the Amsterdam Academy of Sciences, Bierens de Haan has given a list of 553 tables of logarithms. A previous paper of the same kind, containing notices of some of the tables, was published by him in the *Verslagen en Mededeelingen* of the same academy (Afd. Natuurkunde) deel. xv. (1863), p. 15.

of the one above it. To construct this table Briggs, using about thirty places of decimals, extracted the square root of 10 fifty-four times, and thus found that the logarithm of 1·00000 00000 00000 12781 91493 20032 35 was 0·00000 00000 00000 05551 11512 31257 82702, and that for numbers of this form (*i.e.* for numbers beginning with 1 followed by fifteen ciphers, and then by seventeen or a less number of significant figures) the logarithms were proportional to these significant figures. He then by means of a simple proportion deduced that log (1·00000 00000 00000 1) = 0·00000 00000 00000 04342 94481 90325 1804, so that, a quantity 1·00000 00000 00000 x (where x consists of not more than seventeen figures) having been obtained by repeated extraction of the square root of a given number, the logarithm of 1·00000 00000 00000 x could then be found by multiplying x by ·00000 00000 00000 04342.....

To find the logarithm of 2, Briggs raised it to the tenth power, viz. 1024, and extracted the square root of 1·024 forty-seven times, the result being 1·00000 00000 00000 16851 60570 53949 77. Multiplying the significant figures by 4342... he obtained the logarithm of this quantity, viz. 0·00000 00000 00000 07318 55936 90623 9336, which multiplied by 2^{47} gave 0·01029 99566 39811 95265 277444, the logarithm of 1·024, true to 17 or 18 places. Adding the characteristic 3, and dividing by 10, he found (since 2 is the tenth root of 1024) log 2 = ·30102 99956 63981 195. Briggs calculated in a similar manner log 6, and thence deduced log 3.

It will be observed that in the first process the value of the modulus is in fact calculated from the formula.

$$\frac{h}{10^h-1}=\frac{1}{\log_e 10},$$

the value of h being $1/2^{54}$, and in the second process $\log_{10} 2$ is in effect calculated from the formula.

$$\log_{10} 2=\left(2^{\frac{10}{2^{47}}}-1\right)\times\frac{1}{\log_e 10}\times\frac{2^{47}}{10}.$$

Briggs also gave methods of forming the mean proportionals or square roots by differences, and the general method of constructing logarithmic tables by means of differences is due to him.

The following calculation of log 5 is given as an example of the application of a method of mean proportionals. The process consists in taking the geometric mean of numbers above and below 5, the object being to at length arrive at 5·000000. To every geometric mean in the column of numbers there corresponds the arithmetical mean in the column of logarithms. The numbers are denoted by A, B, C, &c., in order to indicate their mode of formation.

	Numbers.	Logarithms.
$A =$	1·000000	0·0000000
$B =$	10·000000	1·0000000
$C = \sqrt{(AB)}$ =	3·162277	0·5000000
$D = \sqrt{(BC)}$ =	5·623413	0·7500000
$E = \sqrt{(CD)}$ =	4·216964	0·6250000
$F = \sqrt{(DE)}$ =	4·869674	0·6875000
$G = \sqrt{(DF)}$ =	5·232991	0·7187500
$H = \sqrt{(FG)}$ =	5·048065	0·7031250
$I = \sqrt{(FH)}$ =	4·958069	0·6953125
$K = \sqrt{(HI)}$ =	5·002865	0·6992187
$L = \sqrt{(IK)}$ =	4·980416	0·6972656
$M = \sqrt{(KL)}$ =	4·991627	0·6982421
$N = \sqrt{(KM)}$ =	4·997242	0·6987304
$O = \sqrt{(KN)}$ =	5·000052	0·6989745
$P = \sqrt{(NO)}$ =	4·998647	0·6988525
$Q = \sqrt{(OP)}$ =	4·999350	0·6989135
$R = \sqrt{(OQ)}$ =	4·999701	0·6989440
$S = \sqrt{(OR)}$ =	4·999876	0·6989592
$T = \sqrt{(OS)}$ =	4·999963	0·6989668
$V = \sqrt{(OT)}$ =	5·000008	0·6989707
$W = \sqrt{(TV)}$ =	4·999984	0·6989687
$X = \sqrt{(WV)}$ =	4·999997	0·6989697
$Y = \sqrt{(VX)}$ =	5·000003	0·6989702
$Z = \sqrt{(XY)}$ =	5·000000	0·6989700

Great attention was devoted to the methods of calculating logarithms during the 17th and 18th centuries. The earlier methods proposed were, like those of Briggs, purely arithmetical, and for a long time logarithms were regarded from the point of view indicated by their name, that is to say, as depending on the theory of compounded ratios. The introduction of infinite series into mathematics effected a great change in the modes of calculation and the treatment of the subject. Besides Napier and Briggs, special reference should be made to Kepler (*Chilias*, 1624) and Mercator (*Logarithmotechnia*, 1668), whose methods were arithmetical, and to Newton, Gregory, Halley and Cotes, who employed series. A full and valuable account of these methods is given in Hutton's "Construction of Logarithms," which occurs in the introduction to the early editions of his *Mathematical Tables*, and also forms tract 21 of his *Mathematical Tracts* (vol. i., 1812). Many of the early works on logarithms were reprinted in the *Scriptores logarithmici* of Baron Maseres already referred to.

In the following account only those formulae and methods will be referred to which would now be used in the calculation of logarithms.

Since

$$\log_e(1+x)=x-\tfrac{1}{2}x^2+\tfrac{1}{3}x^3-\tfrac{1}{4}x^4+\&c.,$$

we have, by changing the sign of x,

$$\log_e(1-x)=-x-\tfrac{1}{2}x^2-\tfrac{1}{3}x^3-\tfrac{1}{4}x^4-\&c.;$$

whence

$$\log_e\frac{1+x}{1-x}=2(x+\tfrac{1}{3}x^3+\tfrac{1}{5}x^5+\&c.),$$

and, therefore, replacing x by $\frac{p-q}{p+q}$,

$$\log_e\frac{p}{q}=2\left\{\frac{p-q}{p+q}+\tfrac{1}{3}\left(\frac{p-q}{p+q}\right)^3+\tfrac{1}{5}\left(\frac{p-q}{p+q}\right)^5+\&c.\right\},$$

in which the series is always convergent, so that the formula affords a method of deducing the logarithm of one number from that of another.

As particular cases we have, by putting $q=1$,

$$\log_e p=2\left\{\frac{p-1}{p+1}+\tfrac{1}{3}\left(\frac{p-1}{p+1}\right)^3+\tfrac{1}{5}\left(\frac{p-1}{p+1}\right)^5+\&c.\right\},$$

and by putting $q=p+1$,

$$\log(p+1)-\log_e p=2\left\{\frac{1}{2p+1}+\tfrac{1}{3}\frac{1}{(2p+1)^3}+\tfrac{1}{5}\frac{1}{(2p+1)^5}+\&c.\right\};$$

the former of these equations gives a convergent series for $\log_e p$, and the latter a very convergent series by means of which the logarithm of any number may be deduced from the logarithm of the preceding number.

From the formula for $\log_e(p/q)$ we may deduce the following very convergent series for $\log_e 2$, $\log_e 3$ and $\log_e 5$, viz.:—

$$\log_e 2=2(7P+5Q+3R),$$
$$\log_e 3=2(11P+8Q+5R),$$
$$\log_e 5=2(16P+12Q+7R),$$

where

$$P=\frac{1}{31}+\tfrac{1}{3}\cdot\frac{1}{(31)^3}+\tfrac{1}{5}\cdot\frac{1}{(31)^5}+\&c.$$

$$Q=\frac{1}{49}+\tfrac{1}{3}\cdot\frac{1}{(49)^3}+\tfrac{1}{5}\cdot\frac{1}{(49)^5}+\&c.$$

$$R=\frac{1}{161}+\tfrac{1}{3}\cdot\frac{1}{(161)^3}+\tfrac{1}{5}\cdot\frac{1}{(161)^5}+\&c.$$

The following still more convenient formulae for the calculation of $\log_e 2$, $\log_e 3$, &c. were given by J. Couch Adams in the *Proc. Roy. Soc.*, 1878, 27, p. 91. If

$$a=\log\frac{10}{9}=-\log\left(1-\frac{1}{10}\right),\quad b=\log\frac{25}{24}=-\log\left(1-\frac{4}{100}\right),$$

$$c=\log\frac{81}{80}=\log\left(1+\frac{1}{80}\right),\quad d=\log\frac{50}{49}=-\log\left(1-\frac{2}{100}\right),$$

$$e=\log\frac{126}{125}=\log\left(1+\frac{8}{1000}\right),$$

then

$$\log 2=7a-2b+3c,\ \log 3=11a-3b+5c,\ \log 5=16a-4b+7c,$$

and

$$\log 7=\tfrac{1}{2}(39a-10b+17c-d)\ \text{or}=19a-4b+8c+e,$$

and we have the equation of condition,

$$a-2b+c=d+2e.$$

By means of these formulae Adams calculated the values of $\log_e 2$, $\log_e 3$, $\log_e 5$, and $\log_e 7$ to 276 places of decimals, and deduced the value of $\log_e 10$ and its reciprocal M, the modulus of the Briggian system of logarithms. The value of the modulus found by Adams is

Mo =	0·43429	44819	03251	82765	11289
	18916	60508	22943	97005	80366
	65661	14453	78316	58646	49208
	87077	47292	24949	33843	17483
	18706	10674	47663	03733	64167
	92871	58963	90656	92210	64662
	81226	58521	27086	56867	03295
	93370	86965	88266	88331	16360
	77384	90514	28443	48666	76864
	65860	85135	56148	21234	87653
	43543	43573	17253	83562	21868
	25				

which is true certainly to 272, and probably to 273, places (*Proc. Roy. Soc.*, 1886, 42, p. 22, where also the values of the other logarithms are given).

If the logarithms are to be Briggian all the series in the preceding formulae must be multiplied by M, the modulus; thus

$$\log_{10}(1+x)=M(x-\tfrac{1}{2}x^2+\tfrac{1}{3}x^3-\tfrac{1}{4}x^4+\&c.),$$

and so on.

As has been stated, Abraham Sharp's table contains 61-decimal

Briggian logarithms of primes up to 1100, so that the logarithms of all composite numbers whose greatest prime factor does not exceed this number may be found by simple addition; and Wolfram's table gives 48-decimal hyperbolic logarithms of primes up to 10,009. By means of these tables and of a factor table we may very readily obtain the Briggian logarithm of a number to 61 or a less number of places or of its hyperbolic logarithm to 48 or a less number of places in the following manner. Suppose the hyperbolic logarithm of the prime number 43,867 required. Multiplying by 50, we have $50 \times 43{,}867 = 2{,}193{,}350$, and on looking in Burckhardt's *Table des diviseurs* for a number near to this which shall have no prime factor greater than 10,009, it appears that

$$2{,}193{,}349 = 23 \times 47 \times 2029;$$

thus

$$43{,}867 = \tfrac{1}{50}(23 \times 47 \times 2029 + 1),$$

and therefore

$$\log_e 43{,}867 = \log_e 23 + \log_e 47 + \log_e 2029 - \log_e 50$$
$$+ \frac{1}{2{,}193{,}349} - \frac{1}{2}\frac{1}{(2{,}193{,}349)^2} + \frac{1}{3}\frac{1}{(2{,}193{,}349)^3} - \&c.$$

The first term of the series in the second line is

0·00000 04559 23795 07319 6286;

dividing this by $2 \times 2{,}193{,}349$ we obtain

0·00000 00000 00103 93325 3457,

and the third term is

0 00000 00000 00000 00003 1590,

so that the series =

0·00000 04559 23691 13997 4419;

whence, taking out the logarithms from Wolfram's table,

$\log_e 43{,}867 = 10{\cdot}68891\ 76079\ 60568\ 10191\ 3661.$

The principle of the method is to multiply the given prime (supposed to consist of 4, 5 or 6 figures) by such a factor that the product may be a number within the range of the factor tables, and such that, when it is increased by 1 or 2, the prime factors may all be within the range of the logarithmic tables. The logarithm is then obtained by use of the formula

$$\log_e(x+d) = \log_e x + \frac{d}{x} - \frac{1}{2}\frac{d^2}{x^2} + \frac{1}{3}\frac{d^3}{x^3} - \&c.,$$

in which of course the object is to render d/x as small as possible. If the logarithm required is Briggian, the value of the series is to be multiplied by M.

If the number is incommensurable or consists of more than seven figures, we can take the first seven figures of it (or multiply and divide the result by any factor, and take the first seven figures of the result) and proceed as before. An application to the hyperbolic logarithm of π is given by Burckhardt in the introduction to his *Table des diviseurs* for the second million.

The best general method of calculating logarithms consists, in its simplest form, in resolving the number whose logarithm is required into factors of the form $1 - {\cdot}1^r n$, where n is one of the nine digits, and making use of subsidiary tables of logarithms of factors of this form. For example, suppose the logarithm of 543839 required to twelve places. Dividing by 10^5 and by 5 the number becomes 1·087678, and resolving this number into factors of the form $1 - {\cdot}1^r n$ we find that

$$543839 = 10^5 \times 5(1-{\cdot}1^2 8)(1-{\cdot}1^3 6)(1-{\cdot}1^4 6)(1-{\cdot}1^6 3)(1-{\cdot}1^7 3)$$
$$\times(1-{\cdot}1^8 5)(1-{\cdot}1^9 7)(1-{\cdot}1^{10} 9)(1-{\cdot}1^{11} 3)(1-{\cdot}1^{12} 2),$$

where $1-{\cdot}1^2 8$ denotes $1-{\cdot}08$, $1-{\cdot}1^3 6$ denotes $1-{\cdot}0006$, &c., and so on. All that is required therefore in order to obtain the logarithm of any number is a table of logarithms, to the required number of places, of ·n, ·9n, ·99n, ·999n, &c., for $n = 1, 2, 3, \ldots 9$.

The resolution of a number into factors of the above form is easily performed. Taking, for example, the number 1·087678, the object is to destroy the significant figure 8 in the second place of decimals; this is effected by multiplying the number by $1-{\cdot}08$, that is, by subtracting from the number eight times itself advanced two places, and we thus obtain 1·00066376. To destroy the first 6 multiply by $1-{\cdot}0006$ giving 1·000063361744, and multiplying successively by $1-{\cdot}00006$ and $1-{\cdot}000003$, we obtain 1·000000357932, and it is clear that these last six significant figures represent without any further work the remaining factors required. In the corresponding antilogarithmic process the number is expressed as a product of factors of the form $1+{\cdot}1^n x$.

This method of calculating logarithms by the resolution of numbers into factors of the form $1-{\cdot}1^r n$ is generally known as Weddle's method, having been published by him in *The Mathematician* for November 1845, and the corresponding method for antilogarithms by means of factors of the form $1+({\cdot}1)^r n$ is known by the name of Hearn, who published it in the same journal for 1847. In 1846 Peter Gray constructed a new table to 12 places, in which the factors were of the form $1-({\cdot}01)^r n$, so that n had the values 1, 2, . . . 99; and subsequently he constructed a similar table for factors of the form $1+({\cdot}01)^r n$. He also devised a method of applying a table of Hearn's form (*i.e.* of factors of the form $1+{\cdot}1^r n$) to the construction of logarithms, and calculated a table of logarithms of factors of the form $1+({\cdot}001)^r n$ to 24 places. This was published in 1876 under the title *Tables for the formation of logarithms and antilogarithms to twenty-four or any less number of places*, and contains the most complete and useful application of the method, with many improvements in points of detail. Taking as an example the calculation of the Briggian logarithm of the number 43,867, whose hyperbolic logarithm has been calculated above, we multiply it by 3, giving 131,601, and find by Gray's process that the factors of 1·31601 are

(1) 1·316 (5) $1{\cdot}(001)^4 002$
(2) 1·000007 (6) $1{\cdot}(001)^5 602$
(3) $1{\cdot}(001)^2 598$ (7) $1{\cdot}(001)^6 412$
(4) $1{\cdot}(001)^3 780$ (8) $1{\cdot}(001)^7 340$

Taking the logarithms from Gray's tables we obtain the required logarithm by addition as follows:—

522	878	745	280	337	562	704	972	= colog 3
119	255	889	277	936	685	553	913	= log (1)
	3	040	050	733	157	610	239	= log (2)
		259	708	022	525	453	597	= log (3)
			338	749	695	752	424	= log (4)
					868	588	964	= log (5)
					261	445	278	= log (6)
						178	929	= log (7)
							148	= log (8)
4·642	137	934	655	780	757	288	464	= $\log_{10}$ 43,867

In Shortrede's *Tables* there are tables of logarithms and factors of the form $1 \pm ({\cdot}01)^r n$ to 16 places and of the form $1 \pm ({\cdot}1)^r n$ to 25 places; and in his *Tables de Logarithmes à 27 Décimales* (Paris, 1867) Fédor Thoman gives tables of logarithms of factors of the form $1 \pm {\cdot}1^r n$. In the *Messenger of Mathematics*, vol. iii. pp. 66-92, 1873, Henry Wace gave a simple and clear account of both the logarithmic and antilogarithmic processes, with tables of both Briggian and hyperbolic logarithms of factors of the form $1 \pm {\cdot}1^r n$ to 20 places.

Although the method is usually known by the names of Weddle and Hearn, it is really, in its essential features, due to Briggs, who gave in the *Arithmetica logarithmica* of 1624 a table of the logarithms of $1+{\cdot}1^r n$ up to $r = 9$ to 15 places of decimals. It was first formally proposed as an independent method, with great improvements, by Robert Flower in *The Radix, a new way of making Logarithms*, which was published in 1771; and Leonelli, in his *Supplément logarithmique* (1802-1803), already noticed, referred to Flower and reproduced some of his tables. A complete bibliography of this method has been given by A. J. Ellis in a paper "on the potential radix as a means of calculating logarithms," printed in the *Proceedings of the Royal Society*, vol. xxxi., 1881, pp. 401-407, and vol. xxxii., 1881, pp. 377-379. Reference should also be made to Hoppe's *Tafeln zur dreissigstelligen logarithmischen Rechnung* (Leipzig, 1876), which give in a somewhat modified form a table of the hyperbolic logarithm of $1+{\cdot}1^r n$.

The preceding methods are only appropriate for the calculation of isolated logarithms. If a complete table had to be reconstructed, or calculated to more places, it would undoubtedly be most convenient to employ the method of differences. A full account of this method as applied to the calculation of the *Tables du Cadastre* is given by Lefort in vol. iv. of the *Annales de l'Observatoire de Paris*.

(J. W. L. G.)

LOGAU, FRIEDRICH, Freiherr von (1604–1655), German epigrammatist, was born at Brockut, near Nimptsch, in Silesia, in June 1604. He was educated at the gymnasium of Brieg and subsequently studied law. He then entered the service of the duke of Brieg. In 1644 he was made "ducal councillor." He died at Liegnitz on the 24th of July 1655. Logau's epigrams, which appeared in two collections under the pseudonym "Salomon von Golaw" (an anagram of his real name) in 1638 (*Erstes Hundert Teutscher Reimensprüche*) and 1654 (*Deutscher Sinngedichte drei Tausend*), show a marvellous range and variety of expression. He had suffered bitterly under the adverse conditions of the time; but his satire is not merely the outcome of personal feeling. In the turbulent age of the Thirty Years' War he was one of the few men who preserved intact his intellectual integrity and judged his contemporaries fairly. He satirized with unsparing hand the court life, the useless bloodshed of the war, the lack of national pride in the German people, and their slavish imitation of the French in customs, dress and speech. He belonged to the *Fruchtbringende Gesellschaft* under the name *Der Verkleinernde*, and regarded himself as a follower of Martin Opitz; but he did not allow such ties to influence his independence or originality.

Logau's *Sinngedichte* were edited in 1759 by G. E. Lessing and K. W. Ramler, who first drew attention to their merits; a second edition appeared in 1791. A critical edition was published by G. Eitner in 1872, who also edited a selection of Logau's epigrams for the *Deutsche Dichter des XVII. Jahrhunderts* (vol. iii., 1870); there is also a selection by H. Oesterley in Kürschner's *Deutsche Nationalliteratur*, vol. xxviii. (1885). See H. Denker, *Beiträge zur literarischen Würdigung Logaus* (1889); W. Heuschkel, *Untersuchungen über Ramlers und Lessings Bearbeitung Logauscher Sinngedichte* (1901).

LOGIA, a title used to describe a collection of the sayings of Jesus Christ (λόγια Ἰησοῦ) and therefore generally applied to the "Sayings of Jesus" discovered in Egypt by B. P. Grenfell and A. S. Hunt. There is some question as to whether the term is rightly used for this purpose. It does not occur in the Papyri in this sense. Each "saying" is introduced by the phrase "Jesus says" (λέγει) and the collection is described in the introductory words of the 1903 series as λόγοι not as λόγια. Some justification for the employment of the term is found in early Christian literature. Several writers speak of the λόγια τοῦ κυρίου or τὰ κυριακὰ λόγια, *i.e.* oracles of (or concerning) the Lord. Polycarp, for instance, speaks of "those who pervert the oracles of the Lord" (Philipp. 7), and Papias, as Eusebius tells us, wrote a work with the title "Expositions of the Oracles of the Lord." The expression has been variously interpreted. It need mean no more (Lightfoot, *Essays on Supernatural Religion*, 172 seq.) than narratives of (or concerning) the Lord; on the other hand, the phrase is capable of a much more definite meaning, and there are many scholars who hold that it refers to a document which contained a collection of the sayings of Jesus. Some such document, we know, must lie at the base of our Synoptic Gospels, and it is quite possible that it may have been known to and used by Papias. It is only on this assumption that the use of the term Logia in the sense described above can be justified.

"The Sayings," to which the term Logia is generally applied, consist of (*a*) a papyrus leaf containing seven or eight sayings of Jesus discovered in 1897, (*b*) a second leaf containing five more sayings discovered in 1903, (*c*) two fragments of unknown Gospels, the former published in 1903, the latter in 1907. All these were found amongst the great mass of papyri acquired by the Egyptian Exploration Fund from the ruins of Oxyrhynchus, one of the chief early Christian centres in Egypt, situated some 120 m. S. of Cairo.

The eight "sayings" discovered in 1897 are as follows:—

1\. . . . καὶ τότε διαβλέψεις ἐκβαλεῖν τὸ κάρφος τὸ ἐν τῷ ὀφθαλμῷ τοῦ [illegible]

2\. [illegible] βασιλείαν [illegible] πατέρα.

3\. [illegible] αὐτοῖς, [illegible] πονεῖ ἡ [illegible] αὐτῶ[ν] [illegible] . . .

[illegible] possibly joins on to 3] . . . [τ]ὴν πτωχείαν.

5\. [illegible] ε[ἰς] [illegible] εὑρήσεις [illegible]

6\. [illegible] αὐτ[οῦ], οὐδὲ [illegible]

7\. [illegible] ἐστηριγμένη [illegible]

8\. [illegible] ας].

Letters in brackets are missing in the original: letters which are [illegible] doubtful.

1\. "[illegible] shalt thou see clearly to cast out the mote that is [illegible]

2\. [illegible] Except ye fast to the world, ye shall in no wise [illegible] God; and except ye make the sabbath a real [illegible] the Father."

3\. [illegible] I stood in the midst of the world and in the [illegible] and I found all men drunken, and none [illegible] and my soul grieveth over the sons of [illegible] in their heart, and see not . . . ."

[illegible] there are two, they are not without [illegible] alone, I say, I am with him. Raise [illegible] find me, cleave the wood and there [illegible]

[illegible] not acceptable in his own country, [illegible] upon them that know him."

[illegible] high hill and [illegible]

[illegible] other ear

The "sayings" of 1903 were prefaced by the following introductory statement:—

οἱ τοῖοι οἱ λόγοι οἱ [. . . οὓς ἐλάλησεν Ἰη(σοῦ)ς ὁ ζῶν κ(ύριο)ς ? . . . καὶ Θωμᾷ καὶ εἶπεν [αὐτοῖς· πᾶς ὅστις ἂν τῶν λόγων τούτ]ων ἀκούσῃ θανάτου οὐ μὴ γεύσηται.

"These are the (wonderful?) words which Jesus the living (Lord) spake to . . . and Thomas and he said unto (them) every one that hearkens to these words shall never taste of death."

The "sayings" themselves are as follows:—

(1) [λέγει Ἰη(σοῦ)ς· μὴ παυσάσθω ὁ ζη[τῶν . . .
ἕως ἂν εὕρῃ καὶ ὅταν εὕρῃ [θαμβηθήσεται
καὶ θαμβηθεὶς βασιλεύσει κα[ὶ βασιλεύσας
ἀναπαήσεται.

(2) λέγει Ἰ[η(σοῦς . . . τίνες . . .
οἱ ἕλκοντες ἡμᾶς [εἰς τὴν βασιλείαν εἰ
ἡ βασιλεία ἐν οὐρα[νῷ ἐστιν;
τὰ πετεινὰ τοῦ οὐρ[ανοῦ καὶ τῶν θηρίων ὅ
τι ὑπὸ τὴν γῆν ἐστ[ὶν ἢ ἐπὶ τῆς γῆς καὶ
οἱ ἰχθύες τῆς θαλά[σσης οὗτοι οἱ ἕλκοντες ὑμᾶς καὶ ἡ βασ[ιλεία τῶν οὐρανῶν
ἐντὸς ὑμῶν [ἐ]στι [καὶ ὅστις ἂν ἑαυτὸν
γνῷ ταύτην εὑρή[σει . . .
ἑαυτοὺς γνώσεσθε [καὶ εἰδήσετε ὅτι υἱοί
ἐστε ὑμεῖς τοῦ πατρὸς τοῦ τ[. . .
γνώσ(εσ)θε ἑαυτοὺς ἐν[. . .
καὶ ὑ εῖς ἐστὲ πτο[

(3) [λέγει Ἰη(σοῦ)ς
οὐκ ἀποκνήσει ἄνθ[ρωπος . . .
ρων ἐπερωτῆσαι πα[. . .
ρων περὶ τοῦ τόπου τῆ[ς . . .
σετε ὅτι πολλοὶ ἔσονται π[ρῶτοι ἔσχατοι καὶ
οἱ ἔσχατοι πρῶτοι καὶ [. . .
σιν.

(4) λέγει Ἰη(σοῦ)ς· [πᾶν τὸ μὴ ἔμπροσ-
θεν τῆς ὄψεώς σου καὶ [τὸ κεκρυμμένον
ἀπὸ σοῦ ἀποκαλυφ(θ)ήσετ[αί σοι. οὐ γάρ ἐστιν κρυπτὸν ὃ οὐ φανε[ρὸν γενήσεται
καὶ τεθαμμένον ὃ ο[ὐκ ἐγερθήσεται.

(5) [ἐξ]ετάζουσιν αὐτὸν ο[ἱ μαθηταὶ αὐτοῦ καὶ
[λέ]γουσιν· πῶς νηστεύ[σομεν καὶ πῶς . . .
[. . .]μεθα καὶ πῶς [. . .
[. . . κ]αὶ τί παρατηρήσ[ομεν . . .
[. . .]ν; λέγει Ἰη(σοῦ)ς· [. . .
[. . .]ειται μὴ ποιεῖτ[ε . . .
[. . .]ης ἀληθείας ἀν[. . .
[. . .]ν ἀ[π]οκεκρ[υ . . .
[. . . μα]κάρι[ός] ἐστιν [. . .
[. . .]ω ἐστ[ι . . .
[. . .]ιν [. . .

1\. "Jesus saith, Let not him who seeks . . . cease until he finds and when he finds he shall be astonished; astonished he shall reach the kingdom and having reached the kingdom he shall rest."

2\. "Jesus saith (ye ask? who are those) that draw us (to the kingdom if) the kingdom is in Heaven? . . . the fowls of the air and all beasts that are under the earth or upon the earth and the fishes of the sea (these are they which draw) you and the kingdom of Heaven is within you and whosoever shall know himself shall find it. (Strive therefore?) to know yourselves and ye shall be aware that ye are the sons of the (Almighty?) Father; (and?) ye shall know that ye are in (the city of God?) and ye are (the city?)."

3\. "Jesus saith, A man shall not hesitate . . . to ask concerning his place (in the kingdom. Ye shall know) that many that are first shall be last and the last first and (they shall have eternal life?)."

4\. "Jesus saith, Everything that is not before thy face and that which is hidden from thee shall be revealed to thee. For there is nothing hidden which shall not be made manifest nor buried which shall not be raised."

5\. "His disciples question him and say, How shall we fast and how shall we (pray?) . . . and what (commandment) shall we keep . . . Jesus saith . . . do not . . . of truth . . . blessed is he . . . ."

The fragment of a lost Gospel which was discovered in 1903 contained originally about fifty lines, but many of them have perished and others are undecipherable. The translation, as far as it can be made out, is as follows:—

1-7\. "(Take no thought) from morning until even nor from evening until morning either for your food what ye shall eat or for your raiment what ye shall put on. 7-13. Ye are far better than the lilies which grow but spin not. Having one garment what do ye (lack)? 13-15. Who could add to your stature? 15-16. He himself will give you your garment. 17-23. His disciples say unto him, When wilt thou be manifest unto us and when shall we see thee? He saith, When ye shall be stripped and not be ashamed . . . 41-46. He said, The key of knowledge ye hid: ye entered not in yourselves, and to them that were entering in, ye opened not."

The second Gospel fragment discovered in 1907 "consists of a single vellum leaf, practically complete except at one of the lower corners and here most of the lacunae admit of a satisfactory solution." The translation is as follows:—

. . . before he does wrong makes all manner of subtle excuse. But give heed lest ye also suffer the same things as they: for the evil doers among men receive their reward not among the living only, but also await punishment and much torment. And he took them and brought them into the very place of purification and was walking in the temple. And a certain Pharisee, a chief priest, whose name was Levi, met them and said to the Saviour, Who gave thee leave to walk in this place of purification, and to see these holy vessels when thou hast not washed nor yet have thy disciples bathed their feet? But defiled thou hast walked in this temple, which is a pure place, wherein no other man walks except he has washed himself and changed his garments neither does he venture to see these holy vessels. And the Saviour straightway stood still with his disciples and answered him, Art thou then, being here in the temple, clean? He saith unto him, I am clean; for I washed in the pool of David and having descended by one staircase I ascended by another and I put on white and clean garments, and then I came and looked upon these holy vessels. The Saviour answered and said unto him, Woe ye blind, who see not. Thou hast washed in these running waters wherein dogs and swine have been cast night and day and hast cleansed and wiped the outside skin which also the harlots and flute-girls anoint and wash and wipe and beautify for the lust of men, but within they are full of scorpions and all wickedness. But I and my disciples who thou sayest have not bathed have been dipped in the waters of eternal life which come from. . . But woe unto thee . . .

These documents have naturally excited considerable interest and raised many questions. The papyri of the "sayings" date from the 3rd century and most scholars agree that the "sayings" themselves go back to the 2nd. The year A.D. 140 is generally assigned as the *terminus ad quem*. The problem as to their origin has been keenly discussed. There are two main types of theory. (1) Some suppose that they are excerpts from an uncanonical Gospel. (2) Others think that they represent an independent and original collection of sayings. The first theory has assumed three main forms. (*a*) Harnack maintains that they were taken from the Gospel according to the Egyptians. This theory, however, is based upon a hypothetical reconstruction of the Gospel in question which has found very few supporters. (*b*) Others have advocated the Gospel of the Hebrews as the source of the "sayings," on the ground of the resemblance between the first "saying" of the 1903 series and a well-authenticated fragment of that Gospel. The resemblance, however, is not sufficiently clear to support the conclusion. (*c*) A third view supposes that they are extracts from the Gospel of Thomas—an apocryphal Gospel dealing with the boyhood of Jesus. Beyond the allusion to Thomas in the introductory paragraph to the 1903 series, there seems to be no tangible evidence in support of this view. The second theory, which maintains that the papyri represent an independent collection of "sayings," seems to be the opinion which has found greatest favour. It has won the support of W. Sanday, H. B. Swete, Rendel Harris, W. Lock, Heinrici, &c. There is a considerable diversity of judgment, however, with regard to the value of the collection. (*a*) Some scholars maintain that the collection goes back to the 1st century and represents one of the earliest attempts to construct an account of the teaching of Jesus. They are therefore disposed to admit to a greater or less extent and with widely varying degrees of confidence the presence of genuine elements in the new matter. (*b*) Sanday and many others regard the sayings as originating early in the 2nd century and think that, though not "directly dependent on the Canonical Gospels," they have "their origin under conditions of thought which these Gospels had created." The "sayings" must be regarded as expansions of the true tradition, and little value is therefore to be attached to the new material.

With the knowledge at our disposal, it is impossible to reach an assured conclusion between these two views. The real problem, to which at present no solution has been found, is to account for the new material in the "sayings." There seems to be no motive sufficient to explain the additions that have been made to the text of the Gospels. It cannot be proved that the expansions have been made in the interests of any sect or heresy. Unless new discoveries provide the clue, or some reasonable explanation can otherwise be found, there seems to be no reason why we should not regard the "sayings" as containing material which ought to be taken into account in the critical study of the teaching of Jesus.

The 1903 Gospel fragment is so mutilated in many of its parts that it is difficult to decide upon its character and value. It appears to be earlier than 150, and to be taken from a Gospel which followed more or less closely the version of the teaching of Jesus given by Matthew and Luke. The phrase "when ye shall be stripped and not be ashamed" contains an idea which has some affinity with two passages found respectively in the Gospel according to the Egyptians and the so-called Second Epistle of Clement. The resemblance, however, is not sufficiently close to warrant the deduction that either the Gospel of the Egyptians or the Gospel from which the citation in 2 Clement is taken (if these two are distinct) is the source from which our fragment is derived.

The second Gospel fragment (1907) seems to be of later origin than the documents already mentioned. Grenfell and Hunt date the Gospel, from which it is an excerpt, about 200. There is considerable difficulty with regard to some of the details. The statement that an ordinary Jew was required to wash and change his clothes before visiting the inner court of the temple is quite unsupported by any other evidence. Nothing is known about "the place of purification" (ἁγνευτήριον) nor "the pool of David" (λίμνη τοῦ Δαυείδ). Nor does the statement that "the sacred vessels" were visible from the place where Jesus was standing seem at all probable. Grenfell and Hunt conclude therefore—"So great indeed are the divergences between this account and the extant and no doubt well-informed authorities with regard to the topography and ritual of the Temple that it is hardly possible to avoid the conclusion that much of the local colour is due to the imagination of the author who was aiming chiefly at dramatic effect and was not really well acquainted with the Temple. But if the inaccuracy of the fragment in this important respect is admitted the historical character of the whole episode breaks down and it is probably to be regarded as an apocryphal elaboration of Matt. xv. 1-20 and Mark vii. 1-23."

See the *Oxyrhynchus Papyri*, part i. (1897), part iv. (1904), part v. (1908). (H. T. A.)

LOGIC (λογική, sc. τέχνη, the art of reasoning), the name given to one of the four main departments of philosophy, though its sphere is very variously delimited. The present article is divided into I. *The Problems of Logic*, II. *History*.

I. *The Problems of Logic.*

Introduction.—Logic is the science of the processes of inference. What, then, is inference? It is that mental operation which proceeds by combining two premises so as to cause a consequent conclusion. Some suppose that we may infer from one premise by a so-called "immediate inference." But one premise can only reproduce itself in another form, *e.g.* all men are some animals; therefore some animals are men. It requires the combination of at least two premises to infer a conclusion different from both. There are as many kinds of inference as there are different ways of combining premises, and in the main three types:—

1. *Analogical Inference*, from particular to particular: *e.g.* border-war between Thebes and Phocis is evil; border-war between Thebes and Athens is similar to that between Thebes and Phocis; therefore, border-war between Thebes and Athens is evil.

2. *Inductive Inference*, from particular to universal: *e.g.* border-war between Thebes and Phocis is evil; all border-war is like that between Thebes and Phocis; therefore, all border-war is evil.

3. *Deductive or Syllogistic Inference*, from universal to particular, *e.g.* all border-war is evil; border-war between Thebes and Athens is border-war; therefore border-war between Thebes and Athens is evil.

[illegible] kinds of inference there are three mental [illegible] being expressed as above in three linguistic [illegible] and the two first are the premises which are [illegible], while the third is the conclusion which is consequent [illegible]. Each proposition consists of two terms, [illegible] predicate, united by the copula. Each in[illegible] three terms. In syllogistic inference the subject [illegible] is the minor term, and its predicate the major term, while between these two extremes the term common to the two premises is the middle term, and the premise containing the middle and major terms is the major premise, the premise containing the middle and minor terms the minor premise. Thus in the example of syllogism given above, "border-war between Thebes and Athens" is the minor term, "evil" the major term, and "border-war" the middle term. Using S for minor, P for major and M for middle, and preserving these signs for corresponding terms in analogical and inductive inferences, we obtain the following formula of the three inferences:—

Analogical.	*Inductive.*	*Deductive or Syllogistic.*
[illegible] is P	S is P	Every M is P
[illegible] is similar to S[1]	Every M is similar to S	S is M
[illegible] is P.	Every M is P.	∴ S is P.

The love of unity has often made logicians attempt to resolve [illegible] three processes into one. But each process has a pecu[illegible] own; they are similar, not the same. Analogical and inductive inference alike begin with a particular premise containing one or more instances; but the former adds a par[illegible] premise to draw a particular conclusion, the latter requires a universal premise to draw a universal conclusion. A citizen [illegible] who had known the evils of the border-war between [illegible] and Phocis would readily perceive the analogy of a [illegible] between Thebes and Athens, and conclude analog[illegible] that it would be evil; but he would have to generalize [illegible] of all border-wars in order to draw the inductive [illegible] that all alike are evil. Induction and deduction differ [illegible] and are in fact opposed, as one makes a particular [illegible] evidence of a universal conclusion, the other makes [illegible] premise evidence of a particular conclusion. Yet [illegible] requiring the generalization of the universal [illegible] there are classes which are whole numbers [illegible] point both differ from inference by analogy, [illegible] from particular premises to a particular [illegible] we may redivide inference into particular [illegible] analogy and universal inference by induction and [illegible] universal inference is what we call reasoning; [illegible] very closely connected, because universal [illegible] become universal premises of deduction. [illegible] in order to deduce, ascending from par[illegible] descending from universal to particular [illegible] so that we may proceed either directly [illegible] by analogical inference, or indirectly [illegible] universal to particular by an inductive-[illegible] might be called "perduction." On [illegible] inductive and deductive inferences [illegible] similar and closely connected processes. [illegible] inference, though different from one [illegible] principle of similarity of which each [illegible] Analogical inference requires that one [illegible] induction that a whole number [illegible] instances, deduction that each [illegible] number or class. Not that these [illegible] or assume, or premise or [illegible] general, or in its applied forms: [illegible] needs the mind to assume. [illegible] not assumed by the inferring [illegible] similarity of things and the [illegible] concludes in the form [illegible] ("similia similibus [illegible] of similarity, each of [illegible] to premise both that [illegible]

and by combining these premises to conclude that this is similarly determined to that. Thus the very principle of inference by similarity requires it to be a combination of premises in order to draw a conclusion.

The three processes, as different applications of the principle of similarity, consisting of different combinations of premises, cause different degrees of cogency in their several conclusions. Analogy hardly requires as much evidence as induction. Men speculate about the analogy between Mars and the earth, and infer that it is inhabited, without troubling about all the planets. Induction has to consider more instances, and the similarity of a whole number or class. Even so, however, it starts from a particular premise which only contains many instances, and leaves room to doubt the universality of its conclusions. But deduction, starting from a premise about all the members of a class, compels a conclusion about every and each of necessity. One border-war may be similar to another, and the whole number may be similar, without being similarly evil; but if all alike are evil, each is evil of necessity. Deduction or syllogism is superior to analogy and induction in combining premises so as to involve or contain the conclusion. For this reason it has been elevated by some logicians above all other inferences, and for this very same reason attacked by others as no inference at all. The truth is that, though the premises contain the conclusion, neither premise alone contains it, and a man who knows both but does not combine them does not draw the conclusion; it is the synthesis of the two premises which at once contains the conclusion and advances our knowledge; and as syllogism consists, not indeed in the discovery, but essentially in the synthesis of two premises, it is an inference and an advance on each premise and on both taken separately. As again the synthesis contains or involves the conclusion, syllogism has the advantage of compelling assent to the consequences of the premises. Inference in general is a combination of premises to cause a conclusion; deduction is such a combination as to compel a conclusion involved in the combination, and following from the premises of necessity.

Nevertheless, deduction or syllogism is not independent of the other processes of inference. It is not the primary inference of its own premises, but constantly converts analogical and inductive conclusions into its particular and universal premises. Of itself it causes a necessity of consequence, but only a hypothetical necessity; if these premises are true, then this conclusion necessarily follows. To eliminate this "if" ultimately requires other inferences before deduction. Especially, induction to universals is the warrant and measure of deduction from universals. So far as it is inductively true that all border-war is evil, it is deductively true that a given border-war is therefore evil. Now, as an inductive combination of premises does not necessarily involve the inductive conclusion, induction normally leads, not to a necessary, but to a probable conclusion; and whenever its probable conclusions become deductive premises, the deduction only involves a probable conclusion. Can we then infer any certainty at all? In order to answer this question we must remember that there are many degrees of probability, and that induction, and therefore deduction, draw conclusions more or less probable, and rise to the point at which probability becomes moral certainty, or that high degree of probability which is sufficient to guide our lives, and even condemn murderers to death. But can we rise still higher and infer real necessity? This is a difficult question, which has received many answers. Some noölogists suppose a mental power of forming necessary principles of deduction a priori; but fail to show how we can apply principles of mind to things beyond mind. Some empiricists, on the other hand, suppose that induction only infers probable conclusions which are premises of probable deductions; but they give up all exact science. Between these extremes there is room for a third theory, empirical yet providing a knowledge of the really necessary. In some cases of induction concerned with objects capable of abstraction and simplification, we have a power of identification, by which, not a priori but in the act of inducing a conclusion, we apprehend that the things signified by its subject and predicate are one and the same thing which cannot exist apart from itself. Thus by combined induction and identification we apprehend that one and one are the same as two, that there is no difference between a triangle and a three-sided rectilineal figure, that a whole must be greater than its part by being the whole, that inter-resisting bodies necessarily force one another apart, otherwise they would not be inter-resisting but occupy the same place at the same moment. Necessary principles, discovered by this process of induction and identification, become premises of deductive demonstration to conclusions which are not only necessary consequents on the premises, but also equally necessary in reality. Induction thus is the source of deduction, of its truth, of its probability, of its moral certainty; and induction, combined with identification, is the origin of the necessary principles of demonstration or deduction to necessary conclusions.

Analogical inference in its turn is as closely allied with induction. Like induction, it starts from a particular premise, containing one or more examples or instances; but, as it is easier to infer a particular than a universal conclusion, it supplies particular conclusions which in their turn become further particular premises of induction. Its second premise is indeed merely a particular apprehension that one particular is similar to another, whereas the second premise of induction is a universal apprehension that a whole number of particulars is similar to those from which the inference starts; but at bottom these two apprehensions of similarity are so alike as to suggest that the universal premise of induction has arisen as a generalized analogy. It seems likely that man has arrived at the apprehension of a whole individual, *e.g.* a whole animal including all its parts, and thence has inferred by analogy a whole number, or class, *e.g.* of animals including all individual animals; and accordingly that the particular analogy of one individual to another has given rise to the general analogy of every to each individual in a class, or whole number of individuals, contained in the second premise of induction. In this case, analogical inference has led to induction, as induction to deduction. Further, analogical inference from particular to particular suggests inductive-deductive inference from particular through universal to particular.

Newton, according to Dr Pemberton, thought in 1666 that the moon moves so like a falling body that it has a similar centripetal force to the earth, 20 years before he demonstrated this conclusion from the laws of motion in the *Principia*. In fact, analogical, inductive and deductive inferences, though different processes of combining premises to cause different conclusions, are so similar and related, so united in principle and interdependent, so consolidated into a system of inference, that they cannot be completely investigated apart, but together constitute a single subject of science. This science of inference in general is logic.

Logic, however, did not begin as a science of all inference. Rather it began as a science of reasoning (λόγος), of syllogism (συλλογισμός), of deductive inference. Aristotle was its founder. He was anticipated of course by many generations of spontaneous thinking (*logica naturalis*). Many of the higher animals infer by analogy: otherwise we cannot explain their thinking. Man so infers at first: otherwise we cannot explain the actions of young children, who before they begin to speak give no evidence of universal thinking. It is likely that man began with particular inference and with particular language; and that, gradually generalizing thought and language, he learnt at last to think and say "all," to infer universally, to induce and deduce, to reason, in short, and raise himself above other animals. In ancient times, and especially in Egypt, Babylon and Greece, he went on to develop reason into science or the systematic investigation of definite subjects, *e.g.* arithmetic of number, geometry of magnitude, astronomy of stars, politics of government, ethics of goods. In Greece he became more and more reflective and conscious of himself, of his body and soul, his manners and morals, his mental operations and especially his reason. One of the characteristics of Greek philosophers is their growing tendency, in investigating any subject, to turn round and ask themselves what should be the method of investigation. In this way the Presocratics and Sophists, and still more Socrates and Plato, threw out hints on sense and reason, on inferential processes and scientific methods which may be called anticipations of logic. But Aristotle was the first to conceive of reasoning itself as a definite subject of a special science, which he called analytics or analytic science, specially designed to analyse syllogism and especially demonstrative syllogism, or science, and to be in fact a science of sciences. He was therefore the founder of the science of logic.

Among the Aristotelian treatises we have the following, which together constitute this new science of reasoning:—

1. The *Categories*, or names signifying things which can become predicates;
2. The *De Interpretatione*, or the enumeration of conceptions and their combinations by (1) nouns and verbs (names), (2) enunciations (propositions);
3. The *Prior Analytics*, on syllogism;
4. The *Posterior Analytics*, on demonstrative syllogism, or science;
5. The *Topics*, on dialectical syllogism; or argument;
6. The *Sophistical Elenchi*, on sophistical or contentious syllogism, or sophistical fallacies.

So far as we know, Aristotle had no one name for all these investigations. "Analytics" is only applied to the *Prior* and *Posterior Analytics*, and "logical," which he opposed to "analytical," only suits the *Topics* and at most the *Sophistical Elenchi*; secondly, while he analyzed syllogism into premises, major and minor, and premises into terms, subject and predicate, he attempted no division of the whole science; thirdly, he attempted no order and arrangement of the treatises into a system of logic, but only of the *Analytics*, *Topics* and *Sophistical Elenchi* into a system of syllogisms. Nevertheless, when his followers had arranged the treatises into the *Organon*, as they called it to express that it is an instrument of science, then there gradually emerged a system of syllogistic logic, arranged in the triple division—terms, propositions and syllogisms—which has survived to this day as technical logic, and has been the foundation of all other logics, even of those which aim at its destruction.

The main problem which Aristotle set before him was the analysis of syllogism, which he defined as "reasoning in which certain things having been posited something different from them of necessity follows by their being those things" (*Prior Analytics*, i. 1). What then did he mean by reasoning, or rather by the Greek word λόγος of which "reasoning" is an approximate rendering? It was meant (cf. *Post. An.* i. 10) to be both internal, in the soul (ὁ ἔσω λόγος, ἐν τῇ ψυχῇ), and external, in language (ὁ ἔξω λόγος): hence after Aristotle the Stoics distinguished λόγος ἐνδιάθετος and προφορικός. It meant, then, both reason and discourse of reason (cf. Shakespeare, *Hamlet*, i. 2). On its mental side, as reason it meant combination of thoughts. On its linguistic side, as discourse it was used for any combination of names to form a phrase, such as the definition "rational animal," or a book, such as the *Iliad*. It had also the mathematical meaning of *ratio*; and in its use for definition it is sometimes transferred to essence as the object of definition, and has a mixed meaning, which may be expressed by "account." In all its uses, however, the common meaning is combination. When Aristotle called syllogism λογος, he meant that it is a combination of premises involving a conclusion of necessity. Moreover, he tended to confine the term λόγος to syllogistic inference. Not that he omitted other inferences (πίστεις). On the contrary, to him (cf. *Prior Analytics*, ii. 24) we owe the triple distinction into inference from particular to particular (παράδειγμα, example, or what we call "analogy"), inference from particular to universal (ἐπαγωγή, induction), and inference from universal to particular (συλλογισμός, syllogism, or deduction). But he thought that inferences other than syllogism are imperfect; that analogical inference is rhetorical induction; and that induction, through the necessary preliminary of syllogism and the sole process of ascent from sense, memory and experience to the principles of science, is itself neither reasoning nor science. To be perfect he thought that all inference must be reduced to syllogism of the first figure, which he regarded as the specially scientific inference. Accordingly, the syllogism appeared to him to be the rational process (μετὰ λόγου), and the demonstrative syllogism from inductively discovered principles to be science [illegible] without his saying it in so many words, [illegible] a logic of deductive reasoning, [illegible] this deductive tendency helped [illegible] The obscurer premises of analogy and [illegible] with the paucity of experience and the back- [illegible] in Aristotle's time would have [illegible] premises. On the other hand, the [illegible] mathematical sciences of his time, and the [illegible] found in Plato's dialogues, provided [illegible] examples of deduction, which is also the [illegible] of analysis. Aristotle's analysis of the [illegible] how to advance by combining his [illegible] trains of deductive reasoning. Nevertheless, the [illegible] remained for logic: what is the nature of all inference, and the special form of each of its three main processes?

As then the reasoning of the syllogism was the main problem of Aristotle's logic, what was his analysis of it? In distinguishing inner and outer reason, or reasoning and discourse, he added that it is not to outer reason but to inner reason in the soul that demonstration and syllogism are directed (*Post. An.* i. 10). One would expect, then, an analysis of mental reasoning into mental judgments ([illegible]) as premises and conclusion. In point of fact, he analysed it into premises, but then analysed a premise into terms, which he divided into subject and predicate, with the addition of the copula "is" or "is not." This analysis, regarded as a whole and as it is applied in the *Analytics* and in the other logical treatises, was evidently intended as a linguistic analysis. So in the *Categories*, he first divided things said (τὰ λεγόμενα) into uncombined and combined, or names and propositions, and then divided the former into categories; and in the *De interpretatione* he expressly excluded mental conceptions and their combinations, and confined himself to nouns and verbs and enunciations, or, as we should say, to names and propositions. Aristotle apparently intended, or at all events has given logicians in general the impression, that he intended to analyse syllogism into propositions as premises, and premise into names as terms. His logic therefore exhibits the curious paradox of being an analysis of mental reasoning into linguistic elements. The explanation is that outer speech is more obvious than inner thought, and that grammar and poetic criticism, rhetoric and dialectic preceded logic, and that out of those arts of language arose the science of reasoning. The sophist Protagoras had distinguished [illegible] kinds of sentences, and Plato had divided the sentence into noun and verb, signifying a thing and the action of a thing. [illegible] had enumerated various means of persuasion, some of which are logical forms, *e.g.* probability and sign, example and [illegible]. Among the dialecticians, Socrates had used inductive [illegible] to obtain definitions as data of deductive arguments [illegible] his opponents, and Plato had insisted on the processes of [illegible] and descending from an unconditional principle by the [illegible] giving and receiving argument. All these points about [illegible] and argument between man and man were ab[illegible] Aristotle's theory of reasoning, and in particular the [illegible] the sentence consisting of noun and verb caused the [illegible] proposition consisting of subject and predicate. At the [illegible] Aristotle was well aware that the science of reasoning is [illegible] and must take up a different position towards [illegible] of thought. In the *Categories* he classified [illegible] as a grammarian by their structure, but [illegible] their signification. In the *De interpretatione*, [illegible] the enunciation, or proposition, from other [illegible] in which there is truth or falsity, he relegated the [illegible] poetry, and founded the logic of the proposi[illegible] he retained the grammatical analysis into [illegible] *Analytics* he took the final step of originating [illegible] the proposition as premise into subject and [illegible] mediated by the copula, and analysed the [illegible] elements. Thus did he become the founder [illegible] linguistic analysis of reasoning as discourse (ὁ ἔξω [illegible] and terms. Nevertheless, the deeper ques[illegible] the logical but mental analysis of reasoning [illegible] its mental premises and conclusion?

[illegible] the founder of logic as a science. But he [illegible] on reasoning as syllogism or deduction, [illegible]; and he laid too much stress on the [illegible] rational discourse into proposition and terms. [illegible] ingrained in technical logic to this day. [illegible] the development of the science, logicians [illegible] correct those defects, and have diverged [illegible] have devoted themselves to induction [illegible] and widened logic till it has become [illegible] method. Others [illegible] analysis of reasoning, and have narrowed logic into a science of conception, judgment and reasoning. The former belong to the school of empirical logic, the latter to the school of conceptual and formal logic. Both have started from points which Aristotle indicated without developing them. But we shall find that his true descendants are the empirical logicians.

Aristotle was the first of the empiricists. He consistently maintained that sense is knowledge of particulars and the origin of scientific knowledge of universals. In his view, sense is a congenital form of judgment (δύναμις σύμφυτος κριτική, *Post. An.* ii. 19); a sensation of each of the five senses is always true of its proper object; without sense there is no science; sense is the origin of induction, which is the origin of deduction and science. The *Analytics* end (*Post. An.* ii. 19) with a detailed system of empiricism, according to which sense is the primary knowledge of particulars, memory is the retention of a sensation, experience is the sum of many memories, induction infers universals, and intelligence is the true apprehension of the universal principles of science, which is rational, deductive, demonstrative, from empirical principles.

This empirical groundwork of Aristotle's logic was accepted by the Epicureans, who enunciated most distinctly the fundamental doctrine that all sensations are true of their immediate objects, and falsity begins with subsequent opinions, or what the moderns call "interpretation." Beneath deductive logic, in the logic of Aristotle and the canonic of the Epicureans, there already lay the basis of empirical logic: sensory experience is the origin of all inference and science. It remained for Francis Bacon to develop these beginnings into a new logic of induction. He did not indeed accept the infallibility of sense or of any other operation unaided. He thought, rather, that every operation becomes infallible by method. Following Aristotle in this order—sense, memory, intellect—he resolved the whole process of induction into three ministrations:—

1. The ministration to sense, aided by observation and experiment.
2. The ministration to memory, aided by registering and arranging the data, of observation and experiment in tables of instances of agreement, difference and concomitant variations.
3. The ministration to intellect or reason, aided by the negative elimination by means of contradictory instances of whatever in the instances is not always present, absent and varying with the given subject investigated, and finally by the positive inference that whatever in the instances is always present, absent and varying with the subject is its essential cause.

Bacon, like Aristotle, was anticipated in this or that point; but, as Aristotle was the first to construct a system of deduction in the syllogism and its three figures, so Bacon was the first to construct a system of induction in three ministrations, in which the requisites of induction, hitherto recognized only in sporadic hints, were combined for the first time in one logic of induction. Bacon taught men to labour in inferring from particular to universal, to lay as much stress on induction as on deduction, and to think and speak of inductive reasoning, inductive science, inductive logic. Moreover, while Aristotle had the merit of discerning the triplicity of inference, to Bacon we owe the merit of distinguishing the three processes without reduction:—

1. Inference from particular to particular by Experientia Literata, in plano;
2. Inference from particular to universal by Inductio, ascendendo;
3. Inference from universal to particular by Syllogism, descendendo.

In short, the comprehensive genius of Bacon widened logic into a general science of inference.

On the other hand, as Aristotle over-emphasized deduction so Bacon over-emphasized induction by contending that it is the only process of discovering universals (*axiomata*), which deduction only applies to particulars. J. S. Mill in his *Logic* pointed out this defect, and without departing from Baconian principles remedied it by quoting scientific examples, in which deduction, starting from inductive principles, applies more general to less general universals, *e.g.* when the more general law of gravitation is shown to include the less general laws of planetary gravitation. Mill's logic has the great merit of copiously exemplifying the principles of the variety of method according to subject-matter. It teaches us that scientific method is sometimes induction, sometimes deduction, and sometimes the consilience of both, either by the inductive verification of previous deductions, or by the deductive explanation of previous inductions.

It is also most interesting to notice that Aristotle saw further than Bacon in this direction. The founder of logic anticipated the latest logic of science, when he recognized, not only the deduction of mathematics, but also the experience of facts followed by deductive explanations of their causes in physics.

The consilience of empirical and deductive processes was an Aristotelian discovery, elaborated by Mill against Bacon. On the whole, however, Aristotle, Bacon and Mill, purged from their errors, form one empirical school, gradually growing by adapting itself to the advance of science: a school in which Aristotle was most influenced by Greek deductive Mathematics, Bacon by the rise of empirical physics at the Renaissance, and Mill by the Newtonian combination of empirical facts and mathematical principles in the *Principia*. From studying this succession of empirical logicians, we cannot doubt that sense, memory and experience are the real origin of inference, analogical, inductive and deductive. The deepest problem of logic is the relation of sense and inference. But we must first consider the mental analysis of inference, and this brings us to conceptual and formal logic.

Aristotle's logic has often been called formal logic; it was really a technical logic of syllogism analysed into linguistic elements, and of science rested on an empirical basis. At the same time his psychology, though maintaining his empiricism, contained some seeds of conceptual logic, and indirectly of formal logic. Intellectual development, which according to the logic of the *Analytics* consists of sense, memory, experience, induction and intellect, according to the psychology of the *De Anima* consists of sense, imagination and intellect, and one division of intellect is into conception of the undivided and combination of conceptions as one (*De An.* iii. 6). The *De Interpretatione* opens with a reference to this psychological distinction, implying that names represent conceptions, propositions represent combinations of conceptions. But the same passage relegates conceptions and their combinations to the *De Anima*, and confines the *De Interpretatione* to names and propositions in conformity with the linguistic analysis which pervades the logical treatises of Aristotle, who neither brought his psychological distinction between conceptions and their combinations into his logic, nor advanced the combinations of conceptions as a definition of judgment (*κρίσις*), nor employed the mental distinction between conceptions and judgments as an analysis of inference, or reasoning, or syllogism: he was no conceptual logician. The history of logic shows that the linguistic distinction between terms and propositions was the sole analysis of reasoning in the logical treatises of Aristotle; that the mental distinction between conceptions (ἔννοιαι) and judgments (ἀξιώματα in a wide sense) was imported into logic by the Stoics; and that this mental distinction became the logical analysis of reasoning under the authority of St Thomas Aquinas. In his commentary on the *De Interpretatione*, St Thomas, after citing from the *De Anima* Aristotle's "duplex operatio intellectus," said, "Additur autem et tertia operatio, scilicet ratiocinandi," and concluded that, since logic is a rational science (*rationalis scientia*), its consideration must be directed to all these operations of reason. Hence arose conceptual logic; according to which conception is a simple apprehension of an idea without belief in being or not being, *e.g.* the idea of man or of running; judgment is a combination of conceptions, adding being or not being, *e.g.* man is running or not running; and reasoning is a combination of judgments: conversely, there is a mental analysis of reasoning into judgments, and judgment into conceptions, beneath the linguistic analysis of rational discourse into propositions, and propositions into terms. Logic, according to this new school, which has by our time become an old school, has to co-ordinate these three operations, direct them, and, beginning with conceptions, combine conceptions into judgments, and judgments into inference, which thus becomes a complex combination of conceptions, or, in modern parlance, an extension of our ideas. Conceptual logicians were, indeed, from the first aware that sense supplies the data, and that judgment and therefore inference contains belief that things are or are not. But they held, and still hold that sensation and conception are alike mere apprehensions, and that the belief that things are or are not arises somehow after sensation and conception in judgment, from which it passes into inference. At first, they were more sanguine of extracting from these unpromising beginnings some knowledge of things beyond ideas. But at length many of them became formal logicians, who held that logic is the investigation of formal thinking, or consistent conception, judgment and reasoning; that it shows how we infer formal truths of consistency without material truth of signifying things; that, as the science of the form or process, it must entirely abstract from the matter, or objects, of thought; and that it does not tell us how we infer from experience. Thus has logic drifted further and further from the real and empirical logic of Aristotle the founder and Bacon the reformer of the science.

The great merit of conceptual logic was the demand for a mental analysis of mental reasoning, and the direct analysis of reasoning into judgments which are the sole premises and conclusions of reasoning and of all mental inferences. Aristotle had fallen into the paradox of resolving a mental act into verbal elements. The Schoolmen, however, gradually came to realize that the result to their logic was to make it a *sermocionalis scientia*, and to their metaphysics the danger of nominalism. St Thomas made a great advance by making logic throughout a *rationalis scientia*; and logicians are now agreed that reasoning consists of judgments, discourse of propositions. This distinction is, moreover, vital to the whole logic of inference, because we always think all the judgments of which our inference consists, but seldom state all the propositions by which it is expressed. We omit propositions, curtail them, and even express a judgment by a single term, *e.g.* "Good!" "Fire!". Hence the linguistic expression is not a true measure of inference; and to say that an inference consists of two propositions causing a third is not strictly true. But to say that it is two judgments causing a third is always true, and the very essence of inference, because we must think the two to conclude the third in "the sessions of sweet silent thought." Inference, in short, consists of actual judgments capable of being expressed in propositions.

Inference always consists of judgments. But judgment does not always consist of conceptions. It is not a combination of conceptions; it does not arise from conceptions, nor even at first require conception. Sense is the origin of judgment. One who feels pained or pleased, who feels hot or cold or resisting in touch, who tastes the flavoured, who smells the odorous, who hears the sounding, who sees the coloured, or is conscious, already believes that something sensible exists before conception, before inference, and before language; and his belief is true of the immediate object of sense, the sensible thing, *e.g.* the hot felt in touch. But a belief in the existence of something is a judgment and a categorical judgment of existence. Sense, then, outer and inner, or sensation and consciousness, is the origin of sensory judgments which are true categorical beliefs in the existence of sensible things; and primary judgments are such true categorical sensory beliefs that things exist, and neither require conception nor are combinations of conceptions. Again, since sense is the origin of memory and experience, memorial and experiential judgments are categorical and existential judgments, which so far as they report sensory judgments are always true. Finally, since sense, memory and experience are the origin of inference, primary inference is categorical and existential, starting from sensory, memorial and experiential judgments as premises, and proceeding to inferential judgments as conclusions, which are categorical and existential, and are true, so far as they depend on sense, memory and experience.

Sense, then, is the origin of judgment; and the consequence is that primary judgments are true, categorical and existential judgments of sense, and primary inferences are inferences from categorical and existential premises to categorical and existential conclusions, which are true so far as they arise from outer and inner sense, and proceed to things similar to sensible things. All other judgments and inferences about existing things, or ideas, or names, whether categorical or hypothetical, are afterthoughts, partly true and partly false.

Sense, then, because it involves a true belief in existence is fitted to be the origin of judgment. Conception on the other hand is the simple apprehension of an idea, particular or universal, but without belief that anything is or is not, and therefore is unfitted to beget judgment. Nor could a combination of conceptions make a difference so fundamental as that between conceiving and believing. The most that it could do would be to cause an ideal judgment, *e.g.* that the idea of a centaur is the idea of a man-horse; and even here some further origin is needed for the addition of the copula "is."

So far from being a cause, conception is not even a condition of all judgments; a sensation of hot is sufficient evidence that hot exists, before the idea of hot is either present or wanted. Conception is, however, a condition of a memorial judgment: in order to remember being hot, we require an idea of hot. Memory, however, is not that idea, but involves a judgment that there previously existed the hot now represented by the idea, which is about the sensible thing beyond the conceived idea; and the cause of this [illegible] So sense, [illegible] though [illegible] al judgment [illegible] things, and [illegible] judgments about the [illegible] beyond conceived [illegible] inference. Starting [illegible] conclusions which are [illegible] of things similar to [illegible]. In rising, however, from [illegible] induction, as we have seen, adds [illegible] a universal premise, every M is [illegible] the universal conclusion, every M is P. [illegible] a universal conception of a class or [illegible] particulars, as a condition. But the [illegible] conception, it is a belief that there is a whole [illegible] similar to those already experienced. The [illegible] class is not, as the conceptual logic assumes, the [illegible] a general idea, but an inference from the analogy [illegible] individual thing, e.g. a whole man, to a whole number [illegible] individuals, e.g. the whole of men. The general idea of all [illegible] the combination that the idea of all men is similar to the [illegible] particular men would not be enough, the universal premise [illegible] in fact are similar to those who have died is required [illegible] the universal conclusion that all men in fact die. Universal [illegible] thus requires particular and universal conceptions as its [illegible]; but, so far as it arises from sense, memory, experience, [illegible] involves generalization, it consists of judgments which do not consist of conceptions, but are beliefs in things existing beyond conception. Inference then, so far as it starts from categorical and existential premises, causes conclusions, or inferential judgments, which require conceptions, but are categorical and existential judgments beyond conception. Moreover, as it becomes more deductive, and causes conclusions further from sensory experience, these inferential judgments become causes of inferential conceptions. For example, from the evidence of molar changes due to the obvious parts of bodies, science first comes to believe in molecular changes due to imperceptible particles, and then tries to conceive the ideas of particles, molecules, atoms, electrons. The conceptual logic supposes that conception always precedes judgment, but the truth is that sensory judgment begins and inferential judgment ends by preceding conception. The supposed triple order—conception, judgment, reasoning—is defective and false. The real order is sensation and sensory judgment, conception, memory and memorial judgment, experience and experiential judgment, inference, inferential judgment, inferential conception. This is not all: inferential conceptions are inadequate, and finally fail. They are often symbolical, that is, we conceive one thing only by another like it, e.g. atoms by minute bodies not nearly small enough. Often the symbol is not like. What idea can the physicist form of intra-spatial ether? What believer in God pretends to conceive Him as He really is? We believe many things that we cannot conceive; as Mill said, the inconceivable is not the incredible, and the point of science is not what we can conceive but what we should believe on evidence. Conception is the weakest, judgment the strongest power of man's mind. Sense before conception is the original cause of judgment, and inference from sense enables judgment to continue after conception ceases. Finally, as there is judgment without conception, so there is conception without judgment. We often say "I understand, but do not decide." But this suspension of judgment is a highly refined act, unfitted to the beginning of thought. Conception begins as a condition of memory, and after a long continuous process of inference ends in mere ideation. The conceptual logic has made the mistake of making ideation a stage in thought prior to judgment.

It was natural enough that the originators of conceptual logic, seeing that judgments can be expressed by propositions, and conceptions by terms, should fall into the error of supposing that, as propositions consist of terms, so judgments consist of conceptions, and that there is a triple mental order—conception, judgment, reasoning—parallel to the triple linguistic order—term, proposition, discourse. They overlooked the fact that man thinks long before he speaks, makes judgments which he does not express at all, or expresses them by interjections, names and phrases before he uses regular propositions, and that he does not begin by conceiving and naming and then proceed to believing and proposing. Feeling and sensation, involving believing or judging, come before conception and language. As conceptions are not always present in judgment, as they are only occasional conditions, and as they are unfitted to cause beliefs or judgments, and especially judgments of existence, and as judgments both precede conceptions in sense and continue after them in inference, it follows that conceptions are not the constituents of judgment, and judgment is not a combination of conceptions. Is there then any analysis of judgment? Paradoxical as it may sound, the truth seems to be that primary judgment, beginning as it does with the simplest feeling and sensation, is not a combination of two mental elements into one, but is a division of one sensible thing into the thing itself and its existence and the belief that it [illegible] as existing, e.g. that hot exists, cold exists, the [illegible] existed exists. Such a judgment has a cause, namely sense, but no mental elements. Afterwards come judgments of complex sense, e.g. that the existing hot is burning or becoming more or less hot, &c. Thus there is a combination of sensations causing the judgment; but the judgment is still a division of the sensible thing into itself and its being, and a belief that it is so determined. Afterwards follow judgments arising from more complex causes, e.g. memory, experience, inference. But however complicated these mental causes, there still remain these points common to all judgment:—(1) The mental causes of judgment are sense, memory, experience and inference, while conception is a condition of some judgments. (2) A judgment is not a combination either of its causes or of its conditions, e.g. it is not a combination of sensations any more than of ideas. (3) A judgment is a unitary mental act, dividing not itself but its object into the object itself and itself as determined, and signifying that it is so determined. (4) A primary judgment is a judgment that a sensible thing is determined as existing; but later judgments are concerned with either existing things, or with ideas, or with words, and signify that they are determined in all sorts of ways. (5) When a judgment is expressed by a proposition, the proposition expresses the results of the division by two terms, subject and predicate, and by the copula that what is signified by the subject is what is signified by the predicate; and the proposition is a combination of the two terms, e.g. border war is evil. (6) A complex judgment is a combination of two judgments, and may be copulative, e.g. you and I are men, or hypothetical, or disjunctive, &c.

Empirical logic, the logic of Aristotle and Bacon, is on the right way. It is the business of the logician to find the causes of the judgments which form the premises and the conclusions of inference, reasoning and science. What knowledge do we get by sense, memory and experience, the first mental causes of judgment? What is judgment, and what its various kinds? What is inference, how does it proceed by combining judgments as premises to cause judgments as conclusions, and what are its various kinds? How does inference draw conclusions more or less probable up to moral certainty? How does it by the aid of identification convert probable into necessary conclusions, which become necessary principles of demonstration? How is categorical succeeded by conditional inference? What is scientific method as a system of inferences about definite subjects? How does inference become the source of error and fallacy? How does the whole process from sense to inference discover the real truth of judgments, which are true so far as they signify things known by sense, memory, experience and inference? These are the fundamental questions of the science of inference. Conceptual logic, on the other hand, is false from the start. It is not the first business of logic to direct us how to form conceptions signified by terms, because sense is a prior cause of judgment and inference. It is not the second business of logic to direct us how out of conceptions to form judgments signified by propositions because the real causes of judgments are sense, memory, experience and inference. It is, however, the main business of logic to direct us how out of judgments to form inferences signified by discourse, and this is the one point which conceptual logic has contributed to the science of inference. But why spoil the further mental analysis of inference by supposing that conceptions are constituents of judgment and therefore of inference, which thus becomes merely a complex combination of conceptions, an extension of ideas? The mistake has been to convert three operations of mind into three processes in a fixed order—conception, judgment, inference. Conception and judgment are decisions; inference alone is a process, from decisions to decision, from judgments to judgment. Sense, not conception, is the origin of judgment. Inference is the process which from judgments about sensible things proceeds to judgments about things similar to sensible things. Though some conceptions are its conditions and some judgments its causes, inference itself in its conclusions causes many more judgments and conceptions. Finally, inference is an extension, not of ideas, but of beliefs, at first about existing things, afterwards about ideas, and even about words; about anything in short about which we think, in what is too fancifully called "the universe of discourse."

Formal logic has arisen out of the narrowness of conceptual logic. The science of inference no doubt has to deal primarily with formal truth or the consistency of premises and conclusion. But as all truth, real as well as formal, is consistent, formal rules of consistency become real rules of truth, when the premises are true and the consistent conclusion is therefore true. The science of inference again rightly emphasizes the formal thinking of the syllogism in which the combination of premises involves the conclusion. But the combinations of premises in analogical and inductive inference, although the combination does not involve the conclusion, yet causes us to infer it, and in so similar a way that the science of inference is not complete without investigating all the combinations which characterize different kinds of inference. The question of logic is how we infer in fact, as well as perfectly; and we cannot understand inference unless we consider inferences of probability of all kinds. Moreover, the study of analogical and inductive inference is necessary to that of the syllogism itself, because they discover the premises of syllogism. The formal thinking of syllogism alone is merely necessary consequence; but when its premises are necessary principles, its conclusions are not only necessary consequents but also necessary truths. Hence the manner in which induction aided by identification discovers necessary principles must be studied by the logician in order to decide when the syllogism can really arrive at necessary conclusions. Again, the science of inference has for its subject the form, or processes, of thought, but not its matter or objects. But it does not follow that it can investigate the former without the latter. Formal logicians say that, if they had to consider the matter, they must either consider all things, which would be impossible, or select some, which would be arbitrary. But there is an intermediate alternative, which is neither impossible nor arbitrary; namely, to consider the general distinctions and principles of all things; and without this general consideration of the matter the logician cannot know the form of thought, which consists in drawing inferences about things on these general principles. Lastly, the science of inference is not indeed the science of sensation, memory and experience, but at the same time it is the science of using those mental operations as data of inference; and, if logic does not show how analogical and inductive inferences directly, and deductive inferences indirectly, arise from experience, it becomes a science of mere thinking without knowledge.

Logic is related to all the sciences, because it considers the common inferences and varying methods used in investigating different subjects. But it is most closely related to the sciences of metaphysics and psychology, which form with it a triad of sciences. Metaphysics is the science of being in general, and therefore of the things which become objects apprehended by our minds. Psychology is the science of mind in general, and therefore of the mental operations, of which inference is one. Logic is the science of the processes of inference. These three sciences, of the objects of mind, of the operations of mind, of the processes used in the inferences of mind, are differently, but closely related, so that they are constantly confused. The real point is their interdependence, which is so intimate that one sign of great philosophy is a consistent metaphysics, psychology and logic. If the world of things is *known* to be partly material and partly mental, then the mind must have powers of sense and inference enabling it to know these things, and there must be processes of inference carrying us from and beyond the sensible to the insensible world of matter and mind. If the whole world of things is matter, operations and processes of mind are themselves material. If the whole world of things is mind, operations and processes of mind have only to recognize their like all the world over. It is clear then that a man's metaphysics and psychology must colour his logic. It is accordingly necessary to the logician to know beforehand the general distinctions and principles of things in metaphysics, and the mental operations of sense, conception, memory and experience in psychology, so as to discover the processes of inference from experience about things in logic.

The interdependence of this triad of sciences has sometimes led to their confusion. Hegel, having identified being with thought, merged metaphysics in logic. But he divided logic into objective and subjective, and thus practically confessed that there is one science of the objects and another of the processes of thought. Psychologists, seeing that inference is a mental operation, often extemporize a theory of inference to the neglect of logic. But we have a double consciousness of inference. We are conscious of it as one operation among many, and of its omnipresence, so to speak, to all the rest. But we are also conscious of the processes of the operation of inference. To a certain extent this second consciousness applies to other operations: for example, we are conscious of the process of association by which various mental causes recall ideas in the imagination. But how little does the psychologist know about the association of ideas, compared with what the logician has discovered about the processes of inference! The fact is that our primary consciousness of all mental operations is hardly equal to our secondary consciousness of the processes of the one operation of inference from premises to conclusions permeating long trains and pervading whole sciences. This elaborate consciousness of inferential process is the justification of logic as a distinct science, and is the first step in its method. But it is not the whole method of logic, which also and rightly considers the mental process necessary to language, without substituting linguistic for mental distinctions.

Nor are consciousness and linguistic analysis all the instruments of the logician. Logic has to consider the things we know, the minds by which we know them from sense, memory and experience to inference, and the sciences which systematize and extend our knowledge of things; and having considered these facts, the logician must make such a science of inference as will explain the power and the poverty of human knowledge.

General Tendencies of Modern Logic

There are several grounds for hope in the logic of our day. In the first place, it tends to take up an intermediate position between the extremes of Kant and Hegel. It does not, with the former, regard logic as purely formal in the sense of abstracting thought from being, nor does it follow the latter in amalgamating metaphysics with logic by identifying being with thought. Secondly, it does not content itself with the mere formulae of thinking, but pushes forward to theories of method, knowledge and science; and it is a hopeful sign to find this epistemological spirit, to which England was accustomed by Mill, animating German logicians such as Lotze, Dühring, Schuppe, Sigwart and Wundt. Thirdly, there is a determination to reveal the psychological basis of logical processes, and not merely to describe them as they are in adult reasoning, but to explain also how they arise from simpler mental operations and primarily from sense. This attempt is connected with the psychological turn given to recent philosophy by Wundt and others, and is dangerous only so far as psychology itself is hypothetical. Unfortunately, however, these merits are usually connected with a less admirable characteristic—contempt for tradition. Writing his preface to his second edition in 1888, Sigwart says: "Important works have appeared by Lotze, Schuppe, Wundt and Bradley, to name only the most eminent; and all start from the conception which has guided this attempt. That is, logic is grounded by them, not upon an effete tradition but upon a new investigation of thought as it actually is in its psychological foundations, in its significance for knowledge, and its actual operation in scientific methods." How strange! The spirit of every one of the three reforms above enumerated is an unconscious return to Aristotle's *Organon*. Aristotle's was a logic which steered, as Trendelenburg has shown, between Kantian formalism and Hegelian metaphysics; it was a logic which in the Analytics investigated the syllogism as a means to understanding knowledge and science: it was a logic which, starting from the psychological foundations of sense, memory and experience, built up the logical structure of induction and deduction on the profoundly Aristotelian principle that "there is no process from universals without induction, and none by induction without sense." Wundt's comprehensive view that logic looks backwards to psychology and forward to epistemology was hundreds of years ago one of the many discoveries of Aristotle.

ideas, and are judgments of memory after sense that something sensible existed, *e.g.* pressure existed: afterwards come judgments of memory after inference, *e.g.* Caesar was murdered. Finally, most judgments are inferential. These are conclusions which primarily are inferred from sensory and memorial judgments; and so far as inference starts from sense or something sensible in the present, and from memory after sense of something sensible in the past, and concludes similar things, inferential judgments are indirect beliefs in being and in existence beyond ideas. When from the sensible pressures between the parts of my mouth, which I feel and remember and judge that they exist and have existed, I infer another similar pressure (*e.g.* of the food which presses and is pressed by my mouth in eating), the inferential judgment with which I conclude is a belief that the latter exists as well as the former (*e.g.* the pressure of food without as well as the sensible pressures within). Inference, no doubt, is closely involved with conception. So far as it depends on memory, an inferential judgment presupposes memorial ideas in its data; and so far as it infers universal classes and laws, it produces general ideas. But even so the part played by conception is quite subordinate to that of belief. In the first place, the remembered datum, from which an inference of pressure starts, is not the conceived idea, but the belief that the sensible pressure existed. Secondly, the conclusion in which it ends is not the general idea of a class, but the belief that a class, represented by a general idea, exists, and is (or is not) otherwise determined (*e.g.* that things pressing and pressed exist and move). Two things are certain about inferential judgment: one, that when inference is based on sense and memory, inferential judgment starts from a combination of sensory and memorial judgment, both of which are beliefs that things exist; the other, that in consequence inferential judgment is a belief that smiliar things exist. There are thus three primary judgments: judgments of sense, of memory after sense, and of inference from sense. All these are beliefs in being and existence, and this existential belief is first in sense, and afterwards transferred to memory and inference. Moreover, it is transferred in the same irresistible way: frequently we cannot help either feeling pressure, or remembering it, or inferring it; and as there are involuntary sensation and attention, so there are involuntary memory and inference. Again, in a primary judgment existence need not be expressed; but if expressed, it may be expressed either by the predicate, *e.g.* "I exist," or by the subject, *e.g.* "I who exist think." There are indeed differences between primary judgments, in that the sensory is a belief in present, the memorial in past, and the inferential in present, past and future existence. But these differences in detail do not alter the main point that all these are beliefs in the existing, in the real as opposed to the ideal, in actual things which are not ideas. In short, a primary judgment is a belief in something existing apart from our idea of it; and not because we have an idea of it, or by comparing an idea with, or referring an idea to, reality; but because we have a sensation of it, or a memory of it or an inference of it. Sensation, not conception, is the origin of judgment.

2. *Different Significations of Being in different Kinds of Judgment.*—As Aristotle remarked both in the *De Interpretatione* and in the *Sophistici Elenchi*, "not-being is thinkable" does not mean "not-being exists." In the latter treatise he added that it is a *fallacia a dicto secundum quid ad dictum simpliciter* to argue from the former to the latter; "for," as he says, "it is not the same thing to be something and to exist absolutely." Without realizing their debt to tradition, Herbart, Mill and recently Sigwart, have repeated Aristotle's separation of the copula from the verb of existence, as if it were a modern discovery that "is" is not the same as "exists." It may be added that they do not quite realize what the copula exactly signifies: it does not signify existence, but it does signify a fact, namely, that something is (or is not) determined, either absolutely in a categorical judgment, or conditionally in a conditional judgment. Now we have seen that all primary judgments signify more than this fact; they are also beliefs in the existence of the thing signified by the subject. But, in the first place, primary judgments signify this existence never by the copula, but sometimes by the predicate, and sometimes by the subject; and, secondly, it does not follow that all judgments whatever signify existence. Besides inference of existence there is inference of non-existence, of things inconsistent with the objects of primary judgments. Hence secondary judgments, which no longer contain a belief that the thing exists, *e.g.* the judgment, "not-being is thinkable," cited by Aristotle; the judgment, "A square circle is impossible," cited by Herbart; the judgment, "A centaur is a fiction of the poets," cited by Mill. These secondary judgments of non-existence are partly like and partly unlike primary judgments of existence. They resemble them in that they are beliefs in being signified by the copula. They are beliefs in things of a sort; for, after all, ideas and names are things; their objects, even though non-existent, are at all events things conceivable or nameable; and therefore we are able to make judgments that things, non-existent but conceivable or nameable, are (or are not) determined in a particular manner. Thus the judgment about a centaur is the belief, "A conceivable centaur is a fiction of the poets," and the judgment about a square circle is the belief, "A so-called square circle is an impossibility." But, though beliefs that things of some sort are (or are not) determined, these secondary judgments fall short of primary judgments of existence. Whereas in a primary judgment there is a further belief, signified by subject or predicate, that the thing is an existing thing in the sense of being a real thing (*e.g.* a man), different from the idea of it as well as from the name for it; in a secondary judgment there is no further belief that the thing has any existence beyond the idea (*e.g.* a centaur), or even beyond the name (*e.g.* a square circle): though the idea or name exists, there is no belief that anything represented by idea or name exists. Starting, then, from this fundamental distinction between judgments of existence and judgments of non-existence, we may hope to steer our way between two extreme views which emanate from two important thinkers, each of whom has produced a flourishing school of psychological logic.

On the one hand, early in the 19th century Herbart started the view that a categorical judgment is never a judgment of existence, but always hypothetical; on the other hand, in the latter part of the century Brentano started the view that all categorical judgments are existential. The truth lies between these contraries. The view of Herbart and his school is contradicted by our primary judgments of and from sense, in which we cannot help believing existence; and it gives an inadequate account even of our secondary judgments in which we no longer indeed believe existence, but do frequently believe that a non-existent thing is (or is not) somehow determined unconditionally. It is true, as Herbart says, that the judgment, "A square circle is an impossibility," does not contain the belief, "A square circle is existent"; but when he goes on to argue that it means, "If a square circle is thought, the conception of impossibility must be added in thought," he falls into a *non-sequitur*. To be categorical, a judgment does not require a belief in existence, but only that something, existent or not, is (or is not) determined; and there are two quite different attitudes of mind even to a non-existent thing, such as a square circle, namely, unconditional and conditional belief. The judgment, "A non-existent but so-called square circle is an impossibility," is an unconditional, or categorical judgment of non-existence, quite different from any hypothetical judgment, which depends on the conditions "if it is thought," or "if it exists," or any other "if." On the other hand, the view of Brentano and his school is contradicted by these very categorical judgments of non-existence; and while it applies only to categorical judgments of existence, it does so inadequately. To begin with the latter objection, Brentano proposed to change the four Aristotelian forms of judgment, A, E, I, O, into the following existential forms:—

A. "There is not an immortal man."
E. "There is not a live stone."
I. "There is a sick man."
O. "There is an unlearned man."

[illegible] and predicate in one [illegible] verb of existence, [illegible] English logicians [illegible] forms, $s\bar{y}=0$, [illegible] but only as [illegible] Bradley says that "S–P [illegible] the ultimate [illegible] never stands for [illegible] follows Bradley, [illegible] as "that which [illegible] words, asserts [illegible] to contain [illegible] in the same [illegible] determined as [illegible] is particularly [illegible] such a judgment [illegible] nor does [illegible] Metaphysically, all [illegible] logically, even [illegible] existing [illegible] their parents [illegible] reality. The normal [illegible] "S is a real P," [illegible] of all categorical [illegible] Brentano's [illegible] even of normal [illegible] it is much more [illegible] of non-existence. [illegible] as "A centaur is a [illegible] there is a centaur, or that [illegible] out, it cannot be [illegible] thing asserted is [illegible] correspondence with [illegible] in imagination; [illegible] to one, then, [illegible] imaginary centaur"; [illegible] imaginary centaur." [illegible] is not to the point. [illegible] imagination, and inside [illegible] But the point is [illegible] not exist beyond the [illegible] man, a real thing [illegible] No amount of [illegible] a categorical judg- [illegible] is mortal," and a [illegible] "A conceivable [illegible] we believe and mean [illegible] the latter we do [illegible] the latter a judg- [illegible] about words; [illegible] case be invented [illegible] that between judg- [illegible] about ideal centaurs. [illegible] natural sense, and call [illegible] latter judgments of [illegible] Bradley supposes, the [illegible] both judgments, but [illegible] definition of a [illegible] To assert [illegible] are not, as he [illegible] asserts a fact and [illegible] "Jupiter is non- [illegible] better than innova- [illegible] belief in the [illegible] some sort is (or is [illegible] judgments are also [illegible] either by the [illegible] beliefs that the [illegible] something conceivable, [illegible] [illegible] says

3. *Particular and Universal Judgments.*—Aristotle, by distinguishing affirmative and negative, particular and universal made the fourfold classification of judgments, A, E, I and O the foundation both of opposition and of inference. With regard to inference, he remarked that a universal judgment means by "all," not every individual we know, but every individual absolutely, so that, when it becomes a major premise, we know therein every individual universally, not individually, and often do not know a given individual individually until we add a minor premise in a syllogism. Whereas, then, a particular judgment is a belief that some, a universal judgment is a belief that all, the individuals of a kind or total of similar individuals, are similarly determined, whether they are known or unknown individuals. Now, as we have already seen, what is signified by the subject may be existing or not, and in either case a judgment remains categorical so long as it is a belief without conditions. Thus, "Some existing men are poets," "All existing men are mortal," "Some conceivable centaurs are human in their forequarters," "All conceivable centaurs are equine in their hindquarters," are all categorical judgments, while the two first are also categorical judgments of existence. Nevertheless these obvious applications of Aristotelian traditions have been recently challenged, especially by Sigwart, who holds in his *Logic* (secs. 27, 36) that, while a particular is a categorical judgment of existence, a universal is hypothetical, on the ground that it does not refer to a definite number of individuals, or to individuals at all, but rather to general ideas, and that the appropriate form of "all M is P" is "if anything is M it is P." This view, which has influenced not only German but also English logicians, such as Venn, Bradley and Bosanquet; destroys the fabric of inference, and reduces scientific laws to mere hypotheses. In reality, however, particular and universal judgments are too closely connected to have such different imports. In opposition, a categorical particular is the contradictory of a universal, which is also categorical, not hypothetical, *e.g.*, "not all M is P" is the contradictory of "all M is P," not of "if anything is M it is P." In inference, a particular is an example of a universal which in its turn may become a particular example of a higher universal. For instance, in the history of mechanics it was first inferred from some that all terrestrial bodies gravitate, and then from these as some that all ponderable bodies, terrestrial and celestial, gravitate. How absurd to suppose that here we pass from a particular categorical to a universal hypothetical, and then treat this very conclusion as a particular categorical to pass to a higher universal hypothetical! Sigwart, indeed, is deceived both about particulars and universals. On the one hand, some particulars are not judgments of existence, *e.g.* "some imaginary deities are goddesses"; on the other hand, some universals are not judgments of non-existence, *e.g.* "every existing man is mortal." Neither kind is always a judgment of existence, but each is sometimes the one and sometimes the other. In no case is a universal hypothetical, unless we think it under a condition; for in a universal judgment about the non-existing, *e.g.* about all conceivable centaurs, we do not think, "If anything is a centaur," because we do not believe that there are any; and in a universal judgment about the existent, *e.g.* about all existing men, we do not think, "If anything is a man," because we believe that there is a whole class of men existing at different times and places. The cause of Sigwart's error is his misconception of "all." So far as he follows Aristotle in saying that "all" does not mean a definite number of individuals he is right; but when he says that we mean no individuals at all he deserts Aristotle and goes wrong. By "all" we mean every individual whatever of a kind; and when from the experience of sense and memory we start with particular judgments of existence, and infer universal judgments of existence and scientific laws, we further mean those existing individuals which we have experienced, and every individual whatever of the kind which exists. We mean neither a definite number of individuals, nor yet an infinite number, but an incalculable number, whether experienced or inferred to exist. We do not mean existing here and now, nor yet out of time and place, but at any time and place (*semper et ubique*)—

past, present and future being treated as simply existing, by what logicians used to call *suppositio naturalis*. We mean then by "all existing" every similar individual whatever, whenever, and wherever existing. Hence Sigwart is right in saying that "All bodies are extended" means "Whatever is a body is extended," but wrong in identifying this form with "If anything is a body it is extended." "Whatever" is not "if anything." For the same reason it is erroneous to confuse "all existing" with a general idea. Nor does the use of abstract ideas and terms make any difference. When Bosanquet says that in "Heat is a mode of motion" there is no reference to individual objects, but "a pure hypothetical form which absolutely neglects the existence of objects," he falls far short of expressing the nature of this scientific judgment, for in his *Theory of Heat* Clerk Maxwell describes it as "believing heat as it exists in a hot body to be in the form of kinetic energy" As Bacon would say, it is a belief that all individual bodies *qua* hot are individually but similarly moving in their particles. When, again, Bradley and Bosanquet speak of the universal as if it always meant one ideal content referred to reality, they forget that in universal judgments of existence, such as "All men existing are mortal," we believe that every individually existing man dies his own death individually, though similarly to other men; and that we are thinking neither of ideas nor of reality; but of all existent individual men being individually but similarly determined. A universal is indeed one whole; but it is one whole of many similars, which are not the same with one another. This is indeed the very essence of distribution, that a universal is predicable, not singly or collectively, but severally and similarly of each and every individual of a kind, or total of similar individuals. So also the essence of a universal judgment is that every individual of the kind is severally but similarly determined. Finally, a universal judgment is often existential; but whether it is so or not it remains categorical, so long as it introduces no hypothetical antecedent about the existence of the thing signified by the subject. It is true that even in universal judgments of existence there is often a hypothetical element; for example, "All men are mortal" contains a doubt whether every man whatever, whenever and wherever existing, must die. But this is only a doubt whether all the things signified by the subject are similarly determined as signified by the predicate, and not a doubt whether there are such things at all. Hence the hypothetical element is not a hypothetical antecedent "If anything is a man," but an uncertain conclusion that "All existing men are mortal." In other words, a categorical universal is often problematic, but a problematic is not the same as a hypothetical judgment.

4. *The Judgment and the Proposition.*—Judgment in general is the mental act of believing that something is (or is not) determined. A proposition is the consequent verbal expression of such a belief, and consists in asserting that the thing as signified by the subject is (or is not) determined as signified by the predicate. But the expression is not necessary. Sensation irresistibly produces a judgment of existence without needing language. Children think long before they speak; and indeed, as mere vocal sounds are not speech, and as the apprehension that a word signifies a thing is a judgment, judgment is originally not an effect, but a cause of significant language. At any rate, even when we have learnt to speak, we do not express all we think, as we may see not only from the fewness of words known to a child, but also from our own adult consciousness. The principle of thought is to judge enough to conclude. The principle of language is to speak only so far as to understand and be understood. Hence speech is only a curtailed expression of thought. Sometimes we express a whole judgment by one word, *e.g.* "Fire!" or by a phrase, *e.g.* "What a fire!" and only usually by a proposition. But even the normal proposition in the syllogistic form *tertii adjacentis*, with subject, predicate and copula, is seldom a complete expression of the judgment. The consequence is that the proposition, being different from a judgment arising after a judgment, and remaining an imperfect copy of judgment, is only a superficial evidence of its real nature. Fortunately, we have more profound evidences, and at least three evidences in all. the linguistic expression of belief in the proposition; the consciousness of what we mentally believe; and the analysis of reasoning, which shows what we must believe, and have believed, as data for inference. In these ways we find that a judgment is both different from, and more than, a proposition. But recent logicians, although they perceive the difference, nevertheless tend to make the proposition the measure of the judgment. This makes them omit sensory judgments, and count only those which require ideas, and even general ideas expressed in general terms. Sigwart, for example, gives as instances of our most elementary judgments, "This is Socrates," "This is snow"—beliefs in things existing beyond ourselves which require considerable inferences from many previous judgments of sense and memory. Worse still, logicians seem unable to keep the judgment apart from the proposition. Herbart says that the judgment "A is B" does not contain the usually added thought that A is, because there is no statement of A's existence; as if the statement mattered to the thought. So Sigwart, in order to reduce universals to hypotheticals, while admitting that existence is usually thought, argues that it is not stated in the universal judgment; so also Bosanquet. But in the judgment the point is not what we state, but what we think; and so long as the existence of A is added in thought, the judgment in question must contain the thought that A exists as well as that A is B, and therefore is a judgment that something is determined both as existing and in a particular manner. The statement only affects the proposition; and whenever we believe the existence of the thing, the belief in existence is part of the judgment thought, whether it is part of the proposition stated or not.

Here Sir William Hamilton did a real service to logic in pointing out that "Logic postulates to be allowed to state explicitly in language all that is implicitly contained in the thought." Not that men should or can carry this logical postulate out in ordinary life; but it is necessary in the logical analysis of judgments, and yet logicians neglect it. This is why they confuse the categorical and the universal with the hypothetical. Taking the carelessly expressed propositions of ordinary life, they do not perceive that similar judgments are often differently expressed, *e.g.* "I, being a man, am mortal," and "If I am a man, I am mortal"; and conversely, that different judgments are often similarly expressed. In ordinary life we may say, "All men are mortal," "All centaurs are figments," "All square circles are impossibilities," "All candidates arriving five minutes late are fined" (the last proposition being an example of the identification of categorical with hypothetical in Keynes's *Formal Logic*). But of these universal propositions the first imperfectly expresses a categorical belief in existing things, the second in thinkable things, and the third in nameable things, while the fourth is a slipshod categorical expression of the hypothetical belief, "If any candidates arrive late they are fined." The four judgments are different, and therefore logically the propositions fully expressing them are also different. The judgment, then, is the measure of the proposition, not the proposition the measure of the judgment. On the other hand, we may go too far in the opposite direction, as Hamilton did in proposing the universal quantification of the predicate. If the quantity of the predicate were always thought, it ought logically to be always stated. But we only sometimes think it. Usually we leave the predicate indefinite, because, as long as the thing in question is (or is not) determined, it does not matter about other things, and it is vain for us to try to think all things at once. It is remarkable that in *Barbara*, and therefore in many scientific deductions, to think the quantity of the predicate is not to the point either in the premises or in the conclusion; so that to quantify the propositions, as Hamilton proposes, would be to express more than a rational man thinks and judges. In judgments, and therefore in propositions, indefinite predicates are the rule, quantified predicates the exception. Consequently, A E I O are the normal propositions with indefinite predicates; whereas propositions with quantified predicates are only occasional forms, which we should use whenever we require to think the quantity of the predicate, *e.g.* (1) in conversion, when we must think that all men are some animals, in order to judge that some animals are men; (2) in syllogisms of the 3rd figure, when the predicate of the minor premise must be particularly quantified in thought in order to become the particularly quantified subject of the conclusion; (3) in identical propositions including definitions, where we must think both that 1 + 1 are 2 and 2 are 1 + 1. But the normal judgment, and therefore the normal proposition, do not require the quantity of the predicate. It follows also that the normal judgment is not an equation. The symbol of equality (=) is not the same as the copula (is); it means "is equal to," where "equal to" is part of the predicate, leaving "is" as the copula.

[illegible] in all judgment we think "is," but in few judgments predicate "equal to." In quantitative judgments we may think $x=y$, or, as Boole proposes, $x=xy=\frac{0}{0}y$, or, as Jevons proposes, $x=xy$, or, as [illegible] proposes, x which is not $y=0$; and equational symbolic logic is useful whenever we think in this quantitative way. But it is a [illegible] of thought. In most judgments all we believe is that x is [illegible], that a thing is (or is not) determined, and that the thing signified by the subject is a thing signified by the predicate, [illegible] that it is the only thing, or equal to everything signified by the predicate. The symbolic logic, which confuses "is" with "is equal to," having introduced a particular kind of predicate into the copula, falls into the mistake of reducing all predication [illegible] of the quantitative; whereas it is more often [illegible], e.g. "I am a man," not "I am equal to a man," [illegible], e.g. "I am white," not "I am equal to white," [illegible], e.g. "I am born in sin," not "I am equal to born [illegible]." Predication, as Aristotle saw, is as various as the categories [illegible]. Finally, the great difficulty of the logic of judgment is [illegible] act behind the linguistic expression, to ascribe [illegible] what is thought, neither more nor less, and to apply [illegible] thought to the logical proposition, without expecting [illegible] propositions. Beneath Hamilton's postulate [illegible] principle of logic—*A rational being thinks only to [illegible] only to understand and be understood.*

Inference

[illegible] of inference have been so fully treated [illegible] that here we may content ourselves with [illegible].

1. *[illegible] of Syllogism arising from False Views of Judgment.*—[illegible] of judgment, which we have been examining, [illegible] false views of inference. On the one hand, [illegible] categorical judgments to an existential form, [illegible] reform the syllogism, with the results that [illegible], of which two are opposed and two [illegible] when it is negative, both premises are negative, [illegible] when it is affirmative, one premise, at least, is [illegible] to infer the universal affirmative that every [illegible] because he is a man, Brentano's existential [illegible] run as follows:—

> [illegible] not a not-mortal man.
> [illegible] not a not-human professor.
> [illegible] not a not-mortal professor.

[illegible] the plan of Sigwart categorical universals [illegible] hypotheticals, the same inference would be a [illegible] syllogism, thus:—

> [illegible] is a man it is mortal.
> [illegible] is a professor it is a man.
> [illegible] is a professor it is mortal.

[illegible] forms, which are certainly not analyses [illegible] of categorical reasoning, break down at [illegible] explain those moods in the third figure, [illegible] from universal premises to a particular [illegible] to infer that some wise men are good [illegible], Brentano's syllogism would be

> [illegible] a not-good professor.
> [illegible] not-wise professor.
> [illegible] not-good (*non-sequitur*).

[illegible] would be the following *non-sequitur*:—

> [illegible] professor, it is good.
> [illegible] professor, it is wise.
> [illegible] good (*non-sequitur*).

[illegible] logicians these reconstructions of [illegible] their respective reductions of [illegible] and hypotheticals are false, [illegible] inference. Sigwart does [illegible] absurdities; he reduces [illegible] and the second to the *modus* [illegible] and then, finding no place for [illegible] necessity; whereas it [illegible] of particular conclusions. [illegible] if all universals were hypo[illegible] existence [illegible]

enough until we remember that all universal affirmative conclusions in all sciences would with their premises dissolve into mere hypothesis. No logic can be sound which leads to the following analysis:—

> If anything is a body it is extended.
> If anything is a planet it is a body
> If anything is a planet it is extended.

Sigwart, indeed, has missed the essential difference between the categorical and the hypothetical construction of syllogisms. In a categorical syllogism of the first figure, the major premise, "Every M whatever is P," is a universal, which we believe on account of previous evidence without any condition about the thing signified by the subject M, which we simply believe sometimes to be existent (*e.g.* "Every man existent"), and sometimes not (*e.g.*, "Every centaur conceivable"); and the minor premise, "S is M," establishes no part of the major, but adds the evidence of a particular not thought of in the major at all But in a hypothetical syllogism of the ordinary mixed type, the first or hypothetical premise is a conditional belief, *e.g.* "If anything is M it is P," containing a hypothetical antecedent, "If anything is M," which is sometimes a hypothesis of existence (*e.g.* "If anything is an angel"), and sometimes a hypothesis of fact (*e.g.* "If an existing man is wise"); and the second premise or assumption, "Something is M," establishes part of the first, namely, the hypothetical antecedent, whether as regards existence (*e.g.* "Something is an angel"), or as regards fact (*e.g.* "This existing man is wise"). These very different relations of premises are obliterated by Sigwart's false reduction of categorical universals to hypotheticals. But even Sigwart's errors are outdone by Lotze, who not only reduces "Every M is P" so "If S is M, S is P," but proceeds to reduce this hypothetical to the disjunctive, "If S is M, S is P^1 or P^2 or P^3," and finds fault with the Aristotelian syllogism because it contents itself with inferring "S is P" without showing what P. Now there are occasions when we want to reason in this disjunctive manner, to consider whether S is P^1 or P^2 or P^3, and to conclude that "S is a particular P"; but ordinarily all we want to know is that "S is P"; *e.g.* in arithmetic, that 2+2 are 4, not any particular 4, and in life that all our contemporaries must die, without enumerating all their particular sorts of deaths. Lotze's mistake is the same as that of Hamilton about the quantification of the predicate, and that of those symbolists who held that reasoning ought always to exhaust all alternatives by equations. It is the mistake of exaggerating exceptional into normal forms of thought, and ignoring the principle that a rational being thinks only to the point.

2. *Quasi-syllogisms.*—Besides reconstructions of the syllogistic fabric, we find in recent logic attempts to extend the figures of the syllogism beyond the syllogistic rules. An old error that we may have a valid syllogism from merely negative premises (*ex omnibus negativis*), long ago answered by Alexander and Boethius, is now revived by Lotze, Jevons and Bradley, who do not perceive that the supposed second negative is really an affirmative containing a "not" which can only be carried through the syllogism by separating it from the copula and attaching it to one of the extremes, thus:—

> The just are not unhappy (*negative*).
> The just are not-recognized (*affirmative*).
> ∴Some not-recognized are not unhappy (*negative*).

Here the minor being the infinite term "not-recognized" in the conclusion, must be the same term also in the minor premise. Schuppe, however, who is a fertile creator of quasi-syllogisms, has managed to invent some examples from two negative premises of a different kind:—

(1)	(2)	(3)
No M is P.	No M is P.	No P is M.
S is not M.	S is not M.	S is not M.
∴Neither S nor M is P.	∴S may be P.	∴S may be P.

But (1) concludes with a mere repetition, (2) and (3) with a contingent "may be," which, as Aristotle says, also "may not be," and therefore *nihil certe colligitur*. The same answer applies to Schuppe's supposed syllogisms from two particular premises:—

(1)	(2)
Some M is P.	Some M is P.
Some S is M.	Some M is S.
∴ Some S may be P.	∴ Some S may be P.

The only difference between these and the previous examples (2) and (3) is that, while those break the rule against two negative premises, these break that against undistributed middle. Equally fallacious are two other attempts of Schuppe to produce syllogisms from invalid moods:—

(1) 1st Fig.	(2) 2nd Fig.
All M is P.	P is M.
No S is M.	S is M.
∴ S may be P.	∴ S is partially identical with P.

In the first the fallacy is the indifferent contingency of the conclusion caused by the *non-sequitur* from a negative premise to an affirmative conclusion; while the second is either a mere repetition of the premises if the conclusion means "S is like P in being M," or, if it means "S is P," a *non-sequitur* on account of the undistributed middle. It must not be thought that this trifling with logical rules has no effect. The last supposed syllogism, namely, that having two affirmative premises and entailing an undistributed middle in the second figure, is accepted by Wundt under the title "Inference by Comparison" (*Vergleichungsschluss*), and is supposed by him to be useful for abstraction and subsidiary to induction, and by Bosanquet to be useful for analogy. Wundt, for example, proposes the following premises:—

Gold is a shining, fusible, ductile, simple body
Metals are shining, fusible, ductile, simple bodies.

But to say from these premises, "Gold and metal are similar in what is signified by the middle term," is a mere repetition of the premises, to say, further, that "Gold may be a metal" is a *non-sequitur*, because, the middle being undistributed, the logical conclusion is the contingent "Gold may or may not be a metal," which leaves the question quite open, and therefore there is no syllogism. Wundt, who is again followed by Bosanquet, also supposes another syllogism in the third figure, under the title of 'Inference by Connexion" (*Verbindungsschluss*), to be useful for induction. He proposes, for example, the following premises:—

Gold, silver, copper, lead, are fusible
Gold, silver, copper, lead, are metals.

Here there is no syllogistic fallacy in the premises; but the question is what syllogistic conclusion can be drawn, and there is only one which follows without an illicit process of the minor, namely, "Some metals are fusible." The moment we stir a step further with Wundt in the direction of a more general conclusion (*ein allgemeinerer Satz*), we cannot infer from the premises the conclusion desired by Wundt, "Metals and fusible are connected"; nor can we infer "All metals are fusible," nor "Metals are fusible," nor "Metals may be fusible," nor "All metals may be fusible," nor any assertory conclusion, determinate or indeterminate, but the indifferent contingent, "All metals may or may not be fusible," which leaves the question undecided, so that there is no syllogism. We do not mean that in Wundt's supposed "inferences of relation by comparison and connexion" the premises are of no further use; but those of the first kind are of no syllogistic use in the second figure, and those of the second kind of no syllogistic use beyond particular conclusions in the third figure. What they really are in the inferences proposed by Wundt is not premises for syllogism, but data for induction parading as syllogism. We must pass the same sentence on Lotze's attempt to extend the second figure of the syllogism for inductive purposes, thus:—

S is M.
Q is M.
R is M.
∴ Every Σ, which is common to S, Q, R, is M.

We could not have a more flagrant abuse of the rule *Ne esto plus minusque in conclusione quam in praemissis.* As we see from Lotze's own defence, the conclusion cannot be drawn without another premise or premises to the effect that "S, Q, R, are Σ, and Σ is the one real subject of M." But how is all this to be got into the second figure? Again, Wundt and B. Erdmann propose new moods of syllogism with convertible premises, containing definitions and equations. Wundt's *Logic* has the following forms:—

(1) 1st Fig.	(2) 2nd Fig.	(3) 3rd Fig.
Only M is P.	$x = y$.	$y = x$.
No S is M.	$z = y$.	$y = z$.
∴ No S is P.	∴ $x = z$.	∴ $x = z$.

Now, there is no doubt that, especially in mathematical equations, universal conclusions are obtainable from convertible premises expressed in these ways. But the question is how the premises must be thought, and they must be thought in the converse way to produce a logical conclusion. Thus, we must think in (1) "All P is M" to avoid illicit process of the major, in (2) "All y is z" to avoid undistributed middle, in (3) "All x is y" to avoid illicit process of the minor. Indeed, it is the very essence of a convertible judgment to think it in both orders, and especially to think it in the order necessary to an inference from it. Accordingly, however expressed, the syllogisms quoted above are, as thought, ordinary syllogisms, (1) being *Camestres* in the second figure, (2) and (3) *Barbara* in the first figure. Aristotle, indeed, was as well aware as German logicians of the force of convertible premises; but he was also aware that they require no special syllogisms, and made it a point that, in a syllogism from a definition, the definition is the middle, and the *definitum* the major in a convertible major premise of *Barbara* in the first figure, *e.g.*:—

The interposition of an opaque body is (essentially) deprivation of light.
The moon suffers the interposition of the opaque earth.
The moon suffers deprivation of light.

It is the same with all the recent attempts to extend the syllogism beyond its rules, which are not liable to exceptions, because they follow from the nature of syllogistic inference from universal to particular. To give the name of syllogism to inferences which infringe the general rules against undistributed middle, illicit process, two negative premises, *non-sequitur* from negative to affirmative, and the introduction of what is not in the premises into the conclusion, and which consequently infringe the special rules against affirmative conclusions in the second figure, and against universal conclusions in the third figure, is to open the door to fallacy, and at best to confuse the syllogism with other kinds of inference, without enabling us to understand any one kind.

3. *Analytic and Synthetic Deduction.*—Alexander the Commentator defined synthesis as a progress from principles to consequences, analysis as a regress from consequences to principles; and Latin logicians preserved the same distinction between the *progressus a principiis ad principiata*, and the *regressus a principiatis ad principia.* No distinction is more vital in the logic of inference in general and of scientific inference in particular; and yet none has been so little understood, because, though analysis is the more usual order of discovery, synthesis is that of instruction, and therefore, by becoming more familiar, tends to replace and obscure the previous analysis. The distinction, however, did not escape Aristotle, who saw that a progressive syllogism can be reversed thus:—

1. *Progression.*	2. *Regression.* (1)	(2)
All M is P	All P is M.	All S is P
All S is M	All S is P	All M is S.
∴ All S is P.	∴ All S is M.	∴ All M is P.

Proceeding from one order to the other, by converting one of the premises, and substituting the conclusion as premise for the other premise, so as to deduce the latter as conclusion, is what he calls circular inference; and he remarked that the process is fallacious unless it contains propositions which are convertible, as in mathematical equations. Further, he perceived that the difference between the progressive and regressive orders extends from mathematics to physics, and that there are two kinds of syllogism: one progressing a priori from real ground to consequent fact (ὁ τοῦ διότι συλλογισμός), and the other regressing a posteriori from consequent fact to real ground (ὁ τοῦ ὅτι συλλογισμός). For example, as he says, the sphericity of the moon is the real ground of the fact of its light waxing; but we can deduce either from the other, as follows:—

1. *Progression.*	2. *Regression.*
What is spherical waxes.	What waxes is spherical.
The moon is spherical.	The moon waxes.
∴ The moon waxes.	∴ The moon is spherical.

These two kinds of syllogism are synthesis and analysis in the ancient sense. Deduction is analysis when it is regressive from consequence to real ground, as when we start from the proposition that the angles of a triangle are equal to two right angles and deduce analytically that therefore (1) they are equal to equal angles made by a straight line standing on another straight line, and (2) such equal angles are two right angles. Deduction is synthesis when it is progressive from real ground to consequence, as when we start from these two results of analysis as principles and deduce synthetically the proposition that therefore the angles of a triangle are equal to two right angles, in the order familiar to the student of Euclid. But the full value of the ancient theory of these processes cannot be appreciated until we recognize that as Aristotle planned them Newton used them. Much of the *Principia* consists of synthetical deductions from definitions and axioms. But the discovery of the centripetal force of the planets to the sun is an analytic deduction from the facts of their motion discovered by Kepler to their real ground, and is so stated by Newton in the first regressive order of Aristotle—P-M, S-P, S-M. Newton did indeed first show synthetically what kind of motions by mechanical laws have their ground in a centripetal force varying inversely as the square of the distance (all P is M); but his next step was, not to deduce synthetically the planetary motions, but to make a new start from the planetary motions as facts established by Kepler's laws and as examples of the kind of motions in question (all S is P); and then, by combining these two premises, one mechanical and the other astronomical, he analytically deduced that these facts of planetary motion have their ground in a centripetal force varying inversely as the squares of the distances of the planets from the sun (all S is M). (See *Principia* I. prop. [illegible] coroll. 6; III. Phaenomena, 4-5; prop. 2.) What Newton [illegible] in short, was to prove by analysis that the planets, revolving by Kepler's astronomical laws round the sun, have motions [illegible] by mechanical laws are consequences of a centripetal [illegible] the sun. This done, as the major is convertible, the [illegible] order—P-M, S-P, S-M—was easily inverted into the [illegible] order—M-P, S-M, S-P; and in this progressive order [illegible] as now taught begins with the centripetal force [illegible] as real ground, and deduces the facts of planetary [illegible]. Thereupon the Newtonian analysis [illegible] synthesis, became forgotten; until at last [illegible] neglecting the *Principia*, had the temerity [illegible] discovery which was really a pure example [illegible] into a mere hypothetical deduction; as [illegible] saying "*Hypotheses non fingo*" started [illegible] centripetal force to the sun, and thence [illegible] facts of planetary motion, which [illegible] the hypothesis. This gross misrepresenta- [illegible] kind of logical fashion. Worse still, [illegible] analytic deduction from consequence [illegible] deduction from ground to conse- [illegible] term "inverse deduction." Wundt [illegible] to make a compromise between the old [illegible] analysis in the very opposite way [illegible] defined it as a regressive process [illegible] ground, according to Wundt it is a pro- [illegible] granted a proposition and deducing [illegible] true verifies the proposition. He [illegible]: one categorical, the other [illegible] he means the ancient analysis [illegible] more general propositions. By the [illegible] new-fangled analysis from a given proposition to more particular propositions, *i.e.* from a hypothesis to consequent facts. But his account of the first is imperfect, because in ancient analysis the more general propositions, with which it concludes, are not mere consequences, but the real grounds of the given proposition; while his addition of the second reduces the nature of analysis to the utmost confusion, because hypothetical deduction is progressive from hypothesis to consequent facts whereas analysis is regressive from consequent facts to real ground. There is indeed a sense in which all inference is from ground to consequence, because it is from logical ground (*principium cognoscendi*) to logical consequence. But in the sense in which deductive analysis is opposed to deductive synthesis, analysis is deduction from real consequence as logical ground (*principiatum* as *principium cognoscendi*) to real ground (*principium essendi*), *e.g.* from the consequential facts of planetary motion to their real ground, *i.e.* centripetal force to the sun. Hence Sigwart is undoubtedly right in distinguishing analysis from hypothetical deduction, for which he proposes the name "reduction." We have only further to add that many scientific discoveries about sound, heat, light, colour and so forth, which it is the fashion to represent as hypotheses to explain facts, are really analytical deductions from the facts to their real grounds in accordance with mechanical laws. Recent logic does scant justice to scientific analysis.

4. *Induction.*—As induction is the process from particulars to universals, it might have been thought that it would always have been opposed to syllogism, in which one of the rules is against using particular premises to draw universal conclusions. Yet such is the passion for one type that from Aristotle's time till now constant attempts have been made to reduce induction to syllogism. Aristotle himself invented an inductive syllogism in which the major (P) is to be referred to the middle (M) by means of the minor (S), thus:—

A, B, C magnets (S) attract iron (P).
A, B, C magnets (S) are all magnets whatever (M).
∴ All magnets whatever (M) attract iron (P).

As the second premise is supposed to be convertible, he reduced the inductive to a deductive syllogism as follows:—

Every S is P.	Every S is P.
Every S is M (convertibly).	Every M is S.
∴ Every M is P.	∴ Every M is P.

In the reduced form the inductive syllogism was described by Aldrich as "*Syllogismus in Barbara cujus minor* (*i.e.* every M is S) *reticetur.*" Whately, on the other hand, proposed an inductive syllogism with the major suppressed, that is, instead of the minor premise above, he supposed a major premise, "Whatever belongs to A, B, C magnets belongs to all." Mill thereupon supposed a still more general premise, an assumption of the uniformity of nature. Since Mill's time, however, the logic of induction tends to revert towards syllogisms more like that of Aristotle. Jevons supposed induction to be inverse deduction, distinguished from direct deduction as analysis from synthesis, *e.g.* as division from multiplication; but he really meant that it is a deduction from a hypothesis of the law of a cause to particular effects which, being true, verify the hypothesis. Sigwart declares himself in agreement with Jevons; except that, being aware of the difference between hypothetical deduction and mathematical analysis, and seeing that, whereas analysis (*e.g.* in division) leads to certain conclusions, hypothetical deduction is not certain of the hypothesis, he arrives at the more definite view that induction is not analysis proper but hypothetical deduction, or "reduction," as he proposes to call it. Reduction he defines as "the framing of possible premises for given propositions, or the construction of a syllogism when the conclusion and one premise is given." On this view induction becomes a reduction in the form: all M is P (hypothesis), S is M (given), ∴ S is P (given). The views of Jevons and Sigwart are in agreement in two main points. According to both, induction, instead of inferring from A, B, C magnets the conclusion "Therefore all magnets attract iron," infers from the hypothesis, "Let every magnet attract iron," to A, B, C magnets, whose given attraction verifies the hypothesis. According to both, again, the hypothesis of a law with which the process starts contains more than is present in the particular data: according to Jevons, it is the hypothesis of a law of a cause from which induction deduces particular effects; and according to Sigwart, it is a hypothesis of the ground from which the particular data necessarily follow according to universal laws. Lastly, Wundt's view is an interesting piece of eclecticism, for he supposes that induction begins in the form of Aristotle's inductive syllogism, S-P, S-M, M-P, and becomes an inductive method in the form of Jevons's inverse deduction, or hypothetical deduction, or analysis, M-P, S-M, S-P. In detail, he supposes that, while an "inference by comparison," which he erroneously calls an affirmative syllogism in the second figure, is preliminary to induction, a second "inference by connexion," which he erroneously calls a syllogism in the third figure with an indeterminate conclusion, is the inductive syllogism itself. This is like Aristotle's inductive syllogism in the arrangement of terms; but, while on the one hand Aristotle did not, like Wundt, confuse it with the third figure, on the other hand Wundt does not, like Aristotle, suppose it to be practicable to get inductive data so wide as the convertible premise, "All S is M, and all M is S," which would at once establish the conclusion, "All M is P." Wundt's point is that the conclusion of the inductive syllogism is neither so much as all, nor so little as some, but rather the indeterminate "M and P are connected." The question therefore arises, how we are to discover "All M is P," and this question Wundt answers by adding an inductive method, which involves inverting the inductive syllogism in the style of Aristotle into a deductive syllogism from a hypothesis in the style of Jevons, thus:—

(1)	(2)
S is P.	Every M is P.
S is M.	S is M.
M and P are connected.	.˙. S is P.

He agrees with Jevons in calling this second syllogism analytical deduction, and with Jevons and Sigwart in calling it hypothetical deduction. It is, in fact, a common point of Jevons, Sigwart and Wundt that the universal is not really a conclusion inferred from given particulars, but a hypothetical major premise from which given particulars are inferred, and that this major contains presuppositions of causation not contained in the particulars.

It is noticeable that Wundt quotes Newton's discovery of the centripetal force of the planets to the sun as an instance of this supposed hypothetical, analytic, inductive method; as if Newton's analysis were a hypothesis of the centripetal force to the sun, a deduction of the given facts of planetary motion, and a verification of the hypothesis by the given facts, and as if such a process of hypothetical deduction could be identical with either analysis or induction. The abuse of this instance of Newtonian analysis betrays the whole origin of the current confusion of induction with deduction. One confusion has led to another. Mill confused Newton's analytical deduction with hypothetical deduction; and thereupon Jevons confused induction with both. The result is that both Sigwart and Wundt transform the inductive process of adducing particular examples to induce a universal law into a deductive process of presupposing a universal law as a ground to deduce particular consequences. But we can easily extricate ourselves from these confusions by comparing induction with different kinds of deduction. The point about induction is that it starts from experience, and that, though in most classes we can experience only some particulars individually, yet we infer all. Hence induction cannot be reduced to Aristotle's inductive syllogism, because experience cannot give the convertible premise, "Every S is M, and every M is S"; that "All A, B, C are magnets" is, but that "All magnets are A, B, C" is not, a fact of experience. For the same reason induction cannot be reduced to analytical deduction of the second kind in the form, S-P, M-S, .˙. M-P; because, though both end in a universal conclusion, the limits of experience prevent induction from such inference as:—

Every experienced magnet attracts iron.
Every magnet whatever is every experienced magnet.
Every magnet whatever attracts iron.

Still less can induction be reduced to analytical deduction of the first kind in the form—P-M, S-P, .˙. S-M, of which Newton has left so conspicuous an example in his *Principia*. As the example shows, that analytic process starts from the scientific knowledge of a universal and convertible law (every M is P, and every P is M), *e.g.* a mechanical law of all centripetal force, and ends in a particular application, *e.g.* this centripetal force of planets to the sun. But induction cannot start from a known law. Hence it is that Jevons, followed by Sigwart and Wundt, reduces it to deduction from a hypothesis in the form "Let every M be P, S is M, .˙. S is P." There is a superficial resemblance between induction and this hypothetical deduction. Both in a way use given particulars as evidence. But in induction the given particulars are the evidence by which we discover the universal, *e.g.* particular magnets attracting iron are the origin of an inference that all do; in hypothetical deduction, the universal is the evidence by which we explain the given particulars, as when we suppose undulating aether to explain the facts of heat and light. In the former process, the given particulars are the data from which we infer the universal; in the latter, they are only the consequent facts by which we verify it. Or rather, there are two uses of induction: inductive discovery before deduction, and inductive verification after deduction. But neither use of induction is the same as the deduction itself: the former precedes, the latter follows it. Lastly, the theory of Mill, though frequently adopted, *e.g.* by B. Erdmann, need not detain us long. Most inductions are made without any assumption of the uniformity of nature; for, whether it is itself induced, or a priori or postulated, this like every assumption is a judgment, and most men are incapable of judgment on so universal a scale, when they are quite capable of induction. The fact is that the uniformity of nature stands to induction as the axioms of syllogism do to syllogism; they are not premises, but conditions of inference, which ordinary men use spontaneously, as was pointed out in *Physical Realism*, and afterwards in Venn's *Empirical Logic*. The axiom of contradiction is not a major premise of a judgment: the *dictum de omni et nullo* is not a major premise of a syllogism: the principle of uniformity is not a major premise of an induction. Induction, in fact, is no species of deduction; they are opposite processes, as Aristotle regarded them except in the one passage where he was reducing the former to the latter, and as Bacon always regarded them. But it is easy to confuse them by mistaking examples of deduction for inductions. Thus Whewell mistook Kepler's inference that Mars moves in an ellipse for an induction, though it required the combination of Tycho's and Kepler's observations, as a minor, with the laws of conic sections discovered by the Greeks, as a major, premise. Jevons, in his *Principles of Science*, constantly makes the same sort of mistake. For example, the inference from the similarity between solar spectra and the spectra of various gases on the earth to the existence of similar gases in the sun, is called by him an induction; but it really is an analytical deduction from effect to cause, thus:—

Such and such spectra are effects of various gases.
Solar spectra are such spectra.
Solar spectra are effects of those gases.

In the same way, to infer a machine from hearing the regular tick of a clock, to infer a player from finding a pack of cards arranged in suits, to infer a human origin of stone implements, and all such inferences from patent effects to latent causes, though they appear to Jevons to be typical inductions, are really deductions which, besides the minor premise stating the particular effects, require a major premise discovered by a previous induction and stating the general kind of effects of a general kind of cause. B. Erdmann, again, has invented an induction from particular predicates to a totality of predicates which he calls "ergänzende Induction," giving as an example, "This body has the colour, extensibility and specific gravity of magnesium; therefore it is magnesium." But this inference contains the tacit major, "What has a given colour, &c., is magnesium," and is a syllogism of recognition. A deduction is often like an induction, in inferring from particulars; the difference is that

parity of reasoning. We return then to the old view of Aristotle, that truth is believing in being; that sense is true of its immediate objects, and reasoning from sense true of its mediate objects; and that logic is the science of reasoning with a view to truth, or *Logica est ars ratiocinandi, ut discernatur verum a falso.* All we aspire to add is that, in order to attain to real truth, we must proceed gradually from sense, memory and experience through analogical particular inference, to inductive and deductive universal inference or reasoning. Logic is the science of all inference, beginning from sense and ending in reason.

In conclusion, the logic of the last quarter of the 19th century may be said to be animated by a spirit of inquiry, marred by a love of paradox and a corresponding hatred of tradition. But we have found, on the whole, that logical tradition rises superior to logical innovation. There are two old logics which still remain indispensable, Aristotle's *Organon* and Bacon's *Novum Organum*. If, and only if, the study of deductive logic begins with Aristotle, and the study of inductive logic with Aristotle and Bacon, it will be profitable to add the works of the following recent German and English authors:—

AUTHORITIES.—J. Bergmann, *Reine Logik* (Berlin, 1879); *Die Grundprobleme der Logik* (2nd ed., Berlin, 1895); B. Bosanquet, *Logic* (Oxford, 1888); *The Essentials of Logic* (London, 1895); F. H. Bradley, *The Principles of Logic* (London, 1883); F. Brentano, *Psychologie vom empirischen Standpunkte* (Vienna, 1874); R. F. Clarke, *Logic* (London, 1889); W. L. Davidson, *The Logic of Definition* (London, 1885); E. Dühring, *Logik und Wissenschaftstheorie* (Leipzig, 1878); B. Erdmann, *Logik* (Halle, 1892); T. Fowler, *Bacon's Novum Organum*, edited, with introduction, notes, &c. (2nd ed., Oxford, 1889); T. H. Green, *Lectures on Logic*, in *Works*, vol. iii. (London, 1886); J. G. Hibben, *Inductive Logic* (Edinburgh and London, 1896); F. Hillebrand, *Die neuen Theorien der kategorischen Schlüsse* (Vienna, 1891); L. T. Hobhouse, *The Theory of Knowledge* (London, 1896); H. Hughes, *The Theory of Inference* (London, 1894); E. Husserl, *Logische Untersuchungen* (Halle, 1891, 1901); W. Jerusalem, *Die Urtheilsfunction* (Vienna and Leipzig, 1895); W. Stanley Jevons, *The Principles of Science* (3rd ed., London, 1879); *Studies in Deductive Logic* (London, 1880); H. W. B. Joseph, *Introduction to Logic* (1906); E. E. Constance Jones, *Elements of Logic* (Edinburgh, 1890); G. H. Joyce, *Principles of Logic* (1908); J. N. Keynes, *Studies and Exercises in Formal Logic* (2nd ed., London, 1887); F. A. Lange, *Logische Studien* (2nd ed., Leipzig, 1894); T. Lipps, *Grundzüge der Logik* (Hamburg and Leipzig, 1893); R. H. Lotze, *Logik* (2nd ed., Leipzig, 1881, English translation edited by B. Bosanquet, Oxford, 1884); *Grundzüge der Logik* ([illegible]) (3rd ed., Leipzig, 1891, English translation by G. T. Ladd, Boston, 1887); Werner Luthe, *Beiträge zur Logik* (Berlin, 1872, 1877); Members of Johns Hopkins University, *Studies in Logic* (edited by C. S. Peirce, Boston, 1883); J. B. Meyer, *Ueberweg's System der Logik*, fünfte vermehrte Auflage (Bonn, 1882); Max Müller, *Science of Thought* (London, 1887); Carveth Read, *On the Theory of Logic* (London, 1878); *Logic, Deductive and Inductive* (2nd ed., London, [illegible]); E. Schröder, *Vorlesungen über die Algebra der Logik* (Leipzig, [illegible], 1895); W. Schuppe, *Erkenntnisstheoretische Logik* (Bonn, [illegible]); *Grundriss der Erkenntnisstheorie und Logik* (Berlin, 1894); R. [illegible], *Discourse on Truth* (London, 1877); Alfred Sidgwick, [illegible] (London, 1883); *The Use of Words in Reasoning* (London, [illegible]); C. Sigwart, *Logik* (2nd ed., Freiburg-i.-Br. and Leipzig, 1889–[illegible], English translation by Helen Dendy, London, 1895); K. [illegible], *Grundlehren der Logik* (Breslau, 1883); J. Veitch, *Institutes of Logic* (Edinburgh and London, 1885); J. Venn, *Symbolic Logic* (London, 1894); *The Principles of Empirical or Inductive Logic* (London, 1889); J. Volkelt, *Erfahrung und Denken* (Hamburg [illegible]); J. Welton, *A Manual of Logic* (London, 1891, [illegible]); W. Windelband, *Präludien* (Freiburg-i.-Br., 1884); W. [illegible], *Logik* (2nd ed., Stuttgart, 1893–1895). Text-books are not [illegible] in this list. (T. CA.)

II. HISTORY

[illegible] cannot dispense with the light afforded by its history so [illegible] counter-solutions of the same fundamental problems [illegible] hold the field. A critical review of some of the chief [illegible] logical theory, with a view to determine development, [illegible] justification.

[illegible] at least for the Western world, in the golden age [illegible] speculation which culminated in Plato and Aristotle. [illegible] logic, it is true, but its priority is more than [illegible] any case no influence upon Greek thought [illegible] The movement which ends in the logic of Aristotle [illegible] self-contained. When we have shaken [illegible] the prejudice that all stars are first seen in the East, Oriental attempts at analysis of the structure of thought may be treated as negligible.

It is with Aristotle that the bookish tradition begins to dominate the evolution of logic. The technical perfection of the analysis which he offers is, granted the circle of presuppositions within which it works, so decisive, that what precedes, even Plato's logic, is not unnaturally regarded as merely preliminary and subsidiary to it. What follows is inevitably, whether directly or indirectly, by sympathy or by antagonism, affected by the Aristotelian tradition.

A. GREEK LOGIC

i. *Before Aristotle*

The physical philosophers.

Logic needs as its presuppositions that thought should distinguish itself from things and from sense, that the problem of validity should be seen to be raised in the field of thought itself, and that analysis of the structure of thought should be recognized as the one way of solution. Thought is somewhat late in coming to self-consciousness. Implied in every contrast of principle and fact, of rule and application, involved as we see after the event, most decisively when we react correctly upon a world incorrectly perceived, thought is yet not reflected on in the common experience. Its so-called natural logic is only the potentiality of logic. The same thing is true of the first stage of Greek philosophy. In seeking for a single material principle underlying the multiplicity of phenomena, the first nature-philosophers, Thales and the rest, did indeed raise the problem of the one and the many, the endeavour to answer which must at last lead to logic. But it is only from a point of view won by later speculation that it can be said that they sought to determine the predicates of the single subject-reality, or to establish the permanent subject of varied and varying predicates.[1] The direction of their inquiry is persistently outward. They hope to explain the opposed appearance and reality wholly within the world of things, and irrespective of the thought that thinks things. Their universal is still a material one. The level of thought on which they move is still clearly pre-logical. It is an advance on this when Heraclitus[2] opposes to the eyes and ears which are bad witnesses "for such as understand not their language" a common something which we would do well to follow; or again when in the incommensurability of the diagonal and side of a square the Pythagoreans stumbled upon what was clearly neither thing nor image of sense, but yet was endowed with meaning, and henceforth were increasingly at home with symbol and formula. So far, however, it might well be that thought, contradistinguished from sense with its illusions, was itself infallible. A further step, then, was necessary, and it was taken at any rate by the Eleatics, when they opposed their thought to the thought of others, as the way of truth in contrast to the way of opinion. If Eleatic thought stands over against Pythagorean thought as what is valid or grounded against what is ungrounded or invalid, we are embarked upon dialectic, or the debate in which thought is countered by thought. Claims to a favourable verdict must now be substantiated in this field and in this field alone. It was Zeno, the controversialist of the Eleatic school, who was regarded in after times as the "discoverer" of dialectic.[3]

Zeno's amazing skill in argumentation and his paradoxical conclusions, particular and general, inaugurate a new era. "The philosophical mind," says Walter Pater,[4] "will perhaps never be quite in health, quite sane or natural again." The give and take of thought had by a swift transformation of values come by something more than its own. Zeno's paradoxes, notably, for example, the puzzle of Achilles and the Tortoise, are still capable of amusing the modern world. In his own age they found him imitators. And there follows the sophistic movement.

---

[1] Cf. Heidel, "The Logic of the Pre-Socratic Philosophy," in Dewey's *Studies in Logical Theory* (Chicago, 1903).

[2] Heraclitus, *Fragmm.* 107 (Diels, *Fragmente der Vorsokratiker*) and 2, on which see Burnet, *Early Greek Philosophy*, p. 153 note (ed. 2).

[3] *e.g.* Diog. Laërt. ix. 25, from the lost *Sophistes* of Aristotle.

[4] *Plato and Platonism*, p. 24.

The sophists have other claims to consideration than their service to the development of logic. In the history of the origins of logic the sophistic age is simply the age of the free play of thought in which men were aware that in a sense anything can be debated and not yet aware of the sense in which all things cannot be so. It is the age of discussion used as a universal solvent, before it has been brought to book by a deliberate unfolding of the principles of the structure of thought determining and limiting the movement of thought itself. The sophists furthered the transition from dialectic to logic in two ways. In the first place they made it possible. Incessant questioning leads to answers. Hair-splitting, even when mischievous in intent, leads to distinctions of value. Paradoxical insistence on the accidents of speech-forms and thought-forms leads in the end to perception of the essentials. Secondly they made it necessary. The spirit of debate run riot evokes a counter-spirit to order and control it. The result is a self-limiting dialectic. This higher dialectic is a logic. It is no accident that the first of the philosophical sophists, Gorgias, on the one hand, is Eleatic in his affinities, and on the other raises in the characteristic formula of his intellectual nihilism[1] issues which are as much logical and epistemological as ontological. The meaning of the copula and the relation of thoughts to the objects of which they are the thoughts are as much involved as the nature of being. It is equally no accident that the name of Protagoras is to be connected, in Plato's view at least, with the rival school of Heracliteans. The problems raised by the relativism of Protagoras are no less fundamentally problems of the nature of knowledge and of the structure of thought. The *Theaetetus* indeed, in which Plato essays to deal with them, is in the broad sense of the word logical, the first distinctively logical treatise that has come down to us. Other sophists, of course, with more practical interests, or of humbler attainments, were content to move on a lower plane of philosophical speculation. As presented to us, for example, in Plato's surely not altogether hostile caricature in the *Euthydemus*, they mark the intellectual preparation for, and the moral need for, the advance of the next generation.

The Sophists.

Among the pioneers of the sophistic age Socrates stands apart. He has no other instrument than the dialectic of his compeers, and he is as far off as the rest from a criticism of the instrument, but he uses it differently and with a difference of aim. He construes the give and take of the debate-game with extreme rigour. The rhetorical element must be exorcised. The set harangue of teacher to pupil, in which steps in argument are slurred and the semblance of co-inquiry is rendered nugatory, must be eliminated. The interlocutors must in truth render an account under the stimulus of organized heckling from their equals or superiors in debating ability. And the aim is heuristic, though often enough the search ends in no overt positive conclusion. Something can be found and something is found. Common names are fitted for use by the would-be users being first delivered from abortive conceptions, and thereupon enabled to bring to the birth living and organic notions.

Socrates.

Aristotle would assign to Socrates the elaboration of two logical functions:—general definition and inductive method.[2] Rightly, if we add that he gives no theory of either, and that his practical use of the latter depends for its value on selection.[3] It is rather in virtue of his general faith in the possibility of construction, which he still does not undertake, and because of his consequent insistence on the elucidation of general concepts, which in common with some of his contemporaries, he may have thought of as endued with a certain objectivity, that he induces the controversies of what are called the Socratic schools as to the nature of predication. These result in the formulation of a new dialectic or logic by Plato. Manifestly Socrates' use of certain forms of argumentation, like their abuse by the sophists, tended to evoke their logical analysis. The use and abuse, confronted one with the other, could not but evoke it.

The one in the many, the formula which lies at the base of the possibility of predication, is involved in the Socratic doctrine of general concepts or ideas. The nihilism of Gorgias from the Eleatic point of view of bare identity, and the speechlessness of Cratylus from the Heraclitean ground of absolute difference, are alike disowned. But the one in the many, the identity in difference, is so far only postulated, not established. When the personality of Socrates is removed, the difficulty as to the nature of the Socratic universal, developed in the medium of the individual processes of individual minds, carries disciples of diverse general sympathies, united only through the practical inspiration of the master's life, towards the identity-formula or the difference-formula of other teachers. The paradox of predication, that it seems to deny identity, or to deny difference, becomes a *pons asinorum*. Knowledge involves synthesis or nexus. Yet from the points of view alike of an absolute pluralism, of a flux, and of a formula of bare identity—and *a fortiori* with any blending of these principles sufficiently within the bounds of plausibility to find an exponent—all knowledge, because all predication of unity, in difference, must be held to be impossible. Plato's problem was to find a way of escape from this impasse, and among his Socratic contemporaries he seems to have singled out Antisthenes[4] as most in need of refutation. Antisthenes, starting with the doctrine of identity without difference, recognizes as the only expression proper to anything its own peculiar sign, its name. This extreme of nominalism for which predication is impossible is, however, compromised by two concessions. A thing can be described as like something else. And a compound can have a λόγος or account given of it by the (literally) adequate enumeration of the names of its simple elements or στοιχεῖα.[5] This analytical λόγος he offers as his substitute for knowledge.[6] The simple elements still remain, sensed and named but not known. The expressions of them are simply the speech-signs for them. The account of the compound simply sets itself taken piecemeal as equivalent to itself taken as aggregate. The subject-predicate relation fails really to arise. Euclides[7] found no difficulty in fixing Antisthenes' mode of illustrating his simple elements by comparison, and therewith perhaps the "induction" of Socrates, with the dilemma; so far as the example is dissimilar, the comparison is invalid; so far as it is similar, it is useless. It is better to say what the thing is. Between Euclides and Antisthenes the Socratic induction and universal definition were alike discredited from the point of view of the Eleatic logic. It is with the other point of doctrine that Plato comes to grips, that which allows of a certainty or knowledge consisting in an analysis of a compound into simple elements themselves not known. The syllable or combination is, he shows, not known by resolution of it into letters or elements themselves not known. An aggregate analysed into its mechanical parts is as much and as little known as they. A whole which is more than its parts is from Antisthenes' point of view inconceivable. Propositions analytical of a combination in the sense alleged do not give knowledge. Yet knowledge is possible. The development of a positive theory of predication has become quite crucial.

Antisthenes.

Plato's logic supplies a theory of universals in the doctrine of ideas. Upon this it bases a theory of predication, which, however, is compatible with more than one reading of the metaphysical import of the ideas. And it sets forth a dialectic with a twofold movement, towards differentiation and integration severally, which amounts to a formulation of inference. The more fully analysed movement, that which proceeds downward from less determinate to more determinate universals, is named Division. Its associations, accordingly, are to the modern ear almost inevitably those of a doctrine of classification only. Aristotle, however, treats it as a dialectical rival to syllogism, and it influenced Galilei and Bacon in their views of inference after the Renaissance. If we add to this logic of "idea," judgment and inference, a doctrine of categories in the modern sense of the word which makes the *Theaetetus*, in which it first occurs, a forerunner of Kant's *Critique of Pure Reason*, we have clearly a very significant contribution to logic even in technical regard. Its general philosophical setting may be said to enhance its value even as logic.

Plato.

(*a*) Of the idea we may say that whatever else it is, and apart from all puzzles as to ideas of relations such as smallness, of negative qualities such as injustice, or of human inventions such as beds, it is opposed to that of which it is the idea as its intelligible formula or law, the truth or validity—Herbart's word—of the phenomenon from the point of view of nexus or system. The thing of sense in its relative isolation is unstable. It is and is not. What gives stability is the insensible principle or principles which it holds, as it were, in solution. These are the ideas, and their mode of being is naturally quite other than that of the sensible phenomena which they order. The formula for an indefinite number of particular things in particular places at particular times, and all of them presentable in sensuous imagery of a given time and place, is not itself presentable in sensuous imagery side by side with the individual members of the group it orders. The law, *e.g.*, of the equality of the radii of a circle cannot be exhibited to sense, even if equal radii may be so exhibited. It is the wealth of illustration with which Plato expresses his meaning, and the range of application which he gives the idea—to the class-

The "Idea."

[1] Nothing is. If anything is, it cannot be known. If anything is known it cannot be communicated.

[2] *Metaphys.* μ. 1078*b* 28 sqq.

[3] Cf. Arist. *Top.* θ. i. 1 *ad fin.*

[4] For whom see Dümmler, *Antisthenica* (1882, reprinted in his *Kleine Schriften*, 1901).

[5] Aristotle, *Metaphys.* 1024*b* 32 sqq.

[6] Plato, *Theaetetus*, 201 E. sqq., where, however, Antisthenes is not named, and the reference to him is sometimes doubted. But cf. Aristotle, *Met.* H 3. 1043*b* 24-28.

[7] Diog. Laërt. ii. 107.

concepts of natural groups objectively regarded, to categories, to aesthetic and ethical ideals, to the concrete aims of the craftsman as well as to scientific laws—that have obscured his doctrine, viz. that wherever there is law, there is an idea.

The one in the many.

(*b*) The paradox of the one in the many is none, if the idea may be regarded as supplying a principle of nexus or organization to an indefinite multiplicity of particulars. But if Antisthenes is to be answered, a further step must be taken. The principle of difference must be carried into the field of the ideas. Not only sense is a principle of difference. The ideas are many. The multiplicity in unity must be established within thought itself. Otherwise the objection stands: man is man and good is good, but to say that man is good is clearly to say the thing that is not. Plato replies with the doctrine of the interpenetration of ideas, obviously not of all with all, but of some with some, the formula of identity in difference within thought itself. Nor can the opponent fairly refuse to admit it, if he affirms the participation of the identical with being, and denies the participation of difference with being, or affirms it with not-being. The *Sophistes* shows among other things that an identity-philosophy breaks down into a dualism of thought and expression, when it applies the predicate of unity to the real, just as the absolute pluralism on the other hand collapses into unity if it affirms or admits any form of relation whatsoever. Identity and difference are all-pervasive categories, and the speech-form and the corresponding thought-form involve both. For proposition and judgment involve subject and predicate and exhibit what a modern writer calls "identity of reference with diversity of characterization." Plato proceeds to explain by his principle of difference both privative and negative predicates, and also the possibility of false predication. It is obvious that without the principle of difference error is inexplicable. Even Plato, however, perhaps scarcely shows that with it, and nothing else but it, error is explained.

Division.

(*c*) Plato's Division, or the articulation of a relatively indeterminate and generic concept into species and sub-species with resultant determinate judgments, presumes of course the doctrine of the interpenetration of ideas laid down in the *Sophistes* as the basis of predication, but its use precedes the positive development of that formula, though not, save very vaguely, the exhibition of it, negatively, in the antinomies of the one and the many in the *Parmenides*. It is its use, however, not the theory of it, that precedes. The latter is expounded in the *Politicus* (260 sqq.) and *Philebus* (16*c* sqq.). The ideal is progressively to determine a universe of discourse till true *infimae species* are reached, when no further distinction in the determinate many is possible, though there is still the numerical difference of the indefinite plurality of particulars. The process [illegible] take as far as possible the form of a continuous disjunction [illegible] contraries. We must bisect as far as may be, but the division [illegible] after all to be into limbs, not parts. The later examples of [illegible] *Politicus* show that the permission of three or more co-ordinate species is not nugatory, and that the precept of dichotomy is merely in order to secure as little of a *saltus* as possible; [illegible] avoid *e.g.* the division of the animal world into men and brutes. [illegible] the middle range of the μέσα of *Philebus* 17*a* that appeals [illegible] not only this but their mediating quality that appeals [illegible]. The *media axiomata* of the one and the *middle* [illegible] other lie in the phrase. Plato's division is never[illegible] syllogism nor *exclusiva*. It is not syllogism [illegible] based on the disjunctive, not on the hypothetical [illegible] so extends horizontally where syllogism strikes downward. Again it is not syllogism because it is [illegible] finally dialectical. It brings in the choice of an [illegible] at each stage, and so depends on a concession for [illegible] proved.[1] Nor is it Bacon's method of exclusions, [illegible] the imputation of being dialectical, if not that of [illegible] cumbrous, in virtue of the cogency of the negative [illegible] Platonic division was, however, offered as the [illegible] of the school. A fragment of the comic poet Epicrates gives a picture of it at work.[2] And the movement of disjunction as truly has a place in the scientific specification of a concept in all its differences as the linking of lower to higher in syllogism. The two are complementary, and the reinstatement of the disjunctive judgment to the more honourable rôle in inference has been made by so notable a modern logician as Lotze.

Combination.

(*d*) The correlative process of Combination is less elaborately sketched, but in a luminous passage in the *Politicus* (§ 278), in explaining by means of an example the nature and use of examples, Plato represents it as the bringing of one and the same element seen in diverse settings to conscious realization, with the result that it is viewed as a single truth of which the terms compared are now accepted as the differences. The learner is to be led forward to the unknown by being made to hark back to more familiar groupings of the alphabet of nature which he is coming to recognize with some certainty. To lead on, ἐπάγειν, is to refer back, ἀνάγειν,[3] to what has been correctly divined of the same elements in clearer cases. Introduction to unfamiliar collocations follows upon this, and, only so, is it possible finally to gather scattered examples into a conspectus as instances of one idea or law. This is not only of importance in the history of the terminology of logic, but supplies a philosophy of induction.

Mental synthesis.

(*e*) Back of Plato's illustration and explanation of predication and dialectical inference there lies not only the question of their metaphysical grounding in the interconnexion of ideas, but that of their epistemological presuppositions. This is dealt with in the Theaetetus (184*b* sqq.). The manifold affections of sense are not simply aggregated in the individual, like the heroes in the Trojan horse. There must be convergence in a unitary principle, soul or consciousness, which is that which really functions in perception, the senses and their organs being merely its instruments. It is this unity of apperception which enables us to combine the data of more than one sense, to affirm reality, unreality, identity, difference, unity, plurality and so forth, as also the good, the beautiful and their contraries. Plato calls these pervasive factors in knowledge κοινά, and describes them as developed by the soul in virtue of its own activity. They are objects of its reflection and made explicit in the few with pains and gradually.[4] That they are not, however, psychological or acquired categories, due to "the workmanship of the mind" as conceived by Locke, is obvious from their attribution to the structure of mind[5] and from their correlation with immanent principles of the objective order. Considered from the epistemological point of view, they are the implicit presuppositions of the construction or συλλογισμός[6] in which knowledge consists. But as ideas,[7] though of a type quite apart,[8] they have also a constitutive application to reality. Accordingly, of the selected "kinds" by means of which the interpenetration of ideas is expounded in the *Sophistes*, only motion and rest, the ultimate "kinds" in the physical world, have no counterparts in the "categories" of the *Theaetetus*. In his doctrine as to ἐν τὸ ποιοῦν or κρῖνον, as generally in that of the activity of the νοῦς ἀπαθής, Aristotle in the *de Anima*[9] is in the main but echoing the teaching of Plato.[10]

[1] *An. Pr.* [illegible] sqq.; cf. 91*b* 12 sqq.

[2] Athenaeus ii. 59*c*. See Usener, *Organisation der wissenschaft. Arbeit* (1884; reprinted in his *Vorträge und Aufsätze*, 1907).

[3] Socrates' reference of a discussion to its presuppositions (Xenophon, *Mem.* iv. 6, 13) is not relevant for the history of the terminology of induction.

[4] *Theaetetus*, 186*c*.

[5] Timaeus, 37*a*, *b* (quoted in H. F. Carlill's translation of the *Theaetetus*, p. 60).

[6] *Theaetetus*, 186*d*.

[7] *Sophistes*, 253*d*.

[8] *Ib. id.*; cf. *Theaetetus*, 197*d*.

[9] Aristotle, *de An.* 430*b* 5, and generally iii. 2, iii. 5.

[10] For Plato's Logic, the controversies as to the genuineness of the dialogues may be treated summarily. The *Theaetetus* labours under no suspicion. The *Sophistes* is apparently matter for animadversion by Aristotle in the *Metaphysics* and elsewhere, but derives stronger support from the testimonies to the *Politicus* which presumes it. The *Politicus* and *Philebus* are guaranteed by the use made of them in Aristotle's Ethics. The rejection of the *Parmenides* would involve the paradox of a nameless contemporary of Plato

ii. *Aristotle.*

Plato's episodic use of logical distinctions[1] is frequent. His recourse to such logical analysis as would meet the requirements of the problem in hand[2] is not rare. In the "dialectical" dialogues the question of method and of the justification of its postulates attains at least a like prominence with the ostensible subject matter. There is even formal recognition of the fact that to advance in dialectic is a greater thing than to bring any special inquiry to a successful issue.[3] But to the end there is a lack of interest in, and therefore a relative immaturity of, technique as such. In the forcing atmosphere, however, of that age of controversy, seed such as that sown in the master's treatment of the uttered λόγος[4] quickly germinated. Plato's successors in the Academy must have developed a system of grammatico-logical categories which Aristotle could make his own. Else much of his criticism of Platonic doctrine[5] does, indeed, miss fire. The gulf too, which the *Philebus*[6] apparently left unbridged between the sensuous apprehension of particulars and the knowledge of universals of even minimum generality led with Speusippus to a formula of knowledge in perception (ἐπιστημονικὴ αἴσθησις). These and like developments, which are to be divined from references in the Aristotelian writings, jejune, and, for the most part, of probable interpretation only, complete the material which Aristotle could utilize when he seceded from the Platonic school and embarked upon his own course of logical inquiry.

Syllogism.

This is embodied in the group of treatises later known as the *Organon*[7] and culminates in the theory of syllogism and of demonstrative knowledge in the *Analytics*. All else is finally subsidiary. In the well-known sentences with which the *Organon* closes[8] Aristotle has been supposed to lay claim to the discovery of the principle of syllogism. He at least claims to have been the first to dissect the procedure of the debate-game, and the larger claim may be thought to follow. In the course of inquiry into the formal consequences from probable premises, the principle of mediation or linking was so laid bare that the advance to the analytic determination of the species and varieties of syllogism was natural. Once embarked upon such an analysis, where valid process from assured principles gave truth, Aristotle could find little difficulty in determining the formula of demonstrative knowledge or science. It must be grounded in principles of assured certainty and must demonstrate its conclusions with the use of such middle or linking terms only as it is possible to equate with the real ground or cause in the object of knowledge. Hence the account of axioms and of definitions, both of substances and of derivative attributes. Hence the importance of determining how first principles are established. It is, then, a fair working hypothesis as to the structure of the *Organon* to place the *Topics*, which deal with dialectical reasoning, before the *Analytics*.[9] Of the remaining treatises nothing of fundamental import depends on their order. One, however, the *Categories*, may be regarded with an ancient commentator,[10] as preliminary to the dialectical inquiry in the *Topics*. The other, on thought as expressed in language (Περὶ ἑρμηνείας) is possibly spurious, though in any case a compilation of the Aristotelian school. If genuine, its naïve theory that thought copies things and other features of its contents would tend to place it among the earliest works of the philosopher.

The logical treatises.

Production in the form of a series of relatively self-contained treatises accounts for the absence of a name and general definition of their common field of inquiry. A more important lack which results is that of any clear intimation as to the relation in which Aristotle supposed it to stand to other disciplines. In his definite classification of the sciences,[11] into First Philosophy, Mathematics and Physics, it has no place. Its axioms, such as the law of contradiction, belong to first philosophy, but the doctrine as a whole falls neither under this head nor yet, though the thought has been entertained, under that of mathematics, since logic orders mathematical reasoning as well as all other. The speculative sciences, indeed, are classified according to their relation to form, pure, abstract or concrete, *i.e.* according to their objects. The logical inquiry seems to be conceived as dealing with the thought of which the objects are objects. It is to be regarded as a propaedeutic,[12] which, although it is in contact with reality in and through the metaphysical import of the axioms, or again in the fact that the categories, though primarily taken as forms of predication, must also be regarded as kinds of being, is not directly concerned with object-reality, but with the determination for the thinking subject of what constitutes the knowledge correlative to being. Logic, therefore, is not classed as one, still less as a branch of one, among the 'ologics, ontology not excepted.

The way in which logical doctrine is developed in the Aristotelian treatises fits in with this view. Doubtless what we have is in the main a reflex of the heuristic character of Aristotle's own work as pioneer. But it at least satisfies the requirement that the inquiry shall carry the plain man along with it. Actual modes of expression are shown to embody distinctions which average intelligence can easily recognize and will readily acknowledge, though they may tend by progressive rectification fundamentally to modify the assumption natural to the level of thought from which he begins. Thus we start[13] from the point of view of a world of separate persons and things, in which thought mirrors these concrete realities, taken as ultimate subjects of predicates. It is a world of communication of thought, where persons as thinkers need to utter in language truths objectively valid for the *mundus communis*. In these truths predicates are accepted or rejected by subjects, and therefore depend on the reflection of fact in λόγοι (propositions). These are combinatory of parts, attaching or detaching predicates, and so involving

and Aristotle who was inferior as a metaphysician to neither. No other dialogue adds anything to the logical content of these.

Granted their genuineness, the relative dating of three of them is given, viz. *Theaetetus*, *Sophistes* and *Politicus* in the order named. The *Philebus* seems to presuppose *Politicus*, 283-284, but if this be an error, it will affect the logical theory not at all. There remains the *Parmenides*. It can scarcely be later than the *Sophistes*. The antinomies with which it concludes are more naturally taken as a prelude to the discussion of the *Sophistes* than as an unnecessary retreatment of the doctrine of the one and the many in a more negative form. It may well be earlier than the *Theaetetus* in its present form. The stylistic argument shows the *Theaetetus* relatively early. The maturity of its philosophic outlook tends to give it a place relatively advanced in the Platonic canon. To meet the problem here raised, the theory has been devised of an earlier and a later version. The first may have linked on to the series of Plato's dialogues of search, and to put the *Parmenides* before it is impossible. The second, though it might still have preceded the *Parmenides* might equally well have followed the negative criticism of that dialogue, as the beginning of reconstruction. For Plato's logic this question only has interest on account of the introduction of an 'Ἀριστοτέλης in a non-speaking part in the *Parmenides*. If this be pressed as suggesting that the philosopher Aristotle was already in full activity at the date of writing, it is of importance to know what Platonic dialogues were later than the début of his critical pupil.

On the stylistic argument as applied to Platonic controversies Janell's *Quaestiones Platonicae* (1901) is important. On the whole question of genuineness and dates of the dialogues, H. Raeder, *Platons philosophische Entwickelung* (1905), gives an excellent conspectus of the views held and the grounds alleged. See also PLATO

[1] *E.g.* that of essence and accident, *Republic*, 454.

[2] *E.g.* the discussion of correlation, *ib.* 437 sqq.

[3] *Politicus*, 285*d*.

[4] *Sophistes*, 261*c* sqq.

[5] *E.g.* in *Nic. Eth.* i. 6.

[6] *Philebus*, 16*d*.

[7] Principal edition still that of Waitz, with Latin commentary, (2 vols., 1844–1846). Among the innumerable writers who have thrown light upon Aristotle's logical doctrine, St Hilaire, Trendelenburg, Ueberweg, Hamilton, Mansel, G. Grote may be named. There are, however, others of equal distinction. Reference to Prantl, *op. cit.*, is indispensable. Zeller, *Die Philosophie der Griechen*, ii. 2, "Aristoteles" (3rd ed., 1879), pp. 185-257 (there is an Eng. trans.), and Maier, *Die Syllogistik des Aristoteles* (2 vols., 1896, 1900) (some 900 pp.), are also of first-rate importance.

[8] *Sophist. Elench* 184, espec. *b* 1-3, but see Maier, *loc. cit.* i. 1

[9] References such as 18*b* 12 are the result of subsequent editing and prove nothing. See, however, ARISTOTLE.

[10] Adrastus is said to have called them πρὸ τῶν τοπικῶν.

[11] *Metaphys.* E. 1.

[12] *De Part. Animal.* A. 1, 639*a* 1 sqq.; cf. *Metaphys.* 1005*b* 2 sqq.

[13] *De Interpretatione* 16*a* sqq.

[illegible] and copula.[1] At this stage we are as much [illegible] with speech-forms as the thought-forms of which they [illegible] symbols, such Plato's analysis, for instance, [illegible] and a verb, whose connexion in time is as yet a [illegible]. The universal of this stage is the universal of fact [illegible] predicable of a plurality of subjects. The [illegible] of judgement as the attribution of one member [illegible] contradiction, which is later so important, is [illegible] difficulties,[2] viz. the contingency [illegible] the solution of which remains in- [illegible]

In [illegible] the Categories is still on the same level of [illegible] grammatico-logical analysis in the more [illegible] which had probably been developed by [illegible] before Aristotle came to think of his [illegible] as "them" rather than "us." It is [illegible] gave the now familiar classification of [illegible] that of thought-categories under- [illegible] from any actual combination of [illegible] to determine the types of pre- [illegible] sequences of fact, we have on the one [illegible] subject, a "first substance" or con- [illegible] be predicated in the first place "second [illegible] that it is a member of a concrete class, [illegible] quantity, quality, correlation, action [illegible] the forms of the Greek language so [illegible] appropriated to the use of the [illegible] voice to express the relation of the [illegible]. In all this the individual is the [illegible]. Truth and error are about the [illegible] attach predicates correctly and in- [illegible] fundamental to the metaphysics in the light [illegible] at last to find its complete justifica- [illegible] to be modified profoundly by what [illegible] at the class-concept behind the class, [illegible] the constitutive formula of a substance, [illegible] requirement that an essential attribute must [illegible] the essence of the substance of which [illegible] such attributes alone are admissible [illegible] view of the strict ideal of science. [illegible] ground of common opinion, and these [illegible] as fundamental to the develop- [illegible]

[illegible] it may prove to be the ultimate method [illegible] a philosophy,[5] starts from probable premises,[6] and deals with them only in [illegible] common principles such as may be reason- [illegible] easily established against challenge. [illegible] which involves contingent matter, [illegible] indetermination, *e.g.* to the physician, [illegible] but the reflection that this is so is [illegible]. We start with what is prima facie [illegible] from the ground of principles clarified by [illegible] and certified by νοῦς. The *Topics* [illegible] an anatomy of argumentation, [illegible] to be Aristotle's own metaphor, a [illegible] points (τόποι) for the conflict of [illegible] victory, though it is a barren [illegible] knowledge. It is in this treatise that [illegible] the conceptual categories"[8] emerge. [illegible] of predication as it is analysed in [illegible] theory of definition that dialectic [illegible] predicate either is expressive of the [illegible] of the subject, viz. that original [illegible] attributes of which the absence [illegible] to the class-name, or it is not. [illegible] the subject or it is not. Here then

[8] *Ib.* 18a 28 sqq.

[illegible] of sense and the

judgement, though still viewed as combinatory, has the type[s] which belong to coherent systems of implication discriminate[d] from those that predicate coincidence or accident, *i.e.* any happening not even derivatively essential from the point of view of the grouping in which the subject has found a place. In the theory of dialectic any predicate may be suggested for a subject, and if not affirmed of it, must be denied of it, if not denied must be affirmed. The development of a theory of the ground on which subjects claim their predicates and disown alien predicates could not be long postponed. In practical dialectic the unlimited possibility was reduced to manageable proportions [in] virtue of the groundwork of received opinion upon which the operation proceeded. It is in the *Topics*, further, that we clearly have a first treatment of syllogism as formal implication, with the suggestion that advance must be made to a view of its use for material implication from true and necessary principles. It is in the *Topics*,[9] again, that we have hints at the devices of an inductive process, which, as dialectical, throw the burden [of] producing contradictory instances upon the other party to the discussion. In virtue of the common-stock of opinion among the interlocutors and their potentially controlling audience this process was more valuable than appears on the face [of] things. Obviously tentative, and with limits and ultimate interpretation to be determined elsewhere, it failed to bear fruit [till] the Renaissance, and then by the irony of fate to the discrediting of Aristotle. In any case, however, definition, syllogism, induction all invited further determination, especially if the[y] were to take their place in a doctrine of truth or knowledge. The problem of analytic, *i.e.* of the resolution of the various forms of inference into their equivalents in that grouping of terms or premises which was most obviously cogent, was a legacy of the *Topics*. The debate-game had sought for diversion and found truth, and truth raised the logical problem on a different plane.

At first the problem of formal analysis only. We proceed with the talk of instances and concern ourselves first wi[th] relations of inclusion and exclusion. The question is as to membership of a class, and the dominant formula is the *dictum de omni et nullo*. Until the view of the individual units with which we are so far familiar has undergone radical revision, the primary inquiry must be into the forms [of] a class-calculus. Individuals fall into groups in virtue of the possession of certain predicates. Does one group include, [or] exclude, or intersect another with which it is compared? We are clearly in the field of the diagrams of the text-books, and much [of] the phraseology is based upon an original graphic representation in extension. The middle term, though conceived as an inter[-]mediary or linking term, gets its name as intermediate in a homogeneous scheme of quantity, where it cannot be of narrower extension than the subject nor wider than the predicate of the conclusion.[10] It is also, as Aristotle adds,[11] middle in position [in] the syllogism that concludes to a universal affirmative.[12] Again, so long as we keep to the syllogism as complete in itself ex[-] without reference to its place in the great structure of knowledge, the nerve of proof cannot be conceived in other than a form[al] manner. In analytic we work with an ethos different from that of dialectic. We presume truth and not probability or concession, but a true conclusion can follow from false premises, and it is only in the attempt to derive the premises in turn from their grounds that we unmask the deception. The passage [to] the conception of system is still required. The *Prior Analytics* then are concerned with a formal logic to be knit into a system of knowledge of the real only in virtue of a formula which is at this stage still to seek. The forms of syllogism, however, are tracked successfully through their figures, *i.e.* through the positions of the middle term that Aristotle recognizes as of actual employment, and all their moods, *i.e.* all differences of affirmative and negative, universal and particular within the figures, the cogent or legitimate forms [of]

Class-concept.

The Prior Analytics.

[9] *Topics* 160a 37–b 5.

[10] This is the explanation of the formal definition of induction, *Prior Analytics*, ii. 23, 68b 15 sqq.

[11] 25b 36.

alone left standing, and the formal doctrine of syllogism is complete. Syllogism already defined[1] becomes through exhibition in its valid forms clear in its principle. It is a speech-and-thought-form (λόγος) in which certain matters being posited something other than the matters posited necessarily results because of them, and, though it still needs to receive a deeper meaning when presumed truth gives way to necessary truth of premises, the notion of the class to that of the class-concept, collective fact to universal law, its formal claim is manifest. "Certain matters being posited." Subject and predicate not already seen to be conjoined must be severally known to be in relation with that which joins them, so that more than one direct conjunction must be given. "Of necessity." If what are to be conjoined are severally in relation to a common third it does perforce relate or conjoin them. "Something other." The conjunction was by hypothesis not given, and is a new result by no means to be reached, apart from direct perception save by use of at least two given conjunctions. "Because of them," therefore. Yet so long as the class-view is prominent, there is a suggestion of a begging of the question. The class is either constituted by enumeration of its members, and, passing by the difficulty involved in the thought of "its" members, is an empirical universal of fact merely, or it is grounded in the class-concept. In the first case it is a formal scheme which helps knowledge and the theory of knowledge not at all. We need then to develop the alternative, and to pass from the external aspect of all-ness to the intrinsic ground of it in the universal καθ' αὑτὸ καὶ ᾗ αὐτό, which, whatsoever the assistance it receives from induction in some sense of the word, in the course of its development for the individual mind, is secured against dependence on instances by the decisive fiat or guarantee of νοῦς, insight into the systematic nexus of things. The conception of linkage needs to be deepened by the realization of the middle term as the ground of nexus in a real order which is also rational.

Problem of Inference.

Aristotle's solution of the paradox of inference, viz. of the fact that in one sense to go beyond what is in the premises is fallacy, while in another sense not to go beyond them is futility, lies in his formula of implicit and explicit, potential and actual.[2] The real nexus underlying the thought-process is to be articulated in the light of the voucher by intelligence as to the truth of the principles of the various departments of knowledge which we call sciences, and at the ideal limit it is possible to transform syllogism into systematic presentation, so that, differently written down, it is definition. But for human thought sense, with its accidental setting in matter itself incognizable is always with us. The activity of νοῦς is never so perfectly realized as to merge implication in intuition.

Nous.

Syllogism must indeed be objective, *i.e.* valid for any thinker, but it is also a process in the medium of individual thinking, whereby new truth is reached. A man may know that mules are sterile and that the beast before him is a mule, and yet believe her to be in foal "not viewing the several truths in connexion."[3] The doctrine, then, that the universal premise contains the conclusion not otherwise than potentially is with Aristotle cardinal. The datum of sense is only retained through the universal.[4] It is possible to take a universal view with some at least of the particular instances left uninvestigated.[5] Recognition that the class-concept is applicable may be independent of knowledge of much that it involves. Knowledge of the implications of it does not depend on observation of all members of the class. Syllogism as formula for the exhibition of truth attained, and construction or what not as the instrumental process by which we reach the truth, have with writers since Hegel and Herbart tended to fall apart. Aristotle's view is other. Both are syllogisms, though in different points of view. For this reason, if for no other, the conception of movement from the potential possession of knowledge to its actualization remains indispensable.

[1] *Prior Analytics*, i. 1. 24*a* 18-20, Συλλογισμὸς δέ ἐστι λόγος ἐν ᾧ τεθέντων τινῶν ἕτερόν τι τῶν κειμένων ἐξ ἀνάγκης συμβαίνει τῷ ταῦτα εἶναι. The equivalent previously in *Topics* 100*a* 25 sqq.

[2] *Prior Analytics*, ii. 21; *Posterior Analytics*, i. 1.

[3] 67*a* 33-37, μὴ συνθεωρῶν τὸ καθ' ἑκάτερον.

[4] 67*a* 39-*b* 3.

[5] 79*a* 4-5.

Whether this is explanation or description, a problem or its solution, is of course another matter.

Posterior Analytics.

In the *Posterior Analytics* the syllogism is brought into decisive connexion with the real by being set within a system in which its function is that of material implication from principles which are primary, immediate and necessary truths. Hitherto the assumption of the probable as true rather than as what will be conceded in debate[6] has been the main distinction of the standpoint of analytic from that of dialectic. But the true is true only in reference to a coherent system in which it is an immediate ascertainment of νοῦς, or to be deduced from a ground which is such. The ideal of science or demonstrative knowledge is to exhibit as flowing from the definitions and postulates of a science, from its special principles, by the help only of axioms or principles common to all knowledge, and these not as premises but as guiding rules, all the properties of the subject-matter, *i.e.* all the predicates that belong to it in its own nature. In the case of any subject-kind, its definition and its existence being avouched by νοῦς, "heavenly body" for example, the problem is, given the fact of a non-self-subsistent characteristic of it, such as the eclipse of the said body, to find a ground, a μέσον which expressed the αἴτιον, in virtue of which the adjectival concept can be exhibited as belonging to the subject-concept καθ' αὑτὸ in the strictly adequate sense of the phrase in which it means also ᾗ αὐτό.[7] We are under the necessity then of revising the point of view of the syllogism of all-ness. We discard the conception of the universal as a predicate applicable to a plurality, or even to all, of the members of a group. To know merely κατὰ παντὸς is not to know, save accidentally. The exhaustive judgment, if attainable, could not be known to be exhaustive. The universal is the ground of the empirical "all" and not conversely. A formula such as the equality of the interior angles of a triangle to two right angles is only scientifically known when it is not of isosceles or scalene triangle that it is known, nor even of all the several types of triangle collectively, but as a predicate of triangle recognized as the widest class-concept of which it is true, the first stage in the progressive differentiation of figure at which it can be asserted.[8]

Three points obviously need development, the nature of definition, its connexion with the syllogism in which the middle term is cause or ground, and the way in which we have assurance of our principles.

Definition.

Definition is either of the subject-kind or of the property that is grounded in it. Of the self-subsistent definition is οὐσίας τις γνωρισμός[9] by exposition of genus and differentia.[10] It is indemonstrable. It presumes the reality of its subject in a postulate of existence. It belongs to the principles of demonstration. *Summa genera* and groups below *infimae species* are indefinable. The former are susceptible of elucidation by indication of what falls under them. The latter are only describable by their accidents. There can here be no true differentia. The artificiality of the limit to the articulation of species was one of the points to which the downfall of Aristotle's influence was largely due. Of a non-self-subsistent or attributive conception definition in its highest attainable form is a recasting of the syllogism, in which it was shown that the attribute was grounded in the substance or self-subsistent subject of which it is. Eclipse of the moon, *e.g.* is privation of light from the moon by the interposition of the earth between it and the sun. In the scientific syllogism the interposition of the earth is the middle term, the cause or "because" (διότι), the residue of the definition is conclusion. The difference then is in verbal expression, way of putting, inflexion.[11] If we pluck

[6] 24*b* 10-11.

[7] *Posterior Analytics*, i. 4 καθ' αὑτὸ means (1) contained in the definition of the subject; (2) having the subject contained in its definition, as being an alternative determination of the subject, crooked, *e.g.* is *per se* of line; (3) self-subsistent; (4) connected with the subject as consequent to ground. Its needs stricter determination therefore.

[8] 73*b* 26 sqq., 74*a* 37 sqq.

[9] 90*b* 16.

[10] *Metaphys.* Z. 12, H. 6 ground this formula metaphysically.

[11] 94*a* 12, 75*b* 32.

conclusions from premises of unlike modality, and that a formal advance of some significance attributable to Theophrastus and Eudemus is the doctrine of the hypothetical and disjunctive syllogisms.

The Stoics.

The Stoics are of more importance. Despite the fact that their philosophic interests lay rather in ethics and physics, their activity in what they classified as the third department of speculation was enormous and has at least left ineffaceable traces on the terminology of philosophy. Logic is their word, and consciousness, impression and other technical words come to us, at least as technical words, from Roman Stoicism. Even inference, though apparently not a classical word, throws back to the Stoic name for a conclusion.[1] In the second place, it is in the form in which it was raised in connexion with the individualistic theory of perception with which the Stoics started, that one question of fundamental importance, viz. that of the criterion of truth, exercised its influence on the individualists of the Renaissance. Perception, in the view of the Stoics, at its highest both revealed and guaranteed the being of its object. Its hold upon the object involved the discernment that it could but be that which it purported to be. Such "psychological certainty" was denied by their agnostic opponents, and in the history of Stoicism we have apparently a modification of the doctrine of φαντασία καταληπτική with a view to meet the critics, an approximation to a recognition that the primary conviction might meet with a counter-conviction, and must then persist undisputed in face of the challenge and in the last resort find verification in the haphazard instance, under varying conditions, in actual working. The controversy as to the self-evidence of perception in which the New Academy effected some sort of conversion of the younger Stoics, and in which the Sceptics opposed both, is one of the really vital issues of the decadence.

Another doctrine of the Stoics which has interest in the light of certain modern developments is their insistence on the place of the [illegible] in knowledge. Distinct alike from thing and mental happening, it seems to correspond to "meaning" as it is used as a technical phrase now-a-days. This anticipation was apparently sterile. Along the same lines is their use of the hypothetical form for the universal judgment, and their treatment of the hypothetical form as the typical form of inference.

The Stoical categories, too, have an historical significance. They are apparently offered in place of those of Aristotle, an acquaintance with whose distinctions they clearly presume. Recognizing a linguistic side to "logical" theory with a natural development in rhetoric, the Stoics endeavour to exercise considerations of language from the contrasted side. They offer pure categories arising in series, each successive one presupposing those that have gone before. Yet the substance, quality, condition absolute (πὼς ἔχον) and condition relative of Stoicism have no enduring influence outside the school, though they recur with eclectics like Galen. The Stoics were too "scholastic" in their speculations.

[illegible]

In Epicureanism logic is still less in honour. The practical end, freedom from the bondage of things with the peace it brings, is all in all, and even scientific inquiry is only in place as a means to this end. Of the apparatus of method the less the better. We are in the presence of a necessary evil. Yet in falling back, with a difference, upon the atomism of Democritus, Epicurus had to face some questions of logic. In the inference from phenomena to further phenomena positive verification must be [illegible]. In the inference from phenomena to their non-phenomenal [illegible] the atoms with their inaccessibility to sense, a different [illegible] validity obtains, that of non-contradiction.[2] He distinguishes between the inference to combination of atoms as [illegible] and inference to special causes beyond the range of [illegible]. In the latter case alternatives may be acquiesced in.[3] The [illegible] of science is as well achieved if we set forth possible [illegible] the actual cause. This pococurantism might [illegible] as an insight into the limitations of inverse [illegible] a belief in the plurality of causes in Mill's sense [illegible] probably it reflects the fact that Epicurus was, [illegible] through Nausiphanes, on the whole dominated [illegible] that produced Pyrrhonism. Democritean physics [illegible] necessarily proved sterile of determinate [illegible] was more than enough to ripen the natural- [illegible] into scepticism. Some reading between [illegible] led the "logic" of Epicurus to have an [illegible] but scarcely because of its deserts.

[illegible] has exercised a more legitimate influence. [illegible] by which the Sceptics enforced their ad- [illegible] of judgment are antiquated in type, [illegible] within the limits of the individualistic [illegible] quite unanswerable. Hume had [illegible] The major premise of syllogism, [illegible] inductively from the particular instances. If there be but one of these uncovered by the generalization, this cannot be sound. If the crocodile moves its upper, not its lower, jaw, we may not say that all animals move the lower jaw. The conclusion then is really used to establish the major premise, and if we still will infer it therefrom we fall into the circular proof.[4] Could Mill say more? But again. The inductive enumeration is either of all cases or of some only. The former is in an indeterminate or infinite subject-matter impossible. The latter is invalid.[5] Less familiar to modern ears is the contention that proof needs a standard or criterion, while this standard or criterion in turn needs proof. Or still more the dialectical device by which the sceptic claims to escape the riposte that his very argument presumes the validity of this or that principle, viz. the doctrine of the equipollence of counter-arguments. Of course the counter-contention is no less valid! So too when the reflection is made that scepticism is after all a medicine that purges out itself with the disease, the disciple of Pyrrho and Aenesidemus bows and says, Precisely! The sceptical suspension of judgment has its limits, however. The Pyrrhonist will act upon a basis of probabilities. Nay, he even treats the idea of cause[6] as probable enough so long as nothing more than action upon expectation is in question. He adds, however, that any attempt to establish it is involved in some sort of dilemma. That, for instance, cause as the correlate of effect only exists with it, and accordingly, cause which is come while effect is still to come is inconceivable.[7] From the subjectivist point of view, which is manifestly fundamental through most of this, such arguments suasory of the Pyrrhonist suspense of judgment (ἐποχή) are indeed hard to answer. It is natural, then, that the central contribution of the Sceptics to the knowledge controversy lies in the modes (τρόποι) in which the relativity of phenomena is made good, that these are elaborated with extreme care, and that they have a modern ring and are full of instruction even to-day. Scepticism, it must be confessed, was at the least well equipped to expose the bankruptcy of the post-Aristotelian dogmatism.

It was only gradually that the Sceptic's art of fence was developed. From the time of Pyrrho overlapping Aristotle himself, who seems to have been well content to use the feints of more than one school among his predecessors, while showing that none of them could claim to get past his guard, down through a period in which the decadent academy under Carneades, otherwise dogmatic in its negations, supplied new thrusts and parries, to Aenesidemus in the late Ciceronian age, and again to Sextus Empiricus, there seems to have been something of plasticity and continuous progress. In this matter the dogmatic schools offer a marked contrast. In especial it is an outstanding characteristic of the younger rivals to Aristotelianism that as they sprang up suddenly into being to contest the claims of the Aristotelian system in the moment of its triumph, so they reached maturity very suddenly, and thereafter persisted for the most part in a stereotyped tradition, modified only when convicted of indefensible weakness. The 3rd century B.C. saw in its first half the close of Epicurus' activity, and the life-work of Chrysippus, the refounder of Stoicism, is complete before its close. And subsequent variations seem to have been of a negligible where not of an eclectic character. In the case of Epicureanism we can happily judge of the tyranny of the literal tradition by a comparison of Lucretius with the recorded doctrine of the master. But the rule apparently obtains throughout that stereotype and compromise offer themselves as the exhaustive alternative. This is perhaps fortunate for the history of doctrine, for it produces the commentator, your Aspasius or Alexander of Aphrodisias, and the substitute for the critic, your Cicero, or your Galen with his attempt at comprehension of the Stoic categories and the like while starting from Aristotelianism. Cicero in particular is important as showing the effect or philosophical eclecticism upon Roman cultivation, and as the often author and always popularizer of the Latin terminology of philosophy.

The cause of the stereotyping of the systems, apart from political conditions, seems to have been the barrenness of science. Logic and theory of knowledge go together, and without living science, theory of knowledge loses touch with life, and logic becomes a perfunctory thing. Under such circumstances speculative interest fritters itself and sooner or later the sceptic has his way. Plato is full of the faith of mathematical physics. Aristotle is optimistic of achievement over the whole range of the sciences. But the divorce of science of nature from mathematics, the failure of biological inquiry to reach so elementary a conception as that of the nerves, the absence of chemistry from the circle of the sciences, disappointed the promise of the dawn and the relative achievement of the noon-day. There is no development. Physical science remains dialectical, and a physical experiment is as rare in the age of Lucretius as in that of Empedocles. The cause of eclecticism is the unsatisfying character of the creeds of such science, in conjunction with the familiar law that, in triangular or plusquam-triangular controversies a common hatred will produce an alliance

[1] [illegible] induction, and [illegible]
[2] [illegible] Adv. Math. vii. 211.
[3] [illegible] vi. 703 sqq., v. 526 sqq. (ed. [illegible]

[4] Sextus Empiricus, *Pyrrhon. Hypotyp.* ii. 195, 196.
[5] Sextus, *op. cit.* ii. 204.
[6] *Op. cit.* iii. 17 sqq., and especially 28.
[7] The point is raised by Aristotle, 954.

based on compromise. A bastard Platonism through hostility to Stoicism may become agnostic. Stoicism through hostility to its sceptical critics may prefer to accept some of the positions of the dogmatic nihilist.

Of the later schools the last to arise was Neoplatonism. The mathematical sciences, at least, had not proved disappointing. For those of the school of Plato who refused the apostasy of the new academy, there was hope either in the mathematical side of the Pythagoreo-Platonic tradition, or in its ritual and theological side. Neoplatonism is philosophy become theosophy, or it is the sermon on the text that God geometrizes. It is of significance in the general history of thought as the one great school that developed after the decadence had set in. In its metaphysic it showed no failure in dialectical constructiveness. In the history of logic it is of importance because of its production of a whole series of commentators on the Aristotelian logic. Not only the *Introduction* of Porphyry, which had lasting effects on the Scholastic tradition, but the commentaries of Themistius, and Simplicius. It was the acceptance of the Aristotelian logic by Neoplatonism that determined the Aristotelian complexion of the logic of the next age. If Alexander is responsible for such doctrines as that of the *intellectus acquisitus*, it is to Porphyry, with his characteristically Platonist preference for the doctrine of universals, and for classification, that we owe the scholastic preoccupation with the realist controversy, and with the *quinque voces*, *i.e.* the Aristotelian predicables as restated by Porphyry.

Neoplatonism.

B. Scholasticism

The living force in the spiritual life of the Roman empire was, after all, not philosophy, but religion, and specifically Christianity. With the extension of Christianity to the Gentile world it at length became necessary for it to orientate itself towards what was best in Greek culture. There is a Stoic element in the ethic of the Pauline epistles, but the theological affinity that the Johannine gospel, with its background of philosophic ideas, exhibits to Platonic and Neoplatonist teaching caused the effort at absorption to be directed rather in that direction. Neoplatonism had accepted the Aristotelian logic with its sharper definition than anything handed down from Plato, and, except the logic of the Sceptics, there was no longer any rival discipline of the like prestige. The logic of the Stoics had been discredited by the sceptical onset, but in any case there was no organon of a fitness even comparable to Aristotle's for the task of drawing out the implications of dogmatic premises. Aristotelian logic secured the imprimatur of the revived Platonism, and it was primarily because of this that it passed into the service of Christian theology. The contact of the Church with Platonism was on the mystical side. Orthodoxy needed to counter heretical logic not with mysticism, itself the fruitful mother of heresies, but with argument. Aristotelianism approved itself as the controversial instrument, and in due course held the field alone. The upshot is what is called Scholasticism. Scholasticism is the Aristotelianism of medieval orthodoxy as taught in the "schools" or universities of Western Europe. It takes form as a body of doctrine drawing its premises from authority, sometimes in secular matters from that of Aristotle, but normally from that of the documents and traditions of systematic theology, while its method it draws from Aristotle, as known in the Latin versions,[1] mainly by Boethius, of some few treatises of the *Organon* together with the *Isagoge* of Porphyry. It dominates the centres of intellectual life in the West because, despite its claim to finality in its principles or premises, and to universality for its method, it represents the only culture of a philosophic kind available to the adolescent peoples of the Western nations just becoming conscious of their ignorance. Christianity was the one organizing principle that pulsed with spiritual life. The vocation of the student could find fulfilment only in the religious orders. Scholasticism embodied what the Christian community had saved from the wreckage of Greek dialectic. Yet with all its effective manipulation of the formal technique of its translated and mutilated Aristotle, Scholasticism would have gone under long before it did through the weakness intrinsic to its divorce of the form and the matter of knowledge, but for two reasons. The first is the filtering through of some science and some new Aristotelian learning from the Arabs. The second is the spread of Greek scholarship and Greek manuscripts westward, which was consequent on the Latin occupation of Constantinople in 1204. It was respited by the opportunity which was afforded it of fresh draughts from the Aristotle of a less partial and purer tradition, and we have, accordingly, a golden age of revived Scholasticism beginning in the 13th century, admitting now within itself more differences than before. It is to the schoolmen of the two centuries preceding the Turkish capture of Constantinople that the controversial refinements usually associated with the name of Scholasticism are attributable. The *Analytics* of Aristotle now entered quite definitely into the logical thought of Scholasticism and we have the contrast of a *logica vetus* and *logica nova*. That other matters, the *parva logicalia* and Mnemonics adapted from Psellus and possibly of Stoic origin, entered too did not outweigh this advantage. Confrontation with the historical Aristotle may have brought but little comfort to the orthodox system, but it was a stimulus to dialectical activity within the schools. It provoked the distinction of what was true *secundum fidem* and what was true *secundum rationem* among even sincere champions of orthodoxy, and their opponents accepted with a smile so admirable a mask for that thinking for themselves to which the revival of hope of progress had spurred them. The pioneers of the Renaissance owe something of their strength to their training in the developments which the system that they overthrew underwent during this period. The respite, however, was short. The flight of Byzantine scholarship westward in the 15th century revealed, and finally, that the philosophic content of the Scholastic teaching was as alien from Aristotle as from the spirit of the contemporary revolt of science, with its cry for a new medicine, a new nautical astronomy and the like. The doom of the Scholastic Aristotle was nevertheless not the rehabilitation of the Greek Aristotle. Between him and the tide of feeling at the Renaissance lay the whole achievement of Arab science. That impatience of authority to which we owe the Renaissance, the Reformation and the birth of Nationalism, is not stilled by the downfall of Aristotle as the *nomen appellativum* of the schools. The appeal is to experience, somewhat vaguely defined, as against all authority, to the book of nature and no other. At last the world undertakes to enlarge the circle of its ideas.

[1] See Jourdain, *Recherches critiques sur l'âge et l'origine des traductions latines d'Aristote* (1843).

C. The Renaissance

Accordingly what is in one sense the revival of classical learning is in another a recourse to what inspired that learning, and so is a new beginning. There is no place for a reformed Aristotelian logic, though the genius of Zabarella was there to attempt it. Nor for revivals of the competing systems, though all have their advocates. Scientific discovery was in the air. The tradition of the old world was too heavily weighted with the Ptolemaic astronomy and the like to be regarded as other than a bar to progress. But from the new point of view its method was inadequate too, its contentment with an induction that merely leaves an opponent silent, when experiment and the application of a calculus were within the possibilities. The transformation of logic lay with the man of science, hindered though he might be by the enthusiasm of some of the philosophers of nature. Henceforth the Aristotelian logic, the genuine no less than the traditional, was to lie on the other side of the Copernican change.

The demand is for a new organon, a scientific method which shall face the facts of experience and justify itself by its achievement in the reduction of them to control. It is a notable feature of the new movement, that except verbally, in a certain licence of nominalist expression, due to the swing of the pendulum away from the realist doctrine of universals, there is little that we can characterize as Empiricism. Facts are opposed to abstract universals. Yes. Particulars to controlling formulae. No. Experience is appealed to as fruitful where the formal employment of syllogism is barren. But it is not mere induction, with its "unanalysed concretes taken as ultimate" that is set up as the substitute for deduction. Rather a scientific process, which as experiential may be called inductive, but which is in other regards deductive as syllogism, is set up in contrast to syllogism and enumeration alike. This is to be seen in Zabarella,[1] in Galilei,[2] and in Bacon. The reformed Aristotelian logic of the first-named with its *inductio demonstrativa*, the mathematico-physical analysis followed by synthesis of the second, the *exclusiva*, or method of exclusions of the last, agree at least in this, that the method of science is one and indivisible, while containing both an inductive and a deductive moment. That what, *e.g.*, Bacon says of his method may run counter to this is an accident of the tradition of the quarrel with realism. So, too, with the scholastic universals. Aristotle's forms had been correlated, though inadequately, with the idea of function. Divorced from this they are fairly stigmatized as mental figments or branded as ghostly entities that can but block the path. But consider Bacon's own doctrine of forms. Or watch the mathematical physicist with his formulae. The faith of science looks outward as in the dawn of Greek philosophy, and subjectivism such as Hume's has as yet no hold. Bacon summing up the movement so far as he understood it, in a rather belated way, has no theory of knowledge beyond the metaphor of the mirror held up to nature. Yet he offers an ambitious logic of science, and the case is typical.

Galilei.

The science of the Renaissance differs from that of the false dawn in Greek times in the fact of fruitfulness. It had the achievement of the old world in the field of mathematics upon which to build. It was in reaction against a dialectic and not immediately to be again entrapped. In scientific method, then, it could but advance, provided physics and mathematics did not again fail of accord. Kepler and Galilei secured it against that disaster. The *ubi materia ibi geometria* of the one is the battle-cry of the mathematico-physical advance. The scientific instrument of the other, with its moments of analysis and construction, *metodo risolutivo* and *metodo compositivo*, engineers the road for the advance. The new method of physics is verifiable by its fruitfulness, and so free of any immediate danger from dialectic. Its germinal thought may not have been new, but, if not new, it had at least needed rediscovery from the beginning. For it was to be at once certain and experiential. A mathematico-physical calculus that would work was in question. The epistemological problem as such was out of the purview. The relation of physical laws to the mind that thought them was for the time a negligible constant. When Descartes, having faithfully and successfully followed the mathematico-physical inquiry of his more strictly scientific predecessors, found himself compelled to raise the question how it was possible for him to know what in truth he seemed to know so certainly, the problem entered on a new phase. The scientific movement had happily been content for the time with a half which, then and there at least, was more than the whole.

Bacon.

Bacon was no mathematician, and so was out of touch with the main army of progress. By temperament he was rather with the Humanists. He was content to voice the cry for the overthrow of the dominant system as such, and to call for a new beginning, with no realist presuppositions. He is with the nominalists of the later Scholasticism and the naturalists of the early Renaissance. He echoes the cry for recourse to nature, for induction, for experiment. He calls for a logic of discovery. But at first sight there is little sign of any greater contribution to the reconstruction than is to be found in Ramus or many another dead thinker. The syllogism is [illegible]tive, belonging to argumentation, and constraining assent where what we want is control of things. It is a mechanical combination of propositions as these of terms which are counters to express concepts often ill-defined. The flight from a cursory survey of facts to wide so-called principles must give way to a [illegible] progress upward from propositions of minimum to those [illegible] generality, and in these consists the fruitfulness of [illegible]. Yet the induction of the Aristotelians, the dialectical [illegible] the *Topics*, content with imperfect enumeration [illegible] throwing the burden of disproof upon the critic, is [illegible] the mercy of a single instance to the contrary. In all this there is but little promise for a new organon. It is neither novel nor instrumental. On a sudden Bacon's conception of a new method begins to unfold itself. It is inductive only in the sense that it is identical in purpose with the ascent from particulars. It were better called exclusiva or elimination of the alternative, which Bacon proposes to achieve, and thereby guarantee his conclusion against the possibility of instance to the contrary.

The three Methods.

Bacon's method begins with a digest into three tables of the facts relevant to any inquiry. The first contains cases of the occurrence of the quality under investigation, colour, *e.g.*, or heat, in varying combinations. The second notes its absence in combinations so allied to certain of these that its presence might fairly have been looked for. The third registers its quantitative variation according to quantitative changes in its concomitants. The method now proceeds on the basis of the first table to set forth the possible suggestions as to a general explanatory formula for the quality in question. In virtue of the remaining tables it rejects any suggestion qualitatively or quantitatively inadequate. If one suggestion, and one alone, survives the process of attempted rejection it is the explanatory formula required. If none, we must begin afresh. If more than one recourse is to be had to certain devices of method, in the enumeration of which the methods of agreement, difference and concomitant variations[3] find a place, beside the crucial experiment, the glaring instance and the like. An appeal, however, to such devices, though a permissible "first vintage" is relatively an imperfection of method, and a proof that the tables need revision. The positive procedure by hypothesis and verification is rejected by Bacon, who thinks of hypothesis as the will o' the wisp of science, and prefers the cumbrous machinery of negative reasoning.

Historically he appears to have been under the dominance of the Platonic metaphor of an alphabet of nature, with a consequent belief in the relatively small number of ultimate principles to be determined, and of Plato's conception of Division, cleared of its dialectical associations and used experientially in application to his own molecular physics. True it is that the rejection of all the co-species is a long process, but what if therein their simultaneous or subsequent determination is helped forward? They, too, must fall to be determined sometime, and the ideal of science is fully to determine all the species of the genus. This will need co-operative effort as described in the account of Solomon's House in the *New Atlantis*.[4] But once introduce the conception of division of labour as between the collector of data on the one hand and the expert of method, the interpreter of nature at headquarters, on the other, and Bacon's attitude to hypothesis and to negative reasoning is at least in part explained. The hypothesis of the collector, the man who keeps a rain-gauge, or the missionary among savages, is to be discounted from as a source of error. The expert on the other hand may be supposed, in the case of facts over which he has not himself brooded in the course of their acquisition, to approach them without any presumption this way or that. He will, too, have no interest in the isolation of any one of several co-ordinate inquiries. That Bacon underestimates the importance of selective and of provisional explanatory hypotheses even in such fields as that of chemistry, and that technically he is open to some criticism from the point of view that negative judgment is derivate as necessarily resting on positive presuppositions, may be true enough. It seems, however, no less true that the greatness of his conception of organized common effort in science has but rarely met with due appreciation.

Forms.

In his doctrine of *forms*, too, the "universals" of his logic, Bacon must at least be held to have been on a path which led forward and not back. His forms are principles whose function falls entirely within knowledge. They are formulae for the control of the activities and the production of the qualities of bodies. Forms are qualities and activities expressed in terms of the ultimates of nature, *i.e.* normally in terms of collocations of matter or modes of motion. (The human soul is still an exception.) Form is bound up with the molecular structure and change of structure of a body, one of whose qualities or activities it expresses in wider relations. A mode of motion, for instance, of a certain definite kind, is the form of heat. It is the recipe for, and at the same time is, heat, much as H_2O is the formula for and is water. Had Bacon analysed bodies into their elements, instead of their qualities and ways of behaviour, he would have been the logician of the chemical formula. Here, too, he has scarcely received his meed of appreciation.

His influence on his successors has rather lain in the general stimulus of his enthusiasm for experience, or in the success with which he represents the cause of nominalism and in certain special devices of method handed down till, through Hume or Herschel, they affected the thought of Mill. For the rest he was too Aristotelian, if we take the word broadly enough, or, as the result of his Cambridge studies.

[1] [illegible] *Erkenntnisproblem*, i. 134 seq., and the [illegible] sqq.

[2] [illegible] *f. wiss. Philo*[illegible]

[3] Bacon, *Novum Organum*, ii. 22, 23; cf. also Aristotle, *Topics* i. 12, 13, ii. 10, 11 (Stewart, ad *Nic. Eth.* 1139*b* 27) and Sextus Empiricus, *Pyrr. Hypot.* iii. 15.

[4] Bacon's *Works*, ed. Ellis and Spedding, iii. 164-165.

too Ramist,[1] when the interest in scholastic issues was fading, to bring his original ideas to a successful market.

Bacon's Logic, then, like Galilei's, intended as a contribution to scientific method, a systematization of discovery by which, given the fact of knowledge, new items of knowledge may be acquired, failed to convince contemporaries and successors alike of its efficiency as an instrument. It was an ideal that failed to embody itself and justify itself by its fruits. It was otherwise with the mathematical instrument of Galilei.

Descartes.

Descartes stands in the following of Galilei. It is concurrently with signal success in the work of a pioneer in the mathematical advance that he comes to reflect on method, generalizes the method of mathematics to embrace knowledge as a whole, and raises the ultimate issues of its presuppositions. In the mathematics we determine complex problems by a construction link by link from axioms and simple data clearly and distinctly conceived. Three moments are involved. The first is an *induction*, *i.e.* an exhaustive enumeration of the simple elements in the complex phenomenon under investigation. This resolution or analysis into simple, because clear and distinct, elements may be brought to a standstill again and again by obscurity and indistinctness, but patient and repeated revision of all that is included in the problem should bring the analytic process to fruition. It is impatience, a perversity of will, that is the cause of error. Upon the analysis there results *intuition* of the simple data. With Descartes intuition does not connote givenness, but its objects are evident at a glance when induction has brought them to light. Lastly we have *deduction* the determination of the most complex phenomena by a continuous synthesis or combination of the simple elements. Synthesis is demonstrative and complete. It is in virtue of this view of derived or mediate knowledge that Descartes speaks of the (subsumptive) syllogism as "of avail rather in the communication of what we already know." Syllogism is not the synthesis which together with analysis goes to constitute the new instrument of science. The celebrated *Regulae* of Descartes are precepts directed to the achievement of the new methodological ideal in any and every subject matter, however reluctant.

It is the paradox involved in the function of intuition, the acceptance of the psychological characters of clearness and distinctness as warranty of a truth presumed to be trans-subjective, that leads to Descartes's distinctive contribution to the theory of knowledge. In order to lay bare the ground of certainty he raises the universal doubt, and, although, following Augustine,[2] he finds its limit in the thought of the doubter, this of itself is not enough. *Cogito, ergo sum.* *That* I think may be admitted. *What* I think may still need validation. Descartes's guarantee of the validity of my clear and distinct perceptions is the veracity of God.[3] Does the existence of God in turn call for proof? An effect cannot contain more than its cause, nor the idea of a perfect Being find adequate source save in the actuality of such a Being. Thus the intuition of the casual axiom is used to prove the existence of that which alone gives validity to intuitions. Though the logical method of Descartes has a great and enduring influence, it is the dualism and the need of God to bridge it, the doctrine of "innate" ideas, *i.e.* of ideas not due to external causes nor to volition but only to our capacity to think, our disposition to develop them, and finally the ontological proof, that affect the thought of the next age most deeply. That essence in the supreme case involves existence is a thought which comes to Spinoza more easily, together with the tradition of the *ordo geometricus*.

D. Modern Logic

i. *The Logic of Empiricism*

The path followed by English thought was a different one. Hobbes developed the nominalism which had been the hallmark of revolt against scholastic orthodoxy, and, when he brings this into relation with the analysis and synthesis of scientific method, it is at the expense of the latter.[4] Locke, when Cartesianism had raised the problem of the contents of consciousness, and the spirit of Baconian positivism could not accept of anything that bore the ill-omened name of innate ideas, elaborated a theory of knowledge which is psychological in the sense that its problem is how the simple data with which the individual is in contact in sensation are worked up into a system. Though he makes his bow to mathematical method, he, even more than Hobbes, misses its constructive character. The clue of mathematical certainty is discarded in substance in the English form of "the new way of ideas."

Hobbes.

With Hobbes logic is a calculus of marks and signs in the form of names. Naming is what distinguishes man from the brutes. It enables him to fix fleeting memories and to communicate with his fellows. He alone is capable of truth in the due conjunction or disjunction of names in propositions. Syllogism is simply summation of propositions, its function being communication merely. Analysis is the sole way of invention or discovery. There is more, however, in Hobbes, than the paradox of nominalism. Spinoza could draw upon him for the notion of genetic definition.[5] Leibnitz probably owes to him the thought of a calculus of symbols, and the conception of demonstration as essentially a chain of definitions.[6] His psychological account of syllogism[7] is taken over by Locke. Hume derived from him the explanatory formula of the association of ideas,[8] which is, however, still with Hobbes a fact to be accounted for, not a theory to account for facts, being grounded physically in "coherence of the matter moved." Finally Mill took from him his definition of cause as sum of conditions,[9] which played no small part in the applied logic of the 19th century.

Locke.

Locke is of more importance, if not for his logical doctrine, at least for the theory of knowledge from which it flows. With Locke the mind is comparable to white paper on which the world of things records itself in ideas of sensation. Simple ideas of sensation are the only points of contact we have with things. They are the atomic elements which "the workmanship of the understanding" can thereafter do no more than systematically compound and the like. It is Locke's initial attribution of the primary rôle in mental process to the simple ideas of sensation that precludes him from the development of the conception of another sort of ideas, or mental contents that he notes, which are produced by reflection on "the operations of our own mind within us." It is in the latter group that we have the explanation of all that marks Locke as a forerunner of the critical philosophy. It contains in germ a doctrine of categories discovered but not generated in the psychological processes of the individual. Locke, however, fails to "deduce" his categories. He has read Plato's *Theaetetus* in the light of Baconian and individualist preconceptions. Reflection remains a sort of "internal sense," whose ideas are of later origin than those of the external sense. His successors emphasize the sensationist elements, not the workmanship of the mind. When Berkeley has eliminated the literal materialism of Locke's metaphors of sense-perception, Hume finds no difficulty in accepting the sensations as present virtually in their own right, any non-sensible ground being altogether unknown. From a point of view purely subjectivist he is prepared to explain all that is to be left standing of what Locke ascribes to the workmanship of the mind by the principle of association or customary conjunction of ideas, which Locke had added a chapter to a later edition of his *Essay* explicitly to reject as an explanatory formula. Condillac goes a step farther, and sees no necessity for the superstructure at all, with its need of explanation valid or invalid. Drawing upon Gassendi for his psychological atomism and upon Hobbes for a thoroughgoing nominalism, he reproduces, as the logical conclusion from Locke's premises, the position of Antisthenes

[1] A notable formula of Bacon's *Novum Organum* ii. 4 § 3 turns out, *Valerius Terminus*, cap. 11, to come from Aristotle, *Post. An.* i. 4 *via* Ramus. See Ellis in Bacon's *Works*, iii. 203 sqq.

[2] *De Civitate Dei*, xi. 26. "Certum est me esse, si fallor."

[3] Cf. Plato, *Republic*, 381E seq.

[4] *Elementa Philosophiæ*, i. 3. 20, i. 6. 17 seq.

[5] Hobbes, *Elementa Philosophiæ*, i. 1. 5.

[6] *Id. ib.* i. 6. 16.

[7] *Id. ib.* i. 4. 8; cf. Locke's *Essay of Human Understanding*, iv. 17.

[8] *Id. Leviathan*, i. 3.

[9] *Id. Elem. Philos.* i. 6. 10.

[illegible] Mill expresses [illegible] such as should satisfy the needs of the [illegible] experimental physics and chemistry as [illegible] the first half of the [illegible] century and [illegible] the moral sciences naturalistically construed. In uniting [illegible] the associationism which he inherited, through his father, from Hume, he revealed at once the strength and weakness of the final conception of naturalism. His rare thoroughness and rarer candour made it at once unnecessary and impossible that the work should be done again.

If judged by what he denies, viz. the formal logic of Hamilton and Mansel, whose Aristotelian and scholastic learning did but accentuate their traditionalism, and whose acquiescence in consistency constituted in Mill's view a discouragement of research, such as men now incline to attribute at the least equally to Hume's idealism, Mill is only negatively justified. [illegible] judged by his positive contribution to the theory of method [illegible] claim to find a more than negative justification for his [illegible] in its success. In the field covered by scholastic logic [illegible] frankly associationist. He aims at describing what he

* Hume, *Treatise of Human Nature*, i. 3. 15.

finds given, without reference to insensible implications of doubtful validity and value. The upshot is a psychological account of what from one aspect is evidence, from the other, belief. So he explains "concepts or general notions"[1] by an abstraction which he represents as a sort of alt-relief operated by attention and fixed by naming, association with the name giving to a set of attributes a unity they otherwise lack. This is manifestly, when all is said, a particular psychological event, a collective fact of the associative consciousness. It can exercise no organizing or controlling function in knowledge. So again in determining the "import" of propositions, it is no accident that in all save existential propositions it is to the familiar rubrics of associationism—co-existence, sequence, causation and resemblance—that he refers for classification, while his general formula as to the conjunctions of connotations is associationist through and through. It follows consistently enough that inference is from particular to particular. Mill holds even the ideas of mathematics to be hypothetical, and in theory knows nothing of a non-enumerative or non-associative universal. A premise that has the utmost universality consistent with this view can clearly be of no service for the establishment of a proposition that has gone to the making of it. Nor again of one that has not. Its use, then, can only be as a memorandum. It is a shorthand formula of registration. Mill's view of ratiocinative process clearly stands and falls with the presumed impossibility of establishing the necessity for universals of another type than his, for what may be called principles of construction. His critics incline to press the point that association itself is only intelligible so far as it is seen to depend on universals of the kind that he denies.

In Mill's inductive logic, the nominalistic convention has, through his tendency to think in relatively watertight compartments,[2] faded somewhat into the background. Normally he thinks of what he calls phenomena no longer as psychological groupings of sensations, as "states of mind," but as things and events in a physical world howsoever constituted and apprehended. His free use of relating concepts, that of sameness, for instance, bears no impress of his theory of the general notion, and it is possible to put out of sight the fact that, taken in conjunction with his nominalism, it raises the whole issue of the possibility of the equivocal generation of formative principles from the given contents of the individual consciousness, in any manipulation of which they are already implied. Equally, too, the deductive character, apparently in intention as well as in actual fact, of Mill's experimental methods fails to recall the point of theory that the process is essentially one from particular to particular. The nerve of proof in the processes by which he establishes causal conjunctions of unlimited application is naturally thought to lie in the special canons of the several processes and the axioms of universal and uniform causation which form their background. The conclusions seem not merely to fall within, but to depend on these organic and controlling formulae. They follow not merely according to them but from them. The reference to the rule is not one which may be made and normally is made as a safeguard, but one which must be made, if thought is engaged in a forward and constructive movement at all. Yet Mill's view of the function of "universal" propositions had been historically suggested by a theory—Dugald Stewart's—of the use of axioms![3] Once more, it would be possible to forget that Mill's ultimate laws or axioms are not in his view intuitions, nor forms constitutive of the rational order, nor postulates of all rational construction, were it not that he has made the endeavour to establish them on associationist lines. It is because of the failure of this endeavour to bring the technique of induction within the setting of his Humian psychology of belief that the separation of his contribution to the applied logic of science from his sensationism became necessary, as it happily was easy. Mill's device rested special inductions of causation upon the laws that every event has a cause, and every cause has always the same effect. It rested these in turn upon a general induction enumerative in character of enormous and practically infinite range and always uncontradicted. Though obviously not exhaustive, the unique extent of this induction was held to render it competent to give practical certainty or psychological necessity. A vicious circle is obviously involved. It is true, of course, that ultimate laws need discovery, that they are discovered in some sense in the medium of the psychological mechanism, and that they are nevertheless the grounds of all specific inferences. But that truth is not what Mill expounds, nor is it capable of development within the limits imposed by the associationist formula.

It is deservedly, nevertheless, that Mill's applied logic has retained its pride of place amid what has been handed on, if in modified shape, by writers, *e.g.*, Sigwart, and Professor Bosanquet, whose theory of knowledge is quite alien from his. He prescribed regulative or limiting formulae for research as it was actually conducted in his world. His grasp of the procedure by which the man of science manipulated his particular concrete problems was admirable. In especial he showed clear understanding of the functions of hypothesis and verification in the investigations of the solitary worker, with his facts still in course of accumulation and needing to be lighted up by the scientific imagination. He was therefore enabled to formulate the method of what Bacon had tended to despise as merely the "first vintage." Bacon spent his strength upon a dream of organization for all future discovery. Mill was content to codify. The difference between Bacon and Mill lies chiefly in this, and it is because of this difference that Mill's contribution, spite of its debt to the Baconian tradition, remains both characteristic and valuable. It is of course possible to criticise even the experimental canons with some severity. The caveats, however, which are relevant within the circle of ideas within which Mill's lesson can be learned and improved on,[4] seem to admit of being satisfied by relatively slight modifications in detail, or by explanations often supplied or easily to be supplied from points brought out amid the wealth of illustration with which Mill accompanied his formal or systematic exposition of method. The critic has the right of it when he points out, for example, that the practical difficulty in the Method of Agreement is not due to plurality of causes, as Mill states, but rather to intermixture of effects, while, if the canon could be satisfied exactly, the result would not be rendered uncertain in the manner or to the extent which he supposes. Again the formula of the Joint-Method, which contemplates the enumeration of cases "which have nothing in common but the absence of one circumstance," is ridiculously unsound as it stands. Or, on rather a different line of criticism, the use of corresponding letters in the two series of antecedents and consequents raises, it is said, a false presumption of correlation. Nay, even the use of letters at all suggests that the sort of analysis that actually breaks up its subject-matter is universally or all but universally applicable in nature, and this is not the case. Finally, the conditions of the methods are either realized or not. If they are realized, the work of the scientist falls entirely within the field of the processes preliminary to the satisfaction of the canon. The latter becomes a mere memorandum or formula of registration. So is it possible "to have the enginer hoist with his own petar." But the conditions are not realized, and in an experiential subject-matter are not realizable. Not one circumstance only in common but "apparently one relevant circumstance only in common" is what we are able to assert. If we add the qualification of relevance we destroy the cogency of the method. If we fail to add it, we destroy the applicability.

The objections turn on two main issues. One is the exaggeration of the possibilities of resolution into separate elements that is due to the acceptance of the postulate of an alphabet of nature. This so soon as noted can be allowed for. It is to the

[1] Mill, *Examination of Sir William Hamilton's Philosophy*, cap. 17.

[2] Cf. Mill, *Autobiography*, p. 159. "I grappled at once with the problem of Induction, postponing that of Reasoning." *Ib.* p. 182 (when he is preoccupied with syllogism), "I could make nothing satisfactory of Induction at this time."

[3] *Autobiography*, p. 181.

[4] The insight, for instance, of F. H. Bradley's criticism, *Principles of Logic*, II. ii. 3, is somewhat dimmed by a lack of sympathy due to extreme difference in the point of view adopted.

[illegible] [tend]ency to think chiefly of [illegible] or subtraction of these [illegible] theoretically premature [illegible] This too can be met by a [illegible] is perhaps of more signi[ficance] [illegible] Mill manifests between the [illegible] [practica]lly applicable to concrete [illegible] [conceptio]n of it as an expression of [illegible] procedure. Mill seems most often [illegible] to formulate in terms of the [illegible] at any rate, if relevance *in proximo* is interpolated in the [illegible] clause of the canon of the Joint-Method, the practical [illegible] of the method is rehabilitated. So too, if the canon [of th]e Method of Agreement is never more than approxi[mate]ly satisfied, intermixture of effects will in practice mean that we at least often do not know the cause or antecedent equivalent of a given effect, without the possibility of an alternative. Finally, it is on the whole in keeping with Mill's presuppositions to admit even in the case of the method of difference that in practice it is approximative and instructive, while the theoretical formula, to which it aims at approaching asymptotically as limit, if exact, is in some sense sterile. Mill may well have himself conceived his methods as practically fruitful and normally convincing with the limiting formula in each case more cogent in form but therewith merely the skeleton of the process that but now pulsed with life.

Enough has been said to show why the advance beyond the letter of Mill was inevitable while much in the spirit of Mill must necessarily affect deeply all later experientialism. After Mill experientialism takes essentially new forms. In part because of what Mill had done. In part also because of what he had left undone. After Mill means after Kant and Hegel and Herbart, and it means after the emergence of evolutionary naturalism. Mill, then, marks the final stage in the achievement of a great school of thought.

ii. *The Logic of Rationalism.*

A fundamental contrast to the school of Bacon and of Locke is afforded by the great systems of reason, owning Cartesian inspiration, which are identified with the names of Spinoza and Leibnitz. In the history of logic the latter thinker is of the more importance. Spinoza's philosophy is expounded *ordine geometrico* and with Euclidean cogency from a relatively small number of definitions, axioms and postulates. But how we reach our assurance of the necessity of these principles is not made specifically clear. The invaluable tractate *De Intellectus emendatione*, in which the agreement with and divergence from Descartes on the question of method could have been fully elucidated, is unhappily not finished. We know that we need to pass from what Spinoza terms *experientia vaga*,[1] where imagination with its fragmentary apprehension is liable to error and neither necessity nor impossibility can be predicated, right up to that which *fictionem terminat*—namely, *intellectio*. And what Spinoza has to say of the requisites of definition and the marks of intellection makes it clear that insight comes with coherence, and that the work of method on the "inductive" side is by means of the unravelling of all that makes for artificial limitation to lay bare what can then be seen to exhibit nexus in the one great system. When all is said, however, the geometric method as universalized in philosophy is rather used by Spinoza than expounded.

Spinoza.

With Leibnitz, on the other hand, the logical problem holds the foremost place in philosophical inquiry.[2] From the purely logical thesis, developed at quite an early stage of his thinking,[3] that in any true proposition the predicate is contained in the subject, the main principles of his doctrine of Monads are derivable with the minimum of help from his philosophy of dynamics. *Praedicatum inest subjecto.* All valid propositions express in the last resort the relation of predicate or predicates to a subject, and this Leibnitz holds after considering the case of relational propositions where either term may hold the position of grammatical subject, A = B and the like. There is a subject then, or there are subjects which must be recognized as not possible to be predicated, but as absolute. For reasons not purely logical Leibnitz declares for the plurality of such subjects. Each contains all its predicates: and this is true not only in the case of truths of reason, which are necessary, and ultimately to be exhibited as coming under the law of contradiction, "or, what comes to the same thing, that of identity," but also in the case of truths of fact which are contingent, though a sufficient reason can be given for them which "inclines" without importing necessity. The extreme case of course is the human subject. "The individual notion of each person includes once for all what is to befall it, world without end," and "it would not have been our Adam but another, if he had had other events." Existent subjects, containing eternally all their successive predicates in the time-series, are substances, which when the problems connected with their activity, or dynamically speaking their force, have been resolved, demand—and supply—the metaphysic of the Monadology.

Leibnitz.

Complex truths of reason or essence raise the problem of definition, which consists in their analysis into simpler truths and ultimately into simple—*i.e.* indefinable ideas, with primary principles of another kind—axioms, and postulates that neither need nor admit of proof. These are identical in the sense that the opposite contains an express contradiction.[4] In the case of non-identical truths, too, there is a priori proof drawn from the notion of the terms, "though it is not always in our power to arrive at this analysis,"[5] so that the question arises, specially in connexion with the possibility of a calculus, whether the contingent is reducible to the necessary or identical at the ideal limit. With much that suggests an affirmative answer, Leibnitz gives the negative. Even in the case of the Divine will, though it be always for the best possible, the sufficient reason will "incline without necessitating." The propositions which deal with actual existence are still of a unique type, with whatever limitation to the calculus.

Leibnitz's treatment of the primary principles among truths of reason as identities, and his examples drawn *inter alia* from the "first principles" of mathematics, influenced Kant by antagonism. Identities some of them manifestly were not. The formula of identity passed in another form to Herbart and therefore to Lotze. In recognizing, further, that the relation of an actual individual fact to its sufficient ground was not reducible to identity, he set a problem diversely treated by Kant and Herbart. He brought existential propositions, indeed, within a rational system through the principle that it must be feasible to assign a sufficient reason for them, but he refused to bring them under the conception of identity or necessity, *i.e.* to treat their opposites as formally self-contradictory. This bore interest in the Kantian age in the treatment alike of cause and effect, and of the ontological proof of existence from essence. Not that the Law of Sufficient Reason is quite free from equivoque. Propositions concerning the *possible* existence of individuals put Leibnitz to some shifts, and the difficulty accounts for the close connexion established in regard to our actual world between the law of sufficient reason and the doctrine of the final cause. This connexion is something of an afterthought to distinguish from the potential contingency of the objectively possible the real contingency of the actual, for which the "cause or reason" of Spinoza[6] could not account. The law, however, is not invalidated by these considerations, and with the degree of emphasis and the special setting that Leibnitz gives the law, it is definitely his own.

If we may pass by the doctrine of the Identity of Indiscernibles, which played a part of some importance in subsequent philosophy, and the Law of Continuity, which as Leibnitz represents it is, if not sheer dogma, reached by something very like a fallacy,

[1] Bacon, *Novum organum*, i. 100.
[2] Russell's *Philosophy of Leibnitz*, capp. 1–5.
[3] See especially remarks on the letter of M. Arnauld (Gerhardt's edition of the philosophical works, ii. 37 sqq.).

[4] Gerhardt, vi. 612, quoted by Russell, *loc. cit.*, p. 19.
[5] Ibid., ii. 62, Russell, p. 33.
[6] Spinoza, ed. van Vloten and Land, i. 46 (*Ethica*, i. 11).

we have as Leibnitz's remaining legacy to later logicians the conception of *Characteristica Universalis* and *Ars Combinatoria*, a universal denoting by symbols and a calculus working by substitutions and the like. The two positions that a subject contains all its predicates and that all non-contingent propositions—*i.e.* all propositions not concerned with the existence of individual facts ultimately analyse out into identities—obviously lend themselves to the design of this algebra of thought, though the mathematician in Leibnitz should have been aware that a significant equation is never an identity. Leibnitz, fresh from the battle of the calculus in the mathematical field, and with his conception of logic, at least in some of its aspects, as a generalized mathematic,[1] found a fruitful inspiration, harmonizing well with his own metaphysic, in Bacon's alphabet of nature. He, too, was prepared to offer a new instrument. That the most important section, the list of forms of combination, was never achieved—this too was after the Baconian example while the mode of symbolization was crude with $a=ab$ and the like—matters little. A new technique of manipulation—it is, of course, no more—had been evolved.

It may be said that among Leibnitz's successors there is no Leibnitzian. The system as a whole is something too artificial to secure whole-hearted allegiance. Wolff's formalism is the bastard outcome of the speculation of Leibnitz, and is related to it as remotely as Scholasticism is to Aristotle. Wolff found a sufficient reason for everything and embodied the results of his inquiries in systematic treatises, sometimes in the vernacular. He also, by a transparent *petitio principii*, brought the law of the sufficient reason under that of non-contradiction. Wolff and his numerous followers account for the charge of dogmatism against "the Leibnitzio-Wolffian school." They are of importance in the history of logic for two reasons only: they affected strongly the German vocabulary of philosophy and they constituted the intellectual environment in which Kant grew to manhood.

A truer continuator of Leibnitz in the spirit was Herbart.

iii. *Kant's Logic.*

Herbart's admitted allegiance, however, was Kantian with the qualification, at a relatively advanced stage of his thinking, that it was "of the year 1828"—that is, after controversy had brought out implications of Kant's teaching not wholly contemplated by Kant himself. The critical philosophy had indeed made it impossible to hark back to Leibnitz or any other master otherwise than with a difference.

Yet it is not a single and unambiguous logical movement that derives from Kant. Kant's lesson was variously understood. Different moments in it were emphasized, with a large diversity of result. As interpreted it was acquiesced in or revolted from and revolt ranged from a desire for some modifications of detail or expression to the call for a radical transformation. Grounds for a variety of developments are to be found in the imperfect harmonization of the rationalistic heritage from the Wolffian tradition which still dominates Kant's pure general logic with the manifest epistemological intention of his transcendental theory. Or again, within the latter in his admission of a duality of thought and "the given" in knowledge, which within knowledge was apparently irreducible, concurrently with hints as to the possibility, upon a wider view, of the sublation of their disparateness at least hypothetically and speculatively. The sense in which there must be a ground of the unity of the supersensible[2] while yet the transcendent use of Reason—*i.e.* its use beyond the limits of experience was denied theoretical validity—was not unnaturally regarded as obscure.

Kant's treatment of technical logic was wholly traditional, and in itself is almost negligible. It is comprised[3] in an early essay on the mistaken subtlety of the syllogistic figures, and a late compilation by a pupil from the introductory matter and running annotations with which the master had enriched his interleaved lecture-room copy of Meyer's *Compendium* of 1752. Wolff's general logic, "the best," said Kant, "that we possess," had been abridged by Baumgarten and the abridgment then subjected to commentation by Meyer. With this traditional body of doctrine Kant was, save for matters of minor detail, quite content. Logic was of necessity formal, dealing as it must with those rules without which no exercise of the understanding would be possible at all. Upon abstraction from all particular methods of thought these rules were to be discerned a priori or without dependence on experience by reflection solely upon the use of the understanding in general. The science of the form of thought abstracted in this way from its matter or content was regarded as of value both as propaedeutic and as canon. It was manifestly one of the disciplines in which a position of finality was attainable. Aristotle might be allowed, indeed, to have omitted no essential point of the understanding. What the moderns had achieved consisted in an advance in accuracy and methodical completeness. "Indeed, we do not require any new discoverers in logic,"[4] said the discoverer of a priori synthesis, "since it contains merely the form of thought." Applied logic is merely psychology, and not properly to be called logic at all. The technical logic of Kant, then, justifies literally a movement among his successors in favour of a formal conception of logic with the law of contradiction and the doctrine of formal implication for its equipment. Unless the doctrine of Kant's "transcendental logic" must be held to supply a point of view from which a logical development of quite another kind is inevitable, Kant's mantle, so far as logic is concerned, must be regarded as having fallen upon the formal logicians.

Formal Logic.

Kant's transcendental teaching is summarily as follows: "Transcendental" is his epithet for what is neither empirical—*i.e.* to be derived from experience—nor yet transcendent—*i.e.* applicable beyond the limits of experience, the mark of experience being the implication of sense or of something which thought contradistinguishes from its own spontaneous activity as in some sense "the given." Those features in our organized experience are to be regarded as transcendentally established which are the presuppositions of our having that experience at all. Since they are not empirical they must be structural and belong to "the mind"—*i.e.* the normal human intelligence, and to like intelligence so far as like. If we set aside such transcendental conditions as belong to sensibility or to the receptive phase of mind and are the presuppositions of juxtaposition of parts, the remainder are ascribable to spontaneity or understanding, to thought with its unifying, organizing or focussing function, and their elucidation is the problem of transcendental analytic. It is still logic, indeed, when we are occupied with the transcendent objects of the discursive faculty as it is employed beyond the limits of experience where it cannot validate its ideas. Such a logic, however, is a dialectic of illusion, perplexed by paralogisms and helpless in the face of antinomies. In transcendental analytic on the other hand we concern ourselves only with the transcendental "deduction" or vindication of the conditions of experience, and we have a logic of cognition in which we may establish our epistemological categories with complete validity. Categories are the forms according to which the combining unity of self-consciousness (synthetic unity of apperception) pluralizes itself through the various functions involved in the constitution of objectivity in different types of the one act of thought, viz. judgment. The clue to the discovery of transcendental conditions Kant finds in the existence of judgments, most manifest in mathematics and in the pure science of nature, which are certain, yet not trifling, necessary and yet not reducible to identities, synthetic therefore and a priori, and so accounted for neither by Locke nor by Leibnitz. "There lies a transcendental condition at the basis of every necessity."

Definition of "Transcendental."

Kant's mode of conceiving the activity of thought in the constitution of objects and of their connexion in experience

[1] *Nouveaux essais*, iv. 2 § 9, 17 § 4 (Gerhardt v. 351, 460).

[2] *Critique of Judgment*, Introd. § 2, *ad. fin.* (*Werke*, Berlin Academy edition, vol. v. p. 176, l. 10).

[3] *Kant's Introduction to Logic and his Essay on the Mistaken Subtlety of the Four Figures*, trans. T. K. Abbott (1885).

[4] *Loc. cit.*, p. 11.

was thought to lie open to an interpretation in conformity with the spirit of his logic, in the sense that the form and the content in knowledge are not merely distinguishable functions within an organic whole, but either separable, or at least indifferent one to the other in such a way as to be clearly independent. Thought as form would thus be a factor or an element in a composite unit. It would clearly have its own laws. It would be the whole concern of logic, which, since in it thought has itself for object, would have no reference to the other term of the antithesis, nor properly and immediately to the knowledge which is compact of thought in conjunction with something which, whatever it may be, is prima facie other than thought. There is too much textual warrant for this interpretation of Kant's meaning. Doubtless there are passages which make against an extreme dualistic interpretation. Even in his "logic" Kant speaks of abstraction from all particular objects of thought rather than of a resolution of concrete thinking into thought and its "other" as separable co-operating factors in a joint product. He spoke throughout, however, as if form and content were mutually indifferent, so that the abstraction of form from content implied nothing of falsification or mutilation. The reserve, therefore, that it was abstraction and not a decomposing that was in question remained to the admirers of his logic quite nugatory. They failed to realize that permissible abstraction from specific contents or methods of knowledge does not obliterate reference to matter or content. They passed easily from the acceptance of a priori forms of thinking to that of forms of a priori thinking, and could plead the example of Kant's logic.

Form of Matter of Thought.

Kant's theory of knowledge, then, needed to be pressed to other consequences for logic which were more consonant with the spirit of the *Critique*. The forms of thought and what gives thought its particular content in concrete acts of thinking could not be regarded as subsisting in a purely external and indifferent relation one to the other. "Laws according to which the subject thinks" and "laws according to which the object is known" cannot be the concern of separate departments of inquiry. As soon divorce the investigation of the shape and material of a mirror from the laws of the incidence of the rays that form images in it, and call it a science of reflection! An important group of writers developed the conception of an adaptation between the two sides of Kant's antithesis, and made the endeavour to establish some kind of correlation between logical forms and the process of "the given." There was a tendency to fall back upon the conception of some kind of parallelism, whether it was taken to be interpretative or rather corrective of Kant's meaning. This device was never remote from the constructions of writers for whom the teaching of Spinoza and Leibnitz was an integral part of their intellectual equipment. Other modes of correlation, however, find favour also, and in some variety. Kant is seldom the sole source of inspiration. His unresolved antithesis[1] is interpreted either diversely or with a difference of emphasis. And the light that later writers bring to bear on Kant's logic and epistemology from other sides of his speculation varies in kind and in degree.

Another logical movement springs from those whom a correlation of fact within the unity of a system altogether failed to satisfy. There must also be development of the correlated terms from a single principle. Form and content must not only correspond one to the other. They must be exhibited as distinguishable moments within a unity which can at one and the same time be seen to be the ground from which the distinction springs and the ground in virtue of which it is over-ruled. Along this line of speculation we have a logic which claims that whatsoever is in one plane or at one stage in the development of thought a residuum that apparently defies analysis must at another stage and on a higher plane be shown so to be absorbed as to fall altogether within thought. This is the view of Hegel upon which logic comes to coincide with the progressive self-unfolding of thought in that type of metaphysic which is known as absolute, *i.e.* all-inclusive idealism. The exponent of logic as metaphysic, for whom the rational is the real is necessarily in revolt against all that is characteristically Kantian in the theory of knowledge, against the transcendental method itself and against the doctrine of limits which constitutes the nerve of "criticism." Stress was to be laid upon the constructive character of the act of thought which Kant had recognized, and without Kant's qualifications of it. In all else the claim is made to have left the Kantian teaching behind as a cancelled level of speculation.

Transcendental method is indeed not invulnerable. A principle is transcendentally "deduced" when it and only it can explain the validity of some phase of experience, some order of truths. The order of truths, the phase of experience and its certainty had to be taken for granted. The sense, for example, in which the irreversibility of sequence which is the more known *in ordine ad hominem* in the case of the causal principle differs from merely psychological conviction is not made fully clear. Even so the inference to the a priori ground of its necessity is, it has been often pointed out, subject to the limitation inherent in any process of reduction, in any regress, that is, from conditionate to condition, *viz.* that in theory an alternative is still possible. The inferred principle may hold the field as explanation without obvious competitor potential or actual. Nevertheless its claim to be the sole possible explanation can in nowise be validated. It has been established after all by dialectic in the Aristotelian sense of the word. But if transcendental method has no special pride of place, Kant's conclusion as to the limits of the competence of intellectual faculty falls with it. Cognition manifestly needs the help of Reason even in its theoretical use. Its speculation can no longer be stigmatized as vaticination *in vacuo*, nor its results as illusory.

Limitation of Transcendental Method.

Finally, to logic as metaphysic the polar antithesis is psychology as logic. The turn of this also was to come again. If logic were treated as merely formal, the stress of the problem of knowledge fell upon the determination of the processes of the psychological mechanism. If alleged a priori constituents of knowledge—such rubrics as substance, property, relation—come to be explained psychologically, the formal logic that has perforce to ignore all that belongs to psychology is confined within too narrow a range to be able to maintain its place as an independent discipline, and tends to be merged in psychology. This tendency is to be seen in the activity of Fries and Herbart and Beneke, and was actualized as the aftermath of their speculation. It is no accident that it was the psychology of apperception and the voluntaryist theory or practice of Herbart, whose logical theory was so closely allied to that of the formal logicians proper, that contributed most

Logic and Psychology.

[1] Or antitheses. Kant follows, for example, a different line of cleavage between form and content from that developed between thought and the "given." And these are not his only unresolved dualities, even in the *Critique of Pure Reason*. For the logical inquiry, however, it is permissible to ignore or reduce these differences.

The determination too of the sense in which Kant's theory of knowledge involves an unresolved antithesis is for the logical purpose necessary so far only as it throws light upon his logic and his influence upon logical developments. Historically the question of the extent to which writers adopted the dualistic interpretation or one that had the like consequences is of greater importance.

It may be said summarily that Kant holds the antithesis between thought and "the given" to be unresolved and within the limits of theory of knowledge irreducible. The dove of thought falls lifeless if the resistant atmosphere of "the given" be withdrawn (*Critique of Pure Reason*, ed. 2 Introd. Kant's *Werke*, ed. of the Prussian Academy, vol. iii. p. 32, ll. 10 sqq.). Nevertheless the thing-in-itself is a problematic conception and of a limiting or negative use merely. He "had woven," according to an often quoted phrase of Goethe, "a certain sly element of irony into his method; . . . he pointed as it were with a side gesture beyond the limits which he himself had drawn." Thus (*loc. cit.* p. 46, ll. 8, 9) he declares that "there are two lineages united in human knowledge, which perhaps spring from a common stock, though to us unknown—namely sense and understanding." Some indication of the way in which he would hypothetically and speculatively mitigate the antithesis is perhaps afforded by the reflection that the distinction of the mental and what appears as material is an external distinction in which the one appears outside to the other. "Yet what as thing-in-itself lies back of the phenomenon may perhaps not be so wholly disparate after all" (ib. p. 278, ll. 26 sqq.)

to the development of the post-Kantian psychological logic. Another movement helped also; the exponents of naturalistic evolution were prepared with Spencer to explain the so-called *a priori* in knowledge as in truth *a posteriori*, if not to the individual at any rate to the race. It is of course a newer type of psychological logic that is in question, one that is aware of Kant's "answer to Hume." Stuart Mill, despite of his relation of antagonism to Hamilton and Mansel, who held themselves to be Kantian in spirit, is still wholly pre-Kantian in his outlook.

Summary. Kant's influence, then, upon subsequent logic is least of all to be measured by his achievement in his professed contribution to technical logic. It may be attributed in some slight degree, perhaps, to incidental flashes of logical insight where his thought is least of what he himself calls logic, *e.g.* his exposition of the significance of synthetic judgments *a priori*, or his explanation of the function of imagery in relation to thought, whereby he offers a solution of the problem of the conditions under which one member of a group unified through a concept can be taken to stand for the rest, or again the way in which he puts his finger on the vital issue in regard to the alleged proof from essence to existence, and illustrations could be multiplied. But much more it belongs to his transformation of the epistemological problem, and to the suggestiveness of his philosophy as a whole for an advance in the direction of a speculative construction which should be able to cancel all Kant's surds, and in particular vindicate a "ground of the unity of the supersensible which lies back of nature with that which the concept of freedom implies in the sphere of practice,"[1] which is what Kant finally asserts.

iv. *After Kant.*

Starting from the obvious antithesis of thought and that of which it is the thought, it is possible to view the ultimate relation of its term as that of mutual indifference or, secondly, as that of a correspondence such that while they retain their distinct character modification of the one implies modification of the other, or thirdly and lastly, as that of a mergence of one in the other of such a nature that the merged term, whichever it be, is fully accounted for in a complete theory of that in which it is merged.

The Formal Logicians. The first way is that of the purely formal logicians, of whom Twesten[2] and in England H. L. Mansel may be regarded as typical. They take thought and "the given" as self-contained units which, if not in fact separable, are at any rate susceptible of an abstraction the one from the other so decisive as to constitute an ideal separation. The laws of the pure activity of thought must be independently determined, and since the contribution of thought to knowledge is form they must be formal only. They cannot go beyond the limits of formal consistency or analytic correctness. They are confined to the determination of what the truth of any matter of thought, taken for granted upon grounds psychological or other, which are extraneous to logic, includes or excludes. The unit for logic is the concept taken for granted. The function of logic is to exhibit its formal implications and repulsions. It is questionable whether even this modest task could be really achieved without other reference to the content abstracted from than Mansel, for example, allows. The analogy of the resolution of a chemical compound with its elements which is often on the lips of those who would justify the independence of thought and the real world, with an agnostic conclusion as to non-phenomenal or trans-subjective reality, is not really applicable. The oxygen and hydrogen, for example, into which water may be resolved are not in strictness indifferent one to the other, since both are members of an order regulated according to laws of combination in definite ratios. Or, if applicable, it is double-edged. Suppose oxygen to be found only in water. Were it to become conscious, would it therefore follow that it could infer the laws of a separate or independent activity of its own? Similarly forms of thinking, the law of contradiction not excepted, have their meaning only in reference to determinate content, even though distributively all determinate contents are dispensable. The extreme formalist is guilty of a fallacy of composition in regard to abstraction.

It does not follow, however, that the laws asserted by the formal logicians are invalid or unimportant. There is a permissible abstraction, and in general they practise this, and although they narrow its range unduly, it is legitimately to be applied to certain characters of thinking. As the living organism includes something of mechanism—the skeleton, for example—so an organic logic doubtless includes determinations of formal consistency. The skeleton is meaningless apart from reference to its function in the life of an organism, yet there are laws of skeleton structure which can be studied with most advantage if other characters of the organism are relegated to the background. To allow, however, that abstraction admits of degrees, and that it never obliterates all reference to that from which it is abstracted, is to take a step forward in the direction of the correlation of logical forms with the concrete processes of actual thinking. What was true in formal logic tended to be absorbed in the correlationist theories.

Those formal logicians of the Kantian school, then, may be summarily dismissed, though their undertaking was a necessary one, who failed to raise the epistemological issue at all, or who, raising it, acquiesced in a naive dualism agnostic of the real world as Kant's essential lesson. They failed to develop any view which could serve either in fact or in theory as a corrective to the effect of their formalism. What they said with justice was said as well or better elsewhere.

Among them it is on the whole impossible not to include the names of Hamilton and Mansel. The former, while his erudition in respect to the history of philosophical opinion has rarely been equalled, was not a clear thinker. His general theory of knowledge deriving from Kant and Reid, and including among other things a *contaminatio* of their theories of perception,[3] in no way sustains or mitigates his narrow view of logic. He makes no effective use of his general formula that to think is to condition. He appeals to the direct testimony of consciousness in the sense in which the appeal involves a fallacy. He accepts an ultimate antinomy as to the finiteness or infinity of "the unconditioned," yet applies the law of the excluded middle to insist that one of the two alternatives must be true, wherefore we must make the choice. And what is to be said of the judgment of a writer who considers the relativity of thought demonstrated by the fact that every judgment unites two members? Hamilton's significance for the history of logic lies in the stimulus that he gave to the development of symbolic logic in England by his new analytic based upon his discovery or adoption of the principle of the quantification of the predicate. Mansel, too, was learned, specially in matters of Aristotelian exegesis, and much that is of value lies buried in his commentation of the dry bones of the *Artis Logicae Rudimenta* of Locke's contemporary Aldrich. And he was a clearer thinker than Hamilton. Formal logic of the extremest rigour is nowhere to be found more adequately expressed in all its strength, and it must be added in all its weakness, than in the writings of Mansel. But if the view maintained above that formal logic must compromise or mitigate its rigour and so fail to maintain its independence, be correct, the logical consistency of Mansel's logic of consistency does but emphasize its barrenness. It contains no germ for further development. It is the end of a movement.

The brief logic of Herbart[4] is altogether formal too. Logical forms have for him neither psychological nor metaphysical reference. We are concerned in logic solely with the systematic

[1] *Critique of Judgment*, Introd. § 2 (*Werke*, v., 276 ll. 9 sqq.); cf. Bernard's "Prolegomena" to his translation of this, pp. xxxviii. sqq.).

[2] *Die Logik, insbesondere die Analytik* (Schleswig, 1825). August Detlev Christian Twesten (1789–1876), a Protestant theologian, succeeded Schleiermacher as professor in Berlin in 1835.

[3] See *Sir William Hamilton: The Philosophy of Perception*, by J. Hutchison Stirling.

[4] *Hauptpunkte der Logik*, 1808 (*Werke*, ed. Hartenstein, i. 465 sqq.), and specially *Lehrbuch der Einleitung in die Philosophie* (1813), and subsequently §§ 34 sqq. (*Werke*, i. 77 sqq.).

clarification of concepts which are wholly abstract, so that they are not merely not ultimate realities, but also in no sense actual moments of our concrete thinking. The first task of logic is to distinguish and group such concepts according to their marks, and from their classification there naturally follows their connexion in judgment. It is in the logic of judgment that Herbart inaugurates a new era. He is not, of course, the first to note that even categorical judgments do not assert the realization of their subject. That is a thought which lies very near the surface for formal logic. He had been preceded too by Maimon in the attempt at a reduction of the traditional types of judgment. He was, however, the first whose analysis was sufficiently convincing to exorcise the tyranny of grammatical forms. The categorical and disjunctive judgment reduce to the hypothetical. By means of the doctrine of the quantification of the predicate, in which with his Leibnitzian conception of identity he anticipated Beneke and Hamilton alike, universal and particular judgments are made to pull together. Modal, impersonal, existential judgments are all accounted for. Only the distinction of affirmative and negative judgments remains unresolved, and the exception is a natural one from the point of view of a philosophy of pluralism. There was little left to be done here save in the way of an inevitable *mutatis mutandis*, even by Lotze and F. H. Bradley. From the judgment viewed as hypothetical we pass by affirmation of the antecedent or denial of the consequent to inference. This point of departure is noteworthy, as also is the treatment of the inductive syllogism as one in which the middle term is resoluble into a group or series (*Reihe*). In indicating specifically, too, the case of conclusion from a copulative major premise with a disjunctive minor, Herbart seems to have suggested the cue for Sigwart's exposition of Bacon's method of exclusions.

Herbart.

That it was the formal character of Herbart's logic which was ultimately fatal to its acceptance outside the school as an independent discipline is not to be doubted. It stands, however, on a different footing from that of the formal logic hitherto discussed, and is not to be condemned upon quite the same grounds. In the first place, Herbart is quite aware of the nature of abstraction. In the second, there is no claim that thought at one and the same time imposes form on "the given" and is susceptible of treatment in isolation by logic. With Herbart the forms of common experience, and indeed all that we can regard as his categories, are products of the psychological mechanism and destitute of logical import. And lastly, Herbart's logic conforms to the exigencies of his system as a whole and the principle of the bare or absolute self-identity of the ultimate "reals" in particular. It is for this reason that it finally lacks real affinity to the "pure logic" of Fries. For at the basis of Herbart's speculation there lies a conception of identity foreign to the thought of Kant with his stress on synthesis, in his thoroughgoing metaphysical use of which Herbart goes back not merely to Wolff but to Leibnitz. It is no mere coincidence that his treatment of all forms of continuance and even his positive metaphysic of "reals" show affinity to Leibnitz. It was in the pressing to its extreme consequences of the conception of uncompromising identity which is to be found in Leibnitz, that the contradictions took their rise which Herbart aimed at solving, by the method of relations and his doctrine of the ultimate plurality of "reals." The logic of relations between conceptual units, themselves unaltered by the relation, seems a kind of reflection of his metaphysical method. To those, of course, for whom the only real identity is identity in difference, while identity without difference, like difference without identity, is simply a limit or a vanishing point, Herbart's logic and metaphysic will alike lack plausibility.

The setting of Herbart's logic in his thought as a whole might of itself perhaps justify separate treatment. His far-reaching influence in the development of later logic must certainly do so. Directly he affected a school of thought which contained one logician of first-rate importance in Moritz Wilhelm Drobisch (1802–1896), professor at Leipzig. In less direct relation stands Lotze, who, although under other influences he developed a different view even in logic, certainly let no point in the doctrine of his great predecessor at Göttingen escape him. A Herbartian strain is to be met with also in the thought of writers much further afield, for example F. H. Bradley, far though his metaphysic is removed from Herbart's. Herbart's influence is surely to be found too in the evolution of what is called *Gegenstandstheorie*. Nor did he affect the logic of his successors through his logic alone. Reference has been made above to the effect upon the rise of the later psychological logic produced by Herbart's psychology of apperception, when disengaged from the background of his metaphysic taken in conjunction with his treatment in his practical philosophy of the judgment of value or what he calls the aesthetic judgment. Emerson's verdict upon a greater thinker—that his was "not a mind to nestle in"—may be true of Herbart, but there can be no doubt as to the stimulating force of this master.

The second way of interpreting the antithesis of thought to what is thought of, was taken by a group of thinkers among whom a central and inspiring figure was Schleiermacher. They in no sense constitute a school and manifest radical differences among themselves. They are agreed, however, in the rejection, on the one hand, of the subjectivist logic with its intrinsic implication that knowledge veils rather than reveals the real world, and, on the other hand, of the logic of the speculative construction with its pretension to "deduce," to determine, and finally at once to cancel and conserve any antithesis in its all-embracing dialectic. They agree, then, in a maintenance of the critical point of view, while all alike recognize the necessity of bringing the thought-function in knowledge into more intimate relation with its "other" than Kant had done, by means of some formula of correlation or parallelism. Such an advance might have taken its cue directly from Kant himself. As an historical fact it tended rather to formulate itself as a reaction towards Kant in view of the course taken by the speculative movement. Thus Schleiermacher's posthumously published *Dialektik* (1839) may be characterized as an appeal from the absolutist element in Schelling's philosophy to the conception of that correlation or parallelism which Schelling had exhibited as flowing from and subsisting within his absolute, and therein as a return upon Kant's doctrine of limits. Schleiermacher's conception of dialectic is to the effect that it is concerned with the principles of the art of philosophizing, as these are susceptible of a relatively independent treatment by a permissible abstraction. Pure thinking or philosophizing is with a view to philosophy or knowledge as an interconnected system of all sciences or departmental forms of knowledge, the mark of knowledge being its identity for all thinking minds. Dialectic then investigates the nexus which must be held to obtain between all thoughts, but also that agreement with the nexus in being which is the condition of the validity of the thought-nexus. In knowing there are two functions involved, the "organic" or animal function of sensuous experience in virtue of which we are in touch with being, directly in inner perception, mediately in outer experience, and the "intellectual" function of construction. Either is indispensable, though in different departments of knowledge the predominant rôle falls to one or other, *e.g.* we are more dependent in physics, less so in ethics. The idea of a perfect harmony of thinking and being is a presupposition that underlies all knowing but cannot itself be realized in knowledge. In terms of the agreement of thought and being, the logical forms of the part of dialectic correspondent to knowledge statically considered have parallels and analogies in being, the concept being correlated to substance, the judgment to causal nexus. Inference, curiously enough, falls under the technical side of dialectic concerned with knowledge in process or becoming, a line of cleavage which Ueberweg has rightly characterized as constituting a rift within Schleiermacher's parallelism.

Logic as the rationale of knowledge.

Schleiermacher.

Schleiermacher's formula obviously ascribes a function in knowledge to thought as such, and describes in a suggestive manner a duality of the intellectual and organic functions resting on a parallelism of thought and being whose collapse into identity it is beyond human capacity to grasp. It is rather, however, a statement of a way in which the relations of the terms of the problem may be conceived than a system of necessity. It may indeed be permitted to doubt whether its influence upon subsequent theory would have been a great one apart from the spiritual force of Schleiermacher's personality. Some sort of correlationist conception, however, was an inevitable development, and the list[1] of those who accepted it in something of the spirit of Schleiermacher is a long one and contains many distinguished names, notably those of Trendelenburg and Ueberweg. The group is loosely constituted however. There was scope for diversity of view and there was diversity of view, according as the vital issue of the formula was held to lie in the relation of intellectual function to organic function or in the not quite equivalent relation of thinking to being. Moreover, few of the writers who, whatsoever it was that they baptized with the name of logic, were at least earnestly engaged in an endeavour to solve the problem of knowledge within a circle of ideas which was on the whole Kantian, were under the dominance of a single inspiration. Beneke's philosophy is a striking instance of this, with application to Fries and affinity to Herbart conjoined with obligations to Schelling both directly and through Schleiermacher. Lotze again wove together many threads of earlier thought, though the web was assuredly his own. Finally it must not be forgotten that the host of writers who were in reaction against Hegelianism tended to take refuge in some formula of correlation, as a half-way house between that and formalism or psychologism or both, without reference to, and often perhaps without consciousness of, the way in which historically it had taken shape to meet the problem held to have been left unresolved by Kant.

Lotze. Lotze on the one hand held the Hegelian "deduction" to be untenable, and classed himself with those who in his own phrase "passed to the order of the day," while on the other hand he definitely raised the question, how an "object" could be brought into forms to which it was not in some sense adapted. Accordingly, though he regards logic as formal, its forms come into relation to objectivity in some sort even within the logical field itself, while when taken in the setting of his system as a whole, its formal character is not of a kind that ultimately excludes psychological and metaphysical reference, at least speculatively. As a logician Lotze stands among the masters. His *flair* for the essentials in his problem, his subtlety of analysis, his patient willingness to return upon a difficulty from a fresh and still a fresh point of view, and finally his fineness of judgment, make his logic[2] so essentially logic of the present, and of its kind not soon to be superseded, that nothing more than an indication of the historical significance of some of its characteristic features need be attempted here.

In Lotze's pure logic it is the Herbartian element that tends to be disconcerting. Logic is formal. Its unit, the logical concept, is a manipulated product and the process of manipulation may be called abstraction. Processes of the psychological mechanism lie below it. The paradox of the theory of judgment is due to the ideal of identity, and the way in which this is evaded by supplementation to produce a non-judgmental identity, followed by translation of the introduced accessories with conditions in the hypothetical judgment, is thoroughly in Herbart's manner. The reduction of judgments is on lines already familiar. Syllogism is no instrumental method by which we compose our knowledge, but an ideal to the form of which it should be brought. It is, as it were, a schedule to be filled in, and is connected with the disjunctive judgment as a schematic setting forth of alternatives, not with the hypothetical, and ultimately the apodictic judgment with their suggestion that it is the real movement of thought that is subjected to analysis. Yet the resultant impression left by the whole treatment is not Herbartian. The concept is accounted for in Kantian terms. There is no discontinuity between the pre-logical or sub-logical conversion of impressions into "first universals" and the formation of the logical concept. Abstraction proves to be synthesis with compensatory universal marks in the place of the particular marks abstracted from. Synthesis as the work of thought always supplies, beside the mere conjunction or disjunction of ideas, a ground of their coherence or non-coherence. It is evident that thought, even as dealt with in pure logic, has an objectifying function. Its universals have objective validity, though this does not involve direct real reference. The formal conception of pure logic, then, is modified by Lotze in such a way as not only to be compatible with a view of the structural and functional adequacy of thought to that which at every point at which we take thinking is still distinguishable from thought, but even inevitably to suggest it. That the unit for logic is the concept and not the judgment has proved a stumbling-block to those of Lotze's critics who are accustomed to think in terms of the act of thought as unit. Lotze's procedure is, indeed, analogous to the way in which, in his philosophy of nature, he starts from a plurality of real beings, but by means of a reductive movement, an application of Kant's transcendental method, arrives at the postulate or fact of a law of their reciprocal action which calls for a monistic and idealist interpretation. He starts, that is in logic, with conceptual units apparently self-contained and admitting of nothing but external relation, but proceeds to justify the intrinsic relation between the matter of his units by an appeal to the fact of the coherence of all contents of thought. Indeed, if thought admits irreducible units, what can unite? Yet he is left committed to his puzzle as to a reduction of judgment to identity, which partially vitiates his treatment of the theory of judgment. The outstanding feature of this is, nevertheless, not affected, viz. the attempt that he makes, inspired clearly by Hegel, "to develop the various forms of judgment systematically as members of a series of operations, each of which leaves a part of its problem unmastered and thereby gives rise to the next."[3] As to inference, finally, the ideal of the articulation of the universe of discourse, as it is for complete knowledge, when its disjunctions have been thoroughly followed out and it is exhaustively determined, carried the day with him against the view that the organon for gaining knowledge is syllogism. The Aristotelian formula is "merely the expression, formally expanded and complete, of the truth already embodied in disjunctive judgment, namely, that every S which is a specific form of M possesses as its predicate a particular modification of each of the universal predicates of M to the exclusion of the rest." Schleiermacher's separation of inference from judgment and his attribution of the power to knowledge in process cannot find acceptance with Lotze. The psychologist and the formal logician do indeed join hands in the denial of a real movement of thought in syllogism. Lotze's logic then, is formal in a sense in which a logic which does not find the conception of synthetic truth embarrassing is not so. It is canon and not organon. In the one case, however, where it recognizes what is truly synthesis, *i.e.* in its account of the concept, it brings the statics of knowledge, so to speak, into integral relation with the dynamics. And throughout, wherever the survival from 1843, the identity bug-bear, is for the moment got rid of in what is really a more liberal conception, the statical doctrine is developed in a brilliant and informing manner. Yet it is in the detail of his logical investigations, something too volatile to fix in summary, that Lotze's greatness as a logician more especially lies.

With Lotze the ideal that at last the forms of thought shall be realized to be adequate to that which at any stage of actual knowledge always proves relatively intractable is an illuminating projection of faith. He takes courage from the reflection that to accept scepticism is to presume the competence of the thought that accepts. He will, however, take no easy way of parallelism. Our human thought pursues devious and circuitous methods. Its forms are not unseldom scaffolding for the house of knowledge rather than the framework of the house itself. Our task is not to realise correspondence with something other than thought,

[1] See Ueberweg, *System of Logic and History of Logical Doctrines*, § 34.

[2] *Drei Bücher der Logik*, 1874 (E.T., 1884). The Book on Pure Logic follows in essentials the line of thought of an earlier work (1843).

[3] *Logic*, Eng. trans. 35 *ad. fin.*

[illegible] explicit those [illegible] [illegible] our apprehension. "However much we may [illegible] [illegible] the forms of thought [illegible] [illegible] knowledge, we must be [illegible] [illegible] these many elements which do not directly [illegible] [illegible] reality [illegible] knowledge of which they are [illegible] [illegible] [illegible] immediately [illegible] The [illegible] [illegible]

[illegible]

[illegible] Hegel. [illegible] Kant's [illegible] single [illegible] Fichte [illegible] single principle [illegible] [illegible] Fichte [illegible] Kant's [illegible] Hegel [illegible]

[illegible] Fichte's Ego [illegible] Hegel [illegible]

[illegible]

[illegible] as the presence in those stages which force the [illegible] [illegible] inadequacy and the [illegible] of contradictions. Contradictions must be annulled by [illegible] with resultant increasing coherence in ascending stages. At each successive stage in our progress fresh contradictions break out, but the ideal of a state in which the thought-process and its other [illegible] [illegible], are at one is permissible as a limiting conception. [illegible] Hegel meant only this he has indeed succeeded in concealing his meaning.

Hegel's treatment of the categories or thought determinations [illegible] arise in the development of the immanent dialectic [illegible] [illegible] flashes of insight, but most of them are in the ordinary view of logic wholly metaphysical. In the stage, however, of his process in which he is concerned with the notion are to be found concept, judgment, syllogism. Of the last he declares that it "is the reasonable and everything reasonable" (*Encyk.* § 181), and has the phantasy to speak of the definition of the Absolute as being "at this stage" simply the syllogism. It is, of course, the rhythm of the syllogism that attracts him. The concept goes out from or utters itself in judgment to return to an enhanced unity in syllogism. Ueberweg (*System* § 101) is, on the whole, justified in exclaiming that Hegel's rehabilitation of syllogism "did but slight service to the Aristotelian theory of syllogism," yet his treatment of syllogism must be regarded as an acute contribution to logical criticism in the technical sense. He insists on its objectivity. The transition from judgment is not brought about by our subjective action. The syllogism of "all-ness" is convicted of a *petitio principii* (*Encyk.* § 190), with consequent lapse into the inductive syllogism, and, finally, since inductive syllogism is involved in the infinite process, into analogy. "The syllogism of necessity," on the contrary, does not presuppose its conclusion in its premises. The detail, too, of the whole discussion is rich in suggestion, and subsequent logicians—Ueberweg himself perhaps, Lotze certainly in his genetic scale of types of judgment and inference, Professor Bosanquet notably in his systematic development of "the morphology of knowledge," and others—have with reason exploited it.

Hegel's logic as a whole, however, stands and falls not with his thoughts on syllogism, but with the claim made for the dialectical method that it exhibits logic in its integral unity with metaphysic, the thought-process as the self-revelation of the Idea. The claim was disallowed. To the formalist proper it was self-condemned in its pretension to develop the content of thought and its rejection of the formula of bare-identity. To the epistemologist it seemed to confuse foundation and keystone, and to suppose itself to build upon the latter in a construction illegitimately appropriative of materials otherwise accumulated. At most it was thought to establish a schema of formal unity which might serve as a regulative ideal. To the methodologist of science in genesis it appeared altogether to fail to satisfy any practical interest. Finally, to the psychologist it spelt the failure of intellectualism, and encouraged, therefore, some form of rehabilitated experientialism.

In the Hegelian school in the narrower sense the logic of the master receives some exegesis and defence upon single points of doctrine rather than as a whole. Its effect upon logic is rather to be seen in the rethinking of the traditional body of logical doctrine in the light of an absolute presupposed as ideal, with the postulate that a regulative ideal must ultimately exhibit itself as constitutive, the justification of the postulate being held to lie in the coherence and all-inclusiveness of the result. In such a logic, if and so far as coherence should be attained, would be found something akin to the spirit of what Hegel achieves, though doubtless alien to the letter of what it is his pretension to have achieved. There is perhaps no serious misrepresentation involved in regarding a key-thought of this type, though not necessarily expressed in those verbal forms, as pervading such logic of the present as coheres with a philosophy of the absolute conceived from a point of view that is intellectualist throughout. All other contemporary movements may be said to be in revolt from Hegel.

v. *Logic from* 1880–1910

Logic in the present exhibits, though in characteristically modified shapes, all the main types that have been found in its past history. There is an intellectualist logic coalescent with an absolutist metaphysic as aforesaid. There is an epistemological logic with sometimes formalist, sometimes methodological leanings. There is a formal-symbolic logic engaged with the elaboration of a relational calculus. Finally, there is what may be termed psychological-voluntaryist logic. It is in the rapidity of development of logical investigations of the third and fourth types and the growing number of their exponents that the present shows most clearly the history of logic in the making. All these movements are logic of the present, and a very brief indication may be added of points of historical significance.

Of intellectualist logic Francis Herbert Bradley[1] (b. 1846) and Bernard Bosanquet[2] (1848) may be taken as typical exponents. The philosophy of the former concludes to an Absolute by the annulment of contradictions, though the ladder of Hegel is conspicuous by its absence. His metaphysical method, however, is like Herbart's, not identifiable with his logic, and the latter has for its central characteristic its thorough restatement of the logical forms traditional in language and the text-books, in such a way as to harmonize with the doctrine of a reality whose organic unity is all-inclusive. The thorough recasting that this involves, even of the thought of the masters when it occasionally echoes them, has resulted in a phrasing uncouth to the ear of the plain man with his world of persons and things in which the former simply think about the latter, but it is fundamentally necessary for Bradley's purpose. The negative judgment, for example, cannot be held in one and the same undivided act to presuppose the unity of the real, project an adjective as conceivably applicable to it and assert its rejection. We need, therefore, a restatement of it. With Bradley reality is the one subject of all judgment immediate or mediate. The act of judgment "which refers an ideal content (recognized as such) to a reality beyond the act" is the unit for logic. Grammatical subject and predicate necessarily both fall under the rubric of the adjectival, that is, within the logical idea or ideal content asserted. This is a meaning or universal, which can have no detached or abstract self-subsistence. As found in judgment it may exhibit differences within itself, but it is not two, but one, an articulation of unity, not a fusion, which could only be a confusion, of differences. With a brilliant subtlety Bradley analyses the various types of judgment in his own way, with results that must be taken into account by all subsequent logicians of this type. The view of inference with which he complements it is only less satisfactory because of a failure to distinguish the principle of nexus in syllogism from its traditional formulation and rules, and because he is hampered by the intractability which he finds in certain forms of relational construction.

Bosanquet had the advantage that his logic was a work of a slightly later date. He is, perhaps, more able than Bradley has shown himself, to use material from alien sources and to penetrate to what is of value in the thought of writers from whom, whether on the whole or on particular issues, he disagrees. He treats the book-tradition, however, a debt to which, nowadays inevitable, he is generous in acknowledging,[3] with a judicious exercise of freedom in adaptation, *i.e.* constructively as datum, never eclectically. In his fundamental theory of judgment his obligation is to Bradley. It is to Lotze, however, that he owes most in the characteristic feature of his logic, viz., the systematic development of the types of judgment, and inference from less adequate to more adequate forms. His fundamental continuity with Bradley may be illustrated by his definition of inference. "Inference is the indirect reference to reality of differences within a universal, by means of the exhibition of this universal in differences directly referred to reality."[4] Bosanquet's *Logic* will long retain its place as an authoritative exposition of logic of this type.

Of epistemological logic in one sense of the phrase Lotze is still to be regarded as a typical exponent. Of another type Chr. Sigwart (*q.v.*) may be named as representative. Sigwart's aim was "to reconstruct logic from the point of view of methodology." His problem was the claim to arrive at propositions universally valid, and so true of the object, whosoever the individual thinker. His solution, within the Kantian circle of ideas, was that such principles as the Kantian principle of causality were justified as "postulates of the endeavour after complete knowledge." "What Kant has shown is not that irregular fleeting changes can never be the object of consciousness, but only that the ideal consciousness of complete science would

[1] *The Principles of Logic* (1883).
[2] *Logic, or The Morphology of Thought* (2 vols., 1888).
[3] *Logic*, Pref. pp. 6 seq.
[4] *Id.* vol. ii. p. 4.

be impossible without the knowledge of the necessity of all events.[1] "The universal presuppositions which form the outline of our ideal of knowledge are not so much laws which the understanding prescribes to nature . . . as laws which the understanding lays down for its own regulation in its investigation and consideration of nature. They are a priori because no experience is sufficient to reveal or confirm them in unconditional universality; but they are a priori . . . only in the sense of presuppositions without which we should work with no hope of success and merely at random and which therefore we must believe." Finally they are akin to our ethical principles. With this coheres his dictum, with its far-reaching consequences for the philosophy of induction, that "the logical justification of the inductive process rests upon the fact that it is an inevitable postulate of our effort after knowledge, that the given is necessary, and can be known as proceeding from its grounds according to universal laws."[2] It is characteristic of Sigwart's point of view that he acknowledges obligation to Mill as well as to Ueberweg. The transmutation of Mill's induction of inductions into a postulate is an advance of which the psychological school of logicians have not been slow to make use. The comparison of Sigwart with Lotze is instructive, in regard both to their agreement and their divergence as showing the range of the epistemological formula.

Of the formal-symbolic logic all that falls to be said here is, that from the point of view of logic as a whole, it is to be regarded as a legitimate praxis as long as it shows itself aware of the sense in which alone form is susceptible of abstraction, and is aware that in itself it offers no solution of the logical problem. "It is not an algebra," said Kant[3] of his technical logic, and the kind of support lent recently to symbolic logic by the *Gegenstandstheorie* identified with the name of Alexius Meinong (b. 1853)[4] is qualified by the warning that the real activity of thought tends to fall outside the calculus of relations and to attach rather to the subsidiary function of denoting. The future of symbolic logic as coherent with the rest of logic, in the sense which the word has borne throughout its history seems to be bound up with the question of the nature of the analysis that lies behind the symbolism, and of the way in which this is justified in the setting of a doctrine of validity. The "theory of the object," itself, while affecting logic alike in the formal and in the psychological conception of it very deeply, does not claim to be regarded as logic or a logic, apart from a setting supplied from elsewhere.

Finally we have a logic of a type fundamentally psychological, if it be not more properly characterized as a psychology which claims to cover the whole field of philosophy, including the logical field. The central and organizing principle of this is that knowledge is in genesis, that the genesis takes place in the medium of individual minds, and that this fact implies that there is a necessary reference throughout to interests or purposes of the subject which thinks because it wills and acts. Historically this doctrine was formulated as the declaration of independence of the insurgents in revolt against the pretensions of absolutist logic. It drew for support upon the psychological movement that begins with Fries and Herbart. It has been chiefly indebted to writers, who were not, or were not primarily, logicians, to Avenarius, for example, for the law of the economy of thought, to Wundt, whose system, and therewith his logic,[5] is a pendant to his psychology, for the volitional character of judgment, to Herbert Spencer and others. A judgment is practical, and not to be divorced without improper abstraction from the purpose and will that informs it. A concept is instrumental to an end beyond itself, without any validity other than its value for action. A situation involving a need of adaptation to environment arises and the problem it sets must be solved that the will may control environment and be justified by success. Truth is the improvised machinery that is interjected, so far as this works. It is clear that we are in the presence of what is at least an important half-truth, which intellectualism with its statics of the rational order viewed as a completely articulate system has tended to ignore. It throws light on many phases of the search for truth, upon the plain man's claim to start with a subject which he knows whose predicate which he does not know is still to be developed, or again upon his use of the negative form of judgment, when the further determination of his purposive system is served by a positive judgment from without, the positive content of which is yet to be dropped as irrelevant to the matter in hand. The movement has, however, scarcely developed its logic[6] except as polemic. What seems clear is that it cannot be the whole solution. While man must confront nature from the human and largely the practical standpoint, yet his control is achieved only by the increasing recognition of objective controls. He conquers by obedience. So truth works and is economical because it is truth. Working is proportioned to inner coherence. It is well that the view should be developed into all its consequences. The result will be to limit it, though perhaps also to justify it, save in its claim to reign alone.

There is, perhaps, an increasing tendency to recognize that the organism of knowledge is a thing which from any single viewpoint must be seen in perspective. It is of course a postulate that all truths harmonize, but to give the harmonious whole in a projection in one plane is an undertaking whose adequacy in one sense involves an inadequacy in another. No human architect can hope to take up in succession all essential points of view in regard to the form of knowledge or to logic. "The great campanile is still to finish."

[1] *Logik* (1873, 1889), Eng. trans. ii. 17.
[2] *Op. cit.* ii. 289.
[3] *Introd. to Logic.*, trans. Abbott, p. 10.
[4] *Ueber Annahmen* (1902, &c.).
[5] *Logik* (1880, and in later editions).

BIBLIOGRAPHY.—Historical: No complete history of logic in the sense in which it is to be distinguished from theoretical philosophy in general has as yet been written. The history of logic is indeed so little intelligible apart from constant reference to tendencies in philosophical development as a whole, that the historian, when he has made the requisite preparatory studies, inclines to essay the more ambitious task. Yet there are, of course, works devoted to the history of logic proper.

Of these Prantl's *Geschichte der Logik im Abendlande* (4 vols. 1855-1870), which traces the rise, development and fortunes of the Aristotelian logic to the close of the middle ages, is monumental. Next in importance are the works of L. Rabus, *Logik und Metaphysik*, i. (1868) (pp. 123-242 historical, pp. 453-518 bibliographical, pp. 514 sqq. a section on apparatus for the study of the history of logic), *Die neuesten Bestrebungen auf dem Gebiete der Logik bei den Deutschen* (1880), *Logik* (1895), especially for later writers § 17. Ueberweg's *System der Logik und Geschichte der logischen Lehren* (4th ed. and last revised by the author, 1874, though it has been reissued later, Eng. trans., 1871) is alone to be named with these. Harms' posthumously published *Geschichte der Logik* (1881) (*Die Philosophie in ihrer Geschichte*, ii.) was completed by the author only so far as Leibnitz. Blakey's *Historical Sketch of Logic* (1851), though, like all this writer's works, closing with a bibliography of some pretensions, is now negligible. Franck, *Esquisse d'une histoire de la logique* (1838) is the chief French contribution to the subject as a whole.

Of contributions towards the history of special periods or schools of logical thought the list, from the opening chapters of Ramus's *Scholae Dialecticae* (1569) downwards (v. Rabus *loc. cit.*) would be endless. What is of value in the earlier works has now been absorbed. The *System der Logik* (1828) of Bachmann (a Kantian logician of distinction) contains a historical survey (pp. 569-644), as does the *Denklehre* (1822) of van Calker (allied in thought to Fries), pp. 12 sqq.; Eberstein's *Geschichte der Logik und Metaphysik bei den Deutschen von Leibniz bis auf gegenwärtige Zeit* (latest edition, 1799) is still of importance in regard to logicians of the school of Wolff and the *origines* of Kant's logical thought. Hoffmann, the editor and disciple of von Baader, published *Grundzüge einer Geschichte der Begriffe der Logik in Deutschland von Kant bis Baader* (1851). Wallace's prolegomena and notes to his *Logic of Hegel* (1874, revised and augmented 1892-1894) are of use for the history and terminology, as well as the theory. Riehl's article entitled *Logik* in *Die Kultur der Gegenwart*, vi. 1. *Systematische Philosophie* (1907), is excellent, and touches on quite modern developments. Liard, *Les Logiciens Anglais Contemporains* (5th ed., 1907), deals only with the 19th-century inductive and formal-symbolic logicians down to Jevons, to whom the book was originally dedicated. Venn's *Symbolic Logic* (1881) gave a careful history and bibliography of that development. The history of the more recent changes is as yet to be found only in the form of unshaped material in the pages of review and *Jahresbericht*. (H. W. B.*)

[6] Yet see *Studies in Logic*, by John Dewey and others (1903).

LOGOCYCLIC CURVE, STROPHOID or **FOLIATE**, a cubic curve generated by increasing or diminishing the radius vector of a variable point Q on a straight line AB by the distance QC of the point from the foot of the perpendicular drawn from the origin to the fixed line. The polar equation is $r\cos\theta = a(1 \pm \sin\theta)$, the upper sign referring to the case when the vector is increased, the lower when it is diminished. Both branches are included in the Cartesian equation $(x^2+y^2)(2a-x) = a^2x$, where a is the distance of the line from the origin. If we take for axes the fixed line and the perpendicular through the initial point, the equation takes the form $y\sqrt{(a-x)} = x\sqrt{(a+x)}$. The curve resembles the folium of Descartes, and has a node between $x=0$, $x=a$, and two branches asymptotic to the line $x=2a$.

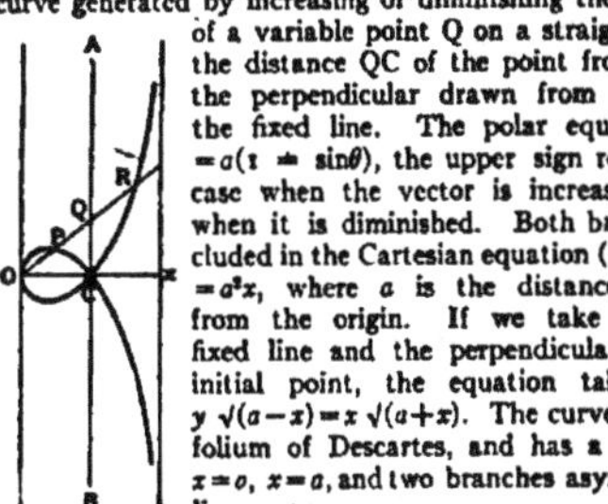

LOGOGRAPHI (λόγος, γράφω, writers of prose histories or tales), the name given by modern scholars to the Greek historiographers before Herodotus.[1] Thucydides, however, applies the term to all his own predecessors, and it is therefore usual to make a distinction between the older and the younger logographers. Their representatives, with one exception, came from Ionia and its islands, which from their position were most favourably situated for the acquisition of knowledge concerning the distant countries of East and West. They wrote in the Ionic dialect, in what was called the unperiodic style, and preserved the poetic character of their epic model. Their criticism amounts to nothing more than a crude attempt to rationalize the current legends and traditions connected with the founding of cities, the genealogies of ruling families, and the manners and customs of individual peoples. Of scientific criticism there is no trace whatever. The first of these historians was probably Cadmus of Miletus (who lived, if at all, in the early part of the 6th century), the earliest writer of prose, author of a work on the founding of his native city and the colonization of Ionia (so Suïdas); Pherecydes of Leros, who died about 400, is generally considered the last. Mention may also be made of the following: Hecataeus of Miletus (550–476); Acusilaus of Argos,[2] who paraphrased in prose (correcting the tradition where it seemed necessary) the genealogical works of Hesiod in the Ionic dialect; he confined his attention to the prehistoric period, and made no attempt at a real history; Charon of Lampsacus (*c.* 450), author of histories of Persia, Libya, and Ethiopia, of annals (ὧροι) of his native town with lists of the prytaneis and archons, and of the chronicles of Lacedaemonian kings; Xanthus of Sardis in Lydia (*c.* 450), author of a history of Lydia, one of the chief authorities used by Nicolaus of Damascus (*fl.* during the time of Augustus); Hellanicus of Mytilene; Stesimbrotus of Thasos, opponent of Pericles and reputed author of a political pamphlet on Themistocles, Thucydides and Pericles; Hippys and Glaucus, both of Rhegium, the first the author of histories of Italy and Sicily, the second of a treatise on ancient poets and musicians, used by Harpocration and Plutarch; Damastes of Sigeum, pupil of Hellanicus, author of genealogies of the combatants before Troy (an ethnographic and statistical list), of short treatises on poets, sophists, and geographical subjects.

On the early Greek historians, see G. Busolt, *Griechische Geschichte* (1893), i. 147-153; C. Wachsmuth, *Einleitung in das Studium der alten Geschichte* (1895); A. Schäfer, *Abriss der Quellenkunde der griechischen und römischen Geschichte* (ed. H. Nissen, 1889); J. B. Bury, *Ancient Greek Historians* (1909), lecture i.; histories of Greek literature by Müller-Donaldson (ch. 18) and W. Mure (bk. iv. ch. 3), where the little that is known concerning the life and writings of the logographers is exhaustively discussed. The fragments will be found, with Latin notes, translation, prolegomena, and copious indexes, in C. W. Müller's *Fragmenta historicorum Graecorum* (1841-1870). See also GREECE: *History, Ancient* (section, "Authorities").

[1] The word is also used of the writers of speeches for the use of the contending parties in the law courts, who were forbidden to employ advocates.

[2] There is some doubt as to whether this Acusilaus was of Peloponnesian or Boeotian Argos. Possibly there were two of the name. For an example of the method of Acusilaus see Bury, *op. cit.* p. 19.

LOGOS (λόγος), a common term in ancient philosophy and theology. It expresses the idea of an immanent reason in the world, and, under various modifications, is met with in Indian, Egyptian and Persian systems of thought. But the idea was developed mainly in Hellenic and Hebrew philosophy, and we may distinguish the following stages:

1. *The Hellenic Logos.*—To the Greek mind, which saw in the world a κόσμος (ordered whole), it was natural to regard the world as the product of reason, and reason as the ruling principle in the world. So we find a Logos doctrine more or less prominent from the dawn of Hellenic thought to its eclipse. It rises in the realm of physical speculation, passes over into the territory of ethics and theology, and makes its way through at least three well-defined stages. These are marked off by the names of Heraclitus of Ephesus, the Stoics and Philo.

It acquires its first importance in the theories of Heraclitus (6th century B.C.), who, trying to account for the aesthetic order of the visible universe, broke away to some extent from the purely physical conceptions of his predecessors and discerned at work in the cosmic process a λόγος analogous to the reasoning power in man. On the one hand the Logos is identified with γνώμη and connected with δίκη, which latter seems to have the function of correcting deviations from the eternal law that rules in things. On the other hand it is not positively distinguished either from the ethereal fire, or from the εἱμαρμένη and the ἀνάγκη according to which all things occur. Heraclitus holds that nothing material can be thought of without this Logos, but he does not conceive the Logos itself to be immaterial. Whether it is regarded as in any sense possessed of intelligence and consciousness is a question variously answered. But there is most to say for the negative. This Logos is not one above the world or prior to it, but in the world and inseparable from it. Man's soul is a part of it. It is *relation*, therefore, as Schleiermacher expresses it, or reason, not speech or word. And it is objective, not subjective, reason. Like a law of nature, objective in the world, it gives order and regularity to the movement of things, and makes the system rational.[3]

The failure of Heraclitus to free himself entirely from the physical hypotheses of earlier times prevented his speculation from influencing his successors. With Anaxagoras a conception entered which gradually triumphed over that of Heraclitus, namely, the conception of a supreme, intellectual principle, not identified with the world but independent of it. This, however, was νοῦς, not Logos. In the Platonic and Aristotelian systems, too, the theory of ideas involved an absolute separation between the material world and the world of higher reality, and though the term Logos is found the conception is vague and undeveloped. With Plato the term selected for the expression of the principle to which the order visible in the universe is due is νοῦς or σοφία, not λόγος. It is in the pseudo-Platonic *Epinomis* that λόγος appears as a synonym for νοῦς. In Aristotle, again, the principle which sets all nature under the rule of thought, and directs it towards a rational end, is νοῦς, or the divine spirit itself; while λόγος is a term with many senses, used as more or less identical with a number of phrases, οὗ ἕνεκα, ἐνέργεια, ἐντελέχεια, οὐσία, εἶδος, μορφή, &c.

In the reaction from Platonic dualism, however, the Logos doctrine reappears in great breadth. It is a capital element in the system of the Stoics. With their teleological views of the world they naturally predicated an active principle pervading it and determining it. This operative principle is called both Logos and God. It is conceived of as material, and is described in terms used equally of nature and of God. There is at the same time the special doctrine of the λόγος σπερματικός, the seminal Logos, or the law of generation in the world, the principle of the active reason working in dead matter. This parts into λόγοι σπερματικοί, which are akin, not to the Platonic ideas, but rather to the λόγοι ἔνυλοι of Aristotle. In man, too, there is a Logos which is his characteristic possession, and which is ἐνδιάθετος, as long as it is a thought resident within his breast,

[3] Cf. Schleiermacher's *Herakleitos der Dunkle*; art. HERACLITUS and authorities there quoted.

but προφορικός when it is expressed as a word. This distinction between Logos as *ratio* and Logos as *oratio*, so much used subsequently by Philo and the Christian fathers, had been so far anticipated by Aristotle's distinction between the ἔξω λόγος and the λόγος ἐν τῇ ψυχῇ. It forms the point of attachment by which the Logos doctrine connected itself with Christianity. The Logos of the Stoics (*q.v.*) is a reason in the world gifted with intelligence, and analogous to the reason in man.

2. *The Hebrew Logos.*—In the later Judaism the earlier anthropomorphic conception of God and with it the sense of the divine nearness had been succeeded by a belief which placed God at a remote distance, severed from man and the world by a deep chasm. The old familiar name Yahweh became a secret; its place was taken by such general expressions as the Holy, the Almighty, the Majesty on High, the King of Kings, and also by the simple word "Heaven." Instead of the once powerful confidence in the immediate presence of God there grew up a mass of speculation regarding on the one hand the distant future, on the other the distant past. Various attempts were made to bridge the gulf between God and man, including the angels, and a number of other hybrid forms of which it is hard to say whether they are personal beings or abstractions. The Wisdom, the Shekinah or Glory, and the Spirit of God are intermediate beings of this kind, and even the Law came to be regarded as an independent spiritual entity. Among these conceptions that of the Word of God had an important place, especially the creative Word of Genesis i. Here as in the other cases we cannot always say whether the Word is regarded as a mere attribute or activity of God, or an independent being, though there is a clear tendency towards the latter. The ambiguity lies in the twofold purpose of these activities: (1) to establish communication with God; (2) to prevent direct connexion between God and the world. The word of the God of revelation is represented as the creative principle (*e.g.* Gen. i. 3; Psalm xxxiii. 6), as the executor of the [illegible] judgments (Hosea vi. 5), as healing (Psalm cvii. 20), as [illegible] of almost personal qualities (Isaiah lv. 11; Psalm [illegible] 15). Along with this comes the doctrine of the angel of [illegible], the angel of the covenant, the angel of the presence, in [illegible] God manifests Himself, and who is sometimes identified [illegible] Yahweh or Elohim (Gen. xvi. 11, 13; xxxii. 29-31; Exod. [illegible] 21), sometimes distinguished from Him (Gen. xxii. [illegible] 7; xxviii. 12, &c.), and sometimes presented [illegible] (Judges ii., vi.; Zech. i.). To this must be [illegible] doctrine of Wisdom, given in the books of Job and [illegible]. At one time it is exhibited as an attribute of God [illegible]. At another it is strongly personified, so as to [illegible] the creative thought of God than a quality (Prov [illegible] it is described as proceeding from God as the [illegible] and objective to Him. In these and [illegible] Job xv. 7, &c.) it is on the way to become [illegible].

[illegible] is partially associated with the Greek in [illegible] the predecessor of Philo, and, according [illegible] of the Alexandrian school. He speaks of [illegible] us of the book of Proverbs. The [illegible] *Wisdom* (generally supposed to be the [illegible] somewhere between Aristobulus [illegible] the Wisdom and with the Logos. It [illegible]. But it represents the former as the [illegible] power or spirit of God, active alike in [illegible] and the ethical domain, and apparently [illegible] Targums, on the other hand, the three [illegible], and the wisdom of God converge [illegible]. In the Jewish theology God is re-[illegible], having no likeness of nature with [illegible] entrance into history. Instead of [illegible] to the world the Targums introduce [illegible] and the *Shechînâ* (real presence). [illegible] as it is also designated, *Dibbûrâ*, is a [illegible] God when direct intercourse with [illegible] passages of the Old Testament where [illegible] of God, the Memra is substituted [illegible] from God, and retains the creaturely [illegible] to have been identified with the [illegible]

3. *Philo.*—In the Alexandrian philosophy, as represented by the Hellenized Jew Philo, the Logos doctrine assumes a leading place and shapes a new career for itself. Philo's doctrine is moulded by three forces—Platonism, Stoicism and Hebraism. He detaches the Logos idea from its connexion with Stoic materialism and attaches it to a thorough-going Platonism. It is Plato's idea of the Good regarded as creatively active. Hence, instead of being merely immanent in the Cosmos, it has an independent existence. Platonic too is the doctrine of the divine architect who seeks to realize in the visible universe the archetypes already formed in his mind. Philo was thus able to make the Logos theory a bridge between Judaism and Greek philosophy. It preserved the monotheistic idea yet afforded a description of the Divine activity in terms of Hellenic thought; the Word of the Old Testament is one with the λόγοι of the Stoics. And thus in Philo's conception the Logos is much more than "the principle of reason, informing the infinite variety of things, and so creating the World-Order"; it is also the divine dynamic, the energy and self-revelation of God. The Stoics indeed sought, more or less consciously, by their doctrine of the Logos as the Infinite Reason to escape from the belief in a divine Creator, but Philo, Jew to the core, starts from the Jewish belief in a supreme, self-existing God, to whom the reason of the world must be subordinated though related. The conflict of the two conceptions (the Greek and the Hebrew) led him into some difficulty; sometimes he represents the Logos as an independent and even personal being, a "second God," sometimes as merely an aspect of the divine activity. And though passages of the first class must no doubt be explained figuratively—for Philo would not assert the existence of two Divine agents—it remains true that the two conceptions cannot be fused. The Alexandrian philosopher wavers between the two theories and has to accord to the Logos of Hellas a semi-independent position beside the supreme God of Judaea. He speaks of the Logos (1) as the agency by which God reveals Himself, in some measure to all men, in greater degree to chosen souls. The appearances recorded in the Old Testament are manifestations of the Logos, and the knowledge of God possessed by the great leaders and teachers of Israel is due to the same source; (2) as the agency whereby man, enmeshed by illusion, lays hold of the higher spiritual life and rising above his partial point of view participates in the universal reason. The Logos is thus the means of redemption; those who realize its activity being emancipated from the tyranny of circumstance into the freedom of the eternal.

4. *The Fourth Gospel.*—Among the influences that shaped the Fourth Gospel that of the Alexandrian philosophy must be assigned a distinct, though not an exaggerated importance. There are other books in the New Testament that bear the same impress, the epistles to the Ephesians and the Colossians, and to a much greater degree the epistle to the Hebrews. The development that had thus begun in the time of Paul reaches maturity in the Fourth Gospel, whose dependence on Philo appears (1) in the use of the allegorical method, (2) in many coincident passages, (3) in the dominant conception of the Logos. The writer narrates the life of Christ from the point of view furnished him by Philo's theory. True, the Logos doctrine is only mentioned in the prologue to the Gospel, but it is presupposed throughout the whole book. The author's task indeed was somewhat akin to that of Philo, "to transplant into the world of Hellenic culture a revelation originally given through Judaism." This is not to say that he holds the Logos doctrine in exactly the same form as Philo. On the contrary, the fact that he starts from an actual knowledge of the earthly life of Jesus

[illegible] the Pentateuch under Gen. vii. 16, [illegible] &c.; the Jerusalem Targum on Numb. vii. 89, &c. For further information regarding the Hebrew *Logos* see, beside Dr Kaufmann Kohler, *s.v.* "Memra," *Jewish Encyc.* viii. 464-465, Bousset, *Die Religion des Judenthums* (1903), p. 341, and Weber, *Jüdische Theologie* (1897), pp. 180-184. The hypostatizing of the Divine Word in the doctrine of the Memra was probably later than the time of Philo, but it was the outcome of a mode of thinking already common in Jewish theology. The same tendency is of course expressed in the "Logos" of the Fourth Gospel.

while Philo, even when ascribing a real personality to the Logos, keeps within the bounds of abstract speculation, leads him seriously to modify the Philonic doctrine. Though the Alexandrian idea largely determines the evangelist's treatment of the history, the history similarly reacts on the idea. The prologue is an organic portion of the Gospel and not a preface written to conciliate a philosophic public. It assumes that the Logos idea is familiar in Christian theology, and vividly summarizes the main features of the Philonic conception—the eternal existence of the Logos, its relation to God (πρὸς τὸν θεόν, yet distinct), its creative, illuminative and redemptive activity. But the adaptation of the idea to John's account of a historical person involved at least three profound modifications:—(1) the Logos, instead of the abstraction or semi-personification of Philo, becomes fully personified. The Word that became flesh subsisted from all eternity as a distinct personality within the divine nature. (2) Much greater stress is laid upon the redemptive than upon the creative function. The latter indeed is glanced at ("All things were made by him"), merely to provide a link with earlier speculation, but what the writer is concerned about is not the mode in which the world came into being but the spiritual life which resides in the Logos and is communicated by him to men. (3) The idea of λόγος as Reason becomes subordinated to the idea of λόγος as Word, the expression of God's will and power, the outgoing of the divine energy, life, love and light. Thus in its fundamental thought the prologue of the Fourth Gospel comes nearer to the Old Testament (and especially to Gen. i.) than to Philo. As speech goes out from a man and reveals his character and thought, so Christ is "sent out from the Father," and as the divine Word is also, in accordance with the Hebrew idea, the medium of God's quickening power.

What John thus does is to take the Logos idea of Philo and use it for a practical purpose—to make more intelligible to himself and his readers the divine nature of Jesus Christ. That this endeavour to work into the historical tradition of the life and teaching of Jesus—a hypothesis which had a distinctly foreign origin—led him into serious difficulties is a consideration that must be discussed elsewhere.

5. *The Early Church.*—In many of the early Christian writers, as well as in the heterodox schools, the Logos doctrine is influenced by the Greek idea. The Syrian Gnostic Basilides held (according to Irenaeus i. 24) that the Logos or Word emanated from the νοῦς, or personified reason, as this latter emanated from the unbegotten Father. The completest type of Gnosticism, the Valentinian, regarded Wisdom as the last of the series of aeons that emanated from the original Being or Father, and the Logos as an emanation from the first two principles that issued from God, Reason (νοῦς) and Truth. Justin Martyr, the first of the sub-apostolic fathers, taught that God produced of His own nature a rational power (δύναμίν τινα λογικήν), His agent in creation, who now became man in Jesus (*Dial. c. Tryph.* chap. 48, 60). He affirmed also the action of the λόγος σπερματικός, (*Apol.* i. 46; ii. 13, &c.). With Tatian (*Cohort. ad. Gr.* chap. 5, &c.) the Logos is the beginning of the world, the reason that comes into being as the sharer of God's rational power. With Athenagoras (*Suppl.* chap. 9, 10) He is the prototype of the world and the energizing principle (ἰδέα καὶ ἐνέργεια) of things. Theophilus (*Ad Autolyc.* ii. 10, 24) taught that the Logos was in eternity with God as the λόγος ἐνδιάθετος, the counsellor of God, and that when the world was to be created God sent forth this counsellor (σύμβουλος) from Himself as the λόγος προφορικός, yet so that the begotten Logos did not cease to be a part of Himself. With Hippolytus (*Refut.* x. 32, &c.) the Logos, produced of God's own substance, is both the divine intelligence that appears in the world as the Son of God, and the idea of the universe immanent in God. The early Sabellians (comp. Eusebius, *Hist. Eccl.* vi. 33; Athanasius, *Contra Arian.* iv.) held that the Logos was a faculty of God, the divine reason, immanent in God eternally, but not in distinct personality prior to the historical manifestation in Christ. Origen, referring the act of creation to eternity instead of to time, affirmed the eternal personal existence of the Logos. In relation to God this Logos or Son was a copy of the original, and as such inferior to that. In relation to the world he was its prototype, the ἰδέα ἰδεῶν and its redeeming power (*Contra Cels.* v. 608; *Frag. de princip.* i. 4; *De princip.* i. 109, 324).

In the later developments of Hellenic speculation nothing essential was added to the doctrine of the Logos. Philo's distinction between God and His rational power or Logos in contact with the world was generally maintained by the eclectic Platonists and Neo-Platonists. By some of these this distinction was carried out to the extent of predicating (as was done by Numenius of Apamea) three Gods:—the supreme God; the second God, or Demiurge or Logos; and the third God, or the world. Plotinus explained the λόγοι as constructive forces, proceeding from the ideas and giving form to the dead matter of sensible things (*Enneads*, v. 1. 8 and Richter's *Neu-Plat. Studien*).

See the histories of philosophy and theology, and works quoted under HERACLITUS, STOICS, PHILO, JOHN, THE GOSPEL OF, &c., and for a general summary of the growth of the Logos doctrine, E. Caird, *Evolution of Theology in the Greek Philosophers* (1904), vol. ii.; A. Harnack, *History of Dogma*; E. F. Scott, *The Fourth Gospel*, ch. v. (1906); J. M. Heinze, *Die Lehre vom Logos in der griech. Philosophie* (1872); J. Réville, *La Doctrine du Logos* (1881); Aal, *Gesch. d. Logos-Idee* (1899); and the *Histories of Dogma*, by A. Harnack, F. Loofs, R. Seeberg. (S. D. F. S.; A. J. G.)

LOGOTHETE (Med. Lat. *logotheta*, Gr. λογοθέτης, from λόγος, word, account, calculation, and τιθέναι, to set, *i.e.* "one who accounts, calculates or ratiocinates"), originally the title of a variety of administrative officials in the Byzantine Empire, *e.g.* the λογοθέτης τοῦ δρόμου, who was practically the equivalent of the modern postmaster-general; and the λογοθέτης τοῦ στρατιωτικοῦ, the logothete of the military chest. Gibbon defines the great Logothete as "the supreme guardian of the laws and revenues," who "is compared with the chancellor of the Latin monarchies." From the Eastern Empire the title was borrowed by the West, though it only became firmly established in Sicily, where the *logotheta* occupied the position of chancellor elsewhere, his office being equal if not superior to that of the *magnus cancellarius*. Thus the title was borne by Pietro della Vigna, the all-powerful minister of the emperor Frederick II., king of Sicily.

See Du Cange, *Glossarium*, s.v. *Logotheta*.

LOGROÑO, an inland province of northern Spain, the smallest of the eight provinces formed in 1833 out of Old Castile; bounded N. by Burgos, Álava and Navarre, W. by Burgos, S. by Soria and E. by Navarre and Saragossa. Pop. (1900) 189,376; area, 1946 sq. m. Logroño belongs entirely to the basin of the river Ebro, which forms its northern boundary except for a short distance near San Vicente; it is drained chiefly by the rivers Tiron, Oja, Najerilla, Iregua, Leza, Cidacos and Alhama, all flowing in a north-easterly direction. The portion skirting the Ebro forms a spacious and for the most part fertile undulating plain, called La Rioja, but in the south Logroño is considerably broken up by offshoots from the sierras which separate that river from the Douro. In the west the Cerro de San Lorenzo, the culminating point of the Sierra de la Demanda, rises 7562 ft., and in the south the Pico de Urbion reaches 7388 ft. The products of the province are chiefly cereals, good oil and wine (especially in the Rioja), fruit, silk, flax and honey. Wine is the principal export, although after 1892 this industry suffered greatly from the protective duties imposed by France. Great efforts have been made to keep a hold upon French and English markets with light red and white Rioja wines. No less than 128,000 acres are covered with vines, and 21,000 with olive groves. Iron and argentiferous lead are mined in small quantities and other ores have been discovered. The manufacturing industries are insignificant. A railway along the right bank of the Ebro connects the province with Saragossa, and from Miranda there is railway communication with Madrid, Bilbao and France; but there is no railway in the southern districts, where trade is much retarded by the lack even of good roads. The town of Logroño (pop. 1900, 19,237) and the city of Calahorra (9475) are separately described. The only other towns with upwards of 5000 inhabitants are Haro (7914), Alfaro (5938) and Cervera del Rio Alhama (5930).

LOGROÑO, the capital of the Spanish province of Logroño, on the right bank of the river Ebro and on the Saragossa-Miranda de Ebro railway. Pop. (1900) 19,237. Logroño is an ancient walled town, finely situated on a hill 1204 ft. high. Its bridge of twelve arches across the Ebro was built in 1138, but has frequently been restored after partial destruction by floods. The main street, arcaded on both sides, and the crooked but highly picturesque alleys of the older quarters are in striking contrast with the broad, tree-shaded avenues and squares laid out in modern times. The chief buildings are a bull-ring which accommodates 11,000 spectators, and a church, Santa Maria de Palacio, called "the imperial," from the tradition that its founder was Constantine the Great (274–337). As the commercial centre of the fertile and well-cultivated plain of the Rioja, Logroño has an important trade in wine.

The district of Logroño was in ancient times inhabited by the *Berones* or *Verones* of Strabo and Pliny, and their *Varia* is to be identified with the modern suburb of the city of Logroño now known as Varea of Barea. Logroño was named by the Romans *Juliobriga* and afterwards *Lucronius*. It fell into the hands of the Moors in the 8th century, but was speedily retaken by the Christians, and under the name of Lucronius appears with frequency in medieval history. It was unsuccessfully besieged by the French in 1521, and occupied by them from 1808 to 1813. It was the birthplace of the dumb painter Juan Fernandez Navarrete (1526–1579).

LOGROSCINO (or Lo Groscino), **NICOLA** (1700?–1763?), Italian musical composer, was born at Naples and was a pupil of Durante. In 1738 he collaborated with Leo and others in the hasty production of *Demetrio*; in the autumn of the same year he produced a comic opera *L'inganno per inganno*, the first of a long series of comic operas, the success of which won him the name of "il Dio dell' opera buffa." He went to Palermo, prob[illegible] as a teacher of counterpoint; as an opera composer he is last heard of in 1760, and is supposed to have died about 1763. Logroscino has been credited with the invention of the concerted operatic finale, but as far as can be seen from the score of *Il Governatore* and the few remaining fragments of other operas, his finales show no advance upon those of Leo. As a musical humorist, however, he deserves remembrance, and may fairly be classed alongside of Rossini.

LOGWOOD (so called from the form in which it is imported), the heart wood of a leguminous tree, *Haematoxylon campechi*[illegible], native of Central America, and grown also in the West Indian Islands. The tree attains a height not exceeding 40 ft., and is said to be ready for felling when about ten years old. The wood, deprived of its bark and the sap-wood, is sent into the market in the form of large blocks and billets. It is very [illegible] and externally has a dark brownish-red colour; [illegible] less deeply coloured within. The best qualities come from Campeachy, but it is obtained there only in small quantity. Logwood is used in dyeing (*q.v.*), in microscopy, in the prepara[illegible] and to a small extent in medicine on account of the [illegible] contains, though it has no special medicinal value, [illegible] inferior to kino and catechu. The wood was introduced into Europe as a dyeing substance soon after the discovery [illegible], but from 1581 to 1662 its use in England was pro[illegible] legislative enactment on account of the inferior dyes [illegible] were produced by its employment.

[illegible] principle of logwood exists in the timber in the form [illegible] which it is liberated as haematoxylin by fer[illegible] [haemat]oxylin, $C_{16}H_{14}O_6$, was isolated by M. E. Chevreul [illegible] a crystalline hydrate, $C_{16}H_{14}O_6+3H_2O$, which is [illegible] very sparingly soluble in cold water, but dissolving [illegible] in alcohol. By exposure to the air, especially [illegible] haematoxylin is rapidly oxidized into haematein, [illegible] development of a fine purple colour. This re[illegible] is exceedingly rapid and delicate, rendering [illegible] test for alkalis. By the action of hydrogen [illegible] haematein is easily reduced to haematoxylin. [illegible] to brazilin, found in brazil-wood. Hae[illegible] and also their oxidation products, haematin [illegible] elucidated by W. H. Perkin and his pupils [illegible] 1909).

[illegible] state of India, in the south-east corner of [illegible] district and Rajputana. Area, 222 [illegible]; estimated gross revenue, £4800. [illegible] nawab, is a Mahommedan, of Afghan [illegible] Amir-ud-din-Ahmad Khan, K.C.I.E., [illegible]'s legislative council, was until [illegible] of the state of Maler Kotla. [illegible] population in 1901 of 2175.

[illegible] **WILHELM** (1808–1872), German [illegible] born on the 21st of February 1808 in Fürth near Nuremberg, and was educated at the universities of Erlangen and Berlin. In 1831 he was appointed vicar at Kirchenlamitz, where his fervent evangelical preaching attracted large congregations and puzzled the ecclesiastical authorities. A similar experience ensued at Nuremberg, where he was assistant pastor of St Egidia. In 1837 he became pastor in Neuendettelsau, a small and unattractive place, where his life's work was done, and which he transformed into a busy and influential community. He was interested in the spiritual condition of Germans who had emigrated to the United States, and built two training homes for missionaries to them. In 1849 he founded the Lutheran Society of Home Missions and in 1853 an institution of deaconesses. Other institutions were added to these, including a lunatic asylum, a Magdalen refuge, and hospitals for men and women. In theology Löhe was a strict Lutheran, but his piety was of a most attractive kind. Originality of conception, vividness of presentation, fertility of imagination, wide knowledge of Scripture and a happy faculty of applying it, intense spiritual fervour, a striking physique and a powerful voice made him a great pulpit force. He wrote a good deal, amongst his books being *Drei Bücher von der Kirche* (1845), *Samenkörner des Gebetes* (over 30 editions) and several volumes of sermons. He died on the 2nd of January 1872.

See his *Life*, by J. Deinzer (3 vols., Gütersloh, 1873, 3rd ed., 1901).

LOHENGRIN, the hero of the German version of the legend of the knight of the swan. The story of Lohengrin as we know it is based on two principal motives common enough in folklore: the metamorphosis of human beings into swans, and the curious wife whose question brings disaster. Lohengrin's guide (the swan) was originally the little brother who, in one version of "the Seven Swans," was compelled through the destruction of his golden chain to remain in swan form and attached himself to the fortunes of one of his brothers. The swan played a part in classical mythology as the bird of Apollo, and in Scandinavian lore the swan maidens, who have the gift of prophecy and are sometimes confused with the Valkyries, reappear again and again. The wife's desire to know her husband's origin is a parallel of the myth of Cupid and Psyche, and bore in medieval times a similar mystical interpretation. The Lohengrin legend is localized on the Lower Rhine, and its incidents take place at Antwerp, Nijmwegen, Cologne and Mainz. In its application it falls into sharp division in the hands of German and French poets. By the Germans it was turned to mystical use by being attached loosely to the Grail legend (see Grail and Perceval); in France it was adapted to glorify the family of Godfrey de Bouillon.

The German story makes its appearance in the last stanzas of Wolfram von Eschenbach's *Parzival*, where it is related how Parzival's son, Loherangrin,[1] was sent from the castle of the Grail to the help of the young duchess of Brabant. Guided by the swan he reached Antwerp, and married the lady on condition that she should not ask his origin. On the breach of this condition years afterwards Loherangrin departed, leaving sword, horn and ring behind him. Between 1283 and 1290, a Bavarian disciple of Wolfram's[2] adopted the story and developed it into an epic poem of nearly 8000 lines, incorporating episodes of Lohengrin's prowess in tournament, his wars with Henry I against the heathen Hungarians and the Saracens,[3] and incidentally providing a detailed picture of the everyday life of people of high condition. The epic of Lohengrin is put by the anonymous writer into the mouth of Wolfram, who is made to relate it during the Contest of the Singers at the Wartburg in proof of his superiority in knowledge of sacred things over Klingsor the magician, and the poem is thus linked on to German

[1] *i.e.* Garin le Loherin (*q.v.*), or Garin of Lorraine.

[2] Elster (*Beiträge*) says that the poem is the work of two poets the first part by a Thuringian wandering minstrel, the second—which differs in style and dialect—by a Bavarian official.

[3] Based on material borrowed from the *Sächsische Weltchronik* (formerly called *Repgowische Chronik* from its dubious assignment to Eime von Repgow), the oldest prose chronicle of the world in German (*c.* 1248 or 1260).

tradition. Its connexion with Parzival implies a mystic application. The consecrated wafer shared by Lohengrin and the swan on their voyage is one of the more obvious means taken by the poet to give the tale the character of an allegory of the relations between Christ, the Church and the human soul. The story was followed closely in its main outlines by Richard Wagner in his opera *Lohengrin*.

The French legend of the knight of the swan is attached to the house of Bouillon, and although William of Tyre refers to it about 1170 as fable, it was incorporated without question by later annalists. It forms part of the cycle of the *chansons de geste* dealing with the Crusade, and relates how Helyas, knight of the swan, is guided by the swan to the help of the duchess of Bouillon and marries her daughter Ida or Beatrix in circumstances exactly parallel to the adventures of Lohengrin and Elsa of Brabant, and with the like result. Their daughter marries Eustache, count of Boulogne, and had three sons, the eldest of whom, Godefroid (Godfrey), is the future king of Jerusalem. But in French story Helyas is not the son of Parzival, but of the king and queen of Lillefort, and the story of his birth, of himself, his five brothers and one sister is, with variations, that of "the seven swans" persecuted by the wicked grandmother, which figures in the pages of Grimm and Hans Andersen. The house of Bouillon was not alone in claiming the knight of the swan as an ancestor, and the tradition probably originally belonged to the house of Cleves.

German Versions.—See *Lohengrin*, ed. Rückert (Quedlinburg and Leipzig, 1858); another version of the tale, *Lorengel*, is edited in the *Zeitschr. für deutsches Altertum* (vol. 15); modern German translation of *Lohengrin*, by H. A. Junghaus (Leipzig, 1878); Conrad von Würzburg's fragmentary *Schwanritter*, ed. F. Roth (Frankfurt, 1861). Cf. Elster, *Beiträge zur Kritik des Lohengrin* (Halle, 1884), and R. Heinrichs, *Die Lohengrindichtung und ihre Deutung* (Hamm i. West., 1905).

French Versions.—Baron de Reiffenberg, *Le Chevalier au cygne et Godfrey de Bouillon* (Brussels, 2 vols., 1846–1848), in *Mon. pour servir à l'hist. de la province de Namur*; C. Hippeau, *La Chanson du chevalier au cygne* (1874); H. A. Todd, *La Naissance du chevalier au cygne, an inedited French poem of the 12th cent.* (Mod. Lang. Assoc., Baltimore, 1889); cf. the Latin tale by Jean de Haute Seille (Johannes de Alta Silva) in his *Dolopathos* (ed. Oesterley, Strassburg, 1873).

English Versions.—In England the story first appears in a short poem preserved among the Cotton MSS. of the British Museum and entitled *Chevelere assigne*. This was edited by G. E. V. Utterson in 1820 for the Roxburghe Club, and again by H. H. Gibbs in 1868 for the Early English Text Society. The E.E.T.S. edition is accompanied by a set of photographs of a 14th-century ivory casket, on which the story is depicted in 36 compartments. An English prose romance, *Helyas Knight of the Swan*, translated by Robert Copland, and printed by W. Copland about 1550, is founded on a French romance *La Génealogie . . . de Godeffroy de Boulin* (printed 1504) and is reprinted by W. J. Thoms in *Early Prose Romances*, vol. iii. It was also printed by Wynkyn de Worde in 1512. A modern edition was issued in 1901 from the Grolier Club, New York.

LOIN (through O. Fr. *loigne* or *logne*, mod. *longe*, from Lat. *lumbus*), that part of the body in an animal which lies between the upper part of the hip-bone and the last of the false ribs on either side of the back-bone, hence in the plural the general term for the lower part of the human body at the junction with the legs, covered by the loin-cloth, the almost universal garment among primitive peoples. There are also figurative uses of the word, chiefly biblical, due to the loins being the supposed seat of male vigour and power of generation. Apart from these uses the word is a butcher's term for a joint of meat cut from this part of the body. The upper part of a loin of beef is known as the "surloin" (Fr. *surlonge*, *i.e.* upper loin). This has been commonly corrupted into "sirloin," and a legend invented, to account for the name, of a king, James I. or Charles II., knighting a prime joint of beef "Sir Loin" in pleasure at its excellence. A double surloin, undivided at the back-bone, is known as a "baron of beef," probably from an expansion of the legend of the "Sir Loin."

LOIRE, the longest river of France, rising in the Gerbier de Jonc in the department of Ardèche, at a height of 4500 ft. and flowing north and west to the Atlantic. After a course of 18 m. in Ardèche it enters Haute-Loire, in which it follows a picturesque channel along the foot of basaltic rocks, through narrow gorges and small plains. At Vorey, where it is joined by the Arzon, it becomes navigable for rafts. Four miles below its entrance into the department of Loire, at La Noirie, river navigation is officially reckoned to begin, and breaking through the gorges of Saint Victor, the Loire enters the wide and swampy plain of Forez, after which it again penetrates the hills and flows out into the plain of Roanne. As in Haute-Loire, it is joined by a large number of streams, the most important being the Coise on the right and the Lignon du Nord or du Forez and the Aix on the left. Below Roanne the Loire is accompanied on its left bank by a canal to Digoin (35 m.) in Saône-et-Loire, thence by the so-called "lateral canal of the Loire" to Briare in Loiret (122 m.). Owing to the exteme irregularity of the river in different seasons these canals form the only certain navigable way. At Digoin the Loire receives the Arroux, and gives off the canal du Centre (which utilizes the valley of the Bourbince) to Chalon-sur-Saône. At this point its northerly course begins to be interrupted by the mountains of Morvan, and flowing north-west it enters the department of Nièvre. Just beyond Nevers it is joined by the Allier; this river rises 30 m. S.W. of the Loire in the department of Lozère, and following an almost parallel course has at the confluence a volume equal to two-thirds of that of the main stream. Above Nevers the Loire is joined by the Aron, along which the canal du Nivernais proceeds northward, and the Nièvre, and below the confluence of the Allier gives off the canal du Berry to Bourges and the navigable part of the Cher. About this point the valley becomes more ample and at Briare (in Loiret) the river leaves the highlands and flows between the plateaus of Gatinais and the Beauce on the right and the Sologne on the left. In Loiret it gives off the canal de Briare northward to the Seine and itself bends north-west to Orléans, whence the canal d'Orléans, following the little river Cens, communicates with the Briare canal. At Orléans the river changes its north-westerly for a south-westerly course. A striking peculiarity of the affluents of the Loire in Loiret and the three subsequent departments is that they frequently flow in a parallel channel to the main stream and in the same valley. Passing Blois in Loir-et-Cher, the Loire enters Indre-et-Loire and receives on the right the Cisse, and, after passing Tours, the three important left-hand tributaries of the Cher, Indre and the Vienne. At the confluence of the Vienne the Loire enters Maine-et-Loire, in its course through which department it is frequently divided by long sandy islands fringed with osiers and willows; while upon arriving at Les Ponts-de-Cé it is split into several distinct branches. The principal tributaries are: left, the Thouet at Saumur, the Layon and the Evre; right: the Authion, and, most important tributary of all, the Maine, formed by the junction of the rivers Mayenne, Sarthe and Loir. Through Loire-Inférieure the river is studded with islands until below Nantes, where the largest of them, called Belle-Ile, is found. It receives the Erdre on the right at Nantes and on the opposite shore the Sèvre-Nantaise, and farther on the canalized Achenau on the left and the navigable Etier de Méan on the right near Saint Nazaire. Below Nantes, between which point and La Martinière (below Pellerin) the channel is embanked, the river is known as the Loire Maritime and widens out between marshy shores, passing Paimbœuf on the left and finally Saint-Nazaire, where it is 1½ m. broad. The length of the channel of the Loire is about 625 m.; its drainage area is 46,700 sq.m. A lateral canal (built in 1881–1892 at a cost of about £1,000,000) known as the Maritime Canal of the Loire between Le Carnet and La Martinière enables large ships to ascend to Nantes. It is 9¾ m. long, and 19½ (capable of being increased to 24) ft. deep. At each end is a lock 405 ft. long by 59 ft. wide. The canal de Nantes à Brest connects this city with Brest.

The Loire is navigable only in a very limited sense. During the drought of summer thin and feeble streams thread their way between the sandbanks of the channel; while at other times a stupendous flood submerges wide reaches of land. In the middle part of its course the Loire traverses the western portion of the undulating Paris basin, with its Tertiary marls, sands and clays, and the [illegible] carried off from these renders its lower channel inconstant; [illegible] of the drainage area is occupied by crystalline rocks, over [illegible] surface of which the water, undiminished by absorption, [illegible] rapidly into the streams. When the flood waters of two or [illegible] tributaries arrive at the same time serious inundations result. Attempts to control the river must have begun at a very early date, and by the close of the middle ages the bed between Orléans and Angers was enclosed by dykes 10 to 13 ft. high. In 1783 a double [illegible] of dykes or levées 23 ft. high was completed from Bec d'Allier [illegible] towards [illegible]. The channel was, however, so much narrowed that the [illegible] embankments are almost certain to give way as soon as the water [illegible] 16 ft. (the average rise is about 14, and in 1846 and 1856 it [illegible] than 22). In modern times embankments, aided by [illegible] operations extending over a large number of years, have [illegible] a depth of 18 ft. in the channel between La Martinière and Nantes. Several towns have constructed special works to defend themselves against the floods; Tours, the most exposed of all, is [illegible] by a circular dyke.

Various schemes for the systematic regulation of the Loire have been discussed. It has been proposed to construct in the upper [illegible] of the several affluents a number of gigantic dams or reservoirs from which the water, stored during flood, could be let off into the river as required. A dam of this kind (built in 1711) at the village of Pinay, about 18 m. above Roanne, and capable of retaining from 350 to 450 million cub. ft. of water, has greatly diminished the force of the floods at Roanne, and maintained the comparative equilibrium of the current during the dry season. Three other dams of modern construction are also in existence, one near Firminy, the other two near St Étienne.

LOIRE, a department of central France, made up in 1793 of the old district of Forez and portions of Beaujolais and Lyonnais, all formerly included in the province of Lyonnais. Pop. (1906) 643,943. Area 1853 sq. m. It is bounded N. by the department of Saône-et-Loire, E. by those of Rhône and Isère, S. by Ardèche and Haute-Loire, and W. by Puy-de-Dôme and Allier. From 1790 to 1793 it constituted, along with that of Rhône, a single department (Rhône-et-Loire). It takes its name from the river which bisects it from south to north. The Rhone skirts the S.E. of the department, about one-eighth of which belongs to its basin. After crossing the southern border the Loire runs through wild gorges, passing the picturesque crag crowned by the old fortress of St Paul-en-Cornillon. At St Rambert it issues into the broad plain of Forez, flows north as far as its confluence with the Aix where the plain ends, and then again traverses gorges till it enters the less extensive plain of Roanne in the extreme north of the department. These two plains, the beds of ancient lakes, are enclosed east and west by chains of mountains running parallel with the river. In the west are the Forez mountains, which separate the Loire basin from that of the Allier; their highest point (Pierre sur Haute, 5381 ft.) is 12 m. W. of Montbrison. They sink gradually towards the north, and are successively called Bois Noirs (4239 ft.), from their woods, and Monts de la Madeleine (3822 to 1640 ft.). In the east the Rhone and Loire basins are separated, by Mont Pilat (4705 ft.) at the north extremity of the Cévennes, and by the hills of Lyonnais, Tarare, Beaujolais and Charolais, none of which rise higher than 3294 ft. Of the affluents of the Loire the most important are the Lignon du Nord, the beautiful valley of which has been called "La Suisse Forezienne," and the Aix on the left, and on the right the Ondaine (on which stand the industrial towns of Chambon-Feugerolles and Firminy), the Furens and the Rhin. The Gier forms a navigable channel to the Rhone at Givors, and has on its banks the industrial towns of St Chamond and Rive-de-Gier. From Mont Pilat descends the Déôme, in the valley of which are the workshops of Annonay (*q.v.*). The climate on the heights is cold and healthy, it is unwholesome in the marshy plain of Forez, mild in the valley of the Rhone. The annual rainfall varies from 39 to 48 in. on the Forez mountains, but only reaches 20 to 24 in. in the vicinity of Montbrison.

The plains of Forez and Roanne are the two most important agricultural districts, but the total production of grain within the department is insufficient for the requirements of the population. The pasture lands of the plain of Forez, the western portion of which is irrigated by the canal of Forez, support a large number of live stock. Good pasturage is also found on the higher levels of the Forez mountains, on the north-eastern plateaus, where oxen of the famous Charolais breed are raised, and on the uplands generally. Wheat and rye are the leading cereal crops; oats come next in importance, barley and colza occupying a relatively small area. The vine is cultivated in the valley of the Rhone, on the lower slopes of the Forez mountains and on the hills west of the plain of Roanne. The forests of Mont Pilat and the Forez chain yield good-sized pines and wood for mining purposes. The so-called Lyons chestnuts are to a large extent obtained from Forez; the woods and pasture lands of Mont Pilat yield medicinal plants, such as mint. Poultry-rearing and bee-keeping are considerable industries. The department is rich in mineral springs, the waters of St Galmier, Sail-sous-Couzan, St Romain-le-Puy and St Alban being largely exported. The chief wealth of the department lies in the coal deposits of the basin of St Étienne (*q.v.*), the second in importance in France; quarrying is also active. Metal-working industries are centred in the S.E. of the department, where are the great manufacturing towns of St Étienne, Rive-de-Gier, St Chamond and Firminy. At St Étienne there is a national factory of arms, in which as many as 10,000 have been employed; apart from other factories of the same kind carried on by private individuals, the production of hardware, locks, edge-tools, common cutlery, chain cables for the mines, files, rails, &c., occupies thousands of hands. Cast steel is largely manufactured, and the workshops of the department supply the heaviest constructions required in naval architecture, as well as war material and machinery of every description. The glass industry is carried on at Rive-de-Gier and St Galmier. St Étienne and St Chamond are centres for the fabrication of silk ribbons, elastic ribbons and laces, and the dressing of raw silks. Between 50,000 and 60,000 people are employed in the last-named industries. The arrondissement of Roanne manufactures cotton stuffs, muslins and the like. That of Montbrison produces table linen. The department has numerous dye-works, flour-mills, paper works, tanyards, brick-works, silk-spinning works and hat factories. It is served by the Paris-Lyon railway, Roanne being the junction of important lines from Paris to Lyons and St Étienne. Within the department the Loire is hardly used for commercial navigation; the chief waterways are the canal from Roanne to Digoin (13 m. in the department), that from Givors to Rive-de-Gier (7 m.) and the Rhone (7 m.).

Loire comprises three arrondissements—St Étienne, Montbrison and Roanne—with 31 cantons and 335 communes. It falls within the region of the XIII. army corps and the *diocèse* and *académie* (educational circumscription) of Lyons, where also is its court of appeal. St Étienne is the capital, other leading towns being Roanne, Montbrison, Rive-de-Gier, St Chamond, Firminy and Le Chambon, all separately noticed. St Bonnet-le-Château, besides old houses, has a church of the 15th and 16th centuries, containing paintings of the 15th century; St Rambert and St Romain-le-Puy have priory churches of the 11th and 12th centuries; and at Charlieu there are remains of a Benedictine abbey founded in the 9th century, including a porch decorated with fine Romanesque carving.

LOIRE-INFÉRIEURE, a maritime department of western France, made up in 1790 of a portion of Brittany on the right and of the district of Retz on the left of the Loire, and bounded W. by the ocean, N. by Morbihan and Ille-et-Vilaine, E. by Maine-et-Loire and S. by Vendée. Pop. (1906) 666,748. Area 2694 sq. m. The surface is very flat, and the highest point, in the north on the borders of Ille-et-Vilaine, reaches only 377 ft. The line of hillocks skirting the right bank of the Loire, and known as the *sillon de Bretagne*, scarcely exceeds 250 ft.; below Savenay they recede from the river, and meadows give place to peat bogs. North of St Nazaire and Grande Brière, measuring 9 m. by 6, and rising hardly 10 ft. above the sea-level, still supplies old trees which can be used for joiners' work. A few scattered villages occur on the more elevated spots, but communication is effected chiefly by the canals which intersect it. The district south of the Loire lies equally low; its most salient feature is the lake of Grandlieu, covering 27 sq. m., and surrounded by low and marshy ground, but so shallow (6½ ft. at most) that drainage would be comparatively easy. The Loire (*q.v.*) has a course of 70 m. within the department. On the left bank a canal stretches for 9 m. between Pellerin, where the dikes which protect the Loire valley from inundation terminate, and Paimbœuf, and vessels drawing 17 or 18 ft. can reach Nantes. The principal towns on the river within the department are Ancenis, Nantes and St Nazaire (one of the most important commercial ports of France) on the right, and Paimbœuf on the left. The chief affluents are, on the right the Erdre and on the left the Sèvre, both debouching at Nantes. The Erdre in its lower course broadens in places into lakes which give it the appearance of a large river. Four miles below Nort it coalesces with the canal from Nantes to Brest. The Sèvre is hemmed in by picturesque hills; at the point where it enters the department it flows past the beautiful town of Clisson with its imposing castle of the 13th century. Apart from the Loire, the only navigable channel of importance within the department is the Nantes and Brest canal, fed by the Isac, a tributary of the Vilaine, which separates Loire-Inférieure from Ille-et-Vilaine and Morbihan. The climate is humid, mild and equable. At Nantes the mean annual temperature is 54·7° Fahr., and there are one hundred and twenty-two rainy days, the annual rainfall being 25·6 in.

Horse and cattle raising prospers, being carried on chiefly in the west of the department and in the Loire valley. Good butter and cheese are produced. Poultry also is reared, and there is a good deal of bee-keeping. Wheat, oats, buckwheat and potatoes are produced in great abundance; leguminous plants are also largely cultivated, especially near Nantes. Wine, cider and forage crops are the chief remaining agricultural products. The woods are of oak in the interior and pine on the coast. The department has deposits of tin, lead and iron. N.W. of Ancenis coal is obtained from a bed which is a prolongation of that of Anjou. The salt marshes, about 6000 acres in all, occur for the most part between the mouth of the Vilaine and the Loire, and on the Bay of Bourgneuf, and salt-refining, of which Guérande is the centre, is an important industry. The granite of the sea-coast and of the Loire up to Nantes is quarried for large blocks. Steam-engines are built for the government at Indret, a few miles below Nantes; the forges of Basse-Indre are in good repute for the quality of their iron; and the production of the lead-smelting works at Couëron amounts to several millions of francs annually. There are also considerable foundries at Nantes, Chantenay, close to Nantes, and St Nazaire, and shipbuilding yards at Nantes and St Nazaire. Among other industries may be mentioned the preparation of pickles and preserved meats at Nantes, the curing of sardines at Le Croisic and in the neighbouring communes, the manufacture of sugar, brushes, tobacco, macaroni and similar foods, soap and chemicals at Nantes, and of paper, sugar and soap at Chantenay. Fishing is prosecuted along the entire coast, particularly at Le Croisic. Among the seaside resorts Le Croisic, Pornichet and Pornic, where there are megalithic monuments, may be mentioned. The department is traversed by the railways of the state, the Orléans company and the Western company. The department is divided into five arrondissements—Nantes, Ancenis, Châteaubriant, Paimbœuf and St Nazaire—45 cantons and 219 communes. It has its appeal court at Rennes, which is also the centre of the *académie* (educational division) to which it belongs.

The principal places are Nantes, the capital, St Nazaire and Châteaubriant, which receive separate treatment. On the west coast the town of Batz, and the neighbouring villages, situated on the peninsula of Batz, are inhabited by a small community possessed of a distinct costume and dialect, and claiming descent from a Saxon or Scandinavian stock. Its members are employed for the most part in the salt marshes N.E. of the town. Guérande has well-preserved ramparts and gates of the 15th century, a church dating from the 12th to the 16th centuries, and other old buildings. At St Philbert-de-Grandlieu there is a church, rebuilt in the 16th and 17th centuries, but preserving remains of a previous edifice belonging at least to the beginning of the 11th century.

LOIRET, a department of central France, made up of the three districts of the ancient province of Orléanais—Orléanais proper, Gâtinais and Dunois—together with portions of those of Île-de-France and Berry. It is bounded N. by Seine-et-Oise, N.E. by Seine-et-Marne, E. by Yonne, S. by Nièvre and Cher, S.W. and W. by Loir-et-Cher and N.W. by Eure-et-Loir. Area, 2629 sq. m. Pop. (1906) 364,999. The name is borrowed from the Loiret, a stream which issues from the ground some miles to the south of Orléans, and after a course of about 7 m. falls into the Loire; its large volume gives rise to the belief that it is a subterranean branch of that river. The Loire traverses the south of the department by a broad valley which, though frequently devastated by disastrous floods, is famed for its rich tilled lands, its castles, its towns and its vine-clad slopes. To the north of the Loire are the Gâtinais (capital Montargis) and the Beauce; the former district is so named from its *gâtines* or wildernesses, of which saffron is, along with honey, the most noteworthy product; the Beauce (*q.v.*), a monotonous tract of corn-fields without either tree or river, has been called the granary of France. Between the Beauce and the Loire is the extensive forest of Orléans, which is slowly disappearing before the advances of agriculture. South of the Loire is the Sologne, long barren and unhealthy from the impermeability of its subsoil, but now much improved in both respects by means of pine plantation and draining and manuring operations. The highest point (on the borders of Cher) is 900 ft. above sea-level, and the lowest (on the borders of Seine-et-Marne) is 220 ft. The watershed on the plateau of Orléans between the basins of the Seine and Loire, which divide Loiret almost equally between them, is almost imperceptible. The lateral canal of the Loire from Roanne stops at Briare; from the latter town a canal (canal de Briare) connects with the Seine by the Loing valley, which is joined by the Orléans canal below Montargis. The only important tributary of the Loire within the department is the Loiret; the Loing, a tributary of the Seine, has a course of 40 m. from south to north, and is accompanied first by the Briare canal and afterwards by that of the Loing. The Essonne, another important affluent of the Seine, leaving Loiret below Malesherbes, takes its rise on the plateau of Orléans, as also does its tributary the Juine. The department has the climate of the Sequanian region, the mean temperature being a little above that of Paris; the rainfall varies from 18·5 to 27·5 in., according to the district, that of the exposed Beauce being lower than that of the well-wooded Sologne. Hailstorms cause much destruction in the Loire valley and the neighbouring regions.

The department is essentially agricultural in character. A large number of sheep, cattle, horses and pigs are reared; poultry, especially geese, and bees are plentiful. The yield of wheat and oats is in excess of the consumption; rye, barley, meslin, potatoes, beetroot, colza and forage plants are also cultivated. Wine in abundance, but of inferior quality, is grown on the hills of the Loire valley. Buckwheat supports bees by its flowers, and poultry by its seeds. Saffron is another source of profit. The woods consist of oak, elm, birch and pine; fruit trees thrive in the department, and Orléans is a great centre of nursery gardens. The industries are brick and tile making, and the manufacture of faience, for which Gien is one of the most important centres in France. The Briare manufacture of porcelain buttons and pearls employs many workmen. Flour-mills are very numerous. There are iron and copper foundries, which, with agricultural implement making, bell-founding and the manufacture of pins, nails and files, represent the chief metal-working industries. The production of hosiery, wool-spinning and various forms of wool manufacture are also engaged in. A large quantity of the wine grown is made into vinegar (vinaigre d'Orléans). The tanneries produce excellent leather; and paper-making, sugar-refining, wax-bleaching and the manufacture of caoutchouc complete the list of industries. The four arrondissements are those of Orléans, Gien, Montargis and Pithiviers, with 31 cantons and 349 communes. The department forms part of the *académie* (educational division) of Paris.

Besides Orléans, the capital, the more noteworthy places, Gien, Montargis, Beaugency, Pithiviers, Briare and St Benoît-sur-Loire, are separately noticed. Outside these towns notable examples of architecture are found in the churches of Cléry (15th century), of Ferrières (13th and 14th centuries) of Puiseaux (12th and 13th centuries) and Meung (12th century). At Germigny-des-Prés there is a church built originally at the beginning of the 9th century and rebuilt in the 19th century, on the old plan and to some extent with the old materials. Yèvre-le-Châtel has an interesting château of the 13th century, and Sully-sur-Loire the fine medieval château rebuilt at the beginning of the 17th century by Maximilien de Béthune, duke of Sully, the famous minister of Henry IV. There are remains of a Gallo-Roman town (perhaps the ancient *Vellaunodunum*) at Triguères and of a Roman amphitheatre near Montbouy.

LOIR-ET-CHER, a department of central France, formed in 1790 from a small portion of Touraine, the Perche, but chiefly from the Dunois, Vendômois and Blésois, portions of Orléanais. It is bounded N. by Eure-et-Loir, N.E. by Loiret, S.E. by Cher, S. by Indre, S.W. by Indre-et-Loire and N.W. by Sarthe. Pop. (1906) 276,019. Area, 2479 sq. m. The department takes its name from the Loir and the Cher by which it is traversed in the north and south respectively. The Loir rises on the eastern border of the Perche and joins the Maine after a course of 195 m.; the Cher rises on the Central Plateau near Aubusson, and reaches the Loire after a course of 219 m. The Loire flows through the [illegible] from north-east to south-west, and divides it into [illegible]. To the south-east is the district of [illegible] the rich wheat-growing country [illegible] stretches to the Loir. Beyond that [illegible] surface of this region, which contains [illegible] department (840 ft.), is varied by [illegible] and orchards. The Sologne was [illegible] of which those in the neighbourhood [illegible] remains. Its soil, once barren and [illegible] has been considerably improved by draining and [illegible] though pools are still very numerous. The district [illegible] by sportsmen. The Cher and Loir traverse [illegible] occasionally bounded by walls of tufa in which [illegible] have been excavated, as at Les Roches in the Loir [illegible] stone, hardened by exposure to the air, is also used [illegible] purposes. The Loire and, with the help of the Berry [illegible] the Cher are navigable. The chief remaining rivers of the department are the Beuvron, which flows into the Loire on the left, and the Sauldre, a right-hand affluent of the Cher. The climate is temperate and mild, though that of the Beauce tends to dryness and that of the Sologne to dampness. The mean annual temperature is between 52° and 53° F.

The department is primarily agricultural, yielding abundance of [illegible] Besides these the chief products are rye, wheat [illegible] thrive on the valley slopes, the vineyards [illegible] of the Cher, which yield fine red [illegible] the Blésois and the Vendômois. In the valleys [illegible] gardens are numerous; the asparagus of [illegible] Vendôme is well-known. The Sologne supplies [illegible] and there are extensive forests around Blois [illegible] of the Loir. Pasture is of good quality in the [illegible] are the chief stock; the Perche breed of horses [illegible] for its combination of lightness and strength. [illegible] of some importance in the Sologne. Formerly the [illegible] Loir-et-Cher was the production of gun-flints. Stone-[illegible] numerous. The chief industries are the cloth-manu-[illegible] Romorantin, and leather-dressing and glove-making at [illegible] lime burning, flour-milling, distilling, saw-milling, [illegible] and the manufacture of "sabots" and boots and [illegible] linen goods, are carried on. The department is [illegible] the Orléans railway.

[illegible] arrondissements are those of Blois, Romorantin and [illegible] 24 cantons and 297 communes. Loir-et-Cher [illegible] the educational division (*académie*) of Paris. Its [illegible] and the headquarters of the V. army corps, to [illegible] which it belongs, are at Orléans. Blois, the capital, [illegible] Romorantin and Chambord are noticed separately. [illegible] those of Blois and Chambord there are numerous [illegible] in the department, of which that of Montrichard [illegible] of the 11th century, that of Chaumont dating [illegible] and 16th centuries, and that of Cheverny (17th [illegible] late Renaissance style are the most important. [illegible] Lassay, Lavardin and Cellettes may also be [illegible] churches wholly or in part of Romanesque archi-[illegible] at Faverolles, Selles-sur-Cher, St Aignan and [illegible] village of Trôo is built close to ancient tumuli [illegible] church of the 12th century, and among [illegible] of a lazar-house of the Romanesque period. [illegible] the church, consisting of a fine choir in the [illegible] the buildings of a Benedictine abbey. At La [illegible] Montoire) is a small Renaissance manor-[illegible] was born in 1524.

[illegible] FIRMIN (1857–), French Catholic [illegible] at Ambrières in French Lorraine of parents [illegible] a long line of resident peasantry, tilled [illegible]. The physically delicate boy was put [illegible] school of St Dizier, without any intention [illegible] but he decided for the priesthood, and in [illegible] Grand Séminaire of Châlons-sur-Marne. Mgr [illegible] of Châlons, afterwards cardinal and arch-[illegible] ordained him priest in 1879. After being *curé* [illegible] in that diocese, Loisy went in May [illegible] a theological degree, to the Institut [illegible] Here he was influenced, as to biblical [illegible] and loyal-minded Abbé Paulin Martin, and as to a vivid consciousness of the true nature, gravity and urgency of the biblical problems and as Attic sense of form by the historical intuition and the mordant irony of Abbé Louis Duchesne. At the governmental institutions, Professors Oppert and Halévy helped further to train him. He took his theological degree in March 1890, by the oral defence of forty Latin scholastic theses and by a French dissertation, *Histoire du canon de l'ancien testament*, published as his first book in that year.

Professor now at the Institut Catholique, he published successively his lectures: *Histoire du canon du N.T.* (1891); *Histoire critique du texte et des versions de la Bible* (1892); and *Les Evangiles synoptiques* (1893, 1894). The two latter works appeared successively in the bi-monthly *L'Enseignement biblique*, a periodical written throughout and published by himself. But already, on the occasion of the death of Ernest Renan, October 1892, the attempts made to clear up the main principles and results of biblical science, first by Mgr d'Hulst, rector of the Institut Catholique, in his article "La Question biblique" (*Le Correspondant*, Jan. 25th, 1893), and then by Loisy himself, in his paper "La Question biblique et l'inspiration des Écritures" (*L'Enseignement biblique*, Nov.–Dec. 1893), promptly led to serious trouble. The latter article was immediately followed by Loisy's dismissal, without further explanation, from the Institut Catholique. And a few days later Pope Leo XIII. published his encyclical *Providentissimus Deus*, which indeed directly condemned not Abbé Loisy's but Mgr d'Hulst's position, yet rendered the continued publication of consistently critical work so difficult that Loisy himself suppressed his *Enseignement* at the end of 1893. Five further instalments of his *Synoptiques* were published after this, bringing the work down to the Confession of Peter inclusively.

Loisy next became chaplain to a Dominican convent and girls' school at Neuilly-sur-Seine (Oct. 1894–Oct. 1899), and here matured his apologetic method, resuming in 1898 the publication of longer articles, under the pseudonyms of Desprès and Firmin in the *Revue du clergé français*, and of Jacques Simon in the lay *Revue d'histoire et de littérature religieuses*. In the former review, a striking paper upon development of doctrine (Dec. 1st, 1898) headed a series of studies apparently taken from an already extant large apologetic work. In October 1899 he resigned his chaplaincy for reasons of health, and settled at Bellevue, somewhat farther away from Paris. His notable paper, "La Religion d'Israel" (*Revue du clergé français*, Oct. 15th, 1900), the first of a series intended to correct and replace Renan's presentation of that great subject, was promptly censured by Cardinal Richard, archbishop of Paris; and though scholarly and zealous ecclesiastics, such as the Jesuit Père Durand and Monseigneur Mignot, archbishop of Albi, defended the general method and several conclusions of the article, the aged cardinal never rested henceforward till he had secured a papal condemnation also. At the end of 1900 Loisy secured a government lectureship at the École des Hautes Études Pratiques, and delivered there a succession courses on the Babylonian myths and the first chapters of Genesis; the Gospel parables; the narrative of the ministry in the synoptic Gospels; and the Passion narratives in the same. The first course was published in the *Revue d'histoire et de littérature religieuses*; and here also appeared instalments of his commentary on St John's Gospel, his critically important *Notes sur la Genèse*, and a *Chronique biblique* unmatched in its mastery of its numberless subjects and its fearless yet delicate penetration.

It was, however, two less erudite little books that brought him a European literary reputation and the culmination of his ecclesiastical troubles. *L'Évangile et l'église* appeared in November 1902 (Eng. trans., 1903). Its introduction and six chapters present with rare lucidity the earliest conceptions of the Kingdom of Heaven, the Son of God, the Church, Christian dogma and Catholic worship; and together form a severely critico-historical yet strongly Catholic answer to Harnack's still largely pietistic *Wesen des Christentums*. It develops throughout the principles that "what is essential in Jesus' Gospel is what occupies the first and largest place in His authentic teaching, the ideas for which He fought and died, and not only that idea which we may consider to be still a living force to-day"; that "it is supremely arbitrary to decree that Christianity must be essentially what the Gospel did not borrow from Judaism, as though what the Gospel owes to Judaism were necessarily of secondary worth"; that "whether we trust or distrust tradition, we know Christ only by means of, athwart and within the Christian tradition"; that "the *essence of Christianity* resides in the fulness and totality of its life"; and that "the adaptation of the Gospel to the changing conditions of humanity is to-day a more pressing need than ever." The second edition was enlarged by a preliminary chapter on the sources of the Gospels, and by a third section for the Son of God chapter. The little book promptly aroused widespread interest, some cordial sympathy and much vehement opposition; whilst its large companion the *Études évangéliques*, containing the course on the parables and four sections of his coming commentary on the Fourth Gospel, passed almost unnoticed. On the 21st of January 1903 Cardinal Richard publicly condemned the book, as not furnished with an *imprimatur*, and as calculated gravely to trouble the faith of the faithful in the fundamental Catholic dogmas. On the 2nd of February Loisy wrote to the archbishop: "I condemn, as a matter of course, all the errors which men have been able to deduce from my book, by placing themselves in interpreting it at a point of view entirely different from that which I had to occupy in composing it." The pope refused to interfere directly, and the nuncio, Mgr Lorenzelli, failed in securing more than ten public adhesions to the cardinal's condemnation from among the eighty bishops of France.

Pope Leo had indeed, in a letter to the Franciscan minister-general (November 1898), and in an encyclical to the French clergy (September 1899), vigorously emphasized the traditionalist principles of his encyclical *Providentissimus* of 1893; he had even, much to his prompt regret, signed the unfortunate decree of the Roman Inquisition, January 1897, prohibiting all doubt as to the authenticity of the "Three Heavenly Witnesses" passage, 1 John v. 7, a text which, in the wake of a line of scholars from Erasmus downwards, Abbé Paulin Martin had, in 1887, exhaustively shown to be no older than the end of the 4th century A.D. Yet in October 1902 he established a "Commission for the Progress of Biblical Studies," preponderantly composed of seriously critical scholars; and even one month before his death he still refused to sign a condemnation of Loisy's *Études évangéliques*.

Cardinal Sarto became Pope Pius X. on the 4th of August 1903. On the 1st of October Loisy published three new books, *Autour d'un petit livre*, *Le Quatrième Évangile* and *Le Discours sur la Montagne*. *Autour* consists of seven letters, on the origin and aim of *L'Évangile et l'Église*; on the biblical question; the criticism of the Gospels; the Divinity of Christ; the Church's foundation and authority; the origin and authority of dogma, and on the institution of the sacraments. The second and third, addressed respectively to a cardinal (Perraud) and a bishop (Le Camus), are polemical or ironical in tone; the others are all written to friends in a warm, expansive mood; the fourth letter especially, appropriated to Mgr Mignot, attains a grand elevation of thought and depth of mystical conviction. *Le Quatrième Évangile*, one thousand large pages long, is possibly over-confident in its detailed application of the allegorical method; yet it constitutes a rarely perfect sympathetic reproduction of a great mystical believer's imperishable intuitions. *Le Discours sur la Montagne* is a fragment of a coming enlarged commentary on the synoptic Gospels. On the 23rd of December the pope ordered the publication of a decree of the Congregation of the Index, incorporating a decree of the Inquisition, condemning Loisy's *Religion d'Israël*, *L'Évangile et l'Église*, *Études évangéliques*, *Autour d'un petit livre* and *Le Quatrième Évangile*. The pope's secretary of state had on the 19th December, in a letter to Cardinal Richard, recounted the causes of the condemnation in the identical terms used by the latter himself when condemning the *Religion d'Israël* three years before. On the 12th of January 1904 Loisy wrote to Cardinal Merry del Val that he received the condemnation with respect, and condemned whatever might be reprehensible in his books, whilst reserving the rights of his conscience and his opinions as an historian, opinions doubtless imperfect, as no one was more ready to admit than himself, but which were the only form under which he was able to represent to himself the history of the Bible and of religion. Since the Holy See was not satisfied, Loisy sent three further declarations to Rome; the last, despatched on the 17th of March, was addressed to the pope himself, and remained unanswered. And at the end of March Loisy gave up his lectureship, as he declared, "on his own initiative, in view of the pacification of minds in the Catholic Church." In the July following he moved into a little house, built for him by his pupil and friend, the Assyriologist François Thureau Dangin, within the latter's park at Garnay, by Dreux. Here he continued his important reviews, notably in the *Revue d'histoire et de littérature religieuses*, and published *Morceaux d'exégèse* (1906), six further sections of his synoptic commentary. In April 1907 he returned to his native Lorraine, to Ceffonds by Montier-en-Der, and to his relatives there.

Five recent Roman decisions are doubtless aimed primarily at Loisy's teaching. The Biblical Commission, soon enlarged so as to swamp the original critical members, and which had become the simple mouthpiece of its presiding cardinals, issued two decrees. The first, on the 27th of June 1906, affirmed, with some significant but unworkable reservations, the Mosaic authorship of the Pentateuch; and the second (29th of May 1907) strenuously maintained the Apostolic Zebedean authorship of the fourth Gospel, and the strictly historical character of the events and speeches recorded therein. The Inquisition, by its decree *Lamentabili sane* (2nd of July 1907), condemned sixty-five propositions concerning the Church's *magisterium*; biblical inspiration and interpretation; the synoptic and fourth Gospels; revelation and dogma; Christ's divinity, human knowledge and resurrection; and the historical origin and growth of the Sacraments, the Church and the Creed. And some forty of these propositions represent, more or less accurately, certain sentences or ideas of Loisy, when torn from their context and their reasons. The encyclical *Pascendi Dominici Gregis* (Sept. 6th, 1907), probably the longest and most argumentative papal utterance extant, also aims primarily at Loisy, although here the vehemently scholastic redactor's determination to piece together a strictly coherent, complete a priori system of "Modernism" and his self-imposed restriction to medieval categories of thought as the vehicles for describing essentially modern discoveries and requirements of mind, make the identification of precise authors and passages very difficult. And on the 21st of November 1907 a papal *motu proprio* declared all the decisions of the Biblical Commission, past and future, to be as binding upon the conscience as decrees of the Roman Congregations.

Yet even all this did not deter Loisy from publishing three further books. *Les Évangiles synoptiques*, two large 8vo volumes of 1009 and 798 pages, appeared "chez l'auteur, à Ceffonds, Montier-en-Der, Haute-Marne," in January 1908. An incisive introduction discusses the ecclesiastical tradition, modern criticism; the second, the first and the third Gospels; the evangelical tradition; the career and the teaching of Jesus; and the literary form, the tradition of the text and the previous commentaries. The commentary gives also a careful translation of the texts. Loisy recognizes two eye-witness documents, as utilized by all three synoptists, while Matthew and Luke have also incorporated Mark. His chief peculiarity consists in clearly tracing a strong Pauline influence, especially in Mark, which there remodels certain sayings and actions as these were first registered by the eye-witness documents. These doctrinal interpretations introduce the economy of blinding the Jews into the parabolic teaching; the declaration as to the redemptive character of the Passion into the sayings; the sacramental, institutional words into the account of the Last Supper, originally, a solemnly simple Messianic meal; and the formal night-trial before Caiaphas into the original Passion-story with its informal, morning

LOKOJA, a town of Nigeria, at the junction of the Niger and Benue rivers, founded in 1860 by the British consul, W. B. [illegible]kie, and subsequently the military centre of the Royal Niger [illegible]ny. It is in the province of Kabba, 250 m. from the mouth [illegible] Niger, and is of considerable commercial importance (see [illegible] KABBA).

[illegible]S, the name given to the English followers of John [illegible] re the adherents of a religious movement which [illegible] the end of the 14th and beginning of the 15th [illegible] extent maintained itself on to the Reforma- [illegible] uncertain origin; some derive it from [illegible]ucer (*C. T.*, Shipman's Prologue):—

[illegible] prechen us somwhat . . .
[illegible] difficultee
[illegible] in our clene corn";

[illegible]rally received explanation derives the words [illegible]n, to sing softly. The word is much older than [illegible] use, there were Lollards in the Netherlands at the [illegible] of the 14th century, who were akin to the Fratricelli, [illegible]ards and other sectaries of the recusant Franciscan type. The earliest official use of the name in England occurs in 1387 in a mandate of the bishop of Worcester against five "poor preachers," *nomine seu ritu Lollardorum confoederatos*. It is probable that the name was given to the followers of Wycliffe because they resembled those offshoots from the great Franciscan movement which had disowned the pope's authority and set before themselves the ideal of *Evangelical poverty*.

The 14th century, so full of varied religious life, made it manifest that the two different ideas of a life of separation from the world which in earlier times had lived on side by side within the medieval church were irreconcilable. The church chose to abide by the idea of Hildebrand and to reject that of Francis of Assisi; and the revolt of Ockham and the Franciscans, of the Beghards and other spiritual fraternities, of Wycliffe and the Lollards, were all protests against that decision. Gradually there came to be facing each other a great political Christendom, whose rulers were statesmen, with aims and policy of a worldly type, and a religious Christendom, full of the ideas of separation from the world by self-sacrifice and of participation in the benefits of Christ's work by an ascetic imitation. The war between the two ideals was fought out in almost every country in Europe in the 14th century. In England Wycliffe's whole life was spent in the struggle, and he bequeathed his work to the Lollards. The main practical thought with Wycliffe was that the church, if true to her divine mission, must aid men to live that life of evangelical poverty by which they could be separate from the world and imitate Christ, and if the church ceased to be true to her mission she ceased to be a church. Wycliffe was a metaphysician and a theologian, and had to invent a metaphysical theory—the theory of *Dominium*—to enable him to transfer, in a way satisfactory to himself, the powers and privileges of the church to his company of poor Christians; but his followers were content to allege that a church which held large landed possessions, collected tithes greedily and took money from starving peasants for baptizing, burying and praying, could not be the church of Christ and his apostles.

Lollardy was most flourishing and most dangerous to the ecclesiastical organization of England during the ten years after Wycliffe's death. It had spread so rapidly and grown so popular that a hostile chronicler could say that almost every second man was a Lollard. Wycliffe left three intimate disciples:—Nicolas Hereford, a doctor of theology of Oxford, who had helped his master to translate the Bible into English; John Ashton, also a fellow of an Oxford college; and John Purvey, Wycliffe's colleague at Lutterworth, and a co-translator of the Bible. With these were associated more or less intimately, in the first age of Lollardy, John Parker, the strange ascetic William Smith, the restless fanatic Swynderly, Richard Waytstract and Crompe. Wycliffe had organized in Lutterworth an association for sending the gospel through all England, a company of poor preachers somewhat after the Wesleyan method of modern times. "To be poor without mendicancy, to unite the flexible unity, the swift obedience of an order, with free and constant mingling among the poor, such was the ideal of Wycliffe's 'poor priests'" (cf. Shirley, *Fasc. Ziz.* p. xl.), and, although proscribed, these "poor preachers" with portions of their master's translation of the Bible in their hand to guide them, preached all over England. In 1382, two years before the death of Wycliffe, the archbishop of Canterbury got the Lollard opinions condemned by convocation, and, having been promised royal support, he began the long conflict of the church with the followers of Wycliffe. He was able to coerce the authorities of the university of Oxford, and to drive out of it the leading Wycliffite teachers, but he was unable to stifle Oxford sympathies or to prevent the banished teachers preaching throughout the country. Many of the nobles, like Lords Montacute and Salisbury, supported the poor preachers, took them as private chaplains, and protected them against clerical interference. Country gentlemen like Sir Thomas Latimer of Braybrooke and Sir Richard Stury protected them, while merchants and burgesses supported them with money. When Richard II. issued an ordinance (July 1382) ordering every bishop to arrest all Lollards, the Commons compelled him to withdraw it. Thus protected, the "poor preachers" won masses of the people to their opinions, and Leicester, London and the west of England became their headquarters.

The organization must have been strong in numbers, but only those who were seized for heresy are known by name, and it is only from the indictments of their accusers that their opinions can be gathered. The preachers were picturesque figures in long russet dress down to the heels, who, staff in hand, preached in the mother tongue to the people in churches and graveyards, in squares, streets and houses, in gardens and pleasure grounds, and then talked privately with those who had been impressed. The Lollard literature was very widely circulated—books by Wycliffe and Hereford and tracts and broadsides—in spite of many edicts proscribing it. In 1395 the Lollards grew so strong that they petitioned parliament through Sir Thomas Latimer and Sir R. Stury to reform the church on Lollardist methods. It is said that the Lollard Conclusions printed by Canon Shirley (p. 360) contain the substance of this petition. If so, parliament was told that temporal possessions ruin the church and drive out the Christian graces of faith, hope and charity; that the priesthood of the church in communion with Rome was not the priesthood Christ gave to his apostles; that the monk's vow of celibacy had for its consequence unnatural lust, and should not be imposed; that transubstantiation was a feigned miracle, and led people to idolatry; that prayers made over wine, bread, water, oil, salt, wax, incense, altars of stone, church walls, vestments, mitres, crosses, staves, were magical and should not be allowed; that kings should possess the *jus episcopale*, and bring good government into the church; that no special prayers should be made for the dead; that auricular confession made to the clergy, and declared to be necessary for salvation, was the root of clerical arrogance and the cause of indulgences and other abuses in pardoning sin; that all wars were against the principles of the New Testament, and were but murdering and plundering the poor to win glory for kings; that the vows of chastity laid upon nuns led to child murder; that many of the trades practised in the commonwealth, such as those of goldsmiths and armourers, were unnecessary and led to luxury and waste. These Conclusions really contain the sum of Wycliffite teaching; and, if we add that the principal duty of priests is to preach, and that the worship of images, the going on pilgrimages and the use of gold and silver chalices in divine service are sinful (*The Peasants' Rising and the Lollards*, p. 47), they include almost all the heresies charged in the indictments against individual Lollards down to the middle of the 15th century. The king, who had hitherto seemed anxious to repress the action of the clergy against the Lollards, spoke strongly against the petition and its promoters, and Lollardy never again had the power in England which it wielded up to this year.

If the formal statements of Lollard creed are to be got from these Conclusions, the popular view of their controversy with

decision by Caiaphas, and its one solemn condemnation of Jesus, by Pilate. Mark's narratives of the sepulture by Joseph of Arimathea and of the empty tomb are taken as posterior to St Paul; the narratives of the infancy in Matthew and Luke as later still. Yet the great bulk of the sayings remain substantially authentic; if the historicity of certain words and acts is here refused with unusual assurance, that of other sayings and deeds is established with stronger proofs; and the redemptive conception of the Passion and the sacramental interpretation of the Last Supper are found to spring up promptly and legitimately from our Lord's work and words, to saturate the Pauline and Johannine writings, and even to constitute an element of all three synoptic Gospels.

Simples Réflexions sur le décret Lamentabili et sur l'encyclique Pascendi, 12mo, 277 pages, was published from Ceffonds a few days after the commentary. Each proposition of the decree is carefully tracked to its probable source, and is often found to modify the latter's meaning. And the study of the encyclical concludes: "Time is the great teacher . . . we would do wrong to despair either of our civilization or of the Church."

The Church authorities were this time not slow to act. On the 14th of February Mgr Amette, the new archbishop of Paris, prohibited his diocesans to read or defend the two books, which "attack and deny several fundamental dogmas of Christianity," under pain of excommunication. The abbé again declared "it is impossible for me honestly and sincerely to make the act of absolute retractation and submission exacted by the sovereign pontiff." And the Holy Office, on the 7th of March, pronounced the major excommunication against him. At the end of March Loisy published *Quelques Lettres* (December 1903–February 1908) which conclude: "At bottom I have remained in my last writin
on the same line as in the earlier ones. I have aimed at establ
ing principally the historical position of the various quest
and secondarily the necessity for reforming more or l
traditional concepts."

Three chief causes appear jointly to have produced
very absolute condemnation. Any frank recogn
abbé's even general principles involves the aba
the identification of theology with scholasticism
specifically ancient thought in general. Th
position, that our Lord himself held the pr
second coming, involves the loss by churc
of directly divine power, since Church ar
still the true fruits and vehicles of hi
cannot thus be immediately founded
self. And the Church policy, as old a
to crush utterly the man who brings
than the bulk of traditional Chri
digest or resist with a fair
authorities the one means to s

BIBLIOGRAPHY.—Autobiog
d'un petit livre (Paris, 1903
account of his literary ac
found in Abbé Albert H
(Paris, 2nd ed., 1902) a
1906), but the latter e
and sadly lacking in
booklets concerning
specially remarkable
(Paris, Nov. 1901)
biblical studies; M
sur les études eccle
and "Critique et
January 1904), the
Camus, bishop o
(Paris, 1902), a
Lagrange, a D
Testament cr
l'Ancien Tes
1903); P. L
fondement
December
Maurice
Januar
et des
Wehrl
1904

discuss the relations between faith and the affirmation
happenings; Paul Sabatier, "Les Derniers Ou
Loisy," in the *Revue chrétienne* (Dôle, 1904) a
Catholicisme et critique (Paris, 1905), a Broad
and a moralist agnostic's delicate apprecia
Évangiles synoptiques by the Abbé Mange
français (Feb. 15, 1908) containing so
tions; a revue by L. in the *Revue bibl*
mixture of unfair insinuation, powerfu
admissions; and a paper by G. P. B
Annales de philosophie chrétienne (
and to refute certain philosophica
book's treatment, especially of t
the Institution of the Church
Annales de philosophie chréti
Italian theologian's fearless
positions; Rev. P. Louis
I. Br. 1905), the ablest o
method by a highly in
many years in Rome;
What we want, by A.
Modernisti (*ibid.* 1
ed. by Lilley (Lo
substantially on
Vangeli Sinott
(Milan, 1908
Professor F
6 arts. in
criticism
Profess
Literat
inter
Ref
1c

clergy,
Wycliffe
out in a
parted from
Spirituales
erlands) for
glish Works of
Soc., vol. lxxiv.,
English verse:

and him
Oxford
stimony of
was dis-
the council of
delegates. The
the document,
order to purge the
convocation proposed
mas Arundel intended
aching. They provided
to be allowed to preach
achers preaching to the laity
clergy, and that Lollard books
were to be searched for and

king a more determined effort was
hitherto its strength had lain among
who were the representatives of the
clergy had been afraid to attack this
new king determined to overawe them,
ted one who had been a personal friend and
en blameless. This was Sir John Oldcastle,
ife, Lord Cobham, "the good Lord Cobham"
people called him. Henry first tried personal
and when that failed directed trial for heresy.
as convicted, but was imprisoned for forty days in
in hope that he might recant. He escaped, and
his co-religionists to his aid. A Lollard plot was
seize the king's person. In the end Oldcastle was burnt
stinate heretic (Dec. 1417). These persecutions were
ly protested against; the wars of Henry V. with France
akened the martial spirit of the nation, and little sympathy
elt for men who had declared that all war was but the
and plundering of poor people for the sake of kings.
king ballads were composed upon the martyr Oldcastle,
this dislike to warfare was one of the chief accusations
ade against him (comp. Wright's *Political Poems*, ii. 244).
But Arundel could not prevent the writing and distribution of
Lollard books and pamphlets. Two appeared about the time
of the martyrdom of Oldcastle—*The Ploughman's Prayer* and
the *Lanthorne of Light*. The *Ploughman's Prayer* declared that true worship consists in three things—in loving God, and dreading God and trusting in God above all other things; and it showed how Lollards, pressed by persecution, became further separated from the religious life of the church. "Men maketh now great stonen houses full of glasen windows, and clepeth thilke thine houses and churches. And they setten in these houses mawmets of stocks and stones, to fore them they knelen privilich and apert and maken their prayers, and all this they say is they worship. . . . For Lorde our belief is that thine house is man's soul." Notwithstanding the repression, Lollardy fastened in new parts of England, and Lollards abounded in Somerset, Norfolk, Suffolk, Essex, Lincoln and Buckinghamshire.

The council of Constance (1414–1418) put an end to the papal schism, and also showed its determination to put down heresy by burning John Huss. When news of this reached England the clergy were incited to still more vigorous proceedings against Lollard preachers and books. 'From this time Lollardy appears banished from the fields and streets, and takes refuge in houses and places of concealment. There was no more wayside preaching, but instead there were *conventicula occulta* in houses, in peasants' huts, in sawpits and in field ditches, where the Bible was read and exhortations were given, and so Lollardy continued. In 1428 Archbishop Chichele confessed that the Lollards seemed as numerous as ever, and that their literary and preaching work went on as vigorously as before. It was found also that many of the poorer rectors and parish priests, and a great many chaplains and curates, were in secret association with Lollards, so much so that in many places processions were not made and worship on saints' days was abandoned. For Lollards were hardened by persecution, and became fa

of their doctrines. Thomas Bagley was accused
in the sacrament a priest made bread into
it can be eaten by rats and mice; that
monks, and the nuns, and the friars
recognized by the church were
confession to the priest was
nd others held that any
te; and that boys

d. Oxford
vigorous
tish
d

the
ressor
up their
and using
memorial
possessions
ne framing of
copal authority,
of ecclesiastical
e sacraments, the
and capital punish-
pared with the Lollard
y had not greatly altered
ecution. All the articles
unishment, are to be found
many writers have held that
ly from what have been called
and more violent Lollards," all
ycliffe himself. Pecock's idea was
e was prepared to impugn came from
owings," viz. that no governance or
d a law of God which is not founded on
umble-minded Christian man or woman is
defaut" to find out the true sense of Scripture,
e so he ought to listen to no arguments to the
where adds a fourth (i. 102), that if a man
k but also keep God's law he shall have a true
of Scripture, even though "no man ellis teche him
These statements, especially the last, show us the
etween the Lollards and those mystics of the 14th century,
Tauler and Ruysbroeck, who accepted the teachings of
of Basel, and formed themselves into the association of the
s of God.

The persecutions were continued down to the reign of Henry VIII., and when the writings of Luther began to appear in England the clergy were not so much afraid of Lutheranism as of the increased life they gave to men who for generations had been reading Wycliffe's *Wickette*. "It is," wrote Bishop Tunstall to Erasmus in 1523, "no question of pernicious novelty, It is only that new arms are being added to the great band of Wycliffite heretics." Lollardy, which continued down to the Reformation, did much to shape the movement in England. The subordination of clerical to laic jurisdiction, the reduction in ecclesiastical possessions, the insisting on a translation of the Bible which could be read by the "common" man were all inheritances bequeathed by the Lollards.

LITERATURE.—*Fasciculi Zizaniorum Magistri Johannis Wyclif cum Tritico*, edited for the Rolls Series by W. W. Shirley (London, 1858); the *Chronicon Angliae, auctore monacho quodam Sancti Albani*, ed. by Sir E. Maunde Thompson (London, 1874); *Historia Anglicana* of Thomas Walsingham, ed. by H. T. Riley, vol. iii. (London, 1869); *Chronicon* of Henry Knighton, ed. by J. R. Lumby (London, 1895); R. L. Poole, *Wycliffe and Movements for Reform* (London, 1889); R. Pecock, *Repressor of overmuch Blaming of the Clergy* (2 vols., London, 1860); F. D. Matthew, *The English Works of John Wyclif* (Early English Text Society, London, 1880); T. Wright, *Political Poems and Songs* (2 vols., London, 1859); G. V. Lechler, *Johann von Wiclif*, ii. (1873); J. Loserth, *Hus und Wycliffe* (Prague, 1884, English translation by J. Evans, London, 1884); D. Wilkins, *Concilia Magnae Britanniae et Hiberniae*, iii. (London, 1773); E. Powell and G. M. Trevelyan, *The Peasants' Rising and the Lollards, a Collection of Unpublished Documents* (London, 1899); G. M. Trevelyan, *England in the Age of Wycliffe* (London, 1898, 3rd ed., 1904); the publications of the Wiclif Society; H. S. Cronin, "The Twelve Conclusions of the Lollards," in the *English Historical Review* (April 1907, pp. 292 ff.); and J. Gairdner, *Lollardy and the Reformation in England* (1908). (T. M. L.)

LOLLIUS, MARCUS, Roman general, the first governor of Galatia (25 B.C.), consul in 21. In 16, when governor of Gaul, he was defeated by the Sigambri (Sygambri), Usipetes and Tencteri, German tribes who had crossed the Rhine. This defeat is coupled by Tacitus with the disaster of Varus, but it was disgraceful rather than dangerous. Lollius was subsequently (2 B.C.) attached in the capacity of tutor and adviser to Gaius Caesar (Augustus's grandson) on his mission to the East. He was accused of extortion and treachery to the state, and denounced by Gaius to the emperor. To avoid punishment he is said to have taken poison. According to Velleius Paterculus and Pliny, he was a hypocrite and cared for nothing but amassing wealth. It was formerly thought that this was the Lollius whom Horace described as a model of integrity and superior to avarice in *Od.* iv. 9, but it seems hardly likely that this Ode, as well as the two Lollian epistles of Horace (i. 2 and 18), was addressed to him. All three must have been addressed to the same individual, a young man, probably the son of this Lollius.

See Suetonius, *Augustus*, 23, *Tiberius*, 12; Vell. Pat. ii. 97. 102; Tacitus, *Annals*, i. 10, iii. 48; Pliny, *Nat. Hist.* ix. 35 (58); Dio Cassius, liv. 6; see also J. C. Tarver, *Tiberius the Tyrant* (1902), pp. 200 foll.

LOLOS, the name given by the Chinese to a large tribe of aborigines who inhabit the greater part of southern Szechuen. Their home is in the mountainous country called Taliang shan, which lies between the Yangtsze river on the east and the Kien ch'ang valley on the west, in south Szechuen, but they are found in scattered communities as far south as the Burmese frontier, and west to the Mekong. There seems no reason to doubt that they were, like the Miaotze, one of the aboriginal tribes of China, driven southwards by the advancing flood of Chinese. The name is said to be a Chinese corruption of Lulu, the name of a former chieftain of a tribe who called themselves Nersu. Their language, like the Chinese, is monosyllabic and probably ideographic, and the characters bear a certain resemblance to Chinese. No literature, however, worthy of the name is known to exist, and few can read and write. Politically they are divided into tribes, each under the government of a hereditary chieftain. The community consists of three classes, the "blackbones" or nobles, the "whitebones" or plebeians, and the *watse* or slaves. The last are mostly Chinese captured in forays, or the descendants of such captives. Within Lolo-land proper, which covers some 11,000 sq.m., the Chinese government exercises no jurisdiction. The Lolos make frequent raids on their unarmed Chinese neighbours. They cultivate wheat, barley and millet, but little rice. They have some knowledge of metals, making their own tools and weapons. Women are said to be held in respect, and may become chiefs of the tribes. They do not intermarry with Chinese.

See A. F. Legendre, "Les Lolos. Étude ethnologique et anthropologique," in *T'oung Pao II.*, vol. x. (1909); E. C. Baber, *Royal Geog. Society Sup. Papers*, vol. i. (London, 1882); F. S. A. Bourne, *Blue Book, China, No. 1* (1888); A. Hosie, *Three Years in Western China* (London, 1897).

LOMBARD LEAGUE, the name given in general to any league of the cities of Lombardy, but applied especially to the league founded in 1167, which brought about the defeat of the emperor Frederick I. at Legnano, and the consequent destruction of his plans for obtaining complete authority over Italy.

Lacking often the protection of a strong ruler, the Lombard cities had been accustomed to act together for mutual defence, and in 1093 Milan, Lodi, Piacenza and Cremona formed an alliance against the emperor Henry IV., in favour of his rebellious son Conrad. The early years of the reign of Frederick I. were largely spent in attacks on the privileges of the cities of Lombardy. This led to a coalition, formed in March 1167, between the cities of Cremona, Mantua, Bergamo and Brescia to confine Frederick to the rights which the emperors had enjoyed for the past hundred years. This league or *concordia* was soon joined by other cities, among which were Milan, Parma, Padua, Verona, Piacenza and Bologna, and the allies began to build a fortress near the confluence of the Tanaro and the

the church may be gathered from the ballads preserved in the *Political Poems and Songs relating to English History*, published in 1859 by Thomas Wright for the Master of the Rolls series, and in the Piers Ploughman poems. *Piers Ploughman's Creed* (see LANGLAND) was probably written about 1394, when Lollardy was at its greatest strength; the ploughman of the *Creed* is a man gifted with sense enough to see through the tricks of the friars, and with such religious knowledge as can be got from the creed, and from Wycliffe's version of the Gospels. The poet gives us a "portrait of the fat friar with his double chin shaking about as big as a goose's egg, and the ploughman with his hood full of holes, his mittens made of patches, and his poor wife going barefoot on the ice so that her blood followed" (*Early English Text Society*, vol. xxx., pref., p. 16); and one can easily see why farmers and peasants turned from the friars to the poor preachers. The *Ploughman's Complaint* tells the same tale. It paints popes, cardinals, prelates, rectors, monks and friars, who call themselves followers of Peter and keepers of the gates of heaven and hell, and pale poverty-stricken people, cotless and landless, who have to pay the fat clergy for spiritual assistance, and asks if these are Peter's priests. "I trowe Peter took no money, for no sinners that he sold. . . . Peter was never so great a fole, to leave his key with such a losell."

In 1399 the Lancastrian Henry IV. overthrew the Plantagenet Richard II., and one of the most active partisans of the new monarch was Arundel, archbishop of Canterbury and the most determined opponent of Lollardy. Richard II. had aided the clergy to suppress Lollardy without much success. The new dynasty supported the church in a similar way and not more successfully. The strength of the anti-clerical party lay in the House of Commons, in which the representatives of the shires took the leading part. Twice the Commons petitioned the crown to seize the temporalities of the church and apply them to such national purposes as relief of taxation, maintenance of the poor and the support of new lords and knights. Their anti-clerical policy was not continuous, however. The court party and the clergy proposed statutes for the suppression of heresy, and twice at least secured the concurrence of the Commons. One of these was the well-known statute *De heretico comburendo* passed in 1401.

In the earlier stages of Lollardy, when the court and the clergy managed to bring Lollards before ecclesiastical tribunals backed by the civil power, the accused generally recanted and showed no disposition to endure martyrdom for their opinions. They became bolder in the beginning of the 15th century. William Sawtrey (Chartris), caught and condemned, refused to recant and was burnt at St Paul's Cross (March 1401), and other martyrdoms followed. The victims usually belonged to the lower classes. In 1410 John Badby, an artisan, was sent to the stake. His execution was memorable from the part taken in it by the prince of Wales, who himself tried to reason the Lollard out of his convictions. But nothing said would make Badby confess that "Christ sitting at supper did give to His disciples His living body to eat." The Lollards, far from daunted, abated no effort to make good their ground, and united a struggle for social and political liberty to the hatred felt by the peasants towards the Romish clergy. Jak Upland (John Countryman) took the place of Piers Ploughman, and upbraided the clergy, and especially the friars, for their wealth and luxury. Wycliffe had published the rule of St Francis, and had pointed out in a commentary upon the rule how far friars had departed from the maxims of their founder, and had persecuted the *Spirituales* (the Fratricelli, Beghards, Lollards of the Netherlands) for keeping them to the letter (cf. Matthews, *English Works of Wyclif hitherto unprinted*, Early Eng. Text Soc., vol. lxxiv., 1880). Jak Upland put all this into rude nervous English verse:

> "Freer, what charitie is this
> To fain that whoso liveth after your order
> Liveth most perfectlie,
> And next followeth the state of the Apostles
> In povertie and pennance:
> And yet the wisest and greatest clerkes of you
> Wend or send or procure to the court of Rome,
> . . . and to be assoiled of the vow of povertie."

The archbishop, having the power of the throne behind him, attacked that stronghold of Lollardy the university of Oxford. In 1406 a document appeared purporting to be the testimony of the university in favour of Wycliffe; its genuineness was disputed at the time, and when quoted by Huss at the council of Constance it was repudiated by the English delegates. The archbishop treated Oxford as if it had issued the document, and procured the issue of severe regulations in order to purge the university of heresy. In 1408 Arundel in convocation proposed and carried the famous *Constitutiones Thomae Arundel* intended to put down Wycliffite preachers and teaching. They provided amongst other things that no one was to be allowed to preach without a bishop's licence, that preachers preaching to the laity were not to rebuke the sins of the clergy, and that Lollard books and the translation of the Bible were to be searched for and destroyed.

When Henry V. became king a more determined effort was made to crush Lollardy. Hitherto its strength had lain among the country gentlemen who were the representatives of the shires. The court and clergy had been afraid to attack this powerful class. The new king determined to overawe them, and to this end selected one who had been a personal friend and whose life had been blameless. This was Sir John Oldcastle, in right of his wife, Lord Cobham, "the good Lord Cobham" as the common people called him. Henry first tried personal persuasion, and when that failed directed trial for heresy. Oldcastle was convicted, but was imprisoned for forty days in the Tower in hope that he might recant. He escaped, and summoned his co-religionists to his aid. A Lollard plot was formed to seize the king's person. In the end Oldcastle was burnt for an obstinate heretic (Dec. 1417). These persecutions were not greatly protested against; the wars of Henry V. with France had awakened the martial spirit of the nation, and little sympathy was felt for men who had declared that all war was but the murder and plundering of poor people for the sake of kings. Mocking ballads were composed upon the martyr Oldcastle, and this dislike to warfare was one of the chief accusations made against him (comp. Wright's *Political Poems*, ii. 244). But Arundel could not prevent the writing and distribution of Lollard books and pamphlets. Two appeared about the time of the martyrdom of Oldcastle—*The Ploughman's Prayer* and the *Lanthorne of Light*. The *Ploughman's Prayer* declared that true worship consists in three things—in loving God, and dreading God and trusting in God above all other things; and it showed how Lollards, pressed by persecution, became further separated from the religious life of the church. "Men maketh now great stonen houses full of glasen windows, and clepeth thilke thine houses and churches. And they setten in these houses mawmets of stocks and stones, to fore them they knelen privilich and apert and maken their prayers, and all this they say is they worship. . . . For Lorde our belief is that thine house is man's soul." Notwithstanding the repression, Lollardy fastened in new parts of England, and Lollards abounded in Somerset, Norfolk, Suffolk, Essex, Lincoln and Buckinghamshire.

The council of Constance (1414–1418) put an end to the papal schism, and also showed its determination to put down heresy by burning John Huss. When news of this reached England the clergy were incited to still more vigorous proceedings against Lollard preachers and books. 'From this time Lollardy appears banished from the fields and streets, and takes refuge in houses and places of concealment. There was no more wayside preaching, but instead there were *conventicula occulta* in houses, in peasants' huts, in sawpits and in field ditches, where the Bible was read and exhortations were given, and so Lollardy continued. In 1428 Archbishop Chichele confessed that the Lollards seemed as numerous as ever, and that their literary and preaching work went on as vigorously as before. It was found also that many of the poorer rectors and parish priests, and a great many chaplains and curates, were in secret association with the Lollards, so much so that in many places processions were never made and worship on saints' days was abandoned. For the Lollards were hardened by persecution, and became fanatics in the statement of their doctrines. Thomas Bagley was accused of declaring that if in the sacrament a priest made bread into God, he made a God that can be eaten by rats and mice; that the pharisees of the day, the monks, and the nuns, and the friars and all other privileged persons recognized by the church were limbs of Satan; and that auricular confession to the priest was the will not of God but of the devil. And others held that any priest who took salary was excommunicate; and that boys could bless the bread as well as priests.

From England Lollardy passed into Scotland. Oxford infected St Andrews, and we find traces of more than one vigorous search made for Lollards among the teaching staff of the Scottish university, while the Lollards of Kyle in Ayrshire were claimed by Knox as the forerunners of the Scotch Reformation.

The opinions of the later Lollards can best be gathered from the learned and unfortunate Pecock, who wrote his elaborate *Repressor* against the "Bible-men," as he calls them. He summed up their doctrines under eleven heads: they condemn the having and using images in the churches, the going on pilgrimages to the memorial or "mynde places" of the saints, the holding of landed possessions by the clergy, the various ranks of the hierarchy, the framing of ecclesiastical laws and ordinances by papal and episcopal authority, the institution of religious orders, the costliness of ecclesiastical decorations, the ceremonies of the mass and the sacraments, the taking of oaths and the maintaining that war and capital punishment are lawful. When these points are compared with the Lollard Conclusions of 1395, it is plain that Lollardy had not greatly altered its opinions after fifty-five years of persecution. All the articles of Pecock's list, save that on capital punishment, are to be found in the Conclusions; and, although many writers have held that Wycliffe's own views differed greatly from what have been called the "exaggerations of the later and more violent Lollards," all these views may be traced to Wycliffe himself. Pecock's idea was that all the statements which he was prepared to impugn came from three false opinions or "trowings," viz. that no governance or ordinance is to be esteemed a law of God which is not founded on Scripture, that every humble-minded Christian man or woman is able without "fail and defaut" to find out the true sense of Scripture, and that having done so he ought to listen to no arguments to the contrary; he elsewhere adds a fourth (i. 102), that if a man be not only meek but also keep God's law he shall have a true understanding of Scripture, even though "no man ellis teche him saue God." These statements, especially the last, show us the connexion between the Lollards and those mystics of the 14th century, such as Tauler and Ruysbroeck, who accepted the teachings of Nicholas of Basel, and formed themselves into the association of the Friends of God.

The persecutions were continued down to the reign of Henry VIII., and when the writings of Luther began to appear in England the clergy were not so much afraid of Lutheranism as of the increased life they gave to men who for generations had been reading Wycliffe's *Wickette*. "It is," wrote Bishop Tunstall to Erasmus in 1523, "no question of pernicious novelty, it is only that new arms are being added to the great band of Wycliffite heretics." Lollardy, which continued down to the Reformation, did much to shape the movement in England. The subordination of clerical to laic jurisdiction, the reduction in ecclesiastical possessions, the insisting on a translation of the Bible which could be read by the "common" man were all inheritances bequeathed by the Lollards.

LITERATURE.—*Fasciculi Zizaniorum Magistri Johannis Wyclif cum Tritico*, edited for the Rolls Series by W. W. Shirley (London, 1858); the *Chronicon Angliae, auctore monacho quodam Sancti Albani*, ed. by Sir E. Maunde Thompson (London, 1874); *Historia Anglicana* of Thomas Walsingham, ed. by H. T. Riley, vol. iii. (London, 1869); *Chronicon* of Henry Knighton, ed. by J. R. Lumby (London, 1895); R. L. Poole, *Wycliffe and Movements for Reform* (London, 1889); R. Pecock, *Repressor of overmuch Blaming of the Clergy* (2 vols., London, 1860); F. D. Matthew, *The English Works of John Wyclif* (Early English Text Society, London, 1880); T. Wright, *Political Poems and Songs* (2 vols., London, 1859); G. V. Lechler, *Johann von Wiclif*, ii. (1873); J. Loserth, *Hus und Wycliffe* (Prague, 1884, English translation by J. Evans, London, 1884); D. Wilkins, *Concilia Magnae Britanniae et Hiberniae*, iii. (London, 1773); E. Powell and G. M. Trevelyan, *The Peasants' Rising and the Lollards, a Collection of Unpublished Documents* (London, 1899); G. M. Trevelyan, *England in the Age of Wycliffe* (London, 1898, 3rd ed., 1904); the publications of the Wiclif Society; H. S. Cronin, "The Twelve Conclusions of the Lollards," in the *English Historical Review* (April 1907, pp. 292 ff.); and J. Gairdner, *Lollardy and the Reformation in England* (1908). (T. M. L.)

LOLLIUS, MARCUS, Roman general, the first governor of Galatia (25 B.C.), consul in 21. In 16, when governor of Gaul, he was defeated by the Sigambri (Sygambri), Usipetes and Tencteri, German tribes who had crossed the Rhine. This defeat is coupled by Tacitus with the disaster of Varus, but it was disgraceful rather than dangerous. Lollius was subsequently (2 B.C.) attached in the capacity of tutor and adviser to Gaius Caesar (Augustus's grandson) on his mission to the East. He was accused of extortion and treachery to the state, and denounced by Gaius to the emperor. To avoid punishment he is said to have taken poison. According to Velleius Paterculus and Pliny, he was a hypocrite and cared for nothing but amassing wealth. It was formerly thought that this was the Lollius whom Horace described as a model of integrity and superior to avarice in *Od.* iv. 9, but it seems hardly likely that this Ode, as well as the two Lollian epistles of Horace (i. 2 and 18), was addressed to him. All three must have been addressed to the same individual, a young man, probably the son of this Lollius.

See Suetonius, *Augustus*, 23, *Tiberius*, 12; Vell. Pat. ii. 97. 102; Tacitus, *Annals*, i. 10, iii. 48; Pliny, *Nat. Hist.* ix. 35 (58); Dio Cassius, liv. 6; see also J. C. Tarver, *Tiberius the Tyrant* (1902), pp. 200 foll.

LOLOS, the name given by the Chinese to a large tribe of aborigines who inhabit the greater part of southern Szechuen. Their home is in the mountainous country called Taliang shan, which lies between the Yangtsze river on the east and the Kien ch'ang valley on the west, in south Szechuen, but they are found in scattered communities as far south as the Burmese frontier, and west to the Mekong. There seems no reason to doubt that they were, like the Miaotze, one of the aboriginal tribes of China, driven southwards by the advancing flood of Chinese. The name is said to be a Chinese corruption of Lulu, the name of a former chieftain of a tribe who called themselves Nersu. Their language, like the Chinese, is monosyllabic and probably ideographic, and the characters bear a certain resemblance to Chinese. No literature, however, worthy of the name is known to exist, and few can read and write. Politically they are divided into tribes, each under the government of a hereditary chieftain. The community consists of three classes, the "blackbones" or nobles, the "whitebones" or plebeians, and the *watse* or slaves. The last are mostly Chinese captured in forays, or the descendants of such captives. Within Lolo-land proper, which covers some 11,000 sq.m., the Chinese government exercises no jurisdiction. The Lolos make frequent raids on their unarmed Chinese neighbours. They cultivate wheat, barley and millet, but little rice. They have some knowledge of metals, making their own tools and weapons. Women are said to be held in respect, and may become chiefs of the tribes. They do not intermarry with Chinese.

See A. F. Legendre, "Les Lolos. Étude ethnologique et anthropologique," in *T'oung Pao II.*, vol. x. (1909); E. C. Baber, *Royal Geog. Society Sup. Papers*, vol. i. (London, 1882); F. S. A. Bourne, *Blue Book, China, No. 1* (1888); A. Hosie, *Three Years in Western China* (London, 1897).

LOMBARD LEAGUE, the name given in general to any league of the cities of Lombardy, but applied especially to the league founded in 1167, which brought about the defeat of the emperor Frederick I. at Legnano, and the consequent destruction of his plans for obtaining complete authority over Italy.

Lacking often the protection of a strong ruler, the Lombard cities had been accustomed to act together for mutual defence, and in 1093 Milan, Lodi, Piacenza and Cremona formed an alliance against the emperor Henry IV., in favour of his rebellious son Conrad. The early years of the reign of Frederick I. were largely spent in attacks on the privileges of the cities of Lombardy. This led to a coalition, formed in March 1167, between the cities of Cremona, Mantua, Bergamo and Brescia to confine Frederick to the rights which the emperors had enjoyed for the past hundred years. This league or *concordia* was soon joined by other cities, among which were Milan, Parma, Padua, Verona, Piacenza and Bologna, and the allies began to build a fortress near the confluence of the Tanaro and the [illegible], which in honour of Pope Alexander III., was called Alessandria. During the absence of Frederick from Italy [illegible] the schism between the pope and the emperor [illegible] Alexander became the leader of the [illegible]. Meetings of the league were held in 1172 and 1173 to strengthen the bond and to concert measures against the emperor, the penalties of the church being invoked to prevent defection. The decisive struggle began when Frederick attacked Alessandria in 1174. The fortress was bravely defended, and the siege was raised on the approach of succour from the allied cities. Negotiations for peace failed, and the emperor, having marched against Milan, suffered a severe defeat at Legnano on the 29th of May 1176. Subsequently Pope Alexander was detached from his allies and made peace with Frederick, after which a truce for six years was arranged between the emperor and the league. Further negotiations ripened into the peace of Constance signed on the 25th of June 1183, which granted almost all the demands of the cities, and left only a shadowy authority to the emperor (see ITALY).

In 1226, when the emperor Frederick II. avowed his intention of restoring the imperial authority in Italy, the league was renewed, and at once fifteen cities, including Milan and Verona, were placed under the ban. Frederick, however, was not in a position to fight, and the mediation of Pope Honorius III. was successful in restoring peace. In 1231 the hostile intentions of the emperor once more stirred the cities into activity. They held a meeting at Bologna and raised an army, but as in 1226, the matter ended in mutual fulminations and defiances. A more serious conflict arose in 1234. The great question at issue, the nature and extent of the imperial authority over the Lombard cities, was still unsettled when Frederick's rebellious son, the German king Henry VII., allied himself with them. Having crushed his son and rejected the proffered mediation of Pope Gregory IX., the emperor declared war on the Lombards in 1236. He inflicted a serious defeat upon their forces at Cortenuova in November 1237 and met with other successes, but in 1238 he was beaten back from before Brescia. In 1239 Pope Gregory joined the cities and the struggle widened out into the larger one of the Empire and the Papacy. This was still proceeding when Frederick died in December 1250 and it was only ended by the overthrow of the Hohenstaufen and the complete destruction of the imperial authority in [illegible]

For a full account of the Lombard League see C. Vignati, *Storia* [illegible] *Lega Lombarda* (Milan, 1866); H. Prutz, *Kaiser* [illegible] (Danzig, 1871–1874); W. von Giesebrecht, [illegible] *Kaiserzeit*, Band v. (Leipzig, 1888); and [illegible] *Geschichte des Lombardenbundes* (Vienna, 1868).

LOMBARDO, the name of a family of Venetian sculptors and [illegible] surname was apparently Solaro, and the [illegible] Lombardo was given to the earliest known, Martino, [illegible] from Lombardy to Venice in the middle of the [illegible] became celebrated as an architect. He had [illegible] and Pietro, of whom the latter (*c.* 1435–1515) [illegible] sculptors and architects of his time, [illegible] (d. 1516) and Tullio (d. 1559) were [illegible] Pietro's work as an architect is seen in [illegible] Vendramini-Calargi palace (1481), the [illegible] façade (1485) of the *scuola* of St Mark [illegible] Cividale del Friuli (1502); but he is now [illegible], often in collaboration with his sons; [illegible] of the doge Mocenigo (1478) in the church [illegible] Paolo at Venice, and a bas-relief for the [illegible] Ravenna, and in 1483 began the beautiful [illegible] church of Sta Maria de' Miracoli at Venice, [illegible] his workshop (see also VENICE for numer- [illegible] work of the Lombardi). Antonio's master- [illegible] of St Anthony making a new-born child [illegible] mother's honour, in the Santo at Padua [illegible] known works are the four kneeling angels [illegible] Venice, a coronation of [illegible] nd two bas-reliefs in the [illegible] y in the Spitzer collection, representing Vulcan's Forge and Minerva disputing with Neptune.

LOMBARDS, or LANGOBARDI, a Suevic people who appear to have inhabited the lower basin of the Elbe and whose name is believed to survive in the modern Bardengau to the south of Hamburg. They are first mentioned in connexion with the year A.D. 5, at which time they were defeated by the Romans under Tiberius, afterwards emperor. In A.D. 9, however, after the destruction of Varus's army, the Romans gave up their attempt to extend their frontier to the Elbe. At first, with most of the Suevic tribes, they were subject to the hegemony of Maroboduus, king of the Marcomanni, but they revolted from him in his war with Arminius, chief of the Cherusci, in the year 17. We again hear of their interference in the dynastic strife of the Cherusci some time after the year 47. From this time they are not mentioned until the year 165, when a force of Langobardi, in alliance with the Marcomanni, was defeated by the Romans, apparently on the Danubian frontier. It has been inferred from this incident that the Langobardi had already moved southwards, but the force mentioned may very well have been sent from the old home of the tribe, as the various Suevic peoples seem generally to have preserved some form of political union. From this time onwards we hear no more of them until the end of the 5th century.

In their own traditions we are told that the Langobardi were originally called Winnili and dwelt in an island named Scadinavia (with this story compare that of the Gothic migration, see GOTHS). Thence they set out under the leadership of Ibor and Aio, the sons of a prophetess called Gambara, and came into conflict with the Vandals. The leaders of the latter prayed to Wodan for victory, while Gambara and her sons invoked Frea. Wodan promised to give victory to those whom he should see in front of him at sunrise. Frea directed the Winnili to bring their women with their hair let down round their faces like beards and turned Wodan's couch round so that he faced them. When Wodan awoke at sunrise he saw the host of the Winnili and said, "*Qui sunt isti Longibarbi?*"—"Who are these long-beards?"—and Frea replied, "As thou hast given them the name, give them also the victory." They conquered in the battle and were thenceforth known as Langobardi. After this they are said to have wandered through regions which cannot now be identified, apparently between the Elbe and the Oder, under legendary kings, the first of whom was Agilmund, the son of Aio.

Shortly before the end of the 5th century the Langobardi appear to have taken possession of the territories formerly occupied by the Rugii whom Odoacer had overthrown in 487, a region which probably included the present province of Lower Austria. At this time they were subject to Rodulf, king of the Heruli, who, however, took up arms against them; according to one story, owing to the treacherous murder of Rodulf's brother, according to another through an irresistible desire for fighting on the part of his men. The result was the total defeat of the Heruli by the Langobardi under their king Tato and the death of Rodulf at some date between 493 and 508. By this time the Langobardi are said to have adopted Christianity in its Arian form. Tato was subsequently killed by his nephew Waccho. The latter reigned for thirty years, though frequent attempts were made by Ildichis, a son or grandson of Tato, to recover the throne. Waccho is said to have conquered the Suabi, possibly the Bavarians, and he was also involved in strife with the Gepidae, with whom Ildichis had taken refuge. He was succeeded by his youthful son Walthari, who reigned only seven years under the guardianship of a certain Audoin. On Walthari's death (about 546?) Audoin succeeded. He also was involved in hostilities with the Gepidae, whose support of Ildichis he repaid by protecting Ustrogotthus, a rival of their king Thorisind. In these quarrels both nations aimed at obtaining the support of the emperor Justinian, who, in pursuance of his policy of playing off one against the other, invited the Langobardi into Noricum and Pannonia, where they now settled.

A large force of Lombards under Audoin fought on the imperial side at the battle of the Apennines against the Ostrogothic king

Totila in 553, but the assistance of Justinian, though often promised, had no effect on the relations of the two nations, which were settled for the moment after a series of truces by the victory of the Langobardi, probably in 554. The resulting peace was sealed by the murder of Ildichis and Ustrogotthus, and the Langobardi seem to have continued inactive until the death of Audoin, perhaps in 565, and the accession of his son Alboin, who had won a great reputation in the wars with the Gepidae. It was about this time that the Avars, under their first Chagun Baian, entered Europe, and with them Alboin is said to have made an alliance against the Gepidae under their new king Cunimund. The Avars, however, did not take part in the final battle, in which the Langobardi were completely victorious. Alboin, who had slain Cunimund in the battle, now took Rosamund, daughter of the dead king, to be his wife.

In 568 Alboin and the Langobardi, in accordance with a compact made with Baian, which is recorded by Menander, abandoned their old homes to the Avars and passed southwards into Italy, were they were destined to found a new and mighty kingdom. (F G M B.)

The Lombard Kingdom in Italy.—In 568 Alboin, king of the Langobards, with the women and children of the tribe and all their possessions, with Saxon allies, with the subject tribe of the Gepidae and a mixed host of other barbarians, descended into Italy by the great plain at the head of the Adriatic. The war which had ended in the downfall of the Goths had exhausted Italy; it was followed by famine and pestilence; and the government at Constantinople made but faint efforts to retain the province which Belisarius and Narses had recovered for it. Except in a few fortified places, such as Ticinum or Pavia, the Italians did not venture to encounter the new invaders; and, though Alboin was not without generosity, the Lombards, wherever resisted, justified the opinion of their ferocity by the savage cruelty of the invasion. In 572, according to the Lombard chronicler, Alboin fell a victim to the revenge of his wife Rosamund, the daughter of the king of the Gepidae, whose skull Alboin had turned into a drinking cup, out of which he forced Rosamund to drink. By this time the Langobards had established themselves in the north of Italy. Chiefs were placed, or placed themselves, first in the border cities, like Friuli and Trent, which commanded the north-eastern passes, and then in other principal places; and this arrangement became characteristic of the Lombard settlement. The principal seat of the settlement was the rich plain watered by the Po and its affluents, which was in future to receive its name from them; but their power extended across the Apennines into Liguria and Tuscany, and then southwards to the outlying dukedoms of Spoleto and Benevento. The invaders failed to secure any maritime ports or any territory that was conveniently commanded from the sea. Ticinum (Pavia), the one place which had obstinately resisted Alboin, became the seat of their kings.

After the short and cruel reign of Cleph, the successor of Alboin, the Lombards (as we may begin for convenience sake to call them) tried for ten years the experiment of a national confederacy of their dukes (as, after the Latin writers, their chiefs are styled), without any king. It was the rule of some thirty-five or thirty-six petty tyrants, under whose oppression and private wars even the invaders suffered. With anarchy among themselves and so precarious a hold on the country, hated by the Italian population and by the Catholic clergy, threatened also by an alliance of the Greek empire with their persistent rivals the Franks beyond the Alps, they resolved to sacrifice their independence and elect a king. In 584 they chose Authari, the grandson of Alboin, and endowed the royal domain with a half of their possessions. From this time till the fall of the Lombard power before the arms of their rivals the Franks under Charles the Great, the kingly rule continued. Authari, "the Long-haired," with his Roman title of Flavius, marks the change from the war king of an invading host to the permanent representative of the unity and law of the nation, and the increased power of the crown, by the possession of a great domain, to enforce its will. The independence of the dukes was surrendered to the king. The dukedoms in the neighbourhood of the seat of power were gradually absorbed, and their holders transformed into royal officers. Those of the northern marches, Trent and Friuli, with the important dukedom of Turin, retained longer the kind of independence which marchlands usually give where invasion is to be feared. The great dukedom of Benevento in the south, with its neighbour Spoleto, threatened at one time to be a separate principality, and even to the last resisted, with varying success, the full claims of the royal authority at Pavia.

The kingdom of the Lombards lasted more than two hundred years, from Alboin (568) to the fall of Desiderius (774)—much longer than the preceding Teutonic kingdom of Theodoric and the Goths. But it differed from the other Teutonic conquests in Gaul, in Britain, in Spain. It was never complete in point of territory: there were always two, and almost to the last three, capitals—the Lombard one, Pavia; the Latin one, Rome; the Greek one, Ravenna; and the Lombards never could get access to the sea. And it never was complete over the subject race: it profoundly affected the Italians of the north; in its turn it was entirely transformed by contact with them; but the Lombards never amalgamated with the Italians till their power as a ruling race was crushed by the victory given to the Roman element by the restored empire of the Franks. The Langobards, German in their faults and in their strength, but coarser, at least at first, than the Germans whom the Italians had known, the Goths of Theodoric and Totila, found themselves continually in the presence of a subject population very different from anything which the other Teutonic conquerors met with among the provincials—like them, exhausted, dispirited, unwarlike, but with the remains and memory of a great civilization round them, intelligent, subtle, sensitive, feeling themselves infinitely superior in experience and knowledge to the rough barbarians whom they could not fight, and capable of hatred such as only cultivated races can nourish. The Lombards who, after they had occupied the lands and cities of Upper Italy, still went on sending forth furious bands to plunder and destroy where they did not care to stay, never were able to overcome the mingled fear and scorn and loathing of the Italians. They adapted themselves very quickly indeed to many Italian fashions. Within thirty years of the invasions, Authari took the imperial title of Flavius, even while his bands were leading Italian captives in leash like dogs under the walls of Rome, and under the eyes of Pope Gregory; and it was retained by his successors. They soon became Catholics; and then in all the usages of religion, in church building, in founding monasteries, in their veneration for relics, they vied with Italians. Authari's queen, Theodelinda, solemnly placed the Lombard nation under the patronage of St John the Baptist, and at Monza she built in his honour the first Lombard church, and the royal palace near it. King Liutprand (712–744) bought the relics of St Augustine for a large sum to be placed in his church at Pavia. Their Teutonic speech disappeared; except in names and a few technical words all traces of it are lost. But to the last they had the unpardonable crime of being a ruling barbarian race or caste in Italy. To the end they are "nefandissimi," execrable, loathsome, filthy. So wrote Gregory the Great when they first appeared. So wrote Pope Stephen IV., at the end of their rule, when stirring up the kings of the Franks to destroy them.

Authari's short reign (584–591) was one of renewed effort for conquest. It brought the Langobards face to face, not merely with the emperors at Constantinople, but with the first of the great statesmen popes, Gregory the Great (590–604). But Lombard conquest was bungling and wasteful; when they had spoiled a city they proceeded to tear down its walls and raze it to the ground. Authari's chief connexion with the fortunes of his people was an important, though an accidental one. The Lombard chronicler tells a romantic tale of the way in which Authari sought his bride from Garibald, duke of the Bavarians, how he went incognito in the embassy to judge of her attractions, and how she recognized her disguised suitor. The bride was the Christian Theodelinda, and she became to the Langobards what Bertha was to the Anglo-Saxons and Clotilda to the Franks.

She became the mediator between the Lombards and the Catholic Church. Authari, who had brought her to Italy, died shortly after his marriage. But Theodelinda had so won on the Lombard chiefs that they bid her as queen choose the one among them whom she would have for her husband and for king. She chose Agilulf, duke of Turin (590–615). He was not a true Langobard, but a Thuringian. It was the beginning of peace between the Lombards and the Catholic clergy. Agilulf could not abandon his traditional Arianism, and he was a very uneasy neighbour, not only to the Greek exarch, but to Rome itself. But he was favourably disposed both to peace and to the Catholic Church. Gregory interfered to prevent a national conspiracy against the Langobards, like that of St Brice's day in England against the Danes, or that later uprising against the French, the Sicilian Vespers. He was right both in point of humanity and of policy. The Arian and Catholic bishops went on for a time side by side; but the Lombard kings and clergy rapidly yielded to the religious influences around them, even while the national antipathies continued unabated and vehement. Gregory, who despaired of any serious effort on the part of the Greek emperors to expel the Lombards, endeavoured to promote peace between the Italians and Agilulf; and, in spite of the feeble hostility of the exarchs of Ravenna, the pope and the king of the Lombards became the two real powers in the north and centre of Italy. Agilulf was followed, after two unimportant reigns, by his son-in-law, the husband of Theodelinda's daughter, King Rothari (636–652), the Lombard legislator, still an Arian though he favoured the Catholics. He was the first of their kings who collected their customs under the name of laws—and he did this, not in their own Teutonic dialect, but in Latin. The use of Latin implies that the laws were to be not merely the personal law of the Lombards, but the law of the land, binding on Lombards and Romans alike. But such rude legislation could not provide for all questions arising even in the decayed state of Roman [illegible]. It is probable that among themselves the Italians [illegible] to their old usages and legal precedents where they were not forbidden by the conquerors' law, and by degrees a good [illegible] of the Roman civil arrangements made their way into the [illegible] code, while all ecclesiastical ones, and they were a large [illegible] were untouched by it.

[illegible] have been much change of property; but appearances [illegible] as to the terms on which land generally was held by [illegible] or the new comers, and as to the relative legal [illegible]. Savigny held that, making allowance for the [illegible] of conquest, the Roman population held [illegible] as they had held it before, and were governed [illegible] and acknowledged exercise of Roman law in [illegible] organization. Later inquirers, including Leo, [illegible] have found that the supposition does not tally [illegible] facts, which point to a Lombard territorial law [illegible] parallel Roman and personal law, to a great [illegible] rights among the Romans, analogous to the [illegible] under the Turks, and to a reduction of the [illegible] class of half-free "aldii," holding immovable [illegible] superior race and privilege, and subject [illegible] the third part of their holdings or the [illegible]. The Roman losses, both of property and [illegible] great at first; how far they continued [illegible] centuries of the Lombard kingdom, or [illegible] between Rome and Lombard gradually [illegible] further question. The legislation of the [illegible] territorial and not a personal law, shows [illegible] to depress or to favour the Romans, [illegible] maintain, in a rough fashion, strict order [illegible] all their subjects.

[illegible] to Liutprand (712–744) the Lombard [illegible] in the irregular fashion of the time, [illegible] sometimes by election, sometimes by [illegible] fitfully to enlarge their boundaries, [illegible] aristocracy of dukes inherent in the [illegible] nation, an element which, though [illegible] embarrassed the power of the crown, [illegible] the nation. Their old enemies the [illegible] Slaves or Huns, ever ready to break [illegible] times called in by mutinous and [illegible] Trent, were constant and serious [illegible] ts, they were always looked upon with dislike and jealousy, even when they had become zealous Catholics, the founders of churches and monasteries; with the Greek empire there was chronic war. From time to time they made raids into the unsubdued parts of Italy, and added a city or two to their dominions. But there was no sustained effort for the complete subjugation of Italy till Liutprand, the most powerful of the line. He tried it, and failed. He broke up the independence of the great southern duchies, Benevento and Spoleto. For a time, in the heat of the dispute about images, he won the pope to his side against the Greeks. For a time, but only for a time, he deprived the Greeks of Ravenna. Aistulf, his successor, carried on the same policy. He even threatened Rome itself, and claimed a capitation tax. But the popes, thoroughly irritated and alarmed, and hopeless of aid from the East, turned to the family which was rising into power among the Franks of the West, the mayors of the palace of Austrasia. Pope Gregory III. applied in vain to Charles Martel. But with his successors Pippin and Charles the popes were more successful. In return for the transfer by the pope of the Frank crown from the decayed line of Clovis to his own, Pippin crossed the Alps, defeated Aistulf and gave to the pope the lands which Aistulf had torn from the empire, Ravenna and the Pentapolis (754–756). But the angry quarrels still went on between the popes and the Lombards. The Lombards were still to the Italians a "foul and horrid" race. At length, invited by Pope Adrian I., Pippin's son Charlemagne once more descended into Italy. As the Lombard kingdom began, so it ended, with a siege of Pavia. Desiderius, the last king, became a prisoner (774), and the Lombard power perished. Charlemagne, with the title of king of the Franks and Lombards, became master of Italy, and in 800 the pope, who had crowned Pippin king of the Franks, claimed to bestow the Roman empire, and crowned his greater son emperor of the Romans (800).

Effects of the Carolingian Conquest.—To Italy the overthrow of the Lombard kings was the loss of its last chance of independence and unity. To the Lombards the conquest was the destruction of their legal and social supremacy. Henceforth they were equally with the Italians the subjects of the Frank kings. The Carolingian kings expressly recognized the Roman law, and allowed all who would be counted Romans to "profess" it. But Latin influences were not strong enough to extinguish the Lombard name and destroy altogether the recollections and habits of the Lombard rule; Lombard law was still recognized, and survived in the schools of Pavia. Lombardy remained the name of the finest province of Italy, and for a time was the name for Italy itself. But what was specially Lombard could not stand in the long run against the Italian atmosphere which surrounded it. Generation after generation passed more and more into real Italians. Antipathies, indeed, survived, and men even in the 10th century called each other Roman or Langobard as terms of reproach. But the altered name of Lombard also denoted henceforth some of the proudest of Italians; and, though the Lombard speech had utterly perished their most common names still kept up the remembrance that their fathers had come from beyond the Alps.

But the establishment of the Frank kingdom, and still more the re-establishment of the Christian empire as the source of law and jurisdiction in Christendom, had momentous influence on the history of the Italianised Lombards. The Empire was the counterweight to the local tyrannies into which the local authorities established by the Empire itself, the feudal powers, judicial and military, necessary for the purposes of government, invariably tended to degenerate. When they became intolerable, from the Empire were sought the exemptions, privileges, immunities from that local authority, which, anomalous and anarchical as they were in theory, yet in fact were the foundations of all the liberties of the middle ages in the Swiss cantons, in the free towns of Germany and the Low Countries, in the Lombard cities of Italy. Italy was and ever has been a land of cities; and, ever since the downfall of Rome and the decay of the municipal system, the bishops of the cities had really been at the head of the peaceful and industrial part of their population.

and were a natural refuge for the oppressed, and sometimes for the mutinous and the evil doers, from the military and civil powers of the duke or count or judge, too often a rule of cruelty or fraud. Under the Carolingian empire, a vast system grew up in the North Italian cities of episcopal "immunities," by which a city with its surrounding district was removed, more or less completely, from the jurisdiction of the ordinary authority, military or civil, and placed under that of the bishop. These "immunities" led to the temporal sovereignty of the bishops; under it the spirit of liberty grew more readily than under the military chief. Municipal organization, never quite forgotten, naturally revived under new forms, and with its "consuls" at the head of the citizens, with its "arts" and "crafts" and "gilds," grew up secure under the shadow of the church. In due time the city populations, free from the feudal yoke, and safe within the walls which in many instances the bishops had built for them, became impatient also of the bishop's government. The cities which the bishops had made thus independent of the dukes and counts next sought to be free from the bishops; in due time they too gained their charters of privilege and liberty. Left to take care of themselves, islands in a sea of turbulence, they grew in the sense of self-reliance and independence; they grew also to be aggressive, quarrelsome and ambitious. Thus, by the 11th century, the Lombard cities had become "communes," commonalties, republics, managing their own affairs, and ready for attack or defence. Milan had recovered its greatness, ecclesiastically as well as politically; it scarcely bowed to Rome, and it aspired to the position of a sovereign city, mistress over its neighbours. At length, in the 12th century, the inevitable conflict came between the republicanism of the Lombard cities and the German feudalism which still claimed their allegiance in the name of the Empire. Leagues and counter-leagues were formed; and a confederacy of cities, with Milan at its head, challenged the strength of Germany under one of its sternest emperors, Frederick Barbarossa. At first Frederick was victorious; Milan, except its churches, was utterly destroyed; everything that marked municipal independence was abolished in the "rebel" cities; and they had to receive an imperial magistrate instead of their own (1158–1162). But the Lombard league was again formed. Milan was rebuilt, with the help even of its jealous rivals, and at Legnano (1176) Frederick was utterly defeated. The Lombard cities had regained their independence; and at the peace of Constance (1183) Frederick found himself compelled to confirm it.

From the peace of Constance the history of the Lombards is merely part of the history of Italy. Their cities went through the ordinary fortunes of most Italian cities. They quarrelled and fought with one another. They took opposite sides in the great strife of the time between pope and emperor, and were Guelf and Ghibelline by old tradition, or as one or other faction prevailed in them. They swayed backwards and forwards between the power of the people and the power of the few; but democracy and oligarchy passed sooner or later into the hands of a master who veiled his lordship under various titles, and generally at last into the hands of a family. Then, in the larger political struggles and changes of Europe, they were incorporated into a kingdom, or principality or duchy, carved out to suit the interest of a foreigner, or to make a heritage for the nephew of a pope. But in two ways especially the energetic race which grew out of the fusion of Langobards and Italians between the 9th and the 12th centuries has left the memory of itself. In England, at least, the enterprising traders and bankers who found their way to the West, from the 13th to the 16th centuries, though they certainly did not all come from Lombardy, bore the name of Lombards. In the next place, the Lombards or the Italian builders whom they employed or followed, the "masters of Como," of whom so much is said in the early Lombard laws, introduced a manner of building, stately, solemn and elastic, to which their name has been attached, and which gives a character of its own to some of the most interesting churches in Italy (R. W. C.)

LOMBARDY, a territorial division of Italy, bounded N. by the Alps, S. by Emilia, E. by Venetia and W. by Piedmont. It is divided into eight provinces, Bergamo, Brescia, Como, Cremona, Mantua, Milan, Pavia and Sondrio, and has an area of 9386 sq. m. Milan, the chief city, is the greatest railway centre of Italy; it is in direct communication not only with the other principal towns of Lombardy and the rest of Italy but also with the larger towns of France, Germany and Switzerland, being the nearest great town to the tunnels of the St Gothard and the Simplon. The other railway centres of the territory are Mortara, Pavia and Mantua, while every considerable town is situated on or within easy reach of the railway, this being rendered comparatively easy owing to the relative flatness of the greater part of the country. The line from Milan to Porto Ceresio is worked in the main by electric motor driven trains, while on that from Lecco to Colico and Chiavenna over-head wires are adopted. The more remote districts and the immediate environs of the larger town are served by steam tramways and electric railways. The most important rivers are the Po, which follows, for the most part, the southern boundary of Lombardy, and the Ticino, one of the largest tributaries of the Po, which forms for a considerable distance the western boundary. The majority of the Italian lakes, those of Garda, Idro, Iseo, Como, Lugano, Varese and Maggiore, lie wholly or in part within it. The climate of Lombardy is thoroughly continental; in summer the heat is greater than in the south of Italy, while the winter is very cold, and bitter winds, snow and mist are frequent. In the summer rain is rare beyond the lower Alps, but a system of irrigation, unsurpassed in Europe, and dating from the middle ages, prevails, so that a failure of the crops is hardly possible. There are three zones of cultivation: in the mountains, pasturage; the lower slopes are devoted to the culture of the vine, fruit-trees (including chestnuts) and the silkworm; while in the regions of the plain, large crops of maize, rice, wheat, flax, hemp and wine are produced, and thousands of mulberry-trees are grown for the benefit of the silkworms, the culture of which in the province of Milan has entirely superseded the sheep-breeding for which it was famous during the middle ages. Milan is indeed the principal silk market in the world. In 1905 there were 490 mills reeling silk in Lombardy, with 35,407 workers, and 276 throwing-mills with 586,000 spindles. The chief centre of silk weaving is Como, but the silk is commercially dealt with at Milan, and there is much exportation. A considerable amount of cotton is manufactured, but most of the raw cotton (600,000 bales) is imported, the cultivation being insignificant in Italy. There are 400 mills in Lombardy, 277 of which are in the province of Milan. The largest linen and woollen mills in Italy are situated at Fara d'Adda. Milan also manufactures motor-cars, though Turin is the principal centre in Italy for this industry. There are copper, zinc and iron mines, and numerous quarries of marble, alabaster and granite. In addition to the above industries the chief manufactures are hats, rope and paper-making, iron-casting, gun-making, printing and lithography. Lombardy is indeed the most industrial district of Italy. In parts the peasants suffer much from *pellagra*.

The most important towns with their communal population in the respective provinces, according to the census of 1901, are Bergamo (46,861), Treviglio (14,897), total of province 467,549, number of communes 306; Brescia (69,210), Chiari (10,749), total of province 541,765, number of communes 280; Como (38,174), Varese (17,666), Cantù (10,725), Lecco (10,352), total of province 594,304, number of communes 510; Cremona (36,848), Casalmaggiore (16,407), Soresina (10,358), total of province 329,471, number of communes 133; Mantua (30,127), Viadana (16,082), Quistello (11,228), Suzzara (11,502), St Benedetto Po (10,908), total of province 315,448, number of communes 68; Milan (490,084), Monza (42,124), Lodi (26,827), Busto Arsizio (20,005), Legnano (18,285), Seregno (12,050), Gallarate (11,952), Codogno (11,925), total of province 1,450,214, number of communes 297; Pavia (33,922), Vigevano (23,560), Voghera (20,442), total of province 504,382, number of communes 221; Sondrio (7077), total of province 130,966, number of communes 78. The total population of Lombardy was 4,334,099. In most of the provinces of Lombardy there are far more villages than in other parts of Italy except Piedmont; this is attributable partly to their mountainous character, partly perhaps to security from attack by sea (contrast the state of things in Apulia).

Previous to the fall of the Roman republic Lombardy formed a part of Gallia Transpadana, and it was Lombardy, Venetia and Piedmont, the portion of the Italian peninsula N. of the Po, [illegible] did not receive citizenship in 89 B.C. but only Latin rights. The gift of full citizenship in 49 B.C. made it a part of Italy proper, and Lombardy and Piedmont formed the 11th region of [illegible] (Transpadana) while Venetia and Istria formed the [illegible]. It was the second of the regions of Italy in size, but the [illegible] number of towns; it appears, however, to have been [illegible] and peaceful, and cultivation flourished in its fertile [illegible]. By the end of the 4th century A.D. the name Liguria [illegible] extended over it, and Milan was regarded as the [illegible]. Stranger still, in the 6th century the old Liguria [illegible] from it, and under the name of *Alpes Cottiae* [illegible] Lombard province of Italy.

[illegible] subsequent history see LOMBARDS and ITALY; [illegible] see ARCHITECTURE. G. T. Rivoira in *Origini* [illegible] (2 vols. Rome, 1901–1907), successfully [illegible] the classical origin of much that had hitherto been [illegible] authorities as "Byzantine." In the development [illegible] architecture and art Lombardy played a great part, [illegible] Bramante and Leonardo da Vinci resided in [illegible] of the 15th century.

[illegible] (called by the natives *Sasak*), one of the Lesser [illegible] in the Dutch East Indies, E. of Java, between [illegible] S. and 115° 46′ and 116° 40′ E., with an area of [illegible] separated from Bali by the Strait of Lombok [illegible] Sumbawa by the Strait of Alas. Rising out of the sea [illegible] precipitous coasts, Lombok is traversed by [illegible] chains. The northern chain is of volcanic formation [illegible] the peak of Lombok (11,810 ft.), one of the [illegible] in the Malay Archipelago. It is surrounded [illegible] with lower summits, and a magnificent lake, [illegible] ft. high. The southern chain rises a little [illegible]. Between the two chains is a broad valley or terrace [illegible] volcanic hills. Forest-clad mountains and [illegible] jungle alternating with rich alluvial plains, [illegible] under an ancient and elaborate system [illegible] the scenery of Lombok exceedingly attractive. [illegible] only for irrigation and the growing of [illegible] quality. In the plains are also grown [illegible] and sugar, katyang (native beans), cotton [illegible] products are exported. To the naturalist [illegible] interest as the frontier island of the [illegible] its cockatoos and megapods or mound-[illegible] bee-eaters and ground thrushes. The [illegible] the aborigines, as no trace of an [illegible]. They are Mahommedans and distinct in [illegible] the Hindu Balinese, who vanquished [illegible]. The island was formerly divided [illegible] Asam Lombok on the W. side, [illegible] in the S.W. and Pagutan [illegible] dated from the conquest by Agong [illegible] 10th century; the union under [illegible] dated from 1850. In July 1894 [illegible] Ampanam, and advanced towards [illegible] Balinese sultan, who had defied [illegible] send the usual delegation to [illegible] expedition were to punish Mataram [illegible] the Sasaks whom the Balinese [illegible] Dutch expedition met with [illegible] were forced back upon [illegible] despatched a much stronger [illegible] in September. Mataram [illegible] the troops stormed the sultan's [illegible] another chieftain's citadel, [illegible] The old sultan of Mataram [illegible] Balinese chiefs were exiled to [illegible] archipelago, whilst the sultan's [illegible]. Thus ended the Balinese [illegible] island was placed under direct [illegible] resident being appointed [illegible] administered from Bali by the [illegible] people, however, are in [illegible] religions, customs and [illegible] Lombok

Balinese frequently occur. Lombok has been divided since 1898 into the West, Middle and East Lombok. Its chief towns are Mataram, Praya and Sisi. On the west coast the harbour of Ampanam is the most frequented, though, on account of heavy breakers, it is often difficult of approach. The Sasaks are estimated at 320,000, the Balinese at 50,000, Europeans number about 40, Chinese 300, and Arabs 170.

See A. R. Wallace, *Malay Archipelago* (London, 1869, and later editions). The famous "Wallace's Line" runs immediately west of Lombok, which therefore has an important part in the work. Captain W. Cool, *With the Dutch in the East* (Amsterdam and London, 1897), in Dutch and English, is a narrative of the events sketched above, and contains many particulars about the folklore and dual religions of Lombok, which, with Bali, forms the last stronghold of Hinduism east of Java.

LOMBROSO, CESARE (1836–1909), Italian criminologist, was born on the 18th of November 1836 at Verona, of a Jewish family. He studied at Padua, Vienna and Paris, and was in 1862 appointed professor of psychiatry at Pavia, then director of the lunatic asylum at Pesaro, and later professor of forensic medicine and of psychiatry at Turin, where he eventually filled the chair of criminal anthropology. His works, several of which have been translated into English, include *L'Uomo delinquente* (1889); *L'Uomo di genio* (1888) *Genio e follia* (1877) and *La Donna delinquente* (1893). In 1872 he had made the notable discovery that the disorder known as *pellagra* was due (but see PELLAGRA) to a poison contained in diseased maize, eaten by the peasants, and he returned to this subject in *La Pellagra in Italia* (1885) and other works. Lombroso, like Giovanni Bovio (b. 1841), Enrico Ferri (b. 1856) and Colajanni, well-known Italian criminologists, and his sons-in-law G. Ferrero and Carrara, was strongly influenced by Auguste Comte, and owed to him an exaggerated tendency to refer all mental facts to biological causes. In spite of this, however, and a serious want of accuracy and discrimination in handling evidence, his work made an epoch in criminology; for he surpassed all his predecessors by the wide scope and systematic character of his researches, and by the practical conclusions he drew from them. Their net theoretical results is that the criminal population exhibits a higher percentage of physical, nervous and mental anomalies than non-criminals; and that these anomalies are due partly to degeneration, partly to atavism. The criminal is a special type of the human race, standing midway between the lunatic and the savage. This doctrine of a "criminal type" has been gravely criticized, but is admitted by all to contain a substratum of truth. The practical reform to which it points is a classification of offenders, so that the born criminal may receive a different kind of punishment from the offender who is tempted into crime by circumstances (see also CRIMINOLOGY). Lombroso's biological principles are much less successful in his work on Genius, which he explains as a morbid, degenerative condition, presenting analogies to insanity, and not altogether alien to crime. In 1899 he published in French a book which gives a résumé of much of his earlier work, entitled *Le Crime, causes et remèdes*. Later works are: *Delitti vecchi e delitti nuovi* (Turin, 1902); *Nuovi studi sul genio* (2 vols. Palermo, 1902); and in 1908 a work on spiritualism (Eng. trans. *After Death—What?* 1909), to which subject he had turned his attention during the later years of his life. He died suddenly from a heart complaint at Turin on the 19th of October 1909.

See Kurella, *Cesare Lombroso und die Naturgeschichte des Verbrechers* (Hamburg, 1892); and a biography, with an analysis of his works, and a short account of their general conclusions by his daughters, Paola Carrara and Gina Ferrero, written in 1906 on the occasion of the sixth congress of criminal anthropology at Turin.

LOMÉNIE DE BRIENNE, ÉTIENNE CHARLES DE (1727–1794), French politician and ecclesiastic, was born at Paris on the 9th of October 1727. He belonged to a Limousin family, dating from the 15th century, and after a brilliant career as a student entered the Church, as being the best way to attain to a distinguished position. In 1751 he became a doctor of theology, though there were doubts as to the orthodoxy of his thesis. In 1752 he was appointed grand vicar to the archbishop of Rouen. After visiting Rome, he was made bishop of Condom

(1760), and in 1763 was translated to the archbishopric of Toulouse. He had many famous friends, among them A. R. J. Turgot, the Abbé A. Morellet and Voltaire, and in 1770 became an academician. He was on three occasions the head of the *bureau de jurisdiction* at the general assembly of the clergy; he also took an interest in political and social questions of the day, and addressed to Turgot a number of *mémoires* on these subjects, one of them, treating of pauperism, being especially remarkable. In 1787 he was nominated as president of the Assembly of Notables, in which capacity he attacked the fiscal policy of Calonne, whom he succeeded as head of the *conseil des finances* on the 1st of May 1787. Once in power, he succeeded in making the parlement register edicts dealing with internal free trade, the establishment of provincial assemblies and the redemption of the *corvée*; on their refusal to register edicts on the stamp duty and the proposed new general land-tax, he persuaded the king to hold a *lit de justice*, to enforce their registration. To crush the opposition to these measures, he persuaded the king to exile the parlement to Troyes (August 15th, 1787). On the agreement of the parlement to sanction a prolongation for two years to the tax of the two *vingtièmes* (a direct tax on all kinds of income), in lieu of the above two taxes, he recalled the councillors to Paris. But a further attempt to force the parlement to register an edict for raising a loan of 120 million *livres* met with determined opposition. The struggle of the parlement against the incapacity of Brienne ended on the 8th of May in its consenting to an edict for its own abolition; but with the proviso that the states-general should be summoned to remedy the disorders of the state. Brienne, who had in the meantime been made archbishop of Sens, now found himself face to face with almost universal opposition; he was forced to suspend the *Cour plénière* which had been set up to take the place of the parlement, and himself to promise that the states-general should be summoned. But even these concessions were not able to keep him in power, and on the 29th of August he had to retire, leaving the treasury empty. On the 15th of December following, he was made a cardinal, and went to Italy, where he spent two years. After the outbreak of the Revolution he returned to France, and took the oath of the Civil Constitution of the Clergy in 1790 (see FRENCH REVOLUTION). He was repudiated by the pope, and in 1791 had to give up the biretta at the command of Pius VI. Both his past and present conduct made him an object of suspicion to the revolutionaries; he was arrested at Sens on the 9th of November 1793, and died in prison, either of an apoplectic stroke or by poison, on the 16th of February 1794.

The chief works published by Brienne are: *Oraison funèbre du Dauphin* (Paris, 1766); *Compte-rendu au roi* (Paris, 1788); *Le Conciliateur*, in collaboration with Turgot (Rome, Paris, 1754). See also J. Perrin, *Le Cardinal Loménie de Brienne . . . épisodes de la Révolution* (Sens, 1896).

LOMOND, LOCH, the largest and most beautiful of Scottish lakes, situated in the counties of Stirling and Dumbarton. It is about 23 m. long; its width varies from 5 m. towards the south end to ¾ m. at the narrows to the north of the Isle of the Vow; its area is 27 sq. m., and the greatest depth 630 ft. It is only 23 ft. above the sea, of which doubtless it was at one time an arm. It contains 30 islands, the largest of which is Inchmurrin, a deer park belonging to the duke of Montrose. Among other islands are Inch Cailliach (the "Island of Women," from the fact that a nunnery once stood there), Inchfad ("Long Island"), Inchcruin ("Round Island"), Inchtavannach ("Monks' Isle"), Inchconnachan ("Colquhoun's Isle"), Inchlonaig ("Isle of the Yews," where Robert Bruce caused yews to be planted to provide arms for his bowmen), Creinch, Torrinch and Clairinch (which gave the Buchanans their war-cry). From the west the loch receives the Inveruglas, the Douglas, the Luss, the Finlas and the Fruin. From Balloch in the south it sends off the Leven to the Clyde; from the east it receives the Endrick, the Blair, the Cashell and the Arklet; and from the north the Falloch. Ben Lomond (3192 ft.), the ascent of which is made with comparative ease from Rowardennan, dominates the landscape; but there are other majestic hills, particularly on the west and north-west banks. The fish are sea-trout, lake-trout, pike and perch. Part of the shore is skirted by the West Highland railway, opened in 1894, which has stations on the loch at Tarbet and Ardlui, and Balloch is the terminus of the lines from Dumbarton and from Stirling via Buchlyvie. Steamers make the tour of the loch, starting from Balloch and calling at Balmaha, Luss, Rowardennan, Tarbet, Inversnaid and Ardlui. Luss has a considerable population, and there is some stone quarried near it. INVERSNAID is the point of arrival and departure for the Trossachs coaches, and here, too, there is a graceful waterfall, fed by the Arklet from the loch of that name, 2½ m. to the east, commemorated in Wordsworth's poem of the "Highland Girl." Inversnaid was in the heart of the Macgregor country, and the name of Rob Roy is still given to his cave on the loch side a mile to the north and to his prison 3 m. to the south. Inversnaid was the site of a fort built in 1713 to reduce the clan to subjection. Craig Royston, a tract lying between Inversnaid and Ben Lomond, was also associated with Rob Roy.

LOMONOSOV, MIKHAIL VASILIEVICH (1711–1765), Russian poet and man of science, was born in the year 1711, in the village of Denisovka (the name of which was afterwards changed in honour of the poet), situated on an island not far from Kholmogori, in the government of Archangel. His father, a fisherman, took the boy when he was ten years of age to assist him in his calling, but the lad's eagerness for knowledge was unbounded. The few books accessible to him he almost learned by heart; and, seeing that there was no chance of increasing his stock of knowledge in his native place, he resolved to betake himself to Moscow. An opportunity occurred when he was seventeen, and by the intervention of friends he obtained admission into the Zaikonospasski school. There his progress was very rapid, especially in Latin, and in 1734 he was sent from Moscow to St Petersburg. There again his proficiency, especially in physical science, was marked, and he was one of the young Russians chosen to complete their education in foreign countries. He accordingly commenced the study of metallurgy at Marburg; he also began to write poetry, imitating German authors, among whom he is said to have especially admired Günther. His *Ode on the Taking of Khotin from the Turks* was composed in 1739, and attracted a great deal of attention at St Petersburg. During his residence in Germany Lomonósov married a native of the country, and found it difficult to maintain his increasing family on the scanty allowance granted to him by the St Petersburg Academy, which, moreover, was irregularly sent. His circumstances became embarrassed, and he resolved to leave the country secretly and to return home. On his arrival in Russia he rapidly rose to distinction, and was made professor of chemistry in the university of St Petersburg; he ultimately became rector, and in 1764 secretary of state. He died in 1765.

The most valuable of the works of Lomonósov are those relating to physical science, and he wrote upon many branches of it. He everywhere shows himself a man of the most varied learning. He compiled a Russian grammar, which long enjoyed popularity, and did much to improve the rhythm of Russian verse.

LOMZA, or LOMZHA, a government of Russian Poland, bounded N. by Prussia and the Polish government of Suwalki, E. by the Russian government of Grodno, S. by the Polish governments of Siedlce and Warsaw and W. by that of Plock. It covers 4666 sq. m. It is mostly flat or undulating, with a few tracts in the north and south-west where the deeply cut valleys give a hilly aspect to the country. Extensive marshes overspread it, especially on the banks of the Narev, which flows from east to south-west, joining the Bug in the south-western corner of the government. The Bug flows along the southern border, joining the Vistula 20 m. below its confluence with the Narev. There are forests in the east of the government. The inhabitants numbered 501,385 in 1872 and 585,033 in 1897, of whom 279,279 were women, and 69,834 lived in towns. The estimated population in 1906 was 653,100. By religion 77½% are Roman Catholics, 15½% Jews and 5½% members of the Orthodox Church. Agriculture is the predominant industry, the chief crops being rye, oats, wheat, barley, buckwheat, peas, potatoes, flax and hemp. Bees are extensively kept, and large numbers of [illegible] are reared. Stock raising is carried [illegible]. The wood trade is important; other in[illegible] of pottery, beer, flour, leather, [illegible] spirits, tobacco and sugar. There is only [illegible] Grodno and Warsaw), the Bug is navig[illegible] floated down the Narev. The govern[illegible] seven districts, of which the chief towns, [illegible] in 1897, are Lomza (q.v.), Ostrolenka [illegible], Ostrów (11,264), Maków (7232), Kolno [illegible].

[illegible] Russia, capital of the government of the [illegible] Narew, 103 m. by rail N.E. from Warsaw. [illegible] 22,428. Lomza is an old town, one [illegible] having been erected before 1000. In the 16th [illegible] brisk trade with Lithuania and Prussia. [illegible] had two citadels, but nevertheless often [illegible] invasions of the Germans and Tatars, and in the [illegible] was twice plundered by the Cossacks of the [illegible] under the dominion of Prussia, and [illegible] 1807 it came under Russian rule.

[illegible] India, in the Poona district of Bombay, [illegible] pass in the Western Ghats, by which [illegible] railway climbs from Bombay to [illegible]. It contains the locomotive works [illegible] place of resort from Bombay during [illegible]

[illegible] port of entry of Middlesex county, [illegible] N.W. of Toronto, on the river [illegible] Canadian Pacific and Michigan [illegible] 1881, but several suburbs, not [illegible] part of the city. The [illegible] a reproduction of that of the great [illegible]. Situated in a fertile agricul[illegible] distributing centre. Among the [illegible] refineries, and factories [illegible] agricultural implements and of railway [illegible] institutions include the Hellmuth [illegible] University (founded in 1878 [illegible] Church of England). London was [illegible]

[illegible] England and of the British Empire, [illegible] world, lying on each side of the [illegible] mouth.[1] The "City," so called [illegible] a small area (673 acres) on the [illegible] the heart of the metropolis, [illegible] boundaries one only, and one of the [illegible] municipal divisions which make up the [illegible] London. The twenty-eight remaining [illegible] Boroughs. The county thus [illegible] (E. to W.) of 16 m., an extreme [illegible] and an area of 74,839 acres or about [illegible] as follows:—

[illegible]—Touching the northern boundary [illegible] to E.—Hammersmith, Kensington, [illegible] St Pancras, Islington, Stoke Newing[illegible]

[illegible]—Fulham, Chelsea, the City of West[illegible] London intervenes), Stepney, Poplar. [illegible] the City and Stepney, and the northern [illegible] (commonly Marylebone), Holborn, [illegible] Bethnal Green.

[illegible]—Wandsworth, Battersea, Lambeth, [illegible] Bermondsey, Deptford, Lewisham, [illegible] with a small part of the north bank).

[illegible] in common use, though their formal [illegible] extended over several districts [illegible] remain familiar. Each borough [illegible]

[illegible] (vol. xix., 1909), an annual publica[illegible] Council, which besides these divisions [illegible] London main drainage area, and the [illegible]

I. Extent and Site

The County of London is bounded N. and W. by Middlesex, E. by Essex and Kent, S. by Kent and Surrey. The Metropolitan police area, or "Greater London," however, embraces the whole of Middlesex, with parts of the other three counties and of Hertfordshire. Its extent is 443,419 acres or nearly 693 sq. m., and its population is about seven millions. Only here and there upon its fringe the identity of this great area with the metropolis is lost to the eye, where open country remains unbroken by streets or close-set buildings.

Site.—North of the Thames, and west of its tributary the Lea, which partly bounds the administrative county on the east, London is built upon a series of slight undulations, only rarely sufficient to make the streets noticeably steep. On the northern boundary of the county a height of 443 ft. is found on the open Hampstead Heath. The lesser streams which flow from this high ground to the Thames are no longer open. Some, however, as well as other natural features effaced by the growth of the city, retain an historical interest through the survival of their names in streets and districts, or through their relation to the original site of London (in the present City). South of the Thames a broken amphitheatre of low hills, approaching the river near Greenwich and Woolwich on the east and Putney and Richmond on the west, encloses a tract flatter than that to the north, and rises more abruptly in the southern districts of Streatham, Norwood and Forest Hill.

In attempting to picture the site of London in its original condition, that is, before any building took place, it is necessary to consider (1) the condition of the Thames unconfined between made banks, (2) the slopes overlooking it, (3) the tributary streams which watered these slopes. The low ground between the slight hills flanking the Thames valley, and therefore mainly south of the present river, was originally occupied by a shallow lagoon of estuarine character, tidal, and interspersed with marshy tracts and certain islets of relatively firm land. Through this the main stream of the Thames pursued an ill-defined course. The tributary streams entered through marshy channels. The natural process of sedimentation assisted the gradual artificial drainage of the marshes by means of embankments confining the river. The breadth of this low tract, from Chelsea downward, was from 2 to 3 m. The line of the foot of the southern hills, from Putney, where it nearly approaches the present river, lies through Stockwell and Camberwell to Greenwich, where it again approaches the river. On the north there is a flat tract between Chelsea and Westminster, covering Pimlico, but from Westminster down to the Tower there is a marked slope directly up from the river bank. Lower still, marshes formerly extended far up the valley of the Lea. The higher slopes of the hills were densely forested (cf. the modern district-name St John's Wood), while the lower slopes, north of the river, were more open (cf. Moor-gate). The original city grew up on the site of the City of London of the present day, on a slight eminence intersected by the Wal- or Wall-brook, and flanked on the west by the river Fleet.

These and other tributary streams have been covered in and built over (in some cases serving as sewers), but it is possible to trace their valleys at various points by the fall and rise of streets crossing them, and their names survive, as will be seen, in various modern applications. The Wallbrook rose in a marsh in the modern district of Finsbury, and joined the Thames close to the Cannon Street railway bridge. A street named after it runs south from the Mansion House parallel with its course. The Fleet was larger, rising in, and collecting various small streams from, the high ground of Hampstead. It passed Kentish Town, Camden Town and King's Cross, and followed a line approximating to King's Cross Road. The slope of Farringdon Road, where crossed by Holborn Viaduct, and of New Bridge Street, Blackfriars, marks its course exactly, and that of Fleet Street and Ludgate Hill its steep banks. The name also appears in Fleet Road, Hampstead. From King's Cross downward the banks were so steep and high that the stream was called

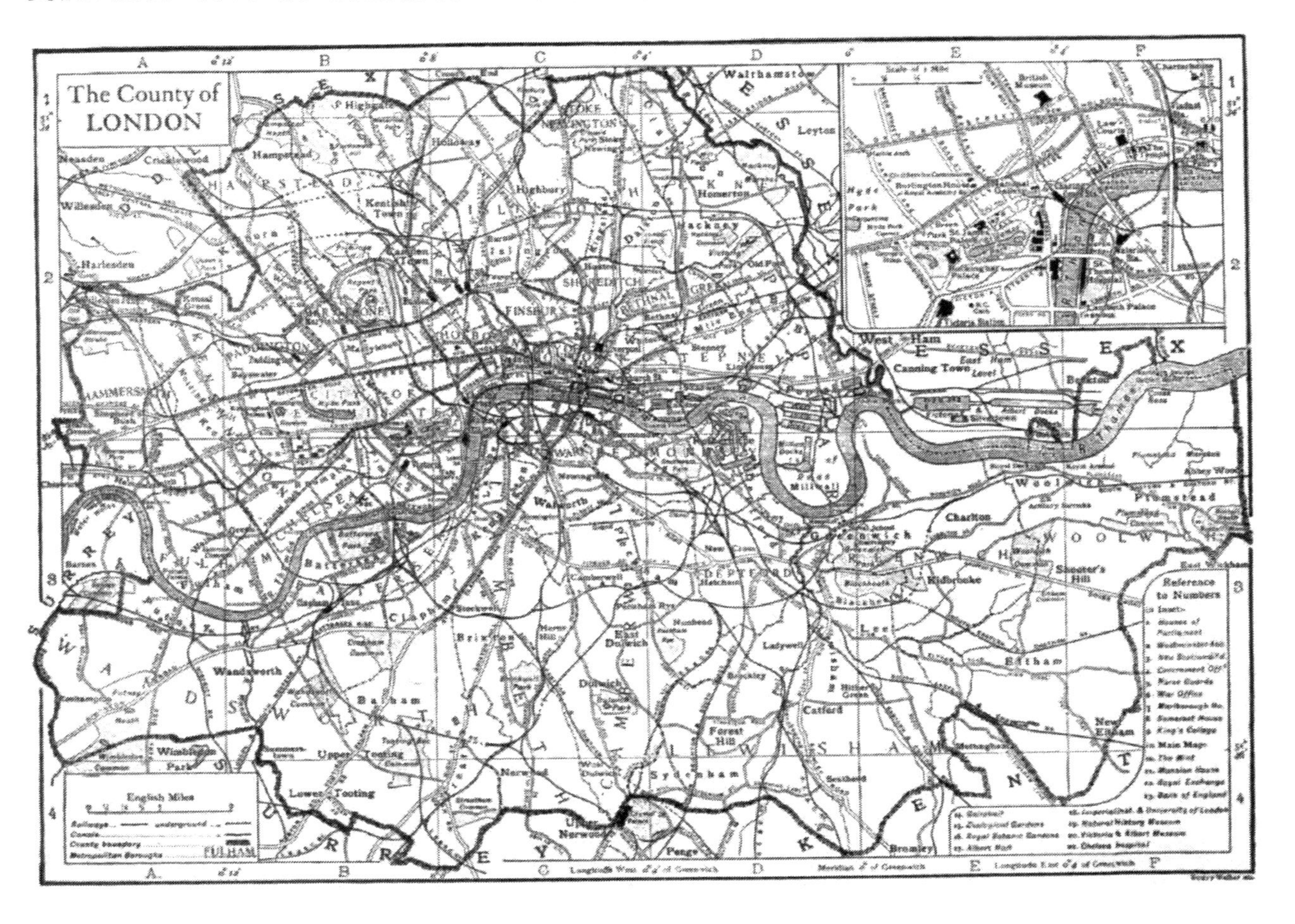

The County of LONDON
Hampstead
Highbury
Holloway
Kentish Town
Hackney
Homerton
Walthamstow
Leyton
Willesden
Harlesden
Shoreditch
Finsbury
West Ham
Canning Town
East Ham
Walworth
Charlton
Plumstead
Greenwich
Kidbrooke
Shooter's Hill
Brixton
East Dulwich
Dulwich
Ladywell
Lee
Eltham
Wandsworth
Balham
Catford
Forest Hill
Sydenham
Upper Tooting
Lower Tooting
Wimbledon Park
Norwood
Upper Norwood
Penge
Bromley
New Eltham
Reference to Numbers
English Miles
FULHAM

Hollow or Hole-bourne, this name surviving in Holborn; and it was fed by numerous springs (Bagnigge Well, Clerkenwell and others) in this vicinity. It entered a creek which was navigable for a considerable distance, and formed a subsidiary harbour for the City, but by the 14th century this was becoming choked with refuse, and though an attempt was made to clear it, and wharves were built in 1670, it was wholly arched over in 1737-1765 below Holborn Bridge. Continuing westward, the most important stream was Tyburn (*q.v.*), which rose at Hampstead, and joined the Thames through branches on either side of Thorney Island, on which grew up the great ecclesiastical foundation of St Peter, Westminster, better known as Westminster Abbey. There is no modern survival of the name of Tyburn, which finds, indeed, its chief historical interest as attaching to the famous place of execution which lay near the modern Marble Arch. The residential district in this vicinity was known at a later date as Tyburnia. The next stream westward was the Westbourne, the name of which is perpetuated in Westbourne Grove and elsewhere in Paddington. It rose on the heights of Hampstead, traversed Paddington, may be traced in the course of the Serpentine lake in Hyde Park, ran parallel to and east of Sloane Street, and joined the Thames close to Chelsea Bridge. The main tributaries of the Thames from the north, to east and west of those described, are not covered, nor is any tributary of importance from the south entirely concealed.

Geology.—London lies within the geological area known as the London basin. Within the confines of Greater London the chalk which forms the basement of this area appears at the surface in isolated patches about Greenwich, while its main line approaches within 10 m. of the City to the south and within 15 to the north-west. In the south and north-west the typical London clay is the principal formation. In the south-east, however, the Blackheath and Woolwich pebble-beds appear, with their belts of Thanet sands bordering the chalk. Valley gravel borders the Thames, with some interruptions, from Kingston to Greenwich, and extends to a wide belt, with ramifications, from Wandsworth south to Croydon, and in a narrower line from Greenwich towards Bromley. Brick earth overlies it from Kensington to Brentford and west thereof, and appears in Chelsea and Fulham, Hornsey and Stoke Newington, and in patches south of the Thames between Battersea and Richmond. The main deposits of alluvium occur below Lambeth and Westminster, and in the valley of the Wandle, which joins the Thames from the south near Putney. In the north and west the clay is interspersed with patches of plateau gravel in the direction of Finchley (where boulder clay also appears), Enfield and Barnet, and of Bagshot sands on Hampstead Heath and Harrow Hill. Gravel is found on the high ground about Richmond Park and Wimbledon. (See further MIDDLESEX.)

Climate.—The climate is equable (though excessive heat is sometimes felt for short periods during the summer) and moist, but healthy. Snow is most common in the early months of the year. The fogs of London have a peculiar and perhaps an exaggerated notoriety. They are apt to occur at all seasons, are common from September to February, and most common in November. The atmosphere of London is almost invariably misty in a greater or less degree, but the denser fogs are generally local and of no long duration. They sometimes cause a serious dislocation of railway and other traffic. Their principal cause is the smoke from the general domestic use of coal. The evil is of very long standing, for in 1306 the citizens petitioned Edward I. to prohibit the use of sea-coal, and he made it a capital offence. The average temperature of the hottest month, July, is 64°·4 F.; of the coldest, January, 37°·9; and the mean annual 50°·4. The mean annual rainfall ranges in different parts of the metropolis from about 20½ to 27½ in.

II. Topography

London as a whole owes nothing in appearance to the natural configuration of its site. Moreover, the splendid building is nearly always a unit; seldom, unless accidentally, a component part of a broad effect. London has not grown up along formal lines; nor is any large part of it laid out according to the conceptions of a single generation. Yet not a few of the great thoroughfares and buildings are individually worthy of London's pre-eminence as a city. The most notable of these fall within a circumscribed area, and it is therefore necessary to preface their consideration with a statement of the broader characteristic divisions of the metropolis.

Characteristic Divisions.—In London north of the Thames, the salient distinction lies between West and East. From the western boundary of the City proper, an area covering the greater part of the city of Westminster, and extending into Chelsea, Kensington, Paddington and Marylebone, is exclusively associated with the higher-class life of London. Within the bounds of Westminster are the royal palaces, the government offices and many other of the finest public buildings, and the wider area specified includes the majority of the residences of the wealthier classes, the most beautiful parks and the most fashionable places of recreation. "Mayfair," north of Piccadilly, and "Belgravia," south of Knightsbridge, are common though unofficial names for the richest residential districts. The "City" bears in the great commercial buildings fringing its narrow streets all the marks of a centre of the world's exchanges. East of it there is an abrupt transition to the district commonly known as the "East End," as distinguished from the wealthy "West End," a district of mean streets, roughly coincident with the boroughs of Stepney and Poplar, Shoreditch and Bethnal Green, and primarily (though by no means exclusively) associated with the problems attaching to the life of the poor. On the Thames below London Bridge, London appears in the aspect of one of the world's great ports, with extensive docks and crowded shipping. North London is as a whole residential: Hackney, Islington and St Pancras consist mainly of dwellings of artisans and the middle classes; while in Hampstead, St Marylebone and Paddington are many terraces and squares of handsome houses. Throughout the better residential quarters of London the number of large blocks of flats has greatly increased in modern times. But even in the midst of the richest quarters, in Westminster and elsewhere, small but well-defined areas of the poorest dwellings occur.

London south of the Thames has none of the grander characteristics of the wealthy districts to the north. Poor quarters lie adjacent to the river over the whole distance from Battersea to Greenwich, merging southward into residential districts of better class. London has no single well-defined manufacturing quarter.

Suburbs.—Although the boundary of the county of London does not, to outward appearance, enclose a city distinct from its suburbs, London outside that boundary may be conveniently considered as suburban. Large numbers of business men and others who must of necessity live in proximity to the metropolis have their homes aloof from its centre. It is estimated that upwards of a million daily enter and leave the City alone as the commercial heart of London, and a great proportion of these travel in and out by the suburban railways. In this aspect the principal extension of London has been into the counties of Kent and Surrey, to the pleasant hilly districts about Sydenham, Norwood and Croydon, Chislehurst and Orpington, Caterham, Redhill and Reigate, Epsom, Dorking and Leatherhead; and up the valley of the Thames through Richmond to Kingston and Surbiton, Esher and Weybridge, and the many townships on both the Surrey and the Middlesex shores of the river. On the west and north the residential suburbs immediately outside the county include Acton and Ealing, Willesden, Highgate, Finchley and Hornsey; from the last two a densely populated district extends north through Wood Green and Southgate to Barnet and Enfield; while the "residential influence" of the metropolis far exceeds these limits, and may be observed at Harrow and Pinner, Bushey and Boxmoor, St Albans, Harpenden, Stevenage and many other places. To the north-east the beauty of Epping Forest attracts numerous residents to Woodford, Chingford and Loughton. The valley of the Lea is also thickly populated, but chiefly by an industrial population working in the numerous factories along this river. The Lea separates the county of London from Essex, but the townships of West Ham and Stratford, Barking and Ilford, Leyton and Walthamstow continue the metropolis in this direction almost without a break. Their population is also largely occupied in local manufacturing establishments; while numerous towns on either bank of the lower Thames share in the industries of the port of London.

Streets.—The principal continuous thoroughfares within the metropolis, though each bears a succession of names, are coincident with the main roads converging upon the capital from all parts of England. On the north of the Thames two great thoroughfares from the west meet in the heart of the City. The northern enters the county in Hammersmith as Uxbridge Road, crosses Kensington and borders the north side of Kensington Gardens and Hyde Park as Bayswater Road. It then bears successively the names of Oxford Street, New Oxford Street and High Holborn; enters the City, becomes known as Holborn Viaduct from the fact that it is there carried over other

of the nuns and the parishioners respectively. The church of St Mary-le-Bow, in Cheapside, is built upon a Norman crypt, and that of St Olave's, Hart Street, which was Pepys's church and contains a modern memorial to him, is of the 15th century. Other ancient churches outside the City are few, but there may be noted St Margaret's, under the shadow of Westminster Abbey; and the beautiful Ely Chapel in Holborn (*q.v.*), the only remnant of a palace of the bishops of Ely, now used by the Roman Catholics. The Chapel Royal, Savoy, near the Strand, was rebuilt by Henry VII. on the site of Savoy Palace, which was erected by Peter, earl of Savoy and Richmond, in 1245, and destroyed in the insurrection of Wat Tyler in 1381. In 1505 Henry VII. endowed here a hospital of St John the Baptist for the poor. The chapel was used as the parish church of St Mary-le-Strand (1564–1717) and constituted a Chapel Royal in 1773; but there are no remains of the rest of the foundation.

Sir Christopher Wren.

The architect to whom, after the great fire of 1666, the opportunity fell of leaving the marks of his influence upon London was Sir Christopher Wren. Had all his schemes been followed out, that influence would have extended beyond architecture alone. He, among others, prepared designs for laying out the City anew. But no such model city was destined to be built; the necessity for haste and the jealous guardianship of rights to old foundations resulted in the old lines being generally followed. It is characteristic of London that St Paul's Cathedral (*q.v.*) should be closely hemmed in by houses, and its majestic west front approached obliquely by a winding thoroughfare. The cathedral is Wren's crowning work. It is the scene from time to time of splendid ceremonies, and contains the tombs of many great men; but in this respect it cannot compete with the peculiar associations of Westminster Abbey. Of Wren's other churches it is to be noted that the necessity of economy usually led him to pay special attention to a single feature. He generally chose the steeple, and there are many fine examples of his work in this department. The steeple of St Mary-le-Bow, commonly called Bow Church, is one of the most noteworthy. This church has various points of interest besides its Norman crypt, from which it took the name of Bow, being the first church in London built on arches. The ecclesiastical Court of Arches sat here formerly. "Bow bells" are famous, and any person born within hearing of them is said to be a "Cockney," a term now applied particularly to the dialect of the lower classes in London. Wren occasionally followed the Gothic model, as in St Antholin. The classic style, however, was generally adopted in the period succeeding his own. Some fine churches belong to this period, such as St Martin's-in-the-Fields (1726), the Corinthian portico of which rises on the upper part of Trafalgar Square; but other examples are regrettable. While the architecture of the City churches, with the exceptions mentioned, is not as a rule remarkable, many are notable for the rich and beautiful wood-carving they contain. A Gothic style has been most commonly adopted in building modern churches; but of these the most notable, the Roman Catholic Westminster Cathedral (see WESTMINSTER), is Byzantine, and built principally of brick, with a lofty campanile. The only other ecclesiastical building to be specially mentioned is Lambeth Palace, opposite to the Houses of Parliament across the Thames. It has been a seat of the archbishops of Canterbury since 1197, and though the present residential portion dates only from the early 19th century, the chapel, hall and other parts are of the 13th century and later (see LAMBETH).

Later churches.

Tower of London.

Among secular buildings, there is none more venerable than the Tower of London (*q.v.*), the moated fortress which overlooks the Thames at the eastern boundary of the City. It presents fine examples of Norman architecture; its historical associations are of the highest interest, and its armoury and the regalia of England, which are kept here, attract great numbers of visitors.

Government buildings.

The Houses of Parliament, with Westminster Abbey and St Margaret's Church, complete the finest group of buildings which London possesses; a group essentially Gothic, for the Houses of Parliament, completed in 1867 from the designs of Barry, are in a late Perpendicular style. They cover a great area, the east front giving immediately upon the Thames. The principal external features are the huge Victoria Tower at the south, and the clock tower, with its well-known chimes and the hour-bell "Big Ben," on the north. Some of the apartments are magnificently adorned within, and the building incorporates the ancient Westminster Hall, belonging to the former royal palace on the site (see WESTMINSTER). The government offices are principally in Whitehall, the fine thoroughfare which connects Parliament Square, in the angle between the Houses and the Abbey, with Trafalgar Square. Somerset House (1776–1786), a massive range of buildings by Sir William Chambers, surrounding a quadrangle, and having its front upon the Strand and back upon the Victoria Embankment, occupies the site of a palace founded by the protector Somerset, *c.* 1548. It contains the Exchequer and Audit, Inland Revenue, Probate, Registrar-General's and other offices, and one wing houses King's College. Other offices are the New Record Office, the repository of State papers and other records, and the Patent Office in Chancery Lane. The Heralds' College or College of Arms, the official authority in matters of armorial bearings and pedigrees, occupies a building in Queen Victoria Street, City, erected subsequently to the great fire (1683). The Royal Courts of Justice or Law Courts stand adjacent to the Inns of Court, facing the Strand at the point where a memorial marks the site of Old Temple Bar (1672), at the entrance to the City, removed in 1878 and later re-erected at Theobald's Park, near Cheshunt, Hertfordshire. The Law Courts (1882) were erected from the designs of G. E. Street, in a Gothic style.

The buildings connected with local government in London are, with one exception modern, and handsome town-halls have been erected for some of the boroughs. The exception is the Guildhall (*q.v.*) of the City Corporation, with its splendid hall, the scene of meetings and entertainments of the corporation, its council chamber, library and crypt (partly opened to the public in 1910). In 1906 the London County Council obtained parliamentary sanction for the erection of a county hall on the south bank of the Thames, immediately east of Westminster Bridge, and in 1908 a design submitted by Mr Ralph Knott was accepted in competition. The style prescribed was English Renaissance. Several of the great livery companies or gilds of the City possess fine halls, containing portraits and other collections of high interest and value. Among the more notable of these halls are those of the Mercers, Drapers, Fishmongers, Clothworkers, Armourers and Stationers.

Royal palaces.

The former royal palaces of Westminster and of Whitehall, of which the fine Jacobean banqueting hall remains, are described under WESTMINSTER. The present London residence of the sovereign is Buckingham Palace, on the west side of St James's Park, with beautiful gardens behind it. Buckingham House was built in 1705 for the duke of Buckinghamshire, and purchased by George III. in 1762. The existing palace was finished by John Nash in 1835, but did not meet with approval, and was considerably altered before Queen Victoria occupied it in 1837. As regards its exterior appearance it is one of the least satisfactory of London's great buildings, though the throne room and other state apartments are magnificent within. The picture gallery contains valuable works of Dutch masters and others. The front of the palace forms the background to the public memorial to Queen Victoria, at the head of the Mall. Provision was made in the design, by Sir Aston Webb, for the extension of the Mall to open upon Trafalgar Square, through gateways in a semicircular range of buildings to be occupied by government offices, and for a wide circular space in front of the Palace, with a statue of the Queen by Thomas Brock in its centre. St James's Palace, at the north side of St James's Park, was acquired and rebuilt by Henry VIII., having been formerly a hospital founded in the 12th century for leprous maidens. It was the royal residence after the destruction of Whitehall by fire in the time of William III. until a fire in 1809 destroyed the greater part. Only the gateway and certain apartments remain of the Tudor building. Marlborough House, adjacent to the palace, was built by the first duke of Marlborough in 1710 from the designs of Wren, came into possession of the Crown in 1817, and has been occupied since 1863 by the prince of Wales. In Kensington (*q.v.*), on the west side of Kensington Gardens, is the palace acquired by William III. as a country seat, and though no longer used by the sovereign, is in part occupied by members of the royal family, and possesses a deeper historical interest than the other royal palaces, as the birth-place of Queen Victoria and her residence in youth.

There are few survivals of ancient domestic architecture in London, but the gabled and timbered front of Staple Inn, Holborn (*q.v.*) is a picturesque fragment. In Bishopsgate Street, City, stood Crosby Hall, which belonged to Crosby Place, the mansion of Sir John Crosby (d. 1475). Richard III. occupied the mansion as duke of Gloucester and Lord Protector (cf. Shakespeare's *Richard III.*, Act i. Sc. 3, &c.). The hall was removed in 1908, in spite of strong efforts to preserve it, which resulted in its re-erection on a site in Chelsea. The hall of the Middle Temple is an admirable example of a refectory of later date (1572).

A fine though circumscribed group of buildings is that in the heart of the City which includes the Bank of England, the Royal Exchange and the Mansion House. The Bank is a characteristic building, quadrilateral, massive and low, but covering a large area, without external windows, and almost wholly unadorned; though the north-west corner is copied from the Temple of the Sibyl at Tivoli. The building is mainly the work of Sir John Soane (*c.* 1788). The first building for the Royal Exchange was erected and presented to the City by Sir Thomas Gresham (1565–1570) whose crest, a grasshopper, appears in the wind-vane above the present building. Gresham's Exchange was destroyed in the great fire of 1666; and the subsequent building was similarly destroyed in 1838. The present building has an imposing Corinthian portico, and encloses a court surrounded by an ambulatory adorned with historical paintings by Leighton, Seymour Lucas, Stanhope Forbes and others. The Mansion House was erected *c.* 1740.

The only other public buildings, beyond those at Westminster, which fall into a great group are the modern museums, the Imperial Institute, London University and other institutions, and Albert Hall, which lie between Kensington Gore and Brompton and Cromwell Roads, and these, together with the National Gallery (in Trafalgar Square) and other art galleries, and the principal scientific, educational and recreative institutions, are considered in Section V.

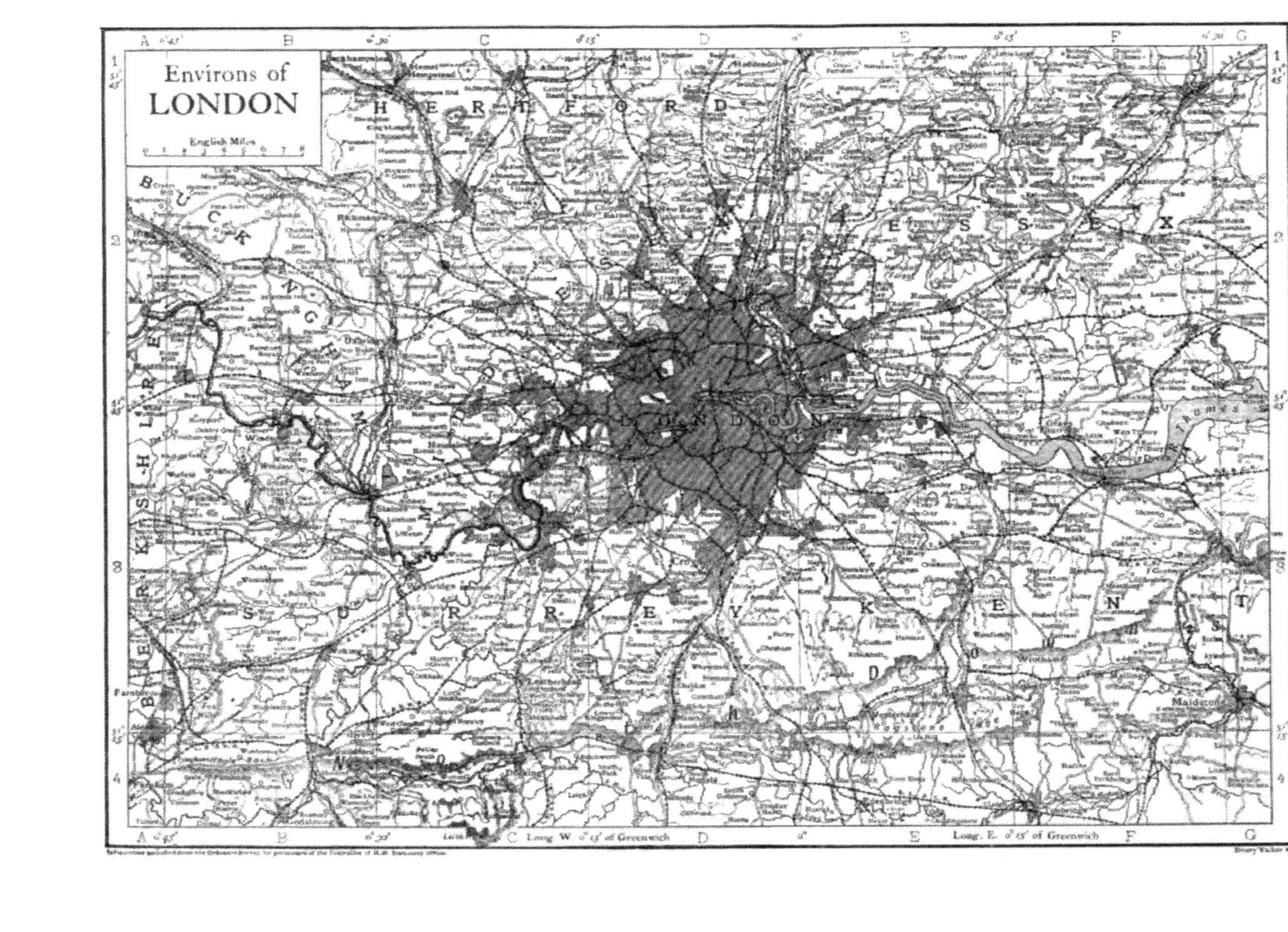
Environs of
LONDON
English Miles
HERTFORD
BUCKINGHAM
MIDDLESEX
ESSEX
LONDON
SURREY
KENT
BERKSHIRE
THAMES
Maidstone
Long. W. 0°15' of Greenwich
Long. E. 0°15' of Greenwich

Monuments and Memorials.—The Monument (1677), Fish Street Hill, City, erected from the designs of Wren in commemoration of the great fire of 1666, is a Doric column surmounted by a gilt representation of a flaming urn. The Nelson Column, the central feature of Trafalgar Square, is from the designs of William Railton (1843), crowned with a statue of Nelson by Baily, and has at its base four colossal lions in bronze, modelled by Sir Edwin Landseer. A statue of the duke of Cambridge, by Captain Adrian Jones, was unveiled in 1907 in front of the War Office, Whitehall. The duke of York's Column, Carlton House Terrace (1833), an Ionic pillar, is surmounted by a bronze statue by Sir Richard Westmacott. The Westminster Column, outside the entrance to Dean's Yard, was erected to the memory of the old pupils of Westminster School who died in the Russian and Indian wars of 1854–1859. The Guards Memorial, Waterloo Place, commemorates the foot guards who died in the Crimea. The Albert Memorial, Kensington Gardens, was erected (1872) by "Queen Victoria and her People to the memory of Albert, Prince Consort," from the designs of Sir Gilbert Scott, with a statue of the Prince (1876) by John Henry Foley beneath a hugeornate Gothic canopy. At the eastern end of the Strand a memorial with statue by Hamo Thorneycroft of William Ewart Gladstone was unveiled in 1905. In Parliament Square and elsewhere are numerous statues, some of high merit, but it cannot be said that statuary occupies an important place in the adornment of streets and open places in London. Cleopatra's Needle, an ancient Egyptian monument, was presented to the government by Mehemet Ali in 1819, brought from Alexandria in 1878, and erected on the Victoria embankment on a pedestal of grey granite.

Nomenclature.—Having regard to the destruction of visible evidences of antiquity in London, both through accidental agencies such as the great fire, and through inevitable modernizing influences, it is well that historical associations in nomenclature are preserved in a great measure unimpaired. The City naturally offers the richest field for study in this direction. The derivations of names may here be grouped into two classes, those having a commercial connexion, and those associated with ancient buildings, particularly the City wall and ecclesiastical foundations. Among examples of the first group, Cheapside is prominent. This modern thoroughfare of shops was in early times the Chepe (O. Eng. *ceap*, bargain), an open place occupied by a market, having, until the 14th century, a space set apart for popular entertainments. There was a Queen Eleanor cross here, and conduits supplied the city with water. Modern Cheapside merges eastward into the street called the Poultry, from the poulterers' stalls "but lately departed from thence," according to Stow, at the close of the 16th century. Cornhill, again, recalls the cornmarket "time out of mind there holden" (Stow), and Gracechurch Street was corrupted from the name of the church of St Benet Grasschurch (destroyed by the great fire, rebuilt, and removed in 1868), which was said to be derived from a herb-market held under its walls. The Jews had their quarter near the commercial centre, their presence being indicated by the street named Old Jewry, though it is probable that they did not reoccupy this locality after their expulsion in 1290. Lombard Street similarly points to the residence of Lombard merchants, the name existing when Edward II. confirmed a grant to Florentine merchants in 1318, while the Lombards maintained their position until Tudor times. Paternoster Row, still occupied by booksellers, takes name from the sellers of prayer-books and writers of texts who collected under the shadow of St Paul's Cathedral. As regards names derived from ancient buildings, instances are the streets called London Wall and Barbican, and those named after the numerous gates. Of those associated with ecclesiastical foundations several occur in the course of this article (Section II., *Ecclesiastical Architecture*, &c.). Such are Austin Friars, Crutched Friars, Blackfriars and Whitefriars. To this last district a curious alternative name, Alsatia, was given, probably in the 17th century, with reference to its notoriety as a hiding-place of debtors. A derivation is suggested from the disputed territory of Alsace, pointing the contrast between this lawless district and the adjacent Temple, the home of the law itself. The name Bridewell came from a well near the Fleet (New Bridge Street), dedicated to St Bride, and was attached to a house built by Henry VIII. (1522), but is most familiar in its application to the house of correction instituted by Edward VI., which remained a prison till 1863. The Minories, a street leading south from Aldgate, takes name from an abbey of nuns of St Clare (*Sorores Minores*) founded in 1293. Apart from the City an interesting ecclesiastical survival is the name Broad Sanctuary, Westminster, recalling the place of sanctuary which long survived the monastery under the protection of which it originally existed. Covent Garden, again, took its name from a convent garden belonging to Westminster. Among the survivals of names of non-ecclesiastical buildings Castle Baynard may be noted; it stood in the City on the banks of the Thames, and was held by Ralph Baynard, a Norman, in the time of William the Conqueror; a later building being erected in 1428 by Humphrey duke of Gloucester. Here Richard III. was acclaimed king, and the mansion was used by Henry VII. and Henry VIII. Its name is kept in a wharf and a ward of the City.

The survival of names of obliterated physical features or characteristics is illustrated in Section I.; but additional instances are found in the Strand, which originally ran close to the sloping bank of the Thames, and in Smithfield, now the central meat market, but for long the "smooth field" where a cattle and hay market was held, and the scene of tournaments and games, and also of executions. Here in 1381 Wat Tyler the rebel was killed by Sir William Walworth during the parley with Richard II. In the West End of London the majority of important street-names are naturally of a later derivation than those in the ancient City, though Charing Cross (*q.v.*) is an instance of an exception. The derivation commonly accepted for Piccadilly is from *pickadil*, a stiff collar or hem in fashion in the early part of the 17th century (Span. *picca*, a spear-head). In Pall Mall and the neighbouring Mall in St James' Park is found the title of a game resembling croquet (Fr. *paille maille*) in favour at or before the time of Charles I., though the Mall was laid out for the game by Charles II. Other names pointing to the existence of pastimes now extinct are found elsewhere in London, as in Balls Pond Road, Islington, where in the 17th century was a proprietary pond for the sport of duck-hunting. An entertainment of another form is recalled in the name of Spring Gardens, St James' Park, where at the time of James I. there was a fountain or spring so arranged as to besprinkle those who trod unwarily on the valve which opened it. Many of the names of the rich residential streets and squares in the west have associations with the various owners of the properties; but Mayfair is so called from a fair held on this ground in May as early as the reign of Charles II. Finally there are several survivals, in street-names, of former private mansions and other buildings. Thus the district of the Adelphi, south of Charing Cross, takes name from the block of dwellings and offices erected in 1768 by the brothers (Gr. *adelphi*) Robert and William Adam, Scottish architects. In Piccadilly Clarendon House, erected in 1664 by Edward Hyde, earl of Clarendon, became Albemarle House when acquired by the duke of Albemarle in 1675. Northumberland House, from which is named Northumberland Avenue, opening upon Trafalgar Square, was built *c.* 1605 by Henry Howard, earl of Northampton, and was acquired by marriage by Algernon Percy, earl of Northumberland, in 1642. It took name from this family, and stood until 1874. Arundel House, originally a seat of the bishops of Bath, was the residence of Thomas Howard, earl of Arundel, whose famous collection of sculpture, the Arundel Marbles, was housed here until presented to Oxford University in 1667. The site of the house is marked by Arundel Street, Strand.

III. Communications

Railways.—The trunk railways leaving London, with their termini, are as follows: (1) *Northern*. The Great Northern, Midland and London & North-Western systems have adjacent termini, namely King's Cross, St Pancras and Euston, in Euston Road, St Pancras. The terminus of the Great Central railway is Marylebone, in the road of that name. (2) *Western*. The terminus of the Great Western railway is Paddington (Praed Street); and that of the London & South-Western, Waterloo, south of the Thames in Lambeth. (3) *Southern*. The London, Brighton & South Coast railway has its western terminus at Victoria, and its central terminus at London Bridge, on the south side of the Thames. The South-Eastern & Chatham railway has four terminal stations, all on or close to the north bank of the river—Victoria, Charing Cross,[1] Holborn Viaduct and Cannon Street (City). St Paul's Station on the Holborn branch is also terminal in part. (4) *Eastern.* The principal terminus of the Great Eastern Railway is in Liverpool Street (City), but the company also uses Fenchurch Street (City), the terminus of the London, Tilbury & Southend railway, and St Pancras. These lines, especially the southern lines, the Great Eastern, Great Northern and South-Western carry a very heavy suburban traffic. Systems of joint lines and running powers are maintained to afford communication between the main lines. Thus the West London Extension line carries local traffic between the North Western and Great Western and the Brighton and South-Western systems, while the Metropolitan Extension through the City connects the Midland and Great Northern with the South-Eastern & Chatham lines.

The railways whose systems are mainly or wholly confined within the metropolitan area are as follows. The North London railway has a terminal station at Broad Street, City, and serves the parts of London implied by its name. The company possesses running powers over the lines of various other companies: thus its trains run as far north as Potter's Bar on the Great Northern line, while it serves Richmond on the west and Poplar on the east. The East London line connects Shoreditch with New Cross (Deptford) by way of the Thames Tunnel, a subway under the river originally built for foot-passengers. The London & India Docks line connects the city with the docks on the north bank of the river as far as North Woolwich. The Metropolitan railway has a line from Baker Street through north-west London to Harrow, continuing to Uxbridge, while the original main line runs on to Rickmansworth, Aylesbury and Verney Junction, but has been worked by the Metropolitan and Great Central companies jointly since 1906. Another line serves the western outskirts (Hammersmith, Richmond, &c.) from the city. Metropolitan trains also connect at New Cross with the south-eastern railway system. This company combines with the Metropolitan District to form the Inner Circle line, which has stations close to all the great railway termini north of the Thames. The Metropolitan District (commonly called the District) system serves Wimbledon, Richmond, Ealing and Harrow on the west, and passes eastward by Earl's Court, South Kensington, Victoria and Mansion House (City) to Whitechapel and Bow. The Metropolitan and the District lines within London are for the most part underground (this feature supplying the title of "the Underground" familiarly applied to both systems); the tunnels being constructed of brick. The earliest part of the system was opened in 1863. Although these railways, as far as concerns the districts they serve, form the fastest method of communication from point to point, their discomfort, arising mainly from the impossibility of proper ventilation, and various other disadvantages attendant upon the use of steam traction, led to a determination to adapt the lines to electrical working. Experiments on a short section of the line were made in 1900, and later schemes were set on foot to electrify the District system and bring under one general control this railway, other lines in deep level "tubes" between Baker Street and Waterloo, between Charing Cross, Euston and Hampstead, and between Hammersmith, [illegible], Piccadilly, King's Cross and Finsbury Park, and the [illegible] United Tramways Company. The Underground Electric [illegible] Company, which acquired a controlling influence over [illegible], undertook the construction of a great power station [illegible], while the Metropolitan Company, which had fallen into [illegible] the District (not without dispute over the system of electri-[illegible]) erected a station at Neasden on the Aylesbury [illegible] traction was gradually introduced on the Metro-[illegible] the District lines in 1906. The former company com-[illegible] Great Western Company as regards the electrification [illegible] of stock for, the lines which they had previously [illegible] Edgware Road by Bishop's Road to Hammer-[illegible] Baker Street & Waterloo railway (known as the [illegible] opened in 1906 and subsequently extended in one [illegible] and in the other to the Elephant and Castle. [illegible] Piccadilly & Brompton line, from Finsbury [illegible] was opened early in 1907, and the Charing [illegible] Hampstead line later in the same year. Deep-[illegible] ("tubes"), communicating with the surface [illegible] familiar in London. The first opened was the [illegible] (1890), subsequently extended to run between [illegible], the Bank (City) and Clapham. Others [illegible] City (1898) running from the terminus of the [illegible] without intermediate stations to the Bank; [illegible] (1900), from the Bank to Shepherd's Bush, [illegible] the Great Northern & City (1904) from [illegible] is an important suburban junction on the [illegible] to Moorgate Street.

[illegible] tramway system of London cannot be [illegible] roughly represented by the boroughs of [illegible] Fulham, the city of Westminster and a [illegible] thereof, and the city of London, the existing streets could not accommodate tram lines along with other traffic over any great distance consecutively, and in point of fact there are few, beyond the embankment line from Blackfriars Bridge to Westminster Bridge, which connects with the southern system. Another line, running south from Islington, uses the shallow-level subway under Kingsway and connects with the embankment line. The northern, western and eastern outskirts and London south of the Thames are extensively served by trams. On the formation of the London County Council there were thirteen tramway companies in existence. Powers under the Tramways Act of 1870 were given to the council, enabling it to acquire possession of these undertakings, and within the county of London they have been for the most part so acquired, and are worked by the council. Outside the county both companies and local authorities own and work tramways. Both electric and horse traction are used; the latter, however, has been in great part displaced by the former. The total mileage for greater London is about 240.

Omnibuses.—The omnibus system is very extensive, embracing all the principal streets throughout the county and extending over a large part of Greater London. The two principal omnibus companies are the London General Omnibus and the London Road Car. The first omnibus ran between the Bank and Paddington in 1829. In 1905 and following years motor omnibuses (worked mostly by internal combustion engines) began to a large extent to supplant horse traction. The principal existing companies adopted them, and new companies were formed to work them exclusively. With their advantages of greater speed and carrying capacity over the horsed vehicles, their introduction was a most important development, though their working at first imposed a severe financial strain on many companies.

Cabs.—The horse-drawn cabs which ply for hire in the streets, or wait at authorized "cab-stands," are of two kinds, the "hansom," a two-wheeled vehicle so named after its inventor (1834) and the "four-wheeler." "Hackney coaches" for hire are first mentioned in 1625, when they were kept at inns, and numbered 20. Until 1832 their numbers were restricted, in 1662 to 400, in 1694 to 700, in 1771 to 1000. In some cases a driver owns his cab, but the majority of vehicles are let to drivers by owners, and the adjustment of terms between them has led to disputes from time to time. In 1894 a dispute necessitated the formulation of the "Asquith award" by the Rt. Hon. H. H. Asquith as home secretary, and subsequent modifications of this were only arrived at, as in 1904, after a strike of the drivers affected. A long-standing cause of complaint on the part of the public has been the common refusal of cab-drivers to accept their legal fares, but, on the other hand, several attempts to introduce cabs with an automatic taximeter failed, until the introduction of motor cabs, of which a few had already been plying for some time when in 1907 a large number, provided with taximeters, were put into service. Subsequently, as the number of "taxicabs" (see MOTOR VEHICLES) increased, that of horse-cabs decreased.

Traffic Problem.—One of the most serious administrative problems met with in London is that of locomotion, especially as regards the regulation of traffic in the principal thoroughfares and at the busiest crossings. The police have powers of control over vehicles and exercise them admirably; their work in this respect is a constant source of wonder to foreign visitors. But this control does not meet the problem of actually lessening the number of vehicles in the main arteries of traffic. At such crossings as that of the Strand and Wellington Street, Ludgate Circus and south of the Thames, the Elephant and Castle, as also in the narrow streets of the City, congestion is often exceedingly severe, and is aggravated when any main street is under repair, and diversion of traffic through narrow side streets becomes necessary. Many street improvements were carried out, it is true, in the last half of the 19th century, the dates of the principal being as follows: 1854, Cannon Street; 1864, Southwark Street; 1870, Holborn Viaduct; 1871, Hamilton Place, Queen Victoria Street; 1876, Northumberland Avenue; 1882, Tooley Street; 1883, Hyde Park Corner; 1884, Eastcheap; 1886, Shaftesbury Avenue; 1887, Charing Cross Road; 1890–1892, Rosebery Avenue. At the beginning of the 20th century several important local widenings of streets were put in hand, as for example between Sloane Street and Hyde Park Corner, in the Strand and at the Marble Arch (1908). At the same period a great work was undertaken to meet the want of a proper central communication between north and south, namely, the construction of a broad thoroughfare, called Kingsway in honour of King Edward VII., from High Holborn opposite Southampton Row southward to the Strand, connexion with which is established at two points through a crescent named Aldwych. The idea of such a thoroughfare is traceable back to the time of William IV. The magnitude of the traffic problem as a whole may be best appreciated by examples of the vast schemes of improvement which from time to time have been put forward by responsible individuals. Thus Sir John Wolfe Barry, as chairman of the Council of the Society of Arts in 1899, proposed to alleviate congestion of traffic by bridges over and tunnels under the streets at six points, namely—Hyde Park Corner, Piccadilly Circus, Ludgate Circus, Oxford Street and Tottenham Court Road, Strand and Wellington Street, and Southwark Bridge and Upper Thames Street. Another scheme seriously suggested in 1904, to meet existing disabilities of communication between north and south by linking the

[1] [illegible] was the scene of a remarkable catastrophe [illegible] roof collapsed, [illegible] theatre,

northern and southern tramway services, [illegible] was opposed Charing Cross terminus of the South Eastern [illegible] and local to the south side of the river, and the construction [illegible] had a in place of the railway bridge. The mere control of [illegible] ing local street improvements and provision of new [illegible] munication between casual points, were felt to miss the [illegible] problem, and in 1903 a Royal Commission was appointed to [illegible] the whole question of locomotion and transport in London, [illegible] evidence being taken from engineers, representatives of the [illegible] railway and other companies, of the County Council, [illegible] councils and police, and others. The commission reported in 19[illegible][1]

Traffic commission 1903. With regard to street improvements the most important recommendation was that of the construction of two main avenues 140 ft. wide, one running west and east, from Bayswater Road to Whitechapel, and passing through the city in the neighbourhood of London Wall, and another from Holloway to the Elephant and Castle, to cross the Thames by a new bridge above Blackfriars. Four lines of surface tramways and four railway lines in shallow tunnels were proposed along these avenues. Many widenings and other improvements of existing thoroughfares, and extensions of tramways were proposed, and detailed recommendations were made as regards urban and suburban railways, and the rehousing of the working population on the outskirts of London. Finally, the commission made the important recommendation that a traffic board should be established for London, to exercise a general supervision of traffic, and to act as a tribunal to which all schemes of railway and tramway construction should be referred.

Thames Steamers.—A local passenger steamboat service on the Thames suffers from the disadvantage that the river does not provide the shortest route between points at any great distance apart, and that the main thoroughfares between east and west do not touch its banks, so that passengers along those thoroughfares are not tempted to use it as a channel of communication. High pier dues, moreover, contributed to the decline of the traffic, and attempts to overcome the disinclination of passengers to use the river (at any rate in winter) show a record of failure. The London, Westminster and Vauxhall Steamboat Company established in 1840 a service of seven steamboats between London Bridge and Vauxhall. This company was bought up by the Citizen and Iron Steamboat Companies in 1865. The City Steamboat Company, established in 1848, began with eight boats, and by 1865 had increased their fleet to seventeen, running from London Bridge to Chelsea. This company was taken over by the London Steamboat Company in 1875. The sinking of the "Princess Alice" in 1878 was a serious blow to the London Steamboat Company, which collapsed, and was succeeded by the River Thames Steamboat Navigation Company, which went into liquidation in 1887. The fleet was bought by a syndicate and sold to the Victoria Steamboat Association. The Thames Steamboat Company then took up the service, but early in 1902 announced that it would be discontinued, although in 1904 it was temporarily resumed. Meanwhile, however, in 1902 the London County Council had promoted a bill in Parliament to enable them to run a service of boats on the Thames. The bill was thrown out on this occasion, but was revived and passed in 1904, and on the 17th of June 1905 the service was put into operation. The boats, however, were worked at a loss, and the service was discontinued in 1909.

Foreign Communications.—A large pleasure traffic is maintained by the steamers of the New Palace Company and others in summer between London Bridge and Southend, Clacton and Harwich, Ramsgate, Margate and other resorts of the Kent coast, and Calais and Boulogne. Passenger steamers sail from the port of London to the principal ports of the British Isles and northern Europe, and to all parts of the world, but the most favoured passenger services to and from Europe and North America pass through other ports, to which the railways provide special services of trains from London. The principal travelling agency in London is that of Messrs Cook, whose head office is at Ludgate Circus. A number of sub-offices of large steamship lines are congregated in Cockspur Street, Trafalgar Square, and several of the principal railway companies have local offices throughout the centre of the metropolis for the issue of tickets and the collection and forwarding of luggage and parcels.

Post Office.—The General Post Office lies in the centre of the City on either side of the street called St Martin's le Grand. The oldest portion of the buildings, Ionic in style, was designed by Sir Robert Smirke and erected in 1829. Here are the central offices of the letter, newspaper and telegraph departments, with the office of the Postmaster General; but the headquarters of the parcels department are at Mount Pleasant, Clerkenwell; those of the Post Office Savings Bank at Blythe Road, West Kensington, and those of the Money Order department in Queen Victoria Street. The postal area is divided into eight districts, commonly designated by initials (which it is customary to employ in writing addresses)—East Central (E.C., the City, north to Pentonville and City Roads, west to Gray's Inn Road and the Law Courts); West Central (W.C., from Euston Road to the Thames, and west to Tottenham Court Road); West (W., from Piccadilly and Hyde Park north to Marylebone and Edg[illegible]

[1] The report appeared in eight volumes, the first of which, containing the general conclusions to which allusion is here made, bore the number, as a blue-book, Cd. 2597.

ance of proper precautions against fire in theatres and places of entertainments. A Salvage Corps is independently maintained by the Insurance Companies.

Cemeteries.—The administrative authorities of cemeteries for the county are the borough councils and the City Corporation and private companies. The large cemetery at Brompton is the property of the government. Kensal Green cemetery, the burial-place of [illegible]ny famous persons, is of great extent, but several large cemeteries [illegible] the metropolis have come into use. Such are that of the [illegible] Necropolis Company at Brookwood near Woking, Surrey, [illegible] of the parishes of St Mary Abbots, Kensington, and St [illegible]over Square, at Hanwell, Middlesex. Crematoria are [illegible] in of the companies' cemeteries, and the Cremation [illegible] borough councils to provide crematoria.

[illegible] EDUCATION AND RECREATION

Elementary education. [illegible] and Foreign School Society (1808) and [illegible] together with the Ragged Schools Union [illegible] organizations providing for [illegible] until 1870. To meet [illegible], increasing as it did [illegible] of these societies, [illegible] institutions. Thus a return [illegible] of accommodating only [illegible] In 1870, however, a [illegible] body carried out [illegible] separ[illegible] tence. In 1903 the [illegible] of the general benefi[illegible] of bringing distin[illegible] County Romf[illegible] trol of Reigate, Epsom, &c., south of it. Pub[illegible] points in numerous shops, railway stations and [illegible] by at many post offices. The District Messenger [illegible] facilities through local offices for the use of [illegible]

IV. POPULATION, PUBLIC HEALTH, &c.

The population of Greater London by the census of [illegible] was 6,581,402.

The following table gives comparisons between the figures of certain census returns for Greater London and its [illegible] component parts, namely, the City, the county and the outer ring (*i.e.* Greater London outside the county). All the figures before those of 1901 are adjusted to these areas.

Year.	City.	County.	Outer Ring.	Greater London.
1801	128,129	831,181	155,334	1,114,644
1841	123,563	1,825,714	286,067	2,235,344
1881	50,569	3,779,728	936,364	4,766,661
1901	26,923	4,509,618	2,044,864	6,581,402

The reason for the decrease in the resident City population is to be found in the rapid extension of business premises, while the widening ramifications of the outer residential areas are illustrated by the increase in the later years of the population of the Outer Ring. The growth and population of London previous to the 19th century is considered under *History, ad fin.*

Aliens. The foreign-born population of London was 60,252 in 1881, and 135,377 in 1901. During 1901, 27,070 aliens (excluding sailors) arrived at the port, and in 1902, 33,060. Of these last Russians and Poles numbered 21,013; Germans, 3386; Austrians and Hungarians, 2197; Dutch, 1902; Norwegians Swedes and Danes, 1341; and Rumanians, 1016. Other nationalities numbered below one thousand each. The foreign-born population shows a large increase in percentage to the whole, being 1·57 in 1881 and 2·98 in 1901. Residents of Irish birth have decreased since 1851; those of Scottish birth have increased steadily, and roughly as the population. German residents are found mainly in the western and west central districts; French mainly in the City of Westminster (especially the district of Soho), St Pancras and St Marylebone; Italians in Holborn (Saffron Hill), Soho and Finsbury; and Russians and Poles in Stepney and Bethnal Green.

Vital Statistics.—The following table shows the average birth-rate and death-rate per thousand at stated periods.

Years.	Births.	Deaths.
1861–1880[1]	35·4	23·4
1891–1900[1]	30·3	19·2
1901–1904[1]	28·5	16·5
1905	27·1	15·6

[1] Average.

A comparison of the death-rate of London and those of other great towns in England and abroad is given here:—

	Average 1895–1904.	1905.
Leicester	16·7	13·3
Brussels	16·7	14·5
Bristol	16·9	14·6
Bradford	17·7	15·2
Leeds	19·1	15·2
LONDON	18·2	15·6
Birmingham	20·2	16·2
Nottingham	18·4	16·5
Newcastle	20·9	16·8
Sheffield	19·6	17·0
Berlin	17·8	17·2
Paris	19·2	17·4
Manchester	22·6	18·0
New York	20·2	18·3
Vienna	20·0	19·0
Liverpool	23·2	19·0
Rome	19·1	20·6
St Petersburg	25·9	25·3

In 1905 the lowest death-rates among the metropolitan boroughs were returned by Hampstead (9·3), Lewisham (11·7), Wandsworth (12·6), Woolwich (12·8), Stoke Newington (12·9), and the highest by Shoreditch (19·7), Finsbury (19·0), Bermondsey (18·7), Bethnal Green (18·6) and Southwark (18·5). A return of the percentage of inhabitants dwelling in over-crowded tenements shows 2·7 for Lewisham, 4·5 for Wandsworth, 5·5 for Stoke Newington, and 6·4 for Hampstead, against 35·2 for Finsbury and 29·9 for Shoreditch.

Sanitation.—As regards sanitation London is under special regulations. When the statutes relating to public health were consolidated and amended in 1875 London was excluded; and the law applicable to it was specially consolidated and amended in 1891. The London County Council is a central sanitary authority; the City and metropolitan boroughs are sanitary districts, and the Corporation and borough councils are local sanitary authorities. The County Council deals directly with matters where uniformity of administration is essential, *e.g.* main drainage, housing of working classes, infant life protection, common lodging-houses and shelters, and contagious diseases of animals. With a further view to uniformity it has certain powers of supervision and control over local authorities, and can make by-laws respecting construction of local sewers, sanitary conveniences, offensive trades, slaughter-houses and dairies, and prevention of nuisances outside the jurisdiction of local authorities. A medical officer of health for the whole county is appointed by the Council, which also pays half the salaries of local medical officers and sanitary inspectors. The Council may also act in cases of default by the local authorities, or may make representations to the Local Government Board respecting such default, whereupon the Board may direct the Council to withhold payment due to the local authority under the Equalization of Rates Act 1894.

The first act providing for a commission of sewers in London dates from 1531. Various works of a more or less imperfect character were carried out, such as the bridging over in 1637 of the river Fleet, which as early as 1307 had become inaccessible to shipping through the accumulation of filth. Scavengers were employed in early times, and sewage was received into wells and pumped into the kennels of the streets. A system of main drainage was inaugurated by the Commissioners of Sewers in 1849, but their work proceeded very slowly. It was carried on more effectively by the Metropolitan Board of Works (1856–1888) which expended over six-and-a-half millions sterling on the work. The London County Council maintained, completed and improved the system. The length of sewers in the main system is about 288 m., and their construction has cost about eight millions. The system covers the county of London, West Ham, Penge, Tottenham, Wood Green, and parts of Beckenham, Hornsey, Croydon, Willesden, East Ham and [illegible]. There are actually two distinct systems, north and south of the Thames, having separate outfall works on the north and south [illegible] of the river, at Barking and Crossness. The clear effluent [illegible] into the Thames, and the sludge is taken 50 m. out to sea. The annual cost of maintenance of the system exceeds £250,000. [illegible] sanitary authorities are concerned only with the supervision of [illegible] drainage, and the construction and maintenance of local [illegible] discharging into the main system. The Thames and the Lea [illegible] have powers to guard against the pollution of the [illegible]

[illegible]—The Metropolitan Asylums Board, though established [illegible] authority for the relief of the sick, insane [illegible] paupers, has become a central hospital [illegible] diseases, with power to receive into [illegible] who are not paupers, suffering from [illegible] diphtheria. Both the Board and the [illegible] powers and duties of sanitary [illegible] regulations. The local sanitary [illegible] of the Infectious Diseases [illegible] which [illegible] [illegible]

for the insane at Tooting Bec (Wandsworth), Ealing (for children); King's Langley, Hertfordshire; Caterham, Surrey; and Darenth, Kent. There are twelve fever hospitals, including northern and southern convalescent hospitals. For smallpox the Board maintains hospital ships moored in the Thames at Dartford, and a land establishment at the same place. There are land and river ambulance services.

There are three regular funds in London for the support of hospitals. (1) King Edward's Hospital Fund (1897) founded by King Edward VII. as Prince of Wales in commemoration of the Diamond Jubilee of Queen Victoria. The League of Mercy, under royal charter, operates in conjunction with the Fund in the collection of small subscriptions. The Order of Mercy was instituted by the King as a reward for distinguished personal service. (2) The Metropolitan Hospital Sunday Fund, founded in 1873, draws the greater part of its revenue from collections in churches on stated occasions. (3) The Metropolitan Hospital Saturday Fund was founded in 1873, and is made up chiefly of small sums collected in places of business, &c. The following is a list of the principal London hospitals, with dates of foundation:—

1. *General Hospitals with Medical Schools* (all of which, with the exception of that of the Seamen's Hospital, are schools of London University):—
   - Charing Cross; Agar Street, Strand (1820).
   - Guy's; St Thomas Street, Southwark (1724).
   - King's College; Lincoln's Inn Fields (1839).
   - London; Whitechapel (1740).
   - Middlesex; Mortimer Street, Marylebone (1745).
   - North London, or University College; Gower Street (1833).
   - Royal Free; Gray's Inn Road (1828; on present site, 1842). London School of Medicine for Women.
   - St Bartholomew's; Smithfield (1123; refounded 1547).
   - St George's; Hyde Park Corner (1733).
   - St Mary's; Paddington (1845).
   - St Thomas'; Lambeth (1213; on present site, 1871).
   - Seamen's Hospital Society; Greenwich (1821).
   - Westminster, facing the Abbey. (1720; on present site, 1834)
2. *General Hospitals without Schools*:—
   - Great Northern Central; Islington (1856; on present site, 1887).
   - Metropolitan; Hackney (1836).
   - Poplar Hospital for Accidents (1854).
   - West London; Hammersmith Road (1856).
3. *Hospitals for Special Purposes*:—
   - Brompton Consumption Hospital (1841).
   - Cancer Hospital; Brompton (1851).
   - City of London Hospital for diseases of the chest; Bethnal Green (1848).
   - East London Hospital for Children and Dispensary for Women; Shadwell (1868).
   - Hospital for Sick Children; Bloomsbury (1852).
   - London Fever Hospital; Islington (1802).
   - National Hospital for Paralysed and Epileptics; Bloomsbury (1859).
   - Royal Hospital for Incurables; Putney (1854).
   - Royal London Ophthalmic Hospital; City Road (1804; on present site, 1899).

(See also separate articles on boroughs.)

Water Supply.—In the 12th century London was supplied with water from local streams and wells, of which Holy Well, Clerk's Well (Clerkenwell) and St Clement's Well, near St Clement's Inn, were examples. In 1236 the magistrates purchased the liberty to convey the waters of the Tyburn from Paddington to the City by leaden pipes, and a great conduit was erected in West Cheap in 1285. Other conduits were subsequently built (cf. Conduit Street off Bond Street, Lamb's Conduit Street, Bloomsbury); and water was also supplied by the company of water-bearers in leathern panniers borne by horses. In 1582 Peter Moris, a Dutchman, erected a "forcier" on an arch of London Bridge, which he rented for 10s. per annum for 500 years. His works succeeded and increased, and continued in his family till 1701, when a company took over the lease. Other forciers had been set up, and in 1609, on an act of 1605, Sir Hugh Myddelton undertook the task of supplying reservoirs at Clerkenwell through the New river from springs near Ware, Hertfordshire; and these were opened in 1613. In 1630 a scheme to bring water from Hoddesdon on the Lea was promoted by aid of a lottery licensed by Charles I. The Chelsea Water Company opened its supply from the Thames in 1721; the Lambeth waterworks were erected in 1783; the Vauxhall Company was established in 1805, the West Middlesex, near Hammersmith, and the East London on the river Lea in 1806, the Kent on the Ravensbourne (Deptford) in 1810, the Grand Junction in 1811, and the Southwark (which amalgamated with the Vauxhall) in 1822.

For many years proposals to amalgamate the working of the companies and displace them by a central public authority were put forward from time to time. The difficulty of administration lay in the fact that of the area of 620 sq. m. constituting what is known as "Water London" (see map in *London Statistics*, vol. xix., issued by the L.C.C., 1909) the London County Council has authority over little more than one-third, and therefore when the Council proposed to acquire the eight undertakings concerned its scheme was opposed not only by the companies but by the county councils and local authorities outside the County of London. The Council had a scheme of bringing water to London from Wales, in view of increasing demands on a stationary supply. This involved impounding the headwaters of the Wye, the Towey and the Usk, and the total cost was estimated to exceed fifteen millions sterling. The capacity of existing sources, however, was deemed sufficient by a Royal Commission under Lord Balfour of Burleigh in 1893, and this opinion was endorsed by a further Commission under Lord Llandaff. The construction of large storage reservoirs was recommended, and this work was put in hand jointly by the New River, West Middlesex and Grand Junction companies at Staines on the Thames. As regards administration, Lord Llandaff's Commission recommended the creation of a Water Trust, and in 1902 the Metropolis Water Act constituted the Metropolitan Water Board to purchase and carry on the undertakings of the eight companies, and of certain local authorities. It consists of 66 members appointed by the London County Council (14), the City of London and the City of Westminster (2 each), the other Metropolitan boroughs (1 each), the county councils of Middlesex, Hertfordshire, Essex, Kent and Surrey (1 each), borough of West Ham (2), various groups of other boroughs and urban districts, and the Thames and the Lea Conservancies. The first election of the Board took place in 1903. The 24th of June, 1904, was the date fixed on which control passed to the Board, and in the meantime a Court of Arbitration adjudicated the claims of the companies for compensation for the acquisition of their properties.

Metropolitan Water Board.

"Water London" is an irregular area extending from Ware in Hertfordshire to Sevenoaks in Kent, and westward as far as Ealing and Sunbury.

A constant supply is maintained generally throughout "Water London," although a suspension between certain hours has been occasionally necessitated, as in 1895 and 1898, when, during summer droughts, the East London supply was so affected. During these periods other companies had a surplus of water, and in 1899 an act was passed providing for the interconnexion of systems. The Thames and Lea are the principal sources of supply, but the Kent and (partially) the New River Company draw supplies from springs. The systems of filtration employed by the different companies varied in efficacy, but both the Royal Commissions decided that water as supplied to the consumer was generally of a very high standard of purity. The expenditure of the Water Board for 1907–1908 amounted to £2,846,265. Debt charges absorbed £1,512,718 of this amount.

Public baths and washhouses are provided by local authorities under various acts between 1846 and 1896, which have been adopted by all the borough councils.

Lighting.—From 1416 citizens were obliged to hang out candles between certain hours on dark nights to illuminate the streets. An act of parliament enforced this in 1661; in 1684 Edward Heming, the inventor of oil lamps, obtained licence to supply public lights; and in 1736 the corporation took the matter in hand, levying a rate. Gas-lighting was introduced on one side of Pall Mall in 1807, and in 1810 the Gas Light & Coke Company received a charter, and developed gas-lighting in Westminster. The City of London Gas Company followed in 1817, and seven other companies soon after. Wasteful competition ensued until in 1857 an agreement was made between the companies to restrict their services to separate localities, and the Gas Light & Coke Company, by amalgamating other companies, then gradually acquired all the gas-lighting north of the Thames, while a considerable area in the south was provided for by another great gas company, the South Metropolitan. Various acts from 1860 onwards have laid down laws as to the quality and cost of gas. Gas must be supplied at 16-candle illuminating power, and is officially tested by the chemists' department of the London County Council. The amalgamations mentioned were effected subsequently to 1860, and there are now three principal companies within the county, the Gas Light & Coke, South Metropolitan and Commercial, though certain other companies supply some of the outlying districts. As regards street lighting, the extended use of burners with incandescent mantles has been of good effect. The Metropolitan Board of Works, and the commissioners of sewers in the City, began experiments with electric light. At the close of the 19th and the beginning of the 20th century a large number of electric light companies came into existence, and some of the metropolitan borough councils, and local authorities within Greater London, also undertook the supply. An extensive use of the light resulted in the principal streets and in shops, offices and private houses.

Fire.—In 1832 the fire insurance companies united to maintain a small fire brigade, and continued to do so until 1866. The brigade was confined to the central part of the metropolis; for the rest, the parochial authorities had charge of protection from fire. The central brigade came under the control of the Metropolitan Board of Works; and the County Council now manages the Metropolitan Fire Brigade, under a chief officer and a staff numbering about 1300. The cost of maintenance exceeds £200,000 annually; contributions towards this are made by the Treasury and the fire insurance companies. The Council controls the provision of fire escapes in factories employing over 40 persons, under an act of 1901; it also compels the maintenance of proper precautions against fire in theatres and places of entertainments. A Salvage Corps is independently maintained by the Insurance Companies.

Cemeteries.—The administrative authorities of cemeteries for the county are the borough councils and the City Corporation and private companies. The large cemetery at Brompton is the property of the government. Kensal Green cemetery, the burial-place of many famous persons, is of great extent, but several large cemeteries outside the metropolis have come into use. Such are that of the London Necropolis Company at Brookwood near Woking, Surrey, and that of the parishes of St Mary Abbots, Kensington, and St George, Hanover Square, at Hanwell, Middlesex. Crematoria are provided at certain of the companies' cemeteries, and the Cremation Act 1902 enabled borough councils to provide crematoria.

V. Education and Recreation

Education.—The British and Foreign School Society (1808) and the National Society (1811), together with the Ragged Schools Union (1844), were the only special organizations providing for the education of the poorer classes until 1870. To meet the demand for elementary education, increasing as it did with population, was beyond the powers of these societies, the churches and the various charitable institutions. Thus a return of 1871 showed that the schools were capable of accommodating only 39% of the children of school-going age. In 1870, however, a School Board had been created in addition, and this body carried out much good work during its thirty-four years of existence. In 1903 the Education (London) Act was passed in pursuance of the general system, put into operation by the Education Act (1902) of bringing education within the scope of municipal government. The County Council was created a local education authority, and given control of secular education in both board and voluntary schools. It appoints an education committee in accordance with a scheme approved by the Board of Education. This scheme must allow of the Council selecting at least a majority of the committee, and must provide for the inclusion of experts and women. Each school or group of schools is under a body of managers, in the appointment of whom the borough council and the County Council share in the following proportions:—(a) *Board or provided schools*: borough council, two-thirds; county council, one-third; (b) *Voluntary or non-provided schools*: the foundation, two-thirds; borough council and county council, each one-sixth. The total number of public elementary schools was 963 in 1905, with 752,487 scholars on the register. Other institutions include higher elementary schools for pupils certified to be able to profit by higher instruction; and schools for blind, deaf and defective children. Instruction for teachers is provided in pupil teachers' centres (preparatory), and in residential and day training colleges. There are about 15 such colleges. Previous to the act of 1903 the County Council had educational powers under the Technical Instructions Acts which enabled it to provide technical education through a special board, merged by the act of 1903 in the education committee. The City and Guilds of London Institute, Gresham College, also maintains various technical institutions. The establishment of polytechnics was provided for by the City of London Parochial Charities Act 1883; the charities being administered by trustees. The model institution was that of Mr Quintin Hogg (1880) in Regent Street, where a striking statue by George Frampton (1906) commemorates him. The general scope of the polytechnics is to give instruction both in general knowledge and special crafts or trades by means of classes, lectures and laboratories, instructive entertainments and exhibitions, and facilities for bodily and mental exercise (gymnasia, libraries, &c.). Other similar institutions exist primarily for special purposes, as the St Bride Foundation Institute, near Fleet Street, in immediate proximity to the great newspaper offices, for the printing trade, and the Herolds' Institute, a branch of the Borough Polytechnic situated in Bermondsey, for the purposes of the leather trade. The County Council also aids numerous separate schools of art, both general and special, such as the Royal School of Art Needlework and the School of Art Woodcarving; the City and Guilds Institute maintains similar establishments at some of its colleges, and art schools are also generally attached to the polytechnics.

Elementary education.

Technical education.

The London County Council maintains a number of industrial schools and reformatories, both in London and in the country, for children who have shown or are likely to be misled into a tendency towards lawlessness. The City Corporation has separate responsibilities in the same direction, but has no schools of its own. The expenditure of the London County Council on education for 1907–1908 was £4,281,291 for elementary education, and £747,962 for higher education.

The work of private philanthropists and philanthropical bodies among the poor of East London, Southwark and Bermondsey, and elsewhere, fails to be noticed at this point. The labours of the regular clergy here lie largely in the direction of social reform, and churches and missions have been established and are maintained by colleges, such as Christ Church, Oxford, schools and other bodies. There are, further, "settlements" where members of the various bodies may reside in order to devote themselves to philanthropical work; and these include clubs, recreation rooms and other institutions for the use of the poor. Such are the Oxford House, Bethnal

Philanthropical institutions.

[illegible] Cambridge House, Camberwell Road; Toynbee Hall, [illegible] House, Canning Town; the Robert [illegible] Southwark; and the Passmore Edwards [illegible]. There are also several women's settlements [illegible]. The People's Palace, Mile End Road, opened [illegible] and an educational institution (called [illegible]) created and subsequently extended mainly through [illegible] the Drapers' Company and of private [illegible].

In early times the priories and other religious houses had generally grammar schools attached to them. Those at St Peter's, Westminster, and St Paul's, attained a fame which has survived, while [illegible] similar foundations lapsed, such as St Anthony's [illegible] Street, City, at which Sir Thomas More, [illegible] and many other men of eminence received [illegible] the schools were re-endowed after the dis[illegible] of the monasteries. St Peter's College or Westminster School [illegible] is unique among English public schools of [illegible] in maintaining its original situation in London. [illegible] foundations have been moved in accord[illegible] either into the country or to sites aloof [illegible]. Thus Charterhouse school, part of the [illegible] Thomas Sutton (1611), was moved from Finsbury [illegible]. St Paul's School occupies modern buildings [illegible] and Christ's Hospital is at Horsham, Sussex. Of [illegible] Merchant Taylors' was founded by the Company of [illegible] and has occupied, since 1875, the premises vacated [illegible] School. The Mercers' School, Dowgate, was origin[illegible] the hospital of St Thomas of Acon, which was sold [illegible] in 1522, on condition that the company [illegible] the school. The City of London School, founded in [illegible] by the City Corporation in 1835, occupies [illegible] on the Victoria Embankment. Dulwich College [illegible] of the College of God's Gift by Edward [illegible] constituted as one of the principal English [illegible]. St Olave's and St Saviour's grammar school, South[illegible] in 1571. Both classical and modern [illegible] a large number of scholarships are maintained [illegible] and exhibitions from the school to the uni[illegible] educational institutions.

[illegible]—The University of London was incorporated [illegible] as an examining body for conferring degrees. [illegible] extended by subsequent charters, and in [illegible] of London Act 1898, it was reorganized [illegible] an examining body. The function of the [illegible] to control the teaching branch, internal [illegible] of the external department to control [illegible] the university extension system [illegible]. The university is governed by a [illegible], chairman of convocation and 54 [illegible] is shared by the Crown, convocation, [illegible] and of Surgeons, the Inns of Court, [illegible] County Council, City Corporation, [illegible] University and King's Colleges and the [illegible] theology, arts, law, music, medicine, [illegible]. The schools of the University [illegible] Gower Street, and King's College, [illegible] of which preparatory schools are con[illegible] and numerous institutions devoted to [illegible] and without London. The university [illegible] formerly belonged to the Imperial [illegible]

[illegible]—The Board of Education directly [illegible] institutions—the Victoria and [illegible], with its branch at Bethnal [illegible] are lent to various institutions [illegible] Royal College of Science, South [illegible] the Royal School of Mines; [illegible] Kingdom and the Museum of [illegible] the Solar Physics Observatory, [illegible] College of Art, South Kensington. [illegible] Street, City, founded in 1597 by [illegible] to its present site in 1843, lectures [illegible] of science, law, divinity, [illegible]

[illegible] and institutions may be [illegible]

[illegible] of British Architects, Conduit [illegible] awards diplomas. [illegible] Preceptors, Bloomsbury, conducts [illegible] education and awards diplomas. [illegible] Engineering is maintained at [illegible]

[illegible]—Middle Temple, Inner Temple, [illegible] board of examiners examines [illegible] Council of Legal Education [illegible] students. [illegible] body [illegible] East, and the Royal College of Surgeons is in Lincoln's Inn Fields. The Society of Apothecaries is in Water Lane, City. The Royal College of Veterinary Surgeons is in Red Lion Square, and the Royal Veterinary College at Camden Town. (The principal hospitals having schools are noted in the list of hospitals, Section VII.)

Military and Naval.—The Royal Military College and the Ordnance College are at Woolwich; the Royal Naval College at Greenwich.

Music.—The principal educational institutions are—the Royal Academy of Music, Tenterden Street, Hanover Square; the Royal College of Music, South Kensington; Guildhall School, City, near the Victoria Embankment; London College, Great Marlborough Street; Trinity College, Manchester Square; Victoria College, Berners Street; and the Royal College of Organists, Bloomsbury.

Scientific Societies.—Numerous learned societies have their headquarters in London, and the following may especially be noticed here. Burlington House, in Piccadilly, built in 1872 on the site of a mansion of the earls of Burlington, houses the Royal Society, the Chemical, Geological, Linnaean and Royal Astronomical Societies, the Society of Antiquaries and the British Association for the Advancement of Science, of which the annual meetings take place at different British or colonial towns in succession. The Royal Society, the most dignified and influential of all, was incorporated by Charles II. in 1663. It originally occupied rooms in Crane Court, City, and was moved in 1780 to Somerset House, where others of the societies named were also located. The Society of Arts, John Street, Adelphi, was established in 1754 for the encouragement of arts, manufactures and commerce. The Royal Institution, Albemarle Street, was founded in 1799, maintains a library and laboratories and promotes research in connexion with the experimental sciences. The Royal Geographical Society, occupying a building close to Burlington House in Savile Row, maintains a map-room open to the public, holds lectures by prominent explorers and geographers, and takes a leading part in the promotion of geographical discovery. The Royal Botanic Society has private gardens in the midst of Regent's Park, where flower shows and general entertainments are held. The Royal Horticultural Society maintains gardens at Wisley, Surrey, and has an exhibition hall in Vincent Square, Westminster. The exhibitions of the Royal Agricultural Society are held at Park Royal, near Willesden. The Zoological Society maintains a magnificent collection of living specimens in the Zoological Gardens, Regent's Park, a popular resort.

Museums, Art Galleries, Libraries.—In the British Museum London possesses one of the most celebrated collections in the world, originated in 1753 by the purchase of Sir Hans Sloane's collection and library by the government. The great building in Bloomsbury (1828–1852) with its massive Ionic portico, houses the collections of antiquities, coins, books, manuscripts and drawings, and contains the reading-rooms for the use of readers. The natural history branch was removed to a building at South Kensington (the Natural History Museum) in 1881, where the zoological, botanical and mineralogical exhibits are kept. Close to this museum is the Victoria and Albert Museum (formerly South Kensington Museum, 1857) for which an extension of buildings, from a fine design by Sir Aston Webb, was begun in 1899 and completed in ten years. Here are collections of pictures and drawings, including the Raphael cartoons, objects of art of every description, mechanical and scientific collections, and Japanese, Chinese and Persian collections, and an Indian section. In the vicinity, also, is the fine building of the Imperial Institute, founded in 1887 as an exhibition to illustrate the resources of all parts of the Empire, as well as an institution for the furtherance of imperial intercourse; though not developed on the scale originally intended. Other museums are Sir John Soane's collection in Lincoln's Inn Fields and the Museum of Practical Geology in Jermyn Street, while the scientific societies have libraries and in some cases collections of a specialized character, such as the museums of the Royal College of Surgeons, the Royal Architectural Society, and the Society of Art and the Parkes Museum of the Sanitary Institute. Among permanent art collections the first place is taken by the National Gallery in Trafalgar Square. This magnificent collection was originated in 1824, and the building dates from 1838, but has been more than once enlarged. The building of the National Portrait Gallery, adjoining it, dates from 1896, but the nucleus of the collection was formed in 1858. The munificence of Sir Henry Tate provided the gallery, commonly named after him, by the Thames near Vauxhall Bridge, which contains the national collection of British art. The Wallace collection of paintings and objects of art, in Hertford House, Manchester Square, was bequeathed to the nation by the widow of Sir Richard Wallace in 1897. Dulwich College possesses a fine series of paintings, of the Dutch and other schools, bequeathed by Sir P. F. Bourgeois in 1811. There are also notable collections of pictures in several of the mansions of the nobility, government buildings, halls of the City Companies and elsewhere. No gallery in London is exclusively or especially devoted to sculpture. Of the periodical art exhibitions that of the Royal Academy is most noteworthy. It is held annually at Burlington House from the first Monday in May to the first Monday in August. It consists mainly of paintings, but includes a few drawings and examples of sculpture. Earlier in each year exhibitions of works by deceased British artists and by old masters are held, and the Gibson and Diploma Galleries are permanent exhibitions. At the Guildhall special exhibitions are held from time to time. There are a number of art galleries in and about Bond Street and Piccadilly, Regent Street and Pall Mall, such as the New Gallery, where periodical exhibitions are given by the New English Art Club, the Royal Society of Painters in Water-Colours, the Royal Institute of Painters in Water-Colours, other societies and art dealers.

Municipal provision of public libraries under acts of 1892 and 1893 is general throughout London, and these institutions are exceedingly popular for purposes both of reference and of loan. The acts are extended to include the provisions of museums and art galleries, but the borough councils have not as a rule availed themselves of this extension. The London County Council administers the Horniman Museum at Forest Hill, Lewisham. The City Corporation maintains the fine Guildhall library and museum. A few free libraries are supported by donations and subscriptions or charities. Besides the Government reference libraries at the British Museum and South Kensington there are other such libraries, of a specialized character, as at the Patent Office and the Record Office. Among lending libraries should be noticed the London Library in St James's Square, Pall Mall.

Theatres and Places of Entertainment.—The principal London theatres lie between Piccadilly and Temple Bar, and High Holborn and Victoria Street, the majority being in Shaftesbury Avenue, the Haymarket, the neighbourhood of Charing Cross and the Strand. At these central theatres successful plays are allowed to "run" for protracted periods, but there are numerous fine houses in other parts of London which are generally occupied by a succession of touring companies presenting either revivals of popular plays or plays successful at the moment in the central theatres. The principal music halls (variety theatres) are in Shaftesbury Avenue, Piccadilly Circus, Leicester Square and the Strand. The Covent Garden theatre is the principal home of grand opera; the building, though spacious, suffers by comparison with the magnificence of opera houses in some other capitals, but during the opera season the scene within the theatre is brilliant. The chief halls devoted mainly to concerts are the Royal Albert Hall, close to the South Kensington museums, and Queen's Hall in Langham Place, Regent Street. For a long time St James's Hall (demolished in 1905) between Regent Street and Piccadilly was the chief concert hall. Oratorio is given usually in the Albert Hall, the vast area of which is especially suited for a large chorus and orchestra, and at the Crystal Palace (*q.v.*). This latter building, standing on high ground at Sydenham, and visible from far over the metropolis, is devoted not only to concerts, but to general entertainment, and the extensive grounds give accommodation for a variety of sports and amusements. Among other popular places of entertainment may be mentioned the exhibition grounds and buildings at Earl's Court; similar grounds at Shepherd's Bush, where a Franco-British Exhibition was held in 1908, an Imperial Exhibition in 1909, and an Anglo-Japanese in 1910, the great Olympia hall, West Kensington; the celebrated wax-work exhibition of Madame Tussaud in Marylebone Road, the Alexandra Palace, Muswell Hill, an institution resembling the Crystal Palace; and the Agricultural Hall, Islington, where agricultural and other exhibitions are held. The well-known Egyptian Hall in Piccadilly was taken down in 1905, and the permanent conjuring entertainment for which (besides picture exhibitions) it was noted was removed elsewhere. Theatres, music halls, concert halls and other places of entertainment are licensed by the County Council, except that the licence for stage-plays is granted by the lord chamberlain under the Theatres Act 1843. The council provides for inspection of places of entertainment in respect of precautions against fire, structural safety, &c. The principal clubs are in and about Piccadilly and Pall Mall (see CLUB). A club for soldiers, sailors and marines in London, called the Union Jack Club, was opened in Waterloo Road by King Edward VII. in 1907.

Parks and Open Spaces: Administration.—The administration of parks and open spaces in and round London, topographical details of the principal of which are given in Section I., is divided between the Office of Works, the London County Council, the City Corporation and the borough councils. The Office of Works controls the Royal parks, the County Council controls the larger parks and open spaces not under Government or City control, and the borough councils the smaller; while the City Corporation controls certain public grounds outside the County of London. There are a few other bodies controlling particular open spaces, as the following list of public grounds exceeding 50 acres (in 1910) will show.—

1. *Under the Office of Works*—	
Green Park	53½ acres
Greenwich Park	185 "
Hyde Park	363¾ "
Kensington Gardens	274¾ "
Regent's Park	472¼ "
St James's Park	93 "
2. *Under the War Office.*—	
Woolwich Common	159 "
3. *Under the London County Council*—	
Avery Hill, Eltham	80 "
Battersea Park	199¼ "
Blackheath	267 "
Bostall Heath and Woods, Woolwich	133¼ "
Brockwell Park, Herne Hill	127¾ acres
Clapham Common	205 "
Clissold Park	54¼ "
Dulwich Park	72 "
Finsbury Park	115 "
Hackney Marsh	339 "
Hainault Forest, Essex	805 "
Hampstead Heath	320¼ "
Ladywell Ground, Lewisham	51¼ "
Marble Hill, Twickenham	66 "
Millfields, Hackney	62¼ "
Parliament Hill	267¼ "
Peckham Rye and Park	113¼ "
Plumstead Common	103 "
Southwark Park	63 "
Streatham Common	66¼ "
Tooting Bec Common	151¼ "
Tooting Graveney Common	66 "
Victoria Park, East London	217 "
Wandsworth Common	155 "
Wormwood Scrubbs	193 "
4. *Under the City Corporation*—	
Burnham Beeches, Buckinghamshire	375 "
Coulsdon Commons, Surrey	347 "
Epping Forest, Essex	5559¼ "
Highgate Woods	69 "
West Ham Park	77 "

Wimbledon and Putney Commons are under a board of conservators. The London County Council's parks and open spaces increased in number from 40 in 1889 to 114 in 1907, and in acreage from 2656 to 5006 in the same years. The expenditure in 1907–1908 was £131,582, which sum included £11,987 for bands. (See also separate articles on boroughs.)

Bathing (at certain hours) and boating are permitted in the ornamental waters in several of the parks, music is provided and much attention is paid to the protection of waterfowl and other birds, while herds of deer are maintained in some places, and also botanical gardens. Surplus plants and cuttings are generally distributed without charge to educational or charitable institutions, and to the poor. Provision is made for cricket, football and other games in a number of the parks. Large gatherings of spectators are attracted to the first-class cricket matches played at Lord's ground, St John's Wood, by the Marylebone Club and the Middlesex County teams, Eton College against Harrow School, and Oxford against Cambridge University; to the Kennington Oval for the matches of the Surrey club, and the Leyton ground for those of the Essex club. In the Crystal Palace grounds the final match for the English Association Football cup is generally played, and huge crowds from both the metropolis and the provinces witness the game. At Queen's Club, West Kensington, the annual Oxford and Cambridge athletic meeting and others take place, besides football matches, and there is covered accommodation for tennis and other games. Professional association football teams are maintained locally in several parts of London, and much popular interest is taken in their matches. Rugby football is upheld by such notable teams as Blackheath and Richmond. Fashionable society takes its pastimes at such centres as the grounds of the Hurlingham and Ranelagh clubs, at Fulham and Barnes respectively, where polo and other games are played; and Rotten Row, the horse-track in Hyde Park, is the favourite resort of riders. In summer, boating on the lovely reaches of the Thames above the metropolis forms the recreation of thousands. The growth of popularity of the cycle, and later of the motor-car, has been a principal factor in the wide development of a tendency to leave London during the "week-end," that is to say, as a rule, for Saturday afternoon and Sunday. With many this is a practice at all seasons, and the railway companies foster the habit by means of tickets at reduced fares to all parts. The watering-places of the Sussex, Kent and Essex coasts, and pre-eminently Brighton, are specially favoured for these brief holidays.

VI. COMMERCE

Port of London.—The extent of the Port of London has been variously defined for different purposes, but for those of the Port Authority it is taken to extend from Teddington Lock to a line between Yantlet Creek in Kent and the City Stone opposite Canvey Isle and in Essex. London Bridge is to outward appearance the up-river limit of the port. There are wharves and a large carrying trade in barges above this point, but below it the river is crowded with shipping, and extensive docks open on either hand.

Towards the close of the 19th century evidence was accumulating that the development of the Port of London was not keeping pace with that of shipping generally. In 1900 a Royal Commission was appointed to investigate the existing administration of the port, the alleged inadequacy of accommodation for vessels and kindred questions, and to advance a scheme of [illegible] showed apprehension to be [illegible] was ascertained, was not kept [illegible] trade was acted as showing [illegible] the administration was found [illegible] The recommendations of the [illegible] a single controlling authority [illegible] Thames Conservancy Watermen's [illegible] the stocks of the companies [illegible] it was advised, should consist [illegible] be nominated by the London [illegible] Corporation of the City (supposing [illegible] responsibilities proposed [illegible] improvements), 5 by the governors [illegible] the mercantile community, 2 by [illegible] each by the Admiralty, [illegible] The remaining members [illegible] e.g. shipowners, barge [illegible] interested, &c. Rival schemes, [illegible] County Council, which [illegible] through a committee, [illegible] suggested that it should appoint [illegible] and by the London [illegible] proposed a Harbour Trust of [illegible] Thames Conservancy also [illegible] a Mansion House [illegible] never and a deputation [illegible] the solution of the matter

[illegible] the condition of the Thames, [illegible] of constructing a dam [illegible] river between Gravesend [illegible] was between three [illegible] be met by a toll, and it [illegible] independent of tides, [illegible] delay of large vessels [illegible] be obviated, that the [illegible] the tides, and the necessity [illegible] abolished. This "barrage [illegible] length, and its theoretical [illegible] The scheme included [illegible] which, incidentally, a high

[illegible] embodying the recommenda- [illegible] certain exceptions, was [illegible] found impossible to carry [illegible] the Port of London Act [illegible] force in 1909. This act [illegible] of a Port Authority, [illegible] below, which took over [illegible] with the docks and other [illegible]

[illegible] the docks owned by them,

[illegible] company had amalgamated [illegible] except the Millwall Docks. [illegible] these docks, with dates of [illegible] St Katherine's (1828; [illegible] West India, covering the [illegible] Isle of Dogs (1802; 121 [illegible] acres), Royal Victoria and [illegible] parallel with the river [illegible] nearly 3 m. in distance [illegible] below London Bridge, con- [illegible] India Docks Company [illegible] the largest steamers trading

[illegible] part of the Isle of Dogs, are

[illegible] (Bermondsey), occupy a [illegible] Limehouse Reach. There [illegible] middle of the 17th century. [illegible] the Greenland, being

[illegible] and through connexions for [illegible] attached to the docks. The [illegible]

building being by Laing, but the Corinthian façade was added by Smirke. It includes a museum containing ancient documents and specimens of articles seized by the customs authorities.

The chief authorities concerned in the government of the Port of London till 1909 were:—

1. *Thames Conservancy.*—For conservancy purposes, regulation of navigation, removal of obstruction, dredging, &c.

2. *City Corporation.*—Port sanitary purposes from Teddington Lock seawards.

3. *Trinity House.*—Pilotage, lighting and buoying from London Bridge seawards.

4. *The Watermen's and Lightermen's Company.*—The licensing authority for watermen and lightermen.

Besides these authorities, the London County Council, the Board of Trade, the Admiralty, the Metropolitan and City Police, police of riparian boroughs, Kent and Essex Fisheries Commissioners, all the dock companies and others played some part in the government and public services of the port.

Port Authority.—The Port of London Authority, as constituted by the act of 1908, is a body corporate consisting of a chairman, vice-chairman, 17 members elected by payers of dues, wharfingers and owners of river craft, 1 member elected by wharfingers exclusively, and 10 members appointed by the following existing bodies—Admiralty (one); Board of Trade (two); London County Council (two from among its own members and two others); City Corporation (one from among its own members and one other); Trinity House (one). The Board of Trade and the County Council must each, under the act, consult with representatives of labour as to the appointment of one of the members, in order that labour may be represented on the Port Authority. The first "elected" members were actually, under the act, appointed by the Board of Trade. The undertakings of the three dock companies mentioned above were transferred to and vested in the Port Authority, an equivalent amount of port stock created under the act being issued to each. The Port Authority has full powers to authorize construction works. All the rights, powers and duties of the Thames Conservancy, so far as concerns the Thames below Teddington Lock, were transferred to the Port Authority under the act, as also were the powers of the Watermen's Company in respect of the registration and licensing of vessels, and the regulation of lightermen and watermen. The Port Authority fixes the port rates, which, however, must not in any two consecutive years exceed one-thousandth part of the value of all imports and exports, or a three-thousandth of the value of goods discharged from or taken on board vessels not within the premises of a dock. Preferential dock charges are prohibited and a port fund established under the act. The authority has powers to borrow money, but for certain purposes in this connexion, as in other matters, it can only act subject to the approval of the Board of Trade.

Commerce.—The following figures may be quoted for purposes of comparison at different periods:—

Value of Exports of Home Produce (1840), £11,586,037; (1874), £60,232,118; (1880), £52,600,929; (1902–1905 average), £60,095,294. *Imports* (1880), £141,442,907; (1902–1905), £174,059,316. These figures point to the fact that London is essentially a mart, and neither is itself, nor is the especial outlet for, a large manufacturing centre; hence imports greatly exceed exports.

Vessels entered and cleared (foreign and colonial trade):—

Year.	Entered.	Cleared.
	Tonnage.	Tonnage.
1694	135,972	81,148
1750	511,680	179,860
1800	796,632	729,554
1841–1850 (average)	1,596,453	1,124,793
1881	5,810,043	4,478,960
1895	8,435,676	6,110,325
1905	10,814,115	7,913,115

In the coastwise trade, in 1881, 38,953 vessels of 4,545,904 tons entered; in 1895, 43,704 vessels of 6,555,618 tons; but these figures include vessels trading within the Thames estuary (ports of London, Rochester, Colchester and Faversham), which later returns do not. Omitting such vessels, therefore, the number which entered in the coastwise trade in 1905 was 16,358 of 6,374,832 tons.

Business.—The City has been indicated as the business centre of the metropolis. Besides the Royal Exchange, in the building of which are numerous offices, including "Lloyd's," the centre of the shipping business and marine insurance, there are many exchanges for special articles. Among these are the Corn Exchange in Mark Lane, where the privilege of a fair was originally granted by Edward I.; the Wool Exchange, Coleman Street; the Coal Exchange, Lower Thames Street; the Shipping Exchange, Billiter Street; and the auction mart for landed property in Tokenhouse Yard. The Hop Exchange is across the river in Southwark. In Mincing Lane are the commercial salerooms. Besides the Bank of England there are many banking houses; and the name of Lombard Street, commemorating the former money dealers of Lombardy, is especially associated with them. The majority of the banks are members of the Clearing House, Post Office Court, where a daily exchange of drafts representing millions of pounds sterling is effected. The Royal Mint is on Tower Hill. The Stock Exchange is in Capel Court, and numbers of brokers have their offices in the vicinity of the Royal Exchange and the Bank of England.

Manufactures and Retail Trade.—No part of London can be pointed out as essentially a manufacturing quarter, and there is a strong tendency for manufacturing firms to establish their factories outside the metropolis. There are, however, several large breweries, among which that of Messrs Barclay & Perkins, on the riverside in Southwark, may be mentioned; engineering works are numerous in East London by the river, where there are also shipbuilding yards; the leather industry centres in Bermondsey, the extensive pottery works of Messrs Doulton are in Lambeth, there are chemical works on the Lea, and paper-mills on the Wandle. Certain industries (not confined to factories) have long been associated with particular localities. Thus, clock-makers and metal-workers are congregated in Finsbury, especially Clerkenwell and in Islington; Hatton Garden, near Holborn Viaduct, is a centre for diamond merchants; cabinet-making is carried on in Bethnal Green, Shoreditch and the vicinity; and large numbers in the East End are employed in the match industry. Silk-weaving is still carried on in the district of Spitalfields (see STEPNEY). West of the City certain streets are essentially connected with certain trades. The old-established collection of second-hand book-shops in Holywell Street was only abolished by the widening of the Strand, and a large proportion then removed to Charing Cross Road. In the Strand, and more especially in Fleet Street and its offshoots, are found the offices of the majority of the most important daily newspapers and other journals. Carriage and motor-car warehouses congregate in Long Acre. In Tottenham Court Road are the showrooms of several large upholstering and furnishing firms. Of the streets most frequented on account of their fashionable shops Bond Street, Regent Street, Oxford Street, Sloane Street and High Street, Kensington, may be selected. In the East End and other poor quarters a large trade in second-hand clothing, flowers and vegetables, and many other commodities is carried on in the streets on movable stalls by costermongers and hawkers.

Markets.—The City Corporation exercises a control over the majority of the London markets, which dates from the close of the 14th century, when dealers were placed under the governance of the mayor and aldermen. The markets thus controlled are:

Central Markets, Smithfield, for meat, poultry, provisions, fruit, vegetables, flowers and fish. These extend over a great area north of Newgate Street and east of Farringdon Road. Beneath them are extensive underground railway sidings. A market for horses and cattle existed here at least as early as the time of Henry II.

Leadenhall Market, Leadenhall Street, City, for poultry and meat. This market was in existence before 1411 when it came into the possession of the City.

Billingsgate Market, by the Thames immediately above the custom house, for fish. Formerly a point of anchorage for small vessels, it was made a free market in 1699.

Smithfield Hay Market.

Metropolitan Cattle Market, Copenhagen Fields, Islington.

Deptford Cattle Market (foreign cattle).

Spitalfields Market (fruit, vegetables and flowers).

Shadwell Market (fish).

Of other markets, the Whitechapel Hay Market and Borough Market, Southwark, are under the control of trustees; and Woolwich Market is under the council of that borough. Covent Garden, the great mart in the west of London for flowers, fruit and vegetables, is in the hands of private owners. It appears to have been used as a market early in the 17th century. Scenes of remarkable activity may be witnessed here and at Billingsgate in the early hours of the morning when the stock is brought in and the wholesale distributions are carried on.

VII. GOVERNMENT

Administration before 1888.—The middle of the 19th century found the whole local administration of London still of a medieval character. Moreover, as complete reform had always been steadily resisted, homogeneity was entirely wanting. Outside the City itself a system of local government can hardly be said to have existed. Greater London (in the sense in which that name might then have been applied) was governed by the inhabitants of each parish in vestry assembled, save that in some instances parishes had elected select vestries under the provisions of the Vestries Act 1831. In neither case had the vestry powers of town management. To meet the needs of particular localities, commissioners or trustees having such powers had been from time to time created by local acts. The resulting chaos was remarkable. In 1855 these local acts numbered 250, administered by not less than 300 bodies, and by a number of persons serving on them computed at 10,448. These persons were either self-elected, or elected for life, or both, and therefore in no degree responsible to the ratepayers. There were two bodies having jurisdiction over the whole metropolis except the City, namely, the officers appointed under the Metropolitan Building Act of 1844, and the Metropolitan Commissioners of Sewers, appointed under the Commissioners of Sewers Act 1848. Neither body was responsible to the ratepayers. To remedy this chaotic state of affairs, the Metropolis Management Act 1855 was passed. Under that act a vestry elected by the ratepayers of the parish was established for each parish in the metropolis outside the City. The vestries so elected for the twenty-two larger parishes were constituted the local authorities. The fifty-six smaller parishes were grouped together in fifteen districts, each under a district board, the members of which were elected by the vestries of the constituent parishes.

Vestries.

A central body, styled the Metropolitan Board of Works, having jurisdiction over the whole metropolis (including the City) was also established, the members of which were elected by the Common Council of the City, the vestries and district boards, and the previously established local board of Woolwich (*q.v.*). Further the area of the metropolis for local government purposes was for the first time defined, being the same as that adopted in the Commissioners of Sewers Act, which had been taken from the area of the weekly bills of mortality. The Metropolitan Board of Works was also given certain powers of supervision over the vestries and district boards, and superseded the commissioners of sewers as authority for main drainage. By an act of the same session it became the central authority for the administration of the Building Acts, and subsequently had many additional powers and duties conferred upon it. The vestries and district boards became the authorities for local drainage, paving, lighting, repairing and maintaining streets, and for the removal of nuisances, &c.

Metropolitan Board of Works.

Acts of 1888 and 1899.—An objection to the Metropolitan Board of Works soon became manifest, inasmuch as the system of election was indirect. Moreover, some of its actions were open to such suspicion that a royal commission was appointed to inquire into certain matters connected with the working of the board. This commission issued an interim report in 1888 (the final report did not appear until 1891), which disclosed the inefficiency of the board in certain respects, and also indicated the existence of corruption. Reform followed immediately. Already in 1884 Sir William Harcourt had attempted to constitute the metropolis a municipal borough under the government of a single council. But in 1888 the Local Government Act, dealing with the area of the metropolis as a separate county, created the London County Council as the central administrative body, possessing not only the powers of an ordinary county council, but also extensive powers of town management, transferred to it from the abolished Board of Works. Here, then, was the central body, under their direct control, which inhabitants of London had hitherto lacked. The question of subsidiary councils remained to be settled. The wealthier metropolitan parishes became discontented with the form of local government to which they remained subject, and in 1897 Kensington and Westminster petitioned to be created boroughs by the grant of charters under the Municipal Corporation Acts. These, however, were inapplicable to London, and it was realized

London County Council.

...of special legislation to bear on special cases (as ... these two boroughs would have demanded) ... be inexpedient as making against homogeneity. ... the London Government Act of 1899 was ... It brought into existence the twenty-eight metropolitan boroughs enumerated at the outset of this ... The county of London may thus be regarded from the ... standpoint as consisting of twenty-nine con... ...ting the City of London. As regards the dis... ... and duties between the County Council and ... and the constitution and working of each, ... principle may be briefly indicated as giving all ... which require uniformity of action throughout ... to the County Council, and powers and duties ... administered to the Borough Councils.

... *Bodies.*—The administrative bodies ... may now be summarized:

...*Council.*—Consists of 118 councillors, 2 elected ... division (but the City of London elects 4); ... chairman, vice-chairman and deputy-chair... Triennial elections of councillors by house... on the rate-books. Aldermen hold office

...*Boroughs.*—Councils consist of a mayor and ... in proportion as 1 to 6. The commonest ... exceeded, are 10 and 60 (see separate ...). Triennial elections.

... *City of London.*—The legislation of 1855, ... government of the small area of the City in ... Corporation. Here at least the medieval ... anomalies with respect to modern conditions, ... other municipal body shares the traditions ... City Corporation. This consists of a Lord ... common councilmen, forming the Court ... is the principal administrative body. ... as including (*a*) duties exercised ... Councils, and by the London County ... is by no means powerless within the ... peculiar duties such as control of markets ... common councilmen, whose institution ... I., takes place annually, the electors ... among the twenty-five wards of the ... each ward (save that the wards of ... share one) is elected for life. The ... by the Court of Aldermen from two ... Court of Common Hall by the Livery, ... members of the ancient trade gilds or ... through their control over the ... had formerly an influence over the ... from the time of Edward III. was

...*ments.*—The Local Government Act ... for non-administrative purposes ... is to say, as a separate county. ... justices, coroners, sheriffs, ... with other counties, except in so far ... modified by the existence of the ... metropolitan police, police courts and ... of quarter-sessions. The powers ... however, are as peculiar in this ... administration, and the act left ... unchanged. Thus the Lord ... authority, and the police of ... bodies, the Metropolitan and

... criminal cases are the Central ... quarter sessions. The Central ... the place of the provincial ... an act of 1834. There are ... Lord Mayor, aldermen and ... the "Old Bailey" sessions... designs of E. W. Mountford ... sessions for the county ... usually, for the north side ... Clerkenwell (Finsbury) ... Causeway, South... was merged with the ... of the Tower was ... the Lord Mayor and

Garden; Clerkenwell; Great Marlborough Street (Westminster); Greenwich and Woolwich; Lambeth; Marylebone; North London, Stoke Newington Road; Southwark; South Western, Lavender Hill (Battersea); Thames, Arbour Street East (Stepney); West Ham; West London, Vernon Street (Fulham); Westminster, Vincent Square; Worship Street (Shoreditch). The police courts of the City are held at the Mansion House, the Lord Mayor or an alderman sitting as magistrate, and at the Guildhall, where the aldermen preside in rotation. The prisons within the metropolis are Brixton, Holloway, Pentonville, Wandsworth and Wormwood Scrubbs. In the county of London there are 12 coroners' districts, 19 petty sessional divisions (the City forming a separate one) and 13 county court districts (the City forming a separate one). The boundaries of these divisions do not in any way correspond with each other, or with the police divisions, or with the borough or parish boundaries. The registration county of London coincides with the administrative county.

Parliamentary Representation.—The London Government Act contains a saving clause by which "nothing in or done under this act shall be construed as altering the limits of any parliamentary borough or parliamentary county." The parliamentary boroughs are thus in many cases named and bounded differently from the metropolitan boroughs. The parliamentary arrangements of each metropolitan borough are indicated in the separate articles on the boroughs. In the following list the boroughs which extend outside the administrative county of London are noted. Each division of each borough, or each borough where not divided, returns one member, save that the City of London returns two members.

(*a*) *North of the Thames.* (1) Bethnal Green—*Divs.*: North-eastern, South-western. (2) Chelsea (detached portion in administrative county of Middlesex, Kensal Town). (3) Finsbury (detached portion in Middlesex, Muswell Hill)—*Divs.*: Holborn, Central, Eastern. (5) Fulham. (6) Hackney—*Divs.*: North, Central, South. (7) Hammersmith. (8) Hampstead. (9) Islington—*Divs.*: Northern, Southern, Eastern, Western. (10) Kensington—*Divs.*: Northern, Southern; (11) City of London. (12) Marylebone—*Divs.*: Eastern, Western. (13) Paddington (extending into Middlesex)—*Divs.*: Northern, Southern. (14) St George's Hanover Square. (15) St Pancras—*Divs.*: Northern, Southern, Eastern, Western. (16) Shoreditch—*Divs.*: Hoxton, Haggerston. (17) Strand. (18) Tower Hamlets—*Divs.*: Bow and Bromley, Limehouse, Mile End, Poplar, St George, Stepney, Whitechapel. (19) Westminster.

A detached portion of the parliamentary division of Hornsey, Middlesex, is in the metropolitan borough of Hackney. London University returns a member.

(*b*) *South of the Thames.* (1) Battersea and Clapham—*Divs.*: Battersea, Clapham. (2) Camberwell (extending into Kent)—*Divs.*: Northern, Peckham, Dulwich. (3) Deptford. (4) Greenwich. (5) Lambeth—*Divs.*: Northern, Kennington, Brixton, Norwood. (6) Lewisham. (7) Newington—*Divs.*: Western, Walworth. (8) Southwark—*Divs.*: Western, Rotherhithe, Bermondsey. (9) Wandsworth. (10) Woolwich.

Part of the Wimbledon parliamentary division of Surrey is in the metropolitan borough of Wandsworth.

Ecclesiastical Divisions and Denominations.—London north of the Thames is within the Church of England bishopric of London, the bishop's palace being at Fulham. In this diocese, which covers nearly the whole of Middlesex and a very small portion of Hertfordshire, are the suffragan bishoprics of Islington, Kensington and Stepney. The bishopric of Southwark was created in 1904, having been previously a suffragan bishopric in the diocese of Rochester. The county contains 612 ecclesiastical parishes. Westminster is the seat of the Roman Catholic archbishopric in England, and Southwark is a bishopric. Among the numerous chapels of dissenting bodies there may be mentioned the City Temple, Congregational, on Holborn Viaduct; the Metropolitan Tabernacle, Baptist, in Southwark, the creation of which was the outcome of the labours of the famous preacher Charles Spurgeon (d. 1892); and Wesley's Chapel, City Road, in the graveyard of which is the tomb of John Wesley; his house, which adjoins the chapel, being open as a memorial museum. In 1903 the Wesleyans acquired the site of the Royal Aquarium, near Westminster Abbey, for the erection of a central hall. The Great Synagogue of the Jews is in St James' Place, Aldgate.

The headquarters of the Salvation Army are in Queen Victoria Street, City. There are numerous foreign churches, among which may be mentioned the French Protestant churches in Monmouth Road, Bayswater and Soho Square; the Greek church of St Sophia, Moscow Road, Bayswater; and the German Evangelical church in Montpelier Place, Brompton Road, opened in 1904. (O. J. R. H.)

VIII. Finance

In addition to the provisions that have been mentioned above (Section VII.), the London Government Act 1899 simplified administration in two respects. The duties of overseers in London had been performed by most diverse bodies. In some parishes overseers were appointed in the ordinary manner; in others the vestry, by local acts and by orders under the Local Government Act 1894, was appointed to act as, or empowered to appoint, overseers, whilst in Chelsea the guardians acted as overseers. The act of 1899 swept away all these distinctions, and constituted the new borough councils in every case the overseers for every parish within their respective boroughs, except that the town clerk of each borough performs the duties of overseers with respect to the registration of electors.[1] Again, with regard to rates, there were in all cases three different rates leviable in each parish—the poor rate, the general rate and the sewers rate—whilst in many parishes in addition there was a separate lighting rate. From the sewers rate and lighting rate, land, as opposed to buildings, was entitled to certain exemptions. Under the act of 1899 all these rates are consolidated into a single rate, called the general rate, which is assessed, made, collected and levied as the poor rate, but the interests of persons previously entitled to exemptions are safeguarded. Further, every precept sent by an authority in London for the purpose of obtaining money (these authorities include the London County Council, the receiver of the Metropolitan Police, the Central Unemployed Body and the Boards of Guardians) which has ultimately to be raised out of a rate within a borough is sent direct to the council of the borough instead of filtering through other authorities before reaching the overseers. The only exceptions to this rule are: (1) precepts issued by the local government board for raising the sums to be contributed to the metropolitan common poor fund; and (2) precepts issued by poor law authorities representing two or more poor-law unions; in both these cases the precept has of necessity to be first sent to the guardians. The metropolitan borough councils make one general rate, which includes the amount necessary to meet their own expenditure, as well as to meet the demands of the various precepting authorities. There was thus raised in the year 1906–1907 a sum of £15,393,956 (in 1898–1899 the amount was £10,401,441); of this £11,012,424 was for central rates, which was subdivided into £7,930,275 for county services and £3,082,149 for local services, leaving a balance of £4,381,532, strictly local rates. The total local expenditure of London for the year 1906–1907 was £24,703,087 (in 1898–1899 it was only £14,768,757), the balance of £9,761,734 being made up by receipts-in-aid and imperial subventions. This expenditure was divided among the following bodies:

London County Council	£9,491,271
Metropolitan Borough Councils	5,009,982
Boards of Guardians	3,587,429
Metropolitan Water Board	2,318,618
Metropolitan Police	1,903,441
City Corporation	1,270,406
Metropolitan Asylums Board	934,463
Central (Unemployed) Body	141,784
Overseers—City of London	34,757
Market Trustees (Southwark)	10,680
Local Government Board—Common Poor Fund	756
	£24,703,087

The total expenditure was equal to a rate in the pound of 11s. 4·4d.; the actual amount raised in rates was equivalent to a rate of 7s. 1·0d., receipts-in-aid were equivalent to a rate of 3s. 2·5d., and imperial subventions to a rate of 1s. 3·4d. Practically the whole amount contributed towards the support of public local expenditure, and a considerable amount of that contributed to public national expenditure is based on the estimated annual value of the immovable property situated within the county of London, which in 1876 was £23,240,070; in 1886 £30,716,719; in 1896 £35,793,672; and in 1909 £44,666,651. The produce of a penny rate was, in the

[1] Over 200 local acts were repealed by schemes made under the act of 1899.

(1) *Rate and Debt Accounts.*

Estimated Income.

Balances		£967,740
Receipts in aid of expenditure (local taxation licences and estate duty, beer and spirit duties, &c.)		513,541
Government grants in aid of education		1,515,663
Interest on loans advanced to local authorities, &c.		586,065
Rents, &c.		427,767
Contributions from revenue-producing undertakings for interest and repayment of debt		685,948
Miscellaneous		3,633
Rate contributions—		
General, for other than education		2,698,610
For education		3,675,694
Special		407,946
		£11,482,607

Estimated Expenditure.

Debt (including management)		£3,905,135
Grants (mostly guardians)		645,913
Pensions		75,665
Establishment charges		232,045
Judicial expenses		52,515
Services—		
Main drainage	£295,650	
Fire brigade	263,575	
Parks and open spaces	140,715	
Bridges, tunnels, ferry	49,925	
Embankments	14,940	
Pauper lunatics	78,870	
Inebriates Acts	14,045	
Coroners	30,925	
Weights and measures	14,830	
Gas testing	13,785	
Building Acts	25,595	
Diseases of Animals Acts	19,260	
Miscellaneous	63,060	
	£1,025,175	
Education	4,837,442	
Steamboats	14,805	
Works Dept.	12,100	5,889,522
Parliamentary expenses		22,678
Miscellaneous		6,214
Total expenditure		10,829,684
Balances		652,923
		£11,482,607

(2) *Revenue Producing Undertakings.*

Estimated Income.

Balances		£4,055
Receipts—		
Working class dwellings	£173,443	
Tramways	2,089,955	
Small Holdings and Allotments	410	
Parks boating	5,100	2,268,908
Transfers		6,214
		£2,279,177

Estimated Expenditure.

Working expenses—		
Working class dwellings	£56,060	
Tramways	1,318,620	
Small Holdings and Allotments	621	
Parks boating	2,965	£1,378,266
Renewals		163,828
Reserve		44,557
Interest on and repayment of debts		685,946
Transfer in relief of rates (parks boating)		2,000
Balances		4,580
		£2,279,177

was part of some more considerable monuments in the forum (*Parentalia*, pp. 265, 266). Holinshed (who was followed by Shakespeare in *2 Henry VI.*, act 4 sc. 6) tells us that when Cade, in 1450, forced his way into London, he first of all proceeded to London Stone, and having struck his sword upon it, said in reference to himself and in explanation of his own action, "Now is Mortimer lord of this city." Mr H. C. Coote, in a paper published in the *Trans. London and Middlesex Arch. Soc.* for 1878, points out that this act meant something to the mob who followed the rebel chief, and was not a piece of foolish acting. Mr Laurence Gomme (*Primitive Folk-Moots*, pp. 155, 156) takes up the matter at this point, and places the tradition implied by Cade's significant action as belonging to times when the London Stone was, as other great stones were, the place where the suitors of an open-air assembly were accustomed to gather together and to legislate for the government of the city. Corroborative facts have been gathered from other parts of the country, and, although more evidence is required, such as we have is strongly in favour of the supposition that the London Stone is a prehistoric monument.

London Stone.

The first London Bridge.

One of the most important questions in the history of London that requires settlement is the date of the building of the first bridge, that is whether it was constructed by Britons or by Romans. If the Britons had not already made the bridge before the Romans arrived it must have been one of the first Roman works. As long as there was no bridge to join the north and south banks of the Thames the great object of Roman rule remained unfulfilled. This object was the completion of a system of roads connecting all parts of the Empire with Rome.

Dion Cassius, who lived in the early part of the 3rd century (*Hist. Rom.* lib. lx. c. 20), states that there was a bridge over the Thames at the time of the invasion of Claudius (A.D. 43), but he places it a little above the mouth of the river ("higher up"). The position is vague, but the mouth of the Thames in these early times may be considered as not far from the present position of London Bridge. Sir George Airy held that this bridge was not far from the site of London Bridge (*Proceedings* of *Institut. Civil Engineers*, xlix. 120), but Dr Guest was not prepared to allow that the Britons were able to construct a bridge over a tidal river such as the Thames, some 300 yds. wide, with a difference of level at high and low water of nearly 20 ft. He therefore suggested that the bridge was constructed over the marshy valley of the Lea, probably near Stratford. It needs some temerity to differ from so great an authority as Dr Guest, but it strikes one as surprising that, having accepted the fact of a bridge made by the Britons, he should deny that these Britons possessed a town or village in the place to which he supposed that Aulus Plautius retired.

As the Welsh word for "bridge" is "pont," and this was taken directly from the Latin, the inference is almost conclusive that the Britons acquired their knowledge of bridges from the Romans. Looking at the stage of culture which the Britons had probably reached, it would further be a natural inference that there was no necessity for a bridge anywhere in Britain before the Roman occupation; but, if Dion's statement is correct, it may be that there is a possible explanation that the increased intercourse with Rome during the hundred years that elapsed between Julius and Claudius Caesar's invasion may have led to the construction of a bridge of some kind across the Thames at London through the influence and under the guidance of Roman traders and engineers. If so, the word "pont" may have been borrowed by the Britons before the commencement of the Roman occupation. Much stronger are the reasons for believing that there was a bridge in Roman times. Remains of villas were found in Southwark, which was evidently a Roman suburb, and it therefore hardly seems likely that a practical people such as the Romans would remain without a bridge. Roach Smith is a strong advocate for the Roman bridge. "It would naturally be erected somewhere near the road into Kent, which I cannot but think [illegible] the site of Old London Bridge, both from its central situation, from the general absence of the foundations of buildings in the approaches on the northern side, and from discoveries recently made in the Thames on the line of the old bridge" (*Archaeologia*, xxix. 160). Smith has, however, still stronger arguments, which he states as follows: "Throughout the entire line of the old bridge, the bed of the river was found to contain ancient wooden piles; and when these piles, subsequently to the erection of the new bridge, were pulled up to deepen the channel of the river, many thousands of Roman coins, with abundance of broken Roman tiles and pottery, were discovered, and immediately beneath some of the central piles brass medallions of Aurelius, Faustina and Commodus. All these remains are indicative of a bridge. The enormous quantities of Roman coins may be accounted for by consideration of the well-known practice of the Romans to make these imperishable monuments subservient towards perpetuating the memory, not only of their conquests, but also of those public works which were the natural result of their successes in remote parts of the world. They may have been deposited either upon the building or repairs of the bridge, as well as upon the accession of a new emperor" (*Archaeological Journal*, i. 113).

At the beginning of the 5th century the Roman legions left Britain, and the *Saxon Chronicle* gives the exact date, stating that never since A.D. 409 "have the Romans ruled in Britain"—the chronicler setting down the Roman sway at 470 winters and dating from Julius Caesar's invasion. We learn that in the year 418 "the Romans collected all the treasures that were in Britain, and hid some of them in the earth, that no man might afterwards find them, and conveyed some with them into Gaul."

2. *Saxon* (449-1066).—We are informed in the *Saxon Chronicle* that about A.D. 449 or 450 the invaders settled in Britain, and in 457 Hengist and Aesc fought against the Britons at Crayford, driving them out of Kent. The vanquished fled to London in terror and apparently found a shelter there. After this entry there is no further mention of London in the *Chronicle* for a century and a half. This silence has been taken by some historians of weight to imply that London practically ceased to exist. Dr Guest asserted "that good reason may be given for the belief that even London itself for a while lay desolate and uninhabited" (*Archaeological Journal*, xix. 219). J. R. Green and Mr Loftie strongly supported this view, and in Sir Walter Besant's *Early London* (1908) the idea of the desolation of the city is taken for granted.

In answer to this contention it may be said that, although the silence of the *Chronicle* is difficult to understand, it is almost impossible to believe that the very existence of the most important city in the country could suddenly cease and the inhabitants disappear without some special notice. Battles and scenes of destruction are so fully described in other instances that one must believe that when nothing is related nothing special occurred. No doubt the coming of the Saxons, which entirely changed the condition of the country, must have greatly injured trade, but although there was not the same freedom of access to the roads, the Londoners had the highway of the river at their doors. Although the Saxons hated towns and refused to settle in London, they may have allowed the original inhabitants to continue their trade on condition that they received some share of the profits or a tribute. The only question really is whether London being an exceptional city received exceptional treatment.

Along the banks of the Thames are several small havens whose names have remained to us, such as Rotherhithe, Lambhith (Lambeth), Chelchith (Chelsea), &c., and it is not unlikely that the Saxons, who would not settle in the city itself, associated themselves with these small open spots. Places were thus founded over a large space which otherwise might have remained unsettled.

Saxon Settlement.

If what is here suggested really occurred it may be that this separation of London from the surrounding country originated the remarkable position of London with its unparalleled privileges, which were continued for many centuries and kept it not only the leader among cities but distinct from all others. Laurence Gomme, in *The Governance of London* (1907), opposes the view that the city was for a time left deserted (a view which, it may be remarked, is a comparatively modern one, probably originating with Dr Guest). H. C. Coote in his *Romans of Britain* elaborated a description of the survival of Roman influence in English institutions, but his views did not obtain much support from London historians. Mr Gomme's contention is to some extent a modification of Mr Coote's view, but it is original in the illustrations that give it force. Londinium was a Roman city, and (as in the case of all such cities) was formed on the model of ancient Rome. It may therefore be expected to retain evidence of the existence of a Pomoerium and Territorium as at Rome. The Pomoerium marked the unbuilt space around the walls. Gomme refers to an open space outside the western wall of Dorchester still called the Pummery as an indication of the Pomoerium in that place; and he considers that the name of Mile End, situated 1 m. from Aldgate and the city walls, marks the extent of the open space around the walls of London known as the Pomoerium. This fact throws a curious light upon the growth of the "Liberties." It has always been a puzzle that no note exists of the first institution of these liberties. If this open space was from the earliest times attached to the city there would be no need when it was built upon for any special act to be passed for its inclusion in London. "The *Territorium* of the city was its special property, and it extended as far as the limits of the territorium of the nearest Roman city or as near thereto as the natural boundaries." This explains the position of Middlesex in relation to London. In connexion with these two features of a Roman city supposed to be found in Ancient London the author argues for the continuity of the city through the changes of Roman and Saxon dominion.

Origin of the Liberties.

One of the most striking illustrations of the probable continuity of London history is to be found in the contrast between York and London. This is only alluded to in Gomme's book, but it is elaborated in an article in the *Cornhill Magazine* (November 1906). These two were the chief Roman cities in Britain, one in the north and the other in the south. They are both equally good examples of important cities under Roman domination. York was conquered and occupied by the Saxons, and there not only are the results of English settlement clear but all records of Roman government were destroyed. In London the Saxon stood outside the government for centuries, and the acceptance of the Roman survival explains much that is otherwise unintelligible.

Gomme finds important evidence of the independence of London in the existence of a merchant law which was opposed to Anglo-Saxon law. He reprints and discusses the celebrated *Judicia Civitatis Lundoniae* of King Æthelstan's reign—"the ordinance" (as it declares itself) "which the bishop and the reeves belonging to London have ordained." He holds that the Londoners passed "their own laws by their own citizens without reference to the king at all," and in the present case of a king who according to Kemble "had carried the influence of the crown to an extent unexampled in any of his predecessors." He adds: "What happened afterwards was evidently this: that the code passed by the Londoners was sent to the king for him to extend its application throughout the kingdom, and this is done by the eleventh section." The view originated by Gomme certainly explains many difficulties in the history of the transition from Roman to English London, which have hitherto been overlooked by historians.

Independence of London.

When the city is next referred to in the *Saxon Chronicle* it appears to have been inhabited by a population of heathens. Under the date 604 we read: "This year Augustine consecrated two bishops: Mellitus and Justus. He sent Mellitus to preach baptism to the East Saxons, whose king was called Sebert, son of Ricole the sister of Æthelbert, and whom Æthelbert had then appointed king. And Æthelbert gave Mellitus a bishop's see in Lundenevic and to Justus he gave Rochester, which is twenty-four miles from Canterbury." The Christianity of the Londoners was of an unsatisfactory character; for, after the death of Sebert, his sons who were heathens stirred up the multitude to drive out their bishop. Mellitus became archbishop of Canterbury, and London relapsed into heathenism. In this, the earliest period of Saxon history recorded, there appears to be no relic of the Christianity of the Britons, which at one time was well in evidence. What became of the cathedral which we may suppose to have existed in London during the later Roman period we cannot tell, but we may guess that it was destroyed by the heathen Saxons. Bede records that the church of St Paul was built by Æthelbert, and from that time to this a cathedral dedicated to St Paul has stood upon the hill looking down on Ludgate.

Arrival of Christianity.

After the driving out of Mellitus London remained without a bishop until the year 656, when Cedda, brother of St Chad of Lichfield, was invited to London by Sigebert, who had been converted to Christianity by Finan, bishop of the Northumbrians. Cedda was consecrated bishop of the East Saxons by Finan and held the see till his death on the 26th of October 664. He was succeeded by Wini, bishop of Winchester, and then came Earconuald (or St Erkenwald), whose shrine was one of the chief glories of old St Paul's. He died on the 30th of April 693, a day which was kept in memory in his cathedral for centuries by special offices. The list of bishops from Cedda to William (who is addressed in the Conqueror's Charter) is long, and each bishop apparently held a position of great importance in the government of the city.

In the 7th century the city seems to have settled down into a prosperous place and to have been peopled by merchants of many nationalities. We learn that at this time it was the great mart of slaves. It was in the fullest sense a free-trading town; neutral to a certain extent between the kingdoms around, although the most powerful of the kings conquered their feebler neighbours. During the 8th century, when a more settled condition of life became possible, the trade and commerce of London increased in volume and prosperity. A change, however, came about towards the end of the century, when the Scandinavian freebooters known as Danes began to harry the coasts. The Saxons had become law-abiding, and the fierce Danes treated them in the same way as in former days they had treated the Britons. In 871 the chronicler affirms that Alfred fought nine great battles against the Danes in the kingdom south of the Thames, and that the West Saxons made peace with them. In the next year the Danes went from Reading to London, and there took up their winter quarters. Then the Mercians made peace with them. In 886 Alfred overcame the Danes, restored London to its inhabitants, rebuilt its walls, reannexed the city to Mercia, and committed it to Ethelred, alderman of Mercia. Then, as the chronicler writes, "all the Angle race turned to him (Alfred) that were not in bondage of the Danish men." In 896 the Londoners came off victorious in their encounters with the Danes. The king obstructed the river so that the enemy could not bring up their ships, and they therefore abandoned them. The Londoners broke up some, and brought the strongest and best to London. In 912 Æthelred, the alderman of the Mercians, who had been placed in authority by Alfred, died, and Edward the Elder took possession of London and Oxford, "and all the lands which thereto belonged."

Danish invasions.

Under Æthelstan we find the city increasing in importance and general prosperity. There were then eight mints at work, a fact which exhibits evidence of great activity and the need of coin for the purposes of trade. The folk-moot met in the precincts of St Paul's at the sound of the bell of the famous bell-tower, which also rang out when the armed levy was required to march under St Paul's banner. For some years after the decisive battle of Brunanburh (A.D. 937) the Danes ceased to trouble the country. Fire, however, was almost as great an enemy to London as the Dane. Fabyan when recording the entire destruction of London by fire in the reign of Æthelred (981) makes this remarkable statement—"Ye shall understand that this daye the cytie of London had more housynge and buyldinge from Ludgate toward Westmynstre and lytel or none wher the chief or hart of the citie is now, except (that) in dyvers places were housyng, but they stod without order."

In the reign of Æthelred II., called the Unready (but more correctly the Redeless), the Danes were more successful in their operations against London, but the inhabitants resisted stoutly. Snorre the Icelander tells us that the Danes fortified Southwark with ditch and rampart, which the English assailed in vain. In 982 London was burnt, and in 994 Olaf and Sweyn (the father of Canute) came with ninety-four ships to besiege it. They tried to set the city on fire, but the townsmen did them more harm than they "ever weened." The chronicler piously adds that "the holy Mother of God on that day manifested her mercy to the townsmen, and delivered them from their foes." The Danes went from the town and ravaged the neighbourhood, so that in the end the king and his witan agreed to give sixteen thousand pounds to be relieved of the presence of the enemy. This was the origin of the Danegelt. In the year 1009 the Danes frequently attacked London, but they had no success, and fared ill in their attempts. The Londoners withstood Sweyn in 1013, but in the end they submitted and gave him hostages. Three years after this, Æthelred died in London, and such of the witan as were there and the townsmen chose Edmund Ironside for king although the witan outside London had elected Canute. [illegible] ships were then at Greenwich on their way to London, where they soon afterwards arrived. The Danes at once set to work to dig a great ditch by Southwark, and then dragged their ships through to the west side of the bridge. They were able after this to keep the inhabitants from going either in or out of the town. In spite of all this, after fighting obstinately both by land and by water, the Danes had to raise the siege of London and [illegible] the ships to the river Orwell. After a glorious reign of seven months Edmund died in London, and Canute became master of England. The tribute which the townsmen of London had to pay was £10,500, about one-seventh of the amount which was paid by all the rest of the English nation. This shows the growing importance of the city. From this time there appears to have been a permanent Danish settlement in London, probably [illegible] referred to below.

[illegible] little more to be said of the history of Saxon London [illegible] Edward the Confessor held his Witanagemot there. [illegible] the Witan which had attended his funeral elected [illegible] Harold, the foremost man in England, and the [illegible] attempted to check the spread of the Norman [illegible] by the Confessor. After his defeat and death [illegible] the Sussex Downs then called Senlac, the duke [illegible] the country at his mercy, but he recognized [illegible] London's position, and moved forward with [illegible] and last.

[illegible] with the history of London during the [illegible] necessary to say something of the counties [illegible] connected with London.

[illegible] London was a distinct political unit, although [illegible] to that one of the kingdoms around [illegible] the most powerful for the time being. [illegible] therefore frequently changed, but [illegible] its identity and individuality all [illegible] seems seldom to have held an inde- [illegible] London first appears as connected [illegible] power was in the hands of the [illegible] Bede, Wini, being expelled from [illegible] took refuge with Wulfhere, king [illegible] he purchased the see of London. [illegible] then have been the overlord of [illegible] afterwards the king of Kent again [illegible] tion here. From the laws of the [illegible] Eadric (673–685) we learn that the [illegible] king of Kent, who exercised a [illegible] men trading with or at London, [illegible] their interests.

[illegible] in which London is chiefly [illegible] question. It is necessary to remember that London is older than these counties, whose names, Middlesex and Surrey, indicate their relative positions to the city and the surrounding county. We have neither record of their settlement nor of the origin of their names. Both must have been peopled from the river. The name Middle Saxons plainly shows that Middlesex must have been settled after the East and West Saxons had given their names to their respective districts. The name Surrey clearly refers to the southern position of the county.

Aldwich.

Reference has already been made to a Danish settlement, and there seems some reason for placing it on the ground now occupied by the parishes of St Clement Danes and St Giles's. For many centuries this district between London and Westminster was a kind of "no man's land" having certain archaic customs. Gomme in his *Governance of London* (1907) gives an account of the connexion of this with the old village of Aldwich, a name that survived in Wych Street, and has been revived by the London County Council in Aldwych, the crescent which leads to Kingsway.

The Conquest.

3. *Norman* (1066–1154).—To return to the condition of things after the great battle. The citizens of London were a divided body, and Duke William knowing that he had many friends in the city saw that a waiting game was the best for his cause in the end. The defeated chiefs retired on the city, led by Ansgar the Staller, under whom as sheriff the citizens of London had marched to fight for Harold at Senlac. They elected Edgar Atheling, the grandson of Edmund Ironside, as king, which the *Saxon Chronicle* says "was indeed his natural right." On hearing of this action William marched towards London, when the citizens sallied forth to meet him. They were repulsed by the Norman horse, but with such loss to the latter that the duke thought it imprudent to lay siege to the city at that time, and he retired to Berkhampstead.[1] It is reported that William sent a private message to Ansgar asking for his support. The result was that Edgar and Earls Edwin and Morkere and "the best men of London" repaired to Berkhampstead, where they submitted themselves and swore fealty to the Conqueror.

Changes in the City.

Thus ends the Saxon period, and the Norman period in London begins with the submission of the citizens as distinct from the action of the rest of the kingdom, which submission resulted soon afterwards in the Conqueror's remarkable charter to William the bishop and Gosfrith the port-reeve, supposed to be the elder Geoffrey de Mandeville. A great change was at once made both in the appearance and in the government of the city under Norman rule. One of the earliest acts of the Conqueror was to undertake the erection of a citadel which should overawe the citizens and give him the command of the city. The Tower was situated at the eastern limit of the city, and not far from the western extremity Castle Baynard was built.

The position of the city grew in importance, but the citizens suffered from severe laws and from serious restrictions upon their liberties. In August 1077 occurred a most extensive fire, such a one, says the *Chronicle*, as "never was before since London was founded." This constant burning of large portions of the city is a marked feature of its early history, and we must remember that, although stone buildings were rising on all sides, these were churches, monasteries, and other public edifices; the ordinary houses remained as before, small wooden structures. The White Tower, the famous keep of the Tower of London, was begun by Gundulph, bishop of Rochester, c. 1078. In 1083 the old cathedral of St Paul's was begun on the site of the church which Æthelbert is said to have founded in 610. But four years afterwards the chronicler tells us "the holy monastery of St Paul, the episcopal see of London, was burnt, and many other monasteries, and the greatest and fairest part of the whole

[1] A valuable article on "The Conqueror's Footprints in Domesday" was published in the *English Historical Review* in 1898 (vol. xiii. p. 17). This article contains an account of Duke William's movements after the battle of Senlac between Enfield, Edmonton, Tottenham and Berkhampstead.

city." In this same year (1087) William the Conqueror died. In 1090 a tremendous hurricane passed over London, and blew down six hundred houses and many churches. The Tower was injured, and a portion of the roof of the church of St Mary-le-Bow, Cheapside, was carried off and fell some distance away, being forced into the ground as much as 20 ft., a proof of the badness of the thoroughfares as well as of the force of the wind. William Rufus inherited from his father a love for building, and in the year 1097 he exacted large sums of money from his subjects with the object of carrying on some of the undertakings he had in hand. These were the walling round of the Tower and the rebuilding of London Bridge, which had been almost destroyed by a flood. In 1100 Rufus was slain, and Henry I. was crowned in London. This king granted the citizens their first real charter, but this was constantly violated. When Stephen seized the crown on the death of Henry I., he tried successfully to obtain the support of the people of London. He published a charter confirming in general terms the one granted by Henry, and commanding that the good laws of Edward the Confessor should be observed. The citizens, however, did not obtain their rights without paying for them, and in 1139 they paid Stephen one hundred marks of silver to enable them to choose their own sheriffs. In this reign the all-powerfulness of the Londoners is brought prominently forward. Stephen became by the shifting fortune of war a prisoner, and the empress Matilda might, if she had had the wisdom to favour the citizens, have held the throne, which was hers by right of birth. She, however, made them her enemies by delivering up the office of justiciary of London and the sheriffwick to her partisan Geoffrey, earl of Essex, and attempting to reduce the citizens to the enslaved condition of the rest of the country. This made her influential enemies, who soon afterwards replaced Stephen upon the throne. The Norman era closes with the death of Stephen in 1154.

Early parishes.

One of the most striking changes in the appearance of Norman London was caused by the rebuilding of old churches and the building of new ones, and also by the foundation of the great monastic establishments. The early history of the parishes of London is one of great difficulty and complexity. Although some of the parishes must be of great antiquity, we have little authentic information respecting them before the Conquest. The dedications of many of the churches indicate their great age, but the constant fires in London destroyed these buildings. The original churches appear to have been very small, as may be judged from their number. It is not easy, however, to understand how it was that when the first parishes were formed so small an area was attached to each. The parish church of which we have the most authentic notice before the Conquest is St Helen's, Bishopsgate. It was in existence many years before the priory of the nuns of St Helen's was founded. Bishop Stubbs in his Introduction to the Historical Works of Ralph de Diceto writes: "St Paul's stood at the head of the religious life of London, and by its side, at some considerable interval, however, St Martin's le Grand (1056), St Bartholomew's, Smithfield (1123) and the great and ancient foundation of Trinity, Aldgate" (1108). The great Benedictine monastery of Black Monks was situated away from the city at Westminster, and it was the only monastic house subject to the rule of St Benedict in the neighbourhood of London, although the houses of nuns, of which there were many dotted over the suburbs of London, were governed by this rule. In course of time there was a widespread desire in Europe for a stricter rule among the monks, and reforms of the Benedictine rule were instituted at Cluni (910), Chartreuse (about 1080) and Citeaux (1098). All these reforms were represented in London.

Religious foundations.

Cluniac Order.—This order was first brought to England by William, earl of Warren (son-in-law of William the Conqueror), who built the first house at Lewes in Sussex about 1077. The priory of Bermondsey in Surrey was founded by Aylwin Child, citizen of London about 1082.

Carthusians.—When this order was brought to England in 1178 the first house was founded at Witham in Somersetshire. In all there were nine houses of the order in England. One of these was the Charterhouse of London which was not founded until 1371 by Sir Walter Manny, K.G.

Cistercians.—It was usual to plant these monasteries in solitary and uncultivated places, and no other house, even of their own order, was allowed to build within a certain distance of the original establishment. This makes it surprising to learn that there were two separate houses of this order in the near neighbourhood of London. A branch of the order came to England about 1128 and the first house was founded at Waverley in Surrey. Very shortly after (about 1134) the abbey of Stratford Langthorne in Essex was founded by William de Montfichet, who endowed it with all his lordship in West Ham. It was not until two centuries afterwards that the second Cistercian house in the immediate neighbourhood of London was founded. This was the Abbey of St Mary Graces, East-Minster or New Abbey without the walls of London, beyond Tower Hill, which Edward III. instituted in 1350 after a severe scourge of plague (the so-called Black Death).

The two great Military Orders—the Knights Hospitallers of St John of Jerusalem and the Templars—followed the Augustinian rule and were both settled in London. The Hospital or Priory of St John was founded in 1100 by Jordan Briset and his wife Muriel, outside the northern wall of London, and the original village of Clerkenwell grew up around the buildings of the knights. A few years after this the Brethren of the Temple of Solomon at Jerusalem or Knights of the Temple came into being at the Holy City, and they settled first on the south side of Holborn near Southampton Row. They removed to Fleet Street or the New Temple in 1184. On the suppression of the order by command of the pope the house in Fleet Street was given in 1313 by Edward II. to Aymer de Valence, earl of Pembroke, at whose death in 1324 the property passed to the knights of St John, who leased the new Temple to the lawyers, still the occupants of the district.

The queen of Henry I. (Matilda or Maud) was one of the chief founders of religious houses, and so great was the number of monasteries built in this king's reign that it was said almost all the labourers became bricklayers and carpenters and there was much discontent in consequence.

Fitz-stephen's description of London.

4. *Plantagenet (1154–1485).*—Henry II. appears to have been to a certain extent prejudiced against the citizens of London on account of their attitude towards his mother, and he treated them with some severity. In 1176 the rebuilding of London Bridge with stone was begun by Peter of Colechurch. This was the bridge which was pulled down early in the 19th century. It consisted of twenty stone arches and a drawbridge. There was a gatehouse at each end and a chapel or crypt in the centre, dedicated to St Thomas of Canterbury, in which Peter of Colechurch was buried in 1205. The large amount of building at this time proves that the citizens were wealthy. Fitzstephen, the monk of Canterbury, has left us the first picture of London. He speaks of its wealth, commerce, grandeur and magnificence—of the mildness of the climate, the beauty of the gardens, the sweet, clear and salubrious springs, the flowing streams, and the pleasant clack of the watermills. Even the vast forest of Middlesex, with its densely wooded thickets, its coverts of game, stags, fallow deer, boars and wild bulls is pressed into the description to give a contrast which shall enhance the beauty of the city itself. Fitzstephen tells how, when the great marsh that washed the walls of the city on the north (Moorfields) was frozen over, the young men went out to slide and skate and sport on the ice. Skates made of bones have been dug up in this district. This sport was allowed to fall into disuse, and was not again prevalent until it was introduced from Holland after the Restoration.

In spite of Fitzstephen's glowing description we must remember that the houses of London were wholly built of wood and thatched with straw or reeds. These houses were specially liable to be destroyed by fire, and in order to save the city from this imminent danger the famous Assize of Building known as "Fitz-Ailwyne's Assize" was drawn up in 1189. In this document the following statement was made: "Many citizens, to avoid such danger, built according to their means, on their ground, a stone house covered and protected by thick tiles against the fury of fire, whereby it often happened that when a fire arose in the city and burnt many edifices and had reached such a house, not being able to injure it, it then became extinguished, so that many neighbours' houses were wholly saved from fire by that house."

Various privileges were conceded to those who built in stone, but no provision was made as to the material to be used in roofing tenements. This Assize, which has been described as the earliest English Building Act, is of great value from an historical point of view, but unfortunately it had little practical effect, and in 1212 what was called "Fitz-Ailwyne's Second Assize," with certain compulsory regulations, was enacted. Thenceforth everyone who built a house was strictly charged not to cover it with reeds, rushes, stubble or straw, but only with tiles, shingle boards or lead. In future, in order to stop a fire, houses could be pulled down in case of need with an alderman's hook and cord. For the speedy removal of burning houses each ward was to provide a strong iron hook, with a wooden handle, two chains and two strong cords, which were to be left in the charge of the bedel of the ward, who was also provided with a good horn, "loudly sounding."

Richard I. was a popular king, but his fighting in the Holy Land cost his subjects much. London had to pay heavily towards his ransom; and, when the king made his triumphal entry into London after his release from imprisonment, a German nobleman is said to have remarked that had the emperor known of the wealth of England he would have insisted on a larger sum. The Londoners were the more glad to welcome Richard back in that the head of the regency, Longchamp, bishop of Ely, was very unpopular from the encroachments he made upon the city with his works at the Tower.

The first charter by which the city claims the jurisdiction and conservancy of the river Thames was granted by Richard I. John granted several charters to the city, and it was expressly stipulated in Magna Charta that the city of London should have all its ancient privileges and free customs. The citizens opposed the king during the wars of the barons. In the year 1215 the barons having received intelligence secretly that they might enter London with ease through Aldgate, which was then in a very ruinous state, removed their camp from Bedford to Ware, and shortly after marched into the city in the night-time. Having succeeded in their object, they determined that so important a gate should no longer remain in a defenceless condition. They therefore spoiled the religious houses and robbed the monastery coffers in order to have means wherewith to rebuild it. Much of the material was obtained from the destroyed houses of the unfortunate Jews, but the stone for the bulwarks was obtained from Caen, and the small bricks or tiles from Flanders.

Allusion has already been made to the great change in the aspect of London and its surroundings made during the Norman period by the establishment of a large number of monasteries. A still more important change in the configuration of the interior of London was made in the 13th century, when the various orders of the friars established themselves there. The Benedictine monks preferred secluded sites; the Augustinians did not cultivate seclusion so strictly; but the friars chose the interior of towns by preference. At the beginning of the 13th century the remarkable evangelical revival, instituted almost simultaneously by St Dominic and St Francis, swept over Europe.

The four chief orders of Mendicant friars were magnificently housed in London:—

Blackfriars.—The Black, Preaching or Dominican Friars came to England in 1221 and their first house was at Oxford. Shortly after this they came to London and settled in Holborn near Lincoln's Inn, where they remained for more than fifty years. In 1276 they removed to the neighbourhood of [illegible] and their house gave a name to a London district [illegible].

[illegible] The Greyfriars, Minorites or Franciscans, first settled [illegible] in 1224 John Ewin made over to them an estate [illegible] ward of Farringdon Within and in the parish of St [illegible] Shambles, where their friary was built. Christ [illegible] Street, occupies the site of the choir of the great [illegible].

[illegible] The house of the Austin Friars or Friars Eremites [illegible] Street Ward in 1253.

[illegible] The Friars of the Blessed Virgin of Mount Carmel [illegible] came to London in 1241, and made their [illegible] Fleet Street and the Thames given by [illegible].

[illegible] orders of friars there were the Crutched [illegible] St Olave, Hart Street (about 1298), and the Friars of the Sac first outside Aldersgate (about 1257) and afterwards in the Old Jewry.

The names of places in London form valuable records of the habitations of different classes of the population. The monasteries and friaries are kept in memory by their names in various parts of London. In the same way the residences of the Jews have been marked. When Edward I. expelled the Jews from England in 1290 the district in which they had lived since William the Conqueror's day came to be called the Old Jewry. On their return after many centuries of exile most of them settled in the neighbourhood of Aldgate and Aldersgate. There is a reminder of them in the names of Jewry Street near the former and of Jewin Street near the latter place. Jewin Street was built on the site of the burying-place of the Jews before the expulsion.

In the middle ages there was a constant succession of pageants, processions and tournaments. The royal processions arranged in connexion with coronations were of great antiquity, but one of the earliest to be described is that of Henry III. in 1236, which was chronicled by Matthew Paris. After the marriage at Canterbury of the king with Eleanor of Provence the royal personages came to London, and were met by the mayor, aldermen and principal citizens to the number of 360, sumptuously apparelled in silken robes embroidered, riding upon stately horses. After the death of Henry III. (1272) the country had to wait for their new king, who was then in the Holy Land. Edward I. came to London on the 2nd of August 1274, when he was received with the wildest expressions of joy. The streets were hung with rich cloths of silk arras and tapestry; the aldermen and principal men of the city threw out of their windows handsful of gold and silver, to signify their gladness at the king's return; and the conduits ran with wine, both white and red.

Dr Jessopp gives a vivid picture of what occurred when King Edward III. entered London in triumph on the 14th of October 1347. He was the foremost man in Europe, and England had reached a height of power and glory such as she had never attained before. Ten years after this, one of the most famous scenes in the streets of London occurred, when Edward the Black Prince brought the French King John and other prisoners after the battle of Poitiers to England. This was a scene unequalled until Henry V. returned from the glorious field of Agincourt in 1415. The mayor and aldermen apparelled in orient-grained scarlet, and four hundred commoners in murrey, well mounted, with rich collars and chains, met the king at Blackheath. At the entrance to London Bridge the towers were adorned with banners of the royal arms, and in the front of them was inscribed *Civitas Regis Justicie.*

During the troubles of the 15th century the authorities had seen the necessity of paying more attention to the security of the gates and walls of the city, and when Thomas Nevill, son of William, Lord Fauconberg, made his attack upon London in 1471 he experienced a spirited resistance. He first attempted to land from his ships in the city, but the Thames side from Baynard's Castle to the Tower was so well fortified that he had to seek a quieter and less prepared position. He then set upon the several gates in succession, and was repulsed at all. On the 11th of May he made a desperate attack upon Aldgate, followed by 500 men. He won the bulwarks and some of his followers entered into the city, but the portcullis being let down these were cut off from their own party and were slain by the enemy. The portcullis was drawn up, and the besieged issued forth against the rebels, who were soon forced to flee.

When Richard, duke of Gloucester, laid his plans for seizing the crown, he obtained the countenance of the lord mayor, Sir Edmund Shaw, whose brother Dr Shaw praised Richard at Paul's Cross. Crosby Hall, in Bishopsgate Street, then lately built, was made the lodging of the Protector. There he acted the accessible prince in the eyes of the people, for the last of the Plantagenets was another of the usurpers who found favour in the eyes of the men of London. His day, however, was short, and with the battle of Bosworth ends Plantagenet London.

5. *Tudor* (*1485–1603*).—It was during this period that the first maps of London were drawn. No representation of the city earlier than the middle of the 16th century has been discovered, although it seems more than probable that some plans must have been produced at an earlier period.[1] The earliest known view is the drawing of Van den Wyngaerde in the Bodleian Library (dated 1550). Braun and Hogenberg's map was published in 1572–1573, and the so-called Agas's map was probably produced soon afterwards, and was doubtless influenced by the publication of Braun and Hogenberg's excellent engraving; Norden's maps of London and Westminster are dated 1593. Some of these maps were pasted upon walls, and must have been largely destroyed by ordinary wear and tear. It is curious that the only two existing copies of Agas's map[2] were published in the reign of James I., although apparently they had not been altered from the earlier editions of Elizabeth's reign which have been lost. By the help of these maps we are able to obtain a clear notion of the extent and chief characteristics of Tudor London. Henry VII. did little to connect his name with the history of London, although the erection of the exquisite specimen of florid Gothic at Westminster Abbey has carried his memory down in its popular name of Henry VII.'s chapel. Soon after this king obtained the throne he borrowed the sum of 3000 marks from the city, and moreover founded the excellent precedent of repaying it at the appointed time. The citizens were so pleased at this unexpected occurrence that they willingly lent the king £6000 in 1488, which he required for military preparations against France. In 1497 London was threatened by the rebels favourable to Perkin Warbeck, who encamped on Blackheath on the 17th of June. At first there was a panic among the citizens, but subsequently the city was placed in a proper state of defence, and the king himself encamped in St George's Fields. On June 22 he entirely routed the rebels; and some time afterwards Perkin Warbeck gave himself up, and was conducted in triumph through London to the Tower.

First maps of London.

As the chief feature of Norman London was the foundation of monasteries, and that of Plantagenet London was the establishment of friaries, so Tudor London was specially characterized by the suppression of the whole of these religious houses, and also of the almost numberless religious gilds and brotherhoods. When we remember that more than half of the area of London was occupied by these establishments, and that about a third of the inhabitants were monks, nuns and friars, it is easy to imagine how great must have been the disorganization caused by this root and branch reform. One of the earliest of the religious houses to be suppressed was the hospital of St Thomas of Acon (or Acre) on the north side of Cheapside, the site of which is now occupied by Mercers' Hall. The larger houses soon followed, and the Black, the White and the Grey Friars, with the Carthusians and many others, were all condemned in November 1538.

Suppression of religious houses.

Love of show was so marked a characteristic of Henry VIII. that we are not surprised to find him encouraging the citizens in the same expensive taste. On the occasion of his marriage with Catherine of Aragon the city was gorgeously ornamented with rich silks and tapestry, and Goldsmiths' Row (Cheapside) and part of Cornhill were hung with golden brocades. When on the eve of St John's Day, 1510, the king in the habit of a yeoman of his own guard saw the famous march of the city watch, he was so delighted that on the following St Peter's Eve he again attended in Cheapside to see the march, but this time he was accompanied by the queen and the principal nobility. The cost of these two marches in the year was very considerable, and, having been suspended in 1528 on account of the prevalence of the sweating sickness, they were soon afterwards forbidden by the king, and discontinued during the remainder of his reign. Sir John Gresham, mayor in 1548, revived the march of the city watch, which was made more splendid by the addition of three hundred light horsemen raised by the citizens for the king's service.

The best mode of utilizing the buildings of the suppressed religious houses was a difficult question left unsolved by Henry VIII. That king, shortly before his death, refounded Rahere's St Bartholomew's Hospital, "for the continual relief and help of an hundred sore and diseased," but most of the large buildings were left unoccupied to be filled by his successor. The first parliament of Edward's reign gave all the lands and possessions of colleges, chantries, &c., to the king, when the different companies of London redeemed those which they had held for the payment of priests' wages, obits and lights at the price of £20,000, and applied the rents arising from them to charitable purposes. In 1550 the citizens purchased the manor of Southwark, and with it they became possessed of the monastery of St Thomas, which was enlarged and prepared for the reception of "poor, sick and helpless objects." Thus was refounded St Thomas's Hospital, which was moved to Lambeth in 1870–1871. Shortly before his death Edward founded Christ's Hospital in the Grey Friars, and gave the old palace of Bridewell to the city "for the lodging of poor wayfaring people, the correction of vagabonds and disorderly persons, and for finding them work." On the death of Edward VI. Lady Jane Grey was received at the Tower as queen, she having gone there by water from Durham House in the Strand. The citizens, however, soon found out their mistake, and the lord mayor, aldermen and recorder proclaimed Queen Mary at Cheapside. London was then gay with pageants, but when the queen made known her intention of marrying Philip of Spain the discontent of the country found vent in the rising of Sir Thomas Wyat, and the city had to prepare itself against attack. Wyat took possession of Southwark, and expected to have been admitted into London; but finding the gates shut against him and the drawbridge cut down he marched to Kingston, the bridge at which place had been destroyed. This he restored, and then proceeded towards London. In consequence of the breakdown of some of his guns he imprudently halted at Turnham Green. Had he not done so it is probable that he might have obtained possession of the city. He planted his ordnance on Hay Hill, and then marched by St James's Palace to Charing Cross. Here he was attacked by Sir John Gage with a thousand men, but he repulsed them and reached Ludgate without further opposition. He was disappointed at the resistance which was made, and after musing a while "upon a stall over against the Bell Savadge Gate" he turned back. His retreat was cut off, and he surrendered to Sir Maurice Berkeley. We have somewhat fully described this historical incident here because it has an important bearing on the history of London, and shows also the small importance of the districts outside the walls at that period.

We now come to consider the appearance of London during the reign of the last of the Tudors. At no other period were so many great men associated with its history; the latter years of Elizabeth's reign are specially interesting to us because it was then that Shakespeare lived in London, and introduced its streets and people into his plays. In those days the frequent visitation of plagues made men fear the gathering together of multitudes. This dread of pestilence, united with a puritanic hatred of plays, made the citizens do all they could to discountenance theatrical entertainments. The queen acknowledged the validity of the first reason, but she repudiated the religious objection provided ordinary care was taken to allow "such plays only as were fitted to yield honest recreation and no example of evil." On April 11, 1582, the lords of the council wrote to the lord mayor to the effect that, as "her Majesty sometimes took delight in those pastimes, it had been thought not unfit, having regard to the season of the year and the clearance of the city from infection, to allow of certain companies of players in London, partly that they might thereby

Tudor London.

[1] "A map of London engraved on copper-plate, dated 1497," which was bought by Ferdinand Columbus during his travels in Europe about 1518–1525, is entered in the catalogue of Ferdinand's books, maps, &c., made by himself and preserved in the Cathedral Library at Seville, but there is no clue to its existence.

[2] One is in the Guildhall Library, and the other among the Pepysian maps in Magdalene College, Cambridge.

attain more dexterity and perfection the better to content her Majesty" (Analytical Index to the *Remembrancia*). When theatres were established the lord mayor took care that they should not be built within the city. The "Theatre" and the "Curtain" were situated at Shoreditch; the "Globe," the "Swan," the "Rose" and the "Hope" on the Bankside; and the Blackfriars theatre, although within the walls, was without the city jurisdiction.

In 1561 St Paul's steeple and roof were destroyed by lightning, and the spire was never replaced. This circumstance allows us to test the date of certain views; thus Wyngaerde's map has the spire, but Agas's map is without it. In 1566 the first stone was laid of the "Burse," which owed its origin to Sir Thomas Gresham. In 1571 Queen Elizabeth changed its name to the Royal Exchange. The Strand was filled with noble mansions washed by the waters of the Thames, but the street, if street it could be called, was little used by pedestrians. Londoners frequented the river, which was their great highway. The banks were crowded with stairs for boats, and the watermen of that day answered to the chairmen of a later date and the cabmen of to-day. The Bankside was of old a favourite place for entertainments, but two only—the bull-baiting and the bear-baiting—were in existence when Agas's map was first planned. On Norden's map,[1] however, we find the gardens of Paris Garden, the bearhouse and the playhouse.

The settled character of the later years of Elizabeth's reign appears to have caused a considerable change in the habits of the people. Many of the chief citizens followed the example of the courtiers, and built for themselves country residences in Middlesex, Essex and Surrey; thus we learn from Norden that Alderman Roe lived at Muswell Hill, and we know that Sir Thomas Gresham built a fine house and planned a beautiful park at Osterley. The maps show us much that remains somewhat the same as it was, but also much that has greatly altered. St Giles's was literally a village in the fields; Piccadilly was "the waye to Redinge," Oxford Street "the way to Uxbridge," Covent Garden an open field or garden, and Leicester Fields lammas land. Moorfields was drained and laid out in walks in Elizabeth's reign. At Spitalfields crowds used to congregate on Easter Monday and Tuesday to hear the Spital sermons preached from the pulpit cross. The ground was originally a Roman Cemetery, and about the year 1576 bricks were largely made from the clayey earth, the recollection of which is kept alive in the name of Brick Lane. Citizens went to Holborn and Bloomsbury for change of air, and houses were there prepared for the reception of children, invalids and convalescents. In the north were sprinkled the outlying villages of Islington, Hoxton and Clerkenwell.

6. *Stuart (1603–1714).*—The Stuart period, from the accession of James I. to the death of Queen Anne, extends over little more than a century, and yet greater changes occurred during those years than at any previous period. The early years of Stuart London may be said to be closely linked with the last years of Elizabethan London, for the greatest men, such as Raleigh, Shakespeare and Ben Jonson, lived on into James's reign. Much of the life of the time was then in the City, but the last years of Stuart London take us to the 18th century, when social life had permanently shifted to the west end. In the middle of the period occurred the civil wars, and then the fire which changed the whole aspect of London. When James came to the throne the term suburbs had a bad name, as all those disreputable persons who could find no shelter in the city itself settled in these outlying districts. Stubbs denounced suburban gardens and garden houses in his *Anatomy of Abuses*, and another writer observed "how happy were cities if they had no suburbs."

The preparations for the coronation of King James were interrupted by a severe visitation of the plague, which killed off as many as 30,578 persons, and it was not till March 15, 1604, that the king, the queen and Prince Henry passed triumphantly from the Tower to Westminster. The lord mayor's shows, which had been discontinued for some years, were revived by order of the king in 1609. The dissolved monastery of the Charterhouse, which had been bought and sold by the courtiers several times, was obtained from Thomas, earl of Suffolk, by Thomas Sutton for £13,000. The new hospital chapel and schoolhouse were begun in 1611, and in the same year Sutton died.

With the death of James I. in 1625 the older history of London may be said to have closed. During the reign of his successor the great change in the relative positions of London within and without the walls had set in. Before going on to consider the chief incidents of this change it will be well to refer to some features of the social life of James's reign. Ben Jonson places one of the scenes of *Every Man in his Humour* in Moorfields, which at the time he wrote the play had, as stated above, lately been drained and laid out in walks. Beggars frequented the place, and travellers from the village of Hoxton, who crossed it in order to get into London, did so with as much expedition as possible. Adjoining Moorfields were Finsbury Fields, a favourite practising ground for the archers. Mile End, a common on the Great Eastern Road, was long famous as a rendezvous for the troops. These places are frequently referred to by the old dramatists; Justice Shallow boasts of his doings at Mile End Green when he was Dagonet in Arthur's Show. Fleet Street was the show-place of London, in which were exhibited a constant succession of puppets, naked Indians and strange fishes. The great meeting-place of Londoners in the day-time was the nave of old St Paul's. Crowds of merchants with their hats on transacted business in the aisles, and used the font as a counter upon which to make their payments; lawyers received clients at their several pillars; and masterless serving-men waited to be engaged upon their own particular bench. Besides those who came on business there were gallants dressed in fashionable finery, so that it was worth the tailor's while to stand behind a pillar and fill his table-books with notes. The middle or Mediterranean aisle was the Paul's Walk, also called the Duke's Gallery from the erroneous supposition that the tomb of Sir Guy Beauchamp, earl of Warwick, was that of the "good" Humphrey, duke of Gloucester. After the Restoration a fence was erected on the inside of the great north door to hinder a concourse of rude people, and when the cathedral was being rebuilt Sir Christopher Wren made a strict order against any profanation of the sacred building. St Paul's churchyard was from the earliest days of printing until the end of the 18th century the headquarters of the book trade, when it shifted to Paternoster Row. Another of the favourite haunts of the people was the garden of Gray's Inn, where the choicest society was to be met. There, under the shadow of the elm trees which Bacon had planted, Pepys and his wife constantly walked. Mrs Pepys went on one occasion specially to observe the fashions of the ladies because she was then "making some clothes."

In those days of public conviviality, and for many years afterwards, the taverns of London held a very important place. The Boar's Head in Great Eastcheap was an inn of Shakespeare's own day, and the characters he introduces into his plays are really his own contemporaries. The "Mermaid" is sometimes described as in Bread Street, and at other times in Friday Street and also in Cheapside. We are thus able to fix its exact position; for a little to the west of Bow church is Bread Street, then came a block of houses, and the next thoroughfare was Friday Street. It was in this block that the "Mermaid" was situated, and there appear to have been entrances from each street. What makes this fact still more certain is the circumstance that a haberdasher in Cheapside living "'twixt Wood Street and Milk Street," two streets on the north side opposite Bread and Friday Streets, described himself as "over against the Mermaid tavern in Cheapside." The Windmill tavern occupies a prominent position in the action of *Every Man in his Humour*.[2] The Windmill stood at the corner of the Old Jewry towards Lothbury, and the Mitre close by the Mermaid in Bread Street. The Mitre in Fleet Street, so intimately associated with Dr Johnson, also existed at this time. It is mentioned in a comedy entitled *Ram Alley* (1611) and Lilly the

[1] This map of London by Norden is dated 1593, as stated above. The same topographer published in his *Middlesex* a map of Westminster as well as this one of the City of London.

[2] Various changes in the names of the taverns are made in the folio edition of this play (1616) from the quarto (1601); thus the Mermaid of the quarto becomes the Windmill in the folio, and the Mitre of the quarto is the Star of the folio.

astrologer frequented it in 1640. At the Mermaid Ben Jonson had such companions as Shakespeare, Raleigh, Beaumont, Fletcher, Carew, Donne, Cotton and Selden, but at the Devil in Fleet Street, where he started the Apollo Club, he was omnipotent. Herrick, in his well-known *Ode to Ben*, mentions several of the inns of the day.

Theatres.

Under James I. the theatre, which established itself so firmly in the latter years of Elizabeth, had still further increased its influence, and to the entertainments given at the many playhouses may be added the masques so expensively produced at court and by the lawyers at the inns of court. In 1613 *The Masque of Flowers* was presented by the members of Gray's Inn in the Old Banqueting House in honour of the marriage of the infamous Carr, earl of Somerset, and the equally infamous Lady Frances, daughter of the earl of Suffolk. The entertainment was prepared by Sir Francis Bacon at a cost of about £2000.

The "West End."

It was during the reign of Charles I. that the first great exodus of the wealthy and fashionable was made to the West End. The great square or piazza of Covent Garden was formed from the designs of Inigo Jones about 1632. The neighbouring streets were built shortly afterwards, and the names of Henrietta, Charles, James, King and York Streets were given after members of the royal family. Great Queen Street, Lincoln's Inn Fields, was built about 1629, and named in honour of Henrietta Maria. Lincoln's Inn Fields had been planned some years before. With the Restoration the separation of fashionable from city life became complete.

When the Civil War broke out London took the side of the parliament, and an extensive system of fortification was at once projected to protect the town against the threatened attack of the royal army. A strong earthen rampart, flanked with bastions and redoubts, surrounded the City, its liberties, Westminster and Southwark, making an immense enclosure.

The Plague.

London had been ravaged by plague on many former occasions, but the pestilence that began in December 1664 lives in history as "the Plague of London." On the 7th of June 1665 Samuel Pepys for the first time saw two or three houses marked with the red cross and the words "Lord, have mercy upon us," on the doors. The deaths daily increased, and business was stopped. Grass grew in the area of the Royal Exchange, at Whitehall, and in the principal streets of the city. On the 4th of September 1665 Pepys writes an interesting letter to Lady Carteret from Woolwich: "I have stayed in the city till above 7400 died in one week, and of them about 6000 of the plague, and little noise heard day or night but tolling of bells." The plague was scarcely stayed before the whole city was in flames, a calamity of the first magnitude, but one which in the end caused much good, as the seeds of disease were destroyed, and London has never since been visited by such an epidemic. On the 2nd of September 1666 the fire broke out at one o'clock in the morning at a house in Pudding Lane. A violent east wind fomented the flames, which raged during the whole of Monday and great part of Tuesday. On Tuesday night the wind fell somewhat, and on Wednesday the fire slackened. On Thursday it was extinguished, but on the evening of that day the flames again burst forth at the Temple. Some houses were at once blown up by gunpowder, and thus the fire was finally mastered. Many interesting details of the fire are given in Pepys's *Diary*. The river swarmed with vessels filled with persons carrying away such of their goods as they were able to save. Some fled to the hills of Hampstead and Highgate, but Moorfields was the chief resort of the houseless Londoner. Soon paved streets and two-storey houses were seen in that swampy place. The people bore their troubles heroically, and Henry Oldenburg, writing to the Hon. Robert Boyle on September 10, says: "The citizens, instead of complaining, discoursed almost of nothing but of a survey for rebuilding the city with bricks and large streets." Within a few days of the fire three several plans were presented to the king for the rebuilding of the city, by Christopher Wren, John Evelyn and Robert Hooke. Wren proposed to build main thoroughfares north and south, and east and west, to insulate all the churches in conspicuous positions, to form the most public places into large piazzas, to unite the halls of the twelve chief companies into one regular square annexed to Guildhall and to make a fine quay on the bank of the river from Blackfriars to the Tower. His streets were to be of three magnitudes—90 ft., 60 ft. and 30 ft. wide respectively. Evelyn's plan differed from Wren's chiefly in proposing a street from the church of St Dunstan's in the East to the cathedral, and in having no quay or terrace along the river. In spite of the best advice, however, the jealousies of the citizens prevented any systematic design from being carried out, and in consequence the old lines were in almost every case retained. But though the plans of Wren and Hooke were not adopted, it was to these two fellows of the Royal Society that the labour of rebuilding London was committed. Wren's great work was the erection of the cathedral of St Paul's, and the many churches ranged round it as satellites. Hooke's task was the humbler one of arranging as city surveyor for the building of the houses. He laid out the ground of the several proprietors in the rebuilding of the city, and had no rest early or late from persons soliciting him to set out their ground for them at once. The first great impetus of change in the configuration of London was given by the great fire, and Evelyn records and regrets that the town in his time had grown almost as large again as it was within his own memory. Although for several centuries attempts had been made in favour of building houses with brick or stone, yet the carpenters continued to be the chief house-builders. As late as the year 1650 the Carpenters' Company drew up a memorial in which they "gave their reasons that tymber buildings were more commodious for this citie than brick buildings were." The Act of Parliament "for rebuilding the city of London" passed after the great fire, gave the *coup de grâce* to the carpenters as house-builders. After setting forth that "building with brick was not only more comely and durable, but also more safe against future perils of fire," it was enacted "that all the outsides of all buildings in and about the city should be made of brick or stone, except doorcases and window-frames, and other parts of the first story to the front between the piers," for which substantial oaken timber might be used "for conveniency of shops." In the winter of 1683–1684 a fair was held for some time upon the Thames. The frost, which began about seven weeks before Christmas and continued for six weeks after, was the greatest on record; the ice was 11 in. thick.

The Great Fire. — Rebuilding. — Wren's scheme.

The revocation of the edict of Nantes in October 1685, and the consequent migration of a large number of industrious French Protestants, caused a considerable growth in the east end of London. The silk manufactories at Spitalfields were then established.

During the short reign of James II. the fortunes of the city were at their lowest, and nowhere was the arrival of the prince of Orange more welcomed.

William III. cared little for London, the smoke of which gave him asthma, and when a great part of Whitehall was burnt in 1691 he purchased Nottingham House and made it into Kensington Palace. Kensington was then an insignificant village, but the arrival of the court soon caused it to grow in importance.

Although the spiritual wants of the city were amply provided for by the churches built by Wren, the large districts outside the city and its liberties had been greatly neglected. The act passed in the reign of Queen Anne for building fifty new churches (1710) for a time supplied the wants of large districts.

7. *Eighteenth Century.*—London had hitherto grown up by the side of the Thames. In the 18th century other parts of the town were more largely built upon. The inhabitants used coaches and chairs more than boats, and the banks of the river were neglected. London could no longer be seen as a whole, and became a mere collection of houses. In spite of this the 18th century produced some of the most devoted of Londoners—men who considered a day lived out of London as one lost out of their lives. Of this class Dr Johnson and Hogarth are striking examples. The exhibitions of vice and cruelty that were

[illegible] the capitals have been superseded by [illegible] by an [illegible] to achieve that such [illegible] of a great [illegible] George I. understand the [illegible] I have lately been [illegible] city of London [illegible] and [illegible] privileges and interests [illegible] lord mayor's [illegible] in Cheapside and attended the [illegible] Queen Anne and the first three Georges [illegible] of these visits to the [illegible] same house opposite Bow church. [illegible] George I. David Barclay, the [illegible] the Quakers, was an apprentice [illegible] became master, and had the [illegible] George II. and George III. as his guests. [illegible] along the front of the house [illegible] hangings of crimson damask [illegible] numbered 108 Cheapside, was pulled [illegible]

[illegible] there was a considerable extension [illegible] the West End. Still, however, the [illegible] remained unbuilt upon. In 1756 [illegible] subsequently the land behind [illegible] (now the British Museum) was [illegible] and when in that year a proposal [illegible] the tenant and the duke of [illegible] In 1772 all beyond Portland [illegible] Street was country. Bedford House [illegible] view of Hampstead and High[illegible] Square was built open to the [illegible] inhabitants might obtain the same [illegible]

[illegible] between Holborn Bridge and Fleet [illegible] Market was removed from [illegible] the present Farringdon Street, [illegible] 25, 1739, the first stone [illegible] Previously the first magistrates [illegible] A frost almost as severe as [illegible] occurred in the winter of 1739- [illegible] the scene of a busy fair. In [illegible] were cleared away, and in [illegible] were taken down and sold. [illegible] Aldersgate 1761, Aldgate [illegible] The statue of Queen [illegible] side of Ludgate was pur[illegible] up against the east end of [illegible] where it still remains. [illegible] London saw the public [illegible] On the 8th February [illegible] great pomp from the [illegible] where it was interred in the [illegible] royal dukes. Pitt was [illegible] on the 10th of October, [illegible]

[illegible] of lighting the streets [illegible] birthday (June 4) 1807, and [illegible] the colonnade before [illegible] the first public place in [illegible] and Grosvenor Square [illegible] the Thames was again [illegible] evening of December 27, [illegible] for a month, a thaw [illegible] January, took place, [illegible] of the frost, so severe [illegible] sheet of ice. There [illegible] road, which was daily [illegible] Royal Exchange [illegible]

larger number of visitors to London than had ever been in it before at one time. The great and continuous increase in the buildings and the enlargement of London on all sides dates from this period.

London within the walls has been almost entirely rebuilt, although in the neighbourhood of the Tower there are still many old houses which have only been refronted. From the upper rooms of the houses may be seen a large number of old tiled roofs.

Unlike many capitals of Europe which have shifted their centres the city of London in spite of all changes and the continual enlargement of the capital remains the centre and head-quarters of the business of the country. The Bank of England, the Royal Exchange and the Mansion House are on the site of Ancient London.

In 1863 on the occasion of the marriage of King Edward VII. (when prince of Wales) the streets of London were illuminated as they had never been before. Among other events which made the streets gay and centred in processions to St Paul's may be specially mentioned the Thanksgiving Day on the 27th of February 1872 for the recovery of the prince of Wales after his dangerous illness; and the rejoicings at the Jubilee of Queen Victoria in 1887, and the Diamond Jubilee in 1897.

The first great emigration of the London merchants westward was about the middle of the 18th century, but only those who had already secured large fortunes ventured so far as Hatton Garden. At the beginning of the 19th century it had become common for the tradesmen of the city to live away from their businesses, but it was only about the middle of the 19th century that it became at all usual for those in the West End to do the same.

During the first half of the 19th century the position of the City Corporation had somewhat fallen in public esteem, and some of the most influential men in the city were unconnected with it, but a considerable change took place in the latter half of the century. Violent attacks were made upon the Livery Companies, but of late years, largely owing to the public spirit of the companies in devoting large sums of money towards the improvement of the several industries in connexion with which they were founded, and the establishment of the City and Guilds of London Technical Institute, a complete change has taken place as to the public estimation in which they are held.

Growth and Population

Medieval Population.

Much has been written upon the population of medieval London, but little certainty has resulted therefrom. We know the size of London at different periods and are able to guess to some extent as to the number of its inhabitants, but most of the figures which have come down to us are mere guesses. The results of the poll-tax have often been considered as trustworthy substitutes for population returns, but Professor Oman has shown that little trust can be placed in these results. As an instance he states that the commissioners of the poll-tax reported that there were only two-thirds as many contributaries in 1381 as in 1377. The adult population of the realm had ostensibly fallen from 1,355,201 to 896,481. These figures were monstrous and incredible.[1]

The Bills of Mortality of the 16th and 17th centuries are of more value, and they have been considered and revised by such able statisticians as John Graunt and Sir William Petty. It was not, however, before the 19th century that accurate figures were obtainable. The circuit of the walls of London which were left by the Romans was never afterwards enlarged, and the population did not overflow into the suburbs to any extent until the Tudor period. Population was practically stationary for centuries owing to pestilences and the large proportion of deaths among infants. We have no materials to judge of the number of inhabitants before the Norman Conquest, but we can guess that there were many open spaces within the walls that were afterwards filled up. It is scarcely worth while to guess as to the numbers in Saxon London, but it is possible that in the early period there were about 10,000 inhabitants, growing later to about 20,000. During the latter part of the Saxon period the numbers of the population of the country began to decay; this decay, however, was arrested by the Norman Conquest. The population increased during ten peaceful years of Henry III., and increased slowly until the death of Edward II., and then it began to fall off, and continued to decrease during the period of the Wars of the Roses and of the Barons until the accession of the first Tudor monarch.

[1] *The Great Revolt of 1381* (Oxford, 1906), p. 27.

The same causes that operated to bring about these changes in the whole kingdom were of course also at work in the case of the City of London.

One of the earliest statements as to the population of London occurs in a letter of about the year 1199 written to Pope Innocent III. by Peter of Blois, then archdeacon of London, and therefore a man of some authority on the subject. He states that the City contained 120 parish churches and 40,000 inhabitants. These numbers have been very generally accepted as fairly correct, and Dr Creighton[1] comes to the conclusion after careful consideration that the population of London from the reign of Richard I. to that of Henry VII. varied within a limit of about forty to fifty thousand inhabitants.

Plagues and Mortality.

Dr Creighton points out that the number given by certain chroniclers of the deaths from the early pestilences in London are incredible; such for instance as the statement that forty or fifty thousand bodies were buried in Charterhouse churchyard at the time of the Black Death in 1348–1349. These numbers have been taken as a basis for calculation of population, and one statistician reasoned that if 50,000 were buried in one churchyard 100,000 should represent the whole mortality of London. If this were allowed the population at this time must have been at least 200,000, an impossible amount.

Although the mortality caused by the different plagues had a great effect upon the population of the country at large the city soon recovered the losses by reason of the numbers who came to London from outside in hopes of obtaining work. Although there were fluctuations in the numbers at different periods there is evidence to show that on the average the amount of forty to fifty thousand fixed by Dr Creighton for the years between 1189 and 1509 is fairly correct. The medieval period closed with the accession of the Tudor dynasty, and from that time the population of London continued to increase, in spite of attempts by the government to prevent it. One of the first periods of increase was after the dissolution of the religious houses; another period of increase was after the Restoration.

A proclamation was issued in 1580 prohibiting the erection within 3 m. of the city gates of any new houses or tenements "where no former house hath been known to have been." In a subsequent proclamation Queen Elizabeth commanded that only one family should live in one house, that empty houses erected within seven years were not to be let and that unfinished buildings on new foundations were to be pulled down. In spite of these restrictions London continued to grow. James I. and Charles I. were filled with the same fear of the increasing growth of London. In 1630 a similar proclamation to that of 1580 was published. During the greater part of the 18th century there was a serious check to the increase of population, but at the end of the century a considerable increase occurred, and in the middle of the 19th century the enormous annual increase became particularly marked. To return to the 16th century when the Bills of Mortality came into existence.[2] Mention is made of these bills as early as 1517, but the earliest series now known dates from 1532.

Bills of Mortality.

Dr Creighton had access to the manuscript returns of burials and christenings for five years from 1578 to 1582 preserved in the library at Hatfield House. The history of the Bills of Mortality which in the early years were intermittent in their publication is of much interest, and Dr Creighton has stated it with great clearness. The Company of Parish Clerks is named in an ordinance of 1581 (of which there is a copy in the Record Office) as the body responsible for the bills, and their duties were then said to be "according to the Order in that behalf heretofore provided." John Bell, clerk to the company, who wrote an essay during the great plague of 1665, had no records in his office of an earlier date than 1593, and he was not aware that his company had been engaged in registering births and deaths before that year. The fire of 1666 destroyed all the documents of the Parish Clerks Company, and in its hall in Silver Street only printed tables from about the year 1700 are to be found. There is a set of Annual Bills from 1658 (with the exception of the years 1756 to 1764) in the library of the British Museum.[3]

These bills were not analysed and general results obtained from them until 1662, when Captain John Graunt first published his valuable *Natural and Political Observations upon the Bills of Mortality*. Sir William Petty followed with his important inquiries upon the population (*Essay on Political Arithmetic*, 1683).

It is not worth while to refer to all the wild guesses that were made by various writers, but Dr Creighton shows the absurdity of one of these calculations made in 1554 by Soranzo, the Venetian ambassador for the information of the doge and senators of Venice. He estimates the population to have been 180,000 persons, which Dr Creighton affirms to be nearly three times the number that we obtain by a moderate calculation from the bills of mortality in 1532 and 1535.

Population in 16th and 17th centuries.

Following on his calculations from 1509, when the population may be supposed to have been about 50,000, Dr Creighton carries on his numbers to the Restoration in the following table:—

1532–1535	62,400	1605	224,275
1563	93,276	1622	272,207
1580	123,034	1634	339,824
1593–1595	152,478	1661	460,000

The numbers for 1661 are those arrived at by Graunt, and they are just about half the population given authoritatively in the first census 1801 (864,845). It therefore took 140 years to double the numbers, while in 1841 the numbers of 1801 were more than doubled.

These numbers were arrived at with much care and may be considered as fairly accurate although some other calculations conflict with a few of the figures. The first attempt at a census was in August 1631 when the lord mayor returned the number of mouths in the city of London and Liberties at 130,268, which is only about half the number given above. This is accounted for by the larger area contained in the bills of mortality compared with that containing only the city and its liberties.[4] Howell's suggestion that the population of London in 1631 was a million and a half need only be mentioned as a specimen of the wildest of guesses.

18th century.

Petty's numbers for 1682 are 670,000 and those of Gregory King for 1696, 530,000. The latter are corroborated by those of 1700, which are given as 550,000. Maitland gives the numbers in 1737 as 725,903. With regard to the relative size of great cities Petty affirms that before the Restoration the people of Paris were more in number than those of London and Dublin, whereas in 1687 the people of London were more than those of Paris and Rome or of Paris and Rouen.

It is not necessary to give any further numbers for the population of the 18th century, as that has been already stated to have been almost stationary. This is proved by Gregory King's figures for 1696 (530,000) when compared with those of the first census for 1801 (864,035). A corroboration is also to be found in the report of the first census for 1801, where a calculation is made of the probable population of the years 1700 and 1750. These are given respectively as 674,350 and 676,250. These figures include (1) the City of London within and (2) without the walls, (3) the City and Liberties of Westminster, (4) the outparishes within the bills of mortality and (5) the parishes not within the bills of mortality. No. 5 is given as 9150 in 1700, and 22,350 in 1750. It is curious to find that already in the 18th century a considerable reduction in the numbers of the city of London is supposed to have taken place, as is seen in the following figures:—

	1700.	1750.
City of London within the walls	139,300	87,000
„ „ without the walls	69,000	57,300

As the increase in Westminster is not great (130,000 in 1700 and 152,000 in 1750) and there is little difference in the totals it will be seen that the amount is chiefly made up by the increase in the parishes without the bills of mortality. The extraordinary growth of London did not come into existence until about the middle of the 19th century (see § IV. above).

GOVERNMENT

Saxon Period.

We know little of the government of London during the Saxon period, and it is only incidentally that we learn how the Londoner had become possessed of special privileges which he continued to claim with success through many centuries. One of the chief of these was the claim to a separate voice in the election of the king. The citizens did not dispute the right of election by the kingdom but they held that that election did not necessarily include the choice of London.

An instance of this is seen in the election of Edmund Ironside, although the Witan outside London had elected Canute. The remarkable instance of this after the Conquest was the election of Stephen, but William the Conqueror did not feel secure until he had the sanction of the Londoners to his kingship, and his attitude towards London when he hovered about the neighbourhood of the city for a time shows that he was anxious to obtain this sanction freely rather than by compulsion. His hopes and expectations were fulfilled when

---

[1] In a valuable paper on "The Population of Old London" in *Blackwood's Magazine* for April 1891.

[2] The old Bills of Mortality, although of value from being the only authority on the subject, were never complete owing to various causes: one being that large numbers of Roman Catholics and Dissenters were not registered in the returns of the parish clerk who was a church officer. The bills were killed by the action of the Registration Act for England and Wales, which came into operation July, 1, 1837. The Weekly Returns of the Registrar-General began in 1840.

[3] "The invention of 'bills of mortality' is not so modern as has been generally supposed, for their proper designation may be found in the language of ancient Rome. Libitina was the goddess of funerals; her officers were the Libitinarii *our* undertakers; her temple in which all business connected with the last rites was transacted, in which the account of deaths—*ratio Libitinae*—was kept, served the purpose of a register office."—*Journal Statistical Society*, xvii. 127 (1854).

[4] The return was made "by special command from the Right Honourable the Lords of His Majesty's Privy Council." The Privy Council were at this time apprehensive of an approaching scarcity of food. The numbers (130,268) were made up as follows: London Within the Walls 71,029, London Without the Walls 40,579, Old Borough of Southwark (Bridge Without) 18,660.

[illegible] him, as already related. [illegible] law for the whole [illegible] is another instance of the [illegible] William the Conqueror [illegible] addressed the bishop and the [illegible] governor and the portreeve [illegible]

[illegible] does not indicate the [illegible] supposed, for Stubbs has [illegible] "although used for the city [illegible] in its character of a Mart or [illegible] of reeve was continued during [illegible] or sheriff has continued to [illegible] several distinct reeves, all ap- [illegible] Some writers have supposed [illegible] in London, but J. H. Round [illegible] after the Conqueror's charter. [illegible] the right of appointing its [illegible] which, however, was recalled [illegible] to be restored by John in [illegible]

[illegible] office of Justiciar was created by [illegible] authority in the city this [illegible] of the privilege of appointing [illegible]

[illegible] great municipal movement over [illegible] as to what was going on [illegible] always willing to wait for an [illegible] they remained ready to take [illegible] occur. Their great oppor- [illegible] engaged abroad as a crusader. [illegible] the 700th anniversary [illegible] popular tradition was founded [illegible] Round writes (*Commune of* [illegible]) that the mayoralty of London [illegible] is an absolute perversion of [illegible] record evidence which com- [illegible] of Richard of Devizes, who [illegible] would King Richard or his [illegible] establishment of the *Commune* in [illegible]

[illegible] John the king's brother and [illegible] became acute. The latter [illegible] who, finding that they [illegible] named the Commune [illegible] A small party of the [illegible] faithful to the chancellor [illegible] Paul's on the 8th of October, [illegible] Rouen as chief justiciar [illegible] appointing a new com- [illegible] Stubbs, in his intro- [illegible] writes: "This done, [illegible] and the Barons swore [illegible] oath of fealty to Richard [illegible] the two archbishops, the [illegible] with the express under- [illegible] they would receive [illegible] important event Mr Round [illegible] out overnight, with [illegible] the capital, streamed [illegible] October at the well- [illegible] from its campanile in [illegible] John take the oath to the [illegible] and then London for the [illegible]

[illegible] then established really [illegible] the manuscripts of the [illegible] Commune proves for [illegible] possessed a fully [illegible] continental pattern. A [illegible] is that the new [illegible] were entirely copied from [illegible] shows that there is con- [illegible] of London derived [illegible] information which [illegible] as to the early [illegible] this we learn that the [illegible] a *mayor* and twelve [illegible] seem for a time [illegible]

[illegible] another document, [illegible] that *alii probi homines* [illegible] to *form* a body of [illegible] an equal number of [illegible] of Skivini and *alii* [illegible] nothing further than [illegible] the germ of the [illegible] that when the city of [illegible] we [illegible]

no king but their mayor," that the king did not occasionally exert his power in suspending the liberties of the city. There were early constant disagreements, and sometimes the king degraded the mayor and appointed a custos or warden in his place. Several instances of this are recorded in the 13th and 14th centuries. It is very important to bear in mind that the mayors of London besides holding a very onerous position were mostly men of great distinction. They often held rank outside the city, and naturally took their place among the rulers of the country. They were mostly representatives of the landed interests as well as merchant princes.

There is no definite information as to when the mayor first received the title of lord. A claim has been set up for Thomas Legge, mayor for the second time in 1354, that he was the first lord mayor, but there is positively no authority whatever for this claim, although it is boldly stated that he was created lord mayor by Edward III. in [illegible] year. Apparently the title was occasionally used, and th[illegible] gradually grew into a prescriptive right. There is no evidenc[illegible] grant, but after 1540 the title had become general.

No record has been found of the date when the alder[illegible] the official advisers of the mayor. The various war[illegible] presided over by an alderman from an early period, [illegible] we cannot fix the time when they were united as a [illegible] of aldermen. Stubbs writes: "The governing [illegible] in the 13th century was composed of the [illegible] aldermen of the wards and two sheriffs."

As we do not find any further evidence [illegible] Commune alluded to of the existence of "[illegible] is possible that aldermen were elected on t[illegible] this title. This, however, is not the opinion [illegible] stated, is inclined to believe that the b[illegible] course of time the Court of Common [illegible] not mentioned as the colleagues of t[illegible] of the 13th century, except in the [illegible] 1189, and this, of course, related spec[illegible] as heads of the wards of the city.

In March 1298–1299 letters were sent [illegible] Commune of the City of London" to the mun[illegible] Caen and Cambray. Although the official form of "[illegible] Commune" was continued until the end of the 13th centu[illegible] was not until early in the 14th century that the form "Ma[illegible] Aldermen and Common Council" came into existence, there is sufficient evidence to show that the aldermen and common council before that time were acting with the mayor as governors of the city. In 1377 it was ordered that aldermen could be elected annually, but in 1384 the rule was modified so as to allow an alderman to be re-elected for his ward at the expiration of his year of office without any interval.

In 1394 the Ordinance respecting annual elections was repealed by the king (Richard II.). Distinct rank was accorded to aldermen, and in the *Liber Albus* we are told that "it is a matter of experience that ever since the year of our Lord 1350, at the sepulture of aldermen, the ancient custom of interment with baronial honours was observed." When the poll-tax of 1379 was imposed the mayor was assessed as an earl and the aldermen as barons.

The government of the city by reeves dates back to a very early period, and these reeves were appointed by the king. The prefix of the various kinds of reeves made but little difference in the duties of the office, although the area of these duties might be different. There was slight difference between the office of sheriff and that of portreeve, which latter does not appear to have survived the Conquest.

Sheriffs.

After the establishment of the Commune and the appointment of a mayor the sheriffs naturally lost much of their importance, and they became what they are styled in *Liber Albus* "the Eyes of the Mayor." When Middlesex was in farm to London the two sheriffs were equally sheriffs of London and Middlesex. There is only one instance in the city records of a sheriff of Middlesex being mentioned as distinct from the sheriffs, and this was in 1283 when Anketin de Betteville and Walter le Blond are described as sheriffs of London, and Gerin as sheriff of Middlesex. By the Local Government Act of 1888 the citizens of London were deprived of all right of jurisdiction over the county of Middlesex, which had been expressly granted by various charters.

In 1383 it was ordained and agreed "that no person shall from henceforth be mayor in the said city if he have not first been sheriff of the said city, to the end that he may be tried in governance and bounty before he attains such estate of the mayoralty."

The two courts—that of aldermen and that of the common council—were probably formed about the same time, but it is remarkable that we have no definite information on the subject. The number of members of the common council varied greatly at different times, but the right to determine the number was indirectly granted by the charter of Edward III. (1341) which enables the city to amend customs and usages which have become hard.

Common Council.

There have also been many changes in the mode of election. The common council were chosen by the wards until 1351, when the appointments were made by certain companies. In 1376 an ordinance was made by the mayor and aldermen, with the assent of the whole commons, to the effect that the companies should select some

[illegible] fur[illegible] the Adr[illegible] pres[illegible] buri[illegible] both [illegible] The [illegible] with [illegible] was [illegible] Carlto[illegible] which [illegible] the last [illegible] frozen [illegible] 1813, w[illegible] of four [illegible] but this [illegible] that the [illegible] was a st[illegible] thronged [illegible] was destr[illegible] opened th[illegible] Sir Willia[illegible]

with whom they were content, and none oth elections of mayors and sheriffs; that the gr not elect more than six, the lesser four and seven companies nominated 156 members election reverted to the wards, but was obt companies in 1467.

The Common Hall was the successor of of which were originally held in the ope Paul's and afterwards in the assemblies of the citizens ar records as *immensa commu civium*. The elections in Common Ha citizens until Edward I.'s reign, citizens to Common Hall by the mayor. In E of mayor, sheriffs and other officers a transferred to liverymen. Various made and now the qualification of corporate offices of lord mayor, s offices in Common Hall is that o company and an enrolled freem aldermen and common councilme

Common Hall.

The recorder, the chief offici formerly appointed by the city Act of 1888 he is no the lord chancellor. appointed by the chancellor. The tr re-elected annually.

Officials of the city.

The chamberlain or com pointed by the livery. He office was probably instit membrancer is appointed

The common hunt, an Courtenay in 1417. Th (1419) and the first reco

Few fundamental alteratio of the city, but in the reign of Ch ceedings were taken against his brother had long entertained d and for the purpose of crushing them tw set up—(1) that a new rate of market tolls had by virtue of an act of common council, and (2) t petition to the king, in which it was alleged that by the prorogation of parliament public justice had been interrupted, had been printed by order of the Court of Common Council. Charles directed a writ *quo warranto* against the corporation of London in 1683, and the Court of King's Bench declared its charter forfeited. Soon afterwards all the obnoxious aldermen were displaced and others appointed in their room by royal commission. When James II. found himself in danger from the landing of the Prince of Orange he sent for the lord mayor and aldermen and informed them of his determination to restore the city charter and privileges, but he had no time to do anything before his flight. The Convention which was summoned to meet on the 22nd of January 1689 was converted by a formal act into a true parliament (February 23). One of the first motions put to the House was that a special Committee should be appointed to consider the violations of the liberties and franchises of all the corporations of the kingdom "and particularly of the City of London." The motion was lost but the House resolved to bring in a bill for repealing the Corporation Act, and ten years later (March 5) the Grand Committee of Grievances reported to the House its opinion (1) that the rights of the City of London in the election of sheriffs in the year 1682 were invaded and that such invasion was illegal and a grievance, and (2) that the judgment given upon the *Quo Warranto* against the city was illegal and a grievance. The committee's opinion on these two points (among others) was endorsed by the House and on the 16th of March it ordered a Bill to be brought in to restore all corporations to the state and condition they were in on the 29th of May 1660, and to confirm the liberties and franchises which at that time they respectively held and enjoyed.[1]

Later history of the corporation.

When the Act for the reform of Municipal Corporations was passed in 1835 London was specially excepted from its provisions. When the Metropolitan Board of Works was formed by the Metropolis Management Act of 1855 the city was affected to a certain extent, but by the Local Government Act of 1888 which founded the London County Council the right of appointing a sheriff for Middlesex was taken away from the city of London.

When the county of Middlesex was dissociated from the city of London one portion was joined to the administrative county of London, and the other to the county of Middlesex.

The lord mayor of London has certain very remarkable privileges which have been religiously guarded and must be of great antiquity. It is only necessary to mention these here, but each of the privileges requires an exhaustive examination as to its origin. They all prove the remarkable position of Old London, and mark it off from all other cities of modern Europe. Shortly stated the privileges are four:

Privileges of the lord mayor.

[1] R. R. Sharpe, *London and the Kingdom* (1894), i. 541.

4th marquess; and (1821–1884), the ceeding as Earl 5th marquess. son Charles Conserva- chairman general 1905) of

offered to him, but he declined so to limit his political activity. His father accepted, at Portland's request, an Irish marquessate, on the understanding that in the future he or his heirs might claim the same rank in the Imperial Legislature; so that Castlereagh was able to sit in the House of Commons as Marquess in 1821–1822. Wilberforce discussed with Pitt the possibility of sending out Castlereagh to India as governor-general, when the friction between Lord Wellesley and the directors became grave; but Pitt objected, as the plan would remove Castlereagh from the House of Commons, which should be "the theatre of his future fame."

In 1802, Castlereagh, at Pitt's suggestion, became president of the Board of Control in the Addington cabinet. He had, hough not in office, taken charge of Irish measures under ddington, including the repression of the Rebellion Bill, and temporary suspension of the Habeas Corpus in 1801, and ued to advocate Catholic relief, tithe reform, state payment olic and dissenting clergy and "the steady application ity in support of the laws." To Lord Wellesley's cy he gave a staunch support, warmly recognized nor-general. On Pitt's return to office (May 1804), ained his post, and, next year, took over also the ary for war and the colonies. Socially and ts of his wife, Lady Emily Hobart, daughter roy, whom he had married in 1794, assisted ise a meeting-place of the party; and his t grew notwithstanding his defects of As a manager of men he had no equal. ving colleagues failed to form a cabinet formidable combination known as eagh acquiesced in the resignation. he Fox-Greville ministry and its vs opposed. His objections to from "Continental entangle- military expenditure were lled "to nail his country's kened by the death of went out in April ce under Portland, at the Foreign priceless oppor- d crippled the ruin of the Alexander with the Tilsit. v the led e.

His Thomas tinued by Tho *London* (1833); Ch *History of London*, illu Grant, *A Comprehensive Hi* Timbs, *Curiosities of London* (18 1876); *Old London Papers, Archaeolog* Loftie, *A History of London* (1883); W. J. (London, 1887); Claude de la Roche Francis, *Lon Social* (Philadelphia, 1902); Sir Walter Besant, *London* (1902–1908)—*Early London, Prehistoric, Roman Norman* (1908); *Mediaeval London*, vol. 1, *Historical* (1906), vol. 2, *Ecclesiastical* (1906); *London in the Time* (1904); *London in the Time of the Stuarts* (1903); *London Eighteenth Century* (1902); H. B. Wheatley, *The Story of London* [Medieval Towns] (London, 1904).

The following are some of the Chronicles of London which have been printed, arranged in order of publication: R. Grafton, *Chronicle 1189–1558* (1809); R. Arnold, *London Chronicle* (1811); *A Chronicle of London from 1089 to 1483 written in the Fifteenth Century* (1827); *William Gregory's Chronicle of London, 1189–1469* (1876); *Historical Collections of a Citizen of London*, edited by James Gairdner (Camden Society, 1876); *Chronicles of London (1300–1516)*, edited by C. L. Kingsford (Oxford, 1905).

Many books have been published on the government of London, of which the following is a selection: *City Law* (1647, 1658); *Lex Londinensis or the City Law* (1680); W. Bohun, *Privilegia Londini* (1723); Giles Jacob, *City Liberties* (1733); *Laws and Customs, Rights, Liberties and Privileges of the City of London* (1765); David Hughson, *Epitome of the Privileges of London* (1816); George Norton, *Commentaries on the History, Constitution and Chartered Franchises of the City of London* (1829, 3rd ed. 1869); *Munimenta Gildhallae Londoniensis*, edited by H. T. Riley—vol. 1, *Liber Albus* (1419), vol. 2, *Liber Custumarum* (1859); *Liber Albus: the White Book of the City of London*, translated by H. T. Riley (1861); H. T. Riley, *Memorials of London and London Life in the 13th, 14th and 15th centuries* (1868); *De Antiquis Legibus Liber. Curante Thoma Stapleton* (Camden Society, 1846); *Chronicles of the Mayors and Sheriffs of London 1188–1274*, translated from the *Liber de Antiquis Legibus* by H. T. Riley. *French Chronicle of London 1259–1343* (1863); *Analytical Index to the Series of Records known as the Remembrancia 1579–1664* (1888); *Calendar of Letter-Books* [*circa 1275–1399*] preserved among the Archives of the Corporation of London at the Guildhall, edited by Reginald R. Sharpe, D.C.L. (1899–1907); W. and R. Woodcock, *Lives of Lord Mayors* (1846); J. F. B. Firth, *Municipal London* (1876); Walter Delgray Birch, *Historical Charters and*

basement bed becomes a thick deposit (60 ft.), forming part of the Oldhaven and Blackheath Beds.

The London Clay is a marine deposit, and its fossils indicate a moderately warm climate, the flora having a tropical aspect. Among the fossils may be mentioned *Panopoea intermedia*, *Ditrupa plana*, *Terebellum personata*, *Conus concinnus*, *Rostellaria ampla*, *Nautilus centralis*, *Belosepia*, foraminifera and diatoms. Fish remains include *Otodus obliquus*, *Sphyroenodus crassidens*; birds are represented by *Halcyornis Toliapicus*, *Lithornis* and *Odontopteryx*, and reptiles by *Chelone gigas*, and other turtles, *Palaeophis*, a serpent and crocodiles. *Hyracotherium leporinum*, *Palaeotherium* and a few other mammals are recorded. Plant remains in a pyritized condition are found in great abundance and perfection on the shore of Sheppey; numerous species of palms, screw pines, water lilies, cypresses, yews, leguminous plants and many others occur; logs of coniferous wood bored through by annelids and *Teredo* are common, and fossil resin has been found at Highgate.

See EOCENE; also W. Whitaker, "The Geology of London and part of the Thames Valley," *Mem. Geol. Survey* (1889), and *Sheet Memoirs of the Geol. Survey, London*, Nos. 314, 315, 268, 329, 332, and *Memoirs on the Geology of the Isle of Wight* (1889).

LONDONDERRY, EARLS AND MARQUESSES OF. The 1st earl of Londonderry was Thomas Ridgeway (*c.* 1565–1631), a Devon man, who was treasurer in Ireland from 1606 to 1616 and was engaged in the plantation of Ulster. Ridgeway was made a baronet in 1611, Baron Ridgeway in 1616 and earl of Londonderry in 1623. The Ridgeways held the earldom until March 1714, when Robert, the 4th earl, died without sons. In 1726 Robert's son-in-law, Thomas Pitt (*c.* 1688–1729), son of Thomas Pitt, "Diamond Pitt," governor at Madras and uncle of the great earl of Chatham, was created earl of Londonderry, the earldom again becoming extinct when his younger son Ridgeway, the 3rd earl of this line, died unmarried in January 1765. In 1796 Robert Stewart (1739–1821), of Mount Stewart, Co. Down, was made earl of Londonderry in the Irish peerage. He had been created Baron Londonderry in 1789 and Viscount Castlereagh in 1795; in 1816 he was advanced to the rank of marquess of Londonderry. The 3rd marquess married the heiress of the Vane-Tempests and took the name of Vane instead of Stewart; the 5th marquess called himself Vane-Tempest and the 6th marquess Vane-Tempest-Stewart.

LONDONDERRY, CHARLES WILLIAM STEWART (VANE), 3RD MARQUESS OF (1778–1854), British soldier and diplomatist, was the son of the 1st marquess by a second marriage with the daughter of the 1st Earl Camden. He entered the army and served in the Netherlands (1794) on the Rhine and Danube (1795), in the Irish rebellion (1798), and Holland (1799), rising to be colonel; and having been elected to parliament for Kerry he became under secretary for war under his half-brother Castlereagh in 1807. In 1808 he was given a cavalry command in the Peninsula, where he brilliantly distinguished himself. In 1809, and again in the campaigns of 1810, 1811, having become a major-general, he served under Wellington in the Peninsula as his adjutant-general, and was at the capture of Ciudad Rodrigo, but at the beginning of 1812 he was invalided home. Castlereagh (see LONDONDERRY, 2nd Marquess of) then sent him to Berlin as minister, to represent Great Britain in the allied British, Russian and Prussian armies; and as a cavalry leader he played an important part in the subsequent fighting, while ably seconding Castlereagh's diplomacy. In 1814 he was made a peer as Baron Stewart, and later in the year was appointed ambassador at Vienna, and was a member of the important congresses which followed. In 1822 his half-brother's death made him 3rd marquess of Londonderry, and shortly afterwards, disagreeing with Canning, he resigned, being created Earl Vane (1823), and for some years lived quietly in England, improving his Seaham estates. In 1835 he was for a short time ambassador at St Petersburg. In 1852, after the death of Wellington, when he was one of the pall-bearers, he received the order of the Garter. He died on the 6th of March 1854. He was twice married, first in 1808 to the daughter of the …l of Darnley, and secondly in 1819 to the heiress of Sir Harry …-Tempest (a descendant of Sir Piers Tempest, who served …gincourt, and heir to Sir Henry Vane, Bart.), when he …ned the name of Vane. Frederick William Robert (1805–

1872), his son by the first marriage, became 4th marquess; and on the latter's death in 1872, George Henry (1821–1884), the eldest son by the second marriage, after succeeding as Earl Vane (according to the patent of 1823), became 5th marquess. In 1884 he was succeeded as 6th marquess by his son Charles Stewart Vane-Tempest-Stewart (b. 1852), a prominent Conservative politician, who was viceroy of Ireland (1886–1889), chairman of the London School Board (1895–1897), postmaster-general (1900–1902), president of the Board of Education (1902–1905) and lord president of the Council (1903–1905).

LONDONDERRY, ROBERT STEWART, 2ND MARQUESS OF (1769–1822), British statesman, was the eldest son of Robert Stewart of Ballylawn Castle, in Donegal, and Mount Stewart in Down, an Ulster landowner, of kin to the Galloway Stewarts, who became baron, viscount, earl and marquess in the peerage of Ireland. The son, known in history as Lord Castlereagh, was born on the 18th of June in the same year as Napoleon and Wellington. His mother was Lady Sarah Seymour, daughter of the earl of Hertford. He went from Armagh school to St John's College, Cambridge, but left at the end of his first year. With Lord Downshire, then holding sway over the County Down, Lord Stewart had a standing feud, and he put forward his son, in July 1790, for one of the seats. Young Stewart was returned, but at a vast cost to his family, when he was barely twenty-one. He took his seat in the Irish House of Commons at the same time as his friend, Arthur Wellesley, M.P. for Trim, but sat later for two close boroughs in England, still remaining member for Down at College Green.

From 1796, when his father became an earl, he took the courtesy title of Viscount Castlereagh, and becoming keeper of the privy seal in Ireland, he acted as chief secretary, during the prolonged absence of Mr Pelham, from February 1797. Castlereagh's conviction was that, in presence of threatened invasion and rebellion, Ireland could only be made safe by union with Great Britain. In Lord Camden, as afterwards in Lord Cornwallis, Castlereagh found a congenial chief; though his favour with these statesmen was jealously viewed both by the Irish oligarchy and by the English politicians who wished to keep the machine of Irish administration in their own hands. Pitt himself was doubtful of the expediency of making an Irishman chief secretary, but his view was changed by the influence of Cornwallis. In suppressing Lord Edward Fitzgerald's conspiracy, and the rebellion which followed in 1798, Castlereagh's vigilance and firmness were invaluable. His administration was denounced by a faction as harsh and cruel—a charge afterwards repudiated by Grattan and Plunket—but he was always on the side of lenity. The disloyal in Ireland, both Jacobins and priest-led, the Protestant zealots and others who feared the consequence of the Union, coalesced against him in Dublin. Even there Castlereagh, though defeated in a first campaign (1799), impressed Pitt with his ability and tact. With Cornwallis he joined in holding out, during the second Union campaign (1800), the prospect of emancipation to the Roman Catholics. They were aided by free expenditure of money and promises of honours, methods too familiar in Irish politics. When the Act of Union was carried through the Irish parliament, in the summer of 1800, Castlereagh's official connexion with his native land practically ended. Before the Imperial Parliament met he urged upon Pitt the measures which he and Cornwallis thought requisite to make the Union effective. In spite of his services and of Pitt's support, disillusion awaited him. The king's reluctance to yield to the Roman Catholic claims was underestimated by Pitt, while Cornwallis imprudently permitted himself to use language which, though not amounting to a pledge, was construed as one. George III. resented the arguments brought forward by Castlereagh—" this young man " who had come over to talk him out of his coronation oath. He peremptorily refused to sanction emancipation, and Pitt and his cabinet made way for the Addington administration. Thereupon Castlereagh resigned, with Cornwallis. He took his seat at Westminster for Down, the constituency he had represented for ten years in Dublin. The leadership of an Irish party was offered to him, but he declined so to limit his political activity. His father accepted, at Portland's request, an Irish marquessate, on the understanding that in the future he or his heirs might claim the same rank in the Imperial Legislature; so that Castlereagh was able to sit in the House of Commons as Marquess in 1821–1822. Wilberforce discussed with Pitt the possibility of sending out Castlereagh to India as governor-general, when the friction between Lord Wellesley and the directors became grave; but Pitt objected, as the plan would remove Castlereagh from the House of Commons, which should be " the theatre of his future fame."

In 1802, Castlereagh, at Pitt's suggestion, became president of the Board of Control in the Addington cabinet. He had, though not in office, taken charge of Irish measures under Addington, including the repression of the Rebellion Bill, and the temporary suspension of the Habeas Corpus in 1801, and continued to advocate Catholic relief, tithe reform, state payment of Catholic and dissenting clergy and " the steady application of authority in support of the laws." To Lord Wellesley's Indian policy he gave a staunch support, warmly recognized by the governor-general. On Pitt's return to office (May 1804), Castlereagh retained his post, and, next year, took over also the duties of secretary for war and the colonies. Socially and politically, the gifts of his wife, Lady Emily Hobart, daughter of a former Irish viceroy, whom he had married in 1794, assisted him to make his house a meeting-place of the party; and his influence in parliament grew notwithstanding his defects of style, spoken and written. As a manager of men he had no equal. After Pitt's death his surviving colleagues failed to form a cabinet strong enough to face the formidable combination known as " All the Talents," and Castlereagh acquiesced in the resignation. But to the foreign policy of the Fox-Greville ministry and its conduct of the war he was always opposed. His objections to the Whig doctrine of withdrawal from " Continental entanglements " and to the reduction of military expenditure were justified when Fox himself was compelled " to nail his country's colours to the mast."

The cabinet of " All the Talents," weakened by the death of Fox and the renewed quarrel with the king, went out in April 1807. Castlereagh returned to the War Office under Portland, but grave difficulties arose, though Canning at the Foreign Office was then thoroughly at one with him. A priceless opportunity had been missed after Eylau. The Whigs had crippled the transport service, and the operations to avert the ruin of the coalition at Friedland came too late. The Tsar Alexander believed that England would no longer concern herself with the Continental struggle, and Friedland was followed by Tilsit. The secret articles of that compact, denied at the time by the Opposition and by French apologists, have now been revealed from official records in M. Vandal's work, *Napoléon et Alexandre*. Castlereagh and Canning saw the vital importance of nullifying the aim of this project. The seizure of the Danish squadron at Copenhagen, and the measures taken to rescue the fleets of Portugal and Sweden from Napoleon, crushed a combination as menacing as that defeated at Trafalgar. The expedition to Portugal, though Castlereagh's influence was able only to secure Arthur Wellesley a secondary part at first, soon dwarfed other issues. In the debates on the Convention of Cintra, Castlereagh defended Wellesley against parliamentary attacks: " A brother," the latter wrote, " could not have done more." The depression produced by Moore's campaign in northern Spain, and the king's repugnance to the Peninsular operations, seemed to cut short Wellesley's career; but early in 1809, Castlereagh, with no little difficulty, secured his friend's appointment as commander-in-chief of the second Portuguese expedition. The merit has been claimed for Canning by Stapleton, but the evidence is all the other way.

Meanwhile, Castlereagh's policy led to a crisis that clouded his own fortunes. The breach between him and Canning was not due to his incompetence in the conduct of the Walcheren expedition. In fact, Castlereagh's ejection was decided by Canning's intrigues, though concealed from the victim, months before

Constitutional … *Round, The* … R. Sharpe, … *the Archives* … *London.* … *tutions* (190… *temp. Henry* …

In conne… on the follow… *the Inns of* … (1848). … *Hon. Artillery* … *of the Hon. Ar*… *History of the* … Thomas A… *and its Liver*… *Companies of* … *City Compan*… *and Compan*… histories … The follo… topography … 1805, 1813, … *Topograph*… *through Lon*… 1844, reprint… *Literary and* … *The Town,* … Peter Cun… and ed. … Wheatley, … by J. W. … Thornbur… *Old and* … by Edwa… *minster,* … *Antiquiti*… 1902); … *Records* … *Committ*…

The … publish… *Bills of* … *Political* … (1687), … 1755), … 1686). … *past* … *of the* … D.D. … Morri… Petty' … (189…)

LON… of the … devel… partly … gravel … scale … on w… times … septar… manu… near S… shire … are of … making … tenaciou… portions. … a few in… sand, par… bonate of … the London … thick; bene… of Essex it is … in thickness, … in the Isle of … here the beds … Alum Bay it is … known as the … sandstone within … In the …

[illegible]atter, not only with Bernadotte but with all [illegible] Castlereagh's avowed intention to take this step without [illegible] or sanction from his cabinet put an end to evasion and [illegible] Blücher was reinforced by the two divisions; the battle of L[illegible] was fought and won, and the allies occupied the French capital. In April 1814 Castlereagh arrived in Paris. He did not disguise his discontent with Napoleon's position at Elba, close to the French coast, though he advised England not to separate herself at this crisis from her allies. His uneasiness led him to summon Wellington from the south to the Embassy in Paris. He hastened himself to London during the visit of the allied sovereigns, and met with a splendid reception. He was honoured with the Garter, being one of the few commoners ever admitted to that order. When the House of Commons offered to the Crown its congratulations upon the treaty of peace, Castlereagh's triumph was signalized by a brilliantly eloquent panegyric from Canning, and by a recantation of his former doubts and denunciations from Whitbread. His own dignified language indicated his country from the charge of selfish ambition.

His appointment as British representative at Vienna, where the Congress was to meet in September, was foreseen; but meanwhile he was not idle. The war with the United States, originating in the non-intercourse dispute and the Orders in Council, did not cease with the repeal of the latter. It lasted through 1814 till the signing of the treaty of Ghent, soon before the flight from Elba. In parliament the ministry, during Castlereagh's absence, had been poorly championed. Canning had thrown away his chance by his unwise refusal of the Foreign Office. None of the ministers had any pretension to lead when Castlereagh was busy abroad and Canning was sulking at home, and Castlereagh's letters to Vansittart, the chancellor of the exchequer, show how these difficulties weighed upon him in facing the position at Vienna, where it was imperative for him to appear. At Vienna he realized at once that the ambition of Russia might be as formidable to Europe and to Great Britain as that of the fallen tyrant. His aim throughout had been to rescue Europe from military domination; and when he found that Russia and Prussia were pursuing ends incompatible with the general interest, he did not hesitate to take a new line. He brought about the secret treaty (Jan. 3, 1815) between Great Britain, Austria and France, directed against the plans of Russia in Poland and of Prussia in Saxony. Through Castlereagh's efforts, the Polish and Saxon questions were settled on the basis of compromise. The threat of Russian interference in the Low Countries was dropped.

While the Congress was still unfinished, Napoleon's escape from Elba came like a thunderclap. Castlereagh had come home for a short visit (Feb. 1815), at the urgent request of the cabinet, just before the flight was known. The shock revived the Great Alliance under the compact of Chaumont. All energies were directed to preparing for the campaign of Waterloo. Castlereagh's words in parliament were, "Whatever measures you adopt or decision you arrive at must rest on your own power and not on reliance on this man." Napoleon promptly published the secret treaty which Castlereagh had concluded with Metternich and Talleyrand, and the last left in the French archives. But Russia and Prussia, though much displeased, saw that, in the face of Bonaparte's return, they dared not weaken the Alliance. British subsidies were again poured out like water. After Napoleon's overthrow, Castlereagh successfully urged his removal to St Helena, where his custodians were charged to treat him "with all the respect due to his rank, but under such precautions as should render his escape a matter of impossibility." Some of the continental powers demanded, after Waterloo, fines and cessions that would have crushed France; but in November a peace was finally concluded, mainly by Castlereagh's endeavours, minimising the penalties exacted, and abandoning on England's part the whole of her share of the indemnity. The war created an economic situation at home which strengthened the Whigs and Radicals, previously discredited by their hostility to a patriotic struggle. In 1816 the Income Tax was remitted, despite Castlereagh's contention that something should first be done to reduce the Debt Charge. His policy, impressed upon

a commodious harbour, its greatest depth being 33 ft. at high
[illegible]e, and 12 ft. at low tide. It is under the jurisdiction of the
[illegible] Society. The port has a considerable shipping trade with
[illegible] Britain, exporting agricultural produce and provisions.
[illegible] services of passenger steamers serve Londonderry from
[illegible]iverpool, Morecambe, Belfast and local coast stations.
[illegible]ndonderry was constituted one of the six county
[illegible]h have separate county councils.
[illegible] of the city, on a hill 803 ft. high, is a remarkable
[illegible] three concentric ramparts, and an interior
[illegible]. It is named the Grianan of Aileach, and
[illegible] O'Neills, kings of Ulster. It was restored
[illegible] of Londonderry, is derived from
[illegible] owes its origin to the monastery
[illegible]6. With the bishopric which
[illegible]ndation, that of Raphoe was
[illegible] to the 11th century the
[illegible]n of the Danes, and was
[illegible]iven from it by Murtagh
[illegible] century. In 1311 it
[illegible]e Burgh. After the
[illegible] of it, it was incor-
[illegible]rry. From this
[illegible]turned to the
[illegible]gun in 1600,
[illegible] the chief
[illegible]e 7th of
[illegible]lly put
[illegible]nd on
[illegible]nest
[illegible]ge

[illegible] Alliance [illegible] matic [illegible] he regarded [illegible] and agreed [illegible] as the Prussian [illegible] of tutelage [illegible] should be excluded [illegible] was the object of the [illegible] nich's idea of extending [illegible] crush "the revolution" [illegible] to take shape, from the [illegible] onward, that Great Britain's [illegible] allies became inevitable. A[illegible] powers Castlereagh from the [illegible] little was he prepared to ac[illegible] emperor Alexander for found[illegible] Europe" upon the inclusive [illegible] ALEXANDER I. of Russia).

Meanwhile financial troubles at home, compl[illegible] resumption of cash payments in 1819, led to acute social [illegible] "Peterloo" and the "Six Acts" were furiously denounced [illegible] though the bills introduced by Sidmouth and Castlereagh were carried in both Houses by overwhelming majorities. The danger that justified them was proved beyond contest by the Cato Street Conspiracy in 1820. It is now admitted by Liberal writers that the "Six Acts," in the circumstances, were tenable and necessary. Throughout, Castlereagh maintained his tranquil ascendancy in the House of Commons, though he had few colleagues who were capable of standing up against Brougham. Canning, indeed, had returned to office and had defended the "Six Acts," but Castlereagh bore the whole burden of parliamentary leadership, as well as the enormous responsibilities of the Foreign Office. His appetite for work caused him to engage in debates and enquiries on financial and legal questions when he might have delegated the task to others. Althorp was struck with his unsleeping energy on the Agricultural Distress Committee; "His exertions, coupled with his other duties—and unfortunately he was always obstinate in refusing assistance—strained his constitution fearfully, as was shown by his careworn brow and increasing paleness." In 1821, on Sidmouth's retirement, he took upon himself the laborious functions of the Home Office. The diplomatic situation had become serious. The policy of "intervention," with which Great Britain had consistently refused to identify herself, had been proclaimed to the world by the famous Troppau Protocol, signed by Russia, Austria and Prussia (see TROPPAU, CONGRESS OF). The immediate occasion was the revolution at Naples, where the egregious Spanish constitution of 1812 had been forced on the king by a military rising. With military revolts, as with paper constitutions of an unworkable type, Castlereagh had no sympathy; and in this particular case the revolution, in his opinion, was wholly without excuse or palliation. He was prepared to allow the intervention of Austria, if she considered her rights under the treaty of 1813 violated, or her position as an Italian Power imperilled. But he protested against the general claim, embodied in the Protocol, of the European powers to interfere, uninvited, in the internal concerns of sovereign states; he refused to make Great Britain, even tacitly, a party to such interference, and again insisted that her part in the Alliance was defined by the letter of the treaties, beyond which she was not prepared to go. In no case, he affirmed, would Great Britain "undertake the moral responsibility for administering a general European police," which she would never tolerate as applied to herself.

To Troppau, accordingly, no British plenipotentiary

the arma
the earl of C
was known
schemes, a
into a co
openly o
sular qu
in fixing
Military
from Wa
Napoleo
approve
main, u
was una
naval a
explain
demned
did not
time w
tracted
was wi
opinion
that, in
remova
troops
learned
in a se
hurt.
not thr
shadow
following
requires
Castlerea
original
league.
rivals sim
and broth
he "was n
lished a len
with him
wronged.
decided ag
name was re
acter and op
Cobbett—to
government i
to the Foreign
had been inch
cheren campai
ministers were
lost faith in W
in 1812, when t
led to Castlerea
1812). The ass
leadership of the
he continued to b
From March 18
truth, the history
minister, during
ministers have ex
wishers admitted
trolled the House o
matist, nobody sav
men or was given
Foreigners saw in hi
of the Allies. At the
of technical knowled
an organizer, the powe
his peculiar combinatio
conciliatory adroitnes
Foreign Office he set.h
in northern Europe

to which the
but
was
was again
himself
Canning, his
mentary,
continental
Naples and
Spanish revolu-
matter with
foreign power
however, the
most critical
against the
question in an
motions of the
Metternich and
attack
to Hanover,
meeting between
A meeting
reagh's opinion
"a practical
had nothing in
question with
concern itself.
he could use the
and he joined
of the emperor
chance to prevent
question. It was,
the matter of
reagh to agree
foreshadowed
pointing out that
recognition of the
and quoting the
ctly applicable.
though he was
pendence *de jure*,
government should
them sooner or
and the means
in restoring

ous life was
foreshadowed
uming. Lord
the toilsome
were struck by
attributed to
employed.
was unwell,
down to
reagh's razors
in a drawer,
He had just
gone"; and,
he moaned
bear a case
prevent his
a shadow of
bilious and
the highest

volumes. Sir Archibald Alison's *Biography* in three volumes came out in 1861, with copious extracts from the manuscripts preserved at Wynyard. It was made the subject of an interesting essay in the *Quarterly Review* for January 1862, reprinted in *Essays by the late Marquis of Salisbury* (London, 1905). A graceful sketch by Theresa, Marchioness of Londonderry (London, 1904), originally brought out in the *Anglo-Saxon Review*, contains some extracts from Castlereagh's unpublished correspondence with his wife, the record of an enduring and passionate attachment which throws a new light on the man. (E. D. J. W.)

LONDONDERRY, a northern county of Ireland in the province of Ulster, bounded N. by the Atlantic, W. by Lough Foyle and Donegal, E. by Antrim and Lough Neagh, and S. by Tyrone. The area is 522,315 acres, or about 816 sq. m. The county consists chiefly of river valleys surrounded by elevated tablelands rising occasionally into mountains, while on the borders of the sea-coast the surface is generally level. The principal river is the Roe, which flows northward from the borders of Tyrone into Lough Foyle below Newton-Limavady, and divides the county into two unequal parts. Farther west the Faughan also falls into Lough Foyle, and the river Foyle passes through a small portion of the county near its north-western boundary. In the south-east the Moyola falls into Lough Neagh, and the Lower Bann from Lough Neagh forms for some distance its eastern boundary with Antrim. The only lake in the county is Lough Finn on the borders of Tyrone, but Lough Neagh forms about 6 m. of its south-eastern boundary. The scenery of the shores of Lough Foyle and the neighbouring coast is attractive, and Castlerock, Downhill, Magilligan and Portstewart are favourite seaside resorts. On the flat Magilligan peninsula, which forms the eastern horn of Lough Foyle, the base-line of the trigonometrical survey of Ireland was measured in 1826. The scenery of the Roe valley, with the picturesque towns of Limavady and Dungiven, is also attractive, and the roads from the latter place to Draperstown and to Maghera, traversing the passes of Evishgore and Glenshane respectively, afford fine views of the Sperrin and Slieve Gallion mountains.

The west of this county consists of Dalradian mica-schist, with some quartzite, and is a continuation of the northern region of Tyrone. An inlier of these rocks appears in the rising ground east of Dungiven, including dark grey crystalline limestone. Old Red Sandstone and Lower Carboniferous Sandstone overlie these old rocks in the south and east, meeting the igneous "green rocks" of Tyrone, and the granite intrusive in them, at the north end of Slieve Gallion. Triassic sandstone covers the lower slope of Slieve Gallion on the south-east towards Moneymore, and rises above the Carboniferous Sandstone from Dungiven northward. At Moneymore we reach the western scarp of the White Limestone (Chalk) and the overlying basalt of the great plateaus, which dip down eastward under Lough Neagh. The basalt scarp, protecting chalk and patches of Liassic and Rhaetic strata, rises to 1260 ft. in Benevenagh north of Limavady, and repeats the finest features of the Antrim coast. A raised shelf with post-glacial marine clays forms the flat land west of Limavady. Haematite has been mined on the south flank of Slieve Gallion.

The excessive rainfall and the cold and uncertain climate are unfavourable for agriculture. Along the sea-coast there is a district of red clay formed by the decomposition of sandstone, and near the mouth of the Roe there is a tract of marl. Along the valleys the soil is often fertile, and the elevated districts of the clay-slate region afford pasture for sheep. The acreage of pasture-land does not greatly exceed that of tillage. Oats, potatoes and turnips are chiefly grown, with some flax; and cattle, sheep, pigs and poultry are kept in considerable numbers. The staple manufacture of the county is linen. The manufacture of coarse earthenware is also carried on, and there are large distilleries and breweries and some salt-works. There are fisheries for salmon and eels on the Bann, for which Coleraine is the headquarters. The deep-sea and coast fisheries are valuable, and are centred at Moville in Co. Donegal. The city of Londonderry is an important railway centre. The Northern Counties (Midland) main line reaches it by way of Coleraine and the north coast of the county, and the same railway serves the eastern part of the county, with branches from Antrim to Magherafelt, and Magherafelt to Cookstown (Co. Tyrone), to Draperstown and to Coleraine, and from Limavady to Dungiven. The Great Northern railway ...ches Londonderry from the south, and the city is also the starting- of the County Donegal, and the Londonderry and Lough railways.

...opulation decreases (152,009 in 1891; 144,404 in 1901) and ...on is extensive, though both decrease and emigration are ...w the average of the Irish counties. Of the total, about ... Roman Catholics, and nearly 30% Presbyterians or

Protestant Episcopalians. Londonderry (pop. 38,892), Coleraine (6958) and Limavady (2692) are the principal towns, while Magherafelt and Moneymore are lesser market towns. The county comprises six baronies. Assizes are held at Londonderry, and quarter sessions at Coleraine, Londonderry and Magherafelt. The county is represented in parliament by two members, for the north and south divisions respectively. The Protestant and Roman Catholic dioceses of Armagh, Derry and Down each include parts of the county.

At an early period the county was inhabited by the O'Cathans or O'Catrans, who were tributary to the O'Neills. Towards the close of the reign of Elizabeth the county was seized, with the purpose of checking the power of the O'Neills, when it received the name of Coleraine, having that town for its capital. In 1609, after the confiscation of the estates of the O'Neills, the citizens of London obtained possession of the towns of Londonderry and Coleraine and adjoining lands, 60 acres out of every 1000 being assigned for church lands. The common council of London undertook to expend £20,000 on the reclamation of the property, and elected a body of twenty-six for its management, who in 1613 were incorporated as the Irish Society, and retained possession of the towns of Londonderry and Coleraine, the remainder of the property being divided among twelve of the great livery companies. Their estates were sequestrated by James I., and in 1637 the charter of the Irish Society was cancelled. Cromwell restored the society to its former position, and Charles II. at the Restoration granted it a new charter, and confirmed the companies in their estates. In the insurrection of 1641 Moneymore was seized by the Irish, and Magherafelt and Bellaghy, then called Vintner's Town, burned, as well as other towns and villages. There are several stone circles, and a large number of artificial caves. The most ancient castle of Irish origin is that of Carrickreagh; and of the castles erected by the English those of Dungiven and Muff are in good preservation. The abbey of Dungiven, founded in 1109, and standing on a rock about 200 ft. above the river Roe, is a picturesque ruin.

LONDONDERRY, or DERRY, a city, county of a city, parliamentary borough (returning one member) and the chief town of Co. Londonderry, Ireland, 4 m. from the junction of the river Foyle with Lough Foyle, and 95 m. N.N.W. of Belfast. Pop. (1901) 38,892. The city is situated on an eminence rising abruptly from the west side of the river to a height of about 120 ft. The eminence is surrounded by hills which reach, a few miles to the north, an elevation of upwards of 1500 ft., and the river and lough complete an admirable picture. The city is surrounded by an ancient rampart about a mile in circumference, having seven gates and several bastions, but buildings now extend beyond this boundary. The summit of the hill, at the centre of the town, is occupied by a quadrangular area from which the main streets diverge. Some old houses with high pyramidal gables remain but are much modernized. The Protestant cathedral of St Columba, in Perpendicular style, was completed from the design of Sir John Vanbrugh in 1633, at a cost of £4000 contributed by the city of London, and was enlarged and restored in 1887. The spire was added in 1778 and rebuilt in 1802. The bishop's palace, erected in 1716, occupies the site of the abbey founded by Columba. The abbot of this monastery, on being made bishop, erected in 1164 Temple More or the "Great Church," one of the finest buildings in Ireland previous to the Anglo-Norman invasion. The original abbey church was called the "Black Church," but both it and the "Great Church" were demolished in 1600 and their materials used in fortifying the city. There is a large Roman Catholic cathedral, erected *c.* 1870 and dedicated to St Eugenius. For Foyle College, founded in 1617, a new building was erected in 1814. This and the Academical Institution, a foundation of 1868, were amalgamated in 1896. Magee College, taking its name from its foundress, Mrs Magee of Dublin, was instituted in 1857 as a training-school for the Presbyterian ministry.

The staple manufacture of the town is linen (especially shirt-making), and there are also shipbuilding yards, iron-foundries, saw-mills, manure-works, distilleries, breweries and flour-mills. The salmon fishery on the Foyle is valuable. The river affords a commodious harbour, its greatest depth being 33 ft. at high tide, and 12 ft. at low tide. It is under the jurisdiction of the Irish Society. The port has a considerable shipping trade with Great Britain, exporting agricultural produce and provisions. Regular services of passenger steamers serve Londonderry from Glasgow, Liverpool, Morecambe, Belfast and local coast stations. In 1898 Londonderry was constituted one of the six county boroughs which have separate county councils.

About 5 m. W. of the city, on a hill 803 ft. high, is a remarkable fort, consisting of three concentric ramparts, and an interior fortification of stone. It is named the Grianan of Aileach, and was a residence of the O'Neills, kings of Ulster. It was restored in 1878.

Derry, the original name of Londonderry, is derived from *Doire*, the "place of oaks." It owes its origin to the monastery founded by Columba about 546. With the bishopric which arose in connexion with this foundation, that of Raphoe was amalgamated in 1834. From the 9th to the 11th century the town was frequently in the possession of the Danes, and was often devastated, but they were finally driven from it by Murtagh O'Brien about the beginning of the 12th century. In 1311 it was granted by Edward II. to Richard de Burgh. After the Irish Society of London obtained possession of it, it was incorporated in 1613 under the name of Londonderry. From this year until the Union in 1800 two members were returned to the Irish parliament. The fortifications, which were begun in 1600, were completed in 1618. In 1688 Derry had become the chief stronghold of the Protestants of the north. On the 7th of December certain of the apprentices in the city practically put themselves and it in a stage of siege by closing the gates, and on the 19th of April 1689 the forces of James II. began in earnest the famous siege of Derry. The rector of Donaghmore, George Walker, who, with Major Baker, was chosen to govern Derry, established fame for himself for his bravery and hopefulness during this period of privation, and the historic answer of "No surrender," which became the watchword of the men of Derry, was given to the proposals of the besiegers. The garrison was at the last extremity when, on the 30th of July, ships broke through the obstruction across the harbour and brought relief. Walker and the siege are commemorated by a lofty column (1828), bearing a statue of the governor, on the Royal Bastion, from which the town standards defied the enemy; and the anniversary of the relief is still observed.

LONG, GEORGE (1800–1879), English classical scholar, was born at Poulton, Lancashire, on the 4th of November 1800, and educated at Macclesfield grammar-school and Trinity College, Cambridge. He was Craven university scholar in 1821 (bracketed with Lord Macaulay and Henry Malden), wrangler and senior chancellor's medallist in 1822 and became a fellow of Trinity in 1823. In 1824 he was elected professor of ancient languages in the new university of Virginia at Charlottesville, U.S.A., but after four years returned to England as the first Greek professor at the newly founded university of London. In 1842 he succeeded T. H. Key as professor of Latin at University College; in 1846–1849 he was reader in jurisprudence and civil law in the Middle Temple, and finally (1849–1871) classical lecturer at Brighton College. Subsequently he lived in retirement at Portfield, Chichester, in receipt (from 1873) of a Civil List pension of £100 a year obtained for him by Gladstone. He was one of the founders (1830), and for twenty years an officer, of the Royal Geographical Society; an active member of the Society for the Diffusion of Useful Knowledge, for which he edited the quarterly *Journal of Education* (1831–1835) as well as many of its text-books; the editor (at first with Charles Knight, afterwards alone) of the *Penny Cyclopaedia* and of Knight's *Political Dictionary*; and a member of the Society for Central Education instituted in London in 1837. He contributed the Roman law articles to Smith's *Dictionary of Greek and Roman Antiquities*, and wrote also for the companion dictionaries of *Biography* and *Geography*. He is remembered, however, mainly as the editor of the *Bibliotheca Classica* series—the first serious attempt to produce scholarly editions of classical texts [illegible] which he contributed the [illegible] [illegible]). He died on the 10th of [illegible]

[illegible] Summary of *Herodotus* (1829); [illegible] Xenophon's *Anabasis* (1831); [illegible] Juvenal and Persius (1867) and [illegible]: a translation with notes of [illegible]; translations of the *Thoughts* [illegible] *Discourses of Epictetus* (1877), [illegible] 1874), 5 vols. See H. J. [illegible] from the *Brighton College* [illegible]

[illegible], American lawyer and [illegible] Buckfield, Oxford county, Maine, [illegible]. He graduated at Harvard in [illegible] Law School and in 1861 was [illegible] at Boston, became active [illegible] was a member of the Massachusetts [illegible] and its speaker in 1876–[illegible] the state in 1879, and governor [illegible] was a member of the National [illegible] from March 1897 to May 1902 [illegible] cabinet, first of President [illegible] Roosevelt. In 1902 he became [illegible] of Harvard College. His [illegible] 1879), *After-Dinner* [illegible] *The New American Navy* (1903).

[illegible] Monmouth county, New Jersey, [illegible] branch of the Shrewsbury [illegible] 30 m. S. of New York [illegible] whom 1431 were foreign-[illegible] 13,298. It is served [illegible] New Jersey, the New York [illegible] and by steamboats to [illegible] vicinity are unusually [illegible] American watering-[illegible] abruptly 20-35 ft. [illegible] which bulkheads and [illegible] from the waves; along [illegible] avenue, 60 ft. wide and [illegible] commands delightful [illegible] above the water [illegible] Ocean Park (about [illegible], one of which is [illegible] Shrewsbury river, where [illegible] principal public institu-[illegible] and the Long Branch [illegible] Monmouth County [illegible]. The southern part of [illegible] some beautiful [illegible] General U. S. Grant [illegible] in another, the [illegible] 1881. In 1909 a [illegible] Park. Adjoining [illegible] Monmouth Beach [illegible]. Before the [illegible] was owned by [illegible] of [illegible]

[illegible]

with Hugh, and by April 1190 had managed to oust him completely from office. In June 1190 he received a commission as legate from Pope Celestine. He was then master in church as well as state. But his disagreeable appearance and manners, his pride, his contempt for everything English made him detested. His progresses through the country with a train of a thousand knights were ruinous to those on whom devolved the burden of entertaining him. Even John seemed preferable to him. John returned to England in 1191, he and his adherents were immediately involved in disputes with William, who was always worsted. At last (June 1191) Geoffrey, archbishop of York and William's earliest benefactor, was violently arrested by William's subordinates on landing at Dover. They exceeded their orders, which were to prevent the archbishop from entering England until he had sworn fealty to Richard. But this outrage was made a pretext for a general rising against William, whose legatine commission had now expired, and whose power was balanced by the presence of the archbishop of Rouen, Walter Coutances, with a commission from the king. William shut himself up in the Tower, but he was forced to surrender his castles and expelled from the kingdom. In 1193 he joined Richard in Germany, and Richard seems to have attributed the settlement soon after concluded between himself and the emperor, to his "dearest chancellor." For the rest of the reign Longchamp was employed in confidential and diplomatic missions by Richard all over the continent, in Germany, in France and at Rome. He died in January 1197. His loyalty to Richard was unswerving, and it was no doubt through his unscrupulous devotion to the royal interest that he incurred the hatred of Richard's English subjects.

Authorities.—Benedictus, *Gesta Henrici*, vol. ii.; Giraldus Cambrensis, *De Vita Galfridi*; Stubbs' Preface to Roger of Hoveden, vol. iii.; L. Bovine-Champeaux, *Notice sur Guillaume de Longchamp* (Évreux, 1885).

LONGCLOTH, a plain cotton cloth originally made in comparatively long pieces. The name was applied particularly to cloth made in India. Longcloth, which is now commonly bleached, comprehends a number of various qualities. It is heavier than cambric, and finer than medium or Mexican. As it is used principally for underclothing and shirts, most of the longcloth sold in Great Britain passes through the hands of the shirt and underclothing manufacturers, who sell to the shopkeepers, though there is still a considerable if decreasing retail trade in piece-goods. The lower kinds of longcloth, which are made from American cotton, correspond in quality to the better kinds of "shirting" made for the East, but the best longcloths are made from Egyptian cotton, and are fine and fairly costly goods.

LONG EATON, an urban district in the Ilkeston parliamentary division of Derbyshire, England, 10 m. E.S.E. of Derby, on the Midland railway. Pop. (1891) 9636; (1901) 13,045. It lies in the open valley of the Trent, at a short distance from the river, and near the important Trent Junction on the Midland railway system. The church of St Lawrence has Norman portions, and an arch and window apparently of pre-Conquest date. The large industrial population of the town is occupied in the manufacture of lace, which extended hither from Nottingham; there are also railway carriage works. To the north is the township of Sandiacre (pop. 2954), where the church has a fine Decorated chancel.

LONGEVITY, a term applied to express either the length or the duration of life in any organism, but, as cases of long duration excite most interest, frequently used to denote a relatively unusual prolongation of life. There is no reason to suppose that protoplasm, the living material of organisms, has a necessarily limited duration of life, provided that the conditions proper to it are maintained, and it has been argued that since every living organism comes into existence as a piece of the protoplasm of a pre-existing living organism, protoplasm is potentially immortal. Living organisms exist, however, as particles or communities of particles of protoplasm (see Life), and as such have a limited duration of life. Longevity, as E. Ray Lankester pointed out in 1869, for practical purposes must be understood to mean the "length of time during which life is exhibited in an individual." The word "individual" must be taken in its ordinary sense as a wholly or partially independent, organized mass produced from a pre-existing organized mass, as otherwise the problem will be confused by arguments as to the meaning of biological individuality.

Empirical Data.—A multitude of observations show that only a very brief life, ranging from a few hours to a few days, is the normal fate of the vast majority of single-celled organisms, whether these be animal or vegetable or on the border-line between the two kingdoms. Death comes to them rapidly from internal or external causes, or the individual life ends in conjugation or division or spore-formation. Under special conditions, natural or artificial, the individual life may be prolonged by desiccation, or freezing, or by some similar arrest of functional activity.

The duration of life among plants is varied. The popular division into annuals, biennials and perennials is not absolute, for natural and artificial conditions readily prolong the lives of annuals and biennials for several seasons, whereas the case of perennials is much complicated by the mode of growth, and the problem of individuality, however we desire to exclude it, obtrudes itself. In the vast majority of cases where a plant is obviously a simple individual, its life is short, ranging from a few days in the case of fungi, to two seasons in the case of biennial herbs. Most of the simple algae are annual, their life enduring only for part of the year; the branching algae are more often perennial, but in their cases not only are observations as to duration lacking, but however simply we may use the term individual, its application is difficult. The larger terrestrial plants with woody tissues which we denote roughly as shrubs and trees have an individuality which, although different from that of a hyacinth or carrot, is usually obvious. Shrubs live from four to ten or more years, and it apparently is the case that odoriferous shrubs such as sage and lavender display the longer duration. Trees with soft wood, such as poplars and willows, last for about fifty years, fruit-trees rather longer. Estimates of the age which large trees can attain, based partly on attempts to count the annual rings, have been given by many writers, and range from about three hundred years in the case of the elm to three to five thousand years in the case of *Sequoia gigantea* of California, and over five thousand years in that of the baobab (*Adansonia digitata*) of Cape Verde. It is impossible to place exact reliance on these estimates, but it is at least certain that very many trees have a duration of life exceedingly great in comparison with the longest-lived animals.

The duration of life amongst multicellular invertebrate animals is little known, except in the frequent instances where it is normally brief. Many sponges and polyps die at the end of the season, leaving winter eggs or buds. The much-branched masses of the larger sponges and compound hydrozoa certainly may be perennial. A sea-anemone (*Actinia mesembryanthemum*), captured in 1828 by Sir John Dalyell, a Scottish naturalist, and then guessed to be about seven years old, lived in captivity in Edinburgh until 1887, the cause of death being unknown. As other instances of great ages attained by sea-anemones are on record, it is plain that these animals, although simple polyps, are long-lived. Echinoderms are inferred to live to considerable ages, as they grow slowly and as there is great difference in size amongst fully adult specimens. On similar reasoning, considerable age is attributed to the larger annulates and crustacea, but the smaller forms in many cases are known to have very short lives. The variation in the length of life of molluscs appears to be great. Many species of gastropods live only a few years; others, such as *Natica heros*, have reached thirty years, whilst the large *Tridacna gigas* is stated to live from sixty to a hundred years. Among insects, the adult stage has usually only a very short duration of life, extending from a few hours to a few months, but the larval stages may last much longer. Including these latter, the range of duration among insects, taking the whole life from hatching to death, appears to lie between the limits of a few weeks in the case of plant-lice to seventeen years in the case of the American *Cicada septemdecim*, the larva of which lives seventeen years, the adult only a month. Most butterflies are annuals, but those which fail to copulate may hibernate and live through a second season, whilst the lives of some have been preserved artificially for seven years. Worker bees and drones do not survive the season, but queens may live from two to five years. In the case of vertebrates, the duration of life appears to be greater among fish and reptiles than among birds and mammals. The ancient Romans have noted that eels, kept in aquaria, could reach the age of sixty years. Estimates based on size and rate of growth have led to the inference that salmon may live to the age of a hundred years, whilst G. L. L. Buffon set down the period of life of carp in ponds as one hundred and fifty years, and there is evidence for a pike having reached the age of over two centuries. More recently it has been claimed that the age of fish can be ascertained exactly by counting the annual rings of the otoliths. No great ages have as yet been recorded by this method, whilst, on the other hand, by revealing great variations of weight and size in fishes with the same number of annual rings, it has thrown doubt on the validity of estimates of age based on size and rate of growth. The evidence as a whole is unsatisfactory, but it is highly probable that in the absence of accidents most fish can attain very great ages. The duration of life among batrachia is little known, but small frogs have been recorded as living over twelve years, and toads up to thirty-six years.

Almost nothing is known as to the longevity of snakes and lizards, but it is probable that no great ages are reached. Crocodiles, alligators and caymans grow slowly and are believed to live very long. There is exact evidence as to alligators in captivity in Europe reaching forty years without signs of senescence, and some of the sacred crocodiles of India are believed to be more than a hundred years old. Chelonians live still longer. A tortoise has lived for eighty years in the garden of the governor of Cape Town, and is believed to be at least two hundred years old. There are records of small land-tortoises that have been kept in captivity for over a century, whilst the very large tortoises of the Galapagos Islands certainly attain ages of at least two centuries and possibly much more. A considerable body of information exists regarding the longevity of birds, and much of this has been brought together by J. H. Gurney. From his lists, which include more than fifty species, it appears that the duration is least in the case of small passerine and picarian birds, where it ranges from eight or nine years (goat-suckers and swifts) to a maximum of twenty-five years, the latter age having been approached by larks, canaries and goldfinch. Gulls have been recorded as living over forty years, ducks and geese over fifty years (the duchess of Bedford has recorded the case of a Chinese goose having been in possession of the same family for fifty-seven years). Parrots frequently live over eighty years, swans nearly as long, ravens and owls rather less, whilst there is excellent evidence of eagles and falcons considerably exceeding a hundred years. Notwithstanding their relatively large size, struthious birds do not reach great ages. The records for cassowaries and rheas do not exceed thirty years, and the maximum for ostriches is fifty years, and that on doubtful evidence.

Exact records regarding the longevity of mammals are surprisingly few. There is no evidence as to Monotremes. The life of Marsupials in captivity is seldom long; a phalanger has lived in the London Zoological Gardens and showed no signs of age at more than ten years old; it may be inferred that the larger forms are capable of living longer. Reliable records as to Edentates do not exist; those in captivity have short lives, but the size and structure of some of the extinct forms suggests that they may have reached a great age. Nothing is known regarding the longevity of Sirenians, except that they do not live long in captivity. In the case of Cetaceans, estimates based on the growth of whale-bone assign an age of several centuries to whale-bone whales; exact records do not exist. More is known regarding Ungulates, as many of these are domesticated, semi-domesticated or are frequently kept in captivity Great length of life has been assigned to the rhinoceros, but the longest actual

with English [illegible]
edition of Cicero [illegible]
August 1879.
Among his ot[illegible]
editions of Herod[illegible]
revised editions [illegible]
Horace (1869); [illegible]
thirteen of Pluta[illegible]
of Marcus Aure[illegible]
Decline of the [illegible]
Matthews, "In [illegible]
Magazine, 1879.

LONG, JOH[illegible] political leader. [illegible] on the 27th of [illegible] 1857, studied [illegible] admitted to th[illegible] in politics as a [illegible] House of Repre[illegible] 1878, lieutenan[illegible] in 1880–1882. [illegible] House of Repr[illegible] was secretary [illegible] McKinley and [illegible] president of th[illegible] publications inc[illegible] *and Other Spee[illegible]*

LONG BRAN[illegible] U.S.A., on the e[illegible] river and on th[illegible] City. Pop. (189[illegible] born and 987 w[illegible] by the Pennsylv[illegible] & Long Branch, [illegible] New York. Th[illegible] good. Long Br[illegible] places. It is sit[illegible] above the beach. [illegible] jetties have been [illegible] or near the edge [illegible] about 5 m. long ([illegible] views of the oce[illegible] for 2 m. The c[illegible] 10 acres), and tw[illegible] Pleasure Bay Par[illegible] operas are given [illegible] tions are the Monm[illegible] Circulating Librar[illegible] Horse Show is hel[illegible] Long Branch, kn[illegible] summer residences [illegible] spent his summer [illegible] Francklyn, Preside[illegible] monument to Garfi[illegible] Long Branch on th[illegible] (incorporated in 19[illegible] War of Independen[illegible] Colonel White, a Bri[illegible] the war, and late in [illegible] place began. Long B[illegible]

LONGCHAMP, WIL[illegible] and bishop of Ely, e[illegible] II.'s reign as official [illegible] deaconry of Rouen. [illegible] the "son of two tra[illegible] Richard, who made hi[illegible] He always showed him[illegible] tinguished himself at Pa[illegible] Henry II.'s attempt to [illegible] On Richard's accession [illegible] dom and bishop of Ely [illegible] 1189), he put the tower [illegible] to share with Hugh de [illegible] the office of chief justici[illegible]

[illegible] which lived for thirty-[illegible] Zoological Gardens. The [illegible] horses, asses and zebras is from [illegible] of individuals reaching [illegible] authenticated. Domestic cattle may [illegible] thirty years, sheep and goats from [illegible] antelopes rather longer, especially in [illegible]. A giraffe has lived for nineteen [illegible] Zoological Gardens. Deer are reputed to [illegible] and records of individuals at the London [illegible] but it is doubtful if they live as long as [illegible]. Camels are long-lived, according to repute, but actual records show no great age; a llama which died in the London [illegible] at the age of seventeen years showed unmistakable [illegible] senility. The hippopotamus is another large ungulate to which great longevity has been assigned, but the longest [illegible] record is the case of a female born in the London Gardens which died in its thirty-fifth year. The duration of life assigned to [illegible] is about twenty years; an Indian wild boar [illegible] the London Zoological Gardens in 1910, and [illegible] was fifteen years old. Elephants are usually [illegible] capable of reaching great ages, but the actual records [illegible] and military animals show that thirty to forty [illegible]. Facts as to rodents are not [illegible]. [illegible] hares and rabbits may live for ten years [illegible] as rats and mice, for five or six years. Bats [illegible] long duration of life, and tropical fruit-bats [illegible] to have lived for seventeen years. No great ages [illegible] recorded for Carnivora, but the average is fairly high. Twenty-five years appears to be a limit very rarely exceeded by [illegible]; domestic cats may live for from twelve [illegible] years, and dogs from sixteen to eighteen years [illegible] as many as thirty-four years have been [illegible] of the smaller forms, but menagerie records show [illegible] between twelve and twenty are frequently reached. [illegible] the London Zoological Gardens, apparently [illegible] at least twelve years old, a [illegible] and a [illegible] nineteen years of age. [illegible] monkeys are unsatisfactory, for these creatures are [illegible] in captivity, and it is practically [illegible] they rarely die of old age. A [illegible] seven years old and a chimpanzee eleven and a half [illegible] in the London Zoological Gardens. [illegible] definitely recorded. [illegible] of the skull and so forth [illegible] specimens that have been killed [illegible] correspondence between the size of [illegible] duration of life, and to set the limits as between seven [illegible] and thirty years.

[illegible] to the human race, there seems to be almost no [illegible] average duration of life has increased with [illegible] the generally improved conditions of life, the [illegible] of the young and of the aged and the advance in [illegible] science for more than [illegible] The expectation of life [illegible] by modern social organization. [illegible] the age of sixty [illegible] is certainly increasing [illegible] a chance of reaching [illegible] one hundred. [illegible]

[illegible]

average duration of life and that centenarians occur more frequently amongst men than amongst most of the lower animals.

Theories of Longevity.—Ray Lankester has pointed out that several meanings are attached to the word longevity. It may be used of an individual, and in this sense has little importance, partly because of the inevitable variability of the individual, and partly because there may be individuals that are abnormal in duration of life, just as there are abnormalities in weight or height. It may be used for the average duration of life of all the individuals of a species and so be another way of expressing the average mortality that affects the species, and that varies not only with structure and constitution but with the kind of enemies, accidents and conditions to which the members of the species are subject. If we reflect on the large incidence of mortality from external causes affecting a species and particularly the young of a species, we shall see that we must conclude that intrinsic, physiological causes can have relatively little weight in determining the average mortality rate. Finally, longevity may be used, and is most conveniently used, to denote the specific potential longevity, that is to say the duration of life that would be attained by normal individuals of a species if the conditions were most favourable. It is necessary to keep in mind these various applications of the term when considering the theoretical explanations that have been associated with the empirical facts.

There is a certain relation between size and longevity. As a general rule small animals do not live so long as larger creatures. Whales survive elephants, elephants live longer than camels, horses and deer, and these again than rabbits and mice. But the relation is not absolute; parrots, ravens and geese live longer than most mammals and than many larger birds. G. L. L. Buffon tried to find a more definite measure of longevity, and believed that it was given by the ratio between the whole period of life and the period of growth. He believed that the possible duration of life was six or seven times that of the period of growth. Man, he said, takes fourteen years to grow, and his duration of life is ninety to one hundred years; the horse has reached its full size at four years of age and may live for a total period of twenty-five to thirty years. M. J. P. Flourens attempted to make Buffon's suggestion more exact; he took the end of the period of growth as the time at which the epiphyses of the long bones united with the bones themselves, and on this basis held that the duration of life was five times the length of the period of growth. The theories of Buffon and Flourens, however, do not apply to all vertebrates and have no meaning in the case of invertebrates. Y. Bunge has suggested that in the case of mammals the period taken by the new-born young to double in weight is an index of the rapidity of growth and is in a definite relation to the possible duration of life. M. Oustalet has discussed the existence of definite relations between duration of life and size, rate of growth, period of gestation and so forth, and found so many exceptions that no general conclusion could be drawn. He finally suggested that diet was the chief factor in determining the span of life. E. Metchnikoff has provided the most recent and fullest criticism and theory of the physiological causes of longevity. He admits that many factors must be involved, as the results vary so much in different kinds of animals. He thinks that too little is known of the physiological processes of invertebrates to draw any valid conclusions in their case. With regard to vertebrates, he calls attention to the gradual reduction of longevity as the scale of life is ascended. On the whole, reptiles live much longer than birds, and birds than mammals, the contrast being specially notable when birds and mammals are compared. He dismisses the effect of the reproductive tax from possible causes of short duration of life, for the obvious reason that longevity is nearly equal in the two sexes, although females have a much greater reproductive drain. He points out that the hind-gut or large intestine is least developed in fishes, relatively small in reptiles, still small but relatively larger in birds and largest in mammals, relatively and absolutely, the caecum or caeca being reckoned as part of the [illegible]. The area of the intestinal tract in question is of little importance in digestion, although a considerable amount of absorption may take place from it. It serves chiefly as a reservoir of waste matter and is usually the seat of extensive putrefactive change. The products of putrefaction are absorbed by the blood and there results a constant auto-intoxication of the body which Metchnikoff believes to be the principal agent in senile degeneration. Mammals, if they escape from enemies, diseases and accidents, fall victims to premature senility as the result of the putrefactive changes in their intestines, and the average mortality of the species is much too high, the normal specific longevity being rarely if ever attained. Metchnikoff urges, and so far probably is followed by all competent authorities, that improvements in the conditions of life, greater knowledge of disease and of hygiene and simplification of habits are tending to reduce the average mortality of man and the domestic animals, and to bring the average longevity nearer the specific longevity. He adds to this, however, a more special theory, which, although it appears rapidly to be gaining ground, is yet far from being accepted. The theory is that duration of life may be prolonged by measures directed against intestinal putrefaction.

The process of putrefaction takes place in masses of badly-digested food, and may be combated by careful dieting, avoidance of rich foods of all kinds and particularly of flesh and alcohol. Putrefaction, however, cannot take place except in the presence of a particular group of bacteria, the entrance of which to the body can be prevented to a certain extent. But it would be impossible or impracticable to secure a sterilized diet, and Metchnikoff urges that the bacteria of putrefaction can be replaced or suppressed by another set of microbes. He found that there was a widely spread popular belief in the advantage of diet consisting largely of products of soured milk and that there was a fair parallel between unusual longevity and such a diet. Experimentally he showed that the presence of the bacilli which produce lactic acid inhibited the process of putrefaction. Accordingly he recommends that the diet of human beings should include preparations of milk soured by cultures of selected lactic acid bacilli, or that the spores of such bacilli should be taken along with food favourable to their development. In a short time the bacilli establish themselves in the large intestine and rapidly stop putrefactive change. The treatment has not yet been persisted in sufficiently long by a sufficient number of different persons to be accepted as universally satisfactory, and there is even more difference of opinion as to Metchnikoff's theory that the chief agent in senile degeneration is the stimulation of phagocytes by the products of putrefaction with the resulting destruction of the specific cells of the tissues. Metchnikoff, however, gave it to the world, not as a proved and completed doctrine, but as the line of inquiry that he himself had found most promising. He has suggested further that if the normal specific longevity were attained by human beings, old and not degenerate individuals would lose the instinct for life and acquire an instinct for death, and that as they had fulfilled the normal cycle of life, they would accept death with the same relieved acquiescence that they now accept sleep.

The various writers whose opinions have been briefly discussed agree in supposing that there is a normal specific longevity, although Metchnikoff alone has urged that this differs markedly from the average longevity, and has propounded a theory of the causes of the divergence. It is common ground that they believe the organism to be wound up, so to say, for a definite period, but have no very definite theory as to how this period is determined. A. Weismann, on the other hand, in a well-known essay on the duration of life, has developed a theory to explain the various fashions in which the gift of life is measured out to different kinds of creatures. He accepts the position that purely physiological conditions set a limit to the number of years that can be attained by each kind of multi-cellular organism, but holds that these conditions leave room for a considerable amount of variation. Duration of life, in fact, according to Weismann, is a character that can be influenced by the environment and that by a process of natural selection can be adapted to the conditions of existence of different species.

If a species is to maintain its existence or to increase, it is obvious that its members must be able to replace the losses caused by death. It is necessary, moreover, for the success of the species, that an average population of full vigour should be maintained. Weismann argues that death itself is an adaptation to secure the removal of useless and worn-out individuals and that it comes as soon as may be after the period of reproductive activity. It is understood that the term reproductive activity covers not merely the production of new individuals but the care of these by the parents until they are self-sufficient. The average longevity, according to Weismann, is adapted to the needs of the species; it is sufficiently long to secure that the requisite number of new individuals is produced and protected. He has brought together a large number of instances which show that there is a relation between duration of life and fertility. Birds of prey, which breed slowly, usually producing an annual brood of no more than one or two, live to great ages, whilst rabbits which produce large litters at frequent invervals have relatively short lives. Allowance has to be made in cases where the young are largely preyed upon by enemies, for this counteracts the effect of high fecundity. In short, the duration of life is so adapted that a pair of individuals on the average succeed in rearing a pair of offspring. Metchnikoff, however, has pointed out that the longevity of such fecund creatures must have arisen independently, as otherwise species subject to high risks of this nature would have ceased to exist and would have disappeared, as many species have vanished in the past of the world's history.

The normal specific longevity, the age to which all normal individuals of a species would survive under the most favourable conditions, must depend on constitution and structure. No doubt selection is involved, as it is obvious that creatures would perish if their constitution and structure were not such that they could live long enough to reproduce their kind. The direct explanation, however, must be sought for in size, complexity of structure, length of period of growth, capacity to withstand the wear and tear of life and such other intrinsic qualities. The average specific longevity, on the other hand, depends on a multitude of extrinsic conditions operating on the intrinsic constitution; these extrinsic conditions are given by the environment of the species as it affects the young and the adults, enemies, diseases, abundance of food, climatic conditions and so forth. It would seem most natural to suppose that in all cases, except perhaps those of intelligent man and the domestic animals or plants he harbours, the average longevity must vary enormously with changing conditions, and must be a factor of greater importance in the survival of the species than the ideal normal specific longevity. It also seems more probable that the reproductive capacity, which is extremely variable, has been adapted to the average longevity of the species, than that, as Weismann supposed, it should itself be the determining cause of the duration of life.

REFERENCES.—G. L. L. Buffon, *Histoire naturelle générale et particulière*, vol. ii. (Paris, 1749); Y. Bunge, *Archiv. f. die gesammte Physiologie*, vol. xcv. (Bonn, 1903); M. J. P. Flourens, *De la longévité humaine et de la quantité de vie sur le globe* (Paris, 1855); J. H. Gurney, *On the Comparative Ages to which Birds live*, *Ibis*, p. 19 (1899); Sir E. Ray Lankester, *Comparative Longevity in Man and the Lower Animals* (London, 1870); E. Metchnikoff, *The Prolongation of Life* (London, 1908); M. Oustalet, *La Nature*, p. 378 (1900); A. Weismann, *Essays upon Heredity* (Oxford, 1889). (P. C. M.)

LONGFELLOW, HENRY WADSWORTH (1807–1882), American poet, was born on the 27th of February 1807, at Portland, Maine. His ancestor, William Longfellow, had immigrated to Newbury, Massachusetts, in 1676, from Yorkshire, England. His father was Stephen Longfellow, a lawyer and United States congressman, and his mother, Zilpha Wadsworth, a descendant of John Alden and of "Priscilla, the Puritan maiden."

Longfellow's external life presents little that is of stirring interest. It is the life of a modest, deep-hearted gentleman, whose highest ambition was to be a perfect man, and, through sympathy and love, to help others to be the same. His boyhood was spent mostly in his native town, which he never ce[illegible]

[illegible] quiet, gave life [illegible]. Here he grew [illegible] once broken, [illegible] on him—

[illegible] most beautiful [illegible]

free rural aspect, its old graveyards and towering elms, its great university, its cultivated society and its vicinity to humane, substantial, busy Boston, were all attractions for such a man. In 1837–1838 several essays of Longfellow's appeared in the *North American Review*, and in 1839 he published *Hyperion: a Romance*, and his first volume of original poetry, entitled *Voices of the Night*. *Hyperion*, a poetical account of his travels, had, at the time of its publication, an immense popularity, due mainly to its sentimental romanticism. At present few persons beyond their teens would care to read it through, so unnatural and stilted is its language, so thin its material and so consciously mediated its sentiment. Nevertheless it has a certain historical importance, for two reasons—(1) because it marks that period in Longfellow's career when, though he had left nature, he had not yet found art, and (2) because it opened the sluices through which the flood of German sentimental poetry flowed into the United States. The *Voices of the Night* contains some of his best minor poems, *e.g.* "The Psalm of Life" and "Footsteps of Angels." In 1842 Longfellow published a small volume of *Ballads and other Poems*, containing some of his most popular pieces, *e.g.* "The Skeleton in Armour," "The Wreck of the Hesperus," "The Village Blacksmith," "To a Child," "The Bridge," "Excelsior." In the same year he paid a third brief visit to Europe, spending the summer on the Rhine. During his return-passage across the Atlantic he wrote his *Poems on Slavery* (1842), with a dedication to Channing. These poems went far to wake in the youth of New England a sense of the great national wrong, and to prepare them for that bitter struggle in which it was wiped out at the expense of the lives of so many of them. In 1843 he married again, his wife being Miss Frances Elizabeth Appleton of Boston, a daughter of Hon. Nathan Appleton, one of the founders of Lowell, and a sister of Thomas G. Appleton, himself no mean poet.

About the same time he bought, and fixed his residence in, the Craigie House, where he had formerly only been a lodger, an old "revolutionary house," built about the beginning of the 18th century and occupied by General Washington in 1776. This quaint old wooden house, in the midst of a large garden and a splendid elms, continued to be his chief residence till the day of his death. Of the lectures on Dante which he delivered about this time, James Russell Lowell says: "These lectures, [illegible] admirable translations, are remembered with [illegible] measure by many who were thus led to learn the full [illegible] of the great Christian poet." Indeed, as a professor, [illegible] was eminently successful. Shortly after the *Poems on Slavery* there appeared in 1843 a more ambitious work, *The Spanish Student, a Play in Three Acts*, a kind of sentimental [illegible] any special merit but good intention. [illegible] it would hardly attract notice; but in those [illegible] times it had considerable popularity, [illegible] the poet's now rapidly widening fame. [illegible] translations of foreign poetry [illegible] by him, [illegible] *The Poets and Poetry of Europe*, appeared in 1845, [illegible] minor poems—songs and sonnets—[illegible] *The Belfry of Bruges*. In 1847 he published at Boston [illegible] of all his works, *Evangeline, a Tale of Acadie*. [illegible] an imitation of Goethe's *Hermann und Dorothea* [illegible], which was derived from Hawthorne's [illegible] simpler than that of the German [illegible] more touching. At the [illegible] a colony of French settlers [illegible] a young couple, on the very [illegible] were separated and carried in different [illegible] each other. The poem [illegible] in search of her lover, and [illegible] an old man on his death-bed, [illegible] she had entered as a nurse. [illegible] one of the most affecting [illegible] one of its most [illegible] "affection that hopes and endures [illegible]." Though written in a metre [illegible] to English ears, the poem immediately attained a wide popularity, which it has never lost, and secured to the dactylic hexameter a recognized place among English metres.

In 1849 Longfellow published a novel of no great merit, *Kavanagh*, and also a volume of poems entitled *The Seaside and the Fireside*, a title which has reference to his two homes, the seaside one on the charming peninsula of Nahant, the fireside one in Cambridge. One of the poems in this collection, "Resignation," has taken a permanent place in literature; another, "Hymn for my Brother's Ordination," shows plainly the nature of the poet's Christianity. His brother, the Rev. Samuel Longfellow, was a minister of the Unitarian Church.

Longfellow's genius, in its choice of subjects, always oscillated between America and Europe, between the colonial period of American history and the Middle and Romantic Ages of European feeling. When tired of the broad daylight of American activity, he sought refuge and rest in the dim twilight of medieval legend and German sentiment. In 1851 appeared *The Golden Legend*, a long lyric drama based upon Hartmann von Aue's beautiful story of self-sacrifice, *Der arme Heinrich*. Next to *Evangeline*, this is at once the best and the most popular of the poet's longer works, and contains many passages of great beauty. Bringing his imagination back to America, he next applied himself to the elaboration of an Indian legend. In 1854 he resigned his professorship. In the following year he gave to the world the Indian Edda, *The Song of Hiawatha*, a conscious imitation, both in subject and metre, of the Finnish epic, the *Kalevala*, with which he had become acquainted during his second visit to Europe. The metre is monotonous and easily ridiculed, but it suits the subject, and the poem is very popular. In 1858 appeared *The Courtship of Miles Standish*, based on a charming incident in the early history of the Plymouth colony, and, along with it, a number of minor poems, included under the modest title, *Birds of Passage*. One of these is "My Lost Youth."

Two events now occurred which served to cast a gloom over the poet's life and to interrupt his activity,—the outbreak of the Civil War, and the tragic fate of his wife, who, having accidentally allowed her dress to catch fire, was burnt to death in her own house in 1861. It was long before he recovered from the shock caused by this terrible event, and in his subsequent published poems he never ventured even to allude to it. When he did in some measure find himself again, he gave to the world his charming *Tales of a Wayside Inn* (1863), and in 1865 his *Household Poems*. Among the latter is a poem entitled "The Children's Hour," which affords a glance into the home life of the widowed poet, who had been left with five children—two sons, Ernest and Charles, and three daughters,

"Grave Alice, and laughing Allegra,
And Edith with golden hair."

A small volume entitled *Flower de Luce* (1867) contains, among other fine things, the beautiful "threnos" on the burial of Hawthorne, and "The Bells of Lynn." Once more the poet sought refuge in medieval life by completing his translation of the *Divina Commedia*, parts of which he had rendered into English as much as thirty years before. This work appeared in 1867, and gave a great impulse to the study of Dante in America. It is a masterpiece of literal translation. Next came the *New England Tragedies* (1868) and *The Divine Tragedy* (1871), which found no large public. In 1868–1869 the poet visited Europe, and was everywhere received with the greatest honour. In 1872 appeared *Three Books of Song*, containing translated as well as original pieces, in 1873 *Aftermath* and in 1875 *The Mask of Pandora, and other Poems*. Among these "other poems" were "The Hanging of the Crane," "Morituri Salutamus" and "A Book of Sonnets." *The Mask of Pandora* is a proof of that growing appreciation of pagan naturalism which marked the poet's later years. Though not a great poem, it is full of beautiful passages, many of which point to the riddle of life as yet unsolved, a conviction which grew ever more and more upon the poet, as the ebulliency of romanticism gave way to the calm of classic feeling. In the "Book of Sonnets" are some of the finest things he ever wrote, especially the five sonnets entitled "Three Friends of Mine." These "three friends" were Cornelius Felton, Louis Agassiz and Charles Sumner, whom he calls

"The noble three,
Who half my life were more than friends to me."

The loss of Agassiz was a blow from which he never entirely recovered; and, when Sumner also left him, he wrote:—

"Thou hast but taken thy lamp and gone to bed;
I stay a little longer, as one stays
To cover up the embers that still burn."

He did stay a little longer; but the embers that still burnt in him refused to be covered up. He would fain have ceased writing, and used to say, "It's a great thing to know when to stop"; but he could not stop, and did not stop, till the last. He continued to publish from time to time, in the magazines, poems which showed a clearness of vision and a perfection of workmanship such as he never had equalled at any period of his life. Indeed it may be said that his finest poems were his last. Of these a small collection appeared under the title of *Keramos, and other Poems* (1878). Besides these, in the years 1875–1878 he edited a collection of *Poems of Places* in thirty-one small volumes. In 1880 appeared *Ultima Thule*, meant to be his last work, and it was nearly so. In October 1881 he wrote a touching sonnet on the death of President Garfield, and in January 1882, when the hand of death was already upon him, his poem, *Hermes Trismegistus*, in which he gives utterance, in language as rich as that of the early gods, to that strange feeling of awe without fear, and hope without form, with which every man of spotless life and upright intellect withdraws from the phenomena of time to the realities of eternity.

In the last years of his life he suffered a great deal from rheumatism, and was, as he sometimes cheerfully said, "never free from pain." Still he remained as sunny and genial as ever, looking from his Cambridge study windows across the Brighton meadows to the Brookline hills, or enjoying the "free wild winds of the Atlantic," and listening to "The Bells of Lynn" in his Nahant home. He still continued to receive all visitors, and to take occasional runs up to Castine and Portland, the homes of his family. About the beginning of 1882, however, a serious change took place in his condition. Dizziness and want of strength confined him to his room for some time, and, although after some weeks he partially recovered, his elasticity and powers were gone. On the 19th of March he was seized with what proved to be peritonitis, and he died on the 24th. The poet was buried two days afterwards near his "three friends" in Mount Auburn cemetery. The regret for his loss was universal; for no modern man was ever better loved or better deserved to be loved.

Longfellow was made an LL.D. of Bowdoin College in 1828, at the age of twenty-one, of Harvard in 1859 and of Cambridge (England) in 1868, and D.C.L. of Oxford in 1869. In 1873 he was elected a member of the Russian Academy of Science, and in 1877 of the Spanish Academy.

In person, Longfellow was rather below middle height, broad shouldered and well built. His head and face were extremely handsome, his forehead broad and high, his eyes full of clear, warming fire, his nose straight and graceful, his chin and lips rich and full of feeling as those of the Praxitelean Hermes, and his voice low, melodious and full of tender cadences. His hair, originally dark, became, in his later years, silvery white, and its wavy locks combined with those of his flowing beard to give him that leonine appearance so familiar through his later portraits. Charles Kingsley said of Longfellow's face that it was the most beautiful human face he had ever seen. A bust to his memory was erected in the Poet's Corner in Westminster Abbey in 1884.

In Longfellow, the poet was the flower and fruit of the man. His nature was essentially poetic, and his life the greatest of his poems. Those who knew only the poems he wrote could form but a faint notion of the harmony, the sweetness, the manliness and the tenderness of that which he lived. What he would have been as a poet, if, instead of visiting Europe in early life and drinking in the spirit of the middle ages under the shadows of cathedral towers, he had, like

[illegible] group of villages, by that time virtually one [illegible] [illegible] called Long Island City, and it was form[illegible] [illegible] that name in 1870. In 1871–1872 the [illegible] [illegible] a commission of which General W. B. Fran[illegible] [illegible]. Political convictions, economic considera[illegible] [illegible] to make the residents in this region la[illegible] [illegible] during the War of Independ[illegible] [illegible] British troops occupied Newtown, a vill[illegible] [illegible] In January 1776 the committee on the state [illegible] [illegible] Congress reported a resolution that "Whereas [illegible] [illegible] the inhabitants of Queens county, in the colony of [illegible] being incapable of resolving to live and die [illegible] [illegible] such persons as voted against sending deputies [illegible] present convention in New York . . . be put out of [illegible] protection of the United Colonies," &c., an action wh[illegible] [illegible] the arrest and imprisonment of many of the accused [illegible].

[illegible] Kelsey, *History of Long Island City* (Long Island City [illegible]).

LONGITUDE (from Lat. *longitudo*, "length"), the angle [illegible] the terrestrial meridian from the pole through a point [illegible] the earth's surface makes with some standard meridian [illegible] that of Greenwich. It is equal to the difference [illegible] local time on the standard meridian, and at the place [illegible] one hour of time corresponding to 15° difference of [illegible]. Formerly each nation took its own capital or principal [illegible] as the standard meridian from which longitudes [illegible] measured. Another system had a meridian passing through [illegible] the island of Ferro, defined as 20° W. of Paris, as the [illegible]. While the system of counting from the capital of [illegible] country is still used for local purposes, the tendency in recent [illegible] is to use the meridian of Greenwich for nautical and [illegible] purposes. France, however, uses the meridian [illegible] Paris observatory as its standard for all nautical and [illegible] purposes (see TIME). In astronomy, the longitude [illegible] is the distance of its projection upon the [illegible] from the vernal equinox, counted in the direction west [illegible] to 360°.

LONGLEY, CHARLES THOMAS (1794–1868), archbishop of [illegible], was born at Rochester, and educated at Westminster [illegible]. He was ordained in 1818, and was appointed [illegible] Oxford, in 1823. In 1827 he received the [illegible] Tytherley, Hampshire, and two years later he [illegible] headmaster of Harrow. This office he held until [illegible] he was consecrated bishop of the new see of Ripon. [illegible] he was translated to the see of Durham, and in [illegible] archbishop of York. In 1862 he succeeded John B[illegible] as archbishop of Canterbury. Soon afterwards the [illegible] connected with the deposition of Bishop Colenso were [illegible] but, while regarding Colenso's opinions as [illegible] as justifiable, he refused to pronounce [illegible] of the case. The chief event of his [illegible] was the meeting at Lambeth, in 1867, of the first [illegible] conference of British, colonial and foreign bishops [illegible] CONFERENCES). His published works include [illegible] sermons and addresses. He died on the 27th of [illegible] Addington Park, near Croydon.

LONGMANS, a firm of English publishers. The founder of the [illegible] Thomas Longman [illegible] (1699–1755), born in 1699, was the [illegible] Longman (d. 1708), a gentleman of Bris[illegible] [illegible] was apprenticed in 1716 to John Osborn, a Londo[illegible] [illegible] the expiration of his apprenticeship he married [illegible] and in August 1724 purchased the stock [illegible] goods of William Taylor, the first publisher [illegible] [illegible] 6d. Taylor's two shops were [illegible] the Black Swan and the Ship, and occupied [illegible] Paternoster Row upon which the present publishing [illegible] Osborn, who afterwards entered into partnership [illegible] held one-sixth of the shares in Ephraim [illegible] *of the Arts and Sciences*, and Thomas [illegible] of the six booksellers who undertook the [illegible] Samuel Johnson's *Dictionary*. In 1754 Thomas

978

love, he has up in and th the W.

The in the the He- Longfe situate 25 m. f legend. thorne, latter *Literat* for two sympa almost which He gr. among fourth father's to dev he was fortuna of a p In ord he went a half tr England and dri The effe it wider and sup it tradit nature a the spirit fell exact the sentim and the su when, in the French faith, whic half-aesthe cratic pagar of dutiful, soon as it be by Napoleor and remained which he pub languages. In Mary Story P a series of tran moral and devo ated in 1835 in In 1835 Long as professor of m On receiving this fifteen months to to the Scandinav visit he lost his w November 1835. On his return to took up his residenc Harvard and to write surroundings entirely

Longman took his nephew into partnership, the title of the firm becoming T. and T. Longman.

Upon the death of his uncle in 1755, Thomas Longman (2) (1730–1797) became sole proprietor. He greatly extended the colonial trade of the firm. He had three sons. Of these, Thomas Norton Longman (3) (1771–1842) succeeded to the business. In 1794 Owen Rees became a partner, and Thomas Brown, who was for many years after 1811 a partner, entered the house as an apprentice. Brown died in 1869 at the age of 92. In 1799 Longman purchased the copyright of Lindley Murray's *English Grammar*, which had an annual sale of about 50,000 copies; he also purchased, about 1800, the copyright, from Joseph Cottle, of Bristol, of Southey's *Joan of Arc* and Wordsworth's *Lyrical Ballads*. He published the works of Wordsworth, Coleridge, Southey and Scott, and acted as London agent for the *Edinburgh Review*, which was started in 1802. In 1804 two more partners were admitted; and in 1824 the title of the firm was changed to Longman, Hurst, Rees, Orme, Brown & Green. In 1814 arrangements were made with Thomas Moore for the publication of *Lalla Rookh*, for which he received £3000; and when Archibald Constable failed in 1826, Longmans became the proprietors of the *Edinburgh Review*. They issued in 1829 Lardner's *Cabinet Encyclopaedia*, and in 1832 M'Culloch's *Commercial Dictionary*.

Thomas Norton Longman (3) died on the 29th of August 1842, leaving his two sons, Thomas (4) (1804–1879) and William Longman (1813–1877), in control of the business in Paternoster Row. Their first success was the publication of Macaulay's *Lays of Ancient Rome*, which was followed in 1849 by the issue of the first two volumes of his *History of England*, which in a few years had a sale of 40,000 copies. The two brothers were well known for their literary talent; Thomas Longman edited a beautifully illustrated edition of the New Testament, and William Longman was the author of several important books, among them a *History of the Three Cathedrals dedicated to St Paul* (1869) and a work on the *History of the Life and Times of Edward III.* (1873). In 1863 the firm took over the business of Mr J. W. Parker, and with it *Fraser's Magazine*, and the publication of the works of John Stuart Mill and J. A. Froude; while in 1890 they incorporated with their own all the publications of the old firm of Rivington, established in 1711. The family control of the firm (now Longmans, Green & Co.) was continued by Thomas Norton Longman (5), son of Thomas Longman (4).

LONGOMONTANUS (or LONGBERG), **CHRISTIAN SEVERIN** (1562–1647), Danish astronomer, was born at the village of Longberg in Jutland, Denmark, on the 4th of October 1562. The appellation Longomontanus was a Latinized form of the name of his birthplace. His father, a poor labourer called Sören, or Severin, died when he was eight years old. An uncle thereupon took charge of him, and procured him instruction at Lemvig; but after three years sent him back to his mother, who needed his help in field-work. She agreed, however, to permit him to study during the winter months with the clergyman of the parish; and this arrangement subsisted until 1577, when the illwill of some of his relatives and his own desire for knowledge impelled him to run away to Viborg. There he attended the grammar-school, defraying his expenses by manual labour, and carried with him to Copenhagen in 1588 a high reputation for learning and ability. Engaged by Tycho Brahe in 1589 as his assistant in his great astronomical observatory of Uraniborg, he rendered him invaluable services there during eight years. He quitted the island of Hveen with his master, but obtained his discharge at Copenhagen on the 1st of June 1597, for the purpose of studying at some German universities. He rejoined Tycho at Prague in January 1600, and having completed the Tychonic lunar theory, turned homeward again in August. He visited Frauenburg, where Copernicus had made his observations, took a master's degree at Rostock, and at Copenhagen found a patron in Christian Friis, chancellor of Denmark, who gave him employment in his household. Appointed in 1603 rector of the school of Viborg, he was elected two years later to a professorship in the university of Copenhagen, and his promotion to the chair of mathematics ensued in 1607. This post he held till his death, on the 8th of October 1647.

Longomontanus, although an excellent astronomer, was not an advanced thinker. He adhered to Tycho's erroneous views about refraction, held comets to be messengers of evil and imagined that he had squared the circle. He found that the circle whose diameter is 43 has for its circumference the square root of 18252—which gives 3·14185 . . . for the value of π. John Pell and others vainly endeavoured to convince him of his error. He inaugurated, at Copenhagen in 1632, the erection of a stately astronomical tower, but did not live to witness its completion. Christian IV. of Denmark, to whom he dedicated his *Astronomia Danica*, an exposition of the Tychonic system of the world, conferred upon him the canonry of Lunden in Schleswig.

The following is a list of his more important works in mathematics and astronomy: *Systematis Mathematici*, &c. (1611); *Cyclometria e Lunulis reciproce demonstrata*, &c. (1612); *Disputatio de Eclipsibus* (1616); *Astronomia Danica*, &c. (1622); *Disputationes quatuor Astrologicae* (1622); *Pentas Problematum Philosophiae* (1623); *De Chronolabio Historico, seu de Tempore Disputationes tres* (1627), *Geometriae quaesita XIII. de Cyclometria rationali et vera* (1631), *Inventio Quadraturae Circuli* (1634); *Disputatio de Matheseos Indole* (1636); *Coronis Problematica ex Mysteriis trium Numerorum* (1637); *Problemata duo Geometrica* (1638); *Problema contra Paulum Guldinum de Circuli Mensura* (1638); *Introductio in Theatrum Astronomicum* (1639); *Rotundi in Plano*, &c. (1644); *Admiranda Operatio trium Numerorum 6, 7, 8*, &c. (1645); *Caput tertium Libri primi de absoluta Mensura Rotundi plani*, &c. (1646).

See E. P. F. Vindingius, *Regia Academia Hauniensis*, p. 212 (1665); R. Nyerup and Kraft, *Almindeligt Litteraturlexikon*, p. 350 (1820); Ch. G. Jöcher, *Allgemeines Gelehrten-lexikon*, ii. 2516, iii. 2111; Jens Worm, *Forsög til et Lexikon over danske, norske og islandske laerde Maend*, p. 617, 1771, &c.; P. Bayle, *Hist. and Crit. Dictionary*, iii. 861 (2nd ed. 1736); J. B. J. Delambre, *Hist. de l'astr. moderne*, i. 262; J. S. Bailly, *Hist. de l'astr. moderne*, ii. 141; J. L. E. Dreyer, *Tycho Brahe*, pp. 126, 259, 288, 291; F. Hoefer, *Hist. de l'astronomie*, p. 371; J. Madler, *Geschichte der Himmelskunde*, i. 195; J. F. Weidler, *Hist. Astronomiae*, p. 451.

LONGSTREET, JAMES (1821–1904), American soldier, lieutenant-general in the Confederate army, was born on the 8th of February 1821 in Edgefield district, South Carolina, and graduated at West Point in 1842. He served in the Mexican War, was severely wounded, and received two brevets for gallantry. In 1861, having attained the rank of major, he resigned when his state seceded, and became a brigadier-general in the Confederate army. In this rank he fought at the first battle of Bull Run, and subsequently at the head of a division in the Peninsular campaign and the Seven Days. This division subsequently became the nucleus of the I. corps, Army of Northern Virginia, which was commanded throughout the war by Longstreet. This corps took part in the battles of second Bull Run and Antietam, and held the left of Lee's front at Fredericksburg. Most of the corps was absent in North Carolina when the battle of Chancellorsville took place, but Longstreet, now a lieutenant-general, returned to Lee in time to take part in the campaign of Gettysburg. At that battle he disapproved of the attack because of the exceptionally strong position of the Federals. He has been charged with tardiness in getting into the action, but his delay was in part authorized by Lee to await an absent brigade, and in part was the result of instructions to conceal his movements, which caused circuitous marching. The most conspicuous fighting in the battle was conducted by Longstreet. In September 1863 he took his corps to the west and bore a conspicuous part in the great battle of Chickamauga. In November he commanded the unsuccessful expedition against Knoxville. In 1864 he rejoined Lee's army in Virginia, and on the 6th of May arrived upon the field of the Wilderness as the Confederate right had been turned and routed. His attack was a model of impetuosity and skill, and drove the enemy back until their entire force upon that flank was in confusion. At this critical moment, as Longstreet in person, at the head of fresh troops, was pushing the attack in the forest, he was fired upon by mistake by his own men and desperately wounded. This mischance stayed the Confederate assault for two hours, and enabled the enemy to provide effective means to meet it. In October 1864 he resumed command of his corps

[illegible] paralysed in his right [illegible] of Reconstruction Longstreet's attitude [illegible] and the discussion of certain [illegible] the responsibility for the Gettysburg [illegible] into extreme unpopularity, and in [illegible] which lasted for many years, much [illegible] by both sides which could be condoned [illegible] His acceptance of a Federal office at New [illegible] into armed conflict with his old [illegible] His admiration for General Grant and his [illegible] party accentuated the ill-feeling of [illegible] But in time his services in former days [illegible] once more "General Lee's war- [illegible] and the people of the South. He held [illegible] being that of minister to [illegible] that of commissioner of Pacific [illegible] McKinley and Roosevelt. In 1896 he [illegible] Appomattox, and in his later years [illegible] Gettysburg, which was published soon [illegible] and reminiscences of his whole [illegible] Longstreet died at Gainesville, Georgia, [illegible]

[illegible] at High Tide, by Helen D. Longstreet [illegible]

[illegible] of Staffordshire, England, on the [illegible] 2½ m. S.E. of Stoke-on-Trent, [illegible] and municipal borough it is included. [illegible] is in the Potteries district, and [illegible] and iron mines. It was governed [illegible] and 30 councillors until under the [illegible] scheme (1908) it became part of the [illegible] in 1910.

[illegible] of a French family which originated [illegible] the "Bastard of Orleans," to whom [illegible] of Longueville in Normandy in [illegible] count of Longueville, was created [illegible] of his brother Louis with Jeanne, [illegible] Philip, count of Baden-Hochberg- [illegible] considerable estates to the house of [illegible] de Longueville (d. 1663), took an [illegible] and for a long time held the royal [illegible] His wife, Anne Geneviève (see [illegible] in the political dissensions of the [illegible] was Jean Louis, the Abbé d'Orléans, [illegible] atist, Charles d'Orléans-Rothelin [illegible] bastard branch of the family.

[illegible] **GENEVIÈVE**, DUCHESSE DE (1619– [illegible] of Henri de Bourbon, Prince de [illegible] Marguerite de Montmorency, and [illegible] Condé. She was born on the 28th [illegible] Vincennes, into which her father [illegible] opposition to Marshal D'Ancre, [illegible] Medici, who was then regent in the [illegible] was educated with great strictness [illegible] in the Rue St Jacques at Paris. [illegible] by the execution of the duc de [illegible] brother, for intriguing against [illegible] mother's cousin the comte de [illegible] in 1635; but her parents [illegible] and being introduced into [illegible] one of the stars of the Hôtel [illegible] centre of all that was learned, [illegible] she was married to the duc [illegible] a widower twice her age. [illegible] Richelieu's death her father [illegible] during the minority of [illegible] the great victory of Rocroy in [illegible] of political importance. [illegible] to Münster, where he was [illegible] and where she charmed the [illegible] the [illegible]

her return she fell in love with the duc de la Rochefoucauld, the author of the *Maxims*, who made use of her love to obtain influence over her brother, and thus win honours for himself. She was the guiding spirit of the first Fronde, when she brought over Armand, Prince de Conti, her second brother, and her husband to the malcontents, but she failed to attract Condé himself, whose loyalty to the court overthrew the first Fronde. It was during the first Fronde that she lived at the Hôtel de Ville and took the city of Paris as god-mother for the child born to her there. The peace did not satisfy her, although La Rochefoucauld won the titles he desired. The second Fronde was largely her work, and in it she played the most prominent part in attracting to the rebels first Condé and later Turenne. In the last year of the war she was accompanied into Guienne by the duc de Nemours, her intimacy with whom gave La Rochefoucauld an excuse for abandoning her, and who himself immediately returned to his old mistress the duchesse de Chevreuse. Thus abandoned, and in disgrace at court, the duchess betook herself to religion. She accompanied her husband to his government at Rouen, and devoted herself to good works. She took for her director M. Singlin, famous in the history of Port Royal. She chiefly lived in Normandy till 1663, when her husband died, and she came to Paris. There she became more and more Jansenist in opinion, and her piety and the remembrance of her influence during the disastrous days of the Fronde, and above all the love her brother, the great Condé, bore her, made her conspicuous. The king pardoned her and in every way showed respect for her. She became the great protectress of the Jansenists; it was in her house that Arnauld, Nicole and De Lane were protected; and to her influence must be in great part attributed the release of Lemaistre De Sacy from the Bastille, the introduction of Pomponne into the ministry and of Arnauld to the king. Her famous letters to the pope are part of the history of PORT ROYAL (*q.v.*), and as long as she lived the nuns of Port Royal des Champs were left in safety. Her elder son resigned his title and estates, and became a Jesuit under the name of the Abbé d'Orléans, while the younger, after leading a debauched life, was killed leading the attack in the passage of the Rhine in 1673. As her health failed she hardly ever left the convent of the Carmelites in which she had been educated. On her death in 1679 she was buried with great splendour by her brother Condé, and her heart, as she had directed, was sent to the nuns of the Port Royal des Champs.

The chief authority for Madame de Longueville's life is a little book in two volumes by Villefore the Jansenist, published in 1738. Victor Cousin has devoted four volumes to her, which, though immensely diffuse, give a vivid picture of her time. See also Sainte-Beuve, *Portraits des femmes* (1840). Her connexion with Port Royal should be studied in Arnauld's *Mémoirs*, and in the different histories of that institution.

LONGUS, Greek sophist and romancer, author of *Daphnis and Chloë*. Nothing is known of his life, and all that can be said is that he probably lived at the end of the 2nd or the beginning of the 3rd century A.D. It has been suggested that the name Longus is merely a misreading of the last word of the title *Λεσβιακῶν ἐρωτικῶν λόγοι δ'* in the Florentine MS.; Seiler also observes that the best MS. begins and ends with *λόγου* (not *λόγγου*) *ποιμενικῶν*. If his name was really Longus, he was probably a freedman of some Roman family which bore it. Longus's style is rhetorical, his shepherds and shepherdesses are wholly conventional, but he has imparted human interest to a purely fanciful picture. As an analysis of feeling, *Daphnis and Chloë* makes a nearer approach to the modern novel than its chief rival among Greek erotic romances, the *Aethiopica* of Heliodorus, which is remarkable mainly for the ingenious succession of incidents. Daphnis and Chloë, two children found by shepherds, grow up together, nourishing a mutual love which neither suspects. The development of this simple passion forms the chief interest, and there are few incidents. Chloë is carried off by a pirate, and ultimately regains her family. Rivals alarm the peace of mind of Daphnis; but the two lovers are recognized by their parents, and return to a happy married life in the country. *Daphnis and Chloë* was the model of *La Sireine* of Honoré d'Urfé, the *Diana enamorada* of

Montemayor, the *Aminta* of Tasso, and *The Gentle Shepherd* of Allan Ramsay. The celebrated *Paul et Virginie* is an echo of the same story.

See J. Dunlop's *History of Prose Fiction* (1888), and especially E. Rohde, *Der griechische Roman* (1900). Longus found an incomparable translator in Jacques Amyot, bishop of Auxerre, whose French version, as revised by Paul Louis Courier, is better known than the original. It appeared in 1559, thirty-nine years before the publication of the Greek text at Florence by Columbani. The chief subsequent editions are those by G. Jungermann (1605), J. B. de Villoison (1778, the first standard text with commentary), A. Coraes (Coray) (1802), P. L. Courier (1810, with a newly discovered passage), E. Seiler (1835), R. Hercher (1858), N. Piccolos (Paris, 1860) and Kiefer (Leipzig, 1904), W. D. Lowe (Cambridge, 1908). A. J. Pons's edition (1878) of Courier's version contains an exhaustive bibliography. There are English translations by G. Thorneley (1733, reprinted 1893), C. V. Le Grice (1803), R. Smith (in Bohn's *Classical Library*), and the rare Elizabethan version by Angel Day from Amyot's translation (ed. J. Jacobs in *Tudor Library*, 1890). The illustrated editions, generally of Amyot's version, are numerous and some are beautiful, Prudhon's designs being especially celebrated.

LONGWY, a fortified town of north-eastern France in the department of Meurthe-et-Moselle, 89 m. N.N.W. of Nancy by rail. Pop. (1906) 8523. Longwy is situated on a plateau overlooking the Chiers, a right-bank affluent of the Meuse, near the frontiers of Belgium and Luxemburg. It comprises an upper and a lower town; the former, on a hill, 390 ft. above the Chiers valley, commands the Luxemburg road, and is strengthened by an enceinte and a few out-lying fortifications. There is garrison accommodation for 5000 men and 800 horses, but the permanent garrison is small. The lower town is the industrial centre. The 17th-century church has a lofty square tower, the hôtel de ville dates from 1730, and there is a fine hospital. Iron is extensively mined in the district, and supplies numerous blast furnaces. Several iron and steel works are in operation, and metal utensils, fire-proof ware and porcelain are manufactured. Longwy (*Longus vicus*) came into the possession of the French in 1678 and was at once fortified by Vauban. It was captured by the Prussians in 1792, 1815 and 1871.

LÖNNROT, ELIAS (1802–1884), Finnish philologist and discoverer of the *Kalevala*, was born at Nyland in Finland on the 9th of April 1802. He was an apothecary's assistant, but entered the university of Åbo in 1822, and after taking his successive degrees became a physician in 1832. But before this, as early as 1827, he had begun to publish contributions to the study of the ancient Finnish language, and to collect the national ballads and folk-lore, a field which was at that time uncultivated. In 1833 he settled as a doctor in the country district of Kajana, and began to travel throughout Finland and the adjoining Russian provinces in his leisure time, collecting songs and legends. In this way he was able to put together the great epic of Finland, the *Kalevala*, the first edition of which he published in 1835; he continued to add to it, and in 1849 issued a larger and completer text. In 1840 Lönnrot issued his important collection of the *Kanteletar*, or folk-songs of ancient Finland, which he had taken down from oral tradition. The *Proverbs of Finland* followed in 1842. In 1853, on the death of Castrén, Lönnrot became professor of the Finnish language and literature at the high school of Helsingfors; he retired from this chair in 1862. He died on the 19th of March 1884.

LONSDALE, EARLS OF. This English earldom is held by the ancient family of Lowther, which traces its descent to Sir Hugh Lowther, who flourished in the reign of Edward I. Sir Hugh's descendant Sir Richard Lowther (1529–1607) received Mary queen of Scots on her flight into England in 1568, and in the two following years was concerned with his brother Gerard in attempts to release her from captivity. He was sheriff of Cumberland and lord warden of the west marches. A house built by Gerard Lowther at Penrith is now the "Two Lions Inn." Sir Richard's eldest son, Sir Christopher Lowther (d. 1617), was the ancestor of the later Lowthers, and another son, Sir Gerard Lowther (d. 1624), was judge of the common pleas in Ireland.

One of Sir Christopher's descendants was Sir John Lowther, Bart. (d. 1706), the founder of the trade of Whitehaven, and another was John Lowther (1655–1700), who was created Viscount Lonsdale in 1696. Before this creation John had succeeded his grandfather, another Sir John Lowther (d. 1675), as a baronet, and had been member of parliament for Westmorland from 1675 to 1696. In 1688 he was serviceable in securing Cumberland and Westmorland for William of Orange; in 1690 he was first lord of the treasury, and he was lord privy seal from March 1699 until his death in July 1700. Lonsdale wrote *Memoirs of the Reign of James II.*, which were printed in 1808 and again in 1857. His family became extinct when his son Henry, the 3rd viscount (1694–1751), died unmarried in March 1751.

James Lowther, 1st earl of Lonsdale (1736–1802), was a son of Robert Lowther (d. 1745) of Maulds Meaburn, Westmorland, who was for some time governor of Barbados, and was descended from Sir Christopher Lowther; through his mother Catherine Pennington, James was a great-grandson of the 1st viscount Lonsdale. He inherited one of the family baronetcies in 1751, and from three sources he obtained immense wealth, being the heir of the 3rd viscount Lonsdale, of Sir James Lowther, Bart. (d. 1755) of Whitehaven, and of Sir William Lowther, Bart. (d. 1756). From 1757 to 1784 he was a member of parliament, exercising enormous influence on elections in the north of England and usually controlling nine seats in the House of Commons, where his nominees were known as "Sir James's ninepins." He secured the election of William Pitt as member for his borough of Appleby in 1781, and his dispute with the 3rd duke of Portland over the possession of the socage manor of Carlisle and the forest of Inglewood gave rise to lengthy proceedings, both in parliament and in the law courts. In 1784 Lowther was created earl of Lonsdale and in 1797 Viscount Lowther with an extended remainder. The earl's enormous wealth enabled him to gratify his political ambitions. Sir N. W. Wraxall (*Historical and Posthumous Memoirs*, ed. H.B. Wheatley, 1884), who gives interesting glimpses of his life, speaks of his "prodigious property" and quotes Junius, who called him "the little contemptible tyrant of the north." He was known as the "bad earl," and Horace Walpole and others speak slightingly of him; he was, however, a benefactor to Whitehaven, where he boasted he owned the "land, fire and water."

He married Mary (1768–1824) daughter of George III.'s favourite, John Stuart, 3rd earl of Bute, but died childless on the 24th of May 1802, when the earldom became extinct; but a kinsman, Sir William Lowther, Bart. (1757–1844), of Swillington, became 2nd viscount Lowther. This viscount, who was created earl of Lonsdale in 1807, is chiefly famous as the friend of Wordsworth and the builder of Lowther Castle, Penrith. His son, William Lowther, 3rd earl of Lonsdale (1787–1872), held several subordinate positions in various Tory ministries, and was lord president of the council in 1852. He died unmarried, and was succeeded by his nephew Henry (1818–1876), whose son Hugh Cecil (b. 1857) succeeded his brother as 6th earl of Lonsdale in 1882.

Other prominent members of the Lowther family are the Right Hon. James William Lowther (b. 1855), who became speaker of the House of Commons in 1905; Sir Gerard Augustus Lowther (b. 1858), who became British ambassador at Constantinople in 1908; and the Right Hon. James Lowther (1840–1904), who was a well-known Conservative member of parliament from 1865 onwards, and chief secretary for Ireland from 1878 to 1880.

LONSDALE, WILLIAM (1794–1871), English geologist and palaeontologist, was born at Bath on the 9th of September 1794. He was educated for the army and in 1810 obtained a commission as ensign in the 4th (King's Own) regiment. He served in the Peninsular War at the battles of Salamanca and Waterloo, for both of which he received medals; and he retired as lieutenant. Residing afterwards for some years at Batheaston he collected a series of rocks and fossils which he presented to the Literary and Scientific Institution of Bath. He became the first honorary curator of the natural history department of the museum, and worked until 1829 when he was appointed assistant secretary and curator of the Geological Society of Lo-

[illegible]**TRIFE**, in botany, the common name of *Lysimachia* [illegible] an erect plant, 2 to 4 ft. high, common on river banks [illegible] the branched stem bears tapering leaves in pairs [illegible] and terminal panicles of rather large deep yellow [illegible] It is a member of the primrose family. *L. nemorum*, [illegible] or wood loosestrife, a low-growing plant with [illegible] stem, and somewhat similar yellow flowers [illegible] singly in the leaf-axils, is frequent in copses. *L.* [illegible] is the well-known creeping jenny or money-wort, [illegible] with widely creeping stem, pairs of shining leaves [illegible] solitary yellow flowers; it is found on banks of rivers [illegible] woods, and is a common rockery plant. Purple loose-[illegible] *Lythrum Salicaria*, belongs to a different family, *Lyth*-[illegible] It is a handsome plant growing 2 to 6 ft. high on river [illegible] ditches, with a branched angled stem bearing whorls [illegible] stalkless leaves and ending in tall tapering [illegible] beautiful rose-purple flowers. The flowers are tri-[illegible] that is to say, exist in three forms which differ in the [illegible] length of the styles and stamens and are known as long-[illegible] and short-styled forms respectively, the [illegible] colour of the pollen also differ. These differences play [illegible] part in the pollination of the flower.

LOOT, [illegible] plunder or spoil taken from an enemy in war, especially [illegible] plunder taken by the victor after the capture [illegible] The word came into English from India. It is adapted [illegible] Hindi *lut*, which is either from Sanskrit *lunt*, to rob, [illegible] *loptra*, booty.

LOPES, FERNÃO [illegible], the patriarch of Portuguese [illegible] was appointed keeper of the royal archives, then [illegible] the castle of St George in Lisbon, by King John I. [illegible] He acted as private secretary to the Infants [illegible] D. Fernando, and when the former ascended the [illegible] Lopes, by letter of the 19th of March 1434, [illegible] of "putting into chronicles the stories of the kings [illegible] as well as the great and lofty actions of the most [illegible] my lord and father" (John I.). The form of the [illegible] its limits, and is a sufficient reply to those [illegible] who have censured Lopes for partiality. Not-[illegible] the official title of chief chronicler of the realm, [illegible] (*Vassallo del Rei*), and received his salary [illegible] King Alphonso V. confirmed him in [illegible] the 3rd of June 1449, and in 1454, after [illegible] in the archives and twenty as chronicler, [illegible] Gomes Eannes de Azurara. The latter [illegible] as "a notable person, a man of [illegible] great authority," and the modern historian [illegible] is not only history in the chronicles of [illegible] poetry and drama as well; there is the [illegible] its enthusiasm, its love of glory." [illegible] the Portuguese Froissart, and that rare [illegible] his subjects live, is common to the [illegible] written in a better-known [illegible] that the general opinion of [illegible] Robert Southey, who called [illegible] the best chronicler of any age [illegible] in order the stories of the [illegible] composed a general chronicle [illegible] appeared under his name, [illegible] for the chronicles of Ruy [illegible] his work with care [illegible] reading of books [illegible] of the archives be-[illegible] churches, both in [illegible] guide in facts, [illegible] of his style.

[illegible] *del Rei D.* [illegible] The third part [illegible]

the same chronicle (Lisbon, 1760). (3) *Chronica do senhor rei D. Fernando* published in the same volume and collection. The British Museum has some important 16th-century MSS. of the chronicles.

See Damião de Goes, *Chronica del Rei Dom Manoel*, part iv. ch. 38; Atalíaia Morato, introduction to vol. iv. of the above collection; Herculano, *Opusculos*, vol. v. (E. Pr.)

LOPEZ, CARLOS ANTONIO (1790–1862), Paraguayan autocrat, was born at Asuncion on the 4th of November 1790, and was educated in the ecclesiastical seminary of that city. He attracted the hostility of the dictator, Francia, and he was forced to keep in hiding for several years. He acquired, however, so unusual a knowledge of law and governmental affairs that on Francia's death in 1840, he obtained an almost undisputed control of the Paraguayan state, which he maintained uninterruptedly until his death on the 10th of September 1862. He was successively secretary of the ruling military *junta* (1840–1841), one of the two consuls (1841–1844), and president with dictatorial powers (1844–1862) by successive elections for ten and three years, and in 1857 again for ten years, with power to nominate his own successor. Though nominally a president acting under a republican constitution, he ruled despotically. His government was in general directed with wise energy towards developing the material resources and strengthening the military power of the country. His jealousy of foreign approach several times involved him in diplomatic disputes with Brazil, England, and the United States, which nearly resulted in war, but each time he extricated himself by skilful evasions.

His eldest son, FRANCISCO SOLANO LOPEZ (1826–1870), was born near Asuncion on the 24th of July 1826. When in his nineteenth year he was made commander-in-chief of the Paraguayan army, during the spasmodic hostilities then prevailing with the Argentine Republic. He was sent in 1853 as minister to England, France and Italy, and spent a year and a half in Europe. He purchased large quantities of arms and military supplies, together with several steamers, and organized a project for building a railroad and establishing a French colony in Paraguay. He also formed the acquaintance of Madame Lynch, an Irish adventuress of many talents and popular qualities, who became his mistress, and strongly influenced his later ambitious schemes. Returning to Paraguay, he became in 1855 minister of war, and on his father's death in 1862 at once assumed the reins of government as vice-president, in accordance with a provision of his father's will, and called a congress by which he was chosen president for ten years. In 1864, in his self-styled capacity of "protector of the equilibrium of the La Plata," he demanded that Brazil should abandon her armed interference in a revolutionary struggle then in progress in Uruguay. No attention being paid to his demand, he seized a Brazilian merchant steamer in the harbour of Asuncion, and threw into prison the Brazilian governor of the province of Matto Grosso who was on board. In the following month (December 1864) he despatched a force to invade Matto Grosso, which seized and sacked its capital Cuyabá, and took possession of the province and its diamond mines. Lopez next sought to send an army to the relief of the Uruguayan president Aguirre against the revolutionary aspirant Flores, who was supported by Brazilian troops. The refusal of the Argentine president, Mitre, to allow this force to cross the intervening province of Corrientes, was seized upon by Lopez as an occasion for war with the Argentine Republic. A congress, hastily summoned, and composed of his own nominees, bestowed upon Lopez the title of marshal, with extraordinary war powers, and on April 13, 1865, he declared war, at the same time seizing two Argentine war-vessels in the bay of Corrientes, and on the next day occupied the town of Corrientes, instituted a provisional government of his Argentine partisans, and summarily announced the annexation to Paraguay of the provinces of Corrientes and Entre Rios. Meantime the party of Flores had been successful in Uruguay, and that state on April the 18th united with the Argentine Republic in a declaration of war on Paraguay. On the 1st of May Brazil joined these two states in a secret alliance, which stipulated that they should unitedly prosecute the war "until the existing government of Paraguay should be overthrown," and "until no arms or elements of war should be left to it." This agreement was literally carried out. The war which ensued, lasting until the 1st of April 1870, was carried on with great stubbornness and with alternating fortunes, though with a steadily increasing tide of disasters to Lopez (see PARAGUAY). In 1868, when the allies were pressing him hard, his mind, naturally suspicious and revengeful, led him to conceive that a conspiracy had been formed against his life in his own capital and by his chief adherents. Thereupon several hundred of the chief Paraguayan citizens were seized and executed by his order, including his brothers and brothers-in-law, cabinet ministers, judges, prefects, military officers, bishops and priests, and nine-tenths of the civil officers, together with more than two hundred foreigners, among them several members of the diplomatic legations. Lopez was at last driven with a mere handful of troops to the northern frontier of Paraguay, where, on the 1st of April 1870, he was surprised by a Brazilian force and killed as he was endeavouring to escape by swimming the river Aquidaban.

LOPEZ DE GÓMARA, FRANCISCO (1510?–1555?), Spanish historian, was educated at the university of Alcalá, where he took orders. Soon after 1540 he entered the household of the famous Cortés, who supplied him with most of the material for his *Historia de las Indias* (1552), and *Crónica de la conquista de Nueva España* (1552). The pleasing style and novel matter enchanted the Spanish public, but the unmeasured laudation of Cortés at the expense of his lieutenants and companions brought about a violent reaction. Though the *Historia* was dedicated to Charles V., both works were forbidden on the 17th of November 1553, and no editions of them were issued between 1554 and 1727. Italian and French versions of his books were published in 1556 and 1578 respectively.

LOP-NOR or **LOB-NOR**, a lake of Central Asia, in the Gobi Desert, between the Astin-tagh (Altyn-tagh) on the south and the Kuruk-tagh on the north. Previous to 1876 it was placed in nearly all maps at 42° 30′ N., a position which agreed with the accounts and the maps of ancient Chinese geographers. In the year mentioned the Russian explorer Przhevalsky discovered two closely connected lake-basins, Kara-buran and Kara-koshun, fully one degree farther south, and considerably east of the site of the old Lop-nor, which lake-basins he nevertheless regarded as being identical with the old Lop-nor of the Chinese. But the water they contained he pronounced to be fresh water. This identification was disputed by Baron von Richthofen, on the ground that the Lop-nor, the "Salt Lake" of the Chinese geographers, could not be filled with fresh water; moreover, being the final gathering basin of the desert stream, the Tarim, it was bound to be salt, more especially as the lake had no outflow. Przhevalsky visited the Lop-nor region again in 1885, and adhered to his opinion. But ten years later it was explored anew by Dr Sven Hedin, who ascertained that the Tarim empties part of its waters into another lake, or rather string of lakes (Avullu-köl, Kara-köl, Tayek-köl and Arka-köl), which are situated in 42° 30′ N., and thus so far justified the views of von Richthofen, and confirmed the Chinese accounts. At the same time he advanced reasons for believing that Przhevalsky's lake-basins, the southern Lop-nor, are of quite recent origin—indeed, he fixed upon 1720 as the probably approximate date of their formation, a date which von Richthofen would alter to 1750. Besides this, Sven Hedin argued that there exists a close inter-relation between the northern Lop-nor lakes and the southern Lop-nor lakes, so that as the water in the one group increases, it decreases to the same proportion and volume in the other. He also argued that the four lakes of northern Lop-nor are slowly moving westwards under the incessant impetus of wind and sandstorm (*buran*). These conclusions were afterwards controverted by the Russian traveller, P. K. Kozlov, who visited the Lop-nor region in 1893–1894—that is, before Dr Sven Hedin's examination. He practically only reiterated Przhevalsky's contention, that the ancient Chinese maps were erroneously drawn, and that the Kara-koshun, in spite of the freshness of its water, was the old Lop-nor, *the* Salt Lake *par excellence* of the Chinese. Finally, in 1900, Dr Sven Hedin, following up the course of [illegible] at the foot of the Kuruk-tagh and [illegible] the now desiccated Kuruk-darya [illegible] other vegetation [illegible] a desiccated salt lake, which he [illegible] Lop-nor of the Chinese geographers, and [illegible] found that the Kara-koshun or Lop-nor of [illegible] extended towards the north, but [illegible] old Lop-nor no longer exists, but in place of a [illegible] of much smaller lakes of newer formation. [illegible] inferred that, owing to the uniform level of the [illegible] sluggish flow of the Tarim, its unceasing tendency to [illegible] reunite, conjoined with the violence and persistency of the [illegible] (mostly from the east and north-east), and the rapid [illegible] growth of the reed-beds in the shallow marshes, the [illegible] waters of the Tarim basin gather now in greater [illegible] in one depression, and now in greater volume in another. [illegible] this view derives support from the extreme shallowness of the lakes in both Sven Hedin's northern Lop-nor and Przhevalsky's southern Lop-nor, together with the uniformly horizontal level of the entire region.

See Delmar Morgan's translation of Przhevalsky's *From Kulja across the Tian-shan to Lop-nor* (London, 1879); Von Richthofen's "Bemerkungen zu den Ergebnissen von Oberst-Leutenant Przhevalskis Reise nach dem Lop-nor" in *Verhandl. der Gesell. f. Erdkunde zu Berlin* (1878), pp. 121 seq.; Sven Hedin's *Scientific Results of a Journey in Central Asia, 1899–1902* (vols. i. and ii., Stockholm, 1905–1906), where Kozlov's share of the controversy is summarized (cl. ii., 270–280). (J. T. Be.)

LOQUAT, JAPANESE PLUM or JAPANESE MEDLAR, known botanically as *Eriobotrya japonica*, small evergreen tree belonging to the natural order Rosaceae, with large thick oval-oblong leaves borne near the ends of the branches, and dark green above with a rusty tomentum on the lower face. The fruit is pear-shaped, yellow, about 1¼ in. long and contains large stony seeds; it has an agreeable acid flavour. The plant is a native of China and Japan, but is widely grown for its fruit and as a decorative plant. It is a familiar object in the Mediterranean region and in the southern United States.

LORAIN, a city of Lorain county, Ohio, U.S.A., on Lake Erie, at the mouth of the Black river, and about 25 m. W. by S. of Cleveland. Pop. (1890) 4863; (1900) 16,028, of whom 4730 were foreign-born and 359 negroes; (1910 census) 28,883. Lorain is served by the New York, Chicago & St. Louis, and the Baltimore & Ohio railways, by the Lake Shore Electric railway, and by several of the more important steamboat lines on the Great Lakes. It has a Carnegie library, the Lake View Hospital and the Saint Joseph's Hospital. There is a good harbour, and the city's chief interests are in the shipping of great quantities of coal, iron-ore, grain and lumber, in the building of large steel vessels, in railway shops, and in the manufacture of iron pipes, gas engines, stoves and automatic steam shovels. The value of the factory products increased from $9,481,388 in 1900 to $14,491,091 in 1905, or 52·8%. The municipality owns and operates the waterworks. A Moravian mission was established here in 1787–1788, and a trading post in 1807, but no permanent settlement was made until several years later. In 1836 the place was incorporated as a village under the name "Charleston", in 1874 the present name was adopted, and in 1896 Lorain became a city of the second class.

LORALAI, a town and district of India, in Baluchistan. The town, which is situated 4700 ft. above the sea, 35 m. by road from the railway station of Harnai, was occupied as a military station in 1886, and has quarters for a native cavalry and a native infantry regiment. Pop. (1901) 3561.

The DISTRICT OF LORALAI was formed in 1903. It consists of a series of long, narrow valleys, hemmed in by rugged mountains, and bordered E. by Dera Ghazi Khan district of the Punjab. Area 7999 sq. m.; pop. (1901) 67,864, of whom the majority are Afghans. The principal crops are wheat and millet; but the chief wealth of the inhabitants is derived from their herds of cattle, sheep and goats.

LORCA, a town of eastern Spain, in the province of Murcia, on the right bank of the river Sangonera (here called the Guadalantin or Guadalentin) and on the Murcia-Baza railway. Pop. (1900) [illegible]. It occupies a height crowned by a medieval fortress, among the foothills of the Sierra del Caño. Its older parts, Moorish in many features and with narrow irregular streets, contrast with the modern parts, which have broad streets and squares and many fine public buildings—theatre, town hall, hospitals, courts of justice and a bridge over the Sangonera. There is an important trade in agricultural products and live stock, as well as manufactures of woollen stuffs, leather, gunpowder, chemicals and porcelain. Silver, sulphur and lead are found in the neighbourhood.

Lorca is the Roman *Eliocroca* (perhaps also the *Ilorci* of Pliny, N.H. iii. 3) and the Moorish *Lurka*. It was the key of Murcia during the Moorish wars, and was frequently taken and retaken. On the 30th of April 1802 it suffered severely by the bursting of the reservoir known as the Pantano de Puentes, in which the waters of the Sangonera were stored for purposes of irrigation (1775–1785); the district adjoining the river, known as the Barrio de San Cristobal, was completely ruined, and more than six hundred persons perished. In 1810 Lorca suffered greatly from the French invasion. In 1886 the Pantano, which was one of the largest of European reservoirs, being formed by a dam 800 ft. long and 160 ft. high, was successfully rebuilt.

LORCH, a town in the Prussian province of Hesse-Nassau, romantically situated on the right bank of the Rhine, 8 m. below Rüdesheim by the railway Frankfort-on-Main-Wiesbaden-Cologne. Pop. (1905) 2269. It has a fine Gothic Roman Catholic church—St Martin's—dating from the 14th century. The slopes of the hills descending to the Rhine are covered with vineyards, which produce excellent wine. In the neighbourhood of Lorch, which was mentioned as early as 832, is the ruined castle of Nollich.

LORCH, a town in the kingdom of Württemberg, on the Rems, 28 m. E. from Stuttgart by the railway to Nördlingen. Pop. (1905) 3033. It possesses a fine Protestant church dating from the 12th century. Its industries include carriage-building and the manufacture of cement and paper. On the Marienberg lying above the town stands the former Benedictine monastery of Lorch, founded about 1108 by Frederick of Hohenstaufen, and in 1563 converted into an Evangelical college. Here Schiller passed a portion of his school days. The church contains several tombs of the Hohenstaufen family. The Roman *limes* began at Lorch and Roman remains have been found in the neighbourhood of the town.

See Kirn, *Führer durch das Kloster Lorch* (Lorch, 1888), and Steimle, *Kastell Lorch* (Heidelberg, 1897).

LORD, JOHN (1810–1894), American historical writer and lecturer, was born in Portsmouth, New Hampshire, on the 27th of December 1810. He was the nephew of Nathan Lord (1792–1870), president of Dartmouth College from 1828 to 1863. He graduated at Dartmouth in 1833, and at Andover Theological Seminary in 1837. His course at the Seminary was interrupted by a period of teaching—at Windham, Connecticut (1834), and at Norwich (1834–1835)—and by a tour in 1836 through New York and Ohio, in which he lectured on the dark ages. He was agent and lecturer for the American Peace Society ([illegible]), and for a brief time was a Congregational pastor in turn at New Marlboro and West Stockbridge, Massachusetts, and at Utica, New York. About 1840 he became a professional lecturer on history. He lectured extensively for fifty years, especially in the United States and Great Britain, and introduced, with success, the mid-day lecture. He was lecturer on history in Dartmouth from 1869 to 1876. He received, in 1864, the degree of LL.D. from the University of the City of New York. From 1854 he made his home in Stamford, Connecticut, where he died on the 15th of December 1894. His works include, besides several school and college histories, *The Old Roman World: the Grandeur and Failure of Civilization* (1867); *Ancient States and Empires* (1869); *Two German Giants: Frederick the Great and Bismarck* (1885); and *Beacon Lights of History* (8 vols., 1884–1896), his chief contribution to historical literature.

See *The Life of John Lord* (1896) by Rev. Alexander S. Twombley, D. D. (in "Beacon Lights of History"), which is based chiefly upon Lord's *Reminiscences of Fifty Years in the Lecture Field.*

LORD (O. Eng. *hlāford, i.e. hlāfweard*, the warder or keeper of bread, *hlāf*, loaf; the word is not represented in any other Teutonic language), in its primary sense, the head of a household, the master of those dependent on him for their daily bread, correlative to O. Eng. *hlāf-ǣta*, loaf-eater, servant; the word frequently occurs in this sense in the Bible, cf. Matt. xxiv. 45. As a term implying the ownership of property, "lord" survives in "lord of the manor" and "landlord." The chief applications are due to its use as the equivalent of Lat. *dominus*, Gr. κύριος and Fr. *seigneur*; thus in the Old Testament it represents *Yahweh*, Jehovah, and in the New Testament κύριος, as a title of Jesus Christ. Selden's words may be quoted for the more general meanings of "lord"; "the name Dominus is . . . to be thought of only as a distinguishing attribute of Greatness and as our English word Lord is; and that without any relation of it to an Interest of property or to servitude, and only as it denotes such Superiours as King or Subjects of the greater Nobility with us and men of special Eminency in other States, known by the names of Heeren, Dons, Sieurs, signiors, seigneurs and the like." It is thus not only a general word for a prince or sovereign, but also the common word for a feudal superior, and particularly of a feudal tenant holding directly of the king, a baron (*q.v.*), hence a peer of the realm, a member of the House of Lords, constituted of the lords temporal and the lords spiritual; this is the chief modern usage. The prefix "lord" is ordinarily used as a less formal alternative to the full title, whether held by right or by courtesy, of marquess, earl or viscount, and is always so used in the case of a baron (which in English usage is generally confined to the holder of a foreign title). Where the name is territorial, the "of" is dropped, thus, the marquess of A., but Lord A. The younger sons of dukes and marquesses have, by courtesy, the title of Lord prefixed to the Christian and surname, *e.g.* Lord John Russell. In the case of bishops, the full and formal title of address is the Lord Bishop of A., whether he be a spiritual peer or not. Many high officials of the British government have the word "lord" prefixed to their titles; some of them are treated in separate articles; for lord privy seal see PRIVY SEAL. In certain cases the members of a board which has taken the place of an office of state are known as lords commissioners or, shortly, lords of the office in question, *e.g.* lords of the treasury, civil or naval lords of the admiralty For lord lieutenant and lord mayor see LIEUTENANT and MAYOR. As the proper form of address "my lord" is used not only to those members of the nobility to whom the title "Lord" is applicable, and to bishops, but also to all judges of the High Court in England, and of the Scottish and Irish Superior Courts, and to lord mayors and lord provosts (see also LADY).

LORD ADVOCATE, or king's advocate, the principal law-officer of the crown in Scotland. His business is to act as a public prosecutor, and to plead in all causes that concern the crown. He is at the head of the system of public prosecutions by which criminal justice is administered in Scotland, and thus his functions are of a far more extensive character than those of the English law-officers of the crown. He is aided by a solicitor-general and by subordinate assistants called advocates-depute. The office of king's advocate seems to have been established about the beginning of the 16th century. Originally he had no power to prosecute crimes without the concurrence of a private party, but in the year 1597 he was empowered to prosecute crimes at his own instance. He has the privilege of pleading in court with his hat on.

[illegible] DONNELLEY & SONS COMPANY, CHICAGO, ON "BRITANNICA INDIA [illegible] RED BY S. D. WARREN & COMPANY, BOSTON, MASS. BINDERS, THE NEW YORK, AND R. R. DONNELLEY & SONS COMPANY, CHICAGO.

END OF SIXTEENTH VOLUME